## Cómo utilizar el diccionario

Todas las **entradas** están ordenadas alfabéticamente y se destacan en negrita.

**dato** ['da·to] *m* **1.** (*detalle*) fact; ...
**dc. d.C.** [des·'pwes de 'kris·to] *abr de* **después de Cristo** AD
**dcha.** [de·'re·ʧa] *abr de* **derecha** R
**de** [de] *prep* **1.** (*posesión*) ...

Los verbos frasales ingleses van justo después del verbo principal y están marcados con un rombo (◆).
Las cifras arábigas *voladas* diferencian **homógrafos**.
Se emplean los signos de la IPA para la transcripción fonética. En español se indica primero la pronunciación latinoamericana. Los puntos centrados indican la división silábica.

**era¹** ['e·ra] *f* era
**era²** ['e·ra] *3. imp de* **ser**
**agradecer** [a·ɣra·de·'ser, -'θer] *irr como* **crecer** *vt* ...
**anillo** [a·'ni·jo, -ʎo] *m* ...

Las indicaciones de las **formas irregulares del plural** y de las **formas irregulares de verbos y adjetivos** están entre paréntesis triangulares. En el apéndice se incluye una lista con modelos de conjugación de los verbos españoles.
Se indica la forma femenina de los sustantivos y adjetivos. Se indica el género de los sustantivos españoles.

**club** <clubs *o* clubes> ...
**merendar** <e→ie> ...
**fotografiar** < *1. pres:* fotografío> ...
**adelgazar** <z→c> ...

**actor, actriz** [ak·'tor, ak·'tris, -'triθ] *m, f* actor *m*, actress *f*; ...
**antiguo, -a** [an·'ti·ɣwo, -a] *adj* ...

Las cifras romanas indican las distintas **categorías gramaticales**. Las cifras arábigas indican las distintas **acepciones**.

**abdominal** [aβ·do·mi·'nal] **I.** *adj* abdominal **II.** *m* DEP sit-up
**abordar** [a·βor·'dar] *vt* **1.** (*persona*) to approach **2.** (*tema*) to discus

La **tilde** sustituye la entrada anterior. El símbolo ▸ introduce el bloque de las locuciones y los proverbios. Las palabras subrayadas permiten una mejor orientación.

**río** ['rri·o] *m* river; ~ **abajo/arriba** downstream/upstream ▸ **cuando el ~ <u>suena</u>, agua lleva** *prov* where there's smoke, there's fire

Se dan numerosas **indicaciones** para dirigir al usuario a la traducción correcta:

- indicaciones de **especialidad**

- **definiciones** o **sinónimos**, **contextos**, **complementos** o **sujetos** típicos de la entrada
- indicaciones de **uso regional** tanto a nivel de la entrada como a nivel de la traducción
- indicaciones de **estilo**

**grabación** [gra·βa·'sjon, -'θjon] *f* recording; TV shooting; COMPUT copying
**bravo, -a** ['bra·βo, -a] *adj* **1.** (*valiente*) brave **2.** (*salvaje*) wild; (*mar*) stormy **3.** *AmL* (*picante*) hot
**porrista** [po·'rris·ta] *mf Méx* DEP fan

**recalentado** [rre·ka·len·'ta·do] *m Méx*, *inf* leftovers *pl*

Si una entrada o un ejemplo no pueden ser traducidos se dará una **explicación** o una **equivalencia aproximada** (≈).

*s. a. (see also)* y *v.t. (véase también)* remiten a una **entrada modelo** para más información.

**pochismo** [po·'ʧis·mo] *m Méx* **1.** *inf* ... *Anglicism introduced into Spanish*
**martes** ['mar·tes] *m inv* Tuesday; ~ **y trece** ≈ Friday the thirteenth; ...
**abril** [a·'βril] *m* April; *v.t.* **marzo** ...

# BARRON'S

## FOREIGN LANGUAGE GUIDES

# SPANISH–ENGLISH
## Pocket Dictionary

---

## Diccionario de bolsillo
### ESPAÑOL–INGLÉS

**BARRON'S Foreign Language Guides**
**Spanish-English Pocket Dictionary**
**Diccionario de bolsillo Español-Inglés**

First edition for the United States and Canada published in 2008 by Barron's Educational Series, Inc.

**Editorial management:** Dr. Meg Tsiris
**Contributors:** Almudena García Hernandez, Eugenio Presno Ruiz, William Steinmetz

**Typesetting:** Mariusz Idzikowski, Poznań; Dörr und Schiller GmbH, Stuttgart

*All inquiries should be addressed to:*
Barron's Educational Series, Inc.
250 Wireless Boulevard
Hauppauge, NY 11788
*www.barronseduc.com*

ISBN-13: 978-0-7641-4005-1
ISBN-10: 0-7641-4005-1
Library of Congress Control Number 2008920657

Printed in China
9 8

**inwards** ['ɪn·wərds] *adv* hacia adentro, para dentro

**I/O** COMPUT *abbr of* **input/output** E/S

**iodine** ['aɪ·ə·daɪn] *n* yodo *m*

All **entries** appear in alphabetical order and are printed in bold type.

**bring** [brɪŋ] <brought, brought> *vt* **1.** ...
◆ **bring about** *vt* **1.** (*cause*) provocar ...

English phrasal verbs come directly after the base verb and are marked with a diamond (◆).

**incense¹** ['ɪn·sents] *n* incienso *m*

**incense²** [ɪn·'sents] *vt* indignar

**flexible** ['flek·sə·bəl] *adj* (*material, policy*) flexible

Raised numbers indicate so-called **homographs.**

The International Phonetic Alphabet is used for all **phonetic transcriptions.** In Spanish, the common Latin-American pronunciation is given first. Centered dots are used for syllable division.

**child** [tʃaɪld] <children> ...

**be** [bi] <was, been>

**uncanny** [ʌn·'kæn·i] *adj* <-ier, -iest> ...

Angle brackets are used to show **irregular plural forms** and **forms of irregular verbs and adjectives**. Model conjugations for Spanish can be found in the appendix.

**abrupt** [ə·'brʌpt] *adj* **1.** (*sudden*) repentino, -a; (*change*) brusco, -a; ...

**instructor** [ɪn·'strʌk·tər] *n* **1.** (*teacher*) instructor(a) *m(f)* ...

**mute** [mjut] **I.** *n* MUS sordina *f* **II.** *adj* mudo, -a

**honey** [hʌn·i] *n* **1.** CULIN miel *f* **2.** (*term of endearment*) cariño *m*

Feminine forms of nouns and adjectives are shown. Spanish nouns are followed by their gender.

Roman numerals are used for the **parts of speech** of a word, and Arabic numerals for **sense divisions**.

**horse** [hɔrs] *n* **1.** ZOOL caballo *m*; **to ride a ~** montar a caballo ... ► **to get sth straight from the ~'s** mouth saber algo de buena tinta; **don't look a gift ~ in the** mouth *prov* a caballo regalado, no le mires el dentado *prov*; ...

The **swung dash** represents the entry word. The ► sign introduces **a block of set expressions, idioms and proverbs**. Key words are underlined as a guide.

Various kinds of **meaning indicators** are used to guide you to the required translation:

**horn** [hɔrn] *n* **1.** ZOOL cuerno *m* **2.** MUS trompa *f* **3.** AUTO bocina *f* ...

**wild** [waɪld] **I.** *adj* **1.** (*animal*) salvaje; (*plant*) silvestre; ...

• **Subject labels**

**celery** ['sel·ə·ri] *n* apio *m*, panul *m* CSur

• **Definitions** or **synonyms,** typical **context partners, subjects** or **objects** of the entry
• **Regional vocabulary and variants**

**juice** [dʒus] *n* **1.** (*drink*) zumo *m* **2.** (*of meat*) jugo *m* **3.** *sl* (*electricity*) luz *f*; (*fuel*) sopa *f* ...

• **Usage Labels**

**ego surfing** *n* COMPUT *introducir en un buscador de Internet el propio nombre*

**Sunday school** *n* REL ≈ catequesis *f inv*

When a word or expression has no direct translation, an **explanation** or **approximate equivalent** is given (≈).

**March** [martʃ] *n* marzo *m*; *s.a.* **April**

*s. a. (see also)* and *v.t. (véase también)* invite the reader to consult a **model entry** for further information.

With the aid of the alphabetical thumb index overleaf (at the edge of the page) you can quickly locate the letter you need to find in the Spanish-English and English-Spanish dictionary. Once you have located the letter you need on the thumb index, simply flip to the correspondingly marked part of the dictionary.

If you are left-handed, you can use the thumb index at the end of this book.

Gracias al índice alfabético del borde derecho (véase al dorso), puede ir directamente a la letra que necesite del diccionario Español-Inglés e Inglés-Español. Una vez localizada en el índice la letra que busca, puede pasar directamente a la parte correspondiente del diccionario.

Si usted es zurdo/a puede utilizar el índice alfabético que hay al final del diccionario.

# Índice

# Contents

# La pronunciación del español – Spanish pronunciation

Remarkable variations are evident in Spanish pronunciation, both within the regions of the Iberian Peninsula and amongst the individual countries in which Spanish is spoken. Surprisingly, these variations are stronger within Spain itself than between the various Spanish-speaking countries in America. In the bilingual regions of the Iberian Peninsula – Catalonia, Valencia, the Balearic Islands, the Basque Provinces, and Galicia – pronunciation of Spanish is strongly influenced by the native languages of these areas. In other regions, it is the phonetic features of a range of dialects that have been mixed into spoken Spanish. Particularly characteristic of Andalusia, for example, is this dialect's particular variant of so-called *ceceo* pronunciation, in which not only the usual *z* and *c*, but also *s* is pronounced θ (as in *think*). So, in Andalusia, the words *la casa* ('the house') and *la caza* ('the hunt') are pronounced in exactly the same way.

In the vernacular pronunciation of some areas of Spain and Spanish America, one encounters aspiration of *s* at the end of a word. In the case of *las casas*, for example, the pronunciation would be **lah kása**, instead of **las kásas**. The *s* can even disappear altogether as is the case in the pronunciation **mímo**, instead of **mísmo** for the word *mismo*. Both phenomena are considered nonstandard and should therefore be avoided.

## Ceceo (θe·'θeo)

This refers to the pronunciation of *z* in all positions and of *c* before *e* or *i* as θ, e.g., paθ for *paz*, θínko for *cinco* or aθeptáble for *aceptable*. Generally speaking, *ceceo* is associated with Spain.

## Pronunciation in Spanish America

Spanish-American pronunciation bears the closest similarity to that of the Andalusian region. Among the phonetic characteristics of Spanish America, the following are the most characteristic:

## Seseo (se·'seo)

**Seseo** refers to the pronunciation of *z* and *c* as *s* (e.g., **pas** instead of paθ for *paz* or **sínko**, instead of θínko for *cinco*). Though this is a characteristic mainly of Spanish America, it also occurs in subregions of Andalusia and on the Canary Islands.

In this dictionary, *seseo* pronunciation is given first and *ceceo* pronunciation is given as a second variant.

## Yeísmo

**Yeísmo** is common not only in Spanish-speaking areas of America but also in various regions of Spain such as Andalusia, the Canary Islands, Extremadura, Madrid, and Castilian subregions. It refers to the pronunciation of *ll* as *y* (e.g., **yovér**, instead of **llovér** for *llover*). However, it would be incorrect to assume that *yeísmo* is a practiced all over Spanish America. As a matter of fact, the standard pronunciation of *ll* is used in the subregions of Chile, Peru, Columbia, and Ecuador.

In this dictionary, *yeísmo* pronunciation is given first and ʎ pronunciation is provided as a second variant.

Also characteristic of Spanish America is the pronunciation of *y* as ʤ (e.g., adʒér, instead of ajér for *ayer*) in Argentina, Uruguay, and subregions of Ecuador and Mexico.

# Símbolos fonéticos del español – Spanish phonetic symbols

## Vowels/Vocales

| Symbol/Símbolo | Graphic representation/Representación gráfica | Examples/Ejemplos |
|---|---|---|
| [a] | a | san, acción |
| [e] | e | pez, saber |
| [i] | i | sí, mirar |
| [o] | o | con |
| [u] | u | tú, dibujo |

## Diphthongs/Diptongos

| Symbol/Símbolo | Graphic representation/Representación gráfica | Examples/Ejemplos | Notes/Notas |
|---|---|---|---|
| [ai] | ai, ay | baile, hay | Pronounced like *i* in *write* |
| [au] | au | auto, causa | Pronounced like *ow* in *how* |
| [ei] | ei, ey | aceite, ley | Pronounced like *a* in *rate* |
| [eu] | eu | deuda | Pronounced similarly to *ay* in *hay* |
| [oi] | oi, oy | boicoteo, hoy | Pronounced like *oi* in *foil* |
| [ja] | ia, ya | envidia, adyacente | Pronounced like *ya* in *yard* |
| [je] | ie, ye | abierto, ayer | Pronounced like *ye* in *yellow* |
| [jo] | io, yo | aleatorio, apoyo | Pronounced like *Yo* in *York* |
| [ju] | iu, yu | ciudad, ayuda | Pronounced like *u* in *fuse* |
| [wa] | ua | adecuado | Pronounced like *wa* in *water* |
| [we] | ue | bueno, cuerda | Pronounced like *wa* in *wake* |
| [wi] | ui | ruido | Pronounced like *wee* in *week* |
| [wo] | uo | arduo | Pronounced like *uo* in *quote* |

## Triphthongs/Triptongos

| Symbol/ Símbolo | Graphic representation/ Representación gráfica | Examples/ Ejemplos | Notes/Notas |
|---|---|---|---|
| [jai] | iái | apreci**ái**s | Pronounced like *yi* in *yikes!* |
| [jei] | iéi | despreci**éi**s | Pronounced like the cheer *yay!* |
| [wai] | uay | Parag**uay** | Pronounced like *why* |
| [wie] | uey | b**uey** | Pronounced like *way* |

## Consonants/Consonantes

| Symbol/ Símbolo | Graphic representation/ Representación gráfica | Examples/ Ejemplos | Notes/Notas |
|---|---|---|---|
| [p] | p | **p**ato | |
| [b] | b, v | **v**acío, **b**ola, hom**b**re | *Used for b and v at the beginning of a word and for b following m.* |
| [β] | b, v | o**bj**eto, pue**b**lo, vi**v**ir | *Used for all positions except b and v at the beginning of a word and for b following m; pronounced like v in never and with both lips touching.* |
| [m] | m, n | ma**m**á | |
| [n] | n | **n**adie, e**n**tre | |
| [ɲ] | ñ | vi**ñ**a, **ñ**ácara | *Pronounced like ny in canyon.* |
| [f] | f | **f**abuloso, ca**f**é | |
| [k] | c, q, k | **c**asa, **c**osa, **C**uba, a**c**tual, **qu**e, **qu**inta, **k**ilo | *Used in the combinations c + a, o, u, c before a consonant and qu + e, i. Also used in a number of words of foreign origin beginning with k.* |
| [g] | g, gu | **g**arra, **g**obierno, **g**ubernamental, **gu**erra, **gu**ija, man**g**o | *Used at the beginning of a word or in the combinations g + a, o, u and gu + e, i. Also used in the middle of a word, preceded by n.* |
| [x] | j, g | **j**usto, ro**j**o, **g**irar, **g**ente, a**g**itar, Mé**x**ico | *Used for j and for the combinations g + e, i except at the end of a word; sometimes also used for x.* |

| Symbol/ Símbolo | Graphic representation/ Representación gráfica | Examples/ Ejemplos | Notes/Notas |
|---|---|---|---|
| [ɣ] | g, gu | paga, agosto, agua, alegre, estigma, alargar, | *Used in the combinations g + a, o, u and gu + e, i in the middle of a word and when not preceded by n.* |
| [t] | t | letra, tío | |
| [d] | d | dedo, conde, caldo | |
| [θ] | c, z | cero, cita, zarza, cruz | *Occurs in the combinations c + e, i as well as in z in all positions in ceceo pronunciation characteristic of Spain.* |
| [l] | l | libro, bloque, sal | |
| [ʎ] | ll | llueve, pollo | *Pronounced similarly to lli in million. Used for ll in all positions.* |
| [s] | s, c | sábado, así, coser, afueras, cebra, cierto, zarza, cruz | *Used for s in all positions; in seseo pronunciation characteristic of Spanish America: for c+e, i and for z in all positions.* |
| [r] | r | caro, prisa, vivir | *Used in the middle or at the end of a word when not preceded by n, l, s.* |
| [rr] | r, rr | roca, honrado | *Used for r when it occurs at the beginning of a word; also used for -rr- and -r- at the beginning of a syllable after n, l, s.* |
| [tʃ] | ch | chino, mucho | |
| [j] | y, ll | cónyuge, inyección, yunque, llueve, pollo | *Used when y occurs at the beginning of a syllable. Also used for ll in yeismo.* |
| [ʃ] | sh | shock | *Like English shock, show.* |
| [w] | u, w | adecuado, bueno, ruido, arduo, windsurf, whisky | *Used as the first element of the diphthongs wa, we, wi, wo; also in w or wh in some words of foreign origin.* |

# English phonetic symbols – Símbolos fonéticos del inglés

## Vowels/Vocales

| | |
|---|---|
| [a] | farm, not |
| [æ] | man, sad |
| [e] | bed, get, hair, dare |
| [ə] | ago, better, actor, anonymous, antivirus |
| [ɜ] | bird, her |
| [i] | beat, bee, me, belief, hobby |
| [ɪ] | it, wish, near |
| [ɔ] | all, law, long, sauce, floor |
| [u] | do, you, soon |
| [ʊ] | look, push, sure, tour |
| [ʌ] | but, son |
| [ã] | genre |

## Diphthongs/Diptongos

| | |
|---|---|
| [aɪ] | life, buy, by |
| [aʊ] | house, now |
| [eɪ] | lame, name |
| [ɔɪ] | boy, oil |
| [oʊ] | rope, piano, road, toe, show, plateau |
| [ju] | accuse, beauty |

## Consonants/Consonantes

| | |
|---|---|
| [b] | been, blind |
| [d] | do, had |
| [ð] | father, this |
| [dʒ] | cartridge, garbage, jam, object |
| [f] | father, wolf |
| [g] | beg, go |
| [h] | house |
| [j] | youth |
| [ʒ] | pleasure |
| [k] | keep, milk |
| [l] | ill, lamp, oil |
| [m] | am, man |
| [n] | manner, no |
| [ŋ] | long, sing, prank |
| [p] | happy, paper |
| [r] | dry, red, current, player, part |
| [s] | sand, stand, yes, cent, capacity |
| [ʃ] | ship, station, fish |
| [t] | fat, tell |
| [t] | butter, water |
| [θ] | death, thank |
| [tʃ] | catch, church |
| [v] | live, voice |
| [w] | water, we, which, will, wore |
| [z] | gaze, these, zeal |

## Signs/Otros símbolos

| | |
|---|---|
| ['] | primary stress |
| [,] | secondary stress |
| [·] | syllable division |

# A

**A, a** *f* (*letra*) A, a; **A de Antonio** A as in Alpha

**a** [a] *prep* **1.** (*dirección*) to; **ir ~ Caracas** to go to Caracas; **llegar ~ Santiago** to arrive in Santiago; **ir ~ casa de alguien** to go to sb's house; **ir ~ la escuela/~l cine** to go to school/to the movies **2.** (*posición*) at; **estar sentado ~ la mesa** to be sitting at the table; **~ la derecha** on the right; **~l sur** (**de**) to the south (of); **~l sol** in the sun **3.** (*distancia*) **~ 10 kilómetros de aquí** 10 kilometers (away) from here **4.** (*tiempo*) at; (*hasta*) until; **~ las tres** at three o'clock; **~ mediodía** at noon; **~ los veinte años** at (the age of) twenty; **~l poco rato** shortly after; **¿~ cuántos estamos?** what's the date? **5.** (*modo*) **~ pie** on foot; **~ mano** by hand; **~ oscuras** in the dark **6.** (*precio*) **¿~ cómo está?** how much is it?; **~ 2 pesos el kilo** (at) 2 pesos a [*o* per] kilo **7.** (*complemento (in)directo, con infinitivo*) to; **dio su fortuna ~ los pobres** he/she gave his/her fortune to the poor; **he visto ~ tu hermano** I've seen your brother; **empezó ~ correr** he/she began to run **8.** (*con verbo, expresiones*) **oler ~ gas** to smell of gas; **jugar ~ los dados** to play dice; **¡~ que llueve mañana!** I bet it'll rain tomorrow!; **~ Pedro le gusta mucho nadar, ¿~ que sí, Pedro?** Pedro likes swimming a lot. Don't you, Pedro?

**abacorar** [a·βa·ko·'rar] *vt AmL* to hound

**abad(esa)** [a·'βað, a·βa·'de·sa] *m(f)* abbot *m,* abbess *f*

**abadía** [a·βa·'di·a] *f* abbey

**abajeño, -a** [a·βa·'xe·ɲo, -a] *adj AmL* coastal

**abajo** [a·'βa·xo] *adv* **1.** (*movimiento*) down; **calle ~** down the street; **cuesta ~** downhill; **de arriba ~** from top to bottom **2.** (*estado*) down (below); (*en casa*) downstairs; **boca ~** face down; **hacia ~** down, downward; **de veinte para ~** twenty or under; **véase más ~** see below

**abalear** [a·βa·le·'ar] *vt Col* to shoot

**abandonar** [a·βan·do·'nar] **I.** *vt* **1.** (*dejar*) to leave; (*desamparar*) to abandon **2.** (*renunciar*) to give up **II.** *vr:* **~se** (*ir desaliñado*) to let oneself go

**abandono** [a·βan·'do·no] *m* **1.** (*abandonamiento*) abandonment **2.** (*renuncia*) renunciation; (*de una idea*) giving-up **3.** (*descuido*) neglect

**abanicar(se)** <c → qu> [a·βa·ni·'kar·(se)] *vt, (vr)* to fan (oneself)

**abanico** [a·βa·'ni·ko] *m* fan; **un ~ de posibilidades** a range of possibilities

**abaratar** [a·βa·ra·'tar] *vt* to make cheaper; (*precios*) to lower; **~ costes** to cut costs

**abarcar** <c → qu> [a·βar·'kar] *vt* (*comprender*) to include; **~ con la vista** to take in

**abarrotar** [a·βa·rro·'tar] *vt* **~ algo de algo** to pack sth with sth

**abarrote** [a·βa·'rro·te] *m Cuba, Méx* grocery store

**abarrotería** [a·βa·rro·te·'ri·a] *f* **1.** *AmL* (*ferretería*) hardware store **2.** *Guat* (*abacería*) retail grocery

**abastecer(se)** [a·βas·te·'ser·(se), -'θer·(se)] *irr como crecer vt, (vr)* **~(se) de** [*o* **con**] **algo** to provide (oneself) with sth

**abastero** [a·βas·'te·ro] *m Chile* (*de carne*) wholesale livestock dealer; *Méx* (*de artículos*) purveyor

**abasto** [a·'βas·to] *m* (*provisiones*) provisions *pl;* **no dar ~ con algo** to be unable to cope with sth

**abati** [a·βa·'ti] *m Arg, Par* (*maíz*) corn; (*bebida*) corn whisky

**abatible** [a·βa·'ti·βle] *adj* **asiento ~** folding chair

**abatido, -a** [a·βa·'ti·do, -a] *adj* dejected

**abatir** [a·βa·'tir] **I.** *vt* **1.** (*árbol*) to fell; (*avión, pájaro*) to shoot down **2.** (*desmontar*) to dismantle **II.** *vr:* **~se** to become dejected

**abdicación** [aβ·di·ka·'sjon, -'θjon] *f* abdication

**abdicar** <c → qu> [aβ·di·'kar] *vt* (*monarca*) to abdicate; (*ideales*) to renounce

**abdomen** [aβ·'do·men] *m* abdomen

**abdominal** [aβ·do·mi·'nal] **I.** *adj* abdominal **II.** *m DEP* sit-up

**abecé** [a·βe·'se, -'θe] *m* ABC, alphabet;

**no saber el** ~ to have no clue

**abecedario** [a·βe·se·'da·rjo, a·βe·θe-] *m* alphabet

**abedul** [a·βe·'dul] *m* BOT birch

**abeja** [a·'βe·xa] *f* bee

**abejorro** [a·βe·'xo·rro] *m* bumblebee
▶ **ser un** ~ to be a pain (in the neck)

**aberración** [a·βe·rra·'sjon, -'θjon] *f* 1. (*desviación*) aberration 2. (*disparate*) absurdity 3. *AmL* (*error*) mistake

**aberrante** [a·βe·'rran·te] *adj* aberrant

**abertura** [a·βer·'tu·ra] *f* 1. (*acción*) opening 2. (*hueco*) hole

**abeto** [a·'βe·to] *m* BOT fir; ~ **rojo** spruce

**abiertamente** [a·βjer·ta·'men·te] *adv* 1. (*francamente*) openly 2. (*patentemente*) clearly

**abierto, -a** [a·'βjer·to, -a] I. *pp de* **abrir** II. *adj* open; (*persona*) open-minded; ~ **a nuevas ideas** open to new ideas

**abismal** [a·βis·'mal] *adj* enormous

**abismo** [a·'βis·mo] *m* GEO abyss; **entre tus opiniones y las mías hay un** ~ there's a world of difference between our opinions

**abjurar** [aβ·xu·'rar] *vi, vt* ~ (**de**) **algo** to renounce sth

**ablandar** [a·βlan·'dar] I. *vt* (*poner blando*) to soften II. *vr:* ~**se** to soften; (*persona*) to relent

**abnegación** [aβ·ne·ɣa·'sjon, -'θjon] *f* self-denial; **con** ~ selflessly

**abnegado, -a** [aβ·ne·'ɣa·do, -a] *adj* selfless

**abochornar** [a·βo·tʃor·'nar] I. *vt* 1. (*calor*) to oppress 2. (*avergonzar*) to embarrass II. *vr* ~**se** to be embarrassed (**de** by)

**abofetear** [a·βo·fe·te·a'ar] *vt* to slap

**abogacía** [a·βo·ɣa·'si·a, -'θi·a] *f* legal profession; **ejercer la** ~ to practice law

**abogado, -a** [a·βo·'ɣa·do, -a] *m, f* 1. JUR lawyer; (*en tribunal*) attorney 2. (*defensor*) advocate

**abogar** <g → gu> [a·βo·'ɣar] *vi* ~ **por algo** to advocate sth

**abolición** [a·βo·li·'sjon, -'θjon] *f* abolition

**abolir** [a·βo·'lir] *irr vt* to abolish

**abolladura** [a·βo·ja·'du·ra, a·βo·ʎa-] *f* dent

**abollar** [a·βo·'jar, -'ʎar] *vt* to dent

**abombarse** [a·βom·'bar·se] *vr* 1. (*abultarse*) to bulge 2. *CSur, Ecua, Nic* (*alimentos*) to go bad

**abominable** [a·βo·mi·'na·βle] *adj* abominable

**abonado, -a** [a·βo·'na·do, -a] *m, f* (*a revistas*) subscriber

**abonar** [a·βo·'nar] I. *vt* 1. (*garantizar*) to guarantee 2. (*pagar*) to pay; ~ **en cuenta** to credit to an account 3. PREN to subscribe to II. *vr:* ~**se** to subscribe (**a** to)

**abono** [a·'βo·no] *m* 1. *t.* TEAT (*para el tren*) season ticket; ~ **mensual** monthly ticket 2. PREN subscription 3. (*pago*) payment; ~ **en cuenta** credit

**abordaje** [a·βor·'da·xe] *m* boarding; **tomar al** ~ to board

**abordar** [a·βor·'dar] *vt* 1. (*persona*) to approach 2. (*tema*) to discuss; (*problema*) to tackle

**aborigen** [a·βo·'ri·xen] I. *adj* aboriginal II. *mf* aborigine

**aborrecer** [a·βo·rre·'ser, -'θer] *irr como crecer vt* to loathe

**abortar** [a·βor·'tar] I. *vi* (*provocado*) to have an abortion; (*espontáneo*) to have a miscarriage II. *vt* to abort

**aborto** [a·'βor·to] *m* (*provocado*) abortion; (*espontáneo*) miscarriage

**abotonar** [a·βo·to·'nar] *vt* to button up

**abr.** *abr de* **abril** Apr.

**abra** ['a·βra] *f AmL* (*desmonte*) clearing

**abrasar** [a·βra·'sar] I. *vi* (*sol*) to scorch II. *vt* 1. (*quemar, dolor*) to burn; (*plantas*) to dry up 2. (*odio*) to consume III. *vr:* ~**se** to burn (up)

**abrasivo** [a·βra·'si·βo] *m* abrasive

**abrazar** <z → c> [a·βra·'sar, -'θar] I. *vt* 1. (*persona*) to embrace 2. (*contener*) to include II. *vr:* ~**se** to embrace (each other)

**abrazo** [a·'βra·so, -θo] *m* embrace; **dar un** ~ **a alguien** to give sb a hug; **un** (**fuerte**) ~ (*en cartas*) best regards

**abrebotellas** [a·βre·βo·'te·jas, -ʎas] *m inv* bottle opener

**abrecartas** [a·βre·'kar·tas] *m inv* letter opener

**abrelatas** [a·βre·'la·tas] *m inv* can opener

**abrevar** [a·βre·'βar] *vt* (*ganado*) to water

**abreviado, -a** [a·βre·'βja·ðo, -a] *adj* abridged

**abreviar** [a·βre·'βjar] **I.** *vt* **1.** (*acortar*) to shorten **2.** (*palabras*) to abbreviate **II.** *vi* to hurry

**abreviatura** [a·βre·βja·'tu·ɾa] *f* abbreviation

**abridor** [a·βri·'ðor] *m* opener

**abrigado, -a** [a·βri·'ɣa·ðo, -a] *adj* (*con ropa*) **estar ~** to be wrapped up warm

**abrigar** <g → gu> [a·βri·'ɣar] *vt* **1.** (*cubrir*) to cover **2.** (*esperanzas*) to cherish

**abrigo** [a·'βri·ɣo] *m* **1.** (*prenda*) coat; **de ~** warm **2.** (*refugio*) shelter; **al ~ de** protected by

**abril** [a·'βril] *m* April; *v. t.* **marzo**

**abrillantado, -a** [a·βri·jan·'ta·ðo, -a; a·βri·ʎan-] *adj* AmL shining; **fruta abrillantada** *Arg* glazed fruit

**abrillantar** [a·βri·jan·'tar, a·βri·ʎan-] *vt* to polish

**abrir** [a·'βrir] *irr* **I.** *vt* **1.** (*algo cerrado*) to open; (*paraguas*) to put up; (*grifo*) to turn on; (*con la llave*) to unlock; **~ de par en par** to open wide **2.** (*túnel*) to dig **3.** (*inaugurar*) to open; (*curso*) to begin ▶ **en un ~ y cerrar de ojos** in the blink of an eye **II.** *vr:* **~se 1.** (*puerta*) to open (**a** onto) **2.** (*confiar*) to confide **3.** *inf* (*irse*) to beat it

**abrochar** [a·βro·'tʃar] *vt* (*con broches*) to fasten; (*con botones*) to button (up); (*cinturón*) fasten

**abrumador(a)** [a·βru·ma·'ðor, -·'ðo·ɾa] *adj* (*agobiador*) overwhelming

**abrumar** [a·βru·'mar] *vt* to overwhelm

**abrupto, -a** [a·'βrup·to, -a] *adj* (*camino*) steep; (*carácter*) abrupt

**absentismo** [aβ·sen·'tis·mo] *m* absenteeism

**absolución** [aβ·so·lu·'sjon, -'θjon] *f* **1.** JUR acquittal **2.** REL absolution

**absolutamente** [aβ·so·lu·ta·'men·te] *adv* absolutely, completely; **~ nada** nothing at all

**absoluto, -a** [aβ·so·'lu·to, -a] *adj* absolute ▶ **en ~** not at all

**absolver** [aβ·sol·'βer] *irr como volver vt* **1.** JUR to acquit **2.** REL to absolve

**absorber** [aβ·sor·'βer] *vt* **1.** (*tierra*) *t.* FÍS to absorb **2.** (*cautivar*) to engross

**absorción** [aβ·sor·'sjon, -'θjon] *f* **1.** (*de líquidos*) *t.* FÍS absorption **2.** ECON takeover

**absorto, -a** [aβ·'sor·to, -a] *adj* **1.** (*pasmado*) amazed **2.** (*entregado*) absorbed

**abstemio, -a** [aβs·'te·mjo, -a] *adj* abstemious, teetotal

**abstención** [aβs·ten·'sjon, -'θjon] *f* *t.* POL abstention

**abstenerse** [aβs·te·'ner·se] *irr como tener vr* (*privarse de*) *t.* POL to abstain (**de** from); **~ del tabaco** to refrain from smoking

**abstinencia** [aβs·ti·'nen·sja, -θja] *f* abstinence; **síndrome de ~** withdrawal symptoms

**abstinente** [aβs·ti·'nen·te] *adj* abstinent

**abstracción** [aβs·trak·'sjon, -'θjon] *f* abstraction

**abstracto, -a** [aβs·'trak·to, -a] *adj* abstract

**abstraer** [aβs·tra·'er] *irr como traer* **I.** *vt* to abstract **II.** *vr* **~se en algo** to be absorbed in sth

**abstraído, -a** [aβs·tra·'i·ðo, -a] *adj* lost in thought; **estar ~ en algo** to be preoccupied by sth

**absurdo** [aβ·'sur·ðo] *m* absurdity

**absurdo, -a** [aβ·'sur·ðo, -a] *adj* absurd

**abuchear** [a·βu·tʃe·'ar] *vt* to boo; (*silbando*) to hiss

**abucheo** [a·βu·'tʃeo] *m* booing; (*silbidos*) hissing

**abuelo, -a** [a·'βwe·lo] *m, f* grandfather *m*, grandmother *f*; **los ~s** the grandparents

**abultado, -a** [a·βul·'ta·ðo, -a] *adj* bulky; (*labios*) thick

**abultar** [a·βul·'tar] **I.** *vi* to take up a lot of room **II.** *vt* *fig* (*exagerar*) to exaggerate

**abundancia** [a·βun·'dan·sja, -θja] *f* abundance; (*de bienes*) plenty; **en ~** in abundance; **vivir en la ~** to be affluent

**abundante** [a·βun·'dan·te] *adj* abundant; (*cosecha*) plentiful; **~ en algo** abounding in sth

**abundar** [a·βun·'dar] *vi* to abound; **~ en algo** to be rich in sth

**aburrido, -a** [a·βu·'rri·ðo, -a] *adj* **1.** *estar* (*harto*) bored (**de** with) **2.** *ser* (*pesado*) boring

**aburrimiento** [a·βu·rriˈmjen·to] *m* **1.** (*tedio*) boredom **2.** (*fastidio*) bore

**aburrir** [a·βuˈrrir] **I.** *vt* **1.** (*hastiar*) to bore **2.** (*fastidiar*) to tire **II.** *vr*: ~**se** to be bored

**abusar** [a·βuˈsar] *vi* **1.** (*usar mal*) ~ **de algo** to misuse sth; ~ **de su salud** to abuse one's health **2.** (*aprovecharse*) ~ **de alguien** to take (unfair) advantage of sb **3.** (*sexualmente*) ~ **de alguien** to sexually abuse sb

**abusivo, -a** [a·βuˈsi·βo, -a] *adj* improper; (*precios*) outrageous

**abuso** [a·ˈβu·so] *m* abuse

**acá** [aˈka] *adv* here; ~ **y allá** here and there; **para** ~ over here; **¡ven** ~**!** come here!

**acabado, -a** [a·kaˈβa·do, -a] *adj* (*completo, sin futuro*) finished

**acabar** [a·kaˈβar] **I.** *vi* **1.** (*terminar*) to end; ~ **bien/mal** to turn out well/badly; **ella acaba de llegar** she's just arrived; ~ **con algo** to finish sth off; ~ **con alguien** to settle with sb **2.** (*finalmente*) ~**ás por comprenderlo** you'll understand it in the end **II.** *vt* to finish; (*consumir*) to finish off **III.** *vr*: ~**se; la mantequilla se ha acabado** there's no butter left; **todo se acabó** it's all over; **¡se acabó!** and that's that!

**academia** [a·kaˈde·mja] *f* **1.** (*corporación*) academy **2.** (*colegio*) (private) school

**académico, -a** [a·kaˈde·mi·ko, -a] *adj* academic

**acaecer** [a·kaeˈser, -ˈθer] *irr como* **crecer** *vi* to happen

**acahual** [a·kaˈwal] *m Méx* sunflower

**acallar** [a·kaˈjar, -ˈʎar] *vt* **1.** (*hacer callar*) to silence **2.** (*apaciguar*) to pacify

**acalorado, -a** [a·ka·loˈra·do, -a] *adj* heated

**acalorarse** [a·ka·loˈrar·se] *vr* **1.** (*sofocarse*) to get hot **2.** (*apasionarse*) to get worked up (**con** over) **3.** (*enfadarse*) to get angry (**por** about)

**acampar** [a·kamˈpar] *vi* to camp

**acantilado** [a·kan·tiˈla·do] *m* cliff

**acantilado, -a** [a·kan·tiˈla·do, -a] *adj* steep

**acaparar** [a·ka·paˈrar] *vt* to hoard

**acapillar** [a·ka·piˈjar, -ˈʎar] *vt Méx* (*atrapar*) to seize

**acariciar** [a·ka·riˈsjar, -ˈθjar] *vt* **1.** (*persona*) to caress **2.** (*plan*) to toy with

**acarrear** [a·ka·rreˈar] *vt* **1.** (*transportar*) to transport **2.** (*ocasionar*) to cause

**acaso** [aˈka·so] **I.** *m* chance; **el** ~ **hizo que...** +*subj* as chance would have it... **II.** *adv* maybe ▶ **por si** ~ (*en caso de*) in case; (*en todo caso*) just in case

**acatar** [a·kaˈtar] *vt* **1.** (*respetar*) to respect **2.** (*obedecer*) to obey **3.** *Col, Guat, PRico* (*caer en cuenta*) to realize

**acatarrarse** [a·ka·taˈrrar·se] *vr* to catch a cold

**acceder** [ak·seˈder, ak·θeˈ-] *vi* **1.** (*consentir*) to agree (**a** to) **2.** (*tener acceso*) to gain access **3.** (*ascender*) to accede; ~ **a un cargo** to take office

**accesible** [ak·seˈsi·βle, ak·θeˈ-] *adj* **1.** (*persona*) approachable **2.** (*lugar*) accessible

**accésit** [akˈse·sit, aɣˈθeˈ-] *m inv* consolation prize

**acceso** [akˈse·so, aɣˈθeˈso] *m* **1.** (*a un lugar*) *t.* COMPUT access; **de fácil** ~ (easily) accessible; **libre** ~ open access **2.** (*ataque*) attack

**accesorio** [ak·seˈso·rjo, aɣ·θeˈ-] *m* (*utensilio*) implement

**accesorio, -a** [ak·seˈso·rjo, -a; aɣ·θeˈ-] *adj* accessory

**accidentado, -a** [ak·si·denˈta·do, -a; aɣ·θiˈ-] **I.** *adj* rugged **II.** *m, f* accident victim

**accidental** [ak·si·denˈtal, aɣ·θiˈ-] *adj* **1.** (*no esencial*) incidental **2.** (*casual*) casual

**accidentarse** [ak·si·denˈtar·se, aɣ·θiˈ-] *vr* to have an accident

**accidente** [ak·si·denˈte, aɣ·θiˈ-] *m* **1.** (*suceso*) accident; **por** ~ by accident; **sufrir un** ~ to have an accident **2.** ~**s geográficos** geographical features

**acción** [akˈsjon, aɣˈθjon] *f* **1.** (*acto*) act; **un hombre de** ~ a man of action; **entrar en** ~ to go into action; **poner en** ~ to put into action **2.** (*influencia*) *t.* MIL, JUR action **3.** FIN share; ~ **común** common share

**accionar** [ak·sjoˈnar, aɣ·θjoˈ-] *vt* TÉC to

operate

**accionista** [akˈsjoˈnisˌta, aɣˈθjo-] *mf* shareholder

**acebo** [aˈseˌβo, aˈθe-] *m* holly

**acechar** [aˈseˌtʃar, aˈθe-] *vt* **1.** (*espiar*) to spy on **2.** (*esperar*) to lie in wait for

**acecho** [aˈseˌtʃo, aˈθe-] *m* spying; **estar al ~** to lie in wait

**aceite** [aˈseiˌte, aˈθei-] *m* oil; **~ comestible** cooking oil ▶ **echar ~ al fuego** to add fuel to the flames

**aceitoso, -a** [aseiˈtoˌso, -a; aθei-] *adj* oily

**aceituna** [aseiˈtuˌna, aθei-] *f* olive

**aceleración** [aseˌleraˈsjon, aˌθeˌleˌraˈθjon] *f* acceleration

**acelerador** [aseˌleraˈdor, aˌθe-] *m* gas pedal; **pisar el ~** to step on the gas

**acelerar** [aseˌleˈrar, aˌθe-] *vt, vi* to accelerate; **¡no aceleres tanto!** don't go so fast!

**acelga** [aˈselˌɣa, aˈθel-] *f* BOT Swiss chard

**acento** [aˈsenˌto, -ˈθenˌto] *m* **1.** LING (*prosódico*) stress **2.** LING (*signo*) accent **3.** (*pronunciación*) accent

**acentuación** [asenˌtwaˈsjon, aˌθenˌtwaˈθjon] *f* (*prosódica*) stress; (*ortográfica*) accentuation

**acentuado, -a** [asenˈtuˌaˌdo, -a; aˌθenˈ-] *adj* **1.** (*al pronunciar*) stressed; (*al escribir*) with an accent **2.** (*marcado*) marked

**acentuar** <*1. pres* acentúo> [asenˈtuˌar, aˌθen-] *vt* **1.** (*al pronunciar*) to stress; (*al escribir*) to write with an accent **2.** (*resaltar*) to highlight

**acepción** [asepˈsjon, aˌθepˈθjon] *f* sense, meaning

**aceptable** [asepˈtaˌβle, aˌθep-] *adj* acceptable

**aceptación** [asepˌtaˈsjon, aˌθepˌtaˈθjon] *f* (*aprobación*) approval

**aceptado** [asepˈtaˌdo, aˌθep-] *interj AmL* (*vale*) OK

**aceptar** [asepˈtar, aˌθep-] *vt* **1.** (*recibir*) to accept **2.** (*aprobar*) to approve

**acequia** [aˈseˌkja, aˈθe-] *f* irrigation ditch

**acera** [aˈseˌra, -ˈθeˌra] *f* sidewalk

**acerca** [aˈserˌka, aˈθer-] *prep* **~ de** (*sobre*) about

**acercamiento** [aserˌkaˈmjenˌto, aˈθer-] *m* approach

**acercar** <*c → qu*> [aserˈkar, aˌθer-] **I.** *vt* **1.** (*poner cerca*) to bring nearer; (*traer*) to bring over **2.** *inf* (*llevar*) to take, to bring **II.** *vr* **~se a alguien/algo** to approach sb/sth

**acero** [aˈseˌro, -ˈθeˌro] *m* steel

**acertado, -a** [aserˈtaˌdo, -a; aˌθer-] *adj* (*atinado*) accurate

**acertar** <*e → ie*> [aserˈtar, aˌθer-] **I.** *vi* **1.** (*dar*) to hit; **~ el blanco** to hit the mark **2.** (*hacer con acierto*) to be right **II.** *vt* **1.** (*dar en el blanco*) to hit **2.** (*adivinar*) to get right

**acertijo** [aserˈtiˌxo, aˌθer-] *m* riddle

**acetona** [aseˈtoˌna, aˌθe-] *f* acetone

**achacoso, -a** [aˌtʃaˈkoˌso, -a] *adj* sickly; **estar ~** to be ailing

**achaque** [aˈtʃaˌke] *m* ailment

**achicar** <*c → qu*> [aˌtʃiˈkar] **I.** *vt* **1.** (*empequeñecer*) to make smaller; (*persona*) to intimidate **2.** (*agua*) to bale out **II.** *vr:* **~se 1.** (*empequeñecerse*) to become smaller **2.** (*persona*) to take fright

**achicharrar** [aˌtʃiˈtʃaˈrrar] **I.** *vt* **1.** (*calor*) to scorch **2.** (*comida*) to burn **II.** *vr:* **~se 1.** (*comida*) to get burnt **2.** (*persona*) to be sweltering

**achichiguar** [aˌtʃiˈtʃiˈɣwar] *vt Méx* (*malcriar*) to spoil

**achicoria** [aˌtʃiˈkoˌrja] *f* chicory

**achinado, -a** [aˌtʃiˈnaˌdo, -a] *adj* (*rasgos*) oriental

**achiote** [aˈtʃjoˌte] *m AmC, Bol, Méx* **1.** BOT annatto tree **2.** (*pigmento*) annatto

**achipolarse** [aˌtʃiˈpoˈlarˌse] *vr Méx* (*personas*) to grow sad

**achiquillado, -a** [aˌtʃiˈkiˈjaˌdo, -a; ˈʎaˌdo, -a] *adj* **1.** *Méx* (*infantil*) childish **2.** *Chile* (*aniñado*) boyish

**achira** [aˈtʃiˌra] *f AmS* BOT canna

**achís** [aˈtʃis] *interj* atchoo

**acholado, -a** [aˈtʃoˈlaˌdo, -a] *adj CSur, Perú, Bol* **1.** (*mestizo*) mestizo **2.** (*acobardado*) intimidated

**acholar** [aˈtʃoˈlar] **I.** *vt Chile, Perú, Bol* (*avergonzar*) to embarrass **II.** *vr:* **~se** *CSur, Perú, Bol* to become intimidated

**achucutado, -a** [a·tʃu·ku·'ta·do, -a] *adj AmL* (*abatido*) depressed

**achumarse** [a·tʃu·'mar·se] *vr Ecua* to get drunk

**achunchar** [a·tʃun·'tʃar] *vt AmL* to humiliate

**acicalarse** [a·si·ka·'lar·se, a·θi-] *vr* to get dressed up

**acidez** [a·si·'des, a·θi·'deθ] *f* acidity; **~ de estómago** MED heartburn

**ácido** ['a·si·do, 'a·θi-] *m t.* QUÍM acid

**ácido, -a** ['a·si·do, -a; 'a·θi-] *adj* **1.** (*agrio*) tart; QUÍM acidic **2.** (*tono*) harsh

**acierto** [a·'sjer·to, a·'θjer-] *m* **1.** (*en el tiro*) accuracy **2.** (*éxito*) success

**acitrón** [a·si·'tron, a·θi-] *m Méx* CULIN candied citron

**aclamación** [a·kla·ma·'sjon, -'θjon] *f* applause

**aclamar** [a·kla·'mar] *vt* to cheer

**aclaración** [a·kla·ra·'sjon, -'θjon] *f* **1.** (*clarificación*) clarification **2.** (*explicación*) explanation

**aclarar** [a·kla·'rar] **I.** *vt* **1.** (*hacer más claro*) to lighten; (*la ropa*) to rinse; **~ la voz** to clear one's throat **2.** (*explicar*) to explain **II.** *vr:* **~se** to be clarified; *inf* (*entender*) to catch on

**aclaratorio, -a** [a·kla·ra·'to·rjo, -a] *adj* explanatory

**acné** [ay·'ne] *m o f* acne

**acobardar** [a·ko·βar·'dar] **I.** *vt* to frighten **II.** *vr:* **~se** (*intimidarse*) to be frightened

**acogedor(a)** [a·ko·xe·'dor, -·'do·ra] *adj* welcoming, inviting

**acoger** <g → j> [a·ko·'xer] *vt* to welcome; (*recibir*) to receive

**acogida** [a·ko·'xi·da] *f* welcome; (*recibimiento*) reception

**acojonado, -a** [a·ko·xo·'na·do, -a] *adj vulg* (*asustado*) scared shitless

**acojonante** [a·ko·xo·'nan·te] *adj vulg* (*fantástico, impresionante*) nasty *sl*

**acojonar** [a·ko·xo·'nar] **I.** *vt vulg* **1.** (*asustar*) to scare the shit out of (sb) **2.** (*impresionar*) to impress **II.** *vr:* **~se** *vulg* (*asustarse*) to be scared shitless; (*acobardarse*) to back down

**acometer** [a·ko·me·'ter] **I.** *vi* to attack **II.** *vt* **1.** (*embestir*) to attack **2.** (*emprender*) to undertake

**acomodado, -a** [a·ko·mo·'da·do, -a] *adj* well-off

**acomodador(a)** [a·ko·mo·da·'dor, -·'do·ra] *m(f)* CINE usher

**acomodar** [a·ko·mo·'dar] **I.** *vt* **1.** (*adaptar*) to adapt **2.** (*colocar*) to place **3.** (*albergar*) to accommodate **II.** *vr:* **~se 1.** (*adaptarse*) to adapt oneself **2.** (*ponerse cómodo*) to make oneself comfortable

**acomodo** [a·ko·'mo·do] *m* **1.** (*arreglo*) arrangement **2.** (*acuerdo*) agreement

**acompañado, -a** [a·kom·pa·'ɲa·do, -a] *adj* accompanied

**acompañante** [a·kom·pa·'ɲan·te] *mf* (*de una dama*) escort; (*en el coche*) passenger

**acompañar** [a·kom·pa·'ɲar] *vt* **1.** (*ir con*) *t.* MÚS to accompany; **~ a alguien a casa** to see sb home **2.** (*hacer compañía*) **~ a alguien** to keep sb company

**acompasado, -a** [a·kom·pa·'sa·do, -a] *adj* MÚS rhythmic

**acomplejado, -a** [a·kom·ple·'xa·do, -a] *adj* full of complexes

**acomplejar** [a·kom·ple·'xar] **I.** *vt* to give (sb) a complex **II.** *vr:* **~se** to get a complex

**aconchar** [a·kon·'tʃar] **I.** *vt Méx* to tell (sb) off **II.** *vr:* **~se** *Chile, Perú* (*sedimentarse*) to settle

**acondicionado, -a** [a·kon·di·sjo·'na·do, -a; -θjo·'na·do, -a] *adj* **bien/mal ~** in good/bad condition

**acondicionar** [a·kon·di·sjo·'nar, -θjo·'nar] *vt* **1.** (*preparar*) to prepare **2.** (*climatizar*) to air-condition

**acongojar** [a·kon·go·'xar] *vt* to distress

**aconsejable** [a·kon·se·'xa·βle] *adj* advisable

**aconsejar** [a·kon·se·'xar] *vt* to advise; **~ algo a alguien** to recommend sth to sb

**acontecer** [a·kon·te·'ser, -'θer] *irr como crecer vi* to happen

**acontecimiento** [a·kon·te·si·'mjen·to, a·kon·te·θi-] *m* event

**acopio** [a·'ko·pjo] *m* store; **hacer ~ de algo** to stock up on sth

**acoplar** [a·ko·'plar] *vt* **1.** (*juntar*) to join **2.** (*piezas*) to fit together **3.** ELEC to connect

**acorazar** <z → c> [a·ko·ra·'sar, -'θar] *vt* to armor-plate

**acordar** <o → ue> [a·kor·'dar] I. *vt* 1. (*convenir*) to agree 2. (*decidir*) to decide II. *vr* ~**se de algo/alguien** to remember sth/sb; **¡acuérdate de decírselo!** remember to tell him/her!

**acorde** [a·'kor·de] I. *adj* agreed; **estar ~ con alguien** to be in agreement with sb; **~ con el medio ambiente** in keeping with the environment II. *m* MÚS chord

**acordeón** [a·kor·de·'on] *m* accordion

**acorralar** [a·ko·rra·'lar] *vt* 1. (*ganado*) to round up 2. (*rodear*) to corner

**acortar** [a·kor·'tar] I. *vt* to shorten; (*duración*) to cut down; **~ camino** to take a short cut II. *vr:* ~**se** to get shorter

**acosar** [a·ko·'sar] *vt* 1. (*perseguir*) to hound 2. (*asediar*) to harass; **~ a alguien a preguntas** to pester sb with questions

**acoso** [a·'ko·so] *m* relentless pursuit; *fig* harassment

**acostar** <o → ue> [a·kos·'tar] I. *vt* to put to bed II. *vr:* ~**se** 1. (*descansar*) to lie down; **estar acostado** to be lying down 2. (*ir a la cama*) to go to bed; ~**se con alguien** to go to bed with sb

**acostumbrado, -a** [a·kos·tum·'bra·do, -a] *adj* accustomed; **mal ~** spoiled

**acostumbrar** [a·kos·tum·'brar] I. *vi* ~ **a hacer algo** to be used to doing sth II. *vr:* ~**se a algo** to get used to sth

**acotación** [a·ko·ta·'sjon, -'θjon] *f* (*cota*) elevation mark

**acre** ['a·kre] *m* acre

**acreditado, -a** [a·kre·di·'ta·do, -a] *adj* reputable

**acreditar** [a·kre·di·'tar] *vt* 1. (*atestiguar*) to vouch for 2. (*autorizar*) to authorize 3. (*dar reputación*) to do credit

**acreedor(a)** [a·kre·e·'dor/a·kre·e·'dor, ·'do·ra] I. *adj* **hacerse ~ a** [o **de**] **algo** to be worthy of sth II. *m(f)* FIN creditor

**acribillar** [a·kri·βi·'jar, -'ʎar] *vt* to riddle (**a** with)

**acrílico, -a** [a·'kri·li·ko, -a] *adj* acrylic

**acriollarse** [a·krjo·'jar·se, -'ʎar·se] *vr AmL* to go native

**acrobacia** [a·kro·'βa·sja, -θja] *f* acrobatics *pl*

**acróbata** [a·'kro·βa·ta] *mf* acrobat

**acrónimo** [a·'kro·ni·mo] *m* acronym

**acta** ['ak·ta] *f* (*de una reunión*) minutes *pl*; **hacer constar en ~** to record in the minutes

**actitud** [ak·ti·'tud] *f* 1. (*corporal*) posture 2. (*disposición*) attitude 3. (*comportamiento*) behavior

**activamente** [ak·ti·βa·'men·te] *adv* actively

**activar** [ak·ti·'βar] *vt* 1. (*avivar*) to stimulate 2. QUÍM, COMPUT to activate

**actividad** [ak·ti·βi·'dad] *f* activity; (*ocupación*) occupation; **~ profesional** profession; **entrar en ~** to become active

**activo** [ak·'ti·βo] *m* FIN assets *pl*; **~ circulante/fijo** current/fixed assets

**activo, -a** [ak·'ti·βo, -a] *adj* active; (*medicamento*) effective

**acto** ['ak·to] *m* 1. (*acción*) action; **hacer ~ de presencia** to put in an appearance 2. (*ceremonia*) ceremony; **~ conmemorativo** commemoration 3. TEAT act ▶ **~ seguido...** immediately after...; **en el ~** immediately, on the spot

**actor, actriz** [ak·'tor, ak·'tris, -'triθ] *m, f* actor *m*, actress *f*; **~ de cine** film actor

**actor(a)** [ak·'tor, ·'to·ra] *m(f)* plaintiff

**actuación** [ak·twa·'sjon, -'θjon] *f* 1. (*conducta*) conduct; **la ~ de la policía** the police action 2. TEAT performance; **~ en directo** live performance

**actual** [ak·tu·'al] *adj* (*de ahora*) present; (*corriente*) current

**actualidad** [ak·twa·li·dad] *f* present; **en la ~** at present; **de ~** topical

**actualizar** <z → c> [ak·twa·li·'sar, -'θar] *vt* to update

**actualmente** [ak·twal·'men·te] *adv* at the moment, currently

**actuar** <*1. pres* actúo> [ak·tu·'ar] *vi* 1. (*hacer*) to work 2. (*tener efecto*) **~ sobre algo** to have an effect on sth 3. TEAT to act

**acuache** [a·'kwa·tʃe] *m Méx* (*compinche*) pal

**acuarela** [a·kwa·'re·la] *f* watercolor

**acuario** [a·'kwa·rjo] *m* aquarium

**Acuario** [a·'kwa·rjo] *m* ASTR Aquarius

**acuático, -a** [a·'kwa·ti·ko, -a] *adj* aquatic; **parque ~** water park

**acuchamarse** [a·ku·tʃa·'mar·se] *vr Ven* (*entristecerse*) to get depressed

**acuchillar** [a·ku·tʃi·'jar, -'ʎar] *vt* (*herir*) to knife; (*matar*) to stab to death

**acudir** [a·ku·'dir] *vi* to go; **~ a una cita** to keep an appointment; **~ a** (*recurrir*) to turn to

**acueducto** [a·kwe·'duk·to] *m* aqueduct

**acuerdo** [a·'kwer·do] *m* **1.** (*convenio*) t. POL agreement; **llegar a un ~** to reach an agreement; **estar de ~ con alguien** to agree with sb; **ponerse de ~** to come to an agreement; **de común ~** by mutual consent **2.** (*decisión*) decision; **tomar un ~** to pass a resolution ▶ **¡de ~!** I agree!, OK!; **de ~ con** in accordance with

**acuerpado, -a** [a·kwer·'pa·do, -a] *adj Bol* (*corpulento*) hefty

**acullicar** [a·ku·ji·'kar, -ʎi·'kar] *vi Arg, Bol, Chile, Perú* to chew coca leaves

**acumuchar** [a·ku·mu·'tʃar] *vt Chile* to pile up

**acumulación** [a·ku·mu·la·'sjon, -'θjon] *f* accumulation; (*de cosas reunidas*) collection

**acumular** [a·ku·mu·'lar] *vt* **1.** (*reunir*) to collect **2.** (*amontonar*) to accumulate

**acunar** [a·ku·'nar] *vt* to rock (to sleep)

**acuñar** [a·ku·'ɲar] *vt* (*monedas*) to mint; (*palabras*) to coin

**acupuntura** [a·ku·pun·'tu·ra] *f* acupuncture

**acurrucarse** <c → qu> [a·ku·rru·'kar·se] *vr* to curl up; (*por el frío*) to huddle up

**acusación** [a·ku·sa·'sjon, -'θjon] *f* **1.** (*inculpación*) accusation **2.** JUR (*en juicio*) charge; (*escrito*) indictment

**acusado, -a** [a·ku·'sa·do, -a] **I.** *adj* (*claro*) pronounced; (*marcado*) marked **II.** *m, f* accused

**acusar** [a·ku·'sar] *vt* **1.** (*culpar*) to accuse (*de* of) **2.** (*en juicio*) to charge **3.** ECON to confirm; **~ recibo de un pedido** to acknowledge receipt of an order

**acusativo** [a·ku·sa·'ti·βo] *m* LING accusative

**acuse** [a·'ku·se] *m* **~ de recibo** acknowledgement of receipt

**acústica** [a·'kus·ti·ka] *f* **1.** (*ciencia*) acoustics + *sing vb* **2.** (*de un sitio*) acoustics + *pl vb*

**acústico, -a** [a·'kus·ti·ko, -a] *adj* acoustic

**acutí** [a·ku·'ti] *m Arg, Par, Urug* ZOOL agouti

**adaptable** [a·dap·'ta·βle] *adj* adaptable

**adaptación** [a·dap·ta·'sjon, -'θjon] *f* adaptation; **la ~ de una obra de teatro al cine** the film version of a play

**adaptador** [a·dap·ta·'dor] *m* TÉC adapter

**adaptar** [a·dap·'tar] **I.** *vt* **1.** (*acomodar*) t. LIT to adapt; **bien adaptado al grupo** well adapted to the group; **~ una novela a la pantalla** to adapt a novel for the screen **2.** (*ajustar*) to adjust; **~ algo a algo** to adapt sth to sth **II.** *vr:* **~se** to adapt

**adecuado, -a** [a·de·'kwa·do, -a] *adj* **1.** (*apto*) appropriate **2.** (*palabras*) fitting

**adecuar** [a·de·'kwar] *vt, vr:* **~se** to adapt

**a. de (J)C.** ['an·tes de (xe·su)·'kris·to] *abr de* **antes de (Jesu)cristo** BC

**adelantado, -a** [a·de·lan·'ta·do, -a] *adj* (*avanzado*) advanced ▶ **por ~** in advance

**adelantamiento** [a·de·lan·ta·'mjen·to] *m* (*del coche*) passing; **realizar un ~** to pass

**adelantar** [a·de·lan·'tar] **I.** *vi* **1.** (*progresar*) to progress; **no adelanto nada en francés** I'm not making any progress in French **2.** (*coche*) to pass **II.** *vt* **1.** (*reloj*) to put forward **2.** (*avanzar*) to move forward; **~ unos pasos** to go forward a few steps **3.** (*coche*) to pass **4.** (*viaje*) to bring forward **5.** (*paga*) to advance **6.** (*ganar*) to gain; **¿qué adelantas con esto?** where does that get you? **III.** *vr:* **~se** (*reloj*) to be fast

**adelante** [a·de·'lan·te] *adv* forward, ahead; **llevar un plan ~** to carry forward a plan; **sacar una familia ~** to provide for a family; **¡~!** come in!; **seguir ~** to go (straight) ahead; **véase más ~** see below

**adelanto** [a·de·'lan·to] *m* progress; (*anticipo*) advance; **~s técnicos** technical innovations

**adelgazar** <z → c> [a·del·ɣa·'sar, -'θar] *vi* to lose weight

**ademán** [a·de·'man] *m* gesture; **hacer ~**

**de salir** to make as if to leave

**además** [a·de·'mas] *adv* besides, moreover

**adentrarse** [a·den·'trar·se] *vr* (*tema*) to study thoroughly; ~ **en algo** to go into sth; (*penetrar*) to penetrate into sth

**adentro** [a·'den·tro] *adv* inside; **mar** ~ out to sea; **el grito le salió de muy** ~ his/her cry came from deep within

**adentros** [a·'den·tros] *mpl* innermost being; **para sus** ~ inwardly; **guardar algo para sus** ~ to keep sth to oneself

**adepto, -a** [a·'dep·to, -a] *m, f* supporter

**aderezar** <z → c> [a·de·re·'sar, -'θar] *vt* 1. (*preparar*) to prepare 2. (*condimentar*) to season; (*ensalada*) to dress

**adeudar** [a·deu·'dar] *vr*: ~**se** to run into debt

**adherir** [a·de·'rir] *irr como sentir* I. *vt* to stick II. *vr*: ~**se** (*pegarse*) to adhere

**adhesión** [a·de·'sjon] *f* 1. (*adherencia*) adhesion 2. (*a una opinión*) adherence, support; ~ **a alguien** support of sb; ~ **a algo** membership in sth

**adhesivo** [a·de·'si·βo] *m* 1. (*sustancia*) adhesive 2. (*pegatina*) sticker

**adhesivo, -a** [a·de·'si·βo, -a] *adj* adhesive

**adicción** [a·dik·'sjon, -a·diɣ·'θjon] *f* addiction; ~ **a las drogas** drug addiction

**adición** [a·di·'sjon, -'θjon] *f t.* MAT addition

**adicional** [a·di·sjo·'nal, -θjo·'nal] *adj* additional

**adicto, -a** [a·'dik·to, -a] I. *adj* addicted; ~ **a las drogas** addicted to drugs II. *m, f* addict

**adiestrar** [a·djes·'trar] *vt* to train

**adinerado, -a** [a·di·ne·'ra·do, -a] *adj* wealthy

**adiós** [a·'djos] I. *interj* (*despedida*) goodbye, bye II. *m* farewell; **decir** ~ **a alguien** to say goodbye to sb

**aditivo** [a·di·'ti·βo] *m* additive

**adivinanza** [a·di·βi·'nan·sa, -θa] *f* riddle

**adivinar** [a·di·βi·'nar] *vt* 1. (*el futuro*) to foretell 2. (*conjeturar*) to guess; **¡adivina cuántos años tengo!** guess how old I am!

**adjetivo** [ad·xe·'ti·βo] *m* adjective; ~ **numeral** numeral

**adjudicar** <c → qu> [ad·xu·di·'kar] I. *vt* (*premio*) to award II. *vr*: ~**se** to appropriate; (*premio*) to win

**adjuntar** [ad·xun·'tar] *vt* to enclose

**adjunto, -a** [ad·'xun·to, -a] *adj* 1. (*junto*) enclosed 2. (*auxiliar*) assistant; **profesor(a)** ~ UNIV associate professor

**administración** [ad·mi·nis·tra·'sjon, -'θjon] *f* 1. (*gestión*) administration; **la** ~ **española** the Spanish authorities; ~ **de una cuenta** managing of an account; ~ **municipal** town/city council 2. (*de medicamentos*) administering 3. *Arg* (*gobierno*) government

**administrador(a)** [ad·mi·nis·tra·'dor] *m(f)* administrator; (*gerente*) manager

**administrar** [ad·mi·nis·'trar] *vt* 1. (*dirigir*) administer; ~ **justicia** to dispense justice 2. (*racionar*) to ration 3. (*medicamentos*) to administer

**administrativo, -a** [ad·mi·nis·tra·'ti·βo, -a] I. *adj* administrative II. *m, f* clerk

**admirable** [ad·mi·'ra·βle] *adj* admirable

**admiración** [ad·mi·ra·'sjon, -'θjon] *f* 1. (*respeto*) admiration 2. (*asombro*) amazement 3. (*signo*) exclamation point

**admirado, -a** [ad·mi·'ra·do, -a] *adj* amazed

**admirador(a)** [ad·mi·ra·'dor, -·'do·ra] *m(f)* admirer

**admirar** [ad·mi·'rar] *vt* 1. (*adorar*) to admire 2. (*asombrar*) to amaze

**admisible** [ad·mi·'si·βle] *adj* admissible

**admisión** [ad·mi·'sjon] *f* ~ **en algo** admission [*o* acceptance] to sth

**admitir** [ad·mi·'tir] *vt* 1. (*aceptar*) to accept 2. (*reconocer*) to recognize 3. (*permitir*) to permit; ~ **una queja** JUR to accept a complaint

**ADN** [a·de·'e·ne] *m abr de* **ácido desoxirribonucleico** DNA

**adobar** [a·do·'βar] *vt* (*con salsa*) to marinate; (*carne*) to pickle

**adobe** [a·'do·βe] *m* adobe

**adolecer** [a·do·le·'ser, -'θer] *irr como crecer vi* (*enfermar*) to get sick; (*padecer*) to suffer; **este chico adolece de falta de imaginación** this boy suffers from a lack of imagination

**adolescencia** [a·do·les·'sen·sja, -'θen·θja] *f* adolescence

**adolescente** [a·do·les·'sen·te, -'θen·te]
I. *adj* adolescent II. *mf* teenager

**adonde** [a·'don·de] *adv* where; **el pueblo
~ iremos es muy bonito** the village
we'll go to is very pretty

**adónde** [a·'don·de] *adv* (*interrogativo*)
where

**adopción** [a·dop·'sjon, -'θjon] *f* adoption

**adoptar** [a·dop·'tar] *vt* to adopt

**adoptivo, -a** [a·dop·'ti·βo, -a] *adj* adopted, foster

**adoquín** [a·do·'kin] *m* cobblestone

**adorable** [a·do·'ra·βle] *adj* adorable

**adorar** [a·do·'rar] *vt* to adore

**adormecer** [a·dor·me·'ser, -'θer] *irr como
crecer* I. *vt* to make sleepy; (*dolor*) to
numb II. *vr*: **~se** to fall asleep

**adormilarse** [a·dor·mi·'lar·se] *vr* to doze

**adornar** [a·dor·'nar] I. *vt* to adorn [*o* to
decorate] II. *vr*: **~se** to adorn oneself

**adorno** [a·'dor·no] *m* adornment; **árbol
de ~** ornamental tree; **la lámpara sólo
está de ~** the lamp is just for decoration;
**estar de ~** *fig* to be for show

**adosado, -a** [a·do·'sa·do, -a] *adj* **casa
adosada** duplex

**adquirir** [ad·ki·'rir] *irr vt* **1.** (*conseguir*) to
acquire; **~ un hábito** to acquire a habit
**2.** (*comprar*) to purchase

**adquisición** [ad·ki·si·'sjon, -'θjon] *f* acquisition; **este coche es una buena ~**
this car is a good buy

**adquisitivo, -a** [ad·ki·si·'ti·βo, -a] *adj* ac-
quisitive; **poder ~** purchasing power

**adrede** [a·'dre·de] *adv* on purpose

**adrenalina** [a·dre·na·'li·na] *f* adrenalin

**Adriático** [a·'drja·ti·ko] *m* GEO Adriatic

**adscribir** [ads·kri·'βir] *irr como escribir*
*vt* to appoint

**aduana** [a·'dwa·na] *f* **1.** (*tasa*) customs
duty; **declaración de ~s** customs declaration; **despacho de ~** customs clearance; **sin ~** duty-free **2.** (*oficina*) customs office

**aduanero, -a** [a·dwa·'ne·ro, -a] I. *adj*
customs *fin* II. *m, f* customs officer

**adulador(a)** [a·du·la·'dor, --'do·ra] *adj*
flattering

**adular** [a·du·'lar] *vt* to flatter

**adulterar** [a·dul·te·'rar] *vt* to falsify; (*alimentos*) to adulterate

**adulterio** [a·dul·'te·rjo] *m* adultery

**adúltero, -a** [a·'dul·te·ro, -a] I. *adj* adulterous II. *m, f* adulterer

**adulto, -a** [a·'dul·to, -a] *adj, m, f* adult

**adverbial** [ad·βer·'βjal] *adj* adverbial

**adverbio** [ad·'βer·βjo] *m* adverb; **~ de
modo/de lugar/de tiempo** adverb of
manner/of place/of time

**adversario, -a** [ad·βer·'sa·rjo, -a] *m, f*
opponent

**adversidad** [ad·βer·si·'dad] *f* **1.** (*contrariedad*) adversity **2.** (*desgracia*) setback

**adverso, -a** [ad·'βer·so, -a] *adj* adverse;
(*clima*) harsh

**advertencia** [ad·βer·'ten·sja, -θja] *f*
**1.** (*amonestación*) warning **2.** (*indicación*) advice

**advertir** [ad·βer·'tir] *irr como sentir vt*
**1.** (*reparar*) to notice; **advirtió mis
intenciones** he/she guessed my intentions **2.** (*indicar*) to point out **3.** (*avisar*) to warn; **~ algo** to draw attention
to sth

**adyacencia** [ad·ja·'sen·sja, -'θen·θja] *f*
*RíoPl* (*proximidad*) proximity; **en las
~s** in the vicinity

**adyacente** [ad·ja·'sen·te, -'θen·te] *adj*
adjacent

**aéreo, -a** [a·'e·reo, -a] *adj* aerial; **base aérea** MIL airbase; **compañía aérea** airline
(company); **por vía aérea** (by) airmail

**aeróbic** [ae·'ro·βik] *m* aerobics + *sing
or pl vb*

**aerodinámico, -a** [ae·ro·di·'na·mi·ko,
-a] *adj* aerodynamic; (*vehículo*) streamlined

**aerolínea** [ae·ro·'li·nea] *f* airline

**aeroplano** [ae·ro·'pla·no] *m* airplane

**aeropuerto** [ae·ro·'pwer·to] *m* airport

**aerosol** [ae·ro·'sol] *m* aerosol; (*espray*)
spray

**afable** [a·'fa·βle] *adj* affable

**afamado, -a** [a·fa·'ma·do, -a] *adj* famous

**afán** [a·'fan] *m* **1.** (*ahínco*) eagerness; **~
de algo** urge for sth; **~ de lucro** profit
motive; **poner mucho ~ en algo** to put
a lot of effort into sth **2.** (*anhelo*) **~ de
algo** longing for sth

**afanador(a)** [a·fa·na·'dor, --'do·ra] *m(f)*

*Arg* (*carterista*) pickpocket

**afanar** [a·fa·'nar] **I.** *vt CSur inf* to steal, to pinch **II.** *vr:* ~**se** (*esforzarse*) to toil (away)

**afección** [a·fek·'sjon, a·fey·'θjon] *f* **1.** MED condition **2.** (*inclinación*) inclination

**afectado, -a** [a·fek·'ta·do, -a] *adj* affected

**afectar** [a·fek·'tar] *vt* **1.** (*influir*) to concern **2.** (*dañar*) to harm **3.** (*impresionar*) to affect

**afectivo, -a** [a·fek·'ti·βo, -a] *adj* **1.** (*de afecto*) affective **2.** (*cariñoso*) affectionate

**afecto** [a·'fek·to] *m* emotion; ~ **a algo/alguien** affection for sth/sb

**afecto, -a** [a·'fek·to, -a] *adj* ~ **a algo/alguien** inclined towards sth/sb

**afectuoso, -a** [a·fek·tu·'o·so, -a] *adj* affectionate; (*cordial*) kind; **afectuosamente** yours affectionately

**afeitado** [a·fei·'ta·do] *m* shave

**afeitar** [a·fei·'tar] **I.** *vt* to shave; **máquina de ~** (*safety*) razor **II.** *vr:* ~**se** to shave

**afgano, -a** [af·'γa·no, -a] *adj, m, f* Afghan

**afianzar** <z → c> [a·fjan·'sar, -'θar] **I.** *vt* (*dar firmeza*) to strengthen **II.** *vr:* ~**se** (*afirmarse*) to become established

**afiche** [a·'fi·tʃe] *m AmL* poster

**afición** [a·fi·'sjon, -'θjon] *f* **1.** (*inclinación*) liking; **tener** [*o* **sentir**] **una ~ hacia** [*o* **a**] **algo** to be fond of sth **2.** (*pasatiempo*) hobby; **hacer algo por ~** to do sth as a hobby **3.** (*hinchada*) fans *pl*

**aficionado, -a** [a·fi·sjo·'na·do, -a; a·fi·θjo-] **I.** *adj* amateur; **ser ~ a tocar la flauta** to be fond of playing the flute **II.** *m, f* **1.** (*entusiasta*) lover; DEP fan **2.** (*no profesional*) amateur

**aficionar** [a·fi·sjo·'nar, a·fi·θjo-] *vt* ~ **a alguien a algo** to get sb interested in sth **II.** *vr* ~**se a algo** (*acostumbrarse*) to take a liking to sth

**afilado, -a** [a·fi·'la·do, -a] *adj* (*cuchillo*) sharp; (*nariz*) pointed; (*cara*) thin

**afilalápices** [a·fi·la·'la·pi·ses, -θes] *m inv* pencil sharpener

**afilar** [a·fi·'lar] **I.** *vt* to sharpen **II.** *vr:* ~**se** to get sharp

**afiliación** [a·fi·lja·'sjon, -'θjon] *f* affilia-

tion; ~ **política** political affiliation

**afiliado, -a** [a·fi·'lja·do, -a] *m, f* member

**afin** [a·'fin] *adj* related

**afinar** [a·fi·'nar] **I.** *vi* (*cantando*) to sing in tune; (*tocando*) to play in tune **II.** *vt* **1.** (*hacer más fino*) to refine; ~ **la puntería** to sharpen one's aim **2.** MÚS to tune

**afinidad** [a·fi·ni·'dad] *f* similarity; ~ **de caracteres** relatedness of character

**afirmación** [a·fir·ma·'sjon, -'θjon] *f* **1.** (*confirmación*) confirmation **2.** (*aseveración*) assertion

**afirmar** [a·fir·'mar] **I.** *vt* **1.** (*decir sí*) to affirm; (*dar por cierto*) to confirm; ~ **con la cabeza** to nod in agreement **2.** (*aseverar*) to state **II.** *vr:* ~**se** to be confirmed; ~**se en algo** to reaffirm sth

**afirmativo, -a** [a·fir·ma·'ti·βo, -a] *adj* affirmative; **en caso ~** if so

**aflicción** [a·flik·'sjon, -γ'θjon] *f* ~ **por algo/alguien** grief for sth/sb

**afligir** <g → j> [a·fli·'xir] **I.** *vt* **1.** (*apenar*) to upset **2.** (*atormentar*) to afflict **II.** *vr* ~**se por algo** to get upset about [*o* over] sth

**aflojar** [a·flo·'xar] **I.** *vi* to slacken **II.** *vt* **1.** (*nudo*) to loosen **2.** (*velocidad*) to reduce; ~ **el paso** to slacken one's pace; **un tira y afloja** a tug-of-war **III.** *vr:* ~**se** to slacken

**aflorar** [a·flo·'rar] *vi* **1.** (*salir*) to come to the surface **2.** (*apuntar*) to appear

**afluencia** [a·'flwen·θja, -sja] *f* abundance; (*gente*) crowd

**afluente** [a·'flwen·te] *m* tributary

**afonía** [a·fo·'ni·a] *f* hoarseness

**afónico, -a** [a·'fo·ni·ko, -a] *adj* hoarse

**aforo** [a·'fo·ro] *m* (*en teatro*) capacity; **la sala tiene un ~ de 300 personas** the hall can seat 300 people

**afortunado, -a** [a·for·tu·'na·do, -a] *adj* fortunate; **¡qué afortunada eres!** how lucky you are!

**afrenta** [a·'fren·ta] *f* affront, insult

**afrentar** [a·fren·'tar] *vt* to insult

**África** ['a·fri·ka] *f* Africa

**africano, -a** [a·fri·'ka·no, -a] *adj, m, f* African

**afroamericano, -a** [a·fro·a·me·ri·'ka·

no] *adj, m, f* Afro-American, African American

**afrodisiaco** [a·fro·di·'sja·ko] *m*, **afrodisíaco** [a·fro·di·'si·a·ko] *m* aphrodisiac

**afrontar** [a·fron·'tar] *vt* to face; ~ **un problema** to tackle a problem

**afuera** [a·'fwe·ra] *adv* outside; ¡~! *inf* get out of here!

**afueras** [a·'fwe·ras] *fpl* outskirts *pl;* ~ **de la ciudad** outskirts of the city

**agachar** [a·ɣa·'tʃar] I. *vt* to lower II. *vr:* ~**se** (*encogerse*) to crouch

**agache** [a·'ɣa·tʃe] *m* 1. *Col* (*mentira*) fib 2. *Cuba* **andar de** ~ to be on the run 3. *Ecua* (*de tapadillo*) **de** ~ on the sly

**agalla** [a·'ɣa·ja, -ʎa] *f* gill; **tener ~s** *fig* to have guts

**agarrada** [a·ɣa·'rra·da] *f inf* fight

**agarrado, -a** [a·ɣa·'rra·do] *adj* stingy

**agarrador** [a·ɣa·rra·'dor] *m* pot holder

**agarrar** [a·ɣa·'rrar] I. *vt* 1. (*tomar*) to take 2. (*asir*) to grasp 3. (*enfermedad*) to catch; ~ **una borrachera** to get drunk; ~ **una pulmonía** to catch pneumonia II. *vr:* ~**se** 1. (*asirse*) to hold on 2. *AmL* (*coger*) to catch; (*frutas*) to pluck

**agarrotar** [a·ɣa·rro·'tar] I. *vt* (*entumecer*) to stiffen up II. *vr:* ~**se** (*entumecerse*) to go numb; (*por el miedo*) to stiffen with fear

**agasajar** [a·ɣa·sa·'xar] *vt* to receive in great style

**agatas** [a·'ɣa·tas] *adv Par, RíoPl* 1. (*con dificultad*) with great difficulty 2. (*casi no*) hardly; ~ **sabe leer** he/she can barely read 3. (*tan sólo*) barely; ~ **hace una hora** barely an hour ago

**agencia** [a·'xen·sja, -θja] *f* 1. (*empresa*) agency; ~ **de noticias/de publicidad/de viajes** news/advertising/travel agency 2. (*sucursal*) branch

**agenciarse** [a·xen·'sjar·se, -'θjar·se] *vr* to get hold of; **agenciárselas** to manage

**agenda** [a·'xen·da] *f* 1. (*calendario*) engagement [*o* date] book; ~ **de bolsillo** pocket diary; **tener una** ~ **apretada** to have a tight schedule 2. (*orden del día*) agenda

**agente** [a·'xen·te] I. *mf* 1. (*representante*) representative; (*de un artista*) agent;

~ **de bolsa** stockbroker 2. (*funcionario*) ~ **de aduanas** customs officer; ~ **de policía** police officer II. *m t.* MED agent

**ágil** [a·'xil] *adj* (*de movimiento*) agile; (*mental*) alert, quick-witted

**agilidad** [a·xi·li·'dad] *f* (*física*) agility; (*mental*) acumen

**agilizar** <z → c> [a·xi·li·'sar, -'θar] *vt* to speed up

**agitación** [a·xi·ta·'sjon, -'θjon] *f* movement; *t.* POL agitation; (*excitación*) excitement

**agitado, -a** [a·xi·'ta·do, -a] *adj* hectic

**agitar** [a·xi·'tar] I. *vt* 1. (*mover*) to move; (*bandera*) to wave 2. (*intranquilizar*) to worry 3. (*sublevar*) to rouse II. *vr:* ~**se** 1. (*moverse*) to move about; (*bandera*) to wave; (*mar*) to get rough 2. (*excitarse*) to get excited

**aglomeración** [a·ɣlo·me·ra·'sjon, -'θjon] *f* agglomeration; ~ **de gente** crowd of people; ~ **urbana** urban sprawl

**ago.** *abr de* **agosto** Aug.

**agobiado, -a** [a·ɣo·'βja·do, -a] *adj* exhausted; **estar** ~ **de trabajo** to be overloaded with work

**agobiante** [a·ɣo·'βjan·te] *adj* overwhelming; (*persona*) tiresome

**agobiar** [a·ɣo·'βjar] I. *vt* 1. (*abrumar*) to overwhelm; ¡**no me agobies!** *inf* don't keep going on at me! 2. (*calor*) to suffocate II. *vr:* ~**se** 1. (*angustiarse*) ~**se por algo** to be weighed down with sth 2. (*sentirse abatido*) to feel overwhelmed

**agobio** [a·'ɣo·βjo] *m* 1. (*carga*) burden 2. (*cansancio*) exhaustion 3. (*opresión*) oppression

**agonia** [a·ɣo·'ni·a] *f* 1. (*del moribundo*) death throes *pl* 2. (*angustia*) anguish

**agónico, -a** [a·'ɣo·ni·ko, -a] *adj* **estar** ~ to be dying

**agonizar** <z → c> [a·ɣo·ni·'sar, -'θar] *vi* to be dying; (*terminar*) to be coming to an end

**agosto** [a·'ɣos·to] *m* August; **hacer su** ~ to make a killing; *v. t.* **marzo**

**agotado, -a** [a·ɣo·'ta·do, -a] *adj* (*producto*) out of stock; (*persona*) exhausted

**agotador(a)** [a·ɣo·ta·'dor, -'do·ra] *adj* exhausting

**agotamiento** [a·ɣo·ta·'mjen·to] *m* exhaustion

**agotar** [a·ɣo·'tar] I. *vt* 1. (*existencias*) to use up; (*mercancía*) to deplete; (*paciencia*) to exhaust 2. (*cansar*) to tire (out) II. *vr:* ~**se** 1. (*mercancía*) to run out; (*pilas*) to run down [*o* out]; (*fuerzas*) to give out; **esta edición se agotó enseguida** this edition sold out immediately 2. (*cansarse*) to wear oneself out

**agraciado, -a** [a·ɣra·'sja·ðo, -a; -'θja·ðo, -a] *adj* 1. (*gracioso*) graceful 2. (*bien parecido*) attractive 3. (*afortunado*) lucky; **salir ~ en la lotería** to win in the lottery

**agradable** [a·ɣra·'ða·βle] *adj* pleasant; ~ **al paladar** tasty; **es ~ a la vista** it is pleasing to the eye; ~ **con alguien** pleasant to sb

**agradar** [a·ɣra·'dar] *vi* to please; **me agrada esta gente** I like these people; **quieres ~ a todos** you want to please everyone

**agradecer** [a·ɣra·de·'ser, -'θer] *irr como* **crecer** *vt* to thank; **te agradezco la invitación** thanks for the invitation; **le ~ía mucho que** +*subj* I'd be very grateful if; **el campo ha agradecido la lluvia** the rain has been good for the fields

**agradecido, -a** [a·ɣra·de·'si·ðo, -a; -'θi·ðo, -a] *adj* (*que agradece*) ~ **por algo** grateful for sth; **le estaría muy ~ si me contestara lo antes posible** I would appreciate it very much if you could reply as soon as possible; **le estoy sumamente ~** I am extremely grateful (to you)

**agradecimiento** [a·ɣra·de·si·'mjen·to, -θi·'mjen·to] *m* gratitude

**agrado** [a·'ɣra·ðo] *m* 1. (*afabilidad*) affability; **tratar a alguien con ~** to treat sb kindly 2. (*complacencia*) willingness; **he recibido con ~ su carta** I was very pleased to receive your letter; **esto no es de mi ~** this isn't to my liking

**agrandar** [a·ɣran·'dar] I. *vt* to make bigger II. *vr:* ~**se** to get bigger

**agrario, -a** [a·'ɣra·rjo, -a] *adj* agrarian; **población agraria** rural population

**agravamiento** [a·ɣra·βa·'mjen·to] *m t.* MED worsening

**agravar** [a·ɣra·'βar] I. *vt* to make worse II. *vr:* ~**se** to worsen

**agraviar** [a·ɣra·'βjar] I. *vt* to offend II. *vr:* ~**se** to be offended

**agravio** [a·'ɣra·βjo] *m* offense; ~ **material** material damage

**agredir** [a·ɣre·'dir] *vt* to attack

**agregado** [a·ɣre·'ɣa·ðo] *m* 1. (*conglomerado*) aggregate 2. (*aditamento*) addition

**agregado, -a** [a·ɣre·'ɣa·ðo, -a] *m, f* UNIV associate professor

**agregar** <g → gu> [a·ɣre·'ɣar] *vt* to add

**agresión** [a·ɣre·'sjon] *f* aggression

**agresividad** [a·ɣre·si·βi·'dad] *f* aggressiveness

**agresivo, -a** [a·ɣre·'si·βo, -a] *adj* aggressive

**agresor(a)** [a·ɣre·'sor] I. *adj* aggressor II. *m(f)* aggressor, assailant

**agreste** [a·'ɣres·te] *adj* 1. (*campestre*) country 2. (*terreno*) rough, wild

**agriar** [a·'ɣrjar] I. *vt* (*alimentos*) to sour; (*persona*) to make bitter II. *vr:* ~**se** (*alimentos*) to turn sour; (*persona*) to become embittered [*o* bitter]

**agrícola** [a·'ɣri·ko·la] *adj* agricultural

**agricultor(a)** [a·ɣri·kul·'tor, -·'to·ra] *m(f)* farmer

**agricultura** [a·ɣri·kul·'tu·ra] *f* agriculture

**agridulce** [a·ɣri·'dul·se, -θe] *adj* bittersweet; CULIN sweet-and-sour

**agrietar** [a·ɣrje·'tar] I. *vt* to crack II. *vr:* ~**se** to crack; (*pared*) to become cracked; (*piel*) to become chapped

**agringarse** <g → gu> [a·ɣrin·'ɣar·se] *vr AmL* to imitate or adopt the customs of a foreigner

**agrio, -a** ['a·ɣrjo, -a] *adj* 1. (*sabor*) sour 2. (*carácter*) bitter

**agrónomo, -a** [a·'ɣro·no·mo, -a] *m, f* agronomist

**agropecuario, -a** [a·ɣro·pe·'kwa·rjo, -a] *adj* agricultural, farming

**agroturismo** [a·ɣro·tu·'ris·mo] *m* agrotourism

**agrupación** [a·ɣru·pa·'sjon, -'θjon] *f* 1. (*agrupamiento*) grouping 2. (*conjunto*) group 3. (*asociación*) society

**agrupar** [a·ɣru·'par] I. *vt* to group (together); ~ **algo por temas** to group sth by subject **II.** *vr*: ~**se** to form a group

**agua** [a·ɣwa] *f* **1.** (*líquido*) water; ~ **de colonia** eau de cologne; ~ **con gas** sparkling water; ~ **del grifo** tap water; ~ **de mar** seawater; ~ **nieve** sleet; ~ **potable** drinking water; **¡hombre al ~!** man overboard!; **claro como el** ~ crystal clear; **esta noche ha caído mucha** ~ it rained a lot last night **2.** *pl* (*mares*) waters *pl*; ~**s interiores** inland waters; ~**s residuales** sewage; ~**s termales** hot baths [*o springs*]; ~**s abajo/arriba** downstream/upstream ▶ **volver las** ~**s a su** <u>cauce</u> to go back to normal; **estoy con el** ~ **hasta el** <u>cuello</u> I'm up to my neck in it; **como** ~ **de** <u>mayo</u> very welcome; **no hallar** ~ **en el** <u>mar</u> to act stupid; **llevar el** ~ **a su** <u>molino</u> to turn things to one's advantage; **sacar** ~ **a las** <u>piedras</u> to make something out of nothing; **estar entre** <u>dos</u> ~**s** to be sitting on the fence; **es** ~ <u>pasada</u> that's water under the bridge; **hacer** ~ (*buque*) to take in water; (*negocio*) to founder

**aguacate** [a·ɣwa·ka·te] *m* avocado

**aguacero** [a·ɣwa·se·ro, -'θe·ro] *m* downpour; **cayó un** ~ there was a cloudburst

**aguachento, -a** [a·ɣwa·'tʃen·to, -a] *adj AmL v.* **aguado**

**aguado, -a** [a·'ɣwa·do, -a] *adj* watered-down; (*fruta*) tasteless

**aguafiestas** [a·ɣwa·'fjes·tas] *mf inv inf* spoilsport, party pooper

**aguafuerte** [a·ɣwa·'fwer·te] *m* etching

**aguaitar** [a·ɣwai·'tar] *vt* **1.** *Arg, Cuba* (*acechar*) to lie in wait for **2.** *Col* (*esperar*) to wait

**aguamiel** [a·ɣwa·'mjel] *f Méx* (*jugo del maguey*) maguey juice

**aguanieve** [a·ɣwa·'nje·βe] *f* sleet

**aguantadero** [a·ɣwan·ta·'de·ro] *m Arg, Urug* hide-out

**aguantar** [a·ɣwan·'tar] **I.** *vt* **1.** (*sostener*) to hold; (*sujetar*) to hold tight; ~ **la risa** to hold back one's laughter **2.** (*soportar*) to bear; **no aguanto más** I can't bear it any more; **no poder** ~ **a alguien** not to be able to stand sb; ~ **la mirada de alguien** to hold sb's stare **3.** (*du-*

*rar*) to last; **este abrigo** ~**á mucho** this coat will last for a long time **II.** *vr*: ~**se 1.** (*contenerse*) to restrain oneself **2.** (*soportar*) to put up with it **3.** (*conformarse*) to resign oneself

**aguante** [a·'ɣwan·te] *m* **1.** (*paciencia*) patience; **tener mucho** ~ to be very patient **2.** (*resistencia*) stamina

**aguar** <gu → gü> [a·'ɣwar] **I.** *vt* **1.** (*mezclar*) to water (down) **2.** (*frustrar*) to spoil **II.** *vr*: ~**se 1.** (*con agua*) to fill with water; **nuestras vacaciones se** ~**on** our vacation was spoiled by rain **2.** (*estropearse*) to be spoiled

**aguardar** [a·ɣwar·'dar] *vt* to wait for; ~ **unos días** to wait a few days; ~ **algo/a alguien** to await sth/sb

**aguardiente** [a·ɣwar·'djen·te] *m* brandy

**aguarrás** [a·ɣwa·'rras] *m* turpentine

**agudeza** [a·ɣu·'de·sa, -θa] *f* **1.** (*del cuchillo*) sharpness; ~ **visual** keenness of sight **2.** (*ingenio*) wittiness

**agudo, -a** [a·'ɣu·do, -a] *adj* **1.** (*afilado*) sharp; **vista aguda** keen sight **2.** (*ingenioso*) witty; (*mordaz*) scathing **3.** (*dolor*) acute **4.** (*sonido*) piercing **5.** (*grave*) severe

**agüero** [a·'ɣwe·ro] *m* omen; **de mal** ~ ill-fated

**aguijón** [a·ɣi·'xon] *m* (*punta*) goad; ZOOL sting, stinger

**águila** ['a·ɣi·la] *f* eagle; ~ **real** golden eagle; **ser un** ~ **para los negocios** *fig* to be sharp in business

**aguinaldo** [a·ɣi·'nal·do] *m* tip (*given at Christmas*)

**aguja** [a·'ɣu·xa] *f* **1.** (*general*) needle; ~ **de punto** knitting needle; ~ **de la iglesia** church steeple; **buscar una** ~ **en un pajar** to look for a needle in a haystack **2.** (*del reloj*) hand; (*de un instrumento*) pointer **3.** FERRO point **4.** CULIN **carne de** ~ rib roast

**agujerear** [a·ɣu·xe·re·'ar] *vt* to make holes in; (*orejas*) to pierce

**agujero** [a·ɣu·'xe·ro] *m* hole; ~ **en la capa de ozono** hole in the ozone layer; **tapar un** ~ to fill a hole

**agujetas** [a·ɣu·'xe·tas] *fpl* stiffness

**aguzar** <z → c> [a·ɣu·'sar, -'θar] *vt* **1.** (*afilar*) to sharpen **2.** (*avivar*) **la**

**atención** to heighten one's attention; ~ **los sentidos** to sharpen one's senses; ~ **la vista** to look more carefully

**ahí** [a·'i] I. *adv* (*lugar*) there; ~ **está** there he/she/it is; ~ **viene** there he/she/it comes; ~ **está el problema** that's the problem; **me voy por** ~ I'm going that way ► ¡~ **es nada**! not bad!; ~ **me las den todas** *inf* I couldn't care less; **por** ~, **por** ~ something like that II. *conj* **de** ~ **que...** that is why...

**ahijado, -a** [a·i·'xa·do, -a] *m, f* godchild

**ahínco** [a·'in·ko] *m* **1.** (*empeño*) effort **2.** (*insistencia*) insistence

**ahogado, -a** [a·o·'ɣa·do, -a] *adj* drowned; **estar ~ de trabajo** *fig* to be snowed under with work

**ahogar** <g → gu> [a·o·'ɣar] I. *vt* **1.** (*en el agua*) to drown **2.** (*asfixiar*) to suffocate II. *vr:* ~**se 1.** (*en el agua*) to drown **2.** (*asfixiarse*) to suffocate; ~**se de calor** to be sweltering (in the heat) **3.** (*motor*) to flood ► ~**se en un vaso de agua** to make mountains out of molehills

**ahondar** [a·on·'dar] *vi* ~ **en algo** (*tema*) to go deeply into sth

**ahora** [a·'o·ra] *adv* now; (*muy pronto*) very soon; ~ **bien** now then; **de** ~ **en adelante** from now on; **hasta** ~ up to now; **por** ~ for the present; ¡~ (**lo entiendo**)! now I've got it!; ~ **mismo vengo** I'm just coming; **acaba de salir** ~ **mismo** he/she has just gone out; ¡**ven** ~ **mismo**! come right now!; ¿**y** ~ **qué**? what now?

**ahorcar(se)** <c → qu> [a·or·'kar(·se)] *vt, (vr)* to hang (oneself)

**ahorita** [a·o·'ri·ta] *adv AmL* right away

**ahorrador(a)** [a·o·rra·'dor, -'do·ra] I. *adj* thrifty II. *m(f)* saver

**ahorrar** [a·o·'rrar] I. *vt* to save; ~ **fuerzas** to save one's energy; ~ **esfuerzos a alguien** to save sb the trouble; **ahórrame explicaciones** spare me your explanations II. *vr:* ~**se** (*evitar*) to save oneself

**ahorrativo, -a** [a·o·rra·'ti·βo, -a] *adj* thrifty

**ahorro** [a·'o·rro] *m* (*cantidad*) saving

**ahuecar** <c → qu> [a·we·'kar] I. *vt* (*vaciar*) to hollow out II. *vr:* ~**se 1.** (*ave*) to ruffle (up) its feathers **2.** (*envanecerse*) to put on airs

**ahulado** [a·u·'la·do] *m AmC, Méx* (*mantel*) oilcloth tablecloth

**ahumado, -a** [a·u·'ma·do, -a] *adj* **1.** (*cristal*) tinted **2.** (*salmón*) smoked

**ahumar** [a·u·'mar] I. *vi* to smoke II. *vt* CULIN to smoke; (*una colmena*) to smoke out

**ahuyentar** [a·u·jen·'tar] *vt* **1.** (*espantar*) to frighten off [o away] **2.** (*dudas*) to dispel

**aimara, aimará** [ai·ma·ra] I. *adj* Aymara II. *mf* Aymara

**aindiado, -a** [a·in·'dja·do, -a] *adj AmL* Indian-looking

**airar** [ai·'rar] *irr* I. *vt* to anger II. *vr:* ~**se** to get angry

**aire** ['ai·re] *m* **1.** (*atmósfera*) air; ~ **acondicionado** air conditioning; **Ejército del Aire** air force; **al** ~ **libre** in the open air; **echar una moneda al** ~ to toss a coin (into the air); **tomar el** ~ to go for a stroll; **dejar una pregunta en el** ~ to leave a question open; **cambiar de** ~**s** to have a change of scene; ¡~! *inf* beat it! **2.** (*viento*) wind; **corriente de** ~ draft; **corre** ~ it's drafty; **hoy hace** ~ it's windy today **3.** (*aspecto*) appearance; **darse** ~**s de grandeza** to have pretensions of grandeur; ¡**tiene unos** ~**s**! he/she is always putting on airs! **4.** (*garbo*) elegance

**airear** [ai·re·'ar] I. *vt* to air II. *vr:* ~**se 1.** (*ventilarse*) to air **2.** (*coger aire*) to get some fresh air

**airoso, -a** [ai·'ro·so, -a] *adj* graceful; **salir** ~ **de algo** to come out of sth with flying colors

**aislado, -a** [ais·'la·do, -a] *adj* isolated

**aislamiento** [ais·la·'mjen·to] *m* **1.** (*retiro*) isolation **2.** *t.* TÉC insulation; ~ **acústico** soundproofing

**aislante** [ais·'lan·te] I. *adj* insulating; **cinta** ~ insulating tape II. *m* insulator

**aislar** [ais·'lar] I. *vt* to isolate; TÉC to insulate; **aislado contra el ruido** soundproof II. *vr:* ~**se** to isolate oneself

**ajedrez** [a·xe·'dres, -'dreθ] *m* DEP chess

**ajeno, -a** [a·'xe·no, -a] *adj* **1.** (*de otro*) somebody else's; **la felicidad ajena**

other people's happiness **2.** *estar* (*ignorante*) ignorant; **estar ~ a** [*o de*] **algo** to be unaware of sth; **vivía ~ a todo lo que pasaba en el mundo** he/she lived unaware of what was happening in the world

**ajetreo** [a.xe.ˈtre.o] *m* (*de personas*) drudgery; (*en un sitio*) bustle

**ají** [a.ˈxi] *m AmS, Ant* **1.** (*arbusto*) pepper (plant) **2.** (*pimentón*) chili; (*de las Indias*) cayenne (pepper)

**ajillo** [a.ˈxi.ʝo, -ʎo] *m* CULIN **al ~** prepared with olive oil and garlic

**ajo** [ˈa.xo] *m* BOT garlic; (*diente*) clove of garlic ▶ **andar** (**metido**) **en el ~** *inf* **estar en el ~** *inf* to be mixed up in it

**ajotar** [a.xo.ˈtar] *vt* **1.** *AmC, Ant* (*azuzar*) to incite **2.** *Cuba* (*desdeñar*) to scorn

**ajuar** [a.ˈxwar] *m* **1.** (*de novia*) trousseau **2.** (*de casa*) furnishings *pl*

**ajustable** [a.xus.ˈta.βle] *adj* adjustable; **sábanas ~s** fitted sheets

**ajustado, -a** [a.xus.ˈta.ðo, -a] *adj* **1.** (*ropa*) tight **2.** (*adecuado*) fitting

**ajustar** [a.xus.ˈtar] **I.** *vi* to fit **II.** *vt* **1.** (*adaptar*) *t.* TÉC to adjust; **~ un vestido** to take in a dress; **~ una correa** to adjust a strap **2.** (*dos piezas*) to fit **III.** *vr:* **~se** (*adaptarse*) to adapt; **no ~se al tema** not to keep to the subject; **~se a la verdad** to stick to the truth

**ajuste** [a.ˈxus.te] *m* **1.** (*adaptación*) adjustment **2.** (*graduación*) graduation; **~ de brillo** brightness control **3.** (*encaje*) fitting **4.** (*acuerdo*) compromise; **~ de cuentas** settling of scores

**ajusticiar** [a.xus.ti.ˈsjar, -ˈθjar] *vt* to execute

**al** [al] = **a + el** *v.* **a**

**ala** [ˈa.la] *f* wing; (*de sombrero*) brim *pl* ▶ **tener demasiadas ~s** to be overconfident; **estar tocado del ~** *inf* to be crazy; **ahuecar el ~** to get going; **cortar las ~s a alguien** to clip sb's wings; **dar ~s a alguien** to encourage sb

**Alá** [a.ˈla] *m* REL Allah

**alabanza** [a.la.ˈβan.sa, -θa] *f* praise; **deshacerse en ~s para con alguien** to shower praises on sb

**alabar** [a.la.ˈβar] **I.** *vt* **~ a alguien por algo** to praise sb for sth; **alabado sea**

**el Señor** praise be to God **II.** *vr:* **~se** to boast

**alabastro** [a.la.ˈβas.tro] *m* alabaster

**alacena** [a.la.ˈse.na, -ˈθe.na] *f* pantry

**alacrán** [a.la.ˈkran] *m* ZOOL scorpion

**ALALC** [a.ˈlalk] *abr de* **Asociación Latinoamericana de Libre Comercio** LAFTA

**alambique** [a.lam.ˈbi.ke] *m* distillery

**alambrada** [a.lam.ˈbra.ða] *f* wire fence; **~ eléctrica** electric fence

**alambre** [a.ˈlam.bre] *m* wire; **~ de espino** barbed wire

**alameda** [a.la.ˈme.ða] *f* (*lugar*) poplar grove

**álamo** [ˈa.la.mo] *m* BOT poplar; **~ temblón** aspen

**alarde** [a.ˈlar.ðe] *m* show; **hacer ~ de algo** to make a show of sth

**alardear** [a.lar.ðe.ˈar] *vi* **~ de algo** to boast about sth

**alargado, -a** [a.lar.ˈɣa.ðo, -a] *adj* elongated

**alargar** <g → gu> [a.lar.ˈɣar] **I.** *vt* **1.** (*extensión*) to lengthen; **~ el cuello** to crane one's neck; **~ la mano** to hold out one's hand **2.** (*duración*) to prolong **II.** *vr:* **~se** (*en la extensión*) to lengthen; **no te alargues** to be brief

**alarido** [a.la.ˈri.ðo] *m* shriek

**alarma** [a.ˈlar.ma] *f* **1.** (*general*) alarm; **falsa ~** false alarm; **dar la ~** to raise the alarm; **ha saltado la ~ del banco** the alarm in the bank has gone off **2.** (*susto*) scare

**alarmar** [a.lar.ˈmar] **I.** *vt* **1.** (*dar la alarma*) to alarm **2.** (*asustar*) to frighten; **noticia alarmante** terrible news **II.** *vr:* **~se** (*inquietarse*) to get worried; (*asustarse*) to be alarmed

**alarmista** [a.lar.ˈmis.ta] *mf* alarmist

**alba** [ˈal.βa] *f* dawn; **al rayar** [*o* **romper**] **el ~** at daybreak

**albacea** [al.βa.ˈse.a, -ˈθe.a] *mf* executor

**albacora** [al.βa.ˈko.ra] *f* Chile, Perú, Méx swordfish

**albahaca** [al.ˈβa.ka/al.βa.ˈa.ka] *f* BOT basil

**albanés, -esa** [al.βa.ˈnes, -·ˈne.sa] *adj, m, f* Albanian

**albañil** [al.βa.ˈɲil] *mf* **1.** (*constructor*) builder **2.** (*artesano*) bricklayer

**albarán** [al.βa.'ran] *m* delivery note, invoice

**albaricoque** [al.βa.ri.'ko.ke] *m* apricot

**albedrío** [al.βe.'dri.o] *m* whim; **libre ~** free will; **a mi ~** just as I like

**albergar** <g → gu> [al.βer.'ɣar] I. *vt* to house II. *vr:* **~se** to lodge

**albergue** [al.'βer.ɣe] *m* refuge; **~ juvenil** youth hostel; **~ de montaña** mountain hut

**albino, -a** [al.'βi.no, -a] *adj, m, f* albino

**albóndiga** [al.'βon.di.ɣa] *f* (*de carne*) meatball

**albornoz** [al.βor.'noθ, -'noθ,] *m* bathrobe

**alborotado, -a** [al.βo.ro.'ta.ðo, -a] *adj* (*excitado*) excited

**alborotar** [al.βo.ro.'tar] I. *vi* to make a racket; (*niños*) to roughhouse II. *vt* 1. (*excitar*) to excite 2. (*desordenar*) to agitate 3. (*sublevar*) to stir up III. *vr:* **~se** 1. (*excitarse*) to get excited 2. (*sublevarse*) to riot

**alboroto** [al.βo.'ro.to] *m* 1. (*vocerío*) racket; (*ruido*) noise 2. (*bulla*) uproar; (*disturbio*) disturbance

**alborozo** [al.βo.'ro.so, -θo] *m* joy

**albufera** [al.βu.'fe.ra] *f* lagoon

**álbum** [al.'βun] *m* <álbum(e)s> album

**albur** [al.'βur] *m* ZOOL (*pez*) bleak ▶ **al ~** at random

**alburear** [al.βu.re.'ar] I. *vt CRI* to disturb II. *vi* 1. Col (*dinero*) to get money 2. Cuba (*engañar*) to deceive

**alcachofa** [al.ka.'tʃo.fa] *f* 1. BOT artichoke 2. (*de ducha*) shower head; (*de regadera*) sprinkler

**alcahuete, -a** [al.ka.'we.te, -a] *m, f* pimp

**alcalde(sa)** [al.'kal.de, al.kal.'de.sa] *m(f)* mayor

**alcaldía** [al.kal.'di.a] *f* (*oficio, oficina*) mayor's office

**alcalino, -a** [al.ka.'li.no, -a] *adj* alkaline

**alcamonero, -a** [al.ka.mo.'ne.ro, -a] *adj* Ven (*entrometido*) nosy; (*de novedades*) newsy

**alcance** [al.'kan.se, -θe] *m* 1. (*distancia*) range; **misil de corto ~** short-range missile; **al ~ de la mano** within reach; **al ~ de todos los bolsillos** within everybody's means; **tener la victoria a su ~** to have victory within one's

grasp 2. (*importancia*) importance; **de mucho/poco ~** of great/little importance ▶ **la noticia de último ~** the latest news; **dar ~ a alguien** to catch up with sb

**alcanfor** [al.kan.'for] *m* camphor

**alcantarilla** [al.kan.ta.'ri.ja, -ʎa] *f* 1. (*cloaca*) sewer 2. (*sumidero*) drain

**alcantarillado** [al.kan.ta.ri.'ja.ðo, -ʎa.ðo] *m* sewer system, drains *pl*

**alcanzar** <z → c> [al.kan.'sar, -'θar] I. *vi* to reach; **el dinero no alcanza para pagar la comida** the money's not enough to pay for the food II. *vt* 1. (*dar alcance*) to catch up (with); **ve tirando, ya te ~é** keep going, I'll catch up with you 2. (*llegar*) to reach; **~ un acuerdo** to reach an agreement; **el disparo le alcanzó en la pierna** he was shot in the leg; **~ fama** to become famous 3. (*entender*) to grasp

**alcaparra** [al.ka.'pa.rra] *f* (*fruto*) caper

**alcatraz** [al.ka.'tras, -'traθ] *m* 1. ZOOL gannet 2. BOT arum

**alcázar** [al.'ka.sar, -θar] *m* MIL fortress

**alce** ['al.se, -θe] *m* ZOOL elk, moose

**alcoba** [al.'ko.βa] *f* bedroom

**alcohol** [al.'kol/al.ko.'ol] *m* alcohol; **bebida sin ~** non-alcoholic drink; **no tomo ~** I don't drink alcohol; **estar bajo los efectos del ~** to be under the influence of alcohol

**alcohólico, -a** [al.'ko.li.ko/al.ko.'o.li.ko, -a] *adj, m, f* alcoholic

**alcoholímetro** [al.ko.'li.me.tro/al.ko.o.'li.me.tro] *m* Breathalyzer®

**alcoholismo** [al.ko.'lis.mo/al.ko.o.'lis.mo] *m* alcoholism

**alcoholizar** <z → c> [al.ko.li.'sar/al.ko.o.li.'sar, -'θar] I. *vt* to get (sb) drunk II. *vr:* **~se** to become an alcoholic

**alcornoque** [al.kor.'no.ke] *m* BOT cork oak; (**pedazo de**) ~ idiot

**alcurnia** [al.'kur.nja] *f* ancestry; **de ~** of noble birth

**aldea** [al.'dea] *f* small village

**aldeano, -a** [al.de.'a.no, -a] *m, f* 1. (*de la aldea*) villager 2. (*inculto*) country bumpkin

**aleación** [a.lea.'sjon, -'θjon] *f* alloy; **~ ligera** light alloy

**aleatorio, -a** [a·lea·'to·rjo, -a] *adj* random, fortuitous

**alegación** [a·le·γa·'sjon, -'θjon] *f* JUR (*declaración*) declaration; (*escrito*) statement

**alegar** <g → gu> [a·le·'γar] *vt* to cite; (*pruebas*) to produce

**alegoría** [a·le·γo·'ri·a] *f* allegory

**alegrar** [a·le·'γrar] I. *vt* 1. (*a personas*) to make happy 2. (*cosas*) to brighten up II. *vr* ~**se de algo** to be glad about sth; **me alegro de verle de nuevo** I'm pleased to see you again; **me alegro (por ti)** I'm so happy for you

**alegre** [a·'le·γre] *adj* 1. (*contento*) happy; (*divertido*) merry; (*color*) bright; **una cara** ~ a cheerful face; **estoy ~ de que** +*subj* I'm pleased that 2. (*frívolo*) frivolous; **llevar una vida** ~ to lead a free-and-easy life 3. *inf* (*achispado*) merry; **estar** ~ to be tipsy

**alegría** [a·le·'γri·a] *f* (*gozo*) happiness; (*buen humor*) cheerfulness; **llevarse una gran** ~ to be very happy

**alejar** [a·le·'xar] I. *vt* 1. (*distanciar*) to remove 2. (*ahuyentar*) to drive away; **aleja estos pensamientos de tu cabeza** banish these thoughts from your mind II. *vr:* ~**se** to move away; (*retirarse*) to withdraw; **todos se alejan de él** everyone avoids him

**aleluya** [a·le·'lu·ja] *interj, m o f* REL hallelujah; **estar de** ~ to rejoice

**alemán** [a·le·'man] *m* German; **decir algo en** ~ to say sth in German

**alemán, -ana** [a·le·'man, -·'ma·na] *adj, m, f* German

**Alemania** [a·le·'ma·nja] *f* Germany; **República Federal de** ~ Federal Republic of Germany

**alentar** <e → ie> [a·len·'tar] I. *vt* to encourage II. *vr:* ~**se** (*animarse*) to take heart

**alergia** [a·'ler·xia] *f* allergy; ~ **al polen** pollen allergy; **esto me da** ~ I'm allergic to this

**alérgico, -a** [a·'ler·xi·ko, -a] *adj* allergic

**alerta** [a·'ler·ta] I. *adj* alert II. *f* alert; ~ **por vibración** TEL vibration alert; **dar la** ~ to give the alarm; **poner en** ~ **a alguien** to put sb on the alert III. *interj*

watch out

**aleta** [a·'le·ta] *f* wing; (*de un buzo*) flipper; (*de un pez*) fin

**alevosía** [a·le·βo·'si·a] *f* treachery; **con** ~ treacherously

**alfabético, -a** [al·fa·'βe·ti·ko, -a] *adj* alphabetic(al); **estar por orden** ~ to be in alphabetical order

**alfabetizar** <z → c> [al·fa·βe·ti·'sar, -'θar] *vt* to teach to read and write

**alfabeto** [al·fa·'βe·to] *m* alphabet

**alfalfa** [al·'fal·fa] *f* BOT alfalfa

**alfarería** [al·fa·re·'ri·a] *f* pottery

**alfarero, -a** [al·fa·'re·ro, -a] *m, f* potter

**alférez** [al·'fe·res, -reθ] *m* MIL second lieutenant

**alfil** [al·'fil] *m* (*ajedrez*) bishop

**alfiler** [al·fi·'ler] *m* 1. (*aguja*) pin 2. (*broche*) brooch; ~ **de corbata** tiepin
▶ **llevo la lección prendida con ~es** I'm hardly prepared for the exam; **no caber un** ~ to be bursting at the seams

**alfombra** [al·'fom·bra] *f* carpet

**alfombrado** [al·fom·'bra·do] *m AmL* carpeting

**alfombrilla** [al·fom·'bri·ja, -·ʎa] *f* 1. (*estera*) mat; ~ **de baño** bath mat 2. COMPUT mousepad

**alforja** [al·'for·xa] *f* bag; (*de caballería*) saddlebag

**alga** ['al·γa] *f* alga

**algarabía** [al·γa·ra·'βi·a] *f* (*griterío*) uproar

**álgebra** ['al·xe·βra] *f* MAT algebra

**álgido, -a** ['al·xi·do, -a] *adj* 1. (*culminante*) **la crisis está en su momento más** ~ the crisis has reached its climax 2. (*muy frío*) freezing

**algo** ['al·γo] I. *pron indef* (*en frases afirmativas*) something; (*en neg., interrog. y condicionales*) anything; ~ **es** ~ it's better than nothing; **¿quieres** ~**?** do you want anything?; **¿apostamos** ~**?** do you want to bet?; **me suena de** ~ it seems familiar to me; **se cree** ~ he/she thinks he/she is something; **por** ~ **lo habrá dicho** he/she must have had a reason for saying it II. *adv* a little; **aún falta** ~ **hasta llegar** there's still a bit to go; ~ **así como** something like

**algodón** [al·γo·'don] *m* 1. (*tejido*) cotton; **una camisa de ~** a cotton shirt; **~ en rama** raw cotton **2.** (*cosmético*) cotton

**alguacil** [al·ɣwa·ˈsil, -ˈθil] *mf* bailiff

**alguien** [ˈal·ɣjen] *pron indef* (*en frases afirmativas*) somebody, someone; (*en interrog. y condicionales*) anybody, anyone; ¿**hay ~ aquí?** is anybody [*o* anyone] there?; **~ me lo ha contado** somebody [*o* someone] told me; **se cree ~** he/she thinks he/she is somebody [*o* someone]

**algún** [al·ˈɣun] *adj v.* **alguno**[1]

**alguno, -a**[1] [al·ˈɣu·no, -a] *adj* <algún> **1.** (*antepuesto*) some; (*en frases neg. e int.*) any; ¿**alguna pregunta?** any questions?; **de alguna manera** somehow; **en algún sitio** somewhere; **alguna vez** sometimes; **algún día** someday **2.** (*postpuesto: ninguno*) no, not any; **en sitio ~** nowhere; **persona alguna** no one

**alguno, -a**[2] [al·ˈɣu·no, -a] *pron indef* somebody, someone; **~s de los presentes** some of those present; **~s ya se han ido** some have already gone; ¿**tienes caramelos? — sí, me quedan ~s** do you have any candy? — yes, I still have some left; **los niños han vuelto a hacer alguna de las suyas** the children have been up to their tricks again

**alhaja** [a·ˈla·xa] *f* (*de piedras preciosas*) piece of jewelry; (*de bisutería*) costume jewelry

**alhajado, -a** [a·la·ˈxa·do, -a] *adj Col* (*rico*) wealthy

**alhajera** [a·la·ˈxe·ra] *f Arg, Chile* jewel box

**aliado, -a** [a·ˈlja·do, -a] **I.** *adj* allied **II.** *m, f* ally

**alianza** [a·li·ˈan·sa, -θa] *f* **1.** (*pacto*) alliance; **Alianza Atlántica** Atlantic Alliance, NATO **2.** (*anillo*) wedding ring

**aliar(se)** <1. pres alío> [a·li·ˈar·(se)] *vt, (vr)* to ally (oneself)

**alias** [ˈa·ljas] *adv, m inv* alias

**alicaído, -a** [a·li·ka·ˈi·do, -a] *adj* weak; (*deprimido*) dejected

**alicates** [a·li·ˈka·tes] *mpl* pliers *pl*

**aliciente** [a·li·ˈsjen·te, -ˈθjen·te] *m* incentive

**aliento** [a·ˈljen·to] *m* **1.** (*respiración*)

breath; **mal ~** bad breath; **sin ~** out of breath; **cobrar ~** to get one's breath back; **esto me quita el ~** this takes my breath away; **tomar ~** to take a breath **2.** (*ánimo*) courage; **dar ~ a alguien** to encourage sb

**aligerar** [a·li·xe·ˈrar] **I.** *vi* to hurry (up) **II.** *vt* **1.** (*cargas*) to lighten **2.** (*acelerar*) to quicken; **~ el paso** to go faster

**alimaña** [a·li·ˈma·ɲa] *f* **1.** (*animal*) pest; **~s** vermin **2.** (*persona*) animal, brute

**alimentación** [a·li·men·ta·ˈsjon, -ˈθjon] *f* **1.** (*nutrición*) food **2.** (*de animales*) feeding **3.** (*de un horno*) stoking; (*de una máquina*) feeding; **~ de energía** energy supply

**alimentar** [a·li·men·ˈtar] **I.** *vi* to be nourishing **II.** *vt* **1.** (*nutrir*) to feed; **~ el odio** to fuel hatred **2.** (*horno*) to stoke; (*máquina*) to feed **III.** *vr* **~se de algo** to live on sth

**alimenticio, -a** [a·li·men·ˈti·sjo, -a; -ˈθjo, -a] *adj* **1.** (*nutritivo*) nourishing **2.** (*alimentario*) food; **industria alimenticia** food industry; **pensión alimenticia** alimony; **productos ~s** foodstuffs *pl*

**alimento** [a·li·ˈmen·to] *m* **1.** (*sustancia*) food; **los ~s** foodstuffs *pl*; **~s congelados** frozen food **2.** (*alimentación*) nourishment; **de mucho/poco ~** full of/lacking nutritional value **3.** *pl* JUR (*asistencia financiera*) alimony

**alineación** [a·li·nea·ˈsjon, -ˈθjon] *f*, **alineamiento** [a·li·nea·ˈmjen·to] *m* **1.** (*general*) alignment **2.** DEP line-up

**alinear** [a·li·ne·ˈar] **I.** *vt* **1.** (*poner en línea*) to line up **2.** DEP to select; (*para un partido*) to field; **país no alineado** POL non-aligned country **II.** *vr:* **~se** to line up

**aliñar** [a·li·ˈɲar] *vt* to season; (*ensalada*) to dress

**aliño** [a·ˈli·ɲo] *m* seasoning; (*para ensalada*) dressing

**alioli** [a·li·ˈo·li] *m* mayonnaise made with olive oil and garlic

**alisar** [a·li·ˈsar] *vt* (*superficie*) to smooth down; (*un terreno*) to level (off); (*el pelo*) to smooth

**aliso** [a·ˈli·so] *m t.* BOT alder

**alistar** [a·lis·ˈtar] *vr:* **~se 1.** (*inscribirse*)

to enroll **2.** MIL to enlist

**aliviar** [a·li·ˈβjar] **I.** vt **1.** (*carga*) to lighten **2.** (*de una preocupación*) to relieve **3.** (*dolor*) to alleviate **II.** vr: ~**se 1.** (*dolor*) to ease off [o up] **2.** (*de una enfermedad*) to recover

**alivio** [a·ˈli·βjo] m **1.** (*aligeramiento*) relief **2.** (*de una enfermedad*) recovery; (*mejoría*) improvement ▶ **ser de** ~ inf to be horrible; **pescar un catarro de** ~ inf to get an awful cold

**allá** [a·ˈja, a·ˈʎa] adv **1.** (*lugar, dirección*) there; **el más** ~ REL the hereafter; **¿cuánto se tarda de aquí** ~? how long does it take to go there?; **ponte más** ~ move further over **2.** (*tiempo*) back; ~ **por el año 1964** around 1964 ▶ **¡**~ **tú!** inf that's your problem!

**allanamiento** [a·ja·na·ˈmjen·to, a·ʎa-] m **1.** (*de un terreno*) leveling **2.** JUR ~ **de morada** breaking and entering

**allanar** [a·ja·ˈnar, a·ʎa-] **I.** vt **1.** (*terreno*) to level (out) **2.** (*dificultades*) to remove **3.** JUR ~ **una casa** to break into a house **II.** vr: ~**se** to agree

**allegado, -a** [a·je·ˈɣa·do, -a; a·ʎe-] **I.** adj close **II.** m, f relative

**allí** [a·ˈji, a·ˈʎi] adv (*lugar, dirección*) there; ~ **cerca de** ~ over there; **¡**~ **viene!** he's/she's just coming!; **hasta** ~ as far as that

**alma** [ˈal·ma] f **1.** (*espíritu*) soul; **agradecer con el** ~ to thank with all one's heart; **me arranca el** ~ it's heartbreaking; **me llega al** ~ I'm deeply touched; **lo siento en el** ~ I'm terribly sorry; **no tener** ~ to be heartless; **fue el** ~ **de la fiesta** he/she was the life and soul of the party **2.** (*ánimo*) spirit ▶ **como** ~ **que lleva el diablo** inf like a bat out of hell; ~ **en pena** lost soul; **se le** **cayó** **el** ~ **a los pies** inf his/her heart sank

**almacén** [al·ma·ˈsen, -ˈθen] m **1.** (*depósito*) warehouse; **tener en** ~ to have in stock **2.** (*tienda*) **grandes almacenes** department store

**almacenaje** [al·ma·se·ˈna·xe, al·ma·θe-] m, **almacenamiento** [al·ma·se·na·ˈmjen·to, al·ma·θe-] m (*de mercancías*) t. COMPUT storage

**almacenar** [al·ma·se·ˈnar, al·ma·θe-] vt t.

COMPUT to store

**almeja** [al·ˈme·xa] f **1.** ZOOL clam **2.** vulg (*vagina*) cunt

**almendra** [al·ˈmen·dra] f (*fruta*) almond

**almendro** [al·ˈmen·dro] m almond tree

**almíbar** [al·ˈmi·βar] m syrup; **melocotón en** ~ peach in syrup

**almidón** [al·mi·ˈdon] m starch; (*cola*) paste

**almidonar** [al·mi·do·ˈnar] vt to starch

**almirante** [al·mi·ˈran·te] mf admiral

**almirez** [al·mi·ˈres, -ˈreθ] m mortar

**almizcle** [al·ˈmis·kle, al·ˈmiθ-] m musk

**almohada** [al·mo·ˈa·da] f pillow ▶ **consultar** **algo con la** ~ inf to sleep on sth

**almohadilla** [al·moa·ˈdi·ja, -ˈdi·ʎa] f (*cojín*) small cushion; (*acerico*) pin cushion

**almorranas** [al·mo·ˈrra·nas] fpl piles pl

**almorzar** [al·mor·ˈsar, -ˈθar] irr como **forzar I.** vi **1.** (*a mediodía*) to have lunch **2.** reg (*desayunar*) to have breakfast **II.** vt **1.** (*a mediodía*) to have for lunch **2.** reg (*desayunar*) to have for breakfast

**almuerzo** [al·ˈmwer·so, -θo] m **1.** (*al mediodía*) lunch; ~ **de negocios** business lunch; **¿qué hay de** ~? what's for lunch? **2.** reg (*desayuno*) breakfast

**aló** [a·ˈlo] interj AmC, AmS TEL hello; ~, **¿quién es?** hello, who's speaking?

**alocado, -a** [a·lo·ˈka·do, -a] adj **1.** (*loco*) crazy **2.** (*imprudente*) reckless

**alojamiento** [a·lo·xa·ˈmjen·to] m **1.** (*lugar*) accommodation **2.** (*acción*) housing

**alojar** [a·lo·ˈxar] **I.** vt **1.** (*albergar*) to accommodate **2.** (*procurar alojamiento*) to house **3.** (*cosa*) to lodge **II.** vr: ~**se** to stay

**alondra** [a·ˈlon·dra] f ZOOL (*ave*) lark

**alopecia** [a·lo·ˈpe·sja, -θja] f alopecia

**Alpes** [ˈal·pes] mpl **los** ~ the Alps + pl vb, Alps

**alpinismo** [al·pi·ˈnis·mo] m mountain climbing

**alpinista** [al·pi·ˈnis·ta] mf mountain climber

**alpaca** [al·ˈpa·ka] f **1.** (*tela*) t. ZOOL alpaca **2.** (*aleación*) nickel silver, German silver

**alpargata** [al·par·ˈɣa·ta] f espadrille

**alpino, -a** [al·'pi·no, -a] *adj* Alpine; **refugio** ~ mountain refuge

**alpiste** [al·'pis·te] *m* 1. (*para pájaros*) birdseed 2. *inf* (*alcohol*) **le gusta mucho el** ~ he's/she's a boozer

**alquilar** [al·ki·'lar] I. *vt* 1. (*dejar*) to rent (out), to let 2. (*tomar en alquiler*) to rent II. *vr:* ~**se** to be let; **se alquila** for rent

**alquiler** [al·ki·'ler] *m* 1. (*acción*) renting, letting; ~ **de coches** car-rental 2. (*precio*) rent, rental

**alquimia** [al·'ki·mja] *f* alchemy

**alquimista** [al·ki·'mis·ta] *mf* alchemist

**alquitrán** [al·ki·'tran] *m* tar

**alrededor** [al·rre·de·'dor] *adv* 1. (*local*) around; ~ **de la plaza** around the square; **un viaje** ~ **del mundo** a trip around the world 2. (*aproximadamente*) ~ **de** around

**alrededores** [al·rre·de·'do·res] *mpl* surroundings *pl*; (*de una ciudad*) outskirts *pl*

**alta** ['al·ta] *f* 1. (*documento*) (certificate of) discharge; **dar el** ~ to discharge; **dar de** ~ **del hospital** to discharge from hospital 2. (*inscripción*) registration; (*ingreso*) membership; **darse de** ~ **en una asociación** to become a member of an association

**altamente** [al·ta·'men·te] *adv* highly; ~ **cualificado** highly qualified

**altanero, -a** [al·ta·'ne·ro, -a] *adj* arrogant, haughty

**altar** [al·'tar] *m* altar

**altavoz** [al·ta·'βoθ, -'βos] *m* loudspeaker

**alteración** [al·te·ra·'sjon, -'θjon] *f* 1. (*cambio*) alteration, change 2. (*perturbación*) disturbance 3. (*turbación*) unrest 4. (*irritación*) irritation

**alterado, -a** [al·te·'ra·do, -a] *adj* upset

**alterar** [al·te·'rar] I. *vt* 1. (*cambiar*) to alter 2. (*perturbar*) to disturb 3. (*turbar*) to upset II. *vr:* ~**se** 1. ~**se por algo** (*aturdirse*) to get upset over sth; (*irritarse*) to be irritated by sth 2. (*cambiar*) to alter

**altercado** [al·ter·'ka·do] *m* argument, altercation *form*

**alternar** [al·ter·'nar] I. *vi* 1. (*turnarse*) to alternate; ~ **en el volante** to take turns at the wheel 2. (*tratar*) ~ **con alguien**

to associate with sb 3. (*en un club*) to go clubbing II. *vt* to alternate; ~ **el trabajo con la diversión** to alternate between periods of work and leisure III. *vr* ~**se en algo** to take turns at sth

**alternativa** [al·ter·na·'ti·βa] *f* alternative; **no le queda otra** ~ **que...** he/she has no other alternative than...

**alternativo, -a** [al·ter·na·'ti·βo, -a] *adj* 1. (*opcional*) alternative 2. (*con alternación*) alternating

**alterne** [al·'ter·ne] *m* **chica de** ~ hostess; **bar de** ~ singles bar

**alterno, -a** [al·'ter·no, -a] *adj* alternate; **en días** ~**s** every other day

**alteza** [al·'te·sa, -θa] *f* (*tratamiento*) nobleness; **Su Alteza Real** His/Her/Your Royal Highness

**altibajos** [al·ti·'βa·xos] *mpl* 1. (*de un terreno*) undulations *pl* 2. (*cambios*) ups *pl* and downs; **es una persona con muchos** ~ **en su estado de ánimo** he's/she's very moody

**altiplanicie** [al·ti·pla·'ni·sje, -θje] *f*, **altiplano** [al·ti·'pla·no] *m* high plateau

**altitud** [al·ti·'tud] *f* height, altitude; **a una** ~ **de 1500 metros** at a height of 1,500 meters

**altivo, -a** [al·'ti·βo, -a] *adj* (*soberbio*) arrogant, haughty

**alto** ['al·to] I. *interj* halt; **¡~ el fuego!** cease fire! II. *m* 1. (*descanso*) stop; ~ **el fuego** ceasefire; **dar el** ~ to order to halt 2. (*altura*) height; **medir 8 metros de** ~ to be 8 meters high 3. (*collado*) hill III. *adv* (*en un lugar elevado*) high (up); **ponlo en lo más** ~ put it as high up as possible ▸ **pasar por** ~ to ignore; **pasar una pregunta por** ~ to overlook a question; **por todo lo** ~ splendidly

**alto, -a** ['al·to, -a] *adj* <más alto *o* superior, altísimo> 1. (*en general*) high; **un** ~ **cargo** a high-ranking position; **notas altas** *mús* high notes; **artículos de cuero de alta calidad** high-quality leather goods; **tener un** ~ **concepto de alguien** to have a high opinion of sb 2. (*persona*) tall; (*edificio*) high, tall 3. (*en la parte superior*) upper; **clase alta** upper class 4. *GEO* (*río*) upper; **la alta montaña** the high mountains

**5.** (*tiempo*) late; **a altas horas de la noche** late at night **6.** (*río*) torrential; (*mar*) rough; **el río está ~** the river is rough **7.** (*sonido*) loud; **hablar en voz alta** to speak loudly

**altoparlante** [al·to·par·'lan·te] *m AmL* loudspeaker

**altramuz** [al·tra·'mus, -'muθ] *m* BOT lupin(e)

**altruista** [al·tru·'is·ta] **I.** *adj* altruistic **II.** *mf* altruist

**altura** [al·'tu·ra] *f* **1.** (*altitud*) height; **de gran ~** high; **de poca ~** low; **a gran ~** at a great height; **una montaña de 2000 metros de ~** a 2,000-meter-high mountain; **el avión pierde ~** the plane is losing altitude **2.** (*estatura*) height **3.** (*de un sonido*) pitch **4.** *pl* (*cielo*) heaven ▶ **estar a la ~ del betún** *inf* to look really stupid; **estar a la ~ de las circunstancias** to rise to the occasion; **estar a la ~ de Valencia** to be in the vicinity of Valencia; **a estas ~s** at this point

**alubia** [a·'lu·βja] *f* bean

**alucinación** [a·lu·si·na·'sjon, -θi·na·'θjon] *f* hallucination

**alucinado, -a** [a·lu·si·'na·do, -a; a·lu·θi·] *adj inf* (*asombrado*) **miraba ~ a la chica** he looked at the girl in amazement; **me quedé ~ al leerlo en el periódico** I was stunned on reading it in the newspaper

**alucinante** [a·lu·si·'nan·te, a·lu·θi·] *adj inf* **1.** (*estupendo*) fantastic **2.** (*increíble*) incredible

**alucinar** [a·lu·si·'nar, a·lu·θi·] **I.** *vi inf* **1.** (*hablando*) to hallucinate; **¡tú alucinas!** *fig* you're crazy! **2.** (*quedar fascinado*) to be fascinated **II.** *vt inf* **1.** (*pasmar*) to amaze **2.** (*fascinar*) to fascinate

**alud** [a·'lud] *m* avalanche; **un ~ de gente** *fig* a throng of people

**aludir** [a·lu·'dir] *vi* (*referirse*) to allude; (*mencionar*) to mention; **darse por aludido** (*ofenderse*) to take it personally; **no darse por aludido** not to take the hint

**alumbrado** [a·lum·'bra·do] *m* lighting; **~ público** street lighting

**alumbrar** [a·lum·'brar] **I.** *vi* (*iluminar*) to give off light; **la lámpara alumbra poco** the lamp doesn't give off much light **II.** *vt* (*iluminar*) to light (up); (*a alguien*) to shine a light on

**aluminio** [a·lu·'mi·njo] *m* aluminum

**alumnado** [a·lum·'na·do] *m* (*de escuela*) pupils *pl*; (*de universidad*) students *pl*

**alumno, -a** [a·'lum·no, -a] *m, f* (*de escuela*) pupil; (*de universidad*) student

**alusión** [a·lu·'sjon] *f* **1.** (*mención*) **~ a algo** mention of sth **2.** (*insinuación*) allusion; **hacer una ~ a algo** to allude to sth

**aluvión** [a·lu·'βjon] *m* (*inundación*) *t. fig* flood

**alza** ['al·sa, -θa] *f* (*elevación*) rise; **estar en ~** (*precios*) to be rising; (*persona*) to be up-and-coming

**alzamiento** [al·sa·'mjento, al·θa-] *m* uprising

**alzar** <z → c> [al·'sar, -'θar] **I.** *vt* **1.** (*levantar*) to lift (up); (*precio*) to raise **2.** (*poner vertical*) to put up **3.** (*construir*) to erect **II.** *vr:* **~se 1.** (*levantarse*) to rise (up); **allí se alza la universidad** the university buildings rise up over there **2.** *AmL* (*sublevarse*) to revolt

**ama** ['a·ma] *f* (*dueña*) mistress; (*propietaria*) owner; **~ de casa** housewife; **~ de llaves** housekeeper

**amabilidad** [a·ma·βi·li·'dad] *f* kindness; **tuvo la ~ de avisarme** he/she was kind enough to warn me

**amable** [a·'ma·βle] *adj* kind; **ser ~ con alguien** to be kind to sb; **¿sería Ud. tan ~ de explicármelo?** would you be so kind as to explain it to me?

**amaestrar** [a·maes·'trar] *vt* to train; (*caballos*) to break in

**amagar** <g → gu> [a·ma·'ɣar] *vt* **1.** (*indicar*) **amagó un golpe** he/she made as if to strike **2.** (*amenazar*) to threaten; **~ a alguien con algo** to threaten sb with sth

**amago** [a·'ma·ɣo] *m* **1.** (*amenaza*) threat **2.** (*indicio*) hint **3.** DEP feint

**amainar** [a·mai·'nar] *vi* to abate

**amalaya** [a·ma·'la·ja] *interj AmL* hopefully

**amalgama** [a·mal·'ɣa·ma] *f* **1.** QUÍM amalgam **2.** (*mezcla*) mixture

**amamantar** [a·ma·man·'tar] *vt* (*bebé*) to breastfeed; (*cachorro*) to suckle

**amanecer** [a·ma·ne·'ser, -'θer] I. *vimpers* to dawn; **está amaneciendo** it's getting light II. *m* dawn; **al ~** at dawn

**amanecida** [a·ma·ne·'si·da, -'θi·da] *f AmL* dawn

**amanerado, -a** [a·ma·ne·'ra·do, -a] *adj* **1.** (*persona*) affected **2.** (*estilo*) mannered

**amansador** [a·man·sa·'dor] *m Méx* (*domador*) horse breaker

**amansar** [a·man·'sar] *vt* **1.** (*animal*) to tame **2.** (*persona*) to subdue; (*sosegar*) to calm down

**amante** [a·'man·te] I. *adj* **soy poco ~ de hablar en público** I don't like speaking in public II. *mf* lover; **un ~ de la naturaleza** a nature-lover

**amañar** [a·ma·'ɲar] I. *vt* **1.** (*asunto*) to fix; **~ una solución** to cook up a solution **2.** (*resultado*) to fake II. *vr* **amañárselas** (**para todo**) to manage to get by (in everything)

**amapola** [a·ma·'po·la] *f* poppy

**amar** [a·'mar] *vt* to love

**amargar** <g > gu> [a·mar·'yar] I. *vt* to make bitter; **~ la vida a alguien** to make life difficult for sb II. *vr*: **~se** to become bitter

**amargo, -a** [a·'mar·yo] *adj* bitter; **la verdad amarga** the painful truth

**amargura** [a·mar·'yu·ra] *f* bitterness; **llorar con ~** to weep bitterly

**amarillento, -a** [a·ma·ri·'jen·to, -a; -'ʎen·to, -a] *adj* yellowish; (*papel*) yellowed

**amarillo, -a** [a·ma·'ri·jo, -ʎo] *adj* **1.** (*color*) yellow **2.** (*pálido*) pale

**amarradero** [a·ma·rra·'de·ro] *m* **1.** (*poste*) post, bollard **2.** NÁUT berth

**amarrar** [a·ma·'rrar] I. *vt* **1.** (*atar*) to tie up **2.** NÁUT to moor ▶ **tener a alguien muy amarrado** *inf* to keep sb under tight control II. *vr*: **~se** *AmL* to get married

**amasar** [a·ma·'sar] *vt* **1.** (*masa*) to knead **2.** (*fortuna*) to amass

**amasijar** [a·ma·si·'xar] *vt AmL inf* (*dar paliza*) to give a beating; (*pegar brutalmente*) to beat to a pulp

**amateur** [a·ma·'ter] I. *adj* amateur II. *mf* <amateurs> amateur

**amatista** [a·ma·'tis·ta] *f* amethyst

**amauta** [a·'mau·ta] *m Bol, Perú* **1.** (*de los incas*) Incan sage **2.** (*autoridad*) village elder

**amazona** [a·ma·'so·na, -'θo·na] *f* **1.** (*mujer*) Amazon **2.** DEP rider

**ámbar** ['am·bar] *adj, m inv* amber

**ambición** [am·bi·'sjon, -'θjon] *f* ambition; **~ de poder** hunger for power; **mi ~ en la vida es...** my ambition in life is...

**ambicioso, -a** [am·bi·'sjo·so, -a; am·bi·'θjo-] *adj* ambitious

**ambientador** [am·bjen·ta·'dor] *m* air freshener

**ambientar** [am·bjen·'tar] I. *vt* **1.** (*novela*) to set; **la novela está ambientada en Lima** the novel is set in Lima **2.** (*fiesta*) to enliven II. *vr*: **~se 1.** (*aclimatarse*) to adjust **2.** (*en una fiesta*) to get into the mood

**ambiente** [am·'bjen·te] *m* **1.** (*aire*) air **2.** (*medio*) surroundings *pl*; **medio ~** environment; **nocivo para el medio ~** harmful to the environment **3.** (*social*) milieu **4.** (*atmósfera*) atmosphere; **dar ~** to create a favorable atmosphere; **no había ~ en la calle** there wasn't much happening in the street

**ambigüedad** [am·bi·ɣwe·'dad] *f* ambiguity; **sin ~es** unambiguous

**ambiguo, -a** [am·'bi·ɣwo, -a] *adj* (*de doble significado*) ambiguous

**ámbito** ['am·bi·to] *m* (*espacio*) area; **en el ~ nacional** on a national level

**ambivalente** [am·bi·β̞a·'len·te] *adj* ambivalent

**ambos, -as** ['am·bos, -as] *adj* both

**ambulancia** [am·bu·'lan·sja, -θja] *f* (*vehículo*) ambulance

**ambulante** [am·bu·'lan·te] *adj* walking; **circo ~** traveling circus; **vendedor ~** peddler; **venta ~** peddling

**ambulatorio** [am·bu·la·'to·rjo] *m* outpatient department

**ameba** [a·'me·βa] *f* ameba

**amedrentar** [a·me·dren·'tar] *vt* **1.** (*asustar*) to scare **2.** (*intimidar*) to intimidate

**amén** [a·'men] *m* amen; **decir ~ a todo** to agree to everything

**amenaza** [a·me·'na·sa, -θa] *f* **1.** (*intimidación*) threat; **bajo la ~ de violencia** under the threat of violence **2.** (*peligro*) menace

**amenazador(a)** [a·me·na·sa·'dor, -·'do·ra; a·me·na·θa-] *adj* **1.** (*tono*) threatening; **gesto ~** threatening gesture **2.** (*que anuncia peligro*) menacing

**amenazar** <z → c> [a·me·na·'sar, -'θar] **I.** *vt* (*intimidar*) to threaten; **el jefe lo ha amenazado con despedirle** the boss has threatened him with dismissal **II.** *vi, vt* (*presagiar*) to threaten; **amenaza tormenta** there's a storm ahead

**amenizar** <z → c> [a·me·ni·'sar, -'θar] *vt* **1.** (*hacer agradable*) to make pleasant **2.** (*entretener*) to entertain

**ameno, -a** [a·'me·no, -a] *adj* **1.** (*agradable*) pleasant **2.** (*entretenido*) entertaining

**América** [a·'me·ri·ka] *f* America; **~ Central** Central America; **~ Latina** Latin America; **~ del Norte/del Sur** North/South America

**americana** [a·me·ri·'ka·na] *f* jacket

**americanismo** [a·me·ri·ka·'nis·mo] *m* LING Americanism

**americano, -a** [a·me·ri·'ka·no] *adj, m, f* (*de América del Sur*) South American; (*estadounidense*) American

**amerindio, -a** [a·me·'rin·djo, -a] *adj, m, f* American Indian, Amerindian

**ametralladora** [a·me·tra·ja·'do·ra, a·me·tra·ʎa-] *f* machine gun

**amigable** [a·mi·'ɣa·βle] *adj* friendly

**amígdala** [a·'miɣ·da·la] *f* tonsil

**amigo, -a** [a·'mi·ɣo, -a] **I.** *adj* **1.** (*amistoso*) friendly; **es muy amiga mía** she's a good friend of mine; **somos (muy) ~s desde la infancia** we've been (close) friends since our childhood **2.** (*aficionado*) **ser ~ de algo** to be fond of sth; **soy ~ de decir las cosas claras** I'm all for calling a spade a spade ▶ **¡y tan ~s!** and that's that! **II.** *m, f* **1.** (*general*) friend; **~ por correspondencia** pen pal; **hacerse ~ de alguien** to make friends with sb; **poner a alguien cara de pocos ~s** to look grimly at sb **2.** (*amante*) lover **3.** (*adepto*) supporter

**amiguete** [a·mi·'ɣe·te] *m* *inf* pal, buddy

**aminorar** [a·mi·no·'rar] **I.** *vi* to diminish **II.** *vt* to reduce; **~ el paso** to slow down

**amistad** [a·mis·'tad] *f* **1.** (*entre amigos*) friendship; **tener ~ con alguien** to be friendly with sb **2.** *pl* (*amigos*) friends *pl*

**amistoso, -a** [a·mis·'to·so, -a] *adj* friendly, amicable; **partido ~** friendly match

**amnesia** [am·'ne·sja] *f* amnesia

**amnistía** [am·nis·'ti·a] *f* amnesty; **Amnistía Internacional** Amnesty International

**amo** ['a·mo] *m* **1.** (*propietario*) owner **2.** (*patrón*) boss; **ser el ~ en algo** to be the boss in sth

**amodorrarse** [a·mo·do·'rrar·se] *vr* to become drowsy [*o* sleepy]

**amoldar** [a·mol·'dar] **I.** *vt* **1.** (*ajustar*) to adjust **2.** (*moldear*) to mold **3.** (*acomodar*) to adapt **II.** *vr:* **~se** to adapt oneself

**amonestación** [a·mo·nes·ta·'sjon, -'θjon] *f* (*advertencia*) warning

**amonestar** [a·mo·nes·'tar] *vt* (*advertir*) to warn; (*reprender*) to reprimand

**amoníaco** [a·mo·'ni·a·ko] *m* ammonia

**amontonar** [a·mon·to·'nar] **I.** *vt* to pile up **II.** *vr:* **~se** to pile up; (*personas*) to crowd together

**amor** [a·'mor] *m* love; **~ al prójimo** love for one's neighbor; **~ propio** self-esteem; **~ a primera vista** love at first sight; **¡~ mío!** my love!; **hacer el ~ con alguien** *inf* to make love with sb; **hacer algo con ~** to do sth lovingly ▶ **por ~ al arte** for nothing; **¡por ~ de Dios!** for God's sake!; **de mil ~es** with the greatest of pleasure

**amoratado, -a** [a·mo·ra·'ta·do, -a] *adj* purple; **un ojo ~** a black eye; **tengo los labios ~s de frío** my lips are blue with cold

**amordazar** <z → c> [a·mor·da·'sar, -'θar] *vt* to gag; *fig* to silence, to gag

**amorfo, -a** [a·'mor·fo, -a] *adj* shapeless, amorphous

**amorío(s)** [a·mo·'ri·o(s)] *m(pl)* *pey* love affair

**amoroso, -a** [a·mo·'ro·so, -a] *adj* **1.** (*de amor*) loving **2.** (*cariñoso*) **~ con al-**

**A**

**guien** affectionate to/towards sb

**amortiguador** [a·mor·ti·ɣwa·'dor] *m* AUTO shock absorber

**amortiguar** <gu → gü> [a·mor·ti·'ɣwar] *vt* (*sonido*) to muffle; (*golpe*) to cushion

**amortización** [a·mor·ti·sa·'sjon, -θa·'θjon] *f* **1.** (*de una deuda*) repayment **2.** (*fiscal*) depreciation

**amortizar** <z → c> [a·mor·ti·'sar, -'θar] *vt* **1.** (*deuda*) to pay off **2.** (*fiscalmente*) to write off **3.** (*inversión*) to recover

**amotinar** [a·mo·ti·'nar] *vr:* ~**se** to rebel

**amparar** [am·pa·'rar] **I.** *vt* to protect; **la constitución ampara la libertad de religión** the constitution guarantees religious freedom **II.** *vr:* ~**se** to seek protection; **se ampara en una ley antigua** he/she has recourse to an old law

**amparo** [am·'pa·ro] *m* (*protección*) protection; **al ~ de la oscuridad** under cover of darkness

**amperio** [am·'pe·rjo] *m* amp

**ampliación** [am·plja·'sjon, -'θjon] *f* **1.** (*engrandecimiento*) enlargement; (*de capital*) increase; (*de un territorio*) expansion; (*de una carretera*) extension **2.** (*de conocimientos*) broadening **3.** (*de un sonido*) amplification; ~ **de RAM** COMPUT RAM expansion

**ampliar** <1. pres amplío> [am·pli·'ar] *vt* **1.** (*hacer más grande*) to enlarge; (*territorio*) to expand; **edición ampliada** extended edition **2.** (*conocimientos*) to broaden **3.** (*sonido*) to amplify

**amplificador** [am·pli·fi·ka·'dor] *m* amplifier

**amplificar** <c → qu> [am·pli·fi·'kar] *vt* to amplify

**amplio, -a** ['am·pljo, -a] *adj* **1.** (*casa*) spacious; (*parque*) extensive **2.** (*vestido*) loose-fitting **3.** (*informe*) detailed; (*experiencia*) wide-ranging; (*red*) extensive; (*interés*) broad; **una derrota amplia** a serious defeat; **en un sentido más ~** in a wider sense

**amplitud** [am·pli·'tud] *f* **1.** (*extensión*) extent; (*de conocimientos*) range; ~ **de miras** broad-mindedness; **de gran ~** wide-ranging **2.** (*de una casa*) roominess; (*de un parque*) extensiveness

**3.** FÍS amplitude

**ampolla** [am·'po·ʝa, -ʎa] *f* **1.** (*burbuja*) blister; **tener ~s en los pies** to have blisters on one's feet **2.** (*garrafa*) flask **3.** (*para inyecciones*) ampoule ▶ **levantar ~s** to get people's backs up

**ampolleta** [am·po·'je·ta, -'ʎe·ta] *f* Arg light bulb

**amputar** [am·pu·'tar] *vt* to amputate

**amuchar** [a·mu·'tʃar] *vt* Arg, Bol, Chile to multiply

**amueblar** [a·mwe·'βlar] *vt* to furnish

**amularse** [a·mu·'lar·se] *vr* Méx (*mercancía*) to become unsalable; (*persona*) to get stubborn

**amuleto** [a·mu·'le·to] *m* amulet

**amurallar** [a·mu·ra·'jar, -'ʎar] *vt* to wall

**anabolizante** [a·na·βo·li·'san·te, -'θan·te] *m* anabolic steroid

**anacardo** [a·na·'kar·do] *m* **1.** BOT cashew tree **2.** (*fruto*) cashew (nut)

**anagrama** [a·na·'ɣra·ma] *m* anagram

**anal** [a·'nal] *adj* anal

**anales** [a·'na·les] *mpl* **1.** HIST annals *pl* **2.** (*de una sociedad*) records *pl*

**analfabetismo** [a·nal·fa·βe·'tis·mo] *m* illiteracy

**analfabeto, -a** [a·nal·fa·'βe·to, -a] *m, f* illiterate (person)

**analgésico** [a·nal·'xe·si·ko] *m* painkiller

**análisis** [a·'na·li·sis] *m inv* **1.** (*general*) *t.* MAT analysis **2.** MED test

**analista** [a·na·'lis·ta] *mf* (*que analiza*) analyst; ~ **de sistemas** COMPUT systems analyst; **el médico mandó las pruebas al** ~ the doctor sent the samples to the laboratory

**analítico, -a** [a·na·'li·ti·ko, -a] *adj* analytic(al)

**analizar** <z → c> [a·na·li·'sar, -'θar] *vt* (*examinar*) *t.* MED to analyze

**analogía** [a·na·lo·'xi·a] *f* analogy; **por ~ con algo** on the analogy of sth

**análogo, -a** [a·'na·lo·ɣo, -a] *adj* analogous

**ananá(s)** [a·na·'na(s)] *m* CSur pineapple

**anaranjado, -a** [a·na·ran·'xa·do, -a] *adj* orange

**anarquía** [a·nar·'ki·a] *f* anarchy

**anarquismo** [a·nar·'kis·mo] *m* anarchism

**anarquista** [a·nar·'kis·ta] *adj, mf* anarchist

**anatomía** [a·na·to·'mi·a] *f* anatomy

**anatómico, -a** [a·na·'to·mi·ko, -a] *adj* **1.** MED anatomical **2.** (*adaptado al cuerpo*) anatomically designed

**anca** ['an·ka] *f* **1.** (*de animal*) haunch; **~s de rana** frogs' legs **2.** (*cadera*) hip **3.** *pl inf* (*nalgas*) backside ▶ **montar a las ~s** to sit behind

**ancestral** [an·ses·'tral, an·θes-] *adj* **1.** (*de los antepasados*) ancestral **2.** (*antiguo*) ancient

**ancho** ['an·tʃo] *m* width; **~ de vía** FERRO gauge [*o* gage]; **tener** [*o* **medir**] **cinco metros de ~** to be five meters wide

**ancho, -a** ['an·tʃo, -a] *adj* wide; (*vestidos*) loose-fitting; **~ de espaldas** broadshouldered; **a lo ~** widthwise **2. en este pueblo estoy a mis anchas** I feel at home in this village; **se queda tan ~ cuando dice tonterías** he remains completely unabashed when he talks nonsense

**anchoa** [an·'tʃoa] *f* anchovy

**anchura** [an·'tʃu·ra] *f* width; (*de un vestido*) looseness

**ancianidad** [an·sja·ni·'dad, an·θja-] *f* old age

**anciano, -a** [an·'sja·no, -a; an·'θja-] **I.** *adj* old **II.** *m, f* old man *m*, old woman *f*

**ancla** ['an·kla] *f* anchor; **echar/levar ~s** to drop/weigh anchor

**anclar** [an·'klar] *vi, vt* to anchor; **estar anclado** to be anchored

**andadas** [an·'da·das] *fpl* **volver a las ~** to revert to old habits

**ándale** ['an·da·le] *interj Méx* (*adiós*) bye; (*deprisa*) come on

**Andalucía** [an·da·lu·'si·a, -'θi·a] *f* Andalusia

**andaluz(a)** [an·da·'lus, -·'lu·sa; -'luθ, -·'lu·θa] *adj, m(f)* Andalusian

**andamiaje** [an·da·'mja·xe] *m,* **andamio** [an·'da·mjo] *m* scaffolding

**andanada** [an·da·'na·da] *f* **por ~s** *Arg* in excess

**andanza** [an·'dan·sa, -θa] *f* (*aventura*) adventure

**andar** [an·'dar] *irr* **I.** *vi* **1.** (*caminar*) to walk; **~ a caballo** to ride (a horse); **~ a**

**gatas** to go on all fours; (*bebés*) to crawl; **~ de prisa** to go quickly; **~ detrás de algo** to be after sth; **desde la estación hay 10 minutos andando** it's 10 minutes walk from the station **2.** (*coche*) to run; (*máquina*) to work **3.** (*estar*) **~ atareado** to be busy; **~ metido en un asunto** to be involved in a matter; **~ haciendo algo** to be doing sth; **te ando llamando desde hace una hora** I've been trying to call you for an hour; **~ mal de dinero** to be short of money; **~emos por los 30 grados** it must be about 30 degrees; **no andes en mi escritorio** don't go rummaging in my desk ▶ **dime con quien andas y te diré quien eres** *prov* a man is known by the company he keeps; **~ a la que salta** to seize the opportunity; **¡anda!** good heavens! **II.** *vt* he andado toda la casa **para encontrarte** I've looked all over the house for you **III.** *m* walk, gait

**andén** [an·'den] *m* FERRO platform

**Andes** ['an·des] *mpl* **los ~** the Andes + *pl vb*

**andinismo** [an·di·'nis·mo] *m AmL* mountaineering, mountain climbing

**andino, -a** [an·'di·no, -a] *adj* Andean

**Andorra** [an·'do·rra] *f* Andorra

**andrajo** [an·'dra·xo] *m* rag

**andrajoso, -a** [an·dra·'xo·so, -a] *adj* ragged

**andurrial** [an·du·'rrjal] *m Arg, Ecua, Perú* muddy road

**anécdota** [a·'nek·do·ta] *f* anecdote

**anemia** [a·'ne·mja] *f* anemia

**anémona** [a·'ne·mo·na] *f* anemone

**anestesia** [a·nes·'te·sja] *f* anesthesia

**anestesiar** [a·nes·te·'sjar] *vt* to anesthetize

**anestésico** [a·nes·'te·si·ko] *m* anesthetic

**anexión** [a·nek·'sjon] *f* annexation

**anexo** [a·'nek·so] *m v.* **anejo**

**anexo, -a** [a·'nek·so, -a] *adj v.* **anejo, -a**

**anfibio** [an·'fi·βjo] *m* amphibian

**anfibio, -a** [an·'fi·βjo, -a] *adj* amphibious

**anfiteatro** [an·fi·te·'a·tro] *m* **1.** (*local*) amphitheater **2.** (*en la universidad*) lecture hall

**anfitrión, -ona** [an·fi·'trjon] *m, f* host *m*, hostess *f*

**ánfora** ['an·fo·ra] *f* (*cántaro*) amphora

**ángel** ['an·xel] *m* angel; **~ de la guarda** guardian angel

**angelical** [an·xe·li·'kal] *adj* angelic(al)

**angina** [an·'xi·na] *f* **~ de pecho** angina (pectoris); **~s** sore throat

**anglicismo** [an·gli·'sis·mo, ·'θis·mo] *m* Anglicism

**angosto, -a** [an·'gos·to, -a] *adj* narrow

**anguila** [an·'gi·la] *f* ZOOL eel

**angula** [an·'gu·la] *f* ZOOL glass eel, elver

**angular** [an·gu·'lar] **I.** *adj* angular; **piedra ~** cornerstone **II.** *m* **gran ~** FOTO wide-angle lens

**ángulo** ['an·gu·lo] *m* **1.** MAT angle; **~ recto** right angle; **en ~** angled; **~ de tiro** DEP angle of fire **2.** (*rincón*) corner **3.** (*de vista*) angle of vision

**angurriento, -a** [an·gu·'rrjen·to, -a] *adj AmL* **1.** *pey* (*glotón*) gluttonous; (*hambriento*) greedy **2.** (*codicioso*) avaricious

**angustia** [an·'gus·tja] *f* **1.** (*temor*) anguish; **~ vital** angst **2.** (*aflicción*) anxiety

**angustiar** [an·gus·'tjar] **I.** *vt* **1.** (*acongojar*) to distress **2.** (*causar temor*) to frighten **3.** (*afligir*) to worry **II.** *vr:* **~se 1.** (*afligirse*) to get worried **2.** (*atemorizarse*) to get scared

**angustioso, -a** [an·gus·'tjo·so, -a] *adj* **1.** (*lleno de angustia*) anguished **2.** (*inquietante*) worrying

**anhelar** [a·ne·'lar] **I.** *vi* to pant **II.** *vt* to long for

**anhelo** [a·'ne·lo] *m* **~ de algo** longing for sth

**anidar** [a·ni·'dar] *vi* (*hacer nido*) to nest

**anilla** [a·'ni·ja, -ʎa] *f* **1.** (*aro*) ring **2.** *pl* DEP rings *pl*

**anillo** [a·'ni·jo, -ʎo] *m* ring; **~ de boda** wedding ring ▶ **venir como ~ al dedo** to be just right; **ese vestido te viene como ~ al dedo** this dress suits you perfectly; **no se me caen los ~s por...** it's not beneath me to...

**ánima** ['a·ni·ma] *f* soul

**animación** [a·ni·ma·'sjon, ·'θjon] *f* **1.** (*acción*) animation **2.** (*viveza*) liveliness **3.** (*actividad*) activity; **había mucha ~ en la calle** the street was very busy

**animado, -a** [a·ni·'ma·do, -a] *adj* **1.** (*persona*) in high spirits; **no estar muy ~** not to be very cheerful **2.** (*lugar*) busy **3.** (*actividad*) lively **4. estar ~ a hacer algo** to be keen on doing sth; **~ por ordenador** COMPUT computer-animated

**animador(a)** [a·ni·ma·'dor, -'do·ra] **I.** *adj* encouraging **II.** *m(f)* **1.** (*artista*) entertainer **2.** (*presentador*) presenter **3.** DEP cheerleader

**animal** [a·ni·'mal] **I.** *adj* **1.** (*de los animales*) animal; **comportamiento ~** animal behavior **2.** (*grosero*) rude **II.** *m* **1.** ZOOL animal; **~es de caza** game; **~ de compañía** pet; **~ de presa** predator; **comer como un ~** *inf* to eat like a horse **2.** *pey* (*persona ignorante*) fool; (*bruta*) brute

**animalada** [a·ni·ma·'la·da] *f inf* **1.** (*disparate*) (piece of) nonsense **2.** (*barbaridad*) disgrace; **¡qué ~!** how outrageous! **3.** (*cantidad*) massive amount

**animar** [a·ni·'mar] **I.** *vt* **1.** (*dinamizar*) to liven up **2.** (*alentar*) to encourage **3.** (*persona*) to cheer up **II.** *vr:* **~se 1.** (*cobrar vida*) to liven up **2.** (*atreverse*) to dare; **¡por fin te has animado a escribir!** so you've finally decided to write!; **¿te animas?** are you up to it? **3.** (*alegrarse*) to cheer up

**ánimo** ['a·ni·mo] *m* **1.** (*espíritu*) spirit; **no estoy con ~s de...** I don't feel like... **2.** (*energía*) energy; (*valor*) courage; **dar ~ to encourage**; **¡~!** cheer up! **3.** (*intención*) intention; **con ~ de...** with the intention of...; **sin ~ de lucro** non-profit-making; **sin ~ de ofender a nadie** without wishing to offend anyone

**aniñado, -a** [a·ni·'na·do, -a] *adj* childlike; *pey* childish

**aniquilar** [a·ni·ki·'lar] *vt* **1.** (*destruir*) to annihilate **2.** (*desanimar*) to shatter

**anís** <anises> [a·'nis] *m* **1.** (*planta*) anise; (*semilla*) aniseed **2.** (*licor*) anisette

**aniversario** [a·ni·βer·'sa·rjo] *m* anniversary; **~ de bodas** wedding anniversary

**ano** ['a·no] *m* ANAT anus

**anoche** [a·'no·tʃe] *adv* last night; **antes de ~** the night before last

**anochecer** [a·no·tʃe·'ser, -'θer] **I.** *irr como crecer vimpers* **anochece** it's getting dark **II.** *m* nightfall; **al ~** at dusk

**anodino, -a** [a·no·ˈdi·no, -a] *adj* (*cosa*) insipid; (*persona*) bland

**anomalía** [a·no·ma·ˈli̯a] *f* anomaly

**anonadar** [a·no·na·ˈdar] **I.** *vt* to astound; (*maravillar*) to overwhelm; **la noticia me dejó anonadado** I was astonished by the news **II.** *vr:* **~se 1.** (*descorazonarse*) to be discouraged **2.** (*aniquilarse*) to be destroyed

**anonimato** [a·no·ni·ˈma·to] *m* anonymity; **mantener el ~** to remain anonymous

**anónimo** [a·ˈno·ni·mo] *m* (*autor*) anonymous author; (*escrito*) anonymous work

**anónimo, -a** [a·ˈno·ni·mo, -a] *adj* anonymous; **sociedad anónima** ECON stock corporation

**anorexia** [a·no·ˈrek·sja] *f* anorexia

**anormal** [a·nor·ˈmal] *adj* abnormal; **~ (físico/síquico)** physically/mentally handicapped

**anotación** [a·no·ta·ˈsjon, -ˈθjon] *f* **1.** (*acción*) annotation; (*en un registro*) record **2.** (*nota*) note

**anotar** [a·no·ˈtar] *vt* to note (down); (*en un registro*) to record

**ansia** [ˈan·sja] *f* **1.** (*angustia*) anguish **2.** (*intranquilidad*) anxiety **3.** (*afán*) longing; **~ de poder** craving for power

**ansiar** <*1. pres* ansío> [an·ˈsjar] *vt* to long for; **el momento ansiado** the long-awaited moment; **~ el regreso de alguien** to long for sb's return

**ansiedad** [an·sje·ˈdad] *f* anxiety

**ansioso, -a** [an·ˈsjo·so, -a] *adj* **1.** (*intranquilo*) anxious **2.** (*anheloso*) eager **3.** (*impaciente*) impatient

**antagónico, -a** [an·ta·ˈɣo·ni·ko, -a] *adj* **1.** (*opuesto*) opposed **2.** (*rival*) antagonistic

**antagonista** [an·ta·ɣo·ˈnis·ta] *mf* antagonist

**antaño** [an·ˈta·ɲo] *adv* long ago

**antártico, -a** [an·ˈtar·ti·ko, -a] *adj* Antarctic; **Océano Glacial Antártico** Antarctic Ocean

**Antártida** [an·ˈtar·ti·da] *f* Antarctica

**ante** [ˈan·te] **I.** *m* **1.** ZOOL elk **2.** (*piel*) suede **II.** *prep* **1.** (*posición*) before **2.** (*en vista de*) in view of **3.** (*adversario*) faced with

**anteanoche** [an·te·a·ˈno·tʃe] *adv* the night before last

**anteayer** [an·te·a·ˈjer] *adv* the day before yesterday

**antebrazo** [an·te·ˈβra·so, -θo] *m* ANAT forearm

**antecedente** [an·te·se·ˈden·te, an·te·θe-] *m pl* history; (*de una persona*) background; **~s penales** criminal record

**anteceder** [an·te·se·ˈder, an·te·θe-] *vt* to precede

**antecesor(a)** [an·te·se·ˈsor, -·ˈso·ra; an·teθe-] *m(f)* **1.** (*en un cargo*) predecessor **2.** (*antepasado*) ancestor

**antelación** [an·te·la·ˈsjon, -ˈθjon] *f* **con ~ in** advance; **con la debida ~** in good time

**antemano** [an·te·ˈma·no] *adv* **de ~** in advance; **calcular de ~** to calculate in advance

**antena** [an·ˈte·na] *f* **1.** ZOOL antenna **2.** (*de televisor*) antenna; **estar en ~** to be on the air; **el programa lleva un año en ~** the program has been running for a year; **estar con las ~s puestas** irón to be all ears

**antepasado, -a** [an·te·pa·ˈsa·do, -a] *m, f* ancestor

**antepenúltimo, -a** [an·te·pe·ˈnul·ti·mo, -a] *adj* antepenultimate, third from last

**anteponer** [an·te·po·ˈner] *irr como* poner **I.** **1.** (*poner delante*) **~ algo a algo** to place sth in front of sth **2.** (*dar preferencia*) to give priority to **II.** *vr:* **~se 1.** (*ponerse delante*) **~se a alguien** to stand in front of sb **2.** (*tener preferencia*) to be preferred

**anteproyecto** [an·te·pro·ˈjek·to] *m* draft

**anterior** [an·te·ˈrjor] **I.** *adj* previous; **la noche ~ había llovido** the night before it had rained; **en la página ~** on the preceding [*o* previous] page **II.** *prep* **~ a** prior to

**anterioridad** [an·te·rjo·ri·ˈdad] *f* anteriority; **con ~ a** prior to, before

**anteriormente** [an·te·rjor·ˈmen·te] *adv* before, previously

**antes** [ˈan·tes] **I.** *adv* **1.** (*de tiempo*) before; (*hace un rato*) just now; (*antiguamente*) formerly; (*primero*) first; **poco ~** shortly before; **piénsate ~ lo que dices**

think before you speak; **ahora como ~** still; **cuanto ~** as soon as possible; **~ de nada** first of all **2.** (*comparativo*) rather **II.** *prep* **~ de** before **III.** *conj* (*temporal*) before; **~ (de) que llegues** before you arrive **IV.** *adj* **el día ~** the previous day

**antiaéreo, -a** [an·tja·'e·reo, -a] *adj* MIL anti-aircraft

**antibalas** [an·ti·'βa·las] *adj inv* bulletproof

**antibiótico** [an·ti·'βjo·ti·ko] *m* antibiotic

**anticiclón** [an·ti·si·'klon, -θi·'klon] *m* anticyclone

**anticipación** [an·ti·si·pa·'sjon, -θi·pa·'θjon] *f* (*de fecha, de suceso*) anticipation

**anticipadamente** [an·ti·si·pa·da·'men·te, an·ti·θi·] *adv* in advance; **jubilar ~ a alguien** to retire sb early

**anticipado, -a** [an·ti·si·'pa·do, -a; an·ti·θi·] *adj* early; **pagar por ~** to pay in advance

**anticipar** [an·ti·si·'par, an·ti·θi·] **I.** *vt* **1.** (*fecha*) to move up **2.** (*suceso*) to anticipate; **no anticipemos los acontecimientos** let's not anticipate events **3.** (*dinero*) to advance; **~ una paga sobre el sueldo** to give an advance on a salary **II.** *vr* **~se a alguien** to beat sb to it; **el verano se ha anticipado este año** summer is early this year

**anticipo** [an·ti·'si·po, -'θi·po] *m* **1.** (*del sueldo*) advance **2.** (*de un pago*) advance payment

**anticonceptivo, -a** [an·ti·kon·sep·'ti·βo, -a; -θep·'ti·βo, -a] *adj* contraceptive, birth-control; **píldora anticonceptiva** oral contraceptive, birth control pill

**anticongelante** [an·ti·kon·xe·'lan·te] *m* antifreeze

**anticonstitucional** [an·ti·kons·ti·tu·sjo·'nal, -θjo·'nal] *adj* unconstitutional

**anticuado, -a** [an·ti·'kwa·do, -a] *adj* old-fashioned

**anticuario, -a** [an·ti·'kwa·rjo, -a] *m, f* antique dealer

**anticucho** [an·ti·'ku·ʧo] *m* Perú kebob

**anticuerpo** [an·ti·'kwer·po] *m* antibody

**antideportivo, -a** [an·ti·de·por·'ti·βo, -a] *adj* unsporting

**antidoping** [an·ti·'do·piŋ] *adj inv* **control ~ drugs** test

**antidoto** [an·'ti·do·to] *m* antidote

**antifaz** [an·ti·'fas, -'faθ] *m* mask

**antiguamente** [an·ti·ywa·'men·te] *adv* once, long ago

**antigüedad** [an·ti·ywe·'dad] *f* **1.** (*edad antigua*) antiquity **2.** (*objeto*) antique; **tener una ~ de 100 años** to be 100 years old **3.** (*en una empresa*) seniority; **tengo 5 años de ~** (**en el trabajo**) I've been in the company's service for 5 years

**antiguo, -a** [an·'ti·ywo, -a] *adj* <antiquísimo> **1.** (*viejo*) old; (*relación*) long-standing **2.** (*anticuado*) antiquated; (*muy anticuado*) ancient **3.** (*de la antigüedad*) ancient **4.** (*anterior*) former **5.** (*en un cargo*) **es el más ~ en esta empresa** he's the most senior member of staff in this firm

**antiinflamatorio, -a** [an·tin·fla·ma·'to·rjo/an·ti·in·fla·ma·'to·rjo] *adj* anti-inflammatory

**antílope** [an·'ti·lo·pe] *m* antelope

**antinatural** [an·ti·na·tu·'ral] *adj* unnatural

**antipatía** [an·ti·pa·'ti·a] *f* antipathy; **~ a alguien** antipathy for sb

**antipático, -a** [an·ti·'pa·ti·ko, -a] *adj* unpleasant

**antirreglamentario, -a** [an·ti·rre·yla·men·'ta·rjo, -a] *adj* unlawful

**antirrobo** [an·ti·'rro·βo] *m* anti-theft device

**antisemita** [an·ti·se·'mi·ta] **I.** *adj* anti-Semitic **II.** *mf* anti-Semite

**antiséptico, -a** [an·ti·'sep·ti·ko] *adj* antiseptic

**antisocial** [an·ti·so·'sjal, -'θjal] *adj* antisocial

**antiterrorista** [an·ti·te·rro·'ris·ta] *adj* antiterrorist; **lucha ~** fight against terrorism

**antítesis** [an·'ti·te·sis] *f inv* antithesis

**antojarse** [an·to·'xar·se] *vimpers* (*encapricharse*) **se me antojó un helado** I felt like having an ice cream; **hace siempre lo que se le antoja** he/she always does as he/she pleases

**antojitos** [an·to·'xi·tos] *mpl* Méx CULIN appetizers *pl*

**antojo** [an·'to·xo] *m* **1.** (*capricho*) whim; **a mi ~** as I please **2.** (*de una embarazada*) craving **3.** *Méx* (*apetito*) appetite

**antología** [an·to·lo·'xi·a] *f* anthology

**antorcha** [an·'tor·tʃa] *f* torch

**antro** ['an·tro] *m* pey dive; **un ~ de corrupción** a den of iniquity

**antropología** [an·tro·po·lo·'xi·a] *f* anthropology

**antropólogo, -a** [an·tro·'po·lo·γo, -a] *m, f* anthropologist

**anual** [a·nu·'al] *adj* annual, yearly; **informe ~** annual report

**anualmente** [a·nwal·'men·te] *adv* annually, yearly

**anuario** [a·nu·'a·rjo] *m* yearbook

**anudar** [a·nu·'dar] **I.** *vt* to knot **II.** *vr:* **~se** to become knotted

**anulación** [a·nu·la·'sjon, -'θjon] *f* (*de una ley*) repeal; (*de una sentencia*) overturning; (*de un matrimonio*) annulment; (*de un contrato*) cancellation

**anular** [a·nu·'lar] **I.** *vt* (*ley*) to repeal; (*sentencia*) to overturn; (*matrimonio*) to annul; (*contrato*) to cancel; (*gol*) to disallow **II.** *adj* (*del anillo*) annular

**anunciar** [a·nun·'sjar, -'θjar] **I.** *vt* **1.** (*comunicar*) to announce; **acaban de ~ la llegada del vuelo** they've just announced the arrival of the flight **2.** (*dar publicidad*) to advertise **II.** *vr:* **~se** (*hacer publicidad*) to be advertised

**anuncio** [a·'nun·sjo, -θjo] *m* **1.** (*de una noticia*) announcement **2.** (*en la TV*) commercial; (*en un periódico*) advertisement, ad

**anverso** [am·'ber·so] *m* obverse

**anzuelo** [an·'swe·lo, -'θwe·lo] *m* **1.** (*para pescar*) (fish-)hook **2.** *inf* (*aliciente*) bait, lure; **echar el ~ a alguien** to lure sb; **morder** [*o* **tragar**] **el ~** to swallow the bait

**añadidura** [a·ɲa·di·'du·ra] *f* addition; **por ~** in addition

**añadir** [a·ɲa·'dir] *vt* to add; **a esto hay que ~ que...** there's also the fact that...

**añares** [a·'ɲa·res] *mpl Arg* ages *pl*

**añejo, -a** [a·'ɲe·xo, -a] *adj* old; (*vino*) mature

**añicos** [a·'ɲi·kos] *mpl* fragments *pl;* **hacer algo ~** to smash sth up

**año** [a·ɲo] *m* year; **~ bisiesto** leap year; **~ luz** light year; **~ natural** calendar year; **la víspera de ~ nuevo** New Year's Eve; **los ~s 60** the sixties; **en el ~ 1960** in 1960; **el ~ de la pera** the year one; **cumplir ~s** to have a birthday; **cumplir 60 ~s** to turn sixty; **¿cuántos ~s tienes?** how old are you?; **Juan le saca cinco ~s a Pepe** Juan is five years older than Pepe; **los ~s no pasan en balde** the years take their toll ▶ **un hombre <u>entrado</u> en ~s** an elderly man; **por él no <u>pasan</u> los ~s** he doesn't seem to get any older; **quitarse ~s** to be older than one admits; **a <u>mis</u> ~s** at my age

**añoranza** [a·ɲo·'ran·sa, -θa] *f* yearning

**añorar** [a·ɲo·'rar] *vt* to yearn for; **~ los viejos tiempos** to long for the old days

**aorta** [a·'or·ta] *f* aorta

**apacible** [a·pa·'si·βle, -'θi·βle] *adj* **1.** (*persona*) placid; (*temperamento*) even **2.** (*tiempo*) mild

**apadrinar** [a·pa·dri·'nar] *vt* **1.** (*ser padrino*) **~ a alguien** (*en un bautizo*) to be sb's godfather; (*en una boda*) to be sb's best man **2.** (*patrocinar*) to sponsor

**apagado, -a** [a·pa·'γa·do, -a] *adj* (*sonido*) muffled; (*persona*) lifeless; (*color*) dull

**apagar** <g → gu> [a·pa·'γar] *vt* (*luz*) to put out; **~ el fuego con una manta** to put out the fire with a blanket; (*radio*) to switch off; (*vela*) to snuff ▶ **estar apagado** to not be in form; **¡papa y <u>vámonos</u>!** that's enough! **II.** *vr:* **~se** (*fuego*) to go out; (*sonido*) to die out

**apagón** [a·pa·'γon] *m* blackout; ELEC power cut

**apalabrar** [a·pa·la·'βrar] *vt* to arrange

**apaleada** [a·pa·le·'a·da] *f Arg, Méx,* **apaleamiento** [a·pa·lea·'mjen·to] *m* (*zurra*) drubbing

**apantallado, -a** [a·pan·ta·'ja·do, -a; -'ʎa·do, -a] *adj Méx* overwhelmed

**apañado, -a** [a·pa·'ɲa·do, -a] *adj* **1.** (*hábil*) skillful **2.** (*adecuado*) suitable; **estás ~ si crees que te voy a ayudar** *inf* you're quite mistaken if you think I'm going to help you

**apañar** [a·pa·'ɲar] **I.** *vt* (*remendar*) to mend **II.** *vr:* **~se** (*arreglárselas*) to manage; **no sé cómo te las apañas** I don't know how you manage

**apaño** [a·ˈpa·ɲo] *m* **1.** (*remiendo*) patch; **encontrar un ~** to find a solution **2.** (*chanchullo*) scam

**aparato** [a·pa·ˈra·to] *m* **1.** (*utensilio*) t. DEP apparatus; **~ indicador** meter; **~ de precisión** precision instrument; **~ de televisión** television set **2.** TEL receiver; **ponerse al ~** to come to the phone **3.** ANAT system; **~ digestivo** digestive system **4.** (*ostentación*) pomp **5.** POL (*de un partido*) machine

**aparatoso, -a** [a·pa·ra·ˈto·so, -a] *adj* **1.** (*ostentoso*) ostentatious **2.** (*desmedido*) excessive

**aparcamiento** [a·par·ka·ˈmjen·to] *m* **1.** (*acción*) parking **2.** (*lugar*) parking lot

**aparcar** <c → qu> [a·par·ˈkar] *vt* **1.** (*coche*) to park **2.** (*decisión*) to put off

**aparecer** [a·pa·re·ˈser, -ˈθer] *irr como* **crecer** I. *vi* to appear; (*algo inesperado*) to turn up; **~ ante la opinión pública** to appear in public II. *vr:* **~se** to appear

**aparejador(a)** [a·pa·re·xa·ˈdor, -·ˈdo·ra] *m(f)* foreman builder *m*, forewoman builder *f*

**aparentar** [a·pa·ren·ˈtar] *vt* to feign; **trata de ~ que es rico** he tries to make out that he's rich; **no aparentas la edad que tienes** you don't look your age

**aparente** [a·pa·ˈren·te] *adj* **1.** (*que parece*) apparent **2.** (*visible*) visible

**aparentemente** [a·pa·ren·te·ˈmen·te] *adv* apparently, seemingly

**aparición** [a·pa·ri·ˈsjon, -ˈθjon] *f* **1.** (*acción*) appearance **2.** (*visión*) apparition

**apariencia** [a·pa·ˈrjen·sja, -θja] *f* appearance; **en ~** apparently; **guardar las ~s** to keep up appearances ▶ **las ~s engañan** appearances can be deceptive

**apartado** [a·par·ˈta·do] *m* **1.** (*párrafo*) paragraph **2.** ADMIN **~ de Correos** post office box

**apartado, -a** [a·par·ˈta·do, -a] *adj* (*lugar*) isolated

**apartamento** [a·par·ta·ˈmen·to] *m* apartment

**apartar** [a·par·ˈtar] I. *vt* **1.** (*separar*) to separate; (*la vista*) to avert **2.** (*a un lado*) to put aside; **~ a alguien para de-**

**cirle algo** to take sb aside to tell him/her sth; **¡aparta la mano del taladro!** take your hand off the drill! **3.** (*de un cargo*) to remove II. *vr:* **~se 1.** (*separarse*) to separate; (*del tema*) to deviate **2.** (*de un camino*) to turn off; **¡apártate!** get out of the way!

**aparte** [a·ˈpar·te] I. *adv* apart; **esta cuestión debe tratarse ~** this question must be dealt with on its own II. *prep* **1.** (*separado*) **él estaba ~ del grupo** he was separated from the group **2.** (*además de*) **~ de** apart from; **~ de esto, perdí las llaves** apart from that, I lost the keys III. *m* paragraph; **punto y ~** new paragraph IV. *adj inv* **1.** (*singular*) special **2.** (*separado*) separate; **en un plato ~** on a separate plate

**apasionado, -a** [a·pa·sjo·ˈna·do, -a] I. *adj* **1.** (*con pasión*) passionate **2.** (*entusiasta*) enthusiastic II. *m, f* enthusiast

**apasionante** [a·pa·sjo·ˈnan·te] *adj* exciting

**apatía** [a·pa·ˈti·a] *f* apathy

**apático, -a** [a·ˈpa·ti·ko, -a] *adj* apathetic

**apátrida** [a·ˈpa·tri·da] *adj* stateless

**apeadero** [a·pea·ˈde·ro] *m* FERRO halt

**apearse** [a·pe·ˈar·se] *vr* (*de un vehículo*) to get out; (*de un caballo*) to dismount

**apechugar** <g → gu> [a·pe·tʃu·ˈɣar] *vi* **~ con** to put up with stoically; **~ con las consecuencias** to suffer the consequences

**apedrear** [a·pe·dre·ˈar] *vt* to throw stones at; (*lapidar*) to stone (to death)

**apegado, -a** [a·pe·ˈɣa·do, -a] *adj* **estar ~ a alguien** to be attached to sb

**apego** [a·ˈpe·ɣo] *m* attachment; **tener un gran ~ a algo** to be very attached to sth

**apelación** [a·pe·la·ˈsjon, -ˈθjon] *f* JUR appeal; **esto no tiene ~** *fig* there's nothing to be done

**apelar** [a·pe·ˈlar] *vi* **1.** (*invocar*) to appeal **2.** (*recurrir*) to turn; (*a algo*) to resort; **~ a todos los medios** to try everything **3.** JUR (*recurrir*) to appeal

**apellidar** [a·pe·ʎi·ˈdar, -ˈʎi·ˈdar] I. *vt* to name II. *vr:* **~se** to be called; **se apellida Martínez** his/her surname is Martínez

**apellido** [a·pe·'ʝi·do, -'ʎi·do] *m* surname; ~ **de soltera** maiden name; **primer ~** father's surname

**apenas** [a·'pe·nas] *adv* 1. (*casi no*) hardly; ~ **había nadie** there was hardly anybody [*o* anyone] there 2. (*tan solo*) just; (*escasamente*) barely; ~ **hace una hora** barely an hour ago; **tengo ~ 10 dólares en el bolsillo** I have just 10 dollars in my pocket

**apéndice** [a·'pen·di·se, -θe] *m* 1. (*de un libro*) appendix; (*tomo separado*) supplement 2. (*complemento*) appendage 3. ANAT appendix

**apendicitis** [a·pen·di·'si·tis, -'θi·tis] *f inv* appendicitis

**aperitivo** [a·pe·ri·'ti·βo] *m* 1. (*bebida*) aperitif 2. (*comida*) appetizer ▶ **¡y ésto es tan solo el ~!** and that's only the beginning!

**apertura** [a·per·'tu·ra] *f* opening; ~ **de un crédito** taking out of a loan

**apestar** [a·pes·'tar] *vi* ~ **a algo** to stink of sth

**apestoso, -a** [a·pes·'to·so, -a] *adj* 1. (*que apesta*) stinking, stinky *inf* 2. (*fastidioso*) annoying

**apetecer** [a·pe·te·'ser, -'θer] *irr como* **crecer** *vi* 1. (*tener ganas de*) to feel like; **¿qué te apetece?** what would you like?; **me apetece un helado** I feel like an ice cream 2. (*gustar*) **una copa de vino siempre apetece** a glass of wine is always welcome

**apetito** [a·pe·'ti·to] *m* 1. (*de comida*) ~ **de algo** appetite for sth; **abrir el ~ ~ de algo** to whet one's appetite 2. (*deseo*) ~ **de algo** desire for sth

**apetitoso, -a** [a·pe·ti·'to·so, -a] *adj* 1. (*que da apetito*) appetizing 2. (*sabroso*) tasty 3. (*deseable*) desirable

**ápice** ['a·pi·se, -θe] *m* apex; **no ceder un ~** *fig* not to yield an inch

**apicultor(a)** [a·pi·kul·'tor, -·'to·ra] *m(f)* beekeeper

**apicultura** [a·pi·kul·'tu·ra] *f* beekeeping, apiculture

**apilar(se)** [a·pi·'lar·(se)] *vt, (vr)* to pile up

**apio** ['a·pjo] *m* celery

**apirularse** [a·pi·ru·'lar·se] *vr* Chile to dress up

**apisonadora** [a·pi·so·na·'do·ra] *f* steamroller

**aplacar** <c → qu> [a·pla·'kar] I. *vt* 1. (*persona*) to calm down 2. (*dolor*) to soothe; (*hambre*) to satisfy; (*sed*) to quench II. *vr:* ~**se** to calm down

**aplanar** [a·pla·'nar] *vt* 1. (*allanar*) to level 2. (*aplastar*) to flatten

**aplastante** [a·plas·'tan·te] *adj* overwhelming; (*derrota*) crushing

**aplastar** [a·plas·'tar] *vt* 1. (*chafar*) to flatten; (*con la mano*) to squash; (*con el pie*) to crush; **el desprendimiento de piedras aplastó a dos personas** the rockfall crushed two people 2. (*derrotar*) to overwhelm

**aplatanarse** [a·pla·ta·'nar·se] *vr* Cuba, PRico (*adoptar las costumbres*) to go native

**aplaudir** [a·plau·'dir] I. *vi* to applaud, to clap II. *vt* 1. (*palmear*) to applaud 2. (*aprobar*) to approve

**aplauso** [a·'plau·so] *m* applause; **digno de ~** *fig* worthy of applause

**aplazamiento** [a·pla·sa·'mjen·to, a·pla·θa-] *m* 1. (*de fecha*) postponement; (*de reunión*) postponement, adjournment 2. (*de decisión*) deferment

**aplazar** <z → c> [a·pla·'sar, -'θar] *vt* 1. (*fecha*) to postpone; (*reunión*) to postpone, to adjourn *(after having begun)*; ~ **el viaje una semana** to postpone the trip by one week 2. (*decisión*) to defer

**aplicación** [a·pli·ka·'sjon, -'θjon] *f* 1. (*de pintura*) application 2. (*utilización*) use; **las múltiples aplicaciones del plástico** the various applications [*o* uses] of plastic

**aplicado, -a** [a·pli·'ka·do, -a] *adj* (*trabajador*) hardworking

**aplicar** <c → qu> [a·pli·'kar] I. *vt* 1. (*poner*) to apply; ~ **dando un ligero masaje** apply, massaging lightly 2. (*utilizar*) to use; ~ **una máquina para un trabajo** to use a machine for a job; ~ **el freno** to apply the brake 3. JUR ~ **una sanción** to impose; **la ley no se puede ~ en este caso** the law is not applicable in this case II. *vr:* ~**se** 1. (*esforzarse*) to apply oneself 2. (*emplearse*) to be used

**aplique** [a·'pli·ke] *m* wall lamp, sconce

**aplomo** [a·'plo·mo] *m* self-confidence, composure; **perder el ~** to lose one's composure

**apocarse** <c → qu> [a·po·'kar·se] *vr* to lose heart

**apodar** [a·po·'dar] I. *vt* to call; (*un apodo*) to nickname II. *vr* **~se...** (*tener el sobrenombre*) to be called ...; (*el apodo*) to be nicknamed...

**apoderado, -a** [a·po·de·'ra·do, -a] *m, f* 1. JUR proxy 2. COM agent

**apoderar** [a·po·de·'rar] I. *vt* to authorize; JUR to grant power of attorney to II. *vr:* **~se** to take possession; **el espía se apoderó del maletín** the spy seized the briefcase

**apodo** [a·'po·do] *m* nickname

**apogeo** [a·po·'xeo] *m* 1. ASTR apogee 2. (*cumbre*) summit; **estar en el ~ de su carrera** to be at the peak of one's career

**apolismado, -a** [a·po·lis·'ma·do, -a] *adj* 1. *AmL* (*magullado*) damaged 2. *Col, Méx, PRico* (*raquítico*) sickly 3. *CRi* (*holgazán*) lazy 4. *Méx, Ven* (*deprimido*) depressed 5. *PRico* (*tonto*) stupid

**apolítico, -a** [a·po·'li·ti·ko, -a] *adj* apolitical

**apología** [a·po·lo·'xi·a] *f* defense

**apoplejía** [a·po·ple·'xi·a] *f* stroke

**aporrear** [a·po·rre·'ar] *vt* (*dar golpes*) to beat; **~ el piano** to bang on the piano; **~ la puerta** to bang [*o* hammer] on the door

**aportación** [a·por·ta·'sjon, -'θjon] *f* 1. (*contribución*) contribution; **~ dineraria** cash contribution; **hacer una ~ a un trabajo** to make a contribution to a job 2. (*donación*) donation

**aportar** [a·por·'tar] *vt* 1. (*contribuir*) to contribute; **he aportado algo a la fiesta** I've made a contribution to the party;. **no aporta nada ir a esa conferencia** it's not worth going to that conference 2. (*información*) to provide

**aposento** [a·po·'sen·to] *m* 1. (*hospedaje*) lodging; **nos dieron ~** they put us up 2. (*cuarto*) room

**aposición** [a·po·si·'sjon, -'θjon] *f* apposition

**apósito** [a·'po·si·to] *m* (*vendaje*) dressing; (*adhesivo*) adhesive tape

**aposta** [a·'pos·ta] *adv* on purpose

**apostar** <o → ue> [a·pos·'tar] I. *vi* **~ por algo/alguien** to back sth/sb II. *vt, vr:* **~se** to bet; **¿qué/cuánto apostamos?** what/how much should we bet?; **¿qué te apuestas a que no lo hace?** I bet you he/she won't do it; **~ doble contra sencillo que...** I bet you two to one that...

**a posteriori** [a pos·te·'rjo·ri] *adv* with hindsight

**apostilla** [a·pos·'ti·ja, -ʎa] *f* marginal note

**apóstol** [a·'pos·tol] *m* apostle

**apóstrofo** [a·'pos·tro·fo] *m* LING apostrophe

**apoteósico, -a** [a·po·te·'o·si·ko, -a] *adj* tremendous; **éxito ~** tremendous success

**apoyar** [a·po·'jar] I. *vt* 1. (*colocar sobre*) to rest; (*contra*) to lean 2. (*fundar*) to base 3. (*patrocinar*) to back; **~ una moción** to support a motion; **~ una reforma** to back a reform II. *vr:* **~se** 1. (*descansar*) to rest; **~se en** [*o* contra] **algo** to lean on sth; **~se con la mano** to support oneself with one's hand 2. (*fundarse*) to be based

**apoyo** [a·'po·jo] *m* 1. (*sostén*) support 2. (*respaldo*) backing, support; (*ayuda*) help; **cuenta con mi ~** you can rely on me

**apreciable** [a·pre·'sja·βle, -'θja·βle] *adj* 1. (*observable*) noticeable; **~ al oído** audible 2. (*considerable*) considerable

**apreciación** [a·pre·sja·'sjon, -θja·'θjon] *f* 1. (*juicio*) assessment 2. (*de una moneda*) appreciation 3. (*del tamaño*) estimation

**apreciado, -a** [a·pre·'sja·do, -a; -'θja·do, -a] *adj* (*en cartas*) **~s Sres** Dear Sirs

**apreciar** [a·pre·'sjar, -'θjar] *vt* 1. (*estimar*) to appreciate; **si aprecias tu vida, ¡desaparece de aquí!** if you value your life, get out of here! 2. (*una moneda*) to appreciate 3. (*tamaño*) to estimate 4. (*captar*) to detect; **de lejos no se aprecia ningún sonido** no sound can be heard from afar; **el médico apreció una contusión en el pecho** the doctor detected bruising in the chest **5.** (*valorar*) to assess

**aprecio** [a·'pre·sjo, -θjo] *m* **1.** (*afecto*) affection; **te tengo un gran ~** I'm very fond of you **2.** (*estima*) esteem; **gran ~** high opinion

**aprehensión** [a·pren·'sjon/a·pre·en·'sjon] *f* **1.** (*acción de coger*) apprehension; (*del botín*) seizure **2.** (*percepción*) perception

**apremiante** [a·pre·'mjan·te] *adj* pressing

**apremiar** [a·pre·'mjar] **I.** *vt* (*acuciar*) to urge (on) **II.** *vi* to be urgent; **el tiempo apremia** time is pressing

**aprender** [a·pren·'der] *vt* to learn; **fácil de ~** easy to learn; **~ a leer** to learn to read; **~ de la historia** to learn from history; **~ de memoria** to learn by heart

**aprendiz(a)** [a·pren·'dis, -·'di·sa, -·'diθ, -·'di·θa] *m(f)* apprentice; **entrar de ~** to become an apprentice; **trabajar de ~** to work as an apprentice

**aprendizaje** [a·pren·di·'sa·xe, -'θa·xe] *m* **1.** (*acción*) learning **2.** (*formación*) apprenticeship

**aprensión** [a·pren·'sjon] *f* **1.** (*recelo*) apprehension; **me da ~ decírtelo** I don't dare tell you **2.** (*asco*) disgust; **me da ~ beber de este vaso** I find it disgusting to drink from this glass **3.** (*temor*) fear

**aprensivo, -a** [a·pren·'si·βo, -a] *adj* overanxious; (*hipocondríaco*) hypochondriac

**apresar** [a·pre·'sar] *vt* to seize; (*delincuente*) to capture

**apresurado, -a** [a·pre·su·'ra·do, -a] *adj* hurried; (*con excesiva prisa*) hasty; **andar con paso ~** to walk quickly

**apresurar** [a·pre·su·'rar] **I.** *vt* (*acelerar*) to speed up; **~ el paso** to quicken one's step **II.** *vr:* **~se** to hurry; **¡no te apresures!** take your time!

**apretado, -a** [a·pre·'ta·do, -a] *adj* **1.** (*oprimido*) oppressed **2.** (*tornillo*) tight; (*vestido*) close-fitting, tight; (*cuerda*) taut; (*personas*) tight-fisted **3.** (*difícil*) **verse** [*o* **estar**] **muy ~** to be in a very difficult situation **4.** (*apurado*) **estar ~ de dinero** to be short of money;

**estar ~ de tiempo** to be short of time

**apretar** <e → ie> [a·pre·'tar] **I.** *vi* **1.** (*calor*) to become oppressive **2.** (*vestido*) to be too tight; **la americana me aprieta por detrás** the jacket is too tight around the back **3.** (*deudas*) **~ a alguien** to weigh heavily on sb **4.** (*esforzarse*) **si aprietas un poco, puedes ganar el partido** if you put more effort into it, you can win the game **5.** (*exigir*) **este profesor aprieta mucho en los exámenes** this professor demands a lot in the examinations **II.** *vt* **1.** (*hacer presión*) to press; **~ un botón** to press a button; **~ algo contra el pecho** to press sth against one's chest; **~ el tubo de la pasta de dientes** to squeeze the toothpaste tube **2.** (*estrechar*) **~ las cuerdas de la guitarra** to tighten the strings of the guitar; **~ los dientes** to grit one's teeth; **~ filas** to close ranks; **~ las manos** to clasp one's hands; **~ el puño** to clench one's fist; **~ un nudo/ un tornillo** to tighten a knot/a screw **III.** *vr:* **~se 1.** (*estrecharse*) to become narrower **2.** (*agolparse*) to crowd together **3.** (*ceñirse*) **~se el cinturón** to tighten one's belt

**apretón** [a·pre·'ton] *m* (*presión*) squeeze

**aprieto** [a·'prje·to] *m* jam, fix; **~ económico** financial difficulties; **estar en un ~** to be in a jam

**a priori** [a pri·'o·ri] *adv* a priori

**aprisa** [a·'pri·sa] *adv* quickly

**aprisionar** [a·pri·sjo·'nar] *vt* **1.** (*atar*) to bind **2.** (*inmovilizar*) to immobilize; (*pillar*) to catch; **quedarse aprisionado en el barro** to be trapped in the mud

**aprobación** [a·pro·βa·'sjon, -'θjon] *f* (*de decisión*) approval; (*de una ley*) passing; **murmullo de ~** murmur of approval

**aprobado** [a·pro·'βa·do] *m* ENS pass; **he sacado un ~ en historia** I've passed history

**aprobar** <o → ue> [a·pro·'βar] **I.** *vt* **1.** (*decisión*) to approve; (*ley*) to pass; **la solicitud fue aprobada** the application was approved **2.** (*examen*) to pass **II.** *vi* ENS to pass

**apronte** [a·'pron·te] *m* AmL preparation

**apropiación** [a·pro·pja·'sjon, -'θjon] *f*

appropriation; **~ indebida** misappropriation

**apropiado, -a** [a·pro·'pja·do, -a] *adj*
**1.** (*adecuado*) suitable; **~ para** algo suitable
for sth **2.** (*oportuno*) appropriate

**apropiar** [a·pro·'pjar] **I.** *vt AmL* (*premio*)
to award; (*encargo*) to assign **II.** *vr* **~se
de algo** to appropriate sth

**aprovechable** [a·pro·βe·'tʃa·βle] *adj* usable

**aprovechado, -a** [a·pro·βe·'tʃa·do, -a] *adj*
(*calculador*) opportunistic

**aprovechamiento** [a·pro·βe·'tʃa·mjen·
to] *m* exploitation

**aprovechar** [a·pro·βe·'tʃar] **I.** *vi* (*valer*)
to be of use ▸ **¡que aproveche!** enjoy your meal!, bon appétit! **II.** *vt* to
make good use of; (*abusar*) to exploit;
**~ una idea** to exploit an idea **III.** *vr:*
**~se 1.** (*sacar provecho*) **~se de algo** to
profit by [*o* from] sth **2.** (*abusar*) to take
advantage; **~se de una mujer** to take
advantage of a woman **3.** (*explotar*) **~se
de alguien** to exploit sb

**aprovisionar** [a·pro·βi·sjo·'nar] *vt* **~ de**
[*o* con] **algo** to supply with sth

**aproximación** [a·prok·si·ma·'sjon] *f*
**1.** (*acercamiento*) approach **2.** (*en una
lotería*) consolation prize

**aproximado, -a** [a·prok·si·'ma·do, -a] *adj*
approximate

**aproximar** [a·prok·si·'mar] **I.** *vt* to bring
nearer; **~ opiniones** to bring opinions
closer together **II.** *vr:* **~se** to approach;
**se aproxima a la realidad** it comes
close to the truth; **las tropas se aproximan** the troops are getting closer

**aptitud** [ap·ti·'tud] *f* **1.** (*talento*) aptitude;
**~ para algo** aptitude for sth **2.** (*conveniencia*) suitability

**apto, -a** ['ap·to, -a] *adj* suitable; **~ para
algo** fit for sth; **la película no es apta
para menores** the film is not suitable
for minors

**apuesta** [a·'pwes·ta] *f* **1.** (*juego*) bet;
**corredor de ~s** bookmaker **2.** (*cantidad*) bid

**apuesto, -a** [a·'pwes·to, -a] *adj* handsome

**apuntador(a)** [a·pun·ta·'dor, -·'do·ra]
*m(f)* TEAT prompter

**apuntar** [a·pun·'tar] **I.** *vi* to appear; (*día*)
to break; **apunta la primavera** spring
is coming **II.** *vt* (*con un arma*) **~ a
algo** to aim at sth; **¡apunten!** take aim!
**2.** (*con el dedo*) **~ a algo** to point at
sth **3.** (*anotar*) to note (down) **4.** (*inscribir*) to enroll; (*en una lista*) to enter
**5.** TEAT to prompt **6.** (*insinuar*) to hint at
**7.** (*indicar*) to point out; **todo apunta
en esta dirección** everything points in
this direction **III.** *vr:* **~se 1.** (*inscribirse*) **~se a algo** to enroll in sth; (*en una
lista*) to enter one's name in sth; **~se
a un club** to join a club **2.** (*tanto*) to
score; (*victoria*) to achieve

**apunte** [a·'pun·te] *m* (*escrito*) note; **tomar ~s** to take notes

**apuñalar** [a·pu·ɲa·'lar] *vt* to stab

**apurado, -a** [a·pu·'ra·do, -a] *adj* **1.** (*falto*) **~ de dinero** hard up; **~ de tiempo** short of time **2.** (*dificultoso*) difficult; **verse ~** to be in trouble **3.** *AmL*
(*apresurado*) hurried; **estar ~** to be
in a hurry

**apurar** [a·pu·'rar] **I.** *vt* **1.** (*vaso*) to drain;
(*plato*) to finish off **2.** (*paciencia*) to exhaust; **~ todos los medios** to try everything **3.** (*atosigar*) to harass; **¡no me
apures, mi paciencia tiene un límite!**
don't hassle me, my patience is limited!
**4.** (*avergonzar*) to embarrass; **me apura decirle que no tengo dinero** I'm
embarrassed to tell him/her that I don't
have any money **5.** *AmL* (*dar prisa*) to
hurry **II.** *vr:* **~se 1.** (*preocuparse*) to
worry; **¡no te apures por eso!** don't
worry about that! **2.** *AmL* (*darse prisa*) to hurry up; **¡no te apures!** there's
no hurry

**apuro** [a·'pu·ro] *m* **1.** (*aprieto*) fix; (*dificultad*) difficulty; **estar en un ~** to be in
a fix; **sacar a alguien de un ~** to get sb
out of a fix **2.** (*estrechez*) financial need;
**sufrir grandes ~s** to be in financial difficulties **3.** (*vergüenza*) embarrassment;
**me da ~ pedirle el dinero** it's embarrassing for me to ask him/her for money
**4.** *AmL* (*prisa*) hurry

**aquel, -ella** [a·'kel, -·'ke·ja, -·'ke·ʎa] **I.** *adj
dem* <aquellos, -as> that, those *pl*;
**aquella casa es nuestra** that house is

ours; ¿qué fue del hombre ~? what became of that man?; ¿estabais de acuerdo en ~ punto? did you agree on that point?; **en aquellos tiempos** in those days **II.** *pron dem v.* **aquél, aquélla, aquello**

**aquí** [a·'ki] *adv* **1.** (*lugar*) here; **(por) ~ cerca** around here; **~ dentro** in here; **éste de ~** this guy here; **¡ah, ~ estás!** oh, there you are!; **andar de ~ para allá** to walk up and down; **de ~ hasta allí hay 10 minutos a pie** it's a 10-minute walk from here; **mejor ir por ~** it's better to go this way **2.** (*de tiempo*) **de ~ en adelante** from now on; **de ~ a una semana** a week from now; **hasta ~** up until now

**ara**[1] [a·ra] *f* altar ▶ **dar la vida en ~s de una idea** to sacrifice one's life for an idea

**ara**[2] ['a·ra] *m AmL* parrot

**árabe** ['a·ra·βe] **I.** *adj* **1.** (*país*) Arab **2.** (*palabra*) Arabic **3.** (*península*) Arabian **4.** (*de los moros*) Moorish **II.** *mf* (*persona*) Arab **III.** *m* (*lengua*) Arabic

**Arabia** [a·'ra·βja] *f* Arabia; **~ Saudita** Saudi Arabia

**arábigo, -a** [a·ra·βi·γo] *adj* Arab; (*número*) Arabic

**arado** [a·'ra·do] *m* plow

**Aragón** [a·ra·'γon] *m* Aragon

**aragonés, -esa** [a·ra·γo·'nes, -·'ne·sa] *adj, m, f* Aragonese

**arancel** [a·ran·'sel, -'θel] *m* tariff; (*impuesto*) duty

**arándano** [a·'ran·da·no] *m* blueberry

**araña** [a·'ra·ɲa] *f* ZOOL spider; **tela de ~** spider web

**arañar(se)** [a·ra·'ɲar(·se)] *vt, vi, (vr)* (*rasguñar*) to scratch (oneself)

**arañazo** [a·ra·'ɲa·so, -θo] *m* scratch; **dar un ~ a alguien** to scratch sb

**arar** [a·'rar] *vt* to plow

**arbitraje** [ar·βi·'tra·xe] *m* **1.** (*juicio*) arbitration **2.** (*en fútbol*) refereeing; (*en tenis*) umpiring

**arbitral** [ar·βi·'tral] *adj* arbitral

**arbitrar** [ar·βi·'trar] *vt* **1.** (*disputa*) **~ algo** to arbitrate in sth **2.** (*medios*) to provide **3.** DEP (*en fútbol*) to referee; (*en tenis*) to umpire

**arbitrariedad** [ar·βi·tra·rje·'dad] *f* **1.** (*cualidad*) arbitrariness **2.** (*acción*) arbitrary act

**arbitrario, -a** [ar·βi·'tra·rjo, -a] *adj* arbitrary

**arbitrio** [ar·'βi·trjo] *m* (*voluntad*) free will; **dejar algo al ~ de alguien** to leave sth to sb's discretion

**árbitro, -a** ['ar·βi·tro, -a] *m, f* **1.** (*mediador*) arbitrator **2.** (*fútbol*) referee; (*tenis*) umpire

**árbol** [ar·βol] *m* **1.** BOT tree; **~ de Navidad** Christmas tree; **~ genealógico** family tree **2.** TÉC (*eje*) shaft ▶ **los ~es no le dejan ver el bosque** he can't see the wood for the trees; **del ~ caído todos hacen leña** *prov* if a man falls, all will tread on him

**arbolado** [ar·βo·'la·do] *m*, **arboleda** [ar·βo·'le·da] *f* woods + *sing or pl vb*

**arbusto** [ar·'βus·to] *m* shrub, bush

**arca** ['ar·ka] *f* chest; (*para dinero*) safe; **las ~s del estado** the treasury ▶ **~ de Noé** Noah's Ark

**arcada** [ar·'ka·da] *f* **1.** ARQUIT arcade **2.** *pl* (*náusea*) heaving

**arcaico, -a** [ar·'kai·ko, -a] *adj* archaic

**arce** ['ar·se, -θe] *m* maple

**arcén** [ar·'sen, -'θen] *m* edge; (*de carretera*) shoulder

**archipiélago** [ar·tʃi·'pje·la·γo] *m* archipelago

**archivador** [ar·tʃi·βa·'dor] *m* **1.** (*mueble*) filing cabinet **2.** (*carpeta*) file

**archivador(a)** [ar·tʃi·βa·'dor, -·'do·ra] *m(f)* archivist

**archivar** [ar·tʃi·'βar] *vt* to file; COMPUT to store; (*asunto: por un tiempo*) to put on file; (*para siempre*) to close the file on

**archivo** [ar·'tʃi·βo] *m* **1.** (*lugar*) archive(s); **constar en los ~s** to be on record **2.** *pl* (*documentos*) archives *pl* **3.** COMPUT file

**arcilla** [ar·'si·ja, -'θi·ʎa] *f* clay

**arco** ['ar·ko] *m* **1.** ARQUIT, MAT arc; **~ de medio punto** arch; **~ iris** rainbow; **~ voltaico** arc lamp **2.** (*arma*) *t.* MÚS bow **3.** *AmL* goal

**arcón** [ar·'kon] *m* large chest

**arder** [ar·'der] *vi* **1.** (*quemar*) to burn; **~ con fuerza** to blaze; **~ sin llama** to smolder; **~ de fiebre** to have a very high temperature; **~ de pasión** to be inflamed with passion; **~ de rabia** to be mad with rage; **me arde la garganta** my throat is burning **2.** + *en, fig* **ardo en deseos de conocerte** I'm dying to get to know you

**ardid** [arˈðið] *m* ruse

**ardiente** [arˈðjen·te] *adj* **1.** (*pasión*) burning **2.** (*persona*) passionate

**ardilla** [arˈði·ʎa, -ʎa] *f* squirrel

**ardor** [arˈðor] *m* **1.** (*calor*) heat; **~ de estómago** heartburn **2.** (*fervor*) ardor; **el ~ de su mirada** the ardor of his/her look

**arduo, -a** [ˈar·ðwo, -a] *adj* arduous

**área** [ˈa·rea] *f t.* MAT area; **un ~ de 200 metros cuadrados** an area of 200 square meters; **~ de descanso** AUTO picnic area; **~ de castigo** DEP penalty area; **~ metropolitana** metropolitan area; **~ de no fumadores** no-smoking area

**arena** [aˈre·na] *f* (*materia*) sand; **~s movedizas** quicksand ▶ **edificar sobre ~** to build on sandy ground

**arenal** [aˈre·nal] *m* sandy area

**arenoso, -a** [a·reˈno·so, -a] *adj* sandy

**arenque** [aˈren·ke] *m* herring; **~s ahumados** kippers *pl*

**arepa** [aˈre·pa] *f AmL* cornmeal griddlecake

**arequipa** [a·reˈki·pa] *f Col, Méx* rice pudding

**arete** [aˈre·te] *m* earring

**argamasa** [ar·yaˈma·sa] *f* mortar

**Argentina** [ar·xenˈti·na] *f* Argentina

**argentino, -a** [ar·xenˈti·no, -a] *adj, m, f* Argentine

**argolla** [arˈɣo·ʎa, -ʎa] *f* **1.** (*anilla*) ring **2.** *Chile, Col, Hond, Méx* (*alianza*) wedding ring

**argot** <argots> [arˈɣo(t)] *m* (*marginal*) slang; (*profesional*) jargon

**argucia** [arˈɣu·sja, -θja] *f* **1.** (*argumento*) fallacy **2.** (*truco*) trick

**argüende** [arˈɣwen·de] *m Méx* (*chisme*) gossip

**argüir** [ar·ɣuˈir] *irr como huir* vt, vi (*alegar*) to argue

**argumentación** [ar·ɣu·men·taˈsjon, -ˈθjon] *f* line of argument

**argumentar** [ar·ɣu·menˈtar] *vi, vt* to

argue

**argumento** [ar·ɣuˈmen·to] *m* **1.** (*razón*) argument; (*razonamiento*) reasoning **2.** CINE plot

**aria** [ˈa·rja] *f* aria

**aridez** [a·riˈðes, -ˈðeθ] *f* aridity

**árido, -a** [ˈa·ri·ðo, -a] *adj* (*terreno*) arid, dry; (*tema*) dry

**Aries** [ˈa·rjes] *m inv* ASTR Aries

**arisco, -a** [aˈris·ko, -a] *adj* (*persona*) surly, unfriendly; (*animal*) skittish

**aristocracia** [a·ris·to·ˈkra·sja, -θja] *f* aristocracy

**aristócrata** [a·ris·ˈto·kra·ta] *mf* aristocrat

**aristocrático, -a** [a·ris·to·ˈkra·ti·ko, -a] *adj* aristocratic

**aritmética** [a·rit·ˈme·ti·ka] *f* arithmetic

**aritmético, -a** [a·rit·ˈme·ti·ko, -a] *adj* arithmetical

**arlequín** [ar·le·ˈkin] *m* harlequin

**arma** [ˈar·ma] *f* **1.** (*instrumento*) weapon, arm; **~s de destrucción masiva** weapons of mass destruction; **un ~ homicida** a murder weapon; **~ blanca** knife; **~ de fuego** firearm; **rendir las ~s** to surrender [*o* lay down] one's arms; **tomar las ~s** to take up arms; **¡apunten ~s!** take aim!; **¡descansen ~s!** order arms! **2.** *pl* (*blasón*) arms *pl* ▶ **ser un ~ de doble filo** to be a double-edged sword; **ser de ~s tomar** to be bold

**armada** [arˈma·ða] *f* **1.** (*fuerzas navales*) navy **2.** (*escuadra*) fleet; HIST armada

**armado, -a** [arˈma·ðo] *adj* armed; **~ de algo** armed with sth

**armador(a)** [ar·maˈðor, -ˈðo·ra] *m(f)* shipowner

**armadura** [ar·maˈðu·ra] *f* **1.** (*de caballero*) armor; **una ~** a suit of armor **2.** (*de edificio*) framework

**armamento** [ar·maˈmen·to] *m* arms *pl*; (*de un país*) armaments *pl*

**armar** [arˈmar] **I.** *vt* **1.** (*ejército*) to arm; **~ a alguien de** [*o* con]... to arm sb with... **2.** TÉC to assemble **3.** *inf* (*jaleo*) to stir up; (*ruido*) to raise; **~la** to start an argument **II.** *vr* **~se** [*o* con] **algo** to arm oneself with sth ▶ **~se de paciencia** to muster one's patience; **~se de valor** to find courage

**armario** [ar·'ma·rjo] *m* cupboard; **~ empotrado** built-in cupboard; **~ (ropero)** wardrobe

**armazón** [ar·ma·'son, -'θon] *m o f* (*armadura*) frame; (*de edificio*) skeleton

**armiño** [ar·'mi·no] *m* **1.** (*animal*) stoat **2.** (*piel*) ermine

**armisticio** [ar·mis·'ti·sjo, -θjo] *m* armistice

**armonía** [ar·mo·'ni·a] *f* harmony; **falta de ~** (*entre personas*) discord; **su comportamiento no estuvo en ~ con la solemnidad del acto** his/her behavior wasn't in keeping with the solemnity of the ceremony

**armónica** [ar·'mo·ni·ka] *f* harmonica, mouth organ

**armónico, -a** [ar·'mo·ni·ko] *adj* harmonic

**armonioso, -a** [ar·mo·'njo·so, -a] *adj* harmonious

**armonizar** <z → c> [ar·mo·ni·'sar, -'θar] **I.** *vi* to harmonize; **~ con** (*colores*) to blend with **II.** *vt* to harmonize; **~ ideas** to reconcile ideas

**árnica** ['ar·ni·ka] *f* BOT arnica

**aro** ['a·ro] *m* **1.** (*argolla*) ring; (*para jugar*) hoop **2.** *Arg* (*arete*) earring **3.** *AmL* (*anillo de boda*) wedding ring ▶ **entrar** [*o* **pasar**] **por el ~** to give in

**aroma** [a·'ro·ma] *m* (*olor*) scent; (*de café*) aroma

**aromático, -a** [a·ro·'ma·ti·ko, -a] *adj* aromatic

**arpa** ['ar·pa] *f* harp

**arpón** [ar·'pon] *m* harpoon

**arqueología** [ar·keo·lo·'xi·a] *f* archeology

**arqueológico, -a** [ar·keo·'lo·xi·ko, -a] *adj* archeological

**arqueólogo, -a** [ar·ke·'o·lo·ɣo, -a] *m, f* archaeologist

**arquero, -a** [ar·'ke·ro, -a] *m, f* **1.** archer **2.** *Arg* DEP goalkeeper

**arquetipo** [ar·ke·'ti·po] *m* archetype

**arquitecto, -a** [ar·ki·'tek·to, -a] *m, f* architect

**arquitectónico, -a** [ar·ki·tek·'to·ni·ko] *adj* architectural

**arquitectura** [ar·ki·tek·'tu·ra] *f* architecture

**arrabal** [a·rra·'βal] *m* (*periferia*) suburb; (*barrio bajo*) slum area; **vivir en los ~es** to live on the outskirts

**arracachada** [a·rra·ka·'tʃa·da] *f* *Col* silliness

**arraigar** <g → gu> [a·rrai·'ɣar] *vi, vr:* **~se** *t. fig* to take root

**arrancar** <c → qu> [a·rran·'kar] **I.** *vt* **1.** (*planta*) to pull up; **el viento arrancó el árbol** the wind uprooted the tree **2.** (*pegatina*) to tear off; (*página*) to tear out **3.** (*muela*) to extract, to pull (out); **el ladrón le arrancó el bolso de la mano** the thief snatched her handbag from her hand; **la corriente arrancó el puente** the current swept away the bridge **4.** (*vehículo, motor*) to start **5.** (*conseguir*) **~ una promesa a alguien** to force a promise out of sb; **~ un secreto a alguien** to get a secret out of sb **II.** *vi* (*vehículo*) to start

**arranque** [a·'rran·ke] *m* **1.** (*comienzo*) start; **en el ~ de la temporada** at the start of the season **2.** AUTO starting; **~ automático** self-starter **3.** (*arrebato*) outburst; **un ~ de cólera** a fit of anger; **en un ~** impulsively **4.** COMPUT boot (up)

**arrasar** [a·rra·'sar] **I.** *vt* (*región*) to devastate **II.** *vi* to triumph; POL to sweep the board

**arrastrado, -a** [a·rras·'tra·do, -a] *adj* poor, miserable

**arrastrar** [a·rras·'trar] **I.** *vt* **1.** (*tirar de*) to pull; (*algo pesado*) to drag; **~on la caja montaña arriba** they dragged the box up the mountain; **el agua arrastra las piedras** the water sweeps the stones along; **el viento arrastra las hojas** the wind sweeps away the leaves; **~ los pies** (*al caminar*) to drag one's feet **2.** (*impulsar*) **~ a alguien a hacer algo** to lead sb to do sth **II.** *vi* to drag **III.** *vr:* **~se 1.** (*reptar*) to crawl; **se por el suelo** to crawl along; **se arrastró hasta la habitación** he/she dragged himself/herself to the room **2.** (*humillarse*) to grovel

**arrastre** [a·'rras·tre] *m* dragging; (*en pesca*) trawling ▶ **estar para el ~** *inf* (*cosa*) to be ruined; (*persona*) to be a wreck

**arre** ['a·rre] *interj* giddy-up

**arreada** [a·rre·'a·da] *f Arg, Chile, Méx* rustling

**arrear** [a·rre·'ar] **I.** *vt* (*ganado*) to drive; *inf* (*golpe*) to give **II.** *vi inf* to hurry along

**arrebatar** [a·rre·βa·'tar] *vt* **1.** (*arrancar*) to snatch (away); ~ **la vida a alguien** to take sb's life; ~ **la victoria a alguien** to snatch victory from sb **2.** (*extasiar*) to captivate

**arrebato** [a·rre·'βa·to] *m* (*arranque*) outburst; **un ~ de cólera** a fit of anger

**arrecho, -a** [a·'rre·t∫o, -a] *adj Col inf* **1.** (*vigoroso*) vigorous **2.** (*cachondo*) horny **3.** (*enfadado*) angry

**arreciar** [a·rre·'sjar, -'θjar] *vi* (*viento*) to get stronger; (*lluvia*) to get heavier; (*críticas*) to intensify

**arrecife** [a·rre·'si·fe, -'θi·fe] *m* reef

**arreglado, -a** [a·rre·'γla·do, -a] *adj* **1.** (*ordenado*) tidy; (*cuidado*) neat **2.** (*elegante*) smart ▶ **¡estamos ~s!** now we're in trouble!; **¡vas ~ si piensas que...!** you're in for a big surprise if you think ...!

**arreglar** [a·rre·'γlar] **I.** *vt* **1.** (*reparar*) to repair; (*ropa*) to mend **2.** (*ordenar*) to tidy up; ~ **la habitación** to tidy up the room; ~ **a los niños para salir** to get the children ready to go outside **3.** (*pelo*) to do **4.** (*resolver*) to sort out, to arrange; ~ **las cuentas con alguien** to get even with sb **5.** MÚS to arrange ▶ **¡ya te ~é yo!** *inf* I'll sort you out! **II.** *vr:* ~**se 1.** (*vestirse*) to get ready **2.** (*componérselas*) to manage; **no sé cómo te las arreglas** I don't know how you manage **3.** (*ponerse de acuerdo*) to come to an agreement; **al final todo se arregló** everything worked out all right in the end

**arreglo** [a·'rre·γlo] *m* **1.** (*reparación*) repair **2.** (*solución*) solution; **no tienes ~** you're a hopeless case; **este trabajo ya no tiene ~** this job is completely botched **3.** (*acuerdo*) agreement; **llegar a un ~** to reach a settlement; **con ~ a lo convenido** as agreed **4.** MÚS arrangement

**arremeter** [a·rre·me·'ter] *vi* (*criticar*) to

attack; ~ **contra alguien** to attack sb

**arrendador(a)** [a·rren·da·'dor, -·'do·ra] *m(f)* (*de casa*) landlord *m*, landlady *f*; (*de terreno*) *t.* JUR lessor

**arrendamiento** [a·rren·da·'mjen·to] *m* **1.** (*alquiler*) rent; (*de terreno*) lease **2.** (*contrato*) contract

**arrendar** <e → ie> [a·rren·'dar] *vt* (*propietario*) to rent, to let; (*inquilino*) to rent, to lease

**arrendatario, -a** [a·rren·da·'ta·rjo, -a] *m, f* (*de una casa*) tenant; (*de un terreno*) *t.* JUR lessee, leaseholder

**arrepentido, -a** [a·rre·pen·'ti·do, -a] *adj* sorry; REL repentant; **estar ~ de algo** to be sorry about sth, to regret sth

**arrepentimiento** [a·rre·pen·ti·'mjen·to] *m* (*lamento*) regret; REL repentance

**arrepentirse** [a·rre·pen·'tir·se] *irr como* **sentir** *vr* (*lamentar*) to regret; REL to repent; ~ **de algo** to regret sth; REL to repent of sth

**arrestar** [a·rres·'tar] *vt* to arrest

**arresto** [a·'rres·to] *m* **1.** (*detención*) arrest; (*reclusión*) imprisonment; **estar bajo ~** to be under arrest; ~ **domiciliario** house arrest **2.** *pl* (*arrojo*) daring; **tener ~s** to be bold

**arria** ['a·rrja] *f AmL* train of pack animals

**arriba** [a·'rri·βa] *adv* **1.** (*posición*) above; (*en una casa*) upstairs; **más ~** higher up; **te espero ~** I'll wait for you upstairs; **la habitación de ~** (*de encima*) the room above; **el piso de ~** (*el último*) the top floor; **de ~ abajo** from top to bottom; (*persona*) from head to foot; **¡manos ~!** hands up! **2.** (*dirección*) up, upwards; **río ~** upstream; **¡~!** get up! **3.** (*cantidad*) **precios de 100 pesos para ~** prices from 100 pesos upwards **4.** *CSur* **de ~** (*gratis*) free (of charge); (*sin merecerlo*) for no reason

**arribar** [a·rri·'βar] *vi* **1.** NÁUT to reach port **2.** *AmL* (*llegar*) to arrive

**arribista** [a·rri·'βis·ta] *mf* arriviste; (*en sociedad*) social climber

**arriesgado, -a** [a·rrjes·'γa·do, -a] *adj* **1.** (*peligroso*) risky, dangerous **2.** (*atrevido*) daring

**arriesgar** <g → gu> [a·rrjes·'γar] **I.** *vt*

**1.** (*vida*) to risk **2.** (*en el juego*) to stake **3.** (*hipótesis*) to venture **II.** *vr:* ~**se** to take a risk; ~**se a hacer algo** to risk doing sth

**arrimar** [a·rri·'mar] **I.** *vt* (*acercar*) to bring closer **II.** *vr:* ~**se** (*acercarse*) to come close(r); ~**se a algo** to move closer to sth

**arrinconar** [a·rrin·ko·'nar] *vt* **1.** (*objeto*) to put in a corner **2.** (*enemigo*) to corner

**arroba** [a·'rro·βa] *f* **1.** COMPUT at, at sign **2.** *AmL* (*unidad de peso*) arroba *unit of weight from 24 to 36 lbs. depending on the region*

**arrodillarse** [a·rro·di·'jar·se, -'ʎar·se] *vr* to kneel (down)

**arrogancia** [a·rro·'ɣan·sja, -θja] *f* arrogance

**arrogante** [a·rro·'ɣan·te] *adj* arrogant

**arrojar** [a·rro·'xar] **I.** *vt* **1.** (*lanzar*) to throw **2.** (*emitir*) to emit, to give off [*o* out] **3.** (*expulsar*) to throw out **4.** *AmL inf* (*vomitar*) to throw up **5.** (*un resultado*) to produce; ~ **beneficios** to yield profits **II.** *vr:* ~**se** to throw oneself; ~**se al agua** to jump into the water

**arrojo** [a·'rro·xo] *m* daring; **con ~** boldly

**arrollador(a)** [a·rro·ja·'dor, -·'do·ra, a·rro·ʎa–] *adj* **1.** (*mayoría*) overwhelming; (*fuerza*) devastating **2.** (*carácter*) irresistible

**arrollar** [a·rro·'jar, -'ʎar] *vt* **1.** (*enrollar*) to roll up **2.** (*atropellar*) to run over **3.** DEP (*derrotar*) to crush

**arrorró** [a·rro·'rro] *m AmS* lullaby

**arroyo** [a·'rro·jo] *m* stream

**arroz** [a·'rros, -roθ] *m* rice; ~ **con leche** rice pudding

**arrozal** [a·rro·'sal, -'θal] *m* rice field

**arruga** [a·'rru·ɣa] *f* (*en la piel*) wrinkle; (*en papel*) crease; **este vestido hace ~s** this dress creases

**arrugar** <g → gu> [a·rru·'ɣar] **I.** *vt* (*piel*) to wrinkle; (*papel*) to crease **II.** *vr:* ~**se** **1.** (*piel*) to wrinkle, to get wrinkled; (*papel*) to crease, to get creased **2.** (*achicarse*) to get scared

**arruinar** [a·rrwi·'nar] **I.** *vt* **1.** (*causar ruina*) to ruin **2.** (*fiesta*) to spoil; (*plan*) to wreck **II.** *vr:* ~**se** to be ruined

**arrullar** [a·rru·'jar, -'ʎar] **I.** *vt* to lull to sleep **II.** *vi* (*paloma*) to coo **III.** *vr:* ~**se** to bill and coo

**arsenal** [ar·se·'nal] *m* arsenal

**arsénico** [ar·'se·ni·ko] *m* arsenic

**arte** ['ar·te] *m o f* (*m en sing, f en pl*) **1.** (*disciplina*) art; ~ **dramático** drama; ~**s plásticas** visual arts; ~**s y oficios** arts and crafts; **bellas ~s** fine arts; **el séptimo ~** the cinema **2.** (*habilidad*) skill; **tiene mucho ~ para la pintura** he's quite a skilled painter **3.** (*maña*) trick; **conseguir algo por malas ~s** to obtain sth by trickery; **desplegó todas sus ~s para convencerlo** she used all her wiles to convince him ▶ **como por ~ de magia** as if by magic

**artefacto** [ar·te·'fak·to] *m* appliance; (*mecanismo*) device; ~ **explosivo** explosive device

**arteria** [ar·'te·rja] *f* **1.** ANAT artery **2.** (*de tráfico*) thoroughfare

**arterio(e)sclerosis** [ar·te·rjos·kle·'ro·sis/ar·te·rjo·es·kle·'ro·sis] *f inv* arteriosclerosis

**artesanal** [ar·te·sa·'nal] *adj* craft; **industria ~** craft industry

**artesanía** [ar·te·sa·'ni·a] *f* **1.** (*arte*) craftsmanship **2.** (*obras*) handicrafts *pl*

**artesano, -a** [ar·te·'sa·no, -a] *m, f* artisan, craftsman *m*, craftswoman *f*

**ártico** ['ar·ti·ko, -a] *m* **1.** (*océano*) Arctic Ocean **2.** (*región*) Arctic

**ártico, -a** ['ar·ti·ko, -a] *adj* Arctic

**articulación** [ar·ti·ku·la·'sjon, -'θjon] *f* **1.** ANAT joint **2.** LING articulation

**articulado, -a** [ar·ti·ku·'la·do, -a] *adj* articulated; **camión ~** tractor-trailer truck

**articular** [ar·ti·ku·'lar] *vt* **1.** TÉC to join together **2.** LING to articulate

**artículo** [ar·'ti·ku·lo] *m* (*objeto*) *t.* PREN article; COM commodity; ~**s de consumo** consumer goods; ~**s de lujo** luxury goods; ~**s de primera necesidad** basic commodities

**artífice** [ar·'ti·fi·se, -θe] *mf* artist; *fig* architect

**artificial** [ar·ti·fi·'sjal, -'θjal] *adj* artificial

**artificio** [ar·ti·fi·'sjo, -θjo] *m* (*habilidad*) skill; (*truco*) trick; **un ~ técnico** a technical contrivance

**artillería** [ar·ti·je·'ri·a, ar·ti·ʎe-] f artillery

**artimaña** [ar·ti·'ma·ɲa] f (sly) trick

**artista** [ar·'tis·ta] mf (de bellas artes) artist; (de circo) artist(e) m(f); **es un ~ en su especialidad** he's an expert in his field

**artístico, -a** [ar·'tis·ti·ko, -a] adj artistic

**artritis** [ar·'tri·tis] f inv arthritis

**artrosis** [ar·'tro·sis] f inv arthrosis

**arzobispo** [ar·so·'βis·po, ar·θo-] m archbishop

**as** [as] m t. fig ace; **un ~ del volante** an ace at the wheel

**asa** ['a·sa] f handle

**asado, -a** [a·'sa·ðo] m 1. CULIN roast 2. Arg (comida) barbecue

**asalariado, -a** [a·sa·la·'rja·ðo, -a] m, f wage earner

**asaltar** [a·sal·'tar] vt 1. (fortaleza) to storm; (banco) to break into, to raid 2. (persona) to attack, to assault 3. (duda) to assail; **me asaltó el pánico** I was overwhelmed by panic

**asalto** [a·'sal·to] m 1. (a una fortaleza) storming; **tomar por** [o **al**] **~** to take by storm 2. (a un banco) raid; **~ a un banco** raid on a bank 3. (a una persona) attack, assault 4. DEP (en boxeo) round

**asamblea** [a·sam·'blea] f assembly; **~ general** general assembly; **~ de trabajadores** workers' meeting

**asar** [a·'sar] I. vt CULIN to roast; **~ a la parrilla** to grill II. vr: **~se** to roast; **en esta casa se asa uno vivo** inf it's absolutely roasting in this house

**ascendencia** [a·sen·'den·sja, as·θen·'den·θja] f (linaje) ancestry, descent; **de ~ escocesa** of Scottish descent

**ascendente** [a·sen·'den·te, as·θen-] adj ascending; **en orden ~** in ascending order

**ascender** <e → ie> [a·sen·'der, as·θen-] I. vi 1. (subir) to rise; DEP to go up; **el equipo asciende a primera (división)** the team goes up to the first division 2. (escalar) to climb 3. (de empleo) to be promoted 4. COM **~ a** (cantidad) to amount to II. vt to promote

**ascendiente** [a·sen·'djen·te, as·θen-] mf (antepasado) ancestor

**ascensión** [a·sen·'sjon, as·θen-] f ascent

**ascenso** [a·'sen·so, as·'θen-] m 1. (de precio) rise 2. (a una montaña) ascent; **el ~ a primera (división)** the promotion to the first division

**ascensor** [a·sen·'sor, as·θen-] m elevator

**asco** ['as·ko] m 1. (sensación) disgust, loathing; **este olor me da ~** this smell makes me feel sick; **las espinacas me dan ~** I hate spinach; **este hombre me da ~** I really detest this man; **hacer ~s a algo** to turn up one's nose at sth; **¡qué ~ de gente!** inf what dreadful people!; **¡qué ~!** how awful! 2. (situación) **estar hecho un ~** (lugar) to be a mess; (persona) to feel low; **estar muerto de ~** to be bored stiff; **ser un ~** to be disgusting

**ascua** ['as·kwa] f ember ▶ **estar en ~s** to be on tenterhooks; **tener a alguien en ~s** to keep sb on tenterhooks

**aseado, -a** [a·se·'a·ðo, -a] adj clean, tidy; (arreglado) smart

**asear** [a·se·'ar] I. vt to clean up II. vr: **~se** to wash (up)

**asediar** [a·se·'djar] vt MIL to besiege

**asedio** [a·'se·djo] m MIL siege

**asegurado, -a** [a·se·ɣu·'ra·ðo, -a] adj, m, f insured

**asegurador(a)** [a·se·ɣu·ra·'ðor, -·'ðo·ra] m(f) insurance agent

**asegurar** [a·se·ɣu·'rar] I. vt 1. (fijar) to secure; **~ una puerta** to secure a door 2. (afirmar) to affirm; **asegura no haber dicho nada** she maintains that she did not say anything 3. (prometer) to assure; **se lo aseguro** I assure you 4. (con un seguro) to insure II. vr: **~se** (comprobar) to make sure; **~se de que funciona** to make sure that it works

**asemejarse** [a·se·me·'xar·se] vr to be alike; **~ a algo** to resemble sth, to be like sth

**asentar** <e → ie> [a·sen·'tar] I. vt (poner) to place; **~ los cimientos** to lay the foundations; **la lluvia ha asentado el polvo** the rain has caused the dust to settle II. vr: **~se** to settle

**asentir** [a·sen·'tir] irr como sentir vi to agree; **~ a algo** to agree to sth; **~ con la cabeza** to nod in agreement

**aseo** [a·'seo] *m* **1.** (*acción*) cleaning; (**cuarto de**) ~ bathroom; ~ **personal** personal hygiene **2.** *pl* (*servicios públicos*) restrooms *pl*

**aséptico, -a** [a·'sep·ti·ko, -a] *adj* MED aseptic; *fig* (*desapasionado*) dispassionate

**asequible** [a·se·'ki·βle] *adj* **1.** (*precio*) reasonable **2.** (*objetivo*) attainable **3.** (*persona*) approachable

**asesinar** [a·se·si·'nar] *vt* to murder; (*personaje público*) to assassinate

**asesinato** [a·se·si·'na·to] *m* murder; (*de personaje público*) assassination

**asesino, -a** [a·se·'si·no, -a] **I.** *adj t. fig* murderous; **ballena asesina** killer whale **II.** *m, f* murderer; (*de personaje público*) assassin; ~ (**a sueldo**) hit man

**asesor(a)** [a·se·'sor, -·'so·ra] **I.** *adj* advisory **II.** *m(f)* adviser, consultant

**asesorar** [a·se·so·'rar] **I.** *vt* to advise **II.** *vr* ~**se en algo** to take advice about sth

**asesoría** [a·se·so·'ri·a] *f* **1.** (*oficio*) consultancy **2.** (*oficina*) consultant's office

**asestar** [a·ses·'tar] *vt* to deal; ~ **una puñalada a alguien** to stab sb

**aseverar** [a·se·βe·'rar] *vt* to affirm; (*asegurar*) to assure; (*con energía*) to assert

**asfaltar** [as·fal·'tar] *vt* to asphalt

**asfalto** [as·'fal·to] *m* asphalt

**asfixia** [as·'fik·sja] *f* suffocation, asphyxia

**asfixiante** [as·fik·'sjan·te] *adj* suffocating; **una atmósfera** ~ a stifling atmosphere; **hace un calor** ~ the heat is suffocating

**asfixiar** [as·fik·'sjar] **I.** *vt* (*persona*) to suffocate; (*humo*) to asphyxiate **II.** *vr:* ~**se** to suffocate

**así** [a·'si] **I.** *adv* **1.** (*de este modo*) accordingly; **lo hizo** ~ he/she did it like this; ~ **es como lo hizo** that's how he/she did it; **yo soy** ~ that's the way I am; **no puedes decir esto** ~ **como** ~ you just can't say that; **¡~ es!** that's right!; **¡~ es la vida!** that's life; **¿no es ~?** isn't it?; **por ~ decirlo** so to speak **2.** (*de extrañeza*) **¿~ que me dejas?** so you're leaving me? **3.** (*de esta medida*) **de grande** this big ▶ ~ **y todo** even so; ~ ~ so-so **II.** *conj* **1.** (*concesiva*) ~ **se esté muriendo de frío...** even though he's/she's freezing... **2.** (*consecutiva*) empe-

zó a llover, ~ **que nos quedamos en casa** it began to rain, so we stayed indoors **III.** *adj inv* like this, like that; **un sueldo** ~ a salary of that amount; **una cosa** ~ something like that

**Asia** [a·'sja] *f* Asia; ~ **menor** Asia Minor

**asiático, -a** [a·'sja·ti·ko, -a] *adj, m, f* Asian, Asiatic

**asidero** [a·si·'de·ro] *m* handle; *fig* pretext

**asiduo, -a** [a·'si·dwo, -a] *adj* frequent; **un** ~ **cliente de este local** a regular in this bar

**asiento** [a·'sjen·to] *m* (*silla*) seat; ~ **delantero** front seat; ~ **trasero** [*o de atrás*] rear seat; **tomar** ~ to take a seat

**asignación** [a·siɣ·na·'sjon, -'θjon] *f* **1.** *t.* COMPUT assignment; (*de recursos*) allocation; ~ **de una tecla** assignment of a key **2.** FIN allowance

**asignar** [a·siɣ·'nar] *vt t.* COMPUT to assign; (*recursos*) to allocate; (*subvención*) to award

**asignatura** [a·siɣ·na·'tu·ra] *f* subject; ~ **pendiente** failed subject

**asilo** [a·'si·lo] *m* **1.** POL asylum; **pedir/ conceder** ~ to seek/to grant political asylum **2.** (*de ancianos*) (old people's) home

**asimetría** [a·si·me·'tri·a] *f* asymmetry

**asimétrico, -a** [a·si·'me·tri·ko, -a] *adj* asymmetric(al)

**asimilar** [a·si·mi·'lar] *vt* to assimilate

**asimismo** [a·si·'mis·mo] *adv* likewise, also

**asir** [a·'sir] *irr* **I.** *vt* to seize **II.** *vr* ~**se a algo** to seize sth

**asistencia** [a·sis·'ten·sja, -θja] *f* **1.** (*presencia*) attendance, presence **2.** (*ayuda*) assistance, help; ~ **médica** medical care; ~ **social** social work

**asistenta** [a·sis·'ten·ta] *f* **1.** (*ayudante*) assistant **2.** (*para limpiar*) cleaning woman

**asistente**[1] [a·sis·'ten·te] *mf* **1.** (*ayudante*) assistant **2.** (*presentes*) **los** ~**s** those present ▶ ~ **social** social worker

**asistente**[2] [a·sis·'ten·te] *m* COMPUT wizard; ~ **de instalacíon** installation wizard; ~ **personal digital** PDA, personal digital assistant

**A**

**asistido, -a** [a·sis·'ti·do, -a] *adj* assisted; **~ por ordenador** computer-assisted; **dirección asistida** power(-assisted) steering; **respiración asistida** artificial respiration

**asistir** [a·sis·'tir] I. *vi* 1. (*ir*) **~ a algo** to attend sth 2. (*estar presente*) to be present; **asistieron unas 50 personas** some 50 people were present 3. (*presenciar*) **~ a algo** to witness sth II. *vt* (*ayudar*) to help, assist; **~ a un enfermo** to care for a patient

**asma** ['as·ma] *f* asthma

**asno** ['as·no] *m* ZOOL donkey, ass

**asociación** [a·so·sja·'sjon, -θja·'θjon] *f* association; **Asociación de Padres de Alumnos** parent-teacher association

**asociar** [a·so·'sjar, -'θjar] I. *vt* 1. *t. POL* to associate; **la asocio con alguien** I associate her with sb 2. (*juntar*) to join II. *vr:* **~se** to associate; COM to become partners, to form a partnership; **~se con alguien** (*hacer compañía*) to join sb

**asolar** <o → ue> [a·so·'lar] *vt* to devastate

**asoleada** [a·so·le·'a·da] *f* Col, Chile, Guat (*insolación*) sunstroke

**asomar** [a·so·'mar] I. *vt* 1. (*mostrar*) to show 2. (*destacar*) to stick out; **~ la cabeza por la ventana** to put one's head out of the window II. *vi* (*verse*) to show; (*aparecer*) to appear; **asoma el día** day is breaking III. *vr:* **~se** (*mostrarse*) to show up; **~se al balcón** to come out onto the balcony; **¡asómate!** stick your head out!

**asombrar** [a·som·'brar] I. *vt* to amaze II. *vr* **~se de algo** to be amazed at sth

**asombro** [a·'som·bro] *m* amazement; **poner cara de ~** to look amazed; **no salir de su ~** not to get over one's amazement

**asombroso, -a** [a·som·'bro·so, -a] *adj* amazing

**asomo** [a·'so·mo] *m* hint; **no pienso en ello ni por ~** I don't give it the slightest thought

**asonancia** [a·so·'nan·sja, -θja] *f* assonance

**asorocharse** [a·so·ro·'tʃar·se] *vr AmS* to get altitude sickness

**aspa** ['as·pa] *f* cross; (*de molino*) sail; **marcar con un ~** to mark with a cross; **en forma de ~** cross-shaped

**aspaviento** [as·pa·'βjen·to] *m* fuss; **hacer ~s** to make a fuss

**aspecto** [as·'pek·to] *m* 1. (*apariencia*) appearance; **tener buen/mal ~** to look/not to look well 2. (*punto de vista*) aspect

**áspero, -a** ['as·pe·ro, -a] *adj* 1. (*superficie*) rough 2. (*persona*) harsh; **tener un carácter ~** to be bad-tempered

**aspiración** [as·pi·ra·'sjon, -'θjon] *f* 1. (*inspiración*) breathing in 2. (*pretensión*) aspiration

**aspiradora** [as·pi·ra·'do·ra] *f* vacuum cleaner; **pasar la ~** to vacuum

**aspirante** [as·pi·'ran·te] *mf* aspirant; (*a un empleo*) applicant

**aspirar** [as·pi·'rar] I. *vt* 1. (*inspirar*) to breathe in, inhale 2. (*aspirador*) to suck in II. *vi* 1. (*inspirar*) to breathe in 2. (*pretender*) to aspire; **~ a mucho en la vida** to have high aims in life

**aspirina®** [as·pi·'ri·na] *f* aspirin®

**asquear** [as·ke·'ar] I. *vt* (*dar asco*) to disgust II. *vr:* **~se** to feel disgusted

**asquerosidad** [as·ke·ro·si·'dad] *f* disgusting mess

**asqueroso, -a** [as·ke·'ro·so, -a] *adj* disgusting; (*sucio*) filthy

**asta** ['as·ta] *f* 1. (*de bandera*) flagpole; **a media ~** at half mast 2. (*cuerno*) horn

**asterisco** [as·te·'ris·ko] *m* asterisk

**asteroide** [as·te·'roi·de] *m* asteroid

**astilla** [as·'ti·ja, -ʎa] *f* splinter; **clavarse una ~** to get a splinter

**astillero** [as·ti·'je·ro, -'ʎe·ro] *m* shipyard

**astro** ['as·tro] *m t. fig* star

**astrología** [as·tro·lo·'xi·a] *f* astrology

**astrólogo, -a** [as·'tro·lo·ɣo, -a] *m, f* astrologer

**astronauta** [as·tro·'nau·ta] *mf* astronaut

**astronomía** [as·tro·no·'mi·a] *f* astronomy

**astrónomo, -a** [as·'tro·no·mo, -a] *m, f* astronomer

**astucia** [as·'tu·sja, -θja] *f* astuteness, shrewdness

**astuto, -a** [as·'tu·to, -a] *adj* astute, shrewd; (*con malicia*) crafty

**asumir** [a·su·'mir] *vt* 1. (*responsabilidad*)

to assume, to take on; (*cargo*) to take over; (*gastos*) to agree to pay **2.** (*suponer*) to assume

**asunto** [a·'sun·to] *m* **1.** (*cuestión*) matter; **ir al ~** to get to the point; **el ~ es que...** the thing is (that)...; **¡~ concluido!** that's the end of it!; **ocúpate de tus ~s** mind your own business **2.** (*negocio*) business; **tener ~s en el extranjero** to have business dealings abroad **3.** (*amorío*) affair **4.** POL **Ministerio/ Ministro de Asuntos Exteriores** State Department/Secretary of State

**asustadizo, -a** [a·sus·ta·'di·θo, -a; -'di·ðo, -a] *adj* jumpy; (*animal*) easily startled

**asustar** [a·sus·'tar] **I.** *vt* to scare, to frighten; **la responsabilidad no me asusta** I'm not afraid of the responsibility **II.** *vr:* **~se** to be scared, to be frightened; **no te asustes** don't be frightened

**atacar** <c → qu> [a·ta·'kar] **I.** *vt* (*embestir*) to attack; **~ por la espalda** to attack from behind **II.** *vi t.* DEP to attack; **~ por las bandas** to attack from the wings

**atadura** [a·ta·'du·ra] *f* **1.** (*acción*) tying **2.** (*cuerda*) rope, string **3.** (*entre personas*) tie, bond

**atajar** [a·ta·'xar] **I.** *vi* to take a short cut **II.** *vt* **1.** (*detener*) to stop **2.** (*cortar el paso*) to head off

**atajo** [a·'ta·xo] *m* short cut; **ir por un ~** to take a short cut

**atalaya** [a·ta·'la·ja] *f* **1.** (*torre*) watchtower **2.** (*lugar*) vantage point

**atañer** <3. pret atañó> [a·ta·'ɲer] *vimpers* **eso no te atañe** that doesn't concern you; **por lo que atañe a tu empleo** as far as your job is concerned

**ataque** [a·'ta·ke] *m* **1.** (*embestida*) attack; **~ por sorpresa** surprise attack; **pasar al ~** to go on the offensive **2.** *t.* MED attack, fit; **~ al corazón** heart attack; **~ de nervios** nervous breakdown; **~ de tos** fit of coughing

**atar** [a·'tar] **I.** *vt* **1.** (*sujetar*) to tie; (*cerrar*) to tie up; (*cautivo*) to bind; **~ a alguien las manos a la espalda** to tie sb's hands behind his/her back; **~ al perro** to tie up the dog **2.** (*comprometer*) **esta profesión te ata mucho** this profession ties you down a lot ▶ **~**

**corto a alguien** to keep a tight rein on sb **II.** *vr:* **~se** to do up; **~se los zapatos** to tie one's shoes

**atardecer** [a·tar·de·'ser, -'θer] **I.** *irr como crecer vimpers* **atardece** it's getting dark **II.** *m* dusk; **al ~** at dusk

**atascar** <c → qu> [a·tas·'kar] **I.** *vt* to block **II.** *vr:* **~se 1.** (*cañería*) to get blocked (up); **el desagüe se ha atascado** the drain is blocked (up) **2.** (*coche*) to get stuck; (*mecanismo*) to jam

**atasco** [a·'tas·ko] *m* **1.** (*de un mecanismo*) blocking; **~ de papel** COMPUT paper jam **2.** (*de tráfico*) traffic jam

**ataúd** [a·ta·'uð] *m* coffin

**ate** [a·te] *m Méx* CULIN *fruit paste*

**ateísmo** [a·te·'is·mo] *m* atheism

**atemorizar** <z → c> [a·te·mo·ri·'sar, -'θar] *vt* to scare, to frighten

**Atenas** [a·'te·nas] *f* Athens

**atenazar** <z → c> [a·te·na·'sar, -'θar] *vt* (*miedo*) to grip; (*duda*) to torment

**atención** [a·ten·'sjon, -'θjon] *f* **1.** (*interés*) attention; **falta de ~** inattentiveness; **digno de ~** noteworthy; **¡~, por favor!** your attention please!; **estamos llamando la ~** we're attracting attention; **llamar la ~ de alguien sobre** [*o* **a**] **algo** to draw sb's attention to sth; **mantener la ~ de alguien** to hold sb's attention; **prestar ~ a algo** to pay attention to sth; **a la ~ de...** for the attention of... **2.** (*cuidado*) attention, care; **~ médica** medical care **3.** (*cortesía*) kindness; **tener muchas atenciones con alguien** to be very nice to sb ▶ **llamar la ~ a alguien** to rebuke sb

**atender** <e → ie> [a·ten·'der] **I.** *vt* **1.** (*prestar atención a*) to pay attention to **2.** (*consejo*) to heed; (*petición*) to comply with; **~ una solicitud** to grant a request **3.** (*cuidar*) **~ a alguien** to care for sb **4.** (*tratar*) to treat **5.** (*despachar*) to wait on, to help; **¿lo atienden?** are you being served? **6.** (*llamada*) to answer; **~ el teléfono** to answer the telephone **II.** *vi* (*prestar atención*) to pay attention

**atenerse** [a·te·'ner·se] *irr como tener vr* **~ a** (*reglas*) to abide by; (*lo dicho*) to stand by, to keep to; **~ a lo seguro**

to play (it) safe; **saber a qué ~** (*en un futuro*) to know what to expect; **si no lo haces, atente a las consecuencias** if you don't do it, you'll bear the consequences

**atentado** [a·ten·'ta·do] *m* attack, assault; (*crimen*) crime; **~ contra alguien** assassination attempt on sb; **~ suicida** suicide attack; **~ terrorista** terrorist attack; **ser víctima de un ~** to be the victim of an assassination attempt

**atentamente** [a·ten·ta·'men·te] *adv* (*carta*) **(muy) ~** (*si la carta empieza "Dear Sir"*) yours truly; (*si la carta empieza "Dear Mr. X"*) sincerely yours

**atentar** [a·ten·'tar] *vi* **~ contra alguien** to make an attempt on sb's life; **~ contra la ley** to break the law

**atento, -a** [a·'ten·to, -a] *adj* **1.** (*observador*) attentive; **estar ~ a la conversación** to follow the conversation closely; **estar ~ al peligro** to be aware of the danger **2.** (*cortés*) kind; **estuvo muy ~ con nosotros** he was very considerate towards us

**atenuante** [a·te·nu·'an·te] *f pl* JUR extenuating circumstances *pl*

**atenuar** <*1. pres* atenúo> [a·te·nu·'ar] *vt* **1.** to attenuate; (*dolor*) to ease **2.** JUR to extenuate

**ateo, -a** [a·'te·o, -a] **I.** *adj* atheistic **II.** *m, f* atheist

**aterrador(a)** [a·te·rra·'dor, -·'do·ra] *adj* terrifying

**aterrar** [a·te·'rrar] *vt* to terrify

**aterrizaje** [a·te·rri·'sa·xe, -·'θa·xe] *m* landing; **~ forzoso** forced landing

**aterrizar** <z → c> [a·te·rri·'sar, -·'θar] *vi* to land

**aterrorizar** <z → c> [a·te·rro·ri·'sar, -·'θar] *vt* **1.** POL, MIL to terrorize **2.** (*causar terror*) to terrify

**atestado** [a·tes·'ta·do] *m* ~ (*policial*) statement

**atestiguar** <gu → gü> [a·tes·ti·'ɣwar] *vt* to testify to

**ático** ['a·ti·ko] *m* attic; (*de lujo*) penthouse

**atinar** [a·ti·'nar] *vi* **1.** (*acertar*) **~ con algo** to hit on sth; **no atiné con la respuesta** I didn't come up with the

answer **2.** (*encontrar*) **~ con algo** to find sth **3.** (*ser capaz*) **~ a hacer algo** to manage to do sth

**atípico, -a** [a·'ti·pi·ko, -a] *adj* atypical

**atisbo** [a·'tis·βo] *m* **un ~ de esperanza** a glimmer of hope

**atizar** <z → c> [a·ti·'sar, -·'θar] *vt* **1.** (*fuego*) to poke; (*pasión*) to rouse **2.** (*bofetada*) to give

**atlántico, -a** [at·'lan·ti·ko, -a] *adj* Atlantic

**Atlántico** [at·'lan·ti·ko] *m* **el ~** the Atlantic

**atlas** ['at·las] *m inv* atlas

**atleta** [at·'le·ta] *mf* athlete

**atlético, -a** [at·'le·ti·ko, -a] *adj* athletic

**atletismo** [at·le·'tis·mo] *m* athletics

**atmósfera** [at·'mos·fe·ra] *f* atmosphere

**atole** [a·'to·le] *m* AmC hot drink prepared with cornmeal

**atolladero** [a·to·ja·'de·ro, a·to·ʎa·] *m* (*apuro*) jam; **estar en un ~** to be in a fix; **sacar a alguien de un ~** to get sb out of a jam

**atolondrado, -a** [a·to·lon·'dra·do, -a] *adj* bewildered

**atomía** [a·to·'mi·a] *f* AmL evil act; **decir ~s** (*decir tonterías*) to talk nonsense

**atómico, -a** [a·'to·mi·ko, -a] *adj* atomic; **refugio ~** fallout shelter

**átomo** ['a·to·mo] *m* atom

**atónito, -a** [a·'to·ni·to, -a] *adj* amazed

**átono, -a** ['a·to·no, -a] *adj* unstressed

**atontado, -a** [a·ton·'ta·do, -a] *adj* **1.** (*tonto*) stupid **2.** (*distraído*) inattentive

**atontar** [a·ton·'tar] **I.** *vt* **1.** (*aturdir*) to stun **2.** (*entontecer*) to bewilder **II.** *vr:* **~se** to be stunned

**atormentar(se)** [a·tor·men·'tar(·se)] *vt, (vr)* (*mortificar*) to torment (oneself)

**atornillador** [a·tor·ni·ja·'dor, -·ʎa·'dor] *m* screwdriver

**atornillar** [a·tor·ni·'jar, -·'ʎar] *vt* to screw down; (*fijar*) to screw on

**atosigar** <g → gu> [a·to·si·'ɣar] *vt* to harass; (*importunar*) to pester

**atracadero** [a·tra·ka·'de·ro] *m* mooring

**atracador(a)** [a·tra·ka·'dor, -·'do·ra] *m(f)* bank robber

**atracar** <c → qu> [a·tra·'kar] **I.** *vi* NÁUT to berth **II.** *vt* **1.** NÁUT to moor **2.** (*asaltar*) to hold up **III.** *vr inf* **~se de algo** to stuff oneself with sth

**atracción** [a·trak·'sjon, -'θjon] *f t.* FÍS attraction; **parque de atracciones** amusement park

**atraco** [a·'tra·ko] *m* hold-up; ~ **a un banco** bank robbery; ~ **a mano armada** armed robbery

**atractivo** [a·trak·'ti·βo] *m* attraction

**atractivo, -a** [a·trak·'ti·βo, -a] *adj* attractive

**atraer** [a·tra·'er] *irr como* traer *vt* to attract; **el cebo atrae a los peces** the bait lures the fish; **sentirse atraído hacia alguien** to feel drawn towards sb

**atrancar** <c → qu> [a·tran·'kar] **I.** *vt* (*puerta*) to bolt **II.** *vr:* ~**se** (*tubo*) to become blocked; (*al hablar*) to get stuck

**atrapar** [a·tra·'par] *vt* to trap; (*ladrón*) to catch; (*animal*) to capture; **el portero atrapó la pelota** the goalkeeper caught the ball

**atrás** [a·'tras] *adv* **1.** (*hacia detrás*) back, backwards; **dar un paso** ~ to take a step backwards [*o* back]; **ir marcha** ~ to back up; **quedar** ~ to fall behind; **volver** ~ to go back; **¡~!** get back! **2.** (*detrás*) back, behind; **rueda de** ~ rear wheel; **dejar** ~ **a los perseguidores** to leave one's pursuers behind; **quedarse** ~ to remain behind; **sentarse** ~ to sit at the back **3.** (*de tiempo*) **años** ~ years ago ▶ **echarse** ~ **de un acuerdo** to back out of an agreement

**atrasado, -a** [a·tra·'sa·do, -a] *adj* **1.** (*en el desarrollo*) behind; (*país*) backward; **viven 20 años** ~**s** they're 20 years behind the times **2.** (*pago*) overdue **3.** (*tarde*) late; **el reloj va** ~ the watch is slow

**atrasar** [a·tra·'sar] **I.** *vt* **1.** (*aplazar*) to postpone **2.** (*reloj*) to put back **II.** *vr:* ~**se** (*retrasarse*) to be late; **el tren se ha atrasado** the train is late

**atraso** [a·'tra·so] *m* **1.** (*de un tren*) delay **2.** (*de un país*) backwardness **3.** FIN arrears *pl*

**atravesar** <e → ie> [a·tra·βe·'sar] **I.** *vt* **1.** (*persona*) **la calle** to cross the street; ~ **un río nadando** to swim across a river; ~ **un momento difícil** to go through a difficult time **2.** (*cuerpo*) ~ **algo con una aguja** to pierce sth

with a needle; **la bala le atravesó el corazón** the bullet went through his/her heart; **una cicatriz le atraviesa el pecho** a scar runs across his/her chest **3.** (*poner de través*) to lay across **II.** *vr:* ~**se 1.** (*ponerse*) **no te atravieses en mi camino** don't get in my way; **se me ha atravesado una miga en la garganta** a crumb has gotten stuck in my throat **2.** (*no soportar*) **se me atraviesa ese tipo** I can't stand that fellow

**atreverse** [a·tre·'βer·se] *vr* to dare; ~ **a hacer algo** to dare to do sth; **¡no te atreverás!** you wouldn't dare!

**atrevido, -a** [a·tre·'βi·do, -a] *adj* **1.** (*persona*) daring **2.** (*insolente*) insolent

**atrevimiento** [a·tre·βi·'mjen·to] *m* **1.** (*audacia*) boldness **2.** (*descaro*) nerve *fig*

**atribuir** [a·tri·βu·'ir] *irr como* huir **I.** *vt* **1.** (*hechos*) to attribute; ~ **la culpa de algo a alguien** to blame sth on sb **2.** (*funciones*) to confer **II.** *vr:* ~**se 1.** (*hechos*) to claim for oneself **2.** (*facultades*) ~**se todo el poder** to assume absolute power

**atributo** [a·tri·'β·u·to] *m t.* LING attribute

**atril** [a·'tril] *m* MÚS music stand; (*de mesa*) lectern

**atrio** ['a·trjo] *m* atrium

**atrocidad** [a·tro·si·'dad, a·tro·θi-] *f* **1.** (*cosa*) atrocity **2.** (*disparate*) foolish remark; **¡no digas ~es!** don't talk nonsense!

**atropellar** [a·tro·pe·'jar, -'ʎar] **I.** *vt* **1.** (*vehículo*) to run over **2.** (*empujar*) to push past **3.** (*agraviar*) to insult **II.** *vr:* ~**se** to rush

**atropello** [a·tro·'pe·jo, -'pe·ʎo] *m* **1.** (*colisión*) collision; (*accidente*) accident **2.** (*empujón*) push **3.** (*insulto*) insult; **¡esto es un ~!** this is preposterous! **4.** (*prisa*) **tomar una decisión sin prisas ni ~s** not to rush a decision

**atroz** [a·'tros, -'troθ] *adj* **1.** (*horroroso*) atrocious **2.** (*cruel*) cruel **3.** (*enorme*) huge

**atufar** [a·tu·'far] *vi inf* to stink

**atún** [a·'tun] *m* tuna (fish)

**aturdido, -a** [a·tur·'di·do, -a] *adj* **1.** (*pasmado*) stunned **2.** (*irreflexivo*) thoughtless

**aturdir** [a·tur·'dir] *vt* 1. (*los sentidos*) to stupefy 2. (*pasmar*) to stun

**audacia** [au·'da·sja, -θja] *f* boldness, audacity

**audaz** [au·'das, -'daθ] *adj* bold, audacious

**audible** [au·'di·βle] *adj* audible

**audición** [au·di·'sjon, -'θjon] *f* 1. (*acción*) hearing 2. TEAT audition

**audiencia** [au·'djen·sja, -θja] *f* 1. TEL audience; **nivel de ~** viewing figures *pl* 2. JUR (*sesión*) hearing; (*sala*) courtroom; (*tribunal*) court

**audífono** [au·'di·fo·no] *m* 1. (*para sordos*) hearing aid 2. *AmL* (*auricular*) receiver

**auditivo, -a** [au·di·'ti·βo, -a] *adj* ANAT hearing

**auditorio** [au·di·'to·rjo] *m* 1. (*público*) audience 2. (*sala*) auditorium

**auge** ['au·xe] *m* (*cumbre*) peak; **en el ~ de su belleza** at the height of her beauty

**augurar** [au·yu·'rar] *vt* to predict

**augurio** [au·'yu·rjo] *m* prediction

**aula** ['au·la] *f* classroom; (*de universidad*) lecture room; **~ magna** main lecture hall

**aullar** [au·'jar, -'ʎar] *irr vi* to howl

**aumentar** [au·men·'tar] **I.** *vi, vt* 1. (*subir*) to increase; (*precios*) to rise, to increase; **~ de peso** to get heavier; **los disturbios aumentan** the disturbances are spreading 2. (*extender*) to extend **II.** *vt* to increase; (*precios*) to raise, to increase

**aumento** [au·'men·to] *m* increase; (*de la temperatura*) rise; (*de valor*) appreciation; (*en la extensión*) expansion; **~ de precio** price increase

**aun** [aun] **I.** *adv* even; **~ así** even so **II.** *conj* **~ cuando** even though

**aún** [a·'un] *adv* still; **~ más** even more; **~ no** yet; **¿~ no ha llegado?** hasn't he/she arrived yet?

**aunar** [au·'nar] *irr como* aullar **I.** *vt* (*unir*) to unite; **~ esfuerzos** to join forces **II.** *vr*: **~se** to unite

**aunque** ['aun·ke] *conj* 1. (*concesivo*) even though; **~ es viejo, aún puede trabajar** although he's old, he can

still work; **~ parezca extraño** however strange it may seem 2. (*adversativa*) but

**aúpa** [a·'u·pa] *interj* up!, get up! ▸ **de ~** *inf* tremendous

**aupar** [au·'par] *irr como* aullar *vt* to lift up

**aura** ['au·ra] *f* aura; **tiene un ~ misteriosa** he/she has a mysterious aura

**aureola** [au·re·'o·la] *f* halo

**auricular** [au·ri·ku·'lar] *m* 1. TEL receiver; **coger/colgar el ~** to pick up/put down the receiver 2. *pl* (*de música*) headphones *pl*

**aurora** [au·'ro·ra] *f* dawn

**auscultar** [aus·kul·'tar] *vt* MED **el médico lo auscultó** the doctor listened to his chest (with a stethoscope)

**ausencia** [au·'sen·sja, -θja] *f* 1. (*estado*) absence 2. (*falta*) lack; **~ de interés** lack of interest 3. PSICO mental blackouts ▸ **brillar por su ~** to be conspicuous by one's absence

**ausentarse** [au·sen·'tar·se] *vr* to go away; **~ de la ciudad** to leave town

**ausente** [au·'sen·te] *adj* 1. (*no presente*) absent; **estar ~** to be absent 2. (*distraído*) distracted

**auspiciar** [aus·pi·'sjar, -'θjar] *vt* 1. (*presagiar*) to predict 2. (*patrocinar*) to back

**austeridad** [aus·te·ri·'dad] *f* austerity

**austero, -a** [aus·'te·ro, -a] *adj* austere

**austral** [aus·'tral] *adj* southern

**Australia** [aus·'tra·lja] *f* Australia

**australiano, -a** [aus·tra·'lja·no, -a] *adj, m, f* Australian

**Austria** ['aus·trja] *f* Austria

**austriaco, -a** [aus·'trja·ko, -a], **austríaco, -a** [aus·'tri·a·ko, -a] *adj, m, f* Austrian

**autenticidad** [au·ten·ti·si·'dad, -θi·'dad] *f* authenticity

**auténtico, -a** [au·'ten·ti·ko, -a] *adj* authentic; **un ~ fracaso** an absolute failure; **es un ~ maestro en su especialidad** he's an absolute expert in his field

**autista** [au·'tis·ta] *adj* autistic

**autobiografía** [au·to·βjo·yra·'fi·a] *f* autobiography

**autobús** [au·to·'βus] *m* bus

**autocar** <autocares> [au·to·'kar] *m* bus

**autocarril** [au·to·ka·'rril] *m Bol, Chile, Nic* divided highway

**autóctono, -a** [au·'tok·to·no, -a] *adj* indigenous

**autodefensa** [au·to·de·'fen·sa] *f* self-defense

**autoescuela** [au·to·es·'kwe·la] *f* driving school

**autógrafo** [au·'to·ɣra·fo] *m* autograph

**autolavado** [au·to·la·'βa·ðo] *m* car wash

**automático** [au·to·'ma·ti·ko] *m* snap fastener

**automático, -a** [au·to·'ma·ti·ko, -a] *adj* automatic; **dispositivo ~** automatic mechanism; **fusil ~** automatic rifle; **la puerta se cierra de modo ~** (*en el metro*) the door closes automatically

**automatizar** <z → c> [au·to·ma·ti·'sar, -'θar] *vt* to automate

**automóvil** [au·to·'mo·βil] *m* car; **~ de carreras** racing car; **~ eléctrico** electrically powered car; **~ todo terreno** all-terrain vehicle; **Salón del Automóvil** motor show

**automovilista** [au·to·mo·βi·'lis·ta] *mf* motorist, driver

**autonomía** [au·to·no·'mi·a] *f* 1. (*personal*) autonomy; **en esta empresa no tengo ~ para tomar decisiones** in this company I cannot make my own decisions 2. (*territorio*) autonomous region

**autonómico, -a** [au·to·'no·mi·ko, -a] *adj* autonomous; **elecciones autonómicas** regional elections

**autónomo, -a** [au·'to·no·mo, -a] *adj* 1. POL autonomous 2. (*trabajador*) self-employed; **trabajar de ~** to be self-employed

**autopista** [au·to·'pis·ta] *f* highway, freeway; **~ de peaje** turnpike

**autopsia** [au·'toβ·sja] *f* MED autopsy

**autor(a)** [au·'tor, -·'to·ra] *m(f)* 1. LIT author; **derechos de ~** royalties 2. (*de un crimen*) perpetrator

**autoridad** [au·to·ri·'dad] *f* 1. (*en general*) authority; **estar bajo la ~ de alguien** to be under sb's control 2. (*pl*) (*policía*) authorities *pl*; **desacato a la ~** contempt (of court) 3. (*experto*) authority

**autoritario, -a** [au·to·ri·'ta·rjo, -a] *adj* authoritarian

**autorización** [au·to·ri·sa·'sjon, -θa·'θjon] *f* authorization

**autorizado, -a** [au·to·ri·'sa·ðo, -a; -'θa·ðo, -a] *adj* 1. (*facultado*) authorized; **persona no autorizada** unauthorized person; **de fuentes autorizadas** from approved sources 2. (*oficial*) official

**autorizar** <z → c> [au·to·ri·'sar, -'θar] *vt* 1. (*consentir*) to approve 2. (*facultar*) to authorize 3. (*dar derecho*) to entitle; **que sea mi jefe no te autoriza para insultarme** even though you're my boss, it doesn't give you the right to insult me

**autorretrato** [au·to·rre·'tra·to] *m* self-portrait

**autoservicio** [au·to·ser·'βi·sjo, -θjo] *m* self-service

**autostopista** [au·tos·to·'pis·ta] *mf* hitchhiker

**autovía** [au·to·'βi·a] *f* divided highway

**auxiliar¹** [auk·si·'ljar] **I.** *adj* assistant **II.** *mf* assistant; **~ administrativo** administrative assistant; **~ de vuelo** flight attendant **III.** *vt* to help

**auxiliar²** [auk·si·'ljar] *m* LING auxiliary verb

**auxilio** [auk·'si·ljo] *m* help; **primeros ~s** first aid; **pedir ~ (a alguien)** to ask for (sb's) help

**avalancha** [a·βa·'lan·tʃa] *f* avalanche

**avance** [a·'βan·se, -θe] *m t.* MIL advance, trailer for sth; **~ informativo** TV news summary

**avanzado, -a** [a·βan·'sa·ðo, -a; a·βan·'θa-] *adj* advanced

**avanzar** <z → c> [a·βan·'sar, -'θar] *vi* 1. (*seguir adelante*) *t.* MIL to advance; **a medida que el tiempo avanzaba** as time went by 2. (*progresar*) to progress; **no ~ nada** not to make any headway

**avaricia** [a·βa·'ri·sja, -θja] *f* 1. (*codicia*) greed 2. (*tacañería*) avarice

**avaricioso, -a** [a·βa·ri·'sjo·so, -a; a·βa·ri·'θjo-] *adj*, **avariento, -a** [a·βa·'rjen·to, -a] *adj* 1. (*codicioso*) greedy 2. (*tacaño*) avaricious

**avaro, -a** [a·'βa·ro, -a] **I.** *adj* miserly **II.** *m, f* miser

**avatares** [a·βa·'ta·res] *mpl* **los ~es de la vida** life's ups and downs

**ave** [a·βe] *f* bird; **~s de corral** poultry; **~ rapaz** [*o* **de rapiña**] bird of prey

**AVE** ['a·βe] *m abr de* **Alta Velocidad Es-**

**pañola** Spanish high-speed train

**avecinarse** [a·βe·si·'nar·se, -θi·'nar·se] *vr* to approach

**avellana** [a·βe·'ʎa·na] *f* hazelnut

**avemaría** [a·βe·ma·'ri·a] *f* Hail Mary

**avena** [a·'βe·na] *f* oats *pl*

**avenida** [a·βe·'ni·da] *f* (*calle*) avenue

**avenido, -a** [a·βe·'ni·do, -a] *adj* **dos personas bien avenidas** two good friends; **una pareja mal avenida** a mismatched couple

**avenir** [a·βe·'nir] *irr como venir* **I.** *vt* to reconcile **II.** *vr:* **~se 1.** (*entenderse*) to get on **2.** (*ponerse de acuerdo*) **~se en algo** to agree on sth; **no ~se a...** not to agree to...

**aventajado, -a** [a·βen·ta·'xa·do, -a] *adj* outstanding

**aventajar** [a·βen·ta·'xar] *vt* (*ser mejor*) to surpass; **~ a todos** to get ahead of everyone

**aventar** <e → ie> [a·βen·'tar] *vt* to blow away; (*el grano*) to winnow

**aventón** [a·βen·'ton] *m Méx inf* push; **dar un ~** to give a lift; **ir de ~** to ride free

**aventura** [a·βen·'tu·ra] *f* adventure; (*amorosa*) affair

**aventurar** [a·βen·tu·'rar] **I.** *vt* to venture; (*algo atrevido*) to dare **II.** *vr:* **~se** to dare

**aventurero, -a** [a·βen·tu·'re·ro, -a] **I.** *adj* adventurous; **espíritu ~** thirst for adventure **II.** *m, f* adventurer

**avergonzado, -a** [a·βer·ɣon·'sa·do, -a; -'θa·do, -a] *adj* embarrassed; **sentirse ~** to be ashamed

**avergonzar** [a·βer·ɣon·'sar, -'θar] *irr* **I.** *vt* to shame **II.** *vr* **~se de** [*o por*] **algo/alguien** to be ashamed of sth/sb

**avería** [a·βe·'ri·a] *f* **1.** AUTO breakdown **2.** (*de mercancía*) damage **3.** TÉC fault

**averiar** <1. *pres* averío> [a·βe·ri·'ar] **I.** *vt* to damage **II.** *vr:* **~se** AUTO to break down; TÉC to fail

**averiguación** [a·βe·ri·ɣwa·'sjon, -'θjon] *f* inquiry

**averiguar** <gu → gü> [a·βe·ri·'ɣwar] *vt* to inquire into; **averigua a qué hora sale el tren** find out (at) what time the train leaves

**aversión** [a·βer·'sjon] *f* aversion

**avestruz** [a·βes·'truθ, -'truθ] *m* ostrich

**aviación** [a·βja·'sjon, -'θjon] *f* **1.** AVIAT aviation; **compañía de ~** airline (company) **2.** MIL air force

**aviador(a)** [a·βja·'dor, --'do·ra] *m(f)* aviator

**aviar** <1. *pres* avío> [a·βi·'ar] **I.** *vt* (*maleta*) to pack; (*mesa*) to set **II.** *vi* **1.** (*apresurar*) **diles que vayan aviando** tell them to get a move on; **estar aviado** (*en un apuro*) to be in a tight spot **2.** *AmS* (*prestar*) to lend

**avicultura** [a·βi·kul·'tu·ra] *f* poultry farming

**avidez** [a·βi·'des, -'deθ] *f* eagerness; **~ de algo** eagerness for sth

**ávido, -a** ['a·βi·do, -a] *adj* eager; **~ de algo** eager for sth

**avinagrarse** [a·βi·na·'ɣrar·se] *vr* (*vino*) to turn sour; (*persona*) to become bitter

**avión** [a·βi·'on] *m* AVIAT airplane; **~ a reacción** jet (plane); **por ~** (*correos*) by airmail; **ir en ~ a La Paz** to fly to La Paz

**avioneta** [a·βjo·'ne·ta] *f* light aircraft

**avisar** [a·βi·'sar] *vt* **1.** (*dar noticia*) to notify; **avísame cuando estés de vuelta** let me know when you're back; **llegar sin ~** to arrive unannounced **2.** (*poner sobre aviso*) to warn **3.** (*llamar*) to call

**aviso** [a·'βi·so] *m* **1.** (*notificación*) notification; (*nota*) notice; (*por altavoz*) announcement; **~ de salida** FERRO departure announcement; **hasta nuevo ~** until further notice; **sin previo ~** without notice **2.** (*advertencia*) warning; **~ de bomba** bomb warning; **estar sobre ~** to be warned; **poner sobre ~** to warn; **servir a alguien de ~** to be a lesson to sb **3.** *AmL* (*en el periódico*) ad(vertisement)

**avispa** [a·'βis·pa] *f* wasp

**avispado, -a** [a·βis·'pa·do, -a] *adj* sharp

**avistar** [a·βis·'tar] *vt* to sight

**avivar** [a·βi·'βar] *vt* to enliven; (*fuego*) to stoke; (*pasión*) to arouse; (*sentidos*) to sharpen; **~ el paso** to increase one's pace

**avizor** [a·βi·'sor, -'θor] *adj* **estar ojo ~** to be alert

**axila** [ak·'si·la] *f* **1.** ANAT armpit **2.** BOT axil

**axioma** [ak·'sjo·ma] *m* axiom

**ay** [ai] *interj* 1. (*de dolor*) ouch 2. (*de sorpresa*) oh; ¡~, qué divertido! oh, how funny! 3. (*de miedo*) oh, my 4. (*de amenaza*) ¡~ si vienes tarde! you'll regret it if you come late!; ~ del que... +*subj* Heaven help anyone who...

**ayer** [a·'jer] *adv* yesterday; ~ (por la) noche last night; ~ hace una semana a week ago yesterday; de ~ acá overnight; ¡parece que fue ~! it seems like only yesterday!; no he nacido ~ I wasn't born yesterday

**ayuda**[1] [a·'ju·da] *f* (*auxilio*) help; eso no me sirve de ninguna ~ that doesn't help me

**ayuda**[2] [a·'ju·da] *m* helper

**ayudado, -a** [a·ju·'da·do, -a] *m, f* Col 1. (*brujo*) witchdoctor; (*de tribu*) medicine man 2. (*endemoniado*) possessed person

**ayudante** [a·ju·'dan·te] *mf* helper; (*cargo*) assistant

**ayudar** [a·ju·'dar] I. *vt* to help; ~ a alguien a levantarse to help sb up; ~ a alguien a salir del coche to help sb to get out of the car; ¡Dios me ayude! God help me!; ¿le puedo ~ en algo? can I help you with anything? II. *vr:* ~se (*valerse de*) to help oneself

**ayunar** [a·ju·'nar] *vi* to fast

**ayunas** [a·'ju·nas] *adv* estar en ~ to have an empty stomach

**ayuno** [a·'ju·no] *m* fast

**ayuntamiento** [a·jun·ta·'mjen·to] *m* 1. (*corporación*) district council; (*de una ciudad*) town/city council 2. (*edificio*) town/city hall

**azabache** [a·sa·'βa·tʃe, a·θa-] *m* jet; ojos de ~ jet-black eyes

**azada** [a·'θa·da, a·'θa-] *f* hoe

**azafata** [a·sa·'fa·ta, a·θa-] *f* AVIAT air hostess; ~ de congresos conference hostess

**azafrán** [a·sa·'fran, a·θa-] *m* saffron

**azahar** [a·'sar, a·sa·'ar; a·'θar, a·θa·'ar] *m* orange blossom

**azalea** [a·sa·'lea, a·θa-] *f* azalea

**azar** [a·'sar, -'θar] *m* 1. (*casualidad*) chance; juegos de ~ games of chance; al ~ at random; por ~ by chance 2. (*im-*previsto) misfortune; los ~es de la vida life's ups and downs

**Azores** [a·'so·res, -θo·res] *fpl* las ~ the Azores + *pl vb*

**azoro** [a·'so·ro, -θo·ro] *m* 1. AmC (*fantasma*) ghost 2. AmC (*aparición*) apparition 3. Méx, Perú, PRico (*azoramiento*) bewilderment

**azotaina** [a·so·'tai·na, a·θo-] *f* spanking

**azotar** [a·so·'tar, a·θo-] *vt* 1. (*con un látigo*) to whip; (*con la mano*) to thrash, to spank; el viento me azota (en) la cara the wind is hitting my face 2. (*producir daños*) to devastate; una epidemia azota la región an epidemic is causing havoc in the region

**azote** [a·'so·te, -'θo·te] *m* 1. (*látigo*) whip 2. (*golpe*) lash; (*en las nalgas*) spank

**azotea** [a·so·'tea, a·θo-] *f* terrace roof
▶ estar mal de la ~ *inf* to be off one's rocker

**azteca** [as·'te·ka, aθ-] I. *adj* Aztec; el equipo ~ (*en fútbol*) Mexico II. *mf* Aztec

**azúcar** [a·'su·kar, a·'θu-] *m* sugar; ~ en polvo icing sugar; tener el ~ muy alto MED to have a very high blood-sugar level

**azucarero** [a·su·ka·'re·ro, a·'θu-] *m* sugar bowl

**azucena** [a·su·'se·na, a·θu·'θe·na] *f* Madonna lily

**azufre** [a·'su·fre, a·'θu-] *m* sulfur

**azul** [a·'sul, a'θul] *adj* blue; ~ celeste sky blue; ~ marino navy blue

**azulado, -a** [a·su·'la·do, -a; a·θu-] *adj* bluish

**azulejo** [a·su·'le·xo, a·θu-] *m* 1. (*para pared*) (glazed) tile 2. ZOOL (*pez*) blue wrasse

**azulgrana** [a·sul·'ɣra·na, a·θul-] *adj* blue and scarlet; el equipo ~ DEP Barcelona Soccer Team

**azuzar** <z → c> [a·su·'sar, a·θu·'θar] *vt* 1. ~ a los perros a uno to set the dogs on sb 2. *fig* (*persona*) to incite, to egg on

# B

**B, b** [be] *f* B, b; **~ de Barcelona** B as in Bravo

**baba** ['ba·βa] *f* spittle; (*del caracol*) slime; **caerse a alguien la ~ por alguien** *inf* to dote on sb

**babero** [ba·'βe·ro] *m* bib

**babosa** [ba·'βo·sa] *f* 1. ZOOL slug 2. *AmL* (*tontería*) stupid thing

**babosada** [ba·βo·'sa·da] *f* *AmC, Méx* (*bobería*) silliness

**babosear** [ba·βo·se·'ar] *vi inf* to drool, to dribble

**baboso, -a** [ba·'βo·so, -a] *adj* 1. (*con babas*) slimy 2. *inf* (*zalamero*) fawning 3. *AmL* (*tonto*) silly

**baca** ['ba·ka] *f* roof rack, luggage rack

**bacalao** [ba·ka·'lao] *m* 1. (*pez*) cod; (*salado*) salt cod 2. MÚS techno music ▶ **cortar el ~** to run the show

**bachatear** [ba·tʃa·te·'ar] *vi AmL* to go out on the town

**bache** ['ba·tʃe] *m* 1. (*en la calle*) pothole 2. (*económico, psíquico*) slump

**bachillerato** [ba·tʃi·je·'ra·to, -ʎe·'ra·to] *m* 1. (*título*) certificate of secondary education 2. (*estudios*) high school education for 14-17-year-olds

**bacilo** [ba·'si·lo, -'θi·lo] *m* bacillus

**bacteria** [bak·'te·rja] *f* bacteria

**badén** [ba·'den] *m* dip; (*en carreteras*) drainage channel

**bádminton** ['bad·min·ton] *m* DEP badminton

**bafle** ['ba·fle] *m* (loud)speaker

**bagaje** [ba·'ɣa·xe] *m* **~ cultural** cultural knowledge

**bagatela** [ba·ɣa·'te·la] *f* trifle

**bagre** ['ba·ɣre] I. *adj* 1. *Bol, Col* (*cursi*) coarse 2. *Guat, Hond, ElSal* (*inteligente*) clever II. *m* 1. *AmL* ZOOL catfish 2. *And* (*antipático*) unpleasant person

**bah** [ba] *interj* 1. (*incredulidad*) never 2. (*desprecio*) that's nothing

**bahía** [ba·'ia] *f* bay

**bailador(a)** [bai·la·'dor, -·'do·ra] I. *adj* dancing II. *m(f)* dancer (of flamenco)

**bailar** [bai·'lar] I. *vi* 1. (*danzar*) to dance 2. (*objetos*) to move; **hacer ~ una**

**peonza** to spin a top ▶ **~ con la más fea** to get the short end of the stick; **otro que tal ~** he/she is just as bad II. *vt* to dance

**bailarín, -ina** [bai·la·'rin, --·'ri·na] I. *adj* dancing II. *m, f* dancer; (*de ballet*) ballet dancer

**baile** ['bai·le] *m* 1. (*acto*) dancing 2. (*danza*) dance 3. (*fiesta*) dance party; (*de etiqueta*) ball

**baja** ['ba·xa] *f* 1. (*disminución*) decrease 2. (*de trabajo*) vacancy; **~ por maternidad** maternity leave; **darse de ~** (*por enfermedad*) to be on sick leave 3. (*en una asociación*) resignation; **dar de ~ a alguien** to expel sb 4. (*documento*) discharge certificate; (*del médico*) doctor's note 5. MIL casualty

**bajada** [ba·'xa·da] *f* 1. (*descenso*) descent; **~ de tipos de interés** ECON fall in interest rates; **~ de bandera** minimum fare 2. (*camino*) way down; (*pendiente*) slope

**bajar** [ba·'xar] I. *vi* 1. (*ir hacia abajo*) to go down; (*venir hacia abajo*) to come down; **~ en ascensor** to take the elevator down 2. (*apearse*) **~ de** (*de un caballo*) to dismount, to get down from; (*de un coche*) to get out of 3. (*disminuir*) to decrease; (*temperatura*) to drop II. *vt* 1. (*transportar*) to bring down; (*coger*) to take down; **~ las persianas** to lower the blinds 2. (*precios*) to lower 3. (*voz*) to lower; (*radio*) to turn down 4. COMPUT to download III. *vr:* **~se** (*descender*) **~se de** (*de un caballo*) to dismount; (*de un coche*) to get out of

**bajativo** [ba·xa·'ti·βo] *m AmL* digestive

**bajo** ['ba·xo] I. *m* 1. (*instrumento*) bass 2. (*persona*) bass player 3. *pl* (*piso*) first floor *Am* 4. *pl* (*parte inferior*) underneath; (*de una prenda*) hemline II. *adv* 1. (*posición*) below 2. (*voz*) quietly III. *prep* 1. (*debajo*) below 2. (*por debajo de*) underneath; **~ llave** under lock and key; **~ la lluvia** in the rain; **~ fianza** on bail

**bajo, -a** <más bajo *o* inferior, bajísimo> ['ba·xo, -a] *adj* 1. *estar* (*posición*) low 2. *ser* (*de temperatura*) low; (*de estatura*) short; **baja tensión** ELEC low tension; **con la cabeza baja** with head lowered; **tener la moral baja** to be in poor spirits **3.** (*voz*) low; (*sonido*) soft **4.** (*comportamiento*) mean **5.** (*clase social*) humble **6.** (*calidad*) poor

**bajón** [ba·'xon] *m* (*descenso*) decline; (*de precios*) drop

**bala** ['ba·la] *f* (*proyectil*) bullet; **~ de fogueo** blank cartridge; **como una ~** like a flash

**balance** [ba·'lan·se, -θe] *m* **1.** COM (*resultado*) balance; **hacer un ~** to draw up a balance **2.** (*comparación*) comparison; **hacer (el) ~** to take stock of the situation

**balancear** [ba·lan·se·'ar, ba·lan·θe-] **I.** *vt* (*mecer*) to sway; (*acunar*) to rock **II.** *vr*: **~se 1.** (*columpiarse*) to swing **2.** NÁUT to roll

**balanceo** [ba·lan·'seo, -'θeo] *m* swaying; NÁUT rocking

**balanza** [ba·'lan·sa, -θa] *f* **1.** (*pesa*) scales *pl* **2.** COM balance; **~ de pagos** balance of payments

**balar** [ba·'lar] *vi* to bleat

**balazo** [ba·'la·so, -θo] *m* **1.** (*tiro*) shot **2.** (*herida*) bullet wound

**balbucir** [bal·βu·'sir, -'θir] *vi*, *vt* to stammer; (*niño*) to babble

**Balcanes** [bal·'ka·nes] *mpl* **los ~** the Balkans

**balcón** [bal'kon] *m* balcony

**balda** ['bal·da] *f* shelf

**baldado, -a** [bal·'da·do, -a] *adj* crippled; *inf* (*muy cansado*) exhausted

**balde** ['bal·de] *m* bucket ▶ **obtener algo de ~** to get sth for nothing; **en ~** in vain

**baldío, -a** [bal·'di·o, -a] *adj* **1.** (*terreno*) uncultivated **2.** (*inútil*) useless; (*en balde*) vain

**baldosa** [bal·'do·sa] *f* paving stone, floor tile

**baldosín** [bal·do·'sin] *m* tile

**balear** [ba·le·'ar] **I.** *vt* AmL **~ a alguien** (*disparar contra*) to shoot at sb; (*herir, matar*) to shoot sb **II.** *vr*: **~se** AmL **1.** (*disparar*) to exchange shots **2.** (*disputar*) to argue **III.** *adj* Balearic **IV.** *mf* native/inhabitant of the Balearic Islands

**Baleares** [ba·le·'a·res] *fpl* **las** (**islas**) **~** the Balearic Islands

**baleo** [ba·'leo] *m* AmL (*disparo*) shot

**balero** [ba·'le·ro] *m* AmL (*juego*) cup-and-ball toy

**ballena** [ba·'je·na, -'ʎe·na] *f* whale

**ballet** <ballets> [ba·'le] *m* ballet

**balneario** [bal·ne·'a·rjo] *m* **1.** (*baños*) spa **2.** (*estación*) health resort

**balón** [ba·'lon] *m* DEP ball ▶ **echar balones fuera** to evade the question

**baloncesto** [ba·lon·'ses·to, -'θes·to] *m* basketball

**balonmano** [ba·lon·'ma·no, ba·lom·'ma·no] *m* handball

**balsa** ['bal·sa] *f* **1.** (*charca*) pool **2.** NÁUT (*barca*) ferry; (*plataforma*) raft; **~ neumática** rubber dinghy ▶ **ser una ~ de aceite** (*mar*) to be as calm as a millpond

**bálsamo** ['bal·sa·mo] *m* balm

**báltico, -a** ['bal·ti·ko, -a] *adj* Baltic; **el mar ~** the Baltic Sea; **los países ~s** the Baltic countries

**baluarte** [ba·'lwar·te] *m* bastion; **un ~ de la libertad** a bulwark of freedom

**balumba** [ba·'lum·ba] *f* AmS (*barullo*) racket

**bambú** [bam·'bu] *m* bamboo

**banal** [ba·'nal] *adj* banal

**banalidad** [ba·na·li·'dad] *f* banality

**banalizar** <z → c> [ba·na·li·'sar, -'θar] *vt* to trivialize

**banana** [ba·'na·na] *f* AmL banana

**banca** ['ban·ka] *f* **1.** (*en el mercado*) stall **2.** AmL (*asiento*) bench **3.** FIN banking; **~ electrónica** electronic banking **4.** (*en juegos*) bank

**bancario, -a** [ban·'ka·rjo, -a] *adj* bank(ing); **cuenta bancaria** bank account

**bancarrota** [ban·ka·'rro·ta] *f* bankruptcy

**banco** ['ban·ko] *m* **1.** (*asiento*) bench **2.** FIN bank; **~ emisor** issuing bank; **Banco Mundial** World Bank **3.** TÉC bench, work table; **~ de pruebas** test bed; *fig* testing ground **4.** (*de peces*) shoal ▶ **~ de datos** COMPUT databank; **~ de sangre** blood bank

**banda** ['ban·da] *f* **1.** (*cinta*) band; (*insignia*) sash; **~ de frecuencia** RADIO fre-

quency band; **~ sonora** CINE soundtrack
**2.** (*pandilla*) gang; **~ terrorista** terrorist
group **3.** (*de música*) band; (*de música
moderna*) group

**bandada** [ban·'da·da] *f* **1.** (*de pájaros*)
flock **2.** (*de personas*) gang

**bandear** [ban·de·'ar] *vt* **1.** AmC (*perseguir a alguien*) to chase; (*herir de gravedad*) to seriously wound **2.** Arg, Par,
Urug (*taladrar*) to drill **3.** Arg, Par, Urug
(*un río*) to cross **4.** Guat (*pretender*) to
court **5.** Urug (*herir con palabras*) to
hurt; (*inculpar*) to charge

**bandeja** [ban·'de·xa] *f* tray; **~ de entrada** in-tray; **~ de salida** out-tray; **servir
en ~** to hand on a plate

**bandera** [ban·'de·ra] *f* flag ▶ **estar hasta la ~** *inf* to be packed full

**banderola** [ban·de·'ro·la] *f* CSur (*ventana*) transom

**bandido, -a** [ban·'di·do, -a] *m, f* **1.** (*criminal*) bandit **2.** (*persona pilla*) rogue

**bando** ['ban·do] *m* **1.** (*edicto*) edict
**2.** (*partido*) faction

**banquero, -a** [ban·'ke·ro, -a] *m, f* banker

**banqueta** [ban·'ke·ta] *f* **1.** (*taburete*)
stool; (*para los pies*) footstool **2.** AmC
(*acera*) sidewalk

**banquete** [ban·'ke·te] *m* banquet

**banquillo** [ban·'ki·jo, -ʎo] *m* bench; JUR
dock

**bañadera** [ba·ɲa·'de·ra] *f* AmL bathtub

**bañado** [ba·'ɲa·do] *m* Arg, Bol, Par
marshland

**bañador** [ba·ɲa·'dor] *m* (*de mujer*) swimsuit; (*de hombre*) swimming trunks

**bañar** [ba·'ɲar] **I.** *vt* **1.** (*lavar*) to bathe
**2.** (*sumergir*) to immerse **3.** (*mar*) to
bathe **4.** (*recubrir*) to coat; **bañado
en sudor** bathed of sweat **II.** *vr:* **~se
1.** (*lavarse*) to take a bath, to bathe
**2.** (*en el mar*) to take a swim

**bañera** [ba·'ɲe·ra] *f* bathtub

**bañista** [ba·'ɲis·ta] *mf* (*en playa*) swimmer; (*en balneario*) guest at a spa

**baño** ['ba·ɲo] *m* **1.** (*acto*) bathing; **~
María** CULIN double boiler; **~ de sangre**
bloodbath **2.** (*cuarto*) bathroom; **ir al ~**
to go to the bathroom **3.** (*de pintura*)
coat; (*de chocolate*) coating **4.** *pl* (*balneario*) spa; **~s termales** hot springs

**bar** [bar] *m* **1.** (*café*) café; (*tasca*) bar
**2.** FÍS bar

**baraja** [ba·'ra·xa] *f* deck of cards; **una
~ de posibilidades** *fig* a range of possibilities

**barajar** [ba·ra·'xar] *vt* **1.** (*naipes*) to
shuffle **2.** (*mezclar*) to mix up **3.** (*posibilidades*) to consider

**barandilla** [ba·ran·'di·ja, -ʎa] *f* (*de balcón*) handrail; (*pasamanos*) banister

**barato** [ba·'ra·to] *adv* cheap(ly)

**barato, -a** [ba·'ra·to, -a] *adj* cheap

**barba** ['bar·βa] *f* **1.** (*mentón*) chin
**2.** (*pelos*) beard; **dejarse ~** to grow a
beard; **por ~** per head ▶ **subirse a las
~s de alguien** to be disrespectful to sb

**barbacoa** [bar·βa·'koa] *f* barbecue

**barbaridad** [bar·βa·ri·'dad] *f* **1.** (*crueldad*) barbarity; **¡qué ~!** how terrible!
**2.** (*disparate*) nonsense

**barbarie** [bar·'βa·rje] *f* savagery

**bárbaro, -a** ['bar·βa·ro] **I.** *adj* **1.** (*cruel*)
savage **2.** *inf* (*estupendo*) tremendous
**II.** *m, f* HIST barbarian

**barbería** [bar·βe·'ri·a] *f* barber's (shop)

**barbero** [bar·'βe·ro] *m* barber

**barbilla** [bar·'βi·ja, -ʎa] *f* chin

**barbo** ['bar·βo] *m* ZOOL barbel

**barbudo, -a** [bar·'βu·do, -a] *adj* bearded

**barca** ['bar·ka] *f* (*small*) boat; **dar un paseo en ~** to take a boat ride

**barchilón, -ona** [bar·tʃi·'lon, --'lo·na] *m, f*
AmL (*curandero*) healer

**barco** ['bar·ko] *m* ship; **~ cisterna** tanker;
**~ de pasajeros** passenger ship; **~ de
vapor** steamer; **~ de vela** sailing ship

**baremo** [ba·'re·mo] *m* range of values

**barniz** [bar·'niθ, -'niθ] *m* polish; (*para
madera*) varnish

**barnizar** ‹z → c› [bar·ni·'sar, -'θar] *vt* to
put a gloss on; (*madera*) to varnish

**barómetro** [ba·'ro·me·tro] *m* barometer

**barón, -onesa** [ba·'ron, ba·ro·'ne·sa] *m, f*
baron *m*, baroness *f*

**barquero, -a** [bar·'ke·ro, -a] *m, f* (*en un
bote*) boatman *m*, boatwoman *f*

**barquillo** [bar·'ki·jo, -ʎo] *m* wafer

**barra** ['ba·rra] *f* **1.** (*pieza*) bar; (*de pan*)
loaf; (*de chocolate*) bar; **~ de labios** lipstick **2.** (*en un bar*) bar **3.** (*raya*) dash;
(*signo gráfico*) slash; MÚS bar **4.** COMPUT

~ **de comandos** taskbar; ~ **de despla-zamiento** scroll bar; ~ **espaciadora** space bar; ~ **inversa** backslash; ~ **de navegación** navigation bar

**barraca** [ba·'rra·ka] *f* **1.** (*casa*) cabin **2.** (*choza*) hut **3.** *AmL* MIL barracks

**barranco** [ba·'rran·ko] *m* **1.** (*despeñade-ro*) cliff **2.** (*cauce*) ravine

**barrenar** [ba·rre·'nar] *vt* to drill

**barrendero, -a** [ba·rren·'de·ro, -a] *m, f* sweeper

**barreño** [ba·'rre·ɲo] *m* washbasin

**barrer** [ba·'rrer] *vt* **1.** (*habitación*) to sweep **2.** *inf* (*derrotar*) to defeat ▶ ~ **para** [*o* hacia] **dentro** to look after number one

**barrera** [ba·'rre·ra] *f* **1.** (*barra*) barrier; ~ **del sonido** sound barrier **2.** DEP wall

**barriada** [ba·'rrja·da] *f* **1.** (*barrio*) district **2.** *AmL* (*barrio pobre*) shanty town

**barricada** [ba·rri·'ka·da] *f* barricade

**barriga** [ba·'rri·ɣa] *f* **1.** (*vientre*) belly **2.** (*de una vasija*) rounded part ▶ **ras-carse la ~** to laze about, to twiddle one's thumbs

**barril** [ba·'rril] *m* (*cuba*) barrel; **cerveza de ~** draught beer

**barrio** ['ba·rrjo] *m* **1.** (*de ciudad*) district, neighborhood; ~ **chino** red-light district; ~ **comercial** business quarter **2.** (*arrabal*) suburb ▶ **irse al otro ~** *inf* to snuff it

**barrizal** [ba·rri·'sal, -'θal] *m* mire

**barro** ['ba·rro] *m* **1.** (*lodo*) mud **2.** (*arci-lla*) clay; **de ~** earthenware

**barroco** [ba·'rro·ko] *m* baroque

**barroco, -a** [ba·'rro·ko] *adj* baroque; *fig* overly elaborate, gaudy *pej*

**barrote** [ba·'rro·te] *m* (*heavy*) bar; **entre ~s** *fig inf* behind bars

**bártulos** ['bar·tu·los] *mpl* belongings *pl*

**barullo** [ba·'ru·jo, -ʎo] *m inf* **1.** (*ruido*) din **2.** (*desorden*) confusion

**basalto** [ba·'sal·to] *m* basalt

**basar** [ba·'sar] **I.** *vt* to ground **II.** *vr* ~**se en algo** (*teoría*) to be based on sth; (*per-sona*) to base oneself on sth

**báscula** ['bas·ku·la] *f* scales *pl*

**base** ['ba·se] *f* **1.** (*fundamento*) basis; ~ **de datos** COMPUT database; **partir de la ~ de que...** to start with the assumption

that... **2.** ARQUIT, MAT base ▶ **a ~ de bien** *inf* really well

**básico, -a** ['ba·si·ko, -a] *adj* (*t. quím*) basic

**basílica** [ba·'si·li·ka] *f* basilica

**bastante** [bas·'tan·te] **I.** *adj* enough; **tengo ~ frío** I'm very cold **II.** *adv* (*sufi-cientemente*) sufficiently; (*considerable-mente*) rather; **con esto tengo ~** this is enough for me

**bastar** [bas·'tar] **I.** *vi* to be enough; **¡bas-ta!** that's enough! **II.** *vr* ~**se** (*uno*) **solo** to be self-sufficient

**bastardo, -a** [bas·'tar·do, -a] **I.** *adj* **1.** (*hijo*) bastard **2.** (*vil*) wicked **II.** *m, f* bastard

**bastidor** [bas·ti·'dor] *m* **1.** TÉC frame-(work); (*de coche*) chassis *inv*; (*de ven-tana*) frame **2.** TEAT wing; **entre ~es** behind the scenes

**basto, -a** ['bas·to, -a] *adj* **1.** (*grosero*) rude; (*vulgar*) coarse **2.** (*superficie*) rough

**bastón** [bas·'ton] *m* **1.** (*para andar*) stick; (*para esquiar*) ski pole **2.** (*de mando*) baton

**bastoncillo** [bas·ton·'si·jo, -'θi·ʎo] *m di-minutivo de* **bastón** small stick; ~ **de algodón** cotton swab, Q–tip®

**bastos** ['bas·tos] *mpl* clubs *pl* (*in Spanish deck of cards*) ▶ **pintan ~** things are getting difficult

**basura** [ba·'su·ra] *f* **1.** (*desperdicios*) garbage; **echar algo a la ~** to throw sth away **2.** (*lo despreciable*) trash

**basurero** [ba·su·'re·ro] *m* **1.** (*vertedero*) garbage dump **2.** (*recipiente*) trashcan

**basurero, -a** [ba·su·'re·ro, -a] *m, f* gar-bage [*o* trash] collector *mf*, garbage man *m*

**bata** ['ba·ta] *f* (*albornoz*) dressing gown; (*de laboratorio*) lab coat; (*de hospital*) white coat

**batacazo** [ba·ta·'ka·so, -θo] *m* **1.** (*golpe*) thump **2.** (*caída*) heavy fall; **se pegó un ~** *inf* he/she came a cropper

**batalla** [ba·'ta·ja, -ʎa] *f* MIL battle; ~ **cam-pal** pitched battle; *fig* bitter dispute

**batallón** [ba·ta·'jon, -'ʎon] *m* **1.** MIL bat-talion **2.** *inf* (*grupo*) group

**batata** [ba·'ta·ta] *f* **1.** (*planta*) sweet potato plant **2.** (*tubérculo*) sweet potato **3.** *CSur* (*susto*) shock **4.** *CSur* (*vergüenza*) embarrassment **5.** *AmL* ~ **de la pierna** calf

**bate** ['ba·te] *m* DEP bat

**batería**[1] [ba·te·'ri·a] *f* **1.** *t.* TÉC battery; ~ **de cocina** pots and pans; **aparcar en** ~ to parallel park; MÚS drums *pl*

**batería**[2] [ba·te·'ri·a] *mf* drummer

**batida** [ba·'ti·da] *f* **1.** (*de cazadores*) beat **2.** (*de policía*) raid **3.** *AmL* (*paliza*) beating, thrashing

**batido** [ba·'ti·do] *m* (*bebida*) milk shake

**batidora** [ba·ti·'do·ra] *f* (*de mano*) whisk; (*eléctrica*) mixer

**batifondo** [ba·ti·'fon·do] *m* *CSur inf* (*alboroto*) uproar; (*disturbio*) commotion; (*zozobra*) uneasiness

**batín** [ba·'tin] *m* (man's) dressing gown

**batir** [ba·'tir] **I.** *vt* **1.** (*golpear, metal*) to beat; (*las olas*) to crash against; ~ **palmas** to clap **2.** (*enemigo*) to defeat; MIL to beat; ~ **un récord** to beat a record **3.** (*un terreno*) to comb **4.** *CSur* (*denunciar*) to inform on **II.** *vr*: ~**se** **1.** (*combatir*) to fight **2.** (*en duelo*) to fight a duel

**batuta** [ba·'tu·ta] *f* MÚS baton ▶ **llevar la** ~ to be in charge

**baúl** [ba·'ul] *m* **1.** (*mueble*) trunk **2.** *AmL* AUT (*portamaletas*) trunk

**bausán, -ana** [bau·'san, -·'sa·na] *adj AmL* (*perezoso*) lazy

**bautismo** [bau·'tis·mo] *m* baptism

**bautizar** <z → c> [bau·ti·'sar, -·'θar] *vt* REL to baptize; (*nombrar*) to christen

**bautizo** [bau·'ti·so, -θo] *m* baptism; (*ceremonia*) christening; (*fiesta*) christening party

**baya** ['ba·ja] *f* berry

**bayeta** [ba·'je·ta] *f* rag, dishcloth

**baza** ['ba·sa, -θa] *f* **1.** (*naipes*) trick; **meter** ~ **en algo** *inf* to butt in on sth **2.** (*provecho*) benefit; **sacar** ~ **de algo** to profit from sth

**bazar** [ba·'sar, -'θar] *m* (*mercado*) bazaar

**bazo** ['ba·so, -θo] *m* ANAT spleen

**beatificar** <c → qu> [bea·ti·fi·'kar] *vt* to beatify

**beato, -a** [be·'a·to, -a] *adj* REL **1.** (*piadoso*) devout **2.** (*beatificado*) beatified

**bebe, -a** ['be·βe, -a] *m, f* *AmL* baby

**bebé** [be·'βe] *m* baby

**bebedor(a)** [be·βe·'dor, -·'do·ra] *m(f)* drinker

**beber** [be·'βer] **I.** *vi, vt* **1.** (*líquido*) to drink; ~ **de la botella** to drink from the bottle; ~ **a sorbos** to sip; ~ **de un trago** to gulp **2.** (*información*) to absorb **II.** *vr*: ~**se** to drink up

**bebida** [be·'βi·da] *f* drink, beverage *form*; ~ **alcohólica** alcoholic drink; ~ **energética** energy drink; **darse a la** ~ to take to drink

**bebido, -a** [be·'βi·do, -a] *adj* (*borracho*) drunk

**beca** ['be·ka] *f* (*de estudios*) grant; (*por méritos*) scholarship; **conceder una** ~ **a alguien** to award a grant to sb

**becario, -a** [be·'ka·rjo, -a] *m, f* grant holder; (*por méritos*) scholarship holder

**becerro** [be·'se·rro, -a; be·'θe-] *m, f* yearling calf

**bechamel** [be·ʃa·'mel] *f* white sauce

**bedel(a)** [be·'del, -·'de·la] *m(f)* beadle, proctor

**begonia** [be·'ɣo·nja] *f* begonia

**beicon** ['bei·kon] *m* bacon

**beige** [beis] *adj* beige

**béisbol** ['beis·βol] *m* DEP baseball

**belduque** [bel·'du·ke] *m* *AmL* pointed sword

**belén** [be·'len] *m* **1.** (*nacimiento*) crib, Nativity scene **2.** *inf* (*confusión*) confusion

**Belén** [be·'len] *m* Bethlehem

**belga** ['bel·ɣa] *adj, mf* Belgian

**Bélgica** ['bel·xi·ka] *f* Belgium

**Belgrado** [bel·'ɣra·do] *m* Belgrade

**belicista** [be·li·'sis·ta, -'θis·ta] **I.** *adj* belligerent **II.** *mf* warmonger

**bélico, -a** ['be·li·ko, -a] *adj* warlike

**beligerante** [be·li·xe·'ran·te] *adj* belligerent

**bellaquear** [be·ja·ke·'ar, be·ʎa-] *vi* **1.** (*persona*) to cheat **2.** *AmL* (*caballo*) to shy

**belleza** [be·'je·sa, -ʎe·θa] *f* beauty

**bello, -a** ['be·jo, -a; -ʎo, -a] *adj* beautiful

**bellota** [be·'jo·ta, -ʎo·ta] *f* acorn

**bembo, -a** ['bem·bo, -a] *adj AmL* thick-lipped

**bemol** [be·'mol] *m* MÚS flat ▶ **tener ~es** to be difficult

**benceno** [ben·'se·no, -·'θe·no] *m* benzene

**bencina** [ben·'si·na, -·'θi·na] *f* benzine; *Arg, Chile, Par, Urug* gasoline

**bendecir** [ben·de·'sir, -·'θir] *irr como decir* *vt* (*sacerdote*) to bless; ~ **la mesa** to say grace

**bendición** [ben·di·'sjon, -·'θjon] *f* **1.** (*acto*) blessing **2.** (*cosa magnífica*) marvel

**bendito, -a** [ben·'di·to, -a] **I.** *adj* **1.** REL blessed; (*agua*) holy; (*santo*) saintly; **¡~ sea!** *inf* thank God! **2.** (*dichoso*) lucky **II.** *m, f* kind soul

**benefactor(a)** [be·ne·fak·'tor, -·'to·ra] **I.** *adj* beneficent **II.** *m(f)* benefactor

**beneficencia** [be·ne·fi·'sen·sja, -·'θen·θja] *f* charity

**beneficiar** [be·ne·fi·'sjar, -·'θjar] **I.** *vt* **1.** (*favorecer*) to benefit **2.** *AmL* (*animal*) to slaughter **II.** *vr:* ~**se** (*sacar provecho*) ~**se de algo** to benefit from sth

**beneficiario, -a** [be·ne·fi·'sja·rjo, -a; be·ne·fi·'θja-] *m, f* beneficiary; ~ **de la pensión** receiver of the pension

**beneficio** [be·ne·fi·'sjo, -·'θjo] *m* **1.** (*bien*) good **2.** (*provecho*) *t.* FIN profit **3.** *AmL* (*matanza*) slaughter

**beneficioso, -a** [be·ne·fi·'sjo·so, -a; be·ne·fi·'θjo-] *adj* **1.** (*favorable*) beneficial **2.** (*útil*) useful **3.** (*productivo*) profitable

**benéfico, -a** [be·'ne·fi·ko, -a] *adj* (*caritativo*) charitable

**beneplácito** [be·ne·'pla·si·to, -·θi·to] *m* (*permiso*) approval

**benévolo, -a** [be·'ne·βo·lo, -a] *adj* **1.** (*favorable*) benevolent **2.** (*clemente*) indulgent

**bengala** [ben·'ga·la] *f* flare; (*pequeña*) sparkler

**benigno, -a** [be·'niɣ·no, -a] *adj* **1.** (*persona*) kind **2.** (*clima*) mild **3.** MED benign

**benjamín, -ina** [ben·xa·'min] *m, f* **1.** (*hijo menor*) youngest child **2.** (*de un grupo*) youngest member

**beodo, -a** [be·'o·do, -a] *adj* drunk

**berberecho** [ber·βe·'re·tʃo] *m* cockle

**berenjena** [be·ren·'xe·na] *f* eggplant

**Berlín** [ber·'lin] *m* Berlin

**berlina** [ber·'li·na] *f* **1.** (*vehículo*) sedan **2.** *AmL* (*pastel*) donut

**berlinés, -esa** [ber·li·'nes, -·'ne·sa] **I.** *adj* Berlin **II.** *m, f* Berliner

**bermudas** [ber·'mu·das] *mpl* Bermuda shorts *pl*

**berrear** [be·rre·'ar] *vi* **1.** (*animal*) to bellow **2.** (*llorar*) to howl **3.** (*chillar*) to screech

**berrinche** [be·'rrin·tʃe] *m inf* **1.** (*llorera*) tantrum **2.** (*enfado*) rage

**berro** ['be·rro] *m* watercress

**berza** ['ber·sa, -θa] *f* cabbage

**besar** [be·'sar] **I.** *vt* to kiss **II.** *vr:* ~**se** to kiss one another

**beso** ['be·so] *m* kiss; **comerse a alguien a ~s** to smother sb with kisses

**bestia¹** ['bes·tja] **I.** *adj* stupid **II.** *mf* (*bruto*) brute; (*grosero*) boor

**bestia²** ['bes·tja] *f* animal; (*salvaje*) (wild) beast

**bestial** [bes·'tjal] *adj* **1.** (*de una bestia*) bestial **2.** (*muy brutal*) brutal **3.** *inf* (*muy intenso*) tremendous; (*muy grande*) huge; (*muy bueno*) marvelous

**bestialidad** [bes·tja·li·'dad] *f* **1.** (*cualidad*) bestiality **2.** (*crueldad*) brutality **3.** *inf* (*gran cantidad*) **una ~ de** lots and lots of

**besugo** [be·'su·ɣo] *m* **1.** ZOOL bream; **ojos de ~** *inf* bulging eyes **2.** *inf* (*persona*) idiot

**besuquear** [be·su·ke·'ar] *vt* to cover with kisses

**betabel** [be·ta·'βel] *f* *Méx* (*remolacha*) beet; ~ **forrajera** fodder beet

**betún** [be·'tun] *m* **1.** QUÍM bitumen **2.** (*para el calzado*) shoe polish

**biaba** ['bja·βa] *f* *Arg, Urug* (*cachetada*) slap; (*paliza*) beating

**bianual** [bi·a·nu·'al] *adj* biannual; BOT biennial

**biberón** [bi·βe·'ron] *m* feeding bottle

**Biblia** ['bi·βlja] *f* Bible

**bíblico, -a** ['bi·βli·ko, -a] *adj* biblical

**bibliografía** [bi·βljo·ɣra·'fi·a] *f* bibliography

**biblioteca** [bi·βljo·'te·ka] *f* **1.** (*local*) library; ~ **de consulta** reference library

**2.** (*estantería*) bookshelves *pl*

**bibliotecario, -a** [bi·βljo·te·'ka·rjo, -a] *m, f* librarian

**bicarbonato** [bi·kar·βo·'na·to] *m* bicarbonate; **~ sódico** baking soda, sodium bicarbonate

**bíceps** ['bi·seps, -θeps] *m inv* ANAT biceps *inv*

**bicho** ['bi·tʃo] *m* **1.** (*animal*) (small) animal; (*insecto*) bug **2.** *inf* (*persona*) **~ raro** weirdo; **mal ~** rogue

**bici** ['bi·si, -θi] *f inf abr de* **bicicleta bike**

**bicicleta** [bi·si·'kle·ta, bi·θi-] *f* bicycle; **~ estática** exercise bike; **~ de montaña** mountain bike

**bicisenda** [bi·si·'sen·da, bi·θi-] *f Arg* bicycle [*o* bike] path

**bidón** [bi·'don] *m* steel drum

**Bielorrusia** [bje·lo·'rru·sja] *f* Byelorussia

**bien** ['bjen] **I.** *m* **1.** (*bienestar*) well-being **2.** (*bondad*) good **3.** (*provecho*) benefit **4.** *pl* ECON goods *pl* **5.** *pl* (*posesiones*) property; (*riqueza*) wealth; **~es inmuebles** real estate **II.** *adv* **1.** (*convenientemente*) properly; (*correctamente*) well; **~ mirado** well thought of; **estar ~ de salud** to be in good health; **estar (a) ~ con alguien** to get on well with sb; **hacer algo ~** to do sth well; **hacer ~ en** +*infin* to do well to +*infin* **¡pórtate ~!** behave yourself!; **te está ~** that serves you right **2.** (*con gusto*) willingly **3.** (*seguramente*) surely **4.** (*muy*) very; (*bastante*) quite; **es ~ fácil** it's very simple **5.** (*asentimiento*) all right; **¡está ~!** OK! ▶ **ahora ~** however **III.** *adj* well-off **IV.** *conj* **1.** (*aunque*) **~ que** although; **si ~** even though **2.** (*o...o*) **~...~...** either... or... **V.** *interj* well done

**bienestar** [bje·nes·'tar] *m* **1.** (*estado*) well-being **2.** (*riqueza*) prosperity; **estado del ~** welfare state

**bienhechor(a)** [bje·ne·'tʃor, -·'tʃo·ra] **I.** *adj* beneficent **II.** *m(f)* benefactor

**bienintencionado, -a** [bjen·in·ten·sjo·'na·do, -a; bjen·in·ten·θjo-] *adj* well-meaning

**bienvenida** [bjem·be·'ni·da] *f* welcome; **dar la ~ a alguien** to welcome sb

**bienvenido, -a** [bjem·be·'ni·do, -a] *adj, interj* welcome; **¡~ a España!** welcome to Spain!

**bife** ['bi·fe] *m CSur* **1.** (*carne*) steak **2.** *inf* (*sopapo*) slap

**bifurcación** [bi·fur·ka·'sjon, -'θjon] *f* fork

**bigamia** [bi·'ya·mja] *f* bigamy

**bigote** [bi·'yo·te] *m* **1.** (*de hombre*) moustache, mustache **2.** *pl* (*de animal*) whiskers *pl*

**bigudí** [bi·yu·'di] *m* (hair) curler

**bikini** [bi·'ki·ni] *m* bikini

**bilingüe** [bi·'lin·gwe] *adj* bilingual

**bilingüismo** [bi·lin·'gwis·mo] *m* bilingualism

**bilis** ['bi·lis] *f inv* ANAT bile

**billar** [bi·'jar, -'ʎar] *m* **1.** (*juego*) billiards; **~ americano** pool **2.** (*mesa*) billiard table

**billete** [bi·'je·te, -'ʎe·te] *m* **1.** (*pasaje*) ticket; **~ de ida y vuelta** roundtrip ticket; **sacar un ~** to get a ticket **2.** FIN bill **3.** (*de lotería*) ticket; **~ premiado** winning ticket

**billetera** [bi·je·'te·ra, bi·ʎe-] *f* billfold

**billón** [bi·'jon, -'ʎon] *m* **1.** ($10^{12}$) trillion **2.** ($10^9$) billion

**binario, -a** [bi·'na·rjo, -a] *adj* binary

**bingo** ['bin·go] *m* (*juego*) bingo; (*sala*) bingo hall

**binoculares** [bi·no·ku·'la·res] *mpl* binoculars *pl*

**binóculo** [bi·'no·ku·lo] *m* pince-nez

**biodegradable** [bio·de·yra·'da·βle] *adj* biodegradable

**biografía** [bjo·yra·'fi·a] *f* biography

**biógrafo** [bi'o·yra·fo] *m CSur* (*cine*) cinema

**biógrafo, -a** [bi'o·yra·fo, -a] *m, f* (*persona*) biographer

**biología** [bio·lo·'xi·a] *f* biology

**biólogo, -a** [bi'o·lo·yo, -a] *m, f* biologist

**biombo** [bi·'om·bo] *m* (folding) screen, bionic

**biopsia** [bi·'oβ·sja] *f* biopsy

**bioquímica** [bio·'ki·mi·ka] *f* biochemistry

**biosfera** [bios·'fe·ra] *f* biosphere

**bipartidismo** [bi··par·ti·'dis·mo] *m* POL two-party system

**biplano** [bi·'pla·no] *m* biplane

**biquini** [bi·'ki·ni] *m* bikini

**birlar** [bir·'lar] *vt inf* (*hurtar*) to swipe

**birome** [bi·'ro·me] *m o f CSur* ballpoint (pen)

**birra** ['bi·rra] *f inf* beer

**birria** ['bi·rrja] *f* **1.** (*persona*) drip; **va hecho una ~** he looks really scruffy **2.** (*objeto*) rubbish, trash; **la película es una ~** the film is rubbish

**birriondo, -a** [bi·'rrjon·do, -a] *adj Méx* **1.** (*callejero*) street; (*animales*) jumpy **2.** (*enamoradizo*) easily infatuated

**biruje** [bi·'ru·xe] *m AmL*, **biruji** [bi·'ru·xi] *m* cold wind

**bis** [bis] **I.** *interj*, *m* MÚS encore **II.** *adv* **1.** MÚS bis **2.** (*piso*) **7 ~ 7A**

**bisabuelo, -a** [bi·sa·'βwe·lo, -a] *m, f* great-grandfather *m*, great-grandmother *f*

**bisagra** [bi·'sa·ɣra] *f* hinge

**biscote** [bis·'ko·te] *m* rusk

**bisexual** [bi·sek·'swal] *adj* bisexual

**bisiesto** [bi·'sjes·to] *adj* **año ~** leap year

**bisílabo, -a** [bi·'si·la·βo, -a] *adj* two-syllable

**bisnieto, -a** [bis·'nje·to, -a] *m, f* great-grandson *m*, great-granddaughter *f*

**bisonte** [bi·'son·te] *m* (*americano*) buffalo; (*europeo*) bison

**bisturí** [bis·tu·'ri] *m* scalpel

**bisutería** [bi·su·te·'ri·a] *f* costume jewelry

**bit** [bit] *m* <bits> COMPUT bit; **~ de parada** stop bit

**bizco, -a** ['bis·ko, -a; 'biθ-] *adj* cross-eyed

**bizcocho** [biθ·'ko·tʃo, biθ-] **I.** *adj Méx* (*cobarde*) cowardly **II.** *m* CULIN sponge cake

**blanca** ['blan·ka] *f* **1.** MÚS half note **2.** (*de dominó*) double-blank ▶ **estar sin ~** *inf* to be broke

**blanco** ['blan·ko] *m* **1.** (*color*) white; **película en ~ y negro** black and white film **2.** (*en un escrito*) blank space; **cheque en ~** blank check **3.** (*diana*) target; **dar en el ~** *fig* to hit the mark ▶ **pasar la noche en ~** to have a sleepless night; **~ del ojo** white of the eye; **quedarse en ~** to go blank

**blanco, -a** ['blan·ko, -a] **I.** *adj* white;

(*tez*) pale **II.** *m, f* white man *m*, white woman *f*

**blando, -a** ['blan·do] *adj* **1.** (*objeto*) soft **2.** (*carácter*) mild; (*blandengue*) soft; (*cobarde*) cowardly

**blanquear** [blan·ke·'ar] **I.** *vi* to whiten **II.** *vt* **1.** (*poner blanco*) to whiten; (*tejido*) to bleach **2.** (*dinero*) to launder

**blasfemar** [blas·fe·'mar] *vi* **1.** REL to blaspheme **2.** (*maldecir*) **~ de algo** to swear about sth

**blasfemia** [blas·'fe·mja] *f* **1.** REL blasphemy **2.** (*injuria*) insult

**blasfemo, -a** [blas·'fe·mo, -a] *adj* blasphemous

**bledo** ['ble·do] *m* BOT goosefoot ▶ **(no) me importa un ~** I couldn't care less

**blindado, -a** [blin·'da·do] *adj* MIL armor-plated; **puerta blindada** reinforced door

**blindaje** [blin·'da·xe] *m* (*armor*) plating

**blindar** [blin·'dar] *vt* to plate

**bloc** [blok] *m* <blocs> (*cuaderno*) note-pad

**blofear** [blo·fe·'ar] *vi AmL* (*engañar*) to bluff

**bloque** ['blo·ke] *m* **1.** block; **~ de viviendas** block of flats **2.** POL bloc ▶ **en ~** en bloc

**bloquear** [blo·ke·'ar] **I.** *vt* **1.** (*el paso*) t. DEP to block; MIL to blockade **2.** (*aislar*) to cut off **3.** TÉC to jam **4.** FIN to freeze **5.** (*obstaculizar*) to obstruct **II.** *vr:* **~se** (*cosa*) to jam; (*persona*) to have a mental block

**bloqueo** [blo·'keo] *m* **1.** (*de paso*) t. DEP blocking; MIL blockade; **~ comercial** COM trade embargo **2.** TÉC (*de un mecanismo*) jamming **3.** (*mental*) block

**blusa** ['blu·sa] *f* blouse

**bluyin** [blu·'jin] <bluyines> *m* blue jeans *pl*

**boa** ['boa] *f* boa

**bobada** [bo·'βa·da] *f* silly thing

**bobina** [bo·'βi·na] *f* ELEC coil; (*de película*) reel

**bobo, -a** [bo·'βo] **I.** *adj* (*tonto*) silly **II.** *m, f* (*tonto*) fool

**boca** ['bo·ka] *f* **1.** ANAT mouth; **~ abajo** face down(ward); **~ arriba** face

up(ward); **estaba tumbada ~ abajo/ arriba** she was lying on her stomach/ on her back; **andar de ~ en ~** to be the subject of gossip **2.** (*abertura*) opening; **~ de metro** subway entrance; **~ de riego** hydrant **3.** (*agujero*) hole; (*de cañón*) muzzle; (*de volcán*) mouth
▶ **quedarse con la ~ abierta** to be dumbfounded; **a pedir de ~** perfectly

**bocacalle** [bo·ka·'ka·je, -ʎe] *f* (*de una calle*) street entrance; (*calle secundaria*) side street

**bocadillo** [bo·ka·'di·jo, -ʎo] *m* **1.** (*sándwich*) sandwich **2.** (*tira cómica*) balloon, bubble

**bocado** [bo·'ka·do] *m* **1.** (*mordisco*) mouthful **2.** (*freno*) bit

**bocajarro** [bo·ka·'xa·rro] *adv* **a ~** (*tirar*) point-blank

**bocanada** [bo·ka·'na·da] *f* puff; **echar ~s** *fig* to boast

**bocaza(s)** [bo·'ka·sa(s), -θa(s)] *mf* (*inv*) loudmouth

**boceto** [bo·'se·to, bo·'θe-] *m* sketch

**boche** ['bo·tʃe] *m* *CSur inf* (*bronca*) telling-off

**bochinche** [bo·'tʃin·tʃe] *m* *AmL* piece of gossip

**bochorno** [bo·'tʃor·no] *m* **1.** METEO sultry weather **2.** (*sofocación*) stifling atmosphere **3.** (*vergüenza*) shame; **me da ~ que esté mirando** it embarrasses me that he/she is looking

**bochornoso, -a** [bo·tʃor·'no·so, -a] *adj* **1.** METEO sultry **2.** (*vergonzoso*) shameful

**bocina** [bo·'si·na, bo·'θi-] *f* **1.** (*de coche*) horn; **tocar la ~** to blow the horn **2.** (*megáfono*) megaphone

**bocio** ['bo·sjo, 'bo·θjo] *m* goiter

**boda** ['bo·da] *f* **1.** (*ceremonia*) wedding **2.** (*fiesta*) wedding reception; **noche de ~s** wedding night

**bodega** [bo·'de·ya] *f* **1.** (*habitación*) wine cellar **2.** (*tienda*) wine shop; (*taberna*) bar **3.** NÁUT (*en un puerto*) storeroom; (*en un buque*) hold

**bodrio** [bo·'drjo] *m* **1.** *inf* (*cosa*) rubbish, trash; **esta película es un ~** this film is rubbish **2.** *AmL* (*confusión*) mess

**BOE** ['boe] *m* *abr de* **Boletín Oficial del**

Estado ≈ The Congressional Record

**bofetada** [bo·fe·'ta·da] *f* smack; **dar una ~ a alguien** to slap sb

**bofia** ['bo·fja] *f* *inf* cops *pl*

**boga** ['bo·ya] *f* (*moda*) vogue; **estar en ~** to be in vogue

**bogavante** [bo·ya·'βan·te] *m* lobster

**bogotano, -a** [bo·yo·'ta·no, -a] **I.** *adj* of/from Bogotá **II.** *m, f* native/inhabitant of Bogotá

**Bohemia** [bo·'e·mja] *f* Bohemia

**bohío** [bo·'i·o] *m* *AmL* rustic hut

**boicot** <boicots> [boi·'ko(t)] *m* boycott

**boicotear** [boi·ko·te·'ar] *vt* to boycott

**boina** ['boi·na] *f* beret

**bol** [bol] *m* (*tazón*) bowl

**bola** ['bo·la] *f* **1.** (*cuerpo*) ball; **~ del mundo** globe; **~ de nieve** snowball **2.** (*canica*) marble **3.** *inf* (*mentira*) fib; (*rumor*) rumor **4.** *pl vulg* (*testículos*) balls *pl*; **en ~s** *inf* naked, in the buff *inf*
▶ **no dar pie con ~** to be unable to do anything right; **ir a su ~** to go one's own way

**bolado** [bo·'la·do] *m* *AmL* (*asunto*) matter

**boleadoras** [bo·lea·'do·ras] *fpl* *CSur* bolas *pl*

**bolear** [bo·le·'ar] *vt* **1.** *CSur* (*cazar*) to hunt; (*atrapar*) to catch with a lasso **2.** *Méx* (*zapatos*) to polish **3.** (*alumno*) to fail

**bolera** [bo·'le·ra] *f* bowling alley

**bolero** [bo·'le·ro] *m* MÚS bolero

**boleta** [bo·'le·ta] *f* *AmL* **1.** (*entrada*) ticket **2.** (*documento*) permit **3.** (*para votar*) ballot (paper)

**boletería** [bo·le·te·'ri·a] *f* *AmL* (*taquilla*) ticket agency [o office]; TEAT box office

**boletero, -a** [bo·le·'te·ro, -a] *m, f* *AmL* (*taquillero*) ticket clerk

**boletín** [bo·le·'tin] *m* **1.** (*publicación*) bulletin **2.** (*informe*) report; **~ de noticias** news report

**boleto** [bo·'le·to] *m* **1.** *AmL* (*entrada*) ticket **2.** (*de quiniela*) coupon **3.** *Arg* (*mentira*) lie

**boliche** [bo·'li·tʃe] *m* **1.** (*bola*) jack **2.** (*bochas*) bowls; (*bolos*) ninepins *pl* **3.** *AmL* (*establecimiento*) grocery shop **4.** *Arg inf* (*bar*) bar

**bólido** [ˈbo·li·do] *m* AUTO racing car

**bolígrafo** [bo·ˈli·ɣra·fo] *m* (ballpoint) pen

**bolillo** [bo·ˈli·jo, -ʎo] *m* **1.** (*de encajes*) bobbin **2.** Col (*de tambor*) drumstick **3.** Méx (*panecillo*) bread roll

**bolívar** [bo·ˈli·βar] *m* FIN bolivar

**Bolivia** [bo·ˈli·βja] *f* Bolivia

**boliviano** [bo·li·ˈβja·no] *m* (*moneda*) boliviano

**boliviano, -a** [bo·li·ˈβja·no, -a] *adj, m, f* Bolivian

**bollería** [bo·ʝe·ˈri·a, bo·ʎe-] *f* (*tienda*) baker's; (*bollos*) buns *pl*, baked goods *pl*

**bollo** [ˈbo·jo, -ʎo] *m* **1.** (*panecillo*) bun; (*pastelillo*) cake **2.** (*abolladura*) dent **3.** (*confusión*) mix-up

**bolo** [ˈbo·lo] *m* DEP skittle; (**juego de**) ~s ≈ ninepins

**bolsa** [ˈbol·sa] *f* **1.** (*saco*) bag **2.** (*bolso*) handbag, purse; ~ **de plástico** plastic bag; ~ **de la compra** shopping bag; ~**s de los ojos** bags under the eyes **3.** FIN stock exchange; ~ **de trabajo** employment bureau; ~ **negra** AmL black market; ~ **de valores** stock exchange **4.** AmL (*bolsillo*) pocket

**bolsillo** [bol·ˈsi·jo, -ʎo] *m* **1.** (*en una prenda*) pocket; **edición de** ~ pocket edition **2.** (*monedero*) purse; **rascarse el** ~ *inf* to pay up

**bolso** [ˈbol·so] *m* bag; (*pequeño*) handbag, purse; (*en una vela*) bulge

**boludo, -a** [bo·ˈlu·do, -a] *inf* **I.** *adj* Arg, Urug (*imbécil*) dummy **II.** *m, f* Arg, Urug (*imbécil*) jerk

**bomba** [ˈbom·ba] **I.** *f* **1.** *t.* MIL bomb; ~ **de relojería** time bomb **2.** TÉC pump; ~ **neumática** air pump **3.** AmL (*bola*) ball **4.** AmL (*pompa*) bubble **5.** AmL *inf* (*borrachera*) **pegarse una** ~ to get drunk ▶ **a prueba de** ~**s** bomb-proof **II.** *adj inf* astounding; **pasarlo** ~ to have a great time

**bombacha** [bom·ˈba·tʃa] *f* CSur (*ropa interior*) panties *pl*

**bombardear** [bom·bar·de·ˈar] *vt* **1.** MIL to bomb **2.** *inf* (*abrumar*) to overwhelm **3.** FÍS to bombard

**bombardeo** [bom·bar·ˈdeo] *m* **1.** MIL bombing **2.** FÍS bombardment

**bombazo** [bom·ˈba·so, -θo] *m* bomb explosion; *inf* (*sensación*) bombshell

**bombear** [bom·be·ˈar] *vt* **1.** (*un líquido*) to pump **2.** (*un balón*) to lob

**bombero** [bom·ˈbe·ro] *m* **1.** (*oficio*) fireman **2.** *pl* (*cuerpo*) fire brigade; **coche de** ~ fire engine

**bombilla** [bom·ˈbi·ja, -ʎa] *f* **1.** ELEC (light) bulb **2.** AmS (*caña*) drinking straw

**bombín** [bom·ˈbin] *m* bowler hat

**bombo** [ˈbom·bo] *m* **1.** MÚS (*tambor*) bass drum; (*en un sorteo*) drum **2.** (*elogio*) exaggerated praise ▶ **tener la cabeza hecha un** ~ to have a splitting headache

**bombón** [bom·ˈbon] *m* **1.** (*golosina*) chocolate **2.** *inf* (*mujer*) **es un** ~ she's gorgeous

**bombona** [bom·ˈbo·na] *f* (*de gas*) cylinder

**bonachón, -ona** [bo·na·ˈtʃon, -·ˈtʃo·na] *adj* **1.** (*buenazo*) kindly **2.** (*crédulo*) naive

**bonaerense** [bo·nae·ˈren·se] **I.** *adj* of/from Buenos Aires province **II.** *mf* native/inhabitant of Buenos Aires province

**bondad** [bon·ˈdad] *f* **1.** (*de bueno*) goodness **2.** (*de amable*) kindness; **tenga la** ~ **de seguirme** so be so kind as to follow me

**bondadoso, -a** [bon·da·ˈdo·so, -a] *adj* good-natured, kind

**bongo** [ˈbon·go] *m* AmL (*canoa*) small canoe; (*balsa*) small raft

**bonificación** [bo·ni·fi·ka·ˈsjon, -ˈθjon] *f* (*gratificación*) bonus

**bonificar** <c → qu> [bo·ni·fi·ˈkar] *vt* (*abonar*) to improve

**bonito** [bo·ˈni·to] **I.** *m* ZOOL bonito **II.** *adv* AmL nicely

**bonito, -a** [bo·ˈni·to, -a] *adj* pretty

**bonitura** [bo·ni·ˈtu·ra] *f* AmL (*hermosura*) beauty

**bono** [ˈbo·no] *m* voucher; COM bond

**bonsái** [bon·ˈsai] *m* <bonsais> bonsai

**boquerón** [bo·ke·ˈron] *m* ZOOL (fresh) anchovy

**boquete** [bo·ˈke·te] *m* opening; (*en pared*) hole

**boquiabierto, -a** [bo·kja·ˈβjer·to, -a] *adj* open-mouthed; **dejar a alguien** ~ *fig* to astonish sb

**boquilla** [bo·'ki·ja, -ʎa] f 1. MÚS mouthpiece 2. (de cigarrillos) cigarette holder 3. TÉC nozzle ▸ **decir** algo de ~ to say sth without meaning it

**borda** ['bor·da] f NÁUT (borde) gunwale; **motor fuera (de)** ~ outboard motor; **echar algo por la** ~ t. fig to throw sth overboard

**bordado** [bor·'da·ðo] m embroidery

**bordar** [bor·'dar] vt to embroider; inf to do superbly

**borde** ['bor·de] I. adj inf (persona) difficult, hostile II. m (de camino) verge; (de mesa) edge; (de río) bank

**bordear** [bor·de·'ar] vt 1. (ir por) to skirt; (en coche) to drive along 2. (estar) to border on 3. (aproximarse) to verge on; **su comportamiento bordea la locura** his/her behavior borders on madness

**bordillo** [bor·'di·jo, -ʎo] m curb

**bordo** ['bor·do] m 1. NÁUT board; **ir a** ~ to go on board 2. Méx (presa) dam

**boreal** [bo·re·'al] adj northern

**borrachera** [bo·rra·'tʃe·ra] f 1. (ebriedad) drunkenness; **agarrar una** ~ to get drunk 2. (juerga) drinking binge

**borracho, -a** [bo·'rra·tʃo, -a] I. adj 1. ser (alcohólico) hard drinking 2. estar (ebrio) drunk; **estar** ~ **como una cuba** inf to be as drunk as a lord; ~ **de algo** fig elated with sth II. m, f drunk

**borrador** [bo·rra·'ðor] m 1. (escrito) rough draft 2. (cuaderno) scribbling pad 3. (utensilio) duster; (esponja) board rubber

**borrar** [bo·'rrar] I. vt 1. (con goma) to rub out; (con esponja) to wipe off 2. (tachar) to cross out; COMPUT to delete 3. (huellas) to remove II. vr: ~**se** to blur; ~**se de algo** to resign from sth

**borrasca** [bo·'rras·ka] f METEO squall; (tempestad) storm

**borrascoso, -a** [bo·rras·'ko·so, -a] adj METEO stormy

**borrego, -a** [bo·'rre·ɣo, -a] m, f 1. (cordero) lamb 2. (persona) meek person 3. AmL (noticia falsa) hoax

**borrón** [bo·'rron] m 1. (mancha) stain 2. (defecto) blemish ▸ **hacer** ~ **y** <u>cuenta nueva</u> to start with a clean

slate

**borroso, -a** [bo·'rro·so, -a] adj (escritura) unclear; (foto) blurred

**Bósforo** ['bos·fo·ro] m Bosphorus

**bosnio, -a** ['bos·njo, -a] adj, m, f Bosnian

**bosque** ['bos·ke] m wood; ~ **frondoso** broad-leaved woodland

**bosquejo** [bos·'ke·xo] m sketch

**bostezar** <z → c> [bos·te·'sar, -'θar] vi to yawn

**bostezo** [bos·'te·so, -θo] m yawn

**bota** ['bo·ta] I. f 1. (calzado) boot; **ponerse las** ~**s** inf to strike it rich 2. (cuba) large barrel II. adj Méx 1. (torpe) dim 2. (borracho) drunk

**botado, -a** [bo·'ta·ðo, -a] adj 1. AmC (malgastador) spendthrift 2. Ecua (resignado) resigned; (resuelto) resolute 3. Guat (tímido) shy 4. Méx (barato) dirt cheap

**botador(a)** [bo·ta·'ðor] adj AmL spendthrift

**botánica** [bo·'ta·ni·ka] f botany

**botánico, -a** [bo·'ta·ni·ko, -a] I. adj botanical II. m, f botanist

**botar** [bo·'tar] I. vi (pelota) to bounce; (persona) to jump ▸ **estar (uno) que bota** to be hopping mad II. vt 1. (pelota) to bounce 2. NÁUT (barco) to launch 3. AmL (tirar) to throw away 4. AmL (expulsar) to fire; **lo** ~**on del colegio** he was expelled from school 5. AmL (derrochar) to squander 6. AmL (extraviar) to lose

**bote** ['bo·te] m 1. (golpe) blow 2. (salto) jump; **pegar un** ~ to jump 3. (de pelota) bounce; **la pelota dio cuatro** ~**s** the ball bounced four times 4. (vasija) jar 5. (en la lotería) jackpot 6. NÁUT boat; ~ **salvavidas** lifeboat ▸ **a** ~ <u>pronto</u> (adj) sudden; (adv) suddenly; <u>chupar</u> **del** ~ inf to feather one's nest; <u>darse</u> **el** ~ inf to beat it; **la** <u>tiene</u> **en el** ~ inf he has her in his pocket

**botella** [bo·'te·ja, -ʎa] f bottle; ~ **de cerveza** bottle of beer

**botija** [bo·'ti·xa] f 1. (vasija) earthenware jug 2. AmL (tesoro) buried treasure

**botín** [bo·'tin] m 1. (calzado) high shoe 2. MIL booty

**botiquín** [bo·ti·'kin] *m* medicine chest; (*de emergencia*) first-aid kit

**botón** [bo·'ton] *m* **1.** (*en vestidos*) button **2.** ELEC knob; ~ **de muestra** sample; *fig* illustration; ~ **de opciones** COMPUT option button **3.** MÚS key **4.** CSur *pey* (*policía*) cop

**botones** [bo·'to·nes] *m inv* errand boy; (*de hotel*) bellhop

**boutique** [bu·'tik] *f* boutique

**bóveda** ['bo·βe·da] *f* ARQUIT vault; ~ **celeste** firmament

**bovino, -a** [bo·'βi·no, -a] *adj* bovine

**box** [boks] *m* **1.** (*para caballos*) stall **2.** AmL (*boxeo*) boxing **3.** AmC (*postal*) mailbox **4.** *pl* AUTO pits *pl*; **entrar en ~es** to make a pit-stop

**boxeador(a)** [bok·sea·'dor, -·'do·ra] *m(f)* boxer

**boxear** [bok·se·'ar] *vi* to box

**boxeo** [bok·'seo] *m* boxing

**boya** ['bo·ja] *f* buoy; (*en una red*) float

**boyante** [bo·'jan·te] *adj* prosperous

**boy scout** <boy scouts> ['boi es·'kaut] *mf* boy scout

**bozal** [bo·'sal, -'θal] *m* **1.** (*de perro*) muzzle **2.** AmL (*cabestro*) halter; (*cuerda*) headstall

**bracero** [bra·'se·ro, -'θe·ro] *m* AmL farmhand; (*peón*) laborer

**braga** ['bra·ɣa] *f pl* (*de mujer*) panties *pl*

**bragueta** [bra·'ɣe·ta] *f* fly

**braille** ['brai·le] *m* Braille

**bramar** [bra·'mar] *vi* (*animal*) to roar; (*persona*) to bluster; (*viento*) to howl

**brandy** ['bran·di] *m* brandy

**branquia** ['bran·kja] *f* gill

**brasa** ['bra·sa] *f* ember; **a la ~** grilled

**brasero** [bra·'se·ro] *m* **1.** (*estufa*) brazier **2.** AmL (*fuego*) fireplace; (*hogar*) hearth

**Brasil** [bra·'sil] *m* (**el**) ~ Brazil

**brasileño, -a** [bra·si·'le·ɲo, -a] *adj, m, f* Brazilian

**brava** ['bra·βa] *f* Cuba (*golpe*) punch; **dar una ~** to intimidate; **a la ~ por las ~s** by force

**bravío** [bra·'βi·o] *m* fierceness

**bravío, -a** [bra·'βi·o, -a] *adj* **1.** (*animal*) wild; (*sin domar*) untamed **2.** (*persona*) impetuous

**bravo** ['bra·βo] *interj* well done

**bravo, -a** ['bra·βo, -a] *adj* **1.** (*valiente*) brave **2.** (*salvaje*) wild; (*mar*) stormy **3.** (*picante*) hot

**brazalete** [bra·sa·'le·te, bra·θa·] *m* (*pulsera*) bracelet; (*banda*) armband

**brazo** ['bra·so, -θo] *m* **1.** ANAT arm; ~ **derecho** *fig* right-hand man; **cruzarse de ~s** to fold one's arms; *fig* to stand by and do nothing; **dar el ~ a torcer** to give in; **ir cogidos del ~** to walk arm-in-arm; **recibir a alguien con los ~s abiertos** to welcome sb with open arms **2.** (*de una silla*) arm **3.** GEO (*del río*) branch **4.** (*poder*) power

**brea** ['brea] *f* tar

**brebaje** [bre·'βa·xe] *m* (*bebida*) brew; (*medicina*) potion

**brecha** ['bre·tʃa] *f* **1.** MIL breach **2.** (*abertura*) opening; (*en una pared*) gap **3.** (*herida*) gash ▶ **estar en la ~** to be in the thick of things

**brécol(es)** ['bre·kol, -·ko·l(es)] *m(pl)* broccoli

**bregar** <g → gu> [bre·'ɣar] *vi* **1.** (*reñir*) to quarrel **2.** (*luchar*) to struggle **3.** (*trabajar*) to slave away

**Bretaña** [bre·'taɲa] *f* Brittany; **Gran ~** Great Britain

**breva** ['bre·βa] *f* **1.** (*higo*) early fig **2.** (*cigarro*) flat cigar **3.** AmL (*tabaco*) chewing tobacco

**breve** ['bre·βe] **I.** *adj* (*de duración*) brief; (*de extensión*) short; **en ~** shortly **II.** *m* PREN short news item

**brevedad** [bre·βe·'dad] *f* (*duración*) brevity; (*extensión*) shortness

**bribón, -ona** [bri·'βon, -·'bo·na] *adj* **1.** (*pícaro*) rascally **2.** (*vago*) idle

**bricolaje** [bri·ko·'la·xe] *m* do-it-yourself

**brida** [bri·'da] *f* **1.** (*de caballo*) bridle **2.** TÉC flange

**brigada**¹ [bri·'ɣa·da] *f* **1.** MIL brigade **2.** (*de policía*) squad

**brigada**² [bri·'ɣa·da] *m* MIL sergeant major

**brillante** [bri·'jan·te, -·'ʎan·te] **I.** *m* diamond **II.** *adj* **1.** (*luz*) bright; (*joya*) sparkling **2.** (*compañía*) brilliant

**brillantez** [bri·jan·'tes, bri·ʎan·'teθ] *f* t.

*fig* brilliance

**brillantina** [bri·jan·'ti·na, bri·ʎan-] *f* brilliantine, hair cream

**brillar** [bri·'jar, -'ʎar] *vi* to shine; **~ por su ausencia** *irón* to be conspicuous by one's absence

**brillo** ['bri·jo, -ʎo] *m* **1.** (*cualidad*) shine; (*reflejo*) glow; **dar ~ a algo** to polish sth **2.** (*gloria*) splendor

**brincar** <c → qu> [brin·'kar] *vi* to hop; (*hacia arriba*) to jump; **~ de alegría** *fig* to jump for joy

**brinco** ['brin·ko] *m* hop; **dar ~s** to hop; **de un ~** in one bound; *AmL* right away

**brindar** [brin·'dar] **I.** *vi* to drink a toast; **~ por alguien** to drink to sb **II.** *vt* to offer

**brindis** ['brin·dis] *m inv* toast; **echar un ~** to drink a toast

**brío** ['bri·o] *m* **1.** (*energía*) spirit **2.** (*pujanza*) drive

**brisa** ['bri·sa] *f* breeze

**británico, -a** [bri·'ta·ni·ko, -a] **I.** *adj* British; **inglés ~** British English **II.** *m, f* Briton

**brizna** ['bris·na, 'briθ-] *f* **1.** (*hebra*) strand; *BOT* blade **2.** (*porción*) scrap **3.** *AmL* (*llovizna*) drizzle

**brocha** ['bro·tʃa] *f* brush; (*de afeitar*) shaving brush; **pintor de ~ gorda** house painter

**broche** ['bro·tʃe] *m* **1.** (*en la ropa*) clasp; (*de adorno*) brooch; **~ de oro** *fig* finishing touch **2.** *AmL* (*sujetapapeles*) paper clip **3.** *pl AmL* (*gemelos*) cufflinks *pl*

**brocheta** [bro·'tʃe·ta] *f* skewer

**broma** ['bro·ma] *f* **1.** (*gracia*) fun, kidding **2.** (*tontería*) joke; **~ pesada** practical joke; **decir algo en ~** to be kidding; **gastar ~s a alguien** to play jokes on sb; **~s aparte...** joking apart...; **estoy de ~** I'm not serious; **no estoy para ~s** I'm in no mood for jokes; **¡ni en ~!** no way!

**bromear** [bro·me·'ar] *vi* to joke, to kid; **¿bromeas?** are you kidding?

**bromista** [bro·'mis·ta] **I.** *adj* fond of jokes **II.** *mf* joker

**bronca** ['bron·ka] *f* **1.** (*riña*) argument **2.** (*reprimenda*) earful **3.** *AmL* (*enfado*) anger

**bronce** ['bron·se, -θe] *m* bronze

**bronceado** [bron·se·a·do, bron·θe-] *m* (*de la piel*) tan

**bronceado, -a** [bron·se·a·do, -a; bron·θe-] *adj* (*piel*) tanned

**bronceador** [bron·sea·'dor, bron·θe-] *m* suntan lotion

**broncear** [bron·se·'ar, bron·θe-] **I.** *vt* (*un objeto*) to bronze; (*la piel*) to tan **II.** *vr:* **~se** to get a (sun)tan

**bronco, -a** ['bron·ko, -a] *adj* **1.** (*voz*) gruff **2.** (*genio*) surly **3.** *AmL* (*caballo*) untamed

**bronquio** ['bron·kjo] *m ANAT* bronchial tube

**bronquitis** [bron·'ki·tis] *f inv MED* bronchitis

**broqueta** [bro·'ke·ta] *f* skewer

**brotar** [bro·'tar] *vi* **1.** *BOT* to sprout; (*semilla*) to germinate **2.** (*agua*) to flow **3.** (*enfermedad*) to break out

**brote** ['bro·te] *m* **1.** *BOT* shoot; **~s de soja** bean sprouts **2.** (*erupción*) outbreak

**bruces** ['bru·ses, 'bru·θes] *adv* **caer de ~** to fall headlong

**bruja** ['bru·xa] *f* witch

**brujería** [bru·xe·'ri·a] *f* witchcraft

**brujo** ['bru·xo] *m* **1.** (*hechicero*) wizard **2.** *AmL* (*curandero*) medicine man

**brújula** ['bru·xu·la] *f* compass; **perder la ~** *fig* to lose one's bearings

**bruma** ['bru·ma] *f* mist

**brumoso, -a** [bru·'mo·so, -a] *adj* misty

**brusco, -a** ['brus·ko, -a] *adj* **1.** (*repentino*) sudden **2.** (*persona*) abrupt

**Bruselas** [bru·'se·las] *f* Brussels

**brutal** [bru·'tal] *adj* **1.** (*violento*) brutal **2.** *inf* (*enorme*) huge **3.** *inf* (*estupendo*) tremendous

**brutalidad** [bru·ta·li·'dad] *f* **1.** (*calidad*) brutality **2.** (*acción*) brutal act, crime **3.** (*cantidad*) huge amount

**bruto** ['bru·to] *m* brute

**bruto, -a** ['bru·to, -a] *adj* **1.** (*brutal*) brutal **2.** (*rudo*) uncouth **3.** (*estúpido*) stupid **4.** (*inculto*) rough **5.** (*tosco*) uncut; **diamante en ~** rough diamond **6.** (*peso*) gross

**buceador(a)** [bu·sea·'dor, -·'do·ra; bu·θea-] *m(f)* diver

**bucear** [bu·se·'ar, bu·θe-] *vi* to dive

**buceo** [buˈseo, -ˈθeo] *m* diving

**buche** [ˈbuˈtʃe] *m* **1.** (*en las aves*) crop **2.** *inf* (*estómago*) belly

**bucle** [ˈbuˈkle] *m* (*onda*) curl; COMPUT loop

**budismo** [buˈdisˈmo] *m* Buddhism

**budista** [buˈdisˈta] *adj, mf* Buddhist

**buen** [bwen] *adj v.* **bueno**

**buenaventura** [bweˈnaˈβenˈtuˈra] *f* **1.** (*suerte*) good luck **2.** (*adivinación*) fortune

**buenazo, -a** [bweˈnaˈso, -a; -θo, -a] *m, f* good-natured person

**bueno** [ˈbweˈno] *interj* OK

**bueno, -a** [ˈbweˈno, -a] *adj* <mejor *o* más bueno, el mejor *o* bonísimo *o* buenísimo> *ante substantivo masc. sing.:* **buen 1.** (*calidad*) good; (*tiempo*) fine; (*constitución*) sound; (*decisión*) right; **~s días** good morning; **buenas tardes/noches** good afternoon/evening; **buen viaje** have a good journey; **hace ~** it's nice weather; **dar algo por ~** to accept sth; **estar de buenas** to be in a good mood; **por las buenas o por las malas** by fair means or foul **2.** (*apropiado*) suitable **3.** (*honesto*) honest; (*bondadoso*) kindly; (*niño*) well-behaved; **es buena gente** he/she is a nice person **4.** (*sano*) healthy **5.** *inf* (*atractivo*) attractive; **está buenísima** she's hot stuff **6.** (*bonito*) fine; **¡buena la has hecho!** *irón* you've done it now!; **¡estaría ~!** *fig* I should think not!

**buey** [bwei] *m* **1.** ZOOL ox **2.** *AmC* (*cornudo*) cuckold

**búfalo** [ˈbuˈfaˈlo] *m* buffalo

**bufanda** [buˈfanˈda] *f* scarf

**bufar** [buˈfar] *vi* **1.** (*resoplar*) to snort; **está que bufa** he/she is really furious **2.** *AmL* (*oler mal*) to stink

**bufete** [buˈfeˈte] *m* **1.** (*escritorio*) desk **2.** (*de abogado*) lawyer's office

**bufido** [buˈfiˈdo] *m* **1.** (*resoplido*) snort **2.** (*exabrupto*) sharp remark

**bufón, -ona** [buˈfon, --ˈfoˈna] *m, f* **1.** (*bromista*) joker **2.** TEAT buffoon

**buhardilla** [bwarˈdiˈja, -ˈʎa] *f* (*vivienda*) garret

**búho** [ˈbuo] *m* ZOOL owl

**buitre** [ˈbwiˈtre] *m* **1.** ZOOL vulture, buz-

zard **2.** *inf* (*persona*) sponger

**bujía** [buˈxiˈa] *f* **1.** (*vela*) candle **2.** AUTO spark plug

**bula** [ˈbuˈla] *f* (*papal*) bull

**bulbo** [ˈbulˈβo] *m* bulb

**bule** [ˈbuˈle] *m* *Méx* BOT gourd

**Bulgaria** [bulˈɣaˈrja] *f* Bulgaria

**búlgaro, -a** [ˈbulˈɣaˈro] *adj, m, f* Bulgarian

**bulimia** [buˈliˈmja] *f* MED bulimia

**bulla** [ˈbuˈja, -ˈʎa] *f* **1.** (*ruido*) racket **2.** *AmL* (*pelea*) brawl

**bullicio** [buˈjisˈjo, -ˈʎiˈθjo] *m* uproar

**bullicioso, -a** [buˈjiˈsjoˈso, -a; buˈʎiˈθjo-] *adj* noisy

**bullir** <3. *pret* bulló> [buˈjir, -ˈʎir] *vi* **1.** (*hervir*) to boil; (*borbotar*) to bubble; **le bulle la sangre (en las venas)** *fig* he/she is a bundle of energy **2.** (*moverse*) to stir

**bulo** [ˈbuˈlo] *m* false rumor

**bulto** [ˈbulˈto] *m* **1.** (*tamaño*) size; **a ~** roughly; **escurrir el ~** *inf* to pass the buck **2.** (*importancia*) importance; **un error de ~** a major error **3.** (*objeto*) mass **4.** (*paquete*) piece of luggage **5.** MED swelling

**búnker** [ˈbunˈker] *m* MIL bunker

**buñuelo** [buˈɲweˈlo] *m* doughnut, donut

**buque** [ˈbuˈke] *m* (*barco*) ship; **~ de carga** freighter; **~ de guerra** warship; **~ insignia** flagship

**buraco** [buˈraˈko] *m* *Arg, Par, Urug* hole

**burbuja** [burˈβuˈxa] *f* bubble

**burbujear** [burˈβuˈxeˈar] *vi* to bubble

**burdel** [burˈdel] *m* brothel

**burdo, -a** [ˈburˈdo, -a] *adj* coarse; (*excusa*) clumsy

**burgués, -esa** [burˈɣes, --ˈɣeˈsa] *adj t. pey* bourgeois, middle-class

**burguesía** [burˈɣeˈsiˈa] *f* bourgeoisie

**burla** [ˈburˈla] *f* **1.** (*mofa*) taunt; **hacer ~ de alguien** to make fun of sb **2.** (*engaño*) hoax

**burlar** [burˈlar] **I.** *vt* to cheat **II.** *vr:* **~se** to joke

**burlón, -ona** [burˈlon, --ˈloˈna] **I.** *adj* mocking **II.** *m, f* **1.** (*mofador*) mocker **2.** (*guasón*) joker

**burocracia** [buˈroˈkraˈsja, -θja] *f* bureaucracy

**burócrata** [bu·'ro·kra·ta] *mf* bureaucrat

**burocrático, -a** [bu·ro·'kra·ti·ko, -a] *adj* bureaucratic

**burrada** [bu·'rra·da] *f inf* silly thing; **decir ~s** to talk nonsense

**burro** ['bu·rro] *m* 1. *AmC* (*escalera*) step ladder 2. *AmC* (*columpio*) swing

**burro, -a** ['bu·rro, -a] I. *m, f* ZOOL donkey; **~ de carga** *t. fig* beast of burden ▶ **apearse del ~** to admit to one's mistake; **no ver tres en un ~** to be as blind as a bat II. *adj* 1. (*tonto*) stupid 2. (*obstinado*) obstinate

**bursátil** [bur·'sa·til] *adj* stock exchange

**bus** [bus] *m t.* COMPUT bus

**busca¹** ['bus·ka] *f* search; **en ~ de alguien** in search of sb

**busca²** ['bus·ka] *m* beeper

**buscar** <c → qu> [bus·'kar] *vi, vt* to look for; **enviar a alguien a ~ algo** to send sb to fetch sth; **ir a ~ algo** to go and look for sth; **me viene a ~ a las 7** he/she is picking me up at 7; **él se lo ha buscado** he brought it on himself; **~ tres pies al gato** to complicate matters; **'se busca'** 'wanted'

**buscavidas** [bus·ka·'βi·das] *mf inv* go-getter

**buseta** [bu·'se·ta] *f* Col, Ven (*pequeño autobús*) minibus

**búsqueda** ['bus·ke·da] *f t.* COMPUT search

**busto** ['bus·to] *m* bust

**butaca** [bu·'ta·ka] *f* armchair; (*de cine*) seat

**butano** [bu·'ta·no] I. *adj* orange II. *m* QUÍM butane (gas)

**buzo** ['bu·so, -θo] *m* diver

**buzón** [bu·'son, -'θon] *m* (*de correos*) mailbox; **~ (electrónico)** COMPUT mailbox

**byte** [bait] *m* COMPUT byte

# C

**C, c** [se, θe] *f* C, c; **~ de Carmen** C as in Charlie

**C/** ['ka·je, -ʎe] *abr de* **calle** St

**cabalgar** <g → gu> [ka·βal·'γar] *vi* to ride horseback

**cabalgata** [ka·βal·'γa·ta] *f* procession, cavalcade

**caballería** [ka·βa·je·'ri·a, -ʎe·'ri·a] *f* 1. (*montura*) mount 2. MIL cavalry

**caballero** [ka·βa·'je·ro, -'ʎe·ro] *m* 1. (*galán*) gentleman 2. HIST knight

**caballerosidad** [ka·βa·je·ro·si·'dad, ka·βa·ʎe-] *f* gentlemanliness

**caballo** [ka·'βa·jo, -ʎo] *m* 1. (*animal*) horse; **a ~** on horseback; **ir a ~** to ride; **~ de batalla** *fig* hobby horse 2. (*ajedrez*) knight 3. AUTO horsepower 4. (*naipes*) queen 5. *inf* (*heroína*) smack

**cabaña** [ka·'βa·ɲa] *f* cabin

**cabecear** [ka·βe·se·'ar, -θe·'ar] I. *vi* 1. (*mover la cabeza*) to shake one's head 2. (*dormitar*) to nod off II. *vt* DEP to head

**cabecera** [ka·βe·'se·ra, -'θe·ra] *f* 1. (*de cama*) head 2. (*del periódico*) masthead; **médico de ~** family doctor

**cabecilla** [ka·βe·'si·ja, -'θi·ʎa] *mf* ringleader

**cabello** [ka·'βe·jo, -ʎo] *m* hair; **se le pusieron los ~s de punta** his/her hair stood on end

**caber** [ka·'βer] *irr vi* (*tener espacio*) **~ en algo** to fit in [*o* into] sth; **no ~ en sí de...** to be beside oneself with...; **esta falda no me cabe** this skirt doesn't fit me

**cabeza** [ka·'βe·sa, -θa] I. *f* 1. *t.* ANAT, TÉC head; **~ de ajo** bulb of garlic; **~ atómica** atomic warhead; **~ abajo** upside down; **~ arriba** upright; **de ~** headfirst; **por ~** a head; **abrirse la ~** to split one's head open; **asentir con la ~** to nod (one's head); **negar con la ~** to shake one's head; **se me va la ~** I feel dizzy; **de la ~ a los pies** from head to toe; **estar mal de la ~** *inf* to be out of one's mind; **levantar ~** to pull through; **métetelo en la ~** get it into your head; **algo se le pasa a alguien por la ~** sth crosses sb's mind; **quitarse algo de la ~** to put sth out of one's mind; **sentar (la) ~** to settle down; **tener la ~ dura** to be stubborn; **traer a alguien de ~** to drive sb crazy; **este chico tiene ~** this boy is clever **2.** (*extremo*) top; **ir en ~** DEP to be in the lead **3.** AGR (*res*) head **II.** *mf* head; **~ de familia** head of the family; **~ rapada** skinhead

**cabezada** [ka·βe·'sa·da, -'θa·da] *f* **dar** [*o* **echar**] **una ~** *inf* to take a nap

**cabezazo** [ka·βe·'sa·so, -θa·θo] *m* blow on the head; DEP header; **darse un ~** to bang one's head

**cabezón, -ona** [ka·βe·'son, -'θon] *adj* **1.** (*de cabeza grande*) with a big head **2.** *inf* (*obstinado*) pigheaded

**cabida** [ka·'βi·da] *f* space; **dar ~ a** to make room for

**cabina** [ka·'βi·na] *f* cabin; (*de gimnasio*) locker; **~ de control** TÉC control room; **~ del piloto** cockpit; **~ de teléfonos** phone booth

**cabinera** [ka·βi·'ne·ra] *f Col* stewardess *f*, flight attendant

**cable** ['ka·βle] *m t.* ELEC (*telegrama*) cable; **se le cruzaron los ~s** *inf* he/she lost control; **echar un ~ a alguien** *inf* to help sb out

**cabo** ['ka·βo] *m* **1.** (*extremo*) end; **al fin y al ~** in the end; **de ~ a rabo** from beginning to end; **llevar a ~** to carry out; **no dejar ningún ~ suelto** to leave no loose ends **2.** GEO cape; **Ciudad del Cabo** Cape Town **3.** MIL corporal **4.** NÁUT rope ▶ **al ~ de** after

**cabra** ['ka·βra] *f* goat; **estar como una ~** *inf* to be off one's rocker

**cabrear** [ka·βre·'ar] **I.** *vt inf* to infuriate; **estar cabreado** to be furious **II.** *vr:* **~se** *inf* to get angry

**cabrón** [ka·'βron] *m* billy goat

**cabrón, -ona** [ka·'βron, -·'βro·na] *m, f vulg* (*insulto*) bastard *m*, bitch *f*

**cábula** ['ka·βu·la] *f* **1.** *Arg, Par* (*amuleto*) amulet **2.** *Arg* (*cábala*) cabal, intrigue **3.** *Chile, Méx, Perú, PRico* (*ardid*) ruse, trick

**caca** ['ka·ka] *f inf* **1.** (*excremento*) poop **2.** (*chapuza*) rubbish

**cacahuete** [ka·ka·'we·te] *m* peanut

**cacalote** [ka·ka·'lo·te] *m AmC* CULIN popcorn

**cacao** [ka·'kao] *m* **1.** (*planta*) cacao; (*polvo, bebida*) cocoa **2.** *inf* (*jaleo*) fuss, todo; **pedir ~** *AmL* to give in

**cacería** [ka·se·'ri·a, ka·θe-] *f* (*partida*) hunting

**cacerola** [ka·se·'ro·la, ka·θe-] *f* saucepan

**cacharpas** [ka·'tʃar·pas] *fpl AmS* odds *m pl* and ends

**cacharro** [ka·'tʃa·rro] *m* **1.** (*recipiente*) pot **2.** *pey inf* (*aparato*) gadget **3.** *pey inf* (*trasto*) piece of junk

**cachear** [ka·tʃe·'ar] *vt* to frisk

**cachete** [ka·'tʃe·te] *m* **1.** (*golpe*) slap **2.** (*carrillo*) (fat) cheek

**cachetear** [ka·tʃe·te·'ar] *vt AmL* to slap

**cachetón, -ona** [ka·tʃe·'ton, -·'to·na] *adj AmL* chubby-cheeked

**cachimba** [ka·'tʃim·ba] *f AmL* (*pipa*) pipe

**cachondeo** [ka·tʃon·'deo] *m* **1.** *inf* (*broma*) joke; **tomar algo a ~** to take sth as a joke; **esto es un ~** this is a joke **2.** (*burla*) farce

**cachondo, -a** [ka·'tʃon·do, -a] **I.** *adj* **1.** *inf* (*sexual*) sexy, horny; **poner a alguien ~** to turn sb on **2.** *inf* (*gracioso*) funny **II.** *m, f inf* (*gracioso*) joker; **es un ~** he's a real laugh

**cachorro, -a** [ka·'tʃo·rro, -a] *m, f* (*de tigre*) cub; (*de perro*) pup(py)

**caco** ['ka·ko] *m inf* burglar

**cacto** ['kak·to] *m* cactus

**cada** ['ka·da] *adj* each; **~ uno/una** each one; **~ hora** hourly; **~ día** daily; **~ vez más/peor** more and more/worse and worse; **¿~ cuánto?** how often?

**cadáver** [ka·'da·βer] *m* corpse; (*de animales*) carcass

**cadena** [ka·'de·na] *f* **1.** *t. fig* chain; **~ alimentaria** BIO food chain; **~ antideslizante** AUTO snow chain; **~ hotelera** hotel chain; **~ humana** human chain; **perpetua** JUR life imprisonment; **trabajo en ~** assembly-line work; **atar un perro con ~** to chain up a dog; **reacción en ~** chain reaction **2.** GEO mountain chain **3.** RADIO, TV network; **~ de sonido** sound system

**cadera** [ka·'de·ra] *f* hip

**caducar** <c → qu> [ka·du·'kar] *vi* **1.** (*documento*) to expire **2.** (*producto*) **la leche está caducada** the milk is past its sell-by date

**caducidad** [ka·du·si·'dad, ka·du·θi-] *f* **fecha de ~** (*de documento*) date of expiry; (*de productos*) use-by date

**caduco, -a** [ka·'du·ko, -a] *adj* senile

**caer** [ka·'er] *irr* **I.** *vi* **1.** (*objeto*) to fall (down); (*precio*) to fall; **~ al suelo** to fall to the ground; **~ en manos de alguien** to fall into sb's hands; **dejarse ~** *inf* to show up; **tu amigo me cae bien/mal** *fig* I like/I don't like your friend; **estar al ~** *inf* to be about to happen **2.** (*encontrarse*) to be (located); **¿por dónde cae Jerez?** whereabouts is Jerez? **3.** (*atacar*) **~ sobre algo/alguien** to fall on sth/sb **II.** *vr:* **~se** to collapse; (*pelo*) to fall out; **se me ha caído el pañuelo** I dropped my handkerchief

**café** [ka·'fe] *m* **1.** (*bebida*) coffee; **~ americano** large black coffee; **~ con leche** coffee with milk; **~ cortado** coffee with a dash of milk; **~ solo** black coffee; **tomar un ~** to have a coffee **2.** (*local*) café

**cafeína** [ka·fe·'i·na] *f* caffeine

**cafetera** [ka·fe·'te·ra] *f* (*jarra*) coffee pot; **~ eléctrica** coffeemaker

**cafetería** [ka·fe·te·'ri·a] *f* café

**cagar** <g → gu> [ka·'ɣar] **I.** *vi* *vulg* to take a shit **II.** *vt* *vulg* to mess up; **¡ya la hemos cagado!** now we really blew it! **III.** *vr:* **~se** *vulg* (*de miedo*) to shit oneself; **¡me cago en diez!** shit!

**caída** [ka·'i·da] *f* **1.** (*acción*) fall; **~ del cabello** hair loss; **~ del sistema** COMPUT system crash; **la ~ del gobierno** the fall of the government **2.** (*de agua*) waterfall

**caimán** [kai·'man] *m* caiman

**Cairo** ['kai·ro] *m* El **~** Cairo

**caja** ['ka·xa] *f* **1.** (*recipiente*) box; **~ fuerte** safe; **~ de herramientas** *t.* COMPUT tool box; **~ negra** AVIAT black box **2.** (*carcasa*) case; **~ de cambios** AUTO gearbox; **~ torácica** ANAT thoracic cavity **3.** FIN fund; **~ de ahorros** savings bank

**cajero, -a** [ka·'xe·ro, -a] *m, f* cashier; **~ automático** cash dispenser

**cajeta** [ka·'xe·ta] *f* **1.** *Arg* (*cepo*) trap **2.** *AmC* CULIN toffee-like candy

**cajetilla** [ka·xe·'ti·ʝa, -ʎa] *f* small box; (*de cigarrillos*) pack of cigarettes

**cajón** [ka·'xon] *m* drawer; **eso es de ~** *inf* that goes without saying

**cajuela** [ka·'xwe·la] *f* *Méx* AUTO trunk

**cal** [kal] *f* lime; **cerrar a ~ y canto** to shut firmly

**cala** ['ka·la] *f* **1.** (*bahía*) cove **2.** NÁUT hold **3.** (*prueba*) probe

**calabacín** [ka·la·βa·'sin, -'θin] *m* zucchini

**calabaza** [ka·la·'βa·sa, -θa] *f* BOT pumpkin
▶ **dar ~s a alguien** (*un suspenso*) to fail sb; (*una negativa*) to brush sb off

**calabozo** [ka·la·'βo·so, -θo] *m* **1.** (*mazmorra*) dungeon **2.** (*celda*) (prison) cell

**calada** [ka·'la·da] *f* *inf* (*de humo*) puff; **¿me das una ~?** will you give me a drag?

**calaguasca** [ka·la·'ɣwas·ka] *f* *Col* CULIN raw brandy

**calamar** [ka·la·'mar] *m* squid

**calambre** [ka·'lam·bre] *m* (*eléctrico*) electric shock; (*muscular*) cramp

**calamidad** [ka·la·mi·'dad] *f* calamity; *inf* (*persona*) disaster

**calar** [ka·'lar] **I.** *vi* to soak in **II.** *vt* **1.** (*líquido*) to soak; **el chaparrón me ha calado la chaqueta** the downpour has drenched my jacket **2.** (*afectar*) **~ a alguien** to make an impression on sb **3.** *inf* (*desenmascarar*) to see through **4.** (*motor*) to stall **III.** *vr:* **~se 1.** (*mojarse*) to get soaked **2.** (*motor*) to stall **3.** (*gorra*) to pull down

**calavera** [ka·la·'βe·ra] *f* skull

**calcar** <c → qu> [kal·'kar] *vt* **1.** (*dibujar*) to trace **2.** (*imitar*) to copy

**calcetín** [kal·se·'tin, kal·θe-] *m* sock

**calcinar(se)** [kal·si·'nar·(se), kal·θi-] *vt, (vr)* to burn

**calcio** ['kal·sjo, -θjo] *m* calcium

**calco** ['kal·ko] *m* **1.** (*de dibujos*) tracing **2.** (*imitación*) imitation

**calculador(a)** [kal·ku·la·'dor, -·'do·ra] *adj* calculating

**calculadora** [kal·ku·la·'do·ra] *f* calculator; **~ de bolsillo** pocket calculator

**calcular** [kal·ku·'lar] *vt* **1.** (*computar*) to calculate **2.** (*aproximadamente*) to estimate; **calculo que llegaré sobre las**

**diez** I reckon that I'll arrive around ten

**cálculo** [ˈkal·ku·lo] *m* 1. *t.* ECON calculation; ~ **mental** mental arithmetic 2. (*suposición*) conjecture 3. MED stone

**caldear** [kal·de·ˈar] I. *vt* (*calentar*) to heat (up) II. *vr*: ~**se** (*calentarse*) to heat up

**caldera** [kal·ˈde·ra] *f* TÉC boiler

**calderilla** [kal·de·ˈri·ja, -ʎa] *f* small change

**caldero** [kal·ˈde·ro] *m* caldron

**calefacción** [ka·le·fak·ˈsjon, -faɣ·ˈθjon] *f* heating

**calendario** [ka·len·ˈda·rjo] *m* calendar

**calentador** [ka·len·ta·ˈdor] *m* heater

**calentamiento** [ka·len·ta·ˈmjen·to] *m* warming; DEP warm-up

**calentar** <e → ie> [ka·len·ˈtar] I. *vi* to be warm II. *vt* 1. (*caldear*) to heat (up) (*con calefacción*) to warm (up) 2. *vulg* (*sexualmente*) to turn on 3. *inf* (*pegar*) to give a good hiding to III. *vr*: ~**se** 1. (*caldearse*) to heat up; DEP to warm up 2. (*enfadarse*) to get angry

**calesita** [ka·le·ˈsi·ta] *f* *Arg, Par* merry-go-round

**caleta** [ka·ˈle·ta] *f* AmL (*barco*) coaster

**calibrar** [ka·li·ˈβrar] *vt* 1. TÉC (*medir*) to gauge, to gage 2. (*graduar*) to calibrate

**calibre** [ka·ˈli·βre] *m* 1. (*diámetro*) caliber; **eso es una mentira de** ~ *inf* that's a huge lie 2. (*instrumento*) gauge, gage

**calidad** [ka·li·ˈdad] *f* quality; **en** ~ **de** as

**cálido, -a** [ˈka·li·do, -a] *adj* (*país*) hot; *fig* warm

**caliente** [ka·ˈljen·te] *adj* 1. (*cálido*) warm; (*ardiente*) hot 2. (*acalorado*) heated

**calificación** [ka·li·fi·ka·ˈsjon, -ˈθjon] *f* 1. (*denominación*) description; (*evaluación*) assessment 2. (*nota*) mark, grade

**calificado, -a** [ka·li·fi·ˈka·do, -a] *adj* qualified; (*reconocido*) well-known

**calificar** <c → qu> [ka·li·fi·ˈkar] *vt* 1. (*definir*) ~ **de algo** to describe as sth 2. (*evaluar*) to assess; ENS to mark, to grade

**calificativo** [ka·li·fi·ka·ˈti·βo] *m* description, qualifier

**California** [ka·li·ˈfor·nja] *f* California

**caligrafía** [ka·li·ɣra·ˈfi·a] *f* calligraphy

**callado, -a** [ka·ˈja·do, -a; ka·ˈʎa-] *adj* (*sin*

*hablar*) silent; (*silencioso*) quiet

**callampa** [ka·ˈjam·pa, ka·ˈʎam-] *f* 1. *Col, Chile, Perú* (*seta*) mushroom 2. *Chile* (*sombrero*) felt hat

**callana** [ka·ˈja·na, -ˈʎa·na] *f* 1. AmS (*vasija*) earthenware pan 2. *Chile* (*reloj*) large pocket watch

**callar** [ka·ˈjar, -ˈʎar] I. *vi, vr* ~**se por algo** (*no hablar*) to keep quiet because of sth; (*enmudecer*) to fall silent due to sth; **¡cállate de una vez!** just shut up! II. *vt* to keep quiet about; **hacer** ~ **a alguien** to make sb keep quiet

**calle** [ˈka·je, -ˈʎe] *f* street; (*de autopista*) *t.* DEP lane; ~ **de dirección única** one-way street; ~ **peatonal** pedestrian street; ~ **arriba/abajo** up/down the street; **hacer la** ~ *inf* to be a streetwalker; **quedarse en la** ~ *inf* to be out of a job

**callejero** [ka·je·ˈxe·ro, ka·ʎe-] *m* street directory

**callejón** [ka·je·ˈxon, ka·ʎe-] *m* alley; ~ **sin salida** blind alley

**callo** [ˈka·jo, -ˈʎo] *m* 1. (*callosidad*) callus; **dar el** ~ *inf* to slave away 2. *pl* CULIN tripe

**calma** [ˈkal·ma] *f* 1. (*silencio*) calm; **¡(con)** ~**!** calm down! 2. *inf* (*indolencia*) indolence

**calmante** [kal·ˈman·te] *m* sedative

**calmar** [kal·ˈmar] I. *vt* 1. (*tranquilizar*) to calm (down) 2. (*dolor*) to relieve II. *vr*: ~**se** to calm down; (*dolor*) to ease off

**caló** [ka·ˈlo] *m* gypsy slang

**calor** [ka·ˈlor] *m* 1. (*de un cuerpo*) warmth 2. (*clima*) heat; ~ **sofocante** stifling heat; **hace mucho** ~ it's very hot 3. (*entusiasmo*) passion

**caloría** [ka·lo·ˈri·a] *f* calorie; **bajo en** ~**s** low-calorie

**calote** [ka·ˈlo·te] *m* RíoPl swindle

**caluma** [ka·ˈlu·ma] *f* Perú Andean gorge

**calumnia** [ka·ˈlum·nja] *f* slander

**caluroso, -a** [ka·lu·ˈro·so, -a] *adj* hot; *fig* warm; **un recibimiento** ~ a warm reception

**calva** [ˈkal·βa] *f* bald patch

**calvario** [kal·ˈβa·rjo] *m* **pasar un** ~ to suffer agonies

**calvicie** [kal·ˈβi·sje, -θje] *f* baldness

**calvo, -a** [ˈkal·βo, -a] *adj* bald

**calzada** [kal·'sa·da, -'θa·da] f (*carretera*) (paved) road

**calzado** [kal·'sa·do, -'θa·do] m footwear

**calzar** <z → c> [kal·'sar, -'θar] **I.** vt **1.** (*zapatos*) to put on; (*cuña*) to wedge **2.** (*llevar puesto*) to wear **II.** vr: ~**se** to put one's shoes on

**calzón** [kal·'son, -'θon] m AmL (*pantalón*) trousers pl, pants pl

**calzoncillo(s)** [kal·son·'si·jo(s), kal·θon·'θi·ʎo(s)] m(pl) men's underpants pl

**calzoneras** [kal·so·'ne·ras, kal·θo-] fpl Méx (*pantalón de montar*) riding pants pl

**cama** ['ka·ma] f bed; ~ **elástica** trampoline

**camaleón** [ka·ma·le·'on] m t. fig chameleon

**cámara** ['ka·ma·ra] **I.** f **1.** FOTO camera; ~ **de vídeo** video camera; **a** ~ **lenta** in slow motion **2.** (*consejo*) house; **Cámara Alta** POL upper house; **Cámara Baja** POL lower house **II.** mf CINE cameraman m, camerawoman f

**camaradería** [ka·ma·ra·de·'ri·a] f comradeship

**camarero, -a** [ka·ma·'re·ro, -a] m, f **1.** (*en restaurantes*) waiter m, waitress f; ¡~! waiter! **2.** (*en la barra*) barman m, barmaid f

**camarón** [ka·ma·'ron] m shrimp, prawn

**camarote** [ka·ma·'ro·te] m NÁUT cabin, berth

**cambiante** [kam·'bjan·te] adj changeable; pey (*veleidoso*) moody

**cambiar** [kam·'bjar] **I.** vi to change; ~ **de casa** to move (house); ~ **de coche** to buy a new car; ~ **de marcha** AUTO to change gear **II.** vt **1.** (*algo comprado*) to (ex)change; ~ **dinero** to change money **2.** (*variar*) to change; ~ **algo de lugar** to move sth **III.** vr (*de ropa*) to change; (*de casa*) to move

**cambiavía** [kam·bja·'βi·a] m AmL FERRO switchman

**cambio** ['kam·bjo] m **1.** (*transformación*) change; ~ **de aceite** AUTO oil change; ~ **climático** climatic change; ~ **de marchas** shift lever, gearshift; **a las primeras de** ~ at the first opportunity; ¿**tiene** ~ **de 100 dólares?** can you change 100 dollars?; **en** ~ however **2.** (*intercambio*)

exchange; **a** ~ **de algo** in exchange for sth **3.** FIN exchange rate; ~ **de divisa** [o **de moneda**] foreign exchange **4.** TÉC gearshift; ~ **de marchas** gearbox, transmission **5.** DEP substitution

**camelia** [ka·'me·lja] f camellia

**camello, -a** [ka·'me·jo, -ʎo] m, f **1.** ZOOL camel **2.** inf (*persona*) drug dealer

**camerino** [ka·me·'ri·no] m TEAT dressing room

**Camerún** [ka·me·'run] m Cameroon

**camilla** [ka·'mi·ja, -ʎa] f stretcher

**camilucho, -a** [ka·mi·'lu·tʃo, -a] m, f AmL Indian day laborer

**caminar** [ka·mi·'nar] **I.** vi **1.** to walk **2.** AmL (*funcionar*) to work **II.** vt (*distancia*) to cover

**caminata** [ka·mi·'na·ta] f long walk

**camino** [ka·'mi·no] m **1.** (*senda*) path; (*estrecho*) track; (*calle*) road; **a medio** ~ halfway (there); **de** ~ **a Londres** on the road to London; **abrirse** ~ to make one's way; **ponerse en** ~ to set out [o off]; **ir por buen/mal** ~ fig to be on the right/wrong track **2.** (*distancia*) way; **está a dos horas de** ~ it's two hours away **3.** (*manera*) way; ~ **de rosas** bed of roses

**camión** [ka·'mjon] m AUTO truck; ~ **de la basura** garbage truck

**camionero, -a** [ka·mjo·'ne·ro, -a] m, f truck driver

**camioneta** [ka·mjo·'ne·ta] f **1.** (*furgoneta*) van; ~ **de reparto** delivery van **2.** AmL (*autobús*) bus

**camisa** [ka·'mi·sa] f **1.** (*prenda*) shirt; ~ **de fuerza** straitjacket; **cambiar de** ~ to change sides **2.** (*funda*) case **3.** (*de reptil*) slough ▶ **meterse en** ~ **de once varas** to bite off more than one can chew

**camiseta** [ka·mi·'se·ta] f (*exterior*) T-shirt; (*interior*) undershirt; DEP shirt

**camisón** [ka·mi·'son] m nightgown

**camote** [ka·'mo·te] m AmL **1.** (*batata*) sweet potato **2.** (*molestia*) nuisance **3.** (*amante*) lover

**camotear** [ka·mo·te·'ar] vi Méx (*vagabundear*) to roam

**campamento** [kam·pa·'men·to] m camp; ~ **de verano** summer camp

**campana** [kam·'pa·na] *f* bell; **~ extractora** (**de humos**) extractor hood; **el coche dio tres vueltas de ~** the car turned over three times

**campanario** [kam·pa·'na·rjo] *m* bell tower

**campante** [kam·'pan·te] *adj inf* (*tranquilo*) calm; **quedarse tan ~** not to bat an eyelid

**campaña** [kam·'pa·na] *f* 1. (*campo*) countryside; **tienda de ~** tent 2. POL campaign; **~ antitabaco** anti-smoking campaign; **~ electoral** electoral [*o* election] campaign 3. COM sales drive

**campar** [kam·'par] *vi* to camp

**campear** [kam·pe·'ar] *vi* 1. *AmL* (*ir de acampada*) to camp 2. *inf* (*arreglárselas*) **ir campeando** to get by

**campechana** [kam·pe·'tʃa·na] *f Méx, Cuba* (*bebida*) cocktail

**campeón, -ona** [kam·pe·'on, -·'o·na] *m, f* champion

**campeonato** [kam·pe·o·'na·to] *m* championship; **de ~** *inf* terrific

**campera** [kam·'pe·ra] *f CSur* Windbreaker®

**campesino, -a** [kam·pe·'si·no, -a] *m, f* man from the country *m*, woman from the country *f*; **los ~s** country people; *t. pey* (*labrador*) peasant

**camping** ['kam·pin] *m* 1. (*campamento*) camping site 2. (*actividad*) **hacer ~** to go camping

**campirano, -a** [kam·pi·'ra·no, -a] *adj* 1. *AmL* (*patán, rural*) rustic 2. *Méx* (*campesino*) peasant 3. *Méx* (*entendido en el campo*) good at farming 4. *Méx* (*que maneja bien caballos*) skilled at handling horses

**campo** ['kam·po] *m* 1. (*terreno*) countryside; (*de cultivo*) field; *t.* DEP **~ de tiro** firing range; **gente del ~** country people 2. *t.* POL, MIL camp; **~ de concentración** HIST concentration camp; **~ de trabajo** work camp 3. *t.* FÍS, COMPUT field; **~ visual** field of vision

**campus** ['kam·pus] *m inv* campus

**camuflaje** [ka·mu·'fla·xe] *m* camouflage

**camuflar** [ka·mu·'flar] *vt t. fig* to camouflage

**cana** ['ka·na] *f* 1. (*pelo*) white hair; **echar**

**una ~ al aire** *fig* to let one's hair down 2. *Arg inf* (*policía*) police 3. *Arg inf* (*prisión*) jail

**Canadá** [ka·na·'da] *m* (**el**) ~ Canada

**canal** [ka·'nal] *m* 1. *t.* ANAT canal 2. GEO, TV channel; **el Canal de la Mancha** the English Channel; **el Canal de Panamá** the Panama Canal

**canalización** [ka·na·li·sa·'sjon, -θa·'θjon] *f* 1. (*de un río*) canalization 2. (*alcantarillado*) sewerage system

**canalizar** <z → c> [ka·na·li·'sar, -'θar] *vt* to canalize; *fig* to channel

**canalla** [ka·'na·ja, -ʎa] *mf pey* swine

**canalón** [ka·na·'lon] *m* gutter

**canana** [ka·'na·na] *f* (*cinturón*) cartridge belt

**Canarias** [ka·'na·rjas] *fpl* **las Islas ~** the Canary Islands

**canario** [ka·'na·rjo] *m* canary

**canasta** [ka·'nas·ta] *f* basket

**canastero, -a** [ka·nas·'te·ro, -a] *m, f Chile* (*panadería*) baker's helper

**cancelar** [kan·se·'lar, kan·θe·] *vt* 1. (*anular*) to cancel; **~ una cita** to cancel an appointment 2. FIN (*una cuenta*) to close; (*una deuda*) to pay (off)

**cáncer** ['kan·ser, -θer] *m* 1. *t. fig* MED cancer 2. ASTR Cancer

**cancerígeno, -a** [kan·se·'ri·xe·no, -a; kan·θe·] *adj* carcinogenic

**canceroso, -a** [kan·se·'ro·so, -a; kan·θe·] *adj* cancerous

**cancha** ['kan·tʃa] *f* 1. DEP (*de deporte*) sports field; (*de tenis*) court 2. *AmL* (*hipódromo*) racetrack 3. *AmL* (*de un río*) broad part of a river 4. *AmL* (*espacio*) space

**canciller** [kan·si·'jer, -θi·'ʎer] *mf* 1. POL chancellor 2. *AmL* (*de Asuntos Exteriores*) foreign minister

**canción** [kan·'sjon, -'θjon] *f* song; (**es**) **siempre la misma ~** (it's) always the same old story

**cancona** [kan·'ko·na] *adj Chile* broadhipped

**candado** [kan·'da·do] *m* padlock

**candelabro** [kan·de·'la·βro] *m* candelabra

**candelejón, -ona** [kan·de·le·'xon, -·'xo·na] *adj Chile, Col, Perú* naïve

**candelilla** [kan·de·'li·ja, -ʎa] f CRi, Chile, Hond (luciérnaga) glow-worm

**candidato, -a** [kan·di·'da·to, -a] m, f applicant; POL candidate; ~ **al título** DEP contender for the title

**candidatura** [kan·di·da·'tu·ra] f (presentación) application; POL candidature

**candil** [kan·'dil] m 1. (lámpara) oil lamp 2. AmL (candelabro) candelabra

**candinga** [kan·'din·ga] f 1. Chile (necedad) absurdity 2. Hond (maraña) mess

**candonga** [kan·'don·ga] f Col (pendiente) earring

**caneca** [ka·'ne·ka] f 1. Col (basurero) trash can 2. Cuba (de agua caliente) hot-water bottle 3. AmL (barril) drum; (balde) bucket

**canela** [ka·'ne·la] f cinnamon

**canfín** [kan·'fin] m AmC (petróleo) gasoline

**cangrejo** [kan·'gre·xo] m crab; ~ **de río** crayfish

**canguro¹** [kan·'gu·ro] m ZOOL kangaroo

**canguro²** [kan·'gu·ro] mf inf baby-sitter

**caníbal** [ka·'ni·βal] adj, mf cannibal

**canica** [ka·'ni·ka] f marble

**canijo, -a** [ka·'ni·xo, -a] adj AmL (malvado) sly

**canilla** [ka·'ni·ja, -ʎa] f Arg, Par, Urug (grifo) tap

**canillera** [ka·ni·'je·ra, -'ʎe·ra] f AmL 1. (espinillera) shin guard 2. (temblor) trembling

**canillita** [ka·ni·'ji·ta, -'ʎi·ta] m AmS newspaper vendor

**canjear** [kan·xe·'ar] vt to exchange

**canoa** [ka·'noa] f 1. t. DEP (bote a remo) canoe 2. AmL (artesa) feeding trough

**canoso, -a** [ka·'no·so, -a] adj grizzled

**cansado, -a** [kan·'sa·do, -a] adj 1. estar (fatigado) tired; (harto) tired 2. ser (fatigoso) tiring; (aburrido) boring; (molesto) tiresome 3. AmL **a las cansadas** at long last

**cansador(a)** [kan·sa·'dor, -·'do·ra] adj Arg 1. ser (fatigoso) tiring 2. ser (aburrido) boring 3. ser (molesto) tiresome

**cansancio** [kan·'san·sjo, -θjo] m 1. (fatiga) tiredness; **estoy muerto de ~** I'm dead tired 2. (hastío) boredom

**cansar** [kan·'sar] I. vi 1. (fatigar) to tire 2. (hastiar) to be tiresome II. vt 1. (fatigar) to tire (out) 2. (hastiar) to bore III. vr: ~**se** 1. (fatigarse) to tire oneself out 2. (hartarse) ~**se de algo** to get tired of sth

**cansera** [kan·'se·ra] f Col (tiempo malgastado) wasted effort

**cantábrico, -a** [kan·'ta·βri·ko, -a] adj Cantabrian; **el Mar Cantábrico** the Bay of Biscay

**cantante** [kan·'tan·te] I. adj **llevar la voz** ~ fig to call the tune II. mf singer

**cantar** [kan·'tar] vi, vt 1. (personas) to sing; (gallo) to crow; (grillo) to chirp; **en menos que canta un gallo** inf in no time at all 2. inf (confesar) to talk 3. inf (oler mal) to stink

**cántaro** ['kan·ta·ro] m pitcher; **llover a** ~**s** to rain cats and dogs

**cantera** [kan·'te·ra] f quarry; DEP young local club players

**cantidad** [kan·ti·'dad] I. f quantity; (número) number; (dinero) sum; **una gran** ~ **de** lots of stuff II. adv inf a lot

**cantimplora** [kan·tim·'plo·ra] f water bottle, canteen

**cantina** [kan·'ti·na] f (en estaciones) buffet; (en cuarteles) canteen

**canto** ['kan·to] m 1. (acción) singing; (canción) song; ~ **de los pájaros** birdsong 2. (arista) edge 3. (de cuchillo) back; (de libro) fore-edge; **poner de** ~ to put on end

**caña** ['ka·ɲa] f 1. AGR reed; (tallo) stalk; ~ **de azúcar** sugar cane 2. (de la pierna) shinbone 3. (de pescar) (fishing) rod 4. (de cerveza) glass

**cáñamo** ['ka·ɲa·mo] m 1. (planta) hemp 2. (tejido) canvas

**cañería** [ka·ɲe·'ri·a] f pipe; ~ **del agua** plumbing

**caño** ['ka·ɲo] m tube; (de la fuente) spout

**cañón** [ka·'ɲon] m 1. (tubo) tube; ~ **de escopeta** barrel 2. MIL cannon 3. GEO canyon; **el Cañón del Colorado** the Grand Canyon

**cañonazo** [ka·ɲo·'na·so, -θo] m cannon shot; inf (en fútbol) powerful shot

**cañonera** [ka·ɲo·'ne·ra] f AmL (pistolera) holster

**caoba** [ka·'o·βa] *f* **1.** (*madera, color*) mahogany **2.** (*árbol*) mahogany tree

**caos** ['ka·os] *m inv* chaos

**caótico, -a** [ka·'o·ti·ko, -a] *adj* chaotic

**capa** ['ka·pa] *f* **1.** *t.* TAUR (*prenda*) cape **2.** (*cobertura*) covering; (*recubrimiento*) layer; (*baño*) coating; **~ aislante** insulating layer; **~ de nieve** covering of snow; **~ de ozono** ozone layer **3.** GEO, MIN stratum ▸ **estar de ~ caída** *inf* to be on the decline

**capacidad** [ka·pa·si·'ðað, ka·pa·θi·] *f* **1.** *t.* FÍS (*cabida*) capacity **2.** (*aptitud*) aptitude; **~ adquisitiva** purchasing power

**capacitado, -a** [ka·pa·si·'ta·ðo, -a; ka·pa·θi-] *adj* **~ para algo** qualified for [*o* to do] sth

**capacitar** [ka·pa·si·'tar, ka·pa·θi·] *vt* **1.** (*formar*) to train; (*preparar*) to prepare **2.** *AmL* JUR (*habilitar*) to capacitate

**capar** [ka·'par] *vt inf* to castrate

**capataz** [ka·pa·'tas, -'taθ] *m* foreman

**capaz** [ka·'pas, -'paθ] *adj* **1.** (*en condiciones*) capable **2.** *AmL* (*tal vez*) perhaps

**capi** [ka·pi] *m* **1.** *AmS* (*maíz*) corn **2.** *Bol* (*harina*) white corn flour

**capilla** [ka·'pi·ja, -ʎa] *f* REL chapel; **~ ardiente** funeral chapel

**capisayo** [ka·pi·'sa·jo] *m Col* (*camiseta*) undershirt

**capital¹** [ka·pi·'tal] **I.** *adj* essential; **pena ~** capital punishment; **de ~ importancia** of prime importance **II.** *m* capital; **~ fijo** fixed capital

**capital²** [ka·pi·'tal] *f* capital (city)

**capitalismo** [ka·pi·ta·'lis·mo] *m* capitalism

**capitalista** [ka·pi·ta·'lis·ta] *adj* capitalist(ic)

**capitán** [ka·pi·'tan] *m* MIL, DEP, AVIAT captain

**capitular** [ka·pi·tu·'lar] *vi* **1.** (*acordar*) to agree to [*o* on] **2.** MIL to surrender

**capítulo** [ka·'pi·tu·lo] *m t.* REL chapter

**capota** [ka·'po·ta] *f* AUTO convertible top

**capotera** [ka·po·'te·ra] *f Hond* (*percha*) clothespin; (*perchero*) coat rack

**capricho** [ka·'pri·tʃo] *m* whim; **darse un**

**~** to allow oneself sth

**caprichoso, -a** [ka·pri·'tʃo·so, -a] *adj* capricious; *pey* (*inconstante*) moody

**Capricornio** [ka·pri·'kor·njo] *m* Capricorn

**cápsula** ['kaβ·su·la] *f* capsule; **~ espacial** AVIAT space capsule

**captar** [kap·'tar] *vt* **1.** (*recoger*) to collect **2.** (*percibir*) to make out; (*comprender*) to grasp

**captura** [kap·'tu·ra] *f* **1.** (*apresamiento*) capture **2.** (*detención*) arrest **3.** (*piezas cobradas*) catch

**capturar** [kap·tu·'rar] *vt* **1.** (*apresar*) to capture **2.** (*detener*) to arrest **3.** (*cazar*) to catch

**capucha** [ka·'pu·tʃa] *f* hood

**capullo** [ka·'pu·jo, -ʎo] *m* **1.** BOT (*de flor*) bud **2.** ZOOL cocoon; **salir del ~** to hatch out **3.** *vulg* (*canalla*) jerk

**cara** ['ka·ra] **I.** *f* **1.** (*rostro*) face; **~ a** face to face; (**no**) **dar la ~ por alguien** (not) to come to sb's defense; **echar en ~** to reproach; **plantar ~ a** to face up to; **partir la ~ a alguien** *inf* to smash sb's face in; **~ de póker** *inf* poker face; **una ~ larga** a long face; **una ~ de pocos amigos** *inf* a sour look; **tener buena/mala ~** to look good/bad **2.** (*lado*) side; (*de una moneda*) face; **~ o cruz** heads or tails **3.** *inf* (*osadía*) nerve; **¡qué ~!** what nerve!; **tener mucha ~** to have some nerve **II.** *prep* (**de**) **~ a** facing; **de ~ al futuro** with an eye to the future **III.** *conj* **de ~ a** +*infin* in order to +*infin*

**caracol** [ka·ra·'kol] *m* **1.** ZOOL snail **2.** (*concha*) conch (shell)

**caracola** [ka·ra·'ko·la] *f* conch

**caracolillo** [ka·ra·ko·'li·jo, -ʎo] *m AmL* high quality small-bean coffee

**carácter** <caracteres> [ka·'rak·ter] *m* **1.** (*en general*) character; (**no**) **tiene ~** he/she has (no) character **2.** (*índole*) nature; **con ~ de** as **3.** *AmL* (*personaje*) character

**característica** [ka·rak·te·'ris·ti·ka] *f* characteristic

**característico, -a** [ka·rak·te·'ris·ti·ko, -a] *adj* characteristic

**caracterizar** <z → c> [ka·rak·te·ri·'sar,

-'θar] **I.** *vt* **1.** (*marcar*) to characterize **2.** TEAT to play **II.** *vr:* **~se** to be
characterized

**caramanchel** [ka·ra·man·'tʃel] *m* **1.** *Perú*
(*cobertizo*) shed **2.** *Chile* (*taberna*)
canteen

**caramba** [ka·'ram·ba] *interj inf* ¡(**qué**)
**~!** (*enfado*) damn!; (*extrañeza*) good
heavens!

**carambola** [ka·ram·'bo·la] *f* cannon; *inf*
(*trampa*) trick

**caramelo** [ka·ra·'me·lo] *m* (*golosina*) candy; (*azúcar*) caramel

**caraota** [ka·ra·'o·ta] *f* *Ven* (*haba*) kidney bean

**carapacho** [ka·ra·'pa·tʃo] *m* **1.** ZOOL car-
apace, shell **2.** *Cuba* CULIN shellfish
cooked in the shell

**caraqueño, -a** [ka·ra·'ke·ɲo, -a] *adj* of/
from Caracas

**carátula** [ka·'ra·tu·la] *f* (*de un disco*) album [*o* CD] cover

**caravana** [ka·ra·'βa·na] *f* **1.** (*remolque*)
trailer **2.** (*embotellamiento*) tailback

**carbón** [kar·'βon] *m* coal; **~ de leña**
[*o* **vegetal**] charcoal; **papel ~** carbon
paper

**carbonato** [kar·βo·'na·to] *m* carbonate

**carbonilla** [kar·βo·'ni·ja, -ʎa] *f* *AmL*
charcoal

**carbono** [kar·'βo·no] *m* carbon; **dióxido
de ~** carbon dioxide

**carburador** [kar·βu·ra·'dor] *m* TÉC carburetor

**carburante** [kar·βu·'ran·te] *m* fuel

**carcajada** [kar·ka·'xa·da] *f* guffaw; **reírse
a ~s** to roar with laughter; **soltar una ~**
to burst out laughing

**carcasa** [kar·'ka·sa] *f* TÉC casing

**cárcel** ['kar·sel, -θel] *f* prison; **tres años
de ~** three years imprisonment; **estar
en la ~** to be in prison

**carcelero, -a** [kar·se·'le·ro, -a; kar·θe·]
*m, f* prison officer, jailer

**carcoma** [kar·'ko·ma] *f* ZOOL woodworm

**cardenal** [kar·de·'nal] *m* **1.** REL cardinal
**2.** (*hematoma*) bruise

**cardiaco, -a** [kar·'dja·ko, -a] *adj*, **cardíaco, -a** [kar·'di·a·ko, -a] *adj* heart; MED
cardiac; **ataque ~** heart attack; **paro ~**

cardiac arrest

**cardinal** [kar·di·'nal] *adj* cardinal; **los cuatro puntos ~es** the four cardinal points

**cardiólogo, -a** [kar·'djo·lo·ɣo, -a] *m, f*
MED cardiologist

**carecer** [ka·re·'ser, -'θer] *irr como crecer*
*vi* **~ de algo** to lack sth

**carencia** [ka·'ren·sja, -θja] *f* lack; (*escasez*) shortage, scarcity; **~ de algo** MED
deficiency in sth

**carente** [ka·'ren·te] *adj* **~ de algo** lacking in sth, devoid of sth; **~ de interés**
uninteresting

**careo** [ka'reo] *m* confrontation

**careta** [ka·'re·ta] *f* mask; **quitar la ~ a
alguien** *t. fig* to unmask sb

**carga** ['kar·ɣa] *f* **1.** (*acto*) loading **2.** (*cargamento*) load; **animal de ~** pack ani-
mal; **buque de ~** freighter **3.** (*obligación*) obligation; **ser una ~ para
alguien** to be a burden on sb **4.** MIL
charge; **~ explosiva** explosive charge;
**~ policial** baton charge; **¡a la ~!** MIL
charge!

**cargado, -a** [kar·'ɣa·do, -a] *adj* (*lleno*) **~
con** [*o* **de**] **algo** loaded with sth; **la batería está cargada** the battery is charged;
**un café muy ~** very strong coffee

**cargamento** [kar·ɣa·'men·to] *m* (*acto*)
loading; (*carga*) load, cargo

**cargar** <g *o* gu> [kar·'ɣar] **I.** *vi* **1.** (*llevar*) **~ con algo** to carry sth **2.** (*atacar*)
**~ contra alguien** to charge at sb **II.** *vt*
**1.** *t.* MIL to load **2.** (*achacar*) to attribute
**3.** FIN (*en una cuenta*) to charge **4.** *inf*a
**Paco le han cargado las mates** Paco
failed Math **5.** COMPUT to load **6.** *AmL*
(*llevar*) to have; **¿cargas dinero?** do
you have any money on you? **III.** *vr:*
**~se 1.** (*llenarse*) **~se de algo** to fill up
with sth **2.** *inf* (*romper*) to smash up;
**¡te la vas a ~!** *fig* you're in for it! **3.** *inf*
(*matar*) to kill

**cargo** ['kar·ɣo] *m* **1.** FIN charge; **~ a
cuenta** debit **2.** (*puesto*) post; **desempeñar un ~** to hold a position **3.** (*cuidado*) **estoy a ~ de las correcciones**
I'm responsible for the corrections; **~ de
conciencia** feeling of guilt

**Caribe** [ka·'ri·βe] *m* **el** (**Mar**) **~** the Caribbean (Sea)

**caribeño, -a** [ka·ri·'βe·ɲo, -a] *adj* Caribbean

**caricatura** [ka·ri·ka·'tu·ra] *f* caricature, cartoon

**caricia** [ka·'ri·sja, -ɵja] *f* caress

**caridad** [ka·ri·'dad] *f* charity; (*limosna*) alms *pl;* **hacer obras de ~** to do works of charity

**caries** ['ka·rjes] *f inv* tooth decay

**carimbo** [ka·'rim·bo] *m Bol* branding iron

**cariño** [ka·'ri·ɲo] *m* affection; (*amor*) love; **hacer algo con ~** to do sth lovingly; **sentir ~ por alguien** to be fond of sb; **¡~ (mío)!** (my) dear!; **hacer ~s** *inf* to caress

**cariñoso, -a** [ka·ri·'ɲo·so, -a] *adj* ~ **con alguien** affectionate [*o* tender] towards sb

**carioca** [ka·'rjo·ka] *adj* of/from Rio de Janeiro; (*brasileño*) Brazilian

**carisma** [ka·'ris·ma] *m* charisma

**caritativo, -a** [ka·ri·ta·'ti·βo, -a] *adj* charitable

**cariz** [ka·'ris, -'riɵ] *m* look; **esto toma buen ~** this is looking good

**carnal** [kar·'nal] *adj* carnal

**carnaval** [kar·na·'βal] *m* carnival

**carnaza** [kar·'na·sa, -ɵa] *f* bait

**carne** ['kar·ne] *f* **1.** (*del cuerpo*) flesh; **ser uña y ~** to be inseparable **2.** (*alimento*) meat; **~ asada** roast meat; **~ de cerdo/vacuna** pork/beef; **~ picada** ground meat ▶ **poner toda la ~ en el** <u>asador</u> to risk all; **~ de gallina** goose bumps *pl;* **ser de ~ y hueso** (*auténtico*) to be real; (*humano*) to be quite human

**carné** [kar·'ne] *m* <carnés> identity card; **~ de identidad** identity card; **~ de conducir** driver's license

**carnear** [kar·ne·'ar] *vt* **1.** *CSur* (*matar: un animal*) to slaughter; (*una persona*) to murder brutally **2.** *Chile* (*engañar*) to cheat **3.** *Méx* (*apuñalar*) to stab (to death)

**carnero** [kar·'ne·ro] *m* **1.** zool ram **2.** *CSur* (*débil*) weakling; (*desertor de huelga*) scab

**carnet** [kar·'ne] *m* <carnets> *v.* **carné**

**carnicería** [kar·ni·se·'ri·a, kar·ni·ɵe-] *f* butcher's (shop); *fig* (*masacre*) massacre

**carnicero, -a** [kar·ni·'se·ro, -a; kar·ni·ɵe-] **I.** *adj* carnivorous; *fig* (*sanguinario*) bloodthirsty **II.** *m, f* butcher

**carnitas** [kar·'ni·tas] *fpl AmC* CULIN barbecued pork

**carnívoro, -a** [kar·'ni·βo·ro, -a] *adj* carnivorous; **animal ~** carnivore

**caro** ['ka·ro] *adv* dear(ly); **esto nos costará ~** *fig* this'll cost us dear

**caro, -a** ['ka·ro, -a] *adj* expensive

**carozo** [ka·'ro·so, -ɵo] *m CSur* stone (*of fruit*)

**carpa** ['kar·pa] *f* **1.** zool carp **2.** (*entoldado*) marquee; **~ del circo** big top **3.** *AmL* (*tienda de campaña*) tent **4.** *AmL* (*puesto de mercado*) market stall

**carpeta** [kar·'pe·ta] *f* folder

**carpincho** [kar·'pin·tʃo] *m AmL* zool capybara

**carpintería** [kar·pin·te·'ri·a] *f* carpentry

**carpintero, -a** [kar·pin·'te·ro, -a] *m, f* carpenter; **pájaro ~** woodpecker

**carpir** [kar·'pir] *vt AmL* to hoe

**carraspear** [ka·rras·pe·'ar] *vi* to clear one's throat

**carrasposo, -a** [ka·rras·'po·so, -a] *adj* *Col, Ecua, Ven* (*áspero*) rough

**carrera** [ka·'rre·ra] *f* **1.** (*movimiento*) run **2.** DEP (*competición*) race; **~ de relevos** relay race; **coche de ~s** racing car **3.** (*profesión*) profession; **~ profesional** career **4.** (*estudios*) degree course; **hacer una ~** to study **5.** (*en medias*) ladder

**carreta** [ka·'rre·ta] *f* wagon

**carrete** [ka·'rre·te] *m t.* FOTO spool, reel; **~ de película** roll of film

**carretera** [ka·rre·'te·ra] *f* (main) road

**carretilla** [ka·rre·'ti·ja, -ʎa] *f* wheelbarrow

**carril** [ka·'rril] *m* (*en la carretera*) lane; **~ de adelantamiento/lento** fast/slow lane

**carro** ['ka·rro] *m* **1.** (*vehículo*) cart; **~ acorazado** [*o* **blindado**] armored car; **¡para el ~!** *inf* hold your horses! **2.** *AmL* (*coche*) car **3.** (*de una máquina*) carriage

**carrocería** [ka·rro·se·'ri·a, ka·rro·ɵe-] *f*

bodywork

**carroña** [ka·'rro·ɲa] f carrion

**carroza** [ka·'rro·sa, -θa] f carriage

**carruaje** [ka·'rrwa·xe] m carriage; (de caballos) coach

**carrusel** [ka·rru·'sel] m (tiovivo) merry-go-round, carousel

**carta** ['kar·ta] f 1. (escrito) letter; ~ **certificada** registered letter; ~ **de presentación** [o **de recomendación**] letter of introduction; **echar una** ~ to mail a letter; **Carta Magna** Magna Carta; **tomar** ~**s en un asunto** to intervene in a matter 2. (naipes) card; **jugar a las** ~**s** to play (at) cards; **echar las** ~**s a alguien** to tell sb's fortune 3. (menú) menu

**cartel** [kar·'tel] m poster; (rótulo) sign; TEAT bill; '**prohibido fijar** ~**es**' ' post no bills'

**cártel** ['kar·tel] m ECON cartel

**cartelera** [kar·te·'le·ra] f notice board; TEAT publicity board; **estar en** ~ to be on

**cartera** [kar·'te·ra] f (de bolsillo) wallet; (de mano) handbag, purse; (escolar) schoolbag; **ministro sin** ~ POL minister without portfolio; ~ **de valores** FIN securities portfolio

**carterista** [kar·te·'ris·ta] mf pickpocket

**cartero, -a** [kar·'te·ro, -a] m, f mailman m, letter carrier

**cartilla** [kar·'ti·ja, -ʎa] f 1. ENS (catón) first reader 2. (cuaderno) notebook; ~ **de ahorros** savings book; ~ **sanitaria** health services card 3. AmL (carnet) identity card

**cartón** [kar·'ton] m 1. (material) cardboard 2. (envase) carton; ~ **de leche** carton of milk

**cartucho** [kar·'tu·tʃo] m t. MIL cartridge; ~ **de tinta** ink cartridge; ~ **de fogueo** blank cartridge

**cartulina** [kar·tu·'li·na] f thin cardboard

**casa** ['ka·sa] f 1. (edificio) house; ~ **adosada** semi-detached house; ~ **de campo** country house 2. (vivienda) flat 3. (hogar) home; **ir a** ~ to go home; **vengo de** ~ I'm coming from home; **en** ~ at home; **estoy en** ~ **de Paco** I'm at Paco's (place); **no parar en** ~ to be always on the go; **todo queda en** ~ it'll

stay in the family; ~ **real** royal family 4. ECON (empresa) firm; ~ **discográfica** record company

**casabe** [ka·'sa·βe] m AmL CULIN cassava bread

**casar** [ka·'sar] I. vi to match II. vt 1. (novios) to marry; **estar casado** to be married; **los recién casados** the newlyweds 2. (combinar) to combine; (piezas) to join together III. vr~**se con alguien** (por la Iglesia/por lo civil) to get married to sb (in church/in a registry office)

**cascabel** [kas·ka·'βel] m (little) bell; **serpiente de** ~ rattlesnake ▶ **poner el** ~ **al gato** to bell the cat

**cascada** [kas·'ka·da] f waterfall; (artificial) cascade

**cascanueces** [kas·ka·'nwe·ses, -θes] m inv nutcracker

**cascar** <c → qu> [kas·'kar] I. vt 1. (romper) to crack; ~ **un huevo** to crack an egg 2. inf (pegar) to clout II. vr: ~**se** to crack; (estropearse) to break III. vi inf (charlar) to chatter

**cáscara** ['kas·ka·ra] f shell; ~ **de huevo** eggshell; ~ **de limón** lemon peel

**cascarón** [kas·ka·'ron] m shell

**cascarudo** [kas·ka·'ru·do] m Arg beetle

**casco** ['kas·ko] m 1. (para cabeza) helmet 2. (pezuña) hoof 3. (de barco) hull 4. (botella) (empty) bottle 5. (de ciudad) center city, downtown; **el** ~ **antiguo** the old city 6. (cascote) piece of rubble 7. pl (auriculares) headphones pl

**caserío** [ka·se·'ri·o] m farmhouse

**casero, -a** [ka·'se·ro, -a] I. adj 1. (de casa) homemade; **remedio** ~ household remedy 2. (hogareño) home-loving II. m, f (propietario) landlord m, landlady f

**caseta** [ka·'se·ta] f hut; (de feria) booth; (de muestras) stand; ~ **del perro** doghouse

**casete¹** [ka·'se·te] m o f (cinta) cassette

**casete²** [ka·'se·te] m 1. (aparato) cassette recorder 2. (pletina) cassette deck

**casi** ['ka·si] adv almost; ~ ~ very nearly

**casilla** [ka·'si·ja, -ʎa] f 1. (en cuadrícula) box; (en tablero) square; (en casillero)

**pigeonhole; sacar a alguien de sus ~s**
*fig* to drive sb crazy

**casillero** [ka·si·'je·ro, -'λe·ro] *m* set of
pigeonholes

**casimba** [ka·'sim·ba] *f AmL* (*hoyo*) well;
(*manantial*) spring; (*barril*) bucket

**casino** [ka·'si·no] *m* casino

**caso** ['ka·so] *m* **1.** (*hecho*) case; **~ aislado** isolated case; **~ de fuerza mayor**
case of force majeure; **¡eres un ~!** *inf*
you're a right one!; **yo, en tu ~...** if I
were you...; **en ~ de +** *infin* in the event
of; **dado** [*o* **llegado**] **el ~** if it comes to
it; **en ~ contrario** otherwise; **en cualquier ~** in any case; **en ningún ~** on
no account; **en último ~** as a last resort;
**en tal ~** in such a case; **en todo ~** in
any case **2.** (*atención*) notice; **hacer ~
a alguien** (*considerar*) to pay attention
to sb; (*obedecer*) to obey sb; (*creer*) to
believe sb

**caspa** ['kas·pa] *f* dandruff

**caspiroleta** [kas·pi·ro·'le·ta] *f AmL* CULIN
eggnog

**casta** ['kas·ta] *f* **1.** (*raza*) race **2.** (*clase
social*) caste

**castaña** [kas·'ta·ɲa] *f* **1.** (*fruto*) chestnut
**2.** *inf* (*golpe*) blow; **darse una ~** to
give oneself a knock **3.** *inf* (*borrachera*)
drunkenness; **coger una ~** to get tight
**4.** *inf* (*rápido*) **a toda ~** flat out

**castaño** [kas·'ta·ɲo] *m* chestnut tree

**castaño, -a** [kas·'ta·ɲo, -a] *adj* brown

**castañuela** [kas·ta·'ɲwe·la] *f* castanet

**castellano** [kas·te·'ja·no, -'λa·no] *m* (*español*) Spanish; (*variedad*) Castilian

**castellano, -a** [kas·te·'ja·no, -a; -'λa·no,
-a] *adj, m, f* Castilian; **la lengua cas-
tellana** the Spanish language

**castidad** [kas·ti·'dad] *f* chastity

**castigar** <g → gu> [kas·ti·'ɣar] *vt* **1.** (*pu-
nir*) **~ por algo** to punish for sth **2.** (*físicamente*) to beat; *fig* to castigate

**castigo** [kas·'ti·ɣo] *m* **1.** (*punición*) punishment **2.** (*aflicción*) affliction

**Castilla** [kas·'ti·ja, -λa] *f* Castile

**castillo** [kas·'ti·jo, -λo] *m t.* NÁUT (*fore*)
castle; **~ de arena** sandcastle; **~ de
naipes** house of cards

**castor** [kas·'tor] *m* beaver

**castrar** [kas·'trar] *vt t.* MED to castrate

**casual** [ka·'swal] *adj* chance

**casualidad** [ka·swa·li·'dad] *f* chance;
**de** [*o* **por**] **~** by chance; **¡qué ~!** what
a coincidence!; **da la ~ que conozco
a tu mujer** it so happens that I know
your wife

**casualmente** [ka·swal·'men·te] *adv* by
chance

**cata** ['ka·ta] *f* sampling; **~ de vinos**
wine-tasting

**catalán** [ka·ta·'lan] *m* (*lengua*) Catalan

**catalán, -ana** [ka·ta·'lan, --'la·na] *adj, m, f*
Catalan, Catalonian

**catalizador** [ka·ta·li·sa·'dor, ka·ta·li·θa·]
*m* catalyst; AUTO catalytic converter

**catalogar** <g → gu> [ka·ta·lo·'ɣar] *vt* to
catalog(ue); **~ a alguien de algo** to classify sb as sth

**catálogo** [ka·'ta·lo·ɣo] *m* catalog(ue)

**Cataluña** [ka·ta·'lu·ɲa] *f* Catalonia

**catapultar** [ka·ta·pul·'tar] *vt* to catapult

**catar** [ka·'tar] *vt* to taste

**catarata** [ka·ta·'ra·ta] *f* **1.** GEO waterfall;
**las ~s del Niágara** the Niagara Falls
**2.** MED cataract

**catarro** [ka·'ta·rro] *m* cold; MED catarrh

**catástrofe** [ka·'tas·tro·fe] *f* catastrophe

**catecismo** [ka·te·'sis·mo, -'θis·mo] *m*
REL catechism

**catedral** [ka·te·'dral] *f* cathedral; **como
una ~** *fig* massive

**catedrático, -a** [ka·te·'dra·ti·ko, -a] *m, f*
ENS professor

**categoría** [ka·te·ɣo·'ri·a] *f* **1.** (*clase*) category **2.** (*calidad*) quality; **de primera
~** first-class; **tener mucha/poca ~** to be
important/unimportant

**catete** [ka·'te·te] *m Chile* **1.** CULIN
pork-broth porridge **2.** (*diablo*) devil

**catolicismo** [ka·to·li·'sis·mo, -'θis·mo] *m*
REL (Roman) Catholicism

**católico, -a** [ka·'to·li·ko, -a] *adj, m, f*
(Roman) Catholic

**catorce** [ka·'tor·se, -θe] *adj inv m* fourteen; *v. t.* **ocho**

**cauce** ['kau·se, -θe] *m* **1.** GEO (*lecho*)
river bed **2.** (*camino*) channel, course;
**~ jurídico** JUR legal action

**cauchal** [kau·'tʃal] *m AmL* rubber plantation

**caucho** ['kau·tʃo] *m* **1.** (*sustancia*) rub-

ber; **árbol del ~** rubber tree **2.** *AmL*
(*neumático*) tire
**caudal** [kau·'dal] *m* **1.** (*de agua*) volume
**2.** (*dinero*) **caja de ~es** safe **3.** (*abun-*
*dancia*) abundance
**caudillaje** [kau·di·'ja·xe, -'ʎa·xe] *m Arg,*
*Chile, Perú pey* (*caciquismo*) rule by
political bosses
**caudillo** [kau·'di·jo, -ʎo] *m* MIL, POL leader
**caula** ['kau·la] *f AmL* (*estratagema*) trick
**causa** ['kau·sa] *f t.* POL (*ideal*) cause; (*mo-*
*tivo*) reason; **a** [*o* **por**] **~ de** on account
of; **la ~ de su despido** the reason for
his/her dismissal
**causar** [kau·'sar] *vt* to cause; **~ daño/**
**problemas** to cause damage/problems;
**~ efecto** to have an effect
**cautela** [kau·'te·la] *f* caution
**cautivar** [kau·ti·'βar] *vt* **1.** (*apresar*) to
capture **2.** (*fascinar*) to captivate
**cautiverio** [kau·ti·'βe·rjo] *m*, **cautividad**
[kau·ti·βi·'dad] *f* captivity
**cautivo, -a** [kau·'ti·βo, -a] *adj, m, f* captive
**cauto, -a** ['kau·to, -a] *adj* cautious
**cava** ['ka·βa] *m* cava *(Champagne from*
*the northeast of Spain)*
**cavar** [ka·'βar] *vi, vt* to dig
**caverna** [ka·'βer·na] *f* cave; (*gruta*) *t.*
MED cavern; **los hombres de las ~s**
cavemen
**caviar** [ka·'βjar] *m* caviar
**cavilar** [ka·βi·'lar] *vt* **~ algo** to ponder
(on) sth
**caza¹** ['ka·sa, -θa] *f* **1.** (*montería*) hunting; **ir de** [*o* **a la**] **~** to go hunting
**2.** (*animales*) game
**caza²** ['ka·sa, -θa] *m* MIL fighter plane
**cazador(a)** [ka·sa·'dor, ka·θa-] **I.** *adj*
hunting **II.** *m(f)* hunter *m,* huntress *f;*
**~ furtivo** poacher
**cazadora** [ka·sa·'do·ra, ka·θa-] *f* bomber
jacket; **~ de piel** leather jacket
**cazar** <z → c> [ka·'sar, -'θar] *vt* **1.** (*atra-*
*par*) to hunt **2.** (*coger*) to catch; (*conse-*
*guir*) to get **3.** *inf* (*engañar*) to take in
**cazo** ['ka·so, -θo] *m* **1.** (*puchero*) saucepan **2.** (*cucharón*) ladle
**cazuela** [ka·'swe·la, -'θwe·la] *f* casserole
**CE** [se·'e, θe·'e] *f* HIST *abr de* **Comuni-**
**dad Europea** EC

**cebada** [se·'βa·da, θe-] *f* barley
**cebar** [se·'βar, θe-] **I.** *vt* **1.** (*engordar*)
to fatten (up) **2.** (*horno*) to stoke (up)
**3.** (*máquina*) to start **II.** *vr:* **~se** (*ira*) to
vent one's anger
**cebo** ['se·βo, θe-] *m* **1.** (*de anzuelo*) bait;
*t. fig* lure **2.** (*en un horno*) fuel
**cebolla** [se·'βo·ja, θe·'βo·ʎa] *f* **1.** BOT (*co-*
*mestible*) onion **2.** BOT (*bulbo*) bulb
**cebra** ['se·βra, 'θe-] *f* zebra; **paso de ~**
AUTO crosswalk
**cecear** [se·se·'ar, θe·θe-] *vi* to pronounce
Spanish 's' as [θ]
**ceder** [se·'der, θe-] **I.** *vi* **1.** (*renunciar*)
to renounce; (*de una pretensión*) to give
up **2.** (*disminuir*) to diminish; **cedió la**
**lluvia** the rain eased off **3.** (*capitular*)
**~ a algo** to give in to sth **4.** (*cuerda*) to
give way **II.** *vt* **1.** (*dar*) to hand over;
(*balón*) to pass **2.** (*transferir*) to transfer
**3.** AUTO **'ceda el paso'** 'yield'
**cedrón** [se·'dron, θe-] *m AmS* BOT lemon
verbena
**cegar** [se·'ɣar, θe-] *irr como* **fregar I.** *vi*
to go [*o* become] blind **II.** *vt* (*quitar la*
*vista*) to blind; **le ciega la ira** he/she is
blinded by rage
**ceguera** [se·'ɣe·ra, θe-] *f t. fig* blindness
**ceja** ['se·xa, 'θe-] *f* (*entrecejo*) eyebrow;
**fruncir las ~s** to knit one's eyebrows;
**tener a alguien entre ~ y ~** *inf* to
have it in for sb
**celador(a)** [se·la·'dor, -'do·ra; θe-] *m(f)*
watchman *m,* watchwoman *f;* (*de cár-*
*cel*) prison guard
**celda** ['sel·da, 'θel-] *f* (*celdilla*) cell; (*en*
*prisión*) prison cell; **~ de castigo** solitary
confinement
**celebración** [se·le·βra·'sjon, θe·le·βra·
'θjon] *f* (*acto*) celebration
**celebrar** [se·le·'βrar, θe-] **I.** *vt* **1.** (*mé-*
*rito*) to celebrate **2.** (*reuniones*) to
hold; **~ una subasta** to hold an auction
**3.** (*alegrarse*) to be delighted; (*aplaudir*)
to applaud **II.** *vr:* **~se** (*fiesta*) to be celebrated; (*reunión*) to be held
**célebre** <celebérrimo> ['se·le·βre, 'θe-]
*adj* **~ por algo** famous for sth
**celebridad** [se·le·βri·'dad, θe-] *f* **1.** (*per-*
*sonaje*) celebrity **2.** (*renombre*) fame

C

**celeste** [se·'les·te, θe-] adj 1. (célico) celestial; **cuerpos ~s** heavenly bodies 2. (color) sky blue

**celestial** [se·les·'tjal, θe-] adj (del cielo) celestial, heavenly

**celibato** [se·li·'βa·to, θe-] m REL celibacy

**celo** ['se·lo, 'θe-] m 1. (afán) zeal 2. pl (por amor) jealousy; **tener ~s** to be jealous 3. pl (envidia) envy 4. ZOOL (macho) rut; (hembra) heat; **estar en ~** (macho) to be in rut; (hembra) to be on heat 5. (cinta) adhesive [o Scotch®] tape

**celoso, -a** [se·'lo·so, -a; θe-] adj 1. (con fervor) ~ **en algo** zealous in sth 2. (exigente) ~ **de algo** conscientious about sth 3. (con celos) jealous 4. (con envidia) envious

**celta** ['sel·ta, 'θel-] I. adj Celtic II. mf Celt

**célula** ['se·lu·la, 'θe-] f BIO, POL cell

**celulitis** [se·lu·'li·tis, θe-] f inv MED cellulitis

**cementerio** [se·men·'te·rjo, θe-] m (camposanto) cemetery

**cemento** [se·'men·to, θe-] m ARQUIT, ANAT cement; ~ **armado** reinforced concrete

**cena** ['se·na, 'θe-] f supper

**cenaduría** [se·na·du·'ri·a, θe-] f Méx eating house (serving only at night)

**cenar** [se·'nar, θe-] I. vi to have dinner II. vt to have for dinner

**cenicero** [se·ni·'θe·ro, θe-] m ashtray

**cenicienta** [se·ni·'sjen·ta, θe·ni·'θjen-] f, **Cenicienta** f t. fig Cinderella

**cenit** [se·'nit, θe-] m zenith

**ceniza** [se·'ni·sa, θe·'ni·θa] f 1. (residuo) ash; **reducir algo a ~s** to reduce sth to ashes 2. pl (restos mortales) ashes pl

**censar** [sen·'sar, θen-] I. vi to carry out a census II. vt to take a census of

**censo** ['sen·so, 'θen-] m census; ~ **electoral** POL electoral roll

**censura** [sen·'su·ra, θen-] f 1. (crítica) censorship 2. (entidad) censor's office 3. POL **moción de ~** motion of censure

**censurar** [sen·su·'rar, θen-] vt to censure; **~on todas las escenas violentas** all the violent scenes were taken out

**centavo** [sen·'ta·βo, θen-] m 1. (centésima parte) hundredth (part) 2. (de dólar) cent, penny 3. AmC, CSur FIN (moneda) centavo

**centavo, -a** [sen·'ta·βo, -a; θen-] adj hundredth; v. t. **octavo**

**centell(e)ar** [sen·te·je·'ar, θen·te·ʎe·'ar; sen·te·'jar, θen·te·'ʎar] vi 1. (relámpago) to flash 2. (fuego) to spark 3. (estrella) to twinkle 4. (ojos) to glitter

**centena** [sen·'te·na, θen-] f hundred

**centenar** [sen·te·'nar, θen-] m hundred

**centenario** [sen·te·'na·rjo, θen-] m centennial

**centenario, -a** [sen·te·'na·rjo, -a; θen-] adj, m, f centenarian

**centeno** [sen·'te·no, θen-] m rye

**centigrado** [sen·'ti·yra·do, θen-] m centigrade; **grado ~** degree centigrade

**centímetro** [sen·'ti·me·tro, θen-] m centimeter

**céntimo** ['sen·ti·mo, -a; 'θen-] I. adj hundredth II. m 1. (parte) hundredth part 2. FIN (moneda) (Euro) cent; CRi, Par, Ven centimo; **estar sin un ~** to be broke

**centinela** [sen·ti·'ne·la; θen-] mf MIL sentry

**centrado, -a** [sen·'tra·do, -a; θen-] adj 1. (en el centro) centered 2. (forma de ser) stable

**central** [sen·'tral, θen-] I. adj central; **estación ~** main station II. f 1. (oficina) head office 2. TÉC (planta) ~ **depuradora** waterworks; ~ **(hidro)eléctrica/nuclear/térmica** (hydro)electric/nuclear/oil-fired power station

**centralismo** [sen·tra·'lis·mo, θen-] m POL centralism

**centralita** [sen·tra·'li·ta, θen-] f TEL switchboard

**centralizar** <z → c> [sen·tra·li·'sar, θen·tra·li·'θar] vt to centralize

**centrar** [sen·'trar, θen-] I. vt 1. TÉC (colocar) to center 2. (concentrar) to concentrate 3. (interés) to focus II. vi, DEP (fútbol) to center III. vr: ~**se** 1. (basarse) to center 2. (interés) to focus

**céntrico, -a** ['sen·tri·ko, -a; 'θen-] adj t. TÉC central; **piso ~** an apartment in the center of town

**centrifugar** <g → gu> [sen·tri·fu·'yar, θen-] vt to spin-dry

**centrífugo, -a** [sen·'tri·fu·γo, -a; θen-] adj centrifugal

**centro** ['sen·tro, 'θen-] m **1.** t. POL, DEP (el medio) center; (de la ciudad) center city, downtown; **~ de gravedad** center of gravity **2.** (institución) center; **~ de enseñanza** teaching institution; **~ comercial** shopping center, mall **3.** ANAT **~ nervioso** nerve center

**Centroamérica** [sen·tro·a·'me·ri·ka, θen-] f Central America

**centroamericano, -a** [sen·tro·a·me·ri·'ka·no, -a; θen-] adj, m, f Central American

**ceñir** [se·'ɲir, θe-] irr **I.** vt (ponerse) to put on; (cinturón) to buckle on **II.** vr: **~se 1.** (ajustarse) to limit oneself; (al hablar) to be brief; **~se al presupuesto** to keep to the budget **2.** (vestido) to be close-fitting **3.** (ponerse) to put on

**ceño** ['se·ɲo, 'θe-] m frown; **fruncir el ~** to frown

**cepa** ['se·pa, 'θe-] f t. BOT (tronco) stump; **de pura ~** real

**cepillar** [se·pi·'jar, θe·pi·'ʎar] **I.** vt **1.** (traje) to brush; TÉC (madera) to plane **2.** AmL inf (adular) to butter up **3.** inf (ganar) to win **II.** vr: **~se 1.** inf (devorar) to polish off **2.** inf (dinero) to squander **3.** inf (matar) to bump off

**cepillo** [se·'pi·jo, θe·'pi·ʎo] m **1.** (para traje) brush; TÉC (para madera) plane; (de limpiar) scrubbing brush; **~ de barrer** broom; **~ de dientes** toothbrush; **pasar el ~** to brush **2.** (en misa) collection box

**cepo** ['se·po, 'θe-] m **1.** (caza) trap; AUTO wheel clamp

**cera** ['se·ra, 'θe-] f wax; **~ de los oídos** earwax; **~ para suelos** wax polish; **museo de ~** wax museum

**cerámica** [se·'ra·mi·ka, θe-] f ceramics pl

**cerca** ['ser·ka, 'θer-] **I.** adv (en el espacio) near; **aquí ~** near here; **mirar de ~** to look closely at **II.** prep **1.** (lugar) **~ de** near **2.** (cantidad) **~ de** about **III.** f fence

**cercanía** [ser·ka·'ni·a, θer-] f **1.** (proximidad) closeness **2.** pl (alrededores) outskirts pl

**cercano, -a** [ser·'ka·no, -a; θer-] adj near

**cercar** <c → qu> [ser·'kar, θer-] vt **1.** (vallar) to fence in **2.** (rodear) to surround

**cerco** ['ser·ko, 'θer-] m **1.** (círculo) circle; (borde) rim **2.** (valla) fence **3.** MIL siege

**cerdo, -a** ['ser·do, -a; 'θer-] **I.** m, f **1.** ZOOL pig; **carne de ~** pork **2.** (insulto) swine **II.** adj (sucio) dirty

**cereales** [se·re·'a·les, θe-] mpl cereals pl, grain

**cerebro** [se·'re·βro, θe-] m **1.** ANAT brain **2.** (inteligencia) brains pl

**ceremonia** [se·re·'mo·nja, θe-] f **1.** (acto) ceremony **2.** (cortesía) formality; **sin ~s** without any fuss

**cereza** [se·'re·sa, θe·'re·θa] f cherry

**cerezo** [se·'re·so, θe·'re·θo] m (árbol) cherry tree; (madera) cherry wood

**cerilla** [se·'ri·ja, θe·'ri·ʎa] f (fósforo) match

**cerillero** [se·ri·'je·ro, θe·ri·'ʎe·ro] m AmL (cajita) matchbox

**cero** ['se·ro, 'θe-] m t. MAT zero; **ocho (grados) bajo/sobre ~** eight below/above zero; **partir de ~** to start from scratch

**cerrado, -a** [se·'rra·do, -a; θe-] adj **1.** estar (no abierto) closed; (con llave) locked; (cielo) overcast; **la puerta está cerrada** the door is closed; **a puerta cerrada** behind closed doors; **aquí huele a ~** it smells stuffy in here **2.** ser (actitud) reserved **3.** ser (denso) dense; **noche cerrada** dark night **4.** ser (acento) broad **5.** ser (curva) sharp **6.** ser (lerdo) thick

**cerradura** [se·rra·'du·ra, θe-] f (dispositivo) lock

**cerrajero, -a** [se·rra·'xe·ro, -a; θe-] m, f locksmith

**cerrar** <e → ie> [se·'rrar, θe-] **I.** vt **1.** (puerta) to close; (con llave) to lock; (carta) to seal; **~ el pico** inf to keep one's trap shut; **~ un archivo** COMPUT to close a file; **~ el paso a alguien** to block sb's way **2.** (agujero) to block (up); (agua) to turn off **3.** (terreno) to close off; (con un cerco) to enclose **4.** (nego-

*ciación*) to conclude **II.** *vi* **1.** (*puerta*) to close **2.** (*acabar*) to end **III.** *vr:* **~se 1.** (*puerta*) **la puerta se cerró sola** the door closed by itself **2.** (*herida*) to heal (up) **3.** (*obstinarse*) to persist **4.** (*el cielo*) to become overcast **5.** (*agruparse*) to crowd together

**cerril** [se·'rril, θe-] *adj* **1.** (*obstinado*) obstinate **2.** (*torpe*) dense

**cerro** ['se·rro, 'θe-] *m* hill; (*peñasco*) crag

**cerrojo** [se·'rro·xo, θe-] *m* bolt; **echar el ~ a la puerta** to bolt the door

**certamen** [ser·'ta·men, θer-] *m* competition

**certeza** [ser·'te·sa, θer·'te·θa] *f* certainty

**certidumbre** [ser·ti·'dum·bre, θer-] *f* certainty

**certificado** [ser·ti·fi·'ka·do, θer-] *m* certificate; **~ de asistencia** certificate of attendance; **~ médico** medical certificate

**certificado, -a** [ser·ti·fi·'ka·do, -a; θer-] *adj* JUR certified; **carta certificada** (*correos*) registered letter

**certificar** [<c → qu>] [ser·ti·fi·'kar, θer-] *vt* **1.** *t.* JUR (*afirmar*) to certify **2.** (*correos*) to register

**cervecería** [ser·βe·se·'ri·a, θer·βe·θe-] *f* **1.** (*bar*) bar **2.** (*fábrica*) brewery

**cervecero, -a** [ser·βe·'se·ro, -a; θer·βe·'θe-] *adj* beer; (*industria*) brewing

**cerveza** [ser·'βe·sa, θer·'βe·θa] *f* beer; **~ de barril** draft beer; **~ negra** dark beer, stout; **~ rubia** lager beer

**cervical** [ser·βi·'kal, θer-] *adj* **1.** ANAT neck **2.** MED cervical

**cesar** [se·'sar, θe-] **I.** *vi* **1.** (*parar*) to stop; **sin ~** ceaselessly **2.** (*en una profesión*) **~ en algo** to leave sth **II.** *vt* **1.** (*pagos*) to stop **2.** (*despedir*) to dismiss, to fire

**cesárea** [se·'sa·rea, θe-] *f* Cesarean, C-section

**cese** ['se·se, 'θe-] *m* **1.** (*que termina*) cessation; (*interrupción*) suspension; **~ de pagos** suspension of payments **2.** (*de obrero*) firing; (*de funcionario*) dismissal; **~ en el cargo** to retire from office

**cesión** [se·'sjon, θe-] *f* **1.** (*entrega*) transfer **2.** JUR cession

**césped** ['ses·ped, 'θes-] *m* grass; **'prohibido pisar el ~'** 'keep off the grass'

**cesta** ['ses·ta, 'θes-] *f* basket

**cesto** ['ses·to, 'θes-] *m t.* DEP basket

**ceta** ['se·ta, 'θe-] *f* Z

**chabola** [tʃa·'βo·la] *f* (*casucha*) shack

**chacal** [tʃa·'kal] *m* jackal

**chacalín** [tʃa·ka·'lin] *m AmC* ZOOL shrimp

**chácara** ['tʃa·ka·ra] *f Par, Nic, Bol* **1.** (*granja*) small farm **2.** MED ulcer

**chacarero, -a** [tʃa·ka·'re·ro] *m, f AmL* farmer; (*trabajador*) farm laborer

**cháchara** ['tʃa·tʃa·ra] *f inf* (*charla*) chatter; **andar** [*o* **estar**] **de ~** to have a chat

**chacra** ['tʃa·kra] *f AmL* (*granja*) small farm; (*finca*) country estate

**chafar** [tʃa·'far] **I.** *vt* **1.** (*aplastar*) to flatten *fig*, to squelch; (*arrugar*) to crease; (*deshacer*) to mess up **2.** (*confundir*) to confuse; **quedar(se) chafado** to be speechless **3.** (*estropear*) to spoil **II.** *vr:* **~se** (*aplastarse*) to be flattened; (*deshacerse*) to be messed up; (*arrugarse*) to be creased

**chaflán** [tʃa·'flan] *m* **1.** (*bisel*) bevel (edge) **2.** (*en una calle*) street corner; (*en un edificio*) house corner

**chagra** ['tʃa·ɣra] *mf Ecua* (*labriego*) peasant

**cháguar** ['tʃa·ɣwar] *m AmS* BOT Paraguayan sisal

**chal** [tʃal] *m* shawl

**chalado, -a** [tʃa·'la·do, -a] *adj inf* crazy

**chalanear** [tʃa·la·ne·'ar] *vt AmL* (*un caballo*) to break in; (*adiestrar*) to train

**chalé** [tʃa·'le] *m* (*casa unifamiliar*) detached family home; (*de campo*) country house; (*villa*) chalet

**chaleco** [tʃa·'le·ko] *m* vest; **~ salvavidas** life jacket

**chalina** [tʃa·'li·na] *f Arg, Col, CRi* (*chal*) narrow shawl

**chamaco, -a** [tʃa·'ma·ko, -a] *m, f Cuba, Méx* **1.** (*muchacho*) boy; (*muchacha*) girl **2.** (*novio*) boyfriend; (*novia*) girlfriend

**chamagoso, -a** [tʃa·ma·'ɣo·so, -a] *adj Méx* (*mugriento*) filthy

**chamico** [tʃa·'mi·ko] *m AmL* BOT thorn apple

**champán** [tʃam·'pan] *m* champagne

**champiñón** [tʃam·pi·'ɲon] *m* mushroom

**champú** [tʃam·'pu] *m* shampoo; **~ anti-**

**caspa** anti-dandruff shampoo

**chamuscar** <c → qu> [tʃa·mus·'kar] I. *vt* (*quemar*) to scorch II. *vr:* ~**se** (*quemarse*) to get scorched

**chance** ['tʃan·se, -θe] *m o f AmC* (*oportunidad*) chance

**chanchería** [tʃan·tʃe·'ri·a] *f AmL* pork butcher's shop

**chancho** ['tʃan·tʃo] *m AmL* pig

**chancho, -a** ['tʃan·tʃo, -a] *adj AmL* **1.** (*marrano*) dirty **2.** (*desaseado*) slovenly

**chanchullo** [tʃan·'tʃu·jo, -ʎo] *m inf* swindle, fiddle

**chancla** ['tʃan·kla] *f* **1.** (*zapato viejo*) old shoe **2.** (*zapatilla*) slipper **3.** (*de playa*) flip flop

**chancleta** [tʃan·'kle·ta] *f* **1.** (*chinela*) slipper **2.** *AmL* (*bebé*) baby girl **3.** *inf* (*persona inepta*) fool

**chanclo** ['tʃan·klo] *m* **1.** (*zueco*) clog **2.** (*de goma*) (rubber) overshoe, galosh

**chándal** ['tʃan·dal] *m* <chándals> tracksuit

**changa** ['tʃan·ga] *f* **1.** *Arg* (*ocupación*) trade **2.** *AmS* (*transporte*) porterage **3.** *AmS, Cuba* (*broma*) joke

**changador** [tʃan·ga·'dor] *m* **1.** *AmS* (*cargador*) carrier **2.** *Arg* (*temporero*) casual worker

**chantaje** [tʃan·'ta·xe] *m* blackmail

**chantajear** [tʃan·ta·xe·'ar] *vt* to blackmail

**chantajista** [tʃan·ta·'xis·ta] *mf* blackmailer

**chantar** [tʃan·'tar] *vt Chile* (*golpe*) to deal

**chapa** ['tʃa·pa] *f* **1.** (*metal*) sheet **2.** (*lámina*) plate **3.** (*contrachapado*) plywood **4.** (*tapón*) (bottle)cap **5.** (*placa*) badge **6.** *AmL* (*cerradura*) lock **7.** *pl* (*juego*) game played with bottle caps

**chaparreras** [tʃa·pa·'rre·ras] *fpl Méx* (*pantalones para montar a caballo*) chaps *pl*

**chaparrón** [tʃa·pa·'rron] *m* **1.** (*lluvia*) downpour; (*chubasco*) cloudburst **2.** *inf* (*cantidad grande*) barrage

**chapetón, -ona** [tʃa·pe·'ton] I. *adj AmL* newly arrived II. *m, f AmL* Spaniard in America

**chapisca** [tʃa·'pis·ka] *f AmC* AGR (*cosecha de maíz*) corn harvest

**chapopote** [tʃa·po·'po·te] *m Ant, Méx* (*asfalto*) asphalt

**chapucero, -a** [tʃa·pu·'se·ro, -a; -'θe·ro, -a] *adj* (*trabajando*) shoddy

**chapulín** [tʃa·pu·'lin] *m* **1.** *AmL* (*langosta*) large cicada **2.** *AmC* (*niño*) child

**chapuza** [tʃa·'pu·sa, -θa] *f* **1.** (*chapucería*) shoddy job **2.** (*trabajo*) odd job

**chapuzón** [tʃa·pu·'son, -'θon] *m* dip; **darse un** ~ to go for a dip

**chaqueta** [tʃa·'ke·ta] *f* jacket; **cambiar de** ~ *fig* to change sides

**chaquetón** [tʃa·ke·'ton] *m* long jacket; (*cazadora*) Windbreaker®

**charanga** [tʃa·'ran·ga] *f* **1.** (*banda*) brass band **2.** *AmL* (*baile*) dance

**charca** ['tʃar·ka] *f* pond

**charco** ['tʃar·ko] *m* puddle, pool

**charcón, -ona** [tʃar·'kon, -·'ko·na] *adj Arg, Bol, Urug* (*flaco*) skinny

**charcutería** [tʃar·ku·te·'ri·a] *f* **1.** (*productos*) cooked or cured pork products *pl* **2.** (*tienda*) ≈ delicatessen

**charla** ['tʃar·la] *f* **1.** (*conversación*) chat; **estar de** ~ to have a chat **2.** (*conferencia*) talk

**charlar** [tʃar·'lar] *vi* **1.** (*conversar*) to chat **2.** (*parlotear*) to chatter

**charlatán, -ana** [tʃar·la·'tan, -·'ta·na] I. *adj* talkative II. *m, f* **1.** (*hablador*) chatterbox **2.** (*chismoso*) gossip **3.** (*vendedor*) hawker

**charol** [tʃa·'rol] *m* **1.** (*barniz*) varnish **2.** (*cuero*) patent leather **3.** *AmL* (*bandeja*) tray

**chárter** ['tʃar·ter] *adj inv* **vuelo** ~ charter flight

**chasco** ['tʃas·ko] *m* (*decepción*) disappointment

**chasco, -a** ['tʃas·ko, -a] *adj CSur* crinkly

**chasis** ['tʃa·sis] *m inv* AUTO chassis

**chasqui** ['tʃas·ki] *m AmS* (*chasque*) messenger

**chasquido** [tʃas·'ki·do] *m* **1.** (*de lengua*) click **2.** (*de la madera*) creak

**chatarra** [tʃa·'ta·rra] *f* **1.** (*metal viejo*) scrap (metal) **2.** (*trastos*) junk **3.** *inf* (*dinero*) change

**chatarrería** [tʃa·ta·rre·'ri·a] *f* junkyard

**chatarrero, -a** [tʃa·ta·'rre·ro, -a] *m, f* junkman *m*, junkwoman *f* chato, -a ['tʃa·to] I. *adj* 1. (*nariz*) snub 2. (*persona*) snub-nosed 3. (*objeto*) blunt; (*aplastado*) flattened II. *m, f inf* (*tratamiento*) kid

chaucha ['tʃau·tʃa] *f AmS* 1. (*judía verde*) green bean 2. (*patata*) new potato 3. *pl* (*calderilla*) small change

chauchera [tʃau·'tʃe·ra] *f Chile, Ecua* (*monedero*) purse

chaval(a) [tʃa·'βal, -·'βa·la] *m(f) inf* (*chico*) kid; (*joven*) young man *m*, young woman *f*

che [tʃe] *interj AmS* hey

checo, -a ['tʃe·ko, -a] I. *adj* Czech; **República Checa** Czech Republic II. *m, f* Czech

chelín [tʃe·'lin] *m* (*moneda*) shilling

chelo ['tʃe·lo] *m* cello

chepa ['tʃe·pa] *f inf* hump ▶ **subirse a la ~ de alguien** to be disrespectful to sb

cheque ['tʃe·ke] *m* check; **~ en blanco** blank check; **~ sin fondo** bounced check; **~ de viaje** traveler's check; **cobrar un ~** to cash a check; **extender un ~** to write a check

chequear [tʃe·ke·'ar] I. *vt AmL* (*comprobar*) to check II. *vr:* **~se** to get a checkup

chequeo [tʃe·'keo] *m* (*de la salud*) checkup; (*de un mecanismo*) service

chequera [tʃe·'ke·ra] *f AmL* checkbook

Chequia ['tʃe·kja] *f* Czech Republic

chévere ['tʃe·βe·re] I. *adj Ven inf* terrific II. *mf Cuba, PRico, Ven* braggart

chica ['tʃi·ka] I. *adj* (*pequeña*) small; (*joven*) young II. *f* 1. (*niña*) girl; (*joven*) young woman 2. (*criada*) maid

chicano, -a [tʃi·'ka·no, -a] *m, f* Chicano (*person of Mexican origin living in the USA*)

chichón [tʃi·'tʃon] *m* bump

chicle ['tʃi·kle] *m* chewing gum

chico ['tʃi·ko] I. *adj* 1. (*pequeño*) small 2. (*joven*) young II. *m* 1. (*niño*) boy; (*joven*) young man 2. (*de los recados*) errand boy

chicote [tʃi·'ko·te] *m AmL* (*látigo*) whip

chiflado, -a [tʃi·'fla·do, -a] *adj inf* crazy

chiflón [tʃi·'flon] *m AmL* (*viento*) gale; (*corriente*) draft; **un ~ de aire** a blast of air

chigüin [tʃi·'ywin] *m AmC* (*niño*) kid

chile ['tʃi·le] *m* (*especia*) chili

Chile ['tʃi·le] *m* Chile

chileno, -a [tʃi·'le·no, -a] *adj, m, f* Chilean

chillar [tʃi·jar, -'ʎar] *vi* 1. (*persona*) to yell; **¡no me chilles!** don't shout at me! 2. (*animal*) to howl; (*frenos*) to screech; (*puerta*) to creak 3. (*colores*) to clash

chillido [tʃi·'ji·do, -·'ʎi·do] *m* 1. (*de persona*) yell 2. (*de animal*) howl; (*de frenos*) screech; (*de puerta*) creak

chilote [tʃi·'lo·te] *m Méx* drink made of chili and pulque (*beverage made of agave*)

chimenea [tʃi·me·'nea] *f* 1. *t.* GEO (*de un edificio*) chimney 2. (*hogar*) fireplace

chimpancé [tʃim·pan·'se, -'θe] *mf* chimpanzee

china ['tʃi·na] *f* 1. (*piedra*) pebble 2. *AmL* (*india*) Indian woman; (*mestiza*) half-caste woman 3. *AmL* (*amante*) mistress

China ['tʃi·na] *f* (la) ~ China

chinchar [tʃin·'tʃar] I. *vt inf* to pester II. *vr:* **~se** *inf* to get upset; **¡chínchate!** so there!, tough luck!

chinche¹ ['tʃin·tʃe] *m o f* ZOOL bedbug

chinche² ['tʃin·tʃe] *mf inf* (*pelmazo*) pain

chincheta [tʃin·'tʃe·ta] *f* thumbtack

chincol [tʃin·'kol] *f AmS* ZOOL crown sparrow

chingar <g → gu> [tʃin·'gar] I. *vt* 1. *inf* (*molestar*) to annoy 2. *inf* (*bebidas*) to drink 3. *vulg* (*joder*) to fuck II. *vr:* **~se** *inf* 1. (*emborracharse*) to get plastered 2. *AmL* (*frustrarse*) to be a washout 3. *AmL* (*fallar*) to fail

chingo, -a ['tʃin·go, -a] *adj* 1. *AmC* (*animal*) with a cropped tail 2. *AmC, Ven* (*chato*) flat-nosed 3. *AmC* (*corto*) short 4. *CRi* (*desnudo*) naked 5. *Ven* (*ansioso*) anxious 6. *Col, Cuba* (*pequeño*) tiny 7. *Nic* (*bajo*) short

chingue ['tʃin·ge] *m Chile* ZOOL skunk

chinita [tʃi·'ni·ta] *f Chile* (*insecto*) ladybug

chino ['tʃi·no] *m AmL* (*indio*) Indian; (*mestizo*) mestizo

**chino, -a** ['tʃi·no, -a] **I.** *adj* Chinese **II.** *m, f* Chinese man *m*, Chinese woman *f* ▸ **engañar a alguien como a un ~** *inf* to take sb for a ride

**chip** [tʃip] *m* COMPUT chip

**chipichipi** [tʃi·pi'tʃi·pi] *m* Méx (*llovizna*) drizzle

**Chipre** ['tʃi·pre] *f* Cyprus

**chiqueo** [tʃi'keo] *m* **1.** *Cuba, Méx* (*mimo*) pampering **2.** *AmC* (*contoneo*) swagger

**chiquillo, -a** [tʃi'ki·jo, -a; -'ki·ʎo, -a] **I.** *adj* young **II.** *m, f* (*niño*) (small) child; (*chico*) (little) boy; (*chica*) (little) girl

**chiringuito** [tʃi·rin'gi·to] *m* kiosk (*selling snacks and drinks*)

**chiripa** [tʃi'ri·pa] *f inf* stroke of luck; (*casualidad*) fluke

**chirola** [tʃi'ro·la] *f* **1.** *Arg* (*moneda*) old coin made of nickel **2.** *Chile* (*moneda*) silver 20 centavo coin **3.** *pl Arg* (*calderilla*) small change

**chirona** [tʃi'ro·na] *f inf* jail, clink *inf*

**chirriar** <*1. pres* chirrío> [tʃi·rri'ar] *vi* **1.** (*metal*) to squeak; (*madera*) to creak **2.** (*pájaros*) to chirp

**chisme** ['tʃis·me] *m* **1.** (*habladuría*) piece of gossip **2.** (*objeto*) thingamajig; **recoge esos ~s** put away those things

**chismoso, -a** [tʃis'mo·so, -a] **I.** *adj* gossiping **II.** *m, f* gossip

**chispa** ['tʃis·pa] *f* **1.** *t.* ELEC spark; **echar ~s** to give off sparks; *fig* to be hopping mad **2.** (*ingenio*) wit **3.** *inf* (*borrachera*) drunkenness **4.** (*una pizca*) **una ~ de...** a bit of...

**chispear** [tʃis·pe'ar] **I.** *vi* **1.** (*centellear*) to spark **2.** (*brillar*) to sparkle **II.** *vimpers* (*lloviznar*) to drizzle

**chiste** ['tʃis·te] *m* (*cuento*) funny story; (*broma*) joke; **~ verde** dirty joke

**chistoso, -a** [tʃis·'to·so, -a] **I.** *adj* funny **II.** *m, f* joker

**chiva** ['tʃi·βa] *f* Col *inf* (*noticia*) (piece of) news

**chivarse** [tʃi·'βar·se] *vr inf* **1.** (*hablar*) to grass **2.** *AmL* (*enojarse*) to get annoyed

**chivatear** [tʃi·βa·te·'ar] *vi* **1.** *Arg, Chile* (*chillar*) to shout **2.** *AmS* (*alborotar*) to make a ruckus

**chivato, -a** [tʃi·'βa·to, -a] *m, f inf* (*informador*) stool pigeon; (*en la escuela*) tell-tale

**chivo, -a** ['tʃi·βo, -a] *m, f* kid; **~ expiatorio** scapegoat

**chocante** [tʃo·'kan·te] *adj* (*raro*) strange; (*sorprendente*) startling

**chocar** <c → qu> [tʃo·'kar] **I.** *vi* (*vehículos*) ~ **contra algo** to collide with sth; (*dar*) to crash into sth; (*coches*) to run into sth **II.** *vt* **1.** (*entrechocar*) ~ **las copas** to clink glasses **2.** (*perturbar*) to startle

**chochear** [tʃo·tʃe·'ar] *vi* **1.** (*por vejez*) to dodder (around) **2.** (*sentir cariño*) to dote

**choclo** ['tʃo·klo] *m* **1.** *AmS* (*maíz*) corn; (*mazorca tierna*) ear of corn **2.** *AmS* CULIN sweet tamale

**chocolate** [tʃo·ko·'la·te] *m* chocolate; *inf* (*hachís*) hash *inf*

**chocolatería** [tʃo·ko·la·te·'ri·a] *f* (*establecimiento*) café specializing in hot chocolate drinks; (*fábrica*) chocolate factory

**chocolatina** [tʃo·ko·la·'ti·na] *f* chocolate bar

**chofer** [tʃo·'fer] *m*, **chófer** ['tʃo·fer] *m* chauffeur

**chollo** ['tʃo·jo, -ʎo] *m inf* **1.** (*suerte*) luck **2.** (*ganga*) bargain **3.** (*trabajo*) cushy job

**cholo, -a** ['tʃo·lo, -a] *m, f* AmL **1.** (*indio*) Indian integrated into Creole society **2.** (*mestizo*) mestizo

**chomba** ['tʃom·ba] *f* Arg (*polo*) polo shirt

**chongo** ['tʃon·go] *m* **1.** Méx *inf* (*trenza*) braid; (*moño*) knot, bun **2.** Chile (*cuchillo*) blunt knife

**chopo** ['tʃo·po] *m* black poplar

**choque** ['tʃo·ke] *m* **1.** (*impacto*) impact; (*colisión*) crash **2.** (*encuentro*) clash

**chorizo** [tʃo·'ri·so, -θo] *m* chorizo (*hard pork sausage*)

**chorizo, -a** [tʃo·'ri·so, -a; -θo, -a] *m, f inf* petty thief

**choro** ['tʃo·ro] *m* **1.** Chile (*mejillón*) large mussel **2.** AmS *inf* (*ladrón*) thief

**chorote** [tʃo·'ro·te] *m* Méx, Ven (*chocolate*) chocolate drink

**chorrada** [tʃo·'rra·da] f 1. inf (tontería) stupid remark 2. inf (cosa superflua) trivial thing

**chorrear** [tʃo·rre·'ar] vi 1. (fluir) to gush (out) 2. (gotear) to drip

**chorro** ['tʃo·rro] m 1. (hilo) trickle; (de ingrediente) drop 2. (torrente) stream; t. TÉC jet; **avión a ~** jet plane

**choza** ['tʃo·sa, -θa] f hut

**chubasco** [tʃu·'βas·ko] m (heavy) shower

**chubasquero** [tʃu·βas·'ke·ro] m raincoat

**chuchería** [tʃu·tʃe·'ri·a] f (dulce) sweet

**chucho** ['tʃu·tʃo] m 1. inf (perro) mutt 2. AmL (escalofrío) shivers pl; (fiebre) fever

**chucrut** [tʃu·'kru] m sauerkraut

**chufa** ['tʃu·fa] f tiger nut

**chufla** ['tʃu·fla] f joke

**chulada** [tʃu·'la·da] f inf (cosa estupenda) cool thing

**chulear** [tʃu·le·'ar] vi, vr: ~se (jactarse) to brag

**chulería** [tʃu·le·'ri·a] f bragging

**chuleta** [tʃu·'le·ta] f 1. (costilla) chop 2. inf (apunte) crib (sheet)

**chuletón** [tʃu·le·'ton] m T-bone steak

**chulo** ['tʃu·lo] m 1. (mal educado) boor 2. inf (proxeneta) pimp

**chulo, -a** ['tʃu·lo, -a] adj 1. (jactancioso) boastful; (presumido) conceited; **ponerse ~** to get cocky 2. inf (elegante) smart

**chungo, -a** ['tʃuŋ·go, -a] adj inf (malo) bad

**chuño** ['tʃu·ɲo] m AmS (fécula) potato flour

**chupa-chups®** [tʃu·pa·'tʃups] m inv lollipop

**chupada** [tʃu·'pa·da] f (paja) suck; (cigarrillo) puff

**chupado, -a** [tʃu·'pa·do, -a] adj 1. (flaco) skinny; (consumido) emaciated 2. inf (fácil) a cinch 3. AmL (borracho) drunk

**chupaflor** [tʃu·pa·'flor] m AmC ZOOL hummingbird

**chupar** [tʃu·'par] I. vt 1. (extraer) to suck out; (aspirar) to suck in; (absorber) to absorb 2. (caramelo) to suck; (helado) to lick 3. (cigarrillo) to smoke, to puff on II. vi 1. inf (mamar) to suckle; ~

**del bote** to line one's pocket 2. AmL inf (beber) to booze III. vr: ~se 1. (secarse) to get very thin 2. inf (aguantar) to sit out, to put up with

**chupe** ['tʃu·pe] m CSur, Ecua, Perú CULIN spicy chowder

**chupete** [tʃu·'pe·te] m 1. (del bebé) pacifier 2. AmL (piruli) lollipop

**churrasco** [tʃu·'rras·ko] m steak

**churro** ['tʃu·rro] m 1. (fritura) ≈ fritter 2. (chapuza) (piece of) shoddy work 3. (suerte) piece of luck 4. Col (persona atractiva) good-looker

**chusma** ['tʃus·ma] f rabble, riffraff

**chutar** [tʃu·'tar] I. vt to shoot; **esto va que chuta** inf it's going well II. vr: ~se inf to shoot up

**chuza** ['tʃu·sa, -θa] f 1. Arg, Urug (lanza) pike 2. Arg (gallo) cock's spur 3. Méx (juego: bolos) strike 4. pl Arg (pelo) rats' tails

**chuzar** <z → c> [tʃu·'sar, -'θar] vt Col to prick

**Cía** ['si·a, 'θi·a] abr de **compañía** Co.

**ciberespacio** [si·βer·es·'pa·sjo, θi·βer·es·'pa·θjo] m cyberspace

**cibernauta** [si·βer·'nau·ta, θi-] mf websurfer, cybernaut

**cibernética** [si·βer·'ne·ti·ka, θi-] f cybernetics pl

**cicatriz** [si·ka·'tris, θi·ka·'triθ] f scar

**cicatrizar** <z → c> [si·ka·tri·'sar, θi·ka·tri·'θar] vt, vi, vr: ~se to heal

**ciclismo** [si·'klis·mo, θi-] m DEP cycling

**ciclista** [si·'klis·ta, θi-] I. adj cycle II. mf cyclist

**ciclo** ['si·klo, 'θi-] m cycle; ~ **económico** economic cycle

**ciclón** [si·'klon, θi-] m cyclone

**ciego, -a** ['sje·ɣo, 'θje-] I. adj 1. (persona) blind; **quedarse ~** to go blind 2. (taponado) blocked II. m, f blind man m, blind woman f III. adv **a ciegas** blindly

**cielo** ['sje·lo, 'θje-] I. m 1. (atmósfera) sky; **como caído del ~** out of the blue 2. REL Heaven 3. (apelativo) darling II. interj ¡~s! good heavens!

**ciempiés** [sjem·'pjes, θjem-] m inv centipede

**cien** [sjen, θjen] adj inv a [o one] hundred; **al ~ por ~** one hundred per cent; v. t. **ochocientos**

**ciencia** ['sjen·sja, 'θjen·θja] f 1. (saber) knowledge; **a ~ cierta** for sure 2. (disciplina) science; **~s políticas** political science; **~s (naturales)** natural science(s)

**ciencia-ficción** ['sjen·sja·fik·'sjon, 'θjen·θja·fiɣ·'θjon] f science fiction

**científico, -a** [sjen·'ti·fi·ko, -a; θjen-] I. adj scientific II. m, f scientist

**ciento** ['sjen·to, 'θjen-] adj <cien> inv [o one] hundred; **el cinco por ~** five per cent; v. t. **ochocientos**

**cierre** ['sje·rre, 'θje-] m 1. (conclusión) closing; (clausura) closure; PREN time of going to press; **~ del ejercicio** close of the financial year; **hora de ~** closing time; **~ centralizado** AUTO central locking 2. Arg (cremallera) zipper

**cierto** ['sjer·to, 'θjer-] adv certainly; **por ~** by the way

**cierto, -a** ['sjer·to, -a; 'θjer-] adj <certísimo> 1. (verdadero) true; (seguro) sure; **estar en lo ~** to be right; **lo ~ es que...** the fact is that... 2. (alguno) a certain; **~ día** one day

**ciervo, -a** ['sjer·βo, -a; 'θjer-] m, f deer

**cifra** ['si·fra, 'θi-] f (guarismo) figure; **~ de negocios** ECON turnover; **~ de ventas** ECON sales figures

**cifrar** [si·'frar, θi-] vt 1. (codificar) to code 2. (calcular) to reckon

**cigarra** [si·'ɣa·rra, θi-] f cicada

**cigarrillo** [si·ɣa·'rri·jo, θi·ɣa·'rri·ʎo] m cigarette

**cigarro** [si·'ɣa·rro, θi-] m cigar

**cigüeña** [si·'ɣwe·ɲa, θi-] f stork

**cilindrada** [si·lin·'dra·da, θi-] f AUTO cubic capacity

**cilindro** [si·'lin·dro, θi-] m cylinder

**cima** ['si·ma, 'θi-] f t. fig summit; **~ del árbol** tree top; **~ del monte** mountain peak

**cimarrón, -ona** [si·ma·'rron, -·'rro·na; θi-] adj AmL wild

**cimbronazo** [sim·bro·'na·so, θim·bro·'na·θo] m AmL 1. (temblor) jolt; (de tierra) earthquake 2. (tirón) yank

**cimiento** [si·'mjen·to, θi-] m foundation

**cinc** [siŋ, θiŋ] m zinc

**cincel** [sin·'sel, θin·'θel] m chisel

**cinco** ['sin·ko, 'θin-] I. adj inv five II. m five; **¡choca esos ~!** give me five!; v. t. **ocho**

**cincuenta** [sin·'kwen·ta, θin-] adj inv fifty; v. t. **ochenta**

**cine** ['si·ne, 'θi-] m 1. (arte) cinema, movies pl; **~ mudo/sonoro** silent/talking films; **~ negro** film noir; **me gusta el ~** I like the movies 2. (sala) cinema, movie theater; **ir al ~** to go to the movies

**cínico, -a** ['si·ni·ko, -a; 'θi-] I. adj cynical II. m, f t. FILOS cynic

**cinismo** [si·'nis·mo, θi-] m cynicism

**cinta** ['sin·ta, 'θin-] f band; **~ adhesiva** adhesive tape; **~ aislante** insulating tape; **~ métrica** tape measure; **~ del pelo** hair ribbon; **~ de vídeo** videotape; **~ virgen** blank tape; **~ transportadora** conveyor belt

**cinto** ['sin·to, 'θin-] m belt

**cintura** [sin·'tu·ra, θin-] f waist

**cinturón** [sin·tu·'ron, θin-] m belt; **ponerse el ~** to fasten one's seatbelt; **apretarse el ~** fig to tighten one' belt

**cipe** ['si·pe, 'θi-] adj AmC sickly, runty

**ciprés** [si·'pres, θi-] m cypress

**circo** ['sir·ko, 'θir-] m (arena) circus; **~ ambulante** traveling circus

**circuito** [sir·ku·'i·to, θir-] m 1. t. ELEC circuit; **~ integrado** integrated circuit; **corto ~** short circuit 2. DEP circuit, track

**circulación** [sir·ku·la·'sjon, θir·ku·la·'θjon] f 1. t. ECON circulation; **~ sanguínea** (blood) circulation; **retirar de la ~** to withdraw from circulation 2. (tránsito) traffic

**circular** [sir·ku·'lar, θir-] I. adj circular II. vi 1. (recorrer) to circulate 2. (personas) to walk (around); (vehículos) to drive (around); **¡circulen!** move along! III. f circular

**circulatorio, -a** [θir·ku·la·'to·rjo, -a; θir-] adj MED circulatory

**círculo** ['θir·ku·lo, 'θir-] m circle; **~ de amistades** circle of friends; **~ vicioso** vicious circle

**circunferencia** [sir·kun·fe·'ren·sja, θir·kun·fe·'ren·θja] f t. MAT circumference

**circunstancia** [sir·kuns·'tan·sja, θir·kuns·'tan·θja] f circumstance; **en estas ~s** in these circumstances

**circunvalación** [sir·kum·ba·la·'sjon, θir·kum·ba·la·'θjon] *f* **carretera de ~** by-pass

**ciruela** [si·'rwe·la, θi-] *f* plum; **~ pasa** prune

**ciruelo** [si·'rwe·lo, θi-] *m* BOT plum tree

**cirugía** [si·ru·'xi·a, θi-] *f* MED surgery; **~ estética** cosmetic surgery

**cirujano, -a** [si·ru·'xa·no, -a; θi-] *m, f* MED surgeon

**cisco** ['sis·ko, θis-] *m* **1.** (*carbón*) coal dust **2.** (*jaleo*) fight

**Cisjordania** [sis·xor·'da·nja, θis-] *f* GEO (the) West Bank

**cisne** ['sis·ne, θis-] *m* swan

**cisterna** [sis·'ter·na, θis-] *f* tank; **barco ~** tanker

**cita** ['si·ta, θi-] *f* **1.** (*convocatoria*) appointment **2.** (*encuentro*) meeting; (*romántico*) date; **~ anual** annual meeting; **~ a ciegas** blind date; **tener una ~ con alguien** to be meeting sb; (*romántica*) to have a date with sb **3.** (*mención*) quotation

**citación** [si·ta·'sjon, θi·ta·'θjon] *f* JUR summons

**citar** [si·'tar, θi-] I. *vt* **1.** (*convocar*) to arrange to meet **2.** (*mencionar*) to quote **3.** JUR to summon II. *vr:* **~se** to arrange to meet

**cítrico, -a** ['si·tri·ko, -a; 'θi-] *adj* citric

**cítricos** ['si·tri·kos, 'θi-] *mpl* citrus fruits *pl*

**ciudad** [sju·'dad, θju-] *f* town; (*más grande*) city; **~ hermanada** twin town; **~ industrial** industrial town [*o* city]; **~ de origen** home town; **~ universitaria** university campus; **~ dormitorio** dormitory town

**ciudadanía** [sju·da·da·'ni·a, θju-] *f* **1.** (*nacionalidad*) citizenship **2.** (*ciudadanos*) citizenry, citizens *pl*

**ciudadano, -a** [sju·da·'da·no, -a; θju-] I. *adj* **1.** (*de la ciudad*) city **2.** (*del ciudadano*) civic II. *m, f* **1.** (*residente*) resident **2.** (*súbdito*) citizen

**cívico, -a** ['si·βi·ko, -a; 'θi-] *adj* (*del ciudadano*) civic

**civil** [si·'βil, θi-] *adj* civil; **derecho ~** civil law; **guerra ~** civil war

**civilización** [si·βi·li·sa·'sjon, θi·βi·li·θa·'θjon] *f* civilization

**civilizar** <z → c> [si·βi·li·'sar, θi·βi·li·'θar] *vt* to civilize

**civismo** [si·'βis·mo, θi-] *m* community spirit, civic-mindedness

**cizaña** [si·'sa·ɲa, θi·'θa-] *f* **1.** BOT darnel **2.** (*enemistad*) discord

**clamar** [kla·'mar] I. *vi* to cry out II. *vt* to demand

**clan** [klan] *m* clan

**clandestino, -a** [klan·des·'ti·no, -a] *adj* secret; **reunión clandestina** secret meeting

**claqué** [kla·'ke] *f* tap dancing

**clara** ['kla·ra] *f* (*del huevo*) white

**claramente** [kla·ra·'men·te] *adv* clearly

**clarear** [kla·re·'ar] I. *vi* **1.** (*amanecer*) to grow light; **al ~ el día** at dawn **2.** (*despejarse*) to clear up II. *vt* to brighten

**clarete** [kla·'re·te] *m* rosé (wine)

**claridad** [kla·ri·'dad] *f* **1.** (*luminosidad*) brightness **2.** (*lucidez*) clarity

**clarificar** <c → qu> [kla·ri·fi·'kar] *vt* **1.** (*iluminar*) to illuminate **2.** (*aclarar*) to clarify

**clarinete** [kla·ri·'ne·te] *m* (*instrumento*) clarinet

**clarividente** [kla·ri·βi·'den·te] *adj* **1.** (*perspicaz*) discerning **2.** (*que percibe*) clairvoyant

**claro** ['kla·ro] I. *interj* of course II. *m* **1.** (*hueco*) gap **2.** (*calvero*) clearing III. *adv* clearly

**claro, -a** ['kla·ro, -a] *adj* **1.** (*iluminado*) bright; **azul ~** light blue **2.** (*evidente*) clear; **poner** [*o* **sacar**] **en ~** to clarify

**clase** ['kla·se] *f* **1.** (*tipo*) kind; **trabajos de toda ~** all kinds of jobs **2.** (*categoría*) class; **~ turista** tourist class; **~ media** middle class **3.** ENS class; (*aula*) classroom; **dar ~s** to teach

**clasicismo** [kla·si·'sis·mo, -'θis·mo] *m* classicism

**clásico, -a** ['kla·si·ko, -a] I. *adj* classical; *fig* classic II. *m, f* classic

**clasificación** [kla·si·fi·ka·'sjon, -'θjon] *f* **1.** (*ordenación*) sorting **2.** *t.* BIO classification

**clasificar** <c → qu> [kla·si·fi·'kar] I. *vt* **~ por algo** (*ordenar*) to sort according to sth; BIO to classify under sth II. *vr:* **~se** to qualify

**clasismo** [kla·'sis·mo] *m* class-consciousness

**claudicar** <c → qu> [klau·di·'kar] *vi* **1.** (*principios*) ~ **de algo** to abandon sth **2.** (*ceder*) to give in

**claustro** ['klaus·tro] *m* ARTE cloister

**claustrofobia** [klaus·tro·'fo·βja] *f* claustrophobia

**cláusula** ['klau·su·la] *f* clause; (*ley*) article

**clausura** [klau·'su·ra] *f* **1.** (*cierre*) closure; **sesión de ~** closing session **2.** REL cloister

**clausurar** [klau·su·'rar] *vt* to close

**clavar** [kla·'βar] *vt* **1.** (*hincar*) to knock in; (*enclavar*) to nail **2.** (*fijar*) to fix; **tener la vista clavada en algo** to have one's eyes set on sth **3.** *inf* (*dar*) to give **4.** *inf* (*cobrar*) to rip off

**clave** ['kla·βe] **I.** *adj inv* key **II.** *f* **1.** (*secreto*) ~ **de algo** key to sth **2.** (*código*) code; ~ **de acceso** password; **en ~** coded **3.** MÚS clef

**clavel** [kla·'βel] *m* carnation

**clavícula** [kla·'βi·ku·la] *f* collar bone

**clavija** [kla·'βi·xa] *f* **1.** TÉC pin; (*enchufe*) plug **2.** MÚS peg ▶ **apretar las ~s a alguien** to put the screws on sb

**clavo** ['kla·βo] *m* **1.** (*punta*) nail; **dar en el ~** to hit the nail on the head **2.** (*especia*) clove

**claxon** ['klak·son] *m* horn

**clemencia** [kle·'men·sja, -θja] *f* mercy

**clemente** [kle·'men·te] *adj* merciful

**cleptómano, -a** [klep·'to·ma·no, -a] *adj, m, f* PSICO kleptomaniac

**clérigo** ['kle·ri·ɣo] *m* clergyman; (*católico*) priest

**clero** ['kle·ro] *m* clergy

**cliché** [kli·'tʃe] *m* **1.** (*tópico*) cliché **2.** FOTO negative

**cliente, -a** ['kljen·te] *m, f* customer; (*de un abogado*) client; ~ **fijo** regular customer

**clientela** [kljen·'te·la] *f* customers *pl*; (*de un abogado*) clients *pl*

**clima** ['kli·ma] *m* **1.** (*atmósfera*) atmosphere **2.** GEO climate

**clínica** ['kli·ni·ka] *f* clinic

**clip** [klip] *m* (*pinza*) clip

**clítoris** ['kli·to·ris] *m inv* clitoris

**cloaca** [klo·'a·ka] *f* sewer

**clon** [klon] *m* BIO clone

**clonar** [klo·'nar] *vt* to clone

**cloro** ['klo·ro] *m* chlorine

**clorofila** [klo·ro·'fi·lja] *f* chlorophyl(l)

**club** <clubs *o* clubes> [kluβ] *m* club; ~ **deportivo** sports club

**cm** [sen·'ti·me·tro, θen-] *abr de* **centímetro** cm.

**coacción** [ko·ak·'sjon, -aɣ·'θjon] *f* coercion

**coaccionar** [ko·ak·sjo·'nar, ko·aɣ·'θjo-] *vt* to coerce

**coagular(se)** [ko·a·ɣu·'lar·(se)] *vt, (vr)* to coagulate

**coágulo** [ko·'a·ɣu·lo] *m* clot

**coalición** [koa·li·'sjon, -'θjon] *f* coalition

**coartada** [koar·'ta·da] *f* alibi

**coartar** [koar·'tar] *vt* (*libertad*) to restrict; (*persona*) to inhibit

**coba** ['ko·βa] *f* lie; **dar ~ a alguien** to suck up to sb

**cobalto** [ko·'βal·to] *m* cobalt

**cobarde** [ko·'βar·de] **I.** *adj* cowardly **II.** *m* coward

**cobardía** [ko·βar·'di·a] *f* cowardice

**cobaya** [ko·'βa·ja] *m o f* guinea pig

**cobija** [ko·'βi·xa] *f* **1.** AmL (*manta*) blanket **2.** *pl* AmL (*ropa de cama*) bedclothes *pl*; **pegarse a alguien las ~s** to oversleep

**cobijar** [ko·βi·xar] **I.** *vt* **1.** (*proteger*) to shelter **2.** (*acoger*) to give shelter to **II.** *vr*: ~**se** to take shelter

**cobo** ['ko·βo] *m* AmC, Ant **1.** ZOOL giant sea snail **2.** (*persona*) unsociable person

**cobra** ['ko·βra] *f* cobra

**cobrar** [ko·'βrar] **I.** *vt* **1.** (*recibir*) to receive; (*suma*) to collect; (*cheque*) to cash; (*sueldo*) to earn; **¿me cobra, por favor?** how much do I owe you? **2.** (*intereses*) to charge; (*deudas*) to recover **3.** (*conseguir*) ~ **ánimos** to gather courage **II.** *vi* **1.** (*sueldo*) to get one's wages **2.** *inf* (*una paliza*) to get a beating; **¡que vas a ~!** you're going to get it! **III.** *vr*: ~**se** to cash up; *fig* to claim

**cobre** ['ko·βre] *m* **1.** QUÍM copper **2.** AmL (*moneda*) copper coin

**cobro** ['ko·βro] *m* **1.** (*acto*) recovery

**2.** FIN (*impuestos*) collection; (*pago*) payment; **llamar a ~ revertido** to reverse the charges **3.** *pl* COM arrears *pl*

**cocaína** [ko·ka·'i·na] *f* cocaine

**cocción** [kok·'sjon, koɣ·'θjon] *f* cooking; (*duración*) cooking time

**cocer** [ko·'ser, -'θer] *irr* **I.** *vt* (*cocinar*) to cook; (*hervir*) to boil **II.** *vi* **1.** (*cocinar*) to cook **2.** (*hervir*) to boil **III.** *vr:* **~se 1.** (*cocinarse*) to be cooked **2.** (*tramarse*) to be going on **3.** *inf* (*pasar calor*) to be sweltering

**cocha** ['ko·tʃa] *f AmS* (*laguna*) lagoon; (*charco*) puddle

**cochayuyo** [ko·tʃa·'ju·jo] *m AmS* BOT rockweed

**coche** ['ko·tʃe] *m* **1.** (*automóvil*) car; **~ de bomberos** fire engine; **~ de carreras** DEP racing car; **ir en ~** to go by car **2.** (*de caballos*) coach, carriage

**coche-cama** <coches-cama> ['ko·tʃe·'ka·ma] *m* FERRO sleeping car

**cochecito** [ko·tʃe·'si·to, -'θi·to] *m* baby carriage

**coche-patrulla** <coches-patrulla> ['ko·tʃe-pa·'tru·ja, -ʎa] *m* patrol car

**cochera** [ko·'tʃe·ra] *f* garage; **~ de tranvías** tram depot

**cochinada** [ko·tʃi·'na·da] *f inf* filthy thing

**cochinillo** [ko·tʃi·'ni·jo, -ʎo] *m* piglet; **~ asado** roast suckling pig

**cochino, -a** [ko·'tʃi·no, -a] **I.** *adj inf* filthy **II.** *m, f* **1.** ZOOL (*macho*) pig; (*hembra*) sow **2.** *inf* (*guarro*) swine

**cocido** [ko·'si·do, ko·'θi-] *m* stew (*made with chickpeas and meat*)

**cocina** [ko·'si·na, ko·'θi·] *f* **1.** (*habitación*) kitchen **2.** (*aparato*) stove **3.** (*arte*) cookery, cooking; **libro de ~** cookbook

**cocinar** [ko·si·'nar, ko·'θi·] *vt, vi* to cook

**cocinero, -a** [ko·si·'ne·ro, -a; ko·'θi·] *m, f* cook

**coco** ['ko·ko] *m* **1.** BOT (*fruto*) coconut; (*árbol*) coconut palm **2.** *inf* (*cabeza*) head; **comerse el ~** to worry **3.** *inf* (*ogro*) bogeyman

**cocodrilo** [ko·ko·'dri·lo] *m* crocodile

**cocoliche** [ko·ko·'li·tʃe] *m Arg, Urug* LING *pidgin Spanish of Italian immigrants*

**cocotero** [ko·ko·'te·ro] *m* coconut palm

**cóctel** <cócteles> ['kok·tel] *m* cocktail

**coctelera** [kok·te·'le·ra] *f* cocktail shaker

**cocuy** [ko·'kuj] *m AmL* **1.** BOT agave **2.** (*bebida alcohólica*) corn whiskey

**cocuyo** [ko·'ku·jo] *m AmL* **1.** ZOOL firefly **2.** AUTO rear light

**codazo** [ko·'da·so, -θo] *m* nudge (with one's elbow)

**codear** [ko·de·'ar] **I.** *vi* to nudge **II.** *vr:* **~se** to rub shoulders [*o* elbows]

**codicia** [ko·'di·sja, -θja] *f* greed; (*algo ajeno*) covetousness; **~ de algo** greed for sth

**codiciar** [ko·di·'sjar, -'θjar] *vt* to covet

**codicioso, -a** [ko·di·'sjo·so, -a; ko·di·'θjo-] *adj* covetous

**codificar** <c → qu> [ko·di·fi·'kar] *vt* to code; *t.* COMPUT to encode

**código** ['ko·di·ɣo] *m* code; **~ de circulación** highway code; **Código Civil** civil code; **~ de barras** bar code; **~ postal** postal code, zip code; **mensaje en ~** coded message

**codillo** [ko·'di·jo, -ʎo] *m* **1.** ZOOL elbow **2.** CULIN knuckle

**codo** ['ko·do] *m* **1.** ANAT elbow; **trabajar ~ a ~** to work side by side; **hablar por los ~s** *inf* to talk nonstop **2.** TÉC (*doblez*) elbow joint **3.** (*de camino*) bend

**codorniz** [ko·dor·'nis, -'niθ] *f* quail

**coetáneo, -a** [koe·'ta·neo, -a] *adj, m, f* contemporary

**cofradía** [ko·fra·'di·a] *f* **1.** (*hermandad*) brotherhood **2.** (*gremio*) guild

**cofre** ['ko·fre] *m* chest; (*baúl*) trunk; (*de joyas*) jewel case

**coger** <g → j> [ko·'xer] **I.** *vt* **1.** (*agarrar*) to take hold, to seize; (*del suelo*) to pick up; (*flores*) to pick; **le cogió del brazo** he/she took him by the arm; **le cogió en brazos** he/she picked him up in his/her arms **2.** (*quitar*) to take away **3.** (*atrapar*) to catch; (*apresar*) to capture **4.** AUTO (*atropellar*) to knock down, to run over **5.** (*hábito*) to acquire; **~ cariño a alguien** to take a liking to sb; **~ el hábito de fumar** to start smoking **6.** (*enfermedad*) to catch; **~ frío** to catch a cold; **ha cogido una gripe** he's/she's caught the flu **7.** (*sorprender*) to find **8.** (*obtener*) to get; **¿vas a ~ el piso?**

are you going to take the apartment?
**9.** (*tomar*) to take; **~ el tren/autobús**
to take the train/bus **10.** *AmL vulg* (*copular*) to screw **II.** *vi* **1.** (*tener sitio*) to
fit **2.** *AmL vulg* (*copular*) to screw

**cognitivo, -a** [koɣ·ni·'ti·βo, -a] *adj* cognitive

**cogote** [ko·'ɣo·te] *m inf* scruff; **estar hasta el ~** *inf* to have had enough

**coherencia** [ko·e·'ren·sja, -θja] *f* coherence

**coherente** [ko·e·'ren·te] *adj* coherent

**cohesión** [ko·e·'sjon] *f* cohesion

**cohete** [ko·'e·te] *m* rocket

**cohibido, -a** [koi·'βi·do, -a] *adj* **1.** (*intimidado*) intimidated **2.** (*inhibido*) inhibited

**coima** ['koi·ma] *f And, CSur* (*soborno*) bribe; (*dinero*) rake-off

**coincidencia** [koin·si·'den·sja, koin·θi·'den·θja] *f* **1.** (*simultaneidad*) coincidence; **¡qué ~!** what a coincidence! **2.** (*acuerdo*) agreement

**coincidir** [koin·si·'dir, koin·θi·] *vi* **1.** (*sucesos*) to coincide **2.** (*toparse*) to meet; **~ con alguien** to meet sb **3.** (*concordar*) to agree; **~ con alguien** to agree with sb

**coipo** ['koi·po] *m Arg, Chile* zool coypu

**coito** ['koi·to] *m* coitus, (sexual) intercourse

**cojear** [ko·xe·'ar] *vi* (*persona*) to limp; (*mueble*) to wobble; *fig* (*tener defecto*) to have a weak point

**cojín** [ko·'xin] *m* cushion

**cojo, -a** ['ko·xo, -a] *adj* (*persona*) lame; (*mueble*) wobbly; **a la pata coja** on one leg

**cojón** [ko·'xon] *m vulg* **1.** *pl* (*testículos*) balls *pl* **2.** *pl* (*interjecciones*) **¡cojones!** damn it!; **es una música de cojones** it's really cool music

**cojonudo, -a** [ko·xo·'nu·do, -a] *adj vulg* fantastic, fucking great *vulg*

**cojudo, -a** [ko·'xu·do, -a] *adj AmL* stupid

**col** [kol] *f* cabbage; **~es de Bruselas** Brussels sprouts

**cola** ['ko·la] *f* **1.** (*de cometa*) *t.* ANAT tail **2.** (*al esperar*) line; **hacer ~** to line up; **ponerse a la ~** to get in line **3.** (*pegamento*) glue

**colaboración** [ko·la·βo·ra·'sjon, -'θjon] *f* collaboration; (*periódico*) contribution

**colaborador(a)** [ko·la·βo·ra·'dor, --'do·ra] **I.** *adj* collaborating **II.** *m(f)* collaborator; LIT contributor

**colaborar** [ko·la·βo·'rar] *vi* **1.** (*cooperar*) to collaborate **2.** LIT to contribute

**colada** [ko·'la·da] *f* (*de ropa*) washing

**coladera** [ko·la·'de·ra] *f Méx* (*alcantarilla*) sewer

**colador** [ko·la·'dor] *m* sieve, strainer

**colapsar** [ko·lap·'sar] **I.** *vt* to bring to a standstill; **~ la red** COMPUT to bring down [*o* to collapse] the net **II.** *vi, vr:* **~se 1.** (*tráfico*) to come to a standstill **2.** MED to collapse

**colapso** [ko·'lap·so] *m* **1.** MED collapse **2.** (*paralización*) standstill

**colar** <o → ue> [ko·'lar] **I.** *vt* (*filtrar*) to filter; (*metal*) to cast **II.** *vi* **1.** (*líquido*) to seep (through); (*aire*) to get in **2.** *inf* (*información*) to be credible; **a ver si cuela** let's see if it comes off **III.** *vr:* **~se 1.** *inf* (*entrar*) to slip in **2.** (*en una cola*) to jump in line [*o* line] **3.** *inf* (*equivocarse*) to be wrong

**colcha** ['kol·tʃa] *f* bedspread

**colchón** [kol·'tʃon] *m* mattress; **~ de agua** water bed

**colchoneta** [kol·tʃo·'ne·ta] *f* (*neumática*) airbed; (*isoterma*) foam mattress; (*de gimnasia*) mat

**colección** [ko·lek·'sjon, -leɣ·'θjon] *f* collection

**coleccionar** [ko·lek·sjo·'nar, ko·leɣ·θjo-] *vt* to collect

**coleccionista** [ko·lek·sjo·'nis·ta, ko·leɣ·θjo-] *mf* collector

**colecta** [ko·'lek·ta] *f* collection (for charity); REL collect

**colectivo** [ko·lek·'ti·βo] *m* **1.** POL collective, group **2.** *Méx* (*microbús*) minibus (*that can be flagged down*)

**colectivo, -a** [ko·lek·'ti·βo, -a] *adj* collective; **acción colectiva** joint action

**colega** [ko·'le·ɣa] *mf* **1.** (*compañero*) colleague **2.** (*homólogo*) counterpart **3.** *inf* (*amigo*) pal, buddy

**colegial(a)** [ko·le·'xjal, -'xja·la] *m(f)* schoolboy *m*, schoolgirl *f*

C

**colegio** [ko·'le·xjo] *m* **1.** ENS school; **ir al ~** to go to school **2.** *AmL* (*universidad*) college; **~ mayor** hall of residence **3.** (*profesional*) association; **~ de abogados** bar association

**cólera¹** ['ko·le·ra] *m* MED cholera

**cólera²** ['ko·le·ra] *f* (*ira*) anger; **acceso de ~** fit of anger

**colesterol** [ko·les·te·'rol] *m* cholesterol

**colgado, -a** [kol·'ɣa·do, -a] *adj* (*cuadro*) hung up; (*bandera*) hung out

**colgador** [kol·ɣa·'dor] *m* hanger; (*gancho*) (coat)hook; (*percha*) coat-hanger

**colgante** [kol·'ɣan·te] **I.** *adj* hanging, **puente ~** (*entre dos lados*) suspension bridge; (*de castillo*) drawbridge **II.** *m* pendant

**colgar** [kol·'ɣar] *irr* **I.** *vt* **1.** (*pender*) **~ algo** to hang sth; (*decorar*) to decorate with sth; **~ el teléfono** to put down the phone **2.** (*dejar*) **~ los libros** to abandon one's studies **3.** (*atribuir*) to attribute **II.** *vi* **1.** (*pender*) to hang; (*lengua*) to droop **2.** TEL (*auricular*) to hang up

**colibrí** [ko·li·'βri] *m* hummingbird

**cólico** ['ko·li·ko] *m* MED colic

**coliflor** [ko·li·'flor] *f* cauliflower

**colilla** [ko·'li·ja, -Áa] *f* cigarette butt

**colín** [ko·'lin] *m* AmC, Ant ZOOL American bobwhite

**colina** [ko·'li·na] *f* hill

**colindar** [ko·lin·'dar] *vi* **~ con algo** to adjoin sth

**colirio** [ko·'li·rjo] *m* eye drops *pl*

**colisión** [ko·li·'sjon] *f* collision

**collage** [ko·'laʃ] *m* ARTE collage

**collar** [ko·'jar, -'Áar] *m* (*adorno*) necklace; **~ de perlas** string of pearls; **~ de perro** dog collar

**colmado** [kol·'ma·do] *m* grocery store

**colmado, -a** [kol·'ma·do, -a] *adj* full; **un año ~ de felicidad** a very happy year

**colmena** [kol·'me·na] *f* beehive

**colmillo** [kol·'mi·jo, -Áo] *m* eyetooth; (*de elefante*) tusk; (*de perro*) fang

**colmo** ['kol·mo] *m* height ► **¡esto es el ~!** this is the last straw!; **para ~** on top of everything

**colocado, -a** [ko·lo·'ka·do, -a] *adj inf* (*bebido*) plastered; (*drogado*) high, stoned

**colocar** <c → qu> [ko·lo·'kar] **I.** *vt*

**1.** (*emplazar*) to place; (*ordenar*) to arrange; (*poner*) to put **2.** COM (*invertir*) to invest; (*mercancías*) to sell **3.** (*empleo*) to find a job for **II.** *vr:* **~se 1.** (*empleo*) to get a steady job **2.** (*sombrero*) to put on **3.** (*posicionarse*) to place oneself **4.** *inf* (*alcohol*) to get plastered; (*drogas*) to get high

**Colombia** [ko·'lom·bja] *f* Colombia

**colombiano, -a** [ko·lom·'bja·no, -a] *adj, m, f* Colombian

**Colón** [ko·'lon] *m* **1.** (*Cristóbal*) Columbus **2.** (*moneda*) colon

**colonia** [ko·'lo·nja] *f* **1.** (*grupo*) colony **2.** (*barrio*) suburb **3.** (*perfume*) cologne

**Colonia** [ko·'lo·nja] *f* Cologne; **agua de ~** eau de cologne

**coloniaje** [ko·lo·'nja·xe] *m AmL* **1.** (*período*) colonial period **2.** (*sistema*) system of colonial government **3.** *pey* (*esclavitud*) slavery

**colonialismo** [ko·lo·nja·'lis·mo] *m* colonialism

**colonización** [ko·lo·ni·sa·'sjon, -θa·'θjon] *f* **1.** (*conquista*) colonization **2.** (*población*) settling

**colonizador(a)** [ko·lo·ni·sa·'dor, -'do·ra; ko·lo·ni·θa·] **I.** *adj* colonizing **II.** *m(f)* **1.** (*conquistador*) colonizer **2.** (*poblador*) settler

**colonizar** <z → c> [ko·lo·ni·'sar, -'θar] *vt* **1.** (*conquistar*) to colonize **2.** (*poblar*) to settle

**colono** [ko·'lo·no, -a] *m* settler; (*labrador*) tenant farmer

**coloquial** [ko·lo·'kjal] *adj* LING colloquial

**coloquio** [ko·'lokjo] *m* conversation; (*científico*) colloquium

**color** [ko·'lor] *m* **1.** (*en general*) color; **un hombre de ~** a dark-skinned man; **nuestros ~es** DEP our team; **sacar los ~es a alguien** to embarrass sb **2.** (*sustancia*) dye **3.** POL (*ideología*) hue ► **verlo todo de ~ de rosa**) to see the world through rose-colored glasses

**colorado, -a** [ko·lo·'ra·do] *adj* (*rojo*) red; **ponerse ~** to blush

**colorante** [ko·lo·'ran·te] *adj, m* coloring

**colorear** [ko·lo·re·'ar] *vt* to color; (*pintar*) to paint

**colosal** [ko·lo·'sal] *adj* colossal

**columna** [ko·'lum·na] *f* column; *fig* pillar; **~ vertebral** ANAT spinal column

**columpiar** [ko·lum·'pjar] **I.** *vt* **1.** (*balancear*) to swing (to and fro) **2.** (*mecer*) to push on a swing **II.** *vr:* **~se** to swing

**columpio** [ko·'lum·pjo] *m* **1.** (*para niños*) swing **2.** *AmL* (*mecedora*) rocking chair

**coma**[1] ['ko·ma] *m* MED coma

**coma**[2] ['ko·ma] *f* LING comma

**comadre** [ko·'ma·dre] *f* **1.** *inf* (*comadrona*) midwife **2.** *inf* (*amiga íntima*) crony **3.** *inf* (*celestina*) go-between

**comadrona** [ko·ma·'dro·na] *f* midwife

**comando** [ko·'man·do] *m* MIL, COMPUT command

**comarca** [ko·'mar·ka] *f* (*zona*) area; (*región*) region

**comba** [kom·ba] *f* **1.** (*curvatura*) bend; (*de madera*) warp **2.** (*cuerda*) skipping rope; (*juego*) skipping; **saltar a la ~** to skip

**combar** [kom·'bar] *vt, vr:* **~se** to bend; (*madera*) to warp

**combate** [kom·'ba·te] *m* **1.** (*lucha*) combat; (*batalla*) battle **2.** DEP match; **~ de boxeo** boxing match; **fuera de ~** out of action

**combatir** [kom·ba·'tir] *vt, vi* to fight

**combinación** [kom·bi·na·'sjon, -'θjon] *f* **1.** (*composición*) combination; **~ ganadora** winning combination **2.** (*de transportes*) connection **3.** (*lencería*) slip

**combinar** [kom·bi·'nar] *vt* **1.** (*componer*) to combine **2.** (*unir*) to unite; **~ ideas** to link ideas **3.** (*coordinar*) to coordinate; MAT to permute

**combustible** [kom·bus·'ti·βle] **I.** *adj* combustible **II.** *m* fuel

**combustión** [kom·bus·'tjon] *f* combustion

**comedia** [ko·'me·dja] *f* **1.** TEAT (*obra*) play; (*divertida*) comedy **2.** CINE comedy **3.** *inf* (*farsa*) farce; **hacer ~** to pretend

**comediante, -a** [ko·me·'djan·te, -a] *m, f* **1.** CINE actor **2.** (*farsante*) fraud

**comedor** [ko·me·'dor] *m* (*sala*) dining room; (*en una empresa*) cafeteria

**comentador(a)** [ko·men·ta·'dor, -·'do·ra] *m(f)* commentator

**comentar** [ko·men·'tar] *vt* **1.** (*hablar*) to talk about; (*hacer comentarios*) to comment on **2.** (*una obra*) to discuss, to review

**comentario** [ko·men·'ta·rjo] *m* **1.** (*general*) comment **2.** *pl* (*murmuraciones*) gossip

**comentarista** [ko·men·ta·'ris·ta] *mf* commentator

**comenzar** [ko·men·'sar, -'θar] *irr como* **empezar** *vt, vi* to begin, to commence; **para ~** to begin with

**comer** [ko·'mer] **I.** *vi* **1.** (*alimentarse*) to eat; **dar de ~ a un animal** to feed an animal; **~ caliente** to have a warm meal **2.** (*almorzar*) to have lunch; **antes/después de ~** before/after lunch **II.** *vt* **1.** (*ingerir*) to eat **2.** *fig* (*consumir*) to consume **3.** (*corroer*) to eat away **4.** (*colores*) to fade **5.** (*en juegos*) to take **III.** *vr:* **~se 1.** (*ingerir*) to eat up; **~se a alguien a besos** to smother sb with kisses; **está para comérsela** she looks a treat **2.** (*corroer*) to eat away **3.** (*colores*) to fade **4.** (*palabras*) to skip; (*al pronunciar*) to slur

**comercial**[1] [ko·mer·'sjal, -'θjal] **I.** *adj* commercial **II.** *mf* sales representative

**comercial**[2] [ko·mer·'sjal, 'θjal] *m* *AmL* (*anuncio*) commercial

**comercializar** <z → c> [ko·mer·sja·li·'sar, -θja·li·'θar] *vt* (*producto*) to market

**comerciante, -a** [ko·mer·'sjan·te, -a; -'θjan·te, -a] *m, f* shopkeeper; (*negociante*) dealer

**comerciar** [ko·mer·'sjar, -'θjar] *vi* **1.** (*tener trato con*) **~ con un país** to trade with a country **2.** (*traficar en*) **~ en algo** to deal in sth

**comercio** [ko·'mer·sjo, -θjo] *m* **1.** (*actividad*) trade; **~ exterior** foreign trade; **~ justo** fair trade; **~ al por mayor** wholesale trade **2.** (*tienda*) shop

**comestibles** [ko·mes·'ti·βles] *mpl* foods; **tienda de ~** grocer's (shop), grocery

**cometa**[1] [ko·'me·ta] *m* ASTR comet

**cometa**[2] [ko·'me·ta] *f* (*de papel*) kite

**cometer** [ko·me·'ter] *vt t.* JUR to commit; (*error*) to make

**comezón** [ko·me·'son, -'θon] *f* (*picor*) itch

**cómic** ['ko·mik] *m* <cómics> comic

**comicios** [ko·'mi·sjos, -θjos] *mpl* elections *pl*

**cómico, -a** ['ko·mi·ko, -a] I. *adj* comedy; (*divertido*) comical II. *m, f* comedian

**comida** [ko·'mi·da] *f* 1. (*alimento*) food; (*plato*) meal; ~ **para animales** pet food; ~ **basura/rápida** junk/fast food; ~ **casera** home-style cooking 2. (*horario*) ~ **principal** main meal (of the day) 3. (*almuerzo*) lunch; ~ **de negocios** business lunch 4. *Col, Perú, Chile* (*cena*) supper

**comienzo** [ko·'mjen·so, -θo] *m* beginning; **al** ~ at first; **a ~s de mes** at the beginning of the month

**comino** [ko·'mi·no] *m* cumin; **no valer un** ~ *inf* not to be worth anything

**comisaría** [ko·mi·sa·'ri·a] *f* (*edificio*) ~ **de policía** police station [*o* precinct]

**comisariato** [ko·mi·sa·'rja·to] *m AmL* company store; (*almacén*) warehouse

**comisario, -a** [ko·mi·'sa·rjo, -a] *m, f* (*de policía*) superintendent, chief of police

**comisión** [ko·mi·'sjon] *f* 1. (*delegación*) commission; (*comité*) committee; **Comisión Europea** European Commission; ~ **permanente** standing committee 2. COM commission; **a** ~ on a commission basis

**comisura** [ko·mi·'su·ra] *f* ANAT commissure; ~ **de los labios** corner of the mouth

**comité** [ko·mi·'te] *m* committee; ~ **de empresa** works committee

**comitiva** [ko·mi·'ti·βa] *f* procession; ~ **fúnebre** cortege

**como** ['ko·mo] I. *adv* 1. (*del modo que*) as, like; **hazlo** ~ **quieras** do it any way you like; ~ **quien dice** so to speak; **blanco** ~ **la nieve** white as snow 2. (*comparativo*) as; **es tan alto** ~ **su hermano** he's as tall as his brother 3. (*aproximadamente*) about; **hace** ~ **un año** about a year ago 4. (*y también*) as well as 5. (*en calidad de*) as; **trabaja** ~ **camarero** he works as a waiter II. *conj* 1. (*causal*) as, since; ~ **no tengo tiempo, no voy** I'm not going because I don't have time 2. (*condicional*) if 3. (*con "si" +subj o con*

"*que*") as if

**cómo** ['ko·mo] I. *adv* 1. (*modal, exclamativo*) how; **¿~ estás?** how are you?; **¿~ (dice)?** sorry?, pardon? 2. (*por qué*) why; **¡~ no!** certainly! II. *m* **el** ~ the how

**cómoda** ['ko·mo·da] *f* chest (of drawers), dresser

**comodidad** [ko·mo·di·'dad] *f* 1. (*confort*) comfort 2. (*conveniencia*) convenience

**comodín** [ko·mo·'din] *m* 1. (*en juegos*) joker 2. (*palabra*) all-purpose word 3. COMPUT wild card

**cómodo, -a** ['ko·mo·do, -a] *adj* 1. **ser** (*cosa*) comfortable; (*conveniente*) convenient 2. **ser** (*perezoso*) lazy 3. **estar** (*a gusto*) comfortable; **¡ponte ~!** make yourself comfortable!

**comoquiera** [ko·mo·'kje·ra] *conj* 1. (*causal*) ~ **que** +*subj* since 2. (*concesiva*) ~ **que** +*subj* in whatever way; ~ **que sea eso** however that may be

**compact disc** ['kom·pak (disk)] *m* compact disc

**compacto, -a** [kom·'pak·to, -a] *adj* compact; (*denso*) dense; (*firme*) firm; **disco** ~ compact disc

**compadecer** [kom·pa·de·'ser, -'θer] *irr como crecer* I. *vt* to feel sorry for II. *vr* ~**se de alguien/algo** to (take) pity (on) sb/sth

**compadre** [kom·'pa·dre] *m* (*amigo*) friend, buddy

**compadrear** [kom·pa·dre·'ar] *vi CSur* (*presumir*) to show off

**compadrito** [kom·pa·'dri·to] *m AmS* braggart

**compaginar** [kom·pa·xi·'nar] I. *vt* (*combinar*) to combine II. *vr:* ~**se** 1. (*combinar*) to combine 2. (*armonizar*) to go together

**compañerismo** [kom·pa·ɲe·'ris·mo] *m* companionship; DEP team spirit

**compañero, -a** [kom·pa·'ɲe·ro, -a] *m, f* 1. (*persona*) companion; (*amigo*) friend; (*pareja*) partner; ~ **de clase** schoolmate; UNIV fellow student; ~ **de piso** roommate; ~ **de trabajo** fellow worker 2. (*cosa*) other one (of a pair)

**compañía** [kom·pa·'ɲi·a] *f* company;

**animal de** ~ pet; **hacer** ~ **a alguien** to keep sb company

**comparación** [kom·pa·ra·'sjon, -'θjon] *f* comparison; **no hay ni punto de** ~ there's no comparison

**comparar** [kom·pa·'rar] **I.** *vt* to compare **II.** *vr:* ~**se** to be compared

**comparativo** [kom·pa·ra·'ti·βo] *m* comparative

**comparecer** [kom·pa·re·'ser, -'θer] *irr como crecer vi* t. JUR to appear (in court)

**compartim(i)ento** [kom·par·ti·'m(j)en·to] *m* compartment

**compartir** [kom·par·'tir] *vt* **1.** (*tener en común*) to share **2.** (*repartirse*) to share (out)

**compás** [kom·'pas] *m* **1.** (*en dibujo*) compass **2.** (*ritmo*) beat; MÚS time **3.** NÁUT compass

**compasión** [kom·pa·'sjon] *f* ~ **de alguien** pity on sb, compassion [*o* sympathy] with sb; **sin** ~ pitiless(ly)

**compasivo, -a** [kom·pa·'si·βo, -a] *adj* compassionate, sympathetic

**compatibilidad** [kom·pa·ti·βi·li·'dad] *f* compatibility

**compatible** [kom·pa·'ti·βle] *adj* compatible

**compatriota** [kom·pa·'trjo·ta] *mf* compatriot, fellow citizen

**compenetración** [kom·pe·ne·tra·'sjon, -'θjon] *f* (mutual) understanding

**compenetrarse** [kom·pe·ne·'trar·se] *vr* (*identificarse*) to reach an understanding

**compensación** [kom·pen·sa·'sjon, -'θjon] *f* compensation

**compensar** [kom·pen·'sar] *vt* ~ **de algo** to compensate for sth

**competencia** [kom·pe·'ten·sja, -θja] *f* **1.** t. COM competition; (*rivalidad*) rivalry; ~ **desleal** unfair competition **2.** (*responsabilidad*) responsibility; **esto (no) es de mi** ~ I'm not responsible for this

**competente** [kom·pe·'ten·te] *adj* competent

**competición** [kom·pe·ti·'sjon, -'θjon] *f* competition

**competidor(a)** [kom·pe·ti·'dor, -·'do·ra] **I.** *adj* competing **II.** *m(f)* t. ECON competitor

**competir** [kom·pe·'tir] *irr como pedir vi* **1.** (*enfrentarse*) ~ **por algo** to compete for sth **2.** (*igualarse*) to rival each other

**competitividad** [kom·pe·ti·ti·βi·'dad] *f* competitiveness

**competitivo, -a** [kom·pe·ti·'ti·βo, -a] *adj* competitive

**compilar** [kom·pi·'lar] *vt* t. COMPUT to compile

**complacer** [kom·pla·'ser, -'θer] *irr como crecer* **I.** *vt* to please **II.** *vr* ~**se en algo** to be pleased to sth

**complaciente** [kom·pla·'sjen·te, -'θjen·te] *adj* **1.** (*servicial*) obliging **2.** (*indulgente*) ~ **con alguien** indulgent towards sb

**complejidad** [kom·ple·xi·'dad] *f* complexity

**complejo** [kom·'ple·xo] *m* complex

**complejo, -a** [kom·'ple·xo, -a] *adj* complex

**complemento** [kom·ple·'men·to] *m* **1.** t. LING complement **2.** *pl* (*accesorio*) accessory

**completamente** [kom·ple·ta·'men·te] *adv* completely

**completar** [kom·ple·'tar] *vt* to complete

**completo, -a** [kom·'ple·to, -a] *adj* (*íntegro*) complete; (*total*) total; (*lleno*) full; (*espectáculo*) sold out; **pensión completa** full board

**complexión** [kom·plek·'sjon] *f* **1.** (*constitución*) constitution, build **2.** *AmL* (*tez*) complexion

**complicación** [kom·pli·ka·'sjon, -'θjon] *f* t. MED (*problema*) complication

**complicar** <c → qu> [kom·pli·'kar] **I.** *vt* (*dificultar*) to complicate **II.** *vr:* ~**se** (*dificultarse*) to get complicated

**cómplice** ['kom·pli·se, -θe] *mf* t. JUR accomplice

**complicidad** [kom·pli·θi·'dad, kom·pli·θi-] *f* complicity

**componente** [kom·po·'nen·te] *m* **1.** t. TÉC component **2.** (*miembro*) member

**componer** [kom·po·'ner] *irr como poner* **I.** *vt* **1.** (*formar*) to put together; (*organizar*) to organize **2.** (*constituir*) to make up **3.** t. MÚS to compose **4.** (*asear*) to arrange **5.** *AmL* (*castrar*) to castrate **6.** *AmL* (*hueso*) to set **II.** *vr:* ~**se 1.** (*constituirse*) to consist **2.** (*arreglarse*) to tidy oneself up **3.** *AmL* (*mejorarse*) to get better

**comportamiento** [kom·por·ta·'mjen·to] *m* conduct, behavior; *t.* TÉC performance

**comportar** [kom·por·'tar] **I.** *vt* to involve; **esto** (**no**) **comporta que** +*subj* this (doesn't) mean(s) that **II.** *vr:* ~**se** to behave

**composición** [kom·po·si·'sjon, -'θjon] *f t.* MÚS composition

**compositor(a)** [kom·po·si·'tor, -·'to·ra] *m(f)* composer

**compra** ['kom·pra] *f* purchase; ~**s** shopping; **ir de** ~**s** to go shopping

**comprador(a)** [kom·pra·'dor, -·'do·ra] *m(f)* buyer; (*cliente*) customer

**comprar** [kom·'prar] *vt* **1.** (*adquirir*) to buy; ~ **al contado** to pay cash; ~ **a plazos** to buy on an installment plan **2.** (*corromper*) to buy off

**comprender** [kom·pren·'der] *vt* **1.** (*entender*) to understand; **hacerse** ~ to make oneself understood; ~ **mal** to misunderstand **2.** (*contener*) to comprise; (*abarcar*) to take in

**comprensible** [kom·pren·'si·βle] *adj* understandable, comprehensible

**comprensión** [kom·pren·'sjon] *f* (*capacidad*) understanding; (*entendimiento*) comprehension

**comprensivo, -a** [kom·pren·'si·βo, -a] *adj* **1.** (*benévolo*) understanding **2.** (*tolerante*) tolerant

**compresa** [kom·'pre·sa] *f* **1.** *t.* MED (*apósito*) compress **2.** (*higiénica*) sanitary napkin [o pad]

**comprimido** [kom·pri·'mi·do] *m* pill

**comprimir** [kom·pri·'mir] *vt t.* FÍS, TÉC to compress

**comprobación** [kom·pro·βa·'sjon, -'θjon] *f* **1.** (*control*) checking **2.** (*verificación*) verification; (*prueba*) proof

**comprobante** [kom·pro·'βan·te] *m* voucher, proof

**comprobar** (o → ue) [kom·pro·'βar] *vt* **1.** (*controlar*) to check **2.** (*verificar*) to verify; (*probar*) to prove

**comprometedor(a)** [kom·pro·me·'te·dor, -·'do·ra] *adj* compromising

**comprometer** [kom·pro·me·'ter] **I.** *vt* **1.** (*implicar*) to involve **2.** (*exponer*) to endanger **3.** (*arriesgar*) to put at risk **4.** (*obligar*) to commit **II.** *vr:* ~**se 1.** (*implicarse*) to compromise oneself **2.** (*obligarse*) to commit oneself

**compromiso** [kom·pro·'mi·so] *m* **1.** (*vinculación*) commitment; (*obligación*) obligation; **visita de** ~ formal visit; **sin** ~ without obligation **2.** (*promesa*) promise **3.** (*acuerdo*) agreement **4.** (*aprieto*) awkward situation **5.** (*cita*) engagement

**compulsar** [kom·pul·'sar] *vt* to compare; JUR to certify

**compulsivo, -a** [kom·pul·'si·βo, -a] *adj* compulsive

**computador** [kom·pu·ta·'dor] *m* computer

**computador(a)** [kom·pu·ta·'dor, -·'do·ra] *adj* computer

**computadora** [kom·pu·ta·'do·ra] *f AmL* computer

**cómputo** ['kom·pu·to] *m* calculation; ~ **de votos** count of votes

**comulgar** <g → gu> [ko·mul·'yar] *vi* REL to take communion; *fig* (*estar de acuerdo*) to agree

**común** [ko·'mun] *adj* common; **de** ~ **acuerdo** by common consent; **sentido** ~ common sense; **fuera de lo** ~ out of the ordinary; **poco** ~ unusual; **por lo** ~ usually

**comunal** [ko·mu·'nal] *adj* communal

**comunicación** [ko·mu·ni·ka·'sjon, -'θjon] *f* **1.** (*en general*) communication **2.** (*conexión*) connection; ~ **telefónica** telephone call **3.** (*de transporte*) link **4.** *pl t.* TEL communications *pl*

**comunicado** [ko·mu·ni·'ka·do] *m* communiqué; ~ **de prensa** press release

**comunicar** <c → qu> [ko·mu·ni·'kar] **I.** *vi* **1.** (*estar unido*) to be joined; (*estar en contacto*) to be connected **2.** (*conectar*) to connect **3.** (*teléfono*) to be busy **II.** *vt* **1.** (*informar*) to inform **2.** (*transmitir*) to communicate **3.** (*unir*) to connect **III.** *vr:* ~**se 1.** (*entenderse*) to communicate **2.** (*relacionarse*) to be connected

**comunicativo, -a** [ko·mu·ni·ka·'ti·βo, -a] *adj* communicative

**comunidad** [ko·mu·ni·'dad] *f* community; **~ de vecinos** residents' association

**comunión** [ko·mu·'njon] *f* communion

**comunismo** [ko·mu·'nis·mo] *m* POL communism

**comunista** [ko·mu·'nis·ta] *adj* POL communist

**comunitario, -a** [ko·mu·ni·'ta·rjo, -a] *adj* 1. (*colectivo*) communal 2. (*municipal*) community 3. POL (*Comunidad Europea*) Community

**con** [kon] I. *prep* 1. (*compañía, modo*) with; **~ el tiempo...** with time... 2. MAT **3 ~ 5** 3 point 5 3. (*actitud*) (**para**) to, towards 4. (*circunstancia*) **~ este tiempo...** in this weather... 5. (*a pesar de*) in spite of II. *conj* + *infin* if; **~ que** +*subj* as long as

**cóncavo, -a** [ˈkon·ka·βo, -a] *adj* concave

**concebir** [kon·se·'βir, kon·θe·-] *irr como pedir* *vt, vi* to conceive; **~ esperanzas** to have hopes

**conceder** [kon·se·'der, kon·θe·-] *vt* (*otorgar*) to grant; (*asignar*) to give; **~ la palabra a alguien** to give sb the floor; **~ un premio** to award a prize

**concejal(a)** [kon·se·'xal, -·'xa·la, kon·θe·-] *m(f)* councilman *m*, councilwoman *f*

**concentración** [kon·sen·tra·'sjon, -θen·tra·'θjon] *f* concentration

**concentrar** [kon·sen·'trar, kon·θen·-] I. *vt* to concentrate II. *vr:* **~se** 1. (*reunirse*) to assemble; (*agruparse*) to gather together 2. (*centrarse*) to concentrate

**concepto** [kon·'sep·to, kon·'θep-] *m* 1. (*noción*) notion; (*plan*) concept 2. (*opinión*) opinion 3. (*motivo*) **bajo ningún ~** on no account 4. (*calidad*) **en ~ de** by way of

**concernir** [kon·ser·'nir, kon·θer·-] *irr como cernir* *vi* to concern; **en** [*o* **por**] **lo que concierne a alguien...** as far as sb is concerned...

**concertar** <e → ie> [kon·ser·'tar, kon·θer·-] I. *vi* *t.* LING to agree II. *vt* (*arreglar*) to arrange

**concesión** [kon·se·'sjon, kon·θe·-] *f* *t.*

concession

**concesionario, -a** [kon·θe·sjo·'na·rjo, -a; kon·θe·-] *m, f* dealer

**concha** [ˈkon·tʃa] *f* 1. (*del molusco*) shell; (*de tortuga*) tortoiseshell 2. AmL (*descaro*) nerve 3. AmL vulg (*vulva*) pussy

**conchabar** [kon·tʃa·'βar] *vt* AmL to hire

**conchudo, -a** [kon·'tʃu·do, -a] *adj* 1. AmL inf (*sinvergüenza*) shameless 2. *Méx, Col* inf (*indolente*) sluggish

**conciencia** [kon·'sjen·sja, -'θjen·θja] *f* 1. (*conocimiento*) awareness 2. (*moral*) conscience; **a ~** conscientiously; (**sin**) **cargo de ~** (without) remorse

**concienciar** [kon·sjen·'sjar, -θjen·'θjar] I. *vt* to make aware II. *vr:* **~se** 1. (*convencerse*) to convince oneself 2. (*sensibilizarse*) to become aware

**concienzudo, -a** [kon·sjen·'su·do, -a; -θjen·'θu·do, -a] *adj* conscientious

**concierto** [kon·'sjer·to, kon·'θjer-] *m* 1. MÚS (*función*) concert; (*obra*) concerto 2. *t.* ECON (*acuerdo*) agreement

**conciliar** [kon·si·'ljar, kon·θi·-] *vt* to reconcile; (*armonizar*) to harmonize; **~ el sueño** *fig* to get to sleep

**concilio** [kon·'si·ljo, -'θi·ljo] *m* *t.* REL council

**conciso, -a** [kon·'si·so, -a; kon·'θi·-] *adj* concise

**concluir** [kon·klu·'ir] *irr como huir* I. *vt* 1. (*terminar*) to complete 2. (*deducir*) **~ de algo** to conclude from sth II. *vi, vr:* **~se** to end; **¡asunto concluido!** that's settled!

**conclusión** [kon·klu·'sjon] *f* conclusion; **llegar a la ~ de que...** to come to the conclusion that...

**concordancia** [kon·kor·'dan·sja, -θja] *f* concordance

**concordar** <o → ue> [kon·kor·'dar] *vi* to coincide

**concordia** [kon·'kor·dja] *f* harmony

**concretar** [kon·kre·'tar] I. *vt* 1. (*precisar*) to put in concrete form 2. (*limitar*) to limit II. *vr:* **~se** to limit oneself

**concretizar** <z → c> [kon·kre·ti·'sar, -'θar] *vt* *v.* **concretar**

**concreto, -a** [kon·'kre·to] *adj* concrete; **en ~** specifically

**concurrido, -a** [kon·ku·'rri·do, -a] *adj* crowded

**concurrir** [kon·ku·'rrir] *vi* **1.** (*en un lugar*) to come together; (*en el tiempo*) to coincide **2.** (*concursar*) ~ **por algo** to compete for sth

**concursante** [kon·kur·'san·te] *mf* **1.** (*aspirante*) candidate **2.** (*participante*) competitor, contestant

**concursar** [kon·kur·'sar] *vi* to compete

**concurso** [kon·'kur·so] *m* **1.** *t.* DEP competition **2.** (*oposición*) (public) competition

**conde(sa)** ['kon·de, kon·'de·sa] *m(f)* count *m*, countess *f*

**condecorar** [kon·de·ko·'rar] *vt* MIL to decorate

**condena** [kon·'de·na] *f* sentence, conviction; **cumplir una** ~ to serve a sentence

**condenado, -a** [kon·de·'na·do, -a] **I.** *adj* inf condemned **II.** *m, f* (*reo*) convicted person, convict

**condenar** [kon·de·'nar] *vt* (*sentenciar*) to condemn

**condensar** [kon·den·'sar] *vt, vr:* ~**se** to condense

**condesa** [kon·'de·sa] *f v.* **conde**

**condición** [kon·di·'sjon, -'θjon] *f* **1.** (*índole*) nature **2.** (*estado*) condition; **a** ~ **de que** +*subj* on condition that, providing **3.** (*situación*) position **4.** (*clase*) social class

**condicional** [kon·di·sjo·'nal, kon·di·θjo·] *adj, m* LING conditional

**condicionar** [kon·di·sjo·'nar, kon·di·θjo·] *vt* (*supeditar*) ~ **a algo** to make conditional on sth

**condimento** [kon·di·'men·to] *m* seasoning, flavoring

**condolencia** [kon·do·'len·sja, -θja] *f* condolence, sympathy

**condolerse** [o → ue] [kon·do·'ler·se] *vr* ~**se de algo** to sympathize with sth

**condón** [kon·'don] *m* inf condom

**condonar** [kon·do·'nar] *vt* (*deuda*) to write off

**cóndor** ['kon·dor] *m* condor

**conducción** [kon·duk·'sjon, --duɣ'θjon] *f* **1.** (*transporte*) transport(ation) **2.** (*coche*) driving; ~ **temeraria** reckless driving

**conducir** [kon·du·'sir, -'θir] *irr como* traducir **I.** *vt* **1.** (*llevar*) to take; (*transportar*) to transport **2.** (*guiar*) to guide **3.** (*arrastrar*) to lead **4.** (*pilotar*) to drive **II.** *vi* **1.** (*dirigir*) to lead **2.** (*pilotar*) to drive

**conducta** [kon·'duk·ta] *f* conduct, behavior

**conducto** [kon·'duk·to] *m* **1.** (*tubo*) pipe **2.** MED canal; ~ **auditivo** ear canal **3.** (*mediación*) channels *pl*

**conductor** [kon·duk·'tor] *m* Fís conductor

**conductor(a)** [kon·duk·'tor, -·'to·ra] **I.** *adj* conductive; **hilo** ~ conductor wire **II.** *m(f)* driver

**conectar** [ko·nek·'tar] **I.** *vt* **1.** (*enlazar*) to connect **2.** (*enchufar*) to plug in **II.** *vi* to communicate

**conejo, -a** [ko·'ne·xo] *m, f* rabbit

**conexión** [ko·nek·'sjon] *f* *t.* TEL connection

**confabularse** [kon·fa·βu·'lar·se] *vr* to plot

**confección** [kon·fek·'sjon, -feɣ·'θjon] *f* making; (*de vestidos*) dressmaking

**confederación** [kon·fe·de·ra·'sjon, -'θjon] *f* confederation

**conferencia** [kon·fe·'ren·sja, -θja] *f* **1.** (*charla*) lecture **2.** (*encuentro*) conference **3.** (*telefónica*) call

**conferir** [kon·fe·'rir] *irr como sentir vt* to confer

**confesar** [e → ie] [kon·fe·'sar] **I.** *vt* **1.** (*admitir*) to confess **2.** REL (*declarar*) to confess **II.** *vr:* ~**se** to confess; ~**se culpable** to admit one's guilt

**confesión** [kon·fe·'sjon] *f* confession

**confesor** [kon·fe·'sor] *m* confessor

**confiado, -a** [kon·fi·'a·do, -a] *adj* **1.** *ser* (*crédulo*) trusting **2.** *estar* (*de sí mismo*) self-confident

**confianza** [kon·fi·'an·sa, -θa] *f* **1.** (*crédito*) trust; **amiga de** ~ close friend **2.** (*esperanza*) confidence **3.** (*en uno mismo*) self-confidence **4.** (*familiaridad*) familiarity

**confiar** <*1. pres* confío> [kon·fi·'ar] **I.** *vi* ~ **en algo/alguien** to trust in sth/sb **II.** *vt* to entrust **III.** *vr* ~**se a alguien** to confide in sb

**confidencia** [kon·fi·'den·sja, -θja] *f* secret

**confidencial** [kon·fi·den·'sjal, -'θjal] *adj* confidential

**confidente** [kon·fi·'den·te] *mf* (*cómplice*) confidant *m*, confidante *f*

**configuración** [kon·fi·yu·ra·'sjon, -'θjon] *f* 1. (*formación*) shaping 2. (*forma*) shape; COMPUT configuration

**configurar** [kon·fi·yu·'rar] I. *vt* to shape; COMPUT to configure II. *vr:* **~se** to take shape

**confirmación** [kon·fir·ma·'sjon, -'θjon] *f t.* REL confirmation

**confirmar** [kon·fir·'mar] I. *vt t.* REL to confirm II. *vr:* **~se** to be confirmed

**confiscar** <c → qu> [kon·fis·'kar] *vt* to confiscate

**confitería** [kon·fi·te·'ri·a] *f* cake [o pastry] shop, candy shop

**conflicto** [kon·'flik·to] *m* conflict

**conformar** [kon·for·'mar] I. *vt* 1. (*dar forma*) to shape 2. (*ajustar*) to adjust II. *vr:* **~se** 1. (*contentarse*) to be satisfied 2. (*ajustarse*) to adjust

**conforme** [kon·'for·me] I. *adj* (*adecuado*) **estar ~ con algo** to be satisfied with sth II. *prep* **~ a** according to III. *conj* (*como*) as

**conformidad** [kon·for·mi·'dad] *f* (*aprobación*) approval

**confort** [kon·'fort] *m* comfort

**confortable** [kon·for·'ta·βle] *adj* comfortable

**confortar** [kon·for·'tar] I. *vt* 1. (*vivificar*) to strengthen 2. (*consolar*) to comfort II. *vr:* **~se** (*consolarse*) to take comfort

**confrontación** [kon·fron·ta·'sjon, -'θjon] *f* 1. (*comparación*) comparison 2. (*enfrentamiento*) confrontation

**confrontar** [kon·fron·'tar] I. *vt* 1. (*comparar*) to compare 2. (*enfrentar*) to confront II. *vr* **~se con alguien** to face up to sb

**confundir** [kon·fun·'dir] I. *vt* 1. (*trastocar*) to mistake 2. (*mezclar*) to mix up 3. (*embrollar*) to confuse II. *vr:* **~se** 1. (*mezclarse*) to mix 2. (*embrollarse*) to get confused

**confusión** [kon·fu·'sjon] *f* confusion

**confuso, -a** [kon·'fu·so, -a] *adj* confused

**congelación** [kon·xe·la·'sjon, -'θjon] *f* 1. (*solidificación*) freezing 2. frost-bite; MED

**congelador** [kon·xe·la·'dor] *m* 1. (*electrodoméstico*) freezer 2. (*de un frigorífico*) freezer compartment

**congelar** [kon·xe·'lar] I. *vt t. fig* to freeze II. *vr:* **~se** (*solidificarse*) to freeze

**congeniar** [kon·xe·'njar] *vi* **~ con** to get on [o along] with

**congénito, -a** [kon·'xe·ni·to, -a] *adj* congenital

**congestión** [kon·xes·'tjon] *f t.* MED congestion

**congoja** [kon·'go·xa] *f* 1. (*pena*) sorrow 2. (*desconsuelo*) anguish

**congola** [kon·'go·la] *f Col* (*pipa de fumar*) pipe

**congregar** <g → gu> [kon·gre·'yar] I. *vt* to bring together II. *vr:* **~se** to gather

**congresista** [kon·gre·'sis·ta] *mf* POL delegate, congressman *m*, congresswoman *f*

**congreso** [kon·'gre·so] *m* 1. POL congress 2. (*reunión*) congress, convention

**congrio** ['kon·grjo] *m* conger eel

**congruencia** [kon·'grwen·sja, -θja] *f* coherence

**conjetura** [kon·xe·'tu·ra] *f* conjecture

**conjugación** [kon·xu·ya·'sjon, -'θjon] *f* conjugation

**conjugar** <g → gu> [kon·xu·'yar] *vt* 1. (*combinar*) to combine 2. LING to conjugate

**conjunción** [kon·xun·'sjon, -'θjon] *f* conjunction

**conjuntamente** [kon·xun·ta·'men·te] *adv* jointly; **~ con** together with

**conjuntar** [kon·xun·'tar] I. *vi* to match; **~ con** to go with II. *vt* to harmonize

**conjuntivitis** [kon·xun·ti·'βi·tis] *f inv* conjunctivitis

**conjunto** [kon·'xun·to] *m* 1. (*totalidad*) whole; **en ~** as a whole 2. TEAT ensemble 3. (*ropa*) outfit 4. MAT set

**conjurar** [kon·xu·'rar] I. *vt* 1. (*invocar*) to beseech 2. (*alejar*) to ward off II. *vr:* **~se** to conspire

**conllevar** [kon·je·'βar, kon·ʎe-] *vt* 1. (*implicar*) to involve 2. (*soportar*) to bear

**conmemoración** [kon·me·mo·ra·'sjon, kom·me-·, -'θjon] *f* commemoration

**conmemorar** [kon·me·mo·'rar, kom·me·mo·'rar] *vt* to commemorate

**conmigo** [kon·'mi·ɣo, kom·'mi·ɣo] *pron pers* with me

**conmoción** [kon·mo·'sjon, kom·mo-, -'θjon] *f* 1. MED concussion 2. *fig* shock

**conmocionar** [kon·mo·sjo·'nar, kom·mo-, -'θjo·'nar] *vt* 1. MED to concuss 2. *fig* to shake

**conmovedor(a)** [kon·mo·βe·'dor, -·'do·ra; kom·mo-] *adj* (*sentimental*) moving

**conmover** <o → ue> [kon·mo·'βer, kom·mo-] I. *vt* (*emocionar*) to move II. *vr:* ~**se** 1. (*emocionarse*) to be moved 2. (*sacudirse*) to be shaken

**cono** ['ko·no] *m* cone; **Cono Sur** GEO Southern Cone (*Argentina, Chile, Paraguay and Uruguay*)

**conocedor(a)** [ko·no·se·'dor, -·'do·ra, ko·no·θe-] I. *adj* ~ **de algo** knowledgeable about sth II. *m(f)* expert

**conocer** [ko·no·'ser, -'θer] *irr como* **crecer** I. *vt* 1. (*saber, tratar*) to know; ~ **de vista** to know by sight; **dar a** ~ to make known 2. (*reconocer*) to recognize 3. (*descubrir*) to get to know 4. (*por primera vez*) to meet; **les conocí en una fiesta** I met them at a party II. *vi* ~ **de algo** to know about sth III. *vr:* ~**se** 1. (*tener trato*) to know each other; **se conocieron en una fiesta** they met at a party 2. (*a sí mismo*) to know oneself

**conocido, -a** [ko·no·'si·do, -a; ko·no·'θi-] I. *adj* (well-)known II. *m, f* acquaintance

**conocimiento** [ko·no·θi·'mjen·to, ko·no·θi-] *m* 1. (*saber*) knowledge 2. (*entendimiento*) understanding 3. (*consciencia*) consciousness 4. *pl* (*nociones*) knowledge

**conque** ['kon·ke] *conj inf* so

**conquista** [kon·'kis·ta] *f* conquest

**conquistador(a)** [kon·kis·ta·'dor, -·'do·ra] *m(f)* conqueror

**conquistar** [kon·kis·'tar] *vt* to conquer

**consagrar** [kon·sa·'ɣrar] I. *vt* (*dedicar*) to dedicate II. *vr:* ~**se** 1. (*dedicarse*) to devote oneself 2. (*acreditarse*) to distinguish oneself

**consciencia** [kon·'sjen·sja, -'θjen·θja] *f* consciousness

**consciente** [kon·'sjen·te, kons·'θjen·te] *adj* conscious; **estar** ~ MED to be conscious; **ser** ~ **de algo** to be aware of sth

**conscripción** [kons·krip·'sjon, -'θjon] *f* Arg (*servicio militar*) conscription

**consecución** [kon·se·ku·'sjon, -'θjon] *f* attainment

**consecuencia** [kon·se·'kwen·sja, -θja] *f* 1. (*efecto*) consequence; **a** ~ **de** as a result of 2. (*coherencia*) consistency

**consecuente** [kon·se·'kwen·te] *adj* consistent

**consecutivo, -a** [kon·se·ku·'ti·βo, -a] *adj* consecutive

**conseguir** [kon·se·'ɣir] *irr como* **seguir** *vt* to get

**consejero, -a** [kon·se·'xe·ro, -a] *m, f* 1. (*guía*) adviser, counselor, consultant 2. (*miembro de un consejo*) member; ~ **delegado** managing director

**consejo** [kon·'se·xo] *m* 1. (*recomendación*) piece of advice 2. (*organismo*) council 3. (*reunión*) meeting

**consenso** [kon·'sen·so] *m* consensus

**consentido, -a** [kon·sen·'ti·do, -a] *adj* spoiled

**consentimiento** [kon·sen·ti·'mjen·to] *m* ~ **para algo** consent to sth

**consentir** [kon·sen·'tir] *irr como* **sentir** I. *vi* (*admitir*) ~ **en algo** to agree to sth II. *vt* 1. (*autorizar*) to allow; (*tolerar*) to tolerate 2. (*mimar*) to spoil 3. (*aguantar*) to put up with

**conserje** [kon·'ser·xe] *mf* 1. (*encargado*) janitor 2. (*hotel*) concierge, receptionist 3. (*portero*) (hall) porter

**conserjería** [kon·ser·xe·'ri·a] *f* 1. (*cargo*) job of caretaker 2. (*oficina*) caretaker's office 3. (*hotel*) reception (desk)

**conserva** [kon·'serβa] *f* canned food; **en** ~ canned

**conservación** [kon·ser·βa·'sjon, -'θjon] *f* 1. (*mantenimiento*) maintenance 2. (*guarda*) conservation 3. (*conserva*) preserving

**conservador(a)** [kon·ser·'·βa·dor] *adj* conservative

**conservar** [kon·ser·'βar] I. *vt* 1. (*mantener*) to maintain 2. (*guardar*) to conserve 3. (*hacer conservas*) to can II. *vr:* ~**se** (*mantenerse*) to keep

**conservatorio** [kon·ser·βa·'to·rjo] *m* conservatory

**considerable** [kon·si·de·'ra·βle] *adj* considerable

**consideración** [kon·si·de·ra·'sjon, -'θjon] *f* 1. (*reflexión*) consideration; **en ~ a** in consideration of 2. (*respeto*) respect

**considerado, -a** [kon·si·de·'ra·do, -a] *adj* 1. (*tenido en cuenta*) considered 2. (*apreciado*) respected 3. (*atento*) considerate

**considerar** [kon·si·de·'rar] *vt, (vr):* **~se** to consider (oneself)

**consigna** [kon·'siɣ·na] *f* 1. MIL motto 2. (*de equipajes*) checkroom

**consignatario, -a** [kon·siɣ·na·'ta·rjo, -a] *m, f* 1. (*destinatario*) addressee 2. COM consignee

**consigo** [kon·'si·ɣo] *pron pers* **tiene el libro ~** he/she has the book with him/her; **llévaselo ~** take it with you

**consiguiente** [kon·si·'ɣjen·te] *adj* resulting; **por ~** consequently

**consistencia** [kon·sis·'ten·sja, -θja] *f* consistency

**consistir** [kon·sis·'tir] *vi* 1. (*componerse*) **~ en algo** to consist of sth 2. (*radicar*) **~ en algo** to lie in sth

**consola** [kon·'so·la] *f* (*mesa*) console table; ELEC console; (*de videojuegos*) video console

**consolar** <o → ue> [kon·so·'lar] *vt, vr:* **~se** to console (oneself)

**consolidación** [kon·so·li·da·'sjon, -'θjon] *f* consolidation

**consolidar** [kon·so·li·'dar] I. *vt* to consolidate II. *vr:* **~se** to be consolidated

**consomé** [kon·so·'me] *m* consommé

**consonancia** [kon·so·'nan·sja, -θja] *f* harmony; **en ~ con** in keeping with

**consonante** [kon·so·'nan·te] *f* LING consonant

**consorcio** [kon·'sor·sjo, -θjo] *m* consortium

**conspiración** [kons·pi·ra·'sjon, -'θjon] *f* conspiracy

**conspirar** [kons·pi·'rar] *vi* to conspire

**constancia** [kons·'tan·sja, -θja] *f* 1. (*firmeza*) constancy 2. (*perseverancia*) perseverance 3. (*certeza*) certainty 4. (*prueba*) proof; **dejar ~ de algo** to

show evidence of sth

**constante** [kons·'tan·te] *adj* constant

**constar** [kons·'tar] *vi* 1. (*ser cierto*) to be clear 2. (*figurar*) to be on record; **hacer ~ algo** to put sth on record 3. (*componerse*) to consist

**constatar** [kons·ta·'tar] *vt* to confirm

**constelación** [kons·te·la·'sjon, -'θjon] *f* constellation

**constipado** [kons·ti·'pa·do] *m* cold

**constipar** [kons·ti·'par] *vr:* **~se** to catch a cold

**constitución** [kons·ti·tu·'sjon, -'θjon] *f* 1. *t.* POL constitution 2. (*composición*) make-up

**constitucional** [kons·ti·tu·sjo'nal, -θjo·'nal] *adj* constitutional

**constituir** [kons·ti·tu·'ir, kons·ti·'twir] *irr como huir vt* 1. (*formar*) to constitute 2. (*ser*) to be

**construcción** [kons·truk·'sjon, -truɣ·'θjon] *f* 1. (*acción*) construction 2. (*edificio*) building

**constructivo, -a** [kons·truk·'ti·βo, -a] *adj* constructive

**constructor(a)** [kons·truk·'tor, --'to·ra] *m(f)* builder

**construir** [kons·tru·'ir/kons·'trwir] *irr como huir vt* (*casa*) to build

**consuelo** [kon·'swe·lo] *m* consolation

**consulado** [kon·su·'la·do] *m* (*lugar*) consulate

**consulta** [kon·'sul·ta] *f* 1. (*acción*) consultation 2. (*de un médico*) surgery; **horas de ~** surgery hours

**consultar** [kon·sul·'tar] *vt* to consult

**consultorio** [kon·sul·'to·rjo] *m* 1. (*establecimiento*) consultancy; (*de un médico*) surgery 2. (*en la radio*) phone-in

**consumar** [kon·su·'mar] *vt* to carry out

**consumición** [kon·su·mi·'sjon, -'θjon] *f* (*bar*) drink; **~ mínima** minimum charge

**consumidor(a)** [kon·su·mi·'dor, --'do·ra] *m(f)* consumer

**consumir** [kon·su·'mir] I. *vt* 1. (*gastar*) to consume 2. (*acabar*) to use 3. (*comer*) to eat II. *vr:* **~se** 1. (*persona*) to waste away 2. (*gastarse*) to be consumed

**consumo** [kon·'su·mo] *m* consumption

**contabilidad** [kon·ta·βi·li·'dad] *f* 1. (*sistema*) accounting 2. (*profesión*) accountancy

**contabilizar** <z → c> [kon·ta·βi·li·'sar, -'θar] *vt* to enter

**contable** [kon·'ta·βle] I. *adj* countable II. *mf* accountant

**contactar** [kon·tak·'tar] *vi, vt* ~ **con alguien** to contact sb

**contacto** [kon·'tak·to] *m* 1. (*tacto*) contact 2. AUTO ignition

**contado** [kon·'ta·do] *m* **pagar al** ~ to pay (in) cash

**contador** [kon·ta·'dor] *m* meter

**contagiar** [kon·ta·'xjar] *vt* to transmit, to infect

**contagio** [kon·'ta·xjo] *m* contagion

**contagioso, -a** [kon·ta·'xjo·so, -a] *adj* contagious

**contaminación** [kon·ta·mi·na·'sjon, -'θjon] *f* pollution

**contaminante** [kon·ta·mi·'nan·te] I. *adj* polluting II. *m* pollutant

**contaminar** [kon·ta·mi·'nar] *vt* 1. (*infestar*) to pollute 2. (*contagiar*) to infect

**contar** <o → ue> [kon·'tar] I. *vi* 1. (*calcular*) to count 2. (+ con: confiar) ~ **con alguien/algo** to rely on sb/sth 3. (+ con: tener en cuenta) ~ **con algo** to expect sth II. *vt* 1. (*numerar*) to count 2. (*narrar*) to tell; **¿qué (te) cuentas?** (*saludo*) how's it going?

**contemplación** [kon·tem·pla·'sjon, -'θjon] *f* 1. (*observación*) contemplation 2. *pl* (*miramientos*) indulgence

**contemplar** [kon·tem·'plar] *vt* 1. (*mirar*) to look at 2. (*considerar*) to consider

**contemporáneo, -a** [kon·tem·po·'ra·neo, -a] *adj, m, f* contemporary

**contenedor** [kon·te·ne·'dor] *m* (*recipiente*) container; (*basura*) dumpster

**contener** [kon·te·'ner] *irr como* tener I. *vt* 1. (*encerrar*) to contain 2. (*refrenar*) to hold back II. *vr*: ~**se** to contain oneself

**contenido** [kon·te·'ni·do] *m* 1. (*lo incluido*) contents *pl* 2. (*concentración*) content

**contentar** [kon·ten·'tar] I. *vt* to satisfy II. *vr*: ~**se** to be contented

**contento, -a** [kon·'ten·to] *adj* (*alegre*) happy; (*satisfecho*) content

**contestación** [kon·tes·ta·'sjon, -'θjon] *f* answer

**contestador** [kon·tes·ta·'dor] *m* answering machine

**contestar** [kon·tes·'tar] I. *vt* to answer II. *vi* to answer; (*replicar*) to answer back

**contexto** [kon·'tes·to] *m* context

**contienda** [kon·'tjen·da] *f* dispute

**contigo** [kon·'ti·yo] *pron pers* with you

**contiguo, -a** [kon·'ti·ɣwo, -a] *adj* adjoining

**continental** [kon·ti·nen·'tal] *adj* continental

**continente** [kon·ti·'nen·te] *m* GEO continent

**continuación** [kon·ti·nwa·'sjon, -'θjon] *f* continuation; **a** ~ (*después*) next; (*en un escrito*) as follows

**continuar** <1. pres continúo> [kon·ti·nu·'ar] *vt, vi* to continue

**continuidad** [kon·ti·nwi·'dad] *f* continuity

**continuo, -a** [kon·'ti·nwo] *adj* continuous

**contorno** [kon·'tor·no] *m* (*de una figura*) outline

**contra¹** ['kon·tra] I. *prep* against; **tener algo en** ~ to object II. *m* **los pros y los** ~**s** the pros and the cons

**contra²** ['kon·tra] *f* (*dificultad*) snag

**contraataque** [kon·tra·'ta·ke/kon·tra·a·'ta·ke] *m* MIL counterattack

**contrabajo** [kon·tra·'βa·xo] *m* (*instrumento*) double bass; (*rock*) bass guitar

**contrabando** [kon·tra·'βan·do] *m* (*comercio*) smuggling; **pasar algo de** ~ to smuggle sth in

**contracción** [kon·trak·'sjon, -traɣ'θjon] *f t.* LING contraction

**contracorriente** [kon·tra·ko·'rrjen·te] *f* crosscurrent

**contradecir** [kon·tra·de·'sir, -'θir] *irr como* decir *vt, (vr):* ~**se** to contradict (oneself)

**contradicción** [kon·tra·dik·'sjon, -diɣ·'θjon] *f* contradiction

**contradictorio, -a** [kon·tra·dik·'to·rjo, -a] *adj* contradictory

**contraer** [kon·tra·'er] *irr como* traer I. *vt* 1. (*encoger*) to contract 2. (*enferme-*

*dad*) to catch, to contract *form* **II.** *vr:* ~**se** to contract

**contraindicación** [kon·tra·in·di·ka·'sjon, -'θjon] *f* MED contraindication

**contramedida** [kon·tra·me·'di·da] *f* countermeasure

**contraoferta** [kon·tra·o·'fer·ta] *f* counteroffer

**contraorden** [kon·tra·'or·den] *f* countermand *form*

**contrapartida** [kon·tra·par·'ti·da] *f* compensation

**contrapeso** [kon·tra·'pe·so] *m* counterweight

**contraproducente** [kon·tra·pro·du·'sen·te, -'θen·te] *adj* counterproductive

**contrariar** <*1. pres* contrarío> [kon·tra·ri·'ar] *vt* (*disgustar*) to upset

**contrariedad** [kon·tra·rje·'dad] *f* **1.** (*inconveniente*) obstacle **2.** (*disgusto*) annoyance

**contrario, -a** [kon·'tra·rjo, -a] **I.** *adj* (*opuesto*) contrary; (*perjudicial*) harmful; **al ~** on the contrary; **en caso ~** otherwise; **de lo ~** or else; **llevar la contraria a alguien** to oppose [*o* contradict] sb **II.** *m, f* opponent

**contrarrestar** [kon·tra·rres·'tar] *vt* to counteract

**contraseña** [kon·tra·'se·ɲa] *f* password

**contrastar** [kon·tras·'tar] **I.** *vi* to contrast **II.** *vt* (*peso*) to verify

**contraste** [kon·'tras·te] *m t.* FOTO contrast

**contratación** [kon·tra·ta·'sjon, -'θjon] *f* contracting

**contratar** [kon·tra·'tar] *vt* **1.** (*trabajador*) to hire; (*artista*) to sign up **2.** (*encargar*) to contract

**contratiempo** [kon·tra·'tjem·po] *m* setback

**contrato** [kon·'tra·to] *m* contract; ~ **de alquiler** lease

**contravenir** [kon·tra·βe·'nir] *irr como venir vt* to contravene

**contribución** [kon·tri·βu·'sjon, -'θjon] *f* **1.** (*aportación*) contribution **2.** (*impuesto*) tax

**contribuir** [kon·tri·βu·'ir] *irr como huir vt, vi* (*ayudar*) to contribute

**contribuyente** [kon·tri·βu·'jen·te] *mf* taxpayer

**contrincante** [kon·trin·'kan·te] *mf* opponent

**control** [kon·'trol] *m* control; (*inspección*) inspection

**controlar** [kon·tro·'lar] **I.** *vt* (*revisar*) to check; (*gobernar*) to control **II.** *vr:* ~**se** to control oneself

**controversia** [kon·tro·'βer·sja] *f* controversy

**controvertido, -a** [kon·tro·βer·'ti·do, -a] *adj* controversial

**contundencia** [kon·tun·'den·sja, -θja] *f* force

**contundente** [kon·tun·'den·te] *adj* contusive; *fig* convincing

**contusión** [kon·tu·'sjon] *f* MED bruise

**convalecencia** [kom·ba·le·'sen·sja, -'θen·θja] *f* convalescence

**convalidación** [kom·ba·li·da·'sjon, -'θjon] *f* **1.** (*de un título*) (re)validation **2.** (*confirmación*) confirmation, recognition

**convalidar** [kom·ba·li·'dar] *vt* **1.** (*título*) to (re)validate **2.** (*confirmar*) to confirm, to recognize

**convencer** <c → z> [kom·ben·'ser, -'θer] **I.** *vt* **1.** (*persuadir*) to persuade **2.** (*satisfacer*) **no me convence ese piso** I'm not at all sure about that flat **II.** *vr:* ~**se** to be convinced

**convencido, -a** [kom·ben·'si·do, -a; -'θi·do, -a] *adj* sure

**convencimiento** [kom·ben·si·'mjen·to, kom·ben·θi-] *m* conviction; **tengo el ~ de que...** I'm convinced that...

**convención** [kom·ben·'sjon, -'θjon] *f* convention

**convencional** [kom·ben·sjo·'nal, kom·ben·θjo-] *adj* conventional

**conveniencia** [kom·be·'njen·sja, -θja] *f* usefulness

**conveniente** [kom·be·'njen·te] *adj* **1.** (*adecuado*) suitable **2.** (*provechoso*) advisable; (*útil*) useful

**convenio** [kom·be·njo] *m* agreement

**convenir** [kom·be·'nir] *irr como venir vi* **1.** (*acordar*) to agree **2.** (*ser oportuno*) to be advisable

**convento** [kom·'ben·to] *m* (*de monjes*) monastery; (*de monjas*) convent

**convergencia** [kom·ber·'xen·sja, -θja] *f* convergence

**converger** <g → j> [kom·ber·'xer] *vi*, **convergir** <g → j> [kom·ber·'xir] *vi* **1.** (*líneas*) to converge **2.** (*coincidir*) to coincide

**conversación** [kom·ber·sa·'sjon, -'θjon] *f* conversation

**conversar** [kom·ber·'sar] *vi* to talk

**conversión** [kom·ber·'sjon] *f* conversion

**convertir** [kom·ber·'tir] *irr como sentir* **I.** *vt* **1.** (*transformar*) ~ **en algo** to turn into sth **2.** COM, TÉC to convert **II.** *vr:* ~**se 1.** (*transformarse*) ~**se en algo** to turn into sth **2.** REL to convert

**convexo, -a** [kom·'bek·so, -a] *adj* convex

**convicción** [kom·bik·'sjon, -biɣ·'θjon] *f* conviction

**convicto, -a** [kom·'bik·to, -a] *adj* convicted

**convidar** [kom·bi·'dar] *vt* to invite

**convincente** [kom·bin·'sen·te, -'θen·te] *adj* convincing

**convivencia** [kom·bi·'βen·sja, -θja] *f* living together; *fig* co-existence

**convivir** [kom·bi·'βir] *vi* to live together; *fig* to coexist

**convocar** <c → qu> [kom·bo·'kar] *vt* **1.** (*citar*) to summon **2.** (*concurso*) to announce

**convocatoria** [kom·bo·ka·'to·rja] *f* **1.** (*citación*) summons **2.** (*de un concurso*) official announcement **3.** (*de una conferencia*) notification

**convulsión** [kom·bul·'sjon] *f* **1.** MED convulsion **2.** POL upheaval **3.** GEO tremor

**conyugal** [kon·ju·'yal] *adj* marital

**cónyuge** ['kon·ju·xe] *mf* spouse

**coña** ['ko·ɲa] *f vulg* (*broma*) joking; **tomar algo a ~** to take sth as a joke; **¡ni de ~!** no way!

**coñac** [ko·'ɲak] *m* <coñacs> cognac

**coñazo** [ko·'ɲa·so, -θo] *m vulg* pain in the ass; **¡esto es un ~!** this is a drag!

**coño** ['ko·ɲo] **I.** *interj vulg* shit! **II.** *m vulg* cunt, pussy; **¿qué ~ te importa?** why the hell does it matter to you?

**cooperación** [ko·pe·ra·'sjon/ko·o·pe·ra·'sjon, -'θjon] *f* cooperation

**cooperar** [ko·pe·'rar/ko·o·pe·'rar] *vi* to cooperate

**cooperativa** [ko·pe·ra·'ti·βa/ko·o·pe·ra·'ti·βa] *f* cooperative, co-op

**cooperativo, -a** [ko·pe·ra·'ti·βo, -a/ko·o·pe·ra·'ti·βo, -a] *adj* cooperative

**coordenada** [kor·de·'na·da/ko·or·de·'na·da] *f* MAT coordinate

**coordinación** [kor·di·na·'sjon/ko·or·di·na·'sjon, -'θjon] *f* coordination

**coordinador(a)** [kor·di·na·'dor/ko·or·di·na·'dor, -·'do·ra] *m(f)* coordinator

**coordinar** [kor·di·'nar/ko·or·di·'nar] *vt* to coordinate

**copa** ['ko·pa] *f* **1.** (*vaso*) glass; **una ~ de vino** a glass of wine; **ir de ~s** to go out for a drink; **tener una ~ de más** to have had one too many **2.** (*de árbol*) top **3.** *t.* DEP (*de sujetador*) cup

**Copenhague** [ko·pe·'na·ɣe] *m* Copenhagen

**copetín** [ko·pe·'tin] *m* **1.** *Méx* (*copa de licor*) glass of liquor; (*aperitivo*) aperitif **2.** *Arg* (*cóctel*) cocktail

**copia** ['ko·pja] *f* copy; FOTO print; **~ de seguridad** COMPUT back-up copy

**copiar** [ko·'pjar] *vt* **1.** (*general*) to copy **2.** (*fotocopiar*) to photocopy, to xerox

**copiloto, -a** [ko·pi·'lo·to, -a] *m, f* AVIAT copilot; AUTO co-driver

**copo** ['ko·po] *m* flake; **~ de nieve** snowflake; **~s de maíz** cornflakes

**copucha** [ko·'pu·tʃa] *f Chile* **1.** (*mentira*) lie **2.** (*vejiga de animal*) bladder

**copular** [ko·pu·'lar] *vi* to copulate

**coquetear** [ko·ke·te·'ar] *vi* to flirt

**coqueto, -a** [ko·'ke·to, -a] *adj* **1.** (*que coquetea*) flirtatious **2.** (*vanidoso*) vain **3.** (*objeto*) pretty

**coracha** [ko·'ra·tʃa] *f AmL* leather bag

**coraje** [ko·'ra·xe] *m* **1.** (*valor*) courage **2.** (*ira*) anger; **dar ~** to make angry

**coral** [ko·'ral] **I.** *adj* (*color*) coral **II.** *m t.* ZOOL coral **III.** *f* (*coro*) choir

**Corán** [ko·'ran] *m* REL Koran

**corazón** [ko·ra·'son, -'θon] *m* **1.** *t. fig* ANAT heart; **de todo ~** with all one's heart; **con el ~ en la mano** with one's heart on one's sleeve; **hacer algo de ~** to do sth willingly; **tener un ~ de oro** to have a heart of gold; **no tener ~** to be heartless; **~ (mío)** darling **2.** BOT core

**corazonada** [ko·ra·so·'na·da, ko·ra·θo·] *f (presentimiento)* hunch

**corbata** [kor·'βa·ta] *f* tie

**corchea** [kor·'tʃea] *f* quaver

**corchete** [kor·'tʃe·te] *m* **1.** *(broche)* hook and eye **2.** TIPO square bracket

**corcho** ['kor·tʃo] *m* cork

**cordel** [kor·'del] *m* cord

**cordero** [kor·'de·ro] *m (carne)* mutton, lamb

**cordero, -a** [kor·'de·ro, -a] *m, f* lamb

**cordial** [kor·'djal] *adj, m* cordial

**cordialidad** [kor·dja·li·'dad] *f* cordiality

**cordillera** [kor·di·'ʝe·ra, -'ʎe·ra] *f* mountain range

**cordillerano, -a** [kor·di·ʝe·'ra·no, -a; kor·di·ʎe-] *adj AmL* GEO Andean

**córdoba** ['kor·do·βa] *m Nic (moneda)* cordoba

**cordobés, -esa** [kor·do·'βes, -·'βe·sa] *adj, m, f* Cordovan

**cordón** [kor·'don] *m* **1.** *(cordel)* cord; *(de zapatos)* shoelace; **~ umbilical** ANAT umbilical cord **2.** MIL cordon

**cordura** [kor·'du·ra] *f (razón)* good sense

**coreografía** [ko·reo·ɣra·'fi·a] *f* choreography

**coreógrafo, -a** [ko·re·'o·ɣra·fo, -a] *m, f* choreographer

**corista** [ko·'ris·ta] *mf* MÚS chorister

**córnea** ['kor·nea] *f* cornea

**córner** ['kor·ner] *m* DEP corner

**corneta** [kor·'ne·ta] *f* cornet; *(en el ejército)* bugle

**corneta** [kor·'ne·ta] *m* cornet player; MIL bugler

**cornudo** [kor·'nu·do, -a] *m inf* cuckold

**cornudo, -a** [kor·'nu·do, -a] *adj (animal)* horned

**coro** ['ko·ro] *m* choir; **a ~** in unison

**corona** [ko·'ro·na] *f* **1.** *(real)* crown; *(de flores)* garland, wreath **2.** *(de los dientes)* crown

**coronar** [ko·ro·'nar] *vt* to crown

**coronel(a)** [ko·ro·'nel, -·'ne·la] *m(f)* colonel

**corotos** [ko·'ro·tos] *mpl AmL (bártulos)* things *pl*

**corporación** [kor·po·ra·'sjon, -'θjon] *f t.* COM corporation

**corporal** [kor·po·'ral] *adj* physical

**corporativo, -a** [kor·po·ra·'ti·βo, -a] *adj* corporate

**corpulento, -a** [kor·pu·'len·to, -a] *adj (persona)* hefty

**corral** [ko·'rral] *m* **1.** *(cercado)* yard; *(redil)* stockyard; *(para gallinas)* chicken run **2.** *(para niños)* playpen

**corralón** [ko·rra·'lon] *m CSur (maderería)* lumberyard

**correa** [ko·'rrea] *f* **1.** *(tira)* strap **2.** *(cinturón)* belt; **~ de transmisión** TÉC driving belt, drive

**corrección** [ko·rrek·'sjon, -reɣ·'θjon] *f* **1.** correction; TIPO proofreading **2.** *(cualidad)* correctness

**correcto, -a** [ko·'rrek·to, -a] *adj* correct

**corrector(a)** [ko·rrek·'tor] **I.** *adj* correcting **II.** *m(f)* TIPO proofreader

**corredor** [ko·rre·'dor] *m* corridor

**corredor(a)** [ko·rre·'dor, -·'do·ra] *m(f)* **1.** DEP runner **2.** COM agent, broker

**correduría** [ko·rre·du·'ri·a] *f* **1.** *(oficio)* brokerage **2.** *(comisión)* commission

**corregir** [ko·rre·'xir] *irr como* **elegir I.** *vt t.* TIPO to correct **II.** *vr:* **~se** *(en la conducta)* to change one's ways

**correlación** [ko·rre·la·'sjon, -'θjon] *f* correlation

**correlativo, -a** [ko·rre·la·'ti·βo, -a] *adj elev* correlative

**correntada** [ko·rren·'ta·da] *f AmL (rápido)* rapids *pl*

**correo** [ko·'rreo] *m* **1.** *(correspondencia)* mail; **~ aéreo** airmail; **~ basura** COMPUT spam; **~ certificado** certified mail; **~ electrónico** e-mail; **~ urgente** special delivery; **echar al ~** to mail **2.** *(persona)* courier

**Correos** [ko·'rreos] *mpl* post office

**correr** [ko·'rrer] **I.** *vi* **1.** *(caminar)* to run; **salir corriendo** to run out; **a todo ~** at top speed **2.** *(conducir)* to go fast **3.** *(líquido)* to flow **4.** *(camino)* to run **5.** *(rumor)* to circulate **6.** *(estar a cargo de)* **eso corre de** [*o* **por**] **mi cuenta** *(gastos)* I'm paying for that **II.** *vt* **1.** *(un mueble)* to move; *(una cortina)* to draw; *(un cerrojo)* to slide **2.** *(tener)* **~ la misma suerte** to suffer the same fate; **corre prisa** it's urgent ► **dejar ~ algo** not to worry about sth **III.** *vr:* **~se 1.** (*mover-se*) to move **2.** *vulg* (*eyacular*) to come **3.** (*colores*) to run

**correspondencia** [ko·rres·pon·'den·sja, -θja] *f* **1.** (*correo, cartas*) mail; **curso por ~** correspondence course **2.** (*equivalente*) correspondence

**corresponder** [ko·rres·pon·'der] **I.** *vi* **1.** (*equivaler*) to correspond **2.** (*armonizar*) to match **3.** (*convenir*) to tally **4.** (*incumbir*) to concern; **no me corresponde criticarlo** it's not for me to criticize him **II.** *vr:* ~**se** (*equivaler, escribir*) to correspond; (*armonizar*) to match

**correspondiente** [ko·rres·pon·'djen·te] *adj* **1.** (*oportuno*) corresponding **2.** (*respectivo*) respective

**corresponsal** [ko·rres·pon·'sal] *mf* correspondent

**corrida** [ko·'rri·da] *f* **1.** TAUR bullfight **2.** (*carrera*) run **3.** *vulg* (*orgasmo*) orgasm

**corriente** [ko·'rrjen·te] **I.** *adj* **1.** (*fluente*) running **2.** (*actual*) current; (*moneda*) valid; **estar al ~ de algo** to be aware of sth; **ponerse al ~ de algo** to get to know about sth **3.** (*ordinario*) ordinary **4.** (*normal*) normal **II.** *f* **1.** (*de fluido*) current; **~ de aire** draft; **~ alterna** alternating current; **hace ~** there's a draft; **ir contra la ~** to swim against the tide; **seguir** [o **llevar**] **la ~ a alguien** to play along with sb **2.** (*tendencia*) tendency

**corrimiento** [ko·rri·'mjen·to] *m* GEO slipping; **~ de tierras** landslide

**corro** ['ko·rro] *m* **1.** (*círculo*) circle, to form a circle; (*hacer sitio*) to make room **2.** (*juego*) ring-around-the-rosy

**corroborar** [ko·rro·βo·'rar] *vt* to corroborate

**corroer** [ko·rro·'er] *irr como* roer *vt* **1.** (*un material*) to corrode **2.** (*una persona*) consume; **el remordimiento lo corroe** he's consumed by remorse

**corromper** [ko·rrom·'per] *vt* **1.** (*descomponer*) to rot **2.** (*sobornar*) to bribe **3.** (*enviciar*) to debauch; (*pervertir*) to corrupt

**corronchoso, -a** [ko·rron·'tʃo·so, -a] *adj* AmL (*basto*) coarse

**corrosca** [ko·'rros·ka] *f* Col broad-brimmed straw hat

**corrosión** [ko·rro·'sjon] *f* corrosion

**corrosivo, -a** [ko·rro·'si·βo, -a] *adj* (*sustancia*) corrosive

**corrupción** [ko·rrup·'sjon, -rruβ·'θjon] *f* **1.** (*descomposición*) decay **2.** (*moral*) corruption

**corrupto, -a** [ko·'rrup·to, -a] *adj* corrupt

**corsé** [kor·'se] *m* corset

**cortacésped** [kor·ta·'ses·ped, -'θes·ped] *m* lawnmower

**cortada** [kor·'ta·da] *f* AmL (*herida*) cut

**cortado** [kor·'ta·do] *m* CULIN coffee with only a little milk

**cortado, -a** [kor·'ta·do, -a] *adj* **1.** (*leche*) sour **2.** (*tímido*) shy

**cortafuegos** [kor·ta·'fwe·ɣos] *m inv* **1.** AGR firebreak, fire lane **2.** COMPUT firewall

**cortar** [kor·'tar] **I.** *vt* **1.** (*tajar*) *t.* COMPUT to cut; (*por el medio*) to cut through; (*en pedazos*) to cut up; (*un traje*) to cut out; (*un árbol*) to cut down; (*leña*) to chop; (*el césped*) to mow; (*pelo*) to trim; **¡corta el rollo!** that's enough! **2.** DEP (*la pelota*) to slice **3.** (*el agua*) to cut off; (*la corriente*) to switch off; (*carretera*) to cut; (*comunicación*) to cut off **II.** *vi* cut; **ha cortado con su novio** *inf* she has split up with her boyfriend **III.** *vr:* ~**se 1.** (*persona*) to cut oneself **2.** (*turbarse*) to become embarrassed; **no se cortó ni un pelo** he/she wasn't embarrassed in the least **3.** (*leche*) to turn **4.** TEL to get cut off

**cortaúñas** [kor·ta·'u·ɲas] *m inv* nail clippers *pl*

**corte¹** ['kor·te] *m* **1.** (*herida*) cut **2.** (*de pelo*) haircut **3.** TÉC section; **~ transversal** cross section **4.** ELEC **~ de corriente** power cut ▶ **hacer a alguien un ~ de mangas** ≈ to give sb the V-sign; **dar ~** to embarrass

**corte²** ['kor·te] *f* court

**cortejar** [kor·te·'xar] *vt* to court

**Cortes** ['kor·tes] *fpl* POL Spanish parliament

**cortés** [kor·'tes] *adj* polite

**cortesía** [kor·te·'si·a] *f* courtesy; (*gentileza*) politeness

**corteza** [kor-'te·sa, -θa] *f* (*de un tronco*) bark; (*del pan*) crust; **la ~ terrestre** GEO the earth's crust

**cortijo** [kor-'ti·xo] *m* (*finca*) country estate; (*casa*) country house

**cortina** [kor-'ti·na] *f* curtain; **correr/descorrer la ~** to draw/to draw back the curtain

**corto, -a** ['kor·to] *adj* **1.** (*pequeño*) short; **~ de vista** short-sighted **2.** (*breve*) brief **3.** (*poco listo*) slow

**cortocircuito** [kor·to·sir·'kwi·to/kor·to·sir·ku·'i·to, kor·to·θir-] *m* ELEC short circuit

**cosa** ['ko·sa] *f* **1.** (*en general*) thing; **eso es ~ tuya/mía** that's your/my affair; **¿sabes una ~?** do you know what?; **no me queda otra ~ que...** I have no alternative but...; **no valer gran ~** not to be worth much; **tal como están las ~s...** as things stand...; **como si tal ~** as if nothing had happened; **esas son ~s de Inés** that's typical of Inés **2.** *pl* (*pertenencias*) things *pl*

**coscacho** [kos·'ka·tʃo] *m AmS inf* (*capón*) rap on the head

**coscorrón** [kos·ko·'rron] *m* (*golpe*) bump

**cosecha** [ko·'se·tʃa] *f* **1.** AGR harvest **2.** (*conjunto de frutos*) crop; **de ~ propia** home-grown

**cosechar** [ko·se·'tʃar] *vi, vt* to harvest

**coser** [ko·'ser] **I.** *vt* **1.** (*un vestido*) to sew; (*un botón*) to sew on; (*un roto*) to sew up; **~ a alguien a balazos** to riddle sb with bullets **2.** MED to stitch (up) **II.** *vi* to sew

**cosmética** [kos·'me·ti·ka] *f* cosmetics *pl*

**cosmopolita** [kos·mo·po·'li·ta] *adj, mf* cosmopolitan

**cosmos** ['kos·mos] *m inv* cosmos

**cosquillas** [kos·'ki·jas, -ʎas] *fpl* **hacer ~** to tickle; **tener ~** to be ticklish; **buscar las ~ a alguien** *fig* to try to stir sb up

**costa** ['kos·ta] *f* **1.** GEO coast **2.** FIN cost; **a toda ~** at any price

**costado** [kos·'ta·do] *m* (*lado*) side; **por los cuatro ~s** through and through

**costalearse** [kos·ta·le·'ar·se] *vr Chile* **1.** (*recibir un costalazo*) to fall heavily **2.** *fig* (*sufrir una decepción*) to be disappointed

**costanera** [kos·ta·'ne·ra] *f Arg* (*paseo marítimo*) jetty

**costar** <o → ue> [kos·'tar] *vi, vt* **1.** (*valer*) to cost; **~ caro** to be expensive; **esto te va a ~ caro** this is going to cost you dear; **cueste lo que cueste** cost what it may **2.** (*ser difícil*) **me cuesta convencerlo** I find it difficult to persuade him

**Costa Rica** [kos·ta·rri·'ka] *f* Costa Rica

**costarriqueño, -a** [kos·ta·rri·'ke·ɲo, -a] *adj, m, f* Costa Rican

**coste** ['kos·te] *m* **1.** (*costo*) cost **2.** (*precio*) price

**costear** [kos·te·'ar] **I.** *vt* to pay for **II.** *vi* NÁUT to sail along the coast of **III.** *vr:* **~se** to cover the expenses

**costero, -a** [kos·'te·ro] *adj* coastal

**costilla** [kos·'ti·ja, -ʎa] *f* **1.** ANAT rib **2.** CULIN chop

**costo** ['kos·to] *m* **1.** (*coste*) cost **2.** *AmL* (*esfuerzo*) effort

**costoso, -a** [kos·'to·so, -a] *adj* **1.** (*en dinero*) expensive **2.** (*en esfuerzo*) difficult

**costra** ['kos·tra] *f* **1.** MED scab **2.** (*corteza*) crust

**costumbre** [kos·'tum·bre] *f* **1.** (*hábito*) habit; **como de ~** as usual **2.** (*tradición*) custom

**costura** [kos·'tu·ra] *f* **1.** (*efecto*) seam **2.** (*acción*) sewing, needlework **3.** (*confección*) dressmaking; **alta ~** haute couture

**cotejar** [ko·te·'xar] *vt* to compare

**cotidiano, -a** [ko·ti·'dja·no, -a] *adj* daily

**cotilla** [ko·'ti·ja, -ʎa] *mf inf* gossip

**cotillear** [ko·ti·je·'ar, ko·ti·ʎe-] *vi inf* to gossip

**cotilleo** [ko·ti·'jeo, -'ʎeo] *m inf* gossip

**cotización** [ko·ti·sa·'sjon, -θa·'θjon] *f* **1.** (*de acciones*) price **2.** (*pago*) contribution

**cotizar** <z → c> [ko·ti·'sar, -'θar] **I.** *vt* FIN **~ a algo** to stand at sth **II.** *vi* to pay contributions **III.** *vr:* **~se 1.** FIN **~ a algo** to sell at sth **2.** (*ser popular*) to be valued

**coto** ['ko·to] *m* (*vedado*) **~ de caza** game [*o* hunting] preserve

**cototo** [ko·'to·to] *m AmL inf* (*chichón*) bump

**coxis** ['kok·sis] *m inv* ANAT coccyx

**coyote** [ko·'jo·te] *m* coyote

**coyuntura** [ko·jun·'tu·ra] *f* (*situación*) situation, circumstances *pl*

**coyuntural** [ko·jun·tu·'ral] *adj* ECON current

**coz** [kos, koθ] *f* (*patada*) kick; **dar coces** to kick

**crack** [krak] *m* 1. ECON crash 2. (*droga*) crack

**cráneo** ['kra·neo] *m* ANAT skull

**cráter** ['kra·ter] *m* crater

**creación** [krea·'sjon, -'θjon] *f* creation

**creador(a)** [krea·'dor,-·'do·ra] I. *adj* creative II. *m(f)* creator

**crear** [kre·'ar] I. *vt* 1. (*hacer*) to create; ~ **archivo** COMPUT to make a new file 2. (*fundar*) to establish II. *vr:* ~**se** to be created

**creatividad** [krea·ti·βi·'dad] *f* creativity

**creativo, -a** [krea·'ti·βo, -a] *adj* creative

**crecer** [kre·'ser, -'θer] *irr* I. *vi* 1. (*aumentar*) to grow, to increase 2. (*luna*) to wax 3. (*agua*) to rise II. *vr:* ~**se** (*persona*) to grow more confident

**creces** ['kre·ses, -θes] *fpl* **con ~** fully

**crecimiento** [kre·si·'mjen·to, kre·θi·] *m t.* ECON growth

**credencial** [kre·den·'sjal, -'θjal] I. *adj* accrediting II. *fpl* credentials

**credibilidad** [kre·di·βi·li·'dad] *f* credibility

**crédito** ['kre·di·to] *m* 1. FIN (*préstamo*) credit; **pedir un ~** to ask for a loan 2. (*fama*) reputation 3. (*confianza*) **dar ~ a algo/alguien** to believe in sth/sb

**credo** ['kre·do] *m* 1. (*creencias*) beliefs *pl* 2. (*oración*) creed

**crédulo, -a** ['kre·du·lo, -a] *adj* credulous

**creencia** [kre·'en·sja, -θja] *f* belief

**creer** [kre·'er] *irr como* leer I. *vi ~* **en Dios/alguien** to believe in God/sb II. *vt* 1. (*dar por cierto*) to believe; **¡quién iba a ~lo!** who would have believed it!; **no te creo** I don't believe you; **hacer ~ algo a alguien** to make sb believe sth 2. (*pensar*) **¡ya lo creo!** I should think so! III. *vr:* ~**se** (*considerarse*) to believe oneself to be

**creíble** [kre·'i·βle] *adj* credible, believable

**creído, -a** [kre·'i·do, -a] *adj inf* (*vanidoso*) conceited

**crema** ['kre·ma] *f* 1. cream; ~ **antiarrugas** anti-wrinkle cream 2. (*natillas*) custard; **la ~ y la nata** *fig* the crème de la crème

**cremallera** [kre·ma·'je·ra, -'ʎe·ra] *f* (*cierre*) zipper

**crematorio** [kre·ma·'to·rjo] *m* crematorium

**crematorio, -a** [kre·ma·'to·rjo, -a] *adj* **horno ~** crematorium

**cremoso, -a** [kre·'mo·so, -a] *adj* creamy

**crepúsculo** [kre·'pus·ku·lo] *m* twilight, dusk; ~ **matutino** dawn

**cresta** ['kres·ta] *f* 1. (*del gallo*) (cocks) comb 2. (*de ola, montaña*) crest 3. (*plumas*) crest 4. (*cabello*) tuft

**Creta** ['kre·ta] *f* Crete

**cretino, -a** [kre·'ti·no, -a] *m, f t. fig* cretin

**creyente** [kre·'jen·te] *mf* believer

**cría** ['kri·a] *f* 1. (*acción*) rearing, raising 2. (*cachorro*) baby animal 3. (*camada*) litter

**criado, -a** [kri·'a·do, -a] *m, f* servant

**criandera** [krjan·'de·ra] *f AmL* wet nurse

**criar** <1. *pres* crío> [kri·'ar] I. *vt* 1. (*alimentar*) to feed; (*mamíferos*) to suckle 2. (*reproducir*) to breed 3. (*educar*) to bring up II. *vr:* ~**se** to grow up

**criatura** [krja·'tu·ra] *f t. fig* creature; (*niño*) child

**criba** ['kri·βa] *f* sieve; *fig* selection process

**cribar** [kri·'βar] *vt* to sieve

**crimen** ['kri·men] *m* crime

**criminal** [kri·mi·'nal] *adj, mf* criminal

**criminalidad** [kri·mi·na·li·'dad] *f* criminality

**crío, -a** ['kri·o, -a] *m, f inf* kid

**criollo, -a** [kri·'o·jo, -a; -·'o·ʎo, -a] *adj, m, f* Creole

**cripta** ['krip·ta] *f* crypt

**críptico, -a** ['krip·ti·ko, -a] *adj* cryptic

**crisis** ['kri·sis] *f inv* crisis; ~ **nerviosa** nervous breakdown

**crispación** [kris·pa·'sjon, -'θjon] *f* (*irritación*) tension

**crispar** [kris·'par] I. *vt* 1. (*exasperar*)

to exasperate **2.** (*contraer*) to contract **II.** *vr:* ~**se 1.** (*exasperarse*) to become exasperated **2.** (*contraerse*) to contract

**cristal** [kris·'tal] *m* **1.** (*cuerpo*) crystal **2.** (*vidrio*) glass

**cristianismo** [kris·tja·'nis·mo] *m* Christianity

**cristiano, -a** [kris·'tja·no, -a] *m inf* **1.** (*persona*) person **2.** (*castellano*) Spanish; **hablar en** ~ *fig* to speak plainly

**cristiano, -a** [kris·'tja·no, -a] *adj, m, f* Christian

**cristo** ['kris·to] *m* crucifix; **todo** ~ *inf* everyone

**Cristo** ['kris·to] *m* Christ

**criterio** [kri·'te·rjo] *m* **1.** (*norma*) criterion **2.** (*discernimiento*) judgment **3.** (*opinión*) opinion

**crítica** ['kri·ti·ka] *f* **1.** (*juicio*) criticism **2.** (*prensa*) review, write-up

**criticar** <c → qu> [kri·ti·'kar] **I.** *vt* to criticize **II.** *vi* to gossip

**crítico, -a** ['kri·ti·ko, -a] **I.** *adj* critical **II.** *m, f* critic

**Croacia** [kro·'a·sja, -θja] *f* Croatia

**croar** [kro·'ar] *vi* to croak

**croata** [kro·'a·ta] *adj, mf* Croat(ian)

**cromo** ['kro·mo] *m* **1.** QUÍM chromium **2.** (*estampa*) (picture) card; ~**s de béisbol** baseball cards; **estar** [*o* **ir**] **hecho un** ~ to look wonderful *iron*

**cromosoma** [kro·mo·'so·ma] *m* chromosome

**crónica** ['kro·ni·ka] *f* **1.** HIST chronicle **2.** (*prensa*) (feature) article; (*reportaje*) report

**crónico, -a** ['kro·ni·ko, -a] *adj t.* MED chronic

**cronista** [kro·'nis·ta] *mf* **1.** HIST chronicler **2.** (*periodista*) journalist

**cronología** [kro·no·lo·'xi·a] *f* chronology, sequence of events

**cronológico, -a** [kro·no·'lo·xi·ko, -a] *adj* chronological

**cronometrar** [kro·no·me·'trar] *vt* to time

**cronómetro** [kro·'no·me·tro] *m* chronometer; DEP stopwatch

**croqueta** [kro·'ke·ta] *f* ≈ croquette

**croquis** ['kro·kis] *m inv* sketch, outline

**cruasán** [krwa·'san/kru·'san] *m* croissant

**cruce** ['kru·se, -θe] *m* **1.** (*acción*) cross-

ing **2.** (*intersección*) crossing, intersection **3.** (*mezcla*) crossing, cross; ~ **de peatones** pedestrian crossing **4.** BIO cross

**crucero** [kru·'se·ro, -'θe·ro] *m* **1.** (*buque*) cruiser **2.** (*viaje*) cruise

**crucial** [kru·'θjal, -'sjal] *adj* crucial

**crucificar** <c → qu> [kru·si·fi·'kar, kru·θi-] *vt* to crucify

**crucifijo** [kru·si·'fi·xo, kru·θi-] *m* crucifix

**crucigrama** [kru·si·'ɣra·ma, kru·θi-] *m* crossword (puzzle)

**crudeza** [kru·'de·sa, -θa] *f* (*rigor*) harshness

**crudo** ['kru·do] *m* crude oil

**crudo, -a** ['kru·do, -a] *adj* **1.** (*sin cocer*) raw **2.** (*tiempo*) harsh

**cruel** [kru·'el] *adj* <crudelísimo> ~ **con alguien** cruel to sb

**crueldad** [krwel·'dad] *f* ~ **con alguien** cruelty to sb

**crujido** [kru·'xi·do] *m* (*de papel*) rustling; (*de madera*) creaking

**crujiente** [kru·'xjen·te] *adj* (*pan*) crunchy

**crujir** [kru·'xir] *vi* (*papel*) to rustle; (*madera*) creak

**cruz** [krus, kruθ] *f* **1.** (*figura*) cross; ~ **gamada** swastika; **Cruz Roja** Red Cross **2.** (*de moneda*) reverse; **¿cara o** ~**?** heads or tails? **3.** (*de animal*) withers *pl* **4.** (*suplicio*) burden; **llevar una** ~ to have a cross to bear

**cruzada** [kru·'sa·da, -'θa·da] *f* crusade

**cruzado, -a** [kru·'sa·do, -a; -'θa·do, -a] *adj* **animal** ~ BIO crossbred animal; **chaqueta cruzada** double-breasted jacket

**cruzar** <z → c> [kru·'sar, -'θar] **I.** *vt, vi* to cross; ~ **los brazos** to cross one's arms **II.** *vr:* ~**se 1.** (*caminos*) to cross **2.** (*encontrarse*) to meet; ~**se con alguien** to pass sb **3.** *t.* MAT to intersect

**cu** [ku] *f* (name of the letter) q

**cuaderno** [kwa·'der·no] *m* notebook; ~ **de bitácora** NÁUT logbook

**cuadra** ['kwa·dra] *f* **1.** (*establo*) stable **2.** (*caballos*) stables *pl* **3.** (*lugar*) pigsty **4.** AmL (*manzana de casas*) block (of houses)

**cuadrado** [kwa·'dra·do] *m t.* ASTR square; **elevar al** ~ to square

**cuadrado, -a** [kwa·'dra·do, -a] *adj*

**1.** (*forma*) square; **tener la cabeza cuadrada** to be pigheaded **2.** (*corpulento*) hefty

**cuadrángulo** [kwa·'dran·gu·lo] *m* quadrangle

**cuadrar** [kwa·'drar] **I.** *vi* **1.** (*convenir*) to fit in **2.** (*coincidir*) to tally **II.** *vt* t. MAT to square **III.** *vr:* ~**se** *inf* (*plantarse*) to dig one's heels in

**cuadrícula** [kwa·'dri·ku·la] *f* grid squares *pl*

**cuadrilla** [kwa·'dri·ja, -ʎa] *f* (*de amigos*) group; (*de maleantes*) gang

**cuadro** ['kwa·dro] *m* **1.** (*cuadrado*) square; **a** ~**s** plaid, check(er)ed **2.** (*pintura*) painting **3.** (*marco*) frame **4.** (*escena*) scene **5.** (*descripción*) description; ~ **sinóptico** synoptic chart **6.** TÉC panel

**cuajada** [kwa·'xa·da] *f* curd

**cuajar** [kwa·'xar] **I.** *vi* **1.** (*espesarse*) to thicken **2.** *inf* (*realizarse*) to come off **II.** *vt* (*leche*) to curdle **III.** *vr:* ~**se** to coagulate; (*leche*) to curdle

**cual** [kwal] *pron rel* **1.** (*explicativo*) **el/la** ~ (*persona*) who, whom; (*cosa*) which; **lo** ~ which; **los/las** ~**es** (*personas*) who, whom; (*cosas*) which; **cada** ~ everyone **2.** (*correlativo*) **hazlo tal** ~ **te lo digo** do it just as I tell you (to); **sea** ~ **sea su intención** whatever his/her intention may be

**cuál** [kwal] **I.** *pron interrog* which (one); **¿~ es el tuyo?** which is yours? **II.** *pron indef* (*distributivo*) ~ **más** ~ **menos** some more, some less

**cualesquier(a)** [kwa·les·'kje·ra] *pron indef pl de* **cualquiera**

**cualidad** [kwa·li·'dad] *f* quality

**cualificación** [kwa·li·fi·ka·'sjon, -'θjon] *f* qualification

**cualificar** <c → qu> [kwa·li·fi·'kar] *vt* to qualify

**cualitativo, -a** [kwa·li·ta·'ti·βo, -a] *adj* qualitative

**cualquiera** [kwal·'kje·ra] **I.** *pron indef* (*ante sustantivo: cualquier*) any; **en un lugar** ~ anywhere; **a cualquier hora** at any time; **cualquier cosa** anything; **de cualquier modo** whichever way; (*de todas maneras*) anyway; **¡~ lo puede**

**hacer!** anybody can do it! **II.** *mf* **ser una** ~ *pey* to be a whore

**cuando** ['kwan·do] *conj* **1.** (*presente, pasado*) when; **de** ~ **en** ~ from time to time **2.** (*futuro; +subj*) when; ~ **quieras** when(ever) you want **3.** (*relativo*) **el lunes es** ~ **no trabajo** I don't work on Mondays **4.** (*condicional*) if; ~ **más** [*o* **mucho**] at (the) most; ~ **menos** at least **5.** (*aunque*) **aun** ~ even if

**cuándo** ['kwan·do] *adv* when

**cuantía** [kwan·'ti·a] *f* amount

**cuantificar** <c → qu> [kwan·ti·fi·'kar] *vt* to quantify

**cuantioso, -a** [kwan·'tjo·so, -a] *adj* substantial

**cuantitativo, -a** [kwan·ti·ta·'ti·βo, -a] *adj* quantitative

**cuanto, -a** ['kwan·to] **I.** *adv* ~ **antes** as soon as possible; ~ **antes mejor** the sooner the better; ~ **más lo pienso, menos me gusta** the more I think about it, the less I like it **II.** *prep* **en** ~ **a** as regards **III.** *conj* (*temporal*) **en** ~ (**que**) as soon as

**cuanto, -a** ['kwan·to, -a] **I.** *pron rel* **1.** (*neutro*) **todo** ~ (that) (which); **tanto...** ~ as much... as; **dije** (**todo**) ~ **sé** I said all that I know **2.** *pl* all those that; **la más hermosa de cuantas conozco** the most beautiful of those I know **II.** *pron indef* **unos** ~**s**/**unas cuantas** some, several

**cuánto** ['kwan·to] *adv* **1.** (*interrogativo*) how much **2.** (*exclamativo*) how; **¡~ llueve!** how hard it's raining!

**cuánto, -a** ['kwan·to, -a] **I.** *adj* **¿~ vino?** how much wine?; **¿~s libros?** how many books?; **¿~ tiempo?** how long?; **¿cuántas veces?** how often? **II.** *pron interrog* how much [*o* many]; **¿~ hay de aquí a Veracruz?** how far is it from here to Veracruz?

**cuarenta** [kwa·'ren·ta] **I.** *adj inv* forty **II.** *m* forty; *v. t.* **ochenta**

**cuarentena** [kwa·ren·'te·na] *f* **1.** (*aislamiento*) quarantine **2.** (*conjunto*) **una** ~ **de veces** about forty times

**cuaresma** [kwa·'res·ma] *f* REL Lent

**cuartel** [kwar·'tel] *m* **1.** MIL (*acuartelamiento*) encampment; ~ **general** headquarters *pl* **2.** MIL (*edificio*) barracks *pl*

**cuartelillo** [kwar·te·'li·jo, -ʎo] *m* police station

**cuarteto** [kwar·'te·to] *m* MÚS quartet

**cuartilla** [kwar·'ti·ja, -ʎa] *f* (*hoja*) sheet of paper

**cuarto** ['kwar·to] *m* **1.** (*habitación*) room; **~ de baño** bathroom; **~ de estar** living room; **~ trastero** lumber room **2.** (*pl*) *inf* (*dinero*) money, dough *inf* **3.** (*de un caballo*) **~s delanteros** forequarters *pl*; **~s traseros** hindquarters *pl*

**cuarto, -a** ['kwar·to, -a] **I.** *adj* fourth **II.** *m, f* quarter; **~ creciente/menguante** first/last quarter; **~s de final** DEP quarterfinal; **un ~ de hora** a quarter of an hour; **es la una y/menos ~** it's a quarter past/to one; *v. t.* **octavo**

**cuarzo** ['kwar·so, -θo] *m* quartz

**cuate, -a** ['kwa·te, -a] *m, f* **1.** *Méx* (*gemelo*) twin **2.** *Guat, Méx* (*amigo*) buddy

**cuatrero, -a** [kwa·'tre·ro, -a] *m, f* rustler

**cuatrimestre** [kwa·tri·'mes·tre] *m* four-month period

**cuatro** ['kwa·tro] *adj inv* four; *v. t.* **ocho**

**cuatrocientos, -as** [kwa·tro·'sjen·tos, -as; kwa·tro·'θjen-] *adj* four hundred; *v. t.* **ochocientos**

**cuba** ['ku·βa] *f* (*tonel*) barrel; **estar como una ~** *inf* (*borracho*) to be plastered

**Cuba** ['ku·βa] *f* Cuba

**cubano, -a** [ku·'βa·no, -a] *adj, m, f* Cuban

**cubertería** [ku·βer·te·'ri·a] *f* cutlery, silverware

**cúbico, -a** ['ku·βi·ko, -a] *adj t.* MAT cubic

**cubierta** [ku·'βjer·ta] *f* **1.** (*cobertura*) cover; (*de libro*) jacket; (*de rueda*) tire; **~ de cama** bedspread **2.** NÁUT deck

**cubierto** [ku·'βjer·to] *m* **1.** *t.* CULIN place setting; **poner un ~** to set a place; **los ~s** the cutlery, the silverware **2.** (*techumbre*) **ponerse a ~** to take cover

**cubierto, -a** [ku·'βjer·to, -a] **I.** *pp de* **cubrir II.** *adj* (*cielo*) overcast

**cubilete** [ku·βi·'le·te] *m* (*en juegos*) cup

**cubismo** [ku·'βis·mo] *m* ARTE cubism

**cubitera** [ku·βi·'te·ra] *f* ice tray

**cubito** [ku·'βi·to] *m* **~ de hielo** ice cube

**cubo** ['ku·βo] *m* **1.** (*recipiente*) bucket; **~ de basura** trashcan **2.** *t.* MAT cube

**cubrir** [ku·'βrir] *irr como* **abrir I.** *vt* **1.** (*tapar*) to cover **2.** (*vacante*) to fill **II.** *vr:* **~se 1.** (*taparse*) to cover oneself **2.** (*cielo*) to become overcast **3.** (*protegerse*) to cover oneself; MIL to take cover

**cucaracha** [ku·ka·'ra·tʃa] *f* cockroach

**cuchara** [ku·'tʃa·ra] *f* spoon; **~ de palo** wooden spoon; **~ sopera** soup spoon

**cucharada** [ku·tʃa·'ra·da] *f* (*porción*) spoonful; **una ~ grande/pequeña** a tablespoonful/teaspoonful; **a ~s** in spoonfuls

**cucharilla** [ku·tʃa·'ri·ja, -ʎa] *f* teaspoon

**cuchichear** [ku·tʃi·tʃe·'ar] *vi* to whisper

**cuchilla** [ku·'tʃi·ja, -ʎa] *f* **1.** (*hoja*) blade; (*de afeitar*) **2.** (*de carnicero*) cleaver, razor blade

**cuchillo** [ku·'tʃi·jo, -ʎo] *m* knife; **~ de cocina** kitchen knife

**cuchitril** [ku·tʃi·'tril] *m* pigsty; *fig* (*habitación*) hole

**cuchuco** [ku·'tʃu·ko] *m* *Col* CULIN pork and barley soup

**cuclillas** [ku·'kli·jas, -ʎas] *fpl* **estar en ~** to be squatting

**cuco** ['ku·ko] *m* cuckoo

**cuco, -a** ['ku·ko, -a] *adj* **1.** (*astuto*) crafty **2.** (*bonito*) pretty

**cuello** ['kwe·jo, -ʎo] *m* **1.** ANAT neck; **~ de botella** *fig* bottleneck; **alargar el ~** to crane one's neck; **estar con el agua al ~** to be in a tight spot **2.** (*de una prenda*) collar; **~ alto** turtleneck; **~ de pico** V-neck; **~ redondo** crew neck

**cuenca** ['kwen·ka] *f* **1.** GEO basin; **~ del río** river basin **2.** (*región*) valley **3.** (*de los ojos*) socket

**cuenco** ['kwen·ko] *m* **1.** (*vasija*) bowl **2.** (*concavidad*) hollow

**cuenta** ['kwen·ta] *f* **1.** (*cálculo*) counting; **~ atrás** countdown; **~s atrasadas** outstanding debts *pl*; **pagar la ~** to pay the bill; **trabajar por ~ propia** to be self-employed; **establecerse por su ~** to set up one's own business; **echar ~s** to reflect; **dar ~ de algo** to report on sth; **ajustar las ~s a alguien** to get even with sb; **ajuste de ~s** act of revenge;

**caer en la** ~ to catch on; **hablar más de la** ~ to talk too much; **a fin de** ~s after all; **en resumidas** ~s in short; **perder la** ~ to lose count **2.** (*en el banco*) account; ~ **corriente** current account; ~ **de crédito** loan account; **abonar en** ~ to credit; **abrir una** ~ to open an account **3.** (*consideración*) **tener en** ~ to bear in mind; **tomar en** ~ to take into consideration; **darse** ~ **de algo** to realize sth **4.** (*de un collar*) bead

**cuentagotas** [kwen·ta·'ɣo·tas] *m inv* dropper; **con** [*o a*] ~ *fig* bit by bit

**cuento** ['kwen·to] *m* LIT (*historieta*) story; ~ **chino** *inf* tall story; ~ **de hadas** fairy tale [*o story*]; ~ **de nunca acabar** never-ending story; **tener mucho** ~ *inf* (*presumir*) to boast a lot; (*exagerar*) to exaggerate everything; **dejarse de** ~s to stop boasting about the bush ▶ **eso es como el** ~ **de la lechera** don't count your chickens before they're hatched; **no venir a** ~ to be beside the point

**cuerda** ['kwer·da] *f* **1.** (*gruesa*) rope; (*delgada*) string; ~ **floja** tightrope; **andar en la** ~ **floja** *fig* to be in an unstable position; **bajo** ~ secretly **2.** (*del reloj*) spring; **dar** ~ **al reloj** to wind up one's watch; **dar** ~ **a alguien** to encourage sb **3.** ANAT ~s **vocales** vocal chords **4.** (*de instrumentos*) string; **juego de** ~s set of strings

**cuerdo, -a** ['kwer·do, -a] *adj* sensible; **estar** ~ to be sane

**cueriza** [kwe·'ri·sa, -θa] *f AmL* (*zurra*) beating

**cuerno** ['kwer·no] *m* **1.** ZOOL horn; **poner a alguien los** ~s *inf* to be unfaithful to sb **2.** *inf* (*exclamativo*) **¡y un** ~! my foot!; **irse al** ~ to be ruined; (*plan*) to fall through; **¡que se vaya al** ~! he/she can go to hell!

**cuero** ['kwe·ro] *m* leather; ~ **cabelludo** scalp; **estar en** ~s *inf* to be stark naked

**cuerpo** ['kwer·po] *m* **1.** (*organismo*) body; (*tronco*) trunk; (*cadáver*) corpse, cadaver; **una foto de** ~ **entero** a full-length photo(graph); **luchar** ~ **a** ~ to fight hand-to-hand; **tomar** ~ to take shape; **estar de** ~ **presente** to lie in state; **hacer de(l)** ~ to relieve oneself;

**haz lo que te pida el** ~ do what you feel like doing **2.** (*objeto, corporación*) body; ~ **de bomberos** fire department; ~ **diplomático** diplomatic corps **3.** (*grosor*) thickness; **tener poco** ~ to be thin ▶ **vivir a** ~ **de rey** to live like a king

**cuervo** ['kwer·βo] *m* raven, crow

**cuesta** ['kwes·ta] *f* slope; ~ **abajo/arriba** downhill/uphill; **un camino en** ~ an uphill road; **llevar algo a** ~s to carry sth on one's back

**cuestión** [kwes·'tjon] *f* question, matter; ~ **de gustos** question of taste; **eso es otra** ~ that's another matter; **la** ~ **es pasarlo bien** the main thing is to enjoy oneself

**cuestionable** [kwes·tjo·'na·βle] *adj* questionable

**cuestionar** [kwes·tjo·'nar] *vt* to question

**cuestionario** [kwes·tjo·'na·rjo] *m* questionnaire

**cuete** ['kwe·te] *m Méx* **1.** (*loncha de carne*) slice of meat **2.** (*borrachera*) drunken spree; **traer un** ~ to be plastered

**cueva** ['kwe·βa] *f* cave

**cuidado** [kwi·'da·ðo] *m* care; **¡**~**!** careful!; **¡**~ **con el escalón!** mind the step!; **de** ~ serious; **eso me tiene sin** ~ I couldn't care less about that

**cuidador(a)** [kwi·da·'ðor] *m(f)* caregiver; *Arg* nurse

**cuidadoso, -a** [kwi·da·'ðo·so, -a] *adj* careful

**cuidar** [kwi·'dar] **I.** *vt* to look after **II.** *vr:* ~**se** to look after oneself; **¡cuídate!** take care!

**culminación** [kul·mi·na·'sjon, -'θjon] *f* culmination

**culminante** [kul·mi·'nan·te] *adj* **punto** ~ high point

**culo** ['ku·lo] *m* bottom; (*de vaso*) bottom; **caer de** ~ to fall on one's backside; *fig* to be amazed; **lamer el** ~ **a alguien** *vulg* to kiss sb's ass; **tonto del** ~ idiot

**culpa** ['kul·pa] *f* fault; JUR guilt; **echar la** ~ **a alguien** to blame sb; **y ¿qué** ~ **tengo yo?** and how am I to blame (for that)?

**culpabilidad** [kul·pa·βi·li·'dad] *f* guilt

**culpable** [kul·'pa·βle] **I.** *adj* guilty; **decla-**

**rar ~** to find guilty **II.** *mf* culprit

**culpar** [kul·'par] **I.** *vt* **~ de** [*o* **por**] **algo** to blame for sth **II.** *vr* **~se de** [*o* **por**] **algo** to be to blame for sth

**cultivar** [kul·ti·'βar] *vt t. fig* AGR to cultivate; **~ la tierra** to farm the land

**cultivo** [kul·'ti·βo] *m* AGR (*acto*) cultivation; (*resultado*) crop; (*de bacterias*) culture; **~ de regadío** irrigated crop

**culto** ['kul·to] *m* worship

**culto, -a** ['kul·to, -a] *adj* educated, cultured

**cultura** [kul·'tu·ra] *f* culture; **~ general** general knowledge

**cultural** [kul·tu·'ral] *adj* cultural

**cuma** ['ku·ma] *f* **1.** *AmC* (*machete*) long knife **2.** *Perú* (*comadre*) godmother

**cumbre** ['kum·bre] *f* **1.** (*cima*) summit **2.** (*reunión*) summit meeting **3.** (*culminación*) height

**cumiche** [ku·'mi·tʃe] *m* *AmC* baby of the family

**cumpleaños** [kum·ple·'a·ɲos] *m inv* birthday

**cumplido** [kum·'pli·do] *m* compliment; **hacer algo por ~** to do sth out of courtesy

**cumplido, -a** [kum·'pli·do, -a] *adj* **1.** (*acabado*) completed; **¡misión cumplida!** mission accomplished! **2.** (*cortés*) courteous

**cumplimentar** [kum·pli·men·'tar] *vt* **1.** (*felicitar*) to congratulate **2.** (*visitar*) to pay one's respects to **3.** (*una orden*) to carry out **4.** (*un impreso*) to complete

**cumplir** [kum·'plir] **I.** *vi* **1.** (*satisfacer*) **~ con su deber/su promesa** to do one's duty/to keep one's promise; **hacer algo sólo por ~** to do sth as a matter of form **2.** (*plazo*) to end **II.** *vt* **1.** (*orden*) to carry out **2.** (*promesa*) to keep **3.** (*plazo*) to keep to **4.** (*una pena*) to serve **5.** (*las leyes*) to observe **6.** (*años*) **en mayo cumplo treinta años** I'm thirty years old in May **III.** *vr:* **~se** to be fulfilled

**cuna** ['ku·na] *f* cradle; **canción de ~** lullaby

**cundir** [kun·'dir] *vi* **1.** (*dar de sí*) to be productive **2.** (*trabajo*) to go well

**cuneta** [ku·'ne·ta] *f* ditch

**cuña** ['ku·ɲa] *f* (*traba*) wedge

**cuñado, -a** [ku·'ɲa·do, -a] *m, f* brother-in-law *m*, sister-in-law *f*

**cuota** ['kwo·ta] *f* **1.** (*porción*) quota; **~ de crecimiento** rate of increase; **~ de mercado** market share **2.** (*contribución*) fee; **~ de socio** membership fee

**cupo** ['ku·po] **I.** *3. pret de* **caber II.** *m* **1.** ECON quota **2.** MIL draft

**cupón** [ku·'pon] *m* coupon; (*de lotería*) lottery ticket

**cúpula** ['ku·pu·la] *f* ARQUIT dome; **~ dirigente** POL top management

**cura¹** ['ku·ra] *m* priest

**cura²** ['ku·ra] *f* **1.** (*curación*) cure **2.** (*tratamiento*) treatment

**curación** [ku·ra·'sjon, -'θjon] *f* treatment

**curado, -a** [ku·'ra·do, -a] *adj* **1.** (*alimento*) cured **2.** *AmL* (*borracho*) drunk

**curandero, -a** [ku·ran·'der·o, -a] *m, f* healer

**curar** [ku·'rar] **I.** *vt* **1.** (*tratar*) to treat; (*sanar*) to cure **2.** (*alimentos*) to cure; (*pieles*) to tan **II.** *vr:* **~se** to recover; **~se en salud** to take precautions

**curativo, -a** [ku·ra·'ti·βo, -a] *adj* curative

**curiosidad** [ku·rjo·si·'dad] *f* curiosity; **despertar la ~ de alguien** to arouse sb's curiosity

**curioso, -a** [ku·'rjo·so, -a] **I.** *adj* curious; **¡qué ~!** how curious! **II.** *m, f* **1.** (*indiscreto*) busybody, snoop **2.** (*mirón*) onlooker, bystander **3.** *AmL* (*curandero*) quack doctor

**currante** [ku·'rran·te] *mf inf* worker

**currar** [ku·'rrar] *vi inf* to work

**currículo** [ku·'rri·ku·lo] *m* curriculum

**curro** ['ku·rro] *m inf* job

**curry** ['ku·rri] *m* curry

**cursar** [kur·'sar] *vt* **1.** (*cursos*) to take **2.** (*orden*) to issue; (*telegrama*) to send; (*solicitud*) to pass on

**cursi** ['kur·si] **I.** *adj inf* affected **II.** *mf inf* affected person

**cursillo** [kur·'si·jo, -ʎo] *m* short course

**cursiva** [kur·'si·βa] *f* italics *pl*

**curso** ['kur·so] *m* **1.** (*transcurso*) course; **~ de agua** watercourse; **estar en ~** to be going on; FIN to be in circulation;

tomar un ~ favorable to go favorably; dar ~ a una solicitud to deal with an application 2. ENS course; ~ acelerado crash course; asistir a un ~ to take part in a course

cursor [kur·'sor] m COMPUT cursor

curtir [kur·'tir] I. vt to tan; fig to harden II. vr: ~se 1. (piel) to become tanned 2. (a la vida dura) to become inured

curva ['kur·βa] f curve

cusma ['kus·ma] f AmS coarse woolen Indian shirt

cúspide ['kus·pi·de] f 1. MAT apex 2. fig pinnacle

custodia [kus·'to·dja] f (guarda) custody; bajo ~ in custody; estar bajo la ~ de alguien to be in sb's care

custodiar [kus·to·'djar] vt to guard

cususa [ku·'su·sa] f AmC uncured rum

cutis ['ku·tis] m inv skin, complexion

cuyo, -a ['ku·jo, -a] pron rel whose; por cuya causa for which reason

# D

D, d [de] f D, d; D de Dolores D as in Delta

D. [don] abr de Don Mr.

Dª ['do·ɲa] abr de Doña Mrs.

dactilar [dak·ti·'lar] adj huellas ~es fingerprints pl

dado¹ ['da·ðo] m die; (jugar a los) ~s (to play) dice

dado² conj 1. (+ inf) ~ que llueve... given that it's raining... 2. (+ subj) ~ que sea posible... assuming it were possible...

dado, -a ['da·ðo, -a] adj (supuesto) given; en el caso ~ in this particular case
► no ser ~ Méx to be brave

daga ['da·ɣa] f dagger; PRico machete

daiquiri [dai·'ki·ri] m CULIN daiquiri

dalia ['da·lja] f dahlia

dálmata ['dal·ma·ta] m ZOOL dalmatian

daltónico, -a [dal·'to·ni·ko, -a] adj color-blind

dama ['da·ma] f 1. (señora) lady; ~ de honor bridesmaid 2. pl (juego) checkers pl

damnificar <c → qu> [dam·ni·fi·'kar] vt (persona) to injure; (cosa) to damage

danés, -esa [da·'nes, -·'ne·sa] I. adj Danish II. m, f Dane

danza ['dan·sa, -θa] f dance

danzar <z → c> [dan·'sar, -'θar] vi, vt to dance

dañar [da·'ɲar] I. vi to harm II. vt (cosa) to damage; (persona) to injure III. vr: ~se to get damaged

dañero, -a [da·'ɲe·ro, -a] adj Ven misleading

dañino, -a [da·'ɲi·no, -a] adj harmful

daño ['da·ɲo] m 1. (perjuicio) damage; ~s y perjuicios JUR damages 2. (dolor) hurt; hacer ~ a alguien to hurt sb; hacerse ~ to hurt oneself

dar [dar] irr I. vt 1. (entregar) to give; ~ forma a algo to shape sth; ~ importancia a algo to consider sth important 2. (producir) la vaca da leche the cow yields milk; este árbol da naranjas this tree bears oranges 3. (celebrar) to give; ~ clases to teach 4. (causar) ~ miedo to be frightening; me das pena I feel sorry for you 5. (película) to show 6. (una noticia) to give; ~ las buenas noches to say goodnight; ~ recuerdos to send one's regards 7. ~ un paseo to take a walk; (encender) to turn on 8. (reloj) to strike 9. (+ 'a') ~ a conocer algo to let sth be known; ~ a entender algo a alguien to let sb know sth II. vi 1. (+ 'a') el balcón da a la calle the balcony faces the street; la ventana da al patio the window opens onto the courtyard 2. (+ 'con') ~ con la solución to find the solution 3. ~ contra algo to hit sth 4. (caer) ~ de espaldas to land on one's back 5. (acertar) ~ en el blanco fig to hit the target; ~ en el clavo fig to hit the nail on the head 6. (+ 'para') da para vivir it's enough to live on 7. (+ 'por' + adj) ~ a alguien por inocente to assume sb is innocent 8. (+ 'por' + vb) le ha dado por dejarse el pelo largo he/she has decided to grow his/her hair long 9. (+ 'que' + vb) ~ que decir/pensar to give cause for comment/thought; ~ que hablar to be the topic of conversation; ~

que hacer to be a lot of work ▶ ¡qué más da! *inf* what does it matter? III. *vr:* ~se 1. (*suceder*) to happen 2. (+ *'a'*) to devote oneself; (*entregarse*) to surrender 3. (+ *'con(tra)'*) ~se con(tra) algo to hit sth 4. (+ *'por'* + *adj*) ~se por vencido to give up 5. (+ *'a'* + *vb*) ~se a conocer (*persona*) to make oneself known; (*noticia*) to become known; ~se a entender to hint 6. (+ *'de'*) ~se de alta/de baja to sign up/off; dárselas de valiente *inf* to pretend to be brave 7. (+ *subst*) ~se un baño to take a bath; ~se cuenta de algo to realize sth; ~se prisa to hurry up

**dardo** ['dar·do] *m* dart

**datar** [da·'tar] *vi, vt* to date

**dátil** ['da·til] *m* date

**dato** ['da·to] *m* 1. (*detalle*) fact; ~s personales personal details 2. (*cantidad*) figure 3. *pl* COMPUT data *pl*; elaborar ~s to compile data

**dC, d.C.** [des·'pwes de 'kris·to] *abr de* después de Cristo AD

**dcha.** [de·'re·tʃa] *abr de* derecha R

**de** [de] *prep* 1. (*posesión*) el reloj ~ mi padre my father's watch 2. (*origen*) from; ser ~ Italia to come from Italy; ~ Caracas a Bogotá from Caracas to Bogotá; un libro ~ Allende a book by Allende 3. (*material, cualidad*) of; ~ oro of gold, golden 4. (*temporal*) from; ~ niño as a child 5. (*finalidad*) máquina ~ lavar washing machine; hora ~ comer mealtime 6. (*causa*) of, from 7. (*condición*) ~ haberlo sabido no habríamos ido if we had known we wouldn't have gone 8. (*partitivo*) dos platos ~ sopa two bowls of soup 9. (+ *nombre propio*) la ciudad ~ Cuzco the city of Cuzco; pobre ~ mí poor me

**deambular** [de·am·bu·'lar] *vi* to wander around

**debajo** [de·'βa·xo] I. *adv* underneath II. *prep* ~ de below, under; (*con movimiento*) under; pasar por ~ de to go under

**debate** [de·'βa·te] *m* 1. POL debate 2. (*charla*) discussion

**debatir** [de·βa·'tir] *vt* 1. POL to debate 2. (*considerar*) to discuss

**deber** [de·'βer] I. *vi* (*suposición*) debe de estar al llegar he/she should arrive soon; deben de ser las nueve it must be nine o'clock II. *vt* 1. (*obligación*) to have to; no ~ías haberlo dicho you shouldn't have said it 2. (*tener que dar*) to owe III. *vr:* ~se 1. (*tener por causa*) ~se a algo to be due to sth; (*gracias a*) to be thanks to sth 2. (*obligación*) to have a duty IV. *m* 1. (*obligación*) duty 2. *pl* (*tareas*) homework

**debido** [de·'βi·do] *prep* ~ a due to

**debido, -a** [de·'βi·do, -a] *adj* como es ~ as is proper

**débil** ['de·βil] *adj* weak; (*sonido*) faint; (*luz*) dim

**debilidad** [de·βi·li·'dad] *f* weakness (por for)

**debilitar** [de·βi·li·'tar] *vt* to weaken

**debitar** [de·βi·'tar] *vt* AmL to debit

**débito** ['de·βi·to] *m* debit; (*deuda*) debt

**debocar** <c → qu> [de·βo·'kar] *vi* Arg, Bol to vomit

**debut** <debuts> [de·'βu(t)] *m* debut; (*teatro*) opening

**debutar** [de·βu·'tar] *vi* to make one's debut

**década** ['de·ka·da] *f* decade

**decadencia** [de·ka·'den·sja, -θja] *f* 1. (*declive*) decay; ~ moral decadence 2. (*de un imperio*) decline

**decadente** [de·ka·'den·te] *adj* (*en declive*) declining; (*moralmente*) decadent

**decaer** [de·ka·'er] *irr como caer vi* to decline; ~ el ánimo to lose heart

**decaído, -a** [de·ka·'i·do, -a] *adj* 1. (*abatido*) downhearted 2. (*débil*) weak

**decano, -a** [de·'ka·no, -a] *m, f* UNIV dean

**decapitar** [de·ka·pi·'tar] *vt* to decapitate

**decatlón** [de·kad·'lon] *m* decathlon

**decena** [de·'se·na, -'θe·na] *f* ten; una ~ de huevos ten eggs

**decencia** [de·'sen·sja, -'θen·θja] *f* decency

**decente** [de·'sen·te, -'θen·te] *adj* 1. (*decoroso*) decent 2. (*honesto*) upright

**decepción** [de·sep·'sjon, -θeβ·'θjon] *f* disappointment

**decepcionante** [de·sep·sjon'an·te, -θeβ·θjon-] *adj* disappointing

**decepcionar** [de·sep·sjo·'nar, -θeβ·θjo·'nar] *vt* to disappoint

**decibel(io)** [de·si·'βel, --'βe·ljo, de·θi-] *m* decibel

**decididamente** [de·si·di·da·'men·te, de·θi-] *adv* **1.** (*resueltamente*) resolutely **2.** (*definitivamente*) decidedly

**decidido, -a** [de·θi·'di·do, -a; de·θi-] *adj* determined

**decidir** [de·si·'dir, de·θi-] **I.** *vi* to decide **II.** *vt* **1.** (*determinar, acordar*) to decide **2.** (*mover a*) to persuade **III.** *vr* ~se por/en contra de algo to decide in favor of/against sth

**décima** ['de·si·ma, de·θi-] *f* tenth

**decimal** [de·si·'mal, de·θi-] *adj, m* decimal

**décimo, -a** ['de·si·mo, -a; de·θi-] **I.** *adj* tenth **II.** *m, f* tenth; (*de lotería*) tenth share of a lottery ticket; *v. t.* **octavo**

**decimonono, -a** [de·si·mo·'no·no, -a; de·θi-], **decimonoveno, -a** [de·si·mo·'βe·no, -a; de·θi-] *adj* nineteenth; *v. t.* **octavo**

**decimoquinto, -a** [de·si·mo·'kin·to, -a; de·θi-] *adj* fifteenth; *v. t.* **octavo**

**decimotercero, -a** [de·si·mo·ter·'se·ro, -a; de·θi·mo·ter·'θe-], **decimotercio, -a** [de·si·mo·'ter·sjo, -a; de·θi·mo·'ter·θjo, -a] *adj* thirteenth; *v. t.* **octavo**

**decir** [de·'sir, -θir] *irr* **I.** *vi* **1.** (*expresar*) ~ algo de alguien to say sth about sb; ~ que sí to say yes; diga [*o* dígame] TEL hello; es [*o* quiere] ~ in other words; ¡no me digas! *inf* really!; ¡quién lo diría! who would have thought it!; y que lo digas you can say that again; y no digamos not to mention **2.** (*llevar escrito*) to say; un letrero que dice 'Bienvenidos' a sign that says "Welcome" **II.** *vt* (*expresar*) to say; (*comunicar*) to tell; dicho y hecho no sooner said than done **III.** *vr* ¿cómo se dice en inglés? how do you say it in English? **IV.** *m* saying ▸ ser un ~ to be a manner of speaking

**decisión** [de·si·'sjon, de·θi-] *f* **1.** (*resolución*) resolution; (*acuerdo*) decision; tomar una ~ to make a decision **2.** (*firmeza*) determination

**decisivo, -a** [de·si·'si·βo, -a; de·θi-] *adj* decisive

**declaración** [de·kla·ra·'sjon, -'θjon] *f* **1.** (*a la prensa*) declaration; hacer declaraciones to make a statement **2.** JUR statement **3.** ~ de la renta income tax return

**declarar** [de·kla·'rar] **I.** *vi* **1.** (*testigo*) to testify, to give evidence **2.** (*a la prensa*) to make a statement **3.** (*manifestar*) to declare; ~ a alguien culpable/inocente to convict/acquit sb **2.** (*ingresos, a aduanas*) to declare **III.** *vr:* ~se (*manifestarse*) to declare oneself; ~se en huelga to go on strike; ~se inocente to plead innocent

**declinación** [de·kli·na·'sjon, -'θjon] *f* **1.** (*disminución*) decline **2.** LING declension

**declinar** [de·kli·'nar] *vi, vt* (*disminuir*) to decline

**declive** [de·'kli·βe] *m* **1.** (*del terreno*) slope; en (fuerte) ~ (steeply) sloping **2.** (*decadencia*) decline

**decodificador** [de·ko·di·fi·ka·'dor] *m* decoder

**decolaje** [de·ko·'la·xe] *m AmL* take-off

**decolar** [de·ko·'lar] *vi AmL* to take off

**decolorar** [de·ko·lo·'rar] **I.** *vt* **1.** QUÍM to discolor **2.** (*el sol*) to bleach **II.** *vr:* ~se to fade

**decoración** [de·ko·ra·'sjon, -'θjon] *f* decoration

**decorado** [de·ko·'ra·do] *m* TEAT set

**decorador(a)** [de·ko·ra·'dor, --'do·ra] *m(f)* decorator; TEAT set designer; ~ de interiores interior designer

**decorar** [de·ko·'rar] *vt* (*adornar*) to decorate

**decorativo, -a** [de·ko·ra·'ti·βo, -a] *adj* decorative

**decoro** [de·'ko·ro] *m* **1.** (*dignidad*) dignity **2.** (*respeto*) respect; guardar el ~ to show respect **3.** (*pudor*) decency; con ~ decently

**decoroso, -a** [de·ko·'ro·so, -a] *adj* **1.** (*decente*) decent **2.** (*digno*) dignified

**decrecer** [de·kre·'ser, -'θer] *irr como* crecer *vi* to decrease; (*nivel, fiebre*) to fall

**decrépito, -a** [de·'kre·pi·to, -a] *adj* **1.** (*persona*) decrepit **2.** (*sociedad*) declining

**decretar** [de·kre·'tar] *vt* to decree

**decreto** [de·'kre·to] *m* decree

**dedal** [de·'dal] *m* thimble

**dedear** [de·de·'ar] *vt Méx* to finger

**dedicación** [de·di·ka·'sjon, -'θjon] *f*
1. (*consagración*) consecration 2. (*entrega*) dedication, commitment

**dedicar** <c → qu> [de·di·'kar] I. *vt*
1. (*destinar*) to dedicate 2. (*consagrar*) to consecrate II. *vr:* ~**se** to devote oneself; ~**se a algo** (*profesionalmente*) to work as sth; ~**se a la enseñanza** to be a teacher; **¿a qué se dedica Ud.?** what do you do?

**dedicatoria** [de·di·ka·'to·rja] *f* dedication

**dedillo** [de·'di·jo, -ʎo] *m inf* **saberse algo al ~** to know sth inside out

**dedo** ['de·do] *m* (*de mano*) finger; (*de pie*) toe; (*pulgar*) thumb ▶ **hacer** [*o* **ir a**] ~ to hitch-hike; **no mover un** ~ to not lift a finger; **nombrar a** ~ to hand-pick

**deducción** [de·duk·'sjon, -duɣ·'θjon] *f t.* ECON deduction; ~ **estándar/por hijo** basic/child tax allowance

**deducir** [de·du·'sir, -'θir] *irr como* **traducir** *vt* 1. (*derivar*) to deduce 2. (*descontar*) to deduct

**defecar** <c → qu> [de·fe·'kar] *vi* to defecate

**defecto** [de·'fek·to] *m* 1. (*carencia*) lack; **en** ~ **de** in the absence of; **en su** ~ (*cosa*) if it is unavailable; (*persona*) in his/her absence 2. (*falta*) defect

**defectuoso, -a** [de·fek·tu·'o·so, -a] *adj* faulty, defective

**defender** <e → ie> [de·fen·'der] I. *vt* 1. (*ideas, intereses*) *t.* JUR to defend 2. (*proteger*) to protect II. *vr:* ~**se** 1. (*contra ataques*) to defend oneself 2. (*arreglárselas*) to get by

**defensa**[1] [de·'fen·sa] *f* 1. (*contra ataques*) *t.* JUR, DEP defense; **en legítima** ~ JUR in self-defense 2. *pl t.* BIO defenses *pl;* **tener** ~**s** to have resistance 3. *Méx* (*paragolpes*) bumper, fender

**defensa**[2] [de·'fen·sa] *mf* DEP defender

**defensiva** [de·fen·'si·βa] *f* (**a la**) ~ (on the) defensive

**defensivo, -a** [de·fen·'si·βo, -a] *adj* defensive

**defensor(a)** [de·fen·'sor, -·'so·ra] I. *adj* defending II. *m(f)* defender

**deferencia** [de·fe·'ren·sja, -θja] *f* (*consideración*) deference; (*cortesía*) courtesy

**deficiencia** [de·fi·'sjen·sja, -θja] *f* 1. (*insuficiencia*) lack 2. (*defecto*) deficiency

**deficiente** [de·fi·'sjen·te, -'θjen·te] I. *adj* 1. (*insuficiente*) lacking 2. (*defectuoso*) deficient II. *mf* ~ **mental** mentally disabled person

**déficit** ['de·fi·sit, -θit] *m inv* 1. FIN ~ (**presupuestario**) (budget) deficit 2. (*escasez*) shortage

**deficitario, -a** [de·fi·si·'ta·rjo, -a; de·fi·θi-] *adj* (*empresa*) loss-making; (*cuenta*) in deficit

**definición** [de·fi·ni·'sjon, -'θjon] *f* (*aclaración*) *t.* TV definition

**definir** [de·fi·'nir] *vt* to define

**definitivo, -a** [de·fi·ni·'ti·βo, -a] *adj* 1. (*irrevocable*) final 2. (*decisivo*) decisive ▶ **en definitiva** in short

**deforestación** [de·fo·res·ta·'sjon, -'θjon] *f* deforestation

**deformación** [de·for·ma·'sjon, -'θjon] *f* 1. (*alteración*) distortion 2. (*desfiguración*) deformation; ~ **física** physical deformity

**deformar** [de·for·'mar] I. *vt* 1. (*alterar*) to distort 2. (*desfigurar*) to deform II. *vr:* ~**se** to become deformed

**deforme** [de·'for·me] *adj* 1. (*imagen*) distorted 2. (*cuerpo*) deformed

**deformidad** [de·for·mi·'dad] *f* deformity

**defraudar** [de·frau·'dar] *vt* 1. (*estafar*) to cheat; ~ **a Hacienda** to evade one's taxes 2. (*decepcionar*) to disappoint

**defunción** [de·fun·'sjon, -'θjon] *f* death

**degeneración** [de·xe·ne·ra·'sjon, -'θjon] *f* degeneration

**degenerar** [de·xe·ne·'rar] *vi* to degenerate

**degollar** <o → ue> [de·ɣo·'jar, -'ʎar] *vt* (*decapitar*) to behead; (*cortar la garganta*) to slit sb's throat

**degradación** [de·ɣra·da·'sjon, -'θjon] *f* (*humillación*) humiliation

**degradante** [de·ɣra·ˈdan·te] *adj* demeaning

**degradar** [de·ɣra·ˈdar] I. *vt* 1. (*en el cargo*) to demote 2. (*calidad*) to worsen; **~ el medio ambiente** to damage the environment 3. (*humillar*) to humiliate II. *vr* to degrade [*o* demean] oneself

**degustación** [de·ɣus·ta·ˈsjon, -ˈθjon] *f* **~ (de vinos)** (wine) tasting

**degustar** [de·ɣus·ˈtar] *vt* to taste

**dehesa** [de·ˈe·sa] *f* pasture

**deidad** [dei·ˈdad] *f* (*dios*) deity

**dejadez** [de·xa·ˈdes, -ˈdeθ] *f* 1. (*falta de aseo*) slovenliness 2. (*pereza*) laziness 3. (*negligencia*) neglect

**dejado, -a** [de·ˈxa·do, -a] *adj* 1. *ser* (*descuidado*) slovenly 2. *estar* (*abatido*) dejected

**dejar** [de·ˈxar] I. *vi* **~ de hacer algo** to stop doing sth; **no dejes de escribirles** don't fail to write them II. *vt* 1. (*en general*) to leave; **~ caer** to drop; **~ claro** to make clear; **~ a deber** to owe; **~ en libertad** to set free; **¡déjanos en paz!** leave us alone! 2. (*abandonar*) to leave; **~ la carrera** to drop out of university 3. (*ganancia*) to give 4. (*permitir*) to allow, to let; **no me dejan salir** they won't let me go out 5. (*entregar*) to give; (*prestar*) to lend; (*en herencia*) to leave III. *vr:* **~se** 1. (*descuidarse*) to neglect oneself 2. (*olvidar*) to forget ► **~se llevar** to let oneself get carried away

**deje** [ˈde·xe] *m* lilt; **se te nota un ~ argentino** you have a slight Argentine accent

**dejo** [ˈde·xo] *m* 1. (*entonación*) lilt; (*acento*) accent 2. (*regusto*) *t. fig* aftertaste

**del** [del] *v.* = **de + el** *v.* **de**

**delantal** [de·lan·ˈtal] *m* apron

**delante** [de·ˈlan·te] I. *adv* 1. (*en la parte delantera*) in front; **de ~** from the front; **abierto por ~** open at the front 2. (*enfrente*) opposite II. *prep* **~ de** in front of; **~ mío** [*o* **de mí**] in front of me

**delantera** [de·lan·ˈte·ra] *f* 1. (*parte anterior*) front (part) 2. (*primera fila*) front row 3. (*distancia*) lead 4. DEP forward line

**delantero** [de·lan·ˈte·ro] *m* (*parte anterior*) front (part)

**delantero, -a** [de·lan·ˈte·ro] *m, f* DEP forward; **~ centro** center forward

**delatar** [de·la·ˈtar] I. *vt* 1. (*denunciar*) to inform on 2. (*manifestar*) to reveal II. *vr:* **~se** to give oneself away

**delegación** [de·le·ɣa·ˈsjon, -ˈθjon] *f* 1. (*comisión*) delegation 2. *Méx* (*comisaría*) police station; (*ayuntamiento*) council

**delegado, -a** [de·le·ˈɣa·do, -a] *m, f* delegate; **~ gubernamental** government representative

**delegar** <g → gu> [de·le·ˈɣar] *vt* **~ algo en alguien** to delegate sth to sb

**deleitar(se)** [de·lei·ˈtar(·se)] *vt, vr* to delight (**con/en** in)

**deleite** [de·ˈlei·te] *m* delight

**deletrear** [de·le·tre·ˈar] *vt* to spell

**delfín** [del·ˈfin] *m* dolphin

**delgado, -a** [del·ˈɣa·do, -a] *adj* thin; (*esbelto*) slender

**deliberado, -a** [de·li·βe·ˈra·do, -a] *adj* 1. (*tratado*) considered 2. (*intencionado*) deliberate

**deliberar** [de·li·βe·ˈrar] *vi, vt* 1. (*reflexionar*) to deliberate 2. (*discutir*) **~ sobre** [*o* **acerca de**] **algo** to discuss sth

**delicadeza** [de·li·ka·ˈde·sa, -ˈθa] *f* 1. (*finura*) delicacy; **con ~** delicately 2. (*miramiento*) attentiveness; **tener la ~ de...** to be thoughtful enough to...

**delicado, -a** [de·li·ˈka·do, -a] *adj* 1. (*fino, frágil*) delicate 2. (*enfermizo*) frail

**delicia** [de·ˈli·sja, -θja] *f* delight

**delicioso, -a** [de·li·ˈsjo·so, -a; -ˈθjo·so, -a] *adj* (*comida*) delicious; (*agradable*) delightful

**delictivo, -a** [de·lik·ˈti·βo, -a] *adj* **acto ~** criminal act

**delimitar** [de·li·mi·ˈtar] *vt* 1. (*terreno*) to mark out 2. (*definir*) to define

**delincuencia** [de·lin·ˈkwen·sja, -ˈθja] *f* crime; **~ juvenil** juvenile delinquency

**delincuente** [de·lin·ˈkwen·te] *adj, mf* criminal

**delinear** [de·li·ne·ˈar] *vt* to draw

**delirar** [de·li·ˈrar] *vi* (*desvariar*) to be delirious

**delirio** [de·ˈli·rjo] *m* delirium; **~s de gran-**

**deza** delusions of grandeur

**delito** [de·'li·to] *m* crime; ~ **común** common offence

**delta** ['del·ta] *m* GEO delta

**demagogia** [de·ma·'ɣo·xja] *f* demagoguery

**demanda** [de·'man·da] *f* 1. (*petición*) request; ~ **de empleo** job application 2. COM demand; **tener mucha** ~ to be in great demand 3. JUR lawsuit; **presentar una** ~ **contra alguien** to bring an action against sb

**demandado, -a** [de·man·'da·do, -a] I. *adj* (*solicitado*) requested II. *m, f* JUR defendant

**demandante** [de·man·'dan·te] I. *adj* JUR **parte** ~ plaintiff II. *mf* claimant; JUR plaintiff

**demandar** [de·man·'dar] *vt* 1. (*pedir*) to ask for; (*solicitar*) to request 2. JUR ~ **por algo** to sue for sth

**demarcación** [de·mar·ka·'sjon, -'θjon] *f* demarcation

**demás** [de·'mas] *adj* other; **y ~...** and other...; **y** ~ and so on; **por lo** ~ otherwise

**demasiado** [de·ma·'sja·do] *adv* (+ *adj*) too; (+ *verbo*) too much

**demasiado, -a** [de·ma·'sja·do] *adj* too much; ~**s** too many; **hace** ~ **calor** it's too hot

**demencia** [de·'men·sja, -θja] *f* dementia; ~ **senil** senile dementia

**demencial** [de·men·'sjal, -'θjal], **demente** [de·'men·te] *adj* insane

**democracia** [de·mo·'kra·sja, -θja] *f* democracy

**demócrata** [de·'mo·kra·ta] I. *adj* democratic II. *mf* democrat

**democrático, -a** [de·mo·'kra·ti·ko, -a] *adj* democratic

**democratizar** <z → c> [de·mo·kra·ti·'sar, -'θar] I. *vt* to democratize II. *vr:* ~**se** to become democratic

**demográfico, -a** [de·mo·'ɣra·fi·ko, -a] *adj* demographic

**demoler** <o → ue> [de·mo·'ler] *vt* to demolish

**demonio** [de·'mo·njo] *m* 1. (*espíritu*) demon 2. (*diablo*) devil ▶ **de mil** ~**s** dreadful; **cómo/dónde/qué** ~**s...** how/where/what the hell...

**demora** [de·'mo·ra] *f* delay

**demorar** [de·mo·'rar] I. *vt* to delay II. *vr* ~**se en hacer algo** to delay in doing sth

**demostración** [de·mos·tra·'sjon, -'θjon] *f* 1. (*prueba*) test 2. (*argumentación*) proof 3. (*exteriorización*) display

**demostrar** <o → ue> [de·mos·'trar] *vt* 1. (*probar*) to demonstrate 2. (*mostrar*) to show

**denegar** [de·ne·'ɣar] *irr como fregar vt* 1. (*negar*) to deny 2. (*rechazar*) to refuse; (*solicitud*) to reject

**denominar** [de·no·mi·'nar] I. *vt* to name II. *vr:* ~**se** to be called

**denotar** [de·no·'tar] *vt* to denote

**densidad** [den·si·'dad] *f* density

**denso, -a** ['den·so, -a] *adj* 1. (*compacto*) dense 2. (*espeso*) thick

**dentadura** [den·ta·'du·ra] *f* teeth *pl;* ~ **postiza** false teeth

**dental** [den·'tal] *adj* dental

**dentera** [den·'te·ra] *f* (*grima*) **dar** ~ **a alguien** to give sb the shivers

**dentista** [den·'tis·ta] *mf* dentist

**dentro** ['den·tro] I. *adv* inside; **desde** ~ from within; **por** ~ inside II. *prep* 1. (*local*) ~ **de** inside 2. (*con movimiento*) ~ **de** into 3. (*temporal*) ~ **de** within

**denuncia** [de·'nun·sja, -θja] *f* 1. (*acusación*) accusation 2. (*injusticia*) denunciation

**denunciar** [de·nun·'sjar, -'θjar] *vt* 1. (*acusar*) ~ **a alguien por algo** to accuse sb of sth 2. (*hacer público*) to expose; (*robo*) to report

**deparar** [de·pa·'rar] *vt* to bring

**departamento** [de·par·ta·'men·to] *m* 1. (*sección*) *t.* UNIV department 2. *AmL* (*apartamento*) apartment

**dependencia** [de·pen·'den·sja, -θja] *f* 1. (*sujeción*) dependency 2. (*sección*) section 3. *pl* rooms *pl*

**depender** [de·pen·'der] *vi* to depend (**de** on); **depende de ti** it's up to you

**dependiente** [de·pen·'djen·te] *adj* dependent (**de** on)

**dependiente, -a** [de·pen·'djen·te, -a] *m, f* dependent; (*de una tienda*) shop assistant

**depilación** [de·pi·la·'sjon, -'θjon] f hair removal

**depilar** [de·pi·'lar] I. vt (con pinzas) to pluck; (con cera) to wax; (afeitarse) to shave II. vr ~se las cejas top pluck one's eyebrows; ~se las piernas (con cera) to wax one's legs; (con maquinilla) to shave one's legs

**deponer** [de·po·'ner] irr como poner vt (destituir) to remove

**deportación** [de·por·ta·'sjon, -'θjon] f deportation

**deportar** [de·por·'tar] vt to deport

**deporte** [de·'por·te] m sport; **hacer ~** to practice sports

**deportista** [de·por·'tis·ta] I. adj sporty II. mf sportsman, sportswoman m

**deportivo, -a** [de·por·'ti·βo, -a] adj sporting; **noticias deportivas** sports news

**depositar** [de·po·si·'tar] I. vt to put; FIN to deposit; (cadáver) to lay out; (confianza) to place II. vr: ~se to settle

**depósito** [de·'po·si·to] m 1. (almacén) warehouse 2. AUTO gas tank 3. FIN deposit

**depravar** [de·pra·'βar] I. vt to corrupt II. vr: ~se to become depraved

**depre** ['de·pre] f inf estar con la ~ to be feeling down

**depredador(a)** [de·pre·da·'dor, -·'do·ra] adj predatory

**depresión** [de·pre·'sjon] f 1. (tristeza) depression 2. ECON, METEO depression; ~ **económica** recession

**depresivo, -a** [de·pre·'si·βo, -a] adj 1. (que deprime) depressing 2. (persona) depressive

**deprimente** [de·pri·'men·te] adj (que deprime) depressing

**deprimir** [de·pri·'mir] I. vt (abatir) to depress II. vr: ~se to become depressed

**deprisa** [de·'pri·sa] adv quickly

**depuradora** [de·pu·ra·'do·ra] f water-treatment plant

**depurar** [de·pu·'rar] vt (purificar) to purify

**derecha** [de·'re·t͡ʃa] f 1. (lado) right-hand side; **a la ~** (estar) on the right; (ir) to the right; **doblar a la ~** to turn right 2. POL right (wing); **de ~(s)** right-wing

**derechista** [de·re·'t͡ʃis·ta] I. adj right-

wing II. mf right-winger

**derecho** [de·'re·t͡ʃo] I. adv straight II. m 1. (legitimidad) right 2. (jurisprudencia, ciencia) **estudiar ~** to study law 3. (de un papel, una tela) right side 4. pl (impuestos) duties pl 5. pl (honorarios) fee(s); ~ **s de autor** copyright

**derecho, -a** [de·'re·t͡ʃo, -a] adj 1. (diestro) right; **lado ~** right-hand side 2. (recto) straight 3. (erguido) upright

**derivado** [de·ri·'βa·do] m derivative

**derivar** [de·ri·'βar] I. vi, vt (proceder) to derive; ~ **hacia algo** to turn towards sth II. vr ~se de algo to come from sth

**dermatólogo, -a** [der·ma·'to·lo·γo, -a] m, f dermatologist

**dérmico, -a** ['der·mi·ko, -a] adj dermal

**derogar** <g → gu> [de·ro·'γar] vt to repeal

**derramamiento** [de·rra·ma·'mjen·to] m spilling; (sangre, lágrimas) shedding (de of)

**derramar** [de·rra·'mar] I. vt (verter) to pour; (sin querer) to spill; (lágrimas, sangre) to shed II. vr: ~se (esparcirse) to spill; ~ **en algo** to leak onto sth

**derrame** [de·'rra·me] m 1. v. **derramamiento** 2. MED hemorrhage

**derrapar** [de·rra·'par] vi to skid

**derretir(se)** [de·rre·'tir(·se)] irr como pedir vt, vr to melt

**derribar** [de·rri·'βar] vt (edificio) to demolish; (puerta) to batter down; (árbol) to fell

**derrocar** <c → qu> [de·rro·'kar] vt (destituir) to remove

**derrochador(a)** [de·rro·t͡ʃa·'dor, -·'do·ra] adj, m(f) spendthrift

**derrochar** [de·rro·'t͡ʃar] vt 1. (despilfarrar) to squander 2. inf (irradiar) to be brimming with

**derroche** [de·'rro·t͡ʃe] m 1. (despilfarro) waste 2. (abundancia) profusion

**derrota** [de·'rro·ta] f defeat

**derrotar** [de·rro·'tar] vt to defeat

**derruir** [de·rru·'ir] irr como huir vt to tear down

**derrumbar** [de·rrum·'bar] I. vt to knock down II. vr: ~se to fall down; (esperanzas) to collapse

**desab(o)rido, -a** [de·sa·'β(o·)ri·do, -a]

*adj* **1.** (*comida*) insipid **2.** (*persona*) disagreeable

**desabrochar(se)** [de·sa·βro·'tʃar(·se)] *vt, vr* to undo; (*cordones*) to untie

**desacato** [de·sa·'ka·to] *m* disrespect (**a** for)

**desacierto** [de·sa·'sjer·to, -'θjer·to] *m* mistake

**desacreditar** [de·sa·kre·di·'tar] *vt* to discredit

**desactivar** [des·ak·ti·'βar] *vt* (*explosivos*) to defuse

**desacuerdo** [de·sa·'kwer·do] *m* disagreement; **estar en ~** to disagree

**desafiar** <*1. pres* desafío> [de·sa·fi·'ar] **I.** *vt* **1.** (*retar*) to challenge **2.** (*hacer frente a*) to defy **II.** *vr:* **~se** to challenge each other

**desafinado, -a** [de·sa·fi·'na·do, -a] *adj* out of tune

**desafinar** [de·sa·fi·'nar] *vi* to sing/play out of tune

**desafío** [de·sa·'fi·o] *m* challenge; (*duelo*) duel

**desafortunado, -a** [de·sa·for·tu·'na·do, -a] *adj* unlucky

**desagradable** [de·sa·γra·'da·βle] *adj* unpleasant

**desagradar** [de·sa·γra·'dar] *vi* to displease

**desagradecido, -a** [de·sa·γra·de·'si·do, -a; -'θi·do, -a] *adj* ungrateful

**desagüe** [de·sa·'γwe] *m* drain

**desahogado, -a** [de·sa·o·'γa·do, -a] *adj* **1.** (*lugar*) spacious **2.** (*adinerado*) well-off

**desahogar** <g → gu> [de·sa·o·'γar] **I.** *vt* **1.** (*aliviar*) to relieve **2.** (*consolar*) to console **II.** *vr* **~se con alguien** to tell one's troubles to sb

**desahogo** [de·sa·'o·γo] *m* **1.** (*alivio*) relief **2.** (*reposo*) rest

**desahuciar** [de·sau·'sjar, -'θjar] *vt* (*inquilino*) to evict

**desajuste** [de·sa·'xus·te] *m* **1.** (*desorden*) imbalance **2.** (*desconcierto*) confusion

**desalentador(a)** [de·sa·len·ta·'dor, -·'do·ra] *adj* discouraging

**desalentar** <e → ie> [de·sa·len·'tar] **I.** *vt* to discourage **II.** *vr:* **~se** to lose heart

**desaliñado, -a** [de·sa·li·'ɲa·do, -a] *adj*

shabby

**desalmado, -a** [de·sal·'ma·do, -a] **I.** *adj* heartless **II.** *m, f* swine

**desalojar** [de·sa·lo·'xar] *vt* (*casa*) to vacate; (*persona*) to eject

**desamparado, -a** [des·am·pa·'ra·do, -a] *adj* defenseless

**desamparar** [des·am·pa·'rar] *vt* **1.** (*dejar*) to abandon **2.** (*desasistir*) to fail to help

**desamparo** [des·am·'pa·ro] *m* **1.** (*desprotección*) defenselessness **2.** (*abandono*) abandonment

**desangrar** [de·san·'grar] **I.** *vt* **1.** (*animales*) to bleed **2.** (*arruinar*) to impoverish, to bleed white **II.** *vr:* **~se** to bleed heavily

**desanimado, -a** [de·sa·ni·'ma·do, -a] *adj* **1.** (*persona*) downhearted **2.** (*lugar*) lifeless

**desanimar** [de·sa·ni·'mar] **I.** *vt* to discourage **II.** *vr:* **~se** to lose heart

**desánimo** [de·'sa·ni·mo] *m* dejection

**desaparecer** [de·sa·pa·re·'ser, -'θer] *irr como crecer vi* to disappear; (*en guerra*) to go missing

**desaparecido, -a** [de·sa·pa·re·'si·do, -a; -'θi·do, -a] *adj* missing

**desaparición** [de·sa·pa·ri·'sjon, -'θjon] *f* disappearance

**desapercibido, -a** [de·sa·per·si·'βi·do, -a; de·sa·per·θi-] *adj* **1.** (*inadvertido*) unnoticed; **pasar ~** to go unnoticed **2.** (*desprevenido*) unprepared; **coger ~** to catch unawares

**desaprensivo, -a** [de·sa·pren·'si·βo, -a] *adj* unscrupulous

**desaprovechar** [de·sa·pro·βe·'tʃar] *vt* to waste

**desarmador** [des·ar·ma·'dor] *m Méx* screwdriver

**desarmar** [des·ar·'mar] *vt* **1.** (*dejar sin armas*) to disarm **2.** (*desmontar*) to take apart

**desarme** [des·'ar·me] *m* disarmament

**desarraigar** <g → gu> [de·sa·rrai·'γar] *vt* **1.** (*árbol, persona*) to uproot **2.** (*costumbre, creencia*) to eradicate

**desarraigo** [de·sa·'rrai·γo] *m* **1.** (*de árbol, persona*) uprooting **2.** (*de costumbre, creencia*) eradication

**desarrollar** [de·sa·rro·'jar, -'ʎar] **I.** *vt* **1.** (*aumentar*) to develop **2.** (*exponer*) to expound **II.** *vr:* ~**se 1.** (*progresar*) to develop **2.** (*ocurrir*) to take place

**desarrollo** [de·sa·'rro·jo, -ʎo] *m* **1.** development; **país en vías de** ~ developing country **2.** (*crecimiento*) growth

**desarticular** [des·ar·ti·ku·'lar] **I.** *vt* **1.** (*mecanismo*) to dismantle **2.** (*grupo*) to break up **II.** *vr:* ~**se 1.** (*mecanismo*) to come apart **2.** (*articulación*) to become dislocated **3.** (*grupo*) to break up

**desasosiego** [de·sa·so·'sje·ɣo] *m* unease

**desastre** [de·'sas·tre] *m* disaster; **ser un** ~ *inf* (*alguien*) to be hopeless; (*algo*) to be a flop

**desastroso, -a** [de·sas·'tro·so, -a] *adj* disastrous

**desatado, -a** [de·sa·'ta·do, -a] *adj* **1.** (*desligado*) untied **2.** (*desenfrenado*) wild

**desatar** [de·sa·'tar] **I.** *vt* **1.** (*soltar*) to untie; (*nudo*) to undo **2.** (*causar*) to unleash **II.** *vr:* ~**se 1.** (*soltarse*) to untie oneself; (*nudo*) to come undone **2.** (*tormenta*) to break; (*crisis*) to erupt

**desatascar** <c → qu> [de·sa·tas·'kar] *vt* to unblock

**desatender** <e → ie> [de·sa·ten·'der] *vt* **1.** (*desoír*) to ignore **2.** (*abandonar*) to neglect

**desatento, -a** [de·sa·'ten·to, -a] *adj* **1.** (*distraído*) inattentive; (*negligente*) careless **2.** (*descortés*) impolite (**con** to)

**desatino** [de·sa·'ti·no] *m* (*error*) mistake; (*torpeza*) blunder

**desatornillador** [des·a·tor·ni·ja·'dor, -ʎa·'dor] *m AmL* screwdriver

**desatornillar** [des·a·tor·ni·'jar, -'ʎar] *vt* to unscrew

**desatrancar** <c → qu> [de·sa·tran·'kar] *vt* to unbolt

**desavenencia** [de·sa·βe·'nen·sja, -θja] *f* **1.** (*desacuerdo*) disagreement **2.** (*discordia*) friction

**desayunar** [de·sa·ju·'nar] **I.** *vi* to have breakfast **II.** *vt* ~ **algo** to have sth for breakfast

**desayuno** [de·sa·'ju·no] *m* breakfast

**desbancar** <c → qu> [des·βan·'kar] *vt* to oust

**desbarajuste** [des·βa·ra·'xus·te] *m* chaos

**desbaratar** [des·βa·ra·'tar] **I.** *vt* **1.** (*desunir, dispersar*) to break up **2.** (*arruinar*) to ruin **II.** *vr:* ~**se 1.** (*separarse*) to break up **2.** (*fracasar*) to fail

**desbloquear** [des·βlo·ke·'ar] *vt* to unblock; FIN to unfreeze

**desbocar** <c → qu> [des·βo·'kar] **I.** *vt* (*enloquecer*) to drive mad **II.** *vr:* ~**se** to go crazy; (*caballo*) to bolt

**desbordamiento** [des·βor·da·'mjen·to] *m* overflowing

**desbordar** [des·βor·'dar] **I.** *vi*, *vr:* ~**se** to overflow **II.** *vt* to exceed

**descabellado, -a** [des·ka·βe·'ja·do, -a; -'ʎa·do, -a] *adj* preposterous

**descafeinado, -a** [des·ka·fei·'na·do, -a] *adj* decaffeinated

**descalcificar** <c → qu> [des·kal·si·fi·'kar, -θi·fi·'kar] *vt* decalcify

**descalificación** [des·ka·li·fi·ka·'sjon, -'θjon] *f* disqualification

**descalificar** <c → qu> [des·ka·li·fi·'kar] *vt* to disqualify

**descalzar** <z → c> [des·kal·'sar, -'θar] *vr:* ~**se** to take one's shoes off

**descalzo, -a** [des·'kal·so, -a; -θo, -a] *adj* barefoot

**descambiar** [des·kam·'bjar] *vt* to change back

**descaminar** [des·ka·mi·'nar] *vr:* ~**se 1.** (*perderse*) to get lost; **ir descaminado** to be on the wrong track **2.** (*descarriarse*) to go astray

**descampado** [des·kam·'pa·do] *m* piece of open ground

**descansar** [des·kan·'sar] *vi* **1.** (*reposar*) to rest **2.** (*recuperarse*) to recover **3.** (*dormir*) to sleep; **¡que descanses!** sleep well! **4.** (*apoyar*) to rest

**descanso** [des·'kan·so] *m* **1.** (*reposo*) rest **2.** (*recuperación*) recovery **3.** (*tranquilidad*) peace **4.** (*pausa*) *t.* DEP break **5.** (*alivio*) relief

**descapotable** [des·ka·po·'ta·βle] *m* convertible

**descarado, -a** [des·ka·'ra·do, -a] *adj* **1.** (*desvergonzado*) shameless **2.** (*evidente*) blatant

**D**

**descarga** [des·'kar·ɣa] *f* **1.** (*de mercancías*) unloading **2.** ELEC, FÍS, FIN discharge **3.** COMPUT download

**descargar** <g → gu> [des·kar·'ɣar] **I.** *vt* **1.** (*carga*) to unload **2.** ELEC, FÍS discharge **3.** COMPUT to download **II.** *vr:* ~**se 1.** (*vaciarse*) to empty; ELEC, FÍS to discharge; (*pila*) to run out **2.** (*librarse*) to unburden oneself; (*desahogarse*) to let off steam

**descaro** [des·'ka·ro] *m* cheek

**descarriarse** <*1. pres* descarrío> [des·ka·rri·'ar·se] *vr* **1.** (*perderse*) to get lost **2.** (*descaminarse*) to go astray

**descarrilar** [des·ka·rri·'lar] *vi* to be derailed

**descartar** [des·kar·'tar] *vt* (*propuesta*) to reject; (*posibilidad*) to rule out

**descendencia** [de·sen·'den·sja, -θen·'den·θja] *f* descendents *pl;* **tener ~** to have offspring

**descendente** [de·sen·'den·te, des·θen-] *adj* **1.** (*en caída*) descending **2.** (*en disminución*) diminishing

**descender** <e → ie> [de·sen·'der, des·θen-] *vi* **1.** (*bajar*) to descend **2.** (*disminuir*) to diminish **3.** (*proceder*) to be descended **II.** *vt* to take down; (*escalera*) to go down

**descendiente** [de·sen·'djen·te, des·θen-] *mf* descendant

**descenso** [de·'sen·so, des·'θen·so] *m* **1.** (*bajada*) descent **2.** (*cuesta*) slope **3.** (*disminución*) decline; ECON downturn

**descentralizar** <z → c> [de·sen·tra·li·'sar, des·θen·tra·li·'θar] *vt* to decentralize

**descifrar** [de·si·'frar, des·θi-] *vt* to decipher

**descocado, -a** [des·ko·'ka·do, -a] *adj* impudent

**descodificador** [des·ko·di·fi·ka·'dor] *m* decoder

**descodificar** <c → qu> [des·ko·di·fi·'kar] *vt* to decode

**descojonante** [des·ko·xo·'nan·te] *adj inf* hilarious

**descojonarse** [des·ko·xo·'nar·se] *vr inf* to die laughing

**descolgar** [des·kol·'ɣar] *irr como* colgar *vt* (*teléfono*) to pick up

**descolorar** [des·ko·lo·'rar], **descolorir** [des·ko·lo·'rir] *vt, vr:* ~**se** *v.* **decolorar**

**descomponer** [des·kom·po·'ner] *irr como* poner **I.** *vt* **1.** (*desordenar*) to mess up **2.** (*separar*) to take apart **3.** (*corromper*) *t.* QUÍM to decompose **II.** *vr:* ~**se 1.** (*desmembrarse*) to come apart **2.** (*corromperse*) to decay

**descomposición** [des·kom·po·si·'sjon, -'θjon] *f* **1.** (*separación*) separation; QUÍM decomposition **2.** (*corrupción*) decay

**descompuesto, -a** [des·kom·'pwes·to, -a] **I.** *pp de* **descomponer II.** *adj* **1.** (*desordenado*) untidy **2.** (*podrido*) rotten

**descomunal** [des·ko·mu·'nal] *adj* enormous

**desconcertar** <e → ie> [des·kon·ser·'tar, des·kon·θer-] *vt* **1.** (*desbaratar*) to ruin **2.** (*pasmar*) to disconcert; **estar desconcertado** to be disconcerted

**desconcierto** [des·kon·'sjer·to, -'θjer·to] *m* **1.** (*desarreglo*) disorder **2.** (*desorientación*) confusion

**desconectar** [des·ko·nek·'tar] **I.** *vt* to disconnect; (*radio, tele*) to switch off **II.** *vi inf* to switch off

**desconfiado, -a** [des·kon·fi·'a·do, -a] *adj* distrustful

**desconfiar** <*1. pres* desconfío> [des·kon·fi·'ar] *vi* ~ **de alguien/algo** to mistrust sb/sth

**descongelar** [des·kon·xe·'lar] **I.** *vt* **1.** (*comida*) to thaw out; (*nevera*) to defrost **2.** FIN to unfreeze **II.** *vr:* ~**se** (*comida*) to thaw out; (*nevera*) to defrost

**descongestionar** [des·kon·xes·tjo·'nar] *vt* to unblock; MED to clear

**desconocer** [des·ko·no·'ser, -'θer] *irr como* crecer *vt* **1.** (*ignorar*) to be unaware of **2.** (*no reconocer*) to not recognize

**desconocido, -a** [des·ko·no·'si·do, -a; -'θi·do, -a] **I.** *adj* unknown; **estar ~** to be unrecognizable **II.** *m, f* stranger

**desconsiderado, -a** [des·kon·si·de·'ra·do, -a] *adj* inconsiderate

**desconsolado, -a** [des·kon·so·'la·do, -a] *adj* disconsolate

**descontado, -a** [des·kon·'ta·do, -a] *adj* (*descartado*) discounted ▶ **dar**

**algo por** ~ to take sth for granted; **por** ~ of course

**descontar** <o → ue> [des·kon·'tar] vt 1. (*restar*) to take away 2. (*descartar*) to disregard

**descontento** [des·kon·'ten·to] m dissatisfaction

**descontento, -a** [des·kon·'ten·to, -a] adj dissatisfied

**descontrol** [des·kon·'trol] m chaos

**descontrolarse** [des·kon·tro·'lar·se] vr (*máquina*) to go out of control; (*persona*) to go wild

**descorazonar** [des·ko·ra·so·'nar, des·ko·ra·θo·] I. vt to discourage II. vr: ~**se** to lose heart

**descorchador** [des·kor·tʃa·'dor] m corkscrew

**descorchar** [des·kor·'tʃar] vt to uncork

**descorrer** [des·ko·'rrer] vt to draw; (*cortinas*) to draw back

**descortés** [des·kor·'tes] adj impolite

**descortesía** [des·kor·te·'si·a] f discourtesy

**descoser** [des·ko·'ser] I. vt to unstitch II. vr: ~**se** to come apart at the seam

**descosido, -a** [des·ko·'si·do] adj **como un** ~ like mad

**descrédito** [des·'kre·di·to] m discredit

**descreído, -a** [des·kre·'i·do, -a] adj skeptical

**describir** [des·kri·'βir] irr como escribir vt 1. (*explicar*) to describe 2. (*trazar*) to trace

**descripción** [des·krip·'sjon, -kriβ·'θjon] f description

**descuartizar** <z → c> [des·kwar·ti·'sar, -'θar] vt to cut up

**descubierto** [des·ku·'βjer·to] m 1. (*lugar*) **al** ~ in the open 2. (*en evidencia*) **poner algo al** ~ to bring sth into the open; **quedar al** ~ to be revealed

**descubierto, -a** [des·ku·'βjer·to, -a] I. pp de **descubrir** II. adj open; (*sin techo*) open-air; (*cielo*) clear

**descubrimiento** [des·ku·βri·'mjen·to] m 1. (*invento*) discovery 2. (*revelación*) disclosure

**descubrir** [des·ku·'βrir] irr como abrir I. vt 1. (*destapar*) to uncover 2. (*encontrar*) to discover 3. (*averiguar*) to

find out 4. (*inventar*) to invent 5. (*desenmascarar*) to unmask II. vr: ~**se** 1. (*salir a la luz*) to come out 2. (*delatarse*) to give oneself away

**descuento** [des·'kwen·to] m discount

**descuidado, -a** [des·kwi·'da·do, -a] adj 1. ser (*despistado*) inattentive; (*sin cuidado*) careless; (*imprudente*) negligent; (*desaseado*) slovenly; (*desaliñado*) untidy 2. estar (*abandonado*) neglected; (*desprevenido*) unprepared

**descuidar** [des·kwi·'dar] I. vi **¡descuida!** don't worry! II. vt to neglect III. vr: ~**se** (*distraerse*) to be distracted

**descuido** [des·'kwi·do] m (*falta de atención*) inattentiveness; (*de cuidado*) carelessness; (*imprudencia*) negligence; **por** ~ inadvertently

**desde** ['des·de] I. prep 1. (*temporal*) since; (*a partir de*) from; ~**... hasta...** from... until...; ~ **ahora/ya** from now on; **¿~ cuándo?** since when?; ~ **entonces** since then; ~ **hace...** for...; ~ **hace poco/mucho** for a short/long time; ~ **hoy/mañana** from today/tomorrow; ~ **el principio** from the beginning 2. (*local*) from II. adv ~ **luego** of course III. conj ~ **que** since

**desdén** [des·'den] m disdain

**desdeñar** [des·de·'ɲar] vt 1. (*despreciar*) to scorn 2. (*rechazar*) to spurn

**desdicha** [des·'di·tʃa] f 1. (*desgracia*) misfortune 2. (*miseria*) misery

**desdichado, -a** [des·di·'tʃa·do, -a] adj unfortunate

**deseable** [de·se·'a·βle] adj desirable

**desear** [de·se·'ar] vt to want; (*sexualmente*) to desire; ~ **suerte a alguien** to wish sb luck; **hacerse** ~ to play hard to get; **¿desea algo más?** would you like anything else?; **dejar mucho que** ~ to leave a lot to be desired

**desecar** <c → qu> [de·se·'kar] I. vt to dry; (*pantano*) to dry out II. vr: ~**se** to dry up

**desechable** [de·se·'tʃa·βle] adj disposable

**desechar** [de·se·'tʃar] vt 1. (*tirar*) to throw away 2. (*descartar*) to rule out; (*desestimar*) to reject

**desechos** [de·'se·tʃos] mpl (*restos*) remains *pl*; (*residuos*) residue; (*basura*) waste

**desembalar** [des·em·ba·'lar] *vt* to unpack

**desembarcar** <c → qu> [des·em·βar·'kar] **I.** *vi* to disembark **II.** *vt* to unload

**desembarco** [des·em·'bar·ko] *m*, **desembarque** [des·em·'bar·ke] *m* landing

**desembocadura** [des·em·bo·ka·'du·ra] *f* mouth

**desembocar** <c → qu> [des·em·bo·'kar] *vi* **1.** (*río*) **~ en** to flow into **2.** (*situación*) **~ en** to result in

**desembolso** [des·em·'bol·so] *m* **1.** (*pago*) payment **2.** (*gasto*) expense

**desembrollar** [des·em·bro·'jar, -'ʎar] *vt inf* **1.** (*madeja*) to untangle **2.** (*asunto*) to sort out

**desembuchar** [des·em·bu·'tʃar] *vi, vt inf* (*confesar*) to come clean (about); **¡desembucha de una vez!** out with it!

**desempacar** <c → qu> [des·em·pa·'kar] *vt AmL* to unpack

**desempaquetar** [des·em·pa·ke·'tar] *vt* to unwrap

**desempate** [des·em·'pa·te] *m* breakthrough

**desempeñar** [des·em·pe·'ɲar] *vt* to carry out; (*cargo*) to hold; (*papel*) to play; (*préstamo*) to pay off

**desempleado, -a** [des·em·ple·'a·do, -a] **I.** *adj* unemployed **II.** *m, f* unemployed person

**desempleo** [des·em·'pleo] *m* unemployment

**desencadenar** [des·en·ka·de·'nar] **I.** *vt* **1.** (*soltar*) to unleash **2.** (*provocar*) to trigger **II.** *vr:* **~se** to break loose

**desencajar** [des·en·ka·'xar] **I.** *vt* to dismantle; MED to dislocate; (*cara*) to distort **II.** *vr:* **~se** to come apart; MED to dislocate

**desencantar** [des·en·kan·'tar] **I.** *vt* (*desilusionar*) to disillusion; (*decepcionar*) to disappoint **II.** *vr:* **~se** to become disillusioned

**desencanto** [des·en·'kan·to] *m* **1.** (*decepción*) disappointment **2.** (*desilusión*) disillusion

**desenchufar** [des·en·tʃu·'far] *vt* to unplug

**desencriptar** [des·eŋ·krip·'tar] *vt* COMPUT to decrypt

**desenfadado, -a** [des·en·fa·'da·do, -a] *adj* **1.** (*desvuelto*) self-assured **2.** (*carácter*) easy-going **3.** (*ropa*) casual

**desenfado** [des·en·'fa·do] *m* openness; (*naturalidad*) naturalness

**desenfocado, -a** [des·en·fo·'ka·do, -a] *adj* out of focus

**desenfrenado, -a** [des·en·fre·'na·do, -a] *adj* frantic

**desenfreno** [des·en·'fre·no] *m* lack of restraint

**desenganchar** [des·en·gan·'tʃar] **I.** *vt* **1.** (*gancho*) to unhook **2.** (*soltar*) to take off **II.** *vr:* **~se** *inf* to get off drugs

**desengañar** [des·en·ga·'ɲar] **I.** *vt* (*desilusionar*) to disillusion **II.** *vr:* **~se** to be disappointed; **pronto te ~ás** you'll soon see the truth

**desengaño** [des·en·'ga·ɲo] *m* disillusion

**desengrasar** [des·en·gra·'sar] *vt* to remove the grease from

**desenlace** [des·en·'la·se, -θe] *m* outcome

**desenmascarar** [des·en·mas·ka·'rar/ des·em·mas·ka·'rar] *vt* to unmask; *fig* to expose

**desenredar** [des·en·rre·'dar] *vt* to unravel; (*pelo*) to untangle

**desenroscar** <c → qu> [des·en·rros·'kar] *vt* to unscrew; (*desenrollar*) to unwind

**desentenderse** <e → ie> [des·en·ten·'der·se] *vr* **1.** (*despreocuparse*) **~ de algo** to want nothing to do with sth; **~ de un problema** to wash one's hands of a problem **2.** (*fingir ignorancia*) **~ de algo** to pretend to not know about sth

**desenterrar** <e → ie> [des·en·te·'rrar] *vt* to dig up; (*cadáver*) to exhume

**desentonar** [des·en·to·'nar] *vi* **1.** (*cantar*) to sing out of tune; (*tocar*) to play out of tune **2.** (*no combinar*) to not match

**desentrañar** [des·en·tra·'ɲar] *vt* to unravel

**desenvolver** [des·em·bol·'βer] *irr como* **volver I.** *vt* **1.** (*desempaquetar*) to unwrap **2.** (*desenrollar*) to unwind; (*desdoblar*) to unfold **II.** *vr:* **~se** (*manejarse*) to handle oneself

**deseo** [de·'se·o] *m* **1.** (*anhelo*) wish **2.** (*necesidad*) need **3.** (*ansia*) longing **4.** (*sexual*) desire

**deseoso, -a** [de·se·'o·so, -a] *adj* **estar ~ de hacer algo** to be eager to do sth

**desequilibrado, -a** [de·se·ki·li·'βra·do, -a] *adj* unbalanced; (*trastornado*) (mentally) disturbed

**desequilibrar** [de·se·ki·li·'βrar] **I.** *vt* **1.** (*descompensar*) to unbalance **2.** (*trastornar*) to disturb **II.** *vr:* **~se 1.** (*descompensarse*) to unbalance **2.** (*psíquicamente*) to become disturbed

**desequilibrio** [de·se·ki·'li·βrjo] *m* **1.** (*falta de equilibrio*) lack of balance; (*descompensación, desproporción*) imbalance **2.** (*trastorno*) disturbance; **~ mental** mental instability

**desertar** [de·ser·'tar] *vi* to desert

**desértico, -a** [de·'ser·ti·ko, -a] *adj* desert

**desertor(a)** [de·ser·'tor, -·'to·ra] *m(f)* deserter

**desesperación** [des·es·pe·ra·'sjon, -'θjon] *f* **1.** (*desmoralización*) desperation, despair; **con ~** desperately **2.** (*enojo*) exasperation

**desesperado, -a** [des·es·pe·'ra·do, -a] *adj* **1.** (*desmoralizado*) desperate; (*situación*) hopeless **2.** (*enojado*) exasperated

**desesperante** [des·es·pe·'ran·te] *adj* **1.** (*sin esperanza*) hopeless **2.** (*exasperante*) exasperating

**desesperar** [des·es·pe·'rar] **I.** *vt* **1.** (*desesperanzar*) to cause to lose hope **2.** (*exasperar*) to exasperate **II.** *vi* to despair **III.** *vr:* **~se 1.** (*desesperanzarse*) to give up hope **2.** (*despecharse*) to despair

**desestimar** [des·es·ti·'mar] *vt* **1.** (*despreciar*) to have a low opinion of **2.** (*rechazar*) to reject

**desfachatez** [des·fa·tʃa·'tes, -'teθ] *f* cheek

**desfallecer** [des·fa·je·'ser, -ʎe·'θer] *irr como crecer vi* **1.** (*debilitarse*) to weaken **2.** (*colapsar*) to collapse; (*desmayarse*) to faint **3.** (*desanimarse*) to lose heart

**desfasado, -a** [des·fa·'sa·do, -a] *adj* (*per-*

*sona*) old-fashioned; (*cosa*) antiquated; **estar ~** to be behind the times

**desfase** [des·'fa·se] *m* (*diferencia*) gap; **~ con la realidad** lack of realism; **¡que ~!** *inf* wild!

**desfavorable** [des·fa·βo·'ra·βle] *adj* unfavorable

**desfavorecer** [des·fa·βo·re·'ser, -'θer] *irr como crecer vt* to discriminate against

**desfigurar** [des·fi·γu·'rar] *vt* **1.** (*afear*) to disfigure **2.** (*deformar*) to deface; (*imagen, realidad*) to distort

**desfiguro** [des·fi·'γu·ro] *m Méx* (*ridiculez*) silly stunt; **hacer un ~** to make a fool of oneself

**desfiladero** [des·fi·la·'de·ro] *m* gorge

**desfilar** [des·fi·'lar] *vi* **1.** (*marchar*) to walk in file **2.** (*salir*) to file out

**desfile** [des·'fi·le] *m* **1.** (*acción*) marching; (*de tropas*) march-past; **~ de modelos** fashion show **2.** (*personas*) procession

**desgana** [des·'γa·na] *f* **1.** (*inapetencia*) lack of appetite **2.** (*desinterés*) lack of enthusiasm

**desgarbado, -a** [des·γar·'βa·do, -a] *adj* gangling

**desgarrador(a)** [des·γa·rra·'dor, -·'do·ra] *adj* heartrending

**desgarrar** [des·γa·'rrar] **I.** *vt* to tear **II.** *vr:* **~se** to tear

**desgarro** [des·'γa·rro] *m* **1.** (*rotura*) tear **2.** *AmL* (*esputo*) spittle

**desgastar** [des·γas·'tar] **I.** *vt* **1.** (*estropear, cansar*) to wear out **2.** (*consumir*) to use up **II.** *vr:* **~se** to wear out; (*color*) to fade

**desgaste** [des·'γas·te] *m* **1.** (*fricción*) wear **2.** (*consumo*) consumption

**desgracia** [des·'γra·sja, -θja] *f* **1.** (*mala suerte*) bad luck; **por ~** unfortunately **2.** (*acontecimiento*) misfortune **3. caer en ~** to fall from grace [*o* into disgrace]

▶ **las ~s nunca vienen solas** *prov* when it rains, it pours *prov*

**desgraciadamente** [des·γra·sja·da·'men·te, des·γra·θja-] *adv* unfortunately

**desgraciado, -a** [des·γra·'sja·do, -a; des·γra·θja-] **I.** *adj* **1.** (*sin suerte*) unlucky **2.** (*infeliz*) miserable **3.** (*con desgracias*) unfortunate **4.** (*pobre*) poor

II. *m, f* **1.** (*sin suerte*) unlucky person **2.** (*infeliz*) poor devil **3.** (*pobre*) poor person

**desgraciar** [des·ɣra·'sjar, -'θjar] I. *vt* **1.** (*estropear*) to ruin **2.** (*disgustar*) to displease II. *vr*: **~se** to be ruined

**desgravable** [des·ɣra·'βa·βle] *adj* tax-deductible

**desgravación** [des·ɣra·'βa·sjon, -θjon] *f* **1.** (*de impuestos*) tax allowance **2.** (*de gastos*) tax relief

**desgravar** [des·ɣra·'βar] *vt* **1.** (*suprimir*) to exempt from **2.** (*reducir*) **~ el tabaco** (*bajar el impuesto*) to reduce the tax on tobacco; (*el arancel*) to reduce the duties on tobacco

**desgreñado, -a** [des·ɣre·'na·ðo, -a] *adj* disheveled

**desguace** [des·'ɣwa·se, -θe] *m* **1.** (*lugar*) junkyard **2.** (*acción*) wrecking

**desguazar** <z → c> [des·ɣwa·'sar, -'θar] *vt* to scrap; (*para reutilizar*) to use sth for scrap

**deshabitado, -a** [des·a·βi·'ta·ðo, -a] *adj* empty

**deshabitar** [des·a·βi·'tar] *vt* to empty; (*edificio*) to abandon; (*casa*) to vacate

**deshacer** [des·a·'ser, -'θer] *irr como hacer* I. *vt* **1.** (*nudo*) to undo; (*cama*) to mess up; (*aparato*) to dismantle; (*maleta*) to unpack; (*error*) to rectify **2.** (*romper*) to break; (*en pedazos*) to tear apart; (*cortar*) to cut up **3.** (*arruinar*) to ruin; (*plan*) to spoil **4.** (*disolver*) to dissolve; (*hielo*) to melt II. *vr*: **~se** **1.** (*descomponerse*) to come apart; (*hielo*) to melt; (*desaparecer*) to disappear **2.** (*romperse*) to break; (*nudo*) to come undone **3.** (*desprenderse*) to come away; **~se de** (*vender*) to offload; (*librarse de, asesinar*) to get rid of

**deshecho, -a** [des·'e·tʃo, -a] I. *pp de* **deshacer** II. *adj* **1.** (*deprimido*) devastated; **dejar a alguien ~** to leave sb shattered **2.** (*cansado*) exhausted

**deshelar** <e → ie> [des·e·'lar] I. *vt* to melt II. *vr*: **~se** (*hielo*) to melt; (*nieve*) to thaw

**desheredar** [des·e·re·'ðar] *vt* to disinherit

**deshidratar** [des·i·ðra·'tar] I. *vt* to dry; (*cuerpo*) to dehydrate II. *vr*: **~se** to dry out; (*cuerpo*) to dehydrate

**deshielo** [des·'je·lo] *m* thawing; METEO, POL thaw

**deshilachar** [des·i·la·'tʃar] *vt, vr*: **~se** to fray

**deshinchar** [des·in·'tʃar] I. *vt* **1.** (*vaciar*) to deflate **2.** (*por una inflamación*) to reduce II. *vr*: **~se** **1.** (*perder aire*) to deflate **2.** (*una inflamación*) to go down

**deshojar** [des·o·'xar] I. *vt* **1.** BOT to strip the leaves from; (*flor*) to pull the petals off **2.** (*libro*) to tear the pages out of II. *vr*: **~se** to lose its leaves/petals/pages

**deshonesto, -a** [des·o·'nes·to, -a] *adj* **1.** (*inmoral*) indecent **2.** (*tramposo*) dishonest

**deshonor** [des·o·'nor] *m*, **deshonra** [des·'on·rra] *f* dishonor; (*afrenta*) disgrace

**deshonrar** [des·on·'rrar] *vt* to disgrace; (*ofender*) to offend; (*humillar*) to humiliate; (*desacreditar*) to bring disgrace on

**deshonroso, -a** [des·on·'rro·so, -a] *adj* disgraceful; (*deshonesto*) dishonest

**deshora** [des·'o·ra] *f* inconvenient time; **venir a ~(s)** (*tarde*) to arrive too late; **dormir a ~s** to sleep at odd hours

**desidia** [de·'si·ðja] *f* **1.** (*descuido*) carelessness **2.** (*pereza*) laziness

**desierto** [de·'sjer·to] *m* **1.** GEO desert **2.** (*despoblado*) wasteland

**desierto, -a** [de·'sjer·to, -a] *adj* **1.** (*sin gente*) deserted **2.** (*árido*) desert

**designación** [de·siɣ·na·'sjon, -'θjon] *f* **1.** (*nombramiento*) appointment **2.** (*nombre*) name

**designar** [de·siɣ·'nar] *vt* **1.** (*dar un nombre*) to designate **2.** (*destinar*) to assign; (*elegir*) to choose; (*fecha*) to set; (*nombrar*) to appoint (**para** to); (*candidato*) to select; (*representante*) to nominate

**designio** [de·'siɣ·njo] *m* **1.** (*plan*) plan **2.** (*propósito*) intention **3.** (*deseo*) wish

**desigual** [de·si·'ɣwal] *adj* **1.** (*distinto*) unequal **2.** (*injusto*) unfair **3.** (*irregular*) uneven **4.** (*inconstante*) inconsistent

**desigualdad** [de·si·ɣwal·'dad] *f* **1.** (*dife-*

*rencia*) inequality **2.** (*injusticia*) unfairness **3.** (*irregularidad*) unevenness

**desilusión** [de·si·lu·'sjon] *f* **1.** (*desengaño*) disappointment **2.** (*desencanto*) disillusion

**desilusionante** [de·si·lu·sjo·'nan·te] *adj* disillusioning

**desilusionar** [de·si·lu·sjo·'nar] **I.** *vt* **1.** (*desencantar*) to disillusion **2.** (*decepcionar*) to disappoint **II.** *vr:* **~se** **1.** (*perder la ilusión*) to become disillusioned; (*ver claro*) to see things for what they are **2.** (*decepcionarse*) to be disappointed

**desinfectante** [des·in·fek·'tan·te] *m* disinfectant

**desinfectar** [des·in·fek·'tar] *vt* to disinfect

**desinflado, -a** [des·in·'fla·do, -a] *adj* flat

**desinflar** [des·in·'flar] **I.** *vt* to deflate **II.** *vr:* **~se** to go down

**desintegración** [des·in·te·ɣra·'sjon, -'θjon] *f* **1.** disintegration; (*erosión*) erosion; QUÍM decomposition **2.** (*territorio, grupo*) breakup

**desintegrar** [des·in·te·'ɣrar] **I.** *vt* to disintegrate; (*grupo, país*) to break up **II.** *vr:* **~se** to disintegrate; (*edificio, muro*) to fall down; QUÍM to decompose; (*grupo*) to break up

**desinterés** [des·in·te·'res] *m* **1.** (*indiferencia*) indifference **2.** (*altruismo*) altruism; (*generosidad*) generosity

**desinteresado, -a** [des·in·te·re·'sa·do, -a] *adj* **1.** (*indiferente*) indifferent **2.** (*altruista*) altruistic; (*generoso*) generous

**desintoxicación** [des·in·tok·si·ka·'sjon, -'θjon] *f* detoxification

**desintoxicar** <c → qu> [des·in·tok·si·'kar] **I.** *vt* to detoxify **II.** *vr:* **~se** **1.** to undergo detoxification; (*de alcohol*) to dry out **2.** *fig* to get away from it all

**desistir** [de·sis·'tir] *vi* ~ **de** (*proyecto*) to give up; (*derecho*) to waive; (*cargo*) to resign

**desleal** [des·le·'al] *adj* (*infiel*) disloyal; (*traidor*) treacherous; (*competencia*) unfair; (*publicidad*) misleading

**deslealtad** [des·leal·'tad] *f* **1.** (*infidelidad*) disloyalty **2.** (*injusticia*) unfairness

**desleír** [des·le·'ir] *irr como reír* *vt, vr:* **~se** to dissolve

**deslenguado, -a** [des·len·'gwa·do, -a] *adj* **1.** (*desvergonzado*) foul-mouthed **2.** (*chismoso*) gossipy

**desligar** <g → gu> [des·li·'ɣar] **I.** *vt* to separate **II.** *vr:* **~se** (*de un compromiso*) to be released; **no poder ~se de algo** to be unable to get out of sth

**desliz** [des·'lis, -'liθ] *m* slip

**deslizante** [des·li·'san·te, -'θan·te] *adj* **1.** (*resbaladizo*) slippery **2.** (*corredizo*) sliding

**deslizar** <z → c> [des·li·'sar, -'θar] **I.** *vt* ~ **la mano sobre algo** to run one's hand over sth; ~ **un sobre por debajo de una puerta** to slip an envelope under the door **II.** *vi* to slip **III.** *vr:* **~se** **1.** (*resbalar*) ~ **sobre algo** to slide over sth **2.** (*escaparse*) to slip away **3.** (*cometer un error*) to slip up

**deslomar** [des·lo·'mar] **I.** *vt* ~ **a alguien** to break sb's back **II.** *vr:* **~se** to break one's back

**deslucido, -a** [des·lu·'si·do, -a; -'θi·do, -a] *adj* (*ropa*) shabby; (*actuación*) lackluster

**deslucir** [des·lu·'sir, -'θir] *irr como lucir* **I.** *vt* **1.** (*estropear*) to ruin; (*metal*) to tarnish; (*tejidos, colores*) to fade **2.** (*desacreditar*) to discredit **II.** *vr:* **~se** **1.** (*fracasar*) to fail **2.** (*deslustrarse*) to lose its shine; (*colores*) to fade; (*metal*) to become dull **3.** (*desacreditarse*) to be discredited

**deslumbrador(a)** [des·lum·bra·'dor, --'do·ra], **deslumbrante** [des·lum·'bran·te] *adj* (*impresionante*) dazzling; (*despampanante*) stunning

**deslumbrar** [des·lum·'brar] *vt* to dazzle

**deslustrar** [des·lus·'trar] *v.* **deslucir**

**desmadrado, -a** [des·ma·'dra·do, -a] *adj* wild

**desmadrarse** [des·ma·'drar·se] *vr* to go wild

**desmadre** [des·'ma·dre] *m* outrageous behavior; (*caos*) chaos

**desmalezar** <z → c> [des·ma·le·'sar] *vt* AmL to weed

**desmantelar** [des·man·te·'lar] *vt* **1.** (*derribar*) to knock down; (*edificio*) to demolish **2.** (*desmontar*) to take apart; (*bomba*) to dismantle

**desmaquillador** [des·ma·ki·ʝa·'dor, des·ma·ki·ʎa-] *m* make-up remover

**desmayado, -a** [des·ma·'ʝa·do, -a] *adj* **1.** (*inconsciente*) unconscious **2.** (*sin fuerza*) exhausted; (*de hambre*) faint with hunger

**desmayar** [des·ma·'ʝar] **I.** *vi* to lose heart **II.** *vr:* ~se to faint

**desmayo** [des·'ma·ʝo] *m* faint; (*desánimo*) dismay

**desmedido, -a** [des·me·'di·do, -a] *adj* excessive

**desmejorar** [des·me·xo·'rar] **I.** *vt* (*estropear*) to ruin; (*gastar*) to wear out **II.** *vi* to deteriorate **III.** *vr:* ~se **1.** (*estropearse*) to be ruined; (*gastarse*) to wear out **2.** (*de salud*) to deteriorate

**desmembrar** <e → ie> [des·mem·'brar] **I.** *vt* **1.** (*desunir*) to break up; (*un cuerpo*) to dismember **2.** (*escindir*) to separate **II.** *vr:* ~se **1.** (*desunirse*) to break up **2.** (*escindirse*) to separate (**de** from)

**desmentir** [des·men·'tir] *irr como sentir vt* (*negar*) to deny; (*contradecir*) to contradict; (*probar que es falso*) to refute

**desmenuzar** <z → c> [des·me·nu·'sar, -'θar] **I.** *vt* **1.** (*deshacer*) to break into small pieces; (*pez*) to flake; (*con un cuchillo*) to chop up; (*con los dedos*) to crumble; (*raspar*) to grate; (*moler*) to grind **2.** (*analizar*) to scrutinize **II.** *vr:* ~se to crumble

**desmerecer** [des·me·re·'ser, -'θer] *irr como crecer* **I.** *vt* to not deserve **II.** *vi* (*decaer*) to decline

**desmesurado, -a** [des·me·su·'ra·do, -a] *adj* **1.** (*enorme*) enormous **2.** (*excesivo*) excessive; (*ambición*) boundless **3.** (*desvergonzado*) shameless; (*descortés*) rude

**desmigajar** [des·mi·ɣa·'xar] *vt, vr:* ~se to crumble

**desmilitarizar** <z → c> [des·mi·li·ta·ri·'sar, -'θar] *vt* to demilitarize

**desmontar** [des·mon·'tar] **I.** *vt* **1.** (*mecanismo*) to disassemble **2.** (*una pieza: quitar*) to detach; (*sacar*) to remove **3.** (*estructura*) to take down **II.** *vi, vr:* ~se to dismount

**desmoralizador(a)** [des·mo·ra·li·sa·'dor, -·'do·ra; des·mo·ra·li·θa-] *adj* **1.** (*que desanima*) demoralizing **2.** (*que corrompe*) corrupting

**desmoralizar** <z → c> [des·mo·ra·li·'sar, -'θar] **I.** *vt* **1.** (*desanimar*) to demoralize **2.** (*corromper*) to corrupt **II.** *vr:* ~se **1.** (*desanimarse*) to lose heart; (*perder la confianza*) to lose one's confidence **2.** (*corromperse*) to be corrupted

**desmoronamiento** [des·mo·ro·na·'mjen·to] *m* ruin; (*edificio*) collapse; (*imperio, ideología*) decline; (*persona*) breakdown; (*sentimiento*) weakening

**desmoronar** [des·mo·ro·'nar] **I.** *vt* to wear away; (*edificio*) to ruin **II.** *vr:* ~se **1.** to fall to pieces; (*edificio, muro*) to fall down; (*imperio, ideología*) to decline; (*persona*) to fall apart

**desnatado** [des·na·'ta·do] *vt* skimmed, low-fat

**desnatar** [des·na·'tar] *vt* to skim

**desnivel** [des·ni·'βel] *m* **1.** (*diferencia de altura*) drop; (*pendiente*) slope **2.** (*desequilibrio*) imbalance **3.** (*altibajo*) unevenness

**desnivelar** [des·ni·βe·'lar] **I.** *vt* **1.** (*terreno*) to make uneven **2.** (*desequilibrar*) to unbalance **II.** *vr:* ~se (*torcerse*) to twist

**desnucar** <c → qu> [des·nu·'kar] **I.** *vt* ~ **a alguien** to break sb's neck **II.** *vr:* ~se to break one's neck

**desnudar** [des·nu·'dar] **I.** *vt* **1.** (*desvestir*) to undress **2.** (*descubrir*) to strip **II.** *vr:* ~se to undress

**desnudez** [des·nu·'des, -'deθ] *f* nudity; *fig* bareness

**desnudo, -a** [des·'nu·do, -a] *adj* **1.** naked, nude **2.** (*despojado*) bare; ~ **de algo** devoid of sth

**desnutrición** [des·nu·tri·'sjon, -'θjon] *f* malnutrition

**desnutrido, -a** [des·nu·'tri·do, -a] *adj* undernourished

**desobedecer** [de·so·βe·de·'ser, -'θer] *irr como crecer vi, vt* to disobey

**desobediencia** [de·so·βe·'djen·sja, -θja] *f* disobedience

**desobediente** [de·so·βe·'djen·te] *adj*

disobedient

**desocupación** [de·so·ku·pa·'sjon, -'θjon] f 1. (paro) unemployment 2. (ociosidad) leisure

**desocupado, -a** [de·so·ku·'pa·do, -a] I. adj 1. (parado) unemployed 2. (vacío) empty; (vivienda) vacant 3. (ocioso) idle II. m, f unemployed person

**desocupar** [de·so·ku·'par] I. vt 1. (abrir paso) to clear 2. (vaciar) to empty; (vivienda) to vacate II. vr: ~se 1. (de una tarea) to get away 2. (quedarse libre) to be vacant III. vi AmL (parir) to give birth

**desodorante** [de·so·do·'ran·te] adj, m deodorant

**desoír** [de·so·'ir] irr como oír vt to not listen to

**desolación** [de·so·la·'sjon, -'θjon] f 1. (devastación) desolation 2. (desconsuelo) distress

**desolado, -a** [de·so·'la·do, -a] adj 1. (desierto) desolate 2. (desconsolado) devastated

**desolar** <o → ue> [de·so·'lar] I. vt to devastate II. vr: ~se to be devastated

**desollar** <o → ue> [de·so·'jar, -'ʎar] vt to skin

**desorbitado, -a** [des·or·βi·'ta·do, -a] adj exaggerated; (precio) exorbitant; (ojos) bulging

**desorbitar** [des·or·βi·'tar] vt, vr: ~se to exaggerate; (asunto) to get out of hand

**desorden** [des·'or·den] m mess; (confusión) chaos

**desordenado, -a** [des·or·de·'na·do, -a] adj jumbled; (persona, suceso) messy

**desordenar** [des·or·de·'nar] vt (turbar) to mess up; (mezclar) to mix up

**desorganización** [des·or·ɣa·ni·sa·'sjon, -θa·'θjon] f lack of organization

**desorganizar** <z → c> [des·or·ɣa·ni·'sar, -'θar] I. vt to disrupt; (planes) to disturb II. vr: ~se to be disorganized

**desorientación** [de·so·rjen·ta·'sjon, -'θjon] f 1. (extravío) disorientation 2. (confusión) confusion 3. (falta de orientación) loss of direction

**desorientar** [de·so·rjen·'tar] I. vt 1. (extraviar) to disorient 2. (confundir) to confuse II. vr: ~se 1. (extraviarse) to

become disoriented 2. (confundirse) to become confused

**desovar** [de·so·'βar] vi to lay eggs; (pez, anfibio) to spawn

**despabilado, -a** [des·pa·βi·'la·do, -a] adj v. espabilado

**despabilar** [des·pa·βi·'lar] v. espabilar

**despachante** [des·pa·'tʃan·te] mf RíoPl customs officer

**despachar** [des·pa·'tʃar] I. vt 1. (enviar) to send; (mercancías) to dispatch 2. (concluir) to finish off 3. (atender) to serve; (vender) to sell 4. (matar) to kill 5. (despedir) to fire II. vi 1. (acabar) to finish 2. (atender) to do business

**despacho** [des·'pa·tʃo] m 1. (oficina) office; (en casa) study 2. (envío) sending; (pedido) dispatch 3. (de un asunto) resolution 4. (de clientes) service 5. (venta) sale 6. (taquilla) ticket office; (tienda) shop

**despacio** [des·'pa·sjo, -θjo] I. adv 1. (lentamente) slowly 2. (calladamente) quietly II. interj take it easy

**despampanante** [des·pam·pa·'nan·te] adj stunning

**desparejado, -a** [des·pa·re·'xa·do, -a] adj odd

**desparpajo** [des·par·'pa·xo] m 1. (desenvoltura) self-confidence; (en el hablar) ease; con ~ confidently 2. (habilidad) skill; con ~ skillfully 3. (frescura) cheek; con ~ flippantly

**desparramar** [des·pa·rra·'mar] I. vt 1. (dispersar) to scatter; (líquido) to spill 2. (malgastar) to waste 3. Arg, Méx, PRico (diluir) to dilute II. vr: ~se 1. (dispersarse) to scatter; (líquido) to spill 2. (divertirse) to enjoy oneself

**despatarrado, -a** [des·pa·ta·'rra·do, -a] adj estar ~ to straddle; (en un sofá) to sprawl (out)

**despavorido, -a** [des·pa·βo·'ri·do, -a] adj terrified

**despecho** [des·'pe·tʃo] m despair

**despectivo, -a** [des·pek·'ti·βo] adj (despreciativo) contemptuous; (desdeñoso) disdainful; (tono) derogatory

**despedazar** <z → c> [des·pe·da·'sar, -'θar] I. vt to smash; (en mil pedazos) to tear to pieces; (con cuchillo/tijeras)

to cut up; (*con las manos*) to tear up
II. *vr*: **~se** to smash; (*en mil pedazos*)
to fall to pieces

**despedida** [des·pe·'di·da] *f* 1. (*separación*) farewell 2. (*acto oficial*) send-off;
(*fiesta*) going-away party; **~ de soltero/
soltera** stag/hen party

**despedir** [des·pe·'dir] *irr como pedir* I. *vt*
1. (*decir adiós*) to say goodbye; **vino a
~me al aeropuerto** he/she came to
the airport to see me off 2. (*echar*) to
throw out; (*de un empleo*) to dismiss
3. (*difundir*) to give off; (*emitir*) to emit
4. (*lanzar*) to launch II. *vr*: **~se** 1. (*decir adiós*) to say goodbye 2. (*dejar un
empleo*) to leave 3. **~se de (hacer)
algo** forget about (doing) sth

**despegado, -a** [des·pe·'γa·do, -a] *adj*
1. (*frío*) distant 2. (*áspero*) unfriendly
3. (*suelto*) unstuck

**despegar** <g → gu> [des·pe·'γar] I. *vt*
to unstick II. *vi* to take off III. *vr*: **~se**
1. (*desprenderse*) to come off; (*deshacerse*) to come apart 3. **~se de alguien**
to lose one's feelings for sb

**despegue** [des·'pe·γe] *m* take-off; (*cohete*) blast-off

**despeinado, -a** [des·pei·'na·do, -a] *adj*
unkempt

**despeinar** [des·pei·'nar] I. *vt* to ruffle
II. *vr* to get one's hair messed up

**despejado, -a** [des·pe·'xa·do, -a] *adj*
1. (*sin nubes/obstáculos*) clear 2. (*ancho*) wide 3. (*listo*) smart 4. (*despierto*) alert; (*cabeza*) clear

**despejar** [des·pe·'xar] I. *vt* 1. (*lugar,
mesa*) to clear; (*sala*) to tidy up 2. (*situación*) to clarify; (*misterio*) to clear up
II. *vr*: **~se** 1. (*cielo, misterio*) to clear
up 2. (*espabilarse*) to wake up; (*mentalmente*) to sharpen one's wits 3. (*un
enfermo*) to improve

**despeje** [des·'pe·xe] *m* DEP clearance

**despellejar** [des·pe·je·'xar, des·pe·ʎe-]
I. *vt* 1. (*desollar*) to flay 2. *inf* (*desvalijar*) to fleece II. *vr*: **~se** to peel

**despelotarse** [des·pe·lo·'tar·se] *vr inf* to
strip off; (*de risa*) to split one's sides

**despeluz(n)ar** [des·pe·lus·'(n)ar, des·
pe·luθ-] I. *vt* 1. (*asustar*) to terrify
2. *Cuba* (*desplumar*) to pluck II. *vr* to

be terrified

**despensa** [des·'pen·sa] *f* 1. pantry
2. *Arg* (*almacén*) shop

**despeñadero** [des·pe·ɲa·'de·ro] *m*
1. GEO precipice 2. (*riesgo*) danger

**despeñar** [des·pe·'ɲar] I. *vt* to throw
down II. *vr*: **~se** to throw oneself
down

**desperdiciar** [des·per·di·'sjar, -'θjar] *vt* to
waste; (*ocasión*) to miss

**desperdicio** [des·per·'di·sjo, -θjo] *m*
1. waste; **no tener ~** to be good from
start to finish 2. *pl* garbage

**desperdigar** <g → gu> [des·per·di·'γar]
*vt*, *vr*: **~se** to scatter

**desperezarse** <z → c> [des·pe·re·'sar·se,
-'θar·se] *vr* to stretch

**desperfecto** [des·per·'fek·to] *m* 1. (*deterioro*) damage 2. (*defecto*) fault

**despertador** [des·per·ta·'dor] *m* alarm
clock

**despertar** <e → ie> [des·per·'tar] I. *vt*,
*vr*: **~se** to wake up II. *m* awakening

**despiadado, -a** [des·pja·'da·do, -a] *adj*
(*inhumano*) ruthless; (*cruel*) cruel

**despido** [des·'pi·do] *m* dismissal; **~ colectivo** mass layoff

**despierto, -a** [des·'pjer·to, -a] *adj* 1. (*insomne*) awake 2. (*listo*) smart; (*mente*) sharp

**despilfarrador(a)** [des·pil·fa·rra·'dor, --
'do·ra] I. *adj* wasteful; (*con el dinero*)
spendthrift II. *m(f)* wasteful person;
(*con el dinero*) spendthrift

**despilfarrar** [des·pil·fa·'rrar] *vt* to waste;
(*dinero*) to squander

**despilfarro** [des·pil·'fa·rro] *m* waste; (*de
dinero*) squandering

**despintar** [des·pin·'tar] I. *vt* 1. (*color*)
to run 2. (*la realidad*) to misrepresent
3. *Chile, PRico* (*apartar la mirada*) to
look away from; (*perder de vista*) to lose
sight of II. *vr*: **~se** (*borrarse*) to fade

**despistado, -a** [des·pis·'ta·do, -a] *adj*,
*m, f* absent-minded

**despistar** [des·pis·'tar] I. *vt* (*confundir*) to confuse; (*desorientar*) to mislead
II. *vr*: **~se** (*perderse*) to get lost; (*desconcertarse*) to become confused

**despiste** [des·'pis·te] *m* 1. (*distracción*)
absentmindedness 2. (*error*) slip

**desplazado, -a** [des·pla·'sa·ðo, -a; -'θa·ðo, -a] *adj* (*no integrado*) out of place; (*trasladado*) displaced

**desplazamiento** [des·pla·sa·'mjen·to, des·pla·θa·-] *m* movement; (*persona*) displacement

**desplazar** <z → c> [des·pla·'sar, -'θar] *vt* 1. (*mover*) to move 2. (*suplantar*) to displace

**desplegable** [des·ple·'ɣa·βle] *adj* folding

**desplegar** [des·ple·'ɣar] *irr como* fregar *vt* 1. (*abrir*) to open out; (*desdoblar*) to unfold 2. MIL to deploy 3. (*desarrollar*) to develop

**despliegue** [des·'plje·ɣe] *m* unfolding, MIL deployment

**desplomarse** [des·plo·'mar·se] *vr* to collapse

**desplumar** [des·plu·'mar] *vt* 1. (*plumas*) to pluck 2. (*robar*) to fleece; ~ **a alguien jugando a las cartas** to clean sb out at cards

**despoblado** [des·po·'βla·ðo] *m* deserted place

**despoblado, -a** [des·po·'βla·ðo, -a] *adj* depopulated

**despoblar** <o → ue> [des·po·'βlar] *vt* to depopulate; (*bosque*) to clear

**despojar** [des·po·'xar] I. *vt* to strip; ~ **de un derecho a alguien** to deprive sb of a right II. *vr:* ~**se** 1. (*desistir*) to give up 2. (*quitar*) to remove; (*ropa*) to take off

**despojo** [des·'po·xo] *m* 1. spoils *pl* 2. *pl* (*restos*) leftovers *pl;* (*mortales*) mortal remains *pl*

**desposeer** [des·po·se·'er] *irr como* leer I. *vt* 1. (*expropiar, destituir*) to dispossess; ~ **a alguien de su cargo** to remove sb from his/her position 2. (*no reconocer*) to not recognize; **la desposeyeron de sus derechos** they deprived her of her rights 3. (*quitar*) to fleece II. *vr:* ~**se** 1. (*renunciar*) to give up 2. (*desapropiarse*) to relinquish

**despostar** [des·pos·'tar] *vt AmS* to joint

**déspota** ['des·po·ta] *mf* despot

**despotismo** [des·po·'tis·mo] *m* despotism

**despotricar** <c → qu> [des·po·tri·'kar] *vi*

*inf* ~ **de algo/alguien** to rant and rave about sth/sb

**despreciable** [des·pre·'sja·βle, -'θja·βle] *adj* contemptible; **nada** ~ to not be sneered at

**despreciar** [des·pre·'sjar, -'θjar] I. *vt* 1. (*menospreciar*) to despise 2. (*rechazar*) to spurn; (*oferta*) to turn down II. *vr:* ~**se** to run oneself down

**despreciativo, -a** [des·pre·sja·'ti·βo, -a; des·pre·θja·-] *adj* disdainful

**desprecio** [des·'pre·sjo, -θjo] *m* contempt

**desprender** [des·pren·'der] I. *vt* 1. (*soltar*) to release 2. (*olor, gas*) to give off 3. (*deducir*) to deduce II. *vr:* ~**se** 1. (*soltarse*) to untie oneself 2. (*deshacerse*) to come undone; (*librarse*) to rid oneself of; (*renunciar*) to part with 3. **de tu comportamiento se desprende que...** your behavior shows that...

**desprendido, -a** [des·pren·'di·ðo, -a] *adj* (*generoso*) generous; (*altruista*) disinterested

**desprendimiento** [des·pren·di·'mjen·to] *m* 1. (*separación*) separation; ~ **de tierras** landslide; ~ **de retina** detached retina 2. (*generosidad*) generosity

**despreocupación** [des·preo·ku·pa·'sjon, -'θjon] *f* 1. (*indiferencia*) indifference 2. (*insensatez*) carelessness

**despreocupado, -a** [des·preo·ku·'pa·ðo, -a] *adj* 1. (*negligente*) careless 2. (*tranquilo*) unconcerned

**despreocuparse** [des·preo·ku·'par·se] *vr* to stop worrying; ~ **de** to neglect

**despresar** [des·pre·'sar] *vt AmS* to carve

**desprestigiar** [des·pres·ti·'xjar] I. *vt* to discredit II. *vr:* ~**se** to fall into discredit; (*la reputación*) to see one's reputation suffer

**desprevenido, -a** [des·pre·βe·'ni·ðo, -a] *adj* unprepared; **coger a alguien** ~ to catch sb unawares

**desproporción** [des·pro·por·'sjon, -'θjon] *f* disproportion

**desproporcionado, -a** [des·pro·por·sjo·'na·ðo, -a; des·pro·por·θjo·-] *adj* disproportionate

**despropósito** [des·pro·'po·si·to] *m* stupid remark

**desproveer** [des·pro·βe·'er] *irr como*
*proveer vt* to deprive

**desprovisto, -a** [des·pro·'βis·to, -a] *adj*
~ **de** lacking

**después** [des·'pwes] I. *adv* after; **una**
**hora** ~ an hour later; ~ **de la torre**
behind the tower; ~ **de todo** after all
II. *conj* ~ **(de) que** +*subj* after

**despuntar** [des·pun·'tar] I. *vi* 1. (*amanecer*) to dawn 2. (*distinguirse*) to
stand out; **despunta en inglés** he/
she excels at English II. *vr*: ~**se** to become blunt

**desquiciado, -a** [des·ki·'sja·ðo, -a; -'θja·
ðo, -a] *adj* disturbed

**desquiciar** [des·ki·'sjar, -'θjar] I. *vt*
1. (*desencajar*) to unhinge 2. (*alterar*) to disturb II. *vr*: ~**se** to become
unstable

**desquitar** [des·ki·'tar] *vt, vr*: ~**se** 1. (*resarcir*) to win back; ~ **de algo** to make
up for sth 2. (*vengar*) to get even with

**desquite** [des·'ki·te] *m* 1. (*satisfacción*)
satisfaction 2. (*venganza*) revenge

**desrielar** [des·rrje·'lar] *vi AmL* to derail

**destacable** [des·ta·'ka·βle] *adj* outstanding

**destacado, -a** [des·ta·'ka·ðo, -a] *adj* outstanding

**destacamento** [des·ta·ka·'men·to] *m*
MIL detail

**destacar** <c → qu> [des·ta·'kar] I. *vi* to
stand out; ~ **en el deporte** to excel
at sports II. *vt* (*realzar*) to emphasize
III. *vr*: ~**se** to stand out

**destajo** [des·'ta·xo] *m* piecework; **trabajar a** ~ *fig* to work hard; **hablar a** ~
to talk nineteen to the dozen; **a** ~ *Arg,
Chile* by guesswork

**destapar** [des·ta·'par] I. *vt* 1. (*abrir*) to
open 2. (*desabrigar*) to uncover 3. (*secretos*) to reveal II. *vr*: ~**se** 1. (*perder
la tapa*) to lose its lid 2. *inf* (*desnudarse*) to strip off 3. (*descubrirse*) to
be revealed

**destartalado, -a** [des·tar·ta·'la·ðo, -a]
*adj* ramshackle

**destellar** [des·te·'jar, -'ʎar] *vi* to sparkle

**destello** [des·'te·jo, -ʎo] *m* 1. (*rayo*)
ray 2. (*reflejo*) glint 3. (*resplandor*)
sparkle

**destemplado, -a** [des·tem·'pla·ðo, -a]
*adj* 1. (*sonido*) out of tune 2. (*voz*)
harsh 3. (*tiempo*) unpleasant 4. (*persona*) bad-tempered

**desteñido, -a** [des·te·'ɲi·ðo, -a] *adj*
(*descolorido*) faded; (*manchado*) discolored

**desteñir** [des·te·'ɲir] *irr como* ceñir I. *vi*
(*descolorarse*) to fade; (*despintar*) to run
II. *vt* 1. (*descolorar*) to fade 2. (*manchar*) to stain III. *vr*: ~**se** (*descolorarse*)
to fade; (*despintar*) to run

**desternillarse** [des·ter·ni·'jar·se, -'ʎar·se]
*vr* ~ **de risa** to laugh one's head off

**desterrar** <e → ie> [des·te·'rrar] *vt*
1. (*exiliar*) to exile 2. (*alejar*) to banish

**destetar** [des·te·'tar] *vt* to wean

**destiempo** [des·'tjem·po] *m* **a** ~ at the
wrong moment

**destierro** [des·'tje·rro] *m* 1. (*pena*) exile
2. (*lugar*) (place of) exile

**destilación** [des·ti·la·'sjon, -'θjon] *f* (*alcohol*) distillation; (*petróleo*) refining

**destilar** [des·ti·'lar] *vi, vt* to distill

**destilería** [des·ti·le·'ri·a] *f* distillery; ~ **de
petróleo** oil refinery

**destinar** [des·ti·'nar] *vt* 1. (*dedicar*) to
dedicate; (*asignar*) to assign 2. (*enviar*) to send 3. (*designar*) to appoint
4. MIL to post

**destinatario, -a** [des·ti·na·'ta·rjo, -a] *m, f*
addressee; (*de mercancías*) consignee

**destino** [des·'ti·no] *m* 1. (*hado*) fate
2. (*empleo*) position 3. (*meta*) destination; **con** ~ **a** to 4. (*finalidad*) purpose

**destitución** [des·ti·tu·'sjon, -'θjon] *f* dismissal; ~ **del cargo** removal from office

**destituir** [des·ti·tu·'ir] *irr como* huir *vt*
to dismiss

**destornillador** [des·tor·ni·ja·'dor, -ʎa·
'dor] *m* screwdriver; ~ **de estrella**
Philips screwdriver

**destornillar** [des·tor·ni·'jar, -'ʎar] *vt* to
unscrew

**destreza** [des·'tre·sa, -θa] *f* skill; ~ **manual** dexterity; **con** ~ skillfully

**destripar** [des·tri·'par] *vt* 1. (*animal*)
to disembowel; (*pez*) to gut 2. (*final*)
to spoil

**destrozar** <z → c> [des·tro·'sar, -'θar] *vt*

D

**1.** (*despedazar*) to smash; (*ropa*) to tear up; (*vehículo*) to smash up **2.** (*emocionalmente*) to shatter; **estar destrozado** to be an emotional wreck **3.** (*físicamente*) to shatter; **estoy destrozado** I'm beat **4.** (*planes*) to ruin

**destrozo** [des·'tro·so, -θo] *m* **1.** (*daño*) damage **2.** (*acción*) destruction

**destrucción** [des·truk·'sjon, -truɣ·'θjon] *f* destruction

**destructivo, -a** [des·truk·'ti·βo, -a] *adj* destructive

**destruir** [des·tru·'ir] *irr como huir vt* **1.** (*destrozar*) to destroy **2.** (*física o moralmente*) to shatter **3.** (*aniquilar*) to annihilate

**desubicado, -a** [de·su·βi·'ka·do, -a] *adj* disoriented

**desunir** [de·su·'nir] I. *vt* **1.** (*separar*) to separate **2.** ~ **a dos personas** to cause discord between two people II. *vr:* ~**se** **1.** (*separarse*) to separate **2.** (*enemistarse*) to fall out

**desuso** [de·'su·so] *m* **caer en** ~ to fall into disuse; (*máquina*) to become obsolete

**desvalido, -a** [des·βa·'li·do, -a] *adj* needy

**desvalijar** [des·βa·li·'xar] *vt* to clean out

**desvalorización** [des·βa·lo·ri·sa·'sjon, -θa·'θjon] *f* depreciation

**desvalorizar** <z → c> [des·βa·lo·ri·'sar, -'θar] *vt* to devalue

**desván** [des·'βan] *m* loft

**desvanecer** [des·βa·ne·'ser, -'θer] *irr como crecer* I. *vt* **1.** (*color*) to tone down **2.** (*dudas*) to dispel; (*sospechas*) to allay II. *vr:* ~**se** to disappear; (*color, esperanza*) to fade; **el entusiasmo se desvaneció pronto** the enthusiasm soon abated

**desvanecimiento** [des·βa·ne·si·'mjen·to, -θi·'mjen·to] *m* **1.** (*desaparición*) disappearance **2.** (*mareo*) faint

**desvariar** <1. *pres* desvarío> [des·βa·ri·'ar] *vi* to talk nonsense; MED to be delirious

**desvarío** [des·βa·'ri·o] *m* craziness; MED delirium

**desvelar** [des·βe·'lar] I. *vt* **1.** (*revelar*) to reveal **2.** (*sueño*) to keep awake II. *vr:*

~**se** to stay awake

**desvelo** [des·'βe·lo] *m* **1.** (*insomnio*) insomnia **2.** (*despabilamiento*) alertness

**desventaja** [des·βen·'ta·xa] *f* disadvantage

**desventura** [des·βen·'tu·ra] *f* misfortune

**desventurado, -a** [des·βen·tu·'ra·do, -a] *adj* unfortunate

**desvergonzado, -a** [des·βer·γon·'sa·do, -θa·do, -a] *adj* shameless; (*descarado*) brazen

**desvergüenza** [des·βer·'γwen·sa, -θa] *f* shamelessness

**desvestir** [des·βes·'tir] *irr como pedir vt, vr:* ~**se** to undress

**desviación** [des·βja·'sjon, -'θjon] *f* **1.** (*torcedura*) deviation; (*columna vertebral*) curvature **2.** (*del tráfico*) diversion; (*bocacalle*) turning

**desviado, -a** [des·βi·'a·do, -a] *adj* deviant

**desviar** <1. *pres* desvío> [des·βi·'ar] I. *vt* (*camino, dinero*) to divert; (*propósito*) to distract; (*cuestión, problema*) to avoid II. *vr:* ~**se** **1.** (*extraviarse*) to get lost **2.** ~**se de** (*camino*) to stray off; (*idea, intención*) to stray from; (*tema*) to depart from **3. se desviaron hacia la izquierda** they turned towards the left

**desvincular** [des·βin·ku·'lar] I. *vt* to dissociate II. *vr:* ~**se** to dissociate oneself

**desvío** [des·'βi·o] *m* detour

**desvirtuar** <1. *pres* desvirtúo> [des·βir·tu·'ar] *vt* **1.** (*tergiversar*) to distort; (*argumento, prueba*) to undermine **2.** (*desmentir: rumor*) to scotch

**detallado, -a** [de·ta·'ja·do, -a; de·ta·'ʎa·do] *adj* detailed; (*lista*) itemized

**detalle** [de·'ta·je, -ʎe] *m* **1.** (*pormenor*) detail; **en** [*o* **al**] ~ in detail; **entrar en** ~**s** to go into details **2.** (*finura*) nice gesture; **qué** ~ **regalarme las flores** it was so kind of you to give me the flowers

**detallista** [de·ta·'jis·ta, -'ʎis·ta] I. *adj* precise; *pey* pedantic II. *mf* **1.** (*minucioso*) perfectionist **2.** (*considerado*) thoughtful person

**detectar** [de·tek·'tar] *vt* to detect

**detective** [de·tek·'ti·βe] *mf* detective

**detector** [de·tek·'tor] *m* detector

**detención** [de·ten·'sjon, -'θjon] *f* 1. (*parada*) stopping 2. (*arresto*) arrest; ~ **ilegal** false imprisonment; ~ **preventiva** preventive detention 3. (*dilación*) delay

**detener** [de·te·'ner] *irr como* tener I. *vt* 1. (*parar*) to stop 2. (*arrestar*) to arrest 3. (*retener*) to keep II. *vr:* ~**se** 1. (*pararse*) to stop 2. (*entretenerse*) ~**se en algo** to spend one's time doing sth

**detenido, -a** [de·te·'ni·do, -a] I. *adj* 1. (*minucioso*) thorough 2. (*arrestado*) arrested II. *m, f* person under arrest

**detenimiento** [de·te·ni·'mjen·to] *m* (*minuciosidad*) care; **con ~** thoroughly

**detergente** [de·ter·'xen·te] *adj, m* detergent; ~ **lavavajillas** dishwashing liquid

**deteriorar** [de·te·rjo·'rar] I. *vt* 1. (*empeorar*) to worsen 2. (*romper*) to break 3. (*gastar*) to wear out II. *vr:* ~**se** 1. (*empeorarse*) to worsen 2. (*estropearse*) to spoil

**deterioro** [de·te·'rjo·ro] *m* 1. (*desmejora*) deterioration; ~ **de calidad** decline in quality 2. (*daño*) damage 3. (*desgaste*) wear and tear

**determinación** [de·ter·mi·na·'sjon, -'θjon] *f* 1. (*fijación*) establishment 2. (*decisión*) decision; **tomar una ~** to make a decision; **con ~** determinedly 3. (*audacia*) determination

**determinado, -a** [de·ter·mi·'na·do, -a] *adj* 1. (*cierto*) *t.* LING definite 2. (*preciso*) specific 3. *estar* determined (**a** to)

**determinante** [de·ter·mi·'nan·te] I. *adj* decisive II. *m* decisive factor

**determinar** [de·ter·mi·'nar] I. *vt* 1. (*fijar*) to establish; (*plazo*) to fix 2. (*decidir*) to decide 3. (*motivar*) to determine II. *vr* decide (**a** to, **por** in favor of)

**detestable** [de·tes·'ta·βle] *adj* loathsome

**detestar** [de·tes·'tar] *vt* to detest

**detonación** [de·to·na·'sjon, -'θjon] *f* 1. (*acción*) detonation 2. (*ruido*) explosion

**detonador** [de·to·na·'dor] *m* detonator

**detonante** [de·to·'nan·te] I. *adj* 1. (*explosivo*) explosive 2. *AmL* (*que molesta*) discordant II. *m* cause

**detonar** [de·to·'nar] *vi, vt* to detonate

**detractor(a)** [de·trak·'tor, -·'to·ra] I. *adj*

denigrating II. *m(f)* detractor

**detrás** [de·'tras] I. *adv* 1. (*local*) behind; **me asaltaron por ~** they attacked me from behind 2. (*por orden*) **el que está ~** the next one II. *prep* ~ **de** 1. (*local*) behind; **ir ~ de alguien** to be looking for sb; **hablar mal (por) ~ de alguien** to criticize sb behind his/her back 2. (*por orden*) after; **uno ~ de otro** one after another

**detrimento** [de·tri·'men·to] *m* 1. (*daño*) harm 2. (*perjuicio*) detriment; **en ~ de alguien** to sb's detriment; **en ~ de su salud** to the detriment of his/her health

**deuda** ['deu·da] *f* 1. (*débito*) debt; ~ **activa/pendiente** productive/outstanding debt; ~ **externa/interna/pública** foreign/internal/national debt; ~ **a pagar** debt due; **cargado de ~s** burdened with debt; **contraer ~s** to get into debt 2. (*moral*) debt; **estar en ~ con alguien** to be indebted to sb; **lo prometido es ~** a promise is a promise

**deudor(a)** [deu·'dor, -·'do·ra] I. *adj* indebted II. *m(f)* debtor

**devaluación** [de·βa·lwa·'sjon, -'θjon] *f* devaluation

**devaluar** <1. *pres* devalúo> [de·βa·lu·'ar] *vt* to devalue

**devaneo** [de·βa·'neo] *m* flirtation

**devastación** [de·βas·ta·'sjon, -'θjon] *f* devastation

**devastar** [de·βas·'tar] *vt* to devastate

**devenir** [de·βe·'nir] *irr como* venir *vi* to occur; ~ **en algo** to become sth

**devoción** [de·βo·'sjon, -'θjon] *f* 1. (*religión*) religious belief; **tener ~ a un santo** to venerate a saint; **con ~** devoutly 2. (*fervor*) fervor 3. (*afición*) attachment

**devolución** [de·βo·lu·'sjon, -'θjon] *f* return; FIN refund; ~ **de impuestos** tax refund; **'no se admiten devoluciones'** "no refunds"

**devolver** [de·βol·'βer] *irr como* volver I. *vt* to return; *fig* to restore; ~ **un favor** to return a favor II. *vi* to throw up III. *vr:* ~**se** *AmL* (*volver*) to return; ~**se a casa** to go back home

**devorar** [de·βo·'rar] *vt* to devour; ~ **la**

**comida** to wolf down one's food

**devoto, -a** [de.'βo.to, -a] **I.** adj **1.** (religioso) devout **2.** (adicto) devoted; **~ admirador** loyal fan **II.** m, f **1.** (creyente) devotee **2.** (admirador) enthusiast

**día** ['di.a] m day; **~ libre/de baja** day off; **al otro ~** by the next day; **un ~ sí y otro no ~ por medio** AmL every other day; **el ~ de mañana** in the future; **un buen ~** [o **el ~ menos pensado**] one fine day; **un ~ de estos** one of these days; **el otro ~** the other day; **en su ~** in his/her day; **hoy (en) ~** nowadays; **hace buen ~** it's nice weather; **de ~** by day; **del ~** today's; **~ a ~** [o **~ tras** [o **por**] ~] day after day; **¡buenos ~s!** good morning!; **¡hasta otro ~!** until another day!; **al ~** up to date

**diabetes** [dja.'βe.tes] f inv diabetes

**diabético, -a** [dja.'βe.ti.ko, -a] adj, m, f diabetic

**diablo** [di.'a.βlo] m devil; **de mil ~s** hellish; **¡vete al ~!** go to hell!; **¿cómo ~s...?** how on earth...?; **¡qué ~s!** hell!; **¡~s!** damn!

**diablura** [dja.'βlu.ra] f prank

**diabólico, -a** [dja.'βo.li.ko, -a] adj diabolic(al)

**diadema** [dja.'de.ma] f diadem; (del pelo) hair band

**diafragma** [dja.'fraγ.ma] m diaphragm

**diagnosis** [djaγ.'no.sis] f inv diagnosis

**diagnosticar** <c → qu> [djaγ.nos.ti.'kar] vt to diagnose

**diagnóstico** [djaγ.'nos.ti.ko] m diagnosis

**diagonal** [dja.γo.'nal] adj, f diagonal; **en ~** diagonally

**diagrama** [dja.'γra.ma] m diagram

**dial** [di.'al] m dial

**dialectal** [dja.lek.'tal] adj dialect

**dialéctica** [dja.'lek.ti.ka] f dialectics pl

**dialecto** [dja.'lek.to] m dialect

**diálisis** [di.'a.li.sis] f inv dialysis

**dialogar** <g → gu> [dja.lo.'γar] vi to talk

**diálogo** [di.'a.lo.γo] m conversation; LIT dialog(ue)

**diamante** [dja.'man.te] m diamond

**diametralmente** [dja.me.tral.'men.te] adv diametrically; **~ opuesto** diametrically opposed

**diámetro** [di.'a.me.tro] m diameter

**diana** [di.'a.na] f **1.** (blanco) target; (centro) bull's-eye; **hacer ~** to hit the bull's-eye **2.** MIL reveille

**diapasón** [dja.pa.'son] m range; (objeto) tuning fork

**diapositiva** [dja.po.si.'ti.βa] f slide

**diariero, -a** [dja.'rje.ro, -a] m, f AmS newspaper vendor

**diario** [di.'a.rjo] m **1.** (periódico) (daily) newspaper **2.** (agenda) diary

**diario, -a** [di.'a.rjo, -a] adj daily; **a ~** daily; **de ~** everyday

**diarismo** [dja.'ris.mo] m AmL journalism

**diarrea** [dja.'rrea] f diarrhea

**dibujante** [di.βu.'xan.te] mf draftsman, draftswoman m, f; (de caricaturas, animaciones) cartoonist

**dibujar** [di.βu.'xar] vt, vi to draw

**dibujo** [di.'βu.xo] m **1.** (acción, resultado) drawing; **~s animados** cartoons **2.** (ilustración) illustration; **con ~s** illustrated **3.** (estampado) pattern

**dic.** abr de **diciembre** Dec.

**diccionario** [dik.sjo.'na.rjo, diγ.θjo-] m dictionary; **~ enciclopédico** encyclopedic dictionary; **~ de inglés-español** English-Spanish dictionary

**dicha** ['di.tʃa] f luck; **nunca es tarde si la ~ es buena** prov better late than never prov

**dicharachero, -a** [di.tʃa.ra.'tʃe.ro, -a] **I.** adj funny **II.** m, f joker

**dicho** ['di.tʃo] m observation; (refrán) saying

**dicho, -a** ['di.tʃo, -a] **I.** pp de **decir II.** adj **dicha gente** the said people; **~ y hecho** no sooner said than done

**dichoso, -a** [di.'tʃo.so, -a] adj happy; irón blessed

**diciembre** [di.'sjem.bre, -'θjem.bre] m December; v. t. **marzo**

**dictado** [dik.'ta.do] m dictation; fig dictate

**dictador(a)** [dik.ta.'dor, -'do.ra] m(f) dictator

**dictadura** [dik.ta.'du.ra] f dictatorship

**dictamen** [dik.'ta.men] m opinion; (informe) report; **~ judicial** legal judgment

**dictaminar** [dik.ta.mi.'nar] vi to render

judgment

**dictar** [dik·'tar] *vt* **1.** (*dictado*) to dictate **2.** (*sentencia*) to pass **3.** (*ley*) to enact **4.** (*discurso*) to give **5.** *AmS* (*clases*) to teach

**didáctico, -a** [di·'dak·ti·ko, -a] *adj* didactic; **material ~** teaching material

**diecinueve** [dje·si·'nwe·βe, dje·θi-] *adj inv m* nineteen; *v. t.* **ocho**

**dieciocho** [dje·si·'o·tʃo, dje·θi-] *adj inv m* eighteen; *v. t.* **ocho**

**dieciséis** [dje·si·'seis, dje·θi-] *adj inv m* sixteen; *v. t.* **ocho**

**dieciseisavo, -a** [dje·si·sei·'sa·βo, dje·θi-] *adj, m, f* (*fraction*) sixteenth; *v. t.* **octavo**

**diecisiete** [dje·si·'sje·te, dje·θi-] *adj inv* seventeen; *v. t.* **ocho**

**diecisieteavo, -a** [dje·si·sje·te·'a·βo, -a; dje·θi-] *adj, m, f* (*fraction*) seventeenth; *v. t.* **octavo**

**diente** ['djen·te] *m* tooth; **~ de leche** milk tooth; **~ picado** decayed tooth; **~s postizos** false teeth; (*ajo*) clove; **~ de león** dandelion; **decir algo entre ~s** to mumble sth; **poner los ~s largos a alguien** to make sb green with envy; **pelar el ~** *AmL inf* to smile flirtatiously; **volar ~** *AmL* to stuff one's face

**diesel** ['dje·sel] *m* diesel

**diestro, -a** ['djes·tro, -a] *adj* <d(i)estrísimo> **1.** (*no zurdo*) right-handed; **a ~ y siniestro** left, right and center **2.** (*hábil*) skillful **3.** (*astuto*) cunning

**dieta** [di·'e·ta] *f* diet; (*equilibrada*) balanced; **a ~** on a diet

**dietético, -a** [dje·'te·ti·ko, -a] *adj* dietary; **régimen ~** diet

**diez** [djes, djeθ] *adj inv m* ten; *v. t.* **ocho**

**diezmar** [djes·'mar, djeθ-] *vt* to decimate

**difamación** [di·fa·ma·'sjon, -'θjon] *f* defamation

**difamar** [di·fa·'mar] *vt* to defame

**difamatorio, -a** [di·fa·ma·'to·rjo, -a] *adj* defamatory

**diferencia** [di·fe·'ren·sja, -θja] *f* **1.** MAT difference; **a ~ de algo** unlike sth **2.** (*desacuerdo*) disagreement; **arreglar (las) ~s** to settle one's differences

**diferencial** [di·fe·ren·'sjal, 'θjal-] **I.** *adj* variable; MAT differential **II.** *f* differential

**diferenciar** [di·fe·ren·'sjar, -'θjar] **I.** *vi* to differentiate **II.** *vt* to distinguish; MAT to differentiate **III.** *vr*: **~se** to differ

**diferendo** [di·fe·'ren·do] *m AmS* dispute

**diferente** [di·fe·'ren·te] **I.** *adj* different; **~s veces** several times **II.** *adv* differently

**diferir** [di·fe·'rir] *irr como* sentir **I.** *vi* to differ; **~ de algo** to be different from sth **II.** *vt* to postpone; **en diferido** pre-recorded

**difícil** [di·'fi·sil, -θil] *adj* difficult; **~ de explicar** difficult to explain; **de ~ acceso** hard to get to

**difícilmente** [di·fi·sil·'men·te, di·fi·θil-] *adv* with difficulty; (*apenas*) hardly

**dificultad** [di·fi·kul·'tad] *f* difficulty; **en ~es** in difficulty; **con ~** with difficulty; **poner ~es a alguien** to put sb in a difficult position

**dificultar** [di·fi·kul·'tar] *vt* to hinder; (*tráfico*) to obstruct

**dificultoso, -a** [di·fi·kul·'to·so, -a] *adj* difficult; (*laborioso*) arduous

**difteria** [dif·'te·rja] *f* diphtheria

**difuminar** [di·fu·mi·'nar] *vt* (*dibujo*) to stump; (*luz*) to diffuse

**difundir** [di·fun·'dir] *vt, vr*: **~se** to spread; (*gas*) to give off; TV, RADIO to broadcast

**difunto, -a** [di·'fun·to, -a] **I.** *adj* deceased; **mi ~ padre** my late father **II.** *m, f* deceased person; **día de ~s** All Souls' Day; **misa de ~s** Requiem (mass)

**difusión** [di·fu·'sjon] *f* dissemination; TV, RADIO broadcast

**difuso, -a** [di·'fu·so, -a] *adj* widespread; (*vago*) diffuse

**digerir** [di·xe·'rir] *irr como* sentir *vt* (*comida*) to digest

**digestión** [di·xes·'tjon] *f* digestion; **corte de ~** stomach cramp

**digestivo, -a** [di·xes·'ti·βo, -a] *adj* digestive; **aparato ~** digestive system

**digital** [di·xi·'tal] *adj* finger; **huellas ~es** fingerprints; COMPUT, TÉC digital

**digitalizar** <z → c> [di·xi·ta·li·'sar, -'θar] *vt* to digitalize

**dígito** ['di·xi·to] *m* digit

**dignarse** [diɣ·'nar·se] *vr~* (a) **hacer algo** to condescend to do sth

**dignidad** [diɣ·ni·'dad] *f* dignity

**digno, -a** ['diɣ·no, -a] *adj* **1.** (*merecedor*) deserving; ~ **de confianza** trustworthy; ~ **de ver** worth seeing **2.** (*adecuado*) fitting **3.** (*noble*) noble

**dilación** [di·la·'sjon, -'θjon] *f* (*aplazamiento*) postponement; (*retraso*) delay; **sin** ~ without delay

**dilapidar** [di·la·pi·'dar] *vt* to squander

**dilatación** [di·la·ta·'sjon, -'θjon] *f* expansion; MED dilation

**dilatar** [di·la·'tar] **I.** *vt* **1.** (*extender*) to expand; MED to dilate **2.** (*prolongar*) to prolong **II.** *vr:* ~**se 1.** (*extenderse*) to expand **2.** (*alargarse*) to be prolonged **3.** *AmL* (*tardar*) to take long

**dilema** [di·'le·ma] *m* dilemma

**diligencia** [di·li·'xen·sja, -θja] *f* **1.** (*esmero*) diligence **2.** (*agilidad*) skill **3.** ADMIN paperwork; ~**s policiales** police proceedings **4.** JUR procedure; ~ **judicial/policial** legal/police procedures

**diligente** [di·li·'xen·te] *adj* diligent

**dilucidar** [di·lu·si·'dar, di·lu·θi·'dar] *vt* to elucidate

**diluir** [di·lu·'ir] *irr como huir vt* to dissolve; (*líquidos, colores*) to dilute; **sin** ~ undiluted

**diluviar** [di·lu·'βjar] *vimpers* to pour down

**diluvio** [di·'lu·βjo] *m* downpour; *fig* shower

**dimanar** [di·ma·'nar] *vi* to emanate

**dimensión** [di·men·'sjon] *f* dimension; *fig* magnitude; **de grandes dimensiones** large; **la** ~ **cultural** the cultural aspect

**diminutivo** [di·mi·nu·'ti·βo] *m* diminutive

**diminuto, -a** [di·mi·'nu·to, -a] *adj* tiny

**dimisión** [di·mi·'sjon] *f* resignation; **presentar la** ~ to resign

**dimitir** [di·mi·'tir] *vi, vt* to resign (**de** from)

**Dinamarca** [di·na·'mar·ka] *f* Denmark

**dinamarqués, -esa** [di·na·mar·'kes, --'ke·sa] **I.** *adj* Danish **II.** *m, f* Dane

**dinámica** [di·'na·mi·ka] *f* dynamics *pl*

**dinámico, -a** [di·'na·mi·ko, -a] *adj* dynamic

**dinamismo** [di·na·'mis·mo] *m* dynamism

**dinamita** [di·na·'mi·ta] *f* dynamite

**dinamitar** [di·na·mi·'tar] *vt* to dynamite

**dinamizar** [di·na·mi·'sar, -'θar] *vt* to vitalize

**dinamo** [di·'na·mo] *f*, **dínamo** ['di·na·mo] *f* dynamo

**dinastía** [di·nas·'ti·a] *f* dynasty

**dineral** [di·ne·'ral] *m* fortune

**dinero** [di·'ne·ro] *m* money; ~ **electrónico** e-cash; ~ **en metálico** [*o* **contante y sonante**] hard cash; ~ **negro** undeclared money; ~ **suelto** loose change; **estar mal de** ~ to be short of money; **de** ~ rich

**dinosaurio** [di·no·'sau·rjo] *m* dinosaur

**dintel** [din·'tel] *m* lintel

**dio** [djo] *3. pret de* **dar**

**diócesis** [di·'o·se·sis, -θe·sis] *f inv* diocese

**dioptría** [djop·'tri·a] *f* diopter

**dios(a)** [djos, 'djo·sa] *m(f)* god, goddess *m, f*

**Dios** [djos] *m* God; **¡~ mío!** my God!; **¡ay ~!** oh dear!; **como ~ lo trajo al mundo** stark naked; **¡(vaya) por ~!** for God's sake!; **todo ~** everyone; ~ **dirá** time will tell; **hacer algo como ~ manda** to do sth properly; **vivir como** ~ to live like a lord

**dióxido** [di·'ok·si·do] *m* dioxide

**diploma** [di·'plo·ma] *m* diploma; ~ **de bachiller(ato)** ≈ *high school diploma;* ~ **universitario** university diploma

**diplomacia** [di·plo·'ma·sja, -θja] *f* diplomacy; (*cuerpo*) diplomatic corps

**diplomado, -a** [di·plo·'ma·do, -a] *adj* qualified

**diplomático, -a** [di·plo·'ma·ti·ko, -a] **I.** *adj* diplomatic **II.** *m, f* diplomat

**diptongo** [dip·'ton·go] *m* diphthong

**diputación** [di·pu·ta·'sjon, -'θjon] *f* deputation; *Méx* (*edificio*) town hall

**diputado, -a** [di·pu·'ta·do, -a] *m, f* member of parliament

**dique** ['di·ke] *m* dike

**dirección** [di·rek·'sjon, -rey·'θjon] *f* **1.** (*rumbo*) direction; ~ **única** one-way; ~ **prohibida** no entry; **en** ~ **contra-**

ria/**opuesta** in the opposite direction; **salir con** ~ **a España** to leave for Spain **2.** ADMIN direction; ~ **central** central control; ~ **general** head office; ~ **comercial** business management **3.** (*guía*) direction; TEAT artistic direction; **bajo la** ~ **de** directed by **4.** (*señas*) address; ~ **comercial** business address; ~ **de correo electrónico** e-mail address **5.** AUTO steering; ~ **asistida** power steering

**directiva** [di·rek·'ti·βa] *f* **1.** (*dirección*) board (of directors) **2.** (*instrucción*) directive

**directivo, -a** [di·rek·'ti·βo, -a] **I.** *adj* managing; **junta directiva** managing committee **II.** *m, f* (*ejecutivo*) director; (*gerente*) manager

**directo, -a** [di·'rek·to, -a] *adj* **1.** (*recto*) straight **2.** (*inmediato, franco*) direct; **en** ~ live; **un tren** ~ a through train; **el camino más** ~ the shortest way

**director(a)** [di·rek·'tor, -·'to·ra] *m(f)* director; (*jefe*) manager; ENS principal; CINE, TEAT director; ~ **administrativo/general/técnico** administrative/managing/technical director; ~ **de departamento** department manager; ~ **de orquesta** conductor; ~ **de tesis** doctoral advisor

**directorio** [di·rek·'to·rjo] *m* **1.** COMPUT directory **2.** (*agenda*) address book; *AmL* telephone book

**directriz** [di·rek·'triθ] *f* guideline, instruction

**dirigente** [di·ri·'xen·te] *mf* leader; **los** ~**s** the leadership

**dirigir** <g → j> [di·ri·'xir] **I.** *vt* **1.** (*coche, buque*) to steer **2.** (*tráfico*) to direct **3.** (*envío, palabras*) to address **4.** (*vista*) to turn **5.** (*empresa*) to manage; (*finca*) to run; (*orquesta, debate*) to conduct **6.** (*por un camino*) to lead **7.** CINE, TEAT, TV to direct **II.** *vr* ~**se a** to head for; ~**se a alguien** to address sb

**discapacitado, -a** [dis·ka·pa·si·'ta·do, -a; dis·ka·pa·θi·] *adj* handicapped

**discernir** [di·ser·'nir, dis·θer-] *irr como* **cernir** *vt*, *vi* to distinguish

**disciplina** [di·si·'pli·na, dis·θi·] *f* discipline

**disciplinado, -a** [di·si·pli·'na·do, -a; dis·

θi-] *adj* disciplined

**disciplinar** [di·si·pli·'nar, dis·θi-] *vt* to discipline

**disciplinario, -a** [di·si·pli·'na·rjo, -a; dis·θi-] *adj* disciplinary; **sanción disciplinaria** disciplinary measure

**discípulo, -a** [di·'si·pu·lo, -a; dis·'θi-] *m, f* disciple

**disc-jockey** <dis yoqueis> [dis 'jo·kei] *mf* disc jockey

**disco** ['dis·ko] *m* **1.** (*aro*) disk **2.** MÚS record **3.** COMPUT disk; ~ **de arranque** boot disk; ~ **duro** hard disk

**discográfico, -a** [dis·ko·'γra·fi·ko, -a] *adj* record

**disconforme** [dis·kon·'for·me] *adj* in disagreement; (*cosas*) incompatible

**disconformidad** [dis·kon·for·mi·'dad] *f* disagreement; (*de cosas*) incompatibility

**discontinuidad** [dis·kon·ti·nwi·'dad] *f* **1.** (*inconstancia*) discontinuity **2.** (*interrupción*) interruption

**discontinuo, -a** [dis·kon·'ti·nwo, -a] *adj* **1.** (*inconstante*) discontinuous **2.** (*interrumpido*) interrupted

**discordancia** [dis·kor·'dan·sja, -θja] *f* disagreement; MÚS discordance

**discordante** [dis·kor·'dan·te] *adj* conflicting; MÚS discordant

**discordia** [dis·'kor·dja] *f* discord

**discoteca** [dis·ko·'te·ka] *f* **1.** (*local*) disco **2.** (*discos*) record collection

**discreción** [dis·kre·'sjon, -'θjon] *f* discretion

**discrepancia** [dis·kre·'pan·sja, -θja] *f* **1.** (*entre cosas*) discrepancy **2.** (*entre personas*) disagreement

**discrepante** [dis·kre·'pan·te] *adj* divergent

**discrepar** [dis·kre·'par] *vi* **1.** (*diferenciarse*) to differ **2.** (*disentir*) to dissent

**discreto, -a** [dis·'kre·to, -a] *adj* discreet

**discriminación** [dis·kri·mi·na·'sjon, -'θjon] *f* discrimination

**discriminar** [dis·kri·mi·'nar] *vt* **1.** (*diferenciar*) to differentiate (between) **2.** (*perjudicar*) to discriminate against

**discriminatorio, -a** [dis·kri·mi·na·'to·rjo, -a] *adj* discriminatory

**disculpa** [dis·'kul·pa] *f* apology; **admi-**

tir una ~ to accept an apology; **pedir ~s** to apologize; **eso no tiene ~** there is no excuse

**disculpar** [dis·kul·'par] I. vt 1. (*perdonar*) to forgive 2. (*justificar*) to justify II. vr: **~se** to apologize

**discurrir** [dis·ku·'rrir] vi 1. (*pensar*) ~ **sobre algo** to ponder sth 2. (*andar*) to roam; (*río*) to flow 3. (*transcurrir*) to pass

**discurso** [dis·'kur·so] m t. LING speech; ~ **de clausura/recepción** closing/opening speech; **pronunciar un ~** to make a speech

**discusión** [dis·ku·'sjon] f 1. (*debate*) discussion 2. (*riña*) argument

**discutible** [dis·ku·'ti·βle] adj 1. (*disputable*) debatable 2. (*dudoso*) doubtful

**discutido, -a** [dis·ku·'ti·do, -a] adj controversial

**discutir** [dis·ku·'tir] vi, vt to argue; (*hablar*) to discuss; **siempre me discutes lo que digo** you always contradict what I say

**disecar** <c → qu> [di·se·'kar] vt to stuff; ANAT to dissect

**disección** [di·sek·'sjon, -seɣ·'θjon] f dissection

**diseminar** [di·se·mi·'nar] vt, vr: **~se** to spread; (*semillas*) to disperse

**disentería** [di·sen·te·'ri·a] f dysentery

**disentir** [di·sen·'tir] irr como sentir vi to dissent

**diseñador(a)** [di·se·ɲa·'dor, -·'do·ra] m(f) 1. (*dibujante*) artist 2. (*decorador*) designer

**diseñar** [di·se·'ɲar] vt 1. (*crear*) to design 2. (*dibujar*) to draw; (*delinear*) to draft 3. (*proyectar*) to plan

**diseño** [di·'se·ɲo] m 1. (*dibujo*) drawing; (*boceto*) sketch; (*esbozo*) outline; ~ **de página** page design 2. (*forma*) design 3. (*en tejidos*) pattern

**disertación** [di·ser·ta·'sjon, -'θjon] f (*escrita*) dissertation; (*oral*) presentation

**disfraz** [dis·'fras, -'fraθ] m disguise; (*en fiestas*) fancy dress; fig pretense

**disfrazar** <z → c> [dis·fra·'sar, -'θar] I. vt, vr to disguise II. vr: **~se de** to disguise oneself as

**disfrutar** [dis·fru·'tar] vi, vt ~ **(de) algo** 1. (*gozar, sacar provecho*) to enjoy 2. (*poseer*) to have 3. (*utilizar*) to use

**disfrute** [dis·'fru·te] m 1. (*goce*) enjoyment 2. (*aprovechamiento*) benefit

**disgregar** <g → gu> [dis·ɣre·'ɣar] vt, vr: **~se** to disintegrate; (*gente*) to disperse

**disgustar** [dis·ɣus·'tar] I. vt 1. (*desagradar*) to displease; **me disgusta** I don't like it 2. (*enfadar*) to anger; (*ofender*) to offend II. vr: **~se** 1. (*enfadarse*) to get angry (**por** about); (*ofenderse*) to be offended (**por** about) 2. (*reñir*) to quarrel (**con** with)

**disgusto** [dis·'ɣus·to] m (*desagrado*) displeasure; **estar a ~** to be ill at ease; (*aflicción*) suffering; (*molestia*) annoyance; (*enfado*) anger; **dar un ~ a alguien** (*afligir*) to cause sb suffering; (*fastidiar*) to annoy sb

**disidencia** [di·si·'den·sja, -θja] f dissent

**disidente** [di·si·'den·te] adj, mf dissident

**disimulación** [di·si·mu·la·'sjon, -'θjon] f 1. (*fingimiento*) pretense 2. (*ocultación*) concealment

**disimular** [di·si·mu·'lar] I. vi to pretend II. vt to conceal; ~ **el miedo** to hide one's fear; **no ~ algo** to not hide sth

**disimulo** [di·si·'mu·lo] m (*fingimiento*) pretense; (*engaño*) deceit; **con ~** furtively

**disipar** [di·si·'par] I. vt (*nubes, niebla*) to disperse; (*dudas*) to dispel II. vr: **~se** to disperse; (*dudas*) to vanish; (*fracasar*) to go up in smoke

**dislexia** [dis·'lek·sja] f dyslexia

**disléxico, -a** [dis·'lek·si·ko, -a] adj, m, f dyslexic

**dislocación** [dis·lo·ka·'sjon, -'θjon] f dislocation

**dislocar** <c → qu> [dis·lo·'kar] vt, vr: **~se** to dislocate

**disminución** [dis·mi·nu·'sjon, -'θjon] f decrease; ~ **de los gastos/precios/producción/ventas** fall in spending/prices/production/sales; ~ **de la natalidad** decline in the birth rate; ~ **de la pena** remission of sentence; **ir en ~** to diminish

**disminuir** [dis·mi·nu·'ir] irr como huir I. vi (*intensidad*) to diminish; (*número*) to decrease **II.** *vt* to diminish; (*precio, sueldo*) to lower; (*velocidad*) to reduce

**disociación** [di·so·sja·'sjon, -θja·'θjon] *f* separation

**disociar** [di·so·'sjar, -'θjar] *vt, vr:* ~**se** to separate

**disoluble** [di·so·'lu·βle] *adj* soluble; (*contrato*) rescindable

**disolución** [di·so·lu·'sjon, -'θjon] *f* dissolution; (*familia*) break-up; (*costumbres*) dissoluteness; (*contrato*) rescission; QUÍM solution

**disolvente** [di·sol·'βen·te] *m* solvent; (*para pintura*) thinner

**disolver** [di·sol·'βer] *irr como* volver *vt, vr:* ~**se** to dissolve; (*reunión*) to break up

**disonancia** [di·so·'nan·sja, -θja] *f* discord; MÚS dissonance

**dispar** [dis·'par] *adj* dissimilar

**disparado, -a** [dis·pa·'ra·do, -a] *adj* salir ~ to rush off

**disparador** [dis·pa·ra·'dor] *m* trigger; FOTO shutter release

**disparar** [dis·pa·'rar] **I.** *vt, vi* to fire (**contra** at) **II.** *vr:* ~**se** (*desbocarse*) to blow one's top; (*arma*) to go off; (*precios*) to shoot up

**disparatado, -a** [dis·pa·ra·'ta·do, -a] *adj* **1.** (*absurdo*) nonsensical **2.** (*desmesurado*) outrageous

**disparate** [dis·pa·'ra·te] *m* **1.** (*acción/comentario/idea*) foolish act/remark/idea **2.** *inf* me gusta un ~ I really love him/her/it; costar un ~ to cost a fortune

**disparidad** [dis·pa·ri·'dad] *f* disparity

**disparo** [dis·'pa·ro] *m* **1.** (*acción*) firing **2.** (*tiro*) shot

**dispensador** [dis·pen·sa·'dor] *m*, **dispensadora** [dis·pen·sa·'do·ra] *f* dispenser

**dispensar** [dis·pen·'sar] *vt* **1.** (*otorgar*) to give out **2.** (*librar*) to release; (*cargo, molestias*) to relieve **3.** (*excusar*) to forgive

**dispensario** [dis·pen·'sa·rjo] *m* dispensary; (*sanitario*) clinic

**dispersar** [dis·per·'sar] **I.** *vt* to spread; (*personas, animales*) to disperse; (*manifestación*) to break up; FÍS to scatter

**II.** *vr:* ~**se** (*semillas*) to be dispersed; (*personas, animales*) to disperse

**dispersión** [dis·per·'sjon] *f* dispersion; FÍS diffusion

**disperso, -a** [dis·'per·so, -a] *adj* scattered

**disponer** [dis·po·'ner] *irr como* poner **I.** *vi* to have (the use) **II.** *vt* **1.** (*colocar*) to place **2.** (*preparar*) to prepare **3.** (*determinar*) to stipulate **III.** *vr:* ~**se 1.** (*colocarse*) to position oneself **2.** (*prepararse*) to get ready

**disponibilidad** [dis·po·ni·βi·li·'dad] *f* availability; *pl* cash

**disponible** [dis·po·'ni·βle] *adj* available

**disposición** [dis·po·si·'sjon, -'θjon] *f* **1.** (*colocación*) arrangement **2.** (*ánimo, salud*) disposition **3.** (*preparativo*) preparation; **estar en ~ de hacer algo** to be ready to do sth **4.** (*disponibilidad*) availability; **de libre ~** freely available; **estoy a su ~** I am at your disposal; **poner a ~** to make available **5.** (*talento*) aptitude (**para** for) **6.** (*resolución*) agreement; ~ **legal** legal provision

**dispositivo** [dis·po·si·'ti·βo] *m* device; ~ **intrauterino** intrauterine device

**dispuesto, -a** [dis·'pwes·to, -a] **I.** *pp de* **disponer II.** *adj* **1.** (*preparado*) ready; **estar ~ a trabajar/negociar** to be prepared to work/negotiate **2.** (*habilidoso*) capable

**disputa** [dis·'pu·ta] *f* argument; (*pelea*) fight; JUR dispute

**disputar** [dis·pu·'tar] **I.** *vi* to argue **II.** *vt, vr:* ~**se** to compete for; ~ **una carrera** to contest a race

**disquete** [dis·'ke·te] *m* floppy disk

**disquetera** [dis·ke·'te·ra] *f* disk drive

**distancia** [dis·'tan·sja, -θja] *f* t. *fig* distance; **¿a qué ~?** how far?; **acortar ~s** to close the gap; **guardar las ~s** to keep one's distance

**distanciado, -a** [dis·tan·'sja·do, -a; -'θja·do, -a] *adj* t. *fig* distant

**distanciamiento** [dis·tan·sja·'mjen·to, dis·tan·θja-] *m fig* distance

**distanciar** [dis·tan·'sjar, -'θjar] **I.** *vt* to distance **II.** *vr:* ~**se** to move away; *fig* to drift apart

**distante** [dis·'tan·te] *adj* t. *fig* distant

**distar** [dis·'tar] *vi* to be distant

**distender** <e → ie> [dis·ten·'der] *vt fig* to relax

**distensión** [dis·ten·'sjon] *f* easing of tension; POL détente

**distinción** [dis·tin·'sjon, -'θjon] *f* 1. (*diferenciación*) distinction; **a ~ de algo** in contrast to sth; **no hacer ~** to make no distinction; **sin ~ de** irrespective of 2. (*claridad*) clarity 3. (*honor*) distinction

**distinguido, -a** [dis·tin·'gi·do, -a] *adj* 1. (*ilustre*) distinguished 2. (*elegante*) refined 3. (*en cartas*) Dear

**distinguir** <gu → g> [dis·tin·'gir] I. *vt* 1. (*diferenciar*) to distinguish; **no ~ lo blanco de lo negro** to not be able to tell left from right 2. (*divisar*) to make out II. *vr*: **~se** (*ser visible/diferente*) to be noticeable/different

**distintivo** [dis·tin·'ti·βo] *m* emblem

**distintivo, -a** [dis·tin·'ti·βo, -a] *adj* distinguishing

**distinto, -a** [dis·'tin·to, -a] *adj* different (**a** from)

**distorsión** [dis·tor·'sjon] *f* distortion

**distorsionar** [dis·tor·sjo·'nar] *vt* to distort

**distracción** [dis·trak·'sjon, -traɣ·'θjon] *f* distraction; (*hobby*) pastime

**distraer** [dis·tra·'er] I. *vt* 1. (*entretener*) to entertain 2. (*despistar*) to distract II. *vr*: **~se** 1. (*entretenerse*) to amuse oneself 2. (*no atender*) to be distracted

**distraído, -a** [dis·tra·'i·do, -a] I. *adj* 1. (*desatento*) distracted 2. (*entretenido*) entertaining 3. *Chile, Méx* (*mal vestido*) badly dressed II. *m, f* **hacerse el ~** to pretend to not notice

**distribución** [dis·tri·βu·'sjon, -'θjon] *f t.* COM, CINE, TEC distribution; FIN sharing out; **~ de beneficios** profit breakdown

**distribuidor** [dis·tri·βwi·'dor] *m* distributor; (*automático*) dispenser; COM dealer; **~ oficial** official dealer; **~ exclusivo** exclusive distributor; **~ industrial** industrial retailer

**distribuidora** [dis·tri·βwi·'do·ra] *f* distribution company

**distribuir** [dis·tri·βu·'ir] *irr como huir*

I. *vt t.* COM to distribute; (*disponer*) to arrange; (*tarea*) to allocate; (*correo*) to deliver II. *vr*: **~se** to divide up

**distributivo, -a** [dis·tri·βu·'ti·βo, -a] *adj* distributive

**distrito** [dis·'tri·to] *m* district; **~ electoral** constituency; **~ industrial** industrial area; **~ judicial** jurisdiction

**disturbio** [dis·'tur·βjo] *m* disturbance

**disuadir** [di·swa·'dir] *vt* to dissuade (**de** from)

**disuasión** [di·swa·'sjon] *f* dissuasion; POL, MIL deterrence

**disuasivo, -a** [di·swa·'si·βo, -a] *adj* dissuasive; POL, MIL deterrent; **poder ~** deterrent

**dita** ['di·ta] *f AmC, Chile* debt

**DIU** ['diu] *m abr de* **dispositivo intrauterino** IUD

**diurético, -a** [dju·'re·ti·ko, -a] *adj* diuretic

**diurno, -a** [di·'ur·no, -a] *adj* daily; **trabajo ~** day work

**divagación** [di·βa·ɣa·'sjon, -'θjon] *f* digression; *pl* ramblings *pl*

**divagar** <g → gu> [di·βa·'ɣar] *vi* to digress; (*al hablar*) to ramble

**diván** [di·'βan] *m* divan

**divergencia** [di·βer·'xen·sja, -θja] *f* divergence

**divergente** [di·βer·'xen·te] *adj* divergent; (*opiniones*) differing

**divergir** <g → j> [di·βer·'xir] *vi t.* MAT to diverge; (*opiniones*) to differ; (*personas*) to disagree

**diversidad** [di·βer·si·'dad] *f* diversity

**diversificación** [di·βer·si·fi·ka·'sjon, -'θjon] *f* diversity; ECON diversification

**diversificar** <c → qu> [di·βer·si·fi·'kar] *vt, vr*: **~se** to diversify

**diversión** [di·βer·'sjon] *f* entertainment; (*pasatiempo*) pastime

**diverso, -a** [di·'βer·so, -a] *adj* distinct; **~s** many

**divertido, -a** [di·βer·'ti·do, -a] *adj* 1. (*alegre*) amusing 2. (*que hace reír*) funny 3. *AmL* (*achispado*) tipsy

**divertir** [di·βer·'tir] *irr como sentir* I. *vt* to amuse II. *vr*: **~se** to amuse oneself; **¡que te diviertas!** enjoy yourself!

**dividendo** [di·βi·'den·do] *m* dividend

**dividir** [di·βi·'dir] I. vt 1. (partir) to divide 2. (distribuir) to distribute 3. (separar) to separate; (sembrar discordia) to disunite 4. (agrupar) to divide up 5. MAT ~ algo entre [o por] dos to divide sth by two II. vr: ~se 1. (partirse) to divide 2. (agruparse) to divide up into 3. (enemistarse) to fall out

**divinidad** [di·βi·ni·'dad] f divinity; (deidad) deity

**divino, -a** [di·'βi·no, -a] adj divine

**divisa** [di·'βi·sa] f currency

**divisar** [di·βi·'sar] vt to make out

**divisible** [di·βi·'si·βle] adj divisible

**división** [di·βi·'sjon] f 1. (partición) t. MAT, MIL division 2. (separación) separation 3. (parte) portion

**divisorio, -a** [di·βi·'so·rjo, -a] adj dividing

**divo, -a** ['di·βo, -a] m, f leading opera singer m,f, diva f

**divorciado, -a** [di·βor·'sja·do, -a; -'θja·do, -a] I. adj divorced II. m, f divorcee

**divorciarse** [di·βor·'sjar·se, -'θjar·se] vr to get divorced

**divorcio** [di·'βor·sjo, -θjo] m divorce

**divulgación** [di·βul·ɣa·'sjon, -'θjon] f disclosure; (publicación) publication; libro de ~ popularizing book

**divulgar** <g → gu> [di·βul·'ɣar] I. vt to spread; (dar a conocer) to make known II. vr: ~se to spread; (conocerse) to become known

**DNI** [de·ne·'i/de·e·ne·'i] m abr de **Documento Nacional de Identidad** ID

**Dña.** ['do·ɲa] abr de **doña** ≈ Ms.

**dobladillo** [do·βla·'di·jo, -ʎo] m hem

**doblaje** [do·'βla·xe] m CINE dubbing

**doblar** [do·'βlar] I. vt 1. (arquear) to bend 2. (plegar) to fold 3. (duplicar) to double 4. CINE to dub 5. (rodear) to go around II. vi 1. (redoblar) to double 2. (torcer) to turn (a towards)

**doble** ['do·βle] adj, mf t. CINE double; ~ nacionalidad dual citizenship; ~ personalidad split personality

**doblegar** <g → gu> [do·βle·'ɣar] I. vt to subdue II. vr: ~se to give in

**doblez** [do·'βles, -'βleθ] m fold

**doce** ['do·se, -θe] adj inv m twelve; v. t. ocho

**doceavo, -a** [do·se·'a·βo, -a; do·θe-] adj (fracción) twelfth; v. t. octavo

**docena** [do·'se·na, -'θe·na] f dozen

**docencia** [do·'sen·sja, -'θen·θja] f teaching; dedicarse a la ~ to be a teacher

**docente** [do·'sen·te, -'θen·te] I. adj teaching II. mf teacher; UNIV professor

**dócil** ['do·sil, -θil] adj docile; (sumiso) obedient

**docilidad** [do·si·li·'dad, do·θi-] f docility; (sumisión) obedience

**docto, -a** ['dok·to, -a] adj learned; ~ en leyes well-versed in the law

**doctor(a)** [dok·'tor, --'to·ra] m(f) doctor

**doctorado** [dok·to·'ra·do] m doctorate; curso de ~ doctoral course

**doctoral** [dok·to·'ral] adj tesis ~ doctoral thesis

**doctorarse** [dok·to·'rar·se] vr to do a doctorate (en in)

**doctrina** [dok·'tri·na] f doctrine

**documentación** [do·ku·men·ta·'sjon, -'θjon] f 1. (estudio) information 2. (documentos) documentation; (del coche) vehicle documents pl

**documentado, -a** [do·ku·men·'ta·do, -a] adj 1. (identificado) documented; (personas) with papers 2. (informado) informed

**documental** [do·ku·men·'tal] adj, m documentary

**documentar** [do·ku·men·'tar] I. vt 1. (probar) to document 2. (instruir) to inform II. vr: ~se to inform oneself

**documento** [do·ku·'men·to] m document; **Documento Nacional de Identidad** identity card

**dogma** ['doɣ·ma] m dogma

**dogmático, -a** [doɣ·'ma·ti·ko, -a] adj dogmatic

**dogo** ['do·ɣo] m bulldog

**dólar** ['do·lar] m dollar

**dolencia** [do·'len·sja, -θja] f ailment

**doler** <o → ue> [do·'ler] I. vi to hurt; me duele la cabeza I have a headache II. vr: ~se de 1. (quejarse) to complain about 2. (arrepentirse) to regret

**dolido, -a** [do·'li·do, -a] adj hurt

**dolor** [do·'lor] m pain; ~ de cabeza headache

**dolorido, -a** [do·lo·'ri·do, -a] *adj* painful; (*apenado*) sad

**doloroso, -a** [do·lo·'ro·so, -a] *adj* painful

**dom.** *abr de* **domingo** Sun.

**domar** [do·'mar] *vt* to tame

**domesticar** <c → qu> [do·mes·ti·'kar] *vt* to domesticate; (*personas*) to bring under control

**doméstico, -a** [do·'mes·ti·ko, -a] *adj* domestic; **vuelo ~** national flight; **animal ~** pet; **gastos ~s** household expenses

**domiciliar** [do·mi·si·'ljar, -θi·'ljar] **I.** *vt* **1.** (*recibo*) to pay by direct debit; (*alquiler*) to pay by standing order; (*nómina*) to pay direct into sb's account **2.** (*dar domicilio*) to house **II.** *vr:* **~se** to reside

**domiciliario, -a** [do·mi·si·'lja·rjo, -a; do·mi·θi-] *adj* home; **arresto ~** house arrest

**domicilio** [do·mi·'si·ljo, -'θi·ljo] *m* residence; (*de empresa*) address; **reparto a ~** home delivery

**dominación** [do·mi·na·'sjon, -'θjon] *f* domination

**dominante** [do·mi·'nan·te] *adj* dominant

**dominar** [do·mi·'nar] **I.** *vi* **1.** (*imperar*) to rule **2.** (*sobresalir*) to stand out **3.** (*predominar*) to predominate **II.** *vt* **1.** (*conocer*) to have a good knowledge of; (*idioma*) to have a good command of **2.** (*reprimir*) to control **3.** (*sobresalir*) to dominate

**domingo** [do·'min·go] *m* Sunday; *v. t.* **lunes**

**dominguero, -a** [do·min·'ge·ro, -a] *m, f pey* Sunday tripper

**dominical** [do·mi·ni·'kal] **I.** *adj* Sunday **II.** *m* Sunday supplement

**dominicano, -a** [do·mi·ni·'ka·no, -a] *adj, m, f* Dominican

**dominio** [do·'mi·njo] *m* **1.** (*dominación*) control **2.** (*poder*) authority **3.** (*territorio*) domain **4.** (*campo*) subject **5.** (*posesión*) ownership; **ser de ~ público** to be common knowledge

**dominó** <dominós> [do·mi·'no] *m* (*juego*) dominoes *pl*

**don** [don] *m* gift; **tener ~ de gentes** to

have a way with people

**don, doña** [don, 'do·ɲa] *m, f* ≈ Mr., ≈ Mrs. *m, f* + *first name*

**donación** [do·na·'sjon, -'θjon] *f* donation

**donaire** [do·'nai·re] *m* grace

**donante** [do·'nan·te] *mf* donor

**donar** [do·'nar] *vt* to donate

**donativo** [do·na·'ti·βo] *m* donation

**doncella** [don·'se·ja, -'θe·ʎa] *f* maid

**donde** ['don·de] *adv* where; **a** [*o* **hacia**] **~...** where... to; **de ~...** where... from; **en ~** where; **estuve ~ Luisa** I was at Luisa's

**dónde** ['don·de] *pron interrog, rel* where; **¿a** [*o* **hacia**] **~?** where to?; **¿de ~?** where from?; **¿en ~?** where?

**dondequiera** [don·de·'kje·ra] *adv* **1.** (*en cualquier parte*) anywhere **2.** (*donde*) wherever

**donut** ['do·nu(t)] *m* <donuts> doughnut

**doña** ['do·ɲa] *f v.* **don**

**doparse** [do·'par·se] *vr* to take drugs

**doping** [do·'pin] *m* drug-taking

**dorada** [do·'ra·da] *f* gilthead

**dorado, -a** [do·'ra·do] *adj* golden

**dorar** [do·'rar] **I.** *vt* to brown **II.** *vr:* **~se** to go brown

**dormilón, -ona** [dor·mi·'lon, -'lo·na] *m, f* sleepyhead

**dormir** [dor·'mir] *irr* **I.** *vi* to sleep; **quedarse dormido** to fall asleep; **~ la siesta** to take a nap; (*pernoctar*) to spend the night **II.** *vr:* **~se** to fall asleep; **se me ha dormido el brazo** my arm fell asleep; (*descuidarse*) to not pay attention

**dormitorio** [dor·mi·'to·rjo] *m* bedroom

**dorsal** [dor·'sal] **I.** *adj* dorsal; **espina ~** backbone **II.** *m DEP* number

**dorso** ['dor·so] *m t. ANAT* back; **véase al ~** please turn over

**dos** [dos] *adj inv* two; **de ~ en ~** two by two; **cada ~ por tres** all the time; **los/las ~** both

**doscientos, -as** [do·'sjen·tos, -as; dos·'θjen·-] *adj* two hundred; *v. t.* **ochocientos**

**dosificar** <c → qu> [do·si·fi·'kar] *vt* to measure out

**dosis** ['do·sis] *f inv* dose; **una buena ~ de paciencia** a lot of patience; (*dro-*

_ga)_ fix _sl_

**dotado, -a** [do·'ta·do, -a] _adj_ gifted

**dotar** [do·'tar] _vt_ ~ **de** [_o_ **con**] **algo** to equip with sth

**dote¹** ['do·te] _m o f_ dowry

**dote²** ['do·te] _f_ gift; ~ **de mando** leadership ability

**doy** [doi] _1. pres de_ **dar**

**Dpto.** [de·par·ta·'men·to] _AmL abr de_ **departamento** administrative district

**Dr(a).** [dok·'tor, -·'to·ra] _abr de_ **doctor(a)** Dr.

**dragón** [dra·'ɣon] _m_ dragon

**drama** ['dra·ma] _m_ drama; TEAT play

**dramático, -a** [dra·'ma·ti·ko, -a] _adj_ dramatic; **autor** ~ playwright

**dramatizar** <z → c> [dra·ma·ti·'sar, -'θar] _vt_ dramatize

**dramaturgo, -a** [dra·ma·'tur·ɣo, -a] _m, f_ playwright

**drástico, -a** ['dras·ti·ko] _adj_ drastic

**drenaje** [dre·'na·xe] _m_ drainage

**drenar** [dre·'nar] _vt_ to drain

**droga** ['dro·ɣa] _f_ drug

**drogadicto, -a** [dro·ɣa·'dik·to, -a] I. _adj_ addicted to drugs II. _m, f_ drug addict

**drogar** <g → gu> [dro·'ɣar] I. _vt_ to drug II. _vr:_ ~**se** to take drugs

**drogodependencia** [dro·ɣo·de·pen·'den·sja, -θja] _f_ drug addiction

**droguería** [dro·ɣe·'ri·a] _f_ drugstore

**dromedario** [dro·me·'da·rjo] _m_ dromedary

**ducha** ['du·t͡ʃa] _f_ shower

**ducharse** [du·'t͡ʃar·se] _vr_ to take a shower

**ducho, -a** ['du·t͡ʃo, -a] _adj_ skilled

**duda** ['du·da] _f_ doubt; **salir de ~s** to dispel one's doubts; **no cabe la menor ~** there is not the slightest doubt; **poner algo en ~** to question sth

**dudar** [du·'dar] I. _vi_ 1. (_desconfiar_) ~ **de algo** to doubt sth 2. (_vacilar_) to hesitate II. _vt_ to doubt

**dudoso, -a** [du·'do·so, -a] _adj_ 1. (_inseguro_) doubtful 2. (_indeciso_) undecided 3. (_sospechoso_) dubious

**duelo** ['dwe·lo] _m_ 1. (_desafío_) duel 2. (_funeral_) mourning

**duende** ['dwen·de] _m_ elf

**dueño, -a** ['dwe·ɲo, -a] _m, f_ owner; (_amo_) boss; **hacerse ~ de algo** (_apro-

_piarse/dominar_) to take possession/command of sth

**dulce** ['dul·se, -θe] I. _adj_ 1. (_sabor_) sweet 2. (_suave_) soft 3. (_agradable_) pleasant 4. (_agua_) fresh II. _m_ 1. (_postre_) dessert 2. (_golosina_) candy

**dulzor** [dul·'sor, -'θor] _m_, **dulzura** [dul·'su·ra, -'θu·ra] _f_ sweetness; (_ternura_) softness

**duna** ['du·na] _f_ dune

**dundera** [dun·'de·ra] _f AmL_ stupidity

**dundo, -a** ['dun·do, -a] _adj AmL_ silly

**dúo** ['duo] _m_ duet

**duodécimo, -a** [duo·'de·si·mo, -a; -'de·θi·mo, -a] _adj_ twelfth; _v. t._ **octavo**

**dúplex** ['du·pleks] _m_ duplex

**duplicado** [du·pli·'ka·do] _m_ duplicate; **por** ~ in duplicate

**duplicar** <c → qu> [du·pli·'kar] _vt, vr:_ ~**se** to duplicate

**duque(sa)** ['du·ke, du·'ke·sa] _m(f)_ duke, duchess _m, f_

**durabilidad** [du·ra·βi·li·'dad] _f_ durability

**duración** [du·ra·'sjon, -'θjon] _f_ length; **de larga** ~ long-term

**duradero, -a** [du·ra·'de·ro, -a] _adj_ long-lasting

**durante** [du·'ran·te] _prep_ during; ~ **una hora** for an hour

**durar** [du·'rar] _vi_ to last; (_permanecer_) to stay

**durazno** [du·'ras·no] _m AmL_ (_fruta_) peach; (_árbol_) peach tree

**dureza** [du·'re·sa, -'re·θa] _f_ hardness; MED hard skin

**duro** ['du·ro] _adv_ hard

**duro, -a** ['du·ro, -a] _adj_ hard; ~ **de oído** hard of hearing; **a duras penas** barely

**DVD** [de·u·βe·'de] _m abr de_ **videodisco digital** DVD

# E

**E** [e], **e** _f_ E, e; **E de España** E as in Echo

**e** [e] _conj_ (_before 'i' or 'hi'_) **Eva ~ Inés** Eva and Inés

**E** ['es·te] _abr de_ **Este** E

**ebanista** [e·βa·'nis·ta] *mf* cabinetmaker

**ébano** ['e·βa·no] *m* ebony

**ebrio, -a** ['e·βrjo, -a] *adj* inebriated; ~ **de** beside oneself with; (*ciego*) blind with

**ebullición** [e·βu·ji·'sjon, -ʎi·'θjon] *f* boiling

**echado, -a** [e·'tʃa·do] *adj* lying down; ~ **para adelante** pushy

**echar** [e·'tʃar] **I.** *vt* **1.** (*tirar*) to throw; (*carta*) to mail; (*a la basura, al suelo*) to throw out; **la suerte está echada** the die is cast **2.** (*verter*) to pour (**en** into) **3.** (*expulsar*) to throw out **4.** (*pelo*) to grow; (*hojas, flores*) to sprout **5.** (*emitir*) to give off; (*humo*) to let out **6.** CINE, TV to show; TEAT to stage **II.** *vi* (*lanzar*) to throw; (*verter*) to pour; ~ **a correr** to break into a run *vr:* ~**se 1.** (*tumbarse*) to lie down **2.** (*lanzarse*) to jump; ~**se sobre algo/alguien** to fall upon sth/sb; ~**se a los pies de alguien** to throw oneself down before sb; ~**se atrás** *fig* to have second thoughts **3.** (*empezar*) to begin; ~**se a llorar** to burst into tears; ~**se a la bebida** to take to drink; ~**se (un) novio** to get a boyfriend

**echarpe** [e·'tʃar·pe] *m AmL* shawl

**eclesiástico, -a** [e·kle·'sjas·ti·ko, -a] *adj* ecclesiastical

**eclipsar** [e·kliβ·'sar] **I.** *vt* **1.** ASTR to eclipse **2.** (*oscurecer*) to darken **3.** *fig* to outshine **II.** *vr:* ~**se 1.** ASTR to be eclipsed **2.** (*decaer*) to decline

**eclipse** [e·'kliβ·se] *m* eclipse

**eco** ['e·ko] *m* **1.** *t. fig* echo; **tener** ~ *fig* to arouse interest; ~**s de sociedad** PREN gossip column **2.** (*repercusión*) consequence; **hacer** ~ to have an impact

**ecografía** [e·ko·ɣra·'fi·a] *f* ultrasound scan

**ecología** [e·ko·lo·'xi·a] *f* ecology

**ecológico, -a** [e·ko·'lo·xi·ko, -a] *adj* ecological; **daños** ~**s** environmental damage; **producción ecológica** organic farming

**ecologismo** [e·ko·lo·'xis·mo] *m* green movement

**ecologista** [e·ko·lo·'xis·ta] **I.** *adj* ecological **II.** *mf* ecologist

**economía** [e·ko·no·'mi·a] *f* **1.** (*situación, sistema*) economy; ~ **de desechos** re-

cycling industry; ~ **forestal** forestry sector; ~ **sumergida** black economy; ~ **de escala** economy of scale; ~ **de oferta** supply-side economy **2.** (*ciencia*) economics; ~ **política/de la empresa** political/business economics **3.** (*ahorro*) saving; **hacer** ~**s** to economize

**económico, -a** [e·ko·'no·mi·ko, -a] *adj* **1.** ECON economic; **año** ~ financial year; **estudiar Ciencias Económicas** to study economics **2.** (*barato*) cheap; (*ahorrador*) economical; (*persona*) thrifty

**economista** [e·ko·no·'mis·ta] *mf* economist

**economizar** <z → c> [e·ko·no·mi·'sar, -'θar] *vi, vt* to economize; **no** ~ **esfuerzos** to spare no effort; ~ **esfuerzos** to save one's efforts

**ecosistema** [e·ko·sis·'te·ma] *m* ecosystem

**ecuación** [e·kwa·'sjon, -'θjon] *f* equation

**ecuador** [e·kwa·'dor] *m* equator

**Ecuador** [e·kwa·'dor] *m* Ecuador

**ecuánime** [e·'kwa·ni·me] *adj* fair

**ecuanimidad** [e·kwa·ni·mi·'dad] *f* impartiality

**ecuatorial** [e·kwa·to·'rjal] *adj* equatorial

**ecuatoriano, -a** [e·kwa·to·'rja·no, -a] *adj, m, f* Ecuadorean

**ecuménico, -a** [e·ku·'me·ni·ko, -a] *adj* universal

**edad** [e·'dad] *f* **1.** age; ~ **para jubilarse** retirement age; ~ **del pavo** adolescence; **mayor de** ~ adult; **menor de** ~ minor; **ser mayor/menor de** ~ to be of/under age; **a la** ~ **de...** at the age of...; **¿qué** ~ **tiene?** how old is he/she?; **de mi** ~ of my age; **de cierta** ~ getting up there (in age); **llegar a la mayoría de** ~ to come of age; **de mediana** ~ middle-aged; **la tercera** ~ old [*o* retirement] age **2.** (*época*) age, era; **la Edad Media** the Middle Ages

**edén** [e·'den] *m* Eden; *fig* paradise

**edición** [e·di·'sjon, -'θjon] *f* edition; ~ **de bolsillo** paperback edition; **la presente** ~ **del Festival de Cine** this year's Film Festival

**edificación** [e·di·fi·ka·'sjon, -'θjon] *f* construction

**edificante** [e·di·fi·'kan·te] *adj* edifying

**edificar** <c → qu> [e·di·fi·'kar] *vt* to build

**edificio** [e·di·'fi·sjo, -θjo] *m* building

**edil(a)** [e·'dil, e·'di·la] *m(f)* councilman, councilwoman *m, f*

**editar** [e·di·'tar] *vt* **1.** (*publicar*) to publish **2.** (*revisar*) to edit

**editor(a)** [e·di·'tor, --'to·ra] *m(f)* **1.** (*que publica*) publisher **2.** (*que revisa*) editor

**editorial¹** [e·di·to·'rjal] **I.** *adj* publishing **II.** *f* publisher

**editorial²** [e·di·to·'rjal] *m* editorial

**Edo.** [es·'ta·do] *Méx, Ven abr de* **Estado** State

**edredón** [e·dre·'don] *m* eiderdown; **~ nórdico** quilt

**educación** [e·du·ka·'sjon, -'θjon] *f* **1.** (*instrucción*) education; **~ de adultos** adult education; **~ ambiental** environmental education; **~ física** ENS physical education; **~ a distancia** distance learning; **~ permanente** permanent education; **Educación General Básica** HIST education for children aged 6 to 14; **educación preescolar** preschool education; **~ vial** road education **2.** (*modales*) manners *pl*; **este niño no tiene ~** this child has no manners

**educado, -a** [e·du·'ka·do, -a] *adj* **1.** (*cortés*) (**bien**) **~** polite; **mal ~** rude **2.** (*culto*) cultivated

**educar** <c → qu> [e·du·'kar] *vt* to educate; (*criar*) to bring up; **debes ~ tu oído** you should train your ear

**educativo, -a** [e·du·ka·'ti·βo, -a] *adj* educational

**edulcorante** [e·dul·ko·'ran·te] *m* sweetener

**EE.UU.** [es·'ta·dos u·'ni·dos] *mpl abr de* **Estados Unidos** USA

**efectivamente** [e·fek·ti·βa·'men·te] *adv* in fact

**efectividad** [e·fek·ti·βi·'dad] *f* effectiveness

**efectivo** [e·fek·'ti·βo] *m* (*dinero*) cash; **en ~** (in) cash; **~ electrónico** electronic cash

**efectivo, -a** [e·fek·'ti·βo, -a] *adj* **1.** (*que* *hace efecto*) effective **2.** (*real*) real; **un éxito ~** a real success; **hacer ~** to put into action; (*cheque*) to cash

**efecto** [e·'fek·to] *m* effect; **~ invernadero** greenhouse effect; **~ retardado** delayed reaction; **~s secundarios** side effects; **hacer ~** to have an effect; **hacer buen ~** (*impresión*) to make a good impression; **tener ~** to take effect; **llevar a ~** to carry out; **en ~** indeed; **para los ~s** effectively; **con ~s retroactivos** retroactively

**efectuar** <*1. pres* efectúo> [e·fek·tu·'ar] **I.** *vt* to carry out; **~ una compra** to make a purchase **II.** *vr:* **~se** (*tener lugar*) to take place; (*realizarse*) to be carried out

**efervescente** [e·fer·βe·'sen·te, -'θen·te] *adj* fizzy; (*pastilla*) dissoluble

**eficacia** [e·fi·'ka·sja, -θja] *f t.* ECON, TÉC efficiency; (*medida*) effectiveness; **con ~** effectively; **sin ~** inefficiently

**eficaz** [e·fi·'kas, -'kaθ] *adj* efficient; (*medida*) effective

**eficiencia** [e·fi·'sjen·sja, -'θjen·θja] *f* efficiency; (*medida*) effectiveness

**eficiente** [e·fi·'sjen·te, -'θjen·te] *adj* efficient; (*medida*) effective

**efusión** [e·fu·'sjon] *f* effusion; **con gran ~** very effusively

**efusivo, -a** [e·fu·'si·βo, -a] *adj* effusive

**Egeo** [e·'xe·o] *m* Aegean

**egipcio, -a** [e·'xip·sjo, -a; -'xiβ·θjo, -a] *adj, m, f* Egyptian

**Egipto** [e·'xip·to] *m* Egypt

**ego** [e·ɣo] *m* ego

**egocéntrico, -a** [e·ɣo·'sen·tri·ko, -a; -'θen·tri·ko, -a] *adj* egocentric

**egoísmo** [e·ɣo·'is·mo] *m* selfishness

**egoísta** [e·ɣo·'is·ta] **I.** *adj* selfish **II.** *mf* egoist

**egresado, -a** [e·ɣre·'sa·do, -a] *m, f Arg, Chile* graduate

**egresar** [e·ɣre·'sar] *vi Arg, Chile* to graduate

**eh** [e] *interj* ¡~! hey!; ¿~? eh?; **no vuelvas a hacerlo, ¿~?** don't do it again, OK?

**ej.** [e·'xem·plo] *abr de* **ejemplo** example

**eje** [e·xe] *m* (*de rueda*) axle; *fig* **~ del debate** crux of the discussion; **ser el ~ de**

**atención** to be the center of attention

**ejecución** [e·xe·ku·'sjon, -'θjon] *f t.* JUR execution; (*proyecto*) implementation; (*pedido*) carrying out; **poner en ~ to** carry out

**ejecutar** [e·xe·ku·'tar] *vt* to execute; (*ley*) to enforce

**ejecutivo, -a** [e·xe·ku·'ti·βo, -a] **I.** *adj t.* JUR executive; **comité ~** executive committee; **poder ~** executive power **II.** *m, f* (*directivo*) executive; (*emplea-do*) manager; **~ de marketing** marketing executive

**ejemplar** [e·xem·'plar] **I.** *adj* exemplary; **un alumno ~** a model student **II.** *m* specimen; (*libro*) copy; (*revista*) issue; **~ de muestra** sample

**ejemplarizar** <z → c> [e·xem·pla·ri·'sar] *vi AmL* to serve as an example

**ejemplificar** <c → qu> [e·xem·pli·fi·'kar] *vt* to exemplify

**ejemplo** [e·'xem·plo] *m* example; **dar buen ~** to set a good example; **po-ner por ~** to give as an example; **por ~** for example; **sin ~** unprecedented; **predicar con el ~** to practice what one preaches; **tomar por ~** to take as an example

**ejercer** <c → z> [e·xer·'ser, -'θer] **I.** *vt* (*profesión*) to practice; (*derechos*) to exercise **II.** *vi* to practice; (*profesor*) to work

**ejercicio** [e·xer·'si·sjo, -'θi·θjo] *m* **1.** (*de una profesión*) practice; **en ~** practicing **2.** DEP, ENS exercise; **tener falta de ~** to be out of practice **3.** ECON **~ contable** tax year; **~** (**económico**) financial year

**ejercitar** [e·xer·si·'tar, -θi·'tar] **I.** *vt* **1.** (*profesión*) to practice; (*actividad*) to carry out **2.** (*adiestrar*) to train **II.** *vr:* **~se** to train

**ejército** [e·'xer·si·to, -θi·to] *m* army; (*fuerzas armadas*) armed forces

**ejote** [e·'xo·te] *m AmC, Méx* string bean

**el** [el], **la** [la], **lo** [lo] <los, las> *art def* **1.** the; **la mesa** the table; **los amigos/as** the friends; **~ azul** the blue one **2.** **lo + adj lo bueno/malo** the good/bad (thing); **lo antes posible** as soon as possible **3.** + *nombres geográficos* **la India** India **4.** + *días de semana* **llegaré el**

**domingo** I'll arrive on Sunday; **los sá-bados no trabajo** I don't work on Sat-urdays **5.** + *nombre propio inf* **he visto a la Carmen** I saw Carmen **6.** + *que* **lo que digo es...** what I'm saying is...

**él** [el] *pron pers, 3. sing m* he; + *prep* him; **el libro es de ~** the book is his

**elaboración** [e·la·βo·ra·'sjon, -'θjon] *f* manufacture; (*de comidas*) preparation; **de ~ casera** homemade

**elaborar** [e·la·βo·'rar] *vt* to manufacture; (*preparar*) to prepare

**elación** [e·la·'sjon] *f AmL* exaltation

**elasticidad** [e·las·ti·si·'dad, -θi·'dad] *f* elasticity

**elástico** [e·'las·ti·ko] *m* elastic

**elástico, -a** [e·'las·ti·ko, -a] *adj* elastic; (*tela*) stretch

**elección** [e·lek·'sjon, -ley·'θjon] *f* (*selec-ción*) choice; **lo dejo a su ~** the choice is yours; POL election; **elecciones ge-nerales/legislativas** general election; **~ parcial** by-election

**electo, -a** [e·'lek·to, -a] *adj* elect

**elector(a)** [e·lek·'tor, -·'to·ra] **I.** *adj* elect-ing **II.** *m(f)* voter

**electorado** [e·lek·to·'ra·do] *m* electorate

**electoral** [e·lek·to·'ral] *adj* electoral

**electricidad** [e·lek·tri·si·'dad, -θi·'dad] *f* electricity

**electricista** [e·lek·tri·'sis·ta, -'θis·ta] *mf* electrician

**eléctrico, -a** [e·'lek·tri·ko, -a] *adj* electric; (*aparato, instalación*) electrical

**electrificar** <c → qu> [e·lek·tri·fi·'kar] *vt*, **electrizar** <z → c> [e·lek·tri·'sar, -'θar] *vt* to electrify

**electrocardiograma** [e·lek·tro·kar·djo·'yra·ma] *m* electrocardiogram

**electrocución** [e·lek·tro·ku·'sjon, -'θjon] *f* electrocution

**electrocutar** [e·lek·tro·ku·'tar] *vt* to elec-trocute

**electrodo** [e·lek·'tro·do] *m* electrode

**electrodoméstico** [e·lek·tro·do·'mes·ti·ko] *m* household appliance

**electrón** [e·lek·'tron] *m* electron

**electrónica** [e·lek·'tro·ni·ka] *f* electron-ics

**electrónico, -a** [e·lek·'tro·ni·ko, -a] *adj* electronic; (*microscopio*) electron;

**correo** ~ e-mail

**elefante, -a** [e·le·'fan·te, -a] *m, f* elephant; ~ **marino** elephant seal

**elegancia** [e·le·'ɣan·sja, -θja] *f* elegance; (*buen gusto*) tastefulness

**elegante** [e·le·'ɣan·te] *adj* elegant; (*con buen gusto*) tasteful

**elegantoso, -a** [e·le·ɣan·'to·so, -a] *adj* *inf* ritzy

**elegir** [e·le·'xir] *irr vi, vt* to choose; **a ~ entre** to be chosen from; POL to elect

**elementado, -a** [e·le·men·'ta·do, -a] *adj* *Chile, Col* bewildered

**elemental** [e·le·men·'tal] *adj* basic

**elemento** [e·le·'men·to] *m* element; ~ **base** basic element; **tener ~s de juicio** to be able to judge; ~ **decisivo** crucial factor; **los ~** the elements; **~s de matemáticas** basic mathematics

**elenco** [e·'len·ko] *m* 1. TEAT cast 2. *AmL* (*personal*) staff 3. *Chile, Perú* (*equipo*) team

**elepé** [e·le·'pe] *m* LP

**elevación** [e·le·βa·'sjon, -'θjon] *f* rise; GEO elevation

**elevado, -a** [e·le·'βa·do, -a] *adj* elevated; (*nivel, estilo*) refined; MAT ~ **a** raised to the power of

**elevador** [e·le·βa·'dor] *m* *AmC* elevator

**elevalunas** [e·le·βa·'lu·nas] *m* *inv* automatic window

**elevar** [e·le·'βar] I. *vt* to raise; (*protesta*) to lodge; MAT ~ **a** to raise to the power of II. *vr:* **~se** to rise; **~se a** (*precio*) to amount to; (*cotización*) to stand at

**eliminación** [e·li·mi·na·'sjon, -'θjon] *f* elimination; (*basura, residuos*) disposal

**eliminar** [e·li·mi·'nar] *vt* 1. to eliminate; ~ **la competencia** to eliminate the competition 2. DEP to knock out; **fueron eliminados en la cuarta prueba** they went out in the fourth round

**eliminatoria** [e·li·mi·na·'to·rja] *f* playoff

**elipse** [e·'lip·se] *f* ellipse

**elite** [e·'li·te] *f,* **élite** [e·'li·te] *f* elite; **de ~** top-class

**elitista** [e·li·'tis·ta] *adj* elitist

**elixir** [e·lik·'sir] *m* elixir

**ella** ['e·ja, -ʎa] *pron pers, 3. sing f* she; + *prep* her; **el abrigo es de ~** the coat is hers

**ellas** ['e·jas, -ʎas] *pron pers, 3. pl f* they; + *prep* them; **el coche es de ~** the car is theirs

**ello** ['e·jo, -ʎo] *pron pers, 3. sing neutro* it; **para ~** for it; **por ~** that is why; **estar en ~** to be doing it; **¡a ~!** let's do it!

**ellos** ['e·jos, -ʎos] *pron pers, 3. pl m* they; + *prep* them; **estos niños son de ~** these children are theirs

**elocuencia** [e·lo·'kwen·sja, -θja] *f* eloquence; **con ~** eloquently

**elocuente** [e·lo·'kwen·te] *adj* eloquent; **las pruebas son ~s** the evidence speaks for itself

**elogiar** [e·lo·'xjar] *vt* to praise

**elogio** [e·'lo·xjo] *m* praise; **hacer ~s** to eulogize; **recibir ~s** to be praised; **digno de ~** praiseworthy

**elote** [e·'lo·te] *m* *AmC* corncob

**eludir** [e·lu·'dir] *vt* to elude; (*preguntas*) to evade; (*responsabilidad*) to shirk

**e-mail** [i·'meil] *m* *abr de* **electronic mail** e-mail

**emanar** [e·ma·'nar] *vi* 1. (*escaparse*) ~ **de** to emanate from *form*; (*líquido*) to ooze from 2. (*originarse*) ~ **de** to stem from

**emancipación** [e·man·si·pa·'sjon, -θi·pa·'θjon] *f* emancipation

**emanciparse** [e·man·si·'par·se, e·man·θi-] *vr* to become emancipated

**embadurnar** [em·ba·dur·'nar] I. *vt* ~ **algo de** [*o* **con**] **algo** to smear sth with sth II. *vr* **~se de** [*o* **con**] **algo** to be smeared with sth

**embajada** [em·ba·'xa·da] *f* embassy

**embajador(a)** [em·ba·xa·'dor, -·'do·ra] *m(f)* ambassador

**embalaje** [em·ba·'la·xe] *m* packaging; (*acción*) packing

**embalar** [em·ba·'lar] I. *vt* to pack II. *vr:* **~se** (*correr*) to dash off

**embalsamar** [em·bal·sa·'mar] *vt* to embalm

**embalsar** [em·bal·'sar] *vt* to dam

**embalse** [em·'bal·se] *m* reservoir; *Arg* dam

**embarazada** [em·ba·ra·'sa·da, -'θa·da] I. *adj* pregnant; **estar ~ de seis meses** to be six months pregnant; **quedarse ~** to get pregnant II. *f* pregnant woman

**embarazo** [em·ba·'ra·so, -θo] *m* pregnancy; **interrupción del ~** abortion; *fig* **causar ~ a alguien** to make sb feel awkward

**embarazoso, -a** [em·ba·ra·'so·so, -a; -'θo·so, -a] *adj* awkward

**embarcación** [em·bar·ka·'sjon, -'θjon] *f* vessel; **~ de recreo** pleasure craft

**embarcadero** [em·bar·ka·'de·ro] *m* pier

**embarcar** <c → qu> [em·bar·'kar] **I.** *vi* to go on board; (*avión*) to board **II.** *vt* (*barco*) to stow; (*avión*) to put on board; (*asunto*) to involve **III.** *vr:* **~se** (*barco*) to embark; (*avión*) to board; (*asunto*) to become involved

**embargar** <g → gu> [em·bar·'ɣar] *vt* to confiscate

**embargo** [em·'bar·ɣo] **I.** *m* confiscation; COM embargo **II.** *conj* **sin ~** however

**embarque** [em·'bar·ke] *m* **1.** (*material*) loading **2.** (*personas*) boarding; **tarjeta de ~** boarding card

**embarrada** [em·ba·'rra·da] *f* Cuba, PRico, And (*desliz*) blunder; (*tontería*) foolishness

**embaucador(a)** [em·bau·ka·'dor, --'do·ra] **I.** *adj* deceitful **II.** *m(f)* cheat

**embaucar** <c → qu> [em·bau·'kar] *vt* to cheat

**embelesar** [em·be·le·'sar] *vi, vt* to captivate

**embellecer** [em·be·je·'ser, -ʎe·'θer] *irr como crecer vt* to beautify

**embestida** [em·bes·'ti·da] *f* onslaught

**embestir** [em·bes·'tir] *irr como pedir* **I.** *vi* to charge **II.** *vt* (*atacar*) to attack; (*coche*) to crash into

**emblema** [em·'ble·ma] *m* emblem; (*logotipo*) logo

**embobar** [em·bo·'βar] **I.** *vt* (*asombrar*) to amaze; (*fascinar*) to fascinate **II.** *vr* **~se en** [*o* **con**] **algo** to be amazed by sth; (*fascinación*) to be fascinated by sth

**embolarse** [em·bo·'lar·se] *vr AmC* to get drunk

**embolia** [em·'bo·lja] *f* embolism; **~ cerebral** brain clot

**embolsar** [em·bol·'sar] *vt* to pocket

**emborrachar** [em·bo·rra·'tʃar] **I.** *vt* to make drunk; CULIN to soak (**con** in) **II.** *vr:* **~se** to get drunk

**emborronar** [em·bo·rro·'nar] *vt* to blot, to smudge

**emboscada** [em·bos·'ka·da] *f* ambush

**embotellado, -a** [em·bo·te·'ja·do, -'ʎa·do] *adj* bottled

**embotellamiento** [em·bo·te·ja·'mjen·to, em·bo·te·ʎa-] *m* **1.** (*de bebidas*) bottling **2.** (*de tráfico*) jam

**embotellar** [em·bo·te·'jar, -'ʎar] **I.** *vt* **1.** (*bebidas*) to bottle **2.** (*tráfico*) to block **II.** *vr:* **~se** (*tráfico*) to get congested

**embrague** [em·'bra·ɣe] *m* clutch

**embriagar** <g → gu> [em·brja·'ɣar] **I.** *vi, vt* **1.** (*emborrachar*) to inebriate **2.** (*enajenar*) to hypnotize **II.** *vr:* **~se** (*emborracharse*) to get drunk

**embriaguez** [em·brja·'ɣes, -'ɣeθ] *f* **1.** (*borrachera*) inebriation; **en estado de ~** inebriated **2.** (*enajenación*) delight

**embrión** [em·bri·'on] *m* embryo

**embrollar** [em·bro·'jar, -'ʎar] **I.** *vt* **1.** (*liar*) to mess up; **embrollas todo lo que tocas** you mess everything up; **lo embrollas más de lo necesario** you're overcomplicating things **2.** *CSur* (*engañar*) to deceive **II.** *vr:* **~se** to get tangled up; **~se en algo** to get involved in sth

**embrollo** [em·'bro·jo, -ʎo] *m* **1.** (*lío*) mess; **meterse en un ~** to get into a mess **2.** (*embuste*) swindle; **no me vengas con ~s** don't try and fool me

**embromado, -a** [em·bro·'ma·do, -a] *adj AmL inf* **1.** (*difícil*) hard **2.** (*molesto*) annoyed

**embromar** [em·bro·'mar] *vt AmL* to annoy

**embroncarse** [em·bron·'kar·se] <c → qu> *vr Arg inf* to get mad

**embrujado, -a** [em·bru·'xa·do, -a] *adj* bewitched; (*casa*) haunted

**embrujar** [em·bru·'xar] *vt* to bewitch

**embudo** [em·'bu·do] *m* funnel; **en forma de ~** funnel-shaped; **aplicar la ley del ~** to apply one-sided rule

**embuste** [em·'bus·te] *m* lie; (*estafa*) swindle

**embustero, -a** [em·bus·'te·ro, -a] **I.** *adj* lying; **¡qué tío más ~!** what a swindler! **II.** *m, f* liar; (*estafador*) swindler

**embute** [em·'bu·te] *m Méx inf* bribe

**embutido** [em·bu·'ti·do] *m* sausage

**embutir** [em·bu·'tir] *vt* to stuff

**emergencia** [e·mer·'xen·sja, -θja] *f* emergency; **estado de ~** state of emergency; **plan de ~** emergency plan

**emergente** [e·mer·'xen·te] *adj* emergent

**emerger** <g → j> [e·mer·'xer] *vi* to emerge; (*submarino*) to surface; **mi jefe emergió de la nada** my boss is a self-made man

**emigración** [e·mi·γra·'sjon, -'θjon] *f* emigration; (*animales*) migration

**emigrante** [e·mi·'γran·te] *mf* emigrant; POL émigré

**emigrar** [e·mi·'γrar] *vi* to emigrate; (*animales*) to migrate

**emilio** [e·'mi·ljo] *m inf* e-mail; **escribir/mandar un ~** to write/send an e-mail

**eminencia** [e·mi·'nen·sja, -θja] *f* Eminence; *fig* expert; **ser una ~ en su campo** to be an expert in one's field

**eminente** [e·mi·'nen·te] *adj* outstanding

**emisión** [e·mi·'sjon] *f* 1. TV, RADIO broadcast; (*de programas*) program 2. FÍS emission; **emisiones contaminantes** pollution

**emisor(a)** [e·mi·'sor] *adj* broadcasting; (*banco*) issuing

**emisora** [e·mi·'so·ra] *f* broadcasting station; **~ clandestina** pirate station; **~ de radio** radio station; **~ de televisión** television station

**emitir** [e·mi·'tir] *vt* 1. TV, RADIO to broadcast 2. FÍS to emit, to give off 3. (*humo*) to let off; (*grito*) to let out; (*dictamen*) to give

**emoción** [e·mo·'sjon, -'θjon] *f* emotion; (*ilusión*) excitement; **lleno de emociones** full of thrills; **palabras llenas de ~** words full of emotion; **llorar de ~** to cry with emotion; **sin ~** without emotion; **sentir una honda ~** to feel a deep emotion; **dar rienda suelta a sus emociones** to give free rein to one's emotions

**emocional** [e·mo·sjo·'nal, e·mo·θjo-] *adj* emotional

**emocionante** [e·mo·sjo·'nan·te, e·mo·θjo-] *adj* exciting; (*conmovedor*) moving

**emocionar** [e·mo·sjo·'nar, e·mo·θjo-] **I.** *vt* 1. (*apasionar*) to excite; **este libro no me emociona** this book doesn't do anything for me 2. (*conmover*) to move; **los espectadores estaban emocionados** the spectators were moved; **tus palabras me ~on** I found your words very moving **II.** *vr:* **~se** to get excited; (*conmoverse*) to get emotional

**emotivo, -a** [e·mo·'ti·βo, -a] *adj* emotional; (*palabras*) moving

**empacar** <c → qu> [em·pa·'kar] *vi, vt AmL* to pack

**empachado, -a** [em·pa·'tʃa·do, -a] *adj* **estoy ~** (*indigestado*) I have indigestion; (*harto*) I'm so full I feel sick

**empachar** [em·pa·'tʃar] **I.** *vt* to give indigestion **II.** *vr:* **~se** to get indigestion; (*comer demasiado*) to eat too much

**empacho** [em·pa·'tʃo] *m* indigestion; **tengo un ~ de dulces** I've eaten too many sweets; (*saturación*) saturation; **tengo un ~ de televisión** I'm sick of watching television

**empadronamiento** [em·pa·dro·na·'mjen·to] *m* registration in local census bureau

**empadronar** [em·pa·dro·'nar] *vt, vr:* **~se** to register (for a census)

**empalagar** <g → gu> [em·pa·la·'γar] **I.** *vi* (*alimento*) to be oversweet **II.** *vr* **~se de** [*o con*] **algo** to get sick of sth

**empalagoso, -a** [em·pa·la·'γo·so, -a] *adj* (*alimento*) oversweet; (*persona*) cloying; (*película*) treacly

**empalmar** [em·pal·'mar] **I.** *vi* **~ con** to meet; (*carretera*) to join up with **II.** *vr:* **~se** to get a hard-on

**empalme** [em·'pal·me] *m* 1. join; (*teléfono*) connection 2. (*erección*) hard-on

**empanada** [em·pa·'na·da] *f* ≈ pie

**empanadilla** [em·pa·na·'di·ja, -ʎa] *f* halfmoon-shaped savory turnover

**empanar** [em·pa·'nar] *vt* to coat in breadcrumbs

**empañetar** [em·pa·ɲe·'tar] *vt AmL* to plaster

**empapar** [em·pa·'par] **I.** *vt* to soak; **la lluvia ha empapado el suelo** the rain has soaked the floor; (*absorber*) to soak up **II.** *vr:* **~se** to get soaked; **~se de**

**algo** *fig* to become versed in sth

**empapelar** [em·pa·pe·'lar] **I.** *vi, vt* to (wall)paper **II.** *vt* **1.** to wrap up **2.** *inf* (*expedientar*) to book

**empaque** [em·'pa·ke] *m AmL* (*cara dura*) cheek

**empaquetar** [em·pa·ke·'tar] *vt* to pack

**emparedado** [em·pa·re·'da·do] *m AmL* sandwich

**emparejar** [em·pa·re·'xar] **I.** *vt* **1.** (*juntar*) to pair up; **ya estoy emparejado** I already have a partner **2.** (*nivelar*) to level **II.** *vr:* **~se** to make a pair

**emparentado, -a** [em·pa·ren·'ta·do, -a] *adj* related (**con** to)

**empastar** [em·pas·'tar] *vt* (*muela*) to fill; (*libro*) to bind

**empaste** [em·'pas·te] *m* filling

**empatar** [em·pa·'tar] **I.** *vi* **1.** DEP to draw; **~ a uno** to draw one-all **2.** POL to tie **II.** *vt* **1.** *AmL* (*cuerdas*) to tie together; **~ mentiras** to tell one lie after another **2.** *CRi, PRico* (*amarrar*) to moor **3.** *Ven, Col* (*importunar*) to annoy

**empate** [em·'pa·te] *m* **1.** DEP draw **2.** POL tie

**empatía** [em·pa·'ti·a] *f* empathy

**empavonar** [em·pa·βo·'nar] **I.** *vt AmL* to grease **II.** *vr:* **~se** *AmC* to get dressed up

**empedernido, -a** [em·pe·der·'ni·do, -a] *adj* incorrigible; (*bebedor*) hardened; (*fumador*) chain; (*solterón*) confirmed

**empeine** [em·'pei·ne] *m* instep

**empelotado, -a** [em·pe·lo·'ta·do, -a] *adj AmL inf* stark naked; *Méx* (*enamorado*) infatuated

**empelotarse** [em·pe·lo·'tar·se] *vr AmL inf* to strip

**empeñar** [em·pe·'ñar] **I.** *vt* to pawn; **~ la palabra** to give one's word **II.** *vr:* **~se** to insist (**en** on); **se empeña en hablar contigo** he/she insists on speaking to you; **no te empeñes** don't go on about it

**empeño** [em·'pe·ño] *m* **1.** (*afán*) determination; **con ~** determinedly; **poner ~ en** to try one's best to; **tengo ~ por** [*o* **en**] **sacar la mejor nota** I'm determined to get the highest mark **2.** (*de objetos*) pawning; **casa de ~s** pawnbroker's

**empeorar** [em·peo·'rar] **I.** *vt* to make worse **II.** *vi, vr:* **~se** to worsen

**empequeñecer** [em·pe·ke·ñe·'ser, -'θer] *irr como* **crecer** *vt* to make smaller; (*quitar importancia*) to trivialize

**emperador** [em·pe·ra·'dor] *m* emperor

**emperatriz** [em·pe·ra·'tris, -'triθ] *f* empress

**emperrarse** [em·pe·'rrar·se] *vr* to be bent dead set on

**empezar** [em·pe·'sar, -'θar] *irr vi, vt* to begin, to start; **empezó de la nada** he/she started with nothing; **¡no empieces!** don't start!; **~ con buen pie** to get off to a good start; **para ~ me leeré el periódico** to begin with, I'll read the newspaper; **para ~ no tengo dinero y, además, no tengo ganas** first of all, I have no money, and what's more, I don't feel like it

**empiezo** [em·'pje·so] *m Col, Ecua, Guat* beginning

**empinado, -a** [em·pi·'na·do, -a] *adj* steep

**empinar** [em·pi·'nar] *vt* to raise; **~ la cabeza** to raise one's head; **~ el codo/una botella** *inf* to take a drink

**empipada** [em·pi·'pa·da] *f AmL* binge

**empiparse** [em·pi·'par·se] *vr AmL* to go on a binge

**empírico, -a** [em·'pi·ri·ko, -a] *adj* empirical

**emplazamiento** [em·pla·sa·'mjen·to, em·pla·θa-] *m* location

**emplazar** <z → c> [em·pla·'sar, -'θar] *vt* to locate; **este monumento no está bien emplazado aquí** this isn't the best place for this monument

**empleado, -a** [em·ple·'a·do, -a] *m, f* employee; **~ de oficina** office worker; **~ de ventanilla** clerk; **los ~s de una empresa** company staff

**empleador(a)** [em·plea·'dor, -·'do·ra] *m(f) AmL* employer

**emplear** [em·ple·'ar] **I.** *vt* **1.** (*medio, técnica, método*) to use; (*tiempo*) to spend; (*dinero*) to invest; **¡podrías ~ mejor el tiempo!** you could make better use of your time!; **¡te está bien empleado!** it serves you right!; **dar algo por bien empleado** to be satisfied with the results of sth; **he empleado todo el dine-**

**ro en la casa** I've put all my money into the house **2.** (*dar trabajo*) to employ; **en estos momentos no estoy empleado** I'm unemployed at the moment **II.** *vr:* ~**se** to be used; ~**se de** [*o como*] **algo** to be employed as sth; ~**se a fondo** to put everything into sth

**empleo** [em·'pleo] *m* employment; (*un trabajo*) job; **pleno** ~ full employment; **no tener** ~ to be out of work; **crear** ~ to create jobs; **solicitud de** ~ job application; **modo de** ~ instructions for use

**emplomadura** [em·plo·ma·'du·ra] *f AmL* filling

**emplomar** [em·plo·'mar] *vt* **1.** *AmL* to fill **2.** *Col, Guat* (*enredar*) to entangle

**empobrecer** [em·po·βre·'ser, -'θer] *irr como crecer* **I.** *vt* to impoverish; **la edad empobrece los reflejos** age slows one's reflexes **II.** *vi, vr:* ~**se** to become poorer; **este terreno se ha empobrecido** this soil has become less fertile

**empobrecimiento** [em·po·βre·si·'mjen·to, -θi·'mjen·to] *m* impoverishment

**empollar** [em·po·'jar, -'ʎar] **I.** *vi* **1.** *inf* (*estudiar*) to work hard **2.** *AmL* (*ampollar*) to blister **II.** *vt* **1.** (*ave*) to brood **2.** *inf* (*estudiarse*) to work hard at

**empollón, -ona** [em·po·'jon, --'jo·na; -'ʎon, --'ʎo·na] *m, f inf* brain

**emponchado, -a** [em·pon·'tʃa·do, -a] *adj* **1.** *AmL* (*astuto*) sharp **2.** *Arg, Ecua, Perú, Urug* (*con poncho*) wearing a poncho **3.** *Arg, Bol, Perú* (*sospechoso*) suspicious

**emporio** [em·'po·rjo] *m AmC* store

**empotrado, -a** [em·po·'tra·do, -a] *adj* built-in

**empotrar** [em·po·'trar] **I.** *vt* to build in **II.** *vr:* ~**se con(tra)** to crash into

**emprendedor(a)** [em·pren·de·'dor, --'do·ra] *adj* enterprising

**emprender** [em·pren·'der] *vt* (*trabajo*) to begin; (*negocio*) to set up; ~ **la marcha** to set out; ~ **la vuelta** to go back; ~ **el vuelo** to take off; **al anochecer la emprendimos hacia la casa** at nightfall we set off back to the house; ~**la con alguien** to take it out on sb; ~**la a insultos con alguien** to begin insulting sb

**empresa** [em·'pre·sa] *f* enterprise; (*com-*

**pañía*) company; **pequeña/mediana** ~ small/medium-sized company; ~ **matriz/pública** parent/state-owned company; ~ **privada** private enterprise; ~ **de mensajería** courier company

**empresarial** [em·pre·sa·'rjal] *adj* business

**empresario, -a** [em·pre·'sa·rjo, -a] *m, f* businessman, businesswoman *m, f*

**empujar** [em·pu·'xar] *vi, vt* to push; (*con violencia*) to shove; (*multitud*) to elbow

**empuje** [em·'pu·xe] *m* **1.** (*acción*) pushing **2.** Fís force **3.** (*energía*) energy; (*resolución*) drive

**empujón** [em·pu·'xon] *m* push; (*violento*) shove; **dar un** ~ **a alguien** to give sb a shove; **entrar en un local a empujones** to push one's way into a place

**empuntar** [em·pun·'tar] **I.** *vt Col, Ecua* to direct towards; ~**las** to beat it **II.** *vr:* ~**se** *Ven* to dig one's heels in

**empuñar** [em·pu·'ɲar] *vt* to grip; ~ **las armas** to take up arms

**empurrarse** [em·pu·'rrar·se] *vr AmC* to get angry

**emulación** [e·mu·la·'sjon, -'θjon] *f* emulation

**emular** [e·mu·'lar] *vt* to emulate

**emulsión** [e·mul·'sjon] *f* emulsion

**en.** *abr de* **enero** Jan.

**en** [en] *prep* **1.** (*lugar: dentro*) in; (*encima de*) on; (*con movimiento*) in, into; **el libro está** ~ **el cajón** the book is in the drawer; **pon el libro** ~ **el cajón** put the book in the drawer; **he dejado las llaves** ~ **la mesa** I left the keys on the table; **coloca el florero** ~ **la mesa** put the vase on the table; ~ **la pared hay un cuadro** there is a painting on the wall; **pon el póster** ~ **la pared** put the poster on the wall; **estar** ~ **el campo/**~ **la ciudad/**~ **una isla** to be in the countryside/in the city/on an island; ~ **España** in Spain; **vacaciones** ~ **el mar** holidays at the seaside; **jugar** ~ **la calle** to play in the street; **estoy** ~ **casa** I'm at home; **trabajo** ~ **una empresa japonesa** I work at a Japanese company **2.** (*tiempo*) in; ~ **el año 2005** in 2005; ~ **mayo** in May; ~ **otra ocasión** on

E

another occasion; ~ **aquellos tiempos** in those times [*o* days]; ~ **un mes** in a month; **lo terminaré** ~ **un momento** I'll finish it in a minute; ~ **todo el día** all [*o* the whole] day **3.** (*modo, estado*) ~ **absoluto** not at all; ~ **construcción** under construction; ~ **flor** in flower; ~ **venta** for sale; ~ **vida** while living; ~ **voz alta** aloud; **de dos** ~ **dos** two at a time; **decir algo** ~ **español** to say something in Spanish; **pagar** ~ **pesos** to pay in pesos **4.** (*medio*) ~ **tren** by train; **lo reconocí** ~ **la voz** I recognized him by his voice **5.** (*ocupación*) **doctor** ~ **filosofía** PhD in Philosophy; **trabajo** ~ **ingeniería** I work in engineering; **estar** ~ **la policía** to be in the police force; **estar** ~ **la mili** to be doing military service; **trabajar** ~ **Correos** to work in the postal service **6.** (*con verbo*) **pienso** ~ **ti** I am thinking of you; **no confío** ~ **él** I don't trust him; **ingresar** ~ **un partido** to join a party; **ganar** ~ **importancia** to gain in importance **7.** (*cantidades*) **aumentar la producción** ~ **un 5%** to increase production by 5%; **me he equivocado sólo** ~ **3 dólares** I was off by just 3 dollars

**enajenación** [e·na·xe·na·ˈsjon, -ˈθjon] *f* derangement; ~ **mental** insanity

**enajenar** [e·na·xe·ˈnar] **I.** *vt* to drive crazy **II.** *vr:* ~**se** to go crazy

**enamoradizo, -a** [e·na·mo·ra·ˈdi·so, -a; -ˈdi·θo, -a] *adj* always falling in love

**enamorado, -a** [e·na·mo·ˈra·do, -a] **I.** *adj* in love (**de** with) **II.** *m, f* lover; **día de los** ~**s** Valentine's Day

**enamorar** [e·na·mo·ˈrar] **I.** *vt* to win the heart of **II.** *vr:* ~**se** (**de**) to fall in love (with)

**enano, -a** [e·ˈna·no, -a] **I.** *adj* tiny **II.** *m, f* **1.** dwarf **2.** *inf* (*niño*) kid

**enardecer** [e·nar·de·ˈser, -ˈθer] *irr como* **crecer** **I.** *vt* to fire with enthusiasm **II.** *vr:* ~**se** to be kindled; ~**se por** to become enthusiastic about

**encabezado** [en·ka·βe·ˈsa·do] *m* Guat, Méx headline

**encabezamiento** [en·ka·βe·sa·ˈmjen·to, -θa·ˈmjen·to] *m* headline; (*de una carta*) letterhead; (*primeras líneas*) opening

**encabezar** <z → c> [en·ka·βe·ˈsar, -ˈθar] *vt* (*lista, grupo*) to head; (*institución*) to be the head of

**encabritarse** [en·ka·βri·ˈtar·se] *vr* to lose one's temper

**encadenar** [en·ka·de·ˈnar] *vt* to chain (up); *fig* to link up

**encajar** [en·ka·ˈxar] **I.** *vi* to fit; **la puerta encaja mal** the door doesn't fit properly; (*datos, hechos*) to fit in; **las dos declaraciones encajan** the two statements fit together; **este chiste no está bien aquí** this joke is uncalled for here **II.** *vt* **1.** to fit; ~ **en algo** to clamp into sth; ~ **dos piezas** to fit two pieces together; ~ **la ventana en el marco** to fit the window into the frame; ~ **el sombrero en la cabeza** to stick a hat on one's head; ~ **la funda en la máquina** to put the covering over the machine **2.** (*dar*) ~ **un golpe a alguien** to hit sb; ~ **una reprimenda a alguien** to give sb a talking-to; ~ **una tarea a alguien** to palm a task off on sb **3.** (*aceptar*) **no** ~ **la muerte de alguien** not to take sb's death well; **no sabes** ~ **una broma** you don't know how to take a joke **III.** *vr:* ~**se 1.** *AmL inf* (*aprovecharse*) to go too far **2.** (*atascarse*) to jam

**encaje** [en·ˈka·xe] *m* lace

**encalambrarse** [en·ka·lam·ˈbrar·se] *vr* *AmL* to cramp up; (*de frío*) to become numb

**encaminar** [en·ka·mi·ˈnar] **I.** *vt* to direct; ~ **sus pasos hacia el pueblo** to head towards the village; ~ **la mirada/la conversación hacia un punto** to direct one's gaze/the conversation towards a point; ~ **los esfuerzos hacia una meta** to focus one's efforts on a goal; ~ **los negocios hacia algo** to steer one's business towards sth **II.** *vr* ~**se a/hacia** to head for/towards; ~**se a la meta** to focus on the goal

**encamotarse** [en·ka·mo·ˈtar·se] *vr* *AmL inf* to fall in love (**de** with)

**encandilar** [en·kan·di·ˈlar] **I.** *vt* to dazzle; **escuchar encandilado** to listen in rapture **II.** *vr:* ~**se 1.** (*luz, emociones*) to light up **2.** *AmL* (*asustarse*) to be scared **3.** *PRico* (*enfadarse*) to get angry

**encanecer** [en·ka·ne·'ser, -'θer] *irr como crecer vi, vr: ~se* to go gray; **pelo encanecido** gray hair

**encantado, -a** [en·kan·'ta·do, -a] *adj* 1. delighted; **¡~ (de conocerle)!** pleased to meet you!; **estoy ~ con mi nuevo trabajo** I love my new job; **estoy ~ de la vida** I am thrilled 2. (*embrujado*) haunted

**encantador(a)** [en·kan·ta·'dor, -·'do·ra] *adj* lovely; (*persona*) charming

**encantamiento** [en·kan·ta·'mjen·to] *m* spell

**encantar** [en·kan·'tar] *vt* (*gustar*) **me encanta viajar** I love to travel; (*cautivar*) to captivate; (*fascinar*) to fascinate

**encanto** [en·'kan·to] *m* charm; **¡es un ~ de niño!** what an adorable child!

**encapricharse** [en·ka·pri·'tʃar·se] *vr* **~se con algo** to be taken by sth; **~se con alguien** to become infatuated with sb

**encapuchado, -a** [en·ka·pu·'tʃa·do, -a] *adj* hooded

**encarar** [en·ka·'rar] **I.** *vt* to bring face to face; (*riesgo, dificultad*) to face up to **II.** *vr:* **~se** to be face to face

**encarcelamiento** [en·kar·se·la·'mjen·to, en·kar·θe·] *m* imprisonment

**encarcelar** [en·kar·se·'lar, en·kar·θe·] *vt* to imprison

**encarecer** [en·ka·re·'ser, -'θer] *irr como crecer vt* to raise the price of

**encarecidamente** [en·ka·re·si·da·'men·te, en·ka·re·θi·] *adv* strongly; **le ruego ~...** I have to insist...

**encarecimiento** [en·ka·re·si·'mjen·to, -θi·'mjen·to] *m* 1. COM price increase 2. (*acentuación*) emphasis; **con ~** insistently

**encargado, -a** [en·kar·'ɣa·do, -a] **I.** *adj* in charge **II.** *m, f* person in charge; **~ de negocios** chargé d'affaires; **~ de campo** groundskeeper; **~ de curso** course director; **~ de obras** site manager; **~ de prensa** press officer

**encargar** <g → gu> [en·kar·'ɣar] **I.** *vt* 1. (*encomendar*) to put in charge; **lo ~on del departamento de ventas** they put him in charge of the sales department; **encargó a su hija a una vecina** he asked a neighbor to look af-

ter his daughter 2. (*comprar*) to order 3. (*mandar*) to ask **II.** *vr* **~se de algo** to take responsibility for sth; **tengo que ~me aún de un par de cosas** I still have to get a couple of things done

**encargo** [en·'kar·ɣo] *m* 1. (*pedido*) order; **~ por anticipado** advance order; **hacer un nuevo ~** to make another order 2. (*trabajo*) job; **traje de ~** tailor-made suit; **de ~** to order; **por ~ de** at the request of; **hacer ~s** to run errands; **tener ~ de hacer algo** to be commissioned to do sth

**encariñado, -a** [en·ka·ri·'ɲa·do, -a] *adj* **estar ~ con algo** to be very attached to sth; **estar ~ con alguien** to be fond of sb

**encariñarse** [en·ka·ri·'ɲar·se] *vr* **~ con algo/alguien** to grow fond of sth/sb

**encarnación** [en·kar·na·'sjon, -'θjon] *f* incarnation

**encarnado, -a** [en·kar·'na·do] *adj* (*color carne*) skin-tone; (*rosado*) pink; (*rojo*) red

**encarnar** [en·kar·'nar] *vt* to represent; CINE, TEAT to play the role of

**encarnizado, -a** [en·kar·ni·'sa·do, -a; ·'θa·do, -a] *adj* bloody

**encarpetar** [en·kar·pe·'tar] *vt AmL* to shelve

**encarrilar** [en·ka·rri·'lar] *vt* to guide

**encasillar** [en·ka·si·'jar, -'ʎar] **I.** *vt* to classify; (*persona, idea*) to pigeon-hole **II.** *vr* **~se en** to limit oneself to

**encausar** [en·kau·'sar] *vt* to prosecute

**encauzar** <z → c> [en·kau·'sar, -'θar] *vt* (*corriente*) to channel; (*debate*) to lead; (*vida*) to sort out

**encéfalo** [en·'se·fa·lo, en·'θe·] *m* brain

**encendedor** [en·sen·de·'dor, en·θen·] *m* lighter

**encender** <e → ie> [en·sen·'der, en·θen·] **I.** *vi* to catch fire; (*motor*) to fire **II.** *vt* to switch on; (*cigarrillo*) to light **III.** *vr:* **~se** 1. (*desencadenarse*) to break out 2. (*arder*) to ignite

**encendido** [en·sen·'di·do, en·θen·] *m* ignition

**encendido, -a** [en·sen·'di·do, -a; en·θen·] *adj* 1. (*conectado*) **estar ~** to be on 2. (*ardiente*) burning; (*cigarrillo*)

E

lighted; (*apasionado*) passionate

**encerado** [en·se'·ra·do, en·θe·] *m* blackboard

**encerar** [en·se'·rar, en·θe·] *vt* to wax

**encerrar** <e → ie> [en·se·'rrar, en·θe·] **I.** *vt* to lock in [*o* up]; ~ **entre paréntesis** to put in parentheses; (*contener*) to contain; **la oferta encerraba una trampa** the was a cacht to the offer **II.** *vr:* ~**se** to lock oneself in

**encerrona** [en·se·'rro·na, en·θe·] *f* trap

**encestar** [en·se·'tar, en·θes·] *vi* to score a basket

**enchastrar** [en·tʃas·'trar] *vt CSur* to dirty

**enchilada** [en·tʃi·'la·da] *f AmC* enchilada

**enchilado, -a** [en·tʃi·'la·do, -a] *adj Méx* **1.** (*bermejo*) ruddy **2.** (*colérico*) angry

**enchilar** [en·tʃi·'lar] **I.** *vt AmC* **1.** CULIN to season with chili **2.** (*molestar*) to annoy **3.** (*decepcionar*) to disappoint **II.** *vr:* ~**se** *AmC* to blow one's top

**enchinar** [en·tʃi·'nar] *Méx* **I.** *vt* to curl **II.** *vr:* ~**se 1.** (*escalofríos*) to get goose bumps **2.** (*acobardarse*) to be frightened

**enchinchar** [en·tʃin·'tʃar] **I.** *vt* **1.** *Guat, RDom* (*incomodar*) to annoy **2.** *Méx* ~ **a alguien** to waste sb's time **II.** *vr:* ~**se 1.** *Arg* (*malhumorarse*) to be in a bad mood **2.** *Guat, Méx, Perú, PRico* (*llenarse de chinches*) to be infested with bugs

**enchironar** [en·tʃi·ro·'nar] *vt* to throw in jail

**enchivarse** [en·tʃi·'βar·se] *vr Col, Ecua* to get furious

**enchufar** [en·tʃu·'far] *vt* **1.** ELEC to plug in **2.** TÉC to connect **3.** (*acoplar*) to couple **4.** ~ **a alguien** to get sth for sb by pulling strings

**enchufe** [en·'tʃu·fe] *m* **1.** (*clavija*) plug **2.** (*toma*) socket **3. tener** ~ to have connections

**enchutar** [en·tʃu·'far] *vt AmC* to introduce; ~ **de algo** to fill with sth

**encía** [en·'si·a, -'θi·a] *f* gum

**enciclopedia** [en·si·klo·'pe·dja, en·θi·] *f* encyclopedia

**enciclopédico, -a** [en·si·klo·'pe·di·ko, -a; en·θi·] *adj* encyclopedic

**encierro** [en·'sje·rro, -'θje·rro] *m* (*reclu-*

*sión*) confinement; (*prisión*) imprisonment; (*aislamiento*) isolation

**encima** [en·'si·ma, -'θi·ma] **I.** *adv* **1.** (*arriba: tocando*) on top; (*sin tocar*) above **2.** (*además*) besides; **te di el dinero y** ~ **una botella de vino** I gave you the money and a bottle of wine into the bargain **3.** *fig* **echarse** ~ **de alguien** to attack sb; **se nos echa el tiempo** ~ time is running out; **quitarse algo de** ~ (*librarse*) to get sth off one's back; **quitar a alguien un peso de** ~ to take a weight off sb's mind; **tener algo** ~ to be saddled with sth; **ya tenemos bastante** ~ we have enough on our plate; **llevaba mucho dinero** ~ he/she had a lot of money on him/her; **por** ~ superficial(ly) **II.** *prep* **1.** (*local: con contacto*) ~ **de** on top of; **con queso** ~ with cheese on top; **el libro está** ~ **de la mesa** the book is on the table; **el rascacielos está por** ~ **de la catedral** the skyscraper is higher than the cathedral; **estar** ~ **de alguien** *fig* to be on sb's case [*o* back] **2.** (*sin contacto*) (**por**) ~ **de** above; **por** ~ **de todo** above all; **por** ~ **de la media** above average **3.** (*con movimiento*) (**por**) ~ **de** over; **pon esto** ~ **de la cama** put this over the bed; **cuelga la lámpara** ~ **de la mesa** hang the light above the table; **¡por** ~ **de mí!** *fig* over my dead body!; **ése pasa por** ~ **de todo** *fig* he only cares about himself

**encina** [en·'si·na, en·'θi·] *f* holm oak

**encinta** [en·'sin·ta, -'θin·ta] *adj* pregnant

**enclave** [en·'kla·βe] *m* enclave

**enclenque** [en·'klen·ke] *adj* (*enfermizo*) sickly; (*débil*) weak

**encoger** <g → j> [en·ko·'xer] **I.** *vi, vt* to shrink **II.** *vr:* ~**se 1.** (*contraerse*) to contract; (*persona*) to cringe; ~**se de hombros** to shrug one's shoulders **2.** (*reducirse*) to shrink

**encolerizar** <z → c> [en·ko·le·ri·'sar, -'θar] **I.** *vt* to incense **II.** *vr:* ~**se** to be incensed

**encomendar** <e → ie> [en·ko·men·'dar] *vt* to recommend; ~ **algo a alguien** to entrust sth to sb

**encomienda** [en·ko·'mjen·da] *f AmL* parcel

**encontrar** ⟨o → ue⟩ [en·kon·'trar] I. *vt* **1.** (*hallar*) to find **2.** (*considerar*) to find II. *vr*: ~**se 1.** (*estar*) to be **2.** (*sentirse*) to feel **3.** ~**se con alguien** to meet sb; (*casualmente*) to run into sb **4.** (*hallar*) to find; ~**se con algo** to come across sth

**encontronazo** [en·kon·tro·'na·so, -θo] *m inf* (*crash*; (*enfrentamiento*) clash

**encorvado, -a** [en·kor·'βa·do, -a] *adj* hunched; (*persona*) stooped

**encorvar** [en·kor·'βar] I. *vt* to bend; (*persona*) to stoop II. *vr*: ~**se** to become bent; (*madera*) to warp; (*persona*) to become hunched

**encuadernación** [en·kwa·der·na·'sjon, -'θjon] *f* binding; (*cubierta*) cover

**encuadernador(a)** [en·kwa·der·na·'dor, -·'do·ra] *m(f)* bookbinder

**encuadernar** [en·kwa·der·'nar] *vt* to bind; **sin** ~ unbound

**encuadrar** [en·kwa·'drar] *vt* **1.** to frame **2.** (*incluir*) to include

**encubierto, -a** [en·ku·'bjer·to, -a] I. *pp de* **encubrir** II. *adj* **una acusación encubierta** a veiled accusation

**encubrir** [en·ku·'brir] *irr como* **abrir** *vt* (*ocultar*) to hide; (*silenciar*) to hush up; (*escándalo, crimen*) to cover up; (*delincuente*) to harbor

**encuentro** [en·'kwen·tro] *m* **1.** (*acción*) encounter; **ir al ~ de alguien** to go to meet sb **2.** (*cita, reunión*) meeting **3.** DEP match

**encuerado, -a** [en·kwe·'ra·do, -a] *adj Cuba, Méx* **1.** (*desharrapado*) shabby **2.** (*desnudo*) naked

**encuerar** [en·kwe·'rar] *vt, vr*: ~**se** *AmL* to undress

**encuerista** [en·kwe·'ris·ta] *mf AmL* stripper

**encuesta** [en·'kwes·ta] *f* opinion poll

**encularse** [en·ku·'lar·se] *vr Arg inf* ~ **por algo** to get ticked off about sth

**enculebrado, -a** [en·ku·'le·bra·do, -a] *adj Col inf* indebted

**encumbrar** [en·kum·'brar] I. *vt* to raise; (*socialmente*) to elevate II. *vr*: ~**se** (*elevarse*) to rise; (*engrandecerse*) to be ennobled

**endeble** [en·'de·βle] *adj* (*débil*) weak;

(*enfermizo*) sickly

**endémico, -a** [en·'de·mi·ko, -a] *adj* endemic

**endemoniado, -a** [en·de·mo·'nja·do, -a] *adj* **1.** (*poseso*) possessed **2.** (*malo*) evil **3.** *inf* (*difícil*) awful; (*travieso*) naughty

**endenantes** [en·de·'nan·tes] *adv AmL inf* a bit before

**enderezar** ⟨z → c⟩ [en·de·re·'sar, -'θar] *vt* to straighten; (*corregir*) to straighten out

**endeudarse** [en·deu·'dar·se] *vr* to get into debt

**endiablado, -a** [en·dja·'βla·do, -a] *adj v.* **endemoniado**

**endibia** [en·'di·βja] *f* endive

**endilgar** ⟨g → gu⟩ [en·dil·'γar] *vt*, **endiñar** [en·di·'ɲar] *vt inf* ~ **algo a alguien** to unload sth onto sb; **me** ~**on el trabajo sucio** I got stuck with the dirty work

**endrogarse** ⟨g → gu⟩ [en·dro·'γar·se] *vr* **1.** *AmL* (*drogarse*) to take drugs **2.** *Méx, Perú* (*endeudarse*) to get into debt

**endulzar** ⟨z → c⟩ [en·dul·'sar, -'θar] *vt* to sweeten

**endurecer** [en·du·re·'ser, -'θer] *irr como* **crecer** I. *vt* **1.** (*poner duro*) to harden; TÉC to chill **2.** (*hacer resistente*) to strengthen; (*mente*) to toughen; (*persona*) to inure II. *vr*: ~**se 1.** (*ponerse duro*) to get tough; (*sentimientos*) to become hardened **2.** (*hacerse resistente*) to be strengthened **3.** (*agudizarse*) to become more intense

**endurecimiento** [en·du·re·si·'mjen·to, -θi·'mjen·to] *m* **1.** (*dureza*) hardness **2.** (*proceso*) hardening **3.** (*resistencia*) harshness

**ene** ['e·ne] *adj inv* ~ **veces** x times

**eneldo** [e·'nel·do] *m* dill

**enema** [e·'ne·ma] *m* enema

**enemigo, -a** [e·ne·'mi·γo, -a] I. *adj* enemy; **país** ~ hostile country II. *m, f* enemy; DEP, POL opponent; ~ **acérrimo** sworn enemy; ~**s mortales** mortal enemies *pl*; **ser** ~ **de algo** to be opposed to sth

**enemistad** [e·ne·mis·'tad] *f* enmity; (*hostilidad*) animosity

**enemistar** [e·ne·mis·'tar] I. *vt* to make

enemies of II. *vr:* ~**se** to become enemies

**energético, -a** [e·ner·'xe·ti·ko, -a] *adj* energy; **valor** ~ calories

**energía** [e·ner·'xi·a] *f* energy; (*fuerza*) force; ~ **nuclear** nuclear energy; ~ **eólica** wind power; **con** ~ *fig* forcefully; **con toda su** ~ with all one's force; **sin** ~ *fig* feebly; **la glucosa da** ~ glucose gives you energy; **emplear todas las** ~**s en algo** to put all one's energies into sth

**enérgico, -a** [e·'ner·xi·ko, -a] *adj* energetic; (*decidido*) firm

**energúmeno, -a** [e·ner·'ɣu·me·no, -a] *m, f inf* berserk; **gritando como un** ~ shouting like a maniac

**enero** [e·'ne·ro] *m* January; *v. t.* **marzo**

**enervante** [e·ner·'βan·te] *adj* annoying

**enésimo, -a** [e·'ne·si·mo, -a] *adj* nth; **por enésima vez** for the umpteenth time

**enfadar** [en·fa·'dar] I. *vt* 1. to anger; **estar enfadado con alguien** to be angry with sb 2. *AmL* to bore II. *vr:* ~**se** to get angry; ~**se con alguien** to get angry with sb

**enfado** [en·'fa·do] *m* anger; (*molestia*) annoyance

**énfasis** ['en·fa·sis] *m inv* emphasis; (*insistencia*) insistence

**enfático, -a** [en·'fa·ti·ko, -a] *adj* emphatic; (*insistente*) insistent

**enfatizar** <z → c> [en·fa·ti·'sar, -'θar] *vt, vi* to emphasize

**enfermar** [en·fer·'mar] I. *vi, vr* to get sick II. *vt* to make sick

**enfermedad** [en·fer·me·'dad] *f* illness; (*específica*) disease

**enfermería** [en·fer·me·'ri·a] *f* infirmary

**enfermero, -a** [en·fer·'me·ro, -a] *m, f* nurse

**enfermizo, -a** [en·fer·'mi·so, -a; -'mi·θo, -a] *adj* sickly; (*morboso*) sick

**enfermo, -a** [en·'fer·mo, -a] I. *adj* ill; ~ **del corazón** suffering heart disease; ~ **de gravedad** seriously ill; **caer** ~ **de algo** to come down with sth; **ponerse** ~ to get ill; **esta situación me pone** ~ this situation is really getting me down II. *m, f* ill person; (*paciente*) patient

**enfilar** [en·fi·'lar] *vt* (*en fila*) to put in a row; (*en línea*) to line up

**enfocar** <c → qu> [en·fo·'kar] *vt* 1. (*ajustar*) to focus; **mal enfocado** out of focus 2. (*iluminar*) to shine light upon 3. (*considerar*) to consider; (*cuestión*) to approach; **no enfocas bien el problema** you're not addressing the issue properly

**enfoque** [en·'fo·ke] *m* (*posición*) stance; (*planteamiento*) approach; (*concepción*) conception

**enfrentamiento** [en·fren·ta·'mjen·to] *m* confrontation; (*pelea*) fight; ~**s callejeros** street-fighting

**enfrentar** [en·fren·'tar] I. *vt* to face II. *vr:* ~**se** 1. (*encararse*) to come face to face 2. (*hacer frente*) to face up to 3. (*pelearse*) to fight; **estar enfrentado a alguien** to be up against sb

**enfrente** [en·'fren·te] I. *adv* opposite; **allí** ~ over there; **la casa de** ~ the house opposite; **tendrás a tu familia** ~ *fig* your family will be against you II. *prep* ~ **de** opposite; ~ **del teatro** opposite the theater; **vivo** ~ **del parque** I live opposite the park; **ponerse** ~ **de alguien** *fig* to be opposed to sb

**enfriamiento** [en·frja·'mjen·to] *m* cooling; (*catarro*) cold

**enfriar** <1. *pres* enfrío> [en·fri·'ar] I. *vi, vt* to cool (down) II. *vr:* ~**se** 1. (*perder calor*) to cool (down) 2. (*calmarse*) to cool off 3. (*acatarrarse*) to catch a cold

**enfundar** [en·fun·'dar] *vt* to sheathe; (*pistola*) to put back in the holster

**enfurecer** [en·fu·re·'ser, -'θer] *irr como* **crecer** I. *vt* to enrage II. *vr:* ~**se** to be furious

**engajado, -a** [en·ga·'xa·do, -a] *adj* Col, CRi curly

**engalanar** [en·ga·la·'nar] I. *vt* (*decorar*) to decorate; (*adornar*) to embellish II. *vr:* ~**se** to get dressed up

**enganchar** [en·gan·'tʃar] I. *vt* 1. (*sujetar*) to hook; (*remolque*) to hitch up 2. (*prender*) to catch on 3. *inf* (*atrapar*) to catch; (*convencer*) to persuade II. *vr:* ~**se** 1. (*sujetarse*) ~**se de algo** to get hooked on sth 2. (*prenderse*) ~**se de** [*o* **con**] **algo** to get caught on sth 3. (*involucrarse*) to get caught up 4. *inf* (*droga*) ~**se a** to get hooked on; **estar engan-**

**chado** to be hooked

**enganche** [en·'gan·tʃe] *m* 1. (*gancho*) hook 2. (*acto*) hooking

**engañabobos** [en·ga·ɲa·'βo·βos] *mf inv inf* con artist

**engañar** [en·ga·'ɲar] I. *vi* to deceive; **las apariencias engañan** appearances can be deceptive II. *vt* 1. (*desorientar*) to confuse 2. (*mentir*) to deceive; (*estafar*) to cheat; **~ a alguien** (*ser infiel*) to cheat on sb; (*burlarse*) to laugh at sb; **~ el hambre** to stave off one's hunger; **dejarse ~** to fall for it III. *vr:* **~se** to deceive oneself; **¡no te engañes con esta oferta!** don't get all excited about this offer!

**engañifa** [en·ga·'ɲi·fa] *f inf*, **engañifla** [en·ga·'ɲi·fla] *f Chile* trap

**engaño** [en·'ga·ɲo] *m* 1. (*mentira*) deceit 2. (*truco*) trick 3. (*ilusión*) illusion

**engañoso, -a** [en·ga·'ɲo·so, -a] *adj* misleading; **publicidad engañosa** false advertising; (*persona*) deceitful

**engaratusar** [en·ga·ra·tu·'sar] *vt AmC, Col* to coax

**engarzar** <z → c> [en·gar·'sar, -'θar] I. *vt* 1. (*trabar*) to join together 2. (*montar*) to set II. *vr:* **~se** *AmL* to get caught up

**engatusar** [en·ga·tu·'sar] *vt* to sweet-talk; **~ a alguien para que haga algo** to coax sb into doing sth

**engavetar** [en·ga·βe·'tar] *vt Guat* to pigeon-hole

**engendrar** [en·xen·'drar] *vt* to beget; *fig* to give rise to

**engendro** [en·'xen·dro] *m* freak

**englobar** [en·glo·'βar] *vt* (*incluir*) to comprise; (*reunir*) to bring together

**engolillarse** [en·go·li·'jar·se, -'ʎar·se] *vr* 1. *Cuba* (*endeudarse*) to get into debt 2. *Perú* (*encolerizarse*) to lose one's temper

**engomar** [en·go·'mar] *vt* to put glue on; (*pelo*) to put gel on

**engordar** [en·gor·'dar] *vi* (*ponerse gordo*) to get fat; (*ganar peso*) to gain weight

**engorroso, -a** [en·go·'rro·so, -a] *adj* awkward; (*molesto*) bothersome

**engranaje** [en·gra·'na·xe] *m* cogs *pl;* TÉC gear

**engrandecer** [en·gran·de·'ser, -'θer] *irr*

*como crecer vt* (*aumentar*) to increase; (*acrecentar*) to enlarge; (*exagerar*) to exaggerate

**engrasar** [en·gra·'sar] *vt* to grease; AUTO, TÉC to lubricate

**engrase** [en·'gra·se] *m* greasing; AUTO, TÉC lubrication

**engreído, -a** [en·gre·'i·do, -a] *adj* conceited; *AmL* (*mimado*) spoiled

**engreír** [en·gre·'ir] *irr como reír vt AmL* to pamper

**engrifarse** [en·gri·'far·se] *vr* 1. *Col* (*volverse altivo*) to become arrogant 2. *Méx* (*irritarse*) to get annoyed

**engualichar** [en·gwa·li·'tʃar] *vt Arg* **~ a alguien** to put a spell on sb; (*al amante*) to have power over sb

**enguandocar** [en·gwan·do·'kar] *vt Col* to adorn; (*recargar*) to overload

**enguaraparse** [en·gwa·ra·'par·se] *vr AmC* to ferment

**engullir** <3. pret engulló> [en·gu·'jir, -'ʎir] *vt* to swallow; (*devorar*) to devour; (*zamparse*) to gobble down

**enharinar** [en·a·ri·'nar] *vt* to coat with flour

**enhebrar** [en·e·'βrar] *vt* to thread

**enhorabuena** [en·o·ra·'βwe·na] *f* congratulations *pl;* **dar la ~ a alguien** to congratulate sb; **estar de ~** to be on top of the world

**enigma** [e·'niɣ·ma] *m* enigma; **descifrar/plantear un ~** to unravel/to pose an enigma

**enigmático, -a** [e·niɣ·'ma·ti·ko, -a] *adj* enigmatic; (*misterioso*) mysterious

**enjabonar** [en·xa·βo·'nar] *vt* to soap

**enjambre** [en·'xam·bre] *m* swarm; *fig* throng

**enjaular** [en·xau·'lar] *vt* to cage

**enjetarse** [en·xe·'tar·se] *vr Arg, Méx* (*enojarse*) to get angry; (*ofenderse*) to take offense

**enjuagar** <g → gu> [en·xwa·'ɣar] *vt* to rinse

**enjuague** [en·'xwa·ɣe] *m* rinse; **~ bucal** mouthwash

**enjugamanos** [en·xu·ɣa·'ma·nos] *m inv AmL* hand-towel

**enjugar** <g → gu> [en·xu·'ɣar] *vt, vr:* **~se** to dry

E

**enjuiciar** [en·xwi·'sjar, -'θjar] *vt* to analyze; JUR to prosecute

**enjutarse** [en·xu·'tar·se] *vr Guat, Ven* (*adelgazar*) to become thin; (*achicarse*) to get smaller; (*encoger*) to shrink

**enjuto, -a** [en·'xu·to, -a] *adj* scrawny

**enlace** [en·'la·se, -θe] *m* 1. connection 2. ELEC, FERRO, COMPUT link 3. (*boda*) wedding

**enlatados** [en·la·'ta·dos] *mpl Col* canned food

**enlatar** [en·la·'tar] *vt* to can; TV **enlatado** prerecorded

**enlazar** <z → c> [en·la·'sar, -'θar] I. *vi* to link up II. *vt* to tie; ELEC, TÉC to connect

**enloquecer** [en·lo·ke·'ser, -'θer] *irr como crecer* I. *vi, vr:* ~se to go crazy; ~ de dolor to be in terrible pain; ~ de rabia to be a lunatic; ~ por alguien to be crazy about sb II. *vt* to drive crazy

**enlozado** [en·lo·'sa·do] *m AmL* glaze

**enlozar** <z → c> [en·lo·'sar] *vt AmL* to enamel

**enmarcar** <c → qu> [en·mar·'kar, emmar·'kar] *vt* to frame

**enmascarar** [en·mas·ka·'rar, em·mas·ka·'rar] I. *vt* (*disfrazar*) to disguise; (*ocultar*) to hide; (*encubrir*) to cover up II. *vr:* ~se to disguise oneself; (*encubrirse*) to cover one's tracks

**enmendar** <e → ie> [en·men·'dar, em·men·'dar] I. *vt* (*corregir*) to correct; (*modificar*) to modify; JUR to amend II. *vr:* ~se to mend one's ways

**enmicar** [en·mi·'kar, em·mi·'kar] <c → qu> *vt Méx* to cover in plastic

**enmienda** [en·'mjen·da, em·'mjen·da] *f* JUR amendment

**enmohecer** [en·mo·e·'ser, em·mo·e·'ser; -'θer] *irr como crecer* *vi, vr:* ~se to go moldy

**enmudecer** [en·mu·de·'ser, em·mu·de·'ser; -'θer] *irr como crecer* I. *vi* to become speechless II. *vt* to silence

**ennegrecer** [en·ne·γre·'ser, -'θer] *irr como crecer* *vi, vr:* ~se to blacken; (*oscurecer*) to darken

**enojar** [e·no·'xar] I. *vt* to anger II. *vr:* ~se to get angry

**enojo** [e·'no·xo] *m* anger

**enojón, -ona** [e·no·'xon, -·'xo·na] I. *adj* Chile, Ecua, Méx touchy II. *m, f* Chile, Ecua, Méx quick-tempered person

**enojoso, -a** [e·no·'xo·so, -a] *adj* annoying

**enorgullecer** [e·nor·γu·je·'ser, -ʎe·'θer] *irr como crecer* I. *vt* to fill with pride II. *vr:* ~se to be proud

**enorme** [e·'nor·me] *adj* huge; *fig* remarkable

**enrabiar** [en·rra·'βjar] I. *vt* to enrage II. *vr:* ~se to lose one's temper

**enraizado, -a** [en·rrai·'sa·do, -a; -'θa·do, -a] *adj* rooted; (*tradición*) deep-seated

**enrastrojarse** [en·rras·tro·'xar·se] *vr AmL* to get dirty

**enredadera** [en·rre·da·'de·ra] *f* climbing plant

**enredar** [en·rre·'dar] I. *vt* (*liar*) to mix up; (*confundir*) to confuse II. *vr:* ~se (*cuerda, asunto*) to get mixed up; (*planta*) to climb

**enredo** [en·'rre·do] *m* tangle; (*engaño*) deceit

**enrejado** [en·rre·'xa·do] *m* grating

**enrevesado, -a** [en·rre·βe·'sa·do, -a] *adj* complicated; (*camino*) winding

**enriquecer** [en·rri·ke·'ser, -'θer] *irr como crecer* I. *vt* to enrich II. *vr:* ~se to get rich

**enriquecimiento** [en·rri·ke·si·'mjen·to, -θi·'mjen·to] *m* enrichment

**enrojecer** [en·rro·xe·'ser, -'θer] *irr como crecer* *vt, vi, vr:* ~se to redden; (*persona*) to blush

**enrolar** [en·rro·'lar] *vt* NÁUT to enroll; MIL to enlist

**enrollar** [en·rro·'jar, -'ʎar] I. *vt* (*cartel*) to roll up; (*cuerda*) to coil II. *vr:* ~se *inf* 1. (*tener rollo*) to go on and on 2. (*ligar*) ~se con alguien to take up with sb 3. (*ser guay*) to get on well

**enroscar** <c → qu> [en·rros·'kar] I. *vt* (*tornillo*) to screw in; (*tapa*) to twist on II. *vr:* ~se to curl up

**enrostrar** [en·rros·'trar] *vt AmL* to throw in one's face

**enrular** [en·rru·'lar] *vt CSur* to curl

**ensalada** [en·sa·'la·da] *f* salad

**ensaladera** [en·sa·la·'de·ra] *f* salad bowl

**ensalzar** <z → c> [en·sal·'sar, -'θar] I. *vt*

to dignify **II.** *vr:* ~**se** to boast

**ensamblar** [en·sam·'blar] *vt* to assemble

**ensanchar** [en·san·'tʃar] *vt, vr:* ~**se** to widen

**ensanche** [en·'san·tʃe] *m* widening

**ensangrentar** <e → ie> [en·san·gren·'tar] *vt* to cover in blood

**ensartar** [en·sar·'tar] *vt* **1.** (*perlas*) to string **2.** (*pinchar*) to skewer

**ensayar** [en·sa·'jar] *vt* to rehearse

**ensayo** [en·'sa·jo] *m* **1.** rehearsal; ~ **general** dress rehearsal **2.** LIT essay **3.** (*prueba*) test; (*experimento*) experiment

**enseguida** [en·se·'ɣi·da] *adv* right away

**ensenada** [en·se·'na·da] *f* **1.** inlet **2.** *Arg* (*corral*) meadow

**enseñanza** [en·se·'ɲan·sa, -θa] *f* **1.** (*sistema*) education; ~ **primaria/secundaria/superior/universitaria** primary/secondary/higher/university education; ~ **privada/pública** private/public education **2.** (*docencia*) teaching; ~ a **distancia** distance learning; ~ **universitaria** university education; **método de** ~ teaching method; **dedicarse a la** ~ to be a teacher **3.** (*lección*) lesson

**enseñar** [en·se·'ɲar] *vt* **1.** (*dar clase*) to teach; (*explicar*) to explain; **ella me enseñó a tocar la flauta** she taught me how to play the flute; **hay que** ~ **con el ejemplo** you have to lead by example; **¡la vida te** ~**á!** life is the best teacher!; **¡ya te** ~**é yo a obedecer!** I'll teach you to be obedient! **2.** (*mostrar*) to show; ~ **el camino a alguien** to show sb the way

**enseres** [en·'se·res] *mpl* belongings *pl*; (*útiles*) tools *pl*

**ensimismarse** [en·si·mis·'mar·se] *vr* **1.** to become absorbed; ~ **en recuerdos/una lectura** to become engrossed in one's memories/reading **2.** *Col, Chile* (*engreírse*) to become vain

**ensombrecer** [en·som·bre·'ser, -'θer] *irr como crecer* **I.** *vt* to darken; *fig* to cast a shadow over **II.** *vr:* ~**se** to darken; *fig* to become sad

**ensopar** [en·so·'par] **I.** *vt AmS* to soak **II.** *vr:* ~**se** *AmS* to get soaked

**ensordecedor(a)** [en·sor·de·se'dor, -·'dor·; en·sor·de·θe-] *adj* deafening

**ensordecer** [en·sor·de·'ser, -'θer] *irr como crecer vi* to go deaf

**ensortijado, -a** [en·sor·ti·'xa·do, -a] *adj* curly

**ensuciar** [en·su·'sjar, -'θjar] **I.** *vt* to dirty **II.** *vr:* ~**se** to get dirty; ~**se de algo** to be stained with sth

**ensueño** [en·'swe·ɲo] *m* dream; **de** ~ fantastic

**entablar** [en·ta·'βlar] *vt* (*conversación*) to strike up; (*negociación*) to begin; (*amistad, comercio*) to establish

**entablillar** [en·ta·βli·'jar, -'ʎar] *vt* to splint

**entallado, -a** [en·ta·'ja·do, -a; en·ta·'ʎa-] *adj* fitted at the waist

**entarimado** [en·ta·ri·'ma·do] *m* floorboards *pl*

**ente** ['en·te] *m* (*ser*) being

**entendederas** [en·ten·de·'de·ras] *fpl inf* **es muy corto de** ~ he's pretty dumb

**entender** <e → ie> [en·ten·'der] **I.** *vi* **1.** (*comprender*) to understand; **si entiendo bien Ud. quiere decir que...** am I right in saying that what you mean is that... **2.** (*saber*) ~ **mucho de algo** to know a lot about sth; **no** ~ **nada de algo** to know nothing about sth **II.** *vt* **1.** (*comprender*) to understand (**por** by); **dar a** ~ **que...** to imply that...; **dar a** ~ **a alguien que...** to lead sb to believe that...; **lo entendieron mal** they misunderstood it; **¿qué entiende Ud. por 'acuerdo'?** what do you understand by 'agreement'?; **ellos ya se harán** ~ they'll soon make themselves understood; **no** ~ **ni jota/papa** *inf* not to understand a thing; **no entiende una broma** he/she can't take a joke **2.** (*creer*) to think; **yo entiendo que sería mejor si** +*subj* I think it would be better if; **yo no lo entiendo así** that's not the way I see it; **tengo entendido que...** (*según creo*) I believe that...; (*según he oído*) I've heard that... **III.** *vr:* ~**se 1.** (*llevarse bien*) to get on **2.** (*ponerse de acuerdo*) to agree; **para el precio entiéndete con mi socio** as regards the price, reach an agreement with my partner **3. ¡yo me entiendo!** I know what I'm doing!; **¡que se las entienda!** let him/ her get on with it!; **pero ¿cómo se entiende?** *inf* but what does it mean?; **eso se entiende por sí mismo** this is self-explanatory **IV.** *m* opinion; **a mi ~** the way I see it

**entendido, -a** [en·ten·'di·do, -a] **I.** *adj* clever; **~ en algo** expert on sth **II.** *m, f* expert; **hacerse el ~** to act smart

**entendimiento** [en·ten·di·'mjen·to] *m* **1.** (*razón*) reason; **obrar con ~** to go about things reasonably; **un hombre de mucho ~** a very reasonable man **2.** (*acuerdo*) agreement

**enterado, -a** [en·te·'ra·do, -a] *adj* **~ de algo** aware of sth; **yo ya estaba ~ del incidente** I already knew about the incident; **no se dio por ~** he pretended he didn't understand

**enteramente** [en·te·ra·'men·te] *adv* wholly

**enterar** [en·te·'rar] **I.** *vt* **1. ~ de algo** to tell about sth **2.** *Méx, CRi, Hond* to pay **II.** *vr* **~se de** (*descubrir*) to find out about; (*saber*) to hear about; **no me enteré de nada hasta que me lo dijeron** I wasn't aware of anything until they told me; **pasa las hojas sin ~se de lo que lee** he/she turns the pages without taking anything in; **¡para que te enteres!** *inf* that'll teach him/her/you!; **para que te enteres...** for your information...

**entereza** [en·te·'re·sa, -'re·θa] *f* (*determinación*) strength (of mind); (*integridad*) integrity

**enternecer** [e·ter·ne·'ser, -'θer] *irr como* **crecer I.** *vt* to move **II.** *vr:* **~se** to be touched

**entero, -a** [en·'te·ro] *adj* whole; **el mundo ~** the whole world; **por ~** completely; **se pasa días ~s sin decir ni una palabra** he/she goes for days at a time without speaking; **el espejo salió ~ de aquí** when the mirror left here it was in one piece; **la comisión entera se declaró a favor** the whole committee declared themselves in favor; **el juego de café no está ~** some of the coffee service is missing

**enterrador(a)** [en·te·rra·'dor] *m(f)* grave-digger

**enterrar** <e → ie> [en·te·'rrar] *vt* to bury; (*poco profundo*) to cover up

**enterratorio** [en·te·rra·'to·rjo] *m AmS* Indian burial ground

**entidad** [en·ti·'dad] *f* organization; **~ aseguradora** insurance firm; **~ crediticia** credit company; **~ jurídica** legal entity; **~ bancaria** bank

**entierro** [en·'tje·rro] *m* burial; (*funeral*) funeral

**entonación** [en·to·na·'sjon, -'θjon] *f* intonation

**entonar** [en·to·'nar] **I.** *vi* **1.** (*canción*) to sing in tune **2.** (*armonizar*) to go well **II.** *vt* (*canción*) to sing

**entonces** [en·'ton·ses, -θes] *adv* then; **desde ~** from then on; **hasta ~** until then; **en** [*o* por] **aquel ~** at that time; **¿y ~ qué pasó?** and what happened next?; **¿pues ~ por qué no vienes?** then why don't you come?; **¡~!** well, then!

**entornar** [en·tor·'nar] *vt* to leave slightly open

**entorno** [en·'tor·no] *m* surroundings *pl*; (*medio ambiente*) environment; (*mundillo*) sphere

**entorpecer** [en·tor·pe·'ser, -'θer] *irr como* **crecer** *vt* (*dificultar*) to hamper; (*sentidos*) to dull

**entrabar** [en·tra·'βar] *vt AmS* to interfere

**entrada** [en·'tra·da] *f* **1.** (*puerta, acción*) entrance; **hacer una ~** to make an entrance; **~ trasera** back door; (*autopista*) (entry) ramp; **prohibida la ~** no entry **2.** (*comienzo*) entry; **~ en funciones** starting date; **~ en vigor** coming into force; **de ~** right from the start; **así de ~ tu idea no me pareció mal** at first your idea didn't strike me as bad **3.** (*ticket*) ticket; **~ gratuita** free entry; **en el estreno hubo una gran ~** the premiere was packed **4.** CULIN first course **5.** (*pelo*) **tiene ~s** his/her hair is receding **6. la ~ del coche** the down-payment on the car; **~s de dinero** income; **~s y salidas** income and costs **7.** COMPUT input

**entrado, -a** [en·'tra·do, -a] *adj* **~ en años** elderly; **entrada la noche** already dark

**entrador(a)** [en·tra·'dor, --'do·ra] *adj*

**1.** AmS (animoso) spirited; (atrevido) daring **2.** Arg (simpático) friendly **3.** AmL (enamoradizo) romantic **4.** Chile (entremetido) interfering **5.** Guat, Nic (compañero) companionable

**entramparse** [en·tram·'par·se] vr to get into debt

**entrante** [en·'tran·te] **I.** adj next **II.** m starter

**entrañable** [en·tra·'ɲa·βle] adj endearing; (recuerdo) fond

**entrañar** [en·tra·'ɲar] vt to involve; (peligro) to entail

**entrañas** [en·'tra·ɲas] fpl entrails pl; **en las ~s de la tierra** in the bowels of the earth

**entrar** [en·'trar] **I.** vi **1.** (pasar) to enter; **~ por la ventana** to come in through the window; **~ por la fuerza** to break in; **el tren entra en la estación** the train enters the station; **me entró por un oído y me salió por otro** it went in one ear and out the other; **~ con buen pie** to start off on the right foot; **¡entre!** come in! **2.** (caber) to fit; **no me entra el anillo** I can't get the ring on; **el corcho no entra en la botella** the cork won't fit into the bottle; **por fin he hecho ~ el tapón** I finally got the lid on **3.** (penetrar) to go in; **el clavo entró en la pared** the nail went into the wall; **¡no me entra en la cabeza!** I can't understand it! **4.** (empezar) to begin; **~ en relaciones** to start a relationship; **el verano entra el 21 de junio** summer begins on the 21st of June; **después entré a trabajar en una casa más rica** afterwards I started working in a wealthier household; **cuando entró de alcalde** when he was elected mayor; **no ~ en detalles** not to go into details; **~ en calor** to warm up; **~ en vigor** to come into force; **me entró la tentación** I was tempted; **me entró un mareo** I became dizzy; **me entró el hambre** I became hungry **5.** (como miembro) **~ en algo** to become a member of sth; **~ en la Academia de Ciencias** to be admitted to the Royal Academy of Science **6.** (formar parte) **en un kilo en-** tran tres panochas you can get three corncobs to the kilo; **eso no entraba en mis cálculos** I hadn't planned on this **7.** COMPUT to access **8.** (dar) **esperemos que no te entre la gripe** we hope you don't get the flu; **le ha entrado la costumbre de...** he/she's gotten into the habit of... **9.** inf (entender) **las matemáticas no me entran** I can't get the hang of mathematics **10.** inf (soportar) **su hermano no me entra** I can't stand his/her brother **11.** inf (relacionarse, tratar) **no sabe ~ a las chicas** he doesn't know how to pick up girls; **a él no sabes como ~le** you don't know how to deal with him **12.** (opinar) **yo en eso no entro** [o **ni entro ni salgo**] inf I have nothing to do with this **II.** vt to put; **~ el coche en el garaje** to put the car into the garage

**entre** ['en·tre] prep **1.** (dos cosas) between; (más de dos cosas) among; **salir de ~ las ramas** to emerge from the branches; **pasar por ~ las mesas** to go between the tables; **~ semana** during the week; **ven ~ las cinco y las seis** come between five and six; **~ tanto** meanwhile; **lo cuento ~ mis amigos** I consider him as one of my friends; **un ejemplo ~ muchos** one of many examples; **el peor ~ todos** the worst of the lot; **llegaron veinte ~ hombres y mujeres** twenty men and women arrived; **se la llevaron ~ cuatro hombres** she was carried off by four men; **lo hablaremos ~ nosotros** we'll talk it over with each other; **~ el taxi y la entrada me quedé sin dinero** what with the taxi and the ticket I had no money left; **¡guárdalo ~ los libros!** keep it with your books; **me senté ~ los dos** I sat down between the two of them **2.** MAT **ocho ~ dos son cuatro** eight divided by two is four

**entreabierto, -a** [en·tre·a·'βjer·to, -a] adj ajar

**entreabrir** [en·tre·a·'βrir] irr como abrir vt to open slightly

**entreacto** [en·tre·'ak·to] m interval

**entrecejo** [en·tre·'sexo, -'θe·xo] m brow

**entrecomillar** [en·tre·ko·mi·'jar, -'ʎar] vt

to put in quotes

**entrecortado, -a** [en·tre·kor·'ta·do, -a] *adj* (*respiración*) uneven; (*voz*) halting

**entrecruzar** <z → c> [en·tre·kru·'sar, -'θar] *vt, vr*: ~**se** to interweave; (*miradas*) to cross

**entredicho** [en·tre·'di·tʃo] *m* **poner algo en** ~ to cast doubt on sth

**entrega** [en·'tre·ɣa] *f* **1.** (*dedicación*) dedication **2.** (*fascículo*) installment; **novela por** ~**s** serialized novel **3.** (*reparto*) delivery; ~ **de premios** giving of prizes; ~ **de títulos** UNIV graduation ceremony; **hacer** ~ **de algo** to hand sth over; ~ **a domicilio** home delivery; **talón de** ~ delivery sheet; **pagadero a la** ~ payable on delivery; ~ **contra reembolso** collect on delivery

**entregar** <g → gu> [en·tre·'ɣar] **I.** *vt* (*dar*) to give; (*correos*) to deliver **II.** *vr*: ~**se** to surrender; ~**se a la bebida** to take to drink; ~**se a la policía** to give oneself up

**entrelazar** <z → c> [en·tre·la·'sar, -'θar] *vt, vr*: ~**se** to (inter)weave

**entremedias** [en·tre·'me·djas] *adv* **1.** (*local*) between **2.** (*temporal*) meanwhile

**entremeses** [en·tre·'me·ses] *mpl* appetizers *pl*

**entremeterse** [en·tre·me·'ser·se, -'θer·se] *vr* to interfere

**entremetido, -a** [en·tre·me·'ti·do, -a] **I.** *adj* interfering **II.** *m, f* busybody

**entremezclar** [en·tre·mes·'klar, en·tre·meθ-] *vt* to intermingle

**entrenador(a)** [en·tre·na·'dor] *m(f)* coach

**entrenamiento** [en·tre·na·'mjen·to] *m* training

**entrenar** [en·tre·'nar] *vt, vr*: ~**se** to train

**entrepierna** [en·tre·'pjer·na] *f* **1.** crotch **2.** *Chile* swimsuit

**entresacar** <c → qu> [en·tre·sa·'kar] *vt* to pick out

**entresuelo** [en·tre·'swe·lo] *m* mezzanine

**entretanto** [en·tre·'tan·to] *adv* meanwhile

**entretecho** [en·tre·'te·tʃo] *m CSur* attic

**entretejer** [en·tre·te·'xer] *vt* to interweave

**entretener** [en·tre·te·'ner] *irr como* tener

**I.** *vt* **1.** (*divertir*) to entertain **2.** (*distraer*) to distract **II.** *vr*: ~**se 1.** (*divertirse*) to amuse oneself **2.** (*tardar*) to delay; **¡no te entretengas!** don't dilly dally! **3.** (*distraerse*) to be distracted

**entretenido, -a** [en·tre·te·'ni·do, -a] *adj* entertaining

**entretenimiento** [en·tre·te·ni·'mjen·to] *m* entertainment; (*pasatiempo*) activity

**entretiempo** [en·tre·'tjem·po] *m* between season

**entrever** [en·tre·'βer] *irr como* ver *vt* to glimpse; (*sospechar*) to surmise

**entrevero** [en·tre·'βe·ro] *m CSur* **1.** (*confusión*) jumble **2.** (*riña*) brawl **3.** (*escaramuza*) skirmish

**entrevista** [en·tre·'βis·ta] *f* **1.** (*prensa, trabajo*) interview **2.** (*reunión*) meeting

**entrevistar** [en·tre·βis·'tar] **I.** *vt* to interview **II.** *vr*: ~**se** to have a meeting

**entristecer** [en·tris·te·'ser, -'θer] *irr como* crecer **I.** *vt* to sadden **II.** *vr*: ~**se** to be saddened

**entrometerse** [en·tro·me·'ter·se] *vr* to interfere

**entrometido, -a** [en·tro·me·'ti·do, -a] *adj, m, f* v. entremetido

**entroncar** <c → qu> [en·tron·'kar] *vi AmL* to connect

**entronque** [en·'tron·ke] *m AmL* connection

**entrucharse** [en·tru·'tʃar·se] *vr Méx* ~ **en algo** to interfere with sth; ~ **de alguien** to fall in love with sb

**entuerto** [en·'twer·to] *m* offense

**entumecerse** [en·tu·me·'ser·se, -'θer·se] *irr como* crecer *vr* to stiffen; (*de frío*) to go numb

**entumecido, -a** [en·tu·me·'si·do, -a; -'θi·do, -a] *adj* stiff; (*de frío*) numb

**enturbiar** [en·tur·'βjar] *vt* to darken

**entusiasmar** [en·tu·sjas·'mar] **I.** *vt* to enthuse **II.** *vr*: ~**se** to get enthusiastic

**entusiasmo** [en·tu·'sjas·mo] *m* enthusiasm

**entusiasta** [en·tu·'sjas·ta] **I.** *adj* enthusiastic **II.** *mf* enthusiast

**enumeración** [e·nu·me·ra·'sjon, -'θjon] *f* enumeration

**enumerar** [e·nu·me·ˈrar] *vt* to enumerate

**enunciado** [e·nun·ˈsja·do, -ˈθja·do] *m* setting out

**enunciar** [e·nun·ˈsjar, -ˈθjar] *vt* to set out; (*expresar*) to state

**envasar** [em·ba·ˈsar] *vt* to package; (*en latas*) to can; (*en botellas*) to bottle

**envase** [em·ˈba·se] *m* **1.** (*paquete*) package; (*recipiente*) container; (*botella*) bottle **2.** (*acción*) packing; ~ **al vacío** vacuum packing

**envejecer** [em·be·xe·ˈser, -ˈθer] *irr como crecer vt, vr:* ~**se** to age

**envenenar** [em·be·ne·ˈnar] *vt* to poison

**envergadura** [em·ber·ɣa·ˈdu·ra] *f* magnitude; **de gran** ~ far-reaching

**envés** [em·ˈbes] *m* back

**enviado, -a** [em·ˈbi·ˈa·do, -a] *m, f* envoy; ~ **especial** special correspondent

**enviar** <*1. pres envío*> [em·bi·ˈar] *vt* to send; ~ **por correo** to mail

**envidia** [em·ˈbi·dja] *f* envy; **tener** ~ **a alguien** to envy sb; **tener** ~ **de algo** to be jealous of sth; **daba** ~ **verlo de lo guapo que iba** it made me envious to see how handsome he looked; **lo corroe la** ~ he is eaten up by jealousy

**envidiable** [em·bi·ˈdja·βle] *adj* enviable

**envidiar** [em·bi·ˈdjar] *vt* to envy

**envidioso, -a** [em·bi·ˈdjo·so, -a] *adj* envious

**envío** [em·ˈbi·o] *m* sending; ~ **a domicilio** home delivery; ~ **contra reembolso** cash on delivery; ~ **urgente** urgent delivery; ~ **con valor declarado** declared value delivery; **gastos de** ~ shipping and handling

**enviudar** [em·bju·ˈdar] *vi* to be widowed

**envoltorio** [em·bol·ˈto·rjo] *m* wrapping

**envoltura** [em·bol·ˈtu·ra] *f* (*capa exterior*) covering

**envolver** [em·bol·ˈβer] *irr como volver vt* (*en papel*) to wrap; ~ **con** [*o en*] **algo** to wrap up in sth; ~ **para regalo** to gift-wrap

**envuelto, -a** [em·ˈbwel·to] *pp de* **envolver**

**enyesar** [en·je·ˈsar] *vt* to plaster

**enzarzar** [en·sar·ˈsar, -θar·ˈθar] *vr:* ~**se en** to get entangled in

**enzima** [en·ˈsi·ma, -ˈθi·ma] *m o f* enzyme

**eólico, -a** [e·ˈo·li·ko, -a] *adj* wind; **central eólica** wind power plant

**epa** [ˈe·pa] *interj AmL* (*saludo*) hi!; (*llamada*) hey!; (*accidente*) (wh)oops!

**épica** [ˈe·pi·ka] *f* epic

**epicentro** [e·pi·ˈsen·tro, -ˈθen·tro] *m* epicenter

**épico, -a** [ˈe·pi·ko, -a] *adj* epic

**epidemia** [e·pi·ˈde·mja] *f* epidemic

**epidermis** [e·pi·ˈder·mis] *f inv* epidermis

**epilepsia** [e·pi·ˈleβ·sja] *f* epilepsy

**epiléptico, -a** [e·pi·ˈlep·ti·ko, -a] *adj, m, f* epileptic

**epílogo** [e·ˈpi·lo·ɣo] *m* epilog(ue)

**episodio** [e·pi·ˈso·djo] *m* episode; (*etapa*) stage

**época** [ˈe·po·ka] *f* **1.** time; ~ **de lluvias** rainy season; **es la** ~ **más calurosa del año** it is the hottest time of the year; **en aquella** ~ at that time **2.** HIST age; **coches de** ~ classic cars *pl;* **muebles de** ~ antique furniture; **trajes de** ~ period costumes *pl;* **un invento que hizo** ~ a revolutionary invention

**epopeya** [e·po·ˈpe·ja] *f* epic

**equidad** [e·ki·ˈdad] *f* fairness; (*precios*) equity

**equilibrado, -a** [e·ki·li·ˈβra·do, -a] *adj* balanced; (*sensato*) sensible

**equilibrar** [e·ki·li·ˈβrar] *vt, vr:* ~**se** to balance

**equilibrio** [e·ki·ˈli·βrjo] *m* balance; **mantener/perder el** ~ to keep/lose one's balance

**equilibrista** [e·ki·li·ˈβris·ta] *mf* tightrope artist

**equino, -a** [e·ˈki·no] *adj* equine

**equipaje** [e·ki·ˈpa·xe] *m* baggage, luggage; **entrega de** ~**s** baggage check-in; **exceso de** ~ excess baggage; **registro de** ~ baggage inspection; **hacer el** ~ to pack; ~ **de mano** hand baggage

**equipal** [e·ki·ˈpal] *m Méx* (*de mimbre*) rustic wicker chair; (*de cuero*) leather chair

**equipamiento** [e·ki·pa·ˈmjen·to] *m* ~ **de serie** standard equipment

**equipar** [e·ki·'par] *vt* to equip

**equiparable** [e·ki·pa·'ra·βle] *adj* comparable

**equiparar** [e·ki·pa·'rar] *vt* 1. (*igualar*) to put on the same level 2. (*comparar*) to compare

**equipo** [e·'ki·po] *m* 1. (*de personas*) team; ~ **gestor** management team; ~ **de investigadores** research team; **trabajo en** ~ teamwork; **carrera por** ~**s** team race; ~ **de casa/de fuera** the home/visiting team 2. (*utensilios*) equipment; ~ **de alta fidelidad** hi-fi system; ~ **productivo** productive equipment; **bienes de** ~ capital goods

**equis** ['e·kis] *inv* I. *adj* X; ~ **dólares** X number of dollars II. *f Col* snake

**equitación** [e·ki·ta·'sjon, -'θjon] *f* horseback riding

**equitativamente** [e·ki·ta·ti·βa·'men·te] *adv* equitably

**equitativo, -a** [e·ki·ta·'ti·βo, -a] *adj* equitable; **hicieron un reparto** ~ **de las ganancias** they split the profits equally

**equivalencia** [e·ki·βa·'len·sja, -θja] *f* equivalence

**equivalente** [e·ki·βa·'len·te] I. *adj* equivalent (**a** to). II. *m* equivalent (**a/de** of)

**equivaler** [e·ki·βa·'ler] *irr como* valer *vi* to be equivalent (**a** to); **lo que equivale a decir que...** which is the same as saying that...

**equivocación** [e·ki·βo·ka·'sjon, -'θjon] *f* mistake; (*error*) error; **por** ~ by mistake

**equivocado, -a** [e·ki·βo·'ka·do, -a] *adj* mistaken; **número** ~ wrong number

**equivocar** <c → qu> [e·ki·βo·'kar] I. *vt* 1. (*confundir*) to get wrong; **equivoqué los sobres de las cartas** I got the envelopes for the letters mixed up 2. (*desconcertar*) to throw II. *vr*: ~**se** 1. (*estar en error*) to be wrong; ~**se en** [*o* **de**] **algo** to be wrong about sth; ~**se de camino** to take the wrong way; ~**se al escribir/al hablar** to make a mistake (when) writing/when speaking; ~**se al leer** to misread; ~**se de número** (**de teléfono**) to dial the wrong number; ~**se de tranvía** to take the wrong tram; ~**se de puerta** to take the wrong door

**equívoco** [e·'ki·βo·ko] *m* (*doble sentido*) ambiguity; (*malentendido*) misunderstanding

**era**[1] ['e·ra] *f* era

**era**[2] ['e·ra] 3. *imp de* **ser**

**erección** [e·rek·'sjon, -rey·'θjon] *f* 1. (*del pene*) erection 2. (*de monumentos*) building

**erecto, -a** [e·'rek·to, -a] *adj* erect; (*cuerpo*) upright

**eres** ['e·res] 2. *pres de* **ser**

**erguido, -a** [er·'yi·do, -a] *adj* upright

**erigir** <g → j> [e·ri·'xir] *vt* 1. (*construir*) to build 2. (*fundar*) to establish

**erizado, -a** [e·ri·'sa·do, -a; e·ri·'θa-] *adj* on end

**erizarse** <z → c> [e·ri·'sar·se, -'θar·se] *vr* (*pelo*) to stand on end

**erizo** [e·'ri·so, -θo] *m* hedgehog; ~ **de mar** sea urchin

**ermita** [er·'mi·ta] *f* hermitage

**ermitaño** [er·mi·'ta·ɲo] *m* hermit crab

**erogación** [e·ro·ya·'sjon, -'θjon] *f* 1. *Arg, Méx, Par* (*pago*) costs *pl* 2. *Ven, Col* (*donativo*) contribution

**erogar** <g → gu> [e·ro·'yar] *vt Arg, Col* (*pagar*) to pay

**erógeno, -a** [e·'ro·xe·no, -a] *adj* erogenous

**erosión** [e·ro·'sjon] *f* GEO erosion

**erosionar** [e·ro·sjo·'nar] *vt* 1. (*desgastar*) to wear away 2. GEO to erode

**erótico, -a** [e·'ro·ti·ko, -a] *adj* erotic

**erotismo** [e·ro·'tis·mo] *m* eroticism

**erradicar** <c → qu> [e·rra·di·'kar] *vt* to eradicate; (*enfermedad*) to stamp out

**errar** [e·'rrar] *irr vi* 1. ~ **en algo** to make a mistake in sth; ~ **en la respuesta** to give the wrong answer; ~ **en el camino** to take the wrong road; *fig* to make the wrong choice 2. (*vagar*) to wander; ~ **por algo** to roam around sth; **ir errando por las calles** to wander the streets

**errata** [e·'rra·ta] *f* errata

**erróneo, -a** [e·'rro·neo, -a] *adj* erroneous form, wrong

**error** [e·'rror] *m* 1. (*falta*) fault; ~ **de cálculo** miscalculation; ~ **de operación** COMPUT operative error; ~ **ortográfico** spelling mistake; ~ **freudiano** Freudian slip; **cometer un** ~ to make a mistake; **has cometido un ~ muy grave** you have made a very serious mistake **2.** (*equivocación*) mistake; (*descuido*) oversight; **estar en el ~** to be wrong; **por ~** by mistake; **~ judicial** miscarriage of justice; **~ de imprenta** misprint **3.** FÍS, MAT error

**eructar** [e·ruk·'tar] *vi* to burp

**eructo** [e·'ruk·to] *m* burp

**erudito, -a** [e·ru·'di·to, -a] *adj* erudite; (*obra*) scholarly **II.** *m, f* scholar

**erupción** [e·rup·'sjon, -ruß·'θjon] *f* **1.** GEO eruption **2.** MED rash

**es** [es] *3. pres de* **ser**

**esa(s)** ['e·sa(s)] *adj, pron dem v.* **ese, -a**

**ésa(s)** ['e·sa(s)] *pron dem v.* **ése**

**esbelto, -a** [es·'ßel·to, -a] *adj* slender; **un hombre ~** a well-proportioned man

**esbozar** <z → c> [es·ßo·'sar, -'θar] *vt* to sketch

**esbozo** [es·'ßo·so, -θo] *m* sketch; (*de un proyecto*) outline

**escabechar** [es·ka·ße·'tʃar] *vt* to marinate

**escabeche** [es·ka·'ße·tʃe] *m* marinade; **en ~** marinated; (*pescado*) pickled

**escabroso, -a** [es·ka·'ßro·so, -a] *adj* (*terreno*) uneven; (*asunto*) thorny

**escabullirse** <3. pret se escabulló> [es·ka·ßu·'ʝir·se, -'ʎir·se] *vr* to slip away

**escacharrar** [es·ka·tʃa·'rrar] *vt, vr:* **~se** *inf* to break (down)

**escafandra** [es·ka·'fan·dra] *f* diving suit; (*espacial*) space suit

**escala** [es·'ka·la] *f* **1.** *t.* MÚS scale; **~ de colores** range of colors, color scale; **~ de cuotas** payment scale; **~ de descuentos** range of discounts; **~ de grados** degree scale; **~ impositiva** tax bracketing; **~ de reproducción** scale of reproduction; **~ de Richter** Richter scale; **~ de salarios** salary scale; **~ de valores** set of values; **a ~** to scale; **hacer ~s** to do scales; **un mapa a ~ 1:100.000** a map with a scale of 1:100,000; **~ milimétrica** millimeter scale **2.** (*medida*) level; **a ~ mundial** on a world scale; **a ~ nacional** on a national scale; **en gran ~** on a large scale; **comprar en gran ~** to buy in bulk; **fabricación en gran ~** large-scale production; **ser de mayor ~** to be on a large

scale **3.** (*parada*) stop; AVIAT stopover; **~ forzada** forced landing; **el avión tuvo que hacer ~ en París** the plane had to land in Paris; **hacer ~ en un puerto** to make a stop at a port **4.** (*escalera*) ladder; **~ de cuerda** rope ladder

**escalada** [es·ka·'la·da] *f* climb; **~ libre** free climbing; **~ en roca** rock climbing; **se produjo una ~ de la violencia** there was an escalation of violence

**escalar** [es·ka·'lar] *vt, vi* to climb

**escaldado, -a** [es·kal·'da·do, -a] *adj* scalded; **salir ~** to learn one's lesson

**escaldadura** [es·kal·da·'du·ra] *f* Arg chafing

**escalera** [es·ka·'le·ra] *f* **1.** (*escalones*) staircase, stairs; AVIAT stairway; **~ abajo** downstairs; **~ arriba** upstairs; **~ de caracol** spiral staircase; **~ mecánica** [*o* **automática**] escalator; **~ de servicio** service stairs **2.** (*escala*) ladder; **~ de bomberos** firemen's ladder; **~ de cuerda** rope ladder; **~ doble** stepladder; **~ de incendios** fire escape; **~ de mano** ladder; **~ de tijera** stepladder; **subir la ~** to go up the ladder **3.** (*naipes*) run; **~ de color real** royal flush

**escalinata** [es·ka·li·'na·ta] *f* staircase

**escalofriante** [es·ka·lo·'frjan·te] *adj* chilling; (*película*) scary

**escalofrío** [es·ka·lo·'fri·o] *m* chill; MED shiver; **al abrir la ventana sentí ~s** I felt a chill when I opened the window; **el libro me produjo ~s** the book sent shivers down my spine; **cierra la puerta, tengo ~s** close the door, I feel chilly

**escalón** [es·ka·'lon] *m* step; (*peldaño*) rung; **subir un ~** *fig* to move up the ladder; **este libro es un ~ hacia el éxito** this book is a stepping stone on the way to success; **descender un ~ en la opinión pública** to go down in the eyes of the public

**escalonado, -a** [es·ka·lo·'na·do, -a] *adj* terraced; (*tarifa*) graded

**escalope** [es·ka·'lo·pe] *m* escalope

**escalpelo** [es·kal·'pe·lo] *m* scalpel

**escama** [es·'ka·ma] *f* scale

**escamado, -a** [es·ka·'ma·do] *adj inf* cautious

**escamar** [es·ka·'mar] **I.** *vt* **1.** (*pescado*)

E

to scale **2.** *inf* to make suspicious **II.** *vr:* ~se *inf* to smell a rat

**escamocha** [es·ka·'mo·tʃa] *f* Méx left-overs *pl*

**escampar** [es·kam·'par] *v impers* **espera hasta que escampe** wait until it clears

**escandalizar** <z → c> [es·kan·da·li·'sar, -'θar] **I.** *vt* to shock **II.** *vr:* ~se to be shocked (**de/por** by)

**escándalo** [es·'kan·da·lo] *m* **1.** scandal; ~ **público** public scandal; **causar** ~ to cause a scandal; **la piedra del** ~ the root of the scandal; **estos precios son un** ~ these prices are outrageous; **tu comportamiento es un** ~ your behavior is a disgrace; **de** ~ scandalous; **¡qué** ~! can you believe it? **2.** (*ruido*) uproar; **armar un** [*o* **dar el**] ~ to make a scene; **se armó un** ~ there was a terrible uproar

**escandaloso, -a** [es·kan·da·'lo·so, -a] *adj* **1.** (*ruidoso*) noisy **2.** (*inmoral*) scandalous **3.** (*precios*) outrageous

**Escandinavia** [es·kan·di·'na·βja] *f* Scandinavia

**escandinavo, -a** [es·kan·di·'na·βo, -a] *adj, m, f* Scandinavian

**escanear** [es·ka·ne·'ar] *vt* to scan

**escáner** [es·'ka·ner] *m* scanner

**escaño** [es·'ka·ɲo] *m* seat

**escapada** [es·ka·'pa·da] *f* escape

**escapar** [es·ka·'par] **I.** *vi* to escape; (*ocultamente*) to get away; **logré** ~ I managed to escape; **es imposible** ~ **a esta ley** it is impossible to dodge this law; ~ **de casa** to run away from home **II.** *vr:* ~se **1.** to escape; (*ocultamente*) to get away; (*agua, gas*) to leak; ~se **de casa** to run away from home; **algunas cosas se escapan al poder de la voluntad** some things are beyond one's power; **no se te escapa ni una** you don't miss a thing **2.** (*sin querer*) **se me ha escapado que te vas a casar** I let it slip that you were getting married; **se escapó un tiro** a shot was let loose; **se me ha escapado su nombre** I've forgotten your name; **se me ha escapado el autobús** I missed the bus; **se me ha escapado la mano** my hand slipped; **se me ha escapado la risa** I couldn't help

laughing; **se me escapó un suspiro** I let out a sigh

**escaparate** [es·ka·pa·'ra·te] *m* **1.** shop window **2.** AmL (*armario*) dresser

**escapatoria** [es·ka·pa·'to·rja] *f* way out

**escape** [es·'ka·pe] *m* leak

**escarabajo** [es·ka·ra·'βa·xo] *m* beetle

**escaramuza** [es·ka·ra·'mu·sa, -θa] *f* skirmish

**escarapelar** [es·ka·ra·pe·'lar] **I.** *vt* **1.** Col, Cri, Méx (*descascarar*) to peel **2.** Col (*manosear*) to handle; (*ajar*) to wear out **II.** *vr:* ~se Méx, Perú **1.** (*atemorizarse*) to be scared **2.** (*temblar*) to shudder

**escarbar** [es·kar·'βar] *vi, vt* ~ (**en**) **algo** to dig sth; *fig* to investigate sth

**escarcha** [es·'kar·tʃa] *f* frost

**escarlata** [es·kar·'la·ta] *adj* scarlet

**escarmentar** <e → ie> [es·kar·men·'tar] **I.** *vi* to learn one's lesson **II.** *vt* to punish

**escarmiento** [es·kar·'mjen·to] *m* lesson

**escarola** [es·ka·'ro·la] *f* curly endive, escarole

**escarpado, -a** [es·kar·'pa·do, -a] *adj* rugged

**escasamente** [es·ka·sa·'men·te] *adv* scarcely

**escasear** [es·ka·se·'ar] *vi* to be scarce

**escasez** [es·ka·'ses, -θeθ] *f* shortage; ~ **de lluvias** lack of rain; ~ **de viviendas** housing shortage; **una región con** ~ **de agua** a region with scarce rainfall; **vivir con** ~ to live in need

**escaso, -a** [es·'ka·so, -a] *adj* insufficient; ~ **de palabras** of few words; **viento** ~ light wind; **andar** ~ **de dinero** to be short of money; **estar** ~ **de tiempo** to be short of time; **tener escasas posibilidades de ganar** to have little chance of winning; **en dos horas escasas** in only two hours

**escatimar** [es·ka·ti·'mar] *vt* to skimp

**escayola** [es·ka·'jo·la] *f* plaster; MED cast

**escayolar** [es·ka·jo·'lar] *vt* to put a cast on; **un brazo escayolado** an arm in a cast

**escena** [e·'se·na, es·'θe-] *f* **1.** (*parte del teatro*) stage; **aparecer en** ~ to appear on stage; **poner en** ~ to stage; **puesta**

en ~ staging; **salir a la ~** to go on stage; **salir de la ~** to go off stage **2.** (*lugar, parte de una obra*) scene; ~ **final** final scene; **cambio de ~** change of scene; ~ **del crimen** scene of the crime; **desaparecer de ~** (*marcharse*) to leave the scene; (*morirse*) to pass away; **poner en ~** to put on stage; **salir a ~** (*aparecer*) to make an appearance **3.** (*arte*) theater; **dedicarse a la ~** to devote oneself to the stage **4.** LIT scene **5.** (*suceso, reproche*) scene; ~ **de celos** display of jealousy; **hacer una ~ ridícula** to make a scene

**escenario** [e·se·ˈna·rjo, es·ˈθe-] *m* **1.** scene; ~ **del crimen** scene of the crime; **un cambio de ~** a change of scene **2.** TEAT stage

**escénico, -a** [e·ˈse·ni·ko, -a; es·ˈθe-] *adj* stage

**escepticismo** [es·sep·ti·ˈsis·mo, es·θep·ti·ˈθis-] *m* skepticism

**escéptico, -a** [es·ˈsep·ti·ko, -a; es·ˈθep-] **I.** *adj* skeptical **II.** *m, f* skeptic

**escindirse** [e·sin·ˈdir·se, es·θin-] *vr* to split (**en** into)

**escisión** [e·si·ˈsjon, es·θi-] *f* MED excision

**esclarecer** [es·kla·re·ˈser, -ˈθer] *irr como crecer vt* to clear up; (*crimen, misterio*) to shed light upon

**esclarecimiento** [es·kla·re·si·ˈmjen·to, -θi·ˈmjen·to] *m* explanation

**esclavitud** [es·kla·βi·ˈtud] *f* slavery

**esclavizar** ‹z → c› [es·kla·βi·ˈsar, -ˈθar] **I.** *vt* to enslave **II.** *vr:* ~**se** to become a slave

**esclavo, -a** [es·ˈkla·βo, -a] **I.** *adj* slave; (*dominado*) dependent; (*obediente*) obedient; **eres esclava de tu familia** you do everything your family wants; **ser ~ del alcohol** to be a slave to alcohol **II.** *m, f* slave; **ser un ~ de algo** *fig* to be dependent on sth

**escoba** [es·ˈko·βa] *f* broom

**escobazo** [es·ko·ˈβa·so, -θo] *m Arg, Chile* **dar un ~ al suelo** to give the floor a quick sweep

**escobilla** [es·ko·ˈβi·ja, -ˈʎa] *f* brush

**escobillar** [es·ko·βi·ˈjar, -ˈʎar] *vi AmL* to tap or shuffle the feet

**escocer** [es·ko·ˈser, -ˈθer] *irr como cocer vi* to sting

**escocés** [es·ko·ˈses, -ˈθes] *m* (Scottish) Gaelic; (*whisky*) Scotch

**escocés, -esa** [es·ko·ˈses, -·ˈse·sa; -ˈθes, -·ˈθe·sa] **I.** *adj* Scottish **II.** *m, f* Scot, Scotsman, Scotswoman *m, f*

**Escocia** [es·ˈko·sja, -θja] *f* Scotland

**escoger** ‹g → j› [es·ko·ˈxer] *vi, vt* to choose; **no has sabido ~** you've made the wrong choice

**escogido, -a** [es·ko·ˈxi·do, -a] *adj* finest; **estos plátanos están ya muy ~s** all the good bananas are gone

**escolar** [es·ko·ˈlar] **I.** *adj* academic; **curso ~** academic year; **edad ~** school age **II.** *mf* schoolboy, schoolgirl *m, f*

**escolaridad** [es·ko·la·ri·ˈdad] *f* schooling; **la ~ es obligatoria** education is compulsory

**escolarización** [es·ko·la·ri·sa·ˈsjon, -θa·ˈθjon] *f* education

**escolarizar** ‹z → c› [es·ko·la·ri·ˈsar, -ˈθar] *vt* to educate

**escollar** [es·ko·ˈjar, -ˈʎar] *vi Arg, Chile* to fail

**escollo** [es·ˈko·jo, -ʎo] *m* pitfall

**escolta** [es·ˈkol·ta] *f* t. MIL escort; (*guardaespaldas*) bodyguard; (*guardia*) guard

**escoltar** [es·kol·ˈtar] *vt* to escort

**escombro(s)** [es·ˈkom·bro(s)] *m(pl)* rubble; **hacer ~** *Arg* to exaggerate

**esconder** [es·kon·ˈder] *vt, vr:* ~**se** to hide; **el fondo del mar esconde muchas riquezas** the ocean bed has many secret treasures

**escondidas** [es·kon·ˈdi·das] *adv* **a ~** secretly; **a ~ del profesor** behind the teacher's back

**escondido(s)** [es·kon·ˈdi·do(s)] *m(pl) AmL* hide and seek

**escondite** [es·kon·ˈdi·te] *m* **1.** (*juego*) hide and seek **2.** (*lugar*) hiding place

**escondrijo** [es·kon·ˈdri·xo] *m* hideout

**escopeta** [es·ko·ˈpe·ta] *f* shotgun; ~ **de aire comprimido** air gun

**escopetear** [es·ko·pe·te·ˈar] *vt* **1.** *Méx* (*con indirectas*) to be snide about **2.** *Ven* (*contestar mal*) to give an unpleasant reply to

**escorchar** [es·kor·ˈtʃar] *vt Arg* to annoy

**escoria** [es·'ko·rja] f scum

**Escorpio** [es·'kor·pjo] m Scorpio

**escorpión** [es·kor·'pjon] m scorpion

**escotado** [es·ko·'ta·do] m neckline

**escotado, -a** [es·ko·'ta·do, -a] adj with a low neckline

**escote** [es·'ko·te] m neckline

**escotilla** [es·ko·'ti·ja, -ʎa] f hatchway

**escozor** [es·ko·'sor, -'θor] m burning

**escrachar** [es·kra·'tʃar] vt **1.** AmL (tachar) to strike out **2.** PRico (estropear) to ruin **3.** Arg inf (arruinar) to wreck

**escracho** [es·'kra·tʃo] m RíoPl **1.** (cara fea) mug inf **2.** (esperpento) fright

**escribanía** [es·kri·βa·'ni·a] f AmL notary

**escribir** [es·kri·'βir] irr **I.** vi, vt write; ~ **algo a mano** to write sth by hand; ~ **algo a máquina** to typewrite sth; **escrito a mano** handwritten; **escrito a máquina** typewritten; **¿cómo se escribe tu nombre?** how do you spell your name? **II.** vr: ~**se** to write (to each other); **se escriben mucho** they write to each other a lot; **estaba escrito que acabarían casándose** it was in their stars to get married

**escrito** [es·'kri·to] m text

**escrito, -a** [es·'kri·to, -a] **I.** pp de **escribir II.** adj written; **por** ~ in writing

**escritor(a)** [es·kri·'tor, -·'to·ra] m(f) writer

**escritorio** [es·kri·'to·rjo] m desk; COMPUT desktop

**escritura** [es·kri·'tu·ra] f **1.** (acto) writing **2.** (signos) script **3.** (documento) deed; ~ **de propiedad/hipoteca** title/mortgage deeds; ~ **de seguro** insurance certificate; ~ **social** company registration; **mediante** ~ in writing

**escriturar** [es·kri·tu·'rar] vt to execute by deed

**escroto** [es·'kro·to] m scrotum

**escrúpulo** [es·'kru·pu·lo] m **1.** (duda) scruple; ~**s de conciencia** pangs of conscience; **ser una persona sin** ~**s** to be completely unscrupulous; **no tener** ~**s en hacer algo** to have no qualms about doing sth **2.** (asco) disgust; **me da** ~ **beber de latas** I think it's disgusting to drink out of cans

**escrupuloso, -a** [es·kru·pu·'lo·so, -a] adj **1.** (meticuloso) scrupulous **2.** (quisquilloso) fussy

**escrutar** [es·kru·'tar] vt (votos) to count

**escrutinio** [es·kru·'ti·njo] m scrutiny; (votos) count

**escuadra** [es·'kwa·dra] f bracket; (para dibujar) set square

**escuadrón** [es·kwa·'dron] m squadron

**escuálido, -a** [es·'kwa·li·do] adj scrawny

**escucha** [es·'ku·tʃa] f listening; ~ **telefónica** telephone tapping; **estar a la** ~ to be listening

**escuchar** [es·ku·'tʃar] **I.** vi to listen; (en secreto) to eavesdrop **II.** vt to listen to; (en secreto) to eavesdrop; ~ **un concierto** to listen to a concert; ~ **una conversación telefónica** to tap into a telephone conversation; ~ **(la) radio** to listen to the radio; **¡escúchame bien!** pay attention to what I'm saying!

**escudar** [es·ku·'dar] **I.** vt to shield **II.** vr ~**se en algo** to use sth as an excuse

**escudo** [es·'ku·do] m **1.** (arma) shield **2.** (moneda) escudo (monetary unit of Chile)

**escudriñar** [es·ku·dri·'ɲar] vt, vi to scrutinize; ~ **en la intimidad de alguien** to invade sb's privacy

**escuela** [es·'kwe·la] f school; (de primaria) primary/elementary school; ~ **de idiomas/conducir/párvulos** language/driving/nursery school; **Escuela de Bellas Artes** School of Fine Arts; ~ **normal** teacher training college; ~ **técnica superior** polytechnic; ~ **taller** workshop; **la vida es la mejor** ~ life is the best teacher; **la** ~ **holandesa/de Durero** the Dutch school/the Dürer school; **su ejemplo ha hecho** ~ his/her work has set an example

**escueto, -a** [es·'kwe·to, -a] adj bare; (lenguaje) concise; **escuetamente** briefly

**escuincle** [es·'kwin·kle, -a] m Méx inf kid

**escuicar** <c → qu> [es·kul·'kar] vt AmC, Col, Méx to go through

**esculpir** [es·kul·'pir] vt to sculpt; ~ **a cincel** to sculpt using a chisel; ~ **en madera** to carve in wood; ~ **una figura en**

**mármol** to sculpt a figure in marble

**escultor(a)** [es·kul·'tor, -·'to·ra] *m(f)* sculptor, sculptress *m, f; ~* **de madera** wood carver

**escultura** [es·kul·'tu·ra] *f* sculpture; *~* **de madera** wood carving

**escultural** [es·kul·tu·'ral] *adj* sculptural; *(bello)* statuesque

**escupidera** [es·ku·pi·'de·ra] *f* chamber pot

**escupir** [es·ku·'pir] **I.** *vi* **1.** to spit **2.** *inf (contar)* to spit it out **II.** *vt* to spit out; *~* **sangre** to spit blood; *~* **fuego** to belch smoke; **escupe lo que sabes** spill the beans

**escurreplatos** [es·ku·rre·'pla·tos] *m inv* plate rack

**escurridizo, -a** [es·ku·rri·'di·so, -a, -'di·θo, -a] *adj* slippery

**escurrido, -a** [es·ku·'rri·do] *adj* **1.** *(flaco)* thin **2.** *Méx, PRico (avergonzado)* embarrassed

**escurridor** [es·ku·rri·'dor] *m* drainer

**escurrir** [es·ku·'rrir] **I.** *vi* to drip; *(verdura)* to drain **II.** *vt* **1.** to drain; *(ropa)* to wring out **2.** *(deslizar)* to slip; *~* **la mano por encima de algo** to run one's hand over sth **III.** *vr:* *~se* **1.** *(resbalar)* to slip **2.** *(escaparse)* to slip out; **el pez se me escurrió de las manos** the fish slipped out of my hands

**ése, ésa, eso** <ésos, -as> *pron dem* that (one); **¿por qué no vamos a otro bar? — ~ no me gusta** why don't we go to another bar? — I don't like that one; **llegaré a eso de las doce** I'll be there at about twelve o'clock; **¡no me vengas con ésas!** come off it!; **¡ni por ésas!** not on your life!; **lejos de eso** just the opposite; **no es eso** it's not that; **por eso (mismo)** that's why; **¡eso sí que no!** definitely not!; *v. t.* **ese, -a**

**ese** ['e·se] *f* ir **haciendo ~s** to stagger from side to side

**ese, -a** ['e·se, -a] **I.** *adj* <esos, -as> that; **¿~ coche es tuyo?** is that car yours?; **el chico ~ no me cae bien** I don't like that boy **II.** *pron dem v.* **ése, ésa, eso**

**esencia** [e·'sen·sja, -θja] *f* essence

**esencial** [e·sen·'sjal, -'θjal] *adj* fundamental; **lo ~** the main thing; **alimento/aceite/elemento ~** essential food/oil/element

**esencialmente** [e·sen·sjal·'men·te, e·sen·θjal-] *adv* essentially

**esfera** [es·'fe·ra] *f* **1.** MAT sphere **2.** *(ámbito)* field; *~* **de actividad** area of activity; *~* **de influencia** sphere of influence; **las altas ~s** the upper classes

**esferográfico** [es·fe·ro·'ɣra·fi·ko, -a] *m AmS* ball-point pen

**esfinge** [es·'fin·xe] *f* sphinx

**esforzar** [es·for·'sar, -'θar] *irr como* **forzar** **I.** *vt* to force; *(vista, voz)* to strain **II.** *vr:* *~se (moralmente)* to strive; *(físicamente)* to make an effort

**esfuerzo** [es·'fwer·so, -θo] *m* effort; **sin ~** effortlessly; **hacer un ~** to make an effort; *(económico)* to tighten one's belt

**esfumarse** [es·fu·'mar·se] *vr:* *~se* to fade away; *inf* to beat it

**esgrima** [es·'ɣri·ma] *f* fencing; **practicar la ~** to do fencing

**esgrimir** [es·ɣri·'mir] *vt* to wield; *(argumento)* to use

**esgrimista** [es·ɣri·'mis·ta] *mf AmL* fencer

**esguince** [es·'ɣin·se, -θe] *m* sprain; **hacerse un ~ en el tobillo** to sprain one's ankle

**eslabón** [es·la·'βon] *m* link; **el ~ perdido** the missing link; *fig* step

**eslavo, -a** [es·'la·βo, -a] *adj, m, f* Slav

**eslogan** [es·'lo·ɣan] *m* slogan

**eslovaco, -a** [es·lo·'βa·ko, -a] **I.** *adj* Slovakian **II.** *m, f* Slovak

**Eslovaquia** [es·lo·'βa·kja] *f* Slovakia

**Eslovenia** [es·lo·'βe·nja] *f* Slovenia

**esloveno, -a** [es·lo·'βe·no, -a] *adj, m, f* Slovene

**esmaltar** [es·mal·'tar] *vt* to enamel

**esmalte** [es·'mal·te] *m* **1.** *(barniz)* varnish; *(en metal, porcelana, dientes)* enamel; **sin ~** mat(te) **2.** *(de uñas)* nail polish **3.** *(color)* smalt

**esmerado, -a** [es·me·'ra·do, -a] *adj* painstaking; *(obra)* professional

**esmeralda** [es·me·'ral·da] *adj, f* emerald

**esmerarse** [es·me·'rar·se] *vr* to make an effort (**en** with)

**esmero** [es·'me·ro] *m* care; **con ~** with great care

**esmirriado, -a** [es·mi·'rria·do, -a] *adj (flaco)* scrawny; *(raquítico)* puny

**esmoquin** [es·'mo·kin] *m* tuxedo

**esnifar** [es·ni·'far] *vt inf* to sniff; *(cocaína)* to snort

**esnob** [es·'noβ] **I.** *adj* snobbish **II.** *mf* snob

**esnobismo** [es·no·'βis·mo] *m* snobbery

**eso** ['e·so] *pron dem v.* **ése**

**esófago** [e·'so·fa·γo] *m* esophagus

**esos** ['e·sos] *adj v.* **ese**

**ésos** ['e·sos] *pron dem v.* **ése**

**esotérico, -a** [e·so·'te·ri·ko, -a] *adj* esoteric

**esoterismo** [e·so·te·'ris·mo] *m* esoteric nature

**espabilada** [es·pa·βi·'la·da] *f Col* blink; **en una ~** in a second

**espabilado, -a** [es·pa·βi·'la·do, -a] *adj* **1.** *(listo)* smart **2.** *(despierto)* awake

**espabilar** [es·pa·βi·'lar] **I.** *vt* **1.** *(despertar)* to wake up **2.** *(avivar)* to sharpen up **II.** *vi* **1.** *(darse prisa)* to hurry up **2.** *(avivar)* to shape up **III.** *vr:* **~se** **1.** *(despertarse)* to wake oneself up **2.** *(avivarse)* to liven up **3.** *AmL (irse)* to head off

**espaciador** [es·pa·sja·'dor, es·pa·'θja-] *m* COMPUT space bar

**espacial** [es·pa·'sjal, -'θjal] *adj* space

**espaciar** [es·pa·'sjar, -'θjar] *vt (sillas)* to separate; *(letras)* to space out; *(visitas)* to stagger

**espacio** [es·'pa·sjo, -θjo] *m* **1.** *t.* ASTR space; *(superficie)* area; **~ exterior/vital** outer/living space; **~ verde** green belt; **a doble ~** double-spaced; **~ virtual** cyberspace; **~ web** web site; **a doble ~** double-spaced; **la bici ocupa demasiado ~** the bike takes up too much room *[o space]* **2.** *(de tiempo)* period; **en el ~ de dos meses** in a period of two months; **por ~ de tres horas** for a three-hour period **3.** *(programa)* program; **~ informativo** news bulletin; **~ publicitario** advertising spot

**espacioso, -a** [es·pa·'sjo·so, -a, es·pa·'θjo-] *adj* spacious, roomy

**espada** [es·'pa·da] *f* sword; *(naipes)* spade

**espadachín, -ina** [es·pa·da·'tʃin, -·'tʃi·na] *m, f* swordsman, swordswoman *m, f*

**espagueti(s)** [es·pa·'ye·ti(s)] *m(pl)* spaghetti

**espalda** [es·'pal·da] *f* **1.** back; **ancho de ~s** broad-shouldered; **ser cargado de ~s** to be hunched; **andar de ~s** to walk backwards; **con las manos en la ~** with one's hands clasped behind one's back; **estar a ~s de alguien** to be behind sb; **estar de ~s a la pared** to have one's back to the wall; **atacar por la ~** to attack from the rear; **coger a alguien por la ~** *fig* to take sb by surprise; **doblar la ~** *fig* to put one's back into a task; **volver la ~ a alguien** *fig* to turn one's back on sb; **hablar a ~s de alguien** to talk behind sb's back; **me caí de ~s al oír eso** *inf* I was astonished to hear that; **tener las ~s muy anchas** *fig* to put up with a lot; **tener las ~s bien guardadas** *inf* to have friends in high places; **la responsabilidad recae sobre mis ~s** the responsibility is on my shoulders; **vivir de ~s a la realidad** to live in the clouds **2.** DEP backstroke; **100 metros ~** 100-meters backstroke; **¿sabes nadar ~?** can you do the backstroke?

**espaldero** [es·pal·'de·ro] *m Ven* bodyguard

**espanglis** [es·'pan·lis] *m* Spanglish

**espantapájaros** [es·pan·ta·'pa·xa·ros] *m inv* scarecrow

**espantar** [es·pan·'tar] **I.** *vt* **1.** *(dar susto)* to shock; *(dar miedo)* to frighten **2.** *(ahuyentar)* to shoo away **II.** *vr* **~se de** *[o por]* **algo** *(personas)* to be scared of sth; *(animales)* to be shooed away

**espanto** [es·'pan·to] *m* **1.** fright; **¡qué ~!** how awful!; **hace un calor de ~** it's terribly hot; **los precios son de ~** prices are outrageous; **estar curado de ~s** *inf* to have been around a few years **2.** *AmL (fantasma)* ghost

**espantosidad** [es·pan·to·si·'dad] *f AmC, Col, PRico* horror

**espantoso, -a** [es·pan·'to·so, -a] *adj* horrible; *(feo)* hideous

**España** [es·'pa·ɲa] *f* Spain

**español** [es·pa·'ɲol] *m* Spanish; **clases**

de ~ Spanish classes; **aprender** ~ to learn Spanish; **traducir al** ~ to translate into Spanish

**español(a)** [es·pa·'ɲol, -·'ɲo·la] **I.** *adj* Spanish; **a la ~a** Spanish-style **II.** *m(f)* Spaniard

**esparadrapo** [es·pa·ra·'dra·po] *m* adhesive tape

**esparcimiento** [es·par·si·'mjen·to, -θi·'mjen·to] *m* **1.** spreading **2.** (*diversión*) fun

**esparcir** <c → z> [es·par·'sir, -'θir] **I.** *vt* to spread out; (*líquido*) to spill; (*noticia*) to spread; **el viento ha esparcido los papeles de la mesa** the wind has blown the papers off the table **II.** *vr:* **~se** to spread out; (*noticias*) to spread

**espárrago** [es·'pa·rra·ɣo] *m* asparagus; ~ **triguero** wild asparagus; **¡vete a freír ~s!** *inf* get lost!; **estar hecho un** ~ *fig* to be as thin as a rake

**espartillo** [es·par·'ti·jo, -·ʎo] *AmL*, **esparto** [es·'par·to] *m* esparto

**espasmo** [es·'pas·mo] *m* spasm

**espasmódico, -a** [es·pas·'mo·di·ko, -a] *adj* spasmodic

**espátula** [es·'pa·tu·la] *f* spatula

**especia** [es·'pe·sja, -θja] *f* spice

**especial** [es·pe·'sjal, -'θjal] *adj* special; (*adecuado*) perfect; (*raro*) peculiar; **edición/comisión/escuela** ~ special edition/committee/school; **en** ~ in particular

**especialidad** [es·pe·sja·li·'dad, es·pe·θja-] *f* specialty; (*rama*) branch

**especialista** [es·pe·sja·'lis·ta, es·pe·θja-] *mf* **1.** specialist **2.** CINE, TV stuntman, stuntwoman *m, f*

**especialización** [es·pe·sja·li·sa·'sjon, -θja·li·θa·'θjon] *f* specialization

**especializar** <z → c> [es·pe·sja·li·'sar, es·pe·θja·li·'θar] *vi, vr:* **~se** to specialize; **personal especializado** skilled staff

**especialmente** [es·pe·sjal·'men·te, es·pe·θjal-] *adv* especially

**especie** [es·'pe·sje, -'pe·θje] *f* **1.** *t.* BOT, ZOOL species *inv;* ~ **amenazada de extinción** endangered species **2.** (*tipo*) kind; **pagar en ~s** to pay in kind

**especificación** [es·pe·si·fi·ka·'sjon, -θi·fi·ka·'θjon] *f* **1.** (*precisión*) specification

**2.** (*explicación*) explanation

**especificar** <c → qu> [es·pe·si·fi·'kar, es·pe·θi-] *vt* (*explicar*) to explain; (*citar*) to specify; (*enumerar*) to enumerate

**específico, -a** [es·pe·'si·fi·ko, -'θi·fi·ko] *adj* specific

**espécimen** [es·'pe·si·men, -θi·men] *m* <**especímenes**> specimen; (*muestra*) sample

**espectacular** [es·pek·ta·ku·'lar] *adj* spectacular

**espectáculo** [es·pek·'ta·ku·lo] *m* **1.** TEAT show; ~ **de variedades** variety show; ~ **deportivo** sporting event **2.** (*visión*) sight **3.** *inf* (*escándalo*) **dar el** ~ to make a scene

**espectador(a)** [es·pek·ta·'dor, -·'do·ra] *m(f)* spectator

**espectro** [es·'pek·tro] *m* specter

**especulación** [es·pe·ku·la·'sjon, -'θjon] *f* speculation

**especulador(a)** [es·pe·ku·la·'dor, -·'do·ra] *m(f)* speculator

**especular** [es·pe·ku·'lar] *vi* **1.** *t.* FIN to speculate; ~ **en la Bolsa** to speculate on the stock market **2.** (*meditar*) to speculate

**especulativo, -a** [es·pe·ku·la·'ti·βo, -a] *adj* speculative; (*teórico*) theoretical

**espejismo** [es·pe·'xis·mo] *m* **1.** (*óptico*) mirage **2.** (*imaginario*) illusion

**espejo** [es·'pe·xo] *m* mirror; ~ **retrovisor** car mirror; **mirarse al** ~ to look at oneself in the mirror

**espeluznante** [es·pe·lus·'nan·te, es·pe·luθ-] *adj* horrific

**espera** [es·'pe·ra] *f* wait; **tuvimos dos horas de** ~ we had a two-hour wait; **a la** ~ waiting; **lista de** ~ waiting list; **esta** ~ **me saca de quicio** this waiting around is really getting to me

**esperanza** [es·pe·'ran·sa, -θa] *f* hope; ~ **de vida** life expectancy; **no tener ~s** to have no hope; **poner las ~s en algo** to put one's hopes into sth; **tener ~s de conseguir un puesto de trabajo** to have hopes of getting a job; **veo el futuro con** ~ I'm hopeful about the future

**esperanzador(a)** [es·pe·ran·sa·'dor, -·'do·ra; -θa·dor, -·'do·ra] *adj* hopeful

**esperanzar** <z → c> [es·pe·ran·'sar, -'θar]

**I.** vt to give hope to **II.** vr ~**se en algo** to become hopeful about sth

**esperar** [es·pe·'rar] **I.** vi **1.** (aguardar) to wait; **hacerse ~** to keep people waiting; **es de ~ que** +subj it is to be expected that; **¡que se espere!** let him/her wait!; **¿a qué esperas?** what are you waiting for?; **espera, que no lo encuentro** hold on, I can't find it; **ganaron la copa tan esperada** they won the long-awaited cup **2.** (confiar) to hope **II.** vt **1.** (aguardar) to wait for; **hace una hora que lo espero** I've been waiting for him for an hour; **hacer ~ a alguien** to keep sb waiting; **la respuesta no se hizo ~** the answer was not long in coming; **me van a ~ al aeropuerto** they're meeting me at the airport; **nos esperan malos tiempos** there are bad times in store for us; **te espera una prueba dura** a hard test awaits you **2.** (un bebé, anticipar) to expect; **ya me lo esperaba** I expected it **3.** (confiar) to hope; **espero que nos veamos pronto** I hope to see you soon; **esperando recibir noticias tuyas...** looking forward to hearing from you...; **espero que sí** I hope so

**esperma** [es·'per·ma] m sperm

**esperpento** [es·per·'pen·to] m fright

**espesar** [es·pe·'sar] **I.** vt (líquido) to thicken **II.** vr: ~**se** (bosque) to become denser

**espeso, -a** [es·'pe·so, -a] adj **1.** thick **2.** Arg, Perú, Ven (molesto) bothersome

**espesor** [es·pe·'sor] m **1.** (grosor) thickness; (nieve) depth **2.** (densidad) density

**espesura** [es·pe·'su·ra] f **1.** thickness; (líquido) density **2.** (bosque) thicket

**espía** [es·'pi·a] mf spy; (de la policía) informer; (infiltrado) infiltrator; ~ **doble** double agent

**espiantar** [es·pjan·'tar] **I.** vi, vr: ~**se** CSur inf (alejarse) to head off; (huir) to escape **II.** vt CSur (hurtar) to steal

**espiar** <1. pres espío> [es·pi·'ar] **I.** vi to spy **II.** vt to spy on; (para la policía) to inform on

**espichar** [es·pi·'tʃar] vt Col inf to squash

**espiga** [es·'pi·ɣa] f ear

**espina** [es·'pi·na] f **1.** (de pescado) bone **2.** BOT thorn **3.** ANAT ~ (**dorsal**) spine **4.** (inconveniente) problem; **esto me da mala** ~ I don't like the look of this **5.** (pesar) frustration; **tener una ~ clavada** to have sth hanging over one

**espinaca** [es·pi·'na·ka] f spinach

**espinal** [es·pi·'nal] adj spinal; **médula** ~ spinal chord

**espinazo** [es·pi·'na·so, -θo] m spinal column

**espinilla** [es·pi·'ni·ja, -ʎa] f **1.** ANAT shin; **dar a alguien una patada en la** ~ to kick sb in the shin **2.** (grano) blackhead

**espino** [es·'pi·no] m **alambre de** ~ barbed wire

**espinoso, -a** [es·pi·'no·so, -a], **espinudo, -a** [es·pi·'nu·do, -a] adj AmC, CSur (planta) thorny; (pescado) bony; (problema) tricky

**espionaje** [es·pjo·'na·xe] m espionage; ~ **industrial** industrial espionage

**espiración** [es·pi·ra·'sjon, -'θjon] f exhalation

**espiral** [es·pi·'ral] **I.** adj spiral; **escalera** ~ spiral staircase **II.** f spiral

**espirar** [es·pi·'rar] **I.** vi to exhale **II.** vt (olor) to give off

**espiritismo** [es·pi·ri·'tis·mo] m spiritualism; **sesión de** ~ séance

**espiritista** [es·pi·ri·'tis·ta] adj spiritualist

**espíritu** [es·'pi·ri·tu] m spirit; (alma) soul; ~ **de compañerismo** brotherly spirit; ~ **emprendedor** hardworking nature; ~ **deportivo** sportsmanship; **el Espíritu Santo** the Holy Spirit

**espiritual** [es·pi·ri·tu·'al] adj spiritual

**espléndido, -a** [es·'plen·di·do, -a] adj **1.** splendid; (día) beautiful; (ocasión, idea, resultado) excellent **2.** (generoso) generous

**esplendor** [es·plen·'dor] m splendor

**esplendoroso, -a** [es·plen·do·'ro·so, -a] adj splendid

**espliego** [es·'plje·ɣo] m lavender

**espolvorear** [es·pol·βo·re·'ar] vt to sprinkle

**esponja** [es·'pon·xa] f sponge; **beber como una** ~ to drink like a fish

**esponjoso, -a** [es·pon·'xo·so, -a] adj

(*masa*) fluffy; (*pan*) light

**espontaneidad** [es·pon·ta·nei·'dad] *f* spontaneity

**espontáneo, -a** [es·pon·'ta·neo, -a] *adj* spontaneous; (*saludo*) natural

**espora** [es·'po·ra] *f* spore

**esporádico, -a** [es·po·'ra·di·ko, -a] *adj* sporadic

**esportivo, -a** [es·por·'ti·βo, -a] *adj AmL* **1.** (*deportivo*) sporting **2.** (*descuidado*) casual

**esposar** [es·po·'sar] *vt* to handcuff

**esposas** [es·'po·sas] *fpl* handcuffs *pl*

**esposo, -a** [es·'po·so, -a] *m, f* husband, wife *m, f*, spouse; **los ~s** husband and wife

**espray** [es·'prai] *m* spray; (*envase*) aerosol

**esprint** [es·'prin(t)] *m* sprint

**espuma** [es·'pu·ma] *f* foam; **~ de afeitar** shaving foam; (*de las olas*) spray; (*de jabón*) lather; (*de cerveza*) head; **crecer como la ~** to grow very quickly

**espumarajo** [es·pu·ma·'ra·xo] *m pey* froth; (*de la boca*) foam

**espumilla** [es·pu·'mi·ja, -ʎa] *f AmL* meringue

**espumoso, -a** [es·pu·'mo·so, -a] *adj* foamy; (*líquido*) sparkling

**esqueje** [es·'ke·xe] *m* cutting

**esquela** [es·'ke·la] *f* notice of death; **~ (mortuoria)** obituary notice

**esquelético, -a** [es·ke·'le·ti·ko, -a] *adj* scrawny; ANAT skeletal

**esqueleto** [es·ke·'le·to] *m* **1.** ANAT skeleton **2.** (*avión, barco*) shell; (*edificio*) framework

**esquema** [es·'ke·ma] *m* (*gráfico*) sketch; (*lista*) summary; **romper los ~s** to shake up sb's ideas

**esquemático, -a** [es·ke·'ma·ti·ko, -a] *adj* schematic

**esquematizar** [es·ke·ma·ti·'sar, -'θar] *vt* to outline

**esquí** [es·'ki] *m* **1.** (*patín*) ski; **~ de fondo** cross-country ski **2.** (*deporte*) skiing; **~ acuático** water-skiing

**esquiador(a)** [es·kja·'dor, -·'do·ra] *m(f)* skier

**esquiar** <*1. pres* esquío> [es·ki·'ar] *vi* to ski

**esquilar** [es·ki·'lar] *vt* to shear

**esquimal** [es·ki·'mal] **I.** *adj* Eskimo; *Can* Inuit; **perro ~** husky **II.** *mf* Eskimo; *Can* Inuit

**esquina** [es·'ki·na] *f* corner; **que hace ~** on the corner; **a la vuelta de la ~** around the corner; **doblar la ~** to turn the corner

**esquinazo** [es·ki·'na·so, -θo] *m inf* **dar ~ a alguien** to avoid sb

**esquivar** [es·ki·'βar] *vt* (*golpe*) to dodge; (*problema*) to shirk; (*persona*) to avoid

**esquivo, -a** [es·'ki·βo, -a] *adj* **1.** (*huidizo*) evasive **2.** (*arisco*) aloof

**esquizofrenia** [es·ki·so·'fre·nja, es·ki·θo-] *f* schizophrenia

**esquizofrénico, -a** [es·ki·so·'fre·ni·ko, -a; es·ki·θo-] *adj, m, f* schizophrenic

**esta** ['es·ta] *adj v.* **este, -a**

**ésta** ['es·ta] *pron dem v.* **éste**

**estabilidad** [es·ta·βi·li·'dad] *f* stability

**estabilización** [es·ta·βi·li·sa·'sjon, -θa·'θjon] *f* stabilization

**estabilizar** <z > c> [es·ta·βi·li·'sar, -'θar] *vt, vr*: **~se** to stabilize

**estable** [es·'ta·βle] *adj* stable; (*trabajo*) steady

**establecer** [es·ta·βle·'ser, -'θer] *irr como* **crecer I.** *vt* **1.** (*fundar*) to establish; (*negocio*) to open; (*principio, récord*) to set; (*escuela*) to found **2.** (*colocar*) to place; (*campamento*) to set up; (*colonos*) to settle; (*conexión*) to establish **II.** *vr* **~se** to settle

**establecimiento** [es·ta·βle·si·'mjen·to, -θi·'mjen·to] *m* establishment

**establo** [es·'ta·βlo] *m* **1.** stable **2.** *Cuba* (*cochera*) depot; (*parking*) garage

**estaca** [es·'ta·ka] *f* post

**estacada** [es·ta·'ka·da] *f* **en la ~** in the lurch

**estación** [es·ta·'sjon, -'θjon] *f* **1.** (*período*) season; **~ de las lluvias** rainy season **2.** RADIO, TV, FERRO station; (*parada*) stop; **~ de autobuses/metro** bus/subway station; **~ central** central station; **~ de destino** destination **3.** (*centro*) **~ meteorológica/espacial** weather/space station; **~ de servicio** gas station

**estacionamiento** [es·ta·sjo·na·'mjen·to, es·ta·θjo-] *m* AUTO (*acción*) parking; (*es-*

*pacio*) parking space; (*lugar*) parking lot; (*edificio*) parking garage

**estacionar** [es·ta·sjo·ˈnar, es·ta·ˈθjo-] **I.** *vt* AUTO to park **II.** *vr*: ~**se 1.** to stabilize **2.** AUTO to park

**estada** [es·ˈta·da] *AmL*, **estadía** [es·ta·ˈdi·a] *f* (*estancia*) stay

**estadio** [es·ˈta·djo] *m* DEP stadium

**estadística** [es·ta·ˈdis·ti·ka] *f* statistics *pl*

**estadístico, -a** [es·ta·ˈdis·ti·ko, -a] **I.** *adj* statistical **II.** *m, f* statistician

**estado** [es·ˈta·do] *m* **1.** (*condición*) condition; **en buen ~** in good condition; (*situación*) state; **~ civil** marital status; **~ gaseoso** gaseous state; **~ de guerra** state of war; **en ~ de embriaguez** in a state of inebriation **2.** POL state; **~ comunitario/miembro/totalitario** community/member/police state

**Estados Unidos** [es·ta·dos·u·ˈni·dos] *mpl* United States of America *pl + sing vb*

**estadounidense** [es·ta·do·u·ni·ˈden·se] **I.** *adj* of/from the US, American **II.** *mf* native/inhabitant of the US, American

**estafa** [es·ˈta·fa] *f* swindle

**estafador(a)** [es·ta·fa·ˈdor, -·ˈdo·ra] *m(f)* swindler

**estafar** [es·ta·ˈfar] *vt* to swindle

**estagnación** [es·taɣ·na·ˈsjon, -ˈθjon] *f* *AmC* stagnation

**estaje** [es·ˈta·xe] *m AmL* piecework

**estajear** [es·ta·xe·ˈar] *vi AmL* to do as piecework

**estajero, -a** [es·ta·ˈxe·ro, -a] *m, f AmL* pieceworker

**estalactita** [es·ta·lak·ˈti·ta] *f* stalactite

**estalagmita** [es·ta·laɣ·ˈmi·ta] *f* stalagmite

**estallar** [es·ta·ˈjar, -ˈʎar] *vi* (*globo*) to burst; (*bomba*) to explode; (*tormenta*) to break; (*revolución, incendio, guerra*) to break out

**estallido** [es·ta·ˈji·do, -ˈʎi·do] *m* explosion; (*globo*) bursting; (*revolución/cólera*) outbreak

**estampa** [es·ˈtam·pa] *f* **1.** (*dibujo*) illustration **2.** (*impresión*) impression

**estampado** [es·tam·ˈpa·do] *m* print; (*diseño*) design; (*en metal*) engraving

**estampado, -a** [es·tam·ˈpa·do, -a] *adj* printed

**estampar** [es·tam·ˈpar] **I.** *vt* (*en papel,*

*tela*) to print; (*con relieve*) to stamp **II.** *vr* ~**se con**(**tra**) **algo** *inf* to crash into sth

**estampilla** [es·tam·ˈpi·ja, -ˈʎa] *f AmL* stamp

**estancamiento** [es·tan·ka·ˈmjen·to] *m* **1.** stagnation **2.** ECON recession

**estancar** <c → qu> [es·tan·ˈkar] **I.** *vt* to stagnate; **aguas estancadas** stagnant water; (*proceso*) to hold up **II.** *vr*: ~**se** (*río*) to be held back; (*negocio*) to falter; **quedarse estancado** to get stuck

**estancia** [es·ˈtan·sja, -ˈθja] *f* **1.** (*permanencia*) stay **2.** (*cuarto*) room **3.** *AmL* (*hacienda*) estate **4.** *Cuba, Ven* (*quinta*) country house

**estanciero, -a** [es·tan·ˈsje·ro, -a; -ˈθje·ro, -a] *m, f CSur, Col, Ven* **1.** (*ganadero*) cattle farmer **2.** (*latifundista*) landowner

**estanco** [es·ˈtan·ko] *m* tobacconist's

**estándar** [es·ˈtan·dar] *adj, m* standard; **tipo ~** standard version

**estandarizar** <z → c> [es·tan·da·ri·ˈsar, -ˈθar] *vt* to standardize

**estanque** [es·ˈtan·ke] *m* pool; (*para regar*) tank

**estanquillo** [es·tan·ˈki·jo, -ˈʎo] *m Méx* shop

**estante** [es·ˈtan·te] *m* shelf

**estantería** [es·tan·te·ˈri·a] *f* shelves *pl*; (*para libros*) bookcase

**estañar** [es·ta·ˈɲar] *vt Ven* to wound

**estaño** [es·ˈta·ɲo] *m* tin; **~ para soldar** solder

**estar** [es·ˈtar] *irr* **I.** *vi* **1.** to be; (*de pie*) to stand; (*tumbado*) to lie; (*colgando*) to hang; **Valencia está en la costa** Valencia is on the coast; **¿está Pepe?** is Pepe there?; **¿está la comida?** is lunch ready? **2.** (*sentirse*) **¿cómo estás?** how are you?; **ya estoy mejor** I'm better **3.** (+ *adjetivo, participio*) ~ **cansado/sentado** to be tired/sitting; **el asado está delicioso** the roast is delicious **4.** (+ *bien, mal*) ~ **mal de azúcar** to be running out of sugar; ~ **mal de dinero** to be short of money; ~ **mal de la cabeza** to be out of one's mind; **eso te está bien empleado** it serves you right; **esa blusa te está bien** that blouse suits you **5.** (+ *a*) ~ **al caer** (*persona*) to be about to arrive; (*suceso*) to be about to happen; ~ **al día** to be up to date; **estamos a uno de enero** it's the first of January; **¿a qué estamos?** what day is it?; **las peras están a 10 pesos el kilo** pears cost 10 pesos a kilo; **las acciones están a 12 dólares** the shares are at 12 dollars; **Caracas está a 40 grados** it is 40 degrees in Caracas **6.** (+ *con*) **estoy con mi novio** I'm with my boyfriend; **estoy contigo en este punto** I agree with you on that point **7.** (+ *de*) ~ **de broma/charla/viaje** to be joking/chatting/traveling; ~ **de mal humor** to be in a bad mood; ~ **de parto** to be in labor; ~ **de pie/suerte** to be standing/lucky; ~ **de secretario** to be working as a secretary; **en esta reunión estoy de más** I'm not needed in this meeting **8.** (+ *en*) **siempre estás en todo** you don't miss a thing **9.** (+ *para*) **hoy no estoy para bromas** today I'm in no mood for jokes; **el tren está para salir** the train is about to leave **10.** (+ *por*) **estoy por llamarle** I think we should call him; **eso está por ver** we don't know that yet; **este partido está por la democracia** this party believes in democracy **11.** (+ *gerundio*) **¿qué estás haciendo?** what are you doing?; **siempre estás viendo la tele** you're always watching TV; **¡lo estaba viendo venir!** I saw it coming! II. *vr*: ~**se** (*permanecer*) to stay; **¡estate quieto!** keep still!; **¡estate callado!** shut up!

**estatal** [es·ta·'tal] *adj* state
**estático, -a** [es·'ta·ti·ko, -a] *adj* static
**estatua** [es·'ta·twa] *f* statue
**estatuilla** [es·ta·'twi·ja, -ʎa] *f* statuette
**estatura** [es·ta·'tu·ra] *f* stature; (*altura*) height; **¿qué ~ tienes?** how tall are you?; **de ~ pequeña** short
**estatus** [es·'ta·tus] *m inv* status
**estatuto** [es·ta·'tu·to] *m* JUR, POL statute
**éste, ésta, esto** <éstos, -as> *pron dem* him, her, this; (a) **éstos no los he visto nunca** I've never seen them; ~ **se cree muy importante** this guy thinks he's very important; **antes yo también tenía una camisa como ésta** I used to

have a shirt like this, too; *v. t.* **este, -a**
**este** ['es·te] *m* east; (*viento*) easterly
**este, -a** ['es·te, -a] I. *adj* <estos, -as> this; ~ **perro es mío** this dog is mine II. *pron dem v.* **éste, ésta, esto**
**estela** [es·'te·la] *f* trail; (*de avión*) slipstream; NÁUT wake
**estelar** [es·te·'lar] *adj* stellar; **invitado/programa ~** star guest/program
**estelaridad** [es·te·la·ri·'dad] *f Chile* stardom
**estepa** [es·'te·pa] *f* steppe
**estera** [es·'te·ra] *f* matting
**estéreo** [es·'te·reo] *adj, m* stereo
**estereotipado, -a** [es·te·reo·ti·'pa·do, -a] *adj* stereotyped; **frase estereotipada** hackneyed expression
**estereotipo** [es·te·reo·'ti·po] *m* stereotype
**estéril** [es·'te·ril] *adj* (*persona*) sterile; (*tierra*) barren; (*trabajo*) mundane; (*esfuerzo*) useless; (*discusión*) pointless
**esterilidad** [es·te·ri·li·'dad] *f* (*persona*) sterility; (*tierra*) barrenness
**esterilizar** [es·te·ri·li·'sar, -'θar] <z → c> *vt* to sterilize
**esterilla** [es·te·'ri·ja, -ʎa] *f* **1.** mat; ~ **de camping** camping mat **2.** *Ecua* **silla de ~** wicker chair
**esterlina** [es·ter·'li·na] *adj* **libra ~** pound sterling
**esternón** [es·ter·'non] *m* sternum, breastbone
**estero** [es·'te·ro] *m* **1.** *AmL* (*pantano*) bog **2.** *Cuba* (*ría*) estuary **3.** *Chile, Ecua* (*arroyo*) stream **4.** *Ven* (*aguazal*) pool
**esteroide** [es·te·'roi·de] *m* steroid
**estética** [es·'te·ti·ka] *f* esthetics
**estético, -a** [es·'te·ti·ko, -a] *adj* esthetic; **cirugía estética** plastic surgery
**estetoscopio** [es·te·tos·'ko·pjo] *m* stethoscope
**estiércol** [es·'tjer·kol] *m* manure
**estigma** [es·'tiɣ·ma] *m* stigma
**estigmatizar** [es·tiɣ·ma·'ti·sar, -θar] <z → c> *vt* to stigmatize
**estilista** [es·ti·'lis·ta] *mf* stylist
**estilístico, -a** [es·ti·'lis·ti·ko, -a] *adj* stylistic
**estilizar** [es·ti·li·'sar, -'θar] <z → c> *vt* to stylize

**estilo** [es·'ti·lo] *m* 1. *t.* ARTE, LIT, DEP style; **al ~ de** in the style of; **~ de vida** lifestyle; **por el ~** like that; **algo por el ~** something similar 2. LING **~ directo/ indirecto** direct/indirect speech

**estilográfica** [es·ti·lo·'γra·fi·ka] *f* fountain pen

**estima** [es·'ti·ma] *f* esteem; **tener a alguien en mucha ~** to hold sb in high esteem

**estimación** [es·ti·ma·'sjon, -'θjon] *f* 1. (*aprecio*) esteem 2. (*evaluación*) estimate; **~ de ventas** sales forecast

**estimado, -a** [es·ti·'ma·do, -a] *adj* **~ Señor** Dear Sir

**estimar** [es·ti·'mar] I. *vt* 1. (*apreciar*) to appreciate 2. (*tasar*) to estimate 3. (*valorar*) **~ en algo** to value at sth 4. (*juzgar*) to consider II. *vr:* **~se en algo** to be valued at sth

**estimulante** [es·ti·mu·'lan·te] *m* stimulant

**estimular** [es·ti·mu·'lar] *vt t.* ECON to stimulate; (*sexualmente*) to excite; (*animar*) to encourage

**estímulo** [es·'ti·mu·lo] *m* incentive; MED stimulus

**estío** [es·'ti·o] *m elev* summer

**esti(p)tiquez** [es·ti(p)·ti·'kes, -'keθ] *f AmL* constipation

**estipulación** [es·ti·pu·la·'sjon, -'θjon] *f* agreement; JUR stipulation

**estipular** [es·ti·pu·'lar] *vt* 1. (*acordar*) to stipulate 2. (*fijar*) to fix

**estirado, -a** [es·ti·'ra·do, -a] *adj* snooty

**estirar** [es·ti·'rar] I. *vi, vr:* **~se** to stretch II. *vt* 1. (*alargar*) to stretch out; (*suma*) to spin out; **~ el bolsillo** to spin out one's resources; **voy a ~ un poco las piernas** I'm going to stretch my legs a little; **~ la pata** to kick the bucket 2. (*alisar*) to smoothen; (*masa*) to roll out 3. (*extender*) to stretch 4. (*tensar*) to tighten

**estirón** [es·ti·'ron] *m* 1. (*tirón*) pull 2. (*crecimiento*) **dar un ~** to shoot up

**estirpe** [es·'tir·pe] *f* stock

**estival** [es·ti·'βal] *adj* summer

**esto** ['es·to] *pron dem v.* **éste**

**estofado** [es·to·'fa·do] *m* (meat) stew

**estofar** [es·to·'far] *vt* to stew

**estoico, -a** [es·'toi·ko, -a] *adj* stoical

**estomacal** [es·to·ma·'kal] *adj* stomach; **trastorno ~** stomach upset

**estómago** [es·'to·ma·γo] *m* stomach; **dolor de ~** stomach-ache

**Estonia** [es·'to·nja] *f* Estonia

**estonio, -a** [es·'to·njo, -a] *adj, m, f* Estonian

**estorbar** [es·tor·'βar] I. *vi* 1. (*obstaculizar*) to get in the way 2. (*molestar*) to be annoying II. *vt* 1. (*obstaculizar*) to hinder 2. (*molestar*) to bother

**estorbo** [es·'tor·βo] *m* 1. (*molestia*) nuisance 2. (*obstáculo*) obstacle

**estornudar** [es·tor·nu·'dar] *vi* to sneeze

**estornudo** [es·tor·'nu·do] *m* sneeze

**estos** ['es·tos] *v.* **este, -a**

**estrabismo** [es·tra·'βis·mo] *m* squint

**estrado** [es·'tra·do] *m* dais; **~ del testigo** witness box

**estrafalario, -a** [es·tra·fa·'la·rjo, -a] *adj inf* 1. (*ropa*) shabby 2. (*extravagante*) outlandish; (*ridículo*) preposterous

**estragón** [es·tra·'γon] *m* tarragon

**estragos** [es·'tra·γos] *m pl* damage

**estrambótico, -a** [es·tram·'bo·ti·ko, -a] *adj* eccentric

**estramonio** [es·tra·'mo·njo] *m* thorn apple

**estrangulación** [es·tran·gu·la·'sjon, -'θjon] *f*, **estrangulamiento** [es·tran·gu·la·'mjen·to] *m* strangulation

**estrangular** [es·tran·gu·'lar] *vt* to strangle

**estraperlista** [es·tra·per·'lis·ta] *mf* black-marketeer

**estraperlo** [es·tra·'per·lo] *m* black market

**estratagema** [es·tra·ta·'xe·ma] *m* ploy

**estrategia** [es·tra·'te·xja] *f* strategy

**estratégico, -a** [es·tra·'te·xi·ko, -a] *adj* strategic

**estrato** [es·'tra·to] *m* stratum

**estrechamente** [es·tre·tʃa·'men·te] *adv* 1. (*íntimamente*) closely 2. (*rigurosamente*) strictly

**estrechar** [es·tre·'tʃar] I. *vt* 1. (*angostar*) to narrow 2. (*abrazar*) to hug; (*mano*) to shake II. *vr:* **~se** 1. (*camino*) to become narrower 2. (*en un asiento*) to squeeze in

**estrechez** [es·tre·'tʃes, -'tʃeθ] *f* 1. (*espacial*) narrowness 2. (*escasez*) shortage;

(*económica*) neediness

**estrecho** [es·'tre·tʃo] *m* strait

**estrecho, -a** [es·'tre·tʃo, -a] *adj* **1.** (*angosto*) narrow; (*amistad*) close; (*ropa, lugar*) tight **2.** (*sexualmente*) prudish

**estregar** [es·tre·'ɣar] *irr como fregar vt v.* **restregar**

**estrella** [es·'tre·ja, -ʎa] *f* **1.** ASTR, CINE star; ~ **fugaz** shooting star; **ver las ~s** *fig* to see stars; **tener buena/mala** ~ to be lucky/unlucky **2.** TIPO asterisk **3.** ~ **de mar** starfish

**estrellado, -a** [es·tre·'ja·do, -a; es·tre·'ʎa·] *adj* **1.** (*esteliforme*) star-shaped **2.** (*cielo*) starry **3.** (*vehículo*) crashed

**estrellar** [es·tre·'jar, -'ʎar] **I.** *adj* star **II.** *vt* to smash; (*coche*) to crash **III.** *vr* ~**se** (**contra** [*o* **en**] **algo**) to crash (into sth)

**estremecedor(a)** [es·tre·me·se·'dor, -·'do·ra, es·tre·me·θe·] *adj* harrowing

**estremecer** [es·tre·me·'ser, -'θer] *irr como crecer* **I.** *vt* to make shudder **II.** *vr:* ~**se** to be shocked; (*temblar*) to shiver

**estremecimiento** [es·tre·me·si·'mjen·to, -θi·'mjen·to] *m* shock; (*de frío, miedo*) shivering

**estrenar** [es·tre·'nar] **I.** *vt* **1.** to use for the first time; (*ropa*) to wear for the first time; (*trabajo*) to start; ~ **un piso** to move into a new apartment; **sin** ~ brand new **2.** CINE, TEAT to premiere **II.** *vr:* ~**se** (*artista*) to make one's debut; (*obra*) to be premiered

**estreno** [es·'tre·no] *m* **1.** (*uso*) first use **2.** (*artista*) debut; (*obra*) premiere

**estreñido, -a** [es·tre·'ɲi·do, -a] *adj* constipated

**estreñimiento** [es·tre·ɲi·'mjen·to] *m* constipation

**estreñir** [es·tre·'ɲir] *irr como ceñir vt* to constipate; **las judías me estriñen** green beans give me constipation

**estrépito** [es·'tre·pi·to] *m* din

**estrepitoso, -a** [es·tre·pi·'to·so, -a] *adj* loud; (*fracaso*) spectacular

**estrés** [es·'tres] *m* stress

**estresante** [es·tre·'san·te] *adj* stressful

**estresar** [es·tre·'sar] *vt* to stress

**estrías** [es·'tri·as] *f pl* grooves *pl*

**estribillo** [es·tri·'βi·jo, -ʎo] *m* chorus

**estribor** [es·tri·'βor] *m* starboard

**estribos** [es·'tri·βos] *m pl* **perder los** ~ to fly off the handle

**estricto, -a** [es·'trik·to, -a] *adj* strict; (*exacto*) exact

**estridente** [es·tri·'den·te] *adj* shrill

**estripazón** [es·tri·pa·'son] *m AmC* **1.** (*apertura*) opening **2.** (*destrozo*) mutilation

**estrofa** [es·'tro·fa] *f* (*poema*) stanza; (*canción*) verse

**estropajo** [es·tro·'pa·xo] *m* scourer

**estropear** [es·tro·pe·'ar] **I.** *vt* to spoil; (*aparato*) to break; (*cosecha*) to ruin **II.** *vr:* ~**se** **1.** (*deteriorarse*) to spoil **2.** (*averiarse*) to break down; (*comida*) to go off; (*planes*) to be spoiled

**estructura** [es·truk·'tu·ra] *f* structure; (*edificio*) framework

**estructural** [es·truk·tu·'ral] *adj* structural

**estructurar** [es·truk·tu·'rar] **I.** *vt* to structure; (*clasificar*) to classify **II.** *vr:* ~**se** to be structured

**estruendo** [es·'trwen·do] *m* **1.** (*ruido*) din **2.** (*alboroto*) uproar

**estrujar** [es·tru·'xar] **I.** *vt* to squeeze; (*papel*) to crumple up; (*machacar*) to crush **II.** *vr:* ~**se** (*apretujarse*) to squeeze together; ~**se los sesos** to rack one's brains

**estuche** [es·'tu·tʃe] *m* case; (*cajita*) little box

**estudiante** [es·tu·'djan·te] *mf* pupil; (*universitario*) student

**estudiantil** [es·tu·djan·'til] *adj* student

**estudiar** [es·tu·'djar] *vi, vt* to study; ~ **para médico** to study to be a doctor; **lo** ~**é** I'll think about it

**estudio** [es·'tu·djo] *m* **1.** (*aprendizaje*) studying **2.** (*obra*) study; (*investigación*) research; **estar en** ~ to be under study **3.** ARTE, TV, TALLER studio **4.** *pl* studies *pl*; **cursar** ~**s** to study; **tener** ~**s** to have an education

**estudioso, -a** [es·tu·'djo·so, -a] **I.** *adj* studious **II.** *m, f* scholar

**estufa** [es·'tu·fa] *f* heater

**estupefacción** [es·tu·pe·fak·'sjon, -fay·'θjon] *f* (*asombro*) amazement; (*sorpresa*) surprise; (*espanto*) fright

**estupefaciente** [es·tu·pe·fa·'sjen·te, -'θjen·te] *m* narcotic; (*ilegal*) drug

**estupefacto, -a** [es·tu·pe·'fak·to, -a] *adj* (*atónito*) amazed; (*espantado*) shocked

**estupendo, -a** [es·tu·'pen·do, -a] *adj* fantastic; **¡~!** great!

**estupidez** [es·tu·pi·'des, -'deθ] *f* stupidity

**estúpido, -a** [es·'tu·pi·do, -a] **I.** *adj* stupid **II.** *m, f* idiot

**estupor** [es·tu·'por] *m* amazement; MED stupor

**esturión** [es·tu·'rjon] *m* sturgeon

**esvástica** [es·'βas·ti·ka] *f* swastika

**etapa** [e·'ta·pa] *f* (*fase*) stage; (*época*) phase; **por ~s** in stages

**etarra** [e·'ta·rra] *mf* ETA member

**etc.** [et·'se·te·ra, et·'θe-] *abr de* **etcétera** etc.

**etcétera** [et·'se·te·ra, et·'θe-] etcetera

**éter** ['e·ter] *m* ether

**etéreo, -a** [e·'te·reo, -a] *adj* ethereal

**eternidad** [e·ter·ni·'dad] *f* eternity; **tardar una ~** to take a lifetime

**eternizar** <z → c> [e·ter·ni·'sar, -'θar] **I.** *vt* to make last forever **II.** *vr* ~**se** (**en algo**) to take ages (doing sth)

**eterno, -a** [e·'ter·no, -a] *adj* eternal

**ética** ['e·ti·ka] *f* ethics

**ético, -a** ['e·ti·ko, -a] *adj* ethical

**etílico, -a** [e·'ti·li·ko, -a] *adj* alcoholic; QUÍM ethyl

**etimología** [e·ti·mo·lo·'xi·a] *f* etymology

**etimológico, -a** [e·ti·mo·'lo·xi·ko, -a] *adj* etymological

**etiqueta** [e·ti·'ke·ta] *f* **1.** label **2.** (*convenciones*) etiquette; **de ~** (*solemne*, *traje*) formal; (*ceremonioso*) ceremonial

**etiquetar** [e·ti·ke·'tar] *vt* to label; (*encasillar*) to stereotype

**etnia** ['ed·nja] *f* ethnic group

**étnico, -a** ['et·ni·ko, -a] *adj* ethnic

**etnología** [et·no·lo·'xi·a] *f* ethnology

**eucalipto** [eu·ka·'lip·to] *m* eucalyptus

**eufemismo** [eu·fe·'mis·mo] *m* euphemism

**euforia** [eu·'fo·rja] *f* euphoria

**eufórico, -a** [eu·'fo·ri·ko, -a] *adj* euphoric

**Eurasia** [eu·'ra·sja] *f* Eurasia

**euro** ['eu·ro] *m* euro

**Europa** [eu·'ro·pa] *f* Europe

**europeo, -a** [eu·ro·'peo, -a] *adj, m, f* European

**Euskadi** [eus·'ka·di] *m* Basque Provinces

**euskera** [eus·'ke·ra], **eusquera** [eus·'ke·ra] *m* Basque language

**eutanasia** [eu·ta·'na·sja] *f* euthanasia

**evacuación** [e·βa·kwa·'sjon, -'θjon] *f* evacuation

**evacuar** [e·βa·'kwar] *vt* (*ciudad*, *población*) to evacuate

**evadir** [e·βa·'dir] **I.** *vt* to avoid; (*peligro*) to avert **II.** *vr:* ~**se** to get away

**evaluación** [e·βa·lwa·'sjon, -'θjon] *f* valuation; ENS assessment

**evaluar** <1. *pres* evalúo> [e·βa·lu·'ar] *vt* to value; ENS to assess

**evangélico, -a** [e·βan·'xe·li·ko, -a] **I.** *adj* evangelical **II.** *m, f* evangelist

**evangelio** [e·βan·'xe·ljo] *m* Gospel

**evaporación** [e·βa·po·ra·'sjon, -'θjon] *f* evaporation

**evaporar** [e·βa·po·'rar] **I.** *vt* to evaporate **II.** *vr:* ~**se 1.** to evaporate **2.** (*desaparecer*) to vanish; (*persona*) to disappear into thin air

**evasión** [e·βa·'sjon] *f* evasion; ~ **de la realidad** escape from reality

**evasiva** [e·βa·'si·βa] *f* evasions; (*pretexto*) excuse

**evasivo, -a** [e·βa·'si·βo, -a] *adj* evasive; (*ambiguo*) non-committal

**evento** [e·'βen·to] *m* event; DEP meeting

**eventual** [e·βen·'twal] *adj* (*posible*) possible; (*accidental*) fortuitous; (*adicional*) extra

**eventualmente** [e·βen·twal·'men·te] *adv* fortuitously; (*tal vez*) possibly

**evidencia** [e·βi·'den·sja, -·θja] *f* evidence; **poner a alguien en ~** to make sb look bad

**evidenciar** [e·βi·den·'sjar, -'θjar] *vt* to show

**evidente** [e·βi·'den·te] *adj* evident; (*prueba*) manifest

**evidentemente** [e·βi·den·te·'men·te] *adv* evidently

**evitar** [e·βi·'tar] **I.** *vt* to avoid; (*prevenir*) to prevent **II.** *vr:* ~**se** to avoid; (*personas*) to avoid each other

**evocación** [e·βo·ka·'sjon, -'θjon] *f* evocation

**evocar** <c → qu> [e·βo·'kar] *vt* to evoke

**evolución** [e·βo·lu·'sjon, -'θjon] *f* 1. *t.* MED progress 2. (*cambio*) transformation 3. BIO evolution

**evolucionar** [e·βo·lu·sjo·'nar, -θjo·'nar] *vi* 1. (*desarrollarse*) to progress 2. (*cambiar*) to transform 3. MED to evolve

**ex** [eks] I. *adj* ex-; ~ **novia** ex-girlfriend II. *mf* ex

**exactitud** [ek·sak·ti·'tud] *f* (*precisión*) accuracy; (*veracidad*) exactitude

**exacto, -a** [ek·'sak·to, -a] *adj* 1. (*preciso*) accurate 2. (*correcto*) correct

**exageración** [ek·sa·xe·ra·'sjon, -'θjon] *f* exaggeration

**exagerado, -a** [ek·sa·xe·'ra·do, -a] I. *adj* exaggerated; (*precio*) steep II. *m, f* **¡eres un ~!** don't exaggerate!

**exagerar** [ek·sa·xe·'rar] *vi, vt* to exaggerate; **¡anda, anda, no exageres tanto!** come on, stop exaggerating!

**exaltación** [ek·sal·ta·'sjon, -'θjon] *f* enthusiasm

**exaltado, -a** [ek·sal·'ta·do, -a] *adj* overexcited; (*violento*) extreme

**exaltarse** [ek·sal·'tar·se] *vr* ~ **con algo** to become excited about sth

**examen** [ek·'sa·men] *m* 1. *t.* MED examination; ~ **de conducir** driving test; ~ **de ingreso** entrance exam; ~ **de selectividad** *university entrance exam*; **presentarse a un ~** to sit for an exam; **someterse a un ~ médico** to have a check-up 2. TÉC test; AUTO check

**examinador(a)** [ek·sa·mi·na·'dor, -·'do·ra] *m(f)* examiner

**examinar** [ek·sa·mi·'nar] I. *vt* 1. *t.* MED, ADMIN, JUR to examine; **para/al ~lo** for/upon examination 2. TÉC, AUTO to inspect II. *vr:* ~**se** to take an exam; **volver a ~se** to retake an exam

**exasperación** [ek·sas·pe·ra·'sjon, -'θjon] *f* exasperation

**exasperante** [ek·sas·pe·'ran·te] *adj* exasperating

**exasperar** [ek·sas·pe·'rar] I. *vt* to exasperate II. *vr:* ~**se** to get exasperated

**excarcelar** [es·kar·se·'lar, es·kar·θe·-] *vt* to release from prison

**excavación** [es·ka·βa·'sjon, -'θjon] *f* excavation; (*arqueológica*) dig

**excavadora** [es·ka·βa·'do·ra] *f* excavator

**excavar** [es·ka·'βar] *vt* to excavate; (*en arqueología*) to dig

**excedencia** [e·se·'den·sja, es·θe·'den·θja] *f* leave

**excedente** [e·se·'den·te, es·θe·-] *adj, m* surplus

**exceder** [e·se·'der, es·θe·-] I. *vi* to be greater; ~ **de algo** to exceed sth II. *vt* (*persona*) to outdo; (*cosa*) to be better than III. *vr:* ~**se** (*pasarse*) to go too far

**excelente** [e·se·'len·te, es·θe·-] *adj* excellent

**excentricidad** [e·sen·tri·si·'dad, es·θen·tri·θi-] *f* eccentricity

**excéntrico, -a** [e·'sen·tri·ko, -a; es·'θen-] *adj, m, f* eccentric

**excepción** [e·sep·'sjon, es·θeβ·'θjon] *f* exception; **de ~** unique; **a** [*o* **con**] ~ **de** with the exception of

**excepcional** [e·sep·sjo·'nal, es·θeβ·θjo-] *adj* exceptional; (*raro*) unusual

**excepto** [e·'sep·to, es·'θep-] *adv* except; **todos ~ yo** everybody except me

**excesivo, -a** [e·se·'si·βo, -a; es·θe·-] *adj* excessive

**exceso** [e·'se·so, -'θe·so] *m* 1. excess; ~ **de alcohol** excessive drinking; ~ **de capacidad** overcapacity; ~ **de equipaje/peso** excess baggage/weight; ~ **de velocidad** speeding; **en** ~ in excess 2. FIN surplus

**excitación** [e·si·ta·'sjon, es·θi·ta·'θjon] *f* excitement; (*sexual*) arousal

**excitar** [e·si·'tar, es·θi-] I. *vt* to incite; (*apetito*) to stimulate; (*sexualmente*) to arouse II. *vr:* ~**se** to become aroused

**exclamación** [es·kla·ma·'sjon, -'θjon] *f* 1. cry 2. LING exclamation; **signo de** ~ exclamation mark

**exclamar** [es·kla·'mar] *vi, vt* to exclaim

**excluir** [es·klu·'ir] *irr como huir vt* to exclude; (*descartar*) to rule out

**exclusión** [es·klu·'sjon] *f* 1. (*eliminación*) exclusion; **con ~ de** excluding 2. (*rechazo*) rejection

**exclusiva** [es·klu·'si·βa] *f* 1. (*privilegio*) sole rights *pl* 2. (*monopolio*) monopoly 3. PREN exclusive

E

**exclusivamente** [es·klu·si·βa·'men·te] *adv* exclusively

**exclusive** [es·klu·'si·βe] *adv* exclusively; **cerrado hasta el 27 de mayo ~** closed up to and including the 26th of May

**exclusivo, -a** [es·klu·'si·βo, -a] *adj* exclusive

**excremento** [es·kre·'men·to] *m* excretion

**exculpar** [es·kul·'par] *vt* to acquit

**excursión** [es·kur·'sjon] *f* excursion; **~ a pie** hike; **ir de ~** to go on an excursion

**excursionista** [es·kur·sjo·'nis·ta] *mf* (*turista*) tourist; (*para un día*) day-tripper; (*a pie*) hiker

**excusa** [es·'ku·sa] *f* 1. (*pretexto*) excuse 2. (*disculpa*) apology 3. (*justificación*) justification

**excusar** [es·ku·'sar] *vt* 1. (*justificar*) to justify 2. (*disculpar*) to excuse 3. (*eximir*) to let off

**exento, -a** [ek·'sen·to, -a] *adj* exempt; **~ de impuestos** tax free

**exfoliar** [es·fo·'ljar] I. *vt* to exfoliate II. *vr*: **~se** (*pintura*) to peel; (*corteza*) to flake

**exhalar** [ek·sa·'lar] *vt* to exhale; (*suspiro*) to let out

**exhaustivo, -a** [ek·saus·'ti·βo, -a] *adj* exhaustive; **de forma exhaustiva** thoroughly

**exhausto, -a** [ek·'saus·to, -a] *adj* exhausted

**exhibición** [ek·si·βi·'sjon, -'θjon] *f* exhibition; (*presentación*) show; **~ cinematográfica/deportiva** film/sports festival

**exhibicionismo** [ek·si·βi·sjo·'nis·mo, -θjo·'nis·mo] *m* indecent exposure

**exhibicionista** [ek·si·βi·sjo·'nis·ta, -θjo·'nis·ta] *mf* flasher

**exhibir** [ek·si·'βir] *vt* to exhibit; (*ostentar*) to show off

**exhumar** [ek·su·'mar] *vt* to exhume

**exigencia** [ek·si·'xen·sja, -θja] *f* 1. (*demanda*) demand 2. (*requisito*) requirement

**exigente** [ek·si·'xen·te] *adj* demanding

**exigir** <g → j> [ek·si·'xir] *vt* to demand

**exil(i)ado, -a** [ek·si·'la·do/ek·si·'lja·do, -a] I. *adj* exiled II. *m, f* exile

**exil(i)ar** [ek·si·'lar/ek·si·'ljar] I. *vt* to exile II. *vr*: **~se** to go into exile

**exilio** [ek·'si·ljo] *m* exile

**eximir** [ek·si·'mir] *vt* to exempt (**de** from)

**existencia** [ek·sis·'ten·sja, -θja] *f* 1. existence 2. *pl* stock

**existencial** [ek·sis·ten·'sjal, -'θjal] *adj* existential

**existir** [ek·sis·'tir] *vi* to exist, to be

**éxito** ['ek·si·to] *m* success; **con ~** successfully; **sin ~** without success; **tener ~** to be successful

**exitoso, -a** [ek·si·'to·so, -a] *adj* successful

**éxodo** ['ek·so·do] *m* exodus; **~ rural** rural depopulation

**exorbitante** [ek·sor·βi·'tan·te] *adj* excessive; (*precio*) exorbitant

**exótico, -a** [ek·'so·ti·ko, -a] *adj* exotic

**exotismo** [ek·so·'tis·mo] *m* exoticism

**expandir** [es·pan·'dir] I. *vt* to spread; (*dilatar*) to expand II. *vr*: **~se** to spread; (*dilatarse*) to expand

**expansión** [es·pan·'sjon] *f* expansion; POL enlargement

**expatriar** <1. pres expatrío> [es·pa·tri·'ar] *vt* to exile; (*quitar la ciudadanía*) to deprive of citizenship

**expectación** [es·pek·ta·'sjon, -'θjon] *f* 1. (*expectativa*) expectation; **con ~** expectantly 2. (*emoción*) excitement

**expectante** [es·pek·'tan·te] *adj* expectant

**expectativa** [es·pek·ta·'ti·βa] *f* 1. (*expectación*) expectation; **estar a la ~ de algo** to be on the lookout for sth 2. (*perspectiva*) prospect; **~ de vida** life expectancy

**expedición** [es·pe·di·'sjon, -'θjon] *f* 1. (*viaje, grupo*) expedition 2. (*remesa*) shipment; (*acción*) shipping 3. (*documento*) issue

**expediente** [es·pe·'djen·te] *m t.* ADMIN file; UNIV record; (*judicial*) proceedings *pl*

**expedir** [es·pe·'dir] *irr como pedir vt* to send; (*pedido*) to ship; (*documento*) to issue

**expeditar** [es·pe·di·'tar] *vt* 1. AmL (*acelerar*) to speed up 2. AmC, Méx (*despachar*) to send

**expendedor(a)** [es·pen·de·'dor, -·'do·ra] I. *adj* **máquina ~a de billetes/tabaco** ticket/cigarette vending machine

**II.** *m(f)* vendor; **~ automático** vending machine

**expendio** [es·'pen·djo] *m And, Méx, Ven* store

**expensas** [es·'pen·sas] *fpl* costs *pl;* **a ~ de** at the expense of; **vivir a ~ de alguien** to live off sb

**experiencia** [es·pe·'rjen·sja, -θja] *f* experience; (**falta de**) **~ laboral** (lack of) work experience; **saber algo por ~ propia** to know sth from experience; (*experimento*) experiment

**experimentado, -a** [es·pe·ri·men·'ta·do, -a] *adj* **1.** experienced **2.** (*probado*) tested; **no ~ en animales** not tested on animals

**experimental** [es·pe·ri·men·'tal] *adj* experimental

**experimentar** [es·pe·ri·men·'tar] **I.** *vi* to experiment **II.** *vt* **1.** (*sentir*) to experience **2.** (*hacer experimentos*) to experiment with; (*probar*) to test **3.** (*en estadísticas*) to register; **~ un aumento/una pérdida** to register an increase/a loss

**experimento** [es·pe·ri·'men·to] *m* experiment

**experto, -a** [es·'per·to, -a] *adj, m, f* expert; (*perito*) specialist

**expirar** [es·pi·'rar] *vi* to expire

**explanada** [es·pla·'na·da] *f* flat area

**explayarse** [es·pla·'jar·se] *vr* to speak at length; **~se con alguien** to talk openly to sb

**explicación** [es·pli·ka·'sjon, -'θjon] *f* **1.** (*aclaración*) explanation **2.** (*motivo*) reason; **dar explicaciones** to justify; **sin dar explicaciones** without giving any reason

**explicar** <c → qu> [es·pli·'kar] **I.** *vt* **1.** (*manifestar*) to tell **2.** (*aclarar*) to explain **3.** (*justificar*) to justify **II.** *vr:* **~se** **1.** (*disculparse*) to apologize **2.** (*expresarse*) to express oneself; **¿me explico?** do I make myself clear?; **no me lo explico** I don't understand it

**explicativo, -a** [es·pli·ka·'ti·βo, -a] *adj* explanatory

**explícito, -a** [es·'pli·si·to, -a; -θi·to, -a] *adj* explicit

**exploración** [es·plo·ra·'sjon, -'θjon] *f* exploration; MED examination

**explorador(a)** [es·plo·ra·'dor] *m(f)* explorer; MIL scout

**explorar** [es·plo·'rar] *vt* to explore; MED to analyze

**explosión** [es·plo·'sjon] *f* **1.** (*estallido*) explosion; **~ demográfica** population boom; **hacer ~** to explode **2.** (*detonación*) detonation; **~ fallida** dud **3.** (*arrebato*) outburst

**explosionar** [es·plo·sjo·'nar] *vi, vt* to explode

**explosivo, -a** [es·plo·'si·βo, -a] *adj, m, f* explosive

**explotación** [es·plo·ta·'sjon, -'θjon] *f* exploitation

**explotar** [es·plo·'tar] **I.** *vi* **1.** to explode **2.** (*persona*) to blow up *inf* **II.** *vt* to exploit; AGR to cultivate; (*empresa*) to manage

**exponente** [es·po·'nen·te] *m* example; MAT exponent

**exponer** [es·po·'ner] *irr como* poner **I.** *vt* **1.** (*mostrar*) to show **2.** (*hablar*) to set out **3.** (*exhibir*) to exhibit **4.** (*arriesgar*) to endanger **II.** *vr:* **~se** **1.** (*descubrirse*) to expose oneself **2.** (*arriesgarse*) to endanger oneself

**exportación** [es·por·ta·'sjon, -'θjon] *f* export

**exportador(a)** [es·por·ta·'dor, -·'do·ra] **I.** *adj* exporting **II.** *m(f)* exporter

**exportar** [es·por·'tar] *vt* to export

**exposición** [es·po·si·'sjon, -'θjon] *f* **1.** (*explicación*) explanation **2.** (*informe*) report **3.** (*exhibición*) exhibition; **~ universal** world('s) fair **4.** FOTO exposure

**exprés** [es·'pres] *adj, m inv* express; **olla ~** pressure cooker

**expresamente** [es·pre·sa·'men·te] *adv* **1.** (*literalmente*) clearly **2.** (*deliberadamente*) expressly

**expresar** [es·pre·'sar] **I.** *vt* to express **II.** *vr:* **~se** to express oneself

**expresión** [es·pre·'sjon] *f* expression

**expresionismo** [es·pre·sjo·'nis·mo] *m* expressionism

**expresionista** [es·pre·sjo·'nis·ta] *adj, mf* expressionist

**expresivo, -a** [es·pre·'si·βo, -a] *adj* expressive; (*afectuoso*) affectionate

**expreso, -a** [es·'pre·so, -a] *adj* express; (*claro*) clear; (**tren**) ~ express train; **enviar por** (**correo**) ~ to send by special delivery

**exprimidor** [es·pri·mi·'dor] *m* squeezer

**exprimir** [es·pri·'mir] *vt* (*fruta*) to squeeze; (*persona*) to bleed (dry)

**expropiación** [es·pro·pja·'sjon, -'θjon] *f* expropriation

**expropiar** [es·pro·'pjar] *vt* to expropriate

**expuesto, -a** [es·'pwes·to, -a] **I.** *pp de* **exponer II.** *adj* **1.** (*peligroso*) exposed **2.** (*sin protección*) exposed **3.** (*sensible*) vulnerable

**expulsar** [es·pul·'sar] *vt* to expel; (*del país*) to deport; (*excluir*) to bar

**expulsión** [es·pul·'sjon] *f* expulsion; (*del país*) deportation

**exquisitez** [es·ki·si·'tes, -'teθ] *f* exquisiteness; (*manjar*) delicacy

**exquisito, -a** [es·ki·'si·to, -a] *adj* exquisite; (*comida*) delicious

**éxtasis** ['eks·ta·sis] *m inv* ecstasy

**extender** <e → ie> [es·ten·'der] **I.** *vt* **1.** (*untar, alisar, propagar*) to spread **2.** (*desplegar*) to unfold; ~ **la mano** to reach out one's hand **3.** (*ensanchar*) to widen; (*agrandar*) to enlarge **II.** *vr:* ~**se 1.** to extend; ~**se por algo** to extend over sth **2.** (*prolongarse*) to last

**extendido, -a** [es·ten·'di·do, -a] *adj* **1.** (*amplio*) widespread; **estar muy** ~ to be very well-known **2.** (*prolongado*) long; (*detallado*) extensive **3.** (*mano, brazos*) outstretched

**extensible** [es·ten·'si·βle] *adj* extensible; **mesa** ~ folding table

**extensión** [es·ten·'sjon] *f* **1.** (*dimensión*) extent; (*longitud, duración*) length; **por** ~ by extension **2.** (*difusión*) spreading **3.** (*ampliación*) *t.* POL expansion **4.** TEL, ELEC extension

**extenso, -a** [es·'ten·so, -a] *adj* extensive

**extenuar** <*1. pres* extenúo> [es·te·nu·'ar] *vt* (*agotar*) to exhaust; (*debilitar*) to weaken

**exterior** [es·te·'rjor] **I.** *adj* **1.** external; (*aspecto*) external; (*espacio*) outer **2.** (*extranjero*) foreign; **Ministerio de Asuntos Exteriores** State Department

**II.** *m* exterior; **en el** ~ abroad

**exteriorizar** <z → c> [es·te·rjo·ri·'sar, -'θar] *vt* (*manifestar*) to show; (*revelar*) to reveal

**exteriormente** [es·te·rjor·'men·te] *adv* externally

**exterminar** [es·ter·mi·'nar] *vt* to exterminate

**exterminio** [es·ter·'mi·njo] *m* extermination

**externo, -a** [es·'ter·no, -a] *adj* external; **de uso** ~ external use only

**extinción** [es·tin·'sjon, -'θjon] *f* **1.** ECOL extinction; **en vías de** ~ threatened by extinction **2.** ~ **de incendios** fire extinguishing **3.** (*contrato*) termination

**extinguir** <gu → g> [es·tin·'gir] **I.** *vt* to terminate; (*apagar*) to extinguish **II.** *vr:* ~**se 1.** ECOL to become extinct; (*finalizar*) to be terminated **2.** (*apagarse*) to be extinguished

**extinto, -a** [es·'tin·to, -a] *adj* **1.** extinct; (*fuego*) extinguished **2.** *AmS, Méx* (*muerto*) deceased

**extintor** [es·tin·'tor] *m* ~ **de incendios** fire extinguisher

**extirpación** [es·tir·pa·'sjon, -'θjon] *f* extraction; (*de un miembro*) amputation

**extirpar** [es·tir·'par] *vt* to extract; (*miembro*) to amputate

**extorsión** [es·tor·'sjon] *f* extortion

**extorsionar** [es·tor·sjo·'nar] *vt* to extort; (*molestar*) to bother

**extra** ['eks·tra] **I.** *adj* extra; **horas** ~**s** overtime; **paga** ~ bonus **II.** *m* **1.** *t.* CINE, TV extra; (*en periódico, revista*) special supplement **2.** (*paga*) bonus **3.** (*ayudante*) helper

**extracción** [es·trak·'sjon, -'θjon] *f* removal; (*diente, mineral*) extraction; ~ **de sangre** drawing of blood

**extraconyugal** [es·tra·kon·ju·'ɣal] *adj* extramarital

**extracto** [es·'trak·to, -a] *m t.* QUÍM extract; (*resumen*) summary

**extractor** [es·trak·'tor] *m* ~ **de humo** exhaust fan

**extradición** [es·tra·di·'sjon, -'θjon] *f* extradition

**extraditar** [es·tra·di·'tar] *vt* to extradite

**extraer** [es·tra·'er] *irr como* traer *vt* to extract

**extraescolar** [es·tra·es·ko·'lar] *adj* extracurricular

**extralimitarse** [es·tra·li·mi·'tar·se] *vr* to go too far

**extranjería** [es·tran·xe·'ri·a] *f* **ley de ~** immigration law

**extranjero, -a** [es·tran·'xe·ro, -a] **I.** *adj* foreign **II.** *m, f* foreigner; (**en**) **el ~** abroad

**extrañar** [es·tra·'ɲar] **I.** *vt* **1.** (*sorprender*) to surprise **2.** (*echar de menos*) to miss **II.** *vr* **~se de algo** to find sth strange

**extrañeza** [es·tra·'ɲe·sa, -θa] *f* strangeness; **causar ~** to cause surprise

**extraño, -a** [es·'tra·ɲo, -a] **I.** *adj* (*raro*) strange; (*peculiar*) peculiar; (*extraordinario*) remarkable **II.** *m, f* stranger

**extraoficial** [es·tra·o·fi·'sjal, -'θjal] *adj* unofficial

**extraordinario, -a** [es·tra·or·di·'na·rjo, -a] *adj* extraordinary; (*muy bueno*) fantastic

**extrarradio** [es·tra·'rra·djo] *m* outskirts *pl*

**extrasensorial** [es·tra·sen·so·'rjal] *adj* extrasensory

**extraterrestre** [es·tra·te·'rres·tre] *adj, mf* extraterrestrial

**extravagancia** [es·tra·βa·'ɣan·sja, -θja] *f* eccentricity

**extravagante** [es·tra·βa·'ɣan·te] **I.** *adj* **1.** (*raro*) odd **2.** (*excéntrico*) eccentric **II.** *mf* eccentric

**extraviado, -a** [es·tra·βi·'a·do, -a] *adj* lost; (*animal*) stray

**extraviar** < *1. pres* extravío> [es·tra·βi·'ar] **I.** *vt* **1.** (*despistar*) to confuse **2.** (*perder*) to lose **II.** *vr:* **~se** to get lost; (*descarriarse*) to stray; *fig* to go astray

**extremado, -a** [es·tre·'ma·do, -a] *adj* (*excesivo*) excessive; (*exagerado*) extreme

**extremar** [es·tre·'mar] *vt* to carry to extremes; (*medidas de seguridad*) to tighten; **~ la prudencia** to be extremely cautious

**extremidad** [es·tre·mi·'dad] *f* limb

**extremismo** [es·tre·'mis·mo] *m* extremism; (*religioso*) fundamentalism

**extremista** [es·tre·'mis·ta] *adj, mf* extremist

**extremo** [es·'tre·mo] *m* (*cabo*) end; (*punto límite*) extreme; **con** [*o* **en**] **~ a lot**

**extremo, -a** [es·'tre·mo, -a] *adj* extreme; (*distante*) furthest

**extrínseco, -a** [es·'trin·se·ko, -a] *adj* extrinsic(al)

**extrovertido, -a** [es·tro·βer·'ti·do, -a] *adj* outgoing

**exuberancia** [ek·su·βe·'ran·sja, -θja] *f* exuberance

**exuberante** [ek·su·βe·'ran·te] *adj* exuberant; (*vegetación*) lush

**eyaculación** [e·ja·ku·la·'sjon, -'θjon] *f* ejaculation

**eyacular** [e·ja·ku·'lar] *vi* to ejaculate

# F

**F, f** ['e·fe] *f* F, f, F, f; **F de Francia** F as in Foxtrot

**fabada** [fa·'βa·da] *f* Asturian bean stew with pork sausage, blood sausage and pork chops

**fábrica** ['fa·βri·ka] *f* factory; **~ de cerveza** brewery; (*de ladrillo, piedra*) masonry; **en** [*o* **ex**] **~** direct from the factory

**fabricación** [fa·βri·ka·'sjon, -'θjon] *f* manufacturing; **~ en masa** mass production

**fabricante** [fa·βri·'kan·te] *mf* manufacturer

**fabricar** <c → qu> [fa·βri·'kar] *vt* to manufacture; **~ cerveza** to brew beer

**fábula** ['fa·βu·la] *f* fable; (*invención*) tale; **¡de ~!** terrific!

**fabuloso, -a** [fa·βu·'lo·so, -a] *adj* fabulous

**facción** [fak·'sjon, -'θjon] *f* **1.** POL faction **2.** *pl* (*facial*) features *pl*

**faceta** [fa·'se·ta, fa·'θe·] *f* facet; (*aspecto*) side

**faceto, -a** [fa·'se·to, -a] *adj* Méx **1.** (*chistoso*) facetious **2.** (*presuntuoso*) cocksure

**facha¹** ['fa·tʃa] *adj, mf* pey inf fascist

**facha²** ['fa·tʃa] *f* inf look; **estar hecho una ~** to look terrible

**fachada** [fa·'tʃa·da] *f* façade; **su buen humor es pura ~** his/her good mood is pure pretense

**facial** [fa·'sjal, -'θjal] *adj* facial

**fácil** ['fa·sil, -θil] *adj* **1.** (*simple*) easy; **es más ~ de decir que de hacer** *prov* easier said than done *prov* **2.** (*cómodo*) undemanding **3.** (*probable*) probable: **es ~ que** +*subj* it is likely that **4.** (*de seducir*) loose

**facilidad** [fa·si·li·'dad, fa·θi·-] *f* **1.** (*sin dificultad*) ease **2.** (*dotes*) facility; **tener ~ para algo** to have an ability for sth; (*idiomas*) to have a flair for languages **3. ~es de pago** payment arrangements *pl*; **ofrecer** [*o* **dar**] **~es a alguien para algo** to facilitate sth for sb

**facilitar** [fa·si·li·'tar, fa·θi·-] *vt* (*favorecer*) to facilitate; (*posibilitar*) to make possible; (*suministrar*) to supply

**fácilmente** [fa·sil·'men·te, fa·θil·-] *adv* easily; (*seguramente*) probably

**factible** [fak·'ti·βle] *adj* feasible

**factor** [fak·'tor] *m* factor; **~ de riesgo** risk factor

**factoría** [fak·to·'ri·a] *f* factory

**factura** [fak·'tu·ra] *f* (*cuenta*) bill; (*recibo*) receipt; **pasar ~** to render an account; **su holgazanería le pasa ahora ~** *inf* he/she is now having to pay the price for his/her idleness; **esta chaqueta es de buena ~** this jacket is well made

**facturación** [fak·tu·ra·'θjon, -'θjon] *f* AVIAT check-in

**facturar** [fak·tu·'rar] *vt* **1.** (*cobrar*) to bill; **~ los gastos de transporte** to bill for transport costs; **nuestra compañía factura tres millones de pesos al mes** our company is bringing in three million pesos a month **2.** (*ganar*) to earn **3. ~** (**el equipaje**) to check in

**facultad** [fa·kul·'tad] *f* **1.** *t.* UNIV faculty; *pl* faculties; **recobró sus ~es** he/she recovered his/her faculties **2.** (*atribuciones*) authority; **tener ~ para hacer algo** to have the authority to do sth; **conceder ~es a alguien** (**para hacer algo**) to authorize sb (to do sth); **este título me faculta para ejercer la abogacía** this qualification entitles me to practice law

**facultar** [fa·kul·'tar] *vt* to authorize

**faena** [fa·e·'na] *f* **1.** task; **~s domésticas** chores *pl* **2.** *inf* dirty trick; **hacer una ~**

**a alguien** to play a dirty trick on sb

**faenar** [fae·'nar] *vi* to work; (*pescar*) to fish

**faenero, -a** [fae·'ne·ro, -a] *m, f* *Chile* field worker

**failear** [fai·le·'ar] *vt* AmC, RíoPl (*documentos*) to file; (*en una carpeta*) to put in a folder

**faisán** [fai·'san] *m* pheasant

**faja** ['fa·xa] *f* corset

**fajada** [fa·'xa·da] *f* **1.** Ant (*ataque*) attack **2.** Arg inf (*paliza*) beating **3.** Ven (*chasco*) disappointment

**fajar** [fa·'xar] **I.** *vt* AmL (*golpear*) to strike **II.** *vr:* **~se** AmL (*pelearse*) to fight

**fajilla** [fa·'xi·ja, -ʎa] *f* AmL wrapper

**fajo** ['fa·xo] *m* bundle; **~ de billetes** wad of bills

**falange** [fa·'lan·xe] *f* phalanx

**falda** ['fal·da] *f* **1.** skirt; **~ pantalón** culottes; **~ plisada** pleated skirt; **~ tubo/recta** straight skirt **2.** (*regazo*) lap **3.** (*de la mesa*) table cover **4.** (*de una montaña*) lower slope

**faldeo** [fal·'deo] *m* Arg, Chile mountainside

**faldero** [fal·'de·ro] *m* womanizer; **perro ~** lapdog

**fálico, -a** ['fa·li·ko, -a] *adj* phallic

**falla** ['fa·ja, -ʎa] *f t.* GEO fault

**fallar** [fa·'jar, -'ʎar] *vi* **1.** to go wrong; (*proyecto*) to fail; (*plan, intento*) to miscarry; **le ~on los nervios** his/her nerves failed him/her; **algo le falla** there is sth wrong with him/her; **no falla nunca** (*cosa*) it never fails; (*persona*) you can always count on her/him; **~ a alguien** to let sb down; (*en una cita*) to stand sb up **2.** JUR to render judgment

**fallecer** [fa·je·'ser, -ʎe·'θer] *irr como crecer vi* to pass away

**fallecido, -a** [fa·je·'si·do, -a; -ʎe·'θi·do, -a] *adj, m, f* deceased

**fallecimiento** [fa·je·si·'mjen·to, -ʎe·θi·'mjen·to] *m* death

**fallido, -a** [fa·'ji·do, -a; fa·'ʎi·-] *adj* (*proyecto*) unsuccessful; (*intento*) abortive; (*deuda*) bad

**fallo** ['fa·jo, -ʎo] *m* **1.** error; (*fracaso*) failure; **~ humano** human error; **este asunto solo tiene un pequeño ~** this

F

matter only has one small shortcoming; TÉC breakdown **2.** JUR sentence **3.** ~ **cardíaco/renal** heart/kidney failure

**falluto, -a** [fa·'ʝu·to, -a; fa·'ʎu-] *adj RíoPl inf* unreliable; (*falso*) two-faced

**falopa** [fa·'lo·pa] *f Arg, Urug inf* drugs *pl*

**falopero, -a** [fa·lo·'pe·ro, -a] *m, f Arg, Urug inf* addict

**falsear** [fal·se·'ar] *vt* to misrepresent; (*verdad*) to distort; (*falsificar*) to counterfeit

**falsedad** [fal·se·'dad] *f* falseness; (*hipocresía*) hypocrisy

**falsificación** [fal·si·fi·ka·'sjon, -'θjon] *f* forgery; ~ **de billetes** counterfeiting of banknotes

**falsificador(a)** [fal·si·fi·ka·'dor, -'do·ra] *m(f)* forger; (*de billetes*) counterfeiter

**falsificar** <c → qu> [fal·si·fi·'kar] *vt* to falsify; (*verdad*) to distort

**falso, -a** [fal·so] *adv* en ~ (*falsamente*) falsely; **jurar en** ~ to commit perjury; **coger a alguien en** ~ to catch sb out [*o* in a lie]; **dar un golpe en** ~ (*movimiento*) to miss the mark; **dar un paso en** ~ (*tropezar*) to stumble; (*equivocarse*) to make a mistake; **sonar** ~ to ring false

**falso, -a** [fal·so, -a] **I.** *adj* false; (*no natural*) artificial **II.** *m, f* liar; (*hipócrita*) hypocrite

**falta** [fal·ta] *f* **1.** (*carencia*) lack; (*ausencia*) absence; ~ **de dinero** shortage of money; ~ **de educación** lack of education; **echar en** ~ to miss; **hacer** ~ to need; **me hace** ~ **dinero** I need money; **¡ni** ~ **que hace!** there is absolutely no need! **2.** (*fallo*) error; ~ **ortográfica** spelling error; **sin** ~**s** with no mistakes; **sin** ~ without fail **3.** DEP foul **4.** JUR default

**faltar** [fal·'tar] *vi* **1.** (*no estar*) to be missing; (*persona*) to be absent; ~ **a clase** to miss class; ~ **a una cita** not to turn up to an appointment; **me faltan mis llaves** my keys are missing **2.** (*necesitarse*) ~ (**por**) **hacer** to be still to be done; **nos falta dinero para...** we do not have enough money to...; **me faltan diez céntimos** I'm ten cents short; **me falta tiempo para hacerlo** I need time to do it; **no falta quien...** there is always sb

who...; **falta** (**por**) **saber si...** we need to know if...; **¡no** ~**ía** [*o* faltaba] **más!** that is the limit!; (*respuesta a agradecimiento*) you are welcome!; (*asentir amablemente*) of course!; **por si algo faltaba...** as if it were not enough already...; **¡lo que faltaba!** that is the last straw! **3.** (*temporal: quedar*) to be left; **faltan cuatro días para tu cumpleaños** your birthday is in four days; **falta poco para las doce** it is nearly twelve o'clock; **faltan diez para las nueve** AmL it is ten to nine; **poco le faltó para llorar** he/she was on the verge of tears **4.** (*no cumplir*) ~ **a una promesa** to break a promise; **nunca falta a su palabra** he/she never goes back on his/her word **5.** (*ofender*) ~ **a alguien** to be disrespectful to sb

**falto, -a** [fal·to, -a] *adj* (*escaso*) ~ **de algo** short of sth; (*desprovisto*) lacking in sth; ~ **de recursos** lacking in resources; ~ **de cariño** lacking affection

**faltón, -ona** [fal·'ton, -·'to·na] *adj inf* **1.** fly-by-night **2.** AmL do-nothing

**fama** [fa·ma] *f* **1.** fame; (*gloria*) glory; **tener** ~ to be famous; **dar** ~ **a algo/alguien** to make sth/sb famous; **unos tienen la** ~ **y otros cardan la lana** *prov* some do all the work while others reap all the glory *prov* **2.** (*reputación*) reputation; **tener** ~ **de...** to have a reputation of being...; **ser de mala** ~ to have a bad reputation

**familia** [fa·'mi·lja] *f* family; (*parentela*) relatives *pl;* ~ **numerosa** large family; **cabeza de** ~ head of the household; ~ **política** in-laws *pl; de buena* ~ from a good family; **eso viene de** ~ that runs in the family; **en** ~ with the family; **ser de la** ~ to be one of the family; **acordarse de la** ~ **de alguien** *inf* to insult sb

**familiar** [fa·mi·'ljar] **I.** *adj* **1.** (*íntimo*) intimate; **asunto** ~ personal matter; **economía** ~ domestic economy **2.** (*conocido*) familiar **II.** *mf* relative

**familiaridad** [fa·mi·lja·ri·'dad] *f* familiarity; (*confianza*) intimacy

**familiarizarse** <z → c> [fa·mi·lja·ri·'sar·se, -'θar·se] *vr* to familiarize oneself (**con** with)

**famoso, -a** [fa·'mo·so, -a] *adj* famous; (*sonado*) talked-of; **~ por algo** famous for sth

**fan** [fan] *mf* <fans> fan

**fanático, -a** [fa·'na·ti·ko, -a] **I.** *adj* fanatical **II.** *m, f* fan; *pey* fanatic; **es una fanática del rock** she is crazy about rock

**fanatismo** [fa·na·'tis·mo] *m* fanaticism

**fané** [fa·'ne] *adj AmL inf* (*arrugado*) crumpled; (*marchito*) withered

**fanfarrón, -ona** [fan·fa·'rron, -·'rro·na] **I.** *adj* swanky **II.** *m, f* swank

**fanfarronear** [fan·fa·rro·ne·'ar] *vi inf* to brag

**fango** ['fan·go] *m* mud

**fantasear** [fan·ta·se·'ar] *vi* to fantasize; (*presumir*) to boast

**fantasía** [fan·ta·'si·a] *f* imagination; (*cosa imaginada*) fantasy; **¡déjate de ~s!** come down to earth!

**fantasioso, -a** [fan·ta·'sjo·so, -a] **I.** *adj* **1.** (*inventado*) fanciful **2.** (*fachendoso*) swanky *inf* **II.** *m, f* show-off

**fantasma** [fan·'tas·ma] *m* **1.** ghost; (*visión*) phantom; **andar como un ~** to be lifeless; **aparecer como un ~** to appear out of nowhere **2.** *inf* boaster

**fantasmada** [fan·tas·'ma·da] *f inf* pose

**fantasmagórico, -a** [fan·tas·ma·'ɣo·ri·ko, -a] *adj* phantasmagorical; TEAT with optical illusion

**fantasmal** [fan·tas·'mal] *adj* phantom

**fantasmón, -ona** [fan·tas·'mon, -·'mo·na] *inf* **I.** *adj* presumptuous **II.** *m, f* show-off

**fantástico, -a** [fan·'tas·ti·ko, -a] *adj* fantastic

**fantochada** [fan·to·'tʃa·da] *f* **1.** (*fantasmada*) pose **2.** (*tontería*) silly act

**fantoche** [fan·'to·tʃe] *m* **1.** (*títere*) puppet **2.** (*mamarracho*) sight

**FAO** ['fao] *f abr de* **Organización para la Agricultura y la Alimentación** FAO

**faramallear** [fa·ra·ma·je·'ar, -ʎe·'ar] *vi Chile, Méx* to brag

**faraón** [fa·ra·'on] *m* Pharaoh

**fardar** [far·'dar] *vi inf* to boast; (*impresionar*) to make an impression

**fardo** ['far·do] *m* package; (*de tela*) bundle

**fardón, -ona** [far·'don, -·'do·na] *adj inf* **1.** (*chulo*) swanky **2.** (*vistoso*) showy; (*coche*) flashy

**farfullar** [far·fu·'jar, -'ʎar] *inf* **I.** *vi* to stutter **II.** *vt* to botch

**faringe** [fa·'rin·xe] *f* pharynx

**faringitis** [fa·rin·'xi·tis] *f inv* pharyngitis

**fariña** [fa·'ri·ɲa] *f AmS* coarse cassava flour

**farmacéutico, -a** [far·ma·'seu·ti·ko, -a; far·ma·'θeu-] **I.** *adj* pharmaceutical; **industria farmacéutica** pharmaceutical industry; **productos ~s** pharmaceutical products **II.** *m, f* druggist

**farmacia** [far·'ma·sja, -'θja] *f* **1.** (*tienda*) drugstore; **~ de guardia** ≈ 24-hour drugstore **2.** (*ciencia*) pharmacy

**fármaco** ['far·ma·ko] *m* drug

**farmacodependencia** [far·ma·ko·de·pen·'den·sja, -'θja] *f* drug dependence

**faro** ['fa·ro] *m* **1.** AUTO headlight; **~ antiniebla** fog light **2.** NÁUT lighthouse

**farol** [fa·'rol] *m* **1.** (*lámpara*) lamp; (*de calle*) streetlight **2.** *inf* (*fanfarronada*) swank; (*patraña*) tall story; **tirarse un ~** to show off **3.** *pl AmL* eyes; **¡adelante con los ~es!** *inf* go for it!

**farola** [fa·'ro·la] *f* street light; (*poste*) lamppost

**farolazo** [fa·ro·'la·so] *m AmC, Méx* swig of liquor

**farolear** [fa·ro·le·'ar] *vi* to swank

**farolero, -a** [fa·ro·'le·ro, -a] *inf* **I.** *adj* bragging **II.** *m, f* show-off

**farrear** [fa·rre·'ar] *inf* **I.** *vi CSur* to paint the town red **II.** *vr*: **~se** *RíoPl* (*dinero*) to blow *inf*

**farrista** [fa·'rris·ta] *adj, mf CSur* fun-loving

**farruto, -a** [fa·'rru·to, -a] *adj Bol, Chile* puny

**farsa** ['far·sa] *f* sham

**farsante** [far·'san·te] **I.** *adj* sham **II.** *mf* charlatan

**FAS** [fas] *fpl* MIL *abr de* **Fuerzas Armadas** the (armed) forces

**fascículo** [fa·'si·ku·lo, fas·'θi-] *m* installment

**fascinación** [fa·si·na·'sjon, fas·θi·na·'θjon] *f* fascination; **sentir ~ por algo** to be fascinated by sth

**fascinador(a)** [fa·si·na·'dor, -·'do·ra, fas·θi-], **fascinante** [fas·θi·'nan·te] adj fascinating; (persona) captivating; (libro) enthralling

**fascinar** [fa·si'nar, fas·θi-] vi, vt to fascinate; (libro) enthrall

**fascismo** [fa·'sis·mo, fas·'θis-] m fascism

**fascista** [fa·'sis·ta, fas·'θis-] I. adj fascist(ic) II. mf fascist

**fase** ['fa·se] f phase

**fast food** [fas fud] m o f fast food

**fastidiado, -a** [fas·ti·'dja·do, -a] adj inf 1. (enfermo) unwell 2. (molesto) annoyed 3. (estropeado) broken; **andar ~ de...** to have a bad...; **ando ~ de dinero/tiempo estos días** I don't have enough money/time these days; **anda ~ de la rodilla** he has a bad knee

**fastidiar** [fas·ti·'djar] inf I. vt 1. (molestar) to annoy; **¡no te fastidia!** you must be kidding! 2. (estropear) ruin II. vr: **~se** 1. (enojarse) to get cross 2. (aguantarse) to put up with it; **¡fastídiate!** get lost!; **¡hay que ~se!** it's unbelievable! 3. AmL (perjudicarse) to harm

**fastidio** [fas·'ti·djo] m 1. (disgusto) bother; **¡vaya ~!** what a nuisance!; (mala suerte) misfortune 2. (aburrimiento) bore

**fastidioso, -a** [fas·ti·'djo·so, -a] adj 1. (molesto) annoying 2. (aburrido) boring 3. (pesado) dull

**fatal** [fa·'tal] I. adj 1. (inevitable) unavoidable; **el momento ~** the fateful moment 2. (muy mal) awful 3. (funesto) fatal; (mortal) mortal; **mujer ~** femme fatale II. adv inf awfully; **el examen me fue ~** my exam was a disaster

**fatalidad** [fa·ta·li·'dad] f misfortune

**fatídico, -a** [fa·'ti·di·ko, -a] adj (terrible) horrible

**fatiga** [fa·'ti·ya] f 1. weariness, fatigue; **~ visual** eye strain 2. pl hardship

**fatigado, -a** [fa·ti·'ya·do, -a] adj worn-out; (sofocado) short of breath

**fatigar** <g → gu> [fa·ti·'yar] I. vt to tire, to fatigue; (molestar) to annoy II. vr: **~se** 1. (agotarse) to wear oneself out; (ojos) to strain 2. (esforzarse) to ex-

ert oneself 3. (sofocarse) to get short of breath

**fatigoso, -a** [fa·ti·'yo·so, -a] adj tiring; (persona) tiresome

**fauces** ['fau·ses, -θes] fpl 1. fauces pl 2. AmL (dientes) teeth

**fauna** ['fau·na] f fauna

**favela** [fa·'βe·la] f 1. AmL shanty 2. pl shanty town

**favor** [fa·'βor] m 1. (servicio) favor; (ayuda) good turn; **por ~** please; **hacer un ~ a alguien** to do sb a favor; **¡hágame el ~ de dejarme en paz!** would you please leave me alone!; **te lo pido por ~** I am begging you; **hagan el ~ de ser puntuales** please be punctual 2. (gracia) favor; **a [o en] ~ de alguien** in sb's favor; **tener a alguien a tu ~** to have sb on your side; **a ~ del viento/de la corriente** with the wind/the current 3. (beneficio) **voto a ~** vote for; **votar a ~ de alguien** to vote for sb; **estar a ~ de algo** to be in favor of sth

**favorable** [fa·βo·'ra·βle] adj favorable; (optimista) promising

**favorecer** [fa·βo·re·'ser, -'θer] irr como **crecer** I. vt 1. (beneficiar) to benefit 2. (ayudar) to help 3. (dar preferencia) to favor 4. (ropa) to become II. vr: **~se** to benefit

**favorecido, -a** [fa·βo·re·'si·do, -a; -'θi·do, -a] adj favored; **has salido ~ en la foto** you came out well in the photo

**favoritismo** [fa·βo·ri·'tis·mo] m nepotism; (parcialidad) favoritism

**favorito, -a** [fa·βo·'ri·to, -a] I. adj favorite; **plato ~** favorite dish II. m, f **~ del público** the public's darling; DEP (the) favorite

**fax** [faks] m inv fax; **mandar un ~ a una empresa/a Suecia** to send a fax to a company/to Sweden

**fayuca** [fa·'ju·ka] f Méx inf black market; **tabaco de ~** contraband tobacco

**fayuquero, -a** [fa·ju·'ke·ro, -a] m, f Méx inf smuggler

**faz** [fas, faθ] f countenance

**fe** [fe] f t. REL faith; **~ en Dios** faith in God; **digno de ~** worthy of trust; **dar ~ a algo/alguien** to vouch for sth/sb; **dar ~ de algo** to certify sth; **tener ~**

**en alguien** to believe in sb; **de buena/mala ~** in good/bad faith; **~ de erratas** errata

**fealdad** |feal·'dad| *f* ugliness

**feb.** *abr de* **febrero** Feb.

**febrero** |fe·'βre·ro| *m* February; *v. t.* **marzo**

**febril** |fe·'βril| *adj* feverish; *(actividad)* hectic; **acceso ~** sudden temperature

**fecal** |fe·'kal| *adj* fecal; **sustancias ~es** fecal matter

**fecha** |'fe·tʃa| *f (data) t.* ECON date; *(señalada)* day; **~ de caducidad** expiration date; *(de comida)* sell-by date; **~ de cierre** closing date; **~ clave** decisive day; **~ de las elecciones** Election day; **~ de entrega** date of delivery; **~ límite** [o **tope**] deadline; **sin ~** undated; **en la ~ fijada** on the agreed day; **hasta la ~** until now, so far; **adelantar/atrasar la ~ de algo** to bring forward/put back the date of sth; **¿cuál es la ~ de hoy?** what is the date today?; **a 30 días ~** at 30 days' sight; **en estas ~s** around this time

**fechable** |fe·'tʃa·βle| *adj* datable

**fechado, -a** |fe·'tʃa·do, -a| *adj* **~ el...** dated...

**fechar** |fe·'tʃar| *vt* to date

**fechoría** |fe·tʃo·'ri·a| *f* prank; JUR misdemeanor

**fécula** |'fe·ku·la| *f* starch

**fecundación** |fe·kun·da·'sjon, -'θjon| *f* fertilization

**fecundar** |fe·kun·'dar| *vt* to fertilize

**fecundidad** |fe·kun·di·'dad| *f* fertility; *(abundancia)* abundance

**fecundo, -a** |fe·'kun·do, -a| *adj* prolific; *(tierra)* fertile; *(campo)* productive

**federación** |fe·de·ra·'sjon, -'θjon| *f* federation

**federado, -a** |fe·de·'ra·do, -a| *adj* federate

**federal** |fe·de·'ral| **I.** *adj* federal; **estado ~** federal state; **república ~** federal republic **II.** *mf* federalist

**federalismo** |fe·de·ra·'lis·mo| *m* federalism

**federalizar** <z → c> |fe·de·ra·li·'sar, -'θar| **I.** *vt* to federalize **II.** *vr:* **~se** to form a federation

**federar** |fe·de·'rar| **I.** *vt* to unite; *(federa-lizar)* to federate **II.** *vr:* **~se** to become a member; *(federalizarse)* to form a federation

**federativo, -a** |fe·de·ra·'ti·βo, -a| *adj* federative

**felación** |fe·la·'sjon, -'θjon| *f* fellatio

**felicidad** |fe·li·si·'dad, fe·li·θi-| *f* happiness; *(dicha)* good fortune; **¡~es!** congratulations!; *(cumpleaños)* happy birthday; **te deseamos muchas ~es** we wish you all the best

**felicitación** |fe·li·si·ta·'sjon, -θi·ta·'θjon| *f* congratulation; *(tarjeta)* greetings card

**felicitar** |fe·li·si·'tar, fe·li·θi-| **I.** *vt* **~ a alguien por algo** to congratulate sb on sth **II.** *vr* **~se por algo** to be glad about sth

**felino, -a** |fe·'li·no, -a| *adj* feline

**feliz** |fe·'lis, -'liθ| *adj* happy; *(exitoso)* fortunate; **¡~ Navidad!** merry Christmas!; **¡~ viaje!** have a good trip!

**felpa** |'fel·pa| *f* plush

**felpeada** |fel·pe·'a·da| *f Arg, Urug, CSur inf* dressing-down

**felpudo** |fel·'pu·do| *m* doormat

**femenino** |fe·me·'ni·no| *m* feminine

**femenino, -a** |fe·me·'ni·no, -a| *adj* **1. equipo ~** women's team **2.** *(afemi-nado)* effeminate **3.** LING feminine

**feminidad** |fe·mi·ni·'dad| *f* femininity

**feminismo** |fe·mi·'nis·mo| *m* feminism; *(movimiento)* feminist movement

**feminista** |fe·mi·'nis·ta| *adj, mf* feminist

**fémur** |'fe·mur| *m* femur

**fenomenal** |fe·no·me·'nal| *adj (extraordi-nario)* incredible; *(estupendo)* terrific

**fenómeno** |fe·'no·me·no| **I.** *adj inv inf* marvelous; **¡~!** terrific! **II.** *m* **1.** *t.* FILOS, MED phenomenon; *(maravilla)* marvel **2.** *(genio)* genius **III.** *adv* marvelously

**feo** |'feo| **I.** *m inf* insult; **hacer un ~ a alguien** to snub sb **II.** *adv AmL* bad, badly

**feo, -a** |'feo, -a| **I.** *adj* **1.** ugly; **dejar ~ a alguien** to show sb up; **la cosa se está poniendo fea** things aren't looking too good **2.** *(malo)* bad; **está muy ~ lo que hiciste** what you did was nasty **II.** *m, f* ugly man, ugly woman *m, f,* ugly child *mf*

**féretro** |'fe·re·tro| *m* coffin

**feria** [ˈferja] f **1.** (*exposición, verbena*) fair; ~ **de muestras** trade fair **2.** (*fiesta*) festival; **puesto de** ~ stand

**feriado, -a** [feˈrjaðo, -a] adj AmL holiday; **día** ~ bank holiday

**ferial** [feˈrjal] **I.** adj fair; **recinto** ~ trade fair pavilion **II.** m fair; (*lugar*) fairground

**feriante** [feˈrjante] mf (*que exhibe*) exhibitor; (*en la verbena*) stall holder; (*que compra*) fairgoer

**fermentación** [fermentaˈsjon, -ˈθjon] f fermentation

**fermentar** [fermenˈtar] vi, vt to ferment

**fermento** [ferˈmento] m fermenting agent

**ferocidad** [ferosiˈðað, feroθi-] f ferocity; (*crueldad*) savagery

**feroz** [feˈros, -ˈroθ] adj fierce; (*cruel*) savage

**férreo, -a** [ˈferreo, -a] adj iron

**ferretería** [ferreteˈria] f hardware store

**ferrocarril** [ferrokaˈrril] m railroad; **por** ~ by rail

**ferrocarrilero, -a** [ferrokarriˈlero, -a] adj AmL inf railroad; **el transporte** ~ rail transport

**ferroviario, -a** [ferroˈβjarjo, -a] **I.** adj railroad **II.** m, f railroad worker

**ferry** [ˈferri] m ferry

**fértil** [ˈfertil] adj fertile; **estar en edad** ~ to be of reproductive age

**fertilidad** [fertiliˈðað] f fertility; (*tierra*) productiveness

**fertilización** [fertilisaˈsjon, -θaˈθjon] f fertilization; ~ **in vitro** in vitro fertilization

**fertilizante** [fertiliˈsante, -ˈθante] m fertilizer

**fertilizar** <z → c> [fertiliˈsar, -ˈθar] vt to fertilize

**ferviente** [ferˈβjente] adj fervent

**fervor** [ferˈβor] m fervor; (*entusiasmo*) enthusiasm; **con** ~ ardently

**festejar** [festeˈxar] vt **1.** to celebrate **2.** AmL (*azotar*) to beat

**festejo** [fesˈtexo] m **1.** celebration **2.** pl public festivities pl

**festín** [fesˈtin] m celebration; (*banquete*) feast

**festinar** [festiˈnar] vt AmC **1.** (*agasajar*) to wine and dine **2.** (*arruinar*) to ruin

**3.** (*apremiar*) to hasten

**festival** [festiˈβal] m festival; ~ **de cine** film festival

**festividad** [festiβiˈðað] f festivity; (*día*) feast

**festivo, -a** [fesˈtiβo, -a] adj **1.** festive; **día** ~ bank holiday **2.** (*humorístico*) humorous; (*persona*) witty

**feta** [ˈfeta] f Arg slice

**fetal** [feˈtal] adj fetal

**fetiche** [feˈtitʃe] m fetish

**fetichismo** [fetiˈtʃismo] m fetishism

**fétido, -a** [ˈfetiðo, -a] adj foul smelling

**feto** [ˈfeto] m fetus

**feúcho, -a** [feˈutʃo, -a] adj inf plain

**feudal** [feuˈðal] adj feudal

**feudalismo** [feuðaˈlismo] m **1.** (*sistema*) feudalism **2.** (*época*) feudal era

**fiabilidad** [fjaβiliˈðað] f **1.** (*persona*) trustworthiness **2.** (*empresa, datos*) reliability

**fiable** [fiˈaβle] adj **1.** (*persona*) trustworthy **2.** (*empresa*) reliable

**fiaca** [fiˈaka] f Arg inf laziness

**fiambre** [fiˈambre] m **1.** CULIN cold meat **2.** inf stiff

**fiambrera** [fjamˈbrera] f (*cesta*) picnic basket; (*para el almuerzo*) lunch pail; (*táper*) Tupperware® container

**fianza** [fiˈansa, -θa] f **1.** (*depósito*) deposit **2.** (*garantía*) security **3.** **en libertad bajo** ~ free on bail

**fiar** <1. pres fío> [fiˈar] **I.** vi **1.** (*al vender*) to give credit **2.** (*confiar*) to trust; **es de** ~ he/she is trustworthy **II.** vt **1.** (*garantizar*) to stand surety for **2.** (*dar crédito*) to sell on credit **3.** (*confiar*) to entrust **III.** vr ~**se de algo/alguien** to trust sth/sb; **no te fíes de lo que dice** don't trust what he/she says

**fiasco** [ˈfjasko] m fiasco

**fibra** [ˈfiβra] f **1.** t. BIO, MED fiber; ~ **muscular** muscle fiber; ~ **de vidrio** fiberglass **2.** (*vigor*) energy; **no tiene** ~ **suficiente para llevar la empresa** he/she doesn't have the drive to run the business

**ficción** [fikˈsjon, -ˈθjon] f **1.** (*simulación*) simulation **2.** (*invención*) invention; LIT, CINE fiction

**ficha** [ˈfitʃa] f **1.** (*de ruleta*) chip; (*de do-*

*minó*) domino; (*de ajedrez*) piece; (*para una máquina*) token **2.** (*tarjeta*) card; ~ **policial** police record; ~ **técnica** technical specifications

**fichaje** [fi·'tʃa·xe] *m* signing (up)

**fichar** [fi·'tʃar] **I.** *vi* **1.** DEP to sign **2.** (*en el trabajo*) to clock in **II.** *vt* **1.** (*registrar*) to enter; **estar fichado** to have a police record; ~ **a alguien** to open a file on sb **2.** DEP to sign up

**fichero** [fi·'tʃe·ro] *m* filing-cabinet; (*caja*) box file; COMPUT file

**ficticio, -a** [fik·'ti·sjo, -a; -θjo, -a] *adj* fictitious

**fidedigno, -a** [fi·de·'diɣ·no, -a] *adj* reliable

**fidelidad** [fi·de·li·'dad] *f* **1.** (*lealtad*) fidelity, faithfulness **2.** (*precisión*) precision; **alta** ~ high fidelity

**fideo** ['fi·deo] *m* fine noodle

**fiebre** ['fje·βre] *f* fever; ~ **del heno** hay fever; ~ **del juego** compulsive gambling; ~ **del oro** gold rush; ~ **palúdica** malaria; **tener** ~ to have a fever; **tener poca** ~ to have a slight temperature

**fiel** [fjel] **I.** *adj* (*persona, retrato*) faithful; (*memoria*) accurate; **ser** ~ **a una promesa** to keep a promise; **siempre me han sido** ~**es** they have always been loyal to me **II.** *m* **los** ~**es** the faithful

**fieltro** ['fjel·tro] *m* felt

**fiera** ['fje·ra] *f* wild animal; (*persona*) animal; (*astuto*) wizard

**fiero, -a** ['fje·ro, -a] *adj* fierce; (*cruel*) cruel

**fierro** ['fje·rro] *m* AmL iron

**fiesta** ['fjes·ta] *f* **1.** (*día*) holiday; **¡Felices Fiestas!** Merry Christmas and a Happy New Year! **hoy hago** ~ I have taken the day off today **2.** (*celebración*) celebration; ~ (**mayor**) festival; **aguar la** ~ to be a wet blanket; **tengamos la** ~ **en paz** let's agree to differ

**fifí** [fi·'fi] *m* AmL playboy

**fifiriche** [fi·fi·'ri·tʃe] *adj* AmL weak

**fig.** [fi·ɣu·ra·'ti·βo] *abr de* **figurado** fig

**figura** [fi·'ɣu·ra] *f* **1.** *t.* ARTE, MAT figure; **las grandes** ~**s del deporte** great sports figures; **un vestido que realza la** ~ a dress that enhances the figure **2.** (*cara, mueca*) face; (*aspecto*) counte-

nance **3.** (*imagen*) image; **se distinguía la** ~ **de un barco** you could make out the shape of a boat

**figurado, -a** [fi·ɣu·'ra·do, -a] *adj* figurative; **en sentido** ~ in a figurative sense; (*lenguaje*) metaphorical

**figurar** [fi·ɣu·'rar] **I.** *vi* **1.** (*encontrarse*) to figure; **no figura en la lista** it is not on the list; **figura en el puesto número tres** he appears in third place **2.** (*destacar*) to stand out **3.** (*aparentar*) to pose; **le gusta un montón** ~ he loves putting on airs **II.** *vt* **1.** (*representar*) to represent **2.** TEAT to appear **3.** (*simular*) to pretend **III.** *vr*: ~**se** to imagine; **¡figúrate!** just think!; **no vayas a** ~**te que...** don't go thinking that...

**figuroso, -a** [fi·ɣu·'ro·so, -a] *adj* Chile, Méx loud-dressing

**fijación** [fi·xa·'sjon, -'θjon] *f* *t. fig* fixation; **tener una** ~ **por alguien** to have a fixation on sb; (*precio, regla*) fixing; (*mirada*) fixedness

**fijador** [fi·xa·'dor] *m* **1.** (*para el pelo*) hair gel **2.** (*de pintura*) fixative **3.** FOTO fixer

**fijar** [fi·'xar] **I.** *vt* **1.** QUÍM to fix; (*residencia, precio*) to establish; ~ **con chinchetas** to stick up with drawing pins; ~ **una placa en la pared** to fix a plaque on the wall; **prohibido** ~ **carteles** bill posters prohibited; ~ **la atención en algo** to concentrate on sth **II.** *vr*: ~**se 1.** (*en un lugar*) to establish oneself **2.** (*atender*) to pay attention; **no se ha fijado en mi nuevo peinado** he/she has not noticed my new hairdo; **ese se fija en todo** nothing escapes him; **fíjate bien en lo que te digo** listen carefully to what I have to say **3.** (*mirar*) to notice; **no se fijó en mí** he/she did not notice me

**fijo, -a** ['fi·xo, -a] **I.** *adj* stable; (*cliente*) regular; (*idea, precio*) fixed; (*mirada*) steady; (*trabajador*) permanent **II.** *adv* with certainty; **saber algo de** ~ to know sth for sure

**fila** ['fi·la] *f* **1.** *t.* MAT row; ~ **de coches** line of cars; **en** ~ **india** in single file; **aparcar en doble** ~ to double-park; **en** ~ in line; **salir de la** ~ to step out of line **2.** MIL rank; **llamar a** ~**s** to draft **3.** *pl* (*de un partido*) ranks *pl*

**filántropo** [fi·'lan·tro·po, -a] *m* philanthropist

**filarmónico, -a** [fi·lar·'mo·ni·ko, -a] *adj* Philharmonic

**filatelia** [fi·la·'te·lja] *f* philately

**filete** [fi·'le·te] *m* filet; (*solomillo*) steak

**filetear** [fi·le·te·'ar] *vt* to filet

**filial** [fi·'ljal] I. *adj* filial II. *f* subsidiary

**film(e)** ['fil·m(e)] *m* film, movie; **~ transparente** plastic wrap

**filmar** [fil·'mar] *vt* to film

**filo** ['fi·lo] *m* 1. (*de cuchillo*) blade; **un arma de dos ~s** a double-edged sword 2. (*entre dos partes*) dividing line 3. *AmC* (*hambre*) hunger

**filología** [fi·lo·lo·'xi·a] *f* philology; **~ hispánica** Hispanic language and literature

**filólogo, -a** [fi·'lo·lo·ɣo, -a] *m, f* philologist

**filoso, -a** [fi·'lo·so, -a] *adj AmL* sharp

**filosofía** [fi·lo·so·'fi·a] *f* philosophy; **tomar las cosas con ~** to be philosophical about things

**filosófico, -a** [fi·lo·'so·fi·ko, -a] *adj* philosophical

**filósofo, -a** [fi·'lo·so·fo, -a] *m, f* philosopher

**filtrar** [fil·'trar] I. *vi* to leak; (*luz*) to filter II. *vt* to filter; (*llamadas*) to screen; (*datos*) to leak; (*noticia*) to percolate III. *vr*: **~se** (*líquido*) to seep; (*luz*) to filter; (*noticia*) to percolate; (*dinero*) to dwindle

**filtro** ['fil·tro] *m* 1. filter; **cigarrillo con ~** filter tip cigarette; **~ solar** sunscreen 2. (*poción*) philter

**filudo, -a** [fi·'lu·do, -a] *adj AmL* sharp

**fin** [fin] *m* 1. (*término*) end; **~ de semana** weekend; **a ~(es) de mes** at the end of the month; **algo toca a su ~** sth is coming to an end; **poner ~ a algo** to put an end to sth; **sin ~** never-ending; **al ~ y al cabo a ~ de cuentas** after all 2. (*propósito*) aim; **~es deshonestos** immoral purposes; **a ~ de que** +*subj* so that

**finado, -a** [fi·'na·do, -a] *m, f* deceased

**final** [fi·'nal] I. *adj* (*producto, resultado*) end; (*fase, examen*) final; (*solución*)

ultimate II. *m* 1. end; (*libro, película*) ending; **película con ~ feliz** film with a happy ending; **al ~ no nos lo dijo** in the end he/she did not tell us 2. (*partido*) final; (*ronda*) finals *pl*

**finalidad** [fi·na·li·'dad] *f* purpose

**finalista** [fi·na·'lis·ta] *mf* finalist

**finalización** [fi·na·li·sa·'sjon, -θa·'θjon] *f* finalization; **~ de contrato** completion of a contract

**finalizar** <z → c> [fi·na·li·'sar, -'θar] I. *vi* to finish; (*plazo*) to end II. *vt* to end; (*discurso*) to conclude

**finalmente** [fi·nal·'men·te] *adv* finally

**financiación** [fi·nan·sja·'sjon, -θja·'θjon] *f* financing, funding; **~ de los partidos** political party financial backing

**financiador(a)** [fi·nan·sja·'dor, --'do·ra, fi·nan·θja-] *m(f)* financial backer

**financiar** [fi·nan·'sjar, -'θjar] *vt* to finance

**financiero, -a** [fi·nan·'sje·ro, -a; -'θje·ro, -a] I. *adj* financial II. *m, f* financier

**financista** [fi·nan·'sis·ta] *mf AmL* financial expert; (*financiador*) financier

**finanzas** [fi·'nan·sas, -θas] *fpl* finance

**finca** ['fin·ka] *f* (*urbana*) (town) property; (*rústica*) (country) estate

**finés, -esa** [fi·'nes] I. *adj* Finnish II. *m, f* Finn

**fingido, -a** [fin·'xi·do, -a] *adj* fake, make-believe; (*persona*) false

**fingir** <g → j> [fin·'xir] *vi, vt* to pretend; (*sentimiento*) to feign

**finiquitar** [fi·ni·ki·'tar] *vt* 1. (*cuenta*) to settle 2. *inf* (*asunto*) to wind up

**finiquito** [fi·ni·'ki·to] *m* settlement; (*documento*) final discharge

**finito, -a** [fi·'ni·to, -a] *adj* finite

**finlandés, -esa** [fin·lan·'des] I. *adj* Finnish II. *m, f* Finn

**Finlandia** [fin·'lan·dja] *f* Finland

**fino, -a** ['fi·no, -a] *adj* 1. (*delgado*) fine 2. (*liso*) smooth 3. (*de calidad*) excellent; (*oro*) refined; (*metal*) precious; (*sentido*) acute; (*paladar*) discriminating 4. (*cortés*) polite; **modales ~s** refined manners 5. (*astuto*) shrewd

**finolis** [fi·'no·lis] *inv inf* I. *adj* la-di-da II. *mf* affected person

**finura** [fi·'nu·ra] *f* 1. (*delgadez*) fineness 2. (*suavidad*) smoothness 3. (*calidad*)

**F**

excellence **4.** (*cortesía*) refinement **5.** (*astucia*) shrewdness

**firma** ['fir·ma] *f* **1.** (*en documentos*) signature **2.** (*de un acuerdo*) signing **3.** (*empresa*) firm

**firmamento** [fir·ma·'men·to] *m* firmament

**firmante** [fir·'man·te] *mf* signatory; **el/la abajo ~** the undersigned

**firmar** [fir·'mar] *vi, vt* to sign; **~ autógrafos** to sign autographs; **~ un cheque** (*para pagar*) to sign a check; (*para cobrar*) to endorse a check; **~ un tratado/un acuerdo** to sign a treaty/an agreement

**firme** ['fir·me] **I.** *adj* (*fijo*) firm; (*estable*) steady; (*seguro*) secure; (*recto*) straight; (*carácter*) resolute; (*amistad*) strong; **con mano ~** with a firm hand; **esta mesa no está ~** this table is unsteady; **es ~ en sus propósitos** he/she is resolute in his/her intentions **II.** *m* road surface **III.** *adv* **de ~** (*fuertemente*) strongly; (*sin parar*) steadily; **el calor aprieta de ~** the heat is intense

**firmeza** [fir·'me·sa, -θa] *f* **1.** solidity; (*mueble*) sturdiness; (*creencia*) firmness; **~ de carácter** resolution **2.** (*perseverancia*) perseverance

**fiscal** [fis·'kal] **I.** *adj* fiscal; (*de impuestos*) tax **II.** *mf* public prosecutor; **Fiscal General del Estado** Attorney General

**fiscalidad** [fis·ka·li·'dad] *f* taxation

**fisgar** <g → gu> [fis·'ɣar] *vi* **~ en algo** to snoop around sth

**fisgón, -ona** [fis·'ɣon, --'ɣo·na] *m, f* nosy parker

**fisgonear** [fis·ɣo·ne·'ar] *vi* **~ en algo** to pry into sth

**física** ['fi·si·ka] *f* physics *pl*

**físicamente** [fi·si·ka·'men·te] *adv* physically

**físico** ['fi·si·ko] *m* physique

**físico, -a** ['fi·si·ko, -a] **I.** *adj* physical; **educación física** physical education **II.** *m, f* physicist

**fisiología** [fi·sjo·lo·'xi·a] *f* physiology

**fisionomía** [fi·sjo·no·'mi·a] *f* v. **fisonomía**

**fisioterapeuta** [fi·sjo·te·ra·'peu·ta] *mf* physiotherapist

**fisioterapia** [fi·sjo·te·'ra·pja] *f* physiotherapy

**fisonomía** [fi·so·no·'mi·a] *f* physiognomy *form*, features *pl*

**fisura** [fi·'su·ra] *f* **1.** crack **2.** MED hairline fracture; (*en el ano*) fissure

**flác(c)ido, -a** ['flak·si·do, -a; 'flaɣ·θi·do, -a] *adj* (*carnes*) flabby; (*piel*) flaccid

**flaco, -a** ['fla·ko, -a] *adj* thin; **punto ~** weak spot

**flacucho, -a** [fla·'ku·tʃo, -a] *adj* skinny

**flamante** [fla·'man·te] *adj inf* flamboyant; **nuevo ~** brand-new

**flamenco** [fla·'men·ko] *m* **1.** ZOOL flamingo **2.** (*cante, baile*) flamenco **3.** (*lengua*) Flemish

**flan** [flan] *m* crème caramel

**flaquear** [fla·ke·'ar] *vi* **1.** (*fuerzas*) to flag; (*salud*) to decline; (*ánimo*) to lose heart; (*demanda*) to slacken **2.** (*en un examen*) to be poor

**flash** [flaʃ] *m inv* flash

**flato** ['fla·to] *m* **1.** **tener ~** to have a stitch **2.** *AmC* melancholy

**flatoso, -a** [fla·'to·so, -a] *adj AmL* apprehensive

**flatulencia** [fla·tu·'len·sja, -θja] *f* flatulence

**flauta** ['flau·ta] *f* (*dulce*) recorder; (*travesera*) flute

**flecha** ['fle·tʃa] *f* arrow

**flechazo** [fle·'tʃa·so, -θo] *m* **1.** (*de flecha*) arrow shot **2.** (*de amor*) love at first sight

**fleco** ['fle·ko] *m* **1.** fringe **2.** *pl* frayed edges *pl*

**flema** ['fle·ma] *f* **1.** (*calma*) imperturbability **2.** (*mucosidad*) phlegm

**flemón** [fle·'mon] *m* conjunctivitis; (*dental*) gumboil

**flequillo** [fle·'ki·jo, -ʎo] *m* fringe

**fleta** ['fle·ta] *f* *AmC* **1.** (*friega*) rubbing **2.** (*zurra*) thrashing; (*castigo*) spanking

**fletar** [fle·'tar] **I.** *vt* **1.** (*avión*) to charter **2.** COM to freight **3.** *AmL* (*vehículo*) to rent **4.** *CSur* (*despedir*) to fire **II.** *vr:* **~se** *AmC* to get annoyed

**flete** ['fle·te] *m* *AmL* (*tarifa*) hire charge

**flexibilidad** [flek·si·βi·li·'dad] *f* flexibility; (*músculo*) suppleness

**flexible** [flek·'si·βle] *adj* flexible; (*múscu-*

*lo*) supple; **horario** ~ flextime

**flexión** [flek·'sjon] *f* flexion

**flexionar** [flek·sjo·'nar] *vt* to flex

**flexo** ['flek·so] *m* flexible table lamp

**flipado, -a** [fli·'pa·do, -a] *adj* freaked; (*drogado*) stoned

**flipante** [fli·'pan·te] *adj* far-out; (*drogas*) mind-bending

**flipar** [fli·'par] *inf* **I.** *vt* **este actor me flipa** I love this actor **II.** *vi, vr:* **~se** (*drogarse*) to be spaced-out

**flojear** [flo·xe·'ar] *vi* to diminish; (*calor*) to ease up; **~ en algo** to be poor at sth

**flojera** [flo·'xe·ra] *f inf* (*debilidad*) weakness; (*pereza*) slackness

**flojo, -a** ['flo·xo, -a] *adj* **1.** (*vino, café, argumento*) weak; (*cuerda*) slack; (*nudo*) loose; (*viento*) light; **estoy ~ en inglés** I am weak in English **2.** *AmL* (*cobarde*) cowardly

**flor** [flor] *f* **1.** BOT flower; (*planta*) flowering plant; **estar en ~** to be in flower [*o* bloom]; **camisa de ~es** flowery shirt; **la ~ de la vida** the prime of life; **la ~ y nata de la sociedad** the cream of society; **la ~ de la canela** *fig* the best **2.** (*piropo*) compliment **3.** (*nivel*) **pasó volando a ~ de tierra** the plane skimmed over the ground; **tengo los nervios a ~ de piel** my nerves are frayed

**flora** ['flo·ra] *f* flora

**florear** [flo·re·'ar] *vi AmL* to flower

**florecer** [flo·re·'ser, -'θer] *irr como crecer* **I.** *vi* to flower, to bloom; (*industria*) to flourish **II.** *vr:* **~se** to grow mold

**floreciente** [flo·re·'sjen·te, -'θjen·te] *adj* flowering; (*industria*) flourishing

**florecimiento** [flo·re·si·'mjen·to, -θi·'mjen·to] *m* flowering; (*industria*) flourishing

**florería** [flo·re·'ri·a] *f CSur, Bol, Perú* florist's

**florero** [flo·'re·ro] *m* vase; (*maceta*) flowerpot

**florido, -a** [flo·'ri·do, -a] *adj* flowery

**florista** [flo·'ris·ta] *mf* florist

**floristería** [flo·ris·te·'ri·a] *f* florist's

**flota** ['flo·ta] *f* fleet

**flotador** [flo·ta·'dor] *m* **1.** float; (*para niños*) rubber ring **2.** *RíoPl inf* roll of fat

**flotar** [flo·'tar] *vi* (*activamente*) to stay afloat; (*pasivamente*) to be suspended; (*en el aire*) to float

**fluctuación** [fluk·twa·'sjon, -'θjon] *f* **1.** fluctuation **2.** (*irresolución*) uncertainty

**fluidez** [flwi·'des, -'deθ] *f* fluidity; **hablar con ~** to speak fluently

**fluido, -a** ['flwi·do, -a] *adj* **1.** (*líquido*) fluid; (*expresión*) fluent **2.** ELEC current

**fluido** ['flwi·do] *m* **1.** (*líquido*) fluid; (*expresión*) fluent **2.** ELEC current

**fluir** [flu·'ir] *irr como huir* *vi* to flow; (*correr*) to run

**flujo** ['flu·xo] *m* **1.** flow; **~ menstrual** menstrual flow; **~ de datos** data flow; **~ de palabras** stream of words **2.** MED discharge

**flúor** ['fluor] *m* fluorine

**fluorescente** [flwo·re·'sen·te, -'θen·te] **I.** *adj* fluorescent; **tubo ~** fluorescent tube **II.** *m* fluorescent light

**fluvial** [flu·'βjal] *adj* fluvial; **puerto ~** river port

**FM** [e·'fe·me/e·fe·'e·me] *f abr de* **Frecuencia Modulada** FM

**FMI** [e·fe·m·e·'i] *m abr de* **Fondo Monetario Internacional** IMF

**fobia** ['fo·βja] *f* aversion; MED phobia

**foca** ['fo·ka] *f* **1.** seal **2.** *pey* whale

**focalizar** <z → c> [fo·ka·li·'sar, -'θar] *vt* to focus on

**foco** ['fo·ko] *m* **1.** Fís, MAT focus **2.** (*centro*) focal point; **~ de infección** source of infection **3.** (*lámpara*) light; (*en estadio*) floodlight; (*en teatro*) spotlight **4.** *AmL* (*bombilla*) light bulb

**fofo, -a** ['fo·fo, -a] *adj* flabby

**fogaje** [fo·'ɣa·xe] *m Arg, Col, PRico, Ven* stifling heat

**fogata** [fo·'ɣa·ta] *f* bonfire

**fogón** [fo·'ɣon] *m* **1.** (*cocina*) stove **2.** *AmL* (*fogata*) fire

**fogueado, -a** [fo·ɣe·'a·do, -a] *adj AmL* expert

**fogueo** [fo·'ɣeo] *m* **bala de ~** blank (cartridge)

**foguerear** [fo·ɣe·re·'ar] *vt Chile, Cuba* to burn off

**F**

**foja** ['fo·xa] *f AmL* sheet; ~ **de servi-cios** record

**folclor(e)** [fol·'klor, -·'klo·re] *m* folklore

**folclórico, -a** [fol·'klo·ri·ko, -a] *adj* folk

**fólder** ['fol·der] *f AmL* folder

**folio** ['fo·ljo] *m* sheet (of paper); (*de un libro*) leaf

**folk** [folk] *m* folk music

**follaje** [fo·'ja·xe, fo·'ʎa-] *m* foliage

**follar** [fo·'jar, -·'ʎar] *vi, vt, vr:* ~**se** to fuck; (*suspender*) to screw up

**folletín** [fo·je·'tin, fo·ʎe-] *m* newspaper serial; **novela de** ~ pulp novel

**folleto** [fo·'je·to, fo·'ʎe-] *m* pamphlet; ~ **publicitario** advertising leaflet

**follón** [fo·'jon, -·'ʎon] *m inf* ruckus; (*lío*) trouble; **armar un** ~ to cause a com-motion

**fome** ['fo·me] *adj Arg, Chile* boring

**fomentar** [fo·men·'tar] *vt* (*empleo*) to promote; (*economía*) to boost; (*discor-dias*) to foment

**fomento** [fo·'men·to] *m* (*empleo*) pro-motion; (*economía*) boosting; (*discor-dias*) fueling

**fondeado, -a** [fon·de·'a·do, -a] *adj AmL* well-heeled

**fondo** ['fon·do] *m* **1.** (*río*) bed; (*valle*) bottom; (*edificio*) depth; **los bajos ~s** the underworld; **tocar** ~ to hit bottom; **al** ~ **del pasillo** at the end of the cor-ridor; **al** ~ **de la casa** at the back of the house; **en el** ~ **de su corazón** in his/her heart of hearts; **en este asunto hay mar de** ~ there are underlying issues in this matter **2.** (*lo esencial*) essence; **artículo de** ~ editorial; **en el** ~ at bot-tom; **ir al** ~ **del asunto** to go to the heart of the matter; **tratar un tema a** ~ to seriously discuss a subject; **hay un** ~ **de verdad en lo que dices** there is sth of truth in what you say **3.** (*de un cuadro*) background; **ruido/música de** ~ background noise/music **4.** DEP long-distance; **corredor de** ~ long-distance runner; **esquiador de** ~ cross-country skier **5.** FIN, POL fund; ~ **común** kitty; **Fondo Monetario Internacional** In-ternational Monetary Fund; **a** ~ **per-dido** non-recoverable **6.** *pl* funds *pl*; ~**s públicos** public funds; **cheque sin**

~**s** bad check

**fonema** [fo·'ne·ma] *m* phoneme

**fonética** [fo·'ne·ti·ka] *f* phonetics *pl*

**fonología** [fo·no·lo·'xi·a] *f* phonology

**fontanería** [fon·ta·ne·'ri·a] *f* plumbing; (*establecimiento*) plumber's

**fontanero, -a** [fon·ta·'ne·ro, -a] *m, f* plumber

**footing** ['fu·tin] *m* jogging; **hacer** ~ to jog

**forajido, -a** [fo·ra·'xi·do, -a] **I.** *adj* out-lawed **II.** *m, f* outlaw

**foráneo, -a** [fo·'ra·neo, -a] *adj* (*de fuera*) outside; (*extraño*) alien

**forastero, -a** [fo·ras·'te·ro, -a] **I.** *adj* (*de fuera*) outside; (*extranjero*) foreign; (*ex-traño*) alien **II.** *m, f* stranger; (*extran-jero*) foreigner

**forcejear** [for·se·xe·'ar, for·θe-] *vi* **1.** (*es-forzarse*) to struggle **2.** (*resistir*) to resist

**forcejeo** [for·se·'xeo, for·θe-] *m* **1.** (*es-fuerzo*) struggle **2.** (*resistencia*) re-sistance

**forense** [fo·'ren·se] **I.** *adj* forensic; **mé-dico** ~ forensic surgeon **II.** *mf* pa-thologist

**forestal** [fo·res·'tal] *adj* forest; **camino** ~ forest track; **repoblación** ~ reforesta-tion; **guarda** ~ forest ranger

**forja** ['for·xa] *f* **1.** (*fragua*) forge **2.** (*ferre-ría*) ironworks *pl* **3.** (*creación*) forging

**forjar** [for·'xar] **I.** *vt* (*fraguar, crear*) to forge; (*inventar*) to invent **II.** *vr:* ~**se** to shape; ~ **ilusiones** to build castles in the air

**forma** ['for·ma] *f* **1.** (*figura*) form, shape; **en** ~ **de gota** in the shape of a drop; **dar** ~ **a** to shape **2.** (*manera*) way; ~ **de comportamiento** demeanor; ~ **de pago** method of payment; **defecto de** ~ JUR defect of form; **de** ~ **libre** freely; **en** ~ **escrita** written; **en** (**buena y**) **debida** ~ duly; **de** ~ **que** so that; **de todas ~s,...** anyway,...; **lo haré de una** ~ **u otra** I will do it one way or another; **no hay** ~ **de abrir la puerta** this door is impossible to open **3.** (*comporta-miento*) manners *pl* **4.** **en** ~ fit; **en baja** ~ off form

**formación** [for·ma·'sjon, -·'θjon] *f*

**1.** (*creación*) creation; GEO formation; **~ de humo** forming of smoke **2.** *t.* MIL (*de personas*) formation; **~ política** political group **3.** (*educación*) education; **~ escolar/de adultos** school/adult education; **~ profesional** vocational training

**formal** [for·'mal] *adj* **1.** (*de la forma*) formal; **requisito ~** formal requirement **2.** (*serio*) serious; (*educado*) educated; (*cumplidor*) reliable **3.** (*oficial*) official; **una invitación ~** a formal invitation; **tiene novio ~** she has a steady boyfriend

**formalidad** [for·ma·li·'ðað] *f* **1.** (*seriedad*) seriousness; (*exactitud*) correctness **2.** *pl* formalities *pl*

**formalizar** <z → c> [for·ma·li·'sar, -'θar] **I.** *vt* **1.** *t.* JUR to formalize; **~ un contrato/una solicitud** to formalize a contract/motion **2.** (*solemnizar*) to solemnize; **~ un noviazgo** (*comprometerse*) to become engaged **II.** *vr:* **~se 1.** (*formarse*) to be formalized **2.** (*volverse formal*) to grow up

**formar** [for·'mar] **I.** *vt* **1.** to form; **~ parte de** to form part of **2.** (*educar*) to train; (*enseñar*) to teach **II.** *vr:* **~se 1.** (*crearse, hacerse*) to form; **~se una idea de algo** to form an impression of sth **2.** (*educarse*) to be educated; **se ha formado a sí mismo** he is self-taught **3.** (*desarrollarse*) to develop

**formatear** [for·ma·te·'ar] *vt* to format

**formato** [for·'ma·to] *m* format; (*tamaño*) size; **~ de datos/texto** data/text format; **~ vertical** vertical format

**formidable** [for·mi·'ða·βle] *adj* **1.** (*estupendo*) fantastic **2.** (*enorme*) enormous **3.** (*temible*) awesome

**fórmula** ['for·mu·la] *f* **1.** formula; **coche de ~ 1** Formula One car **2.** AmL MED prescription

**formular** [for·mu·'lar] *vt* **1.** to formulate; (*demanda*) to file; (*denuncia*) to lodge **2.** MAT, FÍS to express with a formula **3.** AmL (*recetar*) to prescribe

**formulario** [for·mu·'la·rjo] *m* form; (*de fórmulas*) formulary; (*de recetas*) recipe book

**fornicar** <c → qu> [for·ni·'kar] *vi* to forni-

cate; (*adulterio*) to commit adultery

**fornido, -a** [for·'ni·do, -a] *adj* well-built

**foro** ['fo·ro] *m* **1.** (*plaza, internet, romano*) forum **2.** TEAT upstage area

**forofo, -a** [fo·'ro·fo, -a] *m, f* fan

**forrar** [fo·'rrar] **I.** *vt* (*exterior, pared*) to face; (*interior, prenda*) to line; (*butaca*) to upholster; (*libro*) to cover **II.** *vr:* **~se** *inf* to make a packet

**forro** ['fo·rro] *m* **1.** (*exterior, pared*) facing; (*interior, prenda*) lining; (*butaca*) upholstery; (*libro*) cover; **ni por el ~** at all **2.** AmL *inf* rubber

**fortachón, -ona** [for·ta·'tʃon, -·'tʃo·na] *adj inf* beefy

**fortalecer** [for·ta·le·'ser, -'θer] *irr como crecer* **I.** *vt* **1.** (*vigorizar*) to invigorate **2.** (*animar*) to encourage **3.** (*reforzar*) to fortify **II.** *vr:* **~se** to become stronger; (*vigorizarse*) to fortify oneself

**fortaleza** [for·ta·'le·sa, -θa] *f* **1.** (*fuerza*) strength **2.** (*virtud*) fortitude **3.** (*robustez*) robustness **4.** MIL fortress

**fortificación** [for·ti·fi·ka·'sjon, -'θjon] *f* strengthening; MIL fortification

**fortísimo, -a** [for·'ti·si·mo, -a] *adj superl de* **fuerte**

**fortuito, -a** [for·'twi·to, -a/for·tu·'i·to, -a] *adj* fortuitous

**fortuna** [for·'tu·na] *f* (*suerte, capital*) fortune; (*destino*) fate; **por ~** fortunately; (*por casualidad*) luckily; **probar ~** to try one's luck

**forzado, -a** [for·'sa·do, -a; -'θa·do, -a] *adj* (*artificial*) forced; **trabajos ~s** hard labor

**forzar** [for·'sar, -'θar] *irr* **I.** *vt* **1.** (*obligar, esforzar*) to force; (*voz*) to strain; (*puerta, ventana*) to force open; (*acontecimiento*) to bring about **2.** (*violar*) to rape **II.** *vr:* **~se 1.** (*obligarse*) to force oneself **2.** (*esforzarse*) to push oneself

**forzosamente** [for·so·sa·'men·te, for·θo-] *adv* (*inevitablemente*) unavoidably; (*obligatoriamente*) necessarily

**forzoso, -a** [for·'so·so, -a; for·'θo·so, -a] *adj* forced; **aterrizaje ~** forced landing; **venta forzosa** forced sale

**forzudo, -a** [for·'su·do, -a; for·'θu·do, -a] *adj* strong

**fosa** ['fo·sa] *f* **1.** pit; MIL, GEO trench; **~**

**séptica** septic tank **2.** (*sepultura*) grave; **~ común** common grave **3.** ANAT fossa; **~ nasal** nostril

**fosforescente** [fos·fo·re·'sen·te, -res·'θen·te] *adj* phosphorescent; **pintura ~** luminous paint

**fósforo** ['fos·fo·ro] *m* match; QUÍM phosphorus

**fósil** ['fo·sil] *adj, m* fossil

**foso** ['fo·so] *m* **1.** hole; (*alargado*) ditch; MIL trench **2.** MÚS, TEAT orchestra pit

**foto** ['fo·to] *f* photo

**fotocopia** [fo·to·'ko·pja] *f* photocopy

**fotocopiadora** [fo·to·ko·pja·'do·ra] *f* photocopier

**fotocopiar** [fo·to·ko·'pjar] *vt* to photocopy

**fotogénico, -a** [fo·to·'xe·ni·ko, -a] *adj* photogenic

**fotografía** [fo·to·γra·'fi·a] *f* **1.** photograph; **~ aérea** aerial photograph; **~ en color** color photograph; **~ (tamaño) carnet** passport photograph; **álbum de ~s** photo(graph) album **2.** (*arte*) photography

**fotografiar** <*1. pres* fotografío> [fo·to·γra·fi·'ar] **I.** *vi, vt* to photograph **II.** *vr:* **~se** to have one's picture taken

**fotográfico, -a** [fo·to·'γra·fi·ko, -a] *adj* photographic; **máquina fotográfica** camera; **papel ~** photographic paper

**fotógrafo, -a** [fo·to·γra·fo, -a] *m, f* photographer

**fotograma** [fo·to·'γra·ma] *m* **1.** CINE still **2.** FOTO photogram

**fotomatón** [fo·to·ma·'ton] *m* photo booth; (*mecanismo*) photo automaton

**fotomontaje** [fo·to·mon·'ta·xe] *m* photomontage

**fotosíntesis** [fo·to·'sin·te·sis] *f inv* photosynthesis

**FP** [e·fe·'pe] *f abr de* **Formación Profesional** vocational training, technical education

**frac** [frak] *m* <*fracs o fraques*> tails *pl*

**fracasar** [fra·ka·'sar] *vi* to fail; **~ en un examen** to fail an exam; **la película fracasó** the film was a flop

**fracaso** [fra·'ka·so] *m* **1.** (*acción*) failure **2.** (*fiasco*) fiasco **3.** (*desastre*) disaster

**fracción** [frak·'sjon, -'θjon] *f* **1.** (*división*)

division; (*ruptura*) rupture; (*de una cantidad*) splitting up **2.** (*parte*) t. MAT, QUÍM fraction; (*de un objeto*) fragment; (*de una organización*) splinter group; **~ parlamentaria** parliamentary faction

**fractura** [frak·'tu·ra] *f* break; GEO fault; MED fracture; **~ simple/complicada** closed/compound fracture

**fragancia** [fra·'γan·sja, -θja] *f* fragrance; (*perfume*) perfume; (*vino*) bouquet

**fragata** [fra·'γa·ta] *f* frigate

**frágil** ['fra·xil] *adj* fragile; (*constitución, salud*) delicate; (*anciano*) frail; (*carácter*) weak

**fragilidad** [fra·xi·li·'dad] *f* fragility; (*constitución, salud*) delicacy; (*anciano*) frailty; (*carácter*) weakness

**fragmentación** [fraγ·men·ta·'sjon, -'θjon] *f* fragmentation; (*en muchos pedazos*) breaking up; (*cristal*) shattering

**fragmentar** [fraγ·men·'tar] **I.** *vt* to fragment; (*en muchos pedazos*) to break up; (*romper*) to break; (*roca*) to split **II.** *vr:* **~se** (*cristal*) to shatter; (*roca*) to split

**fragmento** [fraγ·'men·to] *m* t. LIT, MÚS fragment; (*cristal*) splinter; (*roca*) chip; (*tejido*) remnant; (*papel*) scrap

**fragua** ['fra·γwa] *f* forge

**fraile** ['frai·le] *m* friar

**frambuesa** [fram·'bwe·sa] *f* raspberry

**francés, -esa** [fran·'ses, --'se·sa; -'θes, --'θe·sa] **I.** *adj* French; **tortilla francesa** plain omelet **II.** *m, f* Frenchman, Frenchwoman *m, f*

**Francia** ['fran·sja, -θja] *f* France

**franco, -a** ['fran·ko, -a] *adj* **1.** (*sincero*) frank **2.** (*generoso*) generous **3.** (*libre*) free; **puerto ~** free port; **~ a bordo** free on board; **~ de derechos** duty-free; **~ en fábrica** ex-factory **4.** (*claro*) patent

**francotirador(a)** [fran·ko·ti·ra·'dor, --'do·ra] *m(f)* sniper

**franela** [fra·'ne·la] *f* **1.** flannel **2.** AmL T-shirt

**franelear** [fra·ne·le·'ar] *vi* Arg, Urug *inf* to pet

**franja** ['fran·xa] *f* **1.** (*guarnición*) border **2.** (*tira*) strip; **~ horaria** time zone

**franquear** [fran·ke·'ar] *vt* **1.** (*carta*) to pay postage on; **a ~ en destino** postage paid at destination **2.** (*abrir*) to clear; **~**

**el paso** to open the way; (*río*) to cross; (*obstáculo*) to get around **3.** (*conceder*) to grant

**franqueo** [fraŋ·'keo] *m* **1.** (*sellos*) postage; **sin ~** without stamps **2.** (*acción: de una carta*) franking; (*de una salida*) opening

**franqueza** [fraŋ·'keˑsa, -ɵa] *f* **1.** (*sinceridad*) frankness; **admitir algo con ~** to openly admit sth **2.** (*generosidad*) generosity **3.** (*familiaridad*) intimacy

**franquicia** [fraŋ·'ki·sja, -ɵja] *f* exemption; **~ postal** free postage; ECON franchise

**frasco** ['fras·ko] *m* **1.** flask; **~ de perfume** perfume bottle; **~ pulverizador** sprayer **2.** *AmL* 2.37 liters

**frase** ['fra·se] *f* sentence; (*locución*) expression; (*refrán*) saying; **~ hecha** idiom; **~ proverbial** proverb

**fraternal** [fra·ter·'nal] *adj* fraternal

**fraternidad** [fra·ter·ni·'dad] *f* fraternity

**fraternizar** <z → c> [fra·ter·ni·'sar, -'ɵar] *vi* **1.** (*unirse*) to mingle with; POL to sympathize with **2.** (*alternar*) to fraternize

**fraude** ['frau·de] *m* fraud; **~ fiscal** tax fraud; **cometer ~** to commit a fraudulent act

**fraudulento, -a** [frau·du·'len·to, -a] *adj* fraudulent; **publicidad fraudulenta** misleading advertising

**frazada** [fra·'sa·da] *f* *AmL* blanket

**frecuencia** [fre·'kwen·sja, -ɵja] *f* t. FÍS frequency; **con ~** frequently

**frecuentar** [fre·kwen·'tar] *vt* to frequent; (*a alguien*) to be in touch with

**frecuente** [fre·'kwen·te] *adj* **1.** (*repetido*) frequent **2.** (*usual*) common

**fregadero** [fre·ɣa·'de·ro] *m* (kitchen) sink

**fregado** [fre·'ɣa·do] *m* **1.** cleaning **2.** *inf* (*lío*) mess; (*pelea*) brawl

**fregado, -a** [fre·'ɣa·do, -a] *adj* **1.** *AmL* (*descarado*) cheeky; (*fastidioso*) tiresome; (*astuto*) sly **2.** *AmC* (*severo*) strict

**fregar** [fre·'ɣar] *irr vt* **1.** (*frotar*) to rub **2.** (*suelo*) to scrub; (*con fregona*) to mop; (*platos*) to wash **3.** *AmL inf* to annoy

**fregona** [fre·'ɣo·na] *f* mop

**freidora** [frei·'do·ra] *f* fryer

**freír** [fre·'ir] *irr* **I.** *vt* to fry; (*en mucho aceite*) to deep-fry **II.** *vr:* **~se 1.** to fry **2.** *inf* to find it hot; **aquí te fríes** it's boiling here

**frenada** [fre·'na·da] *f* *Arg, Chile* sudden braking

**frenar** [fre·'nar] **I.** *vt* to stop; (*impulso, persona*) to restrain; (*desarrollo*) to curb **II.** *vi* to brake; **~ en seco** to slam on the brakes **III.** *vr* **~se en algo** to restrain oneself from sth

**frenazo** [fre·'na·so, -ɵo] *m* sudden braking

**frenesí** [fre·ne·'si] *m* (*exaltación*) frenzy; (*locura*) wildness

**frenético, -a** [fre·'ne·ti·ko, -a] *adj* **1.** (*exaltado*) frenzied; **aplauso ~** frenzied applause **2.** (*loco*) wild **3.** (*furioso*) furious

**freno** ['fre·no] *m* brake; **~ de mano** hand brake; (*contención*) curb; **tirar del ~ a alguien** to hold sb back; **no tener ~** not to hold back

**frente¹** ['fren·te] *f* forehead; **~ a ~** face to face; **fruncir la ~** to frown; **bajó la ~** he/she bowed his/her head

**frente²** ['fren·te] **I.** *m* t. POL, METEO, MIL front; **al ~** (*dirección*) ahead; (*lugar*) in front; **de ~** head-on; **ponerse al ~** to take charge; **estar al ~ de algo** to be in charge of sth; **hacer ~ a alguien** to stand up to sb; **hacer ~ a algo** to face up to sth; **no tener dos dedos de ~** to be as thick as two short planks; **un ~ frío** a cold front **II.** *prep* **1. ~ a** (*enfrente*) opposite; (*delante*) in front of; (*contra*) as opposed to; (*ante*) in the face of **2. en ~ de** opposite

**fresa** ['fre·sa] *f* strawberry

**fresco** ['fres·ko] *m* **1.** freshness; (*frío moderado*) coolness; **salir a tomar el ~** to go out to get some fresh air **2.** ARTE fresco **3.** *AmL* soft drink

**fresco, -a** ['fres·ko, -a] **I.** *adj* **1.** (*frío*) cool; **estar ~** *inf* to be wrong **2.** (*reciente, descansado, desvergonzado*) fresh; **noticia fresca** up-to-date news; **queso ~** cottage cheese **II.** *m, f inf* cheeky person

**frescor** [fres·'kor] *m* freshness; (*frío moderado*) coolness

**frescura** [fres·'ku·ra] *f* 1. freshness; (*frío moderado*) coolness 2. (*desvergüenza*) cheek 3. (*desembarazo*) naturalness; **con ~** freely

**fresquería** [fres·ke·'ri·a] *f AmL store where drinks are made and sold*

**frialdad** [frjal·'dad] *f* 1. (*frío*) coldness 2. (*despego, impasibilidad*) coolness; **me trató con ~** he/she was cool towards me

**fricción** [frik·'sjon, -'θjon] *f* 1. (*resistencia, desavenencia*) friction 2. (*del cuerpo*) rub; (*con linimento*) massage

**friega** ['frje·ɣa] *f* 1. (*fricción*) rub 2. *AmL* (*molestia*) bother 3. *inf* (*zurra*) beating

**friegaplatos** [frje·ɣa·'pla·tos] *m inv* dishwasher

**frigidez** [fri·xi·'des, -'deθ] *f* frigidity

**frígido, -a** ['fri·xi·do, -a] *adj* frigid

**frigorífico** [fri·ɣo·'ri·fi·ko] *m* fridge; (*cámara*) cold store

**frigorífico, -a** [fri·ɣo·'ri·fi·ko, -a] *adj* refrigerated; **camión ~** refrigerated truck

**frijol** [fri·'xol], **fríjol** ['fri·xol] *m AmL* bean

**friki** ['fri·ki] *inf* I. *adj* freaky II. *m* freak

**frío** ['fri·o] *m* cold; **tener ~** to be cold; **hace ~** it is cold; **hace un ~ que pela** it is bitterly cold; **coger ~** to catch cold

**frío, -a** ['fri·o, -a] *adj* 1. cold; (*relación*) cool; (*ambiente*) impersonal 2. (*sin sentimientos*) indifferent; (*impasible*) impassive

**friolento, -a** [frjo·'len·to, -a] *AmL*, **friolero, -a** [frjo·'le·ro, -a] *adj* sensitive to the cold

**frisa** ['fri·sa] *f* 1. *Arg, Chile* (*pelo*) nap 2. *PRico, RDom* (*manta*) blanket

**fritanga** [fri·'tan·ga] *f pey* (greasy) fried food

**frito** ['fri·to] *m* fry

**frito, -a** ['fri·to, -a] I. *pp de* freír II. *adj* 1. (*comida*) fried 2. *inf* (*dormido*) **quedarse ~** to fall fast asleep 3. *inf* (*muerto*) dead; **quedarse ~** to kick the bucket 4. *inf* (*harto*) **estar ~ con algo** to be fed up with sth

**frivolidad** [fri·βo·li·'dad] *f* frivolity; (*trivialidad*) triviality

**frívolo, -a** ['fri·βo·lo, -a] *adj* frivolous

**frondoso, -a** [fron·'do·so, -a] *adj* (*planta, árbol*) leafy; (*bosque*) lush

**frontal** [fron·'tal] *adj* head-on; ANAT frontal

**frontera** [fron·'te·ra] *f* border; **atravesar la ~** to cross the frontier

**fronterizo, -a** [fron·te·'ri·so, -a; -'ri·θo, -a] *adj* frontier; **paso ~** border post; (*país*) border(ing)

**frontón** [fron·'ton] *m* 1. DEP jai alai, pelota 2. ARQUIT pediment

**frotar** [fro·'tar] I. *vt* to rub; (*con cepillo*) to brush; (*con estropajo*) to scrub II. *vr:* **~se** to rub oneself

**fructífero, -a** [fruk·'ti·fe·ro, -a] *adj* fruitful

**fructificar** [<c → qu>] [fruk·ti·fi·'kar] *vi* (*planta*) to bear fruit; (*esfuerzo*) to come to fruition

**fruncir** [<c → z>] [frun·'sir, -'θir] *vt* (*tela*) to shirr; (*labios*) to purse; (*frente*) to wrinkle; **~ el ceño/entrecejo** to frown

**frustración** [frus·tra·'sjon, -'θjon] *f* 1. failure; (*planes*) thwarting; (*esperanza*) frustration 2. (*desilusión*) disappointment

**frustrado, -a** [frus·'tra·do, -a] *adj* frustrated; (*intento*) failed

**frustrar** [frus·'trar] I. *vt* 1. to thwart; (*esperanzas*) to frustrate 2. (*decepcionar*) to discourage II. *vr:* **~se** (*plan*) to fail; (*esperanzas*) to be disappointed

**fruta** ['fru·ta] *f* fruit; **~ del tiempo** seasonal fruit; **~s tropicales** tropical fruits

**frutal** [fru·'tal] I. *adj* fruit; (*planta, árbol*) fruit II. *m* fruit tree

**frutería** [fru·te·'ri·a] *f* greengrocer's

**frutero** [fru·'te·ro] *m* fruit bowl

**frutero, -a** [fru·'te·ro, -a] I. *adj* fruit; **es muy ~** he eats a lot of fruit II. *m, f* fruit seller

**frutilla** [fru·'ti·ja, -ʎa] *f AmL* strawberry

**fruto** ['fru·to] *m* 1. fruit 2. (*hijo*) offspring 3. (*rendimiento*) fruit; (*resultado*) result 4. (*ganancia*) profit; (*provecho*) benefit

**fucsia** ['fuk·sja] I. *adj* fuchsia-colored II. *m* fuchsia III. *f* fuchsia

**fue** [fwe] 1. *3. pret de* ir 2. *3. pret de* ser

**fuego** ['fwe·ɣo] *m* 1. fire; **¿me das ~?** can you give me a light?; **~s artificiales** fireworks; **a ~ lento** over a low heat; *fig* little by little; **prender** [*o* **pegar**] **~ a algo** to set sth on fire; **echar ~ por los**

**ojos** to look daggers at sb; **en el ~ de la discusión** in the heat of the discussion 2. MIL firing; **arma de ~** firearm; **estar entre dos ~s** to be caught in the crossfire

**fuel** [fwel] *m* refined oil

**fuente** ['fwen·te] *f* 1. (*manantial*) spring 2. (*construcción*) fountain 3. (*plato llano*) platter; (*plato hondo*) (serving) dish 4. (*origen*) source; **~s bien informadas** reliable sources

**fuera** ['fwe·ra] I. *adv* 1. (*lugar*) outside; **por ~** on the outside; **de ~** from the outside; **el nuevo maestro es de ~** the new teacher is not from here; **estar ~ de lugar** to be out of place 2. (*dirección*) out; **¡~!** out!; **¡~ con esto!** no way!; **¡~ de mi vista!** out of my sight!; **echar a alguien ~** to throw sb out; **hacia ~** outwards; **salir ~** to go out 3. (*tiempo*) out; **~ de plazo** past the deadline 4. (*de viaje*) away; **me voy ~ una semana** I am going away for a week II. *prep* 1. (*lugar*) out of; **~ de casa** away from home; **~ de juego** offside; **~ de serie** exceptional 2. (*excepto*) **~ de** outside of III. *conj* **~ de que** +*subj* apart from the fact that IV. *m* boo

**fuereño, -a** [fwe·'re·ɲo, -a] I. *adj AmL inf* outside II. *m, f AmL inf* outsider

**fuerte** ['fwer·te] I. *adj* <fortísimo> 1. (*resistente, musculoso*) strong; (*robusto*) tough; **caja ~** safe; **hacerse ~** to entrench oneself; **~ de carácter** strong-willed; **tener un carácter** [*o* **genio**] **muy ~** to be quick-tempered 2. (*intenso*) intense; (*sonido*) loud; (*comida, golpe*) heavy; (*abrazo, beso*) big; **un vino ~** a full-bodied wine 3. (*valiente*) brave 4. (*sólido*) solid; (*duro*) hard; (*tela*) thick 5. (*poderoso*) powerful 6. (*expresión*) nasty; (*palabra*) rude II. *m* 1. (*de una persona*) strong point 2. MIL fort III. *adv* 1. (*con fuerza*) strongly; (*con intensidad*) intensely; **desayunar ~** to have a large breakfast 2. (*en voz alta*) aloud

**fuerza** ['fwer·sa, -θa] *f* 1. *t.* FÍS (*capacidad física*) strength; *t.* FÍS (*potencia*) force; ELEC power; **~ de ánimo** strength of mind; **~ de voluntad** willpower; **sin ~s**

drained; **se le va la ~ por la boca** he/she is all talk 2. (*resistencia*) toughness; (*eficacia*) effectiveness; (*poder*) power; (*intensidad*) intensity; **~ de disuasión** powers of dissuasion; **~ mayor** force majeure 3. (*violencia*) force; **a** [*o* **por**] **la ~** any which way; **por ~** (*por necesidad*) out of necessity; (*con violencia*) by force; **recurrir a la ~** to resort to violence; **a ~ de** by means of; **a ~ de trabajo** through hard work 4. *pl* POL political groups *pl*; MIL forces *pl*; **~s del orden público** forces of law and order; **Fuerzas Armadas** the (armed) forces

**fuete** ['fwe·te] *m AmL* whip

**fuga** ['fu·ɣa] *f* 1. (*de la cárcel*) escape; **darse a la ~** to run away; **~ de capital** flight of capital; **~ de cerebros** brain drain 2. (*escape*) leak; (*de líquido*) leakage; (*de gas*) escape; **la cañería tiene una ~** the pipe has a leak

**fugacidad** [fu·ɣa·si·'dad, -θi·'dad] *f* brevity

**fugarse** <g → gu> [fu·'ɣar·se] *vr* to flee; (*de casa*) to run away; (*para casarse*) to elope; **~ de la cárcel** to escape from prison

**fugaz** [fu·'ɣas, -'ɣaθ] *adj* fleeting; **estrella ~** shooting star

**fugitivo, -a** [fu·xi·'ti·βo, -a] I. *adj* fugitive; (*belleza*) transitory II. *m, f* fugitive; (*de la cárcel*) escapee

**fulana** [fu·'la·na] *f* whore

**fulano, -a** [fu·'la·no, -a] *m, f* 1. (*evitando el nombre*) so-and-so 2. (*persona indeterminada*) John Doe; **no me importa lo que digan ~ y mengano** I do not care what Tom, Dick or Harry say

**fulero, -a** [fu·'le·ro, -a] *adj inf* 1. (*embustero*) lying 2. (*chapucero*) **eres muy ~** you are a bungler

**fulgor** [ful·'ɣor] *m* (*resplandor*) radiance; (*centelleo*) sparkle; (*de una superficie*) gleam

**fulgurante** [ful·ɣu·'ran·te] *adj* rapid; (*dolor*) intense; **su carrera fue ~** he/she rose rapidly in his/her career

**fullería** [fu·ʎe·'ri·a, fu·ʎe·] *f* 1. (*trampa*) trick; (*en el juego*) cheating; **hacer ~s** to cheat 2. (*treta*) ruse

**fullero, -a** [fu·'ʎe·ro, -a; fu·'ʎe·] I. *adj*

**1.** (*tramposo*) tricky **2.** (*astuto*) crafty **II.** *m, f* **1.** (*tramposo*) trickster; (*en el juego*) cheat **2.** (*astuto*) crafty individual

**fulminante** |ful·mi·'nan·te| *adj* **1.** *t.* MED (*inesperado*) sudden **2.** (*explosivo*) explosive; (*mirada*) withering

**fulminar** |ful·mi·'nar| **I.** *vi* to explode **II.** *vt* (*dañar*) to strike down; (*aniquilar*) to destroy; (*matar*) to electrocute

**fumador(a)** |fu·ma·'dor, -·'do·ra| *m(f)* smoker; **no ~** non-smoker; **zona de no ~es** no-smoking area

**fumar** |fu·'mar| *vi, vt, vr:* **~se** to smoke; **~se la clase** to play hooky from school

**fumigar** <g → gu> |fu·mi·'ɣar| *vt* to fumigate

**función** |fun·'sjon, -'θjon| *f* **1.** *t.* BIO, MAT (*rol*) function; **el precio está en ~ de la calidad** the price depends on the quality **2.** (*cargo*) office; (*tarea*) duty; **el ministro en funciones** the acting minister; **entrará en ~ mañana** he/she will start work tomorrow; (*cargo*) he/she will take office tomorrow **3.** (*actuación*) function; CINE showing; TEAT performance; **~ doble** double feature; **~ de noche** late show

**funcional** |fun·sjo·'nal, fun·θjo-| *adj* functional

**funcionalidad** |fun·sjo·na·li·'dad, fun·θjo-| *f* functionality

**funcionamiento** |fun·sjo·na·'mjen·to, fun·θjo-| *m* **1.** (*marcha*) running; **~ administrativo** running of the administration; **~ del mercado** market organization; **poner en ~** to bring into operation **2.** (*rendimiento*) performance; (*manera de funcionar*) operation; (*máquina*) working; **en estado de ~** in working order

**funcionar** |fun·sjo·'nar, fun·θjo-| *vi* to work; **la radio no funciona** the radio does not work; **'no funciona'** "out of order"

**funcionario, -a** |fun·sjo·'na·rjo, -a; fun·θjo-| *m, f* employee; (*público*) civil servant

**funda** |'fun·da| *f* cover; (*libro*) (dust) jacket; (*almohada*) pillowcase; (*butaca*) loose cover; (*gafas*) glasses case; ~

**nórdica** duvet

**fundación** |fun·da·'sjon, -'θjon| *f* foundation

**fundado, -a** |fun·'da·do, -a| *adj* well-founded

**fundador(a)** |fun·da·'dor, -·'do·ra| *adj, m(f)* founder

**fundamental** |fun·da·men·'tal| *adj* fundamental; (*esencial*) essential; (*básico*) basic; (*argumento*) key; (*conocimientos*) rudimentary

**fundamentalismo** |fun·da·men·ta·'lis·mo| *m* fundamentalism

**fundamentalista** |fun·da·men·ta·'lis·ta| *adj, mf* fundamentalist

**fundamentar** |fun·da·men·'tar| *vt* (*basar*) to base; (*establecer*) to establish

**fundamento** |fun·da·'men·to| *m* **1.** (*base*) basis **2.** (*motivo*) grounds; **sin ~** groundless; **hablar sin ~** not to talk seriously **3.** *pl* fundamentals *pl*

**fundar** |fun·'dar| **I.** *vt t.* TÉC to found; (*basar*) to base **II.** *vr:* **~se** (*basarse*) to be founded; (*asentarse*) to be established

**fundición** |fun·di·'sjon, -'θjon| *f* **1.** (*de un metal*) smelting; (*en una forma*) casting **2.** (*taller*) foundry

**fundillo** |fun·'di·jo, -ʎo| *m Méx* bottom

**fundir** |fun·'dir| **I.** *vt* **1.** (*derretir*) to melt; (*dar forma*) to cast **2.** (*unir*) to unite; (*empresas*) to merge **II.** *vr:* **~se** **1.** (*derretirse*) to melt **2.** (*bombilla*) to fuse; (*plomos*) to blow **3.** (*unirse*) to unite; (*empresas*) to merge **4.** *inf* (*gastar*) to squander

**fundo** |'fun·do| *m Chile, Perú* country property

**fúnebre** |'fu·ne·βre| *adj* **1.** (*triste*) mournful; (*sombrío*) gloomy **2.** (*de los difuntos*) funerary; **coche ~** hearse; **pompas ~s** (*ceremonia*) funeral; (*empresa*) undertaker's

**funeral** |fu·ne·'ral| **I.** *adj* funerary **II.** *m* **1.** burial **2.** *pl* funeral

**funeraria** |fu·ne·'ra·rja| *f* funeral parlor

**funesto, -a** |fu·'nes·to, -a| *adj* (*aciago*) ill-fated; (*desgraciado*) terrible

**fungir** <g → j> |fun·'xir| *vi* **1.** *AmL* (*un cargo*) to hold the post **2.** *AmC* (*presumir*) to put on airs

**furgón** |fur·'ɣon| *m* **1.** (*carro*) wagon; (*camioneta*) van **2.** (*para el equipaje*) baggage car; (*para mercancías*) freight car

**furgoneta** [fur·γo·'ne·ta] *f* van

**furia** ['fu·rja] *f* fury; **estaba hecha una ~** she was furious

**furioso, -a** [fu·'rjo·so, -a] *adj* **1.** (*furibundo*) furious **2.** (*loco*) beside oneself **3.** (*violento*) violent; (*tempestad*) raging

**furor** [fu·'ror] *m* **1.** (*ira*) fury; (*locura*) frenzy **2.** (*auge*) craze; **hacer ~** to be the (latest) thing **3.** MED ~ **uterino** nymphomania

**furtivo, -a** [fur·'ti·βo, -a] *adj* furtive; **cazador ~** poacher

**fusible** [fu·'si·βle] *m* fuse

**fusil** [fu·'sil] *m* rifle

**fusilar** [fu·si·'lar] *vt* **lo fusilaron** he was executed by firing squad

**fusión** [fu·'sjon] *f* fusion; (*unión*) union; ECON merger

**fusionar** [fu·sjo·'nar] **I.** *vi* to fuse **II.** *vt, vr:* **~se** to fuse; (*empresas*) to merge

**fustán** [fus·'tan] *m AmL* lady's slip

**fútbol** ['fud·βol] *m* soccer; ~ **americano** football

**futbolín** [fud·βo·'lin] *m* table football

**futbolista** [fud·βo·'lis·ta] *mf* soccer player

**futbolístico, -a** [fud·βo·'lis·ti·ko, -a] *adj* soccer

**fútbol-sala** ['fud·βol·'sa·la] *m* indoor soccer

**fútil** ['fu·til] *adj* trivial

**futileza** [fu·ti·'le·sa] *f Chile* trifle

**futilidad** [fu·ti·li·'ðað] *f* triviality

**futre** ['fu·tre] *m AmL pey* stuck-up person

**futuro** [fu·'tu·ro] *m* future

**futuro, -a** [fu·'tu·ro, -a] **I.** *adj* future **II.** *m, f* intended

# G

**G, g** [xe] *f* (*letra*) G, g; **G de Granada** G as in Golf

**g.** ['gra·mo] *abr de* **gramo** g.

**gabardina** [ga·βar·'ði·na] *f* raincoat

**gabinete** [ga·βi·'ne·te] *m* **1.** (*estudio*) study; ~ **de prensa** press office **2.** POL cabinet

**gacela** [ga·'se·la, ga·'θe-] *f* gazelle

**gaceta** [ga·'se·ta, ga·'θe-] *f* gazette

**gachas** ['ga·tʃas] *fpl* ≈ porridge

**gachí** <gachís> [ga·'tʃi] *f inf* chick

**gachó** [ga·'tʃo] *m inf* bloke

**gafar** [ga·'far] *vt inf* to jinx

**gafas** ['ga·fas] *fpl* glasses *pl;* ~ **de bucear** diving mask; **llevar ~** to wear glasses

**gafe** ['ga·fe] *m* (*cenizo*) jinx; (*aguafiestas*) party-pooper

**gaita** ['gai·ta] *f* bagpipes *pl*

**gajo** ['ga·xo] *m* (*de naranja*) segment

**gala** ['ga·la] *f* **1.** (*fiesta*) gala **2.** (*garbo*) elegance; **hacer ~ de algo** to take pride in sth **3.** *pl* finery

**galáctico, -a** [ga·'lak·ti·ko, -a] *adj* galactic

**galán** [ga·'lan] *m* handsome man; (*novio*) beau

**galante** [ga·'lan·te] *adj* **1.** (*hombre*) gallant **2.** (*mujer*) flirtatious

**galantería** [ga·lan·te·'ri·a] *f* **1.** (*cortesía*) gallantry **2.** (*amabilidad*) politeness **3.** (*cumplido*) compliment

**galápago** [ga·'la·pa·γo] *m* sea turtle

**galardón** [ga·lar·'ðon] *m* prize

**galardonar** [ga·lar·ðo·'nar] *vt* to award a prize to; ~ **a alguien con un título** to confer a title on sb

**galaxia** [ga·'lak·sja] *f* galaxy

**galera** [ga·'le·ra] *f* **1.** galley **2.** *AmL* (*cobertizo*) shed **3.** *AmL* (*de copa*) top hat; (*de hongo*) bowler hat

**galería** [ga·le·'ri·a] *f* **1.** (*corredor, de arte*) *t.* MIN, TEAT gallery **2.** *pl* (*grandes almacenes*) department store; (*centro comercial*) mall **3.** *pl* (*bulevar*) arcade

**galerón** [ga·le·'ron] *m* **1.** *AmS* (*romance*) ballad **2.** *Col, Ven* MÚS folkdance and song **3.** *CRi, ElSal* (*cobertizo*) shed

**galés, -esa** [ga·'les, -·'le·sa] **I.** *adj* Welsh **II.** *m, f* Welshman, Welshwoman *m, f*

**Gales** ['ga·les] *m* Wales

**galgo, -a** ['gal·γo, -a] *m, f* greyhound; **échale un ~!** ¡no way!

**galguerías** [gal·γe·'ri·as] *fpl* candies *pl*

**Galicia** [ga·'li·sja, -θja] *f* Galicia

**galimatías** [ga·li·ma·'ti·as] *m inv* gibberish

G

**gallardía** [ga·jar·'di·a, ga·ʎar-] f (garbo) style; (valentía) bravery

**gallardo, -a** [ga·'jar·do, -a; ga·'ʎar-] adj **1.** (de aspecto) elegant **2.** (garboso) dashing **3.** (valiente) brave. **4.** (generoso) noble

**gallego, -a** [ga·'je·ɣo, -a; ga·'ʎe-] m, f **1.** (de Galicia) Galician **2.** AmS pey Spaniard

**galleta** [ga·'je·ta, -'ʎe·ta] f **1.** (dulce) cookie; (salada) cracker **2.** inf (bofetada) smack

**gallina** [ga·'ji·na, -'ʎi·na] f **1.** hen **2.** inf (cobarde) chicken

**gallinero** [ga·ji·'ne·ro, ga·ʎi-] m (corral) chicken coop

**gallito** [ga·'ji·to, -'ʎi·to] m inf **ser un ~** to be a tough guy; **ponerse ~** to act tough

**gallo** ['ga·jo, -ʎo] m **1.** (ave) cock; **~ de pelea** fighting cock; **en menos que <u>canta</u> un ~** in a flash **2.** (engreído) show-off **3.** MÚS false note; **soltar un ~** to let out a squeak **4.** AmL (fuerte) tough guy

**galón** [ga·'lon] m gallon

**galopar** [ga·lo·'par] vi to gallop

**galope** [ga·'lo·pe] m gallop

**galpón** [gal·'pon] m AmL shed

**galuchar** [ga·lu·'tʃar] vi Col, Cuba, PRico, Ven to gallop

**gama** ['ga·ma] f **1.** range; **una amplia ~ de productos** a wide range of products **2.** MÚS gamut; (escala) scale

**gamba** ['gam·ba] f shrimp

**gamberrada** [gam·be·'rra·da] f act of hooliganism; **hacer ~s** to horse around inf

**gamberro, -a** [gam·'be·rro, -a] m, f hooligan

**gambeta** [gam·'be·ta] f AmL **1.** (distensión) swerve **2.** (evasiva) dodge **3.** (fútbol) dummy; **hacer ~s** to dribble

**gamin, -ina** [ga·'min, -'mi·na] m, f Col urchin

**gamo** ['ga·mo] m fallow deer

**gamonal** [ga·mo·'nal] m AmL local political boss

**gamonalismo** [ga·mo·na·'lis·mo] m AmL caciquism

**gana** ['ga·na] f desire; **tener ~s de hacer**

**algo** to feel like doing sth; **me quedé con las ~s de verlo** I wish I'd been able to see him; **no me da la (real) ~** inf I can't be bothered

**ganadería** [ga·na·de·'ri·a] f **1.** (ganado) livestock **2.** (crianza) livestock farming

**ganadero, -a** [ga·na·'de·ro, -a] **I.** adj livestock **II.** m, f (criador) cattle farmer; (tratante) cattle merchant

**ganado** [ga·'na·do, -a] m **1.** (reses) livestock **2.** ~ **bovino** [o **vacuno**] cattle pl; ~ **cabrío** goats pl; ~ **ovino** sheep inv; ~ **porcino** pigs pl **2.** AmL inf (personas) crowd

**ganador(a)** [ga·na·'dor, -·'do·ra] **I.** adj winning **II.** m(f) winner

**ganancia** [ga·'nan·sja, -θja] f (beneficio) profit; (sueldo) earnings pl

**ganancial** [ga·nan·'sjal, -'θjal] adj profit; **bienes ~es** property acquired by marriage

**ganar** [ga·'nar] **I.** vi to win; (mejorar) ~ **en algo** to improve at sth **II.** vt **1.** (trabajando) to earn; **con ese negocio consiguió ~ mucho dinero** he/she made a lot of money out of that business **2.** (jugando) win; (a alguien) to beat **3.** (adquirir) to gain; (libertad) to win; ~ **peso** to put on weight **4.** (aventajar) ~ **a alguien en algo** to be better than sb at sth **III.** vr: ~**se 1.** (dinero) to earn; **¡te la vas a ~!** inf you're for it **2.** (a alguien) to win over

**ganchillo** [gan·'tʃi·jo, -ʎo] m **1.** (gancho) hook **2.** (labor) crochet; **hacer ~** to crochet

**gancho** ['gan·tʃo] m **1.** (instrumento) hook; **tener ~** to be attractive **2.** DEP (boxeo) hook; (baloncesto) hook shot **3.** (que atrae) bait **4.** AmL (horquilla) hairpin

**gandido, -a** [gan·'di·do, -a] adj Col pey gluttonous

**gandinga** [gan·'din·ga] f Cuba, PRico liver stew

**gandul(a)** [gan·'dul, -·'du·la] **I.** adj lazy **II.** m(f) loafer

**gandulear** [gan·du·le·'ar] vi to loaf around

**ganga** ['gan·ga] f bargain; **a precio de ~** at a bargain price

**ganglio** [ˈgan·gljo] *m* ganglion; **~ linfáti-co** lymph gland

**gangoso, -a** [gan·ˈgo·so, -a] *adj* nasal

**gángster** [ˈgans·ter] *mf* gangster

**gansada** [gan·ˈsa·da] *f* silly thing; **ha-cer ~s** to clown around; **decir ~s** to talk nonsense

**gansear** [gan·se·ˈar] *vi inf* **1.** (*hacer gan-sadas*) to clown around **2.** (*decir gansa-das*) to talk nonsense

**ganso, -a** [ˈgan·so, -a] *m, f* **1.** goose; (*macho*) gander **2.** *inf* dummy; **hacer el ~** to clown around

**ganzúa** [gan·ˈsu·a, -ˈθu·a] *f* picklock

**gañán** [ga·ˈɲan] *m* farmhand; *pey* brute

**garabato** [ga·ra·ˈβa·to] *m* (*al escribir*) scribble; (*al dibujar*) doodle

**garaje** [ga·ˈra·xe] *m* garage

**garante** [ga·ˈran·te] **I.** *adj* responsible **II.** *mf* guarantor

**garantía** [ga·ran·ˈti·a] *f* (*seguridad*) . COM, FIN guarantee; (*caución*) surety; **~s constitucionales** POL constitutional rights

**garantizar** <z → c> [ga·ran·ti·ˈsar, -ˈθar] *vt* to guarantee; JUR to act as guarantor for

**garapiña** [ga·ra·ˈpi·ɲa] *f* **1.** sugar coating **2.** *AmL* iced pineapple drink

**garapiñar** [ga·ra·pi·ˈɲar] *vt* to coat with sugar

**garbanzo** [gar·ˈβan·so, -θo] *m* chickpea

**garbo** [ˈgar·βo] *m* elegance; (*de movi-miento*) grace(fulness); (*de un escri-to*) style

**garete** [ga·ˈre·te] *inf* **ir(se) al ~** to go down the tubes

**garfio** [ˈgar·fjo] *m* hook

**gargajo** [gar·ˈγa·xo] *m inf* phlegm

**garganta** [gar·ˈγan·ta] *f* throat; (*cuello*) neck; **se me hizo un nudo en la ~** I had a lump in my throat

**gargantilla** [gar·γan·ˈti·ja, -ʎa] *f* (short) necklace

**gárgaras** [ˈgar·γa·ras] *fpl* gargles *pl*; **ha-cer ~** to gargle

**gargarear** [gar·γa·re·ˈar] *vi Chile, Guat, Perú* to gargle

**gárgola** [ˈgar·γo·la] *f* gargoyle

**garito** [ga·ˈri·to] *m* nightclub; (*de juego*) gambling den

**garra** [ˈga·rra] *f* **1.** claw; *pey* (*mano*) paw; **caer en las ~s de alguien** to fall into sb's clutches **2.** *pl AmL* (*harapos*) rags *pl* **3.** *inf* **tener ~** to be compelling

**garrafa** [ga·ˈrra·fa] *f* (*pequeña*) carafe; (*grande*) demijohn; **vino de ~** cheap wine

**garrafal** [ga·rra·ˈfal] *adj* (*enorme*) enor-mous; (*fatal*) terrible

**garrapata** [ga·rra·ˈpa·ta] *f* tick

**garrapiña** [ga·rra·ˈpi·ɲa] *f v.* **garrapiña**

**garúa** [ga·ˈru·a] *f AmL* drizzle

**garuar** [ga·ˈrwar] *vimpers AmL* to drizzle

**garza** [ˈgar·sa, -θa] *f* heron

**garzón, -ona** [gar·ˈson, -ˈso·na] *m, f AmL* waiter, waitress *m, f*

**gas** [gas] *m* **1.** gas; **~ natural** natural gas; **bombona/cocina de ~** gas cylinder/ stove; **agua con/sin ~** carbonated/still water **2.** *inf* **dar ~** to accelerate; **ir a todo ~** to go at full speed **3.** *pl* wind

**gasa** [ˈga·sa] *f* gauze; MED lint; (*pañal*) diaper liner

**gaseosa** [ga·se·ˈo·sa] *f* soda

**gaseoso, -a** [ga·se·ˈo·so, -a] *adj* gaseous; (*bebida*) fizzy

**gasfitería** [gas·fi·te·ˈri·a] *f AmL* plumbing

**gasoducto** [ga·so·ˈduk·to] *m* gas pipeline

**gasoil** [gas·ˈoil], **gasóleo** [gas·ˈso·leo] *m* diesel

**gasolina** [ga·so·ˈli·na] *f* gas(oline); **~ súper/sin plomo** premium/unleaded gasoline; **echar ~** to get gas

**gasolinera** [ga·so·li·ˈne·ra] *f* gas station

**gastado, -a** [gas·ˈta·do, -a] *adj* worn out; (*neumático*) bare; (*pila*) used up

**gastar** [gas·ˈtar] **I.** *vt* **1.** to wear out; (*di-nero, tiempo*) to spend; (*electricidad*) to use **2.** (*consumir, usar*) use; **¿qué talla** [o *número*] **gastas?** what size are you? **II.** *vr:* **~se** to run out; (*dinero*) to spend; (*ropa*) to wear out

**gasto** [ˈgas·to] *m* **1.** *pl* (*de dinero*) spend-ing; (*en un negocio*) costs *pl*; (*de fuerza*) *t.* ECON, COM expenditure; **~s adiciona-les** extra charges; **~s pagados** all ex-penses paid; **~s de inscripción** registra-tion fees *pl*; **el ~ público** public expen-diture **2.** (*consumo*) consumption

**gastroenteritis** [gas·tro·en·te·ˈri·tis] *f inv* gastroenteritis

G

**gastronomía** [gas·tro·no·'mi·a] *f* gastronomy

**gastronómico, -a** [gas·tro·'no·mi·ko, -a] *adj* gastronomic

**gatas** ['ga·tas] **andar a ~** to crawl

**gatear** [ga·te·'ar] *vi* to crawl; *AmL* to seduce

**gatera** [ga·'te·ra] *f AmL* vegetable seller

**gatillo** [ga·'ti·jo, -ʎo] *m* trigger; **apretar el ~** to pull the trigger

**gato** ['ga·to] *m* **1.** cat; (*macho*) tomcat; **dar ~ por liebre a alguien** to rip sb off; **aquí hay ~ encerrado** there's something fishy going on here **2.** (*de coche*) jack; (*de carpintero*) vice

**gatuno, -a** [ga·'tu·no, -a] *adj* catlike

**gaucho** ['gau·tʃo] *m AmL* **1.** (*campesino*) gaucho **2.** (*jinete*) skilled horseman

**gaucho, -a** ['gau·tʃo, -a] *adj* **1.** gaucho **2.** (*grosero*) coarse **3.** *AmL* (*astuto*) cunning

**gavilán** [ga·βi·lan] *m* sparrow hawk

**gaviota** [ga·'βjo·ta] *f* (sea)gull

**gay** [gai] *m* gay

**gazpacho** [gas·'pa·tʃo, gaθ-] *m* gazpacho

**GB** [dʒi·ya·'bait] *m* **1.** *abr de* **gigabyte** GB **2.** *abr de* **Gran Bretaña** GB

**géiser** ['xei·ser] *m* geyser

**gel** [xel] *m* gel

**gelatina** [xe·la·'ti·na] *f* gelatin; CULIN (*dulce*) jelly; (*salado*) aspic

**gelatinoso, -a** [xe·la·ti·'no·so, -a] *adj* gelatinous

**gélido, -a** ['xe·li·do, -a] *adj* icy

**gema** ['xe·ma] *f* gem

**gemelo, -a** [xe·'me·lo, -a] *adj, m, f* identical twin; **hermanos ~s** twin brothers

**gemelos** [xe·'me·los] *mpl* **1.** (*anteojos*) binoculars *pl*; **~ de teatro** opera glasses **2.** ANAT calves *pl*

**gemido** [xe·'mi·do] *m* (*de dolor*) groan; (*de pena, de placer*) moan; (*al llorar*) wail

**Géminis** ['xe·mi·nis] *m* Gemini

**gemir** [xe·'mir] *irr como* **pedir** *vi* (*de dolor*) to groan; (*de pena, de placer*) to moan

**gen** [xen] *m* gene

**genealógico, -a** [xe·nea·'lo·xi·ko, -a] *adj* genealogical; **árbol ~** family tree

**generación** [xe·ne·ra·'sjon, -'θjon] *f* generation

**generador** [xe·ne·ra·'dor] *m* generator

**generador(a)** [xe·ne·ra·'dor, -·'do·ra] *adj* productive; **medidas ~as de empleo** employment creation measures; ELEC generating

**general** [xe·ne·'ral] *adj, m* general; **cuartel ~** headquarters; **cultura ~** general knowledge; **por lo** [*o* **en**] **~** in general, generally; **por regla ~** as a (general) rule; **en ~ me siento satisfecho** overall, I'm satisfied; **tengo una idea ~ del tema** I have a general idea about the subject

**generalización** [xe·ne·ra·li·sa·'sjon, -θa·'θjon] *f* generalization; (*difusión*) spread

**generalizar** <z → c> [xe·ne·ra·li·'sar, -'θar] *vt* to generalize; (*difundir*) to spread

**generalmente** [xe·ne·ral·'men·te] *adv* generally; (*ampliamente*) widely

**generar** [xe·ne·'rar] *vt* (*producir*) to generate; (*provocar*) to create

**genérico, -a** [xe·'ne·ri·ko, -a] *adj* generic

**género** ['xe·ne·ro] *m* **1.** BIO genus; **~ humano** mankind **2.** (*clase*) sort **3.** LING gender **4.** LIT, ARTE genre **5.** COM (*artículo*) article; (*mercancía*) goods *pl*

**generosidad** [xe·ne·ro·si·'dad] *f* generosity

**generoso, -a** [xe·ne·'ro·so, -a] *adj* generous

**genética** [xe·'ne·ti·ka] *f* genetics

**genético, -a** [xe·'ne·ti·ko, -a] *adj* genetic

**genial** [xe·'njal] *adj* great; (*idea*) brilliant

**genialidad** [xe·nja·li·'dad] *f* genius

**genio** ['xe·njo] *m* **1.** (*carácter*) character; **tener mal ~** to be bad-tempered **2.** (*persona*) genius **3.** (*duende*) genie

**genital** [xe·ni·'tal] *adj* genital

**genitales** [xe·ni·'ta·les] *mpl* genitals *pl*

**genocidio** [xe·no·'si·djo, -'θi·djo] *m* genocide

**gente** ['xen·te] *f* **1.** people *pl*; **¿qué tal tu ~?** how are your folks? **2.** *AmL* honest people

**gentileza** [xen·ti·'le·sa, -θa] *f* kindness; **¿tendría Ud. la ~ de ayudarme?** would you be so kind as to help me?

**gentío** [xen·'ti·o] *m* crowd

**gentuza** [xen·'tu·sa, -θa] *f* rabble

**genuino, -a** [xe·'nwi·no, -a] *adj* genuine

**geografía** [xeo·γra·'fi·a] *f* geography

**geográfico, -a** [xeo·'γra·fi·ko, -a] *adj* geographical

**geología** [xeo·lo·'xi·a] *f* geology

**geológico, -a** [xeo·'lo·xi·ko, -a] *adj* geological

**geólogo, -a** [xe·'o·lo·γo, -a] *m, f* geologist

**geometría** [xeo·me·'tri·a] *f* geometry

**geométrico, -a** [xeo·'me·tri·ko, -a] *adj* geometric(al)

**geranio** [xe·'ra·njo] *m* geranium

**gerencia** [xe·'ren·sja, -θja] *f* management

**gerente** [xe·'ren·te] *mf* director, general manager; (*pequeña empresa*) manager; (*departamento*) head

**geriatra** [xe·'rja·tra] *mf* geriatrician

**geriatría** [xe·rja·'tri·a] *f* geriatrics *pl*

**geriátrico, -a** [xe·'rja·tri·ko, -a] *adj* geriatric

**germánico, -a** [xer·'ma·ni·ko, -a] *adj*, **germano, -a** [xer·'ma·no, -a] *adj* German; HIST Germanic

**germen** ['xer·men] *m* origin; BIO germ

**germinar** [xer·mi·'nar] *vi* to germinate

**gerundio** [xe·'run·djo] *m* gerund

**gestación** [xes·ta·'sjon, -'θjon] *f* gestation

**gesticular** [xes·ti·ku·'lar] *vi* to gesticulate; (*con la cara*) to pull faces

**gestión** [xes·'tjon] *f* management; (*diligencia*) measure; **hacer gestiones** to take measures

**gestionar** [xes·tjo·'nar] *vt* to manage; (*asunto*) to conduct

**gesto** ['xes·to] *m* gesture; (*con la cara*) expression

**gestor(a)** [xes·'tor, --'to·ra] I. *adj* managing II. *m(f)* agent

**gigabyte** [ʤi·γa·'bait] *m* gigabyte

**gigante** [xi·'γan·te] I. *adj* gigantic II. *m* giant

**gigantesco, -a** [xi·γan·'tes·ko, -a] *adj* gigantic

**gigoló** [ʤi·γo·'lo] *m* gigolo

**gilipollas** [xi·li·'po·jas, -ʎas] *mf inv argot* dimwit

**gilipollez** [xi·li·po·'jes, -'ʎeθ] *f inf* nonsense

**gimnasia** [xim·'na·sja] *f* ENS gym; **hacer ~** to do exercises; DEP gymnastics *pl;* **~ rítmica** rhythm gymnastics

**gimnasio** [xim·'na·sjo] *m* gym

**gimnasta** [xim·'nas·ta] *mf* gymnast

**gimotear** [xi·mo·te·'ar] *vi* to whimper; (*gemir*) to groan

**ginebra** [xi·'ne·βra] *f* gin

**ginecólogo, -a** [xi·ne·ko·lo·γo, -a] *m, f* gynecologist

**gira** ['xi·ra] *f* tour; **estar de ~** to be on tour

**girar** [xi·'rar] I. *vi* 1. (*dar vueltas*) to revolve; **~ en torno a algo** to revolve around sth; (*con rapidez*) to spin 2. (*torcer*) to turn II. *vt* to turn

**girasol** [xi·ra·'sol] *m* sunflower

**giratorio, -a** [xi·ra·'to·rjo, -a] *adj* revolving

**giro** ['xi·ro] *m* turn; COM draft; **~ postal** money order

**gitano, -a** [xi·'ta·no, -a] *adj, m, f* gypsy

**glaciación** [gla·sja·'sjon, -θja·'θjon] *f* glaciation

**glaciar** [gla·'sjar, -'θjar] *m* glacier

**glande** ['glan·de] *m* glans (penis)

**glándula** ['glan·du·la] *f* gland

**global** [glo·'βal] *adj* overall; (*mundial*) global; (*cantidad, valoración*) total; (*informe*) comprehensive

**globalidad** [glo·βa·li·'dad] *f* totality

**globalización** [glo·βa·li·sa·'sjon, -θa·'θjon] *f* globalization

**globo** ['glo·βo] *m* 1. sphere; **~ ocular** eyeball 2. (*mapa*) globe 3. (*para niños*) balloon; (*tebeos*) speech balloon; **~** (**aerostático**) hot-air balloon 4. *inf* rubber

**gloria** ['glo·rja] *f* glory; **estar en la ~** to be in seventh heaven

**glorieta** [glo·'rje·ta] *f* (small) square; (*rotonda*) traffic circle, rotary *reg*

**glosario** [glo·'sa·rjo] *m* glossary

**glotón, -ona** [glo·'ton, --'to·na] I. *adj* gluttonous II. *m, f* glutton

**glotonear** [glo·to·ne·'ar] *vi* to be gluttonous

**glotonería** [glo·to·ne·'ri·a] *f* gluttony

**glucosa** [glu·'ko·sa] *f* glucose

**glúteo** ['glu·teo] *m* gluteus

**gobernador(a)** [go·βer·na·'dor, -·'do·ra]
I. *adj* governing II. *m(f)* governor
**gobernanta** [go·βer·'nan·ta] *f* AmL (*niñera*) nanny; (*institutriz*) governess; (*ama de llaves*) housekeeper
**gobernante** [go·βer·'nan·te] *mf* ruler
**gobernar** <e → ie> [go·βer·'nar] *vt* to govern
**gobierno** [go·'βjer·no] *m* 1. POL government; ~ **autonómico/central** regional/central government 2. (*ministros*) cabinet 3. (*del gobernador*) governorship
**goce** [go·se, -θe] *m* enjoyment
**godo, -a** ['go·do, -a] *m, f* 1. Goth 2. AmC *pey* Spaniard
**gofre** ['go·fre] *m* waffle
**gol** [gol] *m* goal; ~ **del empate** equalizer; **meter un** ~ to score (a goal)
**golazo** [go·'la·so, -θo] *m* great goal
**goleador(a)** [go·lea·'dor, -·'do·ra] *m(f)* goal scorer
**golf** [golf] *m* golf
**golfo** ['gol·fo] *m* gulf
**golfo, -a** ['gol·fo, -a] I. *adj* naughty II. *m, f* 1. (*pilluelo*) urchin 2. (*vagabundo*) tramp
**golondrina** [go·lon·'dri·na] *f* swallow
**golosina** [go·lo·'si·na] *f* candy
**goloso, -a** [go·'lo·so, -a] I. *adj* sweet-toothed; **es una oferta muy golosa** it's a very tempting offer II. *m, f* **ser un** ~ to have a sweet tooth
**golpe** ['gol·pe] *m* 1. (*impacto*) blow; (*choque*) bump; ~ **de Estado** coup (d'état); **abrirse de** ~ to fly open; **dar un** ~ to strike; **me he dado un** ~ **en la cabeza** I banged my head; **me lo tragué de un** ~ I downed it in one gulp 2. (*ruido*) bang 3. (*atraco*) hold-up
**golpear** [gol·pe·'ar] I. *vi* to hit II. *vt* to hit; (*puerta*) to knock on III. *vr* ~**se la cabeza** to bang one's head
**goma** ['go·ma] *f* 1. rubber; ~ **de borrar** eraser; ~ **elástica** elastic band 2. AmL (*resaca*) hangover
**gomaespuma** [go·ma·es·'pu·ma] *f* foam rubber
**gomina®** [go·'mi·na] *f* hair gel
**gominola** [go·mi·'no·la] *f* gumdrop
**góndola** ['gon·do·la] *f* AmL bus
**gordo** ['gor·do] *m* 1. fat 2. (*lotería*) **el**

~ the jackpot
**gordo, -a** ['gor·do, -a] I. *adj* fat; (*tejido*) thick; (*salario, mentira*) big; **ha pasado algo muy** ~ sth serious has happened II. *m, f* fat man, fat woman *m, f*
**gorila** [go·'ri·la] *m* 1. gorilla 2. *inf* (*portero*) bouncer; (*guardaespaldas*) bodyguard; (*matón*) thug
**gorra** ['go·rra] *f* cap; (*para niños*) bonnet; **de** ~ *inf* free
**gorrear** [go·rre·'ar] *vi, vt inf* to scrounge; **¿te puedo** ~ **un cigarrillo?** can I get a cigarette from you?
**gorrinada** [go·rri·'na·da] *f* dirty trick
**gorrino, -a** [go·'rri·no, -a] *m, f* pig
**gorrión** [go·rri·'on] *m* 1. sparrow 2. AmC (*colibrí*) hummingbird
**gorro** ['go·rro] *m* hat; (*de uniforme*) cap; (*para bebés*) bonnet; ~ **de natación** bathing cap
**gorrón, -ona** [go·'rron, -·'rro·na] *m, f* scrounger; AmC selfish person
**gorronear** [go·rro·ne·'ar] *vi v.* gorrear
**gota** ['go·ta] *f* drop; **parecerse como dos** ~**s de agua** to be like two peas in a pod; **no queda ni** ~ **de agua** there's not a drop of water left; ~ **fría** cold front; **la** ~ **que colma el vaso** the last straw
**gotear** [go·te·'ar] I. *vi* to drip; (*salirse*) to leak II. *vimpers* **está goteando** it's drizzling
**goteo** [go·'te·o] *m* drip
**gotera** [go·'te·ra] *f* 1. leak; (*mancha*) stain 2. *pl* AmL outskirts *pl*
**gótico, -a** ['go·ti·ko, -a] *adj* Gothic
**gozada** [go·'sa·da, -'θa·da] *f* *inf* delight
**gozar** <z → c> [go·'sar, -'θar] *vi* to enjoy oneself; ~ **de algo** to enjoy sth; ~ **de una increíble fortuna** to be incredibly wealthy
**gr.** ['gra·mo] *abr de* **gramo** g.
**grabación** [gra·βa·'sjon, -'θjon] *f* recording; TV shooting; COMPUT copying
**grabado** [gra·'βa·do] *m* 1. (*acción*) engraving 2. (*copia*) print 3. (*ilustración*) illustration
**grabador(a)** [gra·βa·'dor] *m(f)* engraver
**grabadora** [gra·βa·'do·ra] *f* tape recorder
**grabar** [gra·'βar] *vt* 1. to record 2. ARTE to engrave; (*en madera*) to cut 3. COMPUT

to copy

**gracia** ['gra·sja, -θja] *f* **1.** *pl* **¡~s!** thanks!; **¡muchas ~s!** thanks a lot!; **~ s a** thanks to **2.** (*chiste*) joke; **no tiene (ni) pizca de ~** it's not the least bit funny; **no me hace nada de ~** I don't find it funny in the least; **la ~ es que...** the funny thing is that...

**gracioso, -a** [gra·'sjo·so, -a; gra·'θjo·] *adj* funny; **no te hagas el ~ conmigo** don't try to play the clown with me

**grada** ['gra·da] *f* **1.** (*de un estadio*) tier; **las ~s** the terraces **2.** *pl* AmL courtyard

**gradación** [gra·da·'sjon, -'θjon] *f* gradation

**grado** ['gra·do] *m* **1.** (*nivel, parentesco, alcohol*) *t.* MAT, LING degree; **~ centígrado** degree centigrade; **~ de confianza** degree of trust; **quemaduras de primer ~** first-degree burns; **en ~ sumo** greatly **2.** ENS year; UNIV degree **3.** MIL rank

**graduable** [gra·du·'a·βle] *adj* adjustable

**graduación** [gra·dwa·'sjon, -'θjon] *f* **1.** (*regulación*) adjustment **2.** (*en grados*) graduation; (*en niveles, de personas*) grading; (*de precios*) regulation; **~ alcohólica** alcohol content **3.** UNIV graduation

**graduado, -a** [gra·du·'a·do, -a] **I.** *adj* graduate(d) **II.** *m, f* graduate; **~ escolar** school diploma

**gradual** [gra·du·'al] *adj* gradual

**gradualmente** [gra·dwal·'men·te] *adv* **1.** (*en grados*) by degrees **2.** (*progresivamente*) gradually

**graduar** <*1. pres* gradúo> [gra·du·'ar] **I.** *vt* **1.** (*regular*) to regulate **2.** TÉC to graduate; **~ la vista a alguien** to test sb's eyesight **3.** (*en niveles*) to classify; (*precios*) to regulate **II.** *vr:* **~se** to graduate

**grafia** [gra·'fi·a] *f* writing; (*ortografía*) spelling

**gráfica** ['gra·fi·ka] *f* graph

**gráfico** ['gra·fi·ko] *m* graph; COMPUT graphic

**gráfico, -a** ['gra·fi·ko, -a] *adj* **1.** (*de la escritura*) written **2.** (*del dibujo*) illustrated; **diccionario ~** visual dictionary; **tarjeta gráfica** graphics card **3.** (*claro*)

graphic **4.** *fig* expressive

**grafito** [gra·'fi·to] *m* graphite

**gragea** [gra·'xea] *f* (sugar-coated) pill

**grajo** ['gra·xo] *m* **1.** rook **2.** AmL (*sobaquina*) body odor

**gral.** [xe·ne·'ral] *adj abr de* **general** gen.

**gramática** [gra·'ma·ti·ka] *f* grammar

**gramatical** [gra·ma·ti·'kal] *adj* grammatical; **regla ~** grammatical rule

**gramilla** [gra·'mi·ja, -ʎa] *f* AmL lawn

**gramo** ['gra·mo] *m* gram

**gran** [gran] *adj v.* **grande**

**granada** [gra·'na·da] *f* **1.** pomegranate **2.** (*de mano*) grenade; (*de artillería*) shell

**granadilla** [gra·na·'di·ja, -ʎa] *f* AmC passionflower

**granate** [gra·'na·te] **I.** *adj* burgundy **II.** *m* garnet

**Gran Bretaña** [gram bre·'ta·ɲa] *f* Great Britain

**grande** ['gran·de] *adj* <*más grande o* mayor, grandísimo> (*ante sust sing:* **gran**) **1.** (*de tamaño*) big; (*número, cantidad, habitación*) large; **gran ciudad** big city; **a gran velocidad** at high speed; **vino gran cantidad de gente** a lot of people came; **tengo un gran interés por...** I'm very interested in...; **no me preocupa gran cosa** I'm not very worried about it **2.** (*de edad*) grown-up **3.** (*moralmente*) great; **un gran hombre** a great man; **una gran idea** a great idea ▶ **pasarlo en ~** to have a great time

**grandeza** [gran·'de·sa, -θa] *f* greatness; (*tamaño*) size

**grandiosidad** [gran·djo·si·'dad] *f* grandeur

**grandioso, -a** [gran·'djo·so, -a] *adj* impressive; (*rimbombante*) grandiose

**grandullón, -ona** [gran·du·'jon, --'jo·na; -'ʎon, --'ʎo·na] *adj* oversized

**granel** [gra·'nel] **a ~** (*sin envase*) loose; (*líquido*) by volume; (*en abundancia*) in abundance

**granero** [gra·'ne·ro] *m* granary; (*de granja*) barn

**granito** [gra·'ni·to] *m* granite

**granizado** [gra·ni·'sa·do, -'θa·do] *m* iced drink; **~ de café** ≈ iced coffee

**granizar** <z → c> [gra·ni·'sar, -'θar] *vimpers* to hail

**granizo** [gra·'ni·so, -θo] *m* hail

**granja** ['gran·xa] *f* farm

**granjero, -a** [gran·'xe·ro, -a] *m, f* farmer

**grano** ['gra·no] *m t.* TÉC grain; (*café*) bean; (*de piel*) pimple; **ir al ~** to get to the point

**granuja** [gra·'nu·xa] *m* (*pilluelo*) rascal; (*bribón*) scoundrel

**grapa** ['gra·pa] *f* 1. (*para papeles*) staple 2. (*licor*) grappa

**grapadora** [gra·pa·'do·ra] *f* stapler

**grapar** [gra·'par] *vt* to staple

**grasa** ['gra·sa] *f* 1. fat; **~ de cerdo** pork fat 2. TÉC oil, grease 3. (*mugre*) grime

**grasiento, -a** [gra·'sjen·to, -a] *adj* fatty; (*de aceite*) greasy

**graso, -a** ['gra·so, -a] *adj* fatty; (*piel*) oily; (*pelo*) greasy

**gratificación** [gra·ti·fi·ka·'sjon, -'θjon] *f* 1. (*recompensa*) reward 2. (*del sueldo*) bonus 3. (*propina*) tip 4. (*satisfacción*) gratification

**gratificante** [gra·ti·fi·'kan·te] *adj* gratifying

**gratificar** <c → qu> [gra·ti·fi·'kar] *vt* 1. (*recompensar*) **~ a alguien por algo** to reward sb for sth 2. (*en el trabajo*) **~ a alguien** to give sb a bonus

**gratinar** [gra·ti·'nar] *vt* to cook au gratin

**gratis** ['gra·tis] *adv* free

**gratitud** [gra·ti·'tud] *f* gratitude

**grato, -a** ['gra·to, -a] *adj* pleasant

**gratuito, -a** [gra·'twi·to, -a] *adj* free

**grava** ['gra·βa] *f* gravel

**gravable** [gra·'βa·βle] *adj* taxable

**gravar** [gra·'βar] *vt* to tax

**grave** ['gra·βe] *adj* serious; (*sonido*) deep; **está ~** he/she is very sick

**gravedad** [gra·βe·'dad] *f* 1. *t.* MED seriousness; **de ~** seriously 2. FÍS gravity 3. MÚS depth

**gravilla** [gra·'βi·ja, -ʎa] *f* gravel

**gravitación** [gra·βi·ta·'sjon, -'θjon] *f* gravitation

**graznar** [gras·'nar, graθ-] *vi* (*cuervo*) to caw; (*ganso*) to honk; (*pato*) to quack

**graznido** [gras·'ni·do, graθ-] *m* (*de cuervo*) caw; (*de ganso*) honk; (*de pato*) quack

**greca** ['gre·ka] *f* AmL coffee machine

**Grecia** ['gre·sja, -θja] *f* Greece

**grecorromano, -a** [gre·ko·rro·'ma·no, -a] *adj* Greco-Roman

**gremio** ['gre·mjo] *m* association; (*sindicato*) trade union

**greña** ['gre·na] *f* matted hair

**griego, -a** ['grje·ɣo] *adj, m, f* Greek

**grieta** ['grje·ta] *f* (*en la pared, una taza*) crack; (*piel*) chap

**grifa** ['gri·fa] *f* dope

**grifo** ['gri·fo] *m* 1. tap; **agua del ~** tap water; **he dejado el ~ abierto** I left the faucet running 2. *Perú, Ecua, Bol* gas station

**grifo, -a** ['gri·fo, -a] *adj inf* stoned

**grillarse** [gri·'jar·se, -'ʎar·se] *vr inf* to go nuts

**grillo** ['gri·jo, -ʎo] *m* ZOOL cricket

**grima** ['gri·ma] *f* **me da ~** (*asco*) it's disgusting; (*dentera*) it gets on my nerves

**gringada** [grin·'ga·da] *f* AmL inf group of gringos; (*faena*) dirty trick

**gringo** ['grin·go] *m* AmL inf gibberish; **hablar en ~** to speak gibberish

**gringo, -a** ['grin·go, -a] *m, f* AmL inf gringo; (*de EE.UU.*) Yank(ee)

**gripa** ['gri·pa] *f* AmL flu

**gripal** [gri·'pal] *adj* flu

**gripe** ['gri·pe] *f* flu; **~ aviar** bird flu

**gris** [gris] *adj, m* gray

**grisáceo, -a** [gri·'sa·seo, -θeo] *adj* grayish

**grisma** ['gris·ma] *f* Chile, Guat, Hond pinch

**gritadera** [gri·ta·'de·ra] *f* Col, Ven loud shouting

**gritar** [gri·'tar] I. *vt* to shout at; (*reprender*) to tell off II. *vi* to shout, to yell

**griterío** [gri·te·'ri·o] *m* uproar

**grito** ['gri·to] *m* shout; **pegar un ~** to shout; **a ~s** in a very loud voice; **a ~ limpio** [*o pelado*] at the top of one's voice; **~ de protesta** cry of protest; **la región está pidiendo a ~s ayuda internacional** the region is crying out for international support; **ser el último ~** to be the (latest) rage

**groenlandés, -esa** [groen·lan·'des, -·'de·sa] I. *adj* Greenland II. *m, f* Greenlander

**Groenlandia** [groen·'lan·dja] f Greenland

**grogui** ['gro·ɣi] adj groggy

**grosella** [gro·'se·ja, -ʎa] f currant

**grosería** [gro·se·'ri·a] f 1. (descortesía) rudeness 2. (ordinariez) vulgarity 3. (observación) rude comment; (palabrota) swearword

**grosero, -a** [gro·'se·ro, -a] adj rude; (ordinario) vulgar

**grosor** [gro·'sor] m thickness

**grotesco, -a** [gro·'tes·ko, -a] adj grotesque

**grúa** ['gru·a] f 1. (máquina) crane 2. (vehículo) wrecker

**grueso, -a** ['grwe·so, -a] adj thick; (persona) stout; **mar gruesa** heavy seas

**grulla** ['gru·ja, -ʎa] f crane

**grumo** ['gru·mo] m lump

**gruñido** [gru·'ɲi·do] m grunt; (queja) grumble; (perro) growl; (puerta) creak

**gruñir** <3. pret gruñó> [gru·'ɲir] vi to grunt; (quejarse) to grumble; (perro) to growl; (puerta) to creak

**gruñón, -ona** [gru·'ɲon, -·'ɲo·na] inf I. adj grumbling II. m, f grumbler

**grupo** ['gru·po] m group; ~ (**industrial**) corporation; ~ **parlamentario** parliamentary group; **trabajo en** ~ group work

**gruta** ['gru·ta] f cave; (artificial) grotto

**guaca** ['gwa·ka] f AmL 1. (tumba) tomb 2. (tesoro) buried treasure 3. (hucha) money box; **hacer** ~ to make money

**guacal** [gwa·'kal] m AmC, Col, Ven gourd

**guacamayo** [gwa·ka·'ma·jo] m macaw

**guacamol(e)** [gwa·ka·'mol, -·'mo·le] m guacamole

**guacamote** [gwa·ka·'mo·te] m Méx manioc

**guachada** [gwa·'tʃa·da] f AmL inf dirty trick

**guachimán** [gwa·tʃi·'man] m AmL watchman

**guacho, -a** ['gwa·tʃo, -a] m, f AmS orphan; (expósito) abandoned child

**guadaña** [gwa·'da·ɲa] f scythe; **la Guadaña** the Grim Reaper

**guagua** ['gwa·ɣwa] f 1. AmC bus 2. CSur baby

**guajiro, -a** [gwa·'xi·ro, -a] adj, m, f Cuba (white) peasant

**guamazo** [gwa·'ma·so] m Méx punch

**guamúchil** [gwa·'mu·tʃil] m вот Méx camachile

**guanábano** [gwa·'na·βa·no] m AmL soursop tree; (fruta) custard apple

**guanaco** [gwa·'na·ko] m guanaco

**guanaco, -a** [gwa·'na·ko, -a] I. adj AmL simple; (lento) slow II. m, f 1. AmL simpleton 2. AmC pey Salvadoran

**guanajo, -a** [gwa·'na·xo, -a] m, f Cuba, PRico turkey

**guandoca** [guan·'do·ka] f Col prison

**guango, -a** ['guan·go, -a] adj Méx baggy

**guano** ['gwa·no] m guano; CSur dung

**guantada** [gwan·'ta·da] f slap; **dar una** ~ **a alguien** to slap sb

**guantazo** [gwan·'ta·so, -θo] m v. **guantada**

**guante** ['gwan·te] m glove

**guantear** [gwan·te·'ar] vt AmL to slap (around)

**guantera** [gwan·'te·ra] f glove compartment

**guaperas** [gwa·'pe·ras] inv inf I. adj good-looking II. m heart-throb

**guaperío** [gwa·pe·'ri·o] m el ~ the jet set

**guapo, -a** ['gwa·po, -a] adj 1. handsome, pretty **estar** [o **ir**] ~ to look smart 2. AmL bully

**guaraca** [gwa·'ra·ka] f AmL (honda) catapult; (látigo) whip

**guaraná** [gwa·ra·'na] f guarana

**guarangada** [gwa·ran·'ga·da] f AmL rude comment

**guaraní** [gwa·ra·'ni] adj, m Guarani; (moneda) guarani

**guarapo** [gwa·'ra·po] m AmL sugar-cane juice; (licor) sugar-cane liquor

**guarda** ['gwar·da] mf guard; (cuidador) keeper; ~ **jurado** security guard

**guardabarros** [gwar·da·'βa·rros] m inv fender

**guardabosque(s)** [gwar·da·'βos·ke(s)] mf (inv) forest ranger; (de caza) gamekeeper

**guardacostas** [gwar·da·'kos·tas] m inv coastguard

**guardaespaldas** [gwar·da·es·'pal·das] mf inv bodyguard

G

**guardameta** [gwar·da·'me·ta] *mf* goal-keeper

**guardar** [gwar·'dar] **I.** *vt* **1.** (*vigilar*) to guard; (*proteger*) to protect **2.** (*conservar, quedarse con*) to keep; ~ **un sitio** to keep a place; ~ **un trozo de pastel a alguien** to save a piece of cake for sb; **¿dónde has guardado las servilletas?** where did you put the napkins?; ~ **algo en el bolsillo** to put sth in one's pocket; ~ **las fuerzas** to save one's strength **3.** COMPUT to save **II.** *vr* ~**se de algo/ alguien** to be on one's guard against sth/sb; ~**se de hacer algo** to be careful not to do sth

**guardarropa** [gwar·da·'rro·pa] *m* check-room; (*armario*) wardrobe

**guardería** [gwar·de·'ri·a] *f* nursery

**guardia¹** ['gwar·dja] *f* **1.** duty; DEP guard; **¿cuál es la farmacia de ~?** which pharmacy is open tonight?; **estar de ~** to be on duty; **estar en ~** to be on one's guard; **bajar la ~** to lower one's guard **2. la Guardia Civil** the Civil Guard; ~ **municipal** [*o* **urbana**] local police

**guardia²** ['gwar·dja] *mf* ~ **civil** civil guard; ~ **municipal** [*o* **urbano**] local policeman; ~ **de tráfico** traffic police-man, -woman *m, f*

**guardián, -ana** [gwar·'djan, -·'dja·na] *m, f* guardian; **perro** ~ watchdog; (*en el zoo*) (zoo)keeper

**guarecerse** [gwa·re·'ser·se, -·'θer·se] *irr como crecer vr* to take refuge; ~**se de la lluvia** to take shelter from the rain

**guarida** [gwa·'ri·da] *f* hideout; (*de animales*) den

**guarnición** [gwar·ni·'sjon, -·'θjon] *f* **1.** CULIN *accompaniment to a main dish* **2.** MIL garrison

**guarro, -a** ['gwa·rro, -a] **I.** *adj* **1.** disgusting; **chiste** ~ dirty joke **2.** (*persona*) dirty; (*moralmente*) smutty **II.** *m, f* pig

**guasa** ['gwa·sa] *f* joke; **estar de** ~ to be joking; **tiene** ~ **que...** +*subj* it's ironic that...

**guasanga** [gwa·'san·ga] *f AmL* hubbub

**guasca** ['gwas·ka] *f AmL* whip

**guasería** [gwa·se·'ri·a] *f Arg, Chile* obscenity

**guaso, -a** ['gwa·so, -a] *adj CSur* peasant;

(*tosco*) coarse

**guata** ['gwa·ta] *f AmL* belly

**Guatemala** [gwa·te·'ma·la] *f* Guatemala

**guatemalteco, -a** [gwa·te·mal·'te·ko, -a] *adj, m, f* Guatemalan

**guay** [gwai] *adj inf* cool

**guayaba** [gwa·'ja·βa] *f* **1.** guava; (*jalea*) guava jelly **2.** *AmL* (*mentira*) lie

**guayabo** [gwa·'ja·βo] *m* guava tree

**guayacán** [gwa·ja·'kan] *m* guaiacum

**Guayana** [gwa·'ja·na] *f* Guyana

**guayarse** [gwa·'jar·se] *vr PRico* to get drunk

**gubernamental** [gu·βer·na·men·'tal] *adj* governmental

**guepardo** [ge·'par·do] *m* cheetah

**güero, -a** ['gwe·ro, -a] *AmL* **I.** *adj* blond(e); (*de piel*) fair **II.** *m, f* blond, blonde *m, f*

**guerra** ['ge·rra] *f* war; **en ~** at war; **la Primera/Segunda Guerra Mundial** the First/Second World War; ~ **quími-ca/psicológica/biológica** chemical/ psychological/biological warfare; **dar mucha ~** *inf* to be a real handful

**guerrero, -a** [ge·'rre·ro, -a] *m, f* warrior

**guerrilla** [ge·'rri·ja, -ʎa] *f* guerrilla band

**guerrillero, -a** [ge·rri·'je·ro, -a, ·ʎe·ro, -a] *m, f* guerrilla (fighter)

**gueto** ['ge·to] *m* ghetto

**guía¹** ['gi·a] *mf* guide; ~ **turístico** tour-ist guide

**guía²** ['gi·a] *f* **1.** (*pauta*) guideline **2.** (*manual*) handbook; ~ **comercial/telefó-nica** trade/telephone directory; ~ **de ferrocarriles** train schedule; ~ **turística** travel guide(book) **3.** TÉC guide **4.** *PRico* (*volante*) steering wheel

**guiar** <*I. pres guío*> [gi·'ar] **I.** *vt* to guide; (*conversación*) to direct **II.** *vr* ~**se por algo** to be guided by sth; **me guío por mi instinto** I follow my instincts

**guijarro** [gi·'xa·rro] *m* pebble

**guillotina** [gi·jo·'ti·na, gi·ʎo-] *f* guil-lotine

**guinda** ['gin·da] *f* morello cherry; **poner la ~ a algo** to top sth off

**guindilla** [gin·'di·ja, -ʎa] *f* chili pepper

**guineo** [gi·'neo] *m AmL* banana

**guiñapo** [gi·'ɲa·po] *m* rag; **estar hecho un ~** to be a wreck

**guiñar** [gi·'ɲar] **I.** *vt* ~ **el ojo a alguien**

to wink at sb **II.** *vi* to wink

**guiño** ['gi·ɲo] *m* wink

**guiñol** [gi·'ɲol] *m* puppet; (*obra*) puppet show

**guión** [gi·'on] *m* **1.** outline; CINE, TV script **2.** LING hyphen; (*en diálogo*) dash

**guionista** [gjo·'nis·ta] *mf* CINE screenwriter; TV scriptwriter

**guiri** ['gi·ri] *mf inf* foreign tourist

**guirigay** [gi·ri·'ɣai] *m* <guirigayes *o* gurigáis> *inf* **1.** (*lenguaje*) gibberish **2.** (*griterío*) uproar; (*barullo*) hubbub

**guirnalda** [gir·'nal·da] *f* garland

**guisado** [gi·'sa·do] *m* stew

**guisante** [gi·'san·te] *m* pea

**guisar** [gi·'sar] *vt* to cook; (*con salsa*) to stew

**guiso** ['gi·so] *m* dish; (*en salsa*) stew

**guita** ['gi·ta] *f* twine; *inf* (*dinero*) dough

**guitarra** [gi·'ta·rra] *f* guitar

**guitarrista** [gi·ta·'rris·ta] *mf* guitarist

**gula** ['gu·la] *f* gluttony

**guripa** [gu·'ri·pa] *m inf* cop

**gurú** [gu·'ru] *m* guru

**gusanillo** [gu·sa·'ni·jo, -ʎo] *m* **matar** el ~ (*comiendo*) to have a snack; (*bebiendo*) to quench one's thirst

**gusano** [gu·'sa·no] *m* worm; (*oruga*) caterpillar

**gustar** [gus·'tar] *vi* **me gusta nadar/el helado** I like swimming/ice cream; **me gustan estos zapatos** I like these shoes; **así me gusta!** ¡well done!; **me gusta tu hermano** I think your brother is handsome; **me gustas** I like you; **me ~ía saber...** I would like to know...

**gustazo** [gus·'ta·θo, -so] *m* great pleasure; **darse el ~ de algo** to treat oneself to sth

**gustillo** [gus·'ti·jo, -ʎo] *m* **1.** (*sabor*) aftertaste **2.** (*sensación*) kick

**gusto** ['gus·to] *m* **1.** (*sentido, sabor*) taste; **una broma de mal ~** a joke in bad taste; **no hago nada a su ~** nothing I do pleases him/her; **~ a algo** taste of sth **2.** (*placer*) pleasure; **con ~** with pleasure; **coger ~ a algo** to take a liking to sth; **estar a ~** to feel comfortable; **tanto ~ en conocerla — el ~ es mío** pleased to meet you — the pleasure is all mine; **cantan que da ~** they sing

wonderfully

**gustoso, -a** [gus·'to·so, -a] *adj* **1.** (*sabroso*) savory **2.** (*agradable*) pleasant; **te acompañaré ~** I'd be glad to accompany you


# H

**H, h** ['a·tʃe] *f* H, h; ~ **de Huelva** H as in Hotel

**haba** ['a·βa] *f* broad bean

**Habana** [a·'βa·na] *f* **La ~** Havana

**habanero, -a** [a·βa·'ne·ro, -a] *adj, m, f* Havanan

**habano** [a·'βa·no] *m* Havana cigar

**haber** [a·'βer] *irr* **I.** *aux* **1.** to have; **ha ido al cine** he/she has gone to the cinema; **he comprado el periódico** I bought the newspaper **2.** *elev* ~ **de hacer algo** to have to do sth; **han de llegar pronto** they should be here soon **3.** (*imperativo*) **no tengo sitio — ¡~ venido antes!** there's no room — you should have come earlier! **II.** *vimpers* **1.** (*ocurrir*) to take place; **ha habido un terremoto** there has been an earthquake; **¿qué hay?** what's the news?; **¿qué hay, Pepe?** how's it going, Pepe? **2.** (*existir, estar*) **hay** there is/are; **había** there was/were; **no hay de qué** not at all; **no hay quien me gane al ping-pong** nobody can beat me at table tennis; **había una vez...** once upon a time there was... **3.** (*obligatoriedad*) **¡hay que ver cómo están los precios!** my God! look at those prices!; **hay que trabajar más** we have to work harder; **no hay que olvidar que...** we must not forget that... **III.** *m* **tener algo en su ~** to have sth (to one's credit)

**habichuela** [a·βi·'tʃwe·la] *f* (kidney) bean; (*blanca*) haricot bean

**hábil** ['a·βil] *adj* **1.** (*diestro*) skilled (**para, en** at) **2.** (*astuto*) shrewd **3.** **días ~es** working days

**habilidad** [a·βi·li·'dad] *f* **1.** (*destreza*) skill **2.** (*facultad*) ability **3.** (*astucia*) shrewdness

**habilidoso, -a** [a·βi·li·'do·so, -a] *adj* ha-

**biloso, -a** [a·βi·'lo·so, -a] *adj AmL* skillful; (*astuto*) shrewd

**habitación** [a·βi·ta·'sjon, -'θjon] *f* room; (*dormitorio*) bedroom; **~ individual** single room

**habitante** [a·βi·'tan·te] *mf* inhabitant; **¿cuántos habitantes tiene Chile?** what is the population of Chile?

**habitar** [a·βi·'tar] **I.** *vi* to live **II.** *vt* to live in

**hábitat** ['a·βi·tat] *m* <hábitats> habitat

**hábito** ['a·βi·to] *m* habit; **he dejado el ~ de fumar** I've given up smoking

**habitual** [a·βi·tu·'al] *adj* regular; **bebedor/cliente ~** regular drinker/client

**habituar** <1. *pres* habitúo> [a·βi·tu·'ar] **I.** *vt* **~ a alguien a algo** to get somebody used to something **II.** *vr* **~se a algo** to get used to sth

**habla** ['a·βla] *f* speech; **quedarse sin ~** to be left speechless; **un país de ~ inglesa** an English-speaking country; **¡Juan al ~!** Juan speaking!; (*manera, dialecto*) way of speaking

**hablado, -a** [a·'βla·do, -a] *adj* spoken; **bien ~** well-spoken; **el francés ~** spoken French; **ser mal ~** to be foulmouthed

**hablador(a)** [a·βla·'dor, -'do·ra] **I.** *adj* talkative **II.** *m(f)* **1.** (*cotorra*) chatterbox **2.** (*chismoso*) gossip

**habladuría** [a·βla·du·'ri·a] *f* rumor; **~s** gossip

**hablante** [a·'βlan·te] *mf* speaker

**hablantina** [a·βlan·'ti·na] *f* Col, Ven chatterbox

**hablar** [a·'βlar] **I.** *vi* **1.** (*decir*) to speak, to talk; **~ a gritos** to shout; **~ entre dientes** to mutter; **déjeme terminar de ~** let me finish what I have to say; **~ claro** to speak frankly; **el autor no habla de este tema** the author does not address this topic; **la policía lo ha hecho ~** the police made him talk; **los números hablan por sí solos** the figures speak for themselves; **¡no ~ás en serio!** you must be joking!; **por no ~ de...** not to mention...; **¡y no se hable más!** and that's an end to it!; **¡ni ~!** no way! **2.** (*conversar*) **~ con alguien** to talk to sb; **~**

**con franqueza** to talk sincerely; **~ por teléfono** to talk on the telephone; **no he podido ~ con él** I haven't managed to speak to him; **~ por los codos** *inf* to talk nineteen to the dozen **III.** *vt* to say; (*idioma*) to speak; **~ a alguien (de algo/alguien)** to talk to sb (about sth/sb); **no me habló en toda la noche** he/she didn't say a word to me all night; **lo hablaré con tu padre** I'll talk about it with your father **III.** *vr:* **~se** to talk to each other; **no se hablan** they are not on speaking terms; **nos hablamos de tú** we are on familiar terms

**hacendoso, -a** [a·sen·'do·so, -a; a·θen-] *adj* hard-working

**hacer** [a·'ser, -'θer] *irr* **I.** *vt* **1.** (*producir*) to make, to manufacture; **la casa está hecha de madera** the house is made of wood **2.** (*realizar*) to do; (*libro*) to write; **¿qué hacemos hoy?** what shall we do today?; **~ una llamada** to make a phone call; **demuestra lo que sabes ~** show us what you can do; **hazlo por mí** do it for me; **a medio ~** half-finished; **hicimos la trayectoria en tres horas** we did the trip in three hours; **lo hecho, hecho está** there's no use crying over spilled milk; **puedes ~ lo que quieras** you can do whatever you want; **¿qué haces por aquí?** what are you doing around here?; **¡me la has hecho!** you've let me in for it; **la ha hecho buena** he's/she's really messed things up **3.** (*pregunta*) to ask; (*observación*) to make; (*discurso*) to make, to give; (*dinero, amigos*) to make; (*ruido*) to make; (*daño*) to cause; **~ destrozos** to wreak havoc; **~ sombra** to cast a shadow; **no puedes ~me esto** you can't do this to me; **¿puedes ~me sitio?** can you fit me in? **4.** (*construir*) to build **5.** (*transformar*) **~ pedazos algo** to smash sth up; **estás hecho un hombre** you're a man now **6.** (*llegar*) **~ puerto** to clear harbor; **~ noche en...** to spend the night in... **7.** (+ *sust*) **~ el amor** to make love; **~ caso a alguien** to pay heed to sb; **~ cumplidos** to pay compliments; **~ deporte** to do sports; **~ frente a algo/alguien** to face up to sth/sb; ~ **la maleta** to pack; ~ **uso de algo** to make use of sth **8.** (+ *verbo*) ~ **creer algo a alguien** to make [*o* have] sb believe sth; ~ **venir a alguien** to make sb come; **hazlo pasar** let him in; **no me hagas contarlo** don't make me say it **9.** (*limpiar*) **hacer las escaleras** *inf* to do the steps **10.** TEAT ~ **una obra** to do [*o* put on] a play; ~ **el papel de Antígona** to play the role of Antigone **11.** ENS (*carrera*) to study, to do; **¿haces francés o inglés?** are you doing French or English? **12.** CULIN (*comida, pastel*) to make; (*patatas*) to do; **quiero la carne bien hecha** I want the meat well done **II.** *vi* **1.** (*convenir*) **eso no hace al caso** that's not relevant **2.** (*oficio*) ~ **de algo** to work as sth **3.** (*con preposición*) **por lo que hace a Juan...** regarding Juan...; **hizo como que no me vio** he/she pretended he/she didn't seen me **III.** *vr:* ~**se 1.** (*volverse*) to become; ~**se del Madrid** to become a Madrid fan **2.** (*crecer*) to grow **3.** (*simular*) to pretend; **se hace a todo** he's/she's always pretending; ~**se la víctima** to act like a victim **4.** (*habituarse*) ~**se a algo** to get used to sth **5.** (*dejarse hacer*) ~**se una foto** to have one's picture taken **6.** (*conseguir*) ~**se respetar** to instill respect; ~**se con el poder** to seize power **7.** (*resultar*) to be; **se me hace muy difícil creer eso** it's very difficult for me to believe that **IV.** *vimpers* **1.** (*tiempo*) **hace frío/calor** it is cold/hot; **hoy hace un buen día** it's a nice day today **2.** (*temporal*) **hace tres días** three days ago; **no hace mucho** not long ago; **desde hace un día** since yesterday

**hacha** ['a·tʃa] *f* axe
**hachís** [xa·'tʃis] *m* hashish
**hacia** ['a·sja, -θja] *prep* **1.** (*dirección*) towards, to; **el pueblo está más** ~ **el sur** the village lies further to the south; **el pueblo está yendo** ~ **Cuzco** the village is on the way to Cuzco; **fuimos** ~ **allí** we went that way; **vino** ~ **mí** he/she came towards me **2.** (*cerca de*) near **3.** (*respecto a*) regarding
**hacienda** [a·'sjen·da, a·'θjen-] *f* **1.** (*finca*) country estate **2.** (*bienes*) ~ **pública**

public finance
**Hacienda** [a·'sjen·da, a·'θjen-] *f* (*ministerio*) Treasury; (*administración*) Internal Revenue Service; **el Ministro de Economía y** ~ the Minister of Finance; **¿pagas mucho a** ~**?** do you pay a lot of tax?
**hacinamiento** [a·si·na·'mjen·to, a·θi-] *m* **1.** (*de haces*) piling **2.** (*de objetos*) stacking; (*de personas*) (over)crowding
**hacinar** [a·si·'nar, a·θi-] **I.** *vt* to pile **II.** *vr:* ~**se** (*personas*) to (over)crowd; (*objetos*) to stack
**hacker** ['xa·ker] *mf* hacker
**hada** ['a·da] *f* fairy; **cuento de** ~**s** fairy tale; ~ **madrina** fairy godmother
**Haití** [ai·'ti] *m* Haiti
**hala** ['a·la] *interj* **1.** (*sorpresa*) wow! **2.** (*prisa*) come on!
**halagar** <g → gu> [a·la·'ɣar] *vt* to flatter
**halago** [a·'la·ɣo] *m* **1.** (*acción*) flattery **2.** (*palabras*) flattering words *pl*, compliment
**halcón** [al·'kon] *m* falcon
**hall** [xol] *m* hall
**hallar** [a·'jar, -'ʎar] **I.** *vt* **1.** (*encontrar*) to find; (*sin buscar*) to come across; (*tierra*) to discover **2.** (*inventar*) to invent **3.** (*averiguar*) to check **4.** (*darse cuenta*) to realize **II.** *vr:* ~**se 1.** (*sitio*) to be **2.** (*estado*) to feel; **se halló con la resistencia de su partido** he/she met opposition from his/her party
**hallazgo** [a·'jas·ɣo, a·'ʎaθ-] *m* **1.** discovery **2.** *pl* findings *pl*
**halterofilia** [al·te·ro·'fi·lja] *f* weightlifting
**hamaca** [a·'ma·ka] *f* **1.** (*cama*) hammock **2.** (*tumbona*) deckchair **3.** AmL (*mecedora*) rocking chair
**hamacar** <c → qu> [a·ma·'kar] *vt, vr:* ~**se** AmS, Guat to rock
**hambre** ['am·bre] *f* **1.** (*apetito*) hunger; **huelga de** ~ hunger strike; **matar el** ~ to satisfy one's hunger; **me ha entrado** (**el**) ~ I'm getting hungry; **morirse de** ~ to die of hunger; **tener** ~ to be hungry **2.** (*de la población*) starvation **3.** (*deseo*) ~ **de algo** longing for sth; ~ **de poder** hunger for power
**hambrear** [am·bre·'ar] *vi AmL* to starve;

(*mendigar*) to be hungry

**hambriento, -a** [am·'brjen·to, -a] *adj* hungry; (*muerto de hambre*) starving; **estar ~ de poder** to be hungry for power

**hambruna** [am·'bru·na] *f* famine

**hamburguesa** [am·bur·'ɣe·sa] *f* hamburger; **~ con queso** cheeseburger

**hamburguesería** [am·bur·ɣe·se·'ri·a] *f* hamburger restaurant

**haragán, -ana** [a·ra·'ɣan, -·'ɣa·na] *m, f* (*persona*) loafer

**harapo** [a·'ra·po] *m* rag

**hardware** ['xard·wer] *m* hardware

**harem** [a·'ren], **harén** [a·'ren] *m* harem

**harina** [a·'ri·na] *f* **1.** CULIN flour; **~ integral** whole-wheat flour; **~ de trigo** wheat flour **2.** (*polvo*) powder

**harinear** [a·ri·ne·'ar] *vimpers* Ven to drizzle

**harmonía** [ar·mo·'ni·a] *f* harmony

**hartar** [ar·'tar] *irr* **I.** *vt* **1.** (*saciar*) **~ a alguien** to give sb their fill **2.** (*fastidiar*) **me harta con sus chistes** I'm getting sick of his/her jokes **II.** *vr:* **-se 1.** (*saciarse*) to eat one's fill; (*en exceso*) to eat too much **2.** (*cansarse*) to get fed up; **~se de reír** to laugh oneself silly; **me he hartado del tiempo que hace en Nueva York** I'm sick of [*o* fed up with] this New York weather

**harto, -a** ['ar·to, -a] **I.** *adj* **1.** (*repleto*) full; (*en exceso*) too full **2.** (*sobrado*) **tengo hartas razones** I have plenty of reasons **3.** (*cansado*) **estar ~ de alguien/algo** to be sick of [*o* fed up with] sb/sth **II.** *adv* (*sobrado*) (more than) enough; (*muy*) a lot of

**hasta** ['as·ta] **I.** *prep* **1.** (*de lugar*) to; **te llevo ~ la estación** I'll give you a lift to the station; **volamos ~ Madrid** we're flying to Madrid; **~ cierto punto** to a certain degree, up to a point **2.** (*de tiempo*) until, up to until; **~ ahora** up to now; **~ el próximo año** up until next year **3.** (*en despedidas*) **¡~ luego!** see you later!; **¡~ la vista!** see you again!; **¡~ la próxima!** until next time! **II.** *adv* even **III.** *conj* **~ cuando come lee el periódico** he/she even reads the newspaper while he's/she's eating; **no con-**

siguió un trabajo fijo ~ que cumplió 40 años he/she didn't get a steady job until he/she was forty

**hastiar** <*1. pres* hastío> [as·ti·'ar] **I.** *vt* **1.** (*aburrir*) to bore **2.** (*hartar, repugnar*) to sicken **II.** *vr* **-se de alguien/algo** to get fed up with sb/sth

**hastío** [as·'ti·o] *m* **1.** (*tedio*) boredom; **¡qué ~!** what a bore! **2.** (*repugnancia*) disgust

**Hawai** [xa·'wai] *m* Hawaii

**hawaiano, -a** [xa·wa·'ja·no, -a] *adj, m, f* Hawaiian

**haya** ['a·ja] *f* beech; (*madera*) beech wood

**haz** [as, aθ] *m* bunch; (*de papeles*) sheaf

**hazaña** [a·'sa·ɲa, a·'θa-] *f* feat, exploit

**hazmerreír** [as·me·rre·'ir, aθ·me-] *m inv* laughing stock; **es el ~ de la gente** he's/she's the butt of everyone's jokes

**he** [e] *1. pres de* **haber**

**hebilla** [e·'βi·ja, -ʎa] *f* buckle

**hebra** ['e·βra] *f* **1.** (*hilo*) thread **2.** (*fibra*) fiber; **tabaco de ~** loose tobacco

**hebreo, -a** [e·'βreo, -a] *adj, m, f* Hebrew

**heces** ['e·ses, 'e·θes] *fpl* (*excrementos*) feces *pl*

**hechicero, -a** [e·tʃi·'se·ro, -a; -'θe·ro, -a] *m, f* **1.** (*brujo*) sorcerer **2.** (*de tribu*) witch doctor

**hechizar** <z → c> [e·tʃi·'sar, -'θar] *vt* **1.** (*encantar*) to cast a spell on **2.** (*fascinar*) captivate, to enchant

**hechizo** [e·'tʃi·so, -θo] *m* spell; **romper el ~** to break the spell

**hecho** ['e·tʃo] *m* **1.** (*circunstancia*) fact **2.** (*acto*) action, deed; **~ delictivo** criminal act **3.** (*suceso*) JUR deed; **exposición de los ~s** statement of events; **lugar de los ~s** scene of the crime; **los ~s que causaron el incendio** the events that gave rise to the fire **▶ de ~** in fact

**hecho, -a** ['e·tʃo, -a] *adj* **1.** (*maduro*) mature; **vino ~** mature wine **2.** (*cocido*) cooked; **me gusta la carne hecha** I like meat well done; **el pollo está demasiado ~** the chicken is overcooked **3.** (*acabado*) finished; **frase hecha** idiom; **traje ~** ready-made suit **4.** (*adulto*) **un hom-**

**bre ~ y derecho** a real man

**hectárea** [ek·ta·re̱a] *f* hectare

**hedonista** [e·do·nis·ta] **I.** *adj* hedonistic **II.** *mf* hedonist

**hedor** [e·dor] *m* stench; **~ a huevos podridos** stench of rotten eggs

**hegemonía** [e·xe·mo·ni̱·a] *f* hegemony

**helada** [e·la·da] *f* frost; **las primeras ~s del año** the first frosts of the year; **anoche cayó una ~** there was a frost last night

**heladera** [e·la·de̱·ra] *f* fridge

**heladería** [e·la·de·ri̱·a] *f* ice cream parlor

**helado** [e·la·do] *m* ice cream; (*sorbete*) sherbe(r)t

**helado, -a** [e·la·do, -a] *adj* **1.** (*frío*) freezing; (*congelado*) frozen; **estoy ~** I'm freezing; **el lago está ~** the lake is frozen; **las cañerías están heladas** the pipes are frozen **2.** (*pasmado*) **me quedé ~** I was left speechless; (*de miedo*) I was petrified **3.** (*altivo*) aloof

**helaje** [e·la·xe] *m Col* frost

**helar** <e → ie> [e·lar] **I.** *vt* **1.** (*congelar*) to freeze **2.** (*pasmar*) to astonish **II.** *vimpers* to freeze; **~se 1.** (*congelarse*) to freeze; **el lago se ha helado** the lake has frozen over **2.** (*morir*) to freeze to death **3.** (*pasar frío*) to be frozen [*o* ice cold]; **~se de frío** to get chilled to the bone

**helecho** [e·le·tʃo] *m* bracken

**hélice** [e·li·se, -θe] *f* propeller

**helicóptero** [e·li·kop·te·ro] *m* helicopter

**helio** [e̱·ljo] *m* helium

**helipuerto** [e·li·pwer·to] *m* heliport

**helvético, -a** [el·βe̱·ti·ko, -a] *adj, m, f* Swiss

**hematoma** [e·ma·to·ma] *m* bruise; MED hematoma

**hembra** [em·bra] *f* t. ZOOL, ELEC, TÉC (*tornillo*) nut

**hemiplejia** [e·mi·ple·xja] *f*, **hemiplejía** [e·mi·ple·xi̱·a] *f* MED hemiplegia, semiparalysis

**hemisferio** [e·mis·fe̱·rjo] *m* hemisphere

**hemorragia** [e·mo·rra·xia] *f* hemorrhage

**hemorroides** [e·mo·rroi·des] *fpl* hemorrhoids *pl*

**heno** [e̱·no] *m* hay; **fiebre del ~** hay fever

**hepatitis** [e·pa·ti·tis] *f inv* hepatitis

**herbicida** [er·βi·si·da, -θi·da] *m* herbicide

**herbívoro** [er·βi̱·βo·ro] *m* herbivore

**herbolario** [er·βo·la·rjo] *m* health food store, herbalist's

**heredar** [e·re·dar] *vt* to inherit; **propiedad heredada** inherited property; **problemas heredados del franquismo** problems handed down from Franco's time

**heredero, -a** [e·re·de̱·ro, -a] *m, f* heir; **el ~ del trono** heir to the throne; **el príncipe ~** the crown prince

**hereditario, -a** [e·re·di·ta̱·rjo, -a] *adj* hereditary; **enfermedad hereditaria** hereditary disease

**herencia** [e·ren·sja, -θja] *f* **1.** JUR inheritance **2.** (*legado*) legacy; **una ~ de la antigüedad** a legacy of the past

**herida** [e·ri·da] *f* **1.** (*lesión*) wound; **tocar a alguien en la ~** *fig* to find somebody's weak [*o* sore] spot **2.** (*ofensa*) affront

**herido, -a** [e·ri·do, -a] **I.** *adj* **1.** (*lesionado*) injured; MIL wounded; **~ de gravedad** seriously injured; MIL mortally wounded **2.** (*ofendido*) hurt, offended **II.** *m, f* injured person; MIL wounded soldier; **los ~s** the wounded; **en el atentado no hubo ~s** nobody was wounded in the attack

**herir** [e·rir] *irr como sentir* **I.** *vt* **1.** (*lesionar*) to injure; MIL to wound **2.** (*golpear*) to hit **3.** (*flecha*) to sink into **4.** (*sol*) to beat down **5.** (*ofender*) to hurt, to offend **II.** *vr:* **~se** to be injured

**hermafrodita** [er·ma·fro·di·ta] *adj, m* hermaphrodite

**hermanastro, -a** [er·ma·nas·tro, -a] *m, f* stepbrother, stepsister *m, f*

**hermandad** [er·man·dad] *f* (*de hombres*) brotherhood; (*de mujeres*) sisterhood

**hermano, -a** [er·ma·no, -a] *m, f* brother, sister *m, f*; **~ de padre** paternal half-brother; **~ político** brother-in-law; **~ de leche** foster brother; **~s siameses** Siamese twins; **mi ~ mayor/pequeño**

my elder/younger brother; **tengo tres ~s** (*sólo chicos*) I have three brothers; (*chicos y chicas*) I have three brothers and sisters; **medio ~** half-brother; **lenguas hermanas** sister tongues

**hermético, -a** [er·'me·ti·ko, -a] *adj* hermetic(al); (*al aire*) airtight; (*al agua*) watertight

**hermoso, -a** [er·'mo·so, -a] *adj* (*paisaje, mujer*) beautiful; (*hombre*) handsome; (*día*) lovely; (*niño*) pretty; (*sanote*) robust

**hermosura** [er·mo·'su·ra] *f* beauty

**hernia** ['er·nja] *f* hernia

**herniarse** [er·'njar·se] *vr* to rupture oneself; *irón* to work very hard; **¡no te herniarás, no!** *irón* don't burst a blood vessel!

**héroe** ['e·roe] *m* hero; (*protagonista*) main character

**heroico, -a** [e·'roi·ko, -a] *adj* heroic

**heroína** [e·ro·'i·na] *f* **1.** (*de héroe*) heroine; (*protagonista*) main character **2.** (*droga*) heroin

**heroinómano, -a** [e·roi·'no·ma·no, -a] *m, f* heroin addict

**herpes** ['er·pes] *m of inv* herpes

**herradura** [e·rra·'du·ra] *f* horseshoe; **camino de ~** bridle path

**herramienta** [e·rra·'mjen·ta] *f* tool; **~ agrícola** agricultural machinery; **caja de (las) ~** tool box

**herrero** [e·'rre·ro] *m* blacksmith

**hervido** [er·'βi·do] *m AmS* stew

**hervir** [er·'βir] *irr como sentir* **I.** *vi* **1.** (*alimentos*) to boil; (*a fuego lento*) to simmer **2.** (*burbujear*) to bubble **3.** (*persona*) to get angry; **~ en cólera** to lose one's temper; **le hierve la sangre** his/her blood is boiling **4.** (*abundar*) **esta calle hierve en rumores** the street is buzzing with rumors **II.** *vt* **1.** (*bullir*) to boil **2.** (*desinfectar*) to sterilize

**hervor** [er·'βor] *m* **1.** (*acción*) boil; **dar un ~ a algo** to bring sth to the boil; **levantar el ~** to come to the boil; **le falta un ~** *fig* he's has a loose screw **2.** (*burbujeo*) bubbling **3.** (*de la juventud*) fervor

**heterogéneo, -a** [e·te·ro·'xe·neo, -a] *adj* heterogeneous

**heterosexual** [e·te·ro·sek·su·'al] *adj, mf* heterosexual

**heterosexualidad** [e·te·ro·sek·swa·li·'dad] *f* heterosexuality

**hibernación** [i·βer·na·'sjon, -'θjon] *f* hibernation

**hibernar** [i·βer·'nar] *vi* to hibernate

**hibisco** [i·'βis·ko] *m* hibiscus

**híbrido, -a** [i·'βri·do, -a] *adj, m, f* hybrid

**hidratante** [i·dra·'tan·te] *adj* moisturizing; **crema ~** moisturizer

**hidratar** [i·dra·'tar] *vt* to moisturize

**hidrato** [i·'dra·to] *m* hydrate

**hidráulico, -a** [i·'drau·li·ko, -a] *adj* hydraulic

**hidroavión** [i·dro·a·βi·'on] *m* seaplane

**hidroeléctrico, -a** [i·dro·e·'lek·tri·ko, -a] *adj* hydroelectric; **central hidroeléctrica** hydroelectric power station

**hidrógeno** [i·'dro·xe·no] *m* hydrogen

**hidrográfico, -a** [i·dro·'ɣra·fi·ko, -a] *adj* hydrographic

**hiedra** ['je·dra] *f* ivy

**hiel** [jel] *f* **1.** (*bilis*) bile **2.** (*amargura*) bitterness; **echar la ~** to sweat blood

**hielera** [je·'le·ra] *f* **1.** *Chile, Méx* ice bucket **2.** *Arg* (*cubitera*) ice cube tray

**hielo** ['je·lo] *m* **1.** ice; **~ en la carretera** black ice; **~ picado** crushed ice; **el barco ha quedado aprisionado en el ~** the ship is trapped in the ice; **capa** [*o* **manta**] **de ~** icecap; **romper el ~** to break the ice **2.** *pl* (*helada*) frost, cold spell

**hiena** ['je·na] *f* hyena

**hierba** ['jer·βa] *f* (*planta, marihuana*) grass; *t.* MED herb; **~ medicinal** medicinal herb; **infusión de ~s** herbal tea; **mala ~** weed; **tenis sobre ~** lawn tennis ► **como la mala ~** like wildfire

**hierbabuena** [jer·βa·'βwe·na] *f* mint

**hierbajo** [jer·'βa·xo] *m* weed

**hierra** ['je·rra] *f AmL* branding

**hierro** ['je·rro] *m* **1.** iron; **edad del ~** Iron Age; **salud de ~** iron constitution; **voluntad de ~** iron will **2.** (*del ganado*) branding iron **3.** (*para marcar*) brand

**hígado** ['i·ɣa·do] *m* liver

**higiene** [i·'xje·ne] *f* hygiene; **~ personal** personal hygiene

**higiénico, -a** [i·'xje·ni·ko, -a] *adj* hygienic;

**compresa higiénica** sanitary napkin; **papel ~** toilet paper

**higienizar** <z → c> [i·xje·ni·'sar, -'θar] *vt* to clean

**higo** ['i·ɣo] *m* 1. (*fruto*) fig; **~ chumbo** prickly pear 2. *inf* (*cosa sin valor*) **esto me importa un ~** I don't give a hoot; **esto no vale un ~** this is pure nonsense 3. (*algo arrugado*) **estar hecho un ~** (*persona*) to be withered (up); (*ropa*) to be crumpled

**higuera** [i·'ɣe·ra] *f* fig tree

**hijastro, -a** [i·'xas·tro, -a] *m, f* stepson, stepdaughter *m, f*

**hijo, -a** ['i·xo, -a] *m, f* 1. (*parentesco*) son, daughter *m, f*; **~ adoptivo** adopted son; **un ~ de papá** Daddy's boy; **~ político** son-in-law; **~ predilecto** (*de una ciudad*) favorite son; **~ de puta** *vulg* bastard; **~ único** only child; **pareja sin ~s** childless couple; **como cualquier ~ de vecino** just like everybody else; **es ~ de Madrid** he's from Madrid 2. *pl* (*descendencia*) children *pl*, offspring

**híjole** ['i·xo·le] *interj Méx inf* Jesus!

**hilacha** [i·'la·t͡ʃa] *f*, **hilacho** [i·'la·t͡ʃo] *m* loose thread

**hilar** [i·'lar] *vt* 1. (*hilo, araña*) to spin 2. (*inferir*) to work out 3. (*cavilar*) to ponder; **~ fino** *fig* to split hairs

**hilera** [i·'le·ra] *f* (*fila, de cosas iguales*) row, line; MIL file; **colocarse en la ~** to get into line

**hilo** ['i·lo] *m* 1. (*para coser*) thread; (*más resistente*) yarn; **~ bramante** twine; **~ dental** dental floss; **~ de perlas** string of pearls; **cortar el ~ de la vida a alguien** *fig* to cut short sb's life; **mover los ~s** *fig* to pull the strings; **pender de un ~** *fig* to hang by a thread 2. (*tela*) linen 3. TÉC wire; **~ conductor** thread 4. (*de un discurso*) gist; **no sigo el ~ de la película** I'm not following the plot of this movie; **perder el ~** (*de la conversación*) to lose the thread of the conversation) 5. **~ musical** piped music, Muzak®

**himen** ['i·men] *m* hymen

**himno** ['im·no] *m* hymn; **~ nacional** national anthem

**hincapié** [in·ka·'pje] *m* hold; **hacer ~ en**

**algo** to emphasize sth

**hincar** <c → qu> [in·'kar] I. *vt* 1. (*clavar*) to stick; **~ el diente en algo** *fig inf* to get one's teeth into sth 2. (*pie*) to get a strong foothold, to stand firmly II. *vr* **~se de rodillas** to kneel down

**hincha** ['in·t͡ʃa] *mf* (*seguidor*) fan

**hinchable** [in·'t͡ʃa·βle] *adj* inflatable; **colchón ~** air mattress

**hinchado, -a** [in·'t͡ʃa·do, -a] *adj* (*pie, madera*) swollen; (*estilo*) verbose; (*persona*) pompous

**hinchar** [in·'t͡ʃar] I. *vt* 1. (*globo*) to blow up; (*neumático*) to inflate; (*estómago*) to swell; **~ la bici** to inflate the bike tires 2. (*exagerar*) to exaggerate; **¡no lo hinches!** come off it! II. *vr:* **~se** 1. (*pierna*) to swell; **se me ha hinchado mucho el pie** my foot's really swollen 2. (*engreírse*) to become conceited 3. *inf* (*de comer*) **~se** (**de algo**) to stuff oneself (with sth) 4. (*hacer mucho*) **~se de mirar/escuchar algo** to look at/to listen to sth non-stop; **~se de insultar a alguien** to go overboard insulting sb

**hinchazón** [in·t͡ʃa·'son, -'θon] *f* (*pie, madera*) swelling

**hindi** ['in·di] *m* Hindi

**hindú** [in·'du] *mf* 1. (*indio*) Indian 2. (*hinduista*) Hindu

**hinduismo** [in·du·'is·mo] *m* Hinduism

**hinojo** [i·'no·xo] *m* fennel

**hipar** [i·'par] *vi* to have the hiccups

**hiperactivo, -a** [i·per·ak·'ti·βo, -a] *adj* hyperactive

**hiperenlace** [i·per·en·'la·se, -θe] *m* hyperlink

**hipermercado** [i·per·mer·'ka·do] *m* superstore

**hipermétrope** [i·per·'me·tro·pe] *adj* farsighted

**hipermetropía** [i·per·me·tro·'pi·a] *f* farsightedness

**hipersensible** [i·per·sen·'si·βle] *adj* hypersensitive

**hipertensión** [i·per·ten·'sjon] *f* high blood pressure

**hipertexto** [i·per·'tes·to] *m* hypertext

**hípica** ['i·pi·ka] *f* (*general*) horsemanship; (*montar*) riding; (*carreras*) horse racing

H

ico, -a [ˈi·pi·ko, -a] *adj* equestrian

ipido [i·ˈpi·ðo] *m* whimper

hipnosis [iβ·ˈno·sis] *f inv* hypnosis

hipnótico, -a [iβ·ˈno·ti·ko, -a] *adj* hypnotic

hipnotizador(a) [iβ·no·ti·sa·ˈðor, -·ˈðo·ra; iβ·no·ti·Ɵa·] *m(f)* hypnotizer

hipnotizar <z → c> [iβ·no·ti·ˈsar, -ˈƟar] *vt* to hypnotize

hipo [ˈipo] *m* 1. (*fisiológico*) hiccup; **tener ~** to have the hiccups 2. (*deseo*) **~ de algo** longing for sth; **...que quita el ~** *fig* ... that takes your breath away

hipocondríaco, -a [i·po·kon·ˈdri·a·ko, -a] *adj, m, f* hypochondriac

hipocrático, -a [i·po·ˈkra·ti·ko, -a] *adj* **el juramento ~** the Hippocratic oath

hipocresía [i·po·kre·ˈsi·a] *f* hypocrisy

hipócrita [i·po·kri·ta] I. *adj* hypocritical II. *mf* hypocrite

hipopótamo [i·po·ˈpo·ta·mo] *m* hippopotamus

hipoteca [i·po·ˈte·ka] *f* mortgage

hipotecar <c → qu> [i·po·te·ˈkar] *vt* to mortgage; **si haces eso ~ás tu libertad** if you do that you're signing away your freedom

hipotensión [i·po·ten·ˈsjon] *f* low blood pressure

hipotenusa [i·po·te·ˈnu·sa] *f* hypotenuse

hipotermia [i·po·ˈter·mja] *f* hypothermia; **muerte por ~** death from hypothermia

hipótesis [i·ˈpo·te·sis] *f inv* hypothesis

hipotético, -a [i·po·ˈte·ti·ko, -a] *adj* hypothetical; **es totalmente ~ que...** we cannot be at all sure that...

hippie [ˈxi·pi], hippy [ˈxi·pi] I. *adj* hippy; **moda ~** hippy style II. *mf* hippy

hirviente [ir·ˈβjen·te] *adj* boiling

hispánico, -a [is·ˈpa·ni·ko, -a] *adj* Hispanic; (*de España*) Spanish; **Filología Hispánica** Spanish Language and Literature

hispano, -a [is·ˈpa·no, -a] I. *adj* Hispanic; (*español*) Spanish II. *m, f* Hispanic; (*español*) Spaniard

Hispanoamérica [is·pa·no·a·ˈme·ri·ka] *f* Spanish America

hispanoamericano, -a [is·pa·no·a·me·ri·ˈka·no, -a] *adj, m, f* Spanish American

hispanohablante [is·pa·no·a·ˈβlan·te] I. *adj* Spanish-speaking; **los países ~s** Spanish-speaking countries II. *mf* Spanish speaker

histeria [is·ˈte·rja] *f* hysteria

histérico, -a [is·ˈte·ri·ko, -a] I. *adj* hysterical II. *m, f* hysterical person

historia [is·ˈto·rja] *f* 1. (*antigüedad*) history; **~ natural** natural history; **~ universal** universal [*o* world] history; **pasar a la ~** (*ser importante*) to go down in history; (*no ser actual*) to be out of date 2. *t. inf* story; **cuenta la ~ completa** tell the whole story; **ésa es la misma ~ de siempre** it's the same old story; **eso sólo son ~s** that doesn't prove anything; **ya sabes la ~** you know what I'm talking about; **¡déjate de ~s!** stop fooling around; **¡no me vengas con ~s!** come off it

historiador(a) [is·to·rja·ˈðor, -·ˈðo·ra] *m(f)* historian

historial [is·to·ˈrjal] I. *adj* historical II. *m* 1. (*antecedentes*) file, record; **~ delictivo** police record 2. (*currículo*) curriculum vitae; **~ profesional** professional background; **este hecho no empañará el ~ de esta institución** this will not tarnish the reputation of this institution; **él tiene un ~ intachable** he has an impeccable record

historiar [is·to·ˈrjar] *vt AmL* to complicate

histórico, -a [is·ˈto·ri·ko, -a] *adj* historical; (*acontecimiento*) historic; **un miembro ~ del partido** a longstanding party member

historieta [is·to·ˈrje·ta] *f* 1. (*anécdota*) anecdote 2. (*con viñetas*) comic strip

hito [ˈi·to] *m* milestone

hobby [ˈxo·βi] *m* <hobbies> hobby

hocico [o·ˈsi·ko, o·ˈƟi·] *m* muzzle; (*de cerdo*) snout; *inf* mug; **caer de ~s** to fall on one's face; **estar de ~s** to be in a bad mood; **meter el ~ en todo** *fig* to stick one's nose in everything

hocicudo, -a [o·si·ˈku·ðo, -a] *adj AmL* 1. (*persona*) thick-lipped 2. (*animal*) long-snouted

hockey [ˈxo·kei] *m* hockey; **~ sobre hielo/hierba** ice/field hockey

hogar [o·ˈɣar] *m* 1. (*casa*) home; **~ del pensionista** old people's home; **~ de** adopción foster home; **artículos para el ~** household items; **persona sin ~** homeless person **2.** (*familia*) family; **la vida del ~** family life; **crear un ~ to** start a family

**hoguera** [o·'ɣe·ra] *f* bonfire; **morir en la ~** to be burnt at the stake

**hoja** ['o·xa] *f* **1.** (*de planta*) leaf; (*pétalo*) petal; **~s del bosque** forest leaves; **árbol sin ~s** leafless tree; **los árboles vuelven a echar ~s** the leaves on the trees are sprouting again **2.** (*de papel*) sheet; **~ de lata** tinplate; **~ volante** leaflet, flyer; **~ de una mesa** (**extensible**) table flap; **pasar la ~** to turn the page; **no hay** [*o* **tiene**] **vuelta de ~** *fig* there's no doubt about it **3.** (*formulario*) form; **~ de estudios** educational record; **~ de pedido** order form; **~ de servicios** service record **4.** (*de arma*) blade; **~ de afeitar** razor blade

**hojalata** [o·xa·'la·ta] *f* tinplate

**hojaldre** [o·'xal·dre] *m* (*pasta*) puff pastry; **pastel de ~** puff pastry

**hojarasca** [o·xa·'ras·ka] *f* fallen leaves

**hojear** [o·xe·'ar] *vt* to browse through

**hojuela** [o·'xwe·la] *f AmC* puff pastry

**hola** ['o·la] *interj* hello

**holán** [o·'lan] *m AmC* canvas

**Holanda** [o·'lan·da] *f* the Netherlands

**holandés, -esa** [o·lan·des, -·'de·sa] **I.** *adj* Dutch; **la escuela holandesa** ARTE the Dutch school **II.** *m, f* Dutchman, Dutchwoman *m, f*

**holgado, -a** [ol·'ɣa·do, -a] *adj* spacious; (*ropa*) loose; **en este coche se va ~** there's lots of space in this car; **ir ~ de tiempo** to have plenty of time

**holgazán, -ana** [ol·ɣa·'san, -·'sa·na, -'θan, -·'θa·na] *m, f* loafer

**holgazanear** [ol·ɣa·sa·ne·'ar, ol·ɣa·θa-] *vi* to loaf around

**holgura** [ol·'ɣu·ra] *f* looseness; **vivir con ~** to live comfortably

**holocausto** [o·lo·'kaus·to] *m* holocaust

**hombre** ['om·bre] **I.** *m* man; (*especie humana*) **el ~** mankind; **el ~ de la calle** *fig* the man in the street; **~ de las cavernas** caveman; **~ de confianza** right-hand man; **~ de estado** statesman; **~ del montón** nobody special; **~ de**

**negocios** businessman; **~ de paja** front man; **el ~ medio** the average man; **el ~ del saco** the boogeyman; **ser ~ de dos caras** to be two-faced; **el ~ del tiempo** the weatherman; **el defensa fue al ~** DEP the defender went for the man; **¡está hecho un ~!** he's become a man!; **hacer un ~ de alguien** to make a man out of sb; **¡~ al agua!** man overboard! **II.** *interj* (*sorpresa*) well, well; (*duda*) well…; **¡~!,** **¿qué tal?** hey! how's it going?; **¡cállate, ~!** c'mon, give it a rest; **¡pero, ~!** but, come on!; **¡sí, ~!** yes, of course!

**hombrera** [om·'bre·ra] *f* shoulder pad; (*de uniforme*) epaulet(te)

**hombro** ['om·bro] *m* shoulder; **ancho de ~s** broad-shouldered; **cargado de ~s** round-shouldered; **encogerse de ~s** to shrug one's shoulders; **llevar algo a ~s** carry sth on one's shoulders; <u>arrimar</u> **el ~** to lend a hand; <u>mirar</u> **a alguien por encima del ~** to snub sb

**homenaje** [o·me·'na·xe] *m* tribute; **hacer una fiesta en ~ de alguien** to celebrate in honor of sb; **rendir ~ a alguien** to pay homage to sb

**homenajear** [o·me·na·xe·'ar] *vt* to pay tribute to

**homeopático, -a** [o·meo·'pa·ti·ko, -a] *adj* homeopathic

**homicida** [o·mi·'si·da, -'θi·da] **I.** *adj* homicidal; **el arma ~** the murder weapon **II.** *mf* murderer

**homicidio** [o·mi·'si·djo, -'θi·djo] *m* homicide; **~ planeado** murder; **~ no planeado** manslaughter; **~ frustrado** attempted murder; **brigada de ~s** murder squad

**homo** ['o·mo] *adj inf* gay

**homogeneidad** [o·mo·xe·nei·'dad] *f* homogeneity

**homogeneizar** [z → c] [o·mo·xe·nei·'sar, -'θar] *vt* **1.** *t.* QUÍM to homogenize **2.** (*uniformar*) to standardize

**homogéneo, -a** [o·mo·'xe·neo, -a] *adj* homogeneous

**homologable** [o·mo·lo·'ɣa·βle] *adj* equivalent

**homologar** [g → gu] [o·mo·lo·'ɣar] **I.** *vt* **1.** ENS to validate **2.** TÉC to authorize **II.** *vr:* **~se** to be officially recognized

H

**ólogo, -a** [o·'mo·lo·γo, -a] **I.** *adj* equivalent **II.** *m, f* counterpart

**omosexual** [o·mo·sek·'swal] *adj, mf* homosexual

**homosexualidad** [o·mo·sek·swa·li·'dad] *f* homosexuality

**honda** ['on·da] *f* sling

**hondo, -a** ['on·do, -a] *adj* deep

**hondonada** [on·do·'na·da] *f* GEO depression

**Honduras** [on·'du·ras] *f* Honduras

**hondureño, -a** [on·du·'re·ɲo, -a] *adj, m, f* Honduran

**honestidad** [o·nes·ti·'dad] *f* honesty

**honesto, -a** [o·'nes·to, -a] *adj* honest

**hongo** ['on·go] *m* fungus; (*comestible*) mushroom

**honor** [o·'nor] *m* honor; **cuestión de ~** matter of honor; **¡palabra de ~!** word of honor!; **¡por mi ~!** on my honor!; **hacer ~ a su fama** to honor his/her name; **es para mí un gran ~** it is a great honor for me; **hacer los ~es** to do the honors

**honorable** [o·no·'ra·βle] *adj* honorable

**honorario, -a** [o·no·'ra·rjo] *adj*, **honorífico, -a** [o·no·'ri·fi·ko, -a] *adj* honorary; **cónsul ~** honorary consul

**honra** ['on·rra] *f* honor; **¡a mucha ~!** I'm proud of it!; **~s fúnebres** funeral proceedings

**honradez** [on·rra·'des, -'deθ] *f* (*honestidad*) honesty; (*integridad*) integrity; **falta de ~** lack of integrity

**honrado, -a** [on·'rra·do, -a] *adj* honorable; (*decente*) upright; **llevar una vida honrada** to lead an honorable life

**honrar** [on·'rrar] **I.** *vt* to honor; **nos honra con su presencia** h/she honors us with his/her presence **II.** *vr* **~se con** [*o de*] **algo** to be an honor for sb

**hora** ['o·ra] *f* **1.** (*del día*) hour; **~s de consulta** surgery hours; **~s extraordinarias** overtime; **~ feliz** happy hour; **~(s) punta** rush hour; **un cuarto de ~** a quarter of an hour; **media ~** half an hour; **una ~ y media** an hour and a half; **a última ~** at the last minute; **a primera/última ~ de la tarde** in the early/late afternoon; **noticias de última ~** last-minute news; **el pueblo está a dos ~s de camino** the village is a two-hour

walk from here; **estuve esperando ~s y ~s** I was waiting for hours and hours; **a la ~** on time **2.** (*de reloj*) time; **¿qué ~ es?** what time is it?, what's the time?; **¿a qué ~ vendrás?** what time are you coming?; **adelantar la ~** to put [*o set*] the clock forward; **poner el reloj en ~** to set one's watch; **retrasar la ~** to put [*o set*] the clock back; **me ha dado [*o tengo*] ~ para el martes** I have an appointment for Tuesday **3.** (*tiempo*) time; **a la ~ de la verdad...** when it comes down to it...; **comer entre ~s** to eat between meals; **estar en ~s bajas** to be feeling down; **no lo dejes para última ~** don't leave it till the last minute; **tener (muchas) ~s de vuelo** *fig* to have alot of experience; **ven a cualquier ~** come at any time; **ya va siendo ~ que tomes tus propias decisiones** it is about time that you made your own decisions

**horario** ['o·ra·rjo] *m* timetable, schedule; (*de consulta*) surgery hours; **~ de atención al público** opening hours; **~ flexible** flextime; **~ de oficina** office hours; **¿qué ~ hacen?** what hours do they work?; **tenemos ~ de tarde** we work evenings; **franja horaria** time zone

**horario, -a** ['o·ra·rjo, -a] *adj* hourly

**horca** ['or·ka] *f* gallows *pl*

**horizontal** [o·ri·son·'tal, o·ri·θon·-] **I.** *adj* horizontal **II.** *f* horizontal position

**horizonte** [o·ri·'son·te, -'θon·te] *m* horizon

**hormiga** [or·'mi·γa] *f* ant; **~ blanca** white ant; **ser una ~** *fig* to be always working

**hormigón** [or·mi·'γon] *m* concrete; **~ armado** reinforced concrete

**hormigueo** [or·mi·'γeo] *m* **1.** (*picor*) pins and needles; **tengo un ~ en la espalda** my back is itching **2.** (*multitud*) swarming

**hormiguero** [or·mi·'γe·ro] *m* **1.** (*de hormigas*) anthill **2.** (*de gente*) swarm; **la plaza era un ~ de gente** the square was crawling with people

**hormiguero, -a** [or·mi·'γe·ro, -a] *adj* related to ants; **oso ~** anteater

**hormona** [or·'mo·na] *f* hormone

**hormonal** [or·mo·'nal] *adj* hormone, hormonal

**hornalla** [or·'na·ja, -ʎa] f AmL 1. (parrilla) barbecue 2. (del fogón) hot plate 3. (horno) oven

**hornear** [or·ne·'ar] vt to bake

**hornillo** [or·'ni·to·pjo, -ʎo] m (cocina) stove; (de una cocina) ring; ~ **de gas** gas ring; ~ **portátil** hot plate

**horno** ['or·no] m 1. oven; ~ **microondas** microwave oven; **recién salido del ~** fresh from the oven; **asar al ~** to oven roast 2. TÉC furnace; ~ **crematorio** cremation furnace; **alto ~** blast furnace; (para cerámica) kiln

**horóscopo** [o·'ros·ko·po] m horoscope

**horquilla** [or·'ki·ja, -ʎa] f (del pelo) bobby pin; (de moño) hairpin

**horrendo, -a** [o·'rren·do, -a] adj v. horroroso

**horrible** [o·'rri·βle] adj 1. (horroroso) horrible; **un crimen ~** a ghastly crime; **una historia ~** a horrible story 2. (muy feo) grotesque

**horripilante** [o·rri·pi·'lan·te] adj horrifying

**horror** [o·'rror] m 1. (miedo, aversión) horror; **tener ~ a algo** to have a horror of sth; **siento ~ a la oscuridad** I'm terrified of the dark; **me da ~ verte con esta corbata** you look terrible with that tie on; **el diseño moderno me parece un ~** I don't like modern design at all; **¡qué ~!** inf how horrible!; **los ~es de la guerra** the atrocities of war 2. inf (mucho) **ganar un ~ de dinero** to earn a lot of money; **hoy hace un ~ de frío** it's freezing cold today; **me cuesta ~es** it's very hard for me; **me gusta ~es el regalo** I absolutely love the gift

**horrorizar** <z → c> [o·rro·ri·'sar, -'θar] I. vt to horrify; **me horrorizó ver el accidente** I was horrified by the accident II. vr ~**se de algo** to be horrified by sth

**horroroso, -a** [o·rro·'ro·so, -a] adj horrifying; **una escena horrorosa** a terrible scene; **su última novela es horrorosa** his/her last novel is awful

**hortaliza** [or·ta·'li·sa, -θa] f vegetable

**hortelano, -a** [or·te·'la·no, -a] m, f truck gardener; ~ **aficionado** amateur gardener

**hortensia** [or·'ten·sja] f BOT hydrangea

**hortera** [or·'te·ra] inf I. adj tasteless II. m vulgar person

**horterada** [or·te·'ra·da] f inf tasteless thing; **esta película es una ~** this movie is so tacky

**hortícola** [or·'ti·ko·la] adj horticultural; **productos ~s** horticultural produce

**hospedaje** [os·pe·'da·xe] m 1. (acción, situación) residence; **dar ~ a alguien** to put sb up 2. (coste) rent

**hospedar** [os·pe·'dar] I. vt to accommodate II. vr: ~**se** to stay

**hospicio** [os·'pi·sjo, -θjo] m 1. (para niños) children's home 2. (para pobres, en un monasterio) hospice

**hospital** [os·pi·'tal] m hospital; ~ **militar** military hospital

**hospitalario, -a** [os·pi·ta·'la·rjo, -a] adj 1. (acogedor) welcoming, hospitable 2. (de hospital) hospital

**hospitalidad** [os·pi·ta·li·'dad] f hospitality

**hospitalización** [os·pi·ta·li·sa·'sjon, -θa·'θjon] f 1. (envío) hospitalization 2. (estancia) stay in hospital

**hospitalizar** <z → c> [os·pi·ta·li·'sar, -'θar] vt to hospitalize; **ayer ~on a mi madre** yesterday my mother went into hospital; **estoy hospitalizado desde el domingo** I've been in hospital since Sunday

**hostal** [os·'tal] m cheap hotel

**hostelería** [os·te·le·'ri·a] f 1. ECON hotel business 2. ENS hotel management; **escuela superior de ~** school of hotel management

**hostelero, -a** [os·te·'le·ro, -a] I. adj hotel II. m, f hotelier

**hostia** ['os·tja] f 1. REL host 2. inf smack; (golpe) bash; **darse una ~** (chocar) to smash

**hostiar** [os·'tjar] vt inf to belt

**hostigante** [os·ti·'yan·te] adj Col (sabor) sickly; (persona) annoying

**hostigoso, -a** [os·ti·'yo·so, -a] adj Chile, Guat, Perú cloying

**hostil** [os·'til] adj hostile; **un recibimiento ~** a hostile reception

**hostilidad** [os·ti·li·'dad] f hostility

**hostión** [os·'tjon] m inf heavy clout

H

~·'tel¦ *m* hotel; ~ **residencia** guest-
~·e

~lero, -a ¦o·te·'le·ro, -a¦ **I.** *adj* ho-
~; **industria hotelera** hotel business
~. *m, f* hotelier, hotelkeeper

~oy ¦oi¦ *adv* today; ~ **(en) día** nowadays;
**llegará de ~ a mañana** it will arrive any
time now; **de ~ en adelante** from now
on; **los niños de ~ (en día)** children
nowadays; **llegará de ~ a mañana** it
will arrive today or tomorrow

**hoyo** ¦'o·jo¦ *m* 1. (*concavidad*) hollow
2. (*agujero*) hole 3. (*sepultura*) grave

**hoyuelo** ¦o·'jwe·lo¦ *m* dimple

**hoz** ¦os, oθ¦ *f* sickle

**huacal** ¦wa·'kal¦ *m And, Méx* wooden box

**huarache** ¦wa·'ra·tʃe¦ *m Méx* sandal; CULIN
*corn dough filled with fried beans*

**huarmi** ¦'war·mi¦ *f AmS* hardworking
woman; (*ama de casa*) housewife

**huasca** ¦'was·ka¦ *f AmL* whip

**huaso, -a** ¦'wa·so, -a¦ *adj, m, f AmS*
peasant

**hubo** ¦'u·βo¦ 3. *pret de* **haber**

**hucha** ¦'u·tʃa¦ *f* 1. (*alcancía*) piggy bank
2. (*ahorros*) savings

**hueco** ¦'we·ko¦ *m* 1. (*agujero*) hole; ~
**del ascensor** elevator shaft; ~ **de la
mano** hollow of the hand 2. (*sitio*)
space; **hazme un ~** move over 3. (*tiempo*) time; **hazme un ~ para mañana**
make time for me tomorrow

**hueco, -a** ¦'we·ko, -a¦ *adj* (*ahuecado*) hollow; (*vacío*) empty; (*sonido*) resonant;
(*tierra*) soft; (*palabras*) empty; (*persona*)
vain; **ponerse ~** to become conceited;
**tener la cabeza hueca** to be dense

**huelga** ¦'wel·ɣa¦ *f* strike; ~ **de advertencia** warning strike; ~ **de brazos caídos** sit-down strike; ~ **general** general
strike; ~ **de hambre** hunger strike; ~
**salvaje** wildcat strike; **convocar una ~**
to call a strike; **declararse en** [*o* **hacer**]
~ to go on strike

**huelguista** ¦wel·'ɣis·ta¦ *mf* striker

**huella** ¦'we·ja, -ʎa¦ *f* 1. (*señal*) mark; ~
**de un animal** animal track; ~ **dactilar**
fingerprint 2. (*vestigio*) trace; (*pasos*)
footsteps; **seguir las ~s de alguien** to
follow sb's footsteps

**huérfano, -a** ¦'wer·fa·no, -a¦ **I.** *adj* or-

phan; **ser ~ de padre** to have no father; **quedarse ~** to become an orphan; **la ciudad se queda huérfana
en invierno** the city empties in winter
**II.** *m, f* orphan

**huerta** ¦'wer·ta¦ *f*, **huerto** ¦'wer·to¦ *m*
(*hortalizas*) vegetable patch; (*frutales*)
orchard; ~ **familiar** allotment

**hueso** ¦'we·so¦ *m* 1. ANAT bone; **carne
sin** ~ boneless meat; **estar en los ~s** to
be a rack of bones; **un ~ duro de roer** a
hard nut to crack; **este profesor es un
~** this teacher's really strict 2. (*de fruto*)
pit 3. *AmL* (*trabajo*) hard work

**huésped** ¦'wes·ped¦ *mf* guest; BIO host

**huesudo, -a** ¦we·'su·do, -a¦ *adj* big-
boned; (*carne*) bony

**hueva** ¦'we·βa¦ *f* roe

**huevada** ¦we·'βa·da¦ *f AmL inf* stupid thing

**huevear** ¦we·βe·'ar¦ *vi AmS inf* to fool
around

**huevo** ¦'we·βo¦ *m* 1. egg; ~ **duro** hard-
boiled egg; ~**s fritos** fried eggs; ~ **pasado por agua** soft-boiled egg; ~**s revueltos** scrambled eggs; **clara de ~** egg
white; **ir pisando ~s** to go very slowly
and/or carefully; **poner un ~** to lay an
egg; *inf* to take a crap; **tener ~s** *inf* to
have guts 2. *vulg* (*testículo*) ball; **¡estoy
hasta los ~s!** I've had it up to here!; **me
importa un ~** I don't give a crap; **¡tiene
~s la cosa!** that's quite something!; **poner algo a alguien a ~** to make sth very
easy for sb; **me costó un ~** (*de dinero*)
it cost loads; (*de dificultades*) it was
damn difficult; **¡y un ~!** like hell!

**huevonear** ¦we·βo·ne·'ar¦ *vi Méx vulg*
to piss around

**huida** ¦u·'i·da¦ *f* flight; ~ **del lugar del
accidente** flight from the scene of the
accident; **no hay ~ posible** there's
no way out

**huir** ¦u·'ir¦ *irr* **I.** *vi* (*escapar*) to flee; ~ **de
casa** to run away from home; **el tiem-
po huye** time flies; **pudieron ~ de sus
perseguidores** they managed to give
their pursuers the slip **II.** *vi, vt* (*evitar*) ~
(**de**) **algo** to keep away from sth; ~ (**de**)
**alguien** to avoid sb

**huiro** ¦'wi·ro¦ *m AmS* seaweed

**hule** ['u·le] *m* 1. oilcloth; (*para la mesa*) tablecloth 2. *AmL* (*caucho*) rubber

**hulero, -a** [u·'le·ro, -a] *m, f AmL* rubber gatherer

**hulla** ['u·ja, -ʎa] *f* fossil coal; **~ blanca** white coal

**humanamente** [u·ma·na·'men·te] *adv* humanly; **hacer todo lo ~ posible** to do everything humanly possible

**humanidad** [u·ma·ni·'dad] *f* 1. (*género humano*) **la ~** mankind; **un crimen contra la ~** a crime against humanity 2. (*naturaleza, caridad humana*) humanity 3. *pl* (*letras*) arts

**humanismo** [u·ma·'nis·mo] *m* humanism

**humanista** [u·ma·'nis·ta] *mf* humanist

**humanitario, -a** [u·ma·ni·'ta·rjo, -a] *adj* humanitarian; **organización humanitaria** humanitarian organization

**humanizar** <z → c> [u·ma·ni·'sar, -'θar] I. *vt* to humanize II. *vr:* **~se** to become human

**humano, -a** [u·'ma·no, -a] *adj* human; (*manera de ser*) humane

**humanoide** [u·ma·'noi·de] *m* humanoid

**humareda** [u·ma·'re·da] *f* cloud of smoke

**humazo** [u·'ma·so, -θo] *m* thick smoke

**humear** [u·me·'ar] *vi* to smoke; (*vapor*) to steam

**humedad** [u·me·'dad] *f* humidity; (*agradable*) moisture; (*desagradable*) dampness

**humedal** [u·me·'dal] *m* wetland

**humedecer** [u·me·de·'ser, -'θer] *irr como crecer vt* to moisten

**húmedo, -a** ['u·me·do, -a] *adj* wet; (*agradable*) moist; (*desagradable*) damp; (*con vapor*) humid; (*aire*) muggy

**humildad** [u·mil·'dad] *f* humility, humbleness; (*social*) lowliness

**humilde** [u·'mil·de] *adj* 1. (*modesto*) humble; **un ~ trabajador** a humble worker 2. (*condición social*) poor; **ser de orígenes ~s** to be of humble origin

**humillación** [u·mi·ʎa·'sjon, -ʎa·'θjon] *f* humiliation; (*vergüenza*) shame

**humillante** [u·mi·'ʎan·te, -'ʎan·te] *adj* humiliating

**humillar** [u·mi·'ʎar, -'ʎar] I. *vt* to humiliate; (*avergonzar*) to shame II. *vr:* **~se** to lower oneself

**humo** ['u·mo] *m* 1. smoke; (*vapor*) steam; **señal de ~** smoke signal; **en ese bar siempre hay ~** it's always smoky in that bar; **la chimenea echa ~** the chimney pours out smoke; **tragar el ~ al fumar** to inhale cigarette smoke 2. *pl* conceit; **bajar los ~s a alguien** to take sb down a peg; **subirse los ~s a la cabeza** to put on airs

**humor** [u·'mor] *m* 1. humor; **~ negro** black humor; **¡pero no tienes sentido del ~ o qué!** don't you have a sense of humor? 2. (*ánimo*) mood; **estar de buen/mal ~** to be in a good/bad mood; **no estoy de ~ para bailar** I'm not in the mood for dancing

**humorado, -a** [u·mo·'ra·do, -a] *adj* **bien/mal ~** (*por un momento*) in a good/bad mood; (*carácter*) even-tempered/bad-tempered

**humorista** [u·mo·'ris·ta] *mf* comic, humorist; (*dibujante*) cartoonist

**humorístico, -a** [u·mo·'ris·ti·ko, -a] *adj* comic

**humus** ['u·mus] *m* humus

**hundido, -a** [un·'di·do, -a] *adj* (*ojos*) deep-set; (*techo*) collapsed; (*persona*) downcast, demoralized

**hundimiento** [un·di·'mjen·to] *m* 1. (*barco*) sinking; (*edificio*) *t.* ECON collapse 2. GEO hollow

**hundir** [un·'dir] I. *vt* 1. (*barco*) to sink; (*suelo*) to cave in; **~ la mano en el agua** to put one's hand in the water; **~ los pies en el barro** to sink one's feet into the mud 2. (*arruinar*) to ruin; (*proyecto*) to cause to fail; (*empresa*) to bankrupt; (*esperanzas*) to destroy; **la crisis económica ha hundido a muchos empresarios** the economic crisis has ruined many businessmen II. *vr:* **~se** 1. (*barco*) to sink; (*edificio*) to collapse; (*suelo*) to cave in; **el rublo se hunde** the ruble is plummeting 2. (*fracasar*) to fail, to lose it; **me he hundido en el tercer set** I lost it in the third set

**húngaro, -a** ['un·ga·ro, -a] *adj, m, f* Hungarian

**Hungría** [un·'gri·a] *f* Hungary

**huracán** [u·ra·'kan] *m* hurricane; (*persona*) whirlwind of energy

H

**...ado, -a** [u·ra·ka·'na·do, -a] *adj* ...stuous; **vientos ~s** hurricane winds

**...o, -a** [u·'ra·ɲo, -a] *adj* **1.** (*insocia...*) unsociable **2.** (*hosco*) surly

**...ar** <g → gu> [ur·'ɣar] I. *vi, vt* **1.** (*re...ver*) ~ **en algo** to poke around in sth; **...el fuego** to poke the fire **2.** (*fisgone...r*) ~ **en algo** to rummage through sth II. *vr* **~se la nariz** to pick one's nose

**...urguetear** [ur·ɣe·te·'ar] *vt AmL* ~ **algo** to rummage around in sth

**hurón, -ona** [u·'ron, -·'ro·na] *m, f* **1.** ferret **2.** *inf* (*husmeador*) nosy parker; (*huraño*) unsociable

**hurra** ['u·rra] *interj* hooray!

**hurtadillas** [ur·ta·'di·ʝas, -ʎas] **a ~** secretly

**hurtar** [ur·'tar] *vt* to steal; (*en tiendas*) to shoplift

**hurto** ['ur·to] *m* stealing; (*en tiendas*) shoplifting; (*cosa*) stolen property

**husmear** [us·me·'ar] I. *vt* (*perro*) to sniff II. *vi* (*perro*) to sniff around; (*fisgonear*) to nose around

**huy** [ui] *interj* (*accidente*) oops!; (*de asombro*) wow!

# I

**I, i** [i] *f* I, i; **~ de Italia** I as in India; **~ griega** y

**I+D** [i mas de] *abr de* **Investigación y Desarrollo** R & D

**ibérico, -a** [i·'βe·ri·ko, -a] *adj* Iberian; **Península Ibérica** Iberian Peninsula

**Iberoamérica** [i·βe·ro·a·'me·ri·ka] *f* Latin America

**iberoamericano, -a** [i·βe·ro·a·me·ri·'ka·no, -a] *adj, m, f* Latin American

**iceberg** [i·se·'βeɣ, i·θe-] *m* <icebergs> iceberg

**icono** [i·'ko·no] *m* REL, COMPUT icon

**ida** ['i·da] *f* departure; **billete de ~** one-way ticket; **billete de ~ y vuelta** return (ticket)

**idea** [i·'dea] *f* **1.** idea; **ni ~** no idea **2.** (*propósito*) intention; **mudar de ~** to change one's mind; **tener ~ de hacer algo** to intend to do sth

**ideal** [i·de·'al] *adj, m* ideal

**idealismo** [i·dea·'lis·mo] *m* idealism

**idealista** [i·dea·'lis·ta] *adj* idealistic

**idealizar** <z → c> [i·dea·li·'sar, -'θar] *vt* to idealize

**idear** [i·de·'ar] *vt* **1.** (*concebir*) to conceive **2.** (*inventar*) to think up **3.** (*un plan*) to devise

**idéntico, -a** [i·'den·ti·ko, -a] *adj* identical; **es ~ a su madre** he looks just like his mother

**identidad** [i·den·ti·'dad] *f* identity; **carné de ~** identity card

**identificación** [i·den·ti·fi·ka·'sjon, -'θjon] *f* identification

**identificar** <c → qu> [i·den·ti·fi·'kar] I. *vt* to identify II. *vr*: **~se** to identify; **~se con alguien/algo** to identify oneself with sb/sth

**ideología** [i·deo·lo·'xi·a] *f* ideology

**idílico, -a** [i·'di·li·ko, -a] *adj* idyllic

**idilio** [i·'di·ljo] *m* idyll; (*relación amorosa*) love affair

**idioma** [i·'djo·ma] *m* language

**idiota** [i·'djo·ta] I. *adj* idiotic, stupid II. *mf* idiot

**idiotez** [i·djo·'tes, -'teθ] *f* idiocy

**ido, -a** ['i·do, -a] *adj inf* crazy

**idolatrar** [i·do·la·'trar] *vt* to worship; (*adorar*) to adore

**ídolo** ['i·do·lo] *m* idol

**idóneo, -a** [i·'do·neo, -a] *adj* apt

**iglesia** [i·'ɣle·sja] *f* church; **casarse por la ~** to have a church wedding

**iglú** [i·'ɣlu] *m* igloo

**ignición** [iɣ·ni·'sjon, -'θjon] *f* ignition

**ignorancia** [iɣ·no·'ran·sja, -θja] *f* ignorance; (*incultura*) lack of culture [*o* education]

**ignorante** [iɣ·no·'ran·te] *adj* **1.** (*desconocedor*) ~ **de algo** ignorant about [*o* of] sth **2.** (*inculto*) uncultured, uneducated

**ignorar** [iɣ·no·'rar] *vt* **1.** (*desconocer*) ~ **algo** to be ignorant of sth **2.** (*no hacer caso*) to ignore

**igual** [i·'ɣwal] I. *adj* **1.** (*idéntico*) identical; (*semejante*) same; MAT equal; **nunca he visto cosa ~** I've never seen anything like it **2.** (*lo mismo*) **¡es ~!** it doesn't matter ► **al ~ que...** as well as... **II.** *mf* equal; **no tiene ~** he/she has no equal **III.** *adv inf* (*quizá*) **~ no viene** he/she might not come

**igualado, -a** [i·ɣwa·'la·do, -a] *adj* (*empatado*) level

**igualar** [i·ɣwa·'lar] **I.** *vt* **1.** (*hacer igual*) to equalize; (*equiparar*) to match **2.** (*allanar*) to flatten (out); (*nivelar*) to level **3.** (*ajustar*) to even out **II.** *vr:* ~**se 1.** (*parecerse*) ~**se a** [*o* con] **alguien** to be similar to sb **2.** (*ponerse al igual*) to make equal, to equate

**igualdad** [i·ɣwal·'dad] *f* equality; (*semejanza*) ~ **de derechos** equal rights; **estar en ~ de condiciones** to be on an equal footing

**igualitario, -a** [i·ɣwa·li·'ta·rjo, -a] *adj* egalitarian

**igualmente** [i·ɣwal·'men·te] **I.** *interj* and the same to you **II.** *adv* equally

**iguana** [i·'ɣwa·na] *f* iguana

**ilegal** [i·le·'ɣal] *adj* illegal, unlawful

**ilegible** [i·le·'xi·βle] *adj* unreadable

**ilegítimo, -a** [i·le·'xi·ti·mo, -a] *adj* (*asunto*) illegal; (*hijo*) illegitimate

**ileso, -a** [i·'le·so, -a] *adj* unharmed, unhurt; **salir** [*o* resultar] **~** to be unscathed

**ilícito, -a** [i·'li·si·to, -a; -θi·to, -a] *adj* illegal, illicit

**ilimitado, -a** [i·li·mi·'ta·do, -a] *adj* unlimited

**ilógico, -a** [i·'lo·xi·ko, -a] *adj* illogical

**iluminación** [i·lu·mi·na·'sjon, -'θjon] *f* illumination; (*alumbrado*) lighting; (*como adorno*) illuminations *pl*

**iluminado, -a** [i·lu·mi·'na·do] *adj* illuminated; (*un monumento*) lit up

**iluminar** [i·lu·mi·'nar] *vt* to illuminate; *fig* to enlighten; (*un monumento*) to light up

**ilusión** [i·lu·'sjon] *f* **1.** (*alegría*) excitement; **ese viaje me hace mucha ~** I'm excited about the journey **2.** (*esperanza*) hope; **hacerse ilusiones** to get one's hopes up **3.** (*sueño*) illusion; (*espejismo*) (optical) illusion

**ilusionar** [i·lu·sjo·'nar] **I.** *vt* **1.** (*entusiasmar*) to excite; **estar ilusionado con algo** to be excited about sth **2.** (*hacer ilusiones*) to raise false hopes **II.** *vr:* ~**se**

(*alegrarse*) to be excited

**ilusionismo** [i·lu·sjo·'nis·mo] *m* illusionism, conjuring

**ilusionista** [i·lu·sjo·'nis·ta] *mf* illusionist

**iluso, -a** [i·'lu·so, -a] *adj* gullible

**ilustración** [i·lus·tra·'sjon, -'θjon] *f* **1.** (*imagen, instrucción*) illustration; (*explicación*) explanation **2.** HIST **la Ilustración** the Enlightenment

**ilustrado, -a** [i·lus·'tra·do, -a] *adj* (*con imágenes*) illustrated

**ilustrar** [i·lus·'trar] *vt* **1.** (*con imágenes*) to illustrate **2.** (*instruir*) to enlighten

**ilustrativo, -a** [i·lus·tra·'ti·βo, -a] *adj* illustrative

**ilustre** [i·'lus·tre] *adj* (*famoso*) illustrious

**imagen** [i·'ma·xen] *f* **1.** (*representación mental*) image; **ser la viva ~ de alguien** to be the spitting image of sb **2.** TV picture

**imaginable** [i·ma·xi·'na·βle] *adj* imaginable

**imaginación** [i·ma·xi·na·'sjon, -'θjon] *f* imagination

**imaginar** [i·ma·xi·'nar] **I.** *vt* to imagine **II.** *vr:* ~**se** (*figurarse*) to imagine, to suppose; **me lo imagino** I can imagine [*o* picture] it

**imaginario, -a** [i·ma·xi·'na·rjo, -a] *adj* imaginary

**imaginativo, -a** [i·ma·xi·na·'ti·βo, -a] *adj* imaginative

**imán** [i·'man] *m* **1.** *t. fig* (*hierro*) magnet **2.** REL imam

**imantar** [i·man·'tar] *vt* to magnetize

**imbatible** [im·ba·'ti·βle] *adj* unbeatable

**imbécil** [im·'be·sil, -θil] *adj, mf* imbecile

**imborrable** [im·bo·'rra·βle] *adj* indelible; (*acontecimiento*) unforgettable

**imbuir** [im·bu·'ir] *irr como huir* **I.** *vt* to imbue **II.** *vr* ~**se de algo** to imbibe sth

**imitable** [i·mi·'ta·βle] *adj* imitable

**imitación** [i·mi·ta·'sjon, -'θjon] *f* imitation

**imitador(a)** [i·mi·ta·'dor, -'do·ra] *m(f)* imitator; (*parodista*) impersonator

**imitar** [i·mi·'tar] *vt* to imitate, to copy; (*parodiar*) to impersonate; **~ una firma** to forge a signature

**impaciencia** [im·pa·'sjen·sja, -'θjen·θja] *f* impatience

**impacientar** [im·pa·sjen·'tar, -θjen·'tar] **I.** *vt* to make impatient **II.** *vr:* **~se** to become impatient

**impaciente** [im·pa·'sjen·te, -'θjen·te] *adj* impatient; **estamos ~s por empezar** we are eager to start

**impactar** [im·pak·'tar] *vt* **1.** (*un acontecimiento*) to make an impact **2.** (*un proyectil*) to strike

**impacto** [im·'pak·to] *m* (*choque*) impact; (*golpe emocional*) shock; (*huella*) damage; *fig* repercussions *pl*; **~ medioambiental** environmental impact

**impago** [im·'pa·ɣo] *m* nonpayment

**impar** [im·'par] *adj* (*número*) odd

**imparable** [im·pa·'ra·βle] *adj* unstoppable

**imparcial** [im·par·'sjal, -'θjal] *adj* impartial; (*sin prejuicios*) unbiased

**imparcialidad** [im·par·sja·li·'dad, -θja·li·'dad] *f* impartiality, fairness

**impartir** [im·par·'tir] *vt* to give; (*conferir*) to impart *form*

**impasible** [im·pa·'si·βle] *adj* impassive

**impecable** [im·pe·'ka·βle] *adj* **1.** *ser* (*correcto*) impeccable **2.** *estar* (*nuevo*) **el motor está ~** the engine is in perfect condition

**impedido, -a** [im·pe·'di·do, -a] *adj* disabled; **estar ~ para algo** to be incapacitated for sth

**impedimento** [im·pe·di·'men·to] *m* **1.** (*que imposibilita algo*) restraint **2.** (*obstáculo*) impediment, hindrance

**impedir** [im·pe·'dir] *irr como pedir vt* **1.** (*imposibilitar*) to prevent, to keep from **2.** (*obstaculizar*) to impede, to hinder

**impenetrable** [im·pe·ne·'tra·βle] *adj* impenetrable

**impensable** [im·pen·'sa·βle] *adj* unthinkable

**imperar** [im·pe·'rar] *vi* to reign; *fig* to prevail

**imperativo** [im·pe·ra·'ti·βo] *m* **1.** LING imperative **2.** *pl* (*necesidad*) imperative

**imperativo, -a** [im·pe·ra·'ti·βo, -a] *adj* imperative

**imperceptible** [im·per·sep·'ti·βle, im·per·θep-] *adj* **1.** (*inapreciable*) imperceptible **2.** (*minúsculo*) minute

**imperdible** [im·per·'di·βle] *m* safety pin

**imperdonable** [im·per·do·'na·βle] *adj* unpardonable, inexcusable

**imperfección** [im·per·fek·'sjon, -'θjon] *f* imperfection, flaw

**imperfecto** [im·per·'fek·to] *m* LING imperfect

**imperfecto, -a** [im·per·'fek·to, -a] *adj* imperfect, flawed

**imperial** [im·pe·'rjal] *adj* imperial

**imperialismo** [im·pe·rja·'lis·mo] *m* POL imperialism

**imperio** [im·'pe·rjo] *m* (*territorio*) empire

**impermeable** [im·per·me·a·βle] **I.** *adj* impermeable **II.** *m* raincoat

**impersonal** [im·per·so·'nal] *adj t.* LING impersonal

**impertinencia** [im·per·ti·'nen·sja, -'nen·θja] *f* (*insolencia*) impertinence, impudence

**impertinente** [im·per·ti·'nen·te] *adj* (*insolente*) impertinent, impudent

**imperturbable** [im·per·tur·'βa·βle] *adj* imperturbable

**ímpetu** ['im·pe·tu] *m* **1.** (*vehemencia*) vehemence **2.** (*brío*) impetus, energy

**impetuoso, -a** [im·pe·tu·o·so, -a] *adj* rash

**implacable** [im·pla·'ka·βle] *adj* implacable; (*riguroso*) relentless

**implantar** [im·plan·'tar] **I.** *vt* **1.** *t.* MED to implant **2.** (*asentar*) to establish **3.** (*instituir*) to found, to institute **4.** (*introducir*) to introduce **II.** *vr:* **~se** to become established

**implementar** [im·ple·men·'tar] *vt AmL* (*método*) to introduce; (*plan*) to implement

**implicación** [im·pli·ka·'sjon, -'θjon] *f* inclusion; (*en un delito*) implication

**implicar** <c → qu> [im·pli·'kar] **I.** *vt* **1.** (*incluir*) to involve **2.** (*significar*) to imply; **eso implica que...** this means that... **II.** *vr:* **~se** to be [*o* become] involved

**implícito, -a** [im·'pli·si·to, -a; -θi·to, -a] *adj* implicit

**implorar** [im·plo·'rar] *vt* (*a alguien*) to implore; (*algo*) to beg

**imponente** [im·po·'nen·te] *adj* (*impresionante*) imposing; (*que infunde respeto*) awesome; (*grandioso*) grand

**imponer** [im·po·'ner] *irr como poner* **I.** *vt* to impose; (*respeto*) to command; **~ a** [*o* **sobre**] **alguien** (*carga, impuestos*) to impose on [*o* upon] sb **II.** *vi* to impress **III.** *vr:* **~se 1.** (*hacerse ineludible*) to become unavoidable **2.** (*hacerse obedecer*) **se impuso a los demás** he/she made his/her authority felt **3.** (*prevalecer*) **~se a algo** to prevail over sth

**impopular** [im·po·pu·'lar] *adj* unpopular

**importación** [im·por·ta·'sjon, -'θjon] *f* **1.** (*acción*) importation **2.** (*producto*) import

**importador(a)** [im·por·ta·'dor, -·'do·ra] *m(f)* importer

**importancia** [im·por·'tan·sja, -θja] *f* **1.** (*interés*) importance; **sin ~** unimportant; **restar** [*o* **quitar**] **~ a algo** to play sth down **2.** (*extensión*) scope, magnitude **3.** (*trascendencia*) significance

**importante** [im·por·'tan·te] *adj* **1.** (*de gran interés*) important **2.** (*dimensión*) considerable **3.** (*cantidad*) significant

**importar** [im·por·'tar] **I.** *vt* (*mercancía*) to import **II.** *vi* to matter, to mind; **no importa la hora que sea** it doesn't matter what time it is; **¿a ti qué te importa?** what does it have to do with you?; **¿te importa esperar?** do you mind waiting?

**importe** [im·'por·te] *m* (*cuantía*) value; (*total*) amount

**importunar** [im·por·tu·'nar] *vt* to pester, to importune *form*

**imposibilitar** [im·po·si·βi·li·'tar] *vt* (*impedir*) to impede, to make impossible

**imposible** [im·po·'si·βle] *adj* **1.** (*irrealizable*) impossible **2.** *inf* (*insoportable*) impossible, unbearable

**imposición** [im·po·si·'sjon, -'θjon] *f* imposition

**impositivo, -a** [im·po·si·'ti·βo, -a] *adj* FIN tax

**impostor(a)** [im·pos·'tor, -·'to·ra] *m(f)* impostor, imposter

**impotencia** [im·po·'ten·sja, -θja] *f* **1.** (*falta de poder*) t. MED impotence **2.** (*incapacidad*) incapacity; (*indefensión*)

helplessness

**impotente** [im·po·'ten·te] *adj* **1.** (*sin poder*) impotent, powerless **2.** (*incapaz*) incapable **3.** (*desvalido*) helpless **4.** MED impotent

**impracticable** [im·prak·ti·'ka·βle] *adj* **1.** (*irrealizable*) unfeasible **2.** (*intransitable*) impassable

**imprecisión** [im·pre·si·'sjon, -θi·'sjon] *f* **1.** (*falta de precisión*) inexactness **2.** (*falta de determinación*) vagueness

**impreciso, -a** [im·pre·'si·so, -a; -'θi·so, -a] *adj* **1.** (*no preciso*) imprecise **2.** (*indefinido*) vague

**impredecible** [im·pre·de·'si·βle, -'θi·βle] *adj* unpredictable; (*suceso*) unforeseeable

**impregnar** [im·preɣ·'nar] **I.** *vt* **1.** (*empapar*) to impregnate, to saturate **2.** (*penetrar*) to penetrate **II.** *vr:* **~se** to become impregnated

**imprenta** [im·'pren·ta] *f* printing; (*taller*) printer's; (*impresión*) print

**imprescindible** [im·pre·sin·'di·βle, im·pres·θin-] *adj* (*ineludible*) essential; (*insustituible*) indispensable

**impresentable** [im·pre·sen·'ta·βle] *adj* unpresentable

**impresión** [im·pre·'sjon] *f* **1.** (*huella*) imprint **2.** TIPO printing, impression; COMPUT print-out **3.** (*sensación*) impression; **cambiar impresiones** to compare notes

**impresionante** [im·pre·sjo·'nan·te] *adj* (*emocionante*) impressive, striking; (*magnífico*) magnificent

**impresionar** [im·pre·sjo·'nar] *vt* to impress

**impresionismo** [im·pre·sjo·'nis·mo] *m* ARTE impressionism

**impreso** [im·'pre·so] *m* **1.** (*formulario*) form **2.** (*envío*) printed matter

**impreso, -a** [im·'pre·so, -a] *pp de* **imprimir**

**impresora** [im·pre·'so·ra] *f* COMPUT printer; **~ de inyección de tinta** ink-jet printer; **~ láser** laser printer

**imprevisible** [im·pre·βi·'si·βle] *adj* unforeseeable; (*persona*) unpredictable

**imprevisto** [im·pre·'βis·to] *m* **1.** (*algo inesperado*) contingency, sth unexpected

**2.** *pl* (*gastos*) unexpected expenses

**imprevisto, -a** [im·pre·'βis·to, -a] *adj* (*no previsto*) unforeseen; (*inesperado*) unexpected

**imprimir** [im·pri·'mir] *irr vt* **1.** TIPO, COMPUT to print **2.** (*editar*) to publish **3.** *t. fig* (*un sello*) to stamp

**improbable** [im·pro·'βa·βle] *adj* improbable, unlikely

**improcedente** [im·pro·se·'den·te, im·proθe-] *adj* **1.** (*inadecuado*) inappropriate **2.** (*antirreglamentario*) irregular; JUR inadmissible

**improductivo, -a** [im·pro·duk·'ti·βo, -a] *adj* **1.** (*no productivo*) unproductive **2.** (*antieconómico*) unprofitable

**impropio, -a** [im·'pro·pjo, -a] *adj* improper, unfitting; (*inadecuado*) inappropriate; **ese comportamiento es ~ en él** that behavior is unusual for him

**improvisación** [im·pro·βi·sa·'sjon, -'θjon] *f* improvisation

**improvisar** [im·pro·βi·'sar] *vt* to improvise; TEAT to ad-lib

**improviso, -a** [im·pro·'βi·so, -a] *adj* unexpected; **de ~** unexpectedly

**imprudencia** [im·pru·'den·sja, -θja] *f* **1.** (*irreflexión*) imprudence, carelessness **2.** JUR **~ temeraria** criminal negligence; (*conduciendo*) reckless driving

**imprudente** [im·pru·'den·te] *adj* **1.** (*irreflexivo*) imprudent; (*insensato*) unwise **2.** (*incauto*) incautious

**impuesto** [im·'pwes·to] *m* FIN tax; **~ sobre la renta** income tax; **~ sobre la propiedad** property tax; **Impuesto sobre el Valor Añadido** Value Added Tax; **libre de ~s** tax-free, duty-free; **sujeto a ~s** taxable, dutiable

**impugnar** [im·puɣ·'nar] *vt* **1.** *t.* JUR to contest **2.** (*combatir*) to dispute; (*una teoría*) to challenge

**impulsar** [im·pul·'sar] *vt* **1.** (*empujar*) to impel **2.** (*estimular*) to motivate; (*promover*) to instigate

**impulsivo, -a** [im·pul·'si·βo, -a] *adj* impulsive

**impulso** [im·'pul·so] *m* (*estímulo*) impulse, stimulus

**impulsor(a)** [im·pul·'sor] *adj* **fuerza ~a** driving force

**impune** [im·'pu·ne] *adj* unpunished

**impunidad** [im·pu·ni·'dad] *f* impunity

**impureza** [im·pu·'re·sa, -'re·θa] *f* impurity

**impuro, -a** [im·'pu·ro, -a] *adj t.* REL impure

**imputar** [im·pu·'tar] *vt* to impute

**inaccesible** [in·ak·se·'si·βle, in·ak·θe-] *adj* inaccessible, unapproachable; (*inalcanzable*) beyond one's reach

**inaceptable** [in·a·sep·'ta·βle, in·a·θep-] *adj* unacceptable

**inactivo, -a** [in·ak·'ti·βo, -a] *adj* inactive; (*volcán*) dormant

**inadecuado, -a** [in·a·de·'kwa·do, -a] *adj* inadequate

**inadmisible** [in·ad·mi·'si·βle] *adj* inadmissible

**inadvertido, -a** [in·ad·βer·'ti·do, -a] *adj* **1.** (*descuidado*) inadvertent; **me cogió ~** it caught me unprepared **2.** (*desapercibido*) unnoticed

**inagotable** [in·a·ɣo·'ta·βle] *adj* inexhaustible; (*persona*) tireless

**inaguantable** [in·a·ɣwan·'ta·βle] *adj* unbearable, intolerable

**inalámbrico, -a** [in·a·'lam·bri·ko, -a] *adj* TEL cordless, wireless

**inalcanzable** [in·al·kan·'sa·βle, -'θa·βle] *adj* unattainable, beyond one's reach

**inalterable** [in·al·te·'ra·βle] *adj* unalterable; (*imperturbable*) impassive

**inalterado, -a** [in·al·te·'ra·do, -a] *adj* unchanged

**inamovible** [in·a·mo·'βi·βle] *adj* fixed, immovable

**inanición** [i·na·ni·'sjon, -'θjon] *f* starvation

**inanimado, -a** [in·a·ni·'ma·do, -a] *adj* inanimate

**inapelable** [in·a·pe·'la·βle] *adj* **1.** JUR unappealable, not open to appeal **2.** (*inevitable*) inevitable

**inapetencia** [in·a·pe·'ten·sja, -θja] *f* loss [*o* lack] of appetite

**inapreciable** [in·a·pre·'sja·βle, -'θja·βle] *adj* **1.** (*imperceptible*) inappreciable **2.** (*de gran valor*) priceless

**inasequible** [in·a·se·'ki·βle] *adj* out of reach

**inaudible** [in·au·'di·βle] *adj* inaudible

**inaudito, -a** [in·au·'di·to, -a] adj 1. (*sin precedente*) unprecedented 2. (*vituperable*) outrageous

**inauguración** [in·au·yu·ra·'sjon, -'θjon] f 1. (*puente, exposición*) opening; (*estatua*) unveiling 2. (*comienzo*) inauguration

**inaugurar** [in·au·yu·'rar] vt 1. (*puente*) to open; (*estatua*) to unveil 2. (*comenzar*) to inaugurate

**inca** ['in·ka] adj, m Inca

**incalculable** [in·kal·ku·'la·βle] adj incalculable

**incandescente** [in·kan·de·'sen·te, -des·'θen·te] adj FÍS (*metal*) incandescent

**incansable** [in·kan·'sa·βle] adj tireless

**incapacidad** [in·ka·pa·si·'dad, in·ka·paθi-] f 1. (*ineptitud*) incompetence 2. (*psíquica*) incapacity; (*física*) disability 3. (*falta de habilidad*) inability, incapability

**incapacitado, -a** [in·ka·pa·si·'ta·do, -a; -θi·'ta·do, -a] adj (*incapaz*) incapacitated; (*incompetente*) incompetent

**incapacitar** [in·ka·pa·si·'tar, -θi·'tar] vt to incapacitate

**incapaz** [in·ka·'pas, -'paθ] adj 1. (*inepto*) incapable 2. JUR (*sin capacidad legal*) incapacitated, incompetent 3. (*sin talento*) inept

**incautarse** [in·kau·'tar·se] vr ~ **de algo** (*confiscar*) to confiscate sth; (*adueñarse*) to appropriate sth

**incauto, -a** [in·'kau·to, -a] adj (*sin cautela*) incautious; (*confiado*) credulous

**incendiar** [in·sen·'djar, in·θen-] I. vt to set fire to II. vr: ~**se** to catch fire

**incendio** [in·'sen·djo, in·'θen-] m fire; ~ **intencionado** arson

**incentivar** [in·sen·ti·'βar, in·θen-] vt to motivate, to offer incentives to

**incentivo** [in·sen·'ti·βo, in·θen-] m incentive

**incertidumbre** [in·ser·ti·'dum·bre, in·θer-] f incertitude

**incesante** [in·se·'san·te, in·θe-] adj incessant

**incesto** [in·'ses·to, in·'θes-] m incest

**incidencia** [in·si·'den·sja, in·θi-] f 1. t. MAT incidence 2. (*consecuencia*) repercussion

**incidente** [in·si·'den·te, in·θi-] m incident

**incidir** [in·si·'dir, in·θi-] vi ~ **en algo** (*consecuencias*) to impinge on [o affect] sth; (*tema*) to touch on sth

**incienso** [in·'sjen·so, -'θjen·so] m incense

**incierto, -a** [in·'sjer·to, -a; in·'θjer-] adj (*dudoso*) doubtful, uncertain; (*falso*) untrue

**incineradora** [in·si·ne·ra·'do·ra, in·θi-] f (*para basuras*) incinerator

**incinerar** [in·si·ne·'rar, in·θi-] vt to incinerate; (*cadáveres*) to cremate

**incisión** [in·si·'sjon, in·θi-] f t. MED incision

**inciso** [in·'si·so, in·'θi-] m (*al relatar*) aside

**incitar** [in·si·'tar, in·θi-] vt (*instigar*) to incite

**inclemencia** [in·kle·'men·sja, -θja] f inclemency

**inclinación** [in·kli·na·'sjon, -'θjon] f 1. (*declive*) slope 2. (*afecto*) ~ **por alguien/algo** inclination for [o to] sb/sth 3. (*tendencias*) propensity, tendency

**inclinado, -a** [in·kli·'na·do, -a] adj inclined; ~ **a algo** inclined to [o towards] sth

**inclinar** [in·kli·'nar] I. vt to incline II. vr: ~**se** 1. (*reverencia*) to bow; (*árboles*) to bend 2. (*propender*) to incline 3. (*preferir*) ~**se por algo** to have a penchant for sth

**incluir** [in·klu·ir] irr como huir vt to include, to enclose, to contain; **todo incluido** all-inclusive

**inclusive** [in·klu·'si·βe] adv inclusively

**incluso** [in·'klu·so] prep including; **han aprobado todos, ~ tú** everybody has passed, even you

**incluso, -a** [in·'klu·so, -a] adj included

**incógnita** [in·'koɣ·ni·ta] f enigma; (*secreto*) secret; **despejar la ~** (*secreto*) to disclose the secret

**incógnito, -a** [in·'koɣ·ni·to] adj incognito

**incoherencia** [in·ko·e·'ren·sja, -θja] f incoherence

**incoherente** [in·ko·e·'ren·te] adj incoherent

**incoloro, -a** [in·ko·'lo·ro, -a] *adj* colorless

**incomodar** [in·ko·mo·'dar] *vt* to inconvenience

**incomodidad** [in·ko·mo·di·'dad] *f* discomfort

**incómodo, -a** [in·'ko·mo·do, -a] *adj* 1. (*inconfortable*) uncomfortable 2. (*molesto*) tiresome

**incomparable** [in·kom·pa·'ra·βle] *adj* incomparable

**incompatible** [in·kom·pa·'ti·βle] *adj* incompatible

**incompetencia** [in·kom·pe·'ten·sja, -θja] *f* incompetence

**incompetente** [in·kom·pe·'ten·te] *adj* incompetent

**incompleto, -a** [in·kom·'ple·to, -a] *adj* incomplete

**incomprensible** [in·kom·pren·'si·βle] *adj* incomprehensible

**incomprensión** [in·kom·pren·'sjon] *f* (*no querer comprender*) unwillingness to understand; (*no poder comprender*) incomprehension

**incomunicado, -a** [in·ko·mu·ni·'ka·do, -a] *adj* incommunicado; **el preso estuvo 6 días** ~ the prisoner spent 6 days in solitary confinement

**incomunicar** <c → qu> [in·ko·mu·ni·'kar] *vt* 1. (*aislar*) to isolate 2. (*bloquear*) to cut off

**inconcebible** [in·kon·se·'βi·βle, -θe·'βi·βle] *adj* 1. (*inimaginable*) inconceivable 2. (*inadmisible*) unacceptable

**inconcluso, -a** [in·kon·'klu·so, -a] *adj* unfinished

**incondicional** [in·kon·di·sjo·'nal, -θjo·'nal] *adj* unconditional

**inconexo, -a** [in·ko·'nek·so, -a] *adj* unconnected

**inconformista** [in·kon·for·'mis·ta] *mf* nonconformist

**inconfundible** [in·kon·fun·'di·βle] *adj* unmistakable

**incongruente** [in·kon·'grwen·te] *adj* incongruous

**inconsciencia** [in·kon·'sjen·sja, -kons·'θjen·θja] *f* 1. (*desmayo*) unconsciousness 2. (*insensatez*) senselessness; (*irresponsabilidad*) thoughtlessness

**inconsciente** [in·kon·'sjen·te, -kons·'θjen·te] *adj* 1. *estar* (*desmayado*) unconscious 2. *ser* (*insensato*) senseless; (*irresponsable*) thoughtless 3. *ser* (*gesto*) involuntary

**inconsistente** [in·kon·sis·'ten·te] *adj* 1. (*irregular*) uneven 2. (*poco sólido*) flimsy; (*argumento*) weak

**inconsolable** [in·kon·so·'la·βle] *adj* inconsolable, broken-hearted

**incontable** [in·kon·'ta·βle] *adj* 1. (*innumerable*) countless 2. LING uncountable

**incontinencia** [in·kon·ti·'nen·sja, -θja] *f* t. MED incontinence

**incontrolado, -a** [in·kon·tro·'la·do, -a] *adj* uncontrolled; (*violento*) violent

**inconveniencia** [in·kom·be·'njen·sja, -θja] *f* (*no adecuado*) inappropriateness

**inconveniente** [in·kom·be·'njen·te] I. *adj* (*no adecuado*) inappropriate II. *m* disadvantage; (*obstáculo*) inconvenience

**incordiar** [in·kor·'djar] *vt* to bother

**incordio** [in·'kor·djo] *m inf* bother, pest

**incorporación** [in·kor·po·ra·'sjon, -'θjon] *f* 1. (*al enderezarse*) straightening up; (*al sentarse*) sitting up 2. (*integración*) incorporation

**incorporar** [in·kor·po·'rar] I. *vt* (*a un grupo*) ~ **a algo** to incorporate in [*o* into] sth II. *vr*: ~**se** 1. (*enderezarse*) to sit up 2. (*en el trabajo*) ~**se al trabajo** to start a new job 3. (*agregarse*) ~**se a algo** to join sth

**incorrecto, -a** [in·ko·'rrek·to, -a] *adj* 1. (*erróneo*) erroneous 2. (*descortés*) impolite

**incorregible** [in·ko·rre·'xi·βle] *adj* incorrigible

**incrédulo, -a** [in·'kre·du·lo, -a] *adj* incredulous

**increíble** [in·kre·'i·βle] *adj* incredible

**incrementar** [in·kre·men·'tar] *vt, vr*: ~**se** to increase

**incremento** [in·kre·'men·to] *m* (*aumento*) increment; (*crecimiento*) increase

**increpar** [in·kre·'par] *vt* to rebuke

**incriminar** [in·kri·mi·'nar] *vt* JUR to incriminate

**incrustación** [in·krus·ta·'sjon, -'θjon] *f* (*proceso*) embedding; ARTE inlaying; MED incrustation

**incrustar** [in·krus·'tar] I. *vt* (*con madera*) to inlay II. *vr:* ~**se** to embed itself; MED to encrust

**incubadora** [in·ku·βa·'do·ra] *f* incubator

**incubar** [in·ku·'βar] *vt, vr:* ~**se** to incubate

**incuestionable** [in·kwes·tjo·'na·βle] *adj* unquestionable

**inculcar** <c → qu> [in·kul·'kar] *vt* (*enseñar*) to instill; (*infundir*) to inculcate

**inculpar** [in·kul·'par] *vt* to accuse

**inculto, -a** [in·'kul·to, -a] *adj* uneducated

**incumbencia** [in·kum·'ben·sja, -θja] *f* responsibility, incumbency *form;* **no es de tu** ~ it's none of your business

**incumbir** [in·kum·'bir] *vi* to concern

**incumplimiento** [in·kum·pli·'mjen·to] *m* non-compliance; ~ **de contrato** breach of contract

**incumplir** [in·kum·'plir] *vt* to breach

**incurable** [in·ku·'ra·βle] *adj* incurable

**incurrir** [in·ku·'rrir] *vi* ~ **en una falta** to commit an error

**incursión** [in·kur·'sjon] *f* incursion, strike

**indagar** <g → gu> [in·da·'ɣar] *vt* ~ **algo** to look into sth

**indebido, -a** [in·de·'βi·do, -a] *adj* wrongful; (*ilícito*) illicit

**indecencia** [in·de·'sen·sja, -'θen·θja] *f* indecency

**indecente** [in·de·'sen·te, -'θen·te] *adj* indecent

**indecisión** [in·de·si·'sjon, in·de·θi·] *f* (*vacilación*) indecision

**indeciso, -a** [in·de·'si·so, -a; 'θi·so, -a] *adj* **1.** (*irresoluto*) irresolute **2.** (*que vacila*) indecisive

**indecoroso, -a** [in·de·ko·'ro·so, -a] *adj* indecorous

**indefenso, -a** [in·de·'fen·so, -a] *adj* defenseless

**indefinidamente** [in·de·fi·ni·da·'men·te] *adv* indefinitely

**indefinido, -a** [in·de·fi·'ni·do, -a] *adj t.* LING indefinite

**indemne** [in·'dem·ne] *adj* (*persona*) unharmed; (*cosa*) undamaged

**indemnización** [in·dem·ni·sa·'sjon, -θa·'θjon] *f* indemnity, indemnification

**indemnizar** <z → c> [in·dem·ni·'sar, -'θar] *vt* (*daños y perjuicios*) to indemnify; ~ **por algo** to indemnify for sth

**independencia** [in·de·pen·'den·sja, -θja] *f* independence; **con ~ de algo** independently of sth

**independiente** [in·de·pen·'djen·te] *adj* independent

**independizar** <z → c> [in·de·pen·di·'sar, -'θar] I. *vt* to make independent II. *vr:* ~**se** to become independent

**indescifrable** [in·de·si·'fra·βle, in·des·θi·'fra·βle] *adj* indecipherable

**indescriptible** [in·des·krip·'ti·βle] *adj* indescribable

**indeseable** [in·de·se·'a·βle] *adj* undesirable

**indestructible** [in·des·truk·'ti·βle] *adj* indestructible

**indeterminación** [in·de·ter·mi·na·'sjon, -'θjon] *f* indeterminacy; (*indecisión*) indecision

**indeterminado, -a** [in·de·ter·mi·'na·do, -a] *adj* indeterminate; (*indeciso*) indecisive

**India** ['in·dja] *f* **la** ~ India; **las** ~**s** the Indies

**indicación** [in·di·ka·'sjon, -'θjon] *f* **1.** (*señal*) indication; (*por escrito*) observation; (*consejo*) advice **2.** *pl* (*instrucciones*) instructions *pl*

**indicado, -a** [in·di·'ka·do, -a] *adj* (*aconsejable*) advisable; (*adecuado*) indicated; **eso es lo más** ~ that is the most suitable

**indicador** [in·di·ka·'dor] *m* indicator; TÉC gauge, gage; ECON index

**indicar** <c → qu> [in·di·'kar] *vt* **1.** TÉC (*aparato*) to register **2.** (*señalar, sugerir*) to indicate; (*mostrar*) to show

**índice** ['in·di·se, -θe] *m* **1.** (*biblioteca, catálogo*) index, catalog; (*libro*) table of contents **2.** (*dedo*) index finger, forefinger **3.** (*estadísticas*) rate; ~ **de audiencia** audience ratings

**indicio** [in·'di·sjo, -θjo] *m* sign; JUR indication; (*vestigio*) trace

**indiferencia** [in·di·fe·'ren·sja, -θja] *f* indifference

**indiferente** [in·di·fe·'ren·te] *adj* indifferent; **me es** ~ it doesn't make any difference to me

**indígena** [in·'di·xe·na] *adj* indigenous, native; (*en Latinoamérica*) Indian

**indigente** [in·di·'xen·te] *mf* destitute person

**indigestar** [in·di·xes·'tar] **I.** *vt* to cause indigestion to **II.** *vr:* ~**se 1.** (*empacharse*) ~**se de** [*o* **por**] **algo** to get indigestion from sth **2.** *inf* (*hacerse antipático*) to be detestable

**indigestión** [in·di·xes·'tjon] *f* MED indigestion

**indignación** [in·diɣ·na·'sjon, -'θjon] *f* indignation

**indignado, -a** [in·diɣ·'na·do, -a] *adj* ~ **por algo** indignant about [*o* at] sth

**indignante** [in·diɣ·'nan·te] *adj* infuriating, outrageous

**indignar** [in·diɣ·'nar] **I.** *vt* to infuriate, to outrage **II.** *vr* ~**se por algo** to become indignant [*o* infuriated] about sth

**indigno, -a** [in·'diɣ·no, -a] *adj* **1.** (*desmerecedor*) unworthy **2.** (*vil*) contemptible

**indio, -a** ['in·djo, -a] **I.** *adj* **1.** (*de la India*) Indian **2.** (*de Norteamérica*) American Indian; (*de América Central, Suramérica*) Indian, Amerindian **II.** *m, f* **1.** (*de la India*) Indian **2.** (*de Norteamérica*) American Indian; (*de América Central, Suramérica*) Indian, Amerindian ▶ **hacer el** ~ (*tonterías*) to fool around [*o* about]

**indirecta** [in·di·'rek·ta] *f* *inf* hint, insinuation; **lanzar** [*o* **soltar**] **una** ~ to drop a hint

**indirecto, -a** [in·di·'rek·to, -a] *adj* indirect

**indisciplinado, -a** [in·di·si·pli·'na·do, -a; in·dis·θi-] *adj* undisciplined

**indiscreción** [in·dis·kre·'sjon, -'θjon] *f* indiscretion

**indiscreto, -a** [in·dis·'kre·to, -a] *adj* imprudent; (*que no guarda secretos*) indiscreet

**indiscutible** [in·dis·ku·'ti·βle] *adj* indisputable

**indispensable** [in·dis·pen·'sa·βle] *adj* indispensable; **lo** (**más**) ~ the most es-

sential; **el requisito** ~ **es...** the key requisite is...

**indisponer** [in·dis·po·'ner] *irr como* poner **I.** *vt* **1.** (*enemistar*) ~ **a uno contra otro** to set one person against another **2.** (*de salud*) to indispose **II.** *vr:* ~**se 1.** (*enemistarse*) to quarrel **2.** (*ponerse mal*) to become indisposed

**indispuesto, -a** [in·dis·'pwes·to, -a] *adj* indisposed; (*reacio*) unwilling

**indistintamente** [in·dis·tin·ta·'men·te] *adv* indiscriminately; **se aplica a todos los niños** ~ it applies to all the children without distinction

**indistinto, -a** [in·dis·'tin·to, -a] *adj* indistinguishable

**individual** [in·di·βi·'dwal] *adj* **1.** (*personal*) personal; (*peculiar*) individual **2.** (*simple*) single

**individualista** [in·di·βi·dwa·'lis·ta] *mf* individualist

**individualizar** <z → c> [in·di·βi·dwa·li·'sar, -'θar] *vt* to individualize

**individuo** [in·di·'βi·dwo] *m* individual; *pey* (*sujeto*) individual, character

**indivisible** [in·di·βi·'si·βle] *adj* indivisible

**indocumentado, -a** [in·do·ku·men·'ta·do, -a] *adj* ~ **estar** ~ to be without papers [*o* means of identification]

**índole** ['in·do·le] *f* nature, kind

**indomable** [in·do·'ma·βle] *adj* (*que no se somete*) indomitable; (*indomesticable*) untameable

**inducir** [in·du·'sir, -'θir] *irr como* traducir *vt* **1.** ELEC (*corriente*) to induce **2.** (*instigar*) to induce; ~ **a error** to lead astray, to mislead

**indudable** [in·du·'da·βle] *adj* undeniable; **es** ~ **que...** it is certain that...

**indulgencia** [in·dul·'xen·sja, -θja] *f* indulgence

**indultar** [in·dul·'tar] *vt* JUR (*perdonar*) to pardon

**indulto** [in·'dul·to] *m* (*perdón total*) pardon; (*perdón parcial*) remission

**indumentaria** [in·du·men·'ta·rja] *f* clothing, clothes *pl;* (*vestir*) dress

**industria** [in·'dus·trja] *f* industry

**industrial** [in·dus·'trjal] *adj* industrial; **polígono** ~ industrial estate, industrial park

**industrializar** <z → c> [in·dus·trja·li·'sar,

-'θar] *vt, vr:* **~se** to industrialize

**inédito, -a** [i·'ne·di·to, -a] *adj* (*no publicado*) unpublished

**ineficacia** [in·e·fi·'ka·sja, -θja] *f* 1. (*sin resultado*) ineffectiveness 2. COM. (*sin rentabilidad*) lack of profitability 3. (*de una persona*) inefficiency

**ineficaz** [in·e·fi·'kas -'kaθ] *adj* 1. (*cosa*) ineffective 2. (*persona*) ineffectual

**ineficiente** [in·e·fi·'sjen·te, -'θjente] *adj* inefficient

**INEM** [i·'nem] *m abr de* **Instituto Nacional de Empleo** *national employment agency*

**ineptitud** [i·nep·ti·'tud] *f* **~ para algo** (*incapacidad*) ineptitude in sth; (*incompetencia*) incompetence in sth

**inepto, -a** [i·'nep·to, -a] *adj* **~ para algo** (*incapaz*) inept at sth; (*incompetente*) incompetent at sth

**inequívoco, -a** [in·e·'ki·βo·ko, -a] *adj* unequivocal; (*inconfundible*) unmistakable

**inercia** [i·'ner·sja, -θja] *f t.* FÍS inertia; **por ~** mechanically

**inerte** [i·'ner·te] *adj* (*sin vida*) inanimate; (*inmóvil*) inert

**inesperado, -a** [in·es·pe·'ra·do, -a] *adj* unexpected

**inestable** [in·es·'ta·βle] *adj* 1. (*frágil*) t. TÉC fragile 2. (*variable*) unstable

**inestimable** [in·es·ti·'ma·βle] *adj* inestimable

**inevitable** [in·e·βi·'ta·βle] *adj* inevitable, unavoidable

**inexacto, -a** [in·ek·'sak·to, -a] *adj* inexact; (*erróneo*) inaccurate

**inexistente** [in·ek·sis·'ten·te] *adj* non-existent

**inexperiencia** [in·es·pe·'rjen·sja, -θja] *f* inexperience

**inexperto, -a** [in·es·'per·to, -a] *adj* inexpert; (*sin experiencia*) inexperienced

**inexplicable** [in·es·pli·'ka·βle] *adj* inexplicable

**inexpresivo, -a** [in·es·pre·'si·βo, -a] *adj* inexpressive

**infalible** [in·fa·'li·βle] *adj* infallible

**infame** [in·'fa·me] *adj* 1. (*vil*) wicked 2. (*muy malo*) vile

**infamia** [in·'fa·mja] *f* infamy; (*deshon-*

*ra*) dishonor

**infancia** [in·'fan·sja, -θja] *f* (*niñez, niños*) childhood

**infantería** [in·fan·te·'ri·a] *f* MIL infantry

**infanticida** [in·fan·ti·'si·da, -'θi·da] **I.** *adj* infanticidal **II.** *mf* person who commits infanticide

**infantil** [in·fan·'til] *adj* 1. (*referente a la infancia*) infant; **trabajo ~** child labor 2. *pey* (*ingenuo*) infantile

**infarto** [in·'far·to] *m* heart attack

**infatigable** [in·fa·ti·'γa·βle] *adj* tireless

**infección** [in·fek·'sjon, -'θjon] *f* contagion; (*afección*) infection

**infeccioso, -a** [in·fek·'sjo·so, -a; -'θjo·so, -a] *adj* infectious; **enfermedad infecciosa** contagious disease

**infectar** [in·fek·'tar] **I.** *vt* (*contagiar*) to transmit; *inf* (*contaminar*) to infect; (*corromper*) to corrupt **II.** *vr:* **~se** 1. (*contagiarse*) **~se de SIDA** to catch AIDS 2. (*inflamarse*) to become infected

**infelicidad** [in·fe·li·si·'dad, -θi·'dad] *f* unhappiness

**infeliz** [in·fe·'lis, -'liθ] *adj* 1. (*no feliz*) unhappy 2. *inf* (*ingenuo*) ingenuous

**inferior** [in·fe·'rjor] **I.** *adj* 1. (*debajo*) lower; **labio ~** lower lip 2. (*de menos calidad*) inferior 3. (*menos*) **~ a algo** lesser than sth 4. (*subordinado*) subordinate **II.** *mf* inferior

**inferioridad** [in·fe·rjo·ri·'dad] *f* inferiority; **estar en ~ de condiciones** to be at a disadvantage

**infernal** [in·fer·'nal] *adj* infernal

**infestar** [in·fes·'tar] *vt* **~ de algo** (*inundar*) to overrun with sth; (*infectar*) to infect with sth; (*corromper*) to corrupt with sth

**infidelidad** [in·fi·de·li·'dad] *f* infidelity, unfaithfulness

**infiel** [in·'fjel] **I.** *adj* <infidelísimo> 1. (*desleal*) unfaithful 2. (*pagano*) heathen **II.** *mf* pagan

**infierno** [in·'fjer·no] *m t.* REL hell; **me mandó al ~** he/she told me to go to hell

**infiltrar** [in·fil·'trar] **I.** *vt* to infiltrate, to penetrate **II.** *vr:* **~se en algo** (*penetrar*) to penetrate sth; (*introducirse*) to infiltrate sth

**infinidad** [in·fi·ni·'dad] *f* 1. (*cualidad de infinito*) infinity 2. (*gran número*) enormous quantity

**infinitivo** [in·fi·ni·'ti·βo] *m* infinitive

**infinito** [in·fi·'ni·to] *m t.* MAT infinity

**infinito, -a** [in·fi·'ni·to, -a] *adj* 1. (*ilimitado*) limitless; (*cosas no materiales*) boundless 2. (*incontable*) infinite

**inflación** [in·fla·'sjon, -'θjon] *f t.* ECON inflation

**inflamable** [in·fla·'ma·βle] *adj* (in)flammable

**inflamación** [in·fla·ma·'sjon, -'θjon] *f* 1. *t.* MED inflammation 2. TÉC ignition

**inflamar** [in·fla·'mar] I. *vt* 1. (*encender*) to ignite 2. (*excitar*) *t.* MED to inflame II. *vr:* ~**se** *t.* MED to become inflamed

**inflar** [in·'flar] I. *vt* 1. (*llenar de aire*) to inflate 2. (*exagerar*) to exaggerate II. *vr* 1. (*hincharse*) ~**se de algo** to swell with sth 2. *inf* (*de comida*) to stuff oneself

**inflexible** [in·flek·'si·βle] *adj* 1. (*rígido*) inflexible 2. (*firme*) firm

**inflexión** [in·flek·'sjon] *f* 1. (*de la voz*) *t.* MAT, LING inflection, inflexion 2. (*torcimiento*) bend

**infligir** <g → j> [in·fli·'xir] *vt* (*dolor*) to inflict; ~ **un castigo** to inflict a punishment; ~ **daño** to cause injury

**influencia** [in·'flwen·sja, -θja] *f* influence; **tener** ~ to be influential

**influenciar** [in·flwen·'sjar, -θjar] *vt* to influence; **dejarse** ~ to be influenced

**influir** [in·flu·'ir] *irr como huir* I. *vi* ~ **en** [*o* **sobre**] **algo** (*contribuir*) to have a hand in sth; (*actuar*) to have an influence on sth II. *vt* to influence

**influyente** [in·flu·'jen·te] *adj* influential

**información** [in·for·ma·'sjon, -'θjon] *f* information; TEL directory assistance

**informal** [in·for·'mal] *adj* 1. (*desenfadado*) informal, casual 2. (*no cumplidor*) unreliable

**informar** [in·for·'mar] I. *vt* to inform II. *vr* ~**se de algo** to find out about sth

**informática** [in·for·'ma·ti·ka] *f* computer [*o* computing] science

**informático, -a** [in·for·'ma·ti·ko, -a] I. *adj* **fallo** ~ computer error II. *m, f* computer expert

**informativo** [in·for·ma·'ti·βo] *m* news

broadcast; **el** ~ **de las nueve** the nine o'clock news

**informativo, -a** [in·for·ma·'ti·βo, -a] *adj* informative; **boletín** ~ (*por escrito, radial*) (news) bulletin

**informatizar** <z → c> [in·for·ma·ti·'sar, -'θar] *vt* to computerize

**informe** [in·'for·me] *m* report

**infortunado, -a** [in·for·tu·'na·do, -a] *adj* unfortunate

**infortunio** [in·for·'tu·njo] *m* misfortune, adversity

**infracción** [in·frak·'sjon, -'θjon] *f* infraction; (*administrativa*) breach; ~ **de tráfico** traffic violation

**infractor(a)** [in·frak·'tor, -·'to·ra] *m(f)* offender

**infraestructura** [in·fra·es·truk·'tu·ra] *f* infrastructure

**infrahumano, -a** [in·fra·u·'ma·no, -a] *adj* subhuman

**infranqueable** [in·fran·ke·'a·βle] *adj* impassable, insurmountable *fig*

**infrarrojo, -a** [in·fra·'rro·xo, -a] *adj* infrared

**infravalorar** [in·fra·βa·lo·'rar] *vt* to undervalue, to underestimate

**infringir** <g → j> [in·frin·'xir] *vt* to infringe; ~ **la ley** to break the law

**infructuoso, -a** [in·fruk·tu·'o·so, -a] *adj* fruitless

**infundado, -a** [in·fun·'da·do, -a] *adj* unfounded

**infundir** [in·fun·'dir] *vt* (*deseo*) to infuse; (*respeto*) to command; (*sospechas*) to instill

**infusión** [in·fu·'sjon] *f* infusion; (*de hierbas*) herb(al) tea

**ingeniar** [in·xe·'njar] I. *vt* to devise II. *vr:* ~**se** to contrive, to manage

**ingeniería** [in·xe·nje·'ria] *f* engineering

**ingeniero, -a** [in·xe·'nje·ro, -a] *m, f* engineer

**ingenio** [in·'xe·njo] *m* (*inventiva*) ingenuity; (*maña*) aptitude

**ingenioso, -a** [in·xe·'njo·so, -a] *adj* 1. (*hábil*) skillful 2. (*listo*) ingenious

**ingenuidad** [in·xe·nwi·'dad] *f* 1. (*inocencia*) candor 2. (*torpeza*) naivety

**ingenuo, -a** [in·'xe·nwo, -a] *adj* ingenuous, candid

**ingerir** [in·xe·'rir] *irr como sentir vt* to ingest; (*medicamentos*) to take

**ingestión** [in·xes·'tjon] *f* ingestion, consumption; (*medicamentos*) taking, intake

**Inglaterra** [in·gla·'te·rra] *f* England

**ingle** ['in·gle] *f* ANAT groin

**inglés, -esa** [in·'gles, -·'gle·sa] **I.** *adj* English **II.** *m, f* Englishman *m*, Englishwoman *f*

**ingratitud** [in·gra·ti·'tuð] *f* ingratitude

**ingrato, -a** [in·'gra·to, -a] *adj* (*persona*) ungrateful; (*tarea*) thankless

**ingravidez** [in·gra·βi·'ðes, -'deθ] *f* weightlessness, lack of gravity

**ingrediente** [in·gre·'djen·te] *m* ingredient

**ingresar** [in·gre·'sar] **I.** *vi* **1.** (*inscribirse*) ~ **en algo** to become a member of sth **2.** (*hospitalizarse*) to be admitted to hospital **II.** *vt* **1.** FIN (*cheque*) to pay in, to deposit **2.** (*hospitalizar*) to hospitalize **3.** (*percibir*) to earn

**ingreso** [in·'gre·so] *m* **1.** (*inscripción*) entry; (*alta*) incorporation; **examen de** ~ entrance exam **2.** (*en una cuenta*) deposit **3.** *pl* (*retribuciones*) income

**inhabilitar** [in·a·βi·li·'tar] *vt* JUR **1.** (*incapacitar*) ~ **para algo** to incapacitate for sth **2.** (*prohibir*) ~ **a** (**hacer**) **algo** to disqualify from (doing) sth

**inhabitado, -a** [in·a·βi·'ta·do, -a] *adj* uninhabited

**inhalador** [in·a·la·'dor] *m* MED inhaler

**inhalar** [in·a·'lar] *vt* t. MED to inhale, to breathe in

**inhibición** [in·i·βi·'sjon, -'θjon] *f* (*represión*) repression; (*abstención*) abstention; MED, JUR inhibition

**inhibir** [in·i·'βir] **I.** *vt* to repress; BIO, JUR to inhibit **II.** *vr* ~**se de algo** to abstain from sth; ~**se de hacer algo** to refrain from doing sth

**inhospitalario, -a** [in·os·pi·ta·'la·rjo, -a] *adj* inhospitable, unfriendly

**inhóspito, -a** [in·'os·pi·to, -a] *adj* inhospitable

**inhumación** [in·u·ma·'sjon, -'θjon] *f* inhumation, burial

**inhumano, -a** [in·u·'ma·no, -a] *adj* (*no humano*) inhuman; (*sin compasión*) inhumane

**iniciación** [i·ni·sja·'sjon, -θja·'θjon] *f* **1.** (*comienzo*) beginning, commencement **2.** (*introducción*) ~ **a** [*o* **en**] **algo** initiation to sth

**iniciado, -a** [i·ni·'sja·do, -a; -'θja·do, -a] **I.** *adj* initiated **II.** *m, f* initiate

**inicial** [i·ni·'sjal, -'θjal] *adj* initial

**iniciar** [i·ni·'sjar, -'θjar] **I.** *vt* **1.** (*comenzar*) to begin **2.** (*introducir*) to initiate; COMPUT to log in [*o* **on**] **II.** *vr*: ~**se 1.** (*comenzar*) to begin **2.** (*introducirse en*) ~ **en algo** to learn sth on one's own

**iniciativa** [i·ni·sja·'ti·βa, i·ni·θja-] *f* initiative

**inicio** [i·'ni·sjo, -θjo] *m* beginning

**inigualable** [in·i·γwa·'la·βle] *adj* incomparable, unrivaled

**inimaginable** [in·i·ma·xi·'na·βle] *adj* unimaginable

**ininteligible** [in·in·te·li·'xen·te] *adj* unintelligible; (*escritura*) illegible

**ininterrumpido, -a** [in·in·te·rrum·'pi·do, -a] *adj* uninterrupted

**injerto** [in·'xer·to] *m* (*brote*) t. MED graft

**injuria** [in·'xu·rja] *f* (*con palabras*) insult, affront; (*con acciones*) harm; JUR slander

**injusticia** [in·xus·'ti·sja, -θja] *f* injustice, unfairness

**injustificado, -a** [in·xus·ti·fi·'ka·do, -a] *adj* unjustified

**injusto, -a** [in·'xus·to, -a] *adj* (*no justo*) unjust, unfair

**inmaculado, -a** [in·ma·ku·'la·do, -a, im·ma-] *adj* immaculate

**inmadurez** [in·ma·du·'res, -reθ; im·ma-] *f* immaturity

**inmaduro, -a** [in·ma·'du·ro, -a; im·ma-] *adj* immature

**inmediaciones** [in·me·dja·'sjo·nes, -'θjo·nes; im·me-] *fpl* surroundings *pl*, vicinity

**inmediatamente** [in·me·dja·ta·'men·te, im·me-] *adv* **1.** (*sin demora*) immediately **2.** (*directamente*) directly

**inmediato, -a** [in·me·'dja·to, -a, im·me-] *adj* **1.** (*sin demora*) immediate; **de** ~ immediately, right away **2.** (*directo*) direct **3.** (*próximo*) adjacent

**inmejorable** [in·me·xo·'ra·βle, im·me-] *adj* unbeatable, excellent

**inmensidad** [in·men·si·'dad, im·men-] *f* **1.** (*extensión*) immensity **2.** (*cantidad*) vastness

**inmenso, -a** [in·'men·so, -a/im·'men·so, -a] *adj* immense

**inmerecido, -a** [in·me·re·'si·do, -a, -'θi·do, -a; im·me- ime-] *adj* undeserved

**inmersión** [in·mer·'sjon, im·mer-] *f* (*sumersión*) immersion

**inmerso, -a** [in·'mer·so, -a/im·'mer·so, -a] *adj* immersed; *fig* involved

**inmigración** [in·mi·γra·'sjon, -'θjon; im·mi-] *f* immigration

**inmigrante** [in·mi·'γran·te, im·mi-] *mf* immigrant

**inmigrar** [in·mi·'γrar, im·mi-] *vi* to immigrate

**inminente** [in·mi·'nen·te; im·mi·'nen·te] *adj* imminent

**inmiscuir** [in·mis·ku·'ir, im·mi-] *irr como huir* **I.** *vt* to put in **II.** *vr:* ~**se** to interfere, to meddle

**inmobiliaria** [in·mo·βi·'lja·rja, im·mo-] *f* real estate agency

**inmobiliario, -a** [in·mo·βi·'lja·rjo, -a; im·mo-] *adj* property

**inmoral** [in·mo·'ral, im·mo-] *adj* immoral

**inmortal** [in·mor·'tal, im·mor-] *adj* immortal

**inmortalidad** [in·mor·ta·li·'dad, im·mor-] *f* immortality

**inmortalizar** <z → c> [in·mor·ta·li·'sar, -'θar; im·mor-] *vt* to immortalize

**inmóvil** [in·'mo·βil, im·mo-] *adj* immobile

**inmovilizar** <z → c> [in·mo·βi·li·'sar, -'θar; im·mo-] *vt* (*paralizar*) to paralyze; ~ **a alguien** to put sb out of action

**inmueble** [in·'mwe·βle, im·'mwe-] *adj, m* property

**inmundo, -a** [in·'mun·do, -a; im·'mun·do, -a] *adj* filthy; (*asqueroso*) disgusting

**inmune** [in·'mu·ne/im·'mu·ne] *adj* immune

**inmunidad** [in·mu·ni·'dad, im·mu·ni-] *f* immunity

**inmunizar** <z → c> [in·mu·ni·'θar, im·mu·ni-] *vt* to immunize

**inmunodeficiencia** [in·mu·no·de·fi·'sjen·sja, -'θjen·θja; im·mu·no-] *f* MED immunodeficiency; **síndrome de ~ adquirida** Acquired Immune Deficiency Syndrome

**inmutable** [in·mu·'ta·βle, im·mu-] *adj* immutable

**inmutar** [in·mu·'tar, im·mu·'tar] **I.** *vt* **1.** (*afectar*) to affect **2.** (*variar*) to alter **II.** *vr:* ~**se** to be affected; **sin ~se** without batting an eyelash

**innato, -a** [in·'na·to, -a] *adj* innate, inborn; **tiene un talento ~** he/she has a natural talent

**innecesario, -a** [in·ne·se·'sa·rjo, -a; in·ne·θe-] *adj* unnecessary

**innegable** [in·ne·'γa·βle] *adj* undeniable

**innovación** [in·no·βa·'sjon, -'θjon] *f* innovation

**innovador(a)** [in·no·βa·'dor, -·'do·ra] *adj* innovative, novel

**innovar** [in·no·'βar] *vt* to innovate

**innumerable** [in·nu·me·'ra·βle] *adj* innumerable

**inocencia** [i·no·'sen·sja, -'θen·θja] *f* (*falta de culpabilidad/malicia*) innocence

**inocentada** [i·no·sen·'ta·da, i·no·θen-] *f* (*engaño*) blunder; (*broma*) **gastar una ~ a alguien** to play a practical joke on sb

**inocente** [i·no·'sen·te, -'θen·te] *adj* innocent

**inocuo, -a** [i·'no·kwo, -a] *adj* innocuous, harmless

**inodoro** [i·no·'do·ro] *m* (*recipiente*) toilet

**inodoro, -a** [i·no·'do·ro, -a] *adj* odorless

**inofensivo, -a** [in·o·fen·'si·βo, -a] *adj* inoffensive

**inolvidable** [in·ol·βi·'da·βle] *adj* unforgettable

**inoportuno, -a** [in·o·por·'tu·no, -a] *adj* (*fuera de lugar*) inappropriate; (*fuera de tiempo*) inopportune, untimely

**inorgánico, -a** [in·or·'γa·ni·ko, -a] *adj* (*no viviente*) inorganic

**inoxidable** [in·ok·si·'da·βle] *adj* rustproof; (*acero*) stainless

**input** ['im·put] *m* <inputs> COMPUT input

**inquietante** [in·kje·'tan·te] *adj* (*preocupante*) worrying; (*perturbador*) disturbing

**inquietar** [in·kje·'tar] **I.** *vt* to worry **II.** *vr*

**~se por algo** to worry about sth

**inquieto, -a** [in·'kje·to, -a] *adj* **1.** *estar* (*intranquilo*) anxious **2.** *ser* (*desasosegado*) restless

**inquietud** [in·kje·'tud] *f* **1.** (*intranquilidad*) anxiety **2.** (*desasosiego*) restlessness **3.** *pl* (*anhelos*) aspirations *pl*

**inquilino, -a** [in·ki·'li·no] *m, f* tenant, lessee

**Inquisición** [in·ki·si·'sjon, -'θjon] *f* Inquisition

**insaciable** [in·sa·'sja·βle, -'θja·βle] *adj* insatiable; (*sed*) unquenchable

**insalubre** [in·sa·'lu·βre] *adj* unhealthy, insalubrious *form*

**insalvable** [in·sal·'βa·βle] *adj* unsalvageable; (*obstáculo*) insuperable

**insano, -a** [in·'sa·no, -a] *adj* **1.** (*insalubre*) unhealthy **2.** (*loco*) insane

**insatisfacción** [in·sa·tis·fak·'sjon, -'θjon] *f* dissatisfaction

**insatisfecho, -a** [in·sa·tis·'fe·tʃo, -a] *adj* dissatisfied

**inscribir** [ins·kri·'βir] *irr como escribir* **I.** *vt* **1.** (*registrar*) to register **2.** (*grabar*) to inscribe; **~ en algo** to inscribe on sth **3.** (*alistar*) to enroll; **~ en algo** to enroll in sth **II.** *vr:* **~se 1.** (*registrarse*) to register; **se inscribió en la oficina de empleo** he registered with the employment agency **2.** *t. UNIV* (*alistarse*) to enroll; **~se en algo** to enroll in sth

**inscripción** [ins·krip·'sjon, -kriβ·'θjon] *f* **1.** (*registro*) registration **2.** (*alistamiento*) *t. UNIV* enrollment; **~ en un curso** registration in a course **3.** (*escrito grabado*) inscription

**inscrito, -a** [ins·'kri·to, -a] *pp de* **inscribir**

**insecticida** [in·sek·ti·'si·da, -'θi·da] *m* insecticide

**insecto** [in·'sek·to] *m* insect

**inseguridad** [in·se·ɣu·ri·'dad] *f* insecurity

**inseguro, -a** [in·se·'ɣu·ro, -a] *adj* insecure

**inseminación** [in·se·mi·na·'sjon, -'θjon] *f* insemination

**insensatez** [in·sen·sa·'tes, -'teθ] *f* **1.** (*falta de sensatez*) foolishness **2.** (*disparate*) stupidity

**insensato, -a** [in·sen·'sa·to, -a] *adj* foolish

**insensibilizar** <z → c> [in·sen·si·βi·li·'sar, -'θar] **I.** *vt* to render insensitive; *MED* to desensitize **II.** *vr:* **~se** (*no sentir*) to become insensitive

**insensible** [in·sen·'si·βle] *adj* (*física o afectivamente*) insensitive

**inseparable** [in·se·pa·'ra·βle] *adj* inseparable

**inserción** [in·ser·'sjon, -'θjon] *f* (*inclusión*) inclusion; **~ social** social insertion

**insertar** [in·ser·'tar] *vt* **1.** (*llave, moneda, texto*) to insert **2.** (*anuncio*) to place

**inservible** [in·ser·'βi·βle] *adj* useless

**insignia** [in·'siɣ·nja] *f* **1.** (*de asociación*) badge; (*honorífica*) decoration; (*militar*) insignia **2.** (*bandera*) flag, ensign

**insignificante** [in·siɣ·ni·fi·'kan·te] *adj* insignificant

**insinuación** [in·si·nwa·'sjon, -'θjon] *f* **1.** (*alusión*) allusion **2.** (*engatusamiento*) insinuation

**insinuar** <1. pres insinúo> [in·si·nu·'ar] **I.** *vt* to insinuate; **¿qué estás insinuando?** what are you insinuating? **II.** *vr:* **~se 1.** (*engatusar*) **~se a alguien** to get in with sb; *inf* (*amorosamente*) to flirt with sb **2.** (*cosa*) to be discernible

**insípido, -a** [in·'si·pi·do, -a] *adj* **1.** (*comida*) insipid **2.** (*persona: aburrida*) dull; (*sin espíritu*) listless

**insistencia** [in·sis·'ten·sja, -θja] *f* **1.** (*perseverancia*) persistence **2.** (*énfasis*) insistence

**insistente** [in·sis·'ten·te] *adj* **1.** (*perseverante*) persistent; (*machacón*) insistent **2.** (*con énfasis*) pressing

**insistir** [in·sis·'tir] *vi* to persist; **~ en algo** (*perseverar*) to persist in sth; (*exigir*) to insist on sth

**insobornable** [in·so·βor·'na·βle] *adj* incorruptible

**insolación** [in·so·la·'sjon, -'θjon] *f* *MED* sunstroke

**insolencia** [in·so·'len·sja, -θja] *f* impertinence, disrespect; (*arrogancia*) arrogance

**insolente** [in·so·'len·te] *adj* impertinent; (*arrogante*) insolent

**insolidario, -a** [in·so·li·'da·rjo, -a] *adj*
(*egoísta*) selfish

**insólito, -a** [in·'so·li·to, -a] *adj* (*inhabitual*) unusual, uncommon

**insoluble** [in·so·'lu·βle] *adj* insoluble

**insolvencia** [in·sol·'βen·sja, -θja] *f* ECON insolvency

**insolvente** [in·sol·'βen·te] *adj* ECON insolvent

**insomnio** [in·'som·njo] *m* MED insomnia, sleeplessness

**insonorizar** <z → c> [in·so·no·ri·'sar, -'θar] *vt* to soundproof

**insoportable** [in·so·por·'ta·βle] *adj* unbearable

**insospechable** [in·sos·pe·'tʃa·βle] *adj* (*imprevisible*) unforeseeable

**insospechado, -a** [in·sos·pe·'tʃa·do, -a] *adj* **1.** (*no esperado*) unexpected **2.** (*no sospechado*) unsuspected, unforeseen

**insostenible** [in·sos·te·'ni·βle] *adj* untenable

**inspección** [ins·pek·'sjon, -'θjon] *f* t. TÉC inspection; (*de equipaje*) check; **Inspección Técnica de Vehículos** motor vehicle inspection

**inspeccionar** [ins·pek·sjo·'nar, -θjo·'nar] *vt* t. TÉC to inspect; (*equipaje*) to check

**inspector(a)** [ins·pek·'tor, -·'to·ra] *m(f)* inspector; ENS school inspector

**inspiración** [ins·pi·ra·'sjon, -'θjon] *f* **1.** (*de aire*) inhalation **2.** (*ideas*) inspiration

**inspirar** [ins·pi·'rar] **I.** *vt* **1.** (*aire*) to inhale **2.** (*ideas, confianza*) to inspire **II.** *vr* **~se en algo/alguien** to be inspired by sth/sb

**instalación** [ins·ta·la·'sjon, -'θjon] *f* **1.** (*acción*) installation; (*de baño*) plumbing **2.** (*lo instalado*) TÉC fitting; (*objeto fijo*) fixture **3.** *pl* (*edificio*) facility

**instalador(a)** [ins·ta·la·'dor, -·'do·ra] *m(f)* installer, fitter

**instalar** [ins·ta·'lar] **I.** *vt* **1.** (*calefacción, teléfono*) to install; (*baño*) to plumb, to fit **2.** (*alojar*) to accommodate **II.** *vr*: **~se** to settle; (*negocio*) to set up; **me instalé en un sillón** I settled into an armchair

**instancia** [ins·'tan·sja, -θja] *f* **1.** (*acción*

*de instar*) urging **2.** (*solicitud*) application; (*petición formal*) petition **3.** JUR instance; **en última ~** *fig* as a last resort

**instantánea** [ins·tan·'ta·nea] *f* FOTO snapshot

**instantáneo, -a** [ins·tan·'ta·neo, -a] *adj* instantaneous; (*efecto, café*) instant

**instante** [ins·'tan·te] *m* instant; **en un ~** in an instant; **a cada ~** constantly; **¡un ~!** one moment!

**instar** [ins·'tar] *vi, vt* to urge; **~ a algo** to press for sth

**instaurar** [ins·tau·'rar] *vt* (*imperio*) to found; (*democracia*) to establish; (*plan*) to implement

**instigar** <g → gu> [ins·ti·'ɣar] *vt* to instigate; (*a algo malo*) to incite

**instintivo, -a** [ins·tin·'ti·βo, -a] *adj* instinctive

**instinto** [ins·'tin·to] *m* instinct

**institución** [ins·ti·tu·'sjon, -'θjon] *f* **1.** (*social*) institution; **~ penitenciaria** prison **2.** (*fundación*) foundation

**institucional** [ins·ti·tu·sjo·'nal, -θjo·'nal] *adj* institutional

**instituir** [ins·ti·tu·'ir] *irr como huir vt* **1.** (*fundar*) to found **2.** (*establecer: comisión*) to set up; (*derecho*) to institute; (*norma*) to introduce

**instituto** [ins·ti·'tu·to] *m* **1.** ENS (*de bachillerato*) secondary school, high school **2.** (*científico*) institute

**instrucción** [ins·truk·'sjon, -'θjon] *f* **1.** (*enseñanza*) teaching; (*en una máquina*) instruction **2.** *pl* (*órdenes*) instructions *pl*, directions *pl*

**instructivo, -a** [ins·truk·'ti·βo, -a] *adj* instructive, educational

**instructor(a)** [ins·truk·'tor, -·'to·ra] **I.** *m(f)* instructor **II.** *adj* instructional

**instruido, -a** [ins·tru·'i·do, -a] *adj* educated

**instruir** [ins·tru·'ir] *irr como huir vt* **1.** (*enseñar*) to teach; (*en una máquina*) to instruct; (*en tarea específica*) to train **2.** (*informar*) to inform

**instrumental** [ins·tru·men·'tal] *adj* t. MÚS instrumental

**instrumento** [ins·tru·'men·to] *m* instrument

**insuficiencia** [in·su·fi·'sjen·sja, -'θjen·θja] *f* insufficiency; MED failure

**insuficiente** [in·su·fi·'sjen·te, -'θjen·te]
I. *adj* insufficient II. *m* ENS fail; **sacar un ~** to get an F

**insufrible** [in·su·'fri·βle] *adj* insufferable

**insular** [in·su·'lar] *adj* insular

**insulina** [in·su·'li·na] *f* insulin

**insulso, -a** [in·'sul·so, -a] *adj* (*comida*) insipid, tasteless; (*persona, película*) dull

**insultante** [in·sul·'tan·te] *adj* insulting

**insultar** [in·sul·'tar] *vt* to insult; (*con injurias*) to abuse

**insulto** [in·'sul·to] *m* insult; (*injuria*) abuse

**insuperable** [in·su·pe·'ra·βle] *adj* insuperable, insurmountable; (*resultado*) unbeatable

**insurrección** [in·su·rrek·'sjon, -'θjon] *f* insurrection

**insustituible** [in·sus·ti·tu·'i·βle] *adj* irreplaceable

**intachable** [in·ta·'tʃa·βle] *adj* irreproachable; (*comportamiento*) faultless

**intacto, -a** [in·'tak·to, -a] *adj* (*no tocado*) untouched; (*no dañado*) intact

**intangible** [in·tan·'xi·βle] *adj* (*intocable, inmaterial*) intangible

**integración** [in·te·ɣra·'sjon, -'θjon] *f* integration

**integral** [in·te·'ɣral] *adj* 1. (*completo*) integral, full 2. (*pan*) wholegrain 3. (*elemento*) integral, intrinsic 4. MAT integral

**integrar** [in·te·'ɣrar] I. *vt* 1. (*constituir*) to constitute, to comprise 2. (*en conjunto*) *t.* MAT to integrate II. *vr:* ~se to integrate

**integridad** [in·te·ɣri·'dad] *f* 1. (*totalidad*) entirety 2. (*honradez*) integrity 3. (*física*) physical well-being

**integrismo** [in·te·'ɣris·mo] *m* (*ideológico*) fundamentalism

**íntegro, -a** ['in·te·ɣro, -a] *adj* (*completo*) whole; (*persona*) honest, upright

**intelectual** [in·te·lek·tu·'al] *adj, mf* intellectual

**inteligencia** [in·te·li·'xen·sja, -θja] *f t.* POL intelligence; **servicio de ~** intelligence agency [*o* bureau]

**inteligente** [in·te·li·'xen·te] *adj* intelligent

**inteligible** [in·te·li·'xi·βle] *adj* comprehen-

sible; (*sonido*) *t.* FILOS intelligible

**intemperie** [in·tem·'pe·rje] *f* (*el aire libre*) **a la ~** out in the open

**intención** [in·ten·'sjon, -'θjon] *f* intention; (*propósito firme*) resolution; **sin ~** unintentionally; **con ~** deliberately; **tener buenas intenciones** to mean well

**intencionado, -a** [in·ten·sjo·'na·do, -a; -θjo·'na·do, -a] *adj* intentional; **bien ~** (*acción*) well-meant; (*persona*) well-meaning; **mal ~** unkind; (*persona*) malicious

**intensidad** [in·ten·si·'dad] *f t.* FÍS intensity; (*de tormenta*) severity; (*de viento*) force

**intensificar** <c → qu> [in·ten·si·fi·'kar] I. *vt* to intensify II. *vr:* ~**se** (*tráfico, calor*) to increase; (*conflicto*) to intensify

**intensivo, -a** [in·ten·'si·βo, -a] *adj* intensive

**intenso, -a** [in·'ten·so, -a] *adj* (*fuerza, olor*) strong; (*frío, calor*) intense

**intentar** [in·ten·'tar] *vt* 1. (*probar*) to attempt, to try 2. (*proponerse*) to intend, to mean

**intento** [in·'ten·to] *m* attempt, try

**intentona** [in·ten·'to·na] *f inf* reckless attempt

**interacción** [in·ter·ak·'sjon, -'θjon] *f* interaction

**interactivo, -a** [in·ter·ak·'ti·βo, -a] *adj* interactive

**intercalar** [in·ter·ka·'lar] *vt* (*en un periódico*) to insert

**intercambiar** [in·ter·kam·'bjar] *vt* to interchange; (*opiniones*) to exchange; (*cosas*) to swap

**intercambio** [in·ter·'kam·bjo] *m* exchange

**interceder** [in·ter·se·'der, -θe·'der] *vi* to intercede; **~ en favor de alguien** to intercede on behalf of sb

**interceptar** [in·ter·sep·'tar, -θep·'tar] *vt* (*comunicaciones*) to cut off; (*el paso de algo*) to intercept

**intercultural** [in·ter·kul·tu·'ral] *adj* intercultural

**interdisciplinar** [in·ter·di·si·pli·'nar, -dis·θi·pli·'nar] *adj*, **interdisciplinario, -a** [in·ter·di·si·pli·'na·rjo, -a; in·ter·dis·θi·] *adj* interdisciplinary

**interés** [in·te·'res] *m* **1.** (*importancia*) concern **2.** (*deseo, atención*) interest; **tengo ~ por saber...** I'm interested in knowing... **3.** (*provecho*) interest; **el ~ público** the public's interest; **esto redunda en ~ tuyo** this redounds to your credit **4.** FIN interest; (*rendimiento*) yield; **un 10% de ~** 10% interest

**interesado, -a** [in·te·re·'sa·do, -a] **I.** *adj* **1.** (*con interés*) interested **2.** (*egoísta*) selfish, self-seeking **II.** *m, f* **1.** the interested party, the person concerned **2.** (*egoísta*) selfish person

**interesante** [in·te·re·'san·te] *adj* interesting

**interesar** [in·te·re·'sar] **I.** *vi* to be of interest **II.** *vr:* **~se 1.** (*mostrar interés*) **~se por algo** to become interested in sth **2.** (*preguntar por*) **~se por algo** to ask about sth

**interferencia** [in·ter·fe·'ren·sja, -θja] *f t.* FÍS, LING interference

**interferir** [in·ter·fe·'rir] *irr como sentir vi t.* FÍS to interfere; **eso no interfiere en mi decisión** that does not influence my decision

**interfono** [in·ter·'fo·no] *m* intercom

**interino, -a** [in·te·'ri·no, -a] **I.** *adj* **1.** (*funcionario*) temporary **2.** POL interim **II.** *m, f* **1.** (*suplente*) stand-in **2.** (*funcionario*) temporary [*o* acting] incumbent; (*maestro*) substitute teacher

**interior** [in·te·'rjor] **I.** *adj* interior; (*sin costa*) inland; **mercado ~** COM (*de la UE*) internal market; **ropa ~** underwear **II.** *m* interior; **Ministerio del Interior** POL Department of the Interior; **en el ~ de...** inside...

**interiores** [in·te·'rjo·res] *mpl* Col (*calzoncillos*) men's underpants *pl*

**interiorizar** <z → c> [in·te·rjo·ri·'sar, -'θar] *vt* to internalize

**interjección** [in·ter·xek·'sjon, -'θjon] *f* LING interjection, exclamation

**interlocutor(a)** [in·ter·lo·ku·'tor, -·'to·ra] *m(f)* speaker, interlocutor *form*

**intermediario, -a** [in·ter·me·'dja·rjo, -a] *m, f* **1.** (*mediador*) mediator, intermediary; (*enlace*) go-between **2.** (*comerciante*) middleman

**intermedio** [in·ter·'me·djo] *m* interval

**intermedio, -a** [in·ter·'me·djo, -a] *adj* **1.** (*capa*) intermediate **2.** (*período de tiempo*) intervening

**interminable** [in·ter·mi·'na·βle] *adj* interminable, endless

**intermitencia** [in·ter·mi·'ten·sja, -θja] *f* **1.** (*calidad*) intermittency **2.** MED intermittence

**intermitente** [in·ter·mi·'ten·te] *m* intermittence; AUTO turn signal

**internacional** [in·ter·na·sjo·'nal, -θjo·'nal] *adj* international

**internado** [in·ter·'na·do] *m* boarding school

**internado, -a** [in·ter·'na·do, -a] *m, f* **1.** (*alumno*) boarder **2.** (*demente*) inmate

**internar** [in·ter·'nar] *vt* **~ en** (*hospital*) to admit to; (*asilo*) to commit to

**internauta** [in·ter·'nau·ta] *mf* COMPUT Internet user

**internet** [in·ter·'net] *f* COMPUT Internet

**interno, -a** [in·'ter·no, -a] *adj* internal; **régimen ~** (*de una empresa*) internal management; (*de un partido*) internal affairs

**interponer** [in·ter·po·'ner] *irr como poner* **I.** *vt* **1.** (*entre varias cosas*) to interpose; (*entre dos cosas: silla*) to place **2.** (*en un asunto*) to intervene **3.** JUR to bring, to lodge **II.** *vr:* **~se** to intervene

**interposición** [in·ter·po·si·'sjon, -'θjon] *f* **1.** (*entre varias cosas*) interposition; (*de una silla*) placing between; (*de un papel*) insertion; (*de alguien*) coming between **2.** (*en un asunto*) intervention **3.** JUR bringing, lodging

**interpretación** [in·ter·pre·ta·'sjon, -'θjon] *f* **1.** (*de texto*) interpretation; (*traducción oral*) interpreting **2.** TEAT performance; MÚS rendering; **escuela de ~** TEAT stage [*o* acting] school

**interpretar** [in·ter·pre·'tar] *vt* **1.** (*texto, traducir oralmente*) to interpret **2.** TEAT to perform; MÚS to render

**intérprete** [in·'ter·pre·te] *mf* (*actor*) performer; (*traductor*) interpreter

**interprofesional** [in·ter·pro·fe·sjo·'nal] *adj* **Salario Mínimo Interprofesional** minimum wage

**interpuesto, -a** [in·ter·'pwes·to, -a] *pp*

*de* **interponer**

**interrelacionado, -a** [in·te·rre·la·sjo·'na·do, -a; -θjo·'na·do, -a] *adj* interrelated

**interrogación** [in·te·rro·ɣa·'sjon, -'θjon] *f* (*signo*) question mark

**interrogante** [in·te·rro·'ɣan·te] *m* question

**interrogar** <g → gu> [in·te·rro·'ɣar] *vt* to question; (*policía*) to interrogate

**interrogatorio** [in·te·rro·ɣa·'to·rjo] *m* interrogation, (cross-)examination

**interrumpir** [in·te·rrum·'pir] *vt* (*cortar*) to interrupt; (*bruscamente al hablar*) to break

**interrupción** [in·te·rrup·'sjon, -rruβ·'θjon] *f* (*corte*) break; **sin ~** uninterruptedly

**interruptor** [in·te·rrup·'tor] *m* ELEC switch

**intersección** [in·ter·sek·'sjon, -'θjon] *f* intersection

**interurbano, -a** [in·ter·ur·'βa·no, -a] *adj* intercity

**intervalo** [in·ter·'βa·lo] *m t.* MÚS interval; **a ~s** at intervals

**intervención** [in·ter·βen·'sjon, -'θjon] *f* **1.** (*participación*) participation **2.** (*en conflicto*) intervention **3.** (*mediación*) mediation **4.** POL intervention **5.** MED operation **6.** (*del teléfono*) tapping

**intervenir** [in·ter·βe·'nir] *irr como* **venir** I. *vi* **1.** (*tomar parte*) to participate **2.** (*en conflicto*) to intervene **3.** (*mediar*) to mediate II. *vt* **1.** MED to operate on **2.** (*incautar*) to seize **3.** (*teléfono*) to tap **4.** COM to audit

**intestinal** [in·tes·ti·'nal] *adj* intestinal

**intestino** [in·tes·'ti·no] *m* **1.** ANAT intestine; **el ~ delgado/grueso** the small/large intestine **2.** *pl* (*tripas*) intestines *pl*, bowels *pl*

**intimar** [in·ti·'mar] *vi* to become intimate [*o* friendly]

**intimidación** [in·ti·mi·da·'sjon, -'θjon] *f* intimidation

**intimidad** [in·ti·mi·'dad] *f* **1.** (*asuntos*) personal matters *pl*; (*privacidad*) privacy **2.** (*vida privada*) private life

**intimidar** [in·ti·mi·'dar] I. *vt* to intimidate II. *vr:* **~se** to be intimidated

**intimidatorio, -a** [in·ti·mi·da·'to·rjo, -a] *adj* intimidating

**íntimo, -a** ['in·ti·mo, -a] *adj* **1.** (*interior,*

*interno*) inner, innermost **2.** (*amigo*) intimate, close **3.** (*velada*) intimate

**intocable** [in·to·'ka·βle] *adj* untouchable

**intolerable** [in·to·le·'ra·βle] *adj* intolerable

**intolerancia** [in·to·le·'ran·sja, -θja] *f* intolerance

**intolerante** [in·to·le·'ran·te] *adj* intolerant

**intoxicación** [in·tok·si·ka·'sjon, -'θjon] *f* (*alimentos*) food poisoning; (*alcohol*) intoxication

**intoxicar** <c → qu> [in·tok·si·'kar] *vt, vr:* **~(se)** to poison

**intranquilizar** <z → c> [in·tran·ki·li·'sar, -'θar] *vt, vr:* **~(se)** to worry

**intranquilo, -a** [in·tran·'ki·lo, -a] *adj* **1.** (*preocupado*) worried, uneasy **2.** (*excitado*) agitated, restless

**intransferible** [in·trans·fe·'ri·βle] *adj* untransferable

**intransigente** [in·tran·si·'xen·te] *adj* intransigent; (*intolerante*) intolerant

**intrascendente** [in·tra·sen·'den·te, -tras-θen·'den·te] *adj* trivial

**intratable** [in·tra·'ta·βle] *adj* (*persona*) impossible

**intrépido, -a** [in·'tre·pi·do, -a] *adj* intrepid

**intriga** [in·'tri·ɣa] *f* **1.** (*maquinación*) intrigue **2.** (*de una película*) suspense

**intrigante** [in·tri·'ɣan·te] *adj* (*película*) gripping

**intrigar** <g → gu> [in·tri·'ɣar] I. *vi* to scheme II. *vt* to intrigue

**introducción** [in·tro·duk·'sjon, -'θjon] *f* introduction; COMPUT (*de datos*) input; (*de mercancías*) launching; (*de libro*) preface

**introducir** [in·tro·du·'sir, -'θir] *irr como* **traducir** I. *vt* (*llave*) to insert, to put in; (*medidas*) to introduce; COMPUT (*datos*) to enter, to input II. *vr:* **~se** (*meterse*) to get in(to); **~se en algo** to enter into sth

**intromisión** [in·tro·mi·'sjon] *f* interference

**introvertido, -a** [in·tro·βer·'ti·do, -a] *adj* introverted

**intruso, -a** [in·'tru·so, -a] *m, f* intruder; (*en reunión*)

**intuición** [in·twi·'sjon, -'θjon] *f* intuition

**intuir** [in·tu·'ir] *irr como* huir *vt* (*presentir*) to sense; **intuyo que...** I have a hunch that...

**intuitivo, -a** [in·twi·'ti·βo, -a] *adj* intuitive

**inundación** [i·nun·da·'sjon, -'θjon] *f* flood(ing)

**inundar** [i·nun·'dar] *vt* to flood

**inusitado, -a** [i·nu·si·'ta·do, -a] *adj* 1. (*no habitual*) unusual, uncommon 2. (*extraordinario*) unwonted

**inusual** [in·u·su·'al] *adj* 1. (*no habitual*) unusual 2. (*extraordinario*) unwonted

**inútil** [in·'u·til] I. *adj* 1. (*que no sirve*) useless 2. (*esfuerzo*) vain 3. (*sin sentido*) futile II. *mf* (*torpe*) incompetent person

**inutilizar** <z → c> [in·u·ti·li·'sar, -'θar] *vt* 1. (*objeto*) to render useless 2. (*al enemigo*) to defeat

**invadir** [im·ba·'dir] *vt* (*país*) to invade; (*entrar en gran número*) to overrun; (*privacidad*) to intrude on; **los hinchas invadieron el campo** the fans invaded the pitch [*o* field]

**invalidar** [im·ba·li·'dar] *vt* to invalidate

**invalidez** [im·ba·li·'des, -'deθ] *f* invalidity; MED disability

**inválido, -a** [im·'ba·li·do, -a] *adj* invalid; MED disabled

**invariable** [im·ba·'rja·βle] *adj t.* MAT invariable

**invasión** [im·ba·'sjon] *f t.* MIL, MED invasion; (*en privacidad*) intrusion

**invasor(a)** [im·ba·'sor, --so·ra] *m(f)* invader

**invencible** [im·ben·'si·βle, -'θi·βle] *adj* invincible; (*insuperable*) unbeatable; (*obstáculo*) insurmountable

**invención** [im·ben·'sjon, -'θjon] *f* invention

**inventar** [im·ben·'tar] *vt* to invent

**inventario** [im·ben·'ta·rjo] *m* inventory

**inventiva** [im·ben·'ti·βa] *f* inventiveness

**invento** [im·'ben·to] *m* invention

**inventor(a)** [im·ben·'tor, --to·ra] *m(f)* inventor

**invernadero** [im·ber·na·'de·ro] *m* greenhouse; **el efecto ~** the greenhouse effect

**invernal** [im·ber·'nal] *adj* winter; (*tiempo*) wintry

**invernar** <e → ie> [im·ber·'nar] *vi* to winter

**inverosímil** [im·be·ro·'si·mil] *adj* implausible; (*que no parece verdad*) improbable, hard to believe

**inversión** [im·ber·'sjon] *f* 1. COM, FIN investment 2. (*efecto de invertir*) inversion

**inverso, -a** [im·'ber·so] *adj* inverse, opposite; **a la inversa** inversely; **y a la inversa** vice versa; **en orden ~** in reverse order

**inversor(a)** [im·ber·'sor, --so·ra] *m(f)* investor

**invertido, -a** [im·ber·'ti·do, -a] *adj* (*al revés*) inverted; (*volcado*) upside-down

**invertir** [im·ber·'tir] *irr como* sentir *vt* 1. (*orden*) to invert 2. (*volcar*) to turn upside down 3. (*dinero*) to invest

**investigación** [im·bes·ti·ɣa·'sjon, -'θjon] *f* 1. (*indagación*) investigation; (*averiguación*) inquiry 2. (*ciencia*) research

**investigador(a)** [im·bes·ti·ɣa·'dor, --do·ra] I. *adj* investigating; **comisión ~a** investigatory commission II. *m(f)* investigator, researcher

**investigar** <g → gu> [im·bes·ti·'ɣar] *vt* 1. (*indagar*) to investigate; (*averiguar*) to inquire 2. (*en la ciencia*) to research

**inviable** [im·bi·'a·βle] *adj* non-viable, unfeasible

**invicto, -a** [im·'bik·to, -a] *adj* unbeaten

**invidente** [im·bi·'den·te] *adj* blind

**invierno** [im·'bjer·no] *m* winter; AmL (*lluvias*) rainy season

**invisibilidad** [im·bi·si·βi·li·'dad] *f* invisibility

**invisible** [im·bi·'si·βle] *adj* invisible

**invitación** [im·bi·ta·'sjon, -'θjon] *f* invitation

**invitado, -a** [im·bi·'ta·do, -a] *m, f* guest

**invitar** [im·bi·'tar] I. *vt* 1. (*convidar*) to invite 2. (*instar*) to press; (*rogar*) to beg II. *vi* to invite; **esta vez invito yo** this time it's on me

**invocar** <c → qu> [im·bo·'kar] *vt* to invoke; (*suplicar*) to implore, to appeal; (*alegar*) to allege

**involucrar** [im·bo·lu·'krar] I. *vt* to involve II. *vr:* **~se** to interfere; (*intervenir*) to become [*o* get] involved

**involuntario, -a** [im·bo·lun·'ta·rjo, -a] *adj* involuntary; (*sin querer*) unintentional

**invulnerable** [im·bul·ne·'ra·βle] *adj* invulnerable

**inyección** [in·jek·'sjon, -'θjon] *f* **1.** MED injection **2.** TÉC fuel injection

**inyectar** [in·jek·'tar] *vt* to inject

**ión** [i·'on] *m* ion

**ir** [ir] *irr* **I.** *vi* **1.** (*general*) to go; ¡**voy!** I'm coming!; ¡**vamos!** let's go!, come on!; ~ **a pie** to go on foot; ~ **en bicicleta** to go by bicycle; ~ **a caballo** to go on horseback; **tengo que ~ a París** I have to go to Paris **2.** (*ir a buscar*) **iré por el pan** I'll go and get the bread **3.** (*progresar*) to go; ¿**cómo va la tesina?** how is the dissertation going?; ¿**cómo te va?** how are things?; **en lo que va de año** so far this year **4.** (*referirse*) **eso no va por ti** I'm not referring to you; ¿**tú sabes de lo que va?** do you know what it is about? **5.** (*interj: sorpresa*) ¡**qué va!** of course not! **6.** (*con verbo*) **iban charlando** they were chatting; **voy a hacerlo** I'm going to do it **II.** *vr:* ~**se 1.** (*marcharse*) to leave **2.** (*dirección*) to go; ~**se por las ramas** to beat about the bush

**ira** ['i·ra] *f* anger

**irascible** [i·ra·'si·βle, --ras'θi·βle] *adj* irascible

**irgo** ['ir·γo] *1. pres de* **erguir**

**irguió** [ir·'γjo] *3. pret de* **erguir**

**iris** ['i·ris] *m inv* ANAT iris; **arco ~** rainbow

**Irlanda** [ir·'lan·da] *f* Ireland

**irlandés, -esa** [ir·lan·'des, --'de·sa] **I.** *adj* Irish **II.** *m, f* Irishman *m*, Irishwoman *f*

**ironía** [i·ro·'ni·a] *f* irony

**irónico, -a** [i·'ro·ni·ko, -a] *adj* ironic

**ironizar** ‹z → c› [i·ro·ni·'sar, -'θar] *vt* to be ironic

**irracional** [i·rra·sjo·'nal, -θjo·'nal] *adj* irrational; **número ~** MAT irrational number

**irreal** [i·rre·'al] *adj* unreal

**irrealizable** [i·rrea·li·'θa·βle, -'θa·βle] *adj* unrealizable, unfeasible

**irrebatible** [i·rre·βa·'ti·βle] *adj* irrefutable

*adj* unrecognizable

**irreflexivo, -a** [i·rre·flek·'si·βo, -a] *adj* reckless; (*persona*) rash

**irrefutable** [i·rre·fu·'ta·βle] *adj* irrefutable

**irregular** [i·rre·γu·'lar] *adj* irregular

**irrelevante** [i·rre·le·'βan·te] *adj* irrelevant

**irremediable** [i·rre·me·'dja·βle] *adj* irremediable

**irreparable** [i·rre·pa·'ra·βle] *adj* irreparable

**irrepetible** [i·rre·pe·'ti·βle] *adj* unique

**irreprimible** [i·rre·pri·'mi·βle] *adj* irrepressible

**irreprochable** [i·rre·pro·'tʃa·βle] *adj* irreproachable

**irresistible** [i·rre·sis·'ti·βle] *adj* (*atractivo*) irresistible

**irrespetuoso, -a** [i·rres·pe·tu·'o·so, -a] *adj* disrespectful

**irrespirable** [i·rres·pi·'ra·βle] *adj* (*por tóxico*) unbreathable; (*aire*) stale, suffocating

**irresponsable** [i·rres·pon·'sa·βle] *adj* irresponsible

**irreverente** [i·rre·βe·'ren·te] *adj* irreverent

**irreversible** [i·rre·βer·'si·βle] *adj* irreversible

**irrevocable** [i·rre·βo·'ka·βle] *adj* irrevocable

**irrisorio, -a** [i·rri·'so·rjo, -a] *adj* derisory; **a precios ~s** at ridiculous prices

**irritable** [i·rri·'ta·βle] *adj* irritable

**irritación** [i·rri·ta·'sjon, -'θjon] *f* **1.** MED (*órgano*) inflammation; (*de piel*) irritation **2.** (*enfado*) irritation

**irritante** [i·rri·'tan·te] *adj* irritating

**irritar** [i·rri·'tar] **I.** *vt* **1.** (*enojar, molestar*) to irritate **2.** MED (*órgano*) to inflame **II.** *vr:* ~**se 1.** (*enojarse*) to become irritated **2.** MED (*órgano*) to become inflamed

**irrompible** [i·rrom·'pi·βle] *adj* unbreakable

**irrumpir** [i·rrum·'pir] *vi* ~ **en algo** to burst into sth

**isla** ['is·la] *f* island

**Islam** [is·'lan] *m* REL Islam

**islámico, -a** [is·'la·mi·ko, -a] *adj* Islamic

**islandés, -esa** [is·lan·'des, -·'de·sa] **I.** *adj* Icelandic **II.** *m, f* Icelander

**Islandia** [is·'lan·dja] *f* Iceland

**isleño, -a** [is·'le·ɲo, -a] *m, f* islander

**islote** [is·'lo·te] *m* islet

**Israel** [i·rra·'el/is·rra·'el] *m* Israel

**israelí** [i·rrae·'li/is·rrae·'li] *adj, mf* Israeli

**Italia** [i·'ta·lja] *f* Italy

**italiano, -a** [i·ta·'lja·no, -a] *adj, m, f* Italian

**itinerancia** [i·ti·ne·'ran·sja, -θja] *f* TEL roaming *no pl*

**itinerante** [i·ti·ne·'ran·te] *adj* itinerant, traveling

**itinerario** [i·ti·ne·'ra·rjo] *m* itinerary, schedule; AVIAT (*vuelo*) route

**ITV** [i·te·'u·βe] *f abr de* **Inspección Técnica de Vehículos** MOT test

**IVA** ['i·βa] *m abr de* **Impuesto sobre el Valor Añadido** VAT

**izar** <z → c> [i·'sar, -'θar] *vt* to hoist

**izda.** *adj,* **izqdo.** [is·'kjer·da, iθ-] *adj abr de* **izquierda, izquierdo** left

**izquierda** [iθ·'kjer·da, iθ-] *f* **1.** (*mano*) left hand **2.** POL left **3.** (*lado*) left side; **a la ~** to the left

**izquierdo, -a** [is·'kjer·do, -a; iθ-] *adj* left; (*zurdo*) left-handed; **levantarse con el pie ~** to get up on the wrong side of the bed

# J

**J, j** ['xo·ta] *f* J, j; **~ de Juan** J as in Juliet

**ja** [xa] *interj* ha

**jabalí** [xa·βa·'li] *m* <jabalíes> wild boar

**jabalina** [xa·βa·'li·na] *f* DEP javelin

**jabón** [xa·'βon] *m* **1.** (*para lavar*) soap; **pastilla de ~** bar of soap **2.** *PRico, Arg* (*susto*) fright ▶ **dar ~ a alguien** to soft-soap sb

**jabonar** [xa·βo·'nar] *vt* to soap

**jacal** [xa·'kal] *m Méx, Ven* hut

**jacinto** [xa·'sin·to, -'θin·to] *m* BOT hyacinth

**jaco** ['xa·ko] *m pey* (*caballo*) nag

**jactancioso, -a** [xak·tan·'sjo·so, -a; -'θjo·so, -a] *adj* boastful

**jactarse** [xak·'tar·se] *vr* **~ de algo** to boast

of [*o* about] sth

**jade** ['xa·de] *m* jade

**jadear** [xa·de·'ar] *vi* to pant

**jaguar** [xa·'ɣwar] *m* ZOOL jaguar

**jagüey** [xa·'ɣwei] *m AmL* (*balsa*) pool; (*cisterna*) cistern

**jaiba** ['xai·βa] **I.** *adj* **1.** *Ant, Méx* (*astuto*) cunning **2.** *Cuba* (*perezoso*) lazy **II.** *f AmL* (*cangrejo*) crab

**jalado, -a** [xa·'la·do, -a] *adj* **1.** *Méx, Ven* (*exagerado*) exaggerated **2.** *AmL* (*demacrado*) emaciated **3.** *AmL* (*obsequioso*) obliging **4.** *AmL* (*borracho*) drunk

**jalar** [xa·'lar] **I.** *vt* **1.** *AmL* (*una cuerda*) to pull **2.** *AmL* (*una persona*) to attract **3.** *inf* (*comer*) to guzzle, to wolf down **II.** *vi Bol, PRico, Urug, Ven* (*largarse*) to clear off **III.** *vr:* **~se** *AmL* to get drunk

**jalea** [xa·'lea] *f* jelly

**jalear** [xa·le·'ar] *vt* (*animar*) to encourage

**jaleo** [xa·'leo] *m* **1.** (*barullo*) commotion; **armar ~** to make a scene **2.** (*desorden*) confusion

**jamás** [xa·'mas] *adv* never; **~ de los jamases** never in your life; **nunca digas nunca ~** never (ever) say never; **nunca ~** never again

**jamelgo** [xa·'mel·yo] *m inf* (*caballo*) nag

**jamón** [xa·'mon] *m* ham; **~ de York** boiled ham; **~ serrano** cured ham ▶ **¡y un ~!** *inf* get away!

**Japón** [xa·'pon] *m* Japan

**japonés, -esa** [xa·po·'nes, -·'ne·sa] *adj, m, f* Japanese

**jaque** ['xa·ke] *m* check; **~ mate** checkmate; **dar ~ to** check ▶ **tener a alguien en ~** *fig* to keep sb in check

**jaqueca** [xa·'ke·ka] *f* (*severe*) headache, migraine

**jara** ['xa·ra] *f Guat, Méx* (*flecha*) arrow

**jarabe** [xa·'ra·βe] *m* syrup; (*para la tos*) cough mixture [*o* syrup]; **~ de arce** maple syrup ▶ **dar ~ de palo a alguien** *inf* to give sb a thrashing

**jarana** [xa·'ra·na] *f* **1.** *inf* (*juerga*) spree **2.** *Méx* MÚS *small guitar* **3.** *AmL* (*burla*) joke **4.** *AmC* (*deuda*) debt **5.** *Col* (*embuste*) trick

**jardín** [xar·'din] *m* garden; **~ de infancia** (*hasta los tres años*) nursery school; (*a* partir de tres años) kindergarten; **los jardines de una ciudad** the municipal parks

**jardinear** [xar·di·ne·'ar] *vt AmL* to garden

**jardinera** [xar·di·'ne·ra] *f* (*maceta*) window box

**jardinería** [xar·di·ne·'ri·a] *f* gardening

**jardinero, -a** [xar·di·'ne·ro, -a] *m, f* gardener

**jareta** [xa·'re·ta] *f CRi, Par* (*bragueta*) fly, zipper

**jarocho, -a** [xa·'ro·tʃo, -a] *adj AmL* (*arrogante*) rude

**jarra** ['xa·rra] *f* jar; (*de agua*) jug, pitcher
▶ **ponerse en ~s** to stand with arms akimbo

**jarro** ['xa·rro] *m* jug, pitcher; **echar un ~ de agua fría** *fig* to pour cold water on

**jarrón** [xa·'rron] *m* vase

**jauja** ['xau·xa] *f* earthly paradise; **para ti la vida es Jauja** you're living in clover

**jaula** ['xau·la] *f* (*para animales*) cage

**jauría** [xau·'ri·a] *f* pack of hounds

**jazmín** [xas·'min, xaθ-] *m* jasmine

**jazz** [dʒas] *m* jazz

**J.C.** [xe·su·'kris·to] *abr de* **Jesucristo** J.C.

**jebe** ['xe·βe] *m AmL* (*caucho*) rubber

**jefatura** [xe·fa·'tu·ra] *f* 1. (*cargo*) leadership 2. (*sede*) **~ del gobierno** seat of government; **~ de policía** police headquarters

**jefazo, -a** [xe·'fa·so, -a; -θo, -θa] *m, f inf* big boss

**jefe, -a** ['xe·fe, -a] *m, f* head, boss; (*de una banda*) leader; **~ de filas** *DEP* team captain; **~ de gobierno** head of the government; **~ de(l) Estado** head of state; **~ redactor** editor-in-chief

**jeque** ['xe·ke] *m* sheik(h)

**jerarca** [xe·'rar·ka] *mf* high official

**jerarquía** [xe·rar·'ki·a] *f* hierarchy

**jerárquico, -a** [xe·'rar·ki·ko, -a] *adj* hierarchical

**jerez** [xe·'res, -'reθ] *m* sherry

**jerga** ['xer·ɣa] *f* jargon

**jeringa** [xe·'rin·ga] *f* (*instrumento*) syringe

**jeringuilla** [xe·rin·'gi·ja, -ʎa] *f* syringe

**jeroglífico** [xe·ro·'ɣli·fi·ko] *m* hieroglyph(ic); (*pasatiempo*) rebus, puzzle

**jersey** [xer·'sei] *m* pullover; **~ de cuello alto** turtleneck sweater

**Jesucristo** [xe·su·'kris·to] *m* Jesus Christ

**Jesús** [xe·'sus] *m* Jesus ▶ **¡~!** (*al estornudar*) bless you!; (*interjección*) good heavens!

**jeta** ['xe·ta] *f inf* (*cara*) mug, dial; **ése tiene una ~ increíble** *fig* what incredible cheek that guy has

**jíbaro, -a** ['xi·β̞a·ro, -a] *adj* 1. *AmL* (*campesino*) country, peasant; (*costumbres, vida*) rural 2. *AmL* (*planta, animal*) wild 3. *Ant, Méx* (*huraño*) shy

**jícama** ['xi·ka·ma] *f Méx* BOT jicama, Mexican turnip

**jícaro** ['xi·ka·ro] *m AmC* (*árbol*) calabash tree

**jilguero** [xil·'ɣe·ro] *m* goldfinch

**jinete** [xi·'ne·te] *m* (*persona*) horseman; (*profesional*) rider

**jinetear** [xi·ne·te·'ar] *vt AmL* to break in (horses)

**jirafa** [xi·'ra·fa] *f* giraffe

**jirón** [xi·'ron] *m* shred; **hacer algo jirones** to tear sth to shreds

**jitomate** [xi·to·'ma·te] *m Méx* (*tomate*) tomato

**JJ.OO.** ['xwe·ɣos o·'lim·pi·kos] *abr de* **Juegos Olímpicos** Olympic Games

**jo** [xo] *interj* 1. (*so*) whoa 2. (*sorpresa*) **¡~!** well, well!

**jockey** ['xo·kei] *m* jockey

**jocoso, -a** [xo·'ko·so, -a] *adj* humorous, jocular

**joder** [xo·'der] I. *vt vulg* 1. (*copular*) to fuck, to screw 2. (*fastidiar*) to be an asshole; **¡no me jodas!** stop being an asshole! 3. (*echar a perder*) to fuck up II. *vi vulg* to fuck III. *vr:* **~se** *vulg* 1. (*fastidiarse*) to get pissed off; **¡jódete!** fuck off! 2. (*echar a perder*) **nuestra amistad se ha jodido** our friendship's gone down the drain; **la tele se ha jodido** the TV is all screwed up IV. *interj vulg* shit

**jodido, -a** [xo·'di·do, -a] I. *pp de* **joder** II. *adj vulg* 1. (*cansado*) beat; **estoy ~** I'm beat 2. (*difícil*) **es ~ tener que trabajar tanto** it's damned hard having to work so much

**jolgorio** [xol·'ɣo·rjo] *m* merriment

**jolín** [xo·'lin] *interj,* **jolines** [xo·'li·nes] *interj* sugar

**jopé** [xo·'pe] *interj* sugar

**jornada** [xor·'na·da] *f* **1.** (*de trabajo*) working day; (*tiempo trabajado*) hours of work; **~ continua** continuous schedule without lunch break, finishing early; **~ partida** split shift; **trabajo media ~** I work half a day [*o* part-time] **2.** (*viaje*) day's journey **3.** *pl* (*congreso, simposio*) conference

**jornal** [xor·'nal] *m* (*paga*) day's wage [*o* pay]

**jornalero, -a** [xor·na·'le·ro, -a] *m, f* day laborer

**joroba** [xo·'ro·βa] *f* (*de persona*) hunched back; (*de camello*) hump

**jorobado, -a** [xo·ro·'βa·do, -a] *adj* hunchbacked

**jorobar** [xo·ro·'βar] **I.** *vt inf* to annoy **II.** *vr:* **~se** *inf* **1.** (*enojarse*) to get annoyed **2.** (*aguantar*) to put up with it; **si no le gusta, ¡que se jorobe!** if he doesn't like it, he can lump it!

**jorongo** [xo·'ron·go] *m Méx* poncho

**jota** ['xo·ta] *f* (*letra*) j ► **no entender** [*o* **saber**] **ni ~** *inf* not to have a clue

**joto** ['xo·to] *m* **1.** *Col* (*paquete*) bundle **2.** *Méx pey* (*homosexual*) queer

**joven** ['xo·βen] **I.** *adj* young; **de muy ~** in early youth **II.** *mf* young man *m,* young woman *f*

**jovial** [xo·'βjal] *adj* cheerful, jovial

**joya** ['xo·ja] *f* (*alhaja*) jewel; **las ~s** jewelry; **esta mujer de la limpieza es una ~** this cleaning lady [*o* cleaner] is a gem

**joyería** [xo·je·'ri·a] *f* (*tienda*) jeweler's (shop)

**joyero** [xo·'je·ro] *m* jewel case

**joyero, -a** [xo·'je·ro, -a] *m, f* jeweler

**juanete** [xwa·'ne·te] *m* (*del pie*) bunion

**jubilación** [xu·βi·la·'sjon, -'θjon] *f* **1.** (*acción*) retirement **2.** (*pensión*) pension

**jubilado, -a** [xu·βi·'la·do, -a] *m, f* pensioner, retiree

**jubilar** [xu·βi·'lar] **I.** *vt* to pension off **II.** *vr:* **~se 1.** (*retirarse*) to retire **2.** *AmC* (*hacer novillos*) to play truant

**júbilo** ['xu·βi·lo] *m* joy, jubilation

**jubiloso, -a** [xu·βi·'lo·so, -a] *adj* jubilant

**judía** [xu·'di·a] *f* BOT bean; **~ verde** green bean

**judicial** [xu·di·'sjal, -'θjal] *adj* judicial

**judío, -a** [xu·'di·o, -a] **I.** *adj* Jewish **II.** *m, f* Jew

**judo** ['dʒu·do] *m* DEP judo

**juego** ['xwe·ɣo] *m* **1.** (*diversión*) game; **~ de mesa** board game; **hacer ~s malabares** to juggle **2.** DEP play; **~ en blanco** zero-zero tie; **~ limpio** fair play; **~ sucio** foul play; **fuera de ~** (*persona*) offside **3.** (*conjunto*) set; **~ de café** coffee set; **hacer ~** to match

**juerga** ['xwer·ɣa] *f* spree; **ayer estuve de ~** *inf* I was (out) partying yesterday

**jueves** ['xwe·βes] *m inv* Thursday; **Jueves Santo** Maundy Thursday; *v. t.* **lunes**

**juez** [xwes, xweθ] *mf t.* JUR judge; **~ de instrucción** JUR examining magistrate; **~ de línea** DEP linesman

**jugada** [xu·'ɣa·da] *f* DEP play **2.** (*jugarreta*) bad turn; **hacer** [*o* **gastar**] **una ~ a alguien** to play a dirty trick on sb

**jugador(a)** [xu·ɣa·'do, -·'do·ra] *m(f) t.* DEP player

**jugar** [xu·'ɣar] *irr* **I.** *vi* **1.** (*a un juego, deporte*) to play; **~ limpio/sucio** to play fair/unfairly; **¿quién juega?** (*juego de mesa*) whose move is it?; (*partido en la TV, radio*) who's playing?; **¿puedo ~?** can I join in? **2.** (*bromear*) to play about **3.** **~ a la bolsa** to speculate on the stock exchange **II.** *vt* **1.** (*un juego, una partida*) to play **2.** (*apostar*) to gamble; **~ fuerte** to play for high stakes **III.** *vr:* **~se 1.** (*la lotería*) to be drawn **2.** (*apostar*) **~se algo** to gamble [*o* to bet] on sth **3.** (*arriesgar*) to risk; **~se el todo por el todo** to stake one's all ► **jugársela a alguien** to take sb for a ride

**jugarreta** [xu·ɣa·'rre·ta] *f inf* dirty trick

**jugo** ['xu·ɣo] *m* **1.** (*de fruta, carne*) juice **2.** (*esencia*) essence; **declaraciones con mucho ~** *fig* important declarations

**jugoso, -a** [xu·'ɣo·so, -a] *adj* juicy

**juguete** [xu·'ɣe·te] *m* toy

**juguetear** [xu·ɣe·te·'ar] *vi* **1.** (*con las llaves, una pelota*) to play **2.** (*los niños*) to romp

**juguetería** [xu·ɣe·te·'ri·a] *f* toyshop

**juguetón, -ona** [xu·ɣe·'ton, -·'to·na] *adj*

playful

**juicio** ['xwi·sjo, -θjo] *m* **1.** (*facultad para juzgar*) reason **2.** (*razón*) sense; **falta de ~** lack of common sense; **recobrar el ~** to come to one's senses; **tú no estás en tu sano ~** you're not in your right mind **3.** (*opinión*) opinion; **a mi ~** to my mind; **emitir un ~ sobre algo** to pass judgment on sth **4.** JUR trial; **llevar a alguien a ~** to take sb to court; **el (día del) Juicio final** REL the Last Judgment

**juicioso, -a** [xwi·'sjo·so, -a; -θjo·so, -a] *adj* (*sensato*) sensible; (*acertado*) fitting

**julepe** [xu·'le·pe] *m AmL* **1.** (*miedo*) scare **2.** (*ajetreo*) drudgery; **dar un ~ a alguien** *inf* to make sb sweat

**julio** ['xu·ljo] *m* **1.** (*mes*) July; *v. t.* **marzo 2.** FÍS joule

**juma** ['xu·ma] *f AmL inf* drunkenness

**jumarse** [xu·'mar·se] *vr Col, Cuba* to get drunk

**junco** ['xun·ko] *m* BOT reed

**jungla** ['xun·gla] *f* jungle

**junio** ['xu·njo] *m* June; *v. t.* **marzo**

**júnior** ['dʒu·njor] *m* <juniors> junior

**junta** ['xun·ta] *f* **1.** (*comité*) committee; (*consejo*) council; **~ directiva** COM board of directors **2.** (*reunión*) meeting; **~ general** general meeting; **~ de accionistas** shareholders' meeting

**juntar** [xun·'tar] **I.** *vt* **1.** (*aproximar*) **~ la mesa a la pared** to move the table over to the wall; **~ las sillas** to put the chairs together **2.** (*unir*) to join **3.** (*reunir: personas*) to assemble; (*objetos*) to put together; (*dinero*) to collect **II.** *vr:* **~se 1.** (*reunirse*) to meet **2.** (*unirse*) to come together **3.** (*aproximarse*) to come closer **4.** (*vivir juntos*) to move in (together)

**junto** ['xun·to] **I.** *adv* **hacerlo todo ~** to do it all at the same time **II.** *prep* **1.** (*local*) **~ a** near to; **estábamos ~ a la entrada** we were at the entrance; **pasaron ~ a nosotros** they walked past us **2.** (*con movimiento*) **~ a** beside; **pon la silla ~ a la mesa** put the chair next to the table **3.** (*con, en compañía de*) **~ con** together with

**junto, -a** ['xun·to, -a] *adj* joined; **nos sen-**

tamos todos **~s** we all sat together

**jura** ['xu·ra] *f* oath; (*acto*) swearing in

**jurado** [xu·'ra·do] *m* **1.** JUR (*miembro*) juror; (*tribunal*) jury **2.** (*de un examen*) qualified examiner **3.** (*de un concurso*) panel member

**jurado, -a** [xu·'ra·do, -a] *adj* qualified; **intérprete ~** sworn interpreter

**juramento** [xu·ra·'men·to] *m* **1.** *t.* JUR (*jura*) oath; **falso ~** perjury; **estar bajo ~** to be on oath; **tomar ~ a alguien** to swear sb in **2.** (*blasfemia*) swearword

**jurar** [xu·'rar] *vi, vt* to swear; **~ por alguien** to swear by sb; **jurársela a alguien** *inf* to swear vengeance on sb

**jurídico, -a** [xu·'ri·di·ko, -a] *adj* legal, lawful

**jurisdicción** [xu·ris·dik·'sjon, -'θjon] *f* **1.** JUR (*potestad*) jurisdiction **2.** (*territorio*) administrative district

**jurisdiccional** [xu·ris·dik·sjo·'nal, -'θjo·'nal] *adj* jurisdictional, judicial; **aguas ~es** territorial waters

**jurisprudencia** [xu·ris·pru·'den·sja, -θja] *f* **1.** (*legislación*) jurisprudence **2.** (*ciencia*) science of law

**jurista** [xu·'ris·ta] *mf* jurist

**justamente** [xus·ta·'men·te] *adv* justly; (*precisamente*) precisely

**justicia** [xus·'ti·sja, -θja] *f* justice; (*derecho*) law; **hacer ~ a alguien** to do sb justice

**justificable** [xus·ti·fi·'ka·βle] *adj* justifiable

**justificación** [xus·ti·fi·ka·'sjon, -'θjon] *f* justification; **no hay ~ para lo que has hecho** there's no excuse for what you've done

**justificante** [xus·ti·fi·'kan·te] *m* (*de ausencia*) note of absence

**justificar** <c → qu> [xus·ti·fi·'kar] **I.** *vt* (*disculpar*) to justify; **mi desconfianza es justificada** my distrust is vindicated **II.** *vr:* **~se** to justify oneself

**justo** ['xus·to] *adv* **1.** (*exactamente*) right; **llegué ~ a tiempo** I arrived just in time **2.** (*escasamente*) scarcely; **tengo ~ para vivir** I have just enough to live on

**justo, -a** ['xus·to, -a] *adj* **1.** (*persona, decisión*) just **2.** (*exacto*) exact; (*acertado*) correct; **el peso ~** the correct weight;

**tener el dinero ~** to have exact change **3.** (*escaso*) **ha venido muy justo el dinero** money's been very tight **4.** (*ajustado*) close-fitting; **este abrigo me viene ~** this coat is rather tight for me

**juvenil** [xu·βe·'nil] **I.** *adj* youthful, young **II.** *mf* DEP **juego con los ~es** I'm in the junior team

**juventud** [xu·βen·'tuð] *f* **1.** (*edad*) youth **2.** (*estado*) early life **3.** (*jóvenes*) young people

**juzgado** [xus·'ɣa·ðo, xuθ-] *m* court; **~ de guardia** police court

**juzgar** <g → gu> [xus·'ɣar, xuθ-] *vt* **1.** (*juez: decidir*) to judge; (*condenar*) to sentence **2.** (*opinar sobre*) to judge; (*considerar*) to consider, to deem; **~ mal a alguien** to misjudge sb; **no te juzgo capaz de hacerlo** I don't think you're capable of doing it

# K

**K, k** [ka] *f* K, k; **~ de Kenia** K as in Kilo

**kaki** [ka·ki] *adj* khaki

**karaoke** [ka·ra·'o·ke] *m* karaoke

**karate** [ka·'ra·te] *m*, **kárate** ['ka·ra·te] *m* DEP karate

**kayak** [ka·'jak] *m* <kayaks> DEP kayak

**keroseno** [ke·ro·'se·no] *m* kerosene

**ketchup** ['ked·ʧup] *m* <ketchups> ketchup

**kg** [ki·lo·'ɣra·mo] *abr de* **kilogramo** kg

**kikiriki** [ki·ki·ri·'ki] *m* cock-a-doodle-doo

**kilo** ['ki·lo] *m* kilo

**kilocaloría** [ki·lo·ka·lo·'ri·a] *f* kilocalorie

**kilogramo** [ki·lo·'ɣra·mo] *m* kilogram

**kilohercio** [ki·lo·'er·sjo, -θjo] *m* kilohertz

**kilolitro** [ki·lo·'li·tro] *m* kiloliter

**kilometraje** [ki·lo·me·'tra·xe] *m* AUTO mileage

**kilométrico, -a** [ki·lo·'me·tri·ko] *adj* kilometric

**kilómetro** [ki·'lo·me·tro] *m* kilometer

**kilovatio** [ki·lo·'βa·tjo] *m* kilowatt

**kinder** ['kin·der] *m inv* AmL, **kindergarten** [kin·der·'ɣar·ten] *m inv* kindergarten, nursery school

**kit** [kit] *m* <kits> kit

**kleenex**® ['kli·neks] *m inv*, **klínex** ['kli·neks] *m inv* Kleenex®, tissue

**km** [ki·'lo·me·tro] *abr de* **kilómetro** km.

**km/h** [ki·'lo·me·tro por 'o·ra] *abr de* **kilómetro por hora** km/h

# L

**L, l** ['e·le] *f* L,l; **~ de Lisboa** L as in Lima

**l** ['li·tro] *abr de* **litro(s)** l

**la** [la] **I.** *art def v.* **el, la II.** *pron pers, f sing* **1.** *objeto directo: f sing* her; (*cosa*) it; **¡tráeme~!** bring her/it to me!; **mi bicicleta y ~ tuya** my bicycle and yours **2.** (*con relativo*) **~ que...** the one that...; **~ cual** which **III.** *m* MÚS A; **en ~ bemol menor** in A flat minor

**laberinto** [la·βe·'rin·to] *m* **1.** (*lugar*) labyrinth, maze **2.** (*maraña*) tangle

**labia** ['la·βja] *f inf* glibness; **tener mucha ~** to be a smooth talker

**labial** [la·'βjal] *adj* labial

**lábil** ['la·βil] *adj* **1.** *t.* QUÍM (*carácter*) labile **2.** (*frágil*) frail

**labio** ['la·βjo] *m* **1.** (*boca*) lip; **estar sin despegar los ~s** to not say a word **2.** (*borde*) rim **3.** *pl* (*vulva*) labia *pl*

**labor** [la·'βor] *f* work; (*de coser*) needlework; (*labranza*) plowing; **no estoy por la ~** I don't feel like it

**laborable** [la·βo·'ra·βle] *adj* **día ~** working day

**laboral** [la·βo·'ral] *adj* labor

**laboratorio** [la·βo·ra·'to·rjo] *m* laboratory, lab

**laborioso, -a** [la·βo·'rjo·so, -a] *adj* hardworking, industrious; (*difícil*) arduous

**labrador(a)** [la·βra·'dor, --do·ra] *m(f)* farmhand

**labranza** [la·'βran·sa, -θa] *f* (*cultivo*) tillage

**labrar** [la·'βrar] *vt* **1.** (*un material*) to work; (*cristal*) to etch; **sin ~** plain **2.** (*cultivar, en jardín*) to work; (*arar*) to plow

**labriego, -a** [la·'βrje·ɣo, -a] *m, f* farm worker

**laburar** [la·βu·'rar] *vi Arg, Urug inf* to work

**laburo** [la·'βu·ro] *m Arg, Urug inf* work

**laca** ['la·ka] *f* 1. (*pintura*) lacquer, shellac 2. (*para el pelo*) hairspray

**lacayo** [la·'ka·jo] *m* footman; *pey* (*adulador*) lackey

**lacho** ['la·tʃo] *m Chile, Perú* (*enamorado*) lover; (*pisaverde*) dandy

**lacio, -a** ['la·sjo, -a; 'la·θjo-] *adj* (*cabello*) straight, lank

**lacónico, -a** [la·'ko·ni·ko, -a] *adj* brief; (*persona*) laconic

**lacra** ['la·kra] *f* 1. (*de una enfermedad*) mark 2. (*vicio*) blight

**lacrar** [la·'krar] *vt* (*cerrar*) to seal

**lacre** ['la·kre] *m* sealing wax

**lacrimógeno, -a** [la·kri·'mo·xe·no, -a] *adj* tear; **gas ~** tear gas

**lactancia** [lak·'tan·sja, -θja] *f* breastfeeding; (*período*) lactation

**lactante** [lak·'tan·te] I. *adj* nursing; **mujer ~** nursing mother II. *mf* nursling

**lácteo, -a** ['lak·te·o, -a] *adj* milk, dairy; *fig* milky; **vía láctea** ASTR Milky Way

**lactosa** [lak·'to·sa] *f* lactose

**ladeado, -a** [la·de·'a·do, -a] *adj* tilted

**ladear** [la·de·'ar] I. *vt* 1. (*inclinar*) to slant 2. (*desviar*) to skirt II. *vr:* **~se** 1. (*inclinarse*) to lean 2. *Chile* (*enamorarse*) **~se de alguien** to fall in love with sb

**ladera** [la·'de·ra] *f* slope, hillside

**ladilla** [la·'di·ja, -ʎa] *f* crab louse

**ladino, -a** [la·'di·no] *adj* cunning

**lado** ['la·do] *m* 1. *t.* MAT side; **a ambos ~s** on both sides; **por el ~ materno** on the mother's side; **ir de un ~ a otro** to go back and forth; **por todos ~s** everywhere; **al ~** nearby; **la casa de al ~** the house next-door; **al ~ de** (*junto a*) beside, next to; **al ~ mío, a mi ~** next to me, by my side; **por un ~..., y por el otro ~...** on the one hand..., and on the other hand... 2. **ir a algún otro ~** to go somewhere else; **~ a ~** side by side 3. (*punto de vista*) side; **el ~ bueno de la vida** the good side of life; **su ~ débil** his/her weak spot 4. (*camino*) direction; **ir por otro ~** to go another way 5. (*partido*) **me puse de tu ~** I sided with you ▸ **dejar de ~ a alguien** to ignore sb; **mirar de ~ a alguien** to look out of the corner of one's eye at sb

**ladrar** [la·'drar] *vi* to bark

**ladrido** [la·'dri·do] *m* bark

**ladrillo** [la·'dri·jo, -ʎo] *m* brick

**ladrón** [la·'dron] *m* (*enchufe*) multiple socket

**ladrón, -ona** [la·'dron, -·'dro·na] *m, f* thief, robber

**lagar** [la·'ɣar] *m* 1. (*aceite*) oil press; (*vino*) winepress 2. (*edificio*) press house

**lagartija** [la·ɣar·'ti·xa] *f* small lizard

**lagarto** [la·'ɣar·to] *m* 1. (*reptil*) lizard 2. *AmL* (*caimán*) alligator

**lago** ['la·ɣo] *m* lake

**lágrima** ['la·ɣri·ma] *f* tear ▸ **deshacerse en ~s** to burst into tears

**lagrimal** [la·ɣri·'mal] *m* corner of the eye

**laguna** [la·'ɣu·na] *f* 1. (*agua salada*) lagoon; (*dulce*) small lake 2. (*omisión*) gap; **~ en la memoria** memory lapse

**laico, -a** ['lai·ko, -a] *adj* lay

**lambiche** [lam·'bi·tʃe] *adj Méx vulg* (*adulador*) ass-kissing

**lameculos** [la·me·'ku·los] *mf inv vulg* kiss-ass

**lamentable** [la·men·'ta·βle] *adj* regrettable

**lamentación** [la·men·ta·'sjon, -'θjon] *f* lamentation

**lamentar** [la·men·'tar] I. *vt* to regret; **lo lamento** I'm sorry II. *vr* **~se de algo** to complain about sth

**lamento** [la·'men·to] *m* lament

**lamer** [la·'mer] *vt* to lick

**lamido** [la·'mi·do] *m* licking

**lámina** ['la·mi·na] *f* 1. (*hojalata*) tin plate; (*hoja de metal*) sheet; (*segmento*) lamina 2. (*ilustración*) print

**laminar** [la·mi·'nar] I. *adj* 1. (*en forma de lámina*) laminar 2. (*formado de láminas*) laminated II. *vt* 1. (*cortar*) to split 2. (*guarnecer*) to laminate

**lámpara** ['lam·pa·ra] *f* lamp, light; **~ fluorescente** fluorescent lamp; **~ de pie** floor lamp

**lamparilla** [lam·pa·'ri·ja, -ʎa] *f* (*luz*) small lamp

**lamparón** [lam·pa·'ron] *m* (*mancha*) grease stain

**lana** ['la·na] *f* 1. (*material, tela*) wool

K
L

**2.** *inf* (*dinero*) dough; **tienen mucha ~** they're loaded

**lanar** [la·'nar] *adj* wool-bearing; **ganado ~** sheep

**lance** [lan·se, 'lan·θe] *m* throw; **~ de amor** love affair; **~ de fortuna** stroke of luck

**lancha** ['lan·tʃa] *f* motorboat; **~ a remolque** barge; **~ de salvamento** lifeboat

**langosta** [lan·'gos·ta] *f* **1.** (*insecto*) locust **2.** (*crustáceo*) lobster

**langostino** [lan·gos·'ti·no] *m* prawn

**langucia** [lan·'gu·sja, -θja] *f* *AmL* hunger

**lánguido, -a** ['lan·gi·do, -a] *adj* **1.** (*débil*) weak **2.** (*espíritu*) languid

**lanilla** [la·'ni·ja, -ʎa] *f* nap

**lanoso, -a** [la·'no·so, -a] *adj*, **lanudo, -a** [la·'nu·do, -a] *adj* woolly; (*oveja*) wool-bearing

**lanza** ['lan·sa, -θa] *f* lance ▶ **romper una ~ en favor de alguien** to stick up for sb

**lanzacohetes** [lan·sa·ko·'e·tes, lan·θa-] *m inv* rocket launcher

**lanzadera** [lan·sa·'de·ra, lan·θa-] *f* shuttle; (*plataforma*) platform, launch(ing) pad

**lanzado, -a** [lan·'sa·do, -a; lan·'θa-] *adj* **1.** (*decidido*) determined; (*emprendedor*) enterprising **2.** (*impetuoso*) impetuous; (*fogoso*) forward

**lanzador(a)** [lan·sa·'dor, lan·'θa-] *m(f)* thrower; (*béisbol*) bowler, pitcher

**lanzallamas** [lan·sa·'ja·mas, lan·θa·ʎa-] *m inv* flamethrower

**lanzamiento** [lan·sa·'mjen·to, lan·θa-] *m* throw; **~ comercial** commercial promotion, product launch; **~ espacial** space launch; **~ de peso** DEP shot put

**lanzamisiles** [lan·sa·mi·'si·les, lan·θa-] *m inv* missile-launcher

**lanzar** <z → c> [lan·'sar, -'θar] **I.** *vt* **1.** (*arrojar*) **~ a algo/alguien** to throw at [*o* to] sth/sb **2.** (*al mercado*) to launch **II.** *vr* **~se a/sobre algo/alguien** to throw oneself at/against sth/sb; **~se al agua** to dive into the water; **~se en paracaídas** to parachute; **~se en picado** to nosedive; **~se a algo** to undertake sth

**lapa** ['la·pa] *f* ZOOL limpet; **pegarse como una ~** *inf* (*persona*) to stick like a leech

**lapicero** [la·pi·'θe·ro, -·'θe·ro] *m* pencil

**lápida** ['la·pi·da] *f* stone tablet, gravestone

**lapidar** [la·pi·'dar] *vt* to stone

**lápiz** ['la·pis, 'la·piθ] *m* pencil; **~ de labios** lipstick; **~ de ojos** eye pencil; **~ de color** crayon

**lapso** ['laβ·so] *m* **1.** (*período*) **~ (de tiempo)** lapse **2.** *v.* **lapsus**

**lapsus** ['laβ·sus] *m inv* blunder

**largar** <g → gu> [lar·'ɣar] **I.** *vt* **1.** (*soltar*) to release **2.** *inf* (*golpe*) to land; (*bofetada*) to let fly **3.** *inf* (*discurso*) to give **II.** *vr:* **~se 1.** (*irse*) to leave; (*de casa*) to leave home **2.** *AmL* (*comenzar*) to begin; **~se a hacer algo** to start to do sth **III.** *vi inf* to yak

**largo** ['lar·ɣo] **I.** *adv* plenty; **tenemos comida para ~** we have plenty of food; **~ y tendido** at length ▶ **a lo ~ de la playa** along the beach; **a lo ~ del día** throughout the day; **¡~ (de aquí)!** clear off! **II.** *m* length; **nadar tres ~s** to swim three lengths of the pool; **diez metros de ~** ten meters long

**largo, -a** ['lar·ɣo, -a] *adj* long; **a ~ plazo a la larga** in the long term [*o* run]; **dar largas a algo** to put off doing sth; **el pantalón te está ~** your pants are too long for you; **ir de ~** to be in a long dress; (*de gala*) to be in formal dress; **pasar de ~** to pass by; *fig* to ignore; **tener las manos largas** (*pegar*) to be free with one's hands; (*robar*) to be light-fingered

**largometraje** [lar·ɣo·me·'tra·xe] *m* full-length [*o* feature] film

**larguero** [lar·'ɣe·ro] *m* DEP crossbar

**largura** [lar·'ɣu·ra] *f* length

**laringe** [la·'rin·xe] *f* larynx

**larva** ['lar·βa] *f* larva

**las** [las] **I.** *art def v.* **el, la II.** *pron pers f pl* **1.** (*objeto directo*) them; **¡míra~!** look at them! **2.** (*con relativo*) **~ que...** the ones that...; **~ cuales** those which

**lascivo, -a** [la·'si·βo, las·'θi·βo, -a] *adj* lascivious

**láser** ['la·ser] *m* laser

**lástima** ['las·ti·ma] *f* pity; **dar ~** to inspire

pity; **su último libro da ~** his/her latest book is pathetic; **¡qué ~!** what a pity!

**lastimar** [las·ti·'mar] **I.** *vt* **1.** (*herir*) to hurt **2.** (*agraviar*) to offend **II.** *vr:* **~se 1.** (*herirse*) to hurt oneself **2.** (*quejarse*) **~se de algo** to complain about sth

**lastimero, -a** [las·ti·'me·ro, -a] *adj,* **lastimoso, -a** [las·ti·'mo·so, -a] *adj* pitiful

**lastre** ['las·tre] *m* (*estorbo*) dead weight; **ser un ~** to be a burden

**lata** ['la·ta] *f* **1.** (*metal*) tin **2.** (*envase*) can **3.** *inf* (*pesadez*) bore; **dar la ~** to be a nuisance; **¡vaya ~!** (*fastidio*) what a pain!

**latazo** [la·'ta·so, -θo] *m inf* **ser un ~** (*pesado*) to be a drag; (*fastidioso*) bother; (*aburrido*) bore; **dar el ~** to be a nuisance

**latear** [la·te·'ar] *vi AmL* to bore; **se pasa el día lateando** he/she spends all day blabbing away

**latente** [la·'ten·te] *adj* latent

**lateral** [la·te·'ral] *adj* lateral

**latido** [la·'ti·do] *m* (*corazón*) heartbeat

**latifundio** [la·ti·'fun·djo] *m* large estate

**latifundista** [la·ti·fun·'dis·ta] *mf owner of a large estate*

**latigazo** [la·ti·'ɣa·so, -'ɣa·θo] *m* (*golpe*) whiplash; (*chasquido*) crack of a whip

**látigo** ['la·ti·ɣo] *m* whip

**latín** [la·'tin] *m* Latin

**latino, -a** [la·'ti·no, -a] **I.** *adj* Latin; **América Latina** Latin America **II.** *m, f* Latin; *AmL* (*latinoamericano*) Latin American

**Latinoamérica** [la·ti·no·a·'me·ri·ka] *f* Latin America

**latinoamericano, -a** [la·ti·no·a·me·ri·'ka·no, -a] *adj, m, f* Latin American

**latir** [la·'tir] *vi* (*corazón*) to beat

**latitud** [la·ti·'tud] *f* latitude; (*extensión*) breadth

**latón** [la·'ton] *m* brass

**latoso, -a** [la·'to·so, -a] *adj* bothersome

**laúd** [la·'ud] *m* MÚS lute

**laureado, -a** [lau·re·'a·do, -a] *adj* (*premiado*) laureate, prize-winning

**laurel** [lau·'rel] *m* (*árbol*) laurel; (*condimento*) bay leaf; **dormirse en los ~es** to rest on one's laurels

**lava** ['la·ßa] *f* (*volcán*) lava

**lavabo** [la·'ßa·ßo] *m* **1.** (*pila*) sink **2.** (*cuarto*) lavatory

**lavacoches** [la·ßa·'ko·tʃes] *m inv* (*instalación*) car wash

**lavadero** [la·ßa·'de·ro] *m* (*de ropa*) laundry; (*en el río*) washing place

**lavado** [la·'ßa·do] *m* wash; **~ en seco** dry-cleaning; MED washing; **~ de cerebro** *fig* brainwashing; **~ de cara** *fig* facelift

**lavadora** [la·ßa·'do·ra] *f* washing machine

**lavanda** [la·'ßan·da] *f* lavender

**lavandería** [la·ßan·de·'ri·a] *f* laundromat

**lavaplatos** [la·ßa·'pla·tos] *m inv* **1.** (*electrodoméstico*) dishwasher **2.** *Col inf* (*fregadero*) (kitchen) sink

**lavar** [la·'ßar] **I.** *vt* to wash; **~ los platos** to do the dishes **II.** *vr:* **~se** to wash; **~se la cabeza** to wash one's hair; **~se los dientes** to brush one's teeth

**lavarropas** [la·ßa·'rro·pas] *f inv Arg* washing machine

**lavativa** [la·ßa·'ti·ßa] *f* (*enema*) enema

**lavatorio** [la·ßa·'to·rjo] *m AmL* washroom

**lavavajillas** [la·ßa·ßa·'xi·jas, -ʎas] *m inv* **1.** (*electrodoméstico*) dishwasher **2.** (*detergente*) dish detergent

**laxante** [lak·'san·te] *m* laxative

**laxo, -a** ['lak·so, -a] *adj* slack; (*moral*) lax

**lazada** [la·'sa·da, -'θa·da] *f* (*de zapato*) bow

**lazo** ['la·so, -'θo] *m* **1.** (*nudo*) bow **2.** (*para caballos*) lasso **3.** (*cinta*) ribbon **4.** (*vínculo*) tie; **~s afectivos** emotional bonds

**le** [le] *pron pers* **1.** *objeto indirecto: m sing* him; *f sing* her; *forma cortés* you; **¡da~ un beso!** give him/her a kiss!; **~ puedo llamar el lunes** I can call you on Monday **2.** *reg, objeto directo: m sing* him **3.** *forma cortés* you

**leal** [le·'al] *adj* loyal

**lealtad** [le·al·'tad] *f* loyalty

**lección** [lek·'sjon, -'θjon] *f* lesson; **tomar lecciones de matemáticas** to take mathematics classes; **dar una ~ a alguien** to teach sb a lesson; **¡que te sirva de ~!** let that be a lesson to you!

**lechada** [le·'tʃa·da] f (argamasa) grout

**lechal** [le·'tʃal] I. adj (cachorro) suckling II. m (cordero) baby lamb

**leche** ['le·tʃe] f 1. (líquido) milk; ~ **en polvo** powdered milk; ~ **entera** whole milk; ~ **desnatada** skimmed milk; ~ **semidesnatada** partially skimmed milk 2. inf (golpe) blow; ¡te doy una ~! I'm going to belt you one! 3. inf (hostia) **ser la** ~ to be too much; **estar de mala** ~ to be in a foul mood; **tener mala** ~ to be vindictive; **a toda** ~ at full speed

**lechería** [le·tʃe·'ri·a] f dairy

**lechero, -a** [le·'tʃe·ro, -a] m, f milkman m, milkwoman f

**lecho** ['le·tʃo] m bed; (río) riverbed

**lechón, -ona** [le·'tʃon, -·'tʃo·na] m, f suckling pig

**lechuga** [le·'tʃu·ɣa] f lettuce ▶ **fresco como una** ~ as fresh as a daisy

**lechuza** [le·'tʃu·sa, -θa] f barn owl

**lectivo, -a** [lek·'ti·βo, -a] adj **día** ~ school day

**lector** [lek·'tor] m COMPUT reader; ~ **de CD** CD player

**lector(a)** [lek·'tor, -·to·ra] m(f) 1. (que lee) reader; (en voz alta) lector 2. (profesor) conversation assistant

**lectorado** [lek·to·'ra·do] m assistantship

**lectura** [lek·'tu·ra] f 1. t. COMPUT (acción) reading 2. (obra) reading material

**leer** [le·'er] irr vt to read; ~ **en voz alta** to read aloud

**legado** [le·'ɣa·do] m legacy

**legajo** [le·'ɣa·xo] m dossier

**legal** [le·'ɣal] adj 1. (determinado por la ley) legal; (conforme a la ley) lawful 2. (fiel) trustworthy

**legalidad** [le·ɣa·li·'dad] f legality; **fuera de la** ~ unlawful

**legalización** [le·ɣa·li·θa·'θjon] f (autorización) legalization

**legalizar** <z → c> [le·ɣa·li·'sar, -'θar] vt 1. (autorizar) to legalize 2. (atestar) to authenticate

**legaña** [le·'ɣa·ɲa] f sleep, rheum; **tienes ~s** you have sleep in your eyes

**legar** <g → gu> [le·'ɣar] vt (legado) to bequeath

**legendario, -a** [le·xen·'da·rjo] adj legendary; (famoso) renowned

**legible** [le·'xi·βle] adj legible

**legión** [le·'xjon] f legion; **hay comida para una** ~ there's enough food to feed an army

**legionario, -a** [le·xjo·'na·rjo, -a] m, f legionnaire

**legionella** [le·xjo·'ne·la] f MED Legionnaire's disease

**legislación** [le·xis·la·'sjon, -'θjon] f legislation

**legislador(a)** [le·xis·la·'dor, -·'do·ra] I. adj legislative II. m(f) 1. (que legisla) legislator 2. AmL (parlamentario) member of parliament

**legislar** [le·xis·'lar] vi to legislate

**legislativo, -a** [le·xis·la·'ti·βo, -a] adj legislative; **poder** ~ legislative power

**legislatura** [le·xis·la·'tu·ra] f 1. (período) term of office 2. AmL (parlamento) legislative body

**legitimación** [le·xi·ti·ma·'sjon, -'θjon] f 1. (legalización) authentication 2. (habilitación) recognition 3. (hijo) legitimization

**legitimar** [le·xi·ti·'mar] vt 1. (dar legitimidad) to authenticate 2. (habilitar) to recognize 3. (hijo) to make legitimate

**legítimo, -a** [le·xi·'ti·mo, -a] adj 1. (legal) legitimate; **defensa legítima** self-defense 2. (verdadero) genuine 3. (hijo) legitimate

**legua** ['le·ɣwa] f league; **a la** ~ miles away

**legumbre** [le·'ɣum·bre] f 1. (planta) legume 2. (seca) pulse

**leído, -a** [le·'i·do, -a] adj 1. (persona) well-read 2. (revista) widely-read

**lejanía** [le·xa·'ni·a] f distance

**lejano, -a** [le·'xa·no, -a] adj faraway; (parentesco) distant; **en un futuro no muy ~** in the not-so-distant future

**lejía** [le·'xi·a] f (para lavar) bleach

**lejos** ['le·xos] I. adv far; ~ **de algo** far from sth; **a lo** ~ in the distance; **de** ~ from afar; **ir demasiado** ~ t. fig to go too far; **es de** ~ **la mejor soprano** she is by far the best soprano; **llegar** ~ fig to go far; **sin ir más** ~ fig to take an obvious example II. prep ~ **de** far from

**lelo, -a** ['le·lo, -a] adj inf 1. ser (tonto) silly, goofy 2. estar (pasmado) stunned;

(*mareado*) dizzy

**lema** ['le·ma] *m* (*tema*) theme; (*mote*) motto

**lencería** [len·se·'ri·a, len·θe·-] *f* **1.** (*ropa interior*) lingerie **2.** (*ropa blanca*) linen

**lengua** ['len·gwa] *f* **1.** ANAT tongue; **lo tengo en la punta de la ~** I have it on the tip of my tongue; **morderse la ~** *t. fig* to bite one's tongue; **sacar la ~ a alguien** to stick one's tongue out at sb; **se me trabó la ~** I got tongue-tied; **tener la ~ demasiado larga** *fig* to talk too much **2.** LING tongue; **~ materna** mother tongue; **~ oficial** official language **3.** (*forma*) tongue; **~ de agua** tongue of water ▶ **tener la ~ de trapo** *inf* to stutter and stammer; **estar con la ~ <u>fuera</u>** to be out of breath; **dar a la ~** to gab; **aquí alguien se ha <u>ido</u> de la ~** sb here has spilled the beans; **tirar a alguien de la ~** to pump sb for information

**lenguado** [len·'gwa·do] *m* sole

**lenguaje** [len·'gwa·xe] *m* language

**lengüeta** [len·'gwe·ta] *f* (*zapato*) tongue; MÚS reed

**lengüetear** [len·gwe·te·'ar] *vi AmL inf* to stick one's tongue out

**lente** ['len·te] *f* **1.** (*gafas*) eyeglasses *pl*; **llevar ~s** to wear glasses **2.** *t.* FOTO (*cristal*) lens; **~ de aumento** magnifying glass

**lenteja** [len·'te·xa] *f* lentil

**lentejuela** [len·te·'xwe·la] *f* sequin, spangle

**lentilla** [len·'ti·ja, -ʎa] *f* contact lens

**lentitud** [len·ti·'tud] *f* slowness; *fig* slow-wittedness; **con ~** slowly

**lento, -a** ['len·to] *adj* slow; *fig* slow-witted; **a paso ~** slowly; **cocinar a fuego ~** to cook over low heat [*o* a low flame]; **quemar a fuego ~** *fig* to burn slowly

**leña** ['le·ɲa] *f* **1.** (*madera*) firewood; **echar ~ al fuego** to add more firewood; *fig* to add fuel to the flames **2.** (*castigo*) beating; **dar ~** to give a beating; **repartir ~** to dish out blows; **recibir ~** to get beaten up ▶ **hacer ~ del <u>árbol</u> caído** to kick somebody when he is down

**leñador(a)** [le·ɲa·'dor, -·'do·ra] *m(f)* woodcutter, lumberjack

**leñazo** [le·'ɲa·so, -θo] *m inf* bash; **darse un ~ en la cabeza** to bash one's head

**Leo** ['le·o] *m* Leo

**león** [le·'on] *m* lion; **~ (marino)** sea lion

**leonera** [leo·'ne·ra] *f* (*habitación*) messy room

**leopardo** [leo·'par·do] *m* leopard

**leotardo(s)** [leo·'tar·do(s)] *m* **1.** (*malla*) leotards *pl* **2.** DEP (*malla*) tights *pl*

**lépero, -a** ['le·pe·ro, -a] **I.** *adj* **1.** *AmC* (*grosero*) coarse; (*vil*) rotten **2.** *Cuba* (*perspicaz*) shrewd **3.** *Ecua inf* (*arruinado*) broke **II.** *m, f AmC* pauper

**lepra** ['le·pra] *f* MED leprosy

**leproso, -a** [le·'pro·so, -a] **I.** *adj* leprous **II.** *m, f* leper

**lerdear** [ler·de·'ar] *vi AmC, Arg* to be sluggish; (*demorarse*) to take a long time

**lerdo, -a** ['ler·do, -a] *adj* slow, sluggish

**les** [les] *pron pers* **1.** *m pl reg* (*objeto directo*) them; (*forma cortés*) you **2.** *mf pl* (*objeto indirecto*) them; (*forma cortés*) you

**lesbiana** [les·'βja·na] *f* lesbian

**lésbico, -a** ['les·βi·ko, -a] *adj* lesbian

**lesear** [le·se·'ar] *vi Chile* to fool around

**lesera** [le·'se·ra] *f AmL* stupidity

**lesión** [le·'sjon] *f* injury

**lesionar** [le·sjo·'nar] **I.** *vt* (*herir*) to injure; (*dañar*) to damage **II.** *vr:* **~se** to get hurt

**letal** [le·'tal] *adj elev* lethal

**letárgico, -a** [le·'tar·xi·ko, -a] *adj* lethargic

**letargo** [le·'tar·ɣo] *m* lethargy

**Letonia** [le·'to·nja] *f* Latvia

**letra** ['le·tra] *f* **1.** (*signo*) letter; **con ~ mayúscula/minúscula** in capitals/small letters; **al pie de la ~** to the letter; **~ por ~** word for word **2.** (*escritura*) handwriting; **de su puño y ~** in his own handwriting **3.** *pl* (*saber*) learning, letters; UNIV arts *pl*; **hombre de ~s** man of letters **4.** MÚS lyrics *pl* **5.** COM **~ (de cambio)** bill of exchange; **~ al portador** draft payable to the bearer

**letrado, -a** [le·'tra·do, -a] *m, f* lawyer

**letrero** [le·'tre·ro] *m* notice, sign

**leucemia** [leu·'se·mja, -'θe·mja] *f* MED leukemia

**levadizo, -a** [le·βa·'di·so, -a; -'di·θo, -a] *adj* **puente ~** drawbridge

L

**levadura** [le·βa·'du·ɾa] *f* leavening yeast; ~ **en polvo** baking powder

**levantamiento** [le·βan·ta·'mjen·to] *m* **1.** (*amotinamiento*) uprising **2.** (*alzar*) lifting

**levantar** [le·βan·'tar] **I.** *vt* **1.** (*alzar*) to lift, to raise; (*del suelo*) to pick up; (*polvo, telón*) to raise; (*un campamento*) to strike; ~ **el vuelo** to take off; **después del fracaso ya no levantó cabeza** he/she never recovered from the fiasco **2.** (*despertar, provocar*) to awaken; **no queremos ~ sospechas** we don't want to arouse suspicion **3.** (*construir*) to build; (*monumento*) to erect; (*muro*) to put up **4.** (*suprimir*) to remove; (*embargo, castigo*) to lift **5.** (*voz, mirada*) to raise; ~ **la voz a alguien** to raise one's voice to sb **II.** *vr:* ~**se 1.** (*de la cama*) to get up; ~**se con el pie izquierdo** *fig* to get out of bed on the wrong side **2.** (*sublevarse*) to rebel **3.** (*viento, telón*) to rise **4.** (*sesión*) to adjourn; **se levanta la sesión** the meeting is closed, court is adjourned

**levante** [le·'βan·te] *m* east; (*viento*) east wind

**levar** [le·'βar] *vt* ~ **anclas** to weigh anchor

**leve** ['le·βe] *adj* (*enfermedad*) mild; (*peso, sanción*) light; (*error*) slight

**levitar** [le·βi·'tar] *vi* to levitate

**léxico** ['lek·si·ko] *m* vocabulary

**ley** [lei] *f* **1.** JUR, REL, FÍS law; **Ley Fundamental** Fundamental Law; ~ **orgánica** constitutional law; **la ~ de la oferta y demanda** the law of supply and demand; **la ~ seca** the Prohibition; **la ~ de la selva la ~ del más fuerte** the law of the jungle; **fuerza de ~** force of law; **proyecto de ~** bill; **hacer algo con todas las de la ~** to do sth properly; **hecha la ~, hecha la trampa** every law has its loophole; **según la ~ vigente** in accordance with the law currently in force; **ser de ~** *inf* to be reliable **2.** (*oro*) legal standard of fineness; (*monedas*) genuine; **oro de ~** standard gold

**leyenda** [le·'jen·da] *f* LIT, REL legend

**liana** [li·'a·na] *f* liana

**liar** <*1. pres* lío> [li·'ar] **I.** *vt* **1.** (*fardo*) to tie up; (*paquete*) to wrap up **2.** (*cigarrillo*) to roll **3.** *inf* (*engañar*) to take in; (*enredar*) to mix up; **¡ahora sí que la hemos liado!** we've really done it now! **II.** *vr:* ~**se 1.** *inf* (*juntarse*) to become lovers **2.** (*embarullarse*) to get complicated **3.** (*ponerse a*) ~**se a golpes con alguien** to start fighting with sb

**libélula** [li·'βe·lu·la] *f* dragonfly

**liberación** [li·βe·ɾa·'sjon, -'θjon] *f* liberation, release

**liberal** [li·βe·'ɾal] *adj t.* POL liberal

**liberalizar** <z → c> [li·βe·ɾa·li·'sar, -'θar] *vt* to liberalize

**liberar** [li·βe·'ɾar] *vt* to liberate, to set free; (*eximir*) to exempt

**libertad** [li·βeɾ·'tad] *f* (*libre arbitrio*) liberty, freedom; ~ **de expresión** freedom of speech; ~ **de prensa** freedom of the press; **en ~ bajo fianza** on bail; **en ~ condicional** on parole; **poner en ~** to set free; **tomarse demasiadas ~es** to take too many liberties

**libertar** [li·βeɾ·'tar] *vt* to liberate

**libertario, -a** [li·βeɾ·'ta·ɾjo, -a] *adj, m, f* libertarian

**libertinaje** [li·βeɾ·ti·'na·xe] *m* libertinage

**libertino, -a** [li·βeɾ·'ti·no, -a] *adj* dissolute

**libido** [li·'βi·do] *f* libido

**libra** ['li·βɾa] *f* pound; ~ **esterlina** pound sterling

**Libra** ['li·βɾa] *f* Libra

**librado, -a** [li·'βɾa·do, -a] *adj* **salir bien ~ de algo** to come out of sth unscathed, to be successful in sth; **salir mal ~** to come out the worse for wear, to fail

**librar** [li·'βɾar] **I.** *vt* (*dejar libre*) ~ **de algo/alguien** to free from sth/sb; (*salvar*) to save from sth/sb **II.** *vi inf* (*tener libre*) **hoy libro** I have today off **III.** *vr* ~**se de algo/alguien** (*deshacerse*) to get rid of sth/sb; (*salvarse*) to escape from sth/sb

**libre** <libérrimo> ['li·βɾe] *adj* free; ~ **de franqueo** no postage necessary; **dar vía ~** to give the green light; **eres bien ~ de hacerlo** you are quite free to do so

**librecambio** [li·βɾe·'kam·bjo] *m* free trade

**librería** [li·βɾe·'ɾi·a] *f* bookshop

**librero, -a** [li·'βɾe·ro] *m, f* bookseller

**libreta** [li·'βre·ta] *f* 1. (*cuaderno*) notebook; (*para notas*) notepad 2. (*de ahorros*) bank book

**libro** [li·βro] *m* book; ~ **de bolsillo** paperback; ~ **de cocina** cookbook; ~ **de consulta** reference book; ~ **de escolaridad** school record; ~ **de texto** textbook ▶ **hablar como un ~ cerrado** not to express oneself clearly

**licencia** [li·'sen·sja, ·'θen·θja] *f* (*permiso*) license; (*para un libro*) authorization; ~ **de conducir** *Méx, Cuba* driver's license

**licenciado, -a** [li·sen·'sja·ðo, -a; li·θen·'θja-] *m, f* 1. (*estudiante*) graduate; ~ **en economía** Economics graduate 2. (*soldado*) discharged soldier

**licenciar** [li·sen·'sjar, -'θjar] I. *vt* (*despedir*) to dismiss; (*soldado*) to discharge II. *vr*: ~**se** to graduate; **se licenció en psicología** he got a degree in psychology

**licenciatura** [li·sen·sja·'tu·ra, li·θen·θja·] *f* (*título*) degree; (*carrera*) university studies *pl*

**lícito, -a** ['li·si·to, -a; -θi·to, -a] *adj* allowed; (*justo*) fair

**licor** [li·'kor] *m* liquor; (*de frutas*) liqueur

**licuadora** [li·kwa·'ðo·ra] *f* (*batidora*) blender; (*para fruta*) liquidizer

**licuar** <*1. pres* licúo> [li·'kwar] *vt* 1. Fís to liquate 2. (*fruta*) to liquefy

**líder** ['li·ðer] *mf* leader; **la empresa ~** the leading company

**liderar** [li·ðe·'rar] *vt* to lead; (*dirigir*) to head; **el equipo que lidera la clasificación** the team at the top of the table

**liderato** [li·ðe·'ra·to] *m*, **liderazgo** [li·ðe·'ras·ɣo, -'raθ·ɣo] *m* leadership; **capacidad de ~** leadership capability

**lidia** ['li·ðja] *f* fight; TAUR bullfight

**liebre** [lje·'βre] *f* hare ▶ **levantar la ~** to let the cat out of the bag; **donde menos se piensa salta la ~** things always happen when you least expect them to

**lienzo** ['ljen·so, -θo] *m* (*tela*) cloth; (*para cuadros*) canvas; (*óleo*) painting

**liga** ['li·ɣa] *f* 1. (*alianza*) *t.* DEP league 2. (*prenda*) suspender, garter

**ligamento** [li·ɣa·'men·to] *m* ANAT ligament

**ligar** <*g → gu*> [li·'ɣar] I. *vi inf* (*tontear*) to flirt II. *vt* 1. (*atar*) to tie 2. (*unir*) to join III. *vr*: ~**se** 1. (*unirse*) to join 2. *inf* (*tontear*) to flirt

**ligereza** [li·xe·'re·sa, -θa] *f* 1. (*rapidez*) swiftness 2. (*levedad*) lightness

**ligero, -a** [li·'xe·ro, -a] *adj* 1. (*leve, ingrávido*) light; **ir muy ~ de ropa** to be scantily clad, not to be wearing much 2. (*ágil*) nimble ▶ **hacer algo a la ligera** to do sth without thinking; **tomarse algo a la ligera** to not take sth seriously

**ligón** [li·'ɣon, -ona] *m* womanizer; **ser un ~** to be a Don Juan

**ligue** ['li·ɣe] *m inf* 1. (*acción*) pick-up; **tener un ~ con alguien** to have an affair with sb 2. (*persona*) chat-up, pick-up

**liguero** [li·'ɣe·ro] *m* garter belt

**liguero, -a** [li·'ɣe·ro, -a] *adj* DEP league

**lija** ['li·xa] *f* sandpaper

**lijadora** [li·xa·'ðo·ra] *f* sander

**lijar** [li·'xar] *vt* to sand

**lila** ['li·la] I. *adj* lilac II. *f* BOT lilac

**lima** ['li·ma] *f* 1. (*instrumento*) file; **rebajar con la ~** to file down 2. BOT (*fruta*) lime; (*árbol*) lime tree ▶ **comer como una ~** *inf* to eat like a horse

**limar** [li·'mar] *vt* to file; *fig* to perfect

**limbo** ['lim·bo] *m* REL limbo; **estar en el ~** (*distraído*) to be distracted; (*no enterarse*) to be oblivious

**limeño, -a** [li·'me·ɲo, -a] I. *adj* of/from Lima II. *m, f* native/inhabitant of Lima

**limitación** [li·mi·ta·'sjon, -'θjon] *f* limitation; (*de una norma*) restriction; **sin limitaciones** unlimited

**limitado, -a** [li·mi·'ta·ðo, -a] *adj* (*poco*) scant; (*medios*) limited; **un número ~** a limited number

**limitar** [li·mi·'tar] I. *vi* ~ **con algo** to border on II. *vt* to limit; (*libertad*) to restrict III. *vr*: ~**se** to confine oneself

**límite** ['li·mi·te] *m* limit; **situación ~** extreme situation; **sin ~s** limitless; **fecha ~ de entrega** delivery deadline

**limítrofe** [li·mi·tro·fe] *adj* bordering; **países ~s** neighboring countries

**limón** [li·'mon] *adj, m* lemon

**limonada** [li·mo·'na·da] *f* lemonade

**limonero** [li·mo·'ne·ro] *m* lemon tree

**limosna** [li·'mos·na] *f* alms *pl;* **pedir ~** to beg

**limosnero, -a** [li·mos·'ne·ro, -a] *m, f AmL* (*pedigüeño*) beggar

**limpiabotas** [lim·pja·'βo·tas] *mf inv* bootblack

**limpiacristales** [lim·pja·kris·'ta·les] *m inv* (*producto*) window cleaning fluid

**limpiador** [lim·pja·'dor] *m* cleaner

**limpiaparabrisas** [lim·pja·pa·ra·'βri·sas] *m inv* windshield wiper

**limpiar** [lim·'pjar] **I.** *vt* to clean; (*dientes*) to brush; **~ el polvo** to dust; **~ en seco** to dry-clean **II.** *vi* to clean **III.** *vr:* **~se** to clean; (*nariz*) to wipe; (*dientes*) to brush

**limpieza** [lim·'pje·sa, -θa] *f* **1.** (*lavar*) washing; (*casa, zapatos*) cleaning; **~ a fondo** thorough cleaning; **señora de la ~** cleaning lady, cleaner **2.** (*estado*) cleanness, cleanliness **3.** (*eliminación*) cleansing; POL purge

**limpio** ['lim·pjo] *adv* (*sin trampas*) fairly; **jugar ~** to play fair ► **¿qué has sacado en ~ de todo este asunto?** what do you make of all this?

**limpio, -a** ['lim·pjo, -a] *adj* clean; (*aire*) pure ► **lo dejaron ~** *inf* (*sin dinero*) they cleaned him out

**limusina** [li·mu·'si·na] *f* AUTO limousine

**linaje** [li·'na·xe] *m* lineage

**lince** ['lin·se, -θe] *m* lynx; **tener ojos de ~** to be sharp-eyed

**linchamiento** [lin·tʃa·'mjen·to] *m* lynching

**linchar** [lin·'tʃar] *vt* to lynch

**lindar** [lin·'dar] *vi* **~ con algo** to border on sth

**lindo, -a** ['lin·do, -a] *adj* pretty; (*niño*) lovely, cute

**línea** ['li·nea] *f* t. MAT, MIL, ECON (*raya*) line; **~ de meta** DEP (*atletismo*) finishing line; **~ recta** straight line **2.** (*renglón*) line; **~ en blanco** blank line; **leer entre ~s** to read between the lines **3.** (*de transporte*) line; (*trayecto*) route; **~ aérea** airline; **~ férrea** railroad line **4.** TEL telephone line; **no hay ~** the line is dead [*o* down] **5.** (*pariente*) line; **por ~ materna** on his mother's side

**6.** (*tipo*) figure; **guardar la ~** to watch one's figure **7.** (*fábrica*) **~ de montaje** assembly line

**lineal** [li·ne·'al] *adj* t. MAT, ARTE linear

**lingote** [lin·'go·te] *m* ingot

**lingüística** [lin·'gwis·ti·ka] *f* linguistics

**lingüístico, -a** [lin·'gwis·ti·ko, -a] *adj* linguistic

**linimento** [li·ni·'men·to] *m* liniment

**lino** ['li·no] *m* **1.** BOT flax **2.** (*tela*) linen

**linterna** [lin·'ter·na] *f* lantern; (*a pila*) flashlight

**lío** ['li·o] *m* **1.** (*embrollo*) mess; **¡déjame de ~s!** don't come to me with your problems!; **hacerse un ~ con algo** to get into a jam with sth **2.** *inf* (*relación*) affair

**lipidia** [li·'pi·dja] *f* **1.** *AmC* (*pobreza*) poverty; (*miseria*) misery **2.** *Cuba, Méx* (*impertinencia*) impertinence

**lipotimia** [li·po·'ti·mja] *f* blackout

**liquidación** [li·ki·da·'sjon, -θjon] *f* **1.** (*de una mercancía*) sale; **~ total** clearance sale **2.** (*de una factura*) payment; (*cuenta*) settlement

**liquidar** [li·ki·'dar] *vt* **1.** *inf* (*acabar*) to liquidate; (*matar*) to kill; **lo ~on** *inf* they bumped him off **2.** (*mercancía*) to sell; **~ las existencias** to sell off all merchandise **3.** (*cerrar*) to close **4.** (*factura*) to settle

**liquidez** [li·ki·'des, 'deθ] *f* **1.** (*agua*) fluidity **2.** COM liquidity

**líquido** ['li·ki·do] *m* **1.** (*agua*) liquid; **~ de frenos** brake fluid **2.** (*saldo*) cash; **~ imponible** taxable income

**líquido, -a** ['li·ki·do, -a] *adj* **1.** (*material*) liquid **2.** (*dinero*) cash; **renta líquida** disposable income

**lira** ['li·ra] *f* **1.** (*moneda*) lira **2.** (*instrumento*) lyre

**lírica** ['li·ri·ka] *f* poetry

**lírico, -a** ['li·ri·ko, -a] *adj* **1.** LIT lyric(al) **2.** MÚS lyrical

**lirio** ['li·rjo] *m* lily

**lirón** [li·'ron] *m* dormouse; **dormir como un ~** to sleep like a log

**Lisboa** [lis·'βoa] *f* Lisbon

**lisboeta** [lis·βo·'e·ta] **I.** *adj* of/from Lisbon **II.** *mf* native/inhabitant of Lisbon

**lisiado, -a** [li·'sja·do, -a] *adj* crippled

**lisiar** [li·'sjar] *vr:* ~**se** to become disabled

**liso, -a** ['li·so, -a] *adj* **1.** (*superficie*) smooth; (*pelo*) straight; **los 100 metros** ~**s** the 100 meter flat race **2.** (*tela*) plain

**lisonjero, -a** [li·son·'xe·ro, -a] **I.** *adj* flattering **II.** *m, f* flatterer

**lista** ['lis·ta] *f* (*enumeración*) list; ~ **de la compra** shopping list; **estar en la** ~ **de espera** to be on the waiting list; **pasar** ~ (*leer*) to take roll call

**listado** [lis·'ta·do] *m* list

**listar** [lis·'tar] *vt* to list

**listillo, -a** [lis·'ti·jo, -a; -ʎo, -a] *m, f* smart aleck

**listín** [lis·'tin] *m* (*de teléfonos*) directory

**listo, -a** ['lis·to, -a] *adj* **1.** *ser* (*inteligente*) clever; (*sagaz*) shrewd; **pasarse de** ~ to be too clever by half **2.** *estar* (*preparado*) ready; ~ **para despegar** ready for takeoff; **estás** ~ **si crees que...** *inf* you have another think coming if you think that...

**listón** [lis·'ton] *m* lath; **poner el** ~ **muy alto** *fig* to set very high standards

**litera** [li·'te·ra] *f* (*cama*) bunk; FERRO couchette; NÁUT berth

**literal** [li·te·'ral] *adj* literal

**literario, -a** [li·te·'ra·rjo, -a] *adj* literary

**literatura** [li·te·ra·'tu·ra] *f* literature

**litigar** <g → gu> [li·ti·'ɣar] *vt t.* JUR to dispute

**litigio** [li·'ti·xjo] *m* **1.** (*disputa*) dispute; **en** ~ in dispute **2.** (*juicio*) lawsuit

**litoral** [li·to·'ral] *m* (*costa*) coast; (*playa*) shore

**litro** ['li·tro] *m* liter; **un** ~ **de leche** a liter of milk

**liturgia** [li·'tur·xja] *f* liturgy

**liviano, -a** [li·'βja·no, -a] *adj* light

**lívido, -a** ['li·βi·do, -a] *adj* **1.** (*amoratado*) livid; ~ **de frío** livid with cold **2.** (*pálido*) ashen

**llaga** ['ja·ɣa, 'ʎa-] *f* (*herida*) wound

**llama** ['ja·ma, 'ʎa-] *f* **1.** (*fuego*) flame **2.** ZOOL llama

**llamada** [ja·'ma·da, ʎa-] *f* **1.** (*voz*) call; ~ **al orden** call to order **2.** (*de teléfono*) phone call; ~ **a cobro revertido** collect call; ~ **interurbana** long-distance call; ~ **local** local call **3.** (*a la puerta golpeando*) knock; (*con el timbre*) ring

**llamado, -a** [ja·'ma·do, ʎa-] *adj* (*conocido como*) called; (*supuesto*) so-called

**llamado** [ja·'ma·do, -a; ʎa-] *m AmS v.* **llamamiento**

**llamador** [ja·ma·'dor, ʎa-] *m* doorknocker

**llamamiento** [ja·ma·'mjen·to, ʎa-] *m* **1.** (*exhortación*) appeal; **hacer un** ~ **a todos** to issue an appeal to all **2.** MIL ~ **a filas** call to arms **3.** JUR (*citación*) summons, subpoena

**llamar** [ja·'mar, ʎa-] **I.** *vt* **1.** (*voz, teléfono*) to call; ~ **a filas** MIL to draft; **te llaman al teléfono** you're wanted on the phone **2.** (*denominar*) to call; **lo llamé idiota** I called him an idiot **3.** (*despertar*) to wake up; ~ **la atención** (*reprender*) to reprimand; (*ser llamativo*) to attract attention; ~ **la atención sobre algo** to draw attention to sth **II.** *vi* (*a la puerta golpeando*) to knock; (*con el timbre*) to ring; **¿quién llama?** who is it? **III.** *vr:* ~**se** to be called; **¿cómo te llamas?** what's your name?

**llamarada** [ja·ma·'ra·da, ʎa-] *f* blaze

**llamativo, -a** [ja·ma·'ti·βo, -a; ʎa-] *adj* (*traje*) flashy; (*color*) loud

**llana** ['ja·na, 'ʎa-] *f* trowel

**llanca** ['jan·ka, 'ʎa-] *f Chile* bluish-green copper ore

**llanito, -a** [ja·'ni·to, -a; ʎa-] *m, f inf* Gibraltarian

**llano** ['ja·no, 'ʎa-] *m* plain

**llano, -a** ['ja·no, -a; 'ʎa-] *adj* **1.** (*liso*) flat; (*terreno*) level **2.** LING paroxytone **3.** (*sencillo*) **el pueblo** ~ the common people

**llanta** ['janta, 'ʎan-] *f* **1.** *AmL* (*rueda*) tire **2.** (*cerco*) (*metal*) rim; ~ **de aleación** alloy wheel

**llanto** ['jan·to, 'ʎan-] *m* crying

**llanura** [ja·'nu·ra, ʎa-] *f* plain

**llave** ['ja·βe, 'ʎa-] *f* **1.** *t. fig* (*instrumento*) key; ~ **de contacto** AUTO ignition key; **ama de** ~**s** housekeeper; ~ **en mano** (*coche*) on the road; **echar la** ~ to lock; **estar bajo** ~ to be under lock and key; **la** ~ **no entra** the key doesn't fit; **meter/sacar la** ~ to put in/pull out the key **2.** (*grifo*) faucet **3.** (*tuerca*) wrench; ~ **inglesa** monkey wrench **4.** (*interruptor*) switch

**llavero** [ja·βe·ro, ʎe-] *m* key ring

**llegada** [je·ɣa·da, ʎe-] *f* arrival; (*meta*) finishing line

**llegar** <g > gu> [je·ɣar, ʎe-] I. *vi* 1. (*al destino, el correo*) to arrive; ~ **a la meta** DEP to reach the finishing line; **estar al** ~ to be about to arrive; ~ **a Madrid/al hotel** to arrive in Madrid/at the hotel; ~ **tarde** to be late; **¡todo llegará!** all in good time!; **¡hasta ahí podíamos** ~! that's the limit! 2. (*recibir*) **no me ha llegado el dinero** I haven't received the money 3. (*durar*) to live; ~ **a viejo** to live to old age; **el enfermo no** ~**á a la primavera** the patient won't make it to spring 4. (*ascender*) to amount to; **no llega a 20 dólares** it's less than 20 dollars 5. (*lograr*) **ese** ~**á lejos** that fellow will go far; ~ **a ser muy rico** to become very rich; **llegamos a recoger 8.000 firmas** we managed to get 8,000 signatures 6. (*ser suficiente*) to be enough 7. (*tocar*) ~ **a** [*o* **hasta**] **algo** to reach sth; **no me llegas ni a la suela de los zapatos** you can't hold a candle to me II. *vr:* ~**se** (*ir*) to go; ~**se por casa de alguien** to stop by sb's house

**llenador(a)** [je·na·dor, -·do·ra, ʎe-] *adj* Csur filling; **esta tarta es muy llenadora** this pie is very filling

**llenar** [je·nar, ʎe-] I. *vt* 1. (*atestar*) to fill; ~ **de algo** to fill with sth 2. (*cumplimentar*) to fill in [*o* out] 3. (*colmar*) ~ **de algo** to overwhelm with sth; **nos llenó de regalos** we were showered with gifts 4. (*satisfacer*) to satisfy II. *vi* (*comida*) to be filling; **la pasta llena mucho** pasta is very filling III. *vr:* ~**se de algo** *inf* (*comida*) to stuff oneself with sth

**lleno** [ʎe·no, ʎe-] *m* (*teatro, auditorio*) full house

**lleno, -a** [ʎe·no, -a; ʎe-] *adj* full; **luna llena** full moon; ~ **de** full of, filled with; **el autobús iba** ~ the bus was full; **estoy** ~ *inf* I'm full

**llevadero, -a** [je·βa·de·ro, -a; ʎe-] *adj* bearable

**llevar** [je·βar, ʎe-] I. *vt* 1. (*a un destino, acompañar*) to take; (*transportar*) to transport; (*en brazos*) to carry; (*comida*)

to take out; ~ **a alguien en el coche** to give sb a lift; ~ **algo a alguien** to take sth to sb; **dos pizzas para** ~, **por favor** two pizzas to go, please 2. (*costar*) to cost; **este trabajo lleva mucho tiempo** this work takes a lot of time 3. (*tener*) ~ **consigo** to be carrying, to have 4. (*conducir*) to lead; ~ **de la mano** to lead by the hand; **esto no lleva a ninguna parte** this isn't getting us anywhere 5. (*ropa*) to wear 6. (*coche*) to drive 7. (*estar*) to have been; **llevo cuatro días aquí** I've been here for four days 8. (*gestionar*) to manage; ~ **las cuentas** to manage the accounts; **el abogado que lleva el caso** the lawyer handling the case 9. (*inducir*) ~ **a algo** to lead to sth, to induce sth; **me llevó a pensar que...** it led me to think that... 10. (*exceder*) to exceed; **te llevo dos años** I'm two years older than you 11. (*tener como ingrediente*) **¿lleva picante?** does it have hot pepper? ► **dejarse** ~ **por algo** to be carried away with sth; **dejarse** ~ **por alguien** to let sb influence you; ~ **las de perder** to be fighting a losing battle; **¿qué tal lo llevas?** how are you holding up? II. *vr:* ~**se** 1. (*coger*) to take; ~**se algo por delante** to crush sth 2. (*ganar*) to win; ~**se la mejor/peor parte** to get the best/worst of it 3. (*estar de moda*) to be in fashion; **ya no se llevan estos zapatos** those shoes are no longer in fashion 4. (*soportarse*) ~**se bien** to get along well; ~**se a matar** to hate each other ► **...y me llevo cuatro** MAT ... and carry four

**lliclla** [ʎik·ja, ʎik·ʎa] *f* Bol, Ecua, Perú blanket (*carried on the back by Indian women*)

**llicta** [ʎik·ta, ʎik-] *f* Bol potato meal cake (*type of hard cake eaten while chewing coca to give flavor to the coca ball*)

**llorar** [jo·rar, ʎo-] I. *vi* to cry; **me lloran los ojos** my eyes are watering; ~ **de alegría** to cry for joy; ~ **por algo/alguien** to cry over sth/sb; *fig* to mourn sth/sb; **lloramos de risa** we laughed until we cried ► **quien no llora no mama** *inf* the squeaky wheel gets the oil *prov* II. *vt* 1. (*lágrimas*) ~ **la muerte de al-**

**guien** to mourn sb's death **2.** (*quejarse*) to whine; (*lamentar*) to bemoan

**llorica** [jo·'ri·ka, ʎo-] *mf inf* crybaby

**lloriquear** [jo·ri·ke·'ar, ʎo-] *vi* to whimper

**lloriqueo** [jo·ri·'keo, ʎo-] *m* whimpering

**lloro(s)** ['jo·ro(s), ʎo-] *m(pl)* crying; **con estos ~s no conseguirás nada** this crying won't get you anywhere

**llorón, -ona** [jo·'ron, -o·na; ʎo-] **I.** *adj* **sauce ~** weeping willow **II.** *m, f* crybaby

**lloroso, -a** [jo·'ro·so, -a; ʎo-] *adj* tearful

**llover** <o → ue> [jo·'βer, ʎo-] *vi, vt, vimpers* to rain; **está lloviendo** it's raining; **llueve a mares** [*o a cántaros*] it's pouring; **siempre llueve sobre mojado** it never rains but it pours; **como llovido del cielo** heaven sent; **me escucha como quien oye ~** *inf* in one ear and out the other; **ya ha llovido mucho desde entonces** *fig* a lot has happened since then

**llovida** [jo·'βi·da, ʎo-] *f AmL* rain; **¡qué ~!** what a downpour!

**llovizna** [jo·'βis·na, ʎo·βiθ·na] *f* drizzle

**lloviznar** [jo·βis·'nar, ʎo·βiθ·'nar] *vimpers* **está lloviznando** it's drizzling

**lluvia** ['ju·βja, 'ʎu-] *f* **1.** (*chubasco*) rain; **~ de estrellas** meteor shower; **época de las ~s** rainy season; **~ ácida** acid rain; **~ radiactiva** fallout; **hubo una ~ de protestas** there was a shower of protests **2.** *AmL* (*ducha*) shower

**lluvioso, -a** [ju·'βjo·so, -a; ʎu-] *adj* rainy

**lo** [lo] **I.** *art def v.* **el, la, lo II.** *pron pers m y neutro sing* **1.** (*objeto: masculino*) him; (*neutro*) it; **¡lláma~!** call him!; **¡haz~!** do it! **2.** (*con relativo*) what; **~ cual** which; **~ que quiero decir es que...** what I mean is that...

**loable** [lo·'a·βle] *adj* commendable

**lobo, -a** ['lo·βo] *m, f* wolf; **~ de mar** old salt; **meterse en la boca del ~** to go into the lion's den; **ser un ~ con piel de oveja** to be a wolf in sheep's clothing; **tener un hambre de ~** to be as hungry as a wolf

**lóbulo** ['lo·βu·lo] *m ANAT* lobe; **~ de la oreja** earlobe

**local** [lo·'kal] **I.** *adj* local **II.** *m* locale; COM

premises *pl*; **~ público** public building

**localidad** [lo·ka·li·'ðad] *f* **1.** (*municipio*) town **2.** (*entrada*) ticket; (*asiento*) seat

**localización** [lo·ka·li·sa·'sjon, -θa·'θjon] *f* (*búsqueda*) finding; AVIAT tracking; **~ de software** COMPUT software localization

**localizar** <z → c> [lo·ka·li·'sar, -'θar] *vt* **1.** (*encontrar*) to find; **~ por teléfono** to get in touch by phone **2.** (*limitar*) to localize; (*fuego, epidemia*) to confine

**locería** [lo·se·'ri·a, loθe-] *f AmL* crockery

**loción** [lo·'sjon, -'θjon] *f* lotion; **~ capilar** hair lotion; **~ bronceadora** suntan lotion; **~ hidratante** moisturizing cream

**loco, -a** ['lo·ko, -a] **I.** *adj* mad, crazy; **a lo ~** a tontas y a locas any old way; **estar ~ de atar** to be raving mad; **estar ~ por la música** to be crazy about music; **estar ~ de contento** to be elated; **estar medio ~** to be not all there; **tener una suerte loca** to be incredibly lucky **II.** *m, f* madman *m*, madwoman *f*; **casa de ~s** *t. fig* madhouse; **cada ~ con su tema** to each his own; **hacerse el ~** to act dumb; **hacer el ~** to act the fool

**locomoción** [lo·ko·mo·'sjon, -'θjon] *f* locomotion

**locomotora** [lo·ko·mo·'to·ra] *f* locomotive

**locro** ['lo·kro] *m AmS* meat and vegetable stew

**locuaz** [lo·'kwas, -'kwaθ] *adj* loquacious; (*charlatán*) talkative

**locución** [lo·ku·'sjon, -'θjon] *f* (*expresión*) phrase

**locura** [lo·'ku·ra] *f* **1.** (*enajenación mental*) madness; **querer con ~** to be madly in love with **2.** (*disparate*) crazy thing; **andar haciendo ~s** to be doing foolish things

**locutor(a)** [lo·ku·'tor, -·'to·ra] *m(f)* speaker

**locutorio** [lo·ku·'to·rjo] *m TEL* telephone booth

**lodazal** [lo·da·'sal, -'θal] *m* quagmire

**lodo** ['lo·do] *m* mud

**lógica** ['lo·xi·ka] *f* logic

**lógico, -a** ['lo·xi·ko, -a] *adj* logical; (*normal*) natural

**logística** [lo·'xis·ti·ka] *f* logistics *pl*

**logístico, -a** [lo·'xis·ti·ko, -a] *adj* logistic

**logopeda** |lo·ɣo·'pe·da| *mf* speech therapist

**logopedia** |lo·ɣo·'pe·dja| *f* speech therapy

**logotipo** |lo·ɣo·'ti·po| *m* logotype; (*de una empresa, un producto*) logo

**logrado, -a** |lo·'ɣra·ðo, -a| *adj* successful, well done

**lograr** |lo·'ɣrar| *vt* to achieve; **logré convencerla** I managed to convince her

**logro** |'lo·ɣro| *m* achievement

**loma** |'lo·ma| *f* hill

**lombriz** |lom·'briθ, -'briθ| *f* worm; **~ intestinal** tapeworm; **~ de tierra** earthworm

**lomo** |'lo·mo| *m* back; (*de libro*) spine; (*solomillo*) loin

**lona** |'lo·na| *f* canvas

**loncha** |'lon·tʃa| *f* slice; (*beicon*) rasher

**londinense** |lon·di·'nen·se| **I.** *adj* London **II.** *mf* Londoner

**Londres** |'lon·dres| *m* London

**longaniza** |lon·ga·'ni·sa, -'ni·θa| *f* spicy pork sausage

**longevidad** |lon·xe·βi·'dad| *f* longevity

**longevo, -a** |lon·'xe·βo, -a| *adj* (*que dura*) long-lived; (*viejo*) very old

**longitud** |lon·xi·'tud| *f* length; **salto de ~** DEP long jump; **cuatro metros de ~** four meters long; **cincuenta grados ~ este/oeste** fifty degrees longitude east/west

**longitudinal** |lon·xi·tu·di·'nal| *adj* **corte ~** longitudinal section

**lonja** |'lon·xa| *f* COM public exchange

**loquera** |lo·'ke·ra| *f* AmL madness

**loro** |'lo·ro| *m* ZOOL parrot; **repetir como un ~** to repeat parrot fashion; **hablar como un ~** to talk non-stop

**los** |los| **I.** *art def v.* **el, la, lo II.** *pron pers m y neutro pl* **1.** (*objeto directo*) them; **¡llama~!** call them! **2.** (*con relativo*) **~ que...** the ones that...; **~ cuales** which

**losa** |'lo·sa| *f* **1.** (*piedra*) slab; (*lápida*) gravestone **2.** (*baldosa*) tile

**lote** |'lo·te| *m* **1.** (*parte*) share; COM lot **2.** (*toqueteo*) **darse** [*o* **pegarse**] **el ~** to get off with

**lotería** |lo·te·'ri·a| *f* lottery; **~ primitiva** weekly lottery; **administración de ~** office selling lottery tickets; **me tocó la ~** I won the lottery; **un décimo de ~** a tenth share of a lottery number; **¡con ese hijo te tocó la ~!** you really struck gold with that son of yours!; **jugar a la ~** to play the lottery

**loza** |'lo·sa, 'lo·θa| *f* earthenware; (*vajilla*) crockery; **~ fina** china

**lubina** |lu·'βi·na| *f* sea bass

**lubricante** |lu·βri·'kan·te| *m* lubricant

**lubricar** <c → qu> |lu·βri·'kar| *vt* to lubricate

**lucero** |lu·'se·ro, -'θe·ro| *m* (*estrella*) bright star

**lucha** |'lu·tʃa| *f* fight; DEP wrestling; **~ cuerpo a cuerpo** hand-to-hand fighting [*o* combat]; **~ contra la droga** the fight against drugs

**luchador(a)** |lu·tʃa·'dor, -·'do·ra| *m(f)* fighter; DEP wrestler

**luchar** |lu·'tʃar| *vi* **~ por algo** to fight for sth, to struggle for sth

**luche** |'lu·tʃe| *m Chile* **1.** (*juego*) hopscotch **2.** BOT, CULIN sea lettuce

**lucidez** |lu·si·'des, lu·θi·'deθ| *f* **1.** (*estado*) lucidity **2.** (*clarividencia*) clarity; (*sagacidad*) clear-headedness

**lúcido, -a** |'lu·si·do, -a; 'lu·θi-| *adj* **1.** (*clarividente*) clear-sighted; (*sagaz*) astute **2.** (*sobrio*) clear-headed

**luciérnaga** |lu·'sjer·na·ɣa, lu·'θjer-| *f* firefly

**lucio** |'lu·sjo, -θjo| *m* pike

**lucir** |lu·'sir, -'θir| *irr* **III. I.** *vi* **1.** (*brillar*) to shine **2.** (*verse*) to look good; **el vestido no le luce** the dress doesn't look good on her; **es un trabajo pesado y que no luce** it's hard work, though it doesn't look it **II.** *vt* (*exhibir*) to display; **lucía un bronceado impecable** he/she was showing off his/her perfect tan **III.** *vr:* **~se 1.** (*exhibirse*) to display **2.** (*destacarse*) to stand out; **¡ahora sí que nos hemos lucido!** *irón* now we've really made a mess of it!

**lucrativo, -a** |lu·kra·'ti·βo, -a| *adj* lucrative; **sin fines ~s** non-profit making

**lucro** |'lu·kro| *m* profit; **organización sin ánimo de ~** non-profit organization

**lúdico, -a** |'lu·di·ko, -a| *adj* relating to games

**luego** |'lwe·ɣo| **I.** *adv* **1.** (*después*)

later; **¡hasta ~!** see you later! **2.** (*entonces*) then **3.** (*por supuesto*) **desde ~** of course **II. conj 1.** (*así que*) and so **2.** (*después de*) **~ que** as soon as

**lugar** [luˈɣar] *m* place; **en primer/segundo ~** first/second; **tener ~** to take place; **en algún ~ de la casa** somewhere in the house; **la observación está fuera de ~** that comment is out of place; **en ~ de** instead of; **yo en ~ de usted...** if I were you...; **no des ~ a que te reprendan** don't give them any cause for reproach

**lúgubre** [ˈlu·ɣu·βre] *adj* gloomy

**lujo** [ˈlu·xo] *m* luxury; **permitirse el ~ de...** to treat oneself to the luxury of...; **con gran ~ de detalles** with a wealth of detail

**lujoso, -a** [luˈxo·so, -a] *adj* luxurious

**lujuria** [luˈxu·rja] *f* lechery, lust

**lujurioso, -a** [lu·xuˈrjo·so, -a] *adj* lecherous

**lumbago** [lumˈba·ɣo] *m* MED lumbago

**lumbar** [lumˈbar] *adj* lumbar

**lumbre** [ˈlum·bre] *f* (*llamas*) fire; (*brasa*) glow

**luminoso, -a** [lu·miˈno·so, -a] *adj* (*brillante*) bright, luminous; (*día*) light; **anuncio ~** illuminated [*o* neon] sign

**luna** [ˈlu·na] *f* **1.** ASTR moon; (*luz*) moonlight; **~ creciente/menguante** waxing/waning moon; **~ llena/nueva** full/new moon; **~ de miel** honeymoon; **media ~** half moon; **a la luz de la ~** in the moonlight; **estar en la ~** to be daydreaming **2.** (*cristal*) plate glass; **~s del coche** car windows

**lunar** [luˈnar] **I.** *adj* lunar **II.** *m* (*en la piel*) mole; (*en una tela*) polka-dot

**lunático, -a** [lu·naˈti·ko, -a] *adj* lunatic

**lunes** [ˈlu·nes] *m inv* Monday; **el ~** on Monday; **el ~ pasado** last Monday; **el ~ viene** next Monday; **el ~ por la noche/al mediodía/por la mañana/por la tarde** Monday night/at noon/morning/afternoon; (*todos*) **los ~** every Monday; **los ~**, on Mondays; **en la noche del ~ al martes** in the small hours of Tuesday; **el ~ entero** all day Monday; **cada dos ~** every other Monday; **hoy es ~, once de marzo** today is Monday,

March 11th

**lupa** [ˈlu·pa] *f* magnifying glass; **mirar con ~** *fig* to examine meticulously

**lustrabotas** [lus·traˈβo·tas] *mf inv AmL* shoeshine

**lustrar** [lusˈtrar] *vt* to polish; (*zapatos*) to shine

**lustro** [ˈlus·tro] *m* lustrum; **en el último ~** *elev* in the last five years

**lustroso, -a** [lusˈtro·so, -a] *adj* shiny; **estar ~** *fig* to be radiant

**luto** [ˈlu·to] *m* mourning; **ir de ~** to wear mourning; **estar de ~ por alguien** to be in mourning for sb

**luxación** [luk·saˈsjon, -ˈθjon] *f* MED dislocation

**Luxemburgo** [luk·semˈbur·ɣo] *m* Luxembourg

**luxemburgués, -esa** [luk·sem·burˈɣes, -ˈɣe·sa] *adj* Luxembourgish, Luxembourgian

**luz** [lus, luθ] *f* **1.** (*resplandor*) light; **~ corta** dipped headlights; **~ larga** full beam; **~ natural** natural light; **~ trasera** tail light; **traje de luces** bullfighter's suit; **a la ~ del día** in daylight; **a media ~** in subdued light; **dar a ~** to give birth; **¡~ de mis ojos!** the apple of my eye!; **sacar a la ~** *fig* to bring to light; **salir a la ~** *fig* to come to light; **a la ~ de los nuevos datos...** in the light of the new data... **2.** (*energía*) electricity; **¡da la ~!** turn on the light!; **se fue la ~** the power went off; **apagar/encender la ~** to turn off/on the light **3.** *pl* (*inteligencia*) intelligence; **el Siglo de las Luces** the Age of Enlightenment; **ser de pocas luces** to be dim-witted; **tener pocas luces** to be stupid; **a todas luces** evidently

# M

**M, m** [ˈeme] *f* M, m; **~ de María** M as in Mike

**Mª** [ma·ˈri·a] *abr de* **María** *abbreviation for the name Mary*

**macabro, -a** [ma·ˈka·βro, -a] *adj* macabre

**macagua** [ma·'ka·ɣwa] *f* 1. *AmS* (*ave*) laughing falcon 2. *Ven* (*serpiente*) large poisonous snake 3. *Cuba* BOT macaw-tree

**macanudo, -a** [ma·ka·'nu·do, -a] *adj AmL inf* fantastic, super

**macarra** [ma·'ka·rra] *m inf* 1. (*chorizo*) roughneck 2. (*chulo*) pimp

**macarrón** [ma·ka·'rron] *m* (*pasta*) macaroni

**macedonia** [ma·se·'ðo·nja, ma·θe·] *f* ~ (**de frutas**) fruit salad

**maceta** [ma·'se·ta, -'θe·ta] *f* 1. (*tiesto*) flowerpot 2. *Chile* (*ramo*) bunch of flowers

**macetero** [ma·se·'te·ro, ma·θe·] *m* flowerpot stand; *AmL* flowerpot

**machacar** <c → qu> [ma·tʃa·'kar] I. *vt* 1. (*triturar*) to pound 2. (*insistir*) to insist on, to harp on 3. *inf* (*destruir*) to crush II. *vr*: ~**se** *inf* to wear oneself out; **machacársela** *vulg* to jerk off

**machete** [ma·'tʃe·te] *m* 1. machete 2. *Arg, Urug, Col* (*chuleta*) crib (sheet)

**machetear** [ma·tʃe·te·'ar] I. *vi, vt Arg, Col inf* (*copiar*) to copy II. *vr*: ~**se** *Méx* (*trabajar*) to work; *inf* (*empollar*) to cram

**machetero, -a** [ma·tʃe·'te·ro, -a] *m, f* 1. *Arg inf* (*copión*) copycat 2. *Méx* (*empollón*) plodder

**machismo** [ma·'tʃis·mo] *m* male chauvinism

**machista** [ma·'tʃis·ta] *adj* (male) chauvinistic

**macho** ['ma·tʃo] *m* 1. ZOOL (*masculino*) male 2. *inf* (*machote*) tough guy

**machote** [ma·'tʃo·te] *m inf* (*hombre*) (tough) guy

**macizo** [ma·'si·so, -'θi·θo] *m* GEO massif

**macizo, -a** [ma·'si·so, -a; -'θi·θo, -a] *adj* 1. (*puerta*) solid; **de plata maciza** of solid silver 2. (*persona*) robust

**macuto** [ma·'ku·to] *m* 1. (*mochila*) backpack; MIL knapsack 2. *Ven* (*de los mendigos*) begging basket

**madeja** [ma·'de·xa] *f* skein

**madera** [ma·'de·ra] *f* (*de los árboles*) wood; ~ **prensada** particle board, chipboard; (*cortada*) timber, lumber; **de ~**

wooden; **¡toca ~!** knock on wood!; **tener ~ de** to have the makings of

**madrastra** [ma·'dras·tra] *f* stepmother

**madre** ['ma·dre] *f* mother; ~ **de alquiler** surrogate mother; ~ **de leche** wet nurse; ~ **política** mother-in-law; **futura** ~ mother-to-be; **¡~ (mía)!** goodness me!; **¡la ~ que te parió!** *inf* you bastard!; **¡viva la ~ que te parió!** *inf* well done!; **¡tu ~!** *inf* up yours! *vulg*; **de puta ~** *vulg* fucking great! *vulg*; **sacar a alguien de** ~ *inf* to drive sb mad [*o* nuts]; **los alquileres se están saliendo de** ~ *inf* rents are becoming ridiculously high

**Madrid** [ma·'drid] *m* Madrid

**madriguera** [ma·dri·'ɣe·ra] *f* 1. (*guarida*) den; (*de conejo*) burrow; (*de ratón*) hole; (*de zorro*) earth 2. (*escondrijo*) lair

**madrileño, -a** [ma·dri·'le·ɲo, -a] *adj* of/from Madrid

**madrina** [ma·'dri·na] *f* (*de bautismo*) godmother; ~ (**de boda**) maid of honor

**madrugada** [ma·dru·'ɣa·da] *f* dawn; **en la** [*o* **de**] ~ in the early morning; **salimos de viaje de** ~ we set off in the early hours; **a las cinco de la** ~ at five in the morning

**madrugador(a)** [ma·dru·ɣa·'dor, -·'do·ra] *adj* **ser muy** ~ to be an early riser [*o* early bird]

**madrugar** <g → gu> [ma·dru·'ɣar] *vi* to get up early ▶ **a quien madruga, Dios le ayuda** *prov* the early bird catches the worm *prov*; **no por mucho** ~ **amanece más temprano** *prov* ≈ everything will happen at its appointed time

**madrugón** [ma·dru·'ɣon] *m* **darse un** ~ to get up very early

**madurar** [ma·du·'rar] I. *vt* 1. (*hacer maduro: fruta*) to ripen; (*persona*) to mature 2. (*reflexionar sobre*) to think over II. *vi* (*volverse maduro: fruta*) to ripen; (*persona*) to mature

**madurez** [ma·du·'res, -'reθ] *f* (*de fruta*) ripeness; (*de persona*) maturity; (*de un plan*) readiness; **estar en la** ~ to be middle-aged

**maduro, -a** [ma·'du·ro, -a] *adj* (*fruta*) ripe; (*persona: prudente*) mature; (*plan*) ready; **una manzana demasiado ma-**

**dura** an overripe apple; **estar a las duras y a las maduras** to take the bad with the good

**maestría** [maes·'tri·a] *f* (*habilidad*) mastery; **con ~** skillfully

**maestro, -a** [ma·'es·tro, -a] **I.** *adj* **obra maestra** masterpiece **II.** *m, f* **1.** (*profesor*) teacher; **la vida es la mejor maestra** life is the best school **2.** (*persona de gran conocimiento*) master **3.** (*capataz*) overseer; **~ de cocina** master chef; **~ de obras** foreman

**mafioso, -a** [ma·'fjo·so, -a] *m, f* Mafioso

**magdalena** [may·da·'le·na] *f* (*pastel*) sweet muffin

**magia** [ma·xja] *f* magic; **como por arte de ~** as if by magic

**mágico, -a** ['ma·xi·ko, -a] *adj* **1.** (*misterioso*) magic; **varita mágica** magic wand **2.** (*maravilloso*) marvelous

**magisterio** [ma·xis·'te·rjo] *m* **dedicarse al ~** to be a teacher; **estudiar ~** to study to become a teacher

**magistrado, -a** [ma·xis·'tra·do, -a] *m, f* JUR (*juez*) magistrate; (*miembro del Tribunal Supremo*) Supreme Court judge

**magistral** [ma·xis·'tral] *adj* (*con maestría*) masterly

**magma** ['may·ma] *m* magma

**magnate** [may·'na·te] *m* tycoon; **~ de la prensa** press baron

**magnesio** [may·'ne·sjo] *m* magnesium

**magnético, -a** [may·'ne·ti·ko, -a] *adj* magnetic

**magnetismo** [may·ne·'tis·mo] *m* magnetism

**magnetizar** <z → c> [may·ne·ti·'sar, -'θar] *vt* to magnetize; (*retener la atención*) to captivate

**magnífico, -a** [may·'ni·fi·ko, -a] *adj* (*excelente*) magnificent

**magnitud** [may·ni·'tud] *f* magnitude

**magnolia** [may·'no·lja] *f* magnolia

**mago, -a** ['ma·yo, -a] *m, f* magician; **los Reyes Magos** the Magi, the Three Wise Men

**magrear** [ma·yre·'ar] *vt vulg* to feel up

**magro** ['ma·yro] *m* (*como el lomo*) tenderloin; *inf* (*carne magra*) lean meat

**magro, -a** ['ma·yro, -a] *adj* lean

**maguey** [ma·'yei] *m AmL* BOT maguey

**magulladura** [ma·yu·ja·'du·ra, ma·yu·ʎa-] *f* bruising

**magullar** [ma·yu·'jar, -ʎar] *vt* to bruise

**mahometano, -a** [ma·o·me·'ta·no, -a] *adj, m, f* Muslim

**mahonesa** [ma·o·ne·sa] *f* mayonnaise

**maíz** [ma·'is, -'iθ] *m* corn

**majadería** [ma·xa·de·'ri·a] *f* (*tontería*) idiocy

**majadero, -a** [ma·xa·'de·ro] *adj* (*porfiado*) pestering; (*imprudente*) foolish; (*loco*) crazy

**majagua** [ma·'xa·ywa] *f Cuba* **1.** (*árbol*) type of linden tree **2.** (*chaqueta*) suit jacket

**majara** [ma·'xa·ra], **majareta** [ma·xa·'re·ta] *adj inf* crazy, nuts

**majarete** [ma·xa·'re·te] *m* **1.** *Cuba* (*galanteador*) Don Juan **2.** *PRico* (*confusión*) commotion **3.** *Ant, Ven* (*postre*) blancmange (*made with corn, milk and sugar*)

**majestad** [ma·xes·'tad] *f* Majesty; **Su Majestad** Your Majesty

**majestuoso, -a** [ma·xes·tu·'o·so, -a] *adj* majestic

**majo, -a** ['ma·xo, -a] *adj* **1.** (*bonito*) lovely; (*guapo*) attractive **2.** (*agradable*) pleasant

**mal** [mal] **I.** *adj v.* **malo II.** *m* **1.** (*daño*) harm; (*injusticia*) wrong; (*sufrimiento*) suffering; **hacer ~ a alguien** to do sb harm **2.** (*lo malo*) bad thing; **el ~ menor** the lesser evil; **menos ~** thank goodness **3.** (*enfermedad*) illness; **~ de montaña** mountain sickness; **~ de vientre** stomach complaint **4.** (*desgracia*) misfortune ▶ **el ~ de ojo** the evil eye; **no hay ~ que por bien no venga** *prov* every cloud has a silver lining **III.** *adv* **1.** (*de mala manera, insuficientemente*) badly; **dejar ~ a alguien** to show sb in a bad light; **estar ~ de dinero** to be badly off; **esto acabará ~** this will end badly; **ir de ~ en peor** to go from bad to worse; **sentar ~** to upset; **ella me cae ~** I don't like her **2.** (*equivocadamente*) wrongly **3.** (+ *a mal*) **tomarse algo a ~** to take sth badly; **estoy a ~ con mi vecino** I'm on bad terms with my neighbor **4.** (*mal que bien*) **~ que bien, el nego-**

M

**cio sigue funcionando** better or worse, the business is still working; **aprobar los exámenes más ~ que bien** to scrape through the exams

**malabarismo** [ma·la·βa·'ris·mo] *m* juggling

**malabarista** [ma·la·βa·'ris·ta] *mf* juggler

**malaconsejar** [mal·a·kon·se·'xar] *vt* to badly advise

**malacostumbrado, -a** [mal·a·kos·tum·'bra·do, -a] *adj* **estar ~** (*mimado*) to be spoiled; (*vicioso*) to have bad habits

**malacostumbrar** [mal·a·kos·tum·'brar] **I.** *vt* **1.** (*mimar*) to spoil **2.** (*educar mal*) to bring up badly **II.** *vr:* **~se** to get into a bad habit

**malapata** [ma·la·'pa·ta] *mf* clumsy oaf; **tener ~** (*poca destreza*) to be maladroit; (*malas intenciones*) to have wicked intentions; (*mala suerte*) to be unlucky; **la cosa tiene ~** *fig* it is ill-starred [*o* fated]

**malaria** [ma·'la·rja] *f* malaria

**malcriado, -a** [mal·kri·'a·do, -a] *adj* (*mal educado*) spoiled

**malcriar** <*1. pres* malcrío> [mal·kri·'ar] *vt* to bring up badly; (*mimar*) to spoil

**maldad** [mal·'dad] *f* evil, wickedness

**maldecir** [mal·de·'sir, -'θir] *irr* **I.** *vt* to curse, to damn **II.** *vi* **1.** (*jurar*) to swear **2.** (*quejarse*) **~ de algo/alguien** to complain about sth/sb

**maldición** [mal·di·'sjon, -'θjon] *f* **1.** (*imprecación*) curse; **me ha caído una ~** a curse has been put on me **2.** (*juramento*) swear word; **soltar una ~ contra alguien** to swear at sb

**maldito, -a** [mal·'di·to] **I.** *pp de* **maldecir II.** *adj* **1.** (*endemoniado*) damned; **¡maldita sea!** *inf* damn (it)!; **¡~ seas!** *vulg* damn you!; **¡maldita la gracia (que me hace)!** I don't find it funny at all! **2.** (*maligno*) wicked; **¡vete, ~!** get out of here!

**maldoso, -a** [mal·'do·so, -a] *adj Méx* wicked

**maleable** [ma·le·'a·βle] *adj* **1.** (*forjable*) malleable; (*flexible*) pliable **2.** (*dócil*) pliant

**maleante** [ma·le·'an·te] *adj* (*delincuen-*

*te*) delinquent; (*persona maligna*) miscreant

**malecón** [ma·le·'kon] *m* dyke; (*rompeolas*) breakwater

**maleducado, -a** [mal·e·du·'ka·do, -a] *adj* ill-mannered; (*niño*) ill-bred; (*mimado*) spoiled; (*descortés*) rude

**maleducar** [mal·e·du·'kar] *vt* to spoil

**maleficio** [ma·le·'fi·sjo, -θjo] *m* (*hechizo*) curse; (*daño*) harm

**maléfico, -a** [ma·'le·fi·ko, -a] *adj* evil

**malentendido** [mal·en·ten·'di·do] *m* misunderstanding

**malestar** [ma·les·'tar] *m* malaise; (*espiritual*) uneasiness

**maleta** [ma·'le·ta] *f* suitcase; **hacer la ~** to pack one's suitcase

**maletera** [ma·le·'te·ra] *f Col, Méx*, **maletero** [ma·le·'te·ro] *m* AUTO trunk

**maletero, -a** [ma·le·'te·ro, -a] *m, f Chile* (*ladrón*) thief

**maletín** [ma·le·'tin] *m* **1.** briefcase; **~ (de viaje)** overnight bag **2.** (*de aseo*) toilet bag

**malévolo, -a** [ma·'le·βo·lo, -a] *adj* malevolent

**maleza** [ma·'le·sa, -θa] *f* weeds *pl;* (*matorral*) thicket

**malgastar** [mal·γas·'tar] *vt* to waste; **~ todo el dinero en tabaco** to squander all the money on cigarettes; **~ una oportunidad** to waste an opportunity

**malhechor(a)** [mal·e·'tʃor(a)] *m(f)* delinquent, wrongdoer

**malherir** [mal·e·'rir] *irr como sentir vt* to seriously injure

**malhumorado, -a** [mal·u·mo·'ra·do, -a] *adj* bad-tempered

**malicia** [ma·'li·sja, -θja] *f* **1.** (*intención malévola*) malice **2.** (*maldad*) wickedness **3.** (*picardía*) mischievousness; **tener mucha ~** to be full of mischief

**malicioso, -a** [ma·li·'sjo·so, -a; -θjo·so, -a] *adj* malicious; (*maligno*) malign

**maligno, -a** [ma·'liɣ·no] *adj* (*pernicioso*) malign; MED malignant

**malinchista** [ma·lin·'tʃis·ta] *mf Méx* person who favors foreign things

**malintencionado, -a** [mal·in·ten·sjo·'na·do, -a, -θjo·'na·do, -a] *adj* unkind

**malinterpretar** [mal·in·ter·pre·'tar] *vt* to

misinterpret

**malla** ['ma·ja, -ʎa] f 1. (de un tejido) mesh, weave; **de ~ ancha/estrecha/fina** open/close/fine weave 2. pl (pantalones) leggings pl 3. AmL (de baño) swimsuit

**Mallorca** [ma·jor·'ka, ma·ʎor-] f Majorca

**mallorquín, -ina** [ma·jor·'kin, ma·ʎor-] adj of/from Majorca

**malo, -a** ['ma·lo, -a] I. adj <peor, pésimo> (precediendo un sustantivo masc. sing: **mal**) 1. (en general) bad; **fumar es ~ para la salud** smoking is bad for your health; **de mala gana** unwillingly; **me gusta la casa, lo ~ es que es demasiado cara** I like the house, the problem is that it is too expensive; **tener mala mano para algo** to have no talent for sth; **tener mala suerte** to be unlucky; **hace un tiempo malísimo** the weather is really bad; **hacer un trabajo de mala manera** to do a job badly 2. ser (falso) false 3. ser (malévolo) nasty; **tener mal genio** to have a bad temper; **una mala persona** a nasty person; **venir de malas** to have a hostile attitude 4. estar (enfermo) ill 5. ser (travieso) naughty 6. estar (estropeado) spoiled; (leche) sour ► **más vale ~ conocido que bueno por conocer** prov better the devil you know II. adv **podemos llegar a un acuerdo por las buenas o por las malas** we can reach an agreement by fair means or foul; **andar a malas** to be on bad terms III. m, f (persona) bad man m, bad woman f; CINE baddie; **los ~s de la peli** the bad guys

**malograr** [ma·lo·'ɣrar] I. vt 1. (desaprovechar) to waste; (frustrar) to frustrate; **has malogrado la ocasión** you have wasted the occasion 2. (estropear) to ruin II. vr: ~**se** 1. (fallar) to fail; **se han malogrado mis esperanzas** my hopes have come to nothing 2. (estropearse) to be ruined

**maloliente** [mal·o·'ljen·te] adj foul-smelling

**malparar** [mal·pa·'rar] vt (persona) to come off badly; **salió malparado de la pelea** he came off worse in the fight

**malpensado, -a** [mal·pen·'sa·do, -a] adj evil-minded; **no seas tan ~** don't be so cynical

**malsano, -a** [mal·'sa·no, -a] adj unhealthy; (moralmente) unwholesome

**malsonante** [mal·so·'nan·te] adj (sonido) jarring; (palabra) nasty

**malta** ['mal·ta] f 1. t. AGR malt 2. Arg (cerveza) beer

**maltratar** [mal·tra·'tar] vt to maltreat; ~ (de palabra) to abuse (verbally)

**maltrato** [mal·'tra·to] m maltreatment, abuse; (insulto) (verbal) abuse

**maltrecho, -a** [mal·'tre·tʃo, -a] adj (golpeado) battered

**malva** ['mal·βa] I. adj mauve II. f mallow; **estar criando ~s** inf to be pushing up daisies; **ser (como) una ~** inf to be meek and mild

**malvado, -a** [mal·'βa·do, -a] adj wicked

**malvender** [mal·βen·'der] vt to sell at a loss

**malversar** [mal·βer·'sar] vt to misappropriate, to embezzle

**Malvinas** [mal·'βi·nas] fpl Falkland Islands pl

**malvón** [mal·'βon] m Arg, Méx, Par, Urug BOT geranium

**mama** ['ma·ma] f (pecho) breast; (ubre) udder

**mamá** [ma·'ma] f inf mom(my)

**mamada** [ma·'ma·da] f 1. (acción) breastfeeding 2. (cantidad mamada) breastfeed 3. AmL (ganga) bargain; **¡vaya ~!** what a bargain! 4. vulg (felación) blow job; **hacer una ~ a alguien** to give sb a blow job

**mamadera** [ma·ma·'de·ra] f AmL baby bottle

**mamar** [ma·'mar] I. vi, vt 1. (en el pecho) to breastfeed 2. vulg **mamársela a alguien** to give sb a blow job II. vr: ~**se** 1. vulg (emborracharse) to get sloshed

**mamarracho** [ma·ma·'rra·tʃo] m inf ridiculous person

**mamífero** [ma·'mi·fe·ro] m mammal

**mamografía** [ma·mo·gra·'fi·a] f MED mammogram, mammography

**mamón, -ona** [ma·'mon] m, f 1. vulg (insulto) jerk 2. AmL inf (borracho) drunk

M

**mampara** [mam·'pa·ra] f screen (door), (room) divider

**mamporro** [mam·'po·rro] m inf clout; **darse un ~ contra algo** to bash oneself against sth

**mamut** <mamuts> [ma·'mut] m mammoth

**manada** [ma·'na·da] f (rebaño de vacas, ciervos) herd; (de peces) shoal; (de lobos) pack; **~ de gente** crowd of people; **pasamos la frontera en ~** we crossed over the border en masse

**manantial** [ma·nan·'tjal] m spring; **~ caliente** hot spring

**manar** [ma·'nar] **I.** vt to flow with; **la herida no paraba de ~ sangre** the wound wouldn't stop flowing with blood **II.** vi **1.** (surgir) to well; **el agua manaba sucia de la fuente** dirty water welled from the fountain **2.** (fluir fácilmente) to flow; **las palabras manaban de su boca** the words flowed from his/her mouth

**manazas** [ma·'nasas, -θas] mf inv inf clumsy person, klutz; **ser un ~** to be clumsy

**mancha** ['man·tʃa] f **1.** (en la ropa, piel) dirty mark; (de tinta) stain; (salpicadura) spot **2.** (toque de color) fleck; **este perro es blanco con ~s negras** this dog is white with black patches

**Mancha** ['man·tʃa] f **el canal de la ~** the (English) Channel

**manchado, -a** [man·'tʃa·do, -a] adj (ropa, mantel) stained; (cara, fruta) dirty

**manchar** [man·'tʃar] **I.** vt to dirty **II.** vr: **~se** (ensuciarse) to get dirty

**mancillar** [man·si·'jar, -θi·'ʎar] vt to sully

**manco, -a** ['man·ko] adj (de un brazo) one-armed; (de una mano) one-handed; **no ser (cojo ni) ~** (ser hábil) to be dexterous; (ser largo de manos) to be light-fingered

**mancomunidad** [man·ko·mu·ni·'dad] f (comunidad) community

**mandamás** [man·da·'mas] mf pey inf big shot

**mandamiento** [man·da·'mjen·to] m **1.** (orden) order; **~ judicial** court order **2.** (precepto) precept **3.** REL commandment

**mandar** [man·'dar] vt **1.** (ordenar) to order; **~ a alguien que** +subj to order sb to; **lo que Ud. mande** whatever you say **2.** (dirigir) to lead; (gobernar) to govern **3.** (encargar) **~ buscar/hacer/venir** to ask to get/do/come **4.** (enviar) to send; **~ al cuerno** inf to send to hell

**mandarina** [man·da·'ri·na] f mandarin, tangerine

**mandatario, -a** [man·da·'ta·rjo, -a] m, f agent; **primer ~** POL head of state

**mandato** [man·'da·to] m **1.** (orden) order; **~ judicial** injunction **2.** POL mandate; **~ parlamentario** parliamentary mandate

**mandíbula** [man·'di·βu·la] f ANAT jaw

**mandil** [man·'dil] m AmL (de caballería) cloth (used to rub down a horse)

**mandinga** [man·'din·ga] m **1.** AmL inf (diablo) devil **2.** Arg inf (muchacho) scamp

**mando** ['man·do] m **1.** (poder) control; MIL command; (del presidente) term of office; **don de ~** leadership qualities; **estar al ~ de** to be in command of; **estar bajo el ~ de alguien** to be under sb's command **2.** (quien lo tiene) **alto ~** MIL high command **3.** TÉC control; **~ a distancia** remote control

**mandón, -ona** [man·'don, -·'do·na] adj bossy

**manecilla** [ma·ne·'si·ja, -'θi·ʎa] f (del reloj) hand; TÉC pointer

**manejable** [ma·ne·'xa·βle] adj user-friendly; (persona) tractable

**manejar** [ma·ne·'xar] **I.** vt **1.** (usar) to use; (máquina) to operate; fig to handle; **~ un cuchillo** to use a knife; **manejas bien las cifras** you are good with numbers; **'¡manéjese con cuidado!'** 'handle with care!' **2.** (dirigir) to handle **3.** (a alguien) to manage; **maneja al marido a su antojo** she can twist her husband around her little finger **4.** AmL (un coche) to drive **II.** vr: **~se** to manage; **saber ~se en la vida** to know how to get on in life

**manejo** [ma·'ne·xo] m **1.** (uso) use; (de una máquina) operation; fig handling **2.** COMPUT management; **~ de la memoria** memory management **3.** AmL (*de un coche*) driving

**manera** [ma·'ne·ra] *f* **1.** (*forma, modo*) manner, way; **~ de decir** way of saying; **~ de pensar** way of thinking; **~ de proceder** way of acting; **es su ~ de ser** that's the way he/she is; **a la ~ de sus abuelos** in the way their grandparents did; **a mi ~** my way; **de la ~ que sea** somehow or other; **de cualquier ~ de todas ~s** anyway; **de esta ~** that way; **de ~ que** (*finalidad*) so that; **¿de ~ que sacaste mala nota?** so you got a bad mark, did you?; **de ninguna ~** no way; **se echó a gritar de tal ~ que...** *inf* he/she started to shout in such a way that...; **de una ~ o de otra** one way or another; **en cierta ~** in a way; **en gran ~** largely; **no hay ~ de...** there is no way that...; **¡qué ~ de llover!** just look at the rain!; **sobre ~** a lot; **primero se lo dije de buena ~** first I said it to him nicely; **contestar de mala ~** to answer rudely; **hacer las cosas de mala ~** to do things badly **2.** *pl* (*modales*) manners *pl*; **¡estas no son ~s!** this is no way to behave!

**manga** ['man·ga] *f* **1.** (*del vestido*) sleeve; **de ~ corta/larga** short-/long-sleeved; **estar en ~s de camisa** to be in shirt-sleeves; **andar ~ por hombro** *inf* to be a mess; **poner algo ~ por hombro** *inf* to turn sth inside out; **sacarse algo de la ~** *fig* to come up with sth; **hacer un corte de ~s a alguien** ≈ to give sb the finger; **tener (la) [o ser de] ~ ancha** *fig* to be lenient; **tienen algo en la manga** they are keeping sth up their sleeve **2.** METEO **~ de viento** tornado; **~ de agua** waterspout **3.** *Arg pey* (*grupo de personas*) mob

**manganeta** [man·ga·'ne·ta] *f Hond* trick

**mangante** [man·'gan·te] *mf inf* (*ladrón*) thief

**manganzón, -ona** [man·gan·'son, -·'so·na; -'θon, -·'θo·na] *m, f AmL* loafer

**mangar** <g → gu> [man·'gar] *vt inf* to swipe; (*en tiendas*) to shoplift

**mangle** ['man·gle] *m AmL* BOT mangrove tree

**mango** ['man·go] *m* **1.** (*puño*) knob; (*alargado*) handle; **tener la sartén por**

**el ~** *fig* to hold the reins **2.** (*árbol*) mango tree; (*fruta*) mango

**mangonear** [man·go·ne·'ar] *inf* **I.** *vi* **1.** (*entrometerse*) to meddle **2.** (*vaguear*) to loaf **II.** *vt* to wangle; **está mangoneando todo** he/she has a finger in every pie

**mangoneo** [man·go·'ne·o] *m inf* **1.** (*entrometimiento*) meddling **2.** (*vagancia*) idleness

**manguera** [man·'ge·ra] *f* (*tubo*) hose

**maní** [ma·'ni] *m* peanut

**manía** [ma·'ni·a] *f* **1.** (*locura*) mania **2.** (*extravagancia*) eccentricity, quirk **3.** (*obsesión*) obsession **4.** *inf* (*aversión*) aversion; **tener ~ a alguien** not to be able to stand sb; **coger ~ a alguien** to take a dislike to sb

**maniaco, -a** [ma·'nja·ko, -a], **maníaco, -a** [ma·'ni·a·ko, -a] *m, f* maniac

**maniatar** [ma·nja·'tar] *vt* **~ a alguien** to tie sb's hands up

**maniático, -a** [ma·'nja·ti·ko, -a] *m, f* **1.** (*extravagante*) fusspot **2.** (*loco*) maniac; **un ~ de la limpieza** a cleaning maniac

**manicomio** [ma·ni·'ko·mjo] *m* psychiatric hospital; *fig* (*casa de locos*) madhouse

**manicura** [ma·ni·'ku·ra] *f* manicure

**manifestación** [ma·ni·fes·ta·'sjon, -'θjon] *f* **1.** (*expresión*) expression; **como ~ de cariño** as an expression of love **2.** (*reunión*) demonstration

**manifestante** [ma·ni·fes·'tan·te] *mf* demonstrator

**manifestar** <e → ie> [ma·ni·fes·'tar] **I.** *vt* **1.** (*declarar*) to declare **2.** (*mostrar*) to show **II.** *vr:* **~se 1.** (*declararse*) to declare oneself; **~se a favor/en contra de algo** to declare oneself for/against sth **2.** (*revelarse*) to show oneself **3.** (*política*) to demonstrate

**manifiesto** [ma·ni·'fjes·to] *m* manifesto

**manifiesto, -a** [ma·ni·'fjes·to, -a] *adj* (*evidente*) manifest; **poner de ~** (*revelar*) to show [*o* make clear]; (*expresar*) to declare

**manigua** [ma·'ni·ɣwa] *f Cuba* jungle

**manija** [ma·'ni·xa] *f* handle

**manilla** [ma·'ni·ja, -ʎa] *f* (*del reloj*) hand

**M**

**manillar** [ma·ni·'ʎar, -ʎar] *m* handlebars *pl*

**maniobra** [ma·ni·'o·βra] *f* 1. (*operación manual*) handling 2. (*ardid*) ploy 3. MIL maneuver; **estar de ~s** to be on maneuvers 4. (*vehículo*) maneuver

**maniobrar** [ma·njo·'βrar] I. *vi* MIL to carry out maneuvers II. *vt* 1. (*manejar*) to handle 2. (*manipular*) to manipulate

**manipulación** [ma·ni·pu·la·'sjon, -'θjon] *f* 1. (*empleo*) use, handling 2. (*alteración*) manipulation

**manipular** [ma·ni·pu·'lar] *vt* 1. (*máquina*) to operate 2. (*alterar*) to manipulate 3. (*interferir*) ~ **algo** to interfere with sth 4. (*manosear*) ~ **algo** to fiddle with sth

**maniquí** <maniquíes> [ma·ni·'ki] *m* (*para ropa*) mannequin

**manirroto, -a** [ma·ni·'rro·to, -a] *adj* spendthrift

**manitas** [ma·'ni·tas] **hacer ~** *inf* to neck; **ser un ~** *inf* to be dexterous, to be good with one's hands

**manito** [ma·'ni·to] *m* *Méx* pal

**manivela** [ma·ni·'βe·la] *f* handle

**manjar** [man·'xar] *m* food; (*exquisitez*) delicacy

**mano** ['ma·no] *f* 1. ANAT hand; **a ~ alzada** (*votación*) by a show of hands; **a ~ armada** armed; **a ~s llenas** in abundance; **alzar la ~ contra alguien** to raise one's hand to sb; **apretón de ~s** handshake; **coger a alguien con las ~s en la masa** to catch sb red-handed; **cogidos de las ~s** hand in hand; **comer de la ~ de alguien** *fig* to eat out of sb's hand; **me lo prometió con la ~ en el corazón** he/she promised me with his/her hand on his/her heart; **echar una ~ a alguien** to give sb a hand; **dejar algo en ~s de alguien** to leave sth in sb's hands; **echar ~ de alguien** to make use of sb; **estar al alcance de la ~** to be within (arm's) reach; **estar ~ sobre ~** *fig* to be idle; **hecho a ~** hand-made; **su vida se le había ido de las ~s** his/her life has gotten out of hand; **se le ha ido la ~** (*desmesura*) he/she has overdone it; (*violencia*) he/she has lost control; **lavarse las ~s** (**en algo**) to wash one's hands of sth; **llevar a alguien de la ~** to lead sb by the hand; *fig* to guide sb; **~**

**a ~** *fig* hand in hand; **¡~s a la obra!** to work!; **meter ~ a alguien** *inf* to touch sb up; **pedir la ~ de alguien** to ask for sb's hand in marriage; **poner la ~ en el fuego por alguien** to stick one's neck out for someone; **echar ~ de algo** to draw on sth; **traer algo entre ~s** to be up to sth; **¡venga esa ~!** let's shake on it! 2. ZOOL (*de un mono*) hand; (*de un perro*) paw; **~ de cerdo** pig's trotter 3. (*lado*) **~ derecha/izquierda** right-/left-hand side; **a** [*o* **de**] **la ~ derecha** on the right(-hand side) 4. (*capa*) coat; **una ~ de pintura** a coat of paint 5. (*trabajador*) hand; **~ de obra** labor 6. (*habilidad*) skill; **tener buena ~ para coser** to be good at sewing; **tener ~ izquierda** to be tactful; **tener ~ con** to have a way with; **~ de santo** sure remedy 7. (*de naipes*) hand; **ser ~** to lead

**manojo** [ma·'no·xo] *m* bunch; **~ de llaves** bunch of keys; **ser un ~ de nervios** to be a bundle of nerves

**manopla** [ma·'no·pla] *f* mitten; (*para lavarse*) washcloth

**manoseado, -a** [ma·no·se·'a·do, -a] *adj* (*sobado*) worn; (*trillado*) hackneyed

**manosear** [ma·no·se·'ar] *vt* to handle; *pey* to paw

**manotazo** [ma·no·'ta·so, -θo] *m* smack

**mansarda** [man·'sar·da] *f* *AmC, AmS* attic

**mansión** [man·'sjon] *f* (*casa suntuosa*) mansion

**manso, -a** ['man·so] *adj* docile; (*animales*) tame; (*aguas*) quiet

**manta¹** ['man·ta] *f* blanket; **a ~** in abundance; **liarse la ~ a la cabeza** (*actuar con decisión*) to take it on oneself to do sth; (*de modo irreflexivo*) to recklessly decide to do sth; **tirar de la ~** to let the cat out of the bag

**manta²** ['man·ta] *mf* (*persona torpe*) oaf

**manteca** [man·'te·ka] *f* 1. (*grasa*) fat; **~ de cerdo** lard 2. *RíoPl* (*mantequilla*) butter

**mantel** [man·'tel] *m* tablecloth

**mantener** [man·te·'ner] *irr como* tener I. *vt* 1. (*conservar, relaciones*) to maintain; (*orden*) to keep; **mantiene la línea** he/she keeps his/her figure; **~ la calma**

to keep calm **2.** (*perseverar*) ~ **algo** to keep sth up **3.** (*sustentar*) to maintain **4.** (*sostener*) to support **5.** (*proseguir*) to continue; ~ **una conversación con alguien** to hold a conversation with sb **II.** *vr:* ~**se 1.** (*sostenerse*) to support oneself **2.** (*continuar*) to continue **3.** (*perseverar*) to keep; **se mantiene en sus trece** *inf* he/she is sticking to his/her guns

**mantenimiento** [man·te·ni·'mjen·to] *m* **1.** (*alimentos*) sustenance **2.** TÉC maintenance; ~ **de datos** COMPUT database update; **sin** ~ maintenance-free **3.** (*de una propiedad*) upkeep

**mantequilla** [man·te·'ki·ja, -ʎa] *f* butter

**mantilla** [man·'ti·ja, -ʎa] *f* **1.** (*de mujer*) mantilla **2.** (*de niño*) swaddling clothes *pl*

**manto** ['man·to] *m* **1.** (*prenda*) cloak **2.** (*capa*) layer; ~ **terrestre** earth's crust

**mantón** [man·'ton] *m* shawl

**manual** [ma·nu·'al] **I.** *adj* manual, hand; **trabajos** ~**es** handicrafts *pl* **II.** *m* manual, handbook; ~ **de instrucciones** instruction manual

**manufacturar** [ma·nu·fak·tu·'rar] *vt* to manufacture

**manuscrito** [ma·nus·'kri·to] *m* manuscript

**manuscrito, -a** [ma·nus·'kri·to, -a] *adj* handwritten

**manutención** [ma·nu·ten·'sjon, -'θjon] *f* **1.** (*alimentos*) keep **2.** TÉC maintenance

**manzana** [man·'sa·na, -'θa·na] *f* **1.** (*fruta*) apple; **sano como una** ~ as fit as a fiddle **2.** (*conjunto de casas*) block; **dar la vuelta a la** ~ to go around the block **3.** *AmL* ANAT (*nuez*) Adam's apple

**manzanilla** [man·sa·'ni·ja, man·θa·'ni·ʎa] *f* **1.** (*planta*) chamomile; (*flor*) chamomile flower; (*infusión*) chamomile tea **2.** (*vino*) manzanilla

**manzano** [man·'sa·no, -'θa·no] *m* apple tree

**maña** ['ma·ɲa] *f* **1.** (*habilidad*) skill, dexterity; **tener** ~ **para algo** to have a knack for sth **2.** (*astucia*) craftiness **3.** *pl* (*caprichos*) whims *pl*; **tiene** ~**s** he/she has his/her little whims ▶ **más**

**vale** ~ **que** <u>fuerza</u> *prov* better brains than brawn

**mañana¹** [ma'·ɲa·na] **I.** *f* (*temprano*) early morning; (*hasta el mediodía*) morning; **a las 5 de la** ~ at 5 a.m.; **de la noche a la** ~ overnight; **por la** ~ in the morning; **todas las** ~**s** every morning; ~ **por la** ~ tomorrow morning **II.** *adv* **1.** (*día*) tomorrow; **¡hasta** ~! see you tomorrow!; ~ **será otro día** tomorrow is another day; **pasado** ~ the day after tomorrow **2.** (*futuro*) tomorrow ▶ **no dejes para** ~ **lo que puedas hacer** <u>hoy</u> *prov* do not leave for tomorrow what you can do today

**mañana²** [ma'·ɲa·na] *m* tomorrow; **el día de** ~ in the future

**mañanero, -a** [ma·ɲa·'ne·ro, -a] *adj* **1.** (*madrugador*) early-rising **2.** (*de la mañana*) morning

**mañero, -a** [ma·'ɲe·ro, -a] *adj* *Arg inf* fussy

**mañoso, -a** [ma·'ɲo·so, -a] *adj* (*hábil*) dexterous, handy

**mapa** ['ma·pa] *m* map; ~ **del tiempo** weather map; **borrar del** ~ (*matar*) to wipe off the face of the earth; **desaparecer del** ~ to vanish into thin air; **no estar en el** ~ *fig* to be out of this world

**mapache** [ma·'pa·tʃe] *m* raccoon

**maqueta** [ma·'ke·ta] *f* **1.** ARQUIT (*scale*) model **2.** (*formato*) format

**maquetación** [ma·ke·ta·'sjon, -'θjon] *f* layout

**maquillaje** [ma·ki·'ja·xe, -ʎa·xe] *m* **1.** (*acción*) application of make-up **2.** (*producto*) make-up

**maquillar** [ma·ki·jar, -ʎar] **I.** *vt* **1.** to apply make-up to **2.** (*disimular*) to disguise **II.** *vr:* ~**se** to put on make-up

**máquina** ['ma·ki·na] *f* **1.** (*artefacto*) machine; ~ **de afeitar** electric shaver [*o* razor]; ~ **de coser/lavar** sewing/washing machine; ~ **de escribir** (*automática*) (electric) typewriter; **a toda** ~ (at) full speed; **escrito a** ~ typed; **hecho a** ~ machine-made **2.** ~ **de tabaco** cigarette dispenser; ~ **tragaperras** *inf* slot-machine

**maquinar** [ma·ki·'nar] *vt* (*urdir*) to scheme

**maquinaria** [ma·ki·'na·rja] *f* (*máquinas*) machinery

**maquinilla** [ma·ki·'ni·ja, -ʎa] *f* (safety) razor

**maquinista** [ma·ki·'nis·ta] *mf* (*conductor*) machinist

**mar** [mar] *m o f* 1. GEO sea; **Mar Antártico** Antarctic Ocean; **Mar Báltico** Baltic Sea; **Mar de Irlanda** Irish Sea; **Mar Mediterráneo** Mediterranean Sea; **Mar del Norte** North Sea; **en alta ~** offshore; **~ adentro** high seas; **~ gruesa/picada/rizada** heavy/rough/choppy sea; *fig* unrest; **por ~** by sea; **hacerse a la ~** to put out to sea; **al otro lado del ~** overseas 2. *inf* **la ~ de...** loads of...; **llueve a ~es** it is raining cats and dogs; **lloró a ~es** he/she cried his/her eyes out; **sudar a ~es** to pour with sweat; **ser la ~ de aburrido** to be excruciatingly boring

**maraña** [ma·'ra·ɲa] *f* (*lío*) mess; **~ de cabello** tangle of hair; **~ de hilo** tangle of threads

**maratón** [ma·ra·'ton] *m o f* marathon

**maravilla** [ma·ra·'βi·ja, -ʎa] *f* (*portento*) marvel; **a las mil ~s de ~** marvelously; **hablar ~s de alguien** to speak extremely well of sb; **hacer ~s** *fig* to work wonders

**maravillar** [ma·ra·βi·'jar, -ʎar] I. *vt* to amaze II. *vr* **~se de algo** to marvel at sth

**maravilloso, -a** [ma·ra·βi·'jo·so, -a; -ʎo·so, -a] *adj* marvelous

**marca** ['mar·ka] *f* 1. (*distintivo*) mark; **~ de agua** watermark; **~ de ganado** brand 2. (*de productos*) brand; **~ registrada** registered trademark; **ropa de ~** designer label 3. (*huella*) impression 4. DEP record

**marcación** *f* **~ por voz** TEL voice dialing

**marcado, -a** [mar·'ka·do] *adj* (*señalado*) marked; (*evidente*) clear

**marcador** [mar·ka·'dor] *m* 1. (*tablero*) scoreboard; **abrir el ~** to open the scoring 2. *Arg* (*rotulador*) marker pen

**marcaje** [mar·'ka·xe] *m* DEP marking, cover(age)

**marcapaso(s)** [mar·ka·'pa·so(s)] *m* (*inv*) pacemaker

**marcar** <c → qu> [mar·'kar] I. *vt* 1. (*señalar*) to mark; (*ganado*) to brand; (*mercancías*) to label; **~ una época** to denote an era; **~ el compás** to beat time 2. (*resaltar*) to emphasize 3. (*teléfono*) to dial 4. DEP **~ un gol** to score a goal; **~ un punto** to score a point 5. DEP (*a un jugador*) to mark, to cover II. *vr*: **~se** to show

**marcha** ['mar·tʃa] *f* 1. (*movimiento*) progress; **poner en ~** to start 2. (*caminata*) hike 3. (*curso*) course; **la ~ de los acontecimientos** the course of events; **sobre la ~** along the way 4. (*velocidad*) gear; **~ atrás** reverse; **a toda ~** at full speed 5. MIL, MÚS march; **~ silenciosa** silent march 6. (*salida*) departure; **¡en ~!** let's go! 7. *inf* (*acción*) action; **¡aquí hay mucha ~!** this is where the action is!; **ir de ~** to go out on the town; **tener ~** to be full of go

**marchar** [mar·'tʃar] I. *vi* 1. (*ir*) to go; **¡marchando!** let's go! 2. (*funcionar*) to work; **~ sobre ruedas** *fig* to go like clockwork II. *vr*: **~se** (*irse*) to leave

**marchitar** [mar·tʃi·'tar] I. *vi* (*plantas*) to wither; (*personas*) to be on the wane II. *vr*: **~se** to wither

**marchito, -a** [mar·'tʃi·to, -a] *adj* withered

**marchoso, -a** [mar·'tʃo·so, -a] *adj inf* fun-loving

**marcial** [mar·'sjal, -'θjal] *adj* martial; **artes ~es** martial arts; **ley ~** martial law

**marciano, -a** [mar·'sja·no, -a; 'θja·no, -a] *adj, m, f* Martian

**marco** ['mar·ko] *m* 1. (*recuadro*) frame; (*armazón*) framework; **el ~ legal** the legal framework 2. (*ambiente*) background

**marea** [ma·'rea] *f* (*mar*) tide; **~ alta** high tide; **~ baja** low tide; **~ creciente** rising tide; **~ menguante** ebb tide; **~ negra** oil slick [*o* spill]; **una ~ humana** a flood of people

**mareado, -a** [ma·re·'a·do, -a] *adj* 1. (*indispuesto*) sick; (*en el mar*) seasick; (*al viajar*) travel-sick; **estoy ~** I feel sick 2. (*aturdido*) dizzy; *fig* confused

**marear** [ma·re·'ar] I. *vt* 1. *inf* (*molestar*)

to pester **2.** MED to nauseate **3.** (*aturdir*) to make dizzy; *fig* to confuse **II.** *vr:* **~se 1.** (*enfermarse*) to feel sick; (*en el mar*) to get seasick; (*al viajar*) to get travel-sick **2.** (*quedar aturdido*) to become dizzy; *fig* to become confused **3.** (*emborracharse*) to get tipsy

**marejada** [ma·re·'xa·da] *f* swell

**maremoto** [ma·re·'mo·to] *m* tidal wave; (*seísmo*) seaquake

**mareo** [ma·'reo] *m* **1.** (*malestar*) nausea; (*en el mar*) seasickness; (*al viajar*) travel-sickness, motion sickness **2.** (*vértigo*) dizziness

**marfil** [mar·'fil] *m* ivory

**margarina** [mar·ɣa·'ri·na] *f* margarine

**margarita** [mar·ɣa·'ri·ta] *f* **1.** BOT daisy; **deshojar la ~** to play 'he/she loves me, he/she loves me not' **2.** (*bebida*) margarita

**margen** ['mar·xen] *m o f* **1.** (*borde*) edge; **el ~ del río** the riverside [*o* riverbank]; **al ~** apart; **dejar al ~** to leave out; **mantenerse al ~ de algo** *fig* to keep out of sth **2.** (*página*) margin **3.** (*libertad*) leeway; **dar ~** to give leeway **4.** (*ganancia*) profit margin; **~ de seguridad** safety margin

**marginado, -a** [mar·xi·'na·do, -a] *adj* **1.** (*excluido*) excluded, marginalized **2.** (*aislado*) isolated

**marginal** [mar·xi·'nal] *adj* **1.** (*al margen*) apart **2.** (*secundario*) secondary

**marginar** [mar·xi·'nar] *vt* (*ignorar algo*) to disregard; (*a alguien*) to marginalize

**maría** [ma·'ri·a] *f inf* (*marihuana*) grass, pot

**mariachi** [ma·'rja·tʃi] *m Méx* mariachi musician

**marica** [ma·'ri·ka] *m vulg* **1.** (*homosexual*) fag(got) **2.** (*cobarde*) sissy **3.** (*insulto grosero*) asshole

**maricón** [ma·ri·'kon] *m vulg v.* **marica**

**mariconada** [ma·ri·ko·'na·da] *f vulg* (*tontería*) dumb thing to do

**marido** [ma·'ri·do] *m* husband

**mariguana** [ma·ri·'ɣwa·na], **marihuana** [ma·ri·'wa·na] *f* marijuana, marihuana

**marimba** [ma·'rim·ba] *f* **1.** MÚS (*de maderas*) marimba; (*tambor*) African drum **2.** *Arg* (*paliza*) beating

**marina** [ma·'ri·na] *f* navy; **la ~ mercante** the merchant marine

**marinero** [ma·ri·'ne·ro] *m* sailor; **~ de agua dulce** *irón* landlubber

**marinero, -a** [ma·ri·'ne·ro, -a] *adj* **1.** (*relativo al mar*) marine; **pueblo ~** coastal town **2.** (*relativo a la marina*) marine; **nudo ~** sailor's knot

**marino** [ma·'ri·no] *m* sailor, seaman

**marino, -a** [ma·'ri·no, -a] *adj* marine

**marioneta** [ma·rjo·'ne·ta] *f* (*títere*) puppet, marionette

**mariposa** [ma·ri·'po·sa] *f* ZOOL butterfly ▶ **¡a otra <u>cosa</u> ~!** let's change the subject!

**mariquita¹** [ma·ri·'ki·ta] *f* (*insecto*) ladybug

**mariquita²** [ma·ri·'ki·ta] *m inf* fag(got)

**marisco** [ma·'ris·ko] *m* seafood

**marisma** [ma·'ris·ma] *f* marsh

**marisquería** [ma·ris·ke·'ri·a] *f* (*tienda*) seafood shop; (*restaurante*) seafood restaurant

**marital** [ma·ri·'tal] *adj* marital; **vida ~** married life

**marítimo, -a** [ma·'ri·ti·mo, -a] *adj* maritime, marine; **ciudad marítima** seaside town

**marmita** [mar·'mi·ta] *f* pot

**mármol** ['mar·mol] *m* marble; **de ~** of marble

**marmota** [mar·'mo·ta] *f* marmot

**marqués, -esa** [mar·'kes, ·-'ke·sa] *m, f* marquis *m*, marquise *f*

**marquesina** [mar·ke·'si·na] *f* (*glass*) canopy, marquee

**marranada** [ma·rra·'na·da] *f inf* filthiness

**marrano** [ma·'rra·no] *m* (*cerdo*) pig; *pey inf* (*hombre sucio*) dirty man; (*grosero*) rude man

**marrano, -a** [ma·'rra·no, -a] *adj* filthy

**marrón** [ma·'rron] *adj* brown

**marroquí** [ma·rro·'ki] *adj, mf* Moroccan

**Marruecos** [ma·'rrwe·kos] *m* Morocco

**marrullero, -a** [ma·rru·'je·ro, a-; -ʎe·ro, -a] *adj* flattering; (*con labia*) glib

**marsopa** [mar·'so·pa] *f* porpoise

**marsupial** [mar·su·'pjal] *m* marsupial

**marta** ['mar·ta] *f* ZOOL marten

**Marte** ['mar·te] *m* Mars

M

**martes** ['mar·tes] *m inv* Tuesday; ~ **y tre·ce** ≈ Friday the thirteenth; *v. t.* **lunes**

**martill(e)ar** [mar·ti·ʎar, -ʎar; mar·ti·je·'ar, -ʎe·'ar] *vt* to hammer

**martillo** [mar·'ti·jo, -ʎo] *m* hammer; **pez** ~ hammerhead; **repetir algo a macha** ~ to repeat sth ad nauseam

**mártir** ['mar·tir] *mf* martyr

**martirio** [mar·'ti·rjo] *m* REL martyrdom; *fig* torture

**martirizar** <z → c> [mar·ti·ri·'sar, -'θar] *vt* to torture

**maruja** [ma·'ru·xa] *f pey inf* housewife *(whose sole interests are her home, family, personal appearance and gossip)*

**marzo** ['mar·so, -θo] *m* March; **en** ~ in March; **a principios/a mediados/a fin(al)es de** ~ at the beginning/in the middle/at the end of March; **el 21 de** ~ 21st of March; **el mes de** ~ **tie·ne 31 días** the month of March has 31 days; **el pasado** ~ **fue muy frío** last March was very cold

**mas** [mas] *conj* LIT but, yet

**más** [mas] **I.** *adv* **1.** *(cantidad)* more; ~ **dinero/zapatos** more money/shoes **2.** *(comparativo)* more; ~ **inteligen·te/complicado** more intelligent/complicated; ~ **grande/pequeño** bigger/smaller; ~ **temprano/tarde** earlier/later; **correr** ~ to run more; **esto me gusta** ~ I like this better; ~ **acá** closer; ~ **adelante** (*local*) further forward [*o* on]; (*temporal*) later; **es** ~ **guapo que tú** he is more handsome than you; **cada día** [*o* **vez**] ~ more and more; **cuanto** ~ **mejor** the more the merrier; ~ **allá de esto** beyond this; ~ **de la cuenta** too much **3.** *(superlativo)* **el/la** ~ the most; **el** ~ **listo de la clase** the smartest in the class; **lo que** ~ **me gusta** what I most like [*o* like most]; **lo que** ~ **quieras** what you most want; **lo** ~ **probable es que llueva** it is likely to rain; **lo** ~ **pronto posible** as early as possible; ~ **que nunca** more than ever; **a** ~ **no poder** to the utmost; **a** ~ **tardar** at the latest; **todo lo** ~ at most **4.** *(con numerales, cantidad)* ~ **de treinta** more than thirty; **son** ~ **de las diez** it is after

ten **5.** *(tan)* **¡está** ~ **guapa!** she looks so beautiful; **¡qué tarde** ~ **apacible!** what a peaceful afternoon! **6.** *(con pronombre interrogativo, indefinido)* **¿algo** ~? anything else?; **no, nada** ~ no, nothing else **7.** *(en frases negativas)* **no puedo** ~ I have had it; **nunca** ~ never again **8.** MAT plus; **tengo tres libros,** ~ **los que he prestado** I have three books, plus those I have lent **9.** *(de más)* **de** ~ spare, more than enough; **hay comida de** ~ there is food to spare; **estar de** ~ not to be needed; **de lo** ~ very **10.** *(más bien)* ~ **bien** rather; **no es muy del·gado; es** ~ **bien gordo** he is not very thin; rather he is fat **11.** *(más o menos)* ~ **o menos** *(aproximadamente)* more or less; **le va** ~ **o menos** he/she is doing so-so; **ni** ~ **ni menos** exactly **12.** *(por más que)* **por** ~ **que lo intento, no consigo dormirme** however hard I try, I cannot sleep ▶ **el** — **allá** the beyond; **el que** ~ **y el que menos** every single one; **quien** ~ **y quien menos** everyone; **es** ~ ~ **aún** what is more; **el no va** ~ (**de la moda**) the latest fashion; **como el que** ~ as well as the next man; **sin** ~ **ni** ~ without more ado; **¿qué** ~ **da?** what difference does it make? **II.** *m* MAT plus sign

**masa** ['ma·sa] *f* **1.** *(pasta)* mixture; *(para hornear)* dough; **coger a alguien con las manos en la** ~ to catch sb red-handed **2.** *(volumen, muchedumbre)* mass; **medios de comunicación de** ~**s** mass media; **en** ~ en masse

**masacrar** [ma·sa·'krar] *vt* to massacre

**masacre** [ma·'sa·kre] *f* massacre

**masaje** [ma·'sa·xe] *m* massage; **dar** ~**s** to massage

**masajista** [ma·sa·'xis·ta] *mf* masseur *m*, masseuse *f*

**mascada** [mas·'ka·da] *f* **1.** *AmL (tabaco)* quid of chewing tobacco **2.** *Col, Cuba, Chile (bocado)* bite **3.** *Méx (pañuelo)* silk kerchief

**mascar** <c → qu> [mas·'kar] *vt (masticar)* to chew

**máscara** ['mas·ka·ra] *f* mask; **quitar la** ~ **a alguien** *fig* to unmask sb; **quitarse la** ~ *fig* to reveal oneself

**mascarilla** [mas·ka·'ri·ja, -ʎa] *f* 1. (*máscara*) mask 2. (*protección*) face mask 3. (*cosmética*) ~ **exfoliante** face scrub; ~ **facial** face pack

**mascota** [mas·'ko·ta] *f* mascot; (*animal de compañía*) pet

**masculinidad** [mas·ku·li·ni·'dad] *f* masculinity

**masculino** [mas·ku·'li·no] *m* LING masculine

**masculino, -a** [mas·ku·'li·no, -a] *adj* (*de hombre*) masculine; **moda masculina** men's fashion

**mascullar** [mas·ku·'jar, -ʎar] *vt* to mumble

**masificación** [ma·si·fi·ka·'sjon, -'θjon] *f* overcrowding

**masita** [ma·'si·ta] *f* AmS CULIN small cake

**masivo, -a** [ma·'si·βo, -a] *adj* (*grande*) massive; (*fuerte*) strong; (*de masas*) mass

**masón, -ona** [ma·'son, -·'so·na] *m, f* Mason, Freemason

**masoquista** [ma·so·'kis·ta] *adj* masochistic

**máster** <másters> ['mas·ter] *m* master's degree

**masticar** <c → qu> [mas·ti·'kar] *vt* to chew; (*meditar*) to ponder

**mástil** ['mas·til] *m* mast, spar; (*poste*) post, pole

**mastín** [mas·'tin] *m* mastiff

**masturbación** [mas·tur·βa·'sjon, -'θjon] *f* masturbation

**masturbarse** [mas·tur·'βar·se] *vr* to masturbate

**mata** ['ma·ta] *f* clump; (*arbusto*) bush

**matadero** [ma·ta·'de·ro] *m* slaughterhouse; **ir al** ~ *fig* to put one's life in danger; **llevar al** ~ *fig* to send sb to his/her death

**matador(a)** [ma·ta·'dor, -·'do·ra] *m(f)* TAUR matador

**matamoscas** [ma·ta·'mos·kas] *m inv* (*insecticida*) fly-spray; (*objeto*) fly-swatter

**matanza** [ma·'tan·sa, -θa] *f* 1. (*el matar*) killing; (*en batallas*) slaughter; **hacer una** ~ to massacre 2. (*carneada*) slaughter; **hacer la** ~ to slaughter an animal

**matar** [ma·'tar] I. *vt* 1. (*quitar la vida*) to kill; ~ **a golpes** to beat to death; ~ **a palos** to club to death; ~ **a puñaladas** to knife [*o* stab] to death; ~ **a tiros** to shoot dead; ~ **a disgustos** to be the death of 2. (*carnear*) to slaughter 3. (*saciar*) to assuage; (*hambre*) to satisfy; (*sed*) to quench 4. (*el tiempo*) to kill II. *vr:* ~**se** 1. (*suicidarse*) to kill oneself 2. (*trabajar sin descanso*) ~**se a trabajar** to work oneself to death; ~**se por algo** to go out of one's way to do sth 3. (*por accidente*) to get killed

**matarife** [ma·ta·'ri·fe] *mf* butcher

**matarratas** [ma·ta·'rra·tas] *m inv* 1. (*raticida*) rat poison 2. *pey inf* (*alcohol de mala calidad*) rotgut, hooch

**matasanos** [ma·ta·'sa·nos] *mf inv, irón inf* quack

**matasellos** [ma·ta·'se·jos, -ʎos] *m inv* postmark

**match** [matʃ] *m* match

**mate** ['ma·te] I. *adj* dull II. *m* 1. (*ajedrez*) mate; **jaque** ~ checkmate 2. (*acabado*) matte 3. *pl inf* (*matemáticas*) math 4. *AmS* (*bebida*) maté

**matemáticas** [ma·te·'ma·ti·kas] *fpl* mathematics

**matemático, -a** [ma·te·'ma·ti·ko, -a] I. *adj* mathematical II. *m, f* mathematician

**materia** [ma·'te·rja] *f* 1. *t.* Fís matter; ~ **gris** ANAT grey matter; ~ **prima** raw material 2. (*tema*) subject, matter; **en** ~ **de** in the matter of 3. *t.* ENS (*disciplina*) subject

**material** [ma·te·'rjal] I. *adj* (*real*) tangible; **daño** ~ physical damage; **el autor** ~ **del hecho** the actual perpetrator of the deed II. *m* material; ~**es de construcción** building materials; ~ **de oficina** office equipment

**materialista** [ma·te·rja·'lis·ta] *adj* materialistic

**materializar** <z → c> [ma·te·rja·li·'sar, -'θar] I. *vt* to bring into being; (*realizar*) to carry out; (*hacer aparecer*) to produce II. *vr:* ~**se** to materialize

**materialmente** [ma·te·rjal·'men·te] *adv* materially; **ser** ~ **posible** to be physically possible

M

**maternal** [ma·ter·'nal] *adj* maternal, motherly

**maternidad** [ma·ter·ni·'dad] *f* maternity; (*hospital*) maternity hospital; (*sala*) maternity ward

**materno, -a** [ma·'ter·no, -a] *adj* maternal; **abuelo ~** maternal grandfather; **lengua materna** mother tongue

**matinal** [ma·ti·'nal] *adj* morning; **sesión ~** (*congreso*) morning session; CINE, TEAT matinee

**matiz** [ma·'tis, -'tiθ] *m* 1. (*gradación*) shade; (*toque*) touch 2. (*sentido*) nuance

**matizar** <z → c> [ma·ti·'sar, -'θar] *vt* 1. (*combinar colores o tonos*) to blend; **~ de rojo** to tinge with red 2. (*graduar*) to tint 3. (*de un sentido*) to tinge

**matón** [ma·'ton] *m* thug

**matorral** [ma·to·'rral] *m* thicket

**matrícula** [ma·'tri·ku·la] *f* 1. (*documento*) registration document 2. (*inscripción*) enrollment; UNIV matriculation 3. AUTO (*placa*) license plate; **número de la ~** license number

**matricular** [ma·tri·ku·'lar] I. *vt* to register; UNIV to enroll II. *vr* **~se en la universidad** to enroll in the university

**matrimonial** [ma·tri·mo·'njal] *adj* matrimonial, marriage; **agencia ~** dating agency

**matrimonio** [ma·tri·'mo·njo] *m* 1. (*institución*) marriage; **contraer ~** to marry 2. (*marido y mujer*) married couple; **cama de ~** double bed

**matriz** [ma·'tris, -'triθ] *f* 1. (*útero*) womb 2. (*molde*) cast 3. TIPO, MAT matrix

**matrona** [ma·'tro·na] *f* (*comadrona*) midwife

**maturrango, -a** [ma·tu·'rran·go, -a] *adj* 1. *AmS* (*mal jinete*) **ser ~** to be a poor rider 2. *Chile* (*tosco*) clumsy

**matutino, -a** [ma·tu·'ti·no, -a] *adj* morning; **sesión matutina** morning session

**maullar** [mau·'jar, -ʎar] *irr como aullar* *vi* to meow

**maullido** [mau·'ji·do, -ʎido] *m* meow

**mausoleo** [mau·so·'leo] *m* mausoleum

**maxilar** [mak·si·'lar] I. *adj* maxillary II. *m* jaw

**máxima** ['mak·si·ma] *f* maxim

**máxime** ['mak·si·me] *adv* particularly

**máximo, -a** ['mak·si·mo, -a] I. *adj* maximum; **rendimiento ~** maximum output; **pon la radio al ~** turn the radio as high as it goes II. *m, f* maximum; **como ~** at most; (*temporal*) at the latest

**mayo** ['ma·jo] *m* May; *v. t.* **marzo**

**mayonesa** [ma·jo·'ne·sa] *f* mayonnaise

**mayor** [ma·'jor] *adj* 1. (*tamaño*) bigger; **la ~ parte** the majority, most; **el ~ barco** the largest boat; **mal ~** greater evil; **~ que** bigger than; **comercio al por ~** wholesale trade 2. (*edad*) older; **~ que** older than; **mi hermano ~** my older [*o* big] brother; **el ~ de mis hermanos** the eldest of my brothers and sisters; **ser ~** to be grown-up; **ser ~ de edad** to be an adult, to be of legal age; **persona ~** elderly person; **los ~es** the adults, the grown-ups; **ya es ~ para esos juguetes** he/she is too old for [*o* has outgrown] those toys 3. MÚS major; **escala en do ~** scale of C major

**mayorcito, -a** [ma·jor·'si·to, -a; -θi·to, -a] *adj inf* **¡si ya eres ~!** what a big boy/girl you are now!

**mayordomo, -a** [ma·jor·'do·mo, -a] *m, f* (*de una mansión*) butler

**mayoría** [ma·jo·'ri·a] *f* majority; **~ de edad** (age of) majority; **llegar a la ~ de edad** to come of age; **~ relativa** relative majority

**mayorista** [ma·jo·'ris·ta] I. *adj* wholesale; **comercio ~** wholesale business II. *mf* wholesaler

**mayoritario, -a** [ma·jo·ri·'ta·rjo, -a] *adj* majority

**mayormente** [ma·jor·'men·te] *adv* especially, particularly

**mayúscula** [ma·'jus·ku·la] *f* capital (letter); **escribirse con ~** to be written with a capital (letter)

**mayúsculo, -a** [ma·'jus·ku·lo, -a] *adj* big; **letra mayúscula** capital letter

**maza** ['ma·sa, -θa] *f* (*porra*) club; (*para machacar*) pestle; (*percusor*) hammer

**mazacotudo, -a** [ma·sa·ko·'tu·do, -a; ma·θa-] *adj AmL* dense

**mazapán** [ma·sa·'pan, ma·θa-] *m* marzipan

**mazmorra** [mas·'mo·rra, maθ-] *f* dungeon

**mazo** ['ma·so, 'ma·θo] *m* **1.** (*martillo*) mallet **2.** (*del mortero*) pestle; (*grande*) sledgehammer

**mazorca** [ma·'sor·ka, -'θor·ka] *f* (*del maíz*) cob; ~ **de maíz** corncob, ear of corn

**me** [me] **I.** *pron pers* **1.** (*objeto directo*) me; **¡míra~!** look at me! **2.** (*objeto indirecto*) me; **da~ el libro** give me the book **II.** *pron reflexivo* ~ **lavo** I wash myself; ~ **voy** I am going; ~ **lavo el pelo** I wash my hair

**meada** [me·'a·da] *f* **1.** *inf* (*pis*) pee; **echar una** ~ to take a piss **2.** (*mancha de orina*) piss; **aquí hay una** ~ **de gato** a cat took a piss here

**meadero** [mea·'de·ro] *m vulg* urinal

**meandro** [me·'an·dro] *m* (*curva*) meander

**mear** [me·'ar] *vi, vr*: ~**se** *inf* to piss; ~**se de risa** to die laughing

**mecánico, -a** [me·'ka·ni·ko, -a] **I.** *adj* mechanical **II.** *m, f* mechanic

**mecanismo** [me·ka·'nis·mo] *m* mechanism; (*dispositivo*) device

**mecanizar** <z → c> [me·ka·ni·'sar, -'θar] *vt* to mechanize

**mecanografía** [me·ka·no·ɣra·'fi·a] *f* typewriting

**mecate** [me·'ka·te] *m AmC, Col, Méx, Ven* rope

**mecedora** [me·se·'do·ra, me·θe-] *f* rocking chair

**mecenas** [me·'se·nas, -'θe·nas] *mf inv* patron

**mecer** <c → z> [me·'ser, -'θer] **I.** *vt* (*balancear*) to rock; (*columpiar*) to swing **II.** *vr*: ~**se** (*balancearse*) to rock; (*columpiarse*) to swing

**mecha** ['me·tʃa] *f* **1.** (*pabilo*) wick; (*de explosivos*) fuse **2.** (*gasa*) swab **3.** (*mechón*) tuft **4.** *pl* (*mechones teñidos*) highlights *pl*, streaks *pl*; **hacerse** ~**s** to have highlights [*o* streaks] put in **5.** *inf* (*prisa*) **a toda** ~ very fast

**mechero** [me·'tʃe·ro] *m* (*encendedor*) lighter

**mechón** [me·'tʃon] *m* tuft

**medalla** [me·'da·ja, -ʎa] *f* medal; ~ (**militar**) military decoration

**medallista** [me·da·'jis·ta, -ʎis·ta] *mf* medal winner, medalist

**medallón** [me·'da·jon, -ʎon] *m* medallion

**media** ['me·dja] *f* **1.** (*promedio*) average **2.** (*calceta*) stocking; *AmL* (*calcetín*) sock

**mediación** [me·dja·'sjon, -'θjon] *f* mediation

**mediado, -a** [me·'dja·do, -a] *adj* **1.** (*medio lleno*) half-full (**de** of) **2.** (*trabajo*) half-completed; **para ~s de semana** by the middle of the week [*o* by midweek]

**mediador(a)** [me·dja·'dor, -·'do·ra] *m(f)* mediator

**mediano, -a** [me·'dja·no, -a] *adj* **1.** (*calidad*) average **2.** (*tamaño*) medium

**medianoche** [me·dja·'no·tʃe] *f* (*hora*) midnight; **a** ~ at midnight

**mediante** [me·'djan·te] *prep* by means of; (*a través de*) through

**mediar** [me·'djar] *vi* **1.** (*intermediar*) to mediate **2.** (*interceder*) ~ **por alguien** to intercede on behalf of sb

**medicación** [me·di·ka·'sjon, -'θjon] *f* medication

**medicamento** [me·di·ka·'men·to] *m* medicine

**medicar** <c → qu> [me·di·'kar] **I.** *vt* to medicate **II.** *vr*: ~**se** to take medicine

**medicina** [me·di·'si·na, -'θi·na] *f* medicine

**medicinal** [me·di·si·'nal, -θi·'nal] *adj* medicinal; **balón** ~ medicine ball; **hierba** ~ medicinal plant

**medición** [me·di·'sjon, -'θjon] *f* measurement

**médico, -a** ['me·di·ko, -a] **I.** *adj* medical; **cuerpo** ~ medical corps **II.** *m, f* doctor; ~ **de cabecera** general practitioner; ~ **forense** forensic surgeon

**medida** [me·'di·da] *f* **1.** (*medición*) measurement **2.** (*dimensión*) measurement; **a la** ~ (*ropa*) made-to-measure; **tomar la(s)** ~(**s**) to take the measurement(s); **hasta cierta** ~ up to a point; **en la** ~ **de lo posible** as far as possible; **a** ~ **que as 3.** (*moderación*) moderation; **con** ~ with care; **sin** ~ without moderation **4.** (*acción*) measure; **tomar ~s** to take measures

**M**

**medidor** [me·di·'dor] *m* **1.** (*instrumento*) gauge **2.** *AmL* (*contador*) meter

**medieval** [me·dje·'βal] *adj* medieval

**medio** ['me·djo] *m* **1.** (*mitad*) middle; **en ~ de** in the middle of; **meterse por ~** to intervene; **quitar de en ~** to get rid of **2.** (*instrumento*) means; **~ de transporte** means of transport; **por ~ de** by means of **3.** PREN, RADIO, TV medium; **los ~s de comunicación** the media **4.** (*entorno*) surroundings *pl*; **~ ambiente** environment **5.** *Cuba* (*moneda*) five cent coin **6.** *pl* (*fuentes*) sources *pl*; (*capital*) means *pl*

**medio, -a** ['me·djo, -a] **I.** *adj* **1.** (*mitad*) half; **a las cuatro y media** at half past four; **litro y ~** one and a half liters; **mi media naranja** *fig* my better half **2.** (*promedio*) **ciudadano ~** average person **II.** *adv* half; **~ vestido** half dressed; **~ dormido** half asleep; **ir a medias** to go halves

**medioambiental** [me·djo·am·bjen·'tal] *adj* environmental

**mediocre** [me·'djo·kre] *adj* mediocre

**mediodía** [me·djo·'di·a] *m* midday; **al ~** at noon

**medir** [me·'dir] *irr como* **pedir I.** *vt* **1.** (*calcular*) to measure; **¿cuánto mides?** how tall are you? **2.** (*sopesar*) to weigh; **~ los riesgos** to weigh up the risks **3.** (*moderar*) to moderate **II.** *vi* to measure **III.** *vr* **~se con alguien** to measure oneself against sb

**meditación** [me·di·ta·'sjon, -'θjon] *f* meditation

**meditar** [me·di·'tar] *vi, vt* to meditate

**mediterráneo, -a** [me·di·te·'rra·neo, -a] *adj* Mediterranean

**Mediterráneo** [me·di·te·'rra·neo] *m* Mediterranean

**medrar** [me·'drar] *vi* (*crecer*) to grow; (*avanzar*) to thrive

**médula** ['me·du·la] *f* **1.** ANAT marrow; **~ espinal** spinal cord **2.** (*meollo*) core; **hasta la ~** to the core

**medusa** [me·'du·sa] *f* jellyfish

**megáfono** [me·'γa·fo·no] *m* megaphone

**mejicano, -a** [me·xi·'ka·no, -a] *adj, m, f* Mexican

**Méjico** ['me·xi·ko] *m* Mexico

**mejilla** [me·'xi·ja, -ʎa] *f* cheek; **poner la otra ~** to turn the other cheek

**mejillón** [me·xi·'jon, -ʎon] *m* mussel

**mejor** [me·'xor] **I.** *adj* **1.** (*compar*) better; **~ que** better than; **es ~ que no vayas +subj** it is better that you don't go; **cambiar a ~** to change for the better; **pasar a ~ vida** to pass away **2.** (*superl*) **el/la/lo ~** the best; **el ~ alumno** the best student **II.** *adv* better; **a lo ~** maybe; **~ que ~** better still [*o* yet]; **en el ~ de los casos** at best

**mejora** [me·'xo·ra] *f* improvement

**mejorable** [me·xo·'ra·βle] *adj* improvable

**mejorar** [me·xo·'rar] **I.** *vt* **1.** (*perfeccionar*) to improve **2.** (*superar*) to surpass; (*subasta*) to outbid **II.** *vi, vr:* **~se** (*enfermo*) to get better; **¡que se mejore!** I hope you get better soon!

**mejoría** [me·xo·'ri·a] *f* improvement

**melancolía** [me·lan·ko·'li·a] *f* melancholy

**melancólico, -a** [me·lan·'ko·li·ko, -a] *adj* melancholic

**melanoma** [me·la·'no·ma] *m* MED melanoma

**melena** [me·'le·na] *f* **1.** (*crin*) mane **2.** (*pelo*) long hair (*shoulder-length or longer, worn loose*); **soltarse la ~** *t. fig* to let one's hair down

**mella** ['me·ja, -ʎa] *f* **hacer ~** to make an impression

**mellizo, -a** [me·'ji·so, -a; -ʎi·θo, -a] *m, f* twin

**melocotón** [me·lo·ko·'ton] *m* peach

**melocotonero** [me·lo·ko·to·'ne·ro] *m* peach tree

**melodía** [me·lo·'di·a] *f* melody

**melódico, -a** [me·'lo·di·ko, -a] *adj* melodic

**melón** [me·'lon] *m* melon; *inf* (*cabeza*) noggin

**melón, -ona** [me·'lon, -ona] *m, f inf* loony

**membrana** [mem·'bra·na] *f* membrane

**membrete** [mem·'bre·te] *m* letterhead

**membrillo** [mem·'bri·jo, -ʎo] *m* (*árbol*) quince tree; (*fruto*) quince; **carne** [*o* **dulce**] **de ~** quince jelly

**memela** [me·'me·la] *f Méx* CULIN thin

*corn tortilla*

**memo, -a** [ˈme·mo, -a] *adj* idiotic

**memorable** [me·mo·ˈra·βle] *adj* memorable

**memoria** [me·ˈmo·rja] *f* **1.** (*facultad, recuerdo*) memory; **a la** [*o* **en**] **~ de** in memory of; **de ~** by heart; **hacer ~** to try and remember; **traer a la ~** to bring to mind; **venir a la ~** to come to mind **2.** (*informe*) report **3.** COMPUT memory **4.** *pl* (*autobiografía*) autobiography

**memorizar** <z → c> [me·mo·ri·ˈsar, -ˈθar] *vt* to memorize

**menaje** [me·ˈna·xe] *m* household furnishings *pl*; **~ de cocina** kitchen utensils

**mención** [men·ˈsjon, -ˈθjon] *f* mention; **digno de ~** worth mentioning; **hacer ~ de** to mention

**mencionar** [men·sjo·ˈnar, -θjo·ˈnar] *vt* to mention

**menda** [ˈmen·da] **I.** *pron pers inf* yours truly; **aquí el** [*o* **este**] **~ no dijo nada** yours truly didn't say anything **II.** *pron indef inf* **un ~** a guy

**mendigar** <g → gu> [men·di·ˈɣar] *vi, vt* **~ algo** to beg for sth

**mendigo, -a** [men·ˈdi·ɣo, -a] *m, f* beggar

**mendrugo** [men·ˈdru·ɣo] *m* (*trozo de pan*) crust

**menear** [me·ne·ˈar] **I.** *vt* to move; (*cabeza*) to shake; **~ la cola** to wag one's tail **II.** *vr:* **~se** to move; *inf* (*apresurarse*) to get a move on

**meneo** [me·ˈneo] *m* (*brusco*) jolt

**menestra** [me·ˈnes·tra] *f* vegetable stew

**mengano, -a** [men·ˈga·no, -a] *m, f* **fulano y ~** so-and-so

**menguante** [men·ˈgwan·te] *f* **1.** (*marea*) ebb; (*estiaje*) low water level **2.** (*mengua*) decrease

**menguar** <gu → gü> [men·ˈgwar] **I.** *vi* to diminish **II.** *vt* to decrease; (*punto*) to reduce

**meningitis** [me·nin·ˈxi·tis] *f inv* MED meningitis

**menisco** [me·ˈnis·ko] *m* ANAT meniscus

**menopausia** [me·no·ˈpau·sja] *f* MED menopause, change of life

**menor** [me·ˈnor] **I.** *adj* **1.** (*tamaño*) smaller; **~ que** smaller than; (*número*) smaller; **al por ~** COM retail; **no dar**

**la ~ importancia a algo** not to give sth the least importance; **Asia Menor** Asia Minor **2.** (*edad*) younger; **~ que** younger than; **~ de edad** underage; **el ~ de mis hermanos** the youngest of my brothers **3.** MÚS minor **II.** *mf* (*persona*) minor; **no apto para ~es** not suitable for children

**menos** [ˈme·nos] **I.** *adv* **1.** (*contrario de más*) less; **a ~ que** unless; **el/la ~** the least; **el coche ~ caro** the least expensive car; **eso es lo de ~** that is the least important thing; **lo ~** the least; **al** [*o* **por lo**] **~** at least; **aún ~** even less; **cuanto ~... (tanto) más** the less... the more; **de ~** short; **echar de ~** to miss; **en ~ de nada** in no time; **ir a ~** to decrease; **~ de 20 personas** fewer than 20 people; **~ de una hora** less than an hour; **~ mal** thank goodness; **¡ni mucho ~!** not at all!; **son las ocho ~ diez** it's ten minutes to eight; **cada vez ~ tiempo/casos** less and less time/fewer and fewer cases **2.** MAT minus **3.** (*excepto*) except; **todo ~ eso** anything but that **II.** *m* MAT minus

**menospreciar** [me·nos·pre·ˈsjar, -ˈθjar] *vt* to underrate; (*subestimar*) to underestimate

**menosprecio** [me·nos·ˈpre·sjo, -θjo] *m* underrating; (*subestimación*) underestimate

**mensaje** [men·ˈsa·xe] *m* message; **~ de error** COMPUT error message; **~ (de) radio** radio communication; **~ de socorro** SOS message

**mensajero, -a** [men·sa·ˈxe·ro, -a] **I.** *adj* messenger; **paloma mensajera** messenger [*o* carrier] pigeon **II.** *m, f* messenger

**menso, -a** [ˈmen·so, -a] *adj Méx* (*necio*) stupid

**menstruación** [mens·trwa·ˈsjon, -ˈθjon] *f* menstruation

**menstruar** <1. *pres* menstrúo> [mens·tru·ˈar] *vi* to menstruate

**mensual** [men·su·ˈal] *adj* monthly

**mensualidad** [men·swa·li·ˈdad] *f* (*pago*) monthly payment; (*compra aplazada*) monthly installment; **~ del alquiler** month's rent

**M**

**menta** ['men·ta] *f* mint; (*infusión*) mint tea; (*extracto*) menthol; **caramelo de ~** mint

**mental** [men·'tal] *adj* mental; **cálculo ~** mental arithmetic

**mentalidad** [men·ta·li·'dad] *f* mentality

**mentalizar** <z → c> [men·ta·li·'sar, -'θar] **I.** *vt* (*preparar*) to prepare (mentally); (*concienciar*) to make aware; **~ a alguien de algo** to make sb aware of sth **II.** *vr:* **~se** (*prepararse*) to prepare oneself (mentally); (*concienciarse*) to make oneself aware

**mentar** <e → ie> [men·'tar] *vt* to mention

**mente** ['men·te] *f* **1.** (*pensamiento*) mind; **tener en (la) ~** to have in mind; **quitarse algo de la ~** to get sth out of one's head; **tengo la ~ en blanco** my mind is a complete blank; **traer a la ~** to bring to mind **2.** (*intelecto*) intellect

**mentecato, -a** [men·te·'ka·to, -a] *adj* silly

**mentir** [men·'tir] *irr como sentir vi* to lie; **miente más que habla** he/she is a compulsive liar; **¡miento!** I tell a lie!, I am wrong!

**mentira** [men·'ti·ra] *f* lie; **~ piadosa** white lie; **¡parece ~!** I can hardly believe it!

**mentiroso, -a** [men·ti·'ro·so, -a] **I.** *adj* (*persona*) lying **II.** *m, f* liar

**mentol** [men·'tol] *m* menthol

**mentón** [men·'ton] *m* chin

**mentor** [men·'tor] *m* mentor

**menú** [me·'nu] *m* <menús> *t.* COMPUT menu

**menudencia** [me·nu·'den·sja, -θja] *f* (*pequeñez*) trifle; (*meticulosidad*) meticulousness

**menudo, -a** [me·'nu·do, -a] *adj* minuscule; (*pequeño y delgado*) slight; **¡menuda película!** what a movie!; **¡~ lío has armado!** what a fuss you have created! ► **a ~** often

**meñique** [me·'ni·ke] *m* little finger, pinky

**meollo** [me·'o·jo, -ʎo] *m* **1.** (*sesos*) brains *pl* **2.** (*médula*) marrow **3.** (*fundamento*) essence, crux

**mequetrefe** [me·ke·'tre·fe] *m inf* good-for-nothing

**meramente** [me·ra·'men·te] *adv* merely

**mercader** [mer·ka·'der] *m* merchant

**mercadillo** [mer·ka·'di·jo, -ʎo] *m* street market, flea market

**mercado** [mer·'ka·do] *m* market; **~ de divisas** foreign exchange market; **~ exterior/interior** overseas/domestic market; **~ alcista/bajista** bull/bear market; **~ de trabajo** labor market; **~ único europeo** European Single Market; **~ de valores** securities market; **hay ~ los sábados** there is a market on Saturdays

**mercancía** [mer·kan·'si·a, -'θi·a] *f* goods *pl*; **tren de ~s** goods [*o* freight] train

**mercante** [mer·'kan·te] *adj* mercantile

**mercantil** [mer·kan·'til] *adj* mercantile

**merced** [mer·'sed, -'θed] *f* mercy; **~ a** thanks to; **estar a ~ de alguien** to be at sb's mercy

**mercenario, -a** [mer·se·'na·rjo, -a; mer·θe-] *adj, m, f* mercenary

**mercería** [mer·se·'ri·a, mer·θe-] *f* notions *pl*; (*tienda*) notions store

**mercurio** [mer·'ku·rjo] *m* mercury

**Mercurio** [mer·'ku·rjo] *m* Mercury

**merecedor(a)** [me·re·se·'dor, -·'do·ra; me·re·θe·] *adj* deserving; **hacerse ~ de algo** to earn sth

**merecer** [me·re·'ser, -'θer] *irr como crecer* **I.** *vt* to deserve; (*valer*) to be worthy of; **merece respeto de nuestra parte** he/she deserves our respect; **no merece la pena** it is not worth it **II.** *vr:* **~se** to deserve

**merecido** [me·re·'si·do, -'θi·do] *m* deserts *pl*; **se llevó su ~** he/she got his/her just deserts

**merendar** <e → ie> [me·ren·'dar] **I.** *vt* to have for tea, to have for an afternoon snack **II.** *vi* to have tea, to have an afternoon snack; (*en el campo*) to picnic **III.** *vr:* **~se** *inf* to wangle; **~se a alguien** to get the better of sb

**merengue** [me·'ren·ge] *m* **1.** (*dulce*) meringue **2.** *CSur inf* (*lío*) mess

**meridiano** [me·ri·'dja·no] *m* meridian

**meridional** [me·ri·djo·'nal] *adj* south

**merienda** [me·'rjen·da] *f* **1.** (*comida por la tarde*) tea, afternoon snack **2.** (*picnic*) picnic; **ir de ~** to go for a picnic

**mérito** ['me·ri·to] *m* merit; (*valor*) worth; **hacer ~s** to prove oneself worthy

**merlo** ['mer·lo] *m AmL* ZOOL wrasse

**merluza** [mer·'lu·sa, -θa] *f* 1. ZOOL hake 2. *inf* (*borrachera*) **coger una buena ~** to get sloshed

**merluzo, -a** [mer·'lu·so, -a; -θo, -a] *adj inf* silly

**mermar** [mer·'mar] *vt* to lessen

**mermelada** [mer·me·'la·da] *f* jam; **~ de naranja** orange marmalade

**mero** ['me·ro] **I.** *adv* 1. *AmC, Méx* (*pronto*) soon 2. *Méx* (*muy*) very 3. *Méx* (*precisamente*) precisely **II.** *m* 1. ZOOL grouper 2. *Méx* (*jefe*) boss

**mero, -a** ['me·ro, -a] *adj* 1. (*sencillo*) simple 2. (*sin nada más*) mere; **la mera verdad** the plain truth 3. *Méx* (*preciso*) precise 4. *Méx* (*propio*) own

**merodear** [me·ro·de·'ar] *vi* to prowl; **~ por un sitio** to hang about a place

**mes** [mes] *m* month; **a principios/a mediados/a fin(al)es de ~** at the beginning/in the middle/at the end of the month; **5.000 pesos al ~** 5,000 pesos a month; **todos los ~es** every month; **el ~ que viene** next month; **el ~ pasado** last month; **hace un ~** a month ago; **con un ~ de anticipo** a month's salary in advance; **tengo el ~** *inf* I have my period

**mesa** ['me·sa] *f* 1. (*mueble*) table; **vino de ~** table wine; **bendecir la ~** to say grace; **poner la ~** to lay [*o* set] the table; **quitar la ~** to clear the table; **en la ~** (*comiendo*) at the table; **¡a la ~!** food's ready!; **servir una ~** to serve a table 2. POL **~ electoral** *officials in charge of a polling station*

**mesero, -a** [me·'se·ro, -a] *m, f Méx* (*camarero*) waiter *m*, waitress *f*

**meseta** [me·'se·ta] *f* GEO plateau

**mesilla** [me·'si·ja, -ʎa] *f* small table; **~ de noche** nightstand

**mesón** [me·'son] *m* inn, tavern

**mesonero, -a** [me·so·'ne·ro, -a] *m, f* innkeeper

**mestizo, -a** [mes·'ti·so, -a; -θo, -a] **I.** *adj* 1. (*entre blancos e indios*) mestizo 2. (*entre dos razas*) mixed-race **II.** *m, f* 1. (*entre blancos e indios*) mestizo

2. (*entre dos razas*) person of mixed race

**mesura** [me·'su·ra] *f* 1. (*moderación*) moderation 2. (*cortesía*) courtesy, civility 3. (*calma*) calm

**meta** ['me·ta] *f t. fig* winning post; (*portería*) goal; **la ~ de su vida** his/her aim in life; **fijarse una ~** to set oneself a goal

**metabolismo** [me·ta·βo·'lis·mo] *m* metabolism

**metafísica** [me·ta·'fi·si·ka] *f* FILOS metaphysics

**metafísico, -a** [me·ta·'fi·si·ko, -a] *adj* metaphysical

**metáfora** [me·'ta·fo·ra] *f* metaphor

**metafórico, -a** [me·ta·'fo·ri·ko, -a] *adj* metaphorical

**metal** [me·'tal] *m* metal; **~ noble** precious metal; **~ pesado** heavy metal; **el vil ~** (*dinero*) filthy lucre

**metálico** [me·'ta·li·ko] *m* **en ~** in cash; **premio en ~** cash prize

**metálico, -a** [me·'ta·li·ko, -a] *adj* metallic

**metalúrgico, -a** [me·ta·'lur·xi·ko, -a] *adj* metallurgical

**metamorfosis** [me·ta·mor·'fo·sis] *f inv* metamorphosis; (*en una persona*) transformation

**metano** [me·'ta·no] *m* methane

**metástasis** [me·'tas·ta·sis] *f inv* MED metastasis

**metedura** [me·te·'du·ra] *f* **¡vaya ~ de pata!** *inf* what a blooper

**meteórico, -a** [me·te·'o·ri·ko, -a] *adj* (*rápido*) meteoric

**meteorito** [me·teo·'ri·to] *m* meteorite

**meteorología** [me·teo·ro·lo·'xi·a] *f* meteorology

**meteorológico, -a** [me·teo·ro·'lo·xi·ko, -a] *adj* meteorological; **informe ~** weather forecast; **estación meteorológica** weather station

**meteorólogo, -a** [me·teo·'ro·lo·ɣo, -a] *m, f* meteorologist

**meter** [me·'ter] **I.** *vt* 1. (*introducir*) to insert; (*poner*) to put; **~ en una caja** to put in a box; **¡mete el enchufe!** put the plug in!; **~ un clavo en la pared** to hammer a nail into the wall; **~ a alguien en la cárcel** to put sb in jail; **~ un**

M

**gol** DEP to score a goal; **~ dinero en el banco** to put money in the bank **2.** *inf* (*encasquetar*) to palm off; (*vender*) to sell; (*enjaretar*) to foist; **le metieron tres meses de cárcel** they gave him/her three months in jail **3.** *inf* (*pegar*) **~ un puñetazo a alguien** to punch sb **4.** (*provocar*) **~ miedo/un susto a alguien** to frighten/startle sb; **~ prisa a alguien** to hurry sb (up) **5.** (*hacer participar*) to involve; **~ a toda la familia en el asunto** to involve the whole family in the matter **6.** (*emplear*) to employ; **~ a uno a trabajar** to put sb to work (**de** as) ▶ **a todo ~** *inf* as fast as possible **II.** *vr:* **~se 1.** (*introducirse*) to put; **~se el dedo en la nariz** to stick one's finger in one's nose; **se le ha metido en la cabeza que...** he/she has gotten it into his/her head that... **2.** (*entrar en un lugar*) to enter; **lo vi ~se en un cine** I saw him go into a movie theater; **~se entre la gente** to mingle with the people; **¿dónde se habrá metido?** where has he/she gotten to? **3.** (*entrar indebidamente*) to enter unlawfully **4.** (*inmiscuirse*) to meddle; **¡no te metas donde no te llaman!** mind your own business! **5.** (*provocar*) **~se con alguien** to provoke sb **6.** (*comenzar un oficio*) **~se a actor** to become an actor

**metiche** [me·'ti·tʃe] *adj Méx* (*entrometido*) meddlesome

**meticuloso, -a** [me·ti·ku·'lo·so, -a] *adj* meticulous

**metido, -a** [me·'ti·do, -a] *adj* **estar ~ en un negocio** to be involved in a business; **~ en carnes** chubby; **~ en años** elderly; **la llave está metida** the key is in

**metódico, -a** [me·'to·di·ko, -a] *adj* methodical

**método** ['me·to·do] *m* method; **un ~ de guitarra** (*libro*) a guitar manual

**metodología** [me·to·do·lo·'xi·a] *f* methodology

**metralla** [me·'tra·ja, -ʎa] *f* **1.** (*munición*) shell; **fuego de ~** shellfire **2.** (*trozos*) shrapnel

**metralleta** [me·tra·'je·ta, -ʎeta] *f* submachine gun

**métrico, -a** ['me·tri·ko, -a] *adj* metric

**metro** ['me·tro] *m* **1.** (*unidad*) meter; **~ cuadrado** square meter; **~ cúbico** cubic meter **2.** (*para medir*) ruler; **~ de cinta** tape measure; **~ plegable** folding ruler **3.** FERRO subway

**metrópoli** [me·'tro·po·li] *f* (*urbe*) metropolis; (*capital*) capital

**metropolitano** [me·tro·po·li·'ta·no] *m* subway

**metropolitano, -a** [me·tro·po·li·'ta·no, -a] *adj* (*de la capital*) metropolitan; (*de urbe*) city

**mexicano, -a** [me·xi·'ka·no, -a] *adj, m, f* v. **mejicano**

**México** ['me·xi·ko] *m* Mexico

**mezcal** [mes·'kal, meθ-] *m Méx* BOT mescal

**mezcla** ['mes·kla, 'meθ-] *f* mixture; **~ explosiva** *t. fig* explosive mixture

**mezclar** [mes·'klar, meθ-] **I.** *vt* **1.** (*unir*) to blend; CULIN (*añadir*) to mix **2.** (*revolver*) to muddle; (*confundir*) to mix up **3.** (*involucrar*) to involve **II.** *vr:* **~se 1.** (*inmiscuirse*) to meddle; **~se entre los espectadores** to mingle with the spectators; **~se con gente de mucho dinero** to mix with wealthy people **2.** (*revolverse*) to mix

**mezcolanza** [mes·ko·'lan·sa, meθ·ko·'lan·θa] *f pey* hodgepodge

**mezquino, -a** [mes·'ki·no, -a; meθ-] *adj* **1.** (*tacaño*) stingy **2.** (*innoble*) ignoble; (*miserable*) small-minded

**mezquita** [mes·'ki·ta; meθ-] *f* mosque

**mi** [mi] **I.** *adj* (*antepuesto*) my; **~ amigo/casa** my friend/house; **~s amigos** my friends **II.** *m inv* MÚS E; **~ mayor** E major; **~ menor** E minor

**mí** [mi] *pron pers* me; **a ~** (*objeto directo*) me; (*objeto indirecto*) to me; **para ~** for me; **¿y a ~ qué?** so what?; **para ~ (que)...** I think (that)...; **por ~** as far as I'm concerned; **por ~ mismo** by myself; **¡a ~ con esas!** don't give me that!; **¡a ~!** (*¡socorro!*) help!

**miau** [mjau] meow

**miche** ['mi·tʃe] *m* **1.** CRi (*pendencia*) brawl **2.** Chile (*juego*) game of marbles

**mico** ['mi·ko] *m* ZOOL long-tailed monkey

**micro** ['mi·kro] *m* (*micrófono*) mike

**microbio** [mi·'kro·βjo] *m* microbe

**microbús** [mi·kro·'βus] *m* minibus

**microchip** [mi·kro·'tʃip] *m* microchip

**microficha** [mi·kro·'fi·tʃa] *f* microfiche

**microfilm** [mi·kro·'film] *m* <microfilm(e)s> microfilm

**micrófono** [mi·'kro·fo·no] *m* microphone

**microonda** [mi·kro·'on·da/mi·'kron·da] *f t.* FÍS (*cocina*) microwave; (**horno**) ~**s** microwave (oven)

**microorganismo** [mi·kro·or·ɣa·'nis·mo] *m* micro-organism

**microscópico, -a** [mi·kros·'ko·pi·ko, -a] *adj* microscopic

**microscopio** [mi·kros·'ko·pjo] *m* microscope; ~ **de 60 aumentos** microscope with x60 magnification; ~ **electrónico** electron microscope

**microtenis** [mi·kro·'te·nis] *m inv AmL* table tennis

**miedo** ['mje·do] *m* fear; **por ~ a** [*o de*] for fear of; **por ~ de que** +*subj* for fear that; **meter ~ a alguien** to frighten sb; **dar ~** to be frightening; **morirse de ~** to be petrified; **el concierto estuvo de ~** the concert was terrific; **hace un frío de ~** *inf* (*terrible*) it is awfully cold

**miedoso, -a** [mje·'do·so, -a] *adj ser* fearful

**miel** [mjel] *f* honey; **luna de ~** honeymoon; **quedarse con la ~ en los labios** to be left wanting more ▶ ~ **sobre** hojuelas even better

**miembro** ['mjem·bro] *m* 1. *pl* (*extremidades*) limbs *pl* 2. (*pene*) ~ (**viril**) male member 3. *t.* LING, MAT (*socio*) member; **no** ~ non-member; ~ **de pleno derecho** full member; **hacerse ~ de** to join

**mientras** ['mjen·tras] I. *adv* meanwhile; ~ (**tanto**) in the meantime II. *conj* ~ (**que**) while; ~ (**que**) +*subj* as long as

**miércoles** ['mjer·ko·les] *m inv* Wednesday; ~ **de ceniza** Ash Wednesday; ~ **santo** Easter Wednesday; *v. t.* **lunes**

**mierda** ['mjer·da] *f vulg* shit; (*porquería*) muck; ¡~! shit!; ¡**una ~!** like hell!; ¡**a la ~!** to hell with it!; ¡(**vete**) **a la ~!** get lost!; ¡**eso te importa una ~!** you don't give a damn about that!; **mandar a alguien a la ~** to tell sb to go to hell; **irse a la ~** to go to the dogs; **no comerse**

**ni** (**una**) ~ to get absolutely nowhere; **el maestro nuevo es una ~** the new teacher is lousy; **es una ~ de coche** the car is a piece of junk

**mies** [mjes] *f* 1. (*cereal maduro*) (ripe) corn 2. (*temporada*) harvest (time) 3. *pl* (*campos*) cornfields *pl*

**miga** ['mi·ɣa] *f* bread (*not the crust*); (*trocito*) crumb; **hacer buenas/malas ~s con alguien** to get along well/badly with sb; **estar hecho ~** (*cansado*) to be shattered; **hacer ~s** to destroy; **esto tiene su ~** (*esencia*) there is something to this

**migaja** [mi·'ɣa·xa] *f* 1. (*trocito*) crumb; **una ~ de algo** a scrap of sth 2. *pl* (*sobras*) leftovers *pl*

**migración** [mi·ɣra·'sjon, -'θjon] *f* ZOOL migration

**migraña** [mi·'ɣra·ɲa] *f* migraine

**mijo** ['mi·xo] *m* millet

**mil** [mil] I. *adj inv* thousand; **dos ~ millones** two billion; **ya se lo he dicho ~ veces** I have already told him/her hundreds of times II. *m* thousand; **~es** thousands; **a ~es** by the thousand; **~es y ~es** thousands and thousands; **varios ~es de dólares** several thousand dollars; **a las ~** very late

**milagro** [mi·'la·ɣro] *m* miracle; **hacer ~s** to work wonders; **contar la vida y ~s de alguien** to tell all the gory details about sb's life; **esta vez se escapó de ~** this time he/she had a lucky escape

**milagroso, -a** [mi·la·'ɣro·so, -a] *adj* miraculous; (*maravilloso*) marvelous

**milenario, -a** [mi·le·'na·rjo, -a] *adj* millennial

**milenio** [mi·'le·njo] *m* millennium

**mili** ['mi·li] *f inf* military service; **ir a** [*o* **hacer**] **la ~** to do military service

**milicia** [mi·'li·sja, -θja] *f* military; ~ **nacional** (*ciudadanos*) militia

**miligramo** [mi·li·'ɣra·mo] *m* milligram

**mililitro** [mi·li·'li·tro] *m* milliliter

**milímetro** [mi·'li·me·tro] *m* millimeter

**militar** [mi·li·'tar] I. *vi* 1. (*cumplir el servicio*) to serve 2. (*en un partido*) to be an active member of; ~ **en favor de/ contra algo** to campaign for/against sth II. *adj* military; **los altos mandos**

**~es** the military high command  **III.** *m* soldier

**milla** ['mi·ja, -ʎa] *f* mile; **~ marina** nautical mile

**millar** [mi·'jar, -ʎar] *m* thousand

**millón** [mi·'jon, -'ʎon] *m* million; **mil millones** a billion; **cuatro millones de habitantes** four million inhabitants

**millonada** [mi·jo·'na·da, mi·ʎo-] *f inf* fortune

**millonario, -a** [mi·jo·'na·rjo, -a; mi·ʎo-] *m, f* millionaire

**milpa** ['mil·pa] *f AmL* **1.** (*campo*) cornfield **2.** (*planta*) corn

**milpiés** [mil·'pjes] *m inv* millipede

**mimar** [mi·'mar] *vt* to indulge; (*excesivamente*) to spoil

**mimbre** ['mim·bre] *m* wicker; **muebles de ~** wicker furniture

**mimeógrafo** [mi·me·'o·ɣra·fo] *m AmL* mimeograph

**mímica** ['mi·mi·ka] *f* **1.** (*facial*) mime **2.** (*señas*) sign language **3.** (*ademanes*) gesticulation

**mimo** ['mi·mo] *m* **1.** (*actor*) mimic **2.** (*caricia*) caress; (*condescendencia*) spoiling; **necesitar mucho ~** to need a lot of affection; **le dan demasiado ~** they spoil him/her; **realizo mi trabajo con ~** I carry out my work with love

**mimoso, -a** [mi·'mo·so, -a] *adj* **1.** (*mimado*) spoiled **2.** *ser* (*cariñoso*) affectionate **3.** *estar* (*apegado*) clinging

**mina** ['mi·na] *f* **1.** MIN mine; **~ de carbón** coal mine; **este negocio es una ~** this business is a gold mine **2.** (*explosivo*) mine **3.** (*de lápiz*) lead

**minar** [mi·'nar] **I.** *vt* **1.** (*excavar, colocar minas*) to mine **2.** (*debilitar*) to undermine **II.** *vr:* **~se** *inf* (*hartarse*) to become fed up

**mineral** [mi·ne·'ral] **I.** *adj* mineral; **agua ~** mineral water **II.** *m* GEO mineral

**minería** [mi·ne·'ri·a] *f* mining

**minero, -a** [mi·'ne·ro, -a] *m, f* miner

**miniatura** [mi·nja·'tu·ra] *f* miniature

**minibús** [mi·ni·'βus] *m* minibus

**minifalda** [mi·ni·'fal·da] *f* miniskirt

**minifundio** [mi·ni·'fun·djo] *m* smallholding

**minigolf** [mi·ni·'ɣolf] *m* miniature golf

**minimizar** <z > c> [mi·ni·mi·'sar, -'θar] *vt* to minimize

**mínimo** ['mi·ni·mo] *m* minimum; **un ~ de respeto** a minimum of respect; **como ~** (*cantidad*) as a minimum; **como ~ podrías llamar por teléfono** you could at least phone; **reducir al ~** to reduce to the bare minimum

**mínimo, -a** ['mi·ni·mo, -a] *adj superl* **1.** **pequeño** minimum; **la mínima obligación posible** the slightest obligation possible; **sin el más ~ ruido** without the least noise; **no ayudar en lo más ~** to be no help at all

**ministerio** [mi·nis·'te·rjo] *m* **1.** (*cartera, edificio*) ministry **2.** (*cargo*) ministerial office

**ministro, -a** [mi·'nis·tro, -a] *m, f* minister; **primera ministra** prime minister; **~ sin cartera** minister without portfolio; **Ministro de Economía y Hacienda** Treasury Secretary; **Ministro de Educación y Ciencia** Education Secretary; **Ministro del Interior** Secretary of the Interior

**minoría** [mi·no·'ri·a] *f* minority; **~ de edad** minority

**minorista** [mi·no·'ris·ta] **I.** *adj* retail **II.** *mf* retailer

**minoritario, -a** [mi·no·ri·'ta·rjo, -a] *adj* minority

**minucioso, -a** [mi·nu·'sjo·so, -a; -θjo·so, -a] *adj* meticulous

**minúscula** [mi·'nus·ku·la] *f* LING lower case; **en ~s** in lower case [*o* small] letters; **escribirse con ~** to be written in lower case

**minúsculo, -a** [mi·'nus·ku·lo, -a] *adj* minuscule, minute; **letra minúscula** lower-case [*o* small] letter

**minusvalía** [mi·nus·βa·'li·a] *f* **1.** (*física*) handicap, disability **2.** COM capital loss

**minusválido, -a** [mi·nus·'βa·li·do, -a] *adj* handicapped

**minusvalorar** [mi·nus·βa·lo·'rar] *vt* to undervalue

**minuta** [mi·'nu·ta] *f* (*cuenta*) lawyer's bill

**minutero** [mi·nu·'te·ro] *m* minute hand

**minuto** [mi·'nu·to] *m* minute; **sin perder un ~** at once; **vuelvo en un ~** I will be right back

**mío, -a** ['mi·o, -a] *pron pos* **1.** (*de mi propiedad*) mine; **la botella es mía** the bottle is mine; **¡ya es ~!** I have it! **2.** (*tras artículo*) **el ~/la mía** mine; **los ~s** (*cosas*) mine; (*parientes*) my family; **ésta es la mía** *inf* this is just what I want; **eso es lo ~** that is my strong point **3.** (*tras sustantivo*) of mine; **una amiga mía** a friend of mine; **¡amor ~!** my darling!; (**no**) **es culpa mía** it's (not) my fault

**miocardio** [mjo·'kar·djo] *m* ANAT myocardium

**miope** [mi·'o·pe] *adj* myopic, short-sighted

**miopía** [mjo·'pi·a] *f* myopia, short-sightedness

**mira** ['mi·ra] *f* **1.** MIL watchtower; **estar en la ~ de alguien** to be in sb's sights **2.** (*mirada*) gaze; **con amplias ~s** broad-minded; **de ~s estrechas** narrow-minded; **con ~s a** with a view to **3.** (*pl*) (*intención*) intention; **con ~s desinteresadas** disinterestedly

**mirada** [mi·'ra·da] *f* look; **~ perdida** faraway look; **devorar con la ~** to gaze hungrily at; **echar una ~ a algo** to glance at sth; **levantar la ~** to look up; **apartar la ~** to look away; **volver la ~ atrás** to look back

**mirado, -a** [mi·'ra·do, -a] *adj* **estar bien/mal ~** (*persona*) to be well-/badly thought of; **bien ~,...** all things considering [*o* considered],...

**mirador** [mi·ra·'dor] *m* (*atalaya*) viewpoint

**miramiento** [mi·ra·'mjen·to] *m* **1.** (*consideración*) consideration; **tener ~ con alguien** to have[*o* show] consideration for sb; **sin ~** inconsiderately; **andar con ~s** to tread carefully **2.** (*cuidado*) discretion; **sin ~** indiscreetly

**mirar** [mi·'rar] **I.** *vt* **1.** (*observar*) to observe; (*ver*) to look at; **~ fijamente a alguien** to stare at sb; **~ algo por encima** to give sth a quick look (over) **2.** (*buscar*) to look for **3.** (*prestar atención*) to watch; **¡pero mira lo que estás haciendo!** but look what you are doing! **4.** (*meditar*) to think about; **mirándolo bien, bien mirado** taking everything into consideration **5.** (*tener en cuenta*) to take into account; **~ el dinero** to be careful of the money **6.** (*estimar*) **~ bien/mal** to have a good/poor opinion of; **~ con buena/mala cara** to approve/disapprove of **II.** *vi* **1.** (*dirigir la vista*) to look; **~ por la ventana** to look out of the window; **~ por un agujero** to look through a hole; **~ atrás** to look back; **~ alrededor** to look around **2.** (*buscar*) to look for; **siempre miramos por nuestros hijos** we always look out for our children **3.** (*dar*) **la casa mira al este** the house faces east **4.** (*de aviso, exclamativo*) **¡mira! ya llega** look! here he/she/it comes; **mira, mira, déjate de tonterías** that is enough, stop being silly; **¡pues, mira por donde...!** surprise, surprise...!; **mire, ya se lo he explicado tres veces** look, I have explained it to you three times already **5.** (*tener en cuenta*) **mira que si se cae este jarrón** just imagine if the vase fell **6.** (*mira que*) **mira que es tonta, ¿eh?** she really is silly, isn't she? ► **ser de mírame y no me toques** to be very delicate **III.** *vr:* **~se** (*verse*) to look at oneself; **~se a los ojos** to look into another's eyes; **~se en el espejo** to look at oneself in the mirror

**mirilla** [mi·'ri·ja, -Aa] *f* (*en la puerta*) peephole; FOTO viewer

**mirlo** ['mir·lo] *m* blackbird

**mirón, -ona** [mi·'ron, -ona] *m, f* (*espectador curioso*) onlooker; *pey* (*de intimidades*) snoop; (*voyeur*) peeping Tom

**misa** ['mi·sa] *f* mass; **~ de difuntos** requiem mass; **ir a ~** to go to mass; **cantar ~** to sing mass; **decir ~** to say mass ► **no saber de la ~ la media** [*o* la mitad] *inf* not to know the half [*o* the first thing] of it; **eso va a ~** *inf* and that's a fact

**miserable** [mi·se·'ra·βle] *adj* **1.** (*pobre*) poor **2.** (*lamentable*) pitiful **3.** (*tacaño*) stingy **4.** (*poco, mísero*) miserable; **un sueldo ~** a miserable wage

**miseria** [mi·'se·rja] *f* **1.** (*pobreza*) poverty; **caer en la ~** to become impoverished; **vivir en la ~** to live in poverty **2.** (*poco dinero*) pittance

**misericordia** [mi·se·ri·'kor·dja] *f* **1.** (*com-*

*pasión*) compassion **2.** (*perdón*) forgiveness

**misericordioso, -a** [mi·se·ri·kor·'djo·so, -a] *adj* **1.** (*que siente*) compassionate **2.** (*que perdona*) forgiving

**mísero, -a** ['mi·se·ro, -a] *adj v.* **miserable**

**misil** [mi·'sil] *m* missile; **~ antiaéreo** anti-aircraft missile

**misión** [mi·'sjon] *f* mission

**misionero, -a** [mi·sjo·'ne·ro, -a] *m, f* missionary

**mismo** ['mis·mo] *adv* **1.** (*incluso*) even **2.** (*manera*) **así ~** in that way **3.** (*justamente*) **ahí ~** just there; **aquí ~** right here; **ayer ~** only yesterday; **nos podemos ver el miércoles ~** we could meet on Wednesday, say

**mismo, -a** ['mis·mo, -a] *adj* **1.** (*idéntico*) **el/lo ~/la misma** the same; **al ~ tiempo** at the same time; **da lo ~** it does not matter; **por lo ~** for that reason; **lo ~ José que María** both José and María; **lo ~ no vienen** they might not come; **quedamos** [*o* **seguimos**] **en las mismas** we are where we were **2.** (*semejante*) **el ~/la misma/lo ~** the same; **llevar la misma falda** to wear an identical skirt **3.** (*reflexivo*) myself; **te perjudicas a ti ~** you harm yourself; **yo misma lo vi** I myself saw him/it; **lo hizo por sí misma** she did it (all) by herself; **lo podemos hacer nosotros ~s** we can do it ourselves **4.** (*precisamente*) **este ~ perro fue el que me mordió** that very dog was the one that bit me; **¡eso ~!** exactly! **5.** (*hasta*) actual; **el ~ embajador asistió a la fiesta** the ambassador himself attended the party

**misterio** [mis·'te·rjo] *m* mystery

**misterioso, -a** [mis·te·'rjo·so, -a] *adj* mysterious

**mística** ['mis·ti·ka] *f* mysticism

**místico, -a** ['mis·ti·ko] *adj* mystical

**mitad** [mi·'tad] *f* **1.** (*parte igual*) half; **~ hombre ~ bestia** half man, half beast; **a ~ de precio** at half price; **mezcla harina y agua, ~ y ~** mix flour and water, half and half [*o* in equal amounts]; **reducir a la ~** to halve **2.** (*medio*) middle; **en ~ del bosque** in the middle of the

forest; **cortar por la ~** to cut in half

**mítico, -a** ['mi·ti·ko, -a] *adj* mythical, mythological

**mitigar** <g → gu> [mi·ti·'ɣar] **I.** *vt* **1.** (*dolores*) to alleviate; (*sed*) to quench; (*hambre*) to take the edge off; (*temperamento*) to pacify; **~ la inquietud de alguien** to put sb's mind at rest **2.** (*colores, luz*) to subdue; (*calor*) to mitigate **II.** *vr:* **~se 1.** (*dolores*) to lessen **2.** (*color, luz*) to become subdued

**mitin** ['mi·tin] *m* political meeting, rally

**mito** ['mi·to] *m* myth

**mitología** [mi·to·lo·'xi·a] *f* mythology

**mitológico, -a** [mi·to·'lo·xi·ko, -a] *adj* mythological

**mitote** [mi·'to·te] *m Méx* **1.** (*jaleo*) uproar; (*caos*) riot **2.** (*danza*) *ritual Aztec dance*

**mixto, -a** ['mis·to, -a] *adj* mixed

**mobiliario** [mo·βi·'lja·rjo] *m* furniture

**mocasín** [mo·ka·'sin] *m* moccasin

**mochila** [mo·'tʃi·la] *f* backpack

**mochuelo** [mo·'tʃwe·lo] *m* small owl; **cargar a alguien con el ~** *inf* to let sb else do all the dirty work

**moción** [mo·'sjon, -'θjon] *f t.* POL motion; **presentar una ~ de censura** to put forward a censure motion

**moco** ['mo·ko] *m* **1.** (*materia*) mucus; (*de la nariz*) snot; **limpiarse los ~s** to wipe one's nose **2.** (*del pavo*) wattle; **no es ~ de pavo** *fig* you can't laugh this one off ▶ **llorar a ~ tendido** *inf* to cry one's eyes out

**mocoso, -a** [mo·'ko·so, -a] *m, f pey* brat

**moda** ['mo·da] *f* fashion; **estar de ~** to be fashionable; **ponerse/pasar de ~** to come into/go out of fashion; **ir a la (última) ~** to follow the (latest) fashion

**modal** [mo·'dal] **I.** *adj* modal **II.** *mpl* manners *pl*; **¡qué ~es son estos!** what manners are these!

**modalidad** [mo·da·li·'dad] *f* form; **~es de un contrato** types of contract

**modelar** [mo·de·'lar] *vt* to model; *fig* to fashion

**modelo** [mo·'de·lo] *mf* **1.** (*de modas*) model **2.** ARTE, FOTO model

**modelo** [mo·'de·lo] *m* **1.** (*ejemplo*) model; **un político ~** a model politician **2.** (*esquema*) design

**módem** [ˈmo.ðen] *m* COMPUT modem

**moderación** [mo.ðe.ɾa.ˈsjon, -ˈθjon] *f* moderation; **comer con ~** to eat in moderation

**moderado, -a** [mo.ðe.ˈɾa.ðo, -a] *adj* (*propuesta, persona, velocidad*) moderate; (*precio, petición*) reasonable

**moderador(a)** [mo.ðe.ɾa.ˈðoɾ] *m(f)* TV, RADIO moderator

**moderar** [mo.ðe.ˈɾaɾ] **I.** *vt* **1.** (*disminuir*) to moderate **2.** TV, RADIO to present; (*debate*) to chair **II.** *vr:* **~se** to calm down

**modernismo** [mo.ðer.ˈnis.mo] *m* modernism

**modernización** [mo.ðer.ni.sa.ˈsjon, -θa.ˈθjon] *f* modernization

**modernizar** <z → c> [mo.ðer.ni.ˈsar, -ˈθar] **I.** *vt* to modernize **II.** *vr:* **~se** to modernize oneself, to come up to date

**moderno, -a** [mo.ˈðer.no, -a] *adj* modern; **edad moderna** present day

**modestia** [mo.ˈðes.tja] *f* modesty; **~ aparte** modesty apart [*o* aside]

**modesto, -a** [mo.ˈðes.to, -a] *adj* modest

**módico, -a** [ˈmo.ði.ko, -a] *adj* modest

**modificación** [mo.ði.fi.ka.ˈsjon, -ˈθjon] *f* (*de plan*) modification; (*de tema*) alteration

**modificar** <c → qu> [mo.ði.fi.ˈkar] *vt* (*plan*) to modify; (*tema*) to alter

**modismo** [mo.ˈðis.mo] *m* idiom

**modista** [mo.ˈðis.ta] *mf* dressmaker

**modisto** [mo.ˈðis.to] *m* fashion designer

**modo** [ˈmo.ðo] *m* **1.** (*manera*) way; **~ de andar/hablar/pensar** way of walking/talking/thinking; **hazlo a tu ~** do it your way; **de este ~** in this way; **de ningún ~** no way; **hacer algo de cualquier ~** to do sth any old how; **encontrar un ~ de resolver el problema** to find a way to solve the problem; **de cualquier ~** no hubieran ido anyway they would not have gone; **de ~ que lo has conseguido** so you have managed it; **utilizar el paraguas a ~ de espada** to use the umbrella as a sword; **en cierto ~** in a way; **de un ~ u otro** one way or another; **de todos ~s es mejor que te vayas** in spite of everything it would be better

for you to go **2.** LING mood **3.** COMPUT mode **4.** *pl* (*comportamiento*) manners *pl*; **decir algo con buenos/malos ~s** to say sth politely/rudely

**modorra** [mo.ˈðo.ra] *f* drowsiness

**modular** [mo.ðu.ˈlar] *vi, vt* to modulate

**módulo** [ˈmo.ðu.lo] *m* **1.** *t.* ARQUIT, ELEC (*de un mueble*) unit **2.** ENS, COMPUT module

**mofar** [mo.ˈfar] *vi, vr:* **~se de algo/alguien** to scoff at sth/sb

**mofeta** [mo.ˈfe.ta] *f* ZOOL skunk

**moflete** [mo.ˈfle.te] *m* chubby cheek

**mogolla** [mo.ˈɣo.ʝa, -ʎa] *m* Col CULIN dark wholegrain bread

**mogollón** [mo.ɣo.ˈʝon, -ˈʎon] *m inf* **1.** (*cantidad*) load(s); **había ~ de público en el pabellón** there were masses of spectators in the pavilion **2.** (*lío*) mess

**moho** [ˈmo(o)] *m* mold; **no** (**dejar**) **criar ~** (*alimentos*) to be eaten immediately; (*un objeto*) to be in constant use

**mohoso, -a** [mo.ˈo.so, -a] *adj* moldy

**mojar** [mo.ˈxar] **I.** *vt* to wet; (*ligeramente*) to moisten; (*el pan*) to dunk **II.** *vr:* **~se 1.** (*con un líquido*) to get wet **2.** *inf* (*comprometerse*) to get involved

**mojarra** [mo.ˈxa.ra] *f* Arg short broad knife

**mojigato, -a** [mo.xi.ˈɣa.to, -a] *adj* (*gazmoño*) prudish; (*hipócrita*) hypocritical

**molar**[1] [mo.ˈlar] **I.** *adj* **1.** (*de muela*) **diente ~** molar **2.** (*de moler*) grinding **II.** *m* molar **III.** *vi inf* (*gustar*) **este libro mola** this book is really cool; **me molan las rubias** I am into [*o* I go for] blonds

**molde** [ˈmol.de] *m* TÉC, CULIN mold; TIPO form; **pan de ~** sliced bread; **romper ~s** to break the mold

**moldear** [mol.de.ˈar] *vt* to mold

**moldura** [mol.ˈdu.ra] *f* **1.** (*listón*) trim **2.** ARQUIT molding

**mole**[1] [ˈmo.le] *f* (*masa*) mass

**mole**[2] [ˈmo.le] *m* Méx CULIN **1.** (*salsa*) sauce; **~ verde** green sauce **2.** (*guiso*) stew

**molécula** [mo.ˈle.ku.la] *f* molecule

**molecular** [mo.le.ku.ˈlar] *adj* molecular

**moler** <o → ue> [mo.ˈler] *vt* **1.** (*café, trigo*) to grind; (*aceitunas*) to press **2.** (*fatigar*) to exhaust; **estoy molido de la**

M

**excursión** the trip has exhausted me

**molestar** [mo·les·'tar] I. *vt* (*estorbar*) to inconvenience; (*fastidiar*) to bother; (*dolores*) to hurt; (*enfadar*) to annoy; **esta camisa me molesta** this shirt annoys me II. *vr*: **~se 1.** (*tomarse la molestia*) to bother; **ni siquiera te has molestado en comprobarlo** you didn't even bother check it; **no tendrías que haberte molestado** you shouldn't have bothered **2.** (*ofenderse*) to take offense; **se ha molestado por tu comentario** he/she has taken offense at what you said

**molestia** [mo·'les·tja] *f* **1.** (*fastidio*) bother; (*por dolores*) discomfort; **ser una ~** to be a nuisance **2.** (*inconveniente*) trouble; **no es ninguna ~ (para mí)** it is no trouble (for me); **tomarse la ~** to take the trouble; **perdonen las ~s** we apologize for the inconvenience caused

**molesto, -a** [mo·'les·to, -a] *adj* **1.** *ser* (*desagradable*) unpleasant; (*fastidioso*) troublesome **2.** *estar* (*enfadado*) ~ **por algo** annoyed about sth; (*ofendido*) hurt by sth

**molinero, -a** [mo·li·'ne·ro, -a] *m, f* miller

**molinillo** [mo·li·'ni·jo, -ʎo] *m* ~ **de café** coffee grinder

**molino** [mo·'li·no] *m* mill; ~ **de papel** paper mill

**mollera** [mo·'je·ra, -'ʎe·ra] *f* (*seso*) brain; **eso no me entra en la ~** I just don't get it; **ser duro de ~** to be stubborn

**molo** ['mo·lo] *m Chile* (*rompeolas*) breakwater; (*dique*) seawall

**molusco** [mo·'lus·ko] *m* mollusk

**momentáneo, -a** [mo·men·'ta·neo, -a] *adj* **1.** (*instantáneo*) momentary **2.** (*provisional*) provisional; **hacer un arreglo ~** to find a provisional solution **3.** (*temporal*) temporary

**momento** [mo·'men·to] *m* **1.** (*instante*) instant, moment; **¡espera un ~!** wait a moment!; **de un ~ a otro** at any time now; **al ~** immediately; **en cualquier** [*o* **en todo**] ~ at any time; **en el ~ adecuado** at the appropriate time; **en este ~ estaba pensando en ti** I was just thinking about you; **de ~, no te puedo decir nada** for the moment, I can't tell

you anything; **en un ~ de flaqueza** in a moment of weakness; **la tensión aumentaba por ~s** the tension was growing ever stronger [*o* stronger and stronger]; **aparecer en el último ~** to arrive at the last moment; **en todo ~ mantuvo la calma** at all times he/she remained calm; **no tengo un ~ libre** I do not have one free moment; **hace un ~ que ha salido** he/she left a moment ago; **a cada ~** all the time **2.** (*período*) period; **atravieso un mal ~** I am going through a bad patch **3.** (*actualidad*) present; **la música del ~** present-day music

**momia** ['mo·mja] *f* mummy

**mona** ['mo·na] *f* **1.** ZOOL female monkey **2.** *inf* (*borrachera*) drunken state; **coger una ~** to get drunk; **estar como una ~** to be drunk; **dormir la ~** to sleep off a hangover ► **aunque la ~ se vista de seda, ~ se queda** *prov* you can't make a silk purse from a sow's ear

**monada** [mo·'na·da] *f* **es una ~ de chica** that girl is a beauty; **¡qué ~ de vestido!** what a gorgeous dress!

**monaguillo, -a** [mo·na·'ɣi·jo, -a; -ʎo, -a] *m, f* altar boy *m*, altar girl *f*

**monarca** [mo·'nar·ka] *mf* monarch

**monarquía** [mo·nar·'ki·a] *f* monarchy

**monárquico, -a** [mo·'nar·ki·ko, -a] *adj* **1.** (*de la monarquía*) monarchic **2.** (*partidario*) monarchist

**monasterio** [mo·nas·'te·rjo] *m* monastery

**monda** ['mon·da] *f* **1.** (*acción*) peeling **2.** (*peladura*) peel ► **ser la ~** *inf* to be terrific

**mondadientes** [mon·da·'djen·tes] *m inv* toothpick

**mondar** [mon·'dar] I. *vt* **1.** (*plátano, patata, palo*) to peel **2.** (*árbol*) to prune II. *vr*: **~se** to peel; **~se los dientes** to clean one's teeth with a toothpick; **~se (de risa)** *inf* to die laughing

**moneda** [mo·'ne·da] *f* **1.** (*pieza*) coin; ~ **de cinco peniques** five pence coin; ~ **de 5/10/25 centavos** nickel/dime/quarter; ~ **suelta** change; **teléfono de ~s** pay phone; **pagar a alguien con la misma ~** *fig* to pay sb back tit for tat; **la otra cara de la ~** the other side of the coin **2.** (*de un país*) currency; ~ **de curso legal** legal tender; ~ **extranjera** foreign currency; ~ **fuerte/débil** strong/weak currency; ~ **nacional** local currency; ~ **única europea** European single currency

**monedero** [mo·ne·'de·ro] *m* purse

**monetario, -a** [mo·ne·'ta·rjo] *adj* monetary; **institución monetaria** monetary institution

**mongólico, -a** [mon·'go·li·ko, -a] *adj* MED of Down's syndrome

**mongolismo** [mon·go·'lis·mo] *m* MED Down's syndrome

**monigote** [mo·ni·'ɣo·te] *m* **hacer ~s** (*figuras humanas*) to draw stick figures; (*borrones*) to doodle

**monitor** [mo·ni·'tor] *m* TÉC monitor; COMPUT (*pantalla*) screen

**monitor(a)** [mo·ni·'tor(a)] *m(f)* (*de un deporte*) coach, trainer; (*de un campamento*) camp leader; ~ **de natación** swimming instructor

**monja** ['mon·xa] *f* nun, sister

**monje** ['mon·xe] *m* monk, brother

**mono** ['mo·no] *m* **1.** ZOOL monkey; **¿tengo ~s en la cara?** *inf* what are you staring at?; **en esta casa soy el último ~** in this house I am a nobody **2.** (*traje*) overalls *pl*; (*de mecánico*) coveralls *pl*; (*de calle*) jumpsuit **3.** *inf* (*de drogas*) withdrawal symptoms *pl*; **tener el ~** to be suffering from withdrawal symptoms

**mono, -a** ['mo·no, -a] *adj* good-looking; (*niño*) cute; (*chica*) pretty; (*vestido*) lovely

**monogamia** [mo·no·'ɣa·mja] *f* monogamy

**monógamo, -a** [mo·'no·ɣa·mo, -a] *adj* monogamous

**monografía** [mo·no·ɣra·'fi·a] *f* monograph

**monólogo** [mo·'no·lo·ɣo] *m* monologue; TEAT soliloquy

**monopatín** [mo·no·pa·'tin] *m* skateboard

**monopolio** [mo·no·'po·ljo] *m* monopoly

**monopolizar** <z → c> [mo·no·po·li·'sar, -'θar] *vt* COM to monopolize, to corner (a market); ~ **la atención de alguien** to monopolize sb's attention

**monosílabo** [mo·no·'si·la·βo] *m* mono-

syllable; **responder con ~s** to answer in monosyllables

**monosílabo, -a** [mo·no·'si·la·βo, -a] *adj* monosyllabic

**monotonía** [mo·no·to·'ni·a] *f* monotony

**monótono, -a** [mo·'no·to·no, -a] *adj* monotonous

**monóxido** [mo·'nok·si·do, -a] *m* monoxide

**monstruo** ['mons·trwo] *m* monster; (*persona fea*) hideous person; (*persona perversa*) fiend; (*artista*) superstar

**monstruosidad** [mons·trwo·si·'dad] *f* monstrosity

**monstruoso, -a** [mons·tru·'o·so, -a] *adj* (*desfigurado*) disfigured; (*terrible*) monstrous; (*enorme*) huge

**monta** ['mon·ta] *f* **de poca ~** unimportant

**montacargas** [mon·ta·'kar·ɣas] *m inv* (freight) elevator

**montaje** [mon·'ta·xe] *m* **1.** TÉC assembly; CINE editing; FOTO montage **2.** (*engaño*) set-up

**montante** [mon·'tan·te] *m* **1.** (*importe*) total **2.** (*de puerta*) jamb; (*de ventana*) mullion

**montaña** [mon·'ta·ɲa] *f* (*monte*) mountain; (*zona*) mountains *pl*; ~ **rusa** big dipper; **la fe mueve ~s** faith will move mountains ▶ **hacer una ~ de un <u>grano de arena</u>** to make a mountain out of a molehill

**montañero, -a** [mon·ta·'ɲe·ro, -a] *m, f* mountaineer

**montañés, -esa** [mon·ta·'ɲes, -·'ɲe·sa] *adj* highlander

**montañismo** [mon·ta·'ɲis·mo] *m* mountaineering

**montañoso, -a** [mon·ta·'ɲo·so, -a] *adj* mountainous

**montar** [mon·'tar] **I.** *vi* **1.** (*subir a una bici, un caballo*) to get on; (*en un coche*) to get in; ~ **en** (*una bici, un caballo*) to get onto; (*en un coche*) to get into **2.** (*ir a caballo*) to ride; ~ **en bici** to ride a bicycle **II.** *vt* **1.** (*subir en un caballo*) to mount **2.** (*ir a caballo*) to ride **3.** (*acaballar, cubrir*) to cover **4.** (*máquina*) to assemble **5.** (*clara de huevo*) to beat;

**M**

(*nata*) to whip 6. (*negocio*) to set up 7. *inf* (*lío*) ~**la** to kick up a fuss; ~ **un número** to make a scene III. *vr*: ~**se** 1. (*subir*) to climb 2. *inf* (*arreglárselas*) **¿cómo te lo montas con el trabajo?** how do you manage with the work?

**monte** ['mon·te] *m* 1. (*montaña*) mountain; **el** ~ **de los Olivos** the Mount of Olives 2. (*bosque*) ~ **alto** woodland; ~ **bajo** scrub; **batir el** ~ (*cazar*) to go hunting; **echarse al** ~ to take to the hills 3. *pl* (*cordillera*) mountain range ▶ **no todo el** ~ **es** <u>orégano</u> *prov* all that glitters is not gold

**montés, -esa** [mon·'tes, -·'te·sa] *adj* wild; **cabra montesa** mountain goat; **gato** ~ wildcat

**montículo** [mon·'ti·ku·lo] *m* mound

**monto** ['mon·to] *m* total

**montón** [mon·'ton] *m* heap; **un** ~ **de ropa** a heap of clothes; **había un** ~ **de gente** there were a lot of people; **tengo problemas a montones** *inf* I have loads of problems; **ser del** ~ to be ordinary

**montura** [mon·'tu·ra] *f* (*arnés*) harness; (*silla*) saddle; (*de gafas*) frame

**monumental** [mo·nu·men·'tal] *adj* (*grande, de importancia*) monumental; (*error*) tremendous

**monumento** [mo·nu·'men·to] *m* memorial; (*grande*) monument; **los** ~**s de una ciudad** the sights of a city; **esta casa es un** ~ **nacional** this house is a listed building; **esta chica es un** ~ this girl is beautiful

**monzón** [mon·'son, -·'θon] *m* monsoon

**moño** ['mo·ɲo] *m* 1. (*pelo*) bun 2. (*lazo*) bow 3. *Col* (*capricho*) whim 4. *Chile* (*pelo*) hair; (*copete*) forelock 5. *inf* **estar hasta el** ~ **de algo** to be fed up to the back teeth with sth

**moqueta** [mo·'ke·ta] *f* carpet

**mora** ['mo·ra] *f* (*del moral*) mulberry; (*de la zarzamora*) blackberry

**morada** [mo·'ra·da] *f* 1. (*casa*) abode 2. (*residencia*) residence 3. (*estancia*) stay

**morado, -a** [mo·'ra·do, -a] *adj* purple; **poner un ojo** ~ **a alguien** to give sb a black eye; **ponerse** ~ (*comiendo*) *inf* to stuff oneself

**moral** [mo·'ral] I. *adj* 1. (*ético*) moral; **código** ~ code of ethics 2. (*espiritual*) spiritual II. *f* morals *pl*; **levantar la** ~ **a alguien** to boost sb's morale; **hay que tener** ~ **para hacer eso** you have to be sure of yourself to do that

**moraleja** [mo·ra·'le·xa] *f* moral

**moratón** [mo·ra·'ton] *m* bruise

**morbo** ['mor·βo] *m* 1. (*enfermedad*) illness 2. (*interés malsano*) morbid fascination; **esto tiene mucho** ~ this has created a lot of unhealthy interest

**morboso, -a** [mor·'βo·so, -a] *adj* (*placer, imaginación*) morbid

**morcilla** [mor·'si·ʝa, -·'θi·ʎa] *f* 1. CULIN blood sausage 2. *Cuba* (*mentira*) lie 3. *inf* (*fastidiar*) **¡que te den** ~! go fly a kite!

**mordaz** [mor·'das, -'daθ] *adj* (*comentario*) caustic; (*crítica*) scathing

**mordaza** [mor·'da·sa, -·'da·θa] *f* gag; **quieren ponerme una** ~ *fig* they want to shut me up

**mordedura** [mor·de·'du·ra] *f* bite

**morder** <o → ue> [mor·'der] I. *vt* 1. (*con los dientes*) to bite; **está que muerde** *inf* he/she is furious 2. *AmL* (*estafar*) to cheat IO; ~ *vr*: **¡no te muerdas las uñas!** don't bite your nails; **tuve que** ~**me la lengua** I had to bite my tongue

**mordida** [mor·'di·da] *f* 1. *Méx inf* (*acción*) bite; (*dinero*) bribe 2. *Arg* *v.* **mordisco**

**mordisco** [mor·'dis·ko] *m* bite, nibble

**mordisquear** [mor·dis·ke·'ar] *vt* ~ **algo** to nibble at sth

**moreno, -a** [mo·'re·no, -a] *adj* brown; (*de piel*) dark-skinned; (*de cabello*) dark-haired; (*de ojos*) brown-eyed

**morete** [mo·'re·te] *m* *AmC*, **moretón** [mo·re·'ton] *m* *inf* bruise

**morfema** [mor·'fe·ma] *m* LING morpheme

**morfina** [mor·'fi·na] *f* morphine

**morgue** ['mor·ɣe] *f* *AmL* morgue

**moribundo, -a** [mo·ri·'βun·do, -a] *adj* dying

**morir** [mo·'rir] *irr* I. *vi* (*perecer*) to die; (*en catástrofe, guerra, accidente*) to be killed; ~ **de hambre/sed** to die of starvation/thirst; ~ **ahogado** (*en agua*) to drown; (*en humo*) to asphyxiate, to suffocate; **~ de viejo** to die of old age **II.** *vr:* **~se 1.** (*perecer*) to die; (*planta*) to wither **2.** (*con 'de'*) **~se de hambre/de sed** to die of starvation/thirst; **~se de frío** to freeze to death; **~se de risa** to die laughing; **~se de pena** to pine away **3.** (*con 'por'*) **me muero (de ganas) por saber lo que te dijo** I am dying to know what she/he said to you; **me muero por ella** I am crazy about her

**mormón, -ona** [mor·'mon, -·'mo·na] *adj, m, f* Mormon

**moro, -a** ['mo·ro, -a] **I.** *adj* Moorish **II.** *m, f* Moor; **~ y cristianos** *Cuba* rice with black beans ▸ **¡no hay ~s en la costa!** the coast is clear!; **ser un ~** *inf* to be chauvinistic

**moroso, -a** [mo·'ro·so, -a] *m, f* debtor in arrears, defaulter

**morral** [mo·'rral] *m* (*de las caballerías*) nosebag

**morrear** [mo·rre·'ar] *vt, vr:* **~se** *vulg* to French-kiss

**morriña** [mo·'rri·ɲa] *f inf* homesickness

**morro** [mo·'rro] *m* **1.** ZOOL (*hocico*) snout **2.** *inf* (*de persona*) (*labios*) lips; (*boca*) mouth; **beber a ~** to drink straight from the bottle; **me caí de ~s** I fell flat on my face; **estar de ~(s)** *fig* to be angry; **torcer el ~** *fig* to pout; **tiene un ~ que se lo pisa** *inf* he/she has a real nerve; **lo hizo así, por el ~** *inf* he/she did it like that, quite brazenly

**morrón** [mo·'rron] *adj* **pimiento ~** sweet red pepper

**morsa** ['mor·sa] *f* walrus

**morse** ['mor·se] *m* Morse code

**mortadela** [mor·ta·'de·la] *f* mortadella, ≈ bologna, ≈ baloney

**mortaja** [mor·'ta·xa] *f* **1.** (*sábana*) shroud; (*vestidura*) burial garments *pl* **2.** *AmL* (*de cigarrillo*) cigarette paper

**mortal** [mor·'tal] **I.** *adj* **1.** (*sujeto a la muerte*) mortal; **los restos ~es** the mortal remains **2.** (*que la causa*) mortal, lethal; **peligro ~** mortal danger **II.** *mf* mortal; **los ~es** mankind

**mortalidad** [mor·ta·li·'dad] *f* (*cualidad*) mortality; (*número*) mortality rate

**mortero** [mor·'te·ro] *m t.* MIL (*cuenco*) mortar

**mortífero, -a** [mor·'ti·fe·ro, -a] *adj* deadly

**mortificar** <c → qu> [mor·ti·fi·'kar] **I.** *vt* **1.** (*atormentar*) to torment **2.** (*humillar*) to mortify **II.** *vr:* **~se 1.** (*atormentarse*) to be tormented **2.** REL to mortify oneself **3.** *Méx* (*avergonzarse*) to be ashamed

**mortuorio, -a** [mor·tu·'o·rjo, -a] *adj* death

**moruno, -a** [mo·'ru·no, -a] *adj* Moorish; **pincho ~** spicy meat kebab

**mosaico** [mo·'sai·ko] *m* mosaic

**mosca** ['mos·ka] *f* ZOOL fly; **por si las ~s** *inf* just in case; **tener la ~ detrás de la oreja** *inf* to be nagged by sth; **estar ~** *inf* (*receloso*) to be suspicious; (*enfadado*) to be cross; **¿qué ~ te ha picado?** what's bugging you?; **~ cojonera** *vulg* pest; **~ muerta** hypocrite

**moscada** [mos·'ka·da] *adj* **nuez ~** nutmeg

**moscovita** [mos·ko·'βi·ta] *adj, mf* Muscovite

**Moscú** [mos·'ku] *m* Moscow

**mosqueado, -a** [mos·ke·'a·do, -a] *adj inf* cross; **estar ~ con alguien** to be cross with sb

**mosquearse** [mos·ke·'ar·se] *vr inf* (*ofenderse*) to take offense; (*enfadarse*) to get angry

**mosqueo** [mos·'keo] *m* anger

**mosquita** [mos·'ki·ta] *f* **~ muerta** hypocrite

**mosquitero** [mos·ki·'te·ro] *m* mosquito net(ting)

**mosquito** [mos·'ki·to] *m* mosquito; (*pequeño*) gnat

**mostaza** [mos·'ta·sa, -'ta·θa] *f* mustard; (*de*) **color ~** mustard(-yellow)

**mosto** ['mos·to] *m* must

**mostrador** [mos·tra·'dor] *m* (*tienda*) counter; (*bar*) bar; (*ventanilla*) window

**mostrar** <o → ue> [mos·'trar] **I.** *vt* (*enseñar*) to show; (*presentar*) to display **II.** *vr:* **~se** to appear; **~se amigo** to be friendly

**mota** ['mo·ta] *f* (*partícula*) speck; **~ (de polvo)** speak of dust

**mote** ['mo·te] *m* **1.** (*apodo*) nickname; **~ cariñoso** pet name **2.** *AmL* (*maíz*) boiled corn

**moteado, -a** [mo·te·'a·do, -a] *adj* (*ojos*) flecked; (*tela*) dotted; (*huevos*) speckled

**motel** [mo·'tel] *m* motel

**motín** [mo·'tin] *m* uprising; (*militar*) mutiny; **un ~ en la cárcel** a prison riot

**motivación** [mo·ti·βa·'sjon, -'θjon] *f* motivation

**motivar** [mo·ti·'βar] *vt* **1.** (*incitar*) to motivate **2.** (*provocar*) to cause

**motivo** [mo·'ti·βo] *m* **1.** (*causa*) reason behind; (*crimen*) motive; **con ~ de...** on the occasion of...; **por este ~** for this reason **2.** (*tela*) motif

**moto** ['mo·to] *f inf* motorbike; **~ acuática** Jet Ski®; **ir en ~** to ride a motorbike; **iba como una ~** *inf* he/she was going like a bat out of hell; **ponerse como una ~** (*enfadado*) to get furious

**motocicleta** [mo·to·si·'kle·ta, -θi·'kle·ta] *f* motorcycle; **ir en ~** to go by motorcycle

**motociclismo** [mo·to·si·'klis·mo, -θi·'klis·mo] *m* motorcycling

**motociclista** [mo·to·si·'klis·ta, -θi·'klis·ta] *mf* motorcyclist

**motoneta** [mo·to·'ne·ta] *f AmL* motor scooter

**motor** [mo·'tor] *m t. fig* motor; **~ de búsqueda** COMPUT search engine; **~ de reacción** jet engine

**motor(a)** [mo·'tor, --'to·ra] *adj* motor

**motora** [mo·'to·ra] *f* motorboat

**motorista** [mo·to·'ris·ta] *mf* **1.** *t.* DEP motorcyclist **2.** (*policía*) motorized policeman

**motorizar** <z → c> [mo·to·ri·'sar, -'θar] *vt* to motorize; **estar motorizado** *inf* to have wheels [*o a car*]

**motosierra** [mo·to·'sje·rra] *f* chain saw

**motriz** [mo·'tris, -'triθ] *adj* driving; **fuerza ~** driving force

**movedizo, -a** [mo·βe·'di·so, -a; -'di·θo, -a] *adj* (*móvil*) moving; **arenas movedizas** quicksand; *fig* dangerous ground

**mover** <o → ue> [mo·'βer] **I.** *vt* **1.** (*desplazar*) to move; **~ archivo** COMPUT move file; **~ la cola** to wag one's tail; **~ la cabeza** (*asentir*) to nod (one's head); (*negar*) to shake one's head **2.** (*incitar*) to rouse **II.** *vr*: **~se** to move; **¡venga,**

**muévete!** come on! get a move on!

**movida** [mo·'βi·da] *f* **1.** *inf* fuss; **¡qué ~!** (*lío*) what a business! **2.** (*ambiente*) scene

**movido, -a** [mo·'βi·do, -a] *adj* **1.** (*foto*) blurred **2.** (*activo*) active; (*vivo*) lively; **he tenido un día muy ~** I have had a very busy day

**móvil** ['mo·βil] **I.** *adj* (*que se mueve*) mobile **II.** *m* **1.** (*crimen*) motive **2.** TEL cell (phone)

**movilidad** [mo·βi·li·'dad] *f* mobility

**movilización** [mo·βi·li·sa·'sjon, -θa·'θjon] *f* **1.** (*recursos, tropas*) mobilization **2.** (*huelga*) industrial action

**movilizar** <z → c> [mo·βi·li·'sar, -'θar] *vt* to mobilize; (*dinero*) to release

**movimiento** [mo·βi·'mjen·to] *m* **1.** *t.* Fís movement; **~ vibratorio** vibratory movement; **poner en ~** to put [*o set*] in motion; **había mucho ~ en las tiendas** the shops were busy **2.** COM movement; **~s bursátiles** stock-market movements

**mozo** ['mo·so, -θo] *m* servant; **~ (de estación)** porter; **~ de hotel** bellboy

**mozo, -a** ['mo·so, -a; -θo, -a] *m, f* (*chico*) lad; (*chica*) girl; (*joven*) young person; **¡pero si estás hecho un ~!** (*a un chico*) what a strapping lad you are!

**mu** [mu] **I.** *interj* (*vaca*) moo **II.** *m* **no decir ni ~** *inf* not to say a word

**mucamo, -a** [mu·'ka·mo, -a] *m, f AmL* (*criado*) servant; (*criada*) maid

**muchacho, -a** [mu·'tʃa·tʃo, -a] *m, f* (*chico*) boy; (*chica*) girl

**muchedumbre** [mu·tʃe·'dum·bre] *f* (*de personas*) crowd; (*de cosas*) collection

**mucho, -a** ['mu·tʃo, -a] **I.** *adj* a lot of; **~ vino** a lot of wine, much wine; **~s libros** a lot of books, many books; **esto es ~ para ella** this is too much for her; **hace ya ~ tiempo que...** it has been a long time since...; **muchas veces** lots of times **II.** *adv* (*intensidad*) very; **trabajar/esforzarse** ~ to work/to try hard; (*cantidad*) a lot; (*mucho tiempo*) for a long time; (*muchas veces*) many times; (*a menudo*) often; **lo sentimos ~** we are very sorry; **no hace ~ estuvo aquí**

he/she was here not long ago; **es con ~ el más simpático** he is by far the most pleasant; **por ~ que se esfuercen, no lo conseguirán** however hard they try, they will not manage it; **ni ~ menos** far from it; **como ~** at (the) most

**mucosa** [mu·'ko·sa] f mucus

**muda** ['mu·ða] f **1.** (*ropa interior*) change of underwear; (*cama*) change of sheets **2.** (*serpiente*) slough, shedding of skin **3.** (*pájaro, pelo*) molt

**mudanza** [mu·'ðan·sa, - θa] f move; **camión de ~s** moving van; **estar de ~** to be in the middle of a move

**mudar** [mu·'ðar] **I.** *vi, vt* to change; ~ (**de**) **pluma** to molt; ~ (**de**) **piel** to slough, to shed **II.** *vr:* ~**se 1.** (*casa*) to move; **nos mudamos (de aquí)** we are moving (away); ~**se a Ecuador** to move to Ecuador **2.** (*ropa*) ~**se (de ropa)** to change clothes

**mudo, -a** ['mu·ðo, -a] *adj* mute; **cine ~** silent movies; **quedarse ~ de asombro** to be speechless with amazement

**mueble** ['mwe·βle] **I.** *m* **1.** (*pieza*) piece of furniture; ~ **bar** drinks cabinet; ~ **de cocina** kitchen unit **2.** *pl* furniture; **con/sin ~s** furnished/unfurnished **II.** *adj* JUR **bienes ~s** movable goods, personal property

**mueca** ['mwe·ka] f face; **hacer ~s** to pull faces; (*de dolor, disgusto*) grimace

**muela** ['mwe·la] f (*diente*) molar; ~**s del juicio** wisdom teeth; ~ **picada** molar with tooth decay; **dolor de ~s** toothache

**muelle** ['mwe·je, -ʎe] *m* **1.** (*resorte*) spring **2.** (*puerto*) wharf; ~ **flotante** floating quay

**muérdago** ['mwer·ða·ɣo] *m* mistletoe

**muerte** ['mwer·te] f death; **pena de ~** death penalty; **condenar a ~** to condemn [*o* sentence] to death; **morir de ~ natural** to die of natural causes; **hasta que la ~ os separe** (*matrimonio*) till death do you part ▶ **de mala ~** lousy, crummy; **a ~** to death; **a ese tipo lo odio a ~** I detest that man; **llevarse un susto de ~** to be scared to death

**muerto, -a** ['mwer·to, -a] **I.** *pp* de **morir II.** *adj* dead; **horas muertas** period of inactivity; **naturaleza muerta** still life; **estar ~ (de cansancio)** to be exhausted; **estar ~ de hambre/sed** to be ravenous/dying of thirst; **caerse ~** to drop dead; **no tener dónde caerse ~** *inf* to be penniless; **punto ~** AUTO neutral **III.** *m, f* dead person; (*difunto*) deceased; (*cadáver*) corpse; **ahora me cargan el ~ a mí** *inf* now they are laying the blame on me; **hacerse el ~** (*quieto, t. fig*) to play dead; **ser un ~ de hambre** to be a nobody

**muesca** ['mwes·ka] f nick; (*ranura*) groove

**muestra** ['mwes·tra] f **1.** (*mercancía*) sample; ~ **gratuita** free sample; **feria de ~s** trade fair **2.** (*prueba*) proof; ~ **de amistad** token of friendship **3.** (*demostración*) demonstration; **dar ~(s) de valor** to give a demonstration of courage **4.** (*de labores*) example **5.** MED ~ **de sangre/orina** blood/urine sample

**muestrario** [mwes·'tra·rjo] *m* collection of samples

**muestreo** [mwes·'treo] *m* sampling

**mugir** <g → j> [mu·'xir] *vi* (*vaca*) to moo

**mugre** ['mu·ɣre] f grime

**mugriento, -a** [mu·'ɣrjen·to, -a] *adj* grubby

**mujer** [mu·'xer] f woman; (*esposa*) wife; ~ **fatal** femme fatale; ~ **de la limpieza** cleaning lady, cleaner; **está hecha toda una ~** she really is grown-up; **esto es cosa de ~es** this is women's stuff

**mujeriego** [mu·xe·'rje·ɣo] *m* womanizer

**mulato, -a** [mu·'la·to, -a] *m, f* mulatto

**mulero, -a** [mu·'le·ro, -a] *m, f* RíoPl *inf* **1.** (*mentiroso*) liar **2.** (*tramposo*) cheat

**muleta** [mu·'le·ta] f **1.** (*apoyo*) crutch; **andar con ~s** to walk with crutches **2.** TAUR red cloth attached to a stick used by a matador

**muletilla** [mu·le·'ti·ja, -ʎa] f (*coletilla*) tag; (*palabra*) pet word; (*frase*) catch phrase

**mullido, -a** [mu·'ji·ðo, -ʎi·ðo] *adj* soft

**mulo, -a** ['mu·lo, -a] *m, f* (*caballo y asna*) hinny; (*asno y yegua*) mule

**multa** ['mul·ta] f fine; **poner una ~ a alguien** to fine sb

**M**

**multar** [mul·'tar] *vt* to fine; **me han multado con 3.000 pesos** I've been fined 3,000 pesos

**multicolor** [mul·ti·ko·'lor] *adj* multicolored; TIPO polychromatic

**multilingüe** [mul·ti·'lin·gwe] *adj* multilingual

**multimedia** [mul·ti·'me·dja] *adj inv* multimedia

**multimillonario, -a** [mul·ti·mi·jo·'na·rjo, -a, mul·ti·mi·ʎo·] *m, f* multimillionaire

**multinacional** [mul·ti·na·sjo·'nal, -θjo·'nal] *adj, f* multinational

**múltiple** ['mul·ti·ple] *adj* multiple; **~s veces** numerous times

**multiplicación** [mul·ti·pli·ka·'sjon, -'θjon] *f t.* MAT multiplication

**multiplicar** <c → qu> [mul·ti·pli·'kar] **I.** *vi, vt* **1.** MAT **~ por algo** to multiply by sth; **tabla de ~** multiplication table **2.** (*reproducir, aumentar*) to multiply **II.** *vr:* **~se 1.** (*reproducirse*) to multiply **2.** (*desvivirse*) to be everywhere at the same time

**múltiplo, -a** ['mul·ti·plo, -a] *adj, m, f* multiple

**multitud** [mul·ti·'tud] *f* **1.** (*cantidad*) multitude; **una ~ de flores** a great number of flowers **2.** (*gente*) multitude, crowd; (*vulgo*) masses *pl*

**multitudinario, -a** [mul·ti·tu·di·'na·rjo, -a] *adj* multitudinous

**multiuso** [mul·ti·'u·so] *adj inv* multipurpose

**mundanal** [mun·da·'nal] *adj*, **mundano, -a** [mun·'da·no, -a] *adj* **1.** (*del mundo*) of the world; (*terrenal*) worldly **2.** (*extravagante*) society

**mundial** [mun·'djal] *adj* world; **campeonato ~ de fútbol** World Cup; **guerra ~** world war; **a nivel ~** worldwide

**mundillo** [mun·'di·jo, -ʎo] *m inf* (*ambiente*) world; **en el ~ de la música** in musical circles

**mundo** ['mun·do] *m* **1.** (*tierra*) earth; (*planeta*) planet; (*globo*) world; **~ profesional** professional world; **el otro ~** the next world; **dar la vuelta al ~** to go around the world; **venir al ~** to be born; **irse de este ~** to die; **ver ~** to travel a

lot; **recorrer medio ~** to visit many countries; **con la mayor tranquilidad del ~** with the utmost calm; **vive en otro ~** *fig* he/she lives in a world of his/her own; **este ~ es un pañuelo** it is a small world; **desde que el ~ es ~** since the world began; **hacer un ~ de algo** to make a mountain out of a molehill; **así va** [*o* **anda**] **el ~** that is the way things are; **no es nada del otro ~** it is nothing out of this world; **por nada del ~** not for the world **2.** (*humanidad*) **todo el ~** everyone, everybody; **a la vista de todo el ~** for the whole world to see **3.** (*experiencia*) worldliness; **Lola tiene mucho ~** Lola is worldly-wise

**munición** [mu·ni·'sjon, -'θjon] *f* ammunition

**municipal** [mu·ni·si·'pal, -θi·'pal] *adj* municipal; **parque ~** municipal park; **término ~** municipality

**municipio** [mu·ni·'si·pjo, -θi·'pjo] *m* **1.** (*población*) municipality, borough **2.** (*ayuntamiento*) town hall **3.** (*concejo*) town council

**muñeca** [mu·'ɲe·ka] *f* **1.** (*brazo*) wrist **2.** (*juguete*) doll; **~ hinchable** inflatable doll **3.** *fig* (*niña*) doll, cutie

**muñeco** [mu·'ɲe·ko] *m* **1.** (*juguete*) doll; **~ articulado** jointed doll; **~ de nieve** snowman **2.** *pey* (*monigote*) puppet

**muñequera** [mu·ɲe·'ke·ra] *f* wristband

**muñón** [mu·'ɲon] *m* stump

**mural** [mu·'ral] *m* mural

**muralla** [mu·'ra·ja, -ʎa] *f* wall

**murciélago** [mur·'sje·la·ɣo, -mur·'θje] *m* bat

**murmullo** [mur·'mu·jo, -ʎo] *m* **1.** (*voz*) whisper; (*cuchicheo*) murmur **2.** (*hojas*) rustling; (*agua*) murmur

**murmuración** [mur·mu·ra·'sjon, -'θjon] *f* (*calumnia*) slander; (*cotilleo*) gossip

**murmurar** [mur·mu·'rar] **I.** *vi, vt* (*entre dientes*) to mutter; (*susurrar*) to murmur; **~ al oído de alguien** to whisper in sb's ear **II.** *vi* **1.** (*gruñir*) to grumble **2.** (*criticar*) to criticize; (*chismorrear*) to gossip **3.** (*agua*) to murmur; (*hojas*) to rustle

**muro** ['mu·ro] *m* wall; **~ de contención** retaining wall; **Muro de las Lamenta-**

**ciones** the Wailing Wall

**mus** [mus] *m* card game

**musa** ['mu·sa] *f* muse

**musaraña** [mu·sa·'ra·ɲa] *f* 1. ZOOL shrew 2. *fig* (*bicho*) small animal; **pensar en las ~s** *fig* to have one's head in the clouds

**muscular** [mus·ku·'lar] *adj* muscular

**musculatura** [mus·ku·la·'tu·ra] *f* musculature

**músculo** ['mus·ku·lo] *m* muscle; **ser ~ puro** to be all muscle

**musculoso, -a** [mus·ku·'lo·so, -a] *adj* muscular

**museo** [mu·'seo] *m* museum

**musgo** ['mus·ɣo] *m* moss

**música** ['mu·si·ka] *f* music; **~ folclórica** traditional music; **~ de cámara** chamber music; **~ ligera** easy listening; **banda de ~** music box; **tener talento para la ~** to be musical

**musical** [mu·si·'kal] I. *adj* musical; **composición ~** musical composition II. *m* musical

**músico, -a** ['mu·si·ko, -a] *m, f* musician; (*compositor*) composer

**musitar** [mu·si·'tar] *vi* (*balbucear*) to mumble; (*susurrar*) to whisper; **~ al oído de alguien** to whisper in sb's ear

**muslo** ['mus·lo] *m* (*persona*) thigh; (*animal*) leg

**mustio, -a** ['mus·tjo, -a] *adj* 1. (*flores*) wilting 2. (*triste*) low

**musulmán, -ana** [mu·sul·'man, -·'ma·na] *adj, m, f* Muslim

**mutación** [mu·ta·'sjon, -'θjon] *f* mutation

**mutilado, -a** [mu·ti·'la·do, -a] *m, f* cripple; **~ de guerra** disabled war veteran

**mutilar** [mu·ti·'lar] *vt* 1. (*cuerpo*) to mutilate 2. (*recortar*) to cut

**mutis** ['mu·tis] *m inv* TEAT exit; **~ por el foro** quick exit; **hacer ~** to exit

**mutualidad** [mu·twa·li·'dad] *f* 1. (*cooperativa*) mutual benefit society 2. (*reciprocidad*) mutuality

**mutuo, -a** ['mu·two, -a] *adj* mutual

**muy** [mwi] *adv* very; **es ~ improbable que...** +*subj* it is very unlikely that...; **~ a pesar mío** much to my dismay; **~ de tarde en tarde** once in a blue moon; **~**

**de mañana** in the very early morning; **le saluda ~ atentamente,** (*en cartas*) sincerely yours,; **es Ud. ~ libre de hacer lo que quiera** you are completely free to do as you please

# N

**N, n** ['e·ne] *f* N, n; **~ de Navarra** N as in November

**nabo** ['na·βo] *m* 1. BOT turnip 2. *vulg* (*pene*) cock

**nácar** ['na·kar] *m* mother-of-pearl, nacre; **de ~** nacreous, pearly

**nacatamal** [na·ka·ta·'mal] *m AmC, Méx* CULIN pork tamale

**nacer** [na·'ser, -θer] *irr como crecer vi* 1. (*venir al mundo*) to be born; **nací el 29 de febrero** I was born on the 29th of February; **haber nacido para la música** to be a natural for music; **volver a ~** to have a very narrow escape 2. ASTR to be created; (*día*) to rise; **nace una estrella** a star is born; **al ~ el día** at the break of day 3. (*originarse*) to stem; (*arroyo*) to begin; (*surgir*) to arise ▶ **nadie nace <u>enseñado</u>** *prov* we all have to learn

**nacido, -a** [na·'si·do, -θi·do, -a] I. *adj* **bien ~** (*origen*) born into a good family; (*comportamiento*) noble II. *m, f* **recién ~** newborn; **los ~s el 2 de abril** those born on the 2nd of April; **un mal ~** a born villain

**nacimiento** [na·si·'mjen·to, na·θi·] *m* 1. (*venida al mundo*) birth; **de ~** by birth; **ciego de ~** born blind; **lugar de ~** birthplace; **partida de ~** birth certificate; (*belén*) Nativity scene 2. (*linaje*) family; **ser de humilde ~** to be of humble birth 3. (*comienzo*) beginning

**nación** [na·'sjon, -'θjon] *f* nation; (**la Organización de**) **las Naciones Unidas** the United Nations (Organization)

**nacional** [na·sjo·'nal, -θjo·'nal] *adj* national; **carretera ~** (*en los Estados Unidos*) highway; **renta ~** national income; **vuelos ~es** domestic flights

**nacionalidad** [na·sjo·na·li·'dad, na·θjo·]

*f* (*ciudadanía*) nationality, citizenship; **ser de ~ española** to have Spanish nationality

**nacionalismo** [na·sjo·na·ˈlis·mo, na·θjo-] *m* nationalism

**nacionalista** [na·sjo·na·ˈlis·ta, na·θjo-] *adj, mf* nationalist

**nacionalizar** <z → c> [na·sjo·na·li·ˈsar, na·θjo·na·li·ˈθar] I. *vt* (*persona*) to naturalize, to nationalize II. *vr* ~**se español** to obtain Spanish nationality

**nada** [ˈna·da] I. *pron indef* nothing; **¡gracias!** — **¡de ~!** thank you! — you're welcome!; **¡pues ~!** well all right then; **por ~ se queja** he/she complains about the slightest thing; **como si ~** as if nothing had happened; **~ menos que el director** the director himself; **no servir para ~** to be useless II. *adv* not at all; **~ más** (*solamente*) only; (*no más*) no more; **¡~ más!** enough!; **~ de ~** absolutely nothing; **no ser ~ difícil** not to be difficult at all; **¡~ de eso!** none of that!; **¡y ~ de llegar tarde!** no arriving late!; **¡casi ~!** hardly anything!; **antes de ~** (*sobre todo*) above all; (*primero*) first of all; **para ~** not in the slightest III. *f* nothing, nothingness; **salir de la ~** to appear out of nowhere

**nadador(a)** [na·da·ˈdor, -·ˈdo·ra] *m(f)* swimmer

**nadar** [na·ˈdar] *vi* to swim

**nadie** [ˈna·dje] *pron indef* nobody, anybody, no one; **no vi a ~** I didn't see anybody, I saw nobody; **no vino ~** nobody came; **tú no eres ~ para decir...** who are you to say ...?; **un don ~** a nobody; **tierra de ~** no man's land

**nado** [ˈna·do] *adv* **a ~** afloat, swimming

**nagual** [na·ˈɣwal] *f* Méx, Hond witch doctor

**nailon** [ˈnai·lon] *m* nylon

**naipe** [ˈnai·pe] *m* (*carta*) (playing) card

**nalga** [ˈnal·ɣa] *f* buttock; ~**s** bottom

**nana** [ˈna·na] *f* 1. (*canción*) lullaby 2. (*niñera*) nanny

**nanay** [na·ˈnai] *interj inf* no way!

**nanotecnología** [na·no·tek·no·lo·ˈxi·a] *f* nanotechnology

**napia(s)** [ˈna·pja(s)] *f(pl) inf* conk

**naranja** [na·ˈran·xa] I. *f* orange ▶ ~**s**

(**de la China**)! no way!; **tu media ~** your better half II. *adj* (**de color**) ~ orange

**naranjada** [na·ran·ˈxa·da] *f* orangeade

**naranjo** [na·ˈran·xo] *m* orange tree

**narcisismo** [nar·si·ˈsis·mo, nar·θi-] *m* narcissism, egoism

**narcisista** [nar·si·ˈsis·ta, nar·θi-] *adj* narcissistic

**narco** [ˈnar·ko] *m inf* drug dealer

**narcótico** [nar·ˈko·ti·ko] *m* narcotic

**narcótico, -a** [nar·ˈko·ti·ko, -a] *adj* narcotic

**narcotraficante** [nar·ko·tra·fi·ˈkan·te] *mf* drug dealer

**narcotráfico** [nar·ko·ˈtra·fi·ko] *m* drug dealing

**nariz** [na·ˈriθ] *f* 1. ANAT nose; ~ **chata** flat nose; ~ **respingona** turned-up nose; ~ **aguileña** aquiline nose; **dar a alguien con la puerta en las narices** to slam the door in sb's face; **sonarse/limpiarse la ~** to blow/wipe one's nose; **no ver más allá de sus narices** *inf* to not be able to see further than the end of one's nose; **quedarse con un palmo de narices** *inf* to be let down; **me da en la ~ que...** I have a funny feeling that... 2. *inf* (*eufemismo por 'cojones'*) **estar hasta las narices** to have had it up to here; **¡(qué) narices!** no way; **tener narices** to be too much; **¡tócate las narices!** would you believe it?

**narración** [na·rra·ˈsjon, -ˈθjon] *f* narration

**narrador(a)** [na·rra·ˈdor, -·ˈdo·ra] *m(f)* narrator; (*que cuenta la historia*) storyteller

**narrar** [na·ˈrrar] *vt* to narrate; (*informar*) to tell

**narrativa** [na·rra·ˈti·βa] *f* literature

**nasal** [na·ˈsal] *adj* nasal

**nata** [ˈna·ta] *f* 1. (*producto*) cream; ~ **montada** whipped cream; **la crema y ~ de la sociedad** the crème de la crème of society 2. (*sobre un líquido*) film

**natación** [na·ta·ˈsjon, -ˈθjon] *f* DEP swimming

**natal** [na·ˈtal] *adj* native, home; **ciudad ~ ~** home town; **país ~** native country [*o* land]

**natalidad** [na·ta·li·'dad] *f* birth; **índice de** ~ birth rate

**natillas** [na·'ti·jas, -ʎas] *fpl* custard

**nativo, -a** [na·'ti·βo, -a] **I.** *adj* native, home; **lengua nativa** native [*o* mother] tongue **II.** *m, f* *AmL* native

**nato, -a** ['na·to, -a] *adj* born; **un triunfador** ~ a born winner

**natural** [na·tu·'ral] *adj* **1.** (*no artificial, sencillo*) natural; (*fruto*) fresh; (*flor*) real; **de tamaño** ~ life-sized; **esto es lo más** ~ **del mundo** (*normal*) it is the most natural thing in the world **2.** (*nacido*) **ser** ~ **de Madrid** to be a native of Madrid

**naturaleza** [na·tu·ra·'le·sa, -θa] *f* **1.** (*campo*) nature; ~ **muerta** still life; **en plena** ~ in the heart of the countryside **2.** (*manera*) nature **3.** (*índole*) type

**naturalidad** [na·tu·ra·li·'dad] *f* naturalness; **lo dijo con mucha** ~ he/she said it very naturally

**naufragar** <g → gu> [nau·fra·'ɣar] *vi* **1.** (*hundirse*) to sink **2.** (*no hundir del todo*) to be wrecked; (*personas*) to be shipwrecked **3.** (*fracasar*) to fall through

**naufragio** [nau·'fra·xjo] *m* (*accidente*) shipwreck

**náufrago, -a** ['nau·fra·ɣo, -a] *m, f* shipwrecked sailor, castaway

**nauseabundo, -a** [nau·sea·'βun·do, -a] *adj* nauseating

**náuseas** ['nau·seas] *fpl* sick feeling; **tengo** ~ I feel sick; **dar** ~ **a alguien** to make sb feel sick

**náutico, -a** ['nau·ti·ko, -a] *adj* nautical; **club** ~ yacht club

**navaja** [na·'βa·xa] *f* (pocket) knife; ~ **automática** switchblade

**navajazo** [na·βa·'xa·θo] *m* **1.** (*golpe*) stabbing **2.** (*herida*) stab [*o* knife] wound, gash

**naval** [na·'βal] *adj* naval

**nave** ['na·βe] *f* **1.** NÁUT, AVIAT ship, vessel; ~ (**espacial**) spaceship, spacecraft **2.** (*en una iglesia*) nave **3.** (*almacén*) warehouse ▶ **quemar las ~s** to burn one's bridges

**navegable** [na·βe·'ɣa·βle] *adj* navigable

**navegación** [na·βe·ɣa·'sjon, -'θjon] *f* navigation

**navegador** [na·βe·ɣa·'dor] *m* COMPUT browser

**navegante** [na·βe·'ɣan·te] *mf* navigator

**navegar** <g → gu> [na·βe·'ɣar] *vi, vt* to navigate; ~ **veinte nudos por hora** to sail at 20 knots an hour; ~ **contra la corriente** to go against the flow; ~ **por la web** to surf the net

**Navidad** [na·βi·'dad] *f* Christmas; **¡feliz** ~**!** merry Christmas!

**navideño, -a** [na·βi·'de·ɲo, -a] *adj* Christmas

**navío** [na·'βi·o] *m* ship

**neblina** [ne·'βli·na] *f* mist; *fig* haze

**necedad** [ne·θe·'dad] *f* stupidity

**necesariamente** [ne·θe·sa·rja·'men·te] *adv* necessarily

**necesario, -a** [ne·θe·'sa·rjo, -a] *adj* necessary

**neceser** [ne·θe·'ser] *m* (*de aseo*) toilet bag; (*de afeitar*) shaving kit; (*de maquillaje*) cosmetic bag

**necesidad** [ne·θe·si·'dad] *f* **1.** (*ser preciso*) need, necessity; **de primera** ~ essential **2.** (*requerimiento*) need; **tener** ~ **de algo** to be in need of sth **3.** *pl* (*evacuación corporal*) **hacer sus ~es** to relieve oneself

**necesitado, -a** [ne·θe·si·'ta·do, -a] **I.** *adj* (*pobre*) needy; **estar** ~ **de amor** to be in need of love **II.** *m, f* poor person; **los ~s** the poor

**necesitar** [ne·θe·si·'tar] *vt* **1.** (*precisar*) to need **2.** (*tener que*) to need to; **necesitas comer algo** you have to eat something

**necio, -a** ['ne·sjo, -a; neθ-] *adj* idiotic

**necrológico, -a** [ne·kro·'lo·xi·ko, -a] *adj* necrological

**néctar** ['nek·tar] *m* nectar

**nectarina** [nek·ta·'ri·na] *f* nectarine

**neerlandés, -esa** [ne(e)r·lan·'des, -·'de·sa] **I.** *adj* Dutch **II.** *m, f* Dutchman *m*, Dutchwoman *f*

**nefasto, -a** [ne·'fas·to, -a] *adj* awful; (*día*) horrible

**negación** [ne·ɣa·'sjon, -'θjon] *f* **1.** (*desmentir*) denial **2.** (*denegar*) refusal **3.** LING negative

**negado, -a** [ne·'ɣa·do, -a] *adj* ~ **para**

**algo** useless at sth

**negar** [ne·'ɣar] *irr como* **fregar** **I.** *vt* **1.** (*desmentir*) to deny **2.** (*rehusar*) to refuse; (*rechazar*) to reject; ~ **con la cabeza** to shake one's head **II.** *vr:* ~**se** to refuse

**negativa** [ne·ɣa·'ti·βa] *f* (*negación*) denial; (*rehusamiento*) refusal; (*rechazo*) rejection

**negativo** [ne·ɣa·'ti·βo] *m* FOTO negative

**negativo, -a** [ne·ɣa·'ti·βo, -a] *adj* negative; **tu respuesta fue negativa** your answer was negative

**negligencia** [ne·ɣli·'xen·sja, -θja] *f* (*descuido*) carelessness; JUR negligence

**negligente** [ne·ɣli·'xen·te] *adj* **1.** (*descuidado*) careless; JUR negligent

**negociable** [ne·ɣo·'θja·βle] *adj* negotiable; **el precio es** ~ the price is open to negotiation

**negociación** [ne·ɣo·sja·'sjon, -θja·'θjon] *f* negotiation; ~ **colectiva** collective bargaining

**negociador(a)** [ne·ɣo·θja·'dor, -·'do·ra] *m(f)* **1.** (*comerciante*) merchant **2.** (*mediador*) negotiator

**negociante** [ne·ɣo·'θjan·te] *mf* (*comerciante*) dealer

**negociar** [ne·ɣo·'sjar, -'θjar] **I.** *vi* (*comerciar*) to deal **II.** *vi, vt* (*dialogar, concertar*) to negotiate

**negocio** [ne·'ɣo·sjo, -θjo] *m* **1.** (*comercio*) business; **hombre/mujer de** ~**s** businessman/businesswoman **2.** (*asunto*) matter ▸ **hacer un** ~ <u>redondo</u> *inf* to do a good bit of business

**negrero, -a** [ne·'ɣre·ro, -a] *m, f* **1.** (*que trata con esclavos*) slave dealer; (*tirano*) slave driver **2.** *CSur* (*aprovechado*) parasite

**negrilla** [ne·'ɣri·ja, -ʎa] *f*, **negrita** [ne·'ɣri·ta] *f* TIPO bold face

**negro, -a** [ne·'ɣro] **I.** *adj* black; ~ **como la boca del lobo** pitch-black; ~ **como el carbón** as black as coal ▸ **estar/<u>ponerse</u>** ~ *inf* to be/get furious; **<u>pasarlas</u> negras** *inf* to have a terrible time; **<u>verse</u>** ~ **para hacer algo** *inf* to have a hard time doing sth; **<u>verlo todo</u>** ~ to be very pessimistic **II.** *m, f* **1.** (*persona*) black; **trabajar como un** ~ *inf* to work like a

slave **2.** (*escritor*) ghost writer **3.** *Arg inf* (*cariño*) darling

**negrura** [ne·'ɣru·ra] *f* blackness

**nene, -a** ['ne·ne, -a] *m, f inf* (*niño*) baby; (*expresión de cariño*) dear

**neocapitalismo** [neo·ka·pi·ta·'lis·mo] *m* ECON neocapitalism

**neoclásico, -a** [neo·'kla·si·ko, -a] *adj* neoclassical

**neón** [ne·'on] *m* neon

**neoyorquino, -a** [neo·jor·'ki·no, -a] *m, f* New Yorker

**nervio** ['ner·βjo] *m* **1.** (*conductor*) nerve; **ataque de** ~**s** nervous breakdown; **ponerse de los** ~**s** to get nervous [*o* flustered]; **estar atacado de los** ~**s** to be a nervous wreck; **tener** ~**s de acero** to have nerves of steel **2.** (*tendón*) sinew **3.** (*ímpetu*) impetus; **esta empresa tiene** ~ this company is dynamic

**nerviosismo** [ner·βjo·'sis·mo] *m* nervousness

**nervioso, -a** [ner·'βjo·so, -a] *adj* **1.** *t.* ANAT nervous; **el sistema** ~ the nervous system **2.** (*intranquilo*) excitable

**neto, -a** ['ne·to] *adj* (*no bruto*) net

**neumático** [neu·'ma·ti·ko] **I.** *adj* pneumatic; **martillo** ~ pneumatic drill **II.** *m* tire

**neumonía** [neu·mo·'ni·a] *f* MED pneumonia

**neurología** [neu·ro·lo·'xi·a] *f* MED neurology

**neurólogo, -a** [neu·'ro·lo·ɣo, -a] *m, f* MED neurologist

**neurona** [neu·'ro·na] *f* ANAT neuron

**neurótico, -a** [neu·'ro·ti·ko, -a] *adj, m, f* neurotic

**neutral** [neu·'tral] *adj, mf* neutral

**neutralidad** [neu·tra·li·'dad] *f* neutrality

**neutralizar** <z → c> [neu·tra·li·'sar, -'θar] **I.** *vt* to neutralize **II.** *vr:* ~**se** to be neutralized

**neutro, -a** ['neu·tro, -a] *adj* **1.** *t.* QUÍM neutral **2.** LING **género** ~ neuter gender

**neutrón** [neu·'tron] *m* FÍS neutron

**nevada** [ne·'βa·da] *f* snowfall; (*tormenta*) snowstorm

**nevado, -a** [ne·'βa·do] *adj* (*cubierto*) snow-covered; (*montaña*) snow-capped

**nevar** <e → ie> [ne·'βar] *vimpers* to snow

**nevera** [ne·'βe·ra] *f* (*frigorífico*) fridge; **este cuarto es una ~** this room is freezing

**neviscar** <c → qu> [ne·βis·'kar] *vimpers* to snow lightly

**nexo** ['nek·so] *m* nexus; LING connective

**ni** [ni] *conj* **~... ~...** neither... nor...; **no fumo ~ bebo** I don't smoke or drink, I neither smoke nor drink; **~ (siquiera)** not even; **¡~ lo pienses!** don't even let it cross your mind!; **sin más ~ más** without any further ado; **~ bien...** *Arg* as soon as...

**Nicaragua** [ni·ka·'ra·ɣwa] *f* Nicaragua

**nicaragüense** [ni·ka·ra·'ɣwen·se] *adj, mf* Nicaraguan

**nicho** ['ni·tʃo] *m* niche

**nicotina** [ni·ko·'ti·na] *f* nicotine

**nido** ['ni·do] *m* **1.** (*nidal*) nest **2.** (*lecho*) den; **~ de ladrones** den of thieves

**niebla** ['nje·βla] *f* fog; **hay ~** it is foggy

**nieto, -a** ['nje·to, -a] *m, f* grandchild, grandson *m*, grand-daughter *f*; **los nietos** the grandchildren

**nieve** ['nje·βe] *f* **1.** (*precipitación*) snow; **copo de ~** snowflake **2.** *inf* (*cocaína*) coke, snow **3.** *AmC* (*helado*) ice cream

**NIF** [nif] *m abr de* **Número de Identificación Fiscal** Fiscal Identity Number

**nimio, -a** ['ni·mjo, -a] *adj* insignificant

**ninfa** ['nin·fa] *f* (*mitología*) *t.* ZOOL nymph

**ningún** [nin·'gun] *adj indef v.* **ninguno**

**ninguno, -a** [nin·'gu·no, -a] **I.** *adj indef* (*precediendo a un sustantivo masculino singular: ningún*) any; **por ningún lado** anywhere; **de ninguna manera** no way; **ninguna vez** never; **en ningún sitio** nowhere; **no hay ningún peligro** there is no danger **II.** *pron indef* anything, nothing; (*personas*) anybody, nobody; **no quiso venir ~** nobody wanted to come

**niña** ['ni·ɲa] *f* **1.** (*chica, persona no adulta*) girl **2.** ANAT pupil; **eres como las ~s de mis ojos** *fig* you are the apple of my eye

**niñera** [ni·'ɲe·ra] *f* nanny; (*canguro*) babysitter

**niñería** [ni·ɲe·'ri·a] *f* **1.** (*de niños*) childish act **2.** *inf* (*pequeñez*) triviality

**niñez** [ni·'ɲeθ] *f* childhood; *fig* infancy

**niño** ['ni·ɲo] *m* boy; **~ bien** *inf* rich kid; **~ mimado** (*favorito*) spoiled child; **~ probeta** test tube baby; **¡no seas ~!** don't act like a child!

**nipón, -ona** [ni·'pon, -·'po·na] *adj* Japanese

**níquel** ['ni·kel] *m* nickel

**niqui** ['ni·ki] *m* (*camiseta*) T-shirt

**nitidez** [ni·ti·'deθ] *f* brightness; FOTO clarity

**nítido, -a** ['ni·ti·do, -a] *adj* bright; FOTO clear

**nitrato** [ni·'tra·to] *m* nitrate

**nítrico, -a** ['ni·tri·ko, -a] *adj* nitric; **ácido ~** nitric acid

**nitrógeno** [ni·'tro·xe·no] *m* nitrogen

**nivel** [ni·'βel] *m* **1.** (*estándar*) standard; **~ de vida** standard of living; **estar al ~ de lo exigido** to rise to the occasion **2.** (*horizontalidad, grado, cota*) level; **~ estilístico** stylistic level; **paso a ~** grade crossing; **sobre el ~ del mar** above sea level

**nivelar** [ni·βe·'lar] **I.** *vt* to level **II.** *vr:* **~se** to level out

**nixtamal** [nis·ta·'mal] *m Méx* corn (specially processed for tortilla-making)

**N**

**NO** [no·ro·'es·te] *abr de* **Noroeste** NW

**no** [no] *adv* **1.** (*respuesta*) no; **¡que ~!** I tell you it isn't! **2.** + *adjetivo* non-; **~ protegido** non-protected **3.** + *verbo* not; **~... nada** not... anything; **~... nadie** not... anyone; **~... nunca** not... ever, never; **~ ya** not only; **ya ~** not any more, no longer; **hoy ~ tengo clase** I don't have class today; **~ tiene más que un abrigo** he/she only has one coat **4.** (*retórica*) **¿~?** isn't he/she?, don't we/they? ▶ **el ~ va más** the best, the state-of-the-art; **tener un ~ sé qué** to have something special; **a ~ ser que** +*subj* unless; **¡a que ~!** do you want to bet?; **¿cómo ~?** of course; **o, si ~** otherwise

**nº** ['nu·me·ro] *abr de* **número** No.

**noble** ['no·βle] **I.** *adj* <nobilísimo> **1.** *t.* QUÍM (*aristócrata*) noble **2.** (*bueno*) upright **3.** (*honesto*) honest **II.** *mf* nobleman *m*, noblewoman *f*

**nobleza** [no·'βle·sa, -θa] *f* **1.** (*linaje, hi-*

*dalguía*) nobility **2.** (*bondad*) uprightness **3.** (*honestidad*) honesty

**noche** [ˈnoˈtʃe] *f* **1.** (*contrario de día*) night; **buenas ~s** (*saludo*) good evening; (*despedida*) good night; **turno de ~** night shift; **media ~** midnight; **a media ~** at midnight; **por la ~** at night; **toda la ~** all night long; **ayer** (**por la**) **~** last night; **hacerse de ~** to get dark; **hacer ~ en** to spend the night in **2.** (*tarde*) evening **3.** (*oscuridad*) darkness; **es de ~** it's dark ▶ **ser como la ~ y el día** to be like night and day; **de la ~ a la mañana** overnight; **pasar la ~ en blanco** to stay up all night

**Nochebuena** [noˈtʃeˈβweˈna] *f* Christmas Eve; **en ~** on Christmas Eve

**Nochevieja** [noˈtʃeˈβjeˈxa] *f* New Year's Eve

**noción** [noˈsjon, -ˈθjon] *f* **1.** (*idea*) idea; **perder la ~ del tiempo** to lose track of the time **2.** *pl* (*fundamentos*) base; **tengo nociones de francés** I know a little French

**nocivo, -a** [noˈθiˈβo, -a] *adj* harmful; **~ para la salud** damaging to health

**noctámbulo, -a** [nokˈtamˈbuˈlo, -a] *adj* **ser ~** to be a night-bird

**nocturno** [nokˈturˈno] *m* MÚS nocturne

**nocturno, -a** [nokˈturˈno, -a] *adj* **1.** (*de noche*) night; **la vida nocturna** nightlife **2.** BOT, ZOOL nocturnal

**nodo** [ˈnoˈdo] *m* node

**nodriza** [noˈdriˈsa, -ˈθa] *f* **1.** (*ama*) wetnurse **2.** (*transporte*) **avión ~** mother airplane; **buque ~** supply ship

**nogal** [noˈɣal] *m*, **noguera** [noˈɣeˈra] *f* walnut tree

**nómada** [ˈnoˈmaˈda] **I.** *adj* nomadic; **pueblo ~** nomadic people **II.** *mf* nomad

**nomás** [noˈmas] *adv AmL* **1.** (*solamente*) only; **~ que** +*subj* unless; **¡pase ~!** come straight in! **2.** (*nada más*) and that was all **3.** (*apenas*) hardly

**nombrado, -a** [nomˈbraˈdo, -a] *adj* famous

**nombramiento** [nomˈbraˈmjenˈto] *m* (*designación*) appointment

**nombrar** [nomˈbrar] *vt* **1.** (*citar*) to quote; (*mencionar*) to mention **2.** (*llamar*) to call **3.** (*designar*) to appoint

**nombre** [ˈnomˈbre] *m* **1.** (*designación*) name; **~ y apellido** name and surname, full name; **~ de pila** primer **~** first name; **~ de soltera** maiden name; **de ~** by name; **~ artístico** stage name; **sin ~** nameless; **en ~ de** on behalf of; **dar su ~** to give one's name; **poner un ~ a alguien** to give sb a name; **llamar a las cosas por su ~** *fig* to call a spade a spade; **tu conducta no tiene ~** your behavior is a disgrace; **reservar a ~ de X** to book in X's name **2.** (*reputación*) reputation; **de ~** famous **3.** LING noun; **~ común** common noun; **~ propio** proper noun

**nomenclatura** [noˈmenˈklaˈtuˈra] *f* nomenclature

**nomeolvides** [noˈmeolˈβiˈdes] *f inv* forget-me-not

**nómina** [ˈnoˈmiˈna] *f* **1.** (*lista*) list; (*de sueldos*) payroll **2.** (*haberes*) salary

**nominación** [noˈmiˈnaˈsjon, -ˈθjon] *f* appointment, nomination

**nominal** [noˈmiˈnal] *adj* **1.** (*relativo al nombre*) nominal; **valor ~** nominal value **2.** LING noun

**nominar** [noˈmiˈnar] *vt* to nominate

**nominativo** [noˈmiˈnaˈtiˈβo] *m* LING nominative

**nominativo, -a** [noˈmiˈnaˈtiˈβo, -a] *adj* nominative

**non** [non] **I.** *adj* odd **II.** *m* odd number; **decir** (**que**) **~es** *fig* to say no

**noquear** [noˈkeˈar] *vt* to knock out

**nordeste** [norˈdesˈte] *m* (*dirección*) North East; (*viento*) northeasterly

**nórdico, -a** [ˈnorˈdiˈko, -a] *adj* northern, northerly

**noreste** [norˈesˈte] *m v.* **nordeste**

**noria** [ˈnoˈrja] *f* **1.** (*para agua*) water wheel **2.** *inf* (*trabajo*) treadmill *fig* **3.** (*columpio*) Ferris wheel

**norma** [ˈnorˈma] *f* rule; (*general*) norm, standard; **~s de circulación** road safety manual; **~ técnica** technical norm; **observar la ~** to follow the rules; **como ~** (*general*) as a rule

**normal** [norˈmal] *adj* normal; **gasolina ~** regular gas

**normalizar** <z → c> [norˈmaˈliˈsar, -ˈθar] *vt* **1.** (*volver normal*) to normalize

2. (*reglar*) to regulate

**normalmente** [nor·mal·'men·te] *adv* normally; (*habitualmente*) usually

**normativa** [nor·ma·'ti·βa] *f* rules *pl;* ~ **comunitaria** POL Community regulations *pl;* **según la ~ vigente** according to current rules

**normativo, -a** [nor·ma·'ti·βo, -a] *adj* normative

**noroeste** [no·ro·'es·te] *m* (*dirección*) North West

**norte** ['nor·te] *m* **1.** (*punto cardinal*) north; **el ~ de España** Northern Spain; **al ~ de** north of **2.** (*guía*) aim; **ha perdido el ~** *fig* he/she has lost his/her way; **sin ~** aimless

**norteamericano, -a** [nor·te·a·me·ri·'ka·no, -a] *adj, m, f* North American; (*de los EE.UU.*) American

**Noruega** [no·'rwe·ɣa] *f* Norway

**noruego, -a** [no·'rwe·ɣo] *adj, m, f* Norwegian

**nos** [nos] **I.** *pron pers* us; **tu primo ~ pegó** your cousin hit us; **~ escribieron una carta** they wrote a letter to us **II.** *pron reflexivo* ourselves, each other

**nosocomio** [no·so·'ko·mjo] *m AmL* hospital

**nosotros, -as** [no·'so·tros, -as] *pron pers, 1. pl* **1.** (*sujeto*) we **2.** (*tras preposición*) us

**nostalgia** [nos·'tal·xja] *f* (*de lugar*) homesickness; (*del pasado*) nostalgia

**nostálgico, -a** [nos·'tal·xi·ko, -a] *adj* (*de un lugar*) homesick; (*del pasado*) nostalgic; **sentimiento ~** sentimental longing

**nota** ['no·ta] *f* **1.** (*anotación*) note; **~ al pie de la página** footnote **2.** (*apunte*) note; **tomar** (**buena**) **~ de algo** to take (good) note of sth **3.** (*aviso*) letter **4.** (*calificación*) mark, grade; **sacar malas ~s** to get bad marks [*o* grades] **5.** (*factura*) receipt **6.** (*cuenta*) bill **7.** (*detalle*) touch; **una ~ individual** a personal touch **8.** MÚS note ▶ **dar la ~** to stand out (in a negative way)

**notable** [no·'ta·βle] **I.** *adj* remarkable; (*suma*) considerable **II.** *m* ENS very good (7 or 8 out of 10 in the Spanish grading system)

**notación** [no·ta·'sjon, -'θjon] *f* **1.** (*sistema*) notation; **~ musical** musical notation **2.** MAT, QUÍM annotation

**notar** [no·'tar] *vt* to notice; (*calor*) to feel; **hacer ~** to point out; **hacerse ~** to stand out

**notaría** [no·ta·'ria] *f* notary's office

**notarial** [no·ta·'rjal] *adj* JUR legal; (*hecho por el notario*) notarial

**notario, -a** [no·'ta·rjo, -a] *m, f* notary

**noticia** [no·'ti·sja, -θja] *f* (piece of) news; **las ~s** the news; **ser ~** to be in the news; **~s de última hora** latest news; **tener ~ de algo** to have heard about sth

**noticiario** [no·ti·'sja·rjo, -'θja·rjo] *m* RADIO, TV news program

**notificación** [no·ti·fi·ka·'sjon, -'θjon] *f* notification; **~ por escrito** written notification

**notificar** <c → qu> [no·ti·fi·'kar] *vt* to notify

**notorio, -a** [no·'to·rjo, -a] *adj* **1.** (*conocido*) well-known **2.** (*evidente*) obvious

**novatada** [no·βa·'ta·da] *f* (*broma*) hazing; **gastar la ~ a alguien** to play a trick on sb; **pagar la ~** to learn the hard way

**novato, -a** [no·'βa·to, -a] *m, f* (*en un lugar*) new guy *m,* new girl *f;* (*en una actividad*) beginner

**novecientos, -as** [no·βe·'θjen·tos, -as] *adj* nine hundred; *v. t.* **ochocientos**

**novedad** [no·βe·'dad] *f* **1.** (*acontecimiento*) new development; **¿hay alguna ~?** anything new?; **las últimas ~es** the latest **2.** (*cosa*) novelty; (*libro*) new publication

**novedoso, -a** [no·βe·'do·so, -a] *adj AmL* novel

**novela** [no·'βe·la] *f* novel; **~ corta** novella; **~ policíaca** detective story; **~ rosa** romance

**novelista** [no·βe·'lis·ta] *mf* novelist

**noveno, -a** [no·'βe·no, -a] *adj, m, f* ninth; *v. t.* **octavo**

**noventa** [no·'βen·ta] *adj inv m* ninety; *v. t.* **ochenta**

**noviazgo** [no·'βjaθ·ɣo] *m* **1.** (*para casarse*) engagement **2.** *inf* (*relación*) relationship

**novicio, -a** [no·'βi·sjo, a; -θjo, -a] *m, f* **1.** REL novice **2.** (*principiante*) beginner

N

**noviembre** |no·'βjem·bre| *m* November; *v. t.* **marzo**

**novillada** |no·βi·'ʝa·da, -'ʎa·da| *f* TAUR bullfight with young bulls and less experienced bullfighters

**novillo, -a** |no·'βi·jo, -a; -ʎo, -a| *m, f* young bull ► **hacer** ~s to play truant

**novio, -a** |'no·βjo, -a| *m, f* **1.** (*para casarse*) bridegroom *m*, bride *f*; **los** ~s (*en la boda*) the bride and groom; (*después de la boda*) the newly-weds; **viaje de** ~s honeymoon **2.** (*en relación amorosa*) boyfriend *m*, girlfriend *f*; **echarse novia** to get a girlfriend ► **compuesta y sin** ~ all dressed up and nowhere to go

**nube** |'nu·βe| *f* cloud ► **bajar de las** ~s to come back down to earth; **estar por las** ~s (*precios*) to be sky-high; **poner** a alguien **por las** ~s to praise sb to the skies

**nublado** |nu·'βla·do| *adj* cloudy

**nublar** |nu·'βlar| I. *vt* **1.** (*nubes*) to cloud **2.** (*mente*) to get confused; (*ojos*) to mist over II. *vr:* ~**se 1.** (*nubes*) to cloud over **2.** (*mente*) to get confused; (*ojos*) to mist over; **se me nubló la vista** my eyes clouded over

**nubosidad** |nu·βo·si·'dad| *f* cloudiness

**nuboso, -a** |nu·'βo·so, -a| *adj* cloudy

**nuca** |'nu·ka| *f* ANAT nape, back of the neck

**nuclear** |nu·kle·'ar| *adj* nuclear; **energía** ~ nuclear energy [*o* power]

**núcleo** |'nu·kleo| *m* **1.** QUÍM nucleus **2.** (*centro*) hub; ~ **urbano** town

**nudillo** |nu·'di·jo, -ʎo| *m* ANAT knuckle

**nudo** |'nu·do| *m* **1.** *t.* NÁUT (*atadura*) knot; ~ **corredizo** slipknot; **deshacer el** ~ to untie the knot **2.** (*madera*) knot; **sin** ~s smooth **3.** (*punto de reunión*) center; ~ **de comunicaciones** communications center; ~ **ferroviario** junction **4.** (*dificultad*) **el** ~ **del problema es...** the crux of the problem is...

**nuera** |'nwe·ra| *f* daughter-in-law

**nuestro, -a** |'nwes·tro, -a| I. *adj pos antepuesto* our; ~ **hijo**/**nuestra hija** our son/daughter; ~ **s nietos** our grandchildren; **por nuestra parte** on our side II. *pron pos* **1.** (*propiedad*) **la casa es nuestra** the house is ours; **¡ya es** ~!

*fig* we got it/him! **2.** *tras artículo* **el** ~/**la nuestra**/**lo** ~ ours; **los** ~s our people; (*parientes*) our family **3.** *tras substantivo* of ours, our; **una amiga nuestra** a friend of ours; **es culpa nuestra** it is our fault

**nuevamente** |nwe·βa·'men·te| *adv* **1.** (*otra vez*) again **2.** (*últimamente*) recently

**Nueva York** |nwe·βa·'jork| *f* New York

**Nueva Zelanda** |nwe·βa·se·'lan·da| *f* New Zealand

**nueve** |'nwe·βe| *adj inv m* nine; *v. t.* **ocho**

**nuevo, -a** |'nwe·βo, -a| *adj* new; **de** ~ again; **sentirse como** ~ to feel like a new man; **¿qué hay de** ~? what's new?; **hasta** ~ **aviso** until further notice

**nuez** |nweθ| *f* **1.** BOT walnut; ~ **de coco** coconut; ~ **moscada** nutmeg; **cascar nueces** to crack nuts **2.** ANAT Adam's apple

**nulidad** |nu·li·'dad| *f* **1.** (*no válido*) nullity; **declarar la** ~ **de algo** to declare sth invalid **2.** *inf* (*persona*) nonentity; **ser una** ~ to be useless

**nulo, -a** |'nu·lo, -a| *adj* **1.** (*inválido*) null; **voto** ~ invalid vote **2.** (*incapaz*) useless; **soy** ~ **para el deporte** I'm no good at sports

**numeración** |nu·me·ra·'sjon, -'θjon| *f* (*sistema*) numbering system

**numeral** |nu·me·'ral| I. *adj* numeral II. *m* LING number

**numerar** |nu·me·'rar| *vt* to number; **sin** ~ unnumbered

**numérico, -a** |nu·'me·ri·ko, -a| *adj* numerical

**número** |'nu·me·ro| *m* **1.** MAT number; ~ **cardinal** cardinal number; ~ **primo** prime number; **en** ~s **redondos** in round numbers; **hacer** ~s to do one's sums **2.** (*cantidad*) number; ~ **de habitantes** number of inhabitants; **sin** ~ innumerable **3.** *t.* LING (*cifra, edición*) number; ~ **de matrícula** enrollment number; ~ **de identificación personal** PIN (personal identification number); ~ **de zapatos** shoe size; ~ **suelto** odd number **4.** (*ejemplar*) copy; ~ **atrasado** back issue **5.** (*actuación*) ~ **de baile** dance number; **montar un** ~ to make a scene

**numeroso, -a** [nu·me·'ro·so, -a] *adj* numerous; **familia numerosa** large family

**nunca** ['nun·ka] *adv* never; ~ **jamás** never ever; **más que** ~ more than ever

**nupcial** [nup·'sjal, -'β·θjal] *adj* nuptial

**nurse** ['nur·se] *f AmL* **1.** (*niñera*) nanny; (*extranjera*) au-pair **2.** (*enfermera*) nurse

**nutria** ['nu·trja] *f* otter

**nutrición** [nu·tri·'sjon, -'θjon] *f* nutrition

**nutrido, -a** [nu·'tri·do, -a] *adj* **1.** (*alimentado*) fed; **bien ~** well-fed; **mal ~** undernourished **2.** (*numeroso*) ample; (*biblioteca*) well-stocked

**nutrir** [nu·'trir] **I.** *vt* **1.** (*alimentar*) to feed; (*piel*) to nourish **2.** (*fortalecer*) to strengthen **II.** *vr* **~se de** [*o* **con**] **algo** to feed off sth

**nutritivo, -a** [nu·tri·'ti·βo, -a] *adj* nutritious; **valor ~** nutritional value

---

# Ñ

**Ñ, ñ** ['e·ɲe] *f* Ñ, ñ

**ña** [ɲa] *f AmC, AmS inf* (*señora*) lady, Missis

**ñangotarse** [ɲan·go·'tar·se] *vr* **1.** *PRico, RDom* (*ponerse en cuclillas*) to squat **2.** *PRico* (*someterse*) to yield **3.** *PRico* (*perder el ánimo*) to lose heart

**ñapango, -a** [ɲa·'pan·go, -a] *adj Col* mestizo, half-breed

**ñata** ['ɲa·ta] *f AmL inf* beak

**ñeque** ['ɲe·ke] **I.** *adj AmC* strong **II.** *m* **1.** *Chile, Ecua, Perú* (*fuerza*) strength; (*energía*) vim **2.** *Perú* (*valor, coraje*) courage

**ño** [ɲo] *m AmC, AmS inf* (*señor*) abbreviated form of 'señor' used only before the first name

**ñoño, -a** ['ɲo·ɲo, -a] **I.** *adj inf* **1.** (*soso*) insipid; (*aburrido*) boring **2.** (*tonto*) inane **3.** (*remilgado*) prudish **II.** *m, f inf* **1.** (*tonto*) idiot **2.** (*aburrido*) bore

**ñu** [ɲu] *m* gnu

---

# O

**O, o** [o] *f* O, o; ~ **de Oviedo** O as in Oscar ▶ **no saber hacer la 'o' con un canuto** not to know a thing

**o, ó** [o] *conj* or; **~...,** **~...** either..., or...; ~ **sea** in other words; ~ **bien** or else

**O** [o·'es·te] *abr de* **oeste** W

**oasis** [o·'a·sis] *m inv* oasis

**obcecar** <c → qu> [oβ·θe·'kar] **I.** *vt* to blind **II.** *vr:* **~se** to be blinded, to stubbornly insist

**obedecer** [o·βe·de·'ser, -θer] *irr como crecer* **I.** *vt* (*orden, a alguien*) to obey; (*instrucciones*) to follow; **hacerse ~** to make people obey **II.** *vi* (*provenir*) to be due; (*responder*) to respond

**obediencia** [o·βe·'djen·sja, -θja] *f* obedience

**obediente** [o·βe·'djen·te] *adj* obedient

**obesidad** [o·βe·si·'dad] *f* obesity

**obeso, -a** [o·'βe·so, -a] *adj* obese

**obispo** [o·'βis·po] *m* REL bishop

**objeción** [oβ·xe·'sjon, -'θjon] *f* objection; ~ **de conciencia** conscientious objection; **poner ~ a algo** to object to sth

**objetar** [oβ·xe·'tar] *vt* to object; **tengo algo que ~** I have an objection

**objetividad** [oβ·xe·ti·βi·'dad] *f* objectivity

**objetivo** [oβ·xe·'ti·βo] *m* **1.** (*finalidad*) goal; **tener como ~** to have as one's goal **2.** FOTO lens **3.** (*blanco*) target

**objetivo, -a** [oβ·xe·'ti·βo, -a] *adj* objective

**objeto** [oβ·'xe·to] *m* **1.** (*cosa*) object; ~ **de lujo** luxury item; ~ **de valor** valuables *pl;* **la mujer ~** woman as an object; **~s perdidos** lost property **2.** (*motivo*) purpose; **con** (**el**) [*o* **al**] ~ **de...** in order to...; **tener por ~** to have as one's aim **3.** LING object

**objetor(a)** [oβ·xe·'tor, -·'to·ra] *m(f)* dissenter; ~ **de conciencia** conscientious objector

**oblicuo, -a** [o·'βli·kwo, -a] *adj* oblique, slanted

**obligación** [o·βli·ɣa·'sjon, -'θjon] *f* **1.** (*deber*) obligation; **contraer una ~** to undertake an obligation; **cumplir con**

**una ~** to fulfill an obligation; **dedicarse a sus obligaciones** to devote oneself to one's duties; **faltar a sus obligaciones** to neglect one's duties; **tener la ~ de hacer algo** to be obliged to do sth **2.** (*deuda*) liability; (*documento*) bond

**obligado, -a** [o.βli.'ɣa.do, -a] *adj* **1.** *estar* obliged **2.** *ser* (*imprescindible*) obligatory

**obligar** <g → gu> [o.βli.'ɣar] **I.** *vt* **1.** (*forzar*) to force; (*comprometer*) to oblige **2.** *Chile, Arg* (*invitar*) to invite to drink **II.** *vr:* **~se** to commit oneself

**obligatorio, -a** [o.βli.ɣa.'to.rjo, -a] *adj* obligatory; **asignatura obligatoria** compulsory subject; **es ~ llevar puesto el casco** helmets must be worn

**oboe** [o.'βoe] *m* MÚS oboe; (*músico*) oboist

**obra** ['o.βra] *f* **1.** (*creación, labor*) work; **~ de arte** work of art; **~ benéfica** charitable act; **~s completas** collected [*o* complete] works; **~ de consulta** reference work; **~ maestra** masterpiece; **~ de teatro** play; **por ~ (y gracia) de** thanks to; **¡manos a la ~!** let's get to work! **2.** (*construcción*) building work; (*lugar en construcción*) construction site; (*edificio*) building; **~s públicas** public works; **mano de ~** labor; **estar en ~s** to be under construction

**obradera** [o.βra.'de.ra] *f Col, Guat, Pan* (*diarrea*) diarrhea

**obrar** [o.'βrar] **I.** *vi* (*actuar*) to act; **~ a tontas y a locas** *inf* to act rashly **II.** *vi, vt* **1.** (*hacer efecto*) to have an effect on; **~ buen efecto** to be effective; **~ sobre alguien/algo** to act on sb/sth **2.** (*construir*) to build **3.** (*hacer*) to do; (*trabajar*) to work; **sin ~** unworked

**obrero, -a** [o.'βre.ro, -a] **I.** *adj* (*relativo al trabajo*) working; (*relativo al obrero*) working-class **II.** *m, f* worker; **~ asalariado** day laborer; **~ especializado** [*o* cualificado] skilled worker; **~ fijo** permanent employee

**obscenidad** [oβs.θe.ni.'dad] *f* obscenity

**obsceno, -a** [oβs.'θe.no, -a] *adj* obscene

**obsequiar** [oβ.se.'kjar] *vt* **1.** (*con atenciones*) to honor; (*con regalos*) to be-

stow **2.** (*agasajar*) to lavish attention on; (*festejar*) to celebrate; **~ con su presencia** to honor with one's presence **3.** *AmL* (*regalar*) to give

**obsequio** [oβ.'se.kjo] *m* **1.** (*regalo*) gift **2.** (*agasajo*) attention; **en ~ de alguien** in honor of sb

**observación** [oβ.ser.βa.'sjon, -'θjon] *f* **1.** (*contemplación, vigilancia*) observation **2.** (*comentario*) remark

**observador(a)** [oβ.ser.βa.'dor, -'do.ra] **I.** *adj* observant **II.** *m(f)* observer

**observar** [oβ.ser.'βar] *vt* **1.** (*contemplar, cumplir*) to observe **2.** (*orden*) to follow; (*normas, plazos*) to adhere to **3.** (*notar*) to notice; **hacer ~ algo a alguien** to bring sth to sb's attention

**observatorio** [oβ.ser.βa.'to.rjo] *m* observatory; **~ astronómico** observatory; **~ meteorológico** weather station

**obsesión** [oβ.se.'sjon] *f* obsession

**obsesionar** [oβ.se.sjo.'nar] **I.** *vt* to obsess; **el fútbol lo obsesiona** he is obsessed with [*o* by] soccer **II.** *vr:* **~se** to be obsessed; **~se con algo/alguien** to be obsessed by [*o* with] sth/sb

**obsesivo, -a** [oβ.se.'si.βo, -a] *adj* obsessive

**obsoleto, -a** [oβ.so.'le.to, -a] *adj* obsolete

**obstaculizar** <z → c> [oβs.ta.ku.li.'sar, -'θar] *vt* to hinder; **~ la carretera** to obstruct [*o* block] the road; **~ el progreso** to hinder progress

**obstáculo** [oβs.'ta.ku.lo] *m* obstacle; DEP hurdle; **salvar un ~** to overcome an obstacle; **poner ~s a alguien** to hinder sb

**obstante** [oβs.'tan.te] *adv* no ~ nevertheless

**obstinado, -a** [oβs.ti.'na.do, -a] *adj* obstinate

**obstinarse** [oβs.ti.'nar.se] *vr* to persist; **~ en su silencio** to remain silent

**obstrucción** [oβs.truk.'sjon, -'θjon] *f* obstruction; MED blockage

**obstruir** [oβs.tru.'ir] *irr como* huir **I.** *vt* **1.** (*el paso, acción*) to obstruct **2.** (*una tubería*) to block **II.** *vr:* **~se** to get blocked

**obtención** [oβ.ten.'sjon, -'θjon] *f* obtaining; QUÍM extraction; **~ de datos** data collection

**obtener** [oβ·te·'ner] *irr como* tener *vt* to obtain; QUÍM to extract; (*resultado, ventaja*) to gain; **difícil de ~** not easily obtainable

**obturar** [oβ·tu·'rar] *vt* to close; (*bloquear*) to block; (*los dientes*) to fill

**obviar** [oβ·'βjar] **I.** *vi* to stand in the way **II.** *vt* (*evitar*) to avoid; (*eliminar*) to remove; **~ un problema** to get around a problem

**obvio, -a** [ˈoβ·βjo, -a] *adj* obvious; **es ~** it's obvious

**oca** [ˈo·ka] *f* **1.** ZOOL goose **2.** (*juego*) ≈ snakes *pl* and ladders

**ocasión** [o·ka·'sjon] *f* occasion; **coche de ~** second hand car; **libros de ~** bargain [*o* cut-price] books; **aprovechar la ~** to make the most of the opportunity; **desperdiciar la ~** to waste the opportunity; **en esta ~** on this occasion; **en ocasiones** sometimes; **con ~ de** on the occasion of

**ocasional** [o·ka·sjo·'nal] *adj* (*no habitual*) occasional; **trabajo ~** temporary work

**ocasionar** [o·ka·sjo·'nar] *vt* **~ algo** to cause sth, to bring about sth

**occidental** [ok·θi·den·'tal] *adj* western

**occidente** [ok·θi·'den·te] *m* GEO west; **el ~** the West

**Oceanía** [o·θe·a·'ni·a] *f* Oceania

**océano** [o·'θea·no] *m* **1.** (*mar*) ocean **2.** *fig* (*cantidad*) sea; **un ~ de gente** a sea of people

**ochenta** [o·'tʃen·ta] **I.** *adj inv* **1.** eighty; **los años ~** the eighties; **un hombre de alrededor de ~ años** a man of about eighty years of age; **una mujer en sus ~ años** a woman in her eighties **2.** (*octogésimo*) eightieth **II.** *m* eighty

**ocho** [ˈo·tʃo] **I.** *adj inv* eight; **jornada de ~ horas** eight-hour day; **~ veces mayor/menor que...** eight times bigger/smaller than...; **a las ~** at eight (o'clock); **son las ~ y media de la mañana/tarde** it is half past eight in the morning/evening; **las ~ y cuarto/menos cuarto** a quarter past/to eight; **a las ~ en punto** at eight o'clock precisely [*o* on the dot]; **el ~ de agosto** the eighth of

August ► **ser más chulo que un ~** *inf* to be a real showoff; **dar igual ~ que ~** not to care less **II.** *m* eight

**ochocientos, -as** [o·tʃo·'θjen·tos, -as] *adj* eight hundred; **esta basílica fue construida hace ~ años** this basilica was built eight hundred years ago; **vinieron más de ochocientas personas** more than eight hundred people came

**ocio** [ˈo·sjo, -θjo] *m* leisure; **horas de ~** spare time

**ocioso, -a** [o·'sjo·so, -a; -'θjo·so, -a] *adj* **1.** *estar* (*inactivo*) idle **2.** *ser* (*inútil*) useless

**ocote** [o·'ko·te] *m* Méx BOT ocote pine

**octágono** [ok·'ta·γo·no] *m* octagon

**octava** [ok·'ta·βa] *f* LIT, MÚS octave

**octavilla** [ok·ta·'βi·ja, -ʎa] *f* (*volante*) leaflet

**octavo, -a** [ok·'ta·βo] **I.** *adj* eighth; **en ~ lugar** in eighth place; (*enumeración*) eighth; **la octava parte** an eighth **II.** *m, f* eighth

**octogésimo, -a** [ok·to·'xe·si·mo, -a] *adj* eightieth; *v. t.* octavo

**octubre** [ok·'tu·βre] *m* October; *v. t.* marzo

**ocular** [o·ku·'lar] *adj* ocular; **examen ~** eye test; **testigo ~** eyewitness

**oculista** [o·ku·'lis·ta] *mf* MED ophthalmologist

**ocultar** [o·kul·'tar] **I.** *vt* (*cosa*) to hide; (*información, delito*) to conceal; **~ la cara entre** [*o* con] **las manos** to cover one's face with one's hands **II.** *vr:* **~se** to hide

**oculto, -a** [o·'kul·to, -a] *adj* (*escondido*) hidden; (*secreto*) secret; **traerse algo ~** to keep sth hidden

**ocupación** [o·ku·pa·'sjon, -'θjon] *f* **1.** (*trabajo*) occupation; **sin ~** unemployed **2.** (*apoderamiento*) *t.* MIL occupation; **zona de ~** occupied zone

**ocupado, -a** [o·ku·'pa·do, -a] *adj* **1.** (*sitio*) occupied **2.** (*persona*) busy **3.** (*línea de teléfono*) busy

**ocupante** [o·ku·'pan·te] **I.** *adj* MIL occupying **II.** *mf* **1.** (*de vehículo*) occupant; (*de tren, avión*) passenger **2.** (*de un edificio*) resident

**ocupar** [o·ku·'par] **I.** *vt* **1.** (*lugar, telé-*

*fono*) *t.* MIL to occupy **2.** (*un cargo*) to hold; (*vacante*) to fill **3.** (*tiempo, espacio, asiento*) to take up **4.** (*a una persona*) to keep busy **II.** *vr* ~**se de** [*o* **con**] **algo** to busy oneself with sth; ~**se de alguien** (*cuidar*) to look after sb; **ella se ocupó de todo** she took care of everything

**ocurrencia** [o·ku·'rren·sja, -θja] *f* (*idea*) idea; **se bañó en el mar en pleno invierno, ¡qué ~!** he/she swam in the sea in the middle of winter, what a thing to do!; **tener la ~ de...** to have the bright idea of...

**ocurrir** [o·ku·'rrir] **I.** *vi* to happen; **¿qué ocurre?** what's wrong?; **¿qué te ocurre?** what's the matter?; **lo que ocurre es que...** the thing is that... **II.** *vr:* ~**se** to occur; **no se me ocurre nada** I can't think of anything; **¿cómo se te ocurrió esa tontería?** what on earth made you think of a stupid thing like that?; **nunca se me hubiese ocurrido pensar que...** I never would have imagined that...

**odiar** [o·'djar] *vt* to hate; ~ **a alguien a muerte** to have an undying hatred for sb, to hate sb's guts *inf*

**odio** ['o·djo] *m* hate, hatred

**odioso, -a** [o·'djo·so, -a] *adj* **1.** (*hostil*) nasty **2.** (*repugnante*) horrible **3.** *AmL* (*fastidioso*) annoying

**odisea** [o·di·'sea] *f* odyssey

**odontólogo, -a** [o·don·'to·lo·γo, -a] *m, f* MED dentist

**oeste** [o·'es·te] *m* **1.** (*punto*) west; **el lejano ~** the wild [*o* far] west; **película del ~** western; **hacia el ~** westward(s); **al ~ de...** west of... **2.** (*viento*) westerly

**ofender** [o·fen·'der] **I.** *vt* (*humillar*) to offend; **hacerse el ofendido** to take offense **II.** *vr:* ~**se** to take offense; **¡no te ofendas conmigo!** don't get angry with me!

**ofensa** [o·'fen·sa] *f* offense

**ofensiva** [o·fen·'si·βa] *f* offensive; **tomar la ~** to go on the offensive

**ofensivo, -a** [o·fen·'si·βo, -a] *adj* **1.** (*hiriente*) offensive **2.** (*dañino*) damaging; ~ **para el medio ambiente** environ-

mentally damaging **3.** (*que ataca*) attacking

**oferta** [o·'fer·ta] *f* **1.** (*propuesta*) offer; ~ **de empleo** job offer; **estar de ~** to be on special offer **2.** COM tender, bid **3.** ECON supply; ~ **y demanda** supply and demand

**ofertar** [o·fer·'tar] *vt* to offer

**oficial** [o·fi·'θjal] *adj* official; **boletín ~** official gazette

**oficial(a)** [o·fi·'θjal, -·'θja·la] *m(f)* **1.** (*oficio manual*) (skilled) worker; (*administrativo*) clerk; ~ **de obra** building worker **2.** MIL officer **3.** (*funcionario*) civil servant

**oficina** [o·fi·'θi·na] *f* office; ~ **de asistencia social** social security office; ~ **de correos** post office; ~ **de empleo** employment agency

**oficinista** [o·fi·si·'nis·ta, o·fiθ-] *mf* office worker

**oficio** [o·'fi·sjo, -θjo] *m* **1.** (*trabajo manual*) trade; ~ **especializado** skilled trade; **ejercer un ~** to have a trade; **sin ~ ni beneficio** out of work **2.** (*profesión*) profession; **gajes del ~** occupational hazards **3.** (*función*) function; **defensor de ~** JUR public defender; **de ~** ex officio **4.** (*escrito*) official document **5.** REL service; **Santo Oficio** Holy Office

**oficioso, -a** [o·fi·'sjo, -a; -θjo·so, -a] *adj* **1.** (*extraoficial*) unofficial **2.** (*servicial*) obliging

**ofrecer** [o·fre·'ser, -θer] *irr como* crecer **I.** *vt* to offer; ~ **un banquete** to give a meal; ~ **grandes dificultades** to present a lot of difficulties; ~ **un sacrificio** to offer up a sacrifice **II.** *vr:* ~**se** (*brindarse*) to offer oneself; **¿qué se le ofrece?** may I help you?

**ofrecimiento** [o·fre·θi·'mjen·to] *m* offer; REL offering

**ofrenda** [o·'fren·da] *f* offering; (*sacrificio*) sacrifice

**oftalmólogo, -a** [of·tal·'mo·lo·γo, -a] *m, f* MED ophthalmologist

**ofuscar** <c → qu> [o·fus·'kar] **I.** *vt* **1.** (*cegar*) to blind **2.** (*la mente*) to confuse; ~ (**la mente**) **a alguien** to confuse sb **II.** *vr* ~**se en algo** to insist on sth

**ogro** [ˈo·ɣɾo] *m t. fig* ogre

**oída** [o·ˈi·ða] *f* **conocer a alguien de ~s** to have heard about sb; **saber algo de ~s** to have heard about sth

**oído** [o·ˈi·ðo] *m* **1.** (*sentido*) hearing; **aprender de ~** to learn by ear; **aplicar el ~** to listen carefully; **aguzar el ~** to prick up one's ears; **tener buen ~** to have a good ear; **duro de ~** hard of hearing **2.** ANAT ear; **~ interno/medio/externo** inner/middle/outer ear; **cerrar los ~s a algo** to turn a deaf ear to sth; **dar ~s a alguien** (*escuchar*) to listen to sb; (*creer*) to believe sb; **llegar a ~s de alguien** to come to sb's notice [*o* attention]; **ser todo ~s** to be all ears ▶ **¡~ al parche!** look out!

**oír** [o·ˈiɾ] *irr vt* (*sentir*) to hear; (*escuchar*) to listen; **¡oye!** hey!; **¿oyes?** do you understand?; **¡oiga!** excuse me!; **¡Dios te oiga!** may your prayers be answered!; **como lo oyes** believe it or not; **~ decir que...** to hear that...; **ya me oirá** he/she hasn't heard the last of me; **no se oye el vuelo de una mosca** you could hear a pin drop ▶ **como quien oye llover** not to be listening

**ojal** [o·ˈxal] *m* **1.** (*para botones*) buttonhole **2.** (*ojete*) eyelet

**ojalá** [o·xa·ˈla] *interj* I hope so, I wish; **¡~ tuvieras razón!** if only you were right!

**ojeada** [o·xe·ˈa·ða] *f* glance; **echar una ~ a algo** to glance at sth

**ojear** [o·xe·ˈaɾ] *vt* **1.** (*mirar con atención*) to stare at **2.** (*pasar la vista*) to glance at

**ojeras** [o·ˈxe·ɾas] *fpl* bags *pl* (under the eyes); **tener ~** to have dark circles under one's eyes

**ojo** [ˈo·xo] **I.** *m* **1.** ANAT eye; **~ morado** black eye; **~s rasgados** almond [*o* slanting] eyes; **~s saltones** bulging eyes; **a ~ by eye; mirar con buenos/malos ~s** to approve/disapprove of; **pasar los ~s por algo** to run one's eyes over sth; **¡qué ~ tienes!** you don't miss a thing!; **tener ~ clínico** to be a good diagnostician; *fig* to be very observant **2.** (*agujero*) hole; **~ de aguja** eye of a needle; **~ de cerradura** keyhole; **~ del huracán** eye of the storm ▶ **donde pone el ~,**

**pone la bala** he/she is a good shot; **no parecerse ni en el blanco de los ~s** to be like night and day; **poner los ~s en blanco** to roll one's eyes; **costar un ~ de la cara** to cost an arm and a leg; **~s que no ven, corazón que no siente** *prov* out of sight, out of mind *prov*; **a ~ de buen cubero** roughly; **mirar con unos ~s redondos como platos** to look wide-eyed; **a ~s cerrados** without thinking; **con los ~s cerrados** with complete confidence; **andar con cien ~s** to be on one's guard; **cuatro ~s** *pey* four-eyes; **cuatro ~s ven más que dos** *prov* two heads are better than one *prov*; **ser el ~ derecho de alguien** to be the apple of sb's eye; **¡dichosos los ~s que te ven!** *irón* it's great to see you after so long!; **a ~s vistas** visibly; **en un abrir y cerrar de ~s** in a flash; **andar con ~** to be careful; **cerrar los ~s a algo** to shut one's eyes to sth; **clavar ~s en algo** to lay eyes on sth; **comerse con los ~s** to devour with one's eyes; **echar el ~ a algo/alguien** to have one's eye on sth/sb; **echar un ~ a algo/alguien** to take a look at sth/sb; (*vigilar*) to keep an eye on sth/sb; **meter algo a alguien por los ~s** to shove sth down sb's throat; **no pegar ~** to not sleep a wink; **sacarle los ~s a alguien** to kill sb; **tener ~** (*cuidado*) to be careful; **~ por ~ (y diente por diente)** *prov* an eye for an eye (a tooth for a tooth) **II.** *interj* (be) careful, look out; **¡~ con ese tipo!** watch out for that guy!

**ojota** [o·ˈxo·ta] *f AmL* (*sandalia*) sandal

**okupa** [o·ˈku·pa] *mf inf* squatter

**ola** [ˈo·la] *f* wave; **~ de calor** heat wave; **~ de frío** cold spell

**olé** [o·ˈle] *interj* ≈ bravo

**oleada** [o·le·ˈa·ða] *f t. fig* wave; **~ de gente** throng of people

**oleaje** [o·le·ˈa·xe] *m* swell, surf

**óleo** [ˈo·le·o] *m* ARTE oil paint; **cuadro al ~** oil painting; **pintar al ~** to paint in oil

**oler** [o·ˈleɾ] *irr* **I.** *vi* to smell; **~ a algo** to smell of sth; **~ bien** to smell good **II.** *vt* to smell; **~ una flor** to smell a flower; **~ el peligro** to smell danger

**olfatear** [ol·fa·te·ˈaɾ] **I.** *vt* to sniff; (*hus-*

*mear*) to smell out **II.** *vi* to sniff; (*curiosear*) to pry

**olfato** [ol·'fa·to] *m* sense of smell; **tener** (**buen**) ~ *fig* to have a good nose [o instinct]

**olimpiada** [o·lim·'pja·da] *f* Olympics + *pl vb*

**olímpico, -a** [o·'lim·pi·ko, -a] *adj* Olympic

**oliva** [o·'li·βa] **I.** *adj* (**verde**) ~ olive (green) **II.** *f* BOT (*fruta*) olive

**olivo** [o·'li·βo] *m* olive tree; **el Monte de los Olivos** REL the Mount of Olives

**olla** ['o·ja, -ʎa] *f* **1.** (*para cocinar*) pot; ~ **exprés** pressure cooker **2.** CULIN stew

**olmo** ['ol·mo] *m* elm

**olor** [o·'lor] *m* smell; **buen** ~ good smell; (*fragancia*) scent; ~ **corporal** body odor; **tener** ~ **a** to smell of

**oloroso, -a** [o·lo·'ro·so] *adj* fragrant

**olote** [o·'lo·te] *m* Méx corncob

**olvidadizo, -a** [ol·βi·ða·'di·so, -a; -'di·θo, -a] *adj* forgetful

**olvidar** [ol·βi·'dar] *vt, vr:* ~**se** to forget; **no** ~ **que...** (*considerar*) to remember that...; **se me ha olvidado tu nombre** I've forgotten your name

**olvido** [ol·'βi·ðo] *m* **1.** (*falta de memoria*) forgetfulness **2.** (*omisión*) oversight, forgetting; **caer en** (**el**) ~ to sink into oblivion; **enterrar en el** ~ to forget forever

**ombligo** [om·'bli·ɣo] *m* navel, belly button *inf*; **el** ~ **del mundo** the center of the world; **contemplarse el** ~ to self-gratify

**omisión** [o·mi·'sjon] *f* **1.** (*supresión*) omission **2.** (*negligencia*) negligence

**omiso, -a** [o·'mi·so, -a] *adj* (*negligente*) negligent; **hacer caso** ~ **de algo** to take no notice of sth

**omitir** [o·mi·'tir] *vt* **1.** (*no hacer*) to fail to do **2.** (*pasar por alto*) to omit

**ómnibus** ['om·ni·βus] *m* AUTO bus

**omnipotente** [om·ni·po·'ten·te] *adj* almighty, omnipotent

**omnipresente** [om·ni·pre·'sen·te] *adj* ubiquitous

**omoplato** [o·mo·'pla·to] *m*, **omóplato** [o·'mo·pla·to] *m* ANAT scapula, shoulder blade

**once** ['on·θe] **I.** *adj inv* eleven ▶ **estar**

**a las** ~ (*ropa*) to be askew **II.** *m* eleven; *v. t.* **ocho**

**ONCE** ['on·θe] *f abr de* **Organización Nacional de Ciegos Españoles** *Spanish national organization for the blind*

**onceno, -a** [on·'θe·no, -a] *adj* eleventh; *v. t.* **octavo**

**onda** ['on·da] *f. t.* FÍS, RADIO wave; ~ **explosiva** [*o* **expansiva**] shockwave; ~**s del pelo** waves *pl* of hair ▶ **¡qué buena** ~! *inf* that's really cool!; **estar en la misma** ~ to be on the same wavelength; **estar en la** ~ **de algo** *inf* (*seguir*) to keep up with sth

**ondear** [on·de·'ar] *vi* (*formar*) to undulate; (*moverse*) to ripple; (*bandera*) to flutter

**ondulado, -a** [on·du·'la·do, -a] *adj* wavy; **cartón** ~ corrugated cardboard

**ONG** [o.e·ne·'xe] *f abr de* **Organización No Gubernamental** NGO

**ONU** ['o·nu] *f abr de* **Organización de las Naciones Unidas** UNO

**onza** ['on·sa, -θa] *f* ounce

**opa** ['o·pa] *mf* CSur **1.** (*retrasado mental*) mental retard **2.** (*simple*) fool

**opacar** <c → qu> [o·pa·'kar] *vt* **1.** AmL (*hacer opaco*) to darken **2.** Méx (*superar*) to outshine

**opaco, -a** [o·'pa·ko, -a] *adj* **1.** (*no transparente*) opaque **2.** (*sin brillo*) dull; (*oscuro*) gloomy **3.** (*persona, voz*) gloomy

**opción** [op·'sjon, -β·'θjon] *f* **1.** (*elección*) choice; (*posibilidad*) option; ~ **del menú** COMPUT menu option **2.** (*derecho*) right **3.** ECON, JUR option; ~ **de compra** option to purchase

**opcional** [op·sjo·'nal, oβ·θjo-] *adj* optional

**OPEP** [o·'pep] *f abr de* **Organización de Países Exportadores de Petróleo** OPEC

**ópera** ['o·pe·ra] *f* opera; **teatro de la** ~ opera house; ~ **prima** CINE, LIT author's first work

**operación** [o·pe·ra·'sjon, -'θjon] *f* **1.** MAT, MED operation; ~ **quirúrgica** surgical operation **2.** (*actividad*) activity; (*negocio*) transaction; ~ **de saneamiento** clean-up operation

**operador(a)** [o·pe·ra·'dor] *m(f)* COMPUT, TEL operator

**operar** [o·pe·'rar] **I.** *vi* **1.** (*actuar*) t. MIL to operate **2.** COM to do business **3.** (*tener efecto*) to take effect **II.** *vt* MED to operate on **III.** *vr:* **~se** to have an operation

**operario, -a** [o·pe·'ra·rjo, -a] *m, f* worker

**operativo, -a** [o·pe·ra·'ti·βo, -a] *adj* **1.** (*efectivo*) operative **2.** COMPUT **sistema ~** operating system

**opinar** [o·pi·'nar] *vi, vt* to think; **~ bien/mal de algo/alguien** to have a good/bad opinion of sth/sb; **¿tú qué opinas de** [*o* **sobre**] **esto?** what do you think about this?; **¿puedo ~?** can I say what I think?

**opinión** [o·pi·'njon] *f* opinion; (*postura*) stance; (*punto de vista*) viewpoint; **en mi ~** in my opinion; **cambiar de ~** to change one's opinion [*o* mind]; **dar su ~** (**sobre algo**) to express an opinion (about sth); **ser de otra/la misma ~** to be of a different/the same opinion; **tener buena/mala ~ de algo/alguien** to have a good/bad opinion of sth/sb

**opio** [o·'pjo] *m* opium

**oponente** [o·po·'nen·te] *mf* opponent

**oponer** [o·po·'ner] *irr como* **poner I.** *vt* **1.** (*enfrentar*) to oppose; (*confrontar*) to confront **2.** (*objetar*) to object; **~ resistencia** to offer resistance **II.** *vr:* **~se 1.** (*rechazar*) to object; **~se a algo** to oppose sth **2.** (*enfrentarse*) to oppose each other **3.** (*obstaculizar*) to hinder **4.** (*ser contrario*) to be opposed **5.** (*estar enfrente*) to be opposite

**oporto** [o·'por·to] *m* CULIN port (wine)

**oportunidad** [o·por·tu·ni·'dad] *f* **1.** (*posibilidad*) chance; (*ocasión*) opportunity; **una segunda ~** a second chance; **aprovechar la ~** to make the most of the opportunity; (**no**) **tener ~ de...** (not) to have the opportunity of... **2.** (*cualidad*) opportuneness; (*temporal*) timeliness; (*adecuación*) appropriateness

**oportuno, -a** [o·por·'tu·no, -a] *adj* **1.** (*adecuado, apropiado*) appropriate; **en el momento ~** at the right moment **2.** (*propicio*) opportune **3.** (*al caso*) relevant

**oposición** [o·po·si·'sjon, -'θjon] *f* **1.** (*resistencia*) t. POL opposition; **encontrar ~** to meet opposition; **presentar ~** to oppose **2.** (*objeción*) objection **3.** (*contraposición*) comparison **4.** (*pl*) UNIV (competitive) examination *(for a public-sector job)*; **por ~** by examination

**opositar** [o·po·si·'tar] *vi* **~ a algo** to sit an examination for sth

**opositor(a)** [o·po·si·'tor, -·'to·ra] **I.** *adj* opposing; **partido ~** opposing party **II.** *m(f)* **1.** (*oponente*) t. POL opponent **2.** (*candidato*) candidate *(in examination for a public-sector job)*

**opresión** [o·pre·'sjon] *f* **1.** (*angustia*) anxiety **2.** (*represión*) oppression **3.** (*presión*) pressure

**opresor(a)** [o·pre·'sor, -·'so·ra] **I.** *adj* oppressive **II.** *m(f)* oppressor

**oprimir** [o·pri·'mir] *vt* **1.** (*presionar*) to press **2.** (*agobiar*) to weigh down **3.** (*reprimir*) to oppress

**optar** [op·'tar] *vi* **1.** (*escoger*) **~ por algo/alguien** to opt for sth/sb **2.** (*aspirar*) to aspire **3.** (*solicitar*) **~ a un cargo** to apply for a position

**optativo, -a** [op·ta·'ti·βo, -a] *adj* optional; (*asignatura*) **optativa** optional subject

**óptica** [op·ti·ka] *f* **1.** FÍS optics *pl* **2.** (*establecimiento*) optician's **3.** (*punto de vista*) viewpoint; **bajo esta ~** according to this point of view

**óptico, -a** [op·ti·ko, -a] **I.** *adj* **1.** ANAT optic; **nervio ~** optic nerve **2.** FÍS optical **II.** *m, f* optician

**optimismo** [op·ti·'mis·mo] *m* optimism

**optimista** [op·ti·'mis·ta] *adj* optimistic

**optimizar** [op·ti·mi·'sar, -'θar] *vt* to optimize

**óptimo** [op·ti·mo] *m* optimum

**óptimo, -a** [op·ti·mo, -a] **I.** *superl de* **bueno II.** *adj* (*very*) best; (*excelente*) excellent

**opuesto, -a** [o·'pwes·to] **I.** *pp de* **oponer II.** *adj* **1.** (*enfrente*) opposite; **al lado ~** on the other side; **en dirección opuesta** in the opposite direction **2.** (*diverso*) different; (*contrario, enfrentado*) opposing; **polo ~** t. *fig* opposite pole; **el sexo ~** the opposite sex **3.** (*enemigo*) enemy

**oración** [o·ra·'sjon, -'θjon] f 1. REL prayer; **decir una ~** to say a prayer 2. (*frase*) sentence; LING clause; **~ coordinada/subordinada** coordinate/subordinate clause; **~ simple/compuesta** simple/compound sentence

**oráculo** [o·'ra·ku·lo] m oracle

**orador(a)** [o·ra·'dor, -·'do·ra] m(f) orator

**oral** [o·'ral] adj oral; **por vía ~** MED orally

**órale** ['o·ra·le] interj Méx (*animar*) come on; (*oiga*) hey; (*acuerdo*) OK, right

**orar** [o·'rar] vi elev **~ por algo** to pray for sth

**órbita** ['or·βi·ta] f 1. ASTR, FÍS orbit; **~ terrestre** terrestrial orbit; **poner en ~** to put into orbit; **estar en ~** fig to be up to date; **estar fuera de ~** fig to be out of touch 2. (*ámbito*) sphere 3. ANAT eye socket; **se me salían los ojos de las ~s** fig I couldn't believe my eyes

**orca** ['or·ka] f killer whale

**orden¹** <órdenes> ['or·den] m 1. (*organización*) t. REL order; **en ~** in order; **llamar al ~** to call to order; **poner en ~** to put in order; **ser persona de ~** to be orderly; fig to be upright 2. (*sucesión*) order; **en** [o **por**] **su** (**debido**) **~** in the right order; **por ~** by order; **por ~ de antigüedad** in order of seniority 3. (*categoría*) rank; **de primer/segundo ~** first-rate/second-rate; **del ~ de** in the order of

**orden²** <órdenes> ['or·den] f 1. (*mandato*) order; **~ de registro** search warrant; **órdenes son órdenes** orders are orders; **¡a la ~!** yes, sir!; **dar/cumplir una ~** to give/obey an order; **estar a las órdenes de alguien** to be at sb's command; **hasta nueva ~** until further notice; **estar a la ~ del día** fig to be the order of the day 2. COM, REL order; **~ de entrega** delivery order; **~ de pago** payment order; **por ~** by order; **por ~ de** to the order of; **entrar en una ~** (*religiosa*) to join a religious order

**ordenado, -a** [or·de·'na·do, -a] adj 1. *estar* (*en orden*) tidy, neat 2. *ser* (*persona*) organized

**ordenador** [or·de·na·'dor] m computer; **~ de a bordo** car computer; **~ personal** personal computer; **~ portátil**

laptop computer; **asistido por ~** computer-aided

**ordenar** [or·de·'nar] vt 1. (*arreglar*) to organize; (*habitación, armario*) to tidy; (*colocar*) to arrange; (*clasificar*) to order 2. (*mandar*) to order 3. REL to ordain

**ordeñar** [or·de·'ɲar] vt to milk

**ordinal** [or·di·'nal] adj, m ordinal

**ordinario, -a** [or·di·'na·rjo, -a] adj 1. (*habitual*) usual; **de ~** usually 2. (*grosero*) rude 3. t. JUR (*regular*) ordinary

**orégano** [o·'re·ɣa·no] m oregano

**oreja** [o·'re·xa] f 1. ANAT ear; **aguzar las ~s** to prick up one's ears; **calentar las ~s a alguien** to box sb's ears; fig to give sb an earful 2. (*lateral*) flap ▶ **ver las ~s al lobo** to have a close shave; **con las ~s gachas** with one's tail between one's legs; **agachar las ~s** to lose heart

**orfanato** [or·fa·'na·to] m orphanage

**orfebre** [or·'fe·βre] mf (*orífice*) goldsmith; (*platero*) silversmith

**orgánico, -a** [or·'ɣa·ni·ko, -a] adj organic; **Ley Orgánica del Estado** basic law

**organillo** [or·ɣa·'ni·jo, -ʎo] m barrel organ

**organismo** [or·ɣa·'nis·mo] m 1. ANAT, BIO organism 2. (*institución*) body; **~ oficial** official body

**organización** [or·ɣa·ni·sa·'sjon, -θa·'θjon] f organization; **Organización del Tratado del Atlántico Norte** North Atlantic Treaty Organization; **Organización No Gubernamental** Non-Governmental Organization

**organizado, -a** [or·ɣa·ni·'sa·do, -a; -·'θa·do, -a] adj organized

**organizador(a)** [or·ɣa·ni·sa·'dor, -θa·'dor] I. adj organizing; **comité ~** organizing committee II. m(f) (*de un evento*) organizer

**organizar** <z → c> [or·ɣa·ni·'sar, -'θar] I. vt to organize; (*una fiesta*) to hold II. vr: **~se** 1. (*asociarse*) to organize oneself 2. (*surgir*) to break out; **¡menuda se organizó!** all hell broke loose! 3. (*ordenar*) to arrange; **~se el tiempo** to organize one's time

**organizativo, -a** [or·ɣa·ni·sa·'ti·βo, -a; or·ɣa·ni·θa·] adj organizing

**órgano** ['or·ɣa·no] m 1. (*organismo*) t.

ANAT organ; **~ judicial** judicial body; **~s sexuales** sexual organs **2.** MÚS organ; **~ electrónico** electric organ

**orgasmo** [or·'γas·mo] *m* orgasm

**orgía** [or·'xi·a] *f* orgy; (*desenfreno*) wildness, disinhibition

**orgullo** [or·'γu·ʝo, -ʎo] *m* **1.** (*satisfacción*) pride; **sentir ~ por alguien/algo** to be proud of sb/sth; **tener el ~ de...** to be proud to...; **~ propio** self-respect **2.** (*soberbia*) arrogance

**orgulloso, -a** [or·γu·'ʝo·so, a; -'ʎo·so, -a] *adj* **1.** *estar* (*satisfecho*) proud; **sentirse ~ de algo/alguien** to feel proud of sth/sb **2.** *ser* proud; (*soberbio*) arrogant

**orientación** [o·rjen·ta·'sjon, -'θjon] *f* **1.** (*situación*) situation **2.** (*posición*) position **3.** (*ajuste*) adjustment **4.** (*asesoramiento*) advice; (*dirección*) management; **~ profesional** [*o* vocacional] guidance **5.** (*tendencia*) inclination; **~ política** political orientation; **~ sexual** sexual orientation

**oriental** [o·rjen·'tal] *adj* **1.** (*del Este*) eastern **2.** (*del Extremo Oriente*) oriental

**orientar** [o·rjen·'tar] **I.** *vt* **1.** (*dirigir*) to direct; **orientado a la práctica** with a practical focus **2.** (*ajustar*) to adjust **3.** (*asesorar*) to advise **4.** (*dirigir*) to manage **II.** *vr:* **~se 1.** (*dirigirse*) to orient oneself; *fig* to find one's bearings; **~se bien** to have a good sense of direction; **se orientó muy bien en el trabajo** he/she settled in well in the job **2.** (*tender*) to tend

**oriente** [o·rjen·te] *m* **1.** GEO east; **Oriente Próximo** the Near East; **el Lejano Oriente** the Far East **2.** (*viento*) easterly

**orificio** [o·ri·'fi·sjo, -θjo] *m* orifice; (*abertura*) opening; **~ de salida** outlet

**origen** [o·'ri·xen] *m* **1.** (*principio*) origin; **texto/idioma de ~** source text/language **2.** (*causa*) cause; **dar ~ a algo** to give rise to sth; **tener su ~ en algo** to have its origins in sth **3.** (*ascendencia*) descent **4.** (*procedencia*) origin; **de ~ español** of Spanish origin

**original** [o·ri·xi·'nal] **I.** *adj* **1.** (*auténtico, creativo*) original; **versión ~** original version **2.** (*originario*) originating

**3.** (*singular*) peculiar **II.** *m* original; **fiel al ~** faithful to the original

**originalidad** [o·ri·xi·na·li·'dad] *f* **1.** (*autenticidad, creatividad*) originality **2.** (*singularidad*) peculiarity

**originar** [o·ri·xi·'nar] **I.** *vt* **1.** (*causar*) to cause **2.** (*provocar*) to provoke **II.** *vr:* **~se 1.** (*tener el origen*) to originate **2.** (*surgir*) to arise **3.** (*proceder*) **~se en algo** to spring from sth

**originario, -a** [o·ri·xi·'na·rjo, -a] *adj* **1.** (*oriundo*) native; **es ~ de Chile** he comes from Chile **2.** (*de origen*) **país ~** country of origin

**orilla** [o·'ri·ja, -ʎa] *f* **1.** (*borde*) edge **2.** (*ribera*) bank; **a ~s del Orinoco** on the banks of the Orinoco **3.** *pl AmL* (*arrabales*) outskirts *pl*

**orillero, -a** [o·ri·'je·ro, -a; -'ʎe·ro, -a] **I.** *adj AmL pey* **1.** (*arrabalero*) low class **2.** (*grosero*) coarse **II.** *m, f AmL pey* **1.** (*arrabalero*) common person **2.** (*grosero*) ill-bred person

**orina** [o·'ri·na] *f* <orines> urine

**orinal** [o·ri·'nal] *m* chamber pot; (*de niño*) potty

**orinar** [o·ri·'nar] **I.** *vi, vt* to urinate **II.** *vr:* **~se** to wet oneself; **~se en la cama** to wet the bed

**orla** ['or·la] *f* (*foto*) graduating-class photo [*o* picture]

**oro** ['o·ro] *m* gold; **~ de ley** fine gold; **bañado en ~** gold-plated; **de ~** gold; **color ~** golden; **hacerse de ~** to make one's fortune ► **prometer a alguien el ~ y el moro** to promise sb the earth; **mi palabra es ~** my word is my honor; **guardar como ~ en paño** to treasure; **no es ~ todo lo que reluce** *prov* all that glitters is not gold *prov*

**orquesta** [or·'kes·ta] *f* MÚS orchestra

**orquídea** [or·'ki·dea] *f* orchid

**ortiga** [or·'ti·γa] *f* nettle

**ortodoncia** [or·to·'don·sja, -θja] *f* MED orthodontics *pl*

**ortodoxo, -a** [or·to·'dok·so, -a] **I.** *adj* orthodox **II.** *m, f* orthodox

**ortografía** [or·to·γra·'fi·a] *f* spelling; **falta de ~** spelling mistake

**ortográfico, -a** [or·to·'γra·fi·ko, -a] *adj* spelling

**O**

**ortopeda** [or·to·'pe·da] *mf* MED orthopedist

**ortopedia** [or·to·'pe·dja] *f* MED orthopedics

**ortopédico, -a** [or·to·'pe·di·ko, -a] *adj* MED orthopedic; **pierna ortopédica** artificial leg

**oruga** [o·'ru·ɣa] *f* **1.** ZOOL caterpillar **2.** TÉC caterpillar track

**orujo** [o·'ru·xo] *m* **1.** (*residuo*) marc **2.** (*aguardiente*) ≈ grappa

**os** [os] **I.** *pron pers* (*objeto directo e indirecto*) you **II.** *pron reflexivo* yourselves; **¿~ marcháis?** are you leaving?

**osadía** [o·sa·'di·a] *f* daring

**osado, -a** [o·'sa·do, -a] *adj* daring

**osar** [o·'sar] *vi* to dare; **¿cómo osas decir esto?** how dare you say that!

**oscilación** [o·si·la·'sjon, os·θi·la·'θjon] *f* **1.** (*vaivén*) oscillation **2.** (*variación*) fluctuation **3.** (*indecisión*) indecision

**oscilar** [o·si·lar, os·θi·'lar] *vi* **1.** (*en vaivén*) to oscillate **2.** (*péndulo*) to swing **3.** (*variar*) to fluctuate

**oscilatorio, -a** [o·si·la·'to·rjo, os·θi·la·'to·rjo, -a] *adj* oscillatory

**oscurecer** [os·ku·re·'ser, -θer] *irr como crecer* **I.** *vimpers* to get dark **II.** *vt* *fig* (*privar de luz*) to darken **III.** *vr:* **~se** *t. fig* (*volverse oscuro*) to darken **IV.** *m* dusk; **al ~** at dusk

**oscurecimiento** [os·ku·re·θi·'mjen·to] *m t. fig* darkening

**oscuridad** [os·ku·ri·'dad] *f* **1.** (*falta de luz*) darkness; **en la ~** in the dark **2.** (*falta de claridad*) obscurity

**oscuro, -a** [os·'ku·ro, -a] *adj* dark; *fig* obscure; **azul ~** dark blue; **a oscuras** in the dark; **de ~ origen** of obscure origin

**óseo, -a** [o·'se·o, -a] *adj* bony

**oso** [o·so] *m* bear; **~ de peluche** teddy bear; **fuerte como un ~** as strong as an ox

**ostensible** [os·ten·'si·βle] *adj* obvious; **hacer ~** to make evident

**ostentar** [os·ten·'tar] *vt* **1.** (*mostrar*) to show; (*jactarse*) to flaunt **2.** (*poseer*) to have; (*puesto, poder*) to hold

**ostentoso, -a** [os·ten·'to·so, -a] *adj* **1.** (*jactancioso*) ostentatious **2.** (*llamativo*) showy

**ostra** [os·tra] *f* oyster ▶ **aburrirse como una ~** *inf* to be bored to death; **¡~s!** *inf*Jesus!

**OTAN** [o·'tan] *f abr de* **Organización del Tratado del Atlántico Norte** NATO

**otitis** [o·'ti·tis] *f inv* MED (*dolor*) earache; (*infección*) ear infection

**otomano, -a** [o·to·'ma·no, -a] *adj, m, f* Ottoman

**otomía** [o·to·'mi·a] *f Arg, Col* atrocity

**otoñal** [o·to·'ɲal] *adj* autumnal

**otoño** [o·'to·ɲo] *m* autumn, fall; **a fin(al) es de ~** at the end of autumn [*o* fall]; **el ~ (de la vida)** the autumn (of one's life)

**otorgar** <g → gu> [o·tor·'ɣar] *vt* **1.** (*conferir*) to confer; **~ poderes** to confer powers **2.** (*conceder*) to concede; (*ayudas*) to offer **3.** (*expedir*) to issue; **~ licencia** to grant a license **4.** (*acceder*) **~ algo** to agree to sth

**otorrinolaringólogo, -a** [o·to·rri·no·la·rin·'go·lo·ɣo, -a] *m, f* MED ear, nose and throat specialist

**otro, -a** ['o·tro, -a] **I.** *adj* another, other; **al ~ día** the next day; **el ~ día** the other day; **en otra ocasión** another time; **la otra semana** the other week; **en ~ sitio** in another place, somewhere else; **otra cosa** another thing; **~ tanto** as much again; **otra vez** again; **¡otra vez será!** maybe another time!; **eso ya es otra cosa** that is much better; **¡hasta otra (vez)!** until the next time! **II.** *pron indef* **1.** (*distinto: cosa*) another (one); (*persona*) someone else; **~s** others; **el ~/la otra/lo ~** the other (one); **ninguna otra persona ningún ~** nobody else; **de un sitio a ~** from one place to another; **no ~ que...** none other than...; **ésa es otra** (*cosa distinta*) that is different **2.** (*uno más*) another; **otras tres personas** three more people; **¡otra, otra!** more!

**ovación** [o·βa·'sjon, -'θjon] *f* ovation; **dar/recibir una ~** to give/receive an ovation

**oval** [o·'βal] *adj*, **ovalado, -a** [o·βa·'la·do, -a] *adj* oval

**ovario** [o·'βa·rjo] *m* ANAT ovary

**oveja** [o·'βe·xa] *f* sheep *inv*; (*hembra*)

ewe; **la ~ negra de la familia** the black sheep of the family ► **cada ~ con su pareja** *prov* birds of a feather flock together *prov*

**ovillo** [o·ˈβi·ʝo, -ʎo] *m* ball; *fig* tangle; **hacerse un ~** (*enredarse*) to get tangled up; (*encogerse*) to curl up into a ball

**ovino, -a** [o·ˈβi·no, -a] *adj* sheep; **ganado ~** sheep *pl*

**ovni** [ˈoβ·ni] *m* UFO

**ovulación** [o·βu·la·ˈsjon, -ˈθjon] *f* ovulation

**óvulo** [ˈo·βu·lo] *m* ANAT ovule

**oxidación** [ok·si·da·ˈsjon, -ˈθjon] *f* **1.** QUÍM oxidation **2.** (*metal*) rusting

**oxidar** [ok·si·ˈdar] I. *vt* **1.** QUÍM to oxidize **2.** (*metal*) to rust; **un hierro oxidado** a piece of rusty iron II. *vr:* **~se 1.** (*metal*) to rust; (*mente*) to go rusty **2.** QUÍM to oxidize

**óxido** [ˈok·si·do] *m* **1.** QUÍM oxide **2.** (*orín*) rust

**oxigenar** [ok·si·xe·ˈnar] I. *vt* **1.** (*cabello*) to bleach **2.** to oxygenate; **agua oxigenada** (hydrogen) peroxide II. *vr:* **~se** *inf* to get some fresh air

**oxígeno** [ok·ˈsi·xe·no] *m* QUÍM oxygen

**oyente** [o·ˈʝen·te] *mf* listener

**ozono** [o·ˈθo·no] *m* QUÍM ozone; **el agujero en la capa de ~** the hole in the ozone layer

# P

**P, p** [pe] *f* P, p; **~ de París** P as in Papa

**pabellón** [pa·βe·ˈʝon, -ˈʎon] *m* **1.** (*tienda*) bell tent **2.** (*bandera*) flag **3.** ARQUIT pavilion

**pacer** [pa·ˈser, -ˈθer] *irr como crecer vi, vt* to graze

**pacha** [ˈpa·ʧa] *f* **1.** *Nic, Méx* (*botella aplanada*) flask **2.** *Nic* (*biberón*) baby's bottle

**pachacho, -a** [pa·ˈʧa·ʧo, -a] *adj Chile* short-legged

**pachanga** [pa·ˈʧaŋ·ga] *f* **1.** *Cuba* (*danza*) Cuban dance **2.** *Col inf* (*fiesta*) party

**pachón, -ona** [pa·ˈʧon, -·ˈʧo·na] *adj AmL* (*peludo*) hairy

**pachucho, -a** [pa·ˈʧu·ʧo, -a] *adj* **1.** *inf* (*persona*) off-color **2.** (*fruta*) overripe

**paciencia** [pa·ˈsjen·sja, -·ˈθjen·θja] *f* patience; **se me ha acabado la ~** I've run out of patience

**paciente** [pa·ˈsjen·te, ˈθjen·te] I. *adj* patient; **ser ~ con alguien** to be patient with sb II. *mf* patient

**pacífico, -a** [pa·ˈsi·fi·ko, -a, -ˈθi·fi·ko, -a] *adj* peaceful

**Pacífico** [pa·ˈsi·fi·ko, -ˈθi·fi·ko] *m* Pacific (Ocean)

**pacifismo** [pa·si·ˈfis·mo, -ˈθi·ˈfis·mo] *m* pacifism

**pacifista** [pa·si·ˈfis·ta, -θi·ˈfista] *adj, mf* pacifist

**pacotilla** [pa·ko·ˈti·ja, -ʎa] *f* **1.** (*calidad inferior*) trashiness; **de ~** (*mercancía*) shoddy; (*restaurante*) second-rate **2.** *AmL* (*chusma*) rabble

**pactar** [pak·ˈtar] I. *vi* to come to an agreement II. *vt* to agree on

**pacto** [ˈpak·to] *m* agreement; (*contrato*) contract; **~ antiterrorista** antiterrorism pact

**padecer** [pa·de·ˈser, -ˈθer] *irr como crecer* I. *vi* to suffer II. *vt* **1.** (*sufrir*) to suffer; **~ algo** to suffer from sth **2.** (*soportar*) to endure

**padecimiento** [pa·de·θi·ˈmjen·to] *m* **1.** (*sufrimiento*) suffering **2.** (*enfermedad*) ailment

**padrastro** [pa·ˈdras·tro] *m* (*marido de madre*) stepfather

**padre** [ˈpa·dre] *m* **1.** *t.* REL father; **¡tu ~!** *inf* up yours! **2.** *pl* (*padre y madre*) parents *pl*

**padrenuestro** [pa·dre·ˈnwes·tro] *m* Lord's Prayer

**padrillo** [pa·ˈdri·jo, -ʎo] *m CSur* stallion

**padrino** [pa·ˈdri·no] *m* (*de bautizo*) godfather; (*de boda*) best man; **tener buenos ~s** *fig* to know the right people

**padrote** [pa·ˈdro·te] *m AmC, Méx* **1.** (*equino*) stallion; (*bovino*) breeding bull **2.** *inf* (*alcahuete*) pimp

**paella** [pa·ˈe·ja, -ʎa] *f* paella (*Spanish dish of rice, meat and fish, flavored and colored with saffron*)

**paellera** [pae·ˈje·ra, -ˈʎera] *f* paella dish

**pág.** [ˈpa·xi·na] *abr de* **página** p.

P

**paga** ['pa·ɣa] *f* **1.** (*sueldo*) pay **2.** (*acto*) payment

**pagano, -a** [pa·'ɣa·no, -a] *adj* pagan

**pagar** <g → gu> [pa·'ɣar] *vt* **1.** (*gastos*) to pay; (*una deuda*) to repay; ~ **un anticipo** to make an advance payment **2.** (*expiar*) to atone for; **¡me las ~ás!** you'll pay for this! **3.** (*recompensar*) to repay; (*una visita*) to return; **¡Dios se lo pague!** God will reward you!

**pagaré** [pa·ɣa·'re] *m* promissory note, IOU

**página** ['pa·xi·na] *f* page; **pasar (la)** ~ to turn the page; **~s blancas** telephone directory; **~s amarillas** TEL yellow pages; ~ **web** COMPUT web site

**pago** ['pa·ɣo] *m* **1.** payment; ~ **adicional** supplement; ~ **inicial** down payment; ~ **a plazos** payment in installments; **día de** ~ pay day; **anticipar el** ~ to pay in advance; **sujeto a** ~ subject to payment; ~ **anticipado** advance payment **2.** *fig* (*recompensa*) reward; **¿éste es el** ~ **que me das?** is this how you repay me? **3.** *Arg, Perú* (*de nacimiento*) home region

**paila** ['pai·la] *f AmL* (*sartén*) frying pan

**país** [pa·'is] *m* country; ~ **comunitario** member state *(of the European Union)*; ~ **industrializado** industrialized country; ~ **limítrofe** neighboring country; ~ **en vías de desarrollo** developing country; ~ **en vías de industrialización** industrializing country

**paisa** ['pai·sa] *m AmL v.* **paisano**

**paisaje** [pai·'sa·xe] *m* landscape

**paisano, -a** [pai·'sa·no, -a] *m, f* **1.** (*no militar*) civilian; **ir de** ~ to be in plain clothes **2.** (*compatriota*) compatriot **3.** (*campesino*) peasant

**Países Bajos** [pa·'i·ses 'βa·xos] *mpl* Netherlands

**paja** ['pa·xa] *f* straw; **no dormirse en las** ~**s** *inf* to be alert; **hacerse una** ~ *vulg* to jerk off

**pajar** [pa·'xar] *m* haystack; (*lugar*) hayloft; **buscar una aguja en un** ~ *fig* to search for a needle in a haystack

**pajarita** [pa·xa·'ri·ta] *f* bow tie

**pájaro** ['pa·xa·ro] *m* bird; ~ **bobo** penguin; ~ **carpintero** woodpecker; **tener**

**la cabeza llena de** ~**s** to be scatter-brained ▶ **más vale** ~ **en mano que ciento volando** *prov* a bird in the hand is worth two in the bush

**pajita** [pa·'xi·ta] *f* (drinking) straw

**pajonal** [pa·xo·'nal] *m CSur* scrubland

**pajuela** [pa·'xwe·la] *f* **1.** *Bol* (*cerilla*) match **2.** *Bol, Col* (*mondadientes*) toothpick

**pajuerano, -a** [pa·xwe·'ra·no, -a] *m, f Arg, Bol, Urug* pey (*paleto*) country bumpkin, hick

**pala** ['pa·la] *f* **1.** (*para cavar*) spade; (*cuadrada*) shovel; ~ **mecánica** mechanical shovel; *AmL* bulldozer **2.** (*del timón*) rudder **3.** (*raqueta*) racket

**palabra** [pa·'la·βra] *f* word; ~ **clave** *t.* COMPUT keyword, password; ~**s cruzadas** crossword; ~**s mayores** strong words; **juego de** ~**s** pun, play on words; **de pocas** ~**s** quiet; **ahorrar** ~**s** not to waste one's words; **coger a alguien la** ~ to take sb at his/her word; **cumplir la** ~ to be as good as one's word; **dirigir la** ~ **a alguien** to speak to sb; **faltar a la** ~ to go back on one's word; **llevar la** ~ to speak; **medir las** ~**s** to choose one's words carefully; **no entender** ~ not to understand a single word; **quitar a alguien la** ~ **de la boca** to take the words right out of sb's mouth ▶ **dejar a alguien con la** ~ **en la boca** to interrupt sb; **a** ~**s necias oídos sordos** *prov* sticks and stones will break my bones, but names will never hurt me *prov*; **decir la última** ~ to have the last word; **de** ~ (*oral*) by word of mouth; (*que cumple sus promesas*) honorable

**palabrota** [pa·la·'βro·ta] *f* swearword

**palacio** [pa·'la·sjo, -θjo] *m* palace; **Palacio de Justicia** law courts; ~ **municipal** town hall

**paladar** [pa·la·'dar] *m* palate; **tener buen** ~ (*vino*) to be smooth on the palate; (*persona*) to have a discerning palate

**paladear** [pa·la·de·'ar] *vt* to savor

**palanca** [pa·'lan·ka] *f* **1.** (*pértiga*) lever; (*palanqueta*) crowbar; ~ **de mando** AVIAT, COMPUT joystick; ~ **de cambio** gearshift **2.** *AmL* (*influencia*) influence; **tener mucha** ~ to have a lot of influence

**palangana** [pa·lan·'ga·na] *f* washbasin

**palanquear** [pa·lan·ke·'ar] *vt AmL*
1. (*apalancar*) to lever 2. (*influenciar*)
to influence

**palco** ['pal·ko] *m* TEAT box

**Palestina** [pa·les·'ti·na] *m* Palestine

**palestino, -a** [pa·les·'ti·no, -a] *adj, m, f*
Palestinian

**paleta** [pa·'le·ta] *f* 1. (*pala*) (small) shovel; (*del albañil*) trowel 2. (*del pintor*)
palette 3. (*de turbinas*) blade 4. (*omóplato*) shoulder blade 5. *Col inf* (*helado*) popsicle

**paletilla** [pa·le·'ti·ja, -ʎa] *f* (*omóplato*)
shoulder blade

**paleto** [pa·'le·to] *m* fallow deer

**paliacate** [pa·lja·'ka·te] *m Méx* large
brightly colored scarf

**paliar** <*1. pres* palío, palio> [pa·'ljar] *vt*
(*enfermedad*) to alleviate

**palidecer** [pa·li·de·'ser, -θer] *irr como
crecer* vi 1. (*persona*) to turn pale
2. (*cosa*) to fade

**pálido, -a** ['pa·li·do, -a] *adj* pale; (*estilo*) flat

**palillo** [pa·'li·jo, -ʎo] *m* (small) stick; (*para
los dientes*) toothpick; (*para el tambor*)
drumstick

**palique** [pa·'li·ke] *m inf* chat; **estar de ~
con alguien** to chat to sb

**paliza** [pa·'li·sa, -θa] *f* beating; *inf* (*esfuerzo*) slog; **dar una buena ~** (*pegar*)
to beat up; (*derrotar*) to thrash; **¡no me
des la ~!** *fig* give me a break!; **pegarse
una ~ con algo** *inf* to exhaust oneself
with sth

**palma** ['pal·ma] *f* 1. (*palmera*) palm
(tree); (*hoja de palmera*) palm leaf; **llevarse la ~** to be the best 2. ANAT palm;
**conocer algo como la ~ de su mano**
*inf* to know sth like the back of one's
hand 3. *pl* (*ruido*) clapping; (*aplauso*)
applause; **tocar las ~s** to clap

**palmada** [pal·'ma·da] *f* (*golpe*) pat

**palmar** [pal·'mar] *vi inf* **-la** to kick the
bucket

**palmera** [pal·'me·ra] *f* palm (tree)

**palmo** ['pal·mo] *m* (hand) span ▶ **dejar a
alguien con un ~ de narices** to disappoint sb badly; **~ a ~** inch by inch

**palo** ['pa·lo] *m* 1. (*bastón*) stick; (*vara*)
pole; (*garrote*) club; (*estaca*) post; **~ de
la escoba** broomstick; **~ de hockey**
hockey stick; **~ de la portería** goalpost
2. (*paliza*) beating; **dar ~s de ciego** *fig*
to grope in the dark; **dar un ~ a alguien**
*fig* to tear a strip off sb; (*cobrar mucho*)
to rip sb off; **echar a alguien a ~s** to
throw sb out; **liarse a ~s con alguien**
to come to blows with sb; **moler a alguien a ~s** to beat sb black and blue
▶ **~ de agua** *AmL* downpour; **no dar
un ~ al agua** not to do a stick of work;
**de tal ~, tal astilla** *prov* like father, like
son; **ser un ~** to be a setback

**paloma** [pa·'lo·ma] *f* (*ave*) pigeon; (*blanca, como símbolo*) dove; **~ mensajera**
carrier pigeon

**palomitas** [pa·lo·'mi·tas] *fpl* CULIN popcorn

**palpable** [pal·'pa·βle] *adj* palpable; (*evidente*) clear

**palpar** [pal·'par] *vt* 1. (*tocar*) to touch
2. (*percibir*) to feel; **se palpaba el
entusiasmo** you could feel the enthusiasm

**palpitar** [pal·pi·'tar] *vi* (*contraerse*) to
shudder; (*corazón, pulso*) to throb

**palta** ['pal·ta] *f AmS* BOT avocado (pear)

**palto** ['pal·to] *m CSur* BOT avocado pear
tree

**paludismo** [pa·lu·'dis·mo] *m* MED malaria

**palurdo, -a** [pa·'lur·do, -a] *m, f* yokel, hick

**pampa** ['pam·pa] *f* GEO pampas + *sing/
pl vb*

**pampear** [pam·pe·'ar] *vi CSur* to travel
over the pampas

**pampero, -a** [pam·'pe·ro] *adj* of/from
the Pampas

**pamplina** [pam·'pli·na] *f inf* (*pamema*)
silly thing

**pan** [pan] *m* bread; **~ de azúcar** sugar
loaf; **~ integral** wholegrain bread; **~
con mantequilla** bread and butter; **~
de molde** sliced bread; **~ rallado** breadcrumbs *pl*; **estar a ~ y agua** to be on (a
strict diet of) bread and water; **ganarse
el ~** to earn one's living ▶ **no sólo de
~ vive el hombre** man cannot live by

**P**

bread alone; **a falta de ~, buenas son** <u>tortas</u> *prov* half a loaf is better than none; (**llamar**) **al ~, ~ y al** <u>vino</u>, **vino** *inf* to call a spade a spade; **ser más** <u>bue-</u> <u>no</u> **que el ~** to be very good-natured; **ser ~** <u>comido</u> *inf* to be dead easy; **con su ~ se lo** <u>coma</u> *inf* that's his/her lookout [*o* problem]

**pana** ['pa·na] *f* corduroy

**panacea** [pa·na·'sea, -'θea] *f* panacea, cure-all

**panadería** [pa·na·de·'ri·a] *f* bakery

**panadero, -a** [pa·na·'de·ro, -a] *m, f* baker

**panal** [pa·'nal] *m* honeycomb

**Panamá** [pa·na·'ma] *m* Panama

**panameño, -a** [pa·na·'me·ɲo, -a] *adj, m, f* Panamanian

**pancarta** [paŋ·'kar·ta] *f* placard

**pancho** ['pan·tʃo] *m Arg* (*perrito calien-te*) hotdog

**pancho, -a** ['pan·tʃo, -a] *adj* calm

**páncreas** ['paŋ·kreas] *m inv* pancreas

**panda**[1] ['pan·da] *m* ZOOL panda

**panda**[2] ['pan·da] *f v.* pandilla

**pandereta** [pan·de·'re·ta] *f*, **pandero** [pan·'de·ro] *m* MÚS tambourine

**pandilla** [pan·'di·ja, -ʎa] *f* band; (*de amigos*) group; **~ de ladrones** gang of thieves

**panecillo** [pa·ne·'si·jo, -'θi·ʎo] *m* roll

**panel** [pa·'nel] *m* panel; **~ de control** control panel

**panela** [pa·'ne·la] *f* 1. (*bizcocho*) corn cake 2. *Col, CRi, Hond* (*azúcar*) brown sugar loaf

**pánfilo, -a** ['pan·fi·lo, -a] *adj* 1. (*fácil de engañar*) gullible 2. (*lento*) slow

**panfleto** [pan·'fle·to] *m* pamphlet; *fig* propaganda

**pánico** ['pa·ni·ko] *m* panic; **tener ~ a algo** to be terrified of sth

**pánico, -a** ['pa·ni·ko, -a] *adj* panic

**panocha** [pa·'no·tʃa] *f*, **panoja** [pa·'no·xa] *f* 1. (*de maíz*) corncob 2. (*espiga*) ear of corn; (*racimo*) cornstalk

**panoli** [pa·'no·li] *adj inf* idiotic

**panorama** [pa·no·'ra·ma] *m* panorama; *fig* outlook

**pantaleta(s)** [pan·ta·'le·ta(s)] *f(pl) Méx, Ven* (*bragas*) panties *pl*

**pantalla** [pan·'ta·ja, -ʎa] *f* 1. (*de la lám-para*) shade 2. (*protección*) screen 3. COMPUT, TV, CINE screen; **~ panorámi-ca** wide screen; **pequeña ~** *inf* TV

**pantalón** [pan·ta·'lon] *m* trousers *pl*, pants *pl*, pair of pants; **~ tejano** [*o* va-quero] jeans *pl*; **llevar los pantalones** *fig* to wear the trousers [*o* pants]

**pantano** [pan·'ta·no] *m* (*ciénaga*) marsh; (*laguna*) swamp

**pantanoso, -a** [pan·ta·'no·so, -a] *adj* marshy

**panteón** [pan·te·'on] *m* 1. HIST pantheon 2. (*sepultura*) tomb; **~ de familia** family vault 3. *AmL* (*cementerio*) cemetery

**pantera** [pan·'te·ra] *f* panther

**pantimedia(s)** [pan·ti·'me·dja(s)] *f(pl) Méx* pantyhose

**pantis** ['pan·tis] *mpl inf* pantyhose

**pantomima** [pan·to·'mi·ma] *f* panto-mime

**pantorrilla** [pan·to·'rri·ja, -ʎa] *f* calf

**pantufla** [pan·'tu·fla] *f* slipper

**panucho** [pa·'nu·tʃo] *m Méx* meat and bean stuffed tortilla

**panza** ['pan·sa, -θa] *f* 1. (*barriga*) belly 2. ZOOL stomach; (*rumiantes*) rumen

**pañal** [pa·'ɲal] *m* diaper; **estar aún en ~es** *fig* to be still in its infancy

**pañetar** [pa·ɲe·'tar] *vt Col* (*una pared*) to plaster

**paño** ['pa·ɲo] *m* (*tejido, trapo*) cloth; **~ de cocina** (*para fregar*) dishcloth; (*para secar*) dish towel ► **~s** <u>meno-</u> <u>res</u> underwear

**pañoleta** [pa·ɲo·'le·ta] *f* fichu

**pañuelo** [pa·'ɲwe·lo] *m* 1. (*moquero*) handkerchief; **el mundo es un ~** it's a small world 2. (*pañoleta*) fichu; (*de cabeza*) headscarf, scarf

**papa**[1] ['pa·pa] *m* pope

**papa**[2] ['pa·pa] *f* 1. *reg, AmL* (*patata*) potato; **no entender ni ~** not to understand a thing 2. *pl* (*comida*) purée

**papá** [pa·'pa] *m inf* dad; **Papá Noel** Santa Claus; **los ~s** mom and dad

**papada** [pa·'pa·da] *f* (*de la persona*) double chin, jowl; (*del animal*) dewlap

**papagayo** [pa·pa·'ɟa·jo] *m* 1. (*loro*) par-rot 2. (*hablador*) chatterbox

**papaya** [pa·'pa·ja] *f* pawpaw, papaya

**papel** [pa·'pel] *m* **1.** (*para escribir, material*) paper; (*hoja*) piece of paper; (*escritura*) piece of writing; ~ **de calcar** tracing paper; ~ **de envolver** wrapping paper; ~ **de regalo** gift-wrap; ~ **de estraza** brown paper; ~ **de aluminio** aluminum [*o* tin] foil; ~ **de seda** tissue paper; ~ **higiénico** toilet paper; ~ **de lija** sandpaper; ~ **moneda** banknotes *pl,* bills *pl;* ~ **pintado** wallpaper; ~ **de plata** silver paper; ~ **reciclado** recycled paper; ~ **secante** blotting paper; ~ **mojado** *fig* worthless scrap of paper **2.** (*rol*) role; ~ **protagonista** leading role; ~ **secundario** supporting role; **hacer su** ~ to play one's part; **hacer buen/mal** ~ to make a good/bad impression **3.** *pl* (*documentos*) documentation; (*de identidad*) identity papers *pl*

**papeleo** [pa·pe·'leo] *m* paperwork

**papelera** [pa·pe·'le·ra] *f* **1.** (*cesto*) wastepaper basket; (*en la calle*) litter bin **2.** (*fábrica*) paper mill

**papelería** [pa·pe·le·'ri·a] *f* stationer's

**papelerío** [pa·pe·le·'ri·a] *m AmL* mass of papers

**papeleta** [pa·pe·'le·ta] *f* (*cédula*) slip of paper; ~ **de propaganda** flier

**papera** [pa·'pe·ra] *f* MED **1.** *pl* (*enfermedad*) mumps *pl* **2.** (*bocio*) goiter

**papilla** [pa·'pi·ja, -ʎa] *f* baby food; **echar la** (**primera**) ~ *inf* to be as sick as a dog; **hacer** ~ **a alguien** *fig* to beat hell out of sb; **estar hecho** ~ *fig* to be smashed to a pulp

**papiro** [pa·'pi·ro] *m* papyrus

**papo** ['pa·po] *m* **1.** *inf* (*bocio*) goiter **2.** (*papada*) double chin, jowl

**paquete** [pa·'ke·te] *m* **1.** *t. fig* (*atado*) packet; ~ **postal** *inf* to parcel **2.** *inf* (*castigo*) **meter un** ~ **a alguien** (*reprender*) to tell sb off; (*castigar*) to punish sb heavily **3.** *vulg* (*genitales*) basket; **marcar** ~ to show one's basket

**paquete, -a** [pa·'ke·te, -a] *adj Arg* smart

**paquetear** [pa·ke·te·'ar] *vi Arg, Urug inf* to show off one's outfit

**paquete-bomba** [pa·'ke·te··'βom·ba] *m* ‹paquetes-bomba› mail [*o* letter] bomb

**par** [par] **I.** *adj* **1.** (*número*) even; ~**es o**

**nones** odds or evens **2.** (*igual*) equal; **a la** ~ at the same time; **sin** ~ without equal ▸ **de** ~ **en** ~ wide open **II.** *m* **1.** (*dos cosas*) pair; **un** ~ **de zapatos/pantalones** a pair of shoes/pants **2.** (*algunos*) **un** ~ **de minutos** a couple of minutes

**para** ['pa·ra] **I.** *prep* **1.** (*destino*) for; **un regalo** ~ **el niño** a present for the child **2.** (*finalidad*) for; **servir** ~ **algo** to be useful for sth; **¿** ~ **qué es esto?** what is this for? **3.** (*dirección*) to; **voy** ~ **Madrid** I'm going to Madrid; **mira** ~ **acá** look over here **4.** (*duración*) for; ~ **siempre** forever; **vendrá** ~ **Navidad/finales de marzo** he/she will come for Christmas/towards the end of March; **estará listo** ~ **el viernes** it will be ready for [*o* by] Friday; **diez minutos** ~ **las once** *AmL* ten to eleven **5.** (*contraposición*) for; **es muy activo** ~ **la edad que tiene** he is very active for his age **6.** (*trato*) ~ (**con**) with; **es muy amable** ~ **con nosotros** he is very kind to us **7.** (+ *estar*) **estar** ~**...** (*disposición*) to be ready to...; (*a punto de*) about to...; **no estoy** ~ **bromas** I'm in no mood for jokes **8.** (*a juicio de*) ~ **mí, esto no es lo mismo** in my opinion, this is not the same **II.** *conj* **1.** + *infin* to; **he venido** ~ **darte las gracias** I came to thank you **2.** ~ **que** +*subj* so that; **te mando al colegio** ~ **que aprendas algo** I send you to school so that you learn sth

**parábola** [pa·'ra·βo·la] *f* **1.** (*alegoría*) parable **2.** MAT curve, parabola

**parabólica** [pa·ra·'βo·li·ka] *f* satellite dish

**parabrisas** [pa·ra·'βri·sas] *m inv* AUTO windshield

**paracaídas** [pa·ra·ka·'i·das] *m inv* parachute

**paracaidismo** [pa·ra·kai·'dis·mo] *m* parachuting

**paracaidista** [pa·ra·kai·'dis·ta] *mf* DEP parachutist; MIL paratrooper

**parachoques** [pa·ra·'tʃo·kes] *m inv* AUTO bumper

**parada** [pa·'ra·da] *f* **1.** (*de un autobús*) stop; ~ **de taxis** taxi rank **2.** (*acción de parar*) stopping; ~ **de una fábrica** fac-

P

tory stoppage; **hacer una ~ para descansar** to make a rest stop

**paradero** [pa·ra·'de·ro] *m* whereabouts; **está en ~ desconocido** his/her whereabouts are unknown

**paradisíaco, -a** [pa·ra·di·'si·a·ko, -a] *adj* heavenly

**parado, -a** [pa·'ra·do, -a] **I.** *adj* **1.** (*que no se mueve*) stationary; **estar ~** to be motionless; **quedarse ~** to remain motionless **2.** (*sin empleo*) unemployed **3.** (*remiso*) slow **4.** (*tímido*) shy **5.** *AmL* standing up ▸ **salir bien/mal ~ de algo** to come out of sth well/badly; **ser el peor ~** to be the worst off **II.** *m, f* unemployed person

**paradoja** [pa·ra·'do·xa] *f* paradox

**parador** [pa·ra·'dor] *m* inn; (*en España*) state-run luxury hotel

**paragolpes** [pa·ra·'ɣol·pes] *m inv AmL* bumper

**parágrafo** [pa·'ra·ɣra·fo] *m* paragraph

**paraguas** [pa·ra·'ɣwas] *m inv* umbrella

**Paraguay** [pa·ra·'ɣwai] *m* Paraguay

**paraguayo, -a** [pa·ra·'ɣwa·jo, -a] *adj, m, f* Paraguayan

**paragüero** [pa·ra·'ɣwe·ro] *m* umbrella stand

**paraíso** [pa·ra·'i·so] *m* **1.** (*en el cielo*) heaven; **~ terrenal** earthly paradise **2.** *Méx* (*gallinero*) henhouse

**paraje** [pa·'ra·xe] *m* (*lugar*) place; (*punto*) spot

**paralelo, -a** [pa·ra·'le·lo, -a] *adj* parallel; **líneas paralelas** parallel lines; **conexión en ~** ELEC parallel connection; **seguir caminos ~s** to develop along similar lines

**parálisis** [pa·'ra·li·sis] *f inv* paralysis

**paralítico, -a** [pa·ra·'li·ti·ko, -a] *adj* (*persona*) paralyzed

**paralización** [pa·ra·li·sa·'sjon, -θa·θjon] *f* (*de un proceso*) halting

**paralizar** <z → c> [pa·ra·li·'sar, -'θar] **I.** *vt* **1.** (*persona*) to paralyze; **el miedo/el frío la paralizó** she was paralyzed by fear/by the cold **2.** (*cosa*) to stop; **~ un transporte** to paralyze a means of transport **II.** *vr* **1.** (*persona*) to be paralyzed **2.** (*cosa*) to stop

**parámetro** [pa·'ra·me·tro] *m* parameter

**páramo** ['pa·ra·mo] *m* **1.** (*terreno desierto*) wilderness; (*infértil*) wasteland **2.** (*lugar desamparado*) exposed place

**paranoia** [pa·ra·'noja] *f* paranoia

**paranoico, -a** [pa·ra·'noi·ko, -a] *adj* paranoid

**parapetarse** [pa·ra·pe·'tar·se] *vr* to protect oneself

**parapeto** [pa·ra·'pe·to] *m* MIL parapet; (*barricada*) barricade

**parapléjico, -a** [pa·ra·'ple·xi·ko, -a] *adj, m, f* paraplegic

**parar** ['pa·rar] **I.** *vi* **1.** (*detenerse, cesar*) to stop; **la máquina funciona sin ~** the machine works non-stop; **mis hijos no me dejan ~** my kids never give me a break; **ha parado de llover** it has stopped raining; **no para (de trabajar)** he/she never stops (working) **2.** (*acabar*) to finish; **ir a ~ a...** to end up in...; **¿dónde iremos a ~?** what's the world coming to?; **¿en qué irá a ~ esto?** where will it all end?; **salir bien/mal parado de algo** to come out of sth well/badly; **¿dónde quieres ir a ~?** what are you getting at? **3.** (*alojarse, estar*) to live; **nunca para en casa** he/she is never at home; **siempre para en el mismo hotel** he/she always stays at the same hotel **II.** *vt* (*detener*) to stop; (*un golpe*) to block; (*un gol*) to save; (*el motor*) to turn off **III.** *vr* **1.** (*detenerse*) to stop; **~se a pensar** to stop and think; **~se a descansar** to stop to rest **2.** *AmL* (*levantarse*) to get up

**pararrayos** [pa·ra·'rra·jos] *m inv* lightning conductor

**parásito** [pa·'ra·si·to] *m t. fig* parasite

**parasol** [pa·ra·'sol] *m* sunshade; (*en el coche*) sun visor

**parcela** [par·'se·la, -'θe·la] *f* plot; **~ edificable** building plot

**parcelar** [par·se·'lar, par·θe·-] *vt* to parcel out

**parche** ['par·tʃe] *m* **1.** (*pegote*) patch; **~ para el ojo** eye patch; **poner un ~** to patch up **2.** (*retoque*) makeshift remedy; (*de pintura*) dab; **poner ~s** to patch up; *fig* to paper over the cracks

**parchís** [par·'tʃis] *m* Parcheesi®

**parcial** [par·'sjal, -'θjal] *adj* **1.** (*incomple-*

*to*) partial **2.** (*arbitrario*) biased

**parco, -a** ['par·ko, -a] *adj* **1.** (*moderado*) moderate; (*sobrio*) frugal **2.** (*escaso*) meager; **~ en palabras** of few words

**pardiez** [par·'djes, -'djeθ] *interj* HIST good gracious

**pardillo** [par·'di·jo, -ʎo] *m* linnet

**pardillo, -a** [par·'di·jo, -a; -ʎo, -a]. **I.** *adj inf* **1.** (*palurdo*) uncouth **2.** (*ingenuo*) simple **II.** *m, f* **1.** (*palurdo*) yokel **2.** (*ingenuo*) simpleton

**pardo, -a** ['par·do, -a] **I.** *adj* grayish-brown; **oso ~** brown bear; **de ojos ~s** brown-eyed **II.** *m, f AmL* mulatto

**parear** [pa·re·'ar] *vt* **1.** (*formar parejas*) to pair; (*atar*) to tie together; (*ropa*) to match up **2.** BIO to mate **3.** (*igualar*) to match

**parecer** [pa·re·'ser, -θer] **I.** *irr como crecer vi* to seem; (*aparentar*) to appear; **parece mayor de lo que es** he/ she seems older than he/she is; **parece mentira que** +*subj* it seems incredible that; **aunque parezca mentira** though it may seem incredible; **parece que va a llover** it looks like rain; **¿qué te parece?** what do you think?; **si te parece bien,...** if you agree,... **II.** *irr como crecer vr* to look alike; **te pareces mucho a tu madre** you look very much like your mother **III.** *m* **1.** (*opinión*) opinion; (*juicio*) judgment; **a mi ~** in my opinion; **esto es cuestión de ~es** this is a matter of opinion **2.** (*aspecto, apariencia*) appearance; **ser de buen ~** to be good-looking; **al ~** apparently

**parecido, -a** [pa·re·'si·do, -'θi·do] *m* similarity, likeness

**parecido, -a** [pa·re·'si·do, -a; -θi·do, -a] *adj* **1.** (*semejante*) similar **2.** (*de aspecto*) **ser bien/mal ~** (*persona*) to be good/bad-looking

**pared** [pa·'red] *f* wall; (*de una montaña*) face; (*separación*) partition; **~ abdominal** stomach wall; **~ maestra** (*load-bearing*) bearing wall ► **entre cuatro ~es** cooped up; **quedarse pegado a la ~** to be put on the spot; **hablar a la ~** to talk to a brick wall; **¡cuidado, que estas ~es oyen!** careful, walls have ears!; **subirse por las ~es** to go up the wall;

(*enfadarse*) to blow one's top; (*estar nervioso*) to be [*o* go] stir crazy

**pareja** [pa·'re·xa] *f* **1.** (*par*) couple; **~ de hecho** common law couple; **~s mixtas** DEP mixed doubles; **hacen buena ~** they make a good couple; **¿dónde está la ~ de este guante?** where is the other glove? **2.** (*compañero*) partner **3.** (*en los dados*) pair

**parentesco** [pa·ren·'tes·ko] *m* relationship, kinship

**paréntesis** [pa·'ren·te·sis] *m inv* **1.** (*signo*) bracket; **poner algo entre ~** to put sth in brackets; **abrir/cerrar el ~** to open/close brackets; *fig* to introduce/ finish a digression **2.** (*interrupción*) interruption; **hicimos un ~ para almorzar** we had a break for lunch

**paridad** [pa·ri·'dad] *f* **1.** FIN, ECON parity **2.** (*igualdad*) equality; (*semejanza*) similarity; **~ de fuerzas** parity of strength

**pariente, -a** [pa·'rjen·te, -a] **I.** *adj* related **II.** *m, f* **1.** (*familiar*) relative; **los ~s** the relations, the relatives; **~lejano/cercano** distant/close relative **2.** *inf* (*marido, mujer*) other half; **mi parienta** my missus

**paripé** [pa·ri·'pe] *m* show; **hacer el ~** to put on a show; (*fingir*) to pretend

**parir** [pa·'rir] **I.** *vt* to give birth to **II.** *vi* to give birth ► **poner a alguien a ~** *inf* to run sb down **P**

**París** [pa·'ris] *m* Paris

**parisiense** [pa·ri·'sjen·se] *adj, mf* Parisian

**parking** ['par·kin] *m* <parkings> parking lot

**parlamentario, -a** [par·la·men·'ta·rjo, -a] *adj* parliamentary; **debate ~** parliamentary debate

**parlamento** [par·la·'men·to] *m* parliament; **Parlamento Europeo** European Parliament

**parlanchín, -ina** [par·lan·'tʃin, --'tʃi·na] *adj inf* talkative

**paro** ['pa·ro] *m* **1.** (*parar: una fábrica*) shutdown; (*de trabajar*) stopping **2.** (*desempleo*) unemployment; **estar en ~** to be unemployed; **cobrar el ~** to be on the dole

**parodia** [pa·'ro·dja] *f* parody

**parpadear** [par·pa·de·'ar] *vi* **1.** (*ojos*) to blink; **sin ~** *fig* without a second thought **2.** (*luz, llama*) to flicker

**parpadeo** [par·pa·'deo] *m* **1.** (*de los ojos*) blinking **2.** (*de luz, llama*) flicker

**párpado** ['par·pa·do] *m* eyelid

**parque** ['par·ke] *m* **1.** (*jardín*) park; **~ de atracciones** amusement park; **~ natural** National Park; **~ zoológico** zoo **2.** (*depósito*) depot; **~ de bomberos** fire department; **~ militar** military depot **3.** (*conjunto*) collection; **~ industrial** industrial park; **~ de maquinaria** pool of machinery; **~ de vehículos** fleet of vehicles, car pool **4.** (*para niños*) playpen

**parqué** [par·'ke] *m* parquet

**parqueadero** [par·kea·'de·ro] *m AmL* parking lot

**parquímetro** [par·'ki·me·tro] *m* parking meter

**parra** ['pa·rra] *f* (grape)vine; **subirse a la ~** (*enfadarse*) to hit the roof; (*darse importancia*) to put on airs

**párrafo** ['pa·rra·fo] *m v.* **parágrafo**

**parranda** [pa·'rran·da] *f* spree; **ir de ~** to go out on the town

**parrilla** [pa·'rri·ja, -ʎa] *f* **1.** (*para la brasa*) grill; (*de un horno*) oven rack **2.** (*establecimiento*) grill(room) **3.** DEP **~** (*de salida*) (starting) grid **4.** *AmL* AUTO roof-rack

**parrillada** [pa·rri·'ja·da, -'ʎa·da] *f* grill; **~ de pescado** grilled fish; **~ de carne** mixed grill

**párroco** ['pa·rro·ko] *m* parish priest

**parroquia** [pa·'rro·kja] *f* **1.** (*territorio, fieles*) parish **2.** (*iglesia*) parish church

**parsimonia** [par·si·'monja] *f* **1.** (*calma*) calm; (*lentitud*) deliberation; **con ~** calmly **2.** (*prudencia*) care; (*moderación*) moderation

**parte¹** ['par·te] *f* **1.** (*porción, elemento*) part; (*de repuesto*) spare (part); **una cuarta ~** a quarter; **de varias ~s** of several parts; **en ~** in part; **en gran ~** largely; **en mayor ~** for the most part; **por ~** bit by bit; **tomar ~ en algo** to be involved in sth **2.** (*repartición*) division; **~ hereditaria** share of the inheritance; **tener ~ en algo** to have a share in sth;

**llevarse la peor/mejor ~** to come off (the) worst/best **3.** (*lugar*) part; **¿a qué ~ vas?** where are you going?; **a ninguna ~** nowhere; **en ninguna ~** nowhere; **en cualquier ~** anywhere; **por todas** (**las**) **~s** everywhere; **en otra ~** somewhere else; **¿de qué ~ de Colombia eres?** which part of Colombia is your family from?; **no llevar a ninguna ~** *fig* to lead nowhere **4.** *t.* JUR (*bando*) party; (*en una discusión*) participant; **~ contratante** contracting party **5.** (*lado*) side; **dale recuerdos de mi ~** give him/her my regards; **estar de ~ de alguien** to be on sb's side; **ponerse de ~ de alguien** to take sb's side; **me tienes de tu ~** I'm on your side; **de ~ a ~** (*de un lado a otro*) from side to side; **por otra ~** on the other hand; (*además*) what's more **6.** (*sección*) section; (*tomo*) volume; (*capítulo*) chapter **7.** TEAT, MÚS (*papel*) part **8.** *pl* (*genitales*) (private) parts *pl*

**parte²** ['par·te] *m* **1.** (*comunicado*) message; **dar ~** to report **2.** RADIO, TV report; **~ meteorológico** weather report

**partición** [par·ti·'sjon, -'θjon] *f* partition; MAT division

**participación** [par·ti·si·pa·'sjon, -θi·pa·'θjon] *f* **1.** (*intervención*) participation; **~ en los beneficios** profit-sharing **2.** (*parte*) share

**participante** [par·ti·si·'pan·te, par·ti·θi-] *mf* participant

**participar** [par·ti·si·'par, par·ti·θi-] *vi* **1.** (*tomar parte*) to participate; **~ en un juego** to take part in a game **2.** (*tener parte*) to have a part; **~ en una herencia** to share in an inheritance

**partícipe** [par·'ti·si·pe, -θi·pe] **I.** *adj* involved **II.** *mf* participant; **hacer a alguien ~ de algo** (*compartir*) to share sth with sb; (*informar*) to inform sb of sth

**participio** [par·ti·'si·pjo, -'θi·pjo] *m* LING participle; **~ activo** [*o* de presente] present participle; **~ pasivo** [*o* de pretérito] past participle

**partícula** [par·'ti·ku·la] *f* **1.** *t.* FÍS, QUÍM particle; **~s de polvo** dust particles **2.** LING particle

**particular¹** [par·ti·ku·'lar] **I.** *adj* **1.** (*pro-*

_pio_) peculiar; (_individual_) individual; (_típico_) typical; (_personal_) personal; **el sabor ~ del azafrán** the special flavor of saffron **2.** (_raro_) peculiar **3.** (_extraordinario_) unusual **4.** (_privado_) private; **envíamelo a mi domicilio ~** send it to my home address **5.** (_determinado_) particular; **un problema ~** a particular problem; **en ~** in particular **II.** _mf_ private individual

**particular²** [par·ti·ku·'lar] _m_ matter

**particularidad** [par·ti·ku·la·ri·'dad] _f_ **1.** (_especialidad_) specialty; (_singularidad_) distinctive feature; (_peculiaridad_) peculiarity **2.** (_rareza_) peculiarity **3.** (_detalle_) detail; (_circunstancia_) circumstance; **las ~es del crimen** the circumstances of the crime

**particularmente** [par·ti·ku·lar·'men·te] _adv_ particularly

**partida** [par·'ti·da] _f_ **1.** (_salida_) departure **2.** (_envío_) consignment **3.** FIN item; **~ doble** double entry **4.** (_certificado_) certificate; **~ de defunción** death certificate **5.** (_juego_) game; **jugar una ~ de ajedrez** to play a game of chess

**partidario, -a** [par·ti·'da·rjo, -a] **I.** _adj_ (_seguidor_) **ser ~ de algo** to be in favor of sth **II.** _m, f_ (_seguidor_) follower; (_afiliado_) member; (_de una idea_) supporter

**partido** [par·'ti·do] _m_ **1.** POL party; **~ de derecha(s)/de izquierda(s)** right-wing/left-wing party; **~ obrero** worker's party **2.** (_grupo_) group; **esta idea tiene mucho ~** this idea has a lot of supporters **3.** DEP (_juego_) match; **~ amistoso** friendly **4.** (_para casarse_) match; **encontrar un buen ~** to make quite a catch **5.** (_determinación_) determination; **tomar ~ a favor de algo/alguien** (_inclinarse_) to lean towards sth/sb **6.** (_provecho_) advantage; **sacar ~ de algo** to put sth to use; **saqué ~ del asunto** I profited from the affair **7.** AmL (_del pelo_) parting

**partir** [par·'tir] **I.** _vt_ **1.** MAT (_dividir_) to divide; **~ por la mitad** to divide into two halves **2.** (_romper_) to break; (_madera_) to chop; (_una nuez_) to crack; **~ la cabeza a alguien** to crack sb's head open

**3.** (_una baraja_) to cut **II.** _vi_ **1.** (_tomar como base_) to start; **a ~ de ahora** from now on; **a ~ de mañana** from tomorrow; **a ~ de las seis** from six o'clock onwards; **a ~ de entonces** since then **2.** (_salir de viaje_) to leave; (_ponerse en marcha_) to start; **partimos de Cádiz a las cinco** we left Cadiz at five o'clock **III.** _vr_ to split; (_cristal_) to crack; **~se (de risa)** _inf_ to split one's sides laughing

**partitura** [par·ti·'tu·ra] _f_ MÚS score; (_hojas_) sheet music

**parto** ['par·to] _m_ birth; **estar de ~** to be in labor

**parvulario** [par·βu·'la·rjo] _m_ kindergarten; (_educación preescolar_) nursery school, preschool

**párvulo, -a** ['par·βu·lo, -a] _m, f_ infant; **escuela de ~s** nursery school, preschool

**pasa** ['pa·sa] _f_ raisin; **estar hecho una ~** _inf_ to be as shriveled as a prune

**pasable** [pa·'sa·βle] _adj_ passable

**pasada** [pa·'sa·da] _f_ **1.** (_paso_) passing; **hacer varias ~s** to make several passes; **de ~** when passing; _fig_ in passing **2.** (_mano_) going-over; (_pintura_) coat; **dar una ~ a algo** to give sth another going-over **3.** _inf_ (_comportamiento_) excess; **¡vaya (mala) ~!** what a thing to do!; **hacer una mala ~ a alguien** to play a dirty trick on sb **4.** _inf_ (_exageración_) **¡es una ~!** it's way over the top!

**pasadizo** [pa·sa·'di·so, -θo] _m_ (_pasillo_) corridor; (_entre dos calles_) alley; **~ secreto** secret passageway

**pasado** [pa·'sa·do] _m_ past; LING past (tense); **en el ~** in the past; **son cosas del ~** it's all in the past

**pasado, -a** [pa·'sa·do, -a] _adj_ **1.** (_de atrás_) past; **el año ~** last year; **~ mañana** the day after tomorrow; **~s dos meses** after two months; **~ de moda** out of fashion **2.** (_estropeado: alimentos_) bad; (_fruta_) overripe; (_leche_) off, sour; (_mantequilla_) rancid; **el yogur está ~ de fecha** the yogurt is past its sell-by date **3.** (_muy cocido_) overcooked; **un huevo ~ por agua** a soft-boiled egg

**pasador** [pa·sa·'dor] _m_ **1.** (_alfiler_) pin; (_imperdible_) safety pin; (_broche_) clip;

P

(*de corbata*) tiepin **2.** (*para el cabello*) hairclip, barrette **3.** (*cerrojo*) bolt **4.** (*colador*) colander

**pasaje** [pa·sa·xe] *m* **1.** (*derecho*) toll **2.** (*billete de avión*) (plane) ticket; (*de barco*) (boat) ticket; (*precio*) fare **3.** (*pasajeros*) passengers *pl* **4.** (*pasillo*) passage; ~ **subterráneo** underground passage **5.** (*estrecho*) strait

**pasajero, -a** [pa·sa·'xe·ro, -a] **I.** *adj* (*transitorio, breve*) passing; (*fugaz*) fleeting **II.** *m, f* (*viajero*) passenger; **tren de ~s** passenger train

**pasamano(s)** [pa·sa·'ma·no(s)] *m(pl)* handrail

**pasamontañas** [pa·sa·mon·'ta·ɲas] *m inv* ski mask

**pasapalos** [pa·sa·'pa·los] *m inv Méx, Ven* appetizer

**pasaporte** [pa·sa·'por·te] *m* passport; **dar (el) ~ a alguien** *inf* (*despedirlo*) to give sb their marching orders; (*matarlo*) to bump sb off

**pasar** [pa·'sar] **I.** *vi* **1.** (*por delante*) to pass; ~ **desapercibido** to go unnoticed; ~ **de largo** to go past; **dejar ~** (*por delante*) to go past; ~ **por encima de** (*un obstáculo*) to overcome; (*una persona*) to overlook; ~ **por alto** *fig* to leave out; **no dejes ~ la oportunidad** don't miss the opportunity **2.** (*por un hueco*) to go through; **el sofá no pasa por la puerta** the sofa won't go through the door; **el Ebro pasa por Zaragoza** the Ebro flows through Zaragoza; ~ **por una crisis** to go through a crisis **3.** (*trasladarse*) to move; **pasemos al comedor** let's go to the dining room **4.** (*acaecer*) to happen; **¿qué pasa?** what's up?; **¿qué te pasa?** what's wrong?; **pase lo que pase** whatever happens; **dejar ~ algo** to allow sth to happen; **lo que pasa es que...** the thing is that... **5.** (*acabar*) to pass; **cuando pasen las vacaciones...** when the holidays are over... **6.** (*el tiempo*) to pass; **lo pasado, pasado** what's done is done **7.** (*aparentar*) to pass for; **pasa por nuevo** it looks new; **hacerse ~ por médico** to pass oneself off as a doctor **8.** (*cambiar*) to go; **paso a explicar por qué** and now I will (go

on to) explain why; ~ **a mayores** to go from bad to worse **9.** (*ser admisible*) to pass; **arreglándolo aún puede ~** if we fix it, it should still be okay **10.** (*no jugar*) to pass **11.** *inf* (*no necesitar*) **yo paso de salir** I don't want to go out; **pasa de todo** he/she couldn't care less about anything **II.** *vt* **1.** (*atravesar*) to cross; ~ **el puente** to cross the bridge; ~ **el semáforo en rojo** to go through a red light **2.** (*por un hueco*) to go through; ~ **la tarjeta por la ranura** to swipe the card through the slot; ~ **algo por debajo de la puerta** to slide sth under the door **3.** (*trasladar*) to transfer; ~ **a limpio** to make a fair copy **4.** (*dar*) to pass; ~ **la pelota** to pass the ball **5.** (*una temporada*) to spend; ~ **el invierno en el Caribe** to spend the winter in the Caribbean; **~lo bien/mal** to have a good/bad time; **~lo en grande** to have a whale of a time; **¡que lo paséis bien!** enjoy yourselves! **6.** (*sufrir*) to experience; ~ **hambre** to go hungry; ~ **frío** to feel the cold; **pasé un mal rato** I went through a difficult time **7.** (*transmitir*) to send; (*dinero*) to give; ~ **un recado** to pass on a message; **me has pasado el resfriado** you've given me your cold; **le paso a la Sra. Ortega** I'll put you through to Mrs. Ortega **8.** (*sobrepasar*) to exceed; **he pasado los treinta** I am over thirty; **te paso en altura** I am taller than you **9.** (*hacer deslizar*) ~ **la mano por la mesa** to run one's hand over the table; ~ **la aspiradora** to vacuum **10.** (*tolerar*) to allow to pass **11.** (*aprobar*) to pass **12.** (*omitir*) to overlook **13.** (*colar*) to strain **14.** (*las hojas de un libro*) to turn **III.** *vr* **1.** (*acabarse*) to pass; **ya se le ~á el enfado** his anger will soon subside; **~se de fecha** to miss a deadline **2.** (*exagerar*) to go too far; **~se de la raya** to go over the line; **~se de listo** to be too clever by half **3.** (*por un sitio*) to visit; **me pasé un rato por casa de mi tía** I popped by my aunt's house for a while; **se me pasó por la cabeza que...** it occurred to me that...; **~se la mano por el pelo** to run one's hand through one's hair **4.** *t.* MIL (*cambiar) to go over **5.** (*olvidarse*) to be forgotten; **se me pasó tu cumpleaños** I forgot your birthday **6.** (*estropearse: alimentos, leche*) to spoil, to go off; (*fruta*) to overripen; (*mantequilla*) to go rancid; (*flores*) to wilt; **se ha pasado el arroz** the rice is overcooked **7.** (*escaparse*) to be missed; **se me pasó la oportunidad** I missed my chance

**pasarela** [pa·sa·'re·la] *f* **1.** (*para desfiles*) catwalk **2.** (*de un barco*) gangway **3.** (*puente provisional*) temporary bridge; (*para peatones*) walkway

**pasatiempo** [pa·sa·'tjem·po] *m* **1.** (*diversión*) pastime; **los pasatiempos del periódico** the games and puzzles section of the newspaper **2.** (*hobby*) hobby

**pascana** [pas·'ka·na] *f* **1.** *AmS* (*etapa de un viaje*) stage **2.** *Arg, Bol, Perú* (*posada*) wayside inn

**Pascua** ['pas·kwa] *f* **1.** (*de resurrección*) Easter; **de ~s a Ramos** once in a blue moon; **hacer la ~ a alguien** *inf* to do the dirty on sb **2.** *pl* (*navidad*) Christmas time; **dar las ~s a alguien** to wish sb a merry Christmas **3.** *pl* (*pentecostés*) Whitsun ▶ **¡y santas ~s!** and that's that!; **estar como una(s) ~(s)** to be over the moon

**pase** ['pa·se] *m* **1.** (*desfile*) parade; (*de moda*) fashion show **2.** DEP pass **3.** *t.* MIL pass; (*licencia*) license; (*para entrar gratis*) free pass; **~ (de transporte)** travel pass **4.** *AmL* (*pasaporte*) passport

**paseandero, -a** [pa·sean·'de·ro, -a] *adj CSur* fond of walking

**pasear** [pa·se·'ar] **I.** *vt* (*en coche*) to take for a ride; (*a pie*) to take for a walk; **~ al perro** to walk the dog **II.** *vi, vr* (*a pie*) to go for a walk; (*en coche*) to go for a drive; (*a caballo*) to ride

**paseo** [pa·'seo] *m* **1.** (*a pie*) walk; (*en coche, a caballo*) ride; (*en barco*) trip; **dar un ~** to go for a walk; **¡vete a ~!** get lost! **2.** (*para pasear*) avenue; **~ marítimo** promenade, esplanade

**pasillo** [pa·'si·jo, -ʎo] *m* (*corredor*) passage; (*entre habitaciones*) corridor, hallway

**pasión** [pa·'sjon] *f* passion; **con ~** passionately; **sin ~** without enthusiasm;

**sentir ~ por el fútbol** to be passionate about soccer

**pasional** [pa·sjo·'nal] *adj* passionate

**pasividad** [pa·si·βi·'dad] *f* passivity, passiveness

**pasivo** [pa·'si·βo] *m* liabilities *pl*; (*en el balance*) debit side

**pasivo, -a** [pa·'si·βo, -a] *adj t.* LING passive; **verbo ~** passive verb; **voz pasiva** passive

**pasmar** [pas·'mar] *vt* (*asombrar*) to astonish; **me has dejado pasmado** you have left me completely stunned

**paso** ['pa·so] *m* **1.** (*acción de pasar*) passing; **ceder el ~** (*a una persona*) to make way; (*en el tráfico*) to yield; **estar de ~** to be passing through; **nadie salió al ~ de sus mentiras** nobody put a stop to his/her lies **2.** (*movimiento*) step; (*progreso*) progress; **ir al ~** to keep in step; **marcar el ~** to mark the rhythm [*o* time]; **a cada ~** at every step; **~ a ~** step by step; **dar un ~ adelante/atrás** to take a step forwards/backwards; **dar un ~ en falso** to trip; *fig* to make a false move; **vive a dos ~s de mi casa** he/she lives very near to my house; **dar todos los ~s necesarios** *fig* to take all the necessary steps **3.** (*velocidad*) pace; **a ~s agigantados** with giant steps; *fig* by leaps and bounds; **a buen ~** quickly; **a ~ de tortuga** at snail's pace; **a este ~ no llegarás** at this speed you'll never get there **4.** (*pasillo*) passage; (*en el mar*) strait; (*entre montañas*) pass; **~ subterráneo** underground passage; **abrirse ~** to open up a path for oneself; *fig* to make one's way; **¡prohibido el ~!** (*pasar*) no thoroughfare!; (*entrar*) no entry!; **salir del ~ (con algo)** to get out of a jam (with sth) **5.** (*para atravesar algo*) crossing; **~ de cebra** zebra crossing; **~ a nivel** level crossing; **¡~!** make way! **6.** (*de un contador*) unit; **marcar los ~s** to count the units

**pasota** [pa·'so·ta] *mf inf* drop-out; **es un ~ total** he doesn't give a damn about anything

**pasta** ['pas·ta] *f* **1.** (*masa*) paste; (*para un pastel*) pastry; (*para paredes*) filler; (*para madera*) putty; **~ de dientes** toothpaste

P

**2.** (*comida italiana*) pasta **3.** (*pastelería*) pastries *pl* **4.** (*encuadernación*) cover; **de ~ dura/blanda** hardback/paperback **5.** *inf* (*dinero*) dough **6.** (*madera*) pulp; **tener ~ para algo** to be cut out for sth; **tener buena ~** to be good-natured

**pastar** [pas·'tar] *vi, vt* to graze

**pastel** [pas·'tel] *m* **1.** (*tarta*) cake; (*bollo*) pastry; (*de carne*) pie; **descubrir el ~** to catch on **2.** (*lápiz*) pastel crayon **3.** (*pintura*) pastel

**pastelería** [pas·te·le·'ri·a] *f* pastry shop

**pastelero, -a** [pas·te·'le·ro, -a] *m, f* (*repostero*) pastry chef

**pastilla** [pas·'ti·ja, -Áa] *f* **1.** (*medicinal*) tablet; **~ contra el dolor** painkiller; **~ para la garganta** throat lozenge; **~ para la tos** cough drop **2.** (*dulce*) candy **3.** (*trozo*) piece; **~ de caldo** stock cube; **~ de jabón** bar of soap; **ir a toda ~** *inf* to go at full speed

**pasto** ['pas·to] *m* **1.** (*pastizal*) pasture **2.** (*hierba*) grass; **~ seco hierba; ser ~ de las llamas** to go up in flames

**pastor** [pas·'tor] *m* **1.** REL minister **2.** ZOOL **perro ~** sheepdog

**pastor(a)** [pas·'tor, ·'to·ra] *m(f)* (*de ganado*) herdsman *m;* (*de ovejas*) shepherd

**pastorear** [pas·to·re·'ar] *vt* **1.** (*el ganado*) to graze **2.** *AmC* (*mimar*) to spoil **3.** *AmL* (*atisbar*) to spy on

**pastoso, -a** [pas·'to·so, -a] *adj* **1.** (*voz*) mellow; **lengua pastosa** furred tongue **2.** *AmL* (*región*) grassy

**pata** ['pa·ta] *f* (*de un perro*) paw; (*de una silla*) leg; **~s de gallo** (*en el rostro*) crow's feet; **~ de palo** wooden leg; **mala ~** *inf* bad luck; **estirar la ~** *inf* to kick the bucket; **ir a ~** *inf* to go on foot; **~s arriba** upside down; **a la ~ coja** hopping; **a cuatro ~s** on all fours; **meter la ~** *inf* to put one's foot in it

**patada** [pa·'ta·da] *f* (*contra algo*) kick; (*en el suelo*) stamp; **dar una ~ contra la pared** to kick the wall; **dar ~s en el suelo** to stamp one's feet; **romper una puerta a ~s** to kick a door down; **echar a alguien a ~s** to kick sb out; **tratar a alguien a ~s** to treat sb like dirt; **a ~s** *fig* by the bucket load

**patalear** [pa·ta·le·'ar] *vi* to kick; (*en el suelo*) to stamp one's feet

**patata** [pa·'ta·ta] *f* potato; **~s fritas** French fries *pl;* **una bolsa de ~s fritas** a bag of potato chips; **tortilla de ~** Spanish omelet; **puré de ~(s)** mashed potatoes **2.** ¡~! (*al hacer una foto*) cheese!

**patatús** [pa·ta·'tus] *m inv inf* (*desmayo*) faint; **le dio un ~** he/she fainted

**patear** [pa·te·'ar] **I.** *vt* **1.** (*dar golpes*) to kick **2.** (*pisotear*) to trample **3.** (*tratar rudamente*) to trample on **II.** *vi* **1.** (*en el suelo*) to stamp **2.** (*andar mucho*) to tramp around

**patentar** [pa·ten·'tar] *vt* to patent

**patente** [pa·'ten·te] **I.** *adj* **1.** (*visible*) clear **2.** (*evidente*) patent; **hacer ~** to establish; (*comprobar*) to prove; (*revelar*) to reveal **II.** *f* **1.** (*documento*) license; (*permiso*) permit; **~ de comercio** business license; **~ de sanidad** bill of health **2.** JUR patent; **~ industrial** industrial patent; **solicitar la ~** to apply for a patent

**patera** [pa·'te·ra] *f* small boat

**paternal** [pa·ter·'nal] *adj* paternal

**paternidad** [pa·ter·ni·'dad] *f* **1.** (*relación*) fatherhood; JUR paternity **2.** (*calidad*) fatherliness

**paterno, -a** [pa·'ter·no, -a] *adj* paternal; **mi abuelo ~** my paternal grandfather

**patero, -a** [pa·'te·ro, -a] *m, f* Chile bootlicker

**patético, -a** [pa·'te·ti·ko, -a] *adj pey* pathetic

**patíbulo** [pa·'ti·βu·lo] *m* scaffold; (*horca*) gallows *pl*

**patilla** [pa·'ti·ja, -Áa] *f* **1.** (*de gafas*) sidepiece; (*de madero*) peg **2.** *pl* (*pelo*) sideburns *pl*

**patín** [pa·'tin] *m* **1.** (*de hielo*) ice skate; (*de ruedas*) roller skate; **patines en línea** rollerblades **2.** TÉC shoe

**patinaje** [pa·ti·'na·xe] *m* (*sobre hielo*) (ice) skating; (*sobre ruedas*) (roller) skating; **~ artístico** (*sobre hielo*) figure skating; **~ de velocidad** speed skating

**patinar** [pa·ti·'nar] *vi* **1.** (*sobre patines de hielo*) to (ice) skate; (*sobre patines de ruedas*) to (roller) skate **2.** (*deslizarse*) to slip; (*un vehículo*) to skid **3.** (*equivocarse*) to slip up

**patinazo** [pa·ti·'na·so, -θo] *m* **1.** (*deslizamiento*) slip; (*de un vehículo*) skid **2.** *inf* (*equivocación*) blunder

**patinete** [pa·ti·'ne·te] *m* scooter

**patio** ['pa·tjo] *m* (*interior*) courtyard; (*entre dos casas*) back yard; ~ **de recreo** playground

**pato, -a** ['pa·to] *m, f* **1.** ZOOL duck; (*macho*) drake **2.** *inf* (*torpe*) clumsy person
▶ **pagar el** ~ *inf* to carry the can

**patógeno, -a** [pa·'to·xe·no, -a] *adj* MED pathogen; **germen** ~ harmful germ

**patojo, -a** [pa·'to·xo, -a] *m, f* Col, Guat kid *inf*

**patológico, -a** [pa·to·'lo·xi·ko, -a] *adj* t. *fig* pathological

**patoso, -a** [pa·'to·so, -a] *adj* **1.** (*soso*) boring **2.** (*torpe*) clumsy

**patraña** [pa·'tra·ɲa] *f* lie, pack of lies

**patria** ['pa·trja] *f* native land; **madre** ~ mother country; *AmL* Spain

**patrimonio** [pa·tri·'mo·njo] *m* **1.** (*herencia*) inheritance; ~ **cultural** cultural heritage **2.** (*riqueza*) wealth

**patriota** [pa·'trjo·ta] *mf* patriot

**patriótico, -a** [pa·'trjo·ti·ko, -a] *adj* patriotic

**patriotismo** [pa·trjo·'tis·mo] *m* patriotism

**patrocinador(a)** [pa·tro·si·na·'dor, -·'do·ra; patroθi-] *m(f)* t. DEP sponsor

**patrocinar** [pa·tro·si·'nar, pa·tro·'θi] *vt* t. DEP to sponsor

**patrocinio** [pa·tro·'si·njo, -·'θi·njo] *m* **1.** (*protección*) patronage **2.** DEP sponsorship

**patrón** [pa·'tron] *m* (*modelo*) model; (*de costura*) pattern

**patrón, -ona** [pa·'tron, -·'tro·na] *m, f* **1.** (*que protege*) patron *m*, patroness *f* **2.** (*jefe*) boss **3.** (*de una casa*) head; (*de una pensión*) landlord *m*, landlady *f*

**patronal** [pa·tro·'nal] **I.** *adj* (*empresario*) employers'; **cierre** ~ lockout **II.** *f* (*asociación*) employers' organization

**patrono, -a** [pa·'tro·no, -a] *m, f* **1.** (*jefe*) boss **2.** (*de un feudo*) landowner **3.** (*miembro del patronato*) board member **4.** REL patron saint

**patrulla** [pa·'tru·ʎa, -ʎa] *f* t. MIL patrol; **estar de** ~ to be on patrol

**patrullar** [pa·tru·'ʎar, -'ʎar] *vi, vt* to patrol

**paturro, -a** [pa·'tu·rro, -a] *adj* Col short and stocky

**paulatino, -a** [pau·la·'ti·no, -a] *adj* gradual

**pausa** ['pau·sa] *f* pause

**pauta** ['pau·ta] *f* **1.** (*modelo*) guide **2.** (*normas*) standard; **marcar la** ~ to set the example [*o* standard] **3.** (*regla*) rule

**pava** ['pa·βa] *f* **1.** ZOOL v. **pavo, -a 2.** *AmL* (*olla*) pot; (*tetera*) tea kettle **3.** *AmL* (*sombrero*) straw hat **4.** And, AmC (*flecos*) fringe

**pavimentar** [pa·βi·men·'tar] *vt* (*con losas*) to pave; (*con asfalto*) to surface

**pavimento** [pa·βi·'men·to] *m* **1.** (*recubrimiento: en una casa*) flooring; (*en una carretera*) surfacing **2.** (*material: en una casa*) floor; (*en una carretera*) surface

**pavo** ['pa·βo] *m inf* (*dólar*) buck

**pavo, -a** ['pa·βo, -a] *m, f* turkey; (*persona*) idiot; ~ **real** peacock; **estar en la edad del** ~ *inf* to be at an awkward stage (*of one's adolescence*); **no es moco de** ~ *inf* it's not to be scoffed at [*o* sneezed]; **ir de** ~ *AmL* to mooch a ride

**pavor** [pa·'βor] *m* terror

**payada** [pa·'ja·da] *f* CSur MÚS improvised song between two competing musicians, accompanied by guitars

**payasada** [pa·ja·'sa·da] *f* clowning; *pey* idiotic behavior

**payaso, -a** [pa·'ja·so, -a] *m, f* clown; **¡deja de hacer el ~!** stop fooling around!

**payo, -a** ['pa·jo, -a] *m, f* non-gypsy (*gypsy term to refer to people who are not gypsies*)

**paz** [pas, paθ] *f* peace; **hacer las paces** to make up; **estar en ~ con alguien** to be even with sb; **¡déjame en ~!** leave me alone!; **¡...y en ~!** ... and that's that!; **que en ~ descanse** may he/she rest in peace

**P.D.** [pos·'da·ta] *abr de* **posdata** P.S.

**pe** [pe] *f* p; **de ~ a pa** *inf* from A to Z

**peaje** [pe·'a·xe] *m* toll

**peatón, -ona** [pea·'ton, -·'to·na] *m, f* pedestrian

**peca** ['pe·ka] *f* freckle

**pecado** [pe·'ka·do] *m* sin; ~ **capital** deadly sin; ~ **original** original sin; **pagar sus** ~**s** to pay for one's sins; **sería un ~ re-chazarlos** it would be a crying shame to reject them

**pecador(a)** [pe·ka·'dor, -·'do·ra] **I.** *adj* sinning **II.** *m(f)* sinner

**pecar** <c → qu> [pe·'kar] *vi* to sin; ~ **por exceso** to go too far; **peca por exceso de confianza** he/she is too confident by half

**pecarí** [pe·ka·'ri] *m* AmL ZOOL peccary

**pecera** [pe·'se·ra, -θe·ra] *f* fish tank; (*en forma de globo*) fishbowl

**pecho** ['pe·tʃo] *m* breast, chest; **dar el** ~ **al bebé** to breastfeed the baby; **a ~ descubierto** (*sin armas*) unarmed; *fig* openly; **tomarse algo muy a ~** to take sth to heart

**pechuga** [pe·'tʃu·ɣa] *f* (*de ave*) breast; ~ **de pollo** chicken breast

**pechugón, -ona** [pe·tʃu·'ɣon] *adj* **1.** AmL (*descarado*) shameless **2.** AmL (*franco*) outspoken

**pecoso, -a** [pe·'ko·so, -a] *adj* freckly

**pectoral** [pek·to·'ral] **I.** *adj* **1.** ANAT pectoral **2.** (*contra la tos*) cough **II.** *m* MED pectoral

**peculiar** [pe·ku·'ljar] *adj* **1.** (*especial*) distinctive **2.** (*raro*) peculiar

**peculiaridad** [pe·ku·lja·ri·'dad] *f* **1.** (*singularidad*) peculiarity **2.** (*distintivo*) distinguishing feature

**pedagogía** [pe·da·ɣo·'xi·a] *f* pedagogy

**pedagógico, -a** [pe·da·'ɣo·xi·ko, -a] *adj* pedagogical

**pedal** [pe·'dal] *m* pedal; **pisar el** ~ AUTO to accelerate

**pedalear** [pe·da·le·'ar] *vi* to pedal

**pedante** [pe·'dan·te] *adj* pretentious, pedantic

**pedazo** [pe·'da·θo] *m* (big) piece; ~ **de papel** piece of paper; **caerse a ~s** to fall apart, to fall to pieces; **hacerse ~s** to fall to pieces; **hacer ~s** to break; (*madera*) to smash up; (*papel*) to tear up; **ser un ~ de pan** to be very good-natured; **¡~ de bruto!** *inf* you brute!

**pederasta** [pe·de·'ras·ta] *m* pederast

**pedestal** [pe·des·'tal] *m* pedestal; (*apoyo*) base; **poner a alguien en un ~** to put

sb on a pedestal

**pediatra** [pe·'dja·tra] *mf* pediatrician

**pediatría** [pe·dja·'tri·a] *f* pediatrics

**pedicura** [pe·di·'ku·ra] *f* pedicure; **hacerse la ~** to get a pedicure

**pedida** [pe·'di·da] *f* ~ **de mano** asking for sb's hand in marriage

**pedido** [pe·'di·do] *m* COM order; (*de un servicio*) reservation; **enviar sobre ~** to supply on request; **a ~** to order

**pedido, -a** [pe·'di·do, -a] *adj* (*solicitado*) requested; (*encargado*) ordered

**pedigrí** [pe·di·'ɣri] *m* pedigree

**pedir** [pe·'dir] *irr vt* **1.** (*rogar*) to ask for; ~ **algo a alguien** to ask sb for sth; ~ **prestado** to borrow; **a ~ de boca** just right; ~ **la mano de alguien** to ask for sb's hand in marriage; ~ **limosna** to beg **2.** (*exigir*) to demand; (*necesitar*) to need; (*solicitar*) to request; ~ **algo** *fig* to be crying out for sth **3.** (*encargar*) to order

**pedo** ['pe·do] *m inf* **1.** (*ventosidad*) fart; **tirarse un ~** to fart **2.** (*borrachera*) drunkenness

**pedrada** [pe·'dra·da] *f* throw of a stone; **matar a alguien a ~s** to stone sb to death

**pedregullo** [pe·dre·'ɣu·jo, -·ʎo] *m* CSur gravel

**pega** ['pe·ɣa] *f* **1.** *inf* (*dificultades*) difficulty; **poner ~s a** to find fault with; **de ~** fake **2.** CSur, Méx *inf* (*trabajo*) job

**pegadizo, -a** [pe·ɣa·'di·so, -a; -di·θo, -a] *adj* (*pegajoso*) sticky; (*enfermedad*) contagious; **melodía pegadiza** catchy tune

**pegajoso, -a** [pe·ɣa·'xo·so, -a] *adj* **1.** (*adhesivo*) sticky, adhesive **2.** (*persona*) tiresome; (*niño*) clinging

**pegamento** [pe·ɣa·'men·to] *m* glue; ~ **en barra** stick glue; ~ **de contacto** bonding cement

**pegar** <g → gu> [pe·'ɣar] **I.** *vt* **1.** (*aglutinar*) to stick; ~ **un sello** to attach a stamp; **no** ~ **ojo** not to sleep a wink **2.** (*muebles*) ~ **la mesilla a la cama** to put the side table right next to the bed **3.** (*contagiar*) to give **4.** (*golpear*) to hit; ~ **una paliza a alguien** to beat sb up **5.** (*un grito*) to let out; (*un tiro*) to fire; ~ **una bofetada** to slap; ~ **un salto** to jump; ~ **un susto a alguien** to frighten sb **6.** COMPUT to paste **7.** *AmL* *inf* (*tener suerte*) to be lucky; ~**la** to get what one wants **8.** *Méx* (*atar*) to tie **II.** *vi* **1.** (*hacer juego*) to go together; **esto no pega ni con cola** this really doesn't go **2.** (*rozar*) ~ **en algo** to brush against sth; (*tocar*) to touch sth **3.** (*golpear*) to beat; **¡cómo pega el sol!** *inf* the sun is burning hot! **4.** *inf* (*currar*) to work hard; **no** ~ **golpe** not to do a thing **III.** *vr* **1.** (*impactar*) ~**se con algo** to bump into sth; ~**se con alguien** to fight with sb **2.** (*quemarse*) to stick to the pot **3.** (*acompañar siempre*) ~**se a alguien** to stick to sb (like glue); (*perseguir*) to follow sb **4.** (*contagiarse*) **se me pegó el sarampión** I caught [*o* got] the measles **5.** *inf* (*engañar*) **pegársela a alguien** *inf* to trick sb **6.** *inf* (*darse*) ~**se la gran vida** to live it up; ~**se un tiro** to shoot oneself

**pegatina** [pe·ɣa·'ti·na] *f* sticker

**pegote** [pe·'ɣo·te] *m* **esa corbata es un** ~ that tie just doesn't go; **tirarse ~s** to show off

**peinado** [pei·'na·do] *m* hairstyle, hairdo

**peinado, -a** [pei·'na·do, -a] *adj* combed

**peinar** [pei·'nar] **I.** *vt* to comb; (*acicalar*) to style **II.** *vr* to comb one's hair; (*arreglar el pelo*) to style [*o* to do] one's hair

**peine** ['pei·ne] *m* comb; **¡te vas a enterar de lo que vale un** ~! *fig* you'll soon find out what's what!

**peineta** [pei·'ne·ta] *f* Spanish ornamental comb

**p.ej.** [por e·'xem·plo] *abr de* **por ejemplo** e.g.

**pela** ['pe·la] *f* *inf* (*dinero*) **no me quedan más** ~ I have no money left

**pelado** [pe·'la·do] *m* *inf* poor wretch

**pelado, -a** [pe·'la·do, -a] *adj* **1.** (*rapado*) shorn **2.** (*escueto*) bare **3.** *inf* (*sin dinero*) broke

**pelambrera** [pe·lam·'bre·ra] *f* mop

**pelapatatas** [pe·la·pa·'ta·tas] *m inv* potato peeler

**pelar** [pe·'lar] **I.** *vt* **1.** (*pelo*) to cut; (*rapar*) to shear; (*frutas*) to peel; **ser duro de** ~ to be a hard nut to crack **2.** *AmL*

*inf* (*dar una paliza*) to beat up **3.** *And inf* (*morir*) ~**la** to kick the bucket **II.** *vr* **1.** (*el pelo*) to have one's hair cut **2.** (*la piel*) to peel **3.** *inf* (*intensificador*) **corre que se las pela** he/she is a really fast runner; **pelárselas por algo** to be crazy about sth

**peldaño** [pel·'da·ɲo] *m* step

**pelea** [pe·'lea] *f* fight; (*verbal*) quarrel, argument; **buscar** ~ to be looking for trouble

**pelear** [pe·le·'ar] **I.** *vi* to fight; (*discutir*) to argue; ~ **por algo** (*trabajar*) to struggle for sth **II.** *vr* **1.** (*con violencia*) ~**se por algo** to fight over sth; (*verbal*) to argue about sth **2.** (*enemistarse*) to fall out

**pelele** [pe·'le·le] *m* **1.** (*muñeco*) rag doll **2.** *inf* (*persona*) puppet

**peletería** [pe·le·te·'ri·a] *f* **1.** (*costura*) furrier's; (*venta*) fur shop **2.** *AmC* (*zapatería*) shoe store

**pelícano** [pe·'li·ka·no] *m* pelican

**película** [pe·'li·ku·la] *f* film, movie; ~ **en blanco y negro** black and white movie; ~ **muda** silent film [*o* movie]; ~ **de suspense** thriller; ~ **de terror** horror film [*o* movie]; ~ **del oeste** western; **de** ~ *inf* sensational; **como de** ~ like sth out of the movies; **poner en** ~ to film; **echar una** ~ to show a film

**peligrar** [pe·li·'ɣrar] *vi* to be in danger; **hacer** ~ to endanger

**peligro** [pe·'li·ɣro] *m* danger; ~ **de incendio** fire risk; **correr** ~ to run a risk; **estar en** ~ **de muerte** to be in mortal danger; **fuera de** ~ out of danger; **poner en** ~ to endanger; **poniendo en** ~ **su propia vida** risking his/her own life

**peligroso, -a** [pe·li·'ɣro·so, -a] *adj* dangerous

**pelillo** [pe·'li·ʎo] *m* *inf* trifle; **¡~s a la mar!** let bygones be bygones!

**pelirrojo, -a** [pe·li·'rro·xo, -a] *adj* red-haired

**pellejo** [pe·'ʝe·xo, -'ʎe·xo] *m* **1.** (*de animal*) hide **2.** (*de persona*) skin; **no tener más que el** ~ to be all skin and bones; **no caber en su** ~ *fig* to be bursting with pride; **si yo estuviera en tu** ~... *inf* if I were in your shoes...; **salvar el** ~ *inf* to save one's skin; **arriesgar el**

~ to risk one's neck **3.** (*odre*) wineskin **4.** (*fruta*) peel; (*salchicha*) skin

**pellizcar** <c → qu> [pe·jis·'kar, -ʎiθ·'kar] **I.** *vt* **1.** (*repizcar*) to pinch **2.** *inf* (*pizcar algo*) to take a pinch of **II.** *vr* to pinch oneself

**pellizco** [pe·'jis·ko, -ʎiθ·ko] *m* **1.** (*pizco*) pinch; **dar un ~ a alguien** to pinch sb **2.** (*poquito: de sal*) pinch; (*de bocadillo*) nibble

**pelma** ['pel·ma] *mf inf*, **pelmazo, -a** [pel·'ma·so, -a; -θo, -θa] *m, f inf* bore, drag

**pelo** ['pe·lo] *m* **1.** (*cabello*) hair; (*de animal*) fur; (*de barba*) whisker; **tener el ~ rubio** to have fair hair; **cortarse el ~** to get one's hair cut; **soltarse el ~** to let one's hair down; *fig* to show one's true colors **2.** (*vello*) down; (*pelusa*) fluff; (*de alfombra*) pile **3.** (+ *al*) **al ~** perfectly; **todo irá al ~** everything will be fine; **venir al ~** to be just right, to happen [*o* come] at just the right time **4.** *inf* (*poco*) **por un ~ te caes** you very nearly fell; **escaparse por un ~** to escape by the skin of one's teeth ► **no tener ~s en la lengua** *inf* not to mince words; **un hombre de ~ en pecho** a real man; **ponerle a uno los ~s de punta** to make one's hair stand on end; **no tocar un ~ (de la ropa) a alguien** *inf* not to lay a finger on sb; **contar algo con ~s y señales** *inf* to describe sth in great detail; **no tener (un) ~ de tonto** *inf* to be nobody's fool; **estar hasta los ~s** *inf* to be fed up; **tomar el ~ a alguien** *inf* to pull sb's leg; **a ~** (*la cabeza descubierta*) bare-headed; (*sin prepararse*) unprepared

**pelota¹** [pe·'lo·ta] *f* **1.** (*balón*) ball; **devolver la ~ a alguien** (*argumentar*) to turn the tables on sb; (*vengarse*) to give sb a taste of their own medicine; **la ~ sigue en el tejado** *fig* things are still up in the air **2.** (*juego*) pelota **3.** *pl vulg* (*testículos*) balls *pl*; **tocar las ~s a alguien** to irritate sb; **tocarse las ~s** to do absolutely nothing; **¡fíjate, que tiene ~s!** I'll tell you one thing, he's got balls!; **¡y esto es así, por ~s!** that's how it is, no arguing! **4.** *vulg* (*desnudo*) **en ~s** stark

naked; **pillar a alguien en ~s** *fig* to catch sb with their pants down ► **hacer la ~ a alguien** to suck up to sb

**pelota²** [pe·'lo·ta] *m inf* crawler

**pelotazo** [pe·lo·'ta·so, -θo] *m* **1.** (*con el pie*) shot; (*tirando*) throw; (*con la raqueta*) stroke **2.** *inf* (*bebida*) slug; **meterse un ~** to have a drink

**pelotear** [pe·lo·te·'ar] *vi* (*tenis*) to toss back and forth; (*fútbol*) to kick around

**pelotera** [pe·lo·'te·ra] *f inf* fight

**pelotón** [pe·lo·'ton] *m* (*de gente*) crowd; (*en carreras*) pack; **~ de ejecución** firing squad

**pelotudo, -a** [pe·lo·'tu·do, -a] *m, f CSur vulg* jerk

**peluca** [pe·'lu·ka] *f* wig

**peluche** [pe·'lu·tʃe] *m* (*juguete*) soft toy; **oso de ~** teddy bear

**peludo, -a** [pe·'lu·do] *adj* **1.** hairy **2.** *AmC inf* (*difícil*) tricky

**peluquería** [pe·lu·ke·'ri·a] *f* hairdresser's; **ir a la ~** to go to the hairdresser's

**peluquero, -a** [pe·lu·'ke·ro, -a] *m, f* hairdresser

**pelusa** [pe·'lu·sa] *f* (*vello*) down; (*tejido*) fluff; (*de polvo*) fluff; **sentir ~** to be jealous

**pelvis** ['pel·βis] *f inv* pelvis

**pena** ['pe·na] *f* **1.** (*tristeza*) sorrow; **ahogar las ~s** to drown one's sorrows **2.** (*lástima*) **ser una ~** to be a pity; **¡qué ~!** what a shame!; **ella me da ~** I feel really sorry for her **3.** (*sanción*) punishment; **~ capital** capital punishment **4.** (*dificultad*) trouble; **a duras ~s** with great difficulty; (*apenas*) scarcely; **sin ~ ni gloria** undistinguished; **valer la ~** to be worth the effort [*o* the trouble] **5.** *AmL* (*vergüenza*) shame; **tener ~** to be ashamed

**penal** [pe·'nal] **I.** *adj* JUR penal; **antecedentes ~es** criminal record **II.** *m* **1.** (*prisión*) prison **2.** *AmL* (*falta*) foul (*inside the penalty area*)

**penalización** [pe·na·li·sa·'sjon, -θa·'θjon] *f* penalization

**penalizar** <z → c> [pe·na·li·'sar, -'θar] *vt* to penalize

**penalti** [pe·'nal·ti] *m* **1.** (*falta*) foul (*inside the penalty area*) **2.** (*sanción*)

**penalty**; **casarse de ~** *inf* to have a shotgun wedding

**penar** [pe·'nar] **I.** *vt* to punish **II.** *vi* **1.** (*padecer*) to suffer **2.** (*ansiar*) **~ por algo** to long for sth

**pendejada** [pen·de·'xa·ða] *f AmL inf* **1.** (*disparate*) stupidity **2.** (*acto cobarde*) cowardly act

**pendejear** [pen·de·xe·'ar] *vi Col, Méx inf* to mess [*o* to fool] around

**pendejo, -a** [pen·'de·xo] *m, f Arg inf* fool

**pender** [pen·'der] *vi* to hang

**pendiente**[1] [pen·'djen·te] **I.** *adj* **1.** (*colgado*) hanging **2.** (*problema, asunto*) unresolved; (*trabajo, pedido*) outstanding; **una cuenta ~ de pago** an outstanding account; **quedar ~ una asignatura** to have one subject left to pass *(as a resit or carried over to next year)* **3.** *inf* (*ocuparse*) **estate ~ del arroz** keep an eye on the rice **4.** (*depender*) **estamos ~s de lo que digan nuestros padres** it all depends on what our parents say **II.** *m* (*de oreja*) earring; (*de nariz*) nose ring

**pendiente**[2] [pen·'djen·te] *f* (*cuesta, del tejado*) slope; **de mucha ~** steep

**pendón** [pen·'don] *m* banner

**péndulo** [pen·du·lo] *m* pendulum

**pene** ['pe·ne] *m* penis

**penetrante** [pe·ne·'tran·te] *adj* **1.** (*profundo*) deep; (*dolor*) fierce **2.** (*frío*) biting; (*hedor*) strong; (*olor*) pervasive **3.** (*sonido*) penetrating; (*grito*) piercing

**penetrar** [pe·ne·'trar] *vi, vt* (*atravesar*) to penetrate

**penicilina** [pe·ni·si·'li·na, pe·ni·θi·] *f* MED penicillin

**península** [pe·'nin·su·la] *f* GEO peninsula; **la Península Ibérica** the Iberian Peninsula

**peninsular** [pe·nin·su·'lar] *adj* peninsular

**penique** [pe·'ni·ke] *m* penny

**penitencia** [pe·ni·'ten·sja, -θja] *f* **1.** (*pena*) punishment **2.** REL penance; **hacer ~** to do penance **3.** (*arrepentimiento*) penitence

**penitenciario, -a** [pe·ni·ten·'sja·rjo, -'θja·rjo] *adj* (*relativo a la penitenciaría*) penitentiary

**penoso, -a** [pe·'no·so, -a] *adj* **1.** (*ar-*

*duo*) laborious **2.** (*dificultoso*) difficult **3.** *AmL* (*vergonzoso*) shameful

**pensado, -a** [pen·'sa·ðo, -a] *adj* **1.** (*reflexionado*) considered; **lo tengo bien ~** I have thought it through thoroughly; **tener ~ hacer algo** to have it in mind to do sth; **el día menos ~ volverá** just when it's least expected he/she will return **2.** (*persona*) **ser un mal ~** to always be ready to think the worst

**pensamiento** [pen·sa·'mjen·to] *m* **1.** (*acción, idea, objeto*) thought **2.** (*intención*) intention **3.** (*mente*) mind; **¿cuándo te vino esa idea al ~?** when did that idea occur to you? **4.** BOT pansy

**pensar** [pen·'sar] *<e ~ ie>* [pen·'sar] **I.** *vi, vt* **1.** (*formar un juicio, reflexionar*) **~ (en) algo** to think (about) sth; **¡ni ~lo!** don't even think about it!; **¡no quiero ni ~lo!** I don't even want to think about it!; **dar mucho que ~** to give people a lot to think about; **esto hay que ~lo bien** this needs to be thought out carefully; **lo hicimos sin ~lo** we did it without thinking; **pensándolo bien** on reflection; **pienso que deberíamos irnos** I think we should go **2.** (*considerar*) to consider **II.** *vi* (*opinar, suponer*) to think; **~ muy mal de alguien** to think very badly of sb **III.** *vt* **1.** (*intención*) to think of; **pensábamos venir este fin de semana** we were thinking of coming this weekend **2.** (*inventar, tramar*) to think up

**pensativo, -a** [pen·sa·'ti·βo, -a] *adj* thoughtful, pensive

**pensión** [pen·'sjon] *f* **1.** (*paga*) pension; **~ de viudez** widow's pension; **aún no cobra la ~** (*no recibe la paga*) he/she doesn't get a pension yet **2.** (*para huéspedes*) guesthouse **3.** (*precio por alojamiento*) (charge for) board and lodging; **~ completa** full board

**pensionista** [pen·sjo·'nis·ta] *mf* (*jubilado*) pensioner

**pentágono** [pen·'ta·yo·no] *m* pentagon

**pentagrama** [pen·ta·'yra·ma] *m* MÚS stave, staff

**Pentecostés** [pen·te·kos·'tes] *m* REL **1.** (*cristiano*) Whitsun **2.** (*judío*) Pentecost

**penúltimo, -a** [pe·'nul·ti·mo, -a] *adj* penultimate, next-to-last

**penumbra** [pe·'num·bra] *f* semi-darkness; ASTR penumbra

**penuria** [pe·'nu·rja] *f* **1.** (*escasez*) scarcity; **pasar muchas ~s** to suffer great hardship **2.** (*pobreza*) poverty

**peña** ['pe·ɲa] *f* **1.** (*roca*) crag **2.** (*grupo*) group; (*de aficionados*) club; *inf* (*de jóvenes*) gang

**peñasco** [pe·'ɲas·ko] *m* boulder

**peñón** [pe·'ɲon] *m* **1.** (*peñasco*) crag; **el Peñón** the Rock (of Gibraltar) **2.** (*monte*) mountain

**peón** [pe·'on] *m* **1.** (*obrero*) unskilled laborer; *Méx* (*aprendiz*) apprentice **2.** (*en ajedrez*) pawn

**peonza** [pe·'on·sa, -θa] *f* (*juguete*) top

**peor** [pe·'or] *adv, adj comp de* **mal(o)** worse; **en matemáticas soy ~ que tú** I am worse at math than you are; **el ~ de la clase** the worst in the class; **y verás, será ~ aún** you'll see, it will get even worse; **en el ~ de los casos** at worst; **pero lo ~ de todo fue...** but the worst thing of all was...; **vas de mal en ~** you're going from bad to worse

**pepinillo** [pe·pi·'ni·jo, -ʎo] *m* gherkin

**pepino** [pe·'pi·no] *m* cucumber; **eso me importa un ~** *inf* I don't give a hoot about that

**pepita** [pe·'pi·ta] *f* seed

**pequeñajo, -a** [pe·ke·'ɲa·xo, -a] *m, f inf* kid

**pequeñez** [pe·ke·'ɲes, -'ɲeθ] *f* **1.** (*tamaño*) littleness **2.** (*bagatela*) trifle

**pequeño, -a** [pe·'ke·ɲo, -a] **I.** *adj* small, little; **ya desde ~ solía venir a este sitio** I've been coming here since I was little; **esta camisa me queda pequeña** this shirt is too small for me **II.** *m, f* little one

**pequinés** [pe·ki·'nes] *m* ZOOL Pekinese

**pequinés, -esa** [pe·ki·'nes, -'ne·sa] *adj, m, f* Pekinese

**pera** ['pe·ra] *f* BOT pear ▶ **pedir ~s al olmo** *inf* to ask for the impossible; **eso es la ~** *inf* that's the limit

**peral** [pe·'ral] *m* pear tree

**percance** [per·'kan·se, -θe] *m* (*contratiempo*) setback

**per cápita** [per 'ka·pi·ta] *adv* per capita; **consumo ~** per capita consumption

**percatarse** [per·ka·'tar·se] *vr* **~ de algo** (*darse cuenta*) to notice sth; (*comprender*) to realize sth

**percepción** [per·sep·'sjon, -θeβ·'θjon] *f* **1.** (*acción*) perception **2.** (*impresión*) impression **3.** FIN receipt

**percha** ['per·tʃa] *f* **1.** (*en el armario*) hanger **2.** (*perchero*) coat stand; (*en la tienda*) clothes rail **3.** *AmC* (*chaqueta*) jacket **4.** *inf* (*tipo*) build; **tener buena ~** to have a good figure

**perchero** [per·'tʃe·ro] *m* **~ (de pared)** coat rack; **~ (de pie)** coat stand

**percibir** [per·si·'βir, per·θi-] *vt* **1.** (*notar*) to perceive **2.** (*darse cuenta*) to notice **3.** (*cobrar*) to receive

**percusión** [per·ku·'sjon] *f* MÚS percussion; **instrumento de ~** percussion instrument

**perdedor(a)** [per·'de·dor, -·'do·ra] *m(f)* loser

**perder** <e → ie> [per·'der] **I.** *vt* **1.** (*en general, peso, costumbre*) to lose; **~ la cuenta** to lose count; **he perdido mis gafas** I lost my glasses; **~ terreno** *fig* to lose ground **2.** (*malgastar*) to waste **3.** (*oportunidad, tren*) to miss **4.** (*ocasionar daños*) to destroy; **esa equivocación nos perdió** that mistake was our undoing; **el juego lo ~á** gambling will be his undoing **II.** *vi* **1.** (*en general*) to lose; **Portugal perdió por 1 a 2 frente a Italia** Portugal lost 2-1 against Italy; **vas a salir perdiendo** you're going to come off worst; **llevar todas las de ~** to be fighting a losing battle; **lo echó todo a ~** he/she spoiled everything; **la comida se echó a ~** the food was completely ruined **2.** (*decaer*) to decline; **~ en salud** to decline in health **III.** *vr* **1.** (*extraviarse*) to get lost; **¡qué se le habrá perdido por allí?** *fig* what is he/she doing there? **2.** (*bailando, leyendo*) to lose oneself **3.** (*desaparecer*) to disappear **4.** (*desperdiciarse*) to be wasted; **se pierde mucha agua por falta de conciencia ecológica** a lot of water is wasted through lack of environmental awareness **5.** (*ocasión*) to miss out; **si no te vienes, tú te lo pierdes** if you don't come, you'll be the one who misses out **6.** (*anhelar*) **~se por algo/alguien** to be crazy about sth/sb

**perdición** [per·di·'sjon, -'θjon] *f* **1.** (*acción*) loss; (*daño*) ruin **2.** (*moral*) perdition

**pérdida** ['per·di·da] *f* loss; **~ de cabello** hair loss; **esto es una ~ de tiempo** this is a waste of time; **es fácil de encontrar, no tiene ~** it's easy to find, you can't miss it; **~s humanas** victims

**perdido, -a** [per·'di·do, -a] *adj* **1.** (*que no se encuentra*) lost; **dar algo/a alguien por ~** to give sth/sb up for lost; *fig* to give up on sth/sb; **estar ~** to be lost **2.** (*vicioso, sin salida*) lost; **estar loco ~** *inf* to be completely insane **3.** (*sucio*) **poner algo ~** *inf* to make sth completely dirty; **ponerse ~ de pintura** *inf* to get covered in paint

**perdiz** [per·'dis, -'diθ] *f* partridge; **...y fueron felices y comieron perdices** ...and they lived happily ever after

**perdón** [per·'don] *m* **1.** (*absolución, indulto*) pardon **2.** (*disculpa*) **¡~!** sorry!; **¿~?** pardon?; **¡con ~!** if you'll excuse me!; **pedir ~ a alguien** to ask for sb's forgiveness; (*disculparse*) to apologize to sb

**perdonar** [per·do·'nar] *vt* **1.** (*ofensa, deuda*) to forgive; (*pecado, pena*) to pardon; **no te perdono** I don't forgive you; **perdona que te interrumpa** forgive me for interrupting; **perdona, ¿puedo pasar?** excuse me, can I come through? **2.** (*obligación*) to let off; **te perdono los 20 dólares** I'll forget about the 20 dollars you owe me **3.** (*dejar pasar*) **no ~ ningún medio** to use all possible means

**perdurar** [per·du·'rar] *vi* **1.** (*todavía*) to persist **2.** (*indefinidamente*) to last for ever; **su recuerdo ~á para siempre entre nosotros** his/her memory will always be with us

**perecedero, -a** [pe·re·se·'de·ro, -a; pe·re·θe-] *adj* **1.** (*pasajero*) transitory **2.** (*alimento*) perishable

**perecer** [pe·re·'ser, -θer] *irr como crecer* *vi* (*morir*) to perish

**peregrinación** [pe·re·γri·na·'sjon, -'θjon] *f* REL pilgrimage

**peregrinar** [pe·re·γri·'nar] *vi* REL to make a pilgrimage

**peregrino, -a** [pe·re·'γri·no, -a] *m, f* pilgrim

**perejil** [pe·re·'xil] *m* BOT parsley

**perenne** [pe·'ren·ne] *adj* everlasting; BOT perennial

**pereza** [pe·'re·sa, -θa] *f* (*gandulería*) laziness; **me dio ~ ir** I didn't feel like going

**perezosa** [pe·re·'so·sa, -'θo·sa] *f* *Arg, Perú, Urug* deck chair

**perezoso, -a** [pe·re·'so·so, -'θo·so] *adj* (*gandul*) lazy; **y ni corto ni ~** *inf* without giving it a thought

**perfección** [per·fek·'sjon, -'θjon] *f* perfection; **hacer algo a la ~** to do sth to perfection

**perfeccionamiento** [per·fek·sjo·na·'mjen·to, -θjo·na·'mjen·to] *m* perfection; (*técnica, sistema*) improvement; (*profesional*) further training

**perfeccionar** [per·fek·sjo·'nar, -θjo·'nar] *vt* to perfect; (*de técnica, sistema*) to improve

**perfeccionista** [per·fek·sjo·'nis·ta, -θjo·'nis·ta] *adj, mf* perfectionist

**perfectamente** [per·fek·ta·'men·te] *adv* perfectly; **sabes ~ que...** you know perfectly well that...

**perfecto** [per·'fek·to] *m* LING perfect tense

**perfecto, -a** [per·'fek·to, -a] *adj* **1.** perfect; **nadie es ~** nobody is perfect; **habla un inglés ~** he/she speaks perfect English; **un ~ caballero** a perfect gentleman; **eres un ~ idiota** you are a complete idiot **2.** LING **pretérito ~** past perfect

**perfil** [per·'fil] *m* **1.** *t. TÉC* (*de cara*) profile; **de ~** in profile **2.** (*contorno*) outline **3.** (*de personalidad*) characteristics *pl*; **el ~ del candidato** the description of the candidate

**perfilar** [per·fi·'lar] **I.** *vt* **1.** (*retocar*) to touch up **2.** (*sacar perfil*) to outline; TÉC to streamline **II.** *vr* **1.** (*distinguirse*) to stand out **2.** (*tomar forma*) to take shape

P

**perforar** [per·fo·'rar] *vt* (*con máquina*) to drill; (*oreja*) to pierce; (*papel*) to punch; (*para decorar, arrancar*) to perforate

**perfumar** [per·fu·'mar] *vt* to perfume; **las flores perfuman la habitación** the smell of flowers fills the room

**perfume** [per·'fu·me] *m* 1. (*sustancia*) perfume 2. (*olor*) fragrance

**perfumería** [per·fu·me·'ri·a] *f* perfume shop

**pericial** [pe·ri·'sjal, -'θjal] *adj* expert; **informe** ~ expert report

**periferia** [pe·ri·'fe·rja] *f* periphery; (*de ciudad*) outskirts *pl*

**perilla** [pe·'ri·ja, -ʎa] *f* goatee ▶ **venir de** ~**s** to be just what was needed

**perímetro** [pe·'ri·me·tro] *m* MAT perimeter

**periódico** [pe·'rjo·di·ko] *m* newspaper

**periódico, -a** [pe·'rjo·di·ko, -a] *adj* periodic; **sistema** ~ QUÍM periodic table

**periodismo** [pe·rjo·'dis·mo] *m* journalism

**periodista** [pe·rjo·'dis·ta] *mf* journalist

**periodístico, -a** [pe·rjo·'dis·ti·ko, -a] *adj* 1. (*de los periodistas*) journalistic 2. (*de los periódicos*) newspaper; **reportaje** ~ newspaper report

**periodo** [pe·'rjo·do] *m*, **período** [pe·'ri·o·do] *m t*. MAT, FÍS, GEO period; ~ **álgido** critical period; ~ **glacial** ice age; ~ **de prueba** trial period

**peripecia** [pe·ri·'pe·sja, -θja] *f* vicissitude; **pasar por muchas** ~**s** to go through many ups and downs

**periquete** [pe·ri·'ke·te] *m* **estoy lista en un** ~ I'll be ready in a jiffy

**periquito** [pe·ri·'ki·to] *m* parakeet

**periscopio** [pe·ris·'ko·pjo] *m* periscope

**perito, -a** [pe·'ri·to, -a] *m, f* (*experto*) expert

**perjudicar** <c → qu> [per·xu·di·'kar] *vt* 1. (*causar daño*) to damage; (*intereses*) to harm; **fumar perjudica la salud** smoking is bad for your health 2. (*causar desventaja*) to disadvantage

**perjudicial** [per·xu·di·'sjal, -'θjal] *adj* 1. (*que causa daño*) harmful 2. (*desventajoso*) disadvantageous

**perjuicio** [per·'xwi·sjo, -θjo] *m* 1. (*daño: de imagen, naturaleza*) harm; (*de obje-*

*to*) damage; **causar** ~**s** to cause harm 2. (*detrimento*) detriment; **ir en** ~ **de alguien** to be to sb's detriment

**perjurio** [per·'xu·rjo] *m* 1. (*en falso*) perjury 2. (*faltar al juramento*) breaking one's word

**perla** ['per·la] *f* pearl; ~ **cultivada** cultured pearl; **eso viene de** ~**s** that is just what was needed

**permanecer** [per·ma·ne·'ser, -θer] *irr como crecer vi* to remain; ~ **quieto** to keep still; ~ **invariable** to remain unchanged; ~ **dormido** to carry on sleeping; ~ **sentado** to remain seated

**permanencia** [per·ma·'nen·sja, -θja] *f* (*estancia*) stay; (*duración*) duration; **lograr la** ~ **en primera** DEP to stay in the first division

**permanente** [per·ma·'nen·te] I. *adj* permanent; **estado** ~ permanent state II. *f* perm

**permeable** [per·me·'a·βle] *adj* permeable

**permisividad** [per·mi·si·βi·'dad] *f* permissiveness

**permisivo, -a** [per·mi·'si·βo, -a] *adj* permissive

**permiso** [per·'mi·so] *m* 1. (*aprobación, autorización*) permission; **me dio** ~ **para hacerlo** he/she gave me permission to do it; **pedir** ~ **a alguien** to ask sb for permission 2. (*licencia*) permit; ~ **de conducir** driver's license; ~ **de residencia/de trabajo** residence/work permit 3. (*vacaciones*) leave; **estar de** ~ MIL to be on leave

**permitir** [per·mi·'tir] I. *vt* 1. (*consentir*) to permit; **¿me permite pasar/entrar/salir?** may I get past/enter/leave?; **no está permitido fumar** smoking is not allowed; **si me permite la expresión** if you will excuse the phrase 2. (*autorizar*) to authorize 3. (*hacer posible, tolerar*) to allow; **esta máquina permite trabajar el doble** this machine allows you to do twice as much work; **no permito que me levantes la voz** I won't allow you to raise your voice to me II. *vr* to allow oneself

**pernera** [per·'ne·ra] *f* (pant) leg

**pernicioso, -a** [per·ni·'sjo·so, -a; -'θjo·so,

-a] *adj* damaging

**pernoctar** [per·nok·'tar] *vi* to spend the night

**pero** ['pe·ro] **I.** *conj* but; (*sin embargo*) however; ¡~ **si todavía es una niña!** but she is still only a child!; ¿~ **qué es lo que quieres?** what do you want? **II.** *m* (*objeción*) objection; **el proyecto tiene sus ~s** there are lots of problems with the project; **sin un ~** no buts; **poner ~s a algo** to object to sth; **¡no hay ~ que valga!** there are no buts about it!; **poner ~ a todo** to object to everything

**peroné** [pe·ro·'ne] *m* fibula

**perpendicular** [per·pen·di·ku·'lar] *adj, f* perpendicular

**perpetrar** [per·pe·'trar] *vt* to perpetrate

**perpetuar** <*1. pres* perpetúo> [per·pe·tu·'ar] **I.** *vt* **1.** (*recuerdo, memoria, nombre*) to preserve **2.** (*situación, error, mentira*) to perpetuate **II.** *vr* to be perpetuated

**perpetuidad** [per·pe·twi·'dad] *f* **1.** (*continuidad*) continuity **2.** (*eternidad*) perpetuity; **a ~** in perpetuity; **condenar a ~** to condemn to life imprisonment

**perpetuo, -a** [per·'pe·two, -a] *adj* **1.** (*incesante*) perpetual; **nieves perpetuas** permanent snow **2.** (*vitalicio*) life; **cadena perpetua** life sentence

**perplejo, -a** [per·'ple·xo, -a] *adj* perplexed

**perra** ['pe·rra] *f* **1.** ZOOL bitch; *v. t.* **perro I. 2.** *inf* (*rabieta*) tantrum; **coger una ~** to throw a tantrum **3.** (*mujer malvada*) bitch **4.** *inf* (*dinero*) penny; **no tener una ~** to be broke

**perrera** [pe·'rre·ra] *f* (*de perros callejeros*) dog pound

**perrito** [pe·'rri·to] *m* ~ **caliente** hot dog

**perro, -a** ['pe·rro] **I.** *m, f* (*macho*) dog; (*hembra*) bitch; ~ **callejero** stray dog; ~ **faldero** lapdog; ~ **lazarillo** guide-dog; **morir como un ~** *inf* to die a lonely death ▶ **se llevan como el ~ y el gato** *inf* they fight like cat and dog; **ser como el ~ del hortelano** to be a dog in the manger; **humor de ~s** *inf* filthy mood; **a ~ flaco todo son pulgas** *prov* misfortunes never come singly; **tiempo de ~s** *inf* filthy weather; ~ **ladrador,**

**poco mordedor** *prov* his bark is worse than his bite; **muerto el ~ se acabó la rabia** *prov* dead dogs don't bite; **ser ~ viejo** *inf* to be an old hand **II.** *adj* lousy; **llevar una vida perra** to lead a wretched life

**persa** ['per·sa] *adj* Persian; **alfombra ~** Persian rug

**persecución** [per·se·ku·'sjon, -'θjon] *f* pursuit; (*acoso*) persecution; ~ **en coche** car chase

**perseguir** [per·se·'ɣir] *irr como seguir vt* to chase; (*contrato, chica*) to pursue; **la policía persigue al fugitivo** the police are pursuing the fugitive; **me persigue la mala suerte** I'm dogged by bad luck; **el jefe me persigue todo el día** the boss is always on my back; **¡qué persigues con esto?** what do you hope to achieve by this?

**perseverancia** [per·se·βe·'ransja, -θja] *f* **1.** (*insistencia*) ~ **en algo** insistence on sth **2.** (*en trabajo, actividad*) ~ **en algo** perseverance in sth **3.** (*firmeza*) resolve

**perseverante** [per·se·βe·'ran·te] *adj* **1.** (*insistente*) insistent **2.** (*constante*) persevering **3.** (*firme*) determined

**perseverar** [per·se·βe·'rar] *vi* **1.** (*insistir*) to insist **2.** (*mantener*) ~ **en algo** to persevere in sth

**Persia** ['per·sja] *f* Persia

**persiana** [per·'sja·na] *f* blind

**persignarse** [per·siɣ·'nar·se] *vr* to cross oneself

**persistencia** [per·sis·'ten·sja, -θja] *f* persistence

**persistente** [per·sis·'ten·te] *adj* persistent

**persistir** [per·sis·'tir] *vi* to persist

**persona** [per·'so·na] *f* person; ~ **de contacto** contact; ~ **(non) grata** persona (non) grata; **en ~** in person; ~ **jurídica** legal entity; ~ **mayor** adult, grown-up; ~ **física** individual; **ser buena/mala ~** to be good/bad; **había muchas ~s** there were a lot of people; **no había ninguna ~ allí** there was nobody there; **ese es una ~ de cuidado** you need to be careful with him

**personaje** [per·so·'na·xe] *m* personality; TEAT, LIT character; **es todo un ~** he/she is a real character

P

**personal** [per·so·'nal] I. *adj* personal; **datos ~es** personal details; **pronombre ~** personal pronoun II. *m* 1. (*plantilla*) personnel; (*en empresa*) staff; **~ docente** teaching staff 2. *inf* (*gente*) people *pl*

**personalidad** [per·so·na·li·'dad] *f* personality

**personalizar** <z → c> [per·so·na·li·'sar, -'θar] *vt* 1. (*hacer personal*) to personalize 2. (*aludir*) to get personal

**personarse** [per·so·'nar·se] *vr* to appear; **~ en juicio** to appear before the court; **persónese ante el director** report to the director

**personificar** <c → qu> [per·so·ni·fi·'kar] *vt* to personify; **personifica la maldad** he/she is evil personified

**perspectiva** [pers·pek·'ti·βa] *f* 1. (*general*) perspective 2. (*vista*) view 3. *pl* (*posibilidad*) prospects *pl*

**perspicacia** [pers·pi·'ka·sja, -θja] *f* insight

**perspicaz** [pers·pi·'kas, -'kaθ] *adj* 1. (*vista*) keen 2. (*persona*) perceptive

**persuadir** [per·swa·'dir] I. *vt* 1. (*inducir*) to encourage; **lo ~é para que no lo haga** I will persuade him not to do it 2. (*convencer*) to persuade II. *vr* to be persuaded

**persuasión** [per·swa·'sjon] *f* (*acto*) persuasion; **emplear todo su poder de ~** to use all one's powers of persuasion

**persuasivo, -a** [per·swa·'si·βo, -a] *adj* persuasive

**pertenecer** [per·te·ne·'ser, -θer] *irr como* **crecer** *vi* (*ser de*) to belong; **esta casa me pertenece** this house belongs to me

**perteneciente** [per·te·ne·'sjen·te, -'θjen·te] *adj* **~ a** belonging to; **los países ~s a la ONU** the countries that are members of the UN; **todo lo ~ al caso** everything that is relevant to the case

**pertenencia** [per·te·'nen·sja, -θja] *f* 1. (*acción*) belonging 2. *pl* (*bienes*) belongings *pl* 3. *pl* (*accesorios*) accessories *pl*

**pértiga** ['per·ti·γa] *f t.* DEP pole; **salto de ~** pole vault; **saltar con ~** to pole vault

**pertinente** [per·ti·'nen·te] *adj* 1. (*opor-*

*tuno*) appropriate 2. (*datos, pregunta, comentario*) relevant, pertinent 3. (*relativo*) **en lo ~ a...** with regard to...

**perturbado, -a** [per·tur·'βa·do, -a] *m, f* **~** (**mental**) mentally disturbed person

**perturbar** [per·tur·'βar] *vt* to disturb; (*confundir*) to confuse

**Perú** [pe·'ru] *m* Peru

**peruano, -a** [pe·'rwa·no, -a] *adj, m, f* Peruvian

**perversidad** [per·βer·si·'dad] *f* (*sexual*) perversity

**perversión** [per·βer·'sjon] *f* 1. (*acción*) perversion 2. (*cualidad*) perversity

**perverso, -a** [per·'βer·so, -a] *adj* (*sexual*) perverse

**pervertido, -a** [per·βer·'ti·do, -a] *adj* perverted

**pervertir** [per·βer·tir] *irr como* **sentir** I. *vt* to corrupt II. *vr* to become corrupt; (*depravarse*) to become perverted

**pesa** ['pe·sa] *f t.* DEP weight; **hacer ~s** to do weight training; **levantamiento de ~s** weightlifting

**pesadez** [pe·sa·'des, -'deθ] *f* 1. (*de objeto*) heaviness 2. (*de movimiento*) slowness, sluggishness 3. (*de sueño*) drowsiness 4. (*de tarea*) boring nature 5. (*de persona*) tiresome nature 6. (*de viaje*) tediousness 7. (*de lectura*) density; (*aburrido*) dullness 8. (*de estómago*) (acid) indigestion

**pesadilla** [pe·sa·'di·ja, -ʎa] *f* nightmare

**pesado, -a** [pe·'sa·do, -a] *adj* 1. (*que pesa*) heavy; **tengo la cabeza pesada** my head feels rather stuffy; **tengo el estómago ~** my stomach is uncomfortably full 2. (*lento*) slow 3. (*molesto*) tiresome 4. (*duro*) hard; **un trabajo ~** hard work 5. (*aburrido*) boring 6. (*sueño*) deep; (*tiempo*) oppressive; (*viaje*) tedious; (*lectura*) heavy going

**pésame** ['pe·sa·me] *m* condolences *pl*; **dar el ~** to offer one's condolences; **reciba mi más sincero ~** please accept my heartfelt condolences

**pesar** [pe·'sar] I. *vi* to weigh; **esta caja pesa mucho** this box is very heavy; **pon encima lo que no pese** put the lightest things on top; **~ sobre alguien** to weigh heavily on sb; (*problemas*) to weigh sb down **II.** *vt* to weigh; (*cantidad concreta*) to weigh out; **¿me puede ~ la fruta?** could you weigh this fruit for me?; **me pesa haberte mentido** I regret having lied to you; **pese a quien pese** come what may; **pese a que...** although... **III.** *m* **1.** (*pena*) sorrow; **muy a ~ mío** to my great sadness **2.** (*remordimiento*) regret ▶ **a ~ de** in spite of

**pesca** ['pes·ka] *f* fishing; (*captura*) capture; **ir de ~** to go fishing; **~ de altura** deep-sea fishing; **~ de arrastre** trawling; **~ de bajura** inshore fishing; **y toda la ~** *fig inf* and all the rest of the crew

**pescadería** [pes·ka·de·'ri·a] *f* (*tienda*) fish market

**pescado** [pes·'ka·ðo] *m* fish

**pescador(a)** [pes·ka·'dor, -·'do·ra] *m(f)* (*de caña*) angler; (*de mar*) fisherman

**pescar** <c → qu> [pes·'kar] *vt* **1.** (*con caña, en barco*) to fish for; **ir a ~ sardinas** to fish for sardines **2.** (*sorprender*) to catch out; (*resfriado*) to catch **3.** *inf* (*novio*) to land **4.** *inf* (*entender*) to understand

**pescuezo** [pes·'kwe·so, -θo] *m* (scruff of the) neck; **retorcer el ~ a alguien** *inf* to wring sb's neck; **salvar el ~** *fig* to save one's skin

**pese** ['pe·se] *adv* **~ a** in spite of, despite

**pesebre** [pe·'se·βre] *m* manger; (*de Navidad*) Nativity scene

**peseta** [pe·'se·ta] *f* peseta

**pesetero, -a** [pe·se·'te·ro, -a] *m, f* money-grubbing; **eres un ~** all you think about is money

**pesimismo** [pe·si·'mis·mo] *m* pessimism

**pesimista** [pe·si·'mis·ta] *adj* pessimistic

**pésimo, -a** ['pe·si·mo, -a] *adj* dreadful

**peso** ['pe·so] *m* **1.** (*de objeto*) weight; **coger/perder ~** to gain/lose weight; **¿qué ~ tiene?** how much does it weigh?; **vender a ~** to sell by weight; **eso cae por su propio ~** that goes without saying **2.** (*pesadez*) heaviness **3.** (*importancia*) weight; **tener una razón de ~** to have a good reason **4.** (*carga*) burden; **llevar el ~ de algo** to bear the burden of sth; **me saco un ~ de encima** that's taken a load off my mind **5.** DEP (*bola*) shot **6.** DEP (*boxeo*) weight

**7.** (*moneda*) peso ▶ **comprar a ~ de oro** to pay way over the odds

**pesquero** [pes·'ke·ro] *m* fishing boat

**pesquisa¹** [pes·'ki·sa] *f* inquiry; **hacer ~s** to make inquiries

**pesquisa²** [pes·'ki·sa] *m* *Arg, Ecua, Par* detective

**pestaña** [pes·'ta·ɲa] *f* eyelash; **quemarse las ~s** *fig* to burn the midnight oil

**pestañear** [pes·ta·'ɲar; pes·ta·ɲe·'ar] *vi* to blink; **sin ~** without batting an eyelid

**peste** ['pes·te] *f* **1.** *t.* MED (*plaga*) plague; **~ bubónica** bubonic plague **2.** (*olor*) stench; **aquí hay una ~ increíble** it really stinks here **3.** (*crítica*) **echar ~s de alguien** to heap abuse on sb

**pestillo** [pes·'ti·jo, -ʎo] *m* bolt; **echar el ~** to shoot the bolt

**petaca** [pe·'ta·ka] *f* **1.** (*para cigarros*) cigarette case; (*para tabaco*) tobacco pouch **2.** *AmL* (*caja*) box; (*baúl*) chest; (*cesto*) basket **3.** *AmC* (*joroba*) hump

**pétalo** ['pe·ta·lo] *m* petal

**petardo** [pe·'tar·ðo] *m* **1.** (*de fiesta*) firecracker; **tirar ~s** to set off firecrackers **2.** *inf* (*persona o cosa mala*) **ser un ~** to be a pain

**petate** [pe·'ta·te] *m* (*de soldado, marinero*) kit bag

**petición** [pe·ti·'sjon, -'θjon] *f* (*ruego, solicitud*) request; (*escrito*) petition; **a ~ de...** at the request of...

**petiso, -a** [pe·'ti·so] *adj* *Arg, Urug* (*pequeño*) small; (*muy pequeño*) tiny; (*enano*) short

**peto** ['pe·to] *m* (*de bebé, delantal*) bib

**petrificar** <c → qu> [pe·tri·fi·'kar] *vt* *t. fig* to petrify

**petróleo** [pe·'tro·leo] *m* **1.** (*carburante*) petroleum, (crude) oil **2.** (*de lámpara*) paraffin

**petrolero** [pe·tro·'le·ro] *m* (*barco*) oil tanker

**petrolífero, -a** [pe·tro·'li·fe·ro, -a] *adj* oil-bearing; **campo ~** oilfield; **industria petrolífera** oil industry

**petulante** [pe·tu·'lan·te] *adj* **1.** (*arrogante*) arrogant **2.** (*insolente*) insolent

**peyorativo, -a** [pe·jo·ra·'ti·βo, -a] *adj* pejorative; **un comentario ~** a derogatory remark

**P**

**peyote** [pe·'jo·te] *m AmL* BOT peyote cactus

**pez** [pes, peθ] *m* ZOOL fish; **estar como ~ en el agua** to be in one's element; **estar ~ en español** *inf* to have no idea of Spanish; **un ~ gordo** a big shot

**pezón** [pe·'son, -'θon] *m* 1. (*de mujer*) nipple 2. (*de animal*) teat

**pezuña** [pe·'su·ɲa, pe·'θu-] *f* 1. (*de vaca, oveja*) hoof 2. *pl inf* (*de persona*) feet *pl*

**piadoso, -a** [pja·'do·so, -a] *adj* 1. (*misericordioso*) merciful; (*bondadoso*) compassionate 2. (*devoto*) pious

**pialar** [pja·'lar] *vt AmL* to lasso

**pianista** [pja·'nis·ta] *mf* pianist

**piano** [pi·'a·no] *m* piano; **~ de cola** grand piano

**piar** <1. pres pío> [pi·'ar] *vi* (*pájaro*) to chirp

**piara** [pi·'a·ra] *f* herd (of pigs)

**PIB** [pe·i·'βe] *m abr de* **Producto Interior Bruto** GDP

**pibe, -a** ['pi·βe, -a] *m, f Arg* (*chico*) boy; (*chica*) girl

**picadero** [pi·ka·'de·ro] *m* (*para adiestrar*) ring; (*escuela*) riding school

**picadillo** [pi·ka·'di·jo, -ʎo] *m* (*carne picada*) ground meat; **hacer ~ a alguien** *inf* to make mincemeat of sb

**picadura** [pi·ka·'du·ra] *f* 1. (*de insecto*) sting; (*de serpiente*) bite 2. (*en ropa, metal*) hole 3. (*caries*) cavity

**picante** [pi·'kan·te] I. *adj* spicy, hot; *fig* risqué II. *m* CULIN spicy food

**picaporte** [pi·ka·'por·te] *m* 1. (*aldaba*) doorknocker 2. (*tirador*) door handle 3. (*pestillo*) latch

**picar** <c → qu> [pi·'kar] I. *vi* 1. (*sol*) to sting 2. (*pimienta*) to be hot 3. (*pez*) to take the bait 4. (*de la comida*) to snack 5. (*tener picazón*) to itch; **me pica la espalda** my back is itchy 6. (*golpear*) **~ a la puerta** to knock on the door 7. (*aspirar*) **~ muy alto** to aim too high II. *vt* 1. (*insecto*) to sting; (*serpiente*) to bite 2. (*ave*) to peck 3. (*desmenuzar*) to chop up; (*carne*) to mince 4. (*ofender*) to irritate; **estar picado con alguien** to be annoyed with sb; **¿qué mosca te ha picado?** what's eating you? 5. (*incitar*)

to goad III. *vr* 1. (*metal*) to rust; (*muela*) to decay; (*vino*) to turn sour 2. (*mar*) to become choppy 3. (*ofenderse*) to become irritated; (*mosquearse*) to become angry; **~se por nada** to get irritated about the slightest thing

**picardía** [pi·kar·'di·a] *f* 1. (*malicia*) roguishness 2. (*travesura*) **una ~** a dirty trick

**picaresco, -a** [pi·ka·'res·ko, -a] *adj* 1. (*astuto*) cunning 2. (*comentario*) mischievous

**pícaro, -a** ['pi·ka·ro, -a] I. *adj* 1. (*granuja*) roguish 2. (*astuto*) cunning 3. (*comentario*) naughty II. *m, f* rogue

**picazón** [pi·ka·'son, -'θon] *f* itch

**picha** [pi·'tʃa] *f vulg* dick, prick

**pichanga** [pi·'tʃan·ga] *f* 1. *Arg* (*vino*) wine (*not fully fermented*) 2. *Bol* (*fácil*) **ser ~** to be a cinch *inf*

**pichichi** [pi·'tʃi·tʃi] *m* DEP top goal-scorer

**pichín** [pi·'tʃin] *m CSur inf* pee

**pichincha** [pi·'tʃin·tʃa] *f* 1. *Arg* (*ganga*) bargain 2. *Chile* (*cantidad pequeña*) tiny bit

**picnic** ['piɣ·nik] *m* picnic

**pico** ['pi·ko] *m* 1. (*del pájaro*) beak 2. *inf* (*boca*) mouth; **¡cierra el ~!** shut up!; **~ de oro** the gift of gab; **alguien se fue del ~** sb let the cat out of the bag 3. (*herramienta*) pickax 4. (*montaña*) peak; **cortado a ~** sheer 5. (*de jarra*) lip 6. (*cantidad*) **llegar a las cuatro y ~** to arrive just after four o'clock; **tiene cuarenta y ~ años** he/she is forty-something; **salir por un ~** to cost a lot

**picor** [pi·'kor] *m* (*en la piel*) itching; (*en la boca*) stinging, burning

**picotazo** [pi·ko·'ta·so, -θo] *m* **pegar un ~** (*ave*) to peck; **arrancar a ~s** to peck off

**picotear** [pi·ko·te·'ar] I. *vi* (*comer*) to nibble II. *vt* to peck

**picudo, -a** [pi·'ku·do, -a] *adj* pointed; (*anguloso*) angular

**pie** [pje] *m* 1. (*extremidad, medida*) foot; **~s planos** flat feet; **¿qué ~ calza Ud.?** what shoe size do you take?; **a ~ de obra** on the spot; **a ~** on foot; **quedarse de ~** to remain standing; **estar de ~** to be standing; **ponerse de ~** to

stand up; **ya sabemos de qué ~ cojea**
*fig* now we know his/her weak spot;
**tener los ~s en el suelo** *fig* to be realistic; **se marchó por su propio ~** he/
she left on his own; **no hacer ~** (*en una
piscina*) to be out of one's depth; **estoy
cansada: no me tengo en ~** I am so
tired I can barely stand; **con buen ~**
*fig* on the right footing; **estar en ~ de
guerra** to be on a war footing; **ya tiene
un ~ en el hoyo** *inf* he/she already has
one foot in the grave **2.** TIPO ~ **de imprenta** imprint; ~ **de página** foot of the
page **3.** (*métrica*) foot **4.** (*trípode*) leg
▶ **hoy no doy ~ con bola** I can't seem
to do anything right today; **no tener ni
~s ni cabeza** to make no sense; **estar
al ~ del cañón** to be ready for action;
**buscar tres ~s al gato** (*daño*) to ask for
trouble; (*complicaciones*) to complicate
matters; **seguir algo al ~ de la letra** to
follow sth to the letter; **andarse con ~s
de plomo** to tread very carefully; **parar
los ~s a alguien** *inf* to put sb in his/her
place; **~s, ¿para qué os quiero?** time
to leave!; **salir por ~s** *inf* to beat it; **de
a ~** ordinary

**piedad** [pje·'dad] *f* REL piety; (*compasión*) pity; **¡ten ~ de nosotros!** have
pity on us!

**piedra** ['pje·dra] *f* stone; ~ **pómez** pumice stone; ~ **preciosa** precious stone;
**cartón** ~ papier-mâché; **Edad de Piedra** Stone Age; **poner la primera ~** to
lay the foundation stone; ~ **angular** *fig*
cornerstone; ~ **filosofal** *fig* philosopher's
stone; ~ **de toque** *fig* touchstone; **no
dejar ~ sobre ~** to raze to the ground;
**quedarse de ~** to be stunned; **tirar la
~ y esconder la mano** to play the innocent; **tirarse ~s a su propio tejado**
to foul one's own nest; **pasar a alguien
por la ~** *inf* to lay sb

**piel** [pjel] *f* (*de persona, fruta*) skin; (*de
animal*) skin, hide; (*con pelo*) fur; (*cuero*) leather; **dejarse la ~ en algo** *inf* to
work oneself into the ground for sth; **un
abrigo de ~es** a fur coat ▶ ~ **de gallina** goose-pimples *pl*

**pienso** ['pjen·so] *m* fodder; ~ **completo**
compound feed

**pierna** ['pjer·na] *f* leg; ~ **ortopédica**
artificial leg; **estirar las ~s** to stretch
one's legs; **con las ~s cruzadas** with
one's legs crossed; **dormir a ~ suelta**
to be fast asleep

**pieza** ['pje·sa, -θa] *f* **1.** (*pedazo*) *t.* MÚS,
TEAT piece; ~ **de recambio** spare part;
**un traje de dos ~s** a two-piece suit;
~ **por ~** piece by piece; **¡menuda ~
está hecho ese!** *inf* what a little rascal he is! **2.** *AmL* (*habitación*) room
▶ **quedarse de una ~** to be absolutely
dumbfounded

**pifia** ['pi·fja] *f* (*error*) blunder

**pigmento** [piɣ·'men·to] *m* pigment

**pijada** [pi·'xa·da] *f* *inf* piece of nonsense

**pijama** [pi·'xa·ma] *m* pajamas *pl*

**pijo** ['pi·xo] *m* *vulg* dick; **¡y un ~!** like
hell!

**pijo, -a** ['pi·xo, -a] *adj* pey, *inf* stuck-up;
**niño** ~ spoiled brat

**pila** ['pi·la] *f* **1.** (*recipiente*) basin; (*lavadero*) sink; (*bautismal*) font; **nombre
de** ~ first name, Christian name **2.** FÍS
battery; **ponerse las ~s** *inf* to get one's
act together **3.** (*montón*) pile; **una ~ de
libros** a pile of books

**pilar** [pi·'lar] *m* **1.** (*columna*) pillar
**2.** (*apoyo*) prop **3.** (*en camino*) milestone

**pilcha** ['pil·tʃa] *f* *CSur* *inf* fine clothes *pl*

**píldora** ['pil·do·ra] *f* pill; **la ~** (*anticonceptiva*) the pill; **dorar la ~ a alguien**
*inf* to sweeten the pill

**pillar** [pi·'jar, -'ʎar] *vt* **1.** (*atropellar*) to
knock down, to run over **2.** (*encontrar*)
to find; (*en flagrante*) to catch; **me pillas de buen humor** you've caught me
in a good mood; **eso no me pilla de
sorpresa** that doesn't surprise me; **tu
casa nos pilla de camino** your house
is on our way **3.** (*entender*) to grasp
**4.** *Arg* (*orinar*) to piss

**pillastre** [pi·'jas·tre, -'ʎas·tre] *m* *inf* rascal

**pillín, -ina** [pi·'jin, --'ji·na; --'ʎin, --'ʎi·na]
*adj* *inf* crafty

**pillo, -a** ['pi·jo, -a; -ʎo, -a] I. *adj* *inf* crafty
II. *m, f* *inf* rascal

**pilmama** [pil·'ma·na] *f* *Méx* nanny

**pilotar** [pi·lo·'tar] *vt* (*barco*) to steer; (*co-*

*che*) to drive; (*avión*) to fly

**piloto¹** [pi·'lo·to] I. *mf* 1. NÁUT navigator; (*oficial*) first mate; (*práctico*) (coast) pilot 2. AVIAT pilot; **poner el ~ automático** to set the automatic pilot 3. AUTO driver; **~ de carreras** racing driver II. *adj* (*de prueba*) test; (*de modelo*) show, model; **piso ~** model apartment

**piloto²** [pi·'lo·to] *m Arg* (*impermeable*) raincoat

**pimentón** [pi·men·'ton] *m* paprika

**pimienta** [pi·'mjen·ta] *f* pepper; **~ en grano** peppercorns *pl*

**pimiento** [pi·'mjen·to] *m* pepper; **me importa un ~** I couldn't care less

**pinacoteca** [pi·na·ko·'te·ka] *f* art gallery

**pinar** [pi·'nar] *m* pine grove

**pincel** [pin·'sel, -'θel] *m* (paint)brush; **estar hecho un ~** to be stylishly dressed

**pincelada** [pin·se·'la·da, pin·θe·-] *f* brushstroke; **dar las últimas ~s** *fig* to apply the finishing touches

**pinchar** [pin·'tʃar] I. *vi* (*rueda*) to get a flat (tire) **~ ni ~ ni cortar** *inf* to not count for anything II. *vt* 1. (*alfiler*) to prick 2. (*estimular*) to prod; (*mortificar*) to wound 3. (*inyección*) to give an injection; **tengo que ir al médico para que me pinche** I have to go the doctor's for an injection 4. (*teléfono*) to tap III. *vr* 1. (*alfiler*) to prick oneself 2. (*rueda*) **se nos ha pinchado una rueda** one of our tires has a flat 3. (*insulina*) to give oneself an injection 4. *inf* (*drogarse*) to shoot up

**pinchazo** [pin·'tʃa·so, -'tʃa·θo] *m* 1. (*espina*) prick; **me dieron unos ~s en el estómago** I had some shooting pains in the stomach 2. (*neumático*) flat (tire)

**pinche** ['pin·tʃe] *mf* (*tapa*) cook's helper

**pinchito** [pin·'tʃi·to] *m* (*tapa*) snack

**pincho** ['pin·tʃo] *m* 1. (*erizo*) sting; (*rosa*) thorn 2. *v.* **pinchito**

**pingo** ['pin·go] *m* 1. *inf* (*harapo*) rag 2. *CSur* (*caballo*) horse ▶ **poner a alguien hecho un ~** to run sb down

**ping-pong** [pin·'pon] *m* ping-pong

**pingüino** [pin·'gwi·no] *m* penguin

**pino** ['pi·no] *m* 1. (*árbol, madera*) pine; **~ piñonero** stone pine 2. DEP handstand ▶ **en el quinto ~** in the back

of beyond

**pinta** ['pin·ta] *f* 1. *t.* ZOOL (*mancha*) spot; (*gota*) drop 2. *inf* (*aspecto*) appearance; **tener ~ de caro** to look expensive; **tener buena ~** (*plato*) to look tasty; (*persona*) to be attractive

**pintada** [pin·'ta·da] *f* (*pared*) (piece of) graffiti

**pintado, -a** [pin·'ta·do] *adj* (*animal*) spotted; **papel ~** wallpaper; **el traje te sienta que ni ~** *inf* the suit really suits you

**pintalabios** [pin·ta·'la·βjos] *m inv* lipstick

**pintar** [pin·'tar] I. *vi* 1. ARTE to paint 2. (*bolígrafo*) to write II. *vt* 1. (*pared*) to paint; (*con dibujos*) to decorate; **~ de azul** to paint blue; **¡recién pintado!** wet paint! 2. (*cuadro*) to paint; **¿qué pinta eso aquí?** *fig* what's that doing here?; **no ~ nada** *fig* (*persona*) to have no influence; (*asunto*) to be completely irrelevant 3. (*describir*) to describe III. *vr* to do one's make-up

**pinto, -a** ['pin·to, -a] *adj* spotted

**pintor(a)** [pin·'tor, -·'to·ra] *m(f)* painter

**pintoresco, -a** [pin·to·'res·ko, -a] *adj* picturesque, colorful

**pintura** [pin·'tu·ra] *f* 1. (*arte, cuadro*) painting; **~ al óleo** oil painting; **~ rupestre** cave painting; **voy a clases de ~** I go to painting classes; **no lo puedo ver ni en ~** *inf* I can't stand him 2. (*color*) paint; **caja de ~s** paint box; **dar una capa de ~ a algo** to give sth a coat of paint

**pinza(s)** ['pin·sa(s), -θa(s)] *f(pl)* 1. (*tenacilla*) tongs *pl*; TÉC pincers *pl* 2. (*para la ropa*) clothespin 3. (*para depilar*) tweezers *pl* 4. (*de cangrejo*) claw

**piña** ['pi·na] *f* 1. (*pino*) pine cone 2. (*fruta*) pineapple

**piñón** [pi·'non] *m* 1. (*pino*) pine nut; **estar a partir un ~ con alguien** *inf* to be thick as thieves 2. TÉC pinion

**pío** [pi·o] *m* cheep; **no decir ni ~** not to say a word; **¡~, ~, ~!** tweet, tweet!

**pío, -a** [pi·o, -a] *adj* pious

**piojo** [pi·xo] *m* louse

**piojoso, -a** [pjo·'xo·so, -a] *adj* louse-infested; (*sucio*) seedy

**piola** ['pjo·la] I. *adj Arg inf* (*astuto*) clever

**II.** *f AmS* (*cuerda*) cord
**pionero, -a** [pjo·'ne·ro, -a] *m, f* pioneer
**pipa** ['pi·pa] *f* **1.** (*fumador*) pipe; **fumar en ~** to smoke a pipe **2.** (*de fruta*) pip, seed **3.** *CRi inf* (*cabeza*) head **4.** *inf* (*muy bien*) **lo pasamos ~** we had a great time
**pipí** [pi·'pi] *m inf* pee *sl*
**pique** ['pi·ke] *m* **1.** (*rivalidad*) rivalry; **menudo ~ se traen entre ellos** they really hate each other **2.** *Arg, Par, Nic* (*camino*) trail **3.** (*hundirse*) **irse a ~** (*barco*) to sink; (*plan*) to fail
**piqueta** [pi·'ke·ta] *f* pickax
**piquete** [pi·'ke·te] *m* (strike) picket
**pira** ['pi·ra] *f* pyre; **~ funeraria** funeral pyre
**pirado, -a** [pi·'ra·do, -a] *adj inf* crazy
**piragua** [pi·'ra·ɣwa] *f* canoe
**pirámide** [pi·'ra·mi·de] *f* pyramid
**piraña** [pi·'ra·ɲa] *f* piranha
**pirarse** [pi·'rar·se] *vr inf* to clear off
**pirata** [pi·'ra·ta] **I.** *mf* pirate **II.** *adj* pirate; **emisora ~** pirate radio station
**pirenaico, -a** [pi·re·'nai·ko, -a] *adj* Pyrenean
**Pirineos** [pi·ri·'neos] *mpl* Pyrenees
**piripi** [pi·'ri·pi] *adj inf* tipsy
**pirómano, -a** [pi·'ro·ma·no, -a] *m, f* pyromaniac
**piropo** [pi·'ro·po] *m inf* flirtatious comment; **echar ~s** to make flirtatious comments
**pirotecnia** [pi·ro·'tey·nja] *f* pyrotechnics
**pirrarse** [pi·'rrar·se] *vr inf* **~ por alguien** to be crazy about sb
**pirueta** [pi·'rwe·ta] *f* pirouette
**piruleta** [pi·ru·'le·ta] *f*, **pirulí** [pi·ru·'li] *m* <pirulís> lollipop
**pis** [pis] *m inf* piss
**pisada** [pi·'sa·da] *f* **1.** (*acción*) footstep **2.** (*huella*) footprint; **seguir las ~s de alguien** *fig* to follow in sb's footsteps
**pisapapeles** [pi·sa·pa·'pe·les] *m inv* paperweight
**pisar** [pi·'sar] *vt* **1.** (*poner el pie*) to step, to tread; **¡no pises las flores!** don't step on the flowers!; **me han pisado en el bus** sb stepped on my foot in the bus; **ir pisando huevos** *fig* to watch one's step; **~ los talones a alguien** *fig* to follow

on sb's heels; **~ fuerte** *fig* to make a big impact **2.** (*entrar*) to enter **3.** (*humillar*) to walk all over **4.** *inf* (*planes*) to pre-empt; **me han pisado el tema** they have stolen my topic
**piscina** [pi·'si·na, pis·'θi·na] *f* swimming pool; **~ cubierta** indoor swimming pool
**Piscis** ['pi·sis, 'pis·θis] *m inv* Pisces
**pisco** ['pis·ko] *m* **1.** (*aguardiente*) strong Peruvian liquor **2.** *Col, Ven* (*pavo*) turkey **3.** *Col pey* (*hombre*) guy
**piso** ['pi·so] *m* **1.** (*pavimento*) floor; (*calle*) surface **2.** (*planta*) floor, story; **de dos ~s** with two floors **3.** (*vivienda*) apartment
**pisotear** [pi·so·te·'ar] *vt* to trample; *fig* to walk all over
**pisotón** [pi·so·'ton] *m* stamp; **dar un ~ a alguien** to tread on sb's foot
**pista** ['pis·ta] *f* **1.** (*huella*) trail; (*indicio*) clue; **seguir la ~ a alguien** to follow sb's trail **2.** (*de circo*) ring; (*para atletismo, coches*) track; (*de tenis*) court; (*de baile*) floor; **~ de aterrizaje** runway; **~ de esquí** ski slope; **~ de hielo** ice rink **3.** (*camino*) trail **4.** COMPUT track
**pistacho** [pis·'ta·tʃo] *m* pistachio
**pistola** [pis·'to·la] *f* **1.** (*arma*) pistol **2.** (*del pintor*) spray gun
**pistolero, -a** [pis·to·'le·ro, -a] *m* gunman
**pistoletazo** [pis·to·le·'ta·so, -'ta·θo] *m* pistol shot; **~ de salida** *fig* starting signal
**pistón** [pis·'ton] *m* **1.** (*émbolo*) piston **2.** (*de arma*) percussion cap **3.** MÚS key
**pita** ['pi·ta] *f* BOT agave, century plant
**pitar** [pi·'tar] **I.** *vi, vt* **1.** (*claxon*) to blow; **me pitan los oídos** my ears are buzzing **2.** *AmS* (*fumar*) to smoke **3.** *Chile* (*engañar*) to cheat **II.** *vi inf* (*deprisa*) **salir pitando** to rush off
**pitido** [pi·'ti·do] *m* whistle
**pitillera** [pi·ti·'je·ra, -'ʎe·ra] *f* cigarette case
**pitillo** [pi·'ti·jo, -ʎo] *m* cigarette
**pito** ['pi·to] *m* **1.** (*silbato*) whistle; (*claxon*) horn; **entre ~s y flautas** *inf* what with one thing and another; **tomar a alguien por el ~ del sereno** *inf* to take no notice of sb **2.** *inf* (*pene*) dick

**pitón** [pi·'ton] *m* **1.** ZOOL python **2.** (*cuerno*) budding horn

**pitorrearse** [pi·to·rre·'ar·se] *vr inf* to make fun

**pitorreo** [pi·to·'rreo] *m inf* joking; **¡esto es un ~!** this is a joke!

**pitufo** [pi·'tu·fo] *m inf* shrimp

**piyama** [pi·'ja·ma] *m AmL* pajamas *pl*

**pizarra** [pi·'sa·rra, -'θa·rra] *f* **1.** (*roca*) slate **2.** (*encerado*) blackboard

**pizarrón** [pi·sa·'rron, pi·θa-] *m AmL* blackboard

**pizca** ['pis·ka, 'piθ-] *f* **1.** *inf* (*poco*) pinch, little bit; **una ~ de sal** a pinch of salt; **ni ~** not a bit; **no tienes ni ~ de vergüenza** you have no shame whatsoever **2.** *Méx* (*cosecha*) harvest

**pizza** ['pi·tsa] *f* pizza

**placa** ['pla·ka] *f* **1.** (*lámina, plancha*) sheet; FOTO plate; COMPUT board; **~ base** COMPUT motherboard **2.** (*cartel*) plaque; **~ conmemorativa** commemorative plaque **3.** MED **~ dental** (*dental*) plaque

**placenta** [pla·'sen·ta, -'θen·ta] *f* placenta

**placentero, -a** [pla·sen·'te·ro, -a; pla·θen-] *adj* pleasant

**placer** [pla·'ser, -'θer] **I.** *m* pleasure **II.** *irr como crecer vi* to please; **¡haré lo que me plazca!** I will do as I please!

**placero, -a** [pla·'se·ro, -a; -'θe·ro, -a] *m, f AmL* street trader

**plácido, -a** ['pla·si·do, -a; -θi·do, -a] *adj* calm

**plaga** ['pla·ɣa] *f* **1.** AGR plague **2.** (*calamidades*) disaster; (*lacra*) blight **3.** (*abundancia*) glut

**plagado, -a** [pla·'ɣa·do -a] *adj* infested; **el texto estaba ~ de faltas** the text was full of mistakes

**plagar** <g → gu> [pla·'ɣar] **I.** *vt* to infest; **~ de algo** to fill with sth **II.** *vr:* **~se** to become infested; **el pueblo se plagó de ratas** the village became infested with rats

**plagiar** [pla·'xjar] *vt* (*copiar*) to plagiarize

**plagio** ['pla·xjo] *m* (*copia*) plagiarism

**plan** [plan] *m* **1.** (*proyecto*) plan; **¿tienes ~ para esta noche?** do you have

any plans for tonight **2.** *inf* (*actitud*) **esto no es ~** it's just not on; **en ~ de...** as...; **está en un ~ que no lo soporto** I can't stand him/her when he/she behaves like this

**plancha** ['plan·tʃa] *f* **1.** (*lámina*) sheet; TIPO plate; COMPUT board **2.** (*para ropa*) iron **3.** *inf* (*desacierto*) blunder **4.** CULIN grill; **a la ~** grilled

**planchar** [plan·'tʃar] *vt* to iron

**planeador** [pla·nea·'dor] *m* AVIAT glider

**planear** [pla·ne·'ar] **I.** *vi* (*ave*) to hover; AVIAT to glide **II.** *vt* to plan

**planeta** [pla·'ne·ta] *m* planet

**planetario** [pla·ne·'ta·rjo] *m* planetarium

**planetario, -a** [pla·ne·'ta·rjo, -a] *adj* planetary

**planicie** [pla·'ni·sje, -θje] *f* plain

**planificación** [pla·ni·fi·ka·'sjon, -'θjon] *f* planning

**planificar** <c → qu> [pla·ni·fi·'kar] *vt* to plan

**plano** ['pla·no] *m* **1.** MAT plane **2.** (*mapa*) map **3.** CINE **primer ~** close-up; **en primer ~** (*delante*) in the foreground **4.** (*totalmente*) **de ~** directly; (*negar*) flatly

**plano, -a** ['pla·no, -a] *adj* flat; **superficie plana** flat surface

**planta** ['plan·ta] *f* **1.** BOT plant; **~ de interior** houseplant; **~ medicinal** medicinal plant; **~ trepadora** climbing plant **2.** (*pie*) sole **3.** (*fábrica*) plant; **~ de energía atómica/hidráulica** atomic/hydraulic power station; **~ incineradora** incineration plant; **~ de reciclaje de basuras** recycling plant **4.** (*piso*) floor, story; **~ baja** ground floor, first floor *Am* **5.** (*aspecto*) **tener buena ~** to be good-looking

**plantación** [plan·ta·'sjon, -'θjon] *f* plantation

**plantar** [plan·'tar] **I.** *vt* **1.** (*bulbo*) to plant **2.** (*clavar*) to stick in; **~ una tienda de campaña** to pitch a tent **3.** *inf* (*golpe*) to land; **~ un tortazo a alguien** to slap sb **4.** *inf* (*cita*) to stand up; **desapareció y me dejó plantado** he/she disappeared and left me standing; **lo ~on en la calle** they chucked him out **II.** *vr:* **~se 1.** (*resistirse*) **~se ante algo**

to stand firm in the face of sth **2.** (*aparecer*) to get to; **se ~on en mi casa en un periquete** they arrived at my house in no time **3.** (*en los naipes*) to stick; **aquí me planto** I'm sticking

**planteamiento** [plan·tea·'mjen·to] *m* **1.** (*enfoque*) approach **2.** MAT solution

**plantear** [plan·te·'ar] I. *vt* **1.** (*asunto, problema*) to approach; **este problema está mal planteado** this problem has been incorrectly formulated **2.** (*causar*) to cause **3.** (*proponer*) to put forward, to pose II. *vr* **1.** (*reflexionar*) to think about **2.** (*cuestión*) to ask oneself; **ahora me planteo si...** now I ask myself whether...

**plantilla** [plan·'ti·ja, -ʎa] *f* **1.** (*empleados*) staff **2.** (*de zapato*) insole **3.** (*patrón*) pattern **4.** (*equipo*) squad

**plantón** [plan·'ton] *m inf* long wait; **dar un ~ a alguien** to stand sb up

**plasma** ['plas·ma] *m* plasma

**plasmar** [plas·'mar] *vt* (*moldear*) to mold

**plasta** ['plas·ta] *mf pey* bore, drag

**plástico** ['plas·ti·ko] *m* plastic; (*para envolver*) plastic wrap

**plástico, -a** ['plas·ti·ko, -a] *adj* **1.** (*materia*) plastic **2.** (*expresivo*) expressive; **las artes plásticas** the plastic arts

**plastificar** <c → qu> [plas·ti·fi·'kar] *vt* to laminate

**plastilina®** [plas·ti·'li·na] *f* modeling clay

**plata** ['pla·ta] *f* **1.** (*metal*) silver; **~ de ley** sterling silver; **bodas de ~** silver wedding anniversary **2.** AmL (*dinero*) money; **¡adiós mi ~!** *CSur inf* what a disaster! ▶ **hablar en ~** to talk bluntly

**plataforma** [pla·ta·'for·ma] *f t.* POL platform; (*petrolífera*) oil rig; **~ de lanzamiento** launch pad

**platal** [pla·'tal] *m AmL* fortune

**plátano** ['pla·ta·no] *m* (*árbol*) banana tree; (*fruta*) banana

**plateado, -a** [pla·te·'a·do] *adj* silver-plated; (*color*) silver

**plática** ['pla·ti·ka] *f* chat; **estar de ~** to be chatting

**platillo** [pla·'ti·jo, -ʎo] *m* **1.** (*de taza*) saucer **2.** (*de balanza*) pan **3.** MÚS cymbal

**platino** [pla·'ti·no] *m* QUÍM platinum

**plato** ['pla·to] *m* **1.** (*vajilla*) plate; (*para taza*) saucer; **tiro al ~** DEP clay pigeon shooting; **pagar los ~s rotos** *fig* to pay the consequences **2.** (*comida*) dish; **~ combinado** *dish usually consisting of meat or fish and vegetables;* **~ fuerte** main dish; *fig* main part

**plató** [pla·'to] *m* CINE (*film*) set

**platónico, -a** [pla·'to·ni·ko, -a] *adj* platonic

**platudo, -a** [pla·'tu·do, -a] *adj AmL* well-heeled

**plausible** [plau·'si·βle] *adj* (*admisible*) acceptable

**playa** ['pla·ja] *f* **1.** (*mar*) beach **2.** AmL (*espacio*) open space; **~ de estacionamiento** parking lot

**playeras** [pla·'je·ras] *fpl* gym shoes *pl*

**plaza** ['pla·sa, -θa] *f* **1.** (*espacio*) square; (*de mercado*) marketplace; (*de toros*) bullring; **~ de abastos** (central) food market **2.** (*asiento*) seat; (*de garaje*) space **3.** (*empleo*) position **4.** (*en instituciones, viajes*) place

**plazo** ['pla·so, -θo] *m* **1.** (*vencimiento*) period; **~ de entrega** delivery date; **a corto/largo ~** in the short/long term; **en el ~ de un mes** within a month; **depósito a ~ fijo** fixed-term deposit; **el ~ vence el día...** the deadline is on... **2.** (*cantidad*) installment; **a ~s** in installments

**plebe** ['ple·βe] *f pey* (*chusma*) rabble

**plebeyo, -a** [ple·'βe·jo, -a] *adj* **1.** *t.* HIST plebeian **2.** (*sin linaje*) common **3.** (*inculto*) uneducated; (*grosero*) uncouth

**plebiscito** [ple·βis·'si·to, -'θi·to] *m* plebiscite

**plegable** [ple·'ɣa·βle] *adj* (*papel*) foldable; (*mueble*) folding; **silla ~** folding chair

**plegar** [ple·'ɣar] *irr como* fregar *vt* (*doblar*) to fold; (*muebles*) to fold away

**plegaria** [ple·'ɣa·rja] *f* prayer

**pleito** ['plei·to] *m* **1.** JUR lawsuit **2.** (*disputa*) dispute

**plenario, -a** [ple·'na·rjo] *adj* plenary; **sesión plenaria** plenary session

**plenitud** [ple·ni·'tud] *f* **1.** (*totalidad*) fullness **2.** (*apogeo*) height; **~ vital** full vigor

**pleno** ['ple·no] *m* plenary session; **apro-**

P

**bar algo en ~** to approve sth in a full session

**pleno, -a** ['ple·no, -a] *adj* full; **~ empleo** full employment; **a plena luz del día** in broad daylight; **en ~ verano** at the height of summer

**pletórico, -a** [ple·'to·ri·ko, -a] *adj* full; **~ de salud** bursting with health

**pliego** ['plje·ɣo] *m* **1.** (*hoja*) sheet **2.** (*documento*) document

**pliegue** ['plje·ɣe] *m t.* GEO fold

**plomero** [plo·'me·ro] *m* Arg plumber

**plomo** ['plo·mo] *m* **1.** (*metal*) lead; **gasolina sin ~** unleaded gas; **caer a ~** to fall heavily **3.** *inf* (*pesado*) **ser un ~** to be a real drag **3.** *pl* ELEC fuse

**pluma** ['plu·ma] *f* **1.** (*ave*) feather; **cambiar la ~** to molt **2.** (*escribir*) pen; **~ estilográfica** fountain pen

**plumaje** [plu·'ma·xe] *m* (*ave*) plumage

**plumear** [plu·me·'ar] *vt* AmC to write

**plumero** [plu·'me·ro] *m* (*para limpiar*) feather duster ► **vérsele el ~ a alguien** to be obvious what sb is up to

**plural** [plu·'ral] I. *adj* plural II. *m* plural; **~ mayestático** royal 'we'

**plus** [plus] *m* **1.** (*gratificación*) bonus **2.** (*ventaja*) advantage

**pluscuamperfecto** [plus·kwam·per·'fek·to] *m* LING pluperfect

**plusmarquista** [plus·mar·'kis·ta] *mf* DEP record holder

**plusvalía** [plus·βa·'li·a] *f* ECON appreciation

**plutonio** [plu·'to·njo] *m* plutonium

**PN** ['pe·so 'ne·to] *m abr de* **peso neto** net weight

**PNB** [pe·ne·'βe, pe·en·e-] *m abr de* **producto nacional bruto** GNP

**población** [po·βla·'sjon, -'θjon] *f* **1.** *t.* BIO (*habitantes*) population; **~ activa** ECON working population **2.** (*localidad: ciudad*) city; (*ciudad pequeña*) town; (*pueblo*) village

**poblado** [po·'βla·do] *m* (*pueblo*) village; (*colonia*) settlement

**poblado, -a** [po·'βla·do, -a] *adj* **1.** (*habitado*) inhabited **2.** (*cejas*) bushy

**poblar** <o → ue> [po·'βlar] I. *vi, vt* **1.** (*colonizar*) to colonize **2.** (*de plantas*) to plant **3.** (*habitar*) to inhabit;

**distintas especies pueblan el fondo del mar** various species inhabit the sea bed II. *vr:* **~se** to fill; **la costa se pobló rápidamente** the coast quickly filled with people

**pobre** ['po·βre] I. *adj* **1.** (*no rico*) poor **2.** (*desgraciado*) unfortunate **3.** (*humilde*) humble **4.** (*exclamaciones*) **¡~ de ti si dices mentiras!** you'll be sorry if you lie! II. *mf* poor person; **los pobres** the poor *pl*

**pobreza** [po·'βre·sa, -θa] *f* (*necesidad*) poverty

**pochismo** [po·'tʃis·mo] *m* Méx **1.** *inf* (*angloamericanismo*) Anglicism introduced into Spanish **2.** *inf* (*característica de los pochos*) characteristic of Americanized Mexicans

**pocho, -a** ['po·tʃo, -a] I. *m, f* Méx *pey* Americanized Mexican II. *adj* **1.** (*fruta*) overripe **2.** (*persona*) off-color

**pocilga** [po·'sil·ɣa, po·'θil-] *f t. fig* pigsty

**pócima** ['po·si·ma, -θi·ma] *f*, **poción** [po·'sjon, -'θjon] *f* potion; *pey* (*brebaje*) brew; **la ~ mágica** the magic potion

**poco** ['po·ko] I. *m* **1.** (*cantidad*) **un ~ de azúcar** a little sugar; **espera un ~** wait a little **2.** *pl* few; **~s de los presentes lo sabían** few of those present knew it; **los ~s que vinieron...** the few who came... II. *adv* little; **escribir ~** to write little; **es ~ simpático** he is not very friendly; **~ a ~** bit by bit, little by little; **a ~ dejamos de creerle** we gradually stopped believing him; **a ~ de llegar...** shortly after arriving...; **~ después** shortly afterwards; **dentro de ~** soon; **desde hace ~** since recently; **hace ~** recently, not long ago; **a ~ que se esfuerce lo conseguirá** with a little bit of effort he/she will get it; **por ~ me estrello** I very nearly crashed; **y por si fuera ~...** and as if that wasn't enough...

**poco, -a** <poquísimo> ['po·ko, -a] *adj* little; **~s** few; **queda poca comida** there's not much food left; **hay pocas colecciones mejores que ésta** there are few collections better than this one; **tiene pocas probabilidades de aprobar** he/she has little chance of passing

**podar** [po·'dar] *vt* to prune

**poder** [po·'der] **I.** *irr vi* to be able to; **puedo** I can; **puedes** you can; **yo a ti te puedo** *inf* I'm stronger than you; **no ~ con el alma** to be completely exhausted; **no puedes cogerlo sin permiso** you can't take it without permission; **no podemos abandonarlo** we can't abandon him; **¡bien pod(r)ías habérmelo dicho!** you could have told me!; **bien puede haber aquí un millón de abejas** there could easily be a million bees here; **no puedo con mi madre** I can't cope with my mother; **la sala se llenó a más no ~** the room filled to bursting point; **de ~ ser, ¿se dudes que lo hará** if it is at all possible, have no doubt that he/she will do it; **no pude menos que preguntar** I couldn't help but asking; **lo menos que puedes hacer es llamar** the least you can do is call; **no puede ser** it is impossible; **a ~ ser** if possible **II.** *irr vimpers* **puede ser** maybe; **¡puede!** maybe!; **¿se puede?** may I (come in)? **III.** *m* **1.** *t.* POL *(autoridad)* power; **~ absoluto** absolute power; **~ ejecutivo** executive power; **~ judicial** judicial power; **~ legislativo** legislative power; **la división de ~es** the separation of powers; **el partido en el ~** the party in power; **subir al ~** to achieve power; **los documentos están en ~ del juez** the documents are in the hands of the judge; **haré todo lo que está en mi ~** I will do everything in my power **2.** *(autorización)* authority; **~ notarial** power of attorney; **por ~es** by proxy; **~ de decisión** decision-making power **3.** *(fuerza)* strength; **~ adquisitivo** ECON buying [o purchasing] power

**poderío** [po·de·'ri·o] *m (fuerza)* strength

**poderoso, -a** [po·de·'ro·so, -a] *adj* **1.** *(influyente)* powerful **2.** *(rico)* wealthy **3.** *(eficaz)* effective

**podio** ['po·djo] *m* podium

**podrido, -a** [po·'dri·do, -a] *adj* **1.** *(descompuesto)* t. *fig* rotten; **estar ~ de dinero** *inf* estar ~ en plata *Arg inf* to be filthy rich **2.** *Arg inf (aburrido)* fed up

**poema** [po·'e·ma] *m* poem; **estar hecho un ~** to be a real sight

**poesía** [poe·'si·a] *f* **1.** *(género)* poetry **2.** *(poema)* poem

**poeta, -isa** [po·'e·ta, poe·'ti·sa] *m, f* poet *m(f)*, poetess *f*

**poético, -a** [po·'e·ti·ko, -a] *adj t. fig* poetic

**póker** ['po·ker] *m* poker; **poner cara de ~** to look poker-faced

**polaco, -a** [po·'la·ko, -a] *adj* Polish

**polar** [po·'lar] *adj* polar; **Círculo Polar Ártico/Antártico** Arctic/Antarctic Circle; **la estrella ~** Polaris, Pole Star

**polaridad** [po·la·ri·'dad] *f* polarity

**polarizar** <z → c> [po·la·ri·'sar, -'θar] *vt t.* FÍS to polarize; *(atención)* to focus

**polea** [po·'lea] *f* pulley

**polémica** [po·'le·mi·ka] *f* controversy, polemic

**polémico, -a** [po·'le·mi·ko, -a] *adj* polemical

**polemizar** <z → c> [po·le·mi·'sar, -'θar] *vi* to argue

**polen** ['po·len] *m* pollen; **alergia al ~** hay fever

**polera** [po·'le·ra] *f* **1.** *Chile (camiseta)* T-shirt **2.** *Arg (de cuello alto)* turtleneck

**poli** ['po·li] *f inf abr de* **policía** cops *pl*

**policía¹** [po·li·'si·a, -'θi·a] *f* police; **agente de ~** police officer; **coche de ~** police car; **comisaría de ~** police station

**policía²** [po·li·'si·a, -'θi·a] *mf* policeman *m*, policewoman *f*; **perro ~** police dog

**policiaco, -a** [po·li·'sja·ko, -a; -'θja·ko, -a] *adj*, **policíaco, -a** [po·li·'si·a·ko, -a] *adj* police; **película/novela policíaca** detective film/novel

**policial** [po·li·'sjal, -'θjal] *adj v.* **policíaco**

**policlínica** [po·li·'kli·ni·ka] *f* hospital

**polideportivo** [po·li·de·por·'ti·βo] *m* sports center

**polifacético, -a** [po·li·fa·'se·ti·ko, -a; po·li·fa·'θe-] *adj* multi-faceted; *(persona)* many-sided

**poligamia** [po·li·'ɣa·mja] *f* polygamy

**políglota** [po·'li·ɣlo·ta] *adj* polyglot

**polígono** [po·'li·ɣo·no] *m* **1.** MAT polygon **2.** *(terreno)* site; **~ industrial** industrial estate [o park]

**polilla** [po·'li·ja, -ʎa] *f* moth

**polinesio, -a** [po·li·'ne·sjo, -a] *adj, m, f* Polynesian

**polio** ['po·ljo] *f inv* MED polio, poliomyelitis

**pólipo** ['po·li·po] *m* MED polyp

**polisemia** [po·li·'se·mja] *f* LING polysemy

**política** [po·'li·ti·ka] *f* politics; **~ interior/exterior** domestic/foreign policy

**político, -a** [po·'li·ti·ko, -a] I. *adj* 1. POL political; **ciencias políticas** political science 2. (*parentesco*) in-law; **hermano ~** brother-in-law; **hermana política** sister-in-law II. *m, f* politician

**póliza** ['po·li·sa, -θa] *f* policy; **~ de seguros** insurance policy

**polizón** [po·li·'son, -'θon] *mf* stowaway

**polla** ['po·ja, -ʎa] *f* 1. *inf* (*chica*) chick 2. *vulg* (*pene*) dick; **¡y una ~!** like hell! 3. *AmL* (*carrera*) horse race

**pollera** [po·'je·ra, -'ʎe·ra] *f* Arg (*falda*) skirt

**pollo** ['po·jo, -ʎo] *m* 1. CULIN chicken; **~ asado** roast chicken 2. *inf* (*mozo*) boy; **¿quién es ese ~?** who's that guy?

**polo** ['po·lo] *m* 1. GEO, FÍS, ASTR pole; **~ norte** North Pole; **~ sur** South Pole 2. DEP polo 3. (*camiseta*) polo neck 4. (*helado*) popsicle

**Polonia** [po·'lo·nja] *f* Poland

**polución** [po·lu·'sjon, -'θjon] *f* pollution

**polvareda** [pol·βa·'re·da] *f* dust cloud; **levantar una ~** *fig* to cause an uproar

**polvo** ['pol·βo] *m* 1. (*suciedad*) dust; **quitar el ~** to dust; **hacer ~** (*algo*) to smash; (*a alguien*) to annihilate; **estoy hecho ~** *inf* I'm exhausted; **hacer morder el ~ a alguien** to humiliate sb 2. (*sustancia*) powder; **levadura en ~** powdered yeast 3. *vulg* (*coito*) screw; **echar un ~** to screw 4. *pl* (*cosmética*) powder

**pólvora** ['pol·βo·ra] *f* gunpowder; **no haber inventado la ~** *inf* to be a bit dim

**polvorín** [pol·βo·'rin] *m* powder magazine; **estamos sentados sobre un ~** *fig* we're sitting on a powder keg

**polvorón** [pol·βo·'ron] *m* crumbly almond shortbread, eaten at Christmas

**polvoso, -a** [pol·'βo·so, -a] *adj AmL* dusty

**pomada** [po·'ma·da] *f* ointment

**pomelo** [po·'me·lo] *m* grapefruit

**pómez** ['po·mes, -meθ] *f* pumice

**pompa** ['pom·pa] *f* 1. (*esplendor*) pomp; (*ostentación*) display; **~s fúnebres** (*funeraria*) funeral parlor 2. (*burbuja*) bubble

**pompis** ['pom·pis] *m inv inf* bottom, tush(y) *sl*

**pompo, -a** ['pom·po, -a] *adj Col, Ecua* (*sin filo*) blunt

**pomposo, -a** [pom·'po·so, -a] *adj* magnificent; (*estilo*) pompous

**pómulo** ['po·mu·lo] *m* cheekbone

**ponche** ['pon·tʃe] *m* punch

**poncho** ['pon·tʃo] *m* poncho

**poncho, -a** ['pon·tʃo, -a] *adj AmL* lazy

**ponderar** [pon·de·'rar] *vt* 1. (*sopesar*) to weigh up 2. (*encomiar*) to praise

**ponencia** [po·'nen·sja, -θja] *f* (*conferencia*) paper; (*informe*) report

**ponente** [po·'nen·te] *mf* (*en conferencia*) speaker

**poner** [po·'ner] *irr* I. *vt* 1. (*colocar*) to put; (*horizontalmente*) to lie; (*inyección*) to give; (*sellos, etiqueta*) to stick on; (*tirita*) to put on; (*huevos*) to lay; **pon la ropa en el tendedero** hang the clothes on the line; **¿dónde habré puesto...?** where can I have put ...?; **lo pongo en tus manos** *fig* I leave it in your hands 2. (*disponer*) to place; (*la mesa*) to lay, to set; **~ algo a disposición de alguien** to make sth available to sb 3. (*encender*) to switch on; **pon el despertador para las cuatro** set the alarm for four o'clock; **~ en marcha** to start 4. (*convertir*) to make; **~ de mal humor a alguien** to put sb in a bad mood; **el sol te pondrá moreno** the sun will give you a tan 5. (*suponer*) to assume; **pongamos (por caso) que no llegue a tiempo** let's consider what happens if he/she doesn't arrive on time 6. (*exponer*) **~ la leche al fuego** to put the milk on the stove; **~ en peligro** to endanger 7. (*contribuir*) to put in; (*juego*) to bet; **pusimos todo de nuestra parte** we did all that we could 8. (*una expresión*) to take on; **~ mala cara** to look angry 9. (*tratar*) to treat; **~ de**

**idiota** *pey* to treat sb like a fool **10.** (*denominar*) to give; **¿qué nombre le van a ~?** what are they going to call him/ her? **11.** (*espectáculo*) to put on; **¿qué ponen hoy en el cine?** what's on at the cinema today? **12.** (*imponer*) to impose; **nos han puesto muchos deberes** they have given us a lot of homework; **~ una multa** to impose a fine; **~ condiciones** to impose conditions **13.** (*instalar*) to install **14.** (*a trabajar*) **tendré que ~te a trabajar** I will have to put you to work **15.** (*añadir*) to add **16.** (*escribir*) to write; **~ entre comillas** to put in inverted commas; **~ la firma** to sign; **~ un anuncio** to place an advertisement; **~ por escrito** to put in writing **17.** (*estar escrito*) to say **18.** (*vestido, zapato*) to put on; **le pusieron el collar** they put its collar on **19.** (*teléfono*) to put through **II.** *vr:* **~se 1.** (*vestido, zapato*) to put on **2.** ASTR to set; **el sol se pone por el oeste** the sun sets in the west **3.** (*comenzar*) to begin; **se puso a llover** it started to rain **4.** (*con adjetivo o adverbio*) to become; **ponte cómodo** make yourself comfortable; **ponte guapo** make yourself look nice

**pongo** ['pon·go] *I. pres de* **poner**

**poni** ['po·ni] *m* pony

**poniente** [po·'njen·te] *m* (*oeste*) west

**popa** ['po·pa] *f* (*barco*) stern; **viento en ~** following wind; **a ~** astern

**popular** [po·pu·'lar] *adj* **1.** (*del pueblo*) folk **2.** (*conocido*) well-known; (*admirado*) popular

**popularidad** [po·pu·la·ri·'ðað] *f* popularity

**popularizar** <z → c> [po·pu·la·ri·'sar, -'θar] *I. vt* to popularize **II.** *vr:* **~se** to become popular

**poquito** [po·'ki·to] *adv* a little; **bébelo ~ a poco** drink it a little bit at a time

**por** [por] *prep* **1.** (*lugar: a través de*) through; (*vía*) via; (*en*) in; **~ aquí** near here; **limpia la botella ~ dentro/ fuera** clean the inside/outside of the bottle; **pasé ~ Madrid** I passed through Madrid; **adelantar ~ la izquierda** to overtake on the left; **volar ~ encima de los Alpes** to fly over the Alps; **la co-**

gió **~ la cintura** he grasped her waist **2.** (*tiempo*) in; **~ la(s) mañana(s)** in the morning; **mañana ~ la mañana** tomorrow morning; **~ la tarde** in the evening; **ayer ~ la noche** last night; **~ fin** finally **3.** (*a cambio de*) for; (*en lugar de*) instead of; (*sustituyendo a alguien*) in place of; **cambié el libro ~ el álbum** I exchanged the book for the album **4.** (*agente*) by; **hecho ~ mí** done by me **5.** MAT (*multiplicación*) by **6.** (*reparto*) per; **toca a cuatro ~ cabeza** it comes out at four each; **el ocho ~ ciento** eight per cent **7.** (*finalidad*) for **8.** (*causa*) because of; (*en cuanto a*) regarding; **lo hago ~ ti** I'm doing it for you; **~ consiguiente** consequently; **~ eso ~ (lo) tanto** therefore, because of that; **~ mí que se vayan** as far as I'm concerned, they can go **9.** (*preferencia*) in favor; **estoy ~ comprarlo** I think I should buy it; **estar loco ~ alguien** to be crazy about sb **10.** (*dirección*) **voy (a) ~ tabaco** I'm going to get some cigarettes **11.** (*pendiente*) **este pantalón está ~ lavar** these pants need to be washed **12.** (*aunque*) however; **~ muy cansado que esté lo haré** however tired I am, I'll get it done **13.** (*medio*) by means of; (*alguien*) through; **poner ~ escrito** to put in writing; **al ~ mayor** wholesale **14.** (*interrogativo*) **¿~ qué?** why? **15.** **~ si acaso** just in case **16.** (*casi*) **~ poco** almost

**porcelana** [por·se·'la·na, por·θe·] *f* porcelain

**porcentaje** [por·sen·'ta·xe, por·θen-] *m* percentage

**porcentual** [por·sen·tu·'al, por·θen-] *adj* percentage

**porche** ['por·tʃe] *m* **1.** (*pórtico*) porch **2.** (*cobertizo*) arcade

**porcino, -a** [por·'si·no, -'θi·no] *adj* pig; **ganado ~** swine *pl*

**porción** [por·'sjon, -'θjon] *f* portion; CULIN serving

**pordiosero, -a** [por·djo·'se·ro, -a] *m, f* beggar

**pormenorizado, -a** [por·me·no·ri·'sa·do, -a; -θa·do, -a] *adj* detailed

**porno** ['por·no] *adj inv m inf* porn

P

**pornografía** [por·no·ɣra·'fi·a] *f* pornography

**pornográfico, -a** [por·no·'ɣra·fi·ko, -a] *adj* pornographic

**poro** ['po·ro] *m* pore

**poroso, -a** [po·'ro·so, -a] *adj* porous

**poroto** [po·'ro·to] *m Chile* bean

**porque** [por·ke] *conj* **1.** (*causal*) because; **lo hizo ~ sí** he/she did it because he/she wanted to **2.** +*subj* (*final*) so that; **recemos ~ llueva** let us pray that it rains

**porqué** [por·'ke] *m* reason

**porquería** [por·ke·'ri·a] *f inf* **1.** (*suciedad*) filth **2.** (*comida*) pigswill **3.** (*cacharro*) piece of junk

**porra** ['po·rra] *f* (*bastón*) truncheon; **¡vete a la ~!** go to hell!

**porrazo** [po·'rra·so, -θo] *m* blow; **de golpe y ~** all of a sudden; **de un ~** in one go

**porrista** [po·'rris·ta] *mf Méx* fan

**porro** ['po·rro] *m inf* (*canuto*) joint

**porrón** [po·'rron] *m glass wine jar with a long spout*

**portaaviones** [por·ta·βi·'o·nes; por·ta·a·βi-] *m inv* aircraft carrier

**portada** [por·'ta·da] *f* TIPO title page; PREN cover

**portaequipaje(s)** [por·ta·e·ki·'pa·xe(s)] *m (inv)* (*baca, en tren*) luggage rack; (*en bicicleta*) carrier

**portafolios** [por·ta·'fo·ljos] *m inv* briefcase

**portal** [por·'tal] *m* (*zaguán*) hall; COMPUT portal; **~ de Belén** REL Nativity scene

**portalámpara** [por·ta·'lam·pa·ra] *m inv* (*de bombilla*) socket

**portaligas** [por·ta·'li·ɣas] *m inv AmL* garter belt

**portamaletas** [por·ta·ma·'le·tas] *m inv* AUTO trunk

**portaminas** [por·ta·'mi·nas] *m inv* mechanical pencil

**portar** [por·'tar] *vr:* ~**se** to behave; ~**se bien con alguien** to treat sb well; **el niño se porta bien/mal** the child is well-/badly behaved; ~**se como un hombre** to act like a man; **nuestro equipo se ha portado** our team performed well

**portátil** [por·'ta·til] *adj* portable; (**ordenador**) ~ laptop

**portavoz** [por·ta·'βos, -'βoθ] *mf* spokesperson, spokesman *m*, spokeswoman *f*

**portazo** [por·'ta·so, -θo] *m* slam (*of the door*); **dar un ~** to slam the door

**porte** ['por·te] *m* **1.** (*transporte*) transport; **~ aéreo** air freight; **gastos de ~** shipping costs; **a ~ debido** carriage forward **2.** (*gastos de transporte*) shipping costs *pl* **3.** (*correo*) postage; **~ suplementario** additional postage **4.** (*aspecto*) appearance; **es un hombre de ~ distinguido** he has a distinguished air

**portento** [por·'ten·to] *m* marvel; **ser un ~ de energía** to be full of energy

**porteño, -a** [por·'te·ɲo, -a] **I.** *adj* of/from Buenos Aires **II.** *m, f* native/inhabitant of Buenos Aires

**portería** [por·te·'ri·a] *f* **1.** (*en edificio*) porter's lodge **2.** DEP goal

**portero, -a** [por·'te·ro, -a] *m, f* **1.** (*conserje*) caretaker; (*en un edificio de viviendas*) porter; **~ automático** intercom **2.** *Arg* (*administrador*) building manager **3.** DEP goalkeeper

**portorriqueño, -a** [por·to·rri·'ke·ɲo, -a] *adj, m, f* Puerto Rican

**Portugal** [por·tu·'ɣal] *m* Portugal

**portugués, -esa** [por·tu·'ɣes, --'ɣe·sa] *adj, m, f* Portuguese

**porvenir** [por·βe·'nir] *m* future; **tener el ~ asegurado** to have a secure future; **un joven de ~** a young man with great prospects

**pos** [pos] **I.** *adv* **ir en ~ de algo/alguien** to pursue sth/sb; **van en ~ del éxito** they are striving for success **II.** *conj Méx inf v.* **pues**

**posada** [po·'sa·da] *f* **1.** (*parador, fonda*) inn; (*pensión*) guest house **2.** (*hospedaje*) lodging; **dar ~ a alguien** to give sb lodging

**posar** [po·'sar] **I.** *vi* (*modelo*) to pose **II.** *vt* (*poner suavemente*) to place; (*mirada*) to rest **III.** *vr:* ~**se** to settle; **el gorrión se posó en la rama** the sparrow alighted on the branch

**posdata** [pos·'da·ta] *f* postscript

**pose** ['po·se] *f* (*postura*) pose

**poseer** [po·'ser/po·se·'er] *irr como leer vt*

to possess, to have

**poseído, -a** [po·se·'i·do, -a] *adj* possessed; **~ de odio** full of hatred

**posesión** [po·se·'sjon] *f* possession; **estar en ~ de algo** to be in possession of sth

**posesivo, -a** [po·se·'si·βo, -a] *adj t.* LING possessive

**poseso, -a** [po·'se·so, -a] I. *adj* possessed II. *m, f* madman *m*, madwoman *f*

**posguerra** [pos·'ɣe·rra] *f* postwar period

**posibilidad** [po·si·βi·li·'dad] *f* 1. (*lo posible*) possibility 2. (*aptitud, facultad*) capability; **esto está por encima de mis ~es** this is beyond my capabilities 3. *pl* (*medios económicos*) means *pl;* **estás viviendo por encima de tus ~es** you are living beyond your means

**posibilitar** [po·si·βi·li·'tar] *vt* to make possible

**posible** [po·'si·βle] *adj* possible; **hacer ~** to make possible; **hacer todo lo ~** to do everything one can; **es muy ~ que lleguen tarde** they may very well arrive late; **es ~ que** +*subj* it is possible that; **es muy ~ que** +*subj* it is very likely that; **¡no es ~!** I can't believe it!; **¿será ~?** surely not?; **si es ~** if possible; **en lo ~** as far as possible; **lo antes ~** as soon as possible

**posiblemente** [po·si·βle·'men·te] *adv* possibly

**posición** [po·si·'sjon, -'θjon] *f t.* MIL position; **la ~ económica** the economic situation; **la ~ geográfica** the geographic location; **en buena ~** in a good position; **mi ~ ante este asunto...** my opinion on this affair...; **tomar ~** to adopt a stance

**positivo** [po·si·'ti·βo] *m* FOTO print

**positivo, -a** [po·si·'ti·βo, -a] *adj t.* MAT, FÍS positive

**poso** ['po·so] *m* sediment; (*de café*) grounds *pl;* (*de vino*) lees *pl*

**posponer** [pos·po·'ner] *irr como poner vt* 1. (*postergar*) to relegate 2. (*aplazar*) to postpone

**postal** [pos·'tal] I. *adj* mail II. *f* postcard

**poste** ['pos·te] *m t.* TEL post; ELEC pylon; **~ indicador** signpost

**póster** ['pos·ter] *m* poster

**postergar** <g → gu> [pos·ter·'ɣar] *vt* (*aplazar*) to postpone; **~ la fecha** to put back the date

**posteridad** [pos·te·ri·'dad] *f* 1. (*descendencia*) descendants *pl;* (*generaciones venideras*) future generations *pl* 2. (*futuro*) posterity; **pasar a la ~** to be remembered by posterity

**posterior** [pos·te·'rjor] *adj* 1. (*de tiempo*) later; **~ a** after 2. (*de lugar*) back; **la parte ~ de la cabeza** the back of the head

**posteriormente** [pos·te·rjor·'men·te] *adv* subsequently, later

**postizo, -a** [pos·'ti·so, -a; -θo, -a] *adj* artificial; **dentadura postiza** false teeth; **pelo ~** wig

**postor(a)** [pos·'tor, -·'to·ra] *m(f)* bidder; **mejor ~** highest bidder

**postrado, -a** [pos·'tra·do, -a] *adj* prostrate; **~ de dolor** (*dolor físico*) in great pain; (*pena*) beside oneself with grief; **~ en cama** laid up in bed

**postre** ['pos·tre] *m* dessert; **a la ~** *fig* in the end, when all is said and done; **llegar a los ~s** *fig* to arrive too late

**postular** [pos·tu·'lar] *vt* 1. (*pedir*) to request; (*donativos*) to collect 2. (*solicitar*) **~ algo** to petition for sth

**póstumo, -a** ['pos·tu·mo, -a] *adj* posthumous; **fama póstuma** posthumous fame

**postura** [pos·'tu·ra] *f* 1. (*colocación*) position; (*del cuerpo*) posture 2. (*actitud*) attitude

**post-venta** [pos·'βen·ta] *adj* after-sales; **servicio ~** after-sales service

**potable** [po·'ta·βle] *adj* drinkable; **agua ~** drinking water

**potaje** [po·'ta·xe] *m* 1. CULIN (*sopa*) soup; (*guiso*) stew (*containing pulses and vegetables*) 2. *inf* (*mezcla*) mixture

**potasio** [po·'ta·sjo] *m* potassium

**pote** ['po·te] *m* pot; (*para plantas*) flowerpot

**potencia** [po·'ten·sja, -θja] *f* 1. (*fuerza*) strength; (*capacidad*) capacity; **~ de carga** capacity; **~ del motor** engine capacity; **~ motriz** motive power 2. (*poder*) power; **gran ~** great power 3. COMPUT **~ de entrada/de salida** input/output

**P**

capacity **4.** FILOS possibility; **en ~** potential **5.** MAT power; **elevar a la cuarta ~** to raise to the power of four

**potencial** [po·ten·'sjal, -'θjal] **I.** *adj* **1.** (*que tiene potencia*) powerful **2.** (*posible*) potential **II.** *m* **1.** (*poder, capacidad*) power; **~ financiero** financial muscle **2.** FÍS potential energy; ELEC potential difference

**potente** [po·'ten·te] *adj* **1.** (*poderoso*) powerful **2.** (*eficiente*) efficient **3.** (*sexualidad*) potent

**potrear** [po·tre·'ar] *vt* **1.** AmL (*domar*) to break **2.** *Guat, Perú* (*pegar*) to beat

**potro** ['po·tro] *m* **1.** ZOOL colt **2.** DEP vaulting horse **3.** (*de tortura*) rack

**poza** ['po·sa, -θa] *f* (*charca*) puddle

**pozo** ['po·so, -θo] *m* **1.** (*manantial*) well **2.** (*hoyo profundo*) shaft; **~ de extracción** extraction shaft; **~ negro** cesspool; **~ petrolífero** oil well; **~ séptico** septic tank; **ser un ~ sin fondo** *fig* to be a bottomless pit **3.** *CSur* (*bache*) pothole

**práctica** ['prak·ti·ka] *f* **1.** (*experiencia*) experience; **adquirir ~** to gain experience; **perder la ~** to get out of practice; **tener ~ en algo** to have experience of sth **2.** (*ejercitación*) practice; **~ profesional** professional practice **3.** (*cursillo*) practical course **4.** (*realización*) practice; **en la ~** in practice; **llevar a la ~** to carry out; **poner en ~** to put into practice **5.** (*costumbre*) practice; **~ judicial** normal legal practice; **la ~ de los negocios** business norms **6.** (*modo*) manner; (*método*) method; **la ~ comercial** business methods

**practicar** <c → qu> [prak·ti·'kar] *vi, vt* to practice; **~ deporte** to play sport, to do sports; **estudió medicina, pero no practica** he/she studied medicine, but he/she doesn't work as a doctor; **~ el español** to practice Spanish

**práctico** ['prak·ti·ko] *m* NÁUT pilot; **~ de puerto** coast pilot

**práctico, -a** ['prak·ti·ko, -a] *adj* practical

**pradera** [pra·'de·ra] *f* grassland, prairie

**prado** ['pra·do] *m* grassy field; (*para ganado*) meadow; (*para pasear*) park

**pragmático, -a** [pray·'ma·ti·ko, -a] *adj* pragmatic

**preámbulo** [pre·'am·bu·lo] *m* introduction, preamble; **sin ~s** *fig* without further ado; **no andarse con ~s** not to beat around the bush

**precalentar** <e → ie> [pre·ka·len·'tar] *vt* to preheat

**precario, -a** [pre·'ka·rjo, -a] *adj* precarious

**precaución** [pre·kau·'sjon, -'θjon] *f* precaution; **tomar precauciones** to take precautions

**precaver** [pre·ka·'βer] **I.** *vt* (*prevenir*) to prevent; (*evitar*) to avoid **II.** *vr* **hay que ~se de todas las eventualidades** you have to be prepared for all eventualities

**precavido, -a** [pre·ka·'βi·do, -a] *adj* cautious

**precedente** [pre·se·'den·te, pre·θe·] **I.** *adj* preceding **II.** *m* precedent; **sentar un ~** to establish a precedent; **sin ~s** unprecedented

**preceder** [pre·se·'der, pre·θe·] *vt* **1.** (*anteceder*) to precede **2.** (*tener primacía*) **~ a algo/alguien** to have priority over sth/sb; **~ en categoría** to have a higher position

**precepto** [pre·'sep·to, -'θep·to] *m* (*mandamiento*) order; (*norma*) precept

**precintar** [pre·'sin·tar, -'θin·tar] *vt* to seal

**precinto** [pre·'sin·to, 'θin·to] *m* seal

**precio** ['pre·sjo, -θjo] *m* price; **~ al consumidor** retail price; **~ al contado** cash price; **~ de fábrica** price ex-works, factory price; **~ al por mayor** wholesale price; **~ recomendado** recommended price; **~ de venta al público** retail price; **a buen ~** for a good price; **a mitad de ~** at half price; **a ~ de oro** for a very high price; **poner el ~** to set the price; **¿qué ~ tiene el libro?** how much does this book cost?; **no tener ~** *fig* to be priceless; **querer conseguir algo a cualquier ~** to want sth at any price; **poner ~ a la cabeza de alguien** to put a price on sb's head

**preciosidad** [pre·sjo·si·'dad, pre·θjo·] *f* lovely thing; **esta chica es una ~** this girl is lovely

**precioso, -a** [pre·'sjo·so, -a; pre·'θjo·] *adj* **1.** (*valioso*) valuable **2.** (*hermo-*

*so)* lovely

**precipicio** [pre·si·'pi·sjo, -θi·'pi·θjo] *m* precipice; **estar al borde del ~** *fig* to be on the brink of disaster

**precipitación** [pre·si·pi·ta·'sjon, -θi·pi·ta·'θjon] *f* **1.** (*prisa*) haste; **con ~** hastily **2.** METEO rainfall

**precipitadamente** [pre·si·pi·ta·da·'men·te, pre·θi-] *adv* hastily

**precipitado, -a** [pre·si·pi·'ta·do, pre·θi-] *adj* hasty

**precipitar** [pre·si·pi·'tar, pre·θi-] I. *vt* **1.** (*arrojar*) to throw down; **le ~on por la ventana** they threw him out of the window **2.** (*apresurar*) to hasten; (*acelerar*) to hurry II. *vr:* **~se 1.** (*arrojarse*) to throw oneself down; **~se sobre algo/alguien** to hurl oneself at sth/sb **2.** (*acontecimientos*) to happen very quickly; (*personas*) to act hastily; **¡no se precipite!** don't be hasty!

**precisamente** [pre·si·sa·'men·te, pre·θi-] *adv* exactly; **¿tiene que ser ~ hoy?** does it have to be today, of all days?; **~ por eso** for that very reason

**precisar** [pre·si·'sar, pre·θi-] *vt* **1.** (*determinar*) to specify; **no lo puedo ~** I can't put my finger on it **2.** (*necesitar*) to need; **preciso tu ayuda** I need your help

**precisión** [pre·si·'sjon, pre·θi-] *f* **1.** (*exactitud*) precision; **~ (de tiro)** accuracy; **instrumento de ~** precision instrument; **hablar con ~** to speak clearly **2.** (*determinación*) clarification; **hacer precisiones** to clarify matters

**preciso, -a** [pre·'θi·so, -a, pre·'θi-] *adj* **1.** (*necesario*) necessary; **es ~ que nos veamos** we need to see each other; **si es ~...** if necessary... **2.** (*exacto*) precise

**precocinado, -a** [pre·ko·si·'na·do, -a, pre·ko·θi-] *adj* pre-cooked

**preconcebido, -a** [pre·kon·se·'βi·do, -a; pre·kon·θe-] *adj* preconceived; **tener ideas preconcebidas** to have preconceived ideas

**precordillera** [pre·kor·di·'je·ra, -'ʎe·ra] *f* *Arg* Andean foothills *pl*

**precoz** [pre·'kos, -'koθ] *adj* precocious; (*diagnóstico, cosecha*) early; **eyacula-**

**ción ~** premature ejaculation

**precursor(a)** [pre·kur·'sor, --'so·ra] I. *adj* preceding II. *m(f)* precursor

**predecesor(a)** [pre·de·se·'sor --'so·ra, -θe·'sor, --'so·ra --so·ra] *m(f)* **1.** (*en el cargo*) predecessor **2.** (*antepasados*) ancestor

**predecir** [pre·de·'sir, -'θir] *irr como* decir *vt* to predict; (*tiempo*) to forecast

**predestinado, -a** [pre·des·ti·'na·do, -a] *adj* predestined

**predeterminar** [pre·de·ter·mi·'nar] *vt* to predetermine

**predicado** [pre·di·'ka·do] *m* LING predicate

**predicar** <c → qu> [pre·di·'kar] *vt* to preach; **~ en desierto** to preach in the wilderness; **~ con el ejemplo** to practice what one preaches

**predicción** [pre·dik·'sjon, -'θjon] *f* prediction

**predilecto, -a** [pre·di·'lek·to, -a] *adj* favorite; **hijo ~** favorite son

**predisponer** [pre·dis·po·'ner] *irr como* poner I. *vt* **1.** (*fijar por anticipado*) to agree beforehand; **venía predispuesto a pelearse** he arrived in a mood for a quarrel **2.** (*influir*) to predispose; **~ a alguien a favor/en contra de alguien** to bias sb in favor of/against sb **3.** (*inclinar*) to make receptive; MED to predispose II. *vr* **1.** (*prepararse*) **~se a algo** to prepare oneself for sth **2.** (*tomar partido*) to have a bias; **~se a favor/en contra de alguien** to be biased in favor of/against sb

**predisposición** [pre·dis·po·si·'sjon, -'θjon] *f* *t.* MED predisposition; (*tendencia*) tendency; **tener ~ a engordar** to have a tendency to put on weight

**predispuesto, -a** [pre·dis·'pwes·to, -a] I. *pp de* predisponer II. *adj* **1.** *ser* (*sensible*) predisposed **2.** *estar* (*prevenido*) prejudiced; **estar (mal) ~ contra alguien** to be prejudiced against sb

**predominar** [pre·do·mi·'nar] *vi, vt* **1.** (*prevalecer*) to predominate; **aquí predomina la corrupción** corruption is very common here; **~ en número** to be most numerous **2.** (*sobresalir*) to stand out; **~ en algo/sobre alguien** to stand

P

out at sth/over sb

**predominio** [pre·do·'mi·njo] *m* 1. (*poder*) predominance 2. (*preponderancia*) preponderance 3. (*superioridad*) ~ **sobre alguien** superiority over sb

**preescolar** [pres·ko'lar/pre·es·ko'lar] *adj* pre-school

**preestreno** [pres·'tre·no/pre·es·'tre·no] *m* preview

**prefabricado, -a** [pre·fa·βri·'ka·do, -a] *adj* prefabricated; **casa prefabricada** prefabricated house

**preferencia** [pre·fe·'ren·sja, -θja] *f* 1. (*elección, trato*) preference; **mostrar ~ por alguien** to show a preference for sb 2. (*predilección*) predilection; **sentir ~ por alguien** to be biased in favor of sb 3. (*prioridad*) priority; ~ **de paso** right of way; **dar ~** to give preference

**preferentemente** [pre·fe·ren·te·'men·te] *adv* preferably

**preferible** [pre·fe·'ri·βle] *adj* preferable; **sería ~ que lo hicieras** it would be best if you did it

**preferiblemente** [pre·fe·ri·βle·'men·te] *adv* preferably

**preferido, -a** [pre·fe·'ri·do, -a] *adj* favorite

**preferir** [pre·fe·'rir] *irr como* sentir *vt* to prefer; **prefiero ir a pie** I prefer to walk; **prefiero que no venga** I would rather he/she didn't come

**prefijar** [pre·fi·'xar] *vt* to decide (in advance), to prearrange

**prefijo** [pre·'fi·xo] *m* 1. LING prefix 2. TEL area code

**pregón** [pre·'ɣon] *m* proclamation

**pregonar** [pre·ɣo·'nar] *vt* 1. (*en público*) to proclaim 2. (*lo que estaba oculto*) to make public; **a los cuatro vientos** *inf* to proclaim for all to hear 3. (*alabar*) to praise publicly

**pregunta** [pre·'ɣun·ta] *f* 1. (*demanda*) question; ~ **capciosa** trick question 2. (*de datos*) inquiry

**preguntar** [pre·ɣun·'tar] I. *vt* to ask; ~ **a alguien la lección** to test sb; ~ **por alguien** to ask after sb II. *vr* ~**se si/cuándo/qué...** to wonder if/when/what...

**prehistórico, -a** [pre·is·'to·ri·ko, -a] *adj*

prehistoric

**prejuicio** [pre·'xwi·sjo, -θjo] *m* prejudice

**prejuzgar** <g → gu> [pre·xus·'ɣar, pre·xuθ-] *vt* to prejudge

**premamá** [pre·ma·'ma] *adj inv* **vestido ~** maternity dress

**prematuro, -a** [pre·ma·'tu·ro, -a] *adj* premature; (*persona*) precocious; **nacimiento ~** premature birth

**premeditación** [pre·me·di·ta·'sjon, -'θjon] *f* premeditation; **con ~** premeditated

**premeditado, -a** [pre·me·di·'ta·do, -a] *adj* premeditated

**premeditar** [pre·me·di·'tar] *vt* (*planear*) to plan; JUR to premeditate

**premiado, -a** [pre·'mja·do, -a] *adj* prize-winning

**premiar** [pre·'mjar] *vt* to reward; (*dar un premio*) to give [o award] a prize to

**premio** ['pre·mjo] *m* 1. (*galardón*) prize; ~ **Nobel** (**de literatura**) Nobel Prize (for/in literature); **conceder un ~** to award a prize 2. (*recompensa*) reward 3. (*lotería*) prize; **el ~ gordo** the jackpot

**premisa** [pre·'mi·sa] *f* (*condición*) premise

**premonición** [pre·mo·ni·'sjon, -'θjon] *f* premonition

**premunir** [pre·mu·'nir] I. *vt AmL* ~ **de algo** to provide with sth II. *vr AmL* ~**se de algo** to provide oneself with sth

**prenda** ['pren·da] *f* 1. (*fianza*) guarantee; **en ~** as security; **soltar ~** to commit oneself; **no soltar ~** *inf* not to say a word 2. (*pieza de ropa*) garment; ~**s interiores** underwear

**prendar** [pren·'dar] I. *vt* 1. (*tomar como prenda*) to take as security 2. (*ganar el afecto*) to captivate 3. *vr* ~**se de alguien** *elev* to fall in love with sb

**prendedor** [pren·de·'dor] *m* (*broche*) brooch, pin; (*de corbata*) tiepin

**prender** [pren·'der] *vt* 1. (*sujetar*) to hold down; (*con alfileres*) to pin; (*en un gancho*) to hang; ~ **un alfiler de corbata** to put a tiepin on 2. (*detener*) to catch 3. (*fuego*) **el coche prendió fuego** the car caught fire 4. *AmL* (*encender*) to light; (*luz*) to turn on; ~ **un cigarrillo**

to light a cigarette

**prensa** ['pren·sa] *f* 1. (*máquina*) press 2. (*imprenta*) printer's, press; **estar en ~** to be at the printer's 3. PREN press; **~ amarilla** tabloids *pl*; **rueda de ~** press conference; **libertad de ~** freedom of the press; **secretario de ~** press secretary; **tener buena/mala ~** *fig* to get a good/bad press

**prensar** [pren·'sar] *vt* to press

**preñada** [pre·'ɲa·da] *adj* (*mujer*) pregnant

**preñar** [pre·'ɲar] *vt* 1. (*mujer*) to make pregnant 2. (*animal*) to impregnate

**preocupación** [preo·ku·pa·'sjon, -'θjon] *f* 1. worry; **~ por algo/alguien** worry about sth/sb; **sin preocupaciones** unworried 2. (*obsesión*) concern; **tu única ~ es el dinero** the only thing you care about is money

**preocupado, -a** [preo·ku·'pa·do, -a] *adj* worried; **~ por algo/alguien** worried about sth/sb; **mi padre anda bastante ~** my father is quite worried

**preocupante** [preo·ku·'pan·te] *adj* worrying

**preocupar** [preo·ku·'par] I. *vt* to worry; **~ a alguien** to make sb worry II. *vr* 1. (*inquietarse*) **~se por algo/alguien** to worry about sth/sb; **¡no te preocupes tanto!** don't worry so much! 2. (*encargarse*) to take care; **no se preocupa de arreglar el asunto** he/she doesn't do anything to solve the problem

**preparación** [pre·pa·ra·'sjon, -'θjon] *f* 1. (*de asunto, comida*) preparation 2. (*formación*) training; **~ académica** education; **sin ~** untrained

**preparado** [pre·pa·'ra·do] *m* preparation

**preparado, -a** [pre·pa·'ra·do, -a] *adj* (*listo*) ready; **tener ~** to have ready

**preparar** [pre·pa·'rar] I. *vt* 1. (*disponer*) to prepare; **~ el camino** to prepare the way; **~ un discurso** to write a speech; **~ las maletas** to pack one's bags 2. QUÍM, ANAT to prepare II. *vr* to get ready; **prepárate para salir** get ready to leave; **se prepara una tormenta** there's a storm brewing

**preparativo** [pre·pa·ra·'ti·βo] *m* preparation

**preparativo, -a** [pre·pa·ra·'ti·βo, -a] *adj* preparatory

**preposición** [pre·po·si·'sjon, -'θjon] *f* preposition

**prepotente** [pre·po·'ten·te] *adj* arrogant

**presa** ['pre·sa] *f* 1. (*acción*) capture; **ser ~ del terror** to be seized by terror 2. (*objeto, de caza*) prey; **animal de ~** prey; **ave de ~** bird of prey 3. (*dique*) dam 4. (*acequia*) channel 5. DEP hold; **~ de brazo** (*judo*) arm hold

**presagiar** [pre·sa·'xjar] *vt* to betoken *form*; **estas nubes presagian tormenta** these clouds mean there will be a storm

**presagio** [pre·'sa·xjo] *m* 1. (*señal*) warning sign 2. (*presentimiento*) premonition

**prescindible** [pre·sin·'di·βle, pres·θin-] *adj* dispensable

**prescindir** [pre·sin·'dir, pres·θin-] *vi* 1. (*renunciar a*) **~ de algo/alguien** to do without sth/sb; **no podemos ~ de él** we can't do without him 2. (*no contar*) **~ de algo/alguien** to disregard sth/sb

**prescribir** [pres·kri·'βir] *irr como escribir* I. *vi* (*plazo*) to expire II. *vt* (*indicar*) *t.* MED to prescribe; **prescrito por la ley** prescribed by law

**prescripción** [pres·krip·'sjon, -kriβ·'θjon] *f* 1. (*indicación*) indication 2. MED prescription 3. (*plazo*) expiry

**presencia** [pre·'sen·sja, -θja] *f* 1. (*asistencia*) presence; **sin la ~ del ministro** without the minister being present; **hacer acto de ~** to put in an appearance 2. (*aspecto*) appearance; **buena ~** good looks

**presencial** [pre·sen·'sjal, -'θjal] *adj* **testigo ~** eyewitness

**presenciar** [pre·sen·'sjar, -'θjar] *vt* 1. (*ver*) to witness 2. (*asistir*) to attend; **10.000 personas ~on el concierto** 10,000 people attended the concert

**presentable** [pre·sen·'ta·βle] *adj* presentable; **ponerse ~** to make oneself presentable

**presentación** [pre·sen·ta·'sjon, -'θjon] *f* 1. (*de una novela, una película*) launch(ing) 2. (*de un número artístico*)

P

presentation; TEAT show **3.** (*de instancia, dimisión*) submission; **el plazo de ~ de solicitudes finaliza hoy** the period for presenting requests ends today **4.** (*de argumentos, documento, propuesta*) presentation **5.** (*de personas*) introduction **6.** (*aspecto*) appearance **7.** AmL (*súplica*) petition

**presentador(a)** [pre·sen·ta·'dor, -·'do·ra] *m(f)* (*de programa*) presenter; (*de telediario*) newsreader

**presentar** [pre·sen·'tar] I. *vt* **1.** (*mostrar*) to show **2.** (*ofrecer*) to offer; **el viaje presenta dificultades** the journey poses difficulties **3.** TV, RADIO to present; TEAT to put on; (*presentador*) to introduce **4.** (*instancia, dimisión*) to submit **5.** (*argumentos*) to put forward; (*pruebas, propuesta*) to submit **6.** (*pasaporte, documento*) to show **7.** (*persona*) to introduce; **te presento a mi marido** may I introduce you to my husband? **8.** (*candidato*) to propose **II.** *vr:* **~se 1.** (*comparecer*) to present oneself; (*aparecer*) to turn up **2.** (*para elecciones*) **~se a** to run for

**presente** [pre·'sen·te] I. *adj* **1.** (*que está*) present; **¡~!** present!; **estar ~** to be present; (*actual*) current **3.** (*este*) **la ~ edición** this edition **4.** (*a considerar*) **ten ~ lo que te he dicho** bear in mind what I have told you **5.** (*en una carta*) **por la ~ deseo comunicarle que...** I write in order to tell you that... **II.** *m* **1.** (*actualidad*) present; **hasta el ~** until now **2.** LING present (tense) **3.** (*regalo*) present, gift

**presentimiento** [pre·sen·ti·'mjen·to] *m* premonition; **tengo el ~ de que...** I have a feeling that...

**presentir** [pre·sen·'tir] *irr como sentir vt* to have a premonition of; **presiento que mañana lloverá** I have a feeling it's going to rain tomorrow

**preservar** [pre·ser·'βar] *vt* to protect

**preservativo** [pre·ser·βa·'ti·βo] *m* condom

**presidencia** [pre·si·'den·sja, -θja] *f* **1.** (*mandato*) presidency; **asumir la ~** to take over the presidency **2.** (*de organización, asamblea: conjunto*) board;

(*individuo*) chairperson, president; **asumir la ~** to take the chair

**presidencial** [pre·si·den·'sjal, -·'θjal] *adj* POL presidential

**presidente** [pre·si·'den·te, -a] *mf* **1.** POL president; **~ del gobierno** prime minister **2.** (*de asociación*) chairperson

**presidiario, -a** [pre·si·'dja·rjo, -a] *m, f* convict

**presidio** [pre·'si·djo] *m* prison

**presidir** [pre·si·'dir] *vt* **1.** (*ocupar presidencia*) to be president of **2.** (*mandar*) to rule

**presión** [pre·'sjon] *f* pressure; **~ arterial** blood pressure; **~ social** social pressure; **grupo de ~** pressure group; **zona de altas presiones** METEO high pressure area; **cerrado a ~** pressurized; **¿a qué ~ llevas las ruedas?** what is your tire pressure?; **estar bajo ~** to be under pressure; **hacer ~ sobre alguien** to put pressure on sb

**presionar** [pre·sjo·'nar] *vt* **1.** (*apretar*) to press **2.** (*coaccionar*) to put pressure on

**preso, -a** ['pre·so, -a] *m, f* prisoner, (prison) inmate

**prestación** [pres·ta·'sjon, -'θjon] *f* **1.** (*de ayuda, servicio*) provision; **~ por desempleo** unemployment benefit **2.** *pl* (*de coche*) features *pl*; **un coche con todas las últimas prestaciones** a car with all the latest features

**prestado, -a** [pres·'ta·do, -a] *adj* borrowed; **dar algo ~** to lend sth; **pedir algo ~** to borrow sth

**prestamista** [pres·ta·'mis·ta] *mf* moneylender

**préstamo** ['pres·ta·mo] *m* **1.** (*acción*) lending **2.** *t.* FIN (*lo prestado: para exposición*) loan; **~ hipotecario** mortgage; **~ a interés fijo** fixed-interest loan

**prestar** [pres·'tar] I. *vt* **1.** (*dejar*) to lend; **¿me prestas la bici, por favor?** can I borrow your bike?; **el banco me ha prestado el dinero** I have borrowed money from the bank **2.** (*dedicar*) **~ ayuda** to help; **~ servicios** to provide services; **~ apoyo** to support **3.** (*declaración*) to make; (*juramento*) to swear **4.** (*atención*) to pay; **~ silencio** to remain silent II. *vr:* ~**se 1.** (*ofrecerse*) to offer oneself; **se prestó a ayudarme** he/she offered to help me **2.** (*avenirse*) to accept **3.** (*dar motivo*) to give rise to; **tus palabras se prestan a confusión** your words lend themselves to misinterpretation

**prestigio** |pres·'ti·xjo| *m* prestige

**prestigioso, -a** |pres·ti·'xjo·so, -a| *adj* prestigious

**presumido, -a** |pre·su·'mi·do, -a| *adj* (*vanidoso*) vain

**presumir** |pre·su·'mir| I. *vi* ~ **de algo** to boast about sth II. *vt* to presume

**presunto, -a** |pre·'sun·to, -a| *adj* (*supuesto*) presumed; **el ~ asesino** the alleged murderer

**presuntuoso, -a** |pre·sun·tu·'o·so| *adj* conceited

**presuponer** |pre·su·po·'ner| *irr como* **poner** *vt* **1.** (*suponer*) to presuppose **2.** (*calcular*) to suppose

**presupuesto** |pre·su·'pwes·to| *m* **1.** POL, ECON budget; ~ **anual** annual budget **2.** (*cálculo*) estimate

**pretender** |pre·ten·'der| *vt* **1.** (*aspirar a*) to aspire to **2.** (*pedir*) to expect; **¿qué pretendes que haga?** what do you want me to do? **3.** (*tener intención*) to mean; **no pretendía molestar** I didn't mean to disturb you **4.** (*intentar*) to try to

**pretendiente** |pre·ten·'djen·te| *m* (*de trabajo*) applicant; (*de mujer*) suitor; (*a la corona*) pretender

**pretensión** |pre·ten·'sjon| *f* **1.** (*derecho*) claim; ~ **económica** financial demand **2.** (*ambición*) ambition; (*aspiración*) aim; **es una persona con muchas pretensiones** he/she is very ambitious

**pretérito** |pre·'te·ri·to| *m* LING past

**pretérito, -a** |pre·'te·ri·to, -a| *adj* past

**pretexto** |pre·'tes·to| *m* pretext

**prevalecer** |pre·βa·le·'ser, -'θer| *irr como* **crecer** *vi* **1.** (*imponerse*) to prevail; **la verdad prevaleció sobre la mentira** truth prevailed over lies **2.** (*predominar*) to predominate; **esta regla prevalece sobre las demás** this rule takes precedence over the others

**prevaricación** |pre·βa·ri·ka·'sjon, -'θjon|

*f* **1.** JUR perversion of the course of justice **2.** (*del deber*) dereliction of duty

**prevención** |pre·βen·'sjon, -·'θjon| *f* **1.** (*precaución*) precaution **2.** *t.* MED (*acción*) prevention; ~ **del cáncer** cancer prevention; ~ **de accidentes** accident prevention

**prevenido, -a** |pre·βe·'ni·do, -a| *adj* **1.** *estar* (*alerta*) **estar** ~ to be prepared **2.** *ser* (*previsor*) prudent ► **hombre ~ vale por dos** *prov* forewarned is forearmed *prov*

**prevenir** |pre·βe·'nir| *irr como* **venir** *vt* **1.** (*protegerse de*) to prevent **2.** (*advertir*) to warn **3.** (*predisponer*) to prejudice; ~ **a alguien a favor de alguien/en contra de alguien** to bias sb in sb's favor/against sb ► **más vale ~ que curar** *prov* prevention is better than cure, a stitch in time saves nine *prov*

**preventivo, -a** |pre·βen·'ti·βo, -a| *adj* preventive, preventative; **medida preventiva** preventive measure; **prisión preventiva** remand

**prever** |pre·'βer| *irr como* **ver** *vt* to foresee

**previo** |'pre·βjo| *m* TV, CINE playback

**previo, -a** |'pre·βjo, -a| *adj* previous; (*sin*) ~ **aviso** (without) prior warning; ~ **pago de la matrícula** on payment of the matriculation fee

**previsible** |pre·βi·'si·βle| *adj* **1.** (*probable*) predictable **2.** (*que se puede prever*) foreseeable; **era** ~ it was to be expected

**previsión** |pre·βi·'sjon| *f* **1.** (*de prever*) prediction; **esto supera todas las previsiones** this surpasses all the predictions **2.** (*precaución*) precaution **3.** (*cálculo*) forecast; **las previsiones económicas** the economic forecasts

**previsor(a)** |pre·βi·'sor, -·'so·ra| *adj* **1.** (*con visión*) far-sighted **2.** (*precavido*) prudent

**previsto, -a** |pre·'βis·to, -a| *adj* predicted; **todo lo necesario está** ~ everything necessary has been prepared

**prieto, -a** |'prje·to, -a| *adj* (*apretado*) tight

**prima** |'pri·ma| *f* **1.** (*pariente*) (girl) cousin; ~ **hermana/segunda** first/second cousin **2.** FIN bonus; (*seguro*) insurance premium

**primacía** [pri·ma·'sia, -'θia] *f* t. MIL, POL supremacy

**primar** [pri·'mar] **I.** *vi* to be of great importance; **en esta escuela prima el orden** in this school the most important thing is good behavior **II.** *vt* to reward

**primario, -a** [pri·'ma·rjo, -a] *adj* primary; **enseñanza primaria** primary education; **necesidades primarias** basic necessities

**primate** [pri·'ma·te] *m* primate

**primavera** [pri·ma·'βe·ra] *f* spring; **estar en la ~ de la vida** *fig* to be in the prime of life

**primaveral** [pri·ma·βe·'ral] *adj* spring(like)

**primer** [pri·'mer] *adj v.* **primero, -a**

**primera** [pri·'me·ra] *f* **1.** AUTO first (gear); **ir en ~** to be in first (gear) **2.** FERRO, AVIAT first class; **viajar en ~** to travel first class

**primero** [pri·'me·ro] *adv* **1.** (*en primer lugar*) first; **~..., segundo...** first..., second...; **~ dice una cosa, luego otra** first he/she says one thing, then another **2.** (*antes*) rather

**primero, -a** [pri·'me·ro, -a] **I.** *adj* (*ante sustantivo masc. sing.*: **primer**) first; **primera calidad** top quality; **primera edición** first edition; **el Primer Ministro** the Prime Minister; **a primera hora (de la mañana)** first thing (in the morning); **a ~s de mes** at the beginning of the month; **de primera** first-rate; **de primera calidad** top quality; **desde un primer momento** from the outset; **en primer lugar** in the first place; **lo ~ es lo ~** first things first; **lo ~ es ahora la familia** the most important thing now is the family **II.** *m, f* first; **el ~ de la clase** the top of the class; **estar entre los ~s** to be among the leaders

**primicia** [pri·'mi·sja, -θja] *f* PREN, TV, RADIO scoop

**primitivo, -a** [pri·mi·'ti·βo, -a] *adj* primitive; **lotería primitiva** Spanish state lottery

**primo** ['pri·mo] *m* **1.** (*pariente*) (boy) cousin; **~ hermano/segundo** first/sec-

ond cousin **2.** *inf* (*ingenuo*) mug; **hacer el ~** to get taken for a ride

**primo, -a** ['pri·mo, -a] *adj* **materia prima** raw material; **número ~** MAT prime number

**primogénito, -a** [pri·mo·'xe·ni·to, -a] *adj, m, f* first-born

**primor** [pri·'mor] *m* **1.** (*habilidad*) skill **2.** (*esmero*) care

**primordial** [pri·mor·'djal] *adj* **1.** (*más importante*) supreme; **este asunto es de interés ~** this affair is of fundamental concern **2.** (*fundamental*) essential, fundamental

**princesa** [prin·'se·sa, -'θe·sa] *f v.* **príncipe, princesa**

**principado** [prin·si·'pa·do, prin·θi·] *m* principality

**principal** [prin·si·'pal, prin·θi·] *adj* **1.** (*más importante*) principal; **el problema ~** the main problem; **lo ~ es que...** the main priority is... **2.** (*esencial*) essential

**principalmente** [prin·si·pal·'men·te, prin·θi·] *adv* mainly, principally

**príncipe, princesa** ['prin·si·pe, -θi·pe; prin·'se·sa, -'θe·sa] *m, f* prince *m*, princess *f*; **~ heredero** crown prince; **el Príncipe de Asturias** the Prince of Asturias *(title held by the heir to the Spanish throne)*; **~ azul** Prince Charming

**principiante** [prin·si·'pjan·te, prin·θi·] *mf* beginner, novice

**principio** [prin·'si·pjo, -'θi·pjo] *m* **1.** (*comienzo*) beginning; **al ~** at the beginning; **ya desde el ~** right from the beginning; **desde un ~** from the first; **a ~s de diciembre** at the beginning of December **2.** (*causa*) cause; (*origen*) origin; **el ~ de la discusión** the cause of the argument **3.** (*de ética*) principle; **sin ~s** unprincipled; **hombre de ~s** a man of principle(s); **por ~** on principle **4.** t. FÍS (*fundamento*) principle

**pringar** <g → gu> [prin·'gar] **I.** *vt* (*manchar*) **~ de/con algo** to smear with sth **II.** *vi AmL* (*lloviznar*) to drizzle **III.** *vr:* **~se** (*mancharse*) **~se de/con algo** to cover oneself with sth

**pringoso, -a** [prin·'go·so, -a] *adj* greasy

**prioridad** [prjo·ri·'dad] *f* **1.** (*anteriori-*

_dad_) priority; **de máxima ~** top priority; **dar ~ a un asunto** to give a matter priority; **tener ~ sobre** to have priority over 2. AUTO (_de paso_) right of way

**prioritario, -a** [prjo·ri'ta·rjo, -a] _adj_ priority; **este plan es ~** this plan has priority

**prisa** ['pri·sa] _f_ hurry; **a toda ~** at full speed; **de ~** quickly; **de ~ y corriendo** (_con demasiada prisa_) in a rush; (_rápidamente_) quickly; **!no corre ~** there's no hurry; **¡date ~!** hurry up!; **meter ~ a alguien** to hurry sb; **tengo ~** I'm in a hurry

**prisión** [pri'sjon] _f_ 1. (_reclusión_) imprisonment; **~ preventiva** remand 2. (_edificio_) prison; **~ de alta seguridad** high-security prison; **estar en ~** to be in prison

**prisionero, -a** [pri·sjo'ne·ro, -a] _m, f_ prisoner; **hacer ~ a alguien** to take sb prisoner

**prisma** ['pris·ma] _m_ (_figura_) prism

**prismáticos** [pris·'ma·ti·kos] _mpl_ binoculars _pl_

**privación** [pri·βa·'sjon, -'θjon] _f_ 1. (_desposesión_) deprivation; **~ de libertad** JUR loss of liberty 2. (_carencia_) privation

**privado, -a** [pri·'βa·do, -a] _adj_ 1. (_reunión, fiesta_) private; (_sesión_) closed 2. (_personal, confidencial_) private; **vida privada** private life; **en ~** in private 3. (_falto_) **~ de...** without...; **~ de medios** without means

**privar** [pri·'βar] I. _vt_ 1. (_desposeer_) to deprive; **~ a alguien de un derecho** to deprive sb of a right 2. (_prohibir_) to forbid 3. (_gustar_) to delight; **está privado por esa chica** he's crazy about that girl II. _vr_ to deny oneself; **no se privan de nada** they don't want for anything

**privatizar** <z → c> [pri·βa·ti·'sar, -'θar] _vt_ to privatize

**privilegiado, -a** [pri·βi·le·'xja·do, -a] _adj_ privileged; (_memoria_) exceptional

**privilegio** [pri·βi·'le·xjo] _m_ privilege; **~ fiscal** tax concession

**pro** [pro] I. _m o f_ 1. (_provecho_) advantage; **valorar los ~s y los contras** to weigh the pros and cons 2. (_de bien_) **un hombre de ~** an honest man

II. _prep_ for

**proa** ['proa] _f_ NÁUT bow; AVIAT nose

**probabilidad** [pro·βa·βi·li·'dad] _f_ 1. (_verosimilitud_) probability; **con toda ~** in all likelihood 2. (_posibilidad_) prospect; **hay ~es de ganar** there is a good chance of winning

**probable** [pro·'βa·βle] _adj_ (_verosímil_) probable; **un resultado ~** a likely result; **lo más ~ es que...** chances are that...

**probablemente** [pro·βa·βle·'men·te] _adv_ probably

**probado, -a** [pro·'βa·do, -a] _adj_ proven

**probador** [pro·βa·'dor] _m_ fitting room

**probar** <o → ue> [pro·'βar] I. _vt_ 1. (_demostrar_) to prove 2. (_experimentar_) to try; (_aparato_) to test 3. (_a alguien_) to test 4. (_vestido_) to try on 5. CULIN to taste; **no he probado nunca una paella** I have never tried paella II. _vi_ (_intentar_) to try

**problema** [pro·'βle·ma] _m_ problem; **~ de liquidez** cash flow problem

**problemático, -a** [pro·βle·'ma·ti·ko, -a] _adj_ problematic

**procedencia** [pro·se·'den·sja, pro·θe·'den·θja] _f_ (_origen_) origin

**procedente** [pro·se·'den·te, pro·θe-] _adj_ 1. (_oportuno_) appropriate 2. (_que viene de_) **~ de** from; **el tren ~ de Nueva York con destino a Chicago** the train from New York to Chicago 3. JUR fitting

**proceder** [pro·se·'der, pro·θe-] I. _m_ 1. (_comportamiento_) behavior 2. (_actuación_) (course of) action II. _vi_ 1. (_familia_) to descend; (_de un lugar_) to come 2. (_actuar_) to act 3. (_ser oportuno_) to be appropriate; **no ~** to be inappropriate; **táchese lo que no proceda** delete as applicable 4. (_pasar a_) to proceed

**procedimiento** [pro·se·di·'mjen·to, pro·θe-] _m_ 1. (_actuación_) procedure; **seguir un ~** to follow a procedure 2. (_método_) method 3. JUR proceedings _pl_

**procesado, -a** [pro·se·'sa·do, -a; pro·θe-] _m, f_ JUR defendant; **el ~** the accused

**procesador** [pro·se·sa·'dor, pro·θe-] _m_ computer; **~ de textos** word processor

**procesamiento** [pro·se·sa·'mjen·to, pro·θe-] _m_ 1. JUR prosecution 2. COMPUT processing

P

**procesar** [pro·se·'sar, pro·θe-] *vt* **1.** JUR to prosecute; **le procesan por violación** he is being prosecuted for rape **2.** TÉC to process

**procesión** [pro·se·'sjon, pro·θe-] *f* **1.** *t.* REL (*marcha*) procession **2.** (*hilera*) line; (*de personas*) procession **3.** *inf* (*preocupación*) **permaneció tranquilo aunque la ~ iba por dentro** he remained outwardly calm, but he was actually rather worried

**proceso** [pro·'se·so, pro·'θe-] *m* **1.** (*método*) process **2.** (*procedimiento*) procedure **3.** JUR (*causa*) trial

**proclamación** [pro·kla·ma·'sjon, -'θjon] *f* proclamation

**proclamar** [pro·kla·'mar] **I.** *vt* **1.** (*hacer público*) to announce; **~ la República** to proclaim a Republic **2.** (*aclamar*) to acclaim **3.** (*sentimiento*) to declare **4.** (*ganador*) to declare; **fue proclamado Premio Nobel** he was awarded the Nobel Prize **II.** *vr* **~se ganador** to declare oneself the winner

**procrear** [pro·kre·'ar] *vt* to procreate

**procurador(a)** [pro·ku·ra·'dor, -·'do·ra] *m(f)* attorney; (*en negocios*) agent

**procurar** [pro·ku·'rar] **I.** *vt* **1.** (*intentar*) to try; **procura que no te oigan** make sure they don't hear you **2.** (*proporcionar*) to obtain **II.** *vr* to secure (for oneself)

**prodigar** <g → gu> [pro·di·'γar] **I.** *vt* **1.** (*malgastar*) to waste **2.** (*dar*) to lavish **II.** *vr* **se prodigó en toda clase de atenciones con nosotros** he attended to our every need; **se prodigó en elogios hacia él** he/she showered him with praise

**prodigio** [pro·'di·xjo] *m* prodigy; **niño ~** child prodigy

**prodigioso, -a** [pro·di·'xjo·so, -a] *adj* **1.** (*sobrenatural*) miraculous **2.** (*extraordinario*) marvelous

**pródigo, -a** ['pro·di·γo, -a] *adj* **1.** (*malgastador*) wasteful; **el hijo ~** the prodigal son **2.** (*generoso*) generous; **la pródiga naturaleza** bountiful nature

**producción** [pro·duk·'sjon, -'θjon] *f* **1.** *t.* TÉC, CINE production; **~ en cadena** assembly line production; **~ en masa** mass production **2.** (*productos*) output

**producir** [pro·du·'sir, -'θir] *irr como* **traducir I.** *vt* **1.** *t.* TÉC, CINE to produce; (*energía*) to generate **2.** (*beneficios*) generate; (*intereses*) to yield **3.** (*alegría, impresión*) to create; (*aburrimiento, miedo*) to produce; (*daño, tristeza*) to cause **II.** *vr:* **~se 1.** (*fabricarse*) to be produced **2.** (*tener lugar*) to take place; **se produjo una crisis** a crisis occurred

**productividad** [pro·duk·ti·βi·'dad] *f* productivity

**productivo, -a** [pro·duk·'ti·βo, -a] *adj* productive

**producto** [pro·'duk·to] *m* **1.** *t.* QUÍM, MAT product; **~s básicos** commodities; **~s alimenticios** foodstuffs *pl;* **~ de belleza** beauty product; **~ de marca** brand-name product; **~s químicos** chemicals *pl;* **~ (semi)manufacturado** manufactured good; **~ derivado** [*o* secundario] by-product **2.** (*de un negocio*) profit; (*de una venta*) proceeds *pl;* **Producto Interior Bruto** Gross Domestic Product; **Producto Nacional Bruto** Gross National Product

**productor(a)** [pro·duk·'tor, -·'to·ra] **I.** *adj* producing **II.** *m(f)* producer

**profano, -a** [pro·'fa·no, -a] *adj* **1.** (*secular*) secular **2.** (*irreverente*) irreverent **3.** (*ignorante*) ignorant; **soy ~ en esta materia** I am not an expert in this subject

**profecía** [pro·fe·'si·a, -'θi·a] *f* prophecy

**profesar** [pro·fe·'sar] *vt* (*religión, doctrina*) to profess

**profesión** [pro·fe·'sjon] *f* **1.** (*empleo*) profession; **de ~** by profession **2.** (*religión, doctrina*) profession

**profesional** [pro·fe·sjo·'nal] **I.** *adj* professional; **ética ~** professional ethics; **secreto ~** trade secret **II.** *mf* professional

**profesor(a)** [pro·fe·'sor, -·'so·ra] *m(f)* (*no universitario*) teacher; (*universitario*) professor; (*catedrático*) senior teacher

**profeta, -isa** [pro·'fe·ta, pro·fe·'ti·sa] *m, f* prophet *m(f)*, prophetess *f;* **nadie es ~ en su tierra** no one is a prophet in his own land

**profundamente** [pro·fun·da·'men·te] *adv* profoundly; **~ ofendido** deeply offended

**profundidad** [pro·fun·di·'dad] *f* depth; **analizar en ~** to analyze in depth; **tener una ~ de cinco metros** to be five meters deep

**profundizar** <z → c> [pro·fun·di·'sar, -'θar] I. *vt* (*hoyo, zanja*) to make deeper; *fig* to study in depth II. *vi* **~ en algo** to study [*o* to go into] sth in depth

**profundo, -a** [pro·'fun·do] *adj* (*hoyo, lago, voz*) deep; (*observación*) incisive; (*pena*) heartfelt; (*pensamiento, misterio*) profound; (*conocimiento*) thorough; **en lo más ~ de mi corazón** from the very bottom of my heart

**profusión** [pro·fu·'sjon] *f* profusion; **con ~ de detalles** with a wealth of details; **hay gran ~ de noticias** there is a lot of news

**progenitor(a)** [pro·xe·ni·'tor, -·'to·ra] *m(f)* **1.** (*antepasado*) for(e)bear **2.** (*mayor*) father *m*, mother *f*; **los ~es** the parents

**programa** [pro·'yra·ma] *m* program; **~ de las clases** (*de la Universidad*) (university) class schedule; **~ de estudios** study plan; **~ de trabajo** work schedule; **~ antivirus** COMPUT antivirus program

**programación** [pro·yra·ma·'sjon, -'θjon] *f* **1.** (*acción*) programming **2.** TV, RADIO program

**programador(a)** [pro·yra·ma·'dor, -·'do·ra] *m(f)* programmer

**programar** [pro·yra·'mar] *vt* to plan; **la conferencia está programada para el domingo** the talk is scheduled for Sunday; **¿qué tienes programado para esta tarde?** what do you have planned for this evening?

**progresar** [pro·yre·'sar] *vi* to make progress; (*enfermedad, ciencia*) to develop; **~ profesionalmente** to progress [*o* get ahead] in one's career

**progresión** [pro·yre·'sjon] *f* **1.** (*avance*) progress **2.** MAT, MÚS progression

**progresista** [pro·yre·'sis·ta] *adj* progressive

**progresivo, -a** [pro·yre·'si·βo, -a] *adj t.* FIN (*que progresa*) progressive; (*que aumenta*) increasing

**progreso** [pro·'yre·so] *m* progress

**prohibición** [pro·i·βi·'sjon, -'θjon] *f* prohibition

**prohibido, -a** [pro·i·'βi·do, -a] *adj* **~ fumar** no smoking; **fruto ~** forbidden fruit; **prohibida la entrada** no entry

**prohibir** [pro·i·'βir] *irr vt* to prohibit, to ban

**prohibitivo, -a** [pro·i·βi·'ti·βo, -a] *adj* prohibitive; **a precio ~** prohibitively expensive

**prójimo** ['pro·xi·mo] *m* (*semejante*) fellow man; **amor al ~** love of one's neighbor

**proletario, -a** [pro·le·'ta·rjo, -a] *adj* proletarian; **barrio ~** working-class area

**proliferación** [pro·li·fe·ra·'sjon, -'θjon] *f* **1.** (*en cantidad*) proliferation; **tratado de no ~ de armas nucleares** nuclear non-proliferation treaty **2.** *t.* MED (*incontrolada*) spread

**proliferar** [pro·li·fe·'rar] *vi* **1.** (*en cantidad*) to proliferate **2.** (*epidemia, rumor*) to spread

**prólogo** ['pro·lo·yo] *m* (*de libro*) foreword; TEAT, DEP prelude

**prolongación** [pro·lon·ga·'sjon, -'θjon] *f* extension; (*de decisión*) postponement

**prolongado, -a** [pro·lon·'ga·do, -a] *adj* prolonged; **un sobre ~** a long envelope

**prolongar** <g → gu> [pro·lon·'gar] I. *vt* to extend; (*decisión*) to postpone; (*un estado*) to prolong II. *vr:* **~se** to continue; (*un estado*) to be prolonged; (*reunión*) to overrun; **las negociaciones se están prolongando demasiado** the negotiations are dragging on for too long

**promediar** [pro·me·'djar] I. *vt* **1.** (*repartir*) to divide in two **2.** (*sacar promedio*) to average out II. *vi* **1.** (*mediar*) to mediate **2.** (*temporal*) **antes de ~ el año** before the year was halfway through

**promedio** [pro·'me·djo] *m* average; **veo la tele un ~ de dos horas al día** I watch an average of two hours' TV a day

**promesa** [pro·'me·sa] *f* promise; REL VOW; **el jefe me ha dado su ~ de que...** the boss has promised me that...

**prometedor(a)** [pro·me·te·'dor, -·'do·ra] *adj* promising

**prometer** [pro·me·'ter] I. *vt* to promise;

REL to vow; **te prometo que lo haré** I promise you I'll do it; **~ el oro y el moro** to promise the earth ▶ **lo prometido es deuda** *prov* a promise is a promise **II.** *vi* **este negocio promete** this business is promising **III.** *vr* (*novios*) to get engaged

**prometido, -a** [pro·me·'ti·do] *m, f* fiancé *m*, fiancée *f*

**promiscuidad** [pro·mis·kwi·'dad] *f* (*sexual*) promiscuity

**promoción** [pro·mo·'sjon, -'θjon] *f* **1.** (*de empresa, categoría, producto*) promotion **2.** (*de licenciados*) year, graduating class; **ser de la misma ~** to have graduated in the same year

**promocionar** [pro·mo·sjo·'nar, -θjo·'nar] *vt* (*empresa, producto*) to promote; **está promocionando su nueva película** she is promoting her new film

**promotor(a)** [pro·mo·'tor] *m(f)* (*patrocinador*) sponsor; (*deportivo, artístico, de espectáculo*) promoter

**promover** <o → ue> [pro·mo·'βer] *vt* **1.** (*querella, escándalo*) to cause; (*proceso*) to advance **2.** (*en el cargo*) to promote

**promulgar** <g → gu> [pro·mul·'ɣar] *vt* to enact; (*divulgar*) to announce

**pronombre** [pro·'nom·bre] *m* LING pronoun

**pronosticar** <c → qu> [pro·nos·ti·'kar] *vt* to forecast

**pronóstico** [pro·'nos·ti·ko] *m* t. ECON forecast; MED prognosis; DEP prediction

**pronto** ['pron·to] **I.** *adv* **1.** (*rápido*) quickly **2.** (*enseguida*) at once **3.** (*temprano*) early ▶ **de ~** suddenly; **¡hasta ~!** see you!; **por de** [*o* **por lo**] **~** for the time being **II.** *conj* **tan ~ como** as soon as

**pronto, -a** ['pron·to, -a] *adj* **1.** (*rápido*) quick; (*despierto*) sharp **2.** (*dispuesto*) ready; **estar ~** *CSur* to be ready

**pronunciación** [pro·nun·sja·'sjon, -θja·'θjon] *f* LING pronunciation

**pronunciado, -a** [pro·nun·'sja·do, -a; -'θja·do, -a] *adj* pronounced; (*pendiente, cuesta*) steep; **acento ~** strong [*o* marked] accent; **una curva pronunciada** a sharp bend; **rasgos ~s** strong features

**pronunciar** [pro·nun·'sjar, -'θjar] **I.** *vt* **1.** (*articular*) to pronounce; **~ un discurso** to make a speech; **~ unas palabras** to say a few words; **~ sentencia** to pass sentence **2.** (*resaltar*) to emphasize **II.** *vr:* **~se 1.** (*opinar*) **~se sobre algo** to state one's opinion on sth **2.** (*acentuarse*) to become more pronounced

**propagación** [pro·pa·ɣa·'sjon, -'θjon] *f* (*multiplicación, reproducción*) propagation

**propaganda** [pro·pa·'ɣan·da] *f* **1.** (*publicidad*) publicity; **hacer ~** to advertise, to publicize **2.** MIL, POL propaganda

**propagar** <g → gu> [pro·pa·'ɣar] **I.** *vt* (*multiplicar*) to propagate; **~ un rumor** to spread a rumor **II.** *vr:* **~se** (*multiplicarse*) to propagate

**propano** [pro·'pa·no] *m* propane

**propasar** [pro·pa·'sar] *vr:* **~se** (*extralimitarse*) to go too far; **~se con alguien** to take liberties with sb

**propenso, -a** [pro·'pen·so, -a] *adj* (*a enfermedades*) susceptible; (*dispuesto*) inclined; **ser ~ a algo** to be prone to sth

**propiamente** [pro·pja·'men·te] *adv* **~ dicho** strictly speaking

**propiciar** [pro·pi·'sjar, -'θjar] *vt* (*favorecer*) to favor; (*posibilitar*) to make possible; **el viento propició la extensión de las llamas** the wind helped the flames to spread

**propicio, -a** [pro·'pi·sjo, -a; -θjo, -a] *adj* **1.** (*favorable*) favorable; **en el momento ~** at the right moment **2.** (*dispuesto*) inclined; **mostrarse (poco) ~ para...** (not) to be prepared to...

**propiedad** [pro·pje·'dad] *f* **1.** (*pertenencia, cualidad*) t. FÍS property; **~ exclusiva** exclusive ownership; **~ intelectual** intellectual property; **~ inmobiliaria** real estate; **un piso de mi ~** an apartment that I own; **tener algo en ~** to own sth; **ser ~ de alguien** to be sb's property **2.** (*corrección*) correctness; (*exactitud*) precision; **expresarse con ~** to speak correctly

**propietario, -a** [pro·pje·'ta·rjo, -a] *m, f* owner; (*terrateniente*) landowner; (*casero*) landlord

**propina** [pro·'pi·na] *f* tip; **dejar ~ to** leave a tip; **de ~** *fig* for good measure

**propinar** [pro·pi·'nar] *vt* (*golpes*) to give

**propio, -a** ['pro·pjo, -a] *adj* **1.** (*de uno mismo*) own; **en defensa propia** in self-defense; **lo he visto con mis ~s ojos** I have seen it with my own eyes; **tengo piso ~** I own my apartment **2.** (*mismo*) same; **lo ~** the same; **el ~ jefe** the boss himself; **nombre ~** LING proper noun **3.** (*característico*) characteristic; **eso (no) es ~ de ti** that is (not) like you **4.** (*apropiado*) proper

**proponer** [pro·po·'ner] *irr como* **poner** **I.** *vt* **1.** (*sugerir, presentar*) to propose; **~ un brindis por alguien** to propose a toast in sb's honor **2.** (*plantear*) to put forward; **~ una cuestión** to set out a matter **II.** *vr* to propose; (*tener intención*) to intend; **¿qué te propones?** what are you trying to do?

**proporción** [pro·por·'sjon, -'θjon] *f* **1.** (*relación, porcentaje*) proportion; **no guardar ~ con algo** to be out of proportion with sth; **en una ~ de 8 a 1** in a ratio of 8 to 1 **2.** *pl* (*dimensión*) proportions *pl*; **un accidente de enormes proporciones** a major accident

**proporcional** [pro·por·sjo·'nal, -θjo·'nal] *adj* proportional; **reparto ~** proportional distribution; **sistema ~** POL proportional representation

**proporcionar** [pro·por·sjo·'nar, -θjo·'nar] *vt* **1.** (*facilitar*) to provide; **~ víveres a alguien** to provide sb with supplies **2.** (*ocasionar*) to cause; **~ disgustos a alguien** to upset sb

**proposición** [pro·po·si·'sjon, -'θjon] *f* **1.** (*propuesta*) proposal; **~ de ley** bill **2.** LING (*oración*) sentence; (*parte*) clause

**propósito** [pro·'po·si·to] **I.** *m* **1.** (*intención*) intention; **buenos ~s** good intentions; **tener el ~ de...** to intend to... **2.** (*objetivo*) objective ▶ **a ~** (*adrede*) on purpose; (*por cierto*) by the way **II.** *prep* **a ~ de** with regard to

**propuesta** [pro·'pwes·ta] *f* proposal; (*oferta*) offer; **a ~ de alguien** on sb's suggestion; **formular una ~** to draw up a proposal

**propulsar** [pro·pul·'sar] *vt* **1.** TÉC to propel **2.** (*fomentar*) to promote

**propulsión** [pro·pul·'sjon] *f* TÉC propulsion; **~ a hélice** propeller power; **~ por reacción** jet propulsion

**prórroga** ['pro·rro·ɣa] *f* **1.** ECON extension **2.** (*aplazamiento*) deferral **3.** DEP extra time, overtime

**prosa** ['pro·sa] *f* prose

**proseguir** [pro·se·'ɣir] *irr como* **seguir** **I.** *vi* to continue **II.** *vt* **1.** (*continuar*) *t.* JUR to continue **2.** (*un fin*) to pursue

**prospecto** [pros·'pek·to] *m* prospectus; (*de un medicamento*) directions *pl* for use

**prosperar** [pros·pe·'rar] *vi* (*florecer*) to thrive; (*tener éxito*) to prosper

**prosperidad** [pros·pe·ri·'dad] *f* (*bienestar*) prosperity; **~ económica** economic prosperity

**próspero, -a** ['pros·pe·ro, -a] *adj* (*floreciente*) thriving; (*con éxito*) prosperous; **¡Próspero Año Nuevo!** Happy New Year!

**próstata** ['pros·ta·ta] *f* prostate

**prostíbulo** [pros·'ti·βu·lo] *m* brothel

**prostitución** [pros·ti·tu·'sjon, -'θjon] *f* prostitution; **ejercer la ~** to be a prostitute

**prostituir** [pros·ti·tu·'ir] *irr como* **huir** **I.** *vt* to prostitute **II.** *vr:* **~se** *t. fig* to prostitute oneself

**prostituto, -a** [pros·ti·'tu·to, -a] *m, f* male prostitute *m*, prostitute *f*

**protagonista** [pro·ta·ɣo·'nis·ta] **I.** *adj* **el papel ~** the leading role **II.** *mf* key participant; CINE, TEAT leading actor *m*, leading actress *f*; LIT main character

**protagonizar** <z → c> [pro·ta·ɣo·ni·'sar, -'θar] *vt* to play; **~ una película** to star in a film

**protección** [pro·tek·'sjon, -'θjon] *f* protection; **~ sanitaria** health cover; **crema de alta ~** high-protection sun cream; **poner a alguien bajo ~** to place sb under protection; **tomar a alguien bajo su ~** to take sb into one's protection

**protector** [pro·tek·'tor] *m* protector; **~ solar** sunscreen

**protector(a)** [pro·tek·'tor, -·'to·ra] **I.** *adj* protective; **casco ~** protective helmet;

P

**sociedad ~a de animales** society for the prevention of cruelty to animals **II.** *m(f)* protector; (*mecenas*) patron

**proteger** <g → j> [pro·te·'xer] **I.** *vt* to protect **II.** *vr:* **~se** [pro·te·'xer] to protect oneself; **~se los ojos** to protect one's eyes

**protegido, -a** [pro·te·'xi·do, -a] **I.** *adj* protected; **~ contra escritura** COMPUT write-protected **II.** *m, f* protégé *m*, protégée *f*

**proteína** [pro·te·'i·na] *f* protein

**prótesis** ['pro·te·sis] *f inv* prosthesis

**protesta** [pro·'tes·ta] *f* protest; JUR objection

**protestante** [pro·tes·'tan·te] *adj, mf* REL Protestant

**protestar** [pro·tes·'tar] **I.** *vi* to protest **II.** *vt* JUR to raise an objection

**protestón, -ona** [pro·tes·'ton, -·'to·na] *adj inf* grumbling

**protocolo** [pro·to·'ko·lo] *m* protocol

**protón** [pro·'ton] *m* proton

**prototipo** [pro·to·'ti·po] *m* prototype

**provecho** [pro·'βe·tʃo] *m* use; (*ventaja*) advantage; (*beneficio*) benefit; **de ~** useful; **nada de ~** nothing of use; **en ~ de alguien** to sb's advantage; **sacar ~ de algo/alguien** to do benefit from sth/sb, to profit from sth/sb; **¡buen ~!** enjoy your meal!, bon appétit!

**provechoso, -a** [pro·βe·'tʃo·so, -a] *adj* beneficial; (*útil*) useful

**proveedor(a)** [pro·βe·'dor/pro·βe·'e·dor] *m(f)* **1.** (*suministrador*) supplier **2.** COMPUT provider

**proveer** [pro·'βer/pro·βe·'er] *irr* **I.** *vi* to provide **II.** *vt:* **~se 1.** (*abastecer*) to supply; **~ de algo** to furnish with sth; (*dotar*) to provide with sth **2.** (*un puesto*) to fill **III.** *vr* to supply oneself; **~se de algo** to provide oneself with sth

**proveniente** [pro·βe·'njen·te] *adj* **el tren ~ de Madrid** the train from Madrid

**provenir** [pro·βe·'nir] *irr como* venir *vi* **~ de** to come from, to stem from

**proverbio** [pro·'βer·βjo] *m* proverb

**provincia** [pro·'βin·sja, -θja] *f* province; *AmS* (*estado*) state

**provisión** [pro·βi·'sjon] *f* (*reserva*) supply; **provisiones** provisions *pl*

**provisional** [pro·βi·sjo·'nal] *adj* provi-

sional; **gobierno ~** provisional government; **medida ~** temporary measure

**provisto, -a** [pro·'βis·to, -a] **I.** *pp de* **proveer II.** *adj* provided; **~ al efecto** provided for the purpose

**provocación** [pro·βo·ka·'sjon, -'θjon] *f* provocation

**provocador** [pro·βo·ka·'dor] *m* stirrer

**provocar** <c → qu> [pro·βo·'kar] **I.** *vt* **1.** (*incitar*) to provoke; **¡no me provoques!** don't provoke me! **2.** (*causar*) *t.* MED to cause, to induce; **~ risa a alguien** to make sb laugh; **~ un cambio** to bring about a change; **~ una guerra** to start a war; **~ un incendio** to start a fire **II.** *vi* AmL (*apetecer*) **(no) me provoca** I (don't) feel like it

**provocativo, -a** [pro·βo·ka·'ti·βo, -a] *adj* provocative

**próximamente** [prok·si·ma·'men·te] *adv* soon

**proximidad** [prok·si·mi·'dad] *f* proximity; **en las ~es** in the vicinity

**próximo, -a** ['prok·si·mo, -a] *adj* **1.** (*cercano*) near, neighboring; (*temporal*) close; **estar ~ a...** to be close to... **2.** (*siguiente*) next; **el ~ año** next year; **el ~ viernes** next Friday; **la próxima vez** the next time; **¡hasta la próxima!** see you soon!

**proyección** [pro·jek·'sjon, -'θjon] *f* **1.** FÍS, ARQUIT, CINE, PSICO projection; (*sesión*) screening **2.** (*influencia*) influence; **una empresa de ~ internacional** a business with a global presence

**proyectar** [pro·jek·'tar] **I.** *vt* **1.** FÍS, FOTO, CINE to project **2.** (*lanzar*) to throw **3.** (*luz*) to shine; (*sombra*) to cast **4.** (*planear*) to plan **5.** *t.* TÉC (*diseñar*) to design **II.** *vr:* **~se 1.** (*luz*) to be shine; (*sombra*) to be cast **2.** PSICO **~se en algo** to project onto sth

**proyectil** [pro·jek·'til] *m* projectile

**proyecto** [pro·'jek·to] *m* plan; **~ de fin de carrera** UNIV final year project; **~ de ley** bill; **en ~** planned

**proyector** [pro·jek·'tor] *m* FOTO, CINE projector; **~ de cine** film projector; **de diapositivas** slide projector; **~ de luz** floodlight

**prudencia** [pru·'den·sja, -θja] *f* prudence

**prudencial** [pru·den·'sjal, -'θjal] *adj* (*razonable*) reasonable

**prudente** [pru·'den·te] *adj* prudent

**prueba** ['prwe·βa] *f* **1.** *t.* TÉC (*test*) test; (*experimento*) experiment; **~ de alcoholemia** Breathalyzer® test; **~ de aptitud** aptitude test; **~ de paternidad** paternity test; **período de ~** trial period; **poner a ~** to try out; **someter a ~** to test; **sufrir una dura ~** to be put through a stern test; **a ~ de agua** waterproof; **a ~ de balas** bullet-proof; **a ~ de robo** theft-proof; **~ de fuego** *fig* acid test **2.** (*comprobación*) proof **3.** (*examen*) exam; **~ de acceso** entry exam **4.** DEP (*competición*) event; **~ clasificatoria/eliminatoria** qualifier/eliminator **5.** TIPO proof; **~ de imprenta** proof **6.** (*testimonio*) piece of evidence; **~ circunstancial** circumstantial evidence; **en ~ de nuestro reconocimiento** as a token of our gratitude; **tener ~s de que...** to have evidence that...

(p)**seudónimo** [seu·'do·ni·mo] *m* pseudonym

(p)**sicoanálisis** [si·ko·a·'na·li·sis] *m* psychoanalysis

(p)**sicoanalista** [si·ko·a·na·'lis·ta] *mf* psychoanalyst

(p)**sicología** [si·ko·lo·'xi·a] *f* psychology; **~ infantil** child psychology

(p)**sicológico, -a** [si·ko·lo·'xi·ko, -a] *adj* psychological

(p)**sicólogo, -a** [si·ko·lo·γo, -a] *m, f* psychologist

(p)**sicópata** [si·'ko·pa·ta] *mf* psychopath

(p)**sicosis** [si·'ko·sis] *f inv* psychosis; **~ colectiva** collective psychosis

(p)**sicosomático, -a** [si·ko·so·'ma·ti·ko, -a] *adj* psychosomatic

(p)**sicoterapia** [si·ko·te·'ra·pja] *f* psychotherapy

(p)**sique** ['si·ke] *f* psyche

(p)**siquiatra** [si·'kja·tra] *mf* psychiatrist

(p)**siquiatría** [si·kja·tri·a] *f* psychiatry

(p)**siquiátrico** [si·'kja·tri·ko] *m* (*hospital*) mental [*o* psychiatric] hospital

(p)**síquico, -a** ['si·ki·ko, -a] *adj* psychic, mental

**púa** ['pu·a] *f* (*de planta*) thorn; (*de animal*) spine, quill; (*del peine*) tooth; (*de*

*tenedor*) prong; MÚS plectrum

**pub** <pubs> [paβ] *m* bar, cocktail lounge

**pubertad** [pu·βer·'tad] *f* puberty

**pubis** ['pu·βis] *m inv* pubis

**publicación** [pu·βli·ka·'sjon, -'θjon] *f* publication

**publicar** <c → qu> [pu·βli·'kar] **I.** *vt* to publish **II.** *vr:* **~se** to be published

**publicidad** [pu·βli·si·'dad, -θi·'dad] *f* **1.** (*carácter público*) publicity; **este programa le ha dado mucha ~** this program has given him/her a lot of publicity **2.** (*propaganda*) advertising; **hacer ~ de algo** to advertise sth

**publicitario, -a** [pu·βli·si·'ta·rjo, -a; pu·βli·θi-] *adj* advertising

**público** ['pu·βli·ko] *m* public; **en ~** in public; **el gran ~** the general public; **para todos los ~s** for all audiences; CINE G-rated; **abierto/cerrado al ~** open/ closed to the public; **hoy hay poco ~** there aren't many people today

**público, -a** ['pu·βli·ko, -a] *adj* public; **deuda pública** national debt; **relaciones públicas** public relations; **el sector ~** the public sector; **transporte ~** public transport; **escándalo ~** public scandal; **hacer ~** to make public; **hacerse ~** to become known; **ser del dominio ~** to be public domain

**pucha** ['pu·tʃa] *interj* CSur ¡**la ~!** damn!

**pucherazo** [pu·tʃe·'ra·so, -θo] *m* **~ electoral** electoral fraud

**puchero** [pu·'tʃe·ro] *m* (*olla*) pot; CULIN stew; **hacer ~s** *inf* (*gestos*) to pout

**pudor** [pu·'dor] *m* (*recato*) shyness; (*vergüenza*) shame

**pudrir** [pu·'drir] *irr* **I.** *vt fig* to rot **II.** *vr:* **~se** *t. fig* to rot; *Arg inf* (*aburrirse*) to get bored; **~se en la cárcel** *inf* to rot in prison

**pueblo** ['pwe·βlo] *m* **1.** (*nación*) people; **un hombre del ~** a man of the people **2.** (*aldea*) village; (*población*) (small) town; **~ costero** seaside town; **~ de mala muerte** *inf* dead-end town; **de ~** from a small town; *pey* small-town

**puente** ['pwen·te] *m* **1.** *t.* NÁUT, ELEC (*construcción, de las gafas*) bridge; **~ levadizo** drawbridge; **~ colgante** suspension bridge; **~ aéreo** (*servicio*) shuttle;

**P**

MIL airlift; ~ **dental** bridge; ~ **de mando** (compass) bridge; **hacer un ~ a un coche** to hot-wire a car **2.** (*fiesta*) long weekend *(a public holiday plus an additional day off)*; **hacer/tener ~** to take/have a long weekend

**puenting** ['pwen·tin] *m* bungee jumping

**puerco, -a** ['pwer·ko, -a] *m, f* **1.** (*cerdo*) pig; (*macho*) hog; (*hembra*) sow; ~ **espín** porcupine **2.** *inf* (*persona sucia u obscena*) pig **3.** *inf* (*canalla*) swine

**puericultor(a)** [pwe·ri·kul·'tor, -·'to·ra] *m(f)* MED pediatrician

**pueril** [pwe·'ril] *adj* infant

**puerro** ['pwe·rro] *m* leek

**puerta** ['pwer·ta] *f* door; ~ **de la calle** front door; ~ **corredera** sliding door; ~ **de servicio** service door; ~ **giratoria** revolving door; **día de ~s abiertas** open day; **quinta** ~ AUTO rear door; **escuchar detrás de la ~** to eavesdrop; **a la ~ de casa** at the front door; **a ~ cerrada** *t.* JUR in private; **a las ~s de la muerte** at death's door; **estar a las ~s** *fig* to be on the brink; **dar a alguien con la ~ en las narices** to slam the door in sb's face; **de ~s adentro** *fig* in private; **ir de ~ en ~** to go from door to door; **cerrar las ~s a alguien** *fig* to block sb's path; **por la ~ grande** *t. fig* in triumph; **tiene todas las ~s abiertas** *fig* he has a wealth of opportunities; **disparo a ~** DEP shot at goal

**puerto** ['pwer·to] *m* **1.** NÁUT harbor; (*ciudad*) port; ~ **deportivo** marina; ~ **franco** free port; ~ **marítimo** seaport; **tomar** ~ to come into port **2.** (*de montaña*) pass **3.** COMPUT port

**puertorriqueño, -a** [pwer·to·rri·'ke·ɲo, -a] *adj, m, f* Puerto Rican

**pues** [pwes] **I.** *adv* **1.** (*entonces*) then; (*así que*) so; **he vuelto a suspender —** ~ **estudia más** I've failed again — well, you should study more; ~ **entonces, nada** well that's it, then **2.** (*ilativo*) so; ~ **bien** okay; **la consecuencia es, ~,...** so the result is... **3.** (*causal*) **estudio inglés — ¡ah, ~ yo también!** I study English — ah, me too!; **¿quién es? — ~ no sé** who is it? — I don't know **4.** (*expletivo*) well; **¿estuvisteis por fin en**

Toledo? — ~ **no/sí** did you end up going to Toledo? — no, I didn't/yes, I did; **¡~ esto no es nada!** this is nothing compared with what's to come! **5.** (*exclamativo*) **¡~ no faltaría más!** (*naturalmente*) but of course!; (*el colmo*) that's all (etc.) we need! **6.** (*interrogativo*) **¿y ~?** and? **7.** (*atenuación*) well; **¿nos vemos mañana? — ~ no sé todavía** shall we meet tomorrow? — well, I'm not sure yet **8.** (*insistencia*) ~ **así es** well that's how it is; ~ **claro** but of course; **¡~ entonces!** for that very reason! **II.** *conj* **no voy de viaje, ~ no tengo dinero** I'm not going on holiday because I don't have any money

**puesta** ['pwes·ta] *f* putting; (*de aves*) laying; ~ **a cero** resetting; ~ **al día** updating; ~ **en escena** TEAT staging; ~ **en hora** setting (*of time*); ~ **en libertad** release; ~ **en marcha** start button; AUTO starter; ~ **en práctica** putting into effect; ~ **a punto** final check; AUTO service; ~ **de sol** sunset

**puesto** ['pwes·to] *m* **1.** (*lugar*) place; (*posición*) position; ~ **de observación** ASTR observation station; MED observation post **2.** (*empleo*) job; (*cargo, posición*) position **3.** (*tenderete*) stall; (*feria de muestras*) stand; (*chiringuito*) open-air bar; ~ **de periódicos** newspaper stand **4.** MIL post **5.** (*guardia*) post; ~ **de socorro** first-aid station

**puesto, -a** ['pwes·to, -a] **I.** *pp de* **poner** **II.** *adj* **1.** *inf* (*arreglado*) **ir muy bien** ~ to be very smartly dressed; **tenerlos muy bien** ~**s** *vulg* to be a real man **2.** *inf* (*entendido*) **estar ~ en un tema** to be well-informed about a subject; ~ **al día** up to date **III.** *conj* ~ **que** given that

**puja** ['pu·xa] *f* (*en una subasta*) bid

**pujar** [pu·'xar] *vi* (*en una subasta*) to bid

**pulcro, -a** <pulquérrimo> ['pul·kro, -a] *adj* (*aseado*) tidy

**pulga** ['pul·ɣa] *f* flea; COMPUT bug; **tener** ~**s** to be restless; **tener malas** ~**s** *inf* to be bad-tempered; **buscar las** ~**s a alguien** *inf* to tease sb

**pulgada** [pul·'ɣa·da] *f* (*medida*) inch

**pulgar** [pul·'ɣar] *adj, m* thumb

**pulir** [puˈlir] *vt* to polish; (*perfeccionar*) to polish up

**pulla** [ˈpuʝa, -ˈʎa] *f* gibe

**pulmón** [pulˈmon] *m* lung; **gritar a pleno ~** to shout at the top of one's lungs

**pulmonar** [pulmoˈnar] *adj* MED pulmonary

**pulmonía** [pulmoˈnia] *f* MED pneumonia

**pulóver** [puˈloβer] *m* AmL pullover

**pulpa** [ˈpulpa] *f* (*de la fruta*) flesh

**pulpero, -a** [pulˈpero, -a] *m, f* AmL grocer

**púlpito** [ˈpulpito] *m* pulpit

**pulpo** [ˈpulpo] *m* octopus

**pulque** [ˈpulke] *m* Méx CULIN *drink made from fermented agave cactus juice*

**pulsación** [pulsaˈsjon, -ˈθjon] *f* 1. ANAT (*latido*) beat, throbbing 2. (*de una tecla*) striking; (*mecanografía*) keystroke

**pulsar** [pulˈsar] *vt* to press; (*teclado*) to strike; **~ el timbre** to ring the bell

**pulsera** [pulˈsera] *f* bracelet; **reloj de ~** wristwatch

**pulso** [ˈpulso] *m* wrist; *fig* steadiness of hand; **a ~** (*sin apoyarse*) freehand; (*por su propio esfuerzo*) on one's own; **con ~** carefully; **tener buen ~** to have a steady hand; **tomar el ~ a alguien** to take sb's pulse; **echar un ~ a alguien** to arm wrestle sb

**pulverizador** [pulβerisaˈdor, -θaˈdor] *m* sprayer; (*atomizador*) atomizing spray

**pulverizar** <z → c> [pulβeriˈsar, -ˈθar] *vt* 1. (*reducir a polvo*) to pulverize 2. (*atomizar*) to atomize

**puma** [ˈpuma] *m* puma

**puna** [ˈpuna] *f* AmS 1. (*altiplano*) Andean plateau 2. (*malestar*) altitude sickness

**punta** [ˈpunta] *f* 1. (*extremo*) end; (*de lengua, iceberg*) tip; (*de tierra*) headland; **hora(s) ~** rush hour; **de ~ a ~** from end to end; **lo tenía en la ~ de la lengua** it was on the tip of my tongue 2. (*pico*) point; **a ~ de navaja** at knifepoint; **a ~ de pistola** at gunpoint; **acabar en ~** to come to a point; **sacar ~** (*afilar*) to sharpen

**puntada** [punˈtada] *f* (*costura*) stitch;

(*pinchazo*) prick; *fig* hint

**puntapié** [puntaˈpje] *m* kick; **pegar un ~ a alguien** to kick sb

**puntería** [punteˈria] *f* (*destreza*) marksmanship; **tener buena/mala ~** to be a good/bad shot

**puntero, -a** [punˈtero, -a] *adj* leading; **tecnología puntera** cutting-edge technology; **el equipo ~** DEP the top team

**puntiagudo, -a** [puntjaˈɣuðo, -a] *adj* (sharp-)pointed

**puntilla** [punˈtiʝa, -ˈʎa] *f* 1. (*encaje*) lace (edging) 2. (*del pie*) **andar/ponerse de ~s** to walk/stand on tiptoe

**punto** [ˈpunto] *m* 1. (*general*) point; **~ álgido** crucial moment; **~ cardinal** point of the compass; **~ clave** key point; **no hay ~ de comparación** there's no comparison; **~ de destino** destination; **~ de ebullición** boiling point; **~ de encuentro** meeting place; **~ fuerte** strong point; **~ de intersección** intersection; **~ muerto** AUTO neutral; **~ de referencia** reference point; **~ de venta** point of sale; **~ de vista** point of view; **ganar por ~s** to win on points; **hasta tal ~ que...** to such a degree that...; **la una en ~** exactly one o'clock; **hasta cierto ~** up to a point; **¿hasta qué ~?** how far?; **a ~ de** on the point of; **está a ~ de llover** it's about to rain; **¡~ en boca!** *inf* mum's the word!; **¡y ~!** *inf* and that's that!; **en su ~** *fig* just right 2. TIPO full stop; **~ y aparte** full stop, new paragraph; **~ y coma** semicolon; **~ final** full stop (*end of paragraph*); **poner ~ final a algo** *fig* to bring sth to an end; **~ y seguido** full stop (*no new paragraph*); **~s suspensivos** suspension points, dot, dot, dot *inf*; **dos ~s** colon; **poner los ~s sobre las íes** *fig* to dot one's i's and cross one's t's 3. (*calceta, labor*) knitting; **chaqueta de ~** knitted jacket; **hacer ~** to knit 4. (*puntada*) stitch; **~ de sutura** MED stitch 5. CULIN **a/en su ~** done 6. (*preparado*) **a ~** ready; **poner a ~** TÉC to fine-tune; (*ajustar*) to adjust 7. COMPUT dot

**puntocom** [puntoˈkom] *f* COMPUT (**compañía**) [*o* **empresa**] ~ dotcom company

**puntuación** [pun·twa·'sjon, -'θjon] *f* **1.** LING punctuation; **signo de ~** punctuation mark **2.** (*calificación*) mark, grade; DEP score; **sistema de ~** scoring system

**puntual** [pun·tu·'al] *adj* **1.** (*concreto*) specific **2.** (*exacto*) precise **3.** (*sin retraso*) punctual

**puntualidad** [pun·twa·li·'dad] *f* punctuality

**puntualizar** <z → c> [pun·twa·li·'sar, -'θar] *vt* to specify; (*aclarar*) to clarify

**puntuar** <1. pres puntúo> [pun·tu·'ar] *vt* **1.** (*un escrito*) to punctuate **2.** (*conseguir puntos*) to score **3.** (*calificar*) to mark, to grade; DEP to score

**punzada** [pun·'sa·da, -θa·da] *f* (*dolor*) sharp pain; (*en los costados*) stitch

**punzante** [pun·'san·te, -θan·te] *adj* **1.** (*puntiagudo*) sharp **2.** (*mordaz*) scathing

**puñado** [pu·'ɲa·do] *m* handful; **a ~s** (*mucho*) by the handful; **un ~** *inf* (*mucho*) a lot

**puñal** [pu·'ɲal] *m* dagger

**puñalada** [pu·ɲa·'la·da] *f* stab; (*herida*) stab wound; *fig* blow; **coser a ~s** to stab repeatedly; **dar una ~ trapera a alguien** *fig* to stab sb in the back

**puñeta** [pu·'ɲe·ta] *f vulg* **1.** (*molestia*) ¡(**qué**) ~(s)**!** hell!; **hacer la ~ a alguien** to screw things up for sb **2.** (*bobada*) stupid thing; ¿**qué ~s estás diciendo?** what the hell are you on about? **3.** *vulg* (*expresión de enfado*) **mandar a alguien a hacer ~s** to tell sb to go to hell; ¡**vete a hacer ~s!** go to hell!

**puñetazo** [pu·ɲe·'ta·so, -θo] *m* punch

**puñetero, -a** [pu·ɲe·'te·ro, -a] *adj inf* damn(ed); **el muy ~ no me ayudó** the bastard didn't help me

**puño** ['pu·ɲo] *m* **1.** (*mano*) fist; **~ cerrado** clenched fist; **con el ~ en alto** with one's fist raised; **apretar los ~s** *fig* to struggle hard; **como un ~** (*huevo, mentira*) enormous; (*casa, habitación*) tiny; **verdades como ~s** fundamental truths; **de su ~ y letra** in his/her own hand; **meter a alguien en un ~** *fig* to intimidate sb **2.** (*mango*) handle; (*pomo*) hilt **3.** (*de la ropa*) cuff; **~ vuel-**

to turned-up cuff

**pupa** ['pu·pa] *f* **1.** (*ampolla*) blister; (*heridilla*) small wound **2.** *inf* (*dolor*) pain; ¡**~!** ouch! **3.** ZOOL pupa

**pupila** [pu·'pi·la] *f* pupil

**pupilo, -a** [pu·'pi·lo, -a] *m, f* ward

**pupitre** [pu·'pi·tre] *m* (*escritorio*) desk

**purasangre** [pu·ra·'san·gre] *adj, m* thoroughbred

**puré** [pu·'re] *m* purée; **~ de patatas** mashed potatoes; **hacer ~** to purée; *fig* to beat to a pulp; **estar hecho ~** *fig* to be knackered

**pureza** [pu·'re·sa, -θa] *f* purity

**purgante** [pur·'yan·te] *adj, m* purgative

**purgar** <g → gu> [pur·'yar] *vt t. fig* to clean; MED to purge; (*evacuar*) to empty; (*aguas*) to drain

**purgatorio** [pur·ya·'to·rjo] *m* purgatory

**purificador** [pu·ri·fi·ka·'dor] *m* purifier; **~ de humos** smoke filter

**purificar** <c → qu> [pu·ri·fi·'kar] **I.** *vt t. fig* to purify **II.** *vr:* **~se** to be purified; *fig* to purify oneself

**puro, -a** ['pu·ro, -a] *adj* pure; (*auténtico*) authentic; **pura lana** pure wool; **la pura verdad** the honest truth; **pura casualidad** sheer chance; **de ~ miedo** from sheer terror; **se cae de ~ bueno/tonto** he is unbelievably kind/stupid

**púrpura** ['pur·pu·ra] *adj, f* purple

**pus** [pus] *m* MED pus

**puta** ['pu·ta] *f vulg* whore; **casa de ~s** brothel; **ir de ~s** to go whoring; **hijo de ~** son of a bitch

**putada** [pu·'ta·da] *f vulg* ¡**qué ~!** what a bloody nuisance!; **hacer una ~ a alguien** to play a dirty trick on sb

**putear** [pu·te·'ar] *vt vulg* (*fastidiar*) to annoy; **estoy puteado** I'm really pissed off; ¡**te han puteado bien!** they've really messed you about!

**puticlub** [pu·ti·'kluβ] *m inf* singles bar

**puto, -a** ['pu·to] *adj vulg* damned; ¡**de puta madre!** terrific!; ¡**qué puta suerte!** (*mala*) what terrible luck!; (*buena*) what incredible luck!; **el ~ coche no arranca** the damn car won't start; **ni puta idea** not a damn clue; **las estoy pasando putas** I'm having a really shitty time

**puzzle** ['pʊs·le, 'puθ-] *m* jigsaw (puzzle)

**PVP** ['pre·sjo de 'βen·ta al 'pu·βli·ko, 'pre·θjo] *m abr de* **Precio de Venta al Público** RRP

# Q

**Q, q** [ku] *f* Q, q; ~ **de Queso** Q as in Quebec

**qm** [kin·'tal 'me·tri·ko] *abr de* **quintal métrico** 100 kg

**que** [ke] I. *pron rel* 1. (*con antecedente: personas, cosas*) that, which (*often omitted when referring to object);* la **pelota ~ está pinchada** the ball that is punctured; **la pelota ~ compraste** the ball you bought; **la historia de ~ te hablé** the story I told you about; **reacciones a las ~ estamos acostumbrados** reactions which we are accustomed to; **el proyecto en el ~ trabajo** the project that I am working on; **la empresa para la ~ trabajo** the company that I work for 2. (*con antecedente: personas*) that, who (*often omitted when referring to the object);* **la mujer que conocí** the woman that [*o* who] I met 3. (*sin antecedente*) **el/la/lo ~...** the one (that/who/which)...; **los ~ hayan terminado** those who have finished; **el ~ quiera, ~ se marche** whoever wants to, can leave; **es de los ~...** he/she/it is the type that...; **el ~ más y el ~ menos** every single one; **es todo lo ~ sé** that's all I know; **lo ~ haces** what you do; **no sabes lo difícil ~ es** you don't know how difficult it is 4. (*con preposición*) **de lo ~ habláis** what you are talking about II. *conj* 1. (*completivo*) that; **me pidió ~ la ayudara** she asked me to help her 2. (*estilo indirecto*) that; **ha dicho ~...** he/she said that... 3. (*comparativo*) **más alto ~** taller than; **lo mismo ~** the same as 4. (*porque*) because; **lo ayudaré, ~ se lo he prometido** I'll help him, because I promised 5. (*de manera que*) **corre ~ vuela** he/she runs like the wind 6. (*o,*

*ya*) ~ **paguen,** ~ **no paguen, eso ya se verá** we'll see whether they pay or not 7. (*frecuentativo*) **y él dale ~ dale** con **la guitarra** and he kept on playing and playing the guitar 8. (*explicativo*) **hoy no vendré, es ~ estoy cansado** I'm not coming in today because I'm tired; **no es ~ no pueda, es ~ no quiero** it's not that I can't, it's that I don't want to; **¿es ~ no puedes venir?** can't you come then? 9. (*enfático*) **¡~ sí/no!** I said "yes"/"no"!; **sí ~ lo hice** I did do it 10. (*de duda*) **¿~ no está en casa?** are you saying he/she isn't at home? 11. (*exclamativo*) **¡~ me canso!** I'm getting tired!; **¡~ sea yo el que tenga que hacerlo!** I would be the one who has to do it! 12. (*con verbo*) **hay ~ trabajar más** you/we/they have to work harder; **tener ~ hacer algo** to have to do something; **dar ~ hablar** to give people something to talk about ▶ **a la ~ llegue** as soon as he/she arrives; **a menos ~ +***subj* unless; **antes (de) ~ +***subj* before; **con tal (de) ~ +***subj* as long as; **por mucho ~ tú digas...** no matter what you say...; **yo ~ tú...** if I were you...

**qué** [ke] *adj, pron interrog* 1. (*general*) what; (*cuál*) which; (*qué clase de*) what kind of; **¿por ~?** why?; **¿en ~ piensas?** what are you thinking about?; **¿para ~?** what for?; **¿de ~ hablas?** what are you talking about?; **¿a ~ esperas?** what are you waiting for?; **¿~ día llega?** what day is he/she arriving?; **¿~ cerveza tomas?** what kind of beer do you drink?; **¿a ~ vienes?** what are you here for?; **¿~ edad tienes?** how old are you? 2. (*exclamativo*) **¡~ alegría/gracia!** how nice/funny!; **¡~ suerte!** what luck! 3. (*cuán*) **¡~ magnífica vista!** what a magnificent view!; **¡mira ~ contento está!** look how happy he is! 4. (*cuánto*) **¡~ de gente!** what a lot of people! ▶ **¿~ tal?** how are you?, how are things?; **¿~ tal si salimos a cenar?** how about going out to dinner?; **¿y ~?** so what?; **¿y a mí ~?** and what about me?; **~, ¿vienes o no?** well, are you coming, or not?

**quebrada** [ke·'βra·da] *f AmL* stream

**quebradizo, -a** [ke·βra·'di·so, -a; -'di·θo,

-a] *adj* **1.** (*objeto*) brittle **2.** (*persona mayor*) frail **3.** (*voz*) faltering

**quebrado** [ke-'βra·do] *m* MAT fraction

**quebrado, -a** [ke-'βra·do, -a] *adj* **1.** (*empresa*) bankrupt; (*terreno*) rough **2.** (*herniado*) ruptured

**quebrantar** [ke-βran·'tar] *vt* **1.** (*romper*) to break; (*cascar*) to crack; (*machacar*) to crush **2.** (*ley, secreto*) to break; (*obligación*) to violate; (*autoridad*) to breach; (*salud*) to debilitate

**quebrar** <e → ie> [ke·'βrar] **I.** *vt* (*romper*) to break **II.** *vi* **1.** (*con alguien*) to break up **2.** COM to go bankrupt **3.** *Méx* (*darse por vencido*) to give in **III.** *vr:* ~**se** MED to rupture oneself; ~**se de dolor** to double over with pain

**quebrazón** [ke·βra·'son] *m AmL* **1.** (*resultado*) breakage **2.** (*acción*) shattering

**quechua** ['ke·tʃwa] **I.** *adj* Quechua **II.** *mf* Quechuan

**quedada** [ke·'da·da] *f inf* **1.** joke **2.** *Méx pey* old maid

**quedado, -a** [ke·'da·do, -a] *adj Arg, Chile* slow

**quedar** [ke·'dar] **I.** *vi* **1.** (*permanecer*) to remain; **los problemas quedan atrás** the problems are a thing of the past; **¿cuánta gente queda?** how many people are left?; ~ **a deber algo** to owe sth **2.** (*sobrar*) to be left; **no nos queda otro remedio que...** there's nothing left for us to do but...; **no queda ningún ejemplar** there are no copies left **3.** (*resultar*) **todo quedó en una simple discusión** it ended up in a mere argument; ~ **acordado** to be arranged; ~ **cojo** to go lame; ~ **eliminado** to be eliminated; ~ **en ridículo** to make a fool of oneself **4.** (*acordar*) ~ **en algo** to agree to sth; **¿en qué habéis quedado?** what have you decided?; **quedamos a las 10** we agreed to meet at 10; **a ver, ¿en qué quedamos?** make up your mind! **5.** (*estar situado*) to lie; **queda por/hacia el norte** it lies to the north; **quedar lejos de aquí** to be a long way from here **6.** (*faltar*) **quedan aún 100 km para llegar a casa** there are still 100 km left before we get home; **aún**

**queda mucho por hacer** there's still a lot to do; **por mí que no quede** I'll do all that I can **7.** (*terminar*) to end; ~ **bien/mal** to turn out well/badly **8.** (+ *por*) ~ **por cobarde** to come across as a coward; **algo queda por ver** sth remains to be seen **9.** (+ *como*) ~ **como un señor** to behave like a real gentleman; ~ **como un idiota** to look like a fool **II.** *vr:* ~**se 1.** (*permanecer*) to stay; ~**se atrás** to stay behind; ~**se colgado** COMPUT to block; **durante la tormenta nos quedamos a oscuras** during the storm the lights went out; **cuando me lo dijo me quedé mudo** when he told me I was speechless **2.** (*resultar*) ~**se ciego** to go blind; ~**se viuda/viudo** to become a widow/widower; **al freír la carne se ha quedado en nada** when the meat was fried it shrunk to almost nothing **3.** (*conservar, adquirir*) **me quedo con el coche pequeño** I'll take the small car; **quédate con el libro** keep the book; ~**se sin nada** to be left with nothing; **entre el mar y la montaña me quedo con el mar** if I have to choose between the sea and the mountains, I'll take the sea **4.** (*burlarse*) ~**se con alguien** to make fun of sb

**quehacer** [ke·a·'ser, -'θer] *m* chores *pl*; **los ~es de la casa** the housework; **dar ~ a alguien** to assign work to sb

**queja** ['ke·xa] *f* complaint

**quejarse** [ke·'xar·se] *vr* ~ **de algo** to complain about sth; (*gemir*) to moan about sth; **se queja del frío** he complains about the cold

**quejica** [ke·'xi·ka] **I.** *adj* complaining; (*por dolor*) moaning; **¡no seas ~, hombre!** stop whining! **II.** *mf* complainer; (*criticón*) picky

**quejido** [ke·'xi·do] *m* moan; (*constante*) lament; ~ **de dolor** cry of pain; **dar ~s** to groan

**quejoso, -a** [ke·'xo·so, -a] *adj* complaining; **estar ~ de alguien** to be annoyed at sb

**quelite** [ke·'li·te] *m Méx* greens *pl*

**quema** ['ke·ma] *f* burning

**quemada** [ke·'ma·da] *f* **1.** *Arg, Méx* (*ridículo*) embarrassment **2.** *Méx* (*que-*

*madura*) burn

**quemado, -a** [ke·'ma·do] *adj* burnt; *fig* exhausted; **este político está ~** *inf* this politician is finished

**quemadura** [ke·ma·'du·ɾa] *f* burn; **~ de primer grado** first-degree burn

**quemar** [ke·'mar] **I.** *vt* to burn; **cuidado, esta sopa quema** be careful, the soup is boiling hot **II.** *vt* **1.** to burn; (*casa*) to burn down; (*planta*) to scorch; **~ un bosque** to set fire to a forest; **este chili quema la garganta/la lengua** this chili burns my throat/tongue **2.** (*fastidiar*) to mess up **3.** *AmC* (*denunciar*) **~ a alguien** to inform against sb **III.** *vr:* **~se 1.** (*arder*) to burn; **el bosque se quema** the forest is on fire; **me he quemado los cabellos** I've singed my hair **2.** (*herir*) to be hurt **3.** (*comida*) to burn; (*ligeramente*) to singe **4.** (*tener calor*) **me estoy quemando** I'm burning up **5.** (*por una pasión*) **~se de amor** to burn with love **6.** (*acertar*) **¡que te quemas!** you're getting warmer!

**quemarropa** [ke·ma·'rro·pa] **disparar a ~** to shoot at close range; **hacerle preguntas a alguien a ~** to fire questions at sb

**quemazón** [ke·ma·'son, -'θon] *f* **1.** (*quema*) burning **2.** (*calor*) intense heat **3. siento una ~ en el estómago** I have a burning sensation in my stomach

**quemo** ['ke·mo] *m Arg* **¡que ~!** how embarrassing!

**quemón** [ke·'mon] *m Méx* dope smoker

**quena** [ke·na] *f* reed flute used in Andean music

**quepo** ['ke·po] *1. pres de* **caber**

**queque** ['ke·ke] *m Chile, Perú, AmC* cake

**querella** [ke·'re·ʝa, -ʎa] *f* dispute; *JUR* lawsuit; **~ criminal** criminal action; **poner una ~ contra alguien** to sue sb

**querencia** [ke·'ren·sja] *f AmL* (*aprecio*) attachment; (*cariño*) affection; (*afición*) liking; **tomar ~ a algo/alguien** to take a liking to sth/sb

**querendón, -ona** [ke·ren·'don,--'do·na] *adj AmL* loving, affectionate

**querer** [ke·'rer] *irr* **I.** *vt* **1.** (*desear*) to desire; (*más suave*) to want; **como tú quieras** as you like; **has ganado, ¿qué más quieres?** you win, what more do you want?; **hacer algo queriendo/sin ~** to do something on purpose/unintentionally; **quisiera tener 20 años menos** I wish I were 20 years younger; **eso es lo que quería decir** that's what I meant to say; **quiero que sepáis que...** I want you to know that ...; **donde quiera que esté** wherever he/she/it may be; **¡por lo que más quieras, deja ese tema!** for God's sake, change the subject! **2.** (*amar*) to like; (*más fuerte*) to love; **te quiero con locura** I'm madly in love with you **3.** (*pedir; precisar*) to require; **estas plantas quieren mucha agua** these plants need a lot of water ▶ **~ es poder** *prov* where there's a will, there's a way; **como quiera que sea** anyhow **II.** *vimpers* **parece que quiere llover** it looks like rain **III.** *m* love

**querido, -a** [ke·'ri·do, -a] **I.** *adj* dear **II.** *m, f* (*amante*) lover; (*como vocativo*) darling

**queroseno** [ke·ro·'se·no] *m* kerosene

**quesadilla** [ke·sa·'di·ʝa, -ʎa] *f* **1.** (*pastel*) cheesecake; (*pastelillo*) pastry **2.** *AmL* (*tortilla*) quesadilla

**queso** [ke·so] *m* **1.** cheese; **~ de bola** Edam cheese **2.** *inf* (*pie*) foot

**quicio** ['ki·sjo, -θjo] *m* **sacar las cosas de ~** to make a mountain out of a molehill; **sacar a alguien de ~** to drive sb up the wall *sl*

**quico** ['ki·ko] *m* toasted corn snack

**quid** [kid] *m* crux; **el ~ de la cuestión** the crux of the matter; **dar en el ~** to hit the nail on the head

**quiebra** ['kje·βra] *f* COM bankruptcy; **dar en ~** to go bankrupt

**quien** [kjen] *pron rel* **1.** (*con antecedente*) who, that (*often omitted when referring to object*); **el chico de ~ te hablé** the boy I told you about; **las chicas con ~es...** the girls with whom ... **2.** (*sin antecedente*) that; **hay ~ dice que...** some people say that...; **no hay ~ lo aguante** nobody can stand him; **~ opine eso...** whoever thinks so...

**quién** [kjen] *pron interrog* who; **¿~ es?** (*llama*) who is it?; **¿~es son tus pa-**

Q

**dres?** who are your parents?; **¿a ~ has visto?** who did you see?; **¿a ~ se lo has dado?** who did you give it to?; **¿~ eres tú para decirme esto?** who are you to tell me this?; **¿por ~ me tomas?** what do you take me for?; **¡~ tuviera 20 años!** If only I were 20!

**quienquiera** <quienesquiera> [kjen·ˈkje·ra] *pron indef* whoever; **~ que sea que pase** whoever it is, come in

**quieto, -a** [kje·to, -a] *adj* **1.** (*tranquilo*) calm **2.** (*parado*) still; **no puede estar nunca ~** he can never keep still; **quedarse ~** to stand still

**quietud** [kje·ˈtud] *f* **1.** (*inmovilidad*) stillness **2.** (*calma*) calm

**quijada** [ki·ˈxa·da] *f* jaw(bone)

**quilate** [ki·ˈla·te] *m* karat

**quilco** [ˈkil·ko] *m* Chile (large) basket

**quilla** [ˈki·ja, -ˈʎa] *f* keel

**quillango** [ki·ˈjan·go, -ˈʎan·go] *m* CSur fur blanket

**quillay** [ki·ˈjai, -ˈʎai] *m* Arg, Chile BOT soapbark tree

**quilo** [ˈki·lo] *m* **1.** (*peso*) kilo(gram) **2.** *inf* (*dinero*) million

**quilombo** [ki·ˈlom·bo] *m* **1.** Chile (*burdel*) whorehouse **2.** Ven (*choza*) hut **3.** Arg (*lío*) mess

**quiltro** [ˈkil·tro] *m* Chile pey mutt

**quimba** [ˈkim·ba] *f* **1.** AmL (*garbo*) grace **2.** AmL (*sandalia*) sandal **3.** *pl* Col (*conflicto*) difficulties *pl*

**quimbo** [ˈkim·bo] *m* Cuba machete

**química** [ˈki·mi·ka] *f* chemistry

**químico, -a** [ˈki·mi·ko, -a] **I.** *adj* chemical; **productos ~s** chemicals *pl* **II.** *m, f* chemist

**quimioterapia** [ki·mjo·te·ˈra·pja] *f* chemotherapy

**quimono** [ki·ˈmo·no] *m* kimono

**quince** [ˈkin·se, -θe] **I.** *adj inv* fifteen; **dentro de ~ días** in two weeks **II.** *m* fifteen; *v. t.* **ocho**

**quincena** [kin·ˈse·na, kin·ˈθe-] *f* two weeks

**quincenal** [kin·se·ˈnal, kin·θe-] *adj* every two weeks; **revista ~** semimonthly journal

**quingos** [ˈkin·gos] *m inv* AmL zigzag

**quiniela** [ki·ˈnje·la] *f* **1.** (*juego*) sports

pools *pl*; (*boleto*) pools coupon; **jugar a las ~s** to do the pools **2.** CSur lottery

**quinientos, -as** [ki·ˈnjen·tos, -as] *adj* five hundred; *v. t.* **ochocientos**

**quino** [ˈki·no] *m* AmL cinchona tree

**quinqué** [kin·ˈke] *m* oil lamp

**quinqui** [ˈkin·ki] *mf inf* crook

**quinta** [ˈkin·ta] *f* **1.** (*casa*) country house **2.** MIL draft

**quintal** [kin·ˈtal] *m* quintal; **~ métrico** 100 kg

**quinteto** [kin·ˈte·to] *m* quintet

**quinto** [ˈkin·to] *m* draftee

**quinto, -a** [ˈkin·to, -a] *adj, m, f* fifth; *v. t.* **octavo**

**quiosco** [ˈkjos·ko] *m* **1.** (*de jardín*) gazebo **2.** (*de periódicos*) news-stand

**quirófano** [ki·ˈro·fa·no] *m* operating room; **pasar por el ~** to be operated on

**quirquincho** [kir·ˈkin·tʃo] *m* CSur **1.** ZOOL small armadillo **2.** (*guitarra*) charango

**quirúrgico, -a** [ki·ˈrur·xi·ko, -a] *adj* surgical

**quiso** [ˈki·so] *3. pret de* **querer**

**quisque** [ˈkis·ke] *pron indef inf*, **quisqui** [ˈkis·ki] *pron indef inf* **todo ~** anyone and everyone; **se lo dijo a todo ~** he told every Tom, Dick and Harry

**quisquilloso, -a** [kis·ki·ˈjo·so, -a; -ˈʎo·so, -a] *adj* (*susceptible*) touchy; (*meticuloso*) fussy

**quiste** [ˈkis·te] *m* cyst

**quitaesmalte** [ki·ta·es·ˈmal·te] *m* nail varnish remover

**quitagusto** [ki·ta·ˈɣus·to] *m* Ecua, Perú killjoy

**quitamanchas** [ki·ta·ˈman·tʃas] *m inv* stain remover

**quitanieves** [ki·ta·ˈnje·βes] *f inv* snowplow

**quitar** [ki·ˈtar] **I.** *vt* **1.** (*piel, funda, obstáculo*) to remove; (*sombrero, tapa, ropa*) to take off; (*botón*) to pull off **2.** (*mancha*) to get out; (*dolor*) to relieve; (*vida*) to take; (*mesa*) to clear; **una capucha de quita y pon** a detachable hood **3.** (*desposeer*) to take; (*robar*) to steal; **me lo has quitado de la boca** you took the words right out of my mouth; **el café me quita el sueño** coffee keeps me up at night; **ese asunto me quita el sueño**

that matter is keeping me awake at night **4.** (*de plan, horario, texto*) to leave out **5.** (*apartar*) to get out of the way; (*mueble*) to remove; **¡quita!** (*no me molestes*) don't bother me!; (*deja eso*) leave that alone!; (*déjate de tonterías*) stop it **6.** MAT to subtract; **quitando dos** taking away two ▶ **ni ~ ni poner en algo** not to have any say in sth **II.** *vr:* **~se** (*sombrero, gafas, ropa*) to take off; (*barba*) to shave off; **~se la vida** to commit suicide; **~se de la bebida** to give up drinking; **~se de encima algo/a alguien** to get rid of sth/sb; **quítate de mi vista** get out of my sight

**quizá(s)** [ki·'sa(s), -'θa(s)] *adv* perhaps, maybe

# R

**R, r** ['e·rre] *f* R, r; **~ de Ramón** R as in Romeo

**rabadilla** [rra·βa·'di·ja, -ʎa] *f* coccyx

**rabanito** [rra·βa·'ni·to] *m* radish

**rábano** ['rra·βa·no] *m* radish; **~ picante** [*o* blanco] horseradish **2.** *inf* **me importa un ~** I couldn't care less; **¡y un ~!** no way!

**rabí** <rabíes> [rra·'βi] *m* rabbi

**rabia** ['rra·βja] *f* **1.** (*furia*) rage; **¡qué ~!** how infuriating! **2.** (*enfado, manía*) **tener ~ a alguien** (*enfado*) to be furious with sb; (*manía*) not to be able to stand sb; **me da ~ sólo pensarlo** just thinking about it makes me mad; **con ~** angrily

**rabiar** [rra·'βjar] *vi* to be furious; **hacer ~ a alguien** to infuriate sb; **~ de...** to be dying of...; **~ de dolor** to be in great pain ▶ **está que rabia** *inf* it's incredibly hot; **a ~** incredibly

**rabieta** [rra·'βje·ta] *f* tantrum; **coger una ~** to throw a tantrum

**rabimocho, -a** [rra·βi·'mo·tʃo, -a] *adj* *AmL* short

**rabino** [rra·'βi·no] *m* rabbi

**rabioso, -a** [rra·'βjo·so, -a] *adj* **1.** furious; **un tema de rabiosa actualidad** a highly topical issue **2.** *inf* (*picante*) really hot

**rabo** ['rra·βo] *m* **1.** (*cola*) tail; **salir con el ~ entre las piernas** to go away with one's tail between one's legs **2.** (*extremo*) end **3.** (*tallo*) stem **4.** *vulg* (*pene*) cock

**rabona** [rra·'βo·na] *f* *CSur inf* **hacer(se) la ~** to play hook(e)y

**rácano, -a** ['rra·ka·no, -a] *adj inf* (*tacaño*) mean; (*gandul*) lazy

**racha** ['rra·tʃa] *f* (*fase*) series; **tener buena/mala ~** to have a good/bad run; **a** [*o por*] **~s** in fits and starts; **~ de aire** gust of wind

**racial** [rra·'sjal, -'θjal] *adj* racial; **disturbios ~es** race riots

**racimo** [rra·'si·mo, rra·'θi-] *m* bunch

**raciocinio** [rra·sjo·'si·njo, -θjo·'θi·njo] *m* **1.** (*facultad, razón*) reason **2.** (*proceso mental*) reasoning

**ración** [rra·'sjon, -'θjon] *f* portion; (*en casa*) helping; (*en restaurante*) plate; **una ~ de patatas fritas** a side of French fries

**racional** [rra·sjo·'nal, rra·θjo·-] *adj* rational; (*razonable*) reasonable

**racionalización** [rra·sjo·na·li·sa·'sjon, -θjo·na·li·θa·'θjon] *f* rationalization

**racionalizar** <z > c> [rra·sjo·na·li·'sar, -θjo·na·li·'θar] *vt* to rationalize

**racionamiento** [rra·sjo·na·'mjen·to, rra·θjo·-] *m* rationing

**racionar** [rra·sjo·'nar, rra·θjo·-] *vt* **1.** (*repartir*) to ration out **2.** (*limitar*) to ration

**racismo** [rra·'sis·mo, -'θis·mo] *m* racism

**racista** [rra·'sis·ta, -'θis·ta] *adj, mf* racist

**radar** [rra·'dar] *m* radar

**radiación** [rra·dja·'sjon, -'θjon] *f* radiation

**radiactividad** [rra·djak·ti·βi·'dad] *f* radioactivity

**radiactivo, -a** [rra·djak·'ti·βo, -a] *adj* radioactive

**radiador** [rra·dja·'dor] *m* radiator

**radial** [rra·'djal] *adj* **1.** radial **2.** *AmL* radio

**radiante** [rra·'djan·te] *adj* radiant; **~ de alegría/felicidad** radiant with joy/happiness; **estás ~ con ese vestido** you look wonderful in that dress

**radiar** [rra·'djar] **I.** *vi* to radiate **II.** *vt*

**1.** (*irradiar*) to radiate **2.** RADIO to broadcast; **un debate radiado** a radio debate **3.** *AmL* (*eliminar*) to delete

**radical** [rra·di·'kal] **I.** *adj* **1.** *t.* BOT, MAT radical **2.** (*fundamental*) drastic **II.** *m* **1.** LING root **2.** MAT, QUÍM, PSICO radical **III.** *mf* POL radical; **~ de derecha** extreme right-winger

**radicalizar** <z → c> [rra·di·ka·li·'sar, -'θar] **I.** *vt* to radicalize **II.** *vr*: **~se** to become radical

**radicar** <c → qu> [rra·di·'kar] *vi* **~ en algo** (*basarse*) to be based on sth; (*consistir*) to consist of sth; **el problema radica en su comportamiento** the problem lies in his/her behavior

**radicheta** [rra·di·'tʃe·ta] *f* *Arg, Urug* chicory

**radio**¹ ['rra·djo] *f* RADIO, TEL **1.** radio; **~ del coche** car radio; **dirigido por ~** radio-controlled; **retransmitir por ~** to send by radio **2.** (*emisora*) radio station; **~ pirata** pirate radio

**radio**² ['rra·djo] *m* **1.** MAT, ANAT radius; **en un ~ de varios kilómetros** within a radius of several kilometers **2.** (*en la rueda*) spoke **3.** (*ámbito*) range; **~ de acción** operational range; *fig* sphere of influence; **~ de alcance** reach

**radioactivo, -a** [rra·djo·ak·'ti·βo, -a] *adj* radioactive

**radioaficionado, -a** [rra·djo·a·fi·sjo·'na·do, -a; -θjo·'na·do, -a] *m, f* radio ham

**radiocomunicación** [rra·djo·ko·mu·ni·ka·'sjon, -'θjon] *f* radio communication

**radiodespertador** [rra·djo·des·per·ta·'dor] *m* radio alarm (clock)

**radiodifusión** [rra·djo·di·fu·'sjon] *f* broadcasting

**radiodifusora** [rra·djo·di·fu·'so·ra] *f* *AmL* radio transmitter

**radioescucha** [rra·djo·es·'ku·tʃa] *mf* listener

**radiografía** [rra·djo·ɣra·'fi·a] *f* **1.** (*técnica*) radiography **2.** (*placa*) radiograph

**radiografiar** <*1. pres* radiografío> [rra·djo·ɣra·fi·'ar] *vt* to radiograph; MED to X-ray

**radiólogo, -a** [rra·'djo·lo·ɣo, -a] *m, f* MED radiologist

**radiopatrulla** [rra·djo·pa·'tru·ja, -ʎa] *f* patrol car

**radiotaxi** [rra·djo·'tak·si] *m* radio taxi

**radioterapia** [rra·djo·te·'ra·pja] *f* MED radiotherapy

**radioyente** [rra·djo·'jen·te] *mf* listener

**R.A.E.** ['rra·e] *f* *abr de* **Real Academia Española** Spanish Royal Academy

**raer** [rra·'er] *irr vt* (*raspar*) to scrape; (*desgastar*) to wear out

**ráfaga** ['rra·fa·ɣa] *f* **1.** (*de aire*) gust **2.** (*de luz, inspiración*) flash

**ragú** <ragús> [rra·'ɣu] *m* ragout

**raído, -a** [rra·'i·do, -a] *adj* (*deslucido*) spoilt; (*gastado*) worn-out

**raíl** [rra·'il] *m* rail

**raíz** [rra·'is, -'iθ] *f* **1.** ANAT, BOT *t. fig* root; **tener sus raíces en un lugar** *fig* to have one's roots in a place **2.** (*causa*) cause; (*origen*) origin; **a ~ de** because of; **tener su ~ en algo** to be due to sth **3.** MAT, LING root; **~ cuadrada/cúbica** square/cube root ▶ **de ~** completely; **arrancar de ~** to destroy

**raja** ['rra·xa] *f* **1.** (*grieta*) crack; (*hendedura*) split **2.** (*abertura*) opening; (*separación*) gap **3.** *vulg* (*vulva*) pussy

**rajada** [rra·'xa·da] *f* *inf* **1.** *Arg* (*fuga*) flight **2.** *Méx* (*cobardía*) chickening out **3.** *Col* (*examen*) fail

**rajadiablo(s)** [rra·xa·'dja·βlos] *m* (*inv*) *Chile* young rogue

**rajante** [rra·'xan·te] *adj* *Arg* definitive

**rajar** [rra·'xar] **I.** *vi inf* (*charlar*) to chatter; **~ de alguien** to slag sb off **II.** *vt* (*cortar*) to cut; (*abrir*) to cut open; (*hender*) to split; (*partir*) to cut up; (*en rajas*) to slice **III.** *vr*: **~se** **1.** (*abrirse*) to split open; (*agrietarse*) to crack **2.** *inf* (*echarse atrás*) to back out

**rajatabla** [rra·xa·'ta·βla] **a ~** (*estrictamente*) strictly; (*exactamente*) to the letter

**raje** ['rra·xe] *m* *Arg* **1.** *inf* (*huída*) flight; **al ~** in a rush **2.** *inf* (*despido*) sacking; **dar el ~ a alguien** to get rid of sb

**rajo** ['rra·xo] *m* *AmC* (*desgarrón*) tear; (*rotura*) rip

**rajón, -ona** [rra·'xon, -·'xo·na] *adj* **1.** *AmC, Méx* (*fanfarrón*) bragging **2.** *AmC* (*ostentoso*) lavish **3.** *Cuba, Méx* (*cobarde*) chicken *inf* **4.** *Méx* (*poco fiable*) unreliable

**ralea** [rra·'lea] *f pey* sort

**ralentí** [rra·len·'ti] *m* **al ~** AUTO ticking over; CINE in slow motion

**rallador** [rra·ja·'dor, rra·ʎa·] *m* grater

**ralladura** [rra·ja·'du·ra, rra·ʎa·] *f* gratings *pl*; **~ de queso** grated cheese

**rallar** [rra·'jar, -'ʎar] *vt* to shred; (*fino*) to grate

**rally(e)** <rallys> ['rra·li] *m* rally

**ralo, -a** ['rra·lo, -a] *adj* 1. scarce; (*cabello*) thin 2. *CSur* (*insustancial*) flimsy

**rama** ['rra·ma] *f t.* BOT, MAT branch; (*sector*) *t.* ECON sector; **~s secas** brushwood; **por la ~ materna/paterna** on the mother's/father's side ▶ **andarse por las ~s** to beat about the bush; **irse por las ~s** to go off on a tangent

**ramada** [rra·'ma·da] *f Chile* festival stand

**ramaje** [rra·'ma·xe] *m* branches *pl*; (*follaje*) foliage

**rambla** ['rram·bla] *f* boulevard

**ramera** [rra·'me·ra] *f pey* whore

**ramificación** [rra·mi·fi·ka·'sjon, -'θjon] *f* ramification

**ramificarse** [rra·mi·fi·'kar·se] <c → qu> *vr* to branch out

**ramillete** [rra·mi·'je·te, -'ʎe·te] *m* bouquet

**ramo** ['rra·mo] *m* (*de flores*) bunch

**rampa** ['rram·pa] *f* ramp; **en ~** sloping

**rampla** ['rram·pla] *f Chile* hand truck

**rana** ['rra·na] *f* frog ▶ **cuando las ~s críen pelo** when pigs fly

**ranchera** [rran·'tʃe·ra] *f AmL* 1. (*canción*) *typical popular Mexican song* 2. (*furgoneta*) station wagon

**ranchería** [rran·tʃe·'ri·a] *f Col* (*chabolas*) shantytown; (*barraca*) bunkhouse

**ranchero, -a** [rran·'tʃe·ro, -a] *m, f* rancher

**rancho** ['rran·tʃo] *m* (*granja*) ranch

**ranciarse** [rran·'sjar·se, -'θjar·se] *vr* to go rancid

**rancio, -a** ['rran·sjo, -a; -θjo, -a] *adj* rancid; (*anticuado*) old-fashioned

**rancotán** [rran·ko·'tan] *adv AmL* in cash

**rango** ['rran·go] *m* (*categoría, puesto*) rank; (*ordenación*) order; **de primer/segundo ~** first/second-level; **de (alto) ~** high-ranking

**rangoso, -a** [rran·'go·so, -a] *adj AmC* 1. (*generoso*) generous 2. (*ostentoso*) ostentatious

**ranura** [rra·'nu·ra] *f* groove; (*junta*) joint; (*fisura*) slot

**rapacidad** [rra·pa·si·'dad, rra·pa·θi·] *f* rapacity

**rapar** [rra·'par] *vt* to shave; **~se el pelo** (*afeitar*) to shave one's head; (*cortar*) to have one's hair cut very short

**rapaz** [rra·'pas, -'paθ] I. *adj* 1. (*ávido*) greedy 2. (*expoliador*) rapacious II. *f* bird of prey

**rapaz(a)** [rra·'pas, -·'pa·sa; -'pa·θ, -·'pa·θa] *m(f)* kid

**rape** [rra·'pe] *m* 1. ZOOL monkfish 2. **al ~** (*pelo*) closely cropped

**rapear** [rra·pe·'ar] *vi* MÚS to rap

**rapidez** [rra·pi·'des, -'deθ] *f* speed; **~ de reflejos** quick reflexes; **con (gran) ~** (very) quickly

**rápido** ['rra·pi·do] *m* 1. (*tren*) express 2. *pl* (*de un río*) rapids *pl*

**rápido, -a** ['rra·pi·do, -a] *adj* 1. (*veloz*) fast 2. (*breve*) quick

**rapiña** [rra·'pi·ɲa] *f* robbery

**raposo, -a** [rra·'po·so, -a] *m, f* 1. ZOOL fox 2. (*astuto*) sly fox

**raptar** [rrap·'tar] *vt* to kidnap

**rapto** ['rrap·to] *m* kidnapping; **~ de un niño** child abduction

**raptor(a)** [rrap·'tor, -·'to·ra] *m(f)* kidnapper

**raque** ['rra·ke] *adj Ven* scrawny

**raqueta** [rra·'ke·ta] *f* 1. DEP (*pala*) bat 2. (*para nieve*) snowshoe

**raquítico, -a** [rra·'ki·ti·ko, -a] *adj inf* (*enclenque*) sickly; (*débil*) weak

**raramente** [rra·ra·'men·te] *adv* (*casi nunca*) rarely, seldom

**rareza** [rra·'re·sa, -θa] *f* 1. (*cualidad*) rarity 2. (*peculiaridad*) peculiarity

**rarífico, -a** [rra·'ri·fi·ko, -a] *adj Chile* implausible

**raro, -a** ['rra·ro, -a] *adj* 1. (*extraño, inesperado*) strange; **¡qué cosa más rara!** how strange! 2. (*inusual*) unusual; (*poco común*) rare; **no es ~ que... +subj** it's not surprising that...

**ras** [rras] *m* level; **a(l) ~ de** on a level with; **a ~ de agua/tierra** at water/ground level; **volar a ~ de suelo** to hedgehop; **al ~** level

**rasante** [rra·'san·te] *f* slope; **cambio de** ~ brow of a hill

**rasar** [rra·'sar] *vt* to level

**rasca** ['rras·ka] *f* 1. *inf* (*frío*) cold; ¡**vaya** ~ **que hace!** it's freezing! 2. *AmL* (*mona*) drunkenness; **pegarse una** ~ to get plastered

**rascacielos** [rras·ka·'sje·los, -'θje·los] *m inv* skyscraper

**rascar** <c → qu> [rras·'kar] **I.** *vt* to scrape; (*con las uñas*) to scratch **II.** *vr:* ~**se** 1. to scratch 2. *AmS* (*achisparse*) to get tipsy

**rascón, -ona** [rras·'kon, -·'ko·na] *adj Méx* troublemaker

**rascuache** [rras·'kwa·tʃe] *adj Méx inf* 1. (*pobre*) wretched 2. (*de baja calidad*) cheap

**rasgar** <g → gu> [rras·'ɣar] **I.** *vt* to tear; (*en dos*) to tear in two; (*en pedazos*) to tear to pieces; (*cortar*) to cut; **ojos rasgados** almond eyes **II.** *vr:* ~**se** 1. to tear 2. *AmL vulg* (*diñarla*) to kick the bucket

**rasgo** ['rras·ɣo] *m* 1. (*del rostro*) feature; (*del carácter*) trait 2. (*trazo*) stroke; **a grandes** ~**s** in outline

**rasguñar** [rras·ɣu·'ɲar] **I.** *vt* 1. (*arañar*) to scratch; (*herir*) to wound; (*cortar*) to cut 2. ARTE to sketch **II.** *vr:* ~**se** (*arañarse*) to scratch oneself; (*herirse*) to wound oneself; ~**se con algo** to graze oneself against sth

**rasguño** [rras·'ɣu·ɲo] *m* (*arañazo*) scratch; (*rasponazo*) scrape; (*excoriación*) chafing; **sin un** ~ unscathed

**raso** ['rra·so] *m* satin

**raso, -a** ['rra·so, -a] *adj* 1. (*liso*) smooth; (*llano*) flat 2. (*cielo*) clear; **al** ~ in the open air 3. (*al borde*) level; **una cucharada rasa** a level spoonful

**raspa** ['rras·pa] *f* 1. backbone 2. *AmL* prostitute; (*ratero*) pickpocket

**raspada** [rras·'pa·da] *f Méx, PRico* scolding

**raspar** [rras·'par] **I.** *vi* (*ser rasposo*) to be rough; (*en sorteos*) to scratch **II.** *vt* 1. (*rascar*) to scratch 2. *AmL inf* (*mangar*) to swipe 3. *AmS inf* (*abroncar*) to yell at **III.** *vr:* ~**se** to scratch oneself

**raspón** [rras·'pon] *m* 1. (*arañazo*) scratch

2. *Col* (*sombrero*) (large) straw hat

**rasposo, -a** [rras·'po·so, -a] *adj* rough

**rasquetear** [rras·ke·te·'ar] *vt* 1. *AmL* (*almohazar*) to groom 2. *Arg* (*raer*) to scrape 3. *AmS* (*caballo*) to curry

**rasquiña** [rras·'ki·ɲa] *f AmL* itch

**rastras** ['rras·tras] *fpl* **a** ~**s** unwillingly; **llevar a alguien a** ~**s** to drag sb along

**rastrear** [rras·tre·'ar] *vt* 1. (*seguir*) to track 2. (*investigar*) to make inquiries about

**rastrero, -a** [rras·'tre·ro, -a] *adj pey* (*canallesco*) base; (*despreciable*) despicable; (*servil*) cringing

**rastrillo** [rras·'tri·jo, -·ʎo] *m* rake

**rastro** ['rras·tro] *m* 1. (*indicio, pista*) trace; **ni** ~ not a trace; **sin dejar** (**ni**) ~ without trace; **seguir el** ~ **a** [*o de*] **alguien** to follow sb's trail 2. (*mercadillo*) flea market

**rastrojo** [rras·'tro·xo] *m* stubble

**rasurar** [rra·su·'rar] *AmL* **I.** *vt* to shave **II.** *vr:* ~**se** to shave

**rata¹** ['rra·ta] *f* ZOOL rat ► **de biblioteca** bookworm; **más pobre que las** ~**s** as poor as a church mouse; **hacerse la** ~ *AmL* to play truant

**rata²** ['rra·ta] *mf inf* (*rácano*) miser

**ratear** [rra·te·'ar] *vt* 1. *inf* (*mangar*) to nick 2. *inf* (*racanear*) ~ **algo** to be stingy with sth

**ratero, -a** [rra·'te·ro, -a] *m, f* petty thief

**raticida** [rra·ti·'si·da, -'θi·da] *m* rat poison

**ratificación** [rra·ti·fi·ka·'sjon, -'θjon] *f* 1. JUR, POL ratification 2. (*confirmación*) confirmation

**ratificar** <c → qu> [rra·ti·fi·'kar] **I.** *vt* 1. (*confirmar*) to confirm 2. JUR, POL to ratify **II.** *vr:* ~**se** JUR, POL to be ratified

**rato** ['rra·to] *m* while; (*momento*) moment; **a** ~**s de** ~ **en** ~ from time to time; **a cada** ~ all the time; **al** (**poco**) ~ shortly after; **todo el** ~ the whole time; **un buen** ~ for quite a time; **pasar un buen/mal** ~ to have a good/bad time; **hacer pasar un mal** ~ **a alguien** to give sb a rough time; **pasar el** ~ to pass the time ► **aún hay para** ~ there's still plenty left to do; **tener para** ~ to have lots to do

**ratón** [rra·'ton] *m* t. COMPUT mouse; ~ **de campo** field mouse ▶ ~ **de biblioteca** bookworm

**ratonera** [rra·to·'ne·ra] *f* 1. (*trampa*) mousetrap; *fig* trap; **caer en la** ~ to fall into the trap 2. (*agujero*) mousehole

**raudal** [rrau·'dal] *m* torrent; ~ **de palabras** flood of words ▶ **a** ~**es** in floods

**raya** [rra·ja] *f* 1. (*línea*) line; (*guión*) dash; **a** ~**s** (*papel*) lined; (*jersey*) striped; **tres en** ~ (*juego*) tic(k)-tac(k)-toe 2. (*del pelo*) part 3. ZOOL ray 4. (*cocaína*) line ▶ **pasar(se) de la** ~ to go too far

**rayar** [rra·'jar] I. *vi* 1. (*lindar*) ~ **con algo** to border on sth 2. (*asemejarse*) ~ **en algo** to come close to sth 3. (*amanecer*) **al** ~ **el día** at the break of day II. *vt* 1. (*con rayas*) to line 2. (*tachar*) to cross out 3. (*arañar*) to scratch III. *vr*: ~**se** to get scratched

**rayo** [rra·jo] *m* 1. (*de luz*) ray; ~ **de luna** shaft of moonlight 2. (*radiación*) ~**s infrarrojos** infrared rays; ~**s X** X-rays; ~ **láser** laser beam 3. (*relámpago*) (bolt of) lightning; **ha caído un** ~ **en la torre** the tower was hit by lightning

**raza** [rra·sa, ·θa] *f* (*casta*) race; (*estirpe*) strain; **de** ~ (*perro*) pedigree; (*caballo*) thoroughbred

**razón** [rra·'son, ·'θon] I. *f* 1. (*discernimiento*) reason; (*entendimiento*) understanding 2. (*razonamiento*) reasoning; (**no**) **atender a razones** (not) to listen to reason 3. (*motivo*) **la** ~ **por la que...** the reason why...; **sin** ~ without justification; **por razones de seguridad** for security reasons; **por una u otra** ~ for one reason or another; **tener razones para...** to have cause to... 4. (*acierto*) **tener** ~ to be right; **tener mucha** ~ to be absolutely right; **dar la** ~ **a alguien** to agree with sb 5. (*información*) information; (*recado*) message; ~ **aquí** inquire here; **pedir** ~ **de alguien** to ask sb for information 6. MAT ratio; **a** ~ **de 2 pesos el kilo** at 2 pesos per kilo ▶ **entrar en** ~ to come to one's senses; **hacer perder la** ~ **a alguien** to make sb lose control II. *prep* **en** ~ **de** (*en cuanto a*) as far as; (*a causa de*) because of

**razonable** [rra·so·'na·βle, rra·θo·] *adj*

(*sensato*) reasonable; (*justo*) fair; (*adecuado*) sufficient

**razonamiento** [rra·θo·na·'mjen·to, rra·θo·] *m* reasoning; **tus** ~**s no son convincentes** your argument is not convincing

**razonar** [rra·θo·'nar, rra·θo·] I. *vi* to reason; (*reflexionar*) to reflect II. *vt* (*exponer*) to show; (*fundamentar*) to establish

**RDSI** [e·rre·de·se·'i/e·rre·de·e·se·'i] *f abr de* **Red Digital de Servicios Integrados** ISDN

**reabrir** [rre·a·'βrir] *irr como abrir vt* to reopen

**reacción** [rre·ak·'sjon, ·aγ·'θjon] *f* reaction; ~ **en cadena** chain reaction; ~ **excesiva** overreaction

**reaccionar** [rre·ak·sjo·'nar, ·aγ·θjo·'nar] *vi* ~ **a** [*o* **ante**] **algo** to react to sth; (*responder*) to respond to sth

**reaccionario, -a** [rre·ak·sjo·'na·rjo, -a; ·aγ·θjo·'na·rjo, -a] *adj, m, f* reactionary

**reacio, -a** [rre·'a·sjo, -a; ·θjo, -a] *adj* reluctant

**reactivar** [rre·ak·ti·'βar] *vt* to reactivate; ECON to boost

**reactivo** [rre·ak·'ti·βo] *m* reagent

**reactor** [rre·ak·'tor] *m* 1. (*motor*) jet engine; (*avión*) jet 2. FÍS reactor

**readaptación** [rre·a·dap·ta·'sjon, ·'θjon] *f* readjustment

**readaptar** [rre·a·dap·'tar] *vt, vr*: ~**se** to readapt; ~ **a algo** to reintegrate into sth

**readmisión** [rre·ad·mi·'sjon] *f* readmission; (*de despedidos*) re-employment

**readmitir** [rre·ad·mi·'tir] *vt* to readmit; (*despedidos*) to re-employ

**reafirmar** [rre·a·fir·'mar] I. *vt* 1. to make firm; (*piel*) to tone up 2. (*apoyar*) to reaffirm II. *vr*: ~**se** to reaffirm; ~**se en algo** to insist on sth

**reagrupar** [rre·a·γru·'par] *vt, vr*: ~**se** to regroup

**reajustar** [rre·a·xus·'tar] *vt* to readjust

**reajuste** [rre·a·'xus·te] *m* readjustment; TÉC, ECON adjustment; ~ **salarial** wage settlement

**real** [rre·'al] *adj* 1. real; **basado en hechos** ~**es** based on a true story 2. (*del rey*) royal

R

**realce** [rre·'al·se, -θe] *m* relief; (*esplendor*) splendor; **dar ~** to highlight

**realengo, -a** [rrea·'len·go, -a] *adj AmL* (*sin amo*) ownerless; (*vagabundo*) stray

**realeza** [rrea·'le·sa, -θa] *f* (*dignidad*) royalty

**realidad** [rrea·li·'dad] *f* reality; **~ virtual** virtual reality; **ajeno a la ~** far removed from reality; **hacer ~** to make come true; **hacerse ~** to happen; **en ~** in fact

**realismo** [rrea·'lis·mo] *m* realism

**realista** [rrea·'lis·ta] I. *adj* realistic II. *mf* realist

**realizable** [rrea·li·'sa·βle, -'θa·βle] *adj* 1. (*practicable*) practical; (*factible*) feasible 2. ECON saleable; **bienes ~s** saleable goods

**realización** [rrea·li·sa·'sjon, -θa·'θjon] *f* 1. (*ejecución*) execution 2. (*materialización*) realization; *t.* ECON realization; (*cumplimiento*) fulfillment; **~ de un pedido** fulfillment of an order

**realizador(a)** [rrea·li·sa·'dor, -·'do·ra; rrea·li·θa·] *m(f)* producer

**realizar** <z → c> [rrea·li·'sar, -'θar] I. *vt* 1. (*efectuar*) to carry out; (*hacer*) to make 2. (*hacer realidad*) to make real; (*sueños*) to fulfill 3. ECON to realize 4. CINE, TV to produce 5. *AmL* (*notar*) to notice II. *vr:* **~se** 1. (*desarrollarse*) to be carried out 2. (*materializarse*) to happen; (*hacerse realidad*) to come true

**realmente** [rre·al·'men·te] *adv* really; (*de hecho*) in fact

**realquilar** [rre·al·ki·'lar] *vt* to sublet

**realzar** <z → c> [rre·al·'sar, -'θar] *vt* 1. (*labrar*) to emboss 2. (*acentuar*) to bring out 3. (*subrayar*) to highlight

**reamargo, -a** [rre·a·'mar·ɣo, -a] *adj AmL* very bitter

**reamigo, -a** [rre·a·'mi·ɣo, -a] *m, f AmL* very close friend; **son ~s del director** they are very close friends of the director

**reanimación** [rre·a·ni·ma·'sjon, -'θjon] *f* 1. revival 2. MED resuscitation; (*posoperatorio*) reanimation; **unidad de ~** intensive care unit

**reanimar** [rre·a·ni·'mar] I. *vt* to revive; (*animar*) to liven up; MED to resuscitate

II. *vr:* **~se** to regain consciousness; (*animarse*) to liven up

**reanudar** [rre·a·nu·'dar] *vt* to resume

**reaparición** [rre·a·pa·ri·'sjon, -'θjon] *f* reappearance; TEAT, CINE comeback

**reapertura** [rre·a·per·'tu·ra] *f* reopening

**reavivar** [rre·a·βi·'βar] *vt*, *vr:* **~se** to revive

**rebaja** [rre·'βa·xa] *f* (*oferta*) sale; (*descuento*) discount; **~s de verano** summer sales; **estar de ~s** to have a sale on

**rebajar** [rre·βa·'xar] I. *vt* 1. (*abaratar*) to reduce 2. (*humillar*) to put down 3. *t.* FOTO (*mitigar*) to soften; (*debilitar*) to weaken; (*bebidas*) to dilute II. *vr:* **~se** 1. (*humillarse*) to be humiliated 2. (*condescender*) to lower oneself

**rebanada** [rre·βa·'na·da] *f* slice

**rebanar** [rre·βa·'nar] *vt* (*hacer rebanadas*) to slice; (*partir*) to cut up

**rebañar** [rre·βa·'ɲar] *vt* to finish off; **~ el plato** to wipe the plate clean

**rebaño** [rre·'βa·ɲo] *m* herd

**rebasar** [rre·βa·'sar] *vt* to exceed; **~ el límite** to overstep the mark; **esto rebasa los límites de mi paciencia** this is trying my patience

**rebatir** [rre·βa·'tir] *vt* (*discutir*) to contest; (*refutar*) to refute; (*rechazar*) to reject

**rebelarse** [rre·βe·'lar·se] *vr* to rebel; (*oponerse*) to be opposed

**rebelde** [rre·'βel·de] I. *adj* 1. (*indócil*) unruly 2. (*insurrecto*) rebellious II. *mf* rebel

**rebeldía** [rre·βel·'di·a] *f* 1. (*cualidad*) rebelliousness 2. (*oposición*) opposition 3. *t.* MIL (*insubordinación*) insubordination

**rebelión** [rre·βe·'ljon] *f* rebellion

**reblandecer** [rre·βlan·de·'ser, -'θer] *irr como crecer* *vt*, *vr:* **~se** to soften

**rebobinar** [rre·βo·βi·'nar] *vt* to rewind

**rebosar** [rre·βo·'sar] *vi* to overflow; **~ de** to be brimming with; **le rebosa el dinero** he/she is rolling in money; (*lleno*) **a ~** (*de*) full to the brim (with)

**rebotar** [rre·βo·'tar] I. *vi* 1. (*botar*) to bounce; (*bala*) to ricochet 2. (*chocar*) **~ en** [*o* contra] **algo** to bump into sth 3. COMPUT to be returned as undeliverable II. *vt* 1. (*botar*) to bounce 2. *inf* (*enfadar*) to anger **III.** *vr:* **~se** *inf* to get angry

**rebote** [rre·'βo·te] *m* bounce; DEP rebound; **de ~** on the rebound

**rebozar** <z > c> [rre·βo·'sar, -'θar] *vt* to coat with breadcrumbs

**rebumbio** [rre·'βum·bjo] *m* Méx commotion

**rebuscado, -a** [rre·βus·'ka·do, -a] *adj* pedantic; (*palabras*) obscure; (*estilo*) contrived

**rebuscar** <c > qu> [rre·βus·'kar] **I.** *vi* to search thoroughly **II.** *vt* to search for **III.** *vr* **rebuscárselas** CSur to get by

**rebuznar** [rre·βus·'nar, rre·βuθ-] *vi* to bray

**recabar** [rre·ka·'βar] *vt* **1.** (*obtener*) to manage to obtain **2.** (*pedir*) to ask for

**recadero, -a** [rre·ka·'de·ro, -a] *m, f* messenger

**recado** [rre·'ka·do] *m* **1.** (*mensaje*) message; **dar un ~ a alguien** to give a message to sb **2.** (*encargo*) errand; **hacer ~s** to do errands

**recaer** [rre·ka·'er] *irr como* caer *vi* **1.** (*enfermedad*) to relapse **2.** (*delito*) to commit a repeat offense; **~ en el mismo error una y otra vez** to repeat the same mistake again and again

**recaída** [rre·ka·'i·da] *f* relapse

**recalar** [rre·ka·'lar] **I.** *vi* AmL to appear **II.** *vt* to soak **III.** *vr:* **~se** to get soaked

**recalcar** <c > qu> [rre·kal·'kar] *vt* to stress

**recalcitrante** [rre·kal·si·'tran·te, rre·kal·θi-] *adj* recalcitrant

**recalentado** [rre·ka·len·'ta·do] *m* Méx *infl*eftovers *pl*

**recalentar** <e > ie> [rre·ka·len·'tar] **I.** *vt* (*comida*) to reheat; (*aparato*) to overheat **II.** *vr:* **~se** to overheat

**recámara** [rre·'ka·ma·ra] *f* **1.** (*para ropa*) dressing room **2.** (*arma*) chamber

**recamarera** [rre·ka·ma·'re·ra] *f* Méx chambermaid

**recambiar** [rre·kam·bi·'ar] *vt* to substitute

**recambio** [rre·'kam·bjo] *m* spare (part); (*envase*) refill

**recapacitar** [rre·ka·pa·si·'tar, -θi·'tar] **I.** *vt* to consider **II.** *vi* to think things over

**recapitulación** [rre·ka·pi·tu·la·'sjon, -'θjon] *f* summary

**recapitular** [rre·ka·pi·tu·'lar] *vt* to summarize

**recargado, -a** [rre·kar·'γa·do, -a] *adj* overelaborate; (*lenguaje*) overblown

**recargar** <g > gu> [rre·kar·'γar] *vt* **1.** (*pila*) to recharge; (*impuesto*) to increase **2.** (*decorar*) to overdecorate **3.** (*carga*) to overload; **~ de trabajo** to overload with work

**recargo** [rre·'kar·γo] *m* (*tasas*) increase; (*sobreprecio*) surcharge; **llamada sin ~** toll-free call

**recatado, -a** [rre·ka·'ta·do, -a] *adj* **1.** (*modesto*) modest **2.** (*cauto*) cautious

**recato** [rre·'ka·to] *m* (*cautela*) caution; (*pudor*) modesty

**recaudación** [rre·kau·da·'sjon, -'θjon] *f* **1.** collection **2.** (*cantidad*) takings *pl*; (*de impuestos*) receipts *pl*

**recaudar** [rre·kau·'dar] *vt* to collect

**recaudería** [rre·kau·de·'ri·a] *f* Méx grocery store

**recelo** [rre·'se·lo, rre·'θe-] *m* mistrust; **mirar algo con ~** to be suspicious of sth

**receloso, -a** [rre·se·'lo·so, -a; rre·'θe-] *adj* distrustful; **estar ~ de alguien** to be suspicious of sb; **ponerse ~** to become suspicious

**recepción** [rre·sep·'sjon, -θeβ·'θjon] *f* reception

**recepcionista** [rre·sep·sjo·'nis·ta, -θeβ·θjo·'nis·ta] *mf* receptionist

**receptividad** [rre·sep·ti·βi·'dad, rre·θep-] *f* receptiveness

**receptivo, -a** [rre·sep·'ti·βo, -a; rre·θep-] *adj* receptive

**receptor** [rre·sep·'tor, rre·θep-] *m* receiver

**receptor(a)** [rre·sep·'tor, -·'to·ra, rre·θep-] *m(f)* recipient

**recesión** [rre·se·'sjon, rre·θe-] *f* recession

**receso** [rre·'se·so] *m* AmL recess

**receta** [rre·'se·ta, rre·'θe-] *f* recipe; MED prescription; **con ~ médica** on prescription

**recetar** [rre·θe·'tar, rre·θe-] *vt* to prescribe

**recetario** [rre·θe·'ta·rjo, rre·θe-] *m* CULIN

R

cookbook; MED prescription pad

**rechazar** <z → c> [rre·tʃa·ˈsar, -ˈθar] vt to reject; (denegar, no tolerar) to refuse; (ataque) to repel

**rechazo** [rre·ˈtʃa·so, -θo] m rejection; (denegación) refusal

**rechinar** [rre·tʃi·ˈnar] I. vi to squeak; (puerta) to creak II. vt ~ **los dientes** to grind one's teeth

**rechistar** [rre·tʃis·ˈtar] vi to grumble; **sin** ~ without complaining

**rechupete** [rre·tʃu·ˈpe·te] **de** ~ delicious

**recibidor** [rre·si·βi·ˈdor, rre·θi-] m lobby; (en casa) entry (hall)

**recibimiento** [rre·si·βi·ˈmjen·to, rre·θi-] m welcome

**recibir** [rre·si·ˈβir, rre·θi-] I. vt to receive; (personas) to welcome; (aceptar) to accept II. vr ~**se de algo** AmL to graduate as sth; (médico, abogado) to qualify as sth

**recibo** [rre·ˈsi·βo, rre·ˈθi-] m receipt; (de la luz, del agua) bill; ~ **de entrega** delivery note; **acusar** ~ to acknowledge receipt

**reciclaje** [rre·si·ˈkla·xe, rre·θi-] m recycling

**reciclar** [rre·si·ˈklar, rre·θi-] vt to recycle

**recién** [rre·ˈsjen, -ˈθjen] adv 1. recently; ~ **pintado** freshly painted; **los** ~ **casados** the newly weds; **el** ~ **nacido** the newborn baby 2. AmL (en cuanto) as soon as

**reciente** [rre·ˈsjen·te, rre·ˈθjen-] adj recent; (nuevo) new; **un libro de** ~ **publicación** a book which has recently been published

**recientemente** [rre·sjen·te·ˈmen·te, rre·θjen-] adv recently

**recinto** [rre·ˈsin·to, rre·ˈθin-] m enclosure; ~ **universitario** university campus; ~ **ferial** fairgrounds

**recio, -a** [ˈrre·sjo, -a; -θjo, -a] adj (fuerte) strong; (rígido) stiff; **en lo más** ~ **del invierno** in the depths of winter

**recipiente** [rre·si·ˈpjen·te, rre·θi-] m container; (de vidrio, barro) vessel

**reciprocidad** [rre·si·pro·si·ˈdad, rre·θi·pro·θi-] f reciprocity

**recíproco, -a** [rre·ˈsi·pro·ko, -a; rre·ˈθi-] adj reciprocal

**recital** [rre·θi·ˈtal, rre·θi-] m concert

**recitar** [rre·si·ˈtar, rre·θi-] vt to recite

**reclamación** [rre·kla·ma·ˈsjon, -ˈθjon] f complaint; (recurso) protest

**reclamar** [rre·kla·ˈmar] I. vi to protest; ~ **por algo** to complain about sth II. vt (pedir) to claim; (deuda) to demand; ~ **daños** to sue for damages

**reclame** [rre·ˈkla·me] m Arg, Urug ad(vertisement)

**reclamo** [rre·ˈkla·mo] m 1. (grito) decoy call; **acudir al** ~ to answer the call 2. COM ad(vertisement)

**reclinar** [rre·kli·ˈnar] vt, vr: ~**se** to lean; (hacia atrás) to lean back; (apoyar(se)) to rest

**recluir** [rre·klu·ˈir] irr como huir I. vt to imprison II. vr: ~**se** to shut oneself away

**reclusión** [rre·klu·ˈsjon] f imprisonment; (aislamiento) seclusion

**recluso, -a** [rre·ˈklu·so, -a] I. adj imprisoned II. m, f prisoner

**recluta** [rre·ˈklu·ta] mf (voluntario) recruit; (obligado) conscript

**reclutamiento** [rre·klu·ta·ˈmjen·to] m recruiting

**reclutar** [rre·klu·ˈtar] vt to recruit

**recobrar** [rre·ko·ˈβrar] I. vt to recover; ~ **el sentido/las fuerzas** to regain consciousness/one's strength; ~ **las pérdidas** to make good one's losses; ~ **las ganas de vivir** to recover one's enthusiasm for life II. vr: ~**se** to recover

**recodo** [rre·ˈko·do] m bend

**recoger** <g → j> [rre·ko·ˈxer] I. vt 1. (buscar) to collect; **te voy a** ~ **a la estación** I'll meet you at the station 2. (coger) to collect; (guardar) to keep; ~ **del suelo** to pick up from the floor; (cosecha) to gather 3. (juntar) to gather together; (cabello) to gather up 4. (acoger) to take in II. vr: ~**se** (a casa) to go home; (a la cama) to go to bed

**recogida** [rre·ko·ˈxi·da] f collection; ~ **de basuras** garbage collection; ~ **de equipajes** baggage claim

**recogido, -a** [rre·ko·ˈxi·do] adj (lugar) secluded

**recolección** [rre·ko·lek·ˈsjon, -leɣ·ˈθjon] f harvest

**recolectar** [rre·ko·lek·'tar] *vt* to gather; (*cosechar*) to harvest

**recomendable** [rre·ko·men·'da·βle] *adj* recommendable

**recomendación** [rre·ko·men·da·'sjon, -'θjon] *f* recommendation; **por ~ de mi médico** on my doctor's advice

**recomendado, -a** [rre·ko·men·'da·do, -a] *adj* recommended

**recomendar** [e → ie] [rre·ko·men·'dar] *vt* to advise; **nos recomendó no salir de casa** he/she advised us not to leave the house

**recompensa** [rre·kom·'pen·sa] *f* reward

**recompensar** [rre·kom·pen·'sar] *vt* to reward; (*por un daño*) to compensate

**reconciliación** [rre·kon·si·lja·'sjon, -θi·lja·'θjon] *f* reconciliation; **en señal de ~** as a sign of reconciliation

**reconciliar** [rre·kon·si·'ljar, rre·kon·θi·] I. *vt* to reconcile II. *vr:* **~se** to be reconciled

**recóndito, -a** [rre·'kon·di·to, -a] *adj* hidden; **la casa está en lo más ~ del bosque** the house is hidden away in the depths of the forest

**reconfortar** [rre·kon·for·'tar] *vt* to comfort

**reconocer** [rre·ko·no·'ser, -'θer] *irr como crecer* I. *vt* 1. (*identificar*) to recognize; **~ a alguien por algo** to recognize sb by sth 2. (*admitir*) to accept; (*error*) to acknowledge; **~ como hijo** to recognize as one's son 3. (*examinar*) to check; MED to examine II. *vr:* **~se** 1. (*declararse*) to admit; **~se culpable** to admit one's guilt 2. (*identificarse*) to recognize oneself

**reconocimiento** [rre·ko·no·si·'mjen·to, -θi·'mjen·to] *m* 1. POL, JUR, COMPUT recognition 2. (*exploración*) inspection; **~ médico** medical examination; **vuelo de ~** reconnaissance flight 3. (*gratitud*) gratefulness; **en ~ de mi labor** in recognition of my work

**reconquista** [rre·kon·'kis·ta] *f* reconquest

**reconquistar** [rre·kon·kis·'tar] *vt* to reconquer; *fig* to win back

**reconstituir** [rre·kons·ti·tu·'ir/rre·kons·ti·'twir] *irr como huir vt* to re-establish

**reconstituyente** [rre·kons·ti·tu·'jen·te] *m* MED restorative

**reconstrucción** [rre·kons·truk·'sjon, -truɣ·'θjon] *f* rebuilding

**reconstruir** [rre·kons·tru·'ir/rre·kons·'trwir] *irr como huir vt* to reconstruct; (*reedificar*) to rebuild

**recontra** [rre·'kon·tra] *AmL inf* **¡idiota! — ¡que te ~!** idiot! — the same to you!

**recontrabueno, -a** [rre·kon·tra·'βwe·no, -a] *adj AmL inf* really good

**recontracaro, -a** [rre·kon·tra·'ka·ro, -a] *adj AmL inf* really expensive

**Recopa** [rre·'ko·pa] *f* Cup-Winners' Cup

**recopilación** [rre·ko·pi·la·'sjon, -'θjon] *f* compilation

**recopilar** [rre·ko·pi·'lar] *vt* to compile

**récord** <*récords*> ['rre·kord] *m* record

**recordar** [o → ue] [rre·kor·'dar] I. *vi, vt* 1. (*acordarse*) to remember 2. (*traer a la memoria, semejar*) to remind; **recuérdale a mamá que me traiga el libro** remind mom to bring me the book; **este paisaje me recuerda a Cuba** this landscape reminds me of Cuba II. *vi, vr:* **~se** *Arg, Méx* (*despertarse*) to wake up

**recorrer** [rre·ko·'rrer] *vt* to cross; (*viajar por*) to travel around; (*trayecto*) to travel; **recorrimos tres kilómetros a pie** we walked three kilometers

**recortar** [rre·kor·'tar] *vt* 1. (*figuras*) to cut out; (*barba, uñas*) to trim; (*quitar*) to cut off 2. (*disminuir*) to cut (down)

**recorte** [rre·'kor·te] *m* 1. (*periódico*) cutting 2. (*rebajamiento*) cut(back); **~ de personal** downsizing

**recostar** [o → ue] [rre·kos·'tar] *vt, vr:* **~se** to rest; **~(se) contra/en algo** to lean against/on sth

**recova** [rre·'ko·βa] *f* 1. *CSur* (*arcadas*) arcade 2. *And, Urug* (*mercado*) market

**recoveco** [rre·ko·'βe·ko] *m* 1. (*escondrijo*) nook 2. **sin ~s** frankly; **persona con ~** complicated person 3. (*vuelta*) bend

**recreación** [rre·krea·'sjon, -'θjon] *f* reproduction; (*diversión*) recreation

**recrear** [rre·kre·'ar] I. *vt* 1. (*reproducir*) to reproduce 2. (*divertir*) to entertain II. *vr:* **~se** to entertain oneself; **se re-**

R

**crea contemplando cuadros** he/she enjoys looking at pictures

**recreativo, -a** [rre·krea·'ti·βo, -a] *adj* recreational; (**salón de juegos**) ~**s** amusement arcade

**recreo** [rre·'kreo] *m* ENS break

**recriminación** [rre·kri·mi·na·'sjon, -'θjon] *f* reproach

**recriminar** [rre·kri·mi·'nar] *vt* to reproach

**recrudecer** [rre·kru·de·'ser, -'θer] *irr como crecer vi, vr:* ~**se** to worsen; (*conflicto*) to intensify

**recta** ['rek·ta] *f* straight; **entrar en la ~ final** to enter the final straight

**rectamente** [rek·ta·'men·te] *adv* justly

**rectangular** [rek·tan·gu·'lar] *adj* rectangular

**rectángulo** [rek·'tan·gu·lo] *m* rectangle

**rectángulo, -a** [rek·'tan·gu·lo, -a] *adj* rectangular

**rectificación** [rek·ti·fi·ka·'sjon, -'θjon] *f* correction

**rectificar** <c → qu> [rek·ti·fi·'kar] *vt* to correct

**rectilíneo, -a** [rek·ti·'li·neo, -a] *adj* rectilinear; (*persona*) rigid

**rectitud** [rek·ti·'tud] *f* (*honradez*) uprightness

**recto**[1] ['rek·to] *adv* straight; **siga todo ~** go straight ahead

**recto**[2] ['rek·to, -a] *m* rectum

**recto, -a** ['rek·to, -a] *adj* straight; (*persona*) upright; **línea recta** straight line; **ángulo ~** right angle

**rector(a)** [rek·'tor, -·'to·ra] *m(f)* rector; UNIV president

**recuadro** [rre·'kwa·dro] *m* box

**recubrimiento** [rre·ku·βri·'mjen·to] *m* covering

**recubrir** [rre·ku·'βrir] *irr como abrir vt* to cover

**recuento** [rre·'kwen·to] *m* count; **hacer el ~ de votos** to count the votes

**recuerdo** [rre·'kwer·do] *m* 1. (*evocación*) memory; **tener un buen ~ de algo** to have good memories of sth 2. (*de un viaje*) souvenir 3. *pl* (*saludos*) regards *pl;* **dales muchos ~s de mi parte** send them my regards

**recuperación** [rre·ku·pe·ra·'sjon, -'θjon] *f* recovery; ~ **de datos** data retrieval;

~ **de las cotizaciones** share price recovery; ~ **de los precios** rally of prices; **examen de** ~ makeup (exam)

**recuperar** [rre·ku·pe·'rar] **I.** *vt* to recover; (*tiempo*) to make up **II.** *vr:* ~**se** to recover (**de** from)

**recurrir** [rre·ku·'rrir] *vi* 1. ~ **a** (*una persona*) to turn to; (*una institución*) to resort to; ~ **a la justicia** to turn to the law 2. JUR to appeal

**recursivo, -a** [rre·kur·'si·βo, -a] *adj* Col resourceful

**recurso** [rre·'kur·so] *m* 1. JUR appeal 2. (*remedio*) solution; **no me queda otro ~ que...** I have no alternative but...; **como último** ~ as a last resort 3. *pl* (*bienes*) means *pl;* **familias sin ~s** families without means 4. *pl* (*reservas*) resources *pl;* ~**s naturales/minerales** natural/mineral resources

**recusar** [rre·ku·'sar] *vt* to reject; JUR to challenge

**red** [rred] *f* 1. net; **caer en las ~es de alguien** to fall into sb's clutches 2. (*sistema*) network; **la Red** the Net; ~ **comercial/vial** business/road network; **una ~ de carteristas** a gang of pickpockets 3. ELEC power lines *pl;* **avería en la** ~ power failure

**redacción** [rre·dak·'sjon, -daɣ·'θjon] *f* 1. ENS writing; **hacer una ~ sobre el mar** to write a composition on the sea 2. PREN editing

**redactar** [rre·dak·'tar] *vt* to write; (*documento*) to edit; (*testamento*) to draw up

**redactor(a)** [rre·dak·'tor, -·'to·ra] *m(f)* writer; PREN editor

**redada** [rre·'da·da] *f* raid

**rededor** [rre·de·'dor] *m* **al** [*o* **en**] ~ (**de**) around

**redistribución** [rre·dis·tri·βu·'sjon, -'θjon] *f* redistribution

**redoble** [rre·'do·βle] *m* drum roll

**redomón** [rre·do·'mon] *adj AmS* half-trained

**redonda** [rre·'don·da] *f* **en tres kilómetros a la** ~ for three kilometers in all directions

**redondear** [rre·don·de·'ar] *vt* to round off; ~ **por defecto/por exceso** to round up/down

**redondel** [rre·don·'del] *m* circle

**redondela** [rre·don·de·la] *f* **1.** *Arg, Chile* round object **2.** *Chile inf* circle

**redondo, -a** [rre·'don·do] *adj* round; (*redondeado*) rounded ▶ **un negocio ~** a great deal; **caer(se) ~** to fall flat; **negarse en ~** to flatly deny

**reducción** [rre·duk·'sjon, -duɣ·'θjon] *f* **1.** reduction; (*rebaja*) discount; (*de personal*) cut **2.** JUR remission

**reducido, -a** [rre·du·'si·do, -a; -'θi·do, -a] *adj* (*pequeño*) small; (*estrecho*) narrow; **tarifas reducidas** reduced rates

**reducidor(a)** [rre·du·θi·'dor, --'do·ra] *m(f) AmS* fence

**reducir** [rre·du·'sir, -'θir] *irr como* traducir I. *vt* **1.** to reduce; (*personal, gastos*) to cut; (*precios*) to lower; **~/quedar reducido a cenizas/escombros** to reduce/ be reduced to ashes/rubble **2.** (*someter*) to subdue; **la policía redujo al agresor** the police overpowered the assailant **3.** (*resumir*) to summarize; (*acortar*) to abbreviate II. *vi* AUTO to downshift III. *vr:* **~se** to come down

**redundancia** [rre·dun·'dan·sja, -θja] *f* redundancy

**redundante** [rre·dun·'dan·te] *adj* redundant

**reeditar** [rre·di·'tar/rre·e·di·'tar] *vt* to re-publish; (*imprimir*) to reprint

**reelección** [rre·lek·'sjon/rre·e·lek·'sjon, -ley·'θjon] *f* re-election

**reelegir** [rre·le·'xir/rre·e·le·'xir] *irr como* elegir *vt* to re-elect

**reembolsar** [rrem·bol·'sar/rre·em·bol·'sar] *vt* to reimburse

**reembolso** [rrem·'bol·so/rre·em·'bol·so] *m* repayment; **enviar algo contra ~** to send sth cash on delivery

**reemplazante** [rrem·pla·'san·te; rre·em-] *mf Méx* replacement

**reemplazar** <z → c> [rrem·pla·'sar/rre·em·pla·'sar, -'θar] *vt* to replace; (*representar*) to substitute

**reemplazo** [rrem·'pla·so/rre·em·'pla·so, -θo] *m* replacement; DEP substitution

**reencontrar** <o → ue> [rre·en·kon·'trar, rre·en-] I. *vt* to find again II. *vr:* **~se** to meet again

**reencuentro** [rren·'kwen·tro/rre·en-'kwen·tro] *m* reunion

**reenviar** <*1. pres* reenvío> [rrem·bi·'ar/rre·em·bi·'ar] *vt* to forward; (*devolver*) to return

**reestructurar** [rres·truk·tu·'rar/rre·es·truk·tu·'rar] *vt* to restructure

**refacción** [rre·fak·'sjon] *f* **1.** *AmL* refurbishment **2.** *Méx* spare (part)

**refaccionar** [rre·fak·sjo·'nar] *vt AmL* to refurbish

**refectorio** [rre·fek·'to·rjo] *m* refectory

**referencia** [rre·fe·'ren·sja, -θja] *f* **1.** reference; **punto de ~** point of reference; **con ~ a** with reference to; **hacer ~ a algo** to refer to sth **2.** *pl* (*informes*) report

**referéndum** <referéndums> [rre·fe·'ren·dun] *m* referendum

**referente** [rre·fe·'ren·te] *adj* regarding; **(en lo) ~ a su queja** with regard to your complaint

**referí** [rre·fe·'ri] *m AmL* referee

**referir** [rre·fe·'rir] *irr como* sentir I. *vt* **1.** (*relatar*) to recount **2.** (*remitir*) to refer II. *vr:* **~se** to refer; **en [o por] lo que se refiere a...** with regard to...

**refinado, -a** [rre·fi·'na·do] *adj* refined

**refinar** [rre·fi·'nar] I. *vt* to refine II. *vr:* **~se** to become refined

**refinería** [rre·fi·ne·'ri·a] *f* refinery

**reflector** [rre·flek·'tor] *m* spotlight

**reflector(a)** [rre·flek·'tor, --'to·ra] *adj* reflective

**reflejar** [rre·fle·'xar] I. *vi, vt* to reflect; **tus palabras reflejan miedo** your words show fear II. *vr:* **~se** to be reflected

**reflejo** [rre·'fle·xo] *m* reflection; MED, PSICO reflex

**reflejo, -a** [rre·'fle·xo, -a] *adj* reflective; **movimiento ~** reflex

**reflexión** [rre·flek·'sjon,] *f* reflection; **sin ~** without thinking

**reflexionar** [rre·flek·sjo·'nar] *vi, vt* to reflect; **reflexiona bien antes de dar ese paso** think carefully before doing that

**reflexivo, -a** [rre·flek·'si·βo, -a] *adj* thoughtful; LING reflexive

**reflujo** [rre·'flu·xo] *m* ebb; MED reflux

**reforma** [rre·'for·ma] *f* **1.** reform; **~ educativa/monetaria** educational/ monetary reform **2.** ARQUIT rebuilding;

R

(*renovación*) renovation; **hacer una ~ en el cuarto de baño** to have one's bathroom refurbished

**reformar** [rre·for·'mar] **I.** *vt* **1.** to reform; **~ su conducta** to change one's ways **2.** ARQUIT to rebuild; (*renovar*) to renovate **II.** *vr:* **~se** to mend one's ways

**reformatorio** [rre·for·ma·'to·rjo] *m* reformatory; **~ para delincuentes juveniles** reform school (for juvenile delinquents)

**reformista** [rre·for·'mis·ta] *adj, mf* reformist

**reforzar** [rre·for·'sar, -'θar] *irr como* forzar **I.** *vt* to reinforce **II.** *vr:* **~se** to be reinforced

**refractar** [rre·frak·'tar] *vt* to refract

**refrán** [rre·'fran] *m* proverb

**refregar** [rre·fre·'ɣar] *irr como* fregar **I.** *vt* **1.** (*frotar*) to rub; (*con cepillo/estropajo*) to scrub **2.** *inf* (*reprochar*) **~ algo a alguien (por las narices)** to rub sb's nose in sth **II.** *vr:* **~se** to rub; **~se los ojos** to rub one's eyes

**refrescante** [rre·fres·'kan·te] *adj* refreshing

**refrescar** [rre·fres·'kar] **I.** *vt* to refresh; **~ la memoria** to refresh one's memory; (*cosas olvidadas*) to brush up; **el baño me ha refrescado** the bath has revived me **II.** *vi* to refresh; (*aire, viento*) to cool down **III.** *vr:* **~se** to cool down; (*tomar el fresco*) to get some fresh air **IV.** *vimpers* **por la tarde refresca** in the evening it gets cooler

**refresco** [rre·'fres·ko] *m* soft drink

**refriega** [rre·'frje·ɣa] *f inf* scuffle

**refrigeración** [rre·fri·xe·ra·'sjon, -'θjon] *f* refrigeration; **~ por aire/agua** air/water-cooling

**refrigerador** [rre·fri·xe·ra·'dor] *m* refrigerator; (*cámara*) cool room; AUTO cooling system

**refrigerador(a)** [rre·fri·xe·ra·'dor, -'do·ra] *adj* **aparato ~** refrigerator; (*para habitaciones*) air-cooling unit

**refrigerar** [rre·fri·xe·'rar] **I.** *vt* to refrigerate; (*habitación*) to air-condition **II.** *vr:* **~se** to cool down

**refrigerio** [rre·fri·'xe·rjo] *m* snack

**refuerzo** [rre·'fwer·so, -θo] *m* **1.** (*viga*) strengthening; (*parche*) patch **2.** (*ayu-*

*da*) support **3.** *pl* MIL reinforcements *pl*

**refugiado, -a** [rre·fu·'xja·do, -a] *m, f* refugee

**refugiarse** [rre·fu·'xjar·se] *vr* to take refuge; **~ de algo** to flee from sth

**refugio** [rre·'fu·xjo] *m* refuge; *t.* MIL shelter; **~** (*montañero*) mountain shelter; **~ nuclear** [*o atómico*] fallout shelter

**refundirse** [rre·fun·'dir·se] *vr* **1.** (*reunirse*) to be joined **2.** *AmC* (*perderse*) to be lost

**refunfuñar** [rre·fun·fu·'ɲar] *vi* to grumble

**refutación** [rre·fu·ta·'sjon, -'θjon] *f* refutation

**refutar** [rre·fu·'tar] *vt* to refute

**regadera** [rre·ɣa·'de·ra] *f* **1.** watering can **2.** *AmC, Col, Méx, Ven* shower

**regaderazo** [rre·ɣa·de·'ra·so] *m Méx* shower

**regadío** [rre·ɣa·'di·o, -a] *m* irrigation; **estos campos son de ~** these fields are irrigated

**regalado, -a** [rre·ɣa·'la·do, -a] *adj* **1.** (*cómodo*) easy; **llevar una vida regalada** to lead a life of luxury **2.** (*barato*) very cheap; **vender algo a precio ~** to sell sth for a knock-down price

**regalar** [rre·ɣa·'lar] *vt* to give

**regaliz** [rre·ɣa·'lis, -'liθ] *m* licorice

**regalo** [rre·'ɣa·lo] *m* **1.** present, gift **2.** (*gusto*) pleasure; **un ~ para la vista** a sight for sore eyes

**regañadientes** [rre·ɣa·ɲa·'djen·tes] **a ~** reluctantly, grudgingly

**regañar** [rre·ɣa·'ɲar] *vt* to scold

**regañina** [rre·ɣa·'ɲi·na] *f* reprimand; **echar una ~ a alguien** to tell sb off; **tener una ~ por algo** to quarrel about sth

**regar** [rre·'ɣar] *irr como* fregar *vt* to water; (*las calles*) to hose down; AGR to irrigate

**regata** [rre·'ɣa·ta] *f* regatta

**regatear** [rre·ɣa·te·'ar] **I.** *vi* **1.** (*mercadear*) to haggle **2.** DEP to dribble **II.** *vt* to haggle over

**regateo** [rre·ɣa·'teo] *m* haggling, dribbling

**regazo** [rre·'ɣa·so, -θo] *m* lap

**regencia** [rre·'xen·sja, -θja] *f* management; POL regency

**regeneración** [rre·xe·ne·ra·'sjon, -'θjon] f regeneration

**regenerar** [rre·xe·ne·'rar] **I.** vt to regenerate; (a alguien) to reform **II.** vr: ~**se** to regenerate; (cabello) to grow back

**regentar** [rre·xen·'tar] vt to manage; POL to govern

**regente** [rre·'xen·te] mf director; (negocio) manager; POL regent

**régimen** ['rre·xi·men] m <regímenes> **1.** (sistema) system; (reglamentos) regulations pl; POL government; ~ **penitenciario** prison system; ~ **abierto** open regime **2.** diet; **a** ~ on a diet

**regimiento** [rre·xi·'mjen·to] m regiment

**región** [rre·'xjon] f region; (espacio) area; ~ **abdominal** abdominal region

**regional** [rre·xjo·'nal] adj regional

**regir** [rre·'xir] irr como elegir **I.** vt **1.** (gobernar) to govern; (dirigir) to direct; (guiar) to lead **2.** LING to take **II.** vr: ~**se** to be guided

**registrador(a)** [rre·xis·tra·'dor, -·'do·ra] adj registering; **caja** ~**a** cash register

**registrar** [rre·xis·'trar] **I.** vt **1.** (examinar) to search **2.** (inscribir; grabar) to record; (empresa, patente) to register **II.** vr: ~**se 1.** (inscribirse) to register **2.** (observarse) to be reported

**registro** [rre·'xis·tro] m **1.** (inspección) search **2.** (medición) measurement **3.** (inscripción, grabación) recording; (inclusión) inclusion; (empresa, patente) registration **4.** (protocolo) record; ~ **de entrada/de salida** note of arrival/departure **5.** (libro) register; ~ **electoral/de la propiedad** electoral/land register **6.** (oficina, archivo) registry; ~ **civil** registry office

**regla** ['rre·γla] f **1.** (instrumento) ruler **2.** (norma) rule; **por** ~ **general** as a general rule; ~ **de tres** rule of three **3.** (periodo) period; **está con la** ~ she has her period ▸ **la excepción confirma la** ~ the exception confirms the rule; **estar/poner en** ~ to be/to put in order

**reglamentación** [rre·γla·men·ta·'sjon, -'θjon] f **1.** (acción) regulation **2.** (reglas) rules pl

**reglamentar** [rre·γla·men·'tar] vt to regulate

**reglamento** [rre·γla·'men·to] m rules pl; (de una organización) regulations pl; ~ **de tráfico** traffic regulations

**regocijo** [rre·γo·'si·xo, -'θi·xo] m delight; (júbilo) rejoicing

**regodeón, -ona** [rre·γo·de·'on] adj Chile, Col inf fussy

**regresar** [rre·γre·'sar] **I.** vi to return, to go back **II.** vt Méx to give back **III.** vr: ~**se** AmL to return

**regresión** [rre·γre·'sjon] f regression

**regresivo, -a** [rre·γre·'si·βo, -a] adj regressive

**regreso** [rre·'γre·so] m return; (**viaje de**) ~ return journey; **estar de** ~ to have returned

**reguero** [rre·'γe·ro] m trail; **expandirse como un** ~ de **pólvora** to spread like wildfire

**regulación** [rre·γu·la·'sjon, -'θjon] f **1.** (reglamentación) regulation; ~ **administrativa** administrative regulations **2.** (organización, ajuste) t. TÉC adjustment

**regulador** [rre·γu·la·'dor] m regulator; (mecanismo) control knob

**regular** [rre·γu·'lar] **I.** vt **1.** (organizar, ajustar) t. TÉC to adjust **2.** (reglamentar) to regulate **II.** adj **1.** regular; **verbos** ~**es** regular verbs **2.** (mediano) average; (mediocre) mediocre; **de tamaño** ~ normal size **III.** adv so-so

**regularidad** [rre·γu·la·ri·'dad] f compliance; **con** ~ regularly; (mediocridad) mediocrity

**regularizar** <z → c> [rre·γu·la·ri·'sar, -'θar] **I.** vt (poner en orden) to regularize; (normalizar) to standardize **II.** vr: ~**se** (regularse) to be regulated; (normalizarse) to become standardized

**regularmente** [rre·γu·lar·'men·te] adv (normalmente) usually

**rehabilitación** [rre·a·βi·li·ta·'sjon, -'θjon] f rehabilitation; (edificio) refurbishment

**rehabilitar** [rre·a·βi·li·'tar] **I.** vt **1.** t. JUR, MED to rehabilitate **2.** (una cosa) to repair; (edificio) to refurbish **II.** vr: ~**se** to be rehabilitated

**rehacer** [rre·a·'ser, -'θer] irr como hacer **I.** vt to redo; (reconstruir) to rebuild;

(*edificio*) to refurbish; (*reparar*) to repair; ~ **su vida con alguien** to rebuild one's life with sb II. *vr* ~**se de una desgracia** to recover from a misfortune

**rehecho, -a** [rre·'e·tʃo, -a] I. *pp de* **rehacer** II. *adj* thickset

**rehén** [rre·'en] *m* hostage

**rehogar** <g → gu> [rre·o·'ɣar] *vt* to sauté

**rehuir** [rre·u·'ir] *irr como* **huir** *vt* to avoid; (*obligación*) to shirk; (*rechazar*) to reject

**rehusar** [rre·u·'sar] *vt* to refuse; (*invitación*) to decline; **¡rehusado!** rejected!

**reimpresión** [rre·im·pre·'sjon] *f* reprint

**reimprimir** [rre·im·pri·'mir] *irr como* **imprimir** *vt* to reprint

**reina** ['rrei·na] *f* queen

**reinado** [rrei·'na·do] *m* reign

**reinar** [rrei·'nar] *vi* to reign; (*ambiente*) *t.* METEO to prevail

**reincidencia** [rre·in·si·'den·sja, -θi·'den·θja] *f* relapse; JUR repeat offense

**reincidente** [rre·in·si·'den·te, rre·in·θi-] I. *adj* repeat II. *mf* repeat offender

**reincidir** [rre·in·si·'dir, rre·in·θi-] *vi* ~ **en algo** to relapse into sth; ~ **en un delito** to repeat an offence

**reincorporar** [rre·in·kor·po·'rar] I. *vt* ~ **a algo** to reincorporate into sth; ~ **a alguien a un puesto** to restore a position II. *vr*: ~**se** to return; (*a una organización*) to rejoin

**reino** ['rrei·no] *m* realm; POL kingdom; **Reino Unido** United Kingdom

**reintegrar** [rre·in·te·'ɣrar] I. *vt* 1. (*reincorporar*) to reintegrate; (*en un cargo*) to reinstate 2. (*devolver*) to return; (*dinero*) to repay; (*desembolsos*) to reimburse II. *vr*: ~**se** to return; (*a una organización*) to rejoin

**reintegro** [rre·in·'te·ɣro] *m* 1. (*reintegración*) reintegration; (*en un cargo*) reinstatement 2. **me tocó un** ~ I won back my stake 3. (*pago*) reimbursement; (*de la cuenta*) withdrawal; (*devolución*) repayment

**reír** [rre·'ir] *irr* I. *vi* to laugh; **echarse a** ~ to burst out laughing; **no me hagas** ~ *fig* don't make me laugh ▶ **el que ríe último ríe mejor** he who laughs last laughs longest [o best] II. *vr* ~**se de**

**algo** to laugh at sth; ~**se a carcajadas** to laugh loudly III. *vt* to laugh at

**reiteradamente** [rrei·te·ra·da·'men·te] *adv* repeatedly

**reiterar** [rrei·te·'rar] I. *vt* to repeat; **reiteró su intención de ayudarme** he/she repeated his/her intention of helping me II. *vr*: ~**se** to repeat; **se reiteró en su decisión de dejar de fumar** he/she reaffirmed his/her decision to stop smoking

**reivindicación** [rrei·βin·di·ka·'sjon, -'θjon] *f* claim (**de** to)

**reivindicar** <c → qu> [rrei·βin·di·'kar] *vt* to claim; (*exigir*) to demand

**reja** ['rre·xa] *f* grill; **entre** ~s *inf* behind bars

**rejego** [rre·'xe·ɣo] *adj AmC, Méx* 1. (*indomable*) wild; (*alzado*) untamed 2. (*intratable*) unmanageable; (*enojadizo*) cranky

**rejilla** [rre·'xi·ja, -ʎa] *f* grating; (*parrilla*) grill

**rejo** [rre·xo] *m AmL* whip

**rejuvenecer** [rre·xu·βe·ne·'ser, -'θer] *irr como* **crecer** I. *vt* to rejuvenate; **este peinado te rejuvenece** this haircut makes you look much younger II. *vr*: ~**se** to be rejuvenated

**relación** [rre·la·'sjon, -'θjon] *f* relationship; **con** ~ **a su petición** with regard to your/his/her request; ~ **calidad-precio** value for money; (**no**) **guardar** ~ **con** to bear (no) relation to; **relaciones públicas** public relations; **mantienen relaciones** they are going out with each other; **mantener relaciones sexuales con alguien** to have a sexual relationship with sb

**relacionar** [rre·la·sjo·'nar, rre·la·θjo-] I. *vt* to relate II. *vr*: ~**se** 1. (*estar relacionado*) to be related 2. (*iniciar relaciones*) to strike up a relationship; (*mantener relaciones*) to mix; ~**se mucho** (*amigos*) to have lots of friends; (*influyentes*) to have lots of contacts

**relajación** [rre·la·xa·'sjon, -'θjon] *f* 1. relaxation 2. (*malas costumbres*) slackness

**relajadura** [rre·la·xa·'du·ra] *f Méx* rupture

**relajar** [rre·la·'xar] I. *vt* to relax; (*suavizar*) to ease II. *vr:* ~**se** to relax; (*suavizarse*) to ease

**relamer** [rre·la·'mer] I. *vt* to lick II. *vr:* ~**se** to lick one's lips; (*animal*) to lick its chops

**relámpago** [rre·'lam·pa·ɣo] *m* flash of lightning

**relance** [rre·'lan·se] *m* 1. *Chile* flirtatious compliment 2. *Col* de ~ in cash

**relatar** [rre·la·'tar] *vt* to report; (*historia*) to tell

**relatividad** [rre·la·ti·βi·'ðað] *f* relativity

**relativo** [rre·la·'ti·βo] *m* relative pronoun; **oración de** ~ relative clause

**relativo, -a** [rre·la·'ti·βo, -a] *adj* relative; **ser** ~ **a algo** to be relative to sth; **un artículo** ~ **a...** an article about...; **pronombre** ~ relative pronoun

**relato** [rre·'la·to] *m* report; LIT story; ~ **corto** short story

**relegar** <g → gu> [rre·le·'ɣar] *vt* ~ **algo a un plano secundario** to push sth into the background

**relevancia** [rre·le·'βan·sja, -θja] *f* relevance

**relevante** [rre·le·'βan·te] *adj* important; (*sobresaliente*) outstanding

**relevar** [rre·le·'βar] I. *vt* 1. (*liberar*) to exempt 2. (*destituir*) to remove; ~ **a alguien de un cargo** to relieve sb of his/her post 3. (*reemplazar*) to place; MIL to relieve; DEP to substitute II. *vr:* ~**se** to take turns

**relevo** [rre·'le·βo] *m* 1. change; **tomar el** ~ **de alguien** to take over from sb 2. (*pl*) DEP relay; **carrera de** ~**s** relay race

**relicario** [rre·li·'ka·rjo] *m AmL* locket

**relieve** [rre·'lje·βe] *m* relief ▶ **poner de** ~ to emphasize

**religión** [rre·li·'xjon] *f* religion

**religioso, -a** [rre·li·'xjo·so, -a] I. *adj* religious II. *m, f* monk(nun) *m(f)*

**reliquia** [rre·'li·kja] *f* relic; (*antigüedad*) collector's item; **una** ~ **de familia** a family heirloom

**rellano** [rre·'ja·no, -'ʎa·no] *m* landing

**rellena** [rre·'je·na, -'ʎe·na] *f Col, Méx* blood sausage

**rellenar** [rre·je·'nar, rre·ʎe-] *vt* 1. ~ **de** [o con] **algo** to fill with sth; CULIN to stuff with sth 2. (*por completo*) to fill up 3. (*completar*) to fill out

**relleno** [rre·'je·no, rre·'ʎe-] *m* filling; CULIN stuffing

**relleno, -a** [rre·'je·no, -a; rre·'ʎe-] *adj* 1. full; CULIN stuffed 2. *inf* chubby

**reloj** [rre·'lox] *m* clock; (*de pulsera*) watch; ~ **despertador** alarm clock; **contra** ~ against the clock

**relojear** [rre·lo·xe·'ar] *vt Arg* 1. (*cronometrar*) to time 2. *inf* (*controlar, espiar*) to keep tabs on; ~ **a alguien de arriba abajo** to look sb up and down

**relojería** [rre·lo·xe·'ri·a] *f* clockmaker's; (*de pulsera*) watchmaker's

**reluciente** [rre·lu·'sjen·te, -'θjen·te] *adj* shining; ~ **de limpio** shiny clean

**relucir** [rre·lu·'sir, -'θir] *irr como* lucir *vi* to shine; (*sobresalir*) to stand out ▶ **sacar algo a** ~ to bring sth up; **salir a** ~ to come up

**relumbrar** [rre·lum·'brar] *vi* to shine; (*sobresalir*) to stand out

**remachado, -a** [rre·ma·'tʃa·ðo] *adj Col* quiet

**remachar** [rre·ma·'tʃar] I. *vt* 1. (*golpear*) to hammer 2. (*sujetar*) to rivet II. *vr:* ~**se** *Col* to remain silent

**remangar** <g → gu> [rre·man·'ɡar] I. *vt* to roll up II. *vr:* ~**se** *t. fig* to roll up one's sleeves

**remanso** [rre·'man·so] *m* (*represa*) pool; (*agua muerta*) stagnant water

**remar** [rre·'mar] *vi* to row

**rematar** [rre·ma·'tar] I. *vt* to finish off; (*terminar de hacer*) to put the finishing touches to; DEP to shoot II. *vi* to end; DEP to shoot

**remate** [rre·'ma·te] *m* 1. conclusion; (*de un producto*) finishing touch 2. DEP shot ▶ **estar** loco **de** ~ to be as mad as a hatter; **para** ~ to top it all off; **por** ~ nothing

**remecer** [rre·me·'ser] *irr como* crecer *vt, vr:* ~**se** *AmL* to shake

**remediar** [rre·me·'djar] *vt* 1. (*evitar*) to prevent; **no puedo** ~**lo** I can't help it 2. (*acabar con*) to finish off; (*reparar*) to repair; (*compensar*) to make up for 3. (*corregir*) to correct

**remedio** [rre·'me·djo] *m* t. MED remedy; (*solución*) solution; **no tener ~** to be a hopeless case; **la crisis no tiene ~** there is no solution to the crisis; **no tenemos** [*o* **no hay**] **más ~ que...** there is no choice but to...; **sin ~** (*inútil*) hopeless; (*sin falta*) inevitable ▶ **es peor el ~ que la enfermedad** *prov* the remedy is worse than the disease; **¿qué ~?** what choice is there?

**rememorar** [rre·me·mo·'rar] *vt* to remember

**remendar** <e → ie> [rre·men·'dar] *vt* to mend; (*con parches*) to patch; (*zurcir*) to darn

**remera** [rre·'me·ra] *f Arg* T-shirt

**remesa** [rre·'me·sa] *f* consignment; FIN remittance

**remezón** [rre·me·'son] *m AmL* shake

**remilgos** [rre·'mil·yos] *mpl* **sin ~** without making a fuss; **hacer ~** to make a fuss

**remite** [rre·'mi·te] *m* sender's name and address

**remitente** [rre·mi·'ten·te] *mf* sender

**remitir** [rre·mi·'tir] **I.** *vt* **1.** (*enviar*) to send; FIN to remit **2.** (*referirse*) to refer **3.** (*de una obligación*) to forgive **4.** (*aplazar*) to postpone **II.** *vi* (*calmarse*) to let up **III.** *vr:* **~se** to refer

**remo** ['rre·mo] *m* oar; (*sin soporte*) paddle; DEP rowing

**remodelación** [rre·mo·de·la·'sjon, -'θjon] *f* redesign

**remodelar** [rre·mo·de·'lar] *vt* to redesign

**remojar** [rre·mo·'xar] **I.** *vt* to soak; (*empapar*) to drench; (*ablandar*) to soften; (*galleta*) to dip **II.** *vr:* **~se** to get wet; (*bañarse*) to have a dip

**remojo** [rre·'mo·xo] *m* soaking; (*baño*) dip; **poner en ~** to leave to soak

**remolacha** [rre·mo·'la·tʃa] *f* beet; (*roja*) beetroot; (*de azúcar*) (sugar) beet

**remolcar** <c → qu> [rre·mol·'kar] *vt* to tow; (*barco*) to tug

**remolienda** [rre·mo·'ljen·da] *f Arg, Urug* binge

**remolino** [rre·mo·'li·no] *m* whirl; (*de agua*) whirlpool; (*de viento, persona*) whirlwind

**remolonear** [rre·mo·lo·ne·'ar] *vi, vr:* **~se** **1.** (*vaguear*) to be lazy **2.** (*evitar*) to shirk

**remolque** [rre·'mol·ke] *m* **1.** (*arrastre*) tow; **llevar a ~** to tow **2.** (*vehículo*) trailer

**remontar** [rre·mon·'tar] **I.** *vt* **1.** (*superar*) to overcome **2.** (*subir*) to go up; **~ el vuelo** to soar **II.** *vr:* **~se** to go back to; **la construcción de la iglesia se remonta al siglo pasado** the construction of the church dates from the past century

**remorder** <o → ue> [rre·mor·'der] *vt* **me remuerde** (**la conciencia**) I feel guilty

**remordimiento** [rre·mor·di·'mjen·to] *m* remorse; **tener ~s** (**de conciencia**) **por algo** to feel remorseful about sth

**remoto, -a** [rre·'mo·to, -a] *adj* remote; **en tiempos ~s** long ago; **ni la más remota posibilidad/idea** not the slightest possibility/idea

**remover** <o → ue> [rre·mo·'βer] **I.** *vt* **1.** (*agitar*) to shake; (*dar vueltas*) to stir; (*ensalada*) to toss **2.** (*mover*) to remove **II.** *vi* to investigate

**remunerable** [rre·mu·ne·'ra·βle] *adj* remunerable

**remuneración** [rre·mu·ne·ra·'sjon, -'θjon] *f* remuneration; (*recompensa*) compensation

**remunerar** [rre·mu·ne·'rar] *vt* to remunerate; **~ a alguien por un servicio** to pay sb for a service; (*recompensar*) to compensate

**renacer** [rre·na·'ser, -'θer] *irr como crecer vi* to revive; **sentirse ~** to feel completely revived

**renacimiento** [rre·na·si·'mjen·to, -θi·'mjen·to] *m* revival; ARTE, LIT renaissance

**renacuajo, -a** [rre·na·'kwa·xo, -a] *m, f* ZOOL tadpole; *pey inf* (*niño pequeño*) shrimp

**renal** [rre·'nal] *adj* renal

**rencor** [rren·'kor] *m* ill feeling; **guardar ~ a alguien** to bear a grudge against sb

**rencoroso, -a** [rren·ko·'ro·so, -a] *adj* (*vengativo*) spiteful; (*resentido*) resentful

**rendición** [rren·di·'sjon, -'θjon] *f* surrender; (*fatiga*) exhaustion

**rendido, -a** [rren·'di·do, -a] *adj* exhausted; (*sumiso*) submissive

**rendija** [rren·'di·xa] *f* crack

**rendimiento** [rren·di·'mjen·to] *m*

**1.** (*productividad*) yield; ECON capacity; **a pleno ~** at full capacity **2.** (*beneficio*) profit; **de gran ~** very profitable **3.** *pl* (*ingresos*) income

**rendir** [rren·ˈdir] *irr como pedir* **I.** *vt* **1.** (*rentar*) to yield; **~ utilidad** to be useful; **~ fruto** to bear fruit **2.** (*trabajar*) to produce; **estas máquinas rinden mucho** these machines are very productive **3.** (*tributar*) to attribute; **~ importancia a algo** to attribute importance to sth **4.** **~ cuentas** to settle the accounts; *fig* to account for one's actions **5.** (*cansar*) to exhaust **II.** *vr:* **~se** to surrender; **~se a la evidencia de algo** to bow to the evidence of sth; **~se a las razones de alguien** to yield to sb's arguments

**renegado, -a** [rre·ne·ˈɣa·do] *inf* **I.** *adj* bad-tempered **II.** *m, f* grouch

**renegar** [rre·ne·ˈɣar] *irr como fregar* **I.** *vi* **~ de algo** (*protestar*) to protest against sth; (*renunciar*) to renounce sth **II.** *vt* (*negar*) to deny; (*detestar*) to detest

**renglón** [rren·ˈɡlon] *m* line

**rengo, -a** [ˈrren·ɡo, -a] *adj CSur* lame

**renguear** [rren·ɡe·ˈar] *vi CSur* (*cojear*) to limp

**renguera** [rren·ˈɡe·ra] *f CSur* limp

**reno** [ˈrre·no] *m* reindeer

**renombrado, -a** [rre·nom·ˈbra·do, -a] *adj* renowned

**renombre** [rre·ˈnom·bre] *m* renown; **una empresa de gran ~** a very well-known company; **una persona de ~** a famous person

**renovación** [rre·no·βa·ˈsjon, -ˈθjon] *f* renewal

**renovar** <o → ue> [rre·no·ˈβar] *vt* to renew; (*casa*) to renovate; (*país*) to modernize; **~ un pedido/aviso** to repeat a request/warning

**renta** [ˈrren·ta] *f* **1.** (*beneficio*) profit; (*ingresos*) income; (*pensión*) pension; **~ per cápita** per capita income **2.** (*alquiler*) rent; **en ~** for rent; **tomar a ~ un negocio** to lease out a business

**rentabilidad** [rren·ta·βi·li·ˈdad] *f* profitability

**rentable** [rren·ˈta·βle] *adj* profitable

**rentar** [rren·ˈtar] *vt AmL* to rent

**rentero, -a** [rren·ˈte·ro, -a] *m, f* **1.** (*arren-*

*datario*) tenant farmer **2.** *Arg* (*contribuyente*) taxpayer

**renuncia** [rre·ˈnun·sja, -θja] *f* **~ a** [*o* **de**] **algo** resignation from sth; **~ al contrato** withdrawal from the contract; **presentar su ~** to resign

**renunciar** [rre·nun·ˈsjar, -ˈθjar] *vi* **~ a algo** (*desistir*) to renounce sth; (*rechazar*) to reject sth; **~ a un cargo** to resign from a post

**reñido, -a** [rre·ˈɲi·do, -a] *adj* **1.** (*lucha, partida*) tough **2.** (*en oposición*) **estar ~ con...** to be incompatible with...

**reñir** [rre·ˈɲir] *irr como ceñir* **I.** *vi* to quarrel **II.** *vt* to scold

**reo, -a** [ˈrreo, -a] **I.** *adj* accused **II.** *m, f* (*culpado*) defendant; (*autor*) culprit; **~ habitual** persistent offender; **~ preventivo** remand prisoner

**reojo** [rre·ˈo·xo] *m* **mirar de ~** (*con hostilidad*) to look askance (at); (*con disimulo*) to look out of the corner of one's eye (at)

**reorganización** [rre·or·ɣa·ni·sa·ˈsjon, -θa·ˈθjon] *f* reorganization; **~ del gobierno** government reshuffle

**reorganizar** <z → c> [rre·or·ɣa·ni·ˈsar, -ˈθar] *vt* to reorganize; (*gobierno*) to reshuffle

**reparación** [rre·pa·ra·ˈsjon, -ˈθjon] *f* repair; (*indemnización*) compensation

**reparar** [rre·pa·ˈrar] **I.** *vt* **1.** (*arreglar*) to repair; **~ el daño** to repair the damage **2.** (*indemnizar*) to compensate **3.** **~ fuerzas** to recover one's strength **II.** *vi* **~ en** (*advertir*) to notice; (*considerar*) to consider; **sin ~ en gastos** regardless of the cost; **no ~ en sacrificios/gastos** to spare no effort/expense

**reparo** [rre·ˈpa·ro] *m* **1.** (*inconveniente*) problem; **sin ~ alguno** without any difficulty; **tener ~s para** to be reluctant [*o* hesitant] to **2.** (*objeción*) objection; **sin ~** without reservation; **no andar con ~s** to have no reservations; **poner ~s a algo** to raise objections to sth

**repartición** [rre·par·ti·ˈsjon, -ˈθjon] *f* **1.** *v.* **repartimiento 2.** *AmL* office

**repartimiento** [rre·par·ti·ˈmjen·to] *m* (*distribución*) distribution; (*división*) division

**repartir** [rre·par·'tir] I. *vt* to distribute; (*correos*) to deliver II. *vr:* ~**se** to divide up

**reparto** [rre·'par·to] *m* distribution; (*división*) division; ~ **postal/a domicilio** mail/home delivery

**repasador** [rre·pa·sa·'dor] *m Arg, Urug* dish cloth

**repasar** [rre·pa·'sar] *vt* to revise; (*cuenta*) to check; (*carta*) to reread; (*ropa*) to mend

**repaso** [rre·'pa·so] *m* 1. (*revisión*) review 2. (*inspección*) check

**repatriar** [rre·pa·'trjar] *vt* to repatriate

**repeinar** [rre·pei·'nar] I. *vt* to comb carefully II. *vr:* ~**se** to comb one's hair carefully

**repelente** [rre·pe·'len·te] I. *adj* 1. (*rechazador*) repellent 2. (*repugnante*) repulsive 3. (*redicho*) affected II. *mf* know-it-all

**repeler** [rre·pe·'ler] *vt* 1. (*rechazar*) to repel; **los imanes se repelen mutuamente** magnets repel one another 2. (*repugnar*) to disgust

**repensar** <e → ie> [rre·pen·'sar] *vt* to reconsider

**repente** [rre·'pen·te] *m* **de** ~ suddenly

**repentino, -a** [rre·pen·'ti·no, -a] *adj* sudden

**repercusión** [rre·per·ku·'sjon] *f* repercussion; **tener gran** ~ to meet with great success

**repercutir** [rre·per·ku·'tir] *vi* ~ **en algo** to have an effect on sth; ~ **en la salud** to affect one's health

**repertorio** [rre·per·'to·rjo] *m* repertoire; (*lista*) list

**repetición** [rre·pe·ti·'sjon, -'θjon] *f* repetition

**repetido, -a** [rre·pe·'ti·do, -a] *adj* repeated; **repetidas veces** again and again; **tengo muchos sellos ~s** I have doubles of lots of my stamps

**repetir** [rre·pe·'tir] *irr como pedir* I. *vi* 1. (*sabor*) to repeat; **los ajos repiten mucho** garlic comes back on me 2. (*plato*) to have second helpings II. *vt* (*reiterar, recitar*) to repeat; ~ **curso** to stay down; ~ **un pedido** to reorder goods III. *vr:* ~**se** to repeat oneself

**repicar** <c → qu> [rre·pi·'kar] *vi, vt* to ring

**repisa** [rre·'pi·sa] *f* shelf; ~ **de chimenea** mantelpiece; ~ **de ventana** window ledge

**replantear** [rre·plan·te·'ar] *vt* to rethink; (*asunto*) to raise again; (*plan*) to revise

**replegar** [rre·ple·'γar] *irr como fregar* I. *vt* 1. (*doblar*) to fold 2. (*para atrás*) to fold back II. *vr:* ~**se** to fall back

**repleto, -a** [rre·'ple·to, -a] *adj* ~ **de algo** full of sth; (*demasiado*) crammed with sth; **el tren está** ~ the train is packed; **estoy** ~ I'm full up

**réplica** ['rre·pli·ka] *f* rebuttal; ARTE replica

**replicar** <c → qu> [rre·pli·'kar] I. *vt* to answer II. *vi* to reply; (*contradecir*) to contradict; **obedecer sin** ~ to obey without argument

**repoblación** [rre·po·βla·'sjon, -'θjon] *f* repopulation; (*de plantas*) replanting; ~ **forestal** reforestation

**repoblar** <o → ue> [rre·po·'βlar] *vt* to repopulate; (*plantas*) to replant; (*árboles*) to reforest

**repollo** [rre·'po·jo, -λo] *m* cabbage

**reponer** [rre·po·'ner] *irr como poner* I. *vt* to replace; (*fuerzas*) to get back II. *vr:* ~**se** to recover

**reportaje** [rre·por·'ta·xe] *m* report; PREN article; ~ **gráfico** illustrated report; (*documental*) documentary

**reportar** [rre·por·'tar] *vt AmL* to report

**reportear** [rre·por·te·'ar] *vt AmL* to interview

**reportero, -a** [rre·por·'te·ro, -a] *m, f* reporter; ~ **gráfico** press photographer

**reposar** [rre·po·'sar] I. *vi* to rest; **aquí reposan los restos mortales de...** here lie the mortal remains of... II. *vt* to settle; ~ **la comida** to let one's food settle III. *vr:* ~**se** to settle; (*vino*) to lie

**reposera** [rre·po·'se·ra] *f AmL* deckchair

**reposición** [rre·po·si·'sjon, -'θjon] *f* 1. replacement; **de existencias** replenishment of stocks; (*mercado, persona*) recovery; (*situación*) stabilization 2. TEAT revival; TV rerun; CINE rerelease

**reposo** [rre·'po·so] *m* peace; (*descanso*)

rest; ~ **en cama** rest in bed

**repostada** [rre·pos·'ta·da] *f AmC* rude reply

**repostar** [rre·pos·'tar] *vt* to stock up with; (*vehículo*) to refuel

**repostería** [rre·pos·te·'ri·a] *f* pastries *pl*; (*pastelería*) pastry shop

**reprender** [rre·pren·'der] *vt* to reprimand

**represalia** [rre·pre·'sa·lja] *f* reprisal; **en ~ por...** in retaliation for...

**representación** [rre·pre·sen·ta·'sjon, ·'θjon] *f* 1. representation; **por** [*o* **en**] ~ **de** representing 2. TEAT performance 3. (*reproducción*) reproduction; (*ilustración*) illustration; ~ **digital** digital display

**representante** [rre·pre·sen·'tan·te] *mf* representative; TEAT, CINE agent, manager; COM dealer

**representar** [rre·pre·sen·'tar] *vt* 1. (*sustituir*) to represent 2. (*actuar*) to act; (*obra*) to perform 3. (*significar*) to mean 4. (*encarnar*) to embody; (*reproducir*) to reproduce; (*ilustrar*) to illustrate

**representativo, -a** [rre·pre·sen·ta·'ti·βo, -a] *adj* representative

**represión** [rre·pre·'sjon] *f* (*contención*) suppression; (*limitación*) repression

**reprimenda** [rre·pri·'men·da] *f* reprimand

**reprimir** [rre·pri·'mir] **I.** *vt* to suppress **II.** *vr:* ~**se** to control oneself

**reprochable** [rre·pro·'tʃa·βle] *adj* reprehensible

**reprochar** [rre·pro·'tʃar] *vt* to reproach

**reproche** [rre·'pro·tʃe] *m* reproach

**reproducción** [rre·pro·duk·'sjon, -duγ·'θjon] *f* reproduction; ~ **radiofónica** radio reproduction; ~ **sexual** sexual reproduction; (*repetición*) repetition; (**de un libro**) copy (of a book); (*documentos*) duplication

**reproducir** [rre·pro·du·'sir, -'θir] *irr como traducir* **I.** *vt* 1. (*procrear*) to reproduce 2. (*repetir*) to repeat; (*copiar*) to reproduce; (*libro*) to print; (*documento*) to duplicate 3. (*representar*) to represent **II.** *vr:* ~**se** to reproduce

**reproductor** [rre·pro·duk·'tor] *m* ~ **de discos compactos** compact disc player

**reptar** [rrep·'tar] *vi* to crawl

**reptil** [rrep·'til] *m* reptile

**república** [rre·'pu·βli·ka] *f* republic

**republicano, -a** [rre·pu·βli·'ka·no, -a] *adj, m, f* republican

**repudiar** [rre·pu·'djar] *vt* to reject; (*parientes*) to disown

**repudio** [rre·'pu·djo] *m* rejection; (*de parientes*) repudiation

**repuesto** [rre·'pwes·to] *m* spare part; **rueda de ~** spare tire

**repuesto, -a** [rre·'pwes·to, -a] *pp de* **reponer**

**repugnancia** [rre·puγ·'nan·sja, -θja] *f* ~ **a algo** repugnance for sth; (*asco*) disgust for sth

**repugnante** [rre·puγ·'nan·te] *adj* disgusting

**repugnar** [rre·puγ·'nar] *vi* to disgust; **me repugna la carne grasosa** fatty meat makes me sick

**repulsión** [rre·pul·'sjon] *f* aversion; (*asco*) disgust

**repulsivo, -a** [rre·pul·'si·βo, -a] *adj* repulsive

**repunte** [rre·'pun·te] *m RíoPl* rise

**reputación** [rre·pu·ta·'sjon, -'θjon] *f* reputation; **tener muy buena/mala ~** to have a very good/bad reputation

**requemar** [rre·ke·'mar] **I.** *vt* (*asar bien*) to roast; (*demasiado*) to burn; ~ **la garganta/la lengua** to burn one's throat/tongue **II.** *vr:* ~**se** to scorch

**requenete** [rre·ke·'ne·te] *adj Ven* (*rechoncho*) tubby

**requerimiento** [rre·ke·ri·'mjen·to] *m* ~ **de algo** demand for sth; (*escrito*) writ for sth; ~ **de información** request for information; **a ~ de...** on the request of...

**requerir** [rre·ke·'rir] *irr como sentir vt* to require; **esto requiere toda la atención** this calls for our fullest attention

**requesón** [rre·ke·'son] *m* cottage cheese

**requetebueno, -a** [rre·ke·te·'βwe·no, -a] *adj AmL inf* really good

**requetecaro, -a** [rre·ke·te·'ka·ro, -a] *adj AmL inf* really expensive

**réquiem** ['rre·kjen] *m* requiem

**requisar** [rre·ki·'sar] *vt* to confiscate

**requisito** [rre·ki·'si·to] *m* requirement; (*condición*) condition; **ser ~ indispen-**

R

**sable** to be absolutely essential; **~ previo** prerequisite; **cumplir con los ~s** to fulfill the requirements

**res** [rres] *f* **1.** beast; **carne de ~** beef **2.** *AmL* head of cattle

**resaca** [rre·'sa·ka] *f* undertow; *inf* hangover

**resaltar** [rre·sal·'tar] *vi, vt* to stand out; **hacer ~** to highlight

**resalte** [rre·'sal·te] *m*, **resalto** [rre·'sal·to] *m* projection, ledge

**resarcir** <c → z> [rre·sar·'sir, ·'θir] I. *vt* to repay; **~ de algo** to compensate for sth II. *vr* **~se de algo** to make up for sth

**resbalada** [rres·βa·'la·da] *f* *AmL inf* slip

**resbaladilla** [rres·βa·la·'di·ja, ·ʎa] *f* *Méx* slide

**resbaladizo, -a** [rres·βa·la·'di·so, ·a; ·θo, ·a] *adj* slippery

**resbalar** [rres·βa·'lar] *vi* to slide; (*sin querer*) to slip; (*coche*) to skid

**resbalín** [rres·βa·'lin] *m* *Chile* slide

**rescatar** [rres·ka·'tar] *vt* **1.** (*prisionero*) to rescue; (*con dinero*) to pay the ransom for; (*un cadáver, algo perdido*) to recover; (*náufrago*) to pick up **2.** (*deuda*) to pay off; *AmL* (*mercancías*) to peddle

**rescate** [rres·'ka·te] *m* recovery; (*prisionero*) rescue; (*con dinero*) ransoming

**rescindir** [rres·sin·'dir, rres·θin·] *vt* (*ley*) to repeal; (*contrato*) to annul

**rescisión** [rresi·'sjon, rresθi·] *f* (*ley*) repeal; (*contrato*) annulment; (*deuda*) cancellation

**resecar** <c → qu> [rre·se·'kar] *vt* to dry out

**resentido, -a** [rre·sen·'ti·do, ·a] *adj* **1.** *estar* (*ofendido*) resentful; (*débil*) worn out **2.** *ser* bitter

**resentimiento** [rre·sen·ti·'mjen·to] *m* resentment

**resentirse** [rre·sen·'tir·se] *irr como sentir vr* **1.** (*ofenderse*) **~ por** [*o* **de**] **algo** to feel resentful about sth **2.** (*sentir dolor*) **~ de** [*o* **con**] **algo** to suffer from sth **3.** (*debilitarse*) to be weakened

**reseña** [rre·'se·ɲa] *f* **1.** (*de un libro*) review **2.** (*de una persona*) description **3.** (*narración*) report

**reseñar** [rre·se·'ɲar] *vt* to summarize; (*libro*) to review; (*persona*) to describe

**resero, -a** [rre·'se·ro, ·a] *m, f* *CSur* cowhand

**reserva** [rre·'ser·βa] *f* **1.** (*previsión*) reservation; **~ de equipajes** *AmL* left luggage; **tener algo en ~** to hold sth in reserve **2.** FIN reserve; (*fondos*) reserves *pl* **3.** (*de plazas*) reservation; **hacer una ~** to book **4.** (*biológica*) reserve; (*para animales*) wildlife reserve **5.** (*vino*) vintage

**reservado, -a** [rre·ser·'βa·do, ·a] *adj* **1.** reserved; (*confidencial*) confidential; **quedan ~s todos los derechos** all rights reserved **2.** (*callado*) reserved; (*cauteloso*) cautious

**reservar** [rre·ser·'βar] I. *vt* **1.** (*plaza*) to reserve **2.** (*guardar*) to put by II. *vr*: **~se** to save oneself

**resfriado** [rres·fri·'a·do] *m* cold

**resfriarse** <3. pres resfría> [rres·fri·'ar·se] *vr* to catch a cold

**resfrío** [rres·'fri·o] *m* *AmL* cold

**resguardar** [rres·ɣwar·'dar] I. *vt* to protect (**de** from) II. *vr* **~se de algo** to protect oneself from sth; **~se tras un muro** to shelter behind a wall

**resguardo** [rres·'ɣwar·do] *m* receipt; **~ de entrega/de transferencia** proof of delivery/transfer

**residencia** [rre·si·'den·sja, ·θja] *f* residence; (*colegio*) boarding school; UNIV dormitory; **~ habitual** usual place of residence; **cambiar de ~** to change one's address; **~ de ancianos** old people's home

**residente** [rre·si·'den·te] *adj, mf* resident; **no ~** non-resident

**residir** [rre·si·'dir] *vi* to reside; **~ en** *fig* to lie in

**residual** [rre·si·du·'al] *adj* residual; **aguas ~es** sewage

**residuo** [rre·'si·dwo] *m* **1.** residue; QUÍM residuum **2.** *pl* waste; **~s industriales/radiactivos** industrial/radioactive waste

**resignación** [rre·siɣ·na·'sjon, ·'θjon] *f* resignation

**resignarse** [rre·siɣ·'nar·se] *vr* to resign oneself (**con, a** to)

**resina** [rre·'si·na] *f* resin

**resistencia** [rre·sis·'ten·sja, ·θja] *f* resistance; **~ a la autoridad** opposition to the authorities; **oponer ~** to offer resistance; **~ física** stamina; **carrera de ~** endurance race

**resistente** [rre·sis·'ten·te] *adj* resistant; **~ al calor/a la luz** heat-/light-resistant

**resistir** [rre·sis·'tir] I. *vi, vt* to resist II. *vr:* **~se** to resist

**resolana** [rre·so·'la·na] *f AmL* 1. (*sol reflejado*) reflection 2. (*lugar a pleno sol*) sunny, windless spot 3. (*resplandor*) sun glare

**resolución** [rre·so·lu·'sjon, -'θjon] *f* 1. (*firmeza*) resolve 2. (*decisión*) decision; POL resolution; **~ judicial** adjudication; **tomar una ~** to reach a decision 3. (*solución*) solution

**resolver** [rre·sol·'βer] *irr como* volver I. *vt* 1. (*acordar*) to agree 2. (*solucionar*) to solve; (*dudas*) to resolve II. *vr:* **~se** 1. (*solucionarse*) to be solved 2. (*decidirse*) to decide

**resonancia** [rre·so·'nan·sja, -θja] *f* resonance; **tener ~** (*suceso*) to have an impact

**resonante** [rre·so·'nan·te] *adj* important; **con éxito ~** with tremendous success

**resonar** <o → ue> [rre·so·'nar] *vi* to resound

**resorte** [rre·'sor·te] *m Méx* elastic

**resortera** [rre·sor·'te·ra] *f Méx* slingshot

**respaldar** [rres·pal·'dar] I. *vt* to support; (*proteger*) to protect II. *vr:* **~se** to lean; (*hacia atrás*) to lean back

**respaldo** [rres·'pal·do] *m* support; (*protección*) protection; **en el ~** on the back

**respectar** [rres·pek·'tar] *vi* (*verbo defectivo*) to regard; **por** [*o* **en**] **lo que respecta a...** with regard to...

**respectivamente** [rres·pek·ti·βa·'men·te] *adv* respectively

**respectivo, -a** [rres·pek·'ti·βo, -a] *adj* respective

**respecto** [rres·'pek·to] *m* (**con**) **~ a** with regard to; **con ~ a eso** in that regard; **a este ~** in this regard

**respetable** [rres·pe·'ta·βle] *adj* respectable; (*notable*) considerable

**respetar** [rres·pe·'tar] *vt* 1. (*honrar*) to respect; **hacerse ~** to command respect

**respeto** [rres·'pe·to] *m* respect; **falta de ~** lack of respect; **tener mucho ~ a las tormentas** to be well aware of the dangers of storms ▶ **faltar al ~ a alguien** to be disrespectful to(wards) sb; **de ~** respectable

**respetuoso, -a** [rres·pe·tu·'o·so, -a] *adj* respectful

**respiración** [rres·pi·ra·'sjon, -'θjon] *f* breathing; (*aliento*) breath; **~ artificial** artificial respiration; **~ boca a boca** mouth to mouth resuscitation

**respirar** [rres·pi·'rar] *vi* to breathe; **~ aliviado** to breathe easily ▶ **¡déjame que respire!** give me a break!; **sin ~** without stopping

**respiratorio, -a** [rres·pi·ra·'to·rjo, -a] *adj* respiratory; **vías respiratorias** air passages

**resplandecer** [rres·plan·de·'ser, -'θer] *irr como* crecer *vi* to shine

**resplandor** [rres·plan·'dor] *m* brightness

**responder** [rres·pon·'der] *vi* 1. (*contestar*) to reply 2. (*contradecir*) to contradict 3. (*corresponder*) to correspond 4. **~ por algo** to answer for sth

**responsabilidad** [rres·pon·sa·βi·li·'dad] *f* responsibility; (*por un daño*) liability

**responsabilizar** <z → c> [rres·pon·sa·βi·li·'sar, -'θar] I. *vt* **~ de algo** to make responsible for sth II. *vr* **~se de algo** to accept the responsibility for sth

**responsable** [rres·pon·'sa·βle] I. *adj* **~ de algo** responsible for sth II. *mf* person in charge; (*culpable*) culprit

**respuesta** [rres·'pwes·ta] *f* answer; **~ negativa** negative reply; **en ~ a su carta del...** in reply to your letter of...

**resquicio** [rres·'ki·sjo, -θjo] *m* 1. (*abertura*) crack 2. (*ocasión*) opening; **~ de esperanza** glimmer of hope

**resta** [rres·ta] *f* subtraction

**restablecer** [rres·ta·βle·'ser, -'θer] *irr como* crecer I. *vt* to re-establish; (*democracia, paz*) to restore II. *vr:* **~se** to recover

**restablecimiento** [rres·ta·βle·si·'mjen·to, -θi·'mjen·to] *m* re-establishment; (*régimen, paz*) restoration

**restante** [rres·'tan·te] I. *adj* remaining; **cantidad ~** remainder **II.** *m* remainder

**restar** [rres·'tar] **I.** *vi* to remain; **restan dos días para...** there are two days left until... **II.** *vt* to take away; MAT to subtract; **~ importancia a algo** to play sth down

**restauración** [rres·tau·ra·'sjon, -'θjon] *f* restoration

**restaurante** [rres·tau·'ran·te] *m* restaurant

**restaurar** [rres·tau·'rar] *vt* to restore

**restitución** [rres·ti·tu·'sjon, -'θjon] *f* return; (*reposición*) replacement

**resto** ['rres·to] *m* rest; MAT remainder; **~s mortales** mortal remains; **los ~s de la torre** the tower ruins; **lo recordaré el ~ de mis días** I will remember him for the rest of my life

**restregar** [rres·tre·'ɣar] *irr como* **fregar** *vt, vr:* **~se** to rub; **~se los ojos** to rub one's eyes

**restricción** [rres·trik·'sjon, -triɣ·'θjon] *f* restriction; (*recorte*) cutback; **sin restricciones** freely

**restringir** <g → j> [rres·trin·'xir] *vt* to restrict

**resucitar** [rre·su·θi·'tar, rre·su·θi-] *vi, vt* to resuscitate

**resuelto, -a** [rre·'swel·to, -a] **I.** *pp de* **resolver II.** *adj* determined

**resultado** [rre·sul·'ta·do] *m* result; **dar buen/mal ~** to work/fail

**resultar** [rre·sul·'tar] *vi* to work; **~ de algo** to result from sth; **~ muerto en un accidente** to be killed in an accident

**resumen** [rre·'su·men] *m* summary; **en ~** in short

**resumidero** [rre·su·mi·'de·ro] *m AmL* (*alcantarilla*) drain; (*pozo ciego*) cesspool

**resumir** [rre·su·'mir] *vt* to summarize

**resurgir** <g → j> [rre·sur·'xir] *vi* to reappear

**resurrección** [rre·su·rrek·'sjon, -reɣ·'θjon] *f* resurrection

**retacón, -ona** [rre·ta·'kon, -·'ko·na] *adj CSur* stubby

**retaguardia** [rre·ta·'ɣwar·dja] *f* rearguard
 ▶ **estar a la ~ de algo** to lag behind sth; **ir a la ~** to bring up the rear; **quedarse en la ~** to stay in the background;

**a** [*o* en] **~** (*tarde*) late

**retar** [rre·'tar] *vt* to challenge

**retardar** [rre·tar·'dar] **I.** *vt* to delay **II.** *vr:* **~se** to be late

**retardo** [rre·'tar·do] *m* delay; **sufrir un ~** to be delayed; **tener ~ con algo** to be late doing sth

**rete** ['rre·te] *adj Méx* very; **su hija es ~ alta** their daughter is very tall

**retención** [rre·ten·'sjon, -'θjon] *f* retention; FIN deduction; **~ fiscal** tax retention

**retener** [rre·te·'ner] *irr como* **tener** *vt* to retain; (*pasaporte*) to withhold; (*detener*) to detain

**reticente** [rre·ti·'sen·te, -'θen·te] *adj* reluctant

**retina** [rre·'ti·na] *f* retina; **desprendimiento de ~** detached retina

**retintín** [rre·tin·'tin] *m* sarcastic tone

**retirada** [rre·ti·'ra·da] *f* abandonment; (*eliminación*) withdrawal; MIL retreat

**retirado, -a** [rre·ti·'ra·do, -a] *adj* **1.** (*lejos*) remote **2.** (*jubilado*) retired

**retirar** [rre·ti·'rar] **I.** *vt* **1.** (*apartar*) to remove; (*dinero*) to withdraw **2.** (*recoger, quitar*) to take away **3.** (*negar*) to deny **II.** *vr:* **~se 1.** (*abandonar*) to withdraw **2.** (*retroceder*) to retreat **3.** (*jubilarse*) to retire

**retiro** [rre·'ti·ro] *m* withdrawal; (*refugio*) retreat

**reto** ['rre·to] *m* challenge

**retobado, -a** [rre·to·'βa·do, -a] *adj* **1.** *AmC, Méx, Ecua* (*respondón*) insolent **2.** *AmC, Cuba, Ecua* (*indómito*) wild **3.** *Arg, Méx, Urug* (*enconado*) ticked off *inf*

**retobar** [rre·to·'βar] **I.** *vt CSur* to cover with leather **II.** *vi Méx* to talk back

**retocar** <c → qu> [rre·to·'kar] *vt* to perfect; FOTO to retouch

**retoñar** [rre·to·'ɲar] *vi* to sprout

**retoque** [rre·'to·ke] *m* alteration; FOTO retouch

**retorcer** [rre·tor·'ser, -'θer] *irr como* **cocer I.** *vt* to twist; (*enroscar*) to twine **II.** *vr:* **~se** to twist; **~ de dolor** to writhe

**retorcido, -a** [rre·tor·'si·do, -a; rre·tor·'θi-] *adj* **1.** (*complicado*) complicated **2.** (*maligno*) twisted; (*mente*) warped

**retórica** [rre·'to·ri·ka] *f* rhetoric
**retornable** [rre·tor·'na·βle] *adj* **botella (no) ~** (non-)returnable bottle
**retornar** [rre·tor·'nar] *vi, vt* to return
**retorno** [rre·'tor·no] *m* return
**retractar** [rre·trak·'tar] **I.** *vt* to take back; JUR to retract **II.** *vr* **~se de algo** to withdraw from sth
**retraer** [rre·tra·'er] *irr como* traer **I.** *vt* **1.** (*encoger*) to withdraw **2.** (*impedir*) to hinder **3.** JUR to retract **II.** *vr*: **~se** to retreat; **~se de algo** to withdraw from sth; **~se a** [*o* **en**] **algo** to withdraw into sth
**retraído, -a** [rre·tra·'i·ðo, -a] *adj* reserved; (*poco sociable*) withdrawn
**retraimiento** [rre·trai·'mjen·to] *m* reserve
**retransmisión** [rre·trans·mi·'sjon] *f* broadcast; **~ deportiva** sports program; **~ en directo/diferido** live/pre-recorded broadcast
**retransmitir** [rre·trans·mi·'tir] *vt* to broadcast
**retrasado, -a** [rre·tra·'sa·ðo, -a] *adj* **1.** (*atrasado*) backward; (*subdesarrollado*) underdeveloped; **~ mental** mentally retarded **2.** (*tarde*) behind schedule
**retrasar** [rre·tra·'sar] **I.** *vt* to delay; (*reloj*) to set back **II.** *vr*: **~se** to be late
**retraso** [rre·'tra·so] *m* **1.** (*demora*) delay; **tener ~ en los pagos** to be in arrears **2.** (*subdesarrollo*) underdevelopment
**retratar** [rre·tra·'tar] *vt* **1.** (*describir*) to depict **2.** (*fotografiar*) to photograph **3.** (*pintar*) to paint a portrait of
**retrato** [rre·'tra·to] *m* portrait ▶ **ser el vivo ~ de alguien** to be the spitting image of sb
**retrete** [rre·'tre·te] *m* (*recipiente*) lavatory; (*habitación*)
**retribución** [rre·tri·βu·'sjon, -'θjon] *f* reward; (*sueldo*) remuneration
**retribuir** [rre·tri·βu·'ir] *irr como* huir *vt* **1.** to remunerate **2.** AmL to compensate
**retroactivo, -a** [rre·tro·ak·'ti·βo, -a] *adj* retroactive
**retroalimentación** [rre·tro·a·li·men·ta·'sjon, -'θjon] *f* feedback
**retroceder** [rre·tro·se·'der, -θe·'der] *vi* to go back

**retroceso** [rre·tro·'se·so, -'θe·so] *m* reversal; MED relapse; (*negociaciones*) setback
**retrógrado, -a** [rre·'tro·γra·ðo, -a] *adj, m, f* reactionary
**retrospectivo, -a** [rre·tros·pek·'ti·βo, -a] *adj* retrospective
**retrovisor** [rre·tro·βi·'sor] *m* rearview mirror; **~ exterior** side mirror
**retumbar** [rre·tum·'bar] *vi* to boom; (*resonar*) to resound
**reuma** ['rreu·ma] *m o f*, **reúma** [rre·'u·ma] *m o f* rheumatism
**reumático, -a** [rreu·'ma·ti·ko, -a] *adj* rheumatic
**reumatismo** [rreu·ma·'tis·mo] *m* rheumatism
**reunificación** [rre·u·ni·fi·ka·'sjon, -'θjon] *f* reunification
**reunificar** <c → qu> [rre·u·ni·fi·'kar] *vt* to reunify
**reunión** [rreu·'njon] *f* meeting; **celebrar una ~** to hold a meeting
**reunir** [rreu·'nir] *irr* **I.** *vt* to assemble; (*unir*) to gather; **~ las cualidades necesarias** to have the necessary qualities **II.** *vr*: **~se** to meet; (*informal*) to get together; (*unirse*) to gather
**revaloración** [rre·βa·lo·ra·'sjon, -'θjon] *f* re-evaluation; FIN revaluation
**revalorización** [rre·βa·lo·ri·sa·'sjon, -θa·'θjon] *f* appreciation
**revancha** [rre·'βan·tʃa] *f* revenge; DEP return match
**revelación** [rre·βe·la·'sjon, -'θjon] *f* revelation
**revelado** [rre·βe·'la·ðo] *m* developing
**revelar** [rre·βe·'lar] *vt* to reveal; FOTO to develop
**revellín** [rre·βe·'jin, -'ʎin] *m* Cuba (*dificultad*) difficulty ▶ **echar ~** to provoke anger
**revenir** [rre·βe·'nir] *irr como* venir *vi, vr*: **~se 1.** (*encoger*) to shrink **2.** (*agriarse*) to sour **3.** (*secarse*) to dry out
**reventa** [rre·'βen·ta] *f* resale; (*entradas*) scalping
**reventadero** [rre·βen·ta·'de·ro] *m* **1.** *Col, Méx* (*hervidero*) bubbling spring **2.** *Chile* (*rompiente*) shoal

R

**reventado, -a** [rre·βen·'ta·ðo, -a] *adj*
**1.** *inf* (*hecho polvo*) wiped out **2.** *Arg*
(*sinuoso*) devious

**reventar** <e → ie> [rre·βen·'tar] **I.** *vi* to
break; (*globo, neumático*) to burst; **lleno hasta ~** full to bursting **II.** *vt* **1.** to
break; (*globo, neumático*) to burst **2.** *inf*
to annoy **III.** *vr:* **~se** to break; (*globo,
neumático*) to burst

**reverbero** [rre·βer·'βe·ro] *m AmL* (*hornillo*) spirit stove

**reverencia** [rre·βe·'ren·sja, -θja] *f* bow

**reverendo** [rre·βe·'ren·do] *m* Reverend

**reversa** [rre·'βer·sa] *f Chile, Col, Méx*
reverse

**reversible** [rre·βer·'si·βle] *adj* reversible

**reversión** [rre·βer·'sjon] *f* reversion

**reverso** [rre·'βer·so] *m* other side

**revertir** [rre·βer·'tir] *irr como sentir vi*
to revert

**revés** [rre·'βes] *m* **1.** (*reverso*) other
side; **al** [*o* **del**] **~** back to front; (*con lo
de arriba abajo*) upside down; (*dentro
para fuera*) inside out; **te has puesto el
jersey del ~** you have put your jumper
on back to front **2.** (*golpe*) blow with
the back of the hand **3.** DEP backhand
**4.** (*infortunio*) setback; **~ de fortuna**
stroke of bad luck

**revirado, -a** [rre·βi·'ra·ðo, -a] *adj Arg,
Urug* nutty

**revire** [rre·'βi·re] *m Arg, Urug inf* crazy
idea; **le dio uno de sus ~s** he/she had
one of his/her crazy ideas

**revisada** [rre·βi·'sa·ða] *f AmL* check

**revisar** [rre·βi·'sar] *vt* to check; TÉC to inspect; (*textos, edición*) to revise

**revisión** [rre·βi·'sjon] *f* check; TÉC inspection; JUR, TIPO revision

**revisor(a)** [rre·βi·'sor, -·'so·ra] *m(f)* inspector; FERRO ticket inspector

**revista** [rre·'βis·ta] *f* magazine; **las ~s del
corazón** the gossip magazines; **~ electrónica** e-zine; **~ especializada** special
interest magazine

**revivir** [rre·βi·'βir] **I.** *vi* to revive **II.** *vt* to
revive; (*evocar*) to relive

**revocar** <c → qu> [rre·βo·'kar] *vt* to
revoke

**revolcar** [rre·βol·'kar] *irr como volcar*
**I.** *vt* (*derribar*) to knock over **II.** *vr* **~se**

**por algo** to roll around in sth

**revolear** [rre·βo·le·'ar] *vt Méx, CSur* to
whirl around

**revoloteo** [rre·βo·lo·'te·o] *m* fluttering

**revoltijo** [rre·βol·'ti·xo] *m* jumble

**revoltoso, -a** [rre·βol·'to·so, -a] **I.** *adj*
mischievous; (*rebelde*) rebellious **II.** *m, f*
troublemaker

**revoltura** [rre·βol·'tu·ra] *f Méx* mixture

**revolución** [rre·βo·lu·'sjon, -'θjon] *f* revolution

**revolucionar** [rre·βo·lu·sjo·'nar, rre·βo·
lu·θjo-] *vt* to revolutionize; (*amotinar*)
to stir up

**revolucionario, -a** [rre·βo·lu·sjo·'na·rjo,
-a; rre·βo·lu·θjo-] *adj, m, f* revolutionary

**revoluta** [rre·βo·'lu·ta] *f AmC* v. **revolución**

**revolvedora** [rre·βol·βe·'do·ra] *f Arg,
Méx* cement mixer

**revolver** [rre·βol·'βer] *irr como volver*
**I.** *vt* **1.** (*mezclar*) to mix; (*desordenar*)
to mess up **2.** (*investigar*) to investigate **II.** *vr:* **~se** to toss and turn; **se me
revuelve el estómago** it makes my
stomach turn

**revólver** [rre·'βol·βer] *m* revolver

**revuelo** [rre·'βwe·lo] *m* disturbance; **causar ~** to disturb

**revuelta** [rre·'βwel·ta] *f* (*tumulto*) disturbance; (*rebelión*) revolt

**revuelto, -a** [rre·'βwel·to, -a] **I.** *pp de*
**revolver II.** *adj* (*agitado*) shaken; (*desordenado*) chaotic; (*tiempo*) unsettled;
(*huevos*) scrambled

**revulsar** [rre·βul·'sar] *vi, vt Méx* to throw
up

**rey** [rrei] *m* king; **los ~es** The King and
Queen; **los Reyes Magos** the Three
Wise Men; **el día de Reyes** Epiphany

**rezagado, -a** [re·sa·'ya·ðo, -a; re·θa-]
*m, f* straggler

**rezar** <z → c> [rre·'sar, -'θar] *vi, vt* to
pray

**rezo** ['rre·so, -θo] *m* prayer

**rezongar** <g → gu> [rre·son·'gar, rre·
θon-] *vi* to grumble

**ría** ['rri·a] *f* ≈ estuary

**riachuelo** [rrja·'tʃwe·lo] *m* stream

**riada** [rri·'a·ða] *f* flood

**ribera** [rri.'βe.ra] *f* (*orilla*) bank; (*tierra*) riverside; (*vega*) fertile plain

**ricamente** [rri.ka.'men.te] *adv* richly; (*con placer*) splendidly

**rico, -a** ['rri.ko, -a] **I.** *adj* **1.** (*acaudalado, abundante*) rich **2.** (*sabroso*) delicious **3.** (*simpático*) lovely **II.** *m, f* (*rico*) rich person; **los ricos** the rich

**ricota** [rri.'ko.ta] *f Arg* ricotta cheese

**ridiculizar** <z → c> [rri.di.ku.li.'sar, -'θar] *vt* to ridicule

**ridículo, -a** [rri.'di.ku.lo, -a] *adj* ridiculous; **poner(se) en ~** to make a fool of (oneself)

**riego** ['rrje.γo] *m* irrigation; **~ sanguíneo** blood flow

**riel** [rrjel] *m* rail

**rienda** ['rrjen.da] *f* rein; **tener las ~s del poder** to hold the reins of power ► **a ~ suelta** wildly; **dar ~ suelta a** to give free rein to; **llevar las ~s** to be in control

**riesgo** ['rrjes.γo] *m* risk; **a ~ de que... +subj** at the risk of...; **por cuenta y ~ propios** at one's own risk and expense; **asumir un ~** to assume a risk; **estar asegurado a todo ~** to have full coverage insurance; **correr un ~** to run a risk

**riesgoso, -a** [rrjes.'γo.so, -a] *adj AmL* (*arriesgado*) risky; (*peligroso*) dangerous

**rifa** ['rri.fa] *f* raffle

**rifar** [rri.'far] *vt* to raffle

**rifle** ['rri.fle] *m* rifle

**rigidez** [rri.xi.'des, -'deθ] *f* rigidity; (*severidad*) strictness

**rígido, -a** ['rri.xi.do, -a] *adj* rigid; (*severo*) strict

**rigor** [rri.'γor] *m* (*severidad*) strictness; (*exactitud*) rigorousness ► **de ~** de rigueur

**riguroso, -a** [rri.γu.'ro.so, -a] *adj* (*severo*) strict; (*exacto*) rigorous

**rima** ['rri.ma] *f* rhyme

**rimar** [rri.'mar] *vi, vt* to rhyme

**rímel®** ['rri.mel] *m* mascara

**rin** [rrin] *m* **1.** *Ven* (*llanta*) rim **2.** *Perú* (*ficha*) telephone token

**rincón** [rrin.'kon] *m* corner; *fig* nook; **por todos los rincones** in every nook and cranny

**rinoceronte** [rri.no.se.'ron.te, rri.no.'θe] *m* rhinoceros

**riña** ['rri.ɲa] *f* quarrel

**riñón** [rri.'ɲon] *m* **1.** kidney **2.** *pl* (*espalda*) lower back ► **costar un ~** to cost an arm and a leg

**riñonera** [rri.ɲo.'ne.ra] *f* fanny pack *inf*

**río** ['rri.o] *m* river; **~ abajo/arriba** downstream/upstream ► **cuando el ~ suena, agua lleva** where there's smoke, there's fire

**rioplatense** [rrio.pla.'ten.se] **I.** *adj* of/ from the River Plate region **II.** *mf* native/inhabitant of the River Plate region

**riqueza** [rri.'ke.sa, -θa] *f* riches *pl*

**risa** [rri.'sa] *f* laughter; **estar muerto de ~** to be laughing one's head off; **tener un ataque de ~** to have a fit of the giggles; **tomar algo a ~** to treat sth as a joke; **¡qué ~!** what a joke!; **no estoy para ~s** I'm in no mood for jokes

**risco** ['rris.ko] *m* crag

**ríspido, -a** ['rris.pi.do, -a] *adj AmL* coarse

**ristra** ['rris.tra] *f* string; **una ~ de ajos/ mentiras** a string of garlic/lies

**risueño, -a** [rri.'swe.ɲo, -a] *adj* smiling

**rítmico, -a** ['rrid.mi.ko, -a] *adj* rhythmic

**ritmo** ['rrid.mo] *m* rhythm

**rito** ['rri.to] *m* ritual; REL rite

**ritual** [rri.tu.'al] *adj, m* ritual

**rival** [rri.'βal] *adj, mf* rival

**rivalidad** [rri.βa.li.'dad] *f* rivalry

**rizado, -a** [rri.'sa.do, rri.'θa-] *adj* curly

**rizo** ['rri.so, -θo] *m* curl; **rizar el ~** to overcomplicate things

**rizo, -a** ['rri.θo, -a] *adj* curly

**robar** [rro.'βar] *vt* **1.** to steal; (*a alguien*) to rob; (*con violencia*) to mug; **me ~on en París** I was robbed in Paris; **me robó la novia** he stole my girlfriend **2.** (*estafar*) to cheat **3.** (*en juegos*) to draw

**roble** ['rro.βle] *m* oak; **estar como un ~** to be as fit as a fiddle

**robo** ['rro.βo] *m* robbery; **~ a mano armada** armed robbery; (*estafa*) swindle; **ser un ~** (*muy caro*) to be a rip-off

**robot** <robots> [rro.'βot] *m* robot; **~ de cocina** food processor

R

**robusto, -a** [rro·'bus·to, -a] *adj* robust

**roca** ['rro·ka] *f* rock

**roce** ['rro·θe, -θe] *m* 1. (*fricción*) brush 2. (*huella*) scrape 3. (*contacto*) contact 4. (*pelea*) scrape

**rochar** [rro·'tʃar] *vt Chile* to catch red-handed

**rochela** [rro·'tʃe·la] *f Col, PRico, Ven* hullabaloo

**rociar** <3. *pres* rocía> [rro·si·'ar, rro·θi·] *vt* to sprinkle

**rocío** [rro·'si·o, -'θi·o] *m* dew

**rock** [rrok] *adj, m* rock

**rocoso, -a** [rro·'ko·so, -a] *adj* rocky; **Montañas Rocosas** Rocky Mountains

**rocote** [rro·'ko·te] *m*, **rocoto** [rro·'ko·to] *m Bol, Ecua, Perú* (large) green pepper

**rodaja** [rro·'da·xa] *f* slice

**rodaje** [rro·'da·xe] *m* shooting

**rodar** <o → ue> [rro·'dar] I. *vi* to roll; (*sobre un eje*) to turn; (*deslizarse*) to slide; ~ **por el suelo** to roll across the floor II. *vt* to roll; (*coche*) to run in; (*película*) to shoot

**rodear** [rro·de·'ar] I. *vi* to go around II. *vt* ~ **de algo** to surround with sth; (*tema*) to avoid III. *vr* ~**se de algo/alguien** to surround oneself with sth/sb

**rodeo** [rro·'deo] *m* 1. (*desvío*) detour; **dar un** ~ to take a detour 2. (*evasiva*) evasion 3. DEP rodeo ▸ **andar(se) con** ~**s** to beat about the bush; **dejarse de** ~**s** to stop beating about the bush; **sin** ~**s** without beating about the bush

**rodilla** [rro·'di·ja, -ʎa] *f* knee; **de** ~ on one's knees; **ponerse de** ~**s** to kneel

**rodillo** [rro·'di·jo, -ʎo] *m* roller; (*de cocina*) rolling pin

**roedor** [rroe·'dor] *m* rodent

**roer** [rro·'er] *irr vt* to gnaw at

**rogar** <o → ue> [rro·'ɣar] *vt* to request; (*con humildad*) to beg; JUR to plead; **le gusta hacerse de** ~ he/she likes playing hard to get

**rojizo, -a** [rro·'xi·so, -a; -θo, -a] *adj* reddish

**rojo, -a** ['rro·xo] *adj* red; (*persona*) redheaded ▸ **al** ~ (**vivo**) red-hot; **poner** ~ **a alguien** to make sb blush; **ponerse** ~ to go red

**rol** [rrol] *m* role; **desempeñar un** ~ to play a role; **juego de** ~ role-playing game

**rollo** ['rro·jo, -ʎo] *m* 1. roll 2. *inf* (*pesadez*) bore; **¡qué** ~ **de película!** what a boring film!; **soltar siempre el mismo** ~ to always come out with the same old stuff 3. *inf* (*tipo de vida*) lifestyle; (*asunto*) affair; **ir a su** ~ to do as one likes; **tener un** ~ **con alguien** *argot* to have a fling with sb; **tener mucho** ~ to be full of crap *sl*; **traerse un mal** ~ to be in a mess; **corta el** ~ cut the crap

**Roma** ['rro·ma] *f* Rome

**romance** [rro·'man·se, -θe] I. *adj* LING Romance II. *m* romance; **tiene un** ~ **con la vecina** he's having an affair with his neighbor

**románico, -a** [rro·'ma·ni·ko, -a] *adj* Romanesque

**romano, -a** [rro·'ma·no] *adj, m, f* Roman

**romanticismo** [rro·man·ti·'sis·mo, -'θis·mo] *m* romanticism

**romántico, -a** [rro·'man·ti·ko, -a] *adj, m, f* romantic

**rombo** ['rrom·bo] *m* rhombus; **en forma de** ~ diamond-shaped

**romería** [rro·me·'ri·a] *f* pilgrimage; (*fiesta*) festival

**romerito** [rro·me·'ri·to] *m Méx* vegetables *pl*

**romero** [rro·'me·ro] *m* rosemary

**romero, -a** [rro·'me·ro, -a] *adj, m, f* pilgrim

**romo, -a** ['rro·mo, -a] *adj* blunt

**rompecabezas** [rrom·pe·ka·'βe·sas, -θas] *m inv* (*juego*) brainteaser; (*acertijo*) riddle

**romper** [rrom·'per] I. *vi* to break; (*separarse*) to break up; **al** ~ **el día** at the break of day; ~ **a llorar** to burst into tears II. *vt* to break; (*cristal*) to shatter; (*plato*) to smash; (*papel, tela*) to tear; (*negociaciones, relaciones*) to break off; ~ **algo a golpes** to bash sth to pieces; ~ **el silencio/el encanto** to break the silence/the spell III. *vr:* ~**se** to break; ~**se la pierna** to break one's leg; ~**se la cabeza** *fig* to rack one's brains

**rompope** [rrom·'po·pe] *m AmC, Ecua, Méx* eggnog

**ron** [rron] *m* rum

**roncar** <c → qu> [rron·'kar] *vi* to snore

**roncear** [rron·se·'ar, rron·θe·] *vt Arg, Chile, Méx* to move by levering

**roncha** ['rron·tʃa] *f* bruise

**ronco, -a** ['rron·ko, -a] *adj* hoarse; (*afónico*) voiceless

**roncón, -ona** [rron·'kon, --'ko·na] *m, f Col, Ven* bragging

**ronda** ['rron·da] *f* round; **pagar una ~** to buy a round

**rondar** [rron·'dar] **I.** *vi* to prowl about; (*patrullando*) to be on patrol **II.** *vt* to surround; **roda los setenta años** he/ she is about seventy years old

**rondín** [rron·'din] *m* **1.** *Bol, Ecua, Perú* (*armónica*) harmonica **2.** *Bol, Chile* (*vigilante*) watchman

**ronquido** [rron·'ki·do] *m* snore

**ronronear** [rron·rro·ne·'ar] *vi* to purr

**roña** ['rro·ɲa] **I.** *f* filth **II.** *mf* stingy

**roñoso, -a** [rro·'ɲo·so, -a] *adj* **1.** (*tacaño*) tight **2.** (*sucio*) filthy **3.** (*sarnoso*) scabby **4.** (*oxidado*) rusty

**ropa** ['rro·pa] *f* clothes *pl*; **~ interior** underwear; **~ de cama** sheets; **cambiar(se) la ~** to change one's clothes; **poner(se) la ~** to get dressed; **~ de abrigo** warm clothing

**ropero** [rro·'pe·ro] *m* wardrobe

**rosa** ['rro·sa] **I.** *adj* pink **II.** *f* BOT rose ▶ **no hay ~ sin espinas** every rose has its thorn

**rosado, -a** [rro·'sa·do, -a] *adj* pink; **vino ~** rosé (wine)

**rosal** [rro·'sal] *m* rosebush

**rosario** [rro·'sa·rjo] *m* rosary

**rosca** ['rros·ka] *f* **1.** TÉC thread; **el tornillo se pasó de ~** the screw broke the thread **2.** (*espiral*) coil **3.** (*aro*) ring; (*bollo*) bread roll; (*torta*) sponge ring; **~ de Reyes** *Méx* cake eaten on Epiphany ▶ **no comerse una ~** not to get off with anyone; **pasarse de ~** to go too far

**roscón** [rros·'kon] *m* sponge ring; **~ de Reyes** cake eaten on Epiphany

**rosedal** [rro·se·'dal] *m Arg, Urug* rose garden

**rosquete** [rros·'ke·te] *adj, m Perú vulg* queer

**rosquilla** [rros·'ki·ja, -ʎa] *f* doughnut ▶ **venderse como ~s** to sell like hot cakes

**rosticería** [rros·ti·se·'ri·a] *f Chile, Méx v.* **rotisería**

**rostro** ['rros·tro] *m* face

**rotación** [rro·ta·'sjon, -'θjon] *f* rotation; **~ de cultivos** crop rotation

**rotería** [rro·te·'ri·a] *f Chile* **1.** (*acción*) inconsiderate act **2.** (*plebe*) the masses

**rotisería** [rro·ti·se·'ri·a] *f Arg* shop that sells roast chicken, beef and other dishes

**roto** ['rro·to] *m* tear; (*agujero*) hole

**roto, -a** ['rro·to, -a] **I.** *pp de* **romper** **II.** *adj* **1.** broken; (*vestido*) torn **2.** (*andrajoso*) wretched **3.** (*destrozado*) destroyed

**rotonda** [rro·'ton·da] *f* traffic circle

**rotoso, -a** [rro·'to·so, -a] **I.** *adj AmL* tattered **II.** *m, f* wretch

**rotulador** [rro·tu·la·'dor] *m* felt-tip pen

**rótulo** ['rro·tu·lo] *m* sign

**rotundo, -a** [rro·'tun·do, -a] *adj* emphatic; (*éxito, palabras*) resounding; **una negativa rotunda** a flat refusal

**rotura** [rro·'tu·ra] *f* (*acción*) breaking; (*parte quebrada*) break; **~ de hueso** fracture; **~ de ligamento** torn ligament

**rouge** [rruʃ] *m Arg, Chile* blusher

**roza** ['rro·sa] *f*, **rozado** [rro·'sa·do, -'θa·do] *m Arg* cleared ground

**rozar** <z → c> [rro·'sar, -'θar] **I.** *vi* to rub; **rozar (por) los cincuenta** to be pushing fifty **II.** *vt* **1.** *t. fig* (*tocar ligeramente*) to brush; **~ la ridiculez** *fig* to border on the ridiculous **2.** (*frotar*) to rub **III.** *vr:* **~se** to rub

**ruana** ['rrwa·na] *f AmS* poncho

**rubéola** [rru·'βeo·la] *f* German measles

**rubí** [rru·'βi] *m* ruby

**rubio, -a** ['rru·βjo, -a] **I.** *adj* fair; **tabaco ~** Virginia tobacco **II.** *m, f* blond, blonde *m, f*

**rublo** ['rru·βlo] *m* ruble

**rubor** [rru·'βor] *m* **1.** (*color*) bright red; (*de vergüenza*) blush **2.** (*vergüenza*) shame; (*bochorno*) embarrassment

**ruborizado, -a** [rru·βo·ri·'sa·do, -a; -'θa·do, -a] *adj* blushing

R

**ruborizar** <z → c> [rru·βo·ri·'sar, -'θar] **I.** *vt* to cause to blush **II.** *vr:* **~se** to blush

**rúbrica** ['rru·βri·ka] *f* signature; (*después del nombre*) flourish

**rubro** ['rru·βro] *m AmL* heading; COM area

**ruca** ['rru·ka] *f Arg, Chile* shack

**ruco, -a** ['rru·ko, -a] *adj AmC* old

**rudimentario, -a** [rru·di·men·'ta·rjo, -a] *adj* rudimentary

**rudo, -a** ['rru·do, -a] *adj* **1.** (*material*) rough; (*sin trabajar*) raw **2.** (*persona tosca*) coarse; (*brusca*) rude; (*torpe*) clumsy

**rueda** ['rrwe·da] *f* **1.** wheel; **~ de repuesto** spare tire **2.** (*de personas, orden*) ring; **~ de prensa** press conference ▶ **todo** <u>marcha</u> **sobre ~s** everything is going smoothly

**ruego** ['rrwe·ɣo] *m* request

**rugby** ['rruɣ·βi] *m* rugby

**rugido** [rru·'xi·do] *m* (*del león*) roar; (*del viento*) howl

**rugir** <g → j> [rru·'xir] *vi* to roar; (*viento*) to howl

**rugoso, -a** [rru·'ɣo·so, -a] *adj* **1.** (*arrugado*) wrinkled **2.** (*áspero*) rough **3.** (*ondulado*) wavy

**ruido** ['rrwi·do] *m* noise; **~ de fondo** background noise ▶ **mucho ~ y pocas** <u>nueces</u> much ado about nothing

**ruidoso, -a** [rrwi·'do·so, -a] *adj* noisy; *fig* sensational

**ruin** [rrwin] *adj* **1.** (*malvado*) wicked; (*vil*) despicable **2.** (*tacaño*) mean

**ruina** ['rrwi·na] *f* **1.** (*destrucción*) destruction; **este hombre está hecho una ~** this man is a wreck **2.** ARQUIT ruin; **convertir una ciudad en ~s** to raze a city to the ground; **declarar una casa en ~s** to condemn a house **3.** (*perdición*) downfall; **causar la ~ de alguien** to cause sb's downfall; **estar en la ~** to be bankrupt; **salvar a alguien de la ~** to save sb from disaster

**ruinoso, -a** [rrwi·'no·so, -a] *adj* **1.** (*edificios*) dilapidated **2.** (*perjudicial*) disastrous; ECON ruinous

**ruiseñor** [rrwi·se·'ɲor] *m* nightingale

**rulenco, -a** [rru·'len·ko, -a] *adj Chile* weak; (*raquítico*) stunted

**rulero** [rru·'le·ro] *m AmS* hair curler

**ruleta** [rru·'le·ta] *f* roulette

**ruletear** [rru·le·te·'ar] *vi AmC, Méx* to drive a taxi

**ruletero, -a** [rru·le·'te·ro, -a] *m, f AmC, Méx* taxi driver

**rulo** ['rru·lo] *m* roller

**ruma** ['rru·ma] *f AmS* **una ~ de...** a pile of...; **~s de...** lots of...

**Rumania** [rru·'ma·nja] *f*, **Rumanía** [rru·ma·'ni·a] *f* Romania

**rumano, -a** [rru·'ma·no] *adj, m, f* Romanian

**rumba** ['rrum·ba] *f* rumba

**rumbo** ['rrum·bo] *m* direction; *t. fig* AVIAT, NÁUT course; **con ~ a** bound [*o* headed] for

**rumiante** [rru·'mjan·te] *m* ruminant

**rumor** [rru·'mor] *m* **1.** (*chisme*) rumor; **corren ~es de que...** it is rumored that... **2.** (*ruido*) murmur; (*del viento*) whistle; (*del bosque*) rustle; **~ de voces** buzz of conversation

**rumorearse** [rru·mo·re·'ar·se] *vr* **se rumorea que...** it is rumored that...

**rundún** [rrun·'dun] *m Arg, Chile, Méx, Perú* (*juguete*) bullroarer

**ruptura** [rrup·'tu·ra] *f* breaking; (*de relaciones*) breaking-off

**rural** [rru·'ral] **I.** *adj* rural; **vida ~** country life **II.** *m* **1.** *AmL t. pey* yokel **2.** *pl Méx* rural police

**Rusia** ['rru·sja] *f* Russia

**ruso, -a** ['rru·so, -a] *adj, m, f* Russian; **ensaladilla rusa** Russian salad

**rústico, -a** ['rrus·ti·ko, -a] **I.** *adj* **1.** (*campestre*) rural; **finca rústica** farmhouse **2.** (*tosco*) rough **II.** *m, f* peasant; *pey* yokel

**ruta** ['rru·ta] *f* route; **~ federal** *AmL* federal highway; **~ de vuelo** flight path

**rutina** [rru·'ti·na] *f* routine

**rutinario, -a** [rru·ti·'na·rjo, -a] *adj* routine; **un hombre ~** a man of habit; (*aburrido*) an unimaginative man

# S

**S, s** ['e·se] *f* S, s; **~ de Soria** S as in Sierra

**S.** [san] *abr de* **San** St

**S.A.** [e·se·'a] *f abr de* **Sociedad Anónima** ≈ Inc.

**sáb.** *abr de* **sábado** Sat.

**sábado** ['sa·βa·ðo] *m* Saturday; *v. t.* **lunes**

**sabana** [sa·'βa·na] *f* savanna(h)

**sábana** ['sa·βa·na] *f* sheet; **~ ajustable** fitted sheet; **se me han pegado las ~s** *inf* I've overslept

**sabandija** [sa·βan·'di·xa] *f* wretch

**sabático, -a** [sa·'βa·ti·ko, -a] *adj* sabbatical

**sabelotodo** [sa·βe·lo·'to·ðo] *mf inv inf* know-it-all

**saber** [sa·'βer] *irr* **I.** *vt* **1.** (*conocer*) to know; **¿sabes mi nombre?** do you know my name?; **~ (mucho) de algo** to know (a lot) about sth; **¿se puede ~ dónde/cómo/quién...?** can sb tell me where/how/who ...?; **vete tú/vaya usted a ~** it's anyone's guess; **(al menos) que yo sepa** as far as I know; **para que lo sepas** for your information; **¡y qué sé yo!** how should I know! **2.** (*poder*) **sabe (hablar) ruso** he/she can speak Russian **3.** (*noticia*) to find out; **lo supe por mi hermano** I heard about it from my brother; **no sé nada de Ana** I have no news of Ana **II.** *vi* **1.** **~ a algo** to taste of sth; **sabe bien/mal** it tastes good/bad **2.** (*agradar*) **me supo a poco** it should have been longer; **me supo mal aquella respuesta** that reply upset me **3.** (*poder*) **~ de algo** to know how to do sth **III.** *vr* to know; **sabérselas todas** *inf* to know all the tricks **IV.** *m* knowledge ▶ **el ~ no ocupa lugar** *prov* you can't know too much

**sabichoso, -a** [sa·βi·'tʃo·so, -a] *adj Cuba, PRico* pedantic; (*sabiondo*) know-it-all

**sabiduría** [sa·βi·ðu·'ri·a] *f* knowledge; (*sensatez*) wisdom

**sabiendas** [sa·'βjen·das] **a ~** knowingly

**sabi(h)ondo, -a** [sa·'βjon·do, -a] *m, f* know-it-all; (*niño*) smarty pants

**sabio, -a** ['sa·βjo, -a] **I.** *adj* wise **II.** *m, f* scholar

**sable** ['sa·βle] *m* saber

**sabor** [sa·'βor] *m* taste (**a** of); **dejar un mal ~ de boca** to leave a nasty taste in one's mouth

**saborear** [sa·βo·re·'ar] *vt* to savor; (*triunfo*) to relish

**sabotaje** [sa·βo·'ta·xe] *m* sabotage

**sabotear** [sa·βo·te·'ar] *vt* to sabotage

**sabroso, -a** [sa·'βro·so, -a] *adj* tasty

**sabueso, -a** [sa·'βwe·so, -a] *m* bloodhound; *fig* sleuth

**sacabuche** [sa·ka·'βu·tʃe] *m Méx* pointed knife

**sacacorchos** [sa·ka·'kor·tʃos] *m inv* corkscrew

**sacapuntas** [sa·ka·'pun·tas] *m inv* pencil sharpener

**sacar** <c → qu> [sa·'kar] **I.** *vt* **1.** (*de un sitio*) to take out, to remove; (*agua*) to draw; (*diente*) to pull (out); (*entrada, billete, votos*) to get; (*mancha*) to remove; (*foto*) to take; (*parte del cuerpo*) to stick out; **~ a bailar** to invite to dance; **~ a alguien de la cama/cárcel** to get sb out of bed/jail; **~ a pasear** to take out for a walk; **¿de dónde lo has sacado?** where did you get it from? **2.** (*de una situación*) to get; **~ adelante** (*persona*) to look after; (*negocio*) to run; (*niño*) to bring up **3.** (*obtener*) to obtain; MIN to extract; **~ en claro** (**de**) to gather (from); **no ~ ni para vivir** not to make enough to live on; **~ a alguien 10 dólares** to squeeze 10 dollars out of sb **4.** (*producto*) to bring out; **~ a la venta** to put on sale [*o the market*]; (*libro*) to publish **5.** (*mostrar*) to show; (*desenterrar*) to unearth; **~ algo a relucir** to bring sth up **II.** *vi* (*tenis*) to serve; (*fútbol: portero*) to take a goal kick; (*fútbol: saque de banda*) to take a throw-in

**sacarina** [sa·ka·'ri·na] *f* saccharin

**sacerdote** [sa·ser·'ðo·te, sa·θer-] *m* priest

**saciar** [sa·'sjar, -'θjar] **I.** *vt* (*hambre, curiosidad*) to satisfy; (*instintos sexuales*) to satiate; (*sed*) to quench **II.** *vr:* **~se** to satiate oneself

**saciedad** [sa·sje·'ðad, sa·θje-] *f* satiation; **repetir hasta la ~** to repeat over and over

**saco** ['sa·ko] *m* 1. sack; ~ **de dormir** sleeping bag; **entrar a** ~ to loot 2. *AmL* (*prenda*) jacket ▸ **en el mismo** ~ in the same boat

**sacón, -ona** [sa·'kon, -·'ko·na] *m, f Méx inf* chicken

**sacramento** [sa·kra·'men·to] *m* sacrament

**sacrificar** <c → qu> [sa·kri·fi·'kar] I. *vt* to sacrifice; *fig* to give up; (*animal*) to slaughter II. *vr* ~**se por algo/alguien** to sacrifice oneself for sth/sb

**sacrificio** [sa·kri·'fi·sjo, -'fi·θjo] *m* sacrifice

**sacrilegio** [sa·kri·'le·xjo] *m* sacrilege

**sacudida** [sa·ku·'di·da] *f* shake; ~ **eléctrica** electric shock; ~ **sísmica** earthquake; **el coche pegaba** ~**s** the car was jolting; **dale una** ~ **a la alfombra** shake the carpet

**sacudir** [sa·ku·'dir] *vt* to shake

**sádico, -a** ['sa·di·ko, -a] I. *adj* sadistic II. *m, f* sadist

**sadomasoquismo** [sa·do·ma·so·'kis·mo] *m* sadomasochism

**safari** [sa·'fa·ri] *m* safari

**sagaz** [sa·'ɣas, -'ɣaθ] *adj* astute

**sagitario** [sa·xi·'ta·rjo] *m* Sagittarius

**sagrado, -a** <sacratísimo> [sa·'ɣra·do] *adj* sacred

**sagú** [sa·'ɣu] *m AmC* arrowroot; (*harina*) sago

**sal** [sal] *f* 1. salt; ~ **marina** sea salt; ~ **gorda** [*o* **gruesa**] *Méx* coarse [*o* rock] salt; ~**es de baño** bath salts 2. (*gracia*) wit; (*encanto*) charm 3. *AmL* (*fario*) bad luck

**sala** ['sa·la] *f* 1. room; (*grande*) hall; ~ **de espera/de estar** waiting/living room 2. *jur* courtroom; **Sala de lo Civil/Penal** Civil/Criminal Court

**salado, -a** [sa·'la·do, -a] *adj* 1. salty 2. (*gracioso*) witty; (*encantador*) charming 3. *AmL* (*infortunado*) unfortunate

**salamanca** [sa·la·'man·ka] *f* 1. *Arg zool* flat-headed salamander 2. *CSur* (*cueva*) natural cave

**salamandra** [sa·la·'man·dra] *f* salamander; ~ **acuática** newt

**salame** [sa·'la·me] *adj Arg inf* fool

**salar** [sa·'lar] *vt* 1. to add salt to; (*para*

*conservar*) to salt 2. *AmL* (*echar a perder*) to spoil

**salarial** [sa·la·'rjal] *adj* wage

**salario** [sa·'la·rjo] *m* wages *pl*

**salchicha** [sal·'tʃi·tʃa] *f* sausage; **perro** ~ *inf* dachshund

**salchichón** [sal·tʃi·'tʃon] *m* ≈ salami

**saldar** [sal·'dar] *vt* (*cuenta*) to pay; (*deuda*) to pay off

**saldo** ['sal·do] *m* balance; (*pago*) payment; ~ **de la cuenta** account balance

**salero** [sa·'le·ro] *m* salt shaker; (*gracia*) wit

**saleroso, -a** [sa·le·'ro·so, -a] *adj inf* (*ingenioso*) witty; (*encantador*) charming

**salida** [sa·'li·da] *f* 1. (*puerta*) way out; **a la** ~ **del teatro** coming out of the theater; **callejón sin** ~ dead end; ~ **de emergencia** emergency exit 2. *aviat, ferro* departure; (*barco*) sailing 3. *astr* rising; ~ **del sol** sunrise 4. *dep* start 5. *com* sale; (*partida*) consignment; ~ **de capital** capital outflow

**salidor, -a** [sa·li·'dor, -·'do·ra] *adj AmL* party-loving; **es muy** ~ he likes to go out a lot

**salina** [sa·'li·na] *f* salt works; (*mina*) salt mine

**salir** [sa·'lir] *irr* I. *vi* 1. (*al exterior*) to go out; (*irse*) to go away; ~ **a dar una vuelta** to go out for a stroll; ~ **con alguien** to go out with sb; ~ **adelante** to make progress; ~ **de un programa** to exit a program 2. (*de viaje*) to leave; (*avión*) to depart; **para** ~ **de dudas...** to clear up any doubts...; ~ **ganando/perdiendo/ileso** to come out the better/the worse/unscathed 3. (*flores, fuente*) to come out; (*sol*) to rise; ~ **a la luz** to come to light; ~ **en la tele** to be on TV 4. **este niño ha salido a su padre** the boy takes after his father 5. *dep* to start 6. (*costar*) to cost II. *vr*: ~**se** to spill; (*líquido*) to overflow; (*leche*) to boil over ▸ ~**se con la suya** to get one's own way

**saliva** [sa·'li·βa] *f* saliva

**salmo** ['sal·mo] *m* psalm

**salmón** [sal·'mon] I. *adj* salmon-pink II. *m* salmon

**salmuera** [sal·'mwe·ra] *f* brine

**salón** [sa·'lon] *m* hall; (*en casa*) living-room; ~ **de actos** assembly hall

**salpicadera** [sal·pi·ka·'de·ra] *f Méx* mud-guard

**salpicar** <c → qu> [sal·pi·'kar] *vt* (*rociar*) to sprinkle; (*pintura*) to splash; (*manchar*) to spatter

**salpicón** [sal·pi·'kon] *m* **1.** ≈ salmagundi **2.** *Col, Ecua* cold drink of fruit juice

**salpimentar** <e → ie> [sal·pi·men·'tar] *vt* to add salt and pepper

**salsa** ['sal·sa] *f* **1.** sauce; (*caldo*) gravy; ~ **verde** parsley sauce (*to accompany fish*); *Méx* sauce made of green tomatoes, chili, garlic and cilantro; ~ **de tomate** tomato sauce **2.** (*gracia*) humor **3.** MÚS salsa ▶ **estar en su propia ~** to be in one's element

**salsamentaría** [sal·sa·men·ta·ri·'a] *f Col* delicatessen

**saltamontes** [sal·ta·'mon·tes] *m inv* grasshopper

**saltar** [sal·'tar] **I.** *vi* **1.** to jump; ~ **de alegría** to jump for joy; ~ **a la cuerda** to skip; ~ **al agua** to jump into the water; ~ **con paracaídas** to make a parachute jump **2.** (*explotar*) to explode; ~ **en pedazos** to break into pieces; ~ **por los aires** to blow up; (*plomos*) to blow; (*chispas*) to fly up **3.** (*desprenderse*) to come off ▶ **estar a la que salta** to look out for an opportunity **II.** *vt* to jump (over); (*animal*) to cover **III.** *vr:* ~**se** to come off; **se me ~on las lágrimas** my eyes filled with tears; (*ley, norma*) to break; (*línea, párrafo*) to skip

**salto** ['sal·to] *m* **1.** jump; **de** [*o* **en**] **un ~** with one jump; **dar un ~** to jump; *fig* to jump with fright; **dar ~s de alegría** to jump for joy; ~ **de altura/longitud** high/long jump; ~ **mortal** somersault; ~ **del potro** vault; ~ **de cama** negligee; ~ **de página** page break **2.** (*omisión*) gap ▶ ~ **de agua** waterfall

**salubridad** [sa·lu·βri·'dad] *f AmL* hygiene

**salud** [sa·'lud] *f* health; **¡~!** (*al estornudar*) bless you!; (*al brindar*) good health!

**saludable** [sa·lu·'da·βle] *adj* healthy

**saludar** [sa·lu·'dar] *vt* **1.** to greet; (*con la mano*) to wave; **estos ya ni se saludan** they don't even speak to each other now **2.** (*recibir*) to welcome **3.** (*mandar saludos*) to send regards to

**saludo** [sa·'lu·do] *m* greeting; **con un cordial ~** yours sincerely; **¡dele ~s de mi parte!** give him/her my regards; **tu madre te manda ~s** your mother sends her love

**salvación** [sal·βa·'sjon, ·'θjon] *f* rescue

**Salvador** [sal·βa·'dor] *m* **El ~** El Salvador

**salvadoreño, -a** [sal·βa·do·'re·ɲo, ·a] *adj, m, f* Salvadoran

**salvaguardar** [sal·βa·ɣwar·'dar] *vt* to safeguard; (*derechos, intereses*) to protect

**salvaje** [sal·'βa·xe] **I.** *adj* (*planta, animal*) wild; (*persona*) uncivilized; (*acto*) savage **II.** *mf* savage; (*persona ruda*) barbarian

**salvamento** [sal·βa·'men·to] *m* rescue

**salvar** [sal·'βar] **I.** *vt* to save; ~ **del peligro** to save from danger; (*foso*) to jump across; (*distancia*) to cover; (*obstáculo, problema*) to overcome; ~ **las apariencias** to keep up appearances **II.** *vr:* ~**se** to save oneself; **¡sálvese quien pueda!** every man for himself!

**salvavidas** [sal·βa·'βi·das] **I.** *m inv* life-belt; **bote ~** lifeboat; **chaleco ~** life-jacket **II.** *mf inv* lifeguard

**salvedad** [sal·βe·'dad] *f* exception; **con la ~ de que...** with the proviso that...

**salvo** ['sal·βo] *prep* except; ~ **que** +*subj* unless

**salvo, -a** ['sal·βo, ·a] *adj* **poner a ~ to** put in a safe place; **sano y ~** safe and sound

**samba** ['sam·ba] *f* samba

**sambumbia** [sam·'bum·bja] *f* **1.** *Col* **volver algo ~** to smash sth to pieces **2.** *Cuba* drink of cane syrup, water and peppers **3.** *Méx* pineapple cordial

**san** [san] *adj* Saint

**sanar** [sa·'nar] **I.** *vi* ~ **de algo** to recover from sth **II.** *vt* to cure

**sanatorio** [sa·na·'to·rjo] *m* sanatorium

**sanción** [san·'sjon, ·'θjon] *f* **1.** (*multa*) penalty; ECON sanction **2.** (*ley*) passing

**sancionar** [san·sjo·'nar, san·θjo·] *vt* (*cas-*

S

*tigar*) to punish; ECON to impose sanctions on; JUR to ratify

**sancochar** [san·ko·'tʃar] *vt AmL* to parboil

**sancocho** [san·'ko·tʃo] *m* 1. *AmC, PRico, Ven* fuss 2. *And, Ven* parboiled meat

**sandalia** [san·'da·lja] *f* sandal

**sándalo** ['san·da·lo] *m* 1. (*árbol*) sandalwood tree 2. (*madera*) sandalwood

**sandez** [san·'des, -'deθ] *f inf* **no decir más que sandeces** to say nothing but foolish things

**sandía** [san·'di·a] *f* watermelon

**sandinista** [san·di·'nis·ta] *adj, mf* Sandinista

**sandunga** [san·'duŋ·ga] *f Col, Chile, PRico inf* celebration

**sándwich** ['san·gwitʃ] *m* toasted sandwich

**saneamiento** [sa·nea·'mjen·to] *m* (*edificio*) repair; (*terreno*) drainage; (*de economía*) reform

**sanear** [sa·ne·'ar] *vt* (*edificio*) to clean up; (*tierra*) to drain; (*economía*) to reform

**sangrar** [san·'grar] I. *vi* to bleed; **estar sangrando por la nariz** to have a nosebleed II. *vt* to bleed; (*dinero*) to bleed dry; (*agua*) to drain off

**sangre** ['san·gre] *f* blood; **a ~ fría** in cold blood; **animales de ~ caliente/fría** warm/cold-blooded animals; (*caballo de*) **pura ~** thoroughbred (horse); **dar** [*o donar*] **~** to give [*o donate*] blood; **hacer ~** to draw blood; **llevar algo en la ~** to have sth in the blood; (*de familia*) to run in the family; **le hierve la ~** his/her blood boils ▶ **sudar ~** to go through hardships; **tener mala ~** to be bad-tempered

**sangría** [san·'gri·a] *f* 1. TIPO indentation 2. (*bebida*) sangria

**sangriento, -a** [san·'grjen·to, -a] *adj* bloody

**sangriligero, -a** [san·gri·li·'xe·ro, -a] *adj AmC* nice

**sangripesado, -a** [san·gri·pe·'sa·do, -a] *adj AmC* disagreeable

**sangrón, -ona** [san·'gron, -·'gro·na] *adj Méx inf* boring; **su novio es un ~, no lo soporto** her boyfriend is a bore, I can't stand him

**sanguaraña** [san·gwa·'ra·ɲa] *f Ecua, Perú* evasion; **déjate de ~s** stop beating around the bush

**sanguijuela** [san·gi·'xwe·la] *f* leech; *pey* bloodsucker

**sanguíneo, -a** [san·'gi·neo, -a] *adj* blood; **grupo ~** blood type

**sanidad** [sa·ni·'dad] *f* health; **~ (pública)** public health

**sanitario, -a** [sa·ni·'ta·rjo, -a] I. *adj* health; (*aparatos, medidas*) sanitary II. *m, f* health worker

**sanitarios** [sa·ni·'ta·rjo] *mpl* bathroom fixtures

**sano, -a** ['sa·no, -a] *adj* healthy; (*no roto*) intact; **cortar por lo ~** to take extreme measures; **salir ~ y salvo** to emerge safe and sound

**santiaguino, -a** [san·tja·'yi·no, -a] I. *adj* of/from Santiago (in Chile) II. *m, f* native/inhabitant of Santiago (in Chile)

**santiamén** [san·tja·'men] *m* **en un ~** in a jiffy

**santidad** [san·ti·'dad] *f* holiness

**santo, -a** ['san·to, -a] I. *adj* holy; (*piadoso*) saintly; **campo ~** cemetery; **Jueves Santo** Maundy Thursday; **Semana Santa** Easter; **Viernes Santo** Good Friday II. *m, f* saint; **día de Todos los Santos** All Saint's Day; **el día de mi ~** my saint's day ▶ **no ser ~ de la devoción de alguien** to not be particularly fond of sb; **ser mano de ~** to be good at everything

**santuario** [san·tu·'a·rjo] *m* 1. (*templo*) shrine; (*capilla*) chapel 2. (*refugio*) sanctuary 3. *Col* (*tesoro*) buried treasure

**saña** ['sa·ɲa] *f* (*ira*) anger; (*rencor*) viciousness; **lo hizo con toda la mala ~** he/she did it with great cruelty

**sapo** ['sa·po] *m* toad

**saque** ['sa·ke] *m* (*fútbol*) goal kick; (*fútbol americano*) kick-off; (*tenis*) serve; **~ de esquina** corner kick

**saquear** [sa·ke·'ar] *vt* to loot

**saqueo** [sa·'keo] *m* looting

**sarampión** [sa·ram·'pjon] *m* measles

**sarape** [sa·'ra·pe] *m Méx* blanket

**sarazo, -a** [sa·'ra·so, -a] *adj Col, Cuba, Méx, Ven* ripening

**sarcasmo** [sar·'kas·mo] *m* sarcasm

**sarcástico, -a** [sar·'kas·ti·ko, -a] *adj* sarcastic

**sardina** [sar·'di·na] *f* sardine; (**estar**) **como ~s en lata** to be packed like sardines

**sargento** [sar·'xen·to] *m* sergeant

**sarpullido** [sar·pu·'ʝi·do, -'ʎi·do] *m* rash

**sarro** ['sa·rro] *m* tartar

**sarta** ['sar·ta] *f* **una ~ de mentiras** a string of lies

**sartén** [sar·'ten] *f* frying pan ▶ **tener la ~ por el <u>mango</u>** to have the whip hand

**sastre, -a** ['sas·tre, -a] *m, f* tailor

**sastrería** [sas·tre·'ri·a] *f* tailor's shop

**satánico, -a** [sa·'ta·ni·ko, -a] *adj* satanic

**satélite** [sa·'te·li·te] *m* satellite

**sátira** ['sa·ti·ra] *f* satire

**satírico, -a** [sa·'ti·ri·ko, -a] **I.** *adj* satirical **II.** *m, f* satirist

**satisfacción** [sa·tis·fak·'sjon, -faɣ·'θjon] *f* satisfaction; (*alegría*) happiness; **a mi entera ~** to my complete satisfaction

**satisfacer** [sa·tis·fa·'ser, -'θer] *irr como* **hacer I.** *vt* to satisfy; (*sed*) to quench; (*demanda*) to settle; (*requisitos*) to meet **II.** *vr:* **~se** to satisfy oneself

**satisfactorio, -a** [sa·tis·fak·'to·rjo, -a] *adj* satisfactory; **no ser ~** to be unsatisfactory; **resulta ~...** it is pleasing...

**satisfecho, -a** [sa·tis·'fe·tʃo, -a] **I.** *pp de* **satisfacer II.** *adj* contented; (*exigencias, deseo sexual*) satisfied; **~ de sí mismo** self-satisfied; **estar ~** (*harto*) to have had enough

**saturación** [sa·tu·ra·'sjon, -'θjon] *f* saturation

**saturar** [sa·tu·'rar] *vt* to saturate

**sauce** ['sau·se, 'sau·θe] *m* willow; **~ llorón** weeping willow

**saúco** [sa·'u·ko] *m*, **sauco** [sau·ko] *m* elder

**saudí** <saudíes> [sau·'di], **saudita** [sau·'di·ta] **I.** *adj* Saudi; **Arabia Saudí** Saudi Arabia **II.** *mf* Saudi

**sauna** ['sau·na] *f* sauna

**savia** ['sa·βja] *f* sap; (*energía*) vitality

**saxofón** [sak·so·'fon] *m*, **saxófono** [sak·'so·fo·no] *m* saxophone

**sazón** [sa·'son, -'θon] *f* **1.** (*condimento*) flavor **2.** (*madurez*) ripeness; **estar en ~** to be ripe ▶ **<u>fuera</u> de ~** out of season; **a la ~** at that time

**sazonar** [sa·so·'nar, sa·θo·-] *vt* to season; (*madurar*) to ripen

**se** [se] *pron pers* **1.** *reflexivo:* *m sing* himself; *f sing* herself; *de cosa* itself; *pl* themselves; *de Ud.* yourself; *de Uds.* yourselves; *de cosa* itself; *pl* themselves; *de Ud.* yourself; *de Uds.* yourselves **2.** *objeto indirecto:* *m sing* to him; *f sing* to her; *a una cosa* to it; *pl* to them; *a Ud., Uds.* to you; **mi hermana ~ lo prestó a su amiga** my sister lent it to her friend **3.** (*impers*) you; **~ aprende mucho aquí** you learn a lot here **4.** (*pasiva*) **~ confirmó la sentencia** the sentence was confirmed; **~ dice que...** it is said that...

**sé** [se] *1. pres de* **saber**

**SE** *abr de* **sudeste** SE

**sebo** ['se·βo] *m* grease; **hacer ~** *Arg inf* to idle

**seca** ['se·ka] *f* *AmL* drought; (*temporada*) dry season

**secador** [se·ka·'dor] *m* (*de ropa*) clothes horse; (*de pelo*) hairdryer

**secadora** [se·ka·'do·ra] *f* tumble dryer

**secante¹** [se·'kan·te] *adj* drying; **línea ~** secant; **papel ~** blotting paper

**secante²** [se·'kan·te] *f* MAT drying

**secar** <c → qu> [se'kar] **I.** *vt* to dry; (*herida*) to heal; (*enjugar*) to wipe **II.** *vr:* **~se** to dry up; (*fuente*) to run dry; (*herida*) to heal up; (*enjugar*) to wipe

**sección** [sek·'sjon, seɣ·'θjon] *f* **1.** (*parte*) section **2.** (*departamento*) branch **3.** (*corte*) cross-section

**seco, -a** ['se·ko, -a] *adj* **1.** dry; **golpe ~** dull blow; **limpiar en ~** to dry clean **2.** (*desecado, río*) dried up; **frutos ~s** dried fruit and nuts **3.** (*marchito*) withered **4.** (*flaco*) skinny **5.** (*tajante*) curt ▶ **a secas** on its own; **en ~** suddenly; **frenar en ~** to pull up sharply

**secreción** [se·kre·'sjon, -'θjon] *f* segregation; (*sustancia*) secretion

**secretaría** [se·kre·ta·'ri·a] *f* **1.** (*oficina*) secretary's office **2.** (*cargo*) secretary position **3.** (*gobierno, organismo*) secretariat

**secretariado** [se·kre·ta·'rja·do] *m* secretary's office; (*cargo*) secretary position

**S**

**secretario, -a** [se·kre·'ta·rjo] *m, f* secretary

**secretear** [se·kre·te·'ar] *vi inf* to exchange secrets

**secreto** [se·'kre·to] *m* secret; (*reserva*) secrecy; ~ **profesional** trade secret; ~ **a voces** open secret; **en** ~ in secret; **mantener en** ~ to keep secret; **guardar un** ~ to keep a secret

**secreto, -a** [se·'kre·to, -a] *adj* secret

**secta** ['sek·ta] *f* sect

**sectario, -a** ['sek·ta·rjo, -a] I. *adj* sectarian; (*fanático*) fanatical II. *m, f* member of a sect; (*fanático*) fanatic

**sector** [sek·'tor] *m* sector; (*grupo*) group; ~ **económico/servicios** economic/service sector; ~ **hotelero** hotel industry; ~ **multimedia/de la informática** multimedia/computing sector

**secuela** [se·'kwe·la] *f* consequence; (*enfermedad*) after-effect; **dejar ~s** to have after-effects

**secuencia** [se·'kwen·sja, -θja] *f* sequence; (*palabras*) word order; ~ **de caracteres** series of characters

**secuestrador(a)** [se·kwes·tra·'dor, -·'do·ra] *m(f)* kidnapper

**secuestrar** [se·kwes·'trar] *vt* to kidnap

**secuestro** [se·'kwes·tro] *m* kidnapping

**secular** [se·ku·'lar] *adj* secular; *fig* age-old

**secundar** [se·kun·'dar] *vt* to second

**secundario, -a** [se·kun·'da·rjo] *adj* secondary; (*cargo*) minor; **papel** ~ supporting role; **esto es** ~ that's of minor importance

**sed** [sed] *f* thirst; **tener** ~ to be thirsty; ~ **de algo** longing for sth; ~ **de venganza/riquezas** thirst for vengeance/riches

**seda** ['se·da] *f* silk; **de** ~ **natural** of pure silk; **como una** ~ (*tacto*) as smooth as silk; (*persona*) sweet-tempered; (*sin tropiezos*) smoothly

**sedante** [se·'dan·te] I. *adj* (*de efecto*) ~ soothing II. *m* sedative

**sedar** [se·'dar] *vt* to sedate

**sede** ['se·de] *f* seat; (*empresa*) headquarters *pl*

**sedentario, -a** [se·den·'ta·rjo, -a] *adj* sedentary

**sediento, -a** [se·'djen·to, -a] *adj* thirsty; ~ **de algo** thirsty for sth

**sedimentación** [se·di·men·ta·'sjon, -'θjon] *f* sedimentation

**sedimento** [se·di·'men·to] *m* sediment

**sedoso, -a** [se·'do·so, -a] *adj* silky

**seducción** [se·duk·'sjon, -duɣ·'θjon] *f* seduction

**seducir** [se·du·'sir, -'θir] *irr como* traducir *vt* to seduce; (*fascinar*) to charm

**seductor(a)** [se·duk·'tor, -·'to·ra] I. *adj* seductive; (*tentador*) tempting; (*idea*) captivating II. *m(f)* seducer; (*encantador*) charmer

**segar** [se·'ɣar] *irr como* fregar *vt* to reap; (*hierba*) to mow

**segmentar** [seɣ·men·'tar] *vt* to divide into segments

**segmento** [seɣ·'men·to] *m* segment

**segregar** <g → gu> [se·ɣre·'ɣar] *vt* to segregate

**seguido, -a** [se·'ɣi·do, -a] *adj* **1.** consecutive; **un año** ~ a whole year **2.** (*recto*) straight; **todo** ~ straight on

**seguidor(a)** [se·ɣi·'dor] *m(f)* supporter; DEP fan

**seguimiento** [se·ɣi·'mjen·to] *m* chase; ~ (*médico*) (medical) follow-up

**seguir** [se·'ɣir] *irr* I. *vt* **1.** to follow; ~ **un curso de informática** to take a computing course **2.** (*perseguir*) to chase **3.** ~ **adelante** to carry on; **¡que sigas bien!** I hope you keep well! II. *vi* **sigue por esta calle** follow this street

**según** [se·'ɣun] I. *prep* according to; ~ **la ley** in accordance with the law II. *adv* **1.** (*como*) as; ~ **lo convenido** as we agreed **2.** (*mientras*) while; **podemos hablar** ~ **vamos andando** we can talk as we walk **3.** (*eventualidad*) ~ it depends; ~ **el trabajo iré o no** I'll go if work permits

**segunda** [se·'ɣun·da] *f* AUTO second gear; FERRO second class ▶ **con ~s** with veiled meaning

**segundo** [se·'ɣun·do] *m* second

**segundo, -a** [se·'ɣun·do, -a] I. *adj* second; **primo** ~ second cousin; **vivir en el** ~ to live on the second floor II. *m, f* second (one); *v. t.* octavo

**seguramente** [se·ɣu·ra·'men·te] *adv* certainly; (*probablemente*) probably

**seguridad** [se·ɣu·ri·ˈðað] f 1. (*protección*) security; **Seguridad Social** Social Security 2. (*certeza*) certainty; **para mayor ~** to be sure of it 3. (*firmeza*) confidence; **habla con mucha ~** he/she speaks with great self-confidence

**seguro** [se·ˈɣu·ro] I. m 1. (*contrato*) insurance; **~ médico** medical [o health] insurance; **~ a riesgo parcial/a todo riesgo** third-party/comprehensive insurance 2. (*mecanismo*) safety device II. adv for sure; **a buen** [o de] **~** surely; **sobre ~** on safe ground

**seguro, -a** [se·ˈɣu·ro, -a] adj 1. (*sin peligro*) safe 2. (*firme*) secure 3. (*sólido*) solid 4. (*convencido*) certain; **~ de sí mismo** confident; **¿estás ~?** are you sure?

**seis** [seis] adj inv m six; v. t. **ocho**

**seiscientos, -as** [sei·ˈsjen·tos, -as; -ˈθjen·tos, -as] adj six hundred; v. t. **ochocientos**

**seísmo** [se·ˈis·mo] m (*temblor*) tremor; (*terremoto*) earthquake

**selección** [se·lek·ˈsjon, -ley·ˈθjon] f selection; **~ nacional** national team

**seleccionar** [se·lek·sjo·ˈnar, -ley·θjo·ˈnar] vt to select

**selectividad** [se·lek·ti·βi·ˈðað] f university entrance exam

**selectivo, -a** [se·lek·ˈti·βo] adj selective; **método ~** selective criterion

**selecto, -a** [se·ˈlek·to, -a] adj select; (*ambiente*) exclusive

**sellar** [se·ˈjar, -ˈʎar] vt 1. (*timbrar*) to stamp 2. (*concluir*) to end 3. (*precintar*) to seal; (*cerrar*) to close

**sello** [ˈse·jo, -ʎo] m 1. stamp; **~ de garantía** seal of guarantee; **esta película lleva el ~ de su director** this film carries the stamp of its director 2. (*precinto*) seal

**selva** [ˈsel·βa] f forest; (*tropical*) jungle; **~ virgen** virgin forest

**semáforo** [se·ˈma·fo·ro] m traffic lights pl

**semana** [se·ˈma·na] f week; **fin de ~** weekend

**semanal** [se·ma·ˈnal] adj weekly

**semanario** [se·ma·ˈna·rjo] m weekly (magazine)

**semanario, -a** [se·ma·ˈna·rjo, -a] adj weekly

**semántica** [se·ˈman·ti·ka] f semantics

**semblante** [sem·ˈblan·te] m face; (*expresión*) appearance; **tener un ~ alegre** to look cheerful

**sembrar** <e → ie> [sem·ˈbrar] vt to sow; (*esparcir*) to scatter; **~ para el futuro** to sow for the future; **~ el terror** to spread terror

**semejante** [se·me·ˈxan·te] I. adj similar; (*tal*) such; **~ persona** such a person II. m fellow man

**semejanza** [se·me·ˈxan·sa, -θa] f similarity; (*física*) resemblance

**semejar** [se·me·ˈxar] I. vi to resemble II. vr: **~se** to look alike; **~se a alguien** to look like sb

**semen** [ˈse·men] m semen

**semental** [se·men·ˈtal] I. adj breeding; **caballo ~** stud II. m stud

**semestral** [se·mes·ˈtral] adj half-yearly

**semestre** [se·ˈmes·tre] m six-month period; UNIV semester

**semicírculo** [se·mi·ˈsir·ku·lo, -ˈθir·ku·lo] m semicircle

**semifinal** [se·mi·fi·ˈnal] f semi-final; **pasar a la ~** to get through to the semi-final

**semilla** [se·ˈmi·ja, -ʎa] f seed

**seminario** [se·mi·ˈna·rjo] m seminary

**sémola** [ˈse·mo·la] f semolina

**senado** [se·ˈna·do] m senate

**senador(a)** [se·na·ˈdor, -·ˈdo·ra] m(f) senator

**sencillamente** [sen·si·ja·ˈmen·te, sen·θi·ʎa-] adv simply

**sencillez** [sen·si·ˈjes, sen·θi·ˈʎeθ] f simplicity; (*naturalidad*) naturalness

**sencillo, -a** [sen·ˈsi·jo, -a; -ˈθi·ʎo, -a] adj simple; (*fácil*) easy; **gente sencilla** unaffected people

**senda** [ˈsen·da] f, **sendero** [sen·ˈde·ro] m path; (*método*) way

**sendos, -as** [ˈsen·dos, -as] adj each of two; **llegamos en ~ coches** we both arrived by car

**senil** [se·ˈnil] adj senile

**senilidad** [se·ni·li·ˈðað] f senility

**seno** [ˈse·no] m 1. (*concavidad*) hollow 2. ANAT, MAT sinus 3. (*matriz*) womb 4. (*pecho*) breast

**S**

**sensación** [sen·sa·'sjon, -'θjon] *f* **1.** (*sentimiento*) feeling **2.** (*novedad*) sensation; **causar ~** to cause a sensation

**sensacional** [sen·sa·sjo·'nal, sen·sa·θjo-] *adj* sensational

**sensacionalismo** [sen·sa·sjo·na·'lis·mo, sen·sa·θjo-] *m* sensationalism

**sensacionalista** [sen·sa·sjo·na·'lis·ta, sen·sa·θjo-] *adj* sensationalist; **prensa ~** tabloid press

**sensatez** [sen·sa·'tes, -'teθ] *f* good sense

**sensato, -a** [sen·'sa·to, -a] *adj* sensible

**sensibilidad** [sen·si·βi·li·'dad] *f* sensitivity

**sensibilizar** <z → c> [sen·si·βi·li·'sar, -'θar] *vt* to sensitize

**sensible** [sen·'si·βle] *adj* sensitive; (*impresionable*) impressionable

**sensiblemente** [sen·si·βle·'men·te] *adv* **1.** (*perceptible*) perceptibly **2.** (*evidente*) markedly

**sensitivo, -a** [sen·si·'ti·βo, -a] *adj* sensory

**sensor** [sen·'sor] *m* sensor

**sensorial** [sen·so·'rjal] *adj* sensory; **órgano ~** sense organ

**sensual** [sen·su·'al] *adj* sensual

**sensualidad** [sen·swa·li·'dad] *f* sensuality

**sentado, -a** [sen·'ta·do, -a] *adj* **dar algo por ~** to take sth for granted

**sentador(a)** [sen·ta·'dor, -·'do·ra] *adj Arg, Chile* becoming

**sentar** <e → ie> [sen·'tar] **I.** *vi* (*ropa*) to suit; **esa chaqueta me sienta bien/mal** that jacket suits/doesn't suit me; **~ bien/mal a alguien** (*comida*) to agree/disagree with sb; **~ como un tiro** to be as welcome as a hole in the head **II.** *vt* to sit; **estar sentado** to be sitting down; **estar bien sentado** *fig* to be well established **III.** *vr:* **~se 1.** to sit down; **¡siéntese!** have a seat! **2.** (*establecerse*) to settle down

**sentencia** [sen·'ten·sja, -θja] *f* sentence; **dictar ~** to pronounce sentence

**sentenciar** [sen·ten·'sjar, -θjar] *vt* (*condenar*) to sentence **2.** (*decidir*) to give one's opinion on [*o* about]

**sentido** [sen·'ti·do] *m* **1.** (*facultad, signi-*

*ficado*) sense; **~ común** common sense; **~ del deber/humor** sense of duty/humor; **doble ~** (*significado*) double meaning; (*dirección*) two-way; **con los cinco ~s (en)** totally absorbed (in); **estar sin ~** to be unconscious; **perder el ~** to lose consciousness; **sexto ~** sixth sense **2.** (*dirección*) direction; **en el ~ de la flecha** in the direction of the arrow; **en el ~ de las agujas del reloj** clockwise; **~ único** one-way

**sentido, -a** [sen·'ti·do, -a] *adj* (*conmovido*) deeply felt; (*sensible*) sensitive

**sentimental** [sen·ti·men·'tal] *adj* sentimental

**sentimentalismo** [sen·ti·men·ta·'lis·mo] *m* sentimentality

**sentimiento** [sen·ti·'mjen·to] *m* feeling; **sin ~s** unfeeling; (*pena*) sorrow; **le acompaño en el ~** please accept my condolences

**sentir** [sen·'tir] *irr* **I.** *vt* to feel; **sin ~** without noticing; (*lamentar*) to be sorry for; **lo siento mucho** I am very sorry; **siento que** +*subj* I'm sorry that **II.** *vr:* **~se** to feel; **~se bien/mal** to feel good/bad **III.** *m* opinion; (*sentimiento*) feeling

**seña** ['se·ɲa] *f* sign; **hacer ~s** to signal; **hablar por ~s** to talk in sign language

**señal** [se·'ɲal] *f* **1.** (*particularidad*) distinguishing mark **2.** (*signo*) sign; **~ de tráfico** road sign; **en ~ de** as a sign of; **dar ~es de vida** *fig* to show oneself **3.** TEL tone; **~ de comunicar** busy signal **4.** (*huella*) mark; **ni ~** no trace **5.** (*adelanto*) deposit; **paga y ~** first payment; **dejar una ~** to leave a deposit

**señalado, -a** [se·ɲa·'la·do, -a] *adj* **una fecha señalada** a special day

**señalar** [se·ɲa·'lar] *vt* **1.** (*anunciar*) to announce **2.** (*marcar, estigmatizar*) to mark **3.** (*mostrar*) to show **4.** (*indicar*) to point out **5.** (*fijar*) to fix

**señalización** [se·ɲa·li·sa·'sjon, -θa·'θjon] *f* signposting

**señalizar** <z → c> [se·ɲa·li·'sar, -'θar] *vt* to signpost

**señor(a)** [se·'ɲor, -·'ɲo·ra] **I.** *adj inf* **1.** (*noble*) lordly **2.** (*enorme*) huge **II.** *m(f)* **1.** (*dueño*) owner **2.** (*hombre*) (gentle)man; (*mujer*) wife; (*dama*)

lady; ¡~as y ~es! ladies and gentlemen!
**3.** (*título*) Mister, Mistress *m, f* **4. el
Señor** Our Lord

**señoría** [se·ɲo·'ri·a] *f* rule; **Su Señoría**
Your Lordship

**señori(a)l** [se·ɲo·'ril/se·ɲo·'rjal] *adj* lordly;
**casa ~** stately home

**señorito, -a** [se·ɲo·'ri·to, -a] *m, f* young
master, young lady *m, f*; (*título*) Master,
Miss *m, f*

**señuelo** [se·'nwe·lo] *m* decoy; *fig* lure

**separación** [se·pa·ra·'sjon, -'θjon] *f* separa-
ration; (*espacio*) distance

**separado** [se·pa·'ra·do] *adv* **por ~** separa-
rately

**separar** [se·pa·'rar] **I.** *vt* **1.** (*desunir*) to
separate; **~ algo de algo** to separate sth
from sth **2.** (*apartar*) to remove **II.** *vr:*
**~se** to separate

**separo** [se·'pa·ro] *m Méx* cell

**sepia** ['se·pja] *f* cuttlefish; **de color
~** sepia

**sept.** *abr de* **septiembre** September

**septentrional** [sep·ten·trjo·'nal] *adj elev*
northern

**septiembre** [sep·'tjem·bre] *m* September;
*v. t.* **marzo**

**séptimo, -a** ['sep·ti·mo, -a] *adj, m, f* seventh; *v. t.* **octavo**

**sepulcral** [se·pul·'kral] *adj* (*silencio*)
deathly

**sepulcro** [se·'pul·kro] *m* tomb

**sepultar** [se·pul·'tar] *vt* to bury; (*cubrir*)
to conceal

**sepultura** [se·pul·'tu·ra] *f* burial; (*tumba*)
grave; **dar ~ a alguien** to bury sb

**sequía** [se·'ki·a] *f* drought

**séquito** ['se·ki·to] *m* retinue

**ser** [ser] *irr* **I.** *aux* **las casas fueron
vendidas** the houses were sold; **era
de esperar** it was to be expected; **es
de esperar que** +*subj* it is to be hoped
that **II.** *vi* **1.** to be; **éramos cuatro**
there were four of us; **¿quién es?** who
is it?; TEL who's calling?; **soy Pepe** it's
me, Pepe; TEL this is Pepe; **es de noche**
it's night time; **son las cuatro** it's four
o'clock; **el que fue director** the former
director; **el concierto es en el pabellón** the concert is in the pavilion; **eso
fue en 2000** that was in 2000; **¿cuán-**

**to es todo?** how much is everything?
**2.** MAT **cuatro y cuatro son ocho** four
and four make eight **3.** (*convertirse*)
**¿qué quieres ~ de mayor?** what do
you want to be when you grow up?; **llegó a ~ ministro** he became a minister;
**¿qué es de él?** what's he doing now?;
**¿qué ha sido de ella?** whatever happened to her? **4.** (+ *de*) **~ de México**
to be from Mexico; **¿de quién es esto?**
whose is this?; **el paquete es de él** the
parcel belongs to him; **el anillo es de
plata** the ring is made of silver; **el coche es de color azul** the car is blue;
**yo soy de los que piensan que...**
I'm one of those who think that...; **de
no haber sido por ti** if it hadn't been
for you; **manera de ~** manner; **razón
de ~** raison d'être **5.** (+ *para*) **la película no es para niños** it's not a film
for children; **¿para quién es el vino?**
who is the wine for?; **no es para ponerse así** there's no need to get so angry; **es como para no hablarte más**
it's enough to never speak to you again
**6.** (+ *que*) **esto es que no lo has visto
bien** you can't have seen it properly;
**es que ahora no puedo** the thing is I
can't at the moment; **si es que merece
la pena** if it's worthwhile; **¡y es que
tenía unas ganas de acabarlo!** I was
longing to finish it!; **a no ~ que** +*subj*
unless **7.** (*futuro*) **¿~á capaz?** will he/
she be up to it? **8.** (*infin*) **todo puede
~** everything is possible; **¡no puede ~!**
that can't be!; **por lo que pueda ~** just
in case **9.** (*indicativo, condicional*) **es
más** what is more; **siendo así** that being so; **es igual** it doesn't matter; **sería
un buen líder** he'd be a fine leader
**10.** (*subj*) **si yo fuera tú** if I were you;
**si no fuera por eso...** if it weren't for
that...; **si por mí fuera** if it were up to
me; **me tratas como si fuera un niño**
you treat me like a child; **sea quien/
lo que sea** whoever/whatever it is;
**por listo que sea...** however clever he
is...; **o sea...** I mean...; **cómprame un
chupa-chups o lo que sea** buy me a
lollipop or something **III.** *m* being; FILOS
life; **~ vivo** living creature; **~ humano**

**S**

human being

**serenarse** [se·re·'nar·se] *vr* to calm down

**serenata** [se·re·'na·ta] *f* serenade

**serenidad** [se·re·ni·'dad] *f* calmness

**sereno, -a** [se·'re·no, -a] *adj* calm; (*sin nubes*) clear

**serial** [se·'rjal] *m* serial

**serie** ['se·rje] *f* 1. *t.* TV series *inv*; **asesino en ~** serial killer; **fuera de ~** outstanding 2. (*gran cantidad*) set; **fabricar en ~** to mass produce

**seriedad** [se·rje·'dad] *f* seriousness; **falta de ~** irresponsibility

**serio, -a** ['se·rjo, -a] *adj* 1. (*grave, sin bromas*) serious; **¿en ~?** are you serious?; **esto va en ~** this is in earnest 2. (*severo*) solemn 3. (*formal*) reliable 4. (*responsable*) trustworthy

**sermón** [ser·'mon] *m* sermon; **echar un ~ a alguien** to preach to sb

**sermonear** [ser·mo·ne·'ar] *vt inf* to lecture

**seropositivo, -a** [se·ro·po·si·'ti·βo, -a] *adj* HIV-positive

**serpentear** [ser·pen·te·'ar] *vi* to creep; *fig* to wind

**serpentina** [ser·pen·'ti·na] *f* streamer

**serpiente** [ser·'pjen·te] *f* snake; **~ de cascabel** rattlesnake

**serranía** [se·rra·'ni·a] *f* mountainous area

**serrano, -a** [se·'rra·no, -a] *adj* highland; **jamón ~** cured ham

**serrar** <e → ie> [se·'rrar] *vt* to saw

**serrín** [se·'rrin] *m* sawdust

**serruchar** [se·rru·'tʃar] *vt Arg, Chile, PRico* to saw

**serrucho** [se·'rru·tʃo] *m* handsaw

**servible** [ser·'βi·βle] *adj* serviceable

**servicial** [ser·βi·'sjal, -'θjal] *adj* obliging

**servicio** [ser·'βi·sjo, -θjo] *m* 1. service; **~ civil sustitutorio** community service; **~ a domicilio** home delivery; **estar de ~** to be on duty; **hacer un ~ a alguien** to do sb a service 2. (*retrete*) lavatory 3. DEP serve

**servidor** [ser·βi·'dor] *m* server

**servidor(a)** [ser·βi·'dor, --'do·ra] *m(f)* servant; **¿quién es el último? — ~** who is last in line? — I am

**servidumbre** [ser·βi·'dum·bre] *f* 1. (*per-*

*sonal*) servants *pl* 2. (*esclavitud*) servitude

**servil** [ser·'βil] *adj* servile

**servilismo** [ser·βi·'lis·mo] *m* servility

**servilleta** [ser·βi·'je·ta, -'ʎe·ta] *f* napkin

**servir** [ser'βir] *irr como pedir* I. *vi* 1. (*ser útil*) to be of use; **no sirve de nada** it's no use; **no sirve para nada** it's useless [*o* no use at all] 2. (*prestar un servicio*) to serve; **¿en qué puedo ~le?** can I help you? II. *vi, vt* (*comida*) to serve; (*bebida*) to pour out III. *vr:* **~se** 1. (*en la mesa*) to help oneself (*to*) 2. **sírvase cerrar la ventana** please close the window

**sésamo** ['se·sa·mo] *m* sesame

**sesear** [se·se·'ar] *vi* to pronounce the Spanish 'c' before 'e' and 'i' and 'z' in all positions as 's'

**sesenta** [se·'sen·ta] *adj inv m* sixty; *v. t.* **ochenta**

**sesera** [se·'se·ra] *f* 1. (*cerebro*) brainpan 2. (*cabeza*) brains *pl*

**sesgar** <g → gu> [ses·'ɣar] *vt* to cut down; (*torcer*) to slant

**sesión** [se·'sjon] *f* 1. (*reunión*) session; **~ a puerta cerrada** private session 2. (*representación*) show(ing); **~ de tarde** matinee

**seso** ['se·so] *m* 1. ANAT brain 2. (*inteligencia*) brains *pl* ▶ **tener sorbido el ~ a alguien** *inf* to have complete control over sb

**set** [set] *m* <sets> service; DEP set

**seta** ['se·ta] *f* mushroom; (*venenosa*) toadstool

**setecientos, -as** [se·te·'sjen·tos, -as; se·te·'θjen-] *adj* seven hundred; *v. t.* **ochocientos**

**setenta** [se·'ten·ta] *adj inv m* seventy; *v. t.* **ochenta**

**setiembre** [se·'tjem·bre] *m v.* **septiembre**

**seto** ['se·to] *m* fence; **~ vivo** hedge

**seudónimo** [seu·'do·ni·mo] *m* pseudonym; (*escritor*) pen name

**severidad** [se·βe·ri·'dad] *f* severity; (*brusquedad*) roughness; (*rigurosidad*) strictness

**severo, -a** [se·'βe·ro, -a] *adj* harsh; (*brusco*) rough; (*riguroso*) strict

**sexismo** [sek·'sis·mo] *m* sexism

**sexista** [sek·'sis·ta] *adj, mf* sexist

**sexo** ['sek·so] *m* sex; **~ seguro** safe sex; ANAT genitals *pl*

**sexto, -a** ['ses·to, -a] *adj, m, f* sixth; *v. t.* **octavo**

**sexual** [sek·su·'al] *adj* sexual; **órganos ~es** sex organs

**sexualidad** [sek·swa·li·'ðad] *f* sexuality

**shock** [ʃok/tʃok] *m* shock

**short** *m AmL* shorts *pl*

**si** [si] *conj* **1.** *(if)* ~ **no** if not; **por ~** *(acaso)* (just) in case...; ~ **bien** although; **como ~...** *+subj* as if...; **¿y si ...?** what if ...?; **¡~ hiciera un poco más de calor!** if only it were a little warmer! **2.** *(protesta, sorpresa)* but; **¡pero ~ ella se está riendo!** but she's laughing! **3.** *(énfasis)* **fíjate ~ es tonto que...** he's so stupid that...

**sí** [si] **I.** *adv* yes; **¡~ que está buena la tarta!** the cake tastes really good!; **¡(claro) que ~!** of course!; **creo que ~** I think so; **¡eso ~ que no!** certainly not!; **porque ~** because that's the way it is; *(lo digo yo)* because I say so; **volver en ~** to regain consciousness **II.** *pron pers m sing* himself; *f sing* herself; *cosa* itself; **a ~ mismo** to himself; **dar de ~** to be extensive; *(tela)* to give; **fuera de ~** beside oneself; **hablar entre ~** to talk among themselves; **por ~** in itself **III.** *m* consent

**siamés, -esa** [sja·'mes, -·'me·sa] *adj* Siamese; **gato ~** Siamese cat; **hermanos siameses** Siamese twins

**Sicilia** [si·'si·lja, si·'θi-] *f* Sicily

**siciliano, -a** [si·si·'lja·no, -a; si·θi-] *adj, m, f* Sicilian

**sicología** [si·ko·lo·'xi·a] *f* v. **(p)sicología**

**sida** ['si·da], **SIDA** ['si·da] *m abr de* **síndrome de inmunodeficiencia adquirida** AIDS

**siderurgia** [si·de·'rur·xja] *f* iron and steel industry

**sidoso, -a** [si·'do·so, -a] **I.** *adj* AIDS **II.** *m, f* AIDS sufferer

**sidra** ['si·dra] *f* cider

**siega** ['sje·ɣa] *f* reaping; *(tiempo)* harvest time

**siembra** ['sjem·bra] *f* sowing; *(tiempo)* sowing time

**siempre** ['sjem·pre] *adv* always; **de ~** always; **a la hora de ~** at the usual time; **una amistad de ~** a lifelong friendship; **¡hasta ~!** see you!; **por ~ (jamás)** for ever (and ever); **~ que** *+subj* as long as

**sien** [sjen] *f* temple

**sierra** ['sje·rra] *f* saw; GEO mountain range

**siervo, -a** ['sjer·βo, -a] *m, f* servant; *(esclavo)* slave

**siesta** ['sjes·ta] *f* siesta; **echar** [*o* **dormir**] **la ~** to have a nap; **(la hora de) la siesta** the hottest part of the day

**siete** ['sje·te] **I.** *adj inv* seven **II.** *m* **1.** seven; *v. t.* **ocho 2.** *AmS, Méx vulg* ass

**sietemesino, -a** [sje·te·me·'si·no, -a] *m, f* baby born 2 months premature

**sífilis** ['si·fi·lis] *f* syphilis

**sigilo** [si·'xi·lo] *m* discretion; *(secreto)* stealth

**sigla** ['si·ɣla] *f* initial; *(acrónimo)* acronym

**siglo** ['si·ɣlo] *m* century; **el ~ XXI** the 21st century; **hace un ~ que no te veo** I haven't seen you for ages

**signatura** [siɣ·na·'tu·ra] *f* catalog number; TIPO signature

**significación** [siɣ·ni·fi·ka·'sjon, -'θjon] *f* meaning; *(importancia)* significance

**significado** [siɣ·ni·fi·'ka·do] *m* meaning

**significar** <c → qu> [siɣ·ni·fi·'kar] *vi, vt* to mean; **¿qué significa eso?** what's the meaning of this?

**signo** ['siɣ·no] *m* sign; **~ de enfermedad** sign of illness; **~ de más/menos/multiplicar** plus/minus/multiplication sign; **~ de puntuación** punctuation mark

**siguiente** [si·'ɣjen·te] **I.** *adj* following; **de la ~ manera** in the following way **II.** *mf* next; **¡el ~!** next please!

**sílaba** ['si·la·βa] *f* syllable

**silbar** [sil·'βar] *vi, vt* to whistle; *(abuchear)* to boo; *(serpiente)* to hiss; *(flecha, bala)* to whiz(z)

**silbato** [sil·'βa·to] *m* whistle

**silbido** [sil·'βi·do] *m* whistle; *(serpiente)* hiss; *(viento)* whistling; **me silban los oídos** I've got a ringing in my ears

**silenciador** [si·len·sja·'dor, si·len·θja-] *m* silencer

**silenciar** [si·len·'sjar, -'θjar] *vt* (*suceso*) to hush up; (*persona*) to silence

**silencio** [si·'len·sjo, -θjo] *m* silence; **en ~** in silence; **guardar ~** to remain silent; **guardar ~ sobre algo** to keep silent about sth; **romper el ~** to break the silence; **¡~!** quiet!

**silencioso, -a** [si·len·'sjo·so, -a; -'θjo·so, -a] *adj* **1.** (*poco hablador*) quiet **2.** (*callado*) silent **3.** (*sin ruido*) soundless; (*motor*) noiseless

**silicona** [si·li·'ko·na] *f* silicone

**silla** ['si·ja, -ʎa] *f* chair; (*montura*) saddle; **~ de ruedas** wheelchair

**sillón** [si·'jon, -'ʎon] *m* armchair

**silueta** [si·'lwe·ta] *f* silhouette

**silvestre** [sil·'βes·tre] *adj* wild

**sima** ['si·ma] *f* abyss

**simbólico, -a** [sim·'bo·li·ko, -a] *adj* symbolic

**simbolismo** [sim·bo·'lis·mo] *m* symbolism

**simbolizar** <z → c> [sim·bo·li·'sar, -'θar] *vt* to symbolize

**símbolo** ['sim·bo·lo] *m* symbol

**simetría** [si·me·'tri·a] *f* symmetry

**simétrico, -a** [si·'me·tri·ko, -a] *adj* symmetrical

**símil** ['si·mil] *m* simile

**similar** [si·mi·'lar] *adj* similar

**similitud** [si·mi·li·'tud] *f* similarity; (*física*) resemblance

**simio** ['si·mjo] *m* ape

**simpatía** [sim·pa·'ti·a] *f* **1.** (*agrado*) liking; **tener ~ por alguien** to have a liking for sb **2.** (*carácter*) friendliness

**simpático, -a** [sim·'pa·ti·ko] *adj* friendly; **hacerse el ~** to ingratiate oneself

**simpatizar** <z → c> [sim·pa·ti·'sar, -'θar] *vi* **1.** (*congeniar*) to get along **2.** (*identificarse*) to sympathize

**simple** [simplísimo >] ['sim·ple] **I.** *adj* **1.** (*sencillo*) simple **2.** (*fácil*) easy **3.** (*mero*) pure; **a ~ vista** with the naked eye **II.** *m* simpleton

**simpleza** [sim·'ple·sa, -θa] *f* trifle; (*tontería*) silliness

**simplicidad** [sim·pli·si·'dad, sim·pli·θi-] *f* simplicity; (*ingenuidad*) plainness

**simplificar** <c → qu> [sim·pli·fi·'kar] *vt* to simplify; MAT to break down

**simposio** [sim·'po·sjo] *m* symposium

**simulación** [si·mu·la·'sjon, -'θjon] *f* simulation; (*fingimiento*) feigning

**simulacro** [si·mu·'la·kro] *m* (*de incendio*) fire drill

**simulador** [si·mu·la·'dor] *m* simulator

**simular** [si·mu·'lar] *vt* to simulate

**simultaneidad** [si·mul·ta·nei·'dad] *f* simultaneity

**simultáneo, -a** [si·mul·'ta·neo, -a] *adj* simultaneous

**sin** [sin] *prep* without; **~ dormir** without sleep; **~ querer** unintentionally; **~ más** nothing more; **estar ~ algo** to be out of sth

**sinagoga** [si·na·'ɣo·ɣa] *f* synagogue

**sincerarse** [sin·se·'rar·se, sin·θe-] *vr* **~ ante alguien** to be completely honest with sb

**sinceridad** [sin·se·ri·'dad, sin·θe-] *f* sincerity; **con toda ~** in all sincerity

**sincero, -a** [sin·'se·ro, -a; sin·'θe-] *adj* sincere; **seré ~ contigo** I'll be honest with you

**sincrónico, -a** [sin·'kro·ni·ko, -a] *adj* synchronous

**sincronizar** <z → c> [sin·kro·ni·'sar, -'θar] *vt* to synchronize

**sindical** [sin·di·'kal] *adj* union

**sindicalismo** [sin·di·ka·'lis·mo] *m* trade unionism; (*doctrina*) syndicalism

**sindicalista** [sin·di·ka·'lis·ta] **I.** *adj* (*sindical*) union **II.** *mf* trade unionist

**sindicato** [sin·di·'ka·to] *m* labor union

**síndrome** ['sin·dro·me] *m* syndrome; **~ de abstinencia** withdrawal symptoms; **síndrome de Down** Down's syndrome; **~ de inmunodeficiencia adquirida** Acquired Immune Deficiency Syndrome

**sinfonía** [sin·fo·'ni·a] *f* symphony

**sinfónico, -a** [sin·'fo·ni·ko, -a] *adj* symphonic; **orquesta sinfónica** symphony orchestra

**singular** [sin·ɡu·'lar] **I.** *adj* **1.** (*único*) singular **2.** (*excepcional*) outstanding; **en ~** in the singular **3.** (*extraño*) peculiar **II.** *m* singular

**singularidad** [sin·ɡu·la·ri·'dad] *f* **1.** (*uni-*

cidad) singularity **2.** (*excepcionalidad*) exceptional nature **3.** (*distinción*) peculiarity

**siniestro** [si·'njes·tro] *m* accident; (*catástrofe*) natural disaster; (*incendio*) fire

**siniestro, -a** [si·'njes·tro, -a] *adj* evil; (*funesto*) disastrous; **un personaje** ~ a sinister character

**sinnúmero** [sin·'nu·me·ro] *m* huge number

**sino** ['si·no] **I.** *m* fate **II.** *conj* **1.** (*al contrario*) but **2.** (*solamente*) **no espero** ~ **que me creas** I only hope that you believe me **3.** (*excepto*) except

**sinónimo** [si·'no·ni·mo] *m* synonym

**sinónimo, -a** [si·'no·ni·mo, -a] *adj* synonymous

**sinopsis** [si·'noβ·sis] *f inv* synopsis; (*esquema*) diagram

**sinrazón** [sin·rra·'son, -'θon] *f* injustice; (*absurdo*) unreasonableness

**sinsentido** [sin·sen·'ti·do] *m* absurdity

**sintáctico, -a** [sin·'tak·ti·ko, -a] *adj* syntactic

**sintaxis** [sin·'tak·sis] *f inv* syntax

**síntesis** ['sin·te·sis] *f inv* synthesis; **en** ~ in a word

**sintético, -a** [sin·'te·ti·ko, -a] *adj* synthetic

**sintetizador** [sin·te·ti·sa·'dor, sin·te·ti·θa-] *m* synthesizer

**sintetizar** <z → c> [sin·te·ti·'sar, -'θar] *vt* to summarize; QUÍM to synthesize

**síntoma** ['sin·to·ma] *m* symptom

**sintomático, -a** [sin·to·'ma·ti·ko, -a] *adj* symptomatic

**sintonía** [sin·to·'ni·a] *f* **1.** (*adecuación*) tuning **2.** (*señal sonora, melodía*) signature tune **3.** (*entendimiento*) **estar en** ~ (**con alguien**) to be on the same wavelength (as sb)

**sintonizar** <z → c> [sin·to·ni·'sar, -'θar] **I.** *vt* to tune in to; ~ **una emisora** to pick up a radio station **II.** *vi* to tune in, curve

**sinuoso, -a** [si·nu·'o·so, -a] *adj* (*curvado*) winding; (*retorcido*) devious

**sinvergüenza** [sim·ber·'ɣwen·sa, -θa] *pey* **I.** *adj* shameless **II.** *mf* lowlife

**síquico, -a** ['si·ki·ko, -a] *adj v.* **(p)síquico**

**siquiera** [si·'kje·ra] *adv* at least; **ni** ~ not even

**sirena** [si·'re·na] *f* siren; (*mujer pez*) mermaid

**sirope** [si·'ro·pe] *m AmC, Col* syrup

**sirviente** [sir·'βjen·te] *mf* servant

**sisar** [si·'sar] *vt* to pilfer

**sisirisco** [si·si·'ris·ko] *m Méx* anus; (*miedo*) fright

**sísmico, -a** ['sis·mi·ko, -a] *adj* seismic; **movimiento** ~ earth tremor

**sismo** ['sis·mo] *m* tremor; (*terremoto*) earthquake

**sistema** [sis·'te·ma] *m* system; ~ **antibloqueo de frenos** antilock brake system; ~ **inmunitario/operativo/solar** immune/operating/solar system; ~ **montañoso** mountain range

**sistemático, -a** [sis·te·'ma·ti·ko, -a] *adj* systematic

**sistematizar** <z → c> [sis·te·ma·ti·'sar, -'θar] *vt* to systematize

**sitio** ['si·tjo] *m* (*lugar*) place; (*espacio*) room; **en cualquier/en ningún** ~ anywhere/nowhere; **en todos los** ~**s** everywhere; **guardar el** ~ **a alguien** to keep sb's place; **hacer** ~ to make room; **ocupar mucho** ~ to take up a lot of room; **poner a alguien en su** ~ to put sb in his/her place; ~ (**de taxis**) *Méx* taxi stand

**sito, -a** ['si·to, -a] *adj* ~ **en** situated in

**situación** [si·twa·'sjon, -'θjon] *f* situation; (*ubicación*) location

**situado, -a** [si·tu·'a·do, -a] *adj* situated

**situar** <*1. pres* sitúo> [si·tu·'ar] **I.** *vt* (*colocar*) to place; (*emplazar*) to locate **II.** *vr:* ~**se** to situate oneself; (*abrirse paso*) to make one's way

**smog** [es·'moɣ] *m* smog

**snorkeling** [es·'nor·ke·lin] *m* snorkeling; **practicar** ~ to snorkel

**so** [so] **I.** *interj* whoa! **II.** *m inf* **¡**~ **imbécil!** you idiot!

**SO** [su·do·'es·te] *abr de* **sudoeste** SW

**soba** ['so·βa] *f inf* **1.** (*a persona*) pawing; (*de un objeto*) fingering **2.** (*zurra*) beating

**sobaco** [so·'βa·ko] *m* armpit

**sobado, -a** [so·'βa·do, -a] *adj* worn; (*papel*) dog-eared; (*tema*) well worn

**sobajar** [so·βa·'xar] *vt Méx* to humiliate

**sobar** [so·'βar] I. *vt* (*persona*) to paw; (*objeto*) to finger II. *vi inf* to sleep

**soberanamente** [so·βe·ra·na·'men·te] *adv* supremely

**soberanía** [so·βe·ra·'ni·a] *f* sovereignty

**soberano, -a** [so·βe·'ra·no, -a] *adj, m, f* sovereign

**soberbia** [so·'βer·βja] *f* (*orgullo*) pride; (*suntuosidad*) magnificence

**soberbio, -a** [so·'βer·βjo, -a] *adj* (*orgulloso*) proud; (*suntuoso*) magnificent

**sobornar** [so·βor·'nar] *vt* to bribe

**soborno** [so·'βor·no] *m* bribe; (*acción*) bribery

**sobra** ['so·βra] *f* 1. surplus; **de ~** more than enough; **saber algo de ~** to know sth only too well 2. *pl* (*desperdicios*) leftovers *pl*; (*restos*) remnants *pl*

**sobrador(a)** [so·βra·'dor, -·'do·ra] *m(f) Arg, Urug* conceited person

**sobrante** [so·'βran·te] I. *adj* spare; (*de más*) excess; COM, FIN surplus II. *m* remainder; (*superávit*) surplus

**sobrar** [so·'βrar] *vi* 1. (*quedar*) to remain; **nos sobra bastante tiempo** we have plenty of time 2. (*abundar*) to be more than enough; **me sobran cinco kilos** I've got five kilos left over 3. (*estar de más*) to be superfluous; **creo que sobras aquí** I think you're not needed here

**sobre** ['so·βre] I. *m* 1. (*carta*) envelope; **un ~ de levadura** a packet of yeast 2. *inf* bed; **irse al ~** to go off to bed II. *prep* 1. (*encima*) on; **~ la mesa** on the table 2. (*cantidad, hora*) **pesar ~ los cien kilos** to weigh about a hundred kilos; **llegar ~ las tres** to arrive at about three o'clock 3. (*acerca*) about; **~ ello** about it 4. (*superioridad*) **el boxeador triunfó ~ su adversario** the boxer triumphed over his opponent 5. MAT out of; **tres ~ cien** three out of a hundred

**sobreabundancia** [so·βre·a·βun·'dan·sja, -θja] *f* superabundance

**sobrealimentación** [so·βre·a·li·men·ta·'sjon, -'θjon] *f* overfeeding

**sobrecarga** [so·βre·'kar·ɣa] *f* excess; ELEC overload; COM surcharge

**sobrecargar** [so·βre·kar·'ɣar] I. *vt* to overload; (*por esfuerzo*) to overburden II. *vr:* **~se** to overload oneself; **~se de trabajo** to take on too much work

**sobrecoger** [so·βre·ko·'xer] I. *vt* (*sorprender*) to take by surprise; (*espantar*) to frighten II. *vr:* **~se** (*asustarse*) to be startled; (*sorprenderse*) to be surprised (**de** by)

**sobredosis** [so·βre·'do·sis] *f inv* overdose

**sobreentender** [so·βre·en·ten·'der] <e → ie> I. *vt* (*presuponer*) to presuppose; (*adivinar*) to infer; **de todo ello sobreentendemos que...** we understand from all this that... II. *vr:* **~se** to be obvious; **aquí queda sobreentendido que...** it is implied here that...

**sobreestimar** [so·βre·es·ti·'mar] *vt* to overestimate

**sobrehumano, -a** [so·βre·u·'ma·no, -a] *adj* superhuman

**sobrellevar** [so·βre·je·'βar, -ʎe·'βar] *vt* to bear; **~ mal/bien** to take badly/well

**sobremanera** [so·βre·ma·'ne·ra] *adv* exceedingly

**sobremesa** [so·βre·'me·sa] *f* 1. (*mantel*) table cover 2. (*postre*) dessert 3. (*tarde*) after-lunch; **programa de ~** afternoon program 4. COMPUT desktop

**sobrenatural** [so·βre·na·tu·'ral] *adj* 1. supernatural; **ciencias ~es** occult sciences 2. (*extraordinario*) incredible

**sobrenombre** [so·βre·'nom·bre] *m* nickname

**sobrentender** <e → ie> [so·βren·ten·'der/so·βre·en·ten·'der] *vt, vr v.* **sobreentender**

**sobrepasar** [so·βre·pa·'sar] *vt* 1. (*en cantidad*) to surpass; (*límite*) to exceed 2. (*aventajar*) to pass; (*récord, al mejor*) to beat

**sobreponer** [so·βre·po·'ner] *irr como* **poner** I. *vt* **~ a algo/alguien** to place above sth/sb; (*anteponer*) to prefer to sth/sb; **~ a alguien a todos los demás** to put sb before everyone else II. *vr:* **~se** 1. (*calmarse*) to pull oneself together 2. (*al enemigo, a una enfermedad*) to overcome; (*al miedo, a un susto*) to recover from

**sobreprecio** [so·βre·'pre·sjo, -θjo] *m* surcharge

**sobresaliente** [so·βre·sa·'ljen·te] I. *adj* outstanding II. *m* ENS distinction

**sobresalir** [so·βre·sa·'lir] *irr como salir vi* to stand out (**de** from); **~ en algo** to be outstanding at sth

**sobresaltar** [so·βre·sal·'tar] I. *vi* to start II. *vt* to startle III. *vr* **~se con** [*o de*] **algo** to be startled at sth

**sobresalto** [so·βre·'sal·to] *m* (*susto*) scare; (*turbación*) sudden shock; **con ~** shocked; **de ~** suddenly

**sobrestimar** [so·βres·ti·'mar] *vt* to overestimate

**sobresueldo** [so·βre·'swel·do] *m* extra pay

**sobretasa** [so·βre·'ta·sa] *f* surcharge

**sobrevenir** [so·βre·βe·'nir] *irr como venir vi* (*epidemia*) to ensue; (*desgracia, guerra*) to happen unexpectedly; (*tormenta*) to break; **me sobrevino una gran tristeza** a feeling of deep sadness came over me

**sobrevida** [soβ·re·'βida] *f* survival time

**sobreviviente** [so·βre·βi·'βjen·te] *mf* survivor

**sobrevivir** [so·βre·βi·'βir] *vi* to survive; (*a alguien*) to outlive

**sobrevolar** <o → ue> [so·βre·βo·'lar] *vt* to fly over

**sobriedad** [so·βrje·'dad] *f* soberness; (*prudencia*) restraint; (*estilo*) plainness

**sobrino, -a** [so·'βri·no, -a] *m, f* nephew, niece *m, f*

**sobrio, -a** ['so·βrjo, -a] *adj* sober; (*prudente*) restrained; (*estilo*) plain

**socar** <c → qu> [so·'kar] *AmC* I. *vt* to compress II. *vr:* **~se** to get drunk

**socavar** [so·ka·'βar] *vt* to dig under; *fig* to undermine

**sociable** [so·'sja·βle, so·'θja-] *adj* sociable; (*afable*) friendly

**social** [so·'sjal, -'θjal] *adj* 1. (*relativo a la sociedad*) society; (*a la convivencia*) social 2. (*estatal*) **asistencia/asistente ~** social worker; **Estado Social** Welfare State

**socialdemócrata** [so·sjal·de·'mo·kra·ta, so·θjal-] I. *adj* social-democratic II. *mf*

social democrat

**socialismo** [so·sja·'lis·mo, so·θja-] *m* socialism

**socialista** [so·sja·'lis·ta, so·θja-] *adj, mf* socialist

**socializar** <z → c> [so·sja·li·'sar, -θja·li·'θar] *vt* to socialize

**sociedad** [so·sje·'dad, so·θje-] *f* 1. (*población, humanidad*) society 2. (*trato*) company; **la ~ con la que tratas** the company you keep 3. (*empresa*) company; **~ anónima** corporation 4. (*asociación*) association

**socio, -a** ['so·sjo, -a; -θjo, -a] *m, f* (*de asociación*) member; (*de empresa*) partner

**socioeconómico, -a** [so·sjo·e·ko·'no·mi·ko, -a; so·θjo-] *adj* socioeconomic

**sociología** [so·sjo·lo·'xi·a, so·θjo-] *f* sociology

**sociólogo, -a** [so·'sjo·lo·γo; so·'θjo-] *m, f* sociologist

**sociopolítico, -a** [so·sjo·po·'li·ti·ko, -a; so·θjo-] *adj* sociopolitical

**socollón** [so·ko·'jon, -'ʎon] *m AmC, Cuba* jolt

**socorrer** [so·ko·'rrer] *vt* to come to the aid of

**socorrido, -a** [so·ko·'rri·do, -a] *adj* helpful; (*útil*) useful

**socorrista** [so·ko·'rris·ta] *mf* lifeguard; (*en piscinas*) pool attendant

**socorro** [so·'ko·rro] *m* help; (*salvamento*) rescue; **puesto de ~** first-aid post; **¡~!** help!

**socoyote** [so·ko·'jo·te] *m Méx* youngest child

**soda** ['so·da] *f* soda water

**sodio** ['so·djo] *m* sodium

**sofá** <sofás> [so·'fa] *m* sofa

**sofá-cama** <sofás-cama> [so·'fa·'ka·ma] *m* sofa-bed

**sofisticado, -a** [so·fis·ti·'ka·do, -a] *adj* sophisticated

**sofocado, -a** [so·fo·'ka·do, -a] *adj* stifled

**sofocante** [so·fo·'kan·te] *adj* stifling; (*ambiente, aire*) suffocating; (*avergonzante*) shameless

**sofocar** <c → qu> [so·fo·'kar] I. *vt* 1. (*asfixiar*) to suffocate 2. (*frenar*) to stifle; (*fuego*) to put out; (*revolución*) to crush

S

**3.** (*avergonzar*) to embarrass **II.** *vr:* **~se**
**1.** (*sonrojarse*) to blush **2.** (*agobiarse*) to get worked up **3.** (*enojarse*) to get angry **4.** (*ahogarse*) to suffocate

**sofoco** [so·'fo·ko] *m* **1.** (*ahogo*) suffocation; (*jadeo*) panting **2.** (*calor*) heat flush

**soga** ['so·ɣa] *f* rope; **estar con la ~ al cuello** to have one's back to the wall

**sois** [sois] *2. pres pl de* **ser**

**soja** ['so·xa] *f* soy; **salsa/semilla/brote de ~** soy sauce/soybean/bean sprout

**sol** [sol] *m* **1.** sun; (*luz*) sunlight; **de ~ a ~** from dawn to dusk; **hace ~** it's sunny; **día de ~** sunny day; **al ~** in the sun; **tomar el ~** to sunbathe **2.** **~ y sombra** brandy and anisette **3.** (*moneda*) sol **4.** *inf* **es un ~** he/she is an angel ▶ **no dejar a alguien ni a ~ ni a <u>sombra</u>** not to leave sb alone

**solamente** [so·la·'men·te] *adv* only; (*expresamente*) expressly

**solapa** [so·'la·pa] *f* lapel; (*libro*) flap

**solapar** [so·la·'par] **I.** *vi* to overlap **II.** *vt* (*cubrir*) to cover up; (*disimular*) to conceal

**solar** [so·'lar] **I.** *adj* solar **II.** *m* **1.** (*terreno*) plot **2.** (*casa*) family seat **3.** *AmC* (*patio*) yard

**soldado, -a** [sol·'da·ðo, -a] *m, f* soldier; **~ raso** private

**soldador** [sol·da·'ðor] *m* soldering iron

**soldador(a)** [sol·da·'ðor, -·'ðo·ra] *m(f)* welder

**soldar** <o → ue> [sol·'dar] **I.** *vt* (*con metal*) to weld; (*unir*) to join **II.** *vr:* **~se** (*herida*) to heal; (*huesos*) to knit together

**soleado, -a** [so·le·'a·ðo, -a] *adj* sunny

**soledad** [so·le·'dad] *f* solitude; (*sentimiento*) loneliness

**solemne** [so·'lem·ne] *adj* solemn; (*discurso*) formal; (*mentira*) monstrous; (*error*) monumental

**solemnidad** [so·lem·ni·'dad] *f* **1.** solemnity **2.** *pl* formalities *pl*

**soler** <o → ue> [so·'ler] *vi* **~ hacer** to be in the habit of doing; **suele ocurrir que...** it often occurs that...; **solemos coger el tren** we usually catch the train; **solíamos coger el tren** we used

to catch the train

**solfeo** [sol·'fe·o] *m* solfeggio; (*fragmento*) sol-fa

**solicitante** [so·li·si·'tan·te, so·li·θi-] *mf* petitioner; (*para un trabajo*) applicant

**solicitar** [so·li·si·'tar, so·li·θi-] *vt* to ask for; (*gestionar*) to solicit; (*un trabajo*) to apply for; **~ un médico** to call for a doctor; (*compañía, atención*) to seek; **te solicitan en todas partes** you're in great demand

**solícito, -a** [so·'li·si·to, -a; so·li·θi-] *adj* diligent; (*cuidadoso*) solicitous

**solicitud** [so·li·si·'tud, so·li·θi-] *f* request; (*formal*) petition; **~ de empleo** job application

**solidaridad** [so·li·da·ri·'dad] *f* solidarity

**solidario, -a** [so·li·'da·rjo, -a] *adj* solidary

**solidarizarse** <z → c> [so·li·da·ri·'sar·se, -'θar·se] *vr* to feel solidarity

**solidez** [so·li·des, -'deθ] *f* solidity; (*estabilidad*) firmness

**solidificar** <c → qu> [so·li·di·fi·'kar] *vt, vr:* **~se** to solidify; *fig* to harden

**sólido** ['so·li·do] *m* solid

**sólido, -a** ['so·li·do, -a] *adj* solid; (*color*) fast; (*precios*) stable; (*voz*) strong

**solista** [so·'lis·ta] *mf* soloist

**solitaria** [so·li·'ta·rja] *f* tapeworm

**solitario** [so·li·'ta·rjo] *m* solitaire

**solitario, -a** [so·li·'ta·rjo, -a] **I.** *adj* alone; (*abandonado*) lonely; (*lugar*) isolated; **en ~** single-handed **II.** *m, f* loner

**sollozar** <z → c> [so·jo·'sar, so·ʎo·'θar] *vi* to sob

**sollozo** [so·'jo·so, -'ʎo·θo] *m* sob

**solo** ['so·lo] *m* solo

**solo, -a** ['so·lo, -a] *adj* **1.** (*persona*) alone; (*sin familia*) orphaned; (*solitario*) lonely; **por sí ~** on one's own; **lo hace como ella sola** she does it as only she can **2.** (*único*) only; **ni una sola vez** not once **3.** (*sin añadir nada*) on its own; (*café*) black; (*alcohol*) straight ▶ **estar más ~ que la <u>una</u>** to be completely on one's own; **más vale ~ que mal <u>acompañado</u>** better to be alone than in bad company

**sólo** ['so·lo] *adv* only; (*expresamente*) expressly; **~ que...** except that...; **tan**

**solsticio** [sols·'ti·sjo, -θjo] *m* solstice

**soltar** [sol·'tar] *irr* **I.** *vt* to let go of; (*liberar*) to free; (*dejar caer*) to drop; (*nudo*) to untie; (*grito, pedo, embrague*) to let out; (*frenos*) to release; (*cinturón*) to undo; (*tacos*) to come out with; *inf* (*dinero*) to cough up; **¡suéltame!** let me go!; ~ **una carcajada** to burst out laughing; ~ **un golpe** to strike; ~ **una bofetada a alguien** to slap sb; **no ~ prenda** to give nothing away **II.** *vr:* ~**se 1.** (*liberarse*) to escape; (*librarse*) to free oneself **2.** (*nudo*) to come undone; (*tiro*) to go off **3.** (*al hablar*) to let oneself go; **se me soltó la lengua** I found my tongue

**soltero, -a** [sol·'te·ro, -a] **I.** *adj* single **II.** *m, f* bachelor, single woman *m, f*

**solterón, -ona** [sol·te·'ron, -'ro·na] *m, f* confirmed bachelor, spinster *m, f*

**soltura** [sol·'tu·ra] *f* ease; (*hablando*) fluency; (*pelo*) looseness

**soluble** [so·'lu·βle] *adj* soluble; ~ **en agua** water-soluble; **café** ~ instant coffee

**solución** [so·lu·'sjon, -'θjon] *f* solution; **este problema no tiene** ~ there's no solution to this problem; **no hay más** ~ there's nothing more to be done

**solucionar** [so·lu·sjo·'nar, so·lu·θjo-] *vt* to solve

**solvencia** [sol·'βen·sja, -θja] *f* trustworthiness; FIN solvency

**solventar** [sol·βen·'tar] *vt* (*problema*) to resolve; (*asunto*) to settle; (*desavenencia*) to end; (*deuda, cuenta*) to pay

**solvente** [sol·'βen·te] *adj, m* solvent

**somatada** [so·ma·'ta·da] *f* AmC blow

**sombra** ['som·bra] *f* **1.** (*proyección*) shadow; ~ **de ojos** eye shadow; ~ **de duda** shadow of doubt; **se ha convertido en mi** ~ he/she follows me everywhere **2.** (*penumbra*) shade; **hacer** [*o* **dar**] ~ to give shade; **hacer** ~ **a alguien** *fig* to put sb in the shade; **a la** ~ **de** in the shade of; **no fiarse ni de su** (**propia**) ~ to be extremely suspicious; **trabajar en la** ~ to work illegally **3.** *pl* darkness **4.** ARTE shading **5.** (*cárcel*) **a la** ~ in the slammer; **poner a la** ~ to lock

up ► **tener mala** ~ to be a nasty bit of work; (*tener mala suerte*) to be unlucky; **¡vete por la ~!** watch how you go!

**sombrero** [som·'bre·ro] *m* hat; ~ **de copa** top hat; ~ **hongo** derby; **quitarse el** ~ **ante algo** to take one's hat off to sth

**sombrilla** [som·'bri·ja, -ʎa] *f* parasol

**sombrío, -a** [som·'bri·o, -a] *adj* shady; (*oscuro*) dark; (*pesimista*) gloomy

**someter** [so·me·'ter] **I.** *vt* **1.** (*dominar*) to force to submit; (*subyugar*) to conquer **2.** (*proyecto, ideas, tratamiento*) to submit **3.** (*subordinar*) to subordinate; **todo está sometido a tu decisión** everything is subject to your decision **II.** *vr:* ~**se** to give in; ~**se a algo** to undergo sth; (*decisión, opinión*) to bow; ~**se a las órdenes/la voluntad de alguien** to bow to sb's orders/will

**somnífero** [som·'ni·fe·ro] *m* sleeping pill

**somnífero, -a** [som·'ni·fe·ro, -a] *adj* sleep-inducing

**somnolencia** [som·no·'len·sja, -θja] *f* drowsiness

**somos** ['so·mos] *1. pres pl de* ser

**son** [son] **I.** *m* sound; (*rumor, voz*) rumor; **venir en ~ de paz** to come in peace ► **bailar al** ~ **que tocan** to toe the line; **hacer algo a su** ~ to do sth one's own way; **sin** ~ for no reason at all **II.** *3. pres pl de* ser

**sonajero** [so·na·'xe·ro] *m* (baby's) rattle

**sonambulismo** [so·nam·bu·'lis·mo] *m* sleepwalking

**sonámbulo, -a** [so·'nam·bu·lo, -a] **I.** *adj* sleepwalking **II.** *m, f* sleepwalker

**sonante** [so·'nan·te] *adj* **dinero contante y** ~ (hard) cash

**sonar** <o → ue> [so·'nar] **I.** *vi* **1.** to ring; (*instrumento*) to be heard; **me suenan las tripas** my stomach is rumbling **2.** *t.* LING, MÚS (*parecerse*) to sound; ~ **a algo** to sound like sth; ~ **a hueco** to sound hollow; **esto me suena** this sounds familiar; (*tal y*) **como suena** as I'm telling you **II.** *vt* to play; (*nariz*) to blow **III.** *vr:* ~**se** to blow one's nose

**sonata** [so·'na·ta] *f* sonata

**sonda** ['son·da] *f* sounding; MED probe

**sondeo** [son·'deo] *m* **1.** investigation; ~

de mercado/la opinión pública market/public opinion survey **2.** MED probing **3.** MIN boring **4.** NÁUT sounding

**songa-songa** ['son·ga·'son·ga] *AmC, Chile, Ecua* **a la** ~ underhand

**songo, -a** ['son·go] *adj Col, Méx* stupid; *(taimado)* sly

**sonido** [so·'ni·do] *m* **1.** sound **2.** *t.* MÚS *(manera de sonar)* tone **3.** FÍS resonance

**sonoro, -a** [so·'no·ro, -a] *adj* **1.** *(que suena)* *t.* FÍS resonant; *(acústico)* acoustic; *(bóveda)* echoing **2.** *(fuerte)* loud; *(agradable)* sonorous; **una voz sonora/poco sonora** a rich/thin voice **3.** LING voiced **4.** CINE **banda sonora** soundtrack

**sonreír** [son·rre·'ir] *irr como* reír **I.** *vi, vr:* ~**se** to smile; ~ **a alguien** to smile at sb; ~ **maliciosamente** to smile maliciously; ~ **de felicidad** to beam with happiness **II.** *vi* to smile; **le sonríe la fortuna** fortune smiles on him/her

**sonrisa** [son·'rri·sa] *f* smile; *(maliciosa)* smirk; ~ **de oreja a oreja** (broad) grin

**sonrojar** [son·rro·'xar] **I.** *vt* to make blush **II.** *vr:* ~**se** to blush

**sonrojo** [son·'rro·xo] *m* blush

**sonsear** [son·se·'ar] *vi CSur* to behave stupidly

**sonsera** [son·'se·ra] *f Arg* foolishness

**sonso, -a** ['son·so, -a] *m, f CSur* stupid

**soñado, -a** [so·'ɲa·do, -a] *adj* dreamt-of

**soñador(a)** [so·ɲa·'dor, -·'do·ra] **I.** *adj* dreamy **II.** *m(f)* dreamer

**soñar** <o → ue> [so·'ɲar] *vi, vt* to dream *(con* of); ~ **despierto** to daydream; **¡ni** ~**lo!** no way!; **siempre he soñado con ser médico** I've always dreamt of being a doctor

**soñoliento, -a** [so·ɲo·'ljen·to, -a] *adj* drowsy

**sopa** ['so·pa] *f* soup; ~**s de leche** bread and milk ▶ **comer la** [*o* **andar a la**] ~ **boba** to live off other people; **estar** ~ to be tight; **ver hasta en la** ~ to see everywhere; **como** [*o* **hecho**] **una** ~ soaked to the skin

**sopera** [so·'pe·ra] *f* soup tureen

**sopero, -a** [so·'pe·ro, -a] **I.** *adj* soup **II.** *m, f* soup plate

**soplar** [so·'plar] **I.** *vi* to blow **II.** *vt* **1.** to

blow on; *(apartar)* to blow away; *(velas)* to blow out; *(hinchar)* to blow up; *(fuego)* to blow on **2.** *(en un examen)* to whisper; TEAT to prompt **3.** *inf(delatar)* to squeal on; *(alumnos)* to tell on **4.** *inf (hurtar)* to swipe; *(cobrar)* to sting for **III.** *vr:* ~**se** *inf(comer)* to wolf down; *(beber)* to knock back

**soplete** [so·'ple·te] *m* blow torch; ~ **soldador** welding torch

**soplo** ['so·plo] *m* **1.** puff; **de un** ~ with one puff; ~ **de viento** breath of wind; **como un** ~ like a flash **2.** *(denuncia)* tip-off

**soplón, -ona** [so·'plon, -·'plo·na] *m, f* tattletale; *(policía)* informer; TEAT prompter

**sopor** [so·'por] *m* lethargy

**soportable** [so·por·'ta·βle] *adj* bearable

**soportar** [so·por·'tar] *vt* to support; *(aguantar)* to stand

**soporte** [so·'por·te] *m* support; *(pilar)* support pillar; *(de madera)* beam; ~ **físico** hardware; ~ **lógico** software

**soprano** [so·'pra·no] **I.** *m* soprano **II.** *f* soprano

**soquete** [so·'ke·te] *m AmL* anklet

**sor** [sor] *f* sister

**sorber** [sor·'βer] *vt* to sip; *(con pajita)* to suck; *(empapar)* to soak up; *(nariz)* to sniff; MED to inhale

**sorbo** ['sor·βo] *m* sip; **beber a** ~**s** to sip; **tomar de un** ~ to drink in one go

**sordera** [sor·'de·ra] *f* loss of hearing; *(total)* deafness

**sordo, -a** ['sor·do, -a] **I.** *adj* **1.** deaf; *(que oye mal)* hard of hearing; ~ **de un oído** deaf in one ear; **hacer oídos** ~**s** to turn a deaf ear; ~ **como una tapia** as deaf as a post; **quedarse** ~ to go deaf **2.** *(silencioso)* noiseless; **un golpe** ~ a dull thud **3.** LING voiceless **II.** *m, f* deaf person; **hacerse el** ~ to pretend not to hear; **no hay peor** ~ **que el que no quiere oír** there are none so deaf as those who will not hear

**sordomudo, -a** [sor·do·'mu·do, -a] **I.** *adj* deaf and dumb **II.** *m, f* deaf mute

**sorprendente** [sor·pren·'den·te] *adj* **1.** unexpected; *(asombroso)* amazing; *(desarrollo, evolución)* surprising; *(no* es ~ que +*subj* it's (hardly) surprising that 2. (*que salta a la vista*) striking; **poseer una estatura** ~ to be surprisingly tall

**sorprender** [sor·pren·'der] I. *vt* 1. (*coger desprevenido*) to take by surprise; (*asombrar*) to startle; (*extrañar*) to surprise; **no me** ~**ía que viniera** I wouldn't be surprised if he/she came 2. (*descubrir*) to come across 3. (*pillar*) to catch II. *vr*: ~**se** to be surprised; ~**se de algo** to be amazed at sth

**sorpresa** [sor·'pre·sa] *f* surprise; (*efecto*) suddenness; (*asombro*) amazement; **coger a alguien de** [*o* **por**] ~ to take sb by surprise

**sorpresivo, -a** [sor·pre·'si·βo, -a] *adj AmL* unexpected

**sortear** [sor·te·'ar] *vt* 1. (*decidir*) to draw lots for; (*rifar*) to raffle 2. (*esquivar*) to avoid

**sorteo** [sor·'teo] *m* drawing of lots; (*rifa*) raffle

**sortija** [sor·'ti·xa] *f* ring

**sosegado, -a** [so·se·'ɣa·do, -a] *adj* (*apacible*) peaceful; (*tranquilo*) calm

**sosegar** [so·se·'ɣar] *irr como* **fregar** I. *vt* to calm II. *vi*, ~**se** (*descansar*) to rest III. *vr*: ~**se** (*calmarse*) to calm down

**sosegate** [so·se·'ɣa·te] *m Arg, Urug* **dar** [*o* **pegar**] **un** ~ **a alguien** to tell sb off

**sosiego** [so·'sje·ɣo] *m* calm; **con** ~ calmly

**soso, -a** ['so·so, -a] *adj* 1. (*sin sal*) unsalted; (*sin sabor*) insipid 2. (*persona*) dull

**sospecha** [sos·'pe·tʃa] *f* supposition; (*desconfianza*) mistrust; (*de crimen*) suspicion; **bajo** ~ **de asesinato** suspected of murder

**sospechar** [sos·pe·'tʃar] I. *vt* (*suponer*) to suppose; (*recelar*) to suspect; **¡ya lo sospechaba!** I thought as much! II. *vi* to be suspicious

**sospechoso, -a** [sos·pe·'tʃo·so, -a] I. *adj* suspicious; **me resulta** ~ **que** +*subj* I find it suspicious that II. *m, f* suspect

**sostén** [sos·'ten] *m AmL* bra

**sostener** [sos·te·'ner] *irr como* **tener** I. *vt* 1. (*sujetar*) to support 2. (*aguantar*) to bear; (*por debajo*) to hold up 3. (*afir-*

*mar*) to maintain; (*idea, teoría*) to stick to 4. (*lucha, velocidad, posición*) to keep up; ~ **una conversación** to have a conversation II. *vr*: ~**se** 1. (*sujetarse*) to hold oneself up 2. (*aguantarse*) to keep going 3. (*en pie*) to stand up 4. **apenas me puedo** ~ (*de puro cansado*) (I'm so tired) I can hardly stand

**sota** ['so·ta] *f* jack

**sótano** ['so·ta·no] *m* (*piso*) basement; (*habitación*) cellar

**sotreta** [so·'tre·ta] *adj Arg, Bol, Urug* (*holgazán*) idle; (*no fiable*) untrustworthy

**soturno, -a** [so·'tur·no, -a] *adj Ven* taciturn

**soy** [soi] *1. pres de* **ser**

**spray** [es·'prai] *m* <**sprays**> spray

**squash** [es·'kwaʃ] *m* squash

**Sr.** [se·'ɲor] *abr de* **señor** Mr.

**Sra.** [se·'ɲo·ra] *abr de* **señora** Mrs.

**Srta.** [se·ɲo·'ri·ta] *f abr de* **señorita** Miss

**Sta.** ['san·ta] *f abr de* **santa** St.

**status** [es·'ta·tus] *m inv* status

**su** [su] *adj* (*de él*) his; (*de ella*) her; (*de cosa, animal*) its; (*de ellos*) their; (*de Ud, Uds.*) your; (*de uno*) one's; ~ **familia** his/her/their family

**suampo** ['swam·po] *m AmC* swamp

**suave** [su·'a·βe] *adj* (*superficie, piel, aterrizaje*) smooth; (*jersey, pelo, droga*) soft; (*viento, noche, curva, subida*) gentle; (*sopa, salsa, temperatura, tabaco*) mild

**suavidad** [swa·βi·'dad] *f* (*superficie, piel, aterrizaje*) smoothness; (*jersey, cabello*) softness; (*viento, caricia, subida, temperatura*) gentleness

**suavizante** [swa·βi·'san·te, -'θan·te] I. *adj* **crema** ~ conditioner II. *m* conditioner; (*para ropa*) fabric softener

**suavizar** [swa·βi·'sar, -'θar] <z → c> *vt* to smooth; (*pelo, piel*) to soften; (*situación*) to ease; (*persona*) to mollify; (*recorrido, trabajo*) to make easy; (*velocidad*) to moderate

**subalimentación** [suβ·a·li·men·ta·'sjon, -'θjon] *f* undernourishment

**subarrendar** <e → ie> [suβ·a·rren·'dar] *vt* (*piso*) to sublet; (*finca*) to sublease

**subasta** [su·'βas·ta] *f* auction; (*de con-*

S

*trato público*) tender; **sacar a ~ pública** to put up for auction

**subastar** [su·βas·'tar] *vt* to auction; (*contrato público*) to put out to tender

**subcampeón, -ona** [suβ·kam·pe·'on, ··'o·na] *m, f* runner-up; **~ mundial** world number two

**subconsciencia** [suβ·kon·'sjen·sja, -'θjen·θja] *f* subconscious

**subconsciente** [suβ·kon·'sjen·te, -'θjen·te] *adj* subconscious

**subcultura** [suβ·kul·'tu·ra] *f* subculture

**subdesarrollado, -a** [suβ·de·sa·rro·'ja·do, -a; -'ʎa·do, -a] *adj* underdeveloped

**subdirector(a)** [suβ·di·rek·'tor, ··'to·ra] *m(f)* assistant director

**súbdito, -a** ['suβ·di·to, -a] *m, f* vassal

**subdividir** [suβ·di·βi·'dir] *vt* to subdivide

**subestimar** [suβ·es·ti·'mar] **I.** *vt* to underestimate **II.** *vr:* **~se** to underestimate oneself

**subida** [su·'βi·da] *f* **1.** (*calle, río*) rise; (*precios, temperaturas, costes*) increase **2.** (*cuesta*) slope; **la calle hace ~** the street slopes **3.** (*ascenso*) ascent; (*en coche, teleférico*) climb; **~ al poder** rise to power

**subir** [su·'βir] **I.** *vi* (*calle, cuesta*) to go up; (*sol, pastel, globo, río*) to rise; **~ a la cima** to climb to the peak; **la marea ha subido** the tide has come in; **sube a por tus cosas** go up and get your things; **~ en algo** to increase by sth; **la gasolina ha subido** gas has gone up; (*al coche*) to get in; (*al caballo, tren, bici*) to get on; **~ a un árbol** to climb a tree **II.** *vt* to go up; (*llevar*) to take up; (*voz, precio, persiana*) to raise; (*música*) to turn up; (*montaña*) to climb; (*brazos*) to lift up; (*cabeza, pesas*) to lift; **~ a un niño en brazos** to lift up a child; **~ al tercer piso** to go up to the third floor **III.** *vr:* **~se** (*coche*) to get in; (*tren, bici*) to get on; **~se a un árbol/a una silla** to climb a tree/onto a chair; **se me ha subido el vino a la cabeza** the wine has gone to my head

**súbito** ['su·βi·to] *adv* **de ~** suddenly; (*inesperadamente*) unexpectedly

**súbito, -a** ['su·βi·to, -a] *adj* sudden; (*inesperado*) unexpected

**subjefe, -a** [suβ·'xe·fe, -a] *m, f* assistant manager

**subjetividad** [suβ·xe·ti·βi·'dad] *f* subjectivity

**subjetivo, -a** [suβ·xe·'ti·βo, -a] *adj* subjective

**subjuntivo** [suβ·xun·'ti·βo] *m* subjunctive

**sublevación** [su·βle·βa·'sjon, -'θjon] *f* uprising

**sublevar** [su·βle·'βar] *vr:* **~se** to revolt

**sublimación** [su·βli·ma·'sjon, -'θjon] *f* praise; PSICO, QUÍM sublimation

**sublimar** [su·βli·'mar] *vt* to praise; PSICO, QUÍM to sublimate

**sublime** [su·'βli·me] *adj* sublime

**subliminal** [su·βli·mi·'nal] *adj* subliminal

**submarinismo** [suβ·ma·ri·'nis·mo/sum·ma·ri·'nis·mo] *m* scuba-diving; **hacer ~** to go scuba-diving

**submarino** [suβ·ma·'ri·no/sum·ma·'ri·no] *m* submarine

**submarino, -a** [suβ·ma·'ri·no, -a/sum·ma·'ri·no, -a] *adj* submarine; (*vida*) underwater

**subnormal** [suβ·nor·'mal] **I.** *adj* subnormal **II.** *mf* subnormal person; **¡eres un ~!** you moron!

**subordinación** [su·βor·di·na·'sjon, -'θjon] *f* subordination; (*obediencia*) obedience

**subordinado, -a** [su·βor·di·'na·do, -a] *adj, m, f* subordinate; **oración subordinada** subordinate clause

**subordinar** [su·βor·di·'nar] *vt* to subordinate

**subrayado** [suβ·rra·'ja·do] *m* underlining

**subrayar** [suβ·rra·'jar] *vt* to underline; (*recalcar*) to emphasize

**subsanar** [suβ·sa·'nar] *vt* (*falta*) to make up for; (*error*) to rectify; (*defecto*) to repair; (*mal*) to remedy; (*dificultad*) to overcome

**subscripción** [suβs·krip·'sjon, -kriβ·'θjon] *f v.* **suscripción**

**subsecretario, -a** [suβ·se·kre·'ta·rjo, -a] *m, f* assistant; POL undersecretary

**subsidiar** [suβ·si·'djar] *vt* to subsidize

**subsidio** [suβ·'si·djo] *m* subsidy; **~ de paro** [*o* **desempleo**] unemployment compensation

**subsiguiente** [suβ·si·'ɣjen·te] *adj* subsequent

**subsistencia** [suβ·sis·'ten·sja, -'θja] *f* subsistence

**subsistente** [suβ·sis·'ten·te] *adj* surviving

**subsistir** [suβ·sis·'tir] *vi* to subsist

**substancia** [suβs·'tan·sja, -θja] *f v.* **sustancia**

**substantivo** [suβs·tan·'ti·βo] *adj, m v.* **sustantivo**

**substitución** [suβs·ti·tu·'sjon, -'θjon] *f v.* **sustitución**

**substraer** [suβs·tra·'er] *irr como* traer *vt v.* **sustraer**

**subsuelo** [suβ·'swe·lo] *m* subsoil

**subterráneo, -a** [suβ·te·'rra·neo, -a] *adj* underground

**subtítulo** [suβ·'ti·tu·lo] *m* subtitle

**subtropical** [suβ·tro·pi·'kal] *adj* subtropical

**suburbano, -a** [suβ·ur·'βa·no] *adj* suburban

**suburbio** [su·'βur·βjo] *m* (poor) suburb; (barrio) slum area; **vivir en los ~s de Lima** to live on the edge of Lima

**subvención** [suβ·βen·'sjon, -'θjon] *f* grant; POL subsidy

**subvencionar** [suβ·βen·sjo·'nar, -θjo·'nar] *vt* to aid; POL to subsidize; ADMIN to finance with a grant

**subversión** [suβ·βer·'sjon] *f* subversion

**subversivo, -a** [suβ·βer·'si·βo, -a] *adj* subversive

**subyacente** [suβ·ja·'sen·te, -'θen·te] *adj elev* underlying; (problema) hidden

**subyugar** <g → gu> [suβ·ju·'ɣar] *vt* to subjugate

**succionar** [suk·sjo·'nar, suɣ·θjo·] *vt* to suck; (tierra, esponja) to soak up

**sucedáneo** [su·se·'da·neo, su·θe·] *m* substitute

**sucedáneo, -a** [su·se·'da·neo, -a; su·θe·] *adj* substitute

**suceder** [su·se·'der, su·θe·] **I.** *vi* **1.** (seguir) to succeed; (en cargo) to follow on **2.** (ocurrir) to happen; **¿qué sucede?** what's happening?; **por lo que pueda ~** just in case; **suceda lo que suceda** whatever happens; **lo más que puede**

**~ es que** +subj the worst thing that can happen is **II.** *vt* to succeed

**sucesión** [su·se·'sjon, su·θe·] *f* succession; (serie) series *inv*

**sucesivo, -a** [su·se·'si·βo, -a; su·θe·] *adj* following; **en lo ~** henceforth; **en dos días ~** on two consecutive days

**suceso** [su·'se·so, su·'θe·so] *m* (hecho) event; (repentino) incident; (crimen) crime; **sección de ~s** accident and crime reports

**sucesor(a)** [su·se·'sor, -·'so·ra; su·θe·] *m(f)* successor; (heredero) heir

**suche** ['su·tʃe] **I.** *adj Ven* bitter **II.** *m Chile* **1.** (subalterno) assistant **2.** (rufián) pimp

**suciedad** [su·sje·'dad, su·θje·] *f* dirtiness; (porquería) dirt

**sucio** ['su·sjo, -θjo] *adv* **jugar ~** to play dirty

**sucio, -a** ['su·sjo, -a; -θjo, -a] *adj* dirty; (jugada) foul; **apuntes en ~** notes in rough; **hacer el trabajo ~** to do the dirty work

**sucucho** [su·'ku·tʃo] *m AmL* shanty

**suculento, -a** [su·ku·'len·to, -a] *adj* tasty; (jugoso) succulent

**sucumbir** [su·kum·'bir] *vi* to succumb; (morir) to die

**sucursal** [su·kur·'sal] *f* department; (de empresa) subsidiary; (de banco, negocio) branch

**sucusumucu** [su·ku·su·'mu·ku] *adv Col, Cuba, PRico* **a lo ~** playing dumb

**Sudamérica** [su·da·'me·ri·ka] *f* South America

**sudamericano, -a** [su·da·me·ri·'ka·no, -a] *adj, m, f* South American

**sudar** [su·'dar] **I.** *vi, vt* to sweat; *inf* (trabajar) to sweat it out; **me sudan los pies** my feet are sweating; **estoy sudando a chorros** I'm dripping with sweat **II.** *vt* to make sweaty; **gano mucho pero lo sudo** I earn good money but I have to work for it

**sudeste** [su·'des·te] *m* south-east

**sudoeste** [su·do·'es·te] *m* south-west

**sudor** [su·'dor] *m* sweat; **con el ~ de mi frente** with the sweat of my brow

**sudoroso, -a** [su·do·'ro·so, -a] *adj* sweaty

**Suecia** ['swe·sja, -θja] *f* Sweden

S

**sueco, -a** ['sweko] I. *adj* Swedish II. *m, f* Swede ▶ **hacerse el ~** to pretend not to hear [*o* see]

**suegro, -a** ['sweɣro, -a] *m, f* father-in-law, mother-in-law *m, f;* **los ~s** the in-laws

**suela** ['swela] *f* sole; **tú no me llegas a la ~ del zapato** you can't hold a candle to me; **como la ~ de un zapato** tough as shoe leather

**suelazo** [swe'laso] *m Chile, Col, Ecua, Ven* hard fall

**sueldo** ['sweldo] *m* pay; (*mensual*) salary; (*semanal*) wage; **~ base** basic salary; **~ fijo** regular wage; **aumento de ~** pay raise

**suelo** ['swelo] *m* **1.** (*de la tierra*) ground; (*de casa*) floor; **está muy hondo, no toco (el) ~** it's very deep, I can't reach the bottom **2.** (*terreno*) land; **~ edificable** building land ▶ **estar por los ~s** (*deprimido*) to feel very down; (*de precio*) to be dirt cheap

**suelto** ['swelto] *m* loose change

**suelto, -a** ['swelto, -a] *adj* **1.** loose; (*broche*) unfastened; (*arroz*) fluffy; (*ropa*) loose-fitting; (*lenguaje*) fluent; (*dinero*) ready; **no dejar ni un cabo ~** to leave no loose ends; **un prisionero anda ~** a prisoner is on the loose; **tener la lengua suelta** to be talkative **2.** (*separado*) separate; **pieza suelta** individual piece

**sueño** ['sweɲo] *m* **1.** sleep; **me cogió el ~** sleep overcame me; **entre ~s** half asleep; **tener el ~ ligero/pesado** to be a light/heavy sleeper **2.** (*cansancio*) sleepiness; **tener ~** to be sleepy; **me entró ~** I got sleepy; **caerse de ~** to be falling asleep; **me quita el ~** it keeps me awake **3.** (*fantasía*) dream; **ni en ~s** not even in your wildest dreams; **los ~s, ~s son** dreams are dreams

**suero** ['swero] *m* whey; MED serum

**suerte** ['swerte] *f* **1.** (*fortuna*) luck; **¡(buena) ~!** good luck!; **estar de ~** to be in luck; **no estar de ~** to be out of luck; **tener buena/mala ~** to be lucky/unlucky; **traer/dar buena/mala ~** to bring/give good/bad luck; **por ~** fortunately; **probar ~** to try one's luck; **ser cuestión de ~** to be a matter of luck; **la**

**~ está echada** the die is cast **2.** (*destino*) fate; **echar algo a ~(s)** to draw lots for sth **3.** (*casualidad*) chance

**suertero, -a** [swer'tero, -a] *adj Ecua, Hond, Perú* lucky

**suéter** ['sweter] *m* sweater

**suficiente** [sufi'sjente, -'θjente] I. *adj* enough; (*presumido*) self-important II. *m* pass

**sufijo** [su'fixo] *m* suffix

**sufragar** <g → gu> [sufra'ɣar] I. *vt* to aid; (*gastos*) to meet; (*tasa*) to pay II. *vi AmL* **~ por alguien** to vote for sb

**sufragio** [su'fraxjo] *m* **1.** (*voto*) vote **2.** (*derecho*) suffrage; **~ universal** universal suffrage **3.** (*sistema*) election

**sufrido, -a** [su'frido, -a] *adj* uncomplaining; **eres demasiado ~** you're too long-suffering; (*marido*) complaisant

**sufrimiento** [sufri'mjento] *m* suffering

**sufrir** [su'frir] *vt* **1.** (*aguantar*) to bear; (*peso*) to support; (*a alguien*) to put up with **2.** (*padecer*) to suffer; (*cambio*) to undergo; (*desengaño, accidente*) to have; (*pena*) to be stricken with; **~ de celos** to suffer from jealousy; **~ quejas** to receive complaints; **~ las consecuencias** to suffer the consequences; **~ una operación** to have an operation

**sugerencia** [suxe'rensja, -θja] *f* suggestion

**sugerir** [suxe'rir] *irr como* sentir *vt* to suggest; (*insinuar*) to hint; (*evocar*) to prompt

**sugestión** [suxes'tjon] *f* suggestion

**sugestionar** [suxestjo'nar] I. *vt* to influence II. *vr:* **~se** to indulge in autosuggestion

**suiche** ['switʃe] *m Méx* switch; AUTO ignition key

**suicida** [swi'sida, swi'θi-] I. *adj* suicidal II. *mf* suicidal person; (*muerto*) person who has committed suicide

**suicidarse** [swisi'darse, swiθi'-] *vr* to commit suicide

**suicidio** [swi'θidjo, swi'θi-] *m* suicide; **intento de ~** suicide attempt

**suite** [swit] *f* suite

**Suiza** ['swisa, -θa] *f* Switzerland

**suizo, -a** ['swiθo, -a; -θo, -a] *adj, m, f* Swiss

**sujetador** [su·xe·ta·'dor] *m* bra

**sujetar** [su·xe·'tar] I. *vt* to hold; (*asegurar*) to support; (*pelo*) to hold in place; **~ por algo** to seize by sth II. *vr:* **~se a algo** to subject oneself; **~se a algo** to abide by sth

**sujeto** [su·'xe·to] *m* individual

**sujeto, -a** [su·'xe·to, -a] *adj* subject; **~ a comprobación/fluctuaciones** subject to checking/fluctuation; **~ a la inflación** affected by inflation

**sulfato** [sul·'fa·to] *m* sulfate

**sulfuro** [sul·'fu·ro] *m* sulfide

**sultán, -ana** [sul·'tan, -·'ta·na] *m, f* sultan, sultana *m, f*

**suma** ['su·ma] *f* adding (up); (*resultado*) total; (*cantidad*) sum

**sumamente** [su·ma·'men·te] *adv* extremely

**sumar** [su·'mar] I. *vt* to add (up) II. *vr* **~se a** to join; (*discusión*) to participate in

**sumario** [su·'ma·rjo] *m* criminal proceedings *pl*

**sumergible** [su·mer·'xi·βle] I. *adj* submersible; (*reloj*) waterproof II. *m* submarine

**sumergir** <g → j> [su·mer·'xir] *vt, vr:* **~se** to submerge

**sumidero** [su·mi·'de·ro] *m* drain; (*de la calle*) sewer

**suministrar** [su·mi·nis·'trar] *vt* to supply; (*abastecer*) to stock

**suministro** [su·mi·'nis·tro] *m* supply; (*abastecimiento*) stock

**sumir** [su·'mir] I. *vt* to sink (**en** into); **~ en la miseria/desesperación a alguien** to plunge sb into poverty/despair II. *vr:* **~se** to sink (**en** into); **~se en el trabajo** to become absorbed in one's work

**sumisión** [su·mi·'sjon] *f* **1.** (*acción*) submission **2.** (*carácter*) submissiveness **3.** (*obediencia*) obedience

**sumo, -a** ['su·mo] *adj* (*más alto*) high(est); (*mayor*) great; **a lo ~** at most; **en grado ~** highly

**sungo, -a** ['sun·go, -a] *adj Col* Black

**suntuosidad** [sun·two·si·'dad] *f* sumptuousness

**suntuoso, -a** [sun·tu·'o·so, -a] *adj* sumptuous; (*opulento*) lavish

**supeditar** [su·pe·di·'tar] I. *vt* **1.** to subordinate **2.** (*someter*) to subdue **2.** (*condicionar*) to condition II. *vr:* **~se** to submit

**súper** ['su·per] I. *adj inf* super II. *m* supermarket III. *f* Premium (gas)

**superabundancia** [su·per·a·βun·'dan·sja, -θja] *f* superabundance

**superación** [su·pe·ra·'sjon, -'θjon] *f* (*de récord*) improvement; (*de situación*) surmounting

**superar** [su·pe·'rar] I. *vt* to surpass; (*límite*) to exceed; (*récord*) to beat; (*prueba*) to pass; (*situación*) to overcome II. *vr:* **~se** to excel oneself

**superávit** [su·pe·'ra·βit] *m* surplus

**superdotado, -a** [su·per·do·'ta·do, -a] *adj* extremely gifted

**superficial** [su·per·fi·'sjal, -'θjal] *adj* superficial; (*detalle*) minor; **herida ~** flesh wound

**superficie** [su·per·'fi·sje, -θje] *f* surface; **~ cultivable** arable area; **salir a la ~** to surface; (*apariencia*) external appearance

**superfluo, -a** [su·per·flwo, -a] *adj* superfluous; (*gastos*) unnecessary

**superior** [su·pe·'rjor] *adj* higher; (*en calidad*) better; (*en inteligencia, rango*) superior; (*excelente*) excellent; **el curso ~ de un río** the upper course of a river; **el piso ~ al mío** the apartment above mine

**superior(a)** [su·pe·'rjor, -·'rjo·ra] *m(f)* superior

**superioridad** [su·pe·rjo·ri·'dad] *f* superiority (**sobre** over); **hablar con un tono de ~** to speak in a superior tone of voice

**superlativo** [su·per·la·'ti·βo] *m* superlative

**superlativo, -a** [su·per·la·'ti·βo, -a] *adj* superlative

**supermercado** [su·per·mer·'ka·do] *m* supermarket

**superpoblación** [su·per·po·βla·'sjon, -'θjon] *f* overpopulation

**superponer** [su·per·po·'ner] *irr como poner vt* to give more importance to; **~ algo a algo** to superimpose sth on sth

**superpotencia** [su·per·po·'ten·sja, -θja] *f* superpower

**superproducción** [su·per·pro·duk·'sjon, -duɣ·'θjon] *f* **1.** COM overproduction **2.** CINE big-budget movie

**supersónico, -a** [su·per·'so·ni·ko, -a] *adj* supersonic

**superstición** [su·pers·ti·'sjon, -'θjon] *f* superstition

**supersticioso, -a** [su·pers·ti·'sjo·so, -a; -'θjo·so, -a] *adj* superstitious

**supervisar** [su·per·βi·'sar] *vt* to supervise

**supervisión** [su·per·βi·'sjon] *f* supervision

**supervisor(a)** [su·per·βi·'sor, -·'so·ra] *m(f)* supervisor; (*funcionario*) inspector

**supervivencia** [su·per·βi·'βen·sja, -θja] *f* survival

**superviviente** [su·per·βi·'βjen·te] **I.** *adj* surviving **II.** *mf* survivor

**suplantar** [su·plan·'tar] *vt* to supplant

**suplementario, -a** [su·ple·men·'ta·rjo, -a] *adj* supplementary; **tomo ~** additional volume

**suplemento** [su·ple·'men·to] *m* **1.** supplement; (*tomo*) supplementary volume; **~ en color** color supplement **2.** (*precio*) extra charge; (*del tren*) excess fare

**suplencia** [su·'plen·sja, -θja] *f* substitution

**suplente** [su·'plen·te] *adj, mf* substitute

**súplica** ['su·pli·ka] *f* plea; (*escrito*) request

**suplicar** <c → qu> [su·pli·'kar] *vt* to implore; **~ algo de rodillas** to beg on one's knees for sth

**suplicio** [su·'pli·sjo, -θjo] *m* torment; **el viaje fue un ~** we had a terrible journey

**suplir** [su·'plir] *vt* **1.** (*completar*) to make up for **2.** (*sustituir*) to substitute

**supo** ['su·po] *3. pret de* **saber**

**suponer** [su·po·'ner] *irr como* **poner** *vt* **1.** (*dar por sentado*) to suppose; **vamos a ~ que...** let's suppose that...; **se supone que...** it is assumed that...; **suponiendo que...** supposing that...; **pongamos que...** let us assume that... **2.** (*figurar*) to imagine; **supongo que sí** I suppose so; **no supongo que...** +*subj*

I don't imagine...; **no lo suponía tan fuerte** I didn't realize he was so strong **3.** (*significar*) to mean; **~ un duro golpe para alguien** to be a real blow for sb; **esto me supone 60 pesos al mes** this amounts to 60 pesos a month for me; **no ~ molestia alguna** to be no trouble

**suposición** [su·po·si·'sjon, -'θjon] *f* supposition; (*presunción*) assumption

**supositorio** [su·po·si·'to·rjo] *m* suppository

**supremacía** [su·pre·ma·'si·a, -'θi·a] *f* supremacy; (*prioridad*) priority

**supremo, -a** [su·'pre·mo] *adj* highest; *fig* supreme; **Tribunal Supremo** Supreme Court

**suprimir** [su·pri·'mir] *vt* **1.** (*poner fin*) to suppress; (*fronteras*) to eliminate; (*controles, obstáculos, amenaza*) to remove; (*regla*) to abolish **2.** (*omitir*) to omit **3.** (*silenciar*) to silence

**supuesto** [su·'pwes·to] *m* assumption; (*hipótesis*) hypothesis

**supuesto, -a** [su·'pwes·to, -a] *adj* (*pretendido*) so-called; (*ladrón, asesino*) alleged; (*testigo, nombre*) assumed; (*causa*) supposed; **por ~** of course; **dar algo por ~** to take sth for granted; **~ que** since

**supurar** [su·pu·'rar] *vi* to suppurate

**sur** [sur] *m* south; (*viento*) south wind; **América del Sur** South America

**surcar** <c → qu> [sur·'kar] *vt* (*tierra*) to plow; (*mares*) to sail

**surco** ['sur·ko] *m* furrow; (*arruga*) wrinkle

**sureste** [sur·'es·te] *m* south-east

**surf** [surf] *m* surfing; **hacer ~** to windsurf

**surgir** <g → j> [sur·'xir] *vi* (*agua*) to gush; (*dificultad, posibilidad*) to arise; (*pregunta*) to come up

**suroeste** [sur·o·'es·te] *m* south-west

**surrealismo** [su·rrea·'lis·mo] *m* surrealism

**surrealista** [su·rrea·'lis·ta] *adj, mf* surrealist

**surtido** [sur·'ti·do] *m* assortment

**surtido, -a** [sur·'ti·do, -a] *adj* **1.** mixed; (*variado*) varied; **galletas surtidas** assorted biscuits **2.** (*bien provisto*) well-stocked

**surtidor** [sur·ti·ðor] *m* gas station; (*aparato*) gas pump

**surtir** [sur·tir] **I.** *vt* ~ **de algo** to supply with sth; ~ **efecto** to work; (*palabras*) to have the desired effect **II.** *vr* ~**se de algo** to provide oneself with sth

**suruco** [su·ru·ko] *m CSur* crap

**surumbo, -a** [su·rum·bo, -a] *adj Guat, Hond* stunned

**surupa** [su·ru·pa] *f Ven* cockroach

**susceptibilidad** [su·sep·ti·βi·li·ðað, sus-·θep-] *f* susceptibility

**susceptible** [su·sep·ti·βle, sus-θep-] *adj* sensitive; (*irritable*) touchy; ~ **de mejora** capable of improvement; **materiales** ~**s de ser reutilizados** material which can be reused

**suscitar** [su·si·tar, sus·θi-] *vt* to cause; (*discusión*) to start; (*escándalo, comentarios*) to provoke; (*odio, conflicto*) to stir up; (*problema*) to raise; (*antipatías, curiosidad*) to arouse

**suscribirse** [sus·kri·'βir·se] *irr como escribir vr* to subscribe (**a** to)

**suscripción** [sus·krip·'sjon, -kriβ·'θjon] *f* subscription; (*de acciones*) taking up

**suscri(p)tor(a)** [sus·krip·'tor, -·'to·ra] *m(f)* subscriber

**suspender** [sus·pen·'der] *vt* **1.** to fail; **he suspendido matemáticas** I've flunked math **2.** (*trabajador, deportista*) to suspend; (*sesión*) to adjourn; (*tratamiento*) to break off; **se ha suspendido la función de esta noche** tonight's show has been called off **3.** ~ **de algo** to hang from sth

**suspensión** [sus·pen·'sjon] *f* **1.** (*acción de colgar*) suspension **2.** (*interrupción: tratamiento*) interruption; (*producción*) break; ~ **de armas** truce; ~ **de la pena** annulment of the penalty; ~ **de pagos** temporary receivership

**suspenso** [sus·'pen·so] *m* **1.** fail; **sacar un** ~ to fail **2.** *AmL* suspense

**suspicacia** [sus·pi·'ka·sja, -θja] *f* suspicion

**suspicaz** [sus·pi·'kas, -'kaθ] *adj* suspicious

**suspirar** [sus·pi·'rar] *vi* to sigh; ~ **por algo** to long for sth

**suspiro** [sus·'pi·ro] *m* sigh

**sustancia** [sus·'tan·sja, -θja] *f* substance; **en** ~ in essence

**sustancial** [sus·tan·'sjal, -'θjal] *adj* vital; (*fundamental*) essential; (*comida*) substantial; (*libro*) meaty

**sustancioso, -a** [sus·tan·'sjo·so, -a; -'θjo·so, -a] *adj* substantial

**sustantivo** [sus·tan·'ti·βo] *m* noun

**sustentar** [sus·ten·'tar] **I.** *vt* to hold up; (*columna*) to support; (*esperanza*) to sustain; (*familia*) to feed **II.** *vr*: ~**se** to sustain oneself; ~**se en algo** to rely on sth

**sustento** [sus·'ten·to] *m* maintenance; (*apoyo*) support

**sustitución** [sus·ti·tu·'sjon, -'θjon] *f* replacement; (*temporal*) substitution

**sustituir** [sus·ti·tu·'ir] *irr como huir vt* to substitute; (*temporalmente*) to stand in for; (*definitivamente*) to replace

**sustituto, -a** [sus·ti·'tu·to, -a] *m, f* substitute

**susto** ['sus·to] *m* scare; **poner cara de** ~ to look scared; **pegarle un** ~ **a alguien** [*o* **darle**] to give sb a fright; **pegarse** [*o* **llevarse**] **un** ~ to get scared; **no ganar para** ~**s** to have one problem after another

**sustraer** [sus·tra·'er] *irr como traer* **I.** *vt* **1.** (*restar*) to subtract **2.** (*robar*) to steal **3.** (*privar*) to remove **4.** (*separar*) to abduct **II.** *vr* ~**se de algo** to get away from sth

**susurrar** [su·su·'rrar] **I.** *vi* to whisper; (*no claro*) to mutter; (*viento*) to murmur **II.** *vr*: ~**se** to be rumored **III.** *vimpers* **se susurra que...** it is rumored that...

**susurro** [su·'su·rro] *m* whisper; (*no claro*) mutter; (*del viento*) murmur

**sutil** [su·'til] *adj* (*sabor*) subtle; (*aroma*) delicate; (*diferencia, ironía*) fine

**sutileza** [su·ti·'le·sa, -θa] *f*, **sutilidad** [su·ti·li·'ðað] *f* **1.** (*de sabor*) subtlety; (*de aroma*) delicacy **2.** (*de diferencia, ironía*) fineness; (*de jugada, sistema*) refinement **3.** (*de persona*) sharpness

**suyo, -a** ['su·jo, -a] *adj, pron* (*de él*) his; (*de ella*) hers; (*de cosa, animal*) its; (*de ellos*) theirs; (*de Ud., Uds.*) yours; (*de uno*) one's; **este encendedor es** ~ this

**S**

lighter is his/hers/theirs; **siempre habla de los ~s** he/she is always talking about his/her family; **darle a alguien lo ~** to give sb what belongs to him/her; *fig* to give sb what he/she deserves; **ya ha hecho otra de las suyas** he/she has been up to his/her tricks again; **Albert es muy ~** Albert keeps to himself; **eso es muy ~** that's typical of him/her; **ir a lo ~** to go one's own way

# T

**T, t** [te] *f* T, t; **~ de Tarragona** T as in Tango

**tabacal** [ta·βa·'kal] *m AmL* tobacco plantation

**tabaco** [ta·'βa·ko] *m* tobacco; (*cigarrillos*) cigarettes *pl*; **~ rubio/de mascar** Virginia/chewing tobacco; **¿tienes ~?** do you have any cigarettes?

**tabanco** [ta·'βaŋ·ko] *m AmC* attic

**taberna** [ta·'βer·na] *f* tavern

**tabique** [ta·'βi·ke] *m* partition; **~ nasal** nasal septum

**tabla** ['ta·βla] *f* 1. board; **~ de cocina/planchar** cutting/ironing board; **~ de surf/windsurf** surfboard/sailboard 2. (*lista*) list; (*cuadro*) table; (*de libro*) table of contents 3. *pl* draw ▶ **a raja ~** to the letter; **hacer ~ rasa de algo** to wipe the slate clean

**tablada** [ta·'βla·da] *f CSur* stockyard

**tablao** [ta·'βlao] *m* stage

**tablero** [ta·'βle·ro] *m* board; **~ de anuncios/ajedrez** bulletin/chess board

**tableta** [ta·'βle·ta] *f* 1. bar 2. *AmL* tablet

**tabloide** [ta·'βloi·de] *m AmL* tabloid

**tablón** [ta·'βlon] *m* 1. plank; (*de anuncios*) bulletin board 2. *AmL* patch; (*grande*) plot

**tabú** [ta·'βu] *m* <tabúes> taboo

**tabulador** [ta·βu·la·'dor] *m* tab

**tacañería** [ta·ka·ɲe·'ri·a] *f* stinginess

**tacaño, -a** [ta·'ka·ɲo, -a] I. *adj* stingy II. *m, f* miser

**tachar** [ta·'tʃar] *vt* to cross out; **~ de algo** to brand as sth; **lo ~on de incompe-**

**tente** they accused him of being incompetent

**tachero** [ta·'tʃe·ro] *m Arg inf* taxi driver

**tacho** [ta·'tʃo] *m* 1. *AmL* (*vasija*) metal basin 2. *AmL* (*hojalata*) tin 3. *AmL* (*cubo*) trash can 4. *Arg inf* taxi; **irse al ~** to collapse

**tachón** [ta·'tʃon] *m* crossing out

**tácito, -a** ['ta·si·to, -a; 'ta·θi-] *adj* tacit

**taciturno, -a** [ta·si·'tur·no, -a; 'ta·θi-] *adj* taciturn; (*melancólico*) glum

**taco** [ta·ko] *m* 1. (*pedazo*) piece 2. (*de billar*) cue 3. (*de bota*) stud 4. (*de papel*) pad; (*calendario*) tear-off desk; (*fajo*) wad 5. (*de jamón*) cube; (*bocado*) bite to eat 6. (*de palabrota*) swear-word; **decir** [*o* **soltar**] **~s** to swear 7. *inf* (*lío*) mess; **estar hecho un ~** to be all mixed up 8. *AmL* (*tacón*) heel 9. *pl inf* years; **¡ya tengo mis 40 ~s!** I'm already past 40!

**tacón** [ta·'kon] *m* heel; **~ de aguja** spike heel; **zapatos de ~ alto** high-heel(ed) shoes

**táctica** ['tak·ti·ka] *f* tactic(s); **ir con ~** to move strategically

**táctico, -a** ['tak·ti·ko, -a] I. *adj* tactical II. *m, f* tactician

**táctil** ['tak·til] *adj* tactile

**tacto** ['tak·to] *m* 1. touch; **sentido del ~** sense of touch; **al ~** to the touch; **ser áspero al ~** to feel rough 2. (*habilidad*) tact; **no tener ~** to be tactless

**tacuache** [ta·'kwa·tʃe] *m Cuba, Méx zoo* almique

**tacuaco, -a** [ta·'kwa·ko, -a] *adj Chile* chubby

**taita** ['tai·ta] *m* 1. *CSur* expert 2. *Arg* bully 3. *Ven* head of the family

**tajada** [ta·'xa·da] *f* 1. (*porción*) slice; (*corte*) cut; **llevarse la mejor ~** to take the lion's share; **sacar ~ de algo** to take advantage of sth 2. *inf* (*ronquera*) **tener una ~** to be hoarse; (*borrachera*) **pilló una buena ~** he/she got smashed

**tajante** [ta·'xan·te] *adj* sharp; (*respuesta*) categorical; (*actitud*) dogmatic; (*medidas*) unequivocal

**tajar** [ta·'xar] *vt* to cut; *AmL* (*afilar*) to sharpen

**tajo** ['ta·xo] *m* 1. cut; **darse un ~ en el**

**dedo** to cut one's finger **2.** GEO gorge **3.** *inf* work; **ir al ~** to go to work

**tal** [tal] **I.** *adj* **1.** (*igual*) such; **en ~ caso** in that case; **no digas ~ cosa** don't say any such thing; **no he dicho nunca ~ cosa** I never said anything of the kind **2.** (*tanto*) so; **la distancia es ~ que...** it's so far away that... **3.** (*cierto*) certain; **un ~ Pérez llamó** somebody called Perez called **II.** *pron* **1.** (*alguien*) **~ o cual** someone or other **2.** (*cosa*) **hablar de ~ y cual** to talk about one thing and another; **y ~** (**y cual**) and so on (and so forth) **III.** *adv* **1.** (*así*) so **2.** (*de la misma manera*) just; **es ~ cual lo buscaba** it's just what I was looking for; **son ~ para cual** they're two of a kind; **estar ~ cual** to be just as it was; **lo dejé ~ cual** I left it just as I found it; **~ y como** just as; **~ y como suena** just as I'm telling you **3.** (*cómo*) **¿qué ~ (te va)?** how are things?; **¿qué ~ si tomamos una copa?** why don't we have sth to drink?; **¿qué ~ es tu nuevo jefe?** what's your new boss like?; **~ y como están las cosas** the way things are now **IV.** *conj* **con ~ de** *+infin* **con ~ de que** *+subj* as long as; **~ vez** maybe

**tala** ['ta·la] *f* felling

**taladrar** [ta·la·'drar] *vt* to drill; **un ruido que taladra los oídos** an ear-splitting noise

**taladro** [ta·'la·dro] *m* drill

**talante** [ta·'lan·te] *m* disposition; (*humor*) mood; **de buen/mal ~** in a good/bad mood; **de buen ~** willingly

**talar** [ta·'lar] *vt* to fell

**talco** ['tal·ko] *m* talc; (*polvos*) talcum powder

**talento** [ta·'len·to] *m* talent; **de gran ~** very talented; **tener ~ para los idiomas** to have a gift for languages

**talentoso, -a** [ta·len·'to·so, -a] *adj* talented

**talero** [ta·'le·ro] *m Arg, Chile, Urug* whip

**talismán** [ta·lis·'man] *m* talisman

**talla** ['ta·ja, -ʎa] *f* **1.** (*madera*) carving; (*piedra*) sculpting; (*diamante*) cutting **2.** (*estatura*) height; (*moral, intelectual*) stature; **ser de poca ~** to be short; **no dar la ~** not to be good enough **3.** (*de ropa*) size; **un abrigo de la ~ 42** a size 42 coat

**tallar** [ta·'jar, -'ʎar] *vt* (*diamante*) to cut; (*madera*) to carve; (*piedra*) to sculpt

**tallarín** [ta·ja·'rin, ta·ʎa-] *m* noodle

**talle** ['ta·je, -ʎe] *m* waist; (*figura*) figure

**taller** [ta·'jer, -'ʎer] *m* **1.** workshop; **~ artesanal** craft workshop; **~es gráficos** printing works **2.** ENS seminar **3.** (*auto*) garage

**tallo** ['ta·jo, -ʎo] *m* stem; (*renuevo*) shoot

**talón** [ta·'lon] *m* **1.** heel; **pisar a alguien los talones** to be hot on sb's heels **2.** check; **hazme un ~ de 10.000 pesos** make me out a check for 10,000 pesos; **~ sin fondos** bad check **3.** (*resguardo*) voucher; (*recibo*) receipt

**tamal** [ta·'mal] *m AmC, Méx* tamale

**tamalada** [ta·ma·'la·da] *f Méx* tamale party

**tamango** [ta·'man·go] *m CSur* coarse leather shoe

**tamaño** [ta·'ma·ɲo] *m* size; **¿de qué ~ es?** what size is it?; **de gran ~** large

**tamaño, -a** [ta·'ma·ɲo, -a] *adj* **1.** (*grande*) such a big **2.** (*pequeño*) such a small **3.** (*semejante*) such a; **tamaña tontería** such a stupid thing; **~ disparate** such an absurd idea

**tambache** [tam·'ba·tʃe] *m Méx inf* bundle; **un ~ de ropa/hojas** a pile of clothes/papers; **hacer ~ a alguien** to play a dirty trick on sb

**tambalear** [tam·ba·le·'ar] *vi, vr:* **~se** to stagger; *fig* to totter

**tambarria** [tam·'ba·rrja] *f Perú* party

**también** [tam·'bjen] *adv* also, as well, too; **yo lo ví ~** I also saw him, I saw him too [*o* as well]

**tambocha** [tam·'bo·tʃa] *f Col, Ven* poisonous red-headed ant

**tambor** [tam·'bor] *m* drum

**tamiz** [ta·'mis, -'miθ] *m* sieve

**tamizar** <z → c> [ta·mi·'sar, -'θar] *vt* to sift

**tampoco** [tam·'po·ko] *adv* not either, nor, neither; **ni puedo ni ~ quiero** I neither can nor do I want to; **~ me gusta éste** I don't like this one either; **si tú no lo haces yo ~** if you don't do it, neither will I

T

**tampón** [tam·'pon] m tampon

**tamuga** [ta·'mu·ɣa] f 1. AmC (fardo) bundle; (mochila) knapsack 2. AmL (marihuana) joint

**tan** [tan] adv so; ~... como... as... as...; **de ~ simpático me resulta insoportable** he/she is so nice I find him/her unbearable; ~ **siquiera una vez** just once

**tanate** [ta·'na·te] m 1. AmC, Méx (cesto) pannier 2. AmC (fardo) bundle 3. pl Méx vulg (testículos) balls pl 4. pl AmC (cachivaches) gear, stuff

**tanda** ['tan·da] f 1. (turno) shift; **estar en la ~ de día** to be on the day shift 2. (serie) series inv; **por ~s** in batches; **en ~s de ocho** in groups of eight 3. (de trabajo, capa) layer

**tanga** ['tan·ga] m thong

**tangente** [tan·'xen·te] f tangent; **salirse** [o **irse**] **por la** ~ to go off on a tangent

**tangible** [tan·'xi·βle] adj tangible; fig concrete

**tango** ['tan·go] m tango

**tano, -a** ['ta·no, -a] adj, m, f Arg, Urug inf Italian

**tanque** ['tan·ke] m 1. MIL tank 2. (cisterna) tanker; (vehículo) road-tanker 3. inf (de cerveza) large glass 4. AmL (estanque) pool

**tanquear** [tan·ke·'ar] vi Col to get gas

**tantear** [tan·te·'ar] vt 1. to calculate; (a ojo) to size up; (tamaño, volumen) to gauge; (precio) to estimate 2. (probar) to try out; (sondear) to sound out; ~ **el terreno** to get the lay of the land 3. (ir a tientas) to grope; **tuvimos que bajar la escalera tanteando** we had to feel our way down the stairs

**tanteo** [tan·'te·o] m 1. (cálculo: cantidad) calculation; (de tamaño, volumen) weighing up; (a ojo) sizing up; (de precio) estimate; **al** [o **por**] ~ by trial and error 2. (sondeo) sounding out 3. DEP (de puntos) score; (de goles) scoring; ~ **final** final score

**tanto** ['tan·to] I. m 1. (cantidad) certain amount; COM rate; ~ **por ciento** percentage; **costar otro** ~ to cost as much again; **un** ~ a bit; **estar un** ~ **harto de algo** to be rather fed up with sth; **estoy un** ~ **sorprendido** I'm somewhat sur-

prised 2. (punto) point; (gol) goal; **un** ~ **a favor de alguien** a point in sb's favor ▶ **estar al** ~ **de algo** to be up to date on sth II. adv 1. so much; **no es para** ~ there's no need to make such a fuss 2. (de duración) so long; **tu respuesta tardó** ~ **que...** your answer took so long that... 3. (comparativo) ~ **mejor/peor** so much the better/worse; ~ **como** as much as; ~ **si llueve como si no...** whether it rains or not... ▶ **¡ni** ~ **tan calvo!** neither one extreme nor the other!; ~... **como...** both... and...; **en** ~ **(que** +subj) as long as; **entre** ~ meanwhile; **por** (lo) ~ therefore; **por lo** ~ **mejor callar** so best keep quiet

**tanto, -a** ['tan·to, -a] I. adj 1. so much; **tantas posibilidades** so many possibilities; **¡hace** ~ **tiempo que no te veo!** I haven't seen you for so long!; ~ **gusto en conocerle** a pleasure to meet you 2. (comparativo) as much, as many; **no tengo** ~ **dinero como tú** I don't have as much money as you; **tenemos** ~s **amigos como ellos** we have many friends as they do 3. pl **en mil novecientos ochenta y** ~s in nineteen eighty-something; **uno de** ~s one of many; **tener 40 y** ~s **años** to be 40-odd years old; **a las tantas de la madrugada** in the wee hours of the morning; **quedarse despierto hasta las tantas** to stay up until all hours ▶ ~ **tienes,** ~ **vales** a man's worth is the worth of his land II. pron dem ~s as many; **coge** ~s **como quieras** take as many as you like; **no llego a** ~ I won't go that far

**tapa** ['ta·pa] f 1. lid; ~ **de rosca** screwtop; **de** ~s **duras** hardback 2. (de zapato) heelpiece 3. CULIN appetizer; **una** ~ **de aceitunas** a side of olives; ~ **de ternera** round of beef

**tapado** [ta·'pa·do] m Arg coat

**tapar** [ta·'par] I. vt 1. to cover; (olla) to put a lid on; (manta) to cover up; (desagüe) to obstruct; (agujero) to fill in; (botella) to put the cap on 2. (ocultar) to hide; **¿te tapo?** am I blocking your view?; **la pared nos tapa el viento** the wall protects us from the wind II. vr: ~**se** (con ropa) to wrap up; (con *mantas*) to cover up; (*completamente*) to hide; (*oídos, nariz*) to get blocked; **~se la cara/los ojos** to cover one's face/eyes

**taparrabo(s)** [ta·pa·'rra·βo(s)] *m (inv)* loincloth

**tape** ['ta·pe] *m* **1.** *Arg, Urug Indian-looking person* **2.** *Cuba, PRico* (*tapa*) lid **3.** *RíoPl* (*cinta*) tape

**tapeo** [ta·'peo] *m* **ir de ~** to go bar-hopping

**tapia** ['ta·pja] *f* wall; (*de jardín*) garden wall; **estar más sordo que una ~** to be as deaf as a doorknob

**tapicería** [ta·pi·se·'ri·a, ta·pi·θe·] *f* **1.** (*tapices*) tapestries *pl* **2.** (*tienda: de tapices*) tapestry shop; (*de muebles*) upholstery; (*taller*) upholsterer's

**tapisca** [ta·'pis·ka] *f AmC* corn harvest

**tapiz** [ta·'pis, -'piθ] *m* tapestry; (*en el suelo*) rug

**tapizar** <z → c> [ta·pi·'sar, -'θar] *vt* to upholster; (*acolchar*) to quilt

**tapón** [ta·'pon] *m* **1.** stopper; (*de fregadero*) drain plug; (*corcho*) cork; AUTO oil drain plug **2.** *inf* short stubby person **3.** MED tampon; (*para el oído*) earplug **4.** (*de tráfico*) traffic jam

**taponar** [ta·po·'nar] *vt* to plug; (*corcho*) to cork; (*plástico*) to seal; (*desagüe*) to clog

**tapujo** [ta·'pu·xo] *m* **andar con ~s** to behave deceitfully; **no andarse con ~s** to speak plainly

**taquear** [ta·ke·'ar] *AmL* **I.** *vi* **1.** *inf* (*jugar*) to shoot pool **2.** (*arma*) to ram **3.** (*llenar*) to stuff **II.** *vr:* **~se** to tap one's heels

**taquería** [ta·ke·'ri·a] *f* **1.** *Cuba* uninhibitedness **2.** *Méx* taco stand

**taquicardia** [ta·ki·'kar·dja] *f* tachycardia

**taquilla** [ta·'ki·ja, -ʎa] *f* **1.** TEAT, CINE box office; DEP gate money; FERRO ticket window; **éxito de ~** box-office hit **2.** (*recaudación*) receipts *pl*

**tara** ['ta·ra] *f* defect; (*peso*) tare

**tarado, -a** [ta·'ra·do, -a] **I.** *adj* crazy **II.** *m, f* nitwit

**tarantín** <tarantines> [ta·ran·'tin] *m* **1.** *Ven* (*tenducha*) stall **2.** *pl AmC, Cuba, PRico* (*cachivaches*) odds and

ends *pl*

**tarántula** [ta·'ran·tu·la] *f* tarantula

**tararear** [ta·ra·re·'ar] *vt* to la-la-la; (*con labios cerrados*) to hum

**tarascón** [ta·ras·'kon] *m AmS* bite; (*herida*) bite wound

**tardanza** [tar·'dan·sa, -θa] *f* delay; **perdona la ~ en escribirte** forgive me for taking so long to write

**tardar** [tar·'dar] *vi* to take time; **~ en llegar** to take a long time to arrive; **~on tres semanas en contestar** it took them three weeks to answer; **~on mucho en arreglarlo** it took them a long time to fix it; **no tardo nada** I won't be long; **no ~é en volver** I'll be right back; **¡no tardes!** don't be gone long!; **a más ~** at the latest

**tarde** ['tar·de] **I.** *f* (*sobremesa*) afternoon; (*tarde-noche*) evening; **por la ~** in the afternoon; **¡buenas ~s!** good afternoon!, good evening!; **los viernes por la ~** Friday evenings **II.** *adv* late; **~ o temprano** sooner or later; **de ~ en ~** now and then; **se me hace ~** it's getting late ▶ **más vale ~ que nunca** better late than never

**tardío, -a** [tar·'di·o, -a] *adj* late; (*lento*) slow; **un consejo ~** a belated piece of advice

**tarea** [ta·'rea] *f* task; (*trabajo*) job; ENS homework; **¿has hecho tus ~s?** have you done your homework?; **~s de la casa** housework

**tareco** [ta·'re·ko] *m Cuba, Ecua, Ven* **1.** (*herramienta*) tool of trade **2.** (*trasto*) old thing

**tarifa** [ta·'ri·fa] *f* rate; (*transporte*) fare

**tarima** [ta·'ri·ma] *f* platform

**tarja** ['tar·xa] *f AmL* business card

**tarjeta** [tar·'xe·ta] *f* **1.** card; **~ de crédito/visita/gráficos** credit/calling/graphics card; **~ de embarque** boarding pass; **~ postal** postcard **2.** COMPUT **~ de memoria** memory chip

**tarro** ['ta·rro] *m* **1.** pot; (*cristal*) jar; (*metal*) tin **2.** *inf* head; **comer el ~ a alguien** to brainwash sb; **¿estás mal del ~?** are you crazy?

**tarta** ['tar·ta] *f* cake; (*pastel*) pie

**tartamudear** [tar·ta·mu·de·'ar] *vi* to stutter

**tartamudo**, **-a** [tar·ta·'mu·do, -a] **I.** *adj* stuttering **II.** *m, f* stutterer

**tasa** ['ta·sa] *f* **1.** (*valoración*) valuation **2.** (*precio, derechos*) fee; (*impuesto*) tax **3.** (*porcentaje*) rate; **~ de desempleo/interés/natalidad** unemployment/interest/birth rate

**tasajear** [ta·sa·xe·'ar] *vt AmL* to cut; (*carne*) to jerk

**tasar** [ta·'sar] *vt* **1.** (*precio*) to fix the price of; (*impuesto*) to tax **2.** (*valorar*) to value; **~ en exceso** to overrate

**tasca** ['tas·ka] *f* bar

**tata** ['ta·ta] *m AmL* daddy

**tatarabuelo**, **-a** [ta·ta·ra·'βwe·lo, -a] *m, f* great-great-grandfather

**tataranieto**, **-a** [ta·ta·ra·'nje·to, -a] *m, f* great-great-grandson

**tatuaje** [ta·tu·'a·xe] *m* tattoo

**tatuar** <*1. pres* tatúo> [ta·tu·'ar] *vt* to tattoo

**tauca** ['tau·ka] *f* **1.** *Bol, Chile, Ecua* heap; **una ~ de papeles** a pile of papers **2.** *Chile* sack

**taurino**, **-a** [tau·'ri·no, -a] *adj* bull-like; (*del toreo*) bullfighting

**Tauro** ['tau·ro] *m* Taurus

**taxi** ['tak·si] *m* taxi

**taxista** [tak·'sis·ta] *mf* taxi driver

**taza** ['ta·sa, -θa] *f* cup; (*grande*) mug; **una ~ de café** a coffee cup; (*con café*) a cup of coffee; (*del wáter*) bowl; (*de fuente*) basin

**te** [te] **I.** *pron pers* you; **¡míra~!** look at yourself! **II.** *pron reflexivo* ~ **vistes** you get dressed; ~ **levantas** you get up; **no ~ hagas daño** don't hurt yourself

**té** [te] *m* tea

**teatral** [tea·'tral] *adj* theatre; (*efecto, experiencia, autor*) stage; *fig* theatrical

**teatro** [te·'a·tro] *m* theater; (*escenario*) stage; **obra de ~** play; **hacer ~** to work in the theater; *fig* to playact; (*exagerar*) to exaggerate

**techar** [te·'tʃar] *vt* to roof

**techo** ['te·tʃo] *m* ceiling; (*tejado*) roof; **vivir bajo el mismo ~** to live under the same roof

**tecla** ['te·kla] *f* key; ~ **de mayúsculas/retroceso/intro** shift/backspace/enter key; **pulsar una ~** to press a key

**teclado** [te·'kla·do] *m* keyboard

**teclear** [te·kle·'ar] *vi* (*piano*) to play; (*ordenador*) to type; (*dedos*) to drum

**técnica** [te·'kni·ka] *f* technique; (*tecnología*) technology

**tecnicismo** [tek·ni·'sis·mo, -θis·mo] *m* technicality; (*término*) technical term

**técnico**, **-a** ['tek·ni·ko, -a] **I.** *adj* technical **II.** *m, f* specialist; TÉC technician; DEP trainer; ~ **de inserción laboral** employment services assistant

**tecnología** [tek·no·lo·'xi·a] *f* technology; (*técnica*) technique; ~ **punta** leading-edge technology

**tecnológico**, **-a** [tek·no·'lo·xi·ko, -a] *adj* technological; (*técnico*) technical; **parque ~** technology park

**tecolote** [te·ko·'lo·te] *m AmC, Méx* owl

**tedioso**, **-a** [te·'djo·so, -a] *adj* tedious

**teja** ['te·xa] *f* roof tile

**tejado** [te·'xa·do] *m* roof; **empezar la casa por el ~** to put the cart before the horse

**tejano**, **-a** [te·'xa·no] *adj, m, f* Texan; **~s** jeans

**tejaván** [te·xa·'βan] *m AmL* **1.** (*cobertizo*) shed **2.** (*corredor*) corridor **3.** (*alero*) eaves *pl* **4.** (*casa*) rustic house with tiled roof

**tejemaneje** [te·xe·ma·'ne·xe] *m inf* **1.** (*actividad*) to-do; **traerse un ~ increíble con los papeles** to make such a fuss with the papers **2.** (*intriga*) scheming; **se deben de traer algún ~** they must be up to sth

**tejer** [te·'xer] *vt* to knit; (*en un telar*) to weave; (*araña*) to spin; (*cesto, trenza*) to plait; (*plan*) to plot

**tejido** [te·'xi·do] *m* tissue; (*tela*) fabric; **los ~s** textiles *pl*

**tela** ['te·la] *f* **1.** fabric; ~ **de araña** spider web; ~ **metálica** wire screen; ~ **de punto** knit; **lo cubrieron con una ~ blanca** they covered it with a white cloth **2.** *inf* matter; **hay ~ para rato** (*para discutir*) there's plenty to talk about; (*para trabajar*) there's a lot to be done; **este problema tiene ~** this isn't an easy problem **3.** *inf* (*dinero*) dough
▶ **poner algo en ~ de juicio** (*dudar*) to question sth; (*tener reparos*) to raise

objections about sth

**telar** [te·'lar] *m* loom

**telaraña** [te·la·'ra·ɲa] *f* spiderweb; **tener ~s en los ojos** *fig* to be blind to what is going on

**tele** ['te·le] *f inf abr de* **televisión** TV; **ver la ~** to watch TV

**teleadicto, -a** [te·le·a·'dik·to, -a] *adj inf* couch potato

**telecabina** [te·le·ka·'βi·na] *f* cable car

**telecomedia** [te·le·ko·'me·dja] *f* sitcom

**telecompra** [te·le·'kom·pra] *f* teleshopping

**telecomunicación** [te·le·ko·mu·ni·ka·'sjon, -'θjon] *f* telecommunication; **ingeniero de Telecomunicaciones** telecommunications engineer

**telediario** [te·le·di·'a·rjo] *m* TV news; **el ~ de las tres** the 3 o'clock news

**teleférico** [te·le·'fe·ri·ko] *m* cable car

**telefonazo** [te·le·fo·'na·so, -θo] *m inf* ring; **dar un ~ a alguien** to give sb a ring

**telefonía** [te·le·fo·'ni·a] *f* telephony

**telefónico, -a** [te·le·'fo·ni·ko, -a] *adj* (*de teléfono*) telephone; (*de telefonía*) telephonic; **cabina/guía/llamada telefónica** phone booth/book/call

**teléfono** [te·'le·fo·no] *m* **1.** telephone; ~ **móvil/público/de tarjeta** cell/public/card phone; ~ **rojo** hotline; (**número de**) ~ phone number; **por** ~ over the phone; **hablar por** ~ to talk on the phone; **llamar por** ~ to telephone **2.** *pl* telephone company

**telegrafiar** <3. *pret* telegrafió> [te·le·ɣra·fi·'ar] *vi, vt* to telegraph

**telegrama** [te·le·'ɣra·ma] *m* telegram

**telenovela** [te·le·no·'βe·la] *f* soap opera

**telenque** [te·'len·ke] **I.** *adj* **1.** *Chile* (*temblón*) shaking; (*enfermizo*) sickly **2.** *ElSal* (*torcido*) crooked **II.** *m Guat* (*cachivache*) junk

**teleobjetivo** [te·le·oβ·xe·'ti·βo] *m* telephoto lens

**telepatía** [te·le·pa·'ti·a] *f* telepathy

**telepático, -a** [te·le·'pa·ti·ko, -a] *adj* telepathic

**telescópico, -a** [te·les·'ko·pi·ko, -a] *adj* telescopic

**telescopio** [te·les·'ko·pjo] *m* telescope

**telespectador(a)** [te·les·pek·ta·'dor, -·'do·ra] *m(f)* TV viewer

**televidente** [te·le·βi·'den·te] *mf v.* **telespectador**

**televisar** [te·le·βi·'sar] *vt* to broadcast; (*en directo*) to televise live

**televisión** [te·le·βi·'sjon] *f* television; ~ **digital** digital television; ~ **de pago** pay-television; ~ **en color** color TV

**televisor** [te·le·βi·'sor] *m* television set

**telón** [te·'lon] *m* curtain

**tema** ['te·ma] *m* theme; **cada loco con su ~** to each his own; **alejarse del ~** to stray from the issue; ~**s de actualidad** current issues

**temario** [te·'ma·rjo] *m* program; (*para examen*) list of topics

**temática** [te·'ma·ti·ka] *f* subjects *pl*

**temblar** <e → ie> [tem·'blar] *vi* to tremble; ~ **de miedo** to tremble with fear; ~ **de frío** to shiver (with cold); ~ **de pensarlo** to shudder just to think of it; ~ **como un flan** to shake like a leaf

**tembleque** [tem·'ble·ke] *m inf* shaking; **me dio un ~** I got the shakes

**temblor** [tem·'blor] *m* tremor; (*escalofrío*) shiver; ~ **de frío** shivers; ~ (**de tierra**) earthquake

**tembloroso, -a** [tem·blo·'ro·so] *adj* shaky

**temer** [te·'mer] **I.** *vt* to fear; (*sospechar*) to be afraid of **II.** *vi* to be afraid; ~ **por alguien** to fear for sb **III.** *vr:* ~**se** to be afraid; **me temo que sí/no** I'm afraid so/not

**temeroso, -a** [te·me·'ro·so, -a] *adj* fearful; ~ **de que... +***subj* fearful that...

**temible** [te·'mi·βle] *adj* fearsome

**temor** [te·'mor] *m* fear; (*sospecha*) suspicion; **por ~ a** for fear of

**témpano** ['tem·pa·no] *m* ice floe; **quedarse como un ~** to be chilled to the bone; **él es como un ~** he is as cold as stone

**temperamental** [tem·pe·ra·men·'tal] *adj* temperamental; (*persona*) spirited

**temperamento** [tem·pe·ra·'men·to] *m* temperament; **tener mucho ~** to have a strong character

**temperante** [tem·pe·'ran·te] **I.** *adj AmS* abstemious **II.** *mf AmS* teetotaler

**temperatura** [tem·pe·ra·'tu·ra] *f* temperature; (*fiebre*) fever

**tempestad** [tem·pes·'tad] *f* storm; (*marejada*) gale; (*agitación*) turmoil

**templado, -a** [tem·'pla·do, -a] *adj* lukewarm; (*moderado*) moderate

**templar** [tem·'plar] **I.** *vt* **1.** (*moderar*) to moderate **2.** (*calentar*) to warm up **II.** *vr:* ~**se 1.** (*moderarse*) to control oneself **2.** (*calentarse*) to get warm **3.** *AmL* (*enamorarse*) to fall in love **4.** *Col, Perú* (*emborracharse*) to get drunk

**temple** ['tem·ple] *m* **1.** courage; **estar de buen/mal ~** to be in a good/bad mood **2.** (*acero*) temper; (*proceso*) tempering **3.** ARTE tempera

**templo** ['tem·plo] *m* temple; **una verdad como un ~** the naked truth

**temporada** [tem·po·'ra·da] *f* season; (*época*) period; ~ **alta/baja** high/low season; **fruta de ~** seasonal fruit; **están pasando por una ~ difícil** they're going through a difficult period

**temporal** [tem·po·'ral] **I.** *adj* temporal; (*no permanente*) temporary; **contrato ~** temporary contract **II.** *m* storm; (*marejada*) stormy seas *pl*

**temporario, -a** [tem·po·'ra·rjo, -a] *adj* *AmL* temporary

**temprano** [tem·'pra·no] *adv* early; **llegar (demasiado) ~** to arrive (too) early

**temprano, -a** [tem·'pra·no, -a] *adj* early; **a edad temprana** at an early age

**tenacidad** [te·na·si·'dad, te·na·θi·] *f* tenacity

**tenaz** [te·'nas, -'naθ] *adj* tenacious; (*resistente*) resistant

**tenaza(s)** [te·'na·sa(s), -θa(s)] *f(pl)* pliers *pl*

**tencha** ['ten·tʃa] *f* *Guat* jail

**tendajón** [ten·da·'xon] *m* *Méx* small shop

**tendear** [ten·de·'ar] *vi* *Méx* to window-shop

**tendencia** [ten·'den·sja, -θja] *f* tendency; **tener ~ a fazer algo** to have a tendency to to sth; ~ **a algo** trend toward sth; ~ **al alza/a la baja** upward/downward trend; **las últimas ~s de la moda** the latest fashion trends

**tender** <e → ie> [ten·'der] **I.** *vt* **1.** (*ropa*)

to hang out; (*cuerda*) to stretch **2.** (*tumbar*) to lay; (*de golpe*) to throw down **3.** ~ **sobre algo** to spread over sth; ~ **la cama/mesa** *AmL* to make the bed/to lay the table **4.** (*aproximar*) to hold out; ~ **la mano a alguien** *fig* to give sb a hand **II.** *vi* to tend; MAT to tend toward; **tiendo a ser optimista** I more of an optimistic type **III.** *vr:* ~**se** to stretch out

**tendido** [ten·'di·do] *m* **1.** (*de un cable*) laying; (*cables*) wiring **2.** *AmL* (*sábanas*) bed linen

**tendón** [ten·'don] *m* tendon

**tenebroso, -a** [te·ne·'βro·so, -a] *adj* dark; (*tétrico*) gloomy

**tenedor** [te·ne·'dor] *m* fork

**tenedor(a)** [te·ne·'dor, -·'do·ra] *m(f)* holder; ~ **de tierras** landowner

**tenencia** [te·'nen·sja, -θja] *f* possession; ~ **ilícita de armas** illegal possession of arms

**tener** [te·'ner] *irr* **I.** *vt* **1.** to have; ~ **los ojos azules** to have blue eyes; ~ **29 años** to be 29 years old; ~ **hambre/sed/calor/sueño** to be hungry/thirsty/hot/sleepy; ~ **poco de tonto** to be no fool; **¿(con que) ésas tenemos?** so that's the way it is?; ~**la tomada con alguien** *inf* to have it in for sb; **no ~las todas consigo** not to be sure of something; **no ~ nada que perder** to have nothing to lose; **no ~ precio** to be priceless; ~ **cariño a alguien** to be fond of sb; ~ **la culpa de algo** to be to blame for sth; **¿tienes frío?** are you cold?; **le tengo lástima** I feel sorry for him/her; **el frasco ya no tiene miel** there's no honey left in the jar; ~ **un niño** to have a baby **2.** (*considerar*) to consider; ~ **por algo** to consider sth; ~ **a alguien en menos/mucho** to think all the less/more of sb; **ten por seguro que...** rest assured that...; **tengo para mí que...** I think that... **3.** (*coger*) to take; **ten esto** take this; (*sujetar*) to hold; ~ **a alguien por el brazo** to hold sb by the arm **4.** (*hacer sentir*) **me tienes preocupado** I'm worried about you; **me tienes loca** you're driving me mad! **II.** *vr:* ~**se 1.** ~**se por algo** to consider oneself sth; ~**se en mucho** to think highly of oneself

**2.** (*sostenerse*) to stand; **~se de pie** to stand; **~se firme** to stand upright; *fig* to stand firm; **estoy que no me tengo** I'm exhausted **3.** (*dominarse*) to control oneself **4.** (*atenerse*) to adhere **III.** *aux* **1.** ( + *participio*) **~ pensado hacer algo** to plan to do sth; **ya tengo comprado todo** I've bought everything already; **~se algo callado** to keep quiet about sth; **ya me lo tenía pensado** I had already thought of that **2. ~ que** to have to; **~ mucho que hacer** to have a lot to do; **¿qué tiene que ver esto conmigo?** what does this have to do with me?

**tenida** [te·'ni·da] *f Chile* meeting; (*traje*) suit; (*uniforme*) uniform

**teniente** [te·'njen·te] *m* lieutenant; **~ coronel** lieutenant-colonel

**tenis** ['te·nis] *m* tennis; **~ de mesa** table tennis

**tenor** [te·'nor] *m* tenor; **a ~ de** according to

**tensar** [ten·'sar] *vt* (*músculo*) to tense; (*cuerda*) to tighten

**tensión** [ten·'sjon] *f* **1.** stress; (*impaciencia*) anxiety; (*cuerda, piel*) tautness; (*nervios, músculos*) tension; **película de ~** a thriller; **estar en ~** (*nervioso*) to be nervous; (*impaciente*) to be anxious **2.** *Fís* tension **3. ~ arterial** blood pressure **4.** ELEC voltage **5.** *pl* strained relations *pl*

**tenso, -a** ['ten·so, -a] *adj* tense; (*cuerda, piel*) taut; (*impaciente*) anxious

**tentación** [ten·ta·'sjon, -·'θjon] *f* temptation; **me dan tentaciones de...** I'm tempted to...; **caer en la ~** to give in to the temptation

**tentáculo** [ten·'ta·ku·lo] *m* tentacle

**tentar** <e → ie> [ten·'tar] *vt* **1.** (*palpar*) to feel **2.** (*atraer*) to tempt; (*seducir*) to entice

**tentativa** [ten·ta·'ti·βa] *f* attempt; **~ de robo** attempted robbery

**tenue** ['te·nwe] *adj* delicate; (*sutil*) subtle; (*débil*) weak; (*luz*) faint

**teñir** [te·'ɲir] *irr como ceñir vt, vr:* **~se** to dye; **~(se) de rojo** to dye red; **~ de tristeza** to tinge with sadness

**teología** [teo·lo·'xi·a] *f* theology

**teólogo, -a** [te·'o·lo·ɣo, -a] **I.** *adj* theo-

logical **II.** *m, f* theologian

**teorema** [teo·'re·ma] *m* theorem

**teoría** [teo·'ri·a] *f* theory; **en ~** in theory

**teórico, -a** [te·'o·ri·ko, -a] *adj* theoretical

**tepache** [te·'pa·tʃe] *m Méx* tepache (*drink made of fermented agave cactus juice, water, pineapple and cloves*)

**tequesquite** [te·kes·'ki·te] *m Méx* rock salt

**tequiche** [te·'ki·tʃe] *m Ven* dish made with toasted corn, coconut milk and butter

**tequila** [te·'ki·la] *m* tequila

**tequio** ['te·kjo] *m AmC, Méx* (*molestia*) bother; (*daño*) harm

**tequioso, -a** [te·'kjo·so, -a] *adj AmC* **1.** (*travieso*) mischievous; (*niño*) trying **2.** (*molesto*) bothersome

**terapeuta** [te·ra·'peu·ta] *mf* therapist

**terapia** [te·'ra·pja] *f* therapy; **~ en** [*o de*] **grupo** group therapy

**tercer** [ter·'ser, -'θer] *adj v.* **tercero**

**tercermundista** [ter·ser·mun·'dis·ta, ter·θer-] *adj* third-world

**Tercer Mundo** [ter·'ser 'mun·do, -'θer] *m* Third World

**tercero** [ter·'se·ro, ter·'θe·] **I.** *m* third party **II.** *adv* third

**tercero, -a** [ter·'se·ro, -a; ter·'θe-] **I.** *adj* ( + *subst m: tercer*) third; **terceras personas** third parties; **en tercer lugar** thirdly; **viven en el ~** they live on the third floor; **tercera edad** retirement years ▶ **a la tercera va la vencida** third time lucky **II.** *m, f* third; *v. t.* **octavo**

**terciar** [ter·'sjar, -'θjar] **I.** *vt AmL* to water down **II.** *vi* to intervene; (*participar*) to take part **III.** *vr, vimpers:* **~se** to arise; **si se tercia** should the occasion arise

**tercio** ['ter·sjo, -θjo] *m* **1.** third; *v. t.* **octavo 2.** (*cerveza*) 1/3 liter bottle

**terciopelo** [ter·sjo·'pe·lo, ter·θjo·-] *m* velvet

**terco, -a** ['ter·ko, -a] *adj* stubborn; (*niño*) unruly; (*animal*) balky; (*cosa*) tough

**tereque** [te·'re·ke] *m Col, RDom, PRico, Ven* utensil

**tergiversar** [ter·xi·βer·'sar] *vt* to misrepresent; (*verdad*) to distort

**termas** ['ter·mas] *fpl* hot baths *pl*

**térmico, -a** ['ter·mi·ko, -a] *adj* thermal; **central térmica** thermal power plant

**terminación** [ter·mi·na·'sjon, -'θjon] *f* termination; (*proyecto*) completion; (*final*) end

**terminal** [ter·mi·'nal] **I.** *adj* terminal; **enfermo ~** terminally ill patient **II.** *m* COMPUT terminal; **III.** *f* terminal; **~ aérea** air terminal; FERRO station

**terminar** [ter·mi·'nar] **I.** *vt* to finish; (*proyecto*) to complete; **¿cuándo terminas?** when will you be done?; (*consumir*) to finish up; (*beber*) to drink up; (*comer*) to eat up **II.** *vi* **1.** (*tener fin*) to finish; (*plazo, contrato*) to end; **~ bien/mal** to have a happy/an unhappy ending; **en punta** to end in a point; **~ de hacer algo** to finish doing sth; (*haber hecho*) to have just done sth; **~ por hacer algo** to end up doing sth; **la escuela termina a las dos** school is out at 2 pm; **el tabaco va a ~ contigo** tobacco is going to be the end of you! **2.** (*estar acabando*) to be ending; **ya termina la película** the film is almost over **3.** (*poner fin*) to put an end to **III.** *vr:* **~se 1.** (*estar acabando*) to be almost over **2.** (*no haber más*) to be no more; **se terminaron las galletas** there aren't any more biscuits (left); **se me está terminando la paciencia** I'm running out of patience

**término** ['ter·mi·no] *m* **1.** (*fin*) end; **dar ~ a algo** to finish sth off; **llevar a ~** to carry out; **poner ~ a algo** to put an end to sth; **en el ~ de quince días** within 15 days **2.** (*linde*) boundary **3.** ADMIN district; **~ municipal** township **4.** LING, MAT term; **en buenos/malos ~s** on good terms/rudely; **en otros ~s** in other words **5.** *pl* (*de un contrato*) terms *pl* ▶ **estar en buenos/malos ~s** to be on good/bad terms; **en ~s generales** generally speaking; **~ medio** compromise; **en primer ~** first of all; **en último ~** as a last resort; **por ~ medio** on the average

**terminología** [ter·mi·no·lo·'xi·a] *f* terminology

**termita** [ter·'mi·ta] *f* termite

**termo** ['ter·mo] *m* thermos

**termómetro** [ter·'mo·me·tro] *m* thermometer

**termostato** [ter·mos·'ta·to] *m*, **termósta-to** [ter·'mos·ta·to] *m* thermostat

**ternejo, -a** [ter·'ne·xo, -a] *adj* Ecua, Perú lively

**ternera** [ter·'ne·ra] *f* beef

**ternero, -a** [ter·'ne·ro, -a] *m, f* calf

**ternura** [ter·'nu·ra] *f* **1.** tenderness; (*dulzura*) sweetness; (*delicadeza*) gentleness **2.** *Chile, Ecua, Guat* (*inmadurez*) greenness

**terquedad** [ter·ke·'dad] *f* obstinacy

**terraplén** [te·rra·'plen] *m* slope

**terráqueo, -a** [te·'rra·keo, -a] *adj* earth; **globo ~** globe

**terrateniente** [te·rra·te·'njen·te] *mf* landowner

**terraza** [te·'rra·sa, -θa] *f* terrace; (*azotea*) flat roof

**terregal** [te·rre·'ɣal] *m Méx* loose topsoil

**terremoto** [te·rre·'mo·to] *m* earthquake

**terrenal** [te·rre·'nal] *adj* worldly

**terreno** [te·'rre·no] *m* land; GEO terrain; (*espacio*) lot; (*parcela*) plot of land; DEP playing field; **~ edificable** buildable land; **vehículo todo ~** all-terrain vehicle; *fig* sphere; **~ desconocido** unfamiliar territory; **en su propio ~** on one's own ground ▶ **ceder/ganar/perder ~** to give up/gain/lose ground; **explorar el ~** to see how the land lies; **preparar el ~ para algo** to pave the way for sth

**terrestre** [te·'rres·tre] **I.** *adj* **1.** (*de la Tierra*) terrestrial **2.** (*en la tierra*) earthly; **animal ~** land animal; **transporte ~** ground transport **3.** (*terrenal*) earthly **II.** *mf* terrestrial

**terrible** [te·'rri·βle] *adj* terrible; **hace un frío ~** it's terribly cold

**territorial** [te·rri·to·'rjal] *adj* territorial

**territorio** [te·rri·'to·rjo] *m t.* ZOOL territory; POL region; JUR district; **en todo el ~ nacional** nationwide

**terror** [te·'rror] *m* terror; **película de ~** horror film; **las arañas me dan ~** I'm terrified of spiders

**terrorismo** [te·rro·'ris·mo] *m* terrorism

**terrorista** [te·rro·'ris·ta] *adj, mf* terrorist

**terso, -a** ['ter·so, -a] *adj* smooth

**tertulia** [ter·'tu·lja] *f* gathering; **estar**

**de** ~ to talk

**tesis** ['te·sis] *f inv* theory; EDUC, FILOS thesis

**tesón** [te·'son] *m* tenacity; **con** ~ diligently

**tesonero, -a** [te·so·'ne·ro, -a] *adj AmL* persevering; (*tenaz*) tenacious

**tesorería** [te·so·re·'ri·a] *f* treasury; (*despacho*) treasurer's office

**tesorero, -a** [te·so·'re·ro, -a] *m, f* treasurer

**tesoro** [te·'so·ro] *m* treasure; ~ (**público**) (public) treasury; **sí,** ~ yes, darling

**testamento** [tes·ta·'men·to] *m* will; **hacer** ~ to make one's will

**testar** [tes·'tar] *vi* to make a will

**testículo** [tes·'ti·ku·lo] *m* testicle

**testificar** <c → qu> [tes·ti·fi·'kar] I. *vt* 1. (*declarar*) to testify; (*documento*) to bear witness 2. (*demostrar*) to give evidence II. *vi* to testify

**testigo** [tes·'ti·yo] I. *mf* witness; ~ **ocular** eyewitness; **ser** ~ **de algo** to witness sth; **poner a alguien por** ~ to cite sb as witness II. *m* baton

**testimonial** [tes·ti·mo·'njal] *adj* attesting; (*que prueba*) evidentiary

**testimoniar** [tes·ti·mo·'njar] I. *vt* 1. (*declarar*) to testify 2. (*afirmar*) to attest 3. (*probar*) to evidence II. *vi* to bear witness

**testimonio** [tes·ti·'mo·njo] *m* 1. (*declaración*) testimony; (*afirmación*) statement; **dar** ~ to bear witness 2. (*prueba*) evidence

**testosterona** [tes·tos·te·'ro·na] *m* testosterone

**teta** ['te·ta] *f inf* breast; (*ubre*) udder; **dar la** ~ to breast-feed

**tétano(s)** ['te·ta·no(s)] *m (inv)* tetanus

**tetera** [te·'te·ra] *f* 1. teapot; (*para hervir*) kettle 2. *AmL* (*pezón*) nipple 3. *AmL v.* **tetero**

**tetero** [te·'te·ro] *m AmL* baby's bottle

**tétrico, -a** ['te·tri·ko, -a] *adj* dismal

**textil** [tes·'til] *adj, m* textile

**texto** ['tes·to] *m* text; (*pasaje*) extract; **libro de** ~ textbook

**textual** [tes·tu·'al] *adj* textual; (*literal*) word-for-word; **con las palabras** ~**es** with those exact words

**textura** [tes·'tu·ra] *f* structure; (*tejido*) weave; GEO, QUÍM texture

**tez** [tes, teθ] *f* complexion; **de** ~ **morena** dark

**ti** [ti] *pron pers* **a** ~ = you; **de** ~ = from you; **para/por** ~ for you

**tianguis** ['tjan·gis] *m inv Méx* street market

**tibia** ['ti·βja] *f* tibia

**tibiarse** [ti·'βjar·se] *vr AmC, Ven* to get cross

**tibiera** [ti·'βje·ra] *f Ven* (*molestia*) irritation; (*fastidio*) nuisance

**tibio, -a** ['ti·βjo, -a] *adj* 1. lukewarm 2. *AmL inf* angry ▶ **poner** ~ **a alguien** to lay in to sb

**tibor** [ti·'βor] *m AmL* chamber pot

**tiburón** [ti·βu·'ron] *m* shark

**tico, -a** ['ti·ko, -a] *adj, m, f AmL inf* Costa Rican

**tiempo** ['tjem·po] *m* 1. time; ~ **libre/ de ocio** spare/leisure time; **al poco** ~ shortly after; **los buenos** ~**s** the good old days; **a** ~ in time; **con** ~ in good time; **a** ~ **parcial** part-time; **todo a su** ~ all in good time; **al** (**mismo**) ~ [**o a un** ~] at the same time; **al** ~ **que** while; **antes de** ~ early; **desde hace mucho** ~ for a long time; **en estos** ~**s** nowadays; **en mis** ~**s** in my time; **en otros** ~**s** in the past; **dar** ~ **al** ~ to give it time; **hace que...** it's a long time since...; **¡cuánto** ~ **sin verte!** long time no see!; **matar el/hacer** ~ to kill time; **perder el** ~ to waste time; **sin perder** ~ losing no time; **si me da** ~ if I have enough time 2. METEO weather; **hoy hace mal** ~ the weather is bad today 3. LING tense 4. DEP (**medio**) ~ half-time; ~ **muerto** time out 5. TÉC stroke; **motor de dos** ~**s** two-stroke engine ▶ **a(l) mal** ~ **buena cara** you have to look on the bright side of things; **el** ~ **es oro** time is money; **el** ~ **no perdona** time and tide wait for no man

**tienda** ['tjen·da] *f* 1. shop, store; **ir de** ~**s** to go shopping 2. ~ (**de campaña**) tent; **montar/desmontar una** ~ to put up/ take down a tent

**tiento** ['tjen·to] *m* **a** ~ gropingly; **con** ~ carefully

**tierno, -a** ['tjer·no, -a] I. *adj* 1. tender; (*blando*) soft; (*pan, dulces*) fresh; (*cari-*

ñoso) affectionate 2. Chile, Ecua, Guat (inmaduro) green II. m, f Guat, Nic newborn

**tierra** ['tje·rra] f 1. earth; ~ **de nadie** no-man's-land; ~**s altas/bajas** highlands/lowlands; **echar por** ~ fig to ruin 2. (firme) mainland; ~ **adentro** inland; **quedarse en** ~ to be left behind 3. (región) land; **Tierra Santa** Holy Land; ~ (natal) native land 4. (hacienda) property

**tierral** [tje·'rral] m AmL cloud of dust

**tieso, -a** ['tje·so, -a] adj (rígido) stiff; (erguido) erect; **dejar** ~ **a alguien** inf (matar) to bump sb off; (sorprender) to dumbfound; **quedarse** ~ (frío) to be frozen stiff; (miedo) to be scared stiff; (morirse) to croak

**tiesto** ['tjes·to] m 1. flowerpot 2. Chile pot

**tifón** [ti·'fon] m typhoon

**tifus** ['ti·fus] m inv typhus

**tigre** ['ti·yre] m tiger; AmL jaguar; And (café) black coffee with a dash of milk; **oler a** ~ to stink

**tigresa** [ti·'yre·sa] m tigress; AmL jaguar

**tijeras** [ti·'xe·ras] f scissors pl; (grandes) shears pl

**tilde** ['til·de] f accent; (de la ñ) tilde

**tiliches** [ti·'li·tʃes] mpl AmC, Méx junk

**tilingo, -a** [ti·'liŋ·go, -a] adj 1. CSur, Méx (atolondrado) silly 2. Arg (demente) soft in the head

**timar** [ti·'mar] vt to con

**timba** ['tim·ba] f AmL belly

**timbre** ['tim·bre] m 1. bell; (de la puerta) doorbell; **han tocado el** ~ somebody rang the bell 2. (sonido) timbre 3. (sello) stamp

**timidez** [ti·mi·'des, -'deθ] f shyness

**tímido, -a** ['ti·mi·do, -a] adj shy

**timón** [ti·'mon] m rudder

**tímpano** ['tim·pa·no] m eardrum

**tina** ['ti·na] f vat; AmL bathtub

**tincanque** [tiŋ·'kaŋ·ke] m Chile inf flip, flick

**tincar** <c → qu> [tiŋ·'kar] vt 1. Chile (presentir) to have a hunch 2. Arg, Chile (pelota) to drive

**tincazo** [tiŋ·'ka·so] m Arg, Ecua inf flick

**tinga** ['tiŋ·ga] f Méx uproar

**tingo** ['tiŋ·go] Méx **del** ~ **al tango** from pillar to post

**tiniebla** [ti·'nje·βla] f darkness

**tino** ['ti·no] m aim; (destreza) skill; **a buen** ~ by guesswork; **sin** ~ recklessly

**tinoso, -a** [ti·'no·so, -a] adj Col, Ven (hábil) skillful; (sensato) sensible

**tinta** ['tin·ta] f ink; ~ **china** Indian ink; **sobre este asunto ha corrido ríos de** ~ much has been written about this matter; **medias** ~**s** half-tones; fig half measures

**tinte** ['tin·te] m 1. (teñidura) dye 2. (colorante) coloring 3. (matiz) tinge

**tinterillo** [tin·te·'ri·jo, -ʎo] m AmL pey inf shyster

**tintero** [tin·'te·ro] m inkwell; **dejar(se) algo en el** ~ to leave sth unsaid

**tinto, -a** ['tin·to, -a] adj dark red; (uvas, vino) red

**tintorería** [tin·to·re·'ri·a] f dry cleaner's

**tío, -a** ['ti·o, -a] m, f 1. uncle, aunt m, f; ~ **abuelo** great-uncle; **tía abuela** great-aunt; **mis** ~**s** my aunt and uncle 2. inf guy, girl m, f; ¡**oye,** ~! hey, man!; ~ **bueno** good-looking guy

**tipear** [ti·pe·'ar] vi AmC, AmS to type

**típico, -a** ['ti·pi·ko, -a] adj typical; **plato** ~ local or traditional dish

**tipo** ['ti·po] m 1. (modelo) model 2. (muestra) sample; (espécimen) type; **un impreso/una carta** ~ a standard form/letter 3. (cuerpo) build; **aguantar el** ~ to hold out; **mover el** ~ inf to get moving; **tener buen** ~ to have a good figure; **él tiene buen** ~ he's well-built 4. (clase) type, kind 5. FIN rate; ~ **de cambio** exchange rate 6. TIPO type

**tipo, -a** ['ti·po, -a] m, f 1. inf guy, girl m, f 2. pey character; ~ **raro** weirdo

**tiquear** [ti·ke·'ar] vt 1. AmC, PRico, Col (chequear) to check 2. Chile (perforar) to punch

**tira** ['ti·ra] f strip; ~ **cómica** comic strip

**tirabuzón** [ti·ra·βu·'son, -'θon] m ringlet

**tirada** [ti·'ra·da] f 1. (edición) print run; **de una** ~ fig without stopping 2. (distancia) stretch

**tiradero** [ti·ra·'de·ro] m Méx garbage dump

**tirado, -a** [ti·'ra·do, -a] I. adj 1. estar

*inf* (*barato*) dirt cheap; (*fácil*) very easy; **ese ejercicio está ~** that exercise is very easy; **dejar ~ a alguien** to leave sb in the lurch **2.** *ser pey* slovenly **II.** *m, f inf* bum

**tiranía** [ti·ra·'ni·a] *f* tyranny

**tiranizar** <z → c> [ti·ra·ni·'sar, -'θar] *vt* to tyrannize

**tirano, -a** [ti·'ra·no, -a] **I.** *adj* tyrannical **II.** *m, f* tyrant

**tirante** [ti·'ran·te] **I.** *adj* **1.** (*tieso*) taut; **el pantalón me está ~** the pants are tight on me **2.** (*conflictivo*) tense **II.** *m* strap; **~s** (*elásticos*) suspenders *pl*

**tirantez** [ti·ran·'tes, -'teθ] *f* strain

**tirar** [ti·'rar] **I.** *vi* **1.** **~ de algo** to pull on sth; (*sacar*) to pull out sth; **tira y afloja** give and take; **~ de la lengua a alguien** to draw sb out; **aquí cada uno tira por su lado** here everyone takes his/her own turn **2.** to attract; **no me tiran los libros** I'm not very interested in books; **~ a rojo** to tend toward red **3.** (*disparar*) to shoot; **~ al blanco** to target shoot ▶ **¿qué tal? — vamos tirando** *inf* how are you? — we're managing **II.** *vt* **1.** (*lanzar*) to throw; **~ piedras a alguien** to throw stones at sb **2.** (*malgastar*) to waste **3.** (*desechar*) to throw away **4.** (*disparar*) to shoot **5.** (*derribar*) to knock down; (*edificio*) to pull down **6.** FOTO to take **7.** (*derramar*) to spill **III.** *vr:* **~se 1.** (*lanzarse*) to throw oneself **2.** (*echarse*) to lie down **3.** (*pasar*) to spend; **~se una hora esperando** to spend an hour waiting **4.** *inf* **~se a alguien** to lay sb

**tiritar** [ti·ri·'tar] *vi* to shiver

**tiro** ['ti·ro] *m* shot; **~ con arco** archery; **a ~ in range**; *fig* accessible; **dar** [*o* **pegar**] **un ~** to fire a shot; **me salió el ~ por la culata** it backfired on me ▶ **sentar a alguien como un ~** (*comida*) to disagree with sb; (*noticia*) to upset sb; **ni a ~s** not on a long shot

**tiroides** [ti·'roi·des] *adj, m inv* (**glándula**) **~** thyroid (gland)

**tiroteo** [ti·ro·'teo] *m* shooting

**titanio** [ti·'ta·njo] *m* titanium

**titeo** [ti·'teo] *m* *Arg, Bol, Urug* (*burla*) mocking; (*tomadura de pelo*) teasing;

**tomar a alguien para el ~** to make fun of sb

**títere** ['ti·te·re] *m* **1.** puppet; **no dejar ~ con cabeza** to spare no one **2.** *pl* puppet show

**titipuchal** [ti·ti·pu·'tʃal] *m* *Méx inf* throng

**titubear** [ti·tu·βe·'ar] *vi* to hesitate

**titubeo** [ti·tu·'βeo] *m* hesitation

**titulación** [ti·tu·la·'sjon, -'θjon] *f* title; (*académica*) qualifications *pl*

**titulado, -a** [ti·tu·'la·do, -a] **I.** *adj* titled **II.** *m, f* degree holder; **~** (**universitario**) university graduate

**titular¹** [ti·tu·'lar] *mf* holder; **~ de acciones** shareholder

**titular²** [ti·tu·'lar] **I.** *m* headline; **ocupar los ~es** to be in all the newspapers **II.** *vt* to title **III.** *vr:* **~se** to be entitled

**título** ['ti·tu·lo] *m* title; (*diploma*) diploma; **~ universitario** university degree; **~ de propiedad** (property) deeds; **a ~ de** by way of; **¿a ~ de qué hace Ud. eso?** why are you doing that?

**tiza** ['ti·sa, -θa] *f* chalk

**tizate** [ti·'sa·te] *m* *Guat, Hond, Nic* chalk

**tiznado, -a** [tis·'na·do, -a] *adj* *AmC* drunk

**tlachique** [tla·'tʃi·ke] *m* *Méx* agave cactus juice

**tlacote** [tla·'ko·te] *m* *Méx* **1.** (*absceso*) boil **2.** (*tumor*) tumor

**tlapalería** [tla·pa·le·'ri·a] *f* *Méx* hardware store

**TLCAN** *abr de* **Tratado de Libre Comercio de América del Norte** NAFTA

**toalla** [to·'a·ja, -ʎa] *f* towel; **~ de lavabo/baño** hand/bath towel; **arrojar la ~** to throw in the towel

**tobillera** [to·βi·'je·ra, -'ʎe·ra] *f* ankle support

**tobillo** [to·'βi·jo, -ʎo] *m* ankle

**tobo** ['to·βo] *m* *Ven* bucket

**tobogán** [to·βo·'yan] *m* slide

**tocadiscos** [to·ka·'dis·kos] *m inv* record player

**tocado** [to·'ka·do] *m* hairdo

**tocado, -a** [to·'ka·do, -a] *adj* touched; **estar ~** (**de la cabeza**) to be not all there

**tocador** [to·ka·'dor] *m* dressing table

**tocar** <c → qu> [to·'kar] **I.** *vt* **1.** (*palpar*) to touch; **¡no lo toques!** don't touch it!;

**~ fondo** to hit bottom **2.** MÚS (to play); (*campana, timbre*) to ring; (*tambor*) to beat; **el reloj tocó las tres** the clock struck three **3.** (*modificar*) to change **II.** *vi* te toca jugar it's your turn; **hoy me toca barrer** today I have to sweep; **toca irse ya** it's time to go; **le tocó a él hacerlo** it fell to him to do it; **le tocó el premio** he/she won the prize; **~** en to verge on **III.** *vr:* **~se** to touch ► **los extremos se tocan** extremes meet

**tocayo, -a** [to·ˈka·jo, -a] *m, f* namesake

**tocineta** [to·si·ˈne·ta] *f Col*, **tocino** [to·ˈsi·no, to·ˈθi·] *m* pork fat; (*carne*) bacon

**todavía** [to·ða·ˈβi·a] *adv* still; **~ no** not yet; **pero ~** however; **es ~ más caro que...** it is even more expensive than...

**todo** [ˈto·ðo] **I.** *pron indef* all; **~ cuanto** [*o* **lo que**]... all...; (*o*) **~ o nada** all or nothing; **ante** [*o* **sobre**] **~** above all; **~ lo contrario** quite the contrary; **después de ~** after all; **con ~** nevertheless; **estar en ~** to be on the ball; **para ~** all-purpose **II.** *adv inf* completely **III.** *m* the whole; **del ~** completely; **no del ~** not entirely

**todo, -a** [ˈto·ðo, -a] *art indef* **1.** (*entero*) all; **toda la familia** the whole family; **toda Argentina** all of Argentina; **en toda Europa** all over Europe; **a toda prisa** [*o* **a ~ correr**] as fast as possible **2.** (*cada*) every; **a toda costa** at all cost; **~ Dios** [*o* **quisqui**] *inf* absolutely everyone; **toda precaución es poca** you can't be careful enough **3.** *pl* all; **a ~s los niños les gusta el chocolate** all children like chocolate; **~s los niños de la clase tomaron chocolate** all of the children in the class had chocolate; **~s y cada uno** each and every one; **a todas horas** at all hours; **en todas partes** everywhere; **de ~s modos** anyway

**todoterreno** [to·do·te·ˈrre·no] **I.** *adj inv* versatile **II.** *m* all-terrain vehicle

**toldillo** [tol·ˈdi·jo, -ʎo] *m Col* mosquito net

**toldo** [ˈtol·do] *m* marquee; (*en balcón*) canopy; (*en tienda*) awning

**tolerancia** [to·le·ˈran·sja, -θja] *f* tolerance

**tolerar** [to·le·ˈrar] *vt* tolerate

**tolete** [to·ˈle·te] *m* **1.** *AmL* (*garrote*) bludgeon **2.** *Col, Cuba* (*trozo*) piece

**tolvanera** [tol·βa·ˈne·ra] *f AmC, Méx* cloud of dust

**toma** [ˈto·ma] *f* **1.** (*adquisición*) taking; **~ de conciencia** awareness; **~ de datos** data acquisition; **~ de decisiones** decision making; **~ de poder** takeover **2.** (*dosis*) dose **3.** TÉC inlet; (*grabación*) take; FOTO shot

**tomacorriente** [to·ma·ko·ˈrrjen·te] *m* **1.** *AmL* (*colector*) collector **2.** *Arg, Perú* (*enchufe*) plug

**tomar** [to·ˈmar] **I.** *vi* **1.** **toma** here you are **2.** **¡vete a ~ por culo!** fuck off! **3.** *AmL* to drink ► **¡toma!** well! **II.** *vt* **1.** (*coger, quitar, llevar, interpretar*) to take (**por** for); (*préstamo*) to borrow; (*decisión*) to make; (*actitud*) to adopt; **~ a la ligera** to take lightly; **~ algo a mal** to take offense at sth; **~ muy a pecho** to take to heart; **~ en serio/a risa** to take seriously/as a joke; **~ conciencia de algo** to become aware of sth; **~ cariño/manía a alguien** to take a like/dislike to sb **2.** (*contratar*) to hire **3.** (*hacerse cargo*) to take over **4.** *AmL* **~la** to get drunk ► **~la con algo/alguien** to take it out on sth/sb **III.** *vr:* **~se 1.** (*coger*) to take **2.** (*beber, comer*) to have; **~se la cena** to have dinner **3.** *AmL* **tomársela** to get drunk

**tomate** [to·ˈma·te] *m* tomato ► **ponerse rojo como un ~** to turn as red as a beetroot

**tómbola** [ˈtom·bo·la] *f* charity raffle

**tomillo** [to·ˈmi·jo, -ʎo] *m* thyme

**tomo** [ˈto·mo] *m* volume; **de cuatro ~s** in four volumes

**tonada** [to·ˈna·da] *f* **1.** tune **2.** *AmL* (*tonillo*) accent

**tonalidad** [to·na·li·ˈdad] *f* **1.** LING intonation **2.** MÚS tonality **3.** ARTE shade

**tonel** [to·ˈnel] *m* barrel; *inf* fatso

**tonelada** [to·ne·ˈla·da] *f* ton

**tónica** [ˈto·ni·ka] *f* tonic water

**tónico** [ˈto·ni·ko] *m* tonic

**tonificar** <c → qu> [to·ni·fi·ˈkar] *vt* to tone up

**tonina** [to·ˈni·na] *f Arg, Urug* dolphin

**tono** [ˈto·no] *m* tone; **~ agudo/grave**

high/low pitch; ~ **mayor/menor** major/minor key; **bajar el** ~ to lower one's voice; **en** ~ **de reproche** reproachfully; **fuera de** ~ out of place; **a** ~ **con** in tune with; **subirse de** ~ to become heated; **de mal** ~ vulgar

**tontear** [ton·te·'ar] *vi* to fool around; *inf* to flirt

**tontería** [ton·te·'ri·a] *f* trifle; (*memez*) stupidity

**tonto, -a** ['ton·to] **I.** *adj* silly; **a tontas y a locas** without thinking; **ponerse** ~ *inf* to get silly; **ser** ~ **del culo** *inf* to be a complete idiot **II.** *m, f* fool; **hacer el** ~ to clown around; **hacerse el** ~ to play dumb

**topacio** [to·'pa·sjo, -θjo] *m* topaz

**topadora** [to·pa·'do·ra] *f Arg, Méx, Urug* bulldozer

**topar(se)** [to·'par·(se)] *vi, vr* ~ **con algo** to run into sth; ~ **con alguien** to bump into sb; ~ **contra algo** to bump against sth

**tope** ['to·pe] **I.** *adj* maximum; **fecha** ~ latest date **II.** *m* **1.** end; **lleno hasta el** ~ [*o* **los** ~**s**] full to bursting; **estoy a** ~ **de trabajo** I'm swamped with work **2.** obstacle; (*puerta*) doorstop

**tópico** [to·'pi·ko] *m* cliché

**tópico, -a** [to·'pi·ko, -a] *adj* trite; **de uso** ~ for external use only

**topinambur** [to·pi·nam·'bur] *m Arg, Bol* Jerusalem artichoke

**topo** ['to·po] *m* mole; **ver menos que un** ~ to be as blind as a bat

**topocho, -a** [to·'po·tʃo, -a] *adj Ven* plump

**topografía** [to·po·ɣra·'fi·a] *f* topography

**topón** [to·'pon] *m* **1.** *Chile, Col, Hond* (*topetazo*) butt **2.** *Col* (*puñetazo*) punch

**topónimo** [to·'po·ni·mo] *m* place name

**toposo, -a** [to·'po·so, -a] *adj Ven* (*entrometido*) meddlesome; (*pedante*) pretentious

**toque** ['to·ke] *m* (*roce, matiz*) touch; (*golpe*) tap; **dar un** ~ **en la puerta** to tap on the door; ~ **de queda** curfew; ~ **de tambor** drumbeat; ~ (**de atención**) warning; **dame un** ~ **más tarde** give me a call later; **dar los últimos** ~**s a algo** to put the finishing touches on sth

**toquetear** [to·ke·te·'ar] *vt inf* to finger

**tórax** ['to·raks] *m inv* thorax

**torbellino** [tor·βe·'ʝi·no, -'ʎi·no] *m* whirlwind; **ser un** ~ to be a bundle of energy

**torcedura** [tor·se·'du·ra, tor·θe-] *f* sprain

**torcer** [tor·'ser, -'θer] *irr como cocer* **I.** *vi* to turn; ~ **a la izquierda** to turn left **II.** *vt* to turn; (*doblar*) to bend **III.** *vr:* ~**se 1.** to bend; **me torcí el tobillo** I've twisted my ankle **2.** (*corromperse*) to go astray; (*fracasar*) to go wrong

**torcido, -a** [tor·'si·do, tor·'θi-] *adj* lopsided; (*encorvado*) crooked

**torear** [to·re·'ar] **I.** *vi* to bullfight **II.** *vt* to bullfight; (*tomar el pelo*) to tease

**toreo** [to·'reo] *m* bullfighting

**torero, -a** [to·'re·ro, -a] **I.** *adj* bullfighting **II.** *m, f* bullfighter; **saltarse algo a la torera** *inf* to blatantly ignore sth

**tormenta** [tor·'men·ta] *f* storm; (*agitación*) turmoil; **una** ~ **en un vaso de agua** a storm in a teacup

**tormento** [tor·'men·to] *m* anguish; (*castigo*) torment

**torna** ['tor·na] *f* **1.** (*devolución*) restitution **2.** (*regreso*) return ▶ **se han cambiado las** ~**s** the shoe's on the other foot; **volver las** ~**s a alguien** to turn the tables on sb; **volverse las** ~**s** to turn the tables

**tornado** [tor·'na·do] *m* tornado

**tornarse** [tor·'nar·se] *vr* to turn

**torneo** [tor·'neo] *m* tournament

**tornillo** [tor·'ni·jo, -ʎo] *m* screw; **apretar los** ~**s a alguien** to put pressure on sb; **te falta un** ~ you have a screw loose

**torno** ['tor·no] *m* lathe; (*de alfarero*) potter's wheel ▶ **en** ~ **a** about; **en** ~ **a ese tema** with regard to this subject

**toro** ['to·ro] *m* **1.** bull; **coger el** ~ **por los cuernos** to take the bull by the horns; **fuerte como un** ~ strong as an ox **2.** *pl* bullfighting; **ir a los** ~**s** to go to bullfights

**torpe** ['tor·pe] *adj* clumsy; (*tonto*) slow

**torpedo** [tor·'pe·do] *m* torpedo

**torpeza** [tor·'pe·sa, -θa] *f* clumsiness; (*tontería*) stupidity

**torre** ['to·rre] *f* tower; ~ **de alta tensión** electricity pylon; ~ **de mando** control

**T**

tower; (*ajedrez*) rook

**torreja** [to·'rre·xa] *f AmL* ≈ French toast

**torrencial** [to·rren·'sjal, -'θjal] *adj* torrential

**torrente** [to·'rren·te] *m* torrent; *fig* flood

**torrentoso, -a** [to·rren·'to·so, -a] *adj AmL* (*lluvia*) torrential; (*caudal*) fast-flowing

**torso** ['tor·so] *m* torso; ARTE bust

**torta** ['tor·ta] *f* **1.** AmL pie **2.** *inf* slap; **darse una ~** to bang oneself; **llevar una ~** to be plastered ▶ **no saber ni ~** *inf* not to know a thing

**tortilla** [tor·'ti·ja, -ʎa] *f* ≈ omelet; *AmL* tortilla ▶ **dar la vuelta a la ~** to change things completely; **se ha vuelto la ~** the tables have turned

**tórtola** ['tor·to·la] *f* turtledove; **tortolitos** lovebirds

**tortuga** [tor·'tu·ɣa] *f* turtle; **a paso de ~** at a snail's pace

**tortura** [tor·'tu·ra] *f* torture

**torturar** [tor·tu·'rar] *vt* to torture

**tos** [tos] *f* cough

**tosco, -a** ['tos·ko, -a] *adj* coarse

**tosedera** [to·se·'de·ra] *f AmL* nagging cough

**toser** [to·'ser] *vi* to cough

**tostada** [tos·'ta·da] *f* toast; *Méx* fried tortilla

**tostador** [tos·ta·'dor] *m* toaster

**tostar** <o → ue> [tos·'tar] **I.** *vt* to roast; (*pan*) to toast **II.** *vr*: **~se** to tan

**total** [to·'tal] **I.** *adj* total; **en ~** in all; **¡ha sido ~!** *inf* it was great! **II.** *m* sum **III.** *adv* so, in the end

**totalidad** [to·ta·li·'dad] *f* totality; **en su ~** in its entirety

**totalitario, -a** [to·ta·li·'ta·rjo, -a] *adj* totalitarian

**totora** [to·'to·ra] *f AmS* reed

**toxicidad** [tok·si·si·'dad, tok·si·θi-] *f* toxicity

**tóxico** ['tok·si·ko] *m* toxic substance

**tóxico, -a** ['tok·si·ko, -a] *adj* toxic

**toxicomanía** [tok·si·ko·ma·'ni·a] *f* drug addiction

**toxicómano, -a** [tok·si·'ko·ma·no, -a] **I.** *adj* addicted to drugs **II.** *m, f* drug addict

**toxina** [tok·'si·na] *f* toxin

**traba** ['tra·βa] *f* **1.** hindrance; **poner**

**~s a...** to put obstacles in the way of... **2.** *AmL* grass; (*efecto*) high

**trabajador(a)** [tra·βa·xa·'dor, --'do·ra] **I.** *adj* hard-working **II.** *m(f)* worker

**trabajar** [tra·βa·'xar] **I.** *vi* to work; **~ de guía** to work as a guide; **en edad de ~** of working age; **~ como un condenado** to work like a slave; **~ por horas** to be paid by the hour; **~ por cuenta propia** to be self-employed; **~ a tiempo completo/parcial** to work full-time/part-time **II.** *vt* to work; (*máquina*) to operate; **tienes que ~ el acento** you have to work on your accent **III.** *vr*: **~se** to work for; (*persona*) to work on

**trabajo** [tra·'βa·xo] *m* work; (*puesto*) job; **~s manuales** handicrafts; **con/sin ~** employed/unemployed; **~ en equipo** teamwork; **~ fijo** steady job; **hacer un buen ~** to do a good job; **tener ~ atrasado** to have a backlog; **¡buen ~!** well done!; **quedarse sin ~** to be let go; **costar ~** to be difficult; **tomarse el ~ de** to take the trouble to; **ahorrarse el ~ de** to spare oneself the trouble of

**trabalenguas** [tra·βa·'len·gwas] *m inv* tongue twister

**trabar** [tra·'βar] **I.** *vt* **1.** (*juntar*) to join **2.** (*impedir*) to impede **II.** *vi* to take hold **III.** *vr*: **~se** to get stuck; **~se la lengua** to get tongue-tied

**trácala** ['tra·ka·la] *f* **1.** *Ecua* (*multitud*) mob **2.** *Méx, PRico* (*fullería*) fraud **3.** *Méx* (*fullero*) trickster

**tracalada** [tra·ka·'la·da] *f* **1.** *AmC, AmS* (*multitud*) crowd **2.** *Méx* (*fullería*) trickery

**tracalero, -a** [tra·ka·'le·ro, -a] *m, f Méx, PRico* cheat

**tracción** [trak·'sjon, -'θjon] *f* drive; **~ delantera/trasera/a cuatro ruedas** front/rear-wheel/four-wheel drive

**tractor** [trak·'tor] *m* tractor

**tradición** [tra·di·'sjon, -'θjon] *f* tradition

**tradicional** [tra·di·sjo·'nal, tra·di·θjo-] *adj* traditional

**traducción** [tra·duk·'sjon, -duɣ·'θjon] *f* translation; **~ al/del inglés** translation into/from English

**traducir** [tra·du·'sir, -'θir] *irr vt* to translate; **~ al/del español** to translate into/

from Spanish

**traductología** [tra·ðuk·to·lo·'xi·a] *f* translation science

**traductor(a)** [tra·ðuk·'tor, -·'to·ra] *m(f)* translator; **~ de bolsillo** pocket-size electronic translating device; **~ jurado** sworn translator

**traer** [tra·'er] *irr* **I.** *vt* **1.** to bring; (*vestido*) to wear; **trae** give it to me; **lo traigo en la cartera** I've got it in my briefcase; **¿qué te trae por aquí?** what brings you here?; **me trae sin cuidado** I couldn't care less; **me la trae floja** *vulg* I don't give a damn **2.** (*ir a por*) to fetch **3.** (*ocasionar*) to cause **4.** (+ *adj*) to have; **~ de cabeza a alguien** *inf* to be driving sb mad **5.** (+ *subst*) **retraso/prisa/hambre** to be late/in a hurry/hungry; **~ cara de...** to look...; **~ a la memoria** to bring to mind **II.** *vr:* **~se** to bring; (*ir a por*) to fetch; **~se algo entre manos** to be up to something; **este examen se las trae** the exam is really tough

**traficante** [tra·fi·'kan·te] *mf* dealer; (*de drogas*) drug dealer; (*de personas, coches*) smuggler

**traficar** <c → qu> [tra·fi·'kar] *vi* to deal; (*con drogas*) to traffic; (*con personas*) to smuggle

**tráfico** ['tra·fi·ko] *m* **1.** (*vial*) traffic; **~ por carretera** road traffic **2.** COM trade; (*drogas*) traffic; (*personas, coches*) smuggling; **~ de influencias** graft

**tragaluz** [tra·ɣa·'lus, -·'luθ] *m* transom; (*grande*) skylight

**traganíqueles** [tra·ɣa·'ni·ke·les] *f inv Nic inf* slot machine

**tragar** <g → gu> [tra·'ɣar] **I.** *vt, vr:* **~se** to swallow; (*historia, mentira*) to fall for; **¡trágame tierra!** I wish the ground would open up and swallow me!; **tuvimos que ~ toda la conferencia** we had to sit through the whole conference **II.** *vt* to down; **~ saliva** to eat crow; **no ~ a alguien** to not be able to stand sb

**tragedia** [tra·'xe·ðja] *f* tragedy

**trágico, -a** ['tra·xi·ko, -a] *adj* tragic; **no te pongas ~** don't get all melodramatic

**trago** ['tra·ɣo] *m* (*sorbo*) swig; (*bebida*) drink; **de un ~** in one gulp; **tomar un ~**

**de más** to have one drink too many; **pasar un mal ~** to have a bad time of it

**traición** [trai·'sjon, -·'θjon] *f* treachery; (*delito*) treason

**traicionar** [trai·sjo·'nar, trai·θjo·] *vt* to betray; **le traicionó su acento** his/her accent gave him/her away

**traicionero, -a** [trai·sjo·'ne·ro, -a; trai·θjo·] **I.** *adj* perfidious; (*acción*) traitorous; (*memoria*) unreliable; (*animal*) dangerous **II.** *m, f* traitor

**traidor(a)** [trai·'ðor, -·'ðo·ra] *m(f)* traitor

**traje** ['tra·xe] *m* dress; (*de hombre*) suit; (*de mujer*) outfit; **~ de noche/de etiqueta** evening dress/suit; **~ típico/de época** regional/period costume

**trajeado, -a** [tra·xe·'a·ðo, -a] *adj* **ir bien/mal ~** to be well/badly dressed

**trajín** [tra·'xin] *m* haulage; (*ajetreo*) rush

**trajinera** [tra·xi·'ne·ra] *f Méx* (*canoa*) ≈ canoe

**trama** ['tra·ma] *f* plot

**tramar** [tra·'mar] *vt* to plot; (*intriga, plan*) to scheme; **¿qué estarán tramando?** what are they up to?; **aquí se está tramando algo** something's cooking here

**tramitar** [tra·mi·'tar] *vt* to attend to; (*negocio*) to transact; (*expediente*) to process; **está tramitando el divorcio** he/she has started divorce proceedings

**trámite** ['tra·mi·te] *m* formality; **en ~s de hacer algo** in the process of doing sth; **pasar por todos los ~s** to go through the whole procedure

**tramo** ['tra·mo] *m* stretch; FERRO section; (*escalera*) flight

**trampa** ['tram·pa] *f* **1.** trap; **caer en la ~** to fall into the trap; **poner una ~** to set a trap **2.** (*trampilla*) trapdoor **3.** (*fullería*) cheating; **hacer ~** to cheat **4.** *inf* (*deuda*) bad debt ▶ **sin ~ ni cartón** with no catches; **hecha la ley hecha la ~** laws are made to be broken

**trampolín** [tram·po·'lin] *m* (*piscina*) diving board

**tramposo, -a** [tram·'po·so, -a] **I.** *adj* cheating **II.** *m, f* swindler; (*fullero*) cheat

**tranca** ['tran·ka] *f* binge; **coger una ~** to get plastered

**trance** ['tran·se, -·θe] *m* trance

**T**

**tranque** ['tran·ke] *m Chile* reservoir

**tranquilidad** [tran·ki·li·'dad] *f* peace; **con ~** calmly; **para mayor ~** to be on the safe side

**tranquilizante** [tran·ki·li·'san·te, -'θan·te] *m* tranquilizer

**tranquilizar** <z → c> [tran·ki·li·'sar, -'θar] **I.** *vt* to calm down; (*con palabras*) to reassure **II.** *vr:* **~se** to calm down

**tranquillo** [tran·'ki·ʝo, -ʎo] *m* **coger el ~ a algo** to get the knack of sth

**tranquilo, -a** [tran·'ki·lo, -a] *adj* calm; (*sereno*) serene; (*despreocupada*) unconcerned; **tú ~** don't worry; **¡déjame ~!** leave me alone!

**transa** ['tran·sa] *f* **1.** *AmL* (*compromiso*) commitment **2.** *Méx* (*engaño*) deceit **3.** *RíoPl* (*transacción*) transaction; (*de droga*) drug dealing

**transacción** [tran·sak·'sjon, -'θjon] *f* **1.** JUR settlement **2.** POL agreement **3.** COM deal **4.** FIN transaction

**transar** [tran·'sar] *vi AmL* to compromise

**transatlántico** [tran·sat·'lan·ti·ko] *m* ocean liner

**transbordar** [trans·βor·'dar] *vt, vi* to transfer

**transbordo** [trans·'βor·do] *m* change; (*mercancías*) transfer; **hay que hacer ~ en el aeropuerto** you have to change planes at the airport

**transcender** <e → ie> [tran·sen·'der, trans·θen·] *vi v.* **trascender**

**transcribir** [trans·kri·'βir] *irr como escribir vt* to transcribe

**transcripción** [trans·krip·'sjon, -kriβ·'θjon] *f* (*acción*) transcription; (*resultado*) transcript

**transcurrir** [trans·ku·'rrir] *vi* to elapse; (*acontecer*) to take place

**transeúnte** [tran·se·'un·te] *mf* passer-by

**transferencia** [trans·fe·'ren·sja, -θja] *f* transfer

**transferir** [trans·fe·'rir] *irr como sentir vt* **1.** (*trasladar*) to transfer **2.** (*posponer*) to postpone **3.** FIN to make over; (*propiedad, derecho*) to transfer

**transformación** [trans·for·ma·'sjon, -'θjon] *f* transformation

**transformar** [trans·for·'mar] *vt* to transform

**transfusión** [trans·fu·'sjon] *f* transfusion

**transgresión** [trans·γre·'sjon] *f* transgression

**transición** [tran·si·'sjon, -'θjon] *f* transition

**transigente** [tran·si·'xen·te] *adj* broadminded; (*tolerante*) tolerant

**transigir** <g → j> [tran·si·'xir] *vi* **~ con algo** to tolerate sth; JUR, POL to compromise

**transistor** [tran·sis·'tor] *m* ELEC transistor

**transitable** [tran·si·'ta·βle] *adj* open to traffic; (*a pie*) passable

**transitar** [tran·si·'tar] *vi* **~ por** to go/walk along; **muy transitado** very busy

**transitivo, -a** [tran·si·'ti·βo, -a] *adj* transitive

**tránsito** ['tran·si·to] *m t.* COM transit; (*circulación*) traffic; **de mucho ~** very busy

**transitorio, -a** [tran·si·'to·rjo, -a] *adj* temporary

**translúcido, -a** [trans·'lu·si·do, -a; -θi·do, -a] *adj* translucent

**transmisión** [trans·mi·'sjon] *f* transmission; (*noticia*) broadcast

**transmisor** [trans·mi·'sor] *m* transmitter

**transmitir** [trans·mi·'tir] *vt* to transmit; (*noticia*) to broadcast

**transparencia** [trans·pa·'ren·sja, -θja] *f* transparency; (*de intención*) openness

**transparentar** [trans·pa·ren·'tar] **I.** *vt* to reveal **II.** *vi, vr:* **~se** to be transparent **III.** *vr:* **~se** (*dejarse ver, adivinar*) to show through

**transparente** [trans·pa·'ren·te] *adj* transparent

**transpirar** [trans·pi·'rar] *vi* to perspire

**transponer** [trans·po·'ner] *irr como poner* **I.** *vt* to move **II.** *vr:* **~se 1.** to move **2.** (*dormirse*) to doze off

**transportar** [trans·por·'tar] **I.** *vt* to transport; (*en brazos*) to carry **II.** *vr:* **~se** to be transported

**transporte** [trans·'por·te] *m* transport; **~ por carretera** road transport; **~s públicos** public transportation

**transportista** [trans·por·'tis·ta] *mf* carrier

**transpuesto, -a** [trans·'pwes·to, -a] **I.** *pp de* **transponer II.** *adj* quedarse

~ **to** doze off

**transversal** [trans·βer·'sal] *adj* crosswise; **calle** ~ cross street

**tranvía** [tram·'bi·a] *m* streetcar

**trapear** [tra·pe·'ar] *vt AmL* to mop

**trapecio** [tra·'pe·sjo, -θjo] *m* trapeze

**trapiche** [tra·'pi·tʃe] *m AmL* sugar mill

**trapichear** [tra·pi·tʃe·'ar] *vi* **1.** *inf* (*enredos*) to be mixed up in shady business; ~ **en los negocios** to have crooked dealings **2.** (*comerciar*) to buy and sell small scale

**trapo** ['tra·po] *m* rag; (*para limpiar*) cleaning cloth; ~ **de cocina** dish towel; **a todo** ~ at top speed; (*música*) on full blast ▶ **tener manos de** ~ to be a butterfingers; **estar hecho un** ~ to be worn out; **sacar los** ~**s sucios a relucir** to wash one's dirty linen in public

**tráquea** ['tra·kea] *f* windpipe

**traquetear** [tra·ke·te·'ar] **I.** *vi* (*chapa, vajilla*) to clatter; (*motor, ametralladora*) to rattle; (*sillas, carro*) to jolt **II.** *vt* to jolt

**tras** [tras] *prep* after; (*espacial*) behind; **ir** ~ **alguien** to go after sb; **poner uno** ~ **otro** to put one after the other

**trasbocar** <c → qu> [tras·βo·'kar] *vt AmC, AmS* to throw up

**trascendencia** [tra·sen·'den·sja, -θen·'den·θja] *f* consequence; **no tener** ~ to be of little importance

**trascendental** [tra·sen·den·'tal, tras·θen·] *adj* important

**trascender** <e → ie> [tra·sen·'der, tras·θen·] *vi* to become known; ~ **a algo** to have a wide effect on sth; ~ **de algo** to go beyond sth

**trasera** [tra·'se·ra] *f* back

**trasero** [tra·'se·ro] *m* hindquarters *pl*; (*persona*) backside

**trasero, -a** [tra·'se·ro, -a] *adj* back; **parte trasera** rear; **rueda trasera** rear wheel

**trasfondo** [tras·'fon·do] *m* background

**trasladar** [tras·la·'dar] **I.** *vt* to move; (*tienda*) to relocate; (*preso, funcionario*) to transfer **II.** *vr:* ~**se** to go; (*mudarse*) to move

**traslado** [tras·'la·do] *m* **1.** movement; (*preso, funcionario*) transfer **2.** (*mudanza*) removal

**trasluz** [tras·'lus, -'luθ] *m* **mirar algo al** ~ to hold sth up to the light

**trasnochar** [tras·no·'tʃar] *vi* to spend a sleepless night; (*ir de juerga*) to have a night out; (*acostarse tarde*) to stay up late

**traspapelar** [tras·pa·pe·'lar] **I.** *vt* to mislay **II.** *vr:* ~**se** to get mislaid

**traspasar** [tras·pa·'sar] *vt* **1.** (*atravesar*) to go through; (*penetrar, perforar*) to pierce; (*líquido*) to soak through; (*límite*) to go beyond **2.** (*pasar a*) to transfer; FIN to make over

**traspaso** [tras·'pa·so] *m* transfer; (*límite*) exceeding

**traspatio** [tras·'pa·tjo] *m AmL* backyard

**traspié(s)** [tras·'pje(s)] *m* (*inv*) stumble; *fig* slip-up; **dar un** ~ to stumble *fig*, to slip up

**trasplantar** [tras·plan·'tar] *vt* to transplant

**trasplante** [tras·'plan·te] *m* transplanting; MED transplant

**trastada** [tras·'ta·da] *f* dirty trick; (*travesura*) prank; **hacer una** ~ **a alguien** to play a prank on sb

**traste** ['tras·te] *m AmL* piece of junk ▶ **dar al** ~ **con algo** to spoil sth; **irse al** ~ to fall through

**trastero** [tras·'te·ro] *m* lumber room

**trasto** ['tras·to] *m* piece of junk; **tus** ~**s** your stuff; **tirarse los** ~**s a la cabeza** to have a knock down drag out fight

**trastornado, -a** [tras·tor·'na·do, -a] *adj* confused; PSICO disturbed

**trastornar** [tras·tor·'nar] **I.** *vt* **1.** to disarrange; (*de arriba abajo*) to turn upside down; (*orden, plan, ideas*) disrupt; (*orden público*) to disturb **2.** PSICO to traumatize; (*por amor*) to lose one's head over sb; **la muerte de su marido la trastornó** she was traumatized by her husband's death; **me trastornan los coches** I'm crazy about cars **II.** *vr:* ~**se 1.** (*enloquecer*) to go mad **2.** (*estropearse*) to fall through

**trasvasijar** [tras·βa·si·'xar] *vt Chile* to decant

**tratable** [tra·'ta·βle] *adj* sociable

**tratado** [tra·'ta·do] *m* treaty; (*científico*) treatise; ~ **de no agresión** non-

T

aggression treaty; **~ comercial** trade agreement

**tratamiento** [tra·ta·'mjen·to] *m* 1. *t.* MED, QUÍM treatment 2. *t.* COMPUT (*elaboración*) processing 3. (*de cortesía*) form of address

**tratante** [tra·'tan·te] *mf* dealer

**tratar** [tra·'tar] **I.** *vt* 1. (*manejar, portarse*) to deal with 2. MED, QUÍM to treat 3. *t.* COMPUT (*elaborar, agua, minerales*) to process 4. (*dirigirse*) to address 5. (*tema, asunto*) to discuss **II.** *vi* 1. **~ de** [*o sobre*] **algo** to be about sth 2. (*intentar*) to try; **trata de concentrarte** try to concentrate 3. (*con alguien*) to have contact with 4. COM to deal **III.** *vr:* **~se** to have to do; **¿de qué se trata?** what's it about?; **tratándose de ti...** in your case...

**tratativas** [tra·ta·'ti·βas] *fpl* Arg, Par negotiations *pl;* **siguen en ~** they are still discussing terms

**trato** ['tra·to] *m* 1. (*comportamiento*) treatment; **malos ~s** abuse; **recibir un buen ~** to be well-treated 2. (*contacto*) contact; **romper el ~ con alguien** to break off relations with sb; **no querer ~s con alguien** to want nothing to do with sb 3. (*pacto*) agreement; (*negocio*) deal; **cerrar un ~ con alguien** to close a deal with sb; **¡~ hecho!** it's a deal!

**trauma** ['trau·ma] *m* trauma

**traumático, -a** [trau·'ma·ti·ko, -a] *adj* traumatic

**traumatismo** [trau·ma·'tis·mo] *m* injury; **~ cervical** traumatism

**través** [tra·'βes] *prep* **a ~ de** across; (*de alguien*) from

**travesti** [tra·'βes·ti] *mf,* **travestí** [tra·βes·'ti] *mf,* **travestido, -a** [tra·βes·'ti·do, -a] *m, f* transvestite

**travesura** [tra·βe·'su·ra] *f* prank

**travieso, -a** [tra·'βje·so, -a] *adj* naughty; **correr a campo traviesa** to run cross-country

**trayecto** [tra·'jek·to] *m* (*trecho*) distance; (*ruta*) route; (*recorrido*) itinerary; **final de ~** end of the line

**trayectoria** [tra·jek·'to·rja] *f* path; ASTRON, FÍS trajectory; (*profesional*) career

**traza** ['tra·sa, -θa] *f* 1. *t.* ARQUIT plan

2. (*habilidad*) ability 3. (*aspecto*) appearance

**trazado** [tra·'sa·do, tra·'θa-] *m* 1. *t.* ARQUIT design 2. (*recorrido*) route; FERRO line

**trazar** <z → c> [tra·'sar, -'θar] *vt* 1. (*líneas*) to trace; (*esquemáticamente*) to outline; (*dibujos*) to sketch 2. *t.* ARQUIT (*plan*) to draw up 3. (*describir*) to describe

**trazo** ['tra·so, -θo] *m* stroke; **de ~s suaves** with soft features

**trébol** ['tre·βol] *m* clover; (*cartas*) clubs *pl*

**trece** ['tre·se, -θe] **I.** *adj inv* thirteen; **seguir en sus ~** to stand firm; **en el siglo ~** in the thirteenth century; **martes y ~** ≈ Friday the thirteenth **II.** *m* thirteen; *v. t.* **ocho**

**trecho** ['tre·tʃo] *m* distance; (*tramo*) stretch

**tregua** ['tre·ɣwa] *f* truce; (*descanso*) respite; **sin ~** relentlessly

**treinta** ['trein·ta] *adj inv m* thirty; *v. t.* **ochenta**

**treintavo, -a** [trein·'ta·βo, -a] *adj* thirtieth; *v. t.* **ochentavo**

**tremendo, -a** [tre·'men·do, -a] *adj* (*temible*) frightful; (*enorme*) tremendous; (*respetable*) imposing; (*niño*) full of mischief ▶ **tomar las cosas a la tremenda** to make such a fuss over things

**tren** [tren] *m* train; **~ interurbano/rápido/directo** intercity/express/through train; **~ de cercanías/de alta velocidad** suburban/high-speed train; **coger el ~** to catch [*o* take] the train; **ir en ~** to go by train; **perder el último ~** *fig* to miss the boat; **~ de lavado** carwash; **~ de vida** lifestyle; **estar como un ~** *inf* to be very good-looking; **hay sangría como para parar un ~** there's plenty of sangria

**trenza** ['tren·sa, -θa] *f* braid

**trenzar** <z → c> [tren·'sar, -'θar] *vt* to plait; (*pelo*) to braid

**trepa¹** ['tre·pa] *f* (*astucia*) cunning

**trepa²** ['tre·pa] *m pey inf* climber

**trepador(a)** [tre·pa·'dor] **I.** *adj* **planta ~a** climbing plant **II.** *m(f)* go-getter

**trepar** [tre·'par] *vi, vt* to climb; (*planta*) to creep

**trepe** ['tre·pe] *m* CRi (*regaño*) scolding; **echar un ~ a alguien por algo** to tell sb off for sth

**trepidar** [tre·pi·'dar] *vi AmL* to hesitate

**tres** [tres] **I.** *adj inv* three; **no me sale ni a la de ~** I just can't do this no matter how I try; **de ~ al cuarto** two-bit; **~ en raya** (*juego*) tic(k)-tac(k)-toe **II.** *m inv* three; *v. t.* **ocho**

**trescientos, -as** [tres·'sjen·tos, -as; -'θjen·tos, -as] *adj* three hundred; *v. t.* **ochocientos**

**triangular** [trian·gu·'lar] *adj* triangular

**triángulo** [tri·'an·ɣu·lo] *m* triangle

**triates** ['trja·tes] *mpl Méx* triplets *pl*

**tribu** ['tri·βu] *f* tribe

**tribuna** [tri·'βu·na] *f* stand; (*en parlamento*) rostrum; **~ de jurados/de la prensa** jury/press box

**tribunal** [tri·βu·'nal] *m* court; **llevar a los ~es** to take to court; **~ examinador** board of examiners

**tributar** [tri·βu·'tar] *vt* to pay; **~ un homenaje a alguien** to pay tribute to sb

**tributario, -a** [tri·βu·'ta·rjo, -a] *adj* tributary; (*imponible*) tax; **agencia tributaria** Inland Revenue

**tributo** [tri·'βu·to] *m* tax; (*homenaje*) tribute

**triciclo** [tri·'si·klo, tri·'θi-] *m* tricycle

**tricolor** [tri·ko·'lor] *adj* tricolor

**tricota** [tri·'ko·ta] *f AmL* sweater

**tridimensional** [tri·di·men·sjo·'nal] *adj* three-dimensional

**trifulca** [tri·'ful·ka] *f* rumpus

**trigal** [tri·'ɣal] *m* wheat field

**trigo** ['tri·ɣo] *m* wheat; **no ser ~ limpio** not to be totally above board

**trigueño, -a** [tri·'ɣe·no, -a] *AmL* **I.** *adj* light brown; (*pelo*) dark blond; (*piel*) olive-skinned **II.** *m, f* colored person

**trilla** ['tri·ja, -ʎa] *f AmL inf* thrashing

**trillar** [tri·'jar, -'ʎar] *vt AmL inf* to beat

**trillizo** [tri·'ji·so, -a; -'ʎi·θo, -a] *m* triplet

**trillo** ['tri·jo, -ʎo] *m AmC* narrow path

**trimestral** [tri·mes·'tral] *adj* three-month; (*cada tres meses*) quarterly

**trimestre** [tri·'mes·tre] *m* quarter; ENS term

**trinar** [tri·'nar] *vi* to warble; **está que trina** *inf* he/she is completely crazy

**trinca** ['trin·ka] *f* **1.** And, CSur (*pandilla*) gang **2.** AmL inf (*embriaguez*)

drunkenness **3.** CSur (*canicas*) game of marbles

**trincar** <c → qu> [trin·'kar] **I.** *vt* **1.** *inf* (*robar*) to steal **2.** *inf* (*pillar*) to nab **3.** AmL (*apretar*) to be too tight **II.** *vr:* **~se** *inf* (*copular*) to screw

**trinchera** [trin·'tʃe·ra] *f* trench

**trineo** [tri·'neo] *m* sled

**trinidad** [tri·ni·'dad] *f* trinity

**trinitaria** [tri·ni·'ta·rja] *f* **1.** pansy **2.** Col, PRico, Ven bougainvillea

**trino** ['tri·no] *m* warble

**trío** ['tri·o] *m* trio

**tripa** [tri·pa] *f* **1.** (*intestino*) gut **2.** *pl* (*vísceras*) entrails *pl*; *fig* insides *pl*; **me suenan las ~s** my stomach's rumbling; **se me revuelven las ~s** it turns my stomach **3.** *inf* (*vientre*) tummy; **echar ~** to get a paunch; **llenar(se) la ~** to eat one's fill

**triple** ['tri·ple] **I.** *adj* triple; (*de tres capas*) three-ply **II.** *m* triple; **ser el ~ de grande** to be three times as large

**triplicar** <c → qu> [tri·pli·'kar] *vt, vr:* **~se** to triple

**trípode** ['tri·po·de] *m* tripod

**tripón, -ona** [tri·'pon, -·'po·na] *m, f* **1.** Méx *inf* little boy or girl; **los tripones** the kids **2.** *inf* (*gordo*) fatty

**tripulación** [tri·pu·la·'sjon, -'θjon] *f* crew

**tripulina** [tri·pu·'li·na] *f Chile* hubbub

**trisca** ['tris·ka] *f AmC* surreptitious sneer

**triscar** <c → qu> [tris·'kar] *vt AmC* to make fun of

**triste** ['tris·te] *adj* sad; **un ~ sueldo** a miserable salary; **ni un ~...** not a single...; **es ~ que no podamos ir** it's too bad we can't go

**tristeza** [tris·'te·sa, -θa] *f*, **tristura** [tris·'tu·ra] *f AmL* sadness

**trituradora** [tri·tu·ra·'do·ra] *f* grinder; TÉC crusher; **~ de carne** meat grinder; **~ de papel** paper shredder; **~ de basura** waste-disposal unit; **~ de hielo** ice crusher

**triturar** [tri·tu·'rar] *vt* to chop; (*moler*) to grind; (*al masticar*) to chew

**triunfador(a)** [trjun·fa·'dor, -·'do·ra] *m(f)* winner

**triunfar** [trjun·'far] *vi* to triumph; **~ en algo** to win at sth; (*tener éxito*) to suc-

**ceed;** ~ **en la vida** to succeed in life

**triunfo** ['trjun·fo] *m* triumph, victory; (*éxito*) success

**trivialidad** [tri·βja·li·'dad] *f* triviality; (*dicho*) trite remark

**triza** ['tri·sa, -θa] *f* shred; **estar hecho ~s** to feel washed out; **hacer ~s** to tear into shreds; **hacerse ~s** to smash to bits

**trocar** [tro·'kar] *irr como* **volcar** *vt* **1.** ~ **por algo** to exchange for sth **2.** *CSur* (*vender*) to sell

**trofeo** [tro·'feo] *m* trophy

**troglodita** [tro·ɣlo·'di·ta] *m* **1.** troglodyte **2.** *inf* lout

**tromba** ['trom·ba] *f* ~ **(de agua)** water spout; (*aguacero*) downpour

**trombón** [trom·'bon] *m* trombone

**trombosis** [trom·'bo·sis] *f inv* thrombosis

**trompa¹** ['trom·pa] *f* **1.** ZOOL trunk; ~ **de Falopio** Fallopian tube **2.** *inf* (*nariz*) conk **3.** *AmL inf* (*labios*) lips *pl* **4.** *inf* drunkenness; **coger una** ~ to get smashed; **estar** ~ to be drunk

**trompa²** ['trom·pa] *mf CSur inf* boss

**trompada** [trom·'pa·da] *f*, **trompazo** [trom·'pa·so, -θo] *m* (*porrazo*) bash; (*choque*) crash

**trompear** [trom·pe·'ar] *AmL, inf* **I.** *vt* to punch **II.** *vr:* ~**se** to get plastered; (*pelearse*) to fight

**trompeta** [trom·'pe·ta] *f* trumpet

**trompicón** [trom·pi·'kon] *m* **1. a trompicones** in fits and starts **2.** *AmC* punch

**trompis** ['trom·pis] *m inv Arg, Urug* punch; **agarrarse a** ~ to start punching each other

**trompiza** [trom·'pi·sa] *f AmS* fight

**trompo** ['trom·po] *m* spinning top

**trompudo, -a** [trom·'pu·do, -a] *adj AmL* thick-lipped

**tronado, -a** [tro·'na·do, -a] *adj inf* **estar** ~ (*loco*) to be cracked; (*arruinado*) to be broke; *AmL* (*drogado*) to be high on drugs

**tronar** <o → ue> [tro·'nar] *vi, vimpers* to thunder

**troncha** ['tron·tʃa] *f Arg, Chile, Perú* slice

**tronchar** [tron·'tʃar] **I.** *vt* (*tronco*) to cut down; (*rama*) to snap; (*vida*) to cut short; (*esperanzas*) to shatter **II.** *vr:* ~**se** to split; ~**se de risa** to split one's sides laughing

**troncho** ['tron·tʃo] *m* **1.** stalk **2.** *CSur* (*trozo*) chunk

**tronco** ['tron·ko] *m* **1.** BOT, ANAT trunk; (*leño*) log; **dormir como un** ~ *inf* to sleep like a log **2.** *inf* buddy; **tranqui** ~ cool it, pal

**tronera** [tro·'ne·ra] *f Méx* chimney

**trono** ['tro·no] *m* throne; *inf* john

**tropa** ['tro·pa] *f* crowd; *pey* horde; MIL troop

**tropel** [tro·'pel] *m* throng; **en** ~ in a mad rush; **salieron en** ~ **del estadio** they came pouring out of the stadium

**tropero** [tro·'pe·ro] *m Arg* cowboy

**tropezar** [tro·pe·'sar, -'θar] *irr como* **empezar I.** *vi* to trip **II.** *vr* ~**se con** to run into

**tropezón** [tro·pe·'son, -'θon] *m* **1.** (*acción*) stumble; **dar un** ~ to trip; **a tropezones** by fits and starts; *fig* falling and rising; **hablaba a tropezones** he/ she spoke falteringly **2.** (*error*) mistake; (*desliz*) lapse **3.** CULIN small chunk, esp of meat

**tropical** [tro·pi·'kal] *adj* tropical

**trópico** ['tro·pi·ko] *m* tropic; **pasar los ~s** *AmC* to have a hard time

**tropiezo** [tro·'pje·so, -θo] *m* **dar un** ~ to trip; (*error*) blunder

**tropilla** [tro·'pi·ja, -ʎa] *f CSur* drove

**trotar** [tro·'tar] *vi* to trot

**trozo** ['tro·so, -θo] *m* piece, bit; **a ~s** in pieces

**trucar** [tru·'kar] *vt* **1.** (*amañar*) to fix; FOTO to alter **2.** AUTO to soup up

**trucha** ['tru·tʃa] *f* **1.** trout; ~ **asalmonada** salmon trout **2.** *AmC* stand

**trucho, -a** ['tru·tʃo, -a] *adj Arg, Col* crafty

**truco** ['tru·ko] *m* trick; **esto tiene** ~ there's a trick to this ▶ **coger el** ~ **a** to get the hang of sth; (*a alguien*) to catch on to sb

**trueno** ['trwe·no] *m* clap of thunder

**trueque** ['trwe·ke] *m* exchange

**trufa** ['tru·fa] *f* truffle

**truncar** <c → qu> [trun·'kar] *vt* to truncate; (*desarrollo*) to stunt; (*esperanzas, ilusiones*) to shatter

**trusa** ['tru·sa] *f Méx, Perú* girdle

**tu** [tu] *art pos* your; ~ **padre/blusa/ libro** your father/blouse/book; ~**s hermanos/as** your brothers/sisters

**tú** [tu] *pron pers* you; **yo que ~** if I were you; **de ~ a ~** on equal footing

**tuba** ['tu·βa] *f* tuba

**tubérculo** [tu·'βer·ku·lo] *m* tuber; MED tubercle

**tuberculosis** [tu·βer·ku·'lo·sis] *f inv* tuberculosis

**tubería** [tu·βe·'ri·a] *f* pipe

**tubo** ['tu·βo] *m* 1. tube; ~ **digestivo** alimentary canal; ~ **de ensayo/escape** test/exhaust tube; **alucinar por un ~** *inf* to really flip; **tenemos trabajo por un ~** *inf* we have loads of work to do 2. *AmL* TEL receiver

**tucán** [tu·'kan] *m* toucan

**tuerca** ['twer·ka] *f* nut

**tuerto, -a** ['twer·to] *adj* one-eyed

**tuétano** ['twe·ta·no] *m* 1. (*médula*) marrow 2. (*corazón, esencia*) core; **hasta los ~s** through and through; **enamorado hasta los ~s** head over heels in love; **llegar al ~ de un asunto** to get to the crux of a matter; **calado hasta los ~s** soaked to the skin

**tufo** ['tu·fo] *m* stink

**tulipa** [tu·'li·pa] *f* tulip-shaped lampshade

**tulipán** [tu·li·'pan] *m* tulip

**tumba** ['tum·ba] *f* 1. grave; **soy una ~** my lips are sealed 2. *AmL* (*tala*) felling of trees; (*claro*) tree clearing

**tumbar** [tum·'bar] I. *vt* 1. to knock down; **estar tumbado** to be lying down 2. *AmL* to fell; (*tierra*) to clear II. *vr:* ~**se** to lie down

**tumbo** ['tum·bo] *m* (*caída*) tumble; (*vaivén*) roll; **dar un ~** to jolt; **ir por la vida dando ~s** to go through life moving from one hardship to another

**tumor** [tu·'mor] *m* tumor

**tumulto** [tu·'mul·to] *m* tumult

**tunda** ['tun·da] *f* beating; **darse una ~** to wear oneself out

**túnel** [tu·'nel] *m* tunnel; ~ **de lavado** car wash

**túnica** ['tu·ni·ka] *f* tunic

**tuntún** [tun·'tun] *m inf* **al (buen) ~** any

old way; **juzgar al buen ~** to jump to conclusions

**tupé** [tu·'pe] *m* pompadour

**tupí** [tu·'pi] *mf AmL* Tupi

**tupido, -a** [tu·'pi·do, -a] *adj* 1. thick 2. *AmL* blocked 3. *Méx* frequent

**tupirse** [tu·'pir·se] *vr AmL* to get blocked up

**turbación** [tur·βa·'sjon, -'θjon] *f* confusion; (*agitación*) concern

**turbante** [tur·'βan·te] *m* turban

**turbar** [tur·'βar] I. *vt* to disturb; (*avergonzar*) to embarrass II. *vr:* ~**se** to be disturbed; (*avergonzarse*) to get embarrassed

**turbina** [tur·'βi·na] *f* turbine

**turbio, -a** ['tur·βjo, -a] *adj* (*líquido*) cloudy; (*asunto*) turbid; (*negocio*) shady

**turbulencia** [tur·βu·'len·sja, -θja] *f* turbulence; (*alboroto*) commotion

**turbulento, -a** [tur·βu·'len·to, -a] *adj* 1. (*agua, aire*) turbulent 2. (*alborotado*) stormy 3. (*rebelde*) disorderly

**turismo** [tu·'ris·mo] *m* 1. tourism; ~ **verde** ecotourism; **industria del ~** tourist trade; **oficina de ~** visitors' bureau; **hacer ~** to travel as a tourist 2. AUTO private car

**turista** [tu·'ris·ta] *mf* tourist

**turístico, -a** [tu·'ris·ti·ko, -a] *adj* tourist; **viaje ~** sightseeing trip

**turnar** [tur·'nar] *vi, vr:* ~**se** to take turns

**turno** ['tur·no] *m* 1. (*laboral*) shift; **cambio de ~** shift change; **estar de ~** to be on duty; ~ **de día/noche** day/night shift 2. (*orden*) turn; **por ~s** by turns; **hacer algo por ~s** to take turns doing sth; **apareció con la novia de ~** he showed up with his latest girlfriend

**turquesa¹** [tur·'ke·sa] I. *adj* turquoise II. *m* (*color*) turquoise blue

**turquesa²** [tur·'ke·sa] *f* MIN (*piedra*) turquoise

**turrón** [tu·'rron] *m* ≈ nougat

**turulato, -a** [tu·ru·'la·to, -a] *adj inf* dazed; **dejar a alguien ~** to leave sb flabbergasted

**tusar** [tu·'sar] I. *vi Guat* to murmur II. *vt AmL* to scalp *fig*

**tuso, -a** ['tu·so, -a] *adj* 1. *Col, PRico* (*pelón*) cropped 2. *Col, Ven* (*viruelas*)

**T**

pockmarked **3.** *PRico* (*rabón*) bob-tailed

**tutear** [tu·te·'ar] **I.** *vt to address in the familiar manner using 'tú'* **II.** *vr:* **~se** to be on familiar terms

**tutela** [tu·'te·la] *f* protection; **bajo la ~ de** under the protection of

**tutelaje** [tu·te·'la·xe] *m CSur, Guat, Méx* guardianship

**tuteo** [tu·'teo] *m* familiar use of 'tú'

**tutilimundi** [tu·ti·li·'mun·di] *m AmL inf* everybody

**tutor(a)** [tu·'tor, -·'to·ra] *m(f)* JUR guardian; ENS tutor

**tutoría** [tu·to·'ri·a] *f* JUR guardianship; ENS tutorship

**tuyo, -a** ['tu·jo, -a] *pron pos* **1.** yours; **el perro es ~** the dog is yours **2.** (*tras artículo*) **el ~/la tuya/lo ~** yours; **mi coche está roto, vamos en el ~** my car isn't working, let's take yours; **los ~s** (*parientes*) your family; **tú a lo ~** you mind your own business; **esto no es lo ~** this isn't your strong point **3.** (*tras subst*) of yours; **una amiga tuya** a friend of yours; **es culpa tuya** it's your fault

# U

**U, u** [u] *f* <úes> U, u; **~ de Uruguay** U as in Uniform

**U** *abr de* **Universidad** U.

**u** [u] *conj ante 'o', 'ho'* or; **diez u once** ten or eleven

**ubicación** [u·βi·ka·'sjon, -'θjon] *f* **1.** location; (*de empresa*) site **2.** *AmL* (*colocación*) placing

**ubicar** <c → qu> [u·βi·'kar] **I.** *vi* **estar ~** to be situated **II.** *vt AmL* to situate; (*guardar*) to place **III.** *vr:* **~se** to be situated

**ubre** [u·'βre] *f* udder

**UCI** ['u·si, -θi] *abr de* **Unidad de Cuidados Intensivos** ICU

**Ud(s).** [us.'ted, -'te·des] *abr de* **usted(es)** you

**UE** [u·'e] *f abr de* **Unión Europea** EU

**úlcera** ['ul·se·ra, 'ul·θe-] *f* ulcer

**ulterior** [ul·te·'rjor] *adj* subsequent

**últimamente** ['ul·ti·ma·'men·te] *adv* recently, lately; (*por último*) lastly

**ultimar** [ul·ti·'mar] *vt* **1.** to complete; (*acuerdo*) to conclude **2.** *AmL* to murder

**ultimátum** [ul·ti·'ma·tun] *m* <inv *o* ultimatos> ultimatum

**último, -a** ['ul·ti·mo, -a] *adj* last; **el ~** the last; **por última vez** for the last time; **la última moda** the latest fashion; **por ~** lastly; **la última fila** the last row; **en el ~ piso** on the top floor; **ocupar la última posición de la tabla** to be at the bottom of the chart ▶ **estar en las últimas** to be at death's door

**ultra** [ul·tra] **I.** *adj* extreme **II.** *mf* neo-fascist **III.** *adv* extremely

**ultracongelado, -a** [ul·tra·kon·xe·'la·do, -a] *adj* deep-frozen

**ultraconservador(a)** [ul·tra·kon·ser·βa·'dor, -·'do·ra] *adj* ultraconservative

**ultrajar** [ul·tra·'xar] *vt* to insult; **~ de palabra** to revile

**ultraje** [ul·'tra·xe] *m* abuse

**ultramar** [ul·tra·'mar] *m* overseas

**ultramarinos** [ul·tra·ma·'ri·nos] *mpl* grocery store

**ultramoderno, -a** [ul·tra·mo·'der·no, -a] *adj* extremely modern

**ultranza** [ul·'tran·sa, -θa] *f* **luchar a ~** to fight to the death; **ser un ecologista a ~** to be a radical ecologist

**ultrarrápido, -a** [ul·tra·'rra·pi·do, -a] *adj* extra fast

**ultrasónico, -a** [ul·tra·'so·ni·ko, -a] *adj* ultrasonic

**ultrasonido** [ul·tra·so·'ni·do] *m* ultrasound

**ultravioleta** [ul·tra·βjo·'le·ta] *adj inv* ultraviolet

**umbilical** [um·bi·li·'kal] *adj* umbilical

**umbral** [um·'bral] *m* threshold; (*principio*) beginning

**umbrío, -a** [um·'bri·o, -a] *adj* shady

**UME** ['u·me] *f abr de* **Unión Monetaria Europea** EMU

**un** [un], **una** ['u·na] <unos, -as> **I.** *art indef* **1.** a; (*ante vocal o h muda*) an; **un perro** a dog; **una chica** a girl **2.** *pl* (*algunos*) some, a few **3.** *pl* (*aproximadamente*) approximately, about; **unos**

**30 pesos** about 30 pesos **II.** *adj v.* **uno, -a**

**unánime** [u·'na·ni·me] *adj* unanimous

**unanimidad** [u·na·ni·mi·'dad] *f* unanimity; **por ~** unanimously

**UNED** [u·'ned] *f abr de* **Universidad Nacional de Educación a Distancia** ≈ OU

**ungir** <g → j> [un·'xir] *vt* to anoint

**ungüento** [un·'gwen·to] *m* salve; MED ointment

**únicamente** [u·ni·ka·'men·te] *adv* solely

**unicameral** [u·ni·ka·me·'ral] *adj* single-chamber

**único, -a** ['u·ni·ko, -a] *adj* only; (*extraordinario*) unique; **hijo ~** only child; **heredero ~** sole heir; **dirección única** one-way

**unicornio** [u·ni·'kor·njo] *m* unicorn

**unidad** [u·ni·'dad] *f* 1. MIL, MAT, TÉC, COMPUT unit; **Unidad de Cuidados Intensivos** [*o de* **Vigilancia Intensiva**] intensive care unit 2. (*armonía*) unity

**unidimensional** [u·ni·di·men·sjo·'nal] *adj* one-dimensional

**unido, -a** [u·'ni·do, -a] *adj* united; **estamos muy ~s** we are very close; **mantenerse ~s** to stay together

**unifamiliar** [u·ni·fa·mi·'ljar] *adj* single-family; (*casa*) detached

**unificación** [u·ni·fi·ka·'sjon, -'θjon] *f* unification; (*uniformización*) standardization

**unificar** <c → qu> [u·ni·fi·'kar] *vt* to unite; (*uniformar*) to standardize; (*posiciones*) to unify

**uniformar** [u·ni·for·'mar] *vt* to standardize

**uniforme** [u·ni·'for·me] *adj, m* uniform

**uniformidad** [u·ni·for·mi·'dad] *f* (*constancia*) regularity; (*similaridad*) uniformity

**uniformizar** <z → c> [u·ni·for·mi·'sar, -'θar] *vt* to standardize; (*mezclar*) to blend

**unilateral** [u·ni·la·te·'ral] *adj* one-sided; POL unilateral

**unión** [u·'njon] *f* 1. *t.* TÉC (*de dos elementos*) joint 2. *t.* ECON, POL (*territorial*) union; **Unión Europea** European Union; **Unión de Repúblicas Socialistas Soviéticas** Union of Soviet Socialist Republics; **~ monetaria** monetary union; **en ~ con** (together) with 3. (*matrimonio*) marriage 4. COM merger 5. (*armonía*) unity ▶ **la ~ hace la fuerza** united we stand

**unir** [u·'nir] **I.** *vt* 1. (*dos elementos*) to join 2. (*territorios, familia*) to unite; (*esfuerzos*) to combine **II.** *vr:* **~se** to unite; ECON to merge; **~se en matrimonio** to marry

**unisex** [u·ni·'seks] *adj* unisex

**unísono** [u·'ni·so·no] *m* unison; **al ~** in unison

**unitario, -a** [u·ni·'ta·rjo, -a] *adj* unitary

**universal** [u·ni·βer·'sal] *adj* 1. (*del universo*) universal 2. (*del mundo*) worldwide; **historia ~** world history 3. (*amplio*) widespread

**universalidad** [u·ni·βer·sa·li·'dad] *f* universality

**universalizar** <z → c> [u·ni·βer·sa·li·'sar, -'θar] *vt* to make universal

**universidad** [u·ni·βer·si·'dad] *f* university; **ir a la ~** to go to college [*o* university]; **Universidad Nacional de Educación a Distancia** ≈ Open University

**universitario, -a** [u·ni·βer·si·'ta·rjo, -a] **I.** *adj* university; **tener estudios ~s** to have studied at university **II.** *m, f* university student

**universo** [u·ni·'βer·so] *m* universe

**unívoco, -a** [u·'ni·βo·ko, -a] *adj* unanimous

**uno** ['u·no] *m* one

**uno, -a** [u·no, -a] **I.** *adj* one; **a la una** at one o'clock; **¡(a la) una, (a las) dos y (a las) tres!** ready, set, go! **II.** *pron indef* 1. one; **cada ~** each (one), every one; **~s cuantos** some; **~..., el otro...** one..., the other...; **~ de tantos** one of many; **aquí hay ~ que pregunta por ti** there's sb here asking for you; **una de dos, o... o...** the choice is simple, either... or....; **una que otra vez** once in a while; **de ~ en ~** one by one; **no acierto una** I can't do anything right; **lo ~ por lo otro** what goes around comes around 2. *pl* some

**untar** [un·'tar] **I.** *vt* to spread; (*mojar*) to dip; (*grasa*) to grease **II.** *vr* **~se de algo**

to become smeared with sth; **~se con/ de algo** (*crema*) to rub sth in

**uña** [ˈu·ɲa] *f* nail; ZOOL claw; **comerse las ~s** to bite one's nails; *fig* to become furious ▶ **ser ~ y carne** to be inseparable; **defenderse con ~s y dientes** to fight tooth and nail to defend oneself

**upa** [ˈu·pa] I. *interj* oops-a-daisy; **llevar a ~ un niño** to carry a child II. *adj Ecua, Perú* idiot

**uranio** [uˈra·njo] *m* uranium

**urbanícola** [ur·βaˈni·ko·la] *mf* city dweller

**urbanidad** [ur·βa·niˈdad] *f* urbanity

**urbanismo** [ur·βaˈnis·mo] *m* town planning

**urbanístico, -a** [ur·βaˈnis·ti·ko, -a] *adj* town-planning; **desarrollo ~** urban development; **plan ~** development plan

**urbanización** [ur·βa·ni·saˈsjon, -θaˈθjon] *f* urbanization; (*residencial*) housing estate

**urbanizar** <z → c> [ur·βa·niˈsar, -ˈθar] *vt* to urbanize

**urbano** [urˈβano] *m* traffic policeman

**urbano, -a** [urˈβa·no, -a] *adj* urban

**urbe** [ˈur·βe] *f* metropolis

**urgencia** [urˈxen·sja, -θja] *f* 1. (*cualidad*) urgency 2. (*caso*) emergency 3. *pl* emergency room

**urgente** [urˈxen·te] *adj* urgent; (*envío*) express; **un pedido ~** a rush order

**urgir** <g → j> [urˈxir] *vi* to be urgent

**urinario** [u·riˈna·rjo] *m* urinal

**urinario, -a** [u·riˈna·rjo, -a] *adj* urinary; **aparato ~** urinary tract

**urna** [ˈur·na] *f* glass case; (*para cenizas*) urn; POL ballot box

**urogallo** [u·roˈɣa·jo, -ʎo] *m* ZOOL capercaillie

**urología** [u·ro·lo·ˈxi·a] *f* urology

**urraca** [uˈrra·ka] *f* magpie; *inf* chatterbox

**URSS** [urs] *f abr de* **Unión de Repúblicas Socialistas Soviéticas** USSR

**urticaria** [ur·tiˈka·rja] *f* hives *pl*

**Uruguay** [u·ruˈɣwai] *m* Uruguay

**uruguayo, -a** [u·ruˈɣwa·jo, -a] *adj, m, f* Uruguayan

**usado, -a** [uˈsa·do, -a] *adj* secondhand; (*gastado*) worn; (*sello*) used

**usanza** [uˈsan·sa, -θa] *f* usage

**usar** [uˈsar] I. *vt* to use; (*ropa, gafas*) to wear; **de ~ y tirar** disposable; **sin ~** brand new II. *vr:* **~se** to use; **esta palabra ya no se usa** this word is no longer in use; **los escotes ya no se usan** low necklines are out of fashion

**usina** [uˈsi·na] *f AmL* (*de gas*) gasworks; (*de electricidad*) power plant

**uso** [ˈu·so] *m* use; (*costumbre*) *t.* LING usage; **de ~ externo** for external application; **hacer ~ de algo** to make use of sth; **una expresión de ~ corriente** an everyday expression

**usted** [usˈted] *pron* 1. *sing* you; **~es** you; **tratar de ~** to address courteously 2. *pl AmL* (*vosotros*) you

**usual** [uˈsu·al] *adj* usual; (*común*) common

**usuario, -a** [uˈsu·a·rjo, -a] *m, f* user

**usura** [uˈsu·ra] *f* usury

**usurero, -a** [u·suˈre·ro, -a] *m, f* usurer

**usurpar** [uˈsur·par] *vt* to usurp

**utensilio** [u·tenˈsi·ljo] *m* utensil; (*herramienta*) tool

**uterino, -a** [u·teˈri·no, -a] *adj* ANAT, MED uterine; **furor ~** nymphomania

**útero** [ˈu·te·ro] *m* uterus; **el cuello del ~** the cervix

**útil** [ˈu·til] I. *adj* useful; (*ayuda*) helpful; **¿en qué puedo serle ~?** can I be of any help to you? II. *mpl* tools *pl*

**utilidad** [u·ti·liˈdad] *f* utility; **ser de ~** to be useful

**utilizable** [u·ti·liˈsa·βle, -ˈθa·βle] *adj* usable

**utilización** [u·ti·li·saˈsjon, -θaˈθjon] *f* utilization

**utilizar** <z → c> [u·ti·liˈsar, -ˈθar] I. *vt* to use; (*tiempo, a alguien*) to make use of sth II. *vr:* **~se** to be used

**utopía** [u·toˈpi·a] *f* utopia

**utópico, -a** [uˈto·pi·ko, -a] *adj* utopian

**uva** [ˈu·βa] *f* grape; **~ pasa** raisin 2. *inf* **estar de mala ~** to be in a bad mood; **tener mala ~** to be bad-tempered

**UVI** [ˈu·βi] *f abr de* **Unidad de Vigilancia Intensiva** ICU

# V

**V, v** ['u·βe] *f* V, v; **~ de Valencia** V as in Victor

**vaca** ['ba·ka] *f* cow; (*carne*) beef; **síndrome de las ~s locas** mad cow disease; **~s gordas/flacas** prosperous/lean period; **ponerse como una ~** to get as fat as a cow

**vacaciones** [ba·ka·'sjo·nes, -'θjo·nes] *fpl* vacation; **de ~** on vacation

**vacante** [ba·'kan·te] **I.** *adj* vacant **II.** *f* vacancy; (*puesto*) unfilled post

**vaciado** [ba·si·'a·do, ba·θi·-] *m* **1.** (*molde*) cast **2.** (*ahuecamiento*) hollowing out **3.** COMPUT dumping

**vaciar** <*I. pres* vacío> [ba·si·'ar, ba·θi·-] *vt* to empty; (*verter*) to pour; (*escultura*) to cast

**vacilación** [ba·si·la·'sjon, -θi·la·'θjon] *f* hesitation; **sin vacilaciones** unhesitatingly

**vacilada** [ba·si·'la·da, ba·θi·-] *f inf* ¡**menuda ~!** cool!; *Méx* (*borrachera*) binge; (*chiste*) joke; (*chiste verde*) dirty joke; (*timo*) rip-off; **me dieron una ~** they really ripped me off

**vacilante** [ba·si·'lan·te, ba·θi·-] *adj* hesitant; (*voz*) faltering

**vacilar** [ba·si·'lar, ba·θi·-] *vi* **1.** (*dudar*) to hesitate **2.** *inf* **~ a alguien** to pull sb's leg; ¡**no me vaciles!** don't give me that!

**vacío** [ba·'si·o, -'θi·o] *m* emptiness; FÍS vacuum; (*abismo*) void; **~ legal** legal void; **~ de poder** political vacuum; **envasado al ~** vacuum-packed

**vacío, -a** [ba·'si·o, -a; -'θi·o, -a] *adj* empty; (*hueco*) hollow; (*insustancial*) insubstantial; **con las manos vacías** empty-handed; **de ~** empty-handed

**vacuna** [ba·'ku·na] *f* (*sustancia*) vaccine; (*vacunación*) vaccination; **poner una ~** to vaccinate

**vacunación** [ba·ku·na·'sjon, -'θjon] *f* vaccination; **cartilla de ~** vaccination certificate

**vacunar** [ba·ku·'nar] **I.** *vt* to vaccinate **II.** *vr*: **~se** to get vaccinated; **se ha vacunado contra la gripe** he/she got vaccinated against flu

**vacuno** [ba·'ku·no] *m* cattle

**vacuno, -a** [ba·'ku·no, -a] *adj* cow; **ganado ~** cattle

**vado** ['ba·do] *m* **~ permanente** keep clear

**vagabundear** [ba·ɣa·βun·de·'ar] *vi* to wander; *pey* to be a tramp

**vagabundo, -a** [ba·ɣa·'βun·do, -a] **I.** *adj* wandering; (*perro*) stray; *fig, pey* vagrant **II.** *m, f* wanderer; *fig* tramp

**vagancia** [ba·'ɣan·sja, -θja] *f* laziness

**vagar** [ba·'ɣar] <g → gu> *vi* to wander

**vagina** [ba·'xi·na] *f* vagina

**vago, -a** ['ba·ɣo] **I.** *adj* lazy; (*impreciso*) vague **II.** *m, f* lazybones; **hacer el ~** to laze about

**vagón** [ba·'ɣon] *m* car; (*de mercancías*) freight car; **~ restaurante** dining car

**vaguear** [ba·ɣe·'ar] *vi* to laze about

**vaguedad** [ba·ɣe·'dad] *f* vagueness

**vahído** [ba·'i·do] *m* dizzy spell

**vaho** ['ba·o] *m* vapor

**vaina** ['bai·na] *f* BOT pod

**vainica** [bai·'ni·ka] *f* CRi string bean

**vainilla** [bai·'ni·ja, -ʎa] *f* vanilla

**vaivén** [bai·'βen] *m* swaying; (*sacudida*) lurch

**vajilla** [ba·'xi·ja, -ʎa] *f* dishes, dishware

**vale** ['ba·le] *m* voucher

**valedero, -a** [ba·le·'de·ro, -a] *adj* valid; (*vigente*) in force

**valedura** [ba·le·'du·ra] *f* Méx (*favor*) favor; (*protección*) protection; (*ayuda*) help

**valenciana** [ba·len·'sja·na] *f* **1.** CSur (*encaje*) fine cotton lace **2.** Méx (*dobladillo*) pant cuff

**valentía** [ba·len·'ti·a] *f* bravery

**valer** [ba·'ler] *irr* **I.** *vt* to cost; (*equivaler*) to equal ▶ **más vale que te olvides de él** you'd best forget him; ¡**vale ya!** that's enough!; ¡**vale!** OK! **II.** *vi* **1.** to be of use; (*tener validez*) to be valid; **no vale** it's no good **2.** (*tener mérito*) to be worthy; **no ~ nada** to be worthless; **~ poco** to be worth little **3.** (*permitirse*) to be allowed **III.** *vr*: **~se 1.** (*servirse*) to make use **2.** (*desenvolverse*) to manage; **ya no puede ~se solo** he can't fend for himself any longer

**valeriana** [ba·le·'rja·na] *f* valerian

**valeroso, -a** [ba·le·'ro·so, -a] *adj* brave

**valía** [ba·'li·a] *f* worth

**validar** [ba·li·'dar] *vt* to validate

**validez** [ba·li·'des, -'deθ] *f* validity; **dar ~ a** to validate; **tener ~** to be valid; (*ley*) to be in force

**válido, -a** [ba·'li·do, -a] *adj* valid

**valiente** [ba·'ljen·te] *adj* brave

**valija** [ba·'li·xa] *f* case; (*del cartero*) mailbag; **~ diplomática** diplomatic bag

**valioso, -a** [ba·'ljo·so, -a] *adj* valuable

**valla** ['ba·ja, -ʎa] *f* (*tapia*) wall; (*alambrada*) fence; DEP hurdle

**vallado** [ba·'ja·do, -ʎa·do] *m* fence

**vallar** [ba·'jar, -'ʎar] *vt* to fence in

**valle** ['ba·je, -ʎe] *m* valley

**vallunco, -a** [ba·'jun·ko, -a; ba·'ʎun-] *adj* AmC rustic

**valona** [ba·'lo·na] *f* Méx **hacer a alguien la ~** *inf* to put in a good word for sb

**valor** [ba·'lor] *m* **1.** bravery; **armarse de ~** to pluck up courage **2.** (*morro*) cheek **3.** (*valía*) value; (*cuantía*) amount **4.** (*significado*) meaning **5.** *pl* FIN securities *pl*; **~es inmuebles** real estate **6.** **~es morales** moral principles; **escala de ~es** scale of values

**valoración** [ba·lo·ra·'sjon, -'θjon] *f* valuation; (*análisis*) assessment

**valorar** [ba·lo·'rar] *vt* to value (**en** at); **valoro muchísimo tu ayuda** I greatly appreciate your help

**valorizar** <z → c> [ba·lo·ri·'sar, -'θar] *vt* v. **valorar**

**vals** [bals] *m* waltz

**válvula** ['bal·βu·la] *f* valve

**vampiro** [bam·'pi·ro] *m* vampire

**vanagloriarse** [ba·na·ɣlo·'rjar·se] *vr* to boast

**vanamente** [ba·na·'men·te] *adv* vainly

**vandalismo** [ban·da·'lis·mo] *m* vandalism

**vándalo, -a** ['ban·da·lo, -a] *adj, m, f* vandal

**vanguardia** [ban·'gwar·dja] *f* forefront; LIT avant-garde; **de ~** ultra-modern

**vanguardista** [ban·gwar·'dis·ta] **I.** *adj* ultra-modern **II.** *mf* pioneer

**vanidad** [ba·ni·'dad] *f* vanity

**vanidoso, -a** [ba·ni·'do·so, -a] *adj* vain

**vano** ['ba·no] *m* space

**vano, -a** ['ba·no, -a] *adj* vain; (*infundado*) groundless

**vánova** ['ba·no·βa] *f* Arg bedspread

**vapor** [ba·'por] *m* steam; **cocer al ~** to steam

**vaporizador** [ba·po·ri·sa·'dor, ba·po·ri·θa-] *m* vaporizer

**vaporizar** <z → c> [ba·po·ri·'sar, -'θar] **I.** *vt* to vaporize; (*spray*) to spray **II.** *vr:* **~se** to vaporize

**vaporizo** [ba·po·'ri·so] *m* Méx, PRico **1.** (*vaho*) vapor; (*para inhalar*) inhalation **2.** (*calor*) sultry heat

**vaporoso, -a** [ba·po·'ro·so, -a] *adj* steamy; (*tela*) light

**vapulear** [ba·pu·le·'ar] *vt* to beat

**vapuleo** [ba·pu·'leo] *m* beating

**vaquería** [ba·ke·'ri·a] *f* AmS cattle-rearing; (*lechería*) dairy

**vaquero, -a** [ba·'ke·ro, -a] **I.** *adj* cattle **II.** *m, f* cowboy, cowgirl *m, f*

**vaquero(s)** [ba·'ke·ro(s)] *m(pl)* jeans *pl*

**vaquetón, -ona** [ba·ke·'ton, -'to·na] *adj* Méx *inf* (*lento*) sluggish; (*vago*) shiftless; (*descarado*) shameless

**vaquilla** [ba·'ki·ja, -ʎa] *f*, **vaquillona** [ba·ki·'jo·na, -'ʎo·na] *f* Arg, Chile, Nic, Perú heifer

**vara** ['ba·ra] *f* stick

**varar** [ba·'rar] *vi* **1.** to run aground **2.** AmL to break down

**varear** [ba·re·'ar] *vt* (*fruta*) to knock down; (*lana*) to sell by the yard

**varejón** [ba·re·'xon] *m* AmS, Nic switch

**variable** [ba·'rja·βle] **I.** *adj* variable; (*carácter*) changeable **II.** *f* variable

**variación** [ba·rja·'sjon, -'θjon] *f* oscillation; MAT, MÚS variation

**variado, -a** [ba·'rja·do, -a] *adj* varied; (*mezclado*) assorted

**variante** [ba·'rjan·te] *f* version; (*variedad*) variety; LING variant

**variar** <1. pres varío> [ba·ri·'ar] *vi, vt* to vary; **y para ~...** and for a change...

**varicela** [ba·ri·'se·la, -'θe·la] *f* chickenpox

**variedad** [ba·rje·'dad] *f* variety; **una gran ~ de** a wide range of ▶ **en la ~ está el gusto** variety is the spice of life

**variopinto, -a** [ba·rjo·'pin·to, -a] *adj* diverse; (*color*) colorful

**varios, -as** [ba·rjos, -as] *adj pl* some; (*diferentes*) several

**variz** [ba·ris, -riθ] *f* varicose vein

**varón** [ba·ron] *m* male

**varonil** [ba·ro·nil] *adj* virile; (*mujer*) mannish

**vasallo, -a** [ba·sa·jo, -a; -ʎo, -a] *m, f* vassal

**vasija** [ba·si·xa] *f* container

**vaso** [ba·so] *m* glass; **un ~ de agua** a glass of water; **~ de papel** paper cup; ANAT vessel

**vástago** [bas·ta·ɣo] *m* scion; **~s** offspring

**vasto, -a** [bas·to, -a] *adj* vast; (*saber*) wide

**váter** [ba·ter] *m* (*recipiente*) toilet; (*habitación*) washroom

**vaticinar** [ba·ti·si·nar, ba·ti·θi-] *vt* to prophesy

**vatio** [ba·tjo] *m* watt; **una bombilla de 100 ~s** a 100-watt bulb

**Vd.** [us·ted] *pron pers abr de* **usted** you

**vda.** [bju·da] *abr de* **viuda** widow

**Vds.** [us·te·des] *pron pers abr de* **ustedes** you

**vecindad** [be·sin·dad, be·θin-] *f* neighborhood

**vecindario** [be·sin·da·rjo, be·θin-] *m* neighborhood

**vecino, -a** [be·si·no, -a; be·θi-] I. *adj* **~ de algo** near sth; **~ a algo** similar to sth II. *m, f* neighbor; (*habitante*) resident

**vector** [bek·tor] *m* vector

**veda** [be·da] *f* prohibition; **levantar la ~ de animales de caza** to open the hunting season

**vedado** [be·da·do] *m* reserve

**vedar** [be·dar] *vt* to ban

**vedette** [be·det/be·de·te] *f* (music hall) star

**vega** [be·ɣa] *f* **1.** fertile plain **2.** *Cuba* tobacco plantation **3.** *Chile* marshland

**vegetación** [be·xe·ta·sjon, -·θjon] *f* vegetation

**vegetal** [be·xe·tal] I. *adj* plant; **aceite ~** vegetable oil; **carbón ~** charcoal II. *m* vegetable

**vegetar** [be·xe·tar] *vi* BOT to grow

**vegetariano, -a** [be·xe·ta·rja·no, -a] *adj, m, f* vegetarian

**vehemencia** [be·men·sja/be·e·men·sja, -·θja] *f* **1.** (*ímpetu*) impetuosity **2.** (*entusiasmo*) eagerness **3.** (*fervor*) vehemence

**vehemente** [be·men·te/be·e·men·te] *adj* impetuous; (*ardiente*) passionate

**vehículo** [be·i·ku·lo] *m* vehicle

**veinte** [bein·te] *adj inv* twenty; *v. t.* **ochenta**

**veintena** [bein·te·na] *f* **una ~ de personas** about twenty people

**vejación** [be·xa·sjon, -·θjon] *f*, **vejamen** [be·xa·men] *m* **1.** (*molestia*) annoyance **2.** (*humillación*) humiliation

**vejar** [be·xar] *vt* to humiliate

**vejatorio, -a** [be·xa·to·rjo, -a] *adj* humiliating

**vejestorio, -a** [be·xes·to·rjo, -a] *m, f pey* old crock

**vejez** [be·xes, -·xeθ] *f* old age; (*envejecimiento*) aging

**vejiga** [be·xi·ɣa] *f* blister; ANAT bladder

**vela** [be·la] *f* **1.** NÁUT sail **2.** (*luz*) candle ► **pasar la noche en ~** to have a sleepless night; **estar a dos ~s** to be broke

**velada** [be·la·da] *f* evening (gathering)

**veladora** [be·la·do·ra] *f AmL* candlestick

**velar** [be·lar] I. *vi* to stay awake; **~ por algo** to watch over sth II. *vt* to keep watch over; **~ a un muerto** to hold a wake III. *vr:* **~se** to blur

**velatorio** [be·la·to·rjo] *m* wake

**velero** [be·le·ro] *m* sailing ship

**veleta** [be·le·ta] *f* weather vane

**veliz** [be·lis] *m Méx* (*de cuero*) valise; (*de metal*) case

**vello** [be·jo, -ʎo] *m* (body) hair

**velludo, -a** [be·ju·do, -a; -ʎu·do, -a] *adj* hairy

**velo** [be·lo] *m* veil; **correr un (tupido) ~ sobre** to draw a veil over

**velocidad** [be·lo·θi·dad] *f* **1.** speed; **~ de transmisión de datos** data transfer rate; **exceso de ~** speeding; **a gran/toda ~** at high/full speed **2.** AUTO gear

**velocímetro** [be·lo·si·me·tro, be·lo·θi-] *m* speedometer

**velódromo** [be·lo·dro·mo] *m* cycle track

V

**veloz** [be·los, -'loθ] *adj* swift; **raudo y ~** in a flash

**vena** ['be·na] *f* 1. vein 2. (*inspiración*) talent 3. *inf* mood; **dar la ~ a uno** to take it into one's head

**venado** [be·na·do] *m* deer; (*carne*) venison

**vencedor(a)** [ben·se·dor, -·do·ra, ben·θe-] I. *adj* winning II. *m(f)* winner

**vencejo** [ben·se·xo, -·θe·xo] *m* swift

**vencer** <c → z> [ben·ser, -'θer] I. *vi* to win; (*plazo*) to expire II. *vt* to win; (*enemigos*) to defeat; (*obstáculo, sueño*) to overcome ▶ **a la tercera va la vencida** third time lucky

**vencimiento** [ben·si·mjen·to, -θi·mjen·to] *m* expiry

**venda** ['ben·da] *f* bandage

**vendaje** [ben·da·xe] *m* bandaging

**vendar** [ben·dar] *vt* to bandage

**vendaval** [ben·da·βal] *m* strong wind; (*huracán*) hurricane

**vendedor(a)** [ben·de·dor, -·do·ra] *m(f)* seller; **~ ambulante** hawker; **~ a domicilio** door-to-door salesman

**vender** [ben·der] I. *vt, vi* to sell II. *vr:* **~se** 1. to sell; **se vende** for sale 2. (*persona*) to give oneself away

**vendimia** [ben·di·mja] *f* grape harvest

**vendimiar** [ben·di·mjar] *vi* to harvest grapes

**veneno** [be·ne·no] *m* poison

**venenoso, -a** [be·ne·no·so, -a] *adj* poisonous

**venerable** [be·ne·ra·βle] *adj* venerable

**veneración** [be·ne·ra·sjon, -·θjon] *f* worship; (*respeto*) veneration

**venerar** [be·ne·rar] *vt* to worship; (*respetar*) to venerate

**venéreo, -a** [be·ne·reo, -a] *adj* venereal

**venezolano, -a** [be·ne·so·la·no, -a; be·ne·θo-] *adj, m, f* Venezuelan

**Venezuela** [be·ne·swe·la, -'θwe·la] *f* Venezuela

**vengador(a)** [ben·ga·dor, -·do·ra] I. *adj* vindictive II. *m(f)* avenger

**venganza** [ben·gan·sa, -θa] *f* vengeance

**vengar** <g → gu> [ben·gar] I. *vt* to avenge; **~ la muerte de alguien** to avenge sb's death II. *vr:* **~se** to take revenge

**vengativo, -a** [ben·ga·ti·βo, -a] *adj* vindictive

**venida** [be·ni·da] *f* arrival; (*vuelta*) return

**venidero, -a** [be·ni·de·ro, -a] *adj* future; **en años venideros** in years to come

**venir** [be·nir] *irr* III. *vi* 1. to come; (*llegar*) to arrive; **vengo (a) por la leche** I've come to fetch the milk; **me vinieron ganas de reír** I felt like laughing; **el mes que viene** next month; **ya viene la primavera** spring is on its way; **vienen a ser unos 300 pesos** it works out at about 300 pesos 2. (*figurar*) to appear; **no viene en la guía** it's not in the guide 3. (*prenda*) to suit 4. (*persistir*) to keep on; **ya te lo vengo advirtiendo hace mucho tiempo** I've been warning you for a long time 5. **me viene muy bien** it comes in very handy; **¿te viene bien mañana?** would tomorrow suit you?; **me viene mal** it doesn't suit me ▶ **a mí eso ni me va ni me viene** to me that's neither here nor there; **¿a qué viene...?** why...? II. *vr:* **~se** to come back; **~se abajo** to collapse; *fig* to fail

**venta** ['ben·ta] *f* sale; **~ al contado** cash sale; **~ a plazos** purchase on an installment plan; **~ al por menor/mayor** retail/wholesale; **en [o a la] ~** for sale

**ventaja** [ben·ta·xa] *f* advantage; **sacar ~ de** to take advantage of; **tener ~ sobre** to have an advantage over

**ventajoso, -a** [ben·ta·xo·so, -a] *adj* advantageous; (*negocio*) profitable

**ventana** [ben·ta·na] *f* window ▶ **tirar la casa por la ~** to go to great expense

**ventanal** [ben·ta·nal] *m* large window

**ventanilla** [ben·ta·ni·ja, -·ʎa] *f* 1. small window; (*de coche*) side window 2. (*taquilla*) ticket office; (*mostrador*) counter

**ventilación** [ben·ti·la·sjon, -·θjon] *f* ventilation

**ventilador** [ben·ti·la·dor] *m* fan

**ventilar** [ben·ti·lar] I. *vt* 1. (*airear*) to ventilate 2. (*resolver*) to clear up II. *vr:* **~se** to air; (*persona*) to get some air

**ventisca** [ben·tis·ka] *f* blizzard

**ventolera** [ben·to·le·ra] *f* gust of wind;

**le ha dado la ~ de...** he/she has taken it into his/her head to...

**ventosa** [ben·'to·sa] *f* sucker

**ventosear** [ben·to·se·'ar] *vi* to break wind

**ventosidad** [ben·to·si·'dad] *f* fart

**ventura** [ben·'tu·ra] *f* fortune; **por ~** fortunately

**veo-veo** ['beo·'βeo] *m* **jugar al ~** to play I-spy

**ver** [ber] *irr* **I.** *vi*, *vt* to see; (*observar*) to watch; (*encontrarse*) to meet; **lo nunca visto** something unheard of; **no veas lo contenta que se puso** you should have seen how happy she was; **a ~** let's see; **bueno, ya ~emos** well, we'll see; **te veo venir** *fig* I know what you're up to; **tener que ~ con** to have to do with; **eso está por ~** [*o* **habrá que ~lo**] that remains to be seen ▶ **tengo un hambre/un sueño que no veo** I'm really tired/hungry; **si te he visto, no me acuerdo** out of sight, out of mind; **¡hay que ~!** it just goes to show!; **hay que ~ lo tranquilo que es** he is such a quiet fellow; **¡vamos a ~!** let's see!; **¡a ~, escuchadme todos!** come on, listen to me everybody!; **¡para que veas!** so there!; **luego ya ~emos** we'll see about that later **II.** *vr*: **~se 1.** (*encontrarse*) to meet **2.** (*estado*) to be; **~se apurado** to be in a jam **3.** (*imaginarse*) to imagine **4.** (*parecer*) **se ve que...** it seems... **5.** *AmL* (*aspecto*) to look **6. véase...** see...; **no se ve ni torta** you can't see a thing **III.** *m* opinion; (*aspecto*) appearance

**vera** ['be·ra] *f* **1.** (*orilla*) bank; **~ de un río** river bank **2.** (*lado*) edge; **a la ~ de** beside

**veracidad** [be·ra·si·'dad, be·ra·θi·] *f* truthfulness; (*declaración*) veracity

**veraneante** [be·ra·ne·'an·te] *mf* vacationer

**veranear** [be·ra·ne·'ar] *vi* to spend the summer

**veraneo** [be·ra·'neo] *m* summer vacation; **lugar de ~** vacation spot

**veraniego, -a** [be·ra·'nje·γo, -a] *adj* summer

**veranillo** [be·ra·'ni·jo, -ʎo] *m* **~ de San Miguel** [*o* **de San Juan** *AmL*] Indian summer

**verano** [be·'ra·no] *m* summer

**veras** ['be·ras] *fpl* **de ~** really

**veraz** [be·'ras, -'raθ] *adj* true; (*persona*) truthful

**verbalizar** <z → c> [ber·βa·li·'sar, -'θar] *vt* to verbalize

**verbena** [ber·'βe·na] *f* street party; BOT verbena

**verbo** ['ber·βo] *m* verb

**verdad** [ber·'dad] *f* truth; **ser ~** to be true; **una ~ a medias** a half truth; **a decir ~** to tell you the truth; **de ~** really; **un héroe de ~** a real hero; **¿~?** isn't it? ▶ **~es con puños** self-evident truths; **decir cuatro ~es a alguien** to give sb a piece of one's mind

**verdaderamente** [ber·da·de·ra·'men·te] *adv* truly

**verdadero, -a** [ber·da·'de·ro, -a] *adj* true; (*real*) real

**verde** ['ber·de] **I.** *adj* green; (*chiste*) dirty; **viejo ~** dirty old man ▶ **~ de envidia** green with envy; **poner ~ a alguien** to badmouth sb **II.** *m* **1.** green; (*del árbol*) foliage **2.** *CSur* (*pasto*) pasture; (*mate*) maté; (*ensalada*) salad **3.** *AmC, Méx* (*campo*) countryside

**verdear** [ber·de·'ar] *vi* *CSur* to drink maté

**verdor** [ber·'dor] *m* greenness

**verdoso, -a** [ber·'do·so, -a] *adj* greenish

**verdugo** [ber·'du·γo] *m* executioner

**verdulero, -a** [ber·du·'le·ro, -a] *m, f* greengrocer

**verdura** [ber·'du·ra] *f* vegetable

**vereda** [be·'re·da] *f* **1.** path **2.** *AmL* sidewalk ▶ **entrar en ~** to start to lead an orderly life

**veredicto** [be·re·'dik·to] *m* verdict

**verga** ['ber·γa] *f* rod; *vulg* cock

**vergajo** [ber·'γa·xo] *m* *vulg* **1.** *AmL* cock **2.** *And* son of a bitch

**vergonzoso, -a** [ber·γon·'so·so, -a; 'θo·so, -a] *adj* shy; (*acción*) disgraceful

**vergüenza** [ber·'γwen·sa, -θa] *f* **1.** (*rubor*) shame; **se me cae la cara de ~** I feel so ashamed; **me da ~...** I'm ashamed to...; **pasar ~** to feel embarrassed; **tener poca ~** to have no shame; **pasar ~ ajena** to be embarrassed for sb

**V**

else **2.** (*pudor*) shyness **3.** (*escándalo*) disgrace **4.** *pl* private parts *pl*

**verídico, -a** [be·'ri·di·ko, -a] *adj* true

**verificación** [be·ri·fi·ka·'sjon, -'θjon] *f* inspection; (*prueba*) testing

**verificar** <c → qu> [be·ri·fi·'kar] *vt* to check; (*controlar*) to verify

**verja** ['ber·xa] *f* grating; (*cerca*) grille; (*puerta*) iron gate

**vermú** [ber·'mu] *m*, **vermut** [ber·'mu] *m* <vermús> **1.** vermouth **2.** *And, CSur* early performance

**vernáculo, -a** [ber·'na·ku·lo, -a] *adj* vernacular

**verosímil** [be·ro·'si·mil] *adj* (*probable*) likely; (*creíble*) credible

**verosimilitud** [be·ro·si·mi·li·'tud] *f* likelihood

**verraco** [be·'rra·ko] *m AmC, CSur* wild boar

**verraquera** [be·rra·'ke·ra] *f AmC, Col inf* drunken bout

**verruga** [be·'rru·ɣa] *f* wart

**versado, -a** [ber·'sa·do, -a] *adj* ~ **en algo** expert in sth

**versar** [ber·'sar] *vi* **1.** to deal (**sobre** with) **2.** *AmC* (*escribir*) to versify; (*charlar*) to chat **3.** *Méx* (*bromear*) to crack jokes

**versátil** [ber·'sa·til] *adj* flexible; (*persona*) versatile

**versículo** [ber·'si·ku·lo] *m* verse

**versión** [ber·'sjon] *f* version; (*descripción*) account; ~ **resumida** abridged version; ~ **original** in the original language

**verso** ['ber·so] *m* line; **en ~** in verse; (*género*) verse

**vértebra** ['ber·te·βra] *f* vertebra

**vertebrado** [ber·te·'βra·do] *m* vertebrate

**vertebral** [ber·te·'βral] *adj* vertebral; **columna ~** spinal column

**vertedero** [ber·te·'de·ro] *m* garbage dump

**verter** <e → ie> [ber·'ter] **I.** *vt* to empty; (*líquido*) to pour; (*sin querer*) to spill; (*basura*) to dump; (*ideas, conceptos*) to transfer **II.** *vi* to flow

**vertical** [ber·ti·'kal] *adj, f* vertical

**vértice** ['ber·ti·se, -θe] *m* vertex

**vertiente** [ber·'tjen·te] *f* **1.** slope **2.** (*punto de vista*) perspective **3.** *And, CSur,*

*Méx* fountain

**vertiginoso, -a** [ber·ti·xi·'no·so, -a] *adj* giddy; (*velocidad*) excessive

**vértigo** ['ber·ti·ɣo] *m* vertigo; **causar ~(s)** to cause dizziness

**vesícula** [be·'si·ku·la] *f* vesicle; ~ **biliar** gall bladder

**vespa®** ['bes·pa] *f* motor scooter

**vespasiana** [bes·pa·'sja·na] *f Arg, Chile* public urinal

**vespertino, -a** [bes·per·'ti·no] *adj* crepuscular

**vestíbulo** [bes·'ti·βu·lo] *m* hall; (*hotel*) lobby

**vestido** [bes·'ti·do] *m* dress; (*ropa*) clothing

**vestidor** [bes·ti·'dor] *m* dressing room

**vestiduras** [bes·ti·'du·ras] *f* <u>rasgarse</u> <u>las</u> ~ to make a great show of being shocked

**vestigio** [bes·'ti·xjo] *m* vestige; (*señal*) trace

**vestimenta** [bes·ti·'men·ta] *f* clothing

**vestir** [bes·'tir] *irr como pedir* **I.** *vt* to wear; (*cuerpo, persona*) to dress; **vestido de pirata** dressed as a pirate ► **vísteme despacio que tengo prisa** *prov* make haste slowly **II.** *vi* to dress; ~ **de blanco** to dress in white; ~ **de uniforme** to wear a uniform; ~ **siempre muy bien** to always be very well-dressed **III.** *vr:* ~**se** to get dressed; ~**se a la moda** to dress according to fashion; ~**se de azul** to dress in blue

**vestuario** [bes·'twa·rjo] *m* wardrobe; TEAT dressing room; DEP changing room

**veta** ['be·ta] *f* vein; (*madera*) grain

**vetar** [be·'tar] *vt* to veto

**vetarro, -a** [be·'ta·rro, -a] *adj Méx inf* old; **ya están muy ~s** they're getting up there

**veterano** [be·te·'ra·no] *m* veteran

**veterano, -a** [be·te·'ra·no, -a] **I.** *adj* experienced; MIL veteran **II.** *m, f* old hand; MIL veteran

**veterinaria** [be·te·ri·'na·rja] *f* veterinary science

**veterinario, -a** [be·te·ri·'na·rjo, -a] *m, f* veterinarian, vet *inf*

**veto** ['be·to] *m* veto

**vez** [bes, beθ] *f* **1.** time; **una ~** once;

**dos veces** twice; **a la ~** at the same time; **a veces** sometimes; **alguna (que otra) ~** occasionally; **de una ~** in one go; *(por fin)* once and for all; **de ~ en cuando** from time to time; **otra ~** again; **por primera ~** for the first time; **aquella ~** on that occasion; **muchas veces** many times; **¿cuántas veces ...?** how many times ...?; **rara ~** seldom; **tal ~** perhaps; **una y otra ~** time and time again; **de una ~ por todas** once and for all **2.** *(turno)* turn; **en ~ de** instead of ▶ **una ~ al año no hace daño** *prov* once won't do any harm

**vía** ['bi·a] *f* road; *(calle)* street; FERRO track; **Vía Láctea** Milky Way; **~ pública** public thoroughfare; **en ~s de** in the process of; **a Dublín ~ Londres** to Dublin via London; **por ~ férrea/aérea/oral** by rail/air/mouth; **por ~ judicial** by legal means

**viable** [bi·'a·βle] *adj* viable

**viada** [bi·'a·ða] *f And* speed

**viaducto** [bja·'ðuk·to] *m* viaduct

**viajante** [bja·'xan·te] *mf* traveling salesman

**viajar** [bja·'xar] *vi* to travel (**en** by, **por** around)

**viaje** [bi·'a·xe] *m* **1.** travel; **estar de ~** to be away; **irse de ~** to go on a trip; **~ de negocios** business trip; **~ organizado** package tour; **~ de ida/ida y vuelta** outgoing/round trip; **¡buen ~!** have a good trip! **2.** *(carga)* load; *(recorrido)* trip; **de un ~** *AmC* in one go **3.** *inf (drogas)* trip

**viajero, -a** [bja·'xe·ro, -a] **I.** *adj* traveling **II.** *m, f* traveler; *(pasajero)* passenger

**vial** [bi·'al] *adj* road; FERRO rail

**viaraza** [bja·'ra·sa] *f AmL* fit of rage; **me dio la ~** I just felt like it

**víbora** ['bi·βo·ra] *f* viper

**viborear** [bi·βo·re·'ar] *vi* **1.** *AmL inf (murmurar)* to backbite **2.** *CSur (serpentear)* to snake

**vibración** [bi·βra·'sjon, -'θjon] *f* vibration

**vibrador** [bi·βra·'ðor] *m* vibrator

**vibrante** [bi·'βran·te] *adj* vibrant

**vibrar** [bi·'βrar] *vi* to vibrate

**vicario** [bi·'ka·rjo] *m* vicar

**vicedirector(a)** [bi·se·ði·rek·'tor, -·'to·ra;

bi·θe-] *m(f)* COM deputy manager

**vicepresidente, -a** [bi·se·pre·si·'ðen·te, -a; bi·θe-] *m, f* vice president

**vicerrector(a)** [bi·se·rrek·'tor, -·'to·ra, bi·θe-] *m(f)* UNIV vice president

**viceversa** [bi·se·'βer·sa, bi·θe-] *adv* vice versa

**vichar** [bi·'tʃar] *vt Arg, Urug (espiar)* to spy on; *(ver)* to peep at; *(buscar con la mirada)* to look around for

**viciado, -a** [bi·'sja·ðo, -a; bi·'θja-] *adj* stuffy

**viciarse** [bi·'sjar·se, -'θjar·se] *vr:* **~se 1.** *(costumbres)* to deteriorate; *(persona)* to get a bad habit **2.** **~se con algo** to become addicted to sth; **~se con la televisión** to get hooked on television

**vicio** ['bi·sjo, -θjo] *m* bad habit; *(adicción)* vice

**vicioso, -a** [bi·'sjo·so, -a; bi·'θjo·-] *adj* dissolute

**vicisitudes** [bi·si·si·'tu·ðes, bi·θi·-] *fpl* ups and downs *pl*

**víctima** ['bik·ti·ma] *f* victim

**victimar** [bik·ti·'mar] *vt AmL* to injure; *(matar)* to kill

**victimario, -a** [bik·ti·'ma·rjo, -a] *m, f AmL* murderer

**victoria** [bik·'to·rja] *f* victory

**victorioso, -a** [bik·to·'rjo·so, -a] *adj* victorious

**vid** [bid] *f* (grape)vine

**vida** ['bi·ða] *f* life; **~ íntima** private life; (grape)**¿cómo te va la ~?** how's life treating you?; **con ~** alive; **salir con ~** to survive; **buscarse la ~** to get by on one's own ▶ **estar entre la ~ y la muerte** to be fighting for one's life; **de por ~** for life

**vidente** [bi·'ðen·te] *mf* sighted person; *(adivino)* clairvoyant

**vídeo** ['bi·ðeo] *m* video recorder

**videocámara** [bi·ðeo·'ka·ma·ra] *f* video camera

**videocasete** [bi·ðeo·ka·'se·te] *m* videocassette

**videoclip** [bi·ðeo·'klip] *m* music video

**videoconferencia** [bi·ðeo·kon·fe·'ren·sja, -θja] *f* video conference

**videojuego** [bi·ðeo·'xwe·ɣo] *m* video game

V

**vidorria** [bi·'do·rrja] *f* **1.** *Chile, RíoPl* (*vida fácil*) easy life **2.** *Col, PRico, Ven* (*vida dura*) dog's life

**vidriera** [bi·'drje·ra] *f* **1.** stained-glass window **2.** *AmL* shop window

**vidrio** ['bi·drjo] *m* glass ▶ **pagar los ~s rotos** to take the rap

**vidurria** [bi·'du·rrja] *f* *Arg inf* life of leisure

**viejera** [bje·'xe·ra] *f* *PRico* **1.** (*vejez*) old age **2.** (*cosa inservible*) old piece of junk

**viejo, -a** ['bje·xo, -a] **I.** *adj* old; (*usado*) used; (*gastado*) worn-out; **hacerse ~** to get old; **Noche Vieja** New year's Eve **II.** *m, f* old man, old woman *m, f*; **mi ~/vieja** my old man/lady; **mis ~s** my folks

**viento** ['bjen·to] *m* **1.** wind; **hace ~** it's windy; **~s alisios** trade winds; **¡vete a tomar ~!** *inf* get lost! **2.** *AmC* MED flatulence ▶ **contra ~ y marea** come hell or high water; **ir ~ en popa** to go swimmingly

**vientre** ['bjen·tre] *m* abdomen; (*matriz*) womb; (*barriga*) belly; **danza del ~** belly-dancing

**viern.** *abr de* **viernes** Fri.

**viernes** ['bjer·nes] *m inv* Friday; *v. t.* **lunes**

**viga** ['bi·ɣa] *f* (*madera*) beam; (*metal*) girder

**vigencia** [bi·'xen·sja, -θja] *f* validity; **estar en ~** to be valid; **entrar en ~** to come into effect

**vigente** [bi·'xen·te] *adj* valid

**vigía¹** [bi·'xi·a] *f* watchtower

**vigía²** [bi·'xi·a] *mf* lookout

**vigilancia** [bi·xi·'lan·sja, -θja] *f* vigilance; **bajo ~** under surveillance

**vigilante** [bi·xi·'lan·te] **I.** *adj* alert **II.** *mf* **1.** guard; (*cárcel*) warden; **~ de seguridad** security guard; *CSur* policeman, policewoman *m, f*

**vigilar** [bi·xi·'lar] *vt* to guard; (*niños*) to watch

**vigilia** [bi·'xi·lja] *f* wakefulness

**vigor** [bi·'ɣor] *m* vigor; **con ~ entrar en ~** to come into effect

**vigorizar** <z → c> [bi·ɣo·ri·'sar, -'θar] *vt* **1.** (*fortalecer*) to strengthen **2.** (*re-*

*vitalizar*) to invigorate **3.** (*animar*) to encourage

**vigoroso, -a** [bi·ɣo·'ro·so, -a] *adj* vigorous

**VIH** [u·βe·i·'a·tʃe] *m abr de* **virus de inmunodeficiencia humana** HIV

**vil** [bil] *adj* vile; (*bajo*) base; (*infame*) despicable

**vileza** [bi·'le·sa, -θa] *f* vileness; (*acción*) vile act

**villa** ['bi·ja, -ʎa] *f* town; (*casa*) villa

**villancico** [bi·jan·'si·ko, bi·ʎan·'θi·ko] *m* (Christmas) carol

**villano, -a** [bi·'ja·no, -a; -'ʎa·no, -a] *adj* villainous

**vilo** ['bi·lo] *adv* (*tener*) **en ~** (to keep) in suspense; **estar en ~** to be up in the air

**vinagre** [bi·'na·ɣre] *m* vinegar; (*persona*) disagreeable person

**vinagrera** [bi·na·'ɣre·ra] *f* **1.** vinegar bottle **2.** *AmL* indigestion

**vinagreta** [bi·na·'ɣre·ta] *f* vinaigrette

**vincha** ['bin·tʃa] *f* *AmS* hair band

**vinchuca** [bin·'tʃu·ka] *f* *Arg, Chile, Par* ZOOL barbeiro, assassin bug

**vinculación** [bin·ku·la·'sjon, -'θjon] *f* link

**vincular** [bin·ku·'lar] *vt* to link; (*unir*) to join; **~ a** [*o* **con**] **algo** to link to sth

**vínculo** ['bin·ku·lo] *m* **1.** (*unión*) tie; **~s familiares** family ties; **los ~s con el extranjero** links with foreign countries **2.** COMPUT link **3.** (*obligación*) bond

**vinería** [bi·ne·'ri·a] *f* *And, CSur* wine store

**vinícola** [bi·'ni·ko·la] **I.** *adj* wine; (*cultivo*) wine-growing **II.** *mf* wine-grower

**vinicultor(a)** [bi·ni·kul·'tor, -·'to·ra] *m(f)* wine producer

**vinicultura** [bi·ni·kul·'tu·ra] *f* wine production

**vino** ['bi·no] *m* wine; **~ rosado/tinto/de mesa** rosé/red/table wine; **~ espumoso/peleón/de la casa** sparkling/cheap/house wine; **~ caliente** hot punch; **~ de Jerez** sherry

**viña** ['bi·ɲa] *f*, **viñedo** [bi·'ɲe·do] *m* vineyard; (*planta*) vine

**viñatero, -a** [bi·ɲa·'te·ro, -a] *m, f* *Arg, Perú* winegrower

**viola** ['bjo·la] *f* MÚS viola; BOT violet

**violación** [bjo·la·'sjon, -'θjon] f violation; (*ley*) breaking; (*contrato*) breach; (*sexual*) rape

**violar** [bjo·'lar] vt **1.** (*forzar*) to rape **2.** (*ley, principio, sepultura*) to violate; (*contrato*) to break

**violencia** [bjo·'len·sja, -θja] f violence; ~ **de género** gender violence; **no** ~ non-violence; **con** ~ by force

**violentar** [bjo·len·'tar] vt to force; (*sexualmente*) to assault

**violento, -a** [bjo·'len·to, -a] adj **1.** violent; (*impetuoso*) impetuous; (*temperamento*) fiery; (*acto*) embarrassing; (*cohibido*) embarrassed; **me resulta** ~ **decirle que no** I find it very hard to say no to him/her **2.** AmL (*de repente*) suddenly

**violeta** [bjo·'le·ta] adj, f violet

**violín** [bjo·'lin] m violin

**violonc(h)elo** [bjo·lon·'se·lo, -'θe·lo/bjo·lon·'tʃe·lo] m cello

**VIP** [bip] m abr de **Very Important Person** VIP; **sala** ~ VIP lounge

**viraje** [bi·'ra·xe] m turn; (*curva*) bend; NÁUT tack

**virar** [bi·'rar] vi, vt to turn; NÁUT to tack

**virgen** [bir·xen] **I.** adj virgin; (*cinta*) blank **II.** f **la Virgen** the Virgin

**virginal** [bir·xi·'nal] adj virginal

**virginidad** [bir·xi·ni·'dad] f virginity

**Virgo** ['bir·ɣo] m Virgo

**viril** [bi·'ril] adj virile; (*enérgico*) vigorous

**viringo, -a** [bi·'rin·go, -a] adj Col (*sin ropa*) naked; (*sin piel*) skinned; (*sin pelo*) hairless

**virrey, -reina** [bi·'rrei] m, f viceroy, vicereine m, f

**virtual** [bir·tu·'al] adj virtual

**virtud** [bir·'tud] f virtue; **en** ~ **de** by virtue of

**virtuoso, -a** [bir·tu·'o·so, -a] adj virtuous; MUS virtuoso

**viruela** [bi·'rwe·la] f smallpox

**virus** ['bi·rus] m inv virus; **virus de inmunodeficiencia humana** human immunodeficiency virus

**viruta** [bi·'ru·ta] f shaving

**visa** ['bi·sa] m o f AmL, **visado** [bi·'sa·do] m visa; ~ **de entrada/salida** entry/exit visa

**vísceras** ['bi·se·ras, 'bis·θe-] fpl entrails pl

**viscosa** [bis·'ko·sa] f viscose

**viscoso, -a** [bis·'ko·so, -a] adj viscous; (*espeso*) thick

**visera** [bi·'se·ra] f peak

**visibilidad** [bi·si·βi·li·'dad] f visibility

**visible** [bi·'si·βle] adj visible

**visillo** [bi·'si·ʎo, -ʎo] m net curtain

**visión** [bi·'sjon] f (*vista*) sight, vision; (*punto de vista*) view

**visita** [bi·'si·ta] f visit; (*visitante*) visitor; ~ **guiada** guided tour; **hacer una** ~ to pay a visit

**visitante** [bi·si·'tan·te] mf visitor

**visitar** [bi·si·'tar] vt to visit

**vislumbrar** [bis·lum·'brar] vt to distinguish

**visón** [bi·'son] m mink

**visor** [bi·'sor] m viewfinder; ~ **de luz infrarroja** infrared sights

**víspera** ['bis·pe·ra] f (*noche*) eve; (*día*) day before

**vista** ['bis·ta] f **1.** (*visión*) sight, vision; **tener la** ~ **cansada** to have eye strain; **al/fuera del alcance de la** ~ within view/out of sight; **a la** ~ visible; **de** ~ by sight; **apartar la** ~ to take one's eyes off; **perder de** ~ to lose sight of; **a primera** ~ at first sight; **a simple** ~ just by looking; **con** ~**s a** with a view to; **en** ~ **de que** in view of; **alzar/bajar la** ~ to look up/down; **volver la** ~ (**atrás**) to look back **2.** (*panorama*) view ▶ ~ **de pájaro** bird's-eye view; **hacer la** <u>**gorda**</u> to turn a blind eye; <u>**tener**</u> ~ to be shrewd

**vistazo** [bis·'ta·so, -θo] m look; **de un** ~ at a glance; **echar** [*o* **dar**] **un** ~ **a algo** to have a (quick) look at sth

**visto, -a** ['bis·to, -a] **I.** pp de **ver II.** adj common; **está muy** ~ that's old hat; **está** ~ **que...** it's clear that... ▶ **nunca** ~ unknown; (*inaudito*) unheard of; ~ **y no** ~ in a flash; **por lo** ~ apparently **III.** conj ~ **que...** since...

**visto bueno** ['bis·to 'βwe·no] m approval; **dar el** ~ **a algo** to give sth the go-ahead

**vistoso, -a** [bis·'to·so, -a] adj colorful; (*llamativo*) striking

**visual** [bi·su·'al] adj visual; **campo** ~ field of vision

V

**visualización** [bi·swa·li·sa·'sjon, -θa·'θjon] *f* visualization; COMPUT visual display

**visualizar** <z → c> [bi·swa·li·'sar, -'θar] *vt* 1. to visualize; COMPUT to display 2. *AmL* (*divisar*) to make out

**vital** [bi·'tal] *adj* vital; **constantes ~es** vital signs

**vitalicio, -a** [bi·ta·'li·sjo, -a; -θjo, -a] *adj* life

**vitalidad** [bi·ta·li·'dad] *f* vitality

**vitalizar** <z → c> [bi·ta·li·'sar, -'θar] *vt* to revitalize; (*fortalecer*) to strengthen

**vitamina** [bi·ta·'mi·na] *f* vitamin; **pobre/ rico en ~s** low/rich in vitamins

**viticultor(a)** [bi·ti·kul·'tor, -·'to·ra] *m(f)* vine grower

**vítor** ['bi·tor] *m* cheer

**vitorear** [bi·to·re·'ar] *vt* to cheer

**vitrina** [bi·'tri·na] *f* glass cabinet; *AmL* shop window

**vituperar** [bi·tu·pe·'rar] *vt* **~ a alguien** to vituperate against sb

**viudedad** [bju·de·'dad] *f*, **viudez** [bju·'des, -'deθ] *f* widowhood

**viudo, -a** ['bju·do, -a] **I.** *adj* widowed; **quedarse ~** to be widowed **II.** *m, f* widower, widow *m, f*

**viva** ['bi·βa] *interj* hurray!

**vivacidad** [bi·βa·si·'dad, bi·βa·θi·] *f* liveliness

**vivar** [bi·'βar] *vt AmL* to cheer

**vivaracho, -a** [bi·βa·'ra·tʃo, -a] *adj*, **vivaz** [bi·'βas, -'βaθ] *adj* vivacious; (*enérgico*) lively

**vivencia** [bi·'βen·sja, -θja] *f* experience

**víveres** ['bi·βe·res] *mpl* provisions *pl*

**vivero** [bi·'βe·ro] *m* nursery; (*de peces*) hatchery

**viveza** [bi·'βe·sa, -θa] *f* liveliness

**vívido, -a** ['bi·βi·do, -a] *adj* vivid

**vivienda** [bi·'βjen·da] *f* 1. residence; **sin ~** homeless; **el problema de la ~** the housing problem 2. *AmL* way of life

**viviente** [bi·'βjen·te] *adj* living

**vivir** [bi·'βir] **I.** *vi* to live; (*estar vivo*) to be alive; (*perdurar*) to live on; **~ a lo grande** to live it up; **~ de rentas** to live off the rent **II.** *vt* to live **III.** *m* life

**vivo, -a** ['bi·βo, -a] *adj* 1. alive; **ser ~ living** being; **al rojo ~** red-hot; **en ~** live; **ser la viva imagen de alguien** to be

the spitting image of sb 2. (*vivaz*) lively 3. (*color*) bright 4. (*avispado*) sharp

**V.O.** [ber·'sjon o·ri·xi·'nal] *abr de* **versión original** original version

**vocablo** [bo·'ka·βlo] *m* word

**vocabulario** [bo·ka·βu·'la·rjo] *m* vocabulary

**vocación** [bo·ka·'sjon, -'θjon] *f* vocation

**vocal** [bo·'kal] **I.** *adj* vocal **II.** *f* vowel

**voceador(a)** [bo·se·a·'dor, -·'do·ra, bo·θe·] *m(f) AmL* news hawker

**vocear** [bo·se·'ar, bo·θe·] **I.** *vi* to shout **II.** *vt* to express; **~ algo** to boast of sth

**vocerío** [bo·se·'ri·o, bo·θe·] *m* clamor

**vocero, -a** [bo·'se·ro, -a] *m, f AmL* spokesperson

**vociferar** [bo·si·fe·'rar, bo·θi·] *vi, vt* to yell

**vodka** ['bod·ka] *m o f* vodka

**vol.** *abr de* **volumen** vol.

**volado, -a** [bo·'la·do] *adj* 1. *inf* (*loco*) crazy 2. *AmL* (*ausente*) absent-minded; (*enamorado*) lovesick 3. *CSur* **~ de genio** *inf* quick-tempered

**volador(a)** [bo·la·'dor, -·'do·ra] *adj* flying

**volandas** [bo·'lan·das] *fpl* **en ~** up in the air; (*deprisa*) in a rush; **llevar en ~** to carry shoulder-high

**volante** [bo·'lan·te] **I.** *adj* flying **II.** *m* 1. AUTO steering wheel; **ir al ~** to be at the wheel 2. (*adorno*) flounce 3. (*escrito*) leaflet 4. *AmL* winger

**volantón** [bo·lan·'ton, -·'to·na] *m AmL* 1. (*cometa*) kite 2. (*voltereta*) somersault; (*acrobacia*) acrobatics *pl*

**volar** <o → ue> [bo·'lar] **I.** *vi* 1. to fly; **echar a ~** to fly off; **el dinero ha volado** the money has vanished 2. (*apresurarse*) to dash 3. *inf* to be high **II.** *vt* to blow up; **hacer ~ una cometa** to fly a kite **III.** *vr:* **~se** to vanish; *AmL* to get mad

**volátil** [bo·'la·til] *adj* 1. (*volador*) flying 2. QUÍM volatile 3. (*inconstante*) unpredictable

**volatilizar** <z → c> [bo·la·ti·li·'sar, -'θar] *vt, vr:* **~se** to volatilize

**volcán** [bol·'kan] *m* 1. volcano; **~ activo/inactivo** active/dormant volcano 2. *AmL* loads *pl*

**volcánico, -a** [bol·'ka·ni·ko, -a] *adj* volcanic

**volcar** [bol·'kar] *irr* **I.** *vi* to overturn **II.** *vt* **1.** to turn over; (*tirar*) to knock over; (*líquido*) to spill **III.** *vr:* ~**se** to overturn; ~**se en** [o **con**] **alguien** to be extremely kind to sb; ~**se en algo** to throw oneself into sth

**voleibol** [bo·lei·'βol] *m* volleyball

**voleiplaya** [bo·lei·'pla·ja] *m* beach volleyball

**voleo** [bo·'leo] *m* **a ~** at random

**voltaje** [bol·'ta·xe] *m* voltage

**voltario, -a** [bol·'ta·rjo, -a] *adj Chile* **1.** (*gastador*) spendthrift; (*dadivoso*) generous **2.** (*obstinado*) self-willed

**volteado** [bol·te·'a·do] *m Méx inf* fag

**voltear** [bol·te·'ar] *AmL* **I.** *vi* **1.** (*torcer*) to turn **2.** (*girarse*) to turn around **3.** (*pasear*) to go for a walk **4.** ~ **a hacer algo** to do sth again **II.** *vt* **1.** (*volcar*) to knock over **2.** (*volver*) to turn; ~ **la espalda a alguien** to turn one's back on sb; ~ **las campanas** to ring the bells **3.** (*lanzar al aire*) to throw into the air **III.** *vr:* ~**se 1.** (*volcar*) to overturn **2.** (*darse la vuelta*) to turn around

**voltereta** [bol·te·'re·ta] *f* handspring; (*en el aire*) somersault

**voltio** ['bol·tjo] *m* volt

**volumen** [bo·'lu·men] *m* (*tamaño*) size; (*cantidad*) amount; (*pelo*) body; FÍS, MAT volume; **a todo ~** (at) full volume; **en dos volúmenes** in two volumes; ~ **de ventas** turnover

**voluminoso, -a** [bo·lu·mi·'no·so, -a] *adj* sizeable

**voluntad** [bo·lun·'tad] *f* will; (*fuerza de voluntad*) will-power; **contra su ~** against one's will; **por propia ~** of one's own free will

**voluntario, -a** [bo·lun·'ta·rjo, -a] **I.** *adj* voluntary **II.** *m, f* volunteer; **ofrecerse ~** to volunteer

**voluntarioso, -a** [bo·lun·ta·'rjo·so, -a] *adj* willing

**voluptuoso, -a** [bo·lup·tu·'o·so, -a] *adj* voluptuous

**volver** [bol·'βer] *irr* **I.** *vi* **1.** (*dar la vuelta*) to go back; ~ **atrás** to turn back **2.** (*regresar*) to return; ~ **a casa** to go home;

~ **en sí** to come to **3.** ~ **a hacer algo** to do sth again **II.** *vt* **1.** (*dar la vuelta*) to turn over; (*poner del revés*) to turn inside out; ~ **la vista a algo** to look back at sth **2.** (*transformar*) to make; ~ **loco a alguien** to drive sb crazy **III.** *vr:* ~**se 1.** to return; ~**se a** [o **hacia**] **algo** to turn (around) towards sth; ~**se contra alguien** to turn against sb **2.** (*convertirse*) to become; ~**se viejo** to grow old

**vomitar** [bo·mi·'tar] **I.** *vi* to vomit **II.** *vt* to bring up

**vomitivo, -a** [bo·mi·'ti·βo] *adj* emetic; *inf* revolting

**vómito** ['bo·mi·to] *m* vomit; (*acción*) vomiting

**voracidad** [bo·ra·si·'dad, bo·ra·θi-] *f* voraciousness; (*avaricia*) greed

**vorágine** [bo·'ra·xi·ne] *f* (*remolino*) whirlpool; (*confusión*) whirl

**voraz** [bo·'ras, -'raθ] *adj* voracious

**vos** [bos] *pron pers AmL* you

**vosear** [bo·se·'ar] *to address in the familiar manner using 'vos'*

**vosotros, -as** [bo·'so·tros, -as] *pron pers, pl* you; **para ~** for you

**votación** [bo·ta·'sjon, -'θjon] *f* vote; **someter a ~** to put to the vote

**votar** [bo·'tar] *vi, vt* to vote (**a, por** for)

**voto** ['bo·to] *m* **1.** vote; (*acción*) voting; ~ **a favor/en contra** vote in favor/against; ~ **en blanco** unmarked ballot; ~ **por correo** mail vote **2.** REL vow

**voy** [boi] *1. pres de* **ir**

**voz** [bos, boθ] *f* **1.** t. LING voice; **aclarar la ~** to clear one's throat; **levantar/bajar la ~** to raise/lower one's voice; **en ~ alta/baja** aloud/softly; **tener ~ en algo** to have a say in sth **2.** (*grito*) shout; **a ~ en grito** at the top of one's voice; **dar voces** to shout

**vozarrón** [bo·sa·'rron, bo·θa-] *m* booming voice

**vudú** [bu·'du] *m* voodoo

**vuelco** ['bwel·ko] *m* turning over; (*cambio*) drastic change

**vuelo** ['bwe·lo] *m* flight; ~ **regular** scheduled flight; **levantar** [o **alzar**] **el ~** to fly off

**vuelta** ['bwel·ta] *f* **1.** (*giro*) turn; **el camión dio una ~ de campana** the

V

truck flipped over; **a la ~ de la esquina** around the corner; **dar la ~** (*rodear*) to go around; (*volver*) to turn back; (*volcar*) to put face down; **dar media ~** to turn around; **dar una ~** to have a walk around; **la cabeza me da ~s** my head is spinning 2. (*regreso*) return; (*viaje*) trip; **a la ~** on the way back; **de ~ a casa** back home; **estar de ~** to be back 3. (*dinero, cambio*) change; **la vida da muchas ~s** life has many ups and downs ▶ **dar muchas ~s a algo** to think over sth again and again

**vuelto** ['bwel·to, -a] *m AmL* change; **dar el ~** to give change

**vuestro, -a** ['bwes·tro, -a] I. *adj* your; **~ coche** your car; **vuestras monedas** your coins II. *pron pos* 1. yours; **¿es ~?** is this yours?; **el ~** yours 2. (*tras subst*) (of) yours; **un amigo ~** a friend of yours

**vulcanizadora** [bul·ka·ni·sa·'do·ra] *f Méx* vulcanizer

**vulgar** [bul·'ɣar] *adj* common; (*ordinario*) vulgar

**vulgaridad** [bul·ɣa·ri·'dad] *f* ordinariness; *pey* vulgarity

**vulgarizar** <z → c> [bul·ɣa·ri·'sar, -'θar] *vt* to popularize

**vulnerable** [bul·ne·'ra·βle] *adj* vulnerable

**vulneración** [bul·ne·ra·'sjon, -'θjon] *f* violation

**vulnerar** [bul·ne·'rar] *vt* to hurt; (*derecho*) to violate

**vulva** ['bul·βa] *f* vulva

# W

**W, w** ['u·βe 'do·βle] *f* W, w; **~ de Washington** W as in Whiskey

**walkie-talkie** ['wal·ki 'tal·ki] *m* walkie-talkie

**wampa** ['wam·pa] *f Méx* swamp

**wáter** ['ba·ter] *m* (*recipiente*) toilet; (*habitación*) washroom

**waterpolo** [ba·ter·'po·lo] *m* water polo

**watt** [bat] *m* watt

**web** [ueb] *m o f* web

**wélter** ['bel·ter] *AmL* I. *adj* **peso ~** welterweight II. *m* welterweight

**whisky** ['wis·ki] *m* whisky

**windsurf** ['win(d)·surf] *m* windsurfing; **tabla de ~** windsurfer

**wing** [win] *m AmL* 1. (*extremo delantero*) winger 2. (*extrema delantera*) wing

**WWW** *abr de* **World Wide Web** WWW

# X

**X, x** ['e·kis] *f* 1. X, x; **~ de xilófono** X as in X-ray; **rayos ~** X-rays *pl* 2. MAT X 3. *fig* x; **le presté x pesos** I lent him/her x pesos

**xenofobia** [se·no·'fo·βja] *f* xenophobia

**xenófobo, -a** [se·'no·fo·βo, -a] *adj* xenophobic

**xilófono** [si·'lo·fo·no] *m* xylophone

**xilografía** [si·lo·ɣra·'fi·a] *f* xylography

**xirgo, -a** ['sir·ɣo, -a] *adj Méx* (*desaseado*) untidy; (*hirsuto*) hairy

**xocoyote** [so·ko·'jo·te] *m Méx* youngest child

# Y

**Y, y** [i 'ɣrje·ɣa] *f* Y, y; **~ de Yema** Y as in Yankee

**y** [i] *conj* and; **¿~ qué?** so what?; **¿~ tu trabajo?** how's work?; **¿~ tu marido?** and how is your husband?; **¿~ mi monedero?** where's my wallet?; **~ eso que...** despite that...; **¡~ tanto!** you bet!

**ya** [ja] I. *adv* (*pasado*) already; (*pronto*) soon; (*ahora*) now; **~ es hora de que cambies** it's time you changed; **~ no fumo** I don't smoke any more; **~, ~** OK; *irón* oh, sure!; **¡ah, ~!** I get it now!; **¡anda ~!** come off it! II. *conj* **~ que** since; (*aprovechando que*) now; **~ por..., ~ por...** either by... or... III. *interj* that's it!

**yacaré** [ja·ka·'re] *m Arg, Bol, Par, Urug* caiman

**yacer** [ja·'ser, -'θer] *irr vi elev* to lie

**yacimiento** [ja·si·'mjen·to, -θi·'mjen·to] *m* deposit

**yagua** ['ja·ɣwa] *f AmL* royal palm; *(fibras)* palm leaf

**yagual** [ja·'ɣwal] *m AmC* padded ring *(for carrying heavy loads on the head)*

**yaguré** [ja·ɣu·'re] *m AmL* skunk

**yanqui** [jan·ki] **I.** *adj* Yankee **II.** *mf* Yank

**yapa** ['ja·pa] *f AmL* bonus; *(objeto)* extra; **de ~** as an addition

**yapar** [ja·'par] *vt AmL* **~ algo** *(el precio)* to give sth as a bonus; *(un objeto)* to add sth as an extra

**yarda** ['jar·da] *f* yard

**yate** ['ja·te] *m* yacht

**yedra** ['je·dra] *f* ivy

**yegua** ['je·ɣwa] *f* ZOOL mare; *AmC* cigar stub

**yema** ['je·ma] *f* yolk; *(de un dedo)* fingertip; BOT young shoot

**yendo** [jen·do] *gerundio de* **ir**

**yerba** ['jer·βa] *f* grass; **~ mate** *AmS* maté herb

**yerbal** [jer·'βal] *m RíoPl*, **yerbatal** [jer·βa·'tal] *m Arg* maté plantation

**yerbatero, -a** [jer·βa·'te·ro, -a] **I.** *adj AmL* maté **II.** *m, f AmS* **1.** *(curandero)* folk healer **2.** *(vendedor)* herbalist; *(de mate)* grower of maté

**yerbear** [jer·βe·'ar] *vi AmL* to drink maté

**yerbera** [jer·'βe·ra] *f RíoPl* maté (tea) gourd

**yerbero, -a** [jer·'βe·ro, -a] *m, f Méx* herb doctor

**yergo** ['jer·ɣo] *1. pres de* **erguir**

**yermo** ['jer·mo] *m* waste land

**yermo, -a** ['jer·mo, -a] *adj* uninhabited; AGR uncultivated

**yerno** ['jer·no] *m* son-in-law

**yérsey** ['jer·sei] *m*, **yersi** [jer·'si] *m AmC, AmS* jersey

**yeso** ['je·so] *m* plaster; GEO gypsum

**yeta** ['je·ta] *f Arg, Urug* bad luck

**yé-yé** [je·'je] *adj inf* cool; **hoy vas muy ~** you look very hip today

**yin** ['jin] *yines m* jeans *pl*

**yira** ['ji·ra] *f Arg, Urug* pey *inf* slut

**yo** [jo] **I.** *pron pers* I; **~ que tú...** if I were you...; **¿quién fue? — ~ no** who was it? — not me; **soy ~,** Susan it's me, Susan; **~ mismo** myself **II.** *m* ego

**yocalla** [jo·'ka·ja, -ʎa] *m Bol (niño callejero)* street urchin; *(mestizo)* half-breed

**yodo** ['jo·do] *m* iodine

**yoga** ['jo·ɣa] *m* yoga

**yogur** ['jo·ɣur] *m* yogurt; **~ natural** plain yogurt

**yolo** ['jo·lo] *m Méx inf* darling; **¡~ mío!** my darling!

**yonqui** ['jon·ki] *mf* junkie

**yoyó** [jo·'jo] *m* yoyo

**yuca** ['ju·ka] *f* yucca

**yudo** ['ju·do] *m* judo

**yugo** ['ju·ɣo] *m* yoke

**yugular** [ju·ɣu·'lar] *f* jugular vein

**yunga** ['jun·ɡa] *mf Bol, Chile, Ecua, Perú* warm valleys native

**yungas** ['jun·ɡas] *fpl Bol, Chile, Ecua, Perú* warm valleys *pl*

**yunque** ['jun·ke] *m* anvil

**yuntas** ['jun·tas] *fpl PRico, Urug, Ven* cufflinks *pl*

**yuppy** ['ju·pi] *mf* yuppie

**yute** ['ju·te] *m* jute

**yuxtaponer** [jus·ta·po·'ner] *irr como* **poner** **I.** *vt (a otra cosa)* to join; *(dos cosas)* to juxtapose **II.** *vr:* **~se** to join together

**yuxtaposición** [jus·ta·po·si·'sjon, -'θjon] *f* juxtaposition

**yuxtapuesto, -a** [jus·ta·'pwes·to, -a] *adj* juxtaposed

**yuyero, -a** [ju·'je·ro, -a] *m, f Arg, CSur* herbalist

**yuyo** ['ju·jo] *m* **1.** *CSur (yerbajo)* weed **2.** *pl Col, Ecua (condimento)* seasoning **3.** *pl Perú (verdura)* herbs *pl* **4.** *AmC (ampolla)* blister

# Z

**Z, z** ['se·ta, 'θe-/'se·da, 'θe-] *f* Z, z; **~ de Zaragoza** Z as in Zulu

**zabuir** [sa·'bwir] *vi PRico* to plunge

**zacatal** [sa·ka·'tal] *m AmC, Méx* pasture

**zacate** [sa·'ka·te] *m AmL* hay

**zafacoca** [sa·fa·'ko·ka] *f* **1.** *AmC, AmS, Méx (pelea)* fight **2.** *Chile (alboroto)* commotion

W
X
Y
Z

**zafacón** [sa·fa·ˈkon] *m* PRico, RDom trash can

**zafado, -a** [sa·ˈfa·do, -a] *adj* Arg sassy

**zafadura** [sa·fa·ˈdu·ra] *f* AmL dislocation

**zafar** [sa·ˈfar, θa-] *vr* **1.** ~se de to get away; (*compromiso*) to get out of **2.** AmL (*dislocarse*) to dislocate

**zafarrancho** [sa·fa·ˈrran·tʃo, θa-] *m* inf (*limpieza*) clearing up; (*riña*) quarrel; (*destrozo*) mess

**zafiro** [sa·ˈfi·ro, θa-] *m* sapphire

**zafo** [ˈθa·fo] *adv* AmL except

**zaga** [ˈsa·ɣa, θa-] *f* **a la ~** behind

**zagal(a)** [sa·ˈɣal, -·ˈɣa·la; θa-] *m(f)* boy, girl *m, f*

**zaino, -a** [ˈsaj·no, -a; ˈθaj-] *adj* treacherous; **mirar a lo ~** to look shifty

**zalamero, -a** [sa·la·ˈme·ro, -a; θa-] **I.** *adj* flattering **II.** *m, f* flatterer

**zambo, -a** [ˈsam·bo, -a; ˈθam-] *adj* bowlegged

**zambullir** <3. pret zambulló> [sam·bu·ˈʎir, θam·bu·ˈʎir] **I.** *vt* to submerge **II.** *vr* ~se to dive; (*en un asunto*) to plunge (**en** into)

**zampar** [sam·ˈpar, θam-] **I.** *vt* to scarf down **II.** *vr* ~se to scoff

**zampón, -ona** [sam·ˈpon, -·ˈpo·na; θam-] *inf* **I.** *adj* greedy **II.** *m, f* glutton

**zanahoria** [sa·na·ˈo·rja, θa-] **I.** *f* carrot **II.** *m* RíoPl idiot

**zanca** [ˈsan·ka, ˈθan-] *f* shank; *inf* long leg

**zancada** [san·ˈka·da, θan-] *f* stride; **dar ~s** to stride

**zancadilla** [san·ka·ˈdi·ja, θan·ka·ˈdi·ʎa] *f* **poner la ~ a alguien** to trip sb up

**zanco** [ˈsan·ko, ˈθan-] *m* stilt

**zancudo** [san·ˈku·do] *m* AmL mosquito; (*ave*) wader

**zancudo, -a** [san·ˈku·do, -a; θan-] *adj* long-legged

**zanganear** [san·ga·ne·ˈar, θan-] *vi* inf to idle

**zángano** [ˈsan·ga·no, ˈθan-] *m* drone; (*vago*) idler

**zanja** [ˈsan·xa, ˈθan-] *f* ditch; AmL watercourse

**zanjar** [san·ˈxar, θan-] *vt* (*asunto*) to settle; (*disputa*) to end

**zapallo** [sa·ˈpa·jo] *m* **1.** AmL (*calabaza*) pumpkin **2.** Arg, Chile (*chiripa*) fluke

**zapata** [sa·ˈpa·ta, θa-] *f* shoe

**zapatear** [sa·pa·te·ˈar, θa-] *vi* to tap dance

**zapatería** [sa·pa·te·ˈri·a, θa-] *f* shoe store; (*taller*) shoemaker's

**zapatero** [sa·pa·ˈte·ro, θa-] *m* shoe rack

**zapatero, -a** [sa·pa·ˈte·ro, -a; θa-] *m, f* shoemaker

**zapatilla** [sa·pa·ˈti·ja, θa·pa·ˈti·ʎa] *f* slipper; (*de deporte*) sneaker

**zapato** [sa·ˈpa·to, θa-] *m* shoe; **un par de ~s** a pair of shoes ► **tú no me llegas a la suela del ~** you can't hold a candle to me

**zapear** [sa·pe·ˈar, θa-] *vt* to channel surf

**zapping** [ˈsa·pin, ˈθa-] *m* channel surfing

**zar, zarina** [sar, θar; sa·ˈri·na, θa-] *m, f* tsar, tsarina *m, f*

**zarandear** [sarande·ˈar, θa-] *vt* to shake hard; AmL to mock

**zarina** [sa·ˈri·na, θa-] *f* v. **zar**

**zarpa** [ˈsar·pa, ˈθar-] *f* paw; *inf* mitt; **echar la ~** to grab

**zarpar** [sar·ˈpar, θar-] *vi* to set sail

**zarrapastroso, -a** [sa·rra·pas·ˈtro·so, -a; θar-] *adj* inf dirty

**zarza** [ˈsar·sa, ˈθar·θa] *f* bramble

**zas** [sas, θas] *interj* whoosh!; (*golpe*) bang!

**zigzag** [siɣ·ˈsaɣ, θiɣ·ˈθaɣ] *m* <zigzags> zigzag

**zigzaguear** [siɣ·sa·ɣe·ˈar, θiɣ·θa-] *vi* to zigzag

**zinc** [sin, θin] *m* zinc

**zíper** [ˈsi·per] *m* Méx zipper

**zócalo** [ˈso·ka·lo, ˈθo-] *m* **1.** skirting board; ARQUIT pedestal **2.** Méx (town) square

**zodíaco** [so·ˈdia·ko, θo-] *m* zodiac

**zombi** [ˈsom·bi, ˈθom-] *m* zombie; **estar ~** to be like a zombie

**zona** [ˈso·na, ˈθo-] *f* zone; (*terreno*) belt; (*área*) region; **~ de influencia** area of influence; **~ verde** green belt

**zoncera** [son·ˈse·ra] *f* AmL, **zoncería** [son·se·ˈri·a] *f* foolishness

**zonzo, -a** [ˈson·so, -a; ˈθon·θo, -a] *adj* dull; AmL stupid

**zoo** [ˈso·o, ˈθo·o] *m* zoo

**zoología** [so·lo·ˈxi·a/so·o·lo·ˈxi·a; θo-] *f* zoology

**zoológico, -a** [so·lo·xi·ko/so·o·'lo·xi·ko, -a; θo-] *adj* zoological; **parque ~** zoo

**zoólogo, -a** [so·'o·lo·γo, -a; θo-] *m, f* zoologist

**zopenco, -a** [so·'pen·ko, -a; θo-] **I.** *adj* oafish **II.** *m, f* dolt

**zopilote** [so·pi·'lo·te] *m Méx* turkey vulture

**zoquete** [so·'ke·te, θo-] *m* blockhead; *Arg* sock

**zorra** ['so·rra, 'θo-] *f* vixen; *inf* whore; (*insulto*) bitch

**zorrillo** [so·'rri·jo] *m AmL* skunk

**zorro** ['so·rro, 'θo-] *m* fox; *inf* (*astuto*) crafty fellow

**zote** ['so·te, 'θo·te] **I.** *adj* foolish **II.** *mf* fool

**zozobra** [so·'so·βra, θo·'θo-] *f* anxiety

**zozobrar** [so·so·'brar, θo·θo-] **I.** *vi* to capsize; (*persona*) to hesitate **II.** *vt* to sink

**zueco** ['swe·ko, 'θwe-] *m* clog

**zumba** ['sum·ba, 'θum-] *f AmL* beating

**zumbado, -a** [sum·'ba·do, -a; θum-] *adj* **estar ~** to be nuts

**zumbar** [sum·'bar, θu-] **I.** *vi* to buzz; **salir zumbando** to zoom off; (*oídos*) to hum **II.** *vt AmL* to throw; (*expulsar*) to chuck out

**zumbido** [sum·'bi··do, θum-] *m* hum; **~ de los oídos** ringing in the ears

**zumo** ['su··mo, 'θu-] *m* juice

**zupay** [su·'pai] *m AmL* devil

**zurcir** <c → z> [sur·'sir, θur·'θir] *vt* to mend; *inf* **¡que te zurzan!** get lost!

**zurdo, -a** ['sur·do, -a; 'θur-] **I.** *adj* left-handed **II.** *m, f* left-handed person

**zurra** ['su·rra, 'θur-] *f* hiding

**zurrar** [su·'rrar, θu-] *vt* to beat

**zurullo** [su·'ru·jo, θu·'ru·ʎo] *m inf* **1.** (*grumo*) lump **2.** (*excremento*) turd *vulg*

Z

# A

**A, a** [eɪ] *n* **1.** (*letter*) A, a *f*; **~ as in Alpha** A de Antonio **2.** SCHOOL ≈ sobresaliente *m*

**a** [ə, *stressed:* eɪ] *indef art before consonant*, **an** [ən, *stressed:* æn] *before vowel* **1.** (*in general*) un, una; **~ car** un coche; **~ house** una casa **2.** (*not translated*) **do you have ~ car?** ¿tienes coche?; **she is ~ teacher** es maestra **3.** (*to express prices, rates*) **$2 ~ dozen** 2 dólares la docena; **$6 ~ week** 6 dólares por semana **4.** (*before person's name*) **~ Mr. Robinson** un tal Sr. Robinson

**aback** [ə·ˈbæk] *adv* **to take sb ~** coger a alguien de improviso; **to be taken ~** quedarse desconcertado (**by** por)

**abandon** [ə·ˈbæn·dən] *vt* (*vehicle, place, person*) abandonar; (*give up: plan*) renunciar a; (*game*) suspender; **to ~ oneself to sth** entregarse a algo

**abandoned** [ə·ˈbæn·dənd] *adj* abandonado, -a; (*person*) desamparado, -a

**abbreviate** [ə·ˈbriː·vi·eɪt] *vt* abreviar

**abbreviation** [ə·ˌbriː·vɪ·ˈeɪ·ʃən] *n* abreviatura *f*

**abdomen** [ˈæb·də·mən] *n* ANAT abdomen *m*

**abdominal** [æb·ˈdɑm·ə·nəl] *adj* abdominal

**abduct** [æb·ˈdʌkt] *vt* secuestrar, plagiar *AmL*

**abduction** [æb·ˈdʌk·ʃən] *n* secuestro *m*, plagio *m AmL*

**abide** [ə·ˈbaɪd] <-d *or* abode, -d *or* abode> *vt* soportar; **I can't ~ her** no la soporto
◆ **abide by** *vt* (*rule, decision*) atenerse a; (*promise*) cumplir

**ability** [ə·ˈbɪl·ə·ti] <-ies> *n* **1.** (*capability*) capacidad *f*; **to the best of one's ~** lo mejor que una pueda **2.** (*talent*) aptitud *f* **3.** *pl* dotes *fpl*

**ablaze** [ə·ˈbleɪz] *adj* en llamas; *fig* resplandeciente

**able** [ˈeɪ·bəl] *adj* capaz; **to be ~ to do sth** (*have ability, manage*) poder hacer algo; (*have knowledge*) saber hacer algo

**able-bodied** *adj* fuerte y sano, -a

**abnormal** [æb·ˈnɔr·məl] *adj* (*feature*) anómalo, -a; (*person*) anormal

**abnormality** [ˌæb·nɔr·ˈmæl·ə·ti] <-ies> *n* anomalía *f*; (*unusualness*) anormalidad *f*

**aboard** [ə·ˈbɔrd] **I.** *adv* a bordo **II.** *prep* a bordo de; **to go ~ a boat/plane** subir a una barca/un avión

**abode** [ə·ˈboʊd] *vi pt, pp of* **abide**

**abolish** [ə·ˈbɑl·ɪʃ] *vt* abolir

**abolition** [ˌæb·ə·ˈlɪʃ·ən] *n* abolición *f*

**abominable** [ə·ˈbɑm·ə·nə·bəl] *adj* abominable

**abomination** [ə·ˌbɑm·ə·ˈneɪ·ʃən] *n* **1.** (*abominable thing*) abominación *f* **2.** (*disgust*) aversión *f*

**Aborigine** [ˌæb·ə·ˈrɪdʒ·ə·ni] *n* aborigen *mf* (de Australia)

**abort** [ə·ˈbɔrt] *vt, vi* MED abortar; COMPUT abandonar

**abortion** [ə·ˈbɔr·ʃən] *n* MED aborto *m*

**about** [ə·ˈbaʊt] **I.** *prep* **1.** (*on subject of*) sobre, acerca de; **a book ~ football** un libro sobre fútbol; **what is the film ~?** ¿de qué trata la película? **2.** (*characteristic of*) **that's what I like ~ him** eso es lo que me gusta de él **3.** (*surrounding*) alrededor de; **the garden ~ the house** el jardín alrededor de la casa **4.** (*in and through*) por; **to go ~ a place** andar por un lugar ► **how ~ that!** ¡vaya!; **how ~ a drink?** ¿qué tal si tomamos algo?; **what ~ it?** (*suggestion*) ¿quieres/queréis?; (*so what?*) ¿y qué? **II.** *adv* **1.** (*approximately*) aproximadamente; **~ my size** más o menos de mi tamaño; **~ 5 years ago** hace unos cinco años; **~ twenty** unos veinte; **to have had just ~ enough of sth** estar harto de algo; **that's ~ it for today** eso es todo por hoy **2.** (*almost*) casi; **to be (just) ~ ready** estar casi listo **3.** (*on the point of*) **to be ~ to do sth** estar a punto de hacer algo **4.** (*around*) **all ~** por todas partes; **to be somewhere ~** estar por aquí

**above** [ə·ˈbʌv] **I.** *prep* **1.** (*on top of*) encima de **2.** (*over*) sobre; **~ suspicion** por encima de toda sospecha **3.** (*greater than, superior to*) por encima de; **~ 3** más de 3; **he is not ~ lying** es muy capaz de mentir; **~ all** sobre todo **II.** *adv* encima; **the floor** ~ la planta de arriba; **up ~ sth** por encima de algo; **see ~** véase más arriba

**abovementioned** *adj* anteriormente mencionado, -a

**abrasive** [ə·'breɪ·sɪv] *adj* abrasivo, -a; (*in manner*) agresivo, -a

**abreast** [ə·'brest] *adv* **two/three ~** en fila de a dos/tres; **to be/keep ~ of sth** estar/mantenerse al corriente de algo

**abroad** [ə·'brɔd] *adv* **from ~** del extranjero; **to be ~** estar en el extranjero; **to go ~** ir al extranjero; **at home and ~** dentro y fuera del país

**abrupt** [ə·'brʌpt] *adj* **1.** (*sudden*) repentino, -a; (*change*) brusco, -a; (*end*) inesperado, -a **2.** (*brusque*) brusco, -a **3.** (*steep*) abrupto, -a

**ABS** [ˌeɪ·bi·'es] *n abbr of* **antilock braking system** ABS *m*

**absence** ['æb·səns] *n* **1.** (*not being present*) ausencia *f*; **in the ~ of** en ausencia de **2.** (*lack of*) carencia *f*; **in the ~ of** a falta de

**absent**[1] ['æb·sənt] *adj* ausente

**absent**[2] [əb·'sent] *vt* **to ~ oneself** ausentarse (**from** de)

**absentee ballot, absentee voting** *n* voto *m* por correo

**absent-minded** *adj* despistado, -a, volado, -a *AmL*

**absolute** ['æb·sə·lut] *adj* **1.** **a.** POL absoluto, -a; (*denial*) rotundo, -a; (*trust, power, confidence*) pleno, -a **2.** CHEM puro, -a

**absolutely** *adv* absolutamente; (*very*) totalmente; **~!** *inf* ¡claro que sí!; **~ not!** ¡de ninguna manera!

**absorb** [əb·'sɔrb] *vt* **1.** (*liquid*) absorber; (*shock*) amortiguar **2.** (*understand*) asimilar **3.** (*engross*) ocupar; **to be ~ed in one's thoughts** estar absorto en sus pensamientos

**absorbent** [əb·'sɔr·bənt] *adj* absorbente

**absorbing** *adj* (*book, story*) apasionante

**absorption** [əb·'sɔrp·ʃən] *n* **1.** (*of liquid*) absorción *f* **2.** (*in book, story*) concentración *f*; (*in work*) dedicación *f* absoluta

**abstention** [əb·'sten·ʃən] *n* **a.** POL abstención *f*

**abstinence** ['æb·stə·nəns] *n* abstinencia *f*

**abstract**[1] ['æb·strækt] **I.** *adj* abstracto, -a **II.** *n* (*summary*) extracto *m*

**abstract**[2] [əb·'strækt] *vt* **1. a.** CHEM extraer **2.** (*summarize*) resumir

**abstracted** [æb·'stræk·tɪd] *adj* distraído, -a

**abstraction** [əb·'stræk·ʃən] *n* **1.** (*concept*) abstracción *f* **2.** (*absent-mindedness*) distracción *f*

**absurd** [əb·'sɜrd] *adj* absurdo, -a

**absurdity** [əb·'sɜr·də·ti] <-ies> *n* **1.** absurdo *m*; (*idea, situation*) ridiculez *f* **2.** (*absurd thing*) disparate *m*

**abundance** [ə·'bʌn·dəns] *n* abundancia *f*

**abundant** [ə·'bʌn·dənt] *adj* abundante

**abuse**[1] [ə·'bjus] *n* **1.** (*insults*) insultos *mpl*, insultadas *fpl AmL* **2.** (*mistreatment*) maltrato *m* **3.** (*misuse*) abuso *m*; **sexual ~** abuso sexual

**abuse**[2] [ə·'bjuz] *vt* **1.** (*insult*) insultar **2.** (*mistreat*) maltratar **3.** (*sexually, misuse*) abusar de

**abusive** [ə·'bju·sɪv] *adj* (*language*) ofensivo, -a; (*person*) agresivo, -a

**abysmal** [ə·'bɪz·məl] *adj* pésimo, -a

**abyss** [ə·'bɪs] *n* **a.** *fig* abismo *m*

**academic** [ˌæk·ə·'dem·ɪk] *adj* **1.** UNIV académico, -a; SCHOOL escolar **2.** (*intellectual*) erudito, -a

**academy** [ə·'kæd·ə·mi] <-ies> *n* **1.** academia *f*; (*prep school*) instituto *m* **2. the Academy Awards** los Óscars

**accelerate** [ək·'sel·ə·reɪt] **I.** *vi* acelerar; (*growth*) acelerarse **II.** *vt* acelerar

**accelerator** [ək·'sel·ə·reɪ·tər] *n* AUTO acelerador *m*, chancleta *f Ven, Col*

**accent** ['æk·sent] **I.** *n* LING acento *m*; LIT énfasis *m inv* **II.** *vt* enfatizar; LING acentuar

**accentuate** [ək·'sen·tʃʊ·eɪt] *vt* acentuar

**accept** [ək·'sept] **I.** *vt* **1.** (*take when offered*) aceptar **2.** (*approve*) aprobar **3.** (*believe*) creer en **4.** (*acknowledge*) reconocer **II.** *vi* aceptar

**acceptable** *adj* aceptable; (*explanation*) admisible

**acceptance** [ək·'sep·təns] *n* aceptación *f*; (*approval*) aprobación *f*

**access** ['æk·ses] **I.** *n* entrada *f*, aproches *mpl AmL*; **a.** COMPUT acceso *m*;

Internet ~ acceso a Internet; **to gain ~ to sth** acceder a algo; **to have ~ to sth** tener acceso a algo; **with easy ~** de fácil acceso II. vt acceder a

**accessible** [əkˈses·ə·bəl] adj accesible

**accessory** [əkˈses·ə·ri] <-ies> n 1. accesorio m 2. LAW cómplice mf

**accident** [ˈæk·sɪ·dənt] n accidente m; ~ **insurance** seguro m contra accidentes; **by ~** sin querer; (by chance) por casualidad

**accidental** [ˌæk·sɪˈden·təl] adj accidental; (discovery) fortuito, -a

**accident-prone** n propenso, -a a tener accidentes

**acclaim** [əˈkleɪm] vt aclamar; **critically ~ed** elogiado por la crítica

**acclamation** [ˌæk·ləˈmeɪ·ʃən] n aclamación f

**acclimate** [əˈk·laɪ·mɪt] I. vi aclimatarse II. vt aclimatar

**accommodate** [əˈkam·ə·deɪt] vt alojar; **to ~ oneself to sth** adaptarse a algo

**accommodation** [əˌkam·əˈdeɪ·ʃən] n 1. pl alojamiento m 2. (on vehicle, plane) asientos mpl

**accompany** [əˈkʌm·pə·ni] <-ie-> vt acompañar

**accomplice** [əˈkam·plɪs] n cómplice mf

**accomplish** [əˈkam·plɪʃ] vt lograr; (finish) concluir; (task) realizar

**accomplished** [əˈkam·plɪʃt] adj consumado, -a

**accomplishment** n 1. (achievement) logro m 2. (completion) conclusión f; (task) realización f 3. (skill) talento m

**accord** [əˈkɔrd] I. n acuerdo m; (treaty) convenio m II. vi **to ~ with sth** concordar con algo

**accordance** [əˈkɔr·dəns] n **in ~ with** conforme a

**accordingly** adv 1. (appropriately) en consecuencia 2. (therefore) por consiguiente

**according to** [əˈkɔr·dɪŋ·tə] prep según; ~ **her/what I read** según ella/lo que leí; **to go ~ plan** salir según lo previsto; ~ **the law** con arreglo a la ley

**accordion** [əˈkɔr·di·ən] n MUS acordeón m, filarmónica f Méx

**account** [əˈkaʊnt] n 1. (with bank) cuenta f 2. (bill) factura f 3. pl (financial records) cuentas fpl; **to keep an ~ of sth** llevar la cuenta de algo 4. **to give an ~ of sth** informar sobre algo 5. **to take sth into ~** tomar [or tener] algo en cuenta; **to take no ~ of sth** no tomar [or tener] en cuenta algo; **on ~ of sth** por causa de algo 6. responsabilidad f; **on one's own ~** por cuenta propia; **on sb's ~** a cuenta de alguien ▶ **to be called to ~** tener que rendir cuentas (**for** de); **to settle ~s with sb** ajustar cuentas con alguien

◆**account for** vt 1. (explain) explicar 2. (constitute) representar

**accountable** [əˈkaʊn·tə·bəl] adj responsable

**accountant** [əˈkaʊn·tənt] n contable mf, contador(a) m(f) And

**account book** n libro m de cuentas

**accumulate** [əˈkjum·jə·leɪt] I. vt acumular II. vi acumularse

**accumulation** [əˌkjum·jəˈleɪ·ʃən] n acumulación f; (quantity) cúmulo m

**accuracy** [ˈæk·jər·ə·si] n precisión f

**accurate** [ˈæk·jər·ɪt] adj 1. (on target) certero, -a 2. (correct) exacto, -a 3. (careful) cuidadoso, -a

**accusation** [ˌæk·juˈzeɪ·ʃən] n acusación f

**accuse** [əˈkjuz] vt acusar; **she is ~d of...** se la acusa de...

**accused** [əˈkjuzd] n **the ~** el acusado, la acusada

**accustomed** [əˈkʌs·təmd] adj 1. acostumbrado, -a; **to be/to grow ~ to doing sth** estar acostumbrado/acostumbrarse a hacer algo 2. (usual) usual

**ace** [eɪs] I. n as m ▶ **to have an ~ up one's sleeve** tener un as en la manga; **to come within an ~** estar a punto (**of** de) II. adj inf experto, -a III. vt sl (exam, interview) bordar

**ache** [eɪk] I. n dolor m II. vi doler

**achieve** [əˈtʃiv] vt lograr; (task) llevar a cabo; (success) alcanzar

**achievement** n logro m; (achieving) realización f

**acid** [ˈæs·ɪd] I. n a. sl ácido m II. adj 1. ácido, -a 2. (sarcastic) mordaz

**acidity** [əˈsɪd·ə·t̬i] n acidez f; fig mordacidad f

**acid rain** n lluvia f ácida

**acid rock** n MUS acid rock m

**acid-washed** adj deslavado, -a, destintado, -a Méx

**acknowledge** [ək'nɑl·ɪdʒ] vt (admit) admitir; (guilt) confesar

**acknowledg(e)ment** n 1. reconocimiento m; (of guilt) confesión f 2. pl agradecimientos mpl

**acne** ['æk·ni] n acné m

**acorn** ['eɪ·kɔrn] n bellota f

**acoustic(al)** [ə·'ku·stɪk(əl)] I. adj acústico, -a II. npl acústica f

**acoustics** [ə·'ku·stɪks] n + sing vb (science) acústica f; + pl vb (of an enclosed space) acústica f

**acquaint** [ə·'kweɪnt] vt to be/become ~ed with conocer

**acquaintance** [ə·'kweɪn·təns] n (relationship) relación f; (person) conocido, -a m, f

**acquire** [ə·'kwaɪr] vt adquirir; to ~ a taste for sth tomarle el gusto a algo

**acquisition** [æk·wɪ·'zɪʃ·ən] n adquisición f

**acquit** [ə·'kwɪt] <-tt-> vt to ~ sb of a charge absolver a alguien de una acusación; to ~ oneself well/badly salir bien/mal parado

**acquittal** [ə·'kwɪt·əl] n absolución f

**acre** ['eɪ·kər] n acre m (4047 metros cuadrados)

**acrobat** ['æk·rə·bæt] n acróbata mf

**acrobatic** [ˌæk·rə·'bæt·ɪk] adj acrobático, -a

**acronym** ['æk·rə·nɪm] n sigla f

**across** [ə·'krɔs] I. prep 1. (on other side of) al otro lado de; just ~ the street justo al otro lado de la calle; ~ from enfrente de 2. (from one side to other) a través de; to walk ~ the bridge cruzar el puente andando II. adv de un lado a otro; to run/swim ~ cruzar corriendo/a nado; to come ~ sth encontrar(se) algo

**across-the-board** adj global

**acrylic** [ə·'krɪl·ɪk] n acrílico m

**acrylic paint** n pintura f acrílica

**act** [ækt] I. n 1. (action) acto m; ~ of charity obra f de caridad; to catch sb in the ~ pillar a alguien in fraganti 2. (performance) número m 3. (pretence) fingimiento m 4. LAW ley f ▶ to get one's ~ together arreglárselas; to get in on the ~ meterse en el asunto II. vi 1. (take action) a. THEAT actuar; to ~ for sb representar a alguien 2. (behave) portarse 3. (take effect) dar resultado 4. (pretend) fingir III. vt THEAT representar; to ~ the fool hacer el tonto

◆**act on** vt obrar de acuerdo con

◆**act out** vt representar

◆**act up** vi inf hacer de las suyas; (machine) fallar; (knee, back) doler

**acting** ['æk·tɪŋ] I. adj en funciones II. n arte m dramático

**action** ['æk·ʃən] n 1. (activeness) acción f; out of ~ inactivo; (machine) fuera de servicio; to spring into ~ ponerse en marcha; to take ~ tomar medidas 2. MIL combate m 3. (motion) movimiento m 4. LAW demanda f; to bring an ~ interponer una demanda (against contra) 5. inf (exciting events) bullicio m ▶ ~s speak louder than words obras son amores y no buenas razones

**action-packed** adj lleno, -a de acción

**activate** ['æk·tə·veɪt] vt a. CHEM activar

**active** ['æk·tɪv] adj activo, -a; to be ~ in sth participar en algo

**actively** adv 1. (in a lively manner) activamente 2. (energetically) enérgicamente 3. (consciously) de forma activa

**activist** ['æk·tə·vɪst] n activista mf

**activity** [æk·'tɪv·ɪ·t̬i] <-ies> n actividad f

**actor** ['æk·tər] n actor m

**actress** ['æk·trɪs] n actriz f

**actual** ['æk·tʃu·əl] adj (real) verdadero, -a; (precise) exacto, -a

**actually** ['æk·tʃu·ə·li] adv en realidad; ~ I saw her yesterday pues la vi ayer

**acupuncture** ['æk·ju·pʌŋk·tʃər] n acupuntura f

**acute** [ə·'kjut] I. adj (pain, disease, hearing, sight, angle) agudo, -a; (anxiety) extremo, -a; (embarrassment) hondo, -a; (difficulties) grande; (shortage) fuerte II. n acento m agudo

**acutely** adv extremadamente; to be ~ aware of sth ser plenamente consciente de algo

**ad** [æd] n inf abbr of **advertisement**

anuncio *m*

**A.D.** [ˌeɪˈdiː] *abbr of* **anno Domini** d.C.

**adapt** [əˈdæpt] **I.** *vt* adaptar **II.** *vi* adaptarse

**adaptable** *adj* adaptable

**adaptation** [ˌæd·æp·ˈteɪ·ʃən] *n* adaptación *f*

**adapter, adaptor** [əˈdæp·tər] *n* adaptador *m;* (*for several plugs*) ladrón *m*

**add** [æd] *vt* **1.** añadir, agregar *AmL* **2.** MATH sumar

◆**add up** *vi, vt* sumar; **to ~ to...** ascender a...

**adder** [ˈæd·ər] *n* víbora *f*

**addict** [ˈæd·ɪkt] *n* adicto, -a *m, f;* **drug ~** drogadicto *m;* **to be a movie ~** ser un apasionado del cine

**addicted** [əˈdɪk·tɪd] *adj* adicto, -a; **to be ~ to sth** ser adicto a algo; *fig* ser muy aficionado a algo

**addiction** [əˈdɪk·ʃən] *n* adicción *f;* **drug ~** drogadicción *f*

**addictive** [əˈdɪk·tɪv] *adj* adictivo, -a

**addition** [əˈdɪʃ·ən] *n* **1.** adición *f;* (*added thing*) añadido *m;* **in ~ (to)** además (de); **an ~ to the family** uno más en la familia **2.** MATH suma *f*

**additional** [əˈdɪʃ·ən·əl] *adj* adicional

**additionally** [əˈdɪʃ·ən·əl·i] *adv* por añadidura; **and ~** y además

**additive** [ˈæd·ɪ·tɪv] *n* aditivo *m*

**address¹** [ˈæd·res] *n* dirección *f*

**address²** [əˈdres] **I.** *vt* **1.** (*letter*) dirigir **2.** (*speak to*) dirigirse a **II.** *n* **form of ~** tratamiento *m*

**addressee** [ˌæd·re·ˈsi] *n* destinatario, -a *m, f*

**adept** [əˈdept] *adj* experto, -a; **to be ~ at sth** ser hábil para algo

**adequate** [ˈæd·ɪ·kwət] *adj* **1.** (*sufficient*) suficiente **2.** (*good enough*) adecuado, -a

**adhere** [æd·ˈhɪr] *vi* adherirse; *fig* aferrarse

**adhesive** [æd·ˈhi·sɪv] *adj* adhesivo, -a

**ad infinitum** [æd·ɪn·fə·ˈnaɪ·təm] *adv* ad infinítum

**adjacent** [əˈdʒeɪ·sənt] *adj* contiguo, -a; MATH adyacente

**adjective** [ˈædʒ·ɪk·tɪv] *n* adjetivo *m*

**adjoining** *adj* (*room*) contiguo, -a; (*field*) colindante

**adjourn** [əˈdʒɜrn] **I.** *vt* aplazar **II.** *vi* **1.** aplazarse **2.** (*go*) desplazarse

**adjust** [əˈdʒʌst] **I.** *vt* **1. a.** TECH ajustar **2.** (*rearrange*) arreglar **3.** (*change*) modificar **II.** *vi* adaptarse (**to** a)

**adjustable** *adj* ajustable

**adjustable wrench** *n* llave *f* inglesa

**adjustment** *n* ajuste *m;* (*mental*) adaptación *f*

**ad lib** [ˌæd·ˈlɪb] *adv* improvisando

**admin** [əd·ˈmɪn] *abbr of* **administration** admón.

**administer** [æd·ˈmɪn·ɪ·stər] *vt* (*funds, estate, medicine*) administrar; (*punishment*) aplicar; (*first aid*) prestar

**administration** [æd·ˌmɪn·ɪ·ˈstreɪ·ʃən] *n* **a.** POL administración *f;* (*time in power*) mandato *m*

**administrative** [æd·ˈmɪn·ɪ·streɪ·tɪv] *adj* administrativo, -a

**administrator** [æd·ˈmɪn·ɪ·streɪ·tər] *n* administrador(a) *m(f)*

**admirable** [ˈæd·mər·ə·bəl] *adj* admirable

**admiral** [ˈæd·mər·əl] *n* almirante *m*

**admiration** [ˌæd·mə·ˈreɪ·ʃən] *n* admiración *f;* **in ~** lleno de admiración

**admire** [əd·ˈmaɪr] *vt* admirar (**for** por)

**admirer** [əd·ˈmaɪr·ər] *n* admirador(a) *m(f)*

**admissible** [æd·ˈmɪs·ə·bəl] *adj* admisible

**admission** [æd·ˈmɪʃ·ən] *n* **1.** (*entry, entrance fee*) entrada; (*to college, organization*) ingreso *m* **2.** (*acknowledgement*) confesión *f*

**admit** [æd·ˈmɪt] <-tt-> **I.** *vt* **1.** (*acknowledge*) reconocer; (*crime*) confesar **2.** (*allow entrance to*) dejar entrar **3.** (*permit*) admitir **II.** *vt* **to ~ to sth** confesarse culpable de algo

**admittance** [æd·ˈmɪt·əns] *n* entrada *f;* **no ~** se prohíbe la entrada

**admittedly** [æd·ˈmɪt·ɪd·li] *adv* es cierto que

**ado** [əˈdu] *n* **1.** (*commotion*) embrollo *m* **2.** (*delay*) demora *f* ▶ **much ~ about nothing** mucho ruido y pocas nueces

**adobe** [ə·ˈdou·bi] *n* adobe *m;* (*building*) construcción *f* de adobe

**adolescence** [ˌæd·əl·ˈes·əns] *n* adolescencia *f*

**adolescent** [ˌæd·əl·'es·ənt] *adj, n* adolescente *mf*

**adopt** [ə·'dɑpt] *vt* adoptar; (*candidate*) nombrar

**adoption** [ə·'dɑp·ʃən] *n* adopción *f*; (*of candidate*) nombramiento *m*

**adorable** [ə·'dɔr·ə·bəl] *adj* encantador(a)

**adoration** [ˌæd·ə·'reɪ·ʃən] *n* adoración *f*

**adore** [ə·'dɔr] *vt* adorar; **I just ~ the theater** me encanta el teatro

**adoring** [ə·'dɔr·ɪŋ] *adj* cariñoso, -a

**adrenaline** [ə·'dren·ə·lɪn] *n* adrenalina *f*

**adrift** [ə·'drɪft] *adv* a la deriva; **to go ~** *fig* fallar

**adult** [ə·'dʌlt] I. *n* adulto, -a *m, f* II. *adj* adulto, -a; (*explicit*) para adultos

**adultery** [ə·'dʌl·tə·ri] <-ies> *n* adulterio *m*

**advance** [əd·'væns] I. *vi* avanzar (**on** hacia) II. *vt* 1. avanzar; (*interest, cause*) promover 2. (*pay*) anticipar III. *n* 1. (*forward movement*) avance *m*; **in ~** por adelantado 2. FIN anticipo *m* 3. *pl* (*flirtation*) insinuaciones *fpl* IV. *adj* adelantado, -a; **without ~ warning** sin previo aviso

**advanced** [əd·'vænst] *adj* avanzado, -a

**advancement** [əd·'væns·mənt] *n* 1. (*improvement*) avance *m* 2. (*promotion*) fomento *m*

**advance notice** *n* aviso *m* (previo)

**advance payment** *n* anticipo *m*

**advantage** [əd·'væn·tɪdʒ] *n* ventaja *f* (**over** sobre); **to take ~** aprovecharse (**of** de)

**adventure** [æd·'ven·tʃər] *n* aventura *f*

**adventurous** [əd·'ven·tʃər·əs] *adj* aventurero, -a; (*decision*) arriesgado, -a

**adverb** ['æd·'vɜrb] *n* adverbio *m*

**adversary** ['æd·vər·ser·i] <-ies> *n* adversario, -a *m, f*

**adverse** [æd·'vɜrs] *adj* adverso, -a; (*reaction*) hostil

**adversity** [æd·'vɜr·sə·ti] <-ies> *n* adversidad *f*

**advertent** [æd·'vɜr·tənt] *adj* atento, -a

**advertise** ['æd·vər·taɪz] I. *vt* anunciar II. *vi* hacer publicidad

**advertisement** [ˌæd·vər·'taɪz·mənt] *n* anuncio *m*, aviso *m* *AmL*; **job ~** oferta *f* de empleo

**advertiser** ['æd·vər·taɪ·zər] *n* anunciante *mf*

**advertising** ['æd·vər·ˌtaɪ·zɪŋ] *n* publicidad *f*

**advice** [æd·'vaɪs] *n* 1. consejo *m*; **a piece of ~** un consejo; **to ask for ~** pedir consejo (**on** sobre); **on her ~** siguiendo su consejo 2. COM aviso *m*

**advisable** [æd·'vaɪ·zə·bəl] *adj* aconsejable; **it is (not) ~** (no) es aconsejable

**advise** [æd·'vaɪz] I. *vt* aconsejar; (*specialist*) asesorar (**on** sobre); **to ~ against** desaconsejar III. *vi* dar un consejo

**adviser, advisor** [əd·'vaɪ·zər] *n* asesor(a) *m(f)*

**advocacy** ['æd·və·kəsi] *n* (*of cause, idea*) defensa *f*

**advocate**[1] ['æd·və·keɪt] *vt* **to ~ (doing sth)** recomendar (hacer algo)

**advocate**[2] ['æd·və·kət] *n* defensor(a) *m(f)*; (*lawyer*) abogado, -a *m, f* defensor(a)

**aerial** ['er·i·əl] I. *adj* aéreo, -a II. *n* antena *f*

**aerobics** [ə·'rou·bɪks] *n* + *sing/pl vb* aeróbic *m*, aerobic *m*; **to do ~** hacer aeróbic

**aerodynamic** [ˌer·ou·daɪ·'næm·ɪk] *adj* aerodinámico, -a

**aerodynamics** *n* + *sing vb* aerodinámica *f*

**aeronautic** ['er·ə·nɔ·t̬ɪk] *adj* aeronáutico, -a

**aeronautics** *n* + *sing vb* aeronáutica *f*

**aerosol** ['er·ə·sɔl] *n* aerosol *m*

**aesthetics** *n* + *sing vb* estética *f*

**afar** [ə·'far] *adv* lejos

**affable** ['æf·ə·bəl] *adj* afable

**affair** [ə·'fer] *n* 1. (*matter*) asunto *m* 2. (*scandal*) escándalo *m* 3. (**to have**) **an ~** (tener) una aventura (**with** con) 4. (*event*) acontecimiento *m*

**affect** [ə·'fekt] *vt* 1. afectar; **to be ~ed by sth** (*be moved*) conmoverse por algo 2. (*simulate*) fingir

**affected** [ə·'fek·tɪd] *adj* (*behavior, accent*) amanerado, -a; (*emotion*) fingido, -a; (*style, smile*) forzado, -a

**affection** [ə·'fek·ʃən] *n* cariño *m*

**affectionate** [ə·'fek·ʃə·nɪt] *adj* cariñoso, -a

**affiliate**[1] [ə·'fɪl·i·eɪt] *vt* afiliar (**with** a)

**affiliate²** [ə·'fɪl·ɪ·ɪt] *n* filial *f*

**affirm** [ə·'fɜrm] *vt* afirmar

**affirmation** [æf·ər·'meɪ·ʃən] *n* afirmación *f*

**affirmative** [ə·'fɜr·mə·tɪv] **I.** *adj* afirmativo, -a **II.** *n* in the ~ afirmativamente

**affix** [ə·'fɪks] *vt* poner; (*stick*) pegar; (*clip*) clavar

**afflict** [ə·'flɪkt] *vt* afligir; **to be ~ed** padecer (**with** de)

**affluent** [ˈæf·lʊ·ənt] *adj* rico, -a; (*lifestyle*) acomodado, -a; (*society*) opulento, -a

**afford** [ə·'fɔrd] *vt* **1.** (*money, time*) permitirse **2.** (*provide*) proporcionar

**affordable** [ə·'fɔr·də·bəl] *adj* asequible

**afforest** [ə·'fɔr·əst] *vt* forestar

**afield** [ə·'fild] *adv* **far/further** ~ muy/más lejos

**afloat** [ə·'floʊt] *adj* a flote

**afoot** [ə·'fʊt] *adj* **there's sth** ~ se está tramando algo

**aforementioned** [ə·ˌfɔr·'men·ʃənd], **aforesaid** [ə·'fɔr·sed] *form* **I.** *adj* dicho, -a **II.** *n inv* **the** ~ el mencionado/la mencionada; (*person*) el susodicho/la susodicha

**afraid** [ə·'freɪd] *adj* **1.** (*scared*) **to be** ~ tener miedo (**of** a); **to be** ~ **of doing** [*or* **to do**] **sth** tener miedo de hacer algo **2.** (*sorry*) **I'm** ~ **so/not** me temo que sí/no

**Africa** [ˈæf·rɪ·kə] *n* África *f*

**African** [ˈæf·rɪ·kən] *adj, n* africano, -a *m, f*

**African American, Afro-American** *adj, n* afroamericano, -a *m, f*

**aft** [æft] *adv* (*go*) a popa; (*be*) en popa

**after** [ˈæf·tər] **I.** *prep* **1.** (*later, following*) después de; ~ **two days** al cabo de dos días; (*shortly*) ~ **breakfast** (poco) después de desayunar; **to have argument** ~ **argument** tener pelea tras pelea; ~ **all** después de todo; **to ask** ~ **sb** preguntar por alguien **2.** (*behind*) detrás de **II.** *adv* después; **soon** ~ poco después **III.** *conj* después de que +*subj*

**afterbirth** *n* placenta *f*

**aftercare** [ˈæf·tər·ker] *n* MED asistencia *f* postoperatoria

**aftereffects** [ˈæf·tər·ɪ·ˌfekts] *npl* (*drugs*) efectos *m pl* secundarios; (*accident*) secuelas *fpl*

**afterglow** *n* **1.** (*after sunset*) arrebol *m*

**2.** PHYS luminiscencia *f*

**after-hours** *adj* fuera de horas

**afterlife** [ˈæf·tər·laɪf] *n* **the** ~ el más allá

**after-market** *n* venta *f* de repuestos y accesorios [*or Méx* de refacción]

**aftermath** [ˈæf·tər·mæθ] *n* secuelas *fpl*

**afternoon** [ˌæf·tər·'nun] **I.** *n* tarde *f*; **this** ~ esta tarde; **in the** ~ por la tarde; **all** ~ toda la tarde; **tomorrow/yesterday** ~ mañana/ayer por la tarde; **4 o'clock in the** ~ las 4 de la tarde; **good** ~! ¡buenas tardes! **II.** *adj* de la tarde; ~ **nap** siesta *f*

**after-shave** [ˈæf·tər·ʃeɪv] *n* aftershave *m*

**aftershock** *n* réplica *f*

**aftertaste** [ˈæf·tər·teɪst] *n a. fig* regusto *m*

**afterward, afterwards** [ˈæf·tər·wərd(z)] *adv* después; **shortly** ~ poco después

**again** [ə·'gen] *adv* otra vez; (*one more time*) de nuevo; **never** ~ nunca más; **once** ~ otra vez; ~ **and** ~ una y otra vez

**against** [ə·'genst] **I.** *prep* **1.** contra; **to be** ~ estar en contra (de); ~ **the light** a contraluz; ~ **the clock** contrarreloj; **to run** ~ **a wall** estrellarse contra una pared; **to lean** ~ **a tree** apoyarse en un árbol **2.** (*protection*) **to protect oneself** ~ **rain** protegerse de la lluvia **3.** (*in comparison with*) **the dollar rose/fell** ~ **the euro** el dólar subió/bajó respecto al euro **II.** *adv* en contra; **9 votes** ~ **9** votos en contra

**age** [eɪdʒ] **I.** *n* **1.** (*of person, object*) edad *f*; **old** ~ vejez *f*; **when I was her** ~ cuando tenía su edad; **to be under** ~ ser menor de edad **2.** (*era*) época *f*; **I haven't seen you in** ~**s!** ¡hace siglos que no te veo! **II.** *vi, vt* envejecer; CULIN madurar

**age bracket** *n see* **age group**

**aged¹** [eɪdʒd] *adj* **de ... años de edad;** CULIN curado, -a; (*wine*) añejo, -a

**aged²** [ˈeɪ·dʒɪd] **I.** *adj* viejo, -a **II.** *n* **the** ~ los ancianos

**age group** *n* grupo *m* de edad

**agency** [ˈeɪ·dʒən·si] <-ies> *n* agencia *f*; **travel** ~ agencia de viajes; **government** ~ organismo gubernamental

**agenda** [ə·'dʒen·də] *n* orden *m* del día; **to be at the top of the** ~ *fig* ser un asunto prioritario

**agent** ['eɪ·dʒənt] n agente mf

**age-old** adj antiguo, -a

**aggravate** ['æg·rə·veɪt] vt agravar; inf fastidiar

**aggravating** adj molesto, -a

**aggravation** [ˌæg·rə·'veɪ·ʃən] n inf fastidio m

**aggregate¹** ['æg·rɪ·gɪt] I. n 1. FIN, ECON conglomerado m; (sum, value) total m 2. MATH suma f II. adj total

**aggregate²** ['æg·rɪ·geɪt] vt sumar

**aggression** [ə·'greʃ·ən] n (feelings) agresividad f; (violence) agresión f

**aggressive** [ə·'gres·ɪv] adj agresivo, -a

**aggressor** [ə·'gres·ər] n agresor(a) m(f)

**agile** ['ædʒ·əl] adj ágil

**agility** [ə·'dʒɪl·ə·ti] n agilidad f

**aging** I. adj envejecido, -a II. n envejecimiento m

**agitation** [ˌædʒ·ɪ·'teɪ·ʃən] n agitación f

**agnostic** [æg·'nas·tɪk] adj, n agnóstico, -a m, f

**ago** [ə·'goʊ] adv a minute/year ~ hace un minuto/año; a long time ~, long ~ hace mucho tiempo; how long ~ was that? ¿cuánto tiempo hace de eso?

**agog** [ə·'gag] adj to watch/listen ~ mirar/escuchar con avidez

**agonizing** ['æg·ə·naɪ·zɪŋ] adj (pain) atroz; (delay, decision) angustiante

**agony** ['æg·ə·ni] <-ies> n agonía f; to be in ~ sufrir fuertes dolores

**agony column** n sección f de desaparecidos

**agrarian** [ə·'grer·i·ən] adj agrario, -a

**agree** [ə·'gri] I. vi 1. estar de acuerdo; to ~ on sth (be in agreement) estar de acuerdo en algo; (reach agreement) acordar algo; to ~ to do sth (reach agreement) acordar hacer algo; (consent) acceder a hacer algo 2. (be good for) to ~ with sb sentar bien a alguien 3. (match up) a. LING concordar II. vt acordar; at the ~d time a la hora fijada

**agreement** n 1. acuerdo m; to be in ~ estar de acuerdo (with con); to reach an ~ llegar a un acuerdo 2. LING concordancia f

**agriculture** ['æg·rɪ·kʌl·tʃər] n agricultura f

**agritourism** [ˌæg·rɪ·'tʊr·ɪzəm] n agroturismo m

**aground** [ə·'graʊnd] adv to run ~ encallar; fig fracasar

**ah** [a] interj ah

**aha** [a·'ha] interj ajá

**ahead** [ə·'hed] adv 1. (in front) delante 2. (with movement) adelante; to go ~ adelantarse 3. (in the future) to look ~ anticiparse

**ahead of** prep 1. (in front of) delante de; (way) ~ sb/sth (muy) por delante de alguien/algo 2. (before) antes de; ~ time antes de tiempo; to be a minute ~ sb llevar un minuto a alguien; to be ~ one's time anticiparse a su época 3. to keep ~ sth estar al tanto de algo

**ahoy** [ə·'hɔɪ] interj land/ship ~! ¡tierra/barco a la vista!

**AI** [ˌeɪ·'aɪ] n abbr of **artificial intelligence** IA

**aid** [eɪd] I. n ayuda f; to/with the ~ of en/con ayuda de; **financial** ~ asistencia f financiera; **hearing** ~ audífono m II. vt ayudar

**aid convoy** n convoy m humanitario

**AIDS** [eɪdz] n abbr of **Acquired Immune Deficiency Syndrome** sida m

**ailing** ['eɪl·ɪŋ] adj enfermo, -a; (company, economy) debilitado, -a

**aim** [eɪm] I. vi (weapon) apuntar (at a); to ~ at [or for] sth tener algo como objetivo II. vt apuntar; to ~ sth at sb/sth (point a weapon) apuntar algo hacia alguien/algo; (direct at) dirigir algo hacia alguien; to be ~ed at doing sth ir encaminado a hacer algo III. n 1. (ability) puntería f 2. (goal) objetivo m

**aimless** ['eɪm·lɪs] adj sin objetivo(s)

**ain't** [eɪnt] inf 1. (to be) see **am not**, **are not**, **is not** 2. (to have) see **have not**, **has not**

**air** [er] I. n aire m; **by** ~ por aire; to travel **by** ~ viajar en avión; to be on the ~ estar en el aire; to have an ~ of confidence/danger envolverle un aire de confianza/peligro ▶ out of thin ~ de la nada; to disappear into thin ~ desaparecer como por arte de magia II. adj aéreo, -a III. vt 1. TV, RADIO emitir 2. (expose to air) airear IV. vi 1. TV, RADIO emitirse 2. (be exposed to air) ventilarse

**air ball** n (*in basketball*) pelota que no toca ni el aro

**air base** n base f aérea

**airborne** ['er·bɔrn] *adj* aerotransportado, -a; **to be ~** volar

**airbrush** n aerógrafo m

**air bus** n aerobús m

**air-conditioned** *adj* climatizado, -a

**air conditioning** n aire m acondicionado

**aircraft** ['er·kræft] n avión m

**airdrome** ['er·droʊm] n aeródromo m

**air-dry** vt secar al aire

**airfare** n precio m del billete de avión [*or Méx, Col* del tiquete]

**airfield** n aeródromo m

**airframe** n armazón m

**airfreight** n carga f aérea

**airhead** n inf cabeza mf hueca

**air lane** n vía f aérea

**airlift** I. n puente m aéreo II. vt aerotransportar

**airline** n línea f aérea, aerolínea f AmL

**airmail** I. n correo m aéreo II. vt enviar por correo aéreo

**air mass** n masa f de aire

**air mattress** n colchón m inflable

**air piracy** n piratería f aérea

**airplane** n avión m

**air pocket** n bolsa f de aire

**air pollution** n contaminación f atmosférica

**airport** n aeropuerto m

**airport terminal** n terminal f aérea

**air pump** n bomba f de aire

**air rifle** n rifle m de aire comprimido

**airship** n zepelín m

**air show** n exhibición f aérea

**airsick** *adj* mareado, -a; **to get ~** marearse (en avión)

**airspace** n espacio m aéreo

**airstrip** n pista f de aterrizaje

**air taxi** n aerotaxi m

**airtight** *adj* hermético, -a

**airtime** n TV tiempo m en antena

**airway** ['er·weɪ] n ruta f aérea; ANAT vía f respiratoria

**airy** ['er·i] *adj* 1. ARCHIT espacioso, -a 2. (*light*) ligero, -a 3. (*lacking substance*) etéreo, -a

**aisle** [aɪl] n pasillo m ▶ to take sb down the ~ llevar al altar a alguien

**ajar** [ə·'dʒar] *adj* entreabierto, -a

**AK** n abbr of **Alaska** Alaska f

**AKA, aka** abbr of **also known as** alias

**akin** [ə·'kɪn] *adj* ~ **to** parecido a

**AL** n abbr of **Alabama**

**Alabama** [ˌæl·ə·'bæm·ə] n Alabama f

**à la mode** [ˌɑ·lɑ·'moʊd] *adj* con helado

**alarm** [ə·'lɑrm] I. n 1. alarma f; **to cause sb ~** alarmar a alguien; **fire ~** alarma de incendios; **burglar ~** dispositivo m antirrobo 2. (*clock*) reloj m despertador II. vt alarmar; **to be ~ed** estar alarmado

**alarming** *adj* alarmante

**Alaska** [ə·'læs·kə] n Alaska f

**albacore** ['æl·bə·kɔr] n ZOOL albacora f

**albino** [æl·'baɪ·noʊ] *adj*, n albino, -a m, f

**album** ['æl·bəm] n álbum m

**alcohol** ['æl·kə·hɔl] n alcohol m

**alcohol-free** *adj* sin alcohol

**alcoholic** [ˌæl·kə·'hɔ·lɪk] *adj*, n alcohólico, -a m, f

**alcoholism** n alcoholismo m

**ale** [eɪl] n cerveza f

**alert** [ə·'lɜrt] I. *adj* despierto, -a; **to keep ~** mantenerse alerta II. n (on the) ~ alerta f; (*alarm*) alarma f III. vt alertar

**alfalfa** [æl·'fæl·fə] n BOT alfalfa f

**alfresco** [æl·'fres·koʊ] *adv* al aire libre

**alga** ['æl·gə] n <algae> pl alga f

**algebra** ['æl·dʒə·brə] n álgebra f

**alias** ['eɪ·li·əs] *adv*, n alias m inv

**alibi** ['æl·ə·baɪ] n coartada f

**alien** ['eɪ·li·ən] I. *adj* (*foreign*) extranjero, -a; (*strange*) extraño, -a; **~ to sb** ajeno a alguien II. n (*foreigner*) extranjero, -a m, f; (*extraterrestrial*) extraterrestre mf

**alienate** ['eɪ·li·ə·neɪt] vt distanciar; (*property*) enajenar

**alienation** [ˌeɪ·li·ə·'neɪ·ʃən] n distanciamiento m; (*of property*) enajenación f

**alight** [ə·'laɪt] I. *adj* **to be ~** estar ardiendo; **to set sth ~** prender fuego a algo; (*with enthusiasm, joy*) resplandeciente II. vi (on branch) posarse; (*from vehicle*) apearse

**alignment** n alineación f; **to be out of ~** no estar alineado

**alike** [ə·'laɪk] I. *adj* **to look ~** parecerse; **Clara and Carl ~** tanto Clara como Carl

**II.** *adv* por igual

**alimony** ['æl·ɪ·moʊ·ni] *n* pensión *f* alimenticia

**alive** [ə·'laɪv] *adj* **1.** to be ~ estar vivo **2.** (*active*) activo, -a; **the wine come** ~ dar vida a algo **3.** (*aware*) to be ~ to sth ser consciente de algo

**alkaline** ['æl·kə·laɪn] *adj* alcalino, -a

**all** [ɔl] **I.** *adj* todo, -a; ~ **the wine** todo el vino; ~ **my sisters** todas mis hermanas **II.** *pron* **1.** (*everybody*) todos, -as; ~ **but him** todos menos él; **once and for** ~ de una vez por todas **2.** (*everything*) todo; **most of** ~ sobre todo; **for** ~ **I know** que yo sepa **3.** (*the whole quantity*) todo, -a; ~ **of Cuba** toda Cuba; ~ **I want is...** lo único que quiero es... **4.** SPORTS **two** ~ dos a dos **III.** *adv* totalmente; **it's** ~ **the same** me da igual

**Allah** ['æl·ə] *n* REL Alá *m*

**all-day** *adj* que dura todo el día

**allegation** [æl·ɪ·'geɪ·ʃən] *n* acusación *f*

**allege** [ə·'ledʒ] *vt* afirmar; **it is** ~d **that...** se dice que...

**alleged** [ə·'ledʒd] *adj* supuesto, -a

**allegedly** [ə·'ledʒ·ɪd·li] *adv* (según) se dice

**allegiance** [ə·'li·dʒəns] *n* lealtad *f*

**allegorical** [æl·ɪ·'gɔr·ɪk·əl] *adj* alegórico, -a

**allegory** ['æl·ɪ·gɔr·i] <-ies> *n* alegoría *f*

**allergic** [ə·'lɜr·dʒɪk] *adj* alérgico, -a

**allergist** ['æl·ər·dʒɪst] *n* alergólogo, -a *m, f*

**allergy** ['æl·ər·dʒi] <-ies> *n* alergia *f*

**alleviate** [ə·'li·vi·eɪt] *vt* aliviar

**alley** ['æl·i] *n* callejón *m;* (*in garden*) paseo *m;* **blind** ~ callejón sin salida ▶ **to be** (**right**) **up one's** ~ ser lo suyo

**alleyway** *n* callejón *m*

**alliance** [ə·'laɪ·əns] *n* alianza *f*

**allied** ['æl·aɪd] *adj* aliado, -a; ~ **with** [*or* **to**] **sth** unido a algo

**alligator** ['æl·ɪ·geɪ·tər] *n* caimán *m*

**alligator pear** *n* aguacate *m*, palta *f Arg, Bol, Chile, Ecua, Perú, Urug*

**all-inclusive** [ɔl·ɪn·'klu·sɪv] *adj* todo incluido; ~ **rate** precio con todo incluido

**alliteration** *n* aliteración *f*

**all-night** *adj* que dura toda la noche; (*open*) abierto, -a toda la noche

**all-nighter** *n inf* **to pull an** ~ tirarse toda la noche (haciendo algo)

**allocate** ['æl·ə·keɪt] *vt* **1.** (*assign*) asignar **2.** (*distribute*) repartir

**allocation** [æl·ə·'keɪ·ʃən] *n* **1.** (*assignment*) asignación *f* **2.** (*distribution*) distribución *f*

**allot** [ə·'lat] <-tt-> *vt* asignar

**allotment** *n* adjudicación *f*

**all-out** [ɔl·'aʊt] *adj* total

**allow** [ə·'laʊ] *vt* **1.** (*permit*) permitir; **to** ~ **sb to do sth** dejar a alguien hacer algo; **smoking is not** ~ed se prohíbe fumar **2.** (*allocate*) asignar; **please – up to 7 days for delivery** entrega en un plazo máximo de 7 días **3.** (*admit*) **to** ~ **that...** reconocer que...

◆**allow for** *vt* tener en cuenta

**allowable** *adj* (*error*) permisible; (*expenses*) deducible

**allowance** [ə·'laʊ·əns] *n* **1.** (*permitted amount*) cantidad *f* permitida **2.** (*pocket money*) paga *f* **3.** (*preparation*) **to make** ~(**s**) **for sth** tener algo en cuenta **4.** (*excuse*) **to make** ~**s for sb** ser indulgente con alguien; **to make** ~**s for sth** tolerar algo

**all-purpose** [ɔl·'pɜr·pəs] *adj* multiuso

**all right** **I.** *adj* bien; **that's** ~ (*after thanks*) de nada; (*after excuse*) no pasa nada; **to be** ~ (*healthy*) estar bien; (*safe*) estar sano y salvo **II.** *interj* de acuerdo **III.** *adv* **1.** (*well*) bien **2.** (*certainly*) con (toda) seguridad **3.** (*in answer*) vale

**allspice** ['ɔl·spaɪs] *n* pimienta *f* de Jamaica

**all-star** *adj* estelar

**all-terrain vehicle** *n* vehículo *m* todoterreno

**allude** [ə·'lud] *vi* aludir (**to** a)

**alluring** [ə·'lʊr·ɪŋ] *adj* (*attractive*) atractivo, -a; (*enticing*) tentador(a)

**all-weather** *adj* para todo tiempo

**ally** ['æl·aɪ] **I.** <-ies> *n* **1.** (*country*) aliado, -a *m, f* **2.** (*supporter*) partidario, -a *m, f* **II.** <-ie-> *vt* **to** ~ **oneself with sb** aliarse con alguien

**alma mater** ['æl·mə·ma·tər] *n* alma máter *f*

**almighty** [ɔl·'maɪ·ti] *adj* todopoderoso, -a

**almond** ['a·mənd] *n* almendra *f;* (*tree*) almendro *m*

**almost** ['ɔl·moʊst] *adv* casi; ~ **half** casi

la mitad; **we're ~ there** casi hemos llegado

**aloe vera** [ˌal·ou·'ver·ə] *n* áloe *m* vera

**aloha** [ə·'lou·ə] *interj* Hawaiian aloha

**alone** [ə·'loun] **I.** *adj* **1.** (*without others*) solo, -a; **to leave ~** dejar en paz **2.** (*unique*) Jane ~ can do that Jane es la única que sabe hacerlo ▶ **let ~** mucho menos **II.** *adv* sólo

**along** [ə·'lɑŋ] **I.** *prep* por; **all ~** a lo largo de; **I lost it ~ the way** lo perdí por el camino; **it's ~ here** está por aquí **II.** *adv* **all ~** todo el tiempo; **to go ~** seguir adelante; **he will be ~ in an hour** llegará en una hora; **come ~!** ¡vente!

**alongside** [ə·'lɑŋ·saɪd] **I.** *prep* junto a **II.** *adv* al lado

**aloof** [ə·'luf] *adj* distante

**aloud** [ə·'laud] *adv* en voz alta

**alphabet** ['æl·fə·bet] *n* alfabeto *m*

**alphabetical** [ˌæl·fə·'bet·ɪ·kəl] *adj* alfabético, -a; **in ~ order** por orden alfabético

**alphabetize** *vt* alfabetizar

**alpine** ['æl·paɪn] *adj* alpino, -a

**already** [ɔl·'red·i] *adv* ya

**alright** ['ɔl·raɪt] *adv see* **all right**

**also** ['ɔl·sou] *adv* también; **~ known as** alias

**altar** ['ɔl·tər] *n* altar *m*

**altar boy** *n* monaguillo *m*

**altar girl** *n* monaguilla *f*

**alter** ['ɔl·tər] **I.** *vt* cambiar; (*paint*) retocar; (*dress, suit*) hacer ajustes a; (*dog, cat*) castrar **II.** *vi* cambiarse

**alteration** [ɔl·tər·'eɪ·ʃən] *n* modificación *f*; (*in house*) reforma *f*

**altercation** [ɔl·tər·'keɪ·ʃən] *n* altercado *m*

**alter ego** ['al·tər·i·gou] *n* **1.** PSYCH álter ego *m* **2.** (*close friend*) amigo *m* íntimo

**alternate** ['ɔl·tər·neɪt] **I.** *vi, vt* alternar **II.** *adj* **1.** (*by turns*) alterno, -a; **on ~ days** en días alternos **2.** (*alternative*) alternativo, -a

**alternating** ['ɔl·tər·neɪ·tɪŋ] *adj* alterno, -a

**alternating current** *n* ELEC corriente *f* alterna

**alternative** [ɔl·'tɜr·nə·tɪv] **I.** *n* alternativa *f*; **to have no ~ but to do sth** no tener otra alternativa que hacer algo

**II.** *adj* alternativo, -a

**alternative-fuel** *adj* compatible con combustibles menos contaminantes

**alternatively** *adv* si no

**alternator** ['ɔl·tər·neɪ·tər] *n* alternador *m*

**although** [ɔl·'ðou] *conj* aunque

**altitude** ['æl·tə·tud] *n* altitud *f*

**alto** ['æl·tou] *n* contralto *mf*

**altogether** [ɔl·tə·'geð·ər] **I.** *adv* (*completely*) totalmente; (*in total*) en total; **not ~** no del todo **II.** *n* **in the ~** en cueros

**altruism** ['æl·tru·ɪz·əm] *n* altruismo *m*

**altruist** ['æl·tru·ɪst] *n* altruista *mf*

**altruistic** [ˌæl·tru·'ɪs·tɪk] *adj* altruista

**aluminum** [ə·'lu·mə·nəm] *n* aluminio *m*

**aluminum foil** *n* papel *m* de plata

**aluminum oxide** *n* alúmina *f*

**always** ['ɔl·weɪz] *adv* siempre

**Alzheimer's disease** ['alts·haɪ·mərz] *n* Alzheimer *m*

**am** [əm, *stressed:* æm] *vi* 1. pers sing *of* **be**

**amateur** ['æm·ə·tʃər] *adj, n* **1.** aficionado, -a *m, f* **2.** *pej* chapucero, -a *m, f*

**amateurish** [ˌæm·ə·'tʃər·ɪʃ] *adj* chapucero, -a

**amaze** [ə·'meɪz] *vt* (*astound*) asombrar; (*surprise*) sorprender

**amazement** *n* asombro *m*; **to stare at sth in ~** quedarse boquiabierto mirando algo; **to my ~** para mi asombro

**amazing** *adj* asombroso, -a, sorpresivo, -a *AmL*; **truly ~** realmente increíble

**Amazon** ['æm·ə·zan] *n* GEO **the ~** el Amazonas

**ambassador** [æm·'bæs·ə·dər] *n* embajador(a) *m(f)*

**amber** ['æm·bər] *n* ámbar *m*

**ambidextrous** [ˌæm·bɪ·'dek·strəs] *adj* ambidextro, -a

**ambient** ['æm·bi·ənt] *adj* ambiental

**ambiguity** [ˌæm·bə·'gju·ə·ti] <-ies> *n* ambigüedad *f*

**ambiguous** [æm·'bɪg·ju·əs] *adj* ambiguo, -a

**ambition** [æm·'bɪʃ·ən] *n* ambición *f*; **she has no ~** no es nada ambiciosa

**ambitious** [æm·'bɪʃ·əs] *adj* ambicioso, -a

**ambulance** ['æm·bju·ləns] *n* ambulancia *f*

**ambush** ['æm·buʃ] I. *vt* tender una emboscada II. *n* <-es> emboscada *f*

**amen** [eɪ·'men] *interj* amén; **~ to that!** ¡así es!

**amend** [ə·'mend] *vt* (*text, constitution*) enmendar; (*plan*) modificar

**amendment** *n* (*to text, constitution*) enmienda *f*; (*to plan*) modificación *f*

**America** [ə·'mer·ɪ·kə] *n* Estados *m* Unidos *pl*; **the ~s** las Américas

**American** [ə·'mer·ɪ·kən] I. *n* americano, -a *m, f*; LING inglés *m* de EEUU *mf*; (*from USA*) estadounidense *mf* II. *adj* americano, -a

**Americanism** *n* americanismo *m*

**amiable** ['eɪ·mi·ə·bəl] *adj* amable

**amicable** ['æm·ɪ·kə·bəl] *adj* amistoso, -a

**amid(st)** [ə·'mɪd(st)] *prep* en medio de, entre

**amiss** [ə·'mɪs] I. *adj* **there's something ~** algo va mal II. *adv* **to take sth ~** tomar algo a mal; **a little courtesy would not go ~** no vendría mal un poco de cortesía

**ammonia** [ə·'moʊn·jə] *n* amoniaco *m*

**ammunition** [ˌæm·jə·'nɪʃ·ən] *n* munición *f*; *fig* argumentos *mpl*

**amnesia** [æm·'ni·ʒə] *n* amnesia *f*

**amnesty** ['æm·nɪ·sti] <-ies> *n* amnistía *f*

**amok** [ə·'mʌk] *adv see* **amuck**

**among(st)** [ə·'mʌn(st)] *prep* entre; **~ friends** entre amigos; (**just**) **one ~ many** (sólo) uno entre tantos; **~ Canadians** entre los canadienses; **~ other things** entre otras cosas

**amorous** ['æm·ər·əs] *adj* amoroso, -a

**amount** [ə·'maʊnt] I. *n* (*quantity*) cantidad *f*; (*of money*) importe *m*; **a check in the ~ of...** un cheque por valor de...; **any ~ of** grandes cantidades de II. *vi* 1. (*add up to*) **to ~ to sth** ascender a algo 2. (*be successful*) **to ~ to sth** llegar a algo

**amp** 1. *abbr of* **ampere** amperio *m* 2. *inf abbr of* **amplifier** bafle *m*

**ampere** ['æm·pɪr] *n* amperio *m*

**ampersand** [ˌæm·pər·'sænd], **ampersat** [ˌæm·pər·'sæt] *n* COMPUT arroba *f*

**amphetamine** [æm·'fet·ə·min] *n* anfetamina *f*

**amphibian** [æm·'fɪb·i·ən] *n* anfibio *m*

**amphibious** [æm·'fɪb·i·əs] *adj* anfibio, -a

**amphitheater** ['æm·fə·θi·ə·tər] *n* anfiteatro *m*

**ample** ['æm·pəl] *adj* 1. (*plentiful*) abundante 2. (*large*) amplio, -a 3. (*enough*) suficiente

**amplifier** ['æm·plə·faɪ·ər] *n* amplificador *m*

**amplify** ['æm·plə·faɪ] <-ie-> *vt* MUS amplificar; (*idea*) desarrollar; (*remark*) aclarar

**amplitude** ['æm·plɪ·tud] *n* amplitud *f*

**amputate** ['æm·pju·teɪt] *vt* amputar

**amuck** [ə·'mʌk] *adv* de forma descontrolada; **to run ~** descontrolarse

**amuse** [ə·'mjuz] *vt* 1. (*entertain*) entretener 2. (*cause laughter*) divertir; **I'm not ~d** no me hace gracia

**amusement** [ə·'mjuz·mənt] *n* 1. (*entertainment*) entretenimiento *m*, (*entertainment*) entretención *f* AmL; **for one's own ~** para entretenerse 2. (*mirth*) diversión *f*; **to conceal one's ~** aguantarse la risa

**amusement park** *n* parque *m* de atracciones

**amusing** *adj* divertido, -a

**an** [ən, *stressed:* æn] *indef art before vowel see* **a**

**anagram** ['æn·ə·græm] *n* anagrama *m*

**anal** ['eɪ·nəl] *adj* anal

**analgesic** [ˌæn·əl·'dʒi·zɪk] I. *adj* analgésico, -a II. *n* analgésico *m*

**analogy** [ə·'næl·ə·dʒi] <-ies> *n* analogía *f*

**analysis** [ə·'næl·ə·sɪs] <-ses> *n* análisis *m inv*; (*psychoanalysis*) psicoanálisis *m inv* ▶ **in the final** [*or* **last**] **~** a fin de cuentas

**analyst** ['æn·ə·lɪst] *n* analista *mf*; **financial ~** analista de inversiones; PSYCH psicoanalista *mf*

**analytic** [ˌæn·ə·'lɪt·ɪk], **analytical** [ˌæn·ə·'lɪt·ɪ·kəl] *adj* analítico, -a

**analyze** ['æn·ə·laɪz] *vt* analizar; PSYCH psicoanalizar

**anarchic** [æn·'ar·kɪk], **anarchical** [æn·'ar·kɪ·kəl] *adj* anárquico, -a

**anarchist** ['æn·ər·kɪst] *adj, n* anarquista *mf*

**anarchy** ['æn·ər·ki] *n* anarquía *f*

**anatomical** [ˌæn·ə·'tam·ɪ·kəl] *adj* anatómico, -a

**anatomy** [ə·'næt̬·ə·mi] <-ies> *n* anatomía *f*

**ancestor** ['æn·ses·tər] *n* precursor(a) *m(f)*; (*of person*) antepasado, -a *m, f*

**ancestral** [æn·'ses·trəl] *adj* ancestral

**anchor** ['æŋ·kər] **I.** *n* ancla *f*; **to be at ~** estar anclado; *fig* sostén *m*; (*news ~*) presentador(a) *m(f)* de noticias **II.** *vt* **1.** NAUT anclar **2.** (*rope, tent*) sujetar **3.** RADIO, TV presentar **III.** *vi* anclar

**anchorman** ['æŋ·kər·mæn] <-men> *n* RADIO, TV presentador *m*

**anchorwoman** ['æŋ·kər·ˌwʊm·ən] <-men> *n* RADIO, TV presentadora *f*

**anchovy** ['æn·tʃoʊ·vi] <-ies> *n* anchoa *f*; (*fresh*) boquerón *m*

**ancient** ['eɪn·ʃənt] *adj* antiguo, -a; *inf* prehistórico, -a; **since ~ times** desde tiempos remotos

**and** [ən, ænd] *conj* y; (*before 'i' or 'hi'*) e; **food ~ drink** comida y bebida; **parents ~ children** padres e hijos; **2 ~ 3 is 5** 2 más 3 son 5; **four hundred ~ twelve** cuatrocientos doce; **more ~ more** cada vez más; **better ~ better** cada vez mejor; **I tried ~ tried** lo intenté una y otra vez ▸ **so on** [*or* **forth**] etcétera

**Andean** ['æn·di·ən] *adj* andino, -a

**Andes** ['æn·diz] *npl* Andes *mpl*

**android** ['æn·drɔɪd] *n* androide *m*

**anecdotal** [ˌæn·ɪk·'doʊt̬·əl] *adj* anecdótico, -a

**anecdote** ['æn·ɪk·doʊt] *n* anécdota *f*

**anemia** [ə·'ni·mi·ə] *n* anemia *f*

**anemic** [ə·'ni·mɪk] *adj* anémico, -a

**anesthesia** [ˌæn·ɪs·'θi·ʒə] *n* anestesia *f*

**anesthetic** [ˌæn·ɪs·'θet̬·ɪk] *n* anestésico *m*; **to be under ~** estar bajo los efectos de la anestesia

**anesthetist** [ə·'nes·θɪ·tɪst] *n* anestesista *mf*

**anesthetize** [ə·'nes·θɪ·taɪz] *vt* anestesiar

**anew** [ə·'nu] *adv* de nuevo

**angel** ['eɪn·dʒl] *n* ángel *m*

**angelic** [æn·'dʒel·ɪk] *adj* angelical

**anger** ['æŋ·ɡər] **I.** *n* enfado *m*, enojo *m* AmL; (*stronger*) ira *f*; **to speak in ~** hablar indignado **II.** *vt* enfadar, enojar AmL

**angina** [æn·'dʒaɪ·nə] *n* angina *f*; **~ pectoris** angina de pecho

**angle** ['æŋ·ɡəl] **I.** *n* **1.** ángulo *m*; **at an ~** (*picture*) torcido, -a; (*hat*) ladeado, -a; **to see sth from a different ~** ver algo desde otro ángulo; **she knows all the ~s** se las sabe todas **2.** (*opinion*) punto *m* de vista **II.** *vt, vi* **1.** (*to fish*) pescar **2.** (*information*) dirigir; **this article is ~d towards teenagers** este artículo se dirige a los adolescentes

**Anglican** ['æŋ·ɡlɪ·kən] *adj, n* anglicano, -a *m, f*; **Anglican Church** Iglesia *f* Anglicana

**Anglophone** *n Can* anglohablante *mf* en Canadá

**Anglo-Saxon** [ˌæŋ·ɡloʊ·'sæk·sən] *adj, n* anglosajón, -ona *m, f*

**angry** ['æŋ·ɡri] *adj* enfadado, -a, enojado, -a AmL; (*crowd*) enfurecido, -a; (*sky*) tormentoso, -a; (*sea*) embravecido, -a; **to make sb ~** enfadar [*or* AmL enojar] a alguien; **to get ~** enfadarse, enojarse AmL (**with** con, **about** por)

**angst** [æŋkst] *n* angustia *f*

**anguish** ['æŋ·ɡwɪʃ] *n* angustia *f*; **to be in ~** estar angustiado (**over** por)

**angular** ['æŋ·ɡjʊ·lər] *adj* angular; (*face*) anguloso, -a

**animal** ['æn·ɪ·məl] **I.** *n a. fig* animal *m* **II.** *adj* animal; (*desires*) carnal

**animate¹** ['æn·ɪ·meɪt] *vt* animar

**animate²** ['æn·ɪ·mɪt] *vt* animado, -a

**animated** *adj* animado, -a; **to become ~** animarse

**animation** [ˌæn·ɪ·'meɪ·ʃən] *n* animación *f*; **computer ~** animación por ordenador [*or* computadora] AmL

**anime** [ə·'nim] *n* anime *m*

**animosity** [ˌæn·ɪ·'mas·ə·t̬i] *n* animosidad *f*

**aniseed, anise seed** ['æn·ɪ·sid] *n* anís *m*

**ankle** ['æŋ·kəl] *n* tobillo *m*

**anklet** ['æŋ·klɪt] *n* **1.** (*chain*) tobillera *f* **2.** (*sock*) calcetín *m* corto

**annex** ['æn·eks] **I.** *n* <-es> **1.** (*building*) edificio *m* anexo **2.** (*of document*) anexo *m* **II.** *vt* (*territory*) anexionar; (*document*) adjuntar

**annexation** [ˌæn·ɪk·'seɪ·ʃən] *n* anexión *f*

**annihilate** [ə·'naɪ·ə·leɪt] *vt* aniquilar

**annihilation** [ə·ˌnaɪ·ə·ˈleɪ·ʃən] n aniquilación f

**anniversary** [ˌæn·ə·ˈvɜr·sə·ri] <-ies> n aniversario m

**annotation** [ˌæn·ə·ˈteɪ·ʃən] n anotación f

**announce** [ə·ˈnaʊns] vt anunciar; (result) comunicar

**announcement** n anuncio m; official ~ comunicado m oficial

**announcer** [ə·ˈnaʊn·sər] n locutor(a) m(f)

**annoy** [ə·ˈnɔɪ] vt molestar, embromar AmL; **to get ~ed** enfadarse [or enojarse] AmL

**annoyance** [ə·ˈnɔɪ·əns] n fastidio m, enojo m AmL

**annoying** adj (noise, fact) molesto, -a, chocante AmL; (person) pesado, -a; **it's ~ to think that...** me da rabia pensar que...; **how ~!** ¡qué fastidio!

**annual** [ˈæn·ju·əl] I. adj anual II. n anuario m; BOT planta f anual

**annually** [ˈæn·ju·ə·li] adv anualmente

**annuity** [ə·ˈnu·ə·ti] <-ies> n renta f anual

**annul** [ə·ˈnʌl] <-ll-> vt anular

**anoint** [ə·ˈnɔɪnt] vt untar

**anointing** n unción f

**anomaly** [ə·ˈnam·ə·li] <-ies> n anomalía f

**anonymity** [ˌæn·ə·ˈnɪm·ɪ·ti] n anonimato m

**anonymous** [ə·ˈnan·ə·məs] adj anónimo, -a; **to remain ~** permanecer en el anonimato

**anorexia** [ˌæn·ə·ˈrek·si·ə] n anorexia f

**anorexic** [ˌæn·ə·ˈrek·sɪk] adj anoréxico, -a

**another** [ə·ˈnʌð·ər] I. pron 1. otro, -a; **it's always one thing or ~** siempre pasa algo 2. (mutual) **one ~** uno a otro; **they love one ~** se quieren II. adj otro, -a; **~ pastry?** ¿otro pastel?; **~ $30** otros 30 dólares

**answer** [ˈæn·sər] I. n 1. (reply) respuesta f; **in ~ to your question** como respuesta a tu pregunta 2. (solution) solución f II. vt responder a; (door) abrir; (need) satisfacer III. vi responder

♦**answer back** vi contestar; **don't ~!** ¡no repliques!

♦**answer for** vt (action, situation) responder de; (person) responder por

♦**answer to** vt 1. (obey) obedecer a 2. (fit) corresponder a

**answerable** [ˈæn·sər·ə·bəl] adj **to be ~ for sth** ser responsable de algo; **to be ~ to sb** tener que rendir cuentas a alguien

**answering machine** n contestador m automático

**ant** [ænt] n hormiga f ▶ **to have ~s in one's pants** ser un manojo de nervios

**antagonistic** [æn·ˌtæg·ə·ˈnɪs·tɪk] adj antagónico, -a

**antagonize** [æn·ˈtæg·ə·naɪz] vt enfadar, enojar AmL

**Antarctic** [ænt·ˈark·tɪk] I. adj antártico, -a II. n **the ~** el Antártico

**Antarctica** [ænt·ˈark·tɪ·kə] n la Antártida

**anteater** [ˈænt·i·tər] n oso m hormiguero

**antelope** [ˈæn·tɪ·loʊp] <-(s)> n antílope m

**antenna** [æn·ˈten·ə] <-nae or -s> n antena f

**anteroom** [ˈæn·tɪ·rum] n antesala f

**anthem** [ˈæn·θəm] n himno m

**anthill** [ˈænt·hɪl] n hormiguero m

**anthropology** [ˌæn·θrə·ˈpal·ə·dʒi] n antropología f

**anti** [ˈæn·ti] I. adj (to be) ~ (estar) en contra II. prep en contra de

**antiabortion** [ˌæn·ti·ə·ˈbɔr·ʃən] adj antiabortista

**antiaging cream** n crema f antiarrugas

**antiaircraft** [ˌæn·ti·ˈer·kræft] adj antiaéreo, -a

**anti-American** adj antiamericano, -a

**antibiotic** [ˌæn·ti·bar·ˈat·ɪk] I. n antibiótico m II. adj antibiótico, -a

**antibody** [ˈæn·tɪ·bad·i] <-ies> n anticuerpo m

**anticipate** [æn·ˈtɪs·ə·peɪt] vt 1. (plan) tener previsto 2. (look forward to) esperar (con ilusión) 3. (act in advance of) anticiparse a

**anticipation** [æn·ˌtɪs·ə·ˈpeɪ·ʃən] n 1. (foresight) previsión f 2. (funds) anticipo m 3. (excitement) ilusión f; **to wait in ~** esperar con gran ilusión

**anticlimax** [ˌæn·tɪ·ˈklaɪ·mæks] <-es> n

decepción f

**antidote** ['æn·tɪ·doʊt] n antídoto m (**to** contra)

**antiestablishment** adj antisistema

**antifreeze** ['æn·tɪ·friz] n anticongelante m

**antihero** [æn·tɪ·'hɪr·oʊ] <-es> n antihéroe m

**antihistamine** [ˌæn·tɪ·'hɪs·tə·ˌmin] n antihistamínico m

**anti-inflammatory** [ˌæn·tɪ·ɪn·'flæm·ə·tɔr·i] adj antiinflamatorio, -a

**Antilles** [æn·'tɪl·iz] npl **the** ~ las Antillas

**antilock braking system** n AUTO sistema m antibloqueo de frenos

**antimatter** ['æn·tɪ·mæt·ər] n antimateria f

**antipasto** [ˌæn·tɪ·'pæs·ti] n entrada f

**antiperspirant** [ˌæn·tɪ·'pɜr·spər·ənt] n antitranspirante m

**antipollution** adj anticontaminante

**antiquated** ['æn·tɪ·kweɪ·tɪd] adj anticuado, -a

**antique** [æn·'tik] I. n antigüedad f; (old-fashioned) antigualla f II. adj antiguo, -a; (old-fashioned) anticuado, -a

**antiquity** [æn·'tɪk·wə·t̬i] <-ies> n antigüedad f

**antirust** [ˌæn·tɪ·'rʌst] adj antioxidante

**anti-Semitism** [æn·tɪ·'sem·ə·tɪz·əm] n antisemitismo m

**antiseptic** [ˌæn·tə·'sep·tɪk] I. n antiséptico m II. adj antiséptico, -a

**antisocial** [ˌæn·tɪ·'soʊ·ʃəl] adj antisocial

**antithetic** [ˌæn·tɪ·'θet̬·ɪk], **antithetical** [ˌæn·tɪ·'θet̬·ɪ·kəl] adj antitético, -a

**antivirus** [ˌæn·tɪ·'vaɪ·rəs] adj COMPUT antivirus inv

**antiwar** [ˌæn·tɪ·'wɔr] adj antibélico, -a

**antiwrinkle cream** [ˌæn·tɪ·'rɪŋ·kəl·ˌkrim] n crema f antiarrugas

**antler** ['ænt·lər] n cuerno m; ~**s** cornamenta f

**anus** ['eɪ·nəs] n ano m

**anvil** ['æn·vɪl] n yunque m

**anxiety** [æŋ·'zaɪ·ə·t̬i] n 1. (concern) inquietud f; PSYCH ansiedad f 2. (desire) ansia f (**to, for** de)

**anxious** ['æŋk·ʃəs] adj 1. (concerned) preocupado, -a (**about** por) 2. (eager) ansioso, -a; **to be** ~ **for sth/to do sth** estar ansioso por algo/por hacer algo

**any** ['en·i] I. adj 1. (some) algún, alguna; **do they have** ~ **money?** ¿tienen dinero?; **do you want** ~ **more soup?** ¿quieres más sopa? 2. (not important which) cualquier; **come at** ~ **time** ven cuando quieras 3. (in negatives) ningún, ninguna; **I don't have** ~ **money** no tengo dinero II. adv 1. (not) **she doesn't come here** ~ **more** ya no viene 2. (at all) **does she feel** ~ **better?** ¿se siente algo mejor? III. pron 1. (some) alguno, alguna; ~ **of you** alguno de vosotros; ~ **but him would have gone** cualquier otro habría ido 2. (in negatives) ninguno, ninguna

**anybody** ['en·i·bad·i] pron indef 1. (someone) alguien, alguna 2. (not important which) cualquiera; ~ **but him** cualquiera menos él; ~ **else** cualquier otro 3. (no one) nadie, ninguno

**anyhow** ['en·i·haʊ] adv 1. (in any case) de todas maneras 2. (well) bueno; ~, **as I was saying...** bueno, como iba diciendo... 3. (disorderly) de cualquier manera

**anyone** ['en·i·wʌn] pron indef see **anybody**

**anyplace** ['en·i·pleɪs] adv 1. (interrogative) en alguna parte; **have you seen my glasses** ~? ¿has visto mis gafas en alguna parte? 2. (affirmative) en cualquier parte; **I can sleep** ~ puedo dormir en cualquier sitio 3. (negative) en ninguna parte; **you won't see this** ~ no verás esto en ningún sitio

**anything** ['en·i·θɪŋ] pron indef 1. (something) algo; ~ **else?** ¿algo más?; **is there** ~ **new?** ¿alguna novedad? 2. (each thing) cualquier cosa; **it is** ~ **but funny** es todo menos gracioso; ~ **and everything** cualquier cosa; **to be as fast as** ~ inf ser rapidísimo 3. (nothing) nada; **hardly** ~ casi nada; **for** ~ (in the world) por nada (del mundo)

**anytime** ['en·i·taɪm] adv a cualquier hora

**anyway(s)** ['en·i·weɪ(z)] adv 1. (in any case) de todas maneras 2. (well) bueno; ~, **as I was saying...** bueno, como iba diciendo...

**anywhere** ['en·i·wer] adv 1. (interrogative) en alguna parte; **are we** ~ **near**

finished yet? *inf* ¿nos queda mucho para terminar? **2.** (*positive*) en cualquier parte; **its value is ~ between $25 and $30** vale entre los 25 y los 30 dólares; **to live miles from ~** vivir en el quinto pino; **~ else** en cualquier otro sitio **3.** (*negative*) en ninguna parte

**apart** [ə·'pɑrt] *adv* **1.** (*separated*) aparte; **all joking ~** bromas aparte; **to be 20 miles ~** estar a 20 millas; **far ~** lejos; **to move ~** apartarse; **you and me ~** excepto tú y yo **2. to be ~ from sth** estar apartado de algo; **to set sth ~** apartar algo; **to stand ~** mantenerse apartado **3. to come ~** desprenderse; **to take sth ~** desmontar algo

**apart from** *prep* **1.** (*except*) excepto; **~ that** excepto eso **2.** (*in addition*) aparte de **3.** (*separate*) separado, -a de; **to live ~ sb** vivir separado de alguien

**apartheid** [ə·'pɑrt·heɪt] *n* apartheid *m*

**apartment** *n* apartamento *m*, departamento *m AmL*

**apathetic** [ˌæp·ə·'θet̮·ɪk] *adj* apático, -a

**apathy** ['æp·ə·θi] *n* apatía *f* (*about* respecto)

**ape** [eɪp] **I.** *n* simio *m* ▶ **to go ~** *inf* irse de la olla **II.** *vt* imitar

**aperitif** [əˌper·ə·'tif] *n* aperitivo *m*

**aperture** ['æp·ər·tʃʊr] *n* rendija *f*; PHOT abertura *f*

**aphrodisiac** [ˌæf·rə·'dɪ·zi·æk] **I.** *n* afrodisíaco *m* **II.** *adj* afrodisíaco, -a

**apiculture** ['æ·pɪ·ˌkʌl·tʃər] *n* apicultura *f*

**apiece** [ə·'pis] *adv* cada uno; (*per person*) por cabeza

**apologetic** [əˌpɑl·ə·'dʒet̮·ɪk] *adj* de disculpa; **to be ~ about sth** disculparse por algo

**apologetically** *adv* disculpándose

**apologize** [ə·'pɑl·ə·dʒaɪz] *vi* disculparse; **to ~ to sb for sth** pedir perdón a alguien por algo; **I (do) ~ if...** pido disculpas si...

**apology** [ə·'pɑl·ə·dʒi] <-ies> *n* disculpa *f*; **to make an ~** disculparse; **please accept my apologies** le ruego (que) me disculpe

**apostrophe** [ə·'pɑs·trə·fi] *n* apóstrofo *m*

**Appalachia** [ˌæp·ə·'leɪ·fə] *n* los Apalaches *mpl*

**appall** [ə·'pɔl] *vt* horrorizar; **to be ~ed** estar horrorizado (*or* por) (**at** de/por)

**appalling** *adj* (*behavior*) escandaloso, -a; (*conditions*) horroroso, -a

**apparatus** [ˌæp·ə·'ræt̮·əs] *n* equipo *m*; **a piece of ~** un aparato

**apparent** [ə·'pær·ənt] *adj* **1.** (*clear*) evidente; **to become ~ that** hacerse evidente que **2.** (*seeming*) aparente; **for no ~ reason** sin motivo aparente

**appeal** [ə·'pil] **I.** *vi* **1.** (*attract*) atraer; **the idea doesn't ~ to me** no me atrae la idea **2.** LAW apelar **II.** *n* **1.** (*attraction*) atractivo *m*; **to have ~** tener gancho *inf* **2.** LAW apelación *f*; **court of ~s** tribunal *m* de apelación **3.** (*request*) petición *f*

**appealing** [ə·'pi·lɪŋ] *adj* (*smile*) atractivo, -a; (*idea*) tentador(a); (*eyes*) suplicante

**appealingly** *adv* (*dress*) con estilo; (*look*) de manera suplicante; (*speak*) con tono suplicante

**appear** [ə·'pɪr] *vi* **1.** (*be seen*) aparecer **2.** (*newspaper*) salir; (*book*) publicarse; (*film*) estrenarse **3.** LAW comparecer (*before* ante) **4.** (*seem*) parecer; **it ~s to me that...** me parece que...; **it ~s so** eso parece

**appearance** [ə·'pɪr·əns] *n* **1.** (*instance of appearing*) aparición *f* **2.** LAW comparecencia *f* **3.** (*looks*) aspecto *m* **4.** (**to keep up**) **~s** (guardar las) apariencias **5.** (*performance*) actuación *f*; **stage ~** aparición *f* en escena ▶ **~s can be deceptive** las apariencias engañan

**append** [ə·'pend] *vt* (*document, note*) adjuntar; (*signature*) añadir

**appendage** [ə·'pen·dɪdʒ] *n* apéndice *m*

**appendicitis** [əˌpen·dɪ·'saɪ·t̮ɪs] *n* apendicitis *f inv*

**appendix** [ə·'pen·dɪks] *n* **1.** <-es> ANAT apéndice *m* **2.** <-dices *or* -es> TYPO apéndice

**appetite** ['æp·ə·taɪt] *n* apetito *m*, antojo *m Méx*, afán *m*

**appetizer** ['æp·ə·taɪ·zər] *n* (*first course*) entrante *m*; (*snack*) aperitivo *m*, botana *f Méx*, pasabocas *m inv Col*

**appetizing** ['æp·ə·taɪ·zɪŋ] *adj* apetitoso, -a

**applaud** [ə·'plɔd] *vi, vt* aplaudir

**applause** [ə·'plɔz] *n* aplauso *m*; **loud ~**

fuerte aplauso

**apple** ['æp·əl] n manzana f ▶ **to be the ~ of sb's eye** ser la niña de los ojos de alguien; **the Big Apple** la Gran Manzana

**apple pie** n pastel m de manzana

**apple polisher** n inf pelota mf, regalado, -a m, f Col, barbero, -a m, f Méx

**applesauce** n compota f de manzana

**apple tree** n manzano m

**appliance** [ə·'plaɪ·əns] n aparato m; **electrical ~** electrodoméstico m

**applicable** [ə·'plɪ·kə·bəl] adj aplicable; **delete where not ~** táchese lo que no proceda; **those rules are not ~ anymore** esas normas ya no están vigentes

**applicant** ['æp·lɪ·kənt] n solicitante mf; (for job) candidato, -a m, f

**application** [,æp·lɪ·'keɪ·fən] n 1. (request) solicitud f; **on ~** mediante solicitud 2. (coating) a. COMPUT aplicación f 3. (use) uso m 4. (perseverance) diligencia f

**application form** n (hoja f de) solicitud f

**applied** [ə·'plaɪd] adj aplicado, -a

**apply** [ə·'plaɪ] I. vi 1. (request) presentarse; (college, company) solicitar plaza; **to ~ for a job** solicitar un puesto 2. (be relevant) **to ~ to sb** concernir a alguien II. vt aplicar; (pressure) ejercer; **to ~ oneself** dedicarse (**to** a)

**appoint** [ə·'pɔɪnt] vt 1. (select) nombrar; **to ~ sb as heir** nombrar a alguien heredero 2. (designate) fijar; **at the ~ed time** a la hora señalada

**appointment** [ə·'pɔɪnt·mənt] n 1. (to position) nombramiento m 2. (meeting) cita f; **dentist's ~** cita f con el dentista; **to keep an ~** acudir a una cita; **by ~ only** previa cita

**appointment book** n libro m de visitas

**appraisal** [ə·'preɪ·zəl] n (evaluation) evaluación f; (estimation) estimación f; (performance, evidence) valoración f; (property) tasación f

**appreciable** [ə·'pri·fə·bəl] adj apreciable; (change) notorio, -a; (progress) considerable

**appreciate** [ə·'pri·fi·eɪt] I. vt 1. (value) apreciar 2. (understand) comprender

3. (be grateful for) agradecer II. vi revalorizarse

**appreciation** [ə·,pri·fi·'eɪ·fən] n 1. (gratitude) agradecimiento m 2. (understanding) aprecio m

**appreciative** [ə·'pri·fə·tɪv] adj agradecido, -a

**apprehend** [,æp·rɪ·'hend] vt form 1. (arrest) detener 2. (comprehend) concebir

**apprehension** [,æp·rɪ·'hen·fən] n 1. (arrest) detención f 2. (fear) temor m (**about** por) 3. form (comprehension) comprensión f

**apprehensive** [,æp·rɪ·'hen·sɪv] adj aprensivo, -a, flatoso, -a AmL; **to be ~ about sth** estar inquieto por algo

**apprentice** [ə·'pren·tɪs] n aprendiz(a) m(f), peón, -ona m, f Méx

**approach** [ə·'proʊtʃ] I. vt 1. (get close to) acercarse a 2. (ask) dirigirse a 3. (deal with) abordar II. vi acercarse III. n 1. (coming) aproximación f; **at the ~ of winter** al acercarse el invierno 2. (access) acceso m 3. (proposition) propuesta f 4. (methodology) enfoque m

**approachable** [ə·'proʊ·tʃə·bəl] adj accesible

**appropriate** [ə·'proʊ·pri·ət] adj ~ (**to the occasion**) apropiado (para la ocasión)

**approval** [ə·'pru·vəl] n aprobación f; **to meet with sb's ~** obtener la aprobación de alguien

**approve** [ə·'pruv] I. vi estar de acuerdo (**of** con) II. vt aprobar

**approvingly** [ə·'pru·vɪŋ·li] adv con aprobación

**approx.** [ə·'prak·sɪ·met·li] n abbr of **approximately** aprox.

**approximate¹** [ə·'prak·sɪ·mət] adj aproximado, -a

**approximate²** [ə·'prak·sɪ·meɪt] vt aproximarse a

**approximately** adv aproximadamente

**approximation** [ə·,prak·sɪ·'meɪ·fən] n aproximación f

**Apr.** ['eɪ·prəl] n abbr of **April** abr.

**apricot** ['eɪ·prɪ·kat] n albaricoque m, chabacano m Méx, damasco m AmS

**April** ['eɪ·prəl] n abril m; **in ~** en abril; **at**

the beginning/end of ~ a principios/ finales de abril; **on** ~ (**the**) **fourth** el cuatro de abril

**apron** [ˈeɪ·prən] n (clothing) delantal m

**apt** [æpt] adj 1. (appropriate) apropiado, -a; (comment) oportuno, -a 2. (clever) inteligente 3. **to be** ~ **to do sth** tener tendencia a hacer algo

**apt.** [əˈpɑrt·mənt] n abbr of **apartment** apto.

**aptitude** [ˈæp·tɪ·tud] n aptitud f

**aquacize** [ˈæk·wə·saɪz] n aeróbic m en el agua

**Aqua-Lung**® [ˈæk·wə·lʌŋ] n escafandra f autónoma

**aquaplaning** [ˌak·wəˈpleɪ·nɪŋ] n ≈ esquí m acuático

**aquarium** [əˈkwer·i·əm] <-s or -ria> n acuario m

**Aquarius** [əˈkwer·i·əs] n ASTR Acuario m

**aquatic** [əˈkwæt·ɪk] adj acuático, -a

**aquatics** npl deportes m acuáticos pl

**aqueduct** [ˈæk·wɪ·dʌkt] n acueducto m

**AR** abbr of **Arkansas** Arkansas f

**Arab** [ˈær·əb] adj, n árabe mf

**Arabian** adj árabe

**Arabic** [ˈær·ə·bɪk] n árabe m

**arbitrary** [ˈar·bɪ·trer·i] adj arbitrario, -a

**arbitrate** [ˈar·bɪ·treɪt] vi, vt mediar

**arbitration** [ˌar·bɪˈtreɪ·ʃən] n mediación f

**arbitrator** [ˈar·bɪ·treɪ·tər] n árbitro, -a m, f

**arc** [ark] I. n arco m II. vi arquearse

**arcade** [arˈkeɪd] n 1. (of shops) galería f comercial 2. (around square) soportales mpl 3. (with games) recreativos mpl

**arch** [artʃ] I. n arco m II. vi arquearse III. vt arquear IV. <-er, -est> adj burlón, -ona

**archaeology** [ˌar·ki·ˈal·ə·dʒi] n arqueología f

**archbishop** [ˌartʃ·ˈbɪʃ·əp] n arzobispo m

**archenemy** <-ies> n archienemigo, -a m, f

**archeologist** [ˌar·ki·ˈal·ə·dʒɪst] n arqueólogo, -a m, f

**archeology** [ˌar·ki·ˈal·ə·dʒi] n see **archaeology**

**archer** [ˈar·tʃər] n arquero, -a m, f

**archery** [ˈar·tʃə·ri] n tiro m con arco

**architect** [ˈar·kə·tekt] n arquitecto, -a m, f;

fig artífice mf

**architecture** [ˈar·kə·tek·tʃər] n arquitectura f

**archive** [ˈar·kaɪv] n archivo m

**archway** [ˈartʃ·weɪ] n (entrance) arco m

**Arctic** [ˈark·tɪk] I. n **the** ~ el Ártico II. adj ártico, -a

**Arctic Circle** n círculo m polar ártico

**Arctic Ocean** n Océano m Glacial Ártico

**ardent** [ˈar·dənt] adj ferviente; (desire, plea) vehemente

**arduous** [ˈar·dʒu·əs] adj arduo, -a

**are** [ər, stressed: ar] vi see **be**

**area** [ˈer·i·ə] n 1. a. MATH, SPORTS área f 2. (field) campo m

**area rug** n alfombra f

**arena** [əˈri·nə] n arena f

**aren't** [arnt] = **are not** see **be**

**Argentina** [ˌar·dʒən·ˈti·nə] n Argentina f

**Argentine** [ˈar·dʒən·tin], **Argentinean** [ˌar·dʒən·ˈtin·i·ən] adj, n argentino, -a m, f

**arguable** [ˈar·gju·ə·bəl] adj discutible

**arguably** adv posiblemente

**argue** [ˈar·gju] I. vi 1. (disagree) discutir, alegar AmL 2. (reason) razonar; **to** ~ **against/for sth** abogar contra/a favor de algo II. vt **to** ~ **that...** sostener que...; **to** ~ **sb into doing sth** persuadir a alguien de hacer algo

**argument** [ˈar·gjə·mənt] n 1. (disagreement) discusión f 2. (reasoning) argumento m 3. LAW alegato m

**argumentative** [ˌar·gjə·ˈmen·tə·tɪv] adj discutidor(a)

**arid** [ˈær·ɪd] adj árido, -a

**Aries** [ˈer·iz] n ASTR Aries m

**arise** [əˈraɪz] <arose, arisen> vi surgir (**from** de)

**arisen** [əˈrɪz·ən] pp of **arise**

**aristocracy** [ˌær·ɪ·ˈstak·rə·si] <-ies> n + sing/pl vb aristocracia f

**aristocrat** [əˈrɪs·tə·kræt] n aristócrata m, f

**aristocratic** [əˌrɪs·tə·ˈkræt·ɪk] adj aristocrático, -a

**arithmetic** [əˈrɪθ·mɪ·tɪk] I. n aritmética f II. adj aritmético, -a

**arithmetical** [ˌær·ɪθ·ˈmet·ɪ·kəl] adj aritmético, -a

**Arizona** [ˌær·ɪ·ˈzoʊ·nə] n Arizona f

**ark** [ark] *n* arca *f*; **Noah's ~** el Arca de Noé

**Arkansas** ['ɑr·kən·sɔ] *n* Arkansas *f*

**arm¹** [ɑrm] *n* **1.** ANAT, GEO brazo *m*; **~ in ~** del brazo **2.** (*sleeve*) manga *f* ▸ to welcome with **open** ~s recibir con los brazos abiertos; **to cost an ~ and a leg** costar un ojo de la cara; **to keep sb at ~'s length** guardar las distancias con alguien

**arm²** [ɑrm] MIL **I.** *vt* armar **II.** *n* arma *f*; **under ~s** en armas; **to lay down one's ~s** rendir las armas; **to take up ~s** tomar las armas (**against** contra); **to be up in ~s about** poner el grito en el cielo contra

**armadillo** [ɑr·mə·'dɪl·oʊ] *n* armadillo *m*

**armaments** ['ɑr·mə·mənts] *npl* armamento *m*

**armchair** ['ɑrm·tʃer] *n* sillón *m*

**armed** [ɑrmd] *adj* armado, -a

**armful** ['ɑrm·fʊl] *n* brazada *f*

**armload** *n* brazada *f*

**armor** ['ɑr·mər] *n* **1.** (*protective covering*) blindaje *m* **2.** MIL, ZOOL armadura *f* **3.** (*tanks*) carros *m pl* blindados

**armored** *adj* (*car*) blindado, -a; (*train*) acorazado, -a

**armpit** ['ɑrm·pɪt] *n* axila *f*, sobaco *m*

**armrest** ['ɑrm·rest] *n* apoyabrazos *m inv*

**arm-wrestle** *vi* echar [*or Col* hacer] un pulso, jugar a las vencidas *Méx*

**arm wrestling** *n* pulso *m*

**army** ['ɑr·mi] <-ies> *n* ejército *m*; *fig* multitud *f*; **to join the ~** alistarse

**aroma** [ə·'roʊ·mə] *n* aroma *m*

**aromatherapy** [ə·roʊ·mə·'θer·ə·pi] *n* aromaterapia *f*

**aromatic** [ˌær·ə·'mæt̬·ɪk] *adj* aromático, -a

**arose** [ə·'roʊz] *pt of* **arise**

**around** [ə·'raʊnd] **I.** *prep* **1.** (*surrounding, approximately*) alrededor de; **~ May 10th** sobre el 10 de mayo; **to go ~ the corner** doblar la esquina **2.** (*move within*) por; **to drive ~ Mexico** viajar (en coche) por México **II.** *adv* **1.** (*all over*) alrededor; **all ~** en todas partes; **for miles ~** en millas a la redonda; **to be the other way ~** ser justo lo contrario **2.** (*aimlessly*) **to walk ~** dar una

vuelta; **to stand/hang ~** estar/andar por ahí; **to have been ~** haber visto mundo; (*be experienced*) tener mucha experiencia **3.** (*near by*) por ahí; **to be still ~** seguir ahí

**arouse** [ə·'raʊz] *vt* suscitar; (*anger*) provocar; (*sexually*) excitar

**arraign** [ə·'reɪn] *vt* hacer comparecer

**arrange** [ə·'reɪndʒ] **I.** *vt* **1.** (*organize*) organizar; (*date*) acordar **2.** (*put in order*) arreglar **II.** *vi* **to ~ (for)** disponer; **to ~ to do sth** quedar en hacer algo

**arrangement** *n* **1.** *pl* preparativos *mpl*; **to make ~s** hacer los preparativos (**for** de) **2.** (*agreement*) acuerdo *m* **3.** (*method of organizing sth*) arreglo *m*

**arrears** [ə·'rɪrz] *npl* FIN atraso *m*

**arrest** [ə·'rest] **I.** *vt* detener; **to ~ sb's attention** captar la atención de alguien **II.** *n* detención *f*; **to be under ~** estar detenido

**arrival** [ə·'raɪ·vəl] *n* llegada *f*; **on his ~** a su llegada; **new ~** recién llegado *m*

**arrive** [ə·'raɪv] *vi* llegar; (*be born*) nacer

**arrogance** ['ær·ə·gəns] *n* arrogancia *f*

**arrogant** ['ær·ə·gənt] *adj* arrogante

**arrow** ['ær·oʊ] *n* flecha *f*, jara *f Guat, Méx*

**arrowroot** *n* maranta *f*

**arson** ['ɑr·sən] *n* incendio *m* provocado

**art** [ɑrt] *n* arte *f*

**artery** ['ɑr·t̬ə·ri] <-ies> *n* arteria *f*

**art gallery** *n* (*for exhibits*) museo *m* de arte; (*for selling*) galería *f* de arte

**arthritic** [ɑr·'θrɪt̬·ɪk] *adj* artrítico, -a

**arthritis** [ɑr·'θraɪ·t̬ɪs] *n* artritis *f inv*

**artichoke** ['ɑr·t̬ɪ·tʃoʊk] *n* alcachofa *f*

**article** ['ɑr·t̬ɪ·kəl] *n* artículo *m*; **~ of clothing** prenda *f* de vestir

**articulate¹** [ɑr·'tɪk·jə·lət] *adj* (*person*) que se expresa muy bien; (*speech*) claro, -a; TECH, ANAT articulado, -a

**articulate²** [ɑr·'tɪk·jə·leɪt] *vt* expresar; (*sound, idea*) articular

**artifact** ['ɑr·t̬ə·fækt] *n* artefacto *m*

**artificial** [ˌɑr·t̬ə·'fɪʃ·əl] *adj* artificial; **~ insemination/intelligence** inseminación *f*/inteligencia *f* artificial

**artificial respiration** *n* respiración *f* asistida

**artillery** [ɑr·'tɪl·ə·ri] *n* artillería *f*

**artisan** [ɑr·tɪ·zən] n artesano, -a m, f

**artist** [ˈɑr·tɪst] n artista mf

**artiste** [ɑr·ˈtist] n THEAT artista mf

**artistic** [ɑr·ˈtɪs·tɪk] adj artístico, -a

**artistry** [ˈɑr·tɪ·stri] n arte f

**arts and crafts** n trabajos m pl manuales

**artsy** [ˈɑrt·si] adj see **arty**

**artwork** [ˈɑrt·wɜrk] n ilustraciones fpl

**arty** [ˈɑr·ti] <-ier, -iest> adj 1. inf relacionado con la creación de objetos decorativos o de obras de arte 2. pej pseudoartístico, -a; (film) pretencioso, -a

**as** [əz, stressed: æz] I. prep como; dressed ~ a clown vestido de payaso; ~ a baby, I was... de bebé, yo era... II. conj 1. (in comparison) como; the same name ~ el mismo nombre que; ~ fast ~ tan rápido como; to eat ~ much ~ sb comer tanto como alguien; ~ soon ~ possible lo antes posible 2. (like) (tal) como; ~ it is tal como es; ~ if it were true como si fuese verdad 3. (because) como 4. (while) mientras 5. (although) aunque ▶ ~ **far** ~ (to the extent that) en la medida en que; (concerning) respecto a; ~ **for me** en lo que a mí respecta III. adv ~ **well** también; ~ **long as** mientras que +subj; ~ **much** as tanto como; ~ **soon** as en cuanto

**ASAP** [ˌeɪ·es·eɪ·ˈpi] abbr of **as soon as possible** lo antes posible

**asbestos** [æs·ˈbes·təs] n amianto m

**ascend** [ə·ˈsend] vt, vi ascender; **in** ~ing **order** en orden ascendente

**ascent** [ə·ˈsent] n 1. (climb) ascenso f 2. (slope) pendiente f

**ascertain** [ˌæs·ər·ˈteɪn] vt 1. (find out) averiguar 2. (make sure) comprobar

**ascot** [ˈæs·kət] n FASHION ≈ fular m

**ash**[1] [æʃ] n (from fire) ceniza f

**ash**[2] [æʃ] n BOT fresno m

**ashamed** [ə·ˈʃeɪmd] adj avergonzado, -a; **to be** ~ **of oneself** avergonzarse de uno mismo

**ashore** [ə·ˈʃɔr] I. adj en tierra II. adv a tierra

**ashtray** [ˈæʃ·ˌtreɪ] n cenicero m

**Asia** [ˈeɪ·ʒə] n Asia f

**Asian** [ˈeɪ·ʒən] adj, n asiático, -a m, f

**Asian American** n residente en EEUU

de origen asiático

**Asiatic** [ˌeɪ·ʒi·ˈæt·ɪk] adj asiático, -a

**aside** [ə·ˈsaɪd] adv a un lado; **to stand** [or **step**] ~ hacerse a un lado; **to leave sth** ~ dejar algo a un lado

**aside from** prep aparte de

**ask** [æsk] I. vt 1. (inquire) preguntar; **to** ~ (sb) **a question about sth** hacer (a alguien) una pregunta acerca de algo 2. (request) pedir; **to** ~ **a favor/sb's advice** pedir un favor/consejo a alguien; **to** ~ **100 dollars for sth** pedir 100 dólares por algo; **to** ~ **too much of sb** pedir demasiado de alguien 3. (invite) invitar; **to** ~ **sb to do sth** invitar a alguien a hacer algo II. vi 1. (inquire) preguntar 2. (request) pedir

♦**ask for** vt (request) pedir

**asking** [ˈæs·kɪŋ] n petición f; **it's yours for the** ~**ing** lo tienes a pedir de boca

**asking price** n precio m de venta

**asleep** [ə·ˈslip] adj dormido, -a; **to be/to fall** ~ estar/quedarse dormido

**asocial** [eɪ·ˈsoʊ·ʃəl] adj asocial; (antisocial) antisocial

**asparagus** [ə·ˈspær·ə·gəs] n espárrago m; (plant) esparraguera f

**aspect** [ˈæs·pekt] n 1. (point of view) punto m de vista 2. (feature) faceta f 3. (direction) orientación f 4. (appearance) aspecto m

**asphyxiation** [əs·ˌfɪk·si·ˈeɪ·ʃən] n asfixia f

**aspic** [ˈæs·pɪk] n áspic m

**aspire** [ə·ˈspaɪr] vi aspirar (to a)

**aspirin** [ˈæs·pə·rɪn] n aspirina f

**ass** [æs] <-es> n 1. vulg culo m, siete m AmS, Méx 2. ZOOL (donkey) asno m 3. inf (idiot) burro, -a m, f; **to make an** ~ **of oneself** hacer el burro ▶ vulg **get your** ~ **in gear!** ¡espabílate!; **move your** ~**!** ¡mueve el culo!; **to work one's** ~ **off** trabajar como un burro

**assassinate** [ə·ˈsæs·ə·neɪt] vt asesinar

**assassination** [ə·ˌsæs·ɪ·ˈneɪ·ʃən] n magnicidio m

**assault** [ə·ˈsɔlt] I. n ataque m; **to make an** ~ **on** asaltar II. vt atacar

**assemble** [ə·ˈsem·bəl] I. vi congregarse II. vt 1. (collect) reunir 2. (put together) armar

**assembly** [ə·'sem·bli] <-ies> n 1. (*meeting*) reunión f 2. TECH montaje m

**assent** [ə·'sent] I. n consentimiento m II. vi asentir (**to** a)

**assert** [ə·'sɜrt] vt afirmar; **to ~ oneself** imponerse

**assertion** [ə·'sɜr·ʃən] n afirmación f

**assertive** [ə·'sɜr·tɪv] adj confiado, -a

**assess** [ə·'ses] vt calcular; (*evaluate*) evaluar

**assessment** n 1. (*calculation*) valoración f 2. (*evaluation*) evaluación f

**asset** ['æs·et] n 1. ventaja f; **he is an ~ to the team** es una valiosa aportación al equipo 2. pl activo m

**assign** [ə·'saɪn] vt 1. asignar, apropiar AmL; **to ~ sb to a position** destinar a alguien a un puesto; **to ~ the blame for sth to sb** atribuir la culpa de algo a alguien 2. LAW ceder

**assignment** n 1. (*task*) tarea f; **foreign ~** cargo m en el extranjero; **an ~ to do sth** un encargo de hacer algo 2. (*attribution*) asignación f

**assimilate** [ə·'sɪm·ə·leɪt] I. vt asimilar II. vi asimilarse

**assist** [ə·'sɪst] I. vt ayudar (**with** con) II. vi ayudar (**with** en)

**assistance** [ə·'sɪs·təns] n asistencia f; **to be of ~** ser de ayuda

**assistant** n 1. (*helper*) ayudante mf, suche m Chile 2. COMPUT asistente m

**assn.** [ə·,sou·si·'eɪ·ʃən] n abbr of **association** asoc.

**associate**[1] [ə·'sou·ʃi·ɪt] adj, n asociado, -a m, f; **business ~** socio, -a m, f

**associate**[2] [ə·'sou·ʃi·eɪt] I. vt asociar; **to ~ oneself with sth** relacionarse con algo II. vi relacionarse

**associate's degree** n (*college*) ≈ primer ciclo m

**association** n asociación f; (*involvement*) colaboración f

**assorted** [ə·'sɔr·t̬ɪd] adj surtido, -a

**assortment** [ə·'sɔrt·mənt] n surtido m

**asst.** [ə·'sɪs·tənt] n abbr of **assistant** ayudante

**assume** [ə·'sum] vt 1. (*suppose*) suponer, asumir AmL; **let's ~ that...** supongamos que... 2. (*alias, identity*) adoptar 3. (*undertake*) asumir; (*power*) tomar

**assumed** [ə·'sumd] adj supuesto, -a

**assumption** [ə·'sʌmp·ʃən] n 1. (*supposition*) supuesto m; **on the ~ that...** en el supuesto de que... 2. (*hypothesis*) suposición f 3. (*of office, power*) toma f

**assurance** [ə·'ʃur·əns] n 1. (*self-confidence*) seguridad f; **to have ~** tener confianza 2. (*promise*) garantía f

**assure** [ə·'ʃur] vt garantizar

**assuredly** adv ciertamente

**asterisk** ['æs·tə·rɪsk] n asterisco m

**astern** [ə·'stɜrn] adv (**to go**) ~ (ir) hacia atrás; ~ **of** detrás de

**asteroid** ['æs·tə·rɔɪd] n asteroide m

**asthma** ['æz·mə] n asma m

**asthmatic** [æz·'mæt̬·ɪk] adj, n asmático, -a m, f

**astigmatism** [ə·'stɪg·mə·tɪz·əm] n astigmatismo m

**astonish** [ə·'stan·ɪʃ] vt asombrar

**astonishing** adj asombroso, -a

**astonishment** n asombro m

**astound** [ə·'staund] vt asombrar; **to be ~ed** quedarse atónito

**astray** [ə·'streɪ] adv **to go** ~ (*letter*) extraviarse; (*person*) descarriarse; **to lead sb ~** llevar a alguien por mal camino

**astride** [ə·'straɪd] adv a horcajadas

**astrologer** [ə·'stral·ə·dʒər] n astrólogo, -a m, f

**astrology** [ə·'stral·ə·dʒi] n astrología f

**astronaut** ['æs·trə·nɔt] n astronauta mf

**astronomer** [ə·'stran·ə·mər] n astrónomo, -a m, f

**astronomical** [,æs·trə·'nam·ɪ·kəl] adj astronómico, -a

**astronomy** [ə·'stran·ə·mi] n astronomía f

**AstroTurf**® ['æs·trou·,tɜrf] n césped m artificial

**astute** [ə·'stut] adj astuto, -a

**asylum** [ə·'saɪ·ləm] n asilo m; **insane ~** manicomio m

**at**[1] [ət, æt] prep 1. (*place*) en; ~ **the dentist's** en el dentista; ~ **home/school** en casa/la escuela 2. (*time*) ~ **Christmas** en Navidad; ~ **night** por la noche; ~ **once** enseguida; **all ~ once** de repente; ~ **present** en este momento; ~ **the time** en el momento; ~ **the same time** al mismo tiempo; ~ **three o'clock** a las tres 3. (*towards*) **to laugh ~ sb** reírse de

alguien; **to look ~** sth/sb mirar algo/a
alguien; **to point ~** sb señalar a alguien
**4.** (*in reaction to*) **~** sb's request a petición de alguien; **to be astonished/annoyed ~** sth estar asombrado/molesto
por algo; **to be mad ~** sb estar enfadado
con alguien **5.** (*in amount of*) **~** all para
nada; **~ \$10 a kilo** a \$10 el kilo; **~ 120
mph** a 120 m/h **6.** (*in state of*) **~ best/
worst** en el mejor/peor de los casos; **~
first** al principio; **~ least** al menos; **~
ease** tranquilo; **to be ~ a loss** estar sin
saber qué hacer **7.** **to be good/bad ~
French** ser bueno/malo en francés ▶ **~
all** en realidad; **nobody ~ all** nadie en
absoluto; **not ~ all!** ¡para nada!; (*as answer to thanks*) de nada

**at²** [æt] (*email*) arroba *f*

**at bat** *n* (*baseball*) turno *m* de bateo

**ate** [eɪt] *pt of* **eat**

**atheism** ['eɪ·θi·ɪz·əm] *n* ateísmo *m*

**atheist** ['eɪ·θi·ɪst] *adj*, *n* ateo, -a *m*, *f*

**athlete** ['æθ·liːt] *n* atleta *mf*

**athletic** [æθ·'let·ɪk] *adj* atlético, -a

**athletics** *npl* atletismo *m*

**Atlanta** [æt·'læn·tə] *n* Atlanta *f*

**Atlantic** [ət·'læn·tɪk] **I.** *n* **the ~** (*Ocean*)
el (Océano) Atlántico **II.** *adj* atlántico, -a

**atlas** ['æt·ləs] <-es> *n* atlas *m inv*

**atmosphere** ['æt·mə·sfɪr] *n* atmósfera *f*;
*fig* ambiente *m*

**atmospheric** [ˌæt·mə·'sfer·ɪk] *adj* atmosférico, -a; *fig* evocador(a)

**atom** ['æt·əm] *n* átomo *m*

**atomic** [ə·'tɑm·ɪk] *adj* atómico, -a

**atrocious** [ə·'troʊ·ʃəs] *adj* atroz

**atrocity** [ə·'trɑs·ə·ți] <-ies> *n* atrocidad *f*

**at sign** *n* arroba *f*

**attach** [ə·'tætʃ] *vt* **1.** (*fix onto*) fijar
**2.** (*connect*) ligar **3.** COMPUT adjuntar
**4.** (*join*) unir; **to be ~ed** to tener mucho
apego a **5.** (*assign*) destinar

**attaché** [ˌæt·ə·'ʃeɪ] *n* agregado, -a *m*, *f*

**attachment** [ə·'tætʃ·mənt] *n* **1.** (*fondness*) apego *m*; **to form an ~ to sb** coger cariño a alguien **2.** (*support*) adhesión *f* **3.** (*union*) fijación *f* **4.** (*attached
device*) accesorio *m* **5.** LAW incautación *f*
**6.** COMPUT anexo *m*

**attack** [ə·'tæk] **I.** *n* ataque *m* **II.** *vt* ata-

car, cachorrear *Col*; (*problem*) afrontar
**III.** *vi* atacar

**attain** [ə·'teɪn] *vt* alcanzar

**attainable** *adj* alcanzable

**attainment** *n* logro *m*

**attempt** [ə·'tempt] **I.** *n* **1.** (*try*) intento *m*; **to make an ~ at doing sth** intentar hacer algo **2.** (*attack*) atentado *m*
**II.** *vt* intentar

**attend** [ə·'tend] **I.** *vt* asistir a **II.** *vi*
asistir

**attendance** [ə·'ten·dəns] *n* (*presence*)
asistencia *f*

**attendant** [ə·'ten·dənt] *n* asistente, -a *m*, *f*

**attention** [ə·'ten·ʃən] *n* **1.** (*maintenance*)
cuidado *m* **2.** (*care, notice*) atención *f*;
**to pay ~** prestar atención; **to turn one's
~s to sth** dirigir la atención hacia algo

**attentive** [ə·'ten·tɪv] *adj* atento, -a; **to be
~ to sb** ser atento con alguien

**attest** [ə·'test] *vt*, *vi* (*demonstrate*) testimoniar; (*authenticate*) atestiguar

**attic** [æt·ɪk] *n* desván *m*, tabanco *m AmC*,
entretecho *m CSur*

**attitude** ['æt·ɪ·tud] *n* **1.** (*opinion*) actitud *f* (**towards** hacia) **2.** (*position*)
postura *f*

**attorney** [ə·'tɜr·ni] *n* abogado, -a *m*, *f*

**attorney-at-law** *n* <attorneys-at-law>
abogado, -a *m*, *f*

**attract** [ə·'trækt] *vt* atraer, jalar *AmL*; **to
be ~ed** sentirse atraído (**by** por)

**attraction** [ə·'træk·ʃən] *n* atracción *f*; (*appeal*) atractivo *m*; **to feel an ~ to sb**
sentirse atraído por alguien

**attractive** [ə·'træk·tɪv] *adj* atractivo, -a

**attribute** [ə·'trɪb·jut] *vt* atribuir; **to ~ sth
to sb** atribuir algo a alguien; **to ~ importance to sth** dar importancia a algo

**ATV** [ˌeɪ·ti·'vi] *n abbr of* **all terrain vehicle** vehículo *m* todoterreno

**at-will** *adj* (*contract, basis*) rescindible
sin previo aviso; (*employee, employment*) cuyo contrato es rescindible sin
previo aviso

**auction** ['ɔk·ʃən] **I.** *n* subasta *f* **II.** *vt*
subastar

**audacious** [ɔ·'deɪ·ʃəs] *adj* **1.** (*bold*) audaz **2.** (*impudent*) descarado, -a

**audible** ['ɔ·də·bəl] *adj* perceptible

**audience** ['ɔ·di·əns] *n* audiencia *f*; (*spec-*

tators) público *m*; (*of book*) lectores *mpl*

**audio** [ˈɔ·dɪ·ou] I. *adj inv* de audio II. *n* audio *m*

**audio-visual** *adj* audiovisual

**audition** [ɔ·ˈdɪʃ·ən] THEAT I. *n* audición *f* II. *vi* hacer una prueba

**auditor** [ˈɔ·də·t̬ər] *n* UNIV oyente *mf*

**auditorium** [ˌɔ·də·ˈtɔr·i·əm] <-s *or* auditoria> *n* auditorio *m*

**Aug.** *n abbr of* **August** ago. *m*

**au gratin** [ou·ˈgra·tən] *adj* gratinado, -a

**August** [ˈɔ·gəst] *n* agosto *m*; *s. a.* **April**

**aunt** [ænt] *n* tía *f*

**au pair** [ou·ˈper] *n* au pair *mf*

**aura** [ˈɔr·ə] *n* aura *f*

**aural** [ˈɔr·əl] *adj* auditivo, -a

**aurora borealis** [ɔ·ˈrɔr·ə·ˌbɔr·i·ˈæl·ɪs] <aurora borealises *or* aurorae boreales> *n* aurora *f* boreal

**austere** [ɔ·ˈstɪr] *adj* austero, -a

**austerity** [ɔ·ˈster·ə·t̬i] <-ies> *n* austeridad *f*

**Australia** [ɔ·ˈstreɪl·jə] *n* Australia *f*

**Australian** *adj, n* australiano, -a *m, f*

**Austria** [ˈɔ·stri·ə] *n* Austria *f*

**Austrian** *adj, n* austriaco, -a *m, f*

**authentic** [ɔ·ˈθen·t̬ɪk] *adj* auténtico, -a

**authenticity** [ˌɔ·θən·ˈtɪs·ə·t̬i] *n* autenticidad *f*

**author** [ˈɔ·θər] I. *n* autor(a) *m(f)*; *fig* creador(a) *m(f)* II. *vt* escribir

**authoritarian** [ə·ˌθɔr·ə·ˈter·i·ən] *adj, n* autoritario, -a *m, f*

**authoritative** [ə·ˈθɔr·ə·teɪ·t̬ɪv] *adj* **1.** (*assertive*) autoritario, -a **2.** (*reliable*) autorizado, -a

**authority** [ə·ˈθɔr·ə·t̬i] <-ies> *n* **1.** (*power*) autoridad *f*; **the authorities** las autoridades *f* **2.** (*permission*) autorización *f* ▶ **to have sth on good ~** saber algo de buena tinta; **to have sth on sb's ~** saber algo a través de alguien

**authorization** [ˌɔ·θər·ɪ·ˈzeɪ·ʃən] *n* autorización *f*

**authorize** [ˈɔ·θə·raɪz] *vt* autorizar

**autobiographical** [ˌɔ·t̬ə·baɪ·ə·ˈgræf·ɪ·kəl] *adj* autobiográfico, -a

**autobiography** [ˌɔ·t̬ə·baɪ·ˈag·rə·fi] *n* autobiografía *f*

**autocross** *n* autocross *m*

**autograph** [ˈɔ·t̬ə·græf] I. *n* autógrafo *m* II. *vt* autografiar

**automated** *adj* automatizado, -a

**automated teller machine** *n* cajero *m* automático

**automatic** [ˌɔ·t̬ə·ˈmæt·ɪk] I. *n* máquina *f*; (*car*) coche *m* automático II. *adj* automático, -a

**automobile** [ˈɔ·t̬ə·mou·bil] *n* automóvil *m*; **~ accident** accidente de coche

**automotive** [ˌɔ·t̬ə·ˈmou·t̬ɪv] *adj inv* automovilístico, -a

**autonomous** [ɔ·ˈtan·ə·məs] *adj* autónomo, -a

**autonomy** [ɔ·ˈtan·ə·mi] *n* autonomía *f*

**autopsy** [ˈɔ·tap·si] <-ies> *n* autopsia *f*

**autumn** [ˈɔ·təm] *n* otoño *m*; **in (the) ~** en (el) otoño

**autumnal** [ɔ·ˈtʌm·nəl] *adj* otoñal

**auxiliary** [ɔg·ˈzɪl·jə·ri] <-ies> *adj, n* auxiliar *mf*

**av.** **1.** *abbr of* **average** media *f* **2.** *abbr of* **avenue** Avda.

**avail** [ə·ˈveɪl] *n* provecho *m*; **to no ~** en vano

**available** [ə·ˈveɪ·lə·bəl] *adj* **1.** (*obtainable*) disponible; **to make sth ~ to sb** poner algo a disposición de alguien **2.** (*free*) libre; **to be ~ to do sth** tener tiempo para hacer algo **3.** (*single*) **to be ~** estar libre y sin compromiso

**avalanche** [ˈæv·ə·læntʃ] *n* avalancha *f*

**avenge** [ə·ˈvendʒ] *vt* vengar; **to ~ oneself** vengarse

**avenue** [ˈæv·ə·nu] *n* **1.** avenida *f*, carrera *f* *AmL* **2.** (*possibility*) vía *f*

**average** [ˈæv·ər·ɪdʒ] I. *n* promedio *m*; **above/below ~** por encima/por debajo de la media; **on ~** por término medio II. *adj* **1.** medio, -a; **~ Joe** un tipo corriente **2.** (*mediocre*) mediocre

**aversion** [ə·ˈvɜr·ʒən] *n* aversión *f* (**to** hacia)

**avert** [ə·ˈvɜrt] *vt* prevenir; (*eyes, thoughts*) apartar

**aviary** [ˈeɪ·vi·er·i] *n* pajarera *f*

**aviation** [ˌeɪ·vi·ˈeɪ·ʃən] *n* aviación *f*

**avid** [ˈæv·ɪd] *adj* ávido, -a

**avocado** [ˌæv·ə·ˈka·dou] <-s *or* -es> *n* aguacate *m*

avoid [ə·'vɔɪd] *vt* evitar; (*when moving*) esquivar; **to ~ doing sth** evitar hacer algo

**avoidable** *adj* evitable

**avoidance** *n* evasión *f*

**await** [ə·'weɪt] *vt* aguardar; **eagerly ~ed** esperado con ansiedad

**awake** [ə·'weɪk] I. <awoke *or* awaked, awoken *or* awaked> *vi* despertarse; **to ~ to sth** *fig* darse cuenta de algo II. *vt* despertar III. *adj* **1.** despierto, -a; **to stay/lie ~** mantenerse despierto **2.** *fig* alerta; **to be ~ to sth** estar alerta ante algo

**awakening** [ə·'weɪ·kə·nɪŋ] *n* despertar *m*

**award** [ə·'wɔrd] I. *n* premio *m*; (*reward*) recompensa *f*; MIL condecoración *f* II. *vt* otorgar; (*grant*) conceder

**aware** [ə·'wer] *adj* **to be ~ that** saber que; **not that I'm ~ of** no, que yo sepa; **to be ~ of sth** ser consciente de algo

**awareness** [ə·'wer·nɪs] *n* conciencia *f*

**away** [ə·'weɪ] *adv* **1.** (*distant*) **5 miles ~** a 5 millas; **far ~** lejos; **to be miles ~** *fig* no prestar atención **2.** (*absent*) fuera; **to be ~ on vacation** estar de vacaciones **3.** (*future*) **it's only a week ~** sólo queda una semana; **right ~!** ¡enseguida! **4.** (*continuously*) **to read/eat ~** leer/comer sin cesar

**away from** *prep* lejos de; **~ the town** lejos del pueblo; **~ each other** alejados el uno del otro; **to stay ~ sth/sb** mantenerse alejado de algo/alguien; **to go ~ sth** alejarse de algo

**awe** [ɔ] *n* sobrecogimiento *m*; **to hold sb in ~** tener un gran respeto por alguien

**awe-inspiring** *adj* imponente

**awesome** ['ɔ·səm] *adj* imponente; *inf* fabuloso

**awful** ['ɔ·fəl] *adj* terrible; **an ~ lot** muchísimo

**awfully** ['ɔ·fə·li] *adv* terriblemente; (*very*) muy; **I'm ~ sorry** lo siento muchísimo

**awhile** [ə·'hwaɪl] *adv* **to wait ~** esperar un rato

**awkward** ['ɔk·wərd] *adj* **1.** (*difficult*) difícil **2.** (*embarrassed*) incómodo, -a; (*question*) delicado, -a **3.** (*inconvenient*) inoportuno, -a **4.** (*clumsy*) torpe

**awl** [ɔl] *n* punzón *m*

**awning** ['ɔ·nɪŋ] *n* toldo *m*

**awoke** [ə·'woʊk] *pt of* **awake**

**awoken** [ə·'woʊ·kən] *pp of* **awake**

**ax(e)** [æks] I. *n* hacha *f*; **the ~** el hacha
▶ **to get the ~** *inf* (*worker*) ser despedido; (*project*) ser anulado II. <axing> *vt* recortar

**axis** ['æk·sɪs] *n* eje *m*

**axle** ['æk·səl] *n* eje *m*, cardán *m AmC, Ven, Col*; **back/front ~** eje trasero/delantero

**aye** |aɪ] *n* the **~s** los votos a favor

**AZ** *n abbr of* **Arizona** Arizona *f*

# B

**B, b** [bi] *n* **1.** (*letter*) B, b *f*; **~ as in Bravo** B de Barcelona **2.** SCHOOL ≈ notable *m*

**babble** ['bæb·əl] *vi* (*baby*) balbucear; (*adult*) parlotear

**babe** [beɪb] *n* **1.** (*woman*) *inf* nena *f* **2.** (*woman*) tía *f* **3.** (*dear*) cariño *m*, mamita *Col*

**baboon** [bæ·'bun] *n* babuino *m*

**baby** ['beɪ·bi] *n* **1.** bebé *m*; **to expect/have a ~** esperar/tener un bebé **2.** (*dear*) nene, -a *m, f*

**baby carriage** *n* cochecito *m* de bebé, carriola *f Méx*

**babysitter** ['beɪ·bɪ·sɪt·ər] *n* canguro *mf*, nana *f Méx*

**bachelor** ['bætʃ·ə·lər] *n* soltero *m*; UNIV licenciado, -a *m, f* (of en)

**back** [bæk] I. *n* **1.** (*opposite of front*) parte *f* trasera; (*hand, paper, envelope*) dorso *m*; (*chair*) respaldo *m*; (*reverse side*) revés *m*; **to know sth ~ to front** al revés; **to know sth ~ to front** saberse algo al derecho y al revés **2.** ANAT espalda *f*; (*animal*) lomo *m*; **to be on one's ~** estar boca arriba; **to break one's ~** deslomarse; **to do sth behind sb's ~** hacer algo a espaldas de alguien; **to turn one's ~ on sb** dar la espalda a alguien **3.** SPORTS defensa *mf* ▶ **to know sth like the ~ of one's hand** conocer algo al dedillo; **to have one's ~ against the wall** estar entre la espada y la pared; **you scratch my ~ and I'll scratch yours** hoy por ti, mañana por mí II. *adj* trasero, -a;

**B**

MED dorsal III. *adv* **1. to be ~** estar de vuelta; **to come ~** volver; **to want sb ~** querer que alguien vuelva; **I want the money ~** quiero que me devuelvan el dinero; **to bring ~ memories** traer viejos recuerdos a la memoria **2.** (*behind*) detrás, atrás; **~ and forth** atrás y adelante; **to look ~** mirar (hacia) atrás; **to sit ~** recostarse **3.** (*in return*) de vuelta **4.** (*into the past*) atrás IV. *vt* respaldar

◆**back away** *vi* echarse atrás
◆**back down** *vi* retirarse
◆**back off** *vi* retroceder; (*personally*) mantener las distancias
◆**back out of** *vt* salir de; *fig* retirarse de
◆**back up** *vt* **1.** (*reverse*) dar marcha atrás **2.** COMPUT hacer copias de seguridad de **3.** (*support*) respaldar

**backbone** *n* columna *f* vertebral; *fig* pilar *m*
**back door** *n* puerta *f* trasera
**backer** ['bæk·ər] *n* partidario, -a *m, f*
**backfire** ['bæk·faɪr] *vi* fallar; (*plan*) fracasar; AUTO petardear, detonar *AmL*
**backgammon** ['bæk·gæm·ən] *n* backgammon *m*
**background** ['bæk·graʊnd] *n* **1.** (*rear view*) fondo *m;* **in the ~** en segundo plano **2.** (*education*) educación *f;* (*training*) formación *f* **3.** (*circumstances*) antecedentes *mpl*
**background music** *n* música *f* de fondo
**backhand** ['bæk·hænd] *n* revés *m*
**backing** ['bæk·ɪŋ] *n* apoyo *m*
**backlash** *n* **1.** (*reaction*) reacción *f* violenta **2.** TYPO barra *f* inversa
**backlog** *n* atraso *m*
**backpack** ['bæk·pæk] I. *n* mochila *f* II. *vi* viajar con mochila
**backpacker** *n* mochilero, -a *m, f*
**back pay** *n* atrasos *m pl* de sueldo
**back seat** *n* asiento *m* trasero
**backside** *n inf* trasero *m*
**backspace** (**key**) *n* tecla *f* de retroceso
**backstabbing** ['bæk·stæb·ɪŋ] *n* habladurías *f pl* a espaldas de alguien, viboreo *m Méx*
**backstage** [bæk·'steɪdʒ] *adv* entre bastidores

**backstory** *n* historia *f* de fondo
**back talk** *n* réplicas *fpl*
**backup** ['bæk·ʌp] *n* **1.** COMPUT copia *f* de seguridad **2.** (*support*) apoyo *m*
**backward** ['bæk·wərd] *adj* **1.** (*to the rear*) hacia atrás **2.** (*slow in learning*) retrasado, -a **3.** (*underdeveloped*) atrasado, -a
**backward(s)** ['bæk·wərdz] *adv* **1.** (*towards the back*) hacia atrás; (*step*) atrás **2.** (*in reverse order*) al revés **3.** (*from better to worse*) a peor **4.** (*into the past*) atrás en el tiempo
**backyard** *n* jardín *m* trasero
**bacon** ['beɪ·kən] *n* beicon *m*, tocino *m AmL*
**bacteria** [bæk·'tɪr·i·ə] *npl* bacteria *f*
**bad** [bæd] <worse, worst> I. *adj* **1.** (*not good*) malo, -a; (*marriage, times*) difícil; (*pain*) fuerte; (*accident, mistake*) grave; **to go ~** echarse a perder; **to feel ~** sentirse mal; **to look ~** tener mal aspecto; **too ~!** ¡qué lástima!; **to use ~ language** decir palabrotas; **~ luck** mala suerte, macacoa *f PRico;* **in ~ taste** de mal gusto; **to have a ~ temper** tener mal carácter; **to have a ~ heart/back** estar mal del corazón/de la espalda **2.** (*harmful*) perjudicial (**for** para) ▸ **to go from ~ to worse** ir de mal en peor II. *adv inf* mal
**bad dream** *n* pesadilla *f*
**badge** [bædʒ] *n* insignia *f*, placa *f Méx*
**badger** ['bædʒ·ər] I. *n* tejón *m* II. *vt* importunar
**badly** ['bæd·li] <worse, worst> *adv* **1.** mal; **to think ~ of sb** pensar mal de alguien; **to come out of sth ~** salir mal parado de algo **2.** (*very much*) desesperadamente
**badminton** ['bæd·mɪn·tən] *n* bádminton *m*
**baffle** ['bæf·əl] I. *vt* **1.** (*confuse*) desconcertar **2.** (*hinder*) impedir II. *n* deflector *m;* (*audio*) bafle *m*
**baffling** *adj* desconcertante
**bag** [bæg] **1.** *n* bolsa *f*, busaca *f Col, Ven;* (*handbag*) bolso *m;* (*sack*) saco *m;* **to pack one's ~s** hacer las maletas; *fig* marcharse **2.** (*under eyes*) ojera *f* II. *vt* <-gg-> **1.** (*groceries*) meter en una bol-

sa **2.** *inf* (*obtain*) agenciarse

**baggage** ['bæg·ɪdʒ] *n* equipaje *m*; **excess ~** exceso *m* de equipaje

**baggage car** *n* vagón *m* de equipaje, breque *m Ecua, Perú, RíoPl*

**baggage check** *n* documentación *f* del equipaje

**baggage claim** *n* recogida *f* del equipaje

**baggy** ['bæg·i] *adj* (*pants*) ancho, -a

**bagpipes** *npl* gaita *f*

**baguette** [bæ·'get] *n* pan *m* francés

**Bahamas** [bə·'ha·məz] *npl* **the ~** las Bahamas

**Bahamian** [bə·'hæ·mi·ən] *adj*, *n* bahameño, -a *m, f*

**bail** [beɪl] *n* fianza *f*; **on ~** bajo fianza

**bait** [beɪt] **I.** *n* cebo *m*; *fig* señuelo *m*; **to swallow the ~** morder el anzuelo **II.** *vt* cebar; (*person*) acosar

**bake** [beɪk] **I.** *vi* cocerse; *inf* (*place*) ser un horno **II.** *vt* hornear; (*harden*) tostar

**baker** ['beɪ·kər] *n* panadero, -a *m, f*

**bakery** ['beɪ·kə·ri] *n* panadería *f*

**baking** *adj* it's ~ **hot** hace un calor asfixiante

**baking powder** *n* levadura *f*

**baking soda** *n* bicarbonato *m* de sodio

**balance** ['bæl·ənts] **I.** *n* **1.** (*device*) balanza *f* **2.** *fig* equilibrio *m*; **to lose one's ~** perder el equilibrio **3.** (*in bank account*) saldo *m* **4.** (*to be paid*) balance *m* **II.** *vi* mantener el equilibrio **III.** *vt* **1.** (*compare*) contrapesar; **to ~ sth against sth** comparar algo con algo **2.** (*keep in a position*) estabilizar **3.** (*achieve equilibrium*) equilibrar; **to ~ the books** hacer cuadrar las cuentas; **to ~ working and having a family** compaginar el trabajo con la familia

**balanced** *adj* equilibrado, -a; **a ~ diet** una dieta equilibrada

**balance sheet** *n* balance *m*

**balcony** ['bæl·kə·ni] *n* balcón *m*

**bald** [bɔld] *adj* **1.** calvo, -a, pelón, -ona *Méx*; **to go ~** quedarse calvo **2.** (*plain*) escueto, -a

**baldness** ['bɔld·nɪs] *n* calvicie *f*, pelada *f CSur*

**bale** [beɪl] **I.** *n* fardo *m* **II.** *vt* embalar

**ball** [bɔl] *n* **1.** *SPORT* pelota *f*; (*big*) balón *m*; **to play ~** jugar a la pelota; *fig* cooperar **2.** (*round form*) bola *f* **3.** (*dance*) baile *m* ▶ **to have a ~** divertirse; **to get the ~ rolling** poner las cosas en marcha

**ballad** ['bæl·əd] *n* balada *f*

**balladeer** [ˌbæl·ə·'dɪr] *n* cantautor(a) *m(f)*

**ballast** ['bæl·əst] *n NAUT* lastre *m*

**ballerina** [ˌbæl·ə·'ri·nə] *n* bailarina *f*

**ballet dancer** *n* bailarín, -ina *m, f*

**ball game** *n* partido *m* de béisbol

**ballistic** [bə·'lɪs·tɪk] *adj* balístico, -a ▶ **to go ~** *sl* ponerse como un basilisco

**balloon** [bə·'lun] **I.** *n* globo *m* ▶ **to go over like a lead ~** fracasar estrepitosamente **II.** *vi* inflarse

**balloonist** *n* ascensionista *mf*

**ballot** ['bæl·ət] *n* **1.** (*paper*) papeleta *f* **2.** (*election*) sufragio *m* **3.** (*process*) votación *f*

**ballot box** *n* urna *f*

**ballot paper** *n* papeleta *f*

**ballpark** *n* estadio *m* de béisbol; **a ~ figure** una cifra aproximada

**ballplayer** *n* jugador(a) *m(f)* de béisbol

**ballpoint (pen)** *n* bolígrafo *m*, birome *m RíoPl*

**ballroom** *n* salón *m* de baile

**balm** [bam] *n MED* bálsamo *m*; *fig* consuelo *m*

**bamboo** [bæm·'bu] *n* bambú *m*

**ban** [bæn] **I.** *n* prohibición *f* **II.** *vt* <-nn-> prohibir; **she was ~ned from driving** le prohibieron conducir

**banal** [bə·'nal] *adj* banal

**banana** [bə·'næn·ə] *n* plátano *m*, banana *f AmL* ▶ **to go ~s** *sl* irse de la olla

**band¹** [bænd] *n* **1.** (*strip, range*) *a.* TEL banda *f* **2.** (*stripe*) franja *f* **3.** (*ribbon*) cinta *f*; **head ~** cinta *f* del pelo; **waist ~** faja *f* **4.** (*ring*) anillo *m*; **wedding ~** alianza *f*

**band²** [bænd] *n MUS* grupo *m*; (*of friends*) pandilla *f*; (*of robbers*) banda *f*

◆**band together** *vi* agruparse

**bandage** ['bæn·dɪdʒ] **I.** *n* vendaje *m* **II.** *vt* vendar

**Band-Aid®** *n* tirita *f*

**bandit** ['bæn·dɪt] *n* bandido, -a *m, f*, carrilano, -a *m, f Chile*

**bandstand** *n* quiosco *m* (de música)

**bandwagon** *n* **to jump on the ~** subirse al carro

**bandwidth** *n* ancho *m* de banda

**bandy** ['bæn·di] **I.** <-ier, -iest> *adj* patizambo, -a **II.** *vt* <-ies, -ied> intercambiar

**bang** [bæŋ] **I.** *n* **1.** golpe *m*; (*explosion*) detonación *f* **2.** **~s** flequillo *m*, pollina *f PRico, Ven* ▸ **to go over with a ~** salir a las mil maravillas **II.** *adv* **1.** **smack ~ in the middle of the road** en el mismísimo centro de la calzada **2. to go ~** estallar **III.** *interj* bang **IV.** *vi* (*make noise*) dar golpes; (*explode*) estallar; (*slam*) cerrarse de golpe **V.** *vt* golpear; **to ~ one's head against/on sth** darse un golpe en la cabeza contra/con algo

**banish** ['bæn·ɪʃ] *vt a. fig* desterrar; **to ~ sth from one's mind** apartar algo de la mente

**banister** ['bæn·ə·stər] *n* pasamano *m*

**bank**[1] [bæŋk] **I.** *n* **1.** FIN banco *m*; GAMES banca *f* **2.** (*storage*) depósito *m*; **blood/data ~** banco de sangre/datos ▸ **to be laughing all the <u>way</u> to the ~** ganar mucha pasta **II.** *vi* **to ~ with** tener una cuenta en; **to ~ on sb/sth for sth** contar con alguien/algo para algo **III.** *vt* depositar

**bank**[2] [bæŋk] **I.** *n* (*edge*) orilla *f* **II.** *vi* AVIAT ladearse

**bank**[3] [bæŋk] *n* (*earth, snow*) montículo *m*; (*fog*) banco *m*; (*clouds*) masa *f*

◆ **bank up I.** *vi* amontonarse **II.** *vt* amontonar

**bank account** *n* cuenta *f* bancaria

**bankbook** *n* libreta *f* bancaria

**bank charges** *n* gastos *m pl* bancarios

**banker** ['bæŋ·kər] *n* banquero, -a *m, f*

**bank holiday** *n* día *m* festivo

**banking** *n* banca *f*

**bank manager** *n* gerente *mf* de banco

**bank note** *n* billete *m*

**bankrupt** ['bæŋk·rʌpt] **I.** *n* quebrado, -a *m, f* **II.** *vt* llevar a la bancarrota **III.** *adj* **to be ~** estar en quiebra; **to go ~** quebrar

**bankruptcy** ['bæŋk·rəp·si] *n* <-ies> bancarrota *f*

**bank transfer** *n* transferencia *f* bancaria

**banner** ['bæn·ər] *n* **1.** (*flag*) bandera *f* **2.** (*placard*) pancarta *f* **3.** (*Internet*) anuncio *m*

**banquet** ['bæŋ·kwət] *n* banquete *m*

**baptism** ['bæp·tɪz·əm] *n* bautismo *m*

**Baptist** ['bæp·tɪst] *n* bautista *mf*; **the Baptist Church** la Iglesia Bautista

**baptize** ['bæp·taɪz] *vt* bautizar

**bar**[1] [bar] **I.** *n* **1.** (*metal, wood*) barra *f*; (*cage, prison*) reja *f*; (*chocolate*) tableta *f*; (*gold*) lingote *m*; (*soap*) pastilla *f*; (*color*) franja *f*; (*sand*) banco *m*; **to be behind ~s** estar entre rejas **2.** (*restriction*) obstáculo *m* **3.** (*nightclub*) bar *m*; (*counter*) barra *f*; (*in store*) mostrador *m* **4.** **task/scroll/space ~** barra de tareas/de desplazamiento/espaciadora **II.** *vt* <-rr-> **1.** (*obstruct*) obstruir; (*door, window*) atrancar; (*way, path*) obstaculizar **2. to ~ sb from doing sth** prohibir a alguien hacer algo **3.** (*exclude*) excluir

**bar**[2] [bar] *prep* excepto; **~ none** sin excepción

**Bar** [bar] *n* abogacía *f*

**barb** [barb] *n* (*insult*) comentario *m* hiriente

**barbaric** [bar·'ber·ɪk] *adj* bárbaro, -a

**barbecue** ['bar·bɪ·kju] *n* barbacoa *f*, parrillada *f Col, Ven*, asado *m Chile*

**barbed** [barbd] *adj* de púas; *fig* mordaz

**barber** ['bar·bər] *n* barbero, -a *m, f*

**bar code** *n* código *m* de barras

**bare** [ber] **I.** *adj* **1.** (*naked*) desnudo, -a; (*uncovered*) descubierto, -a; **with one's ~ hands** con sus propias manos; **the ~ facts** [*or* **truth**] la pura verdad; **the ~ minimum** lo mínimo; **the ~ necessities** las necesidades básicas **2.** (*empty*) vacío, -a; **to be ~ of sth** estar desprovisto de algo **II.** *vt* desnudar

**barefoot** ['ber·fʊt] *adv* descalzo, -a

**barely** ['ber·li] *adv* **1.** (*hardly*) apenas, agatas *Arg, Urug, Par* **2.** (*scantily*) escasamente

**bargain** ['bar·gɪn] **I.** *n* **1.** (*agreement*) trato *m*; **to drive a hard ~** saber regatear; **to strike a ~** cerrar un trato **2.** (*item*) ganga *f*, pichincha *f Arg, Bol, Par, Urug*, mamada *f AmC, Bol, Chile,*

Perú ▶ **into** the ~ por si fuera poco
II. *vi* negociar; (*haggle*) regatear; **to ~
away** malvender

♦**bargain for, bargain on** *vi* contar con

**bargain basement** *n* sección *f* de ofertas

**bargain sale** *n* rebajas *fpl*

**barge** [bardʒ] I. *n* barcaza *f* II. *vt* empujar; **to ~ one's way through sth** abrirse
paso por algo

♦**barge in** *vi* (*intrude*) colarse; **sorry to
~** *fig* disculpe si me entrometo

♦**barge into** *vi* chocar con

♦**barge through** *vi* abrirse paso a empujones

**bar graph** *n* gráfico *m* de barras

**bark**¹ [bark] I. *n* ladrido *m* ▶ **his ~ is
worse than his bite** perro ladrador
poco mordedor *prov* II. *vi* ladrar; (*person*) gritar III. *vt* gritar

♦**bark out** *vt* gritar

**bark**² [bark] *n* (*tree*) corteza *f*

**barkeeper** ['bar·ki·pər] *n* (*owner*) tabernero, -a *m, f;* (*bartender*) camarero, -a *m, f*

**barley** ['bar·li] *n* cebada *f*

**barman** ['bar·mən] *n* <-men> camarero *m*

**barn** [barn] *n* granero *m*

**barnyard** *n* corral *m*

**baroque** [bə·'rouk] *adj a. fig* barroco, -a

**barrage** [bə·'raʒ] *n fig* aluvión *m*

**barrel** ['bær·əl] I. *n* barril *m;* (*gun*) cañón *m* ▶ **to be a ~ of fun** [*or* **laughs**]
ser una panzada de reír; **to have sb
over a ~** tener a alguien en su puño
II. *vi* <-l-> *inf* ir disparado; **to ~ along** ir
a toda pastilla [*or* a mil] *Col, Méx* III. *vt*
<-l-> embarrilar

**barren** ['bær·ən] *adj* (*infertile*) estéril;
(*landscape*) árido, -a; ~ **years** años
perdidos

**barricade** ['bær·ə·keɪd] I. *n* barricada *f*
II. *vt* atrincherar

**barrier** ['bær·i·ər] *n* barrera *f;* **language ~**
barrera lingüística

**barring** ['bar·ɪŋ] *prep* ~ **accidents** a
menos que surja un imprevisto; ~ **complications** a menos que se presenten
complicaciones; ~ **delays** a menos que
se produzcan retrasos

**bartender** ['bar·ten·dər] *n* camarero,
-a *m, f*

**barter** ['bar·tər] I. *n* trueque *m* II. *vi* comerciar III. *vt* cambiar (**for** por)

**base** [beɪs] I. *n* 1. (*lower part*) *a.* MIL
base *f;* (*of a company*) sede *f* 2. (*bottom*) fondo *m* 3. (*support*) apoyo *m*
4. (*basis*) fundamento *m* ▶ **to be off
~** ir desencaminado; **to touch ~** tocar
fondo II. *vt* basar; **to be ~d** (*company*)
tener su sede; (*person*) trabajar (**in** en)
III. *adj* vil; (*metal*) impuro, -a

**baseball** ['beɪs·bɔl] *n* béisbol *m*

**baseless** ['beɪs·lɪs] *adj* sin fundamento;
(*accusation*) infundado, -a

**base pay** *n* salario *m* base

**bash** [bæʃ] I. *n* porrazo *m;* *sl* juerga *f*
II. *vt* (*thing*) golpear; (*person*) pegar

♦**bash into** *vi insep* estrellarse contra

♦**bash up** *vt inf* (*car*) estrellar

**bashful** ['bæʃ·fəl] *adj* tímido, -a

**basic** ['beɪ·sɪk] *adj* básico, -a; **a ~ command of** conocimientos básicos de

**basically** *adv* básicamente

**basil** ['beɪ·zəl] *n* albahaca *f*

**basilica** [bə·'sɪl·ɪ·kə] *n* basílica *f*

**basin** ['beɪ·sɪn] *n* 1. (*for washing*) lavadero *m* 2. (*sink*) lavabo *m* 3. GEO
cuenca *f*

**basis** ['beɪ·sɪs] *n* <bases> base *f;* **on a
weekly ~** semanalmente

**bask** [bæsk] *vi* **to ~ in the sun** tomar
el sol

**basket** ['bæs·kət] *n* cesta *f;* SPORTS canasta *f*

**basketball** ['bæs·kət·bɔl] *n* baloncesto *m*

**bass**¹ [beɪs] *n* MUS bajo *m*

**bass**² [bæs] *n* ZOOL lubina *f*

**bassoon** [bə·'sun] *n* fagot *m*

**bastard** ['bæs·tərd] *n* 1. (*child*) bastardo,
-a *m, f* 2. *vulg* cabrón, -ona *m, f*

**bat**¹ [bæt] I. *n* murciélago *m* ▶ **to have
~s in the belfry** estar mal de la azotea;
**to be as blind as a ~** no ver tres en un
burro II. *vt* **to ~ one's eyelashes** pestañear; (*at sb*) guiñar un ojo

**bat**² [bæt] SPORTS I. *n* bate *m;* (*blow*)
golpe *m* ▶ **right off the ~** al instante
II. *vt, vi* <-tt-> batear

**batch** [bætʃ] *n* <-es> tanda *f;* COM, COMPUT
lote *m*

**bated** ['beɪ·tɪd] *adj* **with ~ breath** conteniendo la respiración

**bath** [bæθ] *n* (*action*) baño *m*, bañada *f Méx*; **to take a ~** bañarse

**bathe** [beɪð] I. *vi* bañarse II. *vt* bañar; (*wound, eyes*) lavar

**bathing** *n* **~ prohibited** prohibido bañarse

**bathing cap** *n* gorro *m* de baño

**bathing suit** *n* bañador *m*, malla *f RíoPl*, vestido *m* de baño *Col*

**bathing trunks** *npl* bañador *m*

**bath mat** *n* alfombrilla *f* de baño

**bathrobe** *n* albornoz *m*, bata *f Col, Méx*

**bathroom** *n* (cuarto *m* de) baño *m*; (*lavatory*) aseo *m*; (*public*) servicio *m*

**bath towel** *n* toalla *f* de baño

**bathtub** *n* bañera *f*, tina *f AmL*

**baton** [bə·'tan] *n* 1. MUS batuta *f* 2. (*of a policeman*) porra *f* 3. SPORTS testigo *m*

**batsman** ['bæts·mən] <-men> *n* bateador *m*

**batter**[1] ['bæt·ər] I. *n* masa *f*; (*for fried food*) rebozado *m* II. *vt* rebozar

**batter**[2] ['bæt·ər] I. *n* SPORTS bateador(a) *m(f)* II. *vt* apalear; (*person, pet*) maltratar; **to ~ the door in** [*or* **down**] echar la puerta abajo III. *vi* **to ~ at the door** aporrear la puerta

**battered** ['bæt·ərd] *adj* 1. maltratado, -a; (*hat, clothes*) estropeado, -a; (*reputation, image*) maltrecho, -a 2. CULIN rebozado, -a

**battery** ['bæt·ə·ri] <-ies> *n* pila *f*; AUTO batería *f*; **a ~ of questions** una sarta de preguntas

**battery charger** *n* cargador *m*

**battle** ['bæt·əl] I. *n* lucha *f*; MIL batalla *f* ▶ **that's half the ~** con eso ya hay medio camino andado; **to fight a losing ~** luchar por una causa perdida II. *vi* pelear; (*nonviolently*) luchar III. *vt* combatir

**battlefield, battleground** *n* campo *m* de batalla

**battleship** *n* acorazado *m*

**batty** ['bæt·i] *adj sl* grillado, -a; **to go ~** volverse majara

**bawl** [bɔl] I. *vi* vociferar; (*weep*) berrear II. *vt* gritar; **to ~ out** echar la bronca

**bay**[1] [beɪ] *n* GEO bahía *f*

**bay**[2] [beɪ] *n* ZOOL caballo *m* zaino

**bay**[3] [beɪ] *vi* (*dog, wolf*) aullar

**bay leaf** *n* hoja *f* de laurel

**bay window** *n* mirador *m*

**bazaar** [bə·'zar] *n* 1. (*market*) bazar *m* 2. (*event*) venta *f* benéfica, bazar *m Col*

**BBQ** ['bar·bɪ·kju] *n abbr of* **barbecue** (*event*) barbacoa *f*, parrillada *f Col, Ven*, asado *m Chile*

**B.C.** [ˌbiˈsi] *adv abbr of* **before Christ** a.C.

**be** [bi] <was, been> I. *vi* 1. **+** *n/adj* (*permanent state, quality, identity*) ser; **she's Spanish/a cook** es española/cocinera; **to ~ a good** ser bueno; **to ~ able to do sth** ser capaz de hacer algo; **what do you want to ~ when you grow up?** ¿qué quieres ser de mayor?; **to ~ married/single** estar [*or* CSur ser] casado/soltero; **to ~ a widow** ser viuda 2. **+** *adj* (*mental and physical states*) estar; **to ~ fat/happy** estar gordo/contento; **to ~ hungry/thirsty** tener hambre/sed; **don't ~ too long** no tardes mucho 3. (*age*) tener; **I'm 21** tengo 21 años 4. **to ~ for/against** sth estar a favor/en contra de algo 5. (*calculation, cost*) **two and two is four** dos y dos son cuatro; **these glasses are $2 each** estos vasos cuestan $2 cada uno; **how much is that?** ¿cuánto es? 6. (*measurement*) medir; (*weight*) pesar 7. (*exist, live*) **there is/are** hay; **to let ~** dejar en paz; **to ~ or not to ~** ser o no ser 8. (*location, situation*) estar; **to ~ in Ohio** estar en Ohio; **to ~ in a bad situation** estar en una mala situación; **I've never ~en in to Mexico** nunca he estado en Méjico 9. (*take place*) ser, tener lugar 10. **+** *on* **to ~ on the pill** tomar la píldora; **to ~ on vacation/on a diet** estar de vacaciones/a régimen II. *impers vb* **it's cloudy** está nublado; **it's sunny** hace sol; **it's two o'clock** son las dos; **it's ~en so long!** ¡cuánto tiempo!; **it's ten minutes by bus to the market** el mercado está a diez minutos en autobús III. *aux vb* 1. (*continuation*) estar; **to ~ doing sth** estar haciendo algo; **you're always complaining** siempre te estás quejando **2.** (*passive*) ser; **to ~ discovered by sb** ser descubierto por alguien; **he was asked...** le preguntaron... **3.** (*future*) **we are to visit Peru in the May** vamos a ir a Perú en mayo; **she's leaving tomorrow** se va mañana; **she was never to see her brother again** nunca más volvería a ver a su hermano; **you are to come here right now** vas a venir aquí ahora mismo **4.** (*tag question*) **she is tall, isn't she?** es alta, ¿verdad?

**beach** [biːtʃ] *n* playa *f*

**bead** [biːd] *n* **1.** (*drop*) gota *f* **2.** *pl* collar *m* de cuentas

**beak** [biːk] *n* pico *m;* *inf* napia *f,* naso *m RíoPl*

**be all** *n* **the ~ (and end all)** la única cosa que importa

**beam** [biːm] **I.** *n* **1.** (*ray*) rayo *m;* **high/low ~** AUTO luces *f pl* largas/cortas, luces altas/bajas *Chile, Col* **2.** ARCHIT viga *f* **II.** *vt* transmitir **III.** *vi* brillar; (*smile*) sonreír

**beaming** *adj* **to be ~** estar radiante

**bean** [biːn] **I.** *n* **1.** (*green*) judía *f* verde, habichuela *f Col*, ejote *m Méx*, chaucha *f RíoPl*, poroto *m* verde *Chile*, vainita *f Ven* **2.** (*dried*) alubia *f* **3. coffee ~** grano *m* de café; **vanilla ~** vaina *f* de vainilla ► *inf* **to be full of ~s** estar lleno de vida; **to not have a ~** estar pelado; **to spill the ~s** descubrir el pastel **II.** *vt sl* dar un mamporro

**beanbag** *n* (*toy*) bolsa rellena de alubias usada como pelota; (*chair*) puf *m*

**bean sprout** *n* brote *m* de soja

**bear¹** [ber] *n* oso, -a *m, f*

**bear²** [ber] <bore, borne> **I.** *vt* **1.** (*carry*) llevar; (*weight, responsibility, blame*) cargar con; (*cost*) correr con **2.** (*have*) tener; **to ~ a resemblance to** parecerse a; **to ~ in mind** tener presente; **to ~ sb a grudge** guardar rencor a alguien **3. to ~ oneself** comportarse **4.** (*tolerate*) soportar **5.** (*give birth to*) tener **6.** *a. fig* (*fruit*) dar **II.** *vi* **to ~ east** dirigirse al este; **to ~ right** torcer a la derecha

◆**bear on** *vt* (*be relevant*) tener que ver con; (*affect*) afectar a

◆**bear up** *vi* aguantar

◆**bear with** *vi* tener paciencia con

**bearable** ['ber·ə·bəl] *adj* soportable

**beard** [bɪrd] *n* barba *f*

**bearded** *adj* barbudo, -a

**bearing** ['ber·ɪŋ] *n* **1.** NAUT rumbo *m;* **to get/lose one's ~s** orientarse/desorientarse **2.** (*behavior*) comportamiento *m* ► **to have some ~ on sth** tener que ver con algo

**beast** [biːst] *n* bestia *f*

**beat** [biːt] <beat, beaten> **I.** *n* **1.** (*heart*) latido *m;* (*pulse*) pulsación *f* **2.** MUS tiempo *m;* (*rhythm*) ritmo *m* **3.** (*police*) ronda *f* **II.** *adj* reventado, -a **III.** *vt* **1.** (*strike*) golpear; (*drum*) tocar **2.** (*wings, record*) *a.* CULIN batir **3. to ~ a path** abrirse paso **4.** (*defeat*) ganar; **to ~ sb in** [*or at*] **sth** superar a alguien en algo **5.** (*arrive before*) **he ~ me to the door** llegó antes que yo a la puerta ► **if you can't ~ them, join them** si no puedes vencerlos, únete a ellos; **that ~s everything** ¡eso es el colmo!; **~ it!** *sl* ¡lárgate!; **it ~s me how/why...** no me entra cómo/por qué... **IV.** *vi* (*rain*) caer; (*person*) golpear; (*heart, pulse*) latir

◆**beat back** *vt* rechazar

◆**beat down** **I.** *vi* (*hail, rain*) caer con fuerza; (*sun*) picar **II.** *vt* (*door*) derribar; **I managed to beat him down to 50 cents** conseguí que me lo dejara a 50 centavos

◆**beat off** *vt* rechazar

◆**beat up (on)** *vt* dar una paliza a

**beaten** ['biːt·ən] *pp of* **beat**

**beating** ['biː·tɪŋ] *n* **1.** (*assault, defeat*) paliza *f,* zumba *f AmL* **2.** (*heart*) latido *m*

**beautician** [bjuː·tɪʃ·ən] *n* esteticista *mf*

**beautiful** ['bjuː·tə·fəl] *adj* precioso, -a

**beauty** ['bjuː·ti] <-ies> *n* **1.** (*property*) belleza *f* **2.** *inf* (*specimen*) maravilla *f* **3.** (*advantage*) **the ~ of** lo bueno de ► **~ is in the eye of the beholder** *prov* todo es según el color del cristal con que se mira; **~ is only skin-deep** la belleza está en el interior

**beauty parlor, beauty salon, beauty shop** *n* salón *m* de belleza

**beauty spot** *n* lugar *m* pintoresco; (*on the skin*) lunar *m*

**beaver** ['biː·vər] **I.** *n* **1.** ZOOL castor *m;* *inf* (**eager**) ~ persona trabajadora **2.** *vulg* coño *m*, panocha *f Col, Méx*, cola *f RíoPl* **II.** *vi* to ~ **away** trabajar como una hormiguita

**became** [bɪ·ˈkeɪm] *pt of* become

**because** [bɪ·ˈkɒz] **I.** *conj* porque; just ~ he's smiling doesn't mean he is in love que sonría no significa que esté enamorado; ~ I said that, I had to leave como dije eso, tuve que irme; not ~ I am sad but... no porque esté triste, sino... **II.** *prep* ~ of por; ~ of me por mi culpa

**beckon** [ˈbek·ən] **I.** *vt* llamar por señas; to ~ sb over hacer señas a alguien para que se acerque **II.** *vi* hacer señas (to a)

**become** [bɪ·ˈkʌm] <became, become> *vi* **1.** (+ *adj*) volverse; (+ *n*) llegar a ser; to ~ angry enfadarse; to ~ famous/ old hacerse famoso/viejo; to ~ sad/ happy ponerse triste/feliz; to ~ interested interesarse (in por) **2.** ~ of ser de; what ever became of her? ¿qué fue de ella?

**becoming** [bɪ·ˈkʌm·ɪŋ] *adj* **1.** (*clothes, haircut*) favorecedor(a), sentador(a) *Arg, Chile* **2.** (*behavior*) apropiado, -a

**becquerel** [bə·ˈkrel] *n* becquerel *m*

**bed** [bed] *n* cama *f*; (*ocean*) fondo *m*; (*river*) lecho *m*; to get out of ~ levantarse de la cama; to go to ~ (with sb) acostarse (con alguien); to make the ~ hacer la cama ▶ a ~ of nails un calvario; a ~ of roses un lecho de rosas; to get up on the wrong side of the ~ levantarse con el pie izquierdo

♦**bed down** *vi* acostarse

**bed and breakfast** *n* pensión *f*

**bedclothes** *npl*, **bedding** [ˈbed·ɪŋ], **bed linen** *n* ropa *f* de cama, cobijas *fpl AmL*

**bedraggled** [bɪ·ˈdræg·əld] *adj* **1.** (*wet*) empapado, -a **2.** (*disheveled*) desaliñado, -a

**bedridden** [ˈbed·rɪd·ən] *adj* postrado, -a en cama

**bedroom** [ˈbed·rum] *n* dormitorio *m*, recámara *f Méx*

**bedside** [ˈbed·saɪd] *n* cabecera *f*

**bedside lamp** *n* lámpara *f* de noche

**bedside table** *n* mesita *f* de noche, no-

chero *m Col, Chile, Urug*, buró *m Méx*

**bedspread** [ˈbed·spred] *n* colcha *f*

**bedtime** [ˈbed·taɪm] *n* hora *f* de acostarse; **it's (way) past your** ~ hace rato que deberías estar durmiendo

**bee** [biː] *n* **1.** abeja *f* **2.** (*group*) círculo *m* ▶ to be a busy ~ *iron* estar muy atareado

**beech** [biːtʃ] *n* haya *f*

**beef** [biːf] **I.** *n* ternera *f*, res *f AmC, Méx*; **ground** ~ carne *f* picada de ternera; **roast** ~ rosbif *m* **II.** *vi sl* refunfuñar (about por)

♦**beef up** *vt* mejorar

**beehive** [ˈbiː·haɪv] *n* colmena *f*

**been** [bɪn] *pp of* be

**beep** [biːp] **I.** *n* pitido *m* **II.** *vi* pitar

**beer** [bɪr] *n* cerveza *f*

**beer belly** *n* barriga *f* cervecera

**beer garden** *n* terraza *f* de verano

**beeswax** [ˈbiːz·wæks] *n* cera *f* de abeja

**beet** [biːt] *n* remolacha *f*, betabel *f Méx*; **to turn as red as a** ~ ponerse rojo como un tomate

**beetle** [ˈbiːt·əl] *n* escarabajo *m*

**before** [bɪ·ˈfɔr] **I.** *prep* **1.** (*earlier, preceding*) antes de; to leave ~ sb salir antes que alguien; ~ doing sth antes de hacer algo; to put sth ~ sth else anteponer algo a algo; ~ Christ antes de Cristo **2.** (*in front of*) delante de; ~ our eyes ante nuestros ojos **II.** *adv* antes; I've seen it ~ lo he visto anteriormente; the day ~ el día anterior; two days ~ dos días antes **III.** *conj* antes de que +*subj*; he spoke ~ she went out habló antes de que ella se fuera; he had a glass ~ he went se tomó una copa antes de irse; it was a week ~ he came pasó una semana antes de que llegara; he'd die ~ he'd tell the truth preferiría morir a decir la verdad

**beforehand** [bɪ·ˈfɔr·hænd] *adv* de antemano

**befriend** [bɪ·ˈfrend] *vt* hacerse amigo de

**beg** [beg] <-gg-> **I.** *vt* rogar; to ~ sb to do sth rogar a alguien que haga algo **II.** *vi* **1.** (*beggar*) pedir (limosna) **2.** (*request*) implorar

♦**beg off** *vi* excusarse (from de)

**began** [bɪ·ˈgæn] *pt of* begin

**beggar** ['beg·ər] n mendigo, -a m, f, limosnero, -a m, f AmL ▶ **~s can't be choosers** a buen hambre no hay pan duro

**begin** [bɪ·'gɪn] <began, begun> I. vt empezar; (conversation) entablar; **to ~ doing sth** empezar a hacer algo II. vi empezar; **to ~ with** en primer lugar

**beginner** [bɪ·'gɪn·ər] n principiante mf; **~'s luck** la suerte del principiante

**beginning** I. n 1. (start) principio m, empiezo m Arg, Col, Ecua, Guat; **at [o in] the ~** al principio; **from ~ to end** de principio a fin 2. (origin) origen m II. adj inicial

**begrudge** [bɪ·'grʌdʒ] vt (envy) tener envidia de

**begun** [bɪ·'gʌn] pp of **begin**

**behalf** [bɪ·'hæf] n **on ~ of** (for) en beneficio de; (from) de parte de

**behave** [bɪ·'heɪv] vi 1. (act) comportarse; **to ~ badly/well** portarse mal/bien; **~ yourself!** ¡pórtate bien! 2. (function) funcionar

**behavior** [bɪ·'heɪv·jər] n comportamiento m

**behind** [bɪ·'haɪnd] I. prep 1. a. fig detrás de; **right ~ sb/sth** justo detrás de alguien/algo; **~ the wheel** al volante; **there is somebody ~ this** hay alguien detrás de todo esto 2. **to be ~ sb (all the way)** estar con alguien/algo (hasta el final) 3. **~ time** retrasado; **to be ~ schedule** ir con retraso 4. **to be ~ sb/the times** estar atrasado con respecto a alguien/la época II. adv detrás; **to fall ~** (be slower) quedarse atrás; (in work, studies) atrasarse; **to leave sb ~** dejar a alguien atrás; **to be ~** estar atrasado (in en) III. n inf trasero m

**behindhand** [bɪ·'haɪnd·hænd] adv **to be ~** estar atrasado

**beige** [beɪʒ] adj beige

**being** ['bi·ɪŋ] I. n ser m II. pres p of **be** III. adj after n **for the time ~** por el momento

**belated** [bɪ·'leɪ·tɪd] adj tardío, -a

**belch** [beltʃ] I. n inf eructo m II. vi inf soltar un eructo

**belfry** ['bel·fri] n campanario m

**Belgian** ['bel·dʒən] adj, n belga mf

**Belgium** ['bel·dʒəm] n Bélgica f

**belief** [bɪ·'lif] n opinión f; REL creencia f; **in the ~ that** con la convicción de que

**believable** [bɪ·'li·və·bəl] adj creíble

**believe** [bɪ·'liv] I. vt creer; **would you ~ it?** ¡no lo puedo creer!; **she couldn't ~ her eyes/ears** no podía dar crédito a sus ojos/oídos; **~ it or not** aunque parezca mentira II. vi creer (in en)

**believer** [bɪ·'li·vər] n 1. REL creyente mf 2. (supporter) partidario, -a m, f (in de)

**belittle** [bɪ·'lɪt·əl] vt menospreciar

**bell** [bel] n campana f; (round) cascabel m; (bicycle, door) timbre m ▶ **as clear as a ~** más claro que el agua; **his name/face rings a ~** me suena su nombre/cara

**bellboy** n botones m inv

**bellhop** n botones mf inv

**bellow** ['bel·oʊ] I. vt gritar II. vi bramar III. n grito m; (of animal) bramido m

**bell pepper** n pimiento m [o pimentón m Col] dulce

**belly** ['bel·i] <-ies> n inf panza f

**bellyache** inf I. n dolor m de barriga II. vi quejarse

**bellybutton** n ombligo m

**belly flop** n panzazo m

**belong** [bɪ·'lɑŋ] vi 1. **to ~ to** pertenecer a; (club) ser socio de; (political party) estar afiliado a 2. **where do these spoons ~?** ¿dónde pongo estas cucharas?; **this doesn't ~ here** esto no va aquí; **they ~ together** están hechos el uno para el otro

**belongings** npl pertenencias fpl

**beloved**[1] [bɪ·'lʌv·ɪd] n amado, -a m, f

**beloved**[2] [bi·'lʌvd] adj amado, -a

**below** [bɪ·'loʊ] I. prep 1. (lower than, underneath) debajo de; **~ us** debajo de nosotros; **the river ~ the town** el río más abajo del pueblo 2. (less than) **~ average** por debajo de la media; **it's 4 degrees ~ zero** estamos a 4 grados bajo cero; **children ~ the age of twelve** menores de doce años II. adv abajo; **from ~** desde abajo; **the family ~** los vecinos de abajo

**belt** [belt] I. n 1. FASHION cinturón m 2. TECH correa f 3. (area) zona f 4. sl (punch) tortazo m II. vt sl zurrar III. vi *sl* correr a todo tren

**bench** [bentʃ] *n* banco *m*; SPORTS banquillo *m*; (*worktable*) mesa *f* de trabajo

**bend** [bend] <bent, bent> I. *n* curva *f*; **to go/be around the** ~ *sl* volverse/estar chiflado III. *vi* doblarse; (*road*) hacer una curva III. *vt* (*arms, legs*) doblar; (*head*) inclinar ▶ **to** ~ **sb's ear** comerle la oreja a alguien

◆**bend back** *vt* doblar hacia atrás

◆**bend down** *vi* inclinarse

◆**bend over** *vi* inclinarse ▶ **to** ~ **backwards (to help sb)** mover cielo y tierra (por alguien)

**beneath** [bɪ'niːθ] I. *prep* 1. (*lower than, underneath*) debajo de 2. (*inferior to*) por debajo de II. *adv* abajo

**benefit** ['ben·ɪ·fɪt] I. *n* beneficio *m*; **to derive (much)** ~ sacar (mucho) provecho (**from** a); **to be of** ~ ser de utilidad (**to** a); **for the** ~ **of sb** a beneficio de alguien II. <-t- *or* -tt-> *vi* beneficiarse (**from** de) III. <-t- *or* -tt-> *vt* beneficiar

**bent** [bent] I. *pt, pp of* **bend** II. *n* inclinación *f* III. *adj* torcido, -a; **to be** ~ **on** (**doing**) **sth** estar empeñado en (hacer) algo

**bereavement** [bɪ'riːv·mənt] *n* muerte *f* de un familiar

**Bermuda** [bər·'mjuː·də] *n* las Bermudas

**Bermuda shorts** *n* bermudas *fpl*

**berry** ['ber·i] <-ies> *n* baya *f*

**berserk** [bər·'sɜrk] *adj* **to go** ~ ponerse como loco (**over** por); **Mary goes** ~ **over chocolate** a Mary le chifla el chocolate

**berth** [bɜrθ] *n* camarote *m*; RAIL litera *f*

**beside** [bɪ·'saɪd] *prep* 1. (*next, in comparison to*) al lado de 2. (*together with*) junto a 3. **to be** ~ **oneself** estar fuera de sí; **to be** ~ **the point** no venir al caso

**besides** [bɪ·'saɪdz] I. *prep* (*in addition to*) además de; (*except for*) excepto II. *adv* además; **nothing** ~ nada más

**best** [best] I. *adj superl of* **good**; **the** ~ el/la mejor; **the** ~ **days of my life** los mejores días de mi vida; **wishes!** ¡felicidades! II. *adv superl of* **well** mejor; **the** ~ lo mejor; **as** ~ **as (as) you can** lo mejor que puedas; **at** ~ como mucho, a lo

mucho *Méx* III. *n* SPORTS récord *m*

**bestial** ['bes·tʃəl] *adj* bestial

**bestiality** [ˌbes·tʃi·'æl·ə·t̬i] *n* bestialidad *f*

**best man** *n* padrino *m* (de boda)

**bestseller** *n* éxito *m* de ventas

**bet** [bet] <bet *or* -ted, bet *or* -ted> I. *n* apuesta *f*; **to make a** ~ hacer una apuesta (**with** con) II. *vt* apostar; **I** ~ **you don't!** ¡a que no lo haces! III. *vi* apostar (**on** por) ▶ **I'll** ~! ¡seguro!; **you** ~! ¡ya lo creo!

**beta version** *n* versión *f* beta

**betray** [bɪ·'treɪ] *vt* 1. traicionar; (*promise*) romper; (*trust*) defraudar; (*husband*) engañar 2. (*reveal*) delatar; **to** ~ **sth to sb** revelar algo a alguien

**betrayal** [bɪ·'treɪ·əl] *n* (*disloyalty*) traición *f*

**better** ['bet̬·ər] I. *adj comp of* **good** mejor; **to be** ~ MED estar mejor; **it's** ~ **that way** es mejor así II. *adv comp of* **well** mejor; **I like this** ~ me gusta más esto; **we'd** ~ **stay here** lo mejor es quedarse aquí; **or** ~ **yet...** o mejor aún... III. *n* el/la mejor; **to change for the** ~ cambiar para bien; **the sooner, the** ~ cuanto antes, mejor; **so much the** ~ tanto mejor ▶ **for** ~ **or (for) worse** para bien o para mal IV. *vt* **to** ~ **oneself** superarse; (*financially*) prosperar

**between** [bɪ·'twin] I. *prep* entre; **to eat** ~ **meals** comer entre horas; ~ **the two of us** entre nosotros dos II. *adv* (**in**) ~ en medio de; (*time*) a mitad de

**beware** [bɪ·'wer] *vi* tener cuidado; ~ **of pickpockets!** ¡cuidado con los carteristas!

**bewilder** [bɪ·'wɪl·dər] *vt* desconcertar

**bewildered** *adj* desconcertado, -a

**bewildering** *adj* desconcertante

**bewilderment** *n* desconcierto *m*, azoro *m Méx, Perú, PRico*

**bewitch** [bɪ·'wɪtʃ] *vt* hechizar; *fig* fascinar

**bewitching** *adj* fascinante

**beyond** [bɪ·'jand] I. *prep* 1. (*on the other side*) más allá de; ~ **the mountain** al otro lado de la montaña 2. (*after*) después de; (*more than*) más de; ~ **lunchtime** después del almuerzo; **to stay** ~ **a week** quedarse más de una semana **3.** (*further*) más allá de; ~ **the reach** fuera del alcance (of de); ~ **belief** increíble; **he is** ~ **help** *a. iron* es un caso perdido; ~ **the shadow of a doubt** sin lugar a dudas **4.** (*difficult*) **to be** ~ ésb ser demasiado para alguien II. *adv* **1.** (*past*) **the house** ~ la casa de más allá **2.** (*future*) **the next ten years and** ~ los próximos diez años y más

**biannual** [ˌbaɪˈæn·jʊ·əl] *adj* semestral

**bias** [ˈbaɪ·əs] I. *n* **1.** (*prejudice*) prejuicio *m* **2.** (*one-sidedness*) parcialidad *f*; **without** ~ imparcialmente II. <-s-> *vt* influir; **to** ~ **sb towards/against sb** predisponer a alguien a favor de/en contra de alguien

**biased** *adj* parcial

**bib** [bɪb] *n* babero *m*

**Bible** [ˈbaɪ·bəl] *n* **the** ~ la Biblia

**bibliographic** [ˌbɪb·li·ə·ˈgræf·ɪk]**, bibliographical** *adj* bibliográfico, -a

**bibliography** [ˌbɪb·li·ˈag·rə·fi] <-ies> *n* bibliografía *f*

**bicarbonate** [ˌbaɪˈkar·bə·nɪt] *n* bicarbonato *m*

**bicarbonate of soda** *n* bicarbonato *m* de soda

**bicentenary** [baɪ·ˈsen·ten·ə·ri] <-ies> *n*, **bicentennial** [baɪ·sen·ˈten·ɪ·əl] I. *n* bicentenario *m* II. *adj* bicentenario, -a

**biceps** [ˈbaɪ·seps] *n inv* bíceps *m inv*

**bicker** [ˈbɪk·ər] *vi* reñir

**bickering** *n* riñas *fpl*

**bicycle** [ˈbaɪ·sɪk·əl] *n* bicicleta *f*; **to ride a** ~ montar en bicicleta; **by** ~ en bicicleta

**bicycle lane** *n* carril *m* bici

**bid** [bɪd] I. *n* **1.** (*offer*) oferta *f* **2.** (*attempt*) intento *m* II. <bid, bid> *vi* hacer una oferta; (*auction*) pujar III. <bid, bid> *vt* **1.** pujar **2.** *form* **to** ~ **sb farewell** despedirse de alguien; **to** ~ **sb welcome** dar la bienvenida a alguien

**bidden** [ˈbɪd·ən] *pp of* bid

**bidder** [ˈbɪd·ər] *n* postor(a) *m(f)*; **to the highest** ~ al mejor postor

**bidding** [ˈbɪd·ɪŋ] *n* FIN puja *f*

**bidet** [bɪˈdeɪ] *n* bidé *m*

**biennial** [baɪˈen·i·əl] *adj, n* bienal *f*

**bifocal** [ˈbaɪ·foʊ·kəl] *adj* bifocal

**big** [bɪg] <-ger, -gest> *adj* **1.** (*in size,*

*amount*) grande; (*before sing noun*) gran; **a** ~ **book** un libro grande; ~ **letters** mayúsculas; **the ~ger the better** cuanto más grande mejor **2.** (*older*) mayor; ~ **boy/sister** chico/hermana mayor **3.** (*significant*) gran(de); **a** ~ **day** un gran día; **a** ~ **decision** una decisión importante ▶ **to have a** ~ **heart** tener un buen corazón; **to have a** ~ **mouth** ser un bocazas; **to think** ~ tener grandes aspiraciones

**bigamy** [ˈbɪg·ə·mi] *n* bigamia *f*

**Big Dipper** *n* **the** ~ el Carro

**bigoted** *adj* intolerante; REL fanático, -a

**big shot** *n* pez *m* gordo

**big toe** *n* dedo *m* gordo del pie

**bike** [baɪk] *n* bici *f*; (*motorcycle*) moto *f*

**biker** [ˈbaɪ·kər] *n inf* motero, -a *m, f*

**bikini** [bɪˈki·ni] *n* bikini *m*

**bilateral** [ˌbaɪˈlæt·ər·əl] *adj* bilateral

**bile** [baɪl] *n* ANAT bilis *f inv*

**bilingual** [baɪˈlɪŋ·gwəl] *adj* bilingüe

**bill** [bɪl] I. *n* **1.** (*invoice*) factura *f*; **phone** ~ factura del teléfono; **the** ~**, please** la cuenta, por favor **2.** (*bank note*) billete *m* **3.** (*bird*) pico *m* **4.** POL, LAW proyecto *m* de ley II. *vt* pasar la cuenta (of deudas)

**bill collector** *n* cobrador(a) *m(f)*

**billfold** *n* cartera *f*

**billiards** [ˈbɪl·jərdz] *n* billar *m*

**billion** [ˈbɪl·jən] *n* mil millones *mpl*

**billy club** *n* porra *f*

**bimonthly** [ˌbaɪˈmʌnθ·li] I. *adj* (*twice a month*) quincenal; (*every two months*) bimestral II. *adv* (*twice a month*) quincenalmente; (*once every two months*) bimestralmente

**bin** [bɪn] *n* **trash** ~ cubo *m* de basura, basurero *m Méx*

**binary** [ˈbaɪ·nə·ri] *adj* binario, -a

**binary code** *n* código *m* binario

**bind** [baɪnd] I. *n inf* lío *m;* **to be in a** ~ estar en un lío II. <bound, bound> *vi* unirse III. <bound, bound> *vt* **1.** (*tie together*) atar; (*book*) encuadernar **2.** (*unite*) unir **3.** (*commit*) vincular

**binder** [ˈbaɪn·dər] *n* (*notebook*) carpeta *f*

**binding** [ˈbaɪn·dɪŋ] *adj* vinculante

**binge** [bɪndʒ] *inf* I. *n* (*drink*) borrachera f, vacilada f Méx; (food) comilona f; **to go on a ~** ir de parranda **II.** vi atiborrarse

**bingo** ['bɪŋ·goʊ] interj, n bingo m

**binoculars** [bɪ·'nak·jə·lərz] npl prismáticos mpl, binoculares mpl AmL

**biochemistry** [,baɪ·oʊ·'kem·ɪ·stri] n bioquímica f

**biodegradable** [,baɪ·oʊ·dɪ·'greɪ·də·bəl] adj biodegradable

**biodiversity** [,baɪ·oʊ·dɪ·'vɜr·sə·t̬i] n biodiversidad f

**bioengineering** [,baɪ·oʊ·en·dʒɪ·'nɪr·ɪŋ] n ingeniería f biológica

**biography** [baɪ·'ag·rə·fi] <-ies> n biografía f

**biological** [,baɪ·ə·'ladʒ·ɪ·kəl] adj biológico, -a

**biologist** [baɪ·'al·ə·dʒɪst] n biólogo, -a m, f

**biology** [baɪ·'al·ə·dʒi] n biología f

**biorhythm** ['baɪ·oʊ·rɪð·əm] n biorritmo m

**bird** [bɜrd] n pájaro m; (larger) ave f; **a strange ~** inf un bicho raro ▶ **~s of a feather flock together** Dios los cría y ellos se juntan; **to kill two ~s with one stone** matar dos pájaros de un mismo tiro

**bird bath** n alberquilla f

**birdcage** n jaula f

**bird flue** n gripe f aviar

**bird's-eye view** n vista f panorámica

**bird watching** n observación f de aves

**birth** [bɜrθ] n nacimiento m, paritorio m Cuba, Ven; MED parto m; **by/from/of ~** de nacimiento; **to give ~ to a child** dar a luz a un bebé

**birth certificate** n certificado m de nacimiento

**birth control** n control m de natalidad

**birthday** ['bɜrθ·deɪ] **I.** n cumpleaños m inv; **happy ~!** ¡feliz cumpleaños! **II.** adj de cumpleaños

**birthrate** n tasa f de natalidad

**biscuit** ['bɪs·kɪt] n bizcocho m

**bisexual** [,baɪ·'sek·ʃʊ·əl] adj, n bisexual mf

**bishop** ['bɪʃ·əp] n obispo m; (chess) alfil m

**bit¹** [bɪt] n **1.** (piece) trozo m; **little ~s**

pedacitos mpl; **to smash sth to ~s** romper algo en pedazos **2.** (some) **a ~ of** un poco de; **a ~ of trouble** un problemilla; **a ~ stupid** un poco tonto; **quite a ~** bastante; **not a ~** en absoluto **3.** (part) parte f; **~ by ~** poco a poco; **to do one's ~** poner su granito de arena **4.** (short time) momentito m

**bit²** [bɪt] n COMPUT bit m

**bit³** [bɪt] pt of **bite**

**bitch** [bɪtʃ] **I.** n **1.** ZOOL perra f **2.** offensive sl zorra f, tusa f AmL, Cuba **3.** sl (difficult matter) putada f **II.** vi sl quejarse (**about** de)

**bitchy** ['bɪtʃ·i] adj sl con mala leche

**bite** [baɪt] **I.** <bit, bitten> vt, vi morder; (insect) picar; **to ~ one's nails/lips** morderse las uñas/los labios **II.** n **1.** (dog) mordisco m; (insect) picadura f **2.** (mouthful) bocado m

**biting** ['baɪ·t̬ɪŋ] adj (wind) cortante; (criticism) mordaz

**bitten** ['bɪt·ən] pp of **bite**

**bitter** ['bɪt̬·ər] adj <-er, -est> **1.** (in taste) agrio, -a **2.** (painful) amargo, -a; **to be ~ about sth** estar amargado por algo **3.** (dispute) encarnizado, -a; (wind) cortante

**bitterly** adv **1.** (resentfully) con rencor **2.** (intensely) intensamente

**bitterness** n **1.** (animosity) amargura f; (resentment) resentimiento m (**towards** contra) **2.** (taste) amargor m

**biweekly** [,baɪ·'wik·li] **I.** adj **1.** (every two weeks) quincenal **2.** (twice a week) bisemanal **II.** adv **1.** (every two weeks) quincenalmente **2.** (twice a week) bisemanalmente

**bizarre** [bɪ·'zar] adj extraño, -a; (clothes) estrafalario, -a

**blab** [blæb] <-bb-> vi inf **1.** (reveal secret) chivarse **2.** (talk too much) irse de la lengua

**blabber** ['blæb·ər] vi irse de la lengua

**blabbermouth** n chivato, -a m, f; (talkative) parlanchín, -ina m, f

**black** [blæk] **I.** adj **1.** (color) negro, -a; **~ man/woman** negro, -a m, f **2.** (dark) oscuro, -a **3.** (hands) mugriento, -a, mugroso, -a Méx ▶ **to beat sb ~ and blue** moler a alguien a palos **II.** vt en-

**B**

negrecer III. *n* 1. negro *m;* **in ~** de negro; **in ~ and white** en blanco y negro 2. (*person*) negro, -a *m, f*
◆**black out** *vi* desmayarse

**blackberry** ['blæk-ˌber-i] <-ies> *n* zarzamora *f;* (*plant*) zarza *f*

**blackbird** *n* mirlo *m*

**blackboard** *n* pizarra *f*

**blacken** ['blæk-ən] I. *vt* ennegrecer; (*slander*) desacreditar II. *vi* ennegrecerse

**black hat** *n* COMPUT sombrero *m* negro

**blackhead** ['blæk-hed] *n* espinilla *f*

**black hole** *n* agujero *m* negro

**blackish** ['blæk-ɪʃ] *adj* negruzco, -a

**black light** *n* luz *f* negra

**blacklist** ['blæk-lɪst] I. *vt* poner en la lista negra II. *n* lista *f* negra

**blackmail** ['blæk-meɪl] I. *n* chantaje *m* II. *vt* chantajear; **to ~ sb into doing sth** chantajear a alguien para que haga algo

**blackmailer** ['blæk-ˌmeɪ-lər] *n* chantajista *m*

**black mark** *n* punto *m* en contra

**black market** *n* mercado *m* negro

**black markete(e)r** *n* estraperlista *mf*

**blackness** ['blæk-nɪs] *n* negrura *f;* (*darkness*) oscuridad *f*

**blackout** ['blæk-aʊt] *n* 1. (*faint*) desmayo *m;* **to have a ~** sufrir un desmayo 2. ELEC apagón *m* 3. (*censorship*) bloqueo *m;* **news ~** bloqueo informativo

**black sheep** *n* oveja *f* negra

**bladder** ['blæd-ər] *n* vejiga *f*

**blade** [bleɪd] *n* (*tool, weapon*) hoja *f;* (*grass*) brizna *f*

**blah** [bla] *inf* I. *adj* pesado, -a II. *interj* bla

**blame** [bleɪm] I. *vt* culpar; **to ~ sb for sth, to ~ sth on sb** echar a alguien la culpa de algo; **to be to ~** tener la culpa (**for** de); **I don't ~ you** te comprendo II. *n* culpa *f;* **to lay the ~ for sth on sb** echar a alguien la culpa de algo

**blameless** ['bleɪm-lɪs] *adj* libre de culpa; (*life*) intachable

**bland** [blænd] *adj* (*mild*) suave; (*dull*) soso, -a

**blank** [blæŋk] I. *adj* 1. (*empty*) en blanco; (*look*) inexpresivo, -a; **to go ~** quedarse en blanco 2. (*complete*) absoluto, -a; (*despair*) completo, -a II. *n*

espacio *m*

**blanket** ['blæŋ-kɪt] I. *n* manta *f*, frisa *f RDom, PRico*, cobija *f Méx;* (*snow*) capa *f* II. *vt* cubrir (**in** con)

**blasphemy** ['blæs-fə-mi] *n* blasfemia *f*

**blast** [blæst] I. *vt* volar; (*criticize*) hacer polvo II. *n* 1. (*detonation*) explosión *f* 2. (*wind*) ráfaga *f* 3. *sl* (*party*) juerga *f*, tambarria *f AmC, AmS;* **to have a ~** pasarlo bomba [*or Méx* padre] ▶ (**at**) **full ~** (*volume*) a todo volumen; (*speed*) a toda marcha

**blasted** *adj inf* maldito, -a

**blastoff** ['blæst-af] *n* despegue *m*

**blaze** [bleɪz] I. *vi* brillar; (*fire*) arder; **to ~ with anger** echar chispas II. *n* (*fire*) fuego *m;* (*flames, light*) llamarada *f*

**blazing** ['bleɪ-zɪŋ] *adj* resplandeciente, -a; (*heat*) abrasador(a); (*fire*) vivo, -a; **to have a ~ temper** tener muy mal carácter

**bleach** [blitʃ] I. *vt* blanquear II. *n* lejía *f;* (*for hair*) decolorante *m*

**bleak** [blik] *adj* (*future*) sombrío, -a; (*weather*) gris; (*landscape*) desolador(a)

**bleary** ['blɪr-i] *adj* <-ier, -iest> (*person*) cansado, -a; (*eyes*) lagañoso, -a

**bleary-eyed** *adj* **to be ~** estar medio dormido

**bleat** [blit] I. *vi* balar; (*complain*) quejarse II. *n* balido *m;* (*complaint*) quejido *m*

**bled** [bled] *pt, pp of* **bleed**

**bleed** [blid] <bled, bled> I. *vi* sangrar; (*color*) destintar II. *vt* **to ~ sb dry** dejar seco a alguien

**bleep** [blip] I. *n* pitido *m* II. *vi* pitar III. *vt* censurar con pitidos

**blemish** ['blem-ɪʃ] I. *n* mancha *f;* **a reputation without ~** una reputación intachable II. *vt* manchar

**blend** [blend] I. *n* mezcla *f* II. *vt* mezclar III. *vi* armonizar; **to ~ in** no desentonar

**blender** ['blen-dər] *n* licuadora *f*

**bless** [bles] *vt* bendecir ▶ (**God**) **~ you!** (*sneeze*) ¡Jesús!

**blessed** ['bles-ɪd] *adj* 1. (*holy*) bendito, -a 2. *inf* dichoso, -a; **the whole ~ day** todo el santo día

**blessing** ['bles-ɪŋ] *n* bendición *f* ▶ **it's**

**a ~ in disguise** no hay mal que por bien no venga

**blew** [blu] *pt of* **blow**

**blimp** [blɪmp] *n* zepelín *m*; (*obese*) obeso, -a *m, f*

**blind** [blaɪnd] I. *n* 1. the ~ los ciegos 2. (*window*) persiana *f* II. *vt* cegar III. *adj* ciego, -a; (*without knowledge*) a tientas; **to be ~ in one eye** ser tuerto; **to be ~ to sth** no (querer) ver algo IV. *adv* a ciegas; **to be ~ drunk** estar más borracho que una cuba

**blind date** *n* cita *f* a ciegas

**blindfold** ['blaɪnd·foʊld] I. *n* venda *f* II. *vt* vendar los ojos a III. *adj* con los ojos vendados

**blinding** *adj* (*light*) cegador(a); (*color*) deslumbrante

**blindman's buff** *n* gallina *f* ciega

**blindness** *n* ceguera *f*

**blind spot** *n* punto *m* ciego

**bling** [blɪŋ] *sl* I. *n* joyas *f pl* llamativas y ostentosas II. *adj pred* (*look, outfit*) recargado, -a; (*person*) emperifollado, -a

**blink** [blɪŋk] I. *vt, vi* **to ~ (one's eyes)** parpadear; **she didn't even ~** ni se inmutó II. *n* parpadeo *m* ▶ **in the ~ of an eye** en un abrir y cerrar de ojos

**blinker** ['blɪŋ·kər] *n* AUTO intermitente *m*, direccional *f* Col, Méx; **to turn on the ~** poner el intermitente

**blissful** ['blɪs·fəl] *adj* feliz

**blister** ['blɪs·tər] *n* burbuja *f*; ANAT ampolla *f*

**blizzard** ['blɪz·ərd] *n* ventisca *f*

**blob** [blab] *n* goterón *m*

**block** [blak] I. *n* 1. (*solid lump, building*) *a.* COMPUT bloque *m*; (*group of buildings*) manzana *f*, cuadra *f* AmL; (*barrier*) *a.* SPORTS bloqueo *m* II. *vt* 1. (*road, pipe*) bloquear; (*progress*) obstaculizar 2. COMPUT **to ~ and copy** seleccionar y copiar

◆**block off** *vt* cortar

◆**block out** *vt* (*name*) suprimir; (*memory*) borrar

◆**block up** I. *vt* tapar II. *vi* atascarse, atorozarse AmC; MED taponarse

**blockade** [bla·keɪd] I. *n* bloqueo *m* II. *vt* bloquear; (*block off*) cortar

**blockage** ['blak·ɪdʒ] *n* obstrucción *f*

**block letters** *n* letras *f pl* mayúsculas de imprenta

**blond(e)** [bland] *adj, n* rubio, -a *m, f*, güero, -a *m, f* Méx, Guat, Ven

**blood** [blʌd] *n* sangre *f* ▶ **to have ~ on one's hands** tener las manos manchadas de sangre; **bad ~** mala sangre; **in cold ~** a sangre fría; **her ~ ran cold** se le heló la sangre; **it makes my ~ boil** hace que me hierva la sangre; **to sweat ~** sudar tinta

**blood clot** *n* coágulo *m* de sangre

**blood donor** *n* donante *mf* de sangre

**blood group** *n* grupo *m* sanguíneo

**blood pressure** *n* tensión *f* arterial

**bloodshed** *n* derramamiento *m* de sangre

**bloodshot** ['blʌd·ʃat] *adj* (*eyes*) rojo, -a

**bloodstained** ['blʌd·steɪnd] *adj* manchado, -a de sangre

**blood test** *n* análisis *m inv* de sangre

**bloodthirsty** ['blʌd·ˌθɜr·sti] *adj* sanguinario, -a

**blood transfusion** *n* transfusión *f* de sangre

**bloody** ['blʌd·i] <-ier, -iest> *adj* ensangrentado, -a; (*battle*) sangriento, -a

**bloom** [blum] I. *n* flor *f* II. *vi* florecer

**blooming** ['blu·mɪŋ] *adj* floreciente

**blossom** ['blas·əm] I. *n* flor *f*; **in ~** en flor; **orange ~** azahar *m* II. *vi* florecer; (*mature*) madurar

**blot** [blat] I. *n* borrón *m*; (*reputation*) mancha *f* II. *vt* emborronar; (*dry*) secar

**blouse** [blaʊs] *n* blusa *f*

**blow**[1] [bloʊ] *n* golpe *m*, zuque *m* Col

**blow**[2] [bloʊ] I. <blew, blown> *vi* soplar; (*tire*) reventar II. *vt* 1. MUS tocar 2. **to ~ one's nose** sonarse la nariz 3. (*tire*) reventar 4. *sl* (*spend*) pulirse 5. (*mess up*) echar a perder ▶ *inf* **it blew my mind!** ¡me dejó de piedra!; **to ~ one's top** [*or* **lid**] salirse de sus casillas

◆**blow away** *vt* (*wind*) arrancar

◆**blow down** *vt* derribar

◆**blow out** I. *vt* apagar II. *vi* apagarse

◆**blow up** I. *vi* (*storm*) levantarse; (*bomb*) explotar II. *vt* (*balloon*) inflar

**blow-by-blow** *adj* **a ~ account** una descripción con todo lujo de detalles

**blow-dry** *vt* secar con secador

**blow dryer** n secador m [or Méx secadora f] (de pelo)

**blowgun** n cerbatana f

**blowjob** n vulg mamada f

**blown** [bloʊn] vt, vi pp of **blow**

**blowout** n 1. (tire) pinchazo m 2. sl fiestón m, pachangón m Méx inf, rumba f Col inf

**blowup** n PHOT ampliación f

**blubber** ['blʌb·ər] vi lloriquear

**blue** [blu] I. adj 1. azul; light/dark/pale/deep ~ azul claro/oscuro/pálido/intenso 2. (sad) triste II. n azul m; **sky** ~ azul cielo; **the door is painted** ~ la puerta está pintada de azul ▸ **out of the** ~ cuando menos se espera

**blueberry** ['blu·ber·i] <-ies> n arándano m

**bluff** [blʌf] I. vi tirarse un farol II. vt engañar III. n 1. farol m, bluff m AmL 2. (cliff) acantilado m IV. <-er, -est> adj campechano, -a

**bluish** ['blu·ɪʃ] adj azulado, -a

**blunder** ['blʌn·dər] I. n error m garrafal, embarrada f AmL II. vi cometer un error garrafal, cagarla inf; **to** ~ **into sth** tropezar con algo

**blunt** [blʌnt] adj 1. (not sharp) desafilado, -a, pompo, -a Ecua, Col 2. (direct) directo, -a

**bluntly** adv sin rodeos

**blur** [blɜr] I. vi <-rr-> desdibujarse II. vt <-rr-> desdibujar; (picture) desenfocar III. n (memory) vago recuerdo m

**blurb** [blɜrb] n propaganda f

**blurred** [blɜrd] adj borroso, -a

**blush** [blʌʃ] I. vi ruborizarse II. n rubor m; (makeup) colorete m

**boar** [bɔr] n cerdo m; (wild) ~ jabalí m

**board** [bɔrd] I. n 1. (wood) tabla f 2. (blackboard) pizarra f; (notice board) a. GAMES tablero m 3. ADMIN junta f; ~ **of trade** Cámara f de Comercio 4. **room and** ~ pensión f completa 5. **on** ~ a bordo ▸ **to take sth on** ~ adoptar algo II. vt (ship, plane) subir a bordo de; (bus, train) subir a III. vi (stay) alojarse; (in school) estar interno

◆**board up** vt entablar

**boarder** ['bɔr·dər] n huésped mf; (at a school) interno, -a m, f

**board game** n juego m de mesa

**boarding house** n pensión f

**boarding pass** n tarjeta f de embarque

**boarding school** n internado m

**boardroom** n sala f de juntas

**boast** [boʊst] I. vi alardear II. vt enorgullecerse de; **this house** ~**s 10 rooms** esta casa cuenta con 10 habitaciones III. n alarde m

**boastful** ['boʊst·fəl] adj fanfarrón, -ona, bocatero, -a AmL

**boat** [boʊt] n barco m; (small) barca f; (large) buque m; **to go by** ~ ir en barco ▸ **to be in the same** ~ estar en la misma situación; **to miss the** ~ perder la oportunidad

**boathouse** n cobertizo m

**bob** [bab] <-bb-> I. vi **to** ~ (up and down) agitarse II. n (movement) meneo m

**bobby pin** n horquilla f, pinza f Col

**body** ['bad·i] <-ies> n 1. ANAT, ASTR, CHEM cuerpo m; (dead) cadáver m; fig (person) 2. ADMIN, POL unidad f; (governing) organismo m 3. (amount) cantidad f 4. AUTO carrocería f ▸ **to keep** ~ **and soul together** sobrevivir; **to throw oneself** ~ **and soul into sth** entregarse a algo en cuerpo y alma; **over my dead** ~ ¡por encima del cadáver!; **to sell one's** ~ prostituirse

**bodybuilding** n culturismo m

**bodyguard** n guardaespaldas mf inv, espaldero, -a m, f Ven

**body language** n lenguaje m corporal

**body lotion** n loción f corporal

**body suit** n body m

**bog** [bag] n ciénaga f

◆**bog down** <-gg-> vt **to get bogged down in sth** atrancarse en algo

**boggle** ['bag·əl] I. vi quedarse atónito II. vt **to** ~ **the mind** ser increíble

**boggy** ['bag·i] <-ier, -iest> adj pantanoso, -a

**bohemian** [boʊ·'hi·mi·ən] adj, n bohemio, -a m, f

**boil** [bɔɪl] I. vi, vt hervir; **a hard/soft** ~**ed egg** un huevo duro/pasado por agua II. n **to bring sth to a** ~ calentar algo hasta que hierva; **to be at a** ~ estar hirviendo

**B**

◆**boil away** vi evaporarse

◆**boil down** I. vi it all boils down to... todo se reduce a... II. vt reducir

◆**boil over** vi 1. CULIN irse 2. (person) perder el control; (situation) estallar

◆**boil up** vt hervir

**boiler** ['bɔɪ·lər] n caldera f

**boiling** adj hirviendo; (day, weather) abrasador(a); I am ~ me estoy asando; to be ~ (mad) estar que echa chispas

**boisterous** ['bɔɪ·stər·əs] adj bullicioso, -a; (sea) enfurecido, -a

**bold** [boʊld] <-er, -est> adj 1. (brave) audaz; (color) llamativo, -a 2. (not shy) atrevido, -a; (cheeky) descarado, -a 3. in ~ en negrita

**boldness** n audacia f

**bole** [boʊl] n (tree) tronco m

**Bolivia** [bə·'lɪv·i·ə] n Bolivia f

**Bolivian** [bə·'lɪv·i·ən] adj, n boliviano, -a m, f

**bolt** [boʊlt] I. vi huir II. vt 1. (lock) cerrar con pestillo 2. (fasten down) atornillar III. n 1. (on a door) pestillo m 2. (screw) tornillo m 3. (of lightning) rayo m ▶ to make a ~ for it correr hacia algo IV. adv ~ upright rígido

◆**bolt down** vt (food) engullir

**bomb** [bam] I. n 1. bomba f; (aerosol) aerosol m 2. sl (failure) fiasco m II. vt bombardear

**bomb crater** n cráter m de bomba

**bombing** n atentado m con bomba; MIL bombardeo m

**bombproof** adj a prueba de bombas

**bomb scare** n alerta f de bomba

**bombshell** ['bam·ʃel] n obús m; (surprise) bombazo m inf

**bond** [band] I. n 1. (connection) vínculo m; (friendship, love) lazo m 2. (obligation) obligación f; to break one's ~ romper sus cadenas 3. FIN bono m II. vt 1. (stick) pegar 2. to ~ (together) vincular III. vi adherirse

**bone** [boʊn] I. n hueso m; (of a fish) espina f ▶ ~ of contention manzana f de la discordia; to feel sth in one's ~s tener un presentimiento de algo II. adj óseo III. adv muy IV. vt deshuesar; (fish) quitar las espinas a

◆**bone up for** vt (exam) empollar

**bonfire** ['ban·faɪr] n hoguera f

**bonk** [baŋk] inf I. vt (hit on head) dar un golpe en la cabeza II. n golpe m en la cabeza

**bonnet** ['ban·ɪt] n gorrito m

**bonus** ['boʊ·nəs] I. n 1. (money) prima f, abono m AmL; (for Christmas) paga f extraordinaria; **productivity ~** plus m 2. (advantage) ventaja f II. adj de regalo

**bony** ['boʊ·ni] adj <-ier, -iest> huesudo, -a; (fish) con muchas espinas

**boo** [bu] I. interj inf bu II. vi, vt abuchear, pifiar Chile, Méx

**boob** [bub] n 1. vulg teta f 2. sl (fool) pringado, -a m, f

**boob tube** n sl caja f tonta

**booger** ['bʊg·ər] n sl 1. (dried mucus) moco m seco 2. (person) desgraciado, -a m, f

**book** [bʊk] I. n libro m; the ~s COM, FIN las cuentas ▶ to be a closed ~ ser un misterio (to para) II. vt 1. (reserve) reservar 2. (register) fichar III. vi reservar

◆**book up** vt ~ed up completo

**bookie** ['bʊk·i] n inf corredor(a) m(f) de apuestas

**booking** ['bʊk·ɪŋ] n reserva f; to make/cancel a ~ hacer/cancelar una reserva

**bookkeeper** n contable mf

**bookkeeping** n contabilidad f

**booklet** ['bʊk·lɪt] n folleto m

**bookmaker** n corredor(a) m(f) de apuestas

**bookmark** n marcador m

**bookseller** n librero, -a m, f; (shop) librería f

**bookshelf** <-shelves> n estante m

**bookshop, bookstore** n librería f

**boom**[1] [bum] ECON I. vi estar en auge II. n boom m III. adj en alza; (time, town) próspero, -a

**boom**[2] [bum] I. n (sound) estruendo m II. vi, vt to ~ (out) tronar

**boom box** n minicadena f, grabadora f Méx, Col

**boomerang** ['bu·mə·ræŋ] I. n bumerán m II. vi it ~ed on her/him le salió el tiro por la culata

**boondocks** n pl the ~ la conchinchina,

la chingada *Méx*

**boost** [bust] I. *n* 1. (*lift*) to give sb a ~ subir a alguien 2. (*increase*) impulso *m* II. *vt* 1. subir; (*process*) estimular 2. *inf* (*promote*) promover

**boot** [but] I. *n* 1. bota *f*; ankle ~ botín *m* 2. *inf* (*kick*) puntapié *m* 3. (*dismissal*) to get the ~ estar despedido; to give sb the ~ echar a alguien 4. COMPUT arranque *m* ▶ to be too <u>big</u> for one's ~s tener muchos humos; to <u>lick</u> sb's ~s hacer la pelota a alguien; to <u>shake</u> in one's ~s cagarse de miedo II. *vt* 1. (*kick*) dar un puntapié 2. *sl* (*fire*) echar 3. COMPUT arrancar ▶ **to** ~ por si fuera poco

♦**boot out** *vt* poner de patitas en la calle

**boot-cut** *adj* de campana

**booth** [buð] *n* cabina *f*; (*fair, market*) caseta *f*

**bootlace** ['but·leɪs] *n* cordón *m*

**bootleg** ['but·leg] <-gg-> *adj* de contrabando; (*recording, software*) pirata

**bootlicker** ['but·lɪk·ər] *n* lameculos *mf inv*, olfa *mf Arg, Par, Urug*

**booze** [buz] *sl* I. *n* bebida *f* alcohólica; to be on the ~ darle al trago II. *vi* empinar el codo, chupar *AmL*

**boozer** ['bu·zər] *n sl* borrachín, -ina *m, f*

**border** ['bɔr·dər] I. *n* 1. POL frontera *f* 2. (*edge*) borde *m* 3. (*in a garden*) arriate *m* II. *adj* fronterizo, -a III. *vt* limitar con

♦**border on** *vt* limitar con; *fig* rayar en

**bordering** *adj* limítrofe

**borderland** ['bɔr·dər·lænd] *n* zona *f* fronteriza

**borderline** ['bɔr·dər·laɪn] I. *n* frontera *f* II. *adj* dudoso, -a

**bore**[1] [bɔr] I. *n* 1. (*thing*) aburrimiento *m*; (*task*) lata *f*; what a ~! ¡qué lata! 2. (*person*) pesado, -a *m, f* II. <bored> *vt* aburrir

**bore**[2] [bɔr] *pp of* **bear**

**bored** *adj* aburrido, -a

**boredom** ['bɔr·dəm] *n* aburrimiento *m*

**boring** ['bɔr·ɪŋ] *adj* aburrido, -a, cansador(a) *Arg, Chile, Urug*

**born** [bɔrn] *adj* 1. nacido, -a; to be ~ nacer; where were you ~? ¿dónde naciste? 2. (*ability*) nato, -a; (*quality,*

*sympathy*) innato, -a ▶ I wasn't ~ <u>yesterday</u> no nací ayer

**borne** [bɔrn] *pt of* **bear**

**borough** ['bɜr·oʊ] *n* municipio *m*

**borrow** ['bar·oʊ] *vt* 1. tomar prestado; (*ask for*) pedir prestado; may I ~ your bag? ¿me prestas tu bolso? 2. MATH llevarse 3. LING tomar

**boss** [bas] I. *n* jefe, -a *m, f*; (*bossy person*) mandón, -ona *m, f* II. *vt inf* to ~ **around** mandonear

**bossy** ['ba·si] <-ier, -iest> *adj* mandón, -ona

**botanical** [bə·'tæn·ɪ·kəl] *adj* botánico, -a

**botany** ['bat·ən·i] *n* botánica *f*

**botch** [batʃ] I. *n* chapuza *f* II. *vt* hacer una chapuza con

**both** [boʊθ] I. *adj, pron* ~ (**of them**) los dos, las dos, ambos, ambas; ~ **of us** nosotros dos II. *adv* ~ **Cathy and Julie** tanto Cathy como Julie; to be ~ **sad and pleased** estar a la vez triste y satisfecho

**bother** ['bað·ər] I. *n* molestia *f*, friega *f AmL*; it is not worth the ~ no vale la pena II. *vi* molestarse; to (**not**) ~ to **do sth** (no) molestarse en hacer algo; **why** ~? ¿para qué molestarse? III. *vt* 1. (*annoy*) molestar; (*body part*) doler 2. (*worry*) preocupar; he doesn't **seem to be** ~ed **by...** no parece que le preocupe...

**bothersome** ['bað·ər·səm] *adj* molesto, -a, tequioso, -a *AmC*, espeso, -a *Perú, Ven*

**bottle** ['bat·əl] I. *n* 1. botella *f*; (*ink, perfume*) frasco *m*; (*baby's*) biberón *m* 2. *inf* the ~ la bebida; to hit the ~ empinar el codo II. *vt* embotellar; (*emotions*) reprimir

**bottled** ['bat·əld] *adj* embotellado, -a

**bottle green** *adj* verde botella

**bottleneck** ['bat·əl·nek] I. *n* cuello *m* de botella II. *vi* embotellarse, trancarse *Col*

**bottle opener** *n* abrebotellas *m inv*

**bottom** ['bat·əm] *n* 1. (*sea, street, glass*) fondo *m*; (*chair*) asiento *m*; (*stairs, page*) pie *m*; to touch ~ hacer pie; *fig* tocar fondo 2. (*lower part*) parte *f* inferior; from top to ~ de arriba (a) abajo

**3.** (*buttocks*) trasero *m* ▶ **from the ~ of one's <u>heart</u>** de todo corazón; **~s up!** ¡al centro y pa'dentro! *inf;* **to get to the ~ of sth** llegar al fondo de algo

**bottomless** [ˈbɒt·əm·lɪs] *adj* **1.** (*without limit*) infinito, -a **2.** (*very deep*) sin fondo; **a ~ pit** *fig* un pozo sin fondo

**bought** [bɔt] *vt pt of* **buy**

**boulder** [ˈboʊl·dər] *n* roca *f*

**boulevard** [ˈbʊl·ə·vard] *n* bulevar *m*

**bounce** [baʊnts] **I.** *vi, vt* rebotar; (*jump*) dar botes **II.** *n* **1.** bote *m;* **to give sb the ~** poner a alguien de patitas en la calle **2.** (*vitality*) vitalidad *f*

◆**bounce back** *vi* recuperarse

**bouncer** [ˈbaʊn·tsər] *n sl* gorila *m*

**bouncing** *adj* robusto, -a

**bound¹** [baʊnd] **I.** *vi* **1.** (*leap*) saltar **2.** (*bounce: ball*) rebotar *AmL* **II.** *n* salto *m;* **with one ~** de un salto

**bound²** [baʊnd] *vt* **to be ~ed by sth** estar rodeado por algo

**bound³** [baʊnd] *adj* **to be ~ for** ir rumbo a; **north/south-bound traffic** tráfico que va hacia el norte/sur

**bound⁴** [baʊnd] **I.** *pt, pp of* **bind II.** *adj* **she's ~ to come** seguro que viene; **to be ~ to do sth** estar obligado a hacer algo; **it was ~ to happen sooner or later** tarde o temprano tenía que suceder

**boundary** [ˈbaʊn·dri] <-ies> *n* (*line*) *a. fig* límite *m;* (*border*) frontera *f*

**boundless** [ˈbaʊnd·lɪs] *adj* (*love, patience*) sin límites; (*energy*) inagotable; (*universe*) infinito, -a

**bounty** [ˈbaʊn·ti] <-ies> *n* **1.** (*reward*) recompensa *f* **2.** (*gift*) regalo *m*

**bouquet** [boʊ·ˈkeɪ] *n* (*flowers*) ramo *m*

**bout** [baʊt] *n* **1.** SPORTS combate *m;* (*fencing*) asalto *m* **2.** (*illness, coughing*) ataque *m*

**boutique** [bu·ˈtik] *n* boutique *f*

**bovine** [ˈboʊ·vaɪn] *adj* (*of cows*) bovino, -a

**bow¹** [boʊ] *n* arco *m;* (*knot*) lazo *m,* moño *m AmL*

**bow²** [baʊ] *n* NAUT proa *f*

**bow³** [baʊ] **I.** *vi* hacer una reverencia (**to** ante); *fig* ceder; **to ~ to sth** someterse a algo ▶ **to ~ and <u>scrape</u>** hacer la pelo-

ta [*or Méx* barba] **II.** *vt* (*head*) agachar **III.** *n* reverencia *f,* venia *f CSur, Col,* caravana *f Méx*

◆**bow out** *vi* retirarse

**bowel** [ˈbaʊ·əl] *n* MED intestino *m* grueso

**bowl¹** [boʊl] *n* **1.** (*dish*) cuenco *m;* **fruit/ salad ~** frutero/ensaladera *f* **2.** (*of toilet*) taza *f;* (*for washing*) palangana *f* **3.** (*stadium*) estadio *m*

**bowl²** [boʊl] SPORTS **I.** *vi* jugar a los bolos; (*throw*) lanzar la bola **II.** *vt* lanzar **III.** *n* bola *f*

**bow-legged** [ˌboʊ·ˈlegd] *adj* (*person*) patizambo, -a, cascorvo, -a *Col*

**bowling** *n* bolos *mpl*

**bowling alley** *n* bolera *f*

**bowling ball** *n* bola *f* de bolos

**bow tie** *n* pajarita *f,* corbatín *m Col,* moñita *f Urug*

**box¹** [baks] **I.** *vi* boxear **II.** *vt* SPORTS boxear con [*or* contra] **III.** *n* sopapo *m*

**box²** [baks] **I.** *n* **1.** (*container*) caja *f;* **tool ~** caja de herramientas **2.** (*rectangular space*) casilla *f;* **dialog ~** cuadro de diálogo **3.** *pej* (*small space*) agujero *m* **4.** THEAT palco *m;* (*booth*) cabina *f* **5.** (*TV*) **the ~** la caja tonta **6.** (*mailbox*) buzón *m* ▶ **to <u>think</u> outside of the ~** tener ideas innovadoras **II.** *vt* poner en una caja

◆**box in** *vt* cerrar el paso a

◆**box up** *vt* poner en una caja

**boxer** [ˈbak·sər] *n* boxeador(a) *m(f);* (*dog*) bóxer *mf*

**boxer shorts** *npl* bóxer *m*

**boxing** [ˈbak·sɪŋ] *n* boxeo *m,* box *m AmL*

**boxing match** *n* combate *m* de boxeo

**boxing ring** *n* cuadrilátero *m*

**box lunch** *n* comida *f* en una fiambrera [*or* en una lonchera *f Col, Méx*]

**box office** *n* taquilla *f,* boletería *f AmL*

**boy** [bɔɪ] **I.** *n* (*child*) niño *m;* (*young man*) chico *m,* muchacho *m,* chamaco, -a *m, f Méx,* pibe *m Arg;* (*boyfriend*) novio *m* ▶ **the old ~ <u>network</u>** el amiguismo, la rosca *Col;* **~s <u>will</u> be ~s** así son los niños **II.** *interj* (**oh**) **~!** ¡vaya!

**boycott** [ˈbɔɪ·kat] **I.** *vt* boicotear **II.** *n* boicot *m*

**boyfriend** [ˈbɔɪ·frend] *n* novio *m*

**bra** [bra] *n* sujetador *m,* brasier *m Col,*

*Méx*, corpiño *m RíoPl*

**brace** [breɪs] I. *vt* to ~ oneself for sth prepararse para algo II. *n* 1. ~s (*for teeth, back*) aparato *m* 2. (*clamp*) abrazadera *f* 3. TYPO llave *f*

**bracelet** ['breɪs·lɪt] *n* pulsera *f*

**bracket** ['bræk·ɪt] I. *n* 1. TYPO paréntesis *m inv*; **angle** ~ corchete *m*; **curly** ~ llave *f*; **in** ~s entre paréntesis 2. (*category*) categoría *f* II. *vt* agrupar; TYPO poner entre paréntesis

**brag** [bræg] <-gg-> II. *vt* to ~ that... jactarse de que... III. *n* chulería *f*; (*person*) fanfarrón, -ona *m, f*

**Braille** [breɪl] *n* braille *m*

**brain** [breɪn] *n* 1. cerebro *m*; ~s sesos *mpl* 2. (*intelligence*) cabeza *f* 3. *inf* (*genius*) lumbrera *f* ▶ to **have** sth on the ~ tener algo metido en la cabeza; to **rack** one's ~ devanarse los sesos

**brain trust** *n* grupo *m* de peritos

**brainwashing** ['breɪn·waʃ·ɪŋ] *n* lavado *m* de cerebro

**brainwave** ['breɪn·weɪv] *n* onda *f* cerebral; *fig* idea *f* genial, lamparazo *m Col*

**brainy** ['breɪ·ni] <-ier, -iest> *adj* inteligente

**brake** [breɪk] I. *n* freno *m*; to put on the ~s frenar; to put a ~ on sth poner freno a algo II. *vi* frenar

**braking** *n* frenado *m*

**bran** [bræn] *n* salvado *m*

**branch** [bræntʃ] I. *n* a. *fig* rama *f*; (*river, road*) ramal *m*; (*company, library*) sucursal *f*; (*union, government department*) delegación *f* II. *vi* echar ramas; (*river, road*) bifurcarse

◆**branch off** *vi* bifurcarse; to ~ from a subject salirse de un tema

◆**branch out** *vi* diversificarse; to ~ on one's own establecerse por su cuenta

**branch office** *n* sucursal *f*

**brand** [brænd] I. *n* 1. COM marca *f* 2. *fig* clase *f* 3. (*mark*) hierro *m* II. *vt* 1. (*label*) tachar ((as) de) 2. (*cattle*) marcar

**brand-new** *adj* nuevo, -a flamante; ~ **baby** recién nacido

**brandy** ['bræn·di] <-ies> *n* brandy *m*; **French** ~ coñac *m*

**brash** [bræʃ] *adj* (*attitude*) chulo, -a; (*col-*

*ors*) chillón, -ona

**brass** [bræs] *n* latón *m*

**brass band** *n* banda *f* de música, orfeón *m Chile*

**brat** [bræt] *n inf* mocoso, -a *m, f*; **he is a spoiled** ~ es un niño mimado, es un sute *Col, Ven*

**brave** [breɪv] I. *adj* valiente II. *vt* afrontar

**bravery** ['breɪ·və·ri] *n* valentía *f*

**brawl** [brɔl] I. *n* pelea *f*, bulla *f AmL* II. *vi* pelearse

**brawling** *n* alboroto *m*

**bray** [breɪ] I. *vi* rebuznar; ~ing laugh risa estridente II. *n* rebuzno *m*

**brazen** ['breɪ·zən] *adj* descarado, -a

**Brazil** [brə·ˈzɪl] *n* Brasil *m*

**Brazilian** [brə·ˈzɪl·jən] *adj, n* brasileño, -a *m, f*

**breach** [britʃ] I. *n* 1. (*infraction*) infracción *f*; (*contract, promise, agreement*) incumplimiento *m*; (*confidence*) abuso *m* 2. (*opening*) brecha *f* II. *vt* (*law*) infringir; (*contract, promise, agreement*) incumplir; (*security*) poner en peligro

**bread** [bred] I. *n* 1. pan *m*; **a loaf of** ~ una barra de pan 2. *sl* (*money*) pasta *f* II. *vt* empanar

**bread and butter** *n* sustento *m*

**breadbasket, breadbox** *n* panera *f*

**breadcrumb** *n* miga *f* (de pan); ~s pan *m* rallado

**breadth** [bredθ] *n* 1. anchura *f*; to be 5 feet in ~ tener 5 pies de ancho 2. *fig* amplitud *f*

**break** [breɪk] I. *n* 1. (*crack, gap*) grieta *f* 2. (*escape*) fuga *f*; to make a ~ correr (for/towards hacia) 3. (*interruption*) interrupción *f*; (*commercial*) pausa *f* 4. (*rest period*) descanso *m*; **coffee/lunch** ~ pausa del café/para comer 5. (*vacation*) vacaciones *fpl* 6. (*divergence*) ruptura *f*; **a** ~ **from sth** un descanso de algo ▶ to **make** a **clean** ~ cortar por lo sano; **give me a** ~! ¡déjame en paz! II. <broke, broken> *vt* 1. romper; to ~ **(in)to pieces** hacer añicos; (*circuit*) cortar; (*strike*) poner fin a; (*habit*) dejar; (*agreement*) incumplir; (*date*) no acudir a; (*code*) descifrar; (*bill*) cambiar 2. (*tell*) decir;

to ~ **the news to sb** dar la noticia a alguien **III.** <broke, broken> vi **1.** romperse; **to ~ into pieces** hacerse añicos; (*wave*) romper; (*fever*) bajar; (*weather*) cambiar **2.** (*interrupt*) **shall we ~ for lunch?** ¿paramos para comer? ▶ **to ~ even** salir sin ganar ni perder; **to ~ free** liberarse; **to ~ loose** soltarse

◆**break away** vi desprenderse; (*faction, region*) escindirse

◆**break down I.** vi **1.** (*stop working*) averiarse **2.** (*marriage*) romperse; (*negotiations*) fracasar **3.** (*physically, psychologically*) derrumbarse **4.** CHEM descomponerse **II.** vt (*door*) echar abajo; (*opposition, resistance*) acabar con; (*process*) dividir

◆**break in** vi **1.** (*burglar*) entrar a robar **2.** (*interrupt*) **to ~ (on)** interrumpir

◆**break into** vt (*car*) entrar a robar; (*business*) introducirse en; **to ~ laughter/tears** echarse a reír/llorar

◆**break off I.** vt partir; (*relationship*) romper **II.** vi **1.** (*become detached*) desprenderse **2.** (*stop speaking*) callarse

◆**break out** vi escaparse; (*prison*) fugarse; (*war, storm, laughing*) estallar; **he broke out in spots** le salieron granos

◆**break through I.** vi penetrar; (*sun*) salir **II.** vt atravesar; **to ~ the crowd** abrirse paso entre la multitud

◆**break up I.** vt (*meeting, strike*) terminar; (*coalition, union*) disolver; (*family*) separar; (*gang, cartel*) desarticular; **break it up!** *inf* ¡basta ya!; **to break sb up** hacer reír a alguien **II.** vi separarse; (*marriage*) fracasar; (*meeting*) terminar

**breakable** ['breɪ·kə·bəl] adj frágil

**breakage** ['breɪ·kɪdʒ] n roturas fpl

**breakaway** ['breɪk·ə·weɪ] adj POL disidente

**breakdown** ['breɪk·daʊn] n **1.** (*collapse*) ruptura f **2.** TECH avería f **3. give me a ~ of the situation** detállame la situación **4.** (*decomposition*) descomposición f **5.** (*nervous*) ~ **crisis** f inv nerviosa

**breakfast** ['brek·fəst] n desayuno m; **to have ~** desayunar

**breaking point** n límite m; **to reach the ~** llegar al límite

**breakneck** ['breɪk·nek] adj vertiginoso, -a

**breakthrough** ['breɪk·θru] n adelanto m

**breakup** ['breɪk·ʌp] n desintegración f; (*family*) separación f; (*group, empire*) disolución f; (*talks*) fracaso m

**breast** [brest] n pecho m; CULIN pechuga f

**breastfeed** ['brest·fid] vt amamantar

**breath** [breθ] n aliento m; **to be out of ~** estar sin aliento; **to be short of ~** ahogarse; **to hold one's ~** contener la respiración; **to take a deep ~** respirar hondo; **to go out for a ~ of fresh air** salir para que le dé a uno el aire ▶ **to take sb's ~ away** dejar a alguien sin habla

**breathalyze** ['breθ·ə·laɪz] vt hacer la prueba de alcoholemia a

**Breathalyzer®** n alcoholímetro m

**breathe** [brið] vi, vt respirar; **to ~ again** [*or* **easily**] respirar tranquilo

**breather** ['bri·ðər] n respiro m

**breathing** n respiración f

**breathless** ['breθ·lɪs] adj sin aliento

**breathtaking** adj imponente

**bred** [bred] pt, pp of **breed**

**breed** [brid] **I.** vt <bred, bred> criar; (*disease, violence*) engendrar **II.** vi <bred, bred> reproducirse; (*violence*) generarse **III.** n tipo m; ZOOL raza f; BOT variedad f

**breeding** n educación f; ZOOL cría f

**breeze** [briz] n (*wind*) brisa f; **to be a ~** ser pan comido, ser un bollo *RíoPl* ▶ **to shoot the ~** estar de palique

**brew** [bru] **I.** n inf (*beer*) birra f **II.** vi **1.** (*beer*) fermentar **2.** (*tea*) reposar; **to let the tea ~** dejar reposar el té **3.** (*storm, trouble*) avecinarse; **there's something ~ing** se está cociendo algo **III.** vt (*beer*) elaborar; (*tea*) hacer

**brewery** ['bru·ə·ri] <-ies> n (*company*) cervecería f, cervecera f *Méx*; (*place*) fábrica f de cerveza

**brewski** ['bru·ski] <-ies *or* -s> n sl birra f, bironga f *RíoPl*

**bribe** [braɪb] **I.** vt sobornar; **to ~ sb into doing sth** sobornar a alguien para que haga algo **II.** n soborno m

**bribery** ['braɪ·bə·ri] n soborno m, coima f *Perú, CSur*, mordida f *Méx*

**brick** [brɪk] n ladrillo m

◆**brick in** vt tapiar

**bricklayer** n albañil mf

**bridal shower** n despedida f de soltera

**bride** [braɪd] n novia f

**bridegroom** ['braɪd·ˌgrum] n novio m

**bridesmaid** ['braɪdz·ˌmeɪd] n dama f de honor

**bridge** [brɪdʒ] n ARCHIT, MED, MUS puente m; GAMES bridge m

**bridge loan** n crédito m puente

**brief** [brif] I. adj (short) breve; (concise) conciso, -a; be ~! ¡sé breve!; in ~ en resumen II. n (instructions) instrucciones fpl III. vt informar; (instructions) dar instrucciones a

**briefcase** ['brif·keɪs] n maletín m

**briefing** n 1. (instructions) instrucciones fpl 2. (session) reunión f informativa; (for reporters) rueda f de prensa

**briefly** adv (for short time) por poco tiempo; (concisely) brevemente; ~,... en resumen,...

**briefness** n brevedad f

**brigade** [brɪ·'geɪd] n brigada f

**bright** [braɪt] I. adj (light, idea, person) brillante; (room) con mucha luz; (day) soleado; (future) prometedor(a); (color) vivo, -a, fuerte; to go ~ red ponerse rojo como un tomate ▶ to look on the ~ side of sth mirar [or ver] el lado bueno de algo II. n ~s AUTO largas fpl, altas fpl And

**brighten (up)** ['braɪt·ən (ʌp)] I. vt iluminar; (become cheerful) animar II. vi hacerse más brillante; (become cheerful) animarse; (eyes, face) iluminarse; (future, weather) mejorar

**brightness** n (lightness) brillo m

**brilliance** ['brɪl·jəns] n 1. (cleverness) brillantez f 2. (brightness) resplandor m

**brilliant** ['brɪl·jənt] adj 1. (color, idea, person) brillante; (sunlight, smile) radiante; (water) resplandeciente 2. inf (excellent) fantástico, -a

**brim** [brɪm] I. n borde m; to fill sth to the ~ llenar algo hasta el borde II. vi <-mm-> to ~ with happiness/energy rebosar de felicidad/energía

◆**brim over** vi a. fig rebosar

**brimful** [ˌbrɪm·'fʊl] adj repleto, -a; (life, confidence) rebosante

**brine** [braɪn] n CULIN salmuera f

**bring** [brɪŋ] <brought, brought> vt 1. (come with, cause) traer; to ~ sb in hacer pasar a alguien; to ~ sth in meter algo; to ~ poverty/fame to a town traer pobreza/fama a un pueblo; to ~ sb luck traer suerte a alguien; to ~ oneself to do sth obligarse a hacer algo 2. (take) llevar 3. LAW interponer; (complaint) formular

◆**bring about** vt (cause) provocar; (achieve) lograr

◆**bring along** vt traer

◆**bring around** vt 1. MED hacer volver en sí 2. (persuade) convencer

◆**bring back** vt 1. (reintroduce) reintroducir 2. (remind) recordar 3. (return) devolver

◆**bring down** vt 1. (reduce) reducir; (temperature) bajar 2. (knock down) tirar; (tree) talar; (government) derrocar 3. (make sad) deprimir

◆**bring forward** vt 1. (to earlier date) adelantar 2. (for discussion) presentar 3. FIN transferir

◆**bring in** vt 1. (introduce) introducir 2. (call in) llamar 3. to ~ a profit reportar un beneficio

◆**bring off** vt inf lograr

◆**bring on** vt (cause) causar; (improve) mejorar

◆**bring out** vt 1. COM introducir (en el mercado); (book) publicar 2. to ~ the best/worst in sb hace salir lo mejor/peor de alguien

◆**bring over** vt 1. (person) convencer 2. (take with) traer

◆**bring up** vt 1. (child) criar 2. (mention) sacar 3. inf (vomit) devolver

**brink** [brɪŋk] n borde m; to drive sb to the ~ of sth llevar a alguien al borde de algo; to be on the ~ of bankruptcy/war estar al borde de la bancarrota/la guerra

**brisk** [brɪsk] adj (pace) rápido, -a; (walk) a paso ligero; (breeze) fresco, -a; (manner, voice) enérgico, -a

**bristle** ['brɪs·əl] vi (fur, hair) erizarse; to ~ with anger enfurecerse

**Britain** ['brɪt·ən] n Gran Bretaña f

**British** ['brɪt·ɪʃ] I. adj británico, -a; ~

English inglés británico **II.** *n pl* **the ~** los británicos

**broad** [brɔd] *adj* **1.** (*wide*) ancho, -a **2.** (*spacious, wide-ranging*) amplio, -a **3.** **a ~ hint** una clara indirecta; **a ~ mind** una mente abierta

**broadcast** ['brɔd·kæst] **I.** *n* programa *m* **II.** *vi, vt* <broadcast *or* broadcasted, broadcast *or* broadcasted> transmitir; (*rumor*) difundir(se)

**broadcasting** *n* TV transmisión *f*; RADIO radiodifusión *f*

**broadcasting station** *n* emisora *f*

**broaden** ['brɔd·ən] **I.** *vi* ampliarse **II.** *vt* (*street*) ensanchar; (*horizons*) ampliar; (*mind*) abrir

**broadly** ['brɔd·li] *adv* **1.** (*generally*) en líneas generales **2.** (*smile*) de oreja a oreja

**broad-minded** *adj* con mentalidad abierta

**broccoli** ['brɑk·ə·li] *n* brócoli *m*, bréncol *m*

**brochure** [broʊ·'ʃʊr] *n* folleto *m*

**broiler** ['brɔɪ·lər] *n* (*grill*) parrilla *f*

**broke** [broʊk] **I.** *pt of* **break** **II.** *adj* *inf* pelado, -a, planchado, -a *Chile* ▶ **to go ~** *inf* arruinarse

**broken** ['broʊ·kən] **I.** *pp of* **break** **II.** *adj* roto, -a; (*interrupted*) interrumpido, -a; **in ~ English** en inglés mal hablado

**broken-down** *adj* averiado, -a, en pana *Chile*, varado, -a *Col*; (*building*) ruinoso, -a

**broken-hearted** *adj* destrozado, -a

**bronchial tubes** *npl* bronquios *mpl*

**bronze** [branz] **I.** *n* bronce *m* **II.** *adj* de bronce; (*hair*) dorado, -a; (*skin*) bronceado, -a

**brooch** [broʊtʃ] *n* broche *m*

**brood** [brud] **I.** *n* ZOOL camada *f*; (*birds*) nidada *f*; *iron* prole *f* **II.** *vi* **to ~ over sth** dar vueltas a algo

**brook** [brʊk] *n* arroyo *m*

**broom** [brum] *n* escoba *f*

**broth** [brɔθ] *n* caldo *m*

**brother** ['brʌð·ər] *n* **1.** hermano *m* **2.** (*friend*) colega *m*

**brother-in-law** <brothers-in-law *or* brother-in-laws> *n* cuñado *m*, con-

cuño *m* AmL

**brotherly** ['brʌð·ər·li] *adj* fraternal

**brought** [brɔt] *pp, pt of* **bring**

**brown** [braʊn] **I.** *n* marrón *m* **II.** *adj* marrón; (*hair*) castaño, -a; (*bread, rice*) integral **III.** *vi* broncearse; CULIN dorarse **IV.** *vt* broncear; CULIN dorar

**brownnose** ['braʊn·noʊz] **I.** *vi* *inf* ser un pelota [*or* lambón] *Col* **II.** *vt* hacer la pelota [*or* Méx barba] a, echar cepillo a *Col*

**brownout** ['braʊn·aʊt] *n* apagón *m* (parcial)

**browse** [braʊz] **I.** *vi* mirar; **to ~ through** echar un vistazo; (*book, magazine*) hojear **II.** *n* ojeada *f*; **to have a ~ through** echar una ojeada a; (*book, magazine*) hojear

**browser** ['braʊ·zər] *n* navegador *m*

**bruise** [bruz] **I.** *n* cardenal *m* **II.** *vt* MED hacerse una contusión en

**brunt** [brʌnt] *n* impacto *m*

**brush** [brʌʃ] **I.** *n* **1.** (*for hair*) cepillo *m* **2.** (*broom*) escoba *f* **3.** (*for painting*) pincel *m*; (*bigger*) brocha *f* **II.** *vt* **1.** (*hair*) cepillar; **to ~ one's teeth** lavarse los dientes **2.** (*touch lightly*) rozar

◆**brush against** *vt* rozar

◆**brush aside** *vt* **1.** (*push to one side*) apartar **2.** (*disregard*) hacer caso omiso de

◆**brush away** *vt* quitar

◆**brush off** *vt* (*dust*) quitar; (*person*) no hacer caso a

**brush-off** *n* **to give sb the ~** dar calabazas a alguien

**brusque** [brʌsk] *adj* brusco, -a

**brusqueness** *n* brusquedad *f*

**Brussels** ['brʌs·əlz] *n* Bruselas *f*

**brutal** ['bruṭ·əl] *adj* brutal; (*words*) cruel; (*truth*) crudo, -a

**brutality** [bru·'tæl·ə·ṭi] *n* (*cruelty*) brutalidad *f*; (*words*) crueldad *f*; (*harshness*) crudeza *f*

**brute** [brut] **I.** *n* bestia *f* **II.** *adj* **~ force** fuerza *f* bruta

**bubble** ['bʌb·əl] **I.** *n* burbuja *f*; (*comic*) bocadillo *m*; **to live in a ~** vivir en una burbuja **II.** *vi* borbotear

**bubble bath** *n* sales *f pl* de baño; (*bath*) baño *m* de espuma

**bubblegum** n chicle m

**bubble-jet printer** n impresora f de inyección

**bubbly** ['bʌb·li] I. n inf champán m II. adj burbujeante; (fig) animado, -a

**buck** [bʌk] n inf dólar m; **to make a fast ~** hacer dinero fácil; **to pass the ~** escurrir el bulto

♦**buck up** vt inf **to buck sb up** levantar el ánimo a alguien; **to ~ one's ideas** espabilarse

**bucket** ['bʌk·ɪt] n cubo m ▶ **a drop in the ~** un grano de arena en el desierto; **to kick the ~** estirar la pata

**bucketful** ['bʌk·ɪt·fʊl] <-s or **bucketsful**> n cubo m (lleno)

**buckle** ['bʌk·əl] I. n hebilla f II. vt 1. (fasten) abrochar 2. (bend) torcer III. vi 1. (fasten) abrocharse 2. (bend) torcerse; (knees) doblarse

♦**buckle down** vi ponerse ya en serio

♦**buckle up** vi abrocharse el cinturón

**bud** [bʌd] I. n BIO brote m; (flower) capullo m II. vi <-dd-> echar brotes

**Buddhism** ['bu·dɪz·əm] n budismo m

**Buddhist** adj, n budista mf

**buddy** ['bʌd·i] n inf colega m, cuate m Méx

**budge** [bʌdʒ] I. vi moverse; (opinion) cambiar de opinión (**from** en) II. vt mover; (opinion) hacer cambiar de opinión a

**budgerigar** ['bʌdʒ·ə·rɪ·ɡar] n periquito m

**budget** ['bʌdʒ·ɪt] I. n presupuesto m II. vt presupuestar; (wages, time) administrar III. vi **to ~ for** presupuestar IV. adj económico, -a

**budget deficit** n déficit m inv presupuestario

**buffalo** ['bʌf·ə·loʊ] <-(es)> n búfalo m

**buffer** ['bʌf·ər] I. n 1. (barrera f) 2. (intermediary) mediador(a) m(f) 3. COMPUT búfer m II. vt proteger

**buffet**¹ [bə·'feɪ] n 1. (meal) buffet m 2. (bar) cafetería f

**buffet**² ['bʌf·ɪt] vt zarandear

**bug** [bʌɡ] I. n 1. ZOOL chinche f; (any insect) bicho m; MED microbio m 3. COMPUT error m II. vt <-gg-> 1. escuchar clandestinamente; (telephone)

pinchar 2. (annoy) chinchar

**bugaboo** ['bʌɡ·ə·bu] n pesadilla f

**buggy** ['bʌɡ·i] n <-ies> cochecito m

**build** [bɪld] I. vt <built, built> 1. (make) construir; (fire) hacer; (car) fabricar 2. (establish) conseguir; (relationship) establecer II. vi <built, built> 1. (construct) edificar 2. (increase) aumentar III. n complexión f

♦**build in** vt incorporar

♦**build on** vt **to build sth on sth** agregar algo a algo

♦**build up** I. vt desarrollar; (accumulate) acumular; **to build sb up** poner a alguien por las nubes II. vi (increase) ir en aumento; (accumulate) acumularse

**builder** ['bɪl·dər] n (company) constructor(a) m(f); (worker) albañil mf

**building** n edificio m

**building permit** n permiso m de obras

**building site** n obra f

**build-up** n 1. (accumulation) acumulación f; (pressure) aumento m 2. (publicity) propaganda f

**built** [bɪlt] I. pp, pt of **build** II. adj **slightly ~** menudo; **well ~** de complexión robusta; **he's/she's (really) built!** ¡vaya un cuerpazo que tiene!

**built-in** adj (cabinets) empotrado, -a; (feature) incorporado, -a; (advantage) intrínseco, -a

**built-up** adj (area) edificado, -a; (heels, shoes) con alza

**bulb** [bʌlb] n 1. BOT bulbo m 2. ELEC bombilla f, bombillo m AmL

**Bulgaria** [bʌl·'ɡer·i·ə] n Bulgaria f

**Bulgarian** [bʌl·'ɡer·i·ən] I. adj búlgaro, -a II. n 1. (person) búlgaro, -a m, f 2. LING búlgaro m

**bulge** [bʌldʒ] I. vi sobresalir; **to ~ with** estar repleto de II. n 1. (swelling) bulto m 2. (increase) alza f

**bulging** adj abultado, -a; (bag, box) repleto, -a; **~ eyes** ojos saltones

**bulimia** [bu·'li·mi·ə] n bulimia f

**bulk** [bʌlk] I. n (magnitude) volumen m; (mass) mole f; **the ~ of** la mayor parte de; **in ~** a granel; ECON al por mayor II. vi **to ~ large** ser importante III. adj (mailing, order) grande; (goods) en grandes cantidades

**B**

**bulky** ['bʌl·ki] <-ier, iest> adj voluminoso, -a; (*heavy*) pesado, -a; (*person*) corpulento, -a

**bull** [bʊl] n 1. (*bovine*) toro m 2. (*male*) macho m; ~ **whale** ballena macho 3. sl chorradas fpl, macanas fpl RíoPl ▶ **to take the ~ by the** <u>horns</u> coger [*or* AmL agarrar] el toro por los cuernos

**bulldog** ['bʊl·dɔg] n bulldog m

**bulldoze** ['bʊl·doʊz] vt 1. ARCHIT demoler 2. fig **to ~ sth through** conseguir algo a la fuerza; **to ~ sb into doing sth** forzar a alguien a hacer algo

**bullet** ['bʊl·ɪt] n bala f

**bulletin** ['bʊl·ə·tɪn] n boletín m

**bulletin board** n tablón m de anuncios

**bulletproof** ['bʊl·ɪt·pruf] adj blindado, -a; (*glass, vest*) antibalas

**bullfight** ['bʊl·faɪt] n corrida f de toros

**bullfighter** ['bʊl·faɪ·tər] n torero, -a m, f

**bullshit** ['bʊl·ʃɪt] sl I. n gilipolleces fpl; **don't give me that ~!** ¡no me vengas con hostias! II. interj y una mierda III. <-tt-> vi decir gilipolleces

**bully** ['bʊl·i] I. <-ies> n matón, -ona m, f II. <-ie-> vt **to ~ sb** (**into doing sth**) intimidar a alguien (para que haga algo) III. interj inf ~ **for you!** ¡bravo!

**bum** [bʌm] I. n 1. (*lazy*) vago, -a m, f 2. (*homeless*) vagabundo, -a m, f 3. *Can* (*buttocks*) culo m II. adj inf chungo, -a; **a ~ job** una porquería de trabajo III. <-mm-> vt sl gorronear [*or* lagartear] Col (off a) IV. vi inf **to ~ off sb** gorronear a alguien; **to ~ around** vagabundear; (*laze around*) pasar el rato

**bumblebee** ['bʌm·bəl·bi] n abejorro m

**bummed out** adj sl depre

**bump** [bʌmp] I. n 1. (*lump*) bulto m; (*head*) chichón m; (*road*) bache m 2. inf (*blow*) porrazo m II. vt chocar contra; **to ~ one's head** darse un golpe en la cabeza (**on/against** con/contra)

♦**bump into** vt insep 1. (*collide with*) chocar contra 2. (*meet accidentally*) topar con

♦**bump off** vt sl cargarse

**bumper** ['bʌm·pər] I. n AUTO parachoques m inv, paragolpes m inv AmL, defensa f Méx II. adj abundante; (*edition*) especial

**bumpkin** ['bʌmp·kɪn] n paleto, -a m, f

**bumpy** ['bʌm·pi] <-ier, iest> adj (*surface*) desigual; (*road*) lleno, -a de baches; (*journey*) movidito inf

**bun** [bʌn] n 1. (*pastry*) bollo m; (*roll*) panecillo m, pancito m CSur 2. (*hair*) moño m, chongo m Méx 3. ~s sl pompis m inv, cola f Col, CSur

**bunch** [bʌntʃ] <-es> I. n 1. (*grapes*) racimo m; (*carrots, keys*) manojo m; (*flowers*) ramo m 2. (*group*) grupo m; (*of friends*) pandilla f 3. **a** (**whole**) ~ **of problems** un montón de problemas II. vt agrupar III. vi **to ~** (**together**) amontonarse

**bundle** ['bʌn·dəl] n (*clothes*) fardo m; (*money*) fajo m ▶ **to be a ~ of** <u>nerves</u> ser un manojo de nervios

**bung** [bʌŋ] I. n tapón m II. vt taponar

**bungalow** ['bʌŋ·gə·loʊ] n bungalow m, bóngalo m AmL

**bungee jumping** ['bʌn·dʒi·ˌdʒʌm·pɪŋ] n puenting m

**bungle** ['bʌŋ·gəl] vt chapucear

**bungler** n chapucero, -a m, f

**bungling** adj torpe

**bunk** [bʌŋk] n litera f, cucheta f RíoPl

♦**bunk down** vi inf irse a sobar

**bunker** ['bʌŋ·kər] n búnker m

**bunny** (**rabbit**) ['bʌn·i·('ræb·ɪt)] n conejito m

**buoyant** ['bɔɪ·jənt] adj (*cheerful*) optimista

**burble** ['bɜr·bəl] vi borbotar; (*talk*) parlotear

**burden** ['bɜr·dən] I. n carga f; **to be a ~ on** [*or* to] **sb** ser una carga para alguien II. vt cargar; fig estorbar

**bureau** ['bjʊr·oʊ] <-s> n 1. (*office*) agencia f; POL departamento m 2. (*chest of drawers*) cómoda f

**bureaucracy** [bjʊ·'rak·rə·si] n burocracia f

**bureaucratic** [ˌbjʊr·ə·'kræt·ɪk] adj burocrático, -a

**burger** ['bɜr·gər] n inf abbr of **hamburger** hamburguesa f

**burglar** ['bɜr·glər] n ladrón, -ona m, f

**burglar alarm** n alarma f antirrobo

**burglarize** ['bɜr·glə·raɪz] vt robar; **five houses have been ~d** han entrado a robar en cinco casas

**burglary** ['bɜr·glə·ri] <-ies> n robo m

**burgle** ['bɜr·gəl] vt see **burglarize**

**burial** ['ber·i·əl] n entierro m

**burial ground** n cementerio m

**burial service** n funerales mpl

**burlesque** [bɜr·'lesk] adj burlesco, -a

**burly** ['bɜr·li] <-ier, -iest> adj fornido, -a

**burn** [bɜrn] I. <burnt or -ed, burnt or -ed> vi 1. (be in flames) quemarse 2. (be hot) arder 3. estar encendido, -a; **he left all the lights ~ing** dejó todas las luces encendidas 4. **to be ~ing to do sth** estar deseando hacer algo; **to ~ with desire** desear ardientemente; **his face ~ed with anger/shame** se puso rojo de furia/vergüenza II. <burnt or -ed, burnt or -ed> vt quemar; (building) incendia; **to be ~ed** (by the sun) quemarse; (injured) sufrir quemaduras III. n quemadura f, quemada f Méx; **severe/minor ~s** quemaduras graves/leves

♦**burn away** I. vi quemarse; (candle) consumirse II. vt quemar

♦**burn down** I. vt incendiar II. vi incendiarse; (fire, candle) apagarse

♦**burn out** vi quemarse; (fire, candle) apagarse; (bulb) fundirse

♦**burn up** vt 1. quemar; (fuel) consumir 2. inf reventar

**burner** ['bɜr·nər] n fogón m; TECH quemador m

**burning** ['bɜr·nɪŋ] adj ardiente; (sun) abrasador; (issue, question) candente; **to be ~ hot** estar ardiendo

**burnt** [bɜrnt] I. pt, pp of **burn** II. adj quemado, -a; **a ~ smell/taste** un olor/sabor a quemado

**burp** [bɜrp] I. n eructo m; **to let out a ~** soltar un eructo II. vi eructar

**burrow** ['bɜr·oʊ] I. n madriguera f II. vt, vi excavar

**burst** [bɜrst] I. n explosión f; **a ~ of laughter** una carcajada; **a ~ of anger** un arranque de cólera II. <burst, burst> vi (balloon, tire) reventar; (storm) desatarse; **to ~ into tears** romper a llorar; **to be ~ing to do sth** morirse de ganas de hacer algo III. <burst, burst> vt reventar

♦**burst in** vi entrar de sopetón

♦**burst out** vi saltar; **to ~ laughing/cry-**ing echarse a reír/llorar

**bury** ['ber·i] <-ie-> vt enterrar; (hide) ocultar

**bus** [bʌs] <-es> n autobús m, camión m Méx, colectivo m Arg, Ven, guagua f Cuba, ómnibus m Perú, Urug; **school ~** autobús escolar; **to catch/miss the ~** coger/perder el autobús; **to go by ~** [or **to take the ~**] ir en autobús ▶ **to miss the ~** perder el autobús

**bus driver** n conductor(a) m(f) de autobús

**bush** [bʊʃ] <-es> n arbusto m; (hair) mata f; (land) **the ~** el monte ▶ **to beat around the ~** andarse con rodeos

**bushy** ['bʊʃ·i] <-ier, -iest> adj tupido, -a; (beard, mustache) espeso, -a; (eyebrows) poblado, -a

**busily** adv afanosamente

**business** ['bɪz·nɪs] n 1. (trade, commerce) negocios mpl; **to be away on ~** estar de viaje de negocios; **to go out of ~** cerrar; **to set up a ~** montar un negocio 2. ~ (sector) industria f; **the frozen food ~** la industria de los congelados 3. <-es> (company) empresa f; **to start up/run a ~** poner/llevar un negocio 4. (matter) asunto m; **an unfinished ~** un asunto pendiente; **it's none of your ~!** ¡no es asunto tuyo!; **mind your own ~!** ¡no te metas donde no te llaman! ▶ ~ **before pleasure** prov antes es la obligación que el placer

**business address** n dirección f comercial

**business card** n tarjeta f comercial

**business hours** n horas f pl de oficina

**businesslike** ['bɪz·nɪs·laɪk] adj 1. (serious) formal 2. (efficient) eficiente

**businessman** <-men> n hombre m de negocios

**business trip** n viaje m de negocios

**businesswoman** <-women> n mujer f de negocios

**busk** [bʌsk] vi tocar un instrumento en la calle

**busker** ['bʌs·kər] n músico, -a m, f callejero, -a

**bus service** n servicio m de autobuses

**bus station** n estación f de autobuses

**bus stop** n parada f de autobús

**bust**[1] [bʌst] *n* ART busto *m*

**bust**[2] [bʌst] **I.** *adj sl* destrozado, -a; (*bankrupt*) en bancarrota; **to go ~** quebrar **II.** *vt inf* **1.** (*break*) destrozar **2.** (*raid*) realizar una redada en ▸ **to ~ one's butt** (*doing sth/to do sth*) partirse la espalda (haciendo algo)

**bustle** ['bʌs·əl] **I.** *vi* **to ~ around** ir y venir; **to ~ with activity** rebosar de actividad **II.** *n* ajetreo *m*; **hustle and ~** bullicio *m*

**busy** ['bɪz·i] <-ier, -iest> *adj* **1.** (*occupied*) atareado, -a; **to be ~ doing sth** estar muy ocupado haciendo algo; **to be ~ with sth** estar ocupado con algo **2.** (*full of activity*) activo, -a; (*exhausting*) agotador(a); (*street*) concurrido, -a; (*day*) ajetreado, -a **3.** TEL ocupado

**busybody** ['bɪz·i,bad·i] <-ies> *n inf* entrometido, -a *m, f*; **to be a ~** ser un metomentodo

**but** [bʌt] **I.** *prep* excepto; **all ~ one** todos excepto uno; **anything ~...** lo que sea menos...; **nothing ~...** nada más que... **II.** *conj* **1.** pero; **he has paper ~ no pen** tiene papel, pero no pluma **2.** **not... but...** no... sino...; **it is not red ~ pink** no es rojo sino rosa **III.** *adv* sólo **IV.** *n* pero *m*; **there are no ~s about it!** ¡no hay peros que valgan!

**butane** ['bju·teɪn] *n* butano *m*

**butcher** ['bʊtʃ·ər] *n* carnicero, -a *m, f*

**butler** ['bʌt·lər] *n* mayordomo *m*

**butt** [bʌt] **I.** *n* **1.** (*rifle*) culata *f*; (*cigarette*) colilla *f* **2.** (*blow with the head*) cabezazo *m* **3.** **to be the ~ of sth** ser el blanco de algo **4.** (*container*) tonel *m* **5.** (*buttocks*) culo *m* **II.** *vt* darse un cabezazo contra

**butter** ['bʌt·ər] **I.** *n* mantequilla *f* **II.** *vt* untar con mantequilla

◆**butter up** *vt* dar coba a, pellizcar *AmL*

**butterfingers** *n inv* manazas *mf inv*

**butterfly** ['bʌt·ər,flaɪ] <-ies> *n* mariposa *f*; *fig* frívolo, -a *m, f* ▸ **to have butterflies in one's stomach** estar con los nervios a flor de piel

**butthead** *n vulg sl* caraculo *mf*

**buttock** ['bʌt·ək] *n* nalga *f*

**button** ['bʌt·ən] **I.** *n* botón *m*; **start ~** botón de inicio; **right/left mouse ~** botón derecho/izquierdo del ratón; **to push a ~** apretar un botón **II.** *vi* abrocharse **III.** *vt* abrochar

◆**button up** *vt* abrochar

**buttonhole** ['bʌt·ən·hoʊl] *n* ojal *m*

**buy** [baɪ] **I.** *n* compra *f*; **a good ~** una ganga **II.** <bought, bought> *vt* **1.** comprar (**from, off** a) **2.** *inf* **did the teacher ~ your excuse?** ¿se tragó el profesor tu excusa?

◆**buy into** *vt* comprar acciones de; *fig* aceptar como válido

◆**buy off** *vt always sep* sobornar

◆**buy up** *vt insep* acaparar

**buyer** ['baɪ·ər] *n* comprador(a) *m(f)*

**buzz** [bʌz] **I.** *vi* **1.** (*hum*) zumbar; (*bell*) sonar; **my ears were ~ing** me zumbaban los oídos **2.** *sl* **to be ~ed** ir borracho **II.** *vt inf* TEL llamar; (*signal to*) dar un toque a **III.** *n* **1.** (*noise*) zumbido *m*; (*low noise*) rumor *m* **2.** *inf* **to give sb a ~** echar a alguien el teléfono **3.** *inf* (*thrill*) subidón *m*

◆**buzz off** *vi inf* largarse

**buzzer** ['bʌz·ər] *n* timbre *m*

**by** [baɪ] **I.** *prep* **1.** (*near*) cerca de; **close** [*or* **near**] **~...** cerca de... **2.** (*at*) junto a; **~ the sea** junto al mar **3.** **~ day/night** durante el día/la noche **4.** (*at the latest*) para; **~ tomorrow/midnight** para mañana/la medianoche; **~ then/now** para entonces/ahora **5.** (*cause*) por; **a novel ~ Joyce** una novela de Joyce; **to be seen ~ sth/sb** ser visto por algo/alguien; **surrounded ~ dogs** rodeado de perros **6.** **~ train/plane/bus** en tren/avión/autobús; **~ hand** a mano; **~ doing sth** haciendo algo **7.** (*through*) **~ chance/mistake** por suerte/error; **what does he mean ~ that?** ¿a qué se refiere con eso? **8.** (*to be*) **~ oneself** (estar) solo **9.** MAT **to divide ~ 6** dividir entre 6; **to increase ~ 10%** aumentar en un 10%; **to multiply ~ 4** multiplicar por 4; **paid ~ the hour/day** pagado por hora/día; **one ~ one** uno a uno **II.** *adv* **1.** (*aside*) cerca; **to put/lay sth ~** poner/dejar algo a mano **2.** **~ and ~** dentro de poco **3.** **to go/pass ~** pasar

**bye** [baɪ], **bye-bye** [,baɪ·'baɪ] *interj inf* adiós

**bylaw** n reglamento m local; (*organization's rule*) estatuto m

**bypass** ['baɪ·pæs] I. n AUTO circunvalación f II. vt evitar

**byproduct** ['baɪ·prad·əkt] n subproducto m; *fig* derivado m

**byroad** ['baɪ·roʊd] n carretera f secundaria

**bystander** ['baɪ·stæn·dər] n espectador(a) m(f)

**byte** [baɪt] n byte m

**byway** ['baɪ·weɪ] n carretera f secundaria

**byword** ['baɪ·wɜrd] n ejemplo m; **to be a ~ for sth** ser sinónimo de algo

# C

**C, c** [si] n 1. (*letter*) C, c f; **~ as in Charlie** C de Carmen 2. SCHOOL ≈ bien m

**C** *after* n *abbr of* **Celsius, centigrade** C

**c.** 1. *abbr of* **circa** (*by numbers*) aprox.; (*by dates*) hacia 2. *abbr of* **cent** cent 3. *abbr of* **cup** taza f (*aprox. 250 ml*)

**C.** *abbr of* **century** s.

**CA** n *abbr of* **California** California f

**cab** [kæb] n taxi m; **by ~** en taxi

**cabaret** [,kæb·ə·'reɪ] n cabaret m

**cabbage** ['kæb·ɪdʒ] n repollo m

**cabbie, cabby** ['kæb·i], **cabdriver** n taxista m

**cabin** ['kæb·ɪn] n cabaña f; NAUT, AVIAT cabina f

**cabin cruiser** n yate m de motor

**cabinet** ['kæb·ɪ·nɪt] n 1. (*cupboard*) armario m; (*glass*) vitrina f 2. + *sing/pl* vb POL gabinete m

**cabinetmaker** n ebanista mf

**cable** ['keɪ·bəl] n cable m

**cable car** n teleférico m

**cable network** n cableado m

**cable railway** n funicular m

**cable television, cable TV** n televisión f por cable

**caboodle** [kə·'bud·əl] n *inf* **the whole (kit and) ~** toda la pesca

**cabriolet** [,kæb·ri·ə·'leɪ] n descapotable m

**cache** [kæʃ] n 1. (*place*) escondite m; (*stockpile*) alijo m 2. COMPUT caché m

**cackle** ['kæk·əl] I. *vi* (*hen*) cacarear; (*laugh*) reírse escandalosamente II. n (*hen*) cacareo m; (*laugh*) risotada f

**cactus** ['kæk·təs] <-es *or* **cacti**> n cactus m *inv*, ulala f *Bol*

**cafe, café** [kæ·'feɪ] n cafetería f

**cafeteria** [,kæf·ɪ·'tɪr·i·ə] n self-service m

**caffeine** [kæ·'fin] n cafeína f

**cage** [keɪdʒ] I. n jaula f II. vt enjaular

**cagey** ['keɪ·dʒi] <-ier, -iest> adj *inf* reservado, -a

**cahoots** [kə·'huts] n **to be in ~** estar compinchado(s) (**with** con)

**cake** [keɪk] n pastel m; **frosted ~** tarta f helada; **sponge ~** bizcocho m, queque m *AmL* ▶ **to sell like hot ~s** venderse como rosquillas

**cal.** n *abbr of* **calorie** cal.

**Cal.** *abbr of* **California** California f

**calamity** [kə·'læm·ə·ti] <-ies> n calamidad f

**calcium** ['kæl·si·əm] n calcio m

**calculate** ['kæl·kjə·leɪt] vt, vi calcular (**at** en)

**calculated** adj 1. (*likely*) probable 2. MATH calculado, -a; **a ~ risk** un riesgo calculado

**calculating** adj calculador(a)

**calculation** [,kæl·kjə·'leɪ·ʃən] n cálculo m

**calculator** ['kæl·kjə·leɪ·tər] n calculadora f

**calendar** ['kæl·ən·dər] n calendario m, exfoliador m *Chile, Méx*

**calendar year** n año m civil

**calf** [kæf] <**calves**> n ZOOL ternero, -a m, f; ANAT pantorrilla f

**caliber** ['kæl·ə·bər] n calibre m

**Calif.** [,kæl·ə·'fɔr·njə] *abbr of* **California** California f

**California** [,kæl·ə·'fɔr·njə] n California f

**call** [kɔl] I. n 1. a. TEL llamada f; **a ~ for help** una llamada de socorro; **to give sb a ~** llamar a alguien (por teléfono) 2. (*visit*) visita f; **to be on ~/on ~** estar de visita/de guardia 3. (*shout*) grito m ▶ **to have a close ~** salvarse por los pelos II. vt 1. (*name, address as*) llamar; **what's that actor ~ed?** ¿cómo se llama ese actor?; **to ~ sb's attention** llamar la atención de alguien;

you ~ **this a party?** ¿a esto lo llamas fiesta? **2.** TEL llamar, telefonear *AmL;* **to ~ sb collect** llamar a alguien a cobro revertido **3.** (*meeting*) convocar; (*strike*) declarar; **to ~ a halt to sth** suspender algo **III.** *vi* **1.** TEL llamar **2.** (*drop by*) pasar **3.** (*shout*) gritar

◆**call back** *vt* **1.** TEL devolver la llamada a **2.** (*ask to return*) hacer volver

◆**call for** *vt insep* **1.** (*come to get*) pasar a recoger **2.** (*ask*) pedir; (*demand, require*) exigir; **this calls for a celebration** esto hay que celebrarlo

◆**call in** *vt* (*ask to come*) llamar

◆**call off** *vt* (*cancel*) suspender

◆**call out I.** *vt* gritar **II.** *vi* gritar; **to call out for sth** *fig* exigir algo

◆**call up** *vt* TEL llamar

**call center** *n* TEL centro *m* de atención de llamadas

**calligraphy** [kə·ˈlɪg·rə·fi] *n* caligrafía *f*

**calling card** *n* tarjeta *f* telefónica

**calm** [kam] **I.** *adj* **1.** (*not nervous*) tranquilo, -a; **to keep ~** mantener la calma **2.** (*peaceful*) pacífico, -a **3.** (*not windy*) sin viento **II.** *n* tranquilidad *f* **III.** *vt* tranquilizar; **to ~ oneself** calmarse

**calorie** [ˈkæl·ə·ri] *n* caloría *f*

**calorie-laden** *adj* rico, -a en calorías

**camcorder** [ˈkæm·kɔr·dər] *n* videocámara *f*

**came** [keɪm] *vi pt of* **come**

**camel** [ˈkæm·əl] *n* **1.** ZOOL camello *m* **2.** (*color*) beige *m*

**camera** [ˈkæm·ər·ə] *n* PHOT, CINE cámara *f*

**camouflage** [ˈkæm·ə·flaʒ] **I.** *n* camuflaje *m* **II.** *vt* camuflar

**camp** [kæmp] **I.** *n* **1.** (*encampment*) campamento *m;* **summer ~** campamento de verano **2.** (*group*) bando *m;* **to go over to the other ~** pasarse al otro bando **II.** *vi* **to ~** (**out**) acampar; **to go ~ing** ir de acampada, campear *AmL*

**campaign** [kæm·ˈpeɪn] **I.** *n* campaña *f;* **~ trail** campaña electoral **II.** *vi* hacer campaña (**for** a favor de)

**camper** [ˈkæm·pər] *n* campista *mf;* AUTO caravana *f*

**campground** *n* camping *m,* campamento *m Col, Méx*

**camping** [ˈkæm·pɪŋ] *n* camping *m;* **to go ~** ir de acampada

**campsite** [ˈkæmp·saɪt] *n* campamento *m,* camping *m*

**campus** [ˈkæm·pəs] <-es> *n* campus *m inv*

**can**[1] [kæn] **I.** *n* **1.** (*container*) lata *f* **2.** *sl* (*toilet*) trono *m* **3.** *inf* (*prison*) trullo *m* **II.** <-nn-> *vt* **1.** enlatar **2.** *sl* **~ it!** ¡basta ya!

**can**[2] [kən] <could, could> *aux* **1.** (*be able to*) poder; **if I could** si pudiera; **I think she ~ help you** creo que ella te puede ayudar; **I could have kissed her** habría podido besarla **2.** (*be permitted to*) poder; **you can't go** no puedes ir; **could I look at it?** ¿podría verlo? **3.** (*know how to*) saber; **~ you swim?** ¿sabes nadar?

**Canada** [ˈkæn·ə·də] *n* Canadá *m*

**Canadian** [kə·ˈneɪ·di·ən] *adj, n* canadiense *mf*

**canal** [kə·ˈnæl] *n* canal *m*

**canalization** [ˌkæn·ə·lɪ·ˈzeɪ·ʃən] *n* canalización *f*

**canary** [kə·ˈner·i] <-ies> *n* canario *m*

**cancel** [ˈkæn·səl] <-ll-, -l-> *vt a.* COMPUT cancelar; (*party, concert*) suspender; (*result, license*) anular

**cancellation** [ˌkæn·sə·ˈleɪ·ʃən] *n* cancelación *f;* (*party, concert*) suspensión *f;* (*license*) anulación *f;* (*contract*) rescisión *f*

**cancer** [ˈkæn·sər] *n* cáncer *m,* cangro *m Col, Guat*

**Cancer** [ˈkæn·sər] *n* Cáncer *m*

**candid** [ˈkæn·dɪd] *adj* franco, -a; (*talk*) sincero, -a; (*picture*) natural

**candidacy** [ˈkæn·dɪ·də·si] *n* candidatura *f*

**candidate** [ˈkæn·dɪ·dət] *n a.* POL candidato, -a *m, f*

**candid camera** *n* cámara *f* indiscreta

**candle** [ˈkæn·dəl] *n* vela *f* ▶ **she can't hold a ~ to him** no le llega ni a la suela del zapato

**candlelight** [ˈkæn·dəl·laɪt] *n* luz *f* de una vela; **by ~** a la luz de las velas

**candlepower** [ˈkæn·dəl·pau·ər] *n* candela *f*

**candlestick** [ˈkæn·dəl·stɪk] *n* candelabro *m*

**candy** ['kæn·di] I. <-ies> n golosinas fpl II. vt escarchar

**candy store** n tienda f de golosinas

**cane** [keɪn] n 1. (plant) caña f 2. (furniture) mimbre m 3. (stick) bastón m

**cane sugar** n azúcar m de caña

**canister** ['kæn·ɪ·stər] n (metal) lata f; (plastic) bote m

**cannabis** ['kæn·ə·bɪs] n cannabis m

**canned** [kænd] adj enlatado, -a; (fruit, vegetables) en conserva; (food, meat, beer) de lata

**cannibal** ['kæn·ɪ·bəl] n caníbal mf

**cannibalism** ['kæn·ɪ·bəl·ɪz·əm] n canibalismo m

**cannibalize** ['kæn·ɪ·bə·laɪz] vt AUTO desguazar

**cannon** ['kæn·ən] n cañón m

**cannot** ['kæn·at] aux = can not see can²

**canny** ['kæn·i] <-ier, -iest> adj (clever) astuto, -a

**canoe** [kə'nu] n canoa f

**canoeing** n piragüismo m

**canon** ['kæn·ən] n REL, MUS canon m

**can opener** ['kæn·ˌoʊ·pə·nər] n abrelatas m inv

**can't** [kænt] = cannot

**canteen** [kæn·'tin] n (container) cantimplora f

**canvas** ['kæn·vəs] <-es> n 1. (cloth) lona f 2. ART lienzo m, holán m AmC

**canvass** ['kæn·vəs] I. vt 1. (information) sondear; **to ~ sth** hacer una encuesta de algo 2. (votes) escrutar II. vi POL hacer campaña

**canyon** ['kæn·jən] n cañón m

**cap¹** [kæp] I. n 1. gorro m; (with peak) gorra f 2. (cover) tapón m 3. (limit) tope m II. <-pp-> vt (limit) limitar; (cover) tapar; **to ~ it all** para colmo

**cap²** [kæp] n abbr of **capital letter** mayúscula f

**capability** [ˌkeɪ·pə·'bɪl·ə·ti] <-ies> n (ability) capacidad f

**capable** ['keɪ·pə·bəl] adj 1. (competent) competente 2. (able) capaz; **to be ~ of doing sth** ser capaz de hacer algo

**capacity** [kə·'pæs·ə·ti] <-ies> n 1. capacidad f; (mental) aptitud f; **seating ~** aforo m; **filled** [or **full**] **to ~** comple-

tamente lleno 2. (output) rendimiento m; **to work at full ~** trabajar a pleno rendimiento

**cape¹** [keɪp] n GEO cabo m

**cape²** [keɪp] n (cloak) capa f

**caper** ['keɪ·pər] n BOT alcaparra f

**capital** ['kæp·ə·təl] I. n 1. (city) capital f 2. TYPO mayúscula f 3. ARCHIT capitel m 4. FIN capital m II. adj 1. (principal) primordial 2. TYPO mayúscula f

**capital investment** n inversión f de capital

**capitalism** ['kæp·ə·təl·ɪz·əm] n capitalismo m

**capitalist** ['kæp·ə·təl·ɪst] adj, n capitalista mf

**capital letter** ['kæp·ə·təl·'le·t̬ər] n mayúscula f; **in ~s** en mayúsculas

**capital punishment** n pena f de muerte

**cappuccino** [ˌkæp·ə·'tʃi·noʊ] n capuchino m

**Capricorn** ['kæp·rɪ·kɔrn] n Capricornio m

**caps.** n abbr of **capital letter** mayúsc.

**capsize** ['kæp·saɪz] vi, vt fig volcar

**capsule** ['kæp·səl] n cápsula f

**captain** ['kæp·tɪn] n capitán, -ana m, f

**caption** ['kæp·ʃən] n TYPO, PUBL título m; CINE subtítulo m

**captivate** ['kæp·tə·veɪt] vt cautivar

**captive** ['kæp·tɪv] adj, n cautivo, -a m, f; **to hold sb ~** tener prisionero a alguien

**captivity** [kæp·'tɪv·ə·ti] n cautiverio m; **to be in ~** estar en cautividad

**capture** ['kæp·tʃər] I. vt 1. (take prisoner) apresar 2. (take possession of) capturar; (city) conquistar 3. (gain) a. ART captar 4. COMPUT recoger II. n captura f; (city) conquista f

**car** [kar] n coche m, carro m AmL; RAIL vagón m

**caramel** ['kar·məl] I. n (sweet) caramelo m II. adj de caramelo

**carat** <-(s)> n see **karat**

**caravan** ['kær·ə·væn] n (travelers) caravana f

**carbon** ['kar·bən] n CHEM carbono m

**carbon dioxide** n see dióxido m de carbono

**carbon monoxide** n monóxido m de carbono

**carburetor** ['kar·bə·reɪ·t̬ər] n carburador *m*

**carcinogenic** [ˌkar·sɪn·ə·ˈdʒen·ɪk] *adj* cancerígeno, -a

**card** [kard] *n* 1. (*greetings*) a. FIN, COMPUT tarjeta *f*; (*index* ~) ficha *f* 2. GAMES carta *f*; **pack of ~s** baraja; **to play ~s** jugar a las cartas 3. (*identity*) carnet *m*; **membership** ~ carnet de socio 4. tarjeta *f* ▸ **to have a ~ up one's sleeve** tener un as en la manga; **to put one's ~s on the table** poner las cartas sobre la mesa; **to play one's ~s right** jugar bien sus cartas

**cardboard** [ˈkard·bɔrd] *n* cartón *m*

**cardiac** [ˈkar·dɪ·æk] *adj* cardíaco, -a; (*disease*) cardiovascular

**cardigan** [ˈkar·dɪ·ɡən] *n* rebeca *f*

**cardinal** [ˈkar·dɪn·əl] *n* REL, ZOOL cardenal *m*; MAT cardinal *m*

**cardinal number** *n* número *m* cardinal

**cardinal points** *npl* puntos *m pl* cardinales

**card index** [ˈkard·ˌɪn·deks] <-es> *n* fichero *m*

**cardiogram** [ˈkar·di·ə·ɡræm] *n* cardiograma *m*

**care** [ker] I. *n* 1. (*attention*) cuidado *m*; **to take ~ of** cuidar de; (*object*) guardar; (*situation*) encargarse de; **take ~ (of yourself)!** ¡cuídate!; **handle with ~** frágil 2. (*worry*) preocupación *f* II. *vi* 1. (*concern*) preocuparse (**about** por); **as if I ~d!** ¿y a mí qué?; **who ~s?** ¿qué más da? 2. (*affection*) importar 3. **to ~ to do sth** estar dispuesto a hacer algo

**career** [kə·ˈrɪr] *n* 1. (*profession*) profesión *f* 2. (*working life*) carrera *f*

**carefree** [ˈker·fri] *adj* despreocupado, -a

**careful** [ˈker·fəl] *adj* 1. (*cautious*) cuidadoso, -a; (*driver*) prudente; **to be ~ of sth** tener cuidado con algo; **to be ~ to do sth** procurar hacer algo 2. (*meticulous*) meticuloso, -a; (*worker*) esmerado, -a

**careless** [ˈker·lɪs] *adj* distraído, -a; (*carefree*) despreocupado, -a

**carelessness** *n* (*lack of attention*) falta *f* de atención; (*of concern*) despreocupación *f*

**caress** [kə·ˈres] I. <-es> *n* caricia *f* II. *vi, vt* acariciar, barbear *AmC*

**caretaker** [ˈker·ˌteɪ·kər] *n* vigilante *mf*, guachimán *m Col, CRi, Chile, Pan, GuinEc, Nic*

**car ferry** <-ies> *n* transbordador *m*

**cargo** [ˈkar·ɡoʊ] <-(e)s> *n* (*goods*) carga *f*; (*load*) cargamento *m*

**Caribbean** [ˌker·ɪ·ˈbi·ən] I. *n* **the** ~ el Caribe II. *adj* caribeño, -a, caribe *AmL*

**caricature** [ˈker·ə·kə·tjʊr] *n* caricatura *f*

**caries** [ˈker·iz] *n* caries *f inv*

**caring** *adj* compasivo, -a

**car insurance** *n* seguro *m* de vehículos

**carnival** [ˈkar·nə·vəl] *n* carnaval *m*, chaya *f Arg, Bol, Chile*

**carnivorous** [kar·ˈnɪv·ər·əs] *adj* carnívoro, -a

**carol** [ˈker·əl] *n* (*song*) villancico *m*

**carp** [karp] <-(s)> *n* ZOOL carpa *f*

**carpenter** [ˈkar·pən·tər] *n* carpintero, -a *m, f*

**carpentry** [ˈkar·pən·tri] *n* carpintería *f*

**carpet** [ˈkar·pət] I. *n* alfombra *f*; (*fitted*) moqueta *f* ▸ **to sweep sth under the ~** correr un velo sobre algo II. *vt* enmoquetar, alfombrar *AmL*

**car rental** *n* alquiler *m* de coches

**carriage** [ˈker·ɪdʒ] *n* (*vehicle*) carruaje *m*

**carrier** [ˈkær·i·ər] *n* 1. (*company*) empresa *f* de transportes 2. MED portador, -a *m(f)*

**carrot** [ˈker·ət] *n* CULIN zanahoria *f*

**carry** [ˈker·i] <-ies, -ied> *vt* 1. (*bear*) llevar; (*bring*) traer; **to ~ a child** esperar un hijo; **to ~ consequences** tener consecuencias 2. (*transport*) transportar 3. MED transmitir

◆**carry along** *vt* llevar

◆**carry away** *vt* 1. (*remove*) arrastrar 2. **to be carried away (by)** (*be overcome*) dejarse llevar (por); (*be enchanted*) entusiasmarse *f*

◆**carry forward** *vt* FIN transferir

◆**carry off** *vt* (*sb*) llevarse; (*sth*) salir airoso de

◆**carry on** I. *vt insep* seguir II. *vi* 1. (*continue*) seguir; **to ~ doing sth** continuar haciendo algo 2. *inf* (*make a fuss*) montar un número

◆**carry out** *vt* (*repairs*) hacer; (*plan, attack*) llevar a cabo; (*job*) realizar; (*or-*

*der*) cumplir

◆**carry over** *vt* **1.** FIN transferir **2.** (*postpone*) posponer

◆**carry through** *vt* **1.** (*support*) sostener **2.** (*complete*) llevar a término

**carryall** ['kær·ɪ·ɔl] *n* bolso *m* grande

**carryover** *n* **1.** FIN pérdida trasladada al ejercicio siguiente **2.** (*remnant*) remanente *m*

**cart** [kart] **I.** *n* carro *m* **II.** *vt* acarrear

**carte blanche** [ˌkart·'blanʃ] *n* carta *f* blanca

**cartel** [kar·'tel] *n* cártel *m*

**cartilage** ['kar·təl·ɪdʒ] *n* cartílago *m*

**carton** [kar·tən] *n* caja *f* de cartón; (*juice, milk*) brik *m*

**cartoon** [kar·'tun] *n* viñeta *f;* CINE dibujos *m pl* animados

**cartridge** [kar·trɪdʒ] *n* cartucho *m,* cachimba *f AmL*

**carve** [karv] **I.** *vt* cortar; (*stone, wood*) tallar; (*meat*) trinchar **II.** *vi* cortar

**carving** *n* escultura *f;* **wood ~** talla *f*

**car wash** <-es> *n* tren *m* de lavado

**cascade** [kæs·'keɪd] *n* cascada *f*

**case¹** [keɪs] *n a.* MED, LING, LAW caso *m;* **in any ~** en cualquier caso; **just in ~** por si acaso; **in ~ it rains** en caso de que llueva

**case²** [keɪs] *n* (*container*) caja *f;* (*jewels, glasses*) estuche *m;* (*camera, guitar*) funda *f*

**casebook** *n* diario *m;* MED registro *m*

**cash** [kæʃ] **I.** *n* dinero *m* en efectivo **II.** *vt* cobrar

◆**cash in** **I.** *vt insep* canjear **II.** *vi* **to ~ on sth** sacar provecho de algo

**cash cow** *n sl* gallina *f* de los huevos de oro

**cashew** ['kæ·u] *n* anacardo *m,* acajú *m Cuba, Méx, PRico, RDom*

**cashier** [kæ·'ʃɪr] *n* cajero, -a *m, f*

**cash register** *n* caja *f* registradora

**casing** ['keɪ·sɪŋ] *n* cubierta *f;* (*machine*) carcasa *f*

**casino** [kə·'si·noʊ] *n* casino *m*

**casserole** ['kæs·ə·roʊl] *n* cazuela *f*

**cassette** [kə·'set] *n* cinta *f*

**cast** [kæst] **I.** *n* **1.** THEAT, CINE reparto *m* **2.** (*mold*) molde *m* **3.** MED escayola *f* **II.** <cast, cast> *vt* **1.** (*throw*) lanzar

**2.** (*direct: vote*) emitir; **to ~ doubt on sth** poner algo en duda; **to ~ a shadow on sth** ensombrecer algo; **to ~ light on sth** proyectar luz sobre algo; *fig* echar luz sobre algo

◆**cast aside**, **cast away** *vt* (*rid oneself of*) dejar de lado; (*free oneself of*) desechar

**casting** ['kæs·tɪŋ] *n* **1.** ART vaciado *m* **2.** THEAT reparto *m* de papeles

**cast-iron** *adj* de hierro fundido; (*evidence*) irrefutable; (*alibi*) a toda prueba; (*promise*) firme

**castle** ['kæs·əl] **I.** *n* castillo *m;* (*chess*) torre *f* ▶ **to build ~s in the air** construir castillos en el aire **II.** *vi* enrocar

**castoff** ['kæst·af] **I.** *n* **~s** ropa desechada *f* **II.** *adj* desechado, -a

**castor** ['kæs·tər] *n* ruedecita *f*

**castrate** [kæs·'treɪt] *vt* castrar, componer *AmL*

**casual** ['kæʒ·u·əl] *adj* **1.** (*relaxed*) relajado, -a **2.** (*chance*) casual; (*meeting*) fortuito, -a **3.** (*not habitual*) de vez en cuando **4.** (*informal*) informal; (*clothes*) informal

**casually** *adv* de forma relajada

**casualty** ['kæʒ·u·əl·ti] <-ies> *n* (*victim*) víctima *f;* MIL baja *f;* (*injured*) herido, -a *m, f*

**cat** [kæt] *n* gato, -a *m, f* ▶ **to let the ~ out of the bag** descubrir el pastel; (*carelessly*) irse de la lengua; **to fight like ~s and dogs** llevarse como (el) perro y (el) gato; **to rain ~s and dogs** llover a cántaros; **has the ~ got your tongue?** ¿te ha comido la lengua el gato?, ¿te comieron la lengua los ratones? *Col, Méx*

**catalog** ['kæt·əl·aɡ] **I.** *n* catálogo *m;* (*repeated events*) serie *f;* **a ~ of mistakes** un error detrás de otro **II.** *vt* catalogar

**catastrophe** [kə·'tæs·trə·fi] *n* catástrofe *f*

**catastrophic** [ˌkæt·ə·'straf·ɪk] *adj* catastrófico, -a

**catcall** ['kæt·kɔl] *n* (*booing*) abucheo *m;* (*whistling*) silbido *m*

**catch** [kætʃ] <-es> **I.** *n* **1.** (*fish*) pesca *f;* **he's a good ~** *fig* es un buen partido **2.** (*door*) pestillo *m;* (*window*) cierre *m* **II.** <caught, caught> *vt* **1.** (*object*) agarrar; (*animal, person*) atrapar; **to ~ sb**

**at a bad moment** pillar a alguien en un mal momento **2.** (*entangle*) involucrar; **to get caught in sth** quedar atrapado en algo; **to get caught up in sth** verse involucrado en algo; **to get caught on sth** engancharse a algo **3.** (*notice*) darse cuenta de; (*hear*) pillar **4.** (*attract*) atraer **5.** (*get*) coger, tomar *AmL*; **to ~ the bus** coger el autobús **6. to ~ sb** (*doing sth*) pillar a alguien (haciendo algo); **to ~ sb red-handed** pillar a alguien con las manos en la masa **7.** *slang* pillar

◆**catch on** *vi* **1.** (*become popular*) ponerse de moda **2.** *inf* (*understand*) pillar

◆**catch up with** *vi* ponerse al día en; (*person*) alcanzar el nivel de

**catch phrase** ['kætʃ·freɪz] *n* eslogan *m*

**catchy** ['kætʃ·i] <-ier, -iest> *adj* pegadizo, -a

**categorical** [ˌkæt̬·ə·ˈgɔr·ɪ·kəl] *adj* categórico, -a

**category** ['kæt̬·ə·gɔr·i] <-ies> *n* categoría *f*

**cater** ['keɪ·t̬ər] *vi* llevar el catering

**catering** ['keɪ·t̬ər·ɪŋ] *n* catering *m*

**caterpillar** ['kæt̬·ər·pɪl·ər] *n* ZOOL oruga *f*

**catfish** *n* siluro *m*, bagre *m Col, Méx*

**cathedral** [kə·ˈθi·drəl] *n* catedral *f*

**Catholic** ['kæθ·ə·lɪk] *adj, n* católico, -a *m, f*

**Catholicism** [kə·ˈθɑl·ə·sɪz·əm] *n* catolicismo *m*

**catsup** ['kætʃ·əp] *n see* **ketchup**

**cattle** ['kæt̬·əl] *npl* ganado *m*; **beef ~** ganado vacuno

**cattle breeder** *n* ganadero, -a *m, f*

**cattle breeding** *n* ganadería *f*

**cattle car** *n* vagón *m* de ganado

**catty** ['kæt̬·i] <-ier, -iest> *adj* (*hurtful*) malicioso, -a

**catwalk** ['kæt·wɔk] *n* FASHION pasarela *f*

**caught** [kɔt] *pt, pp of* **catch**

**cauliflower** ['kɔ·lɪ·flaʊ·ər] *n* coliflor *f*

**cause** [kɔz] **I.** *n* causa *f*; **he is the ~ of all her woes** es el causante de todas sus penas; **this is no ~ for...** esto no justifica... **II.** *vt* provocar; (*harm*) ocasionar; **to ~ sb/sth to do sth** hacer que alguien/algo haga algo

**caution** ['kɔ·ʃən] *n* **1.** (*carefulness*) cau-

tela *f*; **with ~** con cuidado **2.** (*warning*) advertencia *f*; **a note of ~** un aviso; **~!** ¡cuidado!

**cautious** ['kɔ·ʃəs] *adj* prudente (**about** con)

**cave** [keɪv] *n* cueva *f*

**cave dweller** *n* cavernícola *mf*

**cave-in** *n* derrumbamiento *m*

**caveman** ['keɪv·mæn] <-men> *n* cavernícola *m*

**cavern** ['kæv·ərn] *n* caverna *f*

**cavity** ['kæv·ɪ·t̬i] <-ies> *n* **1.** *a.* ANAT cavidad *f*; **nasal ~** fosa *f* nasal **2.** MED caries *f inv*

**cayenne** [kaɪ·ˈen] *n* cayena *f*

**CD** [ˌsi·ˈdi] *n abbr of* **compact disc** CD *m*; **on ~** en CD

**CD-ROM** [ˌsi·di·ˈrɑm] *n abbr of* **compact disc read-only memory** CD-ROM *m*

**cease** [sis] *form* **I.** *vi* cesar; **to ~ to do sth** cesar de (hacer) algo **II.** *vt* suspender; **it never ~s to amaze me** nunca deja de sorprenderme **III.** *n* **without ~** sin cesar

**ceaseless** ['sis·lɪs] *adj* incesante

**ceiling** ['si·lɪŋ] *n* **1.** techo *m* **2.** (*upper limit*) tope *m*; (*on prices*) límite *m* ▶ **to hit the ~** subirse por las paredes

**celebrate** ['sel·ɪ·breɪt] *vi, vt* celebrar

**celebrated** *adj* célebre

**celebration** [ˌsel·ɪ·ˈbreɪ·ʃən] *n* celebración *f*; (*of an event*) conmemoración *f*; **this calls for** (**a**) **~!** ¡esto hay que celebrarlo!

**celebrity** [sə·ˈleb·rə·t̬i] *n* **1.** <-ies> (*person*) famoso, -a *m, f* **2.** (*fame*) celebridad *f*

**celery** ['sel·ə·ri] *n* apio *m*, panul *m CSur*

**celery root** *n* apio *m* nabo

**cell** [sel] *n* **1.** (*prison*) celda *f*, separo *m Méx* **2.** BIO, POL célula *f*; **grey ~s** materia gris

**cellar** ['sel·ər] *n* sótano *m*; (*for wine*) bodega *f*

**cello** ['tʃel·oʊ] <-s *or* -li> *n* violonchelo *m*

**cellophane** ['sel·ə·feɪn] *n* celofán *m*

**cell phone** ['sel·foʊn] *n* móvil *m*, celular *m Col*

**cellular phone** *n* móvil *m*, celular *m Col*

**cellulite** ['sel·jə·laɪt] *n* celulitis *f inv*

**celluloid** ['sel·jʊ·lɔɪd] *n* celuloide *m*

**cellulose** ['sel·jʊ·loʊs] *n* celulosa *f*

**Celsius** ['sel·si·əs] *adj* Celsius

**cement** [sɪ·'ment] I. *n* 1. ARCHIT cemento *m* 2. (*glue*) cola *f* 3. MED empaste *m* II. *vt* 1. (*stabilize*) fortalecer; (*friendship*) consolidar 2. MED empastar

**cemetery** ['sem·ə·ter·i] <-ies> *n* cementerio *m*, panteón *m AmL*

**censor** ['sen·sər] I. *n* censor(a) *m(f)* II. *vt* censurar

**censorship** ['sen·sər·ʃɪp] *n* censura *f*

**censure** ['sen·ʃər] *vt* censurar

**census** ['sen·səs] <-es> *n* censo *m*

**cent** [sent] *n* centavo *m*; (*euro*) céntimo *m*

**centenarian** [ˌsen·tə·'ner·i·ən] *n* centenario, -a *m, f*

**centenary** ['sen·tə·ner·i] <-ies>, **centennial** [sen·'ten·i·əl] *n* centenario *m*

**center** ['sen·tər] I. *n* centro *m*; (*of population*) núcleo *m* II. *vt* centrar; (*efforts*) concentrar

◆**center around** *vi* girar en torno a

◆**center on** *vi* concentrarse en

**centigrade** ['sen·tə·greɪd] *adj* centígrado, -a

**centigram** ['sen·tə·græm] *n* centigramo *m*

**centimeter** ['sen·tə·ˌmi·tər] *n* centímetro *m*

**central** ['sen·trəl] *adj* 1. (*at the middle*) central; **in ~ Boston** en el centro de Boston 2. (*important*) vital (**to** para); **the ~ character** el protagonista 3. (*bank, air conditioning, unit*) central

**century** ['sen·tʃə·ri] <-ies> *n* siglo *m*; **the twentieth ~** el siglo XX

**ceramic** [sə·'ræm·ɪk] *adj* de cerámica

**cereal** ['sɪr·i·əl] *n* cereal *m*; (*breakfast*) cereales

**ceremonial** [ˌser·ə·'moʊ·ni·əl] *adj, n* ceremonial *m*

**ceremony** ['ser·ə·moʊ·ni] <-ies> *n* ceremonia *f*

**certain** ['sɜr·tən] I. *adj* 1. (*sure*) seguro, -a; **for ~** con certeza; **it is quite ~ (that)...** es muy probable que... +*subj*; **to be ~ about sb** confiar en alguien; **to be ~ about sth** estar convencido de algo;

**to feel ~ (that...)** estar convencido (de que...); **to make ~ (that...)** asegurarse (de que...) 2. (*undeniable*) cierto, -a; **it is ~ that...** es cierto que...; **the disaster seemed ~** el desastre parecía inevitable 3. (*specified*) cierto, -a; **to a ~ extent** hasta cierto punto; **a ~ Steve** un tal Steve II. *pron* cierto, -a

**certainly** *adv* desde luego; **~ not!** ¡desde luego que no!; **why, ~!** ¡claro que sí!

**certainty** ['sɜr·tən·ti] <-ies> *n* certeza *f*; **with ~** a ciencia cierta

**certificate** [sər·'tɪf·ɪ·kət] *n* certificado *m*; (*birth, death*) partida *f*; (*ownership, school*) título *m*

**certification** [ˌsɜr·tə·fɪ·'keɪ·ʃən] *n* (*process*) certificación *f*; (*document*) certificado *m*

**certify** ['sɜr·tə·faɪ] <-ie-> *vt* certificar

**cervical** ['sɜr·vɪ·kəl] *adj* cervical; **~ collar** collarín *m*

**cesarean** [sə·'zer·i·ən] *n* **a ~ section** una cesárea

**chador** [tʃə·'dor] *n* chador *m*

**chain** [tʃeɪn] I. *n* 1. **a.** *fig* cadena *f* 2. GEO cordillera *f* II. *vt* encadenar; **to be ~ed to a desk** *fig* estar encerrado en un despacho

**chain mail** *n* cota *f* de malla

**chain reaction** *n* reacción *f* en cadena; **to set off a ~** provocar una reacción en cadena

**chain saw** *n* motosierra *f*

**chain smoker** *n* fumador(a) *m(f)* empedernido, -a

**chair** [tʃer] I. *n* 1. (*seat*) silla *f* 2. (*head*) presidente, -a *m, f* 3. UNIV cátedra *f* II. *vt* presidir

**chairlift** *n* telesilla *m*

**chairman** ['tʃer·mən] <-men> *n* presidente *m*

**chairperson** ['tʃer·ˌpɜr·sən] *n* presidente, -a *m, f*

**chairwoman** <-women> *n* presidenta *f*

**chalet** [ʃæ·'leɪ] *n* chalet *m*

**chalk** [tʃɔk] *n* tiza *f*, gis *m Méx*; GEO caliza

**challenge** ['tʃæl·ɪndʒ] I. *n* desafío *m*; **to pose a ~ to sth** poner algo en tela de juicio II. *vt* 1. (*ask to compete*) desafiar 2. (*question*) cuestionar

**challenging** *adj* desafiante; (*course, task*) exigente; (*book*) que hace pensar

**chamber** ['tʃeɪm·bər] *n a.* ANAT, POL, ECON cámara *f*

**chameleon** [kə·ˈmi·li·ən] *n* camaleón *m*

**chamomile** ['kæm·ə·maɪl] *n ~* (**tea**) manzanilla *f*

**champ** [tʃæmp] **I.** *n inf* campeón, -ona *m, f* **II.** *vi, vt* masticar

**champagne** [ʃæm·ˈpeɪn] **I.** *n* champán *m* **II.** *adj* color champán

**champion** ['tʃæm·pi·ən] **I.** *adj, n* campeón, -ona *m, f* **II.** *vt* defender

**championship** ['tʃæm·pi·ən·ʃɪp] *n* campeonato *m*; (*of cause*) defensa *f*

**chance** [tʃæns] **I.** *n* **1.** (*random*) casualidad *f*; **a ~ encounter** un encuentro casual; **a game of ~** un juego de azar; **to leave nothing to ~** no dejar nada al azar; **by ~** por casualidad **2.** (*likelihood*) probabilidad *f*; **the ~s are that she's already gone** lo más probable es que ya se haya marchado; **on the off ~ that** con la esperanza de que; **to stand a ~ of doing sth** tener posibilidades de hacer algo; **not a ~!** ¡ni de coña! **3.** (*opportunity*) oportunidad *f* (**to do sth** de hacer algo); **to give sb a ~** dar a alguien una oportunidad; **to have the ~** tener la oportunidad; **to miss one's ~** perder la oportunidad; **to jump at the ~** no dejar escapar la oportunidad; **to take a ~** arriesgarse **II.** *vt* arriesgar; **to ~ it** arriesgarse **III.** *vi* ocurrir (por casualidad)

**chancellor** ['tʃæn·sə·lər] *n* canciller *mf*; UNIV rector(a) *m(f)*

**chancy** ['tʃæn·si] <-ier, -iest> *adj* arriesgado, -a

**change** ['tʃeɪndʒ] **I.** *n* **1.** (*alteration*) cambio *m*; **for a ~** para variar **2.** (*coins*) suelto *m*, sencillo *m AmL*, feria *f Méx*; **small ~** calderilla *f inf*; **a dollar in ~** un dólar en monedas; **have you got ~ for a twenty-dollar bill?** ¿tienes cambio de 20 dólares? **3.** (*money returned*) vuelta *f*, vuelto *m AmL*; **no ~ given** no (se) devuelve cambio; **to have exact ~** tener el importe exacto **II.** *vt* cambiar; **to ~ places with sb** *fig* ponerse en el lugar de alguien; **to ~ sth/sb into sth** convertir algo/a alguien en algo; **to ~ trains/**

**gear(s)** cambiar de tren/marcha **III.** *vi* **1.** cambiar; **to ~ into sth** convertirse en algo; **the traffic light ~d back to red** el semáforo se puso en rojo **2.** (*train/plane*) hacer transbordo **3.** (*clothes*) cambiarse (de ropa)

**changeable** ['tʃeɪn·dʒə·bəl] *adj* cambiante

**changeover** ['tʃeɪndʒ·ˌoʊ·vər] *n* transición *f*

**changing** ['tʃeɪn·dʒɪŋ] *adj* cambiante; **~ room** vestuario *m*; (*shop*) probador *m*

**channel** ['tʃæn·əl] **I.** *n a.* TV canal *m*; **irrigation ~** acequia *f*; **through diplomatic ~s** por la vía diplomática **II.** <-ll-, -l-> *vt* canalizar; *fig* encauzar

**chaos** ['keɪ·as] *n* caos *m inv*

**chaotic** [keɪ·ˈat·ɪk] *adj* caótico, -a

**chap** [tʃæp] <-pp-> **I.** *vi* agrietarse, pasparse *RíoPl* **II.** *vt* agrietar

**chapel** ['tʃæp·əl] *n* capilla *f*; **funeral ~** capilla ardiente

**chapter** ['tʃæp·tər] *n* capítulo *m*

**chapter house** *n* UNIV sala *f* de reuniones

**character** ['ker·ək·tər] *n* **1.** (*qualities*) *a.* TYPO carácter *m*; **to be in/out of ~ with sb/sth** ser/no ser típico de alguien/algo **2.** (*moral integrity*) reputación *f* **3.** (*representation*) personaje *m*, carácter *m Col, Méx*; **in the ~ of** en el papel de

**characteristic** [ker·ək·tə·ˈrɪs·tɪk] **I.** *n* característica *f* **II.** *adj* característico, -a; **with her ~ dignity** con la dignidad que la caracteriza

**charcoal** ['tʃar·koʊl] *n* **1.** carbón *m* vegetal **2.** ART carboncillo *m*, carbonilla *f RíoPl*; **to draw in ~** dibujar al carboncillo

**charge** [tʃardʒ] **I.** *n* **1.** (*cost*) precio *m*; **at no extra ~** sin cargo adicional; **free of ~** gratis **2.** LAW cargo *m*; **to bring ~s** presentar cargos (**against** contra) **3.** MIL, ELEC carga *f*; SPORTS ofensiva *f* **4.** (*authority*) responsabilidad *f*; **to be in ~ of sb/sth** tener algo/a alguien a su cargo; **who is in ~ here?** ¿quién es el responsable aquí? **II.** *vi* **1.** FIN cobrar **2.** (*attack*) arremeter; MIL cargar (**at** contra) **3.** ELEC cargarse **III.** *vt* **1.** FIN cobrar; **to ~ sth to**

sb's account cargar algo en la cuenta de alguien **2.** LAW acusar; **she's been ~d with murder** se la acusa de asesinato **3.** ELEC cargar

**chargeable** ['tʃar·dʒə·bəl] *adj* ~ **to the customer** a cargo del cliente; **to be ~ to tax** estar sujeto a impuestos

**charge card** *n* tarjeta *f* de pago

**charged** *adj* cargado, -a

**charisma** [kə·'rɪz·mə] *n* carisma *m*

**charity** ['tʃer·ə·ţi] <-ies> *n* caridad *f*; (*organization*) institución *f* benéfica

**charm** [tʃarm] **I.** *n* encanto *m* **II.** *vt* cautivar; **to ~ sb into doing sth** embelesar a alguien para que haga algo

**charming** ['tʃar·mɪŋ] *adj* encantador(a)

**chart** [tʃart] **I.** *n* **1.** tabla *f* **2.** MUS **the ~s** la lista de éxitos **II.** *vt* trazar

**charter flight** *n* vuelo *m* chárter

**chase** [tʃeɪs] **I.** *n* persecución *f*; (*hunt*) *a. fig* caza *f*; **to give ~** dar caza **II.** *vi* **they ~ed after her** fueron tras ella **III.** *vt* perseguir; **to ~ away sb/sth** ahuyentar a alguien/algo

**chaste** [tʃeɪst] *adj* casto, -a

**chat** [tʃæt] **I.** *n* charla *f*; COMPUT chat *m* **II.** *vi* <-tt-> charlar, versar *AmC*; **to ~ away** estar de cháchara, echar la chorcha *Méx*; COMPUT chatear

**chatroom** *n* foro *m* de chat

**chatter** ['tʃæţ·ər] **I.** *n* cháchara *f* **II.** *vi* charlar

**chatty** ['tʃæţ·i] <-ier, -iest> *adj inf* hablador(a)

**cheap** [tʃip] *adj* barato, -a; **dirt ~** tirado, -a de precio; **~ labor** mano de obra barata

**cheaply** *adv* de forma barata

**cheat** [tʃit] **I.** *n* **1.** (*person*) estafador(a) *m(f)* **2.** (*trick*) trampa *f* **II.** *vi* hacer trampa(s) (**at** en); **to ~ on a test** copiar en un examen **III.** *vt* engañar

**check** [tʃek] **I.** *n* **1.** (*inspection, restraint*) control *m*; **security ~** control de seguridad; **to keep sth in ~** mantener algo bajo control; (*of facts*) verificación *f*; **to run a ~** realizar una inspección **2.** (*deposit receipt*) resguardo *m* **3.** (*paper money*) cheque *m*; **to pay by ~** pagar con cheque **4.** (*bill*) cuenta *f* **5.** (*chess*) jaque *m* **II.** *adj* a

cuadros **III.** *vt* **1.** (*inspect*) comprobar, chequear *AmL* **2.** (*prevent*) frenar **3.** (*deposit*) dejar en consigna; AVIAT facturar **IV.** *vi* **1.** (*examine*) revisar **2.** (*ask*) consultar

♦**check in** *vi* (*airport*) facturar; (*hotel*) registrarse

♦**check out I.** *vi* **to ~ of a room** dejar libre una habitación **II.** *vt* (*investigate*) investigar

♦**check up on** *vt* controlar

**checkbook** ['tʃek·ˌbʊk] *n* talonario *m* de cheques

**checked** *adj* a cuadros

**checkerboard** ['tʃek·ər·ˌbɔrd] *n* tablero *m* de ajedrez

**checkers** ['tʃek·ərz] *n* + *sing vb* damas *fpl*

**check-in** ['tʃek·ɪn] *n* facturación *f*

**checking account** *n* cuenta *f* corriente

**check-in time** *n* hora *f* de facturación

**checklist** ['tʃek·lɪst] *n* lista *f*

**checkmate I.** *n* (*jaque m*) mate *m*; (*defeat*) fracaso *m* **II.** *vt* dar (jaque) mate a; *fig* ganar

**checkout counter** *n* caja *f*

**checkpoint** ['tʃek·pɔɪnt] *n* punto *m* de control

**checkroom** *n* (*for coats*) guardarropa *m*; (*for luggage*) consigna *f*

**checkup** ['tʃek·ʌp] *n* comprobación *f*; MED chequeo *m*

**cheek** [tʃik] *n* mejilla *f*; (*impertinence*) descaro *m*, empaque *m AmL*; **to have the ~ to do sth** tener la cara dura de hacer algo

**cheekbone** ['tʃik·boʊn] *n* pómulo *m*

**cheeky** ['tʃi·ki] <-ier, -iest> *adj* descarado, -a, fregado, -a *AmL* (**to** con)

**cheep** [tʃip] *vi* piar

**cheer** [tʃɪr] **I.** *n* **1.** (*shout*) ovación *f*; **three ~s for the champion!** ¡tres hurras por el campeón!; **to give a ~** vitorear **2.** (*joy*) alegría *f*; **to be of good ~** estar animado **II.** *interj* **~s** salud **III.** *vt* **to ~ for sb** animar a alguien

**cheerful** ['tʃɪr·fʊl] *adj* alegre; (*encouraging*) alentador(a); (*color*) vivo, -a

**cheerfulness** *n* alegría *f*

**cheering I.** *n* aplausos *mpl* **II.** *adj* alentador(a)

**cheerleader** ['tʃɪr·ˌli·dər] *n* animadora *f*

**cheery** ['tʃɪr·i] <-ier, -iest> *adj* alegre

**cheese** [tʃiz] *n* queso *m*; **hard/melted ~** queso curado/fundido

**cheesecake** ['tʃiz·keɪk] *n* tarta *f* de queso

**cheese-paring** ['tʃiz·ˌper·ɪŋ] *n* tacaño, -a *m, f*

**cheesy** ['tʃi·zi] <-ier, -iest> *adj* **1.** como queso **2.** (*cheap and shoddy*) chungo, -a

**cheetah** ['tʃi·tə] *n* guepardo *m*

**chef** [ʃef] *n* jefe, -a *m, f* de cocina

**chemical** ['kem·ɪ·kəl] **I.** *n* sustancia *f* química; (*additive*) aditivo *m* **II.** *adj* químico, -a

**chemist** ['kem·ɪst] *n* químico, -a *m, f*

**chemistry** ['kem·ɪ·stri] *n* química *f*

**cherry** ['tʃer·i] <-ies> *n* cereza *f*; (*tree*) cerezo *m*

**cherry tomato** *n* tomate *m* cherry

**chess** [tʃes] *n* ajedrez *m*

**chessman** <-men>, **chess piece** *n* pieza *f* de ajedrez

**chest** [tʃest] *n* **1.** ANAT pecho *m* **2.** (*trunk*) baúl *m*, petaca *f* AmL; **medicine ~** botiquín *m* ▶ **to get sth off one's ~** desahogarse confesando algo

**chestnut** ['tʃes·nʌt] **I.** *n* castaña *f*; (*tree, color*) castaño *m* **II.** *adj* castaño, -a

**chesty** ['tʃes·ti] <-ier, -iest> *adj inf* pechugona, bustona *Col, Méx*

**chew** [tʃu] *vt* masticar

◆**chew out** *vt sl* echar la bronca a

**chewing gum** ['tʃu·ɪŋ·gʌm] *n* chicle *m*

**chic** [ʃik] *adj* a la moda

**Chicano** [tʃɪ·'ka·noʊ] *n adj* chicano, -a *m, f*

**chick** [tʃɪk] *n* **1.** (*chicken*) pollito, -a *m, f*; (*bird*) polluelo, -a *m, f* **2.** *sl* tía *f*

**chicken** ['tʃɪk·ən] *n* **1.** (*farm bird*) pollo *m*; **fried/roasted/grilled ~** pollo frito/asado/a la brasa **2.** *inf* rajado, -a *m, f*, rajón, -ona *m, f Cuba, Méx*

**chicken feed** *n* **1.** pienso *m* **2.** (*money*) calderilla *f*

**chickenpox** *n* varicela *f*

**chicken run** *n* gallinero *m*

**chickpea** ['tʃɪk·pi] *n* garbanzo *m*

**chicory** ['tʃɪk·ə·ri] *n* BOT endivia *f*

**chief** [tʃif] **I.** *n* jefe, -a *m, f* **II.** *adj* (*top*) primero, -a; (*major*) principal

**chiefly** *adv* principalmente

**child** [tʃaɪld] <children> *pl n* niño, -a *m, f*

**child abuse** ['tʃaɪld·ə·bjus] *n* maltrato *m* infantil; (*sexual*) abuso *m* infantil

**childbearing** *n* maternidad *f*

**childbirth** *n* parto *m*, parición *f AmL*

**child-care** *n* cuidado *m* de los niños

**childhood** *n* infancia *f*

**childish** ['tʃaɪl·dɪʃ] *adj pej* infantil, achiquillado, -a *Méx*

**childless** ['tʃaɪld·lɪs] *adj* sin hijos

**childlike** ['tʃaɪld·laɪk] *adj* infantil

**children** ['tʃɪl·drən] *n pl of* **child**

**child's play** *n fig* juego *m* de niños

**chile, chili** ['tʃɪl·i] <-es> *n* guindilla *f*, chile *m AmL*, ají *m AmS, Ant*

**Chile** ['tʃɪl·i] *n* Chile *m*

**Chilean** [tʃɪ·'leɪ·ən] *adj, n* chileno, -a *m, f*

**chill** [tʃɪl] **I.** *n* **1.** (*coldness*) frío *m*; **to catch a ~** resfriarse; **to take the ~ off of something** caldear algo **2.** (*shiver*) escalofrío *m*; **to send a ~ down someone's spine** dar escalofríos a alguien **II.** *adj* frío, -a; (*frightening*) estremecedor(a) **III.** *vt* enfriar

**chilly** ['tʃɪl·i] <-ier, -iest> *adj a. fig* frío, -a; **to feel ~** tener frío

**chime** [tʃaɪm] **I.** *vi* repicar **II.** *vt* **to ~ eleven** dar las once

**chimney** ['tʃɪm·ni] *n* chimenea *f*, tronera *f Méx*

**chimpanzee** [tʃɪm·'pæn·zi] *n* chimpancé *m*

**chin** [tʃɪn] *n* barbilla *f* ▶ **to keep one's ~ up** no desanimarse

**china** ['tʃaɪ·nə] *n* (*porcelain*) porcelana *f*; (*dishes*) vajilla *f*

**China** ['tʃaɪ·nə] *n* China *f*

**Chinatown** ['tʃaɪ·nə·ˌtoʊn] *n* barrio *m* chino

**Chinese** [tʃaɪ·'niz] **I.** *adj* chino, -a **II.** *n* **1.** (*person*) chino, -a *m, f* **2.** LING chino *m*

**Chinese cabbage** *n* col *f* china

**chink** [tʃɪŋk] **I.** *n* **1.** (*thin opening*) hendidura *f* **2.** (*noise*) tintineo *m* **II.** *vi* tintinear

**chip** [tʃɪp] **I.** *n* **1.** (*flake*) pedazo *m*; (*wood*) astilla *f* **2.** COMPUT chip *m* **3.** (*token*) ficha *f* ▶ *inf* **he's a ~ off the old block** de tal palo, tal astilla; **when the**

~s are <u>down</u> a la hora de la verdad
II. vt <-pp-> desportillar III. vi <-pp->
desportillarse

**chirpy** ['tʃɜr·pi] <-ier, -iest> adj animado, -a

**chitchat** ['tʃɪt·ˌtʃæt] inf I. n cháchara f
II. vi to ~ about sth estar de palique
sobre algo

**chlorine** ['klɔr·in] n cloro m

**chloroform** ['klɔr·ə·fɔrm] n clorofor-
mo m

**chock** [tʃak] n cuña f

**chock-a-block** [ˌtʃak·ə·'blak] adj ~ with
**people** abarrotado de gente

**chocolate** ['tʃak·lət] n chocolate m; **dark**
~ chocolate negro; (candy) bombón m

**choice** [tʃɔɪs] I. n 1. (option) elección f; **to make a** ~ elegir; **to have**
**no** ~ no tener alternativa; **she didn't**
**have much** ~ no tenía muchas opciones 2. (selection) selección f; **a wide** ~
un amplio surtido 3. (selected person
or thing) preferencia f II. adj (top quality) selecto, -a

**choir** ['kwaɪr] n coro m

**choke** [tʃoʊk] I. vi sofocarse II. vt 1. (stifle) estrangular 2. (block) obstruir

♦**choke back** vt ahogar

♦**choke off** vt cortar

♦**choke up** vt obstruir

**choker** ['tʃoʊ·kər] n gargantilla f

**cholesterol** [kə·'les·tə·ral] n colesterol m

**choose** [tʃuz] <chose, chosen> vt, vi
elegir

**choos(e)y** ['tʃu·zi] <-ier, -iest> adj inf
quisquilloso, -a

**chop** [tʃap] I. vt <-pp-> cortar; (wood)
partir; (meat) picar II. vi <-pp-> cortar III. n 1. CULIN chuleta f 2. (blow)
golpe m

♦**chop away** vt cortar

♦**chop down** vt talar

♦**chop off** vt tronchar

**chop-chop** [ˌtʃap·'tʃap] interj inf ¡vamos,
que nos vamos!

**chopper** ['tʃap·ər] n 1. (tool) hacha f
2. inf helicóptero m

**chopsticks** ['tʃap·stɪks] npl palillos mpl

**chord** [kɔrd] n MUS acorde m

**chore** [tʃɔr] n 1. tarea f; **household**
~s quehaceres domésticos 2. (tedious

task) lata f

**choreography** [ˌkɔr·i·'ag·rə·fi] n coreografía f

**chorus** ['kɔr·əs] <-es> n 1. (refrain)
estribillo m 2. + sing/pl vb (singers)
coro m; **in** ~ a coro

**chose** [tʃoʊz] pt of **choose**

**chosen** ['tʃoʊ·zən] pp of **choose**

**Christ** [kraɪst] I. n Cristo m II. interj
sl ¡Dios!, ¡joder! vulg; **for ~'s sake**
¡por Dios!

**christen** ['krɪs·ən] vt 1. (baptize) bautizar
2. (give name to) llamar 3. (use for first
time) estrenar

**christening** ['krɪs·ə·nɪŋ] n bautizo m

**Christian** ['krɪs·tʃən] adj, n cristiano,
-a m, f

**Christianity** [ˌkrɪs·tʃi·'æn·ə·ti] n cristianismo m

**Christmas** ['krɪs·məs] <-es or -ses> n
Navidad f; **at** ~ en Navidad; **Merry**
~! ¡Feliz Navidad!; **Father** ~ Papá Noel

**Christmas carol** n villancico m

**Christmas Day** n día m de Navidad
[or Perú, Chile Pascua]

**Christmas Eve** n Nochebuena f

**chromosome** ['kroʊ·mə·soʊm] n cromosoma m

**chronic** ['kran·ɪk] adj crónico, -a; (liar)
empedernido, -a

**chronicle** ['kran·ɪ·kəl] n crónica f

**chronological** [ˌkran·ə·'ladʒ·ɪ·kəl] adj
cronológico, -a; **in** ~ **order** en orden
cronológico

**chubby** ['tʃʌb·i] <-ier, -iest> adj regor-
dete, -a

**chuck** [tʃʌk] inf I. vt tirar II. n tiro m

**chuckhole** n bache m, pozo m Csur

**chuckle** ['tʃʌk·əl] I. n risita f II. vi reírse

**chug** [tʃʌg] I. <-gg-> vi resoplar II. n
resoplido m

**chum**[1] [tʃʌm] n inf colega mf, cuate m Méx

**chum**[2] [tʃʌm] n (bait) cebo m

**chummy** ['tʃʌm·i] <-ier, -iest> adj inf
simpático, -a; **to get ~ with sb** hacerse
amigo de alguien

**chump** [tʃʌmp] n inf tontorrón, -ona m, f

**chump change** n sl calderilla f

**chunk** [tʃʌŋk] n 1. (cheese, bread, meat)
trozo m, troncho m CSur 2. inf (large

*part*) cacho m

**chunky** ['tʃʌŋ·ki] <-ier, -iest> *adj* (*person*) macizo, -a; CULIN con trocitos

**church** [tʃɜrtʃ] I. *n* iglesia *f;* **to go to ~** ir a misa II. *adj* (*parade, celebration*) religioso, -a

**churchgoer** ['tʃɜrtʃ·ˌgou·ər] *n* practicante *mf*

**churchyard** ['tʃɜrtʃ·ˌjɑrd] *n* cementerio m

**chute** [ʃut] *n* 1. (*sloping tube*) rampa *f;* garbage ~ vertedero m de basuras 2. (*swimming pool*) tobogán m 3. *inf* AVIAT paracaídas m *inv*

**cicada** <-s *or* -dae> [sɪ'keɪdə] *n* cigarra *f*

**cider** ['saɪ·dər] *n* sweet ~ zumo m de manzana

**cigar** [sɪ'gɑr] *n* puro m

**cigar box** <-es> *n*, **cigar case** *n* pitillera *f*

**cigar cutter** *n* cortapuros m *inv*

**cigarette** [ˌsɪg·ə·'ret] *n* cigarrillo m

**cigarette butt** *n* colilla *f*

**cigarette case** *n* pitillera *f*

**cigarette holder** *n* boquilla *f*

**cigarette paper** *n* papel m de fumar, mortaja *f AmL*

**cigarillo** [sɪg·ə·'rɪl·ou] *n* purito m

**cinema** ['sɪn·ə·mə] *n* cine m, biógrafo m *Arg, Chile, Urug*

**cinnamon** ['sɪn·ə·mən] *n* canela *f;* **ground/stick ~** canela en polvo/en rama

**cipher** ['saɪ·fər] *n* clave *f;* **in ~** en clave

**circa** ['sɜr·kə] *prep* hacia; **~ 1850** hacia (el año) 1850

**circle** ['sɜr·kəl] I. *n* círculo m; **to go around in ~s** dar vueltas; **to run around in ~s** *fig* dar vueltas y más vueltas a algo ▶ **to come full ~** volver al punto de partida II. *vt* rodear III. *vi* dar vueltas

**circuit** ['sɜr·kɪt] *n* 1. ELEC, SPORTS circuito m 2. POL distrito m

**circuit board** *n* placa *f* base

**circular** ['sɜr·kjə·lər] *adj*, *n* circular *f*

**circulate** ['sɜr·kjə·leɪt] I. *vt* divulgar II. *vi* circular

**circulation** [ˌsɜr·kju·'leɪ·ʃən] *n* circulación *f;* **to be out of ~** estar fuera de circulación

**circulatory** ['sɜr·kjə·lə·ˌtɔr·i] *adj* circulatorio, -a

**circumstance** ['sɜr·kəm·stæns] *n* circunstancia *f;* **under no ~s** bajo ningún concepto

**circus** ['sɜr·kəs] <-es> *n* circo m

**cirrhosis** [sə·'rou·sɪs] *n* cirrosis *f inv*

**cistern** ['sɪs·tərn] *n* cisterna *f,* jagüel m *AmL*

**citizen** ['sɪt·ɪ·zən] *n* 1. (*subject*) ciudadano, -a *m, f* 2. (*resident of town*) habitante *mf*

**citizens' band** *n* banda *f* ciudadana

**citizenship** ['sɪt·ɪ·zən·ˌʃɪp] *n* ciudadanía *f*

**citrus** ['sɪt·rəs] <citrus *or* citruses> I. *n* cítrico m II. *adj* cítrico, -a

**city** ['sɪt·i] <-ies> I. *n* ciudad *f* II. *adj* urbano, -a

**city hall** *n* ayuntamiento m

**civic** ['sɪv·ɪk] <inv> *adj* cívico, -a; (*authorities*) civil

**civil** ['sɪv·əl] *adj* civil; (*courteous*) cortés

**civil court** *n* Sala *f* de lo Civil

**civilian** [sɪ·'vɪl·jən] <inv> I. *n* civil *mf* II. *adj* civil; (*clothes*) de paisano, -a

**civilization** [ˌsɪv·ə·lɪ·'zeɪ·ʃən] *n* civilización *f*

**civil servant** *n* funcionario, -a *m, f*

**civil service** *n* Administración *f* Pública

**clad** [klæd] I. *adj* vestido, -a II. *vt pt, pp of* **clothe**

**claim** [kleɪm] I. *n* 1. (*assertion*) afirmación *f* 2. (*demand*) demanda *f;* (*insurance*) reclamación *f;* **to put in a ~** presentar una demanda (**for** por) 3. (*right*) derecho m; **to lay ~ to** reivindicar II. *vt* 1. (*assert*) asegurar 2. (*declare ownership, demand*) reclamar; (*right, reward, title*) reivindicar; **to ~ damages** reclamar daños y perjuicios 3. (*require*) requerir III. *vi* **to ~ for** reclamar

**claimant** ['kleɪ·mənt] *n* solicitante *mf*

**clam** [klæm] *n* 1. almeja *f* 2. *sl* dólar m ▶ **to be happy as a ~** estar feliz como una lombriz

**clamber** ['klæm·bər] *vi* trepar

**clammy** ['klæm·i] <-ier, -iest> *adj* (*feet*) sudoroso, -a; (*weather*) bochornoso, -a

**clamp** [klæmp] *vt* (*impose*) imponer

◆**clamp down** *vi* tomar medidas drásticas (**on** contra)

**clan** [klæn] n clan m

**clandestine** [klæn·ˈdes·tɪn] adj clandestino, -a

**clang** [klæŋ] I. vi repicar II. n estruendo m metálico

**clank** [klæŋk] I. vi hacer ruido II. vt hacer sonar III. n ruido m metálico

**clap** [klæp] I. <-pp-> vt aplaudir; **to ~ one's hands** (**together**) hacer palmas II. <-pp-> vi hacer palmas; (applaud) aplaudir III. n (slap) palmada f; (applause) aplauso m

**claptrap** [ˈklæp·træp] n inf chorradas fpl argot

**clarify** [ˈkler·ɪ·faɪ] <-ie-> vt 1. (make clearer) aclarar 2. (explain) explicar

**clarity** [ˈkler·ə·ti] n claridad f

**clash** [klæʃ] I. vi 1. (fight) pelearse; (argue) discutir (**over** por) 2. (compete) enfrentarse; (views) contradecirse; (colors) desentonar II. <-es> n 1. (encounter) enfrentamiento m 2. (contest) contienda f 3. (conflict) conflicto m 4. (incompatibility) choque m 5. (noise) estruendo m

**clasp** [klæsp] I. n cierre m; (of hands) apretón m II. vt 1. (grip) agarrar; **to ~ one's hands** darse un apretón de manos; **to ~ sb in one's arms** estrechar a alguien entre sus brazos 2. (fasten) abrochar

**class** [klæs] I. <-es> n clase f II. vt catalogar (**as** de)

**classic** [ˈklæs·ɪk] I. adj clásico, -a; (typical) típico, -a; inf (joke, story) genial II. n clásico m

**classical** [ˈklæs·ɪ·kəl] adj clásico, -a

**classification** [ˌklæs·ə·fɪ·ˈkeɪ·ʃən] n clasificación f

**classified** [ˈklæs·ɪ·faɪd] <inv> adj clasificado, -a; (confidential) confidencial

**classified advertisement** n anuncio m clasificado

**classify** [ˈklæs·ɪ·faɪ] <-ie-> vt clasificar

**classmate** n compañero, -a m, f de clase

**classroom** n aula f

**clatter** [ˈklæt̬·ər] I. vi hacer ruido II. n estruendo m

**clause** [klɔz] n cláusula f; LING oración f

**claustrophobia** [ˌklɔ·strə·ˈfoʊ·bi·ə] n claustrofobia f

**claustrophobic** adj claustrofóbico, -a

**clavicle** [ˈklæv·ɪ·kəl] n clavícula f

**claw** [klɔ] I. n garra f; (crab, lobster) pinza f; **to show one's ~s** fig sacar las uñas II. vt arañar

**clay** [kleɪ] I. n 1. arcilla f 2. SPORTS tierra f batida II. adj de arcilla

**clean** [klin] I. adj 1. (not dirty, fair, smooth) limpio, -a; **to make a ~ break with sth** romper por completo con algo 2. (morally acceptable) decente; (reputation) sin tacha II. n limpieza f III. adv completamente IV. vt, vi limpiar

◆ **clean out** vt 1. limpiar; (with water) lavar 2. sl (make penniless) dejar sin blanca a

◆ **clean up** I. vt 1. limpiar; (tidy up) ordenar; **to clean oneself up** asearse 2. (eradicate) acabar con II. vi 1. limpiar 2. sl (make profit) barrer con todo

**cleaner** [ˈkli·nər] n limpiador(a) m(f); (substance) producto m de limpieza

**cleaning** [ˈkli·nɪŋ] n limpieza f

**cleaning lady** <-ies>, **cleaning woman** <women> n mujer f de la limpieza

**cleanly** [ˈklen·li] adv limpiamente

**cleanse** [klenz] vt limpiar; (morally) purificar

**clean-shaven** [ˈklin·ˈʃeɪ·vən] adj bien afeitado, -a

**cleansing cream** n leche f limpiadora

**cleansing tissue** n toallita f desmaquilladora

**cleanup** [ˈklin·ʌp] n limpieza f

**clear** [klɪr] I. n **to be in the ~** estar fuera de peligro II. adv claramente; **to get ~** deshacerse (**of** de); **to stand ~** mantenerse a distancia (**of** de) III. adj 1. (transparent, obvious) claro, -a; (picture) nítido, -a; **to make oneself ~** explicarse con claridad; **as ~ as day** más claro que el agua 2. (conscience) tranquilo, -a; **to be ~ of debt** estar libre de deudas IV. vt 1. (make free) despejar; (drain, pipe) desatascar 2. (remove doubts) aclarar; **to ~ one's head** despejar la cabeza 3. (acquit) absolver V. vi (water) aclararse; (weather) despejarse

◆ **clear away** I. vt quitar II. vi irse

◆ **clear off** I. vi inf largarse, jalar Bol,

PRico, Urug **II.** vt liquidar

◆**clear out I.** vt limpiar; (*throw away*) vaciar **II.** vi irse

◆**clear up I.** vt aclarar; (*tidy*) ordenar **II.** vi despejarse

**clearance** ['klɪr·əns] n **1.** (*space*) espacio m libre **2.** (*permission*) autorización f

**clearance sale** n liquidación f

**clearheaded** adj perspicaz

**clearing** ['klɪr·ɪŋ] n claro m

**clearly** ['klɪr·li] adv claramente

**clef** [klef] n MUS clave f

**clench** [klentʃ] vt presionar; (*one's fist*) apretar

**clerical** ['kler·ɪ·kəl] adj **1.** REL clerical **2.** (*of offices*) de oficina; ~ **worker** oficinista mf

**clerk** [klɜrk] n (*in office*) oficinista mf; (*in hotel*) recepcionista mf; (*in shop*) dependiente mf

**clever** ['klev·ər] adj **1.** (*intelligent*) listo, -a **2.** (*skillful*) hábil; (*invention*) ingenioso, -a **3.** pej astuto, -a; **to be too ~ by half** pasarse de listo

**cleverness** n inteligencia f; (*skill*) habilidad f

**cliché** [kli·'ʃeɪ] n cliché m; (*platitude*) tópico m

**click** [klɪk] **I.** n clic m **II.** vi **1.** (*sound*) chasquear **2.** COMPUT pinchar **3.** (*become friendly*) congeniar; (*become popular*) tener éxito **4.** (*become clear*) caer en la cuenta **III.** vt (*tongue*) chasquear; (*heels*) taconear; COMPUT pinchar

**client** ['klaɪ·ənt] n cliente mf

**cliff** [klɪf] n precipicio m; (*on coast*) acantilado m

**climactic** [ˌklaɪ·'mæk·tɪk] adj culminante

**climate** ['klaɪ·mɪt] n clima m; **the ~ of opinion** la opinión general

**climatic** [klaɪ·'mæt·ɪk] adj climático, -a

**climax** ['klaɪ·mæks] **I.** <-es> n clímax m inv **II.** vi culminar; (*sexual*) alcanzar el orgasmo

**climb** [klaɪm] **I.** n subida f; (*to power*) ascenso m **II.** vt (*stairs*) subir; (*tree*) trepar a; (*mountain*) escalar **III.** vi subir

◆**climb down** vi bajar(se) de; fig echarse atrás

**climb-down** ['klaɪm·daʊn] n vuelta f atrás

**climber** ['klaɪ·mər] n **1.** alpinista mf, andinista mf AmL; (*for higher status*) arribista mf **2.** (*plant*) enredadera f

**climbing** ['klaɪ·mɪŋ] **I.** n (*mountains*) alpinismo m, andinismo m AmL; (*rock faces*) escalada f **II.** adj (*plant*) trepador(a); (*boots*) de montaña

**climbing iron** n see **crampon**

**clinch** [klɪntʃ] **I.** <-es> n abrazo m **II.** vt (*settle*) resolver; (*deal*) cerrar

**clincher** ['klɪn·tʃər] n inf factor m decisivo

**cling** [klɪŋ] <clung, clung> vi **to ~ to** (*embrace*) abrazarse a; (*hold*) agarrarse a; fig aferrarse a; (*stick*) adherirse a; (*stay close*) pegarse a; (*follow closely*) no separarse de

**clinging** adj (*clothes*) ajustado, -a; (*person*) pegajoso, -a

**clinic** ['klɪn·ɪk] n clínica f

**clinical** ['klɪn·ɪ·kəl] adj clínico, -a; (*emotionless*) frío, -a

**clink** [klɪŋk] **I.** vt, vi tintinear **II.** n **1.** tintineo m **2.** sl (*prison*) chirona f

**clip¹** [klɪp] n (*fastener*) clip m; (*hair*) horquilla f; (*jewelry*) broche m **II.** <-pp-> vt sujetar

**clip²** [klɪp] <-pp-> **I.** vt **1.** (*cut*) recortar; (*hair, nails*) cortar; (*ticket*) picar **2.** (*reduce*) abreviar **II.** n (*trim*) recorte m; (*extract*) fragmento m

**clipboard** ['klɪp·bɔrd] n portapapeles m inv

**clique** [klik] n pandilla f

**clitoris** ['klɪt·ər·əs] <-es> n clítoris m inv

**cloak** [kloʊk] **I.** n capa f; (*covering*) manto m **II.** vt (*hide*) encubrir

**cloakroom** ['kloʊk·rum] n guardarropa m

**clobber** ['klab·ər] vt sl endiñar

**clock** [klak] **I.** n **1.** reloj m; **alarm ~** despertador m; **around the ~** las 24 horas; **against the ~** contrarreloj **2.** (*speedometer*) velocímetro m; (*odometer*) cuentakilómetros m inv **II.** vt cronometrar; (*reach*) alcanzar

◆**clock in** vi fichar

◆**clock out** vi fichar *(al salir del trabajo)*; inf salir del trabajo

◆**clock up** vt insep (*attain*) alcanzar; (*travel*) recorrer

**clock radio** n radio despertador f

**clockwise** adj, adv en el sentido de las agujas del reloj

**clockwork** n mecanismo m de relojería; **as regular as** ~ como un reloj

**clog** [klɑg] I. <-gg-> vi atascarse II. <-gg-> vt atascar

**clone** [kloʊn] I. n clon m II. vt clonar

**close¹** [kloʊs] I. adj 1. (near) cercano, -a; (friend) íntimo, -a 2. (almost even) raspado, -a 3. (similar) parecido, -a II. adv cerca; (in time) casi; **to move** ~ acercarse

**close²** [kloʊz] I. n (end) fin m II. vt (shut) cerrar; (end) terminar; **to ~ a deal** cerrar un trato III. vi (shut) cerrarse; (end) terminarse

◆**close down** I. vi cerrarse (definitivamente) II. vt cerrar (definitivamente)

◆**close in** vi 1. (surround) rodear 2. (get shorter) acortarse

◆**close off** vt cerrar

◆**close up** I. vi (people) arrimarse; (wound) cicatrizar II. vt cerrar del todo

**closed** adj cerrado, -a; **behind ~ doors** a puerta cerrada

**closed-door** adj a puerta cerrada

**closedown** n cierre m

**close-knit** adj unido, -a

**closely** [ˈkloʊs·li] adv 1. (near) de cerca 2. (intimately) estrechamente 3. (carefully) atentamente

**closet** [ˈklɑz·ɪt] n (cupboard) armario m; (for food) alacena f ▶ **to come out of the** ~ salir del armario

**close to** I. prep cerca de; ~ **doing sth** cerca de hacer algo; ~ **tears** a punto de llorar; **to be** ~ **sb** estar unido a alguien II. adv (almost) casi

**close-up** [ˈkloʊs·ʌp] n primer plano m

**closing** I. adj último, -a; (speech) de clausura II. n 1. (ending) conclusión f; (act) clausura f 2. com cierre m

**closing date** n fecha f límite

**closing time** n hora f de cierre

**closure** [ˈkloʊ·ʒər] n (closing) cierre m; (end) fin m

**clot** [klɑt] I. n coágulo m II. <-tt-> vi cuajar; (blood) coagularse

**cloth** [klɔθ] I. n tela f; (for cleaning) trapo m II. adj de tela

**clothe** [kloʊð] vt vestir; fig revestir de

**clothes** [kloʊz] npl ropa f

**clothes hanger** n percha f

**clotheshorse** n tendedero m plegable

**clothesline** n cuerda f para tender

**clothespin** n pinza f

**clothing** [ˈkloʊ·ðɪŋ] n ropa f; **article of** ~ prenda f

**cloud** [klaʊd] I. n nube f ▶ **every** ~ **has a silver lining** no hay mal que por bien no venga; **to be on** ~ **nine** estar en el séptimo cielo; **to be under a** ~ estar bajo sospecha II. vt a. fig nublar

◆**cloud over** vi nublarse; fig ensombrecerse

**cloudburst** n chaparrón m

**clouded** [ˈklaʊ·dɪd] adj nublado, -a; (liquid) turbio, -a; (mind) confuso, -a

**cloudless** [ˈklaʊd·lɪs] adj despejado, -a

**cloudy** [ˈklaʊ·di] <-ier, -iest> adj nublado, -a; (liquid) turbio, -a

**clout** [klaʊt] I. n 1. inf (hit) tortazo m 2. (power) influencia f II. vt inf dar un tortazo a

**clove** [kloʊv] n clavo m; (garlic) diente m

**clover** [ˈkloʊ·vər] n trébol m

**clown** [klaʊn] I. n payaso, -a m, f II. vi **to** ~ **around** hacer el payaso

**club** [klʌb] n 1. (group) asociación f, club m 2. (team, disco) club 3. (playing card) trébol m

**clubbing** vi **to go** ~ salir de clubs

**clue** [klu] n 1. (evidence) indicio m; (hint) pista f 2. (secret) clave f 3. (idea) idea f; **I don't have a** ~ no tengo ni idea

◆**clue in** vt informar (**on**)

**clueless** [ˈklu·lɪs] adj inf despistado, -a

**clump** [klʌmp] I. n **to** ~ **together** agrupar II. vi **to** ~ **together** agruparse

**clumsy** [ˈklʌm·zi] <-ier, -iest> adj desgarbado, -a; (bungling) torpe

**clung** [klʌŋ] pp, pt of **cling**

**cluster** [ˈklʌs·tər] I. n grupo m; (fruits) racimo m II. vi agruparse

**clutch** [klʌtʃ] I. vi agarrarse (**at a**) II. vt agarrar m n 1. auto embrague m 2. **to be in the ~es of** estar en las garras de; **to come through in the** ~ salir airoso

**clutter** [ˈklʌt·ər] I. n desorden m II. vt

desordenar

**cm** inv abbr of **centimeter** cm

**c'mon** inf = **come on**

**CO** n abbr of **Colorado** Colorado m

**co.** [koʊ] **1.** abbr of **company** cía. **2.** GEO abbr of **county** condado m

**coach** [koʊtʃ] **I.** <-es> n **1.** (bus) autocar m **2.** (carriage) carruaje m **3.** RAIL vagón m **4.** (teacher) profesor(a) m(f) particular; SPORTS entrenador(a) m(f) **II.** vt to ~ sb (in sth) enseñar (algo) a alguien **III.** vi dar clases particulares

**coaching** n preparación f

**coal** [koʊl] n carbón m

**coalition** [ˌkoʊ·ə·ˈlɪʃ·ən] n coalición f

**coarse** [kɔrs] <-r, -st> adj basto, -a; (sand) grueso, -a; (skin) áspero, -a

**coast** [koʊst] n costa f ▶ **the ~ is clear** no hay moros en la costa

**coastal** [ˈkoʊ·stəl] adj costero, -a, abajeño, -a AmL

**coaster** [ˈkoʊ·stər] n **1.** (for glasses) posavasos m inv **2.** (roller coaster) montaña f rusa

**coast guard** [ˈkoʊst·gɑrd] n, **Coast Guard** [ˈkoʊst·gɑrd] n guardacostas mf inv

**coastline** n línea f de costa

**coat** [koʊt] **I.** n **1.** (overcoat) abrigo m, tapado m AmS; (jacket) chaqueta f **2.** (animal's skin) pelaje m **3.** (layer) capa f; (paint) mano f; (chocolate) baño m **II.** vt cubrir (in de)

**coated** [ˈkoʊ·tɪd] adj cubierto, -a

**coat hanger** n percha f

**coating** [ˈkoʊ·tɪŋ] n see **coat I,3**

**coauthor** [koʊ·ˈɔ·θər] **I.** n coautor(a) m(f) **II.** vt escribir conjuntamente

**coax** [koʊks] vt convencer; **to ~ sth out of sb** sonsacarle algo a alguien

**cob** [kɒb] n (corn) mazorca f, elote m AmC, Méx

**cobble** [ˈkæb·əl] **I.** n adoquín m **II.** vt adoquinar; (shoe) remendar

**cobbler** [ˈkæb·lər] n zapatero m remendón

**cobweb** [ˈkæb·web] n telaraña f

**cocaine** [koʊ·ˈkeɪn] n cocaína f

**cock** [kɑk] **I.** n **1.** (chicken) gallo m **2.** vulg (penis) polla f, pichula f Arg, Chile, Perú **II.** vt **1.** (turn) ladear

**2.** (gun) amartillar

**cockfight** n pelea f de gallos

**cockpit** [ˈkɑk·pɪt] n **1.** AVIAT cabina f **2.** MIL campo m de batalla

**cockroach** [ˈkɑk·roʊtʃ] <-es> n cucaracha f, surupa f Ven

**cocktail** [ˈkɑk·teɪl] n cóctel m

**cocky** [ˈkɑk·i] <-ier, -iest> adj gallito, -a

**cocoa** [ˈkoʊ·koʊ] n cacao m; (drink) chocolate m

**coconut** [ˈkoʊ·kə·nʌt] n coco m

**coconut milk** n leche f de coco

**cocoon** [kə·ˈkun] n capullo m

**cod** [kɑd] n inv bacalao m

**code** [koʊd] **I.** n a. LAW código m **II.** vt cifrar

**coded** adj codificado, -a

**codeine** [ˈkoʊ·din] n codeína f

**code name** n nombre m en clave

**code number** n prefijo m

**code word** n palabra f en clave

**codify** [ˈkɑd·ɪ·faɪ] <-ie-> vt codificar

**coed** [ˈkoʊ·ed] adj inf mixto, -a

**coeducation** [ˌkoʊ·edʒ·ʊ·ˈkeɪ·ʃən] n educación f mixta

**coeducational** [ˌkoʊ·edʒ·ə·ˈkeɪ·ʃən·əl] adj mixto, -a

**coerce** [koʊ·ˈɜrs] vt coaccionar

**coexist** [ˌkoʊ·ɪg·ˈzɪst] vi coexistir

**coexistence** [ˌkoʊ·ɪg·ˈzɪs·təns] n coexistencia f

**coffee** [ˈkɔ·fi] n café m

**coffee bean** n grano m de café

**coffee break** n pausa f del café

**coffee-colored** adj de color café

**coffee cup** n taza f de café

**coffee grinder** n molinillo m de café

**coffeehouse** n cafetería f

**coffeemaker** n cafetera f, greca f AmL

**coffeepot** n cafetera f

**coffee shop** n cafetería f

**coffin** [ˈkɔ·fɪn] n ataúd m

**cog** [kɑg] n TECH diente m; (wheel) piñón m

**cognac** [ˈkoʊn·jæk] n coñac m

**cohabit** [koʊ·ˈhæb·ɪt] vi cohabitar

**coherence** [koʊ·ˈhɪr·əns] n coherencia f

**coherent** [koʊ·ˈhɪr·ənt] adj coherente

**coherently** adv coherentemente

**cohesion** [koʊ·ˈhi·ʒən] n cohesión f

**cohesive** [koʊ·ˈhi·sɪv] adj cohesivo, -a

**coil** [kɔɪl] I. n rollo m; ELEC bobina f II. vi enrollarse III. vt enrollar

**coin** [kɔɪn] I. n moneda f; **to toss a ~** echar a cara o cruz III. vt acuñar

**coincide** [ˌkou·ɪn·ˈsaɪd] vi coincidir; (agree) estar de acuerdo

**coincidence** [kou·ˈɪn·sɪ·dəns] n coincidencia f

**coincidental** [kou·ˌɪn·sɪ·ˈden·təl] adj coincidente

**coitus** [ˈkou·ə·təs] n coito m

**coke** [kouk] n 1. (drink) refresco m de cola 2. sl coca f

**col.** [kal] n abbr of **column** columna f

**cold** [kould] I. adj frío, -a; **to be ~** tener frío; **to go ~** enfriarse; **I'm getting cold** me está dando frío; **it's bitterly ~** hace un frío que pela ▶ **to leave sb ~** dejar frío a alguien II. n 1. **the ~** el frío 2. MED resfriado m; **to catch a ~** resfriarse ▶ **to leave sb out in the ~** dejar a alguien al margen

**cold-blooded** adj de sangre fría

**cold feet** n pl, sl miedítis f, culillo m Col, Nic, Ecua, Pan, ElSal

**cold-hearted** adj insensible

**coldish** [ˈkoul·dɪʃ] adj fresquito, -a

**cold turkey** n sl mono m

**collaborate** [kə·ˈlæb·ə·reɪt] vi colaborar

**collaboration** [kə·ˌlæb·ə·ˈreɪ·ʃən] n colaboración f

**collaborator** [kə·ˈlæb·ə·reɪ·tər] n 1. colaborador(a) m(f) 2. pej colaboracionista mf

**collage** [kə·ˈlaʒ] n collage m

**collapse** [kə·ˈlæps] I. vi 1. MED sufrir un colapso; PSYCH hundirse 2. (building) derrumbarse 3. (fail) fracasar II. n 1. MED colapso m 2. (people, building) hundimiento m 3. (failure) fracaso m

**collapsible** [kə·ˈlæp·sɪ·bəl] adj plegable

**collar** [ˈkal·ər] I. n 1. FASHION cuello m 2. (dog, cat) collar m II. vt sl agarrar

**collarbone** n clavícula f

**collateral** [kə·ˈlæt·ər·əl] adj colateral

**colleague** [ˈkal·ig] n colega mf

**collect** [kə·ˈlekt] I. vt 1. (gather) reunir; (money) recaudar; (stamps) coleccionar 2. (pick up) recoger II. vi 1. (gather) reunirse 2. (money) cobrar; (contributions) hacer una colecta [or Col vaca]

III. adj, adv (call) a cobro revertido

**collected** [kə·ˈlek·tɪd] adj sosegado, -a

**collection** [kə·ˈlek·ʃən] n 1. (money) recaudación f; REL colecta f 2. (objects) colección f 3. (large number) montón m 4. (act of getting) recogida f

**collective** [kə·ˈlek·tɪv] I. adj colectivo, -a II. n colectivo m

**collector** [kə·ˈlek·tər] n coleccionista mf; (payments) cobrador(a) m(f)

**college** [ˈkal·ɪdʒ] n colegio m; (university) universidad f

**collide** [kə·ˈlaɪd] vi chocar

**collision** [kə·ˈlɪʒ·ən] n colisión f

**colloquial** [kə·ˈlou·kwi·əl] adj familiar; (language) coloquial

**Colo.** [ˌkal·ə·ˈrad·ou] abbr of **Colorado** Colorado m

**cologne** [kə·ˈloun] n colonia f

**Colombia** [kə·ˈlʌm·bi·ə] n Colombia f

**Colombian** [kə·ˈlʌm·bi·ən] adj, n colombiano, -a m, f

**colon** [ˈkou·lən] n ANAT colon m; LING dos puntos

**colonel** [ˈkɜr·nəl] n coronel mf

**colonization** [ˌkal·ə·nɪ·ˈzeɪ·ʃən] n colonización f

**colonize** [ˈkal·ə·naɪz] vt colonizar

**colony** [ˈkal·ə·ni] <-ies> n colonia f

**color** [ˈkʌl·ər] I. n 1. color m; **what ~ is it?** ¿de qué color es? 2. (vigor) colorido m 3. (dye) tinte m II. vt 1. (change color) colorear; **to ~ a room blue** pintar una habitación de azul 2. (dye) teñir III. vi sonrojarse

**Colorado** [ˌkal·ə·ˈrad·ou] n Colorado m

**colorblind** adj daltónico, -a

**colored** adj coloreado, -a; (pencil, people) de color

**color filter** n filtro m de color

**colorful** [ˈkʌl·ər·fəl] adj 1. (full of color) colorido, -a 2. (lively) vivo, -a; (countryside) pintoresco, -a

**coloring** [ˈkʌl·ər·ɪŋ] n color m; (chemical) colorante m

**colorless** [ˈkʌl·ər·lɪs] adj incoloro, -a; (bland) soso, -a

**color scheme** n combinación f de colores

**colt** [koult] n potro m, potranco m AmL

**column** [ˈkal·əm] n columna f; **spinal ~**

columna vertebral

**coma** ['kou·mə] *n* coma *m;* **to go into a ~** entrar en coma; **to wake up out of one's ~** salir del coma

**comb** [koum] **I.** *n* peine *m;* ZOOL cresta *f* **II.** *vt* **to ~ one's hair** peinarse; **to ~ an area** peinar una zona

**combat** ['kam·bæt] **I.** *n* combate *m* **II.** *vt* luchar contra; (*crime*) combatir; (*desire*) resistir

**combination** [,kam·bə·'neɪ·ʃən] *n* combinación *f*

**combine** [kəm·'baɪn] **I.** *vt* combinar; **to ~ forces** unir fuerzas (**against** contra) **II.** *vi* asociarse

**combined** [kəm·'baɪnd] *adj* combinado, -a; (*efforts*) conjunto, -a

**come** [kʌm] <came, come, coming> *vi* **1.** venir (**towards** hacia); **are you coming to the game with us?** ¿te vienes al partido? **2.** (*arrive*) llegar; **the year to ~** el próximo año; **to ~ to an agreement/a decision** llegar a un acuerdo/una decisión; **to ~ home** volver a casa **3.** (*happen*) pasar; **to ~ to pass** suceder; **~ what may** pase lo que pase; **how ~?** *inf* ¿cómo es?; **nothing came of it** todo quedó en nada **4.** (*become*) hacerse; **to ~ true** hacerse realidad; **to ~ open** abrirse **5.** *inf* (*climax*) correrse, acabar *AmL* ▸ **~ again?** *inf* ¿cómo?; **to ~ clean** ser sincero (**about** acerca de); **to have it coming** tenerlo merecido

◆**come about** *vi* suceder

◆**come across I.** *vt insep* encontrarse con; (*problem*) topar con **II.** *vi* **to ~ with** proporcionar

◆**come along** *vi* **1.** (*hurry*) darse prisa; **~!** ¡venga! **2.** (*go too*) venirse **3.** (*progress*) progresar

◆**come apart** *vi* separarse

◆**come around** *vi* **1.** (*change mind*) cambiar de opinión **2.** MED volver en sí

◆**come at** *vt insep* atacar

◆**come away** *vi* irse; **to ~ from** desprenderse de

◆**come back** *vi* volver; (*be remembered*) volver (a la memoria)

◆**come by I.** *vt insep* conseguir **II.** *vi* visitar

◆**come down** *vi* **1.** bajar; (*roof*) hundirse; (*rain, snow*) caer **2.** (*land*) aterrizar

◆**come forward** *vi* avanzar; **to ~ to do sth** ofrecerse para hacer algo

◆**come from** *vt* ser de; (*family*) descender de; **where do you ~?** ¿de dónde eres?

◆**come in** *vi* **1.** (*enter*) entrar **2.** (*arrive*) llegar **3.** (*fashion*) ponerse de moda **4.** (*be useful*) servir **5.** (*participate*) participar

◆**come into** *vt insep* **1.** (*enter*) entrar en; (*power*) tomar; **to ~ fashion** ponerse de moda **2.** (*inherit*) heredar

◆**come off I.** *vi* **1.** *inf* (*succeed*) triunfar **2.** (*end up*) terminar **3.** (*become detached*) desprenderse **II.** *vt insep* (*complete*) terminar; (*injury*) recuperarse de ▸ **~ it!** ¡anda ya!

◆**come on I.** *vi* **1.** (*improve*) progresar **2.** THEAT, CINE aparecer **3.** (*film, program*) empezar; **I've got a headache coming on** me está empezando a dar dolor de cabeza **II.** *vt insep* encontrarse **III.** *interj* (*hurry*) ¡date prisa!, ¡ándale! *Méx;* (*encouragement*) ¡ánimo!, ¡órale! *Méx;* (*annoyance*) ¡venga ya!

◆**come out** *vi* **1.** **to ~ in favor of/against sth** pronunciarse a favor/en contra de algo **2.** **how did your painting ~?** ¿cómo quedó tu cuadro? **3.** + *n* **to ~ a mess** resultar un desastre **4.** + *adj* **to ~ wrong/right** salir mal/bien **5.** (*become known*) darse a conocer; **to ~ that...** revelarse que... **6.** (*stamp, book, moon, stars*) salir

◆**come over I.** *vi* **1.** (*come nearer*) acercarse **2.** (*visit*) visitar **3.** (*feel*) sentir **II.** *vt* apoderarse de

◆**come through I.** *vi* **1.** (*show*) mostrar **2.** (*arrive*) llegar **3.** (*survive*) sobrevivir **II.** *vt insep* superar

◆**come to I.** *vt insep* **1.** (*reach*) llegar a; **to come down/up to sth** bajar/subir a algo; **to ~ rest** irse a dormir; **to ~ nothing** quedarse en nada **2.** (*amount to*) ascender a **II.** *vi* MED volver en sí

◆**come up** *vi* **1.** (*be mentioned*) mencionarse **2.** (*happen*) suceder; (*holiday*) llegar

◆**come upon** *vt* encontrarse con

**comeback** ['kʌm·bæk] *n* **1.** vuelta *f*

**2.** (*retort*) réplica *f*

**comedian** [kə·ˈmi·di·ən] *n* **1.** humorista *mf* **2.** (*funny person*) payaso, -a *m, f*

**comedown** [ˈkʌm·daʊn] *n inf* **1.** (*anticlimax*) revés *m* **2.** (*decline in status*) humillación *f*

**comedy** [ˈkam·ə·di] <-ies> *n* comedia *f*; (*funny situation*) comicidad *f*

**come-on** [ˈkʌm·ɔn] *n sl* (*sexual*) insinuación *f*

**comet** [ˈkam·ɪt] *n* cometa *m*

**comeuppance** [kʌm·ˈʌp·əns] *n* **to get one's ~** llevarse su merecido

**comfort** [ˈkʌm·fərt] **I.** *n* comodidad *f*; (*mental*) consuelo *m* **II.** *vt* consolar

**comfortable** [ˈkʌm·fər·tə·bəl] *adj* cómodo, -a; **to make oneself ~** ponerse cómodo; (*financially*) acomodado, -a

**comfortably** [ˈkʌm·fər·tə·bli] *adv* cómodamente; **to live ~** vivir de forma acomodada

**comforting** [ˈkʌm·fər·tɪŋ] *adj* reconfortante

**comfy** [ˈkʌm·fi] <-ier, -iest> *adj inf* cómodo, -a

**comic** [ˈkam·ɪk] **I.** *n* cómic *m*; (*person*) cómico, -a *m, f* **II.** *adj* cómico, -a; **~ play** comedia *f*

**comical** [ˈkam·ɪ·kəl] *adj* cómico, -a; (*idea*) divertido, -a

**comic book** *n* tebeo *m*

**comic strip** *n* tira *f* cómica

**coming** [ˈkʌm·ɪŋ] **I.** *adj* **1.** (*next*) próximo, -a; **the ~ year** el año que viene **2.** (*approaching*) venidero, -a **II.** *n* llegada *f*; **~s and goings** idas y venidas

**comma** [ˈkam·ə] *n* coma *f*

**command** [kə·ˈmænd] **I.** *vt* **1. to ~ sb to do sth** ordenar a alguien que haga algo; **to ~ that** mandar que +*subj* **2.** (*have authority*) estar al mando de **3.** (*have*) disponer de **4.** (*view*) tener; (*respect*) imponer; (*sympathy*) inspirar **II.** *n* **1.** (*order*) orden *f*; **at/under sb's ~** a/bajo las órdenes de alguien **2.** (*control*) mando *m*; **to be in ~** estar al mando (**of** de) **3.** COMPUT comando *m* **4.** (*knowledge*) dominio *m*

**commandant** [ˈkam·ən·dænt], **commander** [kə·ˈmæn·dər] *n* comandante *mf*

**commanding** [kə·ˈmæn·dɪŋ] *adj* **1.** (*authoritative*) dominante; (*voice*) imponente **2.** (*considerable*) abrumador(a)

**command key** *n* tecla *f* de comando

**commando** [kə·ˈmæn·doʊ] <-s *or* -es> *n* comando *m*

**commemorate** [kə·ˈmem·ə·reɪt] *vt* conmemorar

**commemorative** [kə·ˈmem·ər·ə·tɪv] *adj* conmemorativo, -a

**commence** [kə·ˈmens] *vi* dar comienzo

**commend** [kə·ˈmend] *vt* **1.** (*praise*) elogiar **2.** (*entrust*) encomendar **3.** (*recommend*) recomendar

**comment** [ˈkam·ent] **I.** *n* comentario *m*; **no ~** sin comentarios **II.** *vi* comentar

**commentary** [ˈkam·ən·ter·i] <-ies> *n* comentario *m*; RADIO, TV comentarios

**commentate** [ˈkam·ən·teɪt] *vi* **to ~ on sth** hacer un reportaje sobre algo

**commentator** [ˈkam·ən·teɪ·tər] *n* comentarista *mf*

**commerce** [ˈkam·ərs] *n* comercio *m*

**commercial** [kə·ˈmɜr·ʃəl] **I.** *adj* comercial; RADIO, TV publicitario, -a **II.** *n* anuncio *m*, comercial *m AmL*

**commercialization** [kə·ˌmɜr·ʃə·lɪ·ˈzeɪ·ʃən] *n* comercialización *f*

**commercialize** [kə·ˈmɜr·ʃə·laɪz] *vt* comercializar

**commission** [kə·ˈmɪʃ·ən] **I.** *vt* (*order*) encargar **II.** *n* **1.** (*order*) encargo *m* **2.** ADMIN, COM comisión *f*

**commissioner** [kə·ˈmɪʃ·ə·nər] *n* comisario, -a *m, f*

**commit** [kə·ˈmɪt] <-tt-> *vt* cometer; **to ~ suicide** suicidarse; **to ~ oneself** comprometerse (**to** a); **to ~ sb to a hospital/to prison** internar a alguien en un hospital/en prisión

**commitment** [kə·ˈmɪt·mənt] *n* **1.** (*dedication*) dedicación *f* **2.** (*obligation*) compromiso *m*

**committee** [kə·ˈmɪt·i] *n* comité *m*

**commode** [kə·ˈmoʊd] *n* **1.** (*drawers*) cómoda *f* **2.** (*toilet*) taza *f*

**common** [ˈkam·ən] *adj* **1.** común; **to be ~ knowledge** ser de dominio público; **by ~ assent** por unanimidad; **for the ~ good** en beneficio común **2.** (*vulgar*) vulgar

**commonly** *adv* normalmente

**commonplace** ['kam·ən·pleɪs] *adj* corriente

**common sense** *n* sentido *m* común; (*solution*) lógico, -a

**communal** [kə·'mju·nəl] *adj* comunal

**communicate** [kə·'mju·nɪ·keɪt] I. *vt* comunicar; MED transmitir II. *vi* comunicarse

**communication** [kə·ˌmju·nɪ·'keɪ·fən] *n* comunicación *f*

**communicative** [kə·'mju·nə·keɪ·tɪv] *adj* comunicativo, -a

**communism** ['kam·jə·nɪz·əm] *n* comunismo *m*

**communist** ['kam·jə·nɪst] *adj, n* comunista *mf*

**community** [kə·'mju·nə·ti] <-ies> *n* **1.** (*of people*) comunidad *f*; **the local ~** el vecindario **2.** (*of animals, plants*) colonia *f* **3.** (*togetherness*) colectividad *f*

**community center** *n* centro *m* social

**commute** [kə·'mjut] I. *vi* desplazarse al trabajo II. *n* desplazamiento *m* al trabajo III. *vt* (*change*) convertir

**compact**[1] ['kam·pækt] I. *adj* compacto, -a II. *vt* condensar III. *n* AUTO utilitario *m*

**compact**[2] ['kam·pækt] *n* (*agreement*) acuerdo *m*

**compact disk** *n* compact *m*

**compact disk player** *n* reproductor *m* de CD

**companion** [kəm·'pæn·jən] *n* **1.** compañero, -a *m, f*; **traveling ~** compañero de viaje **2.** (*guidebook*) guía *f*

**company** ['kʌm·pə·ni] <-ies> *n* **1.** (*firm, enterprise*) empresa *f*; **Duggan and Company** Duggan y Compañía **2.** (*companionship*) compañía *f*; **to keep sb ~** hacer compañía a alguien; **he's been keeping bad ~** va con malas compañías ▶ **two's ~** (**three's a crowd**) *prov* dos son compañía, tres son multitud

**comparable** ['kam·pər·ə·bəl] *adj* comparable; **~ to** equiparable a

**comparative** [kəm·'per·ə·tɪv] *adj* comparativo, -a

**comparatively** *adv* en comparación; (*relatively*) relativamente

**compare** [kəm·'per] I. *vt* comparar (**to**, **with** con) II. *vi* compararse

**comparison** [kəm·'per·ɪ·sən] *n* comparación *f*; **by ~ with** en comparación con; **there's no ~ between the two restaurants** no hay ni punto de comparación entre los dos restaurantes

**compartment** [kəm·'part·mənt] *n* compartimento *m*

**compass** ['kʌm·pəs] <-es> *n* brújula *f*

**compassion** [kəm·'pæʃ·ən] *n* compasión *f*

**compassionate** [kəm·'pæʃ·ə·nɪt] *adj* compasivo, -a

**compatibility** [kəm·ˌpæt·ə·'bɪl·ə·ti] *n* compatibilidad *f*

**compatible** [kəm·'pæt·ə·bəl] *adj* compatible

**compel** [kəm·'pel] <-ll-> *vt* (*force*) obligar

**compelling** *adj* (*reason*) imponente

**compensate** ['kam·pən·seɪt] *vt, vi* compensar; (*for loss, damage*) indemnizar

**compensation** [ˌkam·pen·'seɪ·fən] *n* **1.** (*award*) compensación *f*; (*for loss, damage*) indemnización *f*; **in ~ for** en compensación por **2.** (*recompense*) recompensa *f*; **in ~** como recompensa

**compete** [kəm·'pit] *vi* **1.** (*strive*) competir (**for** por) **2.** (*take part*) participar

**competence** ['kam·pɪ·təns] *n*, **competency** *n* competencia *f*

**competent** ['kam·pɪ·tənt] *adj* competente (**at** en)

**competition** [ˌkam·pə·'tɪʃ·ən] *n* **1.** (*competing*) competencia *f* **2.** (*rivalry*) rivalidad *f* **3.** (*contest*) concurso *m*; **beauty ~** concurso de belleza; **to enter a ~** presentarse a un concurso

**competitive** [kəm·'pet·ɪ·tɪv] *adj* competitivo, -a; **~ sports** deportes de competición

**competitiveness** [kəm·'pet·ə·tɪv·nɪs] *n* competitividad *f*

**competitor** [kəm·'pet·ə·tər] *n* **1.** *a.* ECON competidor(a) *m(f)* **2.** SPORTS rival *mf*; (*participant*) participante *mf*

**compilation** [ˌkam·pə·'leɪ·fən] *n* (*collection*) recopilación *f*

**compile** [kəm·'paɪl] *vt* recopilar; COMPUT compilar

**compiler** [ˌkəm·'pi·lər] *n* COMPUT compilador *m*

**complain** [kəmˈpleɪn] *vi* quejarse (**about, of** de)

**complaint** [kəmˈpleɪnt] *n* 1. queja *f* (**about** sobre) 2. LAW querella *f* 3. (*illness*) enfermedad *f*

**complement** [ˈkam·plɪ·mənt] *vt* complementar

**complementary** [ˌkam·pləˈmen·tə·ri] *adj* complementario, -a

**complete** [kəmˈplit] I. *vt* 1. (*add*) completar 2. (*finish*) terminar; **to ~ doing sth** terminar de hacer algo 3. (*fill out*) rellenar II. *adj* completo, -a

**completely** *adv* totalmente

**completion** [kəmˈpli·fən] *n* finalización *f*; **to be nearing ~** estar a punto de terminarse

**complex** [ˈkam·pleks] I. *adj* complejo, -a II. <-es> *n* PSYCH, ARCHIT complejo *m*; **guilt/inferiority ~** complejo de culpabilidad/inferioridad; **to have a ~** estar acomplejado (**about** por); **I've got a real ~ about spiders** tengo verdadera fobia a las arañas

**complexion** [kəmˈplek·fən] *n* 1. (*skin*) cutis *m inv* 2. (*character*) cariz *m*; (*of people*) aspecto *m*

**complexity** [kəmˈplek·sə·ti] *n* complejidad *f*

**compliant** [kəmˈplaɪ·ənt] *adj* sumiso, -a

**complicate** [ˈkam·plə·keɪt] *vt* complicar; (*make worse*) empeorar

**complicated** *adj* complicado, -a

**complication** [ˌkam·pləˈkeɪ·fən] *n* complicación *f*; **if any ~s arise...** si surge alguna dificultad...

**complicity** [kəmˈplɪs·ə·ti] *n* complicidad *f*

**compliment** [ˈkam·plə·mənt] I. *n* 1. (*praise*) cumplido *m*; (*flirt*) piropo *m*; **to pay/repay a ~** hacer/devolver un cumplido 2. **~s** saludos *mpl* II. *vt* felicitar (**on** por)

**complimentary** [ˌkam·pləˈmen·tə·ri] *adj* 1. (*praising*) positivo, -a 2. (*free*) gratuito, -a

**comply** [kəmˈplaɪ] <-ie-> *vi* cumplir; **to refuse to ~** negarse a obedecer; **to ~ with the law/the rules** acatar la ley/las normas

**component** [kəmˈpou·nənt] *n* compo-

nente *m*; **key ~** pieza clave

**compose** [kəmˈpouz] I. *vi* componer II. *vt* 1. (*music, poetry*) componer 2. (*write*) redactar 3. **to be ~d of sth** constar de algo 4. **to ~ oneself** calmarse

**composed** [kəmˈpouzd] *adj* tranquilo, -a

**composer** [kəmˈpou·zər] *n* compositor(a) *m(f)*

**composition** [ˌkam·pəˈzɪʃ·ən] *n* composición *f*; (*of a group*) formación *f*; SCHOOL redacción *f*

**composure** [kəmˈpou·ʒər] *n* compostura *f*; **to lose/regain one's ~** perder/recobrar la compostura

**compound**[1] [kəmˈpaund] *vt* 1. (*make worse*) agravar 2. (*mix*) combinar 3. **to be ~ed of sth** constar de algo

**compound**[2] [ˈkam·paund] *n* 1. (*mix*) mezcla *f*; CHEM compuesto *m* 2. (*enclosure*) recinto *m*

**comprehend** [ˌkam·prɪˈhend] *vi, vt* comprender

**comprehensible** [ˌkam·prɪˈhen·sə·bəl] *adj* comprensible

**comprehension** [ˌkampriˈhenʃən] *n* comprensión *f*; **beyond ~** incomprensible; **he has no ~ of the size of the problem** no es consciente de la envergadura del problema

**comprehensive** [ˌkam·prɪˈhen·sɪv] *adj* exhaustivo, -a

**compress**[1] [kəmˈpres] *vt* 1. *a.* COMPUT comprimir 2. (*make shorter*) resumir

**compress**[2] [ˈkam·pres] <-es> *n* compresa *f*

**comprise** [kəmˈpraɪz] *vt* (*consist of*) constar de; (*include*) comprender

**compromise** [ˈkam·prə·maɪz] I. *n* 1. (*concession*) transigencia *f*; **to make a ~** hacer una concesión 2. (*agreement*) compromiso *m*; **to reach a ~** llegar a un acuerdo II. *vi* transigir III. *vt* 1. (*betray*) comprometer; **to ~ one's beliefs/principles** dejar de lado sus creencias/principios 2. (*endanger*) poner en peligro; **to ~ one's reputation** poner en entredicho su reputación

**compromising** *adj* comprometido, -a

**compulsion** [kəmˈpʌl·fən] *n* obligación *f*;

**to be under no ~ to do sth** no estar obligado a hacer algo

**compulsive** [kəm·'pʌl·sɪv] *adj* compulsivo, -a

**compulsory** [kəm·'pʌl·sə·ri] *adj* obligatorio, -a; **~ education** enseñanza obligatoria; **~ by law** preceptivo por ley

**compute** [kəm·'pjut] *vt* computar

**computer** [kəm·'pju·tər] *n* ordenador *m*, computador(a) *m(f) AmL;* **by ~** por ordenador

**computer-aided** *adj* asistido, -a por ordenador

**computer game** *n* juego *m* de ordenador

**computer graphics** *n + sing/pl vb* gráficos *m pl* por ordenador [*or AmL* por computadora]

**computerize** [kəm·'pju·tə·raɪz] **I.** *vt* informatizar **II.** *vi* informatizarse

**computer network** *n* red *f* de ordenadores [*or* computadoras] *AmL*

**computer program** *n* programa *m* (de ordenador)

**computer programmer** *n* programador(a) *m(f)*

**computer science** *n* informática *f*

**computer scientist** *n* informático, -a *m, f*

**computer virus** <-es> *n* virus *m inv* informático

**computing** *n* informática *f*

**comrade** ['kɑm·ræd] *n* compañero, -a *m, f*

**comradeship** ['kɑm·ræd·ʃɪp] *n* compañerismo *m*

**con¹** [kɑn] <-nn-> *vt inf* **to ~ sb** (**into doing sth**) engañar a alguien (para que haga algo); **to ~ sb into believing that...** hacer creer a alguien que...; **to ~ sb out of sth** estafar algo a alguien

**con²** [kɑn] *n* (*against*) contra *m;* **the pros and ~s of sth** los pros y los contras de algo

**con³** [kɑn] *n sl* (*convict*) convicto, -a *m, f*

**concave** ['kɑn·keɪv] *adj* cóncavo, -a

**conceal** [kən·'sil] *vt* esconder; (*surprise*) contener; (*truth*) encubrir

**concede** [kən·'sid] **I.** *vt* **1.** (*acknowledge*) admitir **2.** (*surrender*) ceder; **to ~ sth to sb** otorgar algo a alguien **3.** (*per-*

*mit*) conceder **II.** *vi* darse por vencido

**conceited** [kən·'si·tɪd] *adj* vanidoso, -a

**conceivable** [kən·'siv·ə·bəl] *adj* verosímil

**conceive** [kən·'siv] **I.** *vt* concebir; (*devise*) idear; (*arrange*) preparar **II.** *vi* **1.** (*think*) formarse un concepto (**of** de) **2.** (*devise*) imaginar(se)

**concentrate** ['kɑn·sən·treɪt] **I.** *vi* **1.** (*focus attention*) concentrarse (**on** en) **2.** (*gather*) reunirse **II.** *vt* concentrar **III.** *n* concentrado *m*

**concentrated** *adj a. fig* concentrado, -a

**concentration** [ˌkɑn·sən·'treɪ·ʃən] *n* concentración *f* (**on** en, **of** de); **to lose** (**one's**) **~** perder la concentración

**concept** [kən·sept] *n* concepto *m;* **to grasp a ~** coger una idea

**conception** [kən·'sep·ʃən] *n a.* BIO concepción *f*

**conceptual** [kən·'sep·tʃu·əl] *adj* conceptual

**concern** [kən·'sɜrn] **I.** *vt* **1.** (*apply to*) referirse a; **to ~ oneself** interesarse (**about** por) **2.** (*affect*) incumbir; (*be about*) tener que ver con; **to be ~ed** ocuparse (**with** de); **as far as I'm ~ed** por lo que a mí respecta **3.** (*worry*) preocuparse; **to be ~ed** estar preocupado (**about** por) **II.** *n* **1.** (*matter*) asunto *m;* **it's no ~ of mine** eso no es de mi incumbencia; **that's none of your ~** no es asunto tuyo; **to be of ~** interesar **2.** (*worry*) preocupación *f* (**for** por); **a major ~** una grave preocupación; **a matter of ~** un asunto de interés

**concerning** *prep* acerca de

**concert** ['kɑn·sərt] *n* concierto *m;* **~ tour** gira *f;* **in ~** en concierto; (*all together*) conjuntamente

**concerted** [kən·'sɜr·tɪd] *adj* **1.** (*joint*) concertado, -a; (*action*) conjunto, -a; (*exercise*) acordado, -a **2.** (*resolute*) resuelto, -a; (*effort*) enérgico, -a

**concession** [kən·'sɛʃ·ən] *n* **1.** (*tax*) desgravación *f* **2.** (*compromise*) concesión *f*

**concise** [kən·'saɪs] *adj* conciso, -a

**conciseness** *n*, **concision** [kən·'sɪʒ·ən] *n* concisión *f*

**conclude** [kən·'klud] **I.** *vi* concluir; **to**

~ **by doing sth** terminar haciendo algo
II. *vt* 1. (*finish*) finalizar 2. (*decide*)
resolver 3. (*infer*) **to ~ (from sth) that**
deducir (de algo) que 4. (*ratify*) pactar;
(*contract*) firmar

**concluding** *adj* final; (*chapter*) último, -a

**conclusion** [kən·'klu·ʒən] *n* 1. (*end, inference*) conclusión *f*; (*story*) final *m*; **to come to a ~** llegar a una conclusión 2. (*decision*) decisión *f* 3. (*ratification*) ratificación *f*; (*contract*) firma *f* 4. **in ~** en conclusión; **in ~, I would like to...** para terminar, me gustaría...

**conclusive** [kən·'klu·sɪv] *adj* concluyente

**concrete** ['kan·krit] I. *n* hormigón *m*
II. *adj* de hormigón

**concur** [kən·'kɜr] <-rr-> *vi* **to ~ with sb (in sth)** coincidir con alguien (en algo)

**concurrent** [kən·'kʌr·ənt] *adj* concurrente

**concussion** [kən·'kʌʃ·ən] *n* conmoción *f* cerebral

**condemn** [kən·'dem] *vt* condenar; **to be ~ed to death** ser condenado a muerte; (*building*) declarar en ruina

**condemnation** [ˌkan·dem·'neɪ·ʃən] *n* (*reproof*) condena *f*; (*reason*) motivo *m* de crítica

**condensation** [ˌkan·den·'seɪ·ʃən] *n a.* CHEM, PHYS condensación *f*

**condense** [kən·'dens] I. *vt* (*shorten*) sintetizar; (*liquid*) condensar II. *vi* condensarse

**condescend** [ˌkan·dɪ·'send] *vi* **to ~ to do sth** rebajarse a hacer algo

**condescending** [ˌkan·dɪ·'sen·dɪŋ] *adj* condescendiente

**condition** [kən·'dɪʃ·ən] I. *n* condición *f*; (*mental or physical*) estado *m*; **in perfect ~** en perfecto estado; **in peak ~** en condiciones óptimas; **in terrible ~** en un estado deplorable; **to be out of ~** estar en mal estado; (*person*) estar en baja forma; **to be in no ~ to do sth** no estar en condiciones de hacer algo; **to make a ~** poner una condición; **on the ~ that** con la condición de que +*subj* II. *vt* (*train*) preparar; (*influence*) condicionar

**conditional** [kən·'dɪʃ·ə·nəl] *adj, n* con-

dicional *m*

**conditionally** [kən·'dɪʃ·ə·nə·li] *adv* con reservas

**conditioner** [kən·'dɪʃ·ə·nər] *n* (*hair*) acondicionador *m*, bálsamo *m* Col, Méx

**condolences** [kən·'dou·lən·sɪz] *npl* pésame *m*; **to offer one's ~** dar el pésame

**condom** ['kan·dəm] *n* condón *m*

**conduct¹** [kən·'dʌkt] *vt* 1. (*carry out*) llevar a cabo 2. (*direct*) dirigir 3. **to ~ oneself** comportarse 4. ELEC, PHYS conducir

**conduct²** ['kan·dʌkt] *n* 1. (*management*) dirección *f* 2. (*behavior*) conducta *f* (**towards** hacia)

**conductive** [kən·'dʌk·tɪv] *adj* conductor(a)

**conductor** [kən·'dʌk·tər] *n* 1. (*director*) director(a) *m(f)* 2. PHYS, ELEC conductor *m* 3. (*bus, train*) revisor(a) *m(f)*

**cone** [koun] *n* cono *m*; BOT piña *f*

**confection** [kən·'fek·ʃən] *n* form 1. COM confección *f* 2. CULIN dulce *m*

**confectionery** [kən·'fek·ʃə·ner·i] *n* confitería *f*

**confederacy** [kən·'fed·ər·ə·si] <-ies> *n* confederación *f*

**confederate** [kən·'fed·ər·ət] *adj* confederado, -a

**confederation** [kən·ˌfed·ə·'reɪ·ʃən] *n* + *sing/pl vb* POL confederación *f*

**confer** [kən·'fɜr] <-rr-> I. *vi* consultar II. *vt* otorgar

**conference** ['kan·fər·əns] *n* conferencia *f*

**confess** [kən·'fes] I. *vi* confesarse II. *vt* confesar

**confession** [kən·'feʃ·ən] *n* confesión *f*

**confetti** [kən·'fet̬·i] *n* confeti *m*

**confide** [kən·'faɪd] *vt* confiar

**confidence** ['kan·fə·dəns] *n* 1. (*trust*) confianza *f*; **to win sb's ~** ganarse la confianza de alguien; **he certainly doesn't lack ~** desde luego no le falta confianza en sí mismo 2. (*secrecy*) ~**s** confidencia *f*

**confident** ['kan·fə·dənt] *adj* 1. (*sure*) seguro, -a; **to be ~** estar seguro (**about de**) 2. (*self-assured*) confiado, -a; **to be ~ about oneself** tener confianza en uno mismo

**confidential** [ˌkan·fə·'den·ʃəl] *adj* confidencial

**confidentially** [ˌkan·fə·'den·ʃə·li] *adv* confidencialmente

**configuration** [kən·fɪg·jə·'reɪ·ʃən] *n* configuración *f*

**confine** [kən·'faɪn] I. *vt* confinar; **to ~ sth to sth** restringir algo a algo; **to be ~d to doing sth** limitarse a hacer algo II. *n* **the ~s** los confines

**confinement** [kən·'faɪn·mənt] *n (act)* reclusión *f; (state)* confinamiento *m*

**confirm** [kən·'fɜrm] I. *vt* confirmar II. *vi* confirmarse

**confirmation** [ˌkan·fər·'meɪ·ʃən] *n* confirmación *f*

**confirmed** [kən·'fɜrmd] *adj* 1. *(established)* firme 2. *(chronic)* empedernido, -a 3. *(proved)* confirmado, -a

**confiscate** [kən·fə·skeɪt] *vt* confiscar

**conflict**[1] ['kan·flɪkt] *n* conflicto *m; (opinions)* discrepancia *f*

**conflict**[2] [kən·'flɪkt] *vi* chocar **(with** con)

**conflicting** [kən·'flɪk·tɪŋ] *adj* opuesto, -a; *(evidence)* contradictorio, -a

**conform** [kən·'fɔrm] *vi* conformarse; **to ~ to the law** ser conforme a la ley

**conformist** [kən·'fɔr·mɪst] *adj, n* conformista *mf*

**confront** [kən·'frʌnt] *vt* enfrentarse a

**confuse** [kən·'fjuz] *vt* 1. *(perplex)* desconcertar 2. *(mix up)* confundir

**confused** [kən·'fjuzd] *adj (perplexed)* confundido, -a; *(disordered)* confuso, -a

**confusing** [kən·'fju·zɪŋ] *adj* confuso, -a

**confusion** [kən·'fju·ʒən] *n* confusión *f*

**congested** [kən·'dʒes·tɪd] *adj a.* MED congestionado, -a; *(people)* abarrotado, -a

**congestion** [kən·'dʒes·tʃən] *n a.* MED gestión *f; (road)* caravana *f*

**congratulate** [kən·'græʧ·ə·leɪt] *vt* felicitar **(on** por)

**congratulation** [kən·ˌgræʧ·ə·'leɪ·ʃən] *n* felicitación *f;* **~s!** ¡enhorabuena!

**congregate** ['kaŋ·grɪ·geɪt] *vi* congregarse

**congregation** [ˌkaŋ·grɪ·'geɪ·ʃən] *n* congregación *f*

**congress** ['kaŋ·gres] *n* congreso *m*

**congressman** ['kaŋ·gres·mən] *n* <-men> congresista *m*

**congresswoman** *n* <-women> congresista *f*

**conical** ['kan·ɪ·kəl] *adj* cónico, -a

**conjugate** ['kan·dʒə·geɪt] *vt* conjugar

**conjunction** [kən·'dʒʌŋk·ʃən] *n* conjunción *f;* **in ~ with** conjuntamente con

**conjunctivitis** [kən·ˌdʒʌŋk·tə·'vaɪ·tɪs] *n* conjuntivitis *f inv*

**conjure** ['kan·dʒər] *vt* conjurar; *fig* evocar

◆**conjure up** *vt* invocar; *(memories)* evocar

**conk** [kaŋk] *n sl (blow)* coscorrón *m*

◆**conk out** *vi sl* 1. *(break down)* escacharrarse 2. *(person)* quedarse frito

**con man** ['kan·ˌmæn] *n abbr of* **confidence man** estafador *m*

**Conn.** *n abbr of* **Connecticut** *abbr of* **Connecticut**

**connect** [kə·'nekt] I. *vi* conectar(se); **to ~ to the Internet** conectarse a Internet II. *vt* 1. *(join)* conectar 2. *(associate)* asociar **(with** con) 3. *(in tourism)* enlazar

**connected** *adj* conectado, -a; **to be ~d to sb** tener relación con alguien

**Connecticut** [kə·'net·ɪ·kət] *n* Connecticut *m*

**connecting** *adj* comunicado, -a

**connection** [kə·'nek·ʃən] *n* 1. *a.* ELEC, COMPUT conexión *f* 2. *(relation)* relación *f*

**connector** *n* conector *m*

**connoisseur** [ˌkan·ə·'sɜr] *n* entendido, -a *m, f*

**conquer** ['kaŋ·kər] *vt* conquistar; *(problem)* acabar con

**conquest** ['kan·kwest] *n* conquista *f*

**conscience** ['kan·ʃəns] *n* conciencia *f;* **a guilty ~** remordimientos; **to prey on sb's ~** pesar en la conciencia de alguien

**conscientious** [ˌkan·tʃi·'en·tʃəs] *adj* concienzudo, -a; **~ objector** objetor de conciencia

**conscious** ['kan·ʃəs] *adj* 1. *(deliberate)* expreso, -a 2. *(aware)* consciente; **to be/become ~ of sth** ser consciente/darse cuenta de algo

**consciousness** ['kan·ʃəs·nɪs] *n* 1. MED

conocimiento *m;* **to lose/regain ~** perder/recobrar el conocimiento **2.** (*awareness*) conciencia *f;* **political/social ~** conciencia política/social; **to raise one's ~** concienciarse

**consecutive** [kən·'sek·jə·ṭɪv] *adj* consecutivo, -a

**consecutively** *adv* consecutivamente

**consensus** [kən·'sen·səs] *n* consenso *m*

**consent** [kən·'sent] **I.** *n* consentimiento *m;* **by common ~** de común acuerdo **II.** *vi* **to ~ to do sth** consentir en hacer algo

**consequence** ['kan·sɪ·kwənts] *n* consecuencia *f;* **as a ~** como consecuencia; **in ~** por consiguiente

**consequent** ['kan·sɪ·kwənt], **consequential** [,kan·sɪ·'kwen·tʃəl] *adj* consiguiente

**consequently** *adv* por consiguiente

**conservation** [,kan·sər·'veɪ·ʃən] *n* conservación *f;* **environmental ~** preservación *f* del medio ambiente

**conservative** [kən·'sɜr·və·ṭɪv] *adj* **1.** *a.* POL (*traditional*) conservador(a) **2.** (*cautious*) cauteloso, -a

**conservatory** [kən·'sɜr·və·tɔr·i] *n* conservatorio *m*

**conserve** [kən·'sɜrv] *vt* conservar

**consider** [kən·'sɪd·ər] *vt* **1.** (*contemplate*) considerar **2.** (*examine*) examinar **3.** (*show regard for*) tener en cuenta **4.** (*regard as*) **to be ~ed to be the best** ser considerado el mejor; **to ~ that...** creer que...

**considerable** [kən·'sɪd·ə·rə·bəl] *adj* considerable

**considerate** [kən·'sɪd·ər·ət] *adj* considerado, -a

**consideration** [kən·,sɪd·ə·'reɪ·ʃən] *n* consideración *f;* **to take into ~** tener en cuenta

**considered** [kən·'sɪd·ərd] *adj* considerado, -a

**considering** [kən·'sɪd·ər·ɪŋ] **I.** *prep* teniendo en cuenta; **~ the weather** en vista del tiempo **II.** *adv* a pesar de todo **III.** *conj* **~ (that)...** teniendo en cuenta que...

**consist** [kən·'sɪst] *vi* consistir (**of** en)

**consistency** [kən·'sɪs·tən·si] *n* **1.** (*firm-*ness) consistencia *f* **2.** (*coherence*) coherencia *f*

**consistent** [kən·'sɪs·tənt] *adj* consecuente (**with** con)

**consolation** [,kan·sə·'leɪ·ʃən] *n* consuelo *m;* **~ prize** premio de consolación; **if it's of any ~...** si te sirve de consuelo...

**console¹** [kən·'soʊl] *vt* (*comfort*) consolar

**console²** ['kan·soʊl] *n* (*switch panel*) consola *f*

**consolidate** [kən·'sal·ə·deɪt] **I.** *vi* **1.** (*reinforce*) consolidarse **2.** (*unite*) fusionarse **II.** *vt* consolidar

**consonant** ['kan·sə·nənt] *n* consonante *f*

**consortium** [kən·'sɔr·ṭi·əm] *n* <consortiums *or* consortia> consorcio *m*

**conspiracy** [kən·'spɪr·ə·si] <-ies> *n* conspiración *f*

**conspire** [kən·'spaɪr] *vi* conspirar (**against** contra)

**constant** ['kan·stənt] **I.** *n* constante *f* **II.** *adj* **1.** (*continuous, frequent*) constante; **~ use** uso frecuente **2.** (*unchanging*) inalterable

**constantly** *adv* constantemente

**constellation** [,kan·stə·'leɪ·ʃən] *n* constelación *f*

**consternation** [,kan·stər·'neɪ·ʃən] *n* consternación *f*

**constipated** *adj* estreñido, -a

**constitution** [,kan·stə·'tu·ʃən] *n* constitución *f*

**constitutional** [,kan·stə·'tu·ʃə·nəl] *adj* constitucional

**constrain** [kən·'streɪn] *vt* **to be/feel ~ed to do sth** verse/sentirse obligado a hacer algo

**construct** [kən·'strʌkt] **I.** *n* construcción *f* **II.** *vt* construir

**construction** [kən·'strʌk·ʃən] *n* **1.** *a.* LING construcción *f* **2.** (*building*) edificio *m*

**constructive** [kən·'strʌk·ṭɪv] *adj* constructivo, -a

**consul** ['kan·səl] *n* cónsul *mf*

**consulate** ['kan·sə·lət] *n* consulado *m*

**consult** [kən·'sʌlt] *vi, vt* consultar

**consultancy** [kən·'sʌl·tən·si] <-ies> *n* asesoría *f*

**consultant** [kən·'sʌl·tənt] *n* asesor(a) *m(f);* **tax ~** asesor fiscal

**consume** [kən·ˈsum] *vt* consumir; **to be ~d by sth** estar consumido por algo; **to be ~d by envy** estar muerto de envidia

**consumer** [kən·ˈsu·mər] *n* consumidor(a) *m(f)*

**consumption** [kən·ˈsʌmp·ʃən] *n* consumo *m*

**contact** [ˈkɑn·tækt] **I.** *n* contacto *m;* (*connection*) relación *f;* **to have ~s** tener contactos; **to come into ~ with sth** entrar en contacto con algo **II.** *vt* contactar con

**contact lens** *n* lentilla *f*

**contagious** [kən·ˈteɪ·dʒəs] *adj* contagioso, -a

**contain** [kən·ˈteɪn] *vt* contener

**container** [kən·ˈteɪ·nər] *n* recipiente *m;* (*for transport*) contenedor *m*

**contaminate** [kən·ˈtæm·ə·neɪt] *vt* contaminar

**contamination** [kən·ˌtæm·ɪ·ˈneɪ·ʃən] *n* contaminación *f*

**contemplate** [ˈkɑn·tem·pleɪt] *vt* contemplar; **to ~ doing sth** tener la intención de hacer algo

**contemplation** [ˌkɑn·tem·ˈpleɪ·ʃən] *n* contemplación *f*

**contemporary** [kən·ˈtem·pə·rer·i] *adj, n* contemporáneo, -a *m, f*

**contempt** [kən·ˈtempt] *n* desprecio *m;* **to be beneath ~** ser despreciable; **to hold in ~** despreciar

**contend** [kən·ˈtend] *vi* **1.** (*compete*) competir (**for** por) **2.** (*struggle*) luchar (**against** contra)

**content¹** [ˈkɑn·tent] *n* contenido *m*

**content²** [kən·ˈtent] **I.** *vt* satisfacer; **to ~ oneself** contentarse (**with** con) **II.** *adj* satisfecho (**with** con) **III.** *n* **to one's heart's ~** a más no poder

**contented** *adj* satisfecho, -a

**contentious** [kən·ˈten·ʃəs] *adj* conflictivo, -a

**contentment** [kən·ˈtent·mənt] *n* satisfacción *f*

**contest** [ˈkɑn·test] *n* (*competition*) concurso *m;* **sports ~** competición *f* deportiva

**contestant** [kən·ˈtes·tənt] *n* SPORTS contrincante *mf;* POL candidato, -a *m, f;* TV concursante *mf*

**context** [ˈkɑn·tekst] *n* contexto *m*

**continent** [ˈkɑn·tə·nənt] *n* GEO continente *m*

**continental** [ˌkɑn·tə·ˈnen·təl] *adj* continental; **the ~ United States** Estados Unidos continental

**contingency** [kən·ˈtɪn·dʒən·si] <-ies> *n* contingencia *f*

**continual** [kən·ˈtɪn·ju·əl] *adj* continuo, -a

**continually** *adv* continuamente

**continuation** [kən·ˌtɪn·ju·ˈeɪ·ʃən] *n* continuación *f*

**continue** [kən·ˈtɪn·ju] **I.** *vi* seguir; **to ~ to do** [*or* doing] **sth** seguir haciendo algo; **to ~** (**on**) **one's way** seguir su camino; **to be ~d** continuará; **he ~d by saying that...** prosiguió diciendo que... **II.** *vt* **1.** (*go on*) seguir con **2.** (*lengthen*) prolongar

**continuous** [kən·ˈtɪn·ju·əs] *adj* continuo, -a

**contraceptive** [ˌkɑn·trə·ˈsep·tɪv] *n* anticonceptivo *m*

**contract¹** [kən·ˈtrækt] **I.** *vi* contraerse **II.** *vt a.* MED contraer

**contract²** [ˈkɑn·trækt] **I.** *n* contrato *m;* **~ of employment** contrato laboral; **temporary ~** contrato temporal **II.** *vt* contratar

♦**contract out** *vt* subcontratar

**contraction** [kən·ˈtræk·ʃən] *n* contracción *f*

**contradict** [ˌkɑn·trə·ˈdɪkt] **I.** *vi* contradecirse **II.** *vt* contradecir; **to ~ oneself** contradecirse

**contradiction** [ˌkɑn·trə·ˈdɪk·ʃən] *n* contradicción *f*

**contradictory** [ˌkɑn·trə·ˈdɪk·tə·ri] *adj* contradictorio, -a

**contrary** [ˈkɑn·trer·i] **I.** *n* **on the ~** al contrario; **quite the ~!** ¡todo lo contrario!; **to the ~** en contra **II.** *adj* contrario, -a (**to** a)

**contrary to** *prep* al contrario de; **~ all our expectations** contra todo pronóstico

**contrast¹** [kən·ˈtræst] *vt* contrastar

**contrast²** [ˈkɑn·træst] *n* contraste *m;* **by** [*or* **in**] **~** en contraste; **in ~ to** [*or* **with**] a diferencia de

**contribute** [kən·'trɪb·jut] I. *vi* 1. (*money, time*) contribuir (**towards** en) 2. (*participate*) intervenir II. *vt* (*money*) contribuir; (*article*) escribir; (*information*) aportar; **to ~ (sth) to sth** contribuir (con algo) a algo; **to ~ sth towards sth** aportar algo a algo

**contribution** [ˌkan·trɪ·'bju·ʃən] *n* 1. contribución *f* 2. (*for publication*) colaboración *f*

**contributor** [kən·'trɪb·jə·tər] *n* 1. contribuyente *mf* 2. (*writer*) colaborador(a) *m(f)*

**contributory** [kən·'trɪb·jə·tɔr·i] *adj* contributivo, -a

**control** [kən·'troʊl] I. *n* 1. control *m;* **to bring under ~** controlar; **to go out of ~** descontrolarse; **to have/lose ~** tener/ perder el control (**over** sobre) 2. (*leadership*) mando *m;* **to be in ~** mandar 3. **~s** TECH mandos; **to be at the ~s** llevar los mandos II. *vt* <-ll-> *a.* MED, ECON, FIN controlar; (*vehicle*) conducir; (*anger*) dominar

**control panel** *n* panel *m* de control

**controversial** [ˌkan·trə·'vɜr·ʃəl] *adj* polémico, -a

**controversy** ['kan·trə·vɜr·si] *n* <-ies> polémica *f*

**convenience** [kən·'vin·jəns] *n* conveniencia *f;* (*practicality*) comodidad *f;* (*advantage*) ventaja *f*

**convenient** [kən·'vin·jənt] *adj* 1. (*suitable*) conveniente 2. (*practical*) práctico, -a 3. (*close*) bien situado, -a

**convent** ['kan·vənt] *n* convento *m*

**convention** [kən·'ven·ʃən] *n* convención *f;* (*custom*) convenciones *f*

**conventional** [kən·'ven·ʃə·nəl] *adj* convencional

**converge** [kən·'vɜrdʒ] *vi* converger; (*persons*) reunirse

**conversation** [ˌkan·vər·'seɪ·ʃən] *n* conversación *f,* plática *f AmL;* **to strike up a ~** entablar conversación (**with** con)

**conversion** [kən·'vɜr·ʒən] *n* conversión *f*

**convert** [kən·'vɜrt] I. *vi* convertirse II. *vt* convertir

**converter** [kən·'vɜr·tər] *n* ELEC transformador *m*

**convertible** [kən·'vɜr·tə·bəl] I. *n* AUTO descapotable *m* II. *adj a.* FIN, ECON convertible; **~ sofa** sofá cama, convertible *m AmL*

**convex** ['kan·veks] *adj* convexo, -a

**convey** [kən·'veɪ] *vt* 1. (*transport*) transportar; (*electricity*) conducir 2. (*communicate*) transmitir

**convict**[1] ['kan·vɪkt] *n* presidiario, -a *m, f*

**convict**[2] [kən·'vɪkt] *vt* condenar

**conviction** [kən·'vɪk·ʃən] *n* 1. LAW condena *f* 2. (*belief*) convicción *f;* **to have a ~** estar convencido (**about** de)

**convince** [kən·'vɪns] *vt* convencer

**convincing** [kən·'vɪn·sɪŋ] *adj* convincente

**convoy** ['kan·vɔɪ] *n* convoy *m;* **in ~** en caravana

**cook** [kʊk] I. *n* cocinero, -a *m, f* II. *vi* hacerse; **how long does pasta take to ~?** ¿cuánto tarda en hacerse la pasta? ▶ **what's ~ing?** *sl* ¿qué pasa? III. *vt* cocinar, asar; (*meat*) **to ~ lunch** hacer la comida

**cookbook** ['kʊk·bʊk] *n* libro *m* de cocina

**cookery** ['kʊk·ə·ri] *n* cocina *f*

**cookie** ['kʊk·i] *n* 1. (*biscuit*) galleta *f* 2. *sl* (*person*) tipo, -a *m, f* 3. COMPUT cookie *m*

**cooking** ['kʊk·ɪŋ] *n* **to do the ~** hacer la comida

**cool** [kul] I. *adj* 1. (*drink, evening*) fresco, -a; (*color, greeting*) frío, -a 2. (*calm*) tranquilo, -a; **keep ~** tómatelo con calma 3. *inf* (*fashionable*) **to be ~** estar en la onda II. *interj inf* ¡qué guay! III. *n* 1. (*coolness*) fresco *m* 2. (*calm*) calma *f* IV. *vt* enfriar; **just ~ it** *inf* ¡calma! V. *vi* enfriarse; **to ~ down** [*or* **off**] enfriarse; (*become calmer*) calmarse

**cool-headed** [ˌkul·'hed·ɪd] *adj* sereno, -a

**cooling** ['ku·lɪŋ] *adj* refrescante; (*breeze*) fresco, -a

**coolness** ['kul·nɪs] *n* 1. METEO fresco *m* 2. (*unfriendliness*) frialdad *f*

**coop** [kup] I. *n* gallinero *m* II. *vt* encerrar

**cooperate** [koʊ·'ap·ə·reɪt] *vi* cooperar

**cooperation** [koʊ·ˌap·ə·'reɪ·ʃən] *n* cooperación f

**cooperative** [kou·'ap·ər·ə·t̬ɪv] I. n cooperativa f II. adj cooperativo, -a

**coordinate** [ˌkou·'ɔr·dɪn·eɪt] I. n coordenada f II. vi, vt coordinar(se); (match) combinar III. adj coordinado, -a; (equal) igual

**coordination** [ˌkou·ɔr·də·'neɪ·ʃən] n coordinación f

**coordinator** n coordinador(a) m(f)

**cop** [kap] n inf poli mf; **to play ~s and robbers** jugar a polis y cacos

**copartner** ['kou·ˌpart·nər] n copartícipe mf

**cope** [koup] vi aguantar; **to ~ with** poder con; (situation) enfrentarse a; (problem) hacer frente a; (pain) soportar

**copilot** ['kou·ˌpaɪ·lət] n copiloto mf

**copper** ['kap·ər] I. n (metal) cobre m II. adj (color) cobrizo, -a

**copulate** ['kap·jə·leɪt] vi copular

**copulation** [ˌkap·jə·'leɪ·ʃən] n cópula f

**copy** ['kap·i] I. <-ies> n 1. a. COMPUT copia f; (book) ejemplar m; ART imitación f; **hard ~** copia impresa f; (text to be published) original m II. <-ie-> vt 1. a. COMPUT copiar 2. (imitate) imitar III. vi copiar

**copy protection** n protección f contra escritura

**copyright** n derechos m pl de autor

**coral** ['kɔr·əl] I. n coral m II. adj (color) coralino, -a

**cord** [kɔrd] n (rope) cuerda f, piola f AmS; ELEC cable m; **umbilical ~** cordón m umbilical

**cordless** ['kɔrd·lɪs] adj inalámbrico, -a

**cordon** ['kɔr·dən] I. n cordón m; **police ~** cordón policial II. vt acordonar

**corduroy** ['kɔr·də·rɔɪ] n pana f

**core** [kɔr] n 1. (center) centro m; (apple, pear) corazón m; **to the ~** fig hasta la médula; **to be at the ~ of the problem** llegar al quid de la cuestión 2. PHYS núcleo m

**coriander** ['kɔr·i·æn·dər] n cilantro m

**cork** [kɔrk] I. n 1. corcho m 2. (stopper) tapón m II. vt 1. (put stopper) taponar 2. (restrain) contener

**corkscrew** ['kɔrk·skru] n sacacorchos m inv

**corn¹** [kɔrn] n 1. (crop) maíz m, choclo m AmS, abatí m Arg 2. sl (trite) sensiblería f

**corn²** [kɔrn] n MED callo m

**corn bread** n pan m de maíz

**corncob** n mazorca f de maíz

**cornea** ['kɔr·ni·ə] n córnea f

**corner** ['kɔr·nər] I. n 1. (of roads) esquina f; **to be around the ~** estar a la vuelta de la esquina; **to turn the ~** doblar la esquina 2. (of a room) rincón m; **a distant ~ of the globe** un rincón remoto de la tierra; **the four ~s of the world** todos los rincones del mundo 3. SPORTS córner m 4. (difficulty) **to be in a tight ~** estar en un aprieto; **to drive sb into a (tight) ~** poner a alguien entre la espada y la pared 5. (periphery) **out of the ~ of one's eye** con el rabillo del ojo; **out of the ~ of sb's mouth** en la comisura de los labios ▶ **to cut ~s** ahorrar esfuerzos II. vt 1. (hinder escape) acorralar 2. ECON **to ~ the market** acaparar el mercado

**cornered** ['kɔr·nərd] adj acorralado, -a

**cornflakes** ['kɔrn·fleɪks] npl copos m pl de maíz

**corn poppy** <-ies> n amapola f

**cornstarch** n maicena f

**corny** ['kɔr·ni] <-ier, -iest> adj 1. inf viejo, -a 2. (emotive) sensiblero, -a

**corp.** abbr of **corporation** sociedad f anónima

**corporate** ['kɔr·pər·ət] adj colectivo, -a; (of corporation) empresarial

**corporation** [ˌkɔr·pə·'reɪ·ʃən] n + sing/ pl vb 1. FIN sociedad f anónima; **multinational ~** empresa f multinacional [or AmL transnacional] 2. POL ayuntamiento m

**corpse** [kɔrps] n cadáver m

**correct** [kə·'rekt] I. vt corregir II. adj correcto, -a

**correction** [kə·'rek·ʃən] n corrección f; (improvememt) rectificación f

**correction fluid** n líquido m corrector

**correctly** [kə·'rekt·li] adv correctamente

**correspond** [ˌkɔr·ə·'spand] vi 1. (equal) corresponder a 2. (write) mantener correspondencia

**correspondence** [ˌkɔr·ə·'span·dəns] n

correspondencia f; **business ~** correspondencia comercial

**correspondent** [ˌkɔr·ə·ˈspan·dənt] n corresponsal mf; **special ~** enviado, -a m, f especial

**corresponding** [ˌkɔr·ə·ˈspan·dɪŋ] adj correspondiente

**corridor** [ˈkɔr·ɪ·dər] n (passage) pasillo m

**corrosion** [kə·ˈroʊ·ʒən] n corrosión f; fig deterioro m

**corrosive** [kə·ˈroʊ·sɪv] adj corrosivo, -a; fig destructivo, -a

**corrupt** [kə·ˈrʌpt] I. vt 1. (debase) corromper 2. (bribe) sobornar 3. (document) dañar II. vi corromper III. adj corrupto, -a; (document) dañado, -a

**corruption** [kə·ˈrʌp·ʃən] n corrupción f

**cosmetic** [kaz·ˈmet̬·ɪk] I. n cosmético m II. adj cosmético, -a; (superficial) superficial

**cosmonaut** [ˈkaz·mə·nɔt] n cosmonauta mf

**cosmopolitan** [ˌkaz·mə·ˈpal·ɪ·tən] adj, n cosmopolita mf

**cosmos** [ˈkaz·moʊs] n cosmos m inv

**cost** [kɔst] I. vt 1. <cost, cost> costar; **to ~ a fortune** costar un ojo de la cara; **to ~ sb dearly** salir muy caro a alguien fig 2. <costed, costed> calcular el coste de II. n 1. coste m; **at ~** a precio de coste; **at no extra ~** sin costes adicionales; **to cut ~s** [or the ~] recortar costes 2. (sacrifice) (**only**) **at the ~ of doing sth** (sólo) a costa de hacer algo; **at all ~(s)** a toda costa

**costly** [ˈkɔst·li] <-ier, -iest> adj costoso, -a; **to prove ~ a.** fig salir muy caro

**costume** [ˈkas·tum] n 1. traje m; **to dress in ~** ir trajeado 2. (fancy dress) disfraz m

**cot** [kat] n (camp bed) cama f plegable

**cottage** [ˈkat̬·ɪdʒ] n **country ~** casa f de campo

**cottage cheese** n requesón m

**cotton** [ˈkat·ən] n algodón m

**cotton candy** n algodón m de azúcar

**cotton-picking** adj inf **~ fool** tonto, -a m, f de remate

**couch** [kaʊtʃ] <-es> n sofá m

**cough** [kɔf] I. n tos f II. vi toser

**could** [kʊd] pt, pp **can²**

**council** [ˈkaʊn·səl] n consejo m; **city ~** ayuntamiento m

**counsel** [ˈkaʊn·səl] I. <-ll-, -l-> vt aconsejar II. n 1. (advice) consejo m 2. (lawyer) abogado, -a m, f

**count¹** [kaʊnt] n conde m

**count²** [kaʊnt] I. n 1. recuento m; **to keep/lose ~** llevar/perder la cuenta (of de) 2. (sum) total m II. vt 1. (number) contar 2. (consider) considerar; **to ~ sth a success/failure** considerar algo un éxito/fracaso; **to ~ sb as a friend** tener a alguien como amigo III. vi contar; **that's what ~s** eso es lo que cuenta; **to not ~** no tener ni voz ni voto

◆**count on** vt (depend on) contar con

◆**count out** vt always sep contar; **to count sb out** no contar con alguien

**countdown** [ˈkaʊnt·daʊn] n cuenta f atrás

**counter** [ˈkaʊn·tər] I. n 1. (service point) mostrador m; **over the ~** sin receta médica; **under the ~** fig clandestinamente 2. (machine) caja f; TECH contador m II. vt contrarrestar III. adv en contra

**counterattack** [ˈkaʊn·tər·ə·ˌtæk] I. n contraataque m II. vt, vi contraatacar

**counterclockwise** [ˌkaʊn·tər·ˈklak·waɪz] adj en sentido contrario a las agujas del reloj

**counterfeit** [ˈkaʊn·tər·fɪt] I. adj falsificado, -a; (money) falso, -a II. vt falsificar III. n falsificación f

**countermeasure** [ˈkaʊn·tər·ˌmeʒ·ər] n medida f en contra

**counterpart** [ˈkaʊn·tər·ˌpart] n contrapartida f; POL homólogo, -a m, f

**counterproductive** [ˌkaʊn·tər·prə·ˈdʌk·tɪv] adj contraproducente

**counterterrorism** [ˌkaʊn·tər·ˈter·ər·ɪz·əm] n lucha f antiterrorista

**countless** [ˈkaʊnt·lɪs] adj incontable

**country** [ˈkʌn·tri] I. n 1. (rural area) campo m 2. <-ies> POL país m 3. (area) territorio m 4. MUS country m II. adj rural; MUS country

**country folk** n + pl vb gente f de campo

**countryside** [ˈkʌn·tri·saɪd] n campo m,

**verde** *m AmC, Méx*

**county** ['kaʊn·ti] <-ies> *n* condado *m*

**county fair** *n* feria *f* del condado

**coup** [ku] <coups> *n* golpe *m*; **~ de grâce/d'état** golpe de gracia/Estado

**couple** ['kʌp·əl] **I.** *n* **1.** (*a few*) par *m*; **the first ~ of weeks** las primeras dos semanas **2.** + *sing/pl vb* (*two people*) pareja *f*; (*married*) matrimonio *m* **II.** *vt* **1.** RAIL, AUTO enganchar **2.** (*connect*) conectar **3.** (*link*) unir

**coupon** ['ku·pɑn] *n* cupón *m*

**courage** ['kɜr·ɪdʒ] *n* coraje *m*

**courageous** [kə·'reɪ·dʒəs] *adj* valiente; (*act*) valeroso, -a

**courier** ['kʊr·i·ər] **I.** *n* mensajero, -a *m, f* **II.** *adj* **~ service** servicio *m* de mensajería

**course** [kɔrs] *n* **1.** (*direction*) recorrido *m*; (*river*) curso *m*; **to be off ~** *a. fig* desviarse; **to set ~** poner rumbo (**for** hacia); **your best ~ of action would be...** lo mejor que podrías hacer sería... **2.** (*development*) transcurso *m*; **over the ~ of time** con el tiempo *m*; (*treatment*) tratamiento *m* **4.** SPORTS pista *f*; (*golf*) campo *m* **5.** (*part of meal*) plato *m* ▶ **to let sth run its ~** dejar que algo siga su curso; **of ~** por supuesto; **of ~ not** desde luego que no

**court** [kɔrt] *n* **1.** (*room*) juzgado *m* **2.** (*judicial body*) tribunal *m* **3.** SPORTS cancha *f*; (*tennis*) pista *f* **4.** HIST corte *f*

**courteous** ['kɜr·t̬i·əs] *adj* cortés

**courtesy** ['kɜr·t̬ə·si] <-ies> *n* cortesía *f*; (*decency*) decencia *f*

**courthouse** ['kɔrt·haʊs] *n* juzgado *m*

**court of appeals** *n* tribunal *m* de apelación

**court of law** *n* tribunal *m* de justicia

**courtyard** *n* patio *m*

**cousin** ['kʌz·ɪn] *n* primo, -a *m, f*

**cover** ['kʌv·ər] **I.** *n* **1.** (*top*) tapa *f*; (*book*) cubierta *f*; (*magazine*) portada *f* **2.** (*bedding*) colcha *f* **3.** (*concealment*) abrigo *m*; **to break ~** salir al descubierto; **to take ~** guarecerse **II.** *vt* **1.** (*hide*) tapar; (*head*) cubrir; (*book*) forrar **2.** (*keep warm*) abrigar **3.** (*travel*) recorrer **4.** (*include*) incluir ▶ *sl* **to ~ one's ass** cubrirse las espaldas

◆**cover over** *vt* cubrir

◆**cover up** **I.** *vt* tapar **II.** *vi* encubrir (**for** a)

**coverage** ['kʌv·ər·ɪdʒ] *n* cobertura *f*

**coveralls** ['kʌv·ər·ɔlz] *npl* mono *m*

**covered** *adj* cubierto, -a

**covering** *n* capa *f*

**cover letter** *n* carta *f* adjunta

**cover-up** ['kʌv·ər·ʌp] *n* encubrimiento *m*

**cow¹** [kaʊ] *n* **1.** vaca *f* **2.** (*female*) hembra *f*

**cow²** [kaʊ] *vt* intimidar

**coward** ['kaʊ·ərd] *n* cobarde *mf*

**cowardice** ['kaʊ·ər·dɪs] *n* cobardía *f*

**cowboy** ['kaʊ·bɔɪ] *n* vaquero *m*, tropero *m Arg*

**co-worker** ['koʊ·wɜr·kər] *n* compañero, -a *m, f* de trabajo

**cowshed** ['kaʊ·ʃed] *n* establo *m*

**coy** [kɔɪ] <-er, -est> *adj* **1.** (*secretive*) reservado, -a **2.** (*flirtatious*) coqueto, -a

**coyote** [kaɪ·'oʊ·t̬i] *n* coyote *m*

**coziness** ['koʊ·zi·nɪs] *n* comodidad *f*

**cozy** ['koʊ·zi] **I.** <-ier, -iest> *adj* **1.** (*comfortable*) cómodo, -a; (*place*) acogedor(a) **2.** *pej* de conveniencia **II.** <-ies> *n* tapadera *f*

**CPU** [si·pi·'ju] *n abbr of* **central processing unit** CPU *f*

**crab¹** [kræb] *n* cangrejo *m*, jaiba *f AmL*

**crab²** [kræb] <-bb-> *vi* rezongar

**crab louse** *n* ladilla *f*

**crack** [kræk] **I.** *n* **1.** (*fissure*) grieta *f* **2.** (*sound*) crujido *m* **3.** (*drug*) crack *m* **4.** *inf* (*attempt*) intento *m* **II.** *adj* de primera **III.** *vt* **1.** (*break*) romper; (*egg*) cascar; (*nuts*) partir; (*safe*) forzar; (*code*) descifrar; (*joke*) contar **2.** (*resolve*) resolver **3.** (*hit*) pegar **IV.** *vi* **1.** (*break*) rajarse; (*paintwork*) agrietarse **2.** (*break down*) venirse abajo **3.** (*make noise*) chasquear ▶ **to get ~ing** poner manos a la obra

◆**crack up** *vi* (*laugh*) reírse a carcajadas

**crackdown** ['kræk·daʊn] *n* ofensiva *f*

**cracked** [krækt] *adj* rajado, -a; (*lips*) agrietado, -a

**cracker** ['kræk·ər] *n* **1.** (*biscuit*) galleta *f* **2.** COMPUT cracker *mf*

**crackle** ['kræk·əl] **I.** *vi, vt* crujir **II.** *n* crujido *m*; TEL ruido *m*

**crackling** ['kræk·lɪŋ] n crujido m; RADIO ruido m

**cradle** ['kreɪ·dəl] I. n 1. (bed) cuna f; **from the ~ to the grave** durante toda la vida 2. (framework) andamio m II. vt acunar

**craft** [kræft] I. n 1. (means of transport) nave f 2. (skill) arte m 3. (trade) oficio m 4. (ability) destreza f II. vt construir

**craftsman** ['kræfts·mən] <-men> n artesano m

**craft store** n tienda f de artesanía

**crafty** ['kræf·ti] <-ier, -iest> adj astuto, -a

**cram** [kræm] <-mm-> I. vt meter; **to ~ sth with sth** llenar algo de algo II. vi memorizar

**cramp** [kræmp] I. vt poner obstáculos a; **to ~ sb's style** cortar las alas a alguien II. n calambre m

**crampon** ['kræm·pɑn] n crampón m

**cranberry** ['kræn·ˌber·i] <-ies> n arándano m

**crane** [kreɪn] n grúa f; ZOOL grulla f

**crank** [kræŋk] n (person) maniático, -a m, f

**cranky** ['kræŋ·ki] <-ier, -iest> adj maniático, -a

**crap** [kræp] I. <-pp-> vi vulg cagar II. n mierda f III. adj de mierda

**crapper** ['kræp·ər] n vulg cagódromo m ▶ **to go in the ~** irse a la mierda

**crappy** ['kræp·i] <-ier, -iest> adj sl cutre

**crash** [kræʃ] I. n <-es> 1. (accident) accidente m 2. (noise) estrépito m 3. COM crac m 4. COMPUT caída f (del sistema) II. vi 1. (vehicle) chocar; (plane) estrellarse 2. (make noise) retumbar 3. (break) derrumbarse 4. COM colapsarse 5. COMPUT colgarse III. vt 1. (damage) chocar 2. (make noise) hacer ruido

**crash course** n curso m intensivo

**crash landing** n aterrizaje m forzoso

**crate** [kreɪt] I. n cajón m II. vt embalar

**crater** ['kreɪ·tər] n cráter m

**crave** [kreɪv] vt ansiar; (attention) reclamar

**craving** ['kreɪ·vɪŋ] n ansia f

**crawl** [krɔl] vi 1. (go on all fours) gatear

2. (move slowly) arrastrarse 3. **to ~ (up) to sb** hacer la pelota a alguien; **to be ~ing with sth** estar plagado de algo, nadar a crol

**crayfish** ['kreɪ·fɪʃ] n inv cangrejo m de río

**crayon** ['kreɪ·ɑn] I. n lápiz m II. vt colorear III. vi dibujar

**craze** [kreɪz] n manía f

**crazed** [kreɪzd] adj de loco, -a

**crazy** ['kreɪ·zi] <-ier, -iest> adj loco, -a, tarado, -a AmL; **to go ~** volverse loco

**creak** [krik] I. vi crujir; (door) chirriar II. n crujido m; (door) chirrido m

**creaky** ['kri·ki] <-ier, -iest> adj 1. (squeaky) chirriante 2. (decrepit) decrépito, -a

**cream** [krim] I. n 1. FOOD nata f 2. (cosmetic) crema f II. adj 1. (containing cream) cremoso, -a 2. (color) de color crema III. vt (butter) batir; (milk) desnatar; (coffee) añadir crema

**cream cheese** n queso m de untar

**cream-colored** adj de color crema

**creamy** ['kri·mi] <-ier, -iest> adj (smooth) cremoso, -a; (skin) hidratado, -a

**crease** [kris] I. n (fold) arruga f II. vt arrugar III. vi arrugarse

**create** [kri·'eɪt] vt 1. (produce) crear 2. (cause) causar

**creation** [kri·'eɪ·ʃən] n 1. (making) creación f 2. (product) producción f 3. FASHION modelo m

**creative** [kri·'eɪ·t̬ɪv] adj creativo, -a

**creator** [kri·'eɪ·t̬ər] n creador(a) m(f)

**creature** ['kri·tʃər] n criatura f

**credentials** [krɪ·'den·ʃəlz] npl credenciales fpl

**credibility** [ˌkred·ə·'bɪl·ə·t̬i] n credibilidad f

**credible** ['kred·ɪt] I. n 1. (belief) a. FIN crédito m; **to give ~** dar crédito (to a); **on ~** a plazos 2. (recognition) mérito m; **to be a ~ to sb** ser un honor para alguien; **to give ~ to sb** en favor de alguien; **to take (the) ~** atribuirse el mérito (for a) 3. ~s CINE créditos II. vt 1. (believe) creer; **he is ~ed with...** se le atribuye... 2. **to ~ sb with 2000 dollars** abonar 2000 dólares en cuenta a alguien

**creditable** ['kred·ɪ·t̬ə·bəl] adj 1. (believable) digno, -a de crédito 2. (commend-

_able_) digno, -a de elogio

**credit card** _n_ tarjeta _f_ de crédito

**credit slip** _n_ nota _f_ de crédito

**creditworthy** ['kred·ɪt·wɜr·ði] _adj_ solvente

**creep** [krip] **I.** <crept, crept> _vi_ **1.** (_crawl_) arrastrarse; (_snake_) reptar; (_baby_) ir a gatas; (_plant_) trepar **2.** (_move imperceptibly_) deslizarse **II.** _n_ **1.** _sl_ (_sycophant_) pelotillero, -a _m, f_, lambiscón, -ona _m, f Méx_, lambón, -ona _m, f Col_ **2.** _sl_ (_pervert_) pervertido, -a _m, f_ ▶ _inf_ to **give** sb the **~s** poner a alguien la carne de gallina

◆**creep into** _vt insep_ entrar sigilosamente en

◆**creep up** _vi_ acercarse sigilosamente (**on** a)

**creeper** ['kri·pər] _n_ BOT enredadera _f_

**creepy** ['kri·pi] <-ier, -iest> _adj inf_ espeluznante

**cremate** ['kri·meɪt] _vt_ incinerar

**cremation** [krɪ·'meɪ·ʃən] _n_ incineración _f_

**crematorium** [ˌkri·mə·'tɔr·i·əm] <-s _or_ -ria> _n_ crematorio _m_

**crematory** ['kri·mə·tɔr·i] **I.** _n_ crematorio _m_ **II.** _adj_ crematorio, -a

**crepe** [kreɪp] _n_ CULIN crêpe _m o f_

**crept** [krept] _pp, pt of_ creep

**crest** [krest] **I.** _n_ (_peak_) cima _f_; (_wave, bird_) cresta _f_ **II.** _vt_ coronar

**crew** [kru] _n_ + _sing/pl vb_ **1.** NAUT, AVIAT tripulación _f_; RAIL personal _m_; **ground/ flight ~** personal de tierra/de vuelo **2.** _inf_ (_gang_) peña _f_

**crib** [krɪb] _n_ **1.** (_bed_) cuna _f_ **2.** _sl_ (_home_) keli _m_ **3.** _inf_ SCHOOL chuleta _f_, chancho _m Col_, acordeón _m Méx_, machete _m RíoPl_

**cricket** ['krɪk·ɪt] _n_ **1.** SPORTS cricket _m_ **2.** ZOOL grillo _m_, siripita _f Bol_

**crime** [kraɪm] _n_ **1.** LAW delito _m_; (_murder_) crimen _m_; **~ of passion** crimen pasional; **to commit a ~** cometer un delito; **the scene of the ~** la escena del crimen **2.** (_criminal activity_) delincuencia _f_; **~ rate** índice de criminalidad; **organized ~** crimen organizado

**criminal** ['krɪm·ə·nəl] **I.** _n_ delincuente _mf_; (_serious offender_) criminal _mf_ **II.** _adj_ **1.** (_illegal_) delictivo, -a; (_more serious_) criminal **2.** LAW penal; **~ court** juzgado _m_ de lo penal; **~ record** antecedentes penales **3.** _fig_ (_shameful_) vergonzoso, -a; **to be ~ to do sth** ser un crimen hacer algo

**criminality** [ˌkrɪm·ə·'næl·ə·ti] _n_ criminalidad _f_

**crimson** ['krɪm·zən] **I.** _n_ carmesí _m_ **II.** _adj_ **1.** (_color_) carmesí **2.** (_redfaced_) colorado, -a

**crinkle** ['krɪŋ·kəl] **I.** _vt_ arrugar **II.** _vi_ to **~ (up)** arrugarse **III.** _n_ arruga _f_

**cripple** ['krɪp·əl] **I.** _n_ lisiado, -a _m, f_ **II.** _vt_ **1.** (_disable_) lisiar; (_machine, object_) inutilizar **2.** (_paralyze_) paralizar

**crisis** ['kraɪ·sɪs] <crises> _n_ crisis _f inv_ (**over** provocada por); **to go through a ~** atravesar una crisis

**crisp** [krɪsp] **I.** <-er, -est> _adj_ **1.** (_crunchy_) crujiente **2.** (_fresh_) fresco, -a; (_shirt, pants_) recién planchado, -a; (_banknote_) nuevo, -a **3.** (_sharp_) nítido, -a **4.** (_lively_) animado, -a **5.** (_concise_) escueto, -a; (_manner_) seco, -a; (_style_) conciso, -a **II.** _vt_ FOOD tostar ligeramente

**crispy** ['krɪs·pi] <-ier, -iest> _adj_ crujiente

**crisscross** ['krɪs·krɑs] **I.** _vt_ entrecruzar **II.** _vi_ entrecruzarse **III.** _adj_ entrecruzado, -a **IV.** <-es> _n fig_ enredo _m_

**criterion** [kraɪ·'tɪr·i·ən] <-ria> _n_ criterio _m_

**critic** ['krɪt·ɪk] _n_ crítico, -a _m, f_

**critical** ['krɪt·ɪ·kəl] _adj_ crítico, -a; **to be (highly) ~ of sth/sb** criticar (duramente) algo/a alguien; **to be ~ to sth** ser crítico para algo; **to be in ~ condition** estar en estado crítico

**criticism** ['krɪt·ɪ·sɪz·əm] _n_ crítica _f_

**criticize** ['krɪt·ɪ·saɪz] _vt, vi_ criticar

**croak** [kroʊk] **I.** _vi_ **1.** (_crow_) graznar; (_frog_) croar; (_person_) gruñir **2.** _sl_ (_die_) palmar **II.** _vt_ decir con voz ronca **III.** _n_ (_crow_) graznido _m_; (_frog_) croar _m_; (_person_) gruñido _m_

**Croatia** [kroʊ·'eɪ·ʃə] _n_ Croacia _f_

**Croatian** [kroʊ·'eɪ·ʃən] _adj, n_ croata _mf_

**crochet** [kroʊ·'ʃeɪ] _n_ ganchillo _m_

**crockery** ['krɑk·ə·ri] _n_ vajilla _f_ de barro

**crocodile** ['krɑk·ə·daɪl] <-(s)> _n_ cocodrilo _m_

**croissant** [krwa·'saŋ] n croissant m

**crook** [krʊk] I. n 1. (*criminal*) delincuente mf 2. inf (*rogue*) sinvergüenza mf 3. (*curve*) recodo m II. vt doblar

**crooked** ['krʊk·ɪd] adj 1. (*not straight*) torcido, -a; (*back*) encorvado, -a; (*path*) tortuoso, -a 2. inf (*dishonest*) deshonesto, -a

**crop** [krap] I. n 1. AGR cultivo m; (*harvest*) cosecha f 2. (*group*) montón m; **a ~ of lies** una sarta de mentiras II. <-pp-> vt 1. (*cut*) cortar; (*hair*) cortar al uno; (*plant*) podar III. vi AGR darse; (*land*) rendir

◆**crop up** vi surgir

**cross** [krɔs] I. vt 1. cruzar; **to ~ one's legs/fingers** cruzar las piernas/los dedos; **to ~ one's arms** cruzarse de brazos 2. (*oppose*) contrariar 3. (*mark with a cross*) marcar con una cruz II. vi 1. (*intersect*) cruzarse 2. (*go across*) cruzar III. n 1. a. REL cruz f; **to bear one's ~** cargar con su cruz 2. (*streets, roads*) cruce m 3. BIO cruce, cruza f AmL 4. (*mixture*) mezcla f IV. adj enfadado, -a (**about** por); **to get ~** enfadarse (**with** con)

◆**cross out** vt tachar

◆**cross over** vi, vt cruzar

**crossbar** ['krɔs·bar] n travesaño m; (*bicycle*) barra f

**cross-country** adj, adv a campo traviesa

**cross-cultural** adj intercultural

**crosscurrent** n contracorriente f

**cross-dress** vi travestirse

**cross-dresser** n travesti mf

**cross-eyed** adj bizco, -a

**crossfire** n fuego m cruzado; **to be caught in the ~** fig estar entre dos fuegos

**crossing** ['krɔ·sɪŋ] n 1. (*place to cross, journey*) paso m; **border/level/pedestrian ~** paso fronterizo/a nivel/de peatones 2. (*crossroads*) cruce m 3. ARCHIT crucero m

**cross-legged** [ˌkrɔs·'leg·ɪd] adj con las piernas cruzadas

**crossover** n paso m; fig fusión f

**cross-purposes** npl **to be talking at ~** estar hablando de cosas distintas

**cross-reference** n remisión f

**crossroads** n inv cruce m; fig encrucijada f

**cross section** n sección f transversal; fig muestra f representativa

**crosswalk** n paso m de cebra

**crossword** (**puzzle**) n crucigrama m

**crouch** [kraʊtʃ] I. vi **to ~ (down)** agacharse; **to be ~ing** estar en cuclillas II. n **to lower oneself into a ~** agacharse

**crow**[1] [kroʊ] n ZOOL cuervo m ▶ **as the ~ flies** en línea recta

**crow**[2] [kroʊ] <crowed, crowed> I. n grito m (de alegría); (*baby*) gorjeo m; (*cock*) cacareo m II. vi 1. (*cry*) gritar de entusiasmo; (*baby*) gorjear; (*cock*) cacarear 2. (*boast*) alardear

**crowd** [kraʊd] I. n + sing/pl vb 1. (*throng*) multitud f; **there was quite a ~** había mucha gente 2. fig **to stand out from the ~** destacar(se); **to follow the ~** dejarse llevar por los demás 3. inf (*group*) grupo m; **the usual ~** los de siempre 4. fig (*large number*) montón m; **a ~ of things** un montón de cosas 5. (*audience*) público m II. vi aglomerarse; **to ~ into a place** entrar en tropel en un sitio; **to ~ around sb/sth** apiñarse alrededor de alguien/algo III. vt 1. (*fill*) llenar; **to ~ the streets/a stadium** abarrotar las calles/un estadio 2. (*cram*) amontonar 3. inf (*pressure*) atosigar

◆**crowd out** vt 1. (*exclude*) excluir 2. **to be crowded out** estar abarrotado

**crowded** adj lleno, -a; **~ together** amontonados; **the bar was ~** el bar estaba abarrotado

**crowd-pleaser** n inf (*song*) hit m

**crown** [kraʊn] I. n 1. corona f 2. (*peak*) cima f; (*hat, tree*) copa f; (*head*) coronilla f; (*bird*) cresta f 3. (*culmination*) culminación f II. vt 1. (*coronate*) coronar 2. (*complete*) rematar; **the prize ~ed his career** el premio fue la culminación de su carrera 3. inf (*hit*) dar un coscorrón

**crown prince** n príncipe m heredero

**crow's feet** ['kroʊz·fit] npl patas f pl de gallo

**crucial** ['kru·ʃəl] adj crucial (**to** para);

it is ~ that... es de vital importancia que... +*subj*

**crucify** ['kru·sɪ·faɪ] <-ie-> *vt* crucificar; **if she ever finds out, she'll ~ me** si alguna vez lo descubre, me matará

**crude** [krud] **I.** *adj* **1.** (*rudimentary*) rudimentario, -a **2.** (*unrefined*) bruto, -a; (*oil*) crudo, -a **3.** (*vulgar*) basto, -a; (*manners*) grosero, -a **II.** *n* crudo *m*

**cruel** ['kru·əl] <-(l)ler, -(l)lest> *adj* cruel (**to** con)

**cruelty** ['kru·əl·ti] <-ies> *n* crueldad *f* (**to** con); **society for the prevention of ~ to animals** sociedad protectora de animales

**cruise** [kruz] **I.** *n* crucero *m*; **to go on a ~** hacer un crucero **II.** *vi* **1.** NAUT hacer un crucero; (*at constant speed*) ir a una velocidad de crucero **2.** (*police*) patrullar **3.** *inf* (*drive around*) dar una vuelta en coche

**cruising** *adj* de crucero

**crumb** [krʌm] *n* **1.** (*bread*) miga *f* **2.** (*small amount*) pizca *f*; **a small ~ of...** un poco de...

**crumble** ['krʌm·bəl] **I.** *vt* desmenuzar **II.** *vi* (*cliff*) derrumbarse; (*empire*) desmoronarse; (*resistance, opposition*) venirse abajo

**crummy** ['krʌm·i] <-ier, -iest> *adj sl* cutre

**crumple** ['krʌm·pəl] **I.** *vt* arrugar; (*metal*) abollar **II.** *vi* **1.** (*fabric, face*) arrugarse **2.** (*collapse*) desplomarse

**crunch** [krʌntʃ] **I.** *vt* **1.** (*eat*) masticar (haciendo ruido) **2.** (*grind*) triturar **II.** *vi* crujir **III.** <-es> *n* **1.** (*sound*) crujido *m* **2.** (*crisis*) **the ~** la hora de la verdad

**crunchy** ['krʌn·tʃi] <-ier, -iest> *adj* crujiente

**crush** [krʌʃ] **I.** *vt* **1.** (*compress*) aplastar; (*paper*) estrujar; (*dress*) arrugar; (*person*) apretujar **2.** (*grind: garlic*) machacar; (*grapes, olives*) prensar; (*stone*) triturar; (*ice*) picar **3.** (*shock severely*) abatir **4.** (*defeat, suppress*) aplastar; (*rebellion, revolution*) reprimir; (*opponent*) derrotar; (*hopes*) frustrar; (*rumor*) acallar **II.** <-es> *n* **1.** (*throng*) muchedumbre *f*; **there was a great ~** había una gran aglomeración **2.** *inf* (*infatuation*) enamoramiento *m*; **to have a ~ on**

sb encapricharse de alguien
♦**crush up** *vt* triturar

**crushing** *adj* aplastante; (*reply, argument*) contundente

**crust** [krʌst] *n* **1.** CULIN, BOT, GEO corteza *f* **2.** (*layer*) capa *f*; **a ~ of ice/dirt** una capa de hielo/suciedad **3.** ZOOL caparazón *m* **4.** MED costra *f*

**crustacean** [krʌ·'steɪ·ʃən] *n* crustáceo *m*

**crusty** ['krʌs·ti] <-ier, -iest> *adj* **1.** CULIN crujiente **2.** (*person*) malhumorado, -a

**crutch** [krʌtʃ] *n* **1.** muleta *f*; **to be on ~es** andar con muletas **2.** *fig* apoyo *m*

**cry** [kraɪ] **I.** <-ie-> *vi* **1.** (*weep*) llorar; **to ~ for joy** llorar de alegría **2.** (*shout*) gritar; (*animal*) aullar **II.** <-ie-> *vt* (*shout*) gritar ▶ **to ~ one's eyes out** llorar a lágrima viva **III.** *n* **1.** (*weeping*) llanto *m*; **to have a ~** llorar **2.** (*shout*) grito *m*; **to give a ~** dar un grito; **a ~ for help** una llamada de socorro

♦**cry down** *vt* (*decry*) menospreciar

♦**cry for** *vt insep* pedir

♦**cry off** *vi inf* echarse atrás; **to ~ a deal** romper un trato

♦**cry out I.** *vi* gritar; **to ~ against sth** clamar contra algo; **to ~ for sth** pedir algo a gritos **II.** *vt* gritar

**crying** ['kraɪ·ɪŋ] *n* lloro *m*

**crystal** ['krɪs·təl] *n* cristal *m*

**crystalline** ['krɪs·tə·laɪn] *adj* cristalino, -a

**crystallize** ['krɪs·tə·laɪz] *vt, vi* cristalizar; (*plan, thought*) materializar

**CT** *n abbr of* **Connecticut** Connecticut *m*

**ct.** **1.** *abbr of* **cent** centavo *m* **2.** *abbr of* **karat** quilate *m*

**cub** [kʌb] *n* cachorro *m*

**Cuba** ['kju·bə] *n* Cuba *f*

**Cuban** ['kju·bən] *adj, n* cubano, -a *m, f*

**cubbyhole** ['kʌb·ɪ·hoʊl] *n* cuchitril *m*

**cube** [kjub] **I.** *n* cubo *m*; (*cheese*) taco *m*; (*sugar*) terrón *m*; (*ice*) cubito *m*; **~ root** raíz cúbica *f*. **II.** *vt* **1.** CULIN cortar en tacos **2.** MATH elevar al cubo

**cubic** ['kju·bɪk] *adj* (*cube-shaped*) cúbico, -a

**cubicle** ['kju·bɪ·kəl] *n* (*changing room*) probador *m*

**cuckoo** ['ku·ku] **I.** *n* cuco *m* **II.** *adj inf* chiflado, -a

**cuckoo clock** n reloj m de cuco

**cucumber** ['kju·kʌm·bər] n pepino m ▸ (as) <u>cool</u> as a ~ más fresco que una lechuga

**cuddle** ['kʌd·əl] I. vt abrazar II. vi abrazarse III. n abrazo m

**cue** [kju] n 1. THEAT pie m 2. MUS entrada f 3. (billiards) taco m; ~ **ball** bola blanca ▸ to <u>take</u> one's ~ from sb seguir el ejemplo de alguien; (right) on ~ en el momento justo

**cuff** [kʌf] I. n 1. (sleeve) puño m 2. ~s inf (handcuffs) esposas fpl ▸ <u>off</u> the ~ improvisado, -a II. vt inf esposar

**cul-de-sac** ['kʌl·də·sæk] <-s or culs-de-sac> n callejón m sin salida

**culminate** ['kʌl·mɪ·neɪt] vi culminar (in en)

**culmination** [ˌkʌl·mɪ·'neɪ·ʃən] n culminación f

**culprit** ['kʌl·prɪt] n culpable mf

**cult** [kʌlt] n culto m; (sect) secta f

**cultivate** ['kʌl·tə·veɪt] vt cultivar

**cultivated** adj 1. AGR cultivado, -a 2. (person) culto, -a

**cultural** ['kʌl·tʃər·əl] adj cultural

**culture** ['kʌl·tʃər] I. n 1. cultura f 2. AGR cultivo m II. vt cultivar

**cultured** ['kʌl·tʃərd] adj 1. AGR cultivado, -a 2. (intellectual) culto, -a; (taste) refinado, -a

**culture shock** n choque m cultural

**cumin** ['kju·mɪn] n comino m

**cumulative** ['kju·mjə·lə·tɪv] adj 1. (increasing) acumulativo, -a 2. (accumulated) acumulado, -a

**cunning** ['kʌn·ɪŋ] I. adj 1. (ingenious) ingenioso, -a 2. (sly) taimado, -a II. n astucia f

**cunt** [kʌnt] n vulg ANAT coño m

**cup** [kʌp] n 1. (container) taza f; tea ~ taza de té; **egg** ~ huevera f 2. SPORTS copa f; the **World Cup** la copa del mundo

**cupboard** ['kʌb·ərd] n armario m; built-**in** ~ armario empotrado; **kitchen** ~ armario de cocina

**cupful** ['kʌp·fʊl] n taza f; a ~ **of** sugar una taza de azúcar

**curable** ['kjʊr·ə·bəl] adj curable

**curb** [kɜrb] I. vt (anger, passion) dominar; (inflation, appetite) controlar; (expenditure) frenar II. n 1. (control) freno m; to keep a ~ on refrenar; to put a ~ on poner freno (on a) 2. (obstacle) estorbo m 3. (at roadside) bordillo m, cordón m CSur

**curd** [kɜrd] n cuajada f; ~ **cheese** requesón m

**cure** [kjʊr] I. vt curar; (problem) remediar; (leather) curtir II. vi sanar; FOOD curarse III. n cura f; (return to health) curación f

**curfew** ['kɜr·fju] n toque de queda m

**curiosity** [ˌkjʊr·ɪ·'as·ə·ti] <-ies> n curiosidad f ▸ ~ **killed the** <u>cat</u> la curiosidad mató al gato

**curious** ['kjʊr·i·əs] adj curioso, -a; to be ~ sentir curiosidad (about/to por); it is ~ that es curioso que +subj

**curl** [kɜrl] I. n 1. (hair) rizo m 2. (sinuosity) serpenteo m 3. (spiral) espiral f 4. (of lips) mueca f de desprecio II. vi (hair) rizarse; (path) serpentear III. vt (hair) rizar; to ~ **oneself up** acurrucarse ▸ to ~ **one's** <u>lip</u> hacer una mueca de desprecio

**curler** ['kɜr·lər] n rulo m

**curly** ['kɜr·li] <-ier, -iest> adj rizado, -a

**currant** ['kɜr·ənt] n 1. (dried grape) pasa f de Corinto 2. (berry) grosella f

**currency** ['kɜr·ən·si] <-ies> n 1. FIN moneda f; **foreign** ~ divisas; ~ **market** mercado de divisas; ~ **unit** unidad monetaria 2. (acceptance) difusión f; to **gain** ~ extenderse

**current** ['kɜr·ənt] I. adj 1. (present) actual; **in** ~ **use** en uso 2. (latest) último, -a 3. (prevalent) generalizado, -a 4. (valid) vigente II. n 1. a. ELEC corriente f 2. (tendency) tendencia f ▸ to <u>drift</u> with the ~ dejarse llevar por la corriente; to <u>swim</u> against the ~ nadar contra corriente

**currently** adv 1. (at present) actualmente 2. (commonly) comúnmente

**curry** ['kɜr·i] <-ies> n curry m; **chicken** ~ pollo al curry

**curse** [kɜrs] I. n 1. (word) palabrota f, grosería f Col 2. (evil spell) maldición f; to **put a** ~ echar una maldición (on a) II. vt 1. (swear) insultar 2. (wish

**C**

*evil*) maldecir **III.** *vi* (*swear*) soltar palabrotas

**cursor** ['kɜr·sər] *n* cursor *m*

**cursory** ['kɜr·sə·ri] *adj* rápido, -a

**curt** [kɜrt] *adj* (*rudely brief*) seco, -a; (*refusal*) tajante

**curtain** ['kɜr·tən] *n* **1. a.** *fig* cortina *f* **2.** THEAT telón *m*; **to raise/lower the ~** subir/bajar el telón ▶ **it's ~s for you** estás acabado

**curve** [kɜrv] **I.** *n* curva *f* **II.** *vi* estar curvado; (*river, road*) hacer una curva **III.** *vt* curvar

**cushion** ['kʊʃ·ən] **I.** *n* **1.** cojín *m* **2.** (*billiards*) banda *f* **II.** *vt* **1.** (*blow*) amortiguar **2.** (*protect*) proteger

**cushy** ['kʊʃ·i] <-ier, -iest> *adj inf* fácil; **a ~ job** un chollo

**custard** ['kʌs·tərd] *n* ≈ natillas *fpl*

**custody** ['kʌs·tə·di] *n* **1.** (*care*) cuidado *m*; **in the ~ of sb** al cuidado de alguien **2.** (*guardianship*) custodia *f* **3.** LAW detención *f*; **to take into ~** detener

**custom** ['kʌs·təm] *n* **1.** (*tradition*) costumbre *f*; **it is his ~ to get up late** tiene por costumbre levantarse tarde **2.** LAW derecho *m* consuetudinario **3.** ~s (*place*) aduana *f*; (*tax*) aranceles *mpl*; **to get through ~s** pasar por la aduana

**customary** ['kʌs·tə·mer·i] *adj* **1.** (*traditional*) tradicional; **it is ~ to invite...** es costumbre invitar... **2.** (*usual*) habitual

**customer** ['kʌs·tə·mər] *n* **1.** cliente, -a *m, f*; **regular ~** cliente habitual **2.** *inf* (*person*) tío, -a *m, f*

**customer service** *n* servicio *m* de atención al cliente

**custom(s)house** *n* aduana *f*

**cut** [kʌt] **I.** *n* **1.** (*incision*) *a.* FASHION, MED, CINE corte *m*; **to get a ~** cortarse **2.** (*portion*) parte *f*; (*slice*) tajada *f*; **to take one's ~ of sth** sacar tajada de algo; **cold ~s** fiambres **3.** (*decrease*) reducción *f*; **a ~ in production** una disminución de la producción; **a ~ in staff** una reducción de plantilla; **wage/ budget ~** recorte salarial/presupuestario **II.** *adj* cortado, -a; (*glass, diamond*) tallado, -a **III.** <cut, cut, -tt-> *vt* **1.** (*make an incision*) cortar; (*tree*) talar;

(*corn*) segar; **to ~ in half** partir por la mitad; **to ~ to pieces** trocear; **to have one's hair ~** cortarse el pelo **2.** (*cause moral pain*) herir **3.** (*decrease*) reducir; (*costs, budget, wages*) recortar; (*prices*) bajar **4.** shorten, acortar **5.** (*diamond*) tallar; (*benefits*) repartir; (*motor, lights*) apagar; (*class*) saltarse **IV.** <cut, cut, -tt-> *vi* **1.** (*slice*) **this knife ~s well** este cuchillo corta bien; **this cheese ~s easily** este queso se corta con facilidad **2.** GAMES, CINE cortar **3.** **to ~ to the left/right** torcer a la izquierda/derecha **4.** (*morally wound*) herir ▶ **to ~ both ways** ser un arma de doble filo; **to ~ and run** salir pitando

◆**cut across** *vt insep* **1.** (*take short cut*) atajar por **2.** (*transcend*) trascender

◆**cut away** *vt* cortar

◆**cut back** *vt* **1.** (*trim down*) recortar; (*bushes, branches*) podar **2.** (*reduce*) reducir; **to ~ (on) costs** recortar costes

◆**cut down** **I.** *vt* **1.** (*tree*) talar **2.** (*reduce*) reducir; **to ~ expenses** recortar gastos **3.** (*destroy*) destruir **II.** *vi* reducir el consumo (**on** de)

◆**cut in** *vi* **to ~ (on)** interrumpir

◆**cut into** *vt insep* **1.** (*cake*) dar el corte **2.** (*interrupt*) interrumpir

◆**cut off** *vt* **1.** (*sever*) *a.* ELEC, TEL cortar **2.** (*amputate*) amputar **3.** (*interrupt*) interrumpir **4.** (*separate*) aislar; **to cut oneself off** aislarse (**from** de); **to be ~ by the snow** estar incomunicado por la nieve **5.** AUTO cortar el paso a

◆**cut out** **I.** *vt* **1.** (*slice*) cortar **2.** (*suppress*) eliminar **3.** *inf* (*stop*) dejar; **cut it out!** ¡basta ya! **II.** *vi* (*engine*) pararse; (*machine*) apagarse

◆**cut short** *vt* acortar

◆**cut up** **I.** *vt* **1.** (*slice*) cortar en pedazos; (*meat*) trinchar **2.** (*hurt*) herir **II.** *vi* (*clown*) payasear

**cut-and-dried** [ˌkʌt·ən·'draɪd] *adj* preparado, -a de antemano; (*idea*) preconcebido, -a

**cutback** ['kʌt·bæk] *n* **1.** (*reduction*) reducción *f* **2.** CINE flashback *m*

**cute** [kjut] *adj* mono, -a *inf*; (*remark, idea*) ingenioso, -a

**cutey** <-ies>, **cutie** ['kju·ti] *n inf* (*wom-*

*an*) bombón *m; (child)* monada *f*

**cutlery** ['kʌt·lə·ri] *n* cubiertos *fpl*

**cutlet** ['kʌt·lɪt] *n* chuleta *f*

**cutoff** ['kʌt·ɔf] *n a.* TECH corte *m; ~* **date** fecha límite; *~* **point** tope *m*

**cutout** *n* **1.** *(design)* recortable *m* **2.** ELEC cortacircuitos *m inv*

**cut-rate** *adj* rebajado, -a

**cutting** ['kʌt·ɪŋ] **I.** *n* **1.** *(act)* corte *m* **2.** *(piece)* recorte *m; (cloth)* retal *m* **3.** BOT esqueje *m* **II.** *adj* cortante; *fig* hiriente

**cuttlefish** ['kʌt·əl·fɪʃ] *n inv* sepia *f*

**cyanide** ['saɪ·ə·naɪd] *n* cianuro *m*

**cybercafé** ['saɪ·bər·kæ·feɪ] *n* cibercafé *m*

**cybercash** ['saɪ·bər·kæʃ] *n* dinero *m* electrónico

**cybernaut** [,saɪ·bər·'nɔt] *n* cibernauta *mf*

**cybernetics** [,saɪ·bər·'net·ɪks] *n + sing vb* cibernética *f*

**cycle** ['saɪ·kəl] **I.** *n* **1.** *(bike)* bicicleta *f* **2.** *(of life, seasons)* ciclo *m* **3.** ASTR órbita *f* **II.** *vi* ir en bicicleta

**cyclic** ['saɪ·klɪk] *adj*, **cyclical** *adj* cíclico, -a

**cycling** *n* ciclismo *m*

**cyclist** ['saɪ·klɪst] *n* ciclista *mf*

**cyclone** ['saɪ·kloʊn] *n* ciclón *m*

**cylinder** ['sɪl·ɪn·dər] *n* **1.** MATH, AUTO, TECH cilindro *m* **2.** *(container: of gas)* bombona *f*, garrafa *f Arg, Urug, (of water)* tanque *m*

**cylindrical** [sɪ·'lɪn·drɪ·kəl] *adj* cilíndrico, -a

**cynic** ['sɪn·ɪk] *adj, n* cínico, -a *m, f*, valemadrista *mf Méx*

**cynical** ['sɪn·ɪ·kəl] *adj* cínico, -a

**cynicism** ['sɪn·ɪ·sɪz·əm] *n* cinismo *m*

**cypress** ['saɪ·prəs] <-es> *n* ciprés *m*

**Czech** [tʃek] **I.** *n* **1.** *(person)* checo, -a *m, f* **2.** *(language)* checo *m* **II.** *adj* checo, -a

**Czech Republic** *n* República *f* Checa

# D

**D, d** [di] *n* **1.** *(letter)* D, d *f; ~* **as in Delta** D de Dolores **2.** SCHOOL ≈ suficiente *m*

**d** *abbr of* **diameter** d

**dab** [dæb] **I.** <-bb-> *vt* tocar ligeramente **II.** <-bb-> *vi* dar toquecitos *(at a)* **III.** *n* **1.** *(pat)* toque *m* **2.** *(tiny bit)* pizca *f; (liquid)* gota *f*

**dad** [dæd] *n* papá *m*

**daddy** ['dæd·i] *n* papi *m*, tata *m AmL*

**daffodil** ['dæf·ə·dɪl] *n* narciso *m*

**dagger** ['dæɡər] *n* puñal *m ►* **to** **look** *~s* **at sb** fulminar a alguien con la mirada

**daily** ['deɪ·li] **I.** *adj* diario, -a; **on a ~ ba·** **sis** por días **II.** *adv* a diario; **twice ~** dos veces al día **III.** <-ies> *n* diario *m*

**dairy** ['deɪ·ri] **I.** *n* **1.** *(farm)* vaquería *f*, tambo *m Arg* **2.** *(shop)* lechería *f* **II.** *adj* **1.** *(made from milk)* lácteo, -a **2.** *(producing milk)* lechero, -a; *(farm, herd)* de vacas

**dairy farm** *n* vaquería *f*, tambo *m Arg*

**dairy products** *npl* productos *m pl* lácteos

**daisy** ['deɪ·zi] <-ies> *n* margarita *f ►* **to** **feel as** **fresh** **as a ~** sentirse fresco como una rosa; **to be** **pushing up** **daisies** criar malvas

**dam** [dæm] **I.** *n (barrier)* presa *f; (reservoir)* embalse *m* **II.** <-mm-> *vt* represar; *fig* contener

**damage** ['dæm·ɪdʒ] **I.** *vt* **1.** *(harm, hurt)* dañar; *(health, reputation)* perjudicar **2.** *(ruin)* estropear **II.** *n* **1.** *(harm)* daño *m; (to pride, reputation)* perjuicio *m;* **to do ~ to sb/sth** hacer daño a alguien/dañar algo **2.** *pl* LAW daños *m pl* y perjuicios *►* **the ~ is** **done** el daño ya está hecho; **what's the ~?** *inf* ¿qué se debe?

**damn** [dæm] *sl* **I.** *interj* ¡mierda! **II.** *adj* maldito, -a **III.** *vt* **1.** *(God vulg) ~* **it!** ¡me cago en la puta!; *~* **him! he took** **my bike!** ¡ese idiota se ha llevado mi bici! **2.** REL condenar **IV.** *adv* muy; **to** **be ~ lucky** tener una suerte increíble; **you know ~ well that...** sabes perfectamente que... **V.** *n* **I don't give a ~** **what he says!** ¡me importa un comino lo que diga!

**damnation** [dæm·'neɪ·ʃən] *interj* ¡maldición!

**damned** *adj sl* maldito, -a; *(for emphasis)* puto, -a *vulg*

**damp** [dæmp] **I.** *adj* húmedo, -a **II.** *vt*

**1.** (*moisten*) humedecer **2.** *a. fig* PHYS, TECH amortiguar **3. to ~ (down)** (*fire*) sofocar; (*enthusiasm*) apagar

**dampen** ['dæm·pən] *vt* **1.** (*moisten*) humedecer **2.** (*lessen*) desanimar; (*enthusiasm*) apagar; (*expectations*) frustrar **3.** *a. fig* PHYS, TECH amortiguar

**dance** [dæns] **I.** <-cing> *vi* **1.** bailar (**to** al compás de); **to go dancing** ir a bailar; **to ~ with joy** dar saltos de alegría **2.** (*bob*) agitarse; **the daffodils were dancing in the breeze** los narcisos se mecían con la brisa **II.** <-cing> *vt* bailar **III.** *n* baile *m*

**dancer** ['dæn·sər] *n* bailarín, -ina *m, f*

**dancing** ['dæn·sɪŋ] *n* baile *m*

**dandelion** ['dæn·də·laɪ·ən] *n* diente *m* de león

**dandruff** ['dæn·drəf] *n* caspa *f*

**Dane** [deɪn] *n* danés, -esa *m, f*

**danger** ['deɪn·dʒər] *n* peligro *m* (**to** para); **the ~s of sth** los peligros de algo; **to be in ~** correr peligro; **to be out of ~** estar fuera de peligro; **there's no ~ of him knowing that** no hay peligro de que lo sepa

**dangerous** ['deɪn·dʒɜr·əs] *adj* peligroso, -a, riesgoso, -a *AmL*

**dangle** ['dæŋ·gəl] **I.** <-ling> *vi* (*hang*) colgar (**from** de) **II.** <-ling> *vt* **1.** (*hang*) hacer oscilar **2.** (*tempt*) **to ~ sth in front of sb** tentar a alguien con algo

**Danish** ['deɪ·nɪʃ] **I.** *adj* danés, -esa **II.** *n* **1.** (*person*) danés, -esa *m, f* **2.** LING danés *m*

**dare** [der] **I.** <-ring> *vt* **1.** (*risk doing*) atreverse a **2.** (*challenge*) desafiar; **to ~ sb (to do sth)** retar a alguien (a hacer algo) **II.** <-ring> *vi* atreverse; **to ~ to do sth** atreverse a hacer algo; **I don't ~ go there** no me atrevo a ir; **just you ~!** ¡atrévete y verás!; **how ~ you...** ¿cómo te atreves a...? ▶ **don't you ~!** ¡ni se te ocurra! **III.** *n* desafío *m*; **to take a ~** aceptar un reto

**daredevil** ['der·dev·əl] *inf* **I.** *n* balarrasa *mf* **II.** *adj* temerario, -a

**daresay** ['der·seɪ] *vt* suponer

**daring** ['der·ɪŋ] **I.** *adj* **1.** (*courageous*) temerario, -a **2.** (*provocative*) atrevido, -a **II.** *n* osadía *f*

**dark** [dark] **I.** *adj* **1.** (*without light, black*) oscuro, -a; **~ blue** azul oscuro; (*coffee*) solo; (*chocolate*) negro, -a; (*complexion, hair*) moreno, -a **2.** (*depressing*) sombrío, -a; **to have a ~ side** tener un lado oscuro; **to look on the ~ side of things** ver el lado malo de las cosas **3.** (*evil*) tenebroso, -a **4.** (*unknown*) oculto, -a **II.** *n* **1.** (*darkness*) oscuridad *f*; **to be in the ~** estar a oscuras **2.** (*time of day*) **at ~** al caer la noche; **before/after ~** antes/después de que anochezca ▶ **to keep sb in the ~ about sth** ocultar algo a alguien

**darken** ['dar·kən] **I.** *vi* oscurecerse; *fig* ensombrecerse **II.** *vt* oscurecer; *fig* ensombrecer

**darkly** *adv* **1.** (*mysteriously*) misteriosamente **2.** (*gloomily*) tristemente; (*look*) con aire sombrío

**darkness** *n* oscuridad *f*; *fig* tinieblas *fpl*

**darling** ['dar·lɪŋ] **I.** *n* **1.** (*person*) amor *m* **2.** (*term of endearment*) cariño *mf* **II.** *adj* **1.** (*beloved*) querido, -a **2.** (*cute*) mono, -a; **a ~ little room** una monada de habitación

**darn** [darn] *vt* *inf* **~ it!** ¡carajo!; **I'll be ~ed if I'll do it!** ¡no lo hago ni que me maten!

**dart** [dart] **I.** *n* **1.** dardo *m*; **to play ~s** jugar a los dardos; **a game of ~s** una partida de dardos **2.** (*quick run*) movimiento *m* fugaz **II.** *vi* precipitarse (**for** hacia); **to ~ away** salir disparado **III.** *vt* lanzar

**dash** [dæʃ] **I.** <-es> *n* **1.** (*rush*) carrera *f*; **to make a ~ for** precipitarse hacia; **to make a ~ for it** huir precipitadamente **2.** (*pinch*) pizca *f*; **a ~ of color** un toque de color **3.** (*flair*) brío *m* **4.** TYPO guión *m* **II.** *vi* **1.** (*hurry*) precipitarse **2.** (*slam*) romperse (**against** contra) **III.** *vt* (*shatter*) romper; (*hopes*) defraudar; (*to ~ off a note*) escribir una nota corriendo

**dashboard** ['dæʃ·bɔrd] *n* salpicadero *m*

**dashing** ['dæʃ·ɪŋ] *adj* gallardo, -a

**data** ['deɪ·tə] *npl + sing/pl vb a.* COMPUT datos *mpl*

**data bank** *n*, **databank** *n* banco *m* de datos

**database** *n* base *f* de datos

**data file** *n* fichero *m* de datos

**data processing** *n* procesamiento *m* de datos

**date¹** [deɪt] **I.** *n* **1.** (*calendar day*) fecha *f*; **expiration ~** fecha de vencimiento; **what ~ is it today?** ¿cuál es la fecha de hoy?; **to be out of ~** FASHION estar pasado de moda **2.** FIN plazo *f* **3.** (*appointment*) cita *f*; **to have a ~** tener una cita; **to make a ~** quedar (**with** con) **4.** *inf* (*person*) novio, -a *m, f* **II.** *vt* **1.** fechar **2.** *inf* **to ~ sb** salir con alguien **III.** *vi* **1. to ~ back to** remontarse a **2.** FASHION pasarse de moda **3.** (*go out*) salir con alguien

**date²** [deɪt] *n* (*fruit*) dátil *m*

**dated** ['deɪ·tɪd] *adj* anticuado, -a

**daughter** ['dɔ·tər] *n* hija *f*

**daughter-in-law** <daughters-in-law> *n* nuera *f*

**dawn** [dɔn] **I.** *n* alba *m*, amanezca *f Méx*; *fig* nacimiento *m*; **from ~ to dusk** de sol a sol; **at ~** al alba **II.** *vi* amanecer; *fig* nacer; **it ~ed on him that...** cayó en la cuenta de que...

**day** [deɪ] *n* **1.** día *m*; **~ after/by ~** día tras/a día; **all ~ (long)** todo el día; **any ~ now** cualquier día de estos; **by ~** de día; **by the ~** diariamente; **for a few ~s** por unos días; **from this ~ forth** de ahora en adelante; **from one ~ to the next** de un día para otro; **one ~** algún día; **two ~s ago** hace dos días; **the ~ before yesterday** anteayer; **the ~ after tomorrow** pasado mañana; **in the (good) old ~s** en los viejos tiempos **2.** (*working period*) jornada *f*; **to take a ~ off** tomarse un día de descanso ▸ **in this ~ and age** en los tiempos que corren; **to have seen <u>bet</u>ter ~s** haber conocido tiempos mejores; **to call it a ~** dejarlo para otro día; **~ in ~ out** un día sí y otro también

**daybreak** ['deɪ·breɪk] *n* alba *m*

**day camp** *n* campamento *m* de día

**daydream** ['deɪ·drim] *vi* soñar despierto

**daylight** ['deɪ·laɪt] *n* luz *f* del día; **in broad ~** a plena luz del día ▸ **to scare the <u>living</u> ~s out of sb** dar un susto de muerte a alguien

**day shift** *n* turno *m* de día

**daytime** ['deɪ·taɪm] *n* día *m;* **in the ~** de día

**day-to-day** *adj* cotidiano, -a

**day trip** *n* excursión *f*

**daze** [deɪz] **I.** *n* **to be in a ~** estar aturdido **II.** *vt* aturdir

**dazzle** ['dæz·əl] **I.** *vt* deslumbrar **II.** *n* deslumbramiento *m*

**dazzled** *adj* deslumbrado, -a

**dB** *n abbr of* **decibel** dB

**DE** *n abbr of* **Delaware** Delaware *m*

**dead** [ded] **I.** *adj* **1.** (*not alive*) muerto, -a **2.** *inf* (*inactive*) parado, -a; (*fire*) apagado, -a; (*battery*) descargado, -a; (*line*) cortado, -a **3.** *inf* (*boring*) muerto, -a **4.** (*numb*) dormido, -a **5.** (*complete: silence*) profundo, -a; **to be a ~ loss** ser un desastre total; **to come to a ~ stop** pararse en seco **II.** *n* **the ~** los muertos ▸ **in the ~ of night/winter** en plena noche/pleno invierno **III.** *adv* **1.** *inf* (*totally*) completamente; **to be ~ set against/on sth** estar completamente en contra de/decidido a algo **2.** (*directly*) justo; **~ ahead** justo al frente

**dead-end** *adj* sin salida

**dead end** *n* callejón *m* sin salida

**dead heat** *n* empate *m*

**deadline** ['ded·laɪn] *n* fecha *f* límite; **to meet/miss the ~** cumplir/incumplir el plazo

**deadlock** ['ded·lak] *n* punto *m* muerto

**deadly** ['ded·li] **I.** <-ier, -iest> *adj* **1.** mortal; (*weapon*) mortífero, -a; (*silence*) sepulcral **2.** *inf* (*boring*) aburridísimo, -a **II.** <-ier, -iest> *adv* extremadamente

**deaf** [def] **I.** *adj* sordo, -a; **to go ~** quedarse sordo; **to be ~ to sth** *fig* hacer oídos sordos a algo **II.** *npl* **the ~** los sordos

**deafen** ['def·ən] *vt* ensordecer

**deafening** *adj* ensordecedor(a)

**deaf-mute** [ˌdef·'mjut] *n* sordomudo, -a *m, f*

**deafness** *n* sordera *f*

**deal¹** [dil] *n* (*amount*) cantidad *f*; **a great ~** una gran cantidad; **a great ~ of effort** mucho esfuerzo

**deal²** [dil] <dealt, dealt> **I.** *n* **1.** COM negocio *m;* **a big ~** un negocio importante **2.** (*agreement*) pacto *m;* **to do a ~** hacer un trato (**with** con) **3.** GAMES **it's your ~** te toca dar a ti ▶ **big ~!** *iron* ¡menuda cosa!; **it's no big ~!** *sl* ¡no es para tanto! **II.** *vi* **1.** (*do business*) negociar; **to ~ with sb** hacer negocios con alguien; **to ~ in sth** comerciar con algo **2.** GAMES repartir **3.** *sl* (*cope*) arreglárselas (**with** con) **III.** *vt* **1.** GAMES repartir **2.** (*give*) dar

◆**deal out** *vt* repartir

◆**deal with** *vt* (*problem*) ocuparse de; (*person*) tratar con; (*book*) tratar de

**dealer** ['di·lər] *n* COM negociante *mf;* **drug ~** traficante de drogas; **antique ~** marchante de antigüedades

**dealing** ['di·lɪŋ] *n* **1.** COM comercio *m* **2.** **~s** FIN transacciones *fpl* **3.** **~s** (*relations*) relaciones *fpl;* **to have ~s with sb** tratar con alguien

**dealt** [delt] *pt, pp of* **deal**

**dean** [din] *n* UNIV decano, -a *m, f*

**dear** [dɪr] **I.** *adj* **1.** (*loved*) querido, -a; **it is ~ to me** le tengo mucho cariño **2.** (*in letters*) estimado, -a; **Dear Sarah** Querida Sarah **3.** (*expensive*) caro, -a **II.** *adv* caro **III.** *interj* *inf* **oh ~!** ¡Dios mío! **IV.** *n* encanto *m;* **she is a ~** es encantadora; **be a ~ and...** hazme el favor de...

**dearly** *adv* mucho; *fig* caro; **he paid ~ for his success** su éxito le costó caro

**death** [deθ] *n* muerte *f;* **scared/bored to ~** muerto de miedo/aburrimiento ▶ **to be at ~'s door** estar a las puertas de la muerte; **to <u>be</u> the ~ of** acabar con

**deathblow** *n* golpe *m* mortal

**death certificate** *n* certificado *m* de defunción

**deathly** ['deθ·li] *adv, adj* de muerte

**death penalty** *n* pena *f* de muerte

**death rate** *n* tasa *f* de mortalidad

**debatable** [dɪ·'beɪ·t̬ə·bəl] *adj* discutible

**debate** [dɪ·'beɪt] **I.** *n* debate *m* (**over** sobre) **II.** *vt, vi* debatir (**about** acerca de)

**debit** ['deb·ɪt] **I.** *n* débito *m* **II.** *vt* **the bank ~ed my account for the rent** el banco cargó a mi cuenta el alquiler

**debt** [det] *n* deuda *f;* **to be in ~** (*person*) tener deudas; (*business*) estar en números rojos

**debt collector** *n* cobrador(a) *m(f)* (de deudas)

**debtor** ['det̬·ər] *n* deudor(a) *m(f)*

**debug** [ˌdi·'bʌɡ] <-gg-> *vt* COMPUT depurar

**debut** [deɪ·'bju] **I.** *n* debut *m* **II.** *vi* debutar (**in/as** en/como)

**Dec.** *n abbr of* **December** dic.

**decade** ['dek·eɪd] *n* década *f*

**decadence** ['dek·ə·dəns] *n* decadencia *f*

**decadent** ['dek·ə·dənt] *adj* decadente

**decaf** ['di·kæf] *adj, n inf abbr of* **decaffeinated** descafeinado, -a

**decaffeinated** [ˌdi·'kæf·ɪ·neɪ·t̬ɪd] *adj* descafeinado, -a

**decathlon** [dɪ·'kæθ·lən] *n* decatlón *m*

**decay** [dɪ·'keɪ] **I.** *n* (*food*) descomposición *f;* (*building, intellect*) deterioro *m;* (*dental*) caries *f inv;* (*civilization*) decadencia *f* **II.** *vi* (*food*) pudrirse; (*building, intellect*) deteriorarse **III.** *vt* descomponer

**decease** [dɪ·'sis] *n* fallecimiento *m*

**deceased** [dɪ·'sist] *adj, n* difunto, -a *m, f*

**deceit** [dɪ·'sit] *n* engaño *m,* transa *f* Méx

**deceitful** [dɪ·'sit·fəl] *adj* engañoso, -a

**deceive** [dɪ·'siv] *vt* engañar; **to ~ oneself** engañarse a sí mismo ▶ **appearances can ~** las apariencias engañan

**December** [dɪ·'sem·bər] *n* diciembre *m;* *s. a.* **April**

**decency** ['di·sən·si] *n* decencia *f*

**decent** ['di·sənt] *adj* **1.** (*socially acceptable*) decente; **are you ~?** *fig* ¿estás presentable? **2.** *inf* (*kind*) amable **3.** *inf* (*salary, living, wage*) decente

**deception** [dɪ·'sep·ʃən] *n* engaño *m*

**deceptive** [dɪ·'sep·tɪv] *adj* engañoso, -a

**decibel** ['des·ə·bəl] *n* decibelio *m*

**decide** [dɪ·'saɪd] **I.** *vi* decidirse (**on** por) **II.** *vt* decidir

**decimal** ['des·ə·məl] *adj, n* decimal *m*

**decipher** [dɪ·'saɪ·fər] *vt* descifrar

**decision** [dɪ·'sɪʒ·ən] *n* **1.** (*choice, resolution*) decisión *f;* **to make a ~** tomar una decisión **2.** LAW fallo *m*

**decisive** [dɪ·'saɪ·sɪv] *adj* (*factor*) decisivo, -a; (*manner*) categórico, -a; (*victory, defeat*) contundente; (*change*) rotundo, -a

**deck** [dek] **I.** *n* **1.** NAUT cubierta *f*

**2.** (*porch*) terraza *f* **3.** (*cards*) baraja *f* **4.** MUS, ELEC platina *f* II. *vt* adornar; **to ~ oneself out** engalanarse

**deck chair** *n* tumbona *f*, reposera *f Arg*

**declaration** [ˌde·klə·'reɪ·ʃən] *n* declaración *f*

**declare** [dɪ·'kler] I. *vt* declarar; **to ~ war** declarar la guerra (**on** a); **to ~ oneself (to be) bankrupt** declararse en bancarrota II. *vi* declararse

**decline** [dɪ·'klaɪn] I. *vi* **1.** (*price*) bajar; (*power, influence*) disminuir; (*civilization*) decaer; **to ~ in value** disminuir de valor **2.** MED debilitarse **3.** (*refuse*) rehusar II. *vt* **1.** (*refuse*) rehusar **2.** LING declinar III. *n* **1.** (*price, power, influence*) disminución *f*; (*civilization*) decadencia *f*; **to be in ~** estar en declive **2.** MED debilitación *f*

**decode** [ˌdi·'koʊd] *vi, vt* descodificar

**decoder** *n* decodificador *m*

**decompose** [ˌdi·kəm·'poʊz] I. *vi* descomponerse II. *vt* descomponer

**decomposition** [ˌdi·kam·pə·'zɪʃ·ən] *n* descomposición *f*

**decompress** [ˌdi·kəm·'pres] *vt a.* COMPUT descomprimir

**decontaminate** [ˌdi·kən·'tæm·ɪ·neɪt] *vt* descontaminar

**decontamination** [ˌdi·kən·ˌtæm·ɪ·'neɪ·ʃən] *n* descontaminación *f*

**decorate** [ˈdek·ə·reɪt] I. *vt* **1.** (*adorn*) decorar; (*paint*) pintar; (*wallpaper*) empapelar **2.** (*honor*) condecorar II. *vi* (*paint*) pintar; (*wallpaper*) empapelar

**decoration** [ˌdek·ə·'reɪ·ʃən] *n* **1.** decoración *f*; (*ornament*) adorno *m* **2.** (*medal*) condecoración *f*

**decorative** [ˈdek·ər·ə·t̬ɪv] *adj* decorativo, -a

**decorator** [ˈdek·ə·reɪ·t̬ər] *n* decorador(a) *m(f)*

**decoy** [ˈdi·kɔɪ] *n* señuelo *m*; **to act as a ~** hacer de señuelo

**decrease¹** [dɪ·'kris] *vi, vt* disminuir; (*prices*) bajar

**decrease²** [ˈdi·kris] *n* disminución *f*

**decree** [dɪ·'kri] I. *n* decreto *m* II. *vt* decretar

**decrepit** [dɪ·'krep·ɪt] *adj* destartalado, -a; (*person*) decrépito, -a

**dedicate** [ˈded·ɪ·keɪt] *vt* **1.** dedicar; **to ~ oneself/one's life to sth** dedicarse/consagrar su vida a algo **2.** (*formally open*) inaugurar

**dedication** [ˌded·ɪ·'keɪ·ʃən] *n* **1.** (*devotion*) dedicación *f* **2.** (*inscription*) dedicatoria *f*

**deduct** [dɪ·'dʌkt] *vt* deducir

**deductible** *adj* deducible

**deduction** [dɪ·'dʌk·ʃən] *n* deducción *f*; **$1000 after ~s** $1000 netos

**deed** [did] *n* **1.** (*act*) acto *m*; (*remarkable*) hazaña *f* **2.** LAW escritura *f*

**deejay** [ˈdi·dʒeɪ] *n inf* pincha *mf*

**deep** [dip] I. *adj* **1.** (*not shallow: a. intellectually*) profundo, -a; (*color*) intenso, -a; **to ~ breath** respirar hondo; **to be in ~ thought** estar absorto en sus pensamientos **2.** (*extending back*) **the dresser is 2 feet ~** la cómoda tiene 61 cm de fondo **3.** (*extreme: love, disappointment*) gran(de); **to be in ~ trouble** estar metido en un buen lío **4.** (*dark*) oscuro, -a; **~ red** rojo intenso II. *adv* **1.** (*far down*) mucho más abajo; **~ in the forest** en lo más profundo del bosque **2.** (*extremely*) mucho; **to be ~ in debt** estar cargado de deudas ▶ **to go ~ into sth** ahondar en algo

**deep freeze** *n* congelador *m*

**deep-frozen** *adj* ultracongelado, -a

**deep-fry** *vt* freír en abundante aceite

**deeply** *adv* profundamente; (*breathe*) hondo

**deer** [dɪr] *n inv* ciervo *m*

**default** [dɪ·'fɔlt] *n* (*omission*) omisión *f*; **by ~** por defecto; **~ value** valor por defecto

**defeat** [dɪ·'fit] I. *vt* **1.** derrotar; (*hopes*) frustrar; (*proposal*) rechazar II. *n* derrota *f*; (*plans*) fracaso *m*; **to admit ~** darse por vencido

**defecate** [ˈdef·ə·keɪt] *vi* defecar

**defect** [ˈdi·fekt] *n a.* TECH, MED defecto *m*

**defective** [dɪ·'fek·tɪv] *adj* defectuoso, -a

**defend** [dɪ·'fend] *vt, vi a.* LAW, SPORTS defender; **to ~ oneself** defenderse (**from** de)

**defendant** [dɪ·'fen·dənt] *n* (*civil case*) demandado, -a *m, f*; (*criminal case*) acusado, -a *m, f*

**defense** [dɪˈfens] *n a.* LAW, MED, SPORTS defensa *f*; **the body's ~s** las defensas del organismo; **counsel for the ~** abogado(a) *m(f)* defensor(a)

**defenseless** [dɪˈfensˌlɪs] *adj* indefenso, -a

**defense mechanism** *n* PSYCH mecanismo *m* de defensa

**defensive** [dɪˈfensɪv] **I.** *adj* defensivo, -a **II.** *n* **to be/go on the ~** estar/ponerse a la defensiva

**defer** [dɪˈfɜr] <-rr-> *vt* aplazar

**deferred** *adj* aplazado, -a

**defiant** [dɪˈfaɪənt] *adj* (*person*) rebelde; (*attitude*) desafiante

**deficiency** [dɪˈfɪʃənsi] *n* deficiencia *f*

**deficient** [dɪˈfɪʃənt] *adj* deficiente; **to be ~ in sth** carecer de algo

**deficit** [ˈdefˌɪsɪt] *n* déficit *m*

**define** [dɪˈfaɪn] *vt* **1.** (*give definition of*) definir **2.** (*explain*) determinar; (*rights*) formular **3.** (*characterize*) caracterizar

**definite** [ˈdefˌɪnɪt] *adj* **1.** (*certain*) seguro, -a; (*opinion*) claro, -a; **it's ~ that...** no hay duda de que... **2.** (*final*) definitivo, -a

**definitely** *adv* definitivamente

**definition** [ˌdefˌɪˈnɪʃən] *n* definición *f*; **to give ~ to sth** realzar algo; **her ideas lack ~** sus ideas no son muy claras

**definitive** [dɪˈfɪnˌɪˌtɪv] *adj* definitivo, -a, rajante *Arg*

**definitively** *adv* definitivamente

**deflect** [dɪˈflekt] **I.** *vt* desviar **II.** *vi* desviarse (**off** de)

**deflection** [dɪˈflekˌʃən] *n* desviación *f*

**defog** [ˌdiˈfɔg] *vt* desempañar

**defogger** [ˌdiˈfɔˌgər] *n* dispositivo *m* anti-vaho

**deforest** [ˌdiˈfɔrˌɪst] *vt* deforestar

**deforestation** [diˌfɔrˌɪˈsteɪˌʃən] *n* deforestación *f*

**deform** [dɪˈfɔrm] **I.** *vt* deformar **II.** *vi* deformarse

**deformation** [ˌdiˌfɔrˈmeɪˌʃən] *n* deformación *f*

**defraud** [dɪˈfrɔd] *vt* estafar; **to ~ sb (of sth)** estafar (algo) a alguien

**defrost** [ˌdiˈfrɔst] **I.** *vt* deshelar; (*fridge, food*) descongelar; (*windshield*) desempañar **II.** *vi* deshelarse; (*fridge, food*) descongelarse

**defy** [dɪˈfaɪ] *vt* **1.** (*authority, gravity*) desafiar **2.** (*resist*) resistirse a; **it defies description** es indescriptible **3.** (*disobey*) desobedecer

**degenerate**[1] [dɪˈdʒenəˌreɪt] *vi* degenerar (**into** en); (*health*) deteriorarse

**degenerate**[2] [dɪˈdʒenˌərət] *adj, n* degenerado, -a *m, f*

**degeneration** [dɪˌdʒenəˈreɪˌʃən] *n* degeneración *f*

**degrade** [dɪˈgreɪd] **I.** *vt a.* CHEM degradar **II.** *vi* degradarse

**degree** [dɪˈgri] *n* **1.** MATH, METEO, MED grado *m*; **5 ~s below zero** 5 grados bajo cero **2.** (*amount*) nivel *m* **3.** (*extent*) **I agree with you to some ~** estoy de acuerdo contigo hasta cierto punto; **by ~s** gradualmente; **to the last ~** en grado sumo **4.** UNIV título *m*; **to have a ~/master's ~** ser licenciado/tener un máster (**in** en); **to do a ~ in chemistry** estudiar química

**dehydrated** *adj* deshidratado, -a; (*milk*) en polvo; **to become ~** deshidratarse

**deice** [ˌdiˈaɪs] *vt* deshelar

**dejected** *adj* desanimado, -a

**dejection** [dɪˈdʒekˌʃən] *n* desánimo *m*

**Del.** [delˈəˌwer] *n abbr of* **Delaware** Delaware *m*

**delay** [dɪˈleɪ] **I.** *vt* aplazar; **to be ~ed** retrasarse; **to ~ doing sth** posponer hacer algo **II.** *vi* tardar; **to ~ in doing sth** dejar algo para más tarde; **don't ~!** ¡no te entretengas! **III.** *n* tardanza *f*; **without ~** sin dilación; **a two-hour ~** un retraso de dos horas

**delegate**[1] [ˈdelˌɪˌgət] *n a.* POL delegado, -a *m, f*

**delegate**[2] [ˈdelˌɪˌgeɪt] *vt* delegar

**delegation** [ˌdelˌɪˈgeɪˌʃən] *n* delegación *f*

**delete** [dɪˈlit] *vt* borrar; COMPUT suprimir; (*file*) eliminar

**deletion** [dɪˈliˌʃən] *n* **1.** (*action*) eliminación *f* **2.** (*removal*) supresión *f*

**deli** [ˈdelˌi] *n inf see* **delicatessen**

**deliberate**[1] [dɪˈlɪbˌərˌət] *adj* **1.** (*intentional*) deliberado, -a; (*decision*) meditado, -a **2.** (*unhurried*) lento, -a; (*movement*) pausado, -a

**deliberate**[2] [dɪˈlɪbˌəˌreɪt] **I.** *vi* reflexionar (**on** sobre) **II.** *vt* deliberar sobre

**deliberately** adv (*intentionally*) adrede

**deliberation** [dɪˌlɪb·əˈreɪ·ʃən] n 1. (*formal discussion*) deliberación f 2. (*consideration*) reflexión f; **after due ~** después de pensarlo bien 3. (*unhurried manner*) parsimonia f

**delicacy** ['del·ɪ·kə·si] n 1. (*tact*) delicadeza f; **the ~ of the situation** lo delicado de la situación 2. (*food*) manjar m

**delicate** ['del·ɪ·kət] adj 1. (*fragile*) frágil; **to be in ~ health** estar delicado (de salud) 2. (*fine*) primoroso, -a; (*soft*) suave; (*aroma*) exquisito, -a 3. (*balance, situation*) a. PSYCH delicado, -a

**delicatessen** [ˌdel·ɪ·kəˈtes·ən] n delicatessen m o f inv

**delicious** [dɪˈlɪʃ·əs] adj exquisito, -a

**delight** [dɪˈlaɪt] I. n placer m; **to do sth with ~** hacer algo con gusto; **to take ~** disfrutar (**in** con) II. vt encantar; **to be ~ed** estar encantado (**with** con)

**delighted** adj encantado, -a

**delightful** [dɪˈlaɪt·fəl] adj delicioso, -a; (*person*) encantador/a

**delimit** [dɪˈlɪm·ɪt] vt delimitar

**delirious** [dɪˈlɪr·i·əs] adj **to be ~** delirar; **to be ~ with joy** estar delirante de alegría

**deliriously** adv MED delirantemente; fig locamente; **she was ~ happy** estaba loca de alegría

**delirium** [dɪˈlɪr·i·əm] n delirio m

**deliver** [dɪˈlɪv·ər] I. vt 1. (*hand over*) entregar; (*letter, package*) repartir (a domicilio) 2. (*lecture, speech, verdict*) pronunciar 3. (*direct*) **to ~ a blow** asestar un golpe; SPORTS lanzar 4. **to ~ a baby** (*mother*) tener un bebé 5. (*save*) librar 6. (*produce*) **to ~ a promise/the goods** cumplir una promesa/lo acordado II. vi 1. COM **we ~** entrega a domicilio 2. (*give birth*) dar a luz

**delivery** [dɪˈlɪv·ə·ri] n 1. (*distribution*) reparto m; **~ charges** gastos de envío; **~ man/woman** repartidor(a) m(f); **to pay on ~** pagar contra reembolso; **to take ~ of** recibir 2. SPORTS lanzamiento m 3. (*birth*) parto m

**delivery room** n sala f de partos

**delivery service** n servicio m de reparto a domicilio

**delivery truck** n furgoneta f de reparto

**delta** ['del·tə] n delta m

**delude** [dɪˈlud] vt engañar; **to ~ sb into believing sth** hacer creer algo a alguien

**deluge** ['del·judʒ] I. n (*downpour*) diluvio m; (*flood*) inundación f; fig avalancha f II. vt a. fig inundar; **to be ~d with tears** estar bañado en lágrimas; **she is ~d with offers** le llueven las ofertas

**delusion** [dɪˈlu·ʒən] n 1. (*wrong idea*) error m 2. PSYCH alucinación f

**deluxe** [dɪˈlʌks] adj de lujo

**demand** [dɪˈmænd] I. vt 1. exigir; (*a right*) reclamar; **to ~ that...** exigir que... +subj; **she demanded to see...** insistió en ver a... 2. (*ask*) preguntar II. n 1. (*request*) exigencia f; **on ~** a petición; **to make a ~ for** exigir; **to make a ~ that...** hacer una petición de que... +subj; **to make heavy ~s on sb's time** ocupar gran parte del tiempo de alguien; **to meet a ~** satisfacer las exigencias (**for** de); **by popular ~** a petición del público 2. COM demanda f; **to be in ~** tener mucha demanda; (*person*) estar muy solicitado

**demanding** adj exigente

**demean** [dɪˈmin] vt degradar; **to ~ oneself** rebajarse

**dementia** [dɪˈmen·ʃə] n demencia f

**demo** ['dem·oʊ] n inf see **demonstration** COMPUT demo f; (*music*) maqueta f, demo m Méx, Col

**democracy** [dɪˈmæk·rə·si] n democracia f

**democrat** ['dem·ə·kræt] n demócrata mf

**democratic** [ˌdem·əˈkræt̮·ɪk] adj democrático, -a

**demolish** [dɪˈmal·ɪʃ] vt demoler; fig echar por tierra

**demolition** [ˌdem·əˈlɪʃ·ən] n demolición f; fig destrucción f

**demon** ['di·mən] n demonio m; **childhood ~s** fantasmas de la infancia ▶ **to be a ~ at sth** ser un hacha haciendo algo; **to work like a ~** trabajar como una fiera

**demonstrate** ['dem·ən·streɪt] I. vt (*show*) mostrar; (*prove*) demostrar II. vi manifestarse

**demonstration** [ˌdem·ənˈstreɪ·ʃən] n

demostración *f;* POL manifestación *f;* **to hold a ~** manifestarse

**demonstrative** [dɪ'man·strə·tɪv] *adj* **1.** (*illustrative*) concluyente **2.** (*effusive*) efusivo, -a

**demonstrator** ['dem·ən·streɪ·tər] *n* (*protester*) manifestante *mf*

**demoralize** [dɪ'mɔr·ə·laɪz] *vt* desmoralizar

**den** [den] *n* **1.** (*animal*) guarida *f* **2.** *a. iron* (*place for vice*) antro *m* **3.** (*small room*) salita *f*

**denial** [dɪ'naɪ·əl] *n* negación *f;* (*refusal*) negativa *f;* **to issue a ~ of** desmentir

**denim** ['den·ɪm] *n* **1.** (*cloth*) tela *f* vaquera **2. ~s** mono *m*

**Denmark** ['den·mark] *n* Dinamarca *f*

**denominator** [dɪ'nam·ə·neɪ·tər] *n* denominador *m*

**denounce** [dɪ'naʊns] *vt* **1.** (*condemn*) censurar **2.** (*inform*) denunciar

**dense** [dens] *adj* **1.** (*thick*) espeso, -a **2.** (*closely packed*) denso, -a; (*compact*) compacto, -a **3.** (*complex*) difícil

**densely** *adv* densamente

**density** ['den·sə·ʧi] *n* densidad *f;* **to be high/low in ~** ser de alta/baja densidad

**dent** [dent] **I.** *n* abolladura *f; fig* mella *f* **II.** *vt* abollar; *fig* hacer mella en

**dental** ['den·təl] *adj* dental

**dental floss** *n* hilo *m* dental

**dentist** ['den·tɪst] *n* dentista *mf*

**dentistry** ['den·tɪ·stri] *n* odontología *f*

**dentures** ['den·ʧərz] *npl* dentadura *f* postiza

**deny** [dɪ'naɪ] *vt* **1.** negar; (*report*) desmentir; **to ~ having done sth** negar haber hecho algo; **she denies that she saw it** niega haberlo visto **2.** (*refuse*) denegar; **to ~ oneself sth** privarse de algo; **to ~ sb a right** privar a alguien de un derecho **3.** (*disown*) renegar de

**deodorant** [di·'oʊ·dər·ənt] *n* desodorante *m*

**depart** [dɪ·'part] *vi* partir; (*plane*) despegar; (*train*) salir; (*ship*) zarpar

♦**depart from** *vi* desviarse de

**departed I.** *adj* **1.** (*dead*) difunto, -a **2.** (*past*) pasado, -a **II.** *n* **the ~** los difuntos

**department** [dɪ·'part·mənt] *n* **1.** (*division*) departamento *m;* (*of a shop*) sección *f* **2.** ADMIN, POL ministerio *m* **3.** *inf* (*domain*) terreno *m* **4. Department of Motor Vehicles** ≈ Dirección General de Tráfico *f*

**department store** *n* grandes almacenes *mpl,* tienda *f* por departamentos *AmS*

**departure** [dɪ·'par·ʧər] *n* **1.** (*person*) partida *f;* (*vehicle*) salida *f;* (*plane*) despegue *m;* **to make one's ~** marcharse **2.** (*deviation*) desviación *f;* **to be a new ~** ser una novedad (**for** para)

**departure gate** *n* puerta *f* de embarque

**departure lounge** *n* sala *f* de embarque

**departure time** *n* hora *f* de salida

**depend** [dɪ·'pend] *vi* **1.** depender (**on** de); **~ing on the weather** según el tiempo que haga; **he depends on his father for money** depende del dinero de su padre **2.** (*trust*) confiar (**on** en)

**dependable** [dɪ·'pen·də·bəl] *adj* fiable; (*person*) serio, -a

**dependent** [dɪ·'pen·dənt] *adj* dependiente; **to be ~ on** depender de; **to be ~ on drugs** ser drogadicto; **she has two ~ children** tiene dos niños a su cargo

**depict** [dɪ·'pɪkt] *vt* representar

**depiction** [dɪ·'pɪk·ʃən] *n* representación *f*

**depleted** *adj* agotado, -a

**deplorable** [dɪ·'plɔr·ə·bəl] *adj* deplorable

**deplore** [dɪ·'plɔr] *vt* deplorar

**deploy** [dɪ·'plɔɪ] *vt* utilizar; (*troops*) desplegar; (*skills*) demostrar

**deployment** [dɪ·'plɔɪ·mənt] *n* utilización *f;* (*troops*) despliegue *m*

**depopulate** [,di·'pap·jə·leɪt] *vt* despoblar

**deport** [dɪ·'pɔrt] *vt* deportar

**deportation** [,di·pɔr·'teɪ·ʃən] *n* deportación *f*

**deportee** [,di·pɔr·'ti] *n* deportado, -a *m, f*

**depose** [dɪ·'poʊz] *vt* destituir

**deposit** [dɪ·'paz·ɪt] **I.** *vt* **1.** depositar; (*luggage*) guardar en consigna **2.** FIN ingresar; **to ~ $1000** dejar 1000 dólares en depósito **II.** *n* **1.** (*sediment*) sedimento *m* **2.** GEO yacimiento *m* **3.** (*payment*) depósito *m;* **to make/leave a ~** efectuar/dejar un depósito; **to leave**

sth as a ~ dejar algo en garantía; **on ~** en depósito

**depositor** [dɪ·ˈpɑz·ə·tər] n cuentahabiente mf

**deprave** [dɪ·ˈpreɪv] vt pervertir

**depraved** adj depravado, -a

**depreciate** [dɪ·ˈpri·ʃi·eɪt] I. vi depreciarse II. vt depreciar

**depreciation** [dɪ·ˌpri·ʃi·ˈeɪ·ʃən] n depreciación f

**depress** [dɪ·ˈpres] vt 1. (sadden) deprimir; **it ~es me that...** me deprime que... +subj 2. (reduce activity) disminuir; (economy) paralizar; (prices) bajar 3. (press) presionar; (pedal, button) apretar

**depressed** adj deprimido, -a, apolismado, -a Méx, Ven; **to feel ~** sentirse abatido; (period) de depresión; (economy) en crisis

**depressing** adj deprimente

**depression** [dɪ·ˈpreʃ·ən] n 1. PSYCH, FIN depresión f; METEO zona f de bajas presiones 2. (hollow) hoyo m

**deprive** [dɪ·ˈpraɪv] vt privar (of de); (dignity) despojar; (sleep) quitar

**deprived** adj desvalido, -a

**depth** [depθ] n 1. a. fig profundidad f; **in the ~ of winter** en pleno invierno; **the ~s of the ocean** las profundidades del océano 2. (intensity) intensidad f ▶ **in ~** en detalle

**deputize** [ˈdep·jə·taɪz] vi suplir (for a)

**deputy** [ˈdep·jə·ti] n delegado, -a m, f

**derail** [dɪ·ˈreɪl] vi descarrilar; fig fracasar

**derailment** [dɪ·ˈreɪl·mənt] n descarrilamiento m; fig fracaso m

**derange** [dɪ·ˈreɪndʒ] vt perturbar

**deranged** adj trastornado, -a

**derelict** [ˈder·ə·lɪkt] adj (building) abandonado, -a

**derision** [dɪ·ˈrɪʒ·ən] n burla f; **to meet sth with ~** burlarse de algo

**derisory** [dɪ·ˈraɪ·sə·ri] adj irrisorio, -a

**derive** [dɪ·ˈraɪv] I. vt obtener (from de) II. vi derivar (from de)

**derogatory** [dɪ·ˈrɑg·ə·tɔr·i] adj desdeñoso, -a

**descale** [ˌdi·ˈskeɪl] vt desincrustar

**descend** [dɪ·ˈsend] I. vi 1. (go down) descender; (fall) caer 2. (lower one-

self) **to ~ to stealing** rebajarse a robar 3. (come from) provenir (**from** de) II. vt descender; (ladder) bajar

**descendant** [dɪ·ˈsen·dənt] n descendiente mf

**descent** [dɪ·ˈsent] n 1. AVIAT descenso m 2. (decline) declive m 3. (ancestry) origen m

**describe** [dɪ·ˈskraɪb] vt 1. describir; (experience) relatar; **to ~ sb as stupid** calificar a alguien de tonto 2. (draw) trazar

**description** [dɪ·ˈskrɪp·ʃən] n descripción f; **to answer a ~** encajar con una descripción; **of every ~** de todo tipo

**descriptive** [dɪ·ˈskrɪp·tɪv] adj descriptivo, -a

**desert**[1] [ˈdez·ərt] I. vi MIL desertar II. vt 1. MIL desertar de 2. (abandon) abandonar; **to ~ sb** dejar a alguien (**for** por)

**desert**[2] [ˈdez·ərt] n desierto m

**deserted** adj desierto, -a; (person) abandonado, -a

**deserts** [dɪ·ˈzɜrts] npl merecido m; **to get one's just ~** tener su merecido

**deserve** [dɪ·ˈzɜrv] vt merecer; **what have I done to ~ this?** ¿qué he hecho yo para merecer esto?

**deservedly** adv merecidamente

**deserving** adj digno (**of** de)

**design** [dɪ·ˈzaɪn] I. vt 1. (plan) diseñar 2. (intend) concebir II. n 1. (plan) diseño m 2. (sketch) bosquejo m 3. (pattern) motivo m 4. (intention) propósito m; **to do sth by ~** hacer algo adrede 5. **~s** inf malas intenciones fpl III. adj de diseño

**designate** [ˈdez·ɪg·neɪt] vt (appoint) nombrar; (indicate) señalar

**designation** [ˌdez·ɪg·ˈneɪ·ʃən] n (appointment) nombramiento m

**designer** [dɪ·ˈzaɪ·nər] I. n diseñador(a) m(f) II. adj de marca

**desirable** [dɪ·ˈzaɪr·ə·bəl] adj 1. (necessary) conveniente; **it is ~ that...** sería deseable que... +subj 2. (attractive) deseable 3. (popular) codiciado, -a

**desire** [dɪ·ˈzaɪr] I. vt 1. desear; **to ~ sb** desear a alguien; **to ~ that...** desear que... +subj; **I ~ you to leave** le ruego que se vaya II. n 1. (craving) deseo m 2. (request) petición f

**desired** adj deseado, -a

**desk** [desk] n 1. (table) escritorio m; SCH pupitre m 2. (counter) mostrador m

**desk lamp** n flexo m

**desktop** n ~ (**computer**) (ordenador m) portátil m

**desolate**[1] ['des·ə·lət] adj desolado, -a; (prospect) desolador, a; **to feel ~** sentirse desconsolado

**desolate**[2] ['des·ə·leɪt] vt desolar

**despair** [dɪ·'sper] I. n desesperación f; **to be in ~** estar desesperado (**about** por); **to drive sb to ~** desesperar a alguien ▶ **to be the ~ of sb** traer de cabeza a alguien II. vi perder las esperanzas (**of** con)

**despairing** adj desesperado, -a; (glance) de desesperación

**desperate** ['des·pər·ɪt] adj desesperado, -a; (great) extremo, -a; **to be ~ for sth** necesitar algo con suma urgencia

**desperation** [,des·pə·'reɪ·ʃən] n desesperación f; **in ~** en su desesperación; **to drive sb to ~** desesperar a alguien

**despise** [dɪ·'spaɪz] vt despreciar (**for** por)

**despite** [dɪ·'spaɪt] prep a pesar de

**despondent** [dɪ·'spɑn·dənt] adj desalentado, -a; **to feel ~** sentirse desanimado (**about** por)

**dessert** [dɪ·'zɜrt] n postre m

**destination** [,des·tə·'neɪ·ʃən] n destino m

**destine** ['des·tɪn] vt **to be ~d for sth** estar destinado a algo; **we're ~d for Denver** nos dirigimos a Denver; **to be ~d to fail/succeed** estar destinado al fracaso/éxito

**destiny** ['des·tə·ni] n destino m; **to fight one's ~** luchar contra el destino; **to shape one's ~** hacerse su propio destino

**destitute** ['des·tɪ·tut] I. adj necesitado, -a II. n **the ~** los indigentes

**destroy** [dɪ·'strɔɪ] vt 1. (demolish) destruir 2. (kill) matar 3. (ruin) arruinar

**destructible** [dɪ·'strʌk·tə·bəl] adj destructible

**destruction** [dɪ·'strʌk·ʃən] n destrucción f; **mass ~** destrucción en masa

**destructive** [dɪ·'strʌk·tɪv] adj destructivo, -a

**detach** [dɪ·'tætʃ] vt separar

**detachable** adj separable

**detached** adj 1. (separated) separado, -a 2. (aloof) indiferente 3. (impartial) imparcial

**detail** [dɪ·'teɪl] I. n 1. (information, feature) detalle m; **in ~** en detalle; **to go into ~** entrar en detalles 2. (unimportant) minucia f; **gory ~s** iron intimidades fpl II. vt detallar

**detailed** adj detallado, -a

**detain** [dɪ·'teɪn] vt 1. (prisoner) retener 2. (delay) entretener

**detainee** [,di·ter·'ni] n detenido, -a m, f

**detect** [dɪ·'tekt] vt 1. (note) advertir; (presence) percibir 2. (discover) descubrir

**detectable** [dɪ·'tek·tə·bəl] adj perceptible

**detection** [dɪ·'tek·ʃən] n detección f

**detective** [dɪ·'tek·tɪv] n detective mf; (police) agente mf

**detective novel, detective story** n novela f policíaca

**detector** [dɪ·'tek·tər] n detector m

**detention** [dɪ·'ten·ʃən] n detención f; SCHOOL castigo f

**detention home** n correccional m

**deter** [dɪ·'tɜr] <-rr-> vt disuadir

**detergent** [dɪ·'tɜr·dʒənt] n detergente m

**deteriorate** [dɪ·'tɪr·i·ə·reɪt] vi 1. (wear out) deteriorarse 2. (worsen) empeorar

**determinant** [dɪ·'tɜr·mə·nənt] n adj determinante m

**determinate** [dɪ·'tɜr·mə·nɪt] adj determinado, -a

**determination** [dɪ·,tɜr·mɪ·'neɪ·ʃən] n determinación f

**determine** [dɪ·'tɜr·mɪn] I. vi 1. decidirse (**on** por) 2. LAW expirar II. vt 1. (decide) decidir 2. (find out) fijar 3. (influence) determinar

**determined** [dɪ·'tɜr·mɪnd] adj decidido, -a; **to be ~ to do sth** estar resuelto a hacer algo

**deterrent** [dɪ·'tɜr·ənt] I. n freno m; **to act as a ~ to sb** disuadir a alguien II. adj disuasivo, -a

**detest** [dɪ·'test] vt detestar

**detestable** [dɪ·'tes·tə·bəl] adj detestable

**detonate** ['det·ə·neɪt] vi, vt detonar

**detonation** [ˌdet·ə·ˈneɪ·ʃən] n detonación f

**detour** [ˈdiː·tʊr] n desvío m; **to make a ~** dar un rodeo

**detoxify** [diˈtɑk·sɪ·faɪ] vt desintoxicar

**detractor** [dɪ·ˈtræk·tər] n detractor(a) m(f)

**detrimental** [ˌdet·rɪ·ˈmen·təl] adj nocivo, -a

**deuce** [dus] n GAMES dos m; SPORTS empate m

**devalue** [ˌdi·ˈvæl·ju] vt devaluar

**devastate** [ˈdev·ə·steɪt] vt devastar

**devastating** adj (destructive) desolador(a); (powerful) devastador(a); (stunning) abrumador(a)

**devastation** [ˌdev·ə·ˈsteɪ·ʃən] n devastación f

**develop** [dɪ·ˈvel·əp] I. vi (grow) desarrollarse; (advance) progresar; **to ~ into** transformarse en II. vt 1. (expand) desarrollar; (improve) ampliar 2. (create) crear 3. (show) revelar; (illness) contraer 4. PHOT revelar

**developed** adj desarrollado, -a; **~ countries** países desarrollados

**developing** adj **~ countries** países en vías de desarrollo

**development** [dɪ·ˈvel·əp·mənt] n 1. (process) desarrollo m; (growth) crecimiento m; (growth stage) avance m; (skills) evolución f 2. (progress) progreso m 3. (event) acontecimiento m 4. (building of) construcción f; (of land) urbanización f

**deviate** [ˈdi·vi·eɪt] vi apartarse; **to ~ from** desviarse de

**device** [dɪ·ˈvaɪs] n 1. (mechanism) dispositivo m; **input/output ~** dispositivo de entrada/salida 2. (method) recurso m ▶ **to leave sb to their own ~s** abandonar a alguien a su suerte

**devil** [ˈdev·əl] n 1. REL diablo m 2. (evil spirit or person) demonio m; **lucky ~!** ¡qué suerte!; **the poor ~!** ¡pobre diablo! 3. **to have a ~ of a time doing sth** costar un huevo hacer algo inf; **to be full of the ~** estar lleno de coraje ▶ **between the ~ and the deep blue sea** entre la espada y la pared; **to sell one's soul to the ~** vender el alma al diablo; **to go** **to the ~** irse al infierno; **to play the ~ with sth** estropear algo; **speak of the ~** hablando del rey de Roma; **how/who/ what/where the ~...?** ¿cómo/quién/ qué/dónde diablos...?; **like the ~** como el demonio

**devilish** [ˈdev·ə·lɪʃ] adj 1. (evil) diabólico, -a 2. (mischievous) malvado, -a 3. (extreme) extremo, -a

**devil's food cake** n pastel m de chocolate

**devious** [ˈdi·vi·əs] adj 1. (dishonest) taimado, -a 2. (winding) tortuoso, -a

**devise** [dɪ·ˈvaɪz] I. n legado m II. vt idear; LAW legar

**devoid** [dɪ·ˈvɔɪd] adj **to be ~ of** estar desprovisto de

**devolution** [ˌdev·ə·ˈlu·ʃən] n transferencia f

**devote** [dɪ·ˈvoʊt] vt dedicar; **to ~ oneself to sth** dedicarse a algo

**devoted** [dɪ·ˈvoʊ·tɪd] adj dedicado, -a; (husband, mother) devoto, -a

**devotion** [dɪ·ˈvoʊ·ʃən] n (loyalty) lealtad f; (admiration) fervor m; (great attachment) dedicación f; REL devoción f

**devour** [dɪ·ˈvaʊ·ər] vt devorar; **to be ~ed by jealousy** estar consumido por los celos

**devout** [dɪ·ˈvaʊt] adj ferviente; REL devoto, -a

**dew** [du] n rocío m

**dextrose** [ˈdek·stroʊs] n dextrosa f

**diabetes** [ˌdaɪ·ə·ˈbi·tiz] n diabetes f inv

**diabetic** [ˌdaɪ·ə·ˈbeʈ·ɪk] adj, n diabético, -a m, f

**diabolic(al)** [ˌdaɪ·ə·ˈbal·ɪk(əl)] adj diabólico, -a

**diagnose** [ˌdaɪ·əg·ˈnoʊs] I. vi hacer un diagnóstico II. vt diagnosticar

**diagnosis** [ˌdaɪ·əg·ˈnoʊ·sɪs] <-ses> n (process) diagnosis f inv; (result) diagnóstico m

**diagonal** [daɪ·ˈæg·ə·nəl] adj, n diagonal f

**diagram** [ˈdaɪ·ə·græm] n 1. (drawing) diagrama m; (plan) esquema m 2. (chart) gráfico m

**dial** [ˈdaɪ·əl] I. n RADIO dial m II. <-I- or -II-, -I- or -II-> vi marcar, discar Arg, Perú, Urug III. vt TEL marcar; RADIO sintonizar

◆**dial in** *vi* conectar (**to** con)

**dialect** ['daɪ·ə·lekt] *n* dialecto *m*

**dialog(ue)** ['daɪ·ə·lag] *n a.* POL diálogo *m;* **to engage in ~** dialogar

**dial tone** *n* tono *m* de marcado

**dialysis** [daɪ·'æl·ə·sɪs] *n* diálisis *f inv*

**diameter** [daɪ·'æm·ə·t̮ər] *n* diámetro *m*

**diametrically** [,daɪ·ə·'met·rɪ·kə·li] *adv* diametralmente; (*completely*) en su totalidad

**diamond** ['daɪ·ə·mənd] *n* **1.** *a.* GAMES diamante *m* **2.** (*rhombus*) rombo *m* ▶ **a ~ in the rough** un diamante en bruto

**diaper** ['daɪ·pər] *n* pañal *m*

**diaphragm** ['daɪ·ə·fræm] *n* diafragma *m*

**diarrhea** [,daɪ·ə·'ri·ə] *n* diarrea *f*

**diary** ['daɪ·ə·ri] *n* diario *m*

**dice** [daɪs] *npl a.* GAMES, FOOD dados *mpl;* **to roll the ~** tirar los dados ▶ **no ~** ni de coña

**dicey** ['daɪ·si] <-ier, -iest> *adj inf* arriesgado, -a

**dick** [dɪk] *n vulg* **1.** (*penis*) polla *f,* pija *f AmL,* paloma *f Méx, Ven,* pajarito *m RíoPl* **2.** (*person*) gilipollas *mf inv*

**dictate** ['dɪk·teɪt] **I.** *n* dictado *m* **II.** *vi* **1.** (*command*) mandar **2.** (*read*) dictar **III.** *vt* **1.** (*command, read*) dictar **2.** (*make necessary*) imponer

**dictation** [dɪk·'teɪ·ʃən] *n* SCHOOL dictado *m*

**dictator** ['dɪk·teɪ·t̮ər] *n* dictador(a) *m(f)*

**dictatorship** [dɪk·'teɪ·t̮ər·ʃɪp] *n* dictadura *f*

**dictionary** ['dɪk·ʃə·ner·i] *n* diccionario *m*

**did** [dɪd] *pt of* **do**

**didactic** [daɪ·'dæk·tɪk] *adj* didáctico, -a

**diddle around** *vi* pasar el tiempo; (*unproductively*) perder el tiempo

**didn't** ['dɪd·ənt] = **did not** *see* **do**

**die¹** [daɪ] <**dice**> *n* **1.** dado *m* **2.** TECH molde *m* ▶ **the ~ is cast** la suerte está echada

**die²** [daɪ] <**dying, died**> *vi* **1.** morir; **to ~ a violent/natural death** morir de muerte violenta/natural; **I'm dying for a cup of tea** me muero por una taza de té **2.** (*end*) desaparecer; **the secret will ~ with her** se llevará el secreto a la tumba **3.** (*appliance*) estropearse; (*battery*) gastarse ▶ **to ~ hard** persistir; **never say ~!** ¡nunca te rindas!; **to do or ~**

vencer o morir

◆**die away** *vi* desaparecer; (*enthusiasm*) decaer; (*wind*) amainar; (*sound*) apagarse

◆**die back** *vi* secarse

◆**die down** *vi* apagarse

◆**die off** *vi* (*species*) extinguirse; (*customs*) desaparecer

◆**die out** *vi* extinguirse

**dieback** ['daɪ·bæk] *n* muerte *f* de los bosques

**die-hard** *n* intransigente *mf*

**diesel** ['di·zəl] *n* diesel *m*

**diesel engine** *n* motor *m* diesel

**diet** ['daɪ·ət] *n* dieta *f;* **to be/go on a ~** estar/ponerse a dieta

**dietetic** [,daɪ·ə·'tet͡·ɪk] *adj* dietético, -a

**differ** ['dɪf·ər] *vi* **1.** diferenciarse (**from** de) **2.** (*disagree*) discrepar (**about** en)

**difference** ['dɪf·ər·əns] *n* **1.** (*dissimilarity, amount, disagreement*) diferencia *f;* **to pay the ~** pagar la diferencia; **to put aside ~s** dejar de lado las diferencias **2.** (*distinction*) distinción *f;* **that makes all the ~** eso lo cambia todo; **to make a ~** importar; **to not make any ~** dar igual **3.** (*new feature*) singularidad *f*

**different** ['dɪf·ər·ənt] *adj* **1.** (*not the same*) diferente; **to do something ~** romper la rutina **2.** (*distinct*) distinto, -a ▶ **to be as ~ as night and day** ser la noche y el día

**differentiate** [,dɪf·ə·'ren·tʃi·eɪt] *vi, vt* distinguir

**difficult** ['dɪf·ɪ·kəlt] *adj* difícil

**difficulty** ['dɪf·ɪ·kəl·ti] <-ies> *n* dificultad *f;* (*problem*) obstáculo *m;* **to have ~ doing sth** tener problemas para hacer algo

**diffract** [dɪ·'frækt] *vt* difractar

**diffuse¹** [dɪ·'fjuz] **I.** *vi* difundirse **II.** *vt* difundir

**diffuse²** [dɪ·'fjus] *adj* difuso, -a

**diffusion** [dɪ·'fju·ʒən] *n* difusión *f;* CHEM, PHYS dispersión *f*

**dig** [dɪg] **I.** *n* **1.** (*poke*) empujón *m* **2.** (*excavation*) excavación *f* **II.** <-gg-, dug, dug> *vi* **1.** (*excavate*) cavar; **to ~ deeper** *fig* ahondar **2.** (*poke*) empujar **III.** *vt* **1.** (*excavate*) cavar; (*machine*) excavar **2.** (*stab, poke*) clavar; **to ~**

one's elbow into... dar un codazo en...
**3.** *sl* (*like*) molar ▶ **to ~ one's own grave** cavarse su propia tumba

◆**dig in I.** *vi inf* atacar **II.** *vt* **1.** (*bury*) enterrar **2.** (*establish oneself*) instalarse

◆**dig into I.** *vi* clavar ▶ **to dig** (**deeper**) **into one's pockets** poner (más) dinero de su propio bolsillo **II.** *vt always sep inf* atacar ▶ **to dig oneself into a hole** meterse en un problema

◆**dig out** *vt* extraer; (*hole*) excavar

◆**dig up** *vt* **1.** (*from ground*) desenterrar **2.** (*excavate*) excavar **3.** *fig* (*find out*) descubrir

**digest¹** ['daɪ·dʒest] *n* (*of essays*) resumen *m*

**digest²** [daɪ·'dʒest] **I.** *vi* digerirse; (*person*) hacer la digestión **II.** *vt* **1.** (*food*) digerir **2.** *inf* (*understand*) asimilar

**digestible** [daɪ·'dʒes·tə·bəl] *adj* digerible

**digestion** [daɪ·'dʒes·tʃən] *n* digestión *f*

**digger** ['dɪɡ·ər] *n* (*machine*) excavadora *f*

**digit** ['dɪdʒ·ɪt] *n* **1.** dígito *m* **2.** ANAT dedo *m*

**digital** ['dɪdʒ·ɪ·təl] *adj* digital

**digitalize** ['dɪdʒ·ɪ·təl·aɪz] *vt* digitalizar

**dignified** ['dɪɡ·nɪ·faɪd] *adj* (*honorable*) digno, -a; (*solemn*) solemne

**dignity** ['dɪɡ·nə·ţi] *n* (*state*) dignidad *f*; (*respect*) respeto *m*

**digress** [daɪ·'ɡres] *vi* desviarse (**from** de)

**dike** [daɪk] *n* dique *m*

**dilapidated** [dɪ·'læp·ɪ·deɪ·ţɪd] *adj* destartalado, -a

**dilate** ['daɪ·leɪt] **I.** *vi* dilatarse **II.** *vt* dilatar

**dilemma** [dɪ·'lem·ə] *n* dilema *m;* **to be in a ~** estar en un dilema

**diligent** ['dɪl·ɪ·dʒənt] *adj* (*careful*) concienzudo, -a; (*hard-working*) diligente

**dill** [dɪl] *n* eneldo *m*

**dilly-dally** ['dɪl·i·dæl·i] *vi inf* **1.** (*waste time*) perder el tiempo **2.** (*be indecisive*) vacilar

**dilute** [daɪ·'lut] **I.** *vt* diluir **II.** *vi* diluirse **III.** *adj* diluido, -a

**dilution** [daɪ·'lu·ʃən] *n a. fig* disolución *f*

**dim** [dɪm] **I.** <-mm-> *vi* (*lights*) apagarse **II.** *vt* apagar **III.** <-mm-> *adj* **1.** (*not bright*) tenue **2.** (*unclear*) borroso, -a

**3.** (*stupid*) tonto, -a **4.** (*unfavorable*) sombrío, -a

**dime** [daɪm] *n* moneda *f* de diez centavos ▶ **they're a ~ a dozen** los hay a patadas

**dimension** [dɪ·'men·tʃən] *n* dimensión *f*

**diminish** [dɪ·'mɪn·ɪʃ] *vi, vt* disminuir; **to** (**greatly**) **~ in value** perder (mucho) valor

**diminution** [ˌdɪm·ə·'nu·ʃən] *n* disminución *f*

**diminutive** [dɪ·'mɪn·jə·ţɪv] **I.** *n* diminutivo *m* **II.** *adj* diminuto, -a

**dimple** ['dɪm·pəl] *n* hoyuelo *m*

**din** [dɪn] *n* estrépito *m*

**dine** [daɪn] *vi* cenar

**diner** ['daɪ·nər] *n* **1.** (*person*) comensal *mf* **2.** (*restaurant*) bar *m* de carretera

**dinghy** ['dɪŋ·i] *n* <-ies> bote *m*

**dingy** ['dɪn·dʒi] <-ier, -iest> *adj* deslustrado, -a

**dining room** *n* comedor *m*

**dinner** ['dɪn·ər] *n* cena *f*, comida *f AmS*; **to make ~** hacer la cena [*or* el almuerzo *AmS*]

**dinner jacket** *n* esmoquin *m*

**dinner party** *n* cena *f*

**dinner service** *n* vajilla *f*

**dinnertime** *n* hora *f* de cenar

**dinnerware** *n* vajilla *f*

**dinosaur** ['daɪ·nə·sɔr] *n* dinosaurio *m; fig* antigualla *f*

**dip** [dɪp] **I.** *n* **1.** (*dunking*) baño *m* **2.** (*drop*) caída *f* **3.** (*sauce*) salsa *f* **4.** (*swim*) chapuzón *m* **II.** *vi* **1.** (*drop down*) descender; (*prices*) caer **2.** (*slope down*) inclinarse **3.** (*swim*) zambullirse **III.** *vt* **1.** (*immerse*) sumergir; CULIN mojar **2.** (*put into*) meter

◆**dip into** *vt* **1.** *always sep* (*put*) meter **2. to ~ one's savings** echar mano de los ahorros **3. I'll just ~ this store** voy a echar un vistazo en esta tienda

**diphthong** ['dɪf·θaŋ] *n* LING diptongo *m*

**diploma** [dɪ·'plou·mə] *n* diploma *m*

**diplomacy** [dɪ·'plou·mə·si] *n* **1.** POL diplomacia *f* **2.** (*tact*) tacto *m*

**diplomat** ['dɪp·lə·mæt] *n* diplomático, -a *m, f*

**diplomatic** [ˌdɪp·lə·'mæţ·ɪk] *adj* diplomático, -a

**dippy** ['dɪp·i] *adj sl* flipado, -a, ahuevado, -a *Col, Perú, Nic, Pan*

**direct** [dɪ·'rekt] **I.** *vt* **1.** (*point, intend*) dirigir (**at** a); **to ~ sb to a place** indicar a alguien el camino hacia un sitio **2.** (*command*) ordenar **II.** *adj* **1.** (*straight, frank*) directo, -a **2.** (*exact*) exacto, -a; **the ~ opposite** justo lo contrario **III.** *adv* directamente

**direct deposit** *n* depósito *m* directo

**direct hit** *n* blanco *m*

**direction** [dɪ·'rek·ʃən] *n* **1.** dirección *f*; **in the ~ of** en dirección a; **sense of ~** sentido de la orientación **2.** *pl* instrucciones *fpl*; **can you give me ~s?** ¿me puedes indicar el camino?

**directive** [dɪ·'rek·tɪv] *n* directriz *f*, directiva *f AmL*

**directly** [dɪ·'rekt·li] *adv* **1.** (*without deviation*) directamente **2.** (*immediately*) inmediatamente **3.** (*exactly*) exactamente

**director** [dɪ·'rek·tər] *n* director(a) *m(f)*; **board of ~s** junta directiva

**directory** [dɪ·'rek·tə·ri] *n* **1.** guía *f*, directorio *m Méx* **2.** COMPUT directorio *m*

**directory assistance** *n* información *f* (telefónica)

**dirt** [dɜrt] *n* **1.** (*earth*) tierra *f* **2.** (*unclean substance*) suciedad *f* **3.** (*excrement, worthless thing*) porquería *f*; **don't bother with him, he's ~** pasa de él, que es un mierda; **to treat sb like ~** tratar a alguien como a un perro **4.** (*scandal, gossip*) trapos *m pl* sucios *fig* ▶ **to eat ~** tragar mierda *inf*

**dirt cheap** *adj inf* tirado, -a, botado, -a *Méx*

**dirty** ['dɜr·ti] **I.** *vt* ensuciar; **to ~ one's hands** ensuciarse las manos **II.** <-ier, -iest> *adj* **1.** (*not clean, unpleasant*) sucio, -a, chancho, -a *AmL*; **to do the ~ work** hacer el trabajo sucio **2.** (*mean, nasty*) bajo, -a **3.** (*lewd*) obsceno, -a; **~ joke/old man** chiste/viejo verde **III.** *adv* suciamente; **to play ~** jugar sucio

**disability** [ˌdɪs·ə·'bɪl·ə·ti] *n* invalidez *f*

**disable** [dɪs·'eɪ·bəl] *vt* incapacitar; COMPUT deshabilitar

**disabled** **I.** *npl* **the ~** los discapacitados **II.** *adj* incapacitado, -a

**disadvantage** [ˌdɪs·əd·'væn·tɪdʒ] **I.** *n* desventaja *f*; **to be at a ~** estar en desventaja **II.** *vt* perjudicar

**disadvantaged** *adj* desfavorecido, -a

**disadvantageous** [ˌdɪs·ˌæd·væn·'teɪ·dʒəs] *adj* desfavorable

**disagree** [ˌdɪs·ə·'gri] *vi* **1.** (*not agree*) no estar de acuerdo (**on/with** en/con), discrepar *elev* **2.** (*differ*) diferir; **the answers ~** las respuestas no concuerdan **3.** (*food*) sentar mal; **spicy food ~s with me** la comida picante me sienta mal

**disagreeable** [ˌdɪs·ə·'gri·ə·bəl] *adj* desagradable

**disagreement** [ˌdɪs·ə·'gri·mənt] *n* **1.** (*lack of agreement*) desacuerdo *m* **2.** (*argument*) discusión *f* **3.** (*discrepancy*) discrepancia *f*

**disallow** [ˌdɪs·ə·'laʊ] *vt* rechazar; LAW, SPORTS anular

**disappear** [ˌdɪs·ə·'pɪr] *vi* desaparecer; **to ~ from sight/without a trace** desaparecer de la vista/sin dejar rastro

**disappearance** [ˌdɪs·ə·'pɪr·əns] *n* desaparición *f*

**disappoint** [ˌdɪs·ə·'pɔɪnt] *vt* decepcionar, enchilar *AmC*

**disappointed** *adj* decepcionado, -a (**in** con)

**disappointing** *adj* decepcionante

**disappointment** [ˌdɪs·ə·'pɔɪnt·mənt] *n* decepción *f*

**disapproval** [ˌdɪs·ə·'pru·vəl] *n* desaprobación *f*

**disapprove** [ˌdɪs·ə·'pruv] *vi* **to ~ of** desaprobar

**disarmament** [dɪs·'ar·mə·mənt] *n* desarme *m*

**disarray** [ˌdɪs·ə·'reɪ] *n* (*disorder*) desorden *m*; (*confusion*) confusión *f*

**disaster** [dɪ·'zæs·tər] *n* desastre *m*; **~ area** zona *f* catastrófica

**disastrous** [dɪ·'zæs·trəs] *adj* desastroso, -a

**disbelief** [ˌdɪs·bɪ·'lif] *n* incredulidad *f*

**disc** [dɪsk] *n* disco *m*

**discard** [dɪ·'skard] *vt* desechar; GAMES descartar

**discerning** [dɪ·'sɜr·nɪŋ] adj (discriminating) exigente; (acute) perspicaz

**discharge**[1] ['dɪs·tʃardʒ] n 1. (hospital) alta f; (job) despido m; (prison) puesta f en libertad 2. MED secreción f 3. ECON liquidación f 4. ELEC descarga f

**discharge**[2] [dɪs·'tʃardʒ] I. vi 1. (ship) descargar 2. MED segregar II. vt 1. a. LAW (release) liberar 2. MIL, ECON despedir; (duty) cumplir; (debt) liquidar 3. (let out) emitir 4. (cancel) cancelar

**disciple** [dɪ·'saɪ·pəl] n seguidor(a) m(f); REL, PHILOS discípulo, -a m, f

**disciplinary** ['dɪs·ə·plə·ner·i] adj disciplinario, -a

**discipline** ['dɪs·ə·plɪn] I. n disciplina f II. vt disciplinar; to ~ oneself to do sth obligarse a hacer algo

**disc jockey** n pinchadiscos mf inv

**disclaim** [dɪs·'kleɪm] vt 1. (deny) negar 2. LAW renunciar a

**disclose** [dɪs·'kloʊz] vt revelar

**disclosure** [dɪs·'kloʊ·ʒər] n revelación f

**disco** ['dɪs·koʊ] n discoteca f; (music) música f disco

**discolor** [dɪs·'kʌl·ər] I. vi desteñirse II. vt decolorar

**discomfort** [dɪs·'kʌm·fərt] n 1. (uneasiness) malestar m (at respecto a) 2. (inconvenience) molestia f

**disconcert** [ˌdɪs·kən·'sɜrt] vt desconcertar

**disconnect** [ˌdɪs·kə·'nekt] vt (unplug) desenchufar; (phone) desconectar

**disconnected** adj desconectado, -a; (incoherent) inconexo, -a

**disconsolate** [dɪs·'san·sə·lət] adj desconsolado, -a

**discontent** [ˌdɪs·kən·'tent] n descontento m

**discontented** adj descontento, -a

**discontinue** [ˌdɪs·kən·'tɪn·ju] I. vi desistir II. vt suspender

**discord** ['dɪs·kɔrd] n (disagreement) discordia f

**discotheque** ['dɪs·kə·tek] n discoteca f

**discount**[1] ['dɪs·kaʊnt] n descuento m; at a ~ con descuento

**discount**[2] [dɪs·'kaʊnt] vt 1. (price) rebajar 2. (disregard) descartar

**discourage** [dɪs·'skɜr·ɪdʒ] vt desanimar; to ~ sb from doing sth disuadir a alguien de hacer algo

**discouraging** adj desalentador(a)

**discourteous** [dɪs·'kɜr·ti·əs] adj descortés

**discover** [dɪs·'skʌv·ər] vt descubrir

**discovery** [dɪs·'skʌv·ə·ri] <-ies> n descubrimiento m

**discredit** [dɪs·'kred·ɪt] I. n (disrepute) desprestigio m; (disgrace) vergüenza f II. vt desacreditar

**discreditable** [dɪs·'kred·ɪ·tə·bəl] adj deshonroso, -a

**discreet** [dɪs·'skrit] adj discreto, -a

**discrepancy** [dɪs·'skrep·ən·si] <-ies> n discrepancia f

**discretion** [dɪs·'skref·ən] n 1. (behavior) discreción f 2. (judgment) criterio m

**discriminate** [dɪs·'skrɪm·ə·neɪt] vi discernir; to ~ against sb discriminar a alguien

**discrimination** [dɪˌskrɪm·ɪ·'neɪ·ʃən] n 1. (unfair treatment) discriminación f 2. (good judgment) criterio m

**discriminatory** [dɪs·'skrɪm·ɪ·nə·tɔr·i] adj discriminatorio, -a

**discuss** [dɪ·'skʌs] vt discutir; (consider) abordar

**discussion** [dɪ·'skʌf·ən] n discusión f, argumento m AmL

**disdainful** [dɪs·'deɪn·fəl] adj desdeñoso, -a

**disease** [dɪ·'ziz] n enfermedad f

**diseased** adj enfermo, -a

**disembark** [ˌdɪs·ɪm·'bark] vi desembarcar

**disentangle** [ˌdɪs·ɪn·'tæn·gəl] vt 1. (release) librar; to ~ oneself from librarse de 2. (untangle) desenredar

**disfavor** [ˌdɪs·'feɪ·vər] vt desfavorecer

**disgrace** [dɪs·'greɪs] n vergüenza f

**disgraceful** [dɪs·'greɪs·fəl] adj vergonzoso, -a

**disguise** [dɪs·'gaɪz] I. n disfraz m; to be in ~ ir disfrazado II. vt 1. disfrazar; to ~ oneself disfrazarse (as de) 2. (hide) encubrir

**disgust** [dɪs·'gʌst] I. n 1. (repugnance) asco m; in ~ con asco 2. (indignation) indignación f (at por) II. vt 1. (sicken) dar asco 2. (be offensive) indignar

**disgusting** adj 1. (repulsive) repugnan-

**dish** [dɪʃ] <-es> n **1.** (for food) plato m;
**to do the ~es** fregar los platos **2.** TEL parabólica f **3.** sl (person) bombón m
◆**dish out** vt (serve) servir
◆**dish up** vt inf (serve) servir; (offer)
ofrecer

**dish antenna** n parabólica f

**dishcloth** ['dɪʃ·klɑθ] n paño m de cocina,
repasador m Arg, Urug

**dishearten** [dɪs·'hɑr·tən] vt descorazonar

**dishonest** [dɪs·'an·ɪst] adj deshonesto, -a

**dishonor** [dɪs·'an·ər] I. n deshonor f
II. vt **1.** (disgrace) deshonrar **2.** (not
keep) incumplir; (not pay) impagar

**dishwasher** n (appliance, person) lavaplatos m inv

**disillusion** [ˌdɪs·ɪ·'lu·ʒən] I. vt desilusionar II. n desilusión f

**disillusioned** adj desilusionado, -a

**disinclined** [ˌdɪs·ɪn·'klaɪnd] adj to be
~ to do sth tener pocas ganas de hacer algo

**disinfect** [ˌdɪs·ɪn·'fekt] vt desinfectar

**disinfectant** [ˌdɪs·ɪn·'fek·tənt] adj, n desinfectante m

**disinfection** [ˌdɪs·ɪn·'fek·ʃən] n desin-
fección f

**disintegrate** [dɪs·'ɪn·tə·greɪt] I. vi desin-
tegrarse II. vt desintegrar

**disintegration** [dɪs·ˌɪn·tə·'greɪ·ʃən] n desintegración f

**disinterested** [dɪs·'ɪn·trɪ·stɪd] adj desinteresado, -a

**disjointed** [dɪs·'dʒɔɪn·tɪd] adj inconexo, -a

**disk** [dɪsk] n disco m; **hard/start-up ~**
disco duro/de arranque

**dislike** [dɪs·'laɪk] I. vt tener aversión a
II. n aversión f

**dislocate** [dɪs·'lou·keɪt] vt **1.** (displace)
desplazar; fig trastornar **2.** MED dislocarse

**dislodge** [dɪs·'ladʒ] vt desalojar

**dismal** ['dɪz·məl] adj **1.** (depressing) deprime **2.** inf (awful) terrible; (truth)
triste

**dismantle** [dɪs·'mæn·təl] vt desmontar;
(system) desmantelar

**dismay** [dɪs·'meɪ] I. n consternación f

II. vt consternar

**dismiss** [dɪs·'mɪs] vt **1.** (job) despedir
**2.** (reject) descartar **3.** LAW desestimar

**dismissal** [dɪs·'mɪs·əl] n (school) expulsión f; (job) despido m

**dismount** [dɪs·'maunt] vi desmontar(se)

**disobedience** [ˌdɪs·ə·'bi·di·əns] n desobediencia f

**disobedient** [ˌdɪs·ə·'bi·di·ənt] adj desobediente

**disobey** [ˌdɪs·ə·'beɪ] vi, vt desobedecer

**disorder** [dɪs·'ɔr·dər] n **1.** desorden m,
desparramo m CSur **2.** MED trastorno m

**disordered** adj desordenado, -a

**disorderly** [dɪs·'ɔr·dər·li] adj **1.** (untidy)
desordenado, -a **2.** (unruly) escandaloso, -a

**disorganized** [dɪs·'ɔr·gə·naɪzd] adj desorganizado, -a

**disoriented** [dɪs·'ɔr·i·ən·tɪd] adj desorientado, -a

**disown** [dɪs·'oun] vt repudiar

**dispatch** [dɪ·'spætʃ] I. <-es> n (delivery)
envío m II. vt a. fig despachar

**dispel** [dɪ·'spel] <-ll-> vt disipar; (rumor)
desmentir

**dispensable** [dɪ·'spen·sə·bəl] adj prescindible

**dispense** [dɪ·'spens] vt (give out) repartir;
(medicine) administrar
◆**dispense with** vt prescindir de

**dispenser** [dɪ·'spen·sər] n máquina f expendedora

**disperse** [dɪ·'spɜrs] I. vt dispersar II. vi
dispersarse

**dispirited** [dɪ·'spɪr·ɪ·tɪd] adj desanimado, -a

**displace** [dɪs·'pleɪs] vt desplazar; (replace) reemplazar

**display** [dɪ·'spleɪ] I. vt **1.** (show) exhibir **2.** (express) demostrar II. n **1.** (arrangement) exposición f; **firework ~**
exhibición f pirotécnica **2.** (demonstration) demostración f **3.** COMPUT pantalla f

**display window** n escaparate m

**displease** [dɪs·'pliz] vt disgustar; **to be
~d** estar disgustado (**by** con)

**displeasure** [dɪs·'pleʒ·ər] n disgusto m

**disposable** [dɪ·'spou·zə·bəl] adj desechable

**disposal** [dɪ·'spoʊ·zəl] *n* eliminación *f*; (*garbage*) trituradora *f* ▶ **to be at sb's ~** estar a disposición de alguien

**dispose** [dɪ·'spoʊz] I. *vt* 1. (*place*) disponer 2. (*incline*) predisponer II. *vi* **to ~ of** (*throw away*) desechar; (*get rid*) deshacerse de

**dispossess** [ˌdɪs·pə·'zes] *vt* desposeer

**disproportionate** [ˌdɪs·prə·'pɔr·ʃə·nɪt] *adj* desproporcionado, -a

**disprove** [dɪs·'pruv] *vt* refutar

**disputable** [dɪ·'spju·t̬ə·bəl] *adj* discutible

**dispute** [dɪ·'spjut] I. *vt* (*argue*) discutir; (*doubt*) poner en duda II. *vi* discutir (**with/over** con/sobre) III. *n* discusión *f*

**disqualification** [dɪs·ˌkwal·ə·fɪ·'keɪ·ʃən] *n* 1. SPORTS descalificación *f* 2. (*incapacity*) impedimento *m*

**disqualify** [dɪs·'kwal·ə·faɪ] <-ie-> *vt* descalificar (**from** de)

**disquieting** *adj* inquietante

**disregard** [ˌdɪs·rɪ·'gard] I. *vt* desatender II. *n* despreocupación *f*

**disrepair** [ˌdɪs·rɪ·'per] *n* deterioro *m*; **to be in a state of ~** estar en mal estado

**disreputable** [dɪs·'rep·jə·t̬ə·bəl] *adj* de mala fama

**disrepute** [ˌdɪs·rɪ·'pjut] *n* desprestigio *m*

**disrespect** [ˌdɪs·rɪ·'spekt] *n* falta *f* de respeto

**disrespectful** [ˌdɪs·rɪ·'spekt·fəl] *adj* descortés

**disrupt** [dɪs·'rʌpt] *vt* (*disturb*) trastornar; (*interrupt*) interrumpir

**disruption** [dɪs·'rʌp·ʃən] *n* (*disturbance*) perturbación *f*; *fig* (*disorder*) desorganización *f*; (*interruption*) interrupción *f*

**disruptive** [dɪs·'rʌp·tɪv] *adj* perturbador

**dissatisfaction** [dɪs·ˌsæt̬·ɪs·'fæk·ʃən] *n* insatisfacción *f*

**dissatisfied** [dɪs·'sæt̬·ɪs·faɪd] *adj* insatisfecho, -a

**dissect** [dɪ·'sekt] *vt* diseccionar; *fig* examinar

**dissection** [dɪ·'sek·ʃən] *n* disección *f*

**dissent** [dɪ·'sent] I. *n* disconformidad *f* II. *vi* discrepar (**from** de)

**dissident** ['dɪs·ɪ·dənt] *adj, n* disidente *mf*

**dissimilar** [ˌdɪ·'sɪm·ɪ·lər] *adj* distinto (**to** a, de)

**dissimulation** [dɪ·ˌsɪm·jə·'leɪ·ʃən] *n* disimulo *m*

**dissolve** [dɪ·'zalv] I. *vi* disolverse; *fig* (*disappear*) desvanecerse II. *vt* disolver

**dissuade** [dɪ·'sweɪd] *vt* disuadir

**distance** ['dɪs·təns] I. *n* distancia *f*; **his house is within walking ~** se puede ir andando a su casa; **to keep one's ~** guardar las distancias; **in the ~** de lejos II. *vt* **to ~ oneself** distanciarse (**from** de)

**distant** ['dɪs·tənt] *adj* distante; (*relative*) lejano, -a

**distantly** *adv* de lejos; *fig* distantemente

**distasteful** [dɪs·'teɪst·fəl] *adj* desagradable

**distillery** [dɪ·'stɪl·ə·ri] *n* destilería *f*

**distinct** [dɪ·'stɪŋkt] *adj* 1. (*separate*) distinto, -a 2. (*marked*) definido, -a

**distinction** [dɪ·'stɪŋk·ʃən] *n* 1. distinción *f*; **of great ~** de gran renombre 2. (*honors*) sobresaliente *m*

**distinctive** [dɪ·'stɪŋk·tɪv] *adj* característico, -a

**distinguish** [dɪ·'stɪŋ·gwɪʃ] *vi, vt* distinguir; **to ~ oneself** destacar (**in** en)

**distinguishable** *adj* distinguible

**distinguished** *adj* distinguido, -a

**distort** [dɪ·'stɔrt] *vt* torcer; (*facts, truth*) tergiversar

**distortion** [dɪ·'stɔr·ʃən] *n* distorsión *f*

**distract** [dɪ·'strækt] *vt* distraer

**distracted** *adj* distraído, -a

**distraction** [dɪ·'stræk·ʃən] *n* 1. (*disturbance*) distracción *f* 2. (*pastime*) entretenimiento *m*

**distress** [dɪ·'stres] I. *n* 1. aflicción *f* 2. (*danger*) apuro *m* II. *vt* afligir

**distressed** *adj* 1. (*unhappy*) afligido, -a 2. (*in difficulties*) apurado, -a

**distressful, distressing** *adj* 1. (*causing worry*) angustioso, -a 2. (*painful*) doloroso, -a

**distribute** [dɪ·'strɪb·jut] *vt* distribuir; (*share*) repartir

**distribution** [ˌdɪs·trɪ·'bju·ʃən] *n* 1. (*giving out*) reparto *m* 2. (*spread*) distribución *f*

**distributor** [dɪ·'strɪb·jə·t̬ər] *n* distribuidor(a) *m(f)*

**district** ['dɪs·trɪkt] n 1. (defined area) distrito m 2. (region) región f

**district attorney** n fiscal m del distrito

**distrust** [dɪs·'trʌst] I. vt desconfiar de II. n desconfianza f

**distrustful** [dɪs·'trʌst·fəl] adj desconfiado, -a

**disturb** [dɪ·'stɜrb] vt 1. (interrupt) molestar 2. (worry) preocupar 3. (move around) perturbar

**disturbance** [dɪ·'stɜr·bəns] n 1. (interruption) molestia f 2. (incident) disturbio m

**disturbed** adj 1. PSYCH trastornado, -a 2. (restless) inquieto, -a

**disturbing** adj 1. (annoying) molesto, -a 2. (worrying) preocupante

**disunity** [dɪs·'ju·nə·t̬i] n desunión f

**disuse** [dɪs·'jus] n desuso m

**disused** [dɪs·'juzd] adj en desuso

**ditch** [dɪtʃ] I. <-es> n (trench) zanja f; (by a road) cuneta f; **irrigation** ~ acequia f II. vt sl 1. (discard) deshacerse de; (idea) descartar; (boyfriend) cortar con 2. (escape) zafarse de

**dither** ['dɪð·ər] vi inf 1. (indecisive) vacilar 2. (nervous) ponerse nervioso

**ditsy** ['dɪt·si] adj sl empanado, -a, elevado, -a Col

**dive** [daɪv] I. n 1. (in swimming) salto m [or AmL clavado m] de cabeza 2. (submerge) inmersión f 3. to take a ~ caer en picado; **to make a ~ for...** precipitarse hacia... II. vi <dived or dove, dived or dove> 1. (in swimming) tirarse de cabeza 2. (submerge) sumergirse; to ~ under sth bucear por debajo de algo 3. (drop) bajar en picado

**diver** ['daɪ·vər] n buzo mf

**diverge** [dɪ·'vɜrdʒ] vi divergir; to ~ from apartarse de

**divergence** [dɪ·'vɜr·dʒəns] n divergencia f

**diverse** [dɪ·'vɜrs] adj 1. (varied) diverso, -a 2. (not alike) diferente

**diversion** [dɪ·'vɜr·ʃən] n (change of direction) desviación f

**diversity** [dɪ·'vɜr·sə·t̬i] n diversidad f

**divert** [dɪ·'vɜrt] vt 1. (change direction) desviar 2. (distract) distraer

**diverting** [dɪ·'vɜr·t̬ɪŋ] adj ameno, -a

**divide** [dɪ·'vaɪd] I. vt 1. a. MATH dividir (**into** en) 2. (allot) repartir II. vi dividirse; **their paths ~d** sus caminos se separaron ▶ ~ **and conquer** divide y vencerás

◆**divide off** vt always sep dividir

◆**divide out, divide up** vt always sep (re)partir

**divided** adj (opinion) dividido, -a

**dividend** ['dɪv·ɪ·dend] n MATH, FIN dividendo m

**dividing line** n línea f divisoria

**diving** n (jumping) zambullida f; (swimming) buceo m

**diving board** n trampolín m

**diving suit** n escafandra f

**divisible** [dɪ·'vɪz·ə·bəl] adj divisible

**division** [dɪ·'vɪʒ·ən] n 1. a. MIL, MATH, SPORTS división f 2. (splitting up) reparto m 3. (disagreement) discordia f

**divorce** [dɪ·'vɔrs] I. n divorcio m II. vt **to get ~d** divorciarse (**from** de); **he ~d her for infidelity** se divorció de ella por infidelidad III. vi divorciarse

**divorced** adj divorciado, -a

**dizzy** ['dɪz·i] <-ier, -iest> adj 1. (having vertigo) mareado, -a 2. (causing vertigo) vertiginoso, -a 3. sl (silly) lelo, -a

**DJ** ['di·dʒeɪ] n abbr of **disc jockey** DJ mf

**DNA** [di·en·'eɪ] n abbr of **deoxyribonucleic acid** ADN m

**do** [du] I. n the ~s and don'ts el conjunto de normas II. <does, did, done> aux 1. (in questions) ~ **you own a dog?** ¿tienes perro? 2. (in negatives) **Frida ~esn't like olives** a Frida no le gustan las aceitunas 3. (in imperatives) ~ **your homework!** ¡haz los deberes!; ~ **come in!** ¡pero pasa, por favor 4. (for emphasis) **he did ~ it** sí que lo hizo 5. (replacing a repeated verb) **so/neither ~ I** yo también/tampoco; **she speaks more fluently than he ~es** ella habla con mayor fluidez que él 6. (requesting affirmation) ¿verdad?; **you ~n't want to answer, ~ you?** no quieres contestar, ¿verdad? III. <does, did, done> vt 1. (act, carry out) hacer; **to ~ one's best** emplearse a fondo; **to ~ something for sb/sth** hacer algo por alguien/algo **2.** (*deal with*) encargarse de; **if you ~ the washing up, I'll ~ the drying** si tú lavas los platos, yo los seco **3.** (*finish*) terminar **4.** (*put in order*) ordenar; (*clean*) limpiar; (*make neat*) arreglar; **to do one's hair** peinarse **5.** (*Europe, Florida*) visitar **6.** (*be satisfactory*) **I only have beer, will that ~ you?** sólo tengo cerveza, ¿te va bien? **7.** (*sell, offer*) ofrecer algo **8.** (*cook*) cocinar **9.** (*cause*) **to ~ sb a good turn** echar una mano a alguien; **to ~ sb good** sentar bien a alguien **10.** *sl* (*sex*) **to ~** hacerlo ▶ **what's ~ne is ~ne** a lo hecho, pecho; **that ~es it** eso es el colmo **IV.** <does, did, done> *vi* **1.** (*behave, act*) hacer **2.** (*manage*) salir adelante; **to ~ well in school** ir bien en la escuela; **mother and baby are ~ing well** la madre y el bebé se encuentran bien; **how are you ~ing?** ¿qué tal estás? **3.** (*finish with*) **to be ~ne with sb/sth** haber terminado con alguien/algo **4.** (*be satisfactory*) **this behavior just won't ~!** ¡no se puede tolerar este comportamiento! **5.** (*function as*) **it'll ~ for a spoon** servirá de cuchara **6.** *inf* (*going on*) **to be ~ing** pasar **7.** (*treat*) **to ~ badly/well by sb** tratar mal/bien a alguien ▶ **that will never ~** eso no sirve; **that will ~!** ¡ya basta!

◆**do away with** *vi* **1.** (*dispose of*) suprimir **2.** *inf* (*kill*) liquidar

◆**do in** *vt always sep, sl* **1. to do sb in** acabar con alguien **2.** (*ruin*) arruinar **3.** (*exhaust*) agotar

◆**do out** *vt always sep* **1.** (*adorn*) decorar **2. to do sb out of sth** sacar algo a alguien

◆**do over** *vt always sep, inf* (*redo*) volver a hacer

◆**do up** *vt* (*button*) abrochar; (*tie*) anudar; (*shoes*) atarse; (*zipper*) cerrar; (*hair*) arreglar; **to do oneself up** acicalarse

◆**do with** *vi* **1. to have to ~ sth** tener que ver con algo; (*book*) tratar de algo **2.** *inf* **I could ~ a drink** me hace falta tomar algo

◆**do without** *vi* apañarse sin

**doable** ['du·ə·bəl] *n inf* realizable

**dock** [dak] **I.** *n* **1.** NAUT muelle *m* **2.** to

**be in the ~** *fig* estar en apuros **II.** *vt, vi* NAUT atracar

**dockyard** ['dak·jard] *n* astillero *m*

**doctor** ['dak·tər] **I.** *n* **1.** MED médico, -a *m, f*; **to go to the ~'s** ir al médico **2.** UNIV doctor(a) *m(f)* **II.** *vt* (*fix*) **to ~ sth** (**up**) hacer un apaño a algo

**doctorate** ['dak·tər·ət] *n* doctorado *m*

**docudrama** *n* docudrama *m*

**document** ['dak·jə·mənt] **I.** *n* documento *m* **II.** *vt* documentar

**documentary** [‚dak·jə·'men·tə·ri] <-ies> *adj, n* documental *m*

**dodge** [dadʒ] **I.** *vt* esquivar; *fig* eludir; **to ~ doing sth** escaquearse de hacer algo *inf* **II.** *vi* SPORTS regatear **III.** *n* treta *f*

**does** [dʌz] *vt, vi, aux 3. pers sing of* **do**

**doesn't** ['dʌz·ənt] = **does not** *see* **do**

**dog** [dɔg] **I.** *n* **1.** perro, -a *m, f* **2.** *sl* (*ugly*) callo *m*; (*mean*) **the** (**dirty**) **~!** ¡el muy canalla!; (*failure*) fiasco *m* ▶ **he doesn't have a ~'s chance** *inf* no tiene la más remota posibilidad; **every ~ has its day** *prov* a cada uno le llega su momento de gloria; **to lead a ~'s life** llevar una vida de perros; **to be a ~ in the manger** ser como el perro del hortelano; **it's a ~ eat ~ world** este mundo es un lugar despiadado **II.** <-gg-> *vt* perseguir; *fig* acosar

◆**do-gooder** *n inf* tonto, -a de tan bueno, -a *m*

**dog-tired** *adj* hecho, -a polvo

**doing** ['du·ɪŋ] *n* **1. to be** (**of**) **sb's ~** ser cosa de alguien **2. ~s** actividades *fpl*

**do-it-yourself** *n* bricolaje *m*

**doll** [dal] *n* **1.** muñeco, -a *m, f* **2.** *sl* encanto *m*

◆**doll up** *vt* emperifollar; **to doll oneself up** ponerse de punta en blanco

**dollar** ['dal·ər] *n* dólar *m* ▶ **to feel like a million ~s** sentirse a las mil maravillas; **to look like a million ~s** estar despampanante; **to earn a quick ~** ganar dinero fácil

**dollhouse** *n* casa *f* de muñecas

**dollop** ['dal·əp] *n* (*amount*) porción *f*

**dolly** ['dal·i] <-ies> *n childspeak* muñequita *f*

**dolphin** ['dal·fɪn] *n* delfín *m*, bufeo *m Perú*

**domain** [dou·'meın] *n* **1.** POL, COMPUT, MAT dominio *m* **2.** (*scope*) campo *m*; **to be in the public ~** ser de dominio público

**dome** [doum] *n* **1.** ARCHIT cúpula *f* **2.** *sl* cabeza *f*

**domestic** [də·'mes·tık] *adj* **1.** (*of the house*) doméstico, -a **2.** (*home-loving*) casero, -a **3.** (*produce, flight, news*) nacional; (*trade, policy*) interior

**domestic market** *n* mercado *m* nacional

**dominant** ['dam·ə·nənt] *adj* dominante

**dominate** ['dam·ə·neıt] *vi, vt* dominar

**domination** [ˌdam·ə·'neı·ʃən] *n* dominación *f*

**Dominican** [də·'mın·ı·kən] *adj, n* dominicano, -a *m, f*

**Dominican Republic** *n* República *f* Dominicana

**dominion** [də·'mın·jən] *n* dominio *m*; **to have ~ over sb/sth** tener a alguien/algo bajo su dominio

**domino** ['dam·ə·nou] <-es> *n* ~es dominó *m*; **~ effect** efecto dominó

**donate** ['dou·neıt] *vt* donar

**donation** [dou·'neı·ʃən] *n* **1.** (*contribution*) donativo *m* **2.** (*act*) donación *f*

**done** [dʌn] *pp of* **do**

**donkey** ['daŋ·ki] *n a. fig* burro, -a *m, f*

**donkeywork** *n sl* trabajo *m* pesado

**donor** ['dou·nər] *n* donante *mf*

**don't** [dount] = **do not** *see* **do**

**donut** ['dou·nʌt] *n* donut *m*

**doodad** ['du·dæd] *n inf* la cosa esa

**doodle** ['du·dəl] I. *vi* garabatear II. *n* garabato *m*

**doom** [dum] I. *n* (*destiny*) sino *m*; (*death*) muerte *f* II. *vt* condenar

**door** [dɔr] *n* puerta *f*; **front/back ~** puerta principal/trasera; **revolving/sliding ~** puerta giratoria/corredera; **to knock at** [*or* **on**] **the ~** llamar a la puerta; **there's someone at the ~** llaman a la puerta; **to answer the ~** abrir la puerta; **to show sb the ~** echar a alguien; **out of ~s** al aire libre; **behind closed ~s** a puerta cerrada ▶ **to slam the ~ in sb's face** dar a alguien con la puerta en las narices; **to lay sth at sb's ~** echar a alguien la culpa de algo

**doorbell** *n* timbre *m*

**doorjamb** *n* marco *m* de la puerta

**doorkeeper** *n see* **doorman**

**doorknob** *n* pomo *m*

**doorman** <-men> *n* portero *m*

**doormat** *n* felpudo *m*

**doorstep** *n* **to be right on sb's ~** estar a la vuelta de la esquina

**door-to-door** *adj, adv* de puerta en puerta

**doorway** *n* entrada *f*

**dope** [doup] I. *n inf* **1.** (*drugs*) drogas *fpl*; (*marijuana*) maría *f* **2.** SPORTS dopaje *m* **3.** (*person*) capullo, -a *m, f* II. *vt* drogar; SPORTS dopar

**dope dealer**, **dope pusher** *n inf* camello, -a *m, f*

**dop(e)y** ['dou·pi] *adj* <-ier, -iest> *sl* **1.** (*drowsy*) grogui, abombado, -a *AmS* **2.** (*stupid*) lelo, -a

**dormer** *n* buhardilla *f*

**dormitory** ['dɔr·mə·tɔr·i] <-ies> *n* UNIV residencia *f* de estudiantes

**dorsal** ['dɔr·səl] *adj* dorsal

**dosage** ['dou·sıdʒ] *n* dosis *f inv*

**dose** [dous] *n a. fig* dosis *f*

**dossier** ['das·i·eı] *n* expediente *m*

**dot** [dat] *n* **1.** punto *m*; **on the ~** en punto **2. ~s** TYPO puntos *m pl* suspensivos

**doting** *adj* muy cariñoso, -a

**double** ['dʌb·əl] I. *adj* doble; **it is ~ that** es el doble de eso; **~ meaning/life** doble sentido/vida; **in ~ digits** de varias cifras; **a ~ 's'** dos eses; **~ room** habitación doble II. *adv* doble; **to see ~** ver doble; **to fold sth ~** doblar algo por la mitad; **he's ~ your age** te dobla la edad III. *vt* doblar; (*efforts*) redoblar IV. *vi* **1.** duplicarse **2.** CINE, THEAT doblar (**for** a) V. *n* **1.** (*quantity*) doble *m* **2.** (*person*) doble *mf* **3. to play ~s** jugar una partida de dobles ▶ **on** [*or* **at**] **the ~** inmediatamente

◆**double up** *vi* **1.** (*bend over*) retorcerse; **to ~ with laughter** troncharse de risa **2.** (*share room*) compartir habitación

**double bass** <-es> *n* contrabajo *m*

**double bed** *n* cama *f* de matrimonio

**double-check** *vi, vt* comprobar por segunda vez

**double-click** *vi* hacer doble clic; **to ~ on**

the left mouse button hacer doble clic con el botón izquierdo

**double-cross I.** *vt* traicionar **II.** <-es> *n* traición *f*

**double-decker** *n* (*bus*) autobús *m* de dos pisos

**double-edged** *adj a. fig* de doble filo

**double feature** *n* programa *m* doble

**double-park** *vi, vt* aparcar en doble fila

**double talk** *n* palabras *f pl* ambiguas

**double time** *n* COM, ECON paga *f* doble

**doubt** [daʊt] **I.** *n* duda *f*; **no** ~ sin duda; **without a shadow of a** ~ sin lugar a dudas; **there is no** ~ **about it** no cabe la menor duda; **to cast** ~ **on sth** poner algo en tela de juicio **II.** *vt* **1.** (*not believe*) dudar de **2.** (*question*) poner en duda **3.** (*feel uncertain*) dudar; **to** ~ **that** dudar que +*subj*; **to** ~ **if** [*or* whether]... dudar si...; **I** ~ **it very much** lo dudo mucho

**doubtful** ['daʊt·fəl] *adj* **1.** (*person*) indeciso, -a; **to be** ~ **whether to...** dudar si... **2.** (*unlikely*) incierto, -a **3.** (*questionable*) dudoso, -a

**doubtless** ['daʊt·lɪs] *adv* sin duda

**dough** [doʊ] *n* **1.** CULIN masa *f* **2.** *sl* pasta *f*, plata *f* AmS

**doughnut** ['doʊ·nʌt] *n* donut *m*

**dove**[1] [dʌv] *n* paloma *f* blanca

**dove**[2] [doʊv] *pt of* **dive**

**down**[1] [daʊn] *n* (*feathers*) plumón *m*; (*hairs*) pelusa *f*; (*on body*) vello *m*

**down**[2] [daʊn] **I.** *adv* **1.** (*movement*) abajo; **to fall** ~ caerse; **to lie** ~ acostarse **2.** (*from another point*) **to go** ~ **to the lake** bajar al lago; ~ **South** hacia el sur **3.** (*volume, intensity*) **to be worn** ~ estar gastado; **the sun is** ~ se ha puesto el sol; **the price is** ~ el precio ha bajado **4.** (*temporal*) **from 1900** ~ **to the present** desde 1900 hasta el presente; ~ **through the ages** a través de la historia **5.** (*in writing*) **to write/get sth** ~ apuntar algo **6.** (*not functioning*) **to be** ~ no funcionar; (*server*) estar caído; (*telephone lines*) estar cortado ▶ **to be** ~ **on sb** tener manía a alguien **II.** *prep* **to go** ~ **the stairs** bajar las escaleras; **to run** ~ **the slope** correr cuesta abajo

**downcast** ['daʊn·kæst] *adj* alicaído, -a

**downfall** ['daʊn·fɔl] *n* ruina *f*; (*government*) caída *f*

**downgrade** [ˌdaʊn·ˈɡreɪd] **I.** *vt* **1.** (*demote*) bajar de categoría **2.** (*disparage*) minimizar; **to** ~ **the importance** (of de) **II.** *n* bajada *f*; **to be on the** ~ *fig* ir cuesta abajo

**downhearted** [ˌdaʊn·ˈhɑr·tɪd] *adj* descorazonado, -a

**downhill** [ˌdaʊn·ˈhɪl] **I.** *adv* cuesta abajo; **to go** ~ ir cuesta abajo; *fig* ir de mal en peor **II.** *adj* cuesta abajo; **it's all** ~ **from now on** *fig* lo que queda es pan comido *inf*

**download** ['daʊn·loʊd] *vt* bajar(se)

**down-market** *adj* (*neighborhood, newspaper*) popular; (*shop, store*) barato, -a; (*program*) de masas

**down payment** *n* entrada *f*, cuota *f* inicial AmL; **to make a** ~ **on sth** dar la entrada para algo

**downplay** ['daʊn·pleɪ] *vt* restar importancia a

**downpour** ['daʊn·pɔr] *n* chaparrón *m*

**downright** ['daʊn·raɪt] **I.** *adj* (*refusal*) rotundo, -a; (*disobedience*) completo, -a; (*fool*) de remate; **that's** ~ **stupid** eso es una solemne tontería **II.** *adv* completamente; **to be** ~ **difficult** ser dificilísimo; **to refuse** ~ negarse rotundamente

**downside** ['daʊn·saɪd] *n* inconveniente *m*

**downstairs** [ˌdaʊn·ˈsterz] **I.** *adv* abajo; **to go** ~ bajar; **to run** ~ bajar corriendo **II.** *adj* (del piso) de abajo **III.** *n* planta *f* baja

**downstream** [ˌdaʊn·ˈstrim] *adv* río abajo

**Down syndrome** *n* síndrome *m* de Down

**down-to-earth** *adj* realista; (*person*) práctico, -a

**downtown** [ˌdaʊn·ˈtaʊn] **I.** *n* centro *m* (de la ciudad) **II.** *adv* **to go** ~ ir al centro; **to live** ~ vivir en el centro **III.** *adj* (*in the city center*) céntrico, -a; (*related to the city center*) del centro (de la ciudad)

**downturn** ['daʊn·tɜrn] *n* empeoramiento *m*

**downward** ['daʊn·wərd] **I.** *adj* (*movement*) descendente; (*direction*) hacia abajo; (*path*) cuesta abajo; (*tendency, prices*) a la baja **II.** *adv* hacia abajo

**downwards** ['daʊn·wərdz] *adv* hacia abajo

**doz.** *abbr of* **dozen** docena *f*

**doze** [doʊz] **I.** *vi* dormitar; **to ~ off** dormirse **II.** *n* cabezada *f*; **to have a ~** echar un sueño

**dozen** ['dʌz·ən] *n* **1.** (*twelve*) docena *f*; **half a ~** media docena; **two ~ eggs** dos docenas de huevos **2.** (*many*) **~s of times** cientos de veces

**dozy** ['doʊ·zi] *adj* <-ier, -iest> soñoliento, -a

**Dr.** *abbr of* **Doctor** Dr. *m*, Dra. *f*

**drab** [dræb] *adj* <drabber, drabbest> soso, -a; (*existence*) monótono, -a

**draft** [dræft] **I.** *n* **1.** (*air*) corriente *f* de aire **2.** (*drawing*) boceto *m* **3.** (*first version*) borrador *m* **4.** (*beer*) **on ~** de barril **II.** *vt* **1.** (*first version*) redactar el borrador de; (*plan*) trazar **2.** MIL llamar a filas **III.** *adj* (*beer*) de barril

**drafty** ['dræf·ti] *adj* <-ier, -iest> **it's ~ here** hay corriente

**drag** [dræg] **I.** <-gg-> *vt a.* COMPUT arrastrar **II.** <-gg-> *vi* **1.** (*trail along*) arrastrarse por el suelo **2.** (*meeting, time*) hacerse interminable **3.** (*lag behind*) rezagarse **III.** *n* **1.** (*hindrance*) estorbo *m*; **to be a ~ on sb** ser una carga para alguien **2.** *sl* (*boring person*) pelmazo, -a *m, f*; (*boring experience*) lata *f*; **what a ~!** ¡qué rollo! **3. to be in ~** ir vestido de mujer **4.** *inf* (*inhalation*) calada *f*; **to take a ~** dar una calada **5.** *sl* **the main ~** la calle principal

◆**drag along** *vt* arrastrar con dificultad

◆**drag away** *vt* arrancar

◆**drag behind** *vi* seguir con atraso

◆**drag down** *vt* hundir; (*make weak*) debilitar

◆**drag in** *vt* (*person*) involucrar; (*subject*) traer por los pelos

◆**drag on** *vi* hacerse interminable

◆**drag out** *vt* alargar

◆**drag up** *vt* sacar a relucir

**dragon** ['dræg·ən] *n* dragón *m*

**dragonfly** ['dræg·ən·flaɪ] <-ies> *n* libélula *f*, alguacil *m* *RíoPl*

**drain** [dreɪn] **I.** *vt* **1.** AGR, MED drenar;

(*pond*) vaciar; (*food, dishes*) escurrir **2.** (*drink*) apurar **3.** (*exhaust*) agotar **II.** *n* **1.** (*sewer*) alcantarilla *f*, resumidero *m* *AmL*; (*in sink*) desagüe *m* **2.** *fig* to throw sth down the ~ tirar algo por la borda; **to go down the ~** irse al traste **3.** (*outflow*) fuga *f*

◆**drain away** *vi* irse; (*energy*) agotarse

**drainage** ['dreɪ·nɪdʒ] *n* TECH desagüe *m*; **~ system** alcantarillado *m*

**drainboard** *n* escurridero *m*

**drainpipe** *n* tubo *m* de desagüe

**drama** ['dra·mə] *n* **1.** LIT, CINE *a. fig* drama *m* **2.** THEAT arte *m* dramático

**dramatic** [drə·'mæt·ɪk] *adj a. fig* dramático, -a; (*artist, production*) teatral; (*rise, discovery*) espectacular

**drank** [dræŋk] *pt of* **drink**

**drastic** ['dræs·tɪk] *adj* drástico, -a

**draw** [drɔ] **I.** <drew, drawn> *vt* **1.** ART dibujar **2.** (*pull*) arrastrar; (*curtains*) correr; **to ~ sb aside** llevarse a alguien aparte **3.** (*attract*) atraer; **to be ~n toward(s)** sentirse atraído por; **to ~ attention to** llamar la atención sobre **4.** (*elicit*) conseguir (**from** de) **5. to ~ a conclusion** sacar una conclusión **6.** (*take out*) sacar **7.** (*obtain*) obtener; (*salary, pension*) cobrar **8.** (*money*) sacar; **to ~ a check** extender un cheque **9.** SPORTS, GAMES empatar **II.** <drew, drawn> *vi* **1.** ART dibujar **2.** (*move*) **to ~ ahead/away** adelantarse/apartarse **3.** (*approach*) acercarse; **to ~ to a close/an end** finalizar **4.** SPORTS, GAMES empatar **III.** *n* **1.** (*attraction*) atracción *f* **2.** SPORTS, GAMES empate *m* **3.** (*raffle*) sorteo *m*

◆**draw apart** *vi* distanciarse

◆**draw aside** *vt always sep* apartar

◆**draw away** **I.** *vi* (*move off*) alejarse; (*move away*) apartarse; **to ~ from sb** dejar atrás a alguien2 **II.** *vt* apartar

◆**draw down** *vt* bajar

◆**draw in** **I.** *vi* llegar; (*days*) acortarse **II.** *vt* atraer

◆**draw off** *vt* (*boots*) quitarse

◆**draw on** **I.** *vt* **1.** (*use*) usar **2.** (*put on*) ponerse **II.** *vi* **1.** (*time, day*) seguir su curso **2.** (*approach*) acercarse

◆**draw out** **I.** *vt* **1.** (*prolong*) alargar

D

2. (*elicit*) sacar 3. FIN, ECON, COM retirar II. *vi* 1. (*car, bus, train*) salir 2. (*day*) hacerse más largo

♦**draw together** I. *vt* juntar II. *vi* acercarse

♦**draw up** I. *vt* 1. (*draft*) redactar; (*plan*) trazar 2. (*bring near*) arrimar II. *vi* pararse

**drawback** *n* inconveniente *m*

**drawer** [drɔr] *n* cajón *m*

**drawing** *n* dibujo *m*

**drawing room** *n* salón *m*

**drawn** [drɔn] *pp of* draw

**dread** [dred] I. *vt* temer; I ~ **to think...** me da miedo pensar... II. *n* terror *m* III. *adj* aterrador(a)

**dreadful** ['dred·fəl] *adj* 1. (*terrible*) terrible; I feel ~ **about it** me da mucha pena 2. (*bad quality*) fatal

**dreadfully** ['dred·fə·li] *adv* 1. ~ **late** tardísimo 2. (*poorly*) fatal

**dream** [drim] I. *n* sueño *m*; **a bad** ~ una pesadilla; **to be in a** ~ estar en las nubes; **to go like a** ~ ir como la seda; **a** ~ **come true** un sueño hecho realidad; **in your** ~**s!** ¡ni lo sueñes! II. <dreamed *or* dreamt, dreamed *or* dreamt> *vi* soñar; **to** ~ **of** (*doing*) soñar con (hacer) algo; ~ **on!** ¡ni de coña!; I **wouldn't** ~ **of** (**doing**) that no se me pasaría por la cabeza (hacer) eso III. <dreamed *or* dreamt, dreamed *or* dreamt> *vt* soñar; I **never** ~**ed that...** nunca se me había ocurrido que... +*condicional* IV. *adj* ideal; **his** ~ **house** la casa de sus sueños

♦**dream up** *vt* idear

**dreamt** [dremt] *pt, pp of* dream

**dreary** ['drɪr·i] *adj* <-ier, -iest> deprimente

**drench** [drentʃ] *vt* empapar (**in** de)

**dress** [dres] I. *n* <-es> vestido *m* II. *vi* vestirse; **to** ~ **in blue** ir de azul III. *vt* 1. (*put on*) vestir 2. CULIN aliñar 3. (*decorate*) adornar; (*hair*) peinar

♦**dress up** *vi* ponerse elegante; **to** ~ **as** disfrazarse de

**dressing** ['dres·ɪŋ] *n* CULIN aliño *m*

**dressing-down** *n* reprimenda *f*

**dressing gown** *n* bata *f*, albornoz *m*

**dressing table** *n* tocador *m*

**dress rehearsal** *n* ensayo *m* general

**dressy** ['dres·i] *adj* <-ier, -iest> elegante

**drew** [dru] *pt of* draw

**dribble** ['drɪb·əl] I. *vi* (*person*) babear; (*water*) gotear II. *n* (*saliva*) baba *f*; (*water*) chorrito *m*

**dried** [draɪd] I. *pt, pp of* dry II. *adj* seco, -a; ~ **milk** leche en polvo

**dried-up** *adj* seco, -a

**drift** [drɪft] I. *vi* (*move aimlessly*) dejarse llevar II. *n* 1. NAUT deriva *f* 2. *inf* (*sense*) onda *f*; **to catch sb's** ~ captar a alguien

**drill** [drɪl] TECH I. *n* taladro *m* II. *vt, vi* perforar

**drink** [drɪŋk] I. <drank, drunk> *vi* beber; **to** ~ **heavily/in moderation** beber en exceso/con moderación; **to** ~ **to** brindar por II. <drank, drunk> *vt* beber; **to** ~ **a toast** brindar (**to** por) III. *n* bebida *f*; (*alcoholic*) copa *f*; **to have a** ~ tomar algo

♦**drink in** *vt* absorber

**drinkable** ['drɪŋ·kə·bəl] *adj* potable

**drinker** *n* bebedor(a) *m(f)*

**drinking** *n* bebida *f*; (*drunkenness*) alcoholismo *m*

**drinking fountain** *n* fuente *f*

**drinking water** *n* agua *f* potable

**drip** [drɪp] I. <-pp-> *vi* gotear II. <-pp-> *vt* chorrear III. *n* 1. (*act*) goteo *m* 2. (*drop*) gota *f* 3. *sl* (*person*) pánfilo, -a *m, f*

**dripping** ['drɪp·ɪŋ] I. *adj* 1. (*faucet, pipe*) que gotea 2. (*wet*) empapado, -a II. *adv* **to be** ~ **wet** estar chorreando III. *n* ~**s** pringue *m o f*

**drive** [draɪv] I. <drove, driven> *vt* 1. AUTO conducir, manejar *AmL*; (*race car*) pilotar; **to** ~ **sb home** llevar a alguien a casa 2. **to** ~ **sb to** (**do**) **sth** forzar a alguien a (hacer) algo 3. (*render, make*) volver; **to** ~ **sb crazy** sacar a alguien de quicio, mover II. <drove, driven> *vi* 1. (*operate*) conducir, manejar *AmL* 2. (*travel*) ir 3. (*function*) funcionar III. *n* 1. (*journey*) viaje *m*; **to go for a** ~ ir a dar una vuelta en coche 2. (*street*) calle *f* 3. (*driveway*) entrada *f* 4. TECH tracción *f* 5. PSYCH impulso *m*; **to have** ~ ser emprendedor 6. (*campaign*) campaña *f* 7. COMPUT unidad *f* de disco

◆**drive at** vt inf insinuar
◆**drive off** I. vt always sep ahuyentar II. vi irse
◆**drive out** vt expulsar
◆**drive up** vi acercarse
**driven** ['drɪv·ən] pp of **drive**
**driver** ['draɪ·vər] n 1. conductor(a) m(f); **truck ~** camionero, -a m, f; **taxi ~** taxista m f 2. COMPUT driver m
**driver's license** n carné m de conducir
**driving** n conducción f, manejo m AmL
**driving force** n fuerza f motriz
**driving instructor** n profesor(a) m(f) de autoescuela
**driving lessons** npl prácticas f pl de conducir
**driving school** n autoescuela f
**driving test** n examen m de conducir
**drizzle** ['drɪz·əl] METEO I. n llovizna f, garúa f AmL II. vi lloviznar, garuar AmL
**drone** [droʊn] n 1. ZOOL a. fig zángano m 2. (sound) zumbido m
**droop** [drup] I. vi (person) desanimarse II. vt inclinar
**drop** [drap] I. n 1. (liquid) gota f; ~ **by ~** gota a gota; **to have had a ~ too much** llevar una copa de más 2. (trace) pizca f 3. (vertical distance) declive m 4. (decrease) disminución f 5. (fall) caída f ▶ **it's a ~ in the bucket** es una gota de agua en el mar; **at the ~ of a hat** en un abrir y cerrar de ojos II. <-pp-> vt 1. (allow to fall) dejar caer 2. (lower) bajar 3. (give up) renunciar a; **to ~ sb** romper con alguien 4. (leave out) omitir; **let's ~ the subject** cambiemos de tema III. <-pp-> vi 1. (descend) bajar 2. **to ~ into a bar** pasarse por un bar 3. inf (be exhausted) estar agotado, -a ▶ **to let it ~** dejarlo caer; **to let it ~ that...** dar a entender que...
◆**drop behind** vi quedarse atrás
◆**drop by** vi pasarse
◆**drop down** vi caer
◆**drop in** vi inf entrar un momento; **to ~ on sb** pasarse por casa de alguien
◆**drop off** I. vt inf (passenger) dejar II. vi 1. (decrease) disminuir 2. inf (fall asleep) quedarse dormido 3. (fall off) caerse
◆**drop out** vi darse de baja (**of** en)

**drop-down menu** n menú m desplegable
**droplet** ['drap·lət] n gotita f
**drought** [draʊt] n sequía f
**drove**[1] [droʊv] n 1. (animals) rebaño m 2. **~s** inf manada f; **in ~s** a montones
**drove**[2] [droʊv] pt of **drive**
**drown** [draʊn] I. vt a. fig ahogar II. vi 1. ahogarse 2. **to be ~ing in work** estar hasta arriba de trabajo
**drowsy** ['draʊ·zi] <-ier, -iest> adj soñoliento, -a
**drug** [drʌg] I. n fármaco m; (illegal) droga f; **to take ~s** tomar drogas II. <-gg-> vt drogar
**drug addict** n drogadicto, -a m, f
**drug addiction** n drogadicción f
**drug bust** n incautación f de droga
**drug pusher** n camello, -a m, f
**drugstore** n farmacia-droguería f
**drum** [drʌm] n 1. MUS, TECH tambor m; **~s** batería f 2. (for oil) bidón m 3. ANAT tímpano m
**drumstick** n CULIN muslito m
**drunk** [drʌŋk] I. vt, vi pp of **drink** II. adj (inebriated) borracho, -a, jumo, -a AmL; **to be ~** estar borracho; **to get ~** emborracharse III. n borracho, -a m, f
**drunkard** ['drʌŋ·kərd] n borracho, -a m, f
**drunken** ['drʌŋ·kən] adj borracho, -a
**dry** [draɪ] I. <-ier or-er, -iest or-est> adj 1. (not wet) seco, -a; **to go ~** secarse 2. (climate, soil) árido, -a ▶ **to run ~** agotarse II. <-ie-> vt secar III. <-ie-> vi secarse; **to put sth out to ~** sacar algo para que se seque
◆**dry up** I. vi 1. (become dry) secarse 2. inf (become silent) quedarse en silencio 3. (run out) agotarse II. vt secar
**dry cleaner's** n tintorería f
**dryer** ['draɪ·ər] n (for hair) secador m; (for clothes) secadora f
**dry land** n tierra f firme
**dryness** ['draɪ·nɪs] n a. fig sequedad f
**dry run** n prueba f; (tryout) ensayo m
**dual** ['du·əl] adj inv doble
**dual citizenship** n doble nacionalidad f
**dub** [dʌb] <-bb-> vt 1. (film) doblar; **to be ~bed into English** estar doblado al inglés 2. (give sb/sth a nickname) apodar

**dubbing** ['dʌb·ɪŋ] n doblaje m

**dubious** ['du·bi·əs] adj 1. (doubtful) dubitativo, -a 2. (untrustworthy) dudoso, -a

**duchess** ['dʌtʃ·ɪs] n duquesa f

**duck** [dʌk] I. n pato m ► like a ~ to water como pez en el agua II. vi 1. (dip head) agachar la cabeza 2. to ~ out of sth escaquearse de algo III. vt 1. (lower) bajar 2. (avoid) esquivar; fig eludir

**ducky** ['dʌk·i] n sl a pedir de boca

**dude** [dud] n (guy) tío, -a m, f

**due** [du] I. adj 1. (payable) pagadero, -a; (owing) debido, -a; ~ date fecha límite; ECON fecha de vencimiento 2. (appropriate) conveniente; in ~ course a su debido tiempo; with all ~ respect con el debido respeto 3. (expected) esperado, -a; I'm ~ in Mexico City this evening esta noche me esperan en la Ciudad de México 4. ~ to debido a II. n 1. to give sb his/her ~ dar a alguien su merecido 2. ~s (debts) deudas fpl; (subscriptions) deberes mpl; (payment) cuota f

**duel** ['du·əl] n duelo m

**duet** [du·'et] n dúo m

**duffle bag** ['dʌf·əl‚bæg] n talego m

**duffle coat** n trenca f

**dug¹** [dʌg] pt, pp of **dig**

**dug²** [dʌg] n teta f; (cow) ubre f

**duke** [duk] n duque m

**dull** [dʌl] I. adj 1. (boring) aburrido, -a 2. (not bright: sky) gris; (weather) desapacible; (color) apagado, -a; (light) pálido, -a 3. (sound) sordo, -a 4. (not sharp) desafilado, -a II. vt 1. (alleviate) aliviar 2. (desensitize) insensibilizar

**duly** ['du·li] adv 1. (appropriately) debidamente 2. (on time) a su debido tiempo

**dumb** [dʌm] adj 1. often offensive (mute) mudo, -a 2. deaf and ~ sordomudo, -a 2. inf (stupid) estúpido, -a; to play ~ hacerse el tonto

**dumbstruck** ['dʌm·strʌk] adj mudo, -a (de asombro)

**dummy** ['dʌm·i] I. <-ies> n 1. (mannequin) maniquí mf 2. (duplicate) imitación f 3. (fool) tonto, -a II. adj (false) falso, -a

**dump** [dʌmp] I. n 1. (for waste) basurero m 2. fig sl (dirty place) tugurio m II. vt 1. (drop) verter; (get rid of) deshacerse de; (boyfriend) plantar 2. COMPUT volcar III. vi sl to ~ on sb pagarla con alguien

**dumping** n dumping m

**dune** [dun] n duna f

**dungarees** [‚dʌŋ·gə·'riz] npl (workman's) mono m; (jeans) vaqueros mpl

**dungeon** ['dʌn·dʒən] n mazmorra f

**dunk** [dʌŋk] vt mojar

**dup.** n abbr of **duplicate** dup.

**duplicate¹** ['du·plɪ·kət] I. adj inv duplicado, -a m II. n duplicado

**duplicate²** ['du·plɪ·keɪt] vt 1. (replicate) duplicar 2. (copy) copiar

**durability** [‚dʊr·ə·'bɪl·ə·t̬i] n 1. (permanence) permanencia f 2. (life of a product) durabilidad f

**durable** ['dʊr·ə·bəl] adj 1. (hard-wearing) resistente 2. (long-lasting) duradero, -a

**duration** [dʊ·'reɪ·ʃən] n duración f; for the ~ hasta que se acabe

**during** ['dʊr·ɪŋ] prep durante; ~ work/the week durante el trabajo/la semana

**dusk** [dʌsk] n crepúsculo m; at ~ al atardecer

**dust** [dʌst] I. n polvo m ► to bite the ~ morder el polvo; to leave sb in the ~ dejar a alguien atrás II. vi limpiar el polvo

**dust bunny** n inf pelusa f

**duster** ['dʌs·tər] n trapo m

**dust mite** n ácaro m del polvo

**dustpan** n recogedor m

**dustup** n sl bronca f

**dusty** ['dʌs·ti] <-ier, -iest> adj polvoriento, -a; (grayish) ceniciento, -a; ~ brown marrón grisáceo

**Dutch** [dʌtʃ] I. adj holandés, -esa II. n 1. pl the ~ los holandeses 2. LING holandés

**duty** ['du·t̬i] <-ies> n 1. (moral) deber m; (obligation) obligación f; out of ~ por compromiso; to do one's ~ cumplir con su obligación 2. (task) función f 3. (work) tarea f; to do ~ for sb sustituir a alguien; to be on/off ~ estar/no estar de servicio 4. (tax) impuesto m

**duty-free** *adj* libre de impuestos

**duvet** [du·'veɪ] *n* edredón *m* nórdico

**DVD** [ˌdi·vi·'di] *n inv abbr of* **Digital Video Disk** DVD *m*

**dwarf** [dwɔrf] <-s *or* -ves> *n* enano, -a *m, f*

**dwell** [dwel] <dwelt *or* -ed, dwelt *or* -ed> *vi* **to ~ on sth** insistir en algo; **to ~ on a subject** explayarse en un tema

**dwelt** [dwelt] *pp, pt of* **dwell**

**dwindle** ['dwɪn·dəl] *vi* menguar

**dye** [daɪ] **I.** *vt* teñir **II.** *n* tinte *m*

**dyke** [daɪk] *n see* **dike**

**dynamic** [daɪ·'næm·ɪk] *adj* dinámico, -a

**dynamite** ['daɪ·nə·maɪt] *n* dinamita *f*

**dynamo** ['daɪ·nə·moʊ] <-s> *n* dinamo *f*

**dyslexia** [dɪ·'sleksiə] *n* dislexia *f*

**dyslexic** [dɪs·'lek·sɪk] *adj* disléxico, -a

# E

**E, e** [i] *n* **1.** (*letter*) E, e *f;* **~ as in Echo** E de España **2.** MUS mi *m*

**E** *abbr of* **east** E

**each** [itʃ] **I.** *adj* cada **II.** *pron* cada uno, cada una; **$70 ~** 70$ cada uno

**each other** *pron* uno a otro, una a otra; **to help ~** ayudarse mutuamente; **to be made for ~** estar hechos el uno para el otro

**eager** ['i·gər] *adj* ansioso, -a, ávido, -a; **to be ~ to start** estar ansioso por empezar

**eagerness** *n* entusiasmo *m*

**eagle** ['i·gəl] *n* águila *f*

**ear**¹ [ɪr] *n* ANAT oído *m;* (*outer part*) oreja *f;* **~, nose and throat specialist** otorrinolaringólogo, -a *m, f;* **to have a good ~** tener buen oído ► **to play it by ~** *inf* tocarlo de oído, improvisar sobre la marcha

**ear**² [ɪr] *n* BOT espiga *f*

**earache** ['ɪr·eɪk] *n* dolor *m* de oído

**eardrum** *n* tímpano *m*

**ear infection** *n* infección *f* de oído

**earl** [ɜrl] *n* conde *m*

**earlobe** ['ɪr·loʊb] *n* lóbulo *m* de la oreja

**early** ['ɜr·li] **I.** <-ier, -iest> *adj* **1.** (*ahead of time, near the beginning*) temprano,

-a; **to be ~** llegar temprano; **in the ~ 15th century** a principios del siglo XV; **in the ~ morning** de madrugada; **in the ~ afternoon** a primera hora de la tarde; **he is in his ~ twenties** tiene poco más de veinte años; **at an ~ age** a una edad temprana; **to make it an ~ night** acostarse temprano; **the ~ days/years of sth** los primeros tiempos de algo **2.** *form* (*prompt: reply*) rápido, -a; **at your earliest** (**possible**) **convenience** tan pronto como le sea posible **3.** (*first*) primero, -a **II.** *adv* **1.** (*ahead of time*) anticipadamente; **to get up ~** madrugar; **~ in the morning** por la mañana temprano; **an ~ death** una muerte prematura; **the ~ hours** la madrugada **2.** (*soon*) pronto; **as ~ as possible** tan pronto como sea posible; **book your tickets ~** compren sus entradas con tiempo **3.** (*prematurely*) prematuramente; **to die ~** morir joven

**earmark** ['ɪr·mark] *vt* (*put aside*) reservar; (*funds*) destinar

**earmuffs** ['ɪr·mʌfs] *npl* orejeras *fpl*

**earn** [ɜrn] *vt* **1.** (*be paid*) ganar; **to ~ a living** ganarse la vida **2.** (*interest*) devengar

**earnest** ['ɜr·nɪst] **I.** *adj* (*sincere*) sincero, -a **II.** *n* seriedad *f;* **in ~** de verdad

**earnestly** *adv* **1.** (*speak*) seriamente **2.** (*desire*) de todo corazón

**earnings** ['ɜr·nɪŋz] *npl* (*of a person*) ingresos *mpl*

**earphones** ['ɪr·foʊnz] *npl* auriculares *mpl*

**earpiece** ['ɪr·pis] *n* **1.** (*of a phone*) auricular *m* **2.** (*of glasses*) patilla *f*

**earplug** ['ɪr·plʌg] *n* tapón *m* para el oído

**earring** ['ɪr·rɪŋ] *n* pendiente *m,* caravana *f CSur,* candonga *f Col*

**earshot** ['ɪr·ʃat] *n* alcance *m* del oído; **in/ out of ~** al alcance/fuera del alcance del oído; **within ~** al alcance del oído

**earth** [ɜrθ] *n* **1.** (*planet*) Tierra *f;* **on ~** en el mundo **2.** (*soil*) tierra *f* ► **to come back** (**down**) **to ~** bajar de las nubes; **what/who/where/why <u>on</u> ~...?** *inf* ¿qué/quién/dónde/por qué diablos...?

**earthling** ['ɜrθ·lɪŋ] *n* terrícola *mf*

**earthly** ['ɜrθ·li] adj (concerning life on earth) terreno, -a; (existence, paradise) terrenal

**earthquake** ['ɜrθ·kweɪk] n terremoto m, temblor m AmL

**earwax** ['ɪr·wæks] n cerumen m

**ease** [iz] I. n 1. (effortlessness) facilidad f; **to do sth with** ~ hacer algo con facilidad f; (comfort) comodidad f; **to feel at** ~ sentirse cómodo; **to be at** ~ estar a sus anchas; (**stand**) **at** ~! MIL ¡descansen! II. vt 1. (relieve: pain) aliviar; **to** ~ **one's conscience** descargarse la conciencia 2. (burden) aligerar III. vi (pain) aliviarse; (tension, prices) disminuir

◆**ease off** vi, **ease up** vi (pain) aliviarse; (person) relajarse

**easel** ['i·zəl] n caballete m

**easily** ['i·zə·li] adv (without difficulty) fácilmente; **to be** ~ **the best** ser con mucho el mejor

**east** [ist] I. n este m; **further** ~ más hacia el este; **Far East** Extremo m Oriente; **Middle East** Oriente m Medio II. adj del este; ~ **coast** costa f este

**Easter** ['i·stər] n (holiday) Pascua f; **during** ~ en Semana Santa

**Easter Bunny** n conejo m de Pascua

**Easter Day** n Domingo m de Pascua

**Easter egg** n huevo m de Pascua

**Easter holidays** npl vacaciones f pl de Semana Santa

**easterly** ['i·stər·li] adj, adv 1. (towards the east) hacia el este 2. (from the east) del este

**Easter Monday** n lunes m de Pascua

**eastern** ['i·stərn] adj del este, oriental

**Easter Sunday** n Domingo m de Pascua

**East Germany** [,ist·'dʒɜr·mə·ni] n HIST Alemania f oriental

**eastward** ['ist·wərd] adj, adv hacia el este

**eastwards** ['ist·wərdz] adv hacia el este

**easy** ['i·zi] <-ier, -iest> I. adj 1. (simple) fácil; **the hotel is within** ~ **reach of the beach** el hotel está muy cerca de la playa; ~ **to get along with** de trato fácil 2. (relaxed: manner) natural; **an** ~ **disposition** una buena disposición; **to be** ~ **on sb** ser poco severo con alguien II. adv 1. (cautiously) con cuidado; ~ **does it** inf despacito y buena letra 2. (lenient) **to go** ~ **on sb** inf no ser demasiado severo con alguien 3. inf **take it** ~! ¡cálmate! ► ~ **come,** ~ **go** inf tan fácil como viene, se va

**easy chair** n poltrona f

**easy-going** adj (person) de trato fácil

**eat** [it] I. <ate, eaten> vt comer; **to** ~ **breakfast** tomar el desayuno, desayunar; **to** ~ **lunch/dinner** comer/cenar almorzar/comer AmL II. vi comer

◆**eat away** vt (acid) corroer; (termites) carcomer

**eaten** ['i·tən] pp of eat

**eatery** ['i·tə·ri] n inf restaurante m

**eating disorder** n trastorno m alimenticio

**eau de Cologne** [,ou·də·kə·'loun] n (agua f de) colonia f

**eavesdrop** ['ivz·drap] <-pp-> vi **to** ~ **on sth/sb** escuchar algo/a alguien a escondidas

**echelon** ['eʃ·ə·lan] n 1. (strata) nivel m, (of society) capa f 2. MIL escalón m

**echo** ['ek·ou] I. <-es> n eco m II. <-es, -ing, -ed> vi resonar III. <-es, -ing, -ed> vt (repeat) repetir

**eclectic** [ek·'lek·tɪk] I. n form ecléctico, -a m, f II. adj form ecléctico

**eclipse** [ɪ·'klɪps] I. n eclipse m II. vt eclipsar

**ecological** [,i·kə·'ladʒ·ɪ·kəl] adj ecológico, -a

**ecologically** [,i·kə·'ladʒ·ɪk·li] adv ecológicamente; ~ **friendly** ecológico, -a

**ecologist** [i·'kal·ə·dʒɪst] n 1. (expert) ecólogo, -a m, f 2. POL ecologista mf

**ecology** [i·'kal·ə·dʒi] n ecología f

**ecology movement** n movimiento m ecologista

**economic** [,i·kə·'nam·ɪk] adj POL, ECON económico, -a

**economical** [,i·kə·'nam·ɪ·kəl] adj económico, -a

**economics** [,i·kə·'nam·ɪks] npl 1. + sing vb (discipline) economía f 2. + pl vb (matter) aspecto m económico

**economist** [ɪ·'kan·ə·mɪst] n economista mf

**economize** [ɪ·'kan·ə·maɪz] vi ahorrar; **to**

**~ on sth** economizar en algo

**economy** [ɪˈkan·ə·mi] <-ies> n 1. (frugality) ahorro m 2. (monetary assets) economía f

**economy class** n AVIAT clase f turista

**ecstasy** [ˈek·stə·si] <-ies> n (psychological state) éxtasis m inv

**ecstatic** [ekˈstæt̬·ɪk] adj extático, -a; (rapturous) eufórico, -a

**Ecuador** [ˈek·wə·dɔr] n Ecuador m

**Ecuadorian** [ˌek·wəˈdɔr·i·ən] I. n ecuatoriano, -a m, f II. adj ecuatoriano, -a

**ecumenical** [ˌek·juˈmen·ɪ·kəl] adj ecuménico, -a

**eczema** [ˈek·sə·mə] n eczema m

**Eden** [ˈi·dən] n Edén m

**edge** [edʒ] I. n sing 1. (limit) borde m; (of a lake, pond) orilla f; (of a page) margen m; (of a knife) filo m; (of a table) canto m 2. SPORTS ventaja f II. vi to ~ forward ir avanzando

**edgy** [ˈedʒ·i] <-ier, -iest> adj inf nervioso

**edible** [ˈed·ɪ·bəl] adj comestible

**edify** [ˈed·ɪ·faɪ] <-ie-> vt form edificar

**edifying** adj form edificante

**edit** [ˈed·ɪt] vt editar

**edition** [ɪˈdɪʃ·ən] n edición f; (set of books) tirada f

**editor** [ˈed·ɪ·t̬ər] n (of book) editor(a) m(f); (of article) redactor(a) m(f); (of newspaper) director(a) m(f)

**editorial** [ˌed·əˈtɔr·i·əl] I. n editorial m II. adj editorial; ~ staff redacción f

**editor-in-chief** [ˌed·ɪ·t̬ər·ɪnˈtʃif] n redactor(a) m(f) jefe

**educate** [ˈedʒ·əˌkeɪt] vt 1. (bring up) educar 2. (teach) instruir

**educated** [ˈedʒ·əˌkeɪ·t̬ɪd] adj culto, -a

**education** [ˌedʒ·ʊˈkeɪ·ʃən] n 1. SCHOOL educación f 2. (training) formación f 3. (teaching) enseñanza f; (study of teaching) pedagogía f

**educational** [ˌedʒ·ʊˈkeɪ·ʃə·nəl] adj 1. SCHOOL (system) educativo, -a 2. (instructive) pedagógico, -a

**eel** [il] n anguila f

**eerie** [ˈɪr·i] adj, **eery** <-ier, -iest> adj espeluznante

**effect** [ɪˈfekt] I. n 1. (consequence) efecto m; **to have an ~ on sth** afectar

a algo; (result) resultado m; **to take ~** (medicine, alcohol) hacer efecto 2. LAW vigencia f; **to come into** [or **to take**] **~** entrar en vigor 3. **~s** (belongings) efectos mpl II. vt realizar

**effective** [ɪˈfek·tɪv] adj 1. (giving result) efectivo, -a; (medicine) eficaz 2. (operative) vigente; **to become ~** entrar en vigor

**effectively** adv 1. (giving result) eficazmente 2. (really) realmente

**effectiveness** n (efficiency) efectividad f; (of a plan) eficacia f

**effeminate** [ɪˈfem·ə·nɪt] I. adj afeminado, -a II. n afeminado m

**effervescent** [ˌef·ərˈves·ənt] adj 1. efervescente 2. fig eufórico, -a

**efficiency** [ɪˈfɪʃ·ən·si] n 1. (of a person) eficiencia f; (of a method) eficacia f 2. (of a machine) rendimiento m

**efficient** [ɪˈfɪʃ·ənt] adj (person) eficiente

**effigy** [ˈef·ɪ·dʒi] n efigie f

**effort** [ˈef·ərt] n a. PHYS esfuerzo m; **to be worth the ~** valer la pena

**effortless** [ˈef·ərt·lɪs] adj fácil, sin esfuerzo aparente

**e.g.** [ˌiˈdʒi] abbr of **exempli gratia** (= for example) p.ej.

**egalitarian** [ɪˌgæl·ɪˈter·i·ən] adj igualitario, -a

**e-generation** [i·ˌdʒen·ə·ˈreɪ·ʃən] n generación f de internet

**egg** [eg] n huevo m; **fried/boiled ~s** huevos fritos/pasados por agua; **hard-boiled ~** huevo duro; **scrambled ~s** huevos revueltos

**egg cell** n óvulo m

**eggnog** n ponche m de huevo

**eggplant** n berenjena f

**egg roll** n rollito m de primavera

**eggshell** n cáscara f de huevo

**egg yolk** n yema f de huevo

**ego** [ˈi·goʊ] n <-s> 1. PSYCH ego m 2. (self-esteem) amor m propio

**egocentric** [ˌi·goʊˈsen·trɪk] adj egocéntrico, -a

**egoist** [ˈi·goʊ·ɪst] n egoísta mf

**egoistic** [ˌi·goʊ·ˈɪs·tɪk] adj, **egoistical** [ˌi·goʊ·ˈɪs·tɪ·kəl] adj egoísta

**ego surfing** n COMPUT introducir en un buscador de Internet el propio nombre

**egotistic** [ˌiˈgou·ˈtɪs·tɪk] *adj*, **egotistical** [ˌiˈgou·ˈtɪs·tɪ·kəl] *adj* **1.** (*selfish*) egoísta **2.** (*self-important*) egotista

**ego trip** [ˈiˈgou·trɪp] *n* to be on an ~ darse autobombo

**egregious** [ɪˈgriˈdʒəs] *adj* escandaloso, -a

**Egypt** [ˈiˈdʒɪpt] *n* Egipto *m*

**Egyptian** [ɪˈdʒɪpˈʃən] I. *n* egipcio, -a *m, f* II. *adj* egipcio, -a

**eh** [eɪ] *interj* **1.** (*what did you say?*) ¿qué? **2.** (*isn't it; aren't you/they/we?*) ¿verdad?

**eight** [eɪt] I. *adj* ocho *inv;* **there are ~ of us** somos ocho; **it's ~ o'clock** son las ocho; **~ and a quarter/half** ocho y cuarto/media; **~ o'clock** las ocho; **it's ~ o'clock** son las ocho; **it's half past ~** son las ocho y media; **at ~ twenty/thirty** a las ocho y veinte/media II. *n* ocho *m*

**eighteen** [ˌeɪˈtin] I. *adj* dieciocho II. *n* dieciocho *m; s. a.* **eight**

**eighteenth** [ˌeɪˈtinθ] I. *adj* decimoctavo, -a II. *n* **1.** (*order*) decimoctavo, -a *m, f* **2.** (*date*) ocho *m* **3.** (*fraction*) dieciochoavo *m;* (*part*) decimoctava parte *f; s. a.* **eighth**

**eighth** [eɪtθ] I. *adj* octavo, -a; ~ **note** corchea *f* II. *n* **1.** (*order*) octavo, -a *m, f* **2.** (*date*) ocho *m;* **the ~** el día ocho; **the ~ of December** el ocho de diciembre **3.** (*fraction*) octavo *m;* (*part*) octava parte *f* III. *adv* (*in lists*) octavo

**eightieth** [ˈeɪˈtɪ·əθ] I. *adj* octogésimo, -a II. *n* (*order*) octogésimo, -a *m, f;* (*fraction*) octogésimo *m;* (*part*) octogésima parte *f; s. a.* **eighth**

**eighty** [ˈeɪˈti] I. *adj* ochenta *inv;* **he is ~ (years old)** tiene ochenta años II. *n* <-ies> **1.** (*number*) ochenta *m* **2.** (*decade*) **the eighties** los (años) ochenta

**either** [ˈiˈðər] I. *adj* **1.** (*one of two*) ~ **way** de una manera u otra; **I don't like ~ one** no me gusta ninguno de los dos **2.** (*each*) cada; **on ~ side of the river** a cada lado del río *m* II. *pron* cualquiera (de los dos); **which one?** — ~ ¿cuál? — cualquiera III. *adv* tampoco IV. *conj* ~ ... **or** ... o ... o ...

**ejaculate** [ɪˈdʒæk·jʊ·leɪt] I. *vt* (*semen*) eyacular II. *vi* ANAT eyacular

**ejaculation** [ɪˈdʒæk·jʊ·ˈleɪ·ʃən] *n* (*of semen*) eyaculación *f*

**eject** [ɪˈdʒekt] I. *vt* echar, expulsar; (*liquid, gas*) expeler II. *vi* eyectarse

**eke out** [ˈikˌaʊt] *vt* to ~ **a living** ganarse la vida a duras penas

**EKG** [ˌiˈkeɪˈdʒi] *n abbr of* **electrocardiogram** electrocardiograma *m,* electro *m*

**elaborate¹** [ɪˈlæb·ər·ət] *adj* (*complicated*) complicado, -a; (*very detailed: excuse*) rebuscado, -a; (*meal*) de muchos platos

**elaborate²** [ɪˈlæb·ə·reɪt] I. *vt* elaborar II. *vi* entrar en detalles

**elaboration** [ɪˌlæb·ə·ˈreɪ·ʃən] <-(s)> *n* **1.** (*of texts*) explicación *f* **2.** (*complexity*) complicación *f*

**elapse** [ɪˈlæps] *vi form* transcurrir

**elastic** [ɪˈlæs·tɪk] I. *adj* elástico, -a II. *n* (*material*) elástico *m*

**elasticity** [ˌeˈlæ·ˈstɪs·ə·ti] *n a. fig* elasticidad *f*

**elate** [ɪˈleɪt] *vt* regocijar

**elated** *adj* eufórico, -a

**elbow** [ˈel·bou] I. *n* (*of people*) codo *m;* (*of animals*) codillo *m* II. *vt* dar un codazo a

**elbow grease** *n inf* fuerza *f;* **to put some ~ into sth** poner empeño en algo

**elbow room** *n* (*space*) espacio *m*

**elder¹** [ˈel·dər] I. *n* (*senior person*) anciano, -a *m, f* II. *adj* mayor

**elder²** [ˈel·dər] *n* BOT saúco *m*

**elderly** [ˈel·dər·li] I. *adj* anciano, -a II. *n* **the ~** los ancianos

**eldest** [ˈel·dɪst] *adj superl of* **old** mayor; **her ~ (child)** su hijo mayor

**elect** [ɪˈlekt] I. *vt* (*by vote or otherwise*) elegir II. *adj* **the president ~** el presidente *m* electo, la presidenta *f* electa

**election** [ɪˈlek·ʃən] *n* **1.** (*event*) elecciones *fpl* **2.** (*action*) elección *f*

**election campaign** *n* campaña *f* electoral

**election defeat** *n* derrota *f* electoral

**electioneering** [ɪˌlek·ʃə·ˈnɪr·ɪŋ] *n* campaña *f* electoral; *pej* promesas *f pl* electoralistas

**election speech** *n* discurso *m* electoral

**elective** [ɪˈlek·tɪv] I. *adj* (*optional*) optativo, -a II. *n* SCHOOL, UNIV optativa *f*

**electoral** [ɪˈlek·tər·əl] *adj* electoral *m*

**electorate** [ɪˈlek·tər·ət] *n* electorado *m*

**electric** [ɪˈlek·trɪk] *adj* ELEC eléctrico, -a; (*fence*) electrificado, -a; ~ **shock** descarga *f* eléctrica

**electrical** [ɪˈlek·trɪ·kəl] *adj* eléctrico, -a; ~ **tape** cinta *f* aislante

**electrician** [ɪˌlek·ˈtrɪʃ·ən] *n* electricista *mf*

**electricity** [ɪˌlek·ˈtrɪs·ə·ti] *n* electricidad *f*

**electrocute** [ɪˈlek·trə·kjut] *vt* electrocutar

**electrocution** [ɪˌlek·trə·ˈkju·ʃən] *n* electrocución *f*

**electrode** [ɪˈlek·troʊd] *n* electrodo *m*

**electrolysis** [ɪˌlek·ˈtral·ə·sɪs] *n* electrólisis *f*

**electromagnet** [ɪˈlek·troʊ·ˈmæg·nɪt] *n* electroimán *m*

**electromagnetic** [ɪˌlek·troʊ·mæg·ˈnet·ɪk] *adj* electromagnético, -a

**electron** [ɪˈlek·tran] *n* electrón *m*

**electronic** [ɪˌlek·ˈtran·ɪk] *adj* electrónico, -a

**electronics** [ɪˌlek·ˈtran·ɪks] *n + sing vb* electrónica *f*

**electron microscope** *n* microscopio *m* electrónico

**elegance** [ˈel·ɪ·gəns] *n* elegancia *f*

**elegant** [ˈel·ɪ·gənt] *adj* elegante

**elegy** [ˈel·ə·dʒi] *n* elegía *f*

**element** [ˈel·ə·mənt] *n* **1.** *a.* CHEM, MATH elemento *m* **2.** (*factor*) factor *m* **3.** ELEC resistencia *f*

**elemental** [ˌel·ə·ˈmen·təl] *adj* elemental; (*feelings, needs*) primario, -a

**elementary** [ˌel·ə·ˈmen·tə·ri] *adj* elemental; (*course*) básico, -a

**elementary school** *n* escuela *f* (de enseñanza) primaria

**elephant** [ˈel·ə·fənt] *n* elefante *m*

**elevate** [ˈel·ə·veɪt] *vt* (*raise*) elevar; (*prices*) aumentar

**elevated** [ˈel·ə·veɪ·tɪd] *adj* **1.** (*raised*) elevado, -a **2.** (*position*) importante

**elevation** [ˌel·ɪ·ˈveɪ·ʃən] *n* **1.** GEO elevación *f* (del terreno) **2.** ARCHIT alzado *m*

**elevator** [ˈel·ə·veɪ·tər] *n* (*for people*) ascensor *m*, elevador *m* AmL; (*for goods*) montacargas *m inv*

**eleven** [ɪˈlev·ən] **I.** *adj* once **II.** *n* once *m; s. a.* **eight**

**eleventh** [ɪˈlev·ənθ] **I.** *adj* undécimo, -a **II.** *n* **1.** (*order*) undécimo, -a *m, f* **2.** (*date*) once *m* **3.** (*fraction*) onceavo *m;* (*part*) onceava parte *f; s. a.* **eighth**

**eligible** [ˈel·ɪ·dʒə·bəl] *adj* **1.** elegible; ~ **to vote** con derecho a voto **2.** (*desirable*) deseable; **to be ~ for the job** reunir los requisitos necesarios para el puesto

**eliminate** [ɪˈlɪm·ɪ·neɪt] *vt* **1.** (*eradicate*) eliminar **2.** (*exclude from consideration*) descartar

**El Salvador** *n* El Salvador *m*

**else** [els] *adv* **1.** (*in addition*) más; **anyone/anything ~** cualquier otra persona/cosa; **anywhere ~** en cualquier otro lugar; **anyone ~?** ¿alguien más?; **anything ~?** ¿algo más?; **everybody ~** (todos) los demás; **everything ~** todo lo demás; **someone/something ~** otra persona/cosa; **it's something ~!** ¡es algo fuera de serie!; **how ~?** ¿de qué otra forma?; **what/who ~?** ¿qué/quién más? **2.** (*otherwise*) **or ~** si no; **come here or ~!** ¡ven, o ya verás!

**elsewhere** [ˈels·wer] *adv* en otro sitio

**e-mail** [ˈi·meɪl] **I.** *n abbr of* **electronic mail** (mensaje de) correo *m* electrónico, e-mail *m* **II.** *vt* mandar por correo electrónico

**e-mail address** *n* dirección *f* de correo electrónico

**embark** [em·ˈbark] *vi* embarcar(se)

**embarrass** [em·ˈbær·əs] *vt* (*make feel uncomfortable*) avergonzar

**embarrassed** *adj* avergonzado, -a; **to be ~** pasar vergüenza

**embarrassing** *adj* embarazoso, -a, penoso, -a *Méx, Col, Pan, Ven, CRi*

**embarrassment** [em·ˈbær·əs·ment] *n* (*shame*) vergüenza *f*, pena *f Méx, Col, Pan, Ven, CRi*

**embassy** [ˈem·bə·si] <-ies> *n* embajada *f*

**embed** [em·ˈbed] <-dd-> *vt* (*fix*) hincar; (*in rock*) incrustar; (*in memory*) grabar

**embers** [ˈem·bərz] *npl* ascuas *fpl*

**emblem** [ˈem·bləm] *n* emblema *m*

**embody** [em·ˈbad·i] <-ied> *vt* **1.** (*personify*) personificar **2.** (*include*) incorporar

**embolism** ['em·bə·lɪz·əm] n MED embolia f

**embrace** [em·'breɪs] I. vt (hug) abrazar II. vi abrazarse III. n abrazo m

**embroider** [em·'brɔɪ·dər] I. vi bordar II. vt bordar; fig adornar

**embroidery** [em·'brɔɪ·də·ri] n bordado m; ~ **frame** bastidor m

**embryo** ['em·bri·oʊ] n embrión m

**emerald** ['em·ər·əld] I. n esmeralda f II. adj de esmeraldas; (color) esmeralda

**emerge** [ɪ·'mɜrdʒ] vi (come out) salir; (ideas) surgir

**emergency** [ɪ·'mɜr·dʒən·si] I. <-ies> n 1. (dangerous situation) emergencia f; **in an** [or **in case of**] ~ en caso de emergencia; MED urgencia f; ~ **room** sala f de urgencias 3. POL crisis f inv; **national** ~ crisis nacional; **to declare a state of** ~ declarar el estado de excepción II. adj (exit) de emergencia; (services) de urgencia; (brake) de mano; (landing) forzoso, -a; (rations) de reserva; ~ **exit** salida de emergencia; ~ **landing** aterrizaje forzoso

**emerging** adj emergente

**emery board** n lima f de uñas (de esmeril)

**emigrant** ['em·ɪ·grənt] n emigrante mf

**emigrate** ['em·ɪ·greɪt] vi emigrar

**emigration** [ˌem·ɪ·'greɪ·ʃən] n emigración f

**eminent** ['em·ɪ·nənt] adj eminente

**emission** [ɪ·'mɪʃ·ən] n emisión f

**emit** [ɪ·'mɪt] <-tt-> vt (radiation, light) emitir; (smoke) echar

**emoticon** n COMPUT emoticón m

**emotion** [ɪ·'moʊ·ʃən] n 1. (feeling) sentimiento m 2. (affective state) emoción f

**emotional** [ɪ·'moʊ·ʃə·nəl] adj 1. (relating to the emotions) emocional; (involvement, link) afectivo, -a 2. (moving) conmovedor(a) 3. (governed by emotion) emocionado, -a; **to get** ~ emocionarse

**emotionless** adj impasible

**emotive** [ɪ·'moʊ·t̬ɪv] adj emotivo, -a

**empathy** ['em·pə·θi] n empatía f

**emperor** ['em·pər·ər] n emperador m

**emphasis** ['em·fə·sɪs] <emphases> n 1. (importance) énfasis m inv 2. LING

acento m

**emphasize** ['em·fə·saɪz] vt 1. (insist on) poner énfasis en, enfatizar AmL; (fact) hacer hincapié en 2. LING acentuar

**emphatic** [em·'fæt̬·ɪk] adj (forcibly expressive) enfático, -a; (strong) enérgico, -a; **to be** ~ **about sth** hacer hincapié en algo

**empire** ['em·paɪr] n imperio m

**employ** [em·'plɔɪ] vt 1. (give a job to) emplear; **to** ~ **sb to do sth** contratar a alguien para hacer algo 2. (put to use) utilizar

**employee** ['em·plɔɪ·i] n empleado, -a m, f

**employer** [em·'plɔɪ·ər] n empresario, -a m, f

**employment** [em·'plɔɪ·mənt] n (of a person) empleo m

**empower** [em·'paʊ·ər] vt **to** ~ **sb to do sth** (give ability to) capacitar a alguien para hacer algo; (authorize) autorizar a alguien a hacer algo

**empress** ['em·prɪs] n emperatriz f

**emptiness** ['emp·tɪ·nɪs] n vacío m; fig vacuidad f elev

**empty** ['emp·ti] I. <-ier, -iest> adj 1. (with nothing inside) vacío, -a; (truck, ship, train) sin carga; (house) desocupado, -a 2. (threat) vano, -a II. <-ie-> vt (pour) verter; (deprive of contents) vaciar III. <-ie-> vi vaciarse; (river) desembocar

**empty-handed** [ˌemp·ti·'hæn·dɪd] adj con las manos vacías

**emu** ['i·mju] n emú m

**emulate** ['em·jʊ·leɪt] vt emular

**emulsion** [ɪ·'mʌl·ʃən] n 1. a. PHOT emulsión f 2. (paint) pintura f emulsionada

**enable** [ɪ·'neɪ·bəl] vt 1. **to** ~ **sb to do sth** permitir a alguien que haga algo 2. COMPUT activar

**encase** [en·'keɪs] vt encerrar

**enchant** [en·'tʃænt] vt 1. (charm) encantar 2. (bewitch) hechizar

**enchanting** adj encantador(a)

**encircle** [en·'sɜr·kəl] vt rodear

**enclose** [en·'kloʊz] vt 1. (surround) cercar; (field) rodear; **to** ~ **sth in brackets** poner algo entre paréntesis 2. (include) adjuntar, adosar AmL

**enclosed** [en·'kloʊzd] adj 1. (confined)

cerrado, -a; (*garden*) vallado, -a **2.** (*included*) adjunto, -a

**enclosure** [en·'klou·ʒər] *n* **1.** (*enclosed area*) recinto *m*; (*for animals*) corral *m* **2.** (*letter*) documento *m* adjunto

**encode** [en·'koud] *vt a.* COMPUT codificar; LING cifrar

**encompass** [en·'kʌm·pəs] *vt* **1.** (*surround*) rodear **2.** (*include*) abarcar

**encore** ['an·kɔr] **I.** *n* repetición *f*; **as** [*or* **for**] **an** ~ como bis **II.** *interj* otra

**encounter** [en·'kaun·tər] **I.** *vt* encontrar **II.** *n* encuentro *m*; **a close** ~ avistamiento *m*

**encourage** [en·'kɜr·ɪdʒ] *vt* **1.** (*give confidence*) alentar; (*give hope*) animar a alguien a hacer algo **2.** (*support*) fomentar

**encouragement** [en·'kɜr·ɪdʒ·mənt] *n* estímulo *m*; **to give** ~ **to sb** animar a alguien

**encouraging** *adj* alentador(a)

**encyclopedia** [en·,saɪ·klə·'pi·di·ə] *n* enciclopedia *f*

**end** [end] **I.** *n* **1.** (*finish*) fin *m* **2.** (*extremity*) extremo *m* **3.** (*boundary*) límite *m* **4.** (*stop*) fin *m* **5.** ~**s** (*goal*) fin *m*; (*purpose*) intención *f* **6.** (*phone line*) **who is on the other** ~? ¿quién está al otro lado de la línea? **7.** (*death*) muerte *f*; **he is nearing his** ~ está a punto de morir **8.** (*obligation*) **to uphold one's** ~ **of the deal** [*or* **bargain**] cumplir su parte del trato **9.** SPORTS lado *m* **10.** COMPUT tecla *f* de fin ► ~ **of story** punto y final, se acabó; **to be at the** ~ **of one's rope** no poder más; **it's not the** ~ **of the world** no es el fin del mundo; **to go off the deep** ~ *inf* subirse por las paredes; **to make** ~**s meet** llegar a fin de mes; **to put an** ~ **to oneself** [*or* **it all**] acabar con su vida; **in the** ~ a fin de cuentas **II.** *vt* **1.** (*finish*) acabar **2.** (*bring to a stop: reign, war*) poner fin a **III.** *vi* acabar; **to** ~ **in sth** terminar en algo

♦**end up** *vi* terminar; **to** ~ **in prison** acabar en la cárcel; **to** ~ **doing sth** terminar haciendo algo

**endanger** [en·'deɪn·dʒər] *vt* poner en peligro; **an** ~**ed species** una especie en

peligro de extinción

**endeavor** [en·'dev·ər] **I.** *vi* **to** ~ **to do sth** esforzarse por hacer algo **II.** *n* esfuerzo *m*

**ending** ['en·dɪŋ] *n* fin *m*; LING terminación *f*

**endive** ['en·daɪv] *n* CULIN endibia *f*

**endless** ['end·lɪs] *adj* interminable, inacabable

**endorse** [en·'dɔrs] *vt* **1.** (*declare approval for*) aprobar; (*product*) promocionar; (*candidate*) respaldar, apoyar **2.** FIN endosar

**endorsement** *n* **1.** (*support: of a plan*) aprobación *f*; (*of a candidate*) respaldo, apoyo *m*; (*recommendation*) recomendación *f* **2.** FIN endoso *m*

**endowment** *n* **1.** FIN dotación *f* **2.** (*talent*) talento *m*

**endurance** [en·'dur·əns] *n* resistencia *f*

**endure** [en·'dur] **I.** *vt* **1.** (*tolerate*) soportar, aguantar **2.** (*suffer*) resistir **II.** *vi form* durar

**ENE** *abbr of* **east-northeast** ENE

**enema** ['en·ə·mə] <-s *or* enemata> *n* enema *m*

**enemy** ['en·ə·mi] **I.** *n* enemigo, -a *m, f* **II.** *adj* enemigo, -a

**energetic** [,en·ər·'dʒet̬·ɪk] *adj* enérgico, -a; (*active*) activo, -a

**energy** ['en·ər·dʒi] <-ies> *n* energía *f*; **to have the** ~ **to do sth** tener energías para hacer algo

**energy crisis** *n* crisis *f inv* energética

**energy resources** *npl* fuentes *f pl* energéticas [*or* de energía]

**energy-saving** *adj* que ahorra energía

**enforce** [en·'fɔrs] *vt* aplicar; (*law*) hacer cumplir

**enforcement** [en·'fɔrs·mənt] *n* (*of a law*) aplicación *f*; (*of a regulation*) ejecución *f*

**engage** [en·'geɪdʒ] **I.** *vt* **1.** *form* (*hold interest*) atraer **2.** (*put into use*) activar **3.** TECH (*cogs*) engranar; **to** ~ **the clutch** embragar, enclochar *Col, Méx* **4.** MIL (*the enemy*) entablar combate con **II.** *vi* MIL trabar [*or* librar] batalla

**engaged** *adj* **1.** (*to be married*) prometido, -a; **to get** ~ (**to sb**) prometerse (con alguien) **2.** (*occupied*) ocupado, -a

**engagement** [en·'geɪdʒ·mənt] *n* 1. (*appointment*) compromiso *m* 2. (*marriage*) compromiso *m* 3. MIL combate *m*

**engagement ring** *n* anillo *m* de compromiso

**engaging** *adj* atractivo, -a

**engine** ['en·dʒɪn] *n* 1. (*motor*) motor *m;* **diesel/gasoline** ~ motor diesel/de gasolina; **jet** ~ motor a reacción 2. RAIL máquina *f*

**engineer** [,en·dʒɪ·'nɪr] I. *n* 1. (*with a degree*) ingeniero, -a *m, f;* **civil** ~ ingeniero de caminos 2. (*technician*) técnico, -a *m, f* 3. RAIL maquinista *mf* II. *vt* construir; *fig* maquinar

**engineering** [,en·dʒɪ·'nɪr·ɪŋ] *n* ingeniería *f*

**England** ['ɪŋ·glənd] *n* Inglaterra *f*

**English** ['ɪŋ·glɪʃ] I. *n inv* 1. (*language*) inglés *m* 2. *pl* (*people*) ~ los ingleses II. *adj* inglés, -esa; **a movie in** ~ una película en inglés; **an** ~ **class** una clase de inglés

**English Channel** *n* Canal *m* de la Mancha

**English muffin** *n* bollo de pan que se corta en dos y se toma tostado y untado en mantequilla

**English speaker** *n* persona *f* de habla inglesa

**English-speaking** *adj* de habla inglesa

**enjoy** [en·'dʒɔɪ] I. *vt* 1. (*get pleasure from*) disfrutar de; ~ **yourselves!** ¡que lo paséis bien! 2. (*have: health*) poseer; **to** ~ **good health** gozar de buena salud II. *vi* pasarlo bien

**enjoyable** [en·'dʒɔɪ·ə·bəl] *adj* agradable; (*film, book, play*) divertido, -a

**enjoyment** [en·'dʒɔɪ·mənt] *n* disfrute *m*

**enlarge** [en·'lardʒ] *vt* 1. (*make bigger*) agrandar 2. PHOT ampliar

**enlargement** *n* aumento *m;* PHOT ampliación *f*

**enlightenment** [en·'laɪ·tən·mənt] *n* 1. REL iluminación *f* 2. PHILOS **the** (**Age of**) **Enlightenment** el Siglo de las Luces 3. (*explanation*) aclaración *f*

**enlist** [en·'lɪst] I. *vi* MIL alistarse II. *vt* MIL alistar, reclutar

**enormous** [ɪ·'nɔr·məs] *adj* enorme; ~ **difficulties** grandes dificultades *fpl*

**enough** [ɪ·'nʌf] I. *adj* (*sufficient*) suficiente, bastante II. *adv* bastante; **to have seen** ~ haber visto demasiado; **she was kind** [*or* **friendly**] ~ **to help me** tuvo la amabilidad de ayudarme; **oddly** [*or* **strangely**] ~ por extraño que parezca III. *interj* basta IV. *pron* bastante; **more than** ~ más que suficiente; **to have had** ~ (**of sb/sth**) estar harto (de alguien/algo); **as if that weren't** ~ por si fuera poco; **that's** (**quite**) ~! ¡basta ya!; ~ **is** ~ basta y sobra

**enquire** [en·'kwaɪr] *vi, vt see* **inquire**

**enquiry** [en·'kwaɪr·i] <-ies> *n* 1. (*question*) pregunta *f* 2. (*investigation*) investigación *f;* **an** ~ **into sth** una investigación sobre algo

**enraged** [en·'reɪdʒd] *adj* enfurecido, -a

**enrich** [en·'rɪtʃ] *vt* enriquecer

**enroll** <-ll-> *vt*, **enrol** [en·'roʊl] I. *vi* inscribirse; **to** ~ **for/in a course** matricularse para/en un curso II. *vt* inscribir; (*in a course*) matricular

**enrol(l)ment** [en·'roʊl·mənt] *n* inscripción *f;* (*in a course*) matriculación *f*

**en route** [,an·'rut] *adv* en el camino

**ensuing** *adj* siguiente

**en suite bathroom** [,an·swit·'bæθ·rum] *n* baño *m* incorporado

**ensure** [en·'ʃʊr] *vt* asegurar; (*guarantee*) garantizar

**entail** [en·'teɪl] *vt* 1. (*involve*) acarrear 2. (*necessitate*) **to** ~ **doing sth** implicar hacer algo

**entangle** [en·'tæŋ·gəl] *vt* enredar

**enter** ['en·tər] I. *vt* 1. (*go into*) entrar en 2. (*insert*) introducir; (*into a register*) inscribir; COMPUT **to** ~ **data** introducir datos 3. (*compete in*) inscribirse en; **to** ~ **a competition** presentarse a un concurso 4. (*begin*) entrar en; **to** ~ **politics** meterse en el mundo de la política 5. (*make known*) anotar; (*claim*) presentar; (*plea*) formular II. *vi* THEAT entrar

**enter key** *n* COMPUT tecla *f* intro

**enterprise** ['en·tər·praɪz] *n* 1. (*business firm*) empresa *f* 2. (*initiative*) iniciativa *f*

**enterprising** *adj* emprendedor(a)

**entertain** [,en·tər·'teɪn] I. *vt* 1. (*amuse*) entretener 2. (*guests*) recibir 3. (*con-*

sider) considerar **II.** vi (*invite guests*) recibir en casa

**entertaining** adj entretenido, -a; (*person*) divertido, -a

**entertainment** [ˌen·tər·ˈteɪn·mənt] n **1.** (*amusement*) diversión f **2.** (*show*) espectáculo m

**enthusiasm** [en·ˈθu·zɪ·æz·əm] n entusiasmo m; ~ **for sth** entusiasmo por algo

**enthusiastic** [en·ˌθu·zɪ·ˈæs·tɪk] adj entusiasta; **to be ~ about sth** estar entusiasmado con algo

**enticement** n tentación f

**enticing** adj tentador(a); (*smile*) atractivo, -a

**entire** [en·ˈtaɪr] adj **1.** (*whole: life*) todo, -a; **the ~ day** todo el día; **the ~ world** el mundo entero **2.** (*total: commitment, devotion*) total **3.** (*complete*) entero, -a

**entirely** adv enteramente; **she's/he's ~ to blame** la culpa es entera suya; **to agree ~** estar completamente de acuerdo; **to disagree ~** estar del todo en desacuerdo

**entirety** [en·ˈtaɪ·rə·ti] n **in its ~** en su totalidad

**entitle** [en·ˈtaɪ·t̬əl] vt **1.** (*give right*) autorizar; **to ~ sb to a holiday** dar a alguien derecho a vacaciones **2.** (*book*) titular

**entitled** adj **1.** (*person*) autorizado, -a **2.** (*book*) titulado, -a

**entity** [ˈen·t̬ə·ti] <-ies> n form entidad f; **legal ~** persona f jurídica

**entrance**[1] [ˈen·trəns] n (*act of entering; way in*) entrada f

**entrance**[2] [en·ˈtræns] vt (*cast spell*) encantar

**entrance fee** n cuota f de entrada [*or* de inscripción]

**entrance hall** n vestíbulo m

**entrance requirement** n requisito m de entrada

**entrant** [ˈen·trənt] n participante mf

**entrée** [ˈan·treɪ] n plato m principal [*or* fuerte], principio m Col

**entrepreneur** [ˌan·trə·prə·ˈnɜr] n empresario, -a m, f

**entrust** [en·ˈtrʌst] vt confiar; **to ~ sth to sb** [*or* **to ~ sb with sth**] confiar algo a alguien

**entry** [ˈen·tri] <-ies> n **1.** (*act of entering*) entrada f; (*joining an organization*) ingreso m **2.** (*right to enter*) acceso m; **to refuse sb ~** negar el acceso a alguien **3.** (*in dictionary*) entrada f

**entry fee** n cuota f de entrada

**entry-level job** n empleo m raso (*empleo en el nivel más bajo de la jerarquía de una empresa*)

**enunciate** [ɪ·ˈnʌn·si·eɪt] vt **1.** (*sound*) pronunciar, articular **2.** (*theory*) enunciar

**envelop** [en·ˈvel·əp] vt envolver

**envelope** [ˈen·və·loʊp] n sobre m, cierro m Chile

**enviable** [ˈen·vi·ə·bəl] adj envidiable

**envious** [ˈen·vi·əs] adj envidioso, -a; **to be ~ of sb/sth** tener envidia de alguien/algo

**environment** [en·ˈvaɪ·ərn·mənt] n entorno m; **the ~** ECOL el medio ambiente; **working ~** ambiente m de trabajo

**environmental** [en·ˌvaɪ·ərn·ˈmen·təl] adj ambiental; ECOL medioambiental; **~ damage** daños m pl ecológicos

**environs** [en·ˈvaɪ·rənz] npl form alrededores mpl

**envoy** [ˈan·vɔɪ] n enviado, -a m, f

**envy** [ˈen·vi] **I.** n envidia f ▶ **to be green with ~** reconcomerse de envidia **II.** <-ie-> vt envidiar

**enzyme** [ˈen·zaɪm] n enzima f

**epic** [ˈep·ɪk] **I.** n epopeya f **II.** adj épico, -a; **~ poetry** poesía épica

**epicenter** [ˈep·ɪ·sen·tər] n epicentro m

**epilog** [ˈep·ɪ·lag] n epílogo m

**episode** [ˈep·ɪ·soʊd] n episodio m

**epitome** [ɪ·ˈpɪt̬·ə·mi] n **1.** (*embodiment*) personificación f **2.** (*example*) arquetipo m; **the ~ of poor taste** el colmo del mal gusto

**equal** [ˈi·kwəl] **I.** adj (*the same*) igual; (*treatment*) equitativo, -a; **on ~ terms** en igualdad de condiciones **II.** n igual mf **III.** vt **1.** MATH ser igual a **2.** (*match*) igualar

**equality** [ɪ·ˈkwal·ə·ti] n igualdad f

**equalize** [ˈi·kwə·laɪz] vt nivelar

**equalizer** [ˈi·kwə·laɪ·zər] n **1.** MUS ecualizador m **2.** (*in soccer*) gol m del empate

E

**equally** ['i·kwə·li] *adv* igualmente

**equal opportunity** *n* igualdad *f* de oportunidades

**equal(s) sign** *n* MATH signo *m* de igual

**equate** [ɪ·'kweɪt] *vt* equiparar

**equation** [ɪ·'kweɪ·ʒən] *n* ecuación *f*

**equator** [ɪ·'kweɪ·tər] *n* ecuador *m*

**equatorial** [,ek·wə·'tɔr·i·əl] *adj* ecuatorial

**equidistant** [,i·kwɪ·'dɪs·tənt] *adj* equidistante

**equilateral** [,i·kwɪ·'læt·ər·əl] *adj* MATH equilátero, -a

**equip** [ɪ·'kwɪp] <-pp-> *vt* **1.** (*fit out*) equipar; **to ~ sth/sb with sth** proveer algo/a alguien de algo **2.** (*prepare*) preparar

**equipment** [ɪ·'kwɪp·mənt] *n* equipo *m*; **camping ~** accesorios *m pl* de cámping

**equitable** ['ek·wɪ·tə·bəl] *adj* equitativo, -a

**equivalence** [ɪ·'kwɪv·ə·ləns] *n* equivalencia *f*

**equivalent** [ɪ·'kwɪv·ə·lənt] **I.** *adj* equivalente; **to be ~ to sth** equivaler a algo **II.** *n* equivalente *m*

**ESE** *n abbr of* **east-southeast** ESE *m*

**era** ['ɪr·ə] *n* era *f*

**eradicate** [ɪ·'ræd·ɪ·keɪt] *vt* erradicar

**erase** [ɪ·'reɪs] *vt a.* COMPUT borrar; **to ~ a deficit** eliminar un déficit

**eraser** [ɪ·'reɪ·sər] *n* goma *f* de borrar

**erect** [ɪ·'rekt] **I.** *adj* erguido, -a; ANAT erecto, -a **II.** *vt* erigir; (*construct*) construir

**erode** [ɪ·'roʊd] **I.** *vt* erosionar **II.** *vi* erosionarse

**erosion** [ɪ·'roʊ·ʒən] *n* erosión *f*

**erotic** [ɪ·'rɑt·ɪk] *adj* erótico, -a

**err** [ɜr] *vi* errar; **to ~ on the side of sth** pecar (por exceso) de algo ► **to ~ is human** *prov* errar es humano *prov*

**errand** ['er·ənd] *n* recado *m*; **to run an ~** (salir a) hacer un recado

**erratic** [ɪ·'ræt·ɪk] *adj* **1.** (*inconsistent: heartbeat*) irregular; (*behavior*) imprevisible **2.** (*course*) errático, -a

**erroneous** [ɪ·'roʊ·ni·əs] *adj* erróneo, -a; **~ assumption** suposición equivocada

**error** ['er·ər] *n* error *m*; **to do sth in ~** hacer algo por equivocación; **human ~** error humano

**error message** *n* COMPUT mensaje *m* de error

**erupt** [ɪ·'rʌpt] *vi* **1.** (*explode: volcano*) entrar en erupción; *fig* estallar **2.** MED salir

**eruption** [ɪ·'rʌp·ʃən] *n* erupción *f*; *fig* estallido *m*

**escalate** ['es·kə·leɪt] **I.** *vi* (*increase*) aumentar; (*incidents*) intensificarse **II.** *vt* intensificar

**escalator** ['es·kə·leɪ·tər] *n* escalera *f* mecánica

**escapade** [,es·kə·'peɪd] *n* aventura *f*; (*mischievous*) travesura *f*

**escape** [ɪ·'skeɪp] **I.** *vi* escaparse; (*person*) huir de; **to ~ from** escaparse de; **to ~ from a program** COMPUT salir de un programa **II.** *vt* escapar a; (*avoid*) evitar; **to ~ sb('s attention)** pasar desapercibido a alguien **III.** *n* **1.** (*act*) fuga *f* **2.** (*outflow*) escape *m*

**escort** ['es·kɔrt] **I.** *vt* acompañar; (*politician*) escoltar **II.** *n* **1.** (*companion*) acompañante *mf* **2.** (*paid companion*) chico, -a *m, f* de compañía **3.** (*guard*) escolta *f*

**ESOL** ['i·sal] *n abbr of* **English for speakers of other languages** inglés *m* para extranjeros

**esophagus** [ɪ·'saf·ə·gəs] *n* esófago *m*

**ESP** [,i·es·'pi] *n abbr of* **extrasensory perception** percepción *f* extrasensorial

**especially** [ɪ·'speʃ·ə·li] *adv* **1.** (*particularly*) especialmente **2.** (*in particular*) en particular

**espionage** ['es·pi·ə·naʒ] *n* espionaje *m*; **industrial ~** espionaje industrial

**espresso** [ɪ·'spres·oʊ] <-s> *n* café *m* exprés

**essay¹** ['es·eɪ] *n* **1.** LIT ensayo *m* **2.** SCHOOL redacción *f*

**essay²** [e·'seɪ] *vt* **1.** (*try*) intentar hacer **2.** (*test*) probar

**essence** ['es·əns] *n* **1.** esencia *f* **2.** (*in food*) esencia *f*, extracto *m*

**essential** [ɪ·'sen·ʃəl] **I.** *adj* esencial; (*difference*) fundamental **II.** *n* **the ~s** los elementos básicos [*or* esenciales]

**essentially** [ɪ·'sen·ʃə·li] *adv* esencialmente

**essential oil** *n* aceite *m* esencial

**establish** [ɪ·'stæb·lɪʃ] **I.** *vt* **1.** (*found*)

fundar; (*commission, hospital*) crear; (*dictatorship*) instaurar 2. (*set: precedent*) sentar; (*priorities, norm*) establecer; **to ~ a reputation as a pianist** hacerse un nombre como pianista 3. (*determine*) determinar, establecer; (*facts*) verificar; (*truth*) comprobar; **to ~ whether/where...** determinar si/dónde... 4. ADMIN **to ~ residence** fijar la residencia II. *vi* establecerse

**established** [ɪ·'stæb·lɪʃt] *adj* 1. (*founded*) fundado, -a 2. (*fact*) comprobado, -a; (*procedures*) establecido, -a

**establishment** [ɪ·'stæb·lɪʃ·mənt] *n* 1. (*business*) empresa *f;* **family ~** empresa *f* familiar 2. (*organization*) establecimiento *m;* **educational ~** centro *m* educativo; **financial ~** institución *f* financiera; **the Establishment** POL la clase dirigente

**estate** [ɪ·'steɪt] *n* 1. (*piece of land*) finca *f;* **country ~** finca *f,* hacienda *f AmL* 2. LAW (*possessions after death*) patrimonio *m*

**esteemed** *adj* apreciado, -a, valorado, -a; **highly ~** muy apreciado

**esthetics** *n* estética *f*

**estimate**[1] ['es·tɪ·meɪt] *vt* calcular; **to ~ that...** calcular que...

**estimate**[2] ['es·tɪ·mɪt] *n* cálculo *m* (aproximado); **a rough ~** *inf* un cálculo aproximado

**estimated** ['es·tɪ·meɪ·tɪd] *adj* estimado, -a

**estimation** [,es·tɪ·'meɪ·ʃən] *n* opinión *f;* **in my ~** a mi juicio

**Estonia** [es·'tou·ni·ə] *n* Estonia *f*

**Estonian** [es·'tou·ni·ən] I. *adj* estonio, -a II. *n* 1. (*person*) estonio, -a *m, f* 2. LING estonio *m*

**estranged** *adj* (*distance*) distanciado, -a; (*state*) separado, -a

**estrogen** ['es·trə·dʒən] *n* estrógeno *m*

**estuary** ['es·tʃu·er·i] <-ies> *n* estuario *m*

**etc.** *abbr of* **et cetera** etc.

**etch** [etʃ] *vt* grabar (al agua fuerte)

**ETD** *abbr of* **estimated time of departure** hora *f* prevista de salida

**eternal** [ɪ·'tɜr·nəl] *adj* 1. (*lasting forever: life*) eterno, -a 2. (*constant: complaints*) constante, incesante

**eternally** [ɪ·'tɜr·nə·li] *adv* 1. (*forever*) eternamente 2. (*constantly*) constantemente, incesantemente

**eternity** [ɪ·'tɜr·nə·ti] *n* eternidad *f*

**ethical** *adj* ético, -a

**ethics** *n* + *sing vb* ética *f*

**ethnic** ['eθ·nɪk] *adj* étnico, -a; **~ cleansing** limpieza étnica

**ethos** ['i·θas] *n* espíritu *m;* **the working-class ~** los valores de la clase trabajadora

**etiquette** ['et·ɪ·kɪt] *n* etiqueta *f*

**EU** [i·'ju] *n abbr of* **European Union** UE *f*

**Eucharist** ['ju·kər·ɪst] *n* REL **the ~** la Eucaristía

**eulogy** ['ju·lə·dʒi] <-ies> *n form* 1. (*high praise*) elogio *m* 2. LIT panegírico *m*

**euphemism** ['ju·fə·mɪz·əm] *n* eufemismo *m*

**EUR** *n abbr of* **Euro** EUR *m*

**euro** ['jur·ou] *n* euro *m*

**Europe** ['jur·əp] *n* Europa *f*

**European** [jur·ə·'pi·ən] I. *adj* europeo, -a II. *n* europeo, -a *m, f*

**European Union** *n* Unión *f* Europea

**evacuate** [ɪ·'væk·ju·eɪt] *vt* (*people*) evacuar; (*building*) desocupar

**evacuation** [ɪ·,væk·ju·'eɪ·ʃən] *n* evacuación *f;* **~ of the bowels** MED evacuación *f*

**evacuee** [ɪ·,væk·ju·'i] *n* evacuado, -a *m, f*

**evade** [ɪ·'veɪd] *vt* (*responsibility, person*) eludir; (*police*) escaparse de; (*taxes*) evadir

**evaluate** [ɪ·'væl·ju·eɪt] *vt* (*result*) evaluar; (*person*) examinar

**evaluation** [ɪ·,væl·ju·'eɪ·ʃən] *n* evaluación *f;* (*of a book*) crítica *f*

**evangelical** [,i·væn·'dʒel·ɪ·kəl] I. *n* evangélico, -a *m, f* II. *adj* evangélico, -a

**evaporate** [ɪ·'væp·ə·reɪt] I. *vt* evaporar II. *vi* evaporarse; *fig* desaparecer

**evasion** [ɪ·'veɪ·ʒən] *n* 1. (*of tax, responsibility*) evasión *f* 2. (*avoidance*) evasiva *f*

**evasive** [ɪ·'veɪ·sɪv] *adj* evasivo, -a

**eve** [iv] *n* víspera *f;* **on the ~ of** en vísperas de; **Christmas Eve** Nochebuena *f;* **New Year's Eve** Nochevieja *f*

**even** ['i·vən] I. *adj* 1. (*level*) llano, -a;

**E**

(*surface*) liso, -a **2.** (*equalized*) igualado, -a; **to get ~ with sb** ajustar cuentas con alguien **3.** (*of same size, amount*) igual **4.** (*constant, regular*) uniforme; (*rate*) constante **5.** (*fair*) ecuánime **6.** MATH par **II.** *vt* **1.** (*make level*) nivelar; (*surface*) allanar **2.** (*equalize*) igualar **III.** *adv* **1.** (*indicates the unexpected*) incluso; **not ~** ni siquiera **2.** (*despite*) **~ if...** aunque... +*subj*; **~ so...** aun así...; **~ though...** aunque... +*subj* **3.** (*used to intensify*) hasta **4.** **+ comp** (*all the more*) aún

◆**even out I.** *vi* (*prices*) nivelarse **II.** *vt* igualar

◆**even up** *vt* igualar

**evening** [ˈiv·nɪŋ] *n* (*early*) tarde *f*; (*late*) noche *f*; **good ~!** ¡buenas tardes/noches!; **in the ~** por la tarde/noche; **that ~** esa noche; **the previous ~** la noche anterior; **on Monday ~** el lunes por la noche; **during the ~** durante la tarde; **8 o'clock in the ~** las 8 de la tarde; **all ~** (**long**) toda la tarde

**evening class** *n* clase *f* nocturna

**evening dress** *n* (*for woman*) vestido *m* [*or* traje *m*] de noche; (*for man*) traje *m* de etiqueta; **to wear ~** ir de etiqueta

**evening prayer** *n* oración *f* de la tarde

**evenly** [ˈi·vən·li] *adv* **1.** (*calmly*) apaciblemente; **to state sth ~** decir algo sin alterarse **2.** (*equally*) igualmente

**event** [ɪˈvent] *n* **1.** (*happening*) acontecimiento *m*, evento *m* **2.** (*case*) caso *m*; **in any** [*or* **either**] **~** en cualquier caso; **in the ~** (**that**) **it rains** en caso de que llueva

**even-tempered** [ˈi·vən·ˈtem·pərd] *adj* ecuánime

**eventful** [ɪˈvent·fəl] *adj* (*journey, week*) muy movido, -a; (*decision*) memorable

**eventual** [ɪˈven·tʃu·əl] *adj* final

**eventuality** [ɪˈven·tʃuˈæl·ə·ti] <-ies> *n inv* eventualidad *f*

**eventually** [ɪˈven·tʃu·ə·li] *adv* **1.** (*finally*) finalmente **2.** (*some day*) con el tiempo

**ever** [ˈev·ər] *adv* **1.** (*on any occasion*) alguna vez; **have you ~ been to Hawaii?** ¿has estado alguna vez en Hawai?; **for the first time ~** por primera vez; **the**

**hottest day ~** el día mas caluroso; **better than ~** mejor que nunca; **would you ~ dye your hair?** ¿te teñirías el pelo? **2.** (*in negative statements*) nunca, jamás; **nobody has ~ heard of him** nadie ha oído nunca hablar de él; **never ~** nunca jamás; **hardly ~** casi nunca; **nothing ~ happens** nunca pasa nada **3.** (*always*) **~ after** desde entonces; **as ~** como siempre; **~ since...** desde que...; **~ since** (*since then*) desde entonces **4.** (*used to intensify*) **all he ~ does is** +*infin* lo único que hace es +*infin*

**everglade** [ˈev·ər·gleɪd] *n* tierra baja pantanosa cubierta de altas hierbas

**everlasting** [ˌev·ərˈlæs·tɪŋ] *adj* (*undying*) imperecedero, -a; (*gratitude, love*) eterno, -a *f*

**every** [ˈev·ri] *adj* **1.** (*each*) cada; **~ time** cada vez; **her ~ wish** su más mínimo deseo **2.** (*all*) todo, -a; **~ one of them** todos y cada uno de ellos; **in ~ way** de todas las maneras **3.** (*repeated*) **~ other week** una semana sí y otra no; **~ now and then** [*or* **again**] de vez en cuando ▶ **~ little bit helps** *prov* cualquier ayuda es buena

**everybody** [ˈev·riˌbad·i] *pron indef, sing* todos, todo el mundo; **~ but Paul** todos menos Paul; **~ who agrees** todos los que están de acuerdo

**everyday** [ˈev·riˈdeɪ] *adj* diario, -a; (*clothes*) de diario; (*event*) ordinario, -a; (*language*) corriente; (*life*) cotidiano, -a

**everyone** [ˈev·ri·wʌn] *pron see* **everybody**

**everything** [ˈev·ri·θɪŋ] *pron indef, sing* todo; **is ~ all right?** ¿está todo bien?; **~ they drink** todo lo que beben; **to do ~ necessary/one can** hacer todo lo necesario/lo posible; **money isn't ~ la** riqueza no lo es todo

**everywhere** [ˈev·ri·wer] *adv* en todas partes; **~ else** en cualquier otro sitio; **to look ~ for sth** buscar algo por todas partes

**evict** [ɪˈvɪkt] *vt* desahuciar

**eviction** [ɪˈvɪk·ʃən] *n* desahucio *m*

**evidence** [ˈev·ɪ·dəns] *n* **1.** (*sign*) indicios *mpl* **2.** (*proof*) prueba *f* **3.** (*tes-*

timony) testimonio *m* **4.** (*view*) evidencia *f*

**evident** ['ev·ɪ·dənt] *adj* evidente; **to be ~ to sb** ser evidente para alguien; **to be ~ in sth** manifestarse en algo; **it is ~ that...** está claro que...

**evil** ['i·vəl] **I.** *adj* malo, -a; **~ spirit** espíritu maligno **II.** *n* mal *m*; **social ~** lacra *f* social; **good and ~** el bien y el mal

**evocative** [ɪ·'vak·ə·tɪv] *adj* evocador(a); **an ~ image** una imagen sugerente

**evoke** [ɪ·'voʊk] *vt* evocar

**evolution** [ˌev·ə·'lu·ʃən] *n* evolución *f*; *fig* desarrollo *m*

**evolve** [ɪ·'valv] **I.** *vi* (*gradually develop*) desarrollarse; (*animals*) evolucionar; **to ~ into sth** convertirse en algo **II.** *vt* desarrollar

**ewe** [ju] *n* oveja *f*

**ex** [eks] <-es> *n inf* ex *mf*

**exact** [ɪg·'zækt] **I.** *adj* exacto, -a; **the ~ opposite** justo lo contrario **II.** *vt* exigir; **to ~ sth from sb** exigir algo a alguien

**exacting** [ɪg·'zæk·tɪŋ] *adj* exigente

**exactly** [ɪg·'zækt·li] *adv* exactamente; **~ like...** justo como...; **how/what/where ~...** cómo/qué/dónde exactamente...; **I don't ~ agree with that** no estoy del todo de acuerdo en eso; **not ~** no precisamente; **~!** ¡exacto!

**exaggerate** [ɪg·'zædʒ·ə·reɪt] *vi*, *vt* exagerar

**exaggerated** [ɪg·'zædʒ·ə·reɪ·tɪd] *adj* exagerado, -a; **greatly ~** muy exagerado

**exaggeration** [ɪg·ˌzædʒ·ə·'reɪ·ʃən] *n* exageración *f*; **it's no ~ to say that...** no es exagerado decir que...

**exam** [ɪg·'zæm] *n* examen *m*

**examination** [ɪg·ˌzæm·ɪ·'neɪ·ʃən] *n* **1.** (*exam*) examen *m* **2.** (*investigation*) investigación *f*; **medical ~** reconocimiento *m* médico

**examine** [ɪg·'zæm·ɪn] *vt* **1.** (*study*) estudiar **2.** MED hacer un reconocimiento médico de

**examinee** [ɪg·ˌzæm·ɪ·'ni] *n* examinando, -a *m, f*

**examiner** [ɪg·'zæm·ɪn·ər] *n* examinador(a) *m(f)*

**example** [ɪg·'zæm·pəl] *n* (*sample, model*) ejemplo *m*; **for ~** por ejemplo; **to follow sb's ~** seguir el ejemplo de alguien; **to set a good ~** dar (un) buen ejemplo

**exasperating** [ɪg·'zæs·pə·reɪ·tɪŋ] *adj* irritante

**exasperation** [ɪg·ˌzæs·pə·'reɪ·ʃən] *n* exasperación *f*

**excavate** ['ek·skə·veɪt] **I.** *vt* **1.** (*expose*) desenterrar **2.** (*hollow*) excavar **II.** *vi* excavar

**excavation** [ˌek·skə·'veɪ·ʃən] *n* excavación *f*

**exceed** [ɪk·'sid] *vt* exceder; (*outshine*) sobrepasar

**exceedingly** *adv* excesivamente

**excel** [ɪk·'sel] <-ll-> **I.** *vi* sobresalir; **to ~ at** [*or* **in**] **sth** destacar en algo **II.** *vt* **to ~ oneself** lucirse

**excellence** ['ek·sə·ləns] *n* excelencia *f*

**excellent** ['ek·sə·lənt] *adj* excelente

**except** [ɪk·'sept] **I.** *prep* **~ (for)** excepto, salvo, zafo *AmL*; **to do nothing ~ wait** no hacer nada más que esperar **II.** *vt form* exceptuar

**excepting** *prep* excepto, salvo

**exception** [ɪk·'sep·ʃən] *n* excepción *f*; **to be an ~** ser una excepción; **to make an ~** hacer una excepción; **to take ~ (to sth)** ofenderse (por algo)

**exceptional** [ɪk·'sep·ʃə·nəl] *adj* excepcional

**exceptionally** [ɪk·'sep·ʃə·nə·li] *adv* excepcionalmente

**excerpt** ['ek·sɜrpt] *n* extracto *m*

**excess** [ɪk·'ses] <-es> *n* exceso *m*; **to eat to ~** comer en exceso; **in ~ of** superior a

**excess baggage** *n see* **excess luggage**

**excessive** [ɪk·'ses·ɪv] *adj* excesivo, -a; (*claim*) exagerado, -a

**excess luggage** *n* exceso *m* de equipaje

**exchange** [ɪks·'tʃeɪndʒ] **I.** *vt* **1.** (*trade for the equivalent*) cambiar **2.** (*interchange*) intercambiar; **to ~ words** discutir **II.** *n* **1.** (*interchange, trade*) intercambio *m*; **in ~ for sth** a cambio de algo; **~ of (gun)fire** tiroteo *m* **2.** FIN, ECON cambio *m*; **foreign ~** divisas *fpl*

**exchangeable** *adj* cambiable; (*goods*) canjeable; **to be ~ for sth** ser intercambiable por algo

**exchange rate** *n* tipo *m* de cambio

**exchange student** *n* estudiante *mf* de intercambio

**excise** [ek·'saɪz] *vt form* **1.** (*carry out*) quitar; (*tumor*) extirpar **2.** *fig* eliminar, suprimir

**excitable** [ɪk·'saɪ·tə·bəl] *adj* excitable

**excite** [ɪk·'saɪt] *vt* **1.** (*move*) emocionar **2.** (*stimulate*) estimular

**excited** [ɪk·'saɪ·tɪd] *adj* emocionado, -a

**excitement** [ɪk·'saɪt·mənt] *n* emoción *f*; **what ~!** ¡qué emoción!

**exciting** [ɪk·'saɪ·tɪŋ] *adj* emocionante

**exclaim** [ɪk·'skleɪm] *vi, vt* exclamar

**exclamation** [ˌek·sklə·'meɪ·ʃən] *n* exclamación *f*

**exclamation mark** *n*, **exclamation point** *n* signo *m* de exclamación

**exclude** [ɪk·'sklud] *vt* **1.** (*keep out*) excluir; **to ~ sb from a group** excluir a alguien de un grupo **2.** (*possibility*) descartar

**excluding** [ɪk·'sklu·dɪŋ] *prep* excepto, salvo

**exclusion** [ɪk·'sklu·ʒən] *n* exclusión *f*

**exclusive** [ɪk·'sklu·sɪv] I. *adj* exclusivo, -a; **~ interview** entrevista *f* en exclusiva; **~ of** sin; **to be ~ of** no incluir II. *n* exclusiva *f*

**exclusively** *adv* exclusivamente

**excommunication** [ˌeks·kə·ˌmju·nɪ·'keɪ·ʃən] *n* excomunión *f*

**excrement** ['ek·skrə·mənt] *n* excremento *m*

**excruciating** [ɪk·'skru·ʃi·eɪ·tɪŋ] *adj* **1.** agudísimo, -a; (*pain*) atroz, insoportable **2.** (*intense: accuracy*) extenuante

**excursion** [ɪk·'skɜr·ʒən] *n* excursión *f*; **to go on an ~** ir de excursión

**excusable** [ɪk·'skju·zə·bəl] *adj* perdonable

**excuse¹** [ɪk·'skjuz] *vt* **1.** (*justify: behavior*) justificar; (*lateness*) disculpar; **to ~ sb for sth** excusar a alguien por algo **2.** (*forgive*) perdonar; **~ me!** ¡perdón! **3.** (*allow not to attend*) **to ~ sb from sth** dispensar a alguien de algo **4.** (*leave*) **after an hour she ~d herself** después de una hora se disculpó y se fue

**excuse²** [ɪk·'skjus] *n* **1.** (*explanation*) excusa *f*, disculpa *f*, agarradera *f AmL*

**2.** (*pretext*) pretexto *m*; **poor ~** mal pretexto; **to make ~s for sb** justificar a alguien

**execute** ['ek·sɪ·kjut] *vt* **1.** (*carry out*) realizar; (*maneuver*) efectuar; (*plan*) llevar a cabo; (*order*) cumplir **2.** (*put to death*) ejecutar

**execution** [ˌek·sɪ·'kju·ʃən] *n* **1.** (*carrying out*) realización *f* **2.** (*putting to death*) ejecución *f*

**executioner** [ˌek·sɪ·'kju·ʃə·nər] *n* verdugo *m*

**executive** [ɪg·'zek·jʊ·tɪv] I. *n* (*senior manager*) ejecutivo, -a *m, f* II. *adj* ejecutivo, -a; **~ branch** poder ejecutivo

**exempt** [ɪg·'zempt] I. *vt* eximir II. *adj* exento, -a; **to be ~ from** (**doing**) **sth** estar exento de (hacer) algo

**exemption** [ɪg·'zemp·ʃən] *n* exención *f*

**exercise** ['ek·sər·saɪz] I. *vt* **1.** (*muscles*) ejercitar **2.** (*apply: authority, control*) ejercer II. *vi* hacer ejercicio III. *n* **1.** (*physical training*) ejercicio *m*; **to do ~s** hacer ejercicios **2.** SCHOOL, UNIV ejercicio *m* **3.** MIL maniobras *fpl* **4.** (*action, achievement*) acción *f* **5.** (*use*) uso *m*

**exercise book** *n* cuaderno *m*

**exert** [ɪg·'zɜrt] *vt* ejercer; (*apply*) emplear; **to ~ oneself** esforzarse

**exertion** [ɪg·'zɜr·ʃən] *n* **1.** (*application: of authority, influence*) ejercicio *m* **2.** (*physical effort*) esfuerzo *m*

**exhale** [eks·'heɪl] I. *vt* espirar; (*gases, scents*) despedir II. *vi* espirar

**exhaust** [ɪg·'zɔst] I. *vt a. fig* agotar II. *n* (*pipe*) tubo *m* de escape

**exhausted** *adj* agotado, -a

**exhausting** *adj* agotador(a)

**exhaustion** [ɪg·'zɔs·tʃən] *n* agotamiento *m*

**exhaustive** [ɪg·'zɔs·tɪv] *adj* exhaustivo, -a

**exhaust pipe** *n* tubo *m* de escape

**exhaust system** *n* sistema *m* de escape

**exhibit** [ɪg·'zɪb·ɪt] I. *n* **1.** (*display*) objeto *m* expuesto **2.** LAW prueba *f* presentada en juicio II. *vt* (*show*) enseñar; (*rudeness, confidence*) demostrar

**exhibition** [ˌek·sɪ·'bɪʃ·ən] *n* (*display*) exposición *f*; (*performance*) exhibición *f*

▶ **to make an ~ of oneself** ponerse
en ridículo

**exhibitor** [ɪgˈzɪb·ɪ·tər] *n* exposi-
tor(a) *m(f)*

**exhilarating** [ɪgˈzɪl·ə·reɪ·tɪŋ] *adj* estimulante; **an ~ performance** un espectáculo emocionante

**exhilaration** [ɪgˈzɪl·əˈreɪ·ʃən] *n* regocijo *m*

**exhume** [ɪgˈzum] *vt* exhumar

**ex-husband** *n* ex marido *m*

**exile** [ˈek·saɪl] **I.** *n* 1. (*banishment*) exilio *m*; **political ~** exilio político; **to go
into ~** exiliarse 2. (*person*) exiliado,
-a *m, f* **II.** *vt* exiliar

**exist** [ɪgˈzɪst] *vi* 1. (*be*) existir 2. (*live*)
vivir; **to ~ without sth** sobrevivir sin
algo

**existence** [ɪgˈzɪs·təns] *n* 1. (*being*) existencia *f*; **to be in ~** existir 2. (*life*)
vida *f*

**existing** [ɪgˈzɪs·tɪŋ] *adj* existente

**exit** [ˈeg·sɪt] **I.** *n* salida *f*; (*of road*) desvío *m* **II.** *vt* salir de **III.** *vi a.* COMPUT
(*leave*) salir

**exit visa** *n* visado *m* de salida

**exodus** [ˈek·sə·dəs] *n* éxodo *m*

**exorbitant** [ɪgˈzɔr·bə·tənt] *adj* exorbitante; (*demand*) excesivo, -a; (*price*)
desorbitado, -a

**exorcism** [ˈek·sɔr·sɪz·əm] *n* exorcis-
mo *m*

**exotic** [ɪgˈzɑt·ɪk] *adj* exótico, -a

**expand** [ɪkˈspænd] **I.** *vi* 1. (*increase*)
expandirse 2. (*spread*) extenderse
3. PHYS dilatarse **II.** *vt* 1. (*make larger*)
ampliar; (*wings*) extender 2. PHYS dilatar
3. (*elaborate*) desarrollar

**expandable** [ɪkˈspæn·də·bəl] *adj* ex-
pansible

**expansion** [ɪkˈspæn·ʃən] *n* 1. (*spreading
out*) expansión *f*; (*of a metal*) dilatación *f*
2. (*elaboration*) desarrollo *m*

**expatriate¹** [eksˈpeɪ·tri·ət] *n* expatria-
do, -a *m, f*

**expatriate²** [eksˈpeɪ·tri·eɪt] *vt* expatriar

**expect** [ɪkˈspekt] *vt* esperar; (*imagine*)
imaginarse; **to ~ sb to do sth** esperar
que alguien haga algo; **you are ~ed to
return books on time** debes devolver
los libros puntualmente; **to be ~ing** (a
*baby*) esperar un bebé; **I ~ed as much**

ya me lo esperaba; **to ~ that** esperar
que +*subj*

**expectancy** [ɪkˈspek·tən·si] *n* esperanza *f*; **life ~** esperanza *f* de vida

**expectant** [ɪkˈspek·tənt] *adj* expectante; (*look*) de esperanza; **~ mother** futura madre

**expectation** [ˌek·spekˈteɪ·ʃən] *n*
1. (*hope*) esperanza *f* 2. (*anticipation*)
expectativa *f*; **in ~ of sth** en espera
de algo

**expedient** [ɪkˈspi·di·ənt] **I.** *adj* 1. (*advantageous*) conveniente 2. (*necessary*)
necesario, -a **II.** *n* recurso *m*

**expedite** [ˈek·spɪ·daɪt] *vt form* acelerar

**expedition** [ˌek·spɪˈdɪʃ·ən] *n* expedición *f*;
**to be on an ~** estar de expedición; **to
go on an ~** ir de expedición

**expel** [ɪkˈspel] <-ll-> *vt* expeler, arrojar;
(*person*) expulsar; **to ~ sb from school**
expulsar a alguien del colegio

**expenditure** [ɪkˈspen·dɪ·tʃər] *n* (*money*)
gasto *m*; **public ~(s)** gasto público

**expense** [ɪkˈspens] *n* gasto(s) *m(pl)*; **all
~(s) paid** con todos los gastos pagados;
**at great ~** por un precio muy elevado; **at
sb's ~** *a. fig* a costa de alguien

**expense account** *n* cuenta *f* de gastos
de representación

**expensive** [ɪkˈspen·sɪv] *adj* caro, -a

**experience** [ɪkˈspɪr·i·əns] **I.** *n* experiencia *f*; **to have translating ~** tener
experiencia en traducción; **to know
sth from ~** saber algo por experiencia
**II.** *vt* experimentar; **to ~ happiness/
pain** sentir alegría/dolor; **to ~ a loss**
sufrir una pérdida

**experienced** [ɪkˈspɪr·i·ənst] *adj* experimentado, -a

**experiment** [ɪkˈsper·ɪ·mənt] **I.** *n* experimento *m*; **as an ~** como experimento;
**by ~** experimentando **II.** *vi* experimentar; **to ~ with mice** hacer experimentos
con ratones

**experimental** [ɪkˌsper·ɪˈmen·təl] *adj* experimental; **to be still at the ~ stage**
estar todavía en fase experimental

**expert** [ˈek·spɜrt] **I.** *n* experto, -a *m, f*;
**to be a computer ~** ser un experto
en ordenadores [*or AmL* computadoras]
**II.** *adj* 1. (*skilful*) experto, -a; **she's an**

~ **swimmer** es una experta nadadora
**2.** LAW pericial

**expert advice** n **to seek ~** asesorarse
con un experto

**expertise** [ˌek·spər·ˈtiz] n pericia f; (knowledge) conocimientos mpl

**expiration date** n (of a contract) fecha
f de vencimiento; (of food or medicine)
fecha f de caducidad

**expire** [ɪk·ˈspaɪr] I. vi **1.** (contract, license) expirar; (passport, food) caducar
**2.** (die) expirar II. vt espirar

**expiry** [ɪk·ˈspaɪ·ri] n see **expiration**

**explain** [ɪk·ˈspleɪn] I. vt explicar; **to
~ how/what/where/why...** explicar
cómo/qué/dónde/por qué...; **that ~s
everything!** ¡eso lo aclara todo! II. vi
explicar

**explanation** [ˌek·splə·ˈneɪ·ʃən] n explicación f; **by way of ~** como explicación

**explanatory** [ɪk·ˈsplæn·ə·tɔr·i] adj explicativo, -a

**expletive** [ˈək·splɪ·t̬ɪv] n palabrota f

**explicit** [ɪk·ˈsplɪs·ɪt] adj **1.** (exact) explícito, -a; ~ **directions** instrucciones ex-
plícitas **2.** (vulgar) vulgar; ~ **language**
lenguaje m vulgar

**explode** [ɪk·ˈsploʊd] I. vi **1.** (blow up)
explotar; (bomb) estallar; (tire) reventar; **to ~ with anger** montar en cólera **2.** (grow rapidly) dispararse II. vt
(blow up: bomb) hacer explotar; (ball)
reventar

**exploit** [ˈek·splɔɪt] I. vt explotar, pilotear Chile II. n hazaña f

**exploitation** [ˌek·splɔɪ·ˈteɪ·ʃən] n explotación f

**exploration** [ˌek·splɔ·ˈreɪ·ʃən] n **1.** a.
MED exploración f **2.** (examination) estudio m

**exploratory** [ɪk·ˈsplɔr·ə·tɔr·i] adj (voyage)
de exploración; (test) de sondeo; (meeting) preliminar

**explore** [ɪk·ˈsplɔr] I. vt **1.** a. MED, COMPUT
explorar **2.** (examine) analizar; **to ~
sb's past** investigar sobre el pasado de
alguien II. vi explorar

**explorer** [ɪk·ˈsplɔr·ər] n explora-
dor(a) m(f)

**explosion** [ɪk·ˈsploʊ·ʒən] n explosión f;
**population ~** explosión demográfica

**explosive** [ɪk·ˈsploʊ·sɪv] I. adj explosivo,
-a; ~ **device** artefacto explosivo; **an ~
issue** un asunto espinoso; **to have an ~
temper** tener un genio muy vivo II. n
explosivo m

**export** I. [ɪk·ˈspɔrt] vt exportar II. [ˈek·
spɔrt] n **1.** (product) artículo m de exportación **2.** (selling) exportación f; ~
**taxes** aranceles m pl de exportación

**exportation** [ˌek·spɔr·ˈteɪ·ʃən] n exportación f

**expose** [ɪk·ˈspoʊz] vt **1.** (uncover) enseñar **2.** (leave vulnerable to) exponer; **to
~ sb to ridicule** poner a alguien en ridículo **3.** (reveal: person) descubrir; (plot)
desvelar; (secret) sacar a la luz

**exposé** [ˌek·spoʊ·ˈzeɪ] n revelación f

**exposed** [ɪk·ˈspoʊzd] adj **1.** (vulnerable)
expuesto, -a **2.** (uncovered) descubierto,
-a **3.** (unprotected) desprotegido, -a

**exposure** [ɪk·ˈspoʊ·ʒər] n **1.** (contact)
exposición f (to a); ~ **to new ideas**
contacto m con nuevas ideas **2.** MED
hipotermia f; **to die of ~** morir de frío
**3.** a. PHOT exposición f **4.** (revelation)
descubrimiento m **5.** (media coverage)
publicidad f

**exposure meter** n PHOT exposímetro m

**express** [ɪk·ˈspres] I. vt (convey:
thoughts, feelings) expresar; **to ~ oneself** expresarse; **I would like to ~ my
thanks for...** querría expresar mi gratitud por... II. adj **1.** (rapid) rápido,
-a; ~ **train** tren expreso; ~ **mail** correo
urgente **2.** (precise) explícito, -a; **by ~
order** por orden expresa III. n (train)
expreso m IV. adv **to send sth ~** enviar
algo por correo urgente

**expression** [ɪk·ˈspreʃ·ən] n expresión f;
(of love, solidarity) demostración f; **as
an ~ of thanks** en señal de agradecimiento

**expressionist** [ɪk·ˈspreʃ·ə·nɪst] n expresionista mf

**expressionless** [ɪk·ˈspreʃ·ən·lɪs] adj
inexpresivo, -a

**expressive** [ɪk·ˈspres·ɪv] adj expresivo, -a

**expressly** [ɪk·ˈspres·li] adv **1.** (clearly) claramente **2.** (especially) expresamente

**expressway** [ɪkˈspres·weɪ] n autopista f

**ex-prisoner** n ex prisionero, -a m, f

**expulsion** [ɪkˈspʌl·ʃən] n expulsión f

**exquisite** [ˈekˈskwɪ·zɪt] adj 1. (delicate) exquisito, -a 2. (intense) intenso, -a

**extend** [ɪkˈstend] I. vt 1. (enlarge: house) ampliar; (street) alargar 2. (prolong: deadline) prorrogar; (holiday) prolongar 3. (offer) ofrecer; **to ~ one's thanks to sb** dar las gracias a alguien 4. FIN (credit) conceder II. vi extenderse (**beyond** más allá de)

**extended** adj extenso, -a; **~ family** clan m familiar; **an ~ holiday** unas vacaciones prolongadas

**extension** [ɪkˈsten·ʃən] n 1. (increase) extensión f; (of rights) ampliación f; **by ~** por extensión 2. (of a deadline) prórroga f 3. TEL extensión f, supletorio m AmL, anexo m Chile

**extension cord** n alargador m, alargue m RíoPl

**extension ladder** n escalera f extensible

**extensive** [ɪkˈsten·sɪv] adj 1. a. fig extenso, -a; (experience) amplio, -a 2. (large: repair) importante; **~ damage** daños m pl de consideración 3. AGR (farming) extensivo, -a

**extent** [ɪkˈstent] n 1. (size) extensión f; **to its fullest ~** en toda su extensión 2. (degree) alcance m; **to go to the ~ of hitting sb** llegar al extremo de golpear a alguien; **to a great ~** en gran parte; **to the same ~ as...** en la misma medida que...; **to some ~** hasta cierto punto; **to such an ~ that...** hasta tal punto que...; **to what ~...?** ¿hasta qué punto...?

**exterior** [ɪkˈstɪr·i·ər] I. adj exterior II. n 1. (outside surface) exterior m 2. (outward appearance) aspecto m 3. CINE exteriores mpl

**exterminate** [ɪkˈstɜr·mɪ·neɪt] vt exterminar

**extermination** [ɪkˈstɜr·mɪˈneɪ·ʃən] n exterminio m, exterminación f

**external** [ɪkˈstɜr·nəl] I. adj 1. (exterior) externo, -a; (influence) del exterior; (wall) exterior 2. (foreign) exterior 3. MED tópico, -a II. npl las apariencias

**extinct** [ɪkˈstɪŋkt] adj (practice) extinto,

-a; **to become ~** extinguirse

**extinction** [ɪkˈstɪŋk·ʃən] n extinción f

**extinguish** [ɪkˈstɪŋ·gwɪʃ] vt (candle, cigar) apagar; (love, passion) extinguir; (life, memory) apagar; (debt) amortizar

**extinguisher** [ɪkˈstɪŋ·gwɪʃ·ər] n extintor m

**extort** [ɪkˈstɔrt] vt extorsionar; (confession) arrancar

**extortion** [ɪkˈstɔr·ʃən] n extorsión f

**extortionate** [ɪkˈstɔr·ʃə·nɪt] adj abusivo, -a; **~ prices** precios m pl exorbitantes

**extra** [ˈek·strə] I. adj adicional; **~ clothes** ropa f de repuesto; **it costs an ~ $2** cuesta dos dólares más; **meals are ~** el precio no incluye las comidas II. adv (more) más; (extraordinarily) extraordinariamente; **to charge ~ for sth** cobrar algo aparte III. n 1. ECON suplemento m; AUTO extra m 2. CINE extra m

**extract** [ɪkˈstrækt] I. vt 1. (remove) extraer 2. (obtain: information) sacar 3. MATH (square root) sacar II. n 1. (concentrate) extracto m 2. (excerpt) fragmento m

**extraction** [ɪkˈstræk·ʃən] n 1. (removal) extracción f 2. (descent) origen m

**extracurricular** [ˌek·strə·kə·ˈrɪk·jə·lər] adj extraescolar, extracurricular; **~ activities** actividades extraescolares

**extradite** [ˈek·strə·daɪt] vt extraditar

**extradition** [ˌek·strə·ˈdɪʃ·ən] n extradición f

**extramarital** [ˌek·strə·ˈmer·ɪ·t̬əl] adj extramatrimonial

**extraordinary** [ɪkˈstrɔr·də·ner·i] adj 1. a. POL extraordinario, -a 2. (astonishing) asombroso, -a

**extravagant** [ɪkˈstræv·ə·gənt] adj 1. (wasteful) despilfarrador(a) 2. (luxurious) lujoso, -a 3. (exaggerated: praise) excesivo, -a; **~ price** precio m exorbitante 4. (elaborate) extravagante

**extreme** [ɪkˈstrim] I. adj extremo, -a; **an ~ case** un caso extremo; **with ~ caution** con sumo cuidado; **~ pain** dolor agudo; **in the ~ north** en la zona más septentrional; **~ sport** deporte de alto riesgo; **to be ~ in sth** ser extremista en algo II. n extremo m; **at the ~** fig en el peor de los casos; **in the ~** sumamente;

to go from one ~ to the other pasar de un extremo a otro; **to go to ~s** llegar a extremos

**extremely** adv extremadamente; **to be ~ sorry** estar muy arrepentido

**extremist** [ɪkˈstriː·mɪst] **I.** adj extremista **II.** n extremista mf

**extroverted** adj extrovertido, -a

**exuberant** [ɪgˈzuː·bər·ənt] adj **1.** (luxuriant) exuberante **2.** (energetic) desbordante

**exultant** [ɪgˈzʌl·tənt] adj form regocijado, -a, exultante

**ex-wife** n ex mujer f, ex esposa f

**eye** [aɪ] **I.** n **1.** ANAT ojo m; **to blink one's ~s** parpadear; **to keep an ~ on sth/sb** inf echar un ojo a algo/alguien; **to roll one's ~s** poner los ojos en blanco; **to rub one's ~s** restregarse los ojos; **visible to the naked ~** visible a simple vista; **he couldn't take his ~s off the girl** inf no le quitaba ojo a la chica **2.** BOT yema f ▶ **to have ~s in the back of one's head** inf tener ojos en la nuca; **an ~ for an ~, a tooth for a tooth** prov ojo por ojo y diente por diente; **to give sb a black ~** poner a alguien un ojo a la funerala (or negro); **to turn a blind ~ (to sth)** hacer la vista gorda (a algo); **as far as the ~ can see** hasta donde alcanza la vista; **to have a good ~ for sth** tener (buen) ojo para algo; **there's more to this than meets the ~** las apariencias engañan; **to keep one's ~s open** mantener los ojos bien abiertos; **to be able to do sth with one's ~s closed** inf poder hacer algo con los ojos cerrados; (**right**) **before** (or **under**) **my very ~s** delante de mis propios ojos; **to not believe one's ~s** no dar crédito a sus ojos; **to catch sb's ~** llamar la atención de alguien; **to (not) see ~ to ~ with sb** (no) estar de acuerdo con alguien; **in the public ~** a la luz pública **II.** <-ing> vt mirar; (observe) observar; **to ~ sb up and down** mirar a alguien de arriba abajo

**eyeball** [ˈaɪ·bɔl] **I.** n globo m ocular **II.** vt inf mirar de arriba abajo

**eyebrow** n ceja f; **to raise one's ~s at sth** asombrarse ante algo

**eyebrow pencil** n lápiz m de cejas

**eye contact** n contacto m visual

**eyedrops** npl colirio m

**eyelash** <-es> n pestaña f; **false ~es** pestañas f pl postizas

**eyelid** n párpado m

**eyeliner** [ˈaɪ·laɪ·nər] n delineador m de ojos

**eye opener** n inf revelación f

**eyepiece** n ocular m

**eye shadow** n sombra f de ojos

**eyesight** n vista f; **his ~ is failing** le está fallando la vista

**eyesore** n **to be an ~** ofender a la vista

**eyestrain** n vista f cansada

**eyewitness** <-es> n testigo mf ocular

**e-zine** [ˈiː·ziːn] n revista f electrónica

# F

**F, f** [ef] n **1.** (letter) F, f f; **~ as in Foxtrot** F de Francia **2.** MUS fa m

**f** abbr of **feminine** f

**F** abbr of **Fahrenheit** F

**fable** [ˈfeɪ·bəl] n **1.** (story) fábula f **2.** (lie) cuento m

**fabric** [ˈfæb·rɪk] n **1.** (cloth, textile) tejido m; **cotton ~** tela f de algodón **2.** fig **the ~ of society** el tejido social

**fabulous** [ˈfæb·jə·ləs] adj fabuloso, -a; **to look absolutely ~** estar estupendo

**face** [feɪs] **I.** n **1.** a. ANAT cara f; **a happy/sad ~** una cara de felicidad (or de tristeza); **a smiling ~** un rostro sonriente; **to keep a smile on one's ~** no perder la sonrisa; **to keep a straight ~** mantenerse impávido; **to laugh in sb's ~** reírse en la cara de alguien; **to make a ~ (at sb)** hacer una mueca (a alguien); **to tell sth to sb's ~** decir algo a la cara de alguien **2.** (front: of building) fachada f; (of coin) cara f; (of clock) esfera f, carátula f Méx; (of mountain) pared f **3.** (respect, honor) prestigio m; **to lose ~** desprestigiarse; **to save ~** guardar las apariencias ▶ **to fly in the ~ of logic/reason** oponerse abiertamente a la lógica/razón; **on the ~ of it** a primera vista **II.** vt **1.** (turn towards) mirar hacia; **to ~**

**the audience** volverse hacia el público **2.** (*confront*) hacer frente a; **the two teams will ~ each other next week** los dos equipos se enfrentarán la próxima semana; **to ~ the facts** enfrentarse a los hechos; **to ~ one's fears/problems** afrontar los miedos/problemas de uno; **to be ~d with sth** verse frente a algo; **we are ~d with financial problems** estamos pasando por problemas financieros **3.** ARCHIT recubrir **4.** FASHION forrar ▶ **to ~ the music** *inf* afrontar las consecuencias III. *vi* **to ~ towards the street** dar a la calle; **about ~!** ¡media vuelta!

**facecloth** *n* toallita *f*

**face cream** *n* crema *f* facial

**facetious** [fə·ˈsiː·ʃəs] *adj* chistoso, -a, faceto, -a *Méx*; **stop being so ~** deja de hacerte el gracioso

**face value** *n* **1.** ECON valor *m* nominal **2.** *fig* **to take sth at ~** creer algo a pie juntillas

**facility** [fə·ˈsɪl·ə·ti] *n* <-ies> **1.** (*services*) servicio *m* **2.** (*ability, feature*) facilidad *f* **3.** (*building for a special purpose*) complejo *m*

**facing** [ˈfeɪ·sɪŋ] *n* **1.** ARCHIT revestimiento *m* **2.** (*cloth strip*) vuelta *f*

**fact** [fækt] *n* hecho *m*; **the bare ~s** los hechos concretos; **to stick to the ~s** atenerse a los hechos ▶ **~s and figures** *inf* información *f* detallada; **a ~ of life** ley de vida; **the ~s of life** los detalles de la reproducción; **as a matter of ~...** de hecho...; **the ~ of the matter is that ...** la verdad es que...; **in ~** de hecho

**fact-finding** [ˈfækt·faɪn·dɪŋ] *adj* investigador(a)

**factor** [ˈfæk·tər] *n* factor *m*

**factory** [ˈfæk·tə·ri] <-ies> *n* fábrica *f*; **car ~** fábrica de coches

**factual** [ˈfæk·tʃu·əl] *adj* basado, -a en hechos reales; **a ~ error** un error de hecho

**faculty** [ˈfæk·əl·ti] <-ies> *n* **1.** (*teachers*) cuerpo *m* docente **2.** UNIV facultad *f* **3.** (*ability*) facultad *f*

**fad** [fæd] *n* *inf* **1.** (*fashion*) moda *f*; **a passing ~** una moda pasajera **2.** (*obsession*) manía *f*

**fade** [feɪd] I. *vi* **1.** (*lose color*) desteñirse **2.** (*lose intensity: light*) apagarse; (*sound*) debilitarse; (*smile*) borrarse; (*interest*) decaer; (*hope, optimism, memory*) desvanecerse; (*plant, beauty*) marchitarse; (*life*) apagarse **3.** (*disappear*) desaparecer; **to ~ from sight/view** perderse de vista **4.** CINE, TV fundirse II. *vt* desteñir

◆**fade away** *vi* (*hope, memory*) desvanecerse; (*sound, love, grief*) apagarse

◆**fade in** I. *vi* (*picture*) aparecer progresivamente; (*sound*) subir gradualmente II. *vt* (*picture*) hacer aparecer progresivamente; (*sound*) subir gradualmente

◆**fade out** *vi* (*picture*) desaparecer gradualmente; (*sound*) desvanecerse

**fag** [fæg] *n* *offensive sl* (*homosexual*) marica *m*

**faggot** [ˈfæg·ət] *n* *offensive sl* (*homosexual*) marica *m*

**fail** [feɪl] I. *vi* **1.** (*not succeed: person*) fracasar; (*attempt, plan, operation*) fallar; **if all else ~s** como último recurso; **to ~ to do sth** no conseguir hacer algo; **I ~ to see why that matters** no veo qué importancia tiene **2.** SCHOOL, UNIV suspender, ser reprobado *AmL* **3.** TECH, AUTO (*brakes, steering*) fallar; (*engine*) averiarse; (*eyesight, hearing, heart*) fallar **4.** (*crops*) perderse II. *vt* **1.** (*not pass: exam, subject, pupil*) suspender **2.** (*not help*) **her courage ~ed her** le abandonó el coraje III. *n* SCHOOL, UNIV suspenso *m*, reprobado *m AmL* ▶ **without ~** (*definitely*) sin falta; (*always*) sin excepción

**failing** [ˈfeɪ·lɪŋ] I. *adj* (*health*) débil II. *n* (*of mechanism*) defecto *m*; (*of person*) debilidad *f* III. *prep* a falta de

**failure** [ˈfeɪl·jər] *n* **1.** (*lack of success*) fracaso *m*; **to be doomed to ~** estar destinado al fracaso; **the ~ to answer** el no responder **2.** TECH, ELEC (*breakdown*) fallo *m*

**faint** [feɪnt] I. *adj* **1.** (*scent, odor, taste*) leve; (*sound, murmur*) apenas perceptible; (*light, glow*) tenue; (*line, outline, scratch*) apenas visible; (*memory*) confuso, -a; (*smile*) ligero, -a **2.** (*slight: resemblance, sign, suspicion*) vago, -a;

(*chance, hope, possibility*) ligero, -a; **not to have the ~est idea** *inf* no tener ni idea **3.** (*weak*) **to be ~ with hunger** estar desfallecido por el hambre; **to feel ~** sentirse mareado **II.** *vi* desmayarse **III.** *n* desmayo *m*

**fair¹** [fer] **I.** *adj* **1.** (*just: society, trial, wage*) justo, -a; (*price*) razonable; **a ~ share** una parte equitativa; **~ enough** está bien **2.** *inf* (*quite large: amount*) bastante; **it's a ~ size** es bastante grande **3.** (*reasonably good: chance, prospect*) bueno, -a **4.** (*not bad*) aceptable **5.** (*light in color: skin*) blanco, -a, güero, -a *AmL*; (*hair*) rubio, -a **6.** METEO **~ weather** tiempo *m* agradable ▶ **~ is ~** *inf* lo justo es justo **II.** *adv* **to play ~** jugar limpio ▶ **~ and square** (*following the rules*) con todas las de la ley; (*directly*) de lleno

**fair²** [fer] *n* feria *f*; **trade ~** feria comercial

**fair game** *n* caza *f* legal; *fig* objeto *m* legítimo

**fairground** ['fer·graʊnd] *n* parque *m* de atracciones

**fair-haired** [ˌfer'herd] *adj* rubio, -a

**fairly** ['fer·li] *adv* **1.** (*quite*) bastante **2.** (*justly*) con imparcialidad **3.** *liter* (*almost*) prácticamente

**fairness** *n* **1.** (*justice*) justicia *f*; **in (all) ~ ...** para ser justos... **2.** (*of skin*) blancura *f*; (*of hair*) lo rubio

**fairy** ['fer·i] <-ies> *n* **1.** (*creature*) hada *f* **2.** *offensive sl* (*homosexual*) mariquita *m*

**fairy tale** *n* cuento *m* de hadas; *fig* cuento *m* chino

**faith** [feɪθ] *n* fe *f*; **to have/lose ~ in sb/sth** tener fe/perder la fe en alguien/algo; **to put one's ~ in sb/sth** confiar en alguien/algo; **to keep the ~** mantener la fe

**faithful** ['feɪθ·fəl] **I.** *adj* fiel **II.** *n* the **~** los fieles

**faithfully** *adv* **1.** (*loyally: serve*) lealmente **2.** (*exactly: copy, translate*) fielmente

**fake** [feɪk] **I.** *n* **1.** (*painting, jewel*) falsificación *f* **2.** (*person*) impostor(a) *m(f)* **II.** *adj* **~ fur** piel sintética; **~ jewel** joya

falsa **III.** *vt* **1.** (*counterfeit*) falsificar **2.** (*pretend to feel*) fingir **IV.** *vi* fingir

**fall** [fɔl] <fell, fallen> **I.** *vi* **1.** (*drop down*) caerse; (*rain, snow*) caer; (*tree*) venirse abajo; **to ~ flat** (*joke*) no tener gracia; (*plan, suggestion*) no tener éxito; **to ~ down the stairs** caerse por las escaleras; **to ~ flat on one's face** caerse de morros *inf* **2.** (*decrease: prices*) bajar; (*demand*) descender **3.** (*accent, stress*) recaer **4.** (*in rank, on charts*) bajar **5.** (*be defeated*) caer **6.** *liter* (*die in battle*) caer **7.** (*occur*) **to ~ on a Monday** caer en lunes **8.** (*happen: darkness, silence*) caer; **night was ~ing** anochecía **9.** (*belong*) **to ~ into a category** pertenecer a una categoría **10.** (*hang down: hair, cloth*) colgar **11.** (*go down: cliff, ground, road*) descender **12.** + *adj* (*become*) hacerse; **to ~ due** tocar (pagar); **to ~ ill** caer enfermo **13.** (*enter a particular state*) **to ~ madly in love** (**with sb/sth**) enamorarse perdidamente (de alguien/algo); **to ~ out of favor** perder popularidad **II.** *n* **1.** (*drop from a height*) caída *f* **2.** (*decrease*) disminución *f*; **~ in temperature** descenso *m* de la temperatura **3.** (*defeat*) caída *f* **4.** (*autumn*) otoño *m* **5.** **~s** (*waterfall*) cascada *f*; **Niagara Falls** las cataratas del Niágara **6.** REL **the Fall** la Caída **III.** *adj* (*occurring in autumn: festival, sale*) en otoño; (*of autumn: colors, temperatures, weather*) otoñal

◆**fall back** *vi* **1.** (*move backwards: crowd*) quedarse atrás **2.** (*retreat: army*) replegarse **3.** SPORTS (*runner*) perder posiciones

◆**fall behind** *vi* **1.** (*become slower*) quedarse atrás **2.** (*achieve less: team, country*) quedarse rezagado **3.** (*fail to do sth on time*) retrasarse **4.** SPORTS quedarse atrás

◆**fall down** *vi* **1.** (*person*) caerse; (*building*) derrumbarse **2.** (*be unsatisfactory: person, plan*) fallar

◆**fall for** *vt* **to ~ sb** enamorarse de alguien; **to ~ a trick** caer en una trampa

◆**fall in** *vi* **1.** (*into water, hole*) caerse **2.** (*collapse: roof, ceiling*) venirse abajo **3.** MIL formar filas

◆**fall off** vi 1. (*become detached*) desprenderse 2. (*decrease*) reducirse

◆**fall out** vi 1. (*drop out: of container*) caer; (*teeth, hair*) caerse 2. inf (*argue*) pelearse 3. MIL romper filas

◆**fall over** I. vi insep caerse II. vt tropezar con; **to ~ oneself to do sth** inf desvivirse por hacer algo

◆**fall through** vi fracasar

**fallen** ['fɔ·lən] adj caído, -a

**false** [fɔls] adj 1. (*untrue: idea, information*) falso, -a; **~ economy** falso ahorro m; **~ move** movimiento m en falso; **to take a ~ step** dar un paso en falso; **to give a ~ impression** dar una impresión equivocada; **to raise ~ hopes** crear falsas esperanzas 2. (*artificial: beard, eyelashes*) postizo, -a; **a ~ bottom** un doble fondo 3. (*name, address, identity*) falso, -a; **~ accounting** LAW, FIN falsificación f de la contabilidad; **under ~ pretenses** con engaños 4. (*insincere: smile, laugh, manner*) falso, -a; **~ modesty** falsa modestia f

**false teeth** npl dientes m pl postizos

**falsetto** [fɔl'set·oʊ] I. n falsete m II. adv **to sing ~** cantar en falsete

**falsify** ['fɔl·sɪ·faɪ] vt falsificar

**fame** [feɪm] n fama f; **to rise to ~** hacerse famoso

**familiar** [fə·'mɪl·jər] adj 1. (*well-known*) familiar; (*face*) conocido, -a 2. (*acquainted*) familiarizado, -a; **to be ~ with sth** estar familiarizado con algo 3. (*friendly*) de familiaridad; **~ form of address** LING forma f de trato informal; **to be on ~ terms (with sb)** tener un trato de confianza (con alguien)

**familiarize** [fə·'mɪl·jə·raɪz] vt acostumbrar; **to ~ oneself with sth** familiarizarse con algo

**family** ['fæm·ə·li] <-ies> I. n familia f; **to be ~** ser familia; **to run in the ~** venir de familia; **to start a ~** formar una familia II. adj familiar

**family allowance** n Can subsidio m familiar

**family doctor** n médico m de cabecera

**family man** n (*enjoying family life*) hombre m casero; (*with wife and family*) padre m de familia

**family name** n apellido m

**family planning** n planificación f familiar

**family tree** n árbol m genealógico

**famine** ['fæm·ɪn] n hambruna f

**famous** ['feɪ·məs] adj famoso, -a; **to become ~ for sth** hacerse célebre por algo

**famously** adv **to get on ~** llevarse divinamente

**fan¹** [fæn] I. n 1. (*hand-held*) abanico m 2. (*electrical*) ventilador m II. <-nn-> vt (*cool with fan*) abanicar; **to ~ oneself** abanicarse

**fan²** [fæn] n (*admirer: of person*) admirador(a) m(f); (*of team*) hincha mf; (*of music*) fan mf

**fanatic** [fə·'næt̬·ɪk] n 1. entusiasta mf 2. pej fanático, -a m, f

**fanatical** adj fanático, -a

**fan belt** n AUTO correa f del ventilador

**fan club** n club m de fans

**fancy** ['fæn·tsi] I. adj <-ier, -iest> 1. (*elaborate: decoration, frills*) de adorno 2. inf (*expensive*) carísimo, -a; **~ hotel** hotel m de lujo 3. (*whimsical: ideas, notions*) extravagante II. n <-ies> 1. (*liking*) **to take a ~ to sth/sb** quedarse prendado de algo/alguien; **it tickled his ~** le hizo gracia 2. (*imagination*) fantasía f 3. (*whimsical idea*) capricho m III. <-ie-> vt (*imagine*) (*that*)! ¡lo que son las cosas!; **~ meeting you here!** ¡qué casualidad encontrarnos aquí!

**fancy-free** [ˌfæn·tsi·'fri] adj libre

**fang** [fæŋ] n (*of dog, lion*) colmillo m; (*of snake*) diente m

**fan mail** n cartas f pl de admiradores

**fantastic** [fæn·'tæs·tɪk] adj 1. (*excellent*) fantástico, -a 2. (*unbelievable: coincidence*) increíble; (*notion, plan*) absurdo, -a

**fantasy** ['fæn·tə·si] <-ies> n fantasía f

**fanzine** ['fæn·zin] n fanzine m

**far** [far] <farther, farthest or further, furthest> I. adv 1. (*a long distance*) lejos; **how ~ is it from Boston to Maine?** ¿qué distancia hay entre Bos-

**F**

ton y Maine?; **~ from it** todo lo contrario **2.** (*distant in time*) **~ back as I remember...** hasta donde me alcanza la memoria...; **to be not ~ off sth** faltar poco para algo; **so ~** hasta ahora **3.** (*in progress*) **to go too ~** ir demasiado lejos **4.** (*much*) **~ better** mucho mejor; **to be the best by ~** ser el/la mejor con diferencia; **to be ~ too expensive** ser demasiado caro **5.** (*connecting adverbial phrase*) **as ~ as I know...** que yo sepa...; **as ~ as possible** en lo posible ▶ **so ~ so good** hasta ahora todo va bien II. *adj* lejano, -a; **in the ~ distance** a lo lejos; **the ~ left/right** la extrema izquierda/derecha

**faraway** ['fɑr·ə·weɪ] *adj* **a ~ land** una tierra lejana

**fare** [fer] I. *n* **1.** (*for journey*) tarifa *f*; **one way ~** billete *m* [*or* pasaje *m*] sencillo; **round trip ~** billete *m* [*or* pasaje *m*] de ida y vuelta **2.** (*taxi passenger*) pasajero, -a *m*, *f* **3.** CULIN comida *f*; **simple home-style ~** comida *f* casera II. *vi* **to ~ badly/well** salir mal/bien parado

**Far East** *n* **the ~** el Lejano Oriente

**farewell** [ˌfer·'wel] I. *interj form* adiós; **to bid ~ to sb/sth** despedirse de alguien/algo II. *n* despedida *f* III. *adj* de despedida

**far-fetched** [ˌfɑr·'fetʃt] *adj* inverosímil

**farm** [fɑrm] I. *n* (*small*) granja *f*, hacienda *f AmL*, chacra *f CSur, Perú*; (*large*) hacienda *f* II. *vt* cultivar III. *vi* cultivar la tierra

**farmer** ['fɑr·mər] *n* granjero, -a *m*, *f*, hacendado, -a *m*, *f*, chacarero, -a *m*, *f CSur, Perú*

**farm hand** *n* mozo *m* de labranza

**farmhouse** *n* <-s> casa *f* de labranza

**farmyard** *n* corral *m*

**far-off** [ˌfɑr·'ɑf] *adj* (*place, country*) lejano, -a; (*time*) remoto, -a

**far-reaching** [ˌfɑr·'ri·tʃɪŋ] *adj* de grandes repercusiones

**farsighted** [ˌfɑr·'saɪ·tɪd] *adj* (*decision, policy*) con visión de futuro

**far-sighted** *adj* MED hipermétrope

**fart** [fɑrt] *sl* I. *n* pedo *m* II. *vi* tirarse un pedo

*tance*) más allá; **~ away from...** más lejos de...; **~ down/up** más abajo/arriba II. *adj comp of* **far** más lejano, -a

**farthest** ['fɑr·ðɪst] I. *adv superl of* **far** más lejos II. *adj superl of* **far** (*distance*) más lejano, -a; (*time*) más remoto, -a

**fascinate** ['fæs·ə·neɪt] *vt* fascinar

**fascinating** ['fæs·ə·neɪ·tɪŋ] *adj* fascinante

**fascination** [ˌfæs·ə·'neɪ·ʃən] *n* fascinación *f*

**fascist** ['fæʃ·ɪst] I. *n* fascista *mf* II. *adj* fascista

**fashion** ['fæʃ·ən] I. *n* **1.** (*popular style*) moda *f*; **to be in ~** estar de moda; **to be out of ~** estar pasado de moda; **to be all the ~** estar muy de moda; **the latest ~** la última moda **2.** (*manner*) manera *f*; **in the usual ~** como de costumbre II. *vt* dar forma a; (*create*) crear

**fashionable** ['fæʃ·ə·nə·bəl] *adj* (*clothes, style*) moderno, -a; (*nightclub, restaurant*) de moda; (*person, set*) a la moda

**fashion designer** *n* diseñador(a) *m(f)* de moda

**fashion show** *n* desfile *m* de moda

**fast**[1] [fæst] I. <-er, -est> *adj* **1.** (*quick*) rápido, -a; **the ~ lane** el carril de adelantamiento; **to be a ~ worker** trabajar rápido **2.** (*clock*) **to be ~** ir adelantado **3.** (*firmly fixed*) fijo, -a; **to make ~, to make sth ~ (to sth)** fijar algo (a algo) II. *adv* **1.** (*quickly*) rápidamente; **not so ~!** ¡no tan rápido! **2.** (*firmly*) firmemente; **to hold ~ to sth** agarrarse bien a algo **3.** (*deeply*) profundamente; **to be ~ asleep** estar profundamente dormido

**fast**[2] [fæst] I. *vi* (*go without food*) ayunar II. *n* (*period without food*) ayuno *m*

**fasten** ['fæs·ən] *vt* **1.** (*do up*) atar **2.** (*fix securely*) fijar, sujetar; **to ~ one's seatbelt** abrocharse el cinturón **3.** **to ~ sth together** (*with paper clip*) unir algo

**fastener** ['fæs·ə·nər] *n* cierre *m*

**fat** [fæt] I. *adj* **1.** (*quick*) gordo, -a; **to get ~** engordar **2.** (*thick*) grueso, -a **3.** (*large*) grande; **a ~ check** un cheque sustancioso ▶ **~ chance!** *inf* ¡para nada!, ¡ni soñarlo! II. *n* grasa *f*; **animal/vegetable ~** grasa animal/vegetal ▶ **to live off the ~ of the land** vivir a cuerpo de rey

**fatal** ['feɪt·əl] adj 1. (causing death) mortal 2. (disastrous) desastroso, -a 3. liter (consequences) funesto, -a

**fatality** [feɪ·'tæl·ə·t̬i] <-ies> n fatalidad f

**fatally** adv 1. (causing death) mortalmente; ~ ill enfermo de muerte 2. (disastrously) desastrosamente

**fate** [feɪt] n (destiny) destino m; (one's end) suerte f; to meet one's ~ hallar su destino; a ~ worse than death un destino peor que la muerte

**fated** ['feɪ·t̬ɪd] adj predestinado, -a

**fat-free** adj sin grasas

**fathead** ['fæt̬·hed] n sl imbécil mf inf

**father** ['fɑ·ðər] I. n 1. (parent) padre m; to be like a ~ to sb ser como un padre para alguien; on your ~'s side por parte paterna 2. (founder) fundador m 3. ~s liter (ancestors) antepasados mpl ▶ like ~, like son de tal palo, tal astilla II. vt (child) engendrar; (idea) crear

**fatherhood** ['fɑ·ðər·hʊd] n paternidad f

**father-in-law** ['fɑ·ðər·ɪn·lɔ] <fathers-in-law or father-in-laws> n suegro m

**fatherless** ['fɑ·ðər·lɪs] adj huérfano, -a de padre

**fatherly** ['fɑ·ðər·li] adj paternal

**Father's Day** n Día m del Padre

**fatigue** [fə·'tig] I. n 1. (tiredness) cansancio m, fatiga f 2. TECH fatiga f 3. MIL faena f II. vt 1. form (tire) cansar 2. TECH (weaken) debilitar

**fatten** ['fæt̬·ən] vt engordar

**fattening** adj que hace engordar

**fatty** ['fæt̬·i] I. adj 1. (food) graso, -a 2. (tissue) adiposo, -a II. <-ies> n inf gordinflón, -ona m, f

**faucet** ['fɔ·sɪt] n grifo m, bitoque m Chile, Col, Méx, canilla f Río Pl; to turn the ~ on/off abrir/cerrar el grifo

**fault** [fɔlt] I. n 1. (responsibility) culpa f; it's not my ~ yo no tengo la culpa; to be sb's ~ (that...) ser culpa de alguien (que...) 2. (character weakness) debilidad f; to have its ~s tener sus defectos 3. (defect) fallo m 4. GEO falla f 5. SPORTS falta f; double ~ doble falta; foot ~ falta de pie; to call a ~ pitar una falta II. vt encontrar defectos en

**faultless** ['fɔlt·lɪs] adj impecable

**faulty** ['fɔl·ti] adj defectuoso, -a

**favor** ['feɪ·vər] I. n 1. (approval) favor m, aprobación f; to be in ~ of sb/sth estar a favor de alguien/algo; to decide/vote in ~ of (doing) sth decidir/votar a favor de (hacer) algo; to be out of ~ no tener aceptación; to reject sth in ~ of sth else rechazar algo por otra cosa; to find in ~ of sb LAW fallar a favor de alguien; to find ~ with sb caer en gracia a alguien; to win sb's ~ ganarse la simpatía de alguien 2. (advantage) to have sth in one's ~ tener algo a favor 3. (helpful act) favor m, valedura f Méx; to do sb a ~ hacer un favor a alguien; do me a ~! inf ¡hazme el favor! 4. (small gift) detalle m II. vt 1. (prefer) preferir 2. (give advantage to) favorecer

**favorable** ['feɪ·vər·ə·bəl] adj 1. (approving) favorable 2. (advantageous) ventajoso, -a (to a)

**favorite** ['feɪ·vər·ɪt] adj, n favorito, -a m, f

**fawning** ['fɔ·nɪŋ] adj adulador(a)

**fax** [fæks] I. n fax m II. vt mandar por fax

**fax machine** n fax m

**fear** [fir] I. n miedo m; to have a ~ of sth tener miedo de algo; ~ of heights miedo a las alturas; for ~ that por temor a que II. vt 1. (be afraid of) tener miedo de; to have nothing to ~ no tener nada que temer 2. form (feel concern) to ~ (that...) temer (que...) III. vi liter tener miedo; never ~! ¡pierde cuidado!

**fearful** ['fir·fəl] adj 1. (anxious) temeroso, -a; ~ of doing sth temeroso de hacer algo 2. (terrible: pain, accident) terrible 3. inf (very bad: noise, mess) horrendo, -a

**feasibility** [ˌfi·zə·'bɪl·ə·t̬i] n viabilidad f

**feasible** ['fi·zə·bəl] adj 1. (plan) factible 2. (story) plausible

**feast** [fist] I. n 1. (meal) banquete m; a ~ for the eye una fiesta para los ojos 2. REL festividad f II. vi, vt to ~ on sth darse un banquete con algo; to ~ one's eyes on sth regalarse la vista con algo

**feat** [fit] n hazaña f; ~ of agility proeza f de agilidad; ~ of engineering logro m de la ingeniería

**feather** ['feð·ər] I. n pluma f II. vt to ~ one's own nest barrer para dentro

**featherweight** ['feð·ər·weɪt] *n* SPORTS peso *m* pluma

**feature** ['fi·tʃər] I. *n* 1. (*distinguishing attribute*) característica *f*; (*specialty*) peculiaridad *f*; **sb's/sth's best** ~ lo mejor de alguien/algo; **a distinguishing** ~ un rasgo distintivo 2. ~s (*of face*) facciones *fpl* 3. (*in newspaper, magazine*) reportaje *m* 4. CINE largometraje *m* II. *vt* 1. (*have as performer, star*) presentar 2. (*give special prominence to*) ofrecer (como atracción principal); **to** ~ **sth** (*article, report*) destacar algo III. *vi* 1. (*appear*) constar; **to** ~ **in...** constar en... 2. (*be an actor in*) **to** ~ **in a movie** aparecer en una película

**feature film** *n* largometraje *m*

**feature story** *n* reportaje *m*

**February** ['feb·ru·er·i] *n* febrero *m*; *s. a.* **April**

**federal** ['fed·ər·əl] *adj* federal; ~ **republic** república *f* federal

**federation** [fed·ə·'reɪ·ʃən] *n* federación *f*

**fed up** *adj inf* harto, -a; **to be** ~ **with sth/sb** estar harto de algo/alguien

**fee** [fi] *n* (*for doctor, lawyer*) honorarios *mpl*; (*for membership*) cuota *f* de miembro; (*for school, university*) tasas *f pl* de matrícula; **to charge/receive a** ~ **for sth** cobrar/recibir unos honorarios por algo

**feeble** ['fi·bəl] *adj* (*person, attempt*) débil; (*performance*) flojo, -a

**feeble-minded** [,fi·bl·'maɪn·dɪd] *adj* lelo, -a

**feed** [fid] <fed> I. *vt* 1. (*give food to: person, animal*) alimentar; (*plant*) nutrir; (*baby*) amamantar; **to** ~ **the fire** avivar el fuego 2. (*provide food for: family, country*) dar de comer a 3. (*supply*) proporcionar II. *vi* alimentarse; (*baby*) mamar III. *n* 1. (*for farm animals*) pienso *m*; **cattle** ~ pienso para ganado 2. *inf* (*meal*) comida *f* 3. TECH tubo *m* de alimentación

◆**feed on** *vt insep, a. fig* alimentarse de

◆**feed up** *vt* (*person*) alimentar; (*animal*) cebar

**feedback** ['fid·bæk] *n* 1. (*evaluation*) reacción *f*; **positive/negative** ~ reacción *f* positiva/negativa 2. ELEC reali-

**feeder** *n* 1. TECH alimentador *m* 2. (*river*) afluente *m*; ~ **road** carretera *f* de acceso

**feel** [fil] <felt> I. *vi* 1. + *adj/n* (*sensation or emotion*) sentir; **to** ~ **well** sentirse bien; **to** ~ **hot/cold** tener calor/frío; **to** ~ **hungry/thirsty** tener hambre/sed; **to** ~ **certain/convinced** estar seguro/convencido; **to** ~ **as if...** sentirse como si... +*subj*; **to** ~ **like a walk** tener ganas de dar un paseo; **to** ~ **free to do sth** sentirse libre para hacer algo; **to** ~ **one's age** notar el peso de los años; **it** ~s **wonderful/awful** me parece maravilloso/fatal; **how do you** ~ **about him?** ¿qué opinas de él?; **how would you** ~ **if...?** ¿qué te parece si...? 2. + *adj* (*seem*) parecer 3. (*search*) **to** ~ (**around**) **somewhere** buscar palpando por algún sitio II. *vt* 1. (*experience*) experimentar; **not to** ~ **a thing** no sentir nada; **to** ~ **the cold/heat** sentir frío/calor 2. (*think, believe*) **to** ~ (**that**)... creer (que)...; **to** ~ **it appropriate/necessary to do sth** considerar adecuado/necesario hacer algo 3. (*touch*) tocar; (*pulse*) tomar III. *n* 1. (*texture*) textura *f*; **the** ~ **of sth** el tacto de algo 2. (*act of touching*) tacto *m* 3. (*character, atmosphere*) ambiente *m* 4. (*natural talent*) talento *m* natural; **to have a** ~ **for sth** tener talento natural para algo; **to get the** ~ **of sth** acostumbrarse a algo

◆**feel for** *vt* **to** ~ **sb** sentirlo por alguien, compadecer a alguien

**feeling** ['fi·lɪŋ] *n* 1. (*emotion*) sentimiento *m*; **mixed** ~s sentimientos entremezclados [*or* encontrados]; **to hurt sb's** ~s herir los sentimientos de alguien 2. (*sensation*) sensación *f*; **a dizzy** ~ una sensación de vértigo 3. (*impression*) impresión *f*; **to have the** ~ (**that**)... tener la impresión (de que)...; **to have a bad** ~ **about sth/sb** tener un mal presentimiento acerca de algo/alguien 4. (*opinion*) opinión *f*; **to have strong** ~s **about sth** tener firmes convicciones sobre algo 5. (*strong emotion*) sentimiento *m*; **to say sth with** ~ decir algo con emoción 6. (*physical sensation*) sensibilidad *f*

**feet** [fit] *n pl of* **foot**

**fell**[1] [fel] *pt of* **fall**

**fell**[2] [fel] *vt* **1.** (*cut down*) talar **2.** (*knock down: boxer*) derribar

**fell**[3] [fel] *adj* HIST feroz, terrible ▶ **at** [*or* **in**] **one ~ swoop** de un solo golpe

**fellow** ['fel·ou] **I.** *n* **1.** *inf* (*man*) tío *m*; **an odd ~** un tipo raro **2.** UNIV profesor(a) *m(f)* **3.** *form* (*colleague*) compañero, -a *f* **II.** *adj* **~ student** compañero, -a *m, f* de clase

**fellow member** *n* consocio *mf*

**fellowship** ['fel·ou·ʃɪp] *n* **1.** (*comradely feeling*) compañerismo *m* **2.** *form* (*group*) asociación *f*, sociedad *f* **3.** UNIV **research ~** beca *f* de investigación

**felon** ['fel·ən] *n* criminal *mf*

**felony** ['fel·ə·ni] <-ies> *n* crimen *m*

**felt**[1] [felt] *pt, pp of* **feel**

**felt**[2] [felt] **I.** *n* (*material*) fieltro *m* **II.** *adj* de fieltro

**female** ['fi·meɪl] **I.** *adj* femenino, -a; ZOOL, TECH hembra **II.** *n* (*woman*) mujer *f*; ZOOL hembra *f*

**feminine** ['fem·ə·nɪn] **I.** *adj* femenino, -a **II.** *n* LING **the ~** el femenino

**femininity** [ˌfem·ə·'nɪn·ə·ti] *n* feminidad *f*

**feminist** ['fem·ɪ·nɪst] **I.** *n* feminista *mf* **II.** *adj* feminista

**fence** [fens] **I.** *n* (*barrier*) cerca *f*; **to sit on the ~** nadar entre dos aguas **II.** *vi* SPORTS practicar esgrima **III.** *vt* (*enclose*) cercar

**fencer** *n* esgrimista *mf*

**fencing** *n* esgrima *f*

**ferocious** [fə·'rou·ʃəs] *adj* (*battle, criticism*) feroz; (*temper*) violento, -a

**Ferris wheel** ['fer·ɪs·ˌhwil] *n* noria *f*

**ferry** ['fer·i] **I.** *n* (*ship*) ferry *m*; (*smaller*) balsa *f* **II.** *vt* (*in boat*) llevar en barca

**ferryman** <-men> *n* barquero *m*

**fertile** ['fɜr·t̬əl] *adj a. fig* fértil

**fertility** [fər·'tɪl·ə·t̬i] *n* fertilidad *f*

**fertilize** ['fɜr·t̬əl·aɪz] *vt* **1.** BIO fertilizar **2.** AGR abonar

**fertilizer** ['fɜr·t̬əl·aɪ·zər] *n* fertilizante *m*

**festival** ['fes·tɪ·vəl] *n* **1.** (*special event*) festival *m* **2.** REL festividad *f*, fiesta *f*

**festive** ['fes·tɪv] *adj* festivo, -a

**festivity** [fes·'tɪv·ə·t̬i] <-ies> *n* **1.** **festivities** (*festive activities*) festejos *mpl* **2.** (*festival*) fiesta *f*

**fetch** [fetʃ] *vt* **1.** (*bring back*) traer; **to sb sth** (*from somewhere*) traer algo a alguien (de algún sitio) **2.** (*be sold for*) venderse por

**fetching** ['fetʃ·ɪŋ] *adj* atractivo, -a

**fetus** ['fi·t̬əs] *n* feto *m*

**feud** [fjud] **I.** *n* enemistad *f* (heredada); **a family ~** una enemistad entre familias **II.** *vi* pelearse

**fever** ['fi·vər] *n* **1.** MED fiebre *f*; **to have** [*or* **run**] **a ~** tener fiebre **2.** (*excited state*) emoción *f*

**feverish** ['fi·vər·ɪʃ] *adj* **1.** MED con fiebre **2.** (*frantic*) exaltado

**few** [fju] <-er, -est> **I.** *adj det* **1.** (*small number*) pocos, pocas; **one of her ~ friends** uno de sus pocos amigos; **quite a ~ people** bastante gente; **not ~er than 100 people** no menos de 100 personas; **to be ~ and far between** ser poquísimos, ser contadísimos **2.** (*some*) algunos, algunas **II.** *pron* pocos, pocas; **a ~** unos pocos; **I'd like a ~ more** quisiera unos pocos más; **the ~ who have the book** los pocos que tienen el libro; **the happy/lucky ~** los pocos felices/afortunados

**fiancé** [ˌfi·an·'seɪ] *n* prometido *m*

**fiancée** [ˌfi·an·'seɪ] *n* prometida *f*

**fib** [fɪb] <-bb-> *inf* **I.** *vi* decir mentirijillas **II.** *n* mentirijilla *f*, pepa *f* And

**fibber** ['fɪb·ər] *n* mentirosillo, -a *m, f*

**fiber** ['faɪ·bər] *n* **1.** fibra *f* **2.** *fig* carácter *m*

**fiberglass** ['faɪ·bər·ˌglæs] *n* fibra *f* de vidrio

**fickle** ['fɪk·l] *adj* inconstante

**fiction** ['fɪk·ʃən] *n* **1.** *a.* LIT ficción *f* **2.** (*false statement*) invención *f*

**fictional** ['fɪk·ʃə·nəl] *adj* ficticio, -a

**fictitious** [fɪk·'tɪʃ·əs] *adj* **1.** (*false, untrue*) falso, -a **2.** (*imaginary*) ficticio, -a; **~ character** personaje *m* de ficción

**fiddle** ['fɪd·l] **I.** *vi* **1.** (*play the violin*) tocar el violín **2. to ~ (around) with sth** (*fidget with*) juguetear con algo **II.** *n* **1.** (*violin*) violín *m*; **to play the ~** tocar el violín **2.** (*fraud*) trampa *f*

**fidget** ['fɪdʒ·ɪt] **I.** *vi* no parar quieto *inf* **II.** *n* persona *f* inquieta

**fidgety** ['fɪdʒ·ɪ·ti] *adj* inquieto, -a

**fiefdom** ['fif·dəm] *n* feudo *m*

**field** [fild] **I.** *n* **1.** a. ELEC, AGR, SPORTS campo *m*; (*meadow*) prado *m* **2.** + *sing/pl vb* (*contestants*) competidores *mpl*; **to play the ~** *fig* tantear el terreno **3.** (*sphere of activity*) esfera *f*; **it's not my ~** no es mi campo **4.** COMPUT campo *m* **II.** *vt* **1.** (*return*) **to ~ the ball** recoger la pelota; **to ~ a question** sortear una pregunta **2.** (*candidate*) presentar

**field day** *n* **1.** SPORTS día *m* de competición **2.** MIL día de maniobras *fpl* ▶ **to have a ~** divertirse muchísimo

**fielder** ['fil·dər] *n* SPORTS fildeador(a) *m(f)* (*una de las posiciones en béisbol*)

**field glasses** *n* prismáticos *mpl*

**field mouse** *n* ratón *m* de campo

**fieldwork** ['fild·ˌwɜrk] *n* trabajo *m* de campo

**fieldworker** *n* investigador(a) *m(f)* de campo

**fierce** [fɪrs] *adj* <-er, -est> **1.** (*animal*) salvaje **2.** (*competition, opposition*) intenso, -a; (*debate, discussion*) acalorado, -a; (*wind*) fuerte **3.** *inf* (*hard*) difícil

**fiery** ['faɪr·i] *adj* <-ier, -iest> **1.** (*heat*) abrasador(a) **2.** (*passionate*) apasionado, -a **3.** (*very spicy*) muy picante

**fifteen** [ˌfɪf·'tin] **I.** *adj* quince **II.** *n* quince *m*; *s. a.* **eight**

**fifteenth** **I.** *adj* decimoquinto, -a **II.** *n* **1.** (*order*) decimoquinto, -a *m, f* **2.** (*date*) quince *m* **3.** (*fraction*) quinceavo *m*; (*part*) decimoquinta parte *f*; *s. a.* **eighth**

**fifth** [fɪfθ] **I.** *adj* quinto, -a **II.** *n* **1.** (*order*) quinto, -a *m, f* **2.** (*date*) cinco *m* **3.** (*fraction*) quinto *m*; (*part*) quinta parte *f*; *s. a.* **eighth**

**fiftieth** ['fɪf·ti·əθ] **I.** *adj* quincuagésimo, -a **II.** *n* (*order*) quincuagésimo, -a *m, f* (*fraction*) quincuagésimo *m*; (*part*) quincuagésima parte *f*; *s. a.* **eighth**

**fifty** ['fɪf·ti] **I.** *adj* cincuenta **II.** <-ies> *n* cincuenta *m*; *s. a.* **eighty**

**fig** [fɪg] *n* **1.** (*fruit*) higo *m* **2.** (*tree*) higuera *f* ▶ **to be not worth a ~** no valer nada

**fight** [faɪt] **I.** *n* **1.** (*physical*) pelea *f*; (*argument*) disputa *f*; **to put up a ~** defenderse bien **2.** MIL combate *m* **3.** (*struggle*) lucha *f* **4.** (*spirit*) combatividad *f* **II.** <fought, fought> *vi* **1.** (*exchange blows*) pelear; MIL combatir; **to ~ with each other** pelearse; **to ~ with sb** (*against*) luchar contra alguien; (*on same side*) luchar junto a alguien **2.** (*dispute*) discutir; **to ~ about sth** discutir sobre algo **3.** (*struggle to overcome*) luchar (**for/against** por/contra) **III.** *vt* **1.** (*exchange blows with, argue with*) pelearse con **2.** (*wage war, do battle*) luchar con; **to ~ a battle** librar una batalla; **to ~ a duel** batirse en duelo **3.** (*struggle to overcome*) combatir; **to ~ a case** LAW llevar un caso a los tribunales **4.** (*struggle to obtain*) **to ~ one's way through the crowd** hacerse paso entre la multitud; **to ~ one's way to the top** hacerse camino luchando hasta la cima

◆**fight back** **I.** *vi* (*defend oneself*) defenderse; (*counterattack*) contraatacar **II.** *vt* **to ~ one's tears** contener las lágrimas

◆**fight off** *vt* (*repel*) rechazar; (*master, resist*) resistir

**fighter** ['faɪ·tər] *n* **1.** (*person*) luchador(a) *m(f)* **2.** AVIAT caza *m*

**fighting** ['faɪ·tɪŋ] **I.** *n* lucha *f*; (*battle*) combate *m* **II.** *adj* combativo, -a ▶ **there's a ~ chance** that... existen grandes posibilidades de que... +*subj*

**figurative** ['fɪg·jər·ə·tɪv] *adj* **1.** LING figurado, -a **2.** ART figurativo, -a

**figuratively** *adv* en sentido figurado

**figure** ['fɪg·jər] **I.** *n* **1.** (*shape*) figura *f*; **mother ~** figura materna; **to cut a fine ~** causar buena impresión; **to keep one's ~** guardar la línea **2.** ART estatua *f*; (*human being*) figura *f* **3.** (*numeral*) cifra *f*; **to have a head for ~s** ser bueno para los números; **in round ~s** en cifras redondas **4.** (*price*) precio *m* **5.** (*diagram*) figura *f*; (*illustration*) ilustración *f* **II.** *vt* **1.** (*think*) figurarse; **to ~ that...** figurarse que... **2.** (*in diagram*) representar **3.** (*calculate*) calcular **III.** *vi* (*feature*) figurar; **to ~ as sth/sb** figurar como algo/alguien; **that ~s!** es natural

**figure out** vt (*comprehend*) entender; (*work out*) resolver

**figure skating** n patinaje m artístico

**Fiji** ['fi·dʒi] n the ~ **Islands** las Islas Fiji

**file¹** [faɪl] I. n 1. (*folder*) carpeta f 2. (*record*) expediente m; **to open a ~** abrir un expediente; **to keep sth on ~** guardar algo archivado 3. COMPUT fichero m, archivo m 4. (*row*) fila f; **in single ~** en fila india II. vt 1. (*record*) archivar, failear AmC, RíoPl 2. (*present: claim, complaint*) presentar III. vi 1. LAW **to ~ for divorce** presentar una demanda de divorcio 2. (*move in line*) desfilar

**file in** vi entrar en fila

**file out** vi salir en fila

**file²** [faɪl] I. n (*tool*) lima f II. vt limar III. vi **to ~ sth down** limar algo

**file name** n nombre m de archivo [*or* fichero]

**filigree** ['fɪl·ɪ·gri] n filigrana f

**filing** ['faɪ·lɪŋ] n 1. (*archiving*) clasificación f 2. LAW presentación f 3. ~**s** (*bits of metal*) limaduras fpl

**filing cabinet** n archivador m

**fill** [fɪl] I. vt 1. (*make full*) llenar; (*space*) ocupar; **to ~ a vacancy** cubrir una vacante; **to ~ a need** satisfacer una necesidad 2. (*seal*) empastar, emplomar AmL 3. CULIN rellenar 4. (*fulfill: order, requirement*) cumplir II. vi llenarse III. n 1. **to drink/eat one's ~** hartarse de beber/comer 2. (*dirt*) relleno m

**fill in** vt 1. (*seal opening*) llenar 2. (*document*) rellenar 3. (*color in*) colorear 4. (*inform*) informar; **to fill sb in on the details** poner a alguien al corriente de los detalles 5. (*time*) ocupar II. vi to ~ (**for sb**) hacer las veces (de alguien)

**fill out** I. vt (*document*) rellenar II. vi (*put on weight*) engordar

**fill up** I. vt llenar; (*completely*) colmar II. vi llenarse

**fillet** ['fɪl·ɪt] I. n filete m II. vt cortar en filetes

**filling** ['fɪl·ɪŋ] I. n 1. (*substance*) relleno m 2. (*in tooth*) empaste m, emplomadura f AmL II. adj sólido, -a; **to be ~** que llena (el estómago)

**filling station** n gasolinera f, bencine-

ra f Chile, grifo m Perú

**film** [fɪlm] I. n 1. PHOT, CINE película f; **to see** [*or* **watch**] **a ~** ver una película 2. (*fine coating*) capa f; **a ~ of oil** una película de aceite II. vt filmar III. vi rodar

**film buff** n cinéfilo, -a m, f

**film camera** n cámara f cinematográfica

**film star** n estrella f de cine

**film studio** n estudio m de cine

**filter** ['fɪl·tər] I. n filtro m II. vt filtrar III. vi filtrarse

**filter out** I. vi llegar a saberse II. vt quitar filtrando

**filter through** vi filtrarse

**filter paper** n papel m de filtro

**filter tip** n filtro m

**filth** [fɪlθ] n 1. (*dirt*) mugre f 2. (*obscenity*) obscenidad f

**filthy** ['fɪl·θi] I. adj 1. (*very dirty*) inmundo, -a 2. (*obscene*) obsceno, -a II. adv inf **to be ~ rich** estar forrado

**fin** [fɪn] n aleta f

**final** ['faɪ·nəl] I. adj 1. (*last*) final 2. (*irrevocable*) definitivo, -a; **to have the ~ say** (**on sth**) tener la última palabra (sobre algo); **and that's ~** inf y sanseacabó II. n 1. SPORTS final f; **to get** (**through**) **to the ~s** llegar a la final 2. pl UNIV exámenes m de fin de carrera pl

**finale** [fɪ·'næl·i] n final m; **grand ~** gran escena final

**finalist** ['faɪ·nə·lɪst] n finalista mf

**finalize** ['faɪ·nə·laɪz] vt ultimar

**finally** ['faɪ·nə·li] adv 1. (*at long last*) finalmente; (*expressing impatience*) por fin 2. (*in conclusion*) en conclusión

**finance** ['faɪ·næns] vt financiar

**financial** [faɪ·'næn·tʃəl] adj financiero, -a; **sb's ~ affairs** los asuntos financieros de alguien

**finch** [fɪntʃ] n ZOOL pinzón m

**find** [faɪnd] n <found, found> vt 1. (*lost object, person*) encontrar 2. (*locate*) localizar, hallar; **to be nowhere to be found** no encontrarse por ningún sitio; **to ~ no reason why...** no hallar razón alguna por la que...; **to ~ (the) time** sacar tiempo inf; **to ~ the strength (to do sth)** hallar las fuerzas (para hacer algo) 3. (*experience*) sentir; **to ~ oneself**

**alone** sentirse solo **4.** (*conclude*) to ~ **sb guilty/innocent** declarar a alguien culpable/inocente **5.** (*discover*) descubrir **II.** n hallazgo m

◆**find out I.** vt descubrir; (*dishonesty*) desenmascarar; **to ~ when/where/ who...** averiguar cuándo/dónde/ quién... **II.** vi to ~ **about sth/sb** informarse sobre algo/alguien

**finder** ['faɪn·dar] n (*of sth unknown*) descubridor(a) m(f); (*of sth lost*) persona f que encuentra (algo)

**finding** ['faɪn·dɪŋ] n **1.** LAW fallo m **2.** (*recommendation*) recomendación f **3.** (*discovery*) descubrimiento m

**fine¹** [faɪn] **I.** adj **1.** (*slender, light*) fino, -a; (*feature*) delicado, -a; (*nuance*) sutil **2.** (*good*) bueno, -a; (*satisfactory*) satisfactorio, -a; ~ **weather** buen tiempo m; **how are you? — I'm ~, thanks** ¿qué tal estás? — bien, gracias; **to be ~ by sb** estar bien para alguien **3.** (*excellent*) excelente **II.** adv **1.** (*all right*) muy bien; **to feel ~** sentirse bien; **to work ~** funcionar bien **2.** (*fine-grained*) fino, -a

**fine²** [faɪn] **I.** n (*penalty*) multa f, boleta f AmS **II.** vt (*order to pay penalty*) multar

**fine arts** n bellas artes fpl

**finger** ['fɪŋ·gar] **I.** n dedo m; **little/ middle ~** dedo meñique/corazón ▶ **to have sb wrapped around one's <u>little</u> ~** hacer que alguien baile al son que le tocan; **to <u>keep</u> one's ~s crossed** tener los dedos cruzados; **to <u>lay</u> a ~ on sb** poner la mano encima a alguien **II.** vt **1.** (*touch*) manosear **2.** sl (*reveal*) delatar

**fingernail** n uña f

**fingerprint** n huella f dactilar

**fingertip** n punta f del dedo

**finish** ['fɪn·ɪʃ] **I.** n **1.** (*end*) final m, fin m; SPORTS meta f **2.** (*sealing, varnishing: of fabric*) acabado m; (*of furniture*) pulido m **II.** vi terminar(se), acabar(se); **to ~ doing sth** terminar de hacer algo **III.** vt **1.** (*bring to end*) terminar, acabar; **to ~ a sentence** completar una oración **2.** (*make final touches to*) acabar

◆**finish off I.** vt **1.** (*end*) terminar, acabar, rematar; (*use up*) terminar **2.** (*de-*

feat) acabar con **3.** inf (*murder*) liquidar **II.** vi concluir

◆**finish up I.** vi to ~ **at** ir a parar a **II.** vt (*food, drink*) terminar

◆**finish with** vt terminar con; **to ~ sb** romper con alguien

**finished** adj (*product*) terminado, -a, acabado, -a

**finishing line** n, **finishing post** n línea f de meta

**finite** ['faɪ·naɪt] adj a. LING finito, -a

**fir** [fɜr] n abeto m

**fire** ['faɪr] **I.** n **1.** (*flames*) fuego m; (*in fireplace*) lumbre f; (*accidental*) incendio m; **to set sth on ~** prender fuego a algo; **to catch ~** encenderse **2.** TECH calefacción f; (*stove*) hornillo m **3.** MIL **to open ~ on sb** abrir fuego contra alguien; **to be under ~** MIL estar en la línea de fuego; fig ser criticado ▶ **to set the <u>world</u> on ~** hacerse famoso; **to <u>play</u> with ~** jugar con fuego **II.** vt **1.** (*burn*) encender; (*ceramics*) cocer **2.** (*weapon*) disparar **3.** inf (*dismiss*) despedir, botar AmL, fletar Arg **III.** vi **1.** (*with gun*) disparar; **to ~ at sb** disparar contra alguien **2.** AUTO encenderse

**fire alarm** n alarma f contra incendios

**firearm** n arma f de fuego

**firecracker** n petardo m

**fire department** n cuerpo m de bomberos

**fire engine** n coche m de bomberos

**fire escape** n escalera f de incendios

**fire extinguisher** n extintor m

**firefighter** n bombero m

**firefly** n luciérnaga f, cocuyo m AmL

**fire house** n parque m de bomberos

**fireman** <-men> n bombero m

**fireplace** n chimenea f, hogar m

**fireproof** adj a prueba de incendios

**fireside** n hogar m

**fire station** n parque m de bomberos

**firewoman** <-women> n mujer f bombero

**firewood** n leña f

**fireworks** npl **1.** fuegos m artificiales pl [e] **2.** pl, fig explosión f (de cólera)

**firm¹** [fɜrm] **I.** adj **1.** (*secure*) firme; (*strong*) fuerte; **a ~ offer** una oferta en firme **2.** (*dense, solid*) duro, -a **3.** (*res-*

olute) decidido, -a II. *adv* firmemente; **to stand ~** mantenerse firme

**firm²** [fɜrm] *n* (*company*) empresa *f*; *law* ~ bufete *m* de abogados

**first** [fɜrst] I. *adj* (*earliest*) primero, -a; **for the ~ time** por primera vez; **at ~ sight** a primera vista; **the ~ of December/December ~** el primero de diciembre, el uno de diciembre *inf* ▶ **~ and foremost** ante todo II. *adv* primero; (*firstly*) en primer lugar; **~ of all** ante todo; **at ~** al principio; **to go head ~** meterse de cabeza ▶ **~ come ~ served** *inf* por orden de llegada III. *n* **the ~** el primero, la primera

**first aid** *n* primeros auxilios *mpl*

**first class** I. *n* primera clase *f* II. *adv* **to travel ~** viajar en primera

**first-class** *adj* de primera clase

**first floor** *n* planta *f* baja

**firstly** ['fɜrst·li] *adv* en primer lugar

**first name** *n* nombre *m* (de pila)

**first night** *n* noche *f* de estreno

**first-rate** [,fɜrst·'reɪt] *adj* de primer orden

**fish** [fɪʃ] I. <-(es)> *n* **1.** zool pez *m* **2.** culin pescado *m* ▶ (*like*) **a ~ out of water** como pez fuera del agua II. *vi* pescar; **to ~ for compliments** andar a la caza de cumplidos III. *vt* pescar

**fishbone** ['fɪʃ·boʊn] *n* espina *f* (de pescado)

**fishcake** ['fɪʃ·keɪk] *n* croqueta *f* de pescado

**fisherman** ['fɪʃ·ər·mən] <-men> *n* pescador *m*

**fishing** I. *n* pesca *f* II. *adj* pesquero, -a

**fishing line** *n* sedal *m*

**fishpond** ['fɪʃ·pand] *n* estanque *m* para peces

**fishy** ['fɪʃ·i] <-ier, -iest> *adj* **1.** (*taste*) que sabe a pescado; (*smell*) que huele a pescado **2.** *inf* (*dubious*) dudoso, -a ▶ **to smell ~** oler a chamusquina

**fission** ['fɪʃ·ən] *n* phys fisión *f*; bio escisión *f*

**fissure** ['fɪʃ·ər] *n* fisura *f*

**fist** [fɪst] *n* puño *m*; **to clench one's ~s** cerrar los puños

**fistfight** *n* pelea *f*; **to have a ~** liarse a golpes *inf*

**fit¹** [fɪt] I. <-tt-> *adj* **1.** (*apt, suitable*) apto, -a, apropiado, -a; (*competent*) capaz; **~ to eat** bueno para comer **2.** sports en forma **3.** med sano, -a ▶ **to be ~ to be tied** estar fuera de sí II. <-tt-> *vt* **1.** (*adapt*) ajustar **2.** (*clothes*) quedar bien **3.** (*facts*) corresponder con **4.** tech caber en, encajar en III. *vi* <-tt-> **1.** (*be correct size*) ir bien **2.** (*correspond*) corresponder IV. *n* ajuste *m*

◆**fit in** I. *vi* **1.** (*conform*) encajar **2.** (*get along well*) llevarse bien II. *vt* tener tiempo para

◆**fit out** *vt* equipar

◆**fit together** *vi* encajar

◆**fit up** *vt* equipar

**fit²** [fɪt] *n* **1.** med ataque *m*; **coughing ~** acceso *m* de tos **2.** (*outburst of rage*) arranque *m*; **they were in ~s of laughter** se morían de (la) risa

**fitness** ['fɪt·nɪs] *n* **1.** (*good condition*) (buena) condición *f* física; (*health*) (buena) salud *f* **2.** (*competence, suitability*) conveniencia *f*

**fitted** ['fɪt·ɪd] *adj* (*adapted, suitable*) idóneo, -a; (*tailor-made*) a medida

**fitting** ['fɪt·ɪŋ] I. *n* **1.** **~s** (*fixtures*) accesorios *mpl* **2.** (*of clothes*) prueba *f* II. *adj* apropiado, -a

**five** [faɪv] I. *adj* cinco II. *n* cinco *m*; **gimme ~!** *sl* ¡choca esos cinco!; *s. a.* **eight**

**fiver** ['faɪ·vər] *n inf* billete *m* de cinco dólares

**fix** [fɪks] I. *vt* **1.** (*repair*) arreglar **2.** (*fasten*) sujetar; **to ~ one's eyes on sb** fijar los ojos en alguien **3.** (*determine*) fijar **4.** (*arrange*) arreglar **5.** *inf* (*lunch, dinner*) preparar **6.** *inf* (*manipulate: election, result*) amañar **7.** *inf* (*take revenge on*) ajustar las cuentas con; **I'll ~ him** me las pagará **8.** phys, phot (*color*) fijar II. *n* **1.** *inf* (*dilemma*) aprieto *m* **2.** *sl* (*dose of heroin*) chute *m*, pichicata *f Arg*

◆**fix on** *vt* **1.** (*choose*) escoger **2.** (*make definite*) fijar

◆**fix up** *vt* **1.** (*supply with*) **to fix sb up (with sth)** proveer a alguien (de algo) **2.** *inf* (*arrange a date*) **to fix sb up (with sb)** arreglárselo a alguien (con alguien) **3.** (*repair*) arreglar

**fixed** *adj* fijo, -a; **to be of no ~ abode** LAW no tener domicilio permanente

**fixings** *npl inf* guarnición *f*

**fixture** ['fɪkst·ʃər] *n* (*in bathroom and kitchen*) instalación *f* fija; **light ~s** iluminación *f*

**fizz** [fɪz] I. *vi* burbujear II. *n* **1.** (*bubble, frothiness*) efervescencia *f* **2.** (*soda*) gaseosa *f*

**fizzle** ['fɪz·l] *vi* chisporrotear

**fizzy** ['fɪz·i] <-ier, -iest> *adj* (*bubbly*) efervescente; (*carbonated*) gaseoso, -a

**FL** *n*, **Fla.** *n abbr of* **Florida** Florida *f*

**flabby** ['flæb·i] <-ier, -iest> *adj pej* **1.** (*body*) fofo, -a **2.** (*weak*) débil

**flag**[1] [flæg] I. *n* **1.** (*national*) bandera *f*; (*pennant*) estandarte *m*; **to raise a ~** izar una bandera **2.** (*marker*) señalizador *m* II. <-gg-> *vt* (*mark*) señalar; (*label computer data*) etiquetar III. <-gg-> *vi* flaquear

**flag**[2] [flæg] *n* (*stone*) losa *f*

**flagpole** ['flæg·ˌpoʊl] *n* asta *f* (de una bandera)

**flagrant** ['fleɪ·grənt] *adj* flagrante

**flair** [fler] *n* **1.** (*genius*) don *m*, talento *m* **2.** (*style*) estilo *m*

**flake** [fleɪk] I. *vi* (*skin*) pelarse; (*paint*) desconcharse; (*wood*) astillarse; (*plaster*) descascararse II. *n* (*shaving, sliver*) viruta *f*; (*of skin*) escama *f*; (*of snow*) copo *m*

◆**flake out** *vi sl* caer rendido

**flaky** ['fleɪ·ki] <-ier, -iest> *adj* **1.** (*skin*) escamoso, -a; (*paint*) de láminas **2.** *sl* (*strange*) chiflado, -a

**flamboyant** [flæm·ˈbɔɪ·ənt] *adj* (*manner, person*) exuberante; (*air, clothes*) vistoso, -a

**flame** [fleɪm] I. *n* **1.** *(flame) f*; **to be in ~s** arder en llamas; **to burst into ~** estallar en llamas **2.** (*lover*) (*old*) ~ antiguo amor *m* II. *vi* (*blaze, burn*) llamear; (*glare*) brillar

**flaming** ['fleɪ·mɪŋ] *adj* **1.** (*burning*) en llamas **2.** *fig* (*quarrel*) acalorado, -a

**flamingo** [fləˈmɪŋ·goʊ] <-(e)s> *m* flamenco *m*

**flammable** ['flæm·ə·bəl] *adj* inflamable

**flan** [flæn] *n* tarta *f*

**Flanders** ['flæn·dərz] *n* Flandes *m*

**flannel** ['flæn·l] *n* **1.** (*material*) franela *f* **2.** **~s** (*trousers*) pantalones *m pl* de franela

**flap** [flæp] I. <-pp-> *vt* (*wings*) batir; (*shake*) sacudir II. <-pp-> *vi* **1.** (*wings*) aletear; (*flag*) ondear **2.** *inf* (*become nervous*) agitarse III. *n* **1.** (*of cloth*) faldón *m*; (*of skin*) colgajo *m*; (*of pocket, envelope*) solapa *f*; (*of table*) hoja *f* **2.** AVIAT flap *m* **3.** (*of wing*) aleteo *m* **4.** *inf* (*commotion*) jaleo *m*; **to cause a ~** armar un lío

**flare** [fler] I. *n* **1.** (*blaze*) llamarada *f* **2.** (*signal*) cohete *m* de señales **3.** MIL bengala *f* **4.** (*of clothes*) vuelo *m* II. *vi* **1.** (*blaze*) llamear; (*light*) resplandecer III. *vt* **to ~ one's nostrils** resoplar

**flash** [flæʃ] I. *vt* **1.** (*shine: light*) enfocar; **to ~ a light in sb's eyes** dirigir un rayo de luz a los ojos de alguien **2.** (*show quickly*) mostrar (*rápidamente*) **3.** (*communicate*) transmitir; (*smile, look*) lanzar II. *vi* **1.** (*lightning*) relampaguear; *fig* (*eyes*) brillar **2.** *sl* (*expose oneself in public*) exhibirse III. *n* **1.** (*of light*) destello *m*; **~ of lightning** relámpago *m* **2.** PHOT flash *m* ▶ **in a ~** en un instante IV. <-er, -est> *adj sl* llamativo, -a

**flashback** ['flæʃ·bæk] *n* CINE, LIT, THEAT escena *f* retrospectiva, flashback *m*

**flashbulb** ['flæʃ·bʌlb] *n* bombilla *f* de flash

**flasher** ['flæʃ·ər] *n sl* exhibicionista *m*

**flashgun** ['flæʃ·gʌn] *n* disparador *m* de flash

**flashlight** ['flæʃ·laɪt] *n* linterna *f* eléctrica

**flashy** ['flæʃ·i] <-ier, -iest> *adj* ostentoso, -a, llamativo, -a

**flask** [flæsk] *n* CHEM matraz *m*; (*thermos*) termo *m*; **hip ~** petaca *f*

**flat**[1] [flæt] I. *adj* <-tt-> **1.** (*surface*) llano, -a, plano, -a **2.** (*unexciting*) soso, -a **3.** (*drink*) sin gas **4.** (*tire*) desinflado, -a **5.** (*absolute: refusal, rejection*) categórico, -a; **and that's ~** y no hay más que hablar **6.** COM (*not changing*) fijo, -a **7.** MUS desafinado, -a II. <-tt-> *adv* **1.** (*level*) horizontalmente **2.** (*absolutely*) completamente ▶ **to be**

~ **broke** no tener ni un duro; **in five minutes** ~ inf en sólo cinco minutos III. n 1. (*level surface: of sword, knife*) plano m 2. (*low level ground*) llanura f; **salt** ~s salinas fpl 3. (*flat tire*) pinchazo m 4. mus bemol m

**flat²** [flæt] n (*apartment*) piso m, apartamento m Ven, Col, departamento m Méx, CSur

**flat-footed** [ˌflæt·ˈfʊt·ɪd] adj de pies planos

**flatten** [ˈflæt·n̩] vt 1. (*make level*) allanar 2. mus bajar el tono

**flatter** [ˈflæt·ər] vt 1. (*gratify vanity*) adular 2. (*make attractive*) favorecer

**flattering** adj 1. (*clothes, portrait*) que favorece 2. (*remark, description*) halagador(a)

**flattery** [ˈflæt·ə·ri] n adulación f; ~ **will get you nowhere** adulando no conseguirás tu propósito

**flatulence** [ˈflætʃ·ə·ləns] n form flatulencia f

**flavor** [ˈfleɪ·vər] I. n (*taste*) gusto m; (*ice cream, fizzy drink*) sabor m 2. fig sabor m II. vt sazonar

**flavoring** [ˈfleɪ·vər·ɪŋ] n condimento m; (*in industry*) aromatizante m

**flaw** [flɔ] I. n (*in machine*) defecto m; (*in argument, character*) fallo m; (*in cloth*) imperfección f II. vt dañar

**flea** [fli] n pulga f

**flea market** n rastro m

**fled** [fled] pp of **flee**

**fledgeling, fledgling** [ˈfledʒ·lɪŋ] I. n (*young bird*) polluelo m II. adj (*inexperienced*) inexperto, -a

**flee** [fli] <fled> I. vt (*run away from*) huir de II. vi (*run away*) escaparse; liter desaparecer

**fleet** [flit] n 1. naut flota f 2. (*of airplanes*) escuadrón m; **car** ~ parque m móvil

**fleeting** [ˈfli·t̬ɪŋ] adj (*encounter, romance*) pasajero, -a; (*idea*) fugaz

**flesh** [fleʃ] n (*body tissue*) carne f; (*pulp*) pulpa f ▶ **in the** ~ en persona

**flew** [flu] pp, pt of **fly**

**flex** [fleks] I. vt flexionar ▶ **to** ~ **one's muscles** medir sus fuerzas II. n elec cable m

**flexible** [ˈflek·sə·bəl] adj (*material; policy*) flexible

**flick** [flɪk] I. vt chasquear; **to** ~ **the light switch on/off** encender/apagar la luz; **to** ~ **channels** cambiar los canales II. n 1. (*sudden movement, strike*) golpecito m (rápido) 2. sl (*movie*) peli f

**flicker** [ˈflɪk·ər] I. vi parpadear II. n parpadeo m

**flier** [ˈflaɪ·ər] n 1. (*leaflet*) folleto m 2. (*in airplane*) aviador(a) m(f)

**flight** [flaɪt] n 1. (*movement through air*) vuelo m 2. (*group: of birds*) bandada f 3. (*retreat*) huida f; ~ **of investment** fuga f de inversión; **to take** ~ darse a la fuga 4. (*series: of stairs*) tramo m

**flight attendant** n auxiliar mf de vuelo

**flight deck** n 1. (*cockpit*) cabina f de pilotaje 2. (*on aircraft carrier*) cubierta f de aterrizaje

**flight number** n número m de vuelo

**flimsy** [ˈflɪm·zi] <-ier, -iest> adj 1. (*light: dress, blouse*) ligero, -a 2. (*construction*) débil 3. (*argument, excuse*) poco sólido, -a

**fling** [flɪŋ] <flung> I. vt (*throw*) lanzar; **to** ~ **oneself in front of a train** tirarse al tren II. n 1. (*short pleasant time*) rato m de juerga 2. (*relationship*) aventura f (amorosa) 3. inf (*try*) **to have a** ~ **at sth** intentar algo

◆**fling out** vt inf (*throw out*) tirar

**flip** [flɪp] <-pp-> I. vt (*turn over quickly*) dar la vuelta; **to** ~ **a coin** echar a cara o cruz ▶ **to** ~ **one's lid** poner el grito en el cielo II. vi 1. (*turn quickly*) **to** ~ **over** dar una vuelta de campana 2. sl (*go crazy*) perder la chaveta

**flip chart** n rotafolio m

**flip-flop** [ˈflɪp·flap] n chancla f

**flipper** [ˈflɪp·ər] n (*for diving*) a. zool aleta f

**flirt** [flɜrt] I. n (*woman*) coqueta f; (*man*) galanteador m II. vi 1. (*be sexually attracted*) flirtear 2. (*toy with*) **to** ~ **with sth** jugar con algo

**flirtatious** [flɜr·ˈteɪ·ʃəs] adj (*woman*) coqueta; (*man*) galanteador

**float** [floʊt] I. vi 1. (*in liquid, air*) flotar, boyar AmL 2. (*move aimlessly*) moverse sin rumbo 3. econ fluctuar II. vt (*keep* *afloat*) poner a flote **III.** *n* **1.** NAUT flotador *m;* (*for people*) salvavidas *m inv* **2.** (*vehicle*) carroza *f*

♦**float off** *vi* irse a la deriva

**floatation** [floʊˈteɪ·ʃən] *n see* **flotation**

**flock** [flak] **I.** *n* **1.** (*group: of goats, sheep*) rebaño *m;* (*of birds*) bandada *f,* parvada *f AmL;* (*of people*) multitud *f* **2.** REL grey *f* **II.** *vi* congregarse

**flood** [flʌd] **I.** *vt* inundar; **to ~ an engine** AUTO ahogar un motor **II.** *vi* METEO (*town*) inundarse; (*river*) desbordarse; *fig* **refugees have been ~ing in** ha estado llegando un aluvión de refugiados **III.** *n* **1.** METEO inundación *f* **2.** REL **the Flood** el Diluvio **3.** *fig* (*outpouring*) torrente *m;* **~ of tears** mar *m* de lágrimas

**floodlight** [ˈflʌd·laɪt] **I.** *n* foco *m* **II.** *vt irr* iluminar (con focos)

**floor** [flɔr] **I.** *n* **1.** (*of room*) suelo *m;* **dance ~** pista *f* de baile; **to take the ~** (*in debate*) tomar la palabra **2.** (*level in building*) piso *m;* **sea ~** fondo *m* [*or* lecho] del mar *m* **3.** FIN (*lowest limit*) mínimo *m* **II.** *vt* (*knock down*) tumbar; **the question ~ed her** la pregunta la dejó sin respuesta

**floorboard** [ˈflɔr·bɔrd] *n* tabla *f* del suelo

**flooring** *n* solado *m;* **wooden ~** entablado *m*

**flop** [flap] <-pp-> **I.** *vi* **1.** (*fall*) dejarse caer **2.** *inf* (*fail*) fracasar **II.** *n inf* (*failure*) fracaso *m*

**floppy** [ˈflap·i] **I.** <-ier, -iest> *adj* (*ears*) caído, -a; (*hat*) flexible **II.** <-ies> *n* diskette *m*

**Florida** [ˈflɔr·ɪ·də] *n* Florida *f*

**florist** [ˈflɔr·ɪst] *n* florista *mf;* **the ~'s** la floristería

**flour** [ˈflaʊ·ər] **I.** *n* harina *f* **II.** *vt* enharinar

**flourish** [ˈflɜr·ɪʃ] **I.** *vi* florecer **II.** *vt* hacer gala de

**flourishing** *adj* (*place*) esplendoroso, -a; (*business, market, trade*) próspero, -a

**flow** [floʊ] **I.** *vi* fluir, correr **II.** *n* (*of water, ideas*) flujo *m;* (*of goods*) circulación *f* ▶ **to go with the ~** seguir la corriente

**flowchart** *n,* **flow diagram** *n* organigrama *m*

**flower** [ˈflaʊ·ər] **I.** *n* (*plant, bloom*) flor *f;* **to be in ~** estar en flor **II.** *vi* florecer, florear *AmL; fig* desarrollarse

**flower arrangement** *n* arreglo *m* floral

**flowerbed** *n* arriate *m* de flores

**flowerpot** *n* maceta *f*

**flown** [floʊn] *pp of* **fly**[1]

**flu** [flu] *n* gripe *f,* gripa *f Col*

**fluctuation** [ˌflʌk·tʃʊ·ˈeɪ·ʃən] *n* fluctuación *f*

**fluent** [ˈflu·ənt] *adj* (*style, movement*) con fluidez

**fluffy** [ˈflʌf·i] <-ier, -iest> *adj* (*furry: animal*) peludo, -a; (*toy*) de peluche; CULIN (*light*) esponjoso, -a

**fluid** [ˈflu·ɪd] **I.** *n* fluido *m* **II.** *adj* (*liquid*) líquido, -a

**flung** [flʌŋ] *pp, pt of* **fling**

**flunk** [flʌŋk] *vt inf* (*student*) catear, tronar *Méx argot,* rajarse *Col;* (*subject: math, history*) caer a alguien

**fluoride** [ˈflɔr·aɪd] *n* fluoruro *m*

**flurry** [ˈflɜr·i] <-ies> *n* agitación *f;* (*of snow*) ráfaga *f;* **a ~ of excitement** un frenesí

**flush**[1] [flʌʃ] **I.** *vi* (*blush*) ruborizarse **II.** *vt* **to ~ the toilet** tirar de la cadena **III.** *n* (*blush*) rubor *m*

**flush**[2] [flʌʃ] *adj* (*level*) llano, -a

**flushed** [flʌʃt] *adj* emocionado, -a; **~ with success** emocionado con el éxito

**fluster** [ˈflʌs·tər] **I.** *vt* **to ~ sb** poner nervioso a alguien **II.** *n* **to be in a ~** estar nervioso

**flute** [flut] *n* MUS flauta *f*

**flutter** [ˈflʌt·ər] **I.** *n* **1.** (*sound*) revoloteo *m* **2.** *fig* (*nervousness*) agitación *f* **II.** *vi* **1.** (*quiver*) temblar **2.** (*flap*) agitarse **III.** *vt* (*flap*) agitar; **to ~ one's wings** aletear

**fly**[1] [flaɪ] <flew, flown> **I.** *vi* **1.** (*through air*) volar; (*travel by aircraft*) viajar en avión **2.** (*move rapidly*) lanzarse; **to ~ at sb** precipitarse sobre alguien **3.** *inf* (*leave*) salir corriendo ▶ **to ~ high** volar muy alto **II.** *vt* **1.** (*aircraft*) pilotar **2.** (*make move through air*) hacer volar; **to ~ a kite** hacer volar una cometa

♦**fly away** *vi* irse volando

♦**fly in** *vi* **to ~ from somewhere** llegar (en avión) desde algún sitio

**fly²** [flaɪ] n (*insect*) mosca f; **he wouldn't harm a ~** sería incapaz de matar una mosca

**flyer** ['flaɪ·ər] n 1. (*leaflet*) folleto m 2. (*in airplane*) aviador(a) m(f)

**flying** ['flaɪ·ɪŋ] I. n el volar II. adj **to pass an exam with ~ colors** aprobar un examen sin problemas

**flying fish** n pez m volador

**flying saucer** n platillo m volante

**flyover** ['flaɪ·ˌoʊ·vər] n desfile m aéreo

**foam** [foʊm] I. n (*bubbles, foam rubber*) espuma f II. vi **to ~ with rage** echar espuma de (pura) rabia

**foam rubber** n goma espuma f

**focal** ['foʊ·kəl] adj focal; **~ point** foco m

**focus** ['foʊ·kəs] <-es or foci> I. n 1. foco m; **to be in/out of ~** estar enfocado/desenfocado 2. (*center*) centro m; **~ of interest** centro de interés II. <-s- or -ss-> vi enfocar; **to ~ on sth** (*concentrate*) concentrarse en algo III. vt enfocar

**fog** [fɑg] n niebla f; **to be in a ~** *fig* estar confundido

**foggy** ['fɑ·gi] <-ier, -iest> adj 1. (*weather*) nebuloso, -a 2. (*unclear: memory*) vago, -a ▶ **to not have the foggiest** (**idea**) no tener la más remota idea

**foil¹** [fɔɪl] n (*aluminum*) papel m de aluminio

**foil²** [fɔɪl] vt (*cause to fail*) frustrar

**fold¹** [foʊld] I. vt 1. (*bend*) plegar; **to ~ sth back/down** plegar algo 2. (*wrap*) **to ~ sth** (**in sth**) envolver algo (en algo) II. vi 1. (*bend over*) doblarse 2. (*fail, go bankrupt*) fracasar III. n pliegue m

◆**fold up** vt doblar

**fold²** [foʊld] n (*sheep pen*) redil m

**folder** ['foʊl·dər] n a. COMPUT carpeta f, fólder m Col, Méx

**folding** ['foʊl·dɪŋ] adj plegable; **~ door** puerta f plegadiza

**folk** [foʊk] n 1. pl pueblo m; **ordinary ~** gente f corriente; **~ wisdom** sabiduría f popular 2. **~s** (*parents*) viejos mpl

**folk music** n música f folk

**folk song** n canción f popular

**follow** ['fɑl·oʊ] I. vt 1. (*take same route as*) seguir 2. (*happen next*) **to ~ sth** suceder a algo 3. (*understand*) **to ~ sb/**

sth seguir a alguien/algo II. vi 1. (*take same route as*) seguir 2. (*happen next*) suceder

◆**follow on** vi seguir

◆**follow through** I. vt 1. (*study*) investigar 2. (*see through to end*) terminar II. vi SPORTS acompañar (un golpe)

◆**follow up** vt 1. (*consider, investigate*) investigar 2. (*do next*) **to ~ sth by** [or **with**]... hacer algo después de...

**follower** n seguidor(a) m(f)

**following** I. n inv 1. **I'd say the ~** diría lo siguiente 2. (*supporters: of idea*) partidarios, -as m, fpl; (*of doctrine*) seguidores, -as m, fpl II. adj (*next*) siguiente; **the ~ ideas** las siguientes ideas III. prep después de

**follow-up** n seguimiento m

**fond** [fɑnd] <-er, -est> adj 1. (*with liking for*) **he is ~ of...** le gusta... 2. (*loving*) cariñoso, -a; **~ memories** tiernos recuerdos mpl 3. (*hope*) vano, -a

**fondle** ['fɑn·dl] <-ling> vt acariciar

**food** [fud] n comida f ▶ **to give sb ~ for thought** dar a alguien algo en que pensar

**food chain** n cadena f alimentaria

**food poisoning** n intoxicación f por alimentos

**food processor** n procesador m de alimentos

**food stamps** n vales emitidos por el gobierno estadounidense para la compra de comida

**fool** [ful] I. n idiota mf; **to act like a ~** hacer el tonto; **any ~** cualquiera II. vt engañar; **you could have ~ed me!** inf ¡no me lo puedo creer! III. vi (*joke around*) bromear IV. adj inf (*silly*) tonto, -a

**foolish** ['fu·lɪʃ] adj tonto, -a

**foolproof** ['ful·pruf] adj a prueba de tontos

**foot** [fʊt] I. <feet> n 1. (*of person*) pie m; (*of animal*) pata f 2. (*unit of measurement*) pie m (30,48 cm) 3. (*bottom or lowest part*) **at the ~ of one's bed** al pie de la cama; **at the ~ of the page** a pie de página ▶ **to get a ~ in the door** abrirse una brecha, introducirse; **to be back on one's feet** haberse recuperado;

to **have/get** <u>cold</u> **feet** estar/ponerse nervioso; **to get off on the** <u>wrong</u> **~** empezar con mal pie; **to** <u>put</u> **one's ~ down** no ceder; **to** <u>put</u> **one's ~ in it** [*or* **in one's mouth**] meter la pata; **to be** <u>under</u> **sb's feet** estar siempre pegado a alguien II. *vt inf* **to ~ the bill** pagar

**foot-and-mouth disease** *n* fiebre *f* aftosa

**football** ['fʊt·bɔl] *n* **1.** (*sport*) fútbol *m* americano **2.** (*ball*) balón *m* de fútbol americano

**footbridge** ['fʊt·brɪdʒ] *n* puente *m* peatonal

**footer** ['fʊt·ər] *n* pie *m* de página

**footing** ['fʊt·ɪŋ] *n* **1.** **to lose one's ~** resbalar **2.** (*basis*) posición *f*

**footpath** ['fʊt·pæθ] *n* sendero *m*

**footprint** ['fʊt·prɪnt] *n* huella *f*

**footrest** ['fʊt·rest] *n* reposapiés *m inv*

**footstep** ['fʊt·step] *n* paso *m*

**footwear** ['fʊt·wer] *n* calzado *m*

**for** [fɔr] I. *prep* **1.** (*destined for*) para; **this is ~ you** esto es para ti **2.** (*in order to help*) por; **to do sth ~ sb** hacer algo por alguien **3.** (*intention, purpose*) **~ sale/rent** en venta/alquiler; **sth ~ a headache** algo para el dolor de cabeza; **it's time ~ lunch** es hora del almuerzo; **to wait ~ sb** esperar a alguien; **to go ~ a walk** ir a dar un paseo; **fit ~ nothing** bueno para nada; **what ~?** ¿para qué?; **what's that ~?** ¿para qué es eso?; **~ this to be possible** para que esto sea posible **4.** (*to acquire*) **eager ~ power** ávido de poder; **to search ~ sth** buscar algo; **to ask/hope ~ news** pedir/esperar noticias; **to apply ~ a job** solicitar un trabajo **5.** (*towards*) **the train ~ Boston** el tren hacia Boston; **to make ~ home** dirigirse hacia casa **6.** (*distance*) **to walk ~ 8 miles** caminar durante 8 millas **7.** (*time*) **~ now** por ahora; **~ a while/a time** por un rato/un momento; **to last ~ hours** durar horas y horas; **I'm going to be here ~ three weeks** voy a estar aquí durante tres semanas; **I haven't been there ~ three years** hace tres años que no estoy allí; **I have known her ~ three years** la conozco desde hace tres años **8.** (*on date of*) **to have**

sth finished **~ Sunday** acabar algo para el domingo; **to set the wedding ~ May 4th** fijar la boda para el 4 de mayo **9.** (*in support of*) **is he ~ or against it?** ¿está a favor o en contra?; **to fight ~ sth** luchar por algo **10.** (*employed by*) **to work ~ a company** trabajar para una empresa **11.** (*in substitution*) **say hello ~ me** dile hola de mi parte **12.** (*price*) **a check ~ $100** un cheque por valor de cien dólares; **I paid $10 ~ it** pagué diez dólares por ello **13.** (*concerning*) **as ~ me/that** en cuanto a mí/eso; **two are enough ~ me** dos son suficientes para mí; **sorry ~ doing that** perdón por hacer eso; **the best would be ~ me to go** lo mejor sería que me fuese **14.** (*cause*) **excuse me ~ being late** siento llegar tarde; **as the reason ~ one's behavior** como razón por su comportamiento **15.** (*because of*) **to do sth ~ love** hacer algo por amor; **~ fear of doing sth** por miedo a hacer algo; **to cry ~ joy** gritar de alegría **16.** (*despite*) **~ all I know** que yo sepa **17.** (*as*) **~ example** por ejemplo; **he ~ one** empezando por él ▶ **that's kids ~ <u>you</u>!** ¡así son los niños! II. *conj form* pues

**forbid** [fər·'bɪd] <forbade, forbidden> *vt* prohibir; **to ~ sb from doing sth** prohibir a alguien hacer algo

**forbidden** [fər·'bɪd·ən] *pp of* **forbid**

**forbidding** [fər·'bɪd·ɪŋ] *adj* **1.** (*threatening*) que intimida **2.** (*disapproving: frown, look*) severo, -a; (*bearing rain: sky, clouds*) amenazador, a

**force** [fɔrs] I. *n* **1.** (*power*) fuerza *f*; **~ of gravity** PHYS fuerza de la gravedad; **to combine ~s** unir esfuerzos **2.** (*large numbers*) **in ~** en grandes cantidades **3.** (*influence*) influencia *f*; **by ~ of circumstance** debido a las circunstancias; **by ~ of habit** por costumbre; **the ~s of nature** las fuerzas de la naturaleza **4.** (*validity*) validez *f*; **to come into ~** entrar en vigor **5.** MIL **police ~** cuerpo *m* de policía; **Air Force** Fuerzas *f* Aéreas; **the armed ~s** fuerzas *f pl* armadas II. *vt* **1.** (*use power*) forzar; **to ~ a door** forzar una puerta **2.** (*oblige to do*) obligar; **to ~ sb to do sth** obligar a alguien a hacer algo; **to ~ sb into** (**doing**) **sth** forzar a alguien a (hacer) algo; **to ~ sth on sb** imponer algo a alguien

**forced** *adj* (*smile, friendliness*) forzado, -a; **~ landing** aterrizaje *m* forzoso

**force-feed** ['fɔrs·fid] *vt* dar de comer a la fuerza

**forceful** ['fɔrs·fəl] *adj* enérgico, -a

**forcibly** *adv* a la fuerza

**forearm**[1] [fɔr·arm] *n* (*body part*) ante-brazo *m*

**forearm**[2] [ˌfɔr·'arm] *vt liter* (*prepare for battle*) **to ~ oneself** (**against sth**) pre-venirse (contra algo)

**forecast** ['fɔr·kæst] <forecast *or* forecast-ed> **I.** *n* predicción *f*; **weather ~** previ-sión *f* meteorológica **II.** *vt* pronosticar

**forecourt** ['fɔr·kɔrt] *n* patio *m* delantero

**forefinger** ['fɔr·fɪŋ·gər] *n* índice *m*

**forefront** ['fɔr·frʌnt] *n* primer plano *m*

**forego** [fɔr·'gou] <forewent, foregone> *vt see* **forgo**

**foregone** [fɔr·'gan] *pp of* **forego**

**foreground** ['fɔr·graund] **I.** *n* a. ART **the ~** el primer plano *m* **II.** *vt* destacar

**forehand** ['fɔr·hænd] *n* (*tennis shot*) gol-pe *m* de derechas

**forehead** ['fɔr·hed] *n* frente *f*

**foreign** ['fɔr·ɪn] *adj* **1.** (*from another country*) extranjero, -a *m* **2.** (*involving other countries*) exterior; **~ relations** relaciones *f pl* exteriores; **~ trade** co-mercio *m* exterior **3.** (*unknown*) ex-traño, -a; (*uncharacteristic*) impropio, -a **4.** (*not belonging*) ajeno, -a; **a ~ body** un cuerpo extraño

**foreign affairs** *npl* asuntos *m pl* ex-teriores

**foreign correspondent** *n* corresponsal *mf* en el extranjero

**foreign currency** *n* divisa *f*

**foreigner** ['fɔr·ɪ·nər] *n* extranjero, -a *m, f*

**foreign exchange** *n* **1.** (*system*) cambio *m* de divisas **2.** (*currency*) divisa *f*

**foreign policy** *n* política *f* exterior

**foreman** ['fɔr·mən] <-men> *n* (*in fac-tory*) capataz *m*

**foremost** ['fɔr·moust] *adj* **1.** (*most im-portant*) principal **2.** (*furthest forward*) delantero, -a

**forename** ['fɔr·neɪm] *n form* nombre

*m* (de pila)

**foreplay** ['fɔr·pleɪ] *n* juegos *m pl* eróticos preliminares

**forerunner** ['fɔr·rʌn·ər] *n* precursor(a) *m(f)*

**foresee** [fɔr·'si] *irr vt* prever

**foreseeable** *adj* previsible

**foreshadow** [fɔr·'ʃæd·ou] *vt* anunciar

**foresight** ['fɔr·saɪt] *n* previsión *f*

**foreskin** ['fɔr·skɪn] *n* prepucio *m*

**forest** ['fɔr·ɪst] **I.** *n* (*woods*) bosque *m*; (*tropical*) selva *f* **II.** *adj* forestal

**forestall** [fɔr·'stɔl] *vt* anticiparse a

**forester** ['fɔr·ɪ·stər] *n* guardabosques *mf inv*

**forestry** ['fɔr·ɪ·stri] *n* silvicultura *f*

**foretaste** ['fɔr·teɪst] *n* anticipo *m*

**forever** [fɔr·'ev·ər] *adv* **1.** (*for all time*) para siempre **2.** *inf* (*continually*) con-tinuamente

**forewarn** [fɔr·'wɔrn] *vt* prevenir

**forewent** [fɔr·'went] *pp of* **forego**

**foreword** ['fɔr·wɜrd] *n* prefacio *m*

**forfeiture** ['fɔr·fə·tʃər] *n* pérdida *f*

**forgave** [fɔr·'geɪv] *pt of* **forgive**

**forge** [fɔrdʒ] **I.** *vt* **1.** (*make illegal copy*) falsificar **2.** (*metal*) forjar **II.** *vi* **to ~ into the lead** adelantarse mucho **III.** *n* **1.** (*furnace*) fragua *f* **2.** (*smithy*) herrería *f*

**forgery** ['fɔr·dʒə·ri] <-ies> *n* falsifica-ción *f*

**forget** [fɔr·'get] <forgot, forgotten> **I.** *vt* **1.** (*not remember*) olvidar; **to ~ to do sth** olvidarse de hacer algo; **to ~ (that)...** olvidar (que)... **2.** (*leave behind*) **to ~ one's keys** dejarse las llaves **3.** (*stop thinking about*) **to ~ sth/sb** dejar de pensar en algo/alguien **4.** (*give up*) **to ~ sth** dejar algo; **~ it** olvídalo **II.** *vi* **1.** (*not remember*) olvidarse; **to ~ about sth/sb** olvidarse de algo/alguien **2.** (*stop thinking about*) **to ~ about a plan** desistir de un plan **3.** **~ it!** (*no*) ¡ni lo sueñes!

**forgetful** [fɔr·'get·fəl] *adj* olvidadizo, -a

**forgive** [fɔr·'gɪv] <forgave, forgiven> **I.** *vt* **1.** (*pardon*) perdonar; **to ~ sb for sth** perdonar algo a alguien *2.* (*pardon*) **~ me** discúlpeme **II.** *vi* perdonar

**forgiven** *pp of* **forgive**

**forgiveness** *n* perdón *m*

**forgiving** adj misericordioso, -a

**forgo** [fɔr·'goʊ] irr vt privarse de

**forgot** [fər·'gɑt] pt of **forget**

**forgotten** [fər·'gɑtn] I. pp of **forget** II. adj olvidado, -a

**fork** [fɔrk] I. n 1. (cutlery) tenedor m 2. (tool) horca f 3. (in road) bifurcación f 4. pl (on bicycle) horquilla f II. vt coger con tenedor, agarrar con tenedor AmL III. vi (road) bifurcarse

**forked** adj bifurcado, -a

**forklift** [fɔrk·'lɪft] n carretilla f elevadora

**form** [fɔrm] I. n 1. (type, variety) tipo m; **in any way, shape or ~** de cualquier modo 2. (outward shape) forma f; (of an object) bulto m; **to take ~** tomar forma; **in liquid/solid ~** en estado líquido/sólido 3. LING (of word) forma f; **the singular ~** LING el singular 4. (document) formulario m; **an application/entry ~** un formulario de solicitud/admisión; **to fill in a ~** rellenar un formulario 5. SPORTS forma f; **to be in ~** estar en forma; **to be out of ~** estar en baja forma 6. (correct procedure) **in due ~** de la debida forma 7. (mol, a. for baking) molde m II. vt 1. (make) formar; **to ~ a line** formar una cola; **to ~ an opinion** formarse una opinión 2. (shape) moldear 3. (set up) establecer

**formal** ['fɔr·məl] adj (official, ceremonious) formal; **~ dress** traje m de etiqueta; **~ procedures** procedimientos m pl oficiales

**formality** [fɔr·'mæl·ə·ti] <-ies> n formalidad f

**formalize** ['fɔr·mə·laɪz] vt formalizar

**format** ['fɔr·mæt] I. n formato m II. <-tt-> vt COMPUT formatear

**formation** [fɔr·'meɪ·ʃən] n formación f; **in ~** en formación

**formatting** n COMPUT formateo m

**former** ['fɔr·mər] adj 1. (previous) anterior 2. (first of two) primero, -a

**formerly** adv antes; **~ known as** anteriormente conocido como

**formidable** ['fɔr·mə·də·bəl] adj (person) extraordinario, -a; (opponent, task) difícil

**formula** ['fɔr·mjʊ·lə] <-s or -lae> n 1. MATH a. fig fórmula f 2. COM (recipe

for product) receta f 3. (baby milk) leche f para lactantes

**forsake** [fɔr·'seɪk] <forsook, forsaken> vt (abandon) abandonar; (give up) renunciar a

**forsaken** [fɔr·'seɪ·kən] I. pp of **forsake** II. adj abandonado, -a

**forsook** [fɔr·'sʊk] pt of **forsake**

**fort** [fɔrt] n fuerte m

**forte** ['fɔr·teɪ, fɔrt] n (strong point) fuerte m

**forth** [fɔrθ] adv **to go ~** irse; **back and ~** de acá para allá

**forthcoming** [ˌfɔrθ·'kʌm·ɪŋ] adj 1. (happening soon) venidero, -a; (film) de próximo estreno 2. (informative) **to be ~ (about sth)** estar dispuesto a hablar (de algo)

**forthright** ['fɔrθ·raɪt] adj directo, -a

**forthwith** [ˌfɔrθ·'wɪθ] adv form en el acto

**fortieth** ['fɔr·ti·əθ] I. adj cuadragésimo, -a II. n (order) cuadragésimo, -a m, f; (fraction) cuadragésimo m; (part) cuadragésima parte f; s. a. **eighth**

**fortify** ['fɔr·tə·faɪ] <-ie-> vt 1. a. MIL fortificar 2. **fortified with vitamins and minerals** enriquecido con vitaminas y minerales

**fortnight** ['fɔrt·naɪt] n quince días mpl; (business) quincena f

**fortunate** ['fɔr·tʃə·nɪt] adj afortunado, -a; **to be ~ to do sth** tener la suerte de hacer algo

**fortunately** adv afortunadamente

**fortune** ['fɔr·tʃən] n 1. (money) fortuna f; **to be worth a ~** valer una fortuna; **to cost a ~** costar un dineral; **to make a ~** hacer una fortuna 2. form (luck, destiny) suerte f; **good/ill ~** buena/mala suerte; **to tell sb's ~** decir la buenaventura a alguien 3. liter (luck personified) la fortuna

**fortune teller** n adivino, -a m, f

**forty** ['fɔr·ti] I. adj cuarenta II. <-ies> n cuarenta m; s. a. **eighty**

**forward** ['fɔr·wərd] I. adv 1. (towards the front) hacia adelante; **to lean ~** inclinarse hacia adelante; **a step ~** fig un paso hacia adelante 2. (in time) adelante; **to set one's watch/the clock ~** adelantar el reloj; **to look ~ to sth**

esperar algo (con ansia) **II.** adj **1.** (towards the front) hacia adelante; ~ **gear** AUTO marcha f adelante **2.** (in a position close to front) en la parte delantera **3.** (near front of plane) delantero, -a; (ship) de proa **4.** (relating to the future) ~ **buying** compra f a plazos; ~ **planning** planes m pl de futuro **5.** (bold, not modest) descarado, -a **III.** n SPORTS delantero, -a m, f; **center** ~ delantero centro **IV.** vt **1.** (letter, e-mail) remitir; (e-mail) reenviar; **please** ~ por favor, hacer seguir **2.** (help to progress) promover

**forward-looking** adj con miras al futuro

**forwards** ['fɔr·wərdz] adv **1.** (towards the front) hacia adelante **2.** (in time) en adelante

**forwent** [fɔr·'went] pt of **forgo**

**fossil** ['fɑs·əl] n **1.** GEO fósil m **2.** fig inf (person) carca mf

**foster** ['fɑ·stər] vt **1.** (look after) acoger **2.** (encourage) fomentar

**foster child** n hijo, -a m, f acogido, -a

**foster father** n padre m de acogida

**foster home** n casa f de acogida

**foster mother** n madre f de acogida

**fought** [fɔt] pt, pp of **fight**

**foul** [faʊl] **I.** adj **1.** (disagreeable: mood, temper) insoportable; (air) sucio, -a **2.** (rotten: taste) asqueroso, -a; (smell) fétido, -a **3.** (vulgar: language) ordinario, -a **II.** n SPORTS falta f, penal m AmL **III.** vt **1.** (pollute) ensuciar **2.** SPORTS to ~ **sb** hacer una falta a alguien

**foul play** n **1.** SPORTS juego m sucio **2.** (crime) delito m

**found¹** [faʊnd] pt, pp of **find**

**found²** [faʊnd] vt **1.** (establish) fundar **2.** (base) basar **3.** (build) to be ~ed on **sth** estar construido sobre algo

**found³** [faʊnd] vt MIN fundir

**foundation** [faʊn·'deɪ·ʃən] n **1.** pl (of building) cimientos mpl; **to lay the ~(s) (of sth)** poner los cimientos (de algo) **2.** fig (basis) base f **3.** (evidence) fundamento m **4.** (act of establishing) establecimiento m **5.** (organization) fundación f **6.** (make-up) maquillaje m de base

**founder¹** ['faʊn·dər] n (of organization)

fundador(a) m(f)

**founder²** ['faʊn·dər] vi **1.** (sink) hundirse **2.** fig (fail) fracasar

**fountain** ['faʊn·tən] n fuente f

**fountain pen** n pluma f estilográfica

**four** [fɔr] **I.** adj cuatro **II.** n **1.** cuatro m **2.** (group of four) cuarteto m ▶ **to go on all ~s** andar a gatas; s. a. **eight**

**fourteen** [ˌfɔr·'tin] **I.** adj catorce **II.** n catorce m; s. a. **eight**

**fourteenth** **I.** adj decimocuarto, -a **II.** n **1.** (order) decimocuarto, -a m, f **2.** (date) catorce m **3.** (fraction) catorceavo m; (part) catorceava parte f; s. a. **eighth**

**fourth** [fɔrθ] **I.** adj cuarto, -a **II.** n **1.** (order) cuarto, -a m, f **2.** (date) cuatro m **3.** (fraction) cuarto m; (part) cuarta parte f **4.** MUS cuarta f; s. a. **eighth**

**Fourth of July** n Día m de la Independencia de Estados Unidos

**four-wheel drive** n tracción f a las cuatro ruedas

**fox** [fɑks] **I.** n **1.** (animal) zorro m **2.** (fur) piel f de zorro **3.** inf (cunning person) **an old** ~ un viejo zorro **4.** sl (sexy woman) tía f buena **II.** vt **1.** (mystify) mistificar **2.** (trick) engañar

**foyer** ['fɔɪ·ər] n **1.** (in house) vestíbulo m, hall m **2.** (in hotel, theater) vestíbulo m

**fraction** ['fræk·ʃən] n fracción f; **at a ~ of the cost** por parte del costo

**fracture** ['fræk·tʃər] **I.** vt **1.** MED fracturar; **to ~ one's leg** fracturarse la pierna **2.** (break) romper **II.** vi (leg) fracturarse **III.** n MED fractura f

**fragile** ['frædʒ·əl] adj delicado, -a; (object, peace) frágil

**fragment** ['fræg·mənt] **I.** n fragmento m **II.** vi **1.** (break into pieces) fragmentarse **2.** fig (break up) romperse **III.** vt **1.** (break into pieces) fragmentar **2.** fig (break up) romper

**fragrance** ['freɪ·grəns] n fragancia f

**fragrant** ['freɪ·grənt] adj fragante

**frame** [freɪm] **I.** n **1.** (for door, picture) a. COMPUT marco m **2.** pl (spectacles) montura f **3.** (of building) armazón m o f **4.** (body) cuerpo m; **a slight/sturdy** ~ un cuerpo esbelto/robusto **5.** CINE, TV fotograma *m* II. *vt* 1. (*picture*) enmarcar 2. (*conceive: proposal*) elaborar; (*put into words*) 3. *inf* (*falsely incriminate*) incriminar dolosamente

**frame-up** ['freɪm.ʌp] *n inf* montaje *m* (*para inculpar a alguien*)

**framework** ['freɪm.wɜrk] *n* 1. (*supporting structure*) armazón *m* o *f* 2. *fig* (*set of rules, principles*) sistema *m*

**France** [fræns] *n* Francia *f*

**franchise** ['fræn.tʃaɪz] I. *n* franquicia *f* II. *vt* conceder en franquicia

**frank** [fræŋk] I. *adj* franco, -a; **to be ~,...** sinceramente,... II. *vt* franquear

**frankfurter** ['fræŋk.fɜr.tər] *n* salchicha *f* de Frankfurt

**frankly** *adv* sinceramente

**frantic** ['fræn.tɪk] *adj* (*hurry, activity*) frenético, -a; **to be ~ with worry** andar loco de inquietud

**fraud** [frɔd] *n* 1. *a.* LAW fraude *m* 2. (*person*) impostor(a) *m(f)*

**fraudulent** ['frɔ.dʒə.lənt] *adj* fraudulento, -a

**fray¹** [freɪ] *vi* (*rope, cloth*) deshilacharse; **tempers were beginning to ~** la gente estaba perdiendo la paciencia

**fray²** [freɪ] *n* (*fight*) lucha *f*

**freak** [frik] I. *n* 1. (*abnormal person, thing*) monstruo *m;* **a ~ of nature** un fenómeno de la naturaleza 2. (*enthusiast*) fanático, -a *m, f* II. *adj* anormal III. *vi see* **freak out** I

♦**freak out** I. *vi* flipar II. *vt* **to freak sb out** alucinar a alguien

**freckle** ['frek.l] *n* peca *f*

**free** [fri] I. <-r, -est> *adj* 1. (*not constrained: person, country, elections*) libre; **to break ~** (**of sth**) soltarse (de algo); **to break ~ of sb** despegarse de alguien; **to go ~** salir en libertad; **to set sb ~** poner en libertad a alguien 2. (*not affected by*) **to be ~ of sth** no estar afectado por algo 3. (*not busy*) **to be ~ to do sth** estar libre para hacer algo 4. (*not occupied*) libre 5. (*costing nothing*) gratis; **~ ticket** entrada *f* gratis; **~ of charge** gratis; **~ sample** muestra *f* gratuita 6. (*generous*) **to be ~ with sth** dar algo en abundancia ▶ **~ and easy** despreocupado II. *adv* gratis; **~ of**

charge gratis III. *vt* 1. (*release: person*) poner en libertad 2. (*make available*) permitir

**freebie** ['fri.bi] *n* obsequio *m*

**freedom** ['fri.dəm] *n* 1. (*of person, country*) libertad *f;* **~ of the press** libertad *f* de prensa; **~ of speech/thought** libertad *f* de expresión/pensamiento 2. (*right*) derecho *m* 3. (*room for movement*) libertad *f* 4. (*unrestricted use*) usufructo *m*

**free enterprise** *n* libre empresa *f*

**freehold** ['fri.hoʊld] I. *n* plena propiedad *f* II. *adj* de plena propiedad III. *adv* en propiedad absoluta

**free kick** *n* SPORTS tiro *m* libre

**freelance** ['fri.læns] I. *n* freelance *mf* II. *adj* autónomo, -a III. *adv* por cuenta propia IV. *vi* trabajar por cuenta propia

**freely** *adv* 1. (*without obstruction*) libremente 2. (*frankly: speak, criticize*) francamente

**free-range** [ˌfri.'reɪndʒ] *adj* de granja

**free-range chicken** *n* pollo *m* de corral

**free-range egg** *n* huevo *m* de granja

**free speech** *n* libertad *f* de expresión

**freestyle** ['fri.staɪl] *n* estilo *m* libre

**freeware** *n* COMPUT programa *m* de libre distribución

**freeway** *n* autopista *f*

**freewheel** ['fri.hwil] *vi* ir en punto muerto

**free will** *n* libre albedrío *m*

**freeze** [friz] <froze, frozen> I. *vi* 1. (*liquid*) helarse; (*food*) congelarse 2. (*become totally still*) quedarse completamente quieto, -a II. *vt* (*liquid*) helar; (*food, prices*) congelar III. *n* 1. METEO ola *f* de frío 2. ECON congelación *f*

**freezer** *n* congelador *m*, congeladora *f AmS*

**freezing** I. *adj* glacial; **it's ~** hiela; **I'm ~** estoy helado II. *n* congelación *f*

**freight** [freɪt] I. *n* 1. (*type of transportation*) flete *m* 2. (*goods*) mercancías *fpl* 3. (*charge*) porte *m* II. *adv* por flete III. *vt* fletar

**freight car** *n* RAIL vagón *m* de mercancías

**freighter** ['freɪ.tər] *n* 1. (*ship*) buque *m* de carga 2. (*plane*) avión *m* de mercancías

**freight train** n tren m de mercancías

**French** [frentʃ] **I.** adj francés, -esa; **~ speaker** francófono, -a m, f **II.** n **1.** (person) francés, -esa m, f **2.** (language) francés m

**French dressing** n vinagreta f

**French fried potatoes** npl, **French fries** npl patatas f pl fritas

**French horn** n trompa f de llaves

**Frenchman** <-men> n francés m

**French toast** n torrija f

**Frenchwoman** <-women> n francesa f

**frenzy** ['fren·zi] n frenesí m

**frequency** ['fri·kwən·tsi] <-cies> n frecuencia f

**frequent**[1] ['fri·kwənt] adj (occurring often) frecuente, tupido, -a Méx

**frequent**[2] [fri·'kwent] vt (visit regularly) frecuentar

**fresh** [freʃ] adj **1.** (not stale: air, water, food) fresco, -a; (bread) recién hecho, -a **2.** (new) nuevo, -a; **to make a ~ start** volver a empezar **3.** (not tired) como nuevo, -a **4.** inf (disrespectful) descarado, -a

**freshen** ['freʃ·ən] vt refrescar; (one's breath) refrescarse el aliento

**fret**[1] [fret] <-tt-> vi (worry) inquietarse

**fret**[2] [fret] n MUS traste m

**friction** ['frik·ʃən] n **1.** (rubbing) fricción f **2.** fig (disagreement) desavenencia f

**Friday** ['frai·di] n viernes m inv; **on ~s** los viernes; **every ~** todos los viernes; **this** (coming) **~** este (próximo) viernes; **on ~ mornings** los viernes por la mañana; **on ~ night** el viernes por la noche; **last/next ~** el viernes pasado/que viene; **every other ~** un viernes sí y otro no; **on ~ we are going on vacation** el viernes nos vamos de vacaciones

**fridge** [fridʒ] n nevera f, refrigeradora f AmS

**fried** [fraid] adj frito, -a

**fried chicken** n pollo m frito

**fried egg** n huevo m frito

**friend** [frend] n amigo, -a m, f; **to be ~s** ser amigos; **to make ~s (with sb)** hacerse amigo (de alguien); **a ~ of mine/yours/his/hers** un amigo mío/tuyo/suyo

**friendly** ['frend·li] <-ier, -iest> adj (person) simpático, -a, entrador(a) Arg; (house, environment) acogedor(a); (nation) cordial; **to be ~ with sb** llevarse bien con alguien

**friendship** ['frend·ʃip] n amistad f

**fries** [fraiz] npl inf patatas f pl fritas

**fright** [frait] n **1.** (feeling of fear) terror m **2.** (frightening experience) susto m, jabón m Arg, Méx, PRico; **to give sb a ~** dar un susto a alguien

**frighten** ['frait·ən] **I.** vt asustar **II.** vi asustarse

**frightened** adj asustado, -a

**frightful** ['frait·fəl] adj espantoso, -a

**fringe** [frindʒ] **I.** n **1.** (decorative edging) flecos mpl, barbitas f Méx **2.** (edge) margen m; fig **on the ~ of society** al margen de la sociedad **3.** (fringe benefit) extra m **II.** adj secundario, -a

**fringe group** n grupo m marginal

**frisk** [frisk] **I.** vi juguetear **II.** vt cachear

**fritter**[1] ['frit·ər] n CULIN buñuelo m, picarón m AmL

**fritter**[2] ['frit·ər] vt (reduce) **to ~** (away) desperdiciar

**frivolous** ['friv·ə·ləs] adj frívolo, -a

**frizzy** ['friz·i] adj (hair) encrespado, -a

**fro** [froʊ] adv **to and ~** de un lado a otro

**frock** [frak] n vestido m

**frog**[1] [frag] n ZOOL rana f ▶ **to have a ~ in one's throat** tener carraspera

**frog**[2] [frag] n offensive sl (French person) gabacho, -a m, f

**from** [fram] prep **1.** (as starting point) de; **where is he ~?** ¿de dónde es?; **the flight ~ Boston** el vuelo procedente de Boston; **to fly ~ New York to Tokyo** volar de Nueva York a Tokio; **shirts ~ $10** camisas desde 10$; **~ inside** desde dentro **2.** (temporal) **~ day to day** día tras día; **~ time to time** de vez en cuando; **~ that date on(wards)** desde esa fecha **3.** (at distance to) **100 miles ~ the river** a 100 millas del río; **far ~ doing sth** lejos de hacer algo **4.** (one to another) **to go ~ door to door** ir de puerta en puerta; **to tell good ~ evil** distinguir el bien del mal **5.** (originating in) **a card ~ Paul/Corsica** una tarjeta de Paul/Córcega **6.** (in reference to) ~ **what I heard** según lo que he escuchado; **to judge** ~ **appearances** juzgar según las apariencias; **different** ~ **the others** diferente de los demás **7.** (*caused by*) ~ **experience** por experiencia; **to die** ~ **thirst** morirse de sed **8.** (*removed*) **to steal/take sth** ~ **sb** robar/quitar algo a alguien; **to prevent sb** ~ **doing sth** evitar que alguien haga algo; **to keep sth** ~ **sb** mantener algo alejado de alguien

**front** [frʌnt] **I.** n **1.** (*forward-facing part*) frente f; (*of building*) fachada f **2.** PUBL (*outside cover*) cubierta f exterior; (*first pages*) principio m **3.** (*front area*) parte f delantera; **in** ~ delante de **4.** THEAT auditorio m **5.** (*deceptive appearance*) apariencias fpl **6.** MIL frente m; fig **on the domestic/work** ~ en el terreno doméstico/laboral **7.** POL frente m **8.** (*promenade*) paseo m marítimo **9.** METEO frente m **II.** adj **1.** (*at the front*) delantero, -a **2.** (*first*) primero, -a III. vt **1.** (*be head of*) liderar **2.** TV presentar **IV.** vi estar enfrente de; **to** ~ **for** servir de fachada [*or* tapadera]

**front door** n puerta f principal

**front-end** n COMPUT frontal m

**frontier** [frʌnˈtɪr] n **1.** (*border*) a. fig frontera f **2.** (*outlying areas*) **the** ~ los límites

**frontier station** n puesto m fronterizo

**front line** n primera línea f

**front page** n primera página f

**front-runner** n líder mf

**front-wheel drive** n tracción f delantera

**frost** [frɑst] **I.** n (*crystals*) escarcha f; (*on ground*) helada f **II.** vt **1.** (*cover with frost*) cubrir de escarcha **2.** (*cover with icing: cake*) escarchar

**frostbite** [ˈfrɑst·baɪt] n congelación f

**frosted** adj **1.** (*covered with icing*) escarchado, -a **2.** (*opaque: glass*) esmerilado, -a

**frosty** [ˈfrɑsti] <-ier, -iest> adj **1.** (*with frost*) escarchado, -a **2.** (*unfriendly*) frío, -a

**frothy** [ˈfrɑ·θi] <-ier, -iest> adj espumoso, -a

**frown** [fraʊn] **I.** vi **1.** fruncir el ceño **2.** fig (*disapprove of*) **to** ~ **on sth** no

ver algo con buenos ojos **II.** n ceño m fruncido

**froze** [froʊz] pt of freeze

**frozen** [ˈfroʊ·zn] **I.** pp of freeze **II.** adj congelado, -a

**fruit** [frut] n **1.** (*for eating*) fruta f; (*on tree, product*) fruto m **2.** (*results*) fruto m ▶ **to bear** ~ dar fruto; fig dar resultado

**fruitcake** [ˈfrut·keɪk] n **1.** (*cake*) tarta f de frutas **2.** sl (*crazy person*) chiflado, -a m, f

**fruitful** [ˈfrut·fəl] adj (*productive*) provechoso, -a; (*discussion*) productivo, -a

**fruition** [fruˈɪʃ·ən] n **to bring sth to** ~ llevar algo a buen término; **to come to** ~ realizarse

**fruit knife** n cuchillo m de la fruta

**fruitless** [ˈfrut·lɪs] adj infructuoso, -a

**fruit salad** n macedonia f

**fruity** [ˈfru·ti] <-ier, -iest> adj **1.** afrutado, -a **2.** sl (*crazy*) loco, -a, chiflado, -a

**frustrate** [ˈfrʌs·treɪt] <-ting> vt frustrar

**frustrated** adj frustrado, -a

**frustration** [frʌˈstreɪ·ʃən] n frustración f

**fry**[1] [fraɪ] <-ie-> **I.** vt freír **II.** vi **1.** (*be cooked*) freírse **2.** inf (*get burned*) quemarse

**fry**[2] [fraɪ] n **small** ~ (*unimportant person*) don nadie mf; (*young person*) renacuajo, -a m, f inf

**frying pan** n sartén f, paila f AmL

**ft.** abbr of **foot, feet** pie

**fuck** [fʌk] vulg **I.** vt follarse, coger AmL; ~ **you!** ¡jódete!; ~ **that idea** ¡a la mierda esa idea! **II.** vi follar, coger AmL **III.** vt polvo m **IV.** interj joder

**fucked up** adj vulg (*drunk*) pedo mf, rascado, -a Col; (*messed up*) jodido, -a

**fucker** [ˈfʌk·ər] n vulg gilipollas mf inv

**fudge** [fʌdʒ] **I.** n (*candy*) dulce m de azúcar **II.** <-ging> vt (*issue*) esquivar; (*numbers, figures*) falsear

**fuel** [ˈfju·əl] **I.** n combustible m **II.** <-l-> vt **1.** (*provide with fuel*) aprovisionar de combustible **2.** (*increase: tension, controversy*) avivar

**fuel consumption** n AUTO consumo m de gasolina

**fuel gauge** n indicador m del nivel de gasolina

**fulfil** <-ll-> *vt*, **fulfill** [fʊl·ˈfɪl] *vt* (*ambition, task*) realizar; (*condition, requirement*) cumplir; (*need*) satisfacer; (*function, role*) desempeñar; **to ~ oneself** realizarse

**fulfilment** *n*, **fulfillment** *n* (*of condition, requirement*) cumplimiento *m*; (*of function, role*) desempeño *m*; (*satisfaction*) realización *f*

**full** [fʊl] **I.** <-er, -est> *adj* **1.** (*container, space*) lleno, -a; (*vehicle*) completo, -a **2.** (*total: support*) total; (*recovery*) completo, -a; (*member*) de pleno derecho; **to be in ~ dress** estar de gala; **to be in ~ swing** estar en pleno apogeo **3.** (*maximum: employment*) pleno, -a; **~ of mistakes** lleno de errores; **at ~ speed** a toda velocidad **4.** (*rounded*) redondo, -a **5.** (*wide*) amplio, -a **6.** (*wine*) con cuerpo **7.** (*not hungry*) **to be ~** estar lleno **8.** (*conceited*) **to be ~ of oneself** ser un creído **II.** *adv* **1.** (*completely*) completamente **2.** (*directly*) directamente **3.** (*very*) muy; **to know ~ well (that...)** saber muy bien (que...) **III.** *n* **in ~** sin abreviar; **to the ~** al máximo

**fullback** [ˈfʊl·bæk] *n* SPORTS defensa *mf*

**full-blown** [ˌfʊl·ˈbloʊn] *adj* (*disaster, scandal*) auténtico, -a

**full-bodied** [ˌfʊl·ˈbad·ɪd] *adj* (*taste*) fuerte; (*wine*) con mucho cuerpo

**full-grown** *adj* crecido, -a

**full moon** *n* luna *f* llena

**full-page** *adj* de página entera

**full stop** *n* punto *m*; **to come to a ~** paralizarse

**full-time** *adj* de horario completo

**fully** [ˈfʊl·i] *adv* **1.** (*completely*) completamente **2.** (*in detail*) detalladamente **3.** (*at least*) al menos

**fumble** [ˈfʌm·bəl] **I.** *vi* **to ~ around for sth** buscar algo a tientas; **to ~ for words** titubear buscando las palabras **II.** *vt* SPORTS **to ~ the ball** dejar caer la pelota

**fume** [fjum] *vi* **1.** (*be angry*) estar furioso, -a; **to ~ at sb** echar pestes de alguien **2.** (*emit gases*) humear

**fun** [fʌn] **I.** *n* diversión *f*; **to do sth for ~** hacer algo por placer; **to do sth in ~** hacer algo en broma; **to have (a lot of) ~** divertirse (mucho); **have ~ on your**

weekend! ¡pásalo bien el fin de semana!; **have ~!** ¡diviértete!; **to make ~ of sb** reírse de alguien; **what ~!** ¡qué divertido! ► **~ and games** *pej* odisea *f* **II.** *adj* **1.** (*enjoyable*) agradable **2.** (*funny*) divertido, -a

**function** [ˈfʌŋk·ʃən] **I.** *n* **1.** *a.* MATH función *f*; **in my ~ as mayor,...** como alcalde,... **2.** (*formal ceremony*) ceremonia *f* **II.** *vi* funcionar

**functional** [ˈfʌŋk·ʃə·nəl] *adj* **1.** *a.* LING funcional **2.** (*operational, working*) práctico, -a

**fund** [fʌnd] **I.** *n* fondo *m*; **to be short of ~s** ir mal de fondos **II.** *vt* financiar

**fundamental** [ˌfʌn·də·ˈmen·təl] **I.** *adj* fundamental; (*difference*) esencial; (*principles*) básico, -a; **to be of ~ importance** ser de vital importancia **II.** *n* **the ~s** los principios básicos

**fundamentalist** **I.** *n* integrista *mf* **II.** *adj* integrista

**fundamentally** *adv* **1.** (*basically*) fundamentalmente **2.** (*in the most important sense*) esencialmente

**funeral** [ˈfju·nər·əl] *n* entierro *m*; **to attend a ~** asistir a un funeral

**funeral home** *n* funeraria *f*

**funeral parlor** *n* funeraria *f*

**fungus** [ˈfʌŋ·gəs] *n* (*wild mushroom*) hongo *m*; (*mold*) moho *m*

**funky** [ˈfʌŋ·ki] <-ier, -iest> *adj* **1.** (*musty*) **a ~ taste/smell** un sabor/olor raro **2.** *sl* (*cool*) genial **3.** (*music*) funky

**fun-loving** *adj* marchoso, -a

**funnel** [ˈfʌn·əl] **I.** *n* (*tool*) embudo *m* **II.** <-l-> *vt* canalizar

**funny** [ˈfʌn·i] <-ier, -iest> *adj* **1.** (*amusing*) divertido, -a **2.** *inf* (*witty*) gracioso, -a; **to try to be ~** *inf* hacerse el gracioso **3.** (*odd, peculiar*) raro, -a **4.** (*slightly ill*) **to feel ~** no encontrarse bien

**funny bone** *n* *inf* hueso *m* de la alegría

**fur** [fɜr] *n* **1.** (*animal hair*) piel *f* **2.** (*garment*) prenda *f* de pieles

**furious** [ˈfjʊr·i·əs] *adj* (*very angry*) furioso, -a, enchilado, -a *Méx*, caribe *Ant*; **to be ~ about sth** estar furioso por algo

**furl** [fɜrl] *vt* (*flag, sail*) recoger

**furnish** [ˈfɜr·nɪʃ] *vt* **1.** (*supply*) proporcionar; **to ~ sb with sth** suministrar algo a alguien **2.** (*provide furniture for*) amueblar

**furnished** ['fɜr·nɪʃt] *adj* amueblado, -a

**furniture** ['fɜr·nɪ·tʃər] *n* mobiliario *m*; **piece of ~** mueble *m*

**furniture van** *n* camión *m* de mudanzas

**furry** ['fɜr·i] <-ier, -iest> *adj* **1.** peludo, -a **2.** (*looking like fur*) peloso, -a; **~ toy** peluche *m*

**further** ['fɜr·ðər] **I.** *adj comp of* **far 1.** (*greater distance*) más lejano **2.** (*additional*) otro, -a; **until ~ notice** hasta nuevo aviso **II.** *adv comp of* **far 1.** (*greater distance*) más lejos; **~ on** más adelante; **~ and ~** cada vez más lejos **2.** (*more*) más ▶ **to not go any ~** no ir más allá **III.** *vt* fomentar; **to ~ sb's interests** favorecer los intereses de alguien

**furthermore** ['fɜr·ðər·mɔr] *adv* además

**furthest** ['fɜr·ðɪst] **I.** *adj* **1.** *superl of* **far 2.** (*greatest*) mayor **3.** (*at the greatest distance*) más lejano, -a **II.** *adv* **1.** *superl of* **far 2.** (*greatest distance*) más lejos

**fury** ['fjʊr·i] *n* furor *m*; **fit of ~** ataque *m* de furia

**fuse** [fjuz] **I.** *n* **1.** ELEC fusible *m*; **the ~ has blown** han saltado los plomos **2.** (*ignition device, detonator*) espoleta *f*; (*string*) mecha *f* ▶ **to have a short ~** tener mucho genio **II.** *vi* **1.** ELEC fundirse **2.** (*join together*) fusionarse **III.** *vt* **1.** ELEC fundir **2.** (*join*) fusionar

**fuse box** <-es> *n* caja *f* de fusibles

**fusion** ['fju·ʒən] *n* **1.** (*joining together*) fusión *f* **2.** PHYS fusión *f*; **nuclear ~** fusión nuclear

**fuss** [fʌs] **I.** *n* alboroto *m*; **to make a ~** armar un escándalo **II.** *vi* preocuparse; **to ~ over sth/sb** preocuparse en exceso por algo/alguien

**fussy** ['fʌs·i] <-ier, -iest> *adj* **1.** (*overly particular*) puntilloso, -a **2.** (*quick to criticize*) quisquilloso, -a **3.** (*baby*) llorón, -ona

**futile** ['fju·təl] *adj* inútil; **~ attempt** intento *m* en vano

**future** ['fju·tʃər] **I.** *n* **1.** *a.* LING futuro *m*; **to have plans for the ~** tener planes

de futuro; **in the ~ tense** en futuro; **the distant/near ~** el futuro lejano/próximo **2.** (*prospects*) porvenir *m* **II.** *adj* futuro, -a

# G

**G, g** [dʒi] *n* G, g *f*; **~ as in Golf** G de Granada

**g** *abbr of* **gram** g

**Gabon** [gæ·'boʊn] *n* Gabón *m*

**Gabonese** [ˌgæb·oʊ·'niz] **I.** *adj* gabonés, -esa **II.** *n* gabonés, -esa *m, f*

**gadget** ['gædʒ·ɪt] *n* artilugio *m*

**Gaelic** ['geɪ·lɪk] **I.** *n* gaélico *m* **II.** *adj* gaélico, -a

**gag** [gæg] **I.** *n* **1.** (*cloth*) mordaza *f* **2.** (*joke*) broma *f* **II.** <-gg-> *vt* amordazar; (*silence*) hacer callar **III.** <-gg-> *vi inf* (*to joke*) contar chistes

**gage** [geɪdʒ] *n vt see* **gauge**

**gaily** ['geɪ·li] *adv* alegremente

**gain** [geɪn] **I.** *n* **1.** (*increase*) aumento *m*; **~ in weight** aumento de peso **2.** ECON, FIN (*profit*) beneficio *m*; **net ~** beneficio neto **3.** *fig* (*advantage*) ventaja *f* **II.** *vt* **1.** (*obtain*) ganar **2.** (*acquire*) adquirir **3.** (*increase: velocity*) adquirir; **to ~ weight** ganar peso ▶ **to ~ ground** ganar terreno **III.** *vi* **1.** (*benefit*) beneficiarse de, sacar provecho de **2.** (*increase*) aumentar; (*experience, confidence*) adquirir **3.** (*put on weight*) engordar **4.** (*clock, watch*) adelantarse

**gala** ['geɪ·lə] **I.** *n* gala *f* **II.** *adj* (*festive*) de gala

**galaxy** ['gæl·ək·si] <-ies> *n* (*space*) galaxia *f*

**gale** [geɪl] *n* temporal *m*; **a ~-force wind**

un vendaval

**gale warning** n aviso m de temporal

**gall** [gɔl] n 1. (bile) hiel f inv 2. (impertinence) impertinencia f; **to have the ~ to do sth** tener agallas para hacer algo; pej tener la cara de hacer algo

**gallery** ['gæl·ə·ri] <-ries> n 1. (for displaying art) museo m; (for paintings) galería f 2. ARCHIT, THEAT tribuna f

**gallon** ['gæl·ən] n galón m (3,79 l)

**gallop** ['gæl·əp] I. vi galopar II. n galope m; **at a ~** fig al galope

**Gallup poll** ['gæl·əp·poʊl] n sondeo m de la opinión pública

**gamble** ['gæm·bəl] I. n apuesta f II. vi jugar; **to ~ on sth** confiar en algo III. vt (money) jugarse; (one's life) arriesgar

**gambler** ['gæm·blər] n jugador(a) m(f)

**gambling** n juego m

**game**[1] [geɪm] I. n 1. (in sports) partido m; **the Olympic Games** los Juegos Olímpicos 2. (in games) partida f; **~ of chance** juego de azar; **a ~ of chess** una partida de ajedrez ▶ **to beat sb at his/her own ~** ganar a alguien con sus propias armas II. adj (willing) animoso, -a; **to be ~ (to do sth)** animarse (a hacer algo)

**game**[2] [geɪm] n (in hunting) caza f; **big ~** caza mayor

**game show** n concurso m de televisión

**gammon** ['gæm·ən] n jamón m

**gang** [gæŋ] n 1. (criminal group) banda f 2. (organized group) cuadrilla f 3. inf (group of friends) pandilla f, barra f AmL, trinca f And, CSur

**gangly** ['gæŋ·gli] <-ier, -iest> adj larguirucho, -a

**gangster** ['gæŋ·stər] n gángster mf

**gangway** ['gæŋ·weɪ] I. n (gangplank) pasarela f; (ladder) escalerilla f II. interj inf ¡paso!

**gap** [gæp] n 1. (opening) abertura f; (empty space) hueco m; (in text, memory) laguna f 2. (break in time) intervalo m 3. (difference) diferencia f; **age ~** diferencia de edad

**gape** [geɪp] I. vi abrirse; (person) quedarse boquiabierto II. n (look) mirada f pasmada; (yawn) bostezo m

**gaping** adj (hole) enorme; (wound)

abierto, -a

**garage** [gə·'rɑʒ] n 1. (of house) garaje m, cochera f 2. (for repair) taller m

**garage sale** n venta de objetos usados en casa de un particular venta f de garaje Col

**garbage** ['gɑr·bɪdʒ] n basura f; **to take out the ~** sacar la basura

**garbage can** n cubo m [or AmL tacho m] de la basura

**garbage disposal** n triturador m de basura

**garbage dump** n vertedero m

**garbage truck** n camión m de la basura

**garble** ['gɑr·bəl] vt (distort: message) distorsionar

**garbled** adj (distorted: message) distorsionado, -a

**garden** ['gɑr·dən] I. n jardín m; **vegetable ~** huerto m; **botanical ~** jardín m botánico II. vi (with flowers) trabajar en el jardín; (with vegetables) cultivar el huerto

**gardener** ['gɑrd·nər] n 1. (of flowers) jardinero, -a m, f 2. (of vegetables) hortelano, -a m, f

**gardening** ['gɑrd·nɪŋ] n (of flowers) jardinería f; (of vegetables) horticultura f

**garden party** <-ies> n fiesta f al aire libre

**gargle** ['gɑr·gəl] I. vi hacer gárgaras II. n gárgaras fpl

**garlic** ['gɑr·lɪk] n ajo m; **clove of ~** diente m de ajo

**garlic press** <-es> n triturador m de ajos

**garment** ['gɑr·mənt] n prenda f de vestir

**gas** [gæs] I. <-s(s)es> n 1. a. MED, CHEM gas m; **natural ~** gas natural 2. (fuel) gasolina f; **leaded/unleaded ~** gasolina con plomo/sin plomo; **to step on the ~** acelerar 3. (flatulence) gases fpl, ventosidad f II. <-ss-> vt asfixiar con gas

**gaseous** ['gæs·i·əs] adj gaseoso, -a

**gas-guzzler** n inf (vehicle) esponja f, vehículo m de alta consumición

**gash** [gæʃ] <-es> n (deep cut) tajo m; (wound) cuchillada f

**gas heating** n calefacción f de gas

**G**

**gas mask** n máscara f antigás

**gas meter** n contador m del gas

**gasoline** ['gæs·ə·lin] n gasolina f, nafta f CSur

**gasp** [gæsp] I. vi 1. (breathe with difficulty) jadear; **to ~ for air** [or **breath**] hacer esfuerzos para respirar 2. (in shock) dar un grito ahogado II. n jadeo m; **he gave a ~ of astonishment** dio un grito ahogado de asombro ▶ **to be at one's last ~** estar en las últimas

**gas pedal** n acelerador m

**gas pipe** n tubería f de gas

**gas pump** n surtidor m de gasolina

**gas station** n gasolinera f, bomba f And, Ven, estación f de nafta RíoPl, bencinera f Chile, grifo m Perú

**gas stove** n cocina f de gas

**gassy** ['gæs·i] <-ier, -iest> adj 1. (full of gas) lleno, -a de gas 2. (gas-like) gaseoso, -a

**gastritis** [gæ·'strai·təs] n gastritis f inv

**gastroenteritis** [,gæs·trou·,en·tə·'rai·təs] n gastroenteritis f inv

**gastronomy** [gæ·'stran·ə·mi] n gastronomía f

**gate** [geit] n 1. (entrance barrier) puerta f; RAIL barrera f 2. SPORTS entrada f 3. AVIAT puerta f de embarque

**gatecrash** ['geit·kræʃ] I. vt colarse en II. vi colarse

**gatecrasher** n sl (at party, concert) intruso, -a m, f (que se cuela sin pagar o sin haber sido invitado), colado, -a m, f Col

**gatekeeper** n portero, -a m, f; RAIL guardabarrera mf

**gatepost** n poste m

**gateway** n 1. (entrance) entrada f 2. (means of access) puerta f

**gather** ['gæð·ər] I. vt 1. (convene: people) reunir, juntar 2. (harvest) cosechar; (flowers) recoger 3. (information) reunir 4. (muster) **to ~ one's strength** cobrar fuerzas 5. (infer) deducir; **to ~ that...** sacar la conclusión de que... II. vi 1. (convene) reunirse 2. (accumulate: things) amontonarse

**gathering** n reunión f

**gauge** [geidʒ] I. n 1. (measure) medida f 2. (instrument) indicador m 3. RAIL

ancho m de vía II. vt 1. (measure) medir 2. (assess) determinar

**gauntlet** ['gɔnt·lɪt] n guante m; HIST guantelete m

**gauze** [gɔz] n a. MED gasa f

**gave** [geiv] pt of **give**

**gawk** [gɔk] vi papar moscas; **to ~ at** mirar embobado

**gawky** ['gɔ·ki] adj torpe; (tall, awkward) desgarbado, -a

**gay** [gei] I. adj 1. (homosexual) gay 2. (cheerful) alegre II. n (man) gay m; (woman) lesbiana f

**gaze** [geiz] I. vi mirar fijamente II. n mirada f fija

**GB** [,dʒi·'bi] n 1. COMPUT abbr of **gigabyte** GB 2. abbr of **Great Britain** GB

**GDP** [,dʒi·di·'pi] n abbr of **gross domestic product** PIB m

**gear** [gɪr] n 1. TECH engranaje m 2. AUTO marcha f 3. (equipment) equipo m

**gearbox** ['gɪr·baks] <-es> n caja f de cambios

**gearshift** ['gɪr·ʃɪft] n palanca f de cambio

**geezer** ['gi·zər] n sl tío m; **old ~** vejestorio m

**gem** [dʒem] n 1. (jewel) piedra f preciosa 2. (person) joya f fig

**Gemini** ['dʒem·ɪ·nai] n Géminis mf

**gender** ['dʒen·dər] n 1. (sexual identity) sexo m 2. LING género m

**gene** [dʒin] n gen m

**genealogist** [,dʒi·ni·'æl·ə·dʒɪst] n genealogista mf

**gene bank** n banco m genético

**general** ['dʒen·ər·əl] I. adj general; **as a ~ rule** por regla general II. n MIL general mf; **lieutenant ~** teniente mf general; **four-star ~** capitán, -ana m, f general

**general director** n director(a) m(f) general

**general election** n elecciones f pl generales

**generalize** ['dʒen·ər·ə·laiz] vi, vt generalizar

**generally** ['dʒen·ər·ə·li] adv 1. (usually) generalmente 2. (mostly) en general 3. (widely, extensively) por lo general

**general manager** n director(a) m(f) general

**general practitioner** n médico, -a m, f de cabecera

**general store** n tienda f

**general view** n opinión f general

**generate** ['dʒen·ə·reɪt] vt generar

**generation** [ˌdʒen·ə·'reɪ·ʃən] n generación f; **for ~s** durante generaciones

**generator** ['dʒen·ə·reɪ·tər] n a. ELEC generador m

**generous** ['dʒen·ər·əs] adj 1. (magnanimous: person) generoso, -a, rangoso, -a AmS 2. (ample: serving) abundante

**gene therapy** [ˌdʒin·'θer·ə·pi] n terapia f génica

**genetic** [dʒɪ·'net·ɪk] adj genético, -a; **~ disease** enfermedad f genética

**genetically** [dʒɪ·'net·ɪk·ə·li] adj genéticamente; **~ engineered** genéticamente modificado, -a

**geneticist** [dʒɪ·'net·ə·sɪst] n genetista mf

**genitalia** [dʒen·ɪ·'teɪ·li·ə] npl form, **genitals** ['dʒen·ə·təlz] npl genitales mpl

**genitive** ['dʒen·ɪ·tɪv] I. adj genitivo, -a II. n genitivo m

**genius** ['dʒin·jəs] n <-ses> genio mf

**genocide** ['dʒen·ə·saɪd] n genocidio m

**gent** [dʒent] n inf abbr of **gentleman** caballero m

**gentle** ['dʒen·təl] adj 1. (kind) amable; (calm) suave 2. (moderate) moderado, -a; (tap on the door) suave, pasito Col, quedito Méx

**gentleman** ['dʒen·təl·mən] <-men> n 1. (man) señor m; **ladies and gentlemen** señoras y señores 2. (well-behaved man) caballero m

**gentleness** ['dʒen·təl·nɪs] n delicadeza f

**genuine** ['dʒen·ju·ɪn] adj 1. (not fake) genuino, -a 2. (real, sincere) verdadero, -a

**genus** ['dʒi·nəs] <-nera> n BIO género m

**geographer** [dʒi·'ag·rə·fər] n geógrafo, -a m, f

**geography** [dʒi·'ag·rə·fi] n geografía f

**geological** [ˌdʒi·ə·'ladʒ·ɪ·kəl] adj geológico, -a

**geologist** [dʒi·'al·ə·dʒɪst] n geólogo, -a m, f

**geology** [dʒi·'al·ə·dʒi] n geología f

**geometry** [dʒi·'am·ə·tri] n geometría f

**germ** [dʒɜrm] n germen m

**German** ['dʒɜr·mən] I. n 1. (person) alemán, -ana m, f 2. (language) alemán m II. adj alemán, -ana

**Germanic** [dʒər·'mæn·ɪk] adj germánico, -a

**German measles** n + sing vb rubeola f

**German shepherd** n pastor m alemán

**Germany** ['dʒɜr·mə·ni] n Alemania f

**germinate** ['dʒɜr·mə·neɪt] vi, vt germinar

**germination** [ˌdʒɜr·mə·'neɪ·ʃən] n germinación f

**germ warfare** n guerra f bacteriológica

**gerontologist** [ˌdʒer·ən·'tal·ə·dʒɪst] n gerontólogo, -a m, f

**gerund** ['dʒer·ənd] n gerundio m

**gestation** [dʒe·'steɪ·ʃən] n gestación f

**gesticulate** [dʒe·'stɪk·jə·leɪt] vi form gesticular

**gesture** ['dʒes·tʃər] I. n 1. (body movement) gesto m 2. (act) muestra f; **a ~ towards sb** un detalle con alguien II. vi hacer un ademán III. vt indicar con un ademán

**get** [get] I. <got, gotten> vt 1. (obtain) obtener; (a massage) recibir; (a manicure) hacerse; **to ~ the impression that...** dar a alguien la impresión de que... 2. (receive: letter, present) recibir; **to ~ sth from sb** recibir algo de alguien 3. (catch: plane, train) coger; (the flu) pillar, pescar Col; **do you ~ channel 4?** ¿pillas el canal 4?, ¿te entra el canal 4? Col 4. (hear, understand) comprender; (message) captar; (picture) entender; **I don't ~ it** no lo pillo, no agarro la onda 5. (answer) **to ~ the door** inf abrir la puerta; **to ~ the phone** inf coger el teléfono 6. (buy: groceries) comprar 7. (cause to be done) **to ~ sth done** hacer algo; **to ~ sb to do sth** hacer que alguien haga algo 8. (start) **to ~ sb to do sth** conseguir que alguien haga algo 9. inf (irk) repatear; **that really ~s me** eso me afecta realmente 10. inf (start) **to ~ going** poner en marcha; **to ~ cracking** poner manos a la obra II. vi 1. + n/adj (become) volverse; **to ~ married** casarse; **to ~ upset** enfadarse; **to ~ used to sth** acostumbrarse a algo; **to ~ to be sth** llegar a ser algo; **to ~ to**

**like sth** coger afición a algo **2.** (*have opportunity*) **to ~ to do sth** llegar a hacer algo; **to ~ to see sb** lograr ver a alguien **3.** (*travel*) llegar; **to ~ home** llegar a casa

◆**get across** *vt* hacer llegar; **to get a point across to sb** hacer llegar una idea a alguien

◆**get along** *vi* **1.** (*have a good relationship*) llevarse bien **2.** (*manage*) arreglárselas

◆**get around I.** *vt insep* (*avoid*) evitar **II.** *vi* **1.** (*spread*) llegar a **2.** (*travel*) viajar mucho

◆**get at** *vt insep* **1.** (*reach*) llegar a **2.** (*suggest*) apuntar a

◆**get away** *vi* irse

◆**get back** *vt* recuperar

◆**get back at** *vt* vengarse de

◆**get back to** *vt* (*letter*) contestar; (*call*) devolver

◆**get behind** *vi* atrasarse

◆**get by** *vi* (*manage*) arreglárselas

◆**get down I.** *vt always sep* (*disturb*) deprimir **II.** *vi* **1.** (*descend*) bajar **2.** *inf* (*enjoy oneself*) pachanguear *Méx*, rumbear *Col*

◆**get down to** *vt* ponerse con; **to ~ doing sth** ponerse a hacer algo

◆**get in I.** *vi* **1.** (*arrive*) llegar a casa **2.** (*enter*) entrar **3.** (*become member*) ser aceptado **II.** *vt* **1.** (*say*) (lograr) decir **2.** (*bring inside*) llevar dentro **3.** (*accomplish*) lograr

◆**get into** *vt insep* **1.** (*become interested in*) interesarse por **2.** (*involve*) meter; **to get sb into trouble** meter a alguien en problemas

◆**get off I.** *vi* **1.** (*avoid punishment*) librarse **2.** (*leave work*) salir **3.** (*have audacity*) atreverse **4.** *sl* (*have orgasm*) correrse, venirse *Col, Méx* **II.** *vt always sep* **1.** (*shot*) disparar **2.** (*help avoid punishment*) librar de **3.** (*work*) acabar

◆**get on I.** *vi* (*manage*) arreglárselas **II.** *vt sl* **let's get it on** (*enthusiastically begin*) ¡pongamos manos a la obra!; (*have sex*) hagámoslo

◆**get out I.** *vi* **1.** (*leave home*) salir **2.** (*spread*) correr la voz **3.** (*escape*)

escaparse, volarse *Col, Méx* **II.** *vt* (*make leave*) echar

◆**get over** *vt insep* **1.** (*recover from*) recuperarse de; (*illness*) reponerse de; (*difficulty*) superar **2.** (*forget about*) **to ~ sb/sth** olvidarse de alguien/algo

◆**get through I.** *vt* **1.** (*survive*) pasar; (*exam*) aprobar **2.** (*finish*) terminar **II.** *vi* **to ~ to sth/sb** comunicarse con algo/alguien

◆**get together I.** *vi* reunirse **II.** *vt* **1.** (*meet*) juntarse **2.** (*gather*) reunir **3.** (*organize*) preparar

◆**get up I.** *vt* **1.** *always sep* (*wake*) levantarse **2.** (*muster: courage*) conseguir **3.** *insep* (*climb*) subir **4.** *inf* (*dress*) ataviar **II.** *vi* **1.** (*get out of bed*) levantarse **2.** (*rise*) subir

**getaway** ['gɛt·ə·weɪ] *n* fuga *f*

**get-together** ['gɛt·tə·'geð·ər] *n inf* reunión *f*

**get-up** ['gɛt·ʌp] *n inf* atuendo *m*

**ghastly** ['gæst·li] <-ier, -iest> *adj* (*frightful*) horroroso, -a

**gherkin** ['gɜr·kɪn] *n* pepinillo *m*

**ghetto** ['gɛt·oʊ] <-s *or* -es> *n* gueto *m*

**ghetto blaster** *n sl* loro *m* [*or Col, Méx* grabadora *f*] portátil

**ghost** [goʊst] *n a. fig* (*spirit*) fantasma *m*, espanto *m AmL*, azoro *m AmC*; **to believe in ~s** creer en fantasmas ► **not to have a ~ of a <u>chance</u>** no tener ni la más mínima oportunidad

**ghostly** ['goʊst·li] <-ier, -iest> *adj* **1.** (*ghost-like*) fantasmal **2.** (*spooky*) escalofriante

**ghost story** *n* historia *f* de fantasmas

**GI¹** [ˌdʒiː·'aɪ] *n* soldado *m* norteamericano *(especialmente en la II Guerra Mundial)*

**GI²** *abbr of* **government issue** reglamentario, -a

**giant** ['dʒaɪ·ənt] **I.** *n* gigante *m* **II.** *adj* gigantesco, -a

**giddy** ['gɪd·i] <-ier, -iest> *adj* mareado, -a

**gift** [gɪft] *n* **1.** (*present*) regalo *m* **2.** (*talent*) don *m*; **to have the ~ of gab** *inf* tener mucha labia

**gift certificate** *n* vale *m* de [*or* por *un*] regalo

**gifted** *adj* **1.** (*talented: musician*) de (gran) talento **2.** (*intelligent*) brillante; ~ **child** niño *m* superdotado

**gift shop** *n* tienda *f* de regalos

**gig¹** [gɪg] *n sl* (*musical performance*) concierto *m*

**gig²** [gɪg] *n* COMPUT *abbr of* **gigabyte** giga *m*

**gigantic** [dʒaɪˈgæn·tɪk] *adj* gigantesco, -a

**giggle** [ˈgɪg·əl] **I.** *vi* reír(se) tontamente **II.** *n* **1.** (*laugh*) risita *f* **2.** *pl* **to get the ~s** tener un ataque de risa

**gimmick** [ˈgɪm·ɪk] *n* (*trick*) truco *m* (*para vender más*); **sales** ~ truco publicitario

**gimmicky** [ˈgɪm·ɪk·i] *adj* efectista

**gin¹** [dʒɪn] *n* ginebra *f*; ~ **and tonic** gin tonic *m*

**gin²** [dʒɪn] *n* AGR **cotton** ~ desmotadora *f* de algodón

**gin³** [dʒɪn] *n* (*card game*) juego de cartas parecido al rummy

**ginger** [ˈdʒɪn·dʒər] **I.** *n* **1.** (*root spice*) jengibre *m* **2.** (*color*) rojo *m* anaranjado **II.** *adj* rojizo, -a

**gingerbread** [ˈdʒɪn·dʒər·bred] *n* pan *m* de jengibre

**gingerly** [ˈdʒɪn·dʒər·li] *adv* con cautela

**ginger snap** *n* galleta *f* de jengibre

**gipsy** [ˈdʒɪp·si] *n see* **gypsy**

**giraffe** [dʒə·ˈræf] *n* <-(s)> jirafa *f*

**girdle** [ˈgɜr·dəl] *n* **1. a.** *fig* (*belt*) cinturón *m* **2.** (*corset*) faja *f*

**girl** [gɜrl] *n* **1.** (*child*) niña *f*; (*young woman*) chica *f*, piba *f Arg* **2.** the ~s *pl* (*at work*) las compañeras; (*friends*) las amigas

**girlfriend** [ˈgɜrl·frend] *n* **1.** (*of man*) novia *f*, polola *f And* **2.** (*of woman*) amiga *f*

**girlhood** [ˈgɜrl·hʊd] *n* juventud *f*

**girlie** [ˈgɜr·li] *adj* de destape

**girlish** [ˈgɜr·lɪʃ] *adj* de [*or* como una] niña

**Girl Scout** *n* exploradora *f*

**gist** [dʒɪst] *n* **to get the ~ of sth** entender lo básico de algo

**give** [gɪv] **I.** *vt* <gave, given> **1.** (*offer*) dar, ofrecer; (*kiss, signal*) dar; (*a seat*) ceder; **to ~ sb an excuse for sth** dar una excusa a alguien para algo; **given**

the choice... si pudiera elegir...; **to ~ sb something to eat/drink** dar a alguien algo de comer/beber; **don't ~ me that!** *inf* ¡venga ya, tú me la quieres dar con queso!; ~ **me a break!** ¡dame un respiro!; **I don't ~ a damn** *inf* me importa un bledo; **to ~ sb the creeps** producir a alguien escalofríos; **to ~ (it) one's all** [*or* **best**] dar todo de sí mismo; **to ~ anything for sth/to do sth** dar cualquier cosa por algo/por hacer algo; **to ~ one's life to sth** dedicar la vida a algo **2.** (*lecture, performance*) dar; (*speech*) pronunciar; (*strange look*) echar; (*headache, trouble*) producir, dar; **to ~ sb a call** llamar a alguien (por teléfono); **to ~ sth a go** intentar algo **3.** (*organize*) dar, organizar **4.** (*pass on*) contagiar **II.** *vi* <gave, given> **1.** (*offer*) dar, ofrecer **2.** (*stretch*) estirarse, dar de sí; **something will have to ~** *fig* algo tendrá que cambiar **3.** **what ~s?** *inf* ¿qué hay? ▶ **it is better to ~ than to receive** *prov* es mejor dar que recibir *prov* **III.** *n* elasticidad *f*

◆**give away** *vt* **1.** (*for free*) regalar **2.** (*reveal*) revelar **3.** *form* (*bride*) entregar en matrimonio **4.** SPORTS regalar al (equipo) contrario

◆**give back** *vt* devolver, regresar *Méx*

◆**give in I.** *vi* rendirse **II.** *vt* entregar

◆**give off** *vt* emitir; (*odor*) despedir

◆**give out I.** *vt* **1.** (*distribute*) repartir **2.** (*announce*) anunciar **3.** (*emit*) producir; (*noise*) emitir **II.** *vi* **1.** (*run out*) acabar(se) **2.** (*machine*) estropearse; (*legs*) ceder

◆**give up I.** *vt* **1.** (*renounce*) renunciar; **to ~ smoking** dejar de fumar **2.** (*hand over*) ceder **3.** (*lose hope*) **to give sb up for dead** dar a alguien por muerto **4.** (*surrender*) entregar; **to give oneself up (to the police)** entregarse (a la policía) **II.** *vi* **1.** (*quit*) abandonar **2.** (*cease trying to guess*) rendirse

**give-and-take** [ˌgɪv·ən·ˈteɪk] *n* (*compromise*) toma y daca *m*

**giveaway** [ˈgɪv·ə·weɪ] *n* **1.** *inf* (*free gift*) regalo *m* **2.** *inf* (*exposure*) prueba *f* (que delata algo); **the way he dresses is a dead ~** su forma de vestir lo delata

**given** ['gɪv·ən] **I.** *pp of* **give II.** *adj*
**1.** (*specified*) determinado, -a, dado,
-a; **at a ~ time and place** a una hora
y en un lugar determinado **2. to be ~
to** (**doing**) **sth** ser dado a (hacer) algo
**III.** *prep* **~ that** dado que +*subj*, en
el caso de que +*subj*; **~ the chance, I
would go to Japan** si tuviese la oportunidad, iría a Japón **IV.** *n* dato *m* conocido; **that's a ~** eso se sobreentiende

**giver** ['gɪv·ər] *n* donante *mf*

**glacial** ['gleɪ·ʃəl] *adj* GEO glacial

**glacier** ['gleɪ·ʃər] *n* glaciar *m*

**glad** [glæd] <gladder, gladdest> *adj* contento, -a; **to be ~ about sth** alegrarse
de algo; **I'd be ~ to go with you** me
encantaría ir contigo

**gladly** ['glæd·li] *adv* con mucho gusto

**glamorous** ['glæm·ə·rəs] *adj* glamoroso,
-a, atractivo, -a; (*outfit*) sofisticado, -a

**glance** [glæns] **I.** *n* mirada *f*, vistazo *m*;
**at first ~** a primera vista **II.** *vi* **1.** (*look
cursorily*) **to ~ over sth** echar un vistazo
a algo **2.** (*shine*) brillar

♦**glance off** *vi* (chocar y) rebotar

**glare** [gleɪr] **I.** *n* **1.** (*mean look*) mirada *f* (feroz); **to give sb a ~** fulminar
a alguien con la mirada **2.** (*reflection*)
resplandor *m*; **to give off ~** deslumbrar
**II.** *vi* **1.** (*look*) fulminar con la mirada
**2.** (*shine*) resplandecer

**glaring** *adj* **1.** (*obvious: error*) que salta
a la vista; **~ weakness** debilidad *f* mani-
fiesta **2.** (*sun*) deslumbrante **3.** (*hostile:
eyes*) desafiante

**glass** [glæs] <-es> *n* **1.** (*material*) vidrio *m*, cristal *m*; **pane of ~** hoja *f* de
vidrio **2.** (*for drinks*) vaso *m*; **a ~ of
milk** un vaso de leche **3.** (*drink*) copa *f*
**4.** **~s** gafas *fpl*, lentes *fpl* AmL

**glassful** ['glæs·fʊl] *n* vaso *m* (lleno)
(**of** de)

**glasshouse** ['glæs·haʊs] *n* invernadero *m*

**glassworks** *npl* fábrica *f* de vidrio

**glaze** [gleɪz] **I.** *n a.* CULIN glaseado *m*;
(*painting*) barniz *m*; (*pottery*) vidria-
do *m* **II.** *vt* **1.** (*pottery*) vidriar **2.** (*donut*) glasear

**glazier** ['gleɪ·zi·ər] *n* vidriero, -a *m, f*

**gleam** [glim] **I.** *n* reflejo *m*, destello *m*;

**~ of hope** rayo *m* de esperanza **II.** *vi*
brillar, relucir

**glee** [gli] *n* júbilo *m*

**gleeful** ['gli·fəl] *adj* eufórico, -a

**glide** [glaɪd] **I.** *vi* **1.** (*move smoothly*) deslizarse **2.** AVIAT planear **II.** *n*
**1.** (*sliding movement*) deslizamiento *m*
**2.** AVIAT planeo *m*

**glider** ['glaɪ·dər] *n* planeador *m*

**glider pilot** *n* piloto *mf* de planeador

**gliding** ['glaɪ·dɪŋ] *n* vuelo *m* sin motor

**glimmer** ['glɪm·ər] **I.** *vi* brillar tenuemente **II.** *n* (*light*) luz *f* tenue; **~ of hope**
atisbo *m* de esperanza

**glimpse** [glɪmps] **I.** *vt* (*signs*) vislumbrar
**II.** *n* **to catch a ~** of vislumbrar

**glint** [glɪnt] **I.** *vi* destellar **II.** *n* destello *m*

**glisten** ['glɪs·ən] *vi* brillar, relucir

**glitch** [glɪtʃ] <-es> *n* fallo *m*

**glitter** ['glɪt·ər] **I.** *vi* brillar, relucir **II.** *n*
**1.** (*sparkling*) brillo *m*, destello *m*
**2.** (*shiny material*) purpurina *f*

**glittering** *adj* (*sparkling, impressive*) brillante

**glitzy** ['glɪt·si] <-ier, -iest> *adj inf* osten-
tentoso, -a; (*party*) esplendoroso, -a,
suntuoso, -a

**gloat** [gloʊt] **I.** *vi* disfrutar con regocijo;
**to ~ over sth** manifestar (gran) satisfacción por algo; **to ~ at sth** regodearse con
algo **II.** *n* regocijo *m*

**global** ['gloʊ·bəl] *adj* **1.** (*worldwide*) (a
nivel) mundial, global **2.** (*complete*)
global, total, general; COMPUT **~ search
and replace** buscar y reemplazar en
todo el documento

**global warming** *n* calentamiento *m* global

**globe** [gloʊb] *n* (*object*) globo *m*

**globetrotter** ['gloʊb·ˌtrɑt·ər] *n* trotamun-
dos *mf inv*

**gloom** [glum] *n* **1.** (*hopelessness*) pesimismo *m*, melancolía *f* **2.** (*darkness*)
oscuridad *f*

**gloomy** ['glu·mi] <-ier, -iest> *adj* **1.** (*dismal*) lúgubre; (*thoughts*) melancólico,
-a; **to turn ~** abatirse **2.** (*dark: corner,
day*) oscuro, -a

**glorify** ['glɔr·ə·faɪ] <-ie-> *vt* **1.** (*make
seem better*) glorificar **2.** (*honor*) alabar

**glorious** ['glɔr·i·əs] *adj* **1.** (*honorable, illustrious*) glorioso, -a **2.** (*splendid: day, weather*) espléndido, -a **3.** *iron* (*extreme*) enorme

**glory** ['glɔr·i] **I.** *n* **1.** (*honor*) gloria *f*; **to get all the ~ for sth** conseguir toda la gloria por algo **2.** (*splendor*) esplendor *m*; **in all her ~** en todo su esplendor **3.** (*state of delight*) **to be in one's ~** estar en la gloria **4.** (*adoration, praise*) adoración *f* ▶ **be!** (*thank God!*) ¡gracias a Dios! **II.** <-ied> *vi* vanagloriarse; **to ~ in sth** vanagloriarse de algo

**glossary** ['glas·ə·ri] <-ies> *n* PUBL, LIT glosario *m*

**glossy** ['glas·i] **I.** <-ier, -iest> *adj* (*shiny*) brillante, lustroso, -a; (*paper*) satinado, -a **II.** <-ies> *n* PHOT fotografía *f* brillante

**glove** [glʌv] *n* guante *m*; **leather ~s** guantes *m pl* de piel; **a pair of ~s** unos guantes

**glove compartment** *n* AUTO guantera *f*

**glow** [gloʊ] **I.** *n* **1.** (*light*) luz *f* **2.** (*warmth and redness*) ardor *m* **3.** (*good feeling*) sensación *f* grata **II.** *vi* **1.** (*illuminate*) brillar **2.** (*be red and hot*) arder **3.** (*look radiant*) estar radiante

**glower** ['glaʊ·ər] *vi* mirar con el ceño fruncido

**glucose** ['glu·koʊs] *n* glucosa *f*; **~ syrup** jarabe *m* de glucosa

**glue** [glu] **I.** *n* cola *f*, pegamento *m*; **to fix sth with ~** fijar algo con cola; **to sniff ~** esnifar pegamento **II.** *vt* encolar; **to ~ sth together** pegar algo; **to ~ sth on** encolar algo; **to be ~d to sth** *fig* estar pegado a algo

**glue stick** *n* pegamento *m* en barra

**glum** [glʌm] <glummer, glummest> *adj* (*morose, downcast*) taciturno, -a; **to be/feel ~** (**about sth**) estar/sentirse melancólico (por algo)

**gluten** ['glu·tən] *n* gluten *m*

**gnat** [næt] *n* BIO mosquito *m*, jején *m AmS*

**gnaw** [nɔ] **I.** *vi* **1.** (*chew*) **to ~ at** [*or* **on**] **sth** roer algo **2.** (*bother*) atormentar; **to ~ at sb** atormentar a alguien **II.** *vt* (*chew*) roer

**gnawing** *adj* persistente; (*pain*) punzante; (*doubt*) que atormenta

**GNP** [ˌdʒi·en·'pi] *abbr of* **Gross National Product** PNB

**go** [goʊ] **I.** <went, gone> *vi* **1.** (*proceed*) ir; **to ~ (and) do sth** ir a hacer algo; **to ~ home** irse a casa **2.** (*travel*) viajar; **to ~ on a trip** irse de viaje; **to ~ abroad** viajar al extranjero **3.** (*adopt position*) **when I ~ like this, my back hurts** cuando hago esto, me duele la espalda **4.** (*leave*) marcharse; **to have to ~** tener que irse; **when does the bus ~?** ¿a qué hora sale el autobús? **5.** (*do*) hacer; **to ~ camping/fishing/shopping** ir de camping/pesca/compras; **to ~ jogging** hacer footing; **to ~ swimming** ir a nadar **6.** (*attend*) asistir; **to ~ to a concert** ir a un concierto; **to ~ to a movie** ir a ver una película **7.** + *adj or n* (*become*) volverse; **to ~ bankrupt** caer en bancarrota; **to ~ public** hacerse público; **to ~ adrift** fallar; **to ~ bald** quedarse calvo; **to ~ haywire** volverse loco; **to ~ to sleep** dormirse; **to ~ wrong** salir mal **8.** + *adj* (*exist*) **to ~ hungry/thirsty** pasar hambre/sed; **to ~ unnoticed** pasar desapercibido **9.** (*happen*) **to ~ badly/well** ir mal/bien; **the way things are ~ing** tal como van las cosas **10.** (*pass*) pasar; **time seems to ~ faster as you get older** parece que pasa el tiempo más rápido a medida que envejeces **11.** (*begin*) empezar; **ready, set, ~** preparados, listos, ya **12.** (*belong*) pertenecer; **where does this ~?** ¿dónde va esto? **13.** (*fit*) quedar bien; **that old picture would ~ well on that wall** ese viejo cuadro quedaría bien en aquella pared; **two ~es into eight four times** MATH ocho entre dos da cuatro **14.** (*lead*) conducir **15.** (*function*) funcionar; **to get sth to ~** hacer que algo funcione; **to keep a conversation ~ing** mantener una conversación **16.** (*be sold*) venderse; **to ~ for $50** venderse por 50 dólares **17.** (*contribute*) contribuir; **love and friendship ~ to make a lasting relationship** el amor y la amistad contribuyen a hacer duradera una relación **18.** (*sound*) sonar; **the ambulance had**

G

sirens ~ing la ambulancia hacía sonar las sirenas **19.** (*be told*) **as the saying ~es** como dice el refrán **20.** GAMES tocar; **I ~ now** ahora me toca a mí **21.** *inf* (*use the toilet*) **do any of the kids have to ~?** ¿alguno de los niños tiene que ir al lavabo? ▶ **what he says ~es** lo que él dice va a misa; **anything ~es** cualquier cosa vale; **here ~es!** ¡vamos allá! **II.** <went, gone> *vt* **1.** *inf* (*say*) decir; **and then he goes, "Knock it off!"** y entonces es cuando dice: "¡Ya basta!"; **ducks ~ 'quack'** los patos hacen 'cuac' **2.** (*make*) hacer; **to ~ it alone** hacerlo solo **III.** <-es> *n* **1.** (*attempt*) intento *m*; **all in one ~** todo de un tirón **2.** (*a success*) éxito *m*; **to be no ~** ser imposible **3.** (*activity*) actividad *f*; **to be on the ~** trajinar ▶ **from the word ~** desde el principio

◆**go about I.** *vt insep* **1.** (*proceed with*) ocuparse de **2.** (*perform a task*) llevar a cabo **II.** *vi* andar (por ahí)

◆**go after** *vt insep* **1.** (*follow*) seguir; **to ~ sb** ir detrás de alguien **2.** (*chase*) perseguir **3.** (*try to get*) andar tras

◆**go against** *vt insep* **1.** (*contradict*) contradecir **2.** (*oppose*) ir en contra de, oponerse a **3.** (*disobey*) desobedecer

◆**go ahead** *vi* **1.** (*begin*) empezar **2.** (*go before*) ir delante **3.** (*proceed*) seguir adelante; **~!** ¡sigue!

◆**go along** *vi* **1.** (*move onward*) ir hacia delante **2.** (*proceed*) proceder a

◆**go around** *vi* **1.** (*move around*) andar (de acá para allá) **2.** (*move in a curve*) girar **3.** (*rotate*) rotar **4.** (*be in circulation*) estar circulando; **it's going around that...** se dice que...

◆**go away** *vi* **1.** (*travel*) viajar **2.** (*leave*) marcharse **3.** (*disappear*) desaparecer

◆**go back** *vi* **1.** (*move backwards*) retroceder **2.** (*return*) volver, regresarse *AmL* **3.** (*date back*) remontarse

◆**go by** *vi* **1.** (*move past*) pasar (junto a) **2.** (*pass*) transcurrir; **in days gone by** *form* en tiempos pasados; **to let sth ~** no aprovechar algo

◆**go down I.** *vt insep* bajar, descender; **to ~ a mine** MIN bajar a una mina **II.** *vi* **1.** (*set*) caer; (*sun*) ponerse; (*ship*) hun-

dirse; (*plane*) estrellarse; **to ~ on all fours** ponerse [*or* en cuatro patas] a gatas **2.** (*medicine*) tragar **3.** (*decrease*) disminuir; FIN ir a la baja; (*decrease in quality*) empeorar **4.** *sl* (*happen*) pasar; **what's going down, my man?** ¿qué pasa, tío? **5.** (*lose*) perder; SPORTS perder frente a alguien/algo; **to ~ without a fight** rendirse sin luchar **6.** (*travel southward*) ir hacia el sur; **we're going down to Los Angeles for the weekend** vamos a bajar a Los Ángeles por el fin de semana **7.** (*be received*) ser recibido; **to ~ well/badly (with sb)** ser bien/mal recibido (por alguien) **8.** *vulg* (*give oral sex to*) **to ~ on sb** hacer una mamada [*or* mamárselo] a alguien

◆**go for** *vt insep* **1.** (*fetch*) ir a por, ir a buscar **2.** (*try to achieve*) intentar conseguir; (*try to grasp*) intentar alcanzar; **~ it!** ¡a por ello! **3.** (*choose*) elegir **4.** (*attack*) atacar; **to ~ sb with sth** atacar a alguien con algo **5.** (*sell for*) venderse por **6.** *inf* (*like*) molar; (*believe*) creer en

◆**go in** *vi* **1.** (*enter*) entrar **2.** (*belong in*) ir en; **those forks ~ the drawer** esos tenedores van en el cajón

◆**go into** *vt insep* **1.** (*enter*) entrar en **2.** (*fit into*) encajar en; **does two ~ six?** ¿seis es divisible por dos? **3.** (*begin*) empezar; **to ~ a coma/trance** MED entrar en coma/en trance; **to ~ action** pasar a la acción; **to ~ effect** entrar en vigor **4.** (*begin*) **to ~ production** empezar a producirse **5.** (*examine and discuss*) examinar; **to ~ detail** entrar en detalles **6.** (*be used in*) ser utilizado en **7.** (*join*) unirse; **to ~ the military** enrolarse en el ejército **8.** (*crash into*) dar de lleno contra

◆**go off** *vi* **1.** (*explode: bomb*) estallar **2.** (*make sound: alarm clock, siren*) (empezar a) sonar **3.** (*proceed*) marchar **4.** (*leave*) irse **5.** (*digress*) salirse; **to ~ the subject** salirse del tema ▶ **to ~ the deep end** perder los estribos

◆**go on I.** *vi* **1.** (*move on*) seguir su camino, seguir adelante **2.** (*continue*) seguir; (*continue speaking*) continuar **3.** (*go further*) ir más allá; **to ~ ahead** seguir adelante 4. (*extend*) extenderse 5. (*pass*) pasar 6. (*happen*) suceder 7. (*start*) empezar; (*begin functioning*) empezar a funcionar; THEAT, MUS salir (a escena); **the show must ~** el espectáculo debe continuar II. *vt insep* basarse en III. *interj* (*as encouragement*) vamos; (*express disbelief*) anda ya

◆**go out** *vi* 1. (*leave*) salir; **to ~ to dinner** salir a cenar 2. (*on a date*) salir; **to ~ with sb** salir con alguien 3. (*stop working*) estropearse, dañarse; (*light*) apagarse; (*fire*) extinguirse 4. (*recede*) retirarse 5. (*become unfashionable*) pasarse de moda

◆**go over** I. *vt insep* 1. (*examine*) examinar 2. (*cross*) atravesar; **to ~ a border/river/street** cruzar una frontera/un río/una calle 3. (*exceed*) exceder II. *vi* **to ~ to** (*visit*) visitar

◆**go through** *vt insep* 1. (*pass*) pasar por 2. (*experience*) vivir; (*operation*) sufrir 3. (*review, discuss*) repasar 4. (*use up*) gastar

◆**go under** *vi* 1. NAUT (*sink*) hundirse 2. (*move below*) ir por debajo de 3. (*fail*) fracasar; (*be defeated*) ser derrotado

◆**go up** *vi* 1. (*move higher*) subir 2. (*increase*) aumentar; FIN, ECON ascender 3. (*approach*) **to ~ to sb/sth** acercarse a alguien/algo 4. (*travel*) subir, viajar hacia el norte; **to ~ to Baltimore** subir a Baltimore 5. (*be built*) ser construido 6. (*burn up*) arder; **to ~ in flames** ser presa de las llamas

◆**go with** *vt insep* 1. (*accompany*) ir con 2. (*match: clothing, food and drink*) pegar con 3. (*agree with*) estar de acuerdo con 4. (*date*) salir con

◆**go without** *vt insep* pasar sin, prescindir de

**go-ahead** ['goʊ·ə·hed] *n* (*permission*) luz *f* verde

**goal** [goʊl] *n* 1. (*aim*) objetivo *m*, meta *f*; **to achieve/set a ~** conseguir/fijar un objetivo 2. SPORTS (*scoring area*) portería *f*; **to play in ~** ser portero 3. SPORTS (*point*) gol *m*; **to score a ~** marcar un gol; **a penalty ~** un gol de penalty

**goalie** ['goʊ·li] *n inf*, **goalkeeper** ['goʊl·,ki·pər] *n* SPORTS portero, -a *m, f*

**goal line** *n* SPORTS línea *f* de gol

**goalpost** *n* SPORTS poste *m* de la portería

**goat** [goʊt] *n* 1. ZOOL cabra *f*; **~'s milk/cheese** leche *f* /queso *m* de cabra 2. (*scapegoat*) chivo *m* expiatorio

**goatee** [goʊ·'ti] *n* perilla *f*

**gobble** ['gab·əl] I. *vi* 1. (*devour*) jalar 2. (*turkey*) gluglutear II. *vt inf* (*devour*) jalar III. *n* (*of turkey*) gluglú *m*

**go-between** ['goʊ·bə·,twin] *n* mediador(a) *m(f)*; **to act as a ~** hacer de intermediario

**goblin** ['gab·lɪn] *n* duende *m*

**go-cart** ['goʊ·kart] *n* AUTO, SPORTS kart *m*

**god** [gad] *n* 1. REL Dios; **God bless** que Dios te/le... bendiga; **God bless America** Dios bendiga a los EEUU; **God forbid** no lo permita Dios; **God (only) knows** sólo Dios lo sabe; **for God's sake!** ¡por el amor de Dios! 2. REL **Greek/Roman ~s** dioses *m pl* griegos/romanos

**godchild** *n* ahijado, -a *m, f*

**goddaughter** *n* ahijada *f*

**goddess** ['gad·ɪs] <-es> *n* 1. REL diosa *f* 2. (*idolized woman*) musa *f*

**godfather** *n* padrino *m*

**godforsaken** *adj* dejado, -a de la mano de Dios

**godmother** *n* madrina *f*

**godparents** *npl* padrinos *mpl*

**godsend** *n* **to be a ~** (**to sb**) ser un regalo celestial (para alguien)

**godson** *n* ahijado *m*

**goes** [goʊz] *3rd pers sing of* **go**

**go-getter** [,goʊ·'get·ər] *n inf* persona *f* emprendedora

**goggle-eyed** ['gag·əl·aɪd] *adj* con ojos desorbitados; (*person*) con [*or* de] ojos saltones

**goggles** ['gag·əlz] *n* (*glasses*) gafas *fpl*; **safety ~** gafas de protección; **ski/swim ~** gafas de esquí/natación

**going** ['goʊ·ɪŋ] I. *n* 1. (*act of leaving*) ida *f*; (*departure*) salida *f* 2. (*conditions*) **easy/rough ~** condiciones *f pl* favorables/adversas; **while the ~ is good** mientras las condiciones lo permitan 3. (*progress*) progreso *m* ▶ **when the**

G

~ gets <u>tough</u> (the tough get ~) cuando las cosas se ponen feas (los fuertes entran en acción) **II.** *adj* **1.** (*available*) disponible **2.** (*in action*) en funcionamiento; **to get sth** ~ poner algo en funcionamiento **3.** (*current*) actual; ~ **price** precio *m* actual, precio *m* de mercado **III.** *vi aux* **to be** ~ **to do sth** ir a hacer algo

**goings-on** [ˌgoʊ·ɪŋz·ˈɒn] *npl* **1.** (*events*) sucesos *mpl* **2.** (*activities*) tejemanejes *mpl*

**go-kart** [ˈgoʊ·kɑrt] *n see* **go-cart**

**gold** [goʊld] **I.** *n* **1.** (*metal*) oro *m;* **to pan for** ~ lavar oro **2.** SPORTS (*medalla f de*) oro; **to win the** ~ llevarse el oro ▶ **to be good as** ~ portarse como un ángel; **all that glitters is not** ~ *prov* no es oro todo lo que reluce *prov* **II.** *adj* de oro; **a** ~ **ring** un anillo de oro

**golden** [ˈgoʊl·dən] *adj* **1.** (*metal*) de oro **2.** (*color*) dorado, -a **3.** (*very good*) excelente; ~ **anniversary** bodas *f pl* de oro; ~ **oldies** MUS melodías *f pl* de ayer

**goldfish** *n inv* pez *m* de colores

**gold medal** *n* SPORTS medalla *f* de oro

**goldmine** *n* **1.** (*mine*) mina *f* de oro **2.** FIN filón *m*

**golf** [gɑlf] **I.** *n* golf *m;* **to play** ~ jugar al golf; **miniature** ~ minigolf *m* **II.** *vi* jugar al golf

**golf ball** *n* pelota *f* de golf

**golf club** *n* **1.** (*stick*) palo *m* de golf **2.** (*sports association*) club *m* de golf

**golf course** *n* campo *m* de golf

**golfer** [ˈgɑl·fər] *n* golfista *mf*

**gone** [gɒn] **I.** *pp of* **go II.** *adj* **1.** (*absent*) ausente **2.** (*used up*) acabado, -a **3.** *inf* (*dead*) muerto, -a **4.** (*lost: hope*) perdido, -a

**goner** [ˈgɒ·nər] *n sl* **to be a** ~ (*bound to die*) ser hombre muerto; (*broken*) estar para tirar

**goo** [gu] *n inf* (*substance*) sustancia *f* viscosa

**good** [gʊd] **I.** <better, best> *adj* **1.** (*of high quality*) bueno, -a; ~ **ears** buen oído; ~ **eyes** buena vista; ~ **thinking!** ¡buena idea!; **to do a** ~ **job** hacer un buen trabajo; **to be in** ~ **shape** estar en buena forma; **to be/to be not** ~ **enough** ser/no ser lo suficientemente

bueno **2.** (*skilled*) capacitado, -a; **to be** ~ **at** [*or* **in**] sth/doing sth estar capacitado para algo/hacer algo; **to be** ~ **at sth** dár? bien algo; **to be** ~ **with one's hands** ser bueno con las manos **3.** (*pleasant*) placentero, -a; **to have a** ~ **day/evening** tener un buen día/pasar una velada placentera; **to have a** ~ **time** pasarlo/pasárselo bien **4.** (*appealing to senses*) **to feel** ~ sentirse bien; **to have** ~ **looks** ser guapo; **to look** ~ tener buen aspecto; **to smell** ~ oler bien **5.** (*favorable*) **the** ~ **life** la buena vida; ~ **luck** (**in sth**) buena suerte (en algo); ~ **times** buenos tiempos; **to be a** ~ **thing that...** ser bueno que... +*subj* **6.** (*beneficial*) beneficioso, -a; **a** ~ **habit** una buena costumbre; **to be** ~ **for sb/sth** ser bueno para alguien/algo **7.** (*useful*) útil **8.** (*appropriate*) adecuado, -a; (*choice, decision*) correcto, -a; **a** ~ **time to do sth** un buen momento para hacer algo **9.** (*kind*) amable; ~ **deeds/work** buenas obras/buen trabajo **10.** (*moral*) **the Good Book** la Biblia; **a** ~ **name/reputation** un buen nombre/una buena reputación **11.** (*well-behaved*) de buenos modales; **a** ~ **loser** un buen perdedor; **to be on** ~ **behavior** comportarse bien **12.** (*thorough*) completo, -a; **a** ~ **beating** una buena paliza **13.** (*valid*) válido, -a; (*not forged*) auténtico, -a; (*useable*) útil, provechoso, -a; **to be** ~ **for nothing** ser completamente inútil **14.** (*substantial*) sustancial; **a** ~ **many/few** muchos/unos pocos **15.** CULIN en su punto **16.** (*almost, virtually*) **it's as** ~ **as done** está prácticamente terminado; **to be as** ~ **as new** estar como nuevo **17.** (*said to emphasize*) **to be** ~ **and ready** estar listo **18.** (*said to express affection*) **the** ~ **old days** los buenos tiempos **II.** *n* **1.** (*moral force, not evil*) bien *m;* **to be no** ~ ser inútil; **to be up to no** ~ estar tramando algo **2.** (*profit, benefit*) beneficio *m;* **this soup will do you** ~ esta sopa te sentará bien; **for one's own** ~ en beneficio propio; **to do** ~ hacer bien; **to be not much** ~ valer mucho ▶ **for** ~ definitivamente **III.** *adv inf* (*well*) bien **IV.** *interj* **1.** (*to* express *approval*) bien **2.** (*to express surprise, shock*) ~ **God!** ¡Dios mío!; ~ **grief!** ¡madre mía! **3.** (*said as greeting*) ~ **afternoon/evening** buenas tardes; ~ **morning** buenos días; ~ **night** buenas noches

**goodbye I.** *interj* adiós **II.** *n* (*departing word*) adiós *m*; **to say** ~ (**to sb**) decir adiós (a alguien); **to say** ~ despedirse

**good-for-nothing** [ˌgʊd·fər·ˈnʌθ·ɪŋ] **I.** *n* inútil *mf* **II.** *adj* inútil

**Good Friday** *n* Viernes *m* Santo

**good-humored** [ˌgʊd·ˈhju·mərd] *adj* afable

**good-looking** [ˌgʊd·ˈlʊk·ɪŋ] <better-looking, best-looking> *adj* guapo, -a

**good looks** *n* atractivo *m*

**goodly** [ˈgʊd·li] <-ier, -iest> *adj* agradable

**good-natured** <better-natured, best-natured> *adj* **1.** (*pleasant*) afable **2.** (*inherently good*) bonachón, -ona

**goodness** [ˈgʊd·nɪs] **I.** *n* **1.** (*moral virtue*) bondad *f* **2.** (*kindness*) amabilidad *f* **3.** (*quality*) buena calidad *f* **4.** (*said for emphasis*) **my** ~! ¡madre mía!; **for** ~' **sake** ¡por Dios!; **thank** ~! ¡gracias a Dios! **II.** *interj* ~ **gracious!** (*surprise*) ¡Dios mío!; (*annoyance*) ¡vaya por Dios!

**goods** [gʊdz] *npl* (*wares*) productos *mpl*; **to deliver the** ~ entregar la mercancía; *fig* dar la talla

**good-sized** [ˌgʊd·ˈsaɪzd] <better-sized, best-sized> *adj* bastante grande

**good-tempered** [ˌgʊd·ˈtem·pərd] <better-tempered, best-tempered> *adj* irr afable

**goodwill** [ˌgʊd·ˈwɪl] *n* buena voluntad *f*

**goody** [ˈgʊd·i] **I.** <-ies> *n* CULIN golosina *f* **II.** *interj childspeak* qué bien

**gooey** [ˈgu·i] <gooier, gooiest> *adj* (*sticky*) pegajoso, -a; CULIN (*dessert*) empalagoso, -a

**goof** [guf] **I.** *vi sl* pifiarla **II.** *n sl* **1.** (*mistake*) pifia *f* **2.** (*silly person*) bobo, -a *m, f*

**goofy** [ˈgu·fi] <-ier, -iest> *adj sl* bobo, -a

**goose** [gus] <geese> *n* ganso, -a *m, f*

**gooseberry** [ˈgus·ber·i] <-ies> *n* grosella *f* espinosa

**goose bumps** *npl* carne *f* de gallina

**gorge** [gɔrdʒ] **I.** *n* **1.** GEO cañón *m* **2.** ANAT garganta *f* **II.** *vt* **to** ~ **oneself on sth** atiborrarse de algo

**gorgeous** [ˈgɔr·dʒəs] **I.** *adj* **1.** (*attractive: woman, man*) atractivo, -a; (*dress*) precioso, -a **2.** *inf* (*pleasant: weather*) formidable **II.** *n* **hello**, ~! ¡hola, ricura!

**gorilla** [gəˈrɪl·ə] *n* gorila *m*

**gory** [ˈgɔr·i] <-ier, -iest> *adj* **1.** (*bloody*) sangriento, -a **2.** *fig* **the** ~ **details about sth** los detalles morbosos de algo

**gospel** [ˈgas·pəl] *n* REL evangelio *m*; **to spread/preach the** ~ extender/predicar el evangelio; ~ **singer** cantante *mf* de gospel

**gossip** [ˈgas·əp] **I.** *n* **1.** (*rumor*) chismorreo *m*; **the latest** ~ los últimos chismes; ~ **columnist** periodista *mf* de prensa rosa **2.** (*person*) chismoso, -a *m, f* **II.** *vi* (*spread rumors*) chismorrear; **to** ~ **about sb** cotillear acerca de alguien

**gossip column** *n* columna *f* de cotilleo

**got** [gat] *pt of* **get**

**Gothic** [ˈgaθ·ɪk] **I.** *adj* **1.** ARCHIT, LIT gótico, -a; ~ **architecture** arquitectura *f* gótica **2.** (*of Goths*) godo, -a **3.** TYPO ~ **script** escritura *f* gótica **II.** *n* **1.** LING gótico *m* **2.** TYPO letra *f* gótica

**gotten** [ˈgat·ən] *pp of* **get**

**gourmet** [ˈgʊr·meɪ] CULIN **I.** *n* gastrónomo, -a *m, f* **II.** *adj* gastronómico, -a

**govern** [ˈgʌv·ərn] **I.** *vt* **1.** POL, ADMIN (*country*) gobernar; (*organization*) dirigir **2.** (*regulate*) regular; **to** ~ **how/when/what...** regular cómo/cuándo/qué... **3.** LAW (*contract*) regir **4.** (*control*) controlar **5.** LING regir **II.** *vi* POL, ADMIN gobernar

**governing** *adj* directivo, -a

**government** [ˈgʌv·ərn·mənt] *n* (*ruling body*) gobierno *m*, administración *f* Arg; ~ **organization** organización *f* gubernamental; ~ **policy** política *f* estatal

**governor** [ˈgʌv·ər·nər] *n* **1.** POL gobernador(a) *m(f)* **2.** (*of organization*) director(a) *m(f)*; **the board of** ~**s** el consejo de dirección **3.** TECH regulador *m*

**grab** [græb] **I.** <-bb-> *vt* **1.** (*snatch*) quitar; **to** ~ **sth out of sb's hands** quitar algo a alguien de las manos **2.** (*take hold of*) agarrar, hacerse con; **to ~ hold of sth** hacerse con algo **3.** (*arrest*) detener **4.** *inf* (*get, acquire*) conseguir; **to ~ some sleep** dormir un rato; **to ~ sb's attention** captar la atención de alguien; **how does this ~ you?** *inf* ¿qué te parece esto? II.<-bb-> *vi* **1.** (*snatch*) arrebatar **2.** (*hold on*) asir III. *n* **to be up for ~** *sl* estar libre

**grace** [greɪs] I. *n* **1.** (*movement*) elegancia *f*, gracia *f* **2.** (*elegant proportions*) elegancia *f* **3.** REL gracia *f* **4.** (*favor*) favor *m*; **to be in/get into sb's good ~s** congraciarse con alguien; **to fall from ~** caer en desgracia **5.** (*politeness*) cortesía *f* **6.** (*prayer*) bendición *f* (de la mesa); **to say ~** bendecir la mesa **7.** (*leeway*) demora *f* **8.** (*Highness*) **Your/His/Her Grace** su Excelencia **9.** (*sister goddesses*) **the Graces** las Gracias II. *vt* (*honor*) honrar

**grace period** *n* FIN periodo *m* [*or* período] de gracia

**gracious** ['greɪ·ʃəs] I. *adj* **1.** (*kind: host*) hospitalario, -a **2.** (*tactful: humor*) sutil **3.** (*merciful*) clemente II. *interj* **goodness ~** ¡Dios mío!

**grade** [greɪd] I. *n* **1.** SCHOOL curso *m*; **to skip a ~** perder un curso **2.** (*mark*) nota *f*; **good/bad ~s** buenas/malas notas **3.** (*level of quality*) clase *f*, calidad *f*; **high/low ~** alta/baja calidad **4.** GEO pendiente *f* **5.** (*rank*) rango *m* ▸ **make the ~** dar la talla II. *vt* **1.** SCHOOL, UNIV (*evaluate*) evaluar **2.** (*categorize*) clasificar

**grade school** *n* SCHOOL escuela *f* primaria

**grading** ['greɪ·dɪŋ] *n* **1.** (*gradation*) gradación *f* **2.** (*classification*) clasificación *f*

**gradual** ['græʤ·u·əl] *adj* **1.** (*not sudden: erosion, improvement*) gradual **2.** (*not steep: slope*) suave

**gradually** ['græʤ·u·ə·li] *adv* **1.** (*not suddenly: improve*) progresivamente, paulatinamente **2.** (*not steeply*) suavemente

**graduate**[1] ['græʤ·u·ət] *n* **1.** UNIV licenciado, -a *m, f*; **university ~** licenciado *m* universitario **2.** SCHOOL graduado,

-a *m, f* **3.** (*postgraduate*) pos(t)graduado, -a *m, f*

**graduate**[2] ['græʤ·u·eɪt] I. *vi* **1.** UNIV licenciarse; SCHOOL graduarse; **to ~ cum laude** graduarse cum laude **2.** (*move to a higher level*) subir de categoría; **to ~ to...** ascender a... II. *vt* graduar

**graduated** *adj* graduado, -a

**graduate school** *n* escuela *f* de pos(t) grado

**graduation** [græʤ·u·ˈeɪ·ʃən] *n* **1.** SCHOOL, UNIV graduación *f*, egreso *m* *Arg, Chile* **2.** (*promotion*) ascenso *m*

**graft** [græft] I. *n* **1.** BOT, AGR, MED injerto *m*; **a skin ~** un injerto de piel **2.** POL corrupción *f* II. *vt* BOT, AGR, MED injertar III. *vi* POL sobornar

**grain** [greɪn] I. *n* **1.** (*cereal*) cereal *m* **2.** (*smallest piece*) grano *m*; **~ of sand/ salt** grano de arena/sal **3.** (*smallest quantity*) pizca *f* **4.** (*direction of fibers*) fibra *f*; **wood ~** hebra *f* de madera ▸ **to take sth with a ~ of salt** no creerse algo del todo II. *vt* (*granulate*) granular

**gram** [græm] *n* gramo *m*

**grammar** ['græm·ər] *n* gramática *f*

**grammar book** *n* libro *m* de gramática

**grammar school** *n* escuela *f* (de enseñanza) primaria

**grammatical** [grə·ˈmæt·ɪ·kəl] *adj* gramatical

**grand** [grænd] I. *adj* **1.** (*splendid*) magnífico, -a; **to make a ~ entrance** hacer una entrada triunfal; **the Grand Canyon** el Cañón del Colorado **2.** (*excellent*) sublime **3.** (*far-reaching*) importante; **~ ambitions/ideas** grandes ambiciones/ideas **4.** (*large*) grande; **on a ~ scale** a gran escala **5.** (*overall*) **the ~ total** el importe total II. *n* **1.** *inv, sl* (*money*) mil dólares *mpl* **2.** MUS piano *m* de cola; **baby ~** piano *m* de cola

**grandchild** <-children> *n* nieto, -a *m, f*

**granddad** *n inf* (*grandfather*) abuelito *m* **2.** (*old man*) abuelo *m*

**granddaughter** *n* nieta *f*

**grandfather** *n* abuelo *m*

**grand jury** <- -ies> *n* LAW gran jurado *m*

**grandma** *n inf* abuelita *f*

**grandmaster** *n* GAMES (*chess pro*) gran

maestro *m*

**grandmother** *n* abuela *f*

**grandpa** *n inf* abuelito *m*

**grandparents** *npl* abuelos *mpl*

**grand piano** *n* piano *m* de cola

**grandson** *n* nieto *m*

**grandstand** *n* tribuna *f;* ~ **ticket** entrada *f* de tribuna

**granite** ['græn·ɪt] *n* granito *m*

**grannie, granny** ['græn·i] *n* **1.** *inf* abuelita *f* **2.** *inf* (*fussy person*) cascarrabias *mf inv* **3.** *reg: esp. Southern* (*midwife*) matrona *f*

**grant** [grænt] **I.** *n* **1.** UNIV beca *f;* **research** ~ subvención *f* a una investigación; **to give sb a** ~ conceder una beca a alguien **2.** (*a government grant*) subvención *f* **3.** (*from authority*) concesión *f;* **federal** ~ ayuda *f* estatal; **to apply for a** ~ solicitar una subvención **4.** LAW cesión *f* **II.** *vt* **1.** (*allow*) otorgar **2.** (*transfer legally*) ceder; (*asylum*) dar; **to** ~ **sb a pardon** conceder un indulto a alguien **3.** *form* (*consent to fulfill*) **to** ~ **sb a favor** hacer un favor a alguien; **to** ~ **sb a request** acceder a la petición de alguien; **to** ~ **sb a wish** conceder un deseo a alguien **4.** (*admit to*) reconocer, admitir; ~**ed** de acuerdo; **to** ~ **that...** estar de acuerdo en que... +*subj* ▸ **to** <u>take</u> **sth for** ~**ed** dar algo por sentado; **to** <u>take</u> **sb for** ~**ed** no valorar a alguien como se merece

**granulated** ['græn·jə·leɪ·ṭɪd] *adj* (*in grains*) granulado, -a; ~ **sugar** azúcar *m* cristalizado

**grape** [greɪp] *n* (*fruit*) uva *f;* **a bunch of** ~**s** un racimo de uvas

**grapefruit** ['greɪp·fruːt] *n inv* pomelo *m*

**grapevine** *n* vid *f;* (*climbing plant*) parra *f* ▸ **to** <u>hear</u> **sth on the** ~ saber algo por los rumores que corren

**graph**[1] [græf] *n* gráfica *f;* (*diagram*) gráfico *m;* **temperature** ~ gráfico de temperaturas

**graph**[2] [græf] *n* LING grafía *f*

**graphic** ['græf·ɪk] *adj* gráfico, -a; **to describe sth in** ~ **detail** describir algo de forma gráfica

**graphics** *n* + *sing vb* **1.** (*drawings*) artes *f pl* gráficas **2.** COMPUT gráficos *mpl*

**graphics card** *n* tarjeta *f* gráfica

**grapple** ['græp·əl] *vi* **to** ~ **for/with sth** luchar a brazo partido por/con algo

**grasp** [græsp] **I.** *n* **1.** (*grip*) agarre *m* **2.** (*attainability*) alcance *m;* **to be beyond sb's** ~ estar fuera del alcance de alguien **3.** (*understanding*) comprensión *f* **II.** *vt* **1.** (*take firm hold*) agarrar; **to** ~ **sb by the arm/hand** agarrar a alguien del brazo/de la mano **2.** (*understand*) entender **III.** *vi* (*try to hold*) intentar coger

**grasping** *adj* avaro, -a

**grass** [græs] *n* **1.** hierba *f* **2.** (*area of grass*) prado *m;* (*lawn*) césped *m;* **to cut the** ~ cortar el césped **3.** *sl* (*marijuana*) hierba *f inf,* traba *f AmL inf* ▸ **the** ~ **is** (**always**) **greener on the other** <u>side</u> (**of the fence**) *prov* las manzanas siempre parecen mejores en el huerto del vecino *prov*

**grasshopper** ['græs·hɑp·ər] *n* saltamontes *m inv,* chapulín *m AmC, Méx,* saltagatos *m inv AmC, Méx*

**grass snake** *n* culebra *f* de collar

**grate**[1] [greɪt] *n* **1.** (*covering an opening*) rejilla *f* **2.** (*in fireplace, furnace*) hogar *m,* parrilla *f AmS*

**grate**[2] [greɪt] **I.** *vi* **1.** (*annoy: noise*) rechinar; **to** ~ **on sb** irritar a alguien **2.** (*rub together*) rozar; **to** ~ **against each other** rozar uno con otro **II.** *vt* **1.** CULIN rallar **2.** (*one's teeth*) rechinar

**grateful** ['greɪt·fəl] *adj* agradecido, -a; **to be** ~ (**to sb**) **for sth** agradecer algo (a alguien)

**grater** ['greɪ·ṭər] *n* rallador *m*

**gratifying** *adj* gratificante

**grating** ['greɪ·ṭɪŋ] **I.** *n* rejilla *f* **II.** *adj* **1.** (*scraping*) que rasca; (*squeaking*) chirriante **2.** (*annoyingly harsh*) áspero, -a; ~ **voice** voz *f* rasgada

**gratitude** ['græt·ə·tud] *n form* gratitud *f,* reconocimiento *m;* **as a token of my** ~ como muestra de mi gratitud

**gratuitous** [grə·'tu·ə·ṭəs] *adj* **1.** (*unnecessary: criticism, violence*) innecesario, -a, gratuito, -a **2.** (*free*) gratuito, -a

**gratuity** [grə·'tu·ə·ṭi] <-ies> *n form* propina *f*

**grave**[1] [greɪv] *n* tumba *f,* sepultura *f;*

G

**mass** ~ fosa *f* común; **to go to one's ~** irse a la tumba

**grave²** [greɪv] *adj* 1. (*serious: crisis, wound*) grave 2. (*quite important: decision*) importante

**gravel** ['grævəl] *n* 1. (*small stones*) gravilla *f*; GEO grava *f*; **a ~ path** un camino de grava 2. MED arenilla *f*

**gravel pit** *n* gravera *f*

**gravestone** *n* lápida *f*

**graveyard** *n* cementerio *m*

**graving dock** ['greɪvɪŋˌdɑk] *n* dique *m* seco [*or* de carena]

**gravitational** [ˌgrævɪˈteɪʃənəl] *adj* gravitacional; ~ **force** fuerza *f* gravitatoria

**gravity** ['grævəˌti] *n* gravedad *f*; **the law of** ~ la ley de la gravedad

**gravy** ['greɪvi] *n* 1. CULIN salsa hecha con el jugo de la carne 2. *sl* (*easy money*) ganga *f*; **to make some** ~ conseguir un chollo

**gravy boat** *n* salsera *f*

**gray** [greɪ] I. *adj* 1. (*colored gray*) gris; **to be dressed in** ~ ir de gris 2. ~ **weather** tiempo *m* gris 3. *fig* (*gloomy: mood*) triste 4. (*grey-haired*) canoso, -a; **he has started to go** ~ empieza a tener canas 5. (*color of horse*) rucio, -a II. *n* 1. (*color*) gris *m* 2. (*horse*) rucio *m* III. *vi* (*become old*) envejecer

**graying** *adj* con canas

**graze¹** [greɪz] I. *n* roce *m* II. *vt* rozar

**graze²** [greɪz] AGR I. *vi* pastar II. *vt* apacentar

**grease** [gris] I. *n* 1. (*fat*) grasa *f* 2. (*lubricant*) lubricante *m* II. *vt* engrasar; (*in mechanics*) lubricar

**greasepaint** *n* maquillaje *m* teatral

**greasy** ['grisi] <-ier, -iest> *adj* (*food*) grasiento, -a; (*hair, skin*) graso, -a

**great** [greɪt] I. *n* grande *mf*; **Alexander the** ~ Alejandro *m* Magno II. *adj* 1. (*very big*) enorme; **a ~ amount** una gran cantidad; **a ~ deal of time/money** muchísimo tiempo/dinero; **a ~ many people** muchísima gente; **the ~ majority of people** la gran mayoría (de la gente) 2. (*famous and important*) famoso, -a; ~ **minds think alike** las mentes más prestigiosas piensan parecido 3. (*wonderful*) magnífico, -a; **she's ~ at playing**

**tennis** *inf* se le da muy bien el tenis; **to be a ~ one for doing sth** encantar a uno hacer algo; **the ~ thing about sth/ sb is** (**that**) lo mejor de algo/alguien es (que); **I had a ~ time with you** lo he pasado fenomenal contigo; ~**!** ¡estupendo! 4. (*very healthy*) sano, -a; **to feel ~** estar estupendamente 5. (*for emphasis*) **they're ~ friends** son muy amigos; **he's a ~ big...** es un gran(dísimo)... 6. (*good*) excelente

**great-aunt** *n* tía *f* abuela

**greatcoat** *n* sobretodo *m*

**great-grandchild** *n* bisnieto, -a *m, f*

**great-grandparents** *npl* bisabuelos *mpl*

**greatly** ['greɪtli] *adv form* sumamente; **to be ~ impressed** estar muy impresionado

**greatness** ['greɪtnɪs] *n* grandeza *f*

**great-uncle** *n* tío *m* abuelo

**Greece** [gris] *n* Grecia *f*

**greed** [grid] *n* codicia *f*; (*for food*) gula *f*; (*for money*) avaricia *f*; (*for power*) ambición *f*

**greedy** ['gridi] *adj* (*wanting too much*) codicioso, -a; (*wanting food*) glotón, -ona; (*wanting money, things*) avaricioso, -a

**Greek** [grik] I. *n* 1. (*person*) griego, -a *m, f* 2. (*language*) griego *m* II. *adj* griego, -a ▶ **it's all ~ to me** eso me suena a chino

**green** [grin] I. *n* 1. (*color*) verde *m* 2. ~**s** (*green vegetables*) verduras *fpl* 3. (*lawn*) césped *m* 4. SPORTS pista *f* II. *adj* 1. (*green-colored*) verde; **to turn ~** (*traffic lights*) ponerse en verde 2. (*not ripe*) verde, tierno, -a *Chile, Ecua, Guat* 3. (*inexperienced*) novato, -a, verde 4. (*covered with plants*) cubierto, -a de vegetación 5. *fig* (*jealous*) ~ **with envy** verde de envidia 6. ECOL, POL verde

**greenback** *n inf* billete *m* de un dólar

**green belt** *n* cinturón *m* verde

**green card** *n* permiso *m* de residencia y de trabajo

**greenery** ['grinəri] *n* vegetación *f*

**greenhouse** *n* invernadero *m*

**greenhouse effect** *n* **the** ~ el efecto invernadero

**greenish** ['grinɪʃ] *adj* verdoso, -a

**greenness** ['grin·nɪs] n verdor m

**green pepper** [ˌgrin·'pep·ər] n pimiento m verde

**green thumb** n **to have a ~** tener habilidad para la jardinería

**greet** [grit] vt **1.** (welcome) saludar; (receive) recibir; **to ~ each other** saludarse **2.** (react) **to ~ sth** acoger algo **3.** fig (make itself noticeable) presentarse

**greeting** n saludo m; (receiving) recibimiento m

**grenade** [grɪ·'neɪd] n granada f; **hand ~** granada de mano

**grew** [gru] pt of **grow**

**grey** [greɪ] adj, n vi, vt see **gray**

**greyhound** n galgo m

**grid** [grɪd] n parrilla f; SPORTS parrilla de salida

**gridlock** n paralización f del tráfico; fig inactividad f

**grid square** n cuadrícula f

**grief** [grif] n (extreme sadness) aflicción f; (individual mournful feelings) pesar m; (pain) dolor m; **to cause sb ~** causar aflicción a alguien; **to give sb (a lot of) ~** hacer sentir (muy) mal a alguien ▶ **good ~!** inf ¡caramba!

**grievance** ['gri·vəns] n **1.** (complaint) queja f, reivindicación f; **to harbor a ~ against sb** presentar una queja contra alguien **2.** (sense of injustice) injusticia f

**grieve** [griv] I. vi sufrir; **to ~ for sth/sb** llorar por algo/alguien II. vt **1.** (distress) causar dolor; (make sad) afligir; **it ~s me to see your situation** me apena ver tu situación **2.** (mourn) llorar; **to ~ the death of...** llorar la pérdida de...

**grill** [grɪl] I. n **1.** (part of oven) parrilla f; (for barbecue) parrilla f, grill m **2.** (informal restaurant) asador m II. vt (cook) asar a la parrilla

**grille** [grɪl] n rejilla f; (of windows) reja f; (of doors) verja f; (of car) calandra f, parrilla f AmS (rejilla del radiador)

**grilling** ['grɪl·ɪŋ] n inf interrogatorio m

**grim** [grɪm] adj **1.** (very serious: expression) severo, -a **2.** (unpleasant) desagradable; (horrible) horrible; **to feel ~** sentirse muy mal **3.** (without hope) ~ **outlook** mirada f inexorable; **the**

**future looks ~** el futuro parece muy desalentador

**grimy** ['graɪ·mi] <-ier, -iest> adj (face, hands) mugriento, -a; (sooty) sucio, -a

**grin** [grɪn] I. n amplia sonrisa f II. vi (with amusement) sonreír de oreja a oreja; (with glee) sonreír alegremente; (with embarrassment) sonreír nerviosamente; **to ~ impishly at sb** dirigir una sonrisa traviesa a alguien ▶ **to ~ and bear it** poner al mal tiempo buena cara

**grind** [graɪnd] I. n inf **1.** (tiring work) trabajo m pesado **2.** (boring work) rutina f; **the daily ~** la rutina diaria II. <ground, ground> vt **1.** (crush) aplastar; (mill) moler; **to ~ sth (in)to flour/a powder** reducir algo a harina/polvo **2.** (sharpen) afilar III. vi **1.** (pulverize) pulverizar **2.** inf (dance seductively) bailar meneando la cadera **3.** (in skateboarding) girar

**grindstone** ['graɪnd·stoʊn] n muela f, afiladora f ▶ **to keep one's nose to the ~** inf trabajar como un enano

**grip** [grɪp] I. n **1.** (hold) agarre m; fig control m; **to keep a firm ~ on sth** agarrar algo fuertemente; **to be in the ~(s) of sth** estar en poder de algo **2.** (way of holding) asidero m **3.** (bag) maletín m ▶ **to get to ~s with sth** enfrentarse a algo; **to get a ~ on oneself** controlarse II. <-pp-> vt **1.** (hold firmly) agarrar **2.** (overwhelm) **to be ~ped by emotion** estar embargado por la emoción **3.** (interest deeply) absorber la atención de III. vi agarrarse

**gripping** ['grɪp·ɪŋ] adj (exciting: story) apasionante

**gristle** ['grɪs·əl] n cartílago m

**grit** [grɪt] I. n (small stones) arenilla f II. <-tt-> vt (press together) **to ~ one's teeth** a. fig apretar los dientes

**gritty** ['grɪt·i] <-ier, -iest> adj (sandy) con arenilla; (brave: decision) valiente

**grizzly** ['grɪz·li] I. n <-ier, iest> adj gris II. <-ies> n oso m pardo americano

**groan** [groʊn] I. n gemido m II. vi **1.** (make a noise) gemir; **to ~ in pain** gemir de dolor **2.** (express dissatisfaction) gruñir **3.** (complain) quejarse (about de)

**grocer** ['grou·sər] *n* **1.** (*store owner*) tendero, -a *m, f* **2.** (*food store*) tienda *f* de comestibles

**groceries** ['grou·sə·riz] *n pl* provisiones *fpl*, víveres *mpl*

**groggy** ['grag·i] <-ier -iest> *adj* grogui

**groin** [grɔɪn] *n* ingle *f*; (*male sex organs*) entrepierna *f* (del hombre)

**groom** [grum] **I.** *n* **1.** (*for horses*) mozo *m* de cuadra **2.** (*bridegroom*) novio *m* **II.** *vt* **1.** (*clean: an animal*) cepillar; (*a horse*) almohazar **2.** (*prepare: a person*) acicalar

**groove** [gruv] *n* ranura *f*; MUS surco *m*; *fig* onda *f*

**groovy** ['gru·vi] <-ier, -iest> *adj sl* guay

**grope** [group] **I.** *vi* ir a tientas; **to ~ for sth** buscar algo a tientas **II.** *vt* **1.** *sl* (*touch sexually*) sobar **2. to ~ one's way** ir a tientas

**gross** [grous] **I.** *adj* **1.** (*vulgar*) grosero, -a **2.** LAW grave **3.** (*revolting*) asqueroso, -a **4.** (*total*) total; (*without deductions*) bruto, -a **II.** *vt* FIN (*earn before taxes*) ganar en bruto

**gross income** *n* ingreso *m* bruto

**grossly** *adv* (*in a gross manner*) groseramente; (*extremely*) enormemente; **to be ~ unfair** ser completamente injusto

**gross profit** *n* ganancia *f* bruta

**grotto** ['grat·ou] <-oes *or* -os> *n* gruta *f*

**grouch** [grautʃ] **I.** *n* (*grumpy person*) refunfuñón, -ona *m, f* **II.** *vi* refunfuñar; **to ~ about sth/sb** quejarse de algo/alguien

**grouchy** ['grau·tʃi] <-ier, -iest> *adj* malhumorado, -a

**ground**[1] [graund] **I.** *n* **1.** (*the Earth's surface*) tierra *f*; **above/below ~** sobre el nivel del suelo/bajo tierra **2.** (*soil*) suelo *m* **3.** (*area of land*) terreno *m*; **breeding ~** zona *f* de cría **4.** (*reason*) motivo *m*; **to have ~s to do sth** tener motivos para hacer algo; **on the ~s that...** porque... **5.** (*area of knowledge*) tema *m*; **to be on one's own ~** estar en su propio terreno; **to give ~** ceder terreno; **to stand one's ~** mantenerse firme **II.** *vt* **1.** AVIAT no dejar despegar **2.** (*unable to move*) **to be ~ed** estar encallado, -a **3.** *fig inf* no dejar salir

**ground**[2] [graund] **I.** *vt pt of* **grind** **II.** *adj* (*coffee*) molido, -a; (*meat*) picado, -a **III.** *n* ~**s** sedimentos *mpl*; **coffee ~s** poso *m* de café

**ground crew** *n* personal *m* de tierra

**ground floor** *n* planta *f* baja, primer piso *AmS*; **on the ~** en la planta baja, en el primer piso *AmS*; ~ **apartment** entresuelo *m*

**groundless** ['graund·lɪs] *adj* infundado, -a

**groundskeeper** *n* cuidador(a) *m(f)* del terreno de juego

**groundwork** ['graund·wɜrk] *n* trabajo *m* preliminar; (*for further study*) trabajo *m* preparatorio; **to lay the ~ for sth** *fig* establecer las bases de algo

**group** [grup] **I.** *n* **1. a.** CHEM grupo *m*; ~ **photo** foto *f* de grupo; ~ **of trees** arboleda *f*; **to get into ~s** formar grupos **2.** (*specially assembled*) colectivo *m* **3.** (*musicians*) conjunto *m* musical **II.** *vt* agrupar **III.** *vi* agruparse; **to ~ together around sb** agruparse en torno a alguien

**group therapy** <-ies> *n* terapia *f* de grupo

**grow** [grou] <grew, grown> **I.** *vi* **1.** (*increase in size*) crecer; (*flourish*) florecer; **to ~ taller** crecer en estatura **2.** (*increase*) aumentar; **to ~ by 2%** aumentar un 2% **3.** (*develop*) desarrollarse **4.** (*become*) volverse; **to ~ old** hacerse viejo; **to ~ to like sth** llegar a gustarle algo **II.** *vt* **1.** (*cultivate*) cultivar **2.** (*let grow*) dejar crecer; **to ~ a beard** dejarse (crecer la) barba

♦ **grow into** *vt insep* llegar a ser; *fig* acostumbrarse a

♦ **grow up** *vi* (*become adult*) crecer; (*behave like an adult*) madurar; **oh, ~! stop your whining!** ¡a ver si creces de una vez! ¡deja de lloriquear!; **when I grow up I'd like to...** cuando sea mayor me gustaría...

**growing** ['grou·ɪŋ] **I.** *n* crecimiento *m* **II.** *adj* **1.** (*developing*) **a ~ boy/girl** un chico/una chica en edad de crecimiento **2.** ECON que se expande **3.** (*increasing*) que aumenta

**growing pains** *npl* **1.** (*pains in the*

*joints*) dolores *m pl* del crecimiento **2.** (*adolescent emotional problems*) problemas *m pl* de la adolescencia

**growl** [graʊl] **I.** *n* **1.** (*low throaty sound: of a dog*) gruñido *m*; (*of a person*) refunfuño *m* **2.** (*rumble*) ruido *m* sordo **II.** *vi* (*dog*) gruñir; (*person*) refunfuñar

**grown** [groʊn] **I.** *adj* adulto, -a **II.** *pp* of **grow**

**grown-up** ['groʊn.ʌp] *n* adulto, -a *m, f*

**growth** [groʊθ] *n* **1.** (*increase in size*) crecimiento *m* **2.** (*stage of growing*) madurez *f* **3.** (*increase*) aumento *m*; **rate of ~** tasa *f* de crecimiento **4.** (*development*) desarrollo *m* **5.** MED bulto *m*

**grub** [grʌb] **I.** *n sl* (*food*) manduca *f*, mandado *m* Méx **II.** <-bb-> *vi* cavar

**grubby** ['grʌb·i] <-ier, -iest> *adj inf* roñoso, -a

**grudge** [grʌdʒ] *n* rencor *m*, roña *f* Cuba, Méx, PRico; **to have** [*or* hold] **a ~ against sb** guardar rencor a alguien

**grudgingly** ['grʌdʒ·ɪŋ·li] *adv* de mala gana

**grueling** ['gru·lɪŋ] *adj* duro, -a, penoso, -a

**gruesome** ['gru·səm] *adj* horripilante

**gruff** [grʌf] *adj* (*reply*) brusco, -a; **a ~ voice** una voz bronca

**grumble** ['grʌm·bəl] **I.** *n* (*complaint*) queja *f* **II.** *vi* (*person*) quejarse; (*stomach*) sonar; **to ~ about sth/sb** quejarse de algo/alguien

**grumpy** ['grʌm·pi] <-ier, -iest> *adj inf* (*bad tempered*) gruñón, -ona; (*annoyed*) cabreado, -a

**grunt** [grʌnt] **I.** *n* **1.** (*snort*) gruñido *m*; (*groan*) resoplido *m* **2.** *sl* (*soldier*) soldado *mf* **3.** *sl* (*laborer*) currante *mf* [*or* cargaladrillos] *mf* Col **II.** *vi* **1.** (*snort*) gruñir **2.** (*groan*) resoplar

**G-string** ['dʒi·strɪŋ] *n* tanga *m*

**guarantee** [ˌger·ən·'ti] **I.** *n* **1.** (*certainty*) garantía *f*; **there's no ~ that...** no hay ninguna garantía de que... +*subj* **2.** (*for repair or replacement*) garantía *f* **3.** (*a promise*) promesa *f*; **to give sb one's ~** garantizar algo a alguien **4.** (*responsibility for debt*) aval *m* **5.** (*security*) prenda *f* **II.** *vt* **1.** (*promise*) prometer **2.** (*promise to correct faults*) ofrecer

una garantía; **to be ~d for three years** tener una garantía de tres años **3.** (*make certain*) **to ~ that** asegurar que **4.** (*another's debt*) avalar

**guarantor** [ˌger·ən·'tɔr] *n* garante *mf*

**guard** [gɑrd] *n* **1.** (*person*) guardia *mf*; **prison ~** carcelero, -a *m, f*; **security ~** guardia de seguridad; **to be on one's ~** (*against sth/sb*) estar en alerta (contra algo/alguien); **to be under ~** estar bajo guardia y custodia; **to drop one's ~** bajar la guardia; **to keep ~ over sth/ sb** vigilar algo/a alguien **2.** (*in basketball*) base *mf* **3.** (*in football*) escolta *mf* **4.** (*protective device*) resguardo *m* **5.** MIL **the National Guard** la Guardia Nacional **II.** *vt* **1.** (*protect*) proteger; (*prevent from escaping*) vigilar **2.** (*keep secret*) guardar **3.** SPORTS defender

**guard dog** *n* perro *m* guardián

**guard duty** <-ies> *n* guardia *f*

**guarded** ['gɑr·dɪd] *adj* cauteloso, -a

**guardian** ['gɑr·di·ən] *n* **1.** (*responsible person*) guardián, -ana *m, f* **2.** *form* (*protector*) protector(a) *m(f)*

**guardian angel** *n a. fig* ángel *m* de la guarda

**guardianship** *n* **1.** (*being a guardian*) custodia *f* **2.** *form* (*care*) cuidado *m*; **to be in the ~ of sb** estar bajo la tutela de alguien

**Guatemala** [ˌgwa·tə·'ma·lə] *n* Guatemala *f*

**guess** [ges] **I.** *n* conjetura *f*; **a lucky ~** un acierto por casualidad; **to take a ~** adivinar; **to take a wild ~** hacer una conjetura al azar; **your ~ is as good as mine!** ¡vaya Vd. a saber! ► **it's anybody's ~** ¿quién sabe? **II.** *vi* **1.** (*conjecture*) conjeturar; **to ~ right/wrong** adivinar/equivocarse; **~ what I'm doing now?** ¿adivinas qué estoy haciendo ahora?; **to ~ that...** imaginar que...; **how did you ~?** ¿cómo lo has adivinado? **2.** (*believe, suppose*) suponer; (*suspect*) sospechar; **I ~ you're right** supongo que estás en lo cierto **III.** *vt* adivinar ► **to keep sb ~ing** tener a alguien en suspense; **~ what?** ¿sabes qué?

**guesswork** ['ges·wɜrk] *n* conjeturas *fpl*

**guest** [gest] *n* **1.** (*invited person*) invitado, -a *m, f;* **paying ~** (*person renting*) inquilino, -a *m, f;* (*lodger*) huésped *mf* **2.** (*hotel customer*) cliente *mf* ▶ **be my ~** *inf* ¡adelante!

**guesthouse** *n* casa *f* de huéspedes

**guestroom** *n* habitación *f* de invitados

**guidance** ['gaɪ·dəns] *n* (*help and advice*) consejo *m;* (*direction*) orientación *f*

**guide** [gaɪd] **I.** *n* **1.** (*person*) guía *mf;* **tour/mountain ~** guía turístico/de montaña **2.** (*book*) guía *f* **3.** (*help*) orientación *f* **II.** *vt* **1.** (*show*) guiar **2.** (*instruct*) orientar **3.** (*steer, influence*) dirigir

**guidebook** *n* guía *f*

**guided** ['gaɪ·dɪd] *adj* **1.** (*led by a guide*) dirigido, -a; **~ed tour** excursión *f* con guía **2.** (*automatically steered*) teledirigido, -a

**guide dog** *n* perro-guía *m*

**guideline** *n* directriz *f;* (*figure*) pauta *f*

**guiding hand** ['gaɪ·dɪŋ·'hænd] *n fig* mano *f* amiga

**guiding principle** *n* principio *m* rector

**guild** [gɪld] *n* (*of craftsmen*) gremio *m;* **Writers' Guild** asociación *f* de escritores

**guilder** ['gɪl·dər] *n* florín *m* holandés

**guillotine** ['gɪl·ə·tin] *n* guillotina *f*

**guilt** [gɪlt] *n* **1.** (*shame for wrongdoing*) culpabilidad *f* **2.** (*responsibility for crime*) culpa *f;* **to admit one's ~** confesarse culpable

**guiltless** ['gɪlt·lɪs] *adj* inocente

**guilty** ['gɪl·ti] <-ier, -iest> *adj* culpable; **to have a ~ conscience** tener un sentimiento de culpabilidad; **to feel ~ about sth** sentirse culpable por algo; **to plead ~ to a crime** declararse culpable de un crimen

**Guinean I.** *adj* guineano, -a **II.** *n* guineano, -a *m, f*

**guinea pig** *n* conejillo *m* de Indias, cuy *m AmS*

**guitar** [gɪ·'tar] *n* guitarra *f;* **to play the ~** tocar la guitarra

**guitarist** [gɪ·'tar·ɪst] *n* guitarrista *mf*

**gulf** [gʌlf] *n* **1.** (*area of sea*) golfo *m;* **the Gulf of Mexico** el Golfo de Méjico; **the Persian Gulf** el Golfo Pérsico **2.** (*chasm*) abismo *m* **3.** (*difference of*

*opinion*) diferencias *fpl*

**gull**[^1] [gʌl] *n* ZOOL gaviota *f*

**gull**[^2] [gʌl] *vt* **to ~ sb** estafar a alguien

**gullible** ['gʌl·ə·bəl] *adj* crédulo, -a

**gully** ['gʌl·i] <-ies> *n* (*narrow gorge*) barranco *m;* (*channel*) hondonada *f*

**gulp** [gʌlp] **I.** *n* trago *m;* **in one** ~ de un trago **II.** *vt* tragar; (*liquid*) beber **III.** *vi* (*swallow with emotion*) tragar saliva

**gum**[^1] [gʌm] **I.** *n* **1.** (*soft sticky substance*) goma *f;* BOT resina *f* **2.** **chewing ~** chicle *m* **II.** *vt* pegar

◆**gum up** *vt* estropear

**gum**[^2] [gʌm] *n* ANAT encía *f*

**gumdrop** ['gʌm·drap] *n* pastilla *f* de goma

**gun** [gʌn] **I.** *n* **1.** (*weapon*) arma *f* de fuego; (*pistol*) pistola *f;* (*revolver*) revólver *m;* (*rifle*) fusil *m;* **to carry a ~** llevar pistola **2.** SPORTS pistoletazo *m;* **to jump the ~** salir antes de tiempo **3.** (*device*) pistola *f* inyectora **4.** (*person*) pistolero, -a *m, f* ▶ **to stick to one's ~s** mantenerse en sus trece **II.** <-nn-> *vi* (*vehicle*) salir disparado

**gunfight** *n* tiroteo *m*

**gunfire** *n* **1.** (*gunfight*) tiroteo *m;* (*shots*) disparos *mpl* **2.** (*cannon fire*) cañoneo *m*

**gung-ho** ['gʊŋ·hoʊ], **gung ho** *adj sl* entusiasmado, -a

**gunk** [gʊŋk] *n inf* porquería *f*

**gunman** <-men> *n* pistolero *m*

**gunpowder** *n* pólvora *f*

**gunshot** ['gʌn·ʃat] *n* disparo *m*

**gurgle** ['gɜr·gəl] **I.** *n* (*noise of water*) borboteo *m;* (*of baby*) gorjeo *m* **II.** *vi* **1.** (*water*) borbotear **2.** (*baby*) gorjear

**gush** [gʌʃ] **I.** <-es> *n* chorro *m;* *fig* efusión *f;* **a ~ of water** un chorro de agua **II.** *vi* (*any liquid*) chorrear **III.** *vt* derramar a borbollones

**gushing** *adj* (*excesivamente*) efusivo, -a

**gust** [gʌst] *n* (*of wind*) ráfaga *f;* (*of rain*) chaparrón *m* **II.** *vi* soplar

**gusty** ['gʌs·ti] <-ier -iest> *adj* borrascoso, -a

**gut** [gʌt] **I.** *n* **1.** (*intestine*) intestino *m;* **a ~ reaction/feeling** una reacción visceral/un instinto **2.** (*string from animal intestine*) tripa *f* **3.** **~s** *sl* (*bowels*) entrañas *fpl* **4.** ~**s** (*courage*) valor *m*; (*strength of character*) determinación *f* II. <-tt-> *vt* **1.** (*remove the innards*) destripar **2.** (*emotional suffering*) destrozar

**gutless** ['gʌt·lɪs] *adj sl* (*lacking courage*) cobarde; (*lacking enthusiasm*) apático, -a

**gutsy** ['gʌt·si] <-ier, -iest> *adj* **1.** (*brave*) valiente; (*adventurous*) atrevido, -a **2.** (*powerful*) vigoroso, -a

**gutter** ['gʌt·ər] *n* (*on the roadside*) alcantarilla *f*; (*on the roof*) canalón *m*

**guy** [gaɪ] *n inf* (*man*) tío *m*; **hi ~s** ¿qué hay, colegas?

**guzzle** ['gʌz·əl] I. *vt* (*of person: alcohol*) beber como si fuera agua; (*of car: gas*) chupar II. *vi* zampar

**gym** [dʒɪm] *n* **1.** (*gymnasium*) gimnasio *m* **2.** (*school subject*) gimnasia *f*, educación *f* física

**gymnasium** [dʒɪm·'neɪ·zi·əm] *n* gimnasio *m*

**gymnast** ['dʒɪm·næst] *n* gimnasta *mf*

**gymnastic** [dʒɪm·'næs·tɪk] *adj* gimnástico, -a

**gymnastics** [dʒɪm·'næs·tɪks] *npl* gimnasia *f*

**gym shoes** *n* zapatillas *fpl* de deporte

**gynecologist** *n* ginecólogo, -a *m, f*

**gypsy** ['dʒɪp·si] <-ies> I. *n* gitano, -a *m, f* II. *adj* gitano, -a

# H

**H, h** [eɪtʃ] *n* H, h *f*; **~ as in Hotel** H de Huelva

**ha** [ha] *interj a. iron* ¡ajá!

**habit** ['hæb·ɪt] *n* **1.** (*customary practice*) hábito *m*, costumbre *f*; **to do sth out of** ~ hacer algo por costumbre; **to get into the** ~ (**of doing sth**) acostumbrarse (a hacer algo); **to get out of the** ~ **of doing sth** perder la costumbre de hacer algo; **don't make a** ~ **of it** no lo vuelvas una costumbre **2.** (*dress*) hábito *m* **3.** (*addiction*) adicción *f*; **to have a heroin** ~ ser adicto a la heroína

**habitable** ['hæb·ɪ·ṭə·bəl] *adj* habitable

**habitat** ['hæb·ɪ·tæt] *n* hábitat *m*

**habitual** [hə·'bɪtʃ·u·əl] *adj* **1.** (*usual*) habitual **2.** (*describing person*) empedernido, -a; (*liar, drug user*) empedernido, -a

**hack¹** [hæk] I. *vt* **1.** (*chop violently*) cortar a tajos **2.** *sl* (*cope with*) aguantar; **I can't ~ this job** este trabajo me la puede II. *vi* **1.** (*chop*) hacer tajos; **to ~ at sth** cortar algo a tajos **2.** (*cough*) toser (con tos seca)

**hack²** [hæk] *vt* COMPUT **to ~** (**into**) **a system** introducirse ilegalmente en un sistema

**hacker** ['hæk·ər] *n* COMPUT hacker *mf*, pirata *mf* informático, -a

**hacksaw** ['hæk·sɔ] *n* sierra *f* para metales

**had** [hæd, *unstressed:* həd] *pt, pp* of **have**

**haddock** ['hæd·ək] *n* abadejo *m*

**hadn't** ['hæd·ənt] = **had not** *see* **have**

**hag** [hæg] *n* (*woman*) bruja *f*

**haggle** ['hæg·əl] *vi* regatear; **to ~ over sth** regatear el precio de algo

**hail¹** [heɪl] I. *n* METEO granizo *m*; (*of stones, insults*) lluvia *f* II. *vi* granizar

**hail²** [heɪl] I. *vt* **1.** (*call*) llamar; **to ~ a taxi** parar un taxi **2.** (*acclaim*) aclamar **3.** (*welcome*) acoger II. *vi* **to ~ from** (*person*) ser de; (*thing*) proceder de

**hair** [her] *n* **1.** (*on head*) cabello *m*, pelo *m* Col; (*on chest, a. head*) pelo *m*; (*on armpits, legs, pubic*) vello *m*; **to do one's ~** arreglarse el pelo; **to have one's ~ cut** cortarse el pelo; **to wash one's ~** lavarse el pelo **2.** (*on animal*) pelo *m* **3.** (*on plant*) pelusa *f* ► **to make sb's curl** *inf* poner los pelos de punta a alguien; **to get in sb's ~** poner a alguien nervioso; **to split ~s** buscarle tres pies al gato

**hairbrush** <-es> *n* cepillo *m* (del pelo)

**hairclip** *n* pasador *m*, clip *m* para el pelo

**hair conditioner** *n* acondicionador *m* del cabello, bálsamo *m*

**haircut** *n* corte *m* de pelo; **to get a ~** cortarse el pelo

**hairdo** *n inf* peinado *m*

**hairdresser** *n* peluquero, -a *m, f*; **the ~'s** la peluquería

**hair dryer** *n* secador *m* (de pelo)

**hairless** ['her·lɪs] *adj* (*head*) calvo, -a, pelado, -a *AmS*

**hairline** *n* (*edge of the hair*) nacimiento *m* del pelo; **he has a receding ~** tiene entradas

**hairline crack** *n*, **hairline fracture** *n* grieta *f* fina

**hairnet** *n* redecilla *f*

**hairpiece** *n* postizo *m*

**hairpin** *n* horquilla *f*, gancho *m* *AmL*, pinza *f* *Col*

**hairpin curve** *n*, **hairpin turn** *n* curva *f* muy cerrada

**hair-raising** *adj* espeluznante

**hair remover** *n* crema *f* depilatoria

**hair restorer** *n* tónico *m* capilar

**hairstyle** *n* peinado *m*

**hairy** ['her·i] <-ier, -iest> *adj* **1.** (*having much hair*) peludo, -a **2.** *sl* (*difficult, dangerous: escape, problem*) peliagudo, -a

**half** [hæf] **I.** <halves> *n* (*equal part*) mitad *f*; **an apple** media manzana; **in ~** por la mitad; **to cut sth into halves** partir algo por la mitad; **a pound and a ~** una libra y media; **to go halves with sb** ir a medias con alguien; **my better ~** *fig* mi media naranja; **first/second ~** SPORTS primer/segundo tiempo; **the first/second ~ of a century** la primera/segunda mitad de un siglo **II.** *adj* medio, -a; **an hour** media hora; **she's the player she used to be** esta jugadora no es ni sombra de lo que era **III.** *adv* **1.** (*almost*) casi; **to be ~ sure** estar casi seguro **2.** (*partially*) a medias; **~ asleep** medio dormido; **~ cooked** medio crudo; **~ naked** medio desnudo; **~ empty/full** medio vacío/lleno **3.** (*by fifty percent*) **~ as many/much** la mitad; **~ as much again** la mitad más **4.** *inf* (*most*) la mayor parte; **~ (of) the time** la mayor parte del tiempo **5.** (*thirty minutes after*) (at) **~ past three** (a) las tres y media; **at ~ past** a y media **IV.** *pron* la mitad; **only ~ of them came** sólo vino la mitad de ellos

**half and half I.** *adj* **to split sth ~** dividir algo mitad y mitad **II.** *n* (*for coffee*) leche *f* con crema

**halfback** *n* (*in rugby*) medio *m* de melé y medio de apertura; (*in football*) corredor *m*

**half-baked** *adj* **1.** (*food*) medio cocido, -a **2.** *inf* (*plan*) sin sentido, estúpido, -a

**half-dozen** *adj* media docena *f*

**half-empty** *adj* (*glass*) medio vacío, -a

**halfhearted** *adj* poco entusiasta; **a ~ attempt** un intento desganado

**half-price** *n* **at ~** a mitad de precio

**halfway** ['hæf·wei] **I.** *adj* **1.** (*midway*) medio, -a; **~ point** punto medio; **~ stage** etapa *f* intermedia **2.** (*partial*) parcial **II.** *adv* **1.** (*half the distance*) a mitad de camino; **to be ~ through sth** ir por la mitad de algo; **~ through the year** a mediados de año; **~ up** a media cuesta; **to meet sb ~** *fig* llegar a un acuerdo con alguien **2.** (*nearly, partly*) **the proposals only went ~ toward meeting their demands** las propuestas sólo satisfacían en parte sus exigencias

**hall** [hɔl] *n* **1.** (*corridor*) pasillo *m*, corredor *m* **2.** (*entrance room*) vestíbulo *m* **3.** (*large public room*) sala *f*; **concert ~** sala *f* de conciertos; **town** [*or* **city**] **~** ayuntamiento *m* **4.** UNIV colegio *m* mayor; **residence ~** residencia *f* universitaria

**hallelujah** [ˌhæl·ɪ·'lu·jə] **I.** *interj* ¡aleluya! **II.** *n* aleluya *m*

**Halloween** [ˌhæl·ə·'win] *n* víspera *f* de Todos los Santos, Día *f* de las Brujas

**hallucinate** [hə·'lu·sɪ·neit] *vi a. fig* alucinar

**hallucination** [hə·ˌlu·sɪ·'nei·ʃən] *n* alucinación *f*

**hallucinogenic** *adj* alucinógeno, -a

**halo** ['hei·lou] <-s *or* -es> *n* **1.** *a. fig* REL aureola *f* **2.** *a. fig* ASTR halo *m*

**halogen bulb** *n* bombilla *f* halógena

**halt** [hɔlt] **I.** *n* **1.** (*standstill, stop*) parada *f*; **to bring sth/sb to a ~** detener algo/a alguien; **to come** [*or* **grind**] **to a ~** pararse **2.** (*interruption*) interrupción *f* **II.** *vt* (*stop permanently*) parar; (*stop temporarily*) interrumpir **III.** *vi* (*permanently*) parar; (*temporarily*) interrumpirse **IV.** *interj* **~!** ¡alto!

**halve** [hæv] **I.** *vt* **1.** (*lessen*) reducir a la

mitad; (*number*) dividir por dos **2.** (*cut in half*) partir por la mitad **II.** *vi* reducirse a la mitad

**ham** [hæm] *n* **1.** (*cured*) jamón *m* (serrano); (*cooked*) jamón *m* (cocido); **a slice of ~** una loncha *f* [*or Col* tajada *f*] de jamón **2.** (*actor*) histrión *m*

**hamburger** ['hæm·bɜr·gər] *n* **1.** (*patty*) hamburguesa *f* **2.** (*meat*) carne *f* picada

**hammer** ['hæm·ər] **I.** *n* **1.** (*tool*) martillo *m*; **~ blow** *a. fig* martillazo *m*; **to go under the ~** *a. fig* (*painting*) salir a subasta **2.** (*of gun*) percutor *m* **II.** *vt* **1.** (*hit with tool: metal*) martillear; (*nail*) clavar; **to ~ sth into sb** *fig* meter algo en la cabeza a alguien **2.** *inf* SPORTS (*beat easily*) dar una paliza **3.** *inf* (*become very drunk*) **to get ~ed (on sth)** emborracharse (de algo) **III.** *vi* **1.** (*use a hammer*) martillear **2.** (*beat heavily*) golpear

**hammock** ['hæm·ək] *n* hamaca *f*

**hamper¹** ['hæm·pər] *vt* (*hinder*) dificultar; **to ~ sb/sth** poner trabas a alguien/algo

**hamper²** ['hæm·pər] *n* **1.** (*picnic basket*) cesta *f* (*con tapa*) **2.** (*for dirty laundry*) cesto *m* de la ropa

**hamster** ['hæm·stər] *n* hámster *m*

**hamstring** ['hæm·strɪŋ] *n* ANAT tendón *m* de la corva; ZOOL tendón *m* del corvejón

**hand** [hænd] **I.** *n* **1.** ANAT mano *f*; **to be good with one's ~s** tener habilidad manual; **to deliver a letter by ~** entregar una carta en mano; **to do sth by ~** hacer algo a mano; **to shake ~s with sb** estrechar la mano a alguien; **to take sb by the ~** llevar a alguien de la mano; **sword in ~** espada en ristre; **~ in ~** de la mano; **get your ~s off!** ¡no toques!; **~s up!** ¡manos arriba!; **to ask for sb's ~** (**in marriage**) pedir la mano de alguien **2.** (*handy, within reach*) **at ~** muy cerca; **to keep sth close at ~** tener algo a mano; **on ~** (*available to use*) disponible; **to be on ~** (*object*) estar a mano **3.** (*what needs doing now*) **the problem at ~** el problema que nos ocupa; **in ~** (*being arranged*) entre manos;

**preparations are in ~** los preparativos están en marcha **4. ~s** (*responsibility, authority, care*) **to be in good ~s** estar en buenas manos; **to fall into the ~s of sb** caer en manos de alguien; **to put sth into sb's ~s** poner algo en manos de alguien; **at the ~s of sb** (*because of*) a manos de alguien **5.** (*assistance*) **to give (sb) a ~ (with sth)** echar (a alguien) una mano (con algo) **6.** (*control*) **to get out of ~** (*things, situation*) irse de las manos; (*person*) descontrolarse; **to have sth well in ~** tener algo bajo control; **to have a ~ in sth** intervenir en algo **7.** GAMES **to have a good/poor ~** tener una buena/mala mano; **to show one's ~** *a. fig* enseñar las cartas; **a ~ of poker** una mano de póquer **8.** (*on clock*) manecilla *f*; **the hour ~** la aguja de las horas; **the minute ~** el minutero; **the second ~** el segundero **9.** (*manual worker*) obrero, -a *m, f*; (*sailor*) marinero, -a *m, f*; **farm ~** peón, -a *m, f* **10.** (*skillful person*) **old ~** veterano, -a *m, f*; **to be an old ~ at sth** tener mucha experiencia en algo; **to try one's ~ at sth** intentar algo alguna vez **11.** (*applause*) aplauso *m*; **let's have a big ~ for ...** un gran aplauso para... **12.** (*measurement for horses*) palmo *m* de alzada **13.** (*handwriting*) letra *f*; **in his own ~** de su puño y letra ► **to make money ~ over fist** hacer dinero a espuertas [*or* a lo loco]; **to be ~ in glove with sb** ser uña y carne con alguien, meterse a mano al bolsillo; **with a firm ~** con mano dura; **at first ~** de primera mano; **to have one's ~s full** estar muy ocupado; **with a heavy** [*or* **an iron**] **~** con mano dura; **on the one ~ ... on the other (~)...** por un lado..., por otro (lado)...; **to have one's ~s tied** tener las manos atadas; **to have sb eat out of one's ~** meterse a alguien en el bolsillo, poner a alguien a comer de la mano de otro; **to force sb's ~** forzar la mano a alguien; **to get one's ~s on sb** atrapar a alguien, ponerle la mano encima a alguien; **to lay one's ~s on sth** hacerse con algo **II.** *vt* **1.** (*give*) dar; **will you ~ me my bag?** ¿puedes pasarme mi bolso? **2.** (*give credit to*) **you've got to ~ it to him** hay que reconocer que lo hace muy bien

◆**hand back** *vt* devolver

◆**hand down** *vt* **1.** (*knowledge, tradition*) transmitir; (*objects*) pasar **2.** LAW (*judgment*) pronunciar, dictar

◆**hand in** *vt* (*task, document*) entregar

◆**hand on** *vt* (*knowledge*) transmitir; (*object*) pasar

◆**hand out** *vt* **1.** (*distribute*) repartir **2.** (*give: advice*) dar; (*punishment*) aplicar

◆**hand over** *vt* **1.** (*give, submit: money, prisoner*) entregar; (*check*) extender **2.** (*pass: power, authority*) transferir; (*property*) ceder **2.** TEL pasar; **to hand sb over to sb** pasar a alguien con alguien

**handbag** *n* bolso *m*, cartera *f AmL*

**handbook** *n* manual *m*

**handcuff** *vt* esposar

**handcuffs** *npl* esposas *fpl*; **a pair of ~** unas esposas

**handful** ['hænd·fʊl] *n* **1.** *a.* *fig* (*small amount*) puñado *m*; **a ~ of people** un puñado de gente **2.** (*person*) **to be a real ~** (*child*) ser un bicho [*or* terremoto]; (*adult*) ser una buena pieza

**hand grenade** *n* granada *f* de mano

**handgun** *n* pistola *f*

**handicapped** *adj* **physically ~** minusválido, -a; **mentally ~** discapacitado psíquico **II.** *n* **the ~** los minusválidos

**handicap** ['hæn·dɪ·kæp] **I.** *n* **1.** (*disability*) discapacidad *f*; **mental ~** discapacidad *f* mental; **physical ~** invalidez *f* **2.** (*disadvantage*) desventaja *f* **3.** SPORTS hándicap *m* **II.** <-pp-> *vt* perjudicar; **to be ~ped** estar en una situación de desventaja

**handicraft** ['hæn·dɪ·kræft] *n* **1.** (*work*) trabajo *m* artesanal **2.** (*product*) artesanía *f*

**handkerchief** ['hæn·kər·tʃɪf] *n* pañuelo *m*

**handle** ['hæn·dəl] **I.** *n* **1.** (*of pot, basket, bag*) asa *f*; (*of drawer*) tirador *m*; (*of knife*) mango *m* **2.** (*knob*) pomo *m* **3.** *sl* RADIO (*name*) código *m* ▶ **to fly off the ~** *inf* perder los estribos; **to get a ~ on**

sth dar con el clavo [*or* truco] de algo **II.** *vt* **1.** (*touch*) tocar **2.** (*move, transport*) llevar; **~ with care** frágil **3.** (*machine, tool, weapon*) manejar; (*chemicals*) manipular; **I don't know how to ~ her** no sé cómo tratarla **4.** (*direct*) ocuparse de; (*case*) llevar; **I'll ~ this** yo me encargo de esto; **he doesn't know how to ~ other people** (*business*) no sabe dirigir; (*socially*) no tiene don de gentes **5.** (*control*) dominar; (*work, difficult situation*) poder con **III.** *vi* + *adv/prep* responder; **to ~ poorly** no responder bien

**handlebars** *npl* manillar *m*

**handling** *n* **1.** (*management*) manejo *m*; (*of goods*) manipulación *f*; (*of subject*) tratamiento *m* **2.** COM (*fee*) porte *m*

**hand luggage** *n* equipaje *m* de mano

**handmade** *adj* hecho, -a a mano

**hand-operated** *adj* manual

**handout** ['hænd·aʊt] *n* **1.** (*money*) limosna *f* **2.** (*leaflet*) folleto *m* **3.** (*press release*) comunicado *m* de prensa **4.** (*written information*) apuntes *mpl*, hojas *fpl*

**hand-picked** *adj* cuidadosamente seleccionado, -a

**handrail** *n* (*on stairs*) pasamanos *m inv*; (*on bridge*) barandilla *f*

**handshake** *n* apretón *m* de manos

**handsome** ['hæn·səm] *adj* **1.** (*man*) guapo; (*animal, thing*) bello, -a; **the most ~ man** el hombre más apuesto **2.** (*impressive*) magnífico, -a **3.** (*large*) considerable; (*price, salary*) elevado, -a; (*donation*) generoso, -a **4.** (*gracious: gesture*) noble

**hands-on** *adj* **1.** (*practical*) práctico, -a; **~ approach** enfoque práctico **2.** COMPUT manual

**handspring** *n* salto *m* mortal; **backward ~** salto mortal hacia atrás

**handstand** *n* pino *m*; **to do a ~** hacer el pino, pararse en las manos *Col*

**handwriting** *n* letra *f*

**handwritten** *adj* manuscrito, -a

**handy** ['hæn·di] <-ier, -iest> *adj* **1.** (*convenient, available*) a mano; (*nearby*) cercano, -a; **to keep sth ~** tener algo a mano **2.** (*user-friendly*) manejable;

(*form, guide*) sencillo, -a 3. (*skillful*) hábil; **to be ~ with sth** ser mañoso [*or* habilidoso] para algo; **to be ~ around the house** ser un manitas 4. (*convenient*) práctico, -a; (*useful*) útil, venir bien; **to come in ~ (for sb)** venir muy bien (a alguien)

**handyman** ['hæn·dɪ·mæn] <-men> *n* manitas *inv m*

**hang** [hæŋ] **I.** <hung, hung> *vi* 1. (*be suspended*) colgar; (*picture*) estar colgado; **to ~ by/on/from sth** colgar de algo 2. (*lean over or forward*) inclinarse 3. (*float: smoke, fog*) flotar; **to ~ above sb/sth** cernirse sobre alguien/algo; **to leave a question ~ing** dejar una pregunta en el aire 4. (*die*) morir en la horca 5. (*fit, drape: clothes, fabrics*) caer; **to ~ well** tener buena caída 6. *sl* (*be friendly with*) **to ~ with sb** mantenerse con alguien; (*spend time at*) pasársela con alguien ► **~ in there!** ¡aguanta! **II.** <hung, hung> *vt* 1. (*attach*) colgar; (*laundry*) tender; (*door*) colocar; **to ~ wallpaper (on a wall)** empapelar (una pared); **to ~ the curtains** colgar las cortinas 2. (*lights, ornaments, decorations*) adornar 3. (*one's head*) bajar 4. (*execute*) ahorcar ► **to ~ it up** acabar con algo **III.** *n* FASHION caída *f* ► **to get the ~ of sth** *inf* coger el truquillo a algo

◆**hang around I.** *vi* 1. *sl* (*waste time*) perder el tiempo 2. (*wait*) esperar 3. (*idle*) no hacer nada 4. (*be friendly with*) **to ~ with sb** andar por ahí con alguien **II.** *vt insep* rondar; **to ~ a place** andar rondando por un sitio

◆**hang back** *vi* 1. (*be reluctant to move forward*) quedarse atrás 2. (*hesitate*) vacilar

◆**hang behind** *vi* rezagarse

◆**hang on I.** *vi* 1. (*wait briefly*) esperar; **to keep sb hanging on** hacer esperar a alguien; **~!** *inf* ¡espera un momento!; **she's on the other phone — would you like to ~?** está hablando por la otra línea, ¿quiere esperar? 2. (*hold on to*) **to ~ to sth** agarrarse a algo; **~ tight** agárrate fuerte 3. (*persevere*) mantenerse firme; (*resist*) aguantar **II.** *vt insep*

1. (*depend upon*) depender de 2. (*give attention*) estar pendiente de; **to ~ sb's every word** estar pendiente de lo que dice alguien

◆**hang out I.** *vt* (*laundry*) tender **II.** *vi* 1. **let it all ~!** *sl* (*be relaxed*) ¡suéltate la melena! *fig* 2. *sl* (*spend time at*) andar; **where does he ~ these days?** ¿por dónde anda estos días?

◆**hang together** *vi* 1. (*make sense*) ser coherente 2. (*remain associated*) permanecer unidos

◆**hang up I.** *vi* 1. colgar; **to ~ on sb** colgar a alguien 2. *inf* **to get hung up on sth** (*have trouble with*) quedar varado *fig* **II.** *vt* 1. (*curtains, receiver*) colgar 2. (*give up*) **to ~ one's cleats/boxing gloves** *fig* colgar las botas/los guantes 3. (*delay*) causar un retraso a

**hanger** ['hæŋ·ər] *n* (*clothes*) percha *f*, gancho *m* de colgar ropa

**hang-gliding** *n* SPORTS vuelo *m* con ala delta

**hangout** *n sl* guarida *f*; **a favorite ~ of artists** un lugar frecuentado por artistas

**hangover** *n* 1. (*after drinking*) resaca *f*, goma *f AmL*, guayabo *m Col* 2. (*leftover*) vestigio *m*

**hang-up** *n inf* complejo *m*; **to have a ~ about sth** estar acomplejado por algo

**hankie** *n*, **hanky** ['hæŋ·ki] *n inf abbr of* **handkerchief** pañuelo *m*

**Hanukkah** ['ha·nə·kə] *n* Hanukah *m*

**haphazard** [hæp·'hæz·ərd] *adj* 1. (*random, arbitrary*) caprichoso, -a 2. (*badly planned*) hecho, -a de cualquier manera

**happen** ['hæp·ən] *vi* 1. (*occur*) pasar; **if anything ~s to me...** si me ocurre algo...; **these things ~** [*or sl*] **shit ~s** son cosas que pasan; **whatever ~s** pase lo que pase; **what ~ed to your hand?** ¿qué te ha pasado en la mano? 2. (*chance*) **I ~ed to be at home** dio la casualidad de que estaba en casa; **it ~ed (that)...** resultó que...; **he ~s to be my best friend** pues resulta que es mi mejor amigo

**happily** ['hæp·ɪ·li] *adv* 1. (*contentedly*) felizmente; **they lived ~ ever after** fueron felices y comieron perdices 2. (*will-*

*ingly*) con mucho gusto **3.** (*fortunately*) afortunadamente

**happiness** ['hæp·ɪ·nɪs] *n* felicidad *f*

**happy** ['hæp·i] <-ier, -iest> *adj* **1.** (*feeling very good*) feliz; **to be ~ that...** estar contento de que...; **to be ~ to know that...** alegrarse de saber que...; **I'm so ~ for you** me alegro mucho por ti; **to be ~ to do sth** estar encantado de hacer algo; **~ birthday!** ¡feliz cumpleaños!; **many ~ returns (of the day)!** ¡que cumplas muchos más! **2.** (*satisfied*) contento, -a; **to be ~ about sb/sth** estar contento con alguien/algo; **are you ~ with the idea?** ¿te parece bien la idea? **3.** (*fortunate*) afortunado, -a; **a ~ coincidence** una feliz coincidencia **4.** (*suitable: phrase, behavior*) acertado, -a

**harassment** [hə·ˈræs·mənt] *n* **1.** (*pestering*) acoso *m*; **sexual ~** acoso sexual **2.** (*attack*) hostigamiento *m*

**harbor** ['har·bər] **I.** *n* **1.** (*port*) puerto *m*; **fishing ~** puerto pesquero **2.** *fig* (*shelter*) refugio *m* **II.** *vt* **1.** (*give shelter to*) dar cobijo a **2.** (*keep: feelings*) albergar; (*hopes*) abrigar; **to ~ suspicions** tener sospechas; **to ~ a grudge (against sb)** guardar rencor (a alguien) **3.** (*keep in hiding*) esconder; (*criminal*) encubrir

**hard** [hard] **I.** *adj* **1.** (*firm, rigid*) duro, -a; (*rule*) estricto, -a; **~ times** malos tiempos; **to have a ~ time** pasarlo mal; **to give sb a ~ time** hacérselo pasar mal a alguien; **to have ~ luck** tener mala suerte **2.** (*intense, concentrated*) **to take a (good) ~ look at sth** analizar algo detenidamente; **to be a ~ worker** ser muy trabajador **3.** (*forceful*) fuerte **4.** (*difficult, complex*) difícil; **~ landing** AVIAT aterrizaje forzado, -a; **to be ~ to please** ser difícil de contentar; **to learn the ~ way** *fig* aprender a base de errores [*or* palos] **5.** (*severe*) severo, -a **6.** (*hostile, unkind*) **to be ~ on sb/sth** ser duro con alguien/algo **7.** (*extremely cold*) riguroso, -a **8.** (*solid: evidence*) concluyente; (*fact*) innegable; **~ and fast information** información veraz **9.** (*with alcohol*) **~ cider/punch** sidra/ponche fuerte [*or* cargado, -a] **10.** CHEM

(*water*) duro, -a **II.** *adv* **1.** (*forcefully*) fuerte; **to hit sb ~** pegar fuerte a alguien; **to press/pull ~** apretar/estirar con fuerza **2.** (*rigid*) **frozen ~** helado, -a **3.** (*energetically, vigorously*) mucho; **to fight ~** *fig* luchar con todas sus fuerzas; **to study/work ~** estudiar/trabajar mucho; **to try ~ to do sth** esforzarse en hacer algo; **think ~** concéntrate; **to die ~** *fig* tardar en desaparecer **4.** (*intently*) detenidamente; **to look ~ at sth** estudiar algo con detenimiento **5.** (*closely*) muy cerca; **in ~ up** no tener ni un céntimo **6.** (*heavy*) mucho; **it rained ~** llovió fuerte; **to take sth ~** tomarse algo muy mal; **I would be ~ pressed to choose one** me costaría mucho decidirme por uno

**hardback** ['hard·bæk] **I.** *n* (*book*) libro *m* de tapa dura; **in ~** con tapa dura **II.** *adj* con tapa [*or* pasta] dura

**hard-boiled** *adj* (*egg*) duro, -a; (*person*) endurecido, -a

**hard copy** <-ies> *n* COMPUT impresión *f*

**hardcover** *n* (*book*) tapa [*or* pasta] *f* dura

**hard currency** <-ies> *n* FIN moneda *f* fuerte

**hard disk** *n* COMPUT disco *m* duro

**hard drive** *n* COMPUT disco *m* duro

**hard drug** *n* droga *f* dura

**hard-earned** *adj* (*money*) ganado, -a con el sudor de la frente; (*rest, vacation*) merecido, -a

**harden** ['har·dən] **I.** *vt* **1.** (*make more solid, firmer*) endurecer; (*steel*) templar **2.** (*make tougher*) curtir; **to ~ oneself to sth** insensibilizarse a algo; **to become ~ed** curtirse **3.** (*opinions, feelings*) afianzar **II.** *vi* **1.** (*become firmer: character*) endurecerse **2.** (*attitude*) volverse inflexible **3.** (*become confirmed: idea*) confirmarse; (*feeling, intention*) afianzarse

**hard feelings** *npl* resentimiento *m*; **no ~!** ¡olvidémoslo!

**hardly** ['hard·li] *adv* **1.** (*barely*) apenas; **~ anything** casi nada; **~ ever** casi nunca; **she can ~...** apenas puede...; **she can ~ wait until tomorrow** tiene unas ganas locas de que llegue mañana **2.** (*certainly not*) **you can ~ expect him to**

**do that** no puedes esperar que haga eso; **~!** ¡qué va! *inf*

**hardship** ['hard·ʃɪp] *n* (*suffering*) penas *fpl*; (*adversity*) adversidad *f*; (*deprivation*) penuria *f*; **to suffer great ~** pasar muchos apuros

**hardware** *n* **1.** (*household articles*) ferretería *f*; **~ store** ferretero, -a *m, f*; (*home improvement center*) centro *m* de mejoramiento para el hogar **2.** (*articles of metal*) quincallería *f* **3.** COMPUT hardware *m*; **computer ~** soporte *m* físico del ordenador **4.** MIL armamento *m*

**hard-wearing** *adj* resistente

**hard-working** *adj* trabajador(a)

**hare** [her] *n* BIO liebre *f*

**harem** ['her·əm] *n* harén *m*

**harm** [harm] **I.** *n* daño *m*; **to do ~ to sb/ sth** hacer daño a alguien/algo; **to do more ~ than good** hacer más mal que bien; (**to put**) **out of ~'s way** (poner) a salvo; **to see no ~ in sth** no ver nada malo en algo; **I meant no ~** no pretendía hacer daño; **there's no ~ in trying** no se pierde nada con intentarlo **II.** *vt* **1.** (*hurt, ruin*) hacer daño; (*reputation*) perjudicar **2.** (*spoil*) estropear

**harmful** ['harm·fəl] *adj* dañino, -a; (*thing*) nocivo, -a; **to be ~ to sth** ser perjudicial para algo

**harmless** ['harm·lɪs] *adj* (*animal, person*) inofensivo, -a; (*thing*) inocuo, -a; (*fun, joke*) inocente

**harmonium** [har·'mou·ni·əm] *n* MUS armonio *m*

**harmony** ['har·mə·ni] <-ies> *n* armonía *f*; **in ~** (**with sb/sth**) en armonía (con alguien/algo)

**harsh** [harʃ] *adj* **1.** (*severe: parents*) severo, -a; (*punishment*) duro, -a **2.** (*unfair: criticism*) cruel; (*words, reality*) duro, -a **3.** (*unfriendly*) desabrido, -a **4.** (*uncomfortable: light*) fuerte; (*climate, winter*) riguroso, -a; (*terrain*) desolado, -a **5.** (*unaesthetic: color*) chillón, -ona **6.** (*unpleasant to the ear: sound*) discordante; (*voice*) estridente

**harvest** ['har·vɪst] **I.** *n* (*of crops*) cosecha *f*; (*of grapes*) vendimia *f*; (*of vegetables*) recolección *f*; **the apple ~** la cosecha de la manzana **II.** *vt a. fig* co-

sechar; (*grapes*) vendimiar; (*vegetables*) recolectar; **to ~ a field** hacer la cosecha en un campo **III.** *vi* cosechar

**has** [hæz, *unstressed:* həz] *3rd pers sing of* **have**

**has-been** *n inf* vieja gloria *f*; **to be a ~** ser alguien que ya ha pasado a la historia

**hash**[1] [hæʃ] **I.** *vt* CULIN picar **II.** *n* CULIN picadillo *m*

**hash**[2] [hæʃ] *n sl* (*hashish*) chocolate *m inf*

**hash browns** *npl* patatas hervidas y después fritas

**hasn't** ['hæz·ənt] = **has not** *see* **have**

**hassle** ['hæs·əl] **I.** *n inf* (*trouble*) lío *m*; **to give sb a ~** fastidiar a alguien; **it's such a ~** es un jaleo **II.** *vt inf* fastidiar; **to ~ sb to do sth** estar encima a alguien para que haga algo

**haste** [heɪst] *n* prisa *f*; **to make ~** apresurarse; **in ~** de prisa

**hasten** ['heɪ·sən] **I.** *vt* acelerar; **to ~ sb along** dar prisa a alguien **II.** *vi* apresurarse; **to ~ to do sth** apresurarse a hacer algo

**hasty** ['heɪ·sti] <-ier, -iest> *adj* **1.** (*fast*) rápido, -a **2.** (*not thought out*) precipitado, -a; **to make ~ decisions** tomar decisiones irreflexivamente; **to be ~ in doing sth** precipitarse en algo

**hat** [hæt] *n* sombrero *m*; **to pass around the ~** pasar la gorra ▶ **at the <u>drop</u> of a ~** con nada; **to <u>hang</u> one's ~ <u>some</u>where** quedarse a vivir en algún sitio; **to <u>keep</u> sth under one's ~** no decir ni una palabra sobre algo

**hatch**[1] [hætʃ] **I.** *vi* salir del cascarón **II.** *vt* **1.** (*chick*) incubar, empollar **2.** (*devise in secret*) tramar

**hatch**[2] [hætʃ] <-es> *n* trampilla *f*; NAUT escotilla ▶ **<u>down</u> the ~!** ¡salud!

**hatch**[3] [hætʃ] *vt* ART sombrear

**hatchback** ['hætʃ·bæk] *n* AUTO coche *m* con puerta trasera

**hate** [heɪt] **I.** *n* odio *m* **II.** *vt* odiar; **to ~ sb's guts** *sl* odiar a alguien a muerte

**hate crime** *n* delito de carácter xenófobo, racista, antihomosexual, etc.

**hateful** ['heɪt·fəl] *adj* odioso, -a

**hatred** ['heɪ·trɪd] *n* odio *m*

**hat trick** *n* SPORTS tres goles marcados

*por un mismo jugador;* **to score a ~** marcar tres tantos

**haul** [hɔl] I. *vt* 1. (*pull with effort*) arrastrar; **to ~ up the sail** izar la vela; **to ~ a boat out of the water** sacar una barca del agua 2. *inf* (*force to go*) forzar, jalar 3. (*transport goods*) transportar II. *n* 1. (*distance*) trayecto *m;* **in** [*or* **over**] **the long ~** *fig* a la larga 2. (*quantity caught: of fish, shrimp*) redada *f;* (*of stolen goods*) botín *m*

◆**haul up** *vt inf* **to haul up sb before sb** hacer que alguien dé explicaciones a alguien

**haunt** [hɔnt] I. *vt* 1. (*ghost*) aparecerse 2. (*bother, torment*) perseguir; **to be ~ed by sth** estar obsesionado por algo 3. (*frequent*) frecuentar; **to ~ a place** rondar un lugar II. *n* lugar *m* preferido

**haunted** *adj* 1. (*by ghosts*) embrujado, -a 2. (*troubled: look*) angustiado, -a, preocupado, -a

**have** [hæv, *unstressed:* həv] I. <*has, had, had*> *vt* 1. (*own*) tener, poseer; **I have two brothers** tengo dos hermanos; **to ~ sth to do** tener algo que hacer 2. (*engage in*) **to ~ a talk with sb** hablar con alguien 3. (*eat*) **to ~ breakfast/a snack** desayunar/merendar; **to ~ lunch** comer, almorzar *Col;* **to ~ dinner** cenar, comer *Col;* **I ~n't had shrimp in ages!** ¡hace años que no como gambas!; **to ~ some coffee** tomar un poco de café 4. (*give birth to*) **to ~ a child** tener un hijo 5. (*receive*) tener, recibir; **to ~ visitors** tener visita 6. (*show trait*) **to ~ patience/mercy** tener paciencia/compasión; **to ~ doubts/second thoughts** tener dudas/reservas 7. (*cause to occur*) **to ~ dinner ready** tener la cena preparada; **I'll ~ Bob give you a ride home** le pediré [*or* diré] a Bob que te lleve a casa; **I won't ~ him doing that** no dejo que haga esto ▶ **to ~ it in for sb** *inf* tenerla tomada con alguien; **to ~ it in one to do sth** ser capaz de hacer algo; **I didn't think she had it in her!** ¡no pensaba que fuera capaz de eso!; **to ~ had it with sb/sth** *inf* haber tenido más que suficiente de alguien/algo

II. <*has, had, had*> *aux* 1. (*indicates perfect tense*) **he has never been to California** nunca ha estado en California; **we had been swimming** habíamos estado nadando; **had I known you were coming,...** *form* si hubiera sabido que ibas a venir,... 2. (*must*) **to ~ (got) to do sth** tener que hacer algo; **do we ~ to finish this today?** ¿tenemos que acabar esto hoy? III. *n pl* **the ~s and the have-nots** los ricos y los pobres

◆**have back** *vt always sep* **can I have it back?** ¿me lo devuelves?

◆**have in** *vt always sep* invitar; **they had some experts in** llamaron a algunos expertos

◆**have on** *vt always sep* 1. (*wear: clothes*) llevar (puesto); **he didn't have any clothes on** estaba desnudo 2. (*carry*) **to have sth on oneself** llevar algo encima; **have you got any money on you?** ¿llevas dinero contigo?

◆**have out** *vt always sep* 1. (*remove*) sacar 2. *inf* (*argue*) **to have it out with sb** poner las cosas en claro

◆**have over** *vt always sep* invitar

**haven** ['heɪ·vən] *n* refugio *m*

**haven't** ['hæv·ənt] = **have not** *see* **have**

**hawk** [hɔk] I. *n* halcón *m* II. *vt* (*wares*) pregonar III. *vi* carraspear

**hay** [heɪ] *n* heno *m* ▶ **to hit the ~** *inf* acostarse

**hay fever** *n* fiebre *f* del heno

**haystack** *n* almiar *m*

**haywire** *adj inf* **to go/be ~** (*person*) volverse/estar loco; (*machine*) estropearse

**hazard** ['hæz·ərd] I. *n* 1. (*danger*) peligro *m* 2. (*risk*) riesgo *m;* **fire ~** peligro de incendio; **health ~** riesgo para la salud II. *vt* 1. (*dare*) aventurar 2. (*endanger*) arriesgar

**hazard lights** *npl* AUTO luces *f pl* de emergencia

**hazardous** ['hæz·ər·dəs] *adj* (*dangerous*) peligroso, -a; (*risky*) arriesgado, -a

**haze** [heɪz] I. *n* 1. (*mist*) neblina *f;* (*smog*) calima *f* 2. (*mental*) aturdimiento *m* II. *vt* ESP. UNIV hacer novatadas a

**hazelnut** ['heɪ·zəl·nʌt] *n* BOT avellana *f*

**hazy** ['heɪ·zi] <-ier, -iest> *adj* 1. (*with bad visibility*) neblinoso, -a 2. (*con-*

*fused, unclear)* vago, -a

**he** [hi] **I.** *pron pers* **1.** *(male person or animal)* él; **~'s** [*or* **~ is**] **my father** (él) es mi padre; **~'s gone away but ~'ll be back soon** se ha ido, pero volverá pronto; **here ~ comes** ahí viene **2.** *(unspecified sex)* **if somebody comes, ~ will buy it** si alguien viene, lo comprará; **~ who...** *form* aquél que... **II.** *n (of baby)* varón *m; (of animal)* macho *m*

**head** [hed] **I.** *n* **1.** ANAT cabeza *f; to nod one's ~* asentir con la cabeza; **to go straight to sb's ~** *(alcohol, wine)* subírse a la cabeza a alguien **2.** *(unit)* cabeza *f; a* [*or* **per**] **~** por cabeza; **a hundred ~ of cattle** cien cabezas de ganado **3.** *(mind)* **to clear one's ~** aclararse las ideas; **to get sth/sb out of one's ~** sacarse algo/a alguien de la cabeza **4.** *(top: of line)* cabeza *f; (of bed, table)* cabecera; *(of a page, column)* parte *f* superior **5.** BOT cabeza *f;* **a ~ of lettuce** una lechuga **6.** **~s** FIN *(face of coin)* cara *f;* **~s or tails?** ¿cara o cruz? **7.** *(beer foam)* espuma *f* **8.** GEO *(of river)* nacimiento *m* **9.** *(boss)* jefe, -a *m, f* **10.** TECH *(device)* cabezal *m* **11.** COMPUT **read/write ~** cabeza *f* de lectura/escritura **12.** NAUT *(toilet)* baño *m* ▶ **to have one's ~ in the** <u>clouds</u> tener la cabeza [*or* en las nubes] llena de pájaros; **to be ~ over** <u>heels</u> **in love** estar locamente enamorado; **to fall ~ over** <u>heels</u> **in love with sb** enamorarse locamente de alguien; **to bury one's ~ in the** <u>sand</u> hacer como el avestruz; **not to be able to make ~ (n)or tail of sth** no entender ni jota de algo, no encontrarle pies ni cabeza a algo; **~s I win,** <u>tails</u> **you lose** o gano yo o gano yo; **to bang one's ~ against a** <u>wall</u> darse de cabeza contra la pared; **to keep one's ~ above** <u>water</u> mantenerse a flote; **to keep one's ~** <u>down</u> *(avoid attention)* mantenerse al margen; *(work hard)* no levantar la cabeza; **to hold one's ~ high** mantener la cabeza alta; **to** <u>bite</u> **sb's ~ off** echar una bronca a alguien; **to** <u>bring</u> **sth to a ~** llevar algo a un punto crítico; **to** <u>laugh</u> **one's ~ off** desternillarse de risa; **~s** <u>up</u>**!** ¡cuidado!, ¡pilas! *Col,*

¡aguas! *Méx* **vt 1.** *(lead)* encabezar; *(a company, organization)* dirigir; *(team)* capitanear **2.** PUBL encabezar **3.** SPORTS *(ball)* cabecear **III.** *vi* **to ~ (for) home** dirigirse hacia casa

◆**head back** *vi* volver, regresar

◆**head off** **I.** *vt* cortar el paso a **II.** *vi* **to ~ toward** salir hacia

◆**head up** *vt* dirigir

**headache** ['hed-erk] *n* dolor *m* de cabeza

**headband** *n* cinta *f* de pelo

**head cold** *n* resfriado *m*

**header** ['hed-ər] *n* **1.** SPORTS cabezazo *m* **2.** COMPUT cabecera *f*

**headhunter** *n* **1.** ECON cazatalentos *mf inv* **2.** *(warrior)* cazador *m* de cabezas

**headlamp**, **headlight** *n* faro *m*

**headline** **I.** *n* titular *m* ▶ **to** <u>hit</u> **the ~s** salir en primera plana **II.** *vt* titular

**headmaster** *n* director *m* de colegio

**headmistress** <-es> *n* directora *f* de colegio

**head-on** **I.** *adj (collision)* frontal **II.** *adv* frontalmente, de frente

**headphones** *npl* auriculares *mpl*, audífonos *mpl AmL*

**headquarters** *n + sing/pl vb* MIL cuartel *m* general; *(of company)* oficina *f* central; *(of political party)* sede *f; (of the police)* jefatura *f* de policía

**headrest** *n* reposacabezas *m inv*

**headroom** *n* altura *f*

**headscarf** <-scarves> *n* pañuelo *m* para la cabeza

**headset** *n* auriculares *mpl*, audífonos *mpl AmL*

**head start** *n* ventaja *f; to give sb a ~* dar ventaja a alguien

**headway** *n* progreso *m; to make ~* hacer progresos

**heal** [hil] **I.** *vt (wound)* curar; *(differences)* salvar **II.** *vi (wound, injury)* cicatrizar

**health** [helθ] *n* salud *f; to be in good/bad ~* estar bien/mal de salud; **to drink to sb's ~** beber a la salud de alguien

**health care** *n* asistencia *f* sanitaria [*or* médica]

**health center** *n* centro *m* médico

**health certificate** *n* certificado *m* médico

H

**health club** n gimnasio m

**health food** n alimentos m pl naturales

**health food shop** n, **health food store** n tienda f de productos naturales

**health insurance** n seguro m médico

**healthy** ['hel·θi] <-ier, -iest> adj 1. MED sano, -a 2. FIN (strong) próspero, -a; (profit) sustancial 3. (positive: attitude) positivo, -a

**heap** [hip] I. n (pile) pila f, montón m; **a (whole) ~ of work** inf un montón de trabajo II. vt amontonar, apilar

**hear** [hɪr] <heard, heard> I. vt 1. (perceive) oír 2. (be told) enterarse de; **to ~ that...** enterarse de que..., oír que... 3. (listen) escuchar; **Lord, ~ our prayers** REL escúchanos, Señor 4. LAW **to ~ a case** ver un caso; **to ~ a witness** oír a un testigo II. vi 1. (perceive) oír 2. (get news) enterarse; **to ~ of [o about]** sth enterarse de algo

**heard** [hɜrd] pt, pp of **hear**

**hearing** ['hɪr·ɪŋ] n 1. (sense) oído m; **to be hard of ~** ser duro de oído, no oír bien 2. (act) audición f 3. LAW vista f

**hearing aid** n audífono m

**heart** [hart] n 1. ANAT corazón m 2. (center of emotions) **to break sb's ~** partir el corazón a alguien; **to have a cold ~** ser duro de corazón; **to have a change of ~** cambiar de opinión; **to have a good [o kind] ~** tener buen corazón; **to lose ~** desanimarse; **to take ~** animarse; **her ~ sank** se le cayó el alma a los pies 3. (core) centro m; **to get to the ~ of the matter** llegar al fondo de la cuestión 4. CULIN (of lettuce) cogollo m; **artichoke ~s** corazones m pl de alcachofa 5. pl (card suit) corazones mpl; (in Spanish pack) copas fpl ▶ **to one's ~'s content** hasta quedarse satisfecho; **to have a ~ of gold/stone** tener un corazón de oro/piedra, ser todo corazón; **to have one's ~ in the right place** tener buen corazón; **to wear one's ~ on one's sleeve** ir con el corazón en la mano; **with all one's ~** con toda su alma; **to not have the ~ to do sth** no tener el valor para hacer algo; **by ~** de memoria

**heart attack** n ataque m al corazón

**heartbreaking** adj desgarrador(a)

**heartbroken** adj con el corazón partido

**heartburn** n MED acidez f de estómago

**heart disease** n enfermedad f coronaria

**heartening** ['har·tə·nɪŋ] adj alentador(a)

**heartfelt** adj sincero, -a

**heart murmur** n MED soplo m cardíaco

**heart-to-heart** I. n conversación f franca y abierta II. adj franco, -a y abierto, -a

**heat** [hit] I. n 1. (warmth, high temperature) calor m; **to cook sth on a high/low ~** cocinar algo a fuego alto/bajo 2. (heating system) calefacción f; **to turn down/up the ~** bajar/subir la calefacción 3. (emotional state) acaloramiento m; **in the ~ of the argument** en el momento más acalorado de la discusión 4. (sports race) eliminatoria f 5. ZOOL celo m; **to be in ~** estar en celo ▶ **to put the ~ on sb** presionar a alguien; **to take the ~ off sb** dar un respiro a alguien II. vt 1. (make hot) calentar 2. (excite) acalorar III. vi (become hot) calentarse; fig (inflame) acalorarse

♦**heat up** I. vi calentarse II. vt calentar

**heated** adj 1. (window) térmico, -a; (pool) climatizado, -a; (room) caldeado, -a 2. (argument) acalorado, -a

**heater** ['hi·tər] n calefactor m; **water ~** calentador m de agua, radiador m

**heat gauge** n termostato m

**heather** ['heð·ər] n BOT brezo m

**heating** n calefacción f

**heat rash** <-es> n sarpullido m

**heat-resistant** adj, **heat-resisting** adj resistente al calor

**heat stroke** n MED insolación f

**heaven** ['hev·ən] n cielo m; **to go to ~** ir al cielo; **it's ~** fig inf es divino, es fantástico; **to be in (seventh) ~** a. fig estar en el (séptimo) cielo; **the ~s** (sky) el cielo ▶ **what/where/when/who/why in ~'s name...?** ¿qué/dónde/cuándo/quién/por qué demonios...?; **for ~ sake!** ¡por Dios!; **good ~s!** ¡santo cielo!; **~ only knows** sólo Dios lo sabe; **~ help us** que Dios nos ayude; **thank ~s** gracias a Dios

**heavy** ['hev·i] I. adj <-ier, -iest>

**1.** (*weighing a lot*) pesado, -a; ~ **food** comida pesada **2.** (*difficult*) difícil; (*schedule*) apretado, -a **3.** (*strong*) fuerte; ~ **fall** a. ECON fuerte descenso **4.** (*not delicate, coarse*) poco delicado, -a **5.** (*severe*) severo, -a; (*responsibility*) fuerte; (*sea*) grueso, -a; ~ **casualties** muchas bajas **6.** (*abundant*) abundante; (*investment*) cuantioso, -a; ~ **frost/rain** helada/chubasco fuerte; **to go** ~ **on sth** consumir mucho de algo; **the tree was** ~ **with fruit** el árbol estaba cargado de frutas **7.** (*excessive*) ~ **drinker/smoker** bebedor/fumador empedernido **8.** (*thick*) grueso, -a; (*beard*) denso, -a **II.** n <-ies> sl matón m

**heavy-duty** *adj* (*machine*) resistente

**heavy going** *adj* dificultoso, -a

**heavy-handed** *adj* **1.** (*clumsy*) torpe **2.** (*harsh*) duro, -a

**heavyweight I.** *adj* **1.** SPORTS (de la categoría) de los pesos pesados **2.** (*important*) serio, -a e importante **II.** n a. *fig* peso pesado m

**Hebrew** ['hiːbruː] **I.** n **1.** (*person*) hebreo, -a m, f **2.** LING hebreo m **II.** *adj* hebreo, -a

**hectare** ['hekter] n hectárea f

**hectic** ['hektɪk] *adj* ajetreado, -a; ~ **fever** fiebre hé(c)tica; ~ **pace** ritmo intenso

**he'd** [hiːd] = **he had, he would** *see* **have, will**

**hedge** [hedʒ] **I.** n **1.** (*row of bushes*) seto m vivo **2.** FIN (*protection*) cobertura f **II.** *vi* (*avoid action*) dar rodeos; FIN cubrirse **III.** *vt* cercar (con un seto vivo)

**hedgehog** ['hedʒhɒg] n erizo m

**hedgerow** ['hedʒrəʊ] n seto m vivo

**heed** [hiːd] **I.** *vt form* hacer caso de; **to** ~ **advice** seguir los consejos **II.** n **to pay (no)** ~ **to sth, to take (no)** ~ **of sth** (no) prestar atención a algo, hacer caso omiso de algo

**heel** [hiːl] **I.** n **1.** (*of foot*) talón m **2.** (*of shoe*) tacón m, taco m *AmL* **3.** (*of the hand*) base f de la mano **4.** (*of loaf of bread*) cuscurro m, punta f **5.** *inf* (*cad*) canalla m ▸ **to follow close on the** ~**s of sth** seguir inmediatamente a algo; **to be hard on sb's** ~**s** pisar los talones a

alguien; **under the** ~ **of sb/sth** sometido a alguien/algo; **to come to** ~ acceder a obedecer, acudir; **to dig one's** ~**s in** mantenerse en sus trece **II.** *interj* (*to dogs*) ven aquí

**hefty** ['heftɪ] *adj* <-ier, -iest> (*person*) corpulento, -a; (*profit, amount*) cuantioso, -a; (*book*) gordo, -a; (*price increase*) alto, -a

**height** [haɪt] n **1.** (*of person*) estatura f; (*of thing*) altura f **2.** ~**s** (*high places*) alturas *fpl*; **to be afraid of** ~**s** tener vértigo; **to scale (new)** ~**s** *fig* alcanzar (nuevas) cotas **3.** ~**s** (*hill*) cerros *mpl* **4.** (*strongest point*) cima f; **to be at the** ~ **of one's career** estar en la cima de su carrera **5.** (*the greatest degree*) cumbre f; **the** ~ **of stupidity** el colmo de la estupidez

**heighten** ['haɪtən] **I.** *vi* aumentar **II.** *vt* **1.** (*elevate*) elevar **2.** (*increase*) aumentar; **to** ~ **the effect of sth** acentuar el efecto de algo

**heir** [er] n heredero m; **to be (the)** ~ **to sth** ser el heredero de algo; ~ **apparent** heredero forzoso; ~ **to the throne** heredero del trono

**heiress** ['erɪs] n heredera f

**heirloom** ['erluːm] n reliquia f; **family** ~ reliquia familiar

**held** [held] *pt, pp of* **hold**

**helicopter** ['helɪkɒptər] n helicóptero m

**helipad** ['helɪpæd] n plataforma f de aterrizaje de los helicópteros

**heliport** ['helɪpɔːt] n helipuerto m

**hell** [hel] **I.** n **1.** (*place of punishment*) infierno m; ~ **on earth** infierno en vida; **to be (pure)** ~ ser un (auténtico) infierno; **to go to** ~ ir al infierno; **to go through** ~ pasar un calvario; **to make sb's life** ~ *inf* hacer la vida imposible a alguien **2.** *inf* (*as intensifier*) **as cold as** ~ un frío de mil demonios; **as hot as** ~ un calor infernal; **as hard as** ~ duro a más no poder; **to annoy the** ~ **out of sb** molestar horrores a alguien; **to beat the** ~ **out of sb** dar a alguien una paliza de padre y muy señor mío; **to frighten the** ~ **out of sb** dar a alguien un susto de miedo; **to hurt like** ~ hacer un daño

H

de mil demonios; **to run like ~** correr (uno) que se las pela; **a ~ of a decision** una decisión muy importante; **that's a ~ of a way to treat your mother!** ¡qué manera de tratar a tu madre! ▶ **the road to ~ is paved with good intentions** *prov* el camino que lleva al infierno está lleno de buenas intenciones; **come ~ or high water** contra viento y marea; **to have been to ~ and back** haber pasado un calvario; **all ~ broke loose** se armó la gorda; **to catch ~** recibir una bronca; **to do sth for the ~ of it** hacer algo porque sí; **to give sb ~ (for sth)** echar un rapapolvo a alguien (por algo), hacérselas pasar negras a alguien *AmL;* **go to ~!** *inf (leave me alone)* ¡déjame en paz!; *(stronger)* ¡vete a la mierda! *vulg;* **to have ~ to pay** *inf* armarse la gorda; **like ~** *inf* y un cuerno *(emphasis)* ¡demonios! ▶ **what the ~...!** ¡qué diablos...!

**he'll** [hɪl] = **he will** *see* will

**hellish** ['hel·ɪʃ] *adj* infernal; *(experience)* horroroso, -a

**hellishly** *adv* endemoniadamente

**hello** [ha·'loʊ] I. *n* <hellos> *n* hola *m;* **a big ~** un gran saludo II. *interj* 1. *(greeting)* hola; **to say ~ to sb** saludar a alguien 2. *(beginning of phone call)* diga, dígame, aló *AmC, AmS* 3. *(to attract attention)* oiga 4. *(surprise)* anda, ¡ey! **~, ~** pero bueno

**helm** [helm] *n* timón *m;* **to be at the ~** llevar el timón; *fig (lead)* llevar el mando

**helmet** ['hel·mɪt] *n* casco *m;* **crash ~** casco protector

**help** [help] I. *vi* 1. *(assist)* ayudar 2. *(make easier)* facilitar 3. *(improve situation)* mejorar II. *vt* 1. *(assist)* ayudar; **nothing can ~ him now** ya no se puede hacer nada por él; **can I ~ you?** *(in shop)* ¿en qué puedo servirle?; **to ~ sb with sth** ayudar a alguien con algo 2. *(improve)* (ayudar a) mejorar; **this medicine will ~ your headache** esta medicina te aliviará el dolor de cabeza 3. *(contribute to a condition)* contribuir [*or* ayudar] a 4. *(prevent)* evitar; **it can't be ~ed** es así y no hay más remedio; **to**

not be able to ~ doing sth no poder dejar de hacer algo; I can't ~ it no puedo remediarlo; **he can't ~ the way he is** él es así, ¿qué se le va hacer?; **to not be able to ~ but...** no poder menos de... 5. *(take sth)* **to ~ oneself to sth** *(at table)* servirse algo; *(steal)* llevarse III. *n* 1. *(assistance)* ayuda *f;* **to be a ~** ser una ayuda 2. *(servant)* mujer *f* de la limpieza; *(in a shop)* ayudante *mf* IV. *interj* **~!** ¡socorro!; **so ~ me God** y que Dios me asista

◆**help out** *vt* ayudar

**helper** ['hel·pər] *n* ayudante *mf*

**helpful** ['help·fəl] *adj* 1. *(willing to help)* servicial 2. *(useful)* útil

**helping** ['hel·pɪŋ] I. *n (food)* ración *f,* porción *f AmL* II. *adj* **to give sb a ~ hand** echar una mano a alguien

**helpless** ['help·lɪs] *adj* indefenso, -a

**helpline** ['help·laɪn] *n* teléfono *m* de asistencia

**hem** [hem] I. *n* dobladillo *m,* basta *f AmL;* **to take the ~ up/down** meter/sacar [*or* subir/bajar] el dobladillo II. *vt* hacer el dobladillo [*or* la bastilla] a III. *vi* <-mm-> **to ~ and haw** titubear

**hemophilia** [ˌhi·moʊ·'fɪl·i·ə] *n* hemofilia *f*

**hemophiliac** [ˌhi·moʊ·'fɪl·i·æk] *n* hemofílico, -a *m, f*

**hemorrhage** ['hem·ər·ɪdʒ] I. *n* hemorragia *f;* **brain ~** derrame *m* cerebral II. *vi* MED tener una hemorragia

**hemorrhoids** ['hem·ər·ɔɪdz] *npl* hemorroides *fpl*

**hemp** [hemp] *n* cáñamo *m*

**hen** [hen] *n (female chicken)* gallina *f;* *(female bird)* hembra *f*

**hence** [hens] *adv* 1. *(therefore)* de ahí 2. *after n (from now)* dentro de

**hencoop** ['hen·kup] *n,* **henhouse** ['hen·haʊs] *n* gallinero *m*

**hepatitis** [ˌhep·ə·'taɪ·t̬ɪs] *n* hepatitis *f inv*

**heptathlon** [hep·'tæθ·lən] *n* heptatlón *m*

**her** [hɜr] I. *adj pos* su; **~ dress/house** su vestido/casa; **~ children** sus hijos II. *pron pers* 1. *(she)* ella; **it's ~** es ella; **older than ~** mayor que ella; **if I were ~** si yo fuese ella 2. *direct object* la *indirect object* le; **look at ~** mírala;

**I saw** ~ la vi; **he told** ~ **that...** le dijo que...; **he gave** ~ **the pencil** le dio el lápiz (a ella) **3.** *after prep* ella; **it's for/ from** ~ es para/de ella

**herb** [ɜrb] *n* hierba *f*

**herbivorous** [hɜr·'bɪv·ər·əs] *adj* herbívoro, -a

**herd** [hɜrd] **I.** *n* + *sing/pl vb* **1.** (*of animals*) manada *f*; (*of sheep*) rebaño *f* **2.** (*of people*) multitud *f*; **to follow the** ~ seguir a la masa **II.** *vt* (*animals*) llevar en manada; (*sheep*) guardar; **they** ~**ed us into the press room** nos reunieron en la sala de prensa **III.** *vi* ir en manada [*or* rebaño]

**here** [hɪr] **I.** *adv* **1.** (*in, at, to this place*) aquí; **over** ~ acá; **give it** ~ *inf* dámelo; ~ **and there** aquí y allá **2.** (*in introductions*) **here is...** éste está... **3.** (*show arrival*) **they are** ~ ya han llegado **4.** (*now*) **where do we go from** ~? ¿dónde vamos ahora?; ~ **you are**, ~ **you go** (*giving sth*) aquí tienes; **the** ~ **and now** el presente; ~ **goes** *inf* allá voy; ~ **we go** ya estamos otra vez **II.** *interj* (*in roll call*) ¡presente!, ¡aquí!

**hereafter** [hɪr·'æf·tər] **I.** *adv* en lo sucesivo **II.** *n* **the** ~ el más allá

**herewith** [hɪr·'wɪθ] *adv form* adjunto, -a

**heritage** ['her·ɪ·tɪdʒ] *n* **1.** (*objects*) patrimonio *m* histórico **2.** (*tradition*) patrimonio *m* cultural

**hermetic** [hɜr·'met·ɪk] *adj* hermético, -a; ~ **seal** cierre hermético

**hermit crab** *n* cangrejo *m* ermitaño

**hero** ['hɪr·ou] <heroes> *n* **1.** (*brave man*) héroe *m* **2.** (*main character*) protagonista *m* **3.** (*idol*) ídolo *m* **4.** (*sandwich*) sándwich *de carne fría, queso y lechuga*

**heroic** [hɪ·'rou·ɪk] *adj* **1.** (*brave, bold*) heroico, -a; ~ **deed** hazaña *f* **2.** (*epic*) heroico, -a

**heroin** ['her·ou·ɪn] *n* heroína *f*

**heroin addict** *n* MED heroinómano, -a *m, f*

**heroine** ['her·ou·ɪn] *n* (*brave woman*) heroína *f*; (*of film*) protagonista *f*

**heroism** ['her·ou·ɪz·əm] *n* heroísmo *m*

**heron** ['her·ən] <-(s)> *n* garza *f* (real)

**herpes** ['hɜr·piz] *n* herpes *m inv*

**herring** ['her·ɪŋ] <-(s)> *n* arenque *m*

**hers** [hɜrz] *pron pos* (el) suyo, (la) suya, (los) suyos, (las) suyas; **it's not my bag, it's** ~ no es mi bolsa, es la de ella; **this house is** ~ esta casa es suya; **this glass is** ~ este vaso es suyo; **a book of** ~ un libro suyo

**herself** [hɜr·'self] *pron* **1.** *reflexive* se *after prep* sí (misma); **she lives by** ~ vive sola **2.** *emphatic* ella misma; **she hurt** ~ se hizo daño

**he's** [hiz] **1.** = **he is** *see* **be 2.** = **he has** *see* **have**

**hesitant** ['hez·ɪ·tənt] *adj* **1.** (*indecisive*) indeciso, -a; **to be** ~ **about doing sth** no estar decidido a hacer algo **2.** (*shy, uncertain*) vacilante

**hesitantly** *adv* con indecisión

**hesitate** ['hez·ɪ·teɪt] *vi* (*be indecisive*) vacilar, trepidar *AmL*; **to** (**not**) ~ **to do sth** (no) dudar en hacer algo

**hesitation** [ˌhez·ɪ·'teɪ·ʃən] *n* vacilación *f*; **without** ~ sin titubear

**heterogeneous** [ˌhet·ər·ə·'dʒi·ni·əs] *adj* heterogéneo, -a

**heterosexual** [ˌhet·ə·rou·'sek·ʃu·əl] **I.** *n* heterosexual *mf* **II.** *adj* heterosexual

**hexagon** ['hek·sə·gan] *n* hexágono *m*

**hexagonal** [hek·'sæg·ə·nəl] *adv* hexagonal

**hey** [heɪ] *interj inf* eh, oye, órale *Méx*

**heyday** ['heɪ·deɪ] *n* apogeo *m*; **in his/ her/its** ~ en su apogeo

**hi** [haɪ] *interj* hola

**hibernate** ['haɪ·bər·neɪt] *vi* hibernar

**hibernation** [ˌhaɪ·bər·'neɪ·ʃən] *n* hibernación *f*

**hibiscus** [hɪ·'bɪs·kəs] <-es> *n* BOT hibisco *m*

**hiccup, hiccough** ['hɪk·ʌp] **I.** *n* hipo *m*; **to have the** ~**s** tener hipo **II.** *vi* <-p(p)-> tener hipo

**hid** [hɪd] *pt of* **hide²**

**hidden** ['hɪd·ən] **I.** *pp of* **hide² II.** *adj* (*person, thing*) escondido, -a; (*emotion, information*) oculto, -a

**hide¹** [haɪd] *n* (*of an animal*) piel *f*

**hide²** [haɪd] <hid, hidden> **I.** *vi* (*be out of sight*) esconderse, escorarse *Cuba, Hond* **II.** *vt* (*conceal: person, thing*) esconder; (*emotion, information*) ocultar;

to ~ one's face taparse la cara
♦**hide away** vt esconder
♦**hide out** vi, **hide up** vi esconderse
**hide-and-seek** n escondite m; **to play ~** jugar al escondite
**hideaway** ['haɪ·ə·weɪ] n escondite m
**hideous** ['hɪd·i·əs] adj 1. (very unpleasant, ugly) espantoso, -a 2. (terrible) terrible
**hideout** ['haɪd·aʊt] n escondrijo m; **secret ~** guarida f secreta
**hiding**[1] ['haɪ·dɪŋ] n a. fig paliza f
**hiding**[2] ['haɪ·dɪŋ] n **to be in ~** estar escondido; **to go into ~** ocultarse
**hieroglyphics** npl jeroglíficos mpl
**hi-fi** ['haɪ·faɪ] I. n abbr of **high-fidelity** alta fidelidad f II. adj abbr of **high-fidelity** de alta fidelidad
**high** [haɪ] I. adj 1. (elevated) alto, -a; **one yard ~ and three yards wide** una yarda de alto y tres yardas de ancho; **knee/waist-~** hasta la rodilla/cintura; **to fly at ~ altitude** volar a gran altitud 2. (above average) superior; **to have ~ hopes (for sb/sth)** tener grandes esperanzas (puestas en alguien/algo); **to have a ~ opinion of sb** estimar mucho a alguien; **~ blood-pressure/fever** presión/fiebre alta 3. (important, eminent) elevado, -a; **of ~ rank** de alto rango; **to have friends in ~ places** tener amigos en las altas esferas; (regarding job) tener enchufe; **to be ~ and mighty** ser un engreído 4. (under influence of drugs) colocado, -a 5. (of high frequency, shrill: voice) agudo, -a; **a ~ note** una nota alta 6. FASHION **with a ~ neckline/waistline** con escote a (la) caja 7. (at peak, maximum) máximo, -a; **~ noon** mediodía m; **~ priority** alta prioridad ▶ **to leave sb ~ and dry** dejar a alguien colgado II. adv 1. (at or to a great point or height) a gran altura 2. (high or strong) con fuerza ▶ **to search for sth ~ and low** buscar algo por todas partes III. n 1. (high(est) point) punto m máximo; **an all-time ~** un récord de todos los tiempos; **to reach a ~** alcanzar un nivel récord 2. sl (from drugs) **to be on a ~** estar colocado, estar drogado 3. (heaven) **on ~** en el cielo

**highchair** n silla f alta
**high court** n tribunal m superior de justicia
**high-density** adj a. COMPUT de alta densidad
**higher education** n enseñanza f superior
**higher-up** n inf superior m
**high frequency** adj de alta frecuencia
**high-grade** adj (fruit, beef) de primera calidad; (minerals) de alto grado (de pureza)
**high heels** npl tacones m pl altos
**highjack** vt see **hijack**
**high jump** n salto m de altura
**high-level** adj de alto nivel
**highlight** I. n 1. (most interesting part) aspecto m más interesante 2. ~s (in hair) mechas fpl II. vt (draw attention to) destacar; (a problem) señalar
**highlighter** n rotulador m
**highly** ['haɪ·li] adv 1. (very) muy 2. (very well) **to speak ~ of sb** hablar muy bien de alguien
**high-octane** n ~ **gasoline** gasolina de alto octanaje
**high-performance** adj a. AUTO de gran rendimiento
**high-pitched** adj 1. (sloping steeply) escarpado, -a 2. (sound) agudo, -a; **a ~ voice** una voz aguda
**high point** n **the ~** (most successful state) el clímax; (of career) la cima, la cúspide; (most enjoyable state) súmmum m
**high-powered** adj 1. (powerful) de gran potencia 2. (influential, important) poderoso, -a
**high pressure** n METEO presión f alta
**high-pressure** I. adj 1. METEO **a ~ area** una zona de altas presiones 2. (aggressive) enérgico, -a 3. (stressful: job) de mucha responsabilidad, estresante II. vt presionar
**high-protein** adj rico, -a en proteínas
**high-ranking** adj de categoría
**high-resolution** adj COMPUT (image, screen, shot) de alta resolución
**high-risk** adj de alto riesgo; (investment) arriesgado, -a
**high school** n instituto m de enseñanza

secundaria (grados 9 a 12)

**high-speed** *adj* de alta velocidad

**high-spirited** *adj* (*cheerful, lively*) animoso, -a

**high spirits** *npl* buen humor *m*

**high-tech** *adj* de alta tecnología

**high technology** *n* alta tecnología *f*

**high-tension** *adj* ELEC de alta tensión

**high tide** *n* 1. (*of ocean*) marea *f* alta 2. *fig* (*most specific point*) apogeo *m*

**high water** *n* marea *f* alta

**high-water mark** *n* (*showing water level*) línea *f* de pleamar

**highway** ['haɪˌweɪ] *n* carretera *f*

**hijack** ['haɪ.dʒæk] I. *vt* 1. (*take over by force: plane*) secuestrar un avión 2. *fig* (*adopt as one's own*) **to ~ sb's ideas/plans** hacer propias las ideas/los planes de alguien II. *n* secuestro *m*

**hijacker** ['haɪ.dʒæk.ər] *n* secuestrador (a) *m(f)* (aéreo)

**hijacking** ['haɪ.dʒæk.ɪŋ] *n* secuestro *m* (aéreo)

**hike** [haɪk] I. *n* 1. (*long walk*) caminata *f*; **to go on a ~** dar una caminata; **take a ~!** *sl* ¡vete al diablo! 2. (*increase*) aumento *m* II. *vi* ir de excursión (a pie)

**hiker** ['haɪ.kər] *n* excursionista *mf*

**hiking** ['haɪ.kɪŋ] *n* excursionismo *m*

**hilarious** [hɪ.'ler.i.əs] *adj* (*very funny*) divertidísimo, -a

**hill** [hɪl] *n* 1. (*in landscape*) colina *f*; **the ~s** la sierra 2. (*in road*) cuesta *f* 3. (*small heap*) montoncito *m* 4. POL **The Hill** Capitolio *m*, Congreso *m* ▸ **as old as the ~s** tan viejo como el mundo; **to be over the ~** *inf* ser demasiado viejo

**hillbilly** ['hɪl.bɪl.i] <-ies> *n* palurdo, -a *m, f*, montañés *m*

**hillside** ['hɪl.saɪd] *n* ladera *f*

**hilltop** ['hɪl.tap] I. *n* cumbre *f* II. *adj* de la cima

**hilly** ['hɪl.i] <-ier, -iest> *adj* montañoso, -a

**him** [hɪm] *pron pers* 1. (*he*) él; **it's ~** es él; **older than ~** mayor que él; **if I were ~** yo en su lugar 2. *direct object* lo, le *indirect object* le; **she gave ~ the pencil** le dio el lápiz (a él) 3. *after prep* él; **it's for/from ~** es para/de él 4. (*un-*

*specified sex*) **if somebody comes, tell ~ that...** si viene alguien, dile que...

**Himalayas** [ˌhɪm.ə.'leɪ.əz] *npl* el Himalaya

**himself** [hɪm.'self] *pron* 1. *reflexive* se *after prep* sí (mismo); **for ~** para él (mismo); **he lives by ~** vive solo 2. *emphatic* él mismo; **he hurt ~** se hizo daño

**hindrance** ['hɪn.drəns] *n* 1. (*obstruction*) estorbo *m* 2. (*obstacle*) obstáculo *m*

**hindsight** ['haɪnd.saɪt] *n* percepción *f* retrospectiva; **in ~** en retrospectiva

**hinge** [hɪndʒ] I. *n* bisagra *f* II. *vi* **to ~ on/upon sb/sth** depender de alguien/algo

**hint** [hɪnt] I. *n* 1. (*trace: of anger, suspicion*) asomo *m*, atisbo *m* 2. (*allusion*) indirecta *f*; **to drop a ~** lanzar una indirecta; **to take a ~** pillarse una indirecta 3. (*practical tip*) consejo *m* 4. (*slight amount: of salt, curry*) pizca *f* II. *vi* soltar indirectas; **to ~ at sth** hacer alusión a algo

**hip** [hɪp] I. *n* 1. ANAT cadera *f* 2. BOT escaramujo *m* II. *adj sl* (*fashionable*) moderno, -a

**hipbone** ['hɪpˌboʊn] *n* hueso *m* de la cadera

**hip flask** *n* petaca *f*

**hippo** ['hɪp.oʊ] *n inf abbr of* **hippopotamus** hipopótamo *m*

**hippopotamus** [ˌhɪp.ə.'pɑt.ə.məs] <-es *or* -mi> *n* hipopótamo *m*

**hippy** ['hɪp.i] <-ies> *n* hippy *mf*

**hire** [haɪr] I. *n* (*hired person*) contratación *f*; **a new ~** un nuevo empleado II. *vt* (*employ*) contratar, conchabar *AmL*; **to ~ more staff** ampliar la plantilla

◆ **hire out** *vt* alquilar; **to ~ oneself out as sth** trabajar de algo

**his** [hɪz] I. *adj pos* su (de él); **~ car/house** su coche/casa; **~ children** sus hijos II. *pron pos* (el) suyo, (la) suya, (los) suyos, (las) suyas, de él; **it's not my bag, it's ~** no es mi bolsa, es la suya; **this house is ~** esta casa es suya; **this glass is ~** este vaso es suyo; **a book of ~** un libro suyo

**Hispanic** [hɪs.'pæn.ɪk] I. *adj* hispánico,

-a **II.** n hispano, -a m, f

**hiss** [hɪs] **I.** vi **1.** (tea kettle, crowd) silbar **2.** (cat) bufar **II.** vt silbar **III.** n silbido m

**historic** [hɪ·'stɔr·ɪk] adj histórico, -a; **this is a ~ moment...** es un momento clave...

**historical** adj histórico, -a

**history** ['hɪs·tə·ri] n historia f; **to make ~** hacer época; **sb's medical ~** historia médica de alguien

**hit** [hɪt] **I.** n **1.** (blow, stroke) golpe m **2.** inf (shot) tiro m certero **3.** SPORTS punto m; **to score a ~** marcar un tanto [or punto] **4.** (success) éxito m **5.** sl (murder) golpe, atentado m **II.** <-tt-, hit, hit> vt **1.** (strike) golpear, pepenar Méx **2.** (crash into) chocar contra; **to ~ one's head on a shelf** dar con la cabeza contra un estante **3.** (arrive at, reach target) alcanzar **4.** (affect) afectar; **to ~ sb where it hurts** dar a alguien donde más le duele **5.** (reach) tocar; **to ~ rock bottom** fig tocar fondo **6.** (encounter) tropezar con **7.** inf (arrive in or at) llegar a; **to ~ 100 mph** alcanzar las 100 m/h **III.** vi (strike) **to ~ against sth** chocar con algo

◆**hit back** vi devolver el golpe; **to ~ at sb** defenderse de alguien

◆**hit off** vt to hit it off (with sb) hacer buenas migas (con alguien)

◆**hit on** vt **1.** (show sexual interest) ligar con **2.** (think of) dar con

◆**hit out** vi lanzar un ataque

**hit-and-run** adj ~ **attack** MIL ataque relámpago; ~ **driver** conductor que se da a la fuga tras atropellar a alguien

**hitch** [hɪtʃ] **I.** <-es> n **1.** (obstacle) obstáculo m; **technical ~** problema m técnico; **to go off without a ~** salir a pedir de boca **2.** (sudden pull) tirón m **3.** (for a trailer) enganche m **II.** vt **1.** (fasten) atar; **to ~ sth to sth** atar algo a algo **2.** inf (hitchhike) **to ~ a lift** [or ride] hacer dedo [or autostop] **III.** vi inf hacer dedo

◆**hitch up** vt (fasten) to hitch sth up to sth atar algo a algo

**hitcher** ['hɪtʃ·ər] n autostopista mf

**hitch-hiking** n autostop m

**HIV** [ˌeɪtʃ·aɪ·'vi] abbr of human immunodeficiency virus VIH m

**hive** [haɪv] n **1.** (beehive) colmena f **2.** + sing/pl vb (swarm of bees) enjambre m

**hives** [haɪvz] n MED urticaria f

**ho** [hoʊ] interj inf (expressing scorn, surprise) oh!; (attracting attention) oiga!; **land ~!** NAUT ¡tierra a la vista!

**hoagie** ['hoʊ·gi] n sándwich de carne fría, queso y lechuga

**hoard** [hɔrd] **I.** n acumulación f **II.** vt acumular; (food) amontonar

**hoarse** [hɔrs] adj ronco, -a

**hoax** [hoʊks] **I.** <-es> n (joke) broma f de mal gusto; (fraud) engaño m **II.** vt engañar

**hobble** ['hab·əl] vi cojear; **to ~ around** ir cojeando

**hobby** ['hab·i] <-ies> n hobby m

**hockey** ['hak·i] n hockey m

**hodgepodge** ['hadʒ·padʒ] n batiburrillo m

**hog** [hɔg] **I.** n **1.** (pig) puerco m, chancho m AmS **2.** inf (person) egoísta mf ▶ **to live high on the ~** sl vivir como un rajá **II.** <-gg-> vt inf (keep for oneself) acaparar; (food) devorar; **to ~ sb/sth** (all to oneself) acaparar a alguien/algo (para uno mismo)

**hoist** [hɔɪst] vt (raise up) alzar; (flag) enarbolar

**hold** [hoʊld] **I.** n **1.** (grasp, grip) agarre m; **to take ~ of sb/sth** asirse de [or a] alguien/algo **2.** (wrestling) presa f; **no ~s barred** fig sin restricciones **3.** (control) dominio m **4.** NAUT, AVIAT bodega f **5.** (delayed) **to be on ~** estar en espera; TEL **to put sb on ~** poner alguien en espera **6.** (understand) **to get ~ of sth** comprender algo; **to have a ~ of sth** tener idea de algo **7.** (prison cell) prisión f **II.** <held, held> vt **1.** (keep) tener; (grasp) agarrar; **to ~ a gun** sostener un arma; **to ~ hands** agarrarse de la mano; **to ~ sth in one's hand** sostener algo en la mano; **to ~ sb/sth** (tight) sujetar a alguien/algo (con fuerza); **to ~ the door open for sb** aguantar la puerta abierta a alguien **2.** (support) soportar; **to ~ one's head high** mantener la cabeza alta **3.** (*cover up*) **to ~ one's ears/nose** taparse los oídos/la nariz **4.** (*keep, retain*) mantener; **to ~ sb's attention/interest** mantener la atención/el interés de alguien; **to ~ sb hostage** retener a alguien como rehén; **to ~ a note** MUS sostener una nota **5.** (*make keep to*) **to ~ sb to his/her word** [*or promise*] hacer cumplir a alguien su palabra **6.** (*delay, stop*) detener; **~ it!** ¡para!; **to ~ one's breath** contener la respiración; **to ~ one's fire** MIL detener el fuego; **to ~ sb's phone calls** TEL retener las llamadas de alguien **7.** (*contain*) contener; **it ~s many surprises** conlleva muchas sorpresas; **what the future ~s** lo que depara el futuro **8.** (*possess, own*) poseer; (*land, town*) ocupar; **to ~ an account** (**with a bank**) tener una cuenta (en un banco); **to ~ a position** (**as sth**) mantener un puesto (como algo); **to ~** (**down**) **the fort** MIL quedarse al cargo; *fig* hacerse cargo de **9.** (*make happen*) **to ~ a conversation** (**with sb**) mantener una conversación (con alguien); **to ~ an election/a meeting/a news conference** convocar elecciones/una reunión/una rueda de prensa; **to ~ talks** dar charlas **10.** (*believe*) creer; **to be held in great respect** ser muy respetado; **to ~ sb responsible for sth** considerar a alguien responsable de algo; **to ~ sb/sth in contempt** despreciar alguien/algo **III.** *vi* **1.** (*continue*) seguir; **to ~ still** pararse; **to ~ true** seguir siendo válido; **~ tight!** ¡quieto! **2.** (*believe*) sostener

◆**hold against** *vt always sep* **to hold sth against sb** hacerse una mala idea de alguien por algo

◆**hold back I.** *vt* (*keep*) retener; **to ~ information** ocultar información; (*stop*) detener; (*impede development*) parar; **to ~ tears** contener las lágrimas ▸ **there's no holding me back** nada me retiene **II.** *vi* **1.** (*be unforthcoming*) refrenar **2.** (*refrain*) **to ~ from doing sth** abstenerse de hacer algo

◆**hold down** *vt* sujetar; (*control, suppress*) oprimir; **to ~ a job** mantener un trabajo

◆**hold in** *vt* (*emotion*) contener

◆**hold off I.** *vt* (*enemy*) detener; (*reporters*) dar largas a **II.** *vi* mantenerse a distancia; (*wait*) esperar, posponer

◆**hold on** *vi* **1.** (*attach*) agarrarse bien; **to be held on by/with sth** estar sujeto a/con algo **2.** (*manage to keep going*) **to ~** (*tight*) aguantar **3.** (*wait*) esperar

◆**hold onto** *vt insep* **1.** (*grasp*) agarrarse a **2.** (*keep*) guardar

◆**hold out I.** *vt* extender **II.** *vi* **1.** (*offer, chance*) ofrecer **2.** (*manage to resist*) resistir; **to ~ for sth** resistir hasta conseguir algo **3.** (*refuse to give sth*) **to ~ on sb** no acceder a los deseos de alguien

◆**hold over** *vt* **1.** (*defer*) aplazar **2.** (*extend*) alargar

◆**hold to** *vt insep* atenerse a

◆**hold together I.** *vi* mantenerse unidos **II.** *vt* mantener unidos

◆**hold up I.** *vt* **1.** (*raise*) levantar; **to ~ one's hand** levantar la mano; **to be held up by** (**means of**)**/with sth** ser sostenido por (mediante)/con algo; **to hold one's head up high** *fig* mantener la cabeza alta **2.** (*delay*) atrasar **3.** (*rob with violence*) atracar **4.** (*offer as example*) **to hold sb up as an example of sth** mostrar a alguien como ejemplo de algo **II.** *vi* (*weather*) seguir bueno; (*material*) durar

◆**hold with** *vt insep* estar de acuerdo con

**holdall** ['hoʊld·ɔl] *n* bolsa *f* de viaje

**holder** ['hoʊl·dər] *n* **1.** (*device*) soporte *m;* **cigarette ~** boquilla *f* **2.** (*person: of shares, of account*) titular *mf;* (*of title*) poseedor(a) *m(f);* **world record ~** plusmarquista *mf* mundial

**hole** [hoʊl] *n* **1.** (*hollow space*) agujero *m; fig* (*in an argument, sb's reasoning*) laguna *f,* vacío *m;* **to be in the ~** estar endeudado **2.** (*in golf*) hoyo *m* **3.** (*of mouse*) ratonera *f*

◆**hole up** *vi inf* esconderse

**holiday** ['hal·ɪ·deɪ] *n* (*public day off*) día *m* festivo

**holiday resort** *n* centro *m* turístico

**holiness** ['hoʊ·lɪ·nɪs] *n* santidad *f;* **His/Your Holiness** Su Santidad

**holistic** [hoʊ·'lɪs·tɪk] *adj* holístico, -a

**Holland** ['hal·ənd] n Holanda f

**hollow** ['hal·ou] I. adj 1. (empty) hueco, -a 2. (worthless, empty: promise) vano, -a; (victory) vacío, -a; (laughter) falso, -a 3. (sound) sordo, -a II. n hueco m; (valley) hondonada f III. vt to ~ (out) (pumpkin) vaciar; (tree trunk) ahuecar IV. vi (become hollow: tree) ahuecarse

**holly** ['hal·i] n BOT acebo m

**holocaust** ['hal·ə·kɔst] n holocausto m

**hologram** ['hal·ə·græm] n holograma m

**holy** ['hou·li] <-ier, -iest> adj (sacred) santo, -a; (water) bendito, -a

**Holy Communion** n Sagrada Comunión f

**Holy Father** n Santo Padre m

**Holy Scripture** n the ~ las Sagradas Escrituras

**Holy Spirit** n Espíritu m Santo

**homage** ['ham·ɪdʒ] n homenaje m; to pay ~ to sb rendir homenaje a alguien

**home** [houm] I. n 1. (residence) casa f; at ~ en casa; to leave ~ salir [or irse] de casa; away from ~ fuera de casa; make yourself at ~ ponte cómodo, estás en tu casa 2. (family) hogar m 3. (institution) asilo m; (for old people) residencia f; children's ~ orfanato m II. adv 1. (one's place of residence) to be ~ estar en casa; to go/come ~ ir/venir a casa; to take work ~ llevarse trabajo a casa 2. (understanding) to hit ~ causar impacto, dar en el blanco ► to be ~ free tener la victoria asegurada; this is nothing to write ~ about esto no es nada del otro mundo III. adj 1. (from own country) nacional 2. (from own area) local; (team) de casa; (game) en casa; the ~ ground el campo de casa

**home address** n dirección f particular, domicilio m

**homebody** n persona f hogareña

**homecoming** n regreso m (a casa)

**home cooking** n cocina f casera

**home fries** npl CULIN papas f pl fritas

**homeland** n (country of birth) tierra f natal; (of cultural heritage) patria f

**homeless** adj sin hogar II. n + pl vb the ~ los sin techo

**homely** ['houm·li] <-ier, -iest> adj 1. (ugly) feúcho, -a 2. (simple) sencillo, -a 3. (domestic) casero, -a, doméstico, -a

**homemade** adj casero, -a

**homeopath** ['hou·mi·ou·pæθ] n homeópata mf

**homeopathic** [,hou·mi·ou·'pæθ·ɪk] adj homeopático, -a

**homeopathy** [,hou·mi·'ap·ə·θi] n homeopatía f

**homesick** ['houm·sɪk] adj nostálgico, -a; to feel ~ (for) tener morriña (de)

**home team** n equipo m local [or de casa]

**hometown** n ciudad f natal, pueblo m natal

**home truth** n to tell sb a few ~s decir a alguien unas cuantas verdades

**homeward** ['houm·wərd] I. adv de camino a casa II. adj (journey) de regreso

**homework** ['houm·wɜrk] n SCHOOL deberes mpl, tareas fpl Col

**homey** ['hou·mi] <-ier, -iest> adj 1. (cozy) casero, -a 2. sl (home boy or girl) paisano, -a

**homicide** ['ham·ə·saɪd] n 1. (crime) homicidio m 2. (criminal) homicida mf

**homogeneous** adj, **homogenous** [,hou·mou·'dʒi·ni·əs] adj homogéneo, -a

**homosexual** [,hou·mə·'sek·ʃu·əl] I. adj homosexual II. n homosexual mf

**Honduras** [han·'dʊr·əs] n Honduras f

**honest** ['an·ɪst] adj 1. (trustworthy) honesto, -a 2. (truthful) sincero, -a; to be ~ with oneself ser sincero consigo mismo; ~ (to God) inf como Dios manda 3. (fair: wages, day's work) justo, -a, equitativo, -a

**honestly** adv (truthfully) sinceramente; (with honesty) honradamente

**honesty** ['an·ɪ·sti] n 1. (trustworthiness) honestidad f 2. (sincerity) sinceridad f; in all ~ para ser sincero

**honey** ['hʌn·i] n 1. CULIN miel f 2. (term of endearment) cariño m

**honeybee** n abeja f

**honeycomb** n panal m

**honeydew (melon)** n melón m dulce

**honeymoon** n luna f de miel

**honeysuckle** n BOT madreselva f

**honk** [haŋk] I. vi 1. ZOOL graznar 2. AUTO tocar la bocina [or Col el pito] II. n 1. ZOOL graznido m 2. AUTO bocinazo m [or pitazo] m Col

**honor** ['an·ər] I. n 1. (respect) honor m; **in ~ of sb/sth** en honor de alguien/algo; **to be (in) ~ bound to...** estar moralmente obligado a... 2. LAW **Her/His/Your Honor** Su Señoría 3. ~s (distinction) honores mpl; **final ~s** honras f pl fúnebres; **to graduate with ~s** licenciarse [or graduarse] con matrícula de honor II. vt 1. (fulfill: promise, contract) cumplir (con) 2. (confer honor) honrar; **to be ~ed** sentirse honrado

**honorable** adj 1. (worthy of respect: person) honorable; (agreement) honroso, -a 2. (honest) honrado, -a

**honorary** ['an·ə·rer·i] adj 1. (conferred as an honor: title) honorario, -a 2. (without pay) no remunerado, -a

**honor roll** n UNIV, SCHOOL lista f de honor académica

**hood**¹ [hʊd] n 1. (covering for head) capucha f 2. AUTO capó m 3. (on machine) cubierta f

**hood**² [hʊd] n 1. sl (gangster) matón, -ona m, f 2. sl (urban neighborhood) barrio m

**hoof** [hʊf] <hooves or hoofs> n casco m, pezuña f

**hook** [hʊk] I. n 1. (for holding sth) gancho m; (for clothes) percha f; (fish) anzuelo m; **to leave the phone off the ~** dejar el teléfono descolgado 2. (in boxing) gancho m ▶ **by ~ or by crook** por las buenas o por las malas; **to fall for sth ~, line and sinker** tragárselo [or creérselo] todo; **to be off the ~** librarse II. vt 1. (fasten) enganchar 2. (fish) pescar 3. (capture attention) atraer, atrapar III. vi (clothes) abrochar se (con corchetes o ganchitos); (parts) engancharse

◆**hook up** I. vt 1. (hang: curtains) poner 2. (link up) enganchar; (connect) conectar; **to hook sb up with sb** sl (arrange date) reunirse con alguien II. vi (connect) conectarse

**hooked** [hʊkt] adj 1. (nose) ganchudo, -a 2. (fascinated) atrapado, -a 3. (addicted) enganchado, -a

**hooker** ['hʊk·ər] n sl (prostitute) prostituta f, puta f

**hooky** ['hʊk·i] n inf **to play ~** hacer novillos, capar clase Col

**hooligan** ['hu·lɪ·gən] n hooligan mf, vándalo m

**hoot** [hut] I. vi (owl) ulular II. n (of owl) ululato m; (factory whistle) sirena f; (of horn) bocinazo m; (of train) pitido m; **to give a ~ of laughter** soltar una carcajada; **to give a ~ of disgust** dar un grito de repugnancia; **to not give a ~ (about sth)** importar algo un pito a alguien ▶ **to be a (real) ~** inf ser muy cómico

**hop**¹ [hap] n BOT lúpulo m

**hop**² [hap] <-pp-> I. vi 1. (on 1 foot) saltar; fig **to ~ to it** ponerse manos a la obra 2. inf (be busy) **to be ~ping** (city streets, restaurant) tener mucho ajetreo [or movimiento] II. vt inf (bus, train) subir a III. n 1. (leap) salto m; (using only one leg) salto m a la pata coja, brinco m de cojito Méx 2. inf (informal dance) baile m ▶ **a ~, skip and a jump** inf un salto, estar a un paso

**hope** [hoʊp] I. n esperanza f; **to give up ~** perder la(s) esperanza(s) II. vi (wish) esperar; **to ~ for the best** esperar que la suerte lo acompañe a uno

**hopeful** ['hoʊp·fəl] I. adj 1. (person) esperanzado, -a; **to be ~** ser optimista 2. (promising) esperanzador(a) II. n candidato, -a m, f; **young ~s** jóvenes aspirantes mpfls

**hopefully** adv 1. (in a hopeful manner) con ilusión 2. (one hopes) ~! ¡ojalá!; ~ **we'll be in Sweden at 6.00 P.M.** si todo sale bien estaremos en Suecia a las 6 de la tarde

**hopeless** ['hoʊp·lɪs] adj (situation) desesperado, -a; (effort) imposible; **to be ~** inf (person) ser inútil; (service) ser un desastre; **to be ~ at sth** ser negado para algo

**hopelessly** adv 1. (without hope) sin esperanzas 2. (totally, completely) ~ **lost** totalmente perdido

**hopping mad** adj furioso, -a

**horizon** [hə·'raɪ·zən] n a. fig horizonte m

**horizontal** [ˌhɔr·ɪ·'zan·təl] I. adj horizontal II. n horizontal f

**hormone** ['hɔr·moʊn] n hormona f

**horn** [hɔrn] n **1.** ZOOL cuerno m **2.** MUS trompa f **3.** AUTO bocina f ▶ **to lock ~s** (**over sth**) tener un enfrentamiento (por algo); **to toot** [or **blow**] **one's own ~** echarse flores

**hornet** ['hɔr·nɪt] n avispón m

**horoscope** ['hɔr·ə·skoʊp] n horóscopo m

**horrendous** [hɔ·'ren·dəs] adj **1.** (crime) horrendo, -a **2.** (losses) terrible

**horrible** ['hɔr·ə·bəl] adj horrible

**horrid** ['hɔr·ɪd] adj (unpleasant) horrible

**horrific** [hɔ·'rɪf·ɪk] adj horroroso, -a

**horrify** ['hɔr·ə·faɪ] <-ie-> vt horrorizar

**horror** ['hɔr·ər] n horror m, espantosidad f AmC, Col, PRico; **~ film** película f de terror

**horror-stricken** adj, **horror-struck** adj horrorizado, -a

**horse** [hɔrs] n **1.** ZOOL caballo m; **to ride a ~** montar a caballo; **to eat like a ~** comer como una lima [or como un caballo] **2.** SPORTS potro m ▶ **to get sth straight from the ~'s mouth** saber algo de buena tinta; **don't look a gift ~ in the mouth** prov a caballo regalado, no le mires el dentado prov; **to flog a dead ~** perder el tiempo (intentando algo), arar en el mar; **to be on one's high ~** inf tener muchos humos; **hold your ~s!** inf ¡espera un minuto!, ¡no te aceleres!

**horseback** ['hɔrs·bæk] **I.** n **on ~** a caballo **II.** adj **~ riding** equitación f

**horse chestnut** n (tree) castaño m de Indias; (nut) castaña f de Indias

**horseplay** ['hɔrs·pleɪ] n jugueteo(s) m(pl)

**horsepower** inv n caballo m (de vapor)

**horseshoe** n herradura f

**horse van** n remolque m para transportar caballos

**hose** [hoʊz] n **1.** (in garden) manguera f **2.** (in motor) manguera f **3.** (pantyhose) medias f pl pantalón [or Méx de nylon] [or Col veladas]

**hospice** ['has·pɪs] n **1.** (hospital) residencia f para enfermos terminales **2.** (house of shelter) hospicio m

**hospitable** ['has·pɪ·ţə·bəl] adj hospitalario, -a

**hospital** ['has·pɪ·ţəl] n hospital m

**hospitality** [ˌhas·pɪ·'tæl·ə·ţi] n hospitalidad f

**hospitalize** ['has·pɪ·ţə·laɪz] vt hospitalizar

**host¹** [hoʊst] **I.** n **1.** (person who receives guests) anfitrión, -ona m, f **2.** (presenter) presentador(a) m(f) **3.** BIO huésped m **4.** COMPUT servidor m **II.** vt **1.** (party) dar; (event) ser la sede de **2.** TV, RADIO (program) presentar

**host²** [hoʊst] n multitud f

**hostage** ['has·tɪdʒ] n rehén mf; **to take/ hold sb ~** tomar/tener a alguien como rehén

**host country** <-ies> n país m anfitrión

**hostel** ['has·təl] n (inexpensive hotel) hostal m; **youth ~** albergue m juvenil

**hostess** ['hoʊ·stɪs] <-es> n **1.** (woman who receives guests) anfitriona f **2.** (presenter) presentadora f **3.** (in restaurant) mesonera f

**hostile** ['has·təl] adj hostil; **~ aircraft** avión enemigo

**hostility** [ha·'stɪl·ə·ţi] <-ies> n hostilidad f

**hot** [hat] **I.** adj **1.** (very warm: food, water) caliente; (day, weather) caluroso, -a; (climate) cálido, -a; **it's ~** hace calor **2.** (spicy) picante, bravo, -a AmL **3.** inf (skillful) hábil **4.** (dangerous) peligroso, -a **5.** sl (sexually attractive) **to be ~** estar bueno **6.** (exciting: music, party) animado, -a **7.** sl (stolen) robado, -a ▶ **to be all ~ and bothered** estar sulfurado **II.** n **to have the ~s for sb** estar interesado (sentimentalmente) en alguien

**hot air** n fig palabras f pl huecas; **to be full of ~** ser sólo palabrería

**hot dog** n CULIN perrito m caliente, pancho m Arg

**hotel** [hoʊ·'tel] n hotel m

**hotel bill** n factura f del hotel

**hotel staff** n personal m del hotel

**hotfoot** ['hat·fʊt] **I.** adv a toda prisa **II.** vt **to ~ it somewhere** inf ir volando a algún sitio

**hothead** ['hat·hed] n persona f alocada

**hothouse** ['hat·haʊs] **I.** n invernadero f m **II.** adj de invernadero

**hotly** adv apasionadamente

**hot potato** <-oes> n fig patata f caliente

**hot seat** n (*difficult position*) **to be in the ~** estar en la línea de fuego

**hotshot** n sl hacha f

**hot spot** n inf 1. (*popular place*) lugar m concurrido 2. (*nightclub*) club m nocturno

**hot stuff** n 1. (*good*) **to be ~ at sth** ser un as en algo 2. (*sexy*) **to be ~** estar bueno

**hot-tempered** adj irascible

**hot-water bottle** n bolsa f de agua caliente

**hound** [haʊnd] I. n perro m de caza II. vt perseguir

**hour** [aʊr] n 1. (*60 minutes*) hora f; **to be paid by the ~** cobrar por horas 2. **ten minutes to the ~** diez minutos en punto; **till all ~s** hasta [or las tantas] muy tarde; **after ~s** fuera del horario establecido 3. (*time for an activity*) **lunch ~** hora de comer [or almorzar]; **opening ~s** horario m (comercial) 4. (*period of time*) momento m; **at any ~** en cualquier momento; **to keep irregular/regular ~s** llevar un horario variable/regular; **to work long ~s** trabajar hasta muy tarde; **~ after ~** hora tras hora

**hour hand** n manecilla f

**hourly** adv (*every hour*) cada hora; (*pay*) por horas

**house¹** [haʊs] n 1. (*inhabitation*) casa f 2. (*family*) familia f 3. (*business*) empresa f; **it's on the ~** invita la casa 4. (*legislative body*) cámara f 5. (*audience*) público m; **full ~** (teatro m) lleno; **to bring the ~ down** inf ser todo un éxito

**house²** [haʊz] vt 1. (*give place to live*) alojar 2. (*contain*) albergar

**houseboat** n casa f flotante

**housebroken** adj adiestrado, -a

**household** ['haʊs·hoʊld] I. n hogar m II. adj doméstico, -a

**householder** n (*owner*) propietario, -a m, f de una casa; (*head*) cabeza m de familia

**house-hunt** vi inf buscar casa

**housekeeper** ['haʊs·ki·pər] n ama f de llaves

**housekeeping** n organización f doméstica

**houseplant** n planta f de interior

**housewife** <-wives> n ama f de casa

**housework** n tareas f pl del hogar, el oficio m

**housing** ['haʊ·zɪŋ] n (*for living*) vivienda f

**housing conditions** npl condiciones f pl de habitabilidad

**housing development** n urbanización f, condominio m

**housing project** n vivienda f de interés social

**hover** ['hʌv·ər] vi 1. (*stay in air*) cernerse 2. (*wait near*) rondar 3. (*be in an uncertain state*) estar vacilante

**hovercraft** ['hʌv·ər·kræft] <-(s)> n aerodeslizador m

**how** [haʊ] I. adv 1. (*in this way*) como; (*in which way?*) cómo 2. (*in what condition?*) **~ are you?** ¿qué tal?; **~ do you do?** encantado de conocerle 3. (*for what reason?*) **~ come...?** inf ¿cómo es que...? 4. (*suggestion*) **~ about...?** ¿qué tal si... ?; **~ about that!** ¡mira por dónde! 5. (*intensifier*) **~ pretty she looked!** ¡qué guapa estaba!; **and ~!** ¡ni que lo digas!; **well, ~ about that!** (*expressing surprise, approval*) ¡caramba! II. n modo m; **to know the ~(s) and why(s) of sth** saber el cómo y el porqué de algo

**however** [haʊ·ev·ər] I. adv 1. (*no matter how*) por más que +subj; **~ hard she tries...** por mucho que lo intente... 2. (*in whichever way*) como; **do it ~ you like** hazlo como quieras II. conj (*nevertheless*) sin embargo

**howl** [haʊl] I. vi 1. (*person, animal*) aullar; (*wind*) silbar; **to ~ in** [or with] **pain** dar alaridos de dolor 2. (*cry*) chillar; (*child*) berrear 3. sl (*laugh*) morirse de risa II. n 1. (*person, animal*) aullido m 2. (*cry*) chillido m; (*of child*) berrido m

◆**howl down** vt hacer callar a gritos

**howler** ['haʊ·lər] n sl error m garrafal

**howling** adj aullador(a)

**hp** [ˌeɪtʃ·'pi] abbr of **horsepower** CV

**HP** [ˌeɪtʃ·'pi] abbr of **high pressure** alta presión

**HTML** [ˌeɪtʃ·ti·em·'el] COMPUT abbr of **Hypertext Markup Language** HTML

**hub** [hʌb] n 1. (*of wheel*) cubo m 2. fig

(center) centro m

**hubcap** ['hʌb·kæp] n tapacubos m inv, copa m del carro Col

**huckleberry** ['hʌk·əl·ber·i] <-ies> n BOT arándano m

**huddle** ['hʌd·əl] I. vi apiñarse II. n (close group) piña f

♦ **huddle down** vi acurrucarse

♦ **huddle together** vi amontonarse

♦ **huddle up** vi acurrucarse

**huff** [hʌf] I. vi to ~ and puff (breathe loudly) jadear; inf (complain) quejarse II. n inf enfado m; to go off in a ~ enfadarse; to get into a ~ irse ofendido

**huffy** ['hʌf·i] <-ier, -iest> adj 1. (offended) ofendido, -a 2. (touchy) susceptible

**hug** [hʌg] I. <-gg-> vt 1. (embrace) abrazar 2. fig (idea, belief) aferrarse a II. n abrazo m

**huge** [hjudʒ] adj (extremely big) enorme; (impressive) imponente

**hugely** adv enormemente

**hum** [hʌm] <-mm-> I. vi 1. (bee) zumbar 2. (sing) tararear 3. (be full of activity) bullir de animación II. vt tararear III. n zumbido m; (of traffic) murmullo m

**human** ['hju·mən] I. n humano m II. adj humano, -a

**human being** n ser m humano

**humane** [hju·'meɪn] adj humanitario, -a

**humanitarian** [hju·ˌmæn·ə·'ter·i·ən] I. n humanitario, -a m, f II. adj humanitario, -a; ~ **aid** ayuda humanitaria

**humanity** [hju·'mæn·ə·ţi] n humanidad f

**humanly** adv humanamente

**human resources** npl recursos m pl humanos

**human rights** npl derechos m pl humanos

**humble** ['hʌm·bəl] I. adj 1. (meek) humilde; **in my ~ opinion,...** en mi modesta opinión,... 2. (lowly: cottage, furnishings, abode) modesto, -a II. vt humillar

**humid** ['hju·mɪd] adj húmedo, -a

**humidifier** [hju·'mɪd·ɪ·faɪ·ər] n humidificador m

**humidity** [hju·'mɪd·ə·ţi] n humedad f

**humiliate** [hju·'mɪl·i·eɪt] vt (shame) aver-

gonzar, achunchar AmC; (humble) humillar

**humiliating** adj humillante

**humiliation** [hju·ˌmɪl·i·'eɪ·ʃən] n humillación f

**humility** [hju·'mɪl·ə·ţi] n humildad f

**hummingbird** ['hʌm·ɪŋ·bɜrd] n colibrí m, chupaflor m AmC

**humor** ['hju·mər] n 1. (capacity for amusement) humor m; **sense of ~** sentido m del humor 2. form (mood) talante m

**humorous** ['hju·mər·əs] adj (speech) humorístico, -a; (situation) divertido, -a

**hump** [hʌmp] I. n joroba f, petaca f AmC
► **to be over the ~** haber pasado lo más difícil 2. vt vulg (have sex) follar, coger AmL, pichar Col

**humpback** ['hʌmp·bæk] n joroba f

**humpbacked** ['hʌmp·bækt] adj jorobado, -a

**hunch** [hʌntʃ] I. <-es> n presentimiento m; **to have a ~ that...** tener la corazonada de que... II. vi encorvarse III. vt curvar

**hunchback** ['hʌntʃ·bæk] n (person) jorobado, -a m, f

**hundred** ['hʌn·drəd] <-(s)> I. n cien m; **~s of times** cientos de veces II. adj ciento; (before a noun) cien

**hundredth** ['hʌn·drədθ] I. n centésimo m II. adj centésimo, -a

**hung** [hʌŋ] I. pt, pp of **hang** II. adj colgado, -a; ~ **jury** LAW jurado que se disuelve porque no se llega a ningún acuerdo

**Hungarian** [hʌŋ·'ger·i·ən] I. adj húngaro, -a II. n 1. (person) húngaro, -a m, f 2. LING húngaro m

**Hungary** ['hʌŋ·gə·ri] n Hungría f

**hunger** ['hʌŋ·gər] I. n 1. hambre f, filo m AmC 2. fig (desire) ansia f II. vi fig to ~ **after** [or for] ansiar

**hungry** ['hʌŋ·gri] <-ier, -iest> adj 1. (desiring food) hambriento, -a; **to be/go ~** tener/pasar hambre 2. fig (wanting badly) ansioso, -a; **to be ~ for sth** estar ávido de algo

**hunk** [hʌŋk] n 1. (piece) trozo m 2. s. (man) cachas m inv

**hunky dory** [ˌhʌŋ·ki·'dɔr·i] adj sl guay,

**hunt** [hʌnt] **I.** vt **1.** (chase to kill) cazar **2.** (search for) buscar **II.** vi **1.** (chase to kill) cazar; **to go ~ing** ir de caza **2.** (search) to ~ **for** buscar **III.** n **1.** (chase) cacería f **2.** (search) búsqueda f

**hunter** n (person) cazador(a) m(f)

**hunting** n caza f

**hunting season** n temporada f de caza

**hurdle** ['hɜr·dəl] **I.** n **1.** a. SPORTS (fence) valla f, obstáculo m **2.** (difficulty) obstáculo m **II.** vi SPORTS saltar vallas [or obstáculos] **III.** vt SPORTS saltar

**hurdler** n SPORTS vallista mf

**hurdle race** n SPORTS carrera [or obstáculos] de vallas f

**hurl** [hɜrl] vt (throw) lanzar

**hurrah** [hə·'ra] interj, **hurray** [hə·'reɪ] interj hurra

**hurricane** ['hɜr·ɪ·keɪn] n huracán m

**hurried** ['hɜr·id] adj apresurado, -a, apurado, -a AmL

**hurry** ['hɜr·i] <-ie-> **I.** vi darse prisa, apurarse AmL **II.** vt (rush) meter prisas, apurar AmL **III.** n prisa f, apuro m AmL; **to leave in a ~** irse disparado; **to do sth in a ~** hacer algo de prisa; **what's (all) the ~?** ¿a qué viene tanta prisa?

◆**hurry along I.** vi apresurarse **II.** vt always sep meter prisas

◆**hurry away, hurry off I.** vi marcharse de prisa **II.** vt (person) hacer marchar de prisa; (object) hacer llevar de prisa

◆**hurry on** vi continuar rápidamente

◆**hurry up I.** vi darse prisa **II.** vt meter prisa

**hurt** [hɜrt] **I.** <hurt, hurt> vi (physically, emotionally) doler **II.** vt **1.** (wound) herir **2.** (cause pain) lastimar; **it ~s me** me duele **3.** (offend) ofender **4.** (damage) dañar **III.** adj (in pain, injured) dañado, -a; (grieved, distressed) dolido, -a **IV.** n **1.** (pain) dolor m **2.** (offence) ofensa f **3.** (damage) daño m

**hurtful** ['hɜrt·fəl] adj perjudicial

**hurtle** ['hɜr·təl] **I.** vi lanzarse **II.** vt lanzar

**husband** ['hʌz·bənd] **I.** n marido m, esposo m **II.** vt economizar

**hush** [hʌʃ] **I.** n silencio m **II.** interj ~!

¡chitón! **III.** vi callarse **IV.** vt (make silent) hacer callar; (soothe) acallar

◆**hush up** vt encubrir

**hush-hush** adj inf secreto, -a

**hush money** n inf unto m (que se utiliza para comprar el silencio de alguien)

**husky¹** ['hʌs·ki] <-ier, -iest> adj **1.** (low, rough: voice) ronco, -a **2.** (big, strong) fornido, -a; euph (well-built) robusto, -a

**husky²** ['hʌs·ki] <-ies> n perro m esquimal

**hustle** ['hʌs·əl] **I.** vt **1.** (hurry) dar prisa a **2.** (achieve) hacerse con **II.** vi (practice prostitution) prostituirse **III.** n ajetreo m

**hustler** ['hʌs·lər] n **1.** (persuader) camelador(a) m(f) **2.** (prostitute) puto, -a m, f

**hustling** ['hʌs·lɪŋ] n ajetreo m

**hut** [hʌt] n cabaña f

**hutch** [hʌtʃ] <-es> n **1.** (box for animals) jaula f **2.** (cupboard) aparador m

**hybrid** ['haɪ·brɪd] n híbrido, -a m, f

**hydrant** ['haɪ·drənt] n boca f de riego, hidrante m

**hydrocarbon** [,haɪ·droʊ·'kar·bən] **I.** n hidrocarburo m **II.** adj de hidrocarburo

**hydroelectric** [,haɪ·droʊ·ɪ·'lek·trɪk] adj hidroeléctrico, -a

**hydrofoil** ['haɪ·drə·fɔɪl] n hidroala m

**hydrogen** ['haɪ·drə·dʒən] n hidrógeno m

**hydrogen bomb** n bomba f de hidrógeno

**hydroponics** [,haɪ·drə·'pan·ɪks] n + sing vb hidroponía f

**hyena** [haɪ·'i·nə] n hiena f

**hygiene** ['haɪ·dʒin] n higiene f, salubridad f AmL

**hygienic** [,haɪ·dʒi·'en·ɪk] adj higiénico, -a

**hymn** [hɪm] n himno m

**hymnal** ['hɪm·nəl] n, **hymnbook** n himnario m

**hype** [haɪp] **I.** n COM bombo publicitario **II.** vt dar bombo publicitario a

**hypermarket** ['haɪ·pər·mar·kɪt] n hipermercado m

**hypertext** [,haɪ·pər·'tekst] n COMPUT hipertexto m

**hyphen** ['haɪ·fən] n TYPO guión m

**hyphenate** ['haɪ·fə·neɪt] vt separar con guiones

**hypnosis** [hɪp·ˈnoʊ·sɪs] *n* hipnosis *f inv;*
**to be under ~** estar hipnotizado

**hypnotherapy** [ˌhɪp·noʊ·ˈθer·ə·pi] *n* hip-
noterapia *f*

**hypnotist** [ˈhɪp·nə·tɪst] *n* hipnotiza-
dor(a) *m(f)*

**hypnotize** [ˈhɪp·nə·taɪz] *vt* hipnotizar

**hypochondriac** [ˌhaɪ·pə·ˈkan·dri·æk]
I. *n* hipocondríaco, -a *m, f* II. *adj* hipocondríaco, -a

**hypocrite** [ˈhɪp·ə·krɪt] *n* hipócrita *mf*

**hypotenuse** [ˌhaɪ·ˈpat·ə·nus] *n* MATH hipotenusa *f*

**hypothermia** [ˌhaɪ·poʊ·ˈθɜr·mi·ə] *n* hipotermia *f*

**hypothetical** [ˌhaɪ·pə·ˈθet·ɪ·kəl] *adj* hipotético, -a

**hysterectomy** [ˌhɪs·tə·ˈrek·tə·mi] *n* MED
histerectomía *f*

**hysteric** [hɪ·ˈster·ɪk] I. *adj* histérico, -a
II. *n* histérico, -a *m, f*

**hysterical** *adj* histérico, -a

# I

**I, i** [aɪ] *n* I, i *f;* **~ as in India** I de Italia

**I** [aɪ] *pron pers* (*1st person sing*) yo; **~'m
coming** ya voy; **~'ll do it** (yo) lo haré;
**am ~ late?** ¿llego tarde?; **she and ~**
ella y yo; **it was ~ who did that** fui yo
quien lo hizo

**IAEA** *n abbr of* **International Atomic
Energy Agency** OIEA *f*

**ice** [aɪs] I. *n* (*frozen water*) hielo *m*
▶ **to break the ~** *inf* romper el hielo
II. *vt* 1. (*chill a drink*) enfriar con hielo
2. (*put icing on*) escarchar

**Ice Age** *n* era *f* glacial

**iceberg** *n* iceberg *m;* **the tip of the ~** *fig*
la punta del iceberg

**icebox** <-es> *n* 1. (*freezer*) congelador *m* 2. (*fridge*) nevera *f*, refrigeradora *f AmL*

**ice cap** *n* casquete *m* de hielo

**ice-cold** *adj* helado, -a

**ice cream** *n* helado *m*, nieve *f AmC*

**ice cube** [ˈaɪs·kjub] *n* cubito *m* de hielo

**iced** [aɪst] *adj* 1. (*drink*) con hielo
2. (*covered with icing*) escarchado, -a

**ice hockey** *n* hockey *m* sobre hielo

**ice pack** *n* bolsa *f* de hielo

**ice rink** *n* pista *f* de patinaje

**ice-skate** *vi* patinar sobre hielo

**icicle** [ˈaɪ·sɪ·kəl] *n* carámbano *m*

**icing** [ˈaɪ·sɪŋ] *n* glaseado *m*

**icon** [ˈaɪ·kan] *n* icono *m*

**ICU** [ˌaɪ·si·ˈju] *n abbr of* **intensive care
unit** UCI *f*

**icy** [ˈaɪ·si] <-ier, -iest> *adj* 1. (*with ice*)
helado, -a 2. (*unfriendly*) frío, -a

**ID¹** [aɪ·ˈdi] I. *n abbr of* **identification**
identificación *f* II. *vt inf abbr of* **identify** identificar

**ID²** [aɪ·ˈdi] *n abbr of* **Idaho** Idaho *m*

**I'd** [aɪd] 1. = **I would** *see* **would** 2. =
**I had** *see* **have**

**ID card** [aɪ·ˈdi·ˌkard] *n see* **identity card**
carné *m* de identidad

**idea** [aɪ·ˈdi·ə] *n* 1. (*opinion*) idea *f*
2. (*notion*) noción *f*

**ideal** [aɪ·ˈdi·əl] I. *adj* ideal II. *n* ideal *m*

**identical** [aɪ·ˈden·tɪ·kəl] *adj* idéntico, -a,
individual *CSur*

**identifiable** [aɪ·ˌden·tə·ˈfaɪ·ə·bəl] *adj*
identificable

**identification** [aɪ·ˌden·tə·fɪ·ˈkeɪ·ʃən] *n*
identificación *f*

**identification papers** *npl* documentación *f*

**identifier** [aɪ·ˈden·tə·faɪ·ər] *n* COMPUT
identificador *m*

**identify** [aɪ·ˈden·tə·faɪ] <-ie-> *vt* identificar

**identity** [aɪ·ˈden·tə·ti] <-ies> *n* identidad *f*

**identity card** *n* carné *m* de identidad

**ideological** [ˌaɪ·di·ə·ˈlad͡ʒ·ɪ·kəl] *adj* ideológico, -a

**ideology** [ˌaɪ·di·ˈal·ə·d͡ʒi] <-ies> *n* ideología *f*

**idiom** [ˈɪd·i·əm] *n* LING 1. (*phrase*) modismo *m* 2. (*style of expression*) lenguaje *m*

**idiomatic** [ˌɪd·i·ə·ˈmæt·ɪk] *adj* idiomá-
tico, -a

**idiot** [ˈɪd·i·ət] *n* idiota *mf*

**idiotic** [ˌɪd·i·ˈat·ɪk] *adj* tonto, -a

**idle** [ˈaɪ·dəl] I. *adj* 1. (*lazy*) holgazán, -ana 2. (*not busy*) desocupado
-a; (*machine*) parado, -a, desocupado

-a **3.** (*frivolous: pleasures*) frívolo, -a **4.** (*unfounded*) vano, -a; (*gossip*) insustancial **5.** (*ineffective: threat*) inútil **6.** FIN de paro **II.** n AUTO ralentí m **III.** vi (*engine*) marchar al ralentí, funcionar en vacío; (*person*) haraganear

**idol** ['aɪ·dəl] n ídolo m

**idolatry** [aɪ·'dal·ə·tri] n idolatría f

**idolize** ['aɪ·də·laɪz] vt idolatrar

**if** [ɪf] **I.** conj **1.** (*supposing that*) si; ~ **it snows** si nieva; ~ **not** si no; **as** ~ **it were true** como si fuera verdad; ~ **they exist at all** si es que en realidad existen; ~ **A is right, then B is wrong** si A es verdadero, entonces B es falso; **I'll stay, ~ only for a day** me quedaré, aunque sea sólo un día **2.** (*every time that*) ~ **he needs me, I'll help him** si me necesita, le ayudaré **3.** (*whether*) **I wonder ~ he'll come** me pregunto si vendrá **II.** n pero m; **no ~s, ands, or buts!** ¡no hay peros que valgan!

**iffy** ['ɪf·i] <-ier, -iest> adj inf dudoso, -a; (*person*) sospechoso, -a

**igloo** ['ɪg·lu] n iglú m

**ignite** [ɪg·'naɪt] **I.** vi incendiarse **II.** vt form incendiar

**ignition** [ɪg·'nɪʃ·ən] n **1.** AUTO encendido m **2.** form (*causing to burn*) ignición f

**ignition key** n llave f de contacto, suiche m Méx

**ignition switch** <-es> n interruptor m de encendido

**ignorance** ['ɪg·nər·əns] n ignorancia f
► ~ **is** <u>bliss</u> ojos que no ven, corazón que no siente

**ignorant** ['ɪg·nər·ənt] adj ignorante; **to be ~ about sth** desconocer algo

**ignore** [ɪg·'nɔr] vt no hacer caso de, ignorar

**Il.** n, Ill. n abbr of **Illinois** Illinois m

**ill** [ɪl] **I.** adj **1.** (*sick*) enfermo, -a **2.** (*bad*) malo, -a; (*harmful*) nocivo, -a; (*unfavorable*) perjudicial; **an ~ omen** un mal presagio **II.** adv form (*badly*) mal; **to speak ~ of sb** hablar mal de alguien

**I'll** [aɪl] = **I will** see **will**

**ill-advised** [ɪl·əd·'vaɪzd] adj imprudente

**illegal** [ɪ·'li·gəl] adj ilegal

**illegal immigrant** n inmigrante mf ilegal

**illegible** [ɪ·'ledʒ·ə·bəl] adj ilegible

**illegitimate** [ɪl·ɪ·'dʒɪt·ə·mət] adj ilegítimo, -a

**ill-informed** ['ɪl·ɪn·ˌfɔrmd] adj (*wrongly informed*) mal informado, -a

**illiterate** [ɪ·'lɪt·ər·ət] **I.** adj analfabeto, -a; pej, fig inculto, -a **II.** n analfabeto, -a m, f

**ill-mannered** [ˌɪl·'mæn·ərd] adj mal educado, -a

**illness** ['ɪl·nɪs] <-es> n enfermedad f

**illogical** [ɪ·'ladʒ·ɪ·kəl] adj ilógico, -a

**ill-tempered** adj de mal genio

**ill-timed** adj inoportuno, -a

**illuminate** [ɪ·'lu·mə·neɪt] vt iluminar; fig aclarar

**illuminating** [ɪ·'lu·mɪ·neɪ·ʈɪŋ] adj form aclaratorio, -a

**illumination** [ɪ·ˌlu·mɪ·'neɪ·ʃən] n a. ART iluminación f

**illusion** [ɪ·'lu·ʒən] n (*misleading appearance*) apariencia f; (*false impression*) ilusión f

**illustrate** ['ɪl·ə·streɪt] vt ilustrar; fig ejemplificar

**illustration** [ˌɪl·ə·'streɪ·ʃən] n **1.** (*drawing*) ilustración f **2.** (*example*) ejemplo m

**illustrator** ['ɪl·ə·streɪ·ˌʈər] n ilustrador(a) m(f)

**illustrious** [ɪ·'lʌs·tri·əs] adj form ilustre

**I'm** [aɪm] = **I am** see **am**

**image** ['ɪm·ɪdʒ] n **1.** (*likeness*) imagen f **2.** (*picture*) retrato m **3.** (*reputation*) reputación f

**imagery** ['ɪm·ɪdʒ·ri] n LIT imágenes fpl

**imaginable** [ɪ·'mædʒ·ə·nə·bəl] adj imaginable

**imaginary** [ɪ·'mædʒ·ə·ner·i] adj imaginario, -a

**imagination** [ɪ·ˌmædʒ·ə·'neɪ·ʃən] n imaginación f; (*inventiveness*) inventiva f

**imaginative** [ɪ·'mædʒ·ə·nə·ʈɪv] adj imaginativo, -a

**imagine** [ɪ·'mædʒ·ɪn] vt **1.** (*form mental image*) imaginar **2.** (*suppose*) figurarse; ~ **that!** ¡figúratelo!

**imaging** n COMPUT tratamiento m de imágenes

**imbalance** [ˌɪm·'bæl·əns] n desequilibrio m

**imbecile** ['ɪm·bə·sɪl] n imbécil mf

**IMF** [aɪ·em·'ef] n abbr of **International Monetary Fund** FMI m

**imitate** ['ɪm·ɪ·teɪt] vt imitar; (copy) copiar

**imitation** [ˌɪm·ɪ·'teɪ·ʃən] I. n 1. (mimicry) imitación f; **in ~ of sb/sth** a imitación de alguien/algo 2. (copy) reproducción f II. adj de imitación

**immaculate** [ɪ·'mæk·ju·lət] adj 1. (spotless, neat) inmaculado, -a 2. (flawless) impecable

**immature** [ˌɪm·ə·'tʃʊr] adj 1. (young) inmaduro, -a; (people, animals) joven 2. (childish: behavior) infantil

**immaturity** [ˌɪm·ə·'tʃʊr·ə·ti] n inmadurez f

**immeasurable** [ɪ·'meʒ·ər·ə·bəl] adj 1. (boundless) inconmensurable 2. (effect) incalculable

**immediacy** [ɪ·'mi·di·ə·si] n inmediatez f; (nearness) proximidad f

**immediate** [ɪ·'mi·di·ɪt] adj inmediato, -a; **the ~ family** los familiares directos; **in the ~ area** en las inmediaciones; **in the ~ future** en un futuro inmediato

**immediately** adv (time) inmediatamente; **~ after...** justo después de...

**immense** [ɪ·'mens] adj inmenso, -a; (importance) extremo, -a

**immerse** [ɪ·'mɜrs] vt sumergir; **to be ~d in sth** fig estar absorto en algo

**immersion heater** n calentador m de inmersión

**immigrant** ['ɪm·ɪ·grənt] n inmigrante mf

**immigrate** ['ɪm·ɪ·greɪt] vi inmigrar

**immigration** [ˌɪm·ɪ·'greɪ·ʃən] n inmigración f

**imminent** ['ɪm·ɪ·nənt] adj inminente

**immobilize** [ɪ·'moʊ·bə·laɪz] vt inmovilizar

**immodest** [ɪ·'mad·ɪst] adj 1. (conceited) creído, -a 2. (slightly indecent) descarado, -a

**immoral** [ɪ·'mɔr·əl] adj inmoral

**immortal** [ɪ·'mɔr·təl] I. adj 1. (undying) inmortal 2. (remembered forever) imperecedero, -a II. n inmortal mf

**immortality** [ˌɪ·mɔr·'tæl·ə·ti] n inmortalidad f

**immovable** [ɪ·'mu·və·bəl] adj 1. (not moveable) inamovible 2. (not changeable) inalterable

**immune** [ɪ·'mjun] adj 1. MED inmune 2. POL, LAW exento, -a

**immune system** n sistema m inmunológico

**immunity** [ɪ·'mju·nə·ti] n 1. MED inmunidad f 2. **diplomatic ~** inmunidad f diplomática

**immunize** ['ɪm·jə·naɪz] vt inmunizar

**impact** ['ɪm·pækt] I. n 1. (striking contact) choque m; **on ~** por impacto 2. (effect) impacto m II. vt incidir en III. vi **to ~ on sb/sth** impactar en alguien/algo

**impaired** adj (speech, vision, hearing) dañado, -a; (health) perjudicado, -a; **to be visually ~** estar impedido visualmente

**impartial** [ɪm·'par·ʃəl] adj imparcial

**impartiality** [ˌɪm·ˌpar·ʃɪ·'æl·ə·ti] n imparcialidad f

**impassable** [ɪm·'pæs·ə·bəl] adj intransitable; fig infranqueable

**impasse** ['ɪm·pæs] n a. fig callejón m sin salida; **to have reached an ~** haber llegado a un punto muerto [or a un atolladero]

**impassioned** [ɪm·'pæʃ·ənd] adj form apasionado, -a

**impassive** [ɪm·'pæs·ɪv] adj impasible

**impatience** [ɪm·'peɪ·ʃəns] n impaciencia f

**impatient** [ɪm·'peɪ·ʃənt] adj impaciente **to be ~ to do sth** estar impaciente por hacer algo

**impeach** [ɪm·'pitʃ] vt acusar, (someter a un proceso de incapacitación presidencial)

**impeachment** [ɪm·'pitʃ·mənt] n acusación f (proceso de incapacitación presidencial)

**impede** [ɪm·'pid] vt impedir

**imperative** [ɪm·'per·ə·tɪv] I. adj 1. (urgently essential) imprescindible 2. LING imperativo, -a II. n a. LING imperativo m

**imperceptible** [ˌɪm·pər·'sep·tə·bəl] adj imperceptible

**imperfect** [ɪm·'pɜr·fɪkt] I. adj imperfecto, -a II. n LING (pretérito m) imperfecto

**imperfection** [ˌɪm·pər·ˈfek·ʃən] n imperfección f

**imperial** [ɪm·ˈpɪr·i·əl] adj imperial

**imperialism** [ɪm·ˈpɪr·i·ə·lɪz·əm] n imperialismo m

**impersonal** [ˌɪm·ˈpɜr·sə·nəl] adj a. LING impersonal

**impersonate** [ɪm·ˈpɜr·sə·neɪt] vt hacerse pasar por; (imitate) imitar

**impertinent** [ɪm·ˈpɜr·tə·nənt] adj impertinente

**impetuous** [ɪm·ˈpetʃ·u·əs] adj impetuoso, -a

**impetus** [ˈɪm·pɪ·təs] n 1. (push) impulso m 2. (driving force) ímpetu m

**implacable** [ɪm·ˈplæk·ə·bəl] adj form implacable

**implant** [ɪm·ˈplænt] I. n implante m II. vt (add surgically) implantar

**implausible** [ɪm·ˈplɔ·zə·bəl] adj inverosímil

**implement** [ˈɪm·plɪ·mənt] I. n (tool) instrumento m; (small tool) utensilio m II. vt implementar

**implicate** [ˈɪm·plɪ·keɪt] vt 1. (show sb's involvement) implicar 2. (involve) involucrar

**implication** [ˌɪm·plɪ·ˈkeɪ·ʃən] n 1. (hinting at) insinuación f 2. (showing of involvement) implicación f

**implicit** [ɪm·ˈplɪs·ɪt] adj (suggested) implícito, -a

**implore** [ɪm·ˈplɔr] vt implorar; **to ~ sb to do sth** suplicar a alguien que haga algo

**imploring** [ɪm·ˈplɔr·ɪŋ] adj implorante; (voice) suplicante

**imply** [ɪm·ˈplaɪ] <-ie-> vt (suggest) sugerir

**impolite** [ˌɪm·pə·ˈlaɪt] adj descortés; (rude) grosero, -a

**impoliteness** n descortesía f

**import** I. [ɪm·ˈpɔrt] vt ECON, COMPUT importar II. [ˈɪm·pɔrt] n (product) producto m de importación

**importance** [ɪm·ˈpɔr·təns] n importancia f

**important** [ɪm·ˈpɔr·tənt] adj importante

**importantly** adv significativamente

**importation** [ˌɪm·pɔr·ˈteɪ·ʃən] n ECON importación f

**import duty** <-ies> n derecho m de aduana

**impose** [ɪm·ˈpouz] I. vt 1. (implement) imponer 2. (force on) obligar II. vi aprovecharse; **I don't want to ~** no quiero molestar

**imposing** [ɪm·ˈpou·zɪŋ] adj imponente

**imposition** [ˌɪm·pə·ˈzɪʃ·ən] n 1. (forcing, application) imposición f 2. (inconvenience) molestia f

**impossibility** [ɪm·ˌpas·ə·ˈbɪl·ə·t̬i] n imposibilidad f

**impossible** [ɪm·ˈpas·ə·bəl] I. adj (not possible) imposible II. n the ~ lo imposible

**imposter** n, **impostor** [ɪm·ˈpas·tər] n impostor(a) m(f)

**impotence** [ˈɪm·pə·təns] n impotencia f

**impotent** [ˈɪm·pə·tənt] adj impotente

**impound** [ɪm·ˈpaund] vt incautar

**impoverish** [ɪm·ˈpav·ər·ɪʃ] vt (make poor) empobrecer

**impracticable** [ɪm·ˈpræk·tɪ·kə·bəl] adj impracticable

**impractical** [ɪm·ˈpræk·tɪ·kəl] adj poco práctico, -a

**imprecise** [ˌɪm·prɪ·ˈsaɪs] adj impreciso, -a

**impregnable** [ɪm·ˈpreg·nə·bəl] adj (unable to be taken) inexpugnable

**impregnate** [ɪm·ˈpreg·neɪt] vt 1. (inseminate) fecundar 2. (saturate) impregnar

**impress** [ɪm·ˈpres] I. vt 1. (affect) presionar 2. (stamp) estampar; **to ~ sth on** [or **upon**] **sb** (make realize) inculcar algo a alguien II. vi impresionar

**impression** [ɪm·ˈpreʃ·ən] n 1. (general opinion) impresión f; **to be of** [or **under**] **the ~ that...** tener la impresión de que... 2. (feeling) sensación f; **to make an ~ on sb** causar impresión a alguien 3. (imprint) impresión f; fig huella f

**impressionable** [ɪm·ˈpreʃ·ə·nə·bəl] adj impresionable

**impressionism** [ɪm·ˈpreʃ·ə·nɪz·əm] n impresionismo m

**impressive** [ɪm·ˈpres·ɪv] adj impresionante

**imprint** I. [ɪm·ˈprɪnt] vt (stamp) estampar; (paper) imprimir II. [ˈɪm·prɪnt] n 1. (mark) marca f; fig huella f 2. TYPO pie m de imprenta imprison [ɪm·ˈprɪz·ən] vt encarcelar

imprisonment [ɪm·ˈprɪz·ən·mənt] n encarcelamiento m; life ~ cadena f perpetua

improbability [ˌɪm·prab·ə·ˈbɪl·ə·t̬i] n improbabilidad f

improbable [ɪm·ˈprab·ə·bəl] adj improbable

improper [ɪm·ˈprap·ər] adj 1. (incorrect) incorrecto, -a; (showing bad judgment) injusto, -a 2. (not socially decent) indecoroso, -a

improve [ɪm·ˈpruv] vt, vi mejorar

improvement [ɪm·ˈpruv·mənt] n 1. (betterment) mejora f; (progress) progreso m 2. (of illness) mejoría f

improvisation [ɪm·ˌprav·ɪ·ˈzeɪ·ʃən] n improvisación f

improvise [ˈɪm·prə·vaɪz] vi, vt improvisar

imprudent [ɪm·ˈpru·dənt] adj form imprudente

impudence [ˈɪm·pjʊ·dəns] n descaro m

impudent [ˈɪm·pjʊ·dənt] adj impertinente

impulse [ˈɪm·pʌls] n a. ELEC, PHYS, BIO impulso m; to do sth on (an) ~ hacer algo por impulso

impulsive [ɪm·ˈpʌl·sɪv] adj impulsivo, -a

impunity [ɪm·ˈpju·nə·t̬i] n impunidad f

impure [ɪm·ˈpjʊr] adj impuro, -a

impurity [ɪm·ˈpjʊr·ə·t̬i] <-ies> n impureza f

in [ɪn] I. prep 1. (inside, into) en, dentro de; to be ~ bed estar en la cama; there is sth ~ the drawer hay algo dentro del cajón; ~ town/jail en la ciudad/cárcel; ~ Canada/Mexico en Canadá/México 2. (within) ~ sb's face/the picture en el rostro de alguien/la fotografía; ~ the snow/sun en la nieve/el sol; the best ~ New England/town lo mejor de Nueva Inglaterra/de la ciudad 3. (position of) ~ the beginning/end al principio/final; right ~ the middle justo en medio 4. (during) ~ the twenties en los (años) veinte; to be ~ one's thirties estar en los treinta; ~ May/the spring en mayo/primavera; ~ the afternoon por la tarde 5. (at later time) ~ a week/three hours dentro de una semana/tres horas; ~ (the) future en el futuro 6. (in less than) to do sth ~ 4 hours hacer algo en 4 horas 7. (for) he hasn't done that ~ years/a week no ha hecho eso desde hace años/una semana 8. (in situation, state of) ~ fashion de moda; ~ search of sth/sb en busca de algo/alguien; ~ this way de esta manera; when ~ doubt en caso de duda; ~ earnest sinceramente; to be ~ a hurry tener prisa; to be ~ love (with sb) estar enamorado (de alguien); dressed ~ red vestido de rojo 9. (concerning) deaf ~ one ear sordo de un oído; to be interested ~ sth estar interesado en algo; to have faith ~ God tener fe en Dios; to have a say ~ the matter tener algo que decir al respecto; a change ~ attitude un cambio de actitud; a rise ~ prices un aumento de los precios 10. (by) ~ saying sth al decir algo 11. (taking the form of) to speak ~ French hablar en francés; ~ the form of a request en forma de petición 12. (made of) ~ wood/stone de madera/piedra 13. (sound of) ~ a whisper en un murmullo; to speak ~ a loud/low voice hablar en voz alta/baja 14. (aspect of) 6 feet ~ length/height 2 metros de largo/alto 15. (ratio) two ~ six dos de cada seis; to buy sth ~ twos comprar algo de dos en dos; ~ part en parte; ~ tens en grupos de diez 16. (substitution of) ~ your place en tu lugar; ~ lieu of sth form en lugar de algo 17. (as consequence of) ~ return a cambio; ~ reply como respuesta ▶ ~ all con todo; all ~ all en resumen II. adv 1. (inside, into) dentro, adentro; to go ~ entrar; to put sth ~ meter algo 2. (to a place) to be ~ inf estar en casa; to hand sth ~ entregar algo 3. (popular) to be ~ estar de moda ▶ to be ~ for sth inf estar a punto de recibir algo III. adj de moda IV. n the ~s and outs los pormenores

inability [ˌɪn·ə·ˈbɪl·ə·t̬i] n incapacidad f, ineptitud f pey

inaccessible [ˌɪn·æk·ˈses·ə·bəl] adj inaccesible

inaccuracy [ɪn·ˈæk·jər·ə·si] <-ies> n

**1.** (*fact*) error *m* **2.** (*quality*) imprecisión *f*, inexactitud *f*

**inaccurate** [ɪnˈæk·jər·ət] *adj* **1.** (*inexact*) inexacto, -a **2.** (*wrong*) equivocado, -a

**inaction** [ɪnˈæk·ʃən] *n* inacción *f*

**inactive** [ɪnˈæk·tɪv] *adj* inactivo, -a

**inactivity** [ˌɪn·æk·ˈtɪv·ə·ti] *n* inactividad *f*

**inadequate** [ɪnˈæd·ɪ·kwət] *adj* inadecuado, -a; (*inept*) inepto, -a

**inadvertent** [ˌɪn·əd·ˈvɜr·tənt] *adj* involuntario, -a

**inadvisable** [ˌɪn·əd·ˈvaɪ·zə·bəl] *adj* desaconsejable

**inanimate** [ɪnˈæn·ɪ·mət] *adj* inanimado, -a

**inapplicable** [ɪnˈæp·lɪ·kə·bəl] *adj* inaplicable

**inappropriate** [ˌɪn·ə·ˈprou·pri·ət] *adj* inapropiado, -a; (*not suitable*) inadecuado, -a

**inarticulate** [ˌɪn·ɑr·ˈtɪk·jʊ·lət] *adj* **1.** (*unable to express*) incapaz de expresarse **2.** (*unclear*) inarticulado, -a

**inasmuch as** [ˌɪn·əz·ˈmʌtʃ·əz] *conj form* **1.** (*because*) dado que **2.** (*to the extent that*) en tanto que +*subj*

**inattentive** [ˌɪn·ə·ˈten·tɪv] *adj* distraído, -a; **to be ~ to sb/sth** no prestar atención a alguien/algo

**inaudible** [ɪnˈɔ·də·bəl] *adj* inaudible

**inauguration** [ɪnˌɔ·gjʊ·ˈreɪ·ʃən] *n* inauguración *f*

**inauspicious** [ˌɪn·ɔ·ˈspɪʃ·əs] *adj* poco propicio, -a

**inborn** [ˈɪn·bɔrn] *adj* innato, -a

**inbuilt** [ˈɪn·bɪlt] *adj* integrado, -a; *fig* inherente, innato, -a

**Inc.** [ɪŋk] *abbr of* **incorporated** Inc.

**incalculable** [ɪnˈkæl·kjʊ·lə·bəl] *adj* incalculable

**incandescent** [ˌɪn·ken·ˈdes·ənt] *adj* incandescente

**incapable** [ɪnˈkeɪ·pə·bəl] *adj* incapaz; **to be ~ of doing sth** ser incapaz de hacer algo

**incapacity** [ˌɪn·kə·ˈpæs·ə·ti] *n* incapacidad *f*

**incendiary** [ɪnˈsen·di·er·i] *adj a. fig* incendiario, -a

**incense**[1] [ˈɪn·sents] *n* incienso *m*

**incense**[2] [ɪnˈsents] *vt* indignar

**incentive** [ɪnˈsen·tɪv] *n* incentivo *m*

**inception** [ɪnˈsep·ʃən] *n* inicio *m*

**incessant** [ɪnˈses·ənt] *adj* incesante

**incest** [ˈɪn·sest] *n* incesto *m*

**inch** [ɪntʃ] <-es> *n* pulgada *f* ▶ **give someone an ~ and they'll take a mile** *prov* les das la mano y te cogen el brazo *prov;* **to do sth ~ by ~** hacer algo paso a paso

●**inch forward** *vi* avanzar lentamente

**incidence** [ˈɪn·sɪ·dənts] *n* incidencia *f*

**incident** [ˈɪn·sɪ·dənt] *n* incidente *m;* **an isolated ~** un incidente aislado

**incidental** [ˌɪn·sɪ·ˈden·təl] *adj* (*related, of lesser importance*) secundario, -a

**incidentally** *adv* por cierto, a propósito

**incinerate** [ɪnˈsɪn·ə·reɪt] *vt* incinerar

**incinerator** [ɪnˈsɪn·ə·reɪ·tər] *n* incinerador *m*

**incision** [ɪnˈsɪʒ·ən] *n* MED incisión *f*

**incisive** [ɪnˈsaɪ·sɪv] *adj* **1.** (*clear*) incisivo, -a **2.** (*keen, acute*) agudo, -a

**incite** [ɪnˈsaɪt] *vt* instigar

**inclination** [ˌɪn·klɪ·ˈneɪ·ʃən] *n* **1.** (*tendency*) propensión *f* **2.** (*slope*) inclinación *f*

**incline**[1] [ˈɪn·klaɪn] *n* inclinación *f; (of hill, mountain)* inclinación *f*

**incline**[2] [ɪnˈklaɪn] **I.** *vi* **1.** (*tend*) tender **2.** (*lean*) inclinarse **II.** *vt* **1.** (*make sth tend*) predisponer **2.** (*make lean*) inclinar

**inclined** [ɪnˈklaɪnd] *adj* predispuesto, -a; **to be ~ to do sth** estar dispuesto a hacer algo

**inclose** [ɪnˈklouz] *vt see* **enclose**

**include** [ɪnˈklud] *vt* incluir; (*in a letter*) adjuntar

**including** [ɪnˈklu·dɪŋ] *prep* incluso; (*not*) ~ **tax** impuesto (no) incluido; **up to and ~ June 6th** hasta el 6 de junio inclusive

**inclusion** [ɪnˈklu·ʒən] *n* inclusión *f*

**inclusive** [ɪnˈklu·sɪv] *adj* incluido, -a

**incoherent** [ˌɪn·kou·ˈhɪr·ənt] *adj* incoherente

**income** [ˈɪn·kʌm] *n* ingresos *mpl*

**income tax** *n* impuesto *m* sobre la renta

**incoming** [ˈɪn·kʌm·ɪŋ] **I.** *adj* entrante **II.** *interj* MIL se presenta

**incomparable** [ɪn·ˈkam·pər·ə·bəl] *adj* incomparable

**incompatible** [ˌɪn·kəm·ˈpæt̬·ə·bəl] *adj* incompatible

**incompetence** [ɪn·ˈkam·pə·təns] *n*, **incompetency** *n* incompetencia *f*

**incompetent** [ɪn·ˈkam·pə·tənt] I. *adj* incompetente; **mentally ~** deficiente mental II. *n* incompetente *mf*

**incomplete** [ˌɪn·kəm·ˈplit] *adj* incompleto, -a

**incomprehensible** [ˌɪn·kam·prɪ·ˈhen·sə·bəl] *adj* incomprensible

**inconceivable** [ˌɪn·kən·ˈsi·və·bəl] *adj* inconcebible

**inconclusive** [ˌɪn·kən·ˈklu·sɪv] *adj* (*not convincing*) inconcluyente

**inconsequential** [ɪn·ˌkan·sɪ·ˈkwen·ʃəl] *adj* (*illogical*) inconsecuente

**inconsiderate** [ˌɪn·kən·ˈsɪd·ər·ət] *adj* desconsiderado, -a; (*insensitive*) insensible

**inconsistent** [ˌɪn·kən·ˈsɪs·tənt] *adj* 1. (*changeable*) incoherente 2. (*lacking agreement*) contradictorio, -a

**inconsolable** [ˌɪn·kən·ˈsou·lə·bəl] *adj* inconsolable

**inconspicuous** [ˌɪn·kən·ˈspɪk·ju·əs] *adj* desapercibido, -a

**inconstant** [ɪn·ˈkan·stənt] *adj* (*changing*) inconstante

**incontrovertible** [ɪn·ˌkan·trə·ˈvɜr·t̬ə·bəl] *adj* incontrovertible; **~ proof** prueba *f* irrefutable

**inconvenience** [ˌɪn·kən·ˈvin·jəns] I. *n* inconveniencia *f* II. *vt* causar molestias

**inconvenient** [ˌɪn·kən·ˈvin·jənt] *adj* inconveniente; (*time*) inoportuno, -a

**incorporate** [ɪn·ˈkor·pə·reɪt] *vt* 1. (*integrate*) incorporar; (*work into*) integrar 2. (*include*) incluir 3. LAW, ECON constituir

**incorrect** [ˌɪn·kə·ˈrekt] *adj* (*wrong, untrue*) incorrecto, -a; (*diagnosis*) erróneo, -a; **it is ~ that...** no es cierto que...

**incorruptible** [ˌɪn·kə·ˈrʌp·tə·bəl] *adj* (*not able to be corrupted*) incorruptible; (*morally incorruptible*) íntegro, -a

**increase**[1] [ˈɪn·kris] *n* (*raised amount*) incremento *m*; (*willful*) subida *f* 2. **to be on the ~** ir en aumento

**increase**[2] [ɪn·ˈkris] I. *vi* (*become more*)

incrementarse; (*grow*) crecer; **to ~ tenfold/threefold** multiplicarse por diez/tres II. *vt* (*make more*) incrementar; (*make larger*) aumentar

**increasing** *adj* creciente

**increasingly** *adv* cada vez más

**incredible** [ɪn·ˈkred·ə·bəl] *adj* increíble

**incriminate** [ɪn·ˈkrɪm·ɪ·neɪt] *vt* incriminar; **to ~ oneself** autoinculparse

**incubation period** *n* período *m* de incubación

**incur** [ɪn·ˈkɜr] <-rr-> *vt* FIN, ECON (*debt*) contraer; (*costs*) incurrir en; (*losses*) sufrir

**incurable** [ɪn·ˈkjʊr·ə·bəl] *adj* incurable; *fig* incorregible; **he is an ~ romantic** es un romántico empedernido

**indebted** [ɪn·ˈdet̬·ɪd] *adj* 1. (*obliged*) en deuda; **to be ~ to sb** (**for sth**) estar en deuda con alguien (por algo) 2. (*having debt*) endeudado, -a

**indecent** [ɪn·ˈdi·sənt] *adj* indecente, indecoroso, -a

**indecipherable** [ˌɪn·dɪ·ˈsaɪ·frə·bəl] *adj* indescifrable

**indecision** [ˌɪn·dɪ·ˈsɪʒ·ən] *n* indecisión *f*, irresolución *f elev*

**indecisive** [ˌɪn·dɪ·ˈsaɪ·sɪv] *adj* (*unable to make decisions*) indeciso, -a

**indeclinable** [ɪn·dɪ·ˈklaɪ·nə·bəl] *adj* LING indeclinable

**indeed** [ɪn·ˈdid] I. *adv* 1. (*really*) realmente; **this is good news ~!** ¡eso sí que es una buena noticia! 2. (*expresses affirmation*) en efecto II. *interj* ya lo creo; **he's a lovely boy! — ~!** es un chico encantador — ¡ya lo creo!

**indefensible** [ˌɪn·dɪ·ˈfen·sə·bəl] *adj* insostenible; MIL indefendible

**indefinable** [ˌɪn·dɪ·ˈfaɪ·nə·bəl] *adj* indefinible

**indefinite** [ɪn·ˈdef·ə·nɪt] *adj* indefinido, -a; **for an ~ period** por un tiempo indeterminado

**indelible** [ɪn·ˈdel·ə·bəl] *adj* imborrable; (*colors, stains, ink*) indeleble

**indemnify** [ɪn·ˈdem·nɪ·faɪ] <-ie-> *vt* 1. (*insure against damage*) asegurar 2. (*compensate for damage*) indemnizar

**indemnity** [ɪn·ˈdem·nə·t̬i] <-ies> *n form*

**1.** (*insurance for damage*) indemnidad *f*
**2.** (*compensation*) indemnización *f*
**independence** [ˌɪn·dɪ·ˈpen·dəns] *n* independencia *f*
**Independence Day** *n* día *m* de la Independencia
**independent** [ˌɪn·dɪ·ˈpen·dənt] **I.** *adj* independiente **II.** *n* POL diputado, -a *m, f* independiente
**in-depth** [ˈɪn·depθ] *adj* exhaustivo, -a, a fondo
**indescribable** [ˌɪn·dɪ·ˈskraɪ·bə·bəl] *adj* indescriptible
**indestructible** [ˌɪn·dɪ·ˈstrʌk·tə·bəl] *adj* indestructible
**index** [ˈɪn·deks] **I.** *n* **1.** <-es> (*alphabetical list*) índice *m* **2.** <-ices *or* -es> ECON índice *m;* **consumer price ~** índice de precios al consumo **3.** <-ices *or* -es> (*indication*) indicador *m* **4.** <-ices> MATH exponente *m* **II.** *vt* **1.** (*provide with a list*) poner índice a **2.** (*enter in a list*) indexar **3.** ECON **to ~ wages to inflation** equilibrar los sueldos a la inflación
**index card** *n* ficha *f*
**indexer** [ˈɪn·dek·sər] *n* clasificador *m*
**index finger** *n* dedo *m* índice
**Indian** [ˈɪn·di·ən] **I.** *adj* **1.** (*of India*) indio, -a, hindú **2.** (*of America*) indio, -a, indígena **II.** *n* **1.** (*of India*) indio, -a *m, f,* hindú *mf* **2.** (*of America*) indio, -a *m, f,* indígena *mf*
**indicate** [ˈɪn·dɪ·keɪt] *vt* indicar; **to ~ (to sb) that...** señalar a (alguien) que...
**indication** [ˌɪn·dɪ·ˈkeɪ·ʃən] *n* **1.** (*evidence*) indicio *m;* **an ~ of willingness** una muestra de voluntad **2.** *a.* MED indicación *f*
**indicative** [ɪn·ˈdɪk·ə·tɪv] **I.** *adj* indicativo, -a **II.** *n* indicativo *m*
**indicator** [ˈɪn·dɪ·keɪ·tər] *n* indicador *m*
**indices** [ˈɪn·dɪ·siz] *n pl of* **index**
**indict** [ɪn·ˈdaɪt] *vt* **to ~ sb for sth** LAW acusar a alguien de algo
**Indies** [ˈɪn·diz] *npl* Indias *fpl;* **the West ~** las Antillas
**indifference** [ɪn·ˈdɪf·rəns] *n* indiferencia *f*
**indifferent** [ɪn·ˈdɪf·rənt] *adj* (*not interested*) indiferente, valemadrista *inv Méx*

**indigenous** [ɪn·ˈdɪdʒ·ə·nəs] *adj* indígena
**indigestible** [ˌɪn·dɪ·ˈdʒes·tə·bəl] *adj* **1.** (*food*) indigesto, -a **2.** *fig* indigerible
**indigestion** [ˌɪn·dɪ·ˈdʒes·tʃən] *n* indigestión *f;* **to give oneself ~** empacharse
**indignant** [ɪn·ˈdɪg·nənt] *adj* indignado, -a; **to become ~** indignarse
**indignation** [ˌɪn·dɪg·ˈneɪ·ʃən] *n* indignación *f*
**indignity** [ɪn·ˈdɪg·nə·ti] <-ies> *n* (*humiliation*) indignidad *f*
**indirect** [ˌɪn·dɪ·ˈrekt] *adj* indirecto, -a
**indiscreet** [ˌɪn·dɪ·ˈskrit] *adj* indiscreto, -a; (*tactless*) falto, -a de tacto
**indiscretion** [ˌɪn·dɪ·ˈskreʃ·ən] *n* (*lack of discretion*) indiscreción *f*
**indiscriminate** [ˌɪn·dɪ·ˈskrɪm·ə·nɪt] *adj* (*random*) indiscriminado, -a
**indispensable** [ˌɪn·dɪ·ˈspen·sə·bəl] *adj* indispensable
**indistinct** [ˌɪn·dɪ·ˈstɪŋkt] *adj* indistinto, -a
**indistinguishable** [ˌɪn·dɪ·ˈstɪŋ·gwɪ·ʃə·bəl] *adj* indistinguible; (*not perceptible*) imperceptible
**individual** [ˌɪn·dɪ·ˈvɪdʒ·u·əl] **I.** *n* individuo, -a *m, f* **II.** *adj* individual; (*particular*) particular; **an ~ style** un estilo propio
**individualism** [ˌɪn·dɪ·ˈvɪdʒ·u·ə·lɪz·əm] *n* individualismo *m*
**individualist** *n* individualista *mf*
**indivisible** [ˌɪn·dɪ·ˈvɪz·ə·bəl] *adj* indivisible
**indoor** [ˌɪn·ˈdɔr] *adj* interior; (*pool*) cubierto, -a
**indoors** [ˌɪn·ˈdɔrz] *adv* dentro
**induce** [ɪn·ˈdus] *vt* **1.** (*persuade*) *a.* ELEC, PHYS inducir **2.** (*cause*) provocar
**indulge** [ɪn·ˈdʌldʒ] *vt* **1.** (*allow*) consentir **2.** **to ~ oneself in...** darse el lujo de..., permitirse...
**indulgent** [ɪn·ˈdʌl·dʒənt] *adj* **1.** (*lenient*) indulgente **2.** (*tolerant*) tolerante
**industrial** [ɪn·ˈdʌs·tri·əl] **I.** *adj* industrial; (*dispute*) laboral; **for ~ use** para uso industrial **II.** *npl* FIN acciones *f pl* industriales
**industrialist** *n* industrial *mf*
**industrialization** [ɪn·ˌdʌs·tri·ə·lɪ·ˈzeɪ·ʃən]

*n* industrialización *f*

**industrialize** [ɪn·ˈdʌs·tri·ə·laɪz] I. *vi* industrializarse II. *vt* industrializar

**Industrial Revolution** *n* Revolución *f* Industrial

**industrious** [ɪn·ˈdʌs·tri·əs] *adj* trabajador(a)

**industry** [ˈɪn·dəs·tri] *n* 1. (*manufacturing production*) industria *f* 2. <-ies> (*branch*) sector *m*

**inedible** [ɪn·ˈed·ə·bəl] *adj* (*unsuitable as food*) no comestible

**ineffective** [ˌɪn·ɪ·ˈfek·tɪv] *adj* ineficaz

**ineffectual** [ˌɪn·ɪ·ˈfek·tʃʊ·əl] *adj* ineficaz, inútil

**inefficient** [ˌɪn·ɪ·ˈfɪʃ·ənt] *adj* ineficiente

**ineligible** [ɪn·ˈel·ɪdʒ·ə·bəl] *adj* inelegible; **to be ~ for sth** no reunir los requisitos para algo

**inept** [ɪn·ˈept] *adj* (*unskilled*) inepto, -a; **to be ~ at sth** ser inepto para algo

**inequality** [ˌɪn·ɪ·ˈkwal·ə·ti] <-ies> *n* desigualdad *f*

**inequitable** [ɪn·ˈek·wə·tə·bəl] *adj* injusto, -a

**inert** [ɪn·ˈɜrt] *adj* 1. (*not moving*) inerte; *fig* inmóvil 2. PHYS inactivo, -a

**inescapable** [ˌɪn·ɪ·ˈskeɪ·pə·bəl] *adj* ineludible

**inevitable** [ɪn·ˈev·ɪ·tə·bəl] I. *adj* inevitable; (*conclusion, consequence*) inexorable II. *n* **the ~** lo inevitable

**inexact** [ˌɪn·ɪɡ·ˈzækt] *adj* inexacto, -a

**inexcusable** [ˌɪn·ɪk·ˈskju·zə·bəl] *adj* imperdonable

**inexhaustible** [ˌɪn·ɪɡ·ˈzɔs·tə·bəl] *adj* inagotable

**inexpensive** [ˌɪn·ɪk·ˈspen·sɪv] *adj* económico, -a

**inexperienced** [ˌɪn·ɪk·ˈspɪr·i·ənst] *adj* inexperto, -a

**inexplicable** [ˌɪn·ˈək·ˈsplɪk·ə·bəl] I. *adj* inexplicable II. *n* **the ~** lo inexplicable

**infallible** [ɪn·ˈfæl·ə·bəl] *adj* indefectible; (*incapable of being wrong*) infalible

**infamous** [ˈɪn·fə·məs] *adj* 1. (*shocking*) infame 2. (*notorious*) de mala fama

**infancy** [ˈɪn·fən·si] *n* infancia *f*; **from ~** desde niño

**infant** [ˈɪn·fənt] *n* (*very young child*) bebé *m*; **a newborn ~** un recién na-

cido

**infantile** [ˈɪn·fən·taɪl] *adj* infantil

**infant mortality** *n* mortalidad *f* infantil

**infantry** [ˈɪn·fən·tri] *n* + *sing/pl vb* MIL infantería *f*

**infatuated** [ɪn·ˈfætʃ·u·eɪ·tɪd] *adj* encaprichado, -a; **to become ~ with sb/sth** encapricharse con alguien/algo

**infect** [ɪn·ˈfekt] *vt* infectar; *a. fig* (*person*) contagiar

**infection** [ɪn·ˈfek·ʃən] *n* infección *f*; **risk of ~** riesgo *m* de contagio

**infectious** [ɪn·ˈfek·ʃəs] *adj* infeccioso, -a; *a. fig* contagioso, -a

**infer** [ɪn·ˈfɜr] <-rr-> *vt* inferir

**inference** [ˈɪn·fər·əns] *n form* 1. (*conclusion*) conclusión *f* 2. (*process of inferring*) inferencia *f*

**inferior** [ɪn·ˈfɪr·i·ər] I. *adj* inferior II. *n* inferior *mf*

**inferiority** [ɪn·ˌfɪr·i·ˈɔr·ə·ti] *n* inferioridad *f*

**inferiority complex** <-es> *n* complejo *m* de inferioridad

**infernal** [ɪn·ˈfɜr·nəl] *adj* infernal

**inferno** [ɪn·ˈfɜr·noʊ] *n* infierno *m*

**infertile** [ɪn·ˈfɜr·təl] *adj* estéril

**infertility** [ˌɪn·fər·ˈtɪl·ə·ti] *n* esterilidad *f*

**infest** [ɪn·ˈfest] *vt* infestar

**infestation** [ˌɪn·fes·ˈteɪ·ʃən] *n* plaga *f*, infestación *f*

**infidelity** [ˌɪn·fə·ˈdel·ə·ti] *n* infidelidad *f*

**infighting** [ˈɪn·faɪ·tɪŋ] *n* lucha *f* interna

**infiltrate** [ɪn·ˈfɪl·treɪt] *vt* infiltrarse en

**infinite** [ˈɪn·fə·nɪt] *adj* infinito, -a

**infinitesimal** [ˌɪn·fɪn·ɪ·ˈtes·ɪ·məl] *adj form* infinitesimal

**infinitive** [ɪn·ˈfɪn·ə·tɪv] LING I. *n* infinitivo *m* II. *adj* infinitivo, -a

**infinity** [ɪn·ˈfɪn·ə·ti] <-ies> *n* 1. MATH infinito *m* 2. (*huge amount*) infinidad *f*

**infirm** [ɪn·ˈfɜrm] *adj* enfermizo, -a; (*weak*) débil

**infirmary** [ɪn·ˈfɜr·mə·ri] <-ies> *n* 1. (*hospital*) hospital *m* 2. (*room*) enfermería *f*

**inflame** [ɪn·ˈfleɪm] *vt* 1. *a.* MED inflamar 2. (*stir up*) encender

**inflammable** [ɪn·ˈflæm·ə·bəl] *adj* inflamable

**inflammation** [ˌɪn·flə·ˈmeɪ·ʃən] *n* MED inflamación *f*

**inflammatory** [ɪnˈflæm·ə·tɔr·i] *adj*
1. MED inflamatorio, -a 2. (*speech*) incendiario, -a

**inflatable** [ɪnˈfleɪ·t̬ə·bəl] *adj* hinchable

**inflate** [ɪnˈfleɪt] I. *vt* 1. (*fill with air*)
hinchar, inflar 2. ECON (*prices*) disparar
II. *vi* hincharse

**inflated** [ɪnˈfleɪ·t̬ɪd] *adj* 1. (*filled with
air*) hinchado, -a 2. (*exaggerated*) exagerado, -a 3. ECON (*price*) excesivo, -a

**inflation** [ɪnˈfleɪ·ʃən] *n* inflación *f*

**inflationary** *adj* FIN inflacionario, -a

**inflexible** [ɪnˈflek·sə·bəl] *adj* inflexible

**inflict** [ɪnˈflɪkt] *vt* infligir

**influence** [ˈɪn·flu·əns] I. *n* influencia *f*; **to
drive under the ~** *fig* conducir bajo los
efectos del alcohol II. *vt* influir

**influential** [ˌɪn·flu·ˈen·ʃəl] *adj* influyente

**influenza** [ˌɪn·flu·ˈen·zə] *n* gripe *f*

**influx** [ˈɪn·flʌks] *n* influjo *m*

**inform** [ɪnˈfɔrm] I. *vt* informar; **to be
~ed about sth** estar enterado de algo
II. *vi* **to ~ against sb** delatar a alguien

**informal** [ɪnˈfɔr·məl] *adj* informal; (*tone,
manner*) familiar; (*person*) afable

**informant** [ɪnˈfɔr·mənt] *n* informante *mf*

**information** [ˌɪn·fər·ˈmeɪ·ʃən] *n* 1. (*data*)
información *f*; **a lot of/a little ~** mu-
cha/poca información; **to ask for ~**
pedir información; **for further ~** para
más información 2. COMPUT datos *mpl*
3. (*knowledge*) conocimientos *mpl*
4. LAW denuncia *f*

**information science** *n* ciencias *f pl* de
la información

**information superhighway** *n* autopista
*f* de la información

**information technology** *n* tecnologías
*f pl* de la información

**informative** [ɪnˈfɔr·mə·t̬ɪv] *adj* informativo, -a

**informer** [ɪnˈfɔr·mər] *n* informante *mf*,
informador(a) *m(f)*

**infrared** [ˈɪn·frə·ˈred] *adj* infrarrojo, -a

**infrequent** [ɪnˈfri·kwənt] *adj* poco frecuente

**infringe** [ɪnˈfrɪndʒ] I. *vt* LAW infringir
II. *vi* **to ~ on** [*or* **upon**] **sth** usurpar

**infuriate** [ɪnˈfjʊr·i·eɪt] *vt* enfurecer

**infusion** [ɪnˈfju·ʒən] *n a.* MED infusión *f*;

ECON inyección *f*

**ingenious** [ɪnˈdʒin·jəs] *adj* (*creatively
inventive*) inventivo, -a; (*idea, method,
plan*) ingenioso, -a

**ingenuity** [ˌɪn·dʒɪ·ˈnu·ə·t̬i] *n* ingenuidad *f*;
**to use one's ~** utilizar el ingenio

**ingoing** [ˈɪn·goʊ·ɪŋ] *adj* entrante

**ingrained** [ˌɪnˈgreɪnd] *adj* 1. (*embed-
ded: dirt*) incrustado, -a 2. (*deep-seated*) arraigado, -a

**ingratitude** [ɪnˈgræt·ə·tud] *n* ingratitud *f*

**ingredient** [ɪnˈgri·di·ənt] *n* 1. CULIN ingrediente *m* 2. (*component*) *a.* MED
componente *m*

**ingrowing** [ˈɪn·groʊ·ɪŋ] *adj* que crece
hacia dentro (de la piel); **~ toenail**
uñero *m*

**ingrown** [ˈɪn·groʊn] *adj* que crece hacia
dentro (de la piel); **~ toenail** uñero *m*

**inhabit** [ɪnˈhæb·ɪt] *vt* habitar

**inhabitable** *adj* habitable

**inhabitant** [ɪnˈhæb·ɪ·tənt] *n* habitante *mf*

**inhale** [ɪnˈheɪl] I. *vt* aspirar; MED inhalar
II. *vi* inhalar

**inhaler** [ɪnˈheɪ·lər] *n* inhalador *m*

**inherit** [ɪnˈher·ɪt] I. *vt* heredar II. *vi* recibir una herencia

**inheritance** [ɪnˈher·ɪ·təns] *n* herencia *f*;
*fig* legado *m*

**inhibit** [ɪnˈhɪb·ɪt] *vt* (*hinder*) impedir;
(*impair*) inhibir

**inhibition** [ˌɪn·ɪ·ˈbɪʃ·ən] *n* inhibición *f*

**inhospitable** [ɪnˈhas·pɪ·t̬ə·bəl] *adj* inhospitalario, -a; (*place*) inhóspito, -a

**in-house** [ˈɪn·haʊs] COM I. *adj* interno, -a
II. *adv* dentro de la empresa

**inhuman** [ɪnˈhju·mən] *adj* (*not human*)
inhumano, -a

**inhumane** [ˌɪn·hju·ˈmeɪn] *adj* (*cruel*) inhumano, -a, cruel

**initial** [ɪˈnɪʃ·əl] I. *n* inicial *f*; **one's ~s**
las iniciales de uno II. *adj* inicial; (*first*)
primero, -a; **in the ~ phases** en las primeras etapas III. <-ll-, -l-> *vt* marcar
con las iniciales

**initially** [ɪˈnɪʃ·ə·li] *adv* en un principio

**initiate** [ɪˈnɪʃ·i·eɪt] *vt* 1. (*start*) iniciar, dar
comienzo a 2. (*admit to group*) admitir
(como miembro)

**initiation** [ɪ‚nɪʃ·ɪ·ˈeɪ·ʃən] *n* **1.** (*starting*) inicio *m* **2.** (*introducing*) iniciación *f*; (*as a member*) admisión *f*

**initiative** [ɪˈnɪʃ·ə·tɪv] *n* iniciativa *f*; **to show** ~ demostrar iniciativa

**inject** [ɪn·ˈdʒekt] *vt* **1.** a. MED inyectar **2.** (*introduce*) introducir; (*funds, money*) inyectar

**injection** [ɪn·ˈdʒek·ʃən] *n* inyección *f*

**injunction** [ɪn·ˈdʒʌŋk·ʃən] *n* mandato *m*; LAW mandato *m* judicial

**injure** [ˈɪn·dʒər] *vt* **1.** (*wound*) herir, victimar *AmL* **2.** (*do wrong to*) perjudicar

**injured** *adj* **1.** (*wounded*) herido, -a, victimado, -a *AmL* **2.** (*damaged*) dañado, -a **3.** (*wronged*) perjudicado, -a

**injury** [ˈɪn·dʒə·ri] <-ies> *n* (*physical*) lesión *f*, herida *f*

**injustice** [ɪn·ˈdʒʌs·tɪs] *n* injusticia *f*

**ink** [ɪŋk] *n* tinta *f*

**inkling** [ˈɪŋk·lɪŋ] *n* (*suspicion*) sospecha *f*

**inland** [ˈɪn·lənd] **I.** *adj* (*not coastal: sea, shipping*) interior; (*town, village*) del interior *m* **II.** *adv* (*direction*) tierra adentro

**in-laws** [ˈɪn·lɒz] *npl* suegros *mpl*

**inlet** [ˈɪn·let] *n* **1.** GEO ensenada *f*; (*of sea*) cala *f* **2.** TECH entrada *f*

**inmate** [ˈɪn·meɪt] *n* (*prison*) preso, -a *m, f*

**inn** [ɪn] *n* posada *f*

**inner** [ˈɪn·ər] *adj* **1.** (*located in the interior*) interno, -a, interior **2.** (*deep*) íntimo, -a

**innermost** [ˈɪn·ər·moʊst] *adj* más íntimo, -a

**inner tube** *n* cámara *f* de aire

**inning** [ˈɪn·ɪŋ] *n* SPORTS (*part of baseball game*) inning *m*

**innocence** [ˈɪn·ə·səns] *n* inocencia *f*; **in all** ~ inocentemente

**innocent** [ˈɪn·ə·sənt] *adj, n* inocente *mf*; **to be** ~ **of sth** ser inocente de algo; **an** ~ **bystander** un testigo casual

**innovate** [ˈɪn·ə·veɪt] *vi* innovar

**innovation** [‚ɪn·ə·ˈveɪ·ʃən] *n* novedad *f*, innovación *f*

**innovative** [ˈɪn·ə·veɪ·tɪv] *adj* (*model, product*) novedoso, -a; (*person*) innovador(a)

**innuendo** [‚ɪn·ju·ˈen·doʊ] <-(e)s> *n*

**1.** (*insinuation*) insinuación *f*; **to make an** ~ (**about sth**) hacer una insinuación (sobre algo) **2.** (*suggestive remark*) indirecta *f*

**innumerate** [ɪˈnu·mər·ət] *adj* **to be** ~ ser incapaz de realizar cálculos

**inoculate** [ɪˈnak·jə·leɪt] *vt* **to** ~ **sb** (**against sth**) inocular a alguien (contra algo)

**inoculation** [ɪ‚nak·jə·ˈleɪ·ʃən] *n* inoculación *f*

**inoffensive** [‚ɪn·ə·ˈfen·sɪv] *adj* inofensivo, -a

**inoperable** [‚ɪn·ˈap·ər·ə·bəl] *adj* inoperable

**inoperative** [‚ɪn·ˈap·ər·ə·tɪv] *adj* inoperante

**inordinate** [ɪn·ˈɔr·dɪn·ɪt] *adj* desmesurado, -a; **an** ~ **amount of sth** una cantidad excesiva de algo

**input** [ˈɪn·pʊt] **I.** *n* (*contribution*) contribución *f*, aportación *f*; COMPUT entrada *f* **II.** <-tt-> *vt* COMPUT introducir

**inquest** [ˈɪn·kwest] *n* LAW pesquisa *f* judicial; **to hold an** ~ (**into sth**) llevar a cabo una investigación (sobre algo)

**inquire** [ɪn·ˈkwaɪr] **I.** *vi* **1.** (*ask*) preguntar; **to** ~ **about sb** preguntar por alguien; **to** ~ **about sth** pedir información sobre algo **2.** (*investigate*) investigar **II.** *vt* preguntar

**inquiry** [ɪn·ˈkwaɪ·ri] *n* **1.** (*question*) pregunta *f* **2.** (*investigation*) investigación *f*

**inquisitive** [ɪn·ˈkwɪz·ɪ·t̬ɪv] *adj* (*curious*) curioso, -a; (*look, expression*) interrogante; (*child*) preguntón, -ona

**ins and outs** *npl* pormenores *mpl*

**insane** [ɪn·ˈseɪn] *adj* demente; a. fig (*crazy*) loco, -a

**insanitary** [ɪn·ˈsæn·ɪ·ter·i] *adj* antihigiénico, -a

**insanity** [ɪn·ˈsæn·ə·t̬i] *n* **1.** (*mental illness*) demencia *f* **2.** a. fig (*craziness*) locura *f*

**inscription** [ɪn·ˈskrɪp·ʃən] *n* inscripción *f*; (*dedication*) dedicatoria *f*

**insect** [ˈɪn·sekt] *n* insecto *m*; ~ **bite** picadura *f* de insecto

**insecticide** [ɪn·ˈsek·tɪ·saɪd] *n* insecticida *m*

**insecure** [ˌɪn·sɪ·ˈkjʊr] *adj* inseguro, -a

**insensitive** [ɪn·ˈsen·sɪ·tɪv] *adj* insensible

**inseparable** [ɪn·ˈsep·rə·bəl] *adj* inseparable, indisoluble

**insert¹** [ˈɪn·sɜrt] *n* (*page*) encarte *m*

**insert²** [ɪn·ˈsɜrt] *vt* **1.** (*put into*) insertar; (*coins*) introducir **2.** (*add within a text*) intercalar

**in-service** [ˈɪn·sɜr·vɪs] *adj* en funcionamiento

**inside** [ɪn·ˈsaɪd] **I.** *adj* **1.** (*internal*) interno, -a; the ~ door la puerta interior **2.** (*from within: information*) confidencial **II.** *n* **1.** (*internal part or side*) interior *m;* on the ~ por dentro; to turn sth ~ out volver algo del revés; to turn the whole room ~ out *fig* revolver toda la habitación; to know a place ~ out conocer muy bien un lugar **2.** ~s *inf* (*entrails*) tripas *fpl* **III.** *prep* (*within*) (*of*) dentro de; to go ~ the house entrar en casa **IV.** *adv* **1.** (*within something*) dentro; to go ~ entrar **2.** (*internally*) interiormente

**insider** [ˈɪn·saɪ·dər] *n* persona *f* de la casa; (*with special knowledge*) persona *f* enterada

**insight** [ˈɪn·saɪt] *n* **1.** (*capacity*) perspicacia *f* **2.** (*instance*) nueva percepción *f;* to gain ~ into sth/sb entender mejor algo/a alguien

**insignificant** [ˌɪn·sɪg·ˈnɪf·ɪ·kənt] *adj* insignificante; (*trivial*) trivial

**insincere** [ˌɪn·sɪn·ˈsɪr] *adj* poco sincero, -a

**insist** [ɪn·ˈsɪst] **I.** *vi* insistir; to ~ on doing sth obstinarse en hacer algo; if you ~ si insistes **II.** *vt* **1.** (*state*) insistir **2.** (*demand*) exigir

**insistence** [ɪn·ˈsɪs·təns] *n* insistencia *f;* to do sth at sb's ~ hacer algo por insistencia de alguien

**insistent** [ɪn·ˈsɪs·tənt] *adj* insistente; to be ~ (that)... insistir en (que)...

**insofar as** [ˌɪn·soʊ·ˈfar·əz] *adv form* en tanto que +*subj*

**insole** [ˈɪn·soʊl] *n* plantilla *f*

**insolent** [ˈɪn·sə·lənt] *adj* insolente

**insoluble** [ɪn·ˈsal·jə·bəl] *adj* insoluble

**insomnia** [ɪn·ˈsam·ni·ə] *n* insomnio *m*

**insomniac** [ɪn·ˈsam·ni·æk] *n* insomne *mf*

**inspect** [ɪn·ˈspekt] *vt* **1.** (*examine carefully*) inspeccionar, examinar **2.** MIL to ~ the troops pasar revista

**inspection** [ɪn·ˈspek·ʃən] *n* inspección *f;* MIL revista *f*

**inspector** [ɪn·ˈspek·tər] *n* inspector(a) *m(f)*

**inspiration** [ˌɪn·spə·ˈreɪ·ʃən] *n a.* MED inspiración *f*

**inspire** [ɪn·ˈspaɪr] *vt* (*stimulate*) inspirar

**instability** [ˌɪn·stə·ˈbɪl·ə·ṭi] *n* inestabilidad *f*

**instal** <-ll->, **install** [ɪn·ˈstɔl] **I.** *vt* **1.** *a.* TECH, COMPUT instalar **2.** (*place*) colocar; to ~ sb colocar a alguien (en un cargo) **II.** *vr* to ~ oneself instalarse

**installation** [ˌɪn·stə·ˈleɪ·ʃən] *n* instalación *f*

**installment** *n*, **instalment** [ɪn·ˈstɔl·mənt] *n* **1.** RADIO, TV entrega *f* **2.** COM plazo *m;* to pay (for sth) in ~s pagar (algo) a plazos; to be payable in monthly ~s ser pagadero a plazos

**installment plan** *n* compra *f* a plazos

**instance** [ˈɪn·stəns] *n* **1.** (*case*) caso *m;* in this ~ en este caso; for ~ por ejemplo **2.** (*order*) pedido *m;* to do sth at sb's ~ hacer algo a petición de alguien

**instant** [ˈɪn·stənt] **I.** *n* instante *m*, momento *m;* for an ~ por un momento; in an ~ al instante; to do sth this ~ hacer algo inmediatamente **II.** *adj* **1.** (*immediate*) inmediato, -a **2.** CULIN instantáneo, -a; ~ coffee café *m* instantáneo

**instantaneous** [ˌɪn·stən·ˈteɪ·ni·əs] *adj* instantáneo, -a; (*effect, reaction*) inmediato, -a

**instantly** [ˈɪn·stənt·li] *adv* al instante

**instant replay** *n* (*action replay*) repetición *f*

**instead** [ɪn·ˈsted] **I.** *adv* en cambio, en lugar de eso **II.** *prep* ~ of en vez de, en lugar de; ~ of him en su lugar; ~ of doing sth en lugar de hacer algo

**instigate** [ˈɪn·stɪ·geɪt] *vt* **1.** (*initiate*) instigar **2.** (*incite*) incitar

**instil** [ɪn·ˈstɪl] <-ll->, **instill** *vt* to ~ sth (into sb) infundir algo (a alguien)

**instinct** [ˈɪn·stɪŋkt] *n* instinto *m;* to do sth by ~ hacer algo por instinto

**instinctive** [ɪn·ˈstɪŋk·tɪv] *adj* instintivo, -a; (*innate*) innato, -a

**institute** ['ɪn·stɪ·tut] I. *n* academia *f*; (*of education*) instituto *m* II. *vt form* 1. (*establish: system, reform*) instituir 2. (*initiate: steps, measures*) iniciar

**institution** [ɪn·stɪ·'tu·ʃən] *n* 1. (*act*) institución *f*, establecimiento *m* 2. (*society*) asociación *f* 3. (*home*) asilo *m*

**instruct** [ɪn·'strʌkt] *vt* 1. (*teach*) instruir 2. (*order*) ordenar; (*give instructions*) dar instrucciones 3. LAW dar instrucciones

**instruction** [ɪn·'strʌk·ʃən] *n* 1. (*teaching*) instrucción *f* 2. (*order*) orden *f*; to give sb ~s dar órdenes a alguien; to carry out ~s cumplir órdenes 3. ~s (*information on method*) instrucciones *fpl*

**instructive** [ɪn·'strʌk·tɪv] *adj* instructivo, -a

**instructor** [ɪn·'strʌk·tər] *n* 1. (*teacher*) instructor(a) *m(f)*; ski ~ profesor(a) de esquí 2. UNIV profesor(a) *m(f)*

**instrument** ['ɪn·strə·mənt] *n* 1. MUS, LAW instrumento *m* 2. (*tool*) herramienta *f*

**instrumental** [ˌɪn·strə·'men·təl] *adj* 1. MUS instrumental 2. (*greatly influential*) to be ~ in doing sth jugar un papel decisivo en algo

**instrument board** *n*, **instrument panel** *n* AUTO salpicadero *m*; AVIAT, NAUT cuadro *m* de mandos

**insufficient** [ˌɪn·sə·'fɪʃ·ənt] *adj* insuficiente

**insular** ['ɪn·sə·lər] *adj* GEO insular

**insularity** [ˌɪn·sə·'ler·ə·ti] *n* GEO insularidad *f*

**insulate** ['ɪn·sə·leɪt] *vt* aislar; to ~ sth (against sth) aislar algo (de algo)

**insulating** ['ɪn·sə·leɪ·tɪŋ] *adj* aislante

**insulation** [ˌɪn·sə·'leɪ·ʃən] *n* aislamiento *m*

**insult** I. [ɪn·'sʌlt] *vt* insultar II. ['ɪn·sʌlt] *n* insulto *m*, insultada *f AmL* ▶ to add ~ to injury... y por si fuera poco...

**insurance** [ɪn·'ʃʊr·əns] *n* 1. (*financial protection*) seguro *m*; life ~ seguro de vida; to have ~ (against sth) tener un seguro (contra algo); to take out ~ (against sth) hacerse un seguro (contra algo) 2. (*measure*) medida *f* preventiva

**insurance policy** <-ies> *n* póliza *f* de seguros

**insure** [ɪn·'ʃʊr] *vt* asegurar

**insured** [ɪn·'ʃʊrd] I. *adj* asegurado, -a II. *n* the ~ el asegurado

**insurer** [ɪn·'ʃʊr·ər] *n* (*company*) aseguradora *f*

**intact** [ɪn·'tækt] *adj* intacto, -a

**intake** ['ɪn·teɪk] *n* 1. TECH (*mechanical aperture*) toma *f*; fuel ~ toma de combustible 2. (*of air, water*) entrada *f* 3. (*amount taken in*) consumo *m*; the recommended daily ~ of fiber la cantidad diaria recomendada de fibra

**integer** ['ɪn·tɪ·dʒər] *n* MATH número *m* entero

**integral** ['ɪn·tə·grəl] *adj* 1. (*central, essential*) esencial 2. (*part of the whole*) integrante 3. (*complete*) integral

**integrated** ['ɪn·tɪ·greɪ·tɪd] *adj* (*coordinating different elements*) integrado, -a

**integrity** [ɪn·'teg·rə·ti] *n* (*incorruptibility, uprightness*) integridad *f*; a man of ~ un hombre íntegro

**intellect** ['ɪn·təl·ekt] *n* 1. (*faculty*) intelecto *m* 2. (*thinker, intellectual*) intelectual *mf*

**intellectual** [ˌɪn·tə·'lek·tʃu·əl] I. *n* intelectual *mf* II. *adj* intelectual

**intelligence** [ɪn·'tel·ə·dʒəns] *n* inteligencia *f*; artificial ~ inteligencia artificial

**intelligence test** *n* test *m* de inteligencia

**intelligent** [ɪn·'tel·ə·dʒənt] *adj* inteligente

**intend** [ɪn·'tend] *vt* 1. (*aim for, plan*) pretender; I ~ed no harm no quería hacer daño 2. (*earmark, destine*) to be ~ed for sth estar destinado a algo

**intended** [ɪn·'ten·dɪd] I. *adj* (*planned, intentional*) intencional; (*sought*) deseado, -a II. *n inf* prometido, -a *m, f*

**intense** [ɪn·'tens] *adj* 1. (*acute, concentrated, forceful*) intenso, -a; (*feeling, hatred, friendship*) profundo, -a; (*love*) apasionado, -a; (*pain, pressure, wind*) fuerte 2. (*demanding*) agotador(a)

**intensify** [ɪn·'ten·sɪ·faɪ] <-ie-> I. *vt* intensificar; (*joy, sadness*) aumentar; (*pain*) agudizar II. *vi* intensificarse; (*joy, sadness*) aumentar; (*pain*) agudizarse

**intensity** [ɪn·'ten·sə·ti] *n* intensidad *f*

**intensive** [ɪn·'ten·sɪv] *adj* intensivo, -a

**intensive care** *n* cuidados *m pl* intensivos

**intent** [ɪn·'tent] **I.** *n* propósito *m;* **to all ~s and purposes** a efectos prácticos; **with ~** con el objeto de; **with good/evil ~** con buenas/malas intenciones **II.** *adj* **1.** (*absorbed, concentrated, occupied*) abstraído, -a; (*look*) atento, -a; **to be ~ on sth** estar concentrado en algo **2.** (*decided, set*) decidido, -a; **to be/seem ~ on doing sth** estar/parecer resuelto a hacer algo

**intention** [ɪn·'ten·tʃən] *n* intención *f;* **to have no ~ of doing sth** no tener ninguna intención de hacer algo; **with the best of ~s** con la mejor intención

**intentional** [ɪn·'ten·tʃə·nəl] *adj* intencional; (*insult*) deliberado, -a

**interactive** [ˌɪn·tər·'æk·tɪv] *adj* interactivo, -a

**interactive TV** *n* televisión *f* interactiva

**intercept** [ˌɪn·tər·'sept] *vt* interceptar; MATH cortar; **to ~ sb** cerrar el paso a alguien

**interception** [ˌɪn·tər·'sep·ʃən] *n* **1.** (*act of intercepting*) interceptación *f;* MATH intersección *f* **2.** SPORTS (*football play*) intercepción *f*

**interchange** [ˌɪn·tər·'tʃeɪndʒ] **I.** *n* **1.** intercambio *m* **2.** (*of roads*) enlace *m,* periférico *m Méx* **II.** *vt* (*exchange: ideas, knowledge*) intercambiar; COMPUT (*data*) intercambiar

**interchangeable** [ˌɪn·tər·'tʃeɪn·dʒə·bəl] *adj* intercambiable

**intercom** ['ɪn·tər·kam] *n* (*on a plane or ship*) intercomunicador *m;* (*in a building*) portero *m* automático; **through (an) ~** por el interfono; **to speak over the ~** hablar por el portero automático

**intercourse** ['ɪn·tər·kɔrs] *n* **1.** sexual **~** contacto *m* sexual; **to have sexual ~ with sb** tener relaciones sexuales con alguien **2.** *form* social **~** trato *m* social

**interest** ['ɪn·trɪst] **I.** *n* **1.** (*hobby*) interés *m;* **to take an ~ in sth** interesarse por algo **2.** (*curiosity*) **to lose ~ in sb/sth** perder el interés por alguien/algo **3.** **~s** (*profit, advantage*) interés *m;* **a conflict of ~s** un conflicto de intereses;

**to look after the ~s of sb** velar por los intereses de alguien; **to pursue one's own ~s** perseguir los propios intereses; **in the ~ of liberty** en pro de la libertad **4.** (*power to excite attentiveness*) interés *m;* **this is of no ~ to me** eso no me interesa **5.** FIN interés *m;* **~ rate** tipo *m* de interés; **at 5%** con un interés del 5%; **to bear ~** devengar interés; **to earn/pay ~ on sth** percibir/pagar intereses por algo; **to pay back with ~** pagar con intereses; *fig* pagar con creces **6.** (*legal right*) participación *f;* **to have an ~ in sth** tener una participación en algo **II.** *vt* interesar; **may I ~ you in this encyclopedia?** ¿puedo mostrarle esta enciclopedia?

**interested** ['ɪn·trɪ·stɪd] *adj* interesado, -a; **to be ~ in sth/sb** estar interesado en algo/alguien

**interest-free** *adj* FIN sin intereses

**interesting** ['ɪn·trɪ·stɪŋ] *adj* interesante

**interfere** [ˌɪn·tər·'fɪr] *vi* **1.** (*become involved*) interferir; **to ~ between two people** entrometerse entre dos personas **2.** (*disturb*) molestar **3.** RADIO, TECH (*hamper signals*) producir interferencias **4.** SPORTS (*get in way*) obstaculizar

**interference** [ˌɪn·tər·'fɪr·əns] *n* **1.** (*hindrance*) intromisión *f* **2.** RADIO, TECH, SPORTS interferencia *f*

**interim** ['ɪn·tər·ɪm] **I.** *n* ínterin *m* **II.** *adj* provisional; (*payment*) a cuenta; **~ dividend** FIN dividendo *m* a cuenta; **~ coach/manager** entrenador/manager interino

**interior** [ɪn·'tɪr·i·ər] **I.** *adj* **1.** (*inner, inside, internal*) interno, -a; (*lighting*) interior **2.** (*central, inland, remote*) del interior **II.** *n* **1.** (*inside*) interior *m* **2.** POL (*home affairs*) **the U.S. Department of the Interior** el departamento del Interior de EE.UU.

**interior decoration** *n* interiorismo *m*

**interior designer** *n* interiorista *mf*

**intermediate** [ˌɪn·tər·'mi·di·ət] **I.** *adj* intermedio, -a; **~ course** curso *m* de nivel intermedio **II.** *n* intermediario, -a *m, f*

**intermission** [ˌɪn·tər·'mɪʃ·ən] *n* **1.** intermedio *m;* **without ~** sin pausa **2.** CINE, THEAT descanso *m*

**intermittent** [ˌɪn·tər·ˈmɪt·ənt] *adj* intermitente

**intern**[1] [ˈɪn·tɜrn] *n* estudiante *mf* en prácticas; **hospital ~** médico *m* asistente

**intern**[2] [ɪn·ˈtɜrn] I. *vt* recluir II. *vi* MED trabajar como interno, -a; SCHOOL hacer (las) prácticas

**internal** [ɪn·ˈtɜr·nəl] *adj a.* MED interno, -a; **for ~ use only** sólo para uso interno

**international** [ˌɪn·tər·ˈnæʃ·ə·nəl] I. *adj a.* LAW internacional; (*trade*) exterior II. *n* POL Internacional *f*

**internationalize** [ˌɪn·tər·ˈnæʃ·ə·nə·laɪz] *vt* internacionalizar

**Internet** [ˈɪn·tər·net] *n* COMPUT internet *m o f;* **to access the ~** entrar en internet; **over the ~** a través de internet

**internship** *n* prácticas *f pl* como interno, -a *m, f,* pasantía *f* Col

**interplay** [ˈɪn·tər·pleɪ] *n* interacción *f*

**Interpol** [ˈɪn·tər·pal] *n abbr of* **International Criminal Police Organization** Interpol *f*

**interpret** [ɪn·ˈtɜr·prɪt] I. *vt* interpretar II. *vi* interpretar; **to ~ from English into Spanish** interpretar del inglés al español

**interpreter** [ɪn·ˈtɜr·prɪ·tər] *n* intérprete *mf*

**interrogate** [ɪn·ˈter·ə·geɪt] *vt* interrogar

**interrogation** [ɪn·ˌter·ə·ˈgeɪ·ʃən] *n* 1. *a.* COMPUT interrogación *f* 2. LAW interrogatorio *m;* **police ~** interrogatorio policial

**interrogative** [ˌɪn·tə·ˈrag·ə·t̬ɪv] I. *n* LING (*word*) palabra *f* interrogativa II. *adj* LING interrogativo, -a

**interrupt** [ˌɪn·tə·ˈrʌpt] *vi, vt* interrumpir

**interruption** [ˌɪn·tə·ˈrʌp·ʃən] *n* interrupción *f*

**intersection** [ˌɪn·tər·ˈsek·ʃən] *n* 1. (*crossing of lines*) intersección *f* 2. AUTO cruce *m*

**interval** [ˈɪn·tər·vəl] *n a.* MUS intervalo *m;* **at ~s of five minutes** a intervalos de cinco minutos; **at regular ~s** a intervalos regulares

**intervene** [ˌɪn·tər·ˈvin] *vi* 1. (*involve oneself to help*) intervenir; **to ~ militarily/personally** intervenir militarmente/personalmente; **to ~ on sb's behalf** interceder por alguien 2. (*meddle unhelpfully*) **to ~ in sth** mezclarse en algo

3. (*elapse*) sobrevenir

**intervening** *adj* **in the ~ period** en el ínterin

**intervention** [ˌɪn·tər·ˈven·ʃən] *n* intervención *f;* **military ~** MIL intervención militar

**interview** [ˈɪn·tər·vju] I. *n* (*formal conversation*) entrevista *f;* **telephone ~** encuesta *f* telefónica; **to have a job ~** tener una entrevista de trabajo; **to give an ~** conceder una entrevista II. *vt* entrevistar; **to ~ sb about sth** encuestar a alguien sobre algo

**interviewee** [ˌɪn·tər·vju·ˈi] *n* entrevistado, -a *m, f*

**interviewer** [ˈɪn·tər·vju·ər] *n* entrevistador(a) *m(f)*

**intestine** [ɪn·ˈtes·tɪn] *n* intestino *m*

**intimacy** [ˈɪn·tə·mə·si] <-ies> *n* 1. (*familiarity*) intimidad *f* 2. (*sexual relations*) relaciones *f pl* íntimas

**intimate**[1] [ˈɪn·tə·mət] *adj* 1. (*close, sexual*) íntimo, -a; **~ relationship** relaciones *f pl* íntimas; **to be on ~ terms with sb** tener confianza con alguien 2. (*personal: letter*) personal 3. (*link*) estrecho, -a

**intimate**[2] [ˈɪn·tə·meɪt] *vt form* insinuar

**intimidate** [ɪn·ˈtɪm·ɪ·deɪt] *vt* intimidar; **to ~ sb into doing sth** coaccionar a alguien para que haga algo

**intimidating** *adj* intimidante

**intimidation** [ɪn·ˌtɪm·ɪ·ˈdeɪ·ʃən] *n* intimidación *f*

**into** [ˈɪn·tə] *prep* 1. (*to the inside of*) en; (*towards*) hacia; **to walk ~ a place** entrar en un sitio; **to get ~ bed** meterse en la cama; **~ the future** hacia el futuro 2. (*indicating an extent in time or space*) **deep ~ the forest** en lo más profundo del bosque 3. (*against*) contra; **to drive ~ a tree** chocar contra un árbol; **to bump ~ a friend** tropezar con un amigo 4. (*to the state or condition of*) **to burst ~ tears** echarse a llorar; **to grow ~ a woman** hacerse una mujer; **to translate from Spanish ~ English** traducir del español al inglés; **to turn sth ~ sth** convertir algo en algo 5. *inf* (*interested in*) **she's really ~ her new job** está entusiasmada con su nuevo trabajo; **I think they are ~ drugs** creo que andan metidos en drogas **6.** MATH **two goes ~ five two and a half times** cinco dividido entre dos es igual a dos y medio

**intolerable** [ɪn·ˈtal·ər·ə·bəl] *adj* intolerable

**intolerant** [ɪn·ˈtal·ər·ənt] *adj* intolerante; **to be ~ of different opinions** ser intolerante con las opiniones diferentes; **to be ~ of alcohol** MED no tolerar el alcohol

**intoxicate** [ɪn·ˈtak·sɪ·keɪt] **I.** *vt* **1.** *a. fig* (*induce inebriation*) embriagar **2.** MED intoxicar **II.** *vi* **1.** *a. fig* (*cause intoxication*) embriagar **2.** MED intoxicar

**intoxicating** [ɪn·ˈtak·sɪ·keɪ·tɪŋ] *adj* **1.** (*exhilarating, stimulating*) embriagador(a) **2.** (*substance*) estupefaciente; (*causing drunkenness*) alcohólico, -a

**intoxication** [ɪn·ˌtak·sɪ·ˈkeɪ·ʃən] *n* **1.** *a. fig* (*drunkenness*) embriaguez *f* **2.** MED intoxicación *f*

**intransitive** [ɪn·ˈtræn·sɪ·t̬ɪv] *adj* LING, MATH intransitivo, -a

**intravenous** [ˌɪn·trə·ˈvi·nəs] *adj* MED intravenoso, -a; **~ feeding** alimentación *f* por vía intravenosa

**intricate** [ˈɪn·trɪ·kət] *adj* **1.** (*detailed*) intrincado, -a **2.** (*complicated: mechanism*) complejo, -a

**intrigue** [ɪn·ˈtrig] *vt* intrigar; **to be ~d by sth** estar intrigado con algo **II.** *vi* (*plot*) intrigar **III.** [ˈɪn·trig] *n* intriga *f*

**intriguing** [ɪn·ˈtri·gɪŋ] *adj* **1.** (*mysterious*) intrigante **2.** (*fascinating*) fascinante; (*smile*) enigmático, -a

**introduce** [ˌɪn·trə·ˈdus] *vt* **1.** (*acquaint*) presentar; **allow me to ~ myself** permítame que me presente **2.** (*raise interest in subject*) **to ~ sb to sth** iniciar a alguien en algo **3.** (*insert*) introducir; **to ~ sth into sth** introducir algo en algo

**introduction** [ˌɪn·trə·ˈdʌk·ʃən] *n* **1.** (*making first acquaintance*) presentación *f*; **letter of ~** carta *f* de presentación; **to do the ~s** hacer las presentaciones **2.** (*first contact with sth*) iniciación *f* **3.** (*establishment*) introducción *f*; (*of a bill*) presentación *f* **4.** (*insertion*) introducción *f* **5.** (*preface*) prólogo *m*; MUS

introducción *f*

**introductory** [ˌɪn·trə·ˈdʌk·tə·ri] *adj* **1.** (*elementary, preparatory*) de introducción; (*course*) de iniciación **2.** COM (*price*) de lanzamiento **3.** (*beginning*) introductorio, -a; **~ remarks** aclaraciones *f pl* preliminares

**intrude** [ɪn·ˈtrud] **I.** *vi* **1.** (*meddle*) entrometerse; **to ~ into sth** inmiscuirse en algo **2.** (*disturb*) estorbar; **am I intruding?** ¿molesto? **II.** *vt* **to ~ sth on sb** importunar a alguien con algo

**intruder** [ɪn·ˈtru·dər] *n* intruso, -a *m, f*

**intrusion** [ɪn·ˈtru·ʒən] *n* **1.** (*encroachment, infringement*) intrusión *f* **2.** (*meddling*) intromisión *f*

**intrusive** [ɪn·ˈtru·sɪv] *adj* (*noise*) molesto, -a; (*question*) indiscreto, -a; (*person*) entrometido, -a

**intuition** [ˌɪn·tu·ˈɪʃ·ən] *n* intuición *f*

**intuitive** [ɪn·ˈtu·ɪ·tɪv] *adj* intuitivo, -a; **an ~ feeling** una intuición

**invade** [ɪn·ˈveɪd] **I.** *vt* invadir; **to ~ sb's privacy** invadir la intimidad de alguien **II.** *vi* invadir

**invader** [ɪn·ˈveɪ·dər] *n* invasor(a) *m(f)*

**invalid**[1] [ˈɪn·və·lɪd] **I.** *n* (*incapacitated person*) inválido, -a *m, f* **II.** *adj* (*disabled*) inválido, -a *f*

**invalid**[2] [ɪn·ˈvæl·ɪd] *adj* **1.** LAW (*not legally binding*) nulo, -a; **to become ~** caducar **2.** (*unsound*) no válido, -a

**invalidate** [ɪn·ˈvæl·ɪdeɪt] *vt* **1.** (*argument, decision*) invalidar; (*results*) anular **2.** LAW anular; **to ~ a judgment** revocar una sentencia

**invalidity** [ˌɪn·və·ˈlɪd·ə·t̬i] *n* **1.** (*inadmissibility: of a contract*) nulidad *f*; (*of evidence*) invalidez *f* **2.** (*faultiness: of a theory*) invalidez

**invaluable** [ɪn·ˈvæl·ju·ə·bəl] *adj* inestimable; **to be ~ to sb** tener un valor inestimable para alguien

**invariable** [ɪn·ˈver·i·ə·bəl] *adj form* (*custom*) invariable

**invasion** [ɪn·ˈveɪ·ʒən] *n* **1.** MIL invasión *f* **2.** (*interference*) violación *f*; **~ of privacy/of a right** violación de la intimidad/ de un derecho

**invent** [ɪn·ˈvent] *vt* inventar

**invention** [ɪn·ˈven·ʃən] *n* **1.** (*gadget*)

invento *m* **2.** (*creativity*) inventiva *f*
**3.** (*falsehood*) invención *f*

**inventive** [ɪn·ˈven·tɪv] *adj* inventivo, -a

**inventor** [ɪn·ˈven·tər] *n* inventor(a) *m(f)*

**inventory** [ˈɪn·vən·tɔr·i] <-ies> I. *n* **1.** (*catalog*) inventario *m; to draw up an ~* levantar un inventario **2.** (*stock*) stock *m* II. *vt* inventariar III. *adj* (*audit, level, number*) de inventario

**inverse** [ɪn·ˈvɜrs] I. *adj* inverso, -a II. *n the ~ of sth* lo contrario de algo

**invert** [ɪn·ˈvɜrt] *vt* invertir

**invest** [ɪn·ˈvest] I. *vt* **1.** (*put in*) invertir **2.** (*bestow attributes*) investir II. *vi* invertir; *to ~ in sth* invertir en algo

**investigate** [ɪn·ˈves·tɪ·geɪt] *vt* investigar

**investigation** [ɪn·ˌves·tɪ·ˈgeɪ·ʃən] *n* investigación *f*

**investigator** [ɪn·ˈves·tɪ·geɪ·tər] *n* investigador(a) *m(f)*

**investment** [ɪn·ˈvest·mənt] I. *n a. fig* inversión *f; long-term ~s* inversiones *f pl* a largo plazo II. *adj* de inversión

**investor** [ɪn·ˈves·tər] *n* inversor(a) *m(f)*

**invigorating** [ɪn·ˈvɪg·ə·reɪ·tɪŋ] *adj* vigorizante

**invincible** [ɪn·ˈvɪn·sə·bəl] *adj* invencible

**invisible** [ɪn·ˈvɪz·ə·bəl] *adj* invisible

**invitation** [ˌɪn·vɪ·ˈteɪ·ʃən] *n* invitación *f; an ~ to sth* una invitación a algo

**invite**[1] [ˈɪn·vaɪt] *n inf* invitación *f*

**invite**[2] [ɪn·ˈvaɪt] *vt* **1.** (*request to attend*) invitar; *to ~ sb for/to sth* invitar a alguien a algo **2.** (*request*) pedir; *to ~ offers* solicitar ofertas **3.** (*provoke*) buscarse; *to ~ trouble* buscar(se) problemas

**inviting** [ɪn·ˈvaɪ·tɪŋ] *adj* (*attractive*) atractivo, -a, atrayente

**invoice** [ˈɪn·vɔɪs] I. *vt* facturar II. *n* factura *f; ~ for sth* factura de algo

**involuntary** [ɪn·ˈval·ən·ter·i] *adj* involuntario, -a

**involve** [ɪn·ˈvalv] *vt* (*implicate*) implicar, involucrar; *to be ~d in sth* estar metido [*or* envuelto] en algo

**involved** [ɪn·ˈvalvd] *adj* (*implicated*) involucrado, -a

**inward** [ˈɪn·wərd] *adj* **1.** (*inner*) interior, íntimo, -a **2.** (*moving in: flow*) hacia adentro

**inwardly** *adv* interiormente

**inwards** [ˈɪn·wərds] *adv* hacia adentro, para dentro

**I/O** COMPUT *abbr of* input/output E/S

**iodine** [ˈaɪ·ə·daɪn] *n* yodo *m*

**ion** [ˈaɪ·ən] *n* ión *m*

**IOU** [ˌaɪ·oʊ·ˈju] *n inf abbr of* I owe you pagaré *m*

**IQ** [ˌaɪ·ˈkju] *n abbr of* intelligence quotient CI *m*

**IRA** [ˌaɪ·ar·ˈeɪ] *n abbr of* Irish Republican Army IRA *m*

**Iran** [ɪ·ˈræn] *n* Irán *m*

**Iranian** [ɪ·ˈreɪ·ni·ən] I. *n* iraní *mf* II. *adj* iraní

**Iraq** [ɪ·ˈrak] *n* Irak *m*

**Iraqi** [ɪ·ˈrak·i] I. *n* iraquí *mf* II. *adj* iraquí

**Ireland** [ˈaɪr·lənd] *n* Irlanda *f; Republic of ~* República *f* de Irlanda; **Northern ~** Irlanda del Norte

**iris** [ˈaɪ·rɪs] <-es> *n* **1.** BOT lirio *m* **2.** ANAT iris *m*

**Irish** [ˈaɪ·rɪʃ] I. *adj* irlandés, -esa II. *n* **1.** *pl* (*people*) **the ~** los irlandeses **2.** LING irlandés *m; ~ Gaelic* gaélico *m* irlandés

**Irishman** [ˈaɪ·rɪʃ·mən] <-men> *n* irlandés *m*

**Irishwoman** [ˈaɪ·rɪʃ·wʊm·ən] <-women> *n* irlandesa *f*

**irk** [ɜrk] *vt* fastidiar

**iron** [ˈaɪ·ərn] I. *n* **1.** (*metal*) hierro *m*, fierro *m AmL* **2.** (*for pressing clothes*) plancha *f* **3.** SPORTS (*golf club*) hierro *m* II. *vt* planchar; *fig* allanar III. *vi* planchar IV. *adj* de hierro; (*discipline*) férreo, -a

**Iron Age** I. *n* edad *f* del hierro II. *adj* de la edad del hierro

**Iron Curtain** *n* HIST, POL Telón *m* de Acero, Cortina *f* de Hierro

**ironic** [aɪ·ˈran·ɪk] *adj*, **ironical** [aɪ·ˈran·ɪ·kəl] *adj* irónico, -a

**ironing** [ˈaɪ·ər·nɪŋ] *n* planchado *m; to do the ~* planchar

**ironing board** *n* tabla *f* de planchar, burro *m* de planchar *Méx*

**irony** [ˈaɪ·rə·ni] <-ies> *n* ironía *f*

**irrational** [ɪ·ˈræʃ·ə·nəl] *adj* irracional

**irregular** [ɪ·ˈreg·jə·lər] *adj* irregular; (*behavior*) anómalo, -a; (*life*) desordenado, -a

**irrelevance** [ɪrˈrel·ə·vənts] *n*, **irrelevancy** <-ies> *n* irrelevancia *f*

**irrelevant** [ɪrˈrel·ə·vənt] *adj* irrelevante; **to be ~ to sth** no ser relevante para algo

**irreparable** [ɪˈrep·ər·ə·bəl] *adj* irreparable

**irreplaceable** [ˌɪr·ɪˈpleɪ·sə·bəl] *adj* irreemplazable

**irresistible** [ˌɪr·ɪˈzɪs·tə·bəl] *adj* irresistible

**irrespective** [ˌɪr·ɪˈspek·tɪv] *prep* ~ **of** aparte de; ~ **of sth/sb** sin tener en cuenta algo/a alguien

**irresponsible** [ˌɪr·ɪˈspan·sə·bəl] *adj* irresponsable

**irretrievable** [ˌɪr·ɪˈtri·və·bəl] *adj* irrecuperable

**irreverent** [ɪˈrev·ər·ənt] *adj* irreverente

**irreversible** [ˌɪr·ɪˈvɜr·sə·bəl] *adj* irreversible

**irrevocable** [ɪˈrev·ə·kə·bəl] *adj* irrevocable

**irrigate** [ˈɪr·ɪ·ɡeɪt] *vt* **1.** AGR regar **2.** MED irrigar

**irrigation** [ˌɪr·ɪˈɡeɪ·ʃən] **I.** *n* **1.** AGR riego *m* **2.** MED irrigación *f* **II.** *adj* de riego; ~ **canal** acequia *f*

**irrigation plant** *n* planta *f* de riego

**irritable** [ˈɪr·ɪ·tə·bəl] *adj* irritable

**irritant** [ˈɪr·ɪ·tənt] *n* irritante *m*

**irritate** [ˈɪr·ɪ·teɪt] *vt* **1.** (*aggravate*) irritar, molestar **2.** MED irritar

**irritation** [ˌɪr·ɪˈteɪ·ʃən] *n* irritación *f*

**IRS** [ˌaɪ·arˈes] *n abbr of* **Internal Revenue Service** *Oficina de la Renta de EE.UU*

**is** [ɪz] *vt, vi 3rd pers sing of* **to be**

**ISDN** *n abbr of* **integrated services digital network** RDSI *f*

**Islam** [ɪzˈlam] *n* islam *m*

**Islamic** [ɪzˈlam·ɪk] *adj* islámico, -a; ~ **law** ley islámica

**island** [ˈaɪ·lənd] *n* isla *f*; ~ **of calm** *fig* refugio *m* de paz

**islander** [ˈaɪ·lən·dər] *n* isleño, -a *m, f*

**isn't** [ˈɪz·ənt] = **is not**

**isolate** [ˈaɪ·sə·leɪt] *vt* aislar

**isolated** [ˈaɪ·sə·leɪ·tɪd] *adj* (*outlying, disconnected*) aislado, -a

**isolation** [ˌaɪ·sə·ˈleɪ·ʃən] *n* **1.** (*separation*) aislamiento *m* **2.** (*loneliness*) soledad *f*

**isosceles triangle** [aɪˈsas·ə·liz ˈtraɪ·æŋ·ɡəl] *n* MATH triángulo *m* isósceles

**issue** [ˈɪʃ·u] **I.** *n* **1.** (*problem, topic*) cuestión *f*; **side** ~ asunto *m* menor; **the real ~s** las cuestiones de fondo; **the point at** ~ el punto en cuestión; **at** ~ a debate **2.** PUBL (*copy*) número *m*; **latest** ~ último número **3.** FIN, ECON (*of shares, stamps*) emisión *f*; (*of checks*) expedición *f* **4.** *form* (*offspring, children*) descendencia *f* **II.** *vt* **1.** (*supply*) emitir; (*passport*) expedir **2.** (*ultimatum*) presentar **3.** (*publish*) publicar **III.** *vi* **to** ~ **from** (*be born out of*) surgir de; (*come out of*) provenir de

**it** [ɪt] **I.** *pron dem* la, lo *en muchos casos 'it' se omite cuando se refiere a una información ya conocida;* **who was** ~? ¿quién era?; ~'**s in my bag** está en mi bolso; ~'**s Paul who did that** fue Paul quien lo hizo **II.** *pron pers* **1.** él, ella, ello *direct object:* lo, la *indirect object:* le, se; ~ **went off badly** aquello fue mal; **your purse? I took** ~ ¿tu monedero? lo cogí yo; ~'**s your cat, give** ~ **something to eat** es tu gato, dale algo de comer; **I'm afraid of** ~ le tengo miedo; **I fell into** ~ me caí dentro **2.** (*time*) **what time is** ~? ¿qué hora es? **3.** (*weather*) ~'**s cold** hace frío; ~'**s snowing** está nevando **4.** (*distance*) ~'**s 5 miles to town from here** hay 8 km hasta el pueblo **5.** (*empty subject*) ~ **seems that...** parece que... **6.** (*passive subject*) ~ **is said/hoped that...** se dice/espera que...

**IT** [ˌaɪˈti] *n* COMPUT *abbr of* **Information Technology** informática *f*

**Italian** [ɪˈtæl·jən] **I.** *adj* italiano, -a **II.** *n* **1.** (*person*) italiano, -a *m, f* **2.** LING italiano *m*

**italics** [ɪˈtæl·ɪks] *npl* cursiva *f*; **in** ~ en cursiva

**Italy** [ˈɪt·ə·li] *n* Italia *f*

**itch** [ɪtʃ] **I.** *vi* **1.** MED picar **2.** *fig inf* **to** ~**ing to do sth** morirse por hacer algo *fig* **II.** *n* MED comezón *f*, rasquiña *f Arg*

**itchy** [ˈɪtʃ·i] <-ier, -iest> *adj* que pica; **my arm feels** ~ siento picazón en el brazo

**item** [ˈaɪ·təm] *n* **1.** (*thing*) artículo *m*, objeto *m*; ~ **of clothing** prenda *f* de vestir **2.** (*topic*) asunto *m*; ~ **on the agenda** asunto a tratar; ~ **by** ~ punto por punto **3.** COM partida *f* **4.** PUBL noticia *f* **5.** *inf* (*couple*) parejita *f*

**itemize** ['aɪ·tə·maɪz] *vt* detallar

**itinerary** [aɪ·'tɪn·ə·rer·i] <-ies> *n* itinerario *m*

**it'll** ['ɪt·əl] = **it will**

**its** [ɪts] *adj pos* su; ~ **color/weight** su color/peso; ~ **mountains** sus montañas; **the cat hurt** ~ **head** el gato se lastimó la cabeza

**it's** [ɪts] **1.** = **it is 2.** = **it has**

**itself** [ɪt·'self] *pron reflexive* él mismo, ella misma, ello mismo *direct, indirect object:* se *after prep:* sí mismo, -a; **the place** ~ el sitio en sí; **by** ~ solo

**IUD** [,aɪ·ju·'di] *n abbr of* **intrauterine device** DIU *m*

**I've** [aɪv] = **I have** *see* **have**

**ivory** ['aɪ·və·ri] <-ies> *n* marfil *m*

**Ivory Coast** *n* Costa *f* de Marfil

**ivory tower** *n fig* torre *f* de marfil

**ivy** ['aɪ·vi] <-ies> *n* hiedra *f*

# J

**J, j** [dʒeɪ] *n* J, j *f*; ~ **as in Juliet** J de Juan **J** *n* PHYS *abbr of* **joule** J

**jab** [dʒæb] **I.** *n* **1.** (*with a pin*) pinchazo *m*; (*with an elbow*) codazo *m* **2.** (*in boxing*) (*golpe m*) corto *m* **II.** <-bb-> *vt* **to** ~ **a needle into sth** pinchar algo con una aguja **III.** <-bb-> *vi* **to** ~ **at sb/sth** (**with sth**) dar a alguien/algo (con algo)

**jabbering** *n* farfulla *f*

**jack** [dʒæk] *n* **1.** AUTO gato *m* **2.** (*in cards*) jota *f*; (*in a Spanish pack*) sota *f* **3.** *inf* (*anything*) **you don't know** ~! ¡tú no sabes un carajo!

◆**jack up** *vt* **1.** (*object*) levantar **2.** *sl* (*prices*) subir

**jacket** ['dʒæk·ɪt] *n* **1.** (*short coat*) chaqueta *f*, percha *f* AmC, chapona *f* RíoPl, cuácara *f* Chile **2.** (*of a book*) sobrecubierta *f*

**jacket potato** *n* patata *f* asada (con piel)

**jack-in-the-box** ['dʒæk·ɪn·ðə·bɑks] <-xes> *n* caja *f* de sorpresas

**jackpot** ['dʒæk·pɑt] *n* (*premio m*) gordo *m* ▶ **to hit the** ~ *inf* llevarse el gordo

**Jacuzzi®** [dʒə·'ku·zi] *n* jacuzzi® *m*

**jaded** ['dʒeɪ·dɪd] *adj* **to be** ~ **with sth** estar harto de algo

**jagged** ['dʒæɡ·ɪd] *adj* irregular; (*coastline, rocks*) recortado, -a; (*cut, tear*) desigual

**jail** [dʒeɪl] **I.** *n* cárcel *f*, prisión *f*; **to put sb in** ~ encarcelar a alguien **II.** *vt* encarcelar; **she was** ~ed **for life** la condenaron a cadena perpetua

**jailbreak** *n* fuga *f*

**jailer** *n*, **jailor** ['dʒeɪ·lər] *n* carcelero, -a *m, f*

**jam¹** [dʒæm] *n* CULIN mermelada *f*

**jam²** [dʒæm] **I.** *n* **1.** *inf* (*awkward situation*) aprieto *m*; **to get into a** ~ meterse en un lío **2.** (*blockage*) **traffic** ~ atasco *m*; **paper** ~ COMPUT atasco de papel **II.** <-mm-> *vt* **1.** (*cause to become stuck*) atascar; (*door*) obstruir; **to** ~ **sth into sth** embutir algo en algo **2.** (*a wheel*) trabar **III.** <-mm-> *vi* **1.** (*become stuck*) atrancarse; (*brakes*) bloquearse **2.** (*play music*) tocar, improvisar

**jam-packed** [,dʒæm·'pækt] *adj inf* **the streets were** ~ **with people** las calles estaban atestadas de gente

**janitor** ['dʒæn·ɪ·tər] *n* conserje *mf*

**January** ['dʒæn·ju·er·i] <-ies> *n* enero *m*; *s. a.* **April**

**Japan** [dʒə·'pæn] *n* Japón *m*

**Japanese** [,dʒæp·ə·'niz] **I.** *adj* japonés, -esa **II.** *n* **1.** (*person*) japonés, -esa *m, f* **2.** LING japonés *m*

**jar¹** [dʒɑr] *n* (*container*) tarro *m*

**jar²** [dʒɑr] **I.** <-rr-> *vt* (*shake*) sacudir **II.** <-rr-> *vi* (*cause unpleasant feelings*) **to** ~ **on sb's nerves** crispar los nervios a alguien **III.** *n* (*shake*) sacudida *f*

**jargon** ['dʒɑr·ɡən] *n* jerga *f*

**jaundice** ['dʒɔn·dɪs] *n* MED ictericia *f*

**javelin** ['dʒæv·lɪn] *n* (*spear*) jabalina *f*

**jaw** [dʒɔ] *n* **1.** ANAT mandíbula *f* **2.** ~**s** (*mouth*) boca *f*; *fig* fauces *fpl* **3.** ~**s** TECH mordazas *fpl*

**jaywalking** n cruce m imprudente de calzada

**jazz** [dʒæz] n jazz m; ~ **band/club** grupo m/club m de jazz ▶ **and all** that ~ sl y todo ese rollo

◆**jazz up** vt sl crear ambiente

**jazzy** [ˈdʒæz·i] <-ier, -iest> adj 1. MUS de jazz 2. sl (flashy) llamativo, -a

**jealous** [ˈdʒel·əs] adj 1. (envious) envidioso, -a; **to be ~ of sb** tener celos de alguien 2. (fiercely protective) celoso, -a; **to be ~ of sth** ser celoso de algo

**jealousy** [ˈdʒel·ə·si] <-ies> n 1. (possessiveness) celos mpl 2. (envy) envidia f

**jeans** [dʒinz] npl vaqueros mpl; **a pair of ~** vaqueros

**jeep** [dʒip] n jeep m

**jeer** [dʒɪr] I. vt abuchear II. vi mofarse III. n burla f

**jeez** [dʒiz] interj inf (expressing surprise) ¡hala!; (expressing annoyance) ¡vaya, hombre!

**jelly** [ˈdʒel·i] <-ies> n 1. (soft transparent substance) gelatina f 2. (jam) mermelada f

**jellyfish** <-es> n medusa f

**jeopardy** [ˈdʒep·ər·di] n peligro m

**jerk** [dʒɜrk] I. n 1. (jolt) sacudida f 2. (movement) tirón m 3. pej sl (person) gilipollas mf II. vi sacudirse III. vt 1. (shake) sacudir 2. (pull) tirar bruscamente de

**jerky**[1] [ˈdʒɜr·ki] <-ier, -iest> adj (not smooth: ride) dando botes [or tumbos], a tirones Méx

**jerky**[2] [ˈdʒɜr·ki] n CULIN **beef** ~ cecina f

**jersey** [ˈdʒɜr·zi] n 1. (garment) jersey m 2. (sports shirt) camiseta f 3. (cloth) tejido m de punto 4. (type of cow) Jersey f (raza de ganado vacuno)

**Jesuit** [ˈdʒez·u·ɪt] I. n jesuita m II. adj jesuita

**Jesus** [ˈdʒi·zəs] I. n Jesús II. interj inf ¡por Dios!, ¡híjole! AmL

**Jesus Christ** I. n Jesucristo m II. interj inf ¡Dios mío!

**jet**[1] [dʒet] I. n 1. (aircraft) avión m a reacción, jet m 2. (stream) chorro m 3. (nozzle) surtidor m II. <-tt-> vi volar

**jet**[2] [dʒet] n (stone) azabache m

**jet engine** n motor m a reacción

**jet fighter** n caza m a reacción

**jetfoil** n hidroala f a reacción

**jet lag** n desfase m horario, jet lag m

**jet plane** n avión m a reacción

**jet-propelled** adj a reacción

**jet set** n inf **the** ~ la jet-set

**jetty** [ˈdʒet·i] n embarcadero m

**Jew** [dʒu] n judío, -a m, f

**jewel** [ˈdʒu·əl] n 1. (piece of jewelry) a. fig joya f 2. (watch part) rubí m

**jeweler** [ˈdʒu·ə·lər] n, **jeweller** [ˈdʒu·ə·lər] n joyero, -a m, f

**jewelry** [ˈdʒu·əl·ri] n joyas fpl; **a piece of** ~ una joya

**Jewess** [ˈdʒu·ɪs] n offensive judía f

**Jewish** [ˈdʒu·ɪʃ] adj judío, -a

**jiffy** [ˈdʒɪf·i] n inf **in a** ~ en un santiamén

**jigsaw** [ˈdʒɪg·sɔ] n sierra f de vaivén

**jigsaw puzzle** n puzzle m, rompecabezas m inv

**jingle** [ˈdʒɪŋ·gəl] I. vt hacer tintinear II. vi tintinear III. n 1. (noise) tintineo m 2. (in advertisements) jingle m

**jinx** [dʒɪŋks] I. vt gafar II. n gafe f; **to put a** ~ **on sb/sth** echar una maldición a alguien/algo

**jitters** [ˈdʒɪt·ərz] npl inf (nervousness) nervios mpl; **he got the** ~ le entró el canguelo

**jittery** [ˈdʒɪt·ər·i] <-ier, -iest> adj inf nervioso, -a; **he felt** ~ le dió el tembleque

**job** [dʒab] n 1. (piece of work, employment) trabajo m; **to apply for a** ~ presentarse para un trabajo 2. (duty) deber m; **to do one's** ~ cumplir con su deber; **it's not her** ~ no es asunto suyo

**job description** n descripción f del puesto

**job interview** n entrevista f de trabajo

**jobless** [ˈdʒab·lɪs] I. adj desocupado, -a II. npl **the** ~ los parados mpl

**job market** n mercado m laboral

**job rating** n evaluación f del lugar de trabajo

**jobseeker** n demandante mf de empleo

**jock** [dʒak] n 1. sl (athlete) atleta m 2. (jockstrap) suspensorio m

**jockey** [ˈdʒak·i] I. n jockey mf II. vi **to ~ for sth** competir por algo

**jockstrap** n suspensorio m

**jog** [dʒag] I. n 1. (run) trote m; **to go for a ~** hacer footing 2. (nudge) golpe m II. <-gg-> vi correr III. <-gg-> vt **to ~ sb's memory** refrescar la memoria a alguien

◆**jog along** vi inf ir tirando

**jogger** ['dʒag·ər] n persona f que hace footing

**jogging** ['dʒag·ɪŋ] n footing m; **to go (out) ~** hacer footing

**john** [dʒan] n sl (toilet) váter m

**join** [dʒɔɪn] I. vt 1. (connect) juntar, unir; **to ~ hands** cogerse de la mano 2. (come together with sb) reunirse [or juntarse] con 3. (become member of: club) unirse a; (society) ingresar en; (army) alistarse en II. vi 1. (unite) unirse 2. (become member) hacerse socio 3. (participate) **to ~ in sth** tomar parte en algo

**joiner** ['dʒɔɪ·nər] n carpintero, -a m, f

**joint** [dʒɔɪnt] I. adj conjunto, -a II. n 1. ANAT articulación f; **to come out of ~** dislocarse 2. (connection) unión f, juntura f 3. TECH conexión f 4. sl (nightclub) garito m 5. sl (marijuana) porro m

**jointed** adj articulado, -a

**jointly** adv conjuntamente

**joint venture** n empresa f conjunta

**joke** [dʒoʊk] I. n 1. (amusing story) chiste m; (trick, remark) broma f; **to play a ~ on sb** gastar una broma a alguien; **to not be able to take a ~** no aceptar una broma 2. inf (easy thing) **to be no ~** no ser cosa de broma 3. inf (ridiculous thing or person) ridiculez f; **what a ~!** ¡qué farsa! II. vi bromear; **to ~ about sth** hacer bromas sobre algo

**joker** ['dʒoʊ·kər] n 1. (one who jokes) bromista mf 2. inf (annoying person) idiota m 3. (playing card) comodín m

**joking** I. adj jocoso, -a II. n bromas fpl

**jokingly** adv en broma

**jolly** ['dʒal·i] <-ier, -iest> adj (happy: tune) alegre

**jolt** [dʒoʊlt] I. n (sudden jerk) sacudida f II. vt 1. (jerk) sacudir 2. (shock) sobresaltar III. vi dar una sacudida; (vehicle) traquetear

**jostle** ['dʒas·əl] I. vt empujar II. vi

1. (push) empujarse 2. (compete) disputarse; **to ~ for position** luchar por hacerse un hueco

**jot** [dʒat] <-tt-> vt **to ~ sth down** apuntar algo

**jottings** npl apuntes mpl

**journal** ['dʒɜr·nəl] n 1. (periodical) revista f especializada 2. (diary) diario m

**journalism** ['dʒɜr·nə·lɪz·əm] n periodismo m, diarismo m AmL

**journalist** ['dʒɜr·nə·lɪst] n periodista mf

**journey** ['dʒɜr·ni] I. n viaje m II. vi liter viajar

**joy** [dʒɔɪ] n 1. (gladness) alegría f; **to jump for ~** saltar de alegría 2. (cause of joy) placer m

**joyful** ['dʒɔɪ·fəl] adj feliz

**joyless** ['dʒɔɪ·lɪs] adj falto, -a de alegría

**joyous** ['dʒɔɪ·əs] adj liter de júbilo

**joy ride** ['dʒɔɪ·raɪd] n paseo en un coche robado

**joystick** ['dʒɔɪ·stɪk] n 1. AVIAT palanca f de mando 2. COMPUT joystick m

**jubilant** ['dʒu·bɪ·lənt] adj jubiloso, -a; (crowd) exultante

**jubilation** [,dʒu·bɪ·'leɪ·ʃən] n júbilo m

**jubilee** ['dʒu·bə·li] n 1. (anniversary) aniversario m 2. REL jubileo m

**judge** [dʒʌdʒ] I. n 1. LAW juez mf 2. (referee) árbitro m; **panel of ~s** jurado m II. vi a. LAW juzgar; (give one's opinion) opinar III. vt 1. a. LAW juzgar; (question) decidir; (assess) valorar; (consider) considerar; **to ~ that...** opinar que... 2. (as a referee) arbitrar

**judg(e)ment** ['dʒʌdʒ·mənt] n 1. LAW fallo m 2. (opinion) opinión f 3. (discernment) criterio m

**judicial** [dʒu·'dɪʃ·əl] adj judicial

**judiciary** [dʒu·'dɪʃ·i·er·i] n form poder m judicial

**judicious** [dʒu·'dɪʃ·əs] adj form acertado, -a

**judo** ['dʒu·doʊ] n judo m

**jug** [dʒʌg] n 1. (container) jarra f 2. pl vulg (breasts) melones mpl, tetas fpl

**juggernaut** ['dʒʌg·ər·nɔt] n fuerza f irresistible

**juggle** ['dʒʌg·əl] I. vi a. fig hacer juegos malabares II. vt a. fig hacer juegos malabares con

**juggler** n malabarista mf

**jugular vein** n vena f yugular

**juice** [dʒus] n 1. (drink) zumo m 2. (of meat) jugo m 3. sl (electricity) luz f; (fuel) sopa f

**juicy** ['dʒu·si] <-ier, -iest> adj 1. (fruit, steak) jugoso, -a 2. inf (profit) sustancioso, -a 3. (details) picante

**jukebox** ['dʒuk·baks] n máquina f de discos

**July** [dʒu·'laɪ] n julio m; s. a. **April**

**jumble** ['dʒʌm·bəl] I. n revoltijo m II. vt mezclar

**jumbo** ['dʒʌm·boʊ] I. adj gigante m II. n inf gigante, -a m, f

**jump** [dʒʌmp] I. vi 1. (leap) saltar; to ~ up and down pegar saltos 2. (skip) brincar; to ~ for joy brincar de alegría 3. (increase suddenly) subir de golpe II. vt 1. (leap across or over) fig saltar 2. (attack) atacar ▶ to ~ the gun precipitarse III. n (leap) salto m

◆**jump at** vt (an opportunity) no dejar escapar

◆**jump in** vi entrar deprisa

◆**jump up** vi levantarse de un salto

**jumper** ['dʒʌm·pər] n 1. (person, animal) saltador(a) m(f) 2. (dress) pichi m

**jumper cables** npl AUTO cables m pl de arranque

**jumpsuit** n FASHION mono m

**jumpy** ['dʒʌm·pi] <-ier, -iest> adj inf nervioso, -a

**junction** ['dʒʌŋk·ʃən] n cruce m

**June** [dʒun] n junio m; s. a. **April**

**jungle** ['dʒʌŋ·gəl] n 1. (forest) selva f 2. fig (tangled mass) maraña f

**junior** ['dʒun·jər] I. adj 1. (younger) más joven 2. SPORTS juvenil 3. (lower in rank) subalterno, -a; (partner) comanditario, -a II. n 1. (younger person) he is five years my ~ es cinco años menor que yo 2. UNIV, SCHOOL estudiante mf de tercer año

**junk¹** [dʒʌŋk] I. n (objects of no value) trastos mpl, tiliches mpl AmC, Méx II. vt inf tirar a la basura

**junk²** [dʒʌŋk] n (boat) junco m

**junk food** n comida f basura

**junkie** ['dʒʌŋ·ki] n 1. sl (addict) yonqui mf 2. sl (fanatic) fanático, -a m, f

**junk mail** n propaganda f postal

**junkyard** n chatarrería f

**juror** ['dʒʊr·ər] n miembro mf del jurado

**jury** ['dʒʊr·i] n jurado m

**just** [dʒʌst] I. adv 1. (very soon) enseguida; we're ~ about to leave estamos a punto de salir 2. (now) precisamente; to be ~ doing sth estar justamente haciendo algo 3. (very recently) ~ after 10 o'clock justo después de las 10; she's ~ turned 15 acaba de cumplir 15 años 4. (exactly, equally) exactamente, justo; ~ like that justo así; ~ as I expected tal y como yo esperaba; ~ now ahora mismo; not ~ yet todavía no 5. (only) solamente; ~ a minute espera un momento 6. (simply) simplemente; ~ in case lo rains por si llueve 7. (barely) ~ (about), (only) ~ apenas; ~ in time justo a tiempo 8. ~ about (nearly) casi 9. it's ~ as well that... menos mal que... ▶ ~ my luck! ¡me tenía que pasar a mí! II. adj (fair) justo, -a

**justice** ['dʒʌs·tɪs] n 1. justicia f 2. (judge) juez mf

**justifiable** [ˌdʒʌs·tə·'faɪ·ə·bəl] adj justificable

**justification** [ˌdʒʌs·tə·fɪ·'keɪ·ʃən] n justificación f

**justify** ['dʒʌs·tɪ·faɪ] vt justificar; to ~ oneself to sb dar explicaciones a alguien

**justly** ['dʒʌst·li] adv justamente

**jut** [dʒʌt] <-tt-> vi to ~ out sobresalir

**juvenile** ['dʒu·və·naɪl] adj 1. form (young) juvenil 2. pej (childish) infantil

**juxtapose** ['dʒʌk·stə·poʊz] vt yuxtaponer

# K

**K, k** [keɪ] n K, k f; ~ as in **Kilo** K de kilo

**K** 1. COMPUT abbr of **kilobyte** K m 2. (thousand) **$30~** 30.000 dólares

**kaiser roll** ['kaɪ·zər·roʊl] n panecillo con semillas de amapola

**kamikaze attack** n ataque m kamikaze

**kangaroo** [ˌkæn·gə·'ru] <-(s)> n canguro m

**kangaroo court** *n* tribunal *m* desautorizado

**kaput** [ka-'put] *adj inf* (*appliance, car, etc.*) escacharrado, -a, dañado, -a; (*relationship*) finito, -a, acabado, -a

**karat** ['ker-ət] <-(s)> *n* quilate *m*

**karate** [kə-'ra-ţi] *n* kárate *m*

**karate chop** *n* golpe *m* de kárate

**kayak** ['kaɪ-æk] *n* kayak *m*

**kayaking** *n* I love ~ me encanta ir en kayak

**kebab** [kə-'bab] *n* kebab *m*

**keel** [kil] *n* NAUT quilla *f*

**keen** [kin] I. *adj* 1. (*intent, eager*) entusiasta; to be ~ on sth ser aficionado, -a a algo 2. (*perceptive: intelligence*) agudo, -a; to have a ~ sense of smell tener un agudo sentido del olfato 3. (*extreme*) fuerte; a ~ interest un vivo interés II. *n* lamento *m* fúnebre. *vi* lamentarse

**keep** [kip] I. *n* (*livelihood*) subsistencia *f*; to earn one's ~ ganarse el sustento ▶ for ~s para siempre. II. <kept, kept> *vt* 1. (*have: shop*) tener; (*animals*) criar 2. (*store: silence, secret*) guardar; ~ my seat guárdame el sitio; ~ the change quédese con el cambio 3. (*maintain*) mantener; to ~ sb under observation tener a alguien en observación; to ~ one's eyes fixed on sth/sb no apartar los ojos de algo/alguien; to ~ sth going mantener algo a flote *fig* 4. (*detain*) to ~ sb waiting hacer esperar a alguien; to ~ sb in prison tener a alguien en la cárcel; what kept you? ¿qué es lo que te ha entretenido? 5. (*fulfil*) cumplir; to ~ an appointment acudir a una cita; to ~ one's word cumplir su palabra 6. (*record: diary*) escribir; (*accounts*) llevar 7. (*person's expenses*) mantener; to earn enough to ~ oneself ganar lo bastante para mantenerse 8. (*obey, respect*) obedecer; (*law*) observar ▶ to ~ one's <u>balance</u> mantener el equilibrio; to ~ <u>time</u> marcar la hora III. <kept, kept> *vi* 1. *a. fig* (*stay fresh*) conservarse 2. (*stay*) mantenerse; to ~ fit mantenerse en forma; to ~ silent (*about sth*) guardar silencio (sobre algo); to ~ to the left circular por la izquierda; ~ quiet! ¡cállate!; ~ still! ¡estate quieto!

3. (*continue*) to ~ going (*person*) ir tirando; (*machine*) seguir funcionando; to ~ doing sth seguir haciendo algo; he ~s losing his keys siempre pierde las llaves

♦**keep ahead** *vi* seguir en cabeza

♦**keep away** I. *vi* mantenerse alejado, -a; he can't ~ from it no puede dejarlo; ~! ¡no te acerques! II. *vt always sep* mantener alejado, -a

♦**keep back** I. *vi* (*stay away*) to ~ from sth/sb mantenerse alejado de algo/alguien II. *vt* 1. to ~ one's tears contener las lágrimas 2. (*hide*) ocultar 3. (*retain sth*) to keep sth back quedarse con algo; (*slow down*) retrasar algo

♦**keep down** *vt* 1. to keep one's voice down no levantar la voz; to keep prices down controlar los precios 2. (*not vomit*) retener

♦**keep in** I. *vt* (*person*) no dejar salir; (*emotions*) contener II. *vi* to ~ line comportarse bien

♦**keep off** I. *vi* (*stay off*) mantenerse alejado, -a; '~' 'prohibido el paso'; '~ the grass' 'prohibido pisar el césped' II. *vt* 1. mantener alejado, -a; to keep the rain off sth/sb resguardar algo/a alguien de la lluvia; keep your hands off! ¡no lo toques! 2. (*avoid*) evitar

♦**keep on** I. *vi* (*continue*) seguir; to ~ doing sth seguir haciendo algo II. *vt always sep* seguir teniendo; (*not to dismiss*) no despedir

♦**keep out** I. *vi* no entrar; ~! ¡prohibido el paso!; to ~ of trouble no meterse en líos II. *vt* to keep sth/sb out (of sth) no dejar que entre algo/alguien (en algo); to keep the rain/cold out resguardar de la lluvia/del frío

♦**keep together** I. *vt* mantener juntos, -as II. *vi* mantenerse unidos, -as; please, ~ por favor, no se separen

♦**keep up** I. *vt* 1. (*trousers*) sujetar; (*ceiling*) sostener 2. (*continue*) seguir; ~ the good work! ¡sigue así!; keep it up! ¡sigue! 3. (*stop sb sleeping*) tener en vela II. *vi* 1. (*moral*) no decaer 2. (*continue*) seguir; the rain kept up all night *vt* siguió lloviendo durante toda la noche 3. (*to stay level with*) to

~ (with sb/sth) seguir el ritmo (de alguien/algo); **to ~ with the Joneses** *fig* no ser menos que los demás **4.** (*remain informed*) **to ~ with sth** mantenerse al tanto de algo; **to ~ with the times** estar al día

**keeper** ['ki·pər] *n* **1.** (*in charge*) guarda *mf*; (*museum*) conservador(a) *m(f)*; (*jail*) carcelero, -a *m, f* **2.** SPORTS portero, -a *m, f*, arquero, -a *m, f Arg*, golero, -a *m, f Urug*

**keeping** ['ki·pɪŋ] *n* **1.** (*guarding*) cargo *m* **2. in ~ with sth** de acuerdo con algo

**kelp** [kelp] *n* tipo de alga marrón usada en comidas

**kennel** ['ken·əl] *n* **1.** (*doghouse*) perrera *f* **2.** ~s (*boarding*) residencia *f* canina; (*breeding*) criadero *m* de perros

**kept** [kept] **I.** *pt, pp* of **keep II.** *adj* mantenido, -a

**kerosene** ['ker·ə·sin] *n* queroseno *m*

**ketchup** ['ketʃ·əp] *n* ketchup *m*

**kettle** ['ket·əl] *n* tetera *f*, pava *f AmL*; **to put the ~ on** poner agua a hervir

**key¹** [ki] **I.** *n* **1.** (*doors*) llave *f*; **master ~** llave maestra **2. a.** COMPUT tecla *f*; **caps lock ~** tecla de bloqueo de mayúsculas; **to hit a ~** pulsar una tecla **3.** (*list*) clave *f*; (*exercises*) soluciones *fpl* **4.** MUS tono *m*; **in the ~ of C major** en (tono de) do mayor; **to go off ~** desafinar **II.** *adj* (*factor, figure, role*) clave; ~ **decision** decisión *f* clave [*or* fundamental] **III.** *vt* (*type*) **to ~ (in)** teclear

◆**key in** *vt* COMPUT picar, teclear

◆**key up** *vt* emocionar; **to be keyed up** estar emocionado, -a

**key²** [ki] *n* (*island*) cayo *m*

**keyboard** ['ki·bɔrd] *n* teclado *m*

**keyboarding** *n* introducción *f* desde teclado

**keyboard instrument** *n* instrumento *m* de teclado

**keyhole** ['ki·hoʊl] *n* ojo *m* de la cerradura

**key money** *n* adelanto *m*; **as ~** en concepto de adelanto

**keynote address** *n* discurso *m* central

**keynote speech** *n* discurso *m* central

**keypad** ['ki·pæd] *n* COMPUT teclado *m* numérico

**key ring** *n* llavero *m*

**Key West** *n* Cayo Hueso *m*

**KIA** *adj abbr of* **killed in action** fallecido, -a en acto de servicio

**kick** [kɪk] **I.** *n* **1.** (*person*) patada *f*; (*horse*) coz *f*; (*in football*) tiro *m* **2.** (*exciting feeling*) placer *m*; **to do sth for ~s** hacer algo para divertirse; **to get a ~ out of sth** encontrar placer en algo **3.** (*craze*) **he is on an exercise ~ at the moment** ahora le ha dado por hacer ejercicio **II.** *vt* **1.** dar una patada; **to ~ sth open** abrir algo de una patada; **to ~ a ball** chutar una pelota **2.** (*stop*) dejar; **to ~ a habit** dejar un vicio **III.** *vi* **1.** (*person*) dar patadas a; (*horse*) dar coces a; SPORTS chutar **2. to be alive and ~ing** *inf* estar vivito y coleando

◆**kick about, kick around I.** *vi inf* (*hang about*) andar por ahí; (*thing*) andar rodando **II.** *vt* (*a ball*) dar patadas a

◆**kick around** *vt inf* **1.** (*treat badly*) tratar a patadas **2.** (*ponder: idea*) plantearse, dar vueltas a

◆**kick away** *vt* apartar de un golpe

◆**kick back I.** *vt* (*football*) devolver **II.** *vi inf* **1.** (*recoil*) retroceder **2.** *sl* (*give a kickback*) sobornar

◆**kick in** *vt* derribar a patadas; **to kick sb's teeth in** romper la cara a alguien

◆**kick off I.** *vi* (*begin*) empezar, arrancar *inf*; (*in football*) hacer el saque de centro **II.** *vt* quitar de un puntapié

◆**kick out** *vt* **he was kicked out of the party** lo echaron de la fiesta

◆**kick up** *vt* **to ~ dust** *a. fig* levantar polvo

**kickoff** ['kɪk·ɔf] *n* **1.** SPORTS saque *m* inicial **2.** *inf* (*beginning*) arranque *m*

**kid** [kɪd] *n* **1.** (*child*) niño, -a *m, f*, chavito, -a *m, f Méx*, pelado, -a *m, f Col, Ecua*; ~ **brother** hermano *m* pequeño; **as a ~...** de niño... **2.** (*young person*) chico, -a *m, f*, muchacho, -a *m, f* **3.** *sl* (*term of address*) nene, -a *m, f* **4.** ZOOL cría *f*; (*young goat*) cabrito *m* ▶ **that's ~'s stuff** eso está tirado [*or* regalado] *inf* **II.** <-dd-> *vi* bromear; **are you ~ding?** ¿bromeas?; **just ~ding** es broma **III.** *vt* **to ~ sb (about sth)** tomar el pelo a alguien (con algo) **IV.** *vr* **stop ~ding**

**K**

yourself! ¡desengáñate!

**kidnap** ['kɪd·næp] I. <-pp-> vt secuestrar, plagiar AmL II. n secuestro m, plagio m AmL

**kidnapper** ['kɪd·næp·ər] n secuestrador(a) m(f)

**kidnapping** n secuestro m

**kidney** ['kɪd·ni] n riñón m; ~ disease enfermedad f renal

**kidney bean** n judía f, poroto m CSur

**kidney stone** n MED cálculo m renal

**kill** [kɪl] I. n 1. (slaughter) matanza f 2. (hunting) pieza f ▶ to go in for the ~ entrar a matar II. vi matar; thou shalt not ~ (Bible) no matarás III. vt 1. (cause to die) matar; to ~ oneself suicidarse 2. (destroy) acabar con; my feet are ~ing me! ¡los pies me están matando!; to ~ sb with kindness abrumar a alguien con atenciones

♦**kill off** vt exterminar

**killer** ['kɪl·ər] n (sb who kills) asesino, -a m, f; to be a ~ (person) ser un asesino; (disease) cobrar muchas víctimas; the test was a real ~ fig sl el examen ha sido mortal

**killer whale** n orca f

**killing** ['kɪl·ɪŋ] I. n (of a person) asesinato m; (of an animal) matanza f ▶ to make a ~ inf hacer su agosto II. adj 1. (murderous) asesino, -a 2. (exhausting) mortal

**kilo** ['ki·loʊ] n kilo m

**kilobyte** ['kɪl·ə·baɪt] n COMPUT kilobyte m

**kilogram** ['kɪl·ə·græm] n kilogramo m

**kilometer** [kɪ·'lam·ɪ·t̬ər] n kilómetro m

**kilt** [kɪlt] n falda f escocesa, pollera f escocesa CSur

**kin** [kɪn] n next of ~ parientes m pl más cercanos

**kind¹** [kaɪnd] adj amable; to be ~ to sb ser amable con alguien; he was ~ enough to... tuvo la amabilidad de...; would you be ~ enough/so ~ as to...? ¿me haría usted el favor de...?; with ~ regards (in a letter) muchos recuerdos

**kind²** [kaɪnd] I. n 1. (type) clase f; he is not that ~ (of person) no es de esa clase (de personas); what ~ of...? ¿qué

clase de...?; all ~s of... todo tipo de...; to hear/say nothing of the ~ no haber oído/dicho nada parecido 2. (sth similar to) especie f; a ~ of soup una especie de sopa 3. (sth equal to) he repaid her betrayal in ~ pagó su traición con la misma moneda 4. (limited) in a ~ of way en cierta manera 5. (payment) to pay sb in ~ pagar a alguien en especias II. adv inf I ~ of like it bueno, no está mal; he was ~ of sad estaba como triste; "do you like it?" — "~ of" ¿te gusta?" — "no está mal"

**kindergarten** ['kɪn·dər·gar·dən] n guardería f, jardín m infantil Chile, jardín m de infantes RíoPl

**kindle** ['kɪn·dəl] I. vt a. fig encender; to ~ sb's interest despertar el interés de alguien II. vi a. fig encenderse

**kindly** ['kaɪnd·li] I. <-ier, -iest> adj amable II. adv 1. (in a kind manner) amablemente 2. (please) you are ~ requested to leave the building se ruega abandonen el edificio; ~ put that book away! ¡haz el favor de guardar ese libro! 3. (favorably) to take ~ to sth aceptar algo de buen grado

**kindness** ['kaɪnd·nɪs] <-es> n 1. (act of being kind) amabilidad f 2. (kind act) favor m

**kinetic** [kɪ·'net̬·ɪk] adj PHYS cinético, -a

**king** [kɪŋ] n 1. GAMES rey m; the ~ of beasts el rey de la selva 2. (in checkers) dama f

**kingdom** ['kɪŋ·dəm] n reino m; animal/plant ~ reino animal/vegetal; the ~ of God REL el Reino de Dios ▶ to blow sth to ~ come hacer saltar algo en pedazos

**kingfisher** ['kɪŋ·fɪʃ·ər] n ZOOL martín m pescador

**kink** [kɪŋk] n 1. (twist: in a pipe, rope) retorcimiento m; (in hair) rizo m 2. (sore muscle) tortícolis f inv; to have a ~ in one's neck tener tortícolis 3. (problem) fallo m; to iron out (a few) ~s pulir algunos defectos

**kinky** ['kɪŋ·ki] <-ier, -iest> adj 1. (twisted) retorcido, -a 2. (with tight curls) ensortijado, -a 3. (unusual) raro, -a; (involving unusual sexual acts) pervertido, -a

**kiosk** ['ki·ask] n (stand, pavilion) quiosco m

**kipper** ['kɪp·ər] n arenque m ahumado

**kiss** [kɪs] I. <-es> n beso m; ~ of life respiración f boca a boca; ~ of death fig beso de la muerte; to blow sb a ~ lanzar un beso a alguien II. vi besarse III. vt besar; to ~ sb goodnight/goodbye dar un beso de buenas noches/despedida a alguien

**kisser** ['kɪs·ər] n 1. (person) he's a wonderful ~! ¡besa muy bien! 2. sl (mouth) morro m, trompa f

**kiss-off** ['kɪs·ɔf] n sl to give the ~ dar calabazas

**kit** [kɪt] n 1. (set) utensilios mpl; first aid ~ botiquín m de primeros auxilios; tool ~ caja f de herramientas 2. (parts to put together) kit m

**kitchen** ['kɪtʃ·ɪn] n cocina f

**kitchen cabinet** n POL camarilla f

**kitchenette** [,kɪtʃ·ɪ·'net] n cocinita f, rincón m cocina

**kitchen foil** n papel m de aluminio

**kitchen paper** n papel m de cocina

**kitchen sink** n fregadero m, lavaplatos m inv And, pileta f RíoPl

**kitchen towel** n (dishtowel) paño m de cocina

**kitchen unit** n módulo m de cocina

**kite** [kaɪt] n 1. ZOOL milano m 2. (toy) cometa f, volantón m AmL; to fly a ~ hacer volar una cometa; fig tantear el terreno ► go fly a ~! inf ¡vete a freír espárragos!

**kitten** ['kɪt·ən] n gatito, -a m, f

**kitty** ['kɪt·i] <-ies> n 1. (kitten or cat) minino m 2. (money) fondo m

**kiwi** ['ki·wi] n 1. ZOOL, BOT kiwi m 2. inf (New Zealander) neozelandés, -esa m, f

**kJ** abbr of **kilojoule** kJ

**Kleenex®** ['kli·neks] n kleenex® m

**kleptomania** [,klep·toʊ·'meɪ·ni·ə] n cleptomanía f

**kleptomaniac** [,klep·toʊ·'meɪ·ni·æk] n cleptómano, -a m, f

**km/h, kmph** abbr of **kilometers per hour** km/h

**knack** [næk] n habilidad f; to have a ~

for sth tener facilidad para algo; to get the ~ of sth coger el tranquillo a algo, tomar la mano a algo AmL

**knee** [ni] I. n rodilla f; to get down on one's ~s ponerse de rodillas; on your ~s! ¡de rodillas! II. vt to ~ sb dar un rodillazo a alguien

**kneecap** ['ni·kæp] n rótula f

**kneel** [nil] <knelt or kneeled, knelt or kneeled> vi arrodillarse

**knee sock** n media f, calcetín m

**knelt** [nelt] pt of **kneel**

**knew** [nu] pt of **know**

**knickers** ['nɪk·ərz] npl bombachos mpl

**knickknack** ['nɪk·næk] n inf cachivache m

**knife** [naɪf] <knives> I. n 1. (cutting object) cuchillo m 2. (dagger) puñal m; to wield a ~ blandir un puñal elev 3. (in a machine) cuchilla f II. vt apuñalar

**knife-edge** n filo m

**knife sharpener** n afilador m

**knifing** ['naɪ·fɪŋ] n pelea f con navajas

**knight** [naɪt] I. n 1. (man given honorable rank) sir m 2. HIST (man of high social position) caballero m 3. (chess figure) caballo m ► ~ in shining armor príncipe m azul II. vt HIST armar caballero; (give honorable title) conceder el título de 'sir'

**knighthood** n título m de 'sir'

**knit** [nɪt] I. vi (with wool) hacer punto; (with a machine) tejer II. vt (wool) tejer
♦ **knit together** I. vi (combine or join) unirse II. vt fig (join) unir

**knitting** n 1. (the product of knitting) tejido m de punto 2. (material being knitted) labor f de punto 3. (action of knitting) she likes ~ le gusta hacer punto

**knitwear** ['nɪt·wer] n géneros m pl de punto

**knob** [nab] n 1. (round handle: of a door) pomo m; (of a drawer) tirador m 2. (lump) bulto m

**knock** [nak] I. n 1. (blow) golpe m 2. (sound) llamada f 3. fig inf crítica f II. vi 1. (hit) golpear; to ~ on the window/at the door llamar a la ventana/puerta 2. TECH (engine, pipes) martillear III. vt 1. (hit) golpear; to ~ sb dar un

K

golpe a alguien **2.** *inf* (*criticize*) criticar

**◆knock about** *vi, vt see* **knock around**

**◆knock around I.** *vi inf* andar vagando, vagabundear **II.** *vt* (*person*) pegar; (*ball*) golpear

**◆knock back** *vt inf* **1.** (*drink quickly*) pimplar rápidamente **2.** (*surprise*) pasmar

**◆knock down** *vt* **1.** (*cause to fall*) derribar **2.** (*demolish*) demoler **3.** (*reduce*) **to knock the price down** bajar el precio

**◆knock off I.** *vt* **1.** (*cause to fall off*) hacer caer **2.** (*reduce*) rebajar; **to knock $5 off the price** rebajar 5 dólares el precio **3.** *sl* (*murder*) cargarse **4.** (*stop*) **to knock it off** dejarlo; **knock it off!** ¡déjalo! **II.** *vi inf* terminar; **to ~ work at 3 p.m.** soltar a las 3 de la tarde

**◆knock out** *vt* **1.** (*render unconscious*) dejar sin sentido; SPORTS dejar K.O.; (*cause to sleep*) hacer dormir; (*exhaust*) agotar **2.** (*eliminate*) eliminar **3.** (*produce quickly*) hacer en un momento, producir

**◆knock over** *vt* atropellar; (*an object*) volcar

**◆knock together** *vt* construir deprisa, improvisar

**◆knock up I.** *vt sl* (*impregnate*) dejar preñada; **to get knocked up** quedarse preñada **II.** *vi* SPORTS pelotear

**knockdown** *adj* **1.** (*very cheap*) baratísimo, -a; **~ price** precio *m* de saldo; (*at auction*) precio *m* inicial **2.** (*violent: blow*) duro, -a; (*argument*) arrollador(a); (*fight*) violento, -a

**knocker** ['nak·ər] *n* (*on door*) aldaba *f*

**knockout** *n* **1.** (*competition*) eliminatoria *f* **2.** SPORTS (*boxing*) K.O. *m*; **to win sth by a ~** ganar algo por K.O. **3.** *sl* (*attractive*) bombón *m* **II.** *adj* **1.** (*competition*) eliminatorio, -a **2.** (*boxing*) **~ blow** golpe *m* duro; *fig* duro revés *m* **3.** *sl* (*attractive*) macizo, -a

**knot** [nat] **I.** *n* **1.** (*tied join*) **a.** NAUT nudo *m*; **to tie/untie a ~** hacer/deshacer un nudo; (*bow*) lazo *m* **2.** (*chignon*) moño *m*, chongo *m Méx* **3.** (*small group*) corrillo *m* **5.** (*in a*

*wooden board*) nudo *m* ▶ **to tie the ~** *inf* prometerse **II.** <-tt> *vt* anudar

**know** [nou] **I.** <knew, known> *vt* **1.** (*have information*) saber; **to ~ a bit of English** saber un poco de inglés; **she ~s all of their names** se sabe los nombres de todos; **to ~ how to do sth** saber hacer algo; **to ~ all there is to ~ about sth** saber todo lo que hay que saber sobre algo; **to ~ what one is talking about** saber de lo que uno habla; **to ~ sth by heart** saberse algo de memoria; **not to ~ the first thing about sth/sb** no saber nada de algo/alguien; **do you ~ what I mean?** ¿entiendes?; **you ~ what?** *inf* ¿sabes qué? **2.** (*be acquainted*) conocer; **to ~ sb by sight/by name/personally** conocer a alguien de vista/por el nombre/personalmente; **~ing Mary,...** conociendo a Mary,...; **to get to ~ each other** llegar a conocerse (bien) **3.** (*recognize*) conocer, reconocer; **to ~ sb for sth** reconocer a alguien por algo **II.** <knew, known> *vi* **1.** (*be informed*) saber; **as far as I ~** por lo que sé; **to ~ better (than sb)** saber más (que alguien); **to ~ of** [*or* **about**] **sth** saber de algo, estar enterado de algo; **you ~** (*you remember*) ya sabes; (*you understand*) tú ya me entiendes; (**well**) **what do you ~!** *iron* ¡no me digas!; **I ~!** (*I've got an idea!*) ¡ya lo tengo!; (*said to agree with sb*) lo sé **2.** (*be certain*) estar seguro; **one never ~s** nunca se sabe **III.** *n* **to be in the ~ about sth** estar al tanto de algo

**know-how** *n* know-how *m*

**knowing** ['nou·ɪŋ] *adj* astuto, -a; (*grins, look, smile*) de complicidad

**knowingly** *adv* **1.** (*meaningfully*) con conocimiento **2.** (*with full awareness*) a sabiendas

**know-it-all** ['nou·ɪt̬·ɔl] *n inf* sabelotodo *mf*

**knowledge** ['nal·ɪdʒ] *n* **1.** (*body of learning*) conocimiento *m*; **to have a thorough ~ of** sth conocer algo a fondo **2.** (*acquired information*) saber *m*; **to have (no) ~ about sth/sb** (no) saber de algo/alguien; **to my ~** que yo sepa **3.** (*awareness*) conocimiento *m*; **to do**

sth without sb's ~ hacer algo sin que alguien lo sepa

**knowledgeable** ['nal·ɪdʒ·ə·bəl] *adj* entendido, -a

**known** [noʊn] I. *vt, vi pp of* **know** II. *adj* (*expert*) reconocido, -a; (*criminal*) conocido, -a; **no ~ reason** sin razón aparente; **to make sth ~** dar a conocer algo

**knuckle** ['nʌk·əl] *n* nudillo *m*

**kooky** ['ku·ki] <-ier, -iest> *adj sl* majareta

**Koran** [kə·'ræn] *n* **the ~** el Corán

**kosher** ['koʊ·ʃər] *adj* autorizado, -a por la ley judía

**kumquat** ['kʌm·kwat] *n* quinoto *m*, naranja *f* china

**Kwanzaa** ['kwan·zə] *n* kwanzaa *m festival cultural afroamericano*

# L

**L, l** [el] *n* L, l *f*; **~ as in Lima** L de Lisboa

**l** *abbr of* **liter** l.

**LA** [ˌel·'eɪ] *n* **1.** *abbr of* **Los Angeles** Los Ángeles **2.** *abbr of* **Louisiana** Luisiana *f*

**lab** [læb] *n abbr of* **laboratory** laboratorio *m*

**label** ['leɪ·bəl] I. *n* **1.** (*on bottle, clothing*) etiqueta *f* **2.** (*brand name*) marca *f* II. <-l- *or* -ll-, -l- *or* -ll-> *vt* (*affix label*) etiquetar

**labor** ['leɪ·bər] I. *n* **1.** (*work*) trabajo *m*; **manual ~** trabajo manual **2.** ECON (*workers*) mano *f* de obra; **skilled ~** mano de obra cualificada **3.** MED (*childbirth*) parto *m*; **to be in ~** estar de parto II. *vi* **1.** (*work*) trabajar **2.** (*do sth with effort*) esforzarse; **to ~ over sth** esforzarse en algo

**laboratory** ['læb·rə·ˌtɔr·i] <-ies> *n* laboratorio *m*

**Labor Day** *n* Día *m* del Trabajo *(primer lunes de septiembre)*

**laborer** *n* peón *m*

**laborious** [lə·'bɔr·i·əs] *adj* (*task*) laborioso, -a

**labor union** *n* sindicato *m*

**labyrinth** ['læb·ə·rɪnθ] *n* laberinto *m*

**lace** [leɪs] I. *n* **1.** (*cloth*) encaje *m*, cinta *f*; (*edging*) puntilla *f* **2.** (*cord*) cordón *m*; **shoe ~s** cordones *m pl* (de zapatos) II. *vt* **1.** (*fasten*) atar **2.** (*add alcohol to*) echar licor a

♦**lace up** *vt* atar

**lack** [læk] I. *n* falta *f*; **~ of funds** escasez *f* de fondos; **for ~ of ...** por falta de... II. *vt* carecer de; **she ~s talent/experience** le falta talento/experiencia

**lacking** ['læk·ɪŋ] *adj* **he is ~ in talent/experience** le falta talento/experiencia

**lackluster** ['læk·ˌlʌs·tər] *adj* **1.** (*not shiny*) deslustrado, -a **2.** (*dull*) gris

**lad** [læd] *n inf* chico *m*

**ladder** ['læd·ər] *n* **1.** (*for climbing*) escalera *f* (de mano) **2.** (*hierarchy*) escala *f*; **to climb the social ~** subir en la escala social

**laden** ['leɪ·dən] *adj* cargado, -a; **to be ~ with...** estar cargado de...

**ladies' room** *n* servicio *f* [*or* baño *m*] de señoras

**ladle** ['leɪ·dəl] I. *n* cucharón *m*, ramillón *m Col, Ven* II. *vt* (*soup*) servir (con cucharón)

**lady** ['leɪ·di] <-ies> *n* señora *f*; (*aristocratic*) dama *f*; **young ~** señorita *f*; **the ~ of the house** la señora de la casa; **cleaning ~** mujer de la limpieza; **ladies and gentlemen!** ¡señoras y señores!

**lag** [læg] I. *n* (*lapse*) lapso *m* II. <-gg-> *vi* rezagarse; **to ~ behind (sb/sth)** quedarse atrás (con respecto a alguien/algo)

**lager** ['la·gər] *n* cerveza *f* rubia

**lagging** ['læg·ɪŋ] *n* revestimiento *m*

**laid** [leɪd] *pt, pp of* **lay**[1]

**lain** [leɪn] *pp of* **lie**[2]

**laity** ['leɪ·ə·ti] *n* **the ~** el laicado

**lake** [leɪk] *n* lago *m*

**lamb** [læm] *n* **1.** (*animal*) cordero *m* **2.** (*meat*) (carne *f* de) cordero *m*

**lamb chop** *n* chuleta *f* de cordero

**lame** [leɪm] *adj* **1.** (*person, horse*) cojo, -a *B inf* (*argument*) flojo, -a; (*excuse*) débil, poco convincente

**lament** [lə·'ment] I. *n* MUS, LIT elegía *f* II. *vt* lamentar III. *vi* **to ~ over sth** lamentarse de algo

**lamentable** [lə·ˈmən·tə·bəl] *adj* lamentable

**laminated** [ˈlæm·ɪ·neɪ·tɪd] *adj* (*document*) plastificado, -a; (*glass, wood*) laminado, -a

**lamp** [læmp] *n* lámpara *f*; **street ~** farola *f*

**lamppost** [ˈlæmp·poʊst] *n* farola *f*

**lampshade** [ˈlæmp·ʃeɪd] *n* pantalla *f* (de lámpara)

**land** [lænd] I. *n* 1. GEO, AGR tierra *f*; **on ~** en tierra; **to travel by ~** viajar por tierra; **to work (on) the ~** trabajar (en) el campo 2. (*for building*) terreno *m* 3. (*country*) país *m* II. *vi* 1. (*plane, bird*) aterrizar 2. (*arrive by boat*) arribar 3. (*set down, fall on: bird, fly*) posarse 4. (*person, ball*) caer III. *vt* 1. (*bring onto land: aircraft*) (hacer) aterrizar; (*boat*) amarrar 2. (*obtain*) conseguir; **to ~ a job** conseguir un trabajo 3. (*cause*) **to ~ sb in trouble** meter a alguien en un lío

**landing** [ˈlæn·dɪŋ] *n* 1. AVIAT aterrizaje *m*; **to make a ~** realizar un aterrizaje 2. NAUT desembarco *m* 3. (*on staircase*) rellano *m*

**landing gear** *n* AVIAT tren *m* de aterrizaje

**landing strip** *n* pista *f* de aterrizaje

**landlady** [ˈlænd·leɪ·di] <-ies> *n* (*of house*) propietaria *f*; (*of boarding house*) patrona *f*

**landless** *adj* sin tierra

**landlocked** *adj* cercado, -a de tierra; **a ~ country** un país sin acceso al mar

**landlord** *n* (*of house*) propietario *m*; (*of boarding house*) patrón *m*

**landmark** *n* 1. (*object serving as a guide*) mojón *m*; (*point of recognition*) punto *m* destacado, marca *f* 2. (*monument*) monumento *m* histórico II. *adj* (*significant: decision, ruling*) que marca un hito

**land mine** *n* mina *f* terrestre

**landowner** *n* terrateniente *mf*

**land reform** *n* reforma *f* agraria

**landscape** [ˈlænd·skeɪp] I. *n* 1. (*scenery, painting*) paisaje *m* 2. *fig* panorama *m* 3. COMPUT impresión *f* apaisada

II. *vt* ajardinar

**landslide** [ˈlænd·slaɪd] *n* 1. GEO corrimiento *m* de tierras 2. POL victoria *f* arrolladora; **to win by a ~** ganar por mayoría abrumadora

**lane** [leɪn] *n* 1. (*marked strip: on highway*) carril *m*; SPORTS calle *f*; **bus/bike ~** carril bus/de bicicleta; **to change ~s** cambiar de carril 2. (*small road*) vereda *f*

**language** [ˈlæŋ·gwɪdʒ] *n* 1. (*system of communication*) lenguaje *m*; **computer programming ~** lenguaje de programación (de ordenadores); **bad ~** palabrotas *fpl*; **formal/spoken/written ~** lengua formal/oral/escrita 2. (*of particular community*) idioma *m*; **native ~** lengua *f* materna; **the English ~** la lengua inglesa; **to speak the same ~** hablar el mismo idioma

**lank** [læŋk] *adj* 1. (*hair*) lacio, -a 2. (*person*) larguirucho, -a

**lanky** [ˈlæŋ·ki] *adj* desgarbado, -a

**lantern** [ˈlæn·tərn] *n* linterna *f*; (*light*) farol *m*

**lap**[1] [læp] *n* falda *f*

**lap**[2] [læp] SPORTS I. *n* vuelta *f* II. <-pp-> *vt* SPORTS doblar

**lap**[3] [læp] <-pp-> I. *vt* (*drink*) beber dando lengüetazos II. *vi* (*hit gently*) **to ~ against sth** chocar suavemente contra algo

♦**lap up** *vt* 1. (*drink*) beber dando lengüetazos 2. *fig* aceptar entusiasmado; **he lapped up the praise** saboreaba las alabanzas

**lapel** [lə·ˈpel] *n* solapa *f*

**lapse** [læps] I. *n* 1. (*failure*) lapsus *m inv*; **~ of memory** lapsus de memoria 2. (*period*) lapso *m* II. *vi* 1. (*deteriorate*) deteriorarse 2. (*end*) terminar; (*contract*) vencer; (*subscription*) caducar 3. (*revert to*) **to ~ into sth** reincidir en algo; **to ~ into one's native dialect** recurrir al dialecto nativo

**lapsed** [læpst] *adj* (*membership, subscription*) caducado, -a

**laptop** (*computer*) [ˈlæp·tap] *n* (ordenador *m*) portátil *m*

**larch** [lɑrtʃ] *n* BOT alerce *m*

**lard** [lɑrd] *n* manteca *f* de cerdo

**larder** ['lɑr·dər] n despensa f

**large** [lɑrdʒ] adj grande; **a ~ number of people** un gran número de gente; **a ~ family** una familia numerosa ▶ **to be at ~** andar suelto; **by and ~** por lo general

**largely** ['lɑrdʒ·li] adv en gran parte

**large-scale** adj a gran escala

**lark¹** [lɑrk] n (bird) alondra f ▶ **to be up with the ~** levantarse con las gallinas

**lark²** [lɑrk] n 1. (joke) broma f 2. (adventure) **to go on a ~** irse a la aventura

**laryngitis** [ˌler·ɪn·'dʒɑr·t̬ɪs] n laringitis f inv

**laser** ['leɪ·zər] n láser m

**lash¹** [læʃ] <-es> n (eyelash) pestaña f

**lash²** [læʃ] I. <-es> n 1. (whip) látigo m; (flexible part of a whip) tralla f 2. (stroke of whip) latigazo m II. vt 1. (whip) azotar 2. (criticize) vituperar

◆**lash about** vi, **lash around** vi golpear a diestro y siniestro

◆**lash down** vt atar firmemente

◆**lash out** vi **to ~ at sb** atacar a alguien; (verbally) arremeter contra alguien

**last¹** [læst] n (for shoes) horma f

**last²** [læst] I. adj 1. (final: time, opportunity) último, -a; **to have the ~ word** tener la última palabra; **to wait till the ~ minute** (to do sth) esperar hasta el último minuto (para hacer algo) 2. (most recent) último, -a; ~ **week** la semana pasada; ~ **night** anoche II. adv 1. (at the end) por último; ~ **but not least** por último, pero no por eso menos importante 2. (most recent) por última vez III. n **the ~ to do sth** el último en hacer algo; **the second to ~** el penúltimo; **that was the ~ of the cake** era todo lo que quedaba del pastel ▶ **at (long) ~** al fin

**last³** [læst] I. vi durar II. vt **this coat has ~ed me five years** hace cinco años que tengo este abrigo

**lasting** ['læs·t̬ɪŋ] adj duradero, -a

**lastly** ['læst·li] adv por último

**last name** n apellido m

**latch** [lætʃ] <-es> n pestillo m

**late** [leɪt] I. adj 1. (after appointed time) retrasado, -a; **you're ~!** ¡llegas tarde!; **the train was an hour ~** el tren

llegó con una hora de retraso 2. (after the usual time) tardío, -a 3. (towards end of) ~ **night TV show** programa m de televisión de noche; **in the ~ nineteenth century** a finales del siglo XIX 4. (recent: development) reciente; ~**est news** noticias f pl de última hora 5. (deceased) fallecido, -a, difunto, -a II. adv 1. (after usual time) tarde; **too little, too ~** poco y tarde inf; **to work ~** trabajar hasta (muy) tarde 2. (towards end of) ~ **in the day** a última hora del día; ~ **at night** (muy) entrada la noche 3. (recently) **as ~ as the 1980s** aún en los años ochenta; **of ~** últimamente ▶ **better ~ than never** prov más vale tarde que nunca prov

**latecomer** ['leɪt̬ˌkʌm·ər] n persona o cosa que llega tarde

**lately** ['leɪt̬·li] adv (recently) últimamente, ultimadamente Méx; **until ~** hasta hace poco

**later** ['leɪ·t̬ər] I. adj comp of **late** posterior II. adv comp of **late** más tarde; ~ **on** después; **see you ~!** ¡hasta luego!

**latest** ['leɪ·t̬ɪst] I. adj superl of **late** último, -a; **the ~...** el más reciente...; **his ~ movie** su última película; **at the ~** a más tardar II. n **the ~** las últimas noticias; **the ~ in art/physics** lo último en arte/física; **at the (very) ~** a más tardar

**lathe** [leɪð] n torno m

**Latin** ['læt̬·ən] I. adj latino, -a II. n 1. LING latín m 2. (person) latino, -a m, f

**Latin America** n Latinoamérica f, América f Latina

**Latin American** I. adj latinoamericano, -a II. n (person) latinoamericano, -a m, f

**latish** ['leɪ·t̬ɪʃ] I. adj (algo) tardío, -a. II. adv algo tarde

**latitude** ['læt̬·ɪ·tud] n 1. GEO latitud f 2. (freedom) libertad f

**latter** ['læt̬·ər] adj (second of two) **the ~** el último; **in the ~ half of the year** en la segunda mitad del año

**latterly** adv últimamente

**laugh** [læf] I. n 1. (sound) risa f; **to get a ~** hacer reír; **to do sth for a ~** [or for ~s] hacer algo para divertirse 2. (sth *absurd*) ridículo, -a; **his answer was a ~** su respuesta fue ridícula **II.** *vi* reír(se); **to ~ aloud** reírse a carcajadas; **to make sb ~** hacer reír a alguien; **to ~ at sb/sth** *a. fig* reírse de alguien/algo; **to ~ until one cries** llorar de la risa; **don't make me ~** ¡no me hagas reír! ▶ **he who ~s last ~s best** *prov* quien ríe el último, ríe mejor *prov*

**laughable** ['læf·ə·bəl] *adj* de risa

**laughing gas** *n* gas *m* de la risa [*or* hilarante]

**laughter** ['læf·tər] *n* risa(s) *f(pl)*; **to roar with ~** echarse a reír ▶ **~ is the best medicine** *prov* quien canta, sus males espanta *prov*

**launch** [lɔntʃ] **I.** <-ches> *n* **1.** (*boat*) lancha *f* **2.** (*of a boat*) botadura *f* **3.** (*of a missile*) lanzamiento *m* **4.** (*introduction: of exhibition*) inauguración *f* **II.** *vt* **1.** (*set in the water*) botar **2.** (*set in motion: missile*) lanzar **3.** (*start: investigation*) emprender; (*exhibition*) inaugurar

◆**launch into** *vt* emprender

◆**launch out** *vi* lanzarse

**launching pad** *n*, **launch pad** *n* rampa *f* de lanzamiento

**laundry** ['lɔn·dri] *n* **1.** (*dirty clothes*) ropa *f* sucia; **to do the ~** hacer la colada **2.** (*washed clothes*) ropa *f* lavada **3.** <-ies> (*place*) lavandería *f*

**laundry basket** *n* cesto *m* de la ropa sucia

**laundry service** *n* servicio *m* de lavandería

**lavatory** ['læv·ə·tɔr·i] <-ies> *n* lavabo *m*, lavatorio *m AmL*

**lavish** ['læv·ɪʃ] **I.** *adj* (*banquet*) opíparo, -a; (*reception*) fastuoso, -a; (*praise*) abundante **II.** *vt* **to ~ sth on sb** [*or* **to ~ sb with sth**] prodigar algo a alguien

**law** [lɔ] *n* **1.** *a.* PHYS ley *f* **2.** (*legal system*) derecho *m*; (*body of laws*) ley *f*; **~-and-order** la ley y el orden; **his word is ~** lo que él dice va a misa; **to be against the ~** ser ilegal; **to take the ~ into one's own hands** tomarse la justicia por su mano; **the ~ of the jungle** la ley de la selva

**law-abiding** *adj* observante de la ley

**law enforcement** *n* aplicación *f* de la ley

**lawful** ['lɔ·fəl] *adj* (*legal*) legal; (*demands*) legítimo, -a; **~ owner** propietario, -a *m, f* legítimo

**lawless** ['lɔ·lɪs] *adj* sin ley; (*country*) anárquico, -a

**lawn** [lɔn] *n* césped *m*, pasto *m AmL*

**lawn mower** *n* cortacésped *m*

**law school** *n* facultad *f* de derecho

**law student** *n* estudiante *mf* de derecho

**lawsuit** *n* proceso *m* (judicial); **to bring a ~ against sb** presentar una demanda contra alguien

**lawyer** ['lɔ·jər] *n* abogado, -a *m, f*

**lax** [læks] *adj* **1.** (*lacking care*) descuidado, -a; **~ security** seguridad *f* poco rigurosa **2.** (*rules*) poco severo, -a, laxo, -a

**laxative** ['læk·sə·tɪv] **I.** *n* laxante *m* **II.** *adj* laxante

**lay[1]** [leɪ] **I.** *n* **1.** (*situation*) situación *f*; **the ~ of the land** la configuración del terreno; *fig* la situación actual **2.** *vulg* **to be a good ~** tener buen polvo **II.** <laid, laid> *vt* **1.** (*place*) poner; **to ~ sth on/over sth** poner algo en/encima de algo; **to ~ the blame on sb** echar la culpa a alguien **2.** (*install*) colocar; (*cable*) tender; (*pipes*) instalar; **to ~ the foundation for sth** *a. fig* poner los cimientos de algo **3.** (*egg*) poner **4.** *vulg* (*have sex with*) follar **5.** (*state*) presentar; **to ~ sth before sb** poner algo frente a alguien; **to ~ claim to sth** reclamar algo **III.** <laid, laid> *vi* poner huevos

◆**lay about** *vt* **to ~ sb** emprenderla a golpes con alguien

◆**lay aside** *vt* (*put away*) guardar

◆**lay back** *vt* reposar

◆**lay by** *vt* reservar

◆**lay down** *vt* **1.** (*put down*) poner a un lado; (*arms*) deponer; (*life*) sacrificar **2.** (*establish*) estipular; (*law*) dictar

◆**lay into** *vt* *sl* **1.** (*assault*) atacar **2.** (*criticize*) arremeter contra

◆**lay off I.** *vt* despedir (temporalmente) **II.** *vi* *sl* dejar; **to ~ sb** dejar en paz a alguien; **to ~ smoking** dejar de fumar

◆**lay on** *vt* **1.** (*provide: food, drink*) proveer de **2.** *sl* (*reveal*) **to ~ sth on sb** contarle algo a alguien

♦**lay out** vt **1.** (*organize*) organizar **2.** (*explain*) presentar **3.** (*spread out*) extender **4.** inf (*money*) gastar

♦**lay up** vt **1.** (*store*) guardar **2.** (*ship*) desarmar; (*car*) dejar en el garaje **3.** inf (*in bed*) **to be laid up** guardar cama

**lay²** [leɪ] adj **1.** (*not professional*) lego, -a; **in ~ terms** en términos profanos **2.** REL laico, -a

**lay³** [leɪ] pt of **lie²**

**layabout** ['leɪ·ə·baʊt] n inf vago, -a m, f

**layaway** ['leɪ·ə·weɪ] n **to buy/put on ~** comprar/reservar (mediante el pago de un depósito)

**layer¹** ['leɪ·ər] **I.** n **1.** (*of dust, paint*) capa f; **ozone ~** capa de ozono **2.** (*level*) estrato m, capa f **II.** vt acodar

**layer²** ['leɪ·ər] n ZOOL (*hen*) gallina f ponedora

**layered** adj en capas

**layout** ['leɪ·aʊt] n **1.** (*of letter, magazine*) diseño m; (*of town*) trazado m **2.** TYPO maquetación f

**layover** ['leɪ·oʊ·vər] n (*on journey*) parada f; AVIAT escala f

**laziness** ['leɪ·zɪ·nɪs] n holgazanería f

**lazy** ['leɪ·zi] <-ier, -iest> adj (*person*) vago, -a; (*day*) en el/la que no se hace nada, sin hacer nada

**lead¹** [lid] **I.** n **1.** (*front position*) delantera f; **to be in the ~** estar en cabeza; **to hold the ~** llevar la delantera; **to move into the ~** ponerse en cabeza; **to take the ~** tomar la delantera **2.** (*example*) ejemplo m; (*guiding*) iniciativa f; **to follow sb's ~** seguir el ejemplo de alguien **3.** THEAT papel m principal; **to play the ~** representar el papel principal **4.** (*clue, tip*) pista f; **to get a ~ on sth** recibir una pista acerca de algo **5.** (*connecting wire*) cable m, conductor m **6.** (*dog leash*) correa f **II.** <led, led> vt **1.** (*be in charge of*) dirigir; (*discussion, inquiry*) conducir **2.** (*conduct*) conducir, llevar; **to ~ the way** ir primero; *fig* mostrar el camino **3.** (*induce*) inducir; **to ~ sb to do sth** llevar a alguien a hacer algo; **to ~ sb to believe that...** hacer creer a alguien que... **4.** COM, SPORTS (*be ahead of*) liderar **5.** (*live a particular*

*way: life*) llevar; **to ~ a life of luxury** llevar una vida de lujo **III.** <led, led> vi **1.** (*be in charge*) dirigir **2.** (*guide followers*) guiar **3.** (*conduct*) llevar; **to ~ to/into sth** a. *fig* conducir a/hacia algo **4.** (*be ahead*) ser líder; **to ~ by 2 laps** tener una ventaja de 2 vueltas

♦**lead along** vt llevar (de la mano)

♦**lead aside** vt llevar a un lado

♦**lead astray** vt llevar por mal camino

♦**lead away** vt llevar

♦**lead back** vt hacer volver

♦**lead off** **I.** vt (*person*) llevar afuera; (*room*) comunicar con **II.** vi empezar

♦**lead on** vt (*trick, fool*) engañar; (*encourage*) incitar a; **she doesn't want to lead him on** no quiere darle falsas expectativas

**lead²** [led] n **1.** (*metal*) plomo m **2.** (*in pencil*) mina f **3.** NAUT sonda f

**leaded** ['led·əd] adj emplomado, -a; **~ fuel** gasolina f con plomo

**leader** ['li·dər] n **1.** (*of group*) líder mf **2.** (*guide*) guía mf

**leadership** ['li·dər·ʃɪp] n **1.** (*ability to lead*) liderazgo m; **~ qualities** dotes f pl de mando **2.** (*leaders*) dirección f

**lead-free** ['led·fri] adj sin plomo

**leading** ['li·dɪŋ] **I.** adj (*main, principle*) principal **II.** n mando m

**lead pencil** n lápiz m de mina

**lead poisoning** n saturnismo m

**lead singer** n cantante mf principal

**lead story** n PUBL artículo m principal

**leaf** [lif] <leaves> n **1.** (*of plant*) hoja f **2.** (*foliage*) follaje m **3.** (*piece of paper*) hoja f; **~ of paper** hoja de papel **4.** (*thin layer*) **gold/silver ~** baño m en oro/plata f **5.** (*of table*) tablero m ▶ **to shake like a ~** temblar como una pluma; **to turn over a new ~** hacer borrón y cuenta nueva

**leaflet** ['lif·lɪt] n folleto m

**leafy** ['li·fi] <-ier, -iest> adj frondoso, -a

**league** [lig] n **1.** a. SPORTS liga f; **soccer ~** liga de fútbol; **to be/to not be in the same ~ as sb/sth** *fig* estar/no estar a la altura de alguien/algo; **to be out of sb's ~** no tener comparación con alguien **2.** (*measurement*) legua f

**leak** [lik] **I.** n (*of gas, water*) fuga f; (*of in-*

*formation*) filtración *f;* (*in roof*) gotera *f* **II.** *vi* **1.** (*let sth escape*) tener una fuga; (*tire*) perder aire; (*hose, bucket*) perder (agua); (*faucet*) gotear **2.** (*information*) filtrarse **III.** *vt* **1.** (*let escape*) derramar; **to ~ water** perder (agua) **2.** (*information*) filtrar

**leaky** ['li·ki] <-ier, -iest> *adj* que tiene fugas

**lean¹** [lin] **I.** <-ed, -ed> *vi* inclinarse; **to ~ against sth** apoyarse en algo **II.** <-ed, -ed> *vt* apoyar; **to ~ sth against sth** apoyar algo contra algo

◆**lean on** *vt* **1.** (*rely on*) apoyarse en **2.** *sl* (*pressure*) ejercer presión sobre

◆**lean over I.** *vt* inclinarse sobre **II.** *vi* inclinarse

**lean²** [lin] *adj* **1.** (*thin*) flaco, -a; (*face*) enjuto, -a; (*with little fat: meat*) magro, -a **2.** (*efficient: company*) eficiente

**leaning** ['li·nɪŋ] *n* inclinación *f*

**leap** [lip] **I.** <leaped *or* leapt, leaped *or* leapt> *vi* saltar; **to ~ forward** saltar hacia adelante; **to ~ to sb's defense** saltar en defensa de alguien; **his heart ~ed** le dio un vuelco el corazón **II.** <leaped *or* leapt, leaped *or* leapt> *vt* saltar **III.** *n* salto *m;* **to take a ~** dar un salto ▶ **by ~s and bounds** a pasos de gigante; **a ~ in the dark** un salto al vacío

◆**leap out** *vi* saltar

◆**leap up** *vi* (*jump up*) ponerse en pie de un salto

**leapfrog** ['lip·frɔg] **I.** *n* potro *m,* pídola *f;* **to play a game of ~** jugar a saltar al potro, jugar a la pídola, saltar el burro *Méx* **II.** <-gg-> *vt* pasar por encima de

**leapt** [lept] *vt, vi* *pt, pp of* **leap**

**leap year** *n* año *m* bisiesto

**learn** [lɜrn] **I.** <learned, learned> *vt* aprender; **to ~ that** enterarse de que **II.** <learned, learned> *vi* aprender; **to ~ to do sth** aprender a hacer algo; **to ~ from one's mistakes** aprender de los propios errores

**learned** ['lɜr·nɪd] *adj* erudito, -a

**learner** ['lɜr·nər] *n* aprendiz *mf;* **to be a quick ~** aprender rápido

**learning** ['lɜr·nɪŋ] *n* **1.** (*acquisition of knowledge*) aprendizaje *m* **2.** (*extensive knowledge*) saber *m*

**learning disability** *n* <-ies> dificultad *f* de aprendizaje

**lease** [lis] **I.** *vt* alquilar **II.** *n* (*act*) arrendamiento *m* ▶ **a new ~ on life** el comienzo de una nueva vida

**leaseholder** ['lis·hoʊl·dər] *n* arrendatario, -a *m, f*

**leash** [liʃ] *n* correa *f* ▶ **to keep sb on a tight ~** atar corto a alguien

**least** [list] **I.** *adj* mínimo, -a; (*age*) menor **II.** *adv* menos; **the ~ possible** lo menos posible **III.** *n* lo menos; **at** (**the very**) **~** por lo menos, al menos; **not in the ~!** ¡en absoluto!; **to say the ~** para no decir más

**leather** ['leð·ər] *n* cuero *m*

**leathery** ['leð·ə·ri] *adj* (*skin*) curtido, -a; (*meat*) correoso, -a

**leave¹** [liv] **I.** <left, left> *vt* **1.** (*depart from*) salir de; (*school, college*) abandonar; (*work*) dejar; **to ~ home** irse de casa **2.** (*not take away with*) dejar; (*forget*) olvidar(se); **to ~ sth to sb** dejar algo a alguien **3.** (*put in a situation*) **to ~ sb alone** dejar a alguien en paz; **to be left homeless** quedarse sin hogar ▶ **to ~ a lot to be desired** dejar mucho que desear; **to ~ it at that** dejarlo **II.** <left, left> *vi* marcharse, despabilarse *AmL* **III.** *n* partida *f;* **to take** (**one's**) **~** (**of sb**) despedirse (de alguien)

◆**leave behind** *vt* **1.** (*forget*) olvidar **2.** (*progress beyond*) dejar atrás

◆**leave off I.** *vt* **1.** (*give up*) dejar de **2.** (*omit*) omitir **II.** *vi* acabar

◆**leave on** *vt* dejar(se) puesto; (*light*) dejar encendido

◆**leave out** *vt* **1.** (*omit*) omitir **2.** (*exclude*) excluir

◆**leave over** *vt* dejar; **there's nothing left over** no queda nada

**leave²** [liv] *n* permiso *m;* **to go/be on ~** MIL tener/estar de permiso

**lecture** ['lek·tʃər] **I.** *n* *a.* UNIV conferencia *f,* clase *f;* **a ~ on sth** una conferencia acerca de algo; **to give sb a ~** *fig* sermonear a alguien **II.** *vi* (*give a lecture*) dar una conferencia; (*teach*) dar clases **III.** *vt* (*give a lecture*) dar una conferencia a; (*teach*) dar clases a

**lecture notes** *npl* apuntes *m pl* (de clase)

**lecturer** ['lek·tʃər·ər] *n* conferenciante *mf*; UNIV profesor(a) *m(f)* universitario, -a

**lecture tour** *n* gira *f* de conferencias

**led** [led] *pt, pp of* **lead**¹

**LED** [ˌel·iˈdiː] *n abbr of* **light-emitting diode** LED *m*

**ledge** [ledʒ] *n* (*shelf*) repisa *f*; (*on building*) cornisa *f*; (*on cliff*) saliente *m*; **window ~** alféizar *m*

**ledger** ['ledʒ·ər] *n* COM libro *m* mayor

**leek** [liːk] *n* CULIN puerro *m*

**leery** ['lɪr·i] *adj* desconfiado, -a, receloso, -a; **to be ~ of sb/sth** desconfiar de alguien/algo

**leeway** ['liː·weɪ] *n* flexibilidad *f*

**left**¹ [left] *pt, pp of* **leave**¹

**left**² [left] I. *n* 1. (*direction, sight*) izquierda *f*; **the ~ la** izquierda; **to turn to the ~** girar a la izquierda; **on/to the/her ~** en/a la/su izquierda *f*; **on the ~** de izquierda(s) 2. POL izquierda *f* II. *adj* izquierdo, -a III. *adv* a [*or* hacia] la izquierda; **to turn ~** girar hacia la izquierda

**left-hand** *adj* a la izquierda; **~ side** lado *m* izquierdo; **~ turn** curva *f* a la izquierda

**left-handed** *adj* zurdo, -a; **~ scissors** tijeras *f pl* para zurdos

**left-hander** *n* zurdo, -a *m, f*

**leftist** ['lef·tɪst] POL I. *adj* izquierdista II. *n* izquierdista *mf*

**leftovers** ['left·ˌoʊ·vərz] *npl* 1. (*food*) sobras *fpl* 2. (*remaining things*) restos *mpl*

**left wing** *n* POL izquierda *f*

**left-wing** *adj* POL de izquierda

**left-winger** *n* POL izquierdista *mf*

**leg** [leg] *n* 1. (*of person*) pierna *f*; (*of animal, furniture*) pata *f* 2. (*of pants*) pernera *f* 3. CULIN (*of lamb, pork*) pierna *f*; (*of chicken*) muslo *m* 4. (*segment of journey*) etapa *f* ▶ **to be on one's last ~s** estar para el arrastre; **break a ~!** ¡mucha suerte!; **to pull sb's ~** *inf* tomar el pelo a alguien

**legal** ['liː·gəl] *adj* 1. (*in accordance with law*) legal 2. (*concerning the law*) jurídico, -a

**legality** [liːˈgæl·ə·t̬i] *n* legalidad *f*

**legalize** ['liː·gə·laɪz] *vt* legalizar

**legally** ['liː·gə·li] *adv* legalmente

**legend** ['ledʒ·ənd] *n* leyenda *f*; **~ has it that...** dice la leyenda que...

**legendary** ['ledʒ·ənˌder·i] *adj* legendario, -a

**leggings** ['leg·ɪŋz] *npl* mallas *fpl*

**leggy** ['leg·i] <-ier, -iest> *adj* patilargo, -a

**legible** ['ledʒ·ə·bəl] *adj* legible

**legitimacy** [ləˈdʒɪt̬·ə·mə·si] *n* legitimidad *f*

**legitimate**¹ [ləˈdʒɪt̬·ə·mɪt] *adj* 1. (*legal*) legal; **a ~ government** un gobierno legítimo 2. (*reasonable*) válido, -a

**legitimate**² [ləˈdʒɪt̬·ə·meɪt] *vt* legitimar

**legroom** ['leg·rum] *n* espacio *m* para las piernas

**leisure** ['liː·ʒər] *n* 1. ocio *m* 2. **call me at your ~** llámame cuando tengas tiempo

**leisurely** I. *adj* pausado, -a II. *adv* pausadamente

**leisure time** *n* tiempo *m* libre

**lemon** ['lem·ən] *n* 1. (*fruit*) limón *m*; **a slice of ~** una rodaja de limón 2. (*color*) amarillo *m* limón 3. *inf* (*defective object*) patata *f*

**lemonade** [ˌlem·əˈneɪd] *n* limonada *f*

**lemon juice** *n* zumo *m* de limón

**lemon peel** *n* corteza *f* de limón

**lend** [lend] <lent, lent> I. *vt* 1. (*give temporarily*) prestar; **to ~ money to sb** prestar dinero a alguien 2. (*impart, provide*) dar; **to ~ support to a view** apoyar una opinión ▶ **to ~ a hand to sb** echar una mano a alguien; **to ~ one's name to sth** ofrecer su nombre para algo II. *vi* prestar dinero

**lender** ['len·dər] *n* FIN prestamista *mf*

**lending** ['len·dɪŋ] *n* préstamo *m*

**length** [leŋkθ] *n* 1. (*measurement*) longitud *f*; **it's 3 yards in ~** tiene 3 yardas de largo; (*along*) **the ~ of sth** a lo largo de algo 2. (*piece: of pipe, rope*) trozo *m* 3. (*of swimming pool*) largo *m* 4. (*duration*) duración *f*; (*for*) **any ~ of time** (por) cualquier lapso de tiempo; **at ~** al fin, finalmente; **at great ~** detalladamente ▶ **to go to great ~s to do sth** dar el máximo para hacer algo

**lengthen** ['leŋk·θən] I. *vt* 1. (*in time*) prolongar 2. (*physically*) alargar II. *vi* (*physically*) alargarse

**lengthways** ['leŋkθ·weɪz] *adv*, *adj*, **lengthwise** ['leŋkθ·waɪz] *adv*, *adj* a lo largo

**lengthy** ['leŋk·θi] <-ier, -iest> *adj* prolongado, -a; (*speech*) prolijo, -a

**lenience** ['li·ni·əns] *n*, **leniency** *n* indulgencia *f*

**lenient** ['li·ni·ənt] *adj* (*judge*) indulgente; (*punishment*) poco severo, -a

**lens** [lenz] <-es> *n* 1. (*of glasses*) lente *m of*; **contact ~es** lentes *f pl* de contacto, lentillas *fpl* 2. (*of camera*) objetivo *m*; **zoom ~** lente de acercamiento 3. ANAT cristalino *m*

**lent** [lent] *pt*, *pp* of **lend**

**Lent** [lent] *n* Cuaresma *f*

**lentil** ['len·təl] *n* lenteja *f*

**Leo** ['li·oʊ] *n* Leo *m*

**leopard** ['lep·ərd] *n* leopardo *m* ▸ **a ~ can't change its spots** *prov* el árbol que nace torcido jamás sus ramas endereza *prov*, el que nace barrigón ni que lo fajen chiquito *Ven prov*

**leotard** ['li·ə·tard] *n* malla *f*

**lesbian** ['lez·bi·ən] I. *n* lesbiana *f* II. *adj* lésbico, -a

**less** [les] *comp of* **little** I. *adj* (*in degree, size*) menor; (*in quantity*) menos; **sth of ~ value** algo de menor valor; **~ wine/ fat** menos vino/grasa II. *adv* menos; **to drink ~** beber menos; **to see sb ~** ver menos a alguien; **~ than 10** menos de [*or* que] 10; **not him, much ~ her** él no, y mucho menos ella III. *pron* menos; **~ than...** menos que...; **~ and ~** cada vez menos; **the ~ you eat, the ~ you get fat** cuanto menos comas, menos gordo estarás IV. *prep* menos

**lessen** ['les·ən] I. *vi* (*danger*) reducirse; (*pain*) aliviarse II. *vt* (*diminish*) disminuir; (*risk*) reducir; (*pain*) aliviar

**lesser** ['les·ər] *adj comp of* **less** menor; **to a ~ extent** en menor grado

**lesson** ['les·ən] *n* 1. SCHOOL clase *f*; **~s** lecciones *fpl* 2. *fig* lección *f*; **to learn one's ~** aprenderse la lección; **to teach sb a ~** dar a alguien una lección

**lest** [lest] *conj liter* 1. (*for fear that*) no sea que +*subj*; **I didn't do it ~ he should come** no lo hice por si venía 2. (*if*) en caso de que +*subj*

**let**[1] [let] *n* SPORTS let *m*

**let**[2] [let] *vt* <let, let> 1. (*allow*) dejar; **to ~ sb do sth** dejar a alguien hacer algo; **to ~ sb know sth** hacer saber algo a alguien; **to ~ sth pass** pasar algo por alto; **~ him be!** ¡déjalo en paz! 2. (*in suggestions*) **~'s go!** ¡vámonos!; **~'s say...** digamos...; **~ us pray** oremos 3. *inf* (*filler while thinking*) **~'s see** veamos; **~ me think** déjame pensar ▸ **~ alone...** (y) menos aún...; **to ~ sb have it** decir cuatro verdades a alguien; **to ~ sth lie** dejar algo como está; **to ~ it rip** correr

◆**let by** *vt* dejar pasar

◆**let down** *vt* 1. (*disappoint*) decepcionar 2. (*lower*) bajar; (*hair*) soltar; **to let one's hair down** a. *fig* soltarse el pelo

◆**let in** *vt* (*person*) dejar entrar; (*light*) dejar pasar ▸ **to let sb in on sth** revelar un secreto a alguien

◆**let off** *vt* (*forgive*) perdonar; **to let sb off with a fine** poner sólo una multa a alguien

◆**let on** *vi inf* (*divulge*) **to not ~ about sth** callarse algo

◆**let out** *vt* 1. (*release*) dejar salir; (*prisoner*) poner en libertad; (*laugh*) soltar; **to ~ a scream** pegar un grito *inf* 2. (*reveal: secret*) revelar

◆**let up** *vi* 1. (*become weaker, stop*) debilitarse; (*rain*) amainar; (*cold*) suavizarse 2. (*relent*) aflojar; **to ~ on sb** ser menos duro con alguien; **to ~ on the gas** soltar el acelerador

**lethal** ['li·θəl] *adj* letal; (*poison*) mortífero, -a; (*weapon*) mortal

**lethargic** [lɪ·'θar·dʒɪk] *adj* (*lacking energy*) letárgico, -a

**letter** ['leţ·ər] *n* 1. (*message*) carta *f*; **~ of recommendation** carta de recomendación; **~ of credit** letra de crédito 2. (*symbol*) letra *f* ▸ **to the ~** al pie de la letra

**letter bomb** *n* carta *f* bomba

**letterhead** *n* (*logo*) membrete *m*; (*paper*) papel *m* membreteado

**lettering** ['leţ·ər·ɪŋ] *n* caracteres *mpl*

**lettuce** ['leţ·ɪs] *n* lechuga *f*

**leukemia** [luˈkiˑmiˑə] *n* leucemia *f*

**level** [ˈlev·əl] **I.** *adj* **1.** (*horizontal*) horizontal; (*flat*) plano, -a; (*spoonful*) raso, -a **2.** (*having same height*) **to be ~ with sth** estar a la misma altura que algo **3.** (*in same position*) **to be ~ with sb/ sth** estar a la par de alguien/algo **4.** (*of same amount*) igual **5.** (*voice*) mesurado, -a; **to keep a ~ head** no perder la cabeza **II.** *adv* a nivel **III.** *n* **1.** (*position, amount*) nivel *m* **2.** (*height*) altura *f*; **above sea ~** sobre el nivel del mar; **at ground ~** a ras de tierra **3.** (*position in hierarchy*) categoría *f*; **at the (very) highest ~** en el nivel más alto **4.** (*quality of performance*) nivel *m*; **intermediate ~ students** estudiantes *mf pl* de nivel intermedio **5.** (*meaning*) **on another ~** en otro sentido ▸ **to be on the ~** (*business, person*) ser serio **IV.** <-l- *or* -ll-> *vt* **1.** (*smoothen, flatten*) nivelar **2.** (*demolish completely*) arrasar **3.** (*point*) **to ~ sth at sb** apuntar con algo a alguien

◆**level off, level out** *vi* (*aircraft*) nivelarse; (*inflation*) equilibrarse

◆**level up** *vt* igualar

◆**level with** *vt inf* sincerarse con

**lever** [ˈlev·ər] **I.** *n* palanca *f* **II.** *vt* apalancar, palanquear *AmL*

**levy** [ˈlev·i] **I.** <-ies> *n* tasa *f* **II.** <-ie-> *vt* imponer; **to ~ a tax on sth** gravar algo con un impuesto

**lewd** [lud] *adj* (*person*) lascivo, -a; (*gesture, remark*) obsceno, -a

**liability** [ˌlaɪ·ə·ˈbɪl·ə·t̬i] *n* **1.** FIN, LAW responsabilidad *f*; **to accept ~ for sth** hacerse responsable de algo *f* **2.** FIN **liabilities** deudas *fpl*

**liable** [ˈlaɪ·ə·bəl] *adj* **1.** (*prone*) propenso, -a; **to be ~ to do sth** ser propenso a hacer algo **2.** LAW responsable; **to be ~ for sth** ser responsable de algo

**liaison** [ˈli·eɪ·zən] *n* **1.** *a.* LING (*contact*) enlace *m*; (*person*) oficial *mf* de enlace **2.** (*sexual affair*) aventura *f*

**liar** [ˈlaɪ·ər] *n* mentiroso, -a *m, f*

**lib** [lɪb] *n inf abbr of* **liberation** liberación *f*

**libel** [ˈlaɪ·bəl] *n* LAW libelo *m*; PUBL difamación *f*; **to sue sb for ~** demandar a

alguien por difamación

**libelous** [ˈlaɪ·bə·ləs] *adj* LAW, PUBL difamatorio, -a

**liberal** [ˈlɪb·ər·əl] **I.** *adj* **1.** (*tolerant*) *a.* POL liberal **2.** (*generous*) generoso, -a **3.** (*not strict: interpretation*) amplio, -a **II.** *n* liberal *mf*

**liberate** [ˈlɪb·ə·reɪt] *vt* (*free*) liberar; **to ~ oneself from sth/sb** librarse de algo/ alguien

**liberation** [ˌlɪb·ə·ˈreɪ·ʃən] *n* liberación *f*

**liberty** [ˈlɪb·ər·t̬i] *n form* **1.** (*freedom*) libertad *f*; **to take the ~ of doing sth** tomarse la libertad de hacer algo; **to take liberties with sb** tomarse libertades con alguien **2.** **liberties** *pl* (*rights*) derechos *mpl*

**Libra** [ˈli·brə] *n* Libra *m*

**librarian** [laɪ·ˈbrer·i·ən] *n* bibliotecario, -a *m, f*

**library** [ˈlaɪ·brer·i] *n* <-ies> (*place*) biblioteca *f*; **film ~** filmoteca *f*; **newspaper ~** hemeroteca *f*

**lice** [laɪs] *npl see* **louse**

**license** [ˈlaɪ·səns] **I.** *n* **1.** (*document*) licencia *f*, permiso *m*; **driver's ~** carnet *m* [*or* permiso *m*] de conducir; **gun ~** permiso *m* de armas **2.** (*freedom*) libertad *f*; **artistic ~** libertad artística **II.** *vt* autorizar

**licensed** *adj* autorizado, -a; **to be ~ to do sth** tener la autorización para hacer algo

**lick** [lɪk] **I.** *n* **1.** (*with tongue*) lamedura *f* **2.** *inf* (*try*) **to give sth a ~** intentar algo **3.** (*salt stick*) bloque *m* de sal (para el ganado) **II.** *vt* **1.** (*with tongue*) lamer **2.** *sl* (*defeat*) derrotar **3.** *sl* (*beat up*) dar una paliza a

**lid** [lɪd] *n* **1.** (*for container*) tapa *f*, tape *m* Cuba, PRico, *fig* (*limit*) tope *m* **3.** (*eyelid*) párpado *m* ▸ **to keep the ~ on sth** ocultar algo

**lie¹** [laɪ] **I.** <-y-> *vi* mentir; **to ~ about sth** mentir sobre algo **II.** <-y-> *vt* **to ~ oneself out of sth** salvarse de algo por una mentira **III.** *n* mentira *f*, guayaba *f AmL*, boleto *m* Arg; **to be an outright ~** ser de una falsedad total; **to live a ~** vivir en la mentira

**lie²** [laɪ] **I.** <lay, lain> *vi* **1.** (*be lying*

L

*down: person*) estar tumbado; **to ~ in bed** estar acostado en la cama; **to ~ on the ground** estar tumbado en el suelo; **to ~ still** quedarse inmóvil **2.** (*be positioned*) hallarse; **to ~ off the coast** (*boat*) hallarse lejos de la costa; **to ~ to the east of...** quedar al este de...; **to ~ in wait** estar a la espera **3.** *form* (*be buried*) estar enterrado, -a **4.** **to ~ with sb/sth** (*be responsibility of*) corresponder a alguien/algo; (*be the reason for sth*) ser culpa de alguien/algo **5.** SPORTS ubicarse **II.** *n* posición *f*

◆**lie around** *vi* **1.** (*be somewhere*) estar por ahí tirado **2.** (*be lazy*) holgazanear

◆**lie back** *vi* recostarse

◆**lie down** *vi* **1.** (*act*) acostarse **2.** *inf* (*do nothing*) **to ~ on the job** no hacer su trabajo; **to take sth lying down** aceptar algo sin protestar

**lien** [liːn] *n* derecho *m* de retención

**lieu** [luː] *n* **in ~ of** en lugar de

**lieutenant** [luˈtenənt] *n* **1.** MIL teniente *mf* **2.** (*assistant*) lugarteniente *mf*

**life** [laɪf] <lives> *n* **1.** vida *f*; **plant ~** vida vegetal; **private ~** vida privada; **to be full of ~** estar lleno de vida; **to lose one's ~** perder la vida; **to take sb's ~** matar a alguien; **to take one's (own) ~** quitarse la vida, suicidarse **2.** (*existence*) existencia *f*; **to want sth out of ~** querer algo de la vida **3.** (*duration*) vida *f* (útil), duración *f* **4.** *sl* (*prison sentence*) cadena *f* perpetua; **to get ~** ser condenado a cadena perpetua ▶ **to be a matter of ~ and death** ser un asunto de vida o muerte; **to take one's ~ in one's hands** jugarse la vida; **to risk ~ and limb** (**to do sth**) jugarse la vida (para hacer algo); **to lay one's ~ on the line** poner la vida en peligro; **to be the ~ of the party** ser el alma de la fiesta; **to live the good ~** darse la buena vida; **~ is hard!** *iron inf* ¡qué le vamos a hacer!; **to breathe (new) ~ into sth** infundir (nueva) vida a algo; **to bring sth to ~** animar algo; **to come to ~** volver a la vida; **to frighten the ~ out of sb** dar un susto de muerte a alguien; **to give one's ~ for sb/sth** dar la vida por alguien/algo; **to make a new ~** em-

pezar una nueva vida; **for ~** de por vida; **I'm not able for the ~ of me to...** por mucho que lo intente no puedo...; **not on your ~!** *inf* ¡ni hablar!; **that's ~!** ¡así es la vida!; **this is the ~ (for me)!** ¡esto sí es vida!

**lifeboat** *n* bote *m* salvavidas

**life cycle** *n* ciclo *m* vital

**life expectancy** <-ies> *n* esperanza *f* de vida

**life form** *n* forma *f* de vida

**lifeguard** *n* socorrista *mf*, salvavidas *mf inv AmL*

**life insurance** *n* seguro *m* de vida

**life jacket** *n* chaleco *m* salvavidas

**lifeless** [ˈlaɪflɪs] *adj* **1.** (*dead*) sin vida **2.** *fig* flojo, -a

**lifelike** [ˈlaɪflaɪk] *adj* natural

**lifelong** [ˌlaɪfˈlɒŋ] *adj* de toda la vida

**life raft** *n* bote *m* salvavidas

**lifesaver** *n* socorrista *mf*

**life sentence** *n* condena *f* a cadena perpetua

**lifestyle** *n* estilo *m* de vida

**life-threatening** *adj* mortífero, -a

**lifetime** *n* **1.** (*of person*) vida *f*; **in my ~** durante mi vida; **to happen once in a ~** suceder una vez en la vida; **~ guarantee** garantía *f* de por vida **2.** *inf* (*eternity*) eternidad *f*

**lift** [lɪft] **I.** *n* **1.** (*upward motion*) elevación *f* **2.** AVIAT fuerza *f* de ascensión **3.** *fig* (*positive feeling*) ánimos *mpl* **4.** (*hoisting device*) montacargas *m inv* **5.** *inf* (*help*) ayuda *f* **6.** *inf* (*car ride*) viaje *m* en coche (*gratuito*) aventón *m Méx*; **to give sb a ~** llevar (en coche) a alguien **II.** *vi* levantarse **III.** *vt* **1.** (*move upwards*) levantar; (*slightly*) alzar; **to ~ one's eyes** alzar los ojos; **to ~ one's head** levantar la cabeza; **to ~ one's voice to sb** (*yell at*) levantar la voz a alguien **2.** (*stop*) suprimir; **to ~ restrictions** levantar las restricciones **3.** (*encourage*) animar; **to ~ sb's spirits** levantar los ánimos de alguien **4.** (*move by air*) transportar (en avión) **5.** *inf* (*steal*) mangar

◆**lift down** *vt* bajar con cuidado

◆**lift off** *vi* AVIAT despegar

◆**lift up** *vt* alzar; **to ~ one's head** levantar la cabeza

**ligament** [ˈlɪg·ə·mənt] n ligamento m

**light** [laɪt] I. n 1. (energy, brightness) luz f; **by the ~ of the moon** a la luz de la luna 2. (daytime) luz f (de día) 3. (source of brightness) luz f; (lamp) lámpara f; **to turn a ~ off/on** apagar/encender una luz; **~s out** inf (bedtime) hora f de apagar la luz 4. (traffic light) semáforo m 5. (flame) fuego m; **do you have a ~?** ¿tienes fuego? 6. (clarification, insight) comprensión f; **to bring sth to ~** sacar algo a la luz; **to cast** [or **shed**] **~ on sth** arrojar luz sobre algo; **to come to ~** salir a la luz 7. (perspective) perspectiva f; **to see things in a new ~** ver las cosas desde otra perspectiva 8. fig (joy, inspiration) sol m; **you are the ~ of my life** eres mi sol ► **to see the ~ at the end of the** <u>tunnel</u> ver la luz al final del túnel; **to go out like a ~** inf (fall asleep quickly) quedarse dormido enseguida II. adj 1. (not heavy) ligero, -a; **a ~ touch** un pequeño toque 2. (not dark: color) claro, -a; (skin) blanco, -a; (room) luminoso, -a 3. (not serious) ligero, -a; **~ opera** opereta f 4. (not intense: breeze, rain) leve; **to be a ~ sleeper** tener el sueño ligero 5. CULIN frugal; **a ~ meal** una comida ligera 6. (with few calories) bajo, -a en calorías, dietético, -a, light III. adv ligeramente ► **to get off** ~ salir bien parado; **to make ~ of sth** no dar importancia a algo IV. vt <lit or lighted> 1. (illuminate) iluminar; **to ~ the way** mostrar el camino 2. (start burning) encender, prender AmL; **to ~ a cigarette** encender un cigarrillo V. vi <lit or lighted> (catch fire) encenderse

♦**light up** I. vt 1. alumbrar, iluminar 2. (cigarette) encender II. vi 1. (become bright) iluminarse 2. (become animated) animarse; **his face lit up** se le iluminó la cara 3. (start smoking) encender un cigarrillo

**light bulb** n bombilla f, foco m AmL

**lighten** [ˈlaɪ·tən] I. vi 1. (become brighter) clarear 2. (become less heavy) aligerarse; (mood) alegrarse II. vt 1. (make less heavy) aligerar 2. (bleach, make

paler) aclarar

**lighter** [ˈlaɪ·tər] n mechero m, encendedor m AmL

**lightheaded** adj 1. (faint) mareado, -a 2. (excited) delirante

**lighthouse** n faro m

**lighting** [ˈlaɪ·tɪŋ] n iluminación f

**lightly** [ˈlaɪt·li] adv ligeramente; (to rest, touch) levemente; **to take sth ~** tomar algo a la ligera; **to get off ~** salir bien parado

**lightning** [ˈlaɪt·nɪŋ] n relámpago m; **a bolt of ~** un relámpago; **thunder and ~** rayos y centellas

**lightning rod** n pararrayos m inv

**lightweight** I. adj (clothing, material) ligero, -a II. n 1. SPORTS peso m ligero 2. sl (unimpressive person) persona f de poco peso

**light-year** n año m luz; **to be ~s away** inf estar a años luz de distancia

**likable** [ˈlaɪ·kə·bəl] adj simpático, -a

**like**¹ [laɪk] I. vt 1. (find good) **I ~ it** (esto) me gusta; **she ~s apples** le gustan las manzanas; **I ~ swimming** me gusta nadar; **I ~ her** (ella) me cae bien; **he ~s classical music** le gusta la música clásica; **I ~ it when/how...** me gusta cuando/cómo... 2. (desire, want) querer; **I would ~ to go to...** me gustaría ir a...; **would you ~ a cup of tea?** ¿quieres un té?; **I'd ~ to know...** quisiera saber...; **I'd ~ a steak** querría un filete II. ~s n ~s gustos mpl; **sb's ~s and dislikes** las preferencias de alguien

**like**² [laɪk] I. adj semejante; **to be of ~ mind** pensar de la misma manera II. prep 1. **to be ~ sb/sth** ser como alguien/algo; **what was it ~?** ¿cómo fue?; **what does it look ~?** ¿cómo es?, ¿qué aspecto tiene?; **to work ~ crazy** inf trabajar como un burro; **there's nothing ~...** no hay nada que se parezca a... 2. sl **to be ~...** (say) decir ► **~ anything** a más no poder III. conj inf como si +subj; **he speaks ~ he was drunk** habla como si estuviera borracho; **he doesn't do it ~ I do** él no lo hace como yo IV. n 1. (similar things) **toys, games and the ~** juguetes, juegos y cosas por el estilo 2. inf **the ~s of sth/sb**

algo/gente como algo/alguien

**likeable** *adj see* **likable**

**likelihood** ['laɪk·lɪ·hʊd] *n* probabilidad *f;* **in all ~** con toda probabilidad

**likely** ['laɪk·li] I. <-ier, -iest> *adj* probable; **it is ~ (that...)** es probable (que... +*subj*); **to be quite/very ~** ser bastante/muy probable; **to be a ~ story** *iron* ser un cuento chino, ser puro cuento *AmL;* **not ~!** *inf* ¡ni hablar! II. *adv* probablemente; **most/very ~** muy probablemente

**like-minded** *adj* del mismo parecer

**liken** ['laɪ·kən] *vt* comparar; **to ~ sb to sb** comparar alguien con alguien

**likeness** ['laɪk·nɪs] <-es> *n* (*similarity*) semejanza *f*

**likewise** ['laɪk·waɪz] *adv* de la misma forma, asimismo; **to do ~** hacer lo mismo; **thank you for your help — ~** gracias por tu ayuda — lo mismo digo

**liking** ['laɪ·kɪŋ] *n* afición *f;* (*for particular person*) simpatía *f;* **to develop a ~ for sb/sth** tomar cariño a alguien/algo; **it's too sweet for my ~** es demasiado dulce para mi gusto

**lilac** ['laɪ·læk] I. *n* 1. (*bush*) lila *f* 2. (*color*) lila *m* II. *adj* lila

**lily** ['lɪl·i] <-ies> *n* lirio *m;* **water ~** nenúfar *m*

**limb** [lɪm] *n* 1. BOT rama *f* 2. ANAT extremidad *f* ▶ **to be/go out on a ~** (*to do sth*) estar/ponerse en una situación arriesgada (para hacer algo)

**limber** ['lɪm·bər] *adj* (*person*) ágil; (*material*) flexible

**lime**[1] [laɪm] I. *n* 1. (*fruit*) lima *f* 2. (*tree*) limero *m* 3. (*juice*) zumo *m* de lima 4. (*color*) verde *m* lima II. *adj* de color verde lima

**lime**[2] [laɪm] I. *n* CHEM cal *f* II. *vt* abonar con cal

**lime**[3] [laɪm] *n* (*linden tree*) tilo *m*

**limelight** ['laɪm·laɪt] *n* foco *m* proyector; **to be in the ~** estar en el candelero

**limit** ['lɪm·ɪt] I. *n* límite *m;* **speed ~** AUTO límite *m* de velocidad; **to put a ~ on sth** poner un límite a algo; **to overstep the ~** pasarse del límite; **to know no ~s** no tener límites; **within ~s** dentro de ciertos límites; **to be off ~s** (*to sb*)

quedar prohibido el acceso (a alguien) II. *vt* limitar; **to ~ oneself to sth** limitarse a algo

**limitation** [ˌlɪm·ɪ·'teɪ·ʃən] *n* 1. (*lessening*) restricción *f;* (*of pollution, weapons*) limitación *f* 2. **~s** limitaciones *fpl;* **she knows her ~s** ella sabe sus limitaciones 3. LAW prescripción *f*

**limited** ['lɪm·ɪ·tɪd] *adj* limitado, -a; **to be ~ to sth** estar limitado a algo

**limp**[1] [lɪmp] I. *vi* cojear II. *n* cojera *f;* **to walk with a ~** cojear

**limp**[2] [lɪmp] *adj* flojo, -a; (*lettuce*) mustio, -a

**line**[1] [laɪn] <-ning> *vt* revestir; (*clothes*) forrar

**line**[2] [laɪn] I. *n* 1. (*mark*) a. MATH línea *f;* **dividing ~** línea divisoria; **to be in a ~** estar en línea 2. (*for waiting*) fila *f,* cola *f AmL;* **to get in ~** ponerse en fila; **to stand in ~** hacer cola; **to wait in ~** esperar en la cola 3. (*chronological succession*) linaje *m;* **a (long) ~ of disasters/kings** una (larga) sucesión de desastres/reyes 4. (*cord*) cuerda *f;* **clothes ~** cuerda para colgar la ropa 5. TEL línea *f;* **to be/stay on the ~** estar/seguir al habla; **hold the ~!** no cuelgue(s) 6. COMPUT **on ~** en línea; **off ~** desconectado 7. (*defense*) frente *m;* **front ~** línea del frente 8. (*set of tracks*) vía *f;* (*train route*) línea *f;* **the end of the ~** el final de la línea 9. (*transport company*) línea *f;* **cruise ~** línea de cruceros 10. (*of text, poem*) línea *f,* renglón *m;* **to drop sb a ~** *inf* escribir a alguien 11. MUS melodía *f* 12. (*comment*) comentario *m* 13. (*position, attitude*) línea *f;* **~ of reasoning** razonamiento *m;* **to be divided along ethnic ~s** estar dividido según criterios étnicos 14. (*field, pursuit, interest*) especialidad *f;* **what ~ are you in?** ¿a qué se dedica? 15. (*product type*) línea *f;* FASHION línea *f* de moda 16. *sl* (*of cocaine*) raya *f;* **to do a ~ of cocaine, to do ~s** esnifar una raya (de coca) ▶ **somewhere along the ~** en algún momento; **to cross the ~** pasarse de la raya; **to be out of ~** estar fuera de lugar; **to be out of ~ with sb/sth** no estar de acuerdo con alguien/algo II. <-ning> *vt* to ~ **the streets** ocupar las calles

◆**line up** I. *vt* alinear II. *vi* 1. (*stand in row*) alinearse 2. (*wait for sth*) ponerse en fila, hacer cola

**linear** ['lɪn·i·ər] *adj* lineal

**linen** ['lɪn·ɪn] *n* lino *m*; **bed ~s** sábanas *fpl*; **table ~s** mantelería *f*

**liner** ['laɪ·nər] *n* 1. (*lining*) forro *m*; (*garbage bag*) bolsa *f* de basura 2. (*ship*) transatlántico *m*

**linger** ['lɪŋ·gər] *vi* 1. entretenerse; (*film*) hacerse largo; **to ~ over sth** tomarse tiempo para (hacer) algo 2. (*die slowly*) **to ~ on** permanecer, perdurar

**linguist** ['lɪŋ·gwɪst] *n* lingüista *mf*

**lining** ['laɪ·nɪŋ] *n* 1. (*of coat, jacket*) forro *m*; (*of boiler, pipes*) revestimiento *m* 2. ANAT pared *f*

**link** [lɪŋk] I. *n* 1. (*in chain*) eslabón *m* 2. (*connection*) conexión *f*; **rail ~** enlace *m* ferroviario 3. COMPUT vínculo *m*, enlace *m* II. *vt* 1. (*connect*) conectar 2. (*be related to*) relacionar

**linseed** ['lɪn·sid] *n* linaza *f*

**lion** ['laɪ·ən] *n* león *m* ▶ **the ~'s share** la parte del león

**lioness** [laɪ·ə·'nes] <-sses> *n* leona *f*

**lip** [lɪp] *n* 1. ANAT labio *m*; **my ~s are sealed** mis labios están sellados 2. (*rim: of cup, bowl*) borde *m* 3. *sl* (*impudence*) insolencia *f*

**lip service** *n inf* jarabe *m* de pico; **to pay ~ to sth** apoyar algo sólo de boquilla

**lipstick** *n* barra *f* de labios

**liqueur** [lɪ·'kɜr] *n* licor *m*

**liquid** ['lɪk·wɪd] I. *n* líquido *m* II. *adj* líquido, -a

**liquidate** ['lɪk·wɪ·deɪt] *vt a. fig* liquidar

**liquidation** [ˌlɪk·wɪ·'deɪ·ʃən] *n* liquidación *f*; **to go into ~** ECON entrar en liquidación

**liquidize** ['lɪk·wɪ·daɪz] *vt* licuar

**liquidizer** ['lɪk·wɪ·daɪ·zər] *n* licuadora *f*

**Lisbon** ['lɪz·bən] *n* Lisboa *f*

**lisp** [lɪsp] I. *n* ceceo *m* II. *vi* cecear III. *vt* pronunciar ceceando

**list¹** [lɪst] I. *n* lista *f*; **~ price** precio *m* según catálogo; **shopping ~** lista de la compra; **to make a ~ (of sth)** hacer un listado (de algo) II. *vt* 1. (*make a list*)

listar 2. (*enumerate*) enumerar

**list²** [lɪst] NAUT I. *vi* escorar II. *n* escora *f*

**listen** ['lɪs·ən] *vi* 1. (*hear*) escuchar; **to ~ to sth/sb** escuchar algo/a alguien 2. (*pay attention*) estar atento; **to ~ for sth** estar atento para oír algo

◆**listen in** *vi* escuchar (a escondidas); **to ~ on sth** escuchar algo (a escondidas)

**listener** ['lɪs·nər] *n* oyente *mf*

**lit** [lɪt] *pt, pp of* **light**

**litany** ['lɪt·ə·ni] <-ies> *n* letanía *f*

**liter** ['li·tər] *n* litro *m*

**literacy** ['lɪt·ə·rə·si] *n* alfabetización *f*; **~ rate** índice *m* de alfabetización

**literal** ['lɪt·ər·əl] *adj* literal

**literally** ['lɪt·ər·ə·li] *adv* literalmente; **to take sth/sb ~** tomar algo/a alguien al pie de la letra

**literary** ['lɪt·ə·rer·i] *adj* literario, -a

**literate** ['lɪt·ər·ɪt] *adj* 1. (*able to read and write*) que sabe leer y escribir; **to be ~** saber leer y escribir 2. (*well-educated*) culto, -a

**literature** ['lɪt·ər·ə·tʃər] *n* 1. (*novels, poems*) literatura *f*; **nineteenth-century ~** literatura del siglo XIX 2. (*promotional material*) material *m* informativo

**Lithuania** [ˌlɪθ·ʊ·'eɪ·ni·ə] *n* Lituania *f*

**Lithuanian** [ˌlɪθ·ʊ·'eɪ·ni·ə] I. *n* 1. (*person*) lituano, -a *m, f* 2. LING lituano *m* II. *adj* lituano, -a

**litmus test** *n* prueba *m* de tornasol; *fig* prueba *f* de fuego

**litter** ['lɪt·ər] I. *n* 1. (*refuse*) basura *f* 2. ZOOL camada *f* II. *vt* 1. (*make untidy*) ensuciar (tirando basura) 2. *inf* (*scatter*) esparcir; **the floor was ~ed with clothes** el suelo estaba cubierto de ropa

**litter box** *n* bandeja *f* para la arena del gato

**little** ['lɪt·əl] I. *adj* 1. (*in size, age*) pequeño, -a; **a ~ old man/woman** un viejecito/una viejecita; **the ~ ones** *inf* los niños; **my ~ brother/sister** mi hermanito, -a, mi hermano pequeño/ mi hermana pequeña 2. (*in amount*) poco, -a; **a ~ bit (of sth)** un poco de algo); **a ~ something** alguna cosita; (*to eat or drink*) algo (de comer o de beber); **~ hope** pocas esperanzas; **~ by ~** poco a poco **3.** (*in duration*) breve; **for a ~ while** durante un ratito **II.** *n* poco *m;* **a ~ un poco; to know ~** saber poco; **we see ~ of him** lo vemos poco; **to have ~ to say** tener poco que decir **III.** *adv* poco; **~ less than...** poco menos que...; **~ more than an hour** poco más de una hora; **to make ~ of sth** sacar poco en claro de algo

**liturgy** ['lɪt̮·ər·dʒi] <-ies> *n* REL liturgia *f*

**live¹** [laɪv] **I.** *adj* **1.** (*living*) vivo, -a **2.** RADIO, TV en directo; THEAT, MUS en vivo **3.** ELEC que lleva corriente; (*wire*) conectado, -a **4.** (*cartridge*) cargado, -a; (*bomb*) con carga explosiva **II.** *adv* RADIO, TV en directo; THEAT, MUS en vivo

**live²** [lɪv] **I.** *vi* vivir; **long ~ the king!** ¡viva el rey!; **to ~ on sth** (*eat*) alimentarse de algo ▸ **to ~ and let ~** vivir y dejar vivir **II.** *vt* vivir; **to ~ a happy life** llevar una vida feliz

◆**live down** *vt* lograr superar

◆**live in** *vi* vivir en el lugar donde uno trabaja

◆**live on** *vi* vivir; (*tradition*) seguir vivo

◆**live out** *vt* vivir; (*dreams*) realizar

◆**live through** *vt* (*experience*) vivir

◆**live together** *vi* vivir juntos

◆**live up to** *vt* vivir conforme a; **to ~ expectations** estar a la altura de lo esperado

**lively** ['laɪv·li] *adj* (*person, conversation*) animado, -a; (*imagination, interest*) vivo, -a

**liven up** ['laɪ·vən·ʌp] **I.** *vi* animarse **II.** *vt* animar

**liver** ['lɪv·ər] *n* hígado *m*

**livestock** ['laɪv·stak] *n* ganado *m*

**livid** ['lɪv·ɪd] *adj* **1.** (*discolored*) lívido, -a **2.** (*furious*) furioso, -a

**living** ['lɪv·ɪŋ] **I.** *n* **1.** (*livelihood*) vida *f;* **to make a ~** ganarse la vida **2.** (*way of life*) (modo *m* de) vida *f* **3.** *pl* (*people*) **the ~** los vivos **II.** *adj* vivo, -a; (*creature*) viviente

**living conditions** *npl* condiciones *f pl* de vida

**living quarters** *npl* alojamiento *m*

**living room** *n* cuarto *m* de estar, living *m AmL*

**lizard** ['lɪz·ərd] *n* lagarto *m;* (*small*) la-

gartija *f*

**llama** ['la·mə] *n* llama *f*

**load** [loʊd] **I.** *n* **1.** ELEC *a.* *fig* carga *f;* **that took a ~ off my mind!** eso me quitó un (gran) peso de encima **2.** (*amount of work*) cantidad *f* (de trabajo); **a heavy/light ~** mucho/poco trabajo **3.** *inf* (*lots*) montón *m; ~s* [*or* **a ~**] **of...** un montón de... ▸ **to get a ~ of sth** *sl* fijarse en algo **II.** *vt a.* AUTO, PHOT, COMPUT cargar **III.** *vi* cargarse

◆**load down** *vt* recargar; *fig* agobiar

◆**load up I.** *vt* cargar **II.** *vi* cargarse

**loaded** ['loʊ·dɪd] *adj* **1.** (*filled*) cargado, -a **2.** (*unfair: question*) tendencioso, -a **3.** *sl* (*rich*) forrado, -a

**loaf¹** [loʊf] <-loaves> *n* pan *m;* **a ~ of bread** una barra *f* de pan, un pan

**loaf²** [loʊf] *vi* gandulear; **to ~ around** hacer el vago

**loan** [loʊn] **I.** *vt* prestar **II.** *n* préstamo *m,* avío *m AmS*

**lobby** ['lab·i] **I.** <-ies> *n* **1.** ARCHIT vestíbulo *m* **2.** POL grupo *m* de presión **I.** <-ie-> *vi* **to ~ against/for sth** presionar en contra de/en pro de algo **III.** <-ie-> *vt* presionar

**lobbyist** ['lab·i·ɪst] *n* miembro *m* de un grupo de presión

**lobster** ['lab·stər] *n* (*with claws*) bogavante *m;* (*spiny*) langosta *f*

**local** ['loʊ·kəl] **I.** *adj* local; (*people*) del lugar; (*official, police*) municipal; TEL urbano, -a; **~ color** color *m* local **II.** *n* **1.** (*inhabitant*) lugareño, -a *m, f* **2.** (*bus*) autobús *m* de línea; (*train*) tren *m* de cercanías

**local call** *n* llamada *f* local

**local government** *n* administración *f* municipal

**localization** [ˌloʊ·kə·lɪ·'zeɪ·ʃən] *n a.* COMPUT localización *f*

**local time** *n* hora *f* local

**locate** ['loʊ·keɪt] *vt* **1.** (*find*) localizar **2.** (*situate*) situar; **to be ~d near sth** estar situado cerca de algo

**location** [loʊ·'keɪ·ʃən] *n* **1.** (*place*) posición *f* **2.** (*act of locating*) localización *f* **3.** CINE exteriores *mpl;* **to film sth on ~** rodar algo en exteriores

**loch** [lak] *n Scot* **1.** (*lake*) lago *m* **2.** (*in-*

*let)* brazo *m* de mar

**lock**[1] [lak] *n (of hair)* mechón *m*

**lock**[2] [lak] **I.** *n* **1.** *(fastening device)* cerradura *f*, chapa *f Arg, Méx* **2.** *(on canal)* esclusa *f* ▸ **to be under ~ and key** estar cerrado bajo llave **II.** *vt* **1.** *(fasten with lock)* cerrar con llave; *(confine safely: thing)* guardar bajo llave **2.** *(make immovable)* bloquear; **be ~ed** estar bloqueado **III.** *vi* cerrarse con llave

◆**lock away** *vt (jewels, document)* guardar bajo llave; *(person)* encerrar

◆**lock on** *vi*, **lock onto** *vi* MIL localizar y seguir

◆**lock out** *vt* impedir la entrada a; **to lock oneself out** dejarse las llaves dentro

◆**lock up** *vt (jewels, document)* guardar bajo llave; *(person)* encerrar

**locker** ['lak.ər] *n (at train station)* consigna *f* automática; *(at school)* taquilla *f*

**locker room** *n* vestuario *m*, desvestidero *m Col*, vestidor *m Méx*

**lockjaw** ['lak.dʒɔ] *n* MED trismo *m*

**lockout** ['lak.aʊt] *n* cierre *m* patronal

**locksmith** ['lak.smɪθ] *n* cerrajero, -a *m, f*

**locust** ['loʊ.kəst] *n* langosta *f*, chapulín *m Méx*

**lodge** [ladʒ] **I.** *vi* **1.** *(stay in rented room)* alojarse **2.** *(become fixed)* quedarse clavado, -a **II.** *vt* **1.** *(accommodate)* alojar **2.** *(insert)* meter **3.** *(register officially: appeal)* interponer; *(complaint, protest)* presentar **III.** *n* **1.** *(inn)* albergue *m* **2.** *(for organizations)* logia *f*

**lodger** ['ladʒ.ər] *n* inquilino, -a *m, f*

**lodging** ['ladʒ.ɪŋ] *n* **1.** *(accommodations)* alojamiento *m* **2.** **~s** *(room to rent)* habitación *f* de alquiler

**loft** [laft] *n* **1.** *(space under roof)* buhardilla *f*; **hay ~** pajar *m* **2.** *(upstairs living space)* loft *m* **II.** *vt (ball)* lanzar por lo alto

**log**[1] [lɔg] **I.** *n* **1.** *(tree trunk)* tronco *m* **2.** *(firewood)* leño *m* ▸ **to sleep like a ~** dormir como un tronco **II.** <-gg-> *vt* talar **III.** <-gg-> *vi* talar árboles

**log**[2] [lɔg] *inf abbr of* **logarithm** log.

**log**[3] [lɔg] **I.** *n* registro *m* **II.** *vt (record)* registrar

**logarithm** ['lɔ.gə.rɪð.əm] *n* logaritmo *m*

**logic** ['ladʒ.ɪk] *n* lógica *f*

**logical** ['ladʒ.ɪ.kəl] *adj* lógico, -a

**login** ['lɔg.ɪn] *n* COMPUT inicio *m* de sesión

**logo** ['loʊ.goʊ] *n* logo(tipo) *m*

**logoff** ['lɔg.ɔf] *n* COMPUT fin *m* de sesión

**loin** [lɔɪn] **I.** *n* **1.** **~s** *(body area)* bajo vientre *m* **2.** **~s** *liter* the fruit of his **~s** el hijo/la hija de sus entrañas **3.** CULIN lomo *m* **II.** *adj* de lomo

**loiter** ['lɔɪ.tər] *vi* **1.** *(linger)* pasar el rato **2.** *a.* LAW merodear

**loll** [lal] *vi* colgar; **to ~ about** holgazanear

**lollipop** ['lal.i.pap] *n* chupachups® *m inv*

**London** ['lʌn.dən] *n* Londres *m*

**lone** [loʊn] *adj* solitario, -a

**loneliness** ['loʊn.li.nɪs] *n* soledad *f*

**lonely** ['loʊn.li] <-ier, -iest> *adj* **to feel ~** sentirse solo, -a; *(life)* solitario, -a; *(place)* aislado, -a

**loner** ['loʊ.nər] *n* solitario, -a *m, f*

**long**[1] [lɔŋ] **I.** *adj (distance, time, shape)* largo, -a; **to have a ~ way to go** tener mucho camino por recorrer; **it's been a ~ time since...** hace mucho tiempo desde que...; **~ time no see!** *inf* ¡cuánto tiempo (sin verte)! **II.** *adv* **1.** *(a long time)* mucho (tiempo); **~ after/before** mucho después/antes; **~ ago** hace mucho (tiempo); **to take ~ (to do sth)** tardar mucho (en hacer algo); **~ live the king!** ¡viva el rey! **2.** *(for the whole duration)* **all day ~** todo el día; **as ~ as I live** mientras viva; **so ~ as** mientras **3.** *in comparisons* **as ~ as** mientras +*subj*; **to no ~er do sth** ya no hacer algo ▸ **so ~** *inf* ¡hasta luego!

**long**[2] [lɔŋ] *vi* **to ~ for sb** echar de menos a alguien; **to ~ for sth** estar deseando algo; **to ~ to do sth** anhelar hacer algo

**long-distance** **I.** *adj (flight)* de largo recorrido; *(race, runner)* de fondo; *(negotiations, relationship)* a distancia; **~ call** llamada *f* de larga distancia **II.** *adv* **to phone ~** hacer una llamada interurbana

**longing** ['lɔŋ.ɪŋ] **I.** *n* **1.** *(nostalgia)* nostalgia *f* **2.** *(strong desire)* anhelo *m* **II.** *adj* anhelante

**longish** ['lɔŋ.ɪʃ] *adj inf* tirando a largo, -a

L

**longitude** ['lan·dʒə·tud] n longitud f

**long jump** n salto m de longitud, salto m largo AmL

**long-lived** adj (person) longevo, -a

**long-lost** adj perdido, -a hace mucho tiempo

**long-range** adj (missile) de largo alcance; (aircraft) transcontinental; (policy) a largo plazo

**long shot** n 1. (not likely) **to be a ~** ser una posibilidad muy remota 2. (at all) **not by a ~** ni de lejos

**long-sighted** adj 1. (far-sighted) hipermétrope 2. (having foresight) previsor(a)

**long-standing** adj antiguo, -a

**long-suffering** adj sufrido, -a

**long-term** adj (care) prolongado, -a; (loan, memory, strategy) a largo plazo

**long wave** n onda f larga

**long-winded** adj prolijo, -a

**loofa(h)** ['lu·fə] n esponja f vegetal

**look** [lʊk] I. n 1. (act of looking: at person, thing) mirada f; (examination: of book, face) ojeada f; **to take** [or **have**] **a ~ at sth** echar un vistazo a algo 2. (appearance) aspecto m; **good ~s** guapura f 3. (style) look m II. vi 1. (use sight) mirar; **to ~ at sth/sb** mirar algo a alguien; **to ~ out (of) the window** mirar por la ventana; **oh, ~!** ¡mira!; **~ here** ¡oye, tú! 2. (search) buscar; **to ~ for sth/sb** buscar algo a alguien 3. (appear, seem) parecer; **to ~ like sb/sth** parecerse a alguien/algo; **to ~ bad/good** tener mala/buena cara; **to ~ tired** parecer cansado; **to ~ as if...** parecer como si... +subj; **~ alive!** ¡espabila! 4. (face) **to ~ north** mirar [or dar] al norte ► **before you leap** prov mira lo que haces prov III. vt 1. (examine) mirar; **to ~ sb in the eye** mirar a alguien a los ojos [or a la cara] 2. (seem) parecer; **to ~ one's age** aparentar su edad ► **to ~ the other way** hacer la vista gorda

◆**look about** vi mirar alrededor

◆**look after** vi 1. (take care of) cuidar 2. (take responsibility for) encargarse de

◆**look ahead** vi mirar hacia adelante; **looking ahead to...** de cara a...

◆**look around** I. vi 1. (look behind oneself) girarse 2. (look in all directions) mirar alrededor 3. (search) **to ~ for** buscar II. vt (inspect) inspeccionar

◆**look away** vi apartar la mirada

◆**look back** vi 1. (look behind oneself) mirar (hacia) atrás 2. (remember) recordar

◆**look down** vi 1. (from above) mirar hacia abajo; (lower eyes) bajar la vista 2. (feel superior) **to ~ on sth/sb** menospreciar algo/a alguien

◆**look for** vi 1. (search for) buscar 2. (expect) esperar

◆**look forward** vi **to ~ to sth** tener muchas ganas de algo; **I ~ to hearing from you** espero tener pronto noticias suyas

◆**look in** vi **to ~ on sb** ir a ver a alguien

◆**look into** vi investigar

◆**look on** vi 1. (watch) mirar 2. (view) ver

◆**look out** vi 1. (face a particular direction) **to ~ on** (window) dar a 2. (watch out) tener cuidado; **~!** ¡cuidado!; **to ~ for** tener cuidado con; (look for) buscar

◆**look over** vt (report) revisar; (house) inspeccionar

◆**look through** vt 1. (look) mirar por 2. (examine) revisar 3. (peruse) **to ~ sth** echar un vistazo a algo

◆**look to** vi 1. (attend to) mirar por 2. (depend on) depender de 3. (count on) contar con

◆**look up** I. vt 1. (consult) buscar 2. (visit) ir a ver II. vi 1. (raise one's eyes upward) mirar hacia arriba; **to ~ to sb** fig tener a alguien de [or como] ejemplo 2. (improve) mejorar; **things are looking up!** ¡las cosas van mejorando!

**looking glass** <-es> n espejo m

**lookout** ['lʊk·aʊt] n 1. (observation post) puesto m de observación 2. (person) centinela mf; **to be on the ~** estar alerta

**loom** [lum] n (for weaving) telar m

**loony** ['lu·ni] sl I. <-ier, -iest> adj (person) chiflado, -a; (idea) disparatado -a II. <-ies> n loco, -a m, f, chiflado -a m, f

**loop** [lup] I. n 1. (bend) curva f; (of string) lazada f 2. ELEC circuito m cerrado **3.** COMPUT bucle m **4.** (*contraceptive coil*) espiral *f* ▶ **to throw sb for a ~** *sl* dejar a alguien de piedra **II.** *vi* serpentear **III.** *vt* atar con un lazo; **to ~ sth around...** pasar algo alrededor de... ▶ **to ~ the loop** AVIAT rizar el rizo

**loophole** ['lup·hoʊl] *n fig* escapatoria *f*; **legal ~** laguna legal

**loose** [lus] **I.** *adj* **1.** (*not tight: clothing*) holgado, -a; (*knot, rope, screw*) flojo, -a; (*skin*) fláccido, -a **2.** (*not confined*) suelto, -a; **~ change** (dinero *m* ) suelto *m*, sencillo *m AmS* **3.** (*not exact: instructions*) poco preciso, -a; (*translation*) libre **4.** (*not strict or controlled: discipline*) relajado, -a; **~ tongue** lengua *f* desatada **5.** (*sexually immoral*) disoluto, -a **II.** *n* **to be on the ~** estar en libertad **III.** *vt* soltar

**loosely** ['lus·li] *adv* **1.** (*not tightly*) sin apretar **2.** (*not exactly: translate*) libremente; (*speak*) en términos generales **3.** (*not strictly: organized*) de forma flexible

**loosen** ['lu·sən] **I.** *vt* (*belt, knot*) aflojar; (*tongue*) desatar **II.** *vi* aflojarse

**loot** [lut] **I.** *n* **1.** (*plunder*) botín *m* **2.** *sl* (*money*) pasta *f*, lana *f AmL* **II.** *vt, vi* saquear

**looting** *n* saqueo *m*

**lope** [loʊp] *vi* (*person, animal*) andar con paso largo

**lopsided** [ˌlap·ˈsaɪ·dɪd] *adj* **1.** (*leaning to one side*) torcido, -a, chueco, -a *AmL* **2.** (*biased*) parcial

**lord** [lɔrd] *n* señor *m*

**lose** [luz] <lost, lost> **I.** *vt* perder; **to get lost** (*person*) perderse; (*object*) extraviarse **II.** *vi* perder

**loser** ['lu·zər] *n* perdedor(a) *m(f)*

**loss** [lɔs] <-es> *n* pérdida *f*; **to be at a ~** no saber cómo reaccionar; **to be at a ~ for words** no encontrar palabras con que expresarse

**loss-making** *adj* deficitario, -a

**lost** [lɔst] **I.** *pt, pp of* **lose** **II.** *adj* **1.** perdido, -a; **to get ~** perderse; **to give sth/ sb up for ~** dar algo/a alguien por perdido; **to be ~ in a book** estar enfrascado en la lectura de un libro **2.** (*preoccupied*) perplejo, -a; **to be ~ in thought** estar ensimismado

**lot** [lat] *n* **1.** (*for deciding*) **to cast ~s** echar a suertes **2.** (*destiny*) destino *m* **3.** (*plot of land*) terreno *m* **4.** (*in auction*) lote *m* **5.** *inf* (*large quantity*) **a ~ of, lots of** mucho(s); **a ~ of wine** mucho vino; **~s of houses** muchas casas; **I like it a ~** me gusta mucho; **the whole ~** todo

**lotion** ['loʊ·ʃən] *n* loción *f*

**lottery** ['lat·ə·ri] <-ies> *n* lotería *f*, quiniela *f CSur*

**lotus** ['loʊ·təs] <-es> *n* loto *m*

**loud** [laʊd] **I.** *adj* **1.** (*voice*) alto, -a; (*shout*) fuerte **2.** (*noisy*) ruidoso, -a **3.** (*vigorous: complaint*) enérgico, -a **4.** *fig* (*color*) chillón, -ona **II.** *adv* alto; **to laugh out ~** reír a carcajadas

**loudmouth** ['laʊd·maʊθ] *n inf* escandaloso, -a *m, f*

**loudspeaker** [ˌlaʊd·ˈspi·kər] *n* altavoz *m*

**lounge** [laʊndʒ] **I.** *n* **1.** (*room*) salón *m* **2.** (*bar*) bar *m* **II.** *vi* **1.** (*recline*) repanchi(n)garse **2.** (*be idle*) hacer el vago

**louse** [laʊs] *n* **1.** <lice> (*insect*) piojo *m* **2.** <-es> *sl* (*person*) canalla *mf*

**lousy** ['laʊ·zi] <-ier, -iest> *adj* **1.** (*infested with lice*) piojoso, -a **2.** (*of poor quality*) pésimo, -a; **to feel ~** sentirse fatal **3.** (*nasty*) asqueroso, -a

**lout** [laʊt] *n* patán *m*, jallán *m AmC*

**loutish** ['laʊ·tɪʃ] *adj* patán

**love** [lʌv] **I.** *vt* querer, amar; **I ~ swimming, I ~ to swim** me encanta nadar **II.** *n* **1.** (*affection*) amor *m*; **to be in ~** (**with sb**) estar enamorado (de alguien); **to fall in ~** (**with sb**) enamorarse (de alguien); **to make ~ to sb** hacer el amor con alguien **2.** *inf* (*darling*) cariño *m* **3.** (*in tennis*) cero *m* ▶ **not for ~ or money** por nada del mundo **III.** *vi* querer, amar

**love handles** *npl sl* michelines *mpl*, llantas *fpl Col*, lonjas *fpl Méx*

**love-hate relationship** *n* relación *f* de amor y odio

**love letter** *n* carta *f* de amor

**love life** *n* vida *f* amorosa [*or* sentimental]

**lovely** ['lʌv·li] <-ier, -iest> *adj* (*house,*

*present*) bonito, -a; (*weather*) precioso, -a; (*person*) encantador(a)

**lover** ['lʌv·ər] *n* amante *mf*

**lovesick** ['lʌv·sɪk] *adj* locamente enamorado, -a, volado, -a *AmL*

**love song** *n* canción *f* de amor

**love story** *n* historia *f* de amor

**loving** ['lʌv·ɪŋ] *adj* cariñoso, -a

**low¹** [loʊ] **I.** *adj* **1.** (*not high, not loud*) bajo, -a; **to be ~ on sth** (*coffee, gas*) tener poco de algo; **to cook sth on ~ heat** hacer algo a fuego lento **2.** (*poor: opinion, quality*) malo, -a; (*self-esteem*) bajo, -a; (*visibility*) poco, -a; **a ~ trick** una mala jugada **II.** *adv* bajo, -a; **to feel ~** estar deprimido; **stocks are running ~** las existencias están casi agotadas; **the batteries are running ~** se están gastando las pilas **III.** *n* (*minimum*) mínimo *m*; **an all-time ~** un mínimo histórico

**low²** [loʊ] **I.** *vi* (*cow*) mugir **II.** *n* mugido *m*

**low-cal** *adj,* **low-calorie** *adj* bajo, -a en calorías

**low-cut** *adj* escotado, -a

**low-down** *adj inf* bajo, -a; **a ~ trick** una mala jugada

**lower¹** ['loʊ·ər] **I.** *vt* bajar; (*flag, sails*) arriar; (*lifeboat*) echar al agua; **to ~ one's eyes** bajar la vista; **to ~ oneself to do sth** rebajarse a hacer algo **II.** *vi* bajar **III.** *adj* inferior

**lower²** [laʊr] *vi* (*person*) fruncir el ceño

**lower-case** *adj* minúsculo, -a; **in ~ letters** en minúsculas

**low-key** *adj* (*affair*) discreto, -a; (*debate, discussion*) mesurado, -a

**lowly** ['loʊ·li] <-ier, -iest> *adj* humilde

**low-pitched** *adj* (*voice*) grave

**low profile** *n* **to keep a ~** tratar de pasar desapercibido

**low season** *n* temporada *f* baja

**low tide** *n,* **low water** *n* marea *f* baja, bajamar *f*

**lox** [laks] *n* CULIN salmón *m* ahumado

**loyal** ['lɔɪ·əl] *adj* leal; **to remain ~** (**to sb/ sth**) permanecer fiel (a alguien/algo)

**loyalty** ['lɔɪ·əl·ti] <-ies> *n* lealtad *f*

**lubricant** ['lu·brɪ·kənt] *n* lubricante *m*

**lubricate** ['lu·brɪ·keɪt] *vt* lubricar

**luck** [lʌk] *n* suerte *f*; **good/bad ~** buena/ mala suerte; **to bring sb ~** traer suerte a alguien; **to wish sb (good) ~** desear a alguien (buena) suerte; **with any ~** con un poco de suerte; **with no ~** sin éxito ▶ **no such ~!** *inf* ¡qué va!; **to press one's ~** tentar a la suerte

**lucky** ['lʌk·i] <-ier, -iest> *adj* afortunado, -a; **to be ~ in love** tener suerte en el amor; **to be ~ (in that...)** tener la suerte (de que...) +*subj;* **to make a ~ guess** acertar por (pura) casualidad; **~ day** día *m* de suerte; **~ number** número *m* de la suerte

**lucrative** ['lu·krə·tɪv] *adj* lucrativo, -a

**ludicrous** ['lu·dɪ·krəs] *adj* absurdo, -a

**luggage** ['lʌg·ɪdʒ] *n* equipaje *m*

**luggage rack** *n* baca *f*

**lukewarm** [,luk·'wɔrm] *adj* **1.** (*liquid*) tibio, -a **2.** *fig* (*unenthusiastic*) poco entusiasta

**lullaby** ['lʌl·ə·baɪ] <-ies> *n* nana *f*

**lumbar puncture** *n* MED punción *f* lumbar

**lumber¹** ['lʌm·bər] *vi* moverse pesadamente

**lumber²** ['lʌm·bər] **I.** *n* madera *f* **II.** *v* aserrar

**lumberjack** *n* leñador *m*

**luminous** ['lu·mə·nəs] *adj* luminoso, -a

**lump** [lʌmp] **I.** *n* **1.** (*solid mass*) masa *f,* (*of coal*) trozo *m;* (*of sugar*) terrón *m;* ~ **sum** cantidad *f* única **2.** (*swelling: in breast, on head*) bulto *m* ▶ **to have a ~ in one's throat** tener un nudo en la garganta **II.** *vt* <to ~ (together)> agrupar

**lump-sum payment** *n* pago *m* único

**lumpy** ['lʌm·pi] <-ier, -iest> *adj* (*custard, sauce*) grumoso, -a; (*surface*) desigual

**lunacy** ['lu·nə·si] *n* locura *f*

**lunar** ['lu·nər] *adj* lunar

**lunatic** ['lu·nə·tɪk] **I.** *n* loco, -a *m,* ，**II.** *adj* lunático, -a

**lunch** [lʌntʃ] **I.** *n* comida *f*; **to have ~** comer **II.** *vi* comer

**lunch break** *n* descanso *m* para comer

**luncheon** ['lʌn·tʃən] *n form* almuerzo *m*

**luncheon meat** *n* fiambre *de cerdo er conserva*

**lunch hour** *n* hora *f* de comer

**lunchtime** I. *n* hora *f* de comer II. *adj* (*concert*) de mediodía

**lung** [lʌŋ] *n* pulmón *m;* **to shout at the top of one's ~s** decir a voz en grito

**lung cancer** *n* cáncer *m* de pulmón

**lurch** [lɜrtʃ] I. *vi* (*people*) tambalearse; (*car, train*) dar sacudidas II. <-es> *n* sacudida *f* ▶ **to leave sb in the ~** *inf* dejar a alguien colgado

**lure** [lʊr] I. *n* 1. (*attraction*) atractivo *m* 2. (*bait*) cebo *m;* (*decoy*) señuelo *m* II. *vt* atraer; **to ~ sb into a trap** hacer que alguien caiga en una trampa

**lurk** [lɜrk] *vi* merodear, esconderse

**luscious** ['lʌʃ-əs] *adj* 1. (*fruit*) jugoso, -a 2. *inf* (*girl, curves*) voluptuoso, -a; (*lips*) carnoso, -a

**lush** [lʌʃ] I. *adj* (*vegetation*) exuberante II. *n* <-es> *sl* borracho, -a *m, f*

**lust** [lʌst] *n* 1. (*sexual desire*) lujuria *f* 2. (*strong desire*) anhelo *m;* **~ for sth** ansia de algo

**Lutheran** ['lu-θər-ən] I. *adj* luterano, -a II. *n* luterano, -a *m, f*

**Luxembourg** ['lʌk-səm-bɜrg] *n* Luxemburgo *m*

**Luxembourger** *n* luxemburgués, -esa *m, f*

**luxurious** [lʌg-'ʒʊr-i-əs] *adj* lujoso, -a

**luxury** ['lʌk-ʃər-i] <-ies> *n* lujo *m;* **~ apartment** piso *m* de lujo

**lying** ['laɪ-ɪŋ] I. *n* mentiras *fpl* II. *adj* mentiroso, -a

**lyric** ['lɪr-ɪk] I. *adj* lírico, -a II. *n* 1. (*poem*) poema *m* lírico 2. **~s** (*words for song*) letra *f*

**lyricist** ['lɪr-ɪ-sɪst] *n* letrista *mf*

# M

**M, m** [em] *n* M, m *f;* **~ as in Mike** M de María

**M** *n* 1. *abbr of* **male** H 2. *abbr of* **medium** M

**m** 1. *abbr of* **million** millón *m* 2. *abbr of* **minutes** min. 3. *abbr of* **meter** m

**m.** *n abbr of* **mile** milla *f*

**MA** [em-'eɪ] *n* 1. *abbr of* **Master of Arts** máster *m* (*de Humanidades o de Filoso-*

*fía y Letras*) 2. *abbr of* **Massachusetts** Massachusetts *m*

**ma** [mɑ] *n inf* mamá *f*

**ma'am** [mæm] = **madam** (*form of address*) señora *f*

**macabre** [mə-'kɑb-rə] *adj* macabro, -a

**macaroni** [ˌmæk-ə-'roʊ-ni] *n* macarrones *mpl*

**machine** [mə-'ʃin] *n* (*mechanical device*) máquina *f*

**machine gun** *n* ametralladora *f*

**machinery** [mə-'ʃi-nə-ri] *n a. fig* (*machines*) maquinaria *f*

**macho** ['mætʃ-oʊ] *adj* machista

**mackerel** ['mæk-rəl] <-(s)> *n* caballa *f*

**macroeconomics** [ˌmæk-roʊˌek-ə-'nɑm-ɪks] *n* macroeconomía *f*

**mad** [mæd] *adj* 1. (*upset*) furioso, -a 2. (*insane: person*) loco, -a; **to go ~** volverse loco; **to drive sb ~** volver loco a alguien 3. (*enthusiastic*) **to be ~ about sb** estar loco por alguien

**madam** ['mæd-əm] *n* señora *f*

**madden** ['mæd-ən] *vt* enfurecer

**made** [meɪd] *pp, pt of* **make**

**made-up** ['meɪd-ʌp] *adj* (*invented*) inventado, -a

**madhouse** ['mæd-haʊs] *n inf* loquero *m*

**madly** ['mæd-li] *adv* 1. (*frantically*) frenéticamente 2. (*intensely*) **she's ~ in love with him** está locamente enamorada de él

**madman** ['mæd-mən] <-men> *n* loco *m*

**madness** ['mæd-nɪs] *n* locura *f*, loquera *f AmL*

**madwoman** ['mæd-ˌwʊm-ən] <-women> *n* loca *f*

**magazine** ['mæg-ə-zin] *n* 1. (*periodical publication*) revista *f* 2. MIL (*of gun*) recámara *f*

**magic** ['mædʒ-ɪk] I. *n* magia *f;* **as if by ~** como por arte de magia II. *adj* mágico, -a

**magical** *adj* 1. (*power*) mágico, -a 2. (*extraordinary, wonderful*) fabuloso, -a

**magician** [mə-'dʒɪʃ-ən] *n* mago, -a *m, f*

**magistrate** ['mædʒ-ɪ-streɪt] *n juez que se ocupa de los delitos menores*

**magnate** ['mæg-neɪt] *n* magnate *mf*

**magnet** ['mæg-nɪt] *n* imán *m*

M

**magnetic** [mæg·'net·ɪk] *adj* 1. (*force*) magnético, -a 2. (*personality*) atrayente

**magnetism** ['mæg·nə·tɪz·əm] *n* magnetismo *m*

**magnificent** [mæg·'nɪf·ɪ·sənt] *adj* magnífico, -a

**magnify** ['mæg·nɪ·faɪ] <-ie-> *vt* 1. (*make larger*) ampliar; (*voice*) amplificar 2. (*make worse: problem*) exagerar

**magnifying glass** *n* lupa *f*

**magnitude** ['mæg·nɪ·tud] *n* magnitud *f*

**magpie** ['mæg·paɪ] *n* (*bird*) urraca *f*

**mahogany** [mə·'hag·ə·ni] *n* caoba *f*

**maid** [meɪd] *n* 1. (*female servant*) criada *f*, mucama *f AmL* 2. *liter* (*girl, young woman*) doncella *f*

**maiden** ['meɪ·dən] I. *n liter* doncella *f* II. *adj* 1. (*unmarried*) soltera 2. (*first: voyage*) primero, -a

**maiden name** *n* apellido *m* de soltera

**maid of honor** *n* dama *f* de honor

**mail**[1] [meɪl] I. *n a.* COMPUT correo *m*; **electronic** ~ COMPUT correo electrónico; **incoming/outgoing** ~ COMPUT correo entrante/saliente; **by** ~ por correo; **to open the** ~ abrir el correo II. *vt* mandar por correo

**mail**[2] [meɪl] *n* (*armor*) malla *f*

**mailbox** *n* 1. (*for postal deliveries*) buzón *m* 2. COMPUT (**electronic**) ~ buzón *m* electrónico

**mailing list** *n* lista *f* de direcciones (*a las que se envía publicidad o información*)

**mailman** *n* cartero *m*

**maim** [meɪm] *vt* lisiar

**main** [meɪn] I. *adj* (*problem, reason, street*) principal II. *n* 1. (*pipe*) cañería *f* principal; **the water** ~ la cañería maestra; **the gas** ~ la cañería principal de gas 2. (*cable*) cable *m* principal ▶ **in the** ~ en general

**mainframe** ['meɪn·freɪm] *n* COMPUT ordenador *m* central, computadora *f* central *AmL*

**mainland** ['meɪn·lənd] I. *n* continente *m* II. *adj* ~ **China** China continental; ~ **Spain** España peninsular

**mainly** ['meɪn·li] *adv* principalmente

**main office** *n* oficina *f* central

**main road** *n* carretera *f* general

**mainsail** *n* vela *f* mayor

**mainspring** *n* motivo *m* principal

**mainstream** *adj* 1. (*ideology*) dominante 2. (*film, novel*) comercial

**maintain** [meɪn·'teɪn] *vt* 1. (*preserve, provide for*) mantener 2. (*claim*) sostener

**maintenance** ['meɪn·tə·nəns] *n* (*repair work, preservation*) mantenimiento *m*

**majesty** ['mædʒ·ɪ·sti] <-ies> *n* majestuosidad *f*; **Her/His/Your Majesty** su Majestad

**major** ['meɪ·dʒər] I. *adj* 1. (*important, significant*) fundamental 2. (*serious: illness*) grave 3. MUS mayor; **in C** ~ en do mayor II. *n* 1. MIL comandante *m* 2. UNIV especialidad *f*

**Majorca** [mə·'jɔr·kə] *n* Mallorca *f*

**Majorcan** I. *adj* mallorquín, -ina II. *n* mallorquín, -ina *m, f*

**majorette** [ˌmeɪ·dʒər·'et] *n* batonista *f*

**majority** [mə·'dʒɔr·ə·ti] <-ies> *n* 1. (*greater part/number*) mayoría *f* 2. (*most powerful group*) grupo *m* mayoritario 3. (*full legal age*) mayoría *f* de edad; **to reach the age of** ~ alcanzar la mayoría de edad

**make** [meɪk] I. *vt* <made, made> 1. (*produce: coffee, soup, dinner*) hacer; (*product*) fabricar; (*clothes*) confeccionar; (*record*) grabar; (*film*) rodar **to make sth out of sth** hacer algo con algo; **to** ~ **time** hacer tiempo 2. (*cause: trouble*) causar; **to** ~ **noise** hacer ruido; **to** ~ **a scene** montar una escena 3. (*cause to be*) **to** ~ **sb sad** poner triste a alguien; **to** ~ **sb happy** hacer feliz a alguien; **to** ~ **oneself heard/understood** hacerse oír/entender; **to** ~ **sth easy** hacer que algo sea fácil 4. (*perform, carry out*) **to** ~ **a call/reservation** hacer una llamada/reserva; **to** ~ **a decision** tomar una decisión 5. (*force*) obligar; **to** ~ **sb do sth** hacer que alguien haga algo 6. (*amount to, total*) ser; **two plus two** ~**s four** dos y dos son cuatro 7. (*earn, get*) **to** ~ **friends** hacer amigos; **to** ~ **money** (*or ga-nar*) dinero; **to** ~ **a living** ganarse la vida 8. *inf* (*get to, reach*) **to** ~ **it to somewhere** llegar a un sitio; **to** ~ **it** alcanza el éxito **9.** (*make perfect*) **that made my day!** ¡eso me alegró el día! ▸ **to do** (with sth) arreglárselas (con algo) **II.** *vi* (*amount to, total*) **today's earthquake ~s five since the beginning of the year** el terremoto de hoy es el quinto de este año ▸ **to ~ as if to do sth** fingir hacer algo **III.** *n* **1.** (*brand*) marca *f* **2.** (*identification*) ▸ **to get a ~ on sb** identificar [*or* tener] a alguien ▸ **to be on the ~** *sl* (*for money, power*) intentar sacar tajada

◆**make for** *vt insep* (*head for*) dirigirse a

◆**make out I.** *vi* **1.** (*succeed, cope: person*) arreglárselas **2.** *sl* (*kiss passionately*) ▸ **to ~ with sb** darse el lote con alguien **II.** *vt* **1.** (*discern: writing, numbers*) distinguir; (*sth in the distance*) divisar **2.** (*pretend*) **he made himself out to be rich** se hizo pasar por rico **3.** (*write out*) **to ~ a check for $100** extender un cheque por valor de 100 dólares

◆**make up I.** *vt* **1.** (*invent*) inventar **2.** (*prepare*) preparar **3.** (*compensate*) ▸ **to ~ for sth** compensar algo **4.** (*constitute*) constituir **5.** (*decide*) ▸ **to ~ one's mind** decidirse **II.** *vi* reconciliarse

◆**make up to** *vt* ▸ **to make it up to sb** compensar a alguien

**make-believe** ['meɪk·bɪ·ˌliv] *adj* imaginario, -a; (*weapon*) de mentira; **a ~ world** un mundo de fantasía

**maker** ['meɪ·kər] *n* (*manufacturer*) fabricante *mf*

**makeshift** ['meɪk·ʃɪft] *adj* provisional

**make-up** ['meɪk·ʌp] *n* **1.** (*cosmetics*) maquillaje *m;* **to put on ~** maquillarse; **to wear ~** ir maquillado **2.** (*structure*) estructura *f* **3.** (*character*) carácter *m*

**making** ['meɪ·kɪŋ] *n* **1.** (*production*) producción *m;* (*of clothes*) confección *f;* (*of meals*) preparación *f* **2.** **~s** (*essential qualities*) **to have the ~s of sth** tener madera de algo

**malaise** [mæ·'leɪz] *n* malestar *m*

**malaria** [mə·'ler·i·ə] *n* malaria *f*

**male** [meɪl] **I.** *adj* (*hormone, sex*) masculino, -a; (*animal*) macho; **~ chauvinism** machismo *m* **II.** *n* (*person*) varón *m;* (*animal*) macho *m*

**malfunction** [ˌmæl·'fʌŋk·ʃən] **I.** *vi* **1.** (*not work properly*) funcionar mal **2.** (*stop functioning*) fallar **II.** *n* **1.** (*defective functioning*) mal funcionamiento *m* **2.** (*sudden stop*) fallo *m*

**malice** ['mæl·ɪs] *n* malicia *f*

**malicious** [mə·'lɪʃ·əs] *adj* malicioso, -a

**malign** [mə·'laɪn] *adj form* maligno, -a

**malignant** [mə·'lɪg·nənt] *adj* maligno, -a

**mall** [mɔl] *n* centro *m* comercial

**malleable** ['mæl·i·ə·bəl] *adj* maleable

**mallet** ['mæl·ɪt] *n* mazo *m*

**malnutrition** [ˌmæl·nu·'trɪʃ·ən] *n* desnutrición *f*

**malpractice** [ˌmæl·'præk·tɪs] *n* conducta *f* incorrecta; **medical ~** negligencia *f* médica

**malt** [mɔlt] **I.** *n* malta *f* **II.** *vt* maltear

**Malta** ['mɔl·tə] *n* Malta *f*

**maltreatment** [mæl·'trit·mənt] *n* malos tratos *mpl*

**mammal** ['mæm·əl] *n* mamífero *m*

**mammary gland** ['mæm·ə·ri·ˌglænd] *n* glándula *f* mamaria

**mammoth** ['mæm·əθ] *n* mamut *m*

**man** [mæn] **I.** *n* <men> **1.** (*male human*) hombre *m* **2.** (*the human race*) ser *m* humano ▸ **to talk (as) ~ to ~** hablar de hombre a hombre; **as one ~** unánimemente **II.** *vt* <-nn-> (*operate*) encargarse de; (*ship*) tripular; **to ~ a factory** contratar personal para una fábrica; **some volunteers ~ the phones** algunos voluntarios cogen el teléfono **III.** *interj* ¡hombre!; **~, was that cake good!** ¡pues sí que estaba bueno el pastel!

**manage** ['mæn·ɪdʒ] **I.** *vt* **1.** *a.* ECON (*control, be in charge of*) dirigir; (*money, time*) administrar **2.** (*accomplish*) lograr; **to ~ to do sth** conseguir hacer algo **II.** *vi* ▸ **to ~ on a few dollars a day** arreglárselas con un par de dólares al día

**manageable** ['mæn·ɪ·dʒə·bəl] *adj* (*vehicle*) manejable; (*person, animal*) dócil; (*amount*) razonable

**management** ['mæn·ɪdʒ·mənt] *n* **1.** (*direction*) manejo *m* **2.** *a.* ECON dirección *f*, gestión *f*

**manager** ['mæn·ɪ·dʒər] *n* **1.** COM (*administrator*) administrador(a) *m(f);* (*of business unit*) gerente *mf* **2.** (*of performer,*

M

*artist*) representante *mf* artístico, -a; (*of a sports team*) manager *mf*

**managing director** *n* director(a) *m(f)* general

**mandarin** ['mæn·də·rɪn] *n* mandarín *m*

**Mandarin** *n* LING mandarín *m*

**mandate** ['mæn·deɪt] *n a.* POL mandato *m*

**mandatory** ['mæn·də·tɔr·i] *adj form* obligatorio, -a

**mane** [meɪn] *n* (*of horse*) crin *f*; (*of person, lion*) melena *f*

**maneuver** [mə·'nu·vər] **I.** *n a.* MIL maniobra *f* **II.** *vt* hacer maniobrar **III.** *vi* maniobrar

**maneuverable** [mə·'nu·vər·ə·bəl] *adj* maniobrable

**manger** ['meɪn·dʒər] *n* pesebre *m*

**mangle** ['mæŋ·gəl] *vt* (*body, text*) mutilar

**manhandle** ['mæn·hæn·dəl] *vt* 1. (*treat roughly: person*) maltratar 2. (*move by hand: heavy object*) empujar

**manhole** ['mæn·houl] *n* registro *m*, boca *f* de visita *Ven*

**manhood** ['mæn·hʊd] *n* 1. (*adulthood*) edad *f* adulta 2. (*masculinity*) virilidad *f*

**manhunt** ['mæn·hʌnt] *n* persecución *f*

**mania** ['meɪ·ni·ə] *n* (*obsession*) manía *f*

**maniac** ['meɪ·ni·æk] *n* maníaco, -a *m, f*

**manicure** ['mæn·ɪ·kjʊr] *n* manicura *f*

**manifest** ['mæn·ɪ·fest] **I.** *adj form* manifiesto, -a; **to make sth ~** poner algo de manifiesto **II.** *vt form* declarar; **to ~ symptoms of sth** manifestar síntomas de algo

**manifesto** [ˌmæn·ɪ·'fes·toʊ] <-stos *or* -stoes> *n* manifiesto *m*

**manipulate** [mə·'nɪp·jə·leɪt] *vt* manipular

**manipulation** [mə·ˌnɪp·jə·'leɪ·ʃən] *n* manipulación *f*

**manipulative** [mə·ˌnɪp·jə·'lə·t̬ɪv] *adj* manipulador(a)

**mankind** [ˌmæn·'kaɪnd] *n* humanidad *f*

**manly** ['mæn·li] <-ier, -iest> *adj* varonil

**man-made** ['mæn·meɪd] *adj* (*lake*) artificial; (*fiber*) sintético, -a

**manned** [mænd] *adj* AVIAT tripulado, -a

**mannequin** ['mæn·ɪ·kɪn] *n* (*dummy*) maniquí *mf*

**manner** ['mæn·ər] *n* 1. (*way, fashion*) manera *f*; **in the ~ of sb** al estilo de alguien; **in a ~ of speaking** por así decirlo; **a ~ of speaking** una forma de hablar 2. (*behavior*) **~s** modales *mpl*; **it's bad ~s to...** es de mala educación... 3. *form* (*kind, type*) clase *f*; **what ~ of man is he?** ¿qué tipo de hombre es?

**mannerism** ['mæn·ə·rɪz·əm] *n* amaneramiento *m*

**manor** ['mæn·ər] *n* 1. (*house*) casa *f* solariega 2. HIST (*territory*) feudo *m*

**manpower** ['mæn·ˌpaʊ·ər] *n* mano *f* de obra

**mansion** ['mæn·ʃən] *n* mansión *f*

**manslaughter** ['mæn·slɔ·t̬ər] *n* homicidio *m* involuntario

**mantelpiece** ['mæn·təl·pis] *n* repisa *f* de la chimenea

**manual** ['mæn·ju·əl] **I.** *adj* manual; **~ dexterity** habilidad *f* manual **II.** *n* manual *m*; **instruction ~** manual de instrucciones

**manually** ['mæn·ju·ə·li] *adv* manualmente, con las manos

**manufacture** [ˌmæn·ju·'fæk·tʃər] **I.** *vt* (*produce*) fabricar; **~d goods** artículos manufacturados **II.** *n* 1. (*production*) manufactura *f* 2. (*product*) producto *m* manufacturado

**manufacturer** [ˌmæn·ju·'fæk·ʃər·ər] *n* fabricante *mf*; **~'s label** etiqueta *f* de fábrica

**manufacturing** [ˌmæn·jə·'fæk·tʃər·ɪŋ] *adj* (*region, company*) industrial; **~ industry** industria *f* manufacturera

**manure** [mə·'nʊr] *n* abono *m*

**manuscript** ['mæn·ju·skrɪpt] *n* manuscrito *m*

**many** ['men·i] <more, most> **I.** *adj* muchos, muchas; **how ~ bottles?** ¿cuántas botellas?; **too/so ~ people** demasiada/tanta gente; **one too ~** uno de más; **~ times** muchas veces; **as ~ as...** tantos como... **II.** *pron* muchos, muchas; **~ think that...** muchos piensan que...; **so ~** tantos/tantas; **too ~** demasiados/demasiadas

**many-sided** [ˌmen·i·'saɪ·dɪd] *adj* polifacético, -a

**map** [mæp] n 1. (of region, stars) mapa m; (of town) plano m; ~ **of the world** mapamundi m; **road** ~ mapa de carreteras 2. (simple diagram) plano m ▶ **to blow** [or **wipe**] **sth off the** ~ borrar algo del mapa; **to put a town on the** ~ dar a conocer a un pueblo

**◆map out** vt planear, proyectar; **to** ~ **a course/a plan** proyectar un curso/un plan

**maple** ['meɪ·pəl] n (tree) arce m

**maple syrup** n jarabe m de arce

**mar** [mar] <-rr-> vt (ruin) echar a perder

**marathon** ['mær·ə·θɑn] n a. fig maratón m o f

**marble** ['mar·bəl] n 1. (stone) mármol m; ~ **table** mesa f de mármol 2. (glass ball) canica f, bolita f CSur; **to play** ~**s** jugar a las canicas

**marble cake** n pastel de molde con chocolate

**march** [martʃ] I. <-es> n a. MIL marcha f; **funeral** ~ marcha fúnebre; **a 20 mile** ~ una marcha de 32 km; **to be on the** ~ estar en marcha II. vi a. MIL marchar; (parade) desfilar; **to** ~ **into a country** invadir un país

**March** [martʃ] n marzo m; s. a. **April**

**mare** [mer] n yegua f

**margarine** ['mar·dʒər·ɪn] n margarina f

**margin** ['mar·dʒɪn] n a. TYPO margen m; **narrow** ~ margen reducido; ~ **of error** margen de error

**marina** [mə·'ri·nə] n puerto m deportivo

**marinate** ['mær·ɪ·neɪt] vt marinar

**marine** [mə·'rin] I. adj (of the sea) marino, -a; NAUT marítimo, -a; MIL naval II. n infante m de marina

**marital** ['mær·ɪ·təl] adj marital f; ~ **problems** problemas m pl conyugales

**mark¹** [mark] I. n 1. (spot, stain) mancha f; (scratch) marca f; (trace) huella f; **to leave one's** ~ **on sth/sb** fig dejar sus huellas en algo/alguien 2. (written sign) raya f 3. (required standard) norma f; **to be up to the** ~ ser satisfactorio 4. (target) blanco m; **to hit the** ~ dar en el blanco 5. (starting line) línea f de salida; **on your** ~, **get set, go!** ¡preparados, listos, ya! 6. LING signo m; **punctuation** ~ signo de puntuación ▶ **to**

**be wide of the** ~ fallar por mucho, estar lejos de la verdad II. vt 1. (make a spot, stain) manchar 2. (make written sign, indicate) marcar; **the bottle was** ~**ed 'poison'** la botella llevaba la etiqueta 'veneno' 3. (characterize) distinguir; **to** ~ **sb as sth** distinguir a alguien como algo 4. (commemorate) conmemorar; **to** ~ **the beginning/end of sth** conmemorar el principio/final de algo; **to** ~ **the 10th anniversary** celebrar el 10º aniversario

**◆mark down** vt 1. (reduce prices) rebajar 2. (jot down) apuntar 3. SCHOOL **to mark sb down** bajar las calificaciones de alguien 4. fig (assess) **to mark sb down as sth** catalogar a alguien como algo

**◆mark off** vt 1. (divide land) demarcar 2. (cross off) tachar

**◆mark out** vt trazar

**◆mark up** vt aumentar

**mark²** [mark] n FIN marco m

**marked** [markt] adj 1. (improvement, difference) marcado, -a 2. (with distinguishing marks) marcado, -a 3. (liable to be attacked) **to be a** ~ **man/woman** estar en el punto de mira

**marker** ['mar·kər] n 1. (sign, symbol) señal f 2. (pen) rotulador m 3. SPORTS (indicator) marcador m

**market** ['mar·kɪt] I. n mercado m; **the housing** ~ el mercado inmobiliario; **the stock** ~ la bolsa de valores; **on the** ~ a la venta II. vt comercializar

**marketing** n 1. (discipline) marketing m 2. (commercialization) comercialización f

**marketplace** n 1. ECON mercado m 2. (square) plaza f (del mercado)

**market research** n estudio m de mercado

**market trader** n comerciante mf

**marking** n (identification) señal f; (on animal) pinta f

**marksmanship** ['marks·mən·ʃɪp] n puntería f

**markup** ['mark·ʌp] n margen m de ganancia

**marmalade** ['mar·mə·leɪd] n mermelada f (de cítricos)

M

**marquee** [mar·'ki] *n* 1. (*rooflike structure*) marquesina *f* 2. (*scrolling text*) letrero con el nombre de los artistas en la fachada de un teatro u otro local

**marriage** ['mær·ɪdʒ] *n* 1. (*wedding*) boda *f* 2. (*relationship, state*) matrimonio *m;* **he is a relative by ~** es pariente político 3. *fig* (*of organizations*) unión *f*

**married** *adj* (*person*) casado, -a; **~ couple** matrimonio *m*

**married name** *n* apellido *m* de casada

**marrow** ['mær·ou] *n* MED médula *f*

**marry** ['mær·i] <-ie-> I. *vt* 1. (*become husband or wife*) **to ~ sb** casarse con alguien; **to get married** (**to sb**) casarse (con alguien) 2. (*priest*) casar II. *vi* casarse

**Mars** [marz] *n* Marte *m*

**marsh** [marʃ] <-es> *n* ciénaga *f*

**marshal** ['mar·ʃəl] *n* 1. LAW alguacil *mf* 2. (*police or fire officer*) comisario, -a *m, f*

**marshland** ['marʃ·lænd] *n* pantanal *m*

**marshmallow** ['marʃ·mel·ou] *n* 1. (*sweet*) dulce *m* de malvavisco, carlotina *f Ven* 2. (*plant*) malvavisco *m*

**marshy** ['mar·ʃi] <-ier, -iest> *adj* pantanoso, -a

**martial** ['mar·ʃəl] *adj* marcial

**martial arts** *n* SPORTS artes *m pl* marciales

**martial law** *n* ley *f* marcial; **to impose ~ on a country** imponer la ley marcial en un país

**Martian** ['mar·ʃən] I. *adj* marciano II. *n* marciano, -a *m, f*

**martyr** ['mar·t̬ər] I. *n* mártir *mf* II. *vt* martirizar

**marvel** ['mar·vəl] I. *n* 1. (*thing*) maravilla *f* 2. (*person*) joya *f* II. <-ll-, -l-> *vi* **to ~ that...** maravillarse de que... +*subj*; **to ~ at sb/sth** maravillarse de alguien/algo

**marvel(l)ous** ['mar·və·ləs] *adj* maravilloso, -a; **to feel ~** sentirse espléndido

**marzipan** ['mar·zɪ·pæn] *n* mazapán *m*

**mascara** [mæ·'skær·ə] *n* rímel *m*

**mascot** ['mæs·kat] *n* mascota *f*

**masculine** ['mæs·kjə·lɪn] *adj a.* LING masculino, -a

**mash** [mæʃ] I. *n* 1. AGR (*animal feed*) afrecho *m,* salvado *m* 2. (*fermentable mixture*) malta *f* II. *vt* machacar; **to ~ potatoes** hacer puré de patatas

**mask** [mæsk] I. *n a. fig* máscara *f;* **oxygen ~** máscara de oxígeno II. *vt* enmascarar; **to ~ sth with sth** encubrir algo con algo

**masked** *adj* enmascarado, -a

**masochist** ['mæs·ə·kɪst] *n* masoquista *mf*

**mason** ['meɪ·sən] *n* 1. (*stonecutter*) cantero *m* 2. (*bricklayer*) albañil *m* 3. (*Freemason*) masón, -ona *m, f*

**masonry** ['meɪ·sən·ri] *n* 1. (*occupation*) albañilería *f* 2. (*stonework*) mampostería *f* 3. (*Freemasonry*) masonería *f*

**mass** [mæs] *n* 1. *a.* PHYS masa *f* 2. (*formless substance*) bulto *m* 3. (*large quantity*) montón *m;* **the ~ of the people** la muchedumbre II. *vi* (*gather*) juntarse; (*troops*) concentrarse III. *adj* de masas

**Mass** [mæs] *n* misa *f;* **to attend ~** ir a misa

**massacre** ['mæs·ə·kər] I. *n* (*killing*) *a. fig* masacre *f* II. *vt* (*kill*) *a. fig* masacrar

**massage** [mə·'sadʒ] I. *n* masaje *m;* **to give sb a ~** dar a alguien un masaje; **water ~** hidromasaje *m* II. *vt* 1. dar masajes a 2. *fig* manipular

**masseur** [mæ·'sɜr] *n* masajista *m*

**masseuse** [mæ·'sɜz] *n* masajista *f*

**massive** ['mæs·ɪv] *adj* masivo, -a, enorme; **~ amounts of money** grandes cantidades de dinero

**mass media** *n* **the ~** los medios de comunicación de masas

**mass production** *n* fabricación *f* en serie

**mast** [mæst] *n* 1. NAUT mástil *m* 2. (*flag pole*) asta *m;* **at half ~** a media asta 3. RADIO, TV antena *f*

**master** ['mæs·tər] I. *n* 1. (*of house*) señor *m;* (*of slave*) amo *m;* (*of dog*) dueño *m* 2. (*one who excels*) maestro *m* 3. (*instructor*) instructor *m* 4. (*master copy*) original *m* ▶ **to be one's own ~** no depender de nadie II. *vt* 1. (*cope with*) vencer; **to ~ one's fear of flying** superar el miedo a volar 2. (*become*

**proficient at**) dominar

**master copy** <-ies> n original m

**masterful** ['mæs·tər·fəl] adj 1. (authoritative) autoritario, -a 2. (skillful) magistral

**master key** n llave f maestra

**masterly** ['mæs·tər·li] adj magistral

**mastermind** ['mæs·tər·maɪnd] I. n cerebro m II. vt (activity) planear; (crime) ser el cerebro de

**Master of Arts** n licenciado, -a m, f con máster (en Humanidades o en Filosofía y Letras)

**masterpiece** n obra f maestra

**master switch** <-es> n interruptor m principal

**masturbate** ['mæs·tər·beɪt] I. vi masturbarse II. vt masturbar

**mat¹** [mæt] n 1. (on floor) estera f; (decorative) tapiz m; **bath ~** alfombra f de baño 2. (on table) salvamanteles m inv 3. SPORTS (in gymnastics) colchoneta f

**mat²** adj, **matte** [mæt] adj mate

**match¹** [mætʃ] <-es> n 1. (for making fire) cerilla f, fósforo m; **box of ~es** caja de fósforos

**match²** [mætʃ] I. n 1. (competitor) contrincante mf; **to be no ~ for sb** no poder competir con alguien; **to meet one's ~** encontrar la horma de su zapato 2. (similarity) **to be a good ~** combinar bien 3. (in marriage) **to make a good ~** casarse bien 4. SPORTS partido m; **wrestling ~** combate m de lucha libre II. vi (harmonize: design, color) armonizar, pegar; (description) coincidir III. vt 1. (have same color) hacer juego con 2. (equal) igualar

**matchbox** ['mætʃ·bɑks] <-es> n caja f de cerillas, cerillero m AmL

**matching** ['mætʃ·ɪŋ] adj que hace juego

**match point** n SPORTS bola f de partido

**matchstick** ['mætʃ·stɪk] n cerilla f, fósforo m

**mate¹** [meɪt] I. n 1. (partner) pareja f 2. ZOOL (male) macho m; (female) hembra f 3. NAUT oficial m de a bordo II. vi aparearse III. vt aparear

**mate²** [meɪt] n GAMES mate m

**material** [mə·'tɪr·i·əl] I. n 1. PHILOS, PHYS materia f 2. (physical substance) mate-

rial m; **raw ~** materia f prima 3. (information) **publicity ~** material m publicitario 4. (textile) tejido m 5. **~s** (equipment) materiales mpl II. adj 1. (physical) material; **~ damage** daño m material 2. (important) importante

**materialize** [mə·'tɪr·i·ə·laɪz] vi 1. (take physical form) materializarse 2. (hope, idea) realizarse

**maternal** [mə·'tɜr·nəl] adj 1. (feeling) maternal 2. (relative) materno, -a

**maternity** [mə·'tɜr·nə·t̬i] n maternidad f

**maternity leave** n baja f por maternidad

**math** [mæθ] n inf abbr of **mathematics** mates fpl

**mathematical** [ˌmæθ·ə·'mæt̬·ɪ·kəl] adj matemático, -a

**mathematician** [ˌmæθ·ə·mə·'tɪʃ·ən] n matemático, -a m, f

**mathematics** [ˌmæθ·ə·'mæt̬·ɪks] n matemáticas fpl

**matinee** ['mæt̬·ə·neɪ] n CINE primera sesión f; THEAT función f de tarde

**mating** ['meɪ·t̬ɪŋ] n apareamiento m

**matriculation** [mə·ˌtrɪk·jə·'leɪ·ʃən] n matrícula f

**matrimony** ['mæt̬·rə·moʊ·ni] n matrimonio m

**matrix** ['meɪ·trɪks] <-ices> n a. MATH matriz f

**matted** adj enmarañado, -a

**matter** ['mæt̬·ər] I. n 1. (subject) materia f; (question, affair) asunto m; **the ~ at hand** el asunto a tratar; **it's a ~ of life or death** es una cuestión de vida o muerte; **money ~s** asuntos financieros; **a ~ of opinion** una cuestión de opinión 2. **~s** (situation) situación f; **to make ~s worse** por si eso fuera poco; **to help ~s** mejorar las cosas 3. (wrong) problema m; **what's the ~ with you?** ¿qué te pasa? 4. (material) material m; **advertising ~** material publicitario 5. (amount) **a ~ of...** cosa de...; **in a ~ of seconds** en cuestión de segundos 6. (substance) materia f II. vi importar; **it really ~s to me** me importa mucho; **no ~ what they say** digan lo que digan; **it doesn't ~ if...** no importa si...

**matter-of-fact** [ˌmæt̬·ər·əv·'fækt] adj

M

(*practical*) práctico, -a

**mattress** ['mæt·rɪs] *n* colchón *m*

**mature** [mə·'tʃʊr] **I.** *adj* **1.** (*person, attitude*) maduro, -a; (*animal*) adulto, -a **2.** (*wine*) añejo, -a; (*cheese*) curado, -a; (*fruit*) maduro, -a **3.** FIN vencido, -a **II.** *vi* **1.** *a. fig* madurar **2.** FIN vencer **III.** *vt* (*cheese, ham*) curar; (*wine*) añejar

**maturity** [mə·'tʃʊr·ə·t̬i] *n* <-ies> **1.** (*of person, attitude*) madurez *f*; **to come to ~** llegar a la madurez **2.** FIN vencimiento *m*

**mauve** [moʊv] *adj* malva

**maximize** ['mæk·sɪ·maɪz] *vt* maximizar

**maximum** ['mæk·sɪ·məm] **I.** *n* máximo *m*; **to do sth to the ~** hacer algo al máximo **II.** *adj* máximo, -a; **this car has a ~ speed of 100 mph** este coche alcanza una velocidad máxima de 160 km/h

**may**[1] [meɪ] <might, might> *aux* **1.** *form* (*be allowed*) poder; **~ I come in?** ¿puedo pasar?; **~ I ask you a question?** ¿puedo hacerte una pregunta? **2.** (*possibility*) ser posible; **it ~ rain** puede que llueva; **be that as it ~** en cualquier caso **3.** (*hope, wish*) **~ she rest in peace** que en paz descanse

**may**[2] [meɪ] *n* (*bush*) espino *m*; (*flower*) flor *f* de espino

**May** [meɪ] *n* mayo *m; s. a.* **April**

**maybe** ['meɪ·bi] *adv* (*perhaps*) quizás

**mayday** ['meɪ·deɪ] *n* S.O.S. *m*

**mayhem** ['meɪ·hem] *n* caos *m inv*

**mayonnaise** [ˌmeɪ·ə·'neɪz] *n* mayonesa *f*

**mayor** ['meɪ·ər] *n* alcalde(sa) *m(f)*

**maypole** ['meɪ·poʊl] *n* mayo *m (palo)*

**maze** [meɪz] *n* laberinto *m*

**MD** [ˌem·'di] *n* **1.** *abbr of* **Doctor of Medicine** Dr. *m*, Dra. *f* **2.** *abbr of* **Maryland** Maryland *m*

**me** [mi] *pron* **1.** me; **look at ~** mírame; **she saw ~** me vio; **he told ~ that...** me dijo que... **2.** (*after verb 'to be'*) yo; **it's ~** soy yo; **she is older than ~** ella es mayor que yo **3.** (*after prep*) mí; **is this for ~?** ¿es para mí esto?

**ME** [meɪn] *n abbr of* **Maine** Maine *m*

**meadow** ['med·oʊ] *n* pradera *f*

**meager** ['mi·gər] *adj* escaso, -a

**meal**[1] [mil] *n* comida *f*; **a heavy/light ~** una comida pesada/ligera

**meal**[2] [mil] *n* (*flour*) harina *f*

**mealtime** ['mil·taɪm] *n* hora *f* de comer

**mean**[1] [min] *adj* **1.** (*unkind*) vil; **to be ~ to sb** tratar mal a alguien; **to have a ~ streak** tener muy mala uva *inf* **2.** *sl* (*excellent*) de la hostia

**mean**[2] [min] <meant, meant> *vt* **1.** (*signify: word, event*) significar; **does that name ~ anything to you?** ¿te suena ese nombre? **2.** (*express, indicate: person*) querer decir; **what do you ~?** ¿a qué te refieres?; **I ~ what I say** digo lo que pienso **3.** (*intend for particular purpose*) destinar; **to be meant for sth** estar destinado a algo; **to be meant for each other** estar hechos el uno para el otro **4.** (*intend*) pretender; **to ~ to do sth** tener la intención de hacer algo; **to ~ well** tener buenas intenciones; **I ~ to say...** quiero decir... ▶ **to ~ business** *inf* hablar muy en serio

**meaning** ['mi·nɪŋ] *n* significado *m*; **to give sth a whole new ~** dar a algo un significado completamente nuevo; **what is the ~ of this?** ¿qué significa esto?; **to have ~ for sb** tener significado para alguien

**meaningful** ['mi·nɪŋ·fəl] *adj* **1.** (*difference, change*) significativo, -a **2.** (*look, smile*) expresivo, -a **3.** (*relationship*) importante

**meaningless** ['mi·nɪŋ·lɪs] *adj* sin sentido

**means** [minz] *npl* **1.** (*instrument, method*) medio *m*; **~ of transport** medio de transporte **2.** *pl* (*resources*) medios *mpl*; **by ~ of sth** por medio de algo **3.** *pl* (*income*) recursos *mpl*; **a person of ~** una persona acaudalada; **private ~** fondos *m pl* privados; **to live beyond one's ~** vivir por encima de sus posibilidades ▶ **by all ~!** ¡por supuesto!; **by no ~** de ninguna manera

**meant** [ment] *pt, pp of* **mean**

**meantime** ['min·taɪm] **I.** *adv* mientras tanto **II.** *n* **in the ~** mientras tanto

**meanwhile** ['min·hwaɪl] *adv* mientras tanto

**measles** ['mi·zəlz] *n* sarampión *m*

**measure** ['meʒ.ər] I. vt medir II. vi medir; **the box ~s 4 in. by 4 in. by 6 in.** la caja mide 10 cm por 10 cm por 15 cm III. n 1. (size) medida f 2. (measuring instrument) metro m; (ruler) regla f 3. (proof) medición f 4. ~s (action) medidas fpl; **to take ~s to do sth** tomar medidas para hacer algo 5. (degree, amount) grado m 6. MUS compás m

**measured** adj (response) moderado, -a; (voice, tone) comedido, -a

**measurement** ['meʒ.ər.mənt] n 1. (size) medida f 2. (dimension of body) medida; **to take sb's ~s** tomar a alguien las medidas 3. (act of measuring) medición f

**measuring cup** n vaso m medidor

**measuring spoon** n cuchara f medidora

**meat** [mit] n 1. (food) carne f 2. fig (essence) sustancia f 3. fig (target) **this guy is fresh ~** ese tío es carne fresca

**meatball** n albóndiga f

**meat grinder** n picadora f de carne

**meat loaf** n pastel m de carne

**Mecca** ['mek.ə] n REL La Meca

**mechanic** [mɪ'kæn.ɪk] n mecánico, -a m, f

**mechanical** adj 1. (relating to machines) mecánico, -a 2. (without thinking) mecánico, -a

**mechanics** [mɪ'kæn.ɪks] npl 1. AUTO, TECH mecánica f 2. inf (how things are organized) mecanismo m

**mechanism** ['mek.ə.nɪz.əm] n mecanismo m

**medal** ['med.əl] n medalla f

**medalist** ['med.əl.ɪst] n medallista mf

**medallion** [mə'dæl.jən] n medallón m

**meddle** ['med.əl] vi **to ~ in sth** entrometerse en algo

**media** ['mi.di.ə] n 1. pl of **medium** 2. **the ~** los medios; **the mass ~** los medios de comunicación de masas

**mediate** ['mi.di.eɪt] vi mediar (between entre)

**mediator** ['mi.di.eɪ.tər] n mediador(a) m(f)

**medic** ['med.ɪk] n médico, -a m, f

**medical** ['med.ɪ.kəl] I. adj médico, -a II. n inf reconocimiento m médico

**medical history** n historial m clínico

**Medicare** ['med.ɪ.ker] n programa de asistencia sanitaria para personas mayores de 65 años

**medicate** ['med.ɪ.keɪt] vt (treat medically) medicar

**medication** [ˌmed.ɪ'keɪ.ʃən] <-(s)> n medicamento m

**medicine** ['med.ɪ.sɪn] n 1. (substance) medicamento m 2. (medical knowledge) medicina f 3. (remedy) remedio m ▶ **to give sb a taste of his/her own ~** pagar a alguien con su misma moneda

**medicine cabinet** n botiquín m

**medieval** [ˌmi.di'i.vəl] adj medieval

**mediocre** [ˌmi.di'oʊ.kər] adj mediocre

**meditate** ['med.ɪ.teɪt] vi (engage in contemplation) meditar

**Mediterranean** [ˌmed.ɪ.tə'reɪ.ni.ən] I. n Mediterráneo m II. adj mediterráneo, -a

**Mediterranean Sea** n mar m Mediterráneo

**medium** ['mi.di.əm] I. adj 1. (not big or small) mediano, -a 2. CULIN a punto II. n 1. <media or -s> (method) medio m 2. COMPUT soporte m; **data ~** soporte de datos 3. <-s> (spiritualist) médium mf

**M**

**medium-dry** adj semi seco, -a

**medium-rare** adj CULIN poco hecho, -a

**meek** [mik] adj manso, -a

**meet** [mit] <met, met> I. vt 1. (encounter) encontrarse con; (intentionally) reunirse con; (for first time) conocer a; **to arrange to ~ sb** quedar con alguien 2. (wait for: at train station, airport) ir a buscar a alguien 3. (confront: opponent) enfrentarse con; (problem) tropezar con 4. (fulfill) reunir; (cost) correr con; (demand) atender; (obligation) cumplir con II. vi 1. (encounter) encontrarse; (intentionally) reunirse; (for first time) conocerse; **to arrange to ~** quedar 2. (join: lines) unirse 3. SPORTS enfrentarse

◆**meet with** vt insep reunirse con; **to ~ success** tener éxito

**meeting** ['mi.t̬ɪŋ] n 1. (gathering) reunión f; **to call a ~** convocar una reunión **2.** POL mitin *m* **3.** (*casual*) encuentro *m*

**meeting point** *n* punto *m* de encuentro

**melody** ['mel·ə·di] <-ies> *n* melodía *f*

**melon** ['mel·ən] *n* melón *m*; (*watermelon*) sandía *f*

**melt** [melt] **I.** *vt* (*metal*) fundir; (*ice, chocolate*) derretir **II.** *vi* **1.** (*metal*) fundirse; (*ice, chocolate*) derretirse **2.** *fig* enternecerse

**meltdown** ['melt·daυn] *n* fusión *f*

**melting point** *n* punto *m* de fusión

**melting pot** *n a. fig* crisol *m*

**member** ['mem·bər] *n* miembro *mf*; (*of society, club*) socio, -a *m, f*

**membership** *n* (*state of belonging*) calidad *f* de miembro; (*to society, club*) calidad *f* de socio; **to apply for ~ to a club** solicitar ingreso en un club

**membership card** *n* carnet *m* de socio

**membrane** ['mem·breɪn] *n* membrana *f*

**memo** ['mem·oυ] *n abbr of* **memorandum 1.** (*message*) memorándum *m* **2.** (*note*) nota *f*

**memoir** ['mem·war] *n* **1.** (*record of events*) memoria *f* **2.** *pl* (*autobiography*) memorias *fpl*

**memorable** ['mem·ər·ə·bəl] *adj* memorable

**memorial** [mə·'mɔr·i·əl] **I.** *n* monumento *m* conmemorativo **II.** *adj* conmemorativo, -a

**Memorial Day** *n* Día *m* de los Caídos

**memorize** ['mem·ə·raɪz] *vt* memorizar

**memory** ['mem·ə·ri] <-ies> *n* **1.** (*ability to remember*) memoria *f*; **to recite sth from ~** recitar algo de memoria **2.** (*remembered event*) recuerdo *m*; **to bring back memories** evocar recuerdos **3.** COMPUT memoria *f*

**men** [men] *n pl of* **man**

**menace** ['men·əs] *n* **1.** (*threat*) amenaza *f* **2.** (*child*) demonio *m*, peligro *m*

**menacing** *adj* amenazador(a)

**mend** [mend] **I.** *n* **1.** (*repair*) reparación *f* **2.** (*patch*) remiendo *m* **II.** *vt* **1.** (*repair*) reparar **2.** (*darn: socks*) zurcir **III.** *vi* (*improve*) mejorar; (*broken bone*) soldarse

**menopause** ['men·ə·pɔz] *n* menopausia *f*

**men's room** ['menz·rum] *n* lavabo *m* de hombres

**mental** ['men·təl] *adj* **1.** (*of the mind*) mental **2.** *offensive sl* (*crazy*) chiflado, -a

**mentally** *adv* mentalmente; **~ disturbed** trastornado, -a

**mention** ['men·ʃən] **I.** *n* mención *f*; **to make ~ of sth** mencionar algo **II.** *vt* mencionar; **don't ~ it!** ¡no hay de qué!; **not to ~...** sin contar...

**menu** ['men·ju] *n* **1.** (*list of dishes*) carta *f*; (*fixed meal*) menú *m* **2.** COMPUT menú

**menu bar** *n* barra *f* de menús

**meow** [mi·'aυ] **I.** *n* miau *m* **II.** *vi* maullar

**mercenary** ['mɜr·sə·ner·i] **I.** *n* <-ies> mercenario, -a *m, f* **II.** *adj* mercenario, -a

**merchant** ['mɜr·tʃənt] *n* comerciante *mf*

**merchant marine** *n* marina *f* mercante

**merchant ship** *n* mercante *m*

**merciful** ['mɜr·sɪ·fəl] *adj* misericordioso, -a

**merciless** ['mɜr·sɪ·lɪs] *adj* despiadado, -a

**mercury** ['mɜr·kjə·ri] *n* mercurio *m*

**Mercury** ['mɜr·kjə·ri] *n* Mercurio *m*

**mercy** ['mɜr·si] *n* **1.** (*compassion*) compasión *f*; **to have ~ on sb** tener compasión de alguien **2.** (*forgiveness*) misericordia *f*; **to be at the ~ of sb** estar a merced de alguien; **to plead for ~** pedir clemencia

**mere** [mɪr] *adj* mero, -a; **a ~ formality** una simple formalidad

**merely** ['mɪr·li] *adv* solamente

**merge** [mɜrdʒ] **I.** *vi* unirse; ECON, POL fusionarse **II.** *vt* unir; ECON, POL, COMPUT fusionar

**merger** ['mɜr·dʒər] *n* ECON fusión *f*

**meridian** [mə·'rɪd·i·ən] *n* meridiano *m*

**merit** ['mer·ɪt] **I.** *n* **1.** (*virtue*) cualidad *f* **2.** (*advantage*) ventaja *f* **3.** *pl* (*commendable quality or act*) mérito *m*; **to achieve sth on one's own ~s** conseguir algo por mérito propio **II.** *vt* merecer

**merry** ['mer·i] <-ier, -iest> *adj* alegre

**merry-go-round** ['mer·i·goυ·raυnd] *n* tiovivo *m*

**mesmerize** ['mez·mə·raɪz] vt hipnotizar

**mesmerizing** [mez·'mer·ɪk] adj hipnótico, -a

**mess** [mes] <-es> n 1. (confusion) confusión f; (disorganized state) desorden m; **to be in a ~** estar revuelto; **to make a ~ of sth** echar a perder algo 2. (things) caos m inv 3. (trouble) lío m, merengue m Arg

♦**mess around** vi 1. (joke) hacer el tonto 2. (waste time) pasar el rato

♦**mess up** vt inf 1. (make untidy) desordenar 2. (dirty) ensuciar 3. (screw up) echar a perder II. vi cagarla inf

**message** ['mes·ɪdʒ] n mensaje m; **error ~** comput mensaje m de error

**messenger** ['mes·ɪn·dʒər] n mensajero, -a m, f

**mess-up** n inf follón m

**messy** ['mes·i] <-ier, -iest> adj 1. (untidy) desordenado, -a 2. (dirty) sucio, -a

**met** [met] vi, vt pt of **meet**

**metal** ['met̬·əl] I. n (element) metal m II. adj metálico, -a

**metal detector** n detector m de metales

**metallic** [mə·'tæl·ɪk] adj metálico, -a

**metaphor** ['met̬·ə·fɔr] n metáfora f

**meteorite** ['mi·t̬i·ə·raɪt] n meteorito m

**meteorological** [ˌmi·t̬i·ər·ə·'ladʒ·ɪ·kəl] adj meteorológico, -a

**meteorology** [ˌmi·t̬i·ə·'ral·ə·dʒi] n meteorología f

**meter**[1] ['mi·t̬ər] n contador m, medidor m AmL; **(parking) ~** parquímetro m; **(taxi) ~** taxímetro m

**meter**[2] ['mi·t̬ər] n metro m

**method** ['meθ·əd] n método m

**methodical** [mə·'θad·ɪ·kəl] adj metódico, -a

**metric(al)** ['met·rɪk] adj métrico, -a

**metro**[1] ['met·rou] n rail (subway) metro m

**metro**[2] ['met·rou] adj abbr of **metropolitan** metropolitano, -a

**metropolis** [mə·'trap·ə·lɪs] <-es> n metrópoli f

**metropolitan** [ˌmet·rə·'pal·ə·tən] adj metropolitano, -a

**Mexican** ['mek·sɪ·kən] adj, n mexicano, -a m, f

**Mexico** ['mek·sɪ·kou] n México m; **New ~** Nuevo México

**Mexico City** n Ciudad f de México

**MI** ['mɪʃ·ɪ·gən] n abbr of **Michigan** Michigan m

**MIA** [ˌem·aɪ·'eɪ] abbr of **missing in action** desaparecido, -a en combate

**mic** [maɪk] n inf 1. abbr of **microphone** 2. abbr of **mike**

**mice** [maɪs] n pl of **mouse**

**microbe** ['maɪ·kroub] n microbio m

**microbiology** [ˌmaɪ·krou·baɪ·'al·ə·dʒi] n microbiología f

**microchip** ['maɪ·krou·ˌtʃɪp] n microchip m

**microorganism** [ˌmaɪ·krou·'ɔr·gə·nɪz·əm] n microorganismo m

**microphone** ['maɪ·krə·foun] n micrófono m

**microprocessor** ['maɪ·krou·ˌpras·es·ər] n microprocesador m

**microscope** ['maɪ·krə·skoup] n microscopio m

**microscopic** [ˌmaɪ·krə·'skap·ɪk] adj microscópico, -a

**microwave** ['maɪ·krou·weɪv] n 1. (wave) microonda f 2. (oven) microondas m inv

**midday** [ˌmɪd·'deɪ] n mediodía m; **at ~** al mediodía; **~ meal** almuerzo m

**middle** ['mɪd·əl] I. n (center) medio m; **in the ~ of sth** en medio de algo; **in the ~ of the night** en plena noche II. adj 1. (equidistant) central 2. (medium) medio, -a

**middle-aged** adj de mediana edad

**Middle Ages** npl Edad f Media

**middle-class** adj de la clase media

**Middle East** n Oriente m Medio

**middleman** ['mɪd·əl·mæn] <-men> n intermediario m

**middle name** n segundo nombre m

**middle-of-the-road** adj moderado, -a

**middling** ['mɪd·lɪŋ] adj inf 1. (average) mediano, -a 2. (not very good) regular, flojo, -a

**Mideast** n Oriente m Medio

**midget** ['mɪdʒ·ɪt] I. n enano, -a m, f II. adj en miniatura

**midlife crisis** [ˌmɪd·'laɪf·'kraɪ·sɪs] n crisis f inv de los cuarenta

**midnight** ['mɪd·naɪt] n medianoche f

**midst** [mɪdst] n **in the ~ of** en medio de

**midsummer** [,mɪd·'sʌm·ər] n pleno verano m

**midterm** [,mɪd·'tɜrm] I. n UNIV (exam) parcial m II. adj de mitad del trimestre; **~ vacation** vacaciones f pl de mitad de trimestre

**midway** [,mɪd·'weɪ] I. adv a medio camino II. n feria f (con juegos de azar, espectáculos...)

**midweek** [,mɪd·'wik] adv entre semana

**midwife** ['mɪd·waɪf] <-wives> n comadrona f

**miffed** [mɪft] adj ofendido, -a; **to be ~ at sb** estar picado con alguien

**might**[1] [maɪt] pt of **may**; **it ~ be that...** podría ser que... +subj; **how old ~ she be?** ¿qué edad tendrá?

**might**[2] [maɪt] n **1.** (power) poder m **2.** (strength) fuerza f

**mighty** ['maɪ·ti] <-ier, -iest> adj **1.** (powerful) fuerte **2.** (great) enorme

**migraine** ['maɪ·ɡreɪn] <-(s)> n migraña f

**migrate** ['maɪ·ɡreɪt] vi emigrar

**migration** [maɪ·'ɡreɪ·ʃən] <-(s)> n (person) emigración f; (animal) migración f

**mike** [maɪk] n inf micro m

**mild** [maɪld] <-er, -est> adj **1.** (not severe) apacible; (criticism) moderado, -a; (penalty) leve **2.** (in taste) suave **3.** METEO templado, -a

**mildly** ['maɪld·li] adv **1.** (gently) suavemente **2.** (slightly) ligeramente

**mile** [maɪl] n milla f (1,61 km); **to walk for ~s (and ~s)** andar kilómetros y kilómetros ▶ **to smell sth a ~ away** ver algo a la legua

**mileage** ['maɪ·lɪdʒ] n AUTO kilometraje m

**milestone** ['maɪl·stoʊn] n **1.** (marker) mojón m **2.** fig hito m

**militant** ['mɪl·ɪ·tənt] I. adj militante II. n militante mf

**military** ['mɪl·ɪ·ter·i] I. n **the ~** los militares II. adj militar

**military academy** n academia f militar

**military police** n policía f militar

**military service** n servicio m militar

**milk** [mɪlk] I. n leche f II. vt **1. to ~ a cow** ordeñar una vaca **2.** fig inf (exploit) **to ~ sb dry** chupar la sangre a alguien

**milk chocolate** n chocolate m con leche

**milkman** <-men> n lechero m

**milkshake** n batido m, malteada f Méx

**milk tooth** n diente m de leche

**milky** ['mɪl·ki] <-ier, -iest> adj **1.** (color) lechoso, -a **2.** (coffee) con mucha leche

**mill** [mɪl] I. n **1.** (for grain) molino m; (for coffee) molinillo m **2.** (factory) fábrica f (de tejidos) II. vt (grain) moler

**millennium** [mɪ·'len·i·əm] <-s or -ennia> n milenio m

**miller** ['mɪl·ər] n molinero, -a m, f

**milligram** ['mɪl·ɪ·ɡræm] n miligramo m

**milliliter** ['mɪl·ɪ·li·t̬ər] n mililitro m

**millimeter** ['mɪl·ɪ·mi·t̬ər] n milímetro m

**million** ['mɪl·jən] <-(s)> n millón m; **two ~ people** dos millones de personas; **a ~ times** inf un millón de veces; **to be one in a ~** ser único

**millionaire** [,mɪl·jə·'ner] n millonario, -a m, f

**millipede** ['mɪl·ɪ·pid] n milpiés m inv

**mimic** ['mɪm·ɪk] I. vt <-ck-> imitar II. n imitador(a) m(f)

**min. 1.** abbr of **minute** min. **2.** abbr of **minimum** mín.

**mince** [mɪns] I. vt **1.** (shred) picar **2.** (use tact) **to not ~ words** no andarse con rodeos II. n carne f picada

**mincemeat** n **1.** (meat) carne f picada **2.** (fruit) picadillo m de fruta ▶ **to make ~ of sb/sth** sl hacer picadillo a alguien/algo

**mind** [maɪnd] I. n **1.** (brain) mente f; **to be out of one's ~** estar fuera de juicio **2.** (thought) pensamiento m; **to bear sth in ~** tener algo presente; **to bring sth to ~** recordar algo **3.** (intention) intención f; **to change one's ~** cambiar de parecer; **to have sth in ~** tener pensado algo; **to make up one's ~** decidirse **4.** (consciousness) conciencia f; **this will take your ~ off (of) it** esto te distraerá **5.** (opinion) opinión f; **to be of the same ~** ser de la misma opinión;

to give sb a piece of one's ~ cantar las cuarenta a alguien II. vt 1. (be careful of) tener cuidado con; ~ **what you're doing!** ¡cuidado con lo que haces! 2. (look after) estar al cuidado de; **don't ~ me** no te preocupes por mí 3. (bother) sentirse molesto por; **do you ~ my smoking?** ¿te molesta si fumo?; **would you ~ opening the window?** ¿haces el favor de abrir la ventana?; **I wouldn't ~ a beer** no me vendría mal una cerveza III. vi **never ~!** ¡no importa!; **I don't ~** me es igual; **if you don't ~, I prefer...** si no te importa, prefiero...; **would you ~ if...** ¿te importa si...?

**mindful** ['maɪndfəl] adj form cuidadoso, -a; **to be ~ of sth** tener presente algo

**mindless** ['maɪnd·lɪs] adj 1. (job) mecánico, -a 2. (violence) gratuito, -a 3. (heedless) descuidado, -a

**mine**[1] [maɪn] pron pos (el) mío, (la) mía, (los) míos, (las) mías; **it's not his bag, it's ~** no es su bolsa, es la mía

**mine**[2] [maɪn] I. n MIN, MIL mina f; **a ~ of information** fig una fuente abundante de información II. vt 1. MIN extraer 2. MIL minar III. vi MIN explotar minas; **to ~ for silver/gold** buscar plata/oro

**minefield** ['maɪn·fild] n 1. campo de minas 2. fig terreno m minado

**miner** ['maɪ·nər] n minero, -a m, f

**mineral** ['mɪn·ər·əl] adj, n mineral m

**mineral water** n agua f mineral

**minestrone** [ˌmɪn·ɪ·'stroʊ·ni] n sopa f de verduras

**mingle** ['mɪŋ·gəl] I. vi mezclarse (**with** con) II. vt mezclar

**miniature** ['mɪn·i·ə·tʃər] n miniatura f

**minibus** ['mɪn·i·bʌs] n microbús m

**minimal** ['mɪn·ɪ·məl] adj mínimo, -a

**minimize** ['mɪn·ɪ·maɪz] vt minimizar; fig menospreciar

**minimum** ['mɪn·ɪ·məm] I. <-s or minima> n mínimo m; **to reduce sth to a ~** reducir algo al mínimo II. adj mínimo, -a; ~ **requirements** requisitos m pl básicos

**mining** ['maɪ·nɪŋ] n minería f

**miniskirt** ['mɪn·i·skɜrt] n minifalda f

**minister** ['mɪn·ɪ·stər] n 1. POL ministro, -a m, f 2. REL pastor m

**ministry** ['mɪn·ɪ·stri] <-ies> n 1. REL sacerdocio m 2. POL ministerio m

**minivan** ['mɪn·i·væn] n vehículo m mixto, minivan m Col, Méx

**minor** ['maɪ·nər] I. adj (not great) pequeño, -a; (role) secundario, -a; (detail) sin importancia; ~ **offense** delito m de menor cuantía; **B** ~ MUS si m menor II. n 1. (person) menor mf de edad 2. UNIV asignatura f secundaria

**Minorca** [mɪ·'nɔr·kə] n Menorca f

**Minorcan** adj, n menorquín, -ina m, f

**minority** [maɪ·'nɔr·ə·ti] <-ies> n minoría f; **to be in the ~** estar en minoría

**mint**[1] [mɪnt] n 1. (herb) hierbabuena f 2. (candy) caramelo m de menta

**mint**[2] [mɪnt] I. n FIN casa f de la moneda II. vt acuñar III. adj (coin) de reciente acuñación; (stamp) nuevo, -a

**minus** ['maɪ·nəs] I. prep 1. a. MATH menos; **5 ~ 2 equals 3** 5 menos 2 igual a 3; ~ **ten degrees Celsius** diez grados bajo cero 2. inf (without) sin II. adj MATH menos III. n MATH (signo m) menos m

**minute**[1] ['mɪn·ɪt] n 1. (sixty seconds) minuto m 2. (moment) momento m; **any ~** de un momento a otro; **at the last ~** a última hora; **in a ~** en seguida; **this very ~** ahora mismo; **to the ~** puntual; **wait a ~** espera un segundo 3. ~**s** (of meeting) acta(s) f(pl)

**minute**[2] [maɪ·'nut] adj diminuto, -a

**minute hand** n minutero m

**miracle** ['mɪr·ə·kəl] n milagro m

**miraculous** [mɪ·'ræk·jə·ləs] adj milagroso, -a

**mirror** ['mɪr·ər] I. n espejo m II. vt reflejar

**misbehave** [ˌmɪs·bɪ·'heɪv] vi portarse mal

**misbehavior** [ˌmɪs·bɪ·'heɪv·jər] n mala conducta f

**misc.** adj abbr of **miscellaneous** diverso, -a

**miscalculate** [ˌmɪs·'kæl·kjə·leɪt] vt, vi calcular mal

**miscalculation** [ˌmɪs·kæl·kjə·'leɪ·ʃən] n error m de cálculo

**miscarriage** [ˌmɪs·kær·ɪdʒ] n MED aborto m (espontáneo)

**miscarry** ['mɪs·kær·i] <-ied, -ying> vi

M

1. MED abortar 2. *fig* fracasar

**mischief** ['mɪs·tʃɪf] *n* 1. (*naughtiness*) travesura *f* 2. to get (oneself) into ~ meterse en problemas 3. (*wickedness*) malicia *f*

**mischievous** ['mɪs·tʃə·vəs] *adj* 1. (*naughty*) travieso, -a 2. (*malicious*) malicioso, -a; ~ rumors rumores *m pl* malintencionados

**misconception** [,mɪs·kən·'sep·ʃən] *n* idea *f* equivocada

**misconduct** [,mɪs·'kan·dʌkt] *n* (*misbehavior*) mala conducta *f*

**miser** ['maɪ·zər] *n* avaro, -a *m, f*

**miserable** ['mɪz·rə·bəl] *adj* 1. (*unhappy*) triste 2. (*unpleasant*) lamentable 3. (*inadequate*) mísero, -a; a ~ amount una miseria

**miserably** *adv* 1. (*unhappily*) tristemente; to feel ~ sentirse abatido 2. (*completely*) to fail ~ fallar miserablemente

**misery** ['mɪz·ə·ri] *n* 1. (*unhappiness*) infelicidad *f* 2. (*suffering*) sufrimiento *m* 3. (*extreme poverty*) miseria *f*, lipidia *f AmC*

**misfire** [,mɪs·'faɪr] *vi* 1. (*weapon*) encasquillarse 2. (*engine*) fallar

**misfit** ['mɪs·fɪt] *n* inadaptado, -a *m, f*

**misfortune** [,mɪs·'fɔr·tʃən] *n* infortunio *m*

**misguided** [mɪs·'gaɪ·dɪd] *adj* desencaminado, -a

**mishap** ['mɪs·hæp] *n form* percance *m*

**mishear** [,mɪs·'hɪr] *vt irr* oír mal

**misinform** [,mɪs·ɪn·'fɔrm] *vt* informar mal, desinformar *Méx*

**misjudge** [,mɪs·'dʒʌdʒ] *vt* juzgar mal

**mislead** [,mɪs·'lid] *vt irr* 1. (*deceive*) engañar 2. to let oneself be misled dejarse engañar

**misleading** *adj* engañoso, -a

**misplace** [,mɪs·'pleɪs] *vt* (*lose*) extraviar

**misprint** ['mɪs·,prɪnt] *n* errata *f*

**mispronounce** [,mɪs·prə·'naʊns] *vt* pronunciar mal

**misread** [,mɪs·'rid] *vt irr* 1. (*read badly*) leer mal 2. (*interpret badly*) malinterpretar

**misrepresent** [,mɪs·,rep·rɪ·'zent] *vt* tergiversar

**miss¹** [mɪs] *n* (*form of address*) señorita *f*

**miss²** [mɪs] I. <-es> *n* fallo *m* II. *vi* fallar III. *vt* 1. (*not hit*) fallar 2. (*not catch*) perder; to ~ the bus perder el bus; to ~ a deadline no cumplir con una fecha límite 3. (*avoid*) evitar 4. (*not notice*) no fijarse en; you didn't ~ much no te has perdido nada 5. (*not hear*) no oír 6. (*overlook*) saltarse; to ~ a meeting faltar a una reunión 7. (*not take advantage*) dejar pasar; to ~ an opportunity perder una oportunidad 8. (*regret absence*) echar de menos 9. (*notice loss*) echar en falta

◆**miss out** *vi* perdérselo

**missile** ['mɪs·əl] *n* (*rocket*) misil *m*; (*projectile*) proyectil *m*

**missing** ['mɪs·ɪŋ] *adj* 1. (*lost: person*) desaparecido, -a; (*thing or object*) perdido, -a 2. (*absent*) ausente

**mission** ['mɪʃ·ən] *n a.* REL (*task*) misión *f*; peace ~ misión de paz; rescue ~ operación *f* de rescate; his ~ in life su misión en la vida; ~ accomplished misión cumplida

**missionary** ['mɪʃ·ə·ner·i] <-ies> *n* misionero, -a *m, f*

**Mississippi** [mɪs·ɪ·'sɪ·pi] *n* Misisipí *m*

**Missouri** [mɪ·'zʊr·i] *n* Misuri *m*

**misspell** [,mɪs·'spel] *vt irr* escribir mal

**mist** [mɪst] *n* 1. (*light fog*) neblina *f*; to be shrouded in ~ estar cubierto por la neblina 2. (*condensation*) vaho *m*

**mistake** [mɪ·'steɪk] I. *n* error *m*; typing ~ errata *f*; to learn from one's ~s aprender de los propios errores; to make a ~ cometer un error; by ~ por error II. *vt irr* confundir

**mistaken** [mɪ·'steɪ·kən] I. *pp of* mistake II. *adj* (*belief*) equivocado, -a; (*identity*) confundido, -a; to be (very much) ~ estar (muy) equivocado

**Mister** ['mɪs·tər] *n* señor *m*

**mistook** [mɪ·'stʊk] *pt of* mistake

**mistreat** [mɪs·'trit] *vt* maltratar

**mistress** ['mɪs·trɪs] *n* 1. (*sexual partner*) amante *f* 2. (*woman in charge*) ama *f*; the ~ of the house la dueña de la casa

**mistrust** [,mɪs·'trʌst] I. *n* desconfianza *f* II. *vt* to ~ sb/sth recelar de alguien/algo

**mistrustful** [ˌmɪsˈtrʌstfəl] *adj* receloso, -a; **to be ~ of sb/sth** recelar de alguien/algo

**misty** [ˈmɪsti] <-ier, -iest> *adj* (*foggy*) neblinoso, -a; (*window, glasses*) empañado, -a

**misunderstand** [ˌmɪsˌʌnˈdərˈstænd] *vt irr* entender mal

**misunderstanding** *n* 1. (*failure to understand*) malentendido *m* 2. (*disagreement*) desacuerdo *m*

**misuse** [ˌmɪsˈjus] *n* 1. (*wrong use*) mal uso *m* 2. (*abuse*) abuso *m*

**mitten** [ˈmɪtən] *n* manopla *f*

**mix** [mɪks] **I.** *n* mezcla *f* **II.** *vt* 1. CULIN (*ingredients*) mezclar; (*cocktails*) preparar 2. (*combine*) combinar; **to ~ business with pleasure** combinar los negocios con el placer **III.** *vi* 1. (*combine*) mezclarse 2. (*socially*) **to ~ well** llevarse bien

◆**mix up** *vt* 1. (*confuse*) confundir 2. (*put in wrong order*) revolver

**mixed** *adj* 1. mezclado, -a; **person of ~ race** mestizo, -a *m, f* 2. (*contradictory*) contradictorio, -a

**mixer** [ˈmɪksər] *n* (*machine*) batidora *f*

**mixture** [ˈmɪksˈtʃər] *n* mezcla *f*

**mix-up** [ˈmɪksˈʌp] *n* confusión *f*

**MMR** [ˌememˈar] *n* MED *abbr of* **measles, mumps and rubella** SPR *f*

**MN** [ˌmɪnˈɪˈsouˈtə] *n abbr of* **Minnesota** Minnesota *f*

**MO** *n* 1. *abbr of* **modus operandi** procedimiento *m* 2. *abbr of* **Missouri** Misuri *m* 3. *abbr of* **money order** giro *m*

**moan** [moʊn] **I.** *n* 1. (*sound*) gemido *m* 2. (*complaint*) quejido *m* **II.** *vi* 1. gemir; **to ~ with pain** gemir de dolor 2. (*complain*) lamentarse (**about** de)

**mob** [mab] **I.** *n + sing/pl vb* 1. (*crowd*) muchedumbre *f*; **angry ~** turba *f* 2. *inf* **the Mob** la mafia **II.** <-bb-> *vt* acosar; **he was ~bed by his fans** sus fans se aglomeraron en torno a él

**mobile** [ˈmoʊˈbəl] **I.** *n a.* TEL móvil *m* **II.** *adj* (*able to move*) móvil; **to be ~** *inf* tener coche

**mobile home** *n* caravana *f*

**mobster** [ˈmabˈstər] *n* gángster *mf*

**mock** [mak] **I.** *adj* 1. (*imitation*) artificial 2. (*fake*) ficticio, -a; **~ approval** aprobación simulada **II.** *vi* burlarse (**at** de) **III.** *vt* 1. (*ridicule*) mofarse de 2. (*imitate*) remedar

**mode** [moʊd] *n* 1. *a.* LING, PHILOS (*manner*) modo *m* 2. *form* (*fashion*) moda *f*; **in ~** de moda

**model** [ˈmadəl] **I.** *n* (*version, example*) *a.* ART modelo *m*; (*of car, house*) maqueta *f* **II.** *adj* modélico, -a; **a ~ student** un alumno modelo **III.** <-ll-> *vt* 1. modelar 2. (*show clothes*) desfilar **IV.** *vi* hacer de modelo

**modem** [ˈmouˈdəm] *n* COMPUT módem *m*

**moderate¹** [ˈmadˈərˈət] *adj* 1. (*average*) mediano, -a 2. *a.* POL (*not extreme: speed*) moderado, -a; (*increase*) mesurado, -a; (*price*) módico, -a

**moderate²** [ˈmadˈəˈreɪt] **I.** *vt* moderar **II.** *vi* 1. (*act as moderator*) hacer de moderador 2. (*become less extreme*) moderarse

**moderation** [ˌmadˈəˈreɪˈʃən] *n* moderación *f*; **in ~** con moderación

**moderator** [ˈmadˈəˈreɪˈtər] *n* moderador(a) *m(f)*

**modern** [ˈmadˈərn] *adj* moderno, -a

**modernize** [ˈmadˈərˈnaɪz] *vt* modernizar

**modest** [ˈmadˈɪst] *adj* modesto, -a

**modesty** [ˈmadˈɪˈsti] *n* modestia *f*

**modification** [ˌmadˈɪˈfɪˈkeɪˈʃən] *n* modificación *f*

**modify** [ˈmadˈɪˈfaɪ] <-ie-> *vt a.* LING modificar

**modular** [ˈmadʒˈəˈlər] *adj* modular; (*construction*) por módulos

**module** [ˈmadʒˈul] *n* módulo *m*

**moist** [mɔɪst] *adj* húmedo, -a

**moisten** [ˈmɔɪˈsən] **I.** *vt* humedecer **II.** *vi* humedecerse

**moisture** [ˈmɔɪsˈtʃər] *n* humedad *f*

**moisturizer** *n* hidratante *m*

**molar¹** [ˈmouˈlər] *n* muela *f*

**molar²** [ˈmouˈlər] *adj* CHEM molar

**mold¹** [moʊld] **I.** *n* molde *m* **II.** *vt* moldear

**mold²** [moʊld] *n* BOT moho *m*

**moldy** [ˈmoʊlˈdi] <-ier, -iest> *adj* mohoso, -a

**mole¹** [moʊl] *n* ANAT lunar *m*

M

**mole²** ['moʊl] *n* **1.** ZOOL topo *m* **2.** (*spy*) topo *mf*

**molecular** [mə·'lek·jə·lər] *adj* molecular

**molecule** ['mal·ɪ·kjul] *n* molécula *f*

**molehill** ['moʊl·hɪl] *n* topera *f*

**mollusk** ['mal·əsk] *n* molusco *m*

**molten** ['moʊl·tən] *adj* fundido, -a

**mom** [mam] *n inf* mamá *f*

**moment** ['moʊ·mənt] *n* momento *m*; **at the ~** por el momento; **at any ~** en cualquier momento; **at the last ~** en el último momento; **in a ~** enseguida; **not for a ~** ni por un momento; **the ~ that...** en cuanto... +*subj*

**momentarily** [ˌmoʊ·mən·'ter·ɪ·li] *adv* **1.** (*briefly*) por un momento **2.** (*soon*) en un momento

**momentary** ['moʊ·mən·ter·i] *adj* momentáneo, -a

**momentous** [moʊ·'men·təs] *adj* (*fact*) trascendental; (*day*) memorable

**momentum** [moʊ·'men·təm] *n* PHYS momento *m*; *fig* impulso *m*; **to gather ~** coger velocidad

**monarch** ['man·ərk] *n* monarca *mf*

**monarchy** ['man·ər·ki] <-ies> *n* monarquía *f*

**monastery** ['man·ə·ster·i] <-ies> *n* monasterio *m*

**Monday** ['mʌn·di] *n* lunes *m inv*

**monetary** ['man·ə·ter·i] *adj* monetario, -a

**money** ['mʌn·i] *n* dinero *m*; **to be short of ~** ir escaso de dinero; **to change ~** cambiar dinero; **to make ~** hacer dinero; **to raise ~** recolectar fondos ▶ **~ doesn't grow on trees** *prov* el dinero no cae del cielo *prov*

**money order** *n* giro *m* postal

**monitor** ['man·ɪ·tər] I. *n* **1.** COMPUT monitor *m*; **15-inch ~** monitor de 15 pulgadas **2.** (*person*) supervisor(a) *m(f)* II. *vt* controlar; **to ~ sb/sth closely** seguir a alguien/algo de muy cerca

**monk** [mʌŋk] *n* monje *m*

**monkey** ['mʌn·ki] *n* mono, -a *m, f*

**monkey wrench** *n* <-es> llave *f* inglesa

**monkfish** *n* rape *m*

**monogamy** [mə·'nag·ə·mi] *n* monogamia *f*

**monologue** ['man·ə·lag] *n* monólogo *m*

**monopolize** [mə·'nap·ə·laɪz] *vt* monopolizar

**monopoly** [mə·'nap·ə·li] <-ies> *n* monopolio *m*

**monorail** ['man·oʊ·reɪl] *n* monorraíl *m*

**monotonous** [mə·'nat·ən·əs] *adj* monótono, -a

**monotony** [mə·'nat·ən·i] *n* monotonía *f*

**monsoon** [man·'sun] *n* monzón *m*

**monster** ['man·stər] *n* monstruo *m*

**monstrous** ['man·strəs] *adj* **1.** (*big*) enorme **2.** (*awful*) monstruoso, -a

**month** [mʌnθ] *n* mes *m*

**monthly** ['mʌnθ·li] I. *adj* mensual II. *adv* mensualmente

**monument** ['man·jə·mənt] *n* monumento *m*

**monumental** [ˌman·jə·'men·təl] *adj* (*very big*) monumental

**moo** [mu] I. <-s> *n* mugido *m* II. *vi* mugir

**mood¹** [mud] *n* humor *m*; **in a good ~** de buen humor; **to not be in the ~ to do sth** no tener ganas de hacer algo

**mood²** [mud] *n* LING modo *m*

**moody** ['mu·di] <-ier, -iest> *adj* **1.** (*changeable*) voluble **2.** (*bad-tempered*) malhumorado, -a

**moon** [mun] *n* luna *f*; **full/new ~** luna llena/nueva ▶ **once in a blue ~** de higos a brevas; **to be over the ~** estar como un niño con zapatos nuevos

**moonlight** I. *n* luz *f* de la luna II. *vi inf* estar pluriempleado

**moonlit** *adj* iluminado, -a por la luna

**moor¹** [mʊr] *n* (*area*) páramo *m*

**moor²** [mʊr] *vt* NAUT amarrar

**mooring** ['mʊr·ɪŋ] *n* amarra *f*

**moose** [mus] *n* ZOOL alce *m* americano

**mop** [map] I. *n* **1.** (*for cleaning*) fregona *f*, trapeador *m Chile, Méx* **2.** **a ~ of hair** una mata de pelo II. <-pp-> *vt* fregar

**moped** ['moʊ·ped] *n* ciclomotor *m*

**moral** ['mɔr·əl] I. *adj* moral; **~ support** apoyo moral II. *n* **1.** (*message*) moraleja *f* **2.** **~s** (*standards*) moralidad *f*

**morale** [mə·'ræl] *n* moral *f*

**morality** [mɔ·'ræl·ə·ți] <-ies> *n* moralidad *f*

**moralize** ['mɔr·ə·laɪz] *vi* moralizar

**more** [mɔr] *comp of* **much, many** I. *adj* más; ~ **money/coins** más dinero/monedas; **a few ~ coins** unas pocas monedas más; **no ~ money at all** nada más de dinero; **some ~ money** un poco más de dinero II. *adv* más; ~ **beautiful than me** más guapo que yo; **to drink (a bit/much)** ~ beber (un poco/mucho) más; **once** ~ una vez más; **never** ~ nunca más; ~ **than 10** más de 10 III. *pron* más; ~ **and** ~ más y más; **to have** ~ **than sb** tener más que alguien; **to cost** ~ **than sth** costar más que algo; **what** ~ **does he want?** ¿qué más quiere? ▶ **all the** ~ tanto más

**moreover** [mɔr·'ou·vər] *adv form* además

**morgue** [mɔrg] *n* depósito *m* (de cadáveres)

**Mormon** ['mɔr·mən] *n* mormón, -ona *m, f*

**morning** ['mɔr·nɪŋ] I. *n* mañana *f*; **good ~!** ¡buenos días!; **that ~** esa mañana; **the ~ after** la mañana siguiente; **every ~** cada mañana; **every Monday ~** cada lunes por la mañana; **(early) in the ~** por la mañana (temprano); **6 o'clock in the ~** las 6 de la mañana; **from ~ until night** de la mañana a la noche II. *interj inf* ¡buenas!

**morning-after pill** [,mɔr·nɪŋ·'æf·tər·,pɪl] *n* píldora *f* del día después

**morning sickness** *n* náuseas *f pl* matutinas

**moron** ['mɔr·ɑn] *n* capullo, -a *m, f*

**morsel** ['mɔr·səl] *n* (*of food*) bocado *m*

**mortal** ['mɔr·təl] I. *adj* mortal; ~ **danger** peligro *m* de muerte II. *n liter* mortal *mf*

**mortality** [mɔr·'tæl·ə·t̮i] *n form* mortalidad *f*

**mortar** ['mɔr·tər] *n a.* MIL, TECH mortero *m*

**mortgage** ['mɔr·gɪdʒ] I. *n* hipoteca *f* II. *vt* hipotecar

**mortify** ['mɔr·tə·faɪ] *vt* <-ie-> (*embarrass*) avergonzar

**mortuary** ['mɔr·tʃu·er·i] *n* tanatorio *m*

**mosaic** [mou·'zeɪ·ɪk] *n* mosaico *m*

**Moscow** ['mɑs·kau] *n* Moscú *m*

**Moslem** ['mɑz·ləm] *adj, n* musulmán,

-ana *m, f*

**mosque** [mɑsk] *n* mezquita *f*

**mosquito** [mə·'ski·t̮ou] <-(e)s> *n* mosquito *m*, zancudo *m AmL*

**moss** [mɑs] <-es> *n* musgo *m*

**mossy** ['mɑs·i] <-ier, -iest> *adj* musgoso, -a

**most** [moust] *superl of* **many, much** I. *adj* la mayoría de; ~ **people** la mayoría de la gente; **for the ~ part** en su mayor parte II. *adv* más; **the ~ beautiful** el más bello, la más bella; **what I want** ~ lo que más quiero; ~ **of all** más que nada; ~ **likely** muy probablemente III. *pron* la mayoría; **at the (very)** ~ a lo sumo; ~ **of them** la mayoría de ellos; ~ **of the time** la mayor parte del tiempo; **to make the** ~ **of sth/of oneself** sacar el máximo partido a [*or de*] algo/sí mismo

**mostly** ['moust·li] *adv* 1. (*mainly*) sobre todo 2. (*usually*) en general

**motel** [mou·'tel] *n* motel *m*, hotel-garaje *m AmL*

**moth** [mɔθ] *n* polilla *f*

**mothball** ['mɔθ·bɔl] *n* bola *f* de naftalina

**moth-eaten** ['mɔθ·ˌi·tən] *adj* apolillado, -a

**mother** ['mʌð·ər] I. *n* madre *f* II. *vt* mimar

**motherhood** *n* maternidad *f*

**mother-in-law** *n* suegra *f*

**motherly** ['mʌð·ər·li] *adj* maternal

**mother tongue** *n* lengua *f* materna

**motion** ['mou·ʃən] I. *n* 1. (*movement*) movimiento *m*; **in slow** ~ a cámara lenta; **to put sth in** ~ poner algo en marcha 2. (*proposal*) moción *f* II. *vt* indicar con un gesto; **to** ~ **sb to do sth** indicar a alguien que haga algo III. *vi* hacer señas

**motionless** *adj* inmóvil

**motion picture** *n* película *f*

**motivate** ['mou·tə·veɪt] *vt* 1. (*cause*) motivar 2. (*arouse interest of*) animar

**motivation** [,mou·tə·'veɪ·ʃən] *n* 1. (*reason*) motivo *m* 2. (*ambition*) motivación *f*

**motive** ['mou·tɪv] *n* motivo *m*

**motor** ['mou·tər] I. *n a. fig* motor *m*

M

**II.** *adj a.* PHYS motor, motriz

**motorbike** *n* moto *f*

**motorboat** *n* lancha *f* motora

**motorcycle** *n* motocicleta *f*

**motorcycling** *n* motociclismo *m*

**motorcyclist** *n* motociclista *mf*

**motor home** *n* autocaravana *f*

**motorist** ['mou·tər·ɪst] *n* conductor(a) *m(f)*

**motor racing** *n* automovilismo *m*

**motor vehicle** *n form* automóvil *m*

**motto** ['mɑt·ou] <-(e)s> *n* lema *m*

**mound** [maund] *n* 1. (*elevation*) montículo *m* 2. (*heap*) montón *m*

**mount** [maunt] **I.** *n* 1. (*horse*) montura *f* 2. (*frame*) marco *m* **II.** *vt* 1. (*get on: horse*) montar; **to ~ a ladder** subirse a una escalera 2. (*organize*) organizar; **to ~ a rescue** organizar un rescate **III.** *vi* montarse

**mountain** ['maun·tən] *n* 1. GEO montaña *f* 2. *inf* (*amount*) montón *m* ▶ **to** **move** **~s** mover cielo y tierra

**mountain bike** *n* bicicleta *f* de montaña

**mountaineer** [,maun·tə·'nɪr] *n* montañero, -a *m, f*

**mountaineering** *n* montañismo *m*

**mountainous** ['maun·tə·nəs] *adj* GEO montañoso, -a

**mountain range** *n* GEO sierra *f*

**mourn** [mɔrn] **I.** *vi* lamentarse **II.** *vt* llorar la muerte de

**mourner** ['mɔr·nər] *n* doliente *mf*

**mourning** ['mɔr·nɪŋ] *n* luto *m*

**mouse** [maus] <mice> *n* ZOOL, COMPUT ratón *m*

**mouse pad** *n* COMPUT alfombrilla *f* del ratón

**mousetrap** *n* ratonera *f*

**moustache** ['mʌs·tæʃ] *n* bigote *m*

**mouth**[1] [mauθ] *n* 1. (*of person, animal*) boca *f;* **to shut one's ~** *inf* cerrar el pico 2. (*opening*) abertura *f;* (*of bottle, jar, well*) boca *f;* (*of cave*) entrada *f;* (*of river*) desembocadura *f* ▶ **it made her ~ wa-ter** se le hizo la boca agua con eso

**mouth**[2] [mauð] *vt* 1. (*form words silently*) articular 2. (*say insincerely*) soltar; **to ~ an excuse** soltar la excusa de rigor

**mouthful** ['mauθ·ful] *n* (*of food*) bocado *m;* (*of drink*) sorbo *m*

**mouthpiece** *n* TEL micrófono *m*

**mouthwash** *n* enjuague *m* bucal

**mouthwatering** *adj* apetitoso, -a

**move** [muv] **I.** *n* 1. (*movement*) movimiento *m;* **to be on the ~** (*traveling*) estar de viaje; (*very busy*) no parar; **to get a ~ on** darse prisa 2. (*change of abode*) mudanza *f;* (*change of job*) traslado *m* 3. GAMES jugada *f;* **it's your ~** te toca (a ti) 4. (*action*) paso *m;* **to make the first ~** dar el primer paso **II.** *vi* 1. (*change position*) moverse; (*make progress*) hacer progresos 2. (*in games*) mover 3. (*change abode*) mudarse; (*change job*) cambiar de trabajo ▶ **~ it!** *inf* ¡apúrate! **III.** *vt* 1. (*change position*) mover; (*reschedule*) cambiar la fecha de 2. (*cause emotions*) conmover; **to be ~d by sth** estar conmovido por algo

◆**move away I.** *vi* mudarse **II.** *vt* apartar

◆**move back I.** *vi* retirarse **II.** *vt* colocar más atrás

◆**move down** *vi, vt* bajar

◆**move in** *vi* 1. (*move into abode*) instalarse 2. (*intervene*) intervenir 3. (*advance to attack*) avanzar; **to ~ on enemy territory** invadir territorio enemigo

◆**move on** *vi* 1. (*leave*) partir 2. (*continue to move*) seguir adelante; **to ~ to another subject** pasar a otro tema

◆**move out** *vi* 1. (*stop inhabiting*) dejar la casa 2. (*depart*) irse

◆**move over I.** *vi* (*make room*) dejar sitio; (*on seat*) correrse hacia un lado **II.** *vt* mover a un lado

◆**move up I.** *vi* 1. (*make room*) hacer sitio; (*on seat*) correrse hacia un lado 2. (*increase*) subir 3. (*advance*) ascender **II.** *vt* subir

**movement** ['muv·mənt] *n* 1. *a.* MUS (*act*) movimiento *m* 2. FIN, COM actividad *f* 3. (*tendency*) tendencia *f*

**movie** ['mu·vi] *n* película *f;* **the ~s** el cine

**movie camera** *n* cámara *f* cinematográfica

**moviegoer** *n* cinéfilo, -a *m, f*

**movie star** *n* estrella *f* de cine

**movie theater** *n* cine *m*
**moving** ['mu·vɪŋ] *adj* **1.** (*that moves*) móvil; ~ **stairs** escaleras mecánicas **2.** (*motivating*) motriz; **the ~ force** la fuerza motriz **3.** (*causing emotion*) conmovedor(a)
**mow** [moʊ] <mowed, mown *or* mowed> *vt* (*grass*) cortar; (*hay*) segar
**mower** ['moʊ·ər] *n* (*for lawn*) cortacésped *m*
**mown** [moʊn] *pp of* **mow**
**MP** [ˌem·'pi] *n abbr of* **Military Police** policía *f* militar
**mpg** *n abbr of* **miles per gallon** millas *f pl* por galón
**mph** [ˌem·pi·'eɪtʃ] *abbr of* **miles per hour** m/h
**Mr.** ['mɪs·tər] *n abbr of* **Mister** Sr.
**Mrs.** ['mɪs·ɪz] *n* Sra.
**MS** [ˌem·'es] **1.** *abbr of* **Mississippi** Misisipí *m* **2.** *abbr of* **Master of Science** máster *m*
**Ms.** [mɪz] *n forma de tratamiento que se aplica tanto a mujeres solteras como casadas*
**MT** *n abbr of* **Montana** Montana *f*
**Mt.** *abbr of* **Mount** mte.
**much** [mʌtʃ] <more, most> **I.** *adj* mucho, mucha; **how ~ milk?** ¿cuánta leche?; **too/so ~ water** demasiada/tanta agua; **as ~ as** tanto como; **three times as ~** tres veces más **II.** *adv* mucho; **~ better** mucho mejor; **thank you very ~** muchas gracias; **to be very ~ surprised** estar muy sorprendido; **~ to my astonishment** para gran sorpresa mía **III.** *pron* mucho; **~ of the day** la mayor parte del día; **I don't think ~ of it** no le doy mucha importancia
**muck** [mʌk] *n* (*dirt*) suciedad *f*
**mucky** ['mʌk·i] <-ier, -iest> *adj inf* guarro, -a
**mud** [mʌd] *n* barro *m* ▶ **to drag sb's name through the ~** ensuciar el nombre de alguien
**muddle** ['mʌd·əl] **I.** *vt* **1.** (*mix up*) desordenar **2.** (*confuse*) confundir **II.** *n* desorden *m*
**muddy** ['mʌd·i] **I.** <-ier, -iest> *adj* (*dirty*) lleno, -a de barro; (*water*) turbio, -a **II.** *vt* (*make dirty*) manchar de barro ▶ **to ~ the waters** complicar las cosas
**mudslide** *n* (*flow*) avalancha *f* de lodo
**muffin** ['mʌf·ɪn] *n especie de magdalena*
**muffle** ['mʌf·əl] *vt* amortiguar
**mug¹** [mʌg] *n* tazón *m;* (*for beer*) jarra *m*
**mug²** [mʌg] **I.** *n inf* jeta *f,* escracho *m RíoPl* **II.** <-gg-> *vt* atracar
**mugger** ['mʌg·ər] *n* atracador(a) *m(f)*
**muggy** ['mʌg·i] <-ier, -iest> *adj* bochornoso, -a
**mule** [mjul] *n* (*animal*) mulo, -a *m, f* ▶ **as stubborn as a ~** terco como una mula
**mull** [mʌl] *vt* **to ~ sth over** meditar algo
**multicolored** [ˌmʌl·ti·'kʌl·ərd] *adj* multicolor
**multilingual** [ˌmʌl·ti·'lɪŋ·gwəl] *adj* plurilingüe
**multimedia** [ˌmʌl·ti·'mi·di·ə] *adj* multimedia *inv*
**multimillionaire** [ˌmʌl·ti·mil·jə·'ner] *n* multimillonario, -a *m, f*
**multinational** [ˌmʌl·ti·'næʃ·ə·nəl] *adj, n* multinacional *f*
**multiplayer** ['mʌl·ti·pleɪ·ər] *adj* (*computer game*) multijugador
**multiple** ['mʌl·ţə·pəl] *adj* múltiple
**multiplication** [ˌmʌl·tə·plɪ·'keɪ·ʃən] *n* multiplicación *f*
**multiply** ['mʌl·tə·plaɪ] <-ie-> **I.** *vt* multiplicar **II.** *vi* multiplicarse
**multipurpose** [ˌmʌl·ti·'pɜr·pəs] *adj* multiuso
**multitude** ['mʌl·tə·tud] *n* multitud *f;* **the ~s** *liter* las masas
**mum** [mʌm] *adj* **to keep ~** *inf* guardar silencio
**mumble** ['mʌm·bəl] *vi* hablar entre dientes
**mummy** ['mʌm·i] <-ies> *n* momia *f*
**mumps** [mʌmps] *n* MED paperas *fpl*
**munch** [mʌntʃ] *vi, vt* masticar
**mural** ['mjʊr·əl] *n* mural *m*
**murder** ['mɜr·dər] **I.** *n* (*killing*) asesinato *m;* LAW homicidio *m;* **to commit ~** cometer un asesinato; **this job is ~** *fig* este trabajo es matador; **he gets away with ~** *fig* se le consiente cualquier cosa **II.** *vt* (*kill*) asesinar, ultimar *AmL*

**murderer** ['mɜr·dər·ər] n (*killer*) asesino, -a m, f; LAW homicida mf, victimario, -a m, f AmL

**murderous** ['mɜr·dər·əs] adj 1. mortífero, -a 2. (*instinct, look*) asesino, -a; (*plan*) criminal 3. inf (*heat*) insufrible

**murky** ['mɜr·ki] <-ier, -iest> adj (*water, past*) turbio, -a; (*night*) nublado, -a

**murmur** ['mɜr·mər] I. vi, vt murmurar II. n murmullo m

**muscle** ['mʌs·əl] n ANAT músculo m

**muscular** ['mʌs·kjə·lər] adj 1. (*pain, contraction*) muscular 2. (*arms, legs*) musculoso, -a

**muse** [mjuz] I. vi to ~ (on sth) cavilar (sobre algo) II. n musa f

**museum** [mju·'zi·əm] n museo m

**mushroom** ['mʌʃ·rum] n champiñón m; (*wild*) seta f

**music** ['mju·zɪk] n 1. (*art*) música f 2. (*notes*) partitura f

**musical** ['mju·zɪ·kəl] adj, n musical m

**music box** n caja f de música

**musician** [mju·'zɪʃ·ən] n músico, -a m, f

**music stand** n atril m

**Muslim** ['mʌz·ləm] n musulmán, -ana m, f

**mussel** ['mʌs·əl] n mejillón m

**must** [mʌst] I. aux 1. (*obligation*) deber; ~ you leave so soon? ¿tienes que irte tan pronto?; you ~n't do that no debes hacer eso 2. (*probability*) deber de; I ~ have lost it debo de haberlo perdido; you ~ be hungry supongo que tendrás hambre II. n cosa f imprescindible; this book is an absolute ~ este es un libro de lectura obligada

**mustache** ['mʌs·tæʃ] n bigote m

**mustard** ['mʌs·tərd] n mostaza f

**mustn't** ['mʌs·ənt] = must not s. must

**mutant** ['mju·tənt] adj mutante

**mutation** [mju·'teɪ·ʃən] n mutación f

**mute** [mjut] I. n MUS sordina f II. adj mudo, -a

**mutiny** ['mju·tɪ·ni] n <-ies> motín m

**mutter** ['mʌt·ər] I. vi 1. (*talk*) murmurar 2. (*complain*) refunfuñar II. vt murmurar

**mutton** ['mʌt·ən] n carne f de oveja

**mutual** ['mju·tʃu·əl] adj (*understanding*) mutuo, -a; (*friend, interest*) común

**muzzle** ['mʌz·əl] I. n 1. (*of horse,*

*dog*) hocico m 2. (*for dog*) bozal m 3. (*of gun*) boca f II. vt (*dog*) poner un bozal a

**my** [maɪ] I. adj pos mi; ~ dog/house mi perro/casa; ~ children mis hijos; this car is ~ own este coche es mío; I hurt ~ foot/head me he hecho daño en el pie/la cabeza II. interj ¡madre mía!

**myopia** [maɪ·'oʊ·pi·ə] n miopía f

**myopic** [maɪ·'ɑp·ɪk] adj form 1. (*shortsighted*) miope 2. fig corto, -a de miras

**myself** [maɪ·'self] pron reflexive 1. (*direct, indirect object*) me; I hurt ~ me hice daño; I deceived ~ me engañé a mí mismo; I bought ~ a handbag me compré un bolso 2. emphatic yo (mismo, misma); my brother and ~ mi hermano y yo; I'll do it ~ lo haré yo mismo; I did it (all) by ~ lo hice (todo) yo solo 3. after prep mí (mismo, misma); I said to ~ me dije (a mí mismo); I am ashamed of ~ estoy avergonzado de mí mismo; I live by ~ vivo solo

**mysterious** [mɪ·'stɪr·i·əs] adj misterioso, -a

**mystery** ['mɪs·tə·ri] <-ies> n misterio m

**mystic** ['mɪs·tɪk] adj místico, -a

**mystical** ['mɪs·tɪ·kəl] adj místico, -a

**myth** [mɪθ] n mito m

**mythical** ['mɪθ·ɪ·kəl] adj 1. (*legendary*) mítico, -a 2. (*supposed*) supuesto, -a

**mythology** [mɪ·'θɑl·ə·dʒi] n <-ies> mitología f

# N

**N, n** [en] n N, n f; ~ as in November N de Navarra

**n** abbr of **noun** n m

**N** abbr of **north** N m

**nab** [næb] <-bb-> vt inf (*person*) pillar, pescar; (*thing*) agarrar

**nag¹** [næg] n (*horse*) jamelgo m

**nag²** [næg] I. <-gg-> vi 1. (*pester*) fastidiar; to ~ at sb dar la lata a alguien inf 2. (*scold*) regañar 3. (*complain*) quejarse II. <-gg-> vt 1. (*pester*) fastidiar 2. (*scold*) regañar, dar la lata a inf III. n *inf* quejica *mf*

**nagging** ['næg·ɪŋ] I. *n* quejas *fpl* II. *adj* 1. (*pain, ache*) persistente 2. (*pestering: husband, wife*) refunfuñón, -ona

**nail** [neɪl] I. *n* 1. (*tool*) clavo *m* 2. ANAT uña *f* II. *vt* (*fasten*) clavar

**nail-biting** *adj fig* angustioso, -a

**nail clippers** *npl* cortaúñas *m inv*

**nail file** *n* lima *f* de uñas

**nail polish** *n* esmalte *m* de uñas

**nail scissors** *npl* tijeras *f pl* para uñas

**naive** [na·'iv] *adj* ingenuo, -a

**naked** ['neɪ·kɪd] *adj* 1. (*unclothed*) desnudo, -a 2. (*aggression*) manifiesto, -a; (*ambition*) puro, -a

**name** [neɪm] I. *n* 1. nombre *m;* (*surname*) apellido *m;* **by ~** de nombre; **to know sb by ~** conocer a alguien de oídas; **under the ~ of...** bajo el seudónimo de...; **to call sb ~s** llamar a alguien de todo 2. (*reputation*) fama *f;* **to make a ~ for oneself** hacerse un nombre II. *vt* 1. (*call*) poner nombre a 2. (*list*) nombrar

**name day** *n* santo *m;* **today is my ~** hoy es mi santo

**namely** ['neɪm·li] *adv* a saber

**nameplate** ['neɪm·pleɪt] *n* placa *f* con el nombre

**nanny** ['næn·i] <-ies> *n* niñera *f*, nurse *f AmL*

**nap**¹ [næp] *n* (*sleep*) siesta *f;* **to take a ~** echarse una siesta

**nap**² [næp] *n* (*on fabric*) pelo *m*

**napkin** ['næp·kɪn] *n* servilleta *f*

**narcotic** [nar·'kɑt·ɪk] I. *n* narcótico *m* II. *adj* narcótico, -a

**narrate** ['nær·eɪt] *vt* 1. (*tale, story*) narrar, relatar 2. TV (*documentary*) hacer de comentarista de

**narrator** ['nær·eɪ·t̬ər] *n* narrador(a) *m(f);* TV comentarista *mf*

**narrow** ['nær·oʊ] I. <-er, -est> *adj* 1. (*thin*) estrecho, -a 2. (*small: margin*) escaso, -a, reducido, -a II. *vi* estrecharse; (*gap*) reducirse III. *vt* (*reduce width of*) estrechar; (*gap*) reducir

**narrowly** *adv* (*barely*) por poco

**narrow-minded** [,nær·oʊ·'maɪn·dɪd] *adj* de mentalidad cerrada

**nasal** ['neɪ·zəl] *adj* nasal; (*voice*) gangoso, -a

**nasty** ['næs·ti] <-ier, -iest> *adj* 1. (*bad: person*) malvado, -a; (*habit*) feo, -a; (*smell, taste*) asqueroso, -a; (*surprise*) desagradable 2. (*dangerous*) peligroso, -a 3. (*serious*) serio, -a; (*accident*) grave

**nation** ['neɪ·ʃən] *n* (*country*) nación *f*, país *m*

**national** ['næʃ·ə·nəl] I. *adj* nacional II. *n* ciudadano, -a *m, f;* **foreign ~** extranjero, -a *m, f*

**national anthem** *n* himno *m* nacional

**national holiday** *n* fiesta *f* nacional

**nationalism** ['næʃ·ə·nə·lɪz·əm] *n* nacionalismo *m*

**nationality** [,næʃ·ə·'næl·ə·t̬i] <-ies> *n* nacionalidad *f;* **to adopt American/Spanish ~** adoptar la nacionalidad estadounidense/española

**nationwide** [,neɪ·ʃən·'waɪd] *adv* (*operate*) a nivel nacional

**native** ['neɪ·t̬ɪv] I. *adj* 1. (*indigenous*) nativo, -a; (*plant, animal*) autóctono, -a, originario, -a 2. (*of place of origin*) nativo, -a, natural; **~ country** país *m* natal 3. (*indigenous*) indígena 4. (*original*) nativo, -a; (*innate*) innato, -a; (*language*) materno, -a II. *n* nativo, -a *m, f*, natural *mf;* **to speak English like a ~** hablar el inglés como un nativo

**native American** *n* indígena *mf* americano, -a

**native speaker** *n* hablante *mf* nativo, -a

**NATO** ['neɪ·t̬oʊ] *n abbr of* **North Atlantic Treaty Organization** OTAN *f*

**natter** ['næt̬·ər] *vi inf* charlar

**natural** ['nætʃ·ər·əl] I. *adj* 1. natural; **~ father** padre *m* natural 2. (*usual, to be expected*) normal II. *n* 1. *inf* **to be a ~ for sth** tener un talento innato para algo 2. MUS nota *f* natural

**natural childbirth** *n* parto *m* natural

**natural gas** *n* gas *m* natural

**natural history** *n* historia *f* natural

**naturalist** ['nætʃ·ər·ə·lɪst] I. *n* naturalista *mf* II. *adj* naturalista

**naturally** *adv* naturalmente

**natural resources** *npl* recursos *m pl* naturales

**natural science(s)** n(pl) ciencias f pl naturales

**natural selection** n selección f natural

**nature** ['neɪ·tʃər] n 1. (environment) naturaleza f 2. (quality) naturaleza f; **things of this ~** cosas de esta índole; **it's in the ~ of things** es natural; **to be in sb's ~** estar en la naturaleza de alguien ▶ **second ~** hábito muy arraigado en una persona

**nature conservation** n conservación f natural

**nature lover** n amante mf de la naturaleza

**nature reserve** n reserva f natural

**naught** [nɔt] pron liter nada f; **to be all for ~** quedarse en nada

**naughty** ['nɔ·ți] <-ier, -iest> adj (child) desobediente, travieso, -a

**nausea** ['nɔ·zi·ə] n 1. náusea f 2. fig repugnancia f

**nauseating** ['nɔ·zi·eɪ·țɪŋ] adj nauseabundo, -a

**nautical** ['nɔ·țɪ·kəl] adj náutico, -a

**nautical mile** n milla f marina

**naval** ['neɪ·vəl] adj naval; **~ battle/force** batalla f/fuerza f naval

**navel** ['neɪ·vəl] n ombligo m ▶ **to contemplate one's ~** rascarse el ombligo

**navigate** ['næv·ɪ·geɪt] I. vt 1. (steer) llevar; AUTO guiar 2. (sail) navegar por 3. (cross) atravesar 4. COMPUT **to ~ the Internet** navegar por la red, surfear II. vi NAUT, AVIAT navegar; AUTO guiar, hacer de copiloto

**navigation** [ˌnæv·ɪ·ˈgeɪ·ʃən] n navegación f

**navigator** ['næv·ɪ·geɪ·țər] n navegante mf; AUTO copiloto mf

**navy** ['neɪ·vi] I. <-ies> n (military) **the Navy** la Marina II. adj (color) azul marino

**nay** [neɪ] I. adv form no II. n (negative vote) voto m en contra

**NC** [ˌnɔrθˌkær·ə·ˈlaɪ·nə] n abbr of **North Carolina** Carolina f del Norte

**ND** [ˌnɔrθˌdə·ˈkoʊ·də] n abbr of **North Dakota** Dakota f del Norte

**NE** 1. abbr of **Nebraska** Nebraska f 2. abbr of **New England** Nueva Inglaterra f 3. abbr of **northeast** NE m

**near** [nɪr] I. adj 1. (spatial) cercano, -a 2. (temporal) próximo, -a; **in the ~ future** en un futuro próximo 3. (dear) **a ~ and dear friend** un amigo íntimo 4. (similar: portrait) parecido, -a 5. **that was a ~ miss** faltó poco II. adv (spatial or temporal) cerca; **to be ~** estar cerca; **to come ~** aproximarse, acercarse; **~ at hand** a mano; **to come ~er to sb/sth** acercarse más a alguien/algo III. prep 1. (in proximity to) **~ (to)** cerca de; **~ (to) the house** cerca de la casa; **~ the end of the film** hacia el final de la película 2. (almost) **it's ~ midnight** es casi medianoche 3. (about ready to) **to be ~ to doing sth** estar a punto de hacer algo IV. vt acercarse a; **it is ~ing completion** está casi terminado

**nearby** [ˌnɪr·ˈbaɪ] I. adj cercano, -a II. adv cerca; **is it ~?** ¿está cerca?

**Near East** n Oriente m Próximo

**nearly** ['nɪr·li] adv casi; **~ certain** casi seguro; **to be ~ there** estar casi ahí; **to very ~ do sth** estar a punto de hacer algo; **she's ~ as tall as her father** es casi tan alta como su padre

**near-sighted** [ˌnɪr·ˈsaɪ·țɪd] adj a. fig miope

**neat** [nit] adj 1. (orderly, well-ordered) cuidado, -a, ordenado, -a; **~ appearance** apariencia f cuidada; **~ and tidy** ordenado 2. (deft) cuidadoso, -a; **~ solution** solución f exacta 3. sl (excellent) guay inf

**neatly** adv 1. (with care) cuidadosamente 2. (in orderly fashion) de forma ordenada 3. (deftly) con estilo

**necessarily** [ˌnes·ɪ·ˈser·ə·li] adv necesariamente; **not ~** no necesariamente

**necessary** ['nes·ɪ·ser·i] adj necesario, -a; **a ~ evil** un mal necesario; **strictly ~** estrictamente necesario; **that won't be ~** no será necesario; **to do what is ~** hacer lo que es necesario; **if ~** si es necesario

**necessity** [nə·ˈses·ə·ți] <-ies> n (need) necesidad f; **in case of ~** en caso de necesidad; **when the ~ arises** cuando surja la necesidad; **by ~** por necesidad; **bare ~** primera necesidad

**neck** [nek] I. n 1. ANAT cuello m; (nape) nuca f 2. FASHION (also of bottle, violin) cuello *m* ▸ **to be up to one's ~ in sth** *inf* estar (metido) hasta el cuello en algo **II.** *vi inf* besuquearse

**necklace** ['nek·lɪs] *n* collar *m*

**neckline** ['nek·laɪn] *n* escote *m*

**necktie** *n* corbata *f*

**née** [neɪ] *adj* de soltera

**need** [nid] **I.** *n* necesidad *f;* **in ~** necesitado, -a; **basic ~s** necesidades básicas; **~ for sb/sth** necesidad de alguien/ algo; **to be in ~ of sth** necesitar (de) algo; **if ~(s) be** si es necesario; **there's no ~ to shout so loud** no hace falta gritar tanto **II.** *vt* **1.** (*require*) necesitar; **to ~ sb to do sth** necesitar que alguien haga algo **2.** (*ought to need*) **to ~ sth** no necesitar (de) algo **3.** (*must, have*) **to ~ to do sth** tener que hacer algo; **~ we/I/you?** ¿nos/ me/te hace falta?

**needed** *adj* necesario, -a

**needle** ['ni·dəl] **I.** *n* aguja *f;* **hypodermic ~** jeringa *f;* **knitting ~** aguja *f* de hacer punto; **~ and thread** aguja e hilo; **to thread a ~** enhebrar una aguja ▸ **it's like looking for a ~ in a** haystack es como buscar una aguja en un pajar **II.** *vt* (*prick*) pinchar; (*annoy*) provocar

**needless** ['nid·lɪs] *adj* innecesario, -a; **~ to say...** no hace falta decir...

**needy** ['ni·di] <-ier, -iest> *adj* necesitado, -a

**negate** [nɪ·'geɪt] *vt* negar

**negation** [nɪ·'geɪ·fən] *n* negación *f*

**negative** ['neg·ə·tɪv] **I.** *adj* **1.** (*not positive*) negativo, -a; **~ answer** respuesta *f* negativa **2.** *a.* MED negativo, -a; **~ pole** polo *m* negativo; **~ number** número *m* negativo **II.** *n* **1.** (*rejection*) negativa *f* **2.** (*saying no*) negación *f* **3.** PHOT negativo *m* **III.** *vt* negar

**neglect** [nɪ·'glekt] **I.** *vt* desatender; **to ~ to do sth** descuidar hacer algo **II.** *n* negligencia *f;* (*poor state*) deterioro *m*

**neglected** *adj* descuidado, -a; (*undervalued*) infravalorado, -a; **~ child** niño, -a *m, f* abandonado, -a

**neglectful** [nɪ·'glekt·fəl] *adj* negligente

**negligence** ['neg·lɪ·dʒəns] *n a.* LAW negligencia *f*

**negligible** ['neg·lɪ·dʒə·bəl] *adj* insignificante

**negotiable** [nɪ·'goʊ·fi·ə·bəl] *adj* negociable; **non~** no negociable

**negotiate** [nɪ·'goʊ·fi·eɪt] **I.** *vt* **1.** (*discuss*) negociar **2.** (*convert into money*) **to ~ securities** negociar títulos **II.** *vi* negociar; **to ~ on sth** negociar algo

**negotiation** [nɪ·goʊ·fi·'eɪ·fən] *n* negociación *f*

**negotiator** [nɪ·'goʊ·fi·eɪ·ţər] *n* negociador(a) *m(f)*

**Negro** ['ni·groʊ] <-es> *n offensive* negro, -a *m, f*

**neigh** [neɪ] **I.** *n* relincho *m* **II.** *vi* relinchar

**neighbor** ['neɪ·bər] **I.** *n* vecino, -a *m, f;* (*fellow human*) prójimo, -a *m, f* **II.** *vi* to **~ on sth** lindar con algo

**neighborhood** ['neɪ·bər·hʊd] *n* **1.** (*surroundings*) vecindario *m;* (*people*) vecinos *mpl;* **in the ~** en el vecindario **2.** (*vicinity*) alrededores *mpl;* **in the ~ of the airport** en los alrededores del aeropuerto **3.** (*approximately*) **in the ~ of** alrededor de

**neighboring** ['neɪ·bər·ɪŋ] *adj* (*nearby*) cercano, -a; (*bordering*) adyacente; **~ house** casa *f* adyacente; **~ country** país *m* vecino

**neighborly** ['neɪ·bər·li] *adj* amable

**neither** ['ni·ðər] **I.** *pron* ninguno, -a; **~ which one? — ~ (of them)** ¿cuál? — ninguno (de los dos) **II.** *adv* ni; **~... nor...** ni... ni... **III.** *conj* tampoco; **if he won't eat, ~ will I** si él no come, yo tampoco **IV.** *adj* ningún, -una; **~ book is good** ninguno de los dos libros es bueno

**neon** ['ni·an] *n* neón *m*

**neo-Nazi** [ˌni·oʊ·'nat·si] *n* neonazi *mf*

**neon sign** *n* letrero *m* de neón

**nephew** ['nef·ju] *n* sobrino *m*

**Neptune** ['nep·tun] *n* Neptuno *m*

**nerd** [nɜrd] *n pej sl* **1.** (*awkward person*) empollón, -ona *m, f m* **2.** (*foolish person*) pardillo, -a *m, f*

**nerve** [nɜrv] *n* **1.** ANAT nervio *m* **2.** **~s** nerviosismo *m;* **to be a bundle of ~s** *fig* ser un puñado de nervios; **to get on sb's ~s** *inf* poner los nervios de punta a alguien **3.** (*courage*) **to lose one's ~**

N

perder el valor; **to have the ~ to do sth** *inf* tener el morro de hacer algo **4.** (*apprehension*) **~s** ansiedad *f*

**nervous** ['nɜr·vəs] *adj* (*jumpy*) nervioso, -a; (*edgy*) ansioso, -a; **to make sb ~** poner nervioso a alguien; **to be ~ about sth** estar nervioso por algo

**nervous breakdown** *n* ataque *m* de nervios

**nervousness** *n* (*condition*) nerviosismo *m;* (*fearfulness*) ansiedad *f*

**nervous system** *n* sistema *m* nervioso

**nervy** ['nɜr·vi] <-ier, -iest> *adj* **1.** (*rude*) descarado, -a **2.** (*courageous*) atrevido, -a

**nest** [nest] **I.** *n* nido *m;* **to leave the ~** dejar el nido *f* **II.** *vi* anidar

**nest egg** *n* ahorros *mpl*

**net**[1] [net] **I.** *n* **1.** (*material*) malla *f;* mosquito **2.** (*for fishing*) *a.* SPORTS red *f* **II.** <-tt-> *vt* (*catch: fish*) pescar

**net**[2] [net] **I.** *adj* **1.** ECON neto, -a; **~ income** ingreso *m* neto **2.** (*weight*) neto, -a **II.** *vt* **to ~ sth** ganar algo en neto

**Net** [net] *n* COMPUT **the ~** la red

**Netherlands** ['neð·ər·ləndz] *n* **the ~** los Países Bajos, Holanda *f*

**nett** [net] *adj, vt see* **net**[1] **I.**, **net**[2]

**netting** ['net·ɪŋ] *n* **1.** (*net*) malla *f* **2.** SPORTS red *f*

**nettle** ['net·əl] **I.** *n* ortiga *f* **II.** *vt* irritar

**network** ['net·wɜrk] **I.** *n* **1.** COMPUT, TEL red *f;* **computer ~** red informática **2.** TV cadena *f* **II.** *vt* **1.** (*link together*) conectar **2.** (*broadcast*) retransmitir **III.** *vi* interconectar

**networking** *n* COMPUT interconexión *f*

**neurological** [ˌnʊr·ə·'lɑdʒ·ɪ·kəl] *adj* neurológico, -a

**neuron** ['nʊr·ɑn] *n* neurona *f*

**neurosurgeon** [ˌnʊr·oʊ·'sɜr·dʒən] *n* neurocirujano, -a *m, f*

**neurosurgery** [ˌnʊr·oʊ·'sɜr·dʒə·ri] *n* neurocirugía *f*

**neurotic** [nʊ·'rɑt·ɪk] *adj* neurótico, -a

**neuter** ['nu·tər] **I.** *adj* neutro, -a **II.** *vt* **1.** (*castrate: male*) castrar **2.** (*sterilize: female*) esterilizar **3.** (*neutralize*) neutralizar

**neutral** ['nu·trəl] **I.** *adj* **1.** (*uninvolved*) neutral; **to remain ~** mantenerse al margen **2.** *a.* CHEM, ELEC neutro, -a **3.** (*unemotional*) objetivo, -a **II.** *n* AUTO punto *m* muerto

**neutrality** [nu·'træl·ə·t̬i] *n* neutralidad *f*

**neutralize** ['nu·trə·laɪz] *vt* neutralizar

**neutron** ['nu·trɑn] *n* neutrón *m*

**never** ['nev·ər] *adv* nunca, jamás; **~ again!** ¡nunca más!; **~ fear!** ¡no te preocupes!; **well I ~ (did)** ¡no me digas!; **as ~ before** como nunca; **~ ever** nunca jamás; **~ mind** qué más da

**never-ending** ['nev·ər·'en·dɪŋ] *adj* interminable

**nevermore** *adv* nunca más

**nevertheless** [ˌnev·ər·ðə·'les] *adv* sin embargo, no obstante

**new** [nu] *adj* **1.** (*latest, recent*) nuevo, -a, reciente; **~ technology** tecnología *f* punta **2.** (*changed*) nuevo, -a; **~ boy/girl** SCHOOL novato, -a *m, f* **3.** (*inexperienced*) nuevo, -a, novato, -a; **she's ~ to the job** es nueva en el trabajo **4.** (*in new condition*) nuevo, -a; **brand ~** nuevo flamante **5.** (*fresh*) fresco, -a; **~ blood** *fig* sangre *f* fresca **6.** (*new*) fresco, -a, reciente

**newbie** ['nu·bi] *n* novato, -a *m, f*

**newborn** *adj* reciente; **~ baby** recién nacido, -a *m, f*

**New Caledonia** *n* Nueva Caledonia *f*

**newcomer** *n* **1.** (*just arrived*) recién llegado, -a *m, f* **2.** (*stranger*) nuevo, -a *m, f* **3.** (*beginner*) principiante *mf;* novato, -a *m, f*

**New England** *n* Nueva Inglaterra *f*

**Newfoundland** ['nu·fən·lənd] *n* Terranova *f*

**newish** ['nu·ɪʃ] *adj inf* bastante nuevo, -a

**newly** ['nu·li] *adv* **1.** (*discovered, diagnosed, released*) recientemente **2.** (*named, phrased*) de otra manera

**newly-wed** ['nu·li·wed] *npl* recién casados *mpl*

**New Mexico** [ˌnu·'mek·sɪ·koʊ] *n* Nuevo México *m*

**new moon** *n* luna *f* nueva

**New Orleans** [ˌnu·'ɔr·li·ənz] *n* Nueva Orleans *f*

**news** [nuz] *n + sing vb* **1.** noticias *fpl;* **bad/good ~** malas/buenas noticias; **to**

**break the ~ to sb** dar la noticia a alguien; **when the ~ broke** cuando se supo la noticia; **really! that's ~ to me** ¿de veras? no lo sabía **2.** (*broadcast*) noticias *fpl*, informativo *m*; **to be ~ ser** noticia ► **no ~ is good ~** *prov* si no hay noticias, buena señal

**news agency** <-ies> *n* agencia *f* de noticias

**newscast** *n* informativo *m*

**newsflash** <-es> *n* noticia *f* de última hora

**newsgroup** *n* COMPUT foro *m* de discusión

**news item** *n* noticia *f*

**newsletter** *n* nota *f* de prensa

**newspaper** *n* periódico *m*

**news report** *n* reportaje *m* informativo

**newsroom** *n* sala *f* de redacción

**newsstand** *n* quiosco *m*

**newsworthy** *adj* de interés periodístico

**newsy** ['nu·zi] <-ier, -iest> *adj* lleno, -a de noticias

**New Year** *n* **1.** año *m* nuevo; **Happy ~** feliz año nuevo **2.** (*opening weeks of year*) principios *m pl* de año

**New Year's Day** *n* día *m* de año nuevo

**New Year's Eve** *n* nochevieja *f*

**New York** [,nu·'jɔrk] *n* Nueva York *f*

**New Yorker** *n* neoyorquino, -a *m, f*

**New Zealand** [,nu·'zi·lənd] *n* Nueva Zelanda *f*

**New Zealander** *n* neozelandés, -esa *m, f*

**next** |nekst| **I.** *adj* **1.** (*in location*) siguiente; **the ~ day** próximo, -a, que viene; **the ~ day** el día siguiente; **~ month** el mes que viene; **the ~ thing** el siguiente paso; **(the) ~ time** la próxima vez **3.** (*following in order*) siguiente; **to be ~ ser** el siguiente; **~ to sth/sb** cerca de algo/alguien **II.** *adv* **1.** (*afterwards, subsequently*) después, luego **2.** (*almost as much*) **~ to** después de **3.** (*again, once more*) de nuevo **4.** (*almost*) casi; **~ to impossible** casi imposible **5.** (*second*) **the ~ best thing** lo segundo mejor **III.** *prep* **1.** (*beside*) **~ to** junto a; **my room is ~ to yours** mi habitación está al lado de la tuya **2.** (*almost*) casi; **to cost ~ to nothing** no valer casi nada

**next door** [,nekst·'dɔr] *adv* al lado

**next of kin** *n* pariente *mf* cercano, -a

**nexus** ['nek·səs] *n inv* nexo *m*

**NF** *n abbr of* **Newfoundland** Terranova *f*

**NH** [,nu·'hæmp·ʃər] *n abbr of* **New Hampshire** New Hampshire

**Niagara Falls** [naɪ·æg·rə·'fɔlz] *n* (**the**) **~** las cataratas del Niágara

**nib** [nɪb] *n* punta *f*; (*of pen*) plumilla *f*

**nibble** ['nɪb·əl] **I.** *n* mordisco *m*, bocado *m*; **to take a ~ (at sth)** dar un mordisco (a algo) **II.** *vt* **1.** (*bite*) mordisquear; (*rat*) roer **2.** (*pick at*) picar **III.** *vi a. fig* picar

**Nicaragua** [,nɪk·ə·'rag·wə] *n* Nicaragua *f*

**Nicaraguan** *n adj* nicaragüense *mf*

**nice** [naɪs] **I.** *adj* **1.** (*pleasant, agreeable*) bueno, -a; **~ one!, ~ work!** *inf* ¡bien hecho!; **~ weather** buen tiempo *m*; **it is ~ to do sth** es agradable hacer algo **2.** (*amiable*) simpático, -a; (*kind*) amable; **to be ~ to sb** ser amable con alguien; **it is/was ~ of sb to do sth** es/fue un detalle por parte de alguien hacer algo **3.** *iron inf* (*unpleasant*) **that's a ~ thing to say to your brother** ¡vaya cosa bonita para decirle a un hermano! **4.** (*subtle*) sutil, delicado, -a; (*fine*) fino, -a **II.** *adv* bien

**nicely** ['naɪs·li] *adv* **1.** (*well, satisfactorily*) bien **2.** (*having success*) espléndidamente **3.** (*pleasantly, politely*) amablemente

**nicety** ['naɪ·sə·ti] <-ies> *n* **1.** (*subtle distinction*) sutileza *f* **2.** (*precision*) precisión *f* **3.** (*precise differentiations*) **niceties** matices *mpl*; (*in negative sense*) nimiedades *fpl*

**niche** [nɪtʃ] *n* **1.** (*alcove*) nicho *m* **2.** (*desired job*) buen puesto *m*; (*suitable position*) buena posición *f*

**nick** [nɪk] **I.** *n* (*chip in surface*) mella *f* ► **in the ~ of time** por los pelos **II.** *vt* **1.** (*chip*) mellar; (*cut*) cortar **2.** *sl* (*cheat*) engañar

**nickel** ['nɪk·əl] *n* **1.** CHEM níquel *m* **2.** (*coin*) moneda *f* de cinco centavos

**nickname** ['nɪk·neɪm] *n* apodo *m*

**nicotine** ['nɪk·ə·tin] *n* nicotina *f*

**niece** [nis] *n* sobrina *f*

**nifty** ['nɪf·ti] <-ier, -iest> *adj sl* (*stylish*)

chulo, -a; (*skilful*) hábil

**niggardly** ['nɪg·ərd·li] *adj* (*stingy*) tacaño, -a; (*meager*) miserable

**nigger** ['nɪg·ər] *n offensive sl* negraco, -a *m, f*

**niggle** ['nɪg·əl] I. *vi* fastidiar II. *vt* 1. (*nag*) reparar en minucias 2. (*irritate*) enfurecer, irritar

**niggling** ['nɪg·lɪŋ] *adj* (*irritating*) molesto, -a

**night** [naɪt] *n* noche *f;* **good ~!** ¡buenas noches!; **last ~** anoche; **10 (o'clock) at ~** las 10 de la noche; **the ~ before** la noche anterior; **~ and day** día y noche; **during the ~** durante la noche; **during Tuesday ~** durante la noche del martes; **to work ~s** trabajar de noche

**night bird** ['naɪt·bɜrd] *n* 1. ZOOL pájaro *m* nocturno 2. (*person*) noctámbulo, -a *m, f,* trasnochador(a) *m(f)*

**night blindness** *n* ceguera *f* nocturna

**nightcap** *n* (*cap*) gorro *m* de dormir

**nightclothes** *npl* ropa *f* de dormir

**nightclub** *n* club *m* (nocturno)

**nightdress** <-es> *n* camisón *m*

**nightfall** *n* atardecer *m*

**nightgown** *n* camisón *m*

**nightie** ['naɪ·ti] *n inf* camisón *m*

**nightingale** ['naɪ·tɪŋ·geɪl] *n* ruiseñor *m*

**nightlight** *n* lamparilla *f*

**nightlong** *adv* durante toda la noche

**nightly** ['naɪt·li] I. *adv* cada noche II. *adj* (*visits, TV program*) de todas las noches

**nightmare** ['naɪt·mer] *n* pesadilla *f*

**nightmarish** ['naɪt·mer·ɪʃ] *adj* espeluznante

**night-nurse** *n* enfermera *f* de noche

**night school** *n* escuela *f* nocturna

**night shift** *n* turno *m* de noche

**nightshirt** *n* camisa *f* de dormir

**nightstand** *n* mesita *f* de noche

**night watchman** *n* vigilante *m* nocturno, nochero *m* CSur

**nihilism** ['naɪ·ə·lɪz·əm] *n* nihilismo *m*

**nihilistic** [ˌnaɪ·ə·lɪs·tɪk] *adj* nihilista

**nil** [nɪl] *n* (*nothing, zero*) nada *f,* cero *m*

**Nile** [naɪl] *n* **the ~** el Nilo

**nimble** ['nɪm·bəl] *adj* (*agile*) ágil; (*quick and light in movement*) diestro, -a; (*quick-thinking*) listo, -a

**nine** [naɪn] I. *adj* nueve *inv* ▶ **~ times out of ten** casi siempre II. *n* nueve *m; s. a.* **eight**

**9-11, 9/11** [naɪn·ɪ·'lev·ən] *n* el 11-S *m*

**nineteen** [ˌnaɪn·'tin] I. *adj* diecinueve II. *n* diecinueve *m; s. a.* **eight**

**nineteenth** I. *adj* decimonoveno, -a II. *n* 1. (*order*) decimonoveno, -a *m, f* 2. (*date*) diecinueve *m* 3. (*fraction*) diecinueveavo *m;* (*part*) diecinueveava parte *f; s. a.* **eighth**

**ninetieth** ['naɪn·ti·əθ] I. *adj* nonagésimo, -a II. *n* (*order*) nonagésimo, -a *m, f;* (*fraction*) noventavo *m;* (*part*) noventava parte *f; s. a.* **eighth**

**ninety** ['naɪn·ti] I. *adj* noventa II. <-ies> *n* noventa *m; s. a.* **eighty**

**ninth** [naɪnθ] I. *adj* noveno, -a II. *n* 1. (*order*) noveno, -a *m, f* 2. (*date*) nueve *m* 3. (*fraction*) noveno *m;* (*part*) novena parte *f; s. a.* **eighth**

**nip** [nɪp] I. <-pp-> *vt* 1. (*bite*) mordisquear 2. (*pinch, squeeze: pliers*) pellizcar 3. (*remove: dead leaves*) arrancar ▶ **to ~ sth in the bud** *fig* cortar algo de raíz II. *n* 1. (*sip*) traguito *m* 2. (*pinch, tight squeeze*) pellizco *m* 3. (*bite*) mordisquito *m* 4. (*coldness*) helada *f*

**nipple** ['nɪp·əl] *n* ANAT pezón *m;* (*teat*) tetilla *f,* tetera *f AmL*

**nippy** ['nɪp·i] <-ier, -iest> *adj inf* helado, -a

**nit** [nɪt] *n* ZOOL liendre *f*

**nitpicking** ['nɪt·pɪk·ɪŋ] I. *adj inf* criticón, -ona II. *n inf* pega *f*

**nitrate** ['naɪ·treɪt] *n* nitrato *m*

**nitric** ['naɪ·trɪk] *adj* nítrico, -a

**nitrite** ['naɪ·traɪt] *n* nitrito *m*

**nitrogen** ['naɪ·trə·dʒən] *n* nitrógeno *m*

**nitroglycerin(e)** [ˌnaɪ·troʊ·'glɪs·ər·ɪn] *n* nitroglicerina *f*

**nitrous** ['naɪ·trəs] *adj* nitroso, -a

**nitty-gritty** [ˌnɪt·i·'grɪt·i] *n inf* **the ~** el meollo; **to get down to the ~** ir al grano

**nitwit** ['nɪt·wɪt] *n inf* idiota *mf*

**NJ** [ˌnu·'dʒɜr·zi] *n abbr of* **New Jersey** Nueva Jersey *f*

**NM** [ˌnu·'mek·sɪ·koʊ] *n abbr of* **New Mexico** Nuevo México *m*

**NNE** *abbr of* **north-northeast** NNE *m*

**NNW** *abbr of* **north-northwest** NNO *m*

**no** [nou] **I.** *adj* **1.** (*not to any degree*) no; ~ **parking** prohibido estacionar; ~ **way** de ninguna manera; ~ **can do** *inf* no se puede; ~ **less than sth/sb** nada menos que algo/alguien **2.** (*equivalent to a negative sentence*) no; (*emphasizes previous statement's falsity*) no **II.** *n* <-(e)s> *n* (*denial, refusal*) no *m*; **to not take ~ for an answer** no admitir un no por respuesta **III.** *interj* (*word used to deny*) no; (*emphasizes distress*) qué me dices

**no., No.** *abbr of* **number** núm., n°

**Nobel prize** [ˌnou·belˈpraɪz] *n* premio *m* nobel

**nobility** [nou·ˈbɪl·ə·t̬i] *n* **1.** + *sing/pl vb* (*aristocracy*) nobleza *f* **2.** (*nobleness of character*) generosidad *f*; (*selflessness*) altruismo *m*

**noble** [ˈnou·bəl] **I.** *adj* **1.** noble; (*action*) generoso, -a; ~ **act** acto *m* noble **2.** (*splendid*) majestuoso, -a **3.** (*excellent*) magnífico, -a; (*horse*) noble **II.** *n* noble *mf*

**nobleman** [ˈnou·bəl·mən] <-men> *n* aristócrata *m*

**noble-minded** *adj* honesto, -a

**nobly** [ˈnou·bli] *adv* noblemente

**nobody** [ˈnou·bad·i] **I.** *pron indef, sing* nadie; **we saw ~** (*else*) no vimos a nadie (más); **he told ~** no se lo dijo a nadie **II.** *n inf* don nadie *m*; **those people are nobodies** esas personas son un cero a la izquierda

**nocturnal** [nak·ˈtɜr·nəl] *adj form* nocturno, -a

**nod** [nad] **I.** *n* cabezada *f*, inclinación *f* de cabeza **II.** <-dd-> *vt* **to ~ one's head** asentir con la cabeza; **to ~ one's head at sth** indicar algo con la cabeza **III.** <-dd-> *vi* **1.** asentir con la cabeza; **to ~ to sb** saludar a alguien con una inclinación de cabeza **2.** *inf* (*when sleepy*) dar cabezadas

◆ **nod off** *vi* quedarse dormido

**nodding** [ˈnad·ɪŋ] *adj* **to have only a ~ acquaintance with sth** conocer algo sólo por encima

**node** [noud] *n* **1.** ANAT (*tissue*) ganglio *m* **2.** BOT (*on a stem*) nódulo *m* **3.** COMPUT

nodo *m*

**nodule** [ˈnadʒ·ul] *n* ANAT, BOT nódulo *m*

**no-go area** [nou·gou·ˈer·i·ə] *n* MIL zona *f* prohibida

**nohow** [ˈnou·hau] *adv sl* de ninguna manera

**noise** [nɔɪz] *n* **1.** (*sound*) ruido *m*; **to make a ~** hacer ruido **2.** (*loud, unpleasant sounds*) estruendo *m* **3.** ELEC interferencia *f* ▶ **to make ~ about sth** *inf* quejarse mucho de algo

**noise barrier** *n* barrera *f* del sonido

**noiseless** [ˈnɔɪz·lɪs] *adj* silencioso, -a

**noise pollution** *n* contaminación *f* acústica

**noise prevention** *n* prevención *f* del ruido

**noisy** [ˈnɔɪ·zi] <-ier, -iest> *adj* **1.** (*making noise: crowd*) ruidoso, -a **2.** (*full of noise: restaurant, street*) bullicioso, -a **3.** ELEC (*signal*) acústico, -a

**nomad** [ˈnou·mæd] *n* nómada *mf*

**nomadic** [nou·ˈmæd·ɪk] *adj* nómada

**no man's land** [ˈnou·mænz·lænd] *n* tierra *f* de nadie

**nominal** [ˈnam·ə·nəl] *adj* **1.** (*in name*) nominal **2.** (*small: sum*) pequeño, -a

**nominally** [ˈnam·ə·nə·li] *adv* nominalmente

**nominate** [ˈnam·ə·neɪt] *vt* **1.** (*propose*) proponer; (*for an award*) nominar **2.** (*appoint*) nombrar

**nomination** [ˌnam·ə·ˈneɪ·ʃən] *n* **1.** (*proposal*) propuesta *f* **2.** (*appointment*) nombramiento *m*; (*for an award*) nominación *f*

**nominative** [ˈnam·ə·nə·t̬ɪv] **I.** *n* nominativo *m* **II.** *adj* nominativo, -a

**nominee** [ˌnam·ə·ˈni] *n* candidato, -a *m, f*; (*for an award*) nominado, -a *m, f*

**nonagenarian** [ˌnan·ə·dʒə·ˈner·i·ən] *adj* nonagenario, -a

**nonalcoholic** [ˌnan·æl·kə·ˈhal·ɪk] *adj* sin alcohol

**nonaligned** [ˌnan·ə·ˈlaɪnd] *adj* no alineado, -a

**nonchalant** [ˌnan·fə·ˈlant] *adj* despreocupado, -a

**nonconformist** [ˌnan·kən·ˈfɔr·mɪst] *adj* inconformista

**nonconformity** [ˌnan·kən·ˈfɔr·mə·t̬i] *n*

**N**

inconformidad f

**non-deposit bottle** [ˌnɑn·dɪ·ˈpɑz·ɪt·ˈbɑt·əl] n envase m no retornable

**nondescript** [ˌnɑn·dɪ·ˈskrɪpt] adj sin nada de particular; (person) anodino, -a; (color) indefinido, -a

**none** [nʌn] I. pron 1. (nobody) nadie, ninguno, -a; ~ **of them** ninguno de ellos; ~ **of you helped me** ninguno de vosotros me ayudó 2. (not any) ninguno, -a 3. (not any) nada; ~ **of that!** ¡déjate de eso! II. adv 1. (not) ~ **the less** sin embargo; **to be** ~ **the wiser** seguir sin entender nada 2. (not very) **it's** ~ **too soon** ya era hora; **it's** ~ **too warm** no hace mucho calor

**nonentity** [nɑn·ˈen·tə·ti] <-ies> n 1. (person) cero m a la izquierda 2. (insignificance) insignificancia f

**non-iron** [ˌnɑn·ˈaɪ·ərn] adj que no necesita plancha

**nonplus** [ˌnɑn·ˈplʌs] <-ss-> vt dejar perplejo; **to be ~sed** quedarse perplejo

**nonprofit** [ˌnɑn·ˈprɑf·ɪt] adj no lucrativo, -a

**nonrefundable** [ˌnɑn·rɪ·ˈfʌn·də·bəl] adj no reembolsable; ~ **down payment** pago m a fondo perdido

**nonresident** [ˌnɑn·ˈrez·ɪ·dənt] adj no residente

**nonsense** [ˈnɑn·sens] I. n tonterías fpl; **to talk** ~ inf decir tonterías II. interj tonterías

**nonsensical** [ˌnɑn·ˈsen·sɪ·kəl] adj absurdo, -a

**nonskid** [ˌnɑn·ˈskɪd] adj antideslizante

**nonsmoking** adj para no fumadores

**nonstop** [ˌnɑn·ˈstɑp] I. adj 1. (without stopping, direct) sin parar; (flight) directo, -a 2. (uninterrupted) incesante II. adv sin pausa

**noodle**[1] [ˈnu·dəl] n fideo m

**noodle**[2] [ˈnu·dəl] n 1. (head) coco m 2. (person) tontolaba mf

**nook** [nʊk] n liter rincón m

**noon** [nun] n mediodía m; **at** ~ a mediodía; **about** ~ alrededor de mediodía

**no one** [ˈnoʊ·wʌn] pron see **nobody**

**noose** [nus] n 1. (loop of rope) soga f 2. (for catching) lazo m

**nope** [noʊp] adv inf no

**nor** [nɔr] conj 1. (and also not) tampoco; ~ (**do**) **I** ni yo tampoco 2. (not either) ni

**Nordic** [ˈnɔr·dɪk] adj nórdico, -a

**norm** [nɔrm] n norma f

**normal** [ˈnɔr·məl] adj normal; **as (is)** ~ como es normal

**normalize** [ˈnɔr·mə·laɪz] a. COMPUT I. vt normalizar II. vi normalizarse

**normally** [ˈnɔr·mə·li] adv normalmente

**north** [nɔrθ] I. n 1. (cardinal point) norte m; **to lie 3 miles to the** ~ estar a 5 km al norte de algo; **to go/drive to the** ~ ir/viajar hacia el norte; **further** ~ más al norte 2. GEO norte m; **in the** ~ **of France** en el norte de Francia 3. (of sth) del norte, septentrional; ~ **wind** viento m del norte; ~ **coast** costa f norte; **the North Sea** El Mar del Norte; **North Star** Estrella f Polar; **the North Pole** el Polo Norte

**North America** n América f del Norte

**North American** I. n norteamericano, -a m, f II. adj norteamericano, -a

**North Carolina** [ˌnɔrθ·kær·ə·ˈlaɪ·nə] n Carolina f del Norte

**North Dakota** [ˌnɔrθ·də·ˈkoʊ·də] n Dakota f del Norte

**northeast** [ˌnɔrθ·ˈist] n nordeste m

**northeastern** [ˌnɔrθ·ˈi·stərn] adj nororiental

**northerly** [ˈnɔr·ðər·li] adj del norte

**northern** [ˈnɔr·ðərn] adj del norte, norteño, -a, nortino, -a Chile, Perú; ~ **hemisphere** hemisferio m norte; ~ **lights** aurora f boreal

**northerner** [ˈnɔr·ðər·nər] n norteño, -a m, f

**northernmost** adj más septentrional

**Northern Territory** n territorio m norte

**North Pole** [ˈnɔrθ·poʊl] n **the** ~ el Polo Norte

**North Sea** n Mar m del Norte

**North-South divide** n ECON división f Norte-Sur

**northward** [ˈnɔrθ·wərd] adv hacia el norte

**northwest** [ˌnɔrθ·ˈwest] I. n noroeste m; **to the** ~ (**of**) al noroeste (de) II. adj del noroeste; ~ **Texas** el noroeste de Texas III. adv en dirección noroeste

**northwesterly** [ˌnɔrθˈwesˑtərˑli] adj en dirección noroeste; (from the northwest) del noroeste

**Northwest Territories** n pl territorios m pl del noroeste

**Norway** [ˈnɔrˌwei] n Noruega f

**Norwegian** [nɔrˈwiˑdʒən] I. adj noruego, -a II. n 1. (person) noruego, -a m, f 2. LING noruego m

**nose** [nouz] I. n 1. ANAT nariz f; (of animal) hocico m; **to blow one's ~** sonarse la nariz 2. AVIAT morro m ▶ **to follow one's ~** inf (trust instincts) guiarse por su olfato; (go straight ahead) seguir adelante; **to have a (good) ~ for sth** tener buen olfato para algo; **to poke one's ~ into sth** inf meter las narices en algo; **to rub sb's ~ in it** restregar algo a alguien por las narices; **right out from under sb's ~** inf delante de las narices de alguien II. vi fisgonear III. vt **to ~ one's way in/out/up** entrar/salir/pasar lentamente

**nosebag** [ˈnouzˌbæg] n morral m

**nosebleed** n hemorragia f nasal

**nose cone** n AVIAT cabeza f

**nosedive** vi 1. AVIAT descender en picado 2. FIN caer en picado

**nose job** n inf arreglo m de nariz

**nosey** [ˈnouˑzi] <-ier, -iest> adj see nosy

**nosh** [naʃ] I. n inf papeo m II. vi papear

**nostalgia** [naˈstælˑdʒə] n nostalgia f

**nostalgic** [naˈstælˑdʒɪk] adj nostálgico, -a

**nostril** [ˈnasˑtrəl] n ventana f de la nariz

**nosy** [ˈnouˑzi] <-ier, -iest> adj fisgón, -ona

**not** [nat] adv no; **it's a woman, ~ a man** es una mujer, no un hombre; **he's asked me ~ to do it** me ha pedido que no lo haga; **~ all the children like singing** no les gusta cantar a todos los niños; **~ me!** ¡yo no!; **why ~?** ¿por qué no?; **he is ~ ugly** no es feo; **or ~** o no; **~ at all** (nothing) en absoluto; (no need to thank) de nada; **~ only... but also...** no sólo... sino también; **~ just** [or **simply**] no sólo; **~ much** no mucho

**notable** [ˈnouˑtəˑbəl] adj 1. (remarkable)

notable 2. (eminent) eminente

**notably** [ˈnouˑtəˑbli] adv notablemente

**notary** [ˈnouˑtəˑri] <-ies> n ~ **(public)** notario, -a m, f

**notation** [nouˈteiˑʃən] n MATH, MUS notación f

**notch** [natʃ] <-es> n I. vt 1. (cut) hacer una muesca 2. (achieve) conseguir II. n 1. (cut) muesca f; (hole) agujero m 2. (degree) punto m 3. (narrow valley) valle m

**note** [nout] I. n 1. (annotation) nota f; **to take ~** tomar nota 2. LIT apunte m 3. MUS nota f; (sound) tono m; **to strike the right ~** fig dar con el tono apropiado 4. (money) billete m 5. (importance) **of ~** form notable; **nothing of ~** nada importante II. vt form anotar; (mention) observar; **to ~ (that)...** hacer notar (que)...

**notebook** [ˈnoutˑbʊk] n cuaderno m

**noted** [ˈnouˑtɪd] adj célebre; **to be ~ for sth** ser conocido por algo

**notepad** [ˈnoutˑpæd] n bloc m

**notepaper** [ˈnoutˌpeiˑpər] n papel m de carta

**noteworthy** [ˈnoutˌwɜrˑði] adj form de interés; **nothing/something ~** nada/algo digno de atención

**nothing** [ˈnʌθˑɪŋ] I. pron indef, sing 1. (no objects) nada; **~ happens** no pasa nada; **we saw ~ (else/more)** no vimos nada (más); **~ new** nada nuevo 2. (not anything) **~ came of it** no salió nada (de ahí); **~ doing!** inf ¡para nada!; **fit for ~** bueno para nada; **to make ~ of it** no darle importancia; **there is ~ to laugh at** no tiene ninguna gracia 3. (not important) **that's ~!** ¡no es nada! 4. (only) **~ but** tan sólo; **she is ~ if not patient** es paciente por encima de todo; **~ much** poca cosa II. adv **~ less than** ni más ni menos que III. n 1. nada f 2. MATH, SPORTS cero m; **three to ~** tres a cero

**nothingness** [ˈnʌθˑɪŋˑnɪs] n (emptiness) vacío m; (worthlessness) nada f

**notice** [ˈnouˑtɪs] I. vt 1. (see) ver; (perceive) fijarse en; **to ~ (that)...** darse cuenta de (que)... 2. (recognize) reconocer II. vi darse cuenta III. n

**1.** (*attention*) interés *m*; **to take ~ of sb/sth** prestar atención a alguien/algo; **that escaped my ~** se me pasó por alto **2.** (*display*) letrero *m*; (*in newspaper, magazine*) anuncio *m* **3.** (*warning*) aviso *m*; **to give sb ~** (**of sth**) avisar a alguien (de algo); **at short ~** a corto plazo; **at a moment's ~** a un momento; **until further ~** hasta nuevo aviso **4.** LAW preaviso *m*; **to give (in) one's ~** presentar la dimisión; **to give sb their ~** despedir a alguien

**noticeable** ['nou·tɪs·ə·bəl] *adj* (*change, improvement*) evidente; (*difference, increase, lack of friendliness*) notable

**notifiable** ['nou·tə·faɪ·ə·bəl] *adj* (*disease*) que hay que notificar

**notification** [ˌnou·tə·fɪ·ˈkeɪ·ʃən] *n* notificación *f*

**notify** ['nou·tə·faɪ] <-ie-> *vt* informar; **to ~ sb of sth** notificar algo a alguien

**notion** ['nou·ʃən] *n* **1.** (*idea*) noción *f*; **to have some ~ of sth** tener algunas nociones de algo; **to have no ~ of sth** no tener ni idea de algo **2.** (*silly idea*) burrada *f*

**notional** ['nou·ʃə·nəl] *adj form* teórico, -a

**notoriety** [ˌnou·tə·ˈraɪ·ə·ti] *n* mala fama *f*

**notorious** [nou·ˈtɔr·i·əs] *adj* de mala reputación; (*thief*) bien conocido, -a; **she's a ~ liar** tiene fama de mentirosa; **to be ~ for sth** tener mala fama por algo

**notwithstanding** [ˌnat·wɪθ·ˈstæn·dɪŋ] *form* **I.** *prep* a pesar de **II.** *adv* no obstante

**nougat** ['nu·gət] *n* ≈ turrón *m*

**nought** [nɔt] *pron see* **naught**

**noun** [naʊn] *n* nombre *m*; LING sustantivo *m*

**nourish** ['nɜr·ɪʃ] *vt* alimentar

**nourishing** ['nɜr·ɪʃ·ɪŋ] *adj* nutritivo, -a; (*rich*) rico, -a

**nourishment** *n* **1.** (*food*) alimento *m* **2.** (*providing with food*) alimentación *f*

**Nova Scotia** [ˌnou·və·ˈskou·ʃə] *n* Nueva Escocia *f*

**novel**[1] ['nav·əl] *n* LIT novela *f*

**novel**[2] ['nav·əl] *adj* (*new*) novedoso, -a

**novelist** ['nav·ə·lɪst] *n* novelista *mf*

**novelty** ['nav·əl·ti] <-ies> *n* **1.** (*newness*) novedad *f* **2.** (*innovation*) innovación *f*

**November** [nou·ˈvem·bər] *n* noviembre *m*; *s. a.* **April**

**novice** ['nav·ɪs] *n* novato, -a *m, f*; REL novicio, -a *m, f*

**now** [naʊ] **I.** *adv* **1.** ahora; **just ~** ahora mismo **2.** (*currently*) actualmente **3.** (*then*) entonces; **any time ~** en cualquier momento; (**every**) **~ and then** de vez en cuando **4.** (*give emphasis*) **~, where did I put her book?** ¿se puede saber dónde he puesto su libro?; **~ we're talking!** ¡parece que empezamos a entendernos!; **~ then** ¡vamos a ver! ▸ (**it's**) **~ or never** (es) ahora o nunca **II.** *n* (*present*) presente *m*; **before ~** antes; **by ~** ahora ya; **for ~** por ahora; **as of ~** a partir de ahora **III.** *conj* **~** (**that**)... ahora que...

**nowadays** ['nau·ə·deɪz] *adv* hoy en día

**nowhere** ['nou·hwer] *adv* en ninguna parte; **to appear out of ~** aparecer de la nada; **to be going ~** *a. fig* no llevar a ninguna parte

**noxious** ['nak·ʃəs] *adj form* nocivo, -a; (*very unpleasant*) desagradable

**nozzle** ['naz·əl] *n* tobera *f*; (*of a gas pump*) inyector *m*; (*of a gun*) boquilla *f*

**NT** *abbr of* **Northwest Territories** Northwest Territories (Canadá)

**nuance** ['nu·ans] *n* matiz *m*

**nub** [nʌb] *n* **1.** (*point*) quid *m* **2.** (*piece*) trozo *m*

**nubile** ['nu·bɪl] *adj* núbil

**nuclear** ['nu·kli·ər] *adj* nuclear

**nucleic acid** [nu·ˈkli·ɪk·æs·ɪd] *n* ácido *m* nucleico

**nucleus** ['nu·kli·əs] <-ei *or* -es> *n* núcleo *m*

**nude** [nud] *adj* desnudo, -a

**nudge** [nʌdʒ] **I.** *vt* dar un codazo a; *fig* empujar **II.** *n* (*push*) codazo *m*

**nudism** ['nu·dɪz·əm] *n* nudismo *m*

**nudist** ['nu·dɪst] *adj* nudista

**nudity** ['nu·də·ti] *n* desnudez *f*

**nugget** ['nʌg·ɪt] *n* MIN pepita *f*

**nuisance** ['nu·səns] *n* molestia *f*

**nuke** [nuk, njuk] *vt sl* **1.** MIL bombardear

con armas atómicas **2.** (*cook*) cocinar en el microondas

**null** [nʌl] *adj* nulo, -a; **~ and void** sin efecto

**nullification** [ˌnʌl·ɪ·fɪ·ˈkeɪ·ʃən] *n* anulación *f*

**nullify** [ˈnʌl·ɪ·faɪ] <-ie-> *vt* anular

**numb** [nʌm] **I.** *adj* entumecido, -a; **to go ~** entumecerse **II.** *vt* entumecer; (*desensitize*) insensibilizar

**number** [ˈnʌm·bər] **I.** *n* **1.** MATH número *m*; (*symbol*) cifra *f*; **telephone ~** número de teléfono **2.** (*amount*) cantidad *f*; (**a**) **small/large ~(s) (of children)** (una) pequeña/gran cantidad (de niños); **for a ~ of reasons** por una serie de razones; **to be 3 in ~** ser 3; **to be few in ~** ser pocos **3.** PUBL, MUS, THEAT número *m* ▶ **to be (the) ~ one** ser el mejor **II.** *vt* **1.** (*assign a number to*) poner número a; **to ~ sth from... to...** numerar algo del... al... **2.** (*count*) contar **3.** (*amount to*) sumar; **each group ~s 10 members** cada grupo tiene 10 miembros

**numbering** *n* numeración *f*

**numberless** *adj* innumerable

**numbness** [ˈnʌm·nɪs] *n* **1.** (*on part of body*) entumecimiento *m* **2.** (*lack of feeling*) insensibilidad *f*

**numeracy** [ˈnu·mər·ə·si] *n* capacidad *f* para la aritmética

**numeral** [ˈnu·mər·əl] *n* número *m*

**numeration** [ˌnu·mə·ˈreɪ·ʃən] *n form* numeración *f*

**numerical** [nu·ˈmer·ɪ·kəl] *adj* numérico, -a; **in ~ order** por orden numérico

**numeric keypad** [nu·ˌmer·ɪk·ˈki·pæd] *n* COMPUT teclado *m* numérico

**numerous** [ˈnu·mər·əs] *adj* numeroso, -a

**nun** [nʌn] *n* monja *f*

**nunnery** [ˈnʌn·ə·ri] <-ies> *n* convento *m* de monjas

**nuptial** [ˈnʌp·ʃəl] *adj* nupcial

**nurse** [nɜrs] **I.** *n* **1.** MED enfermero, -a *m, f* **2.** (*nanny*) niñera *f*; (*wet nurse*) nodriza *f* **II.** *vt* **1.** (*care for*) cuidar **2.** (*nurture*) nutrir **3.** (*harbor*) abrigar **4.** (*breastfeed*) amamantar **III.** *vi* dar de mamar

**nursery** [ˈnɜr·sə·ri] <-ies> *n* (*school*) guardería *f*

**nursery rhyme** *n* canción *f* infantil

**nursery school** *n* parvulario *m*, jardín *m* de infancia

**nursing I.** *n* enfermería *f* **II.** *adj* de enfermería

**nurture** [ˈnɜr·tʃər] **I.** *vt* alimentar; (*a plant*) cuidar **II.** *n* nutrición *f*

**nut** [nʌt] *n* **1.** BOT nuez *f* **2.** TECH tuerca *f* **3.** *sl* (*madman*) chiflado, -a *m, f*; (*enthusiast*) entusiasta *mf*

**nutcracker** [ˈnʌt·ˌkræk·ər] *n* cascanueces *m inv*

**nuthatch** <-es> *n* trepatroncos *m inv*

**nuthouse** <-s> *n sl* manicomio *m*

**nutmeg** *n* nuez *f* moscada

**nutrient** [ˈnu·tri·ənt] **I.** *n* nutriente *m* **II.** *adj* nutritivo, -a

**nutrition** [nu·ˈtrɪʃ·ən] *n* nutrición *f*

**nutritionist** [nu·ˈtrɪʃ·ə·nɪst] *n* nutricionista *mf*

**nutritious** [nu·ˈtrɪʃ·əs] *adj*, **nutritive** [ˈnu·trɪ·ʧɪv] *adj* nutritivo, -a

**nuts** [nʌts] **I.** *npl vulg* cojones *mpl* **II.** *adj* **to be ~** estar chiflado; **to go ~** volverse loco

**nutshell** [ˈnʌt·ʃel] *n* cáscara *f* de nuez ▶ **in a ~** en resumidas cuentas

**nutty** [ˈnʌt·i] <-ier, -iest> *adj* **1.** (*cake*) con nueces; (*flavor*) de nuez **2.** *sl* (*crazy*) chiflado, -a; **to be (as) ~ as a fruit-cake** estar más loco que una cabra

**nuzzle** [ˈnʌz·əl] **I.** *vt* acariciar con el hocico **II.** *vi* acurrucarse; **to ~ closer** arrimarse

**NV** [nə·ˈva·də] *abbr of* **Nevada** Nevada *f*

**NW** *abbr of* **northwest** NO *m*

**NY** [ˌnu·ˈjɔrk] *abbr of* **New York** Nueva York *f*

**nylon** [ˈnaɪ·lən] *n* nailon *m*

**nymph** [nɪmf] *n* ninfa *f*

**nymphomaniac** [ˌnɪm·fou·ˈmeɪ·ni·æk] *n* ninfómana *f*

# O

**O, o** [oʊ] *n* **1.** (*letter*) O, o *f*; **~ as in Oscar** O de Oviedo **2.** (*zero*) cero *m*

**oak** [oʊk] n (tree, wood) roble m

**oar** [ɔr] n remo m

**oarsman** ['ɔrz·mən] <-men> n remero m

**oarswoman** ['ɔrz·wʊm·ən] <-women> n remera f

**oasis** [oʊ·'eɪ·sɪs] <-es> n oasis m inv

**oath** [oʊθ] n juramento m; **under** ~ bajo juramento

**oats** [oʊts] npl avena f

**obedience** [oʊ·'bi·di·əns] n obediencia f

**obedient** [oʊ·'bi·di·ənt] adj obediente

**obese** [oʊ·'bis] adj obeso, -a

**obesity** [oʊ·'bi·sə·ti] n obesidad f

**obey** [oʊ·'beɪ] vt (person) obedecer; (order, the law) cumplir

**object¹** ['ab·dʒɪkt] n 1. (unspecified thing) objeto m 2. (purpose, goal) propósito m, objetivo m; **the** ~ **of the exercise is...** el objeto del ejercicio es... 3. (obstacle) **money is no** ~ el dinero no importa 4. LING complemento m

**object²** [əb·'dʒekt] I. vi oponerse II. vt objetar; **to** ~ **that...** objetar que...

**objection** [əb·'dʒek·ʃən] n objeción f; **to raise** ~**s to sth** protestar contra algo

**objective** [əb·'dʒek·tɪv] I. n objetivo m II. adj objetivo, -a

**objector** n objetor(a) m(f)

**obligation** [ab·lə·'geɪ·ʃən] n obligación f; **to be under an** ~ **to do sth** tener la obligación de hacer algo

**oblige** [ə·'blaɪdʒ] vt 1. (force) obligar 2. (perform service for) hacer un favor a

**obliging** [ə·'blaɪ·dʒɪŋ] adj servicial, comedido, -a AmL

**oblivion** [ə·'blɪv·i·ən] n olvido m; **to fall into** ~ caer en el olvido

**oblivious** [ə·'blɪv·i·əs] adj inconsciente; ~ **of sth** inconsciente de algo

**oblong** ['ab·lɑŋ] adj rectangular, oblongo, -a

**obnoxious** [əb·'nak·ʃəs] adj detestable

**obscene** [əb·'sin] adj (indecent) obsceno, -a

**obscenity** [əb·'sen·ə·ti] <-ies> n obscenidad f, indecencia f

**obscure** [əb·'skjʊr] I. adj oscuro, -a II. vt 1. (from vision) oscurecer 2. (from understanding) complicar

**observant** [əb·'zɜr·vənt] adj observador(a); (of one's duty) cumplidor(a)

**observation** [ab·zər·'veɪ·ʃən] n 1. (act of seeing) observación f; LAW vigilancia f; **to keep sth/sb under** ~ vigilar algo/a alguien; **under** ~ MED en observación 2. (remark) comentario m, observación f

**observation tower** n atalaya f

**observatory** [əb·'zɜr·və·tɔr·i] n observatorio m

**observe** [əb·'zɜrv] vt 1. (watch closely) observar; (notice) observar; **to** ~ **sb doing sth** ver a alguien haciendo algo 2. (remark) comentar 3. (obey: rules) observar; (silence, religious holiday) guardar

**observer** [əb·'zɜr·vər] n observador(a) m(f)

**obsess** [əb·'ses] vt obsesionar; **to be** ~**ed by sb/sth** obsesionarse por alguien/algo

**obsession** [əb·'sef·ən] n obsesión f

**obsessive** [əb·'ses·ɪv] adj obsesivo, -a

**obsolete** [ab·sə·'lit] adj obsoleto, -a

**obstacle** ['ab·stə·kəl] n obstáculo m; **an insurmountable** ~ un obstáculo insalvable; **to overcome an** ~ superar un obstáculo

**obstinate** ['ab·stə·nɪt] adj obstinado, -a

**obstruct** [əb·'strʌkt] vt 1. (block) obstruir; (traffic) bloquear; (view) tapar 2. (hinder: progress) obstaculizar

**obstruction** [əb·'strʌk·ʃən] n 1. (action) a. MED, POL obstrucción f 2. (impediment) obstáculo m

**obstructive** [əb·'strʌk·tɪv] adj (tactic, attitude) obstruccionista; (person) que pone obstáculos

**obtain** [əb·'teɪn] vt obtener; **to** ~ **sth from sb/sth** obtener algo de alguien/algo

**obtainable** [əb·'teɪ·nə·bəl] adj que se puede conseguir

**obtrusive** [əb·'tru·sɪv] adj form (question, presence) inoportuno, -a; (noise) molesto, -a; (color, design) (demasiado) llamativo, -a

**obtuse** [ab·'tus] adj obtuso, -a

**obvious** ['ab·vi·əs] adj obvio, -a; **for** ~

**reasons** por razones obvias; **it is ~ to me that...** me doy perfecta cuenta de que...; **to make sth ~ to sb** hacer algo patente a alguien

**obviously** *adv* obviamente, claramente; **~,...** como es lógico,...

**occasion** [ə·'keɪ·ʒən] *n* **1.** (*particular time*) ocasión *f;* **on ~** de vez en cuando; **on one ~** en una ocasión; **on several ~s** en varias ocasiones **2.** (*event*) acontecimiento *m;* **on the ~ of...** con motivo de... **3.** (*reason*) motivo *m;* **to give ~ to sth** dar lugar a algo **4.** (*opportunity*) ocasión; **should the ~ arise** si se presenta la ocasión

**occasional** [ə·'keɪ·ʒə·nəl] *adj* ocasional; **I smoke an ~ cigarette** fumo un cigarrillo de vez en cuando

**occasionally** *adv* ocasionalmente, de vez en cuando

**Occident** ['ɑk·sə·dənt] *n* **the ~** Occidente

**occidental** [ˌɑk·sə·'den·təl] *adj* occidental

**occupancy rate** *n* tasa *f* de ocupación

**occupant** ['ɑk·jə·pənt] *n form* **1.** (*of building, vehicle*) ocupante *mf;* (*tenant*) inquilino, -a *m, f* **2.** (*of post*) titular *mf*

**occupation** [ˌɑk·jə·'peɪ·ʃən] *n* **1.** *a.* MIL ocupación *f* **2.** (*profession*) profesión *f* **3.** (*pastime*) pasatiempo *m*

**occupational** [ˌɑk·jə·'peɪ·ʃə·nəl] *adj* profesional

**occupier** ['ɑk·jə·paɪ·ər] *n* (*of territory, building*) ocupante *mf;* (*tenant*) inquilino, -a *m, f*

**occupy** ['ɑk·ju·paɪ] <-ie-> *vt* **1.** (*room, position*) *a.* MIL ocupar; **the bathroom's occupied** el lavabo está ocupado **2.** (*engage*) **to be occupied with sth** estar ocupado con algo; **to keep sb occupied** mantener a alguien ocupado; **to ~ oneself** entretenerse **3.** (*hold*) **to ~ a post** ocupar un cargo **4.** (*dwell in*) **to ~ a house** vivir en una casa **5.** (*employ*) dar trabajo

**occur** [ə·'kɜr] <-rr-> *vi* **1.** (*happen*) ocurrir; (*change, problem*) producirse; (*symptom*) presentarse; **to ~ once every two years** tener lugar una vez cada dos años **2.** (*come into mind*) **to ~ to**

**sb** ocurrírsele a alguien; **did it ever ~ to you that...?** ¿no se te ha ocurrido nunca que...?

**occurrence** [ə·'kɜr·əns] *n* **1.** (*event*) acontecimiento *m;* **an unexpected ~** un suceso inesperado **2.** (*case*) caso *m* **3.** (*incidence: of disease*) incidencia *f*

**ocean** ['oʊ·ʃən] *n* océano *m*

**Oceania** [ˌoʊ·ʃi·'er·ni·ə] *n* Oceanía *f*

**oceanic** [ˌoʊ·ʃi·'æn·ɪk] *adj* oceánico, -a

**o'clock** [ə·'klɑk] *adv* **it's one ~** es la una; **it's two ~** son las dos

**octagon** ['ɑk·tə·gən] *n* octógono *m*

**octane** ['ɑk·teɪn] *n* octano *m*

**octave** ['ɑk·tɪv] *n* LIT, MUS octava *f*

**October** [ɑk·'toʊ·bər] *n* octubre *m; s. a.* **April**

**octogenarian** [ˌɑk·toʊ·dʒɪ·'ner·i·ən] **I.** *adj* octogenario, -a **II.** *n* octogenario, -a *m, f*

**octopus** ['ɑk·tə·pəs] <-es *or* -pi> *n* pulpo *m*

**oculist** ['ɑk·jə·lɪst] *n* oculista *mf*

**odd** [ɑd] *adj* **1.** (*strange*) extraño, -a; **an ~ person/thing** una persona/cosa rara; **how (very) ~!** ¡qué raro!; **it is ~ that...** es raro que +*subj;* **to look ~** tener un aspecto extraño **2.** (*number*) impar **3.** (*approximately*) **30 ~ people** 30 y pico personas **4.** (*occasional*) ocasional; **at ~ times** algunas veces **5.** (*unmatched: glove, sock*) suelto, -a

**oddly** *adv* **1.** (*in a strange manner*) de forma extraña **2.** (*curiously*) curiosamente; **~ enough** por extraño que parezca

**odds** [ɑdz] *npl* (*probability*) probabilidades *fpl;* **the ~ against/in favor of sth** las probabilidades en contra/a favor de algo; **the ~ are against us** tenemos las de perder; **the ~ are in his favor** tiene todas las de ganar; **the ~ are that...** lo más seguro es que +*subj* ▶ **~ and ends** *inf* (*bits*) cosas *f pl* sueltas; **against all (the) ~** contra todo pronóstico; **to be at ~ with sb** estar en desacuerdo con alguien

**odor** ['oʊ·dər] *n* (*smell*) olor *m;* (*fragrance*) aroma *m*

**odorless** *adj form* inodoro, -a

**odyssey** ['ɑd·ɪ·si] *n* odisea *f*

**of** [əv, *stressed:* ʌv] *prep* **1.** de **2.** (*belonging to*) de; **the works ~ Twain** las obras de Twain; **a friend ~ mine/ theirs** un amigo mío/de ellos **3.** (*done by*) de; **it's kind ~ him** es amable de su parte **4.** (*representing*) de; **a drawing ~ Paul** un dibujo de Paul **5.** (*without*) **a tree bare ~ leaves** un árbol sin hojas; **free ~ charge** sin cargo; **free ~ tax** libre de impuestos; **to cure sb ~ a disease** curar a alguien de una enfermedad **6.** (*with*) **a man ~ courage** un hombre de valor; **a city ~ wide avenues** una ciudad con amplias avenidas **7.** (*away from*) **to be north ~ Atlanta** estar al norte de Atlanta **8.** (*temporal*) **the 4th ~ May** el 4 de mayo **9.** (*to*) **it is ten/ (a) quarter ~ two** son las dos menos diez/cuarto **10.** (*consisting of*) de; **a ring ~ gold** un anillo de oro; **to smell/ to taste ~ cheese** oler/saber a queso **11.** (*characteristic*) **with the patience ~ a saint** con la paciencia de un santo; **this idiot ~ a plumber** el idiota del fontanero **12.** (*concerning*) **his love ~ jazz** su amor por el jazz; **to know sb ~ sb's past** saber algo del pasado de alguien; **to approve ~ sb's idea** estar de acuerdo con la idea de alguien; **what has become ~ him?** ¿qué ha sido de él?; **what do you think ~ him?** ¿qué piensas de él? **13.** (*cause*) **because ~ sth/sb** a causa de algo/alguien; **to die ~ grief** morir de pena; **it happened ~ itself** sucedió de por sí **14.** (*a portion of*) **there's a lot ~ it** hay mucho de eso; **one ~ the best** uno de los mejores; **the best ~ friends** los mejores amigos; **many ~ them came** muchos de ellos vinieron; **there are five ~ them** hay cinco de ellos; **he knows the five ~ them** los conoce a los cinco; **two ~ the five** dos de los cinco; **he ~ all people knows that** él lo sabe mejor que nadie; **today ~ all days** precisamente hoy **15.** (*to amount of*) **80 years ~ age** 80 años de edad

**off** [ɔf] **I.** *prep* **1.** (*near*) **to be just ~ the main road** estar muy cerca de la carretera principal **2.** (*away from*) **to take sth ~ the shelf** coger algo del estante; **keep ~ the grass** prohibido pisar el césped **3.** (*down from*) **to fall/jump ~ a ladder** caer/saltar de una escalera; **to get ~ the train** bajarse del tren **4.** (*from*) **to eat ~ a plate** comer de un plato; **to cut a piece ~ the cheese** cortar un pedazo del queso; **to take 10 dollars ~ the price** rebajar 10 dólares del precio **5.** (*stop using*) **to be ~ caffeine/drugs** dejar la cafeína/las drogas **6.** (*as source of*) **to run ~ batteries** funcionar con pilas **II.** *adv* **1.** (*not on*) **to switch/turn sth ~** apagar algo; **it's ~ between them** *fig* lo han dejado **2.** (*away*) **the town is 5 miles ~ to the east** el pueblo está 8 km más al este; **not far ~** no lejos (de); **a way's ~** a bastante distancia; **to drive/ run ~** irse en coche/corriendo; **~ with him** fuera con él; **it's time I was ~** ya debería haber salido **3.** (*removed*) **the lid is ~** la tapa está fuera; **with one's coat ~** con el abrigo quitado; **~ with that hat!** ¡quítate el sombrero! **4.** (*free from work*) **to get ~ at 4:00 p.m.** salir (del trabajo) a las cuatro; **to get a day ~** tener un día libre **5.** (*completely*) **to kill ~** exterminar; **to pay sth ~** acabar de pagar **6.** COM **5% ~** 5% de descuento **7.** (*until gone*) **to walk ~ the dinner** caminar para bajar la comida; **to sleep ~ the wine** dormir el vino **8.** (*separating*) **to fence sth ~** cercar algo ▶ **straight** [*or* **right**] **~** de bat enseguida; **~ and on** on and ~ de cuando en cuando **III.** *adj* **1.** (*not on: light*) apagado, -a; (*faucet*) cerrado, -a; (*water*) cortado, -a **2.** (*canceled: engagement, wedding, deal*) suspendido, -a **3.** (*free from work*) **to be ~ at 5:00 p.m.** salir (del trabajo) a las cinco; **I'm ~ on Mondays** los lunes estoy libre **4.** (*provided for*) **to be well ~** tener dinero; **to be not well ~** andar mal de dinero **5.** (*substandard*) **to be ~ one's game** SPORTS estar en mala forma **6.** *inf* **to go ~ on sb** echar la bronca a alguien

**off-center** *adj* **1.** (*diverging from the center*) descentrado, -a **2.** (*unconventional*) poco convencional

**off chance** ['ɔf·tʃæns] *n* **on the ~** por si acaso

**off-color** [ˌɒfˈkʌl·ər] *adj* 1. (*unwell*) indispuesto, -a; **to feel ~** encontrarse mal; **to look ~** tener mala cara 2. (*in bad taste: joke*) subido, -a de tono

**off-duty** *adj* fuera de servicio

**offend** [əˈfend] I. *vi* 1. (*cause displeasure*) ofender 2. (*violate*) **to ~ against sth** atentar contra algo 3. LAW infringir la ley; (*commit a crime*) cometer un delito II. *vt* ofender; **to be ~ed by sth** ofenderse por algo

**offender** [əˈfen·dər] *n* infractor(a) *m(f)*; (*guilty of crime*) delincuente *mf*; **first ~** delincuente sin antecedentes; **previous** [*or* **repeat**] **~** reincidente *mf*

**offense** [əˈfens] *n* 1. (*crime*) delito *m*; **minor ~** infracción *f*; **traffic ~** infracción de tráfico 2. (*affront*) atentado *m*; **an ~ against sth** un atentado contra algo 3. (*upset feeling*) ofensa *f*; **to cause ~** (**to sb**) ofender (a alguien); **to take ~** (**at sth**) ofenderse (por algo); **no ~** (**intended**) *inf* sin ánimo de ofender 4. SPORTS ofensiva *f*

**offensive** [əˈfen·sɪv] I. *adj* 1. (*remark, joke*) ofensivo, -a; (*language, word*) grosero, -a; (*tone*) desagradable; **to be ~ to sb** insultar a alguien 2. (*disagreeable: smell*) repugnante II. *n* MIL ofensiva *f*; **to go on the ~** pasar a la ofensiva

**offer** [ˈɒ·fər] I. *vt* 1. (*proffer: help, advice, money*) ofrecer; **to ~ sb sth** ofrecer algo a alguien; **to ~ an apology** pedir disculpas; **can I ~ you a drink?** ¿quiere tomar algo?; **to ~ a good price for sth** ofrecer un buen precio por algo; **to ~ a reward** ofrecer una recompensa; **to ~ an explanation** dar una explicación; **to ~ shelter** dar cobijo; **to have much to ~** tener mucho que ofrecer 2. (*give: gift*) dar 3. (*volunteer*) **to ~ to do sth** ofrecerse para [*or a*] hacer algo 4. (*excuse*) presentar; (*opinion*) expresar II. *n* 1. (*proposal*) propuesta *f*; (*of help*) ofrecimiento *m*; (*of a job*) oferta *f*; **that's my last ~** es mi última oferta; **to make** [*or* **put in**] **an ~ of $1000 for sth** ofrecer 1000 dólares por algo

**offering** [ˈɒ·fər·ɪŋ] *n* 1. (*thing given*) ofrecimiento *m* 2. (*contribution*) donativo *m* 3. REL (*sacrifice*) ofrenda *f*

**offhand** [ˌɒfˈhænd] I. *adj* 1. (*without previous thought*) improvisado, -a; **an ~ remark** una observación que no viene al caso 2. (*uninterested*) brusco, -a; **to be ~ about sth** pasar (de algo) *inf* II. *adv* de improviso; **to judge sb/sth** juzgar algo/a alguien a la ligera; **~, I'd say...** así de pronto, yo diría...

**office** [ˈɒ·fɪs] *n* 1. (*of a company*) oficina *f*; (*room in house*) despacho *m*; **they've got ~s in Los Angeles and Miami** tienen oficinas en Los Ángeles y Miami; **to stay at the ~** quedarse en la oficina; **doctor's ~** consultorio *m*; **lawyer's ~** bufete *m* 2. POL (*authoritative position*) cargo *m*; **to hold ~** ocupar un cargo; **to be in ~** (*person*) estar en funciones; (*party*) estar en el poder; **to be out of ~** haber dejado el cargo; **to take ~** entrar en funciones 3. REL oficio *m*

**office building** *n* bloque *m* de oficinas

**office hours** *npl* horas *f pl* de oficina

**officer** [ˈɒ·fɪ·sər] *n* 1. MIL oficial *mf* 2. (*policeman*) policía *mf*; **police ~** agente *mf* de policía 3. (*in organization*) directivo, -a *m, f*; (*in political party*) dirigente *mf* 4. (*official*) funcionario, -a *m, f*

**office staff** *n* personal *m* de oficina

**office supplies** *npl* artículos *m pl* de oficina

**office worker** *n* oficinista *mf*

**official** [əˈfɪʃ·əl] I. *n* 1. POL oficial *mf* 2. (*civil servant*) funcionario, -a *m, f* II. *adj* oficial

**officially** [əˈfɪʃ·ə·li] *adv* oficialmente

**off-key** MUS I. *adv* **to play/sing ~** desafinar II. *adj* desafinado, -a

**off-limits** *adj* fuera de los límites (permitidos)

**offline** [ˌɒfˈlaɪn] *adj* COMPUT sin conexión

**off-peak** [ˌɒfˈpik] *adj* (*fare, rate*) fuera de las horas punta

**off-putting** [ˈɒfˌpʊt·ɪŋ] *adj* 1. (*smell, manner, appearance, person*) desagradable 2. (*experience*) desalentador(a)

**off-road vehicle** *n* vehículo todoterreno *m*

**off-season** [ˈɒfˌsi·zən] *n* temporada *f* baja

**offset** [ˈɒf·set] I. *n* 1. (*compensation*) compensación *f* 2. BOT vástago *m*

**II.** <offset, offset> *vt* (*compensate*) compensar

**offshore** [ˌɔfˈʃɔr] **I.** *adj* **1.** (*from the shore: breeze, wind*) terral **2.** (*at sea*) a poca distancia de la costa; ~ **fishing** pesca de bajura; ~ **oilfield** yacimiento *m* petrolífero marítimo **3.** (*in foreign country*) en el exterior **II.** *adv* mar adentro; **to anchor** ~ anclar a cierta distancia de la costa

**offside** [ˌɔfˈsaɪd] SPORTS **I.** *n* fuera de juego *m* **II.** *adj* en fuera de juego

**offspring** [ˈɔfsprɪŋ] *n inv* **1.** (*animal young*) cría *f* **2.** *pl* (*children*) prole *f*

**off-white** [ˌɔfˈhwaɪt] *adj* de color hueso

**often** [ˈɔfən] *adv* a menudo; **we ~ go there** solemos ir allí; **as ~ as** siempre que; **as ~ as not** la mitad de las veces; **every so ~** alguna que otra vez; **how ~?** ¿cuántas veces?; **more ~ ~ that...** no es frecuente que +*subj*; **more ~ than not** la mayoría de las veces

**oh** [oʊ] *interj* **1.** oh; ~ **dear!** ¡Dios mío!; ~ **no!** ¡ay, no!; ~ **well** bueno; ~ **yes?** ¿ah, sí? **2.** (*by the way*) ah

**OH** [oʊˈhaɪˌoʊ] *n abbr of* **Ohio** Ohio *m*

**oil** [ɔɪl] **I.** *n* **1.** (*lubricant*) aceite *m*; **sunflower** ~ aceite de girasol **2.** (*petroleum*) petróleo *m*; **to strike** ~ encontrar petróleo **3.** (*grease*) grasa *f* **II.** *vt* engrasar

**oil field** *n* yacimiento *m* petrolífero

**oil level** *n* TECH nivel *m* de aceite

**oil painting** *n* óleo *m*

**oil pipeline** *n* oleoducto *m*

**oil-producing** *adj* productor(a) de petróleo

**oil production** *n* producción *f* de petróleo

**oil rig** *n* plataforma *f* petrolífera

**oilskin** *n* **1.** (*cloth*) hule *m* **2.** ~**s** (*clothing*) impermeable *m*

**oil slick** *n* marea *f* negra

**oil tanker** *n* NAUT petrolero *m*

**oil well** *n* pozo *m* de petróleo

**oily** [ˈɔɪli] <-ier, -iest> *adj* **1.** (*oil-like*) oleoso, -a **2.** (*greasy: hands*) grasiento, -a; (*food*) aceitoso, -a; (*skin, hair*) graso, -a

**ointment** [ˈɔɪntˌmənt] *n* MED pomada *f*

**OK¹, okay** [ˌoʊˈkeɪ] *inf* **I.** *adj* **1.** (*acceptable*) **is it ~ with you if...?** ¿te importa si...?; **it's ~ with me** por mí no hay problema **2.** (*not bad*) **to be ~** no estar mal **II.** *interj* vale *inf*, okey *AmL inf*, órale *Méx* **III.** <OKed, okayed> *vt* **to ~ sth** dar el visto bueno a algo **IV.** *n* visto bueno *m*; **to give** (**sb/sth**) **the** ~ dar (a alguien/algo) el visto bueno **V.** *adv* bastante bien

**OK²** [ˌoʊ-klə-ˈhoʊ-mə] *n abbr of* **Oklahoma** Oklahoma *f*

**old** [oʊld] **I.** *adj* **1.** (*not young*) viejo, -a; ~ **people** la gente mayor; **to grow** ~**er** envejecer **2.** (*not new*) viejo, -a; (*food*) pasado, -a; (*wine*) añejo, -a; (*furniture, house*) antiguo, -a **3.** (*denoting an age*) **how ~ are you?** ¿cuántos años tienes?; **he's five years** ~ tiene cinco años; **she's three years** ~**er than I** me lleva tres años **4.** (*former: job, partner*) antiguo, -a **5.** (*of long standing*) de siempre; ~ **friend** viejo amigo; **the same** ~ **faces** las mismas caras de siempre **II.** *n* (*elderly people*) **the** ~ los viejos, los ancianos *AmL*; **young and** ~ grandes y chicos

**old age** *n* vejez *f*; **to reach** ~ llegar a viejo

**old-fashioned** [ˌoʊldˈfæʃˌənd] *adj pej* **1.** (*not modern: clothes*) pasado, -a de moda; (*views*) anticuado, -a **2.** (*traditional*) tradicional

**old school** *adj* de la vieja escuela

**olive** [ˈɑlɪv] *n* **1.** (*fruit*) oliva *f*, aceituna *f* **2.** (*tree*) olivo *m*

**Olympic** [oʊˈlɪmˌpɪk] *adj* olímpico, -a; **the Olympic Games** SPORTS los Juegos Olímpicos

**omelet(te)** [ˈɑmˌlət] *n* tortilla *f*

**omen** [ˈoʊˌmen] *n* indicio *m*, augurio *m*

**omission** [oʊˈmɪʃˌən] *n* omisión *f*

**omit** [oʊˈmɪt] <-tt-> *vt* (*person, information*) omitir; **to ~ any reference to sb/sth** evitar toda referencia a alguien/algo

**omnivorous** [ɑmˈnɪvˌərˌəs] *adj* omnívoro, -a

**on** [ɑn] **I.** *prep* **1.** (*place*) sobre, en; ~ **the table** sobre la mesa; ~ **the wall** en la pared; **to be ~ the plane** estar en el avión; **to hang ~ a branch** colgar de una rama; **to have** sth ~ **one's mind** *fig* tener algo en mente **2.** (*by means of*) to go ~ **the train** ir en tren; **to go** ~ **foot** ir a pie; **to keep a dog** ~ **a leash** llevar (a) un perro con correa **3.** (*source of*) con; **to run** ~ **gas** funcionar con gasolina; **to live** ~ **$2,000 a month** vivir con 2.000 dólares al mes **4.** MED **to be** ~ **drugs** tomar medicamentos **5.** (*spatial*) ~ **the right/left** a la derecha/izquierda; ~ **the corner/back of** sth en la esquina/la parte posterior de algo; **a house** ~ **the river** una casa junto al río **6.** (*temporal*) ~ **Sunday** el domingo; ~ **Sundays** los domingos; **at 2:00 p.m.** ~ **the dot** a las dos en punto de la tarde **7.** (*at time of*) **to leave** ~ **time** salir a tiempo; ~ **her arrival** a su llegada; ~ **arriving there** al llegar allí; **to finish** ~ **schedule** acabar puntualmente **8.** (*about*) sobre; **a lecture** ~ **Shakespeare** una conferencia sobre Shakespeare; **to compliment sb** ~ sth felicitar a alguien por algo; **to be there** ~ **business** estar ahí por negocios **9.** (*through medium of*) ~ **TV/video/CD** en televisión/vídeo/CD; **to speak** ~ **the radio/the phone** hablar en la radio/por teléfono; **to work** ~ **a computer** trabajar con un ordenador; **to play** sth ~ **the flute** tocar algo con la flauta **10.** (*with basis in*) ~ **the principle that** en el supuesto de que; **to do** sth ~ **purpose** hacer algo a propósito **11.** (*in state of*) ~ **sale** en venta; **to set** sth ~ **fire** prender fuego a algo; **to go** ~ **vacation/a trip** ir de vacaciones/de viaje; ~ **the whole** en general **12.** (*involved in*) **to work** ~ **a project** trabajar en un proyecto; **to be** ~ **page 10** estar en la página 10; **two** ~ **each side** dos en [*or* a] cada lado **13.** (*because of*) ~ **account of** sth/sb a causa de algo/alguien; **to depend** ~ sb/sth depender de alguien/algo **14.** (*against*) **to turn** ~ sb volverse contra alguien; **to cheat** ~ sb hacer trampa [*or* engañar] a alguien **15.** (*paid by*) **to buy** sth ~ **credit** comprar algo a crédito; **this is** ~ **me** *inf* esto corre por mi cuenta **II.** *adv* **1.** (*covering one's body*) **to put a hat** ~ ponerse un sombrero; **to have** sth ~

llevar algo (puesto); **to try** ~ sth probarse algo **2.** (*connected to* sth) **to screw** sth ~ enroscar algo **3.** (*aboard*) **to get** ~ **a train** subir a un tren; **to get** ~ **a horse** montarse en un caballo **4.** (*not stopping*) **to keep** ~ **doing** sth seguir haciendo algo; **to get** ~ **with** sth ponerse a hacer algo **5.** (*in forward direction*) hacia delante; **to move** ~ avanzar; **to urge sb** ~ *fig* animar a alguien; **from that day** ~ desde aquel día; **later** ~ más tarde; **and so** ~ y así sucesivamente **6.** (*in operation*) **to turn** ~ encender; (*tap*) abrir **7.** (*performing*) en escena; **to go** ~ salir a escena ▶ ~ **and off** de vez en cuando; ~ **and** ~ sin parar **III.** *adj* **1.** (*functioning: light*) encendido, -a; (*faucet*) abierto, -a; (*brake*) puesto, -a; **to leave the light** ~ dejar la luz encendida **2.** (*scheduled*) **what's** ~ **at the movies this week?** ¿qué dan en el cine esta semana? **3.** THEAT (*performing*) **to be** ~ estar en escena; (*performing well*) hacerlo muy bien **4.** (*job*) **to be** ~ **duty** estar de servicio; (*doctor*) estar de guardia **5.** (*good: day*) bueno, -a **6.** (*acceptable*) **you're** ~! ¡de acuerdo!

**once** [wʌns] **I.** *adv* **1.** (*one time*) una vez; ~ **a week** una vez por [*or* a la] semana; ~ **in a lifetime** una vez en la vida; (*every*) ~ **in a while** de vez en cuando; ~ **again** de nuevo; ~ **and for all** de una vez por todas; **just for** ~ sólo una vez; ~ **more** (*one more time*) otra vez; (*again, as before*) una vez más; ~ **or twice** una o dos veces; **at** ~ (*simultaneously*) al mismo tiempo; (*immediately*) en seguida **2.** *liter* (*at one time past*) hace tiempo; ~ **upon a time there was...** *liter* érase una vez... **II.** *conj* una vez que +*subj*; **but** ~ **I'd arrived,...** pero una vez que llegué... ▶ **at** ~ en seguida

**oncoming** ['ɒnˌkʌm·ɪŋ] *adj* que se aproxima; (*traffic, vehicle*) que viene en dirección contraria

**one** [wʌn] **I.** *n* (*number*) uno *m* ▶ (**all**) **in** ~ todo en uno; **as** ~ *form* a la vez; **in** ~ de una sola pieza **II.** *adj* **1.** *numeral* un, uno, -a; ~ **hundred** cien; **it's** ~ **o'clock** es la una; **as** ~ **man** todos a

O

una; **~ man out of** [*or* **in**] **two** uno de cada dos hombres **2.** *indef* un, uno, -a; **we'll meet ~ day** nos veremos un día de estos; **~ winter night** una noche de invierno **3.** (*sole*) único, -a; **her ~ and only hope** su única esperanza **4.** (*single*) mismo, -a, único, -a; **all files on the ~ disk** todos los archivos en un único disco **III.** *pron pers* **1.** *impers, no pl* **what can ~ do?** ¿qué puede hacer uno?; **to wash ~'s face** lavarse la cara **2.** (*person*) **no ~** nadie; **every ~** cada uno; **the little ~s** los pequeños; **the ~ who...** el que...; **I for ~** al menos yo **3.** (*particular thing or person*) **any ~** cualquiera; **this ~** éste; **which ~?** ¿cuál de ellos?; **the ~ on the table** el que está en la mesa; **the thinner ~** el más fino

**one-armed** [ˌwʌnˈɑːrmd] *adj* manco, -a

**one-eyed** [ˌwʌnˈaɪd] *adj* tuerto, -a

**one-handed I.** *adv* con una sola mano **II.** *adj* manco, -a

**one-night stand** [ˌwʌnˈnaɪtˈstænd] *n sl* (*relationship*) ligue *m* de una noche

**one-piece** (**swimsuit**) [ˈwʌnˈpiːs] *n* bañador *m*

**oneself** [wʌnˈself] *pron reflexive* **1.** se *emphatic* sí (mismo, misma); **to deceive ~** engañarse a sí mismo; **to express ~** expresarse **2.** (*same person*) uno mismo

**one-sided** [ˌwʌnˈsaɪdɪd] *adj* (*contest*) desigual; (*decision*) unilateral; (*view, account*) parcial

**one-way street** [ˌwʌnˈweɪˈstrɪt] *n* calle *f* de sentido único

**one-way ticket** *n* billete *m* sencillo

**ongoing** [ˈɑnˌgoʊɪŋ] *adj* en curso

**onion** [ˈʌnjən] *n* cebolla *f*

**online** *adj, adv* COMPUT en línea

**onlooker** [ˈɑnˌlʊkər] *n* espectador(a) *m(f)*; **there were many ~s at the accident site** había muchos curiosos en el lugar del accidente

**only** [ˈoʊnli] **I.** *adj* único, -a; **the ~ glass he had** el único vaso que tenía; **the ~ way of doing sth** la única manera de hacer algo; **I'm not the ~ one** no soy el único; **the ~ thing is...** la única cosa es... **II.** *adv* sólo, nomás *AmL*; **not ~... but also** no sólo... sino también; **I can ~**

**say...** sólo puedo decir...; **he has ~ two** sólo tiene dos; **~ Paul can do it** sólo Paul puede hacerlo; **I've ~ just eaten** acabo de comer ahora mismo **III.** *conj inf* sólo que

**onset** [ˈɑnset] *n* comienzo *m*; (*of winter*) llegada *f*; (*of illness*) aparición *f*

**onside** [ˈɑnˈsaɪd] *adj* SPORTS **to be ~** (*player*) estar en posición correcta

**onto** [ˈɑntu] *prep*, **on to** *prep* **1.** (*in direction of*) sobre; **to put sth ~ the chair** poner algo sobre la silla; **to step ~ the road** pisar la calzada; **to come ~ a subject** tocar un tema **2.** (*connected to*) **to hold ~ sb's arm** aferrarse al brazo de alguien; **to be ~ sb** ver a alguien su juego

**onward** [ˈɑnwərd] **I.** *adj* hacia delante **II.** *adv* hacia delante; **from today ~** de hoy en adelante

**oops** [ups] *interj inf* ¡huy!

**ooze** [uz] *vi* **1.** (*seep out*) exudar; **to ~ with sth** rezumar algo **2.** *fig* (*be full of*) rebosar

**open** [ˈoʊpən] **I.** *adj* **1.** (*not closed*) abierto, -a; **wide ~** completamente abierto; **to push sth ~** abrir algo de un empujón **2.** (*undecided*) sin concretar; **to keep one's options ~** dejar abiertas todas las alternativas **3.** (*not secret, public: scandal*) público, -a; (*hostility*) abierto, -a, manifiesto, -a; **to be an ~ book** *fig* ser un libro abierto; **an ~ secret** una cosa sabida **4.** (*unfolded: map*) desplegado, -a **5.** (*frank: person*) abierto, -a; **to welcome sb with ~ arms** recibir a alguien con los brazos abiertos **6.** (*accessible to all*) abierto, -a; (*discussion*) abierto, -a al público; (*session*) a puertas abiertas; (*trial*) público, -a **7.** (*willing to listen to new ideas*) abierto, -a de mente; **to have an ~ mind** tener una actitud abierta **8.** (*still available: job*) vacante **II.** *n* **1.** (*outdoors, outside*) (**out**) **in the ~** al aire libre **2.** (*not secret*) **to get sth** (**out**) **in the ~** sacar algo a la luz **III.** *vi* **1.** (*door, window, box*) abrirse **2.** (*shop*) abrir **IV.** *vt* **1.** (*door, box, shop*) abrir; **to ~ the door to sth** *fig* abrir la puerta a algo; **to ~ sb's eyes** (**to sb/sth**) *fig* abrir a alguien los ojos (sobre alguien/algo); **to ~ fire (on sb)** abrir fuego (contra alguien) **2.** (*reveal feelings*) **to ~ one's heart to sb** abrir su corazón a alguien

◆**open up I.** *vi* **1.** (*unfold*) abrirse **2.** (*shop*) abrir **3.** (*become wider*) ensancharse **II.** *vt* abrir; (*map*) desplegar

**open-air** [ˌoʊ·pən·'er] *adj* al aire libre

**open-ended** [ˌoʊ·pən·'en·dɪd] *adj* (*contract*) de duración indefinida; (*question*) abierto, -a

**opener** ['oʊ·pə·nər] *n* abridor *m*, destapador *m AmL*; **bottle ~** abrebotellas *m inv*; **can ~** abrelatas *m inv*

**opening** ['oʊ·pə·nɪŋ] *n* **1.** (*gap, hole*) abertura *f*; (*in forest*) claro *m* **2.** (*job opportunity*) vacante *f* **3.** (*beginning*) apertura *f*; (*of book, film*) principio *m* **4.** (*ceremony*) inauguración *f*; (*new play, film*) estreno *m*

**opening balance** *n* FIN saldo *m* de apertura

**opening bid** *n* oferta *f* inicial

**opening night** *n* THEAT noche *f* del estreno

**openly** ['oʊ·pən·li] *adv* **1.** (*frankly*) honestamente **2.** (*publicly*) abiertamente

**open-minded** [ˌoʊ·pən·'maɪn·dɪd] *adj* (*accessible to new ideas*) de actitud abierta

**openness** ['oʊ·pən·nəs] *n* franqueza *f*

**open-source** *adj* de software libre

**opera** ['ɑp·rə] *n* ópera *f*

**operate** ['ɑp·ə·reɪt] **I.** *vi* **1.** (*work, run*) funcionar **2.** (*have or produce an effect*) actuar, surtir efecto **3.** (*perform surgery*) operar (**on** a) **4.** (*be in business*) operar **II.** *vt* **1.** (*work*) manejar **2.** (*run, manage*) llevar, tener

**operating** ['ɑp·ə·reɪ·tɪŋ] *adj* **1.** ECON (*profit, costs*) de explotación **2.** TECH (*speed*) de funcionamiento **3.** MED de operaciones; **~ room** quirófano *m*

**operation** [ˌɑp·ə·'reɪ·ʃən] *n* **1.** (*way of working*) funcionamiento *m;* **to be in ~** estar en funcionamiento; **to come into ~** (*machines*) entrar en funcionamiento **2.** *a.* MED, MIL, MATH operación *f*

**operational** [ˌɑp·ə·'reɪ·ʃə·nəl] *adj* **1.** (*relating to operations*) operativo, -a **2.** (*working*) **to be ~** estar en funcio-

namiento

**operative** ['ɑp·ər·ə·tɪv] **I.** *n* (*worker*) operario, -a *m, f* **II.** *adj* **1.** (*rules*) en vigor **2.** MED quirúrgico

**operator** ['ɑp·ə·reɪ·tər] *n* **1.** (*person*) operador(a) *m(f);* TEL telefonista *mf;* **machine ~** maquinista *mf* **2.** (*company*) empresa *f;* **a tour ~** un(a) agente de viajes

**opinion** [ə·'pɪn·jən] *n* opinión *f*

**opinionated** [ə·'pɪn·jə·neɪ·tɪd] *adj pej* dogmático, -a

**opinion poll** *n* encuesta *f* de opinión

**opium** ['oʊ·pi·əm] *n* opio *m*

**opponent** [ə·'poʊ·nənt] *n* **1.** POL opositor(a) *m(f)* **2.** SPORTS contrincante *mf,* rival *mf*

**opportunity** [ˌɑp·ər·'tu·nə·ti] <-ies> *n* oportunidad *f*

**oppose** [ə·'poʊz] *vt* **1.** (*be against*) oponerse a **2.** (*resist*) combatir

**opposed** *adj* opuesto, -a; **to be ~ to sth** oponerse a algo, estar en contra de algo

**opposing** *adj* contrario, -a

**opposite** ['ɑp·ə·zɪt] **I.** *n* contrario *m;* **quite the ~!** ¡todo lo contrario! ▶ **~s attract** los extremos se atraen **II.** *adj* **1.** (*absolutely different*) contrario, -a; **the ~ sex** el sexo opuesto **2.** (*facing*) de enfrente; **~ to sth** enfrente de algo **III.** *adv* (*facing*) enfrente; **they live ~** viven enfrente **IV.** *prep* enfrente de, frente a; **~ to sth** enfrente de algo; **~ me** frente a mí; **to sit ~ one another** estar sentados uno enfrente al otro

**opposition** [ˌɑp·ə·'zɪʃ·ən] *n* **1.** POL oposición *f* **2.** (*contrast*) contraposición *f* (**to** a) **3.** (*opponent*) adversario, -a *m, f;* ECON competencia *f*

**oppression** [ə·'preʃ·ən] *n* **1.** (*submission*) opresión *f* **2.** (*feeling*) agobio *m*

**oppressive** [ə·'pres·ɪv] *adj* **1.** (*harsh: regime, measures*) opresivo, -a **2.** (*burdensome*) agobiante

**opt** [ɑpt] *vi* optar (**for** por)

**optic** ['ɑp·tɪk] *adj* óptico, -a

**optical** ['ɑp·tɪ·kəl] *adj* óptico, -a

**optician** [ɑp·'tɪʃ·ən] *n* MED óptico, -a *m, f*

**optics** ['ɑp·tɪks] *n* óptica *f*

**optimism** ['ɑp·tə·mɪz·əm] *n* optimismo *m*

**optimist** ['ap·tə·mɪst] *n* optimista *mf*

**optimistic** [,ap·tə·'mɪs·tɪk] *adj* optimista

**optimum** ['ap·tə·məm] *adj* óptimo, -a

**option** ['ap·ʃən] *n* 1. (*choice*) *a.* ECON opción *f* 2. (*possibility*) posibilidad *f*

**optional** ['ap·ʃə·nəl] *adj* opcional; (*subject*) optativo, -a

**or** [ɔr] *conj* o; (*before o, ho*) u; (*between numbers*) ó; **seven ~ eight** siete u ocho; **6 ~ 7** 6 ó 7; **either... ~...** o... o...; **to ask whether ~ not sb is coming** preguntar si alguien viene o no; **I can't read ~ write** no sé leer ni escribir

**OR** *n* 1. *abbr of* **operating room** quirófano *m*, sala *f* de operaciones 2. *abbr of* **Oregon** Oregón *m*

**oracle** ['ɔr·ə·kəl] *n* oráculo *m*

**oral** ['ɔr·əl] *adj* oral

**orange** ['ɔr·ɪndʒ] I. *n* naranja *f* II. *adj* naranja

**orangeade** [,ɔr·ɪndʒ·'eɪd] *n* naranjada *f*

**orange juice** *n* zumo *m* de naranja

**orange peel** *n* cáscara *f* de naranja

**orange tree** *n* naranjo *m*

**orbit** ['ɔr·bɪt] I. *n* 1. ASTR órbita *f*; **to go into ~** entrar en órbita 2. (*range of action, field*) campo *m* de influencia II. *vt* orbitar alrededor de

**orbital** ['ɔr·bɪ·ʈəl] *adj* orbital; **~ trajectory** trayectoria *f* orbital

**orchard** ['ɔr·tʃərd] *n* huerto *m*

**orchestra** ['ɔr·kɪ·strə] *n* orquesta *f*

**orchestral** [ɔr·'kes·trəl] *adj* orquestal

**orchestra pit** *n* foso *m* orquestal

**orchid** ['ɔr·kɪd] *n* orquídea *f*

**ordeal** [ɔr·'dil] *n* calvario *m*

**order** ['ɔr·dər] I. *n* 1. (*sequence*) orden *m*; **to put sth in ~** poner en orden algo; **in alphabetical ~** por orden alfabético 2. (*instruction*) *a.* LAW, REL orden *f*; **to give/receive an ~** dar/recibir una orden; **by ~ of sb** por orden de alguien 3. (*working condition, satisfactory arrangement*) orden *m*; **to keep ~** mantener el orden; **the car is in perfect working ~** el coche funciona perfectamente bien; **to be out of ~** no funcionar; (*toilet*) estar fuera de servicio; **are your immigration papers in ~?** ¿tienes los papeles de inmigración en regla? 4. (*appropriate behavior*) out

of **~** improcedente 5. (*purpose*) **in ~ (not) to** para (no) +*infin*; **in ~ for, in ~ that** para que +*subj* 6. COM pedido *m*; **to put in an ~ for sth** hacer un pedido de (*or* encargar) algo; **made to ~** hecho por encargo II. *vi* pedir; **are you ready to ~?** ¿ya han decidido qué van a pedir? III. *vt* 1. (*command*) **~ sb to do sth** ordenar a alguien que haga algo; **to ~ sb out** echar a alguien 2. (*request goods or service*) encargar 3. (*arrange*) ordenar, poner en orden

**order form** *n* hoja *f* de pedidos

**orderly** ['ɔr·dər·li] <-ies> I. *n* 1. (*hospital attendant*) celador(a) *m(f)* 2. MIL ordenanza *mf* II. *adj* 1. (*tidy*) ordenado, -a 2. (*well-behaved*) disciplinado, -a

**ordinal (number)** ['ɔr·də·nəl] *n* ordinal *m*

**ordinary** ['ɔr·də·ner·i] I. *n* **out of the ~** fuera de lo común II. *adj* normal, corriente; **in the ~ way...** normalmente...

**ordnance** ['ɔrd·nəns] *n* artillería *f*

**ore** [ɔr] *n* mena *f*; **iron ~** mineral *m* de hierro

**Oregon** ['ɔr·ɪ·gən] *n* Oregón *m*

**organ** ['ɔr·gən] *n* órgano *m*

**organ donor** *n* donante *mf* de órganos

**organic** [ɔr·'gæn·ɪk] *adj* 1. (*disease, substance, compound*) orgánico, -a 2. (*produce, farming method*) biológico, -a 3. (*fundamental: part*) inherente 4. (*systematic: change*) sistemático, -a

**organism** ['ɔr·gə·nɪz·əm] *n* organismo *m*

**organist** ['ɔr·gə·nɪst] *n* organista *mf*

**organization** [,ɔr·gə·nɪ·'zeɪ·ʃən] *n* organización *f*

**organizational** [,ɔr·gə·nɪ·'zeɪ·ʃə·nəl] *adj* organizativo, -a

**organize** ['ɔr·gə·naɪz] I. *vt* organizar II. *vi* organizarse

**organizer** *n* 1. (*person*) organizador(a) *m(f)* 2. COMPUT agenda *f* electrónica

**orgasm** ['ɔr·gæz·əm] *n* orgasmo *m*

**orgy** ['ɔr·dʒi] <-ies> *n* orgía *f*

**Orient** ['ɔr·i·ənt] *n* **the ~** (el) Oriente

**oriental** [,ɔr·i·'en·tal] *adj* oriental

**orientation** [,ɔr·i·en·'teɪ·ʃən] *n* orientación f

**origin** ['ɔr·ə·dʒɪn] n origen m

**original** [ə·'rɪdʒ·ɪ·nəl] I. n original m II. adj 1. (new, unusual) original 2. (first) originario, -a

**originality** [ə·ˌrɪdʒ·ɪ·'næl·ə·t̬i] n originalidad f

**originally** [ə·'rɪdʒ·ɪ·nə·li] adv 1. (initially) originariamente 2. (unusually) con originalidad

**originate** [ə·'rɪdʒ·ɪ·neɪt] I. vi originarse II. vt crear

**ornament** ['ɔr·nə·mənt] n adorno m

**ornamental** [ˌɔr·nə·'men·t̬əl] adj ornamental, decorativo, -a

**ornithology** [ˌɔr·nə·'θal·ə·dʒi] n ornitología f

**orphan** ['ɔr·fən] n huérfano, -a m, f, guacho, -a m f Arg, Chile

**orphanage** ['ɔr·fə·nɪdʒ] n orfanato m, orfelinato m

**orthodontist** [ˌɔr·θə·'dan·tɪst] n ortodoncista mf

**orthodox** ['ɔr·θə·daks] adj ortodoxo, -a

**orthographic(al)** [ˌɔr·θə·'græf·ɪk(·əl)] adj ortográfico, -a

**orthography** [ɔr·'θag·rə·fi] n ortografía f

**ostrich** ['as·trɪtʃ] n avestruz f

**other** ['ʌð·ər] I. adj 1. (different) otro, -a 2. (remaining) **the ~ one** el otro; **the ~ three** los otros tres; **any ~ questions?** ¿alguna otra pregunta? 3. (being vague) **some ~ time** en algún otro momento; **the ~ day** el otro día; **every ~ day** un día sí y otro no II. pron 1. (people) **the ~s** los otros, los demás; **no ~ than he** form nadie excepto él 2. (different ones) **each ~** uno a(l) otro, mutuamente; **some eat, ~s drink** algunos comen, otros beben 3. **sing** (either/or) **to choose one or the ~** escoger uno u otro 4. (being vague) **someone or ~** alguien III. adv de otra manera; **somehow or ~** de una manera u otra

**otherwise** ['ʌð·ər·waɪz] I. adj form distinto, -a II. adv 1. (differently: behave, act) de otro modo 2. (in other ways) **~,...** por lo demás,... III. conj si no

**ouch** [autʃ] interj ay

**ought** [ɔt] aux 1. (have as duty) deber; **you ~ to do it** deberías hacerlo 2. (be

likely) tener que; **he ~ to be here** tendría que [or debería] estar aquí; **they ~ to win** merecerían ganar 3. (probability) **she ~ to have arrived by now** debe de haber llegado ya

**ounce** [auns] n 1. (weight) onza f (28,4 g) 2. (of decency, common sense) pizca f

**our** [aur] adj pos nuestro, -a; **~ house** nuestra casa; **~ children** nuestros hijos

**ours** [aurz] pron pos el nuestro, la nuestra; **it's not their bag, it's ~** no es su bolsa, es la nuestra; **a book of ~** un libro nuestro; **~ is bigger** el nuestro es mayor

**ourselves** [aur·'selvz] pron reflexive 1. nos emphatic nosotros mismos, nosotras mismas; **we hurt ~** nos lastimamos 2. after prep nosotros, -as (mismos, mismas)

**out** [aut] I. adj 1. (absent: person) fuera 2. (released: book, news) publicado, -a 3. BOT (in blossom) en flor 4. (visible) **the moon is ~** ha salido la luna 5. (finished) **before the week is ~** antes de que acabe la semana 6. (not functioning: fire, light) apagado, -a 7. SPORTS (out of bounds) fuera 8. (unfashionable) pasado, -a de moda 9. (not possible) **to be ~** estar descartado, ser imposible II. adv 1. (not inside) fuera, afuera; **to go ~** salir fuera; **get ~!** ¡fuera! 2. (outside) afuera; **keep ~!** prohibido el paso; **to eat ~** comer fuera 3. (remove) **to cross ~ words** tachar palabras; **to get a stain ~** sacar una mancha; **to put ~ a fire** apagar un fuego 4. (away) **to be ~** (person) no estar; **to be ~ at sea** estar mar adentro; **the tide is going ~** la marea está bajando 5. (unconscious) **to pass ~** perder el conocimiento; **to be ~ cold** estar fuera de combate ▶ **to be ~ and about** (on the road) estar en camino; (healthy) estar repuesto; **~ with it!** ¡desembucha! III. prep 1. (towards outside) **~ of** fuera de; **to go ~ of the room** salir de la habitación; **to take sth ~ of a box** sacar algo de una caja; **to look ~ of the window** mirar por la ventana 2. (outside from) **~ of sight/ of reach** fuera de vista/de alcance; **to**

O

**drink ~ of a glass** beber de un vaso; **to be ~ of it** estar en otra onda *inf* **3.** (*away from*) **to be ~ of town/the country** estar fuera de la ciudad/del país; **to get ~ of the rain** resguardarse de la lluvia; **~ of the way!** ¡quita de en medio! **4.** (*without*) **to be ~ of money/work** estar sin dinero/trabajo; **~ of breath** sin aliento; **~ of order** averiado, -a; **his dog is ~ of control** su perro está fuera de control **5.** (*from*) **made ~ of wood/steel** hecho de madera/acero; **to copy sth ~ of a file** copiar algo de un archivo; **to get sth ~ of sb** sacar algo a alguien; **in 3 cases ~ of 10** en 3 de cada 10 casos **6.** (*because of*) **to do sth ~ of politeness** hacer algo por cortesía

**outboard (motor)** ['aʊt·bɔrd] *n* fueraborda *m*

**outbreak** ['aʊt·breɪk] *n* (*of the flu, violence*) brote *m*; (*of war*) estallido *m*

**outburst** ['aʊt·bɜrst] *n* arrebato *m*

**outcast** ['aʊt·kæst] *n* paria *mf*; **social ~** marginado, -a *m, f* de la sociedad

**outclass** [,aʊt·'klæs] *vt* superar, aventajar

**outcome** ['aʊt·kʌm] *n* **1.** (*result*) resultado *m* **2.** (*consequence*) consecuencia *f*

**outcry** ['aʊt·kraɪ] <-ies> *n* gran protesta *f*

**outdated** [aʊt·'deɪ·tɪd] *adj* anticuado, -a, pasado, -a de moda

**outdo** [aʊt·'du] *vt irr* superar, mejorar; **to ~ sb in sth** superar a alguien en algo; **to ~ oneself** mejorarse

**outdoor** ['aʊt·'dɔr] *adj* al aire libre; (*clothing*) de calle; (*plants*) de exterior

**outer** ['aʊ·tər] *adj* exterior; **~ ear** oído *m* externo

**outermost** ['aʊ·tər·moʊst] *n* más exterior

**outfit** ['aʊt·fɪt] *n* **1.** (*clothing*) conjunto *m* **2.** (*team*) equipo *m*

**outgoing** ['aʊt·goʊ·ɪŋ] *adj* **1.** (*sociable*) sociable, extrovertido, -a **2.** (*departing: president*) saliente

**outgrow** [aʊt·'groʊ] *vt irr* **1.** (*become bigger than*) crecer más que; **she's ~n her pants** se le han quedado pequeños los pantalones **2.** (*habit*) pasar de la edad de

**outing** ['aʊ·tɪŋ] *n* excursión *f*

**outlast** [,aʊt·'læst] *vt* **to ~ sth** durar más que algo; **to ~ sb** sobrevivir a alguien

**outlaw** ['aʊt·lɔ] **I.** *n* forajido, -a *m, f* **II.** *vt* (*product, practice*) prohibir; (*person*) proscribir

**outlet** ['aʊt·let] *n* **1.** ECON punto *m* de venta; **retail ~** tienda *f* al por menor **2.** (*means of expression*) válvula *f* de escape **3.** (*vent: for air*) respiradero *m*; (*for water*) desagüe *m* **4.** ELEC toma *f* de corriente

**outline** ['aʊt·laɪn] **I.** *n* **1.** (*draft*) esbozo *m* **2.** (*shape*) perfil *m* **3.** (*general description*) resumen *m* **II.** *vt* **1.** (*draw outer line of*) perfilar **2.** (*describe*) describir a grandes trazos; (*summarize*) resumir

**outlive** [,aʊt·'lɪv] *vt* sobrevivir a

**outlook** ['aʊt·lʊk] *n* **1.** (*prospects*) perspectivas *fpl* **2.** (*attitude*) punto *m* de vista **3.** (*view*) vista *f*

**outnumber** [,aʊt·'nʌm·bər] *vt* superar en número a

**out-of-date** [,aʊt·əv·'deɪt] *adj* anticuado, -a

**out-of-the-way** [,aʊt·əv·ðə·'weɪ] *adj* apartado, -a

**outplay** [,aʊt·'pleɪ] *vt* jugar mejor que

**output** ['aʊt·pʊt] *n* ECON producción *f*; (*of machine*) rendimiento *m*

**output device** *n* COMPUT dispositivo *m* de salida

**outrage** ['aʊt·reɪdʒ] **I.** *n* **1.** (*atrocity*) atrocidad *f* **2.** (*scandal*) escándalo *m* **II.** *vt* (*offend*) ultrajar

**outrageous** [aʊt·'reɪ·dʒəs] *adj* **1.** (*shocking: behavior*) escandaloso, -a; (*person*) atrevido, -a **2.** (*cruel, violent*) atroz

**outright** ['aʊt·raɪt] **I.** *adj* (*disaster, defeat*) total; (*winner*) indiscutible **II.** *adv* **1.** (*defeat, ignore*) totalmente; (*win*) indiscutiblemente **2.** (*declare, ask*) descaradamente

**outset** ['aʊt·set] *n* principio *m*

**outshine** [,aʊt·'ʃaɪn] *vt irr* eclipsar

**outside** [aʊt·'saɪd] **I.** *adj* **1.** (*external*) externo, -a, exterior; (*world*) exterior; **the ~ door** la puerta exterior **2.** (*not likely*) **an ~ chance that...** una posibilidad remota de que... +*subj* **3.** (*extreme*) extremo, -a **II.** *n* **1.** (*external* part or side) exterior m; **judging from the ~** a juzgar por el aspecto exterior **2.** (at most) **at the ~** a lo más **III.** prep **1.** (not within) fuera de; **to wait ~ the door** esperar en la puerta; **~ business hours** fuera de horas de oficina **2.** (besides) además de **IV.** adv (outdoors) fuera, afuera; **to go ~** salir fuera; **to go ~ the house** salir de casa; **to live an hour ~ Detroit** vivir a una hora de Detroit

**outsider** [ˌaʊtˈsaɪ·dər] n (person not from a group) persona f de fuera

**outskirts** [ˈaʊtˈskɜrts] npl afueras fpl; **on the ~** en las afueras

**outsourcing** [ˈaʊtˌsɔrˈsɪŋ] n externalización f

**outstanding** [ˌaʊtˈstæn·dɪŋ] adj **1.** (excellent) destacado, -a **2.** FIN (debt) pendiente (de pago) **3.** (unsolved) por resolver

**outstretched** [ˌaʊtˈstretʃt] adj extendido, -a

**outthink** [ˌaʊtˈθɪŋk] irr vt ser más listo que

**outward** [ˈaʊt·wərd] **I.** adj **1.** (visible: indication) externo, -a **2.** (exterior: appearance, beauty) exterior **3.** (apparent: similarities, differences) aparente **II.** adv hacia fuera

**outwardly** [ˈaʊt·wərd·li] adv aparentemente

**outwards** [ˈaʊt·wərdz] adv hacia fuera

**oval** [ˈoʊ·vəl] **I.** n óvalo m **II.** adj ovalado, -a, oval

**Oval Office** n the ~ el despacho oval

**ovary** [ˈoʊ·və·ri] <-ies> n ovario m

**ovation** [oʊ·ˈveɪ·ʃən] n ovación f

**oven** [ˈʌv·ən] n horno m

**ovenproof** [ˈʌv·ən·pruf] adj refractario, -a

**oven-ready** [ˌʌv·ən·ˈred·i] adj listo, -a para hornear

**over** [ˈoʊ·vər] **I.** prep **1.** (above) encima de, por encima de; **the bridge ~ the freeway** el puente sobre la autopista; **to fly ~ the sea** volar sobre el mar **2.** (on) **to drive ~ sth** arrollar algo; **to spread a cloth ~ the table** extender un mantel sobre la mesa **3.** (across) **to go ~ the bridge** cruzar el puente; **the house ~ the road** la casa de enfrente; **it rained**

all ~ **New England** llovió por toda Nueva Inglaterra **4.** (behind) **to look ~ sb's shoulder** mirar por encima del hombro de alguien **5.** (during) durante; **~ the winter** durante el invierno; **~ time** con el tiempo; **~ a two-year period** durante un período de dos años **6.** (more than) **to speak for ~ an hour** hablar más de una hora; **~ 150** más de 150; **children ~ 14** niños mayores de 14 (años); **~ and above that** además de eso **7.** (through) **I heard it ~ the radio** lo oí por la radio; **to hear sth ~ the noise** escuchar algo a pesar del ruido; **what came ~ him?** ¿qué le picó? inf **8.** (in superiority to) **to have command ~ sth** tener mando sobre algo; **to have an advantage ~ sb** tener ventaja sobre alguien **9.** (about) **~ sth** acerca de algo **10.** (for checking) **to go ~ a text** revisar un texto; **to watch ~ a child** cuidar a un niño **11.** (past) **to be ~ the worst** haber pasado lo peor **12.** MATH **4 ~ 12 equals a third** 4 entre 12 es igual a un tercio **II.** adv **1.** (moving above: go, jump) por encima; **to fly ~ the city** sobrevolar la ciudad **2.** (at a distance) **to move sth ~** apartar algo; **~ here** acá; **~ there** allá; **~ the road** cruzando la calle **3.** (moving across) **to come ~ here** venir para acá; **to go ~ there** ir para allá; **he has flown ~ to Europe** se ha ido a Europa; **he swam ~ to me** nadó hacia mí; **he went ~ to the enemy** fig se cambió al bando enemigo **4.** (on a visit) **come ~ tonight** pásate por aquí esta noche **5.** (changing hands) **to pass/hand sth ~** pasar/dar algo **6.** (downwards) **to fall ~** caerse; **to knock sth ~** tirar algo **7.** (another way up) **to turn the page ~** pasar la página **8.** (in exchange) **to change ~** intercambiar **9.** (completely) **to look for sb all ~** buscar a alguien por todos lados; **to think sth ~** pensar algo (detalladamente) **10.** (again) **to count them ~ again** contarlos otra vez; **I repeated it ~ and ~** lo repetí una y otra vez; **to do sth all ~** hacer algo desde el principio **11.** (more) **children 14 and ~** niños de 14 años en adelante **12.** RADIO, AVIAT **~** cambio; **~ and out** cambio y corto

O

III. *adj* 1. (*finished*) acabado, -a; **it's all ~** se acabó; **the snow is ~** se acabó la nieve 2. (*remaining*) restante; **there are three left ~** quedan tres

**overall** ['ou·vər·ɔl] I. *adj* 1. (*general*) global 2. (*above all others*) total; **~ winner** campeón absoluto II. *adv* en conjunto III. *n* ~s mono *m;* **a pair of ~s** un peto

**overboard** ['ou·vər·bɔrd] *adv* al agua; **to fall ~** caer al agua; **man ~!** ¡hombre al agua!; **to go ~** *inf* exagerar

**overbook** [ˌou·vər·'buk] *vt* sobrecontratar, sobrevender *Col*

**overcast** ['ou·vər·kæst] *adj* nublado, -a

**overcharge** [ˌou·vər·'tʃardʒ] *vi* cobrar de más

**overcoat** ['ou·vər·kout] *n* abrigo *m*

**overcome** [ˌou·vər·'kʌm] *irr* I. *vt* 1. (*defeat*) vencer 2. (*cope with*) superar II. *vi irr* vencer; **we shall ~** venceremos

**overconfident** [ˌou·vər·'kan·fə·dənt] *adj* demasiado seguro, -a de sí mismo, -a

**overcrowded** [ˌou·vər·'krau·dɪd] *adj* abarrotado, -a

**overdo** [ˌou·vər·'du] *vt* 1. **to ~ things** pasarse; (*work too hard*) trabajar demasiado 2. *inf* (*exaggerate*) exagerar

**overdone** [ˌou·vər·'dʌn] *adj* (*overexaggerated*) exagerado, -a

**overdose** ['ou·vər·dous] *n* sobredosis *f inv*

**overdraft** ['ou·vər·dræft] *n* FIN descubierto *m*

**overdraw** [ˌou·vər·'drɔ] *irr vi, vt* girar en descubierto

**overdue** [ˌou·vər·'du] *adj* 1. (*late*) atrasado, -a; **to be ~** llevar retraso 2. FIN (*debt*) pendiente (de pago)

**overestimate¹** [ˌou·vər·'es·tɪ·mɪt] *n* sobreestimación *f*

**overestimate²** [ˌou·vər·'es·tə·meɪt] *vt* sobreestimar

**overexcited** [ˌou·vər·ɪk·'saɪ·tɪd] *adj* sobreexcitado, -a

**overflow** [ˌou·vər·'flou] I. *n* (*excess: of liquid, people*) exceso *m* II. *vi* rebosar; (*river*) desbordarse

**overgrown** [ˌou·vər·'groun] *adj* (*garden*) abandonado, -a

**overhang** [ˌou·vər·'hæn] *irr* I. *n* (*cliff*) saliente *m;* ARCHIT alero *m* II. *vt* **to ~ sth** sobresalir por encima de algo

**overhead** [ˌou·vər·'hed] I. *n* gastos *m pl* generales II. *adj* de arriba, encima de la cabeza; **~ cable** cable *m* aéreo; **~ light** luz *f* de techo

**overhear** [ˌou·vər·'hɪr] *irr vt* oír por casualidad

**overheat** [ˌou·vər·'hit] I. *vt* sobrecalentar II. *vi* recalentarse

**overjoyed** [ˌou·vər·'dʒɔɪd] *adj* encantado, -a

**overland** ['ou·vər·lænd] *adj* terrestre; **~ vehicle** vehículo *m* todoterreno; **by ~ mail** por vía terrestre

**overlap** ['ou·vər·læp] *n* superposición *f*

**overleaf** ['ou·vər·lif] *adv* al dorso

**overload¹** ['ou·vər·loud] *n* 1. ELEC sobrecarga *f* 2. (*of work*) exceso *m*

**overload²** [ˌou·vər·'loud] *vt* ELEC sobrecargar; **to be ~ed with sth** *fig* estar agobiado de algo

**overlook** [ˌou·vər·'luk] I. *n* vista *f* II. *vt* 1. (*look out onto*) tener vistas a 2. (*not notice*) pasar por alto 3. (*forget*) olvidar

**overnight** [ˌou·vər·'naɪt] I. *adj* de noche *f;* **~ stay** estancia *f* de una noche; **~ delivery** envío *m* para la mañana siguiente II. *adv* durante la noche; **to stay ~** pasar la noche

**overpass** ['ou·vər·pæs] *n* paso *m* elevado

**overpay** [ˌou·vər·'peɪ] *irr vt* pagar de más

**overpopulated** [ˌou·vər·'pap·jə·leɪ·tɪd] *adj* superpoblado, -a

**overpower** [ˌou·vər·'pau·ər] *vt* dominar

**overpowering** [ˌou·vər·'pau·ər·ɪŋ] *adj* (*person, attack*) abrumador(a); (*taste, smell*) muy fuerte

**overrate** [ˌou·vər·'reɪt] *vt* sobrevalorar

**overreact** [ˌou·vər·ri·'ækt] *vi* reaccionar de forma exagerada

**overreaction** [ˌou·vər·ri·'æk·ʃən] *n* reacción *f* exagerada

**override** [ˌou·vər·'raɪd] I. *n* anulación *f* de automatismo II. *vt* 1. (*not accept*) anular 2. (*interrupt*) cancelar

**overriding** [ˌou·vər·'raɪ·dɪŋ] *adj* primordial

**overrule** [ˌouˑvərˈrul] *vt* anular; **to ~ an objection** LAW rechazar una objeción

**overrun** [ˌouˑvərˈrʌn] **I.** *vt irr* **1.** (*invade*) invadir; **to be ~ with sth** estar plagado de algo **2.** (*budget*) exceder **II.** *vi irr* prolongarse más de lo previsto

**overseas** [ˌouˑvərˈsiz] **I.** *adj* extranjero, -a; (*trade*) exterior **II.** *adv* **to go/travel ~** ir/viajar al extranjero

**oversee** [ˌouˑvərˈsi] *irr vt* supervisar

**overshadow** [ˌouˑvərˈʃædˑou] *vt* **1.** (*cast shadow over*) ensombrecer **2.** (*make insignificant*) eclipsar

**oversight** [ˈouˑvərˈsaɪt] *n* **1.** (*omission*) descuido *m* **2.** (*supervision*) supervisión *f*

**oversleep** [ˌouˑvərˈslip] *irr vi* quedarse dormido

**overspend** [ˌouˑvərˈspend] *vi* gastar demasiado

**overstaffed** [ˌouˑvərˈstæft] *adj* con exceso de personal

**overstay** [ˌouˑvərˈsteɪ] *vt* **to ~ one's welcome** quedarse más de lo conveniente

**overstep** [ˌouˑvərˈstep] *irr vt* sobrepasar
▶ **to ~ the mark** pasarse de la raya

**overtake** [ˌouˑvərˈteɪk] *irr* **I.** *vt* **1.** AUTO adelantar **2.** (*in contest*) superar **II.** *vi* adelantar

**overthrow** [ˌouˑvərˈθrou] **I.** *n* POL derrocamiento *m* **II.** *vt irr* POL derrocar

**overtime** [ˈouˑvərˈtaɪm] *n* **1.** (*work*) horas *f pl* extra **2.** SPORTS prórroga *f*

**overturn** [ˌouˑvərˈtɜrn] **I.** *vi* volcar, voltearse *AmL* **II.** *vt* volcar; POL derrumbar

**overview** [ˈouˑvərˈvju] *n* perspectiva *f* general

**overweight** [ˌouˑvərˈweɪt] *adj* **to be ~** pesar más de la cuenta

**overwhelm** [ˌouˑvərˈwelm] *vt* **1.** (*overcome by force*) abrumar, sobrecoger **2.** (*swamp*) inundar

**overwhelming** [ˌouˑvərˈwelˑmɪŋ] *adj* abrumador(a); **~ grief** dolor inconsolable

**overwork** [ˌouˑvərˈwɜrk] **I.** *n* agotamiento *m* **II.** *vi* trabajar demasiado

**ovum** [ˈouˑvəm] <ova> *n* óvulo *m*

**owe** [ou] **I.** *vt* deber **II.** *vi* tener deudas

**owing** [ˈouˑɪŋ] *adj* por pagar

**owing to** *prep* debido a

**owl** [aul] *n* búho *m*, tecolote *m AmC, Méx*; **barn ~** lechuza *f*

**own** [oun] **I.** *adj* propio, -a; **with one's ~ eyes** con sus propios ojos ▶ **in one's ~ right** por derecho propio; **to do one's ~ thing** ir a su aire; **in one's ~ time** en su tiempo libre; **to hold one's ~** mantenerse firme **II.** *vt* poseer ▶ **as if one ~ed the place** como Pedro por su casa
◆**own up** *vi* confesar

**owner** [ˈouˑnər] *n* propietario, -a *m, f*

**ownership** [ˈouˑnərˈʃɪp] *n* posesión *f*; **to be under private ~** ser de propiedad privada

**ox** [aks] <-en> *n* buey *m*

**oxidize** [ˈakˑsɪˈdaɪz] **I.** *vi* oxidarse **II.** *vt* oxidar

**oxygen** [ˈakˑsɪˈdʒən] *n* oxígeno *m*

**oyster** [ˈɔɪˈstər] *n* ostra *f*

**oz** *n abbr of* **ounce** onza *f (28,4 g)*

**ozone** [ˈouˑzoun] *n* ozono *m*

**ozone layer** *n* capa *f* de ozono

# P

**P, p** [pi] <-'s> *n* P, p *f*; **~ as in Papa** P de París

**p** *abbr of* **page** pág. *f*

**pa** [pa] *n inf* papá *m*

**PA** *n abbr of* **Pennsylvania** Pensilvania *f*

**p.a.** [ˌpiˑˈeɪ] *abbr of* **per annum** por año

**pace** [peɪs] **I.** *n* **1.** (*speed*) velocidad *f*; **to set the ~** marcar el ritmo; **to keep ~ with sth** avanzar al mismo ritmo que algo; **to keep up/stand the ~** llevar/mantener el ritmo **2.** (*step*) paso *m*; **to quicken one's ~** acelerar el paso **II.** <pacing> *vt* **1.** (*walk up and down*) pasearse por **2.** (*measure in strides*) medir a pasos

**pacemaker** [ˈpeɪsˈmeɪˈkər] *n* MED marcapasos *m inv*

**Pacific** [pəˈsɪfˈɪk] **I.** *n* **the ~** el Pacífico; **the ~ Ocean** el Océano Pacífico **II.** *adj* del Pacífico

**pacifier** [ˈpæsˑəˈfaɪˈər] *n* (*for baby*) chupete *m*

**pacifist** ['pæs·ə·fɪst] *adj, n* pacifista *mf*

**pacify** ['pæs·ə·faɪ] <-ie-> *vt* 1. (*establish peace*) pacificar 2. (*calm*) calmar

**pack** [pæk] I. *n* 1. (*bundle*) fardo *m;* (*backpack*) mochila *f;* (*packet*) paquete *m;* (*of cigarettes*) cajetilla *f* 2. (*group*) grupo *m;* (*of wolves, hounds*) manada *f; inf* (*of lies*) montón *m,* sarta *f* II. *vi* (*luggage*) hacer las maletas III. *vt* 1. (*fill: box, train*) llenar 2. (*wrap*) envasar; (*put in packages*) empaquetar; **to ~ one's suitcase** hacer la maleta

◆**pack in** I. *vt* 1. (*put in*) meter 2. *inf* (*stop*) dejar; **pack it in!** ¡déjalo! 3. (*attract audience*) captar II. *vi* apiñar

◆**pack off** *vt inf* **to pack sb off** deshacerse de alguien

◆**pack up** I. *vt* 1. (*put away*) guardar 2. *inf* (*finish*) terminar II. *vi inf* (*stop work*) dejar de trabajar

**package** ['pæk·ɪdʒ] *n* paquete *m;* **software ~** paquete de software II. *vt* (*pack*) empaquetar

**package deal** *n* acuerdo *m* global con concesiones mutuas

**packaging** *n* 1. (*wrapping*) embalaje *m* 2. (*action*) envasado *m*

**packet** ['pæk·ɪt] *n* 1. (*parcel*) paquete *m;* (*of cigarettes*) cajetilla *f* 2. *inf* (*money*) dineral *m*

**packing** *n* (*action, material*) embalaje *m*

**pad¹** [pæd] I. *n* 1. (*cushion*) almohadilla *f;* **knee ~** rodillera *f;* **mouse ~** COMPUT alfombrilla *f* (del ratón); **shin ~** espinillera *f;* **shoulder ~** hombrera *f* 2. (*of paper*) bloc *m* II. <-dd-> *vt* 1. acolchar 2. (*inflate: the budget*) inflar

**pad²** [pæd] <-dd-> *vi* (*walk*) andar silenciosamente

**padded** *adj* acolchado, -a

**padding** *n a. fig* relleno *m*

**paddle** ['pæd·əl] I. *n* 1. (*type of oar*) canalete *m* 2. (*act of paddling*) chapoteo *m* II. *vt* 1. (*row*) remar 2. (*spank*) zurrar III. *vi* (*row*) remar

**padlock** ['pæd·lak] *n* candado *m*

**page¹** [peɪdʒ] *n* (*in book*) a. COMPUT página *f;* **front ~** primera plana *f*

**page²** [peɪdʒ] I. *n* 1. (*of knight*) paje *m* 2. (*in hotel*) botones *m inv* II. *vt* (*by pager*) llamar (a alguien) al busca

**page layout** *n* diseño *m* de página

**pager** ['peɪ·dʒər] *n* busca *m*

**paid** [peɪd] I. *pt, pp of* **pay** II. *adj* pagado, -a

**pain** [peɪn] *n* 1. dolor *m;* **to be in ~** estar sufriendo; **I have a ~ in my foot** me duele el pie 2. **~s** (*great care*) gran cuidado *m;* **to be at ~s to do sth** esmerarse en hacer algo ▶ *inf* **to be a ~ in the backside** [*or vulg* **ass**] ser un plomo

**painful** ['peɪn·fəl] *adj* 1. (*physically*) doloroso, -a 2. (*emotionally*) angustioso, -a

**painkiller** ['peɪn·ˌkɪl·ər] *n* analgésico *m*

**painless** ['peɪn·lɪs] *adj* 1. (*not painful*) indoloro, -a 2. *fig* (*easy*) fácil

**painstaking** ['peɪnz·ˌteɪ·kɪŋ] *adj* (*research*) laborioso, -a; (*search*) exhaustivo, -a

**paint** [peɪnt] I. *n* pintura *f* II. *vi* pintar III. *vt* pintar

**paintbrush** <-es> *n* (*for pictures*) pincel *m;* (*for walls*) brocha *f*

**painter** ['peɪn·tər] *n* pintor(a) *m(f)*

**painting** *n* 1. (*painted picture*) cuadro *m* 2. (*art*) pintura *f*

**paint stripper** *n* quitapintura *m*

**pair** [per] I. *n* 1. (*things*) par *m* (**of** de); **a ~ of glasses** unas gafas; **a ~ of scissors** unas tijeras; **a ~ of pants** un pantalón 2. (*people, animals*) pareja *f;* **in ~s** de dos en dos II. *vi* aparearse

**pajamas** [pə·'dʒɑ·məz] *npl* pijama *m;* **in** (**one's**) **~** en pijama

**Pakistan** ['pæk·ɪ·stæn] *n* Paquistán *m*

**Pakistani** I. *n* paquistaní *mf* II. *adj* paquistaní

**pal** [pæl] *n inf* 1. (*friend*) amigo, -a *m, f* 2. (*form of address*) tío, -a *m, f,* colega *mf*

**palace** ['pæl·əs] *n* palacio *m*

**palate** ['pæl·ət] *n* paladar *m*

**pale** [peɪl] I. *adj* 1. (*lacking color*) pálido, -a; **to look ~** tener mal color 2. (*not dark*) claro, -a II. *vi* palidecer

**paleness** ['peɪl·nɪs] *n* palidez *f*

**paleontology** [ˌper·li·an·'tal·ə·dʒi] *n* paleontología *f*

**Palestine** ['pæl·ə·staɪn] *n* Palestina *f*

**Palestinian** I. *n* palestino, -a *m, f* II. *adj*

**palestino, -a**

**palette** ['pæl·ɪt] n ART paleta f

**palm**[1] [pam] **I.** n (of hand) palma f; **to read sb's ~** leer la mano a alguien **II.** vt **1.** (hide) escamotear **2.** (steal) robar

**palm**[2] [pam] n (tree) palmera f

**◆palm off** vt **to palm sth off on sb** encajar algo a alguien; **to palm sb off with sth** apartar a alguien con algo

**palmtop** n COMPUT palmtop m

**pamper** ['pæm·pər] vt mimar

**pamphlet** ['pæm·flɪt] n folleto m; POL panfleto m

**pan**[1] [pæn] n (for cooking) cazuela f; **frying ~** sartén f

**pan**[2] [pæn] vi CINE panoramizar

**◆pan out** vi inf (develop) resultar; **to ~ well** salir bien

**Panama** ['pæn·ə·ma] n Panamá m

**Panama City** n Ciudad f de Panamá

**Panamanian** [,pæn·ə·'meɪ·ni·ən] **I.** adj panameño, -a **II.** n panameño, -a m, f

**Pan-American** ['pæn·ə·'mer·ɪ·kən] adj panamericano, -a

**pancake** ['pæn·keɪk] n crep m, panqueque m AmL

**panda** ['pæn·də] n panda m

**pane** [peɪn] n cristal m; **window ~** hoja f de cristal de una ventana

**panel** ['pæn·əl] n **1.** (wooden) tabla f; (metal) placa f **2.** FASHION paño m **3.** (of cartoon strip) tabla f **4.** (team) panel m; (in exam) tribunal m **5.** (instrument board) panel m; **instrument ~** AUTO, AVIAT cuadro m de mandos

**panel discussion** n mesa f redonda

**paneling** n paneles mpl

**panelist** ['pæn·ə·lɪst] n (in discussion) miembro mf de una mesa redonda

**panic** ['pæn·ɪk] **I.** n pánico m; **to be in a ~** estar nervioso **II.** <-ck-> vi ponerse nervioso

**panicky** ['pæn·ɪ·ki] <-ier, iest> adj (person) inquieto, -a; (feeling) de pánico

**panic-stricken** adj preso, -a del pánico

**panoramic** [,pæn·ə·'ræm·ɪk] adj panorámico, -a; **~ view** vista f panorámica

**pansy** ['pæn·zi] <-ies> n **1.** BOT pensamiento m **2.** offensive sl (wimp) nenaza f; (homosexual) maricón m

**pant** [pænt] **I.** vi jadear **II.** vt decir jadeando

**panther** ['pæn·θər] n **1.** pantera f **2.** (puma) puma m

**panties** ['pæn·tiz] npl bragas fpl

**pantomime** ['pæn·tə·maɪm] n **1.** (gestures) gestos mpl **2.** (mime) pantomima f **3.** (performer) mimo mf

**pantry** ['pæn·tri] <-ies> n despensa f

**pants** [pænts] npl **1.** (trousers) pantalones mpl **2.** (underpants) calzoncillos mpl **▸ to be caught with one's ~ down** inf ser cogido en fuera de juego

**pantsuit** n traje m pantalón (de mujer)

**pantyhose** npl medias fpl

**papal** ['peɪ·pəl] adj papal

**paper** ['peɪ·pər] **I.** n **1.** papel m; **a sheet of ~** una hoja de papel; **to put sth down on ~** poner algo por escrito; **on ~** (in writing) sobre papel; (in theory) sobre el papel **2.** (newspaper) periódico m **3.** (official document) **~s** papeles mpl **4.** (academic discourse) conferencia f; **to give a ~** dar un discurso **II.** vt (walls) empapelar

**paperback** ['peɪ·pər·bæk] n libro m de bolsillo

**paper bag** n bolsa f de papel

**paper clip** n sujetapapeles m inv, clip m

**paper cup** n vaso m de papel

**paperknife** <-knives> n abrecartas m inv

**paper mill** n fábrica f de papel

**paper money** n papel m moneda

**paper napkin** n servilleta f de papel

**paper-thin** adj fino, -a como el papel

**paperweight** n pisapapeles m inv

**paperwork** n trabajo m administrativo, papeleo m inf

**paprika** [pæ·'pri·kə] n pimentón m dulce

**par** [par] n **1.** (standard) **to be on a ~ with sb** estar al mismo nivel que alguien; **below ~** por debajo de la media; **to feel below ~** no sentirse del todo bien **2.** (in golf) par m **3.** FIN (face value) valor m nominal; **at/above/below ~** a/sobre/bajo la par

**par.** abbr of **paragraph** párrafo m

**parachute** ['pær·ə·ʃut] n paracaídas m inv

**parade** [pə·'reɪd] **I.** n desfile m **II.** vi

**desfilar III.** vt **1.** (exhibit) lucir **2.** fig (show off) ostentar; **to ~ one's knowledge** hacer alarde de erudición

**paradise** ['pær·ə·daɪs] n paraíso m

**paradox** ['pær·ə·daks] <-es> n paradoja f

**paragliding** ['pær·ə‚glaɪ·dɪŋ] n parapente m

**paragraph** ['pær·ə·græf] n LING párrafo m

**Paraguay** ['pær·ə·gwaɪ] n Paraguay m

**Paraguayan** ['pær·ə·ˈgwaɪ·ən] **I.** adj paraguayo, -a **II.** n paraguayo, -a m, f

**parallel** ['pær·ə·lel] **I.** adj a. MATH paralelo, -a (**to** a) **II.** n **1.** MATH paralela f **2.** GEO paralelo m **3.** ELEC **in ~** en paralelo **4.** (similarity) similitud f **5. without ~** sin igual

**parallel bars** npl SPORTS barras f pl paralelas

**paralysis** [pə·ˈræl·ə·sɪs] <-ses> n parálisis f inv

**paralytic** [‚pær·ə·ˈlɪt̬·ɪk] adj MED paralítico, -a

**paralyze** ['pær·ə·laɪz] vt paralizar

**paramedic** [‚pær·ə·ˈmed·ɪk] n paramédico, -a m, f

**paramilitary** [‚pær·ə·ˈmɪl·ɪ·ter·i] adj paramilitar

**paranoid** ['pær·ə·nɔɪd] adj paranoico, -a

**paraphrase** ['pær·ə·freɪz] **I.** vt parafrasear **II.** n (reformulation) paráfrasis f inv

**parasite** ['pær·ə·saɪt] n a. fig parásito m

**paratrooper** ['pær·ə‚tru·pər] n MIL paracaidista mf

**paratroops** ['pær·ə·trups] npl MIL paracaidistas mpl

**parboil** ['par·bɔɪl] vt CULIN sancochar

**parcel** ['par·səl] n **1.** (package) paquete m **2.** (of land) terreno m, parcela f

**parcel post** n servicio m de paquetería

**parched** adj **1.** (dried-out) seco, -a **2.** fig inf (thirsty) **to be ~** estar muerto de sed

**pardon** ['par·dən] **I.** vt (forgive) disculpar; (prisoner) indultar; **~ me for interrupting** siento interrumpir; (I beg your) **~?** (requesting repetition) ¿cómo dice?; **~ me!** (after interrupting) ¡perdone!; (after burping) ¡perdón!; (requesting to pass) ¡disculpe! **II.** n indulto m

**parent** ['per·ənt] n (father) padre m; (mother) madre f; **~s** padres mpl

**parental** [pə·ˈren·t̬əl] adj de los padres

**parent company** <-ies> n sociedad f matriz

**parenthesis** [pə·ˈren·θə·sɪs] <-ses> n **1.** TYPO paréntesis m inv; **in parentheses** en [or entre] paréntesis **2.** (remark) paréntesis m

**parenthood** ['per·ənt·hʊd] n (of man) paternidad f; (of woman) maternidad f

**Paris** ['pær·ɪs] n París m

**parish** ['pær·ɪʃ] <-es> n **1.** REL parroquia f **2.** (in Louisiana) condado m

**Parisian** [pə·ˈri·ʒən] n parisino, -a m, f

**parity** ['pær·ɪ·t̬i] <-ies> n paridad f

**park** [park] **I.** n **1.** parque m **2.** (stadium) **baseball ~** estadio m de béisbol **3.** AUTO (posición f de) estacionamiento m **II.** vt (vehicle) aparcar, estacionar **III.** vi aparcar, estacionar

**parking** n aparcamiento m, estacionamiento m

**parking brake** n freno m de mano

**parking fine** n multa f de aparcamiento

**parking lot** n aparcamiento m

**parking meter** n parquímetro m

**parking space** n sitio m (de aparcamiento), estacionamiento m AmL

**parking ticket** n multa f de aparcamiento

**parkway** ['park·weɪ] n avenida f ajardinada

**Parl.** abbr of **Parliament** Parlamento m

**parliament** ['par·lə·mənt] n parlamento m

**parliamentary** [‚par·lə·ˈmen·tə·ri] adj parlamentario, -a

**parlor** ['par·lər] n **1.** (store) **beauty ~** salón m de belleza; **pizza ~** pizzería f **2.** (in house) salón m

**parody** ['pær·ə·di] **I.** <-ies> n **1.** (humorous) parodia f **2.** (poor imitation) burda imitación f **II.** <-ie-> vt parodiar

**parole** [pə·ˈroʊl] **I.** n LAW libertad f condicional; **to be out on ~** estar en libertad condicional **II.** vt **to be ~d** ser puesto en libertad condicional

**parquet** [par·ˈkeɪ] n parqué m

**parrot** ['pær·ət] **I.** n loro m, papagayo m **II.** vt pej repetir como un loro

**parsley** ['pars·li] *n* perejil *m*

**parsnip** ['pars·nɪp] *n* CULIN chirivía *f*

**part** [part] **I.** *n* **1.** (*not the whole*) parte *f* (of de); **the easy/hard ~** la parte fácil/difícil; **in ~** en parte; **for the most ~** en la mayor parte **2.** (*component*) componente *m*; **spare ~s** piezas *f pl* sueltas **3.** (*area, region*) zona *f*; **in these ~s** *inf* por aquí **4.** (*in ratios, measure*) parte *f* **5.** (*role*) papel *m*; **to want no ~ in sth** no querer tener nada que ver en algo **6.** (*episode, chapter*) capítulo *m* **7.** CINE, THEAT papel *m*; **to play the ~ of the King** desempeñar el papel del rey **8.** (*in hair*) raya *f* ▶ **for my ~** por mi parte; **to take sb's ~** tomar partido por alguien; **on sb's ~** de parte de alguien **II.** *adv* parcialmente; **to be ~ African** ser en parte africano **III.** *vt* **1.** (*detach, split*) separar; **to ~ sb from sb/sth** separar a alguien de alguien/algo **2.** (*divide*) partir, dividir; **to ~ sth in two** partir algo en dos; **to ~ sb's hair** hacer la raya (del pelo) a alguien **IV.** *vi* **1.** (*separate*) separarse **2.** (*say goodbye*) despedirse

**partake** [par·'teɪk] *vi irr* **1.** (*participate*) **to ~ in sth** tomar parte en algo **2.** **to ~ of sth** (*eat*) comer algo; (*drink*) beber algo

**parted** *adj* **1.** (*opened: lips*) entreabierto, -a **2.** (*separated*) **to be ~ from sb** estar separado de alguien

**partial** ['par·ʃəl] *adj* **1.** (*incomplete*) parcial **2.** (*biased*) parcial

**partially** *adv* parcialmente, en parte

**participant** [par·'tɪs·ə·pənt] *n* participante *mf*

**participate** [par·'tɪs·ə·peɪt] *vi* participar

**participation** [par·tɪs·ə·'peɪ·ʃən] *n* participación *f*

**participle** ['par·tɪ·sɪ·pəl] *n* participio *m*

**particle** ['par·tɪ·kəl] *n* PHYS, LING partícula *f*

**particular** [pər·'tɪk·jə·lər] **I.** *adj* **1.** (*particular*) particular; **no ~ reason** ninguna razón en concreto; **in ~** en especial **2.** (*fussy, meticulous*) quisquilloso, -a; (*demanding*) exigente; **he is very ~ about his appearance** es muy maniático con su imagen **II.** *n* detalle *m*

**particularly** [pər·'tɪk·jə·lər·li] *adv* espe-cialmente, particularmente

**parting** ['par·tɪŋ] **I.** *n* **1.** (*separation*) separación *f* **2.** (*saying goodbye*) despedida *f* **II.** *adj* de despedida; **~ words** palabras *f pl* de despedida

**partisan** ['par·tɪ·zən] *n* (*supporter*) partidario, -a *m, f*

**partition** [par·'tɪʃ·ən] *n* **1.** (*wall*) tabique *m* **2.** (*of country*) división *f* **3.** COMPUT partición *f*

**partly** ['part·li] *adv* en parte, en cierto modo

**partner** ['part·nər] *n* **1.** (*companion*) compañero *m* **2.** COM socio, -a *m, f* **3.** (*in relationship, sports*) pareja *f*

**partnership** ['part·nər·ʃɪp] *n* **1.** (*association*) asociación *f* **2.** COM sociedad *f* (colectiva)

**part ownership** *n* copropiedad *f*

**part-time** [,part·'taɪm] *adj* a tiempo parcial

**part-time job** *n* empleo *m* a tiempo parcial

**part-timer** *n* (*worker*) empleado, -a *m, f* a tiempo parcial; (*student*) estudiante *mf* a tiempo parcial

**party** ['par·ti] **I.** *n* <-ies> **1.** fiesta *f*; **to have** [*or* **throw**] **a ~** hacer una fiesta **2.** + *sing/pl vb* POL partido *m*; **opposition/ruling ~** partido en la oposición/en el poder **3.** + *sing/pl vb* (*group*) grupo *m*; **to make a reservation for a ~ of two/eight** reservar una mesa para dos/ocho **4.** *a.* LAW parte *f*; **the guilty ~** la parte inculpada; **to be a ~ to sth** ser partícipe en algo **5.** *inf* (*person*) individuo *m* **II.** <-ie-> *vi* ir de fiesta

**party headquarters** *n* POL sede *f* del partido

**party line** *n* **1.** TEL línea *f* de varios abonados **2.** POL línea *f* política del partido

**party politics** *npl* política *f* de partidos

**party pooper** *n sl* aguafiestas *mf inv*

**pass** [pæs] **I.** *n* <-es> **1.** **mountain ~** puerto *m* [*or* paso *m*] de montaña **2.** (*in football, soccer*) pase *m* **3.** (*in exam, class*) aprobado *m* **4.** (*authorization*) pase *m*; (*for festival, concert*) entrada *f* **5.** (*for bus, train*) abono *m* (de transportes) **6.** SCHOOL (*permit to leave class*) permiso *m* **II.** *vt* **1.** (*go past*) pasar;

(*cross*) cruzar **2.** (*exceed: a limit*) sobrepasar **3.** (*hand to*) **to ~ sth to sb** pasar algo a alguien **4.** (*in football, soccer*) pasar **5.** (*exam, class*) aprobar **6.** POL (*bill, law*) aprobar **III.** *vi* **1.** (*move by*) pasar; **we often ~ed on the stairs** a menudo nos cruzábamos en la escalera **2.** (*come to an end*) desaparecer; **it'll soon ~** se olvidará pronto **3.** (*in exam*) aprobar **4.** (*elapse: time*) pasar, transcurrir

◆**pass away** *vi euph* (*die*) fallecer *elev*

◆**pass by** *vi* **1.** (*elapse*) pasar **2.** (*go past*) pasar de largo

◆**pass off** **I.** *vt* **1.** (*treat as unimportant*) disimular **2.** (*give appearance of*) **he tried to pass himself off as an expert** intentó hacerse pasar por experto **II.** *vi* **1.** (*take place successfully*) tener lugar **2.** (*fade away, wear off*) desaparecer

◆**pass on** *vi* **1.** (*continue moving*) seguir su camino; **to ~ to a different topic** pasar a un tema diferente **2.** (*die*) fallecer *elev* **II.** *vt* **1.** BIO (*transmit*) contagiar **2.** (*information, advice*) pasar **3.** (*refer*) **to pass sb on to sb** poner a alguien con alguien

◆**pass out** *vi* (*faint*) perder el conocimiento

◆**pass over** *vt* pasar por alto

◆**pass through** *vt* pasar por

◆**pass up** *vt* desperdiciar

**passage** ['pæs·ɪdʒ] *n* **1.** (*corridor*) pasillo *m*; (*path*) pasadizo *m* **2.** LIT, MUS pasaje *m* **3.** (*onward journey*) viaje *m* **4.** (*sea voyage*) travesía *f*

**passageway** ['pæs·ɪdʒ·weɪ] *n* pasillo *m*

**passbook** ['pæs·bʊk] *n* libreta *f* de ahorros

**passenger** ['pæs·ən·dʒər] *n* pasajero, -a *m, f*

**passenger list** *n* lista *f* de pasajeros

**passerby** [ˌpæs·ər·'baɪ] <**passersby**> *n* transeúnte *mf*

**passing** ['pæs·ɪŋ] **I.** *adj* **1.** (*going past*) que pasa **2.** (*brief: fad, infatuation*) pasajero, -a; (*glance*) rápido, -a; (*remark*) de pasada **II.** *n euph* (*death*) fallecimiento *m elev*

**passion** ['pæʃ·ən] *n* (*emotion*) pasión *f*

**passionate** ['pæʃ·ə·nɪt] *adj* (*emotional*) apasionado, -a

**passive** ['pæs·ɪv] *adj* pasivo, -a

**passport** ['pæs·pɔrt] *n* pasaporte *m*; *fig* **sb's ~ to success** su llave hacia el éxito

**password** ['pæs·wɜrd] *n* COMPUT contraseña *f*

**past** [pæst] **I.** *n* pasado *m*; **to be a thing of the ~** ser una cosa del pasado; **sb with a ~** alguien con historia; **simple ~** LING pasado *m* simple **II.** *adj* pasado, -a; **the ~ week** la semana pasada; **in ~ times** en otros tiempos; **that's ~ history** eso pertenece a la historia **III.** *prep* **1.** (*temporal*) después de; **ten/quarter/half ~ two** dos y diez/cuarto/media **2.** (*spatial*) después de **3.** (*beyond*) **to be ~ thirty** pasar de los treinta; **~ belief** increíble; **~ description** indescriptible; **I'm ~ that now** *iron* ya he superado eso **IV.** *adv* por delante; **to go/run/march ~ (sb/sth)** ir/correr/pasar por delante (de alguien/algo)

**pasta** ['pɑs·tə] *n* CULIN pasta *f*

**past continuous** *n* LING pasado *m* continuo

**paste** [peɪst] **I.** *n* pasta *f* **II.** *vt a.* COMPUT pegar

**pasteurize** ['pæs·tʃə·raɪz] *vt* pasteurizar

**past participle** *n* LING participio *m* pasado

**past perfect** *n* LING pretérito *m* perfecto

**pastry** ['peɪ·stri] <**-ies**> *n* **1.** (*dough*) masa *f* **2.** (*sweet bun*) pastel *m*

**past tense** *n* LING tiempo *m* pasado

**pasture** ['pæs·tʃər] **I.** *n* AGR pasto *m* **II.** *vt* apacentar **III.** *vi* pacer

**pasty** ['peɪ·sti] <**-ier, -iest**> *adj* (*texture*) pastoso, -a

**pat¹** [pæt] **I.** <**-tt-**> *vt* (*touch softly*) dar palmaditas a; **to ~ sb on the back** *fig* felicitar a alguien **II.** *n* **1.** (*tap*) palmadita *f* **2.** (*of butter*) porción *f*

**pat²** [pæt] *adj pej* (*answer*) fácil

**patch** [pætʃ] **I.** *n* **1.** (*piece of cloth*) a. COMPUT parche *m* **2.** (*of land*) parcela *f* de tierra; (*of fog*) zona *f* **3.** *inf* (*phase*) fase *f* **II.** *vt* (*hole*) remendar

◆**patch up** *vt* **1.** (*mend*) hacer un arreglo provisional a **2.** *fig* (*friendship*) arreglar; **to patch things up** hacer las paces

**patchy** ['pætʃ·i] <**-ier, -iest**> *adj* (*performance, novel*) desigual; (*weather*) variable; (*results*) irregular

**pâté** [pɑ·'teɪ] *n* paté *m*

**patent** ['pæt·ənt] **I.** *n* LAW patente *f* **II.** *adj* (*unconcealed*) evidente, patente **III.** *vt* LAW patentar

**paternal** [pə·'tɜr·nəl] *adj* paternal; ~ **grandfather** abuelo paterno; ~ **grandmother** abuela paterna

**paternity leave** *n* permiso *m* de paternidad

**path** [pæθ] *n* **1.** (*footway, trail*) camino *m*; **bike** ~ carril *m* bicicleta; **to clear a** ~ abrir un sendero; **to follow a** ~ seguir una senda **2.** (*way*) trayecto *m*; **to cross sb's** ~ tropezar con alguien **3.** COMPUT ruta *f*

**pathetic** [pə·'θet·ɪk] *adj* **1.** (*arousing sympathy*) conmovedor(a); **a** ~ **sight** una escena lastimosa **2.** (*arousing scorn*) patético, -a; **a** ~ **performance** una pésima actuación

**pathfinder** ['pæθ·faɪn·dər] *n* explorador(a) *m(f)*

**pathway** ['pæθ·weɪ] *n* sendero *m*

**patience** ['peɪ·ʃəns] *n* paciencia *f*

**patient** ['peɪ·ʃənt] **I.** *adj* paciente; **to be** ~ **with sb** tener paciencia con alguien; **just be** ~! ¡ten paciencia! **II.** *n* MED paciente *m/f*

**patio** ['pæt·i·oʊ] <-s> *n* **1.** (*paved area*) *área pavimentada contigua a una casa* **2.** (*courtyard*) patio *m*

**patriot** ['peɪ·tri·ət] *n* patriota *m/f*

**patriotic** [peɪ·tri·'ɑṭ·ɪk] *adj* patriótico, -a

**patrol** [pə·'troʊl] **I.** <-ll-> *vi* patrullar **II.** <-ll-> *vt* patrullar por **III.** *n* patrulla *f*; **to be on** ~ patrullar

**patrol car** *n* coche *m* patrulla

**patrol duty** *n* servicio *m* de patrulla

**patrolman** *n* policía *m*

**patronize** ['peɪ·trə·naɪz] *vt* **1.** (*be customer*) ser cliente de **2.** (*treat condescendingly*) tratar con condescendencia

**patronizing** ['peɪ·trə·naɪ·zɪŋ] *adj* condescendiente

**patter** ['pæṭ·ər] **I.** *n* **1.** (*of rain*) golpeteo *m* **2.** (*talk*) labia *f* **II.** *vi* (*make sound*) golpetear

**pattern** ['pæṭ·ərn] *n* **1.** (*model*) modelo *m* **2.** ART (*design, motif*) diseño *m* **3.** FASHION patrón *m*

**paunch** [pɔntʃ] *n* barriga *f*

**pauper** ['pɔ·pər] *n* indigente *m/f*

**pause** [pɔz] **I.** *n* pausa *f* **II.** *vi* hacer una pausa

**pave** [peɪv] *vt* pavimentar; **to** ~ **the way for sth** *fig* preparar el terreno para algo

**pavement** ['peɪv·mənt] *n* calzada *f*

**pavilion** [pə·'vɪl·jən] *n* pabellón *m*

**paw** [pɔ] *n* pata *f*; (*of cat, lion*) garra *f*, zarpa *f*; *fig inf* (*of person*) manaza *f*

**pawn**¹ [pɔn] *n* GAMES peón *m*; *fig* títere *m*

**pawn**² [pɔn] *vt* empeñar

**pawnbroker** ['pɔn·broʊ·kər] *n* prestamista *m/f* (sobre prenda), agenciero, -a *m, f Chile*; **the** ~**'s** la casa de empeños

**pawn shop** *n* casa *f* de empeños

**pay** [peɪ] **I.** *n* paga *f* **II.** <paid, paid> *vt* **1.** (*with money*) pagar; **to** ~ **cash** pagar al contado; **to** ~ **one's debts** liquidar las deudas de uno **2.** (*be worthwhile for*) ser provechoso, -a **3.** (*give, render*) **to** ~ **attention** (**to sb/sth**) prestar atención (a alguien/algo); **to** ~ **a call** (**on sb**), **to** ~ (**sb**) **a call** hacer una visita (a alguien); **to** ~ **sb a compliment** hacer un cumplido a alguien **III.** <paid, paid> *vi* **1.** (*settle, recompense*) pagar **2.** (*benefit*) ser provechoso, -a

◆**pay back** *vt* devolver

◆**pay in** *vt* ingresar

◆**pay off I.** *vt* **1.** (*debt*) liquidar **2.** *inf* (*bribe*) sobornar **II.** *vi fig* merecer la pena

◆**pay out I.** *vt* (*money*) desembolsar **II.** *vi* pagar

◆**pay up** *vi* pagar (lo que se debe)

**payable** ['peɪ·ə·bəl] *adj* pagadero, -a; **to make a check** ~ **to sb** extender un cheque a favor de alguien

**payback** ['peɪ·bæk] *n* FIN (*return on investment*) restitución *f*, retorno *m* de la inversión; (*equaling the sum invested*) amortización *f*

**paycheck** *n* cheque *m* del salario

**pay deal** *n* acuerdo *m* salarial

**pay desk** *n* caja *f*

**payee** [peɪ·'i] *n* beneficiario, -a *m, f*

**payer** ['peɪ·ər] *n* pagador(a) *m(f)*; **bad** ~ moroso, -a *m, f*

P

**pay freeze** n congelación f salarial

**paying** adj rentable

**payment** ['peɪ·mənt] n **1.** (sum of cash) pago m **2.** (installment) plazo m

**payoff** ['peɪ·ɔf] n **1.** (payment) pago m; (debt payment) liquidación f **2.** inf (bribe) soborno m, coima f CSur, mordida f Méx **3.** inf (positive result) beneficios mpl; (on bet) ganancias fpl

**pay-per-view** n pago m por visión

**pay phone** n teléfono m público

**pay raise** n aumento m de sueldo

**payroll** n nómina f

**payslip** n nómina f

**pay-TV** n televisión f de pago

**PC** [ˌpiː·ˈsiː] n abbr of **personal computer** PC m, pecé f

**PDT** n abbr of **Pacific Daylight Time** Hora f del Pacífico

**PE** [ˌpiː·ˈiː] abbr of **physical education** educación f física

**pea** [piː] n guisante m

**peace** [piːs] n **1.** (absence of war) a. REL paz f **2.** (social order) orden m público; **to keep the ~** mantener el orden; **to make ~** hacer las paces **3.** (tranquility) tranquilidad f; **~ of mind** tranquilidad de ánimo; **~ and quiet** paz y tranquilidad; **to give sb no ~** no dejar a alguien en paz; **to leave sb in ~** dejar a alguien en paz ▶ **to be at ~ with the** world estar satisfecho de la vida; **speak now or forever hold your ~** que hable ahora o que calle para siempre

**peaceful** ['piːs·fəl] adj **1.** (calm, quiet: animal) manso, -a; (place, person) tranquilo, -a **2.** (non-violent) pacífico, -a

**peacekeeper** n (soldier) soldado mf en misión de paz

**peace-loving** adj amante de la paz

**peacemaker** ['piːs·ˌmeɪ·kər] n conciliador(a) m(f)

**peacemaking** ['piːs·ˌmeɪ·kɪŋ] n (between countries) pacificación f; (between friends) conciliación f

**peace movement** n movimiento m pacifista

**peace negotiations** npl negociaciones f pl de paz

**peace pipe** n pipa f de la paz

**peacetime** n tiempo m de paz

**peace treaty** <-ies> n tratado m de paz

**peach** [piːtʃ] <-es> n **1.** (fruit) melocotón m, durazno m Arg, Chile **2.** (tree) melocotonero m, duraznero m Arg, Chile

**peach tree** n melocotonero m, duraznero m Arg, Chile

**peacock** ['piː·kak] n **1.** ZOOL pavo m real **2.** (vain person) engreído, -a m, f ▶ **to strut like a ~** pavonearse

**peak** [piːk] **I.** n **1.** (mountain top) cima f **2.** (highest point, summit) punto m máximo; (of a roof) pico m; **to be at the ~ of one's career/power** estar en la cúspide de su carrera/poder **II.** adj máximo, -a

**peal** [piːl] **I.** n **1.** (sound: of bell) repique m; (of thunder) trueno m; **a ~ of laughter** una carcajada **2.** (set) ~ **of bells** carillón m **II.** vi (thunder) tronar; (bell) repiquetear

**peanut** ['piː·nʌt] n **1.** (nut) cacahuete m, maní m AmL, cacahuate m Méx **2.** inf **to pay ~s** pagar una miseria

**peanut butter** n manteca f de cacahuete

**pear** [per] n pera f

**pearl** [pɜrl] n **1.** (jewel) perla f **2.** fig (a drop) gota f **3.** fig (a fine example) joya f ▶ **to cast one's ~s before the** swine prov echar margaritas a los cerdos prov

**pear tree** n peral m

**peasant** ['pez·ənt] n **1.** (poor farmer) campesino, -a m, f **2.** pej inf (crude person) paleto, -a m, f

**pebble** ['peb·əl] n guijarro m

**peck** [pek] **I.** n **1.** (of bird) picotazo m **2.** inf (quick kiss) besito m **II.** vt **1.** (bird) picar, picotear **2.** (kiss) dar un besito **III.** vi picar

**peckish** ['pek·ɪʃ] adj irritable

**peculiar** [pɪ·ˈkjul·jər] adj **1.** (strange) extraño, -a, raro, -a **2.** (belonging to) propio, -a, peculiar

**pedal** ['ped·əl] **I.** n pedal m **II.** <-l- or -ll-, -l- or -ll-> vi pedalear

**pedal bin** n cubo m de la basura (con pedal)

**pedal boat** n pedaleta f

**peddler** ['ped·lər] n vendedor(a) m(f)

ambulante

**pedestrian** [pə·'des·tri·ən] **I.** n peatón, -ona m, f **II.** adj (for walkers) peatonal

**pedestrianize** [pə·'des·tri·ə·naɪz] vt convertir en zona peatonal

**pediatrician** [ˌpi·di·ə·'trɪʃ·ən] n MED pediatra mf

**pediatrics** [ˌpi·di·'æt·rɪks] n MED pediatría f

**pedigree** ['ped·ɪ·gri] **I.** n (genealogy: of animal) pedigrí m **II.** adj (animal) de raza

**pedophile** ['ped·ə·faɪl] n pederasta m, pedófilo m

**pee** [pi] sl **I.** n pis m; **to take a ~** hacer pis **II.** vi hacer pis **III.** vt **to ~ oneself** mearse encima

**peek** [pik] **I.** n mirada f rápida **II.** vi **1.** (look) mirar furtivamente; **to ~ at sth** echar una mirada furtiva a algo **2.** (become visible) asomar

**peel** [pil] **I.** n piel f; (of fruit) cáscara f; (peelings) mondas fpl **II.** vt (fruit) pelar; (skin) levantar **III.** vi (person) pelarse; (paint) descharse; (bark) descortezarse

◆**peel off I.** vt (paint) quitar; (bark) descortezar; (clothes) quitarse **II.** vi (come off: paper) despegarse; (paint) desconcharse; (skin) pelarse

**peeler** ['pi·lər] n pelapatatas m inv

**peelings** ['pi·lɪŋz] npl (of fruit) pelauras fpl

**peep¹** [pip] **I.** n (sound: of bird) pío m; **to not say a ~** no decir ni pío **II.** vi piar

**peep²** [pip] **I.** n (look) vistazo m; **to have a ~ at sth** echar una ojeada a algo **II.** vi **1.** (look quickly) mirar rápidamente **2.** (become visible) asomar

**peephole** ['pip·houl] n mirilla f

**peer¹** [pɪr] vi **to ~ at sth** escudriñar algo; **to ~ into the distance** fijar la mirada en la distancia

**peer²** [pɪr] n (equal) igual mf, par mf; **to have no ~s** no tener par

**peg** [peg] **I.** n **1.** (for coat) colgador m **2.** (in furniture, for tent) estaquilla f **II.** <-gg-> vt **1.** (with pegs) enclavijar **2.** ECON fijar; **to ~ prices** congelar precios **3.** inf (throw) lanzar

◆**peg away** vi inf darle duro; **to ~ at sth**

persistir en algo

◆**peg out** vt señalar con estacas

**pejorative** [pɪ·'dʒɔr·ə·tɪv] adj peyorativo, -a

**pelican** ['pel·ɪ·kən] n pelícano m

**pellet** ['pel·ɪt] n **1.** (small ball) bolita f **2.** inf (animal excrement) cagadita f **3.** (gunshot) perdigón m

**pelt¹** [pelt] n (of animal) pellejo m; (fur) piel f

**pelt²** [pelt] **I.** vt (throw) lanzar **II.** vi **1.** (rain) llover a cántaros **2.** (run, hurry) apresurarse; **to ~ after sb** salir disparado tras alguien **III.** n **1.** (smack) golpe m **2.** (quick pace) paso m ligero; **at full ~** a todo correr

**pen¹** [pen] **I.** n (fountain pen) pluma f; (ballpoint pen) bolígrafo m, birome f Arg; **felt-tip ~** rotulador m **II.** <-nn-> vt escribir

**pen²** [pen] n **1.** (enclosure) corral m; **pig ~** pocilga f **2.** inf (jail) **the ~** el talego m

**penalty** ['pen·əl·ti] <-ies> n **1.** LAW pena f; **death ~** pena de muerte **2.** (punishment) castigo m **3.** SPORTS castigo m; (in soccer) penalti m

**penalty area** n SPORTS área f (de penalti)

**penalty box** <-es> n (in ice hockey) banquillo m

**penalty kick** n SPORTS (tiro m de) penalti m

**pencil** ['pen·səl] n lápiz m

**pencil case** n estuche m (para lápices)

**pencil sharpener** n sacapuntas m inv, tajalápiz m Col

**pendant** ['pen·dənt] **I.** n colgante m **II.** adj colgante

**pending** ['pen·dɪŋ] adj pendiente; **~ deal** negocio m pendiente; **patent ~** patente en trámite

**penetrate** ['pen·ɪ·treɪt] vt **1.** (move into or through) penetrar; **to ~ a market** introducirse en un mercado **2.** (spread through) impregnar, calar en

**penetrating** adj penetrante

**penguin** ['peŋ·gwɪn] n pingüino m

**penholder** ['pen·houl·dər] n portalápices m inv

**penicillin** [ˌpen·ɪ·'sɪl·ɪn] n penicilina f

**peninsula** [pə·'nɪn·sə·lə] n península f

P

**penis** ['piːnɪs] <-nises *or* -nes> *n* pene *m*

**penitence** ['penɪtəns] *n* REL penitencia *f*

**penitentiary** [ˌpenɪˈtenˌtʃəri] *n* prisión *f* penitenciaria

**penknife** ['pennaɪf] <-knives> *n* navaja *f*

**penniless** ['penɪlɪs] *adj* to be ~ no tener un duro

**Pennsylvania** [ˌpensɪlˈveɪniːə] *n* Pensilvania *f*

**penny** ['peni] *n* centavo *m* ▶ to **pinch pennies** apretarse el cinturón

**pen pal** *n* amigo, -a *m, f* por correspondencia

**pension** ['penʃən] I. *n* FIN pensión *f;* to **draw a** ~ cobrar una pensión II. *vt* to ~ **sb off** jubilar a alguien

**pensioner** ['penʃənər] *n* pensionista *mf*

**pension fund** *n* fondo *m* de pensiones

**pentagon** ['pentəgən] *n* pentágono *m*

**pentathlon** [pen'tæθlən] *n* pentatlón *m*

**penthouse** ['penthaʊs] *n* ático *m* de lujo

**pent-up** [ˌpentˈʌp] *adj* (*emotion*) contenido, -a, reprimido, -a

**penultimate** [pɪˈnʌltəmət] *adj* penúltimo, -a

**people** ['piːpəl] *n* 1. *pl* (*plural of person*) gente *f;* city/country ~ gente de ciudad/de campo 2. (*nation, ethnic group*) pueblo *m;* ~'s **republic** república *f* popular 3. *pl* (*ordinary citizens*) ciudadanos, -as *m, fpl;* of/by/for the ~ del/por/para el pueblo

**pepper** ['pepər] I. *n* 1. (*spice*) pimienta *f* 2. (*vegetable*) pimiento *m* II. *vt* 1. (*add pepper*) poner [*or* echar] pimienta a 2. (*pelt*) to ~ **sb with questions** acribillar a alguien a preguntas

**peppercorn** ['pepərkɔrn] *n* grano *m* de pimienta

**pepper mill** *n* molinillo *m* de pimienta

**peppermint** ['pepərmɪnt] *n* 1. (*mint plant*) menta *f* 2. (*sweet*) caramelo *m* de menta

**pep talk** *n inf* to **give sb a** ~ dar ánimos a alguien

**per** [pɜr] *prep* 1. (*for a*) por; **$5 ~ pound/hour** $5 por libra/hora 2. (*in*

*a*) por, a; **100 miles ~ hour** 100 millas por hora 3. *form* **as ~...** (*as stated in*) de acuerdo con...; **as ~ usual** como siempre

**per annum** *adv* al año, por año

**per capita** *adj, adv* per cápita

**perceive** [pər'siv] *vt* 1. (*see*) ver; (*sense*) percibir, notar; to ~ **that...** percibir que... 2. (*view, regard*) considerar; **how do the young ~ the old?** ¿qué piensan los jovenes de los viejos?

**percent** [pər'sent] *n* porcentaje *m;* **25 ~** 25 por ciento

**percentage** [pər'sentɪdʒ] *n* 1. (*proportion*) porcentaje *m;* **what ~...?** ¿qué porcentaje...?; to **get a ~ of sth** recibir un tanto por ciento de algo 2. (*advantage*) tajada *f* inf

**percentage point** *n* punto *m* porcentual

**perception** [pər'sepʃən] *n* 1. percepción *f* 2. (*insight*) perspicacia *f,* agudeza *f*

**perceptive** [pər'septɪv] *adj* perspicaz, agudo, -a

**perch**[1] [pɜrtʃ] I. <-es> *n* (*for birds*) percha *f* II. *vi* (*person*) sentarse; (*bird*) posarse

**perch**[2] [pɜrtʃ] *n* (*fish*) perca *f*

**percussion** [pər'kʌʃən] *n* MUS percusión *f*

**percussionist** *n* MUS percusionista *mf*

**perennial** [pə'reniːəl] *adj* 1. BOT perenne 2. (*constant*) constante

**perfect**[1] ['pɜrfɪkt] I. *adj* perfecto, -a; (*calm*) total; **in ~ condition** en perfecto estado; **the ~ crime** el crimen perfecto; to **be a ~ stranger** ser un completo desconocido; to **be far from ~** estar (muy) lejos de ser perfecto II. *n* LING perfecto *m*

**perfect**[2] [pər'fekt] *vt* perfeccionar

**perfection** [pər'fekʃən] *n* perfección *f;* to ~ **a la perfección**

**perfectly** *adv* perfectamente; ~ **clear** completamente claro

**perforate** ['pɜrfəreɪt] *vt* perforar; (*ticket*) picar

**perform** [pər'fɔrm] I. *vt* 1. MUS, THEAT, TV interpretar 2. (*do, accomplish*) realizar; to ~ **one's duty** cumplir con su deber; **to ~ miracles** hacer milagros; **to ~ a task** llevar a cabo una tarea **II.** vi **1.** THEAT actuar; MUS tocar **2.** (*operate*) funcionar

**performance** [pərˈfɔr·məns] n **1.** (*of play*) representación f; (*by actor*) actuación f; **to give a ~** hacer una representación **2.** SPORTS actuación f

**performer** [pərˈfɔr·mər] n **1.** THEAT artista mf; **star ~** estrella f **2.** (*achiever*) **top ~** (*at work*) empleado, -a m, f modelo; **bad ~** (*at school*) mal(a) estudiante mf; (*at work*) mal(a) trabajador(a) m(f)

**perfume** [pərˈfjum] **I.** n perfume m **II.** vt perfumar

**perhaps** [pərˈhæps] adv quizá(s), tal vez

**peril** [ˈper·əl] n form peligro m; **to be in ~** correr peligro

**perilous** [ˈper·ə·ləs] adj form peligroso, -a

**perimeter** [pəˈrɪm·ə·t̬ər] n perímetro m

**period** [ˈpɪr·i·əd] **I.** n **1.** **a.** GEO período m; **in/over a ~ of sth** en/durante un período de algo **2.** ECON plazo m **3.** SCHOOL (*lesson*) hora f **4.** (*distinct stage*) época f **5.** (*menstruation*) período m, regla f; **to have one's ~** tener la regla **6.** LING punto m final **II.** interj ¡y punto! **II.** interj

**periodical** [ˌpɪr·i·ˈɑd·ɪ·kəl] **I.** n (*general*) publicación f periódica **II.** adj periódico, -a

**peripheral** [pəˈrɪf·ər·əl] **I.** adj **1.** (*importance, role*) secundario, -a **2.** **a.** ANAT, COMPUT periférico, -a **II.** n COMPUT periférico m

**periscope** [ˈper·ɪ·skoʊp] n periscopio m

**perish** [ˈper·ɪʃ] vi liter **1.** (*die*) perecer **2.** (*disappear: motivation, hope*) desaparecer

**perishable** [ˈper·ɪʃ·ə·bəl] adj perecedero, -a elev

**perjury** [ˈpɜr·dʒə·ri] n perjurio m

**perk** [pɜrk] n inf abbr of **perquisite 1.** (*advantage*) ventaja f **2.** (beneficio m) extra m

◆ **perk up I.** vi **1.** (*cheer up*) alegrarse **2.** (*improve*) mejorar **II.** vt (*cheer up*) alegrar

**perm** [pɜrm] **I.** n inf (*hair*) permanente f **II.** vt **to ~ one's hair** hacerse la

---

permanente

**permanent** [ˈpɜr·mə·nənt] adj (*job*) fijo, -a; (*damage*) irreparable; (*exhibition, situation, position*) permanente; (*ink*) indeleble

**permission** [pərˈmɪʃ·ən] n permiso m

**permit¹** [ˈpɜr·mɪt] n **1.** permiso m (por escrito); **to hold a ~** tener un permiso **2.** **fishing/gun/building ~** licencia f de pesca/armas/construcción

**permit²** [pərˈmɪt] <-tt-> **I.** vt permitir; **I will not ~ you to go there** no te permito que vayas allí **II.** vi **weather ~ing** si el tiempo no lo impide; **if time ~s** si hay tiempo

**perpendicular** [ˌpɜr·pən·ˈdɪk·ju·lər] adj perpendicular

**perpetual** [pərˈpetʃ·u·əl] adj (*lasting forever*) perpetuo, -a

**perplex** [pərˈpleks] vt desconcertar

**persecute** [ˈpɜr·sɪ·kjut] vt **a.** POL perseguir

**persecution** [ˌpɜr·sɪ·ˈkju·ʃən] n persecución f

**persevere** [ˌpɜr·sə·ˈvɪr] vi perseverar

**persist** [pərˈsɪst] vi (*continue: cold, heat, rain*) continuar; (*habit, belief, doubts*) persistir

**persistence** [pərˈsɪs·təns] n **1.** (*of cold, belief*) persistencia f **2.** (*of person*) insistencia f

**persistent** [pərˈsɪs·tənt] adj **1.** (*cold, belief*) persistente **2.** (*person*) insistente

**person** [ˈpɜr·sən] <people or form -s> n (*human*) **a.** LING persona f; **per ~** por persona

**personal** [ˈpɜr·sə·nəl] adj **1.** (*property*) privado, -a; (*data, belongings, account*) personal **2.** (*done in person*) en persona **3.** (*matter*) privado, -a, personal; (*life*) privado, -a **4.** **to get ~** llevar las cosas al plano personal; **it's nothing ~** no es nada personal **5.** (*bodily, physical: appearance*) personal; (*hygiene*) íntimo, -a

**personal computer** n ordenador m personal, computadora f personal AmL

**personality** [ˌpɜr·sə·ˈnæl·ə·t̬i] n <-ies> **1.** (*character*) personalidad f **2.** (*famous person*) personalidad f, figura f

**personally** adv **1.** (*in person*) personal-

**P**

mente 2. (*as offensive*) **to take sth ~** ofenderse con [*or* por] algo 3. (*referring to oneself*) ~... personalmente... 4. (*referring to sb's character*) como persona; **I don't like him ~** no me gusta como persona

**personnel** [ˌpɜr·sə·ˈnel] *n pl* (*staff, employees*) personal *m*

**personnel department** *n* departamento *m* de personal

**personnel director** *n* director(a) *m(f)* de personal

**perspective** [pər·ˈspek·tɪv] *n* perspectiva *f*

**perspiration** [ˌpɜr·spə·ˈreɪ·ʃən] *n* transpiración *f*

**perspire** [pər·ˈspaɪr] *vi* transpirar

**persuade** [pər·ˈsweɪd] *vt* convencer; **to ~ sb into/out of sth** convencer/disuadir a alguien de algo; **to ~ sb to do sth** convencer a alguien de que haga algo

**persuasion** [pər·ˈsweɪ·ʒən] *n* 1. (*act*) persuasión *f* 2. (*conviction*) creencia *f*

**persuasive** [pər·ˈsweɪ·sɪv] *adj* (*person, manner*) persuasivo, -a; (*argument*) convincente

**Peru** [pə·ˈru] *n* Perú *m*

**Peruvian** [pə·ˈru·vi·ən] I. *adj* peruano, -a II. *n* peruano, -a *m, f*

**perverse** [pər·ˈvɜrs] *adj* perverso, -a

**perversion** [pər·ˈvɜr·ʒən] *n* (*sexual*) perversión *f*; (*of the truth*) distorsión *f*

**pervert¹** [ˈpɜr·vɜrt] *n* (*sexual*) pervertido, -a *m, f*

**pervert²** [pər·ˈvɜrt] *vt* pervertir

**pessimism** [ˈpes·ə·mɪz·əm] *n* pesimismo *m*

**pessimist** *n* pesimista *mf*

**pessimistic** [ˌpes·ə·ˈmɪs·tɪk] *adj* pesimista

**pest** [pest] *n* 1. (*animal*) plaga *f* 2. *inf* (*person*) pesado, -a *m, f*

**pest control** *n* (*insects*) fumigación *f*

**pester** [ˈpes·tər] *vt* molestar

**pesticide** [ˈpes·tə·saɪd] *n* pesticida *m*

**pet** [pet] I. *n* 1. (*house animal*) animal *m* doméstico, mascota *f* 2. *pej* (*favorite person*) mimado, -a *m, f*; **he's the teacher's ~** es el mimado del profesor II. *adj* 1. **my ~ cat** el gato que tengo de mascota, mi gato 2. (*favorite: project,*

*theory*) favorito, -a III. <-tt-> *vi* besarse y acariciarse

**petal** [ˈpet·əl] *n* BOT pétalo *m*

**peter** [ˈpi·tər] *vi* **to ~ out** (*trail, track, path*) desaparecer; (*conversation, interest*) decaer

**petition** [pə·ˈtɪʃ·ən] I. *n* 1. POL petición *f* 2. LAW demanda *f* II. *vi* POL **to ~ for sth** elevar una petición solicitando algo

**petrified** *adj* 1. GEO petrificado, -a 2. (*terrified*) aterrorizado, -a

**petrify** [ˈpet·rɪ·faɪ] <-ies> I. *vi* GEO petrificarse II. *vt* (*terrify*) aterrorizar

**petroleum** [pə·ˈtrou·li·əm] *n* petróleo *m*, canfín *m* *AmC*

**pet shop** *n* ≈ pajarería *f*

**petticoat** [ˈpet·i·kout] *n* enagua *f*, combinación *f*, fondo *m* *Méx*

**petty** [ˈpet·i] <-ier, -iest> *adj* 1. *pej* (*detail, amount*) trivial, insignificante 2. LAW menor

**pew** [pju] *n* banco *m* (de iglesia)

**pg.** *abbr of* **page** pág. *f*

**phantom** [ˈfæn·təm] I. *n* fantasma *m* II. *adj* 1. (*ghostly*) fantasmal 2. (*imaginary*) ilusorio, -a

**pharmaceutical** I. *adj* farmacéutico, -a II. *n* ~**s** fármacos *mpl*

**pharmacist** [ˈfar·mə·sɪst] *n* farmacéutico, -a *m, f*

**pharmacy** [ˈfar·mə·si] <-ies> *n* farmacia *f*

**pharynx** [ˈfær·ɪŋks] <pharynges> *n* faringe *f*

**phase** [feɪz] *n* (*stage*) fase *f*; (*period*) etapa *f*; **to go through a ~** pasar por una etapa

◆ **phase in** *vt* introducir paulatinamente

◆ **phase out** *vt* (*service*) retirar progresivamente; (*product*) dejar de producir paulatinamente

**PhD** [ˌpi·eɪtʃ·ˈdi] *n abbr of* **Doctor of Philosophy** 1. (*award*) doctorado *m* 2. (*person*) Dr. *m*, Dra. *f*

**pheasant** [ˈfez·ənt] <-(s)> *n* faisán *m*

**phenomenal** *adj* (*success, achievement*) espectacular; (*strength*) increíble

**phenomenon** [fə·ˈnam·ə·nan] <phenomena *or* -s> *n* fenómeno *m*

**phew** [fju] *interj inf* ¡uf!

**philosopher** [fɪ·ˈlas·ə·fər] *n* filósofo,

-a *m, f*

**philosophize** [fɪ·'las·ə·faɪz] *vi* filosofar

**philosophy** [fɪ·'las·ə·fi] *n* filosofía *f*

**phobia** ['fou·bi·ə] *n* PSYCH fobia *f*

**phone** [foun] I. *n* teléfono *m;* **to hang up the ~** colgar el teléfono; **to pick up the ~** coger el teléfono; **to be on the ~** estar hablando por teléfono II. *vt* llamar (por teléfono), telefonear

◆**phone back** *vt* volver a llamar (por teléfono)

◆**phone in** I. *vi* llamar (por teléfono); **to ~ sick** llamar (por teléfono) para dar parte de enfermo II. *vt* llamar por teléfono

◆**phone up** *vt* llamar (por teléfono)

**phone book** *n* guía *f* (telefónica), directorio *m Col, Méx*

**phone booth** <-es> *n* cabina *f* (telefónica)

**phone call** *n* llamada *f* (telefónica)

**phone number** *n* número *m* (de teléfono), teléfono *m*

**phonetic** [fə·'net·ɪk] *adj* fonético, -a; **~ transcription** transcripción *f* fonética

**phonetics** [fə·'net·ɪks] *n* fonética *f*

**phony** ['fou·ni] <-ier, -iest> *adj inf (person, address)* falso, -a; *(documents)* falsificado, -a

**phosphorescent** [fas·fə·'res·ənt] *adj* fosforescente

**phosphorus** ['fas·fər·əs] *n* fósforo *m*

**photo** ['fou·tou] <-s> *n inf abbr of* **photograph** foto *f*

**photo album** *n* álbum *m* de fotos

**photocopier** [fou·tou·'kap·i·ər] *n* fotocopiadora *f*

**photocopy** ['fou·tou·kap·i] I. <-ies> *n* fotocopia *f* II. *vt* fotocopiar

◆**photo finish** *n* SPORTS foto *f* finish

**photoflash** *n* flash *m*

**photograph** ['fou·tou·græf] I. *n* fotografía *f;* **color ~** fotografía en color; **to take a ~** sacar una fotografía (**of** de) II. *vt* fotografiar

**photograph album** *n* álbum *m* de fotos

**photographer** [fə·'tag·rə·fər] *n* fotógrafo, -a *m, f*

**photographic** [fou·tə·'græf·ɪk] *adj* fotográfico, -a

**photography** [fə·'tag·rə·fi] *n* fotografía *f*

**photojournalism** [fou·tou·'dʒɜr·nə·lɪz·əm] *n* periodismo *m* gráfico

**photometer** [fou·'tam·ɪ·tər] *n* fotómetro *m*

**photomontage** [fou·tou·man·'taʒ] *n* fotomontaje *m*

**photo reporter** *n* reportero, -a *m, f* fotográfico, -a

**photosynthesis** [fou·tou·'sɪn·θɪ·sɪs] *n* fotosíntesis *f*

**phrasal verb** [frei·zəl·'vɜrb] *n* LING verbo *m* con partícula

**phrase** [freɪz] I. *n* frase *f; (idiomatic expression)* expresión *f* II. *vt* **to ~ sth well/badly** expresar algo bien/mal

**phrase book** *n* libro *m* de frases

**physical** ['fɪz·ɪ·kəl] I. *adj* físico, -a; **to be in poor ~ condition** estar en bajo estado de forma; **to have a ~ disability** sufrir una discapacidad física; **~ exercise** ejercicio *m* físico II. *n* MED reconocimiento *m* médico

**physical education** *n* educación *f* física

**physician** [fɪ·'zɪʃ·ən] *n* médico, -a *m, f*

**physicist** ['fɪz·ɪ·sɪst] *n* físico, -a *m, f*

**physics** ['fɪz·ɪks] *n* física *f*

**physique** [fɪ·'zik] *n* físico *m*

**pianist** ['pi·æn·ɪst] *n* pianista *mf*

**piano** [pi·'æn·ou] <-s> *n* piano *m*

**pick** [pɪk] I. *vt* 1. *(select)* elegir 2. *(harvest: fruit, vegetables)* recoger 3. *(touch)* tocar; **to ~ one's nose** hurgarse la nariz 4. *(steal)* robar; **to ~ a lock** forzar una cerradura; **to ~ sb's pocket** robar algo del bolsillo de alguien 5. *(provoke)* **to ~ a fight** (**with sb**) buscar camorra (con alguien) II. *n* 1. *(selection)* elección *f; (of people)* selección *f;* **to take one's ~** elegir; **to have one's ~** poder elegir 2. *(pickax)* pico *m*

◆**pick off** *vt (shoot)* abatir (a tiros)

◆**pick on** *vt insep* 1. *(victimize)* meterse con 2. *(select)* **to ~ sb for sth** escoger a alguien para algo

◆**pick out** *vt* 1. *(choose)* elegir 2. *(recognize)* distinguir

◆**pick over** *vt* ir revolviendo y examinando

◆**pick up** I. *vt* 1. *(lift)* levantar; **to ~ the phone** coger el teléfono; **to ~ the pieces** *fig* empezar de nuevo 2. *(get)* conseguir; *(conversation)* captar; **to ~**

**a bargain** conseguir una ganga; **to ~ an illness** pillar una enfermedad *inf*; **to ~ speed** coger velocidad; **to ~ the bill** [*or* **tab**] *inf* pagar la cuenta 3. (*collect*) recoger; **to pick sb up** recoger a alguien 4. (*clean: one's room, the living room*) ordenar 5. (*buy*) adquirir 6. (*detect: noise, signal*) detectar 7. (*learn*) aprender 8. *sl* (*sexually*) **to pick sb up** ligarse a alguien 9. *inf* (*halt*) detener; (*arrest*) arrestar 10. *inf* (*earn*) ganar **II.** *vi* 1. (*improve*) mejorar; (*numbers*) ir a mejor; MED reponerse 2. (*continue*) continuar; **to ~ where one left off** reanudar donde uno lo dejó

**pickax** ['pɪk·æks] *n* (*tool*) pico *m*, azadón *m* de pico

**picket** ['pɪk·ɪt] *n* 1. (*stake*) estaca *f* 2. (*striker*) a. MIL piquete *m*

**picket line** *n* piquete *m*; **to be on the ~** participar en un piquete

**pickle** ['pɪk·əl] *n* 1. (*pickled item*) encurtido *m* 2. (*pickled cucumber*) pepinillo *m* en vinagre al eneldo **II.** *vt* (*vegetables*) conservar en vinagre; (*fish*) conservar en escabeche

**pickled** *adj* 1. (*vegetables*) encurtido, -a; (*fish*) en escabeche 2. *fig sl* (*drunk*) borracho, -a; **to get ~** emborracharse

**pickpocket** ['pɪk·ˌpak·ɪt] *n* carterista *mf*, bolsista *mf* AmC, Méx

**pickup** *n* 1. *inf* (*collection*) recogida *f*, recolección *f* 2. (*increase*) aumento *m*

**pickup truck** *n* camioneta *f* con plataforma

**picnic** ['pɪk·nɪk] *n* picnic *m*; **to go on a ~** ir de picnic; **to be no ~** *fig* no ser nada agradable

**picnicker** *n* excursionista *mf*

**picture** ['pɪk·tʃər] **I.** *n* 1. (*image*) imagen *f*; (*painting*) pintura *f*; **to draw a ~** hacer un dibujo; **to paint a ~** pintar un cuadro 2. (*photo*) fotografía, foto *f*; **to take a ~** sacar una foto 3. (*film*) película *f* 4. (*mental image*) imagen *f* 5. *fig* (*description*) representación *f*; **to paint a ~ of sth** representar algo; **to paint a very black ~** pintar un panorama muy negro ▶ **a ~ is worth a thousand words** *prov* una imagen vale más que mil palabras; **to get the ~** entender

**II.** *vt* imaginarse

**picture book** *n* libro *m* ilustrado

**picture frame** *n* marco *m* (para cuadro)

**picture gallery** *n* galería *f* de arte

**picture postcard** *n* (tarjeta *f*) postal *f*

**picturesque** [ˌpɪk·tʃə·ˈresk] *adj* (*scenic*) pintoresco, -a

**pidgin** ['pɪdʒ·ɪn] *n* LING pidgin *m*

**pie** [paɪ] *n* tarta *f*, pay *m* AmS ▶ (**as**) **easy as ~** pan comido

**piece** [pis] *n* 1. (*small unit: of wood, metal, food*) trozo *m*; (*of land*) terreno *m*; **a ~ of paper** (*scrap*) un trozo de papel; (*sheet*) una hoja; **in one ~** en una sola pieza; **to break sth to/in ~s** hacer algo pedazos; **to tear sth into ~s** desgarrar algo 2. (*item, one of set*) unidad *f*; **~ of luggage** bulto *m*; **~ of clothing** prenda *f* de vestir 3. (*in games*) pieza *f* 4. (*with mass nouns*) **a ~ of advice** un consejo 5. ART, MUS pieza *f* 6. (*coin*) moneda *f*; **a 50 cent ~** una moneda de 50 centavos ▶ **to be a ~ of cake** *inf* ser pan comido

**piece rate** *n* precio *m* por unidad

**piecework** ['pis·wɜrk] *n* trabajo *m* a destajo

**pieceworker** *n* trabajador(a) *m(f)* a destajo

**pier** [pɪr] *n* 1. (*at the water*) muelle *m* 2. ARCHIT (*pillar*) columna *f*, pilar *f*; (*buttress*) contrafuerte *m*

**pierce** [pɪrs] **I.** *vt* (*perforate*) perforar; **to ~ a hole in sth** agujerear algo; **to have one's ears ~d** hacerse agujeros en las orejas **II.** *vi* (*drill*) **to ~ through sth** atravesar algo

**piercing I.** *adj* 1. (*wind*) cortante; **it's ~ cold** hace un frío que pela 2. (*eyes, gaze, look*) penetrante; (*question, reply, wit*) punzante 3. (*cry*) desgarrador(a) **II.** *n* piercing *m*

**pig** [pɪg] *n* 1. ZOOL cerdo *m* 2. *inf* (*person*) cochino, -a *m, f*; **to be a ~** ser un cerdo 3. *offensive sl* (*policeman*) madero *m* ▶ **to make a ~ of oneself** ponerse como un cerdo

◆ **pig out** <-gg-> *vi sl* ponerse morado; **to ~ out on sth** comer demasiado de algo

**pigeon** ['pɪdʒ·ən] *n* (*bird*) paloma *f*

**pigeonhole** ['pɪdʒ·ən·hoʊl] **I.** *n* casilla f II. vt to ~ sb/sth encasillar a alguien/algo

**piggyback** ['pɪɡ·i·bæk] n to carry sb/ride ~ llevar/montar a caballito

**piggy bank** n alcancía f en forma de cerdito

**pigheaded** [ˌpɪɡ·'hed·ɪd] adj testarudo, -a

**piglet** ['pɪɡ·lɪt] n cochinillo m

**pigment** ['pɪɡ·mənt] n pigmento m

**pigsty** ['pɪɡ·staɪ] n a. fig, pej pocilga f

**pigtail** ['pɪɡ·teɪl] n (hair) trenza f

**pile** [paɪl] I. n 1. (stack) pila f 2. (heap) montón m; to have ~s of sth inf tener montones de algo; ELEC pila f II. vt amontonar

◆**pile in** vi ~! ¡todos dentro, que nos vamos!

◆**pile on** vt 1. (enter) entrar desordenadamente 2. (heap) amontonar 3. inf (exaggerate) to (really) pile it on exagerar (mucho)

◆**pile up** I. vi 1. (accumulate) acumularse 2. (form a pile) apilarse II. vt amontonar

**piles** npl inf almorranas fpl

**pileup** ['paɪl·ʌp] n accidente m múltiple

**pilfer** ['pɪl·fər] vt ratear

**pilgrim** ['pɪl·ɡrɪm] n peregrino, -a m, f

**pilgrimage** ['pɪl·ɡrə·mɪdʒ] n peregrinación f

**pill** [pɪl] n 1. pastilla f, píldora f; the ~ (contraception) la píldora 2. inf (pesky person) pesado, -a m, f ▶ to sweeten [or sugar] the ~ dorar la píldora

**pillage** ['pɪl·ɪdʒ] I. vt saquear II. n saqueo m

**pillar** ['pɪl·ər] n 1. ARCHIT pilar m, columna f 2. fig (of support) sostén m, puntal m; to be a ~ of strength ser firme como una roca

**pillow** ['pɪl·oʊ] n 1. (for bed) almohada f 2. (cushion) cojín m

**pillowcase** n funda f de almohada

**pilot** ['paɪ·lət] I. n 1. AVIAT piloto mf 2. NAUT práctico mf 3. TV programa m piloto 4. TECH (flame) piloto m II. vt 1. (plane) pilotar 2. (boat) guiar

**pilot boat** n bote m del práctico

**pilot burner** n (on boiler) piloto m (de una caldera)

**pilot light** n piloto m

**pilot plant** n planta f piloto

**pilot program** n programa m piloto

**pilot's license** n licencia f de vuelo

**pilot survey** n estudio m experimental

**pimp** [pɪmp] n proxeneta mf, chulo m (de putas) inf

**pimple** ['pɪm·pəl] n grano m

**pimply** ['pɪm·pli] <-ier, -iest> adj lleno, -a de granos

**pin** [pɪn] I. n 1. (needle) alfiler m; tie ~ alfiler m de corbata 2. (brooch) prendedor m 3. pl, fig (legs) patas fpl ▶ to have ~s and needles sentir un hormigueo II. <-nn-> vt (attach with a pin) to ~ sth on prender algo con un alfiler

◆**pin down** vt 1. (define) precisar 2. (locate) concretar 3. (pressure to decide) presionar (a alguien) para que se defina 4. (restrict movement) inmovilizar

◆**pin up** vt (attach using pins) recoger con alfileres; (on the wall) fijar con chinchetas; to ~ one's hair recogerse el pelo con horquillas

**PIN** [pɪn] n abbr of personal identification number PIN m (número de identificación personal)

**pinball machine** n (máquina f de) petacos mpl

**pincers** ['pɪn·sərz] npl 1. ZOOL pinzas fpl 2. (tool) tenazas fpl

**pinch** [pɪntʃ] I. vt 1. (with fingers) pellizcar 2. (be too tight) apretar 3. inf (steal) birlar 4. vi (with fingers) estrujar III. n 1. (nip) pellizco m; to give sb a ~ dar un pellizco a alguien 2. (small quantity) pizca f

**pine¹** [paɪn] n pino m

**pine²** [paɪn] vi 1. (waste away) to ~ (away) languidecer 2. (long for) to ~ for sb suspirar por alguien

**pineapple** ['paɪn·æp·əl] n (fruit) piña f

**pinecone** n piña f

**pine needle** n aguja f de pino

**pine tree** n pino m

**ping** [pɪŋ] I. n (sound: of bell) tintín m; (of glass, metal) sonido m metálico II. vi tintinear

**pink** [pɪŋk] I. n (color) rosa m ▶ to be in the ~ rebosar de salud II. adj rosado, -a

**pinkie** ['pɪŋ·ki] n inf dedo m meñique

P

**pinpoint** ['pɪn·pɔɪnt] I. vt (location, reason) indicar con toda precisión II. adj exacto, -a; ~ **accuracy** gran precisión f

**pinprick** ['pɪn·prɪk] n pinchazo m

**pinstripe** ['pɪn·straɪp] n (stripe) raya f fina; (suit) traje m de raya diplomática

**pint** [paɪnt] n pinta f (0,47 l); **a ~ of beer/milk** una pinta de cerveza/leche

**pinup** ['pɪn·ʌp] n (poster) póster m (de una persona atractiva)

**pioneer** [ˌpaɪ·ə·'nɪr] n pionero, -a m, f; fig pionero, -a m, f

**pious** ['paɪ·əs] adj REL a. iron piadoso, -a

**pip** [pɪp] n BOT pepita f

**pipe** [paɪp] I. n 1. TECH (tube) tubo m; (for gas, water) cañería f, tubería f 2. (for smoking) pipa f, cachimba f AmL 3. MUS (wind instrument) ~**s** gaita f II. vt (transport) transportar por tuberías

◆**pipe down** vi inf (be quiet) callarse; (become quieter) calmarse

**pipe dream** n sueño m imposible

**pipeline** ['paɪp·laɪn] n tubería f; **oil ~** oleoducto m; **gas ~** gasoducto m; **to be in the ~** fig estar tramitándose

**piper** ['paɪ·pər] n gaitero, -a m, f

**piping** ['paɪ·pɪŋ] n (pipes) tubería f

**piracy** ['paɪ·rə·si] n NAUT, COM piratería f

**pirate** ['paɪ·rət] I. n pirata m II. adj pirata; ~ **copy** copia f pirata

**Pisces** ['paɪ·siz] n Piscis m

**piss** [pɪs] vulg I. n meada f; (**to have**) **to take a ~** (tener ganas de) mear II. vi mear III. vt **to ~ one's pants** mearse encima

**pissed** [pɪst] adj vulg sl, **pissed off** adj sl **to be ~** (angry) estar de mala leche

**pistachio** [pɪ·'stæʃ·i·oʊ] <-s> n pistacho m, pistache m Méx

**pistol** ['pɪs·təl] n pistola f

**piston** ['pɪs·tən] n TECH pistón m

**pit¹** [pɪt] n 1. (in ground) hoyo m; (on metal) muesca f; (on face) marca f; **in the ~ of one's stomach** en la boca del estómago 2. (mine) mina f 3. the ~**s** pl, fig inf lo peor 4. THEAT (seating area) patio m de asientos; (orchestral area) platea f 5. the ~**s** pl SPORTS los boxes

**pit²** [pɪt] <-tt-> I. n (of fruit) hueso m II. vt CULIN deshuesar

**pitch¹** [pɪtʃ] I. n 1. (in baseball) lanza-

miento m 2. (slope) grado m de inclinación; **low/steep ~** pendiente f suave/pronunciada 3. (volume) volumen m 4. MUS, LING tono m 5. (spiel) rollo m, **sales ~** labia f para vender; **to make a ~** soltar un rollo II. vt 1. (throw) lanzar 2. SPORTS (throw) tirar 3. (fix level of sound) **this tune is ~ed (too) high/low** esta afinación es (demasiado) alta/baja 4. (direct at: speech, advertisement) **to ~ sth at sb** diseñar algo para alguien 5. (set up) **to ~ camp/a tent** montar el campamento/una tienda (de campaña) 6. (sell forcefully: product) vender (de forma agresiva) III. vi 1. (fall headlong) caerse de morros inf 2. (boat) cabecear 3. SPORTS (throw baseball) lanzar 4. (slope) inclinarse

◆**pitch in** vi inf contribuir

**pitch²** [pɪtʃ] n (bitumen) brea f

**pitch-black** [ˌpɪtʃ·'blæk] adj (extremely dark) muy oscuro, -a; (very black) muy negro, -a

**pitcher¹** ['pɪtʃ·ər] n (jug: large) cántaro m (smaller) jarra f

**pitcher²** ['pɪtʃ·ər] n (in baseball) lanzador(a) m(f)

**pitchfork** ['pɪtʃ·fɔrk] n horca f

**pitfall** ['pɪt·fɔl] n escollo m

**pith** [pɪθ] n 1. BOT médula f 2. fig (main point) meollo m

**pithy** ['pɪθ·i] <-ier, -iest> adj (remark) sucinto, -a

**pitiful** ['pɪt·ɪ·fəl] adj 1. (terrible) lamentable; **a ~ sight** una escena patética 2. (unsatisfactory) insatisfactorio, -a; ~ **excuse** excusa f pobre

**pitiless** ['pɪt·ɪ·lɪs] adj despiadado, -a

**pit stop** n 1. (in racing) parada f en boxes 2. fig (quick stop) parada f rápida

**pity** ['pɪt·i] I. n 1. (compassion) compasión f; **to feel ~ for sb** compadecerse de alguien; **to take ~ on sb** apiadarse de alguien 2. (shame) (it's a) ~ **that...** (es una) lástima que...; **what a ~!** ¡qué pena! II. <-ies, -ied> vt compadecerse de

**pivot** ['pɪv·ət] I. n 1. TECH eje m 2. (focal point) punto m central, pivote m II. vi pivotar

**pizza** ['pit·sə] *n* pizza *f*

**placard** ['plæk·ard] *n* pancarta *f*

**placate** ['pleɪ·keɪt] *vt* **1.** (*soothe*) aplacar **2.** (*appease*) apaciguar

**place** [pleɪs] I. *n* **1.** (*location, area*) lugar *m*; ~ **of birth** lugar de nacimiento; **people in high** ~**s** gente *f* bien situada; **to be in** ~ estar en su sitio; *fig* estar listo; **if I were in your** ~,... yo en tu lugar...; **in** ~ **of sb/sth** en vez de alguien/algo; **it is not your** ~ **to say that** no eres quién para decir eso **2.** *inf* (*house*) casa *f*; **at my** ~ en mi casa **3.** (*building*) edificio *m* **4.** (*commercial location*) local *m* **5.** (*position*) posición *f*; **to take first/second** ~ quedar en primer/segundo lugar; **in the first** ~ primero; **in the second** ~ segundo **6.** (*seat*) sitio *m*; (*in theater*) localidad *f*; **is this** ~ **taken?** ¿está ocupado este sitio?; **to change** ~**s with sb** cambiar el sitio con alguien; **to save sb a** ~ guardar un sitio a alguien **7.** MATH **decimal** ~ decimal *m* **8.** *inf* (*in location*) **any** ~ en/a cualquier sitio; **every** ~ en todas partes; **some** ~ (a) algún sitio; **no** ~ en ningún sitio ▶ **to fall into** ~ encajar; **to go** ~**s** *inf* (*become successful*) llegar lejos; **to know one's** ~ saber cuál es el lugar de uno; **to put sb in his/her** ~ poner a alguien en su sitio; **all over the** ~ por todas partes; **to feel out of** ~ sentirse fuera de lugar II. *vt* **1.** (*position, put*) colocar; **to** ~ **sth somewhere** colocar algo en un sitio; **to** ~ **an advertisement in the newspaper** poner un anuncio en el periódico; **to** ~ **sth on the agenda** apuntar algo en la agenda **2.** (*impose*) imponer; **to** ~ **an embargo on sth** prohibir algo; **to** ~ **a limit on sth** poner un límite a algo; **to** ~ **sb under arrest** arrestar a alguien **3.** (*ascribe*) poner; **to** ~ **the blame on sb** echar la culpa a alguien; **to** ~ **one's hopes on sb/sth** poner sus esperanzas en alguien/algo; **to** ~ **one's faith in sb** depositar su confianza en alguien **4.** (*arrange for*) hacer; **to** ~ **an order for sth** hacer un pedido de algo; **to** ~ **a bet** hacer una apuesta; **to** ~ **sth at sb's disposal** poner algo a disposición de alguien **5.** (*appoint to a position*) to

~ **sb in charge (of sth)** poner a alguien a cargo de (algo); **to** ~ **sth under the control of sb** poner algo bajo el control de alguien; **to** ~ **sb under pressure** someter a alguien a presión; **to** ~ **sth above sth** poner algo por encima de algo; **to be** ~**d first/second** SPORTS quedar en primer/segundo lugar III. *vi* SPORTS clasificarse

**place card** *n* tarjeta *f* (indicadora del puesto que se ocupa)

**place mat** *n* salvamanteles *m inv*

**placement** ['pleɪs·mənt] *n* colocación *f*

**place name** *n* topónimo *m*

**plague** [pleɪg] I. *n* peste *f*; (*infestation of insects*) plaga *f*; (*source of annoyance*) pesadez *f*; **the** ~ la peste; **to avoid sb like the** ~ huir de alguien como de la peste II. *vt* fastidiar; **to** ~ **sb for sth** acosar a alguien por algo

**plaice** [pleɪs] *inv n* (*fish*) platija *f*

**plain** [pleɪn] I. *adj* **1.** sencillo, -a; (*monochrome*) de un solo color; (*without additions*) sin aditivos; ~ **yogur** *m* natural **2.** (*uncomplicated*) fácil; ~ **and simple** liso y llano **3.** (*clear, obvious*) evidente; **it is** ~ **that...** es evidente que...; **to be** ~ **enough** estar lo suficientemente claro; **to make sth** ~ dejar algo claro; **to be** ~ **with sb** ser franco con alguien **4.** (*mere, pure*) puro, -a; **the** ~ **truth** la pura verdad **5.** (*not pretty*) sin atractivo; **a** ~ **girl** una chica más bien fea II. *adv inf* (*downright*) y punto; ~ **awful** horrible III. *n* GEO llanura *f*; **the great Plains** la grandes llanuras (norteamericanas)

**plainclothes** *n* LAW (*of policeman*) ropa *f* de paisano

**plainly** ['pleɪn·li] *adv* **1.** (*simply*) simplemente **2.** (*clearly*) claramente; (*obviously*) evidentemente; **to be** ~ **visible** ser muy visible **3.** (*undeniably*) sin duda

**plaintiff** ['pleɪn·tɪf] *n* LAW demandante *mf*

**plait** [plæt] I. *n* trenza *f* II. *vt* trenzar

**plan** [plæn] I. *n* **1.** (*scheme, program*) plan *m*; **to draw up a** ~ elaborar un plan; **to go according to** ~ ir de acuerdo con lo previsto; **to change** ~**s** cambiar de planes; **do you have any** ~**s for this**

weekend? ¿tienes planes para este fin de semana? **2.** FIN, ECON (*policy*) seguro *m;* **healthcare ~** seguro *m* médico; **savings ~** plan *m* de ahorro **3.** (*diagram*) plano *m* II. <-nn-> *vt* **1.** (*work out in detail*) planificar; (*prepare*) preparar **2.** (*intend*) proponerse; **to ~ to do sth** proponerse hacer algo III. <-nn-> *vi* **1.** (*prepare*) hacer proyectos; **to ~ carefully** hacer proyectos detallados **2.** (*reckon with*) **to ~ on sth** tener pensado algo

**plane¹** [pleɪn] I. *n* (*level surface*) nivel *m;* MATH plano *m* II. *adj* plano, -a; MATH llano, -a; **~ angle** ángulo *m* plano

**plane²** [pleɪn] *n* (*airplane*) avión *m;* **by ~** en avión

**plane³** [pleɪn] I. *n* (*tool*) cepillo *m* (de carpintero) II. *vt* cepillar

**planet** [ˈplæn.ɪt] *n* planeta *m;* **~ Earth** la Tierra; **~ Jupiter** el planeta Júpiter

**planetarium** [ˌplæn·ɪˈter·i·əm] <-s *or* -ria> *n* planetario *m*

**plank** [plæŋk] *n* tabla *f*

**planner** *n* planificador(a) *m(f);* **city ~** urbanista *mf*

**planning** *n* planificación *f*

**plant** [plænt] I. *n* **1.** BOT planta *f* **2.** (*factory*) fábrica *f* **3.** (*machinery*) maquinaria *f* II. *vt* **1.** AGR (*put in earth*) plantar; **to ~ sth with sth** sembrar algo de algo **2.** (*put*) colocar; **to ~ oneself somewhere** *inf* meterse en algún sitio; **to ~ a bomb** poner una bomba; **to ~ a secret agent** introducir un agente secreto **3.** *inf* (*incriminate*) **to ~ evidence on sb** colocar pruebas para incriminar a alguien III. *adj* vegetal; **~ life** vida *f* vegetal

**plantation** [plænˈteɪ.ʃən] *n* plantación *f;* (*of trees*) arboleda *f*

**plaque** [plæk] *n* **1.** (*on building*) placa *f* **2.** MED sarro *m*

**plaster** [ˈplæs·tər] I. *n a.* MED yeso *m* II. *vt* (*wall, ceiling*) enyesar

**plasterboard** [ˈplæs·tər·bɔrd] *n* cartón *m* de yeso (y fieltro)

**plaster cast** *n* MED escayola *f*

**plastered** *adj sl* (*drunk*) borracho, -a

**plasterer** *n* yesero, -a *m, f*

**plastic** [ˈplæs·tɪk] I. *n* **1.** (*material*) plás-

tico *m* **2.** *inf* (*credit card*) tarjeta *f* (de crédito) II. *adj* **1.** (*made from plastic*) de plástico **2.** *pej* (*artificial*) artificial

**plastic surgery** *n* cirugía *f* plástica

**plate** [pleɪt] I. *n* **1.** (*dinner plate*) plato *m* **2.** (*panel, sheet*) lámina *f;* **steel ~** lámina de acero **3.** AUTO **license ~** (*placa f de la*) matrícula *f* **4.** (*layer of metal*) capa *f;* **gold ~** capa de oro **5.** (*picture in book*) ilustración *f* ▶ **to have a lot on one's ~** tener muchos asuntos entre manos II. *vt* **to ~ sth with gold/silver** chapar algo en oro/plata

**plated** *adj* (*coated in metal*) chapeado, -a; (*jewelry*) chapado, -a

**plateful** [ˈpleɪt·fʊl] *n* plato *m*

**plate glass** *n* vidrio *m*

**plate rack** *n* portaplatos *m inv*

**platform** [ˈplæt·fɔrm] *n* **1.** *a.* COMPUT plataforma *f* **2.** RAIL andén *m* **3.** (*stage*) escenario *m* **4.** (*means for expressing view*) medio *m* **5.** POL (*policy*) programa *m* electoral

**platinum** [ˈplæt·nəm] *n* platino *m*

**platonic** [pləˈtan·ɪk] *adj* platónico, -a

**platter** [ˈplæt̬·ər] *n* **1.** (*large dish*) fuente *f* **2.** (*food*) plato *m* fuerte ▶ **to give sth to sb on a ~** servir algo a alguien en bandeja

**platypus** [ˈplæt̬·ɪ·pəs] <-es> *n* ornitorrinco *m*

**play** [pleɪ] I. *n* **1.** (*recreation*) juego *m;* **to be at ~** estar en juego **2.** SPORTS juego *m;* **to be in/out of ~** estar en/fuera de juego **3.** SPORTS (*move*) jugada *f;* **foul ~** juego sucio; **to make a bad/good ~** hacer una mala/buena jugada **4.** THEAT obra *f* de teatro **5.** (*free movement*) juego *m* **6.** (*interaction*) juego *m;* **to bring sth into ~** poner algo en juego; **to come into ~** entrar en juego II. *vi* **1.** *a.* SPORTS jugar; **to ~ for a team** jugar en un equipo; **to ~ fair/rough** jugar limpio/sucio **2.** (*perform*) actuar **3.** MUS tocar III. *vt* **1.** (*participate in game, sport*) jugar; **to ~ bridge/soccer** jugar al bridge/al fútbol; **to ~ a card** jugar una carta; **to ~ a match/a round** jugar un partido/una ronda **2.** (*perform a role*) interpretar; **to ~ the clown** [*or* **fool**] hacer el payaso **3.** MUS (*instrument*) tocar; (*recording: CD, tape, video, DVD*) poner; **do you have to ~ the music so loud?** ¿es necesario que pongas la música tan alta?

◆**play down** *vt* quitar importancia a

◆**play on** I. *vt* 1. (*exploit*) **to ~ sb's weakness** aprovecharse de la debilidad de alguien 2. (*phrase, word*) jugar con II. *vi* (*keep playing*) SPORTS, GAMES seguir jugando; MUS seguir tocando

◆**play up** I. *vt* (*exaggerate: problem, difficulty*) exagerar II. *vi inf* **to ~ to sb** (*flatter*) dar coba a alguien

**play-act** ['pleɪ·ækt] *vi* 1. THEAT actuar 2. *fig* hacer teatro

**playback** ['pleɪ·bæk] *n* (*of tape*) reproducción *f*

**playboy** ['pleɪ·bɔɪ] *n* playboy *m*

**player** ['pleɪ·ər] *n* 1. SPORTS jugador(a) *m(f)*; **card ~** jugador(a) *m(f)* de cartas; **soccer ~** futbolista *mf*; **tennis ~** tenista *mf* 2. MUS instrumentista *mf*; **cello ~** violoncelista *mf*; **flute ~** flautista *mf* 3. THEAT actor *m*, actriz *f* 4. **CD ~** reproductor *m* de CD; **record ~** tocadiscos *m inv* 5. *sl* (*important person*) peso *m* pesado

**playful** ['pleɪ·fəl] *adj* 1. (*full of fun*) juguetón, -ona 2. (*comment, tone*) de guasa

**playground** ['pleɪ·graʊnd] *n* 1. (*at school*) patio *m*; (*in park*) campo *m* de recreo 2. *fig* (*resort*) lugar *m* de recreo

**playgroup** ['pleɪ·grup] *n* guardería *f*

**playing card** *n* carta *f*, naipe *m*

**playing field** *n* terreno *m* de juego

**playoff** ['pleɪ·ɔf] *n* desempate *m*; **~ match** partido *m* de desempate; **the ~s** las eliminatorias *fpl*

**playpen** ['pleɪ·pen] *n* parque *m*

**playroom** ['pleɪ·rum] *n* cuarto *m* de jugar

**playtime** ['pleɪ·taɪm] *n* SCHOOL recreo *m*

**playwright** ['pleɪ·raɪt] *n* dramaturgo, -a *m, f*

**plea** [pli] *n* 1. (*appeal*) petición *f*, súplica *f*; **to make a ~ for help** pedir ayuda 2. LAW alegato *m*; **to enter a ~ of not guilty** declararse inocente

**plead** [plid] <-ed *or* pled, -ed *or* pled>

I. *vi* 1. (*implore, beg*) implorar, suplicar; **to ~ for forgiveness** suplicar perdón 2. LAW **to ~ innocent** (**to a charge**) declararse inocente (de un cargo) II. *vt* 1. LAW **to ~ sb's case** defender el caso de alguien 2. (*claim as pretext*) pretextar; **to ~ ignorance of sth** pretextar su ignorancia en algo

**pleading** ['pli·dɪŋ] I. *n* 1. (*entreaty, appeal*) súplicas *fpl* 2. LAW alegato *m* II. *adj* (*look, tone*) suplicante

**pleasant** ['plez·ənt] *adj* 1. (*pleasing*) agradable; **what a ~ surprise!** ¡qué agradable sorpresa!; **have a ~ journey!** ¡buen viaje! 2. (*friendly*) amable

**please** [pliz] I. *vt* 1. (*make happy*) complacer; **to be hard to ~** ser difícil de contentar 2. *inf* (*do as one wishes*) **~ yourself** haz lo que te parezca II. *vi* 1. (*be agreeable*) eager **to ~** deseoso de agradar 2. (*think fit, wish*) **you can do as you ~** como usted quiera; **to do whatever one ~s** hacer todo lo que se quiera III. *interj* por favor; **if you ~** form con su permiso; **more potatoes? — (yes) ~** ¿más patatas? — sí, por favor; **oh, ~!** (*in annoyance*) ¡oh, por favor!

**pleased** *adj* 1. (*satisfied, contented*) satisfecho, -a (**with** de); **to be ~ about sth** estar contento de algo 2. (*happy, glad*) contento, -a; **I'm ~ to inform you that ...** me complace informarle de que...; **(I'm very) ~ to meet you** encantado de conocerle 3. (*willing*) **to be ~ to do sth** estar encantado de hacer algo

**pleasing** *adj* agradable; **~ news** buenas noticias *fpl*

**pleasurable** ['pleʒ·ər·ə·bəl] *adj* grato, -a

**pleasure** ['pleʒ·ər] *n* 1. (*feeling of enjoyment*) placer *m*; **it was such a ~ to meet you** ha sido un placer conocerle; **to take ~ in sth/in doing sth** disfrutar de algo/haciendo algo; **with ~** con mucho gusto 2. (*source of enjoyment*) placer *m*

**pleat** [plit] *n* pliegue *m*

**pleb** [pleb] *n inf abbr of* **plebian** plebeyo, -a *m, f*

**pled** [pled] *pt, pp of* **plead**

**pledge** [pledʒ] I. *n* 1. (*solemn promise*) promesa *f* solemne; **to fulfill a ~** cumplir un compromiso **2.** (*symbolic sign of promise*) **a ~ of good faith** una garantía de buena fe **3.** (*promised donation*) donativo *m* prometido **4.** (*pawned item*) prenda *f* **II.** *vt* **1.** (*promise*) prometer; **to ~ loyalty** jurar lealtad; **to ~ to do sth** prometer hacer algo; **to ~ that...** prometer que... **2.** (*give as security*) **to ~ money** dar dinero como garantía

**plentiful** ['plen·tɪ·fəl] *adj* abundante

**plenty** ['plen·ti] **I.** *n* **1.** (*abundance*) abundancia *f*; **land of ~** tierra *f* de abundancia; **food in ~** comida *f* en abundancia **2.** (*a lot*) **~ of time** tiempo *m* de sobra **II.** *adv* suficientemente; **~ more** mucho más

**pliers** ['plaɪ·ərz] *npl* alicates *mpl*; **a pair of ~** unos alicates

**plight** [plaɪt] *n* apuro *m*

**plod** [plad] <-dd-> *vi* **1.** (*walk heavily*) andar con paso pesado **2.** (*do without enthusiasm*) **to ~ through one's work** trabajar sin ganas

**plonk** [plaŋk] *n vt* see **plunk**

**plop** [plap] **I.** *n* plaf *m*; **to fall with a ~** caerse haciendo plaf **II.** <-pp-> *vi* (*fall*) **to ~ onto the bed** dejarse caer sobre la cama

**plot** [plat] **I.** *n* **1.** (*conspiracy, secret plan*) conspiración *f*; **the ~ thickens** *iron* el asunto se complica **2.** (*story line*) argumento *m* **3.** (*small piece of land*) terreno *m*; **a ~ of land** un terreno; **building ~** solar *m* **II.** <-tt-> *vt* **1.** (*conspire*) tramar **2.** (*create*) **to ~ a story line** idear un argumento **3.** (*graph, line*) trazar; **to ~ a course** planear una ruta **III.** <-tt-> *vi* **to ~ against sb** conspirar contra alguien; **to ~ to do sth** planear hacer algo

**plotter** ['plat·ər] *n* **1.** (*person*) conspirador(a) *m(f)* **2.** COMPUT plotter *m*

**plough** [plaʊ] *n vt, vi* see **plow**

**plow** [plaʊ] **I.** *n* arado *m* ▸ **to put one's hand to the ~** ponerse manos a la obra **II.** *vt* **1.** AGR arar **2.** (*move through*) **to ~ one's way through sth** abrirse paso por algo **3.** (*invest*) **we ~d into the sea** nos zambullimos en el mar **3.** (*begin abruptly*) **to ~ into sth** emprender algo

paso por algo

**ploy** [plɔɪ] *n* **1.** (*activity*) aventura *f* **2.** (*tactics*) estratagema *f*

**pluck** [plʌk] **I.** *n* **1.** (*sharp pull*) tirón *m* **2.** (*courage*) valor *m*; **it takes a lot of ~** hace falta mucho valor **II.** *vt* **1.** (*remove quickly*) arrancar **2.** (*remove hair, feathers*) **to ~ a chicken** desplumar un pollo; **to ~ one's eyebrows** depilarse las cejas **3.** MUS puntear

**plucky** ['plʌk·i] <-ier, -iest> *adj* valiente

**plug** [plʌg] **I.** *n* **1.** ELEC enchufe *m* **2.** (*stopper*) tapón *m* **3.** (*spark plug*) bujía *f* **II.** <-gg-> *vt* **1.** (*connect*) conectar; ELEC enchufar **2.** (*stop up, close*) **to ~ a hole** tapar un agujero **3.** (*publicize*) anunciar

♦**plug away** *vi* **to ~ (at sth)** perseverar (en algo)

♦**plug in** *vt* conectar; ELEC enchufar

**plug-in** *n* COMPUT plug-in *m*, enchufe *m*

**plum** [plʌm] **I.** *n* **1.** (*fruit*) ciruela *f* **2.** (*opportunity, reward*) chollo *m* **II.** *adj* (*color*) de color ciruela

**plumber** ['plʌm·ər] *n* fontanero, -a *m, f*, plomero, -a *m, f AmL*

**plumbing** ['plʌm·ɪŋ] *n* fontanería *f*

**plummet** ['plʌm·ɪt] *vi* caer en picado

**plump** [plʌmp] *adj* (*person*) rollizo, -a; (*animal*) gordo, -a

♦**plump up** *vt* **1.** (*pillow*) sacudir **2.** (*chicken*) cebar

**plum tree** *n* ciruelo *m*

**plunder** ['plʌn·dər] **I.** *n* **1.** (*stolen goods*) botín *m* **2.** (*act of plundering*) saqueo *m* **II.** *vt* **1.** (*village, city*) saquear **2.** (*goods, gold, treasures*) robar

**plunderer** ['plʌn·dər·ər] *n* saqueador(a) *m(f)*

**plunge** [plʌndʒ] **I.** *n* **1.** (*sharp decline*) caída *f* **2.** (*dive*) zambullida *f* de cabeza **II.** *vi* **1.** (*fall suddenly*) precipitarse **2.** (*leap, enter*) **we ~d into the sea** nos zambullimos en el mar **3.** (*begin abruptly*) **to ~ into sth** emprender algo

**plunger** ['plʌn·dʒər] *n* (*of syringe*) émbolo *m*; (*for drain, toilet*) desatascador *m*

**plunk** [plʌŋk] **I.** *n* inf (*sound*) ruido *m* sordo **II.** *vt* inf (*set down heavily*) dejar caer pesadamente

**pluperfect** ['plu·ˌpɜr·fɪkt] *n* LING pluscuamperfecto *m*

**plural** ['plʊr·əl] I. *n* plural *m*; **in the ~** en plural; **second person ~** segunda persona del plural II. *adj* 1. *a.* LING plural 2. (*multiple*) múltiple

**plus** [plʌs] I. *prep* más; **5 ~ 2 equals 7** 5 más 2 igual a 7 II. *conj* además III. <-es> *n* 1. (*mathematical symbol*) signo *m* más 2. (*advantage*) ventaja *f* a favor IV. *adj* 1. (*above zero*) positivo, -a; **~ 8** más 8; **~ two degrees** dos grados positivos 2. (*more than*) algo más de; **200 ~** más de 200 3. (*advantageous*) **the ~ side** (**of sth**) el lado positivo (de algo)

**plush** [plʌʃ] I. *adj* (*luxurious*) lujoso, -a, elegante II. <-es> *n* felpa *f*

**Pluto** ['plu·t̮oʊ] *n* Plutón *m*

**plutonium** [plu·'toʊ·ni·əm] *n* plutonio *m*

**ply¹** [plaɪ] *n* (*of cloth, wood*) capa *f*; **two-~ rope** cuerda *f* de dos cabos

**ply²** [plaɪ] <-ie-> *vt* 1. **to ~ one's trade** ejercer su profesión 2. **to ~ sb with questions** acosar a alguien a preguntas 3. (*sell*) **to ~ drugs** traficar con drogas; **to ~ one's wares** vender su mercancía

**plywood** ['plaɪ·wʊd] *n* contrachapado *m*

**PM** [ˌpiˈem] *n* 1. *abbr of* **postmortem** autopsia *f* 2. *abbr of* **prime minister** primer ministro *m*, primera ministra *f*

**P.M.** [ˌpiˈem] *abbr of* **post meridiem** p.m.; **one ~** la una de la tarde; **ten ~** las diez de la noche

**pneumatic** [nu·ˈmæt̮·ɪk] *adj* neumático, -a

**pneumonia** [nu·ˈmoʊn·jə] *n* neumonía *f*

**poach¹** [poʊtʃ] *vt* (*eggs*) escalfar; (*fish*) cocer

**poach²** [poʊtʃ] *vt, vi* (*animals*) cazar furtivamente; (*fish*) pescar furtivamente

**poacher** ['poʊ·tʃər] *n* (*hunter*) cazador(a) *m(f)* furtivo, -a; (*fisherman*) pescador(a) *m(f)* furtivo, -a

**poaching** ['poʊ·tʃɪŋ] *n* (*hunting*) caza *f* furtiva; (*fishing*) pesca *f* furtiva

**POB** *n abbr of* **post office box** apdo. *m* de correos

**pocket** ['pak·ɪt] I. *n* 1. (*in pants, jacket*) bolsillo *m*, bolsa *f* AmC, Méx; **inside ~** bolsillo interior; **to pay for sth out of**

one's own ~ pagar algo de su bolsillo 2. (*isolated group, area*) **a ~ of resistance** un foco de resistencia; **~ of turbulence** AVIAT, METEO racha *f* de turbulencias 3. (*in pool table*) tronera *f* ▸ **to have sth/sb in one's ~** tener algo/a alguien en el bolsillo II. *vt* 1. (*put in pocket*) **to ~ sth** meterse algo en el bolsillo 2. (*keep for oneself*) apropiarse de III. *adj* (*dictionary*) de bolsillo

**pocketbook** ['pak·ɪt·bʊk] *n* 1. (*handbag*) bolso *m*, cartera *f* AmL 2. (*billfold*) monedero *m* 3. (*book*) libro *m* de bolsillo

**pocket calculator** *n* calculadora *f* de bolsillo

**pocketknife** <-knives> *n* navaja *f*

**pocket money** *n* dinero *m* para gastos personales

**pocket-sized** *adj* de bolsillo

**pod** [pad] *n* BOT vaina *f*

**podium** ['poʊ·di·əm] <-s *or* -dia> *n* podio *m*

**poem** ['poʊ·əm] *n* poema *m*

**poet** ['poʊ·ət] *n* poeta *mf*

**poetry** ['poʊ·ɪ·tri] *n a. fig* poesía *f*

**point** [pɔɪnt] I. *n* 1. (*sharp end*) punta *f* 2. GEO cabo *m* 3. (*particular place*) punto *m*; **boiling/freezing ~** punto *m* de ebullición/congelación; **starting ~** punto de partida 4. (*particular time*) momento *m*; **to get to the ~ that...** llegar al extremo de...; **at this ~ in time** en este momento 5. (*significant idea*) cuestión *f*; **that's just the ~!** ¡eso es lo importante!; **to be beside the ~** no venir al caso; **to get to the ~** ir al grano; **to make one's ~** expresar su opinión; **to miss the ~** no captar lo relevante; **~ taken** de acuerdo; **~ by ~** punto por punto 6. (*purpose*) finalidad *f*; **what's the ~?** ¿qué sentido tiene? 7. (*characteristic*) **sb's strong/weak ~s** los puntos fuertes/débiles de alguien 8. (*in score, result*) punto *m*; **percentage ~** puntos *m pl* porcentuales; **to win (sth) on ~s** (*in boxing*) ganar (algo) por puntos 9. MATH **decimal ~** coma *f*, punto *m* decimal AmL ▸ **to make a ~ of doing sth** procurar de hacer algo II. *vi* (*with finger*) señalar; (*indicate*) **to ~ to sth** indicar algo III. *vt* 1. (*aim*) apun-

**P**

tar; **the man had ~ed a knife at him** el hombre le había amenazado con un cuchillo; **to ~ a finger at sb** a. fig señalar con el dedo a alguien **2.** (direct) señalar; **to ~ sth toward sth/sb** dirigir algo hacia algo/alguien

♦**point out** vt **1.** (show) indicar **2.** (inform of) **to point sth out to sb** advertir a alguien de algo; **to ~ that...** señalar que...

**point-blank** [ˌpɔɪntˈblæŋk] adv **1.** (fire) a quemarropa **2.** (ask) a bocajarro; **to refuse** ~ negarse rotundamente

**pointed** ['pɔɪn·tɪd] adj **1.** (implement, stick) puntiagudo, -a **2.** fig (question) directo, -a; (remark) intencionado, -a

**pointer** ['pɔɪn·tər] n **1.** (for blackboard) puntero m; (of clock) aguja f, manecilla f **2.** COMPUT puntero m; **mouse ~** puntero del ratón **3.** (advice, tip) consejo m

**pointless** ['pɔɪnt·lɪs] adj inútil

**point of no return** n inf punto m sin retorno

**point of view** <points of view> n punto m de vista

**poise** [pɔɪz] n **1.** (composure) aplomo m; **to lose/regain one's ~** perder/recobrar la serenidad **2.** (elegance) porte m

**poised** adj **1.** (suspended) suspendido, -a; **~ in the air** suspendido, -a en el aire **2.** (ready) preparado, -a **3.** (calm) sereno, -a

**poison** ['pɔɪ·zən] **I.** n veneno m; **rat ~** matarratas m inv; **to take ~** envenenarse ▶ **what's your ~?** fig ¿qué tomas? **II.** vt **1.** (give poison to) envenenar **2.** (spoil, corrupt) emponzoñar

**poison gas** n gas m tóxico

**poisoning** n envenenamiento m

**poison ivy** n BOT hiedra f venenosa

**poisonous** ['pɔɪ·zə·nəs] adj venenoso, -a; fig ~ **atmosphere** ambiente m pernicioso; ~ **remark** comentario m malicioso

**poke¹** [poʊk] n reg: esp. Southern (bag) bolsa f, saco m

**poke²** [poʊk] **I.** n (push) empujón m; (with elbow) codazo m **II.** vt **1.** (with finger) dar con la punta del dedo en; (with elbow) dar un codazo a; **to ~ a hole in sth** hacer un agujero en algo; **to ~**

~ **one's nose into sb's business** meter las narices en los asuntos de alguien **2.** (emerge) asomar **III.** vi **to ~ at sth/ sb** dar a algo/alguien; **to ~ through** (sth) salirse (de algo)

**poker¹** ['poʊ·kər] n (card game) póquer m

**poker²** ['poʊ·kər] n (fireplace tool) atizador m

**poky** ['poʊ·ki] <-ier, -iest> adj inf **1.** (slow) lerdo, -a **2.** (small) diminuto, -a; **a ~ little room** un cuartucho

**Poland** ['poʊ·lənd] n Polonia f

**polar** ['poʊ·lər] adj GEO, MATH polar

**polar bear** n oso m polar

**polar icecap** n casquete m polar

**polarity** [poʊ·ˈlær·ə·ti] n polaridad f

**pole¹** [poʊl] n palo m; **fishing ~** caña f de pescar; **telephone ~** poste m de teléfonos

**pole²** [poʊl] n **1.** GEO, ELEC polo m **2.** fig bando m; **to be ~s apart** ser polos opuestos

**Pole¹** [poʊl] n (person) polaco, -a m, f

**Pole²** [poʊl] n GEO **the North/South ~** el Polo Norte/Sur

**pole vault** n salto m con pértiga

**police** [pə·ˈlis] n policía f

**police car** n coche m de policía

**police dog** n perro m policía

**police escort** n escolta f policial; **under** ~ con escolta policial

**police force** n cuerpo m de policía

**policeman** [pə·ˈlis·mən] <-men> n policía m, guardia m

**police officer** n policía mf, guardia m

**police patrol** n patrulla f policial

**police raid** n redada f, arreada f Arg

**police record** n **1.** (file) expediente m **2.** (history of convictions) antecedentes m pl penales

**police state** n estado m policíaco

**police station** n comisaría f (de policía)

**policewoman** [pə·ˈlis·ˌwʊm·ən] <-women> n (mujer f) policía f

**policy¹** ['pal·ə·si] <-ies> n **1.** POL, ECON política f; **company** ~ política de empresa **2.** (principle) principio m; **my ~ is to tell the truth** tengo por norma decir la verdad

**policy²** ['pal·ə·si] <-ies> n FIN póliza f;

**insurance ~** póliza de seguros

**policyholder** ['pɑl·ə·si·ˌhoʊl·dər] *n* asegurado, -a *m, f*

**policy maker** *n* responsable *mf* de los principios políticos de un partido

**policy number** *n* número *m* de póliza

**policy owner** *n* titular *mf* de una póliza

**polio** [ˌpoʊ·li·oʊ] *n* MED polio *f*

**polish** ['pɑl·ɪʃ] I. *n* 1. (*substance: for furniture*) cera *f*; (*for shoes*) betún *m*; (*for silver*) abrillantador *m*; (*for nails*) esmalte *m* 2. (*sophisticated, refined style*) refinamiento *m* II. *vt* 1. (*make shine*) sacar brillo a; (*shoes, silver*) limpiar 2. *fig* (*refine*) pulir

♦**polish off** *vt* (*food*) despacharse; (*work, opponent*) liquidar

♦**polish up** *vt* 1. (*polish to a shine*) dar brillo a 2. (*improve, brush up*) perfeccionar

**Polish** ['poʊ·lɪʃ] I. *adj* polaco II. *n* LING polaco *m*

**polished** *adj* 1. (*shiny*) pulido, -a 2. *fig* (*sophisticated*) distinguido, -a; **~ manners** modales *m pl* refinados; **a ~ performance** una actuación impecable

**polite** [pə·'laɪt] *adj* 1. (*courteous*) atento, -a 2. (*cultured*) educado, -a; (*refined*) fino, -a 3. (*superficially courteous*) correcto, -a

**politeness** *n* cortesía *f*, educación *f*

**political** [pə·'lɪt·ɪ·kəl] *adj* político, -a

**politically correct** *adj* políticamente correcto, -a

**politician** [ˌpɑl·ə·'tɪʃ·ən] *n* político, -a *m, f*

**politics** *n pl* 1. (*government*) política *f*; **to go into ~** dedicarse a la política; **to talk ~** hablar de política 2. (*intrigue*) **company ~** intrigas en la empresa

**poll** [poʊl] I. *n* 1. (*public survey*) encuesta *f*; **opinion ~** sondeo *m* de la opinión pública; **to conduct a ~** hacer una encuesta 2. *pl* (*elections*) **to go to the ~s** acudir a las urnas 3. (*number of votes cast*) votos *mpl* II. *vt* 1. (*record the opinion*) sondear; **half the people ~ed** la mitad de los encuestados 2. (*receive*) **to ~ votes** obtener votos

**pollen** ['pɑl·ən] *n* polen *m*

**polling place** *n* colegio *m* electoral

**pollutant** [pə·'lu·tənt] *n* agente *m* contaminador

**pollute** [pə·'lut] *vt* 1. ECOL contaminar 2. *fig* (*corrupt*) corromper

**polluter** [pə·'lu·tər] *n* contaminador(a) *m(f)*

**pollution** [pə·'lu·ʃən] *n* contaminación *f*

**polo** ['poʊ·loʊ] *n* SPORTS polo *m*

**polo shirt** *n* polo *m*

**polystyrene** [ˌpɑl·i·'staɪ·rin] *n* (espuma *f* de) poliestireno *m*

**polytechnic** [ˌpɑl·i·'tek·nɪk] *n* escuela *f* politécnica

**polyunsaturated fats** *npl*, **polyunsaturates** [ˌpɑl·i·ʌn·'sætʃ·ə·rəts] *npl* grasas *f pl* poliinsaturadas

**polyurethane** [ˌpɑl·i·'jʊr·ə·θeɪn] *n* poliuretano *m*

**pomp** [pɑmp] *n* pompa *f*

**pompous** ['pɑm·pəs] *adj* 1. pomposo, -a 2. (*pretentious*) ostentoso, -a

**pond** [pɑnd] *n* (*natural*) charca *f*; (*man-made*) estanque *m*; **fish ~** vivero *m*

**ponder** ['pɑn·dər] I. *vt* sopesar; **to ~ whether/why...** preguntarse si/por qué... II. *vi* reflexionar; **to ~ on sth** meditar sobre algo

**ponderous** ['pɑn·dər·əs] *adj* 1. (*movement*) pesado, -a 2. (*style*) laborioso, -a

**pony** ['poʊ·ni] <-ies> *n* poni *m*

**ponytail** ['poʊ·ni·teɪl] *n* coleta *f*

**poo** [pu] *sl* I. *n* caca *f* II. *vi* hacer caca

**poodle** ['pu·dəl] *n* caniche *m*, perro *m* de lanas

**pool¹** [pul] *n* 1. (*of water*) charca *f*; (*of oil, blood*) charco *f* 2. (*man-made*) estanque *m*; **swimming ~** piscina *f*, pileta *f* RíoPl

**pool²** [pul] I. *n* 1. (*common fund*) fondo *m* común 2. (*common supply*) reserva *f*; **car ~** parque *m* de automóviles 3. SPORTS billar *m* americano; **to play (a game of) ~** jugar al billar II. *vt* (*money, resources*) hacer un fondo común; (*information*) compartir

**poor** [pʊr] *adj* 1. (*lacking money*) pobre 2. (*attendance, harvest*) escaso, -a; (*memory, performance*) malo, -a; **~ visibility** visibilidad *f* escasa; **to be ~ at sth** no estar fuerte en algo; **to be in ~ health** estar mal de salud; **to be a ~ los-**

P

er no saber perder; **to have ~ eyesight** tener mala vista; **to have ~ hearing** ser duro de oído; **to do a ~ job of (doing) sth** hacer algo mal **3.** (*deserving of pity*) pobre; **you ~ thing!** ¡pobrecito!

**poorly** ['pʊr·li] **I.** *adv* **1.** (*resulting from poverty*) pobremente **2.** (*inadequately*) mal; **~ dressed** mal vestido; **to think ~ of sb** tener mala opinión de alguien **II.** *adj* to feel **~** encontrarse mal

**pop¹** [pap] **I.** *adj* popular; **~ culture** cultura *f* pop **II.** *n* MUS (música *f*) pop *m*

**pop²** [pap] *n inf* (*father*) papá *m*

**pop³** [pap] **I.** *n* **1. the ~ of a champagne cork** el taponazo de una botella de champán **2.** (*soda pop*) gaseosa *f*; **orange ~** naranjada *f* **II.** <-pp-> *vi* **1.** (*explode*) estallar; (*burst*) reventar; **to let the cork ~** hacer saltar el tapón **2.** (*come, go quickly*) **to ~ upstairs** subir un momento; **to ~ out for sth** salir un momento a por algo **III.** <-pp-> *vt* (*make burst*) hacer estallar; **to ~ popcorn** hacer palomitas

◆**pop in** *vi* entrar un momento en

◆**pop out** *vi* salir; **to ~ from somewhere** salir de pronto de un sitio; **to ~ for sth** salir un momento a hacer algo

◆**pop up** *vi* (*appear*) aparecer; **to ~ out of nowhere** surgir de la nada

**popcorn** ['pap·kɔrn] *n* palomitas *f pl* (de maíz), pororó *m* CSur, cacalote *m* AmC, Méx

**pope** [poʊp] *n* REL **1.** (*Catholic*) papa *m* **2.** (*Orthodox*) pope *m*

**poplar** ['pap·lər] *n* álamo *m*

**popper** ['pap·ər] *n* **1.** (*for making popcorn*) recipiente para hacer palomitas **2.** *inf* (*drug*) popper *m*

**poppy** ['pap·i] <-ies> *n* amapola *f*

**popular** ['pap·jə·lər] *adj* **1.** (*liked*) popular; **he is ~ with girls** tiene éxito con las chicas **2.** (*by the people*) popular; **~ elections** elecciones *f pl* democráticas; **~ support** el apoyo del pueblo; **by ~ request** a petición del público **3.** (*widespread*) generalizado, -a

**popularity** [ˌpap·jə·ˈlær·ə·t̬i] *n* popularidad *f*

**population** [ˌpap·jə·ˈleɪ·ʃən] *n* población *f*; **the working ~** la población activa

**population density** *n* densidad *f* de población

**population explosion** *n* explosión *f* demográfica

**populous** ['pap·jʊ·ləs] *adj* populoso, -a

**porcelain** ['pɔr·sə·lɪn] *n* porcelana *f*

**porch** [pɔrtʃ] *n* **1.** (*over entrance*) porche *m*; (*church*) pórtico *m* **2.** (*verandah*) veranda *f*

**porcupine** ['pɔr·kjʊ·paɪn] *n* puercoespín *m*

**pore** [pɔr] *n* poro *m*

**pork** [pɔrk] *n* (carne *f* de) cerdo *m*, (carne *f* de) puerco *m* Méx, (carne *f* de) chancho *m* Chile, Perú

**porn** [pɔrn] *n abbr of* **pornography** porno *m*

**pornographic** [ˌpɔr·nə·ˈgræf·ɪk] *adj* pornográfico, -a

**pornography** [pɔr·ˈnag·rə·fi] *n* pornografía *f*

**porous** ['pɔr·əs] *adj* poroso, -a

**porpoise** ['pɔr·pəs] *n* marsopa *f*

**porridge** ['pɔr·ɪdʒ] *n* ≈ gachas *f pl* de avena

**port¹** [pɔrt] *n* **1.** NAUT (*harbor*) puerto *m*; **to come into ~** tomar puerto; **to leave ~** zarpar **2.** COMPUT puerto *m*; **parallel/ serial ~** puerto paralelo/serial

**port²** [pɔrt] *n* AVIAT, NAUT (*left side*) babor *m*; **to ~** a babor

**port³** [pɔrt] *n* (*wine*) oporto *m*

**portable** ['pɔr·t̬ə·bəl] *adj* portátil

**porter** ['pɔr·t̬ər] *n* mozo *m* de equipajes; (*on expedition*) porteador *m*

**portfolio** [pɔrt·ˈfoʊ·li·oʊ] *n* **1.** (*case*) portafolio(s) *m* (*inv*) **2.** (*of drawings*) carpeta *f* de trabajos **3.** FIN, POL cartera *f*; **minister without ~** Can ministro, -a *m, f* sin cartera

**portion** ['pɔr·ʃən] **I.** *n* **1.** (*part*) parte *f* **2.** (*serving*) ración *f*; (*of cake, cheese*) trozo *m* **II.** *vt* to **~ out sth** repartir algo

**portly** ['pɔrt·li] <-ier, -iest> *adj* corpulento, -a

**portrait** ['pɔr·trɪt] **I.** *n* ART, LIT retrato *m* **II.** *adj* TYPO de formato vertical

**portraitist** *n* retratista *mf*

**portray** [pɔr·ˈtreɪ] *vt* **1.** ART (*person*) retratar; (*object*) pintar; (*scene, environ-*

ment) representar **2.** *fig* describir

**portrayal** [pɔr'treɪ·əl] *n* **1.** ART retrato *m* **2.** *fig* descripción *f*

**Portugal** ['pɔr·tʃə·gəl] *n* Portugal *m*

**Portuguese** [,pɔr·tʃə'giz] **I.** *adj* portugués, -esa **II.** *n* **1.** (*person*) portugués, -esa *m, f* **2.** LING portugués *m*

**pose¹** [poʊz] *vt* (*difficulty, problem*) plantear; (*question*) formular; **to ~ a threat to sb** representar una amenaza para alguien

**pose²** [poʊz] **I.** *vi* **1.** ART, PHOT posar **2.** (*pretend to be*) **to ~ as sb/sth** hacerse pasar por alguien/algo **II.** *n* (*body position*) pose *f*

**poser** ['poʊ·zər] *n inf* (*question*) pregunta *f* difícil; (*problem*) dilema *m*

**posh** [pɑʃ] *adj inf* (*stylish: area*) elegante; (*car, hotel, restaurant*) de lujo, pijo, -a *pey*

**position** [pə'zɪʃ·ən] **I.** *n* **1.** *a.* MIL, SPORTS posición *f*; **they took up their ~s** ocuparon sus puestos; **to be in ~** estar en su sitio; **to be out of ~** estar fuera de lugar **2.** (*rank*) posición *f*, puesto *m*; (*social*) rango *m*; (*job*) puesto *m* (de trabajo); **the ~ of director** el cargo de director; **a ~ of responsibility** un puesto de responsabilidad **3.** (*opinion*) postura *f*; **to take a ~ on sth** adoptar una postura sobre algo **4.** (*situation*) situación *f*; **financial ~** situación económica; **to be in a ~ to do sth** estar en condiciones de hacer algo; **to be in no ~ to do sth** no estar en condiciones de hacer algo **II.** *vt* (*place*) colocar; MIL apostar

**positive** ['pɑz·ɪ·tɪv] *adj* **1.** *a.* ELEC, MATH positivo, -a **2.** MED **HIV ~** seropositivo, -a **3.** (*certain*) definitivo, -a; (*proof*) concluyente; **to be ~ about sth** estar seguro de algo; (**absolutely**) **~!** ¡segurísimo!

**positively** *adv* **1.** (*think*) positivamente; **to answer ~** contestar afirmativamente; **to think ~** pensar en positivo **2.** (*completely*) totalmente; **to ~ refuse to do sth** negarse rotundamente a hacer algo

**possess** [pə'zes] *vt* **1.** (*own, have*) poseer **2. to ~ sb** (*anger, fear*) apoderarse de alguien; (*evil spirit*) poseer a alguien

**possessed** [pə'zest] *adj* poseso, -a, poseído, -a; **to be ~ with sth** estar obsesionado con algo

**possession** [pə'zeʃ·ən] *n* **1.** (*having*) posesión *f*; **illegal ~ of arms** tenencia *f* ilícita de armas; **to take ~ of sth** tomar posesión de algo; **to come into ~ of sth** hacerse dueño de algo; **to gain ~ of sth** apoderarse de algo; **to be in sb's ~** estar en poder de alguien **2.** (*item of property*) bien *m* **3.** POL dominio *m* **4.** SPORTS **to be in ~ of the ball** llevar la bola

**possessive** [pə'zes·ɪv] *adj* posesivo, -a; **to be ~ about sb** comportarse de manera posesiva con alguien

**possibility** [,pɑs·ə·'bɪl·ə·ti] *n* <-ies> **1.** (*sth feasible*) posibilidad *f* **2.** (*likelihood*) perspectiva *f*; **within the realm of ~** dentro de lo posible; **is there any ~ (that)...?** ¿hay alguna posibilidad de que +*subj*...?

**possible** ['pɑs·ə·bəl] *adj* posible; **as clean/good as ~** lo más limpio/lo mejor posible; **as far as ~** en lo posible; **as soon as ~** lo antes posible; **if ~** si es posible

**possibly** ['pɑs·ə·bli] *adv* **1.** (*perhaps*) quizás, posiblemente; **could you ~ help me?** ¿sería tan amable de ayudarme? **2.** (*by any means*) **we did all that we ~ could** hicimos todo lo posible; **I couldn't ~ do it** me es totalmente imposible hacerlo

**post¹** [poʊst] **I.** *n* correo *m* **II.** *vt* **1.** (*letter, package*) echar (al correo); **to ~ sth to sb** enviar algo por correo a alguien **2.** (*inform*) **to keep sb ~ed on sth** tener a alguien al corriente de algo

**post²** [poʊst] *n* (*job*) puesto *m* (de trabajo); **to apply for a teaching ~** solicitar un empleo de profesor; **to take up a ~** entrar en funciones; **to desert one's ~** MIL desertar del puesto

**post³** [poʊst] **I.** *n* **1.** *a.* SPORTS poste *m*; **starting/finishing ~** línea *f* de salida/de meta **2.** *inf* (*goalpost*) poste *m* (de la portería) **II.** *vt* **~ no bills** prohibido fijar carteles

**postage** ['poʊ·stɪdʒ] *n* franqueo *m*; **~ and handling** gastos *m pl* de envío

**postal** ['poʊ·stəl] *adj* postal

**post card** *n* (tarjeta *f*) postal *f*

**poster** ['poʊ·stər] n 1. (*picture*) póster m 2. (*notice*) cartel m

**postgraduate** [,poʊst·'grædʒ·u·ɪt] I. n postgraduado, -a m, f; II. adj de postgrado; ~ **studies** (estudios m pl de) postgrado m

**posting** ['poʊ·stɪŋ] n destino m

**postman** ['poʊst·mən] <-men> n cartero m

**postmark** ['poʊst·mɑrk] I. n matasellos m inv II. vt matasellar

**post meridiem** adv see **P.M.**

**postmortem** [,poʊst·'mɔr·təm] n autopsia f; **to carry out a ~** realizar una autopsia

**post office** n (oficina f de) correos m

**post office box** n apartado m de correos, casilla f postal CSur

**postpone** [poʊst·'poʊn] vt aplazar, posponer

**postponement** n aplazamiento m

**postscript** ['poʊst·skrɪp] n 1. (*at end of letter*) pos(t)data f 2. fig epílogo m; **as a ~ to sth** como colofón de algo

**posture** ['pɑs·tʃər] I. n postura f, actitud f II. vi tomar una postura, adoptar una actitud

**postwar** [,poʊst·'wɔr] adj de (la) posguerra

**pot¹** [pɑt] I. n 1. (*container*) bote m 2. (*for cooking*) olla f; **~s and pans** cacharros mpl 3. (*of food*) tarro m; (*of drink*) jarro m; (*for coffee*) cafetera f; (*for tea*) tetera f 4. maceta f, tiesto m 5. inf GAMES **to win the ~** llevarse el bote 6. (*common fund*) fondo m común 7. inf (*a lot*) montón m; **~s of money** montones de dinero 8. fig (*beer belly*) barriga f inf II. <-tt-> vt 1. (*put in a pot: food*) conservar en un tarro; **to ~ (up)** (*plants*) plantar 2. (*shoot*) cazar 3. SPORTS (*ball*) meter (en la tronera)

**pot²** [pɑt] n sl (*marijuana*) hierba f, maría f, mota f Méx; **to smoke ~** fumar maría

**potato** [pə·'teɪ·toʊ] <-es> n patata f, papa f AmL; **sweet ~** batata f; **baked ~** patata al horno; **mashed ~es** puré m de patatas; **fried/roast(ed) ~s** patatas fritas/asadas

**potato chips** npl patatas f pl fritas (en

bolsa), papas f pl chip AmL

**potato masher** n pasapurés m inv

**potato peeler** n pelapatatas m inv, pelapapas m inv AmL

**potent** ['poʊ·tənt] adj potente; (*drink, poison, symbol*) fuerte; (*motive*) poderoso, -a

**potential** [pə·'ten·ʃəl] I. adj 1. posible 2. LING, PHYS potencial II. n potencial m; **to have (a lot of) ~** tener (un gran) potencial

**potentially** [pə·'ten·ʃə·li] adv potencialmente

**pothole** ['pɑt·hoʊl] n 1. (*in road*) bache m, pozo m CSur 2. (*underground hole*) sima f

**pot roast** n estofado m

**potshot** ['pɑt·ʃɑt] n tiro m al azar

**potted** ['pɑt·ɪd] adj 1. (*plant*) en tiesto, en maceta 2. (*food*) en conserva

**potter** ['pɑt·ər] n alfarero, -a m, f; **~'s wheel** torno m de alfarero

**pottery** ['pɑt·ə·ri] n 1. (*art*) cerámica f 2. <-ies> (*workshop*) alfarería f

**potty** ['pɑt·i] <-ies> n (*for baby*) orinal m; **to go (to the) ~** (*small child*) (ir a) hacer pis

**pouch** [paʊtʃ] n 1. a. ANAT, ZOOL bolsa f 2. (*handbag*) bolso m; (*for mail*) valija f; **tobacco ~** petaca f

**poultry** ['poʊl·tri] n 1. (*birds*) aves f pl de corral 2. (*meat*) carne f de ave

**pounce** [paʊns] I. n (*spring*) salto m II. vi 1. (*jump*) saltar; **to ~ on sth** abalanzarse sobre algo 2. fig **to ~ on an opportunity** no dejar escapar una oportunidad

**pound¹** [paʊnd] n 1. (*weight*) libra f (*454 g*); **by the ~** por libras 2. (*currency*) libra f; **~ sterling** libra esterlina

**pound²** [paʊnd] n (*for cars*) depósito m; (*for dogs*) perrera f; (*for sheep*) redil m

**pound³** [paʊnd] I. vt 1. (*hit repeatedly*) aporrear; (*beat*) golpear; (*with a hammer*) martillear; **the waves ~ed the ship** las olas batían contra el barco 2. (*walk heavily*) patear; **I could hear him ~ing the floor upstairs** podía oír sus pasos en el piso de arriba 3. (*crush*) machacar; (*meat*) golpear, ablandar 4. MIL batir; **to ~ sth to**

**rubble** reducir algo a escombros II. *vi* 1. (*beat*) dar golpes; (*on a door, table*) aporrear; (*heart, pulse*) latir con fuerza; **my head is ~ing!** ¡la cabeza me va a estallar! 2. (*run*) **to ~ downstairs** bajar corriendo 3. *fig* **to ~ away at sth** insistir en algo

**pounding** *n* 1. (*noise*) golpeteo *m;* (*of heart*) fuerte latido *m;* (*of sea*) embate *m;* (*in head*) martilleo *m* 2. (*crushing*) trituración *f* 3. (*attack*) ataque *m; a. fig* (*beating*) paliza *f inf;* **to take a ~** *a. fig* llevarse una paliza; **the film took a heavy ~** la película tuvo muy malas críticas

**pour** [pɔːr] I. *vt* 1. (*cause to flow*) verter; **to ~ coffee/wine** echar café/vino; **to ~ sb sth** servir algo a alguien 2. (*give in large amounts*) verter; (*money, resources*) invertir; **to ~ time into** sth dedicar tiempo a algo; **to ~ energy into sth** volcarse en algo II. *vi* 1. (*flow in large amounts: water*) fluir; (*letters, messages*) llegar en grandes cantidades; **to ~ into sth** (*sunshine*) entrar a raudales en algo; **refugees are ~ing into the country** no cesan de llegar refugiados al país 2. *impers* **it's ~ing** llueve a cántaros

♦ **pour in** *vi* llegar en abundancia

♦ **pour out** I. *vt* 1. (*from container*) verter; (*cause to flow quickly: smoke, water*) echar 3. (*tell*) **to ~ sth to sb** revelar algo a alguien II. *vi* (*liquid*) salir; (*people*) salir en tropel

**pout** [paʊt] I. *vi* hacer un mohín II. *vt* **to ~ one's lips** hacer un mohín III. *n* mohín *m*

**poverty** ['pɑv·ər·t̬i] *n* 1. (*lack of money*) pobreza *f* 2. *fig* (*lack of ideas, imagination*) escasez *f*

**poverty-stricken** ['pɑv·ər·t̬i·strɪk·ən] *adj* muy pobre

**POW** [ˌpiː·oʊ·ˈdʌb·əl·ju] *n abbr of* **prisoner of war** prisionero, -a *m, f* de guerra

**powder** ['paʊ·dər] I. *n* 1. (*dust*) polvo *m;* **to crush** [*or* **reduce**] **sth to a ~** reducir algo a polvo 2. (*makeup*) polvos *mpl;* **talcum ~** polvos (de) talco II. *vt* 1. (*cover with powder*) empolvar; **to ~ one's face** empolvarse; **to ~ one's**

**nose** *fig* ir al servicio 2. (*sprinkle*) espolvorear

**powdered** *adj* en polvo; **~ sugar** azúcar *m* glas

**powdery** ['paʊ·də·ri] *adj* como de polvo

**power** ['paʊ·ər] I. *n* 1. (*ability to control*) poder *m;* **to be within one's ~ to do sth** estar en manos de alguien hacer algo 2. (*country, organization, person*) potencia *f* 3. (*right*) derecho *m* 4. (*ability*) capacidad *f;* **sb's ~s of concentration/persuasion/observation** la capacidad de concentración/persuasión/observación de alguien 5. (*strength*) fuerza *f* 6. (*electricity*) electricidad *f;* **to cut** (**off**) **the ~** cortar la corriente 7. (*energy*) energía *f* 8. MATH potencia *f;* **two to the ~ of five** dos elevado a la quinta potencia II. *vt* impulsar

**powerboat** *n* lancha *f* fuera borda

**power brakes** *npl* AUTO frenos *m pl* asistidos, servofrenos *mpl*

**power cable** *n* cable *m* de energía eléctrica

**powerful** ['paʊ·ər·fəl] *adj* 1. (*influential, mighty*) poderoso, -a 2. (*physically strong*) fuerte 3. (*having a great effect*) convincente 4. (*anger, jealousy*) intenso, -a 5. (*able to perform well*) potente

**powerfully** ['paʊ·ər·fə·li] *adv* 1. (*using great force*) con potencia 2. (*argue, speak*) de forma convincente

**powerless** ['paʊ·ər·lɪs] *adj* impotente; **to be ~ against sb** no poder hacer nada contra alguien

**power line** *n* línea *f* eléctrica

**power plant** *n* central *f* eléctrica; **nuclear ~** central *f* nuclear

**power station** *n* central *f* eléctrica

**power steering** *n* dirección *f* asistida

**pox** [pɑks] *n* MED (*chickenpox*) varicela *f;* (*smallpox*) viruela *f;* (*syphilis*) sífilis *f inv*

**pp.** *abbr of* **pages** págs.

**PR** [piː·ˈɑr] *n* 1. *abbr of* **public relations** relaciones *f pl* públicas 2. GEO *abbr of* **Puerto Rico** Puerto Rico *m*

**practicable** ['præk·tɪ·kə·bəl] *adj form* factible

**practical** ['præk·tɪ·kəl] I. *adj* práctico, -a

II. n examen m práctico

**practical joke** n broma f pesada, trastada f

**practically** ['præk·tɪk·li] adv 1. (almost) casi 2. (of a practical nature) to be ~ based basarse en la práctica; to be ~ minded tener sentido práctico

**practice** ['præk·tɪs] I. n 1. (act of practicing) práctica f; to be out of ~ estar desentrenado; ~ makes perfect se aprende con la práctica 2. (custom, regular activity) costumbre f; standard ~ práctica f habitual 3. (training session) entrenamiento m 4. (of a profession) ejercicio m 5. (business, office) bufete m; (medical) consulta f II. vt 1. (do, carry out) practicar 2. (improve skill) hacer ejercicios de; to ~ the piano estudiar el piano 3. (work in: medicine, law) ejercer ▶ to ~ what one **preaches** predicar con el ejemplo III. vi 1. (improve skill) practicar; SPORTS entrenarse 2. (work in profession) ejercer; to ~ as a doctor ejercer de médico

**practiced** ['præk·tɪst] adj (experienced, skilled) experto, -a; a ~ liar un mentiroso consumado

**practicing** ['præk·tɪs·ɪŋ] adj (doctor, lawyer) en ejercicio; (Catholic, Jew) practicante

**practitioner** [præk·'tɪʃ·ə·nər] n (of a skill) profesional mf; (doctor) médico, -a m, f; **legal** ~ abogado, -a m, f

**praise** [preɪz] I. vt 1. (express approval) elogiar 2. (worship) alabar II. n 1. (expression of approval) elogio m 2. (worship) alabanza f

**praiseworthy** ['preɪz·ˌwɜr·ði] adj loable

**prank** [præŋk] n broma f; to play a ~ on sb gastar una broma a alguien

**prattle** ['præt·əl] I. vi parlotear; (child) balbucear II. n parloteo m; (of child) balbuceo m

**prawn** [prɔn] n gamba f

**pray** [preɪ] I. vi 1. REL rezar 2. (hope) to ~ for sth rezar para obtener [or que ocurra] algo II. vt suplicar; and what, ~ tell, are you doing? ¿qué estás haciendo, si se puede saber?

**prayer** [prer] n 1. REL oración f; to say a ~ [or one's ~s] rezar 2. (action of

praying) rezo m 3. ~s (church service) morning/evening ~s misa matinal/vespertina 4. fig (hope) súplica f

**praying mantis** ['preɪ·ɪŋ·'mæn·tɪs] n mantis f inv religiosa

**preach** [pritʃ] I. vi predicar; to ~ at sb pej sermonear a alguien II. vt 1. REL (a sermon, the Gospel) predicar 2. (advocate) abogar por ▶ to **practice** what you ~ predicar con el ejemplo

**preacher** ['pri·tʃər] n predicador(a) m(f)

**precarious** [prɪ·'ker·i·əs] adj precario, -a

**precaution** [prɪ·'kɔ·ʃən] n precaución f

**precautionary** [ˌprɪ·'kɔ·ʃə·ner·i] adj de precaución; ~ measure medida f preventiva

**precede** [prɪ·'sid] vt preceder

**precedence** ['pres·ə·dəns] n 1. (priority) prioridad f; to take ~ over sb tener prioridad sobre alguien 2. (order of priority) preferencia f

**precedent** ['pres·ə·dent] n precedente m; to set a ~ (for sth/doing sth) sentar un precedente (para algo/hacer algo)

**preceding** [prɪ·'si·dɪŋ] adj precedente; the ~ day el día anterior

**precinct** ['pri·sɪŋkt] n 1. (police district) distrito m policial 2. (electoral district) distrito m 3. form (environs) alrededores mpl

**precious** ['preʃ·əs] adj 1. (valuable: stone, metal) precioso, -a 2. (beloved: child, pet) querido, -a 3. (affected) afectado, -a; (person) amanerado, -a

**precipice** ['pres·ə·pɪs] n precipicio m

**précis** [prei·'si] I. n resumen m II. vt form resumir

**precise** [prɪ·'saɪs] adj preciso, -a

**precisely** adv 1. (exactly) precisamente; ~! ¡eso es! 2. (carefully) meticulosamente

**precision** [prɪ·'sɪʒ·ən] n 1. (accuracy) precisión f 2. (meticulous care) exactitud f

**preclude** [prɪ·'klud] vt form excluir

**precocious** [prɪ·'koʊ·ʃəs] adj precoz

**precociousness** n, **precocity** [prɪ·'kas·ə·ti] n form precocidad f

**preconceived** [ˌpri·kən·'sivd] adj preconcebido, -a

**preconception** [ˌpri·kən·'sep·ʃən] n idea

*f* preconcebida

**precondition** [ˌpriːkənˈdɪʃən] *n* condición *f* previa

**predate** [priːˈdeɪt] *vt* preceder

**predator** [ˈpredətər] *n* depredador *m*

**predatory** [ˈpredəˌtɔːri] *adj* depredador(a)

**predecessor** [ˈpredəˌsesər] *n* predecesor(a) *m(f)*; (*ancestor*) antepasado, -a *m, f*

**predestination** [priːˌdestɪˈneɪʃən] *n* predestinación *f*

**predicament** [prɪˈdɪkəmənt] *n* apuro *m*

**predict** [prɪˈdɪkt] *vt* predecir

**predictable** [prɪˈdɪktəbəl] *adj* previsible

**prediction** [prɪˈdɪkʃən] *n* 1. (*forecast*) pronóstico *m* 2. (*act of predicting*) predicción *f*

**predominance** [prɪˈdɑmənəns] *n* predominio *m*

**predominant** [prɪˈdɑmənənt] *adj* predominante

**predominate** [prɪˈdɑməneɪt] *vi* predominar

**preemptive** [priːˈemptɪv] *adj* 1. (*right*) prioritario, -a 2. (*attack*) preventivo, -a

**prefab** [ˈpriːfæb] *adj inf abbr of* **prefabricated** prefabricado, -a

**prefabricate** [priːˈfæbrɪkeɪt] *vt* prefabricar

**preface** [ˈprefɪs] *n* prefacio *m*

**prefect** [ˈpriːfekt] *n* prefecto *m*

**prefer** [prɪˈfɜr] <-rr-> *vt* preferir

**preferable** [ˈprefərəbəl] *adj* preferible

**preferably** [ˈprefərəbli] *adv* preferentemente, preferiblemente

**preference** [ˈprefərəns] *n* 1. (*liking better*) preferencia *f* 2. (*priority*) preferencia *f*

**preferential** [ˌprefəˈrenʃəl] *adj* preferente; ECON preferencial

**preferred** [prɪˈfɜrd] *adj* preferido, -a

**prefix** [ˈpriːfɪks] <-es> *n* prefijo *m*

**pregnancy** [ˈpregnənsi] *n* 1. (*condition: woman*) embarazo *m*; ZOOL preñez *f* 2. (*period of time*) embarazo *m*

**pregnancy test** *n* prueba *f* de embarazo

**pregnant** [ˈpregnənt] *adj* 1. (*woman*) embarazada; (*animal*) preñado; **to become ~** (*woman*) quedarse embarazada; **to get sb ~** dejar embarazada a alguien 2. *fig* (*silence, pause*) muy significativo, -a

**prehistoric** [ˌpriːhɪˈstɔrɪk] *adj* prehistórico, -a

**prehistory** [ˌpriːˈhɪstəri] *n* prehistoria *f*

**prejudge** [ˌpriːˈdʒʌdʒ] *vt* prejuzgar

**prejudice** [ˈpredʒədɪs] *n* 1. (*preconceived opinion*) prejuicio *m* 2. (*bias*) parcialidad *f*; LAW perjuicio *m*

**prejudiced** [ˈpredʒədɪst] *adj* (*person*) lleno, -a de prejuicios; (*attitude, judgment, opinion*) parcial; **to be ~ in favor of/against sb** estar predispuesto a favor de/contra alguien

**prejudicial** [ˌpredʒəˈdɪʃəl] *adj form* perjudicial

**preliminary** [prɪˈlɪmɪˌneri] I. *adj* preliminar II. <-ies> *n* 1. (*introduction*) preparativos *mpl* 2. SPORTS (*heat*) rondas *f pl* previas 3. *form* (*preliminary exam*) examen *m* preliminar

**prelude** [ˈpreljud] *n* preludio *m*

**premarital** [ˌpriːˈmærɪtəl] *adj* prematrimonial

**premature** [ˌpriːməˈtʃʊr] *adj* prematuro, -a

**premeditated** [ˌpriːˈmedɪˌteɪtɪd] *adj* premeditado, -a

**premier** [prɪˈmɪr] *n* POL primer ministro *m*, primera ministra *f*

**première** [prɪˈmɪr] *n* estreno *m*

**premise** [ˈpremɪs] *n* 1. (*of argument*) premisa *f*; **on** [*or* **under**] **the ~ that...** en el supuesto de que... 2. *pl* (*land and building on it*) recinto *m*

**premium** [ˈpriːmiəm] I. *n* 1. (*insurance payment*) prima *f* 2. (*extra charge*) recargo *m*; (*high price*) precio *m* con prima [*or* inflado] 3. (*bonus*) prima *f* 4. (*importance*) **to put a ~ on sth** darle (gran) importancia a algo 5. (*gasoline*) súper *f* II. *adj* de primera calidad

**preoccupation** [ˌpriːˌɑkjəˈpeɪʃən] *n* preocupación *f*

**preoccupied** [priːˈɑkjuˌpaɪd] *adj* preocupado, -a

**preoccupy** [priːˈɑkjuˌpaɪ] <-ie-> *vt* preocupar

**P**

**prep** [prep] I. *adj abbr of* **preparatory** preparatorio, -a II. *n inf abbr of* **preparation** preparación *f*

**prepaid** [ˌpriːˈpeɪd] *adj* pagado, -a por adelantado; **~ phone** [*or* **calling**] **card** tarjeta (telefónica) de prepago

**preparation** [ˌprepəˈreɪʃən] *n* **1.** (*getting ready*) preparación *f* **2.** (*substance*) preparado *m* **3.** *pl* (*measures*) preparativos *mpl*

**preparatory** [prɪˈpærətɔːrɪ] *adj* preliminar, preparatorio, -a

**prepare** [prɪˈper] I. *vt* preparar; **to ~ sb for sth** preparar a alguien para algo II. *vi* prepararse; **to ~ for action** prepararse para actuar

**prepared** [prɪˈperd] *adj* **1.** (*ready*) listo, -a **2.** (*willing*) dispuesto, -a **3.** (*food, speech*) preparado, -a de antemano

**prepay** [ˌpriːˈpeɪ] *vt irr* pagar por adelantado

**prepayment** [ˌpriːˈpeɪmənt] *n* pago *m* por adelantado

**preposition** [ˌprepəˈzɪʃən] *n* preposición *f*

**preschool** [ˈpriːskuːl] I. *n* jardín *m* de infancia II. *adj* preescolar

**prescribe** [prɪˈskraɪb] I. *vt* **1.** MED recetar; (*rest, diet*) recomendar **2.** *form* (*order*) prescribir; **~d by law** establecido por la ley II. *vi* MED hacer una receta

**prescription** [prɪˈskrɪpʃən] *n* **1.** MED receta *f*; **only available with a ~** sólo con receta médica; **to make out a ~** extender una receta **2.** *form* (*act of prescribing*) prescripción *f*

**presence** [ˈprezəns] *n* **1.** (*attendance*) presencia *f*; **~ of mind** presencia de ánimo; **in sb's ~** en presencia de alguien; **in my ~** delante de mí; **your ~ is requested** se ruega su asistencia; **to make one's ~ felt** hacerse notar **2.** (*personality*) carisma *m*

**present¹** [ˈprezənt] I. *n* presente *m* ▶ **at ~** en este momento; **for the ~** por ahora II. *adj* **1.** (*current: address, generation*) actual; **at the ~ moment** [*or* **time**] en este momento; **the ~ year** el año en curso; **in the ~ case** en este caso; **up to the ~ time** hasta la fecha **2.** (*in attendance*) presente; **to be ~**

**at sth** asistir a algo; **all those ~** todos los presentes

**present²** [ˈprezənt] *n* (*gift*) regalo *m*; **to give sb a ~** hacer un regalo a alguien; **I got it as a ~** me lo regalaron

**present³** [prɪˈzent] *vt* **1.** (*give*) presentar; **to ~ one's apologies to sb** *form* presentar sus disculpas a alguien; **to ~ one's credentials** presentar sus credenciales; **to ~ sth** (**to sb**) entregar algo (a alguien) **2.** (*introduce*) presentar; **to ~ sb to sb** presentar alguien a alguien; **may I ~ my wife?** permítame presentarle a mi esposa **3.** (*to an audience: play, musical, concert*) presentar; **~ing X as Julius Caesar** con X en el papel de Julio César; **to ~ a paper at a conference** presentar una ponencia en un congreso **4.** (*confront*) **to ~ sb with sth** enfrentar a alguien con algo; **to be ~ed with a complicated situation** verse frente a una situación complicada **5.** (*constitute*) constituir; **to ~ a problem for sb** significar [*or* suponer] un problema para alguien **6.** (*offer*) ofrecer; (*view, atmosphere*) presentar **7.** (*exhibit: argument, plan, theory*) exponer; (*check, passport, ticket*) presentar; **to ~ a petition to sb** elevar una petición a alguien *elev* **8.** MIL **to ~ arms** presentar armas **9.** (*appear*) **to ~ oneself for sth** presentarse a algo

**presentable** [prɪˈzentəbəl] *adj* presentable; **to make oneself ~** arreglarse

**presentation** [ˌprezənˈteɪʃən] *n* **1.** (*act*) presentación *f*; (*of theory, dissertation*) exposición *f*; **to make** [*or* **give**] **a ~** hacer una exposición; **on ~ of this voucher** al presentar este vale **2.** (*of prize, award*) entrega *f*

**present-day** [ˌprezəntˈdeɪ] *adj* actual; **~ Boston** el Boston de hoy (en) día

**presenter** [prɪˈzentər] *n* presentador(a) *m(f)*

**presently** [ˈprezəntli] *adv* **1.** (*soon*) pronto; **I'll be there ~** voy enseguida **2.** (*now*) ahora

**present participle** *n* LING participio *m* presente

**present tense** *n* LING tiempo *m* presente

**preservation** [ˌprezərˈveɪʃən] *n* **1.** (*of*

*building*) conservación *f;* **to be in a poor/good state of ~** estar en mal/buen estado de conservación **2.** (*of species, custom*) preservación *f*

**preservative** [prɪˈzɜrvəˌtɪv] **I.** *adj* preservativo, -a **II.** *n* conservante *m;* **without artificial ~s** sin conservantes (artificiales)

**preserve** [prɪˈzɜrv] **I.** *vt* **1.** (*maintain: customs, peace*) mantener; (*dignity, sense of humor, building*) conservar; (*appearance, silence*) guardar **2.** (*food*) conservar **3.** (*protect*) proteger; **to ~ sb from sth** proteger a alguien de algo **II.** *n* **1.** ~s (*jam*) confitura *f* **2.** (*reserve*) coto *m,* vedado *m;* **wildlife ~** reserva *f* de animales *m; fig* (*domain*) terreno *m;* **to be the ~ of the rich** ser dominio exclusivo de los ricos

**preserved** *adj* **1.** (*maintained*) conservado, -a; **to be badly ~** estar mal conservado **2.** (*food*) en conserva; **~ food** conservas *fpl*

**presidency** [ˈprezɪdənsi] *n* **1.** (*office of president*) POL presidencia *f;* (*of company*) dirección *f* **2.** (*tenure as president*) mandato *m* (presidencial)

**president** [ˈprezɪdənt] *n* POL presidente, -a *m, f;* (*of company*) director(a) *m(f)*

**presidential** [ˌprezɪˈdenˌtʃəl] *adj* presidencial

**press** [pres] **I.** *vt* **1.** (*push: button, switch*) pulsar; (*doorbell*) tocar; (*trigger*) apretar; **to ~ sth down** apretar algo **2.** (*squeeze*) apretar; **the crowd ~ed us against the locked door** la multitud nos apretujaba contra la puerta cerrada **3.** (*flatten: flowers, grapes, olives*) prensar **4.** (*extract juice*) exprimir **5.** (*iron: shirt, dress*) planchar **6.** MUS (*album, disk*) imprimir **7.** (*try to force*) presionar; **to ~ sb to do sth** presionar a alguien para que haga algo; **to ~ sb for payment** acosar a alguien para que pague **8.** (*find difficult*) **to be (hard) ~ed to do sth** tener dificultad para hacer algo **9.** (*be short of*) **to be ~ed for money/time** andar escaso de dinero/tiempo **10.** (*pursue*) insistir; **to ~ a claim/one's case** insistir en una petición/sus argumentos; **to ~ a point** insistir en algo

**11.** LAW **to ~ charges** presentar cargos **II.** *vi* **1.** (*push*) apretar; **to ~ hard** apretar fuerte; **to ~ on the brakes** pisar el freno **2.** (*crowd*) apiñarse; **to ~ through the crowd** abrirse paso entre el gentío; **to ~ down (on sth)** hacer presión (sobre algo) **3.** (*be urgent*) urgir; **time is ~ing** el tiempo apremia **4.** (*put under pressure*) hacer presión; **to ~ for sth** insistir para conseguir algo **III.** *n* **1.** (*push*) presión *f;* (*with hand*) apretón *m;* **at the ~ of a button** apretando un botón **2.** (*ironing*) planchado *m;* **to give sth a ~** planchar algo **3.** (*crush*) apiñamiento *m* **4.** (*machine*) prensa *f;* **printing ~** imprenta *f;* **to be in ~** estar en prensa; **to go to ~** (*newspaper, book*) ir a imprenta **5.** PUBL **the ~** la prensa; **to have bad/good ~** (*publicity*) tener mala/buena prensa

◆ **press on** *vi* seguir adelante

**press agency** *n* agencia *f* de prensa

**press card** *n* acreditación *f* de prensa

**press conference** *n* rueda *f* de prensa; **to hold a ~** dar una rueda de prensa

**press coverage** *n* cobertura *f* periodística

**pressing** **I.** *adj* (*issue, matter*) urgente; (*need*) apremiante **II.** *n* (*of clothes*) planchado *m;* (*of records, fruits*) prensado *m*

**press office** *n* oficina *f* de prensa

**press release** *n* comunicado *m* de prensa; **to issue a ~** emitir un comunicado

**pressure** [ˈpreʃər] **I.** *n* **1.** *a.* PHYS presión *f;* **high/low ~** presión alta/baja; **to put ~ on sth** hacer presión sobre algo; **at full ~** a toda presión; **to be under ~** *a. fig* estar bajo presión **2.** (*influence*) presión *f;* **to put ~ on sb (to do sth)** presionar a alguien (para que haga algo); **under the ~ of circumstances** presionado por las circunstancias **3.** ~s (*stressful circumstances*) **the ~s of life/work** tensiones en la vida/el trabajo **4.** MED tensión *f;* **blood ~** tensión arterial **5.** PHYS (*force*) presión *f* **II.** *vt* **to ~ sb to do sth** presionar a alguien para que haga algo

**pressure cooker** *n* olla *f* a presión

**pressure gauge** *n* manómetro *m*

**pressure group** *n* POL grupo *m* de presión

**pressurize** ['preʃ·ə·raɪz] *vt* **1.** (*control air pressure*) presurizar **2.** *inf* (*person, government*) presionar; **to ~ sb into doing sth** forzar a alguien a hacer algo

**prestige** [pre·'stiːʒ] *n* prestigio *m*

**prestigious** [pre·'strdʒ·əs] *adj* prestigioso, -a

**presumably** [prɪ·'zuː·mə·bli] *adv* presumiblemente

**presume** [prɪ·'zuːm] **I.** *vt* **1.** (*suppose*) suponer; **to ~ that...** imaginarse que...; **~d dead** dado por muerto; **to be ~d innocent** ser presuntamente inocente **2.** (*dare*) **to ~ to do sth** atreverse a hacer algo **II.** *vi* **1.** (*be presumptuous*) presumir; **I don't wish to ~, but...** no quisiera parecer impertinente, pero... **2.** (*assume*) **Dr Smith, I ~?** usted debe de ser el Dr. Smith

**presumption** [prɪ·'zʌmp·ʃən] *n* **1.** (*assumption*) suposición *f*; **the ~ of innocence** LAW la presunción de inocencia **2.** *form* (*arrogance*) presunción *f* **3.** (*daring*) atrevimiento *m*

**presumptuous** [prɪ·'zʌmp·tʃu·əs] *adj* **1.** (*arrogant*) impertinente **2.** (*forward*) osado, -a

**pretax** [,pri·'tæks] *adj* antes de impuestos, bruto, -a

**pretend** [prɪ·'tend] **I.** *vt* **1.** (*make believe*) fingir; **to ~ to be interested** fingir interés; **to ~ to be dead** hacerse el muerto; **to ~ to be sb** hacerse pasar por alguien **2.** (*claim*) pretender; **I don't ~ to know** no pretendo saber **II.** *vi* fingir; **he's just ~ing** sólo está fingiendo

**pretender** *n* pretendiente *mf*

**pretense** ['pri·tens] *n* **1.** (*simulation*) fingimiento *m*, apariencia *f*; **to make a ~ of sth** fingir algo; **to make no ~ of sth** no disimular algo **2.** (*pretext*) pretexto *m*; **under (the) ~ of...** con el pretexto de...; **to do sth under false ~s** hacer algo bajo un falso pretexto **3.** (*claim*) pretensión *f*; **to make no ~ to objectivity/innocence** no pretender ser totalmente objetivo/inocente

**pretentious** [prɪ·'ten·ʃəs] *adj* pretencioso, -a

**pretext** ['pri·tekst] *n* pretexto *m*; **a ~ for doing sth** un pretexto para hacer

algo; **on the ~ that...** con el pretexto de que...; **under the ~ of doing sth** so pretexto de hacer algo *elev*

**pretty** ['prɪt·i] **I.** *adj* <-ier, -iest> **1.** (*beautiful: thing*) bonito, -a, lindo, -a *AmL*; (*child, woman*) guapo, -a, lindo, -a *AmL*; **not a ~ sight** nada agradable de ver **2.** *inf* (*considerable*) menudo, -a; **~ mess** menudo lío *m* **II.** *adv* **1.** (*quite*) bastante **2.** **~ much** más o menos; **to be ~ much the same** ser prácticamente lo mismo; **~ well everything** casi todo

**prevail** [prɪ·'veɪl] *vi* **1.** (*triumph*) prevalecer; **to ~ over/against sth** prevalecer sobre/contra algo; **to ~ over/against sb** triunfar sobre/contra alguien **2.** (*predominate*) predominar; (*conditions, situation*) imperar **3.** (*convince*) **to ~ (up) on sb (to do sth)** *form* convencer a alguien (para que haga algo)

**prevailing** *adj* predominante; (*atmosphere, feelings*) reinante; **under the ~ circumstances** en las circunstancias actuales

**prevent** [prɪ·'vent] *vt* **1.** (*hamper*) impedir; **to ~ sb from doing sth** impedir que alguien haga algo **2.** (*avoid*) prevenir; (*confusion, panic, crime*) evitar

**prevention** [prɪ·'ven·ʃən] *n* prevención *f*; **for the ~ of crime** para evitar la delincuencia ► **is better than cure** *prov* más vale prevenir que curar *prov*

**preventive** [prɪ·'ven·tɪv] *adj* preventivo, -a

**preview** ['pri·vjuː] *n* CINE, THEAT preestreno *m*; (*of TV program, exhibition*) adelanto *m*

**previous** ['pri·vi·əs] *adj* **1.** (*former*) anterior; **on the ~ day/week** el día/ la semana anterior; **no ~ experience required** no se necesita experiencia **2.** (*prior*) previo, -a

**previously** *adv* **1.** (*beforehand*) previamente **2.** (*formerly*) anteriormente; **to have met sb ~** haber visto a alguien antes

**prey** [preɪ] *n* **1.** (*animal*) presa *f*; **bird of ~** ave *f* de presa **2.** (*person*) víctima *f*; **to be easy ~ for sb** ser presa fácil para alguien; **to fall ~ to** (*animal*) ser presa de; (*person*) ser víctima de

**price** [praɪs] I. *n* 1. COM precio *m;* oil ~s, the ~ of oil el precio del petróleo; **to ask a high/low ~** pedir un precio alto/bajo; **to be the same ~** valer [*or* costar] lo mismo; **to go up/down in ~** subir/bajar de precio; **to name a ~** pedir un precio; **what ~ are apples?** ¿a cuánto están las manzanas? 2. FIN (*of stocks*) cotización *f,* precio *m* 3. *fig* (*disadvantage*) precio *m;* **the ~ of fame** el precio de la fama; **beyond** [*or* **without**] **~** sin precio; **to set a high ~ on sth** valorar mucho algo ▶ **to set a ~ on one's head** poner precio a la cabeza de alguien; **at any ~** a toda costa; **not at any ~** por nada del mundo; **to pay a heavy ~** pagarlo caro; **to pay the ~** pagar caro; **at a ~** a un precio muy alto II. *vt* 1. (*mark with price tag*) poner el precio a 2. (*fix price*) poner precio a; **to be reasonably ~d** tener un precio razonable

**price bracket** *n* gama *f* de precios

**price control** *n* control *m* de precios

**priceless** ['praɪs·lɪs] *adj* 1. (*invaluable*) incalculable; **to be ~** no tener precio 2. *fig* (*funny*) divertidísimo, -a; **that's ~!** ¡eso es para partirse de risa! *inf*

**price list** *n* lista *f* de precios

**price tag** *n* 1. (*label*) etiqueta *f* (del precio) 2. *inf* (*cost*) precio *m*

**pricey** ['praɪ·si] *adj* <pricier, priciest> *inf* (*object*) carillo, -a; (*shop*) carero, -a

**pricing** ['praɪ·sɪŋ] *n* fijación *f* de precios

**prick** [prɪk] I. *vt* 1. (*jab*) pinchar, picar; **to ~ sb's conscience** hacer que a alguien le remuerda la conciencia 2. (*mark with holes*) agujerear 3. (*listen: animal*) **to ~ one's ears** levantar las orejas; (*person*) aguzar el oído II. *vi* 1. (*pin*) pinchar 2. (*hurt: eyes, skin*) escocer III. *n* 1. (*act, pain*) pinchazo *m* 2. (*mark*) agujero *m* 3. *vulg* (*penis*) polla *f,* pija *f* RíoPl 4. *vulg* (*idiot*) gilipollas *m inv*

**prickle** ['prɪk·əl] I. *n* 1. (*thorn: of plant*) pincho *m;* (*of animal*) púa *f* 2. (*tingle*) picor *m;* **to feel a ~ of excitement** sentir un cosquilleo de emoción II. *vi* 1. (*cause prickling sensation*) picar 2. (*tingle*) sentir picor 3. (*prick*) pinchar III. *vt* (*prick*) pinchar, picar

**prickly** ['prɪk·li] <-ier, -iest> *adj*

1. (*thorny: plant*) espinoso, -a; (*animal*) con púas 2. (*tingling*) que pica; (*beard*) que pincha; **~ sensation** picor *m*

**pride** [praɪd] I. *n* 1. (*proud feeling*) orgullo *m;* **to take ~ in sth** enorgullecerse de algo; (*one's work*) esmerarse en algo; **to be sb's ~ and joy** ser el orgullo de alguien 2. (*self-respect*) amor *m* propio; **to hurt sb's ~** herir el orgullo de alguien; **to swallow one's ~** tragarse el orgullo 3. (*arrogance*) soberbia *f* II. *vt* **to ~ oneself on** (**doing**) **sth** enorgullecerse de (hacer) algo; **to ~ oneself that...** preciarse de que...

**priest** [prist] *n* REL cura *m*

**priesthood** ['prist·hʊd] *n* REL 1. (*position, office*) sacerdocio *m;* **to enter the ~** ser ordenado sacerdote 2. (*priests in general*) clero *m*

**primarily** [praɪ·ˈmer·ə·li] *adv* principalmente

**primary** ['praɪ·mer·i] I. *adj* 1. (*principal*) fundamental; (*aim*) prioritario, -a 2. (*basic*) primario, -a; (*industry*) de base, primario, -a II. <-ies> *n* POL elecciones *f pl* primarias

**primary school** *n* escuela *f* (de enseñanza) primaria

**prime** [praɪm] I. *adj* 1. (*main*) principal; (*objective*) prioritario, -a; **of ~ importance** de importancia primordial 2. (*first-rate*) excelente; (*beef*) de primera calidad; **in ~ condition** en perfecto estado II. *n* 1. (*best stage*) apogeo *m elev;* **to be in one's ~, to be in the ~ of life** estar en la flor de la vida 2. (*prime number*) número *m* primo III. *vt* 1. (*apply undercoat: surface*) aplicar una capa de base sobre 2. (*prepare for exploding: gun, pump, motor*) cebar 3. (*brief*) informar; (*prepare*) **to ~ sb for doing sth** preparar a alguien para hacer algo 4. (*make drunk*) emborrachar

**prime minister** *n* POL primer(a) ministro, -a *m, f*

**prime number** *n* MATH número *m* primo

**primer** ['praɪ·mər] *n* 1. (*paint*) (pintura *f* de) imprimación *f;* **a ~ coat** una primera mano 2. (*explosive*) cebo *m* 3. (*textbook*) manual *m;* (*for learning to read*) cartilla *f*

**prime time** n RADIO, TV horas f pl de máxima audiencia

**primitive** ['prɪm·ɪ·tɪv] I. adj a. ART, HIST, ZOOL primitivo, -a II. n ART, HIST, SOCIOL primitivo, -a m, f

**primrose** ['prɪm·roʊz] n, **primula** ['prɪm·jə·lə] n BOT prímula f, primavera f

**prince** [prɪns] n príncipe m; **crown ~** príncipe heredero; **Prince Charming** príncipe azul; **Prince of Wales** Príncipe de Gales

**princess** ['prɪn·sɪs] n princesa f

**principal** ['prɪn·sə·pəl] I. adj principal II. n (head of a school) director(a) m(f)

**principle** ['prɪn·sə·pəl] n principio m; **in ~** en principio; **on ~** por principio

**print** [prɪnt] I. n 1. (handwriting) texto m impreso; (type) **bold ~** negrita f 2. (printed form) **to appear in ~** publicarse; **to go out of ~** agotarse 3. (of artwork) copia f; (engraving) grabado m; PHOT positivo m 4. (printed pattern) estampado m 5. ~s inf (fingerprints) huella f II. vt 1. (publish) publicar 2. (put into printed form) imprimir 3. COMPUT (make printout of) imprimir 4. PHOT positivar 5. (mark fabric) estampar III. vi 1. (appear in printed form) imprimirse 2. (write in unjoined letters) escribir con letra de imprenta

**printer** ['prɪn·tər] n COMPUT impresora f; **inkjet/laser ~** impresora de chorro de tinta/láser

**printing** n 1. (art) imprenta f 2. (action) impresión f

**printing press** n prensa f, imprenta f

**printout** ['prɪnt·aʊt] n COMPUT impresión f, listado m

**print run** n tirada f

**prior** ['praɪ·ər] I. adv form (before) antes; **~ to doing sth** antes de hacer algo II. adj form 1. (earlier) previo, -a; **without ~ notice** sin previo aviso 2. (preferred) preferente III. n REL prior m

**priority** [praɪ·ˈɔr·ə·t̬i] I. n <-ies> n 1. (being most important) prioridad f; (in time) anterioridad f 2. pl (order of importance) prioridades fpl; **to set priorities** establecer un orden de prioridades II. adj 1. (of utmost importance)

prioritario, -a 2. (claim, right) a. FIN preferente

**priory** ['praɪ·ə·ri] n priorato m

**prism** ['prɪz·əm] n prisma m

**prison** ['prɪz·ən] n prisión f; **to go to ~** ir a la cárcel

**prison camp** n campo m de prisioneros

**prison cell** n celda f

**prisoner** ['prɪz·ə·nər] n preso, -a m, f; MIL prisionero, -a m, f; **to hold sb ~** detener a alguien

**prison inmate** n recluso, -a m, f

**privacy** ['praɪ·və·si] n intimidad f; **I'd like some ~** me gustaría estar a solas

**private** ['praɪ·vət] I. adj 1. (not public) privado, -a 2. (confidential) confidencial; **he's a very ~ person** es una persona muy reservada 3. (intimate) íntimo, -a; **~ parts** partes f pl pudendas II. n 1. ~s inf (genitals) partes fpl 2. MIL soldado m raso

**privately** ['praɪ·vət·li] adv 1. (in private) en privado 2. (secretly) en secreto 3. (personally) personalmente

**privatization** [ˌpraɪ·və·tɪ·ˈzeɪ·ʃən] n privatización f

**privatize** ['praɪ·və·taɪz] vt privatizar

**privilege** ['prɪv·ə·lɪdʒ] I. n 1. (special right) privilegio m 2. (honor) honor m II. vt **to be ~d to do sth** tener el privilegio de hacer algo

**privileged** adj 1. (special) privilegiado, -a 2. (confidential) confidencial

**privy** ['prɪv·i] n (toilet) retrete m

**prize¹** [praɪz] I. n 1. (in competition) premio m; **to take home a ~** ganar un premio 2. (reward) recompensa f II. adj 1. inf (first-rate) de primera 2. (prize winning) premiado, -a III. vt apreciar; **to ~ sth highly** estimar algo mucho

**prize²** [praɪz] vt see **pry²**

**prize list** n lista f de premiados

**prize money** n SPORTS premio m en metálico

**pro¹** [proʊ] adj inf abbr of **professional** profesional

**pro²** [proʊ] I. adv a favor II. n inf pro m, **the ~s and cons of sth** los pros y los contras de algo III. prep pro IV. adj favorable

**probability** [ˌprɑb·ə·ˈbɪl·ə·t̬i] n probabilidad *f*; **in all ~** sin duda

**probable** ['prɑb-ə-bəl] *adj* 1. (*likely*) probable 2. (*credible*) verosímil 3. LAW **~ cause** motivo *m* razonable

**probably** *adv* probablemente

**probation** [prou-'beɪ-ʃən] *n* 1. (*at work*) período *m* de prueba 2. LAW libertad *f* condicional

**probe** [proub] I. *vi* (*examine*) investigar; **to ~ into the possibilities** tantear las posibilidades; **to ~ into sb's private life** indagar en la vida privada de alguien II. *vt* 1. (*examine*) investigar 2. MED sondar III. *n* 1. (*examination, investigation*) investigación *f* 2. MED, AVIAT sonda *f*

**problem** ['prɑb-ləm] *n* problema *m*

**problematic** [ˌprɑb-lə-'mæt-ɪk] *adj*, **problematical** [ˌprɑb-lə-'mæt-ɪ-kəl] *adj* 1. (*creating difficulty*) problemático, -a 2. (*questionable, disputable*) dudoso, -a

**procedure** [prə-'si-dʒər] *n* procedimiento *m*

**proceed** [prou-'sid] *vi* 1. (*move along*) seguir; **to ~ with sth** avanzar con algo; **to ~ against sb** proceder contra alguien; AVIAT (*to a gate*) dirigirse a 2. (*come from*) **to ~ from** provenir de, proceder de 3. (*start, begin*) **to ~ with sth** empezar con algo; **to ~ to do sth** ponerse a hacer algo

**proceedings** [prou-'si-dɪŋz] *npl* 1. LAW proceso *m* 2. *form* (*events*) actos *mpl* 3. *form* (*minutes of meeting*) actas *fpl*

**proceeds** ['prou-sidz] *n* ingresos *mpl*

**process[1]** ['prɑs-es] I. *n* proceso *m*; **in the ~** mientras tanto; **to be in the ~ of doing sth** estar en vías de hacer algo II. *vt* 1. a. TECH, COMPUT procesar 2. PHOT revelar

**process[2]** [prə-'ses] *vi form* desfilar

**processing** ['prɑs-es-ɪŋ] *n* 1. a. TECH, COMPUT procesamiento *m*; **data ~** procesamiento de datos 2. PHOT revelado *m*

**procession** [prə-'seʃ-ən] *n* 1. desfile *m*; **to go in ~** desfilar- 2. REL procesión *f* 3. *fig* serie *f*

**processor** [prɑ-'ses-ər] *n* COMPUT procesador *m*

**pro-choice** *adj* proabortista

**proclaim** [prou-'kleɪm] *vt form* proclamar; **to ~ war** declarar la guerra

**procrastinate** [prou-'kræs-tə-neɪt] *vi* dejar para más tarde

**procreate** ['prou-kri-eɪt] *vi form* procrearse

**prod** [prɑd] I. *n* (*poke*) golpe *m*; (*with sharp object*) pinchazo *m*; **to give sb a ~** *fig* dar un empujón a alguien II. <-dd-> *vt* 1. (*poke*) golpear; (*with sharp object*) pinchar 2. (*encourage, urge on*) **to ~ sb** (*into doing sth*) estimular a alguien (para que haga algo)

**prodigy** ['prɑd-ə-dʒi] *n* prodigio *m*; **child ~** niño, -a *m, f* prodigio

**produce[1]** [prə-'dus] I. *vt* 1. (*create*) producir; (*manufacture*) fabricar 2. (*give birth to*) dar a luz 3. CINE, THEAT, TV realizar, producir 4. (*show*) mostrar; **to ~ a knife** sacar un cuchillo; **to ~ one's passport** enseñar el pasaporte 5. (*cause*) causar; **to ~ results** producir resultados II. *vi* BOT (*bear fruit*) dar frutos

**produce[2]** ['prou-dus] *n* AGR productos *m pl* agrícolas; **the ~ section** (*in grocery store*) la sección de frutas y verduras

**producer** [prə-'du-sər] *n* productor(a) *m(f)*

**product** ['prɑd-əkt] *n* 1. a. MATH producto *m* 2. (*result*) resultado *m*

**production** [prə-'dʌk-ʃən] *n* 1. (*of goods*) fabricación *f*; (*output of factory*) producción *f* 2. CINE, THEAT, TV producción *f*

**production costs** *npl* costes *m pl* de producción

**production line** *n* cadena *f* de montaje

**production manager** *n* encargado, -a *m, f* de producción

**productive** [prə-'dʌk-tɪv] *adj* productivo, -a; (*writer*) prolífico, -a

**productivity** [ˌprou-dək-'tɪv-ə-t̬i] *n* productividad *f*

**profane** [prou-'feɪn] *adj* 1. (*blasphemous*) blasfemo, -a 2. *form* (*secular*) profano, -a

**profanity** [prou-'fæn-ə-t̬i] *n* 1. (*blasphemy*) blasfemia *f* 2. (*obscene language*) blasfemia *f* 3. (*obscene word*) palabrota *f*

**profess** [prə-'fes] *vt* 1. (*declare*) profesar;

to ~ **little enthusiasm** manifestar poco entusiasmo **2.** (*pretend*) **to ~ to be sth** pretender ser algo **3.** (*religion, Catholicism*) profesar

**professed** [prə·'fest] *adj* **1.** (*self-acknowledged*) declarado, -a **2.** (*alleged*) supuesto, -a

**profession** [prə·'feʃ·ən] *n* **1.** (*occupation*) profesión *f*; **the teaching ~** la docencia **2.** (*declaration*) declaración *f*

**professional** [prə·'feʃ·ə·nəl] **I.** *adj* **1.** (*related to profession*) profesional **2.** (*competent*) profesional **II.** *n* profesional *mf*

**professor** [prə·'fes·ər] *n* UNIV profesor(a) *m(f)*

**proficiency** [prə·'fɪʃ·ən·si] *n* competencia *f*

**proficient** [prə·'fɪʃ·ənt] *adj* competente

**profile** ['prou·faɪl] **I.** *n* **1.** (*side view*) perfil *m*; **in ~** de perfil **2.** (*description*) descripción *f*; **user ~** COMPUT perfil *m* de usuario ▶ **to keep a low ~** tratar de pasar inadvertido **II.** *vt* (*describe*) describir

**profit** ['praf·ɪt] **I.** *n* **1.** FIN beneficio *m* **2.** (*advantage*) provecho *m* **II.** *vi* **1.** (*benefit*) beneficiarse; **to ~ by sth** sacar provecho de algo **2.** (*make a profit*) ganar

**profitability** [,praf·ɪ·tə·'bɪl·ə·ti] *n* rentabilidad *f*

**profitable** ['praf·ɪ·tə·bəl] *adj* **1.** FIN rentable **2.** (*advantageous*) provechoso, -a

**profit and loss** *n* FIN pérdidas *f pl* y ganancias *fpl*

**profiteering** *n pej* especulación *f*

**profit-making** *adj* lucrativo, -a; **~ movie** película *f* taquillera

**profit margin** *n* margen *m* de beneficio

**profound** [prə·'faund] *adj* profundo, -a

**prognosis** [prag·'nou·sɪs] *n* pronóstico *m*

**program** ['prou·græm] **I.** *n a.* COMPUT programa *m* **II.** <-mm-> *vt a.* COMPUT programar

**programmable** ['prou·græm·ə·bəl] *adj* programable

**programmer** *n a.* COMPUT programador(a) *m(f)*

**programming** *n a.* COMPUT programa-

ción *f*

**progress**[1] ['prag·res] *n* progreso *m*; **to make ~** avanzar; **to be in ~** estar en curso

**progress**[2] [prou·'gres] *vi* **1.** (*improve*) progresar **2.** (*continue onward*) avanzar

**progression** [prə·'greʃ·ən] *n* **1.** (*development*) desarrollo *m*; (*of disease*) evolución *f* **2.** MATH (*series*) progresión *f*

**progressive** [prə·'gres·ɪv] *adj* **1.** (*by successive stages*) progresivo, -a; (*disease*) degenerativo, -a **2.** POL progresista **3.** (*modern*) moderno, -a **4.** MUS progresivo, -a **5.** LING continuo, -a

**prohibit** [prou·'hɪb·ɪt] *vt* **1.** (*forbid*) prohibir **2.** (*prevent*) impedir

**prohibition** [,prou·ə·'bɪʃ·ən] *n* **1.** (*ban*) prohibición *f* **2.** HIST **Prohibition** la Ley Seca

**prohibitive** [prou·'hɪb·ɪ·tɪv] *adj* prohibitivo, -a

**project**[1] ['pradʒ·ekt] *n* **1.** (*undertaking, plan*) proyecto *m* **2.** SCHOOL, UNIV (*essay*) trabajo *m* **3.** (*social housing*) ≈viviendas *f pl* de protección oficial

**project**[2] [prə·'dʒekt] *vt* **1.** (*forecast*) pronosticar **2.** (*propel*) impulsar **3.** PSYCH proyectar; **to ~ sth onto sb** proyectar algo en alguien **4.** (*promote*) promover; **to ~ oneself** promocionarse

**projection** [prə·'dʒek·ʃən] *n* **1.** (*forecast*) pronóstico *m* **2.** PSYCH proyección *f*

**projectionist** *n* proyeccionista *mf*

**project manager** *n* coordinador(a) *m(f)* de proyectos, gestor(a) *m(f)* de proyectos

**projector** [prə·'dʒek·tər] *n* proyector *m*

**prolific** [prou·'lɪf·ɪk] *adj* **1.** (*producing a lot*) prolífico, -a **2.** (*having many offspring*) prolífico, -a

**prolong** [prou·'laŋ] *vt* prolongar; (*agony*) alargar

**prom** [pram] *n* (*school dance*) baile *m*

**promenade** [,pram·ə·'neɪd] *n form* (*walk*) paseo *m*

**prominent** ['pram·ə·nənt] *adj* **1.** (*conspicuous*) prominente **2.** (*teeth, chin*) saliente **3.** (*distinguished, well-known*) importante; (*position*) destacado, -a

**promiscuous** [prə·'mɪs·kju·əs] *adj* promiscuo, -a

**promise** ['pram·ɪs] **I.** vt (*pledge, have potential*) prometer; **to ~ to do sth** prometer hacer algo **II.** vi (*pledge*) prometer; **I ~!** ¡lo prometo! **III.** n **1.** (*pledge*) promesa f; **to make a ~** prometer; **~s, ~s!** *iron* ¡promesas, promesas! **2.** (*potential*) posibilidad f; **a young person of ~** un joven con porvenir; **to show ~** demostrar aptitudes

**promising** adj prometedor(a)

**promote** [prə·'moʊt] vt **1.** (*in army, company, organization*) ascender; (*soccer team*) subir **2.** (*encourage*) promover **3.** (*advertise*) promocionar

**promoter** n promotor(a) m(f)

**promotion** [prə·'moʊ·ʃən] n **1.** (*in army, company, organization*) ascenso m **2.** (*encouragement, advertising*) promoción f

**promotional material** n material m de promoción

**prompt** [prampt] **I.** vt **1.** (*spur*) provocar; **to ~ sb to do sth** estimular a alguien para que haga algo **2.** THEAT apuntar **II.** adj (*quick*) rápido, -a **III.** adv puntualmente **IV.** n **1.** COMPUT línea f de comandos **2.** THEAT (*prompter*) apuntador(a) m(f)

**prompter** ['pramp·tər] n THEAT apuntador(a) m(f)

**promptly** ['prampt·li] adv **1.** (*quickly*) rápidamente **2.** inf (*immediately afterward*) de inmediato

**prone** [proʊn] **I.** adj **to be ~ to doing sth** ser propenso a hacer algo **II.** adv boca abajo; **to lie ~ on the floor/table** estar tumbado boca abajo sobre el suelo/la mesa

**prong** [praŋ] n (*of fork*) diente m; (*of antler*) punta f

**pronoun** ['proʊ·naʊn] n LING pronombre m

**pronounce** [prə·'naʊns] vt **1.** (*speak*) pronunciar **2.** (*declare*) declarar; (*judgment*) dictaminar

**pronounced** adj pronunciado, -a; (*accent*) marcado, -a

**pronunciation** [prə·ˌnʌn·si·'eɪ·ʃən] n LING pronunciación f

**proof** [pruf] **I.** n a. LAW prueba f; **the bur-** den of ~ el peso de la evidencia ▶ **the ~ of the pudding is in the eating** prov no se sabe si algo es bueno hasta que se prueba **II.** adj (*alcoholic strength*) de graduación **III.** vt impermeabilizar

**proofread** ['pruf·ˌrid] vt irr TYPO, PUBL corregir, revisar

**prop** [prap] **I.** n **1.** (*support*) apoyo m **2.** THEAT objeto m de atrezzo **II.** <-pp-> vt sostener, apuntalar; **to ~ sth up with sth** aguantar algo con [or contra] algo

**propaganda** [ˌprap·ə·'gæn·də] n propaganda f

**propagate** ['prap·ə·geɪt] **I.** vt **1.** BOT propagar **2.** (*make known: lie, rumor*) difundir **II.** vi propagarse

**propagation** [ˌprap·ə·'geɪ·ʃən] n **1.** BOT, PHYS propagación f **2.** (*of lies, rumors*) difusión f

**propel** [prə·'pel] <-ll-> vt propulsar

**propellant** [prə·'pel·ənt] n propelente m

**propeller** [prə·'pel·ər] n hélice f

**proper** ['prap·ər] adj **1.** (*appropriate: time, place, method*) apropiado, -a; (*use*) correcto, -a **2.** (*socially respectable*) **to be ~ to do sth** ser apropiado hacer algo **3.** (*itself*) verdadero, -a; **it's not in Boston ~** no está en Boston propiamente dicho **4.** (*real*) verdadero, -a; **a ~ job** un trabajo de verdad

**properly** ['prap·ər·li] adv **1.** (*correctly*) correctamente; **~ speaking** hablando como es debido **2.** (*behave*) como es debido **3.** (*politely*) educadamente

**proper name** n, **proper noun** n nombre m propio

**property** ['prap·ər·ti] <-ies> n **1.** (*possession*) propiedad f; LAW (*house, land*) bien m inmueble **2.** (*house*) inmueble m; (*land*) terreno m **3.** a. COMPUT (*attribute*) propiedad f

**prophecy** ['praf·ə·si] <-ies> pl n profecía f

**prophesy** ['praf·ə·saɪ] <-ie-> vt (*predict*) predecir; REL profetizar

**prophet** ['praf·ɪt] n adivino, -a m, f; REL profeta, -isa m, f

**prophetic** [prə·'fet·ɪk] adj profético, -a

**proponent** [prə·'poʊ·nənt] n defensor(a) m(f)

**proportion** [prə·'pɔr·ʃən] n **1.** (*relation-*

P

ship) proporción *f;* **the ~ of** A **to** B el porcentaje entre A y B; **to be out of ~ to sth** estar desproporcionado con algo; **to be in ~ to sth** estar en proporción con algo; **to keep a sense of ~** mantener un sentido de la proporción **3.** (*part*) parte *f* proporcional **3.** ~s (*size*) dimensiones *fpl*

**proportional** [prə·'pɔr·ʃə·nəl] *adj* proporcional; **inversely ~** inversamente proporcional

**proportioned** *adj* **well~** bien proporcionado

**proposal** [prə·'poʊ·zəl] *n* **1.** (*suggestion*) propuesta *f;* **to put forward a ~** presentar una proposición **2.** (*offer of marriage*) proposición *f;* **to make a marriage ~** hacer una petición de mano

**propose** [prə·'poʊz] **I.** *vt* **1.** (*put forward*) proponer; **to ~ a toast** proponer un brindis **2.** (*intend*) **to ~ to do sth** tener la intención de hacer algo **3.** (*nominate*) nombrar **II.** *vi* (*offer marriage*) **to ~** (**to sb**) declararse (a alguien)

**proposer** [prə·'poʊ·zər] *n* **1.** (*suggester*) autor(a) *m(f)* de una moción **2.** (*nominator*) proponente *mf*

**proposition** [ˌprɑp·ə·'zɪʃ·ən] **I.** *n* **1.** (*theory, argument*) proposición *f* **2.** (*business*) ofrecimiento *m* **3.** (*suggestion*) sugerencia *f* **II.** *vt* hacer proposiciones deshonestas a

**proprietary** [prə·'praɪ·ə·ter·i] *adj* **1.** (*owning property*) propietario, -a **2.** ECON (*name, brand*) registrado, -a

**proprietor** [prə·'praɪ·ə·tər] *n* propietario, -a *m, f*

**proprietress** [prə·'praɪ·ə·trɪs] *n* propietaria *f*

**propriety** [prə·'praɪ·ə·ti] <-ies> *n* **1.** (*correctness*) corrección *f*, propiedad *f* **2.** **proprieties** (*standard of conduct*) convenciones *f pl* sociales; **to observe the proprieties** atenerse al decoro

**propulsion** [prə·'pʌl·ʃən] *n* propulsión *f*

**proscribe** [proʊ·'skraɪb] *vt* proscribir

**proscription** [proʊ·'skrɪp·ʃən] *n form* proscripción *f*

**prose** [proʊz] *n* prosa *f*

**prosecute** ['prɑs·ɪ·kjut] **I.** *vt* **1.** LAW **to ~ sb** (**for sth**) procesar a alguien (por algo)

**2.** *form* (*pursue, follow up*) proseguir **II.** *vi* interponer

**prosecuting** *adj* acusador(a)

**prosecution** [ˌprɑs·ɪ·'kju·ʃən] *n* **1.** LAW (*proceedings*) proceso *m* **2.** LAW (*the prosecuting party*) **the ~** la acusación **3.** *form* (*of campaign, inquiry*) seguimiento *m*

**prosecutor** ['prɑs·ɪ·kju·tər] *n* LAW fiscal *mf*

**prospect** ['prɑs·pekt] **I.** *n* **1.** (*possibility*) posibilidad *f;* **the ~ of sth** la probabilidad de algo **2.** ~s (*chances*) perspectivas *fpl* **3.** ECON (*potential customer*) posible cliente *mf;* (*potential employee*) candidato, -a *m, f* **4.** *liter* (*view*) panorama *m;* **a ~ of/over sth** una vista de/sobre algo **II.** *vi* MIN buscar

**prospective** [prə·'spek·tɪv] *adj* posible; (*candidate, student*) futuro, -a

**prospector** ['prɑs·pek·tər] *n* MIN prospector(a) *m(f)*

**prospectus** [prə·'spek·təs] *n* prospecto *m;* UNIV folleto *m* informativo

**prosper** ['prɑs·pər] *vi* prosperar

**prosperity** [prɑ·'sper·ə·ti] *n* prosperidad *f*

**prosperous** ['prɑs·pər·əs] *adj* próspero, -a; (*business*) exitoso, -a

**prostitute** ['prɑs·tə·tut] **I.** *n* prostituta *f* **II.** *vt a. fig* **to ~ oneself** prostituirse

**prostitution** [ˌprɑs·tɪ·'tu·ʃən] *n* prostitución *f*

**protagonist** [proʊ·'tæg·ə·nɪst] *n* (*main character*) protagonista *mf*

**protect** [prə·'tekt] *vt* proteger

**protection** [prə·'tek·ʃən] *n* (*defense*) protección *f;* **to be under sb's ~** estar bajo la protección de alguien

**protection factor** *n* factor *m* de protección

**protective** [prə·'tek·tɪv] *adj* **1.** (*giving protection*) proteccionista; **~ custody** detención *f* preventiva **2.** (*wishing to protect: instinct*) protector(a)

**protector** [prə·'tek·tər] *n* **1.** (*person*) protector(a) *m(f)* **2.** (*device*) (aparato *m*) protector *m*

**protein** ['proʊ·tin] *n* proteína *f*

**protest**[1] ['proʊ·test] *n* **1.** (*complaint*) protesta *f;* **in ~** en señal de protesta

**2.** (*demonstration*) manifestación *f* de protesta

**protest²** [prou·ˈtest] **I.** *vi* protestar; **to ~ about/against sth** protestar por/en contra de algo **II.** *vt* (*show dissent*) protestar en contra de

**Protestant** [ˈprɑt·ɪ·stənt] *n* protestante *mf*

**protester** *n* manifestante *mf*

**protest march** *n* marcha *f* de protesta

**protest vote** *n* voto *m* de protesta

**protocol** [ˈprou·tə·kɔl] *n a.* COMPUT protocolo *m*

**prototype** [ˈprou·tə·taɪp] *n* prototipo *m*

**protracted** [prou·ˈtræk·tɪd] *adj* prolongado, -a

**protractor** [prou·ˈtræk·tər] *n* (*for measuring angles*) transportador *m* (de grados)

**protruding** *adj* prominente; (*ears*) que sobresale

**proud** [praud] *adj* **1.** (*pleased*) orgulloso, -a; **to be ~ of sth/sb** enorgullecerse de algo/alguien; **to be ~ to do sth** tener el honor de hacer algo **2.** (*having self-respect*) digno, -a **3.** (*arrogant*) arrogante

**provable** [ˈpru·və·bəl] *adj* demostrable

**prove** [pruv] <**proved**, **proved** *or* **proven**> **I.** *vt* (*verify: theory*) probar; (*innocence, loyalty*) demostrar; **to ~ sb innocent** probar la inocencia de alguien **II.** *vi* (*be established*) resultar; **to ~ to be sth** resultar ser algo

**proven** [ˈpru·vən] **I.** *vi*, *vt pp of* **prove** **II.** *adj* (*verified*) comprobado, -a, probado, -a

**proverb** [ˈprɑv·ɜrb] *n* refrán *m*, proverbio *m*; **as the ~ goes...** como dice el refrán...

**provide** [prə·ˈvaɪd] **I.** *vt* **1.** proveer; **to ~ sb with sth** proveer a alguien de algo **2.** *form* LAW estipular **II.** *vi* **1.** (*prepare*) **to ~ for sth** hacerse cargo de algo **2.** (*support*) **to ~ for one's family/children** mantener a su familia/hijos **3.** (*mandate*) prever

**provided** *conj* **~ that...** con tal (de) que... +*subj*

**providence** [ˈprɑv·ə·dəns] *n* providencia *f*

**provider** *n* **1.** (*person*) proveedor(a) *m(f)*

**2.** COMPUT (*for Internet services*) proveedor *m* (de Internet)

**providing** *conj* **~ (that)...** con tal (de) que... +*subj*

**province** [ˈprɑv·ɪns] *n* POL, ADMIN provincia *f*

**provincial** [prə·ˈvɪn·tʃəl] *adj* **1.** POL, ADMIN provincial **2.** (*unsophisticated*) provinciano, -a

**provision** [prə·ˈvɪʒ·ən] **I.** *n* **1.** (*act of providing*) suministro *m* **2.** (*thing provided*) provisión *f* **3.** (*preparation*) previsiones *fpl*; **to make ~s for sth** tomar medidas de previsión para algo **4.** LAW (*in will, contract*) disposición *f* **II.** *vt* abastecer

**provisional** [prə·ˈvɪʒ·ə·nəl] *adj* provisional

**proviso** [prə·ˈvaɪ·zou] <-s> *n* condición *f*; **with the ~ that...** con la condición de que +*subj*

**provocation** [ˌprɑv·ə·ˈkeɪ·ʃən] *n* provocación *f*

**provocative** [prə·ˈvɑk·ə·t̬ɪv] *adj* **1.** (*sexually*) provocativo, -a **2.** (*thought-provoking: idea, question*) estimulante, provocador, -a **3.** (*causing anger*) provocador(a)

**provoke** [prə·ˈvouk] *vt* **1.** (*make angry*) provocar **2.** (*discussion*) motivar; (*crisis*) causar

**provoking** *adj* (*irritating*) irritante

**prowl** [praul] **I.** *vt* vagar por; **to ~ the streets for victims** merodear por las calles en busca de víctimas **II.** *vi* **to ~ (around)** rondar por

**proximity** [prɑk·ˈsɪm·ə·t̬i] *n form* proximidad *f*; **to be in (close) ~ to sth** estar (muy) cerca de algo

**proxy** [ˈprɑk·si] <-ies> *n* apoderado, -a *m*, *f*; **to do sth by ~** hacer algo por poderes

**prudent** [ˈpru·dənt] *adj* prudente

**prune¹** [prun] *vt* podar; **to ~ (back) costs** reducir gastos

**prune²** [prun] *n* (*dried plum*) ciruela *f* pasa

**pry¹** [praɪ] <pries, pried> *vi* (*be nosy*) husmear; **to ~ into sth** entrometerse en algo; **to ~ around** curiosear

**pry²** [praɪ] *vt* **to ~ sth off** arrancar algo; **to**

**~ sth open** abrir algo por la fuerza

**PS** [ˌpiˈes] *abbr of* **postscript** P.D.

**psalm** [sam] *n* REL salmo *m*

**pseudonym** [ˈsuˈdəˈnɪm] *n* seudónimo *m*

**PST** *n abbr of* **Pacific Standard Time** Hora *f* del Pacífico

**psychiatric** [ˌsaɪˈkiˈætˈrɪk] *adj* psiquiátrico, -a

**psychiatrist** [saɪˈkaɪˈəˈtrɪst] *n* psiquiatra *mf*

**psychiatry** [saɪˈkaɪˈəˈtri] *n* psiquiatría *f*

**psychic** [ˈsaɪˈkɪk] **I.** *adj* **1.** (*with occult powers*) parapsicológico, -a **2.** (*of the mind*) psíquico, -a **II.** *n* vidente *mf*

**psycho** [ˈsaɪˈkoʊ] *n sl* (*crazy person*) psicópata *mf*

**psychoanalysis** [ˌsaɪˈkoʊˈəˈnælˈəˈsɪs] *n* psicoanálisis *m inv*

**psychoanalyst** [ˌsaɪˈkoʊˈænˈəˈlɪst] *n* psicoanalista *mf*

**psychological** [ˌsaɪˈkəˈlɑdʒˈɪˈkəl] *adj* psicológico, -a

**psychologist** [saɪˈkalˈəˈdʒɪst] *n* psicólogo, -a *m, f*

**psychology** <-ies> *n* (*science, mentality*) psicología *f*

**psychopath** [ˈsaɪˈkəˈpæθ] *n* psicópata *mf*

**psychopathic** [ˌsaɪˈkəˈpæθˈɪk] *adj* psicopático, -a

**psychotherapist** [ˌsaɪˈkoʊˈθerˈəˈpɪst] *n* psicoterapeuta *mf*

**psychotherapy** [ˌsaɪˈkoʊˈθerˈəˈpi] *n* psicoterapia *f*

**pt.** *n* **1.** *abbr of* **part** parte *f* **2.** *abbr of* **pint** pinta *f* (≈ 0,47 litros) **3.** *abbr of* **point** punto *m*

**PTA** [ˌpiˈtiˈeɪ] *n abbr of* **Parent Teacher Association** asociación *f* de padres y maestros

**pub** [pʌb] *n* pub *m*

**puberty** [ˈpjuˈbərˈti] *n* pubertad *f*

**public** [ˈpʌbˈlɪk] **I.** *adj* **1.** (*of/for the people, provided by state*) público, -a **2.** (*done openly*) abierto, -a; **to go ~ with sth** revelar algo **II.** *n* **1.** (*people collectively, audience*) público *m;* **in ~** en público **2.** (*ordinary people*) gente *f* de la calle

**public appearance** *n* aparición *f* pública

**public appointment** *n* designación *f* pública

**publication** [ˌpʌbˈlɪˈkeɪˈʃən] *n* publicación *f*

**public defender** *n* LAW defensor(a) *m(f)* de oficio

**public health service** *n* servicio *m* sanitario

**public holiday** *n* fiesta *f* oficial

**publicity** [pʌbˈlɪsˈəˈti] *n* **1.** publicidad *f* **2.** (*attention*) **to attract ~** atraer la atención

**publicize** [ˈpʌbˈlɪˈsaɪz] *vt* promocionar

**public library** <-ies> *n* biblioteca *f* pública

**publicly** *adv* (*openly*) en público

**public opinion** *n* opinión *f* pública

**public property** *n* bienes *m pl* públicos

**public prosecutor** *n* fiscal *mf*

**public relations** *npl* relaciones *f pl* públicas

**public school** *n* escuela *f* pública

**public sector** *n* sector *m* público

**public servant** *n* funcionario, -a *m, f*

**public service** *n* funcionariado *m*

**public-spirited** [ˌpʌbˈlɪkˈspɪrˈɪˈt̬ɪd] *adj* solidario, -a

**public transportation** *n* transporte *m* público

**publish** [ˈpʌbˈlɪʃ] *vt* (*book, author, result*) publicar; (*information*) divulgar

**publisher** *n* **1.** (*company*) editorial *f* **2.** (*person*) editor(a) *m(f)*

**publishing** *n* industria *f* editorial

**puck** [pʌk] *n* SPORTS disco *m*

**pudding** [ˈpʊdˈɪŋ] *n* (*baked*) pudin *m;* **vanilla ~** crema *f* de vainilla; **rice ~** arroz *m* con leche

**puddle** [ˈpʌdˈəl] *n* charco *m*

**pudgy** [ˈpʊdʒˈi] <-ier, -iest> *adj* rechoncho, -a

**Puerto Rican** [ˌpwerˈt̬əˈriˈkən] **I.** *n* portorriqueño, -a *m, f* **II.** *adj* portorriqueño, -a

**Puerto Rico** [ˌpwerˈt̬əˈriˈkoʊ] *n* Puerto Rico *m*

**puff** [pʌf] **I.** *vi* **1.** (*blow*) soplar **2.** (*be out of breath*) jadear **3. to ~ on a pipe/cigar/cigarette** dar una calada a una pipa/un cigarro/un cigarrillo **II.** *vt* **1.** (*smoke*) soplar; (*cigarette smoke*) echar **2.** (*praise: product, book*) dar bombo a **3.** (*say while panting*) resoplar **III.** *n* **1.** *inf* (*breath, wind*) soplo *m*; (*of dust, smoke*) bocanada *f* **2.** (*drag, breathing-in*) calada *f* **3.** (*quilt*) edredón *m* **4.** *inf* (*speech, praise*) bombo *m*

◆**puff out** *vt* **1.** (*expand*) inflar **2.** (*exhaust*) dejar sin aliento

◆**puff up I.** *vt* inflar **II.** *vi* hincharse

**puff pastry** *n* hojaldre *m*

**puffy** ['pʌf·i] <-ier, -iest> *adj* hinchado, -a

**puke** [pjuk] *sl* **I.** *vt* vomitar **II.** *vi* vomitar; **he makes me (want to) ~!** ¡me da asco!

**pull** [pʊl] **I.** *vt* **1.** (*draw*) tirar de, jalar *AmL*; (*trigger*) apretar **2.** *inf* (*take out: gun, knife*) sacar **3.** MED (*extract*) sacar **4.** SPORTS, MED (*strain: muscle*) forzar **5.** (*attract: business, customers*) atraer ▸ **to ~ a fast one (on sb)** *inf* hacer una jugarreta (a alguien) **II.** *vi* **1.** (*exert force*) tirar **2. to ~ on a beer** dar un trago a una cerveza; **to ~ on a cigarette** dar una calada a un cigarrillo **3.** *inf* (*hope for success*) **to be ~ing for sb/sth** estar con alguien/algo **III.** *n* **1.** (*act of pulling*) tirón *m* **2.** *inf* (*influence*) influencia *f* **3.** (*on knob, handle*) tirador *m* **4.** (*attraction*) atracción *f*; (*power to attract*) atractivo *m*, tirón *m* **5.** (*of cigarette*) chupada *f*; (*of drink*) trago *m*

◆**pull apart** *vt insep* **1.** (*break into pieces*) separar **2.** (*separate using force*) hacer pedazos

◆**pull away I.** *vi* (*vehicle*) alejarse **II.** *vt* arrancar; **to pull sth away from sth** arrancar algo a algo

◆**pull back I.** *vi* **1.** (*move out of the way*) retirarse **2.** (*not proceed, back out*) dar marcha atrás **II.** *vt* retener

◆**pull down** *vt* **1.** (*move down*) bajar **2.** (*demolish*) tirar [*or* echar] abajo **3.** (*drag down, hold back*) **to pull sb down** arrastrar a alguien **4.** *inf* (*earn wages*) ganar

◆**pull in I.** *vi* (*vehicle*) llegar **II.** *vt* **1.** (*attract*) atraer **2.** (*arrest*) detener

◆**pull off I.** *vt inf* (*succeed*) lograr; **to**

**pull it off** lograrlo, vencer **II.** *vi* (*leave*) arrancar

◆**pull out I.** *vi* **1.** (*move out to pass*) salirse; (*drive onto road*) meterse **2.** (*leave*) dejar **3.** (*withdraw*) retirarse **II.** *vt* (*take out*) sacar

◆**pull over I.** *vt* (*cause to fall*) volcar **2.** (*police*) parar **II.** *vi* hacerse a un lado

◆**pull through** *vi* reponerse

◆**pull together** *vt* **1.** (*regain composure*) **to pull oneself together** recobrar la compostura **2.** (*organize, set up*) organizar

◆**pull up I.** *vt* **1.** (*raise*) levantar **2.** (*plant*) arrancar **II.** *vi* parar

**pull-down menu** *n* COMPUT menú *m* desplegable

**pulley** ['pʊl·i] <-s> *n* TECH polea *f*

**pullover** ['pʊl·oʊ·vər] *n* jersey *m*, suéter *m*

**pull-up** *n* (*exercise*) flexión *f* en una barra horizontal

**pulp** [pʌlp] *n* **1.** (*soft wet mass*) pasta *f*; (*for making paper*) pulpa *f* de papel; **to beat sb to a ~** *inf* hacer papilla a alguien **2.** (*of fruit*) pulpa *f* **3.** (*literature*) literatura *f* barata

**pulpit** ['pʊl·pɪt] *n* REL púlpito *m*

**pulsate** ['pʌl·seɪt] *vi* palpitar

**pulse¹** [pʌls] **I.** *n* **1.** ANAT pulso *m*; (*heartbeat*) latido *m*; **to take sb's ~** tomar el pulso a alguien **2.** (*single vibration*) pulsación *f* **II.** *vi* latir

**pulse²** [pʌls] *n* CULIN legumbre *f*

**pumice** ['pʌm·ɪs] *n* ~ (**stone**) piedra *f* pómez

**pump** [pʌmp] **I.** *n* bomba *f*; (*for fuel*) surtidor *m* **II.** *vt* bombear

**pumpkin** ['pʌmp·kɪn] *n* calabaza *f*

**pun** [pʌn] *n* juego *m* de palabras

**punch¹** [pʌntʃ] **I.** *vt* **1.** (*hit*) pegar; **to ~ sb out** *sl* dar una paliza a alguien **2.** (*push: button, key*) pulsar **3.** (*pierce*) perforar; (*ticket*) picar; **to ~ holes in sth** hacer agujeros a algo; **to ~ the clock** [*or* **card**] fichar, marcar **II.** *vi* **1.** (*hit*) pegar **2.** (*employee*) **to ~ in/out** fichar (al entrar/al salir) **III.** <-es> *n* **1.** (*hit*) puñetazo *m* **2.** (*tool for puncturing*) punzón *m*; (**hole**) ~ perforadora *f*; (**ticket**) ~

**P**

máquina *f* de picar billetes **3.** *fig (strong effect)* fuerza *f* ▶ **to beat sb to the ~** ganar a alguien por la mano; **to roll with the ~es** saber arreglárselas

**punch²** [pʌntʃ] *n (beverage)* ponche *m*

**punch line** *n* gracia *f* (de un chiste)

**punctual** ['pʌŋk·tʃu·əl] *adj* puntual

**punctuality** [ˌpʌŋk·tʃu·'æl·ə·ti] *n* puntualidad *f*

**punctuation** [ˌpʌŋk·tʃu·'eɪ·ʃən] *n* LING puntuación *f*

**punctuation mark** *n* signo *m* de puntuación

**puncture** ['pʌŋk·tʃər] **I.** *vt* **1.** *(pierce)* pinchar; *(abscess)* reventar; *(lung)* perforar **2.** *fig (sb's confidence, self-esteem, ego)* minar **II.** *vi (tire, ball)* pincharse **III.** *n (tire, ball)* pinchazo *m;* **to have a ~** *(driver)* pinchar

**pungent** ['pʌn·dʒənt] *adj (sharp)* punzante; *(taste)* fuerte

**punish** ['pʌn·ɪʃ] *vt* castigar

**punishable** *adj liter* punible

**punishment** ['pʌn·ɪʃ·mənt] *n* **1.** *(for misbehavior or crime)* castigo *m;* **capital ~** pena *f* capital; **to inflict a ~ on sb** castigar a alguien **2.** *(rough use)* maltrato *m*

**punitive** ['pju·nɪ·tɪv] *adj form* punitivo, -a

**punk** [pʌŋk] **I.** *n* **1.** *(punk rocker)* punk *mf* **2.** *(troublemaker)* gamberro, -a *m, f* **II.** *adj* **1.** *(music, style)* punk **2.** *(poor quality)* de pacotilla

**punt¹** [pʌnt] SPORTS **I.** *vt (in football)* despejar **II.** *vi (in football)* despejar

**punt²** [pʌnt] **I.** *vi (in boat)* ir en batea **II.** *n (boat)* batea *f*

**punt³** [pʌnt] *vi* GAMES jugar contra la banca

**puny** ['pju·ni] <-ier, -iest> *adj (person)* enclenque; *(attempt)* lastimoso, -a

**pup** [pʌp] **I.** *n* **1.** *(baby dog)* cachorro, -a *m, f* **2.** *(baby animal)* cría *f* **II.** <-pp-> *vi* parir

**pupa** ['pju·pə] <pupas *or* pupae> *n* BIO crisálida *f,* pupa *f*

**pupate** ['pju·peɪt] *vi* BIO convertirse en crisálida

**pupil¹** ['pju·pəl] *n* SCHOOL alumno, -a *m, f*

**pupil²** ['pju·pəl] *n* ANAT pupila *f*

**puppet** ['pʌp·ɪt] *n a. fig* títere *m*

**puppeteer** [pʌp·ə·'tɪr] *n* titiritero, -a *m, f*

**puppy** ['pʌp·i] <-ies> *n* cachorro, -a *m, f*

**purchase** ['pɜr·tʃəs] **I.** *vt* **1.** *(buy)* comprar, adquirir **2.** NAUT **to ~ the anchor** levar el ancla **II.** *n* **1.** *(act of buying)* compra *f;* **to make a ~** hacer una adquisición **2.** *(hold)* agarre *m;* **to get a ~ on sth** agarrarse a [*or de*] algo

**purchaser** *n (buyer)* comprador(a) *m(f)*

**purchasing** *n* compras *fpl*

**purchasing power** *n* poder *m* adquisitivo

**pure** [pjʊr] *adj* puro, -a; **~ air** aire *m* puro; **~ gold** oro *m* puro; **~ and simple** simple y llano

**purée** [pjʊ·'reɪ] *n* puré *m*

**purely** ['pjʊr·li] *adv* **1.** *(completely)* puramente; **~ by chance** por pura casualidad **2.** *(simply)* meramente; **~ and simply** simple y llanamente

**purge** [pɜrdʒ] **I.** *vt* **1.** MED, POL purgar **2.** *a.* REL *(crime, sin)* expiar **II.** *n* MED, POL purga *f*

**purify** ['pjʊr·ə·faɪ] *vt (cleanse)* purificar; *(language, water)* depurar

**puritan** ['pjʊr·ɪ·tən] *n a. fig* puritano, -a *m, f*

**puritanical** [ˌpjʊr·ɪ·'tæn·ɪ·kəl] *adj* puritano, -a

**purity** ['pjʊr·ɪ·ti] *n* pureza *f*

**purple** ['pɜr·pəl] *adj (reddish)* púrpura; *(bluish)* morado, -a; **to be ~ with rage** estar lívido de rabia

**purpose** ['pɜr·pəs] *n* **1.** *(goal)* intención *f; for the ~* al efecto; **I did that for a ~** hice eso por algo; **for that very ~** precisamente por eso; **for practical ~s** a efectos prácticos; **not to the ~** que no viene al caso; **to have a ~ in life** tener una meta en la vida **2.** *(motivation)* **(strength of) ~** resolución *f* **3.** *(use)* utilidad *f; to no ~* inútilmente; **to serve a ~** servir de algo; **what's the ~ of...?** ¿para qué sirve...? ▶ **on ~** a propósito

**purposeful** ['pɜr·pəs·fəl] *adj* **1.** *(determined)* decidido, -a **2.** *(meaningful)* con sentido 3. (*intentional*) intencionado, -a

**purposely** ['pɜr·pəs·li] *adv* a propósito

**purr** [pɜr] **I.** *vi* (*cat*) ronronear; (*engine*) zumbar **II.** *n* (*of cat*) ronroneo *m*; (*of engine*) zumbido *m*

**purse** [pɜrs] **I.** *n* **1.** (*handbag*) bolso *m*, cartera *f AmL*, bolsa *f Méx* **2.** (*wallet*) monedero *m* **3.** (*funds*) **to be beyond one's ~** estar por encima de las posibilidades de uno **4.** (*prize*) premio *m* en efectivo **II.** *vt* (*lips*) apretar

**pursue** [pər·'su] *vt* **1.** (*chase*) perseguir **2.** (*seek to find*) buscar; (*dreams, goals*) luchar por; (*rights, peace*) reivindicar **3.** (*follow: plan*) seguir; **to ~ a matter** seguir un caso **4.** (*work towards*) **to ~ a career** dedicarse a una carrera profesional

**pursuer** [pər·'su·ər] *n* perseguidor(a) *m(f)*

**pursuit** [pər·'sut] *n* **1.** (*chase*) persecución *f*; **police ~** persecución policial; **to be in ~ of sth** ir tras algo; (*knowledge, happiness*) ir en busca de algo **2.** (*activity*) actividad *f*; **outdoor ~s** actividades al aire libre

**purveyor** [pər·'veɪ·ər] *n* ECON proveedor(a) *m(f)*

**pus** [pʌs] *n* MED pus *m*, postema *f Méx*

**push** [pʊʃ] **I.** *vt* **1.** (*shove*) empujar; **to ~ one's way through sth** abrirse paso a empujones por algo; **to ~ sth to the back of one's mind** intentar no pensar en algo; **to ~ the door open** abrir la puerta de un empujón; **to ~ sb out of the way** apartar a alguien a empujones **2.** (*force*) **to ~ one's luck** tentar a la suerte; **to ~ sb too far** sacar a alguien de quicio **3.** (*coerce*) obligar; **to ~ sb to do** [*or* **into doing**] **sth** presionar a alguien para que haga algo; **to ~ oneself** exigirse demasiado **4.** (*insist*) insistir en; **to ~ sb for sth** apremiar a alguien para algo **5.** (*press: button*) apretar; (*brakes, gas pedal*) pisar **6. to be ~ing 30** rondar los 30 (años) **II.** *vi* **1.** (*force movement*) empujar **2.** (*press*) apretar **3.** (*insist*) presionar; **to ~ for sth** presionar para (conseguir) algo **III.** <-es> *n* **1.** (*shove*) empujón *m*; **to give sb a ~** *fig* dar un empujón a alguien **2.** (*press*)

at the ~ of a button apretando un botón **3.** (*strong action*) impulso *m*; (*will to succeed*) empuje *m* **4.** (*strong effort*) esfuerzo *m*; **to make a ~ for sth** hacer un esfuerzo para algo **5.** MIL (*military attack*) ofensiva *f*

◆**push along** *vi inf* largarse

◆**push around** *vt inf* mangonear *inf*

◆**push away** *vt* apartar

◆**push back** *vt* (*move backwards*) hacer retroceder; (*hair*) echar hacia atrás

◆**push down** *vt* **1.** (*knock down*) derribar **2.** (*press down*) apretar **3.** ECON (*price, interest rate*) hacer bajar

◆**push forward I.** *vt* **1.** (*force forward*) empujar hacia delante **2.** (*promote*) promocionar **II.** *vi* **1.** (*advance*) avanzar **2.** (*continue*) **to ~ (with sth)** seguir (con algo)

◆**push in** *vt* **1.** (*nail*) empujar (hacia adentro) **2.** (*force in*) **to push one's way in** colarse *inf*

◆**push off** *vi inf* largarse

◆**push on I.** *vi* **1.** (*continue despite problems*) **to ~ (with sth)** seguir adelante (con algo) **2.** (*continue traveling*) **we pushed on to Veracruz** seguimos hasta Veracruz **II.** *vt* **1.** (*activate*) apresurar **2.** (*urge on*) **to push sb on to do sth** empujar a alguien a hacer algo

◆**push out** *vt* (*force out*) **to push sb out (of sth)** echar a alguien (de algo) **2.** (*get rid of*) eliminar; **to push competitors out of the market** eliminar a los competidores del mercado

◆**push over** *vt always sep* (*thing*) volcar; (*person*) hacer caer

◆**push through I.** *vi* abrirse paso entre **II.** *vt* (*help to succeed*) llevar a buen término

◆**push up** *vt* **1.** (*move higher*) levantar; *fig* (*help*) dar un empujón **2.** (*price, interest rate*) hacer subir

**pushcart** ['pʊʃ·kart] *n* carretilla *f* de mano

**pusher** *n sl* camello *mf*

**pushover** ['pʊʃ·ou·vər] *n* **1.** (*easy success*) **to be a ~** ser pan comido **2.** (*easily influenced*) **to be a ~** ser muy fácil de convencer

**pushpin** ['pʊʃ·pɪn] *n* chincheta *f*

P

**push-start** *vi* AUTO arrancar empujando el coche

**pushup** ['puʃ.ʌp] *n* SPORTS flexión *f* de brazos; **to do ~s** hacer flexiones

**pushy** ['puʃ.i] *adj* avasallador(a), insistente

**puss** [pus] <-es> *n* (*cat*) minino, -a *m, f*; **Puss in Boots** el gato con botas

**pussy** ['pus.i] <-ies> *n* **1.** (*cat*) ~ (**cat**) minino, -a *m, f* **2.** *vulg* conejo *m*, concha *f AmL*

**put** [put] <-tt-, put, put> I. *vt* **1.** (*place*) poner; (*in box, hole*) meter; ~ **the spoons next to the knives** pon las cucharas junto a los cuchillos; **to ~ sth to one's lips** llevarse algo a los labios; ~ **it there!** (*shake hands*) ¡chócala!; **to ~ sth in the oven** meter algo en el horno **2.** (*add*) echar; **to ~ sugar/ salt in sth** echar azúcar/sal a algo; **to ~ the date on sth** poner la fecha en algo; **to ~ sth on a list** apuntar algo en una lista **3.** (*direct*) **to ~ pressure on sb** presionar a alguien; **to ~ one's heart into sth** poner todo el afán de uno en algo; **to ~ one's mind to sth** poner los cinco sentidos en algo; **to ~ one's trust/ hope in sb** depositar la confianza/las esperanzas de uno en alguien **4.** (*invest*) **to ~ sth into sth** invertir algo en algo; **to ~ energy/time into sth** dedicar energía/tiempo a algo **5.** (*bet*) apostar; **to ~ money on sth** jugarse dinero a algo **6.** (*cause to be*) **to ~ sb in a good mood** poner a alguien de buen humor; **to ~ sb in danger** poner a alguien en peligro; **to ~ oneself in sb's place** [*or* **shoes**] ponerse en el lugar de alguien; **to ~ into practice** poner en práctica; **to ~ sb on the train** acompañar a alguien hasta el tren; **to ~ sth right** arreglar algo; **to ~ sb to bed** acostar a alguien; **to ~ sth to good use** hacer buen uso de algo; **to ~ sb to shame** avergonzar a alguien; **to ~ a stop to sth** poner fin a algo; **to ~ sb to work** poner a alguien a trabajar **7.** (*impose*) **to ~ an idea in sb's head** meter una idea en la cabeza a alguien; **to ~ a tax on sth** gravar algo con un impuesto **8.** (*attribute*) **to ~ the blame on sb** echar la culpa a alguien;

**to ~ emphasis on sth** conceder especial importancia a algo **9.** (*present*) **to ~ a question** plantear una pregunta; **to ~ sth to discussion** someter algo a debate; **to ~ sth to a vote** someter algo a votación; **to ~ a proposal before a committee** presentar una propuesta ante un comité; **I ~ it to you that...** mi opinión es que... **10.** (*express*) decir; **as John ~ it** como dijo John; **to ~ one's feelings into words** expresar sus sentimientos con palabras; **to ~ sth into Spanish** traducir algo al español; **to ~ sth in writing** poner algo por escrito **11.** (*judge, estimate*) **I ~ the number of visitors at 2,000** calculo que el número de visitantes ronde los 2.000; **I'd ~ her at about 35** calculo que tiene unos 35 años; **to ~ sb on a level with sb** poner a alguien al mismo nivel que alguien **II.** *vi* NAUT **to ~ to sea** zarpar

◆**put about** <-tt-> *irr* **I.** *vt* NAUT hacer virar **II.** *vi* NAUT virar

◆**put across** <-tt-> *irr vt* (*make understood*) comunicar; **to put sth across to sb** hacer entender algo a alguien

◆**put aside** <-tt-> *irr vt* **1.** (*place to one side*) dejar a un lado **2.** (*save*) ahorrar; (*time*) reservar **3.** (*give up*) **to put sth aside** dejar algo **4.** (*reject*) rechazar

◆**put away** <-tt-> *irr vt* **1.** (*save*) ahorrar **2.** *inf* (*eat a lot*) zamparse **3.** (*remove*) guardar **4.** *inf* (*imprison*) **to put sb away** encerrar a alguien **5.** *sl* (*kill*) matar

◆**put back** <-tt-> *irr vt* **1.** (*return*) volver a poner en su sitio **2.** (*postpone*) posponer **3.** SCHOOL (*not be promoted*) **to put sb back a year** hacer repetir curso a alguien **4.** (*set earlier: watch*) atrasar

◆**put by** <-tt-> *irr vt* ahorrar

◆**put down** <-tt-> *irr vt* **1.** (*set down*) dejar; **to not be able to put a book down** no poder parar de leer un libro **2.** (*lower*) bajar; **to put one's arm/feet down** bajar el brazo/los pies; **to put sb/ sth down somewhere** dejar a alguien/ algo en un sitio **3.** (*attribute*) **to put sth down to sb** atribuir algo a alguien **4.** (*write*) escribir; **to put sth down on paper** poner algo por escrito **5.** (*assess*) catalogar; **I put her down as 30** le echo 30 años **6.** (*register*) **to put sb down for sth** inscribir a alguien en algo **7.** FIN (*prices*) disminuir **8.** ECON (*leave as deposit*) dejar en depósito **9.** (*stop: rebellion, opposition*) reprimir **10.** *sl* (*humiliate*) menospreciar **11.** (*have killed: animal*) sacrificar

◆**put forward** <-tt-> *irr vt* **1.** (*offer for discussion: subject*) proponer; (*idea, plan*) exponer; **to ~ a proposal** hacer una propuesta **2.** (*advance: event*) adelantar; **to put the clock forward** adelantar el reloj

◆**put in** <-tt-> *irr* **I.** *vt* **1.** (*place inside*) meter **2.** (*add*) poner; **to ~ a comma/a period** añadir una coma/un punto **3.** (*say*) decir; (*remark*) hacer; **to put a word in** intervenir en la conversación; **to ~ a good word for sb** hablar bien de alguien **4.** AGR (*plant: vegetables, trees*) plantar **5.** TECH (*install*) instalar **6.** (*invest: money*) poner; (*time, effort*) dedicar; **to ~ overtime** hacer horas extra **7.** (*submit: claim, request*) presentar; (*candidate*) presentarse; **to put oneself in for sth** inscribirse para algo **8.** (*make*) **to ~ an appearance** hacer acto de presencia **II.** *vi* **1.** (*apply*) **to ~ for sth** solicitar algo **2.** NAUT (*dock*) hacer escala

◆**put into** <-tt-> *irr vt* **1.** (*place inside*) meter **2. to put sth into sth** (*add*) añadir algo a algo **3.** (*dress in*) **to put sb into sth** vestir a alguien de algo **4.** TECH (*install*) instalar **5.** FIN (*deposit*) **to put money into a bank** ingresar dinero en un banco **6.** (*invest*) **to put sth into sth** (*money*) invertir algo en algo; (*time, effort*) dedicar algo a algo **7.** (*cause to be*) **to put a plan into operation** [*or inf* **action**] poner un plan en marcha **8.** (*institutionalize*) **to put sb into sth** meter a alguien en algo; **to put sb into prison** meter a alguien en la cárcel

◆**put off** <-tt-> *irr vt* **1.** (*turn off: lights, TV*) apagar; (*take off: sweater, jacket*) quitarse **2.** (*delay*) posponer; **to put sth off for a week** aplazar algo una semana **3.** *inf* (*make wait*) entretener; **to put sb off with excuses** dar largas a alguien *inf*

**4.** (*repel*) alejar; (*food, smell*) dar asco a **5.** (*disconcert*) desconcertar **6.** (*distract*) distraer; **to put sb off sth** distraer a alguien de algo

◆**put on** <-tt-> *irr vt* **1.** (*place upon*) **to put sth on sth** poner algo sobre algo **2.** (*attach*) **to put sth on sth** poner algo a algo **3.** (*wear: shirt, shoes*) ponerse; **to ~ make-up** maquillarse **4.** (*turn on*) encender; **to ~ Mozart** poner (música de) Mozart **5.** (*use*) **to ~ the brakes** frenar; **to put the handbrake on** poner el freno de mano **6.** (*perform: film*) dar; (*play*) poner en escena **7.** (*provide: dish*) servir; **to ~ a party** dar una fiesta **8.** (*begin boiling: water, soup, potatoes*) calentar **9.** (*assume: expression*) adoptar; **to ~ a frown** fruncir el ceño; **to ~ airs** darse aires **10.** (*pretend*) fingir; (*accent*) afectar **11.** (*be joking with*) **to put sb on** tomar el pelo a alguien **12.** (*gain: weight*) engordar **13.** TEL (*place sth on the* (**tele**)**phone** pasar el teléfono a alguien; **to put sb on to sb** poner a alguien con alguien; **I'll put him on** le paso con él **14.** (*inform*) **to put sb on to sb** hablar a alguien de alguien

◆**put out** <-tt-> *irr* **I.** *vt* **1.** (*take outside*) **to put the dog out** sacar al perro **2.** (*extend*) extender; **to ~ one's hand** tender la mano **3.** (*extinguish: fire*) extinguir; **to ~ a cigarette** apagar un cigarrillo **4.** (*turn off: lights, TV*) apagar **5.** (*eject*) expulsar **6.** (*publish: newsletter, magazine*) publicar; (*announcement*) hacer público **7.** (*spread: rumor*) **to put it out that...** hacer correr la voz de que... **8.** (*produce industrially*) producir **9.** (*sprout: leaves*) echar **10.** (*contract out*) **to put sth out to subcontract** subcontratar **11.** (*inconvenience*) molestar **12.** (*offend*) **to be ~** ofenderse **13.** (*dislocate*) dislocar; **to ~ one's shoulder** dislocarse el hombro **14.** NAUT botar **II.** *vi* NAUT zarpar

◆**put over** <-tt-> *irr vt* **1.** (*place higher*) **to put sth over sth** poner algo por encima de algo **2.** (*make understood: idea, plan*) comunicar **3.** (*fool*) **to put sth over on sb** engañar a alguien

◆**put through** <-tt-> *irr vt* **1.** (*insert*

*through*) **to put sth through sth** hacer pasar algo por algo **2.** (*complete, implement*) llevar a cabo; (*proposal*) hacer aceptar **3.** (*send*) mandar; **to put sb through college** mandar a alguien a la universidad **4.** TEL poner; **to ~ a telephone call to Montreal** contactar con un número de Montreal; **to put a call through** pasar una llamada **5.** *inf* (*make endure*) **to put sb through sth** someter a alguien a algo

♦**put together** <-tt-> *irr vt* **1.** (*join*) juntar; (*collection*) reunir; (*assemble*) ensamblar; (*machine, model, radio*) montar; (*pieces*) acoplar **2.** *fig* (*connect: facts, clues*) relacionar **3.** (*list*) hacer; (*team*) formar; (*meal*) preparar **4.** MATH sumar

♦**put up** <-tt-> *irr* **I.** *vt* **1.** (*hang up*) colgar; (*notice*) fijar **2.** (*raise*) levantar; (*one's collar*) subirse; (*flag*) izar; (*umbrella*) abrir; **to put one's hair up** recogerse el pelo **3.** (*build*) construir; (*tent*) montar **4.** (*increase: prices*) subir **5.** (*make available*) **to put sth up for sale** poner algo a la [*or* en] venta; **to put sth up for auction** sacar algo a subasta pública **6.** (*give shelter*) alojar; **I can put you up for a week** te puedes quedar una semana en casa **7.** (*provide: funds*) aportar; **to ~ the money for sth** poner el dinero para algo **8.** (*show opposition*) **to ~ opposition** oponerse; **to ~ a struggle** [*or* **fight**] oponer resistencia **II.** *vi* **1.** (*sleep at*) alojarse; **to ~ at a hotel** hospedarse en un hotel **2.** (*tolerate unwillingly*) **to ~ with sb/sth** soportar a alguien/algo

**put-on** *n sl* burla *f*; (*joke*) broma *f*

**putrefy** ['pjuː·trə·faɪ] <-ie-> *vi* pudrirse

**putt** [pʌt] SPORTS **I.** *vi* patear **II.** *n* golpe *m* corto (al hoyo), put *m AmL*

**putter¹** ['pʌt·ər] *n* (*golf club*) putter *m*

**putter²** ['pʌt·ər] *n* entretenerse; **to ~ around the house** pasearse por la casa

**putty** ['pʌt·i] *n* masilla *f*

**put-up** *adj inf* **a ~ job** un asunto fraudulento

**put-upon** *adj inf* explotado, -a

**puzzle** ['pʌz·əl] **I.** *vt* dejar perplejo, -a **II.** *vi* **to ~ over sth** dar vueltas a algo

**III.** *n* **1.** (*game*) rompecabezas *m inv*, **jigsaw ~ puzzle** *m*; **crossword ~** crucigrama *m* **2.** (*mystery*) misterio *m*, enigma *m*; **to solve a ~** resolver un enigma

**puzzled** *adj* perplejo, -a

**puzzling** *adj* desconcertante

**pylon** ['paɪ·lɑn] *n* ELEC torre *f* de alta tensión

**pyramid** ['pɪr·ə·mɪd] *n* pirámide *f*

**Pyrenees** ['pɪr·ə·ˌniz] *npl* **the ~** los Pirineos

**Pyrex®** ['paɪ·reks] **I.** *n* pyrex *m* **II.** *adj* de pyrex

**pyromaniac** *n* pirómano, -a *m, f*

**python** ['paɪ·θən] <-(ons)> *n* pitón *f*

# Q

**Q, q** [kju] *n* Q, q *f*; **~ as in Quebec** Q de queso

**Q** *abbr of* **Queen** reina *f*

**Q-Tip®** *n* bastoncillo *m* (para los oídos)

**quack¹** [kwæk] **I.** *n* (*of duck*) graznido *n* **II.** *vi* graznar

**quack²** [kwæk] *pej* **I.** *n* **1.** (*doctor*) ma tasanos *m inv* **2.** (*charlatan*) fantasmón -ona *m, f inf* **II.** *adj* falso, -a

**quadrangular** [kwa·ˈdræŋ·gjə·lər] *ad* cuadrangular

**quadratic** [kwa·ˈdræt·ɪk] *adj* cuadráti co, -a

**quadrilateral** [ˌkwad·rɪ·ˈlæt·ər·əl] *n* cua drilátero *m*

**quadruped** ['kwad·rə·ped] *n* cuadrúpe do *m*

**quadruple** [kwa·ˈdru·pəl] **I.** *vt* cuadru plicar **II.** *vi* cuadruplicárse **III.** *a* cuádruple

**quadruplet** [kwa·ˈdru·plɪt] *n* cuatrill zo, -a *m, f*

**quaint** [kweɪnt] *adj* **1.** (*charming*) pir toresco, -a **2.** *pej* (*strange*) raro, - **3.** (*pleasantly unusual*) singular

**quake** [kweɪk] **I.** *n* **1.** (*shaking*) ten blor *m* **2.** *inf* (*earthquake*) terreme to *m* **II.** *vi* **1.** (*move*) estremecers **2.** (*shake*) temblar; **to ~ with fear** ten blar de miedo

**Quaker** ['kweɪ·kər] *n* cuáquero, -a *m,*

**the ~s** los cuáqueros

**qualification** [ˌkwɑl·ə·fɪ·ˈkeɪ·ʃən] *n*
**1.** (*document*) título *m*; (*exam*) calificación *f*; **academic ~** título académico; **her ~s are very good** está muy cualificada **2.** (*limiting criterion*) restricción *f*; (*condition*) reserva *f*; (*change*) matización *f*; **without ~** sin reservas

**qualified** [ˈkwɑl·ɪ·faɪd] *adj* **1.** (*trained*) titulado, -a; (*certified*) certificado, -a; (*by the state*) homologado, -a **2.** (*competent*) capacitado, -a **3.** (*limited*) limitado, -a

**qualify** [ˈkwɑl·ɪ·faɪ] <-ie-> **I.** *vi* **1.** (*meet standards*) **to ~ for sth** estar habilitado para algo; (*have qualifications*) estar acreditado para algo **2.** (*complete training*) titularse **3.** SPORTS clasificarse **II.** *vt* **1.** (*give credentials*) acreditar **2.** (*make eligible*) habilitar; **to ~ sb to do sth** dar derecho a alguien para hacer algo **3.** (*explain and limit*) limitar; **to ~ a remark** matizar un comentario **4.** LING (*modify*) calificar

**qualifying** [ˈkwɑl·ɪ·faɪ·ɪŋ] *adj* **1.** (*limiting*) matizador(a) **2.** SPORTS (*testing standard*) clasificatorio, -a; **~ round** eliminatoria *f* **3.** LING (*modifying*) calificativo, -a

**quality** [ˈkwɑl·ɪ·t̬i] **I.** <-ies> *n* **1.** (*degree of goodness*) calidad *f*; **~ of life** calidad de vida **2.** (*characteristic*) cualidad *f*; **artistic ~** cualidades *f pl* artísticas **II.** *adj* de calidad

**quality time** *n* tiempo *m* para relacionarse en especial los momentos, escasos pero intensos, que una persona dedica a sus hijos

**quantify** [ˈkwɑn·tə·faɪ] <-ie-> *vt* cuantificar

**quantitative** [ˈkwɑn·tə·teɪ·t̬ɪv] *adj* cuantitativo, -a

**quantity** [ˈkwɑn·tə·t̬i] <-ies> *n* **1.** (*amount*) cantidad *f*; **a large/small ~ of sth** una gran/pequeña cantidad de algo **2.** (*large amounts*) cantidades *fpl*; **to buy in ~** comprar al por mayor

**quantity discount** *n* descuento *m* por grandes cantidades

**quarantine** [ˈkwɔr·ən·ˌtin] **I.** *n* cuarentena *f*; **to be/place under ~** estar/

poner en cuarentena **II.** *vt* **to ~ sb/an animal** poner en cuarentena a alguien/a un animal

**quarrel** [ˈkwɔr·əl] **I.** *n* disputa *f* **II.** <-ll-> *vi* reñir, pelearse

**quarrelsome** [ˈkwɔr·əl·səm] *adj* **1.** (*belligerent*) pendenciero, -a **2.** (*grumbly*) enojadizo, -a, enojón, -ona *Méx*

**quarry**[1] [ˈkwɔr·i] **I.** <-ies> *n* (*rock pit*) cantera *f* **II.** <-ie-> *vt* extraer

**quarry**[2] [ˈkwɔr·i] <-ies> *n* (*prey*) presa *f*

**quart** [kwɔrt] *n* cuarto *m* de galón

**quarter** [ˈkwɔr·t̬ər] **I.** *n* **1.** (*one fourth*) cuarto *m*; **three ~s** tres cuartos; **a ~ of a century/an hour** un cuarto de siglo/de hora; (**a**) **~ to three** las tres menos cuarto; (**a**) **~ past three** las tres y cuarto **2.** (*25 cents*) un cuarto de dólar **3.** *a.* FIN, SCHOOL trimestre *m* **4.** (*neighborhood*) barrio *m*; (*area*) zona *f*; **at close ~s** de cerca; **all ~s of the earth** en todos los confines de la tierra **5.** **~s** (*unspecified group or person*) círculos *mpl*; **in certain ~s** en ciertos círculos; **in high ~s** en altas esferas **6.** SPORTS cuarto *m* **7.** (*mercy*) cuartel *m*; **to give ~** dar cuartel; **to ask for ~** pedir cuartel **II.** *vt* **1.** (*cut into four*) cuartear; **to ~ sb** descuartizar a alguien **2.** (*give housing*) alojar; **to be ~ed with sb** estar alojado en casa de alguien **III.** *adj* cuarto; **~ hour** un cuarto de hora

**quarterfinal** *n* SPORTS cuarto *m* de final

**quarterly** [ˈkwɔr·t̬ər·li] **I.** *adv* trimestralmente **II.** *adj* trimestral

**quartet** *n*, **quartette** [kwɔr·ˈtet] *n* MUS cuarteto *m*

**quartz** [kwɔrts] **I.** *n* cuarzo *m* **II.** *adj* de cuarzo; **~ crystal** cristal de cuarzo

**quash** [kwɑʃ] *vt* **1.** (*suppress*) suprimir; (*rumor*) acallar; **to ~ sb's dreams/plans** aplastar los sueños/planes de alguien **2.** LAW (*annul: conviction, verdict, sentence*) anular; (*law, bill, writ*) derogar

**quaver** [ˈkweɪ·vər] **I.** *vi* temblar **II.** *n* temblor *m*

**quay** [ki] *n* muelle *m*

**queasy** [ˈkwi·zi] <-ier, -iest> *adj* **1.** (*nauseous*) mareado, -a **2.** *fig* (*unsettled*) intranquilo, -a; **with a ~ conscience**

con la conciencia intranquila

**queen** [kwin] **I.** n **1.** (*monarch*) reina *f*; **~ of hearts/diamonds** (*cards*) reina de corazones/diamantes **2.** *offensive sl* (*gay man*) loca *f* **II.** vt **1.** (*make queen*) **to ~ sb** coronar reina a alguien **2.** (*in chess*) coronar

**queen bee** n ZOOL abeja *f* reina

**queer** [kwɪr] <-er, -est> adj **1.** (*strange*) extraño, -a; **to have ~ ideas** tener ideas raras **2.** *offensive sl* (*homosexual*) maricón

**quell** [kwel] vt (*unrest, rebellion, protest*) sofocar; **to ~ sb's anger** calmar la rabia de alguien

**quench** [kwentʃ] vt **1.** (*satisfy*) satisfacer; (*thirst*) saciar **2.** (*put out*) sofocar; **to ~ a fire** apagar un incendio **3.** (*suppress*) suprimir; **to ~ sb's desire** apagar el deseo de alguien

**query** [ˈkwɪr·i] **I.** <-ies> n pregunta *f* **II.** <-ie-> vt **1.** *form* (*dispute*) cuestionar; (*doubt*) poner en duda **2.** (*ask*) preguntar

**quest** [kwest] n búsqueda *f*; **the ~ for the truth/an answer** la búsqueda de la verdad/una respuesta

**question** [ˈkwes·tʃən] **I.** n **1.** (*inquiry*) pregunta *f*; **frequently asked ~s** a COMPUT preguntas frecuentes; **to pop the ~ to sb** proponer matrimonio a alguien **2.** (*doubt*) duda *f*; **without ~** sin duda; **to be beyond ~** estar fuera de duda **3.** (*issue*) cuestión *f*; **to be a ~ of time/ money** ser una cuestión de tiempo/ dinero; **to raise a ~** plantear un problema; **to be out of the ~** ser totalmente imposible; **there's no ~ of sb doing sth** sería imposible que alguien hiciera algo **4.** SCHOOL, UNIV (*test problem*) pregunta *f*; **to do a ~** resolver una pregunta **II.** vt **1.** (*ask*) preguntar **2.** (*interrogate*) interrogar **3.** (*doubt*) cuestionar

**questionable** [ˈkwes·tʃə·nə·bəl] adj discutible

**questioner** n interrogador(a) *m(f)*

**questioning I.** n interrogatorio *m;* **to be taken in for ~** ser detenido para ser interrogado **II.** adj inquisidor(a); **to have a ~ mind** ser inquisitivo

**question mark** n signo *m* de interrogación

**questionnaire** [ˌkwes·tʃə·ˈner] n cuestionario *m*

**queue** [kju] n COMPUT cola *f*

**quibble** [ˈkwɪb·əl] **I.** n **1.** (*petty argument*) sutileza *f*; **a ~ over sth** una objeción acerca de algo **2.** (*criticism*) pega *f* **II.** vi poner peros a; **to ~ over sth** quejarse por algo

**quiche** [kiʃ] n quiche *f*

**quick** [kwɪk] **I.** <-er, -est> adj **1.** (*fast*) rápido, -a; **~ as lightning** (*veloz*) como un rayo; **to be ~ to do sth** hacer algo con rapidez **2.** (*short*) corto, -a; **the ~est way** el camino más corto **3.** (*hurried*) apresurado, -a; **to say a ~ good-bye/hello** decir un adiós/hola apresurado **4.** (*smart*) vivo, -a; **~ thinking** pensamiento ágil; **to have a ~ mind** tener una mente vivaz; **to have a ~ temper** tener mal genio **II.** <-er, -est> adv rápidamente; **~!** ¡rápido!; **as ~ as possible** tan pronto como sea posible **III.** n carne *f* viva; **to bite/cut nails to the ~** deja las uñas en carne viva

**quick-acting** [ˌkwɪk·ˈæk·tɪŋ] adj de efecto rápido

**quicken** [ˈkwɪk·ən] **I.** vt (*make faster*) apresurar; **to ~ the pace** acelerar el paso **II.** vi **1.** (*increase speed*) acelerarse **2.** (*become more active*) avivarse

**quick-freeze** [ˈkwɪk·friz] vt irr congela rápidamente

**quickie** [ˈkwɪk·i] n inf **1.** (*quick sex*) quiqui *m*, palito *m* Méx **2.** (*fast drink*) copa *f* rápida

**quickly** [ˈkwɪk·li] adv rápidamente

**quickness** [ˈkwɪk·nɪs] n **1.** (*speed*) rapidez *f* **2.** (*liveliness*) viveza *f*; **~ of mind** mente *f* rápida

**quicksand** [ˈkwɪk·sænd] n arenas *f p* movedizas

**quicksilver** n see **mercury** mercurio *m*

**quick-tempered** adj irascible

**quick-witted** adj perspicaz

**quiet** [ˈkwaɪ·ət] **I.** n **1.** (*silence*) silencio *m* **2.** (*lack of activity*) sosiego *m*; **peace and ~** paz y tranquilidad **II.** <-er, -est> adj **1.** (*not loud*) silencioso, -a; **to speak in a ~ voice** hablar en voz baja **2.** (*not talkative*) callado, -a; **t**

keep ~ mantenerse callado 3. (*secret*) secreto, -a; **to have a ~ word with sb** hablar en privado con alguien; **to keep ~ about sth** mantenerse callado respecto a algo 4. (*unostentatious*) discreto, -a 5. (*unexciting*) tranquilo, -a

♦**quiet down** I. *vi* 1. (*quiet*) callarse 2. (*calm*) calmarse II. *vt* 1. (*silence*) hacer callar 2. (*calm (down)*) calmar

**quietly** ['kwaɪət·li] *adv* 1. (*not loudly*) silenciosamente; **to speak ~** hablar en voz baja 2. (*peacefully*) tranquilamente

**quietness** ['kwaɪ·ət·nɪs] *n* tranquilidad *f*

**quill** [kwɪl] *n* 1. (*feather, pen*) pluma *f* 2. (*of porcupine*) púa *f*

**quilt** [kwɪlt] *n* edredón *m*

**quince** [kwɪns] *n* membrillo *m*

**quinine** ['kwaɪ·naɪn] *n* quinina *f*

**quintet(te)** [kwɪn·'tet] *n* quinteto *m*

**quintuple** [kwɪn·'tup·əl] *form* I. *adj* quíntuplo, -a II. *vt* quintuplicar III. *vi* quintuplicarse

**quintuplet** [kwɪn·'tʌp·lɪt] *n* quintillizo, -a *m, f*

**quip** [kwɪp] *n* ocurrencia *f*

**quirk** [kwɜrk] *n* 1. (*habit*) excentricidad *f* 2. (*oddity*) rareza *f* 3. (*sudden twist or turn*) **a ~ of fate** un capricho del destino

**quit** [kwɪt] <quit *or* quitted, quit *or* quitted> I. *vi* (*resign*) dimitir II. *vt* 1. (*resign*) dejar 2. (*stop*) parar; (*smoking*) dejar de 3. COMPUT salir de

**quite** [kwaɪt] *adv* 1. (*fairly*) bastante; **~ a bit** mucho, bastantito *Méx*; **~ a distance** una distancia considerable; **~ something** una cosa notable 2. (*completely*) ~ **wrong** totalmente equivocado; **not ~** no tanto; **not ~ as clever/rich as ...** no tan inteligente/rico como...

**quits** [kwɪts] *adj inf* en paz; **to be ~ (with sb)** estar en paz con alguien; **to call it ~** hacer las paces

**quitter** *n* desertor, -a *m, f,* rajado, -a *Méx*

**quiver**[1] ['kwɪv·ər] I. *n* (*shiver*) estremecimiento *m* II. *vi* temblar

**quiver**[2] ['kwɪv·ər] *n* (*for arrows*) aljaba *f*

**quiz** [kwɪz] I. <-es> *n* encuesta *f* II. *vt* interrogar

**quizmaster** ['kwɪz·ˌmæs·tər] *n* moderador(a) *m(f)*

**quiz show** *n* concurso *m* (de TV)

**quota** ['kwoʊ·tə] *n* 1. (*fixed amount allowed*) cuota *f* 2. (*proportion*) parte *f*

**quotation** [kwoʊ·'teɪ·ʃən] *n* 1. (*repeated words*) cita *f* 2. FIN cotización *f*

**quotation marks** *npl* comillas *fpl*

**quote** [kwoʊt] I. *n* 1. *inf* (*quotation*) cita *f* 2. ~s (*quotation marks*) comillas *fpl* 3. (*estimate*) presupuesto *m* 4. FIN cotización *f* II. *vt* 1. citar 2. (*name*) nombrar 3. FIN cotizar; **a ~d company** una empresa que cotiza en bolsa III. *vi* (*repeat exact words*) citar; **to ~ from sb** citar a alguien

**quotient** ['kwoʊ·ʃənt] *n* 1. MATH cociente *m* 2. (*factor*) coeficiente *m;* **intelligence ~** coeficiente de inteligencia

# R

**r, R** [ar] *r,* R *f;* **~ as in Romeo** R de Ramón

**R** CINE *abbr of* **restricted** *clasificación de cine para mayores de 17 años*

**R.** *abbr of* **River** r.

**rabbi** ['ræb·aɪ] *n* rabino *m*

**rabbit** ['ræb·ɪt] *n* conejo, -a *m, f*

**rabble** ['ræb·əl] *n* muchedumbre *f*

**rabid** ['ræb·ɪd] *adj* 1. (*furious*) furibundo, -a 2. (*fanatical*) fanático, -a 3. (*suffering from rabies*) rabioso, -a

**rabies** ['reɪ·biz] *n* rabia *f;* **to carry ~** tener la rabia

**raccoon** [ræ·'kun] *n* mapache *m*

**race**[1] [reɪs] I. *n* carrera *f;* **a ~ against time** una carrera contra reloj; **100-meter ~** carrera de cien metros lisos; **to run a ~** participar en una carrera II. *vi* 1. (*move quickly*) correr; SPORTS competir 2. (*engine*) acelerarse III. *vt* 1. (*compete against*) competir con; **to ~ sb home** echar una carrera hasta casa a alguien 2. (*enter for race: horse*) hacer correr

**race**[2] [reɪs] *n* 1. (*ethnic*) raza *f* 2. (*species*) especie *f* 3. (*lineage*) estirpe *f*

**racecar** *n* coche *m* de carreras, carro *m*

de carreras *Col*

**racehorse** ['reɪs,hɔrs] *n* caballo *m* de carreras

**racer** ['reɪ·sər] *n* 1. (*person*) corredor(a) *m(f)* 2. (*bicycle*) bicicleta *f* de carreras

**race relations** *npl* relaciones *f pl* interraciales

**racetrack** ['reɪs·træk] *n* (*for cars*) circuito *m;* (*for runners*) estadio *m;* (*for bicycles*) velódromo *m;* (*for horses*) hipódromo *m*

**racial** ['reɪ·ʃəl] *adj* racial

**racing** I. *n* carreras *fpl* II. *adj* de carreras

**racing bicycle** *n*, **racing bike** *n inf* bicicleta *f* de carreras

**racism** ['reɪ·sɪz·əm] *n* racismo *m*

**racist** ['reɪ·sɪst] *adj* racista

**rack** [ræk] *n* 1. (*framework, shelf*) estante *m;* **luggage ~** portaequipajes *m inv;* **dish ~** escurreplatos *m inv* 2. (*bar for hanging things on*) barra *f;* **towel ~** portatoallas *m inv* 3. CULIN **~ of lamb/beef** costillar *m* de cordero/ternera 4. (*torture instrument*) potro *m;* **to be on the ~** *fig* estar en ascuas

**racket** ['ræk·ɪt] *n* 1. SPORTS raqueta *f* 2. *inf* (*loud noise*) barullo *m;* **to make a ~** armar un alboroto 3. (*scheme*) chanchullo *m*

**racketeer** [,ræk·ə·'tɪr] *n* timador(a) *m(f)*

**racy** ['reɪ·si] <-ier, -iest> *adj* (*film, novel*) atrevido, -a

**radar** ['reɪ·dar] *n* radar *m*

**radar trap** *n* detector *m* de velocidad

**radial** ['reɪ·di·əl] *adj* radial; TECH en estrella

**radiant** ['reɪ·di·ənt] *adj* radiante

**radiate** ['reɪ·di·eɪt] *vt* 1. (*emit*) irradiar 2. (*display: happiness, enthusiasm*) mostrar

**radiation** [,reɪ·di·'eɪ·ʃən] *n* radiación *f*

**radiation therapy** *n* radioterapia *f*

**radiator** ['reɪ·di·eɪ·tər] *n* radiador *m*

**radical** ['ræd·ɪ·kəl] I. *n a.* CHEM, MATH radical *m* II. *adj* (*change, idea*) radical; (*measures*) drástico, -a

**radio** ['reɪ·di·oʊ] I. *n* radio *f* II. *vt* (*information*) radiar; (*person*) llamar por radio

**radioactive** [,reɪ·di·oʊ·'æk·tɪv] *adj* radiactivo, -a

**radioactivity** [,reɪ·di·oʊ·æk·'tɪv·ə·ţi] *n* radiactividad *f*

**radiographer** *n* radiógrafo, -a *m, f*

**radiography** [,reɪ·di·'ag·rə·fi] *n* radiografía *f*

**radio ham** *n* radioaficionado, -a *m, f*

**radiologist** [,reɪ·di·'al·ə·dʒɪst] *n* radiólogo, -a *m, f*

**radiology** [,reɪ·di·'al·ə·dʒi] *n* radiología *f*

**radio station** *n* emisora *f* de radio, estación *f* de radio *AmL*

**radio telescope** *n* radiotelescopio *m*

**radiotherapy** [,reɪ·di·oʊ·'θer·ə·pi] *n* radioterapia *f*

**radish** ['ræd·ɪʃ] <-es> *n* rábano *m*

**radius** ['reɪ·di·əs] <-dii> *n* radio *m*

**raffle** ['ræf·əl] I. *n* rifa *f* II. *vt* rifar

**raft**[1] [ræft] (*vessel*) I. *n* balsa *f* II. *vi* ir en balsa

**raft**[2] [ræft] *n* (*large quantity*) *inf* montón *m;* **a ~ of options** un montón de opciones

**rafter** ['ræf·tər] *n* ARCHIT viga *f*

**rag** [ræg] I. *n* 1. (*old cloth*) trapo *m* 2. *pl* (*worn-out clothes*) harapos *mpl* 3. *pej sl* (*newspaper*) periodicucho *m* II. <-gg-> *vt sl* tomar el pelo a

**rage** [reɪdʒ] I. *n* 1. (*anger*) furia *f;* **to be in a ~** estar hecho una furia 2. (*fashion*) **to be all the ~** ser el último grito II. *vi* 1. (*express fury*) enfurecerse; **to ~ at sb/sth** enfurecerse con alguien/algo 2. (*continue: battle*) continuar con pleno vigor; (*wind, storm*) bramar; (*fire*) arder furiosamente

**ragged** ['ræg·ɪd] *adj* 1. (*torn: clothes*) hecho, -a jirones 2. (*wearing worn clothes*) andrajoso, -a 3. (*rough*) recortado, -a 4. (*irregular*) irregular

**raging** ['reɪ·dʒɪŋ] *adj* (*gale*) furioso, -a; (*fire*) incontenible

**raid** [reɪd] I. *n* 1. MIL incursión *f* 2. (*attack*) ataque *m* 3. (*robbery*) asalto *m* 4. (*by police*) redada *f* II. *vt* 1. MIL invadir 2. (*attack*) atacar 3. (*by police*) hacer una redada en

**rail** [reɪl] I. *n* 1. (*of fence*) valla *f;* (*of balcony, stairs*) barandilla *f* 2. (*railway system*) ferrocarril *m;* **by ~** en tren, por ferrocarril 3. (*track*) raíl [*or* rail] *m*, riel *m AmL* II. *vt* **to ~ sth in** [*or* **off**] cercar algo

**railing** ['reɪ·lɪŋ] *n* 1. (*post*) valla *f*; **iron ~** verja *f* 2. (*of stairs*) pasamanos *m* inv

**railroad** ['reɪl·roʊd] *n* 1. (*system*) ferrocarril *m* 2. (*track*) línea *f* de ferrocarril

**railroad line** *n* vía *f* del tren

**railroad station** *n* estación *f* de ferrocarril

**railway** ['reɪl·weɪ] *n* ferrocarril *m*

**rain** [reɪn] I. *n* lluvia *f*; **~ shower** chubasco *m*; **the ~s** la temporada de lluvias II. *vi* llover

♦**rain out** *vt* **to be rained out** cancelarse por lluvia

**rainbow** *n* METEO arco *m* iris

**rain cloud** *n* nube *f* de lluvia

**raincoat** *n* gabardina *f*, piloto *m Arg*

**raindrop** *n* gota *f* de lluvia

**rainfall** *n* precipitación *f*

**rain forest** *n* selva *f* tropical

**rainproof** I. *adj* impermeable II. *vt* impermeabilizar

**rainstorm** *n* tormenta *f* de lluvia

**rainwater** *n* agua *f* de lluvia

**rainy** ['reɪ·ni] *adj* <-ier, -iest> lluvioso, -a; **the ~ season** la temporada de las lluvias

**raise** [reɪz] I. *n* (*of wages, prices*) aumento *m* II. *vt* 1. (*lift*) levantar; (*periscope, window*) subir; (*arm, hand, leg*) levantar; (*flag*) izar; (*anchor*) levar 2. (*stir up*) provocar 3. (*increase: wages, awareness*) aumentar; (*bet*) subir; MATH elevar; (*standards*) mejorar 4. (*promote*) ascender 5. (*introduce: subject, problem*) plantear 6. FIN recaudar 7. (*build*) erigir; (*monument*) levantar 8. (*bring up, cultivate*) cultivar 9. (*end: embargo*) levantar 10. (*contact*) llamar, contactar *Méx, Col*; **to ~ the alarm** dar la voz de alarma

**raisin** ['reɪ·zən] *n* pasa *f*

**rake¹** [reɪk] *n* (*tool*) rastrillo *m*

**rake²** [reɪk] *n* (*dissolute man*) vividor *m*

♦**rake in** *vt sl* (*money*) amasar; **to be raking it in** estar forrándose

♦**rake up** *vt* 1. (*gather*) reunir 2. *fig* (*refer to*) sacar a relucir

**rally** ['ræl·i] <-ies> I. *n* 1. (*race*) rally *m* 2. POL mitin *m* II. *vi* 1. MED mejorar; FIN

reputar 2. MIL agruparse; **to ~ behind sb** apoyar a alguien III. *vt* 1. MIL reagruparse 2. (*support*) apoyar

**ram** [ræm] I. *n* 1. (*male sheep*) carnero *m*; (*astrology*) Aries *m* 2. MIL ariete *m* II. *vt* <-mm-> (*hit*) embestir contra

**ramble** ['ræm·bəl] I. *n* (*walk*) caminata *f*; **to go for a ~** ir de excursión II. *vi* 1. (*person*) pasear; (*river*) serpentear; (*plant*) trepar 2. (*in speech*) divagar

**rambler** ['ræm·blər] *n* 1. (*walker*) excursionista *mf* 2. BOT rosa *f* trepadora

**rambling** ['ræm·blɪŋ] I. *n* **~s** (*speech*) divagaciones *fpl* II. *adj* 1. (*estate, house*) laberíntico, -a 2. (*speech*) divagante 3. (*rose*) trepador(a) 4. (*roaming*) errante

**ramp** [ræmp] *n* 1. (*sloping way*) rampa *f* 2. AUTO (*on-ramp*) carril *m* de incorporación; (*off-ramp*) carril *m* de salida

**rampage** ['ræm·peɪdʒ] I. *n* destrozos *mpl*; **to be on the ~** ir arrasando todo II. *vi* arrasar

**rampant** ['ræm·pənt] *adj* (*disease, growth*) exuberante; (*inflation*) galopante

**ran** [ræn] *pt of* **run**

**ranch** [ræntʃ] I. <-es> *n* granja *f*, rancho *m* II. *vi* (*run a ranch*) llevar una granja

**rancher** ['ræn·tʃər] *n* 1. (*owner*) hacendado, -a *m, f*, ranchero, -a *m, f Méx* 2. (*worker*) granjero, -a *m, f*

**rancid** ['ræn·sɪd] *adj* rancio, -a

**rancor** ['ræŋ·kər] *n* rencor *m*

**R & D** [ˌar·ənd·ˈdi] *abbr of* **Research and Development** I+D

**random** ['ræn·dəm] I. **n at ~** al azar II. *adj* aleatorio, -a

**rang** [ræŋ] *pt of* **ring²**

**range** [reɪndʒ] I. *n* 1. (*variety*) variedad *f* 2. (*scale*) gama *f*; **the full ~ of sth** la gama completa de algo 3. (*extent*) distancia *f* 4. (*maximum capability*) alcance *m*; **out of ~** fuera del alcance; **within ~** al alcance 5. (*field*) ámbito *m*, campo *m*; **shooting ~** campo *m* de tiro 6. (*pasture*) pradera *f* 7. MUS extensión *f* 8. GEO cadena *f*; **mountain ~** cordillera *f*; (*shorter*) sierra *f* II. *vi* 1. (*vary*) variar 2. (*extend*) extenderse

**R**

3. (*rove*) deambular

**ranger** ['reɪn·dʒər] n guardabosque mf

**rank¹** [ræŋk] I. n 1. (*status*) rango m 2. MIL graduación f; **the ~s** las tropas II. vi clasificarse; **to ~ above sb** estar por encima de alguien III. vt 1. (*classify*) clasificar 2. (*arrange*) situar

**rank²** [ræŋk] adj 1. (*smelling unpleasant*) fétido, -a 2. (*absolute*) total; (*beginner*) absoluto, -a

**ranking** ['ræn·kɪŋ] n clasificación f

**rankle** ['ræn·kəl] vi doler; **to ~ with sb** estar resentido con alguien; **it ~s that...** duele que... +subj

**ransom** ['ræn·səm] I. n rescate m; **to hold sb (for) ~** secuestrar a alguien y pedir rescate; fig chantajear a alguien II. vt rescatar

**rant** [rænt] I. n despotrique m II. vi despotricar; **to ~ and rave** despotricar

**rap** [ræp] I. n 1. (*knock*) golpe m seco 2. MUS rap m II. vt golpear III. vi 1. (*talk*) charlar 2. MUS rapear

**rape¹** [reɪp] I. n 1. (*of person*) violación f 2. (*of city*) saqueo m II. vt 1. (*person*) violar 2. (*city*) saquear

**rape²** [reɪp] n BOT, AGR colza f

**rapeseed oil** n aceite m de colza

**rapid** ['ræp·ɪd] adj (*quick*) rápido, -a

**rapist** ['reɪ·pɪst] n violador(a) m(f)

**rapture** ['ræp·tʃər] n éxtasis m inv

**rapturous** ['ræp·tʃər·əs] adj (*expression*) extasiado, -a; (*applause*) entusiasta

**rare¹** [rer] adj 1. (*uncommon: animal, coin, disease*) raro, -a 2. (*exceptional: genius, sense of honor*) único, -a

**rare²** [rer] adj CULIN poco hecho, -a

**rarely** ['rer·li] adv raramente, raras veces

**rarity** ['rer·ə· t̬i] <-ies> n rareza f

**rascal** ['ræs·kəl] n granuja mf

**rash¹** [ræʃ] n 1. MED sarpullido m 2. (*outbreak: of burglaries, etc*) racha f

**rash²** [ræʃ] adj (*decision*) precipitado, -a; (*move*) impulsivo, -a

**rasher** ['ræʃ·ər] n loncha f (de beicon)

**raspberry** ['ræz·ber·i] <-ies> n 1. (*fruit*) frambuesa f 2. sl SPORTS (*wound*) rasponazo m

**rat** [ræt] I. n 1. (*animal*) rata f 2. (*person*) canalla mf ▶ **I smell a ~** aquí hay gato encerrado II. vi (*betray*) dela-

tar; **to ~ on sb** chivatear a alguien Col, Cuba, PRico

**rate** [reɪt] I. n 1. (*speed*) velocidad f; **at this ~** a este ritmo; **at one's own ~** a su propio ritmo 2. (*proportion*) índice m, tasa f; **birth/death ~** tasa f de natalidad/mortalidad; **unemployment ~** índice m de desempleo 3. (*price*) precio m; **~ of exchange** cambio m, interest ~ tipo m de interés ▶ **at any ~** de todos modos II. vt calificar; **to ~ sb/sth as sth** considerar algo/a alguien como algo III. vi **to ~ as** ser considerado como

**rather** ['ræð·ər] I. adv 1. (*somewhat*) ~ **sleepy** medio dormido 2. (*more exactly*) más bien 3. (*on the contrary*) más bien 4. (*very*) bastante 5. (*in preference to*) I would ~ **stay here** preferiría quedarme aquí; ~ **you than me!** ¡no quisiera estar en tu lugar! II. interj por supuesto

**ratify** ['ræt̬·ə·faɪ] vt ratificar

**rating** ['reɪ·t̬ɪŋ] n 1. (*estimation*) evaluación f 2. pl TV, RADIO índice m de audiencia

**ratio** ['reɪ·ʃi·oʊ] n proporción f

**ration** ['ræʃ·ən] I. n 1. (*fixed allowance*) ración f 2. ~**s** (*total amount allowed*) raciones fpl; **food ~s** víveres mpl II. vt racionar

**rational** ['ræʃ·ə·nəl] adj 1. (*able to reason*) racional 2. (*sensible*) razonable

**rationalization** [ˌræʃ·ə·nə·lɪ·'zeɪ·ʃən] n racionalización f

**rationalize** ['ræʃ·ə·nə·laɪz] vt racionalizar

**rationing** n racionamiento m

**rat poison** n raticida m

**rat race** n **the ~** la lucha para sobrevivir

**rattle** ['ræt̬·əl] I. n 1. (*noise*) ruido m; (*of carriage*) traqueteo m 2. (*for baby*) sonajero m II. vi hacer ruido; (*carriage*) traquetear III. vt 1. (*making noise*) hacer sonar 2. (*make nervous*) poner nervioso, -a

**rattlesnake** ['ræt̬·əl·sneɪk] n serpiente f de cascabel

**ravage** ['ræv·ɪdʒ] vt hacer estragos en

**rave** [reɪv] I. adj inf (*review*) elogioso, -a II. vi desvariar; **to ~ about sth/sb** poner algo/a alguien por las nubes; **to**

**~ against sb/sth** despotricar contra alguien/algo

**raven** ['reɪ·vən] n cuervo m

**ravenous** ['ræv·ə·nəs] adj (person, animal) hambriento, -a; (appetite) voraz

**ravine** [rə·'vin] n barranco m

**raving** ['reɪ·vɪn] I. adj (success) total; **a ~ madman** un loco de remate II. adv **to be ~ mad** estar como una cabra III. npl desvaríos mpl

**raw** [rɔ] adj 1. (uncooked) crudo, -a 2. (unprocessed: sewage) sin tratar; (data) en sucio; **~ material** materia prima 3. (sore) en carne viva 4. (inexperienced) novato, -a 5. (unrestrained) salvaje 6. (weather) crudo, -a

**ray**[1] [reɪ] n 1. (of light) rayo m 2. (trace) resquicio m

**ray**[2] [reɪ] n (fish) raya f

**razor** ['reɪ·zər] I. n navaja f de afeitar; **electric ~** maquinilla f de afeitar II. vt afeitar

**razor-sharp** adj 1. (knife) muy afilado, -a 2. (person) agudo, -a

**RC** [ˌɑr·'si] 1. abbr of **Red Cross** Cruz f Roja 2. abbr of **Roman Catholic** católico, -a m, f

**Rd.** abbr of **road** C/

**re** [reɪ] n MUS re m

**reach** [ritʃ] I. n 1. (range) alcance m; **to be within (sb's) ~** a. fig estar al alcance (de alguien); **to be out of (sb's) ~** a. fig estar fuera del alcance de alguien) 2. (of river) tramo m; **the upper/lower ~es of the Amazon** la parte alta/baja del Amazonas II. vt 1. (stretch out) alargar, extender 2. (arrive at: city, country) llegar a 3. (attain) alcanzar; (agreement) llegar a; **to ~ 80** cumplir (los) 80 (años) 4. (extend to) llegar a 5. (communicate with) ponerse en contacto con III. vi **to ~ for sth** alargar la mano para tomar algo

◆**reach down** vi **to ~ to** (land) extenderse hasta; (clothes) llegar hasta

◆**reach out** vi tender la(s) mano(s); **to ~ for sth** estirar la mano para agarrar algo

**react** [rɪ·'ækt] vi reaccionar; **to ~ to sth** reaccionar ante algo; MED reaccionar a algo; **to ~ against sth** reaccionar

contra algo

**reaction** [rɪ·'æk·ʃən] n 1. a. CHEM reacción f; **chain ~** reacción en cadena 2. MED efecto m

**reactionary** [rɪ·'æk·ʃə·ner·i] adj reaccionario, -a

**reactor** [rɪ·'æk·tər] n reactor m

**read**[1] [rid] I. n lectura f II. vt <read, read> 1. leer; **to ~ sth aloud** leer algo en voz alta; **to ~ sb a story** leer un cuento a alguien 2. (decipher) descifrar; **to ~ sb's mind** [or **thoughts**] adivinar los pensamientos de alguien; **to ~ sb's palm** leer la mano a alguien; **to ~ sb like a book** conocer a alguien como la palma de la mano; **~ my lips!** ¡léeme los labios! 3. (interpret) interpretar 4. (inspect) inspeccionar; (meter) leer 5. (understand) entender; **I don't ~ you** no te sigo III. vi <read, read> (person) leer; (book, magazine) leerse

◆**read off** vt leer (de un tirón)

◆**read on** vi seguir leyendo

◆**read out** vt 1. (read aloud) leer en voz alta 2. COMPUT (data) sacar

◆**read over** vt releer

◆**read through** vt leer de principio a fin

**read**[2] [red] adj leído, -a; **little/widely ~** poco/muy leído

**readable** ['ri·də·bəl] adj 1. (legible) legible 2. (easy to read) ameno, -a

**reader** ['ri·dər] n 1. (person) lector(a) m(f) 2. (book) libro m de lectura 3. TECH lector m

**readership** ['ri·dər·ʃɪp] n lectores mpl

**readily** ['red·ə·li] adv 1. (promptly) de buena gana 2. (easily) fácilmente

**readiness** ['red·i·nɪs] n 1. (willingness) (buena) disposición f 2. (preparedness) preparación f

**reading** ['ri·dɪn] n 1. lectura f 2. (interpretation) interpretación f 3. TECH medición f

**reading glasses** npl gafas f pl para leer

**reading lamp** n lámpara f portátil

**readjust** [ˌri·ə·'dʒʌst] I. vt a. TECH reajustar II. vi (objects) reajustarse; (people) readaptarse

**readjustment** [ˌri·ə·'dʒʌst·mənt] n TECH reajuste m

**ready** ['red·i] I. adj <-ier, -iest> 1. (pre-

R

pared*) listo, -a; **to get ~ (for sth)** prepararse (para algo); **to get sth ~** preparar algo **2.** (*willing*) dispuesto, -a **3.** (*available*) disponible; **~ cash** dinero *m* en efectivo; **~ at hand** a mano **4.** (*quick, prompt*) vivo, -a; **to find ~ acceptance** tener inmediata aceptación ▶ **~, set, go!** SPORTS ¡preparados, listos, ya! **II.** *n* **at the ~** a punto **III.** *vt* preparar

**real** [rɪl] **I.** *adj* **1.** (*actual*) real; **for ~** de verdad **2.** (*genuine*) auténtico, -a; **the ~ thing** [*or* **deal**] lo auténtico; **a ~ man** *iron* un hombre como Dios manda **II.** *adv inf* muy

**realist** ['rɪ·lɪst] *n* realista *mf*

**realistic** [ˌrɪ·ə·'lɪs·tɪk] *adj* realista

**reality** [rɪ·'æl·ə·t̬i] *n* realidad *f*; **to come back to ~** volver a la realidad; **to face ~** enfrentarse a la realidad; **to become a ~** hacerse realidad; **in (all) ~** en realidad

**reality television** *n*, **reality TV** *programación televisiva basada en la vida real*

**realization** [ˌrɪ·ə·lɪ·'zeɪ·ʃən] *n* **1.** (*awareness*) comprensión *f* **2. a.** FIN realización *f*

**realize** ['rɪ·ə·laɪz] **I.** *vt* **1.** (*be aware of*) ser consciente de; (*become aware of*) darse cuenta de **2.** (*achieve*) realizar **3.** (*fulfill*) cumplir **4.** FIN realizar; (*acquire*) liquidar **II.** *vi* (*notice*) darse cuenta; (*be aware of*) ser consciente

**really** ['rɪ·ə·li] **I.** *adv* **1.** (*genuinely*) de verdad **2.** (*actually*) en realidad **3.** (*very*) muy **II.** *interj* **1.** (*surprise and interest*) ¿ah sí? **2.** (*annoyance*) pero bueno **3.** (*disbelief*) ¿de veras?

**realm** [relm] *n* **1.** (*kingdom*) reino *m* **2.** (*area of interest*) campo *m*

**realtor** ['rɪ·əl·tər] *n* agente *mf* inmobiliario, -a

**reap** [rip] *vi, vt* cosechar

**reappear** [ˌrɪ·ə·'pɪr] *vi* reaparecer

**reapply** [ˌrɪ·ə·'plaɪ] **I.** *vi* **to ~ for sth** volver a presentar una solicitud para algo **II.** *vt* (*paint*) dar otra capa de

**rear¹** [rɪr] **I.** *adj* (*light*) trasero, -a; (*leg, wheel*) posterior **II.** *n* **1.** (*back part*) parte *f* trasera **2.** *inf* (*buttocks*) trasero *m* **3.** MIL retaguardia *f*

**rear²** [rɪr] **I.** *vt* **1.** (*bring up: child, animals*) criar **2.** (*raise*) **to ~ one's head**

levantar la cabeza **II.** *vi* (*horse*) encabritarse

**rearmost** ['rɪr·moʊst] *adj* último, -a

**rearrange** [ˌrɪ·ə·'reɪndʒ] *vt* **1.** (*system*) reorganizar **2.** (*furniture*) colocar de otra manera **3.** (*meeting*) volver a concertar

**rearview mirror** *n* retrovisor *m*

**rear-wheel drive** *n* tracción *f* trasera

**reason** ['ri·zən] *n* **1.** (*motive*) motivo *m*; **the ~ why...** el motivo por el que...; **for no particular ~** sin ningún motivo en concreto; **for some ~** por algún motivo **2.** (*common sense*) sensatez *f*; **within ~** dentro de lo razonable; **to listen all ~** atender a razones; **to be beyond all ~** no tener ninguna lógica **3.** (*sanity*) razón *f*; **to lose one's ~** perder la razón **II.** *vt* razonar **III.** *vi* razonar; **to ~ from sth** discurrir partiendo de algo

**reasonable** ['ri·zə·nə·bəl] *adj* **1.** (*sensible*) sensato, -a; (*demand*) razonable **2.** (*inexpensive*) moderado, -a

**reasonably** ['ri·zə·nə·bli] *adv* **1.** (*fairly*) razonablemente **2.** (*acceptably*) bastante

**reasoning** ['ri·zə·nɪŋ] *n* razonamiento *m*

**reassemble** [ˌrɪ·ə·'sem·bəl] *vt* (*machine*) volver a montar; (*people*) volver a reunir

**reassurance** [ˌrɪ·ə·'ʃʊr·əns] *n* (*comfort*) palabras *f pl* tranquilizadoras

**reassure** [ˌrɪ·ə·'ʃʊr] *vt* tranquilizar

**reassuring** [ˌrɪ·ə·'ʃʊr·ɪŋ] *adj* tranquilizador(a)

**rebate** ['ri·beɪt] *n* **1.** (*refund*) reembolso *m*; **tax ~** devolución *f* de impuestos **2.** (*discount*) rebaja *f*

**rebel¹** ['reb·əl] **I.** *n* rebelde *mf* **II.** *adj* rebelde

**rebel²** [rɪ·'bel] <-ll-> *vi* rebelarse

**rebellion** [rɪ·'bel·jən] *n* rebelión *f*

**rebellious** [rɪ·'bel·jəs] *adj* rebelde

**reboot** [ˌrɪ·'but] *vt* COMPUT reiniciar

**rebound** [rɪ·'baʊnd] **I.** *vi* **1.** (*bounce back: ball*) rebotar **2.** (*in basketball*) rebotear **II.** *vt* rebotar **III.** *n* **1.** (*basketball*) rebote **2.** *fig* **to marry on the ~** casarse por despecho

**recall** [rɪ·'kɔl] **I.** *vt* **1.** (*remember*) recordar **2.** ECON retirar (del mercado) **II.** vi recordar **III.** n **1.** (*memory*) memoria f **2.** ECON retirada f (del mercado)

**recap**[1] ['riː·kæp] <-pp-> vi, vt inf abbr of **recapitulate** recapitular

**recap**[2] [riː·'kæp] <-pp-> vt AUTO recauch(ut)ar, reencauchar AmC

**recede** [rɪ·'siːd] vi **1.** (*move backward: sea*) retirarse; (*tide*) bajar; (*fog*) desvanecerse **2.** (*diminish*) disminuir; (*prices*) bajar

**receding hairline** n entradas fpl

**receipt** [rɪ·'siːt] n **1.** (*document*) recibo m **2.** ~s COM ingresos mpl **3.** (*act of receiving*) recepción f; **payment on** ~ pago m al recibo; **on** ~ **of...** al recibo de...; **to acknowledge** ~ **of** acusar recibo de

**receive** [rɪ·'siːv] **I.** vt **1.** (*be given*) a. TEL, RADIO recibir; (*pension, salary*) percibir **2.** (*react to: proposal, suggestion*) acoger; **the book was well/badly** ~d el libro tuvo buena/mala acogida **3.** (*injury*) sufrir **II.** vi SPORTS recibir

**receiver** [rɪ·'siː·vər] n **1.** TEL auricular m, tubo m AmL, fono m Chile **2.** RADIO receptor m **3.** SPORTS receptor(a) m(f)

**recent** ['riː·sənt] adj reciente; **in** ~ **times** en los últimos tiempos

**recently** adv recientemente

**reception** [rɪ·'sep·ʃən] n **1.** (*welcome*) acogida f **2.** (*in hotel*) recepción f

**reception desk** n (mesa f de) recepción

**receptionist** [rɪ·'sep·ʃə·nɪst] n recepcionista mf

**receptive** [rɪ·'sep·tɪv] adj receptivo, -a

**recess** ['riː·ses] **I.** <-es> n **1.** POL suspensión f de actividades, receso m AmL **2.** SCHOOL recreo m **3.** ARCHIT hueco m **4.** MED fosa f **5.** often pl (*place*) lugar m recóndito **II.** vi prorrogar; (*meeting, session*) suspender

**recession** [rɪ·'sef·ən] n **1.** (*retreat*) retroceso m **2.** ECON recesión f

**recharge** [riː·'tʃɑrdʒ] **I.** vt recargar **II.** vi recargarse

**rechargeable** [riː·'tʃɑr·dʒə·bəl] adj recargable

**recipe** ['res·ə·pi] n a. fig receta f

**recipient** [rɪ·'sɪp·i·ənt] n (*of letter*) destinatario, -a m, f; (*of transplant*) recep-

tor(a) m(f)

**reciprocal** [rɪ·'sɪp·rə·kəl] adj **1.** a. LING, MATH recíproco, -a **2.** (*reverse*) mutuo, -a

**recital** [rɪ·'saɪ·təl] n **1.** MUS recital m **2.** (*description*) relación f

**recite** [rɪ·'saɪt] **I.** vt **1.** (*repeat*) recitar **2.** (*list*) enumerar **II.** vi dar un recitado

**reckless** ['rek·lɪs] adj imprudente; LAW temerario, -a

**reckon** ['rek·ən] **I.** vt **1.** (*calculate*) calcular **2.** (*consider*) considerar; **to** ~ **(that)...** creer (que)...; **I** ~ **not** me parece que no; **what do you** ~? ¿qué opinas? **3.** (*judge*) estimar **II.** vi inf calcular

◆**reckon with** vt insep tener en cuenta; **she is a force to be reckoned with** es alguien a quien hay que tener muy en cuenta

◆**reckon without** vt insep no tener en cuenta

**reckoning** ['rek·ə·nɪŋ] n **1.** (*calculation*) cálculo m; **to be out in one's** ~ calcular mal **2.** (*settlement*) ajuste m de cuentas

**reclaim** [rɪ·'kleɪm] vt **1.** (*claim back: title, rights*) reclamar **2.** (*reuse: land*) recuperar; (*material*) reciclar **3.** (*reform*) regenerar

**recline** [rɪ·'klaɪn] **I.** vi apoyarse; **to** ~ **on** reclinarse contra [or en] **II.** vt reclinar

**recliner** [rɪ·'klaɪ·nər] n asiento m reclinable

**recognition** [ˌrek·əg·'nɪʃ·ən] n a. COMPUT reconocimiento m; **voice** ~ reconocimiento de voz; **in** ~ **of** en reconocimiento de

**recognizable** ['rek·əg·naɪ·zə·bəl] adj reconocible

**recognize** ['rek·əg·naɪz] vt reconocer

**recognized** ['rek·əg·naɪzd] adj reconocido, -a

**recoil**[1] [rɪ·'kɔɪl] vi **1.** (*draw back*) echarse atrás; **to** ~ **in horror** retroceder de miedo; **to** ~ **from doing sth** rehuir hacer algo **2.** (*gun*) retroceder

**recoil**[2] ['rɪ·kɔɪl] n retroceso m

**recollect** [ˌrek·ə·'lekt] vi, vt recordar

**recollection** [ˌrek·ə·'lek·ʃən] n recuerdo m; **to have no** ~ **of sth** no recordar algo

R

**recommend** [ˌrek·ə·'mend] *vt* recomendar

**recommendable** *adj* recomendable

**recommendation** [ˌrek·ə·mən·'deɪ·ʃən] *n* (*suggestion*) recomendación *f*; **on sb's** ~ por recomendación de alguien

**reconcile** ['rek·ən·saɪl] *vt* 1. (*person*) reconciliar; **to become ~d with sb** reconciliarse con alguien 2. (*difference, fact*) conciliar; **to be ~d to sth** aceptar algo

**reconciliation** [ˌrek·ən·ˌsɪl·i·'eɪ·ʃən] *n* 1. (*restoration of good relations*) reconciliación *f* 2. (*making compatible*) conciliación *f*

**reconnaissance** [rɪ·'kan·ə·səns] *n* reconocimiento *m*

**reconsider** [ˌri·kən·'sɪd·ər] I. *vt* reconsiderar II. *vi* recapacitar

**reconstruct** [ˌri·kən·'strʌkt] *vt* 1. (*building*) reconstruir 2. (*life*) rehacer; (*crime, event*) reconstituir

**reconstruction** [ˌri·kən·'strʌk·ʃən] *n* 1. (*of building*) reconstrucción *f* 2. (*of crime, event*) reconstitución *f*

**record**[1] ['rek·ərd] I. *n* 1. (*account*) relación *m*; (*document*) documento *m*; **medical** ~ historial *m* médico; **to say sth off the** ~ decir algo extraoficialmente 2. (*sb's past*) antecedentes *mpl*; **to have a good** ~ tener un buen historial; **to have a clean** ~ no tener antecedentes 3. ~**s** archivos *mpl* 4. MUS disco *m*; **to make a** ~ grabar un disco 5. SPORTS récord *m*; **to break a** ~ batir un récord 6. LAW acta *f* II. *adj* récord; **to do sth in** ~ **time** hacer algo en un tiempo récord

**record**[2] [rɪ·'kɔrd] I. *vt* 1. (*store*) archivar 2. *a.* COMPUT registrar; MUS grabar 3. LAW hacer constar en acta II. *vi* grabar

**record-breaking** *adj* que bate todos los récords

**recorded** [rɪ·'kɔr·dɪd] *adj* registrado, -a; (*history*) documentado, -a; (*music*) grabado, -a

**recorder** [rɪ·'kɔr·dər] *n* 1. (*tape recorder*) grabadora *f* 2. MUS flauta *f* dulce

**record holder** *n* SPORTS plusmarquista *mf*

**recording** *n* (*of sound*) grabación *f*

**record label** *n* sello *m* discográfico

**record player** *n* tocadiscos *m inv*

**recount**[1] [rɪ·'kaʊnt] *vt* 1. (*narrate*) contar 2. (*count again*) volver a contar

**recount**[2] ['ri·kaʊnt] *n* POL recuento *m*

**recover** [rɪ·'kʌv·ər] I. *vt a.* COMPUT recuperar; **to ~ one's composure** recobrar su compostura II. *vi* (*regain health*) recuperarse

**re-cover** [ˌri·'kʌv·ər] *vt* retapizar

**recovery** [rɪ·'kʌv·ə·ri] <-ies> *n a.* MED, ECON recuperación *f*; **to be beyond** ~ ser irrecuperable

**recreate** [ˌri·kri·'eɪt] *vt* recrear

**recreation**[1] [ˌri·kri·'eɪ·ʃən] *n* (*of conditions, situation*) recreación *f*

**recreation**[2] [ˌrek·ri·'eɪ·ʃən] *n* 1. *a.* SCHOOL recreo *m* 2. (*pastime*) diversión *f*

**recreational** [ˌrek·ri·'eɪ·ʃə·nəl] *adj* recreativo, -a

**recreation room** *n* salón *m* recreativo

**recruit** [rɪ·'krut] I. *vt* MIL reclutar; (*employee*) contratar II. *n* MIL recluta *mf*

**recruitment** *n* MIL reclutamiento *m*; ECON contratación *f*

**rectangle** ['rek·tæŋ·gəl] *n* rectángulo *m*

**rectangular** [rek·'tæŋ·gjə·lər] *adj* rectangular

**rectify** ['rek·tə·faɪ] *vt* rectificar

**rector** ['rek·tər] *n* 1. SCHOOL director(a) *m(f)* 2. UNIV rector(a) *m(f)*

**recur** [rɪ·'kɜr] *vi* repetirse

**recurrence** [rɪ·'kɜr·əns] *n* repetición *f*

**recurrent** [rɪ·'kɜr·ənt] *adj* (*dream, motif*) recurrente; (*costs, expenses*) constante

**recurring** *adj* recurrente

**recycle** [ˌri·'saɪ·kəl] *vt* reciclar

**recycling** *n* reciclaje *m*

**red** [red] I. <-dd-> *adj* rojo, -a; (*hair*) pelirrojo, -a; (*wine*) tinto; **to be** [*or* **go**] ~ ruborizarse II. *n* rojo *m*; **to be in the** ~ FIN estar en números rojos ▶ **to** <u>see</u> ~ salir de sus casillas

**red blood cell** *n* glóbulo *m* rojo

**Red Crescent** *n* **the** ~ la Media Luna Roja

**Red Cross** *n* **the** ~ la Cruz Roja

**red deer** *n inv* ciervo *m*

**redden** ['red·ən] I. *vi* enrojecerse; (*person*) ruborizarse II. *vt* enrojecer

**reddish** ['red·ɪʃ] *adj* rojizo, -a

**redecorate** [ˌri·'dek·ə·reɪt] *vt* redecorar; (*paint*) volver a pintar; (*wallpaper*) volver a empapelar

**redeem** [rɪ'diːm] *vt* **1.** *a.* REL (*person, soul*) redimir; (*situation*) salvar; **to ~ oneself** redimirse **2.** FIN (*policy, share*) liquidar; (*pawned item*) desempeñar; (*debt*) pagar **b.** (*fulfill: promise*) cumplir

**Redeemer** [rɪ'diːmər] *n* REL **the ~** el Redentor

**redeeming** [rɪ'diːmɪŋ] *adj* redentor(a)

**redemption** [rɪ'dempʃən] *n* **1.** *a.* REL redención *f* **2.** FIN (*of policy, share*) liquidación *f*

**redevelop** [ˌriːdɪ'veləp] *vt* reurbanizar

**red-haired** [ˌred'herd] *adj* pelirrojo, -a

**red-handed** [ˌred'hændɪd] *adj* **to catch sb ~** pillar a alguien con las manos en la masa

**redhead** ['redhed] *n* pelirrojo, -a *m, f*

**red-headed** *adj* pelirrojo, -a

**red herring** *n fig* pista *f* falsa

**red-hot** [ˌred'hɑt] *adj* **1.** (*extremely hot*) candente; **to be ~** estar al rojo vivo **2.** (*exciting*) apasionante **3.** (*up-to-the-minute: information*) de última hora

**redirect** [ˌriːdɪ'rekt] *vt* reorientar; (*traffic*) desviar

**red light** *n* semáforo *m* en rojo

**red-light district** *n* barrio *m* de mala fama

**red meat** *n* carne *f* roja

**redneck** ['redˌnek] *n campesino blanco de la clase baja rural, de los estados del Sur*

**redness** ['rednɪs] *n* rojez *f*

**redo** [ˌriː'duː] *vt irr* rehacer

**redouble** [riː'dʌbəl] *vt* redoblar; **to ~ one's efforts** redoblar los esfuerzos

**red pepper** *n* pimiento *m* rojo

**Red Sea** *n* **the ~** el Mar Rojo

**redskin** *n offensive* piel *mf* roja

**red tape** *n* papeleo *m*

**reduce** [rɪ'duːs] *vt* **1.** (*diminish*) reducir; (*price*) rebajar **2.** **to ~ sb to tears** hacer llorar a alguien; **to ~ sth to rubble/ashes** reducir algo a escombros/cenizas; **to be ~d to doing sth** verse forzado a hacer algo **3.** MATH (*fraction*) simplificar

**reduced** [rɪ'duːst] *adj* (*lower*) reducido, -a; (*price*) rebajado, -a

**reduction** [rɪ'dʌkʃən] *n* reducción *f*; (*in price*) rebaja *f*

**redundancy** [rɪ'dʌndənsi] <-ies> *n* redundancia *f*

**redundant** [rɪ'dʌndənt] *adj* (*superfluous*) superfluo, -a; LING redundante

**red wine** *n* vino *m* tinto

**reed** [riːd] *n* **1.** (*plant*) junco *m*, totora *f AmS* **2.** (*straw*) caña *f* **3.** MUS lengüeta *f*

**reef** [riːf] *n* **1.** (*ridge*) arrecife *m* **2.** (*mine*) filón *m*

**reel**[1] [riːl] *n* (*storage or winding device*) carrete *m*; (*for film, rope, tape*) bobina *f*

**reel**[2] [riːl] *vi* **1.** (*move unsteadily*) tambalearse **2.** (*recoil*) retroceder

**re-elect** [ˌriːɪ'lekt] *vt* reelegir

**re-enter** [ˌriːˈentər] *vt* **1.** (*go in again*) volver a entrar en **2.** COMPUT teclear de nuevo

**re-entry** [ˌriːˈentri] <-ies> *n* reingreso *m*

**ref** [ref] *n* **1.** *inf abbr of* **referee** árbitro, -a *m, f* **2.** *abbr of* **reference** referencia *f*

**refectory** [rɪ'fektəri] <-ies> *n* refectorio *m*

**refer** [rɪ'fɜːr] <-rr-> *vt* **to refer sth to sb** (*article*) remitir algo a alguien; **to ~ a patient to a specialist** mandar a un paciente a un especialista

**referee** [ˌrefə'riː] *n* SPORTS árbitro, -a *m, f*, referí *m AmL*

**reference** ['refərəns] *n* **1.** (*consultation*) consulta *f* **2.** (*source*) referencia *f* **3.** (*allusion*) alusión *f*; **with ~ to what was said** en alusión a lo que se dijo **4.** ADMIN (*number*) número *m* de referencia **5.** (*for job application*) referencias *fpl*

**reference book** *n* libro *m* de consulta

**reference library** *n* biblioteca *f* de consulta

**reference number** *n* **1.** (*in document, on book*) número *m* de referencia **2.** (*on product*) número *m* de serie

**referendum** [ˌrefə'rendəm] <-s *or*-da> *n* referéndum *m*

**refill**[1] [riː'fɪl] *vt* (*fill again*) rellenar

**refill**[2] ['riːfɪl] *n* (*replacement*) recambio *m*

R

**refine** [rɪ'faɪn] vt 1. (*oil, sugar*) refinar 2. (*technique*) perfeccionar

**refined** [rɪ'faɪnd] adj 1. (*oil, sugar*) refinado, -a 2. (*sophisticated*) sofisticado, -a 3. (*very polite*) fino, -a

**refinery** [rɪ'faɪ·nə·ri] <-ies> n refinería f

**reflation** [ˌri'fleɪ·ʃən] n reflación f

**reflect** [rɪ'flekt] I. vt reflejar II. vi 1. (*cast back light*) reflejarse 2. (*contemplate*) reflexionar

**reflection** [rɪ'flek·ʃən] n 1. (*image*) reflejo m 2. (*thought*) reflexión f; ~s on sth reflexión acerca de algo; on ~ pensándolo bien 3. *fig* to be a fair ~ of sth ser un fiel reflejo de algo

**reflective** [rɪ'flek·tɪv] adj 1. (*surface*) reflector(a) 2. (*thoughtful*) reflexivo, -a

**reflector** [rɪ'flek·tər] n (*mirror*) reflector m; (*of bicycle, car*) captafaros m inv

**reflex** [rɪ'fleks] <-es> I. n reflejo m II. adj reflejo, -a

**reflexive** [rɪ'flek·sɪv] adj 1. (*independent of will*) reflejo, -a 2. LING reflexivo, -a

**reform** [rɪ'fɔrm] I. vt reformar II. vi reformarse III. n reforma f

**reformation** [ˌref·ər'meɪ·ʃən] n reforma f; **the Reformation** la Reforma

**reformer** n reformador(a) m(f)

**refract** [rɪ'frækt] vt PHYS refractar

**refraction** [rɪ'fræk·ʃən] n refracción f

**refrain**[1] [rɪ'freɪn] vi *form* abstenerse; **to ~ from doing sth** abstenerse de hacer algo

**refrain**[2] [rɪ'freɪn] n MUS estribillo m

**refresh** [rɪ'freʃ] vt refrescar; **to ~ oneself** refrescarse

**refreshing** adj 1. (*drink*) refrescante 2. (*change, difference*) reconfortante

**refreshment** [rɪ'freʃ·mənt] n 1. (*drink*) refresco m 2. (*food*) refrigerio m

**refrigerate** [rɪ'frɪdʒ·ə·reɪt] vt refrigerar

**refrigerator** [rɪ'frɪdʒ·ə·reɪ·tər] n nevera f, refrigerador m

**refuel** [rɪ'fju·əl] <-ll-, -l-> I. vi repostar combustible II. vt reabastecer de combustible; *fig* renovar

**refuge** ['ref·judʒ] n refugio m; **to take ~ in sth** refugiarse en algo

**refugee** [ˌref·ju'dʒi] n refugiado, -a m, f

**refugee camp** n campo m de refugiados

**refund**[1] [rɪ'fʌnd] vt reembolsar

**refund**[2] ['ri·fʌnd] n reembolso m

**refusal** [rɪ'fju·zəl] n negativa f

**refuse** [rɪ'fjuz] I. vi negarse II. vt (*request, gift*) rechazar; (*permission, entry*) denegar; **to ~ sb sth** negar algo a alguien

**regain** [rɪ'geɪn] vt (*freedom, possession*) recuperar; (*consciousness, health*) recobrar

**regal** ['ri·gəl] adj regio, -a

**regard** [rɪ'gard] I. vt 1. (*consider*) considerar; **to ~ sb highly** tener muy buena opinión de alguien 2. *form* (*watch*) contemplar 3. (*concerning*) **as ~s...** respecto a... II. n *form* 1. (*consideration*) consideración f; **to pay no ~ to sth** no prestar atención a algo; **with ~ to...** en cuanto a... 2. (*respect*) respeto m, estima f 3. (*point*) respecto m; **in this ~** con respecto a esto 4. **~s** (*in messages*) recuerdos mpl; **with kind ~s** muchos saludos

**regarding** prep en cuanto a

**regardless** [rɪ'gard·lɪs] I. adv a pesar de todo; **to press on ~** seguir cueste lo que cueste II. adj indiferente; **~ of...** sin tener en cuenta...

**regenerate** [rɪ'dʒen·ə·reɪt] I. vt regenerar II. vi regenerarse

**regeneration** [rɪˌdʒen·ə·'reɪ·ʃən] n regeneración f

**regime** [rə·'ʒim] n régimen m

**regiment** ['redʒ·ə·mənt] n 1. MIL regimiento m 2. *fig* multitud f

**region** [rɪ'dʒən] n 1. GEO, ANAT región f; **in the ~ of 30** alrededor de 30 2. (*administrative area*) provincia f

**regional** ['ri·dʒə·nəl] adj regional

**register** ['redʒ·ɪ·stər] I. n registro m; **class ~** lista f de la clase II. vt registrar; (*car*) matricular; (*voter*) inscribir; (*letter, package*) certificar III. vi 1. (*record*) inscribirse; UNIV matricularse 2. (*be understood*) **the information didn't ~ with him** no registró la información

**registered** ['redʒ·ɪ·stərd] adj registrado, -a; (*nurse*) diplomado, -a; (*student*) matriculado, -a; (*letter, package*) certificado, -a

**registration** [ˌredʒ·ɪ·'streɪ·ʃən] n 1. (*act*)

**inscripción** f 2. AUTO matrícula f 3. UNIV matriculación f

**registration fee** n cuota f de inscripción; UNIV matrícula f

**registration number** n matrícula f

**registry** ['redʒɪstri] n registro m

**regret** [rɪ'gret] I. <-tt-> vt lamentar; **to ~ doing sth** arrepentirse de haber hecho algo II. n arrepentimiento m; **to have ~s** tener remordimientos; **to have no ~s about sth** no arrepentirse de algo; **much to my ~** muy a mi pesar; **to send one's ~s** enviar sus condolencias

**regretful** [rɪ'gret·fəl] adj arrepentido, -a

**regretfully** adv lamentablemente

**regrettable** [rɪ'gret·ə·bəl] adj lamentable

**regroup** [ˌri·'grup] I. vt reagrupar II. vi reagruparse

**regular** ['reg·jə·lər] adj 1. (pattern) regular; (appearance, customer) habitual; (procedure) normal; **to have ~ meetings** tener reuniones periódicas 2. (gas) normal 3. LING regular

**regularity** [ˌreg·jʊ·'ler·ə·t̬i] n regularidad f

**regularly** adv con regularidad

**regulate** ['reg·jʊ·leɪt] vt 1. (supervise) reglamentar 2. (adjust) regular

**regulation** [ˌreg·jʊ·'leɪ·ʃən] n 1. (rule) regla f; **safety ~s** reglamento m de seguridad; **in accordance with (the) ~s** de acuerdo con el reglamento 2. (adjustment) regulación f

**regulator** ['reg·jʊ·leɪ·t̬ər] n regulador m

**regulatory** ['reg·jə·lə·tɔr·i] adj regulador(a)

**rehab** ['ri·hæb] n inf abbr of **rehabilitation** rehabilitación f

**rehabilitate** [ˌri·hə·'bɪl·ə·teɪt] vt rehabilitar

**rehabilitation** [ˌri·hə·ˌbɪl·ə·'teɪ·ʃən] n rehabilitación f

**rehearsal** [rɪ·'hɜr·səl] n ensayo m

**rehearse** [rɪ·'hɜrs] vt, vi ensayar

**reign** [reɪn] I. vi 1. (be monarch) reinar 2. fig (be dominant) imperar II. n 1. (sovereignty) reinado m 2. (rule) régimen m

**reimburse** [ˌri·ɪm·'bɜrs] vt reembolsar

**reimbursement** n reembolso m

**rein** [reɪn] n rienda f ▶ **to keep sb on a tight ~** atar corto a alguien, tener a alguien controlado; **to hold the ~s** sujetar las riendas

**reincarnation** [ˌri·ɪn·kar·'neɪ·ʃən] n reencarnación f

**reindeer** ['reɪn·dɪr] n inv reno m

**reinforce** [ˌri·ɪn·'fɔrs] vt a. MIL reforzar; (argument) fortalecer

**reinforcement** n refuerzo m

**reject**[1] [rɪ·'dʒekt] vt a. MED, TECH rechazar; (application, request) desestimar; (accusation) negar

**reject**[2] ['ri·dʒekt] n 1. (cast-off) artículo m defectuoso 2. (person) persona f rechazada

**rejection** [rɪ·'dʒek·ʃən] n rechazo m

**rejoice** [rɪ·'dʒɔɪs] vi regocijarse; **to ~ in doing sth** regocijarse haciendo algo; **I ~d to see that...** me alegré al ver que...

**rejoicing** n regocijo m

**rejoin** [ˌri·'dʒɔɪn] I. vt (join again) volver a unirse con; (regiment) reincorporarse a II. vi reunirse

**rejuvenate** [rɪ·'dʒu·və·neɪt] vt rejuvenecer

**relapse** [rɪ·'læps] I. n MED recaída f II. vi a. MED recaer

**relate** [rɪ·'leɪt] I. vt 1. (establish connection) relacionar 2. (tell) contar II. vi 1. (be connected with) **to ~ to sb/sth** estar relacionado con alguien/algo 2. (understand) **to ~ to sth/sb** comprender algo/a alguien

**related** adj 1. (linked) relacionado, -a 2. (in same family) emparentado, -a; **to be ~ to sb** estar emparentado con alguien

**relating to** prep acerca de

**relation** [rɪ·'leɪ·ʃən] n 1. (link) relación f; **in ~ to** en relación a; **to bear no ~ to sb/sth** no tener relación con alguien/algo 2. (relative) pariente mf 3. **~s** (contact) relaciones fpl

**relationship** [rɪ·'leɪ·ʃən·ʃɪp] n 1. (link) relación f 2. (family connection) parentesco m 3. (between two people) relaciones fpl; **to be in a ~ with sb** tener una relación con alguien; **business ~s** relaciones comerciales

R

**relative** ['rel·ə·tɪv] I. *adj* relativo, -a II. *n* pariente *mf*

**relatively** *adv* relativamente

**relativity** [,rel·ə·'tɪv·ə·t̬i] *n* relatividad *f*

**relax** [rɪ·'læks] I. *vi* relajarse; (*rules*) suavizarse; **relax!** ¡cálmate! II. *vt* relajar; (*rules*) suavizar; **to ~ one's efforts** disminuir sus esfuerzos

**relaxation** [,ri·læk·'seɪ·ʃən] *n* relajación *f*

**relaxed** *adj* relajado, -a

**relay** ['ri·leɪ] I. *vt* (*information*) pasar; TV retransmitir II. *n* 1. (*group*) turno *m*; **to work in ~s** trabajar por turnos 2. SPORTS carrera *f* de relevos 3. ELEC relé *m*

**release** [rɪ·'lis] I. *vt* 1. (*set free*) poner en libertad 2. (*cease to hold*) soltar; PHOT disparar 3. (*allow to escape: gas*) emitir 4. (*weaken: pressure*) aliviar 5. (*make public: information*) anunciar; (*book*) publicar; (*film*) estrenar; (*CD*) poner a la venta II. *n* 1. (*of prisoner*) excarcelación *f*; (*of hostage*) liberación *f* 2. PHOT disparador *m* 3. (*escape*) escape *m* 4. (*publication*) publicación *f*; (*of film*) estreno *m*; **press ~** comunicado *m* de prensa

**relegate** ['rel·ə·geɪt] *vt* relegar

**relent** [rɪ·'lent] *vi* (*person*) ceder; (*wind, rain*) amainar

**relentless** [rɪ·'lent·lɪs] *adj* (*pursuit, opposition*) implacable; (*pressure*) incesante; (*criticism*) despiadado, -a

**relevance** ['rel·ə·vəns] *n* pertinencia

**relevant** ['rel·ə·vənt] *adj* pertinente

**reliability** [rɪ·ˌlaɪ·ə·'bɪl·ə·t̬i] *n* 1. (*dependability*) seguridad *f* 2. (*trustworthiness*) fiabilidad *f*

**reliable** [rɪ·'laɪ·ə·bəl] *adj* 1. (*credible*) fidedigno, -a; (*authority*) serio, -a; (*evidence*) fehaciente 2. (*trustworthy*) de confianza

**reliance** [rɪ·'laɪ·əns] *n* 1. (*dependence*) dependencia *f* 2. (*belief*) confianza *f*

**reliant** [rɪ·'laɪ·ənt] *adj* **to be ~ on sb/sth** depender de alguien/algo

**relic** ['rel·ɪk] *n* a. *fig* reliquia *f*

**relief** [rɪ·'lif] I. *n* 1. (*relaxation*) alivio *m*; **what a ~!** ¡menos mal! 2. (*aid*) socorro *m* 3. (*replacement*) relevo *m* 4. a. GEO relieve *m* 5. **tax ~** desgravación *f* fiscal II. *adj* 1. de relevo; (*driver*) su-

plente 2. GEO en relieve

**relief worker** *n* trabajador (a) *m(f)* de una organización humanitaria

**relieve** [rɪ·'liv] *vt* 1. (*assist*) socorrer 2. (*alleviate: pain*) aliviar; (*suffering*) mitigar; (*one's mind*) tranquilizar 3. (*urinate, defecate*) **to ~ oneself** hacer sus necesidades

**relieved** *adj* aliviado, -a

**religion** [rɪ·'lɪdʒ·ən] *n* religión *f*

**religious** [rɪ·'lɪdʒ·əs] *adj* religioso, -a

**relish** ['rel·ɪʃ] I. *n* 1. (*enjoyment*) gusto *m*; **with ~** con gusto 2. (*enthusiasm*) entusiasmo *m* 3. CULIN condimento *m* II. *vt* deleitarse en

**reload** [,ri·'loʊd] I. *vt* recargar II. *vi* recargar

**relocate** [ri·'loʊ·keɪt] I. *vi* trasladarse II. *vt* trasladar

**reluctance** [rɪ·'lʌk·təns] *n* desgana *f*; **with ~** de mala gana

**reluctant** [rɪ·'lʌk·tənt] *adj* reacio, -a; **to be ~ to do sth** tener pocas ganas de hacer algo

**rely** [rɪ·'laɪ] *vi* **to ~ on** [*or* **upon**] (*trust*) confiar en; (*depend on*) depender de

**remain** [rɪ·'meɪn] *vi* 1. (*stay*) quedar(se) 2. (*continue*) permanecer; **to ~ seated** quedarse sentado; **to ~ unsolved** seguir sin solucionarse; **much ~s to be done** queda mucho por hacer; **the fact ~s that...** sigue siendo un hecho que...; **it ~s to be seen** (*who/what/how*) está por ver (quién/qué/cómo)

**remainder** [rɪ·'meɪn·dər] *n* a. MATH resto *m*; **the ~ of sb's life** lo que queda de la vida de alguien

**remaining** [rɪ·'meɪ·nɪŋ] *adj* restante

**remains** [rɪ·'meɪnz] *npl* restos *mpl*

**remand** [rɪ·'mænd] I. *vt* **to ~ sb to prison** [*or* **in custody**] poner a alguien en prisión preventiva; **to ~ sb on bail** poner a alguien en libertad bajo fianza II. *n* **to be on ~** estar en prisión preventiva

**remark** [rɪ·'mark] I. *vi* **to ~ on sth** hacer observaciones sobre algo II. *n* observación *f*; **to make ~s about sb/sth** hacer comentarios sobre alguien/algo

**remarkable** [rɪ·'mar·kə·bəl] *adj* extraordinario, -a; (*coincidence*) singular

**remarry** [,ri·'mær·i] <-ie-> *vi* volver a

casarse

**remedy** ['rem·ə·di] I. <-ies> n 1. remedio m; **to be beyond ~** no tener remedio 2. LAW (**legal**) **~** recurso m (legal) II. vt remediar

**remember** [rɪ'mem·bər] vt 1. (recall) recordar 2. (commemorate) conmemorar

**remind** [rɪ'maɪnd] vt recordar; **to ~ sb to do sth** recordar a alguien que haga algo; **he ~s me of you** me recuerda a ti; **that ~s me,...** por cierto,...

**reminder** [rɪ'maɪn·dər] n 1. (note) recordatorio m 2. (warning) advertencia f 3. (memento) recuerdo m

**reminisce** [rem·ə·'nɪs] vi rememorar

**remission** [rɪ'mɪʃ·ən] n remisión f

**remit** [rɪ'mɪt] <-tt-> vt form 1. (send) remitir; (money) enviar 2. LAW perdonar

**remittance** [rɪ'mɪt·əns] n giro m

**remorse** [rɪ'mɔrs] n remordimiento m; **without ~** sin remordimientos

**remorseful** [rɪ'mɔrs·fəl] adj arrepentido, -a

**remote** [rɪ'moʊt] adj <-er, -est> (place, possibility) remoto, -a

**remote control** n mando m a distancia, control m remoto Col

**remote-controlled** adj teledirigido, -a

**removal** [rɪ'mu·vəl] n 1. (of stain, problem) eliminación f 2. (extraction) extracción f

**remove** [rɪ'muv] vt 1. (take away) quitar; (clothes) quitarse 2. (get rid of) eliminar; (cork, dent) sacar; (entry, name) borrar; (doubts, fears) disipar; (problem) solucionar; **to ~ one's hair** depilarse 3. (dismiss from job) destituir

**remover** [rɪ'mu·vər] n 1. agente mf de mudanzas 2. **stain ~** quitamanchas m inv 3. **nail polish ~** quitaesmalte

**rename** [ri·'neɪm] vt poner un nuevo nombre a

**render** ['ren·dər] vt form 1. (make) hacer; **to ~ sb speechless** dejar a alguien mudo 2. (perform) representar; MUS interpretar 3. (give: thanks) ofrecer; (aid, service) prestar; (judgment) emitir 4. (translate) traducir 5. (homage) rendir

**rendezvous** ['ran·deɪ·vu] n inv 1. (meeting) cita f 2. (place) lugar m de reunión

**renew** [rɪ'nu] vt 1. (begin again: membership, passport) renovar 2. (mend) recuperar

**renewable** [rɪ'nu·ə·bəl] adj renovable

**renewed** [rɪ'nud] adj renovado, -a

**renounce** [rɪ'naʊns] vt renunciar a

**renovate** ['ren·ə·veɪt] vt restaurar, renovar

**renovation** [ren·ə·'veɪ·ʃən] n renovación f

**renowned** [rɪ'naʊnd] adj renombrado, -a

**rent¹** [rent] n (rip) rasgadura f

**rent²** [rent] I. vt (apartment, car, video) alquilar; (land) arrendar II. n alquiler m; **for ~** se alquila

**rent-a-car** n (car) coche m de alquiler; (agency) agencia f de alquiler de coches

**rental** ['ren·təl] I. n alquiler m II. adj de alquiler

**rent-free** adj exento, -a de alquiler

**reopen** [ri·'oʊ·pən] I. vt reabrir II. vi reabrirse

**reorder** [ri·'ɔr·dər] vt 1. (reorganize) reordenar 2. COM hacer un nuevo pedido de

**reorganize** [ri·'ɔr·gə·naɪz] I. vt reorganizar II. vi reorganizarse

**rep** [rep] n inf 1. abbr of **representative** representante mf de ventas 2. THEAT abbr of **repertory** repertorio m

**Rep.** 1. abbr of **Republic** Rep. 2. abbr of **Republican** republicano, -a

**repair** [ri·'per] I. vt 1. (machine) reparar; (clothes) arreglar 2. (set right: damage) enmendar II. n 1. (mending: of machine) reparación f; (of clothes) arreglo m; **to be beyond ~** no tener arreglo; **to be under ~** estar en reparación 2. (state) **to be in good/bad ~** estar en buen/mal estado

**repair kit** n caja f de herramientas

**repairman** <-men> n (for cars) mecánico m; (for television) técnico m

**repair shop** n taller m de reparaciones

**repatriate** [ri·'peɪ·tri·eɪt] vt repatriar

**repay** [rɪ'peɪ] <repaid> vt (money) de-

R

volver; (*debts*) liquidar; **to ~ money to sb** reintegrar dinero a alguien; **to ~ a debt** pagar una deuda

**repayable** [rɪ·'peɪ·ə·bəl] *adj* reembolsable

**repayment** [rɪ·'peɪ·mənt] *n* reembolso *m*

**repeat** [rɪ·'pit] I. *vt* (*say or do again*) repetir II. *vi* (*happen again*) repetirse; (*taste*) repetir

**repeated** *adj* repetido, -a

**repel** [rɪ·'pel] <-ll-> I. *vt* 1. (*ward off*) rechazar 2. MIL, PHYS repeler 3. (*disgust*) repugnar

**repellent** [rɪ·'pel·ənt] I. *n* repelente *m* II. *adj* repugnante

**repentance** [rɪ·'pen·təns] *n* arrepentimiento *m*

**repetition** [ˌrep·ə·'tɪʃ·ən] *n* repetición *f*

**replace** [rɪ·'pleɪs] *vt* 1. (*take the place of*) reemplazar; (*person*) sustituir 2. (*put back*) reponer

**replacement** [rɪ·'pleɪs·mənt] I. *n* 1. (*person*) sustituto, -a *m, f*; (*part*) recambio *m* 2. MIL reemplazo *m* 3. (*act of substituting*) sustitución *f* II. *adj* de repuesto

**replay**[1] [ˌri·'pleɪ] *vt* 1. SPORTS volver a jugar 2. MUS volver a tocar 3. TV repetir

**replay**[2] ['ri·pleɪ] *n* 1. SPORTS, TV repetición; **instant ~** repetición *f* instantánea 2. MUS reproducción *f*

**reply** [rɪ·'plaɪ] I. <-ied> *vt* contestar II. <-ied> *vi* 1. (*verbally*) contestar 2. (*react*) responder III. <-ies> *n* respuesta *f*

**report** [rɪ·'pɔrt] I. *n* (*account*) informe *m*; PUBL noticia *f*; (*longer*) reportaje *m*; **to give a ~** presentar un informe II. *vt* 1. (*recount*) relatar; (*discovery*) anunciar; **to ~ that...** informar que...; **nothing to ~** sin novedades 2. (*denounce*) denunciar III. *vi* 1. (*make results public*) presentar un informe 2. (*arrive at work*) presentarse; **to ~ sick** dar parte de enfermedad

**report card** *n* cartilla *f* escolar

**reporter** [rɪ·'pɔr·tər] *n* reportero, -a *m, f*

**represent** [ˌrep·rɪ·'zent] *vt* (*act for; depict*) representar

**representative** [ˌrep·rɪ·'zen·tə·tɪv] I. *adj*

1. *a.* POL representativo, -a 2. (*typical*) típico, -a II. *n* 1. *a.* COM representante *mf* 2. LAW apoderado, -a *m, f* 3. POL diputado, -a *m, f*

**repress** [rɪ·'pres] *vt* reprimir

**repression** [rɪ·'preʃ·ən] *n* represión *f*

**repressive** [rɪ·'pres·ɪv] *adj* represivo, -a

**reprimand** ['rep·rə·mænd] I. *vt* reprender II. *n* reprimenda *f*

**reprint**[1] [ˌri·'prɪnt] *vt* reimprimir

**reprint**[2] ['ri·prɪnt] *n* reimpresión *f*

**reprisal** [rɪ·'praɪ·zəl] *n* represalia *f*; **to take ~s** tomar represalias

**reproach** [rɪ·'proʊtʃ] I. *vt* reprochar II. *n* reproche *m*; **beyond ~** intachable

**reproachful** [rɪ·'proʊtʃ·fəl] *adj* acusador(a)

**reprocess** [ˌri·'pras·es] *vt* reprocesar

**reprocessing plant** *n* ECOL, TECH planta *f* reprocesadora

**reproduce** [ˌri·prə·'dus] I. *vi* reproducirse II. *vt* reproducir

**reproduction** [ˌri·prə·'dʌk·ʃən] *n* reproducción *f*

**reproductive** [ˌri·prə·'dʌk·tɪv] *adj* reproductor(a)

**reprove** [rɪ·'pruv] *vt* reprender

**reproving** [rɪ·'pru·vɪŋ] *adj* reprobatorio, -a

**reptile** ['rep·taɪl] *n* reptil *m*

**republic** [rɪ·'pʌb·lɪk] *n* república *f*

**republican** [rɪ·'pʌb·lɪ·kən] I. *n* republicano, -a *m, f* II. *adj* republicano, -a

**repugnance** [rɪ·'pʌg·nəns] *n* repugnancia *f*

**repugnant** [rɪ·'pʌg·nənt] *adj* repugnante

**repulse** [rɪ·'pʌls] I. *vt* 1. (*disgust*) repulsar 2. (*ward off*) rechazar II. *n* repulsa *f*

**repulsion** [rɪ·'pʌl·ʃən] *n* repulsión *f*

**repulsive** [rɪ·'pʌl·sɪv] *adj* repulsivo, -a

**reputable** ['rep·jə·tə·bəl] *adj* acreditado, -a

**reputation** [ˌrep·ju·'teɪ·ʃən] *n* reputación *f*; **to have a good/bad ~** tener buena/mala fama

**repute** [rɪ·'pjut] *n* reputación *f*

**request** [rɪ·'kwest] I. *n* petición *f*; ADMIN solicitud *f*; **on ~** a petición; **to make a ~ for sth** pedir algo II. *vt* pedir; ADMIN solicitar

**require** [rɪˈkwaɪr] *vt* 1. (*need*) necesitar 2. (*demand*) exigir; **to ~ sb to do sth** exigir a alguien que haga algo

**requirement** [rɪˈkwaɪrˌmənt] *n* requisito *m*

**rerun** [ˌriˈrʌn] *vt irr* CINE, TV repetir; THEAT reestrenar

**resale** [ˈriˈseɪl] *n* reventa *m*

**reschedule** [ˌriˈskedʒˌul] *vt* reprogramar

**rescue** [ˈresˌkju] I. *vt* (*save*) rescatar II. *n* rescate *m;* **to come to sb's ~** rescatar a alguien

**research** [ˈriˈsɜrtʃ] I. *n* investigación *f* II. *vi, vt* investigar

**researcher** *n* investigador(a) *m(f)*

**resemblance** [rɪˈzemˌbləns] *n* parecido *m*

**resemble** [rɪˈzemˌbəl] *vt* parecerse a

**resent** [rɪˈzent] *vt* **to ~ sth** sentirse molesto por algo

**resentful** [rɪˈzentˌfəl] *adj* (*person*) resentido, -a; (*expression*) de resentimiento

**resentment** [rɪˈzentˌmənt] *n* resentimiento *m*

**reservation** [ˌrezərˈveɪˌʃən] *n* 1. (*booking*) reserva *f* 2. (*doubt*) reserva *f;* **to have ~s about sth** tener ciertas dudas sobre algo

**reserve** [rɪˈzɜrv] I. *n* 1. reserva *f;* **to have sth in ~** tener algo en reserva 2. SPORTS suplente *mf* II. *vt* reservar

**reserved** *adj* reservado, -a

**reservoir** [ˈrezərˌvwar] *n* 1. (*tank*) depósito *m* 2. (*lake*) embalse *m*

**reset** [ˌriˈset] *vt irr* 1. (*machine*) reajustar; COMPUT reiniciar 2. (*jewel*) reengastar

**reshuffle** [ˌriˈʃʌfˌəl] *vt* (*a government*) reorganizar; (*cards*) volver a barajar

**residence** [ˈrezˌɪˌdəns] *n* 1. (*home*) domicilio *m* 2. (*act*) residencia *f*

**residence permit** *n* permiso *m* de residencia

**resident** [ˈrezˌɪˌdənt] I. *n* residente *mf* II. *adj* residente

**residential** [ˌrezˌɪˈdenˌʃəl] *adj* residencial

**resign** [rɪˈzaɪn] I. *vi* 1. (*leave job*) dimitir 2. GAMES abandonar II. *vt* (*leave: job*) dimitir de; **to ~ oneself to sth** resignarse a algo

**resignation** [ˌrezˌɪgˈneɪˌʃən] *n* 1. (*from job*) dimisión *f* 2. (*conformity*) resignación *f*

**resigned** [rɪˈzaɪnd] *adj* resignado, -a

**resilient** [rɪˈzɪlˌjənt] *adj* (*material*) elástico, -a; (*person*) resistente

**resist** [rɪˈzɪst] I. *vt* resistir; **to ~ doing sth** resistirse a hacer algo II. *vi* resistir

**resistance** [rɪˈzɪsˌtəns] *n* resistencia *f*

**resistant** [rɪˈzɪsˌtənt] *adj* resistente

**resistor** [rɪˈzɪsˌtər] *n* resistencia *f*

**resolution** [ˌrezəˈluˌʃən] *n a.* COMPUT, PHOT, TV resolución *f*

**resort** [rɪˈzɔrt] *n* 1. (*use*) recurso *m;* **as a last ~** como último recurso 2. (*for holidays*) lugar *m* de veraneo; **ski ~** estación *f* de esquí

**resound** *adj* 1. (*noise*) resonante 2. (*failure, success*) rotundo, -a

**resource** [ˈriˈsɔrs] I. *n* 1. (*asset*) recurso *m* 2. (*natural*) **~s** recursos *m pl* naturales 3. (*resourcefulness*) inventiva *f* II. *vt* financiar

**resourceful** [rɪˈsɔrsˌfəl] *adj* ingenioso, -a

**respect** [rɪˈspekt] I. *n* 1. (*relation*) respeto *m* 2. (*esteem*) estima *f;* **with all due ~** con el debido respeto 3. (*point*) respecto *m;* **in all/many/some ~s** desde todos/muchos/algunos puntos de vista; **in every ~** en todos los sentidos; **in this ~** a este respecto; **with ~ to** con respecto a II. *vt* respetar

**respectable** [rɪˈspekˌtəˌbəl] *adj* 1. (*person*) respetable 2. (*behavior*) decente 3. (*performance, result*) aceptable

**respected** [rɪˈspekˌtəd] *adj* respetado, -a

**respectful** [rɪˈspektˌfəl] *adj* respetuoso, -a

**respectfully** [rɪˈspektˌfəˌli] *adv* respetuosamente

**respecting** [rɪˈspekˌtɪŋ] *prep* respecto a

**respective** [rɪˈspekˌtɪv] *adj* respectivo, -a

**respectively** *adv* respectivamente

**respirator** [ˈresˌpəˌreɪˌtər] *n* respirador *m*

**respiratory** [ˈresˌpərˌəˌtɔrˌi] *adj* respiratorio, -a

**respond** [rɪˈspand] *vi* 1. (*answer*) contestar 2. (*react*) responder

**response** [rɪˈspans] *n* 1. (*answer*) respuesta *f* 2. (*reaction*) reacción *f*

**responsibility** [rɪˌspanˌsəˈbɪlˌəˌti] *n* responsabilidad *f*

R

**responsible** [rɪˈspɒn·sə·bəl] adj responsable; **to be ~ for sth/to sb** ser responsable de algo/ante alguien

**responsive** [rɪˈspɒn·sɪv] adj (person) receptivo, -a; (mechanism) sensible; **to be ~ to sth** MED responder a algo

**rest¹** [rest] I. vt 1. (cause to repose) descansar 2. (support) apoyar II. vi 1. (cease activity) descansar 2. (remain) quedar 3. (be supported) apoyarse; **to ~ on sth** (theory) basarse en algo ▸ **you can ~ assured that...** esté seguro de que... III. n 1. (period of repose) descanso m; **to come to ~** detenerse; **at ~** (not moving) en reposo; (dead) en paz 2. MUS pausa f 3. (support) apoyo m

**rest²** [rest] n resto m; **the ~** (the other people) los demás; (the other things) lo demás; **for the ~** por lo demás

**restaurant** [ˈres·tər·ənt] n restaurante m

**restful** [ˈrest·fəl] adj tranquilo, -a, relajante

**rest home** n residencia f de ancianos

**restless** [ˈrest·lɪs] adj 1. (agitated) inquieto, -a 2. (impatient) impaciente

**restoration** [ˌres·tə·ˈreɪ·ʃən] n 1. (act of restoring: of building, painting) restauración f; (of communication, peace) restablecimiento m 2. (return to owner) restitución f

**restore** [rɪˈstɔr] vt 1. (reestablish: building, painting) restaurar; (communication, peace) restablecer; **to ~ sb's faith in sth** hacer que alguien recupere la fe en algo; **to ~ sb to health** devolver la salud a alguien; **to ~ sb to power** volver a colocar a alguien en el poder 2. form (return to owner) restituir

**restrain** [rɪˈstreɪn] vt (person, animal) contener; (temper, ambition) dominar; (trade) restringir; **to ~ sb from doing sth** impedir que alguien haga algo; **to ~ oneself** contenerse

**restrained** [rɪˈstreɪnd] adj (person) comedido, -a; (criticism, policy) moderado, -a

**restraint** [rɪˈstreɪnt] n 1. (self-control) dominio m de sí mismo; **to exercise ~** form mostrarse comedido 2. (restriction) restricción f

**restrict** [rɪˈstrɪkt] vt (limit) restringir; **to ~ oneself** limitarse

**restricted** adj 1. (limited) restringido, -a; (document) confidencial; (parking) limitado, -a; **entry is ~ to...** sólo se permite la entrada a... 2. (small: space) reducido, -a; (existence, horizon) limitado, -a

**restriction** [rɪˈstrɪk·ʃən] n restricción f; **speed ~** límite m de velocidad; **to impose ~s on sth** imponer restricciones a algo

**restrictive** [rɪˈstrɪk·tɪv] adj restrictivo, -a

**restring** [ˌriˈstrɪŋ] irr vt (instrument, tennis racket) volver a encordar; (necklace) reensartar

**rest room** n aseos mpl, baños mpl Col

**restructuring** n reestructuración f

**result** [rɪˈzʌlt] I. n a. MATH, SPORTS, POL resultado m; (of exam) nota f; **to get ~s** obtener buenos resultados; **with no ~** sin resultado; **as a ~ of** a consecuencia de; **as a ~** por consiguiente II. vi **to ~ from** ser consecuencia de; **to ~ in** ocasionar

**resume** [rɪˈzum] I. vt 1. (start again: work, journey) reanudar; (speech) proseguir con 2. form (duties) volver a asumir II. vi form proseguir

**résumé** [ˈrez·u·meɪ] n 1. (summary) resumen m 2. (for jobs) currículum m (vitae)

**resumption** [rɪˈzʌmp·ʃən] n (of journey, work) reanudación f

**resurrection** [ˌrez·ə·ˈrek·ʃən] n resurrección f

**retail** [ˈri·teɪl] COM I. n venta f al por menor II. vt vender al por menor III. vi venderse al detalle; **this product ~s at $5** el precio de venta al público de este producto es 5 dólares

**retail business** n comercio m minorista

**retailer** n minorista mf

**retail price** n COM precio m de venta al público

**retail trade** n ECON comercio m minorista

**retain** [rɪˈteɪn] vt 1. form (keep: power) retener; (right) reservarse; (title) revalidar 2. (not lose: dignity) mantener; (color) conservar 3. (hold in place: water) contener **4.** (*remember*) retener

**retake¹** [ˌriˈteɪk] *vt irr* **1.** (*recapture: town*) volver a tomar; **to ~ the lead** recuperar el liderazgo **2.** SCHOOL, UNIV (*exam*) volver a presentarse a **3.** CINE volver a rodar; PHOT volver a hacer

**retake²** [ˈriˈteɪk] *n* CINE toma *f* repetida

**retaliate** [rɪˈtæl·i·eɪt] *vi* tomar represalias

**retaliation** [rɪˌtæl·i·ˈeɪ·ʃən] *n* represalias *fpl*

**retard** [rɪˈtɑrd] *vt form* (*growth, development*) retardar; (*journey*) retrasar; **mentally ~ed person** retrasado, -a *m, f* mental

**retarded** *adj* **1.** *offensive* (*mentally ill*) retrasado mental **2.** *sl* (*very stupid*) retrasado

**retch** [retʃ] *vi* tener arcadas [*or* náuseas]

**retentive** [rɪˈten·tɪv] *adj* retentivo, -a; **he's very ~** tiene muy buena memoria

**rethink¹** [ˌriˈθɪŋk] *vt irr* replantearse

**rethink²** [ˈriˈθɪŋk] *n* replanteamiento *m*

**reticent** [ˈret·ə·sənt] *adj* reticente

**retina** [ˈret·nə] <*s or* -nae> *n* retina *f*

**retire** [rɪˈtaɪr] **I.** *vi* **1.** (*stop working*) jubilarse; (*soldier, athlete*) retirarse **2.** *form* (*withdraw*) retirarse **3.** SPORTS (*from a race*) abandonar **II.** *vt* (*stop working*) jubilar **2.** MIL (*soldier*) retirar

**retired** *adj* jubilado, -a; (*soldier, athlete*) retirado, -a

**retirement** [rɪˈtaɪr·mənt] *n* **1.** (*act of retiring*) retiro *m*; (*from race*) abandono *m* **2.** (*after working*) jubilación *f*; **to be in ~** estar jubilado; **to come out of ~** salir de su retiro **3.** MIL retirada *f*

**retiring** *adj* **1.** (*reserved*) reservado, -a **2.** (*worker, official*) saliente

**retrace** [rɪˈtreɪs] *vt* repasar; **to ~ one's steps** volver sobre sus pasos

**retract** [rɪˈtrækt] **I.** *vt* **1.** (*statement, offer*) retirar **2.** (*claws*) retraer; (*wheels*) replegar **II.** *vi* **1.** (*withdraw statement, offer*) retractarse **2.** (*be withdrawn: claws*) retraerse; (*wheels*) replegarse

**retractable** [rɪˈtræk·tə·bəl] *adj* retráctil

**retrain** [ˌriˈtreɪn] **I.** *vt* reconvertir **II.** *vi* hacer un curso de perfeccionamiento

**retreat** [rɪˈtrit] **I.** *vi* retroceder **II.** *n* **1.** (*withdrawal*) *a.* MIL retirada *f* **2.** (*safe place*) refugio *m* **3.** (*seclusion*) retiro *m*; **to go on a ~** hacer un retiro espiritual

**retrial** [ˈriˈtraɪl] *n* nuevo juicio *m*

**retribution** [ˌret·rəˈbju·ʃən] *n form* castigo *m* justo; **divine ~** justicia *f* divina

**retrieval** [rɪˈtri·vəl] *n* (*finding*) *a.* COMPUT recuperación *f*

**retrieve** [rɪˈtriv] *vt* **1.** (*get back*) *a.* COMPUT recuperar **2.** (*make amends for: error*) enmendar **3.** (*repair: loss*) reparar **4.** SPORTS (*in tennis*) devolver

**retrospect** [ˈret·rə·spekt] *n* **in ~** mirando hacia atrás

**retrospective** [ˌret·rə·ˈspek·tɪv] *adj* **1.** (*looking back*) retrospectivo, -a **2.** LAW retroactivo, -a

**return** [rɪˈtɜrn] **I.** *n* **1.** (*going back*) regreso *m*; (*home, to work, to school*) vuelta *f*; **on his ~** a su regreso **2.** (*to previous situation*) retorno *m*; **a ~ to sth** un restablecimiento de algo **3.** MED (*of illness*) recaída *f* **4.** (*giving back*) devolución *f* **5.** (*recompense*) recompensa *f* **6.** FIN (*proceeds*) ganancia *f*; (*interest*) rédito *m* **7.** ~**s** POL resultados *m pl* de las elecciones **8.** COMPUT (tecla *f* de) retorno **9.** FIN declaración *f* ► **many happy ~s!** ¡feliz cumpleaños!; **by ~ mail** a vuelta de correo; **in ~ for sth** a cambio de algo **II.** *adj* (*coming back: flight, journey*) de vuelta **III.** *vi* **1.** (*come back*) volver; (*home*) regresar a **2.** (*reappear*) volver a aparecer **IV.** *vt* **1.** (*give back*) devolver **2.** (*reciprocate*) corresponder a; (*compliment, favor, ball*) devolver; **to ~ sb's call** devolver la llamada a alguien **3.** (*send back*) volver a colocar; ~ **to sender** devuélvase al remitente **4.** FIN (*yield*) dar; (*profit*) proporcionar **5.** ECON (*income*) declarar

**return journey** *n* viaje *m* de vuelta

**return key** *n* COMPUT tecla *f* de retorno

**return ticket** *n* billete *m* de vuelta

**reunification** [ˌri·ju·nə·fɪˈkeɪ·ʃən] *n* reunificación *f*

**reunion** [ˌriˈjun·jən] *n* **1.** (*meeting*) reunión *f* **2.** (*after separation*) reencuentro *m*

**reunite** [ˌri·juˈnaɪt] **I.** *vt* **1.** (*bring together*) volver a unir **2.** (*friends*) reconciliar **II.** *vi* reunirse

R

**reusable** [ˌriˈjuːzəbəl] *adj* reutilizable

**reuse** [ˌriˈjuːz] *vt* volver a usar

**reveal** [rɪˈviːl] *vt* **1.** (*divulge: secret, identity*) revelar; **he ~d his identity** desveló su identidad **2.** (*uncover*) descubrir

**revealing** [rɪˈviːlɪŋ] *adj* revelador(a)

**revelation** [ˌrevəˈleɪʃən] *n* revelación *f*

**reveler** *n*, **reveller** *n* juerguista *mf*

**revenge** [rɪˈvendʒ] **I.** *n* **1.** (*retaliation*) venganza *f*; **in ~ (for sth)** como venganza (por algo); **to take ~ (on sb) for sth** tomar venganza (en [*or* de] alguien) de [*or* por] algo **2.** SPORTS revancha *f* **II.** *vt* vengar; **to ~ oneself** vengarse de alguien

**revenue** [ˈrevəˌnuː] *n* **1.** (*income*) ingresos *mpl* **2.** (*of government*) rentas *f pl* públicas; **tax ~** declaración *f* de renta

**revere** [rɪˈvɪr] *vt* venerar

**reverence** [ˈrevərəns] *n* veneración *f*; **to pay ~ to sth/sb** rendir homenaje a algo/alguien

**reverend** [ˈrevərənd] *adj* reverendo, -a

**reverent** [ˈrevərənt] *adj* reverente

**reverse** [rɪˈvɜrs] **I.** *vt* **1.** (*turn other way*) volver al revés; (*order*) invertir; (*judgment*) revocar; **to ~ the charges** TEL llamar a cobro revertido **II.** *vi* (*order, situation*) invertirse **III.** *n* **1. the ~** lo contrario; **in ~** a la inversa **2.** AUTO (*gear*) marcha *f* atrás **3.** (*setback*) revés *m* **4.** (*the back*) reverso *m*; (*of cloth*) revés *m*; (*of document*) dorso *m* **IV.** *adj* **1.** (*inverse*) inverso, -a **2.** (*opposite: direction*) contrario, -a

**reversible** [rɪˈvɜrsəbəl] *adj* **1.** (*jacket*) reversible **2.** (*decision*) revocable

**review** [rɪˈvjuː] **I.** *vt* **1.** (*consider*) analizar **2.** (*reconsider*) reexaminar; (*salary*) reajustar **3.** (*look over: notes*) revisar **4.** (*criticize: book, play, film*) hacer una crítica de **5.** MIL (*inspect*) pasar revista a **6.** (*study again*) repasar **II.** *n* **1.** (*examination*) análisis *m inv*; **to come under ~** ser examinado **2.** (*reconsideration*) revisión *f*; **to come up for ~** estar pendiente de revisión **3.** (*summary*) resumen *m* **4.** (*criticism: of book, play, film*) crítica *f*

**reviewer** [rɪˈvjuːər] *n* crítico, -a *m, f*

**revise** [rɪˈvaɪz] *vt* (*alter: text, law*) revisar;

(*opinion*) cambiar de

**revision** [rɪˈvɪʒən] *n* **1.** (*of text, law*) revisión *f*; (*of policy*) modificación *f* **2.** (*book*) edición *f* corregida

**revival** [rɪˈvaɪvəl] *n* **1.** MED reanimación *f* **2.** (*rebirth: of interest*) renacimiento *m*; (*of idea, custom*) restablecimiento *m*; (*of economy*) reactivación *f* **3.** CINE, THEAT reestreno *m*

**revive** [rɪˈvaɪv] **I.** *vt* **1.** MED reanimar **2.** (*resurrect: interest*) hacer renacer; (*idea, custom*) restablecer; (*economy*) reactivar; (*conversation*) reanimar **3.** CINE, THEAT reestrenar **II.** *vi* **1.** (*be restored to life*) volver en sí **2.** (*be restored: country, interest*) resurgir; (*tradition*) restablecerse; (*style*) volver a estar de moda; (*trade, economy*) reactivarse

**revocation** [ˌrevəˈkeɪʃən] *n* **1.** (*of license*) suspensión *f* **2.** (*of law, decision*) revocación *f*

**revoke** [rɪˈvoʊk] *vt* **1.** (*cancel: decision, order*) revocar **2.** (*license*) suspender

**revolt** [rɪˈvoʊlt] POL **I.** *vi* rebelarse, alzarse *AmL*; **to ~ against sb/sth** sublevarse contra alguien/algo **II.** *vt* repugnar a; **it ~s me** me da asco **III.** *n* (*uprising*) revuelta *f*; **to rise in ~ against sb/sth** alzarse contra alguien/algo

**revolting** [rɪˈvoʊltɪŋ] *adj* (*disgusting*) repugnante; **to look ~** tener un aspecto horrible

**revolution** [ˌrevəˈluːʃən] *n a.* POL revolución *f*

**revolutionary** [ˌrevəˈluːʃəˌnerˌi] *adj* revolucionario, -a

**revolutionize** [ˌrevəˈluːʃəˌnaɪz] *vt* revolucionar

**revolve** [rɪˈvalv] *vi* girar; **to ~ on an axis** girar en torno a un eje

**revolving** *adj* giratorio, -a

**revolving door** *n* puerta *f* giratoria

**revulsion** [rɪˈvʌlʃən] *n* repulsión *f*

**reward** [rɪˈwɔrd] **I.** *n* recompensa *f* **II.** *vt* recompensar

**rewarding** *adj* gratificante

**rewind** [ˌriˈwaɪnd] *irr* **I.** *vt* (*tape*) rebobinar; (*clock, watch*) dar cuerda a **II.** *vi* rebobinarse

**rewound** [ˌriˈwaʊnd] *pt of* **rewind**

**rhetorical** [rɪˈtɔrɪkəl] *adj* retórico, -a

**rheumatism** ['ru·mə·tız·əm] *n* reumatismo *m*

**rhino** ['raı·nou] *n inf abbr of* **rhinoceros** rinoceronte *m*

**rhinoceros** [raı·'nɑs·ər·əs] <-(es)> *n* rinoceronte *m*

**rhombus** ['rɑm·bəs] <-es *or* -i> *n* rombo *m*

**rhubarb** ['ru·bɑrb] *n* ruibarbo *m*

**rhyme** [raım] I. *n* 1. (*similar sound*) rima *f;* **in** ~ en verso 2. (*poem*) poesía *f* II. *vi* rimar

**rhythm** ['rıð·əm] *n* ritmo *m*

**RI** *n abbr of* **Rhode Island** Rhode Island *m*

**rib** [rıb] I. *n* 1. (*bone*) costilla *f;* **to dig sb in the ~s** dar a alguien un codazo en el costado 2. NAUT cuaderna *f* II. <-bb-> *vt inf* tomar el pelo a

**ribbon** ['rıb·ən] *n* (*long strip*) cinta *f;* **to be cut to ~s** estar hecho jirones

**rib cage** *n* tórax *m*

**rice** [raıs] *n* arroz *m*

**rice pudding** *n* arroz *m* con leche

**rich** [rıtʃ] I. <-er, -est> *adj* 1. (*person*) rico, -a; (*soil*) fértil; **to become ~** enriquecerse; **to be ~ in** abundar en algo 2. (*stimulating: life, experience, history*) rico, -a 3. (*food*) pesado, -a 4. (*intense: color*) brillante; (*flavor*) intenso, -a **II. the ~s** los ricos

**rid** [rıd] <rid *or* ridded, rid> *vt* **to ~ sth/sb of sth** librar algo/a alguien de algo; **to be ~ of sth/sb** estar libre de algo/alguien; **to get ~ of sb/sth** deshacerse de alguien/algo

**ridden** ['rıd·ən] *pp of* **ride**

**riddle¹** ['rıd·əl] *n* 1. (*conundrum*) adivinanza *f* 2. *fig* (*mystery*) misterio *m;* **to speak in ~s** hablar en clave

**riddle²** ['rıd·əl] *vt* acribillar; **to be ~d with mistakes** estar plagado, -a de errores

**ride** [raıd] I. *n* (*on horse, motorcycle, car*) paseo *m;* **to give sb a ~** llevar a alguien ▶ **to take sb for a ~** *sl* tomar el pelo a alguien II. <rode, ridden> *vt* 1. (*sit on*) **to ~ a bike** montar en bicicleta; **to ~ a horse** montar a caballo; **can you ~ a bike?** ¿sabes montar en bici? 2. *inf* (*tease*) meterse con; **to ~ sb about sth** meterse con alguien por algo

III. <rode, ridden> *vi* 1. (*on horse, bicycle*) montar; **to ~ on a horse** montar a caballo; **to ~ by bicycle** ir en bicicleta 2. (*do well*) **to ~ high** alcanzar popularidad 3. *inf* (*take no action*) **to let sth ~** dejar pasar algo

◆**ride out** *vt a. fig* aguantar

◆**ride up** *vi* (*person*) acercarse; (*dress*) subirse

**rider** ['raı·dər] *n* (*on horse*) jinete *m,* amazona *f;* (*on bicycle*) ciclista *mf;* (*on motorcycle*) motociclista *mf*

**ridge** [rıdʒ] *n* 1. GEO cresta *f* 2. METEO sistema *m* de altas presiones 3. (*of roof*) caballete *m*

**ridicule** ['rıd·ɪ·kjul] I. *n* burlas *fpl;* **to be an object of ~** ser el hazmerreír II. *vt* ridiculizar

**ridiculous** [rı·'dık·ju·ləs] *adj* ridículo, -a

**riding** *n* equitación *f*

**rifle¹** ['raı·fəl] *n* fusil *m,* rifle *m*

**rifle²** ['raı·fəl] I. *vt* 1. (*plunder*) saquear 2. (*steal*) robar II. *vt* revolver III. *vi* **to ~ through sth** rebuscar en algo

**rifle range** *n* campo *m* de tiro

**rift** [rıft] *n* 1. (*in earth*) fisura *f* 2. *fig* ruptura *f;* **to heal the ~** cerrar la brecha

**rig** [rıg] <-gg-> I. *vt* 1. (*falsify*) amañar 2. NAUT aparejar II. *n* 1. TECH (*oil*) ~ plataforma *f* petrolífera 2. (*truck*) camión *m* 3. NAUT aparejo *m* 4. *inf* (*clothing*) atuendo *m*

**rigging** ['rıg·ıŋ] *n* 1. (*of result*) pucherazo *m;* **ballot ~** fraude *m* electoral 2. NAUT jarcia *f*

**right** [raıt] I. *adj* 1. (*correct*) correcto, -a; (*ethical*) justo, -a; **to be ~ (about sth)** tener razón (en algo); **to do sth the ~ way** hacer algo correctamente; **to do the ~ thing** hacer lo que se debe hacer; **to be in the ~ place at the ~ time** estar en el lugar indicado en el momento indicado 2. (*direction*) derecho, -a; **a ~ hook** SPORTS un gancho de derecha 3. POL de derechas 4. (*well*) bueno, -a; **to be not (quite) ~ in the head** *inf* no estar muy bien de la cabeza II. *n* 1. (*entitlement*) derecho *m;* **to have the ~ to do sth** tener el derecho de hacer algo 2. (*morality*) **to be in the ~** tener razón 3. (*right side*) derecha *f* 4. POL

**R**

**the Right** la derecha III. *adv* 1. (*correctly*) correctamente; **to do ~** obrar bien 2. (*straight*) directamente; **~ away** inmediatamente 3. (*to the right*) hacia la derecha 4. (*precisely*) precisamente; **~ here** justo aquí; **to be ~ behind sb** estar inmediatamente detrás de alguien IV. *vt* 1. (*rectify*) rectificar; (*mistake*) enmendar 2. (*straighten*) enderezar V. *interj* de acuerdo, órale *Méx*

**right angle** *n* ángulo *m* recto

**right-angled** ['raɪt·ˌæŋ·gəld] *adj* en ángulo recto

**rightful** ['raɪt·fəl] *adj* legítimo, -a

**right-hand** [ˌraɪt·'hænd] *adj* **on the ~ side** a la derecha

**right-handed** [ˌraɪt·'hæn·dɪd] *adj* diestro, -a

**right-hander** *n* 1. (*person*) diestro, -a *m, f* 2. (*punch*) derechazo *m*

**rightly** *adv* 1. (*correctly*) correctamente; **if I remember ~** si recuerdo bien 2. (*justifiably*) con razón; (**whether**) **~ or wrongly** con razón o sin ella

**right-minded** [ˌraɪt·'maɪn·dɪd] *adj* sensato, -a

**right of way** <-rights> *n* (*on road*) preferencia *f*

**right-wing** [ˌraɪt·'wɪŋ] *adj* POL de derechas

**rigid** ['rɪdʒ·ɪd] *adj* 1. (*stiff*) rígido, -a; **to be ~ with fear/pain** estar paralizado, -a de miedo/dolor 2. (*inflexible*) inflexible; (*censorship*) estricto, -a 3. (*intransigent*) intransigente

**rigorous** ['rɪg·ər·əs] *adj* riguroso, -a

**rim** [rɪm] I. *n* 1. (*of cup, bowl*) canto *m* 2. (*frame for eyeglasses*) montura *f* 3. GEO borde *m*; **the Pacific ~** los países de la costa del Pacífico II. <-mm-> *vt* 1. (*surround*) bordear 2. (*frame*) enmarcar

**rind** [raɪnd] *n* (*of fruit*) cáscara *f*; (*of bacon, cheese*) corteza *f*

**ring**[1] [rɪŋ] I. *n* 1. (*small circle*) círculo *m*; (*of people*) corro *m*; (*around eyes*) ojera *f* 2. (*jewelry*) anillo *m* 3. (*arena*) ruedo *m*; (*in boxing*) cuadrilátero *m*; (*in circus*) pista *f* II. *vt* (*surround*) rodear; **to be ~ed by sth** estar cercado, -a con algo

**ring**[2] [rɪŋ] I. *n* 1. (*metallic sound*) sonido *m* metálico; (*of bell*) toque *m* 2. (*telephone call*) llamada *f*; **to give sb a ~** llamar a alguien (por teléfono) II. <rang, rung> *vt* (*bell*) tocar; (*alarm*) hacer sonar III. <rang, rung> *vi* (*telephone, bell*) sonar

◆**ring out** *vi* resonar

◆**ring up** *vt* COM (*at cash register*) **to ~ sb up** registrar la compra de alguien en la registradora

**ring finger** *n* dedo *m* anular

**ringing** I. *n* repique *m* II. *adj* sonoro, -a

**ringleader** ['rɪŋ·ˌli·dər] *n* cabecilla *mf*

**ringlet** ['rɪŋ·lɪt] *n* tirabuzón *m*

**ringside** ['rɪŋ·saɪd] I. *n* **to be at the ~** estar junto al cuadrilátero II. *adj* (*seats*) de primera fila

**ringtone** *n* TEL tono *m* (del móvil)

**rink** [rɪŋk] *n* pista *f* de patinaje

**rinse** [rɪns] I. *vt* (*dishes, clothes*) enjuagar; (*hands*) lavar II. *n* 1. (*wash*) enjuague *m*; **cold/hot ~** aclarado *m* frío/caliente 2. (*hair coloring*) reflejos *mpl*

**riot** ['raɪ·ət] I. *n* disturbio *m*; **to be a ~** *sl* ser la monda II. *vi* causar disturbios III. *adv* **to run ~** *fig* desmandarse; **to let one's imagination run ~** dar rienda suelta a su imaginación

**rioter** *n* alborotador(a) *m(f)*

**riot gear** *n* uniforme *m* antidisturbios

**rioting** *n* disturbios *mpl*

**rip** [rɪp] I. <-pp-> *vi* rasgarse II. <-pp-> *vt* rasgar; **to ~ sth open** abrir algo de un rasgón III. *n* rasgón *m*

◆**rip down** *vt* arrancar

◆**rip off** *vt* 1. (*remove*) arrancar 2. *sl* (*swindle*) timar

◆**rip out** *vt* arrancar

◆**rip up** *vt* romper

**RIP** [ˌar·aɪ·'pi] *abbr of* **rest in peace** D.E.P.

**ripe** [raɪp] *adj* 1. (*fruit*) maduro, -a; **at the ~ old age of 80** a la avanzada edad de 80 2. (*ready*) **the time is ~ for...** es el momento oportuno de...

**ripen** ['raɪ·pən] I. *vt* hacer madurar II. *vi* madurar

**rip-off** ['rɪp·ɔf] *n sl* timo *m*

**ripple** ['rɪp·əl] I. *n* onda *f* II. *vt* rizar

III. *vi* rizarse

**riptide** ['rɪp·taɪd] *n* corriente *f* de resaca

**rise** [raɪz] I. *n* 1. (*increase*) subida *f*; **to be on the ~** ir en aumento; **to give ~ to sth** dar lugar a algo; **to get** [*or* **take**] **a ~ out of sb** burlarse de alguien 2. (*incline*) cuesta *f* II. <rose, risen> *vi* 1. (*arise*) levantarse 2. (*become higher: ground*) subir (en pendiente); (*temperature*) aumentar; (*river*) crecer 3. (*go up: smoke*) subir; (*moon, sun*) salir; (*building*) elevarse 4. (*improve socially*) ascender; **to ~ to fame** alcanzar la fama 5. (*rebel*) sublevarse

**risen** ['rɪz·ən] *pp of* **rise**

**riser** ['raɪ·zər] *n* (*person*) **early ~** madrugador(a) *m(f)*; **late ~** dormilón, -ona *m, f*

**rising** ['raɪ·zɪŋ] I. *n* levantamiento *m* II. *adj* (*in number*) creciente; (*in status*) ascendente; (*floodwaters*) en aumento; (*sun*) naciente

**risk** [rɪsk] I. *n* 1. (*chance*) riesgo *m*; **to run the ~ of sth** correr el riesgo de algo 2. (*danger*) peligro *m*; **at one's own ~** bajo su propia responsabilidad; **to be at ~** correr peligro II. *vt* arriesgar; **to ~ doing sth** arriesgarse a hacer algo; **to ~ one's life** poner la propia vida en peligro

**risky** ['rɪs·ki] <-ier, -iest> *adj* arriesgado, -a, riesgoso, -a *AmL*

**rite** [raɪt] *n* rito *m*; **last ~s** extremaunción *f*; **~s of passage** rito de paso

**ritual** ['rɪtʃ·u·əl] I. *n* ritual *m* II. *adj* ritual

**rival** ['raɪ·vəl] I. *n* rival *mf* II. *adj* competidor(a) III. <-ll-, -l-> *vt* competir con

**rivalry** ['raɪ·vəl·ri] *n* rivalidad *f*

**river** ['rɪv·ər] *n* río *m*

**river bed** *n* lecho *m* de un río

**riverside** ['rɪv·ər·saɪd] *n* ribera *f*

**riveting** ['rɪv·ɪ·t̬ɪŋ] *adj* fascinante

**roach** [roʊtʃ] <-es> *n inf* (*cockroach*) cucaracha *f*

**road** [roʊd] *n* 1. (*between towns*) carretera *f*; (*in town*) calle *f*; (*route*) camino *m*; **by ~** por carretera; **to be on the ~** (*fit for driving*) estar en circulación; (*traveling by road*) estar en camino; (*performing on tour*) estar de gira 2. *fig* sendero *m*; **to be on the ~ to recovery** estar reponiéndose ▶ **all ~s lead to Rome** *prov* todos los caminos llevan a Roma *prov*; **to get sth on the ~** *inf* empezar (con) algo

**road accident** *n* accidente *m* de circulación

**roadblock** *n* control *m* de carretera

**road hog** *n inf* loco, -a *m, f* del volante

**road map** *n* mapa *m* de carreteras

**road rage** *n* furia *f* al volante

**road safety** *n* seguridad *f* vial

**roadside** ['roʊd·saɪd] *n* borde *m* de la carretera

**road sign** *n* señal *f* de tráfico

**road-test** *vt* **to ~ a car** someter un coche a una prueba de carretera

**roadway** ['roʊd·weɪ] *n* calzada *f*

**roam** [roʊm] I. *vi* vagar II. *vt* vagar por

**roar** [rɔr] I. *vi* (*lion, person*) rugir; (*cannon*) tronar; **to ~ with laughter** reírse a carcajadas II. *vt* vociferar III. *n* (*of lion, person*) rugido *m*; (*of engine*) estruendo *m*

**roaring** I. *adj* rugiente; (*thunder*) estruendoso, -a; (*fire*) furioso, -a II. *adv* completamente

**roast** [roʊst] I. *vt* 1. (*food*) asar; (*coffee*) tostar 2. (*poke fun at*) burlarse de II. *vi* (*food*) asarse; (*person*) achicharrarse III. *n* 1. (*meat*) asado *m* 2. (*party*) asado *m* IV. *adj* (*meat*) asado, -a; (*coffee*) tostado, -a

**roasting** ['roʊs·tɪŋ] I. *n* 1. (*baking*) asado *m* 2. *inf* (*telling off*) **to give sb a ~** echar una bronca a alguien II. *adj* abrasador(a) III. *adv* **~ hot** abrasador(a)

**rob** [rab] <-bb-> *vt* 1. (*person, house*) robar; **to ~ sb of sth** robar algo a alguien 2. (*deprive*) **to ~ sb of sth** privar a alguien de algo

**robber** ['rab·ər] *n* ladrón, -ona *m, f*; **bank ~** atracador (a) *m(f)* de bancos

**robbery** ['rab·ə·ri] <-ies> *n* robo *m*

**robe** [roʊb] *n* (*formal*) toga *f*; (*dressing gown*) traje *m*; (*after bath*) albornoz *m*; (*of a priest*) sotana *f*

**robin** ['rab·ɪn] *n* ZOOL petirrojo *m*

**robot** ['roʊ·bat] *n* (*machine*) robot *m*

R

robotics [rou·'bɑt·ɪks] npl robótica f

rock[1] [rak] n 1. GEO roca f 2. (music) rock m ▶ to be stuck between a ~ and hard place estar entre la espada y la pared; as solid as a ~ duro como una piedra; whisky on the ~s whisky con hielo

rock[2] [rak] I. vt 1. (swing) mecer 2. (shock) sacudir II. vi balancearse

rock band n grupo m de rock

rock bottom n fondo m; to hit ~ tocar fondo; to be at ~ estar por los suelos

rock climber n escalador(a) m(f)

rock climbing n escalada f en roca

rocker ['rak·ər] n 1. (chair) mecedora f 2. inf (musician, fan) roquero, -a m, f

rockery ['rak·ə·ri] <-ies> n jardín m rocoso

rocket ['rak·ɪt] I. n 1. (weapon) misil m 2. (vehicle for space travel) cohete m espacial 3. (firework) cohete m II. vi (costs, prices) dispararse

Rockies ['rak·iz] n the ~ las Rocosas

rocking chair ['rak·ɪŋ] n mecedora f, columpio m AmL

rock music n música f rock

rock salt n sal f gema

rock star n estrella f del rock

rocky[1] ['rak·i] <-ier, -iest> adj rocoso, -a; (ground) pedregoso, -a

rocky[2] ['rak·i] <-ier, -iest> adj (unstable) inestable

Rocky Mountains n Montañas f pl Rocosas

rod [rad] n (stick) varilla f; (fishing rod) caña f de pescar

rode [roud] pt of ride

rodent ['rou·dənt] n roedor m

rodeo ['rou·di·ou] <-s> n rodeo m

roe[1] [rou] n (fish eggs) hueva f

roe[2] [rou] <-(s)> n (deer) corzo, -a m, f

roger ['radʒ·ər] interj RADIO recibido

rogue [roug] I. n 1. (rascal) pícaro, -a m, f 2. (villain) bribón, -ona m, f II. adj (animal) solitario, -a; (trader, company) deshonesto, -a

role n, rôle [roul] n 1. THEAT papel m; to play a ~ THEAT hacer un papel; fig desempeñar un papel

role model n modelo m a imitar

role play n juego m de imitación

role reversal n inversión m de papeles

roll [roul] I. n 1. (turning over) volereta f 2. (swaying movement) balanceo m; to be on a ~ fig tener buena suerte 3. (cylinder: of cloth, paper) rollo m; (film) carrete m 4. (noise: of drum) redoble m 5. (catalog of names) padrón m; (for elections) censo m; to call the ~ pasar lista 6. (bread) panecillo m II. vt 1. (push: ball, barrel) hacer rodar; (dice) tirar; to ~ one's eyes poner los ojos en blanco 2. (form into cylindrical shape) to ~ sth into sth enrollar algo en algo; all ~ed into one todo unido en uno 3. (make: cigarette) liar III. vi 1. (move) rodar; (with undulating motion) ondular 2. (be in operation) funcionar

♦roll back vt 1. (cause to retreat) hacer retroceder 2. ECON reducir 3. (return to previous state) hacer recular

♦roll in vi llegar en abundancia

♦roll on vi seguir rodando; (time) pasar

♦roll out I. vt 1. (flatten) estirar; (pastry) extender 2. (unroll) desenrollar 3. COM (new product) lanzar II. vi (wake up) despertarse

♦roll over vi (movement) dar vueltas

♦roll up I. vi inf aparecer II. vt enrollar; (sleeves) arremangarse

roll bar n AUTO barra f protectora antivuelco

roller ['rou·lər] n 1. TECH rodillo m 2. (for hair) rulo m

Rollerblade® n patín m en línea

roller coaster n montaña f rusa

roller skate I. n patín m de ruedas II. vi patinar

rolling pin n rodillo m

roll-on ['roul·an] adj (deodorant) de bola

Roman ['rou·mən] I. adj romano, -a; (alphabet) latino, -a; (religion) católico, -a II. n romano, -a m, f

Roman Catholic I. n católico, -a m, f II. adj católico, -a; the ~ Church la Iglesia católica romana

romance [rou·'mæns] n 1. (love affair) romance m 2. (novel) novela f rosa; (film) película f de amor 3. (glamour) romanticismo m

Romania [rou·'meɪ·ni·ə] n Rumanía f

**Romanian** [rou-'merˑniˑən] I. *adj* rumano, -a II. *n* 1. (*person*) rumano, -a *m, f* 2. LING rumano *m*

**romantic** [rou-'mænˑtɪk] *adj a.* LIT, ART romántico, -a

**Rome** [roum] *n* Roma *f* ▸ ~ was not built in a <u>day</u> *prov* no se ganó Zamora en una hora *prov;* <u>when</u> in ~ (do as the <u>Romans</u>) *prov* allí donde fueres haz lo que vieres *prov*

**roof** [ruf] <-s> I. *n* (*of house*) tejado *m;* (*of car*) techo *m;* (*of tree*) copa *f* ▸ to <u>go</u> through the ~ (*prices*) estar por las nubes; (*person*) subirse por las paredes; to <u>hit</u> the ~ subirse por las paredes II. *vt* techar

**roof garden** *n* azotea *f* con flores y plantas

**rooftop** ['ruf·tap] *n* techo *m*

**rook** [rʊk] *n* 1. (*bird*) grajo *m* 2. (*in chess*) torre *f*

**rookie** ['rʊk·i] *n sl* novato, -a *m, f*

**room** [rum] I. *n* 1. (*in house*) habitación *m;* ~ and board pensión *f* completa 2. (*space*) espacio *m;* to <u>make</u> ~ for sb/sth hacer sitio para alguien/algo; there's no more ~ for anything else ya no cabe nada más; ~ for improvement posibilidad *f* de mejorar; there is no ~ for doubt no cabe duda II. *vi* to ~ with sb compartir alojamiento con alguien

**roomie** *n inf* (*in same room*) compañero, -a *m, f* de habitación; (*in same apartment*) compañero, -a *m, f* de piso

**roommate** ['rum·meɪt] *n* (*in same room*) compañero, -a *m, f* de habitación; (*in same apartment*) compañero, -a *m, f* de piso

**room service** *n* servicio *m* de habitaciones

**roomy** ['ru·mi] <-ier, -iest> *adj* amplio, -a

**rooster** ['ru·stər] *n* gallo *m*

**root** [rut] *n* 1. *a.* BOT, LING, MATH raíz *f;* to <u>take</u> ~ *a. fig* arraigar 2. (*source*) causa *f;* the ~ of all evil la esencia de todos los males; the ~ of the problem is that... el problema radica en que...

**root vegetable** *n* tubérculo *m*

**rope** [roup] I. *n* 1. (*cord*) cuerda *f;* (*of* *pearls*) sarta *f* 2. ~s (*in boxing*) cuerdas *fpl* 3. (*for capital punishment*) soga *f* ▸ to <u>learn</u> the ~s aprender el oficio; to have sb <u>on</u> the ~s tener a alguien contra las cuerdas II. *vt* atar con una cuerda

**rope ladder** *n* escalera *f* de cuerda

**rose**[1] [rouz] I. *n* 1. (*flower, color*) rosa *f* 2. (*on watering can*) roseta *f* 3. ARCHIT rosetón *m* ▸ to <u>come</u> up smelling of ~s aparecer contento; <u>coming</u> up ~s a pedir de boca II. *adj* rosa

**rose**[2] [rouz] *pt of* **rise**

**rosebud** ['rouz·bʌd] *n* capullo *m*

**rose garden** *n* rosaleda *f*

**rosemary** ['rouz·merˑi] *n* romero *m*

**roster** ['ras·tər] *n* lista *f*

**rostrum** ['ras·trəm] <-s *or* rostra> *n* (*for conductor*) estrado *m;* (*for public speaker*) tribuna *f*

**rosy** ['rou·zi] <-ier, -iest> *adj* 1. (*rose-colored*) rosado, -a 2. (*optimistic: viewpoint*) optimista; (*future*) prometedor(a)

**rot** [rat] I. *n* putrefacción *f* II. <-tt-> *vi* pudrirse III. *vt* pudrir

**rotate** ['rou·teɪt] I. *vt* 1. (*turn around*) dar vueltas a 2. (*alternate*) alternar; (*duties*) turnarse en; AGR cultivar en rotación II. *vi* girar; to ~ around sth girar alrededor de algo

**rotation** [rou·'teɪ·ʃən] *n a.* ASTR, AGR rotación *f*

**rote** [rout] *n* by ~ de memoria

**rotor** ['rou·tər] *n* rotor *m*

**rotten** ['rat·ən] *adj* 1. (*food*) podrido, -a; to <u>go</u> ~ pudrirse 2. *inf* (*nasty: behavior*) despreciable 3. *inf* (*performance, book*) malísimo, -a

**rough** [rʌf] I. *adj* 1. (*uneven: road*) desigual; (*surface*) áspero, -a 2. (*poorly made: work*) chapucero, -a 3. (*harsh: voice*) bronco, -a 4. (*imprecise*) aproximado, -a; ~ work borrador *m* 5. (*unrefined: person, manner*) tosco, -a 6. (*stormy: sea*) agitado, -a; (*weather*) tempestuoso, -a 7. (*difficult*) difícil; (*treatment*) duro, -a; to be ~ on sb *inf* ser injusto con alguien II. *n* 1. (*sketch*) borrador *m* 2. SPORTS the ~ el rough ▸ to take the ~ with the <u>smooth</u> es

tar a las duras y a las maduras III. *adv*
**to play** ~ jugar duro; **to live** ~ vivir a
la intemperie

**rough-and-tumble** *n* riña *f*; *fig* juegos
*m pl* bruscos

**roughen** ['rʌf.ən] *vt* poner áspero

**roughly** *adv* 1. (*approximately*) aproximadamente; ~ **speaking** por así decirlo
2. (*aggressively*) bruscamente

**roulette** [ruˈlet] *n* ruleta *f*

**round** [raʊnd] I. <-er, -est> *adj* 1. (*circular: object, number*) redondo, -a; (*arch*) de medio punto 2. (*not angular*)
arqueado, -a 3. (*sonorous*) sonoro, -a
II. *n* 1. (*circle*) círculo *m* 2. (*series*) serie *f*; (*of shots*) descarga *f* 3. ~**s** (*route*)
recorrido *m*; MIL ronda *f*; MED visita *f*
4. (*time period: of elections*) vuelta *f*; (*in
card games*) mano *f*; SPORTS eliminationria *f*; (*in boxing*) asalto *m* 5. (*of drinks*)
ronda *f*; **this** ~ **is on me** esta ronda la
pago yo 6. (*of ammunition*) bala *f* III. *vt*
1. (*movement*) redondear; (*corner*) doblar 2. MATH aproximar

◆**round down** *vt* MATH redondear por
defecto

◆**round off** *vt* 1. (*finish*) rematar
2. (*smooth*) pulir 3. MATH redondear

◆**round out** *vt* acabar; **to** ~ **a list** completar una lista

◆**round up** *vt* 1. MATH redondear por exceso 2. (*gather*) reunir; (*cattle*) rodear

**roundabout** ['raʊnd.ə.baʊt] *adj* indirecto, -a; **to take a** ~ **route** ir dando
un rodeo

**round-the-clock** *adv* las veinticuatro horas; **to work** ~ trabajar día y noche

**round trip** *n* viaje *m* de ida y vuelta; ~
**ticket** billete *m* de ida y vuelta

**roundup** ['raʊnd.ʌp] *n* 1. AGR rodeo *m*
2. (*by police*) redada *f*

**rouse** [raʊz] *vt* 1. (*awaken*) despertar
2. (*activate*) provocar; **to** ~ **sb to do sth**
animar a alguien a hacer algo

**rousing** ['raʊ.zɪŋ] *adj* (*welcome*) caluroso, -a; (*speech*) vehemente

**route** [raʊt] I. *n* 1. (*way*) ruta *f*; (*of parade, bus*) recorrido *m*; (*to success*) camino *m* 2. (*delivery path*) recorrido *m*;
**to have a paper** ~ hacer un reparto de
periódicos 3. (*road*) carretera *f* II. *vt* **to**

~ **sth via New York** mandar algo vía
Nueva York

**routine** [ruˈtin] I. *n* 1. *a.* COMPUT rutina *f*
2. (*of dancer*) número *m* II. *adj* 1. (*regular*) habitual; (*inspection*) de rutina
2. (*uninspiring*) rutinario, -a

**row**[1] [roʊ] *n* 1. (*line: of houses, cars*)
hilera *f*; (*of people, of seats*) fila *f*; **to
stand in a** ~ estar en la fila 2. (*succession*) sucesión *f*; **three times in a** ~ tres
veces consecutivas

**row**[2] [roʊ] I. *vi* remar II. *vt* (*boat*) llevar;
**to** ~ **sb across the lake** llevar a alguien
en bote al otro lado del lago

**rowboat** ['roʊ.boʊt] *n* bote *m* de remos

**rowdy** ['raʊ.di] <-ier, -iest> *adj* 1. (*noisy*)
alborotador(a) 2. (*quarrelsome*) pendenciero, -a

**rower** ['roʊ.ər] *n* remero, -a *m, f*

**rowing** *n* SPORTS remo *m*

**royal** ['rɔɪ.əl] *adj* 1. (*of monarch*) real;
**the** ~ **we** el plural mayestático 2. *fig*
regio, -a; (*welcome*) espléndido, -a

**royalty** ['rɔɪ.əl.ti] <-ies> *n* 1. (*sovereignty*) realeza *f*; **to treat sb like** ~ tratar a
alguien a cuerpo de rey 2. **royalties**
(*payment*) derechos *m pl* de autor

**RSVP** [ˌar.es.viˈpi] *vi abbr of* **répondez
s'il vous plaît (= please reply)** s.r.c.

**rub** [rʌb] I. *n* 1. (*act of rubbing*) frotamiento *m*; **to give sth a** ~ frotar algo
2. *liter* (*difficulty*) dificultad *f*; **there's
the** ~ ahí está el quid de la cuestión
II. <-bb-> *vt* frotar; (*one's eyes*) restregarse; (*one's hands*) frotarse; **to** ~ **sth
clean** lustrar algo III. <-bb-> *vi* rozar

◆**rub down** *vt* 1. (*smooth*) pulir; (*horse*)
almohazar 2. (*dry*) secar frotando

◆**rub in** *vt* 1. (*spread on skin*) aplicar frotando 2. *inf* (*keep reminding*) reiterar;
*pej* insistir en

◆**rub off** I. *vi* (*become clean: stain*) irse
II. *vt* (*dirt*) quitar frotando

◆**rub out** *vt* (*remove: writing*) borrar;
(*dirt*) quitar

**rubber** ['rʌb.ər] *n* 1. (*material*) goma *f*,
hule *m Méx* 2. *sl* (*condom*) goma *f*,
forro *m RíoPl*

**rubber band** *n* goma *f* (elástica), caucho *m Col*

**rubbernecker** *n sl* mirón, -ona *m, f*

**rubber-stamp** I. vt (*decision*) dar el visto bueno a II. n (*device*) sello m de goma

**rubber tree** n árbol m del caucho

**rubbery** <-ier, -iest> adj (*texture*) parecido a la goma; (*food*) correoso, -a

**rubbish** [ˈrʌb.ɪʃ] n inf tonterías fpl

**rubble** [ˈrʌb.əl] n escombros mpl

**rubella** [ruˈbel.ə] n MED rubéola f

**ruby** [ˈru.bi] <-ies> n rubí m

**rudder** [ˈrʌd.ər] n AVIAT, NAUT timón m

**rudderless** adj a. fig sin timón

**ruddy** [ˈrʌd.i] <-ier, -iest> adj 1. (*cheeks*) rubicundo, -a 2. (*light*) rojizo, -a

**rude** [rud] adj 1. (*impolite*) grosero, -a 2. (*vulgar*) vulgar; (*joke*) verde 3. (*sudden*) brusco, -a; (*surprise*) desagradable 4. liter (*unrefined*) tosco, -a

**rudimentary** [ˌru.dəˈmen.tə.ri] adj rudimentario, -a

**rue** [ru] vt liter lamentar

**ruffle** [ˈrʌf.əl] I. vt 1. (*agitate: hair*) alborotar; (*clothes*) fruncir; (*feathers*) erizar 2. (*upset*) alterar II. n volante m

**rug** [rʌg] n (*small carpet*) alfombra f

**rugby** [ˈrʌg.bi] n rugby m

**rugged** [ˈrʌg.ɪd] adj 1. (*uneven: cliff, mountains*) escarpado, -a; (*landscape, country*) accidentado, -a; (*ground*) desigual 2. (*tough: face*) de facciones duras; (*construction, vehicle*) resistente

**ruin** [ˈru.ɪn] I. vt 1. (*bankrupt*) arruinar 2. (*destroy: city, building*) destruir 3. (*spoil: dress, surprise*) estropear II. n 1. (*bankruptcy, downfall*) ruina f; **drugs will be his ~** las drogas serán su ruina 2. pl (*remains*) ruinas fpl

**rule** [rul] I. n 1. (*law*) regla f; (*principle*) norma f; **~s and regulations** reglamento m; **~s of the road** normas f pl de tráfico; **to be the ~** ser la norma; **to break a ~** infringir una norma; **to play (it) by the ~s** obedecer las reglas; **it is against the ~s** va contra las normas; **as a ~** por lo general 2. (*control*) gobierno m 3. (*measuring device*) regla f ▶ **a ~ of thumb** una regla general II. vt 1. (*govern: country*) gobernar; (*company*) dirigir 2. (*control*) dominar 3. (*draw*) trazar con una regla 4. LAW

(*decide*) dictaminar III. vi 1. (*control*) gobernar; (*monarch*) reinar 2. (*predominate*) imperar 3. LAW **to ~ for/against sb/sth** fallar a favor/en contra de alguien/algo

◆**rule out** vt descartar

**rule book** n reglamento m

**ruler** n 1. (*governor*) gobernante mf; (*sovereign*) soberano, -a m, f 2. (*measuring device*) regla f

**ruling** [ˈru.lɪŋ] I. adj 1. (*governing*) gobernante; (*class*) dirigente; (*monarch*) reinante 2. (*primary*) dominante II. n fallo m; **the final ~** la sentencia definitiva

**rum** [rʌm] n ron m

**rumble** [ˈrʌm.bəl] I. n 1. (*sound*) ruido m sordo; (*of thunder*) estruendo m 2. sl (*fight*) pelea f II. vi hacer un ruido sordo; (*thunder*) retumbar; **my stomach is ~ing** me suenan las tripas

**rumbling** I. n (*sound*) ruido m sordo; (*of thunder*) estruendo m; **there were ~s of war** se hablaba de una posible guerra II. adj retumbante

**rummy** [ˈrʌm.i] n GAMES rummy m

**rumor** [ˈru.mər] I. n rumor m II. vt **it is ~ed that...** se rumorea que...

**rump** [rʌmp] n 1. (*back end: of horse*) grupa f; (*of bird*) rabadilla f 2. (*cut of beef*) cuarto m trasero 3. iron (*buttocks*) trasero m

**run** [rʌn] I. n 1. (*jog*) **to break into a ~** echar a correr; **to go for a ~** salir a correr 2. (*trip*) viaje m; (*of train*) trayecto m; **to go for a ~ in the car** ir a dar una vuelta en el coche 3. (*series*) racha f; (*of books*) tirada f 4. (*demand*) demanda f; **a sudden ~ on the dollar** una súbita presión sobre el dólar; **a ~ on the banks** un pánico bancario 5. (*type*) categoría f 6. (*direction, tendency*) dirección f; **the ~ of events** el curso de los acontecimientos 7. (*enclosure for animals*) corral m 8. (*hole in tights*) carrera f 9. SPORTS (*in baseball, cricket*) carrera f 10. CINE, THEAT permanencia f en cartel ▶ **in the long ~** a la larga; **in the short ~** a corto plazo; **on the ~** deprisa y corriendo; **to be on the ~** huir de la justicia II. vi <ran, run> 1. (*move fast*) correr; **to ~ for the bus** correr para no perder el autobús; **to ~ for help** correr en busca de ayuda; **~ for your lives!** ¡sálvese quien pueda! **2.** (*operate*) funcionar; **to ~ smoothly** ir sobre ruedas *fig* **3.** (*go, travel*) ir; **to ~ off the road** salirse de la carretera; **to ~ ashore/onto the rocks** NAUT embarrancar **4.** (*extend*) extenderse; **the road ~s along the coast** la carretera bordea la costa **5.** (*last*) **to ~ for two hours** durar dos horas; **to ~ and ~** ser el cuento de nunca acabar *inf* **6.** (*be*) existir **7.** (*flow: river*) fluir; (*make-up*) correrse; (*nose*) gotear *inf* **8.** (*enter election*) presentarse, postularse *AmL*; **to ~ for election/Presi-dent** presentarse a las elecciones/como candidato a presidente **9.** + *adj* (*be*) **to ~ dry** (*river*) secarse; **to ~ short** (*water*) escasear **10.** (*say*) decir III. *vt* <ran, run> **1.** (*move fast*) **to ~ a race** participar en una carrera **2.** (*enter in race: candidate, horse*) presentar **3.** (*drive*) llevar; **to ~ sb home** llevar a alguien a casa; **to ~ a truck into a tree** chocar contra un árbol con un camión **4.** (*pass*) pasar **5.** (*operate*) poner en marcha; (*car*) llevar; (*computer program*) ejecutar; (*engine*) hacer funcionar; **to ~ a washing machine** poner una lavadora **6.** (*manage, govern*) dirigir, pilotear *AmL*; **to ~ a farm** tener una granja; **to ~ a government** estar al frente de un gobierno; **to ~ a household** llevar una casa **7.** (*conduct*) realizar; (*experiment, test*) llevar a cabo **8.** (*provide: course*) organizar **9.** (*let flow*) dejar correr; (*bath*) preparar **10.** (*show: article*) publicar; (*series*) emitir **11.** (*smuggle*) pasar de contrabando **12.** (*not heed: blockade*) romper; (*red light*) saltar(se) (en rojo) **13.** (*incur*) exponerse a; (*risk*) correr **14.** (*perform tasks*) **to ~ errands** hacer recados

◆**run about** *vi* andar de un lado para otro
◆**run across** I. *vi* cruzar corriendo II. *vt* toparse con
◆**run after** *vt* correr tras
◆**run along** *vi* marcharse
◆**run away** *vi* escaparse; (*water*) de-rramarse
◆**run away with** *vt* apoderarse de
◆**run back** *vi* volver corriendo
◆**run down** I. *vi* (*clock*) parar; (*battery*) gastarse II. *vt* **1.** (*run over*) atropellar **2.** (*disparage*) hablar mal de **3.** (*capture*) capturar
◆**run in** I. *vi* entrar corriendo II. *vt* **1.** AUTO rodar **2.** *sl* (*capture*) detener
◆**run into** *vt* dar con; AUTO chocar con
◆**run off** I. *vi* escaparse; (*water*) derramar-se II. *vt* **1.** (*water*) dejar correr **2.** TYPO tirar **3.** (*make quickly*) hacer deprisa
◆**run on** *vi* **1.** (*continue to run*) seguir corriendo **2.** (*conversation*) continuar
◆**run out of** *vi* quedarse sin
◆**run over** I. *vi* (*person*) irse; (*fluid*) rebosar II. *vt* AUTO atropellar a
◆**run through** *vt* **1.** (*station*) pasar sin parar por **2.** (*money*) derrochar
◆**run up** I. *vi* **1.** subir corriendo **2.** **to ~ against difficulties** tropezar con dificultades II. *vt* **1.** (*flag*) izar **2.** (*make quickly*) hacer deprisa **3.** **to ~ debts** endeudarse

**runaround** [ˈrʌn·ə·raʊnd] *n* **to give sb the ~** traer a alguien al retortero
**runaway** [ˈrʌn·ə·weɪ] *adj* **1.** (*train*) fuera de control; (*person*) fugitivo, -a; (*horse*) desbocado, -a **2.** (*enormous: success*) arrollador(a)
**rundown** [ˌrʌn·ˈdaʊn] I. *n* **1.** (*report*) resumen *m;* **to give sb the ~ on sth** poner a alguien al tanto de algo **2.** (*reduction*) disminución *f;* (*of staff*) reducción *f* II. *adj* **1.** (*building, town*) mal conservado, -a **2.** (*person*) debilitado, -a
**rung**¹ [rʌŋ] *n* **1.** (*ladder*) peldaño *m* **2.** (*level*) nivel *m*
**rung**² [rʌŋ] *pp* of **ring**²
**run-in** [ˈrʌn·ɪn] *n* **1.** *inf* (*argument*) altercado *m* **2.** (*prelude*) etapa *f* previa
**runner** [ˈrʌn·ər] *n* **1.** SPORTS (*person*) corredor(a) *m(f);* (*horse*) caballo *m* de carreras **2.** (*messenger*) mensajero, -a *m, f* **3.** (*smuggler*) contrabandista *mf;* **drug ~** camello *m* **4.** (*rail*) riel *m;* (*on sledge*) patín *m* **5.** (*stem*) tallo *m* rastrero **6.** (*long rug*) alfombrilla *f* estrecha
**runner-up** [ˌrʌn·ər·ˈʌp] *n* subcampeón, -ona *m, f*

**running** I. n 1. (action of a runner) carrera f 2. (operation) acción f; (of a machine) funcionamiento m; **the day-to-day ~ of the business** el día a día del negocio m II. adj 1. (consecutive) sucesivo, -a; (day) consecutivo, -a 2. (ongoing) continuado, -a 3. (operating) que está funcionando 4. (flowing) que fluye

**runny** ['rʌn·i] <-ier, -iest> adj líquido, -a; (sauce) acuoso, -a

**run-off** ['rʌn·ɔf] n 1. POL desempate m 2. SPORTS segunda vuelta f

**run-through** ['rʌn·θru] n THEAT, MUS ensayo m (rápido); **to have a ~ of sth** ensayar algo

**run-up** ['rʌn·ʌp] n 1. SPORTS carrerilla f 2. (prelude) período m previo; **the ~ to sth** el preludio de algo

**runway** ['rʌn·wei] n pista f

**rupture** ['rʌp·tʃər] I. vi romperse II. vt romper; **to ~ oneself** herniarse III. n 1. (act of bursting) ruptura f 2. (hernia) hernia f, relajadura f Méx

**rural** ['rʊr·əl] adj rural

**ruse** [ruz] n treta f

**rush¹** [rʌʃ] n BOT junco m

**rush²** [rʌʃ] I. n 1. (hurry) prisa f; **to be in a ~** tener prisa; **to leave in a ~** salir corriendo 2. (charge, attack) ataque m; (surge) ola f; (of air) corriente f; (of customers) oleada f; **there's been a ~ on oil** ha habido una fuerte demanda de aceite; **gold ~** fiebre f del oro 3. (dizziness) mareo m II. vi ir deprisa III. vt 1. (do quickly) hacer precipitadamente 2. (hurry) apresurar 3. (attack) asaltar

◆**rush at** vt precipitarse hacia

◆**rush out** I. vi (leave) salir precipitadamente II. vt (publish) publicar con urgencia

**rush hour** n hora f punta

**Russia** ['rʌʃ·ə] n Rusia f

**Russian** ['rʌʃ·ən] I. adj ruso, -a II. n 1. (person) ruso, -a m, f 2. (language) ruso m

**rust** [rʌst] I. n 1. (decay) oxidación f 2. (substance) herrumbre f 3. (color) color m herrumbre II. vi oxidarse III. vt oxidar

**rust-colored** adj de color herrumbre

**rustle** ['rʌs·əl] I. vi (leaves) susurrar; (paper) crujir II. vt 1. (leaves) hacer susurrar; (paper) hacer crujir 2. (steal: cattle) robar III. n (of leaves) susurro m; (of paper) crujido m

**rustler** ['rʌs·lər] n ladrón, -ona m, f de ganado

**rustproof** ['rʌst·pruf] adj inoxidable

**rusty** ['rʌs·ti] <-ier, -iest> adj 1. (metal) oxidado, -a 2. (in skill) falto, -a de práctica; **my Spanish is a bit ~** tengo bastante olvidado el castellano

**rut¹** [rʌt] n bache m ▶ **to be stuck in a ~** estar metido en la rutina

**rut²** [rʌt] n ZOOL celo m

**ruthless** ['ruθ·lɪs] adj (person) despiadado, -a; (ambition) implacable; **to be ~ in doing sth** hacer algo sin piedad

**rye** [rai] n centeno m

# S

**S** [es], **s** n S, s f; **~ as in Sierra** S de Soria

**s** [es] abbr of **second** s m

**S** [es] n abbr of **south** S m

**sabotage** ['sæb·ə·taʒ] I. vt sabotear II. n sabotaje m

**saccharin** ['sæk·ər·ɪn] n sacarina f

**sachet** [sæ·'ʃei] n bolsita f

**sack¹** [sæk] I. n 1. (large bag) saco m; **a ~ of potatoes** un saco de patatas; (bag) bolsa f 2. sl **to hit the ~** irse al catre; **to get the ~** ser despedido; **to give sb the ~** despedir a alguien II. vt despedir

**sack²** [sæk] I. n (plundering) saqueo m II. vt (plunder) saquear

**sacred** ['sei·krɪd] adj sagrado, -a; **is nothing ~ to you?** ¿no tienes respeto por nada?

**sacrifice** ['sæk·rə·fais] I. vt sacrificar; (time, money) renunciar a II. n sacrificio m; **at the ~** en detrimento (**of** de)

**sacrilege** ['sæk·rə·lɪdʒ] n sacrilegio m

**sacrilegious** [ˌsæk·rə·'lɪdʒ·əs] adj sacrílego, -a

**SAD** [ˌes·ei·'di] n abbr of **seasonal affective disorder** trastorno m afectivo estacional

**sad** [sæd] <-dd-> *adj* **1.** (*unhappy*) triste; **it is ~ that** es una pena que +*subj*; **to make sb ~** poner triste a alguien; **to become ~** entristecerse **2.** (*pathetic*) patético, -a **3.** (*deplorable*) lamentable; **~ to say** lamentablemente

**sadden** ['sæd·ən] *vt* entristecer; **to be deeply ~ed** estar muy afligido

**sadistic** [sə·'dɪs·tɪk] *adj* sádico, -a

**sadness** ['sæd·nɪs] *n* tristeza *f*

**safari** [sə·'far·i] *n* safari *m*; **to go on ~** irse de safari

**safe** [seɪf] I. *adj* **1.** (*free of danger*) seguro, -a; (*driver*) prudente; **at a ~ distance** a una distancia prudencial; **it is not ~ to...** es peligroso... +*infin*; **just to be ~** por precaución **2.** (*secure*) salvo, -a; **to feel ~** sentirse a salvo; **in a ~ place** en un lugar seguro **3.** (*certain*) seguro, -a; **a ~ bet** una apuesta segura **4.** (*trustworthy*) de fiar; **to be in ~ hands** estar en buenas manos ► **to be on the ~ side** para mayor seguridad; **it is better to be ~ than sorry** más vale prevenir que curar; **~ and sound** sano y salvo II. *n* caja *f* fuerte

**safe-deposit box** *n* caja *f* de seguridad

**safeguard** ['seɪf·gard] I. *vt* salvaguardar II. *vi* proteger (**against** contra) III. *n* salvaguardia *f*; **as a ~ against sth** para evitar algo

**safekeeping** [,seɪf·'ki·pɪŋ] *n* custodia *f*; **to be in sb's ~** estar bajo la custodia de alguien

**safe sex** [seɪf·'seks] *n* sexo *m* seguro

**safety** ['seɪf·ti] *n* seguridad *f*; (*on gun*) seguro *m*; **a place of ~** un lugar seguro; **for her ~** para su seguridad

**safety belt** *n* cinturón *m* de seguridad

**safety curtain** *n* telón *m* de seguridad

**safety glass** *n* vidrio *m* inastillable

**safety margin** *n* margen *m* de seguridad

**safety net** *n* red *f* (de seguridad); *fig* protección *f*

**safety pin** *n* imperdible *m*

**safety regulations** *npl* normas *f pl* de seguridad

**safety valve** *n* válvula *f* de seguridad

**sag** [sæg] I. <-gg-> *vi* **1.** (*droop*) combarse, achiguarse *Arg, Chile* **2.** (*sink*)

hundirse; (*spirit*) decaer; (*interest*) decrecer II. *n* (*fall*) caída *f*

**Sagittarius** [,sædʒ·ə·'ter·i·əs] *n* Sagitario *m*

**said** [sed] I. *pp, pt of* **say** II. *adj* dicho, -a

**sail** [seɪl] I. *n* **1.** NAUT vela *f* **2.** (*windmill*) aspa *f* ► **to set ~** zarpar (**for** hacia); **under full ~** a toda vela II. *vi* **1.** (*travel*) navegar **2.** (*move smoothly*) deslizarse **3.** **to ~ through sth** hacer algo con facilidad ► **to ~ against the wind** nadar a contracorriente III. *vt* (*navigate*) cruzar; **to ~ the seas** surcar los mares

**sailboard** ['seɪl·bɔrd] *n* tabla *f* de windsurf

**sailboat** ['seɪl·bout] *n* barco *m* de vela

**sailing** *n* **1.** NAUT navegación *f* **2.** SPORTS vela *f* **3.** (*departure*) salida *f*

**sailor** ['seɪ·lər] *n* marinero, -a *m, f*; SPORTS navegante *mf*

**saint** [seɪnt, sənt] *n* santo, -a *m, f*

**saintly** ['seɪnt·li] *adj* santo, -a

**sake¹** [seɪk] *n* **for the ~ of** por ► **for Christ's ~! for goodness ~!** ¡por Dios!; **for old times' ~** por los viejos tiempos

**sake²** *n*, **saki** ['sa·ki] *n* sake *m*

**salable** ['seɪ·lə·bəl] *adj* vendible

**salad** ['sæl·əd] *n* ensalada *f*, verde *m CSur*

**salami** [sə·'la·mi] *n* salami *m*, salame *m CSur*

**salaried** ['sæl·ə·rid] *adj* asalariado, -a

**salary** ['sæl·ə·ri] *n* sueldo *m*

**sale** [seɪl] *n* **1.** (*act of selling*) venta *f*; **the ~s** las rebajas; **benefit ~** venta benéfica *f* **2.** (*auction*) subasta *f* ► **to put sth up for ~** poner algo en venta; **on ~** en venta

**saleable** ['seɪ·lə·bəl] *adj see* **salable**

**sales executive** *n* ejecutivo, -a *m, f* de ventas

**salesman** *n* dependiente *m*; (*for company*) representante *m*

**salesperson** *n* vendedor(a) *m(f)*

**saleswoman** *n* dependienta *f*; (*for company*) representante *f*

**saliva** [sə·'laɪ·və] *n* saliva *f*

**salmon** ['sæm·ən] *n* salmón *m*; **smoked ~** salmón ahumado

**saloon** [sə·'lun] *n* bar *m*

**salt** [sɔlt] I. *n* sal *f*; **bath ~s** sales de baño; **bath/smelling ~s** sales de baño/aromáticas ▶ **to take sth with a grain of ~** creerse la mitad de algo; **to rub ~ in a wound** hurgar en una herida II. *vt* 1. echar sal; (*preserve*) salar 2. (*season*) sazonar con sal III. *adj* salado, -a; (*butter*) con sal

**salt water** *n* agua *f* salada

**salty** ['sɔl·ti] *adj* salado, -a

**Salvadorian** [ˌsæl·və·'dɔr·i·ən] *adj, n* salvadoreño, -a *m, f*

**salvage** ['sæl·vɪdʒ] I. *vt* salvar II. *n* (*retrieval*) salvamento

**salvation** [sæl·'veɪ·ʃən] *n* salvación *f*

**salve** [sæv] I. *n* ungüento *m*; *fig* bálsamo *m* II. *vt* curar; (*conscience*) tranquilizar

**same** [seɪm] I. *adj* 1. (*identical*) **the ~** igual (**as que**) 2. (*not another*) **the ~** el mismo, la misma **at the ~ time** al mismo tiempo ▶ **to be one and the ~** ser lo mismo; **by the ~ token** del mismo modo II. *pron* 1. (*nominal*) **the ~** el mismo, la misma lo mismo *neuter;* **she's much the ~** sigue igual; **it's always the ~** siempre es lo mismo 2. (*adverbial*) **it's all the ~ to me** me da igual; **it's not the ~ as before** ya no es lo mismo; **all the ~ de** todas formas; **~ to you** igualmente III. *adv* igual; **they are spelled the ~** se deletrean igual

**sameness** *n* igualdad *f*; (*monotony*) monotonía *f*

**sample** ['sæm·pəl] I. *n* muestra *f*; **free/urine ~** muestra gratuita/de orina II. *vt* 1. (*try*) probar 2. (*survey*) tomar muestras

**sanatorium** [ˌsæn·ə·'tɔr·i·əm] <-s *or* -ria> *n* sanatorio *m*

**sanction** ['sæŋk·ʃən] I. *n* LAW, POL sanción *f* II. *vt* 1. (*approve*) aprobar 2. (*penalize*) sancionar

**sanctity** ['sæŋk·tə· t̬i] *n* inviolabilidad *f*; REL santidad *f*

**sanctuary** ['sæŋk·tʃu·er·i] *n* <-ies> 1. REL santuario *m*; (*around altar*) sagrario *m* 2. (*refuge*) refugio *m*; (*for animals*) reserva *f*; **wildlife ~** reserva natural

**sand** [sænd] I. *n* arena *f*; **grain of ~** grano *m* de arena ▶ **the ~s of time are running out** el tiempo se agota II. *vt* 1. (*make smooth*) lijar; (*floor*) pulir 2. (*cover with sand*) enarenar

**sandal** ['sæn·dəl] *n* sandalia *f*, quimba *f AmL*

**sandbag** ['sænd·bæg] *n* saco *m* de arena

**sandbank** ['sænd·bæŋk] *n*, **sandbar** ['sænd·bar] *n* banco *m* de arena

**sandcastle** *n* castillo *m* de arena

**sand dune** *n* duna *f*

**sandpaper** ['sænd·peɪ·pər] *n* papel *m* de lija

**sandwich** ['sænd·wɪtʃ] <-es> *n* bocadillo *m*

**sandy** ['sæn·di] *adj* <-ier, -iest> arenoso, -a; (*hair*) rojizo, -a

**sane** [seɪn] *adj* 1. (*not mad*) cuerdo, -a 2. (*sensible*) sensato, -a

**sang** [sæŋ] *pt of* **sing**

**sanitary** ['sæn·ɪ·ter·i] *adj* sanitario, -a; (*clean*) higiénico, -a

**sanitation** [ˌsæn·ɪ·'teɪ·ʃən] *n* saneamiento *m*

**sanity** ['sæn·ə· t̬i] *n* cordura *f*; (*decision*) sensatez *f*

**sank** [sæŋk] *pt of* **sink**

**Santa Claus** *n* Papá *m* Noel

**sap[1]** [sæp] *n* 1. BOT savia *f* 2. (*vitality*) vitalidad *f*

**sap[2]** [sæp] <-pp-> *vt* (*weaken*) socavar

**sap[3]** [sæp] *n sl* (*fool*) papanatas *mf inv*

**sapling** ['sæp·lɪŋ] *n* pimpollo *m*

**sarcasm** ['sar·kæz·əm] *n* sarcasmo *m*

**sarcastic** [sar·'kæs·tɪk] *adj* sarcástico, -a

**sardine** [sar·'din] *n* sardina *f* ▶ **to be packed (in) like ~s** estar como sardinas en lata

**sash[1]** [sæʃ] <-es> *n* faja *f*

**sash[2]** [sæʃ] <-es> *n* ARCHIT marco *m*

**sat** [sæt] *pt, pp of* **sit**

**Satan** ['seɪ·tən] *n* Satanás *m*

**satchel** ['sætʃ·əl] *n* cartera *f*, busaca *f Col, Ven*

**satellite** ['sæt̬·ə·laɪt] I. *n* satélite *m* II. *adj* por satélite

**satin** ['sæt·ən] I. *n* raso *m* II. *adj* satinado, -a

**satire** ['sæt·aɪr] *n* sátira *f*

**satirical** [sə·'tɪr·ɪ·kəl] *adj* satírico, -a

**satirize** ['sæt·ə·raɪz] *vt* satirizar

**satisfaction** [ˌsæt·ɪs·'fæk·ʃən] *n* satisfacción *f* (**to** para); (*compensation*) compensación *f*

**satisfactory** [ˌsæt·ɪs·'fæk·tə·ri] *adj* satisfactorio, -a; SCHOOL suficiente

**satisfy** ['sæt·əs·faɪ] <-ie-> *vt* 1. (*person, desire*) satisfacer; (*condition*) cumplir; (*debt*) saldar 2. (*convince*) convencer (**that** de que)

**satisfying** *adj* satisfactorio, -a

**Saturday** ['sæt·ər·deɪ] *n* sábado *m*; *s. a.* Friday

**Saturn** ['sæt·ərn] *n* Saturno *m*

**sauce** [sɔs] *n* salsa *f*; **tomato ~** salsa de tomate

**sauceboat** *n* salsera *f*

**saucepan** ['sɔs·pæn] *n* cacerola *f*

**saucer** ['sɔ·sər] *n* platillo *m*

**saucy** ['sɔ·si] *adj* <-ier, -iest> descarado, -a

**sauna** ['sɔ·nə] *n* sauna *f*

**sausage** ['sɔ·sɪdʒ] *n* salchicha *f*; (*cured*) salchichón *m*

**sausage meat** *n* carne *f* de salchicha

**savage** ['sæv·ɪdʒ] I. *adj* 1. (*fierce*) salvaje 2. (*bad-tempered*) de mal carácter II. *n* salvaje *mf*

**save¹** [seɪv] I. *vt* 1. (*rescue*) salvar; **~ sb's life** salvar la vida a alguien; **to ~ face** salvar las apariencias; **to ~ one's own skin** salvar el pellejo 2. (*keep*) COMPUT guardar 3. (*collect*) coleccionar 4. (*avoid wasting*) ahorrar 5. (*reserve*) reservar II. *vi* ahorrar (**for** para); **to ~ on** guardar

**save²** [seɪv] *prep* **~** (**for**) salvo; **all ~ the youngest** todos salvo los más jóvenes

**saver** ['seɪ·vər] *n* ahorrador(a) *m(f)*

**saving** ['seɪ·vɪn] I. *n* 1. ahorro *m* 2. (*rescue*) rescate *m* II. *prep* excepto

**savings account** ['seɪ·vɪŋz·ə·ˌkaʊnt] *n* cuenta *f* de ahorros

**savings bank** *n* caja *f* de ahorros

**savior** ['seɪv·jər] *n* salvador(a) *m(f)*

**savor** ['seɪ·vər] I. *n* 1. (*taste*) sabor *m* 2. (*pleasure*) gusto *m* II. *vt* saborear

**savory** ['seɪ·və·ri] *adj* 1. (*salty*) salado, -a 2. (*appetizing*) apetitoso, -a

**saw¹** [sɔ] *pt of* see

**saw²** [sɔ] I. *n* sierra *f*; **power ~** sierra

eléctrica II. <sawed, sawed *or* sawn> *vt* serrar

**saw³** [sɔ] *n* dicho *m*

**sawdust** ['sɔ·dʌst] *n* serrín *m*

**sawn** [sɔn] *pp of* saw

**saxophone** ['sæk·sə·foʊn] *n* saxofón *m*

**say** [seɪ] I. <said, said> *vt* decir (**to** a, **that** que); **to ~ where/when** decir dónde/cuándo; **to ~ sth to sb's face** decir algo a alguien a la cara; **~ no more!** ¡no diga(s) más!; **to have something/nothing to ~** tener algo/no tener nada que decir; **people ~ that...** se dice que...; **the said lady** dicha señora; (**let's**) **~...** digamos... ▶ **when all is said and done** a fin de cuentas; **having said that** una vez dicho eso; **to ~ when** decir basta; **you don't ~ (so)!** ¡no me digas!; **you said it!** ¡dímelo a mí! II. <said, said> *vi* **I'll ~!** ¡ya lo creo!; **I must ~...** debo admitir...; **not to ~...** incluso...; **that is to ~...** es decir... III. *n* parecer *m*; **to have a ~** tener voz y voto (**in** en)

**saying** ['seɪ·ɪn] *n* dicho *m*; **as the ~ goes** como dice el refrán; **it goes without ~** ni qué decir tiene

**say-so** ['seɪ·soʊ] *n inf* 1. (*authority*) autoridad *f*; **to have the ~** tener la última palabra 2. (*approval*) visto bueno *m*; **to get the ~** obtener el visto bueno

**scab** [skæb] *n* (*wound*) costra *f*; BOT, ZOOL roña *f*

**scald** [skɔld] I. *vt* 1. (*burn*) escaldar 2. (*clean*) esterilizar II. *n* MED escaldadura *f*

**scalding** ['skɔl·dɪn] *adj* que escalda; **~ hot** hirviendo

**scale¹** [skeɪl] *n* ZOOL escama *f*; TECH, MED sarro *m*

**scale²** [skeɪl] *n* (*for weighing*) platillo *m*; **~s** balanza *f*; (*bigger*) báscula *f* ▶ **to tip the ~s** inclinar la balanza

**scale³** [skeɪl] I. *n* (*range, magnitude, proportion*) a. MUS escala *f*; **on a large/small ~** a gran/pequeña escala; **to ~** a escala II. *vt* 1. (*climb*) escalar 2. TECH, ARCHIT reducir a escala

◆**scale down** *vt* reducir

**scallop** ['skal·əp] *n* ZOOL vieira *f*

**scalp** [skælp] I. *n* (*head skin*) cuero *m* cabelludo II. *vt* (*resell*) revender

**scaly** ['sker·li] adj <-ier, -iest> escamoso, -a; (skin) reseco, -a

**scam** [skæm] n sl timo m

**scamper** ['skæm·pər] vi corretear

**scan** [skæn] I. <-nn-> vt 1. (scrutinize) escudriñar 2. (look through) dar un vistazo; (newspaper) hojear 3. MED explorar 4. COMPUT escanear II. n COMPUT escaneo m; MED escáner m

**scandal** ['skæn·dəl] n 1. (public outrage) escándalo m; to cover up a ~ tapar un escándalo; what a ~! ¡qué vergüenza! 2. (gossip) chismorreo m; to spread ~ difundir habladurías

**Scandinavia** [ˌskæn·dɪ·'neɪ·vi·ə] n Escandinavia f

**Scandinavian** adj, n escandinavo, -a m, f

**scanner** ['skæn·ər] n COMPUT, MED escáner m

**scanning** n escaneo m

**scapegoat** ['skeɪp·ɡoʊt] n cabeza mf de turco

**scar** [skar] I. n 1. MED (on skin) cicatriz f; to leave a ~ dejar cicatriz 2. (mark of damage) señal f II. <-rr-> vi cicatrizar

**scarce** [skers] adj escaso, -a; to make oneself ~ esfumarse

**scarcely** ['skers·li] adv (barely) apenas; (certainly not) ni mucho menos

**scare** [sker] I. vt asustar, julepear Arg, Par, Urug, acholar Chile, Perú; to be ~d stiff estar muerto de miedo; to ~ sb shitless acojonar a alguien II. vi asustarse III. n susto m, julepe m AmL; to have a ~ llevarse un sobresalto; to give sb a ~ dar un susto a alguien

**scarecrow** ['sker·kroʊ] n espantapájaros m inv

**scarf** [skarf, pl skarvz] <-ves or -s> n bufanda f; (around head) pañuelo m

**scarlet** ['skar·lət] adj, n escarlata f

**scarlet fever** n escarlatina f

**scary** ['sker·i] adj <-ier, -iest> que da miedo; (movie) de miedo

**scat** [skæt] interj inf fuera

**scathing** ['skeɪ·ðɪŋ] adj mordaz

**scatter** ['skæt·ər] I. vt esparcir; to ~ sth with sth salpicar algo con algo II. vi dispersarse

**scatterbrain** ['skæt·ər·breɪn] n cabeza mf de chorlito

**scatterbrained** adj atolondrado, -a

**scattered** adj disperso, -a; (sporadic) esporádico, -a

**scene** [sin] n 1. THEAT, CINE escena f; (setting) escenario m; a. fig behind the ~s entre bastidores; to make a ~ montar una escena 2. (locality) lugar m; the ~ of the crime la escena del crimen 3. (view) vista f 4. (milieu) mundo m; the art ~ el mundo del arte; this is/ isn't my ~ esto es/no es lo mío

**scenery** ['si·nə·ri] n paisaje m; THEAT, CINE decorado m; to blend into the ~ conseguir pasar inadvertido

**scent** [sent] I. n 1. (aroma) aroma m 2. (in hunting) rastro m; to be on the ~ estar sobre la pista (of de); to put [or throw] sb off the ~ despistar a alguien 3. (perfume) perfume m II. vt 1. (smell) oler 2. (sense) intuir 3. (perfume) perfumar

**sceptic** ['skep·tɪk] n see skeptic

**sceptical** adj see skeptical

**schedule** ['skedʒ·ul] I. n 1. (timetable) horario m; bus/flight ~ horario de autobuses/vuelos; to stick to a ~ seguir un horario; everything went according to ~ todo fue según lo previsto 2. (plan) programa m 3. FIN inventario m II. vt 1. (plan) programar 2. (list) hacer una lista

**scheduled** adj programado, -a; (flight) regular

**scheme** [skim] n 1. (structure) esquema m 2. (plot) treta f

**scheming** ['ski·mɪŋ] adj intrigante

**schizophrenia** [ˌskɪt·sə·'fri·ni·ə] n esquizofrenia f

**schizophrenic** [ˌskɪt·sə·'fren·ɪk] adj, n esquizofrénico, -a m, f

**scholar** ['skal·ər] n 1. (erudite) erudito, -a m, f 2. (scholarship holder) becario, -a m, f

**scholarship** ['skal·ər·ʃɪp] n 1. (learning) erudición f 2. (grant) beca f

**school**[1] [skul] I. n escuela f, colegio m; primary ~ escuela primaria; secondary ~ instituto m, liceo m Chile, Méx; dancing ~ escuela de baile; driving ~ autoescuela; to go to ~ ir al colegio II. adj escolar

**S**

**school²** [skul] *n* ZOOL banco *m*

**school board** *n* consejo *m* escolar

**schooling** *n* enseñanza *f*

**schoolmate** *n* compañero, -a *m, f* de clase

**schoolteacher** *n* profesor(a) *m(f)*

**science** ['saɪ·əns] **I.** *n* ciencia *f* **II.** *adj* de ciencias

**science fiction I.** *n* ciencia ficción *f* **II.** *adj* de ciencia ficción

**scientific** [ˌsaɪ·ən·'tɪf·ɪk] *adj* científico, -a

**scientist** *n* científico, -a *m, f*

**scissors** ['sɪz·ərz] *npl* tijeras *fpl*; **a pair of ~** unas tijeras

**scoff** [skaf] *vi* (*mock*) burlarse (**at** de)

**scold** [skoʊld] *vt* regañar

**scone** [skoʊn] *n* bollo *m*

**scoop** [skup] *n* (*utensil*) cucharón *m*; (*amount*) cucharada *f*

**scoot** [skut] *vi* largarse; **to ~ over** escabullirse

**scooter** ['sku·tər] *n* (*toy*) patinete *m*; (*vehicle*) scooter *m*

**scope** [skoʊp] *n* **1.** (*range*) alcance *m* **2.** (*possibilities*) posibilidades *fpl*

**scorch** [skɔrtʃ] **I.** *vt* chamuscar **II.** *vi* chamuscarse **III.** *n* <-es> quemadura *f*

**scorching** *adj* abrasador(a); **it's ~ hot** hace un calor abrasador

**score** [skɔr] **I.** *n* **1.** SPORTS (*points*) puntuación *f*; **to keep (the) ~** llevar la cuenta **2.** SPORTS tanto *m* **3.** SCHOOL nota *f* **4.** (*twenty*) veintena *f*; **~s of people** mucha gente **5.** MUS partitura *f* **II.** *vt* **1.** (*goal, point*) marcar; (*triumph, victory*) obtener; (*drugs*) pillar **2.** (*cut*) cortar **III.** *vi* **1.** SPORTS marcar un tanto **2.** *sl* (*succeed*) triunfar; (*sex*) mojar; (*drugs*) pillar

**scoreboard** ['skɔr·bɔrd] *n* marcador *m*

**Scorpio** ['skɔr·pi·oʊ] *n* Escorpio *m*

**scorpion** ['skɔr·pi·ən] *n* escorpión *m*

**Scot** [skat] *n* escocés, -esa *m, f*

**Scotch** [skatʃ] **I.** *n* whisky *m* escocés **II.** *adj* escocés, -esa

**scot-free** [ˌskat·'fri] *adv* **1.** (*without punishment*) impunemente; **to get away** [*or* **off**] **~** salir impune **2.** (*unharmed*) sin un rasguño

**Scotland** ['skat·lənd] *n* Escocia *f*

**Scots** [skats] *adj see* **Scottish**

**Scotsman** ['skats·mən] <-men> *n* escocés *m*

**Scotswoman** ['skats·ˌwʊm·ən] <-women> *n* escocesa *f*

**Scottish** ['skat·ɪʃ] *adj* escocés, -esa

**scout** [skaʊt] **I.** *n* explorador(a) *m(f)*, scout *mf Méx*; **talent ~** cazatalentos *mf inv* **II.** *vi* **to ~ ahead** reconocer el terreno; **to ~ around for** buscar

**scowl** [skaʊl] *vi* fruncir el ceño

**scrabble** ['skræb·əl] *vi* escarbar

**scram** [skræm] <-mm-> *vi sl* largarse, rajarse *AmC*; **~!** ¡largo!

**scramble** ['skræm·bəl] **I.** *vi* (*struggle*) luchar; **to ~ for sth** esforzarse por algo **II.** *vt* **1.** (*mix*) revolver; **~d eggs** huevos revueltos **2.** (*encrypt*) codificar **III.** *n* **1.** (*rush*) carrera *f*; (*chase*) persecución *f* **2.** (*struggle*) pelea *f*, rebatinga *f Méx*

**scrap¹** [skræp] **I.** *n* **1.** (*piece*) trozo *m*; (*amount*) pizca *f*; **not a ~ of truth** ni un ápice de verdad **2.** *pl* (*food*) sobras *fpl* **3.** (*metal*) chatarra *f* **II.** <-pp-> *vt* (*get rid of*) desechar; (*abandon*) descartar; (*abolish*) abolir; (*car*) desguazar, deshuesar *Méx*

**scrap²** [skræp] **I.** *n* (*fight*) bronca *f*, agarrón *m Méx* **II.** <-pp-> *vi* pelearse

**scrapbook** ['skræp·bʊk] *n* álbum *m* de recortes

**scrape** [skreɪp] **I.** *vt* **1.** (*remove layer*) raspar; (*dirt*) limpiar **2.** (*graze*) rozar; (*scratch*) rascar **3.** (*rub against*) rozar **II.** *vi* **1.** (*rub against*) rozar **2.** (*make noise*) chirriar **3.** (*economize*) ahorrar **III.** *n* **1.** (*act*) raspado, -a *m, f* **2.** (*skin*) rozadura *f* **3.** (*sound*) chirrido *m* **4.** (*situation*) lío *m*

**scrap iron** *n* chatarra *f*

**scrappy¹** ['skræp·i] <-ier, -iest> *adj* (*knowledge*) superficial; (*performance, game*) irregular

**scrappy²** ['skræp·i] <-ier, -iest> *adj* (*ready to fight*) pendenciero, -a, peleonero, -a *Méx*

**scratch** [skrætʃ] **I.** *n* **1.** (*on skin*) arañazo *m*, rayón *m AmL* **2.** (*mark*) raya *f* **3.** (*start*) principio *m*; **from ~** desde cero **II.** *vt* **1.** (*cut*) arañar **2.** (*mark*) rayar **3.** (*relieve itch*) rascar **4.** (*erase*) tachar **5.** (*exclude*) retirar **III.** *vi* **1.** (*cat*) arañar **2.** (*relieve itch*) rascarse **IV.** *adj* improvisado, -a

**scratchy** ['skrætʃ·i] <-ier, -iest> *adj* **1.** (*record, voice*) rayado, -a **2.** (*irritating*) áspero, -a

**scrawl** [skrɔl] **I.** *vt* garabatear **II.** *n* garabato *m*

**scream** [skrim] **I.** *n* grito *m*; (*animal or shrill cry*) chillido *m* ▶ **to be a ~** ser la monda **II.** *vi* gritar; (*shrilly*) chillar; **to ~ with laughter** reír a carcajadas **III.** *vt* gritar; (*abuse, obscenities*) lanzar

**screech** [skritʃ] **I.** *n* chillido *m* **II.** *vi* chillar (**with** de)

**screen** [skrin] **I.** *n* **1.** TV, CINE, COMPUT pantalla *f*; **split/touch ~** pantalla dividida/táctil **2.** (*framed panel*) biombo *m*; (*for protection*) a. *fig* cortina *f* **II.** *vt* **1.** (*conceal*) ocultar **2.** (*shield*) proteger **3.** (*examine*) examinar; (*revise*) revisar **4.** TV emitir; CINE proyectar

◆**screen off** *vt* separar con un biombo

**screening** *n* **1.** CINE proyección *f*; TV emisión *f* **2.** (*testing*) prueba *f* **3.** MED chequeo *m*

**screw** [skru] **I.** *n* **1.** tornillo *m*; **to tighten/loosen a ~** apretar/aflojar un tornillo **2.** (*turn*) vuelta *f* **3.** (*propeller*) hélice *f* **4.** (*twisted piece*) rosca *f* **5.** **I had a good ~ last night** menudo polvo eché anoche; **she's a great ~** qué polvo tiene ▶ **he's got a ~** [*or a few* **~s**] **loose** *inf* le falta (más de) un tornillo; **to put the ~s** apretar las tuercas (**on** a) **II.** *vt* **1.** (*with a screw*) atornillar; (*by twisting*) enroscar **2.** *sl* (*cheat*) timar **3.** *vulg* follarse, coger *AmL*; **~ you!** ¡vete a la mierda! **III.** *vi* **1.** (*turn*) enroscarse; (*become attached*) atornillarse **2.** (*sex*) echar un polvo, echarse un palo *Méx*

◆**screw up** *sl* **I.** *vt* (*mess, injure*) joder **II.** *vi* cagarla

**screwdriver** ['skru·ˌdrai·vər] *n* (*tool*) destornillador *m*, desarmador *m AmL*

**screwed** *adj* jodido, -a

**screw top** *n* tapón *m* de rosca

**scribble** ['skrɪb·əl] **I.** *vt, vi* garabatear **II.** *n* garabatos *mpl*

**Scripture** ['skrɪp·tʃər] *n* Sagrada Escritura *f*

**scriptwriter** ['skrɪpt·ˌrai·tər] *n* guionista *mf*

**scroll** [skroʊl] **I.** *n* (*roll*) rollo *m* **II.** *vi* desplazarse (**to** a); **to ~ down/up** bajar/subir

**scrounge** [skraʊndʒ] *vt, vi* gorronear

**scrounger** ['skroʊn·dʒər] *n* gorrón, -ona *m, f*, pedinche *mf Méx*

**scrub¹** [skrʌb] <-bb-> **I.** *vt* **1.** (*clean*) fregar **2.** (*cancel*) cancelar **II.** *vi* fregar; **to ~ at** restregar **III.** *n* (*act*) fregado *m*

**scrub²** [skrʌb] *n* matorral *m*

**scrubber** ['skrʌb·ər] *n* fregón, -ona *m, f*

**scruff** [skrʌf] *n* cogote *m*; **to grab sb by the ~ of the neck** coger a alguien por el cogote

**scruffy** ['skrʌf·i] <-ier, -iest> *adj* desaliñado, -a, fachoso, -a *Méx*

**scrumptious** ['skrʌmp·ʃəs] *adj* de rechupete

**scrunch** [skrʌntʃ] **I.** *vi, vt* crujir **II.** *n* crujido *m*

**scrutinize** ['skru·tə·naiz] *vt* escudriñar; (*votes*) escrutar; (*text*) revisar

**scuba diving** ['sku·bə·ˌdai·vɪŋ] *n* submarinismo *m*

**scuff** [skʌf] **I.** *vt* **1.** (*roughen*) raspar **2.** (*drag*) arrastrar **II.** *n* rozadura *f*

**scuffle** ['skʌf·əl] **I.** *n* refriega *f* **II.** *vi* pelearse

**sculpture** ['skʌlp·tʃər] **I.** *n* escultura *f* **II.** *vt* esculpir

**scum** [skʌm] *n* (*people*) escoria *f*

**scurry** ['skɜr·i] <-ie-> *vi* corretear

**scuttle¹** ['skʌt·əl] *vi* (*run*) corretear; **~ away** escabullirse

**scuttle²** ['skʌt·əl] *vt* (*sink*) hundir; (*plan*) echar por tierra

**sea** [si] *n* mar *m o f*; **at the bottom of the ~** en el fondo del mar; **by ~** por mar; **by the ~** junto al mar; **out at ~** en alta mar; **open ~, high ~s** mar abierto; **a ~ of people** un mar de gente

**seafood** ['si·fud] *n* marisco *m*

**seafront** ['si·frʌnt] *n* playa *f*; (*promenade*) paseo *m* marítimo, malecón *m Méx*

**seagull** ['si·gʌl] *n* gaviota *f*

**seal¹** [sil] *n* ZOOL foca *f*

**seal²** [sil] *n* **1.** (*wax*) sello *m*; (*goods, door*) precinto *m* ▶ **~ of approval** aprobación *f* **II.** *vt* a. *fig* sellar; (*with tape*) precintar

S

**sea level** n nivel m del mar

**sea lion** n león m marino

**seam** [sim] I. n 1. (*stitching*) costura f; **to come** [*or* **fall**] **apart at the ~s** descoserse; *fig* rebosar de gente 2. (*junction*) juntura f. MIN veta f II. vt (*sew*) coser

**seamy** ['si·mi] <-ier, -iest> adj sórdido, -a

**search** [sɜrtʃ] I. n a. COMPUT búsqueda f; (*building*) registro m, esculco m Col, Méx; (*person*) registro m; **to go in ~ en busca (of** de) II. vi a. COMPUT **to ~ (for)** buscar; **to ~ high and low** buscar por todas partes; **~ and replace** buscar y reemplazar III. vt 1. a. COMPUT buscar en; (*building, baggage*) registrar, escular Col, Méx; (*person*) cachear 2. (*examine*) examinar; **to ~ one's memory** hacer memoria ► **~ me!** ¡a mí que me registren!

♦**search out** vt encontrar; (*information*) averiguar

**search function** n función f de búsqueda

**searching** adj 1. (*penetrating*) inquisitivo, -a 2. (*exhaustive*) minucioso, -a

**searchlight** ['sɜrtʃ·laɪt] n reflector m

**search party** <-ies> n equipo m de salvamento

**search warrant** n orden f de registro [*or* AmL de allanamiento]

**searing** adj (*heat*) abrasador(a); (*pain*) punzante

**sea salt** n sal f marina

**seashell** ['si·ʃel] n concha f

**seashore** ['si·ʃɔr] n costa f; (*beach*) playa f

**seasick** ['si·sɪk] adj mareado, -a; **to get ~** marearse

**seasickness** ['si·sɪk·nɪs] n mareo m

**seaside** ['si·saɪd] I. n costa f; (*beach*) playa f II. adj costero, -a; **a ~ resort** un lugar de veraneo costero, un balneario AmL

**season** ['si·zən] I. n 1. (*of year*) estación f 2. (*epoch*) a. SPORTS temporada f; **Season's Greetings** Felices Fiestas; **the fishing/pear ~** la temporada de pesca/las peras; **to be in ~** estar en sazón; **out of ~** fuera de temporada; **high/low ~**

temporada alta/baja 3. **to be in ~** estar en celo; **the mating ~** la época de celo II. vt CULIN sazonar; (*salt and pepper*) salpimentar

**seasonal** ['si·zə·nəl] adj estacional; **~ affective disorder** trastorno afectivo estacional 2. (*temporary*) temporal; **~ worker** temporero, -a m, f 3. (*food*) del tiempo

**seasoning** ['si·zə·nɪŋ] n condimento m, yuyos mpl Ecua, Perú

**season ticket** n abono m de temporada

**seat** [sit] I. n 1. (*furniture*) asiento m; (*bicycle*) sillín m; THEAT butaca f; **back ~** asiento trasero; **is this ~ free/taken?** ¿está libre/ocupado este asiento?; **to hold a ~** guardar el sitio (**for** a); **to take one's ~** sentarse 2. (*ticket*) entrada f 3. (*buttocks*) trasero m 4. POL escaño m, banca f Arg, Par, Urug 5. (*center*) sede f ► **to fly by the ~ of one's pants** dejarse guiar por el instinto II. vt sentar; ARCHIT, TECH asentar

**seat belt** n cinturón m de seguridad; **to fasten one's ~** abrocharse el cinturón

**seating** n (*seats*) asientos mpl; **~ capacity** número de plazas; **~ for two thousand** aforo de dos mil personas

**seawater** ['si·ˌwɔ·tər] n agua f de mar

**seaweed** ['si·wid] n algas fpl, huiro m Chile

**seaworthy** ['si·ˌwɜr·ði] adj en condiciones de navegar

**secluded** [sɪ·'klu·dɪd] adj aislado, -a; (*life*) solitario, -a

**second¹** ['sek·ənd] I. adj 1. segundo, -a; **every ~ girl** una de cada dos chicas; **every ~ week** una semana sí y otra no; **to be ~** ser el segundo; **the ~ biggest town** la segunda ciudad más grande 2. (*another*) otro, -a; **to give sb a ~ chance** dar a alguien una segunda oportunidad; **to have ~ thoughts** tener dudas (**about** acerca de); **on ~ thought** pensándolo bien; **to have a ~ helping** repetir 3. **the ~ floor** el primero, el segundo AmL II. n 1. AUTO segunda f 2. **may I have ~s?** ¿puedo repetir? III. adv en segundo lugar

**second²** ['sek·ənd] n segundo m; **per**

**~ por segundo; at that very ~** en ese preciso instante; **just a ~!** ¡un segundo!; **it won't take (but) a ~!** ¡sólo será un momento!

**secondary** ['sek·ən·der·i] *adj* secundario, -a; **to be ~** ser de menor importancia (**to** que); (*industry*) derivado, -a

**secondary school** *n* 1. (*school*) instituto *m*, liceo *m Chile, Méx* 2. (*education*) enseñanza *f* secundaria

**second best** *n* segundo, -a *m, f*

**second class** *n* segunda *f* clase

**second-class** I. *adj* de segunda clase; (*mail*) regular; (*hotel, service*) de segunda categoría; (*goods*) de calidad inferior II. *adv* RAIL en segunda

**second cousin** *n* primo, -a *m, f* segundo, -a

**secondly** *adv* en segundo lugar

**second-rate** [,sek·ənd·'reɪt] *adj* mediocre

**secrecy** ['si·krə·si] *n* secreto *m*; **in ~** en secreto

**secret** ['si·krɪt] I. *n* 1. secreto *m*; **an open ~** un secreto a voces; **to let sb in on a ~** revelar un secreto a alguien 2. (*mystery*) misterio *m* II. *adj* secreto, -a; **to keep sth ~** ocultar algo (**from** a)

**secretary** ['sek·rə·ter·i] <-ies> *n* secretario, -a *m, f*; POL ministro, -a *m, f*, secretario, -a *Méx*

**secretive** ['si·krɪ·t̬ɪv] *adj* reservado, -a

**sect** [sekt] *n* secta *f*

**section** ['sek·ʃən] I. *n* 1. a. MIL, MUS, PUBL sección *f*; (*object*) parte *f*; (*city*) distrito *m*; (*document*) párrafo *m*; LAW artículo *m*; (*road*) tramo *m* 2. (*group*) sector *m* 3. (*cut*) corte *m* II. *vt* (*cut*) seccionar; (*divide*) dividir

**sector** ['sek·t̬ər] *n* sector *m*; **public/private ~** sector público/privado

**secure** [sɪ·'kjʊr] I. *adj* <-rer, -est> 1. (*safe, confident*) seguro, -a; **to be ~** estar protegido (**from** contra); **to feel ~** sentirse seguro (**about** respecto a); **to be ~ in the knowledge that...** tener la certeza de que...; **to be financially ~** tener estabilidad económica 2. (*fixed*) firme; (*foundation*) sólido, -a II. *vt* 1. (*obtain*) obtener 2. (*make firm*) asegurar; *fig* afianzar 3. (*make safe*) proteger

**security** [sɪ·'kjʊr·ə·t̬i] <-ies> *n* 1. (*safety*) seguridad *f*; **~ risk** peligro *m* para la seguridad 2. (*stability*) estabilidad *f*; **~ of employment** estabilidad laboral 3. (*safeguard*) salvaguardia *f* 4. (*of payment*) garantía *f*

**security guard** *n* guarda jurado *mf*

**sedation** [sɪ·'deɪ·ʃən] *n* sedación *f*; **under ~** sedado

**sedative** ['sed·ə·t̬ɪv] *adj, n* sedante *m*

**seduce** [sɪ·'dus] *vt* seducir; **to ~ sb into doing sth** inducir a alguien a hacer algo

**seduction** [sɪ·'dʌk·ʃən] *n* seducción *f*; **~s** atractivo *m*

**seductive** [sɪ·'dʌk·t̬ɪv] *adj* atrayente; (*person*) seductor(a); (*offer*) tentador(a)

**see** [si] <saw, seen> I. *vt* 1. ver; **to ~ sth with one's own eyes** ver algo con sus propios ojos; **it is worth ~ing** vale la pena verlo; **you were ~n entering the building** se os vio entrar en el edificio; **to ~ a little/a lot of sb** ver a alguien poco/a menudo; **~ you around!** ¡nos vemos!; **~ you (later)!** ¡hasta luego!; **as I ~ it...** a mi modo de ver...; **I don't ~ him doing that** no lo veo capaz de hacer eso; **I could ~ it coming** lo veía venir; **to ~ how/what/if...** ver cómo/qué/si...; **Mr. Brown will ~ you now** el Sr. Brown le recibirá ahora 2. **to be ~ing sb** salir con alguien 3. (*accompany*) acompañar a 4. (*perceive*) darse cuenta de; **I don't ~ what you mean** no entiendo lo que quieres decir; **to ~ sth in a new light** cambiar de opinión respecto a algo 5. **~ that you are ready when we come** procura estar listo cuando vengamos II. *vi* ver; **as far as the eye can ~** hasta donde alcanza la vista; **as far as I can ~** por lo que veo; **~ for yourself!** ¡véalo usted mismo!; **let me ~** ¿a ver?; **let's ~** vamos a ver; **you'll ~ ya verás;** I ~ **ya veo; you ~?** ¿entiendes? ▶ **he can't ~ further than the end of his nose** no puede ver más allá de sus narices

♦**see about** *vt inf* encargarse de; (*consider*) pensarse ▶ **we'll soon ~ that!** ¡eso ya lo veremos!

♦**see in** *vt* (*welcome*) hacer pasar

S

◆**see off** vt despedir

◆**see out** vt (to door) acompañar hasta la puerta

◆**see through** vt 1. (not be deceived by) calar inf 2. (sustain) mantener a flote

◆**see to** vt encargarse de; **to ~ it that...** asegurarse de que...

**seed** [sid] I. n 1. BOT semilla f; (fruit) pepita f, pepa f AmL; (seeds) simiente f 2. (beginning) germen m; **to sow the ~s of doubt/discord** sembrar la duda/discordia II. vt 1. AGR sembrar 2. **to ~ a project with money** aportar capital a un proyecto

**seedy** ['si·di] <-ier, -iest> adj 1. (dubious) sórdido, -a 2. (unwell) pachucho, -a

**seeing** I. conj ~ (that) en vista de (que) II. n visión f; ~ **is believing** ver para creer

**seek** [sik] <sought> vt 1. (look for, try to obtain) buscar; (help) pedir; (job) solicitar; **to ~ one's fortune** probar suerte 2. (attempt) tratar de

**seem** [sim] vi parecer; **it ~s that...** parece que...; **so it ~s, so it would ~** eso parece; **they ~ed to like the idea** parecía que les gustaba la idea; **to ~ as if...** parecer como si... +subj; **it is not all that it ~s** no es lo que parece; **things aren't always what they ~** las apariencias engañan

**seeming** adj aparente

**seemingly** adv aparentemente

**seen** [sin] pp of **see**

**seep** [sip] vi filtrarse

◆**seep away** vi escurrirse

**see-through** ['si·θru] adj transparente

**segregate** ['seg·rə·geɪt] vt segregar; (girls and boys) separar

**segregation** [ˌseg·rə·'geɪ·ʃən] n segregación f

**seize** [siz] vt 1. (grasp) agarrar, cachar Arg, Nic, Urug, acapillar Méx; (opportunity) no dejar escapar; (initiative, power) tomar; (criminal) detener; (property) confiscar; (drugs, weapons) incautar; **to ~ sb by the arm/by the throat** agarrar a alguien del brazo/por el cuello 2. (overcome) **he was ~d by fear** el miedo se apoderó de él 3. (understand) captar

◆**seize up** vi (stop) paralizarse; (muscles) agarrotarse; COMPUT colgarse

**seizure** ['si·ʒər] n (drugs) incautación f; (property) confiscación f

**seldom** ['sel·dəm] adv rara vez

**select** [sə·'lekt] I. vt seleccionar; (gift, wine) escoger II. adj (high-class) selecto, -a; (product) de primera calidad

**selection** [sə·'lek·ʃən] n selección f; (range) gama f; (food, drinks) surtido m

**selective** [sə·'lek·tɪv] adj selectivo, -a

**self** [self] n <selves> uno mismo, una misma; **his better ~** su mejor parte; **one's other ~** su alter ego; **the ~** el yo

**self-adhesive** adj autoadhesivo, -a

**self-assured** adj seguro, -a de sí mismo, -a

**self-centered** adj egocéntrico, -a

**self-complacent** adj pej engreído, -a

**self-composed** adj sereno, -a; **to remain ~** no perder la serenidad

**self-confessed** adj confeso, -a; **she's a ~ coward** se confiesa cobarde

**self-confidence** n confianza f en uno mismo; **to have ~** confiar en sí mismo

**self-conscious** adj 1. (shy) tímido, -a 2. (unnatural) afectado, -a

**self-contained** adj 1. (community) autosuficiente; (apartment) con cocina y cuarto de baño 2. (reserved) reservado, -a

**self-control** n autocontrol m

**self-critical** adj autocrítico, -a

**self-deception** n engaño a sí mismo

**self-defeating** adj contraproducente

**self-defense** n defensa f personal; LAW legítima defensa

**self-destruct** vi autodestruirse

**self-discipline** n autodisciplina f

**self-employed** I. adj **to be ~** trabajar por cuenta propia II. n **the ~** los autónomos

**self-esteem** n amor m propio

**self-explanatory** adj clarísimo, -a

**self-expression** n expresión f personal

**self-important** adj presuntuoso, -a

**self-indulgent** adj indulgente consigo mismo, -a

**self-inflicted** adj autoinfligido, -a

**elf-interest** *n* interés *m* personal

**elfish** ['sel·frʃ] *adj* egoísta

**elfishness** *n* egoísmo *m*

**elfless** ['self·lɪs] *adj* desinteresado, -a

**elf-pity** *n* autocompasión *f*

**elf-portrait** *n* autorretrato *m*

**elf-possessed** *adj* sereno, -a

**elf-preservation** *n* instinto *m* de supervivencia

**elf-reliant** *adj* independiente

**elf-respect** *n* amor *m* propio; **to lose all ~** perder la dignidad

**elf-respecting** *adj* **every ~ man** todo hombre que se precie

**elf-righteous** *adj* farisaico, -a; (*tone*) de superioridad moral

**elf-sacrifice** *n* abnegación *f*

**elf-satisfied** *adj* engreído, -a

**elf-service** *adj, n* **~ (store)** autoservicio *m;* **~ restaurant** self-service *m*

**elf-sufficient** *adj* independiente; ECON autosuficiente

**elf-taught** *adj* autodidacta

**elf-willed** *adj* obstinado, -a, voltario, -a *Chile*

**ell** [sel] **I.** *vt* <sold, sold> **1.** vender (**for** por); **to ~ sth at half price** vender algo a mitad de precio **2.** (*make accepted*) convencer ▶ **to ~ oneself short** no hacerse valer **II.** *vi* <sold, sold> (*product*) venderse (**at, for** a); (*company, shop*) estar en venta

**sell off** *vt* liquidar; (*industry*) privatizar

**sell out I.** *vi* COM, FIN agotarse; *fig* venderse **II.** *vt* liquidar

**ellable** *adj* vendible

**ell-by date** ['sel·baɪ.deɪt] *n* fecha *f* límite de venta

**eller** *n* vendedor(a) *m(f)*

**elves** [selvz] *n pl of* **self**

**emi** ['sem·i] *n* **1.** (*truck*) trailer *m* **2.** *pl* SPORTS semifinal *f*

**emicircle** ['sem·ɪ.sɜr·kəl] *n* semicírculo *m*

**emicircular** [.sem·ɪ·'sɜr·kjə·lər] *adj* semicircular

**emicolon** ['sem·ɪ.koʊ·lən] *n* punto y coma *m*

**emiconductor** [.sem·ɪ·kən·'dʌk·tər] *n* semiconductor *m*

**seminar** ['sem·ə·nar] *n* seminario *m*

**semolina** [.sem·ə·'li·nə] *n* sémola *f*

**senate** ['sen·ɪt] *n* POL senado *m;* UNIV consejo *m*

**senator** ['sen·ə·tər] *n* senador(a) *m(f)*

**send** [send] *vt* <sent, sent> **1.** enviar, mandar; **to ~ sth by mail** enviar algo por correo; **to ~ sb to prison** mandar a alguien a la cárcel; **~ her my regards** dale recuerdos de mi parte **2.** (*propel*) lanzar **3.** RADIO transmitir ▶ **to ~ sb packing** mandar a alguien a freír espárragos

**send away** *vt* **1.** (*dismiss*) despedir **2.** (*send*) enviar

**send back** *vt* mandar de vuelta

**send for** *vt* (*person*) llamar; (*assistance*) pedir; (*goods*) encargar

**send in** *vt* **1.** (*send*) mandar **2.** (*let in*) hacer pasar

**send off** *vt* mandar

**send on** *vt* **1.** (*in advance*) mandar por adelantado **2.** (*forward*) remitir

**send out** *vt* **1.** (*ask to leave*) echar **2.** (*send on errand*) mandar **3.** (*dispatch*) enviar **4.** (*signal, rays*) emitir; (*smell, heat*) despedir

**send up** *vt* **1.** (*drive up*) hacer subir **2.** (*mock*) parodiar

**sender** *n* remitente *mf*

**senile** ['si·naɪl] *adj* senil

**senior** ['sin·jər] **I.** *adj* **James Smith, Senior** James Smith, padre; **to be ~ to sb** estar por encima de alguien **II.** *n* **1.** (*age*) mayor *mf;* **she is two years my ~** me lleva dos años **2.** (*rank*) superior *mf*

**senior citizen** *n* jubilado, -a *m, f*

**senior partner** *n* socio, -a *m, f* mayoritario, -a

**sensation** [sen·'seɪ·ʃən] *n* sensación *f;* **to be a ~** ser un éxito; **to cause a ~** hacer furor

**sensational** [sen·'seɪ·ʃə·nəl] *adj* sensacional; *pej* sensacionalista

**sense** [sens] **I.** *n* **1.** sentido *m;* **~ of hearing/sight/smell/taste/touch** oído *m*/vista *f*/olfato *m*/gusto *m*/tacto *m;* **to make ~** tener sentido; **there's no ~ in doing...** no tiene sentido hacer...; **to have no ~ of occasion** ser in-

**S**

oportuno; **to lose all ~ of time** perder la noción del tiempo; **in every ~** en todos los sentidos; **in a ~** en cierto modo; **in no ~** de ninguna manera 2. (*sensation*) sensación *f* 3. *pl* PSYCH juicio *m*; **to come to one's ~s** recobrar el conocimiento; (*see reason*) entrar en razón 4. **common ~** sentido común; **to have enough** [*or the good*] **~ to...** tener la sensatez de... II. *vt* sentir; **to ~ that...** darse cuenta de que...

**senseless** ['sens·lɪs] *adj* 1. (*pointless*) sin sentido 2. MED inconsciente

**sense organ** *n* órgano *m* sensorial

**sensibility** [ˌsen·sə·'bɪl·ə·t̬i] *n* sensibilidad *f*; **to offend sb's sensibilities** herir la sensibilidad de alguien

**sensible** ['sen·sə·bəl] *adj* (*person, decision*) sensato, -a

**sensibly** *adv* prudentemente; (*decide*) acertadamente; (*dress*) con ropa cómoda

**sensitive** ['sen·sɪ·t̬ɪv] *adj* 1. (*sympathetic*) sensible 2. (*touchy*) susceptible (*about* a) 3. (*delicate*) delicado, -a

**sent** [sent] *pp, pt of* **send**

**sentence** ['sen·t̬əns] I. *n* 1. LAW sentencia *f*; (*punishment*) condena *f*; **life ~** cadena perpetua; **to serve a ~** cumplir condena 2. LING frase *f* II. *vt* condenar

**sentimental** [ˌsen·t̬ə·'men·t̬əl] *adj* sentimental (*about* con); *pej* sensiblero, -a

**separable** ['sep·ər·ə·bəl] *adj* separable

**separate¹** ['sep·ər·ɪt] *adj* separado, -a; **to remain a ~ entity** ser una entidad independiente; **a ~ piece of paper** un papel aparte; **to go one's ~ ways** ir por caminos distintos

**separate²** ['sep·ə·reɪt] I. *vt* separar II. *vi* separarse

**separated** *adj* separado, -a

**September** [sep·'tem·bər] *n* septiembre *m*; *s. a.* **April**

**septic** ['sep·tɪk] *adj* séptico, -a

**sequel** ['si·kwəl] *n* secuela *f*; (*follow-up*) continuación *f*

**sequence** ['si·kwəns] *n a.* CINE secuencia *f*; (*events*) sucesión *f*

**sequin** ['si·kwɪn] *n* lentejuela *f*

**Serb** [sɜrb] *adj, n* serbio, -a *m, f*

**Serbia** ['sɜr·bi·ə] *n* Serbia *f*

**Serbian** ['sɜr·bi·ən] *n see* **Serb**

**Serbo-Croat** [ˌsɜr·bou·krou·'æt] *n* se bocroata *m*

**sergeant** ['sar·dʒənt] *n* sargento *mf*

**serial** ['sɪr·i·əl] I. *n* serial *m*; TV serie II. *adj* (*in series*) consecutivo, -a; **~ parts**) por entregas

**series** ['sɪr·iz] *n inv* (*sequence*) serie (*succession*) sucesión *f*

**serious** ['sɪr·i·əs] *adj* 1. (*earnest*) ser -a; (*problem, injury*) grave; (*argumen* importante; (*debt, amount*) considerab 2. (*determined*) firme; **to be ~** ir en s rio (*about* con)

**seriously** *adv* 1. (*in earnest*) en ser 2. (*ill, damaged*) gravemente 3. *i* (*very*) muy

**sermon** ['sɜr·mən] *n a. fig* sermón *m*; **deliver a ~** dar un sermón

**serpent** ['sɜr·pənt] *n* serpiente *f*

**servant** ['sɜr·vənt] *n* criado, -a *m, f*, m camo, -a *m, f* AmL

**serve** [sɜrv] I. *n* SPORTS saque *m* II. 1. (*attend*) atender 2. (*provide*) ser 3. (*be enough for*) servir para; **if n memory ~s me right** si la memori no me falla ▶ **it ~s him/her righ** ¡se lo merece! III. *vi* servir (*as de* SPORTS sacar

◆**serve up** *vt* CULIN servir; *fig* ofrecer

**server** ['sɜr·vər] *n* 1. (*spoon*) cucha *f* de servir 2. (*tray*) bandeja *f*; (*dis* fuente *f* 3. (*waiter*) camarero, -a *m,* 4. COMPUT servidor *m*

**service** ['sɜr·vɪs] *n* 1. *a.* SPORTS servicio *n* **train ~** servicio de trenes; **to be of** ser de utilidad 2. TECH mantenimie to *m*; AUTO revisión *f* 3. (*set*) vajilla **tea ~** juego *m* de té ▶ **to be at sb** ~ estar al servicio de alguien; **to be i** ~ estar en uso

**service area** *n* área *f* de servicio

**service center** *n* (*repairs*) centro *m* c reparaciones

**service charge** *n* gastos *m pl* de se vicio

**service road** *n* vía *f* de acceso

**service station** *n* estación *f* de servici

**serving** ['sɜr·vɪŋ] *n* (*portion*) ración *f*

**sesame** ['ses·ə·mi] *n* sésamo *m*

**session** ['seʃ·ən] *n* 1. sesión *f*; **to be i**

~ estar reunido **2.** SCHOOL trimestre *m*; **morning/afternoon** ~ sesión de mañana/tarde

**et** [set] **I.** *adj* **1.** (*ready*) listo, -a; **to get** ~ prepararse (**to** para) **2.** (*fixed*) fijo, -a **3.** (*assigned*) asignado, -a **II.** *n* **1.** (*people*) grupo *m*; (*cups, chess*) juego *m*; (*kitchen utensils*) batería *f*; (*glasses*) cristalería *f*; (*tools*) set *m*; (*teeth*) dentadura *f* **2.** (*collection*) colección *f* **3.** CINE plató *m* **4.** (*TV*) televisor *m* **5.** (*tennis*) set *m* **III.** *vt* <set, set> **1.** (*place*) poner, colocar; **a house that is** ~ **on a hill** una casa situada sobre una colina **2.** (*give*) dar; (*task*) imponer; (*problem*) plantear **3. to** ~ **sth on fire** prender fuego a algo; **to** ~ **sth in motion** poner algo en movimiento **4.** (*adjust*) ajustar; (*prepare*) preparar; (*table*) poner **5.** (*fix*) fijar; (*record*) establecer **IV.** *vi* **1.** MED soldarse **2.** (*cement*) endurecerse; (*Jell-O, cheese*) cuajar; (*sun*) ponerse

**set about** *vt* emprender; **to** ~ **doing sth** comenzar a hacer algo

**set against** *vt* **1.** (*compare*) comparar **2. to set sb against** poner a alguien en contra de

**set apart** *vt* **1.** (*distinguish*) diferenciar **2.** (*reserve*) reservar

**set aside** *vt* **1.** (*save*) reservar; (*money*) ahorrar **2.** (*put to side*) dejar de lado; **to set one's differences aside** dejar a un lado sus diferencias

**set back** *vt* **1.** (*delay*) retrasar **2.** (*place away*) apartar **3.** (*cost*) salir por

**set down** *vt* **1.** (*place on surface*) posar **2.** (*write*) poner por escrito

**set off** **I.** *vi* salir (**for** hacia) **II.** *vt* **1.** (*explosive*) detonar **2.** (*start*) causar **3.** (*enhance*) resaltar

**set out** **I.** *vi* **1.** *see* **set off 2.** (*intend*) tener la intención (**to** de) **II.** *vt* **1.** (*display*) disponer **2.** (*explain*) exponer (**for** a)

**set to** *vi* (*begin working*) ponerse manos a la obra

**set up** *vt* **1.** (*prepare*) poner **2.** (*establish*) establecer; (*arrange*) disponer; (*cause*) causar; (*committee, corporation*) crear **3. to set oneself** dárselas (**as** de) **4.** (*provide*) proveer **5.** (*de-*

*ceive*) jugársela

**setback** ['set·bæk] *n* revés *m*; **to experience a** ~ tener un contratiempo

**settee** [se·'ti] *n* sofá *m*

**setting** ['set·ɪŋ] *n* **1.** (*sun*) puesta *f* **2.** (*scenery*) escenario *m*; (*surroundings*) entorno *m* **3.** TECH ajuste *m*

**settle** ['set·əl] **I.** *vi* **1.** (*residence*) establecerse **2.** (*get comfortable*) ponerse cómodo, -a **3.** (*calm down*) calmarse; (*weather, situation*) normalizarse **4.** (*decide*) llegar a un acuerdo **5.** (*pay*) saldar las cuentas **6.** (*accumulate*) acumularse; (*snow*) cuajar **7.** (*bird*) posarse **II.** *vt* **1.** (*calm down*) calmar **2.** (*decide*) acordar **3.** (*conclude*) finalizar; (*resolve*) resolver **4.** (*pay*) pagar; (*account*) liquidar **5.** (*colonize*) colonizar ▶ **that** ~**s it!** ¡ya no hay más que decir!

◆**settle down** *vi* **1.** (*calm down*) calmarse **2.** (*residence*) establecerse

◆**settle for** *vt* contentarse con

◆**settle in** *vi* acostumbrarse

◆**settle on** *vt* (*decide*) decidir; (*agree*) acordar

◆**settle up** *vi* ajustar cuentas

**settled** ['set·əld] *adj* **1.** (*established*) establecido, -a; **to feel** ~ sentirse cómodo **2.** (*calm*) calmado, -a **3.** (*fixed*) fijo, -a

**settlement** ['set·əl·mənt] *n* **1.** (*resolution*) resolución *f* **2.** (*agreement*) acuerdo *m* **3.** FIN, ECON liquidación *f* **4.** (*town*) asentamiento *m*

**settler** ['set·lər] *n* colono, -a *m, f*

**set-to** ['set·tu] *n* bronca *f*; **to have a** ~ tener una bronca (**with** con)

**seven** ['sev·ən] *adj, n* siete *m*; *s. a.* **eight**

**seventeen** [ˌsev·ən·'tin] *adj, n* diecisiete *m*; *s. a.* **eight**

**seventeenth** [ˌsev·ən·'tinθ] **I.** *adj* decimoséptimo, -a **II.** *n* **1.** (*order*) decimoséptimo, -a *m, f* **2.** (*date*) diecisiete *m* **3.** (*fraction*) diecisieteavo *m*; *s. a.* **eighth**

**seventh** ['sev·ənθ] **I.** *adj* séptimo, -a **II.** *n* **1.** (*order*) séptimo, -a *m, f* **2.** (*date*) siete *m* **3.** (*fraction*) séptimo *m*; *s. a.* **eighth**

**seventy** ['sev·ən·ti] **I.** *adj* setenta *inv* **II.** *n* <-ies> setenta *m*; *s. a.* **eighty**

**several** ['sev·ər·əl] **I.** *adj* varios, -as; ~

**S**

times varias veces; (*distinct*) distintos, -as **II.** *pron* varios, -as; ~ **of us** algunos de nosotros; **we've got** ~ tenemos varios

**severe** [sə·'vɪr] *adj* (*problem, illness*) grave; (*pain*) fuerte; (*criticism, punishment, person*) severo, -a; (*weather*) riguroso, -a

**sew** [soʊ] <sewed, sewn *or* sewed> *vt, vi* coser; **hand** ~**n** cosido a mano

◆**sew up** *vt* **1.** *a.* MED coser **2.** (*arrange*) arreglar; (*deal*) cerrar

**sewage** ['su·ɪdʒ] *n* aguas *f pl* residuales

**sewer** ['su·ər] *n* alcantarilla *f*

**sewing** ['soʊ·ɪŋ] **I.** *n* costura *f* **II.** *adj* de costura

**sewn** [soʊn] *pp of* **sew**

**sex** [seks] <-es> *n* sexo *m;* **to have** ~ tener relaciones sexuales

**sex appeal** *n* atractivo *m*

**sex discrimination** *n* discriminación *f* sexual

**sex education** *n* educación *f* sexual

**sexism** ['sek·sɪz·əm] *n* sexismo *m*

**sexist** *adj, n* sexista *mf*

**sex life** *n* vida *f* sexual

**sexual** ['sek·ʃu·əl] *adj* sexual

**sexuality** [,sek·ʃu·'æl·ə·ti] *n* sexualidad *f*

**sexually** *adv* sexualmente; **to be ~ abused** ser víctima de abusos sexuales

**sexy** ['sek·si] <-ier, -iest> *adj* sexy; (*exciting*) flipante *argot*

**shabby** ['ʃæb·i] <-ier, -iest> *adj* **1.** (*worn*) deteriorado, -a **2.** (*ragged*) desharrapado, -a, encuerado, -a *Méx Cuba* **3.** (*substandard*) de mala calidad

**shack** [ʃæk] *n* choza *f,* ruca *f Arg, Chile,* jacal *m Méx*

**shade** [ʃeɪd] **I.** *n* **1.** (*shadow*) sombra *f;* ART sombreado *m;* **in the** ~ **of** a [oren] la sombra de **2.** (*covering*) pantalla *f* **3.** *pl* (*blind*) persiana *f* **4.** (*variation*) matiz *m;* (*color*) tono *m* **5.** (*small amount*) pizca *f* **6.** *pl, inf* (*sunglasses*) gafas *f pl* de sol **II.** *vt* (*cast shadow*) dar sombra a; (*protect*) resguardar; ART sombrear

**shading** *n* sombreado *m*

**shadow** ['ʃæd·oʊ] **I.** *n* **1.** *a. fig* sombra *f;* **the ~s** las tinieblas **2.** (*trace*) pizca *f;* **without a** ~ **of a doubt** sin lugar a dudas ▶ **to have ~s under one's eyes**

tener ojeras; **to be a** ~ **of one's former self** no ser ni la sombra de lo que fue; **t be afraid of one's own** ~ tener mied de su propia sombra; **to cast a** ~ **ove** ensombrecer; **to be under sb's** ~ esta a la sombra de alguien **II.** *vt* **1.** ART som brear **2.** (*darken*) ensombrecer **3.** (*fo low*) seguir

**shadowy** <-ier, -iest> *adj* **1.** (*dark*) os curo, -a **2.** (*vague*) impreciso, -a

**shady** ['ʃeɪ·di] <-ier, -iest> *adj* sombrea do, -a; (*dubious*) turbio, -a; (*characte* sospechoso, -a

**shaft** [ʃæft] *n* **1.** (*of tool*) mango *i* **2.** TECH eje *m* **3.** (*ray*) rayo *m* ▶ **to giv sb the** ~ joder a alguien

**shaggy** ['ʃæg·i] <-ier, -iest> *adj* peludc -a; (*coat*) lanudo, -a

**shake** [ʃeɪk] **I.** *n* **1.** (*wobble*) sacudi da *f;* (*quiver*) temblor *m* **2.** (*milk*) bati do *m,* malteada *f AmL* **3.** (*handshake* apretón *m* **4.** *pl* (*trembling*) temble que *m;* **to get the ~s** entrarle el tem bleque ▶ **in two ~s of a lamb's tai** en un santiamén **II.** <shook, shaken> *vt* **1.** (*joggle*) agitar; (*person*) sacudir **to ~ hands** darse la mano; **to ~ one'** **head** negar con la cabeza **2.** (*unsettle* debilitar **3.** (*worry*) desconcertar ▶ ~ **leg** mover el culo **III.** <shook, shaken> *vi* (*tremble*) temblar; '~ **well before opening**' 'agitar antes de abrir'; **let's ~ on it** chócala

◆**shake off** *vt* librarse de

◆**shake out** *vt* sacudir

◆**shake up** *vt* **1.** (*reorganize*) reorgani zar **2.** (*upset*) desconcertar

**shaken** ['ʃeɪ·kən] *vi, vt pp of* **shake**

**shakily** ['ʃeɪ·kɪ·li] *adv* de forma temblo rosa

**shaking** ['ʃeɪ·kɪŋ] *adj* tembloroso, -a

**shaky** ['ʃeɪ·ki] <-ier, -iest> *adj* **1.** (*jerky* tembloroso, -a **2.** (*wavering*) inseguro -a **3.** (*unstable*) inestable

**shall** [ʃæl] *aux* **1.** (*future*) **we ~ win the match** ganaremos el partido **2.** (*ough to*) **he ~ call his mother** debería llamar a su madre

**shallow** ['ʃæl·oʊ] *adj* **1.** (*not deep*) poco profundo, -a **2.** (*superficial*) superficial

**sham** [ʃæm] *pej* **I.** *n* **1.** (*fake*) frau

de *m* **2.** (*impostor*) impostor(a) *m(f)*
**3.** (*cover*) funda *f* **II.** *adj* falso, -a; (*deal*)
fraudulento, -a; (*marriage*) simulado, -a
**III.** <-mm-> *vt, vi* fingir

**hame** [ʃeɪm] **I.** forma *f*; **to get out of ~**
perder la forma; **to take ~** adquirir forma; **in the ~** en forma (**of** de); **in bad/
good ~** en mala/buena forma; **to get
into ~** ponerse en forma **II.** *vt* **1.** (*form*)
dar forma a **2.** (*influence*) condicionar

**hame** [ʃeɪm] *n* **1.** vergüenza *f*,
pena *f AmC*; **to die of ~** morirse de vergüenza; **to feel no ~** no tener vergüenza; **to put sb to ~** avergonzar a alguien;
**~ on you!** ¡debería darte vergüenza!; **to
bring ~** deshonrar (**on** a) **2.** (*pity*) pena,
**what a ~!** ¡qué pena!; **what a ~ that...**
qué pena que... +*subj*; **it's a crying ~** es
una verdadera lástima

**hameful** [ʃeɪm·fəl] *adj* vergonzoso, -a,
penoso, -a *AmC*; **it's ~ that...** es una
vergüenza que... +*subj*

**hameless** [ʃeɪm·lɪs] *adj* descarado, -a,
concluido, -a *AmL*

**hampoo** [ʃæm·ˈpu] *n* champú *m*

**hape** [ʃeɪp] **I.** *n* forma *f*; **to get out of ~**
perder la forma; **to take ~** adquirir for-
ma; **in the ~** en forma (**of** de); **in bad/
good ~** en mala/buena forma; **to get
into ~** ponerse en forma **II.** *vt* **1.** (*form*)
dar forma a **2.** (*influence*) condicionar

**hare** [ʃer] **I.** *n* **1.** parte *f*; **to do one's
~** hacer su parte (**of** de) **2.** FIN acción *f*;
**stocks and ~s** acciones y participaciones
**II.** *vi, vt* compartir; (*divide*) repartir

**hark** [ʃark] <-(s)> *n* tiburón *m*; (*person*)
timador(a) *m(f)*

**harp** [ʃarp] **I.** *adj* **1.** (*cutting*) afilado, -a;
(*pointed*) puntiagudo, -a **2.** (*curve*)
cerrado, -a; (*pain, cry*) agudo, -a; (*look*)
penetrante; (*tongue*) viperino, -a **3.** (*astute*) astuto, -a; (*perceptive*) perspicaz **4.** (*sudden*) súbito, -a; (*abrupt*)
abrupto, -a; (*marked*) pronunciado, -a
**5.** (*distinct*) nítido, -a **6.** MUS sostenido, -a **II.** *adv* **1.** (*exactly*) en punto
**2.** (*suddenly*) de repente; **to pull up ~**
frenar en seco

**harpen** [ʃar·pən] *vt* **1.** (*blade*) afilar;
(*pencil*) sacar punta a **2.** (*intensify*)
agudizar; (*appetite*) abrir

**harpener** [ʃar·pən·ər] *n* afilador *m*, afiladora *f Méx*; **pencil ~** sacapuntas *m inv*

**harp-eyed** [ʃarp·ˈaɪd] *adj* observador(a)

**harp-tongued** *adj* mordaz

**harp-witted** *adj* agudo, -a

**hatter** [ʃæt·ər] **I.** *vi* hacer añicos **II.** *vt*

(*smash*) hacer añicos; (*hopes, dreams,
unity*) destruir

**shattering** *adj* tremendo, -a

**shatterproof** [ʃæt·ər·ˌpruf] *adj* inastillable

**shave** [ʃeɪv] **I.** *n* afeitado *m*, rasura-
da *f Méx* ▶ **to have a close ~** librarse
por los pelos **II.** *vi* afeitarse **III.** *vt* afeitar,
rasurar *Méx*

**shaven** [ʃeɪ·vən] *adj* afeitado, -a; (*head*)
rapado, -a

**shaver** [ʃeɪ·vər] *n* maquinilla *f* de afeitar,
rasuradora *f Méx*

**shawl** [ʃɔl] *n* chal *m*

**she** [ʃi] *pron pers* (*female*) ella; **~'s my
mother** (ella) es mi madre

**shed**[1] [ʃed] *n* cobertizo *m*, galera *f AmL*

**shed**[2] [ʃed] <shed, shed> *vt* (*cast off*)
quitarse; (*hair, weight*) perder; (*skin*)
mudar; (*blood, tears*) derramar; (*light*)
emitir

**sheep** [ʃip] *n* oveja *f*; (*ram*) carnero *m*
▶ **black ~** oveja negra

**sheepdog** [ʃip·dɔg] *n* perro *m* pastor

**sheepish** [ʃi·pɪʃ] *adj* tímido, -a

**sheepskin** [ʃip·skɪn] *n* piel *f* de borrego

**sheer** [ʃɪr] *adj* **1.** (*pure*) puro, -a; (*agony,
lunacy*) total; **~ coincidence** pura coincidencia **2.** (*vertical*) escarpado, -a;
(*drop*) en picado **3.** (*thin*) fino, -a

**sheet** [ʃit] *n* **1.** (*bed*) sábana *f*; (*paper*)
hoja *f*; (*metal, stamps*) plancha *f*; (*glass*)
lámina *f* **2.** (*information*) folleto *m*
**3.** (*layer*) capa *f*

**sheik(h)** [ʃik] *n* jeque *m*

**shelf** [ʃelf], *pl* **shelves** *n* estante *m*; **~s** estantería *f*; GEO arrecife *m*

**shell** [ʃel] *n* (*nut, egg*) cáscara *f*; (*shellfish,
snail*) concha *f*; (*crab, turtle*) capara-
zón *m*; (*house*) estructura *f*; (*ship*) casco *m*; TECH armazón *m* ▶ **to come** [*or*
**bust**] **out of one's ~** salir del cascarón

◆ **shell out** *vt, vi inf* (*pay*) aflojar; **to ~ for**
apoquinar para

**shellfish** [ʃel·fɪʃ] *n* CULIN marisco *m*

**shelling** *n* bombardeo *m*

**shelter** [ʃel·tər] **I.** *n* refugio *m*; **to take
~** refugiarse **II.** *vt* resguardar **III.** *vi*
refugiarse

**sheltered** *adj* protegido, -a; *pej* sobre-
protegido, -a

S

**shield** [ʃiːld] I. n (*armor*) escudo m; (*animal*) caparazón m; (*machine*) revestimiento m II. vt proteger

**shift** [ʃɪft] I. vt (*change*) mover; (*reposition*) cambiar de sitio; (*gears, lanes*) cambiar; **to ~ the blame** echar la culpa (**onto** a); **to ~ one's ground** cambiar de opinión II. vi moverse; (*wind*) cambiar III. n 1. (*change*) cambio m 2. (*work*) turno m; **to work in ~s** trabajar por turnos

**shifting** adj movedizo, -a; (*values*) cambiante

**shift key** n tecla f de las mayúsculas

**shifty** [ʃɪfti] <-ier, -iest> adj sospechoso, -a

**shin** [ʃɪn] n ANAT espinilla f

**shine** [ʃaɪn] I. n brillo m ▶ **to take a ~** sentir simpatía (**to** por) II. <shone or shined, shone or shined> vi 1. (*moon, star*) brillar; (*metal*) relucir; (*light*) alumbrar; (*eyes*) resplandecer 2. (*be gifted*) destacar III. <shone or shined, shone or shined> vt **to ~ a light at** alumbrar

**shiner** [ʃaɪnər] n inf ojo m morado

**shining** [ʃaɪnɪŋ] adj 1. (*gleaming*) reluciente, abrillantada, -a AmL; (*eyes*) resplandeciente 2. (*outstanding*) magnífico, -a

**shiny** [ʃaɪni] <-ier, -iest> adj brillante

**ship** [ʃɪp] I. n barco m; **passenger ~** buque m de pasajeros; **sailing ~** velero m II. vt <-pp-> 1. (*send*) **to ~** (**freight**) enviar (mercancías) por barco 2. (*transport*) transportar

◆ **ship out** vi embarcarse

**shipwreck** I. n naufragio m; (*remains*) restos m pl de un naufragio II. vt **to be ~ed** naufragar; fig estar hundido

**shipyard** n astillero m

**shirk** [ʃɜːrk] vt, vi **to ~** (**away from**) sth escaquearse de algo

**shirker** [ʃɜːrkər] n vago, -a m, f

**shirt** [ʃɜːrt] n camisa f ▶ **to lose one's ~** perder hasta la camisa; **keep your ~ on!** ¡no te sulfures!

**shirtsleeve** [ʃɜːrtsliːv] n **to be in ~s** estar en mangas de camisa

**shit** [ʃɪt] inf I. n 1. mierda f 2. (*nonsense*) gilipolleces fpl, pendeja-

das fpl AmL 3. (*nothing*) nada; **to no know ~** no tener ni zorra idea (**abou** de); **I don't give a ~!** ¡me importa u carajo! ▶ **to beat the ~ out of s** moler a alguien a palos; **to frighte the ~ out of sb** acojonar a alguien; **t be in deep ~** estar muy jodido; **no ~** ¡no jodas! II. interj mierda III. <shi shit> vi, vt cagar; **to ~ oneself** [*or* **one'** **pants**] cagarse

**shitty** [ʃɪti] <-ier, -iest> adj 1. (*un pleasant*) de mierda 2. (*sick*) hecho -a una mierda

**shiver** [ʃɪvər] I. vi temblar; **to ~ wit** cold tiritar de frío II. n escalofrío m; t **feel a ~** tener un escalofrío; **to give s the ~s** dar escalofríos a alguien

**shock**[1] [ʃɑk] I. n 1. (*surprise*) conmo ción f, batata f CSur; **look of ~** mirada d asombro; **to give sb a ~** dar un disgust a alguien 2. inf ELEC descarga f 3. ME shock m 4. (*explosion, earthquake* sacudida f II. vt 1. (*appall*) horroriza 2. (*scare*) asustar III. vi impactar

**shock**[2] [ʃɑk] n (*hair*) mata f

**shock absorber** [ʃɑkəbˌsɔːrbər] n amor tiguador m

**shocker** [ʃɑkər] n (*surprising news* bombazo m

**shocking** [ʃɑkɪŋ] adj 1. (*distressing* espantoso, -a 2. (*surprising*) chocant 3. (*offensive*) escandaloso, -a

**shockproof** [ʃɑkpruːf] adj impertur bable

**shock wave** n onda f expansiva; fi conmoción f

**shod** [ʃɑd] pt, pp of **shoe**

**shoddy** [ʃɑdi] <-ier, -iest> adj (*goods* de muy mala calidad; (*treatment*) mez quino, -a

**shoe** [ʃuː] I. n zapato m; **athletic ~** zapatillas f pl de deporte ▶ **if I were** **in your ~s** si estuviera en tu luga II. <shod, shod or shodden> vt calzar

**shoelace** n cordón m; **to tie one's ~** atarse los cordones

**shoe polish** n betún m

**shoestring** [ʃuːstrɪŋ] n cordón m; **on a** **~** con poquísimo dinero

**shone** [ʃoʊn] pt, pp of **shine**

**shoo** [ʃuː] I. interj fuera II. vt espantar

**hook** [ʃʊk] n pt of **shake**

**hoot** [ʃut] I. <shot, shot> vi 1. (fire) a. PHOT disparar (at a); **to ~ to kill** tirar a matar 2. (aim) apuntar (for a) 3. SPORTS chutar 4. CINE rodar ▶ **to ~ for the moon** [or **the stars**] ir a por todas II. <shot, shot> vt 1. disparar 2. CINE rodar; PHOT tomar 3. (glance) lanzar; (goal, basket) meter; (drugs) meterse ▶ **to ~ the breeze** cotillear; **to ~ darts** lanzar miradas asesinas (at a); **to ~ the works** tirar la casa por la ventana III. n 1. (hunt) cacería f 2. CINE rodaje m; PHOT sesión f 3. BOT retoño m

**shoot down** vt (aircraft) derribar

**shoot off** I. vt **to shoot one's mouth off** cotorrear II. vi (vehicle) salir como un bólido

**shoot out** vi salir disparado

**shoot up** vi 1. (expand) crecer mucho; (child) pegar un estirón 2. (drugs) chutarse

**shooting** [ˈʃuːtɪŋ] n 1. (killing) asesinato m 2. (firing) tiroteo m 3. (hunting) caza f; **to go ~** ir de caza 4. SPORTS tiro m al blanco

**shooting star** n estrella f fugaz

**shop** [ʃɑp] I. n tienda f; **book ~** librería f; (workshop) taller m ▶ **to set up ~** establecerse (as como); **to talk ~** hablar de trabajo II. <-pp-> vi hacer compras

**shopaholic** [ˌʃɑp·ə·ˈhɔ·lɪk] n comprador(a) compulsivo, -a m

**shopkeeper** n comerciante mf

**shoplifter** [ˈʃɑp·lɪf·tər] n ladrón, -ona m, f

**shoplifting** n robo m (en tiendas)

**shopper** n comprador(a) m(f)

**shopping** [ˈʃɑp·ɪŋ] n compra f; (purchases) compras; **to go ~** ir de tiendas

**shopping cart** n carrito m de la compra

**shopping center** n centro m comercial

**shopping list** n lista f de la compra

**shopping mall** n centro m comercial

**shore** [ʃɔr] n costa f; (beach) orilla f; **on ~** a tierra

**shoreline** n orilla f

**short** [ʃɔrt] I. adj 1. (not long) corto, -a; (memory) malo, -a; (vowel) breve 2. (not tall) bajo, -a, petizo, -a CSur, Bol 3. (not enough) escaso, -a; **to be** [or

**run**] **~** andar escaso (**on** de); **to be ~ of breath** quedarse sin aliento; **to be in ~ supply** escasear II. n 1. CINE cortometraje m 2. ELEC cortocircuito m III. adv **to cut ~** interrumpir bruscamente; **to stop ~** parar en seco; **to fall ~** quedarse corto; **to fall ~ of** no alcanzar

**shortage** [ˈʃɔr·tɪdʒ] n falta f; (water) escasez f

**short circuit** n cortocircuito m

**shortcoming** [ˈʃɔrt·kʌm·ɪŋ] n defecto m

**shortcut key** n tecla f rápida

**shorten** [ˈʃɔr·tən] I. vt acortar II. vi acortarse

**shorthand** [ˈʃɔrt·hænd] n taquigrafía f

**short-lived** adj efímero, -a; (happiness) pasajero, -a

**shortly** [ˈʃɔrt·li] adv dentro de poco; **~ after** poco después

**shorts** [ʃɔrts] npl 1. (pants) pantalón m corto; **a pair of ~** unos pantalones cortos 2. (underpants) calzoncillos mpl; **boxer ~** boxers mpl

**short-sleeved** adj de manga corta

**short-staffed** adj falto, -a de personal

**short story** n narración m corta

**short-tempered** adj irascible

**short-term** adj a corto plazo

**shot¹** [ʃɑt] I. n 1. (gun) tiro m, baleo m AmC; **to fire a ~** pegar un tiro 2. (person) tirador(a) m(f) 3. SPORTS tiro m; (tennis) golpe m 4. PHOT foto f; CINE toma f 5. inf (try) intento m; **to have** [or **take**] **a ~** probar suerte (at con) 6. (alcohol) chupito m ▶ **a ~ in the arm** un estímulo; **a ~ in the dark** un palo de ciego; **not by a long ~** ni por asomo II. pp, pt of **shoot**

**shot²** [ʃɑt] adj (worn out) hecho, -a polvo

**shotgun** [ˈʃɑt·gʌn] n escopeta f

**shot put** n lanzamiento m de peso

**should** [ʃʊd] aux 1. (advisability) **to insist that sb ~ do sth** insistir en que alguien debería hacer algo; (why) **~ I...?** ¿(por qué) debería...? 2. **I ~ be so lucky!** ¡ojalá! 3. **I ~ like to see her** me gustaría verla; **we ~ like to invite you** nos gustaría invitarle

**shoulder** [ˈʃoʊl·dər] I. n 1. ANAT hombro m; **~ to ~** hombro con hombro; **to**

S

glance over one's ~ mirar por encima del hombro; **to lift a burden off one's ~s** quitarse un peso de encima **2.** CULIN paletilla f **3.** (road) arcén m, banquina f Arg, Urug, berma f Col ▸ **to rub ~s** codearse (**with** con); **to stand ~ to ~** apoyar (**with** a) **II.** vt **1.** empujar; **to ~ one's way** abrirse paso a empujones **2.** (carry) llevar a hombros; (responsibility) cargar con

**shoulder blade** n omóplato m

**shoulder pad** n hombrera f

**shoulder strap** n tirante m

**shout** [ʃaʊt] **I.** n grito m ▸ **to give sb a ~** dar un toque a alguien **II.** vi gritar (**at** a); **to ~ for help** pedir auxilio a gritos ▸ **to give sth to ~ about** dar una gran alegría **III.** vt gritar; (slogans) corear

◆**shout down** vt hacer callar a gritos

◆**shout out** vt gritar

**shouting** n griterío m

**shove** [ʃʌv] **I.** n empujón m, pechada f Arg, Chile; **to give sth a ~** dar un empujón a algo **II.** vt **1.** (push) empujar; **to ~ one's way through** abrirse paso a empujones; **to ~ sb about** [or around] abusar de alguien **2.** vulg **~ it** (**up your ass**)! ¡métetelo por el culo! **III.** vi empujar; **to ~ along** largarse

◆**shove off** vi (go away) largarse

**shovel** [ʃʌv·əl] n (tool) pala f; (machine) excavadora f

**show** [ʃoʊ] **I.** n **1.** (expression) demostración f; **~ of solidarity** muestra f de solidaridad **2.** (exhibition) exposición f; **fashion ~** desfile m de modelos; **slide ~** pase m de diapositivas; **to be on ~** estar expuesto **3.** (play) espectáculo m; TV programa m; THEAT representación f; **quiz ~** concurso m ▸ **~ of hands** voto a mano alzada; **let's get the ~ on the road** vamos manos a la obra; **to put on a good ~** hacer un buen papel; **the ~ must go on** el espectáculo debe continuar; **to run the ~** llevar la voz cantante **II.** <showed, shown> vt **1.** (display) mostrar; (slides) pasar; ART exponer **2.** (express) demostrar; (enthusiasm) expresar **3.** (expose) exponer **4.** (point out) señalar; (statistics) indicar **5.** (prove) probar; **to ~ sb that...** demos-

trar a alguien que... **6.** (escort) guiar; **t ~ sb to the door** acompañar a alguie hasta la puerta **7.** (project) proyectar; ▸ poner **III.** vi<showed, shown> **1.** (t visible) verse **2.** (film) proyectarse; (ar ist) exponer; (work of art) estar expues to, -a **3.** inf (arrive) aparecer

◆**show around** vt guiar

◆**show in** vt hacer pasar

◆**show off** **I.** vt lucir **II.** vi alardear, com padrear Arg, Urug

◆**show out** vt acompañar hasta la puert

◆**show up** **I.** vi **1.** inf (arrive) aparece **2.** (be apparent) ponerse de manifiest **II.** vt **1.** (expose) descubrir; **to shov sb up as** (being) **sth** demostrar qu alguien es algo **2.** (embarrass) pone en evidencia

**showdown** [ʃoʊ·daʊn] n enfrentamien to m

**shower** [ʃaʊ·ər] **I.** n **1.** ducha f, llu via f Arg, Chile, Nic **2.** (rain) chapa rrón m; (sparks, insults) lluvia **II.** ▸ ducharse; (spray) regar **III.** vt **1.** (spra derramar; **to ~ sb** regar a alguien (**witl** de) **2. to ~ sb with gifts** colmar de re galos a alguien

**shower gel** n gel m de ducha

**showery** [ʃaʊ·ə·ri] adj lluvioso, -a

**showground** n recinto m ferial

**showing** n **1.** (exhibition) exposición **2.** (broadcasting) proyección f **3.** (per formance) actuación f

**shown** [ʃoʊn] pp of **show**

**showy** [ʃoʊ·i] <-ier, -iest> adj llama tivo, -a

**shrank** [ʃræŋk] vt, vi pt of **shrink**

**shred** [ʃred] **I.** <-dd-> vt cortar en tiras (document) triturar **II.** n tira f; (hope truth) pizca f; **to be in ~s** estar hecho jirones; **to tear to ~s** hacer trizas

**shredder** [ʃred·ər] n trituradora f

**shriek** [ʃrik] **I.** n chillido m **II.** vt, vi chillar; **to ~ with laughter** reírse a carcajadas

**shrink** [ʃrɪŋk] **I.** n loquero, -a m, _ **II.** <shrank or shrunk, shrunk or shrunken> vt encoger; (costs) re ducir **III.** <shrank or shrunk, shrunk or shrunken> vi disminuir; (clothes) encoger; **to ~ from** (**doing**) **sth** rehuir (hacer) algo

**shrivel** ['ʃrɪv·əl] <-ll-, -l-> I. vi (fruit, plant) secarse; (skin) arrugarse; (person) consumirse II. vt (fruit) secar; (skin) arrugar

♦**shrivel up** vi see **shrivel** I

**shrub** [ʃrʌb] n arbusto m

**shrug** [ʃrʌg] I. n encogimiento m de hombros II. <-gg-> vt, vi to ~ (one's **shoulders**) encogerse de hombros

♦**shrug off** vt 1. (ignore) negar importancia a 2. (overcome) superar

**shrunk** [ʃrʌŋk] pp, pt of **shrink**

**shudder** ['ʃʌd·ər] I. vi vibrar; (person) estremecerse; **to ~ at the memory of sth** temblar al recordar algo II. n vibración f; (person) estremecimiento m; **it sent a ~ down my spine** hizo que me estremeciera

**shuffle** ['ʃʌf·əl] I. n (cabinet, management) reestructuración f; **with a ~** arrastrando los pies II. vt (papers) revolver; (cards) barajar; (cabinet, management) reestructurar; (feet) arrastrar III. vi (cards) barajar; (feet) arrastrar los pies

**shush** [ʃʊʃ] inf I. interj silencio II. vt hacer callar III. vi callarse

**shut** [ʃʌt] I. <shut, shut> vt cerrar; **to ~ one's ears** hacer oídos sordos (**to** a); **to ~ one's finger in the door** pillarse el dedo con la puerta II. <shut, shut> vi (door, window) cerrarse; (shop, factory) cerrar III. adj cerrado, -a; **to slam a door ~** cerrar la puerta de un portazo

♦**shut away** vt encerrar; **to shut oneself away** recluirse

♦**shut down** I. vt 1. (shop, factory) cerrar; (airport) paralizar 2. (turn off) apagar II. vi (shop, factory) cerrar; (engine) apagarse

♦**shut in** vt encerrar

♦**shut off** vt 1. (turn off) apagar 2. (isolate) aislar

♦**shut out** vt 1. (block out) ahuyentar 2. (exclude) dejar fuera

♦**shut up** I. vt 1. (confine) encerrar 2. inf (silence) hacer callar II. vi inf callarse

**shuttle** ['ʃʌt·əl] I. n (bus, train) enlace m; (plane) puente m aéreo II. vt transportar III. vi AVIAT volar (regularmente)

**shuttle flight** n puente m aéreo

**shy** [ʃaɪ] <-er, -est> adj 1. (timid) tímido, -a 2. (lacking) escaso, -a

**shyness** n timidez f

**sick** [sɪk] <-er, -est> adj 1. (ill) enfermo, -a; **to feel ~** sentirse mal; **to get ~** caer enfermo; **to be off ~** estar de baja 2. (nauseated) **to get ~** vomitar; **to feel ~ to one's stomach** tener el estómago revuelto; **alcohol makes me ~** el alcohol me sienta fatal 3. (disgusted) asqueado, -a (**about** de) 4. (angry) furioso, -a; **to be ~ and tired** estar (más que) harto (**of** de) 5. inf cruel; (joke) de mal gusto

**sickbay** n enfermería f

**sickening** ['sɪk·ən·ɪŋ] adj 1. (repulsive) repugnante 2. (annoying) ofensivo, -a

**sick leave** ['sɪk·liːv] n baja f por enfermedad; **to be on ~** estar de baja por enfermedad

**sickness** ['sɪk·nɪs] n enfermedad f; (nausea) mareo m

**sick pay** n subsidio m de enfermedad

**side** [saɪd] n 1. (surface) lado m; (of page) cara f; **at the ~** en el lado (**of** de); **at sb's ~** al lado de alguien; **by ~** uno al lado de otro; **from all ~(s)** de todas partes; **from ~ to ~** de lado a lado; **on the ~** aparte; **to leave sth on one ~** dejar algo a un lado 2. (edge) límite m; (river) ribera f; (road) arcén m; **on all ~(s)** por todas partes 3. (in dispute) **to take ~s** tomar partido; **to take sb's ~** ponerse de parte de alguien; **to be on the ~** ser partidario (**of** de); **to have sth on one's ~** tener algo a su favor; **on my father's ~** por parte de padre 4. (aspect) aspecto m; (story) versión f ▶ **the other ~ of the** coin la otra cara de la moneda; **to be on the** safe **~** para mayor seguridad

**sideboard** ['saɪd·bɔrd] n aparador m, bufet m AmL

**side dish** n acompañamiento m

**side effect** n efecto m secundario

**sideline** ['saɪd·laɪn] n 1. SPORTS (line) línea f; (area) banda f; **on the ~s** fig al margen; **from the ~s** desde fuera 2. (secondary activity) actividad f secundaria

S

**side road** n carretera f secundaria

**sidestep** ['saɪd·step] <-pp-> I. vt esquivar II. vi dar un paso hacia un lado

**side street** n calle f lateral

**sidetrack** ['saɪd·træk] I. vt distraer II. n vía f muerta; fig cuestión f secundaria

**sidewalk** ['saɪd·wɔk] n acera f, vereda f AmL, banqueta f Guat, Méx

**sieve** [sɪv] I. n colador m; (flour) tamiz m II. vt colar; (flour) tamizar

**sigh** [saɪ] I. n suspiro m; **to let out a ~ of relief** soltar un suspiro de alivio II. vi suspirar; **to ~ with relief** suspirar aliviado

**sight** [saɪt] n 1. vista f; (gun) mira f; **to be out of (one's) ~** no estar a la vista; **to come into ~** aparecer; **to catch ~ of** vislumbrar; **to know sb by ~** conocer a alguien de vista; **to lose ~ of sth** perder algo de vista; (forget) no tener presente algo; **at first ~** a primera vista; **within ~** a la vista (of de); **get out of my ~!** inf ¡fuera de mi vista!; **at the ~ of** al ver 2. pl (attractions) lugares m pl de interés ▶ **to be a ~ for sore eyes** ser una alegría para los ojos; **out of ~, out of mind** ojos que no ven, corazón que no siente; **~ unseen** sin haber visto; **I never buy anything ~ unseen** nunca compro nada sin verlo bien antes; **out of ~!** ¡fabuloso!

**sightseeing** ['saɪt·si·ɪŋ] n turismo m; **to go ~** visitar los lugares de interés

**sightseer** ['saɪt·si·ər] n turista mf

**sign** [saɪn] I. n 1. (gesture) señal f; **to make a ~** hacer un gesto (**to** a); **as a ~ that** como señal de que 2. (signpost) indicador m; (signboard) letrero m 3. (symbol) símbolo m 4. MATH, ASTR, MUS signo m; **a ~ that** un signo de que 5. (trace) rastro m; **they couldn't find any ~ of him** no encontraron ni rastro de él. II. vt 1. (signature) firmar 2. (employ) contratar; SPORTS fichar 3. (gesticulate) indicar; **to ~ sb to do sth** indicar a alguien que haga algo 4. (in sign language) decir por señas III. vi 1. (signature) firmar; SPORTS fichar (**with** por); **~ here, please** firme aquí, por favor; **to ~ for sth** firmar el recibo de algo 2. (gesticulate) gesticular; **to ~ to sb that...**

indicar con señas a alguien que...

◆**sign in** I. vi firmar en el registro de entrada II. vt firmar por

◆**sign off** vi inf terminar; RADIO, TV cerrar la emisión

◆**sign on** I. vi firmar un contrato; **to ~ for sth** inscribirse en algo; **he has signed on for courses in Japanese** se ha apuntado a clases de japonés II. vt contratar

◆**sign out** vi firmar en el registro de salida

◆**sign over** vt firmar un traspaso; **to sign property over to sb** poner una propiedad a nombre de alguien

◆**sign up** I. vi apuntarse II. vt contratar

**signal** ['sɪg·nəl] I. n 1. (gesture) a. AUTO, RAIL, COMPUT seña f; **to give sb a ~ to do sth** hacer una señal a alguien para que haga algo 2. (indication) signo m; **to be a ~ that** ser signo de que 3. ELEC, RADIO señal f II. <-ll-, -l-> vt 1. (indicate) indicar (**that** que) 2. (gesticulate) hacer señas; **he ~ed them to be quiet** les hizo señas de que se callaran III. <-ll-, -l-> vi hacer una señal

**signature** ['sɪg·nə·tʃər] n firma f

**significance** [sɪg·'nɪf·ə·kəns] n (importance) importancia f; (meaning) significado m

**significant** [sɪg·'nɪf·ə·kənt] adj 1. (important) importante; (difference) notable 2. (meaningful) significativo, -a

**signify** ['sɪg·nə·faɪ] form I. <-ie-> vt 1. (mean) significar 2. (indicate) indicar II. <-ie-> vi (matter) tener importancia

**sign language** ['saɪn·ˌlæŋ·gwɪdʒ] n lenguaje m por señas; (deaf) lenguaje m de signos

**signpost** I. n señal f II. vt señalizar

**silence** ['saɪ·ləns] I. n silencio m II. vt silenciar; (person) hacer callar

**silent** ['saɪ·lənt] adj silencioso, -a; LING, CINE mudo, -a; **to be ~** no decir nada (**on** sobre); **to fall ~** callarse

**silently** adv silenciosamente; (without speaking) en silencio

**silicon** ['sɪl·ɪ·kən] n silicio m

**silk** [sɪlk] n seda f; **~ scarf** pañuelo m de seda

**silky** ['sɪl·ki] <-ier, -iest> *adj* sedoso, -a; (*fur, voice*) suave

**sill** [sɪl] *n* (*door*) umbral *m*; (*window*) alféizar *m*

**silly** ['sɪl·i] <-ier, -iest> *adj* (*person*) tonto, -a, dundo, -a *AmC, Col*; (*idea*) estúpido, -a; **it was ~ of her to...** fue una estupidez por su parte...; **to look ~** parecer ridículo; **to laugh oneself ~** desternillarse de risa

**silver** ['sɪl·vər] I. *n* plata *f* II. *adj* de plata; (*color*) plateado, -a

**silverware** ['sɪl·vər·wer] *n* (*cutlery*) cubertería *f* de plata; (*dishes, trays*) vajilla *f* de plata

**similar** ['sɪm·ə·lər] *adj* similar

**similarity** [ˌsɪm·ə·'ler·ə·t̬i] *n* semejanza *f*

**simile** ['sɪm·ə·li] *n* símil *m*

**simmer** ['sɪm·ər] I. *vi* hervir a fuego lento; *fig* estar a punto de estallar II. *vt* cocer a fuego lento III. *n* ebullición *f* lenta; **to bring sth to a ~** poner algo a hervir; **at a ~** hirviendo a fuego lento

♦**simmer down** *vi inf* tranquilizarse

**simple** ['sɪm·pəl] *adj* **1.** (*not difficult*) fácil **2.** (*not elaborate*) sencillo, -a **3.** (*honest*) honesto, -a **4.** (*ordinary*) normal **5.** (*foolish*) simple

**simple-minded** [ˌsɪm·pəl·'maɪn·dɪd] *adj inf* (*dumb*) tonto, -a; (*naive*) ingenuo, -a

**simplicity** [sɪm·'plɪs·ə·t̬i] *n* **1.** (*plainness*) sencillez *f* **2.** (*ease*) simplicidad *f*

**simplification** [ˌsɪm·plə·fɪ·'keɪ·ʃən] *n* simplificación *f*

**simply** ['sɪm·pli] *adv* **1.** (*not elaborately*) sencillamente **2.** (*just*) simplemente **3.** (*absolutely*) completamente

**simulation** [ˌsɪm·jʊ·'leɪ·ʃən] *n* simulación *f*; (*of feeling*) fingimiento *m*

**simultaneous** [ˌsaɪ·məl·'teɪ·ni·əs] *adj* simultáneo, -a

**sin** [sɪn] I. *n* pecado *m* ▶ **to be as ugly as ~** ser más feo que Picio II. *vi* <-nn-> pecar

**since** [sɪns] I. *adv* (*ever*) **~** desde entonces; **long ~** hace mucho; **not long ~** hace poco II. *prep* desde III. *conj* **1.** desde que; **it's been a week now ~ I came back** ya ha pasado una semana desde que llegué **2.** (*because*)

puesto que

**sincere** [sɪn·'sɪr] *adj* sincero, -a

**sincerely** *adv* sinceramente

**sine** [saɪn] *n* seno *m*

**sing** [sɪŋ] <sang, sung> I. *vi* cantar (**to** para) II. *vt* cantar

♦**sing out** *vt* **to ~ sb's name** llamar a alguien a voces

**singer** ['sɪŋ·ər] *n* cantante *mf*

**singing** *n* canto *m*

**single** ['sɪŋ·gəl] I. *adj* **1.** (*one only*) único, -a; (*blow*) solo, -a; (*figure*) de un solo dígito; **not a ~ person/thing** nadie/nada; **not a ~ soul** ni un alma; **every ~ thing** cada cosa **2.** (*unmarried*) soltero, -a **3.** (*bed, room*) individual II. *n* **1.** (*bill*) billete *m* de un dólar **2.** MUS single *m* **3.** (*baseball*) sencillo *m*

♦**single out** *vt* señalar

**single-minded** *adj* resuelto, -a

**single-parent family** <-ies> *n* familia *f* monoparental

**singleton** ['sɪŋ·gəl·tən] *n* persona *f* soltera

**singly** ['sɪŋ·gli] *adv* uno por uno

**sink** [sɪŋk] <sank *or* sunk, sunk> I. *n* (*kitchen*) fregadero *m*; (*bathroom*) lavabo *m* II. *vi* **1.** (*in water*) hundirse; **to ~ to the bottom** hundirse hasta el fondo **2.** (*drop*) caer; **to ~ to the ground** caer al suelo **3.** (*decline: a. price, level*) bajar; **to ~ in sb's estimation** perder la estima de alguien; **to ~ into depression** sumirse en la depresión; **to ~ into oblivion** caer en el olvido ▶ **to ~ or swim** a su suerte III. *vt* **1.** (*submerge*) hundir **2.** (*ruin*) destruir **3.** (*invest*) invertir (**into** en)

♦**sink back** *vi* repantigarse

**sink in** *vi* **1.** (*go into surface*) penetrar; (*liquid*) calar **2.** (*be understood*) entenderse

**sinking** ['sɪŋ·kɪŋ] *n* hundimiento *m*

**sinner** ['sɪn·ər] *n* pecador(a) *m(f)*

**sip** [sɪp] I. <-pp-> *vt, vi* sorber II. *n* sorbo *m*; **to have a ~** dar un sorbo

**sir** [sɜr] *n* señor *m*

**siren** ['saɪ·rən] *n* sirena *f*

**sis** [sɪs] *n inf abbr of* **sister** hermana *f*

**sissy** ['sɪs·i] <-ier, -iest> *adj* <-ies> *n* mariquita *m*

S

**sister** ['sɪs·tər] n a. REL hermana f; ~ **company** empresa f asociada

**sister-in-law** ['sɪs·tər·ɪn·ˌlɔ] <sisters-in-law> n cuñada f, concuña f AmL

**sit** [sɪt] <sat, sat> I. vi 1. sentarse; (be seated) estar sentado, -a 2. ART posar 3. inf (babysit) cuidar (**for** a) 4. (perch) posarse; (eggs) empollar 5. (be placed) estar; **to ~ on the shelf** estar en el estante; **to ~ in Congress** ser diputado 6. (fit) **to ~ well/badly** caer [or sentar] bien/mal ► **to be ~ting pretty** estar bien situado; **to ~ tight** no moverse; (opinion) no dar el brazo a torcer II. vt sentar

◆**sit around** vi estar sin hacer nada

◆**sit back** vi 1. (in chair) ponerse cómodo 2. (do nothing) cruzarse de brazos

◆**sit down** I. vi sentarse; (be sitting) estar sentado II. vt sentar

◆**sit in** vi 1. (attend) asistir como oyente 2. **to ~ for sb** sustituir a alguien 3. (hold sit-in) hacer una sentada

◆**sit on** vt inf (information) guardar para sí; (secret) no revelar; (idea, plan) acabar con

◆**sit out** vt 1. (not join) no tomar parte en; **to ~ a dance** no bailar 2. (sit through) aguantar hasta el final

◆**sit through** vt aguantar hasta el final

◆**sit up** vi 1. (sit erect) sentarse derecho; ~! ¡siéntate derecho! 2. (pay attention) atender

**sitcom** ['sɪt·kɑm] n inf abbr of **situation comedy** comedia f de situación

**site** [saɪt] I. n 1. (place) sitio m 2. (vacant land) solar m; **building ~** obra f 3. GEO, HIST yacimiento m 4. COMPUT página f, sitio; **Web ~** página [or sitio] web m. vt situar

**sit-in** ['sɪt·ɪn] n sentada f; **to hold a ~** hacer una sentada

**sitting duck** n inf blanco m fácil

**sitting room** n salón m

**situate** ['sɪtʃ·u·eɪt] vt ubicar; (in context) situar

**situated** ['sɪtʃ·u·eɪ·tɪd] adj situado, -a; **to be ~ near the station** estar ubicado cerca de la estación; **to be well/badly ~** estar bien/mal situado

**situation** [ˌsɪtʃ·u·ˈeɪ·ʃən] n situación f;

**according to the ~** conforme a la situación

**sit-up** ['sɪt·ʌp] n **to do ~s** hacer abdominales

**six** [sɪks] adj, n seis m; **in ~ figures** por encima de cien mil

**sixteen** [sɪk·ˈstin] adj, n dieciséis m; s. a. **eight**

**sixteenth** [ˌsɪk·ˈstinθ] I. adj decimosexto, -a II. n 1. (order) decimosexto, -a m, f 2. (date) dieciséis m 3. (fraction) dieciseisavo m; s. a. **eighth**

**sixth** [sɪksθ] I. adj sexto, -a II. n 1. (order) sexto, -a m, f 2. (date) seis m 3. (fraction) sexto m; s. a. **eighth**

**sixtieth** ['sɪk·sti·əθ] I. adj sexagésimo, -a II. n (order) sexagésimo, -a m, f; (fraction) sesentavo m; s. a. **eighth**

**sixty** ['sɪk·sti] adj, n <-ies> sesenta m; s. a. **eighty**

**size**[1] [saɪz] n (person, thing, space) tamaño m; (problem) magnitud f; (clothes) talla f; (shoes) número m; **to be the same ~** ser de las mismas dimensiones (**as** que); **to increase/decrease in ~** aumentar/disminuir de tamaño

◆**size up** vt evaluar

**size**[2] [saɪz] n cola f

**skate**[1] [skeɪt] SPORTS I. n patín m II. vi patinar; **to ~ over an issue** tocar un tema muy por encima

**skate**[2] [skeɪt] n (fish) raya f

**skateboard** ['skeɪt·bɔrd] n monopatín m

**skateboarder** n skater mf

**skater** n patinador(a) m(f); **figure ~** patinador(a) m(f) artístico, -a

**skating rink** n pista f de patinaje

**skeleton** ['skel·ɪ·tən] n ANAT esqueleto m, cacastle m AmC, Méx; **to be reduced to a ~** quedarse en los huesos; (boat, plane) armazón m; (building) estructura f; (book, report) esquema m ► **to have ~s in one's closet** tener un secreto vergonzoso

**skeleton key** n llave f maestra

**skeptic** ['skep·tɪk] n escéptico, -a m, f

**skeptical** adj escéptico, -a

**sketch** [sketʃ] I. n 1. ART boceto m 2. (draft) borrador m 3. (outline) esquema m 4. THEAT, TV sketch m II. vt hacer un borrador de; ART hacer un boceto de

**III.** *vi* ART hacer bocetos

**sketchy** ['sketʃ·ɪ] <-ier, -iest> *adj* (*vague*) impreciso, -a; (*incomplete*) incompleto, -a

**skewer** ['skjuː·ər] **I.** *n* pincho *m* **II.** *vt* ensartar

**ski** [skiː] **I.** *n* esquí *m*; **on ~s** con esquís **II.** *vi* esquiar; **to ~ down a slope** bajar una pista esquiando

**ski boot** *n* bota *f* de esquí

**skid** [skɪd] **I.** <-dd-> *vi* **1.** (*on ice*) patinar, colear *AmC, Ant*; **to ~ to a halt** AUTO derrapar; **to ~ off the road** derrapar y salirse de la carretera **2.** (*slide*) deslizarse (**along, across** sobre) **II.** *n* AUTO derrape *m* ▶ **to be on the ~s** andar de capa caída

**skier** ['skiː·ər] *n* esquiador(a) *m(f)*

**skiing** *n* esquí *m*; **~ equipment** equipo *m* de esquiar; **~ lesson** clase *f* de esquí

**ski instructor** *n* monitor(a) *m(f)* de esquí

**ski jump** *n* salto *m* de esquí; (*runway*) trampolín *m*

**ski lift** *n* telesquí *m*; (*with chairs*) telesilla *m*

**skill** [skɪl] *n* **1.** (*ability*) habilidad *f*; **to involve some ~** requerir cierta destreza **2.** (*technique*) técnica *f*; **communication ~s** facilidad *f* de comunicación; **language ~s** habilidad *f* para los idiomas; **negotiating ~s** artes *f pl* de negociación

**skilled** *adj* **1.** (*trained*) preparado, -a; (*skillful*) hábil, habiloso, -a *Chile, Perú* **2.** (*requiring skill*) cualificado, -a; **~ labor** mano de obra *f* cualificada

**skillful** ['skɪl·fəl] *adj* hábil, tinoso, -a *Col, Ven*

**skim** [skɪm] <-mm-> **I.** *vt* **1.** CULIN espumar; (*milk*) desnatar **2.** (*move above*) rozar **II.** *vi* **to ~ over** pasar rozando; **to ~ through** *fig* hojear

**skin mask** *n* pasamontañas *m inv*

**skin** [skɪn] **I.** *n* **1.** piel *f*; (*fruit*) cáscara *f*; **to be soaked to the ~** estar calado hasta los huesos **2.** TECH revestimiento *m* **3.** (*milk*) nata *f* ▶ **to be all ~ and bone(s)** estar en los huesos; **it's no ~ off his/her back** ni le va ni le viene; **by the ~ of one's teeth** por los pelos; **to**

**jump out of one's ~** pegarse un susto de muerte; **to get under sb's ~** afectar a alguien **II.** <-nn-> *vt* despellejar

**skincare** *n* cuidado *m* de la piel

**skin-deep** *adj* epidérmico, -a; (*beauty*) superficial

**skinhead** ['skɪn·hed] *n* cabeza *mf* rapada

**skinny** ['skɪn·ɪ] **I.** <-ier, -iest> *adj* flaco, -a, charcón, -ona *Arg, Bol, Urug* **II.** *n sl* verdad *f*

**skip** [skɪp] **I.** <-pp-> *vi* **1.** saltar (**from/to** de/a); (*rope*) saltar a la comba **2.** (*CD*) saltarse **II.** <-pp-> *vt* saltarse; **to ~ class** faltar a clase; **to ~ rope** saltar a la comba; **to ~ a grade** saltarse un curso **III.** *n* brinco *m*

**skipper** ['skɪp·ər] **I.** *n* NAUT patrón, -ona *m, f*; *inf* jefe, -a *m, f* **II.** *vt* (*aircraft*) pilotar; (*team*) capitanear

**ski rack** *n* portaesquís *m inv*

**ski resort** *n* estación *f* de esquí

**skirt** [skɜrt] **I.** *n* falda *f*, pollera *f AmL* **II.** *vt* evitar; (*path, road*) rodear

**ski slope** *n* pista *f* de esquí

**skull** [skʌl] *n* calavera *f*; ANAT cráneo *m* ▶ **to be bored out of one's ~** estar más aburrido que una ostra

**sky** [skaɪ] <-ies> *n* cielo *m*; **under blue skies** bajo el cielo azul ▶ **the ~'s the limit** todo es posible; **to praise to the skies** poner por las nubes

**sky-blue** [ˌskaɪ·bluː] *adj* azul celeste *inv*

**skydiving** ['skaɪˌdaɪ·vɪŋ] *n* caída *m* libre

**sky-high** [ˌskaɪ·ˈhaɪ] **I.** *adv* por las nubes; **to go ~** (*prices*) dispararse **II.** *adj* (*prices*) astronómico, -a

**skyjack** ['skaɪ·dʒæk] *vt* secuestrar

**skylight** ['skaɪ·laɪt] *n* tragaluz *m*

**skyline** ['skaɪ·laɪn] *n* (*horizon*) horizonte *m*

**skyscraper** ['skaɪ·skreɪ·pər] *n* rascacielos *m inv*

**slab** [slæb] *n* (*stone*) losa *f*; (*concrete*) bloque *m*; (*wood*) tabla *f*; (*cake, cheese*) trozo *m*; (*chocolate*) tableta *f*

**slack** [slæk] **I.** *adj* (*rope, piece of work*) flojo, -a; (*muscle*) flácido, -a; (*student*) vago, -a; (*paying*) negligente; (*period, season*) de poca actividad **II.** *n* COM período *m* de inactividad ▶ **to cut sb some ~** *sl* dar más tiempo a alguien **III.** *vi* hacer el vago

**slacken** ['slæk·ən] **I.** *vt* aflojar; (*speed, vigilance*) reducir; (*pace*) aflojar **II.** *vi* aflojarse, petaquearse *Col*; (*demand, intensity*) disminuir

**slacker** ['slæk·ər] *n* vago, -a *m, f*

**slackness** ['slæk·nɪs] *n* 1. (*negligence*) negligencia *f*; (*discipline*) relajamiento *m* 2. COM inactividad *f* 3. (*laziness*) pereza *f*

**slacks** [slæks] *npl* pantalón *m* de sport

**slam** [slæm] **I.** <-mm-> *vt* 1. (*strike*) golpear; **to ~ the door** dar un portazo 2. (*criticize*) poner por los suelos **II.** <-mm-> *vi* cerrarse de golpe; **to ~ against/into** chocar contra/con **III.** *n* (*door*) portazo *m*

**slammer** ['slæm·ər] *n* chirona *f*, cana *f AmS*, bote *m Méx*, guandoca *f Col*

**slander** ['slæn·dər] **I.** *n* calumnia *f* **II.** *vt* calumniar

**slang** [slæŋ] *n* argot *m*

**slangy** <-ier, -iest> *adj* argótico, -a

**slant** [slænt] **I.** *vi* inclinarse **II.** *vt* (*make diagonal*) inclinar **III.** *n* 1. (*slope*) inclinación *f*; **on a ~** en pendiente 2. (*perspective*) perspectiva *f*

**slanting** *adj* inclinado, -a; (*eyes*) rasgado, -a

**slap** [slæp] **I.** *n* palmada *f*; **a ~ in the face** una bofetada, una biaba *Arg, Urug*, un bife *Arg, Urug*, *fig* un insulto **II.** <-pp-> *vt* dar una palmada, guantear *AmL*; **to ~ the book onto the table** tirar el libro en la mesa **III.** *adv* de lleno; **to drive ~** chocar de lleno (**into** contra)

◆**slap down** *vt* 1. tirar 2. (*silence*) hacer callar

**slapdash** ['slæp·dæʃ] *adj* chapucero, -a

**slash** [slæʃ] **I.** *vt* 1. (*cut*) rajar; **to ~ one's wrists** cortarse las venas 2. (*prices, spending*) rebajar drásticamente; (*budget*) recortar drásticamente **II.** *n* 1. (*cut*) corte *m* 2. (*swinging blow*) latigazo *m* 3. FASHION raja *f* 4. TYPO barra *f*

**slate** [sleɪt] **I.** *n* 1. pizarra *f*; POL lista *f* de candidatos ▶ **to wipe the ~ clean** hacer borrón y cuenta nueva **II.** *vt* (*schedule*) programar

**slaughter** ['slɔ·tər] **I.** *vt* (*animal*) matar, beneficiar *AmL*, carnear *CSur*, (*person*) masacrar; *fig* dar una paliza a **II.** *n* (*animal*) matanza *f*, beneficio *AmL*, carneada *f Arg, Chile, Par, Urug*; (*person*) masacre *f*; *fig* paliza *f*

**Slav** [slav] *adj, n* eslavo, -a *m, f*

**slave** [sleɪv] **I.** *n* esclavo, -a *m, f* ▶ **to be a ~ to fashion** ser un esclavo de la moda **II.** *vi* trabajar como un burro

**slavery** ['sleɪ·və·ri] *n* esclavitud *f*

**Slavic** ['sla·vɪk] *adj, n* eslavo, -a *m, f*

**sleaze** [sliz] *n* sordidez *f*; POL corrupción *f*

**sleazy** ['sli·zi] <-ier, -iest> *adj* sórdido, -a; (*person*) con mala pinta; POL corrupto, -a

**sled** [sled] *n* trineo *m*

**sledge** [sledʒ], **sledgehammer** ['sledʒ·ˌhæm·ər] *n* almádena *f*

**sleek** [slik] *adj* (*fur, hair*) lacio, -a y brillante; (*car*) de líneas elegantes; (*person*) muy aseado, -a

**sleep** [slip] **I.** *n* 1. sueño *m;* **to go** [*or* **get**] **to ~** dormirse; **to fall into a deep ~** dormirse profundamente; **to (not) lose ~** (no) perder el sueño (**over** por); **to put sb to ~** dormir a alguien 2. *inf* (*substance*) legañas *fpl;* **to rub the ~ from one's eyes** quitarse las legañas **II.** <slept, slept> *vi* dormir; **to ~ sound(ly)** dormir profundamente; **~ tight!** ¡que duermas bien! ▶ **to ~ on it** consultarlo con la almohada

◆**sleep around** *vi* acostarse con cualquiera

◆**sleep in** *vi* dormir hasta tarde

◆**sleep off** *vt* **to sleep it off** dormir la mona [*or AmL* la cruda]

◆**sleep out** *vi* dormir al aire libre

◆**sleep through** *vt* **to ~ noise** no despertarse con el ruido; **to ~ the entire trip** dormir durante todo el viaje

◆**sleep together** *vi* dormir juntos; (*sex*) acostarse juntos

**sleeper** ['sli·pər] *n* 1. **to be a heavy/light ~** tener el sueño profundo/ligero 2. RAIL coche *m* cama

**sleeping bag** *n* saco *m* de dormir

**sleeping car** *n* coche *m* cama

**sleeping pill** *n* somnífero *m*

**sleepless** ['slip·lɪs] *adj* insomne; (*night*) en vela

**sleepwalk** ['slip·ˌwɔk] *vi* caminar dormido, -a; **he ~s** es sonámbulo

**sleepwalker** ['slip·ˌwɔ·kər] *n* sonámbulo, -a *m, f*

**sleepy** ['sli·pi] <-ier, -iest> *adj* **1.** (*drowsy*) somnoliento, -a **2.** (*quiet*) aletargado, -a

**sleepyhead** ['sli·pi·hed] *n* dormilón, -ona *m, f*

**sleet** [slit] **I.** *n* aguanieve *f* **II.** *vi* **it is ~ing** cae aguanieve

**sleeve** [sliv] *n* **1.** (*shirt*) manga *f*; **to roll up one's ~s** arremangarse **2.** (*cover*) manguito *m* **3.** (*record*) funda *f* ▶ **to have** sth up one's **~** tener algo en la manga

**sleeveless** ['sliv·lɪs] *adj* sin mangas

**sleigh** [sleɪ] *n* trineo *m*

**slender** ['slen·dər] *adj* delgado, -a; (*rod, branch*) fino, -a; (*majority, resources*) escaso, -a; (*chance*) remoto, -a

**slept** [slept] *pt, pp of* **sleep**

**slice** [slaɪs] **I.** *n* (*bread*) rebanada *f*; (*ham*) loncha *f*; (*meat*) tajada *f*; (*cake, pizza*) trozo *m*; (*cucumber, lemon*) rodaja *f*; (*credit, profits*) parte *f* ▶ **to get a ~ of the pie** sacar tajada **II.** *vt* cortar ▶ **any way you ~ it** lo mires por donde lo mires

♦**slice off** *vt* cortar; (*reduce*) reducir en

♦**slice up** *vt* cortar

**sliced** *adj* (*bread*) en rebanadas; (*ham*) en lonchas; (*meat*) fileteado, -a; (*cake*) troceado; (*cucumber, lemon*) en rodajas

**slick** [slɪk] **I.** <-er, -est> *adj* (*person*) hábil, *pej* astuto; (*performance*) pulido, -a **II.** *n* (*oil*) marea *f* negra

**slide** [slaɪd] **I.** <slid, slid> *vi* (*glide*) deslizarse; (*slip*) resbalar; **the door ~s open/shut** la puerta se abre/se cierra corriéndola; **to ~ back into one's old habits** volver a las viejas costumbres **II.** <slid, slid> *vt* deslizar **III.** *n* **1.** (*act*) deslizamiento *m* **2.** (*incline*) rampa *f*; (*playground*) tobogán *m*; **water ~** tobogán acuático **3.** PHOT diapositiva *f* **4.** GEO desprendimiento *m* **5.** FIN caída *f*

**slide projector** *n* proyector *m* de diapositivas

**slide rule** *n* regla *f* de cálculo

**sliding** *adj* (*sunroof*) corredizo, -a; (*door*) corredero, -a

**slight** [slaɪt] **I.** <-er, -est> *adj* (*person*) delgado, -a; (*chance*) escaso, -a; (*error*) pequeño, -a; **the ~est thing** la menor tontería; **not in the ~est** en absoluto; **not to have the ~est** (*idea*) no tener ni la menor idea **II.** *n* desaire *m* **III.** *vt* despreciar

**slightly** *adv* un poco; **to be ~ familiar with sth** conocer algo muy poco

**slim** [slɪm] **I.** <slimmer, slimmest> *adj* (*person*) delgado, -a; (*cigarette, book*) fino, -a; (*chance*) escaso, -a **II.** <-mm-> *vi* adelgazar; (*diet*) hacer régimen

**slimebag, slimeball** *n sl* asqueroso, -a *m, f*

**slimy** ['slaɪ·mi] <-ier, -iest> *adj* viscoso, -a; *fig* asqueroso, -a

**sling** [slɪŋ] <slung, slung> **I.** *n* **1.** (*bandage*) cabestrillo *m* **2.** (*for baby*) canguro *m* **3.** (*weapon*) honda *f* **II.** *vt* **1.** (*fling*) lanzar, aventar *Méx* **2.** (*hang*) colgar

**slink** [slɪŋk] <slunk> *vi* **to ~ away** [*or* **off**] escabullirse

**slip** [slɪp] <-pp-> **I.** *n* **1.** (*slipping*) resbalón *m* **2.** (*mistake*) error *m*; **~ of the tongue** lapsus *m* **3.** COM resguardo *m* **4.** (*underwear*) combinación *f* **5.** BOT esqueje *m* ▶ **to give the ~** dar esquinazo **II.** *vi* **1.** (*slide*) resbalarse **2.** (*move*) deslizarse; **to ~ into a pub** colarse en un bar **3.** (*decline*) decaer; **to ~ into a depression** caer en una depresión **III.** *vt* **1.** (*put*) deslizar; **to ~ a note/some money** pasar una nota/dinero disimuladamente (**to** a); **to ~ in a comment** dejar caer un comentario **2.** (*escape*) escabullirse de; **to ~ sb's attention** pasar desapercibido por alguien; **it ~ped my mind** se me olvidó

♦**slip away** *vi* **1.** (*leave unnoticed*) escabullirse (**from** de) **2.** (*pass*) pasar rápidamente **3.** (*die*) morirse

♦**slip by** *vi* pasar rápidamente; (*unnoticed*) pasar inadvertido, -a

♦**slip down** *vi* dejarse caer

♦**slip in** *vi* colarse

♦**slip off** **I.** *vi* **1.** (*leave*) escabullir-

S

se **2.** (*fall off*) caerse **II.** vt (*clothes*) quitarse

◆**slip on** vt (*clothes*) ponerse

◆**slip out 1.** (*leave*) escabullirse **2.** (*say*) escaparse; **the name slipped out** se me escapó el nombre

◆**slip up** vi equivocarse

**slip-on** ['slɪp·ən] adj (*shoes*) sin cordones

**slippery** ['slɪp·ə·ri] <-ier, -iest> adj (*surface*) resbaladizo, -a; (*soap*) escurridizo, -a; (*character*) <u>que</u> no es de fiar ▶ **to be on the ~ slope** encontrarse en un terreno resbaladizo

**slipshod** ['slɪp·ʃad] adj chapucero, -a

**slip-up** ['slɪp·ʌp] n desliz m

**slit** [slɪt] **I.** <slit, slit> vt cortar; **to ~ one's wrists** cortarse las venas **II.** n (*opening*) rendija f; (*tear*) raja f

**slither** ['slɪð·ər] vi deslizarse (**down/on** por/sobre)

**sliver** ['slɪv·ər] n (*lemon*) rodajita f; (*cake*) trocito m; (*glass, wood*) astilla f

**slob** [slab] n dejado, -a m, f

**slog** [slag] inf **I.** <-gg-> vi (*walk*) avanzar con gran esfuerzo **II.** <-gg-> vt (*hit*) golpear **III.** n esfuerzo m

**slogan** ['slou·gən] n eslogan m

**slop** [slap] <-pp-> inf **I.** n (*food*) aguachirle f **II.** vi derramarse; **to ~ about** [or **around**] salpicarlo todo **III.** vt derramar

**slope** [sloup] **I.** n inclinación f; (*up*) cuesta f; (*down*) declive m; (*ski*) pista f **II.** vi inclinarse; **to ~ down** descender, bajar; **to ~ up** ascender, subir **III.** vt inclinar

**sloping** adj inclinado, -a; (*shoulders*) caído, -a

**sloppiness** n falta f de cuidado

**sloppy** ['slap·i] <-ier, -iest> adj (*messy*) descuidado, -a

**slot** [slat] **I.** n **1.** (*opening*) ranura f **2.** TV espacio m **II.** <-tt-> vt encajar (**in** en)

**slot machine** ['slat·mə·ʃin] n tragaperras f inv

**slouch** [slautʃ] **I.** vi **1.** (*bend*) encorvarse **2.** (*walk*) ir arrastrando los pies **II.** n to be <u>no</u> ~ no ser manco

**Slovakia** [slou·'va·ki·ə] n Eslovaquia f

**Slovene** ['slou·vin] **I.** adj esloveno, -a **II.** n **1.** esloveno, -a m, f **2.** LING es-

loveno m

**Slovenia** [slou·'vi·ni·ə] n Eslovenia f

**Slovenian** n see **Slovene**

**slovenly** ['slʌv·ən·li] adj descuidado, -a

**slow** [slou] **I.** adj **1.** lento, -a; **to be ~ to do sth** tardar en hacer algo; **to be** (**10 minutes**) **~** ir (10 minutos) retrasado **2.** (*stupid*) torpe, guanaco, -a AmL **II.** vi ir más despacio; **to ~ to a halt** detenerse gradualmente **III.** vt frenar

◆**slow down I.** vi **1.** (*speed*) reducir **2.** (*be less active*) moderar el ritmo de vida **II.** vt ralentizar

**slowly** adv lentamente; **~ but surely** lento pero seguro

**slow motion** n cámara f lenta; **in ~** a cámara lenta

**slowpoke** ['slou·pouk] n tortuga f

**slow-witted** adj perezoso, -a

**sluggish** ['slʌg·ɪʃ] adj (*person*) perezoso, -a, conchudo, -a Méx; (*progress, pace*) lento, -a; (*market*) flojo, -a

**sluice** [slus] **I.** n (*gate*) compuerta f **II.** vt regar; **to ~ down** enjuagar

**slum** [slʌm] n suburbio m

**slump** [slʌmp] **I.** n ECON (*decline*) depresión f; **~ in prices** súbita caída de precios; (*recession*) recesión f **II.** vi desplomarse; (*prices*) caer

**slung** [slʌŋ] pt, pp of **sling**

**slunk** [slʌŋk] pt, pp of **slink**

**slur** [slɜr] n **1.** (*insult*) calumnia f **2.** (*in speech*) pronunciación f incomprensible

**slurp** [slɜrp] inf **I.** vt, vi sorber **II.** n sorbetón m

**slush** [slʌʃ] n **1.** (*snow*) nieve f medio derretida **2.** (*sentimentality*) sentimentalismo m

**slushy** adj <-ier, -iest> **1.** (*snow*) a medio derretir **2.** (*sentimental*) sentimentaloide

**slut** [slʌt] n puta f

**sly** [slaɪ] adj **1.** (*secretive*) sigiloso, -a; (*smile*) sutil; **on the ~** a hurtadillas **2.** (*crafty*) astuto, -a, songo, -a Col, Méx

**smack** [smæk] **I.** vt **1.** (*slap*) dar un manotazo a **2.** (*hit*) golpear; **to ~ one's lips** relamerse los labios **II.** n inf **1.** (*slap*) bofetada f; (*soft blow*) palmada f **2.** (*kiss*) besazo m **3.** (*noise*) ruidazo m **III.** *adv* **1.** (*loudly*) haciendo un fuerte ruido **2.** (*directly*) justamente; **~ in the middle** justo en el medio

**small** [smɔl] **I.** *adj* **1.** pequeño, -a; (*person*) bajo, -a, petizo, -a *CSur, Bol*; (*young*) joven; **on a ~ scale** a pequeña escala **2.** TYPO minúscula; **with a ~ 'c'** con 'c' minúscula ► **it's a ~ world** el mundo es un pañuelo *prov* **II.** *n* **the ~ of the back** la región lumbar

**small change** *n* calderilla *f*, chaucha *f Bol, Chile, Perú*, chirolas *fpl Arg*

**small-minded** [ˌsmɔlˈmaɪn·dɪd] *adj* estrecho, -a de miras

**smallpox** [ˈsmɔl·pɑks] *n* viruela *f*

**small-scale** *adj* a pequeña escala

**smart** [smɑrt] **I.** *adj* **1.** (*clever*) inteligente **2.** (*elegant*) elegante **3.** (*quick*) rápido, -a; **at a ~ pace** rápidamente **II.** *vi* escocer; **my eyes ~** me pican los ojos **III.** *n* escozor m

**smarten** [ˈsmɑr·tən] **I.** *vt* **to ~ up** arreglar **II.** *vi* **to ~ up** arreglarse

**smash** [smæʃ] **I.** *vt* (*break*) romper, quebrar *AmL*; (*crush*) destruir; (*glass*) hacer pedazos; (*record*) pulverizar **II.** *vi* **1.** (*break*) romperse, quebrarse *AmL*; (*glass*) hacerse pedazos **2.** (*strike*) chocar (**into** contra) **III.** *n* **1.** (*sound*) estruendo m **2.** (*accident*) colisión *f*

♦**smash in** *vt* forzar; **to smash sb's face in** partir la cara a alguien

♦**smash up** *vt* hacer pedazos; (*car*) destrozar

**smashed** *adj inf* borracho, -a; **to get ~** emborracharse

**smattering** [ˈsmæt·ər·ɪŋ] *n* nociones *fpl*

**smear** [smɪr] **I.** *vt* **1.** (*spread*) untar **2.** (*attack*) desprestigiar **II.** *n* **1.** (*blotch*) mancha *f* **2.** (*accusation*) calumnia *f*

**smell** [smel] <smelled *or* smelt, smelled *or* smelt> **I.** *vi, vt* oler; (*animal*) olfatear; (*stink*) apestar **II.** *n* **1.** (*sense*) olfato m **2.** (*odor*) olor m; (*stink*) peste *f* **3.** (*trace*) sabor m; **the ~ of victory** el sabor del triunfo

**smelly** [ˈsmel·i] *adj* <-ier, -iest> apestoso, -a

**smelt¹** [smelt] *vt* MIN fundir

**smelt²** [smelt] *pt, pp of* **smell**

**smile** [smaɪl] **I.** *n* sonrisa *f*; **to be all ~s** ser todo, -a sonrisas; **to give sb a ~** sonreír a alguien **II.** *vi* sonreír; **to ~ at/about** reírse de; **to ~ on sb/sth** mirar con buenos ojos a alguien/algo

**smiling** *adj* sonriente

**smirk** [smɜrk] **I.** *vi* sonreír afectadamente **II.** *n* sonrisa *f* afectada

**smog** [smɑg] *n* niebla *f* y humo

**smoke** [smoʊk] **I.** *n* humo m; (*cigarette*) pitillo m ► **where there's ~, there's fire** cuando el río suena, agua lleva; **to go up in ~** esfumarse **II.** *vt* **1.** fumar, pitar *AmS*; **to ~ a pipe** fumar en pipa **2.** CULIN ahumar ► **to ~ the peace pipe** fumar la pipa de la paz; **put that in your pipe and ~ it!** ¡métetelo donde te quepa! **III.** *vi* echar humo; (*tobacco*) fumar, pitar *AmS*

♦**smoke out** *vt* (*scandal*) destapar

**smoke bomb** *n* bomba *f* de humo

**smoked** *adj* ahumado, -a; **~ salmon** salmón ahumado

**smoke detector** *n* detector m de humo

**smokeless** [ˈsmoʊk·lɪs] *adj* sin humo; (*tobacco*) de mascar

**smoker** *n* fumador(a) m(f); **to be a heavy ~** fumar como un carretero

**smoking** *n* fumar m; **to give up ~** dejar de fumar; **~ ban** prohibición de fumar

**smoky** [ˈsmoʊ·ki] *adj* <-ier, -iest> **1.** (*filled with smoke*) lleno, -a de humo **2.** (*producing smoke*) humeante **3.** CULIN ahumado, -a

**smolder** [ˈsmoʊl·dər] *vi* **1.** arder sin llama; (*cigarette*) consumirse lentamente **2.** *fig* arder

**smooch** [smutʃ] **I.** *vi* besuquearse **II.** *n* **to have a ~** besuquearse

**smooth** [smuð] **I.** *adj* liso, -a; (*skin, texture, landing, drink*) suave; (*sea, flight*) tranquilo, -a; **as ~ as silk** suave como la seda; **to be a ~ talker** tener un pico de oro **II.** *vt* allanar

♦**smooth down** *vt* alisar

♦**smooth over** *vt* (*difficulty*) solucionar

**smoothie** *n*, **smoothy** [ˈsmu·ði] *n inf* zalamero, -a m, f

**smooth-shaven** *adj* bien afeitado, -a

**smother** [ˈsmʌð·ər] *vt* **1.** (*suffocate*) ahogar **2.** (*suppress*) contener **3.** **to be**

S

~ed estar cubierto (**in** de)

**smudge** [smʌdʒ] I. *vt* (*smear*) emborronar; (*reputation*) destruir II. *vi* mancharse; (*make-up*) correrse III. *n* mancha *f*

**smudgy** ['smʌdʒ·i] *adj* <-ier, -iest> manchado, -a

**smug** [smʌg] *adj* <-gg-> presumido, -a; **to be ~** presumir (**about** de)

**smuggle** ['smʌg·əl] *vt* pasar de contrabando

**smuggling** ['smʌg·lɪŋ] *n* contrabando *m*

**smutty** ['smʌt·i] *adj* <-ier, -iest> obsceno, -a; (*joke*) verde

**snack** [snæk] I. *n* refrigerio *m,* puntal *m AmL;* **to have a ~** tomarse un tentempié II. *vi* picar

**snack bar** *n* cafetería *f*

**snag** [snæg] I. *n* 1. (*problem*) dificultad *f;* **to hit a ~** tropezar con una dificultad 2. (*clothes*) enganchón *m* II. <-gg-> *vt* enganchar; (*cause problems*) causar problemas III. <-gg-> *vi* engancharse (**on** en)

**snail** [sneɪl] *n* caracol *m* ► **at a ~'s pace** a paso de tortuga

**snail mail** *n* correo *m* ordinario

**snake** [sneɪk] I. *n* serpiente *f* II. *vi* serpentear, viborear *Arg, Urug*

**snap** [snæp] <-pp-> I. *n* 1. (*sound*) chasquido *m* 2. (*fastener*) cierre *m* automático 3. **a cold ~** una ola de frío 4. **a ginger ~** una galleta de jengibre 5. PHOT foto *f* II. *adj* repentino, -a III. *vi* 1. (*break*) romperse 2. **to ~ back** recolocarse; **to ~ at sb** (*bite*) intentar morder a alguien; (*answer*) contestar a alguien de forma brusca IV. *vt* 1. (*break*) romper 2. (*sound*) chasquear; **to ~ one's fingers** chasquear los dedos 3. PHOT fotografiar

◆**snap out** *vi* **to ~ of sth** quitarse algo de encima; **~ of it!** ¡anímate!

◆**snap up** *vt* lanzarse sobre

**snappy** ['ʃnæp·i] *adj* <-ier, -iest> 1. *inf* FASHION de lo más elegante; **to be a ~ dresser** vestir con elegancia 2. (*quick*) rápido, -a; **make it ~!** ¡date prisa!

**snarl¹** [snɑrl] I. *vi* gruñir II. *n* gruñido *m*

**snarl²** [snɑrl] *n* 1. (*tangle*) enredo *m*

2. (*traffic jam*) atasco *m*

**snarl-up** ['snɑrl·ʌp] *n* atasco *m*

**snatch** [snætʃ] I. *vt* 1. (*grab*) agarrar; **to ~ sth** (**away**) arrebatar algo (**from** a) 2. (*steal*) robar; **to ~ victory** hacerse con el triunfo 3. (*kidnap*) secuestrar II. *vi* quitar algo de las manos; **to ~ at** tratar de arrebatar III. <-es> *n* 1. **to make a ~ at** intentar arrebatar 2. (*kidnapping*) secuestro *m* 3. *vulg* coño *m*

◆**snatch up** *vt* agarrar

**snazzy** ['snæz·i] *adj* <-ier, -iest> de lo más elegante

**sneak** [snik] I. *vi* moverse furtivamente; **to ~ in/out** entrar/salir a hurtadillas; **to ~ away** [*or* **off**] escabullirse II. *vt* hacer furtivamente; **to ~ a look at** mirar con disimulo

**sneaker** ['sni·kər] *n pl* zapatillas *f pl* de deporte

**sneaking** *adj* 1. (*slight*) ligero, -a 2. (*secret*) secreto, -a

**sneaky** ['sni·ki] *adj* <-ier, -iest> furtivo, -a

**sneer** [snɪr] I. *vi* (*mock*) mofarse (**at** de) II. *n* expresión *f* desdeñosa

**sneering** ['snɪr·ɪŋ] *adj* burlón, -ona

**sneeze** [sniz] I. *vi* estornudar ► **that's not something to be ~d at** no es de despreciar II. *n* estornudo *m*

**snicker** ['snɪk·ər] I. *vi* reírse con disimulo (**at** de) II. *n* risa *f* disimulada

**snide** [snaɪd] *adj* vil

**sniff** [snɪf] I. *vi* (*inhale*) sorber; **to ~ at** oler; (*disdain*) despreciar; **to go ~ing around** husmear (**for** en busca de) ► **not to be ~ed at** no ser de despreciar II. *vt* olfatear; (*person*) oler III. *n* **to have a ~** oler; **to catch a ~ of** captar el olor de

◆**sniff out** *vt* descubrir; (*by smelling*) encontrar olfateando

**sniffer dog** ['snɪf·ər·ˌdɔg] *n* perro *m* rastreador

**sniffle** ['snɪf·əl] I. *vi* 1. (*sniff*) sorberse los mocos 2. (*cry*) lloriquear II. *npl* **to have the ~s** estar acatarrado

**snip** [snɪp] I. *vt* cortar II. *n* 1. (*cut*) tijeretazo *m* 2. (*cloth*) recorte *m*

**sniper** ['snaɪ·pər] *n* francotirador(a) *m(f)*

**snitch** [snɪtʃ] *inf* I. *vi* chivarse (**on**

de) II. vt (*steal*) birlar III. <-es> n
1. (*thief*) caco mf 2. (*tattletale*) soplón,
-ona m, f

**snivel** ['snɪv·əl] I. <-ll-, -l-> vi (*cry*) lloriquear II. n lloriqueo m

**snobbish** ['snab·ɪʃ] <more, most> adj
esnob

**snoop** [snup] pej, inf I. n fisgón, -ona m, f
II. vi fisgonear; **to ~ around** husmear

**snooty** ['snu·t̪i] <-ier, -iest> adj presumido, -a, pituco, -a AmS

**snooze** [snuz] inf I. vi echar una cabezada; (*lightly*) dormitar II. n cabezada f

**snore** [snɔr] MED I. vi roncar II. n ronquido m

**snort** [snɔrt] I. vi resoplar II. vt (*inhale*)
esnifar III. n bufido m

**snot** [snat] n moco m

**snotty** ['snat̪·i] <-ier, -iest> adj inf 1. lleno, -a de mocos 2. (*rude*) petulante

**snout** [snaʊt] n hocico m; (*person*) napia f

**snow** [snoʊ] I. n 1. METEO nieve f; **a
blanket of ~** un manto de nieve 2. (*cocaine*) nieve f II. vi nevar
◆**snow in** vt to be snowed in estar aprisionado por la nieve
◆**snow under** vt to be snowed under
estar desbordado (**with** de)

**snowball** ['snoʊ·bɔl] I. n bola f de nieve
▶ **to not have a ~'s chance in hell
(of doing sth)** no tener ni la más remota posibilidad (de hacer algo) II. vi fig
aumentar progresivamente

**snowboard** n snowboard m

**snowbound** ['snoʊ·baʊnd] adj aprisionado, -a por la nieve

**snowfall** n nevada f; (*snowstorm*) tormenta f de nieve, nevazón m Arg, Chile,
Ecua

**snowflake** n copo m de nieve

**snowman** n muñeco m de nieve

**snowmobile** n moto f de nieve, trineo
m motorizado

**snowstorm** n tormenta f de nieve

**snow tire** n neumático m de nieve

**snowy** ['snoʊ·i] adj (*region, season*) de
mucha nieve; (*street, field*) cubierto,
-a de nieve; (*hair, flowers*) blanco, -a
como la nieve

**snub** [snʌb] I. <-bb-> vt hacer el vacío

II. n desaire m

**snub-nosed** adj (*person*) de nariz respingona

**snuff** [snʌf] I. vt 1. (*put out*) apagar
2. inf (*end*) acabar con II. n rapé m

**snug** [snʌg] adj (*cozy*) acogedor(a);
(*warm*) calentito, -a; (*tight*) ajustado, -a

**snuggle** ['snʌg·əl] vi acurrucarse (**up to**
contra)

**so** [soʊ] I. adv 1. (*same way*) tan,
tanto; **~ do/did I** yo también; **~ to
speak** por así decirlo 2. (*like that*) así;
**~ they say** eso dicen; **is that ~?** ¿de
verdad?; **I hope/think ~** eso espero/
creo 3. (*degree*) tan, tanto; **~ late** tan
tarde; **~ many books** tantos libros; **not
~ ugly as that** no tan feo como eso;
**would you be ~ kind as to...?** ¿sería tan amable de...? 4. (*in order that*)
para; **I bought the book ~ that he
would read it** compré el libro para que
él lo leyera 5. (*result*) así; **and ~ she
won** y así ganó ▶ **and ~ on** [*or* **forth**]
etcétera; **or ~** más o menos II. conj
1. (*therefore*) por (lo) tanto 2. (*afterwards*) ~ (**then**) **he told me...** y entonces me dijo... 3. (*summing up*) así que;
**~ what?** ¿y qué?; **~ now** entonces; **~,
as I was saying...** entonces, como iba
diciendo... III. interj **~ that's why!**
¡conque era eso!

**soak** [soʊk] I. vt remojar, ensopar AmS
II. vi (*lie in liquid*) estar en remojo III. n
remojo m
◆**soak in** vi penetrar
◆**soak up** vt absorber; (*money, resources*) agotar; (*people*) embelesar;
(*sun*) tomar

**soaking** I. n remojo m; **to get a good ~**
calarse hasta los huesos II. adj ~ (**wet**)
empapado, -a

**so-and-so** ['soʊ·ən·soʊ] n (*person*) fulano m; (*thing*) movida f

**soap** [soʊp] I. n jabón m ▶ **soft ~**
coba f II. vt enjabonar

**soap opera** n telenovela f

**soapy** ['soʊ·pi] <-ier, -iest> adj 1. (*full
of lather*) lleno, -a de jabón 2. (*like
soap*) jabonoso, -a 3. (*flattering*) zalamero, -a

**soar** [sɔr] vi llegar muy alto; (*house*) elevarse mucho; (*temperature, prices*) subir bruscamente; (*hopes*) renacer; (*bird, plane*) remontar el vuelo

**sob** [sab] I. <-bb-> *vi* sollozar II. <-bb-> *vt* decir sollozando III. *n* sollozo *m*

**sober** ['souˑbər] *adj* sobrio, -a; (*mood, atmosphere, expression*) serio, -a; (*attire*) sencillo, -a; (*colors*) discreto, -a; (*assessment*) sensato, -a

◆**sober up** *vi* (*less drunk*) espabilar la borrachera; (*serious*) ponerse serio

**sob story** *n* dramón *m*

**so-called** [ˌsouˑ'kɔld] *adj* presunto, -a

**soccer** ['sak·ər] *n* fútbol *m*

**sociable** ['souˑfəˑbəl] *adj* sociable

**social** ['souˑfəl] *adj* social

**socialist** *n* socialista *mf*

**socialize** ['souˑfəˑlaɪz] I. *vi* alternar con la gente II. *vt* PSYCH socializar; POL, ECON nacionalizar

**social science** *n* ciencia *f* social

**social security** *n* seguridad *f* social

**society** [səˑ'saɪˑəˑt̬i] *n* 1. (*all people*) sociedad *f;* **high ~** alta sociedad; **to be a menace to ~** ser una amenaza para la sociedad 2. (*organization*) asociación *f*

**sociolinguistics** [ˌsouˑsiˑouˑlɪŋˑ'gwɪsˑtɪks] *n* sociolingüística *f*

**sociology** [ˌsouˑsiˑ'alˑəˑdʒi] *n* sociología *f*

**sock¹** [sak] *n* calcetín *m,* media *f* AmL; **knee-high ~** calcetín largo ► **to knock sb's ~s off** dejar a alguien con la boca abierta

**sock²** [sak] I. *vt* (*hit*) dar una piña ► **~ it to 'em!** ¡a por ellos! II. *n* tortazo *m*

**socket** ['sakˑɪt] *n* 1. ELEC enchufe *m,* tomacorriente *m* Arg, Perú; **double/triple ~** enchufe de dos/tres entradas 2. (*eye*) cuenca *f;* (*tooth*) alvéolo *m*

**sod** [sad] *n* césped *m*

**sodden** ['sadˑən] *adj* empapado, -a

**sofa** ['souˑfə] *n* sofá *m*

**soft** [sɔft] *adj* 1. (*not hard*) blando, -a 2. (*smooth*) suave; **~ as silk** suave como la seda 3. (*mild*) ligero, -a; (*drug*) blando, -a 4. (*not bright*) suave; (*lighting, light*) tenue 5. (*sound, music*) agradable; (*voice*) dulce 6. (*lenient*) indulgente; **to go ~** ser muy indulgente (**on** con) 7. (*easy*) fácil; **a ~ target** un blanco fácil

8. (*currency*) débil

**soft-boiled** [ˌsɔftˑ'bɔɪld] *adj* pasado, -a por agua

**soften** ['sɔˑfən] I. *vi* ablandarse; (*butter, ground*) reblandecerse, amelocharse Méx II. *vt* (*butter*) reblandecer; (*skin, color, voice, opinion, words*) suavizar; (*effect*) mitigar; (*blow*) amortiguar

◆**soften up** *vt* ablandar

**soft-hearted** ['sɔftˑˌharˑt̬ɪd] *adj* bondadoso, -a

**softie** ['sɔfˑt̬i] *n* blandengue *mf*

**softly** *adv* 1. (*not roughly*) suavemente; (*shine*) tenuemente 2. (*quietly*) silenciosamente

**softness** ['sɔftˑnɪs] *n* blandura *f;* (*smoothness*) suavidad *f*

**software** ['sɔftˑwer] *n* software *m;* **accounting ~** programa *m* de contabilidad

**softy** ['sɔfˑt̬i] *n* blandengue *mf*

**soggy** ['sagˑi] <-ier, -iest> *adj* empapado, -a

**soil¹** [sɔɪl] *n* AGR suelo *m;* **fertile ~** tierra *f* fértil

**soil²** [sɔɪl] I. *vt form* (*stain*) manchar; (*clothing, shoes*) ensuciar II. *vi* ensuciarse

**solar** ['souˑlər] *adj* solar

**sold** [sould] *pt, pp of* **sell**

**soldier** ['soulˑdʒər] *n* soldado *mf;* (*officer*) militar *mf;* **old ~** veterano *m*

**sole¹** [soul] *adj* (*only*) único, -a; (*exclusive*) exclusivo, -a

**sole²** [soul] *n* (*foot*) planta *f;* (*shoe*) suela *f*

**sole³** [soul] <-(s)> *n* (*fish*) lenguado *m;* **filet of ~** filete de lenguado

**solely** ['soulˑli] *adv* únicamente

**solemn** ['salˑəm] *adj* solemne; (*person, appearance*) serio, -a

**solicit** [səˑ'lɪsˑɪt] I. *vt* solicitar II. *vi* ofrecer por la calle servicios sexuales

**solid** ['salˑɪd] I. *adj* 1. (*hard*) sólido, -a; (*table, door*) robusto, -a; (*meal*) pesado, -a; **to be (as) ~ as a rock** ser duro como una piedra 2. (*not hollow*) macizo, -a 3. (*true*) real; (*facts*) verídico, -a; (*evidence*) sustancial; (*argument*) sólido, -a; (*reasons*) de peso; (*conviction*) firme; (*agreement*) concreto, -a 4. (*uninter-*

rupted) ininterrumpido, -a; (*hour, day, week*) entero, -a **II.** *adv* **to be packed/ frozen** ~ estar abarrotado/como un témpano **III.** *n* sólido *m*

**solidify** [sə'lɪd·ə·faɪ] <-ie-, -ying> **I.** *vi* solidificarse; *fig* concretarse **II.** *vt* solidificar; *fig* reforzar

**solidly** *adv* firmemente; (*unanimously*) unánimemente

**solitary** ['sal·ə·ter·i] *adj* **1.** (*alone, single*) solitario, -a **2.** (*isolated*) solo, -a, íngrimo, -a *AmL*; (*unvisited*) apartado, -a; **to go for a ~ walk** ir a pasear solo

**solo** ['soʊ·loʊ] **I.** *adj* solo, -a **II.** *adv* a solas; **to go ~** lanzarse como solista **III.** *n* MUS solo *m*

**soloist** ['soʊ·loʊ·ɪst] *n* solista *mf*

**soluble** ['sal·jə·bəl] *adj* soluble

**solution** [sə'lu·ʃən] *n* solución *f*

**solve** [salv] *vt* resolver

**solvent** ['sal·vənt] **I.** *n* disolvente *m* **II.** *adj* FIN solvente; CHEM disolvente

**somber** ['sam·bər] *adj* (*mood*) sombrío, -a; (*color*) oscuro, -a

**some** [sʌm] **I.** *adj indef* **1.** *pl* (*several*) algunos, -as; **~ apples** algunas manzanas; **~ people think...** algunos piensan... **2.** (*imprecise*) algún, alguna; (**at**) **~ place** (en) algún lugar; **~ day** algún día; (**at**) **~ time** (en) algún momento; **for ~ time** durante un tiempo; **~ other time** en algún otro momento; **~ time ago** hace algún tiempo; **in ~ way or another** de una u otra manera; **to have ~ idea** tener alguna idea (**of** de) **3.** (*amount*) un poco de, algo de; **~ more tea** un poco más de té; **to have ~ money** tener algo de dinero; **to ~ extent** hasta cierto punto **II.** *pron indef* **1.** *pl* (*several*) algunos; **I would like ~** quisiera algunos; **~ like it, others don't** a unos les gusta, a otros no **2.** (*part of it*) algo **III.** *adv* (*about*) unos, unas; **~ more apples** unas manzanas más; **~ more wine** un poco más de vino

**somebody** ['sʌm·bad·i] *pron indef* alguien; **~ else** otra persona, otro; **~ or other** alguien

**somehow** ['sʌm·haʊ] *adv* **1.** (*through unknown methods*) de alguna manera **2.** (*for an unclear reason*) por algún

motivo **3.** (*come what may*) de un modo u otro

**someone** ['sʌm·wʌn] *pron* ver **somebody**

**someplace** ['sʌm·pleɪs] *adv* en algún lugar

**somersault** ['sʌm·ər·sɔlt] **I.** *n* salto *m* mortal **II.** *vi* dar un salto mortal; (*vehicle*) dar una vuelta de campana

**something** ['sʌm·θɪŋ] **I.** *pron indef, sing* **1.** algo; **~ else/nice** algo más/bonito; **~ or other** alguna cosa; **one can't have ~ for nothing** quien algo quiere, algo le cuesta **2. or ~** o algo así; **six-foot-~** dos metros y pico; **his name is Paul ~** es Paul no sé qué **II.** *n* **a little ~** una cosita; **a certain ~** cierta cosa ▸ **that is really ~!** ¡ésa sí que es buena! **III.** *adv* **~ around \$10** alrededor de 10\$; **~ over/ under \$10** algo más/menos de 10\$

**sometime** ['sʌm·taɪm] *adv* en algún momento; **~ soon** pronto

**sometimes** ['sʌm·taɪmz] *adv* a veces

**somewhat** ['sʌm·hwat] *adv* algo; **to feel ~ better** sentirse un poco mejor

**somewhere** ['sʌm·hwer] *adv* **1.** (*be*) en alguna parte; (*go*) a alguna parte; **to be/ go ~ else** estar en/ir a otra parte; **to get ~** *fig* progresar; **or ~** o así **2.** (*roughly*) alrededor de; **she is ~ around 40** ronda los 40; **he earns ~ around \$40,000** gana unos 40.000\$

**son** [sʌn] *n* hijo *m*

**song** [sɔŋ] *n* canción *f*; (*act*) canto *m* ▸ **~ and dance** (*excuse*) rollo *m*; (**to go**) **for a ~** (venderse) a precio de saldo

**songbook** *n* cancionero *m*

**son-in-law** ['sʌn·ɪn·lɔ] <sons-in-law> *n* yerno *m*

**soon** [sun] *adv* pronto, mero *AmC, Méx*; **~ after** poco después de; **how ~...?** ¿para cuándo...?; **as ~ as possible** lo antes posible; **I would just as ~...** preferiría...

**soot** [sʊt] *n* hollín *m*

**soothing** *adj* tranquilizador(a); (*pain-relieving*) analgésico, -a; (*balsamic*) reparador(a)

**sophisticated** [sə·'fɪs·tə·keɪ·tɪd] *adj* **1.** (*refined*) sofisticado, -a **2.** (*cultured*) culto, -a

S

**sophomore** ['saf·ə·mɔr] *n* estudiante *mf* de segundo año

**sopping** ['sap·ɪŋ] *inf* I. *adj* empapado, -a II. *adv* ~ **wet** empapado, -a

**soppy** ['sap·i] <-ier, -iest> *adj* sensiblero, -a

**sore** [sɔr] I. *adj* 1. (*aching*) dolorido, -a; **to be in ~ need of** necesitar a toda costa; **a ~ point** *fig* un punto delicado 2. *inf* (*offended*) resentido, -a; (*aggrieved*) resentido, -a; **~ loser** mal perdedor II. *n* MED llaga *f*; *fig* recuerdo *m* doloroso; **to open an old ~** abrir una vieja herida

**sorely** ['sɔr·li] *adv* form muy; **he will be ~ missed** lo echarán mucho de menos

**sorrow** ['sar·ou] *n* pena *f*; **to feel ~** sentirse apenado (**over** por); **to my ~** muy a mi pesar

**sorry** ['sar·i] I. <-ier, -iest> *adj* 1. triste, apenado, -a; **to be ~ that** sentir que +*subj*; **to feel ~ for oneself** compadecerse de sí mismo; **to feel ~** tener lástima (**for** de) 2. (*regretful*) arrepentido, -a; **I'm** (**very**) **~** lo siento (mucho) (**about** por); **to say ~** pedir perdón 3. (*wretched, pitiful*) desgraciado, -a; (*choice*) desafortunado, -a; (*figure*) lastimoso, -a II. *interj* ~**!** ¡perdón!; ~**?** ¿cómo dice?

**sort** [sɔrt] I. *n* 1. (*type*) tipo *m*; (*kind*) especie *f*; (*variety*) clase *f*; **flowers of all** ~**s** toda clase de flores; **something/nothing of the** ~ algo/nada por el estilo; **he was a friend of** ~**s** se le podía considerar amigo; **to not be the** ~ **to do sth** no ser de los que hacen algo; **I know your** ~**!** ¡sé de qué pie calzas! 2. ~ **of** en cierto modo; (*not exactly*) más o menos; **I** ~ **of feel that...** en cierto modo pienso que...; **that's** ~ **of difficult to explain** es algo difícil de explicar ▶ **out of** ~**s** pachucho II. *vt* clasificar; COMPUT ordenar; **to** ~ **in ascending/descending order** poner en orden ascendente/descendente III. *vi* **to** ~ **through** revisar

◆**sort out** *vt* 1. (*resolve*) solucionar; (*details*) aclarar 2. (*arrange*) clasificar; (*choose*) separar 3. (*tidy up*) arreglar

**SOS** [ˌes·ou·'es] *n* SOS *m*

**so-so** ['sou·sou] *inf* I. *adj* regular II. *adv*

ni fu ni fa, así así

**sought** [sɔt] *pt, pp of* **seek**

**soul** [soul] *n* 1. alma *f*; **bless his/her ~** que en paz descanse; **not a ~** ni un alma; **to be the ~ of discretion** ser la discreción en persona 2. MUS soul *m*

**soul-searching** *n* examen *m* de conciencia; **after much ~** tras mucha reflexión

**sound**[1] [saund] I. *n* 1. *a.* LING, PHYS sonido *m*; **there wasn't a ~ to be heard** no se oía nada; **by the ~ of it** según parece; **I don't like the ~ of that** no me huele nada bien 2. (*radio, TV*) volumen *m*; **to turn the ~ down/up** bajar/subir el volumen II. *vi* 1. sonar 2. (*seem*) parecer III. *vt* (*alarm*) hacer sonar; (*bell, car horn*) tocar

**sound**[2] [saund] I. *adj* 1. (*healthy*) sano, -a; (*robust*) fuerte; (*character, health*) bueno, -a; (*basis*) sólido, -a; **to be of ~ mind** estar en su sano juicio; **to be safe and ~** estar sano y salvo 2. (*trustworthy*) digno, -a de confianza; (*competent*) competente 3. (*thorough*) profundo, -a; **to be a ~ sleeper** tener el sueño profundo II. *adv* **to be ~ asleep** dormir profundamente

**sound**[3] [saund] *vt* NAUT sondear; MED auscultar

**sound**[4] [saund] *n* (*channel*) estrecho *m*; (*inlet*) brazo *m* de mar

◆**sound out** *vt* tantear

**soundproof** ['saund·pruf] I. *vt* insonorizar II. *adj* insonorizado, -a

**soup** [sup] *n* sopa *f*; (*clear*) caldo *m*; **home-made/instant ~** sopa casera/instantánea

**sour** ['sau·ər] I. *adj a. fig* agrio, -a; (*milk*) cortado, -a; **to go ~** agriarse; (*milk*) cortarse II. *vt* agriar; *fig* amargar III. *vi* agriarse; (*milk*) cortarse; (*person*) amargarse

**source** [sɔrs] *n* fuente *f*; **according to government** ~**s** según fuentes gubernamentales; **from a reliable ~** de una fuente fiable; **to list one's** ~**s** hacer la bibliografía; **a ~ of inspiration** una fuente de inspiración

**south** [sauθ] I. *n* sur *m*; **to lie 5 miles to the ~** quedar a 8 km al sur (**of** de);

**to go/drive to the ~** ir hacia el sur; **further** ~ más al sur; **in the ~ of Bolivia** en el sur de Bolivia **II.** *adj* del sur, meridional; **~ wind** viento del sur; **~ coast** costa sur

**South Africa** *n* Sudáfrica *f*

**South African** *adj, n* sudafricano, -a *m, f*

**South America** *n* América *f* del Sur

**South American** *adj, n* sudamericano, -a *m, f*

**southbound** ['saυθ·baυnd] *adj* hacia el sur

**southerly** ['sʌð·ər·li] **I.** *adj* (*location*) en el sur; **in a ~ direction** en dirección sur **II.** *n* viento *m* meridional

**southern** ['sʌð·ərn] *adj* del sur; **the ~ part of the country** la parte sur del país

**southerner** ['sʌð·ər·nər] *n* sureño, -a *m, f*

**South Pole** *n* Polo *m* Sur

**southward(s)** ['saυθ·wərd(z)] *adv* hacia el sur

**souvenir** [ˌsu·və·'nɪr] *n* recuerdo *m*

**Soviet Union** *n* Unión *f* Soviética

**sow**[1] [soυ] <sowed, sown *or* sowed> *vt, vi* AGR sembrar ▶ **as you ~, so shall you <u>reap</u>** lo que siembres cosecharás

**sow**[2] [saυ] *n* (*pig*) cerda *f* ▶ **you can't make a silk purse out of a ~'s <u>ear</u>** no se le puede pedir peras al olmo

**sown** [soυn] *pp of* **sow**

**sox** [saks] *npl* calcetines *mpl*

**soy** [sɔɪ] *n* soja *f*

**spa** [spa] *n* **1.** (*spring*) manantial *m* **2.** (*town*) ciudad *f* balnearia **3.** (*health center*) balneario *m*

**space** [speɪs] **I.** *n* espacio *m*; **parking ~** plaza *f* de aparcamiento; **in a short ~ of time** en un breve espacio de tiempo; **leave some ~ for dessert** deja hueco para tu postre **II.** *vt* espaciar

**space bar** *n* barra *f* espaciadora

**space probe** *n* sonda *f* espacial

**space-saving** *adj* que ocupa poco espacio

**spaceship** ['speɪs·ʃɪp] *n* nave *f* espacial

**space shuttle** *n* transbordador *m* espacial

**space station** *n* estación *f* espacial

**spacing** ['speɪ·sɪŋ] *n* espaciamiento *m*; TYPO espacio *m*; **double ~** doble es-

pacio

**spacious** ['speɪ·ʃəs] *adj* espacioso, -a

**spade** [speɪd] *n* pala *f*; GAMES pica *f* ▶ **to <u>call</u> a ~ a ~** llamar al pan, pan y al vino, vino

**spaghetti** [spə·'ɡet·i] *n* espaguetis *mpl*

**Spain** [speɪn] *n* España *f*

**spam** [spæm] COMPUT **I.** *n* COMPUT spam *m* **II.** *vt* enviar spam

**Spam**® [spæm] *n* fiambre de cerdo enlatado

**spambot** ['spæmbɒt] *n* spambot *m*

**span**[1] [spæn] *pt of* **spin**

**span**[2] [spæn] **I.** *n* **1.** (*time*) lapso *m*; (*project*) duración *f* **2.** ARCHIT luz *f* **3.** AVIAT, NAUT envergadura *f* **II.** <-nn-> *vt* **1.** (*cross*) atravesar **2.** (*include*) abarcar

**spangled** *adj* con lentejuelas; *fig* salpicado, -a (**with**)

**Spaniard** ['spæn·jərd] *n* español(a) *m(f)*

**Spanish** ['spæn·ɪʃ] **I.** *adj* español(a); **~ speaker** hispanohablante *mf* **II.** *n* **1.** (*people*) español(a) *m(f)*; **the ~** los españoles **2.** LING español *m*

**spank** [spæŋk] *vt* zurrar

**spanking** ['spæŋ·kɪŋ] **I.** *n* zurra *f*, fleta *f AmC* **II.** *adj* **~ new** nuevo flamante

**spare** [sper] **I.** *vt* **1.** (*pardon*) perdonar; **to ~ sb sth** ahorrar algo a alguien; **to ~ no effort** no escatimar esfuerzos **2.** (*do without*) prescindir de; (*time*) disponer de **II.** *adj* **1.** (*additional*) de repuesto; (*room, minute*) libre **2.** (*remaining*) sobrante **III.** *n* (*part*) repuesto *m*

**spare time** *n* tiempo *m* libre

**spare tire** *n* rueda *f* de repuesto; *iron* michelín *m*

**spark** [spark] **I.** *n* **1.** chispa *f* **2.** (*small amount*) pizca *f*; **not even a ~ ni una pizca** (**of** de) **II.** *vt* (*debate, protest, problems*) desencadenar; (*interest*) suscitar; **to ~ sb into action** hacer que alguien se mueva

**sparkle** ['spar·kəl] **I.** *n* destello *m*, brillo *m* **II.** *vi* (*eyes*) brillar; (*fire*) chispear; (*sea*) destellar

**sparkler** ['spark·lər] *n* **1.** (*firework*) bengala *f* **2.** *inf* (*diamond*) diamante *m*

**sparkling** ['spark·lɪŋ] *adj* (*light, dia-*

S

*mond*) brillante; (*conversation, wit*) chispeante

**spark plug** ['spark·plʌg] *n* bujía *f*

**sparrow** ['sper·ou] *n* gorrión *m*

**sparse** [spars] *adj* escaso, -a

**spat¹** [spæt] *pt, pp of* **spit**

**spat²** [spæt] **I.** *n* (*quarrel*) rencilla *f* **II.** <-tt-> *vi* (*quarrel*) reñir

**spate** [speɪt] *n* racha *f*; (*of letters, inquiries*) aluvión *m*

**spatial** ['speɪ·ʃəl] *adj* espacial

**spatter** ['spæt·ər] **I.** *vt, vi* salpicar (**with** de) **II.** *n* salpicadura *f*, salpicada *f Méx*; **~ of rain** cuatro gotas

**spawn** [spɔn] **I.** *n* ZOOL hueva(s) *f(pl)* **II.** *vt* generar **III.** *vi* desovar

**speak** [spik] <spoke, spoken> **I.** *vi* hablar (**to** con, **on behalf of** por); **so to ~** por así decir; **generally ~ing** en términos generales; **scientifically ~ing** desde el punto de vista científico; **strictly ~ing** en realidad **II.** *vt* hablar; (*say*) decir; **to ~ dialect/English** hablar dialecto/inglés; **to ~ one's mind** hablar claro; **to ~ the truth** decir la verdad; **to not ~ a word** no decir ni una palabra

◆**speak for** *vi* **1.** (*represent*) hablar por; **speaking for myself** en lo que a mí respecta; **it speaks for itself** habla por sí solo **2.** (*advocate, support*) hablar en favor de

◆**speak out** *vi* expresarse; **to ~ against** denunciar

◆**speak up** *vi* **1.** (*state*) decir lo que se piensa; **to ~ for sth** hablar a favor de algo **2.** (*more loudly*) hablar más alto

**speaker** *n* **1.** hablante *mf* **2.** (*orator*) orador(a) *m(f)* **3.** (*loudspeaker*) altavoz *m*

**speaking** **I.** *n* habla *f*; (*public*) oratoria *f* **II.** *adj* hablante; (*tour*) comentado, -a; **to not be on ~ terms** no dirigirse la palabra

**spear** [spɪr] **I.** *n* lanza *f*; (*for throwing*) jabalina *f*; (*for fishing*) arpón *m* **II.** *vt* (*fork*) pinchar

**spearhead** ['spɪr·hed] *n a. fig* punta *f* de lanza

**special** ['speʃ·əl] **I.** *adj* especial; (*aptitude, character*) excepcional; **nothing ~** nada especial **II.** *n* TV programa *m*

especial; CULIN especialidad *f* del día; COM oferta *f* especial

**specialist** ['speʃ·ə·lɪst] *n* especialista *mf*

**specialize** ['speʃ·ə·laɪz] *vi* especializarse (**in** en)

**specially** *adv* especialmente; **a ~ good wine** un vino especialmente bueno

**specialty** ['speʃ·əl·ti] *n* <-ies> especialidad *f*

**species** ['spi·ʃiz] *n inv* especie *f*

**specific** [spə·'sɪf·ɪk] *adj* específico, -a; **to be ~** dar detalles; **to be ~ to sth** ser propio de algo

**specifically** *adv* (*expressly*) expresamente; (*ask, mention*) explícitamente; (*particularly*) específicamente

**specification** [ˌspes·ə·fɪ·'keɪ·ʃən] *n* especificación *f*

**specify** ['spes·ə·faɪ] <-ie-> *vt* especificar

**specimen** ['spes·ə·mən] *n* **1.** (*blood, urine*) muestra *f*; (*plant, animal, product*) ejemplar *m*; **a ~ copy** un ejemplar de muestra **2.** (*person*) espécimen *m*

**speck** [spek] *n* punto *m*; (*dust*) mota *f*; **not a ~** ni pizca (of aire)

**specs** [speks] *npl inf* **1.** *abbr of* **spectacles** gafas *fpl* **2.** *abbr of* **specifications** especificaciones *fpl*

**spectacle** ['spek·tə·kəl] *n* **1.** espectáculo *m*; **to make a real ~ of oneself** dar el espectáculo **2.** *pl* (*glasses*) gafas *fpl*, lentes *fpl AmL*; **a pair of ~** unas gafas

**spectacular** [spek·'tæk·ju·lər] **I.** *adj* espectacular **II.** *n* programa *m* especial

**spectator** [spek·'teɪ·tər] *n* espectador(a) *m(f)*

**spectrum** ['spek·trəm] <-ra *or* -s> *n* **1.** PHYS espectro *m* **2.** (*range*) gama *f*; **the political ~** el espectro político

**speculation** [ˌspek·ju·'leɪ·ʃən] *n* especulación *f*; **stock-market ~** especulación bursátil

**sped** [sped] *pt, pp of* **speed**

**speech** [spitʃ] <-es> *n* **1.** (*capacity*) habla *f*; **to lose/regain the power of ~** perder/recobrar el habla **2.** (*words*) palabras *fpl* **3.** (*public talk*) discurso *m*; **to make** [*or* **give**] **a ~** pronunciar un discurso

**speech defect** *n* defecto *m* del habla

**speechless** ['spitʃ·lɪs] *adj* mudo, -a; **to**

**leave sb ~** dejar a alguien sin palabras

**speech therapist** n logopeda mf

**speed** [spid] I. n 1. (velocity) velocidad f; **at a ~ of** a una velocidad de 2. (quickness) rapidez f 3. (gear) marcha f 4. PHOT sensibilidad f 5. (drug) speed m II. vi <sped or speeded, sped or speeded> 1. (go fast) ir de prisa; **to ~ by** pasar volando 2. (hasten) apresurarse, AUTO ir con exceso de velocidad III. vt <sped or speeded, sped or speeded> acelerar

**◆speed up** <sped or speeded, sped or speeded> I. vi (car) acelerar; (process) acelerarse; (person) darse prisa, apurarse AmL II. vt (process) acelerar, expeditar AmL; (person) apresurar

**speedboat** ['spid·boʊt] n lancha f motora

**speed bump** n banda f rugosa

**speeding** n exceso m de velocidad

**speed limit** n límite f de velocidad

**speedy** ['spi·di] <-ier, -iest> adj veloz

**spell¹** [spel] <spelled or spelt, spelled or spelt> (language) I. vt 1. deletrear; **how do you ~ it?** ¿cómo se deletrea? 2. significar; **this ~s trouble** esto significa problemas II. vi escribir; **to ~ well** escribir sin faltas

**◆spell out** vt deletrear; fig explicar de forma sencilla (for a)

**spell²** [spel] n (magic) encanto m; **to be under a ~** estar hechizado

**spell³** [spel] n 1. (period) temporada f 2. (turn) turno m

**spellbound** ['spel·baʊnd] adj hechizado, -a; fig fascinado, -a

**spelling** n ortografía f; **~ mistake** falta f de ortografía

**spelt** [spelt] pp, pt of **spell**

**spend** [spend] <spent, spent> I. vt (use up) agotar; (money) gastar; (time) pasar; **to ~ time doing sth** dedicar tiempo a hacer algo II. vi gastar

**spending** n gasto m; **public ~** el gasto público

**spending money** n dinero m para gastos personales

**spending spree** n derroche m de dinero; **to go on a ~** gastar dinero a lo loco

**spent** [spent] I. pp, pt of **spend** II. adj

(used) gastado, -a

**sperm** [spɜrm] <-(s)> n esperma m o f

**spew** [spju] vi, vt vomitar

**sphere** [sfɪr] n esfera f; **~ of influence** ámbito m de influencia

**spherical** ['sfɪr·ɪ·kəl] adj esférico, -a

**spice** [spaɪs] I. n 1. CULIN especia f, olor m Chile 2. (excitement) picante m; **to give ~ to sth** dar sabor a algo (to a); **the ~ of life** la sal de la vida II. vt condimentar

**spicy** ['spaɪ·si] <-ier, -iest> adj 1. (seasoned) condimentado, -a 2. (sensational) picante

**spider** ['spaɪ·dər] n araña f

**spike** [spaɪk] I. n 1. (object) pincho m 2. pl (shoes) zapatillas f pl con clavos 3. (increase) pico m 4. SPORTS remate m II. vt 1. **to ~ a drink** echar alcohol a una bebida 2. (injure) pinchar 3. (secure) clavar 4. SPORTS rematar

**spiky** ['spaɪ·ki] <-ier, -iest> adj 1. (sharp) puntiagudo, -a; (hair) de punta 2. inf chinchoso, -a

**spill** [spɪl] I. n 1. derrame m; **oil ~** vertido m de petróleo 2. inf (fall) caída f; **to take a ~** tener un accidente II. vt <spilled or spilt, spilled or spilt> derramar III. vi derramarse

**◆spill over** vi derramarse

**spilt** [spɪlt] pp, pt of **spill**

**spin** [spɪn] I. n vuelta f; **to go [or take the car] for a ~** dar un paseo (en coche) II. vt <spun, spun> girar; (clothes) centrifugar; (ball) dar efecto a; (wool, cotton) hilar; (story, tale) contar III. vi <spun, spun> girar; (wool, cotton) hilar

**◆spin out** vi (car) salirse de la calzada

**spinach** ['spɪn·ɪtʃ] n espinacas fpl

**spine** [spaɪn] n 1. (person) columna f vertebral; (animal) espina f dorsal 2. (spike) púa f 3. BOT espina f

**spiral** ['spaɪ·rəl] I. n espiral f II. adj en espiral; (staircase) de caracol III. vi <-ll-, -l-> (increase) dispararse; (decrease) caer; **to ~ out of control** descontrolarse

**spire** [spaɪr] n ARCHIT aguja f

**spirit** ['spɪr·ɪt] n 1. (ghost) espíritu m; **the ~ of the age** el espíritu de la época;

S

**that's the ~!** ¡muy bien! **2.** *pl* (*mood*) ánimo *mpl*; **to be in high/low ~s** estar animado/desanimado **3.** *pl* (*alcohol*) licor *m*

**spirited** *adj* enérgico, -a; (*discussion*) animado, -a; (*person*) animoso, -a, entrador(a) *AmS*

**spiritual** ['spɪr·ɪ·tʃu·əl] *adj* espiritual

**spit**¹ [spɪt] BIOL **I.** *n inf* saliva *f* **II.** *vi* <spat, spat> escupir; (*crackle*) chisporrotear **III.** *vt* escupir
◆**spit out** *vt* escupir; (*say angrily*) soltar; **spit it out!** ¡desembucha!

**spit**² [spɪt] *n* **1.** CULIN asador *m* **2.** (*sandbar*) banco *m* de arena

**spite** [spaɪt] **I.** *n* rencor *m*; **out of ~** por despecho; **in ~ of** a pesar de **II.** *vt* fastidiar

**spiteful** ['spaɪt·fəl] *adj* rencoroso, -a

**spitting image** *n* vivo *m* retrato

**splash** [splæʃ] **I.** *n* **1.** (*sound*) chapoteo *m* **2.** (*drops*) salpicadura *f*; **a ~ of color** una mancha de color ▶ **to make a (big) ~** causar sensación **II.** *vt, vi* salpicar
◆**splash down** *vi* amerizar

**splatter** ['splæt̬·ər] *vi, vt* salpicar

**splendid** ['splen·dɪd] *adj* espléndido, -a

**splendor** ['splen·dər] *n* esplendor *m*; *pl* maravillas *fpl*

**splint** [splɪnt] **I.** *n* tablilla *f* **II.** *vt* entablillar

**splinter** ['splɪn·tər] **I.** *n* astilla *f* **II.** *vi* astillarse

**split** [splɪt] **I.** *n* **1.** (*crack*) grieta **2.** (*clothes*) desgarrón **3.** (*division*) división *f* **II.** *vt* <split, split> **1.** (*divide*) dividir; (*atom*) desintegrar; **to ~ sth between two people** repartir algo entre dos personas **2.** (*crack*) agrietar; **to ~ one's head open** abrirse la cabeza ▶ **to ~ one's sides laughing** partirse de risa; **to ~ hairs** buscarle tres pies al gato **III.** *vi* <split, split> **1.** (*divide*) dividirse **2.** (*crack*) agrietarse **3.** (*leave*) largarse
◆**split off I.** *vt* separar **II.** *vi* separarse
◆**split up I.** *vt* partir **II.** *vi* separarse (**with** de)

**split-up** ['splɪt·ʌp] *n* ruptura *m*

**splutter** ['splʌt̬·ər] **I.** *vi* (*person*) farfullar;

(*candle, engine*) chisporrotear **II.** *n* (*candle, engine*) chisporroteo *m*

**spoil** [spɔɪl] **I.** *vt* <spoiled *or* spoilt, spoiled *or* spoilt> estropear, salar *AmL*; (*party*) aguar; (*child*) consentir, engreír *AmL*, papachar *Méx* **II.** *vi* <spoiled *or* spoilt, spoiled *or* spoilt> estropearse **III.** *n* **1.** *pl* (*profits*) botín *m* **2.** (*debris*) escombros *mpl*

**spoilsport** ['spɔɪl·spɔrt] *n* aguafiestas *mf inv*

**spoilt I.** *pp, pt of* **spoil II.** *adj* mimado, -a, engreído, -a *AmL*

**spoke**¹ [spoʊk] *pt of* **speak**

**spoke**² [spoʊk] *n* (*wheel*) radio *m*; **to put a ~ in sb's wheel** poner trabas a alguien

**spoken** *pp of* **speak**

**spokesperson** ['spoʊks·ˌpɜr·sən] *n* portavoz *mf*, vocero, -a *m, f AmL*

**sponge** [spʌndʒ] **I.** *n* **1.** ZOOL esponja *f* **2.** (*person*) gorrón, -ona *m, f* **II.** *vi* gorronear
◆**sponge down** *vt* limpiar con una esponja
◆**sponge off** *vt inf* vivir a costa de

**sponge cake** *n* bizcocho *m*

**sponger** *n* gorrón, -ona *m, f*, sablero, -a *m, f Chile*

**sponsor** ['spɑn·sər] **I.** *vt* patrocinar **II.** *n* patrocinador(a) *m(f)*, propiciador(a) *m(f) AmL*

**spontaneous** [spɑn·ˈteɪ·ni·əs] *adj* espontáneo, -a

**spooky** ['spu·ki] <-ier, -iest> *adj inf* que da miedo

**spoon** [spun] *n* cuchara *f*; (*amount*) cucharada *f*

**spoonful** ['spun·fʊl] <-s *or* spoonsful> *n* cucharada *f*

**sport** [spɔrt] *n* **1.** deporte *m* **2.** **to be a good/poor ~** ser buena/mala gente GAMES, SPORTS ser buen/mal perdedor

**sporting** *adj* deportivo, -a, esportivo *m* -a *AmL*

**sports car** *n* deportivo *m*

**sportsman** ['spɔrts·mən] *n* deportista *m*

**sportsmanship** *n* deportividad *f*

**sports page** *n* página *f* de deportes

**sportswear** *n* ropa *f* de deporte

**sportswoman** ['spɔrts·ˌwʊm·ən] *n* de

portista f

**sporty** ['spɔr·ʈi] <-ier, -iest> adj deportivo, -a

**spot** [spat] I. n 1. (mark) mancha f 2. (pattern) lunar m 3. (skin) grano m 4. (place) lugar m; on the ~ in situ; (at once) en el acto 5. TV, RADIO espacio m ▶ to really hit the ~ venir de perlas; to have a soft ~ tener debilidad (for por); to put sb on the ~ poner a alguien en un aprieto II. <-tt-> vt 1. (see) divisar 2. (speckle) manchar

**spot check** n control m al azar

**spotless** ['spat·lɪs] adj inmaculado, -a

**spotlight** ['spat·laɪt] I. n foco m ▶ to be in the ~ ser el centro de atención II. <spotlighted or spotlit, spotlighted or spotlit> vt iluminar

**spotted** adj con manchas; (pattern) de lunares

**spotty** ['spaʈ·i] <-ier, -iest> adj 1. (skin) con granos 2. (inconsistent) irregular

**spout** [spaʊt] I. n (kettle) pitorro m; (jar) pico m; (tube) caño m; (jet) chorro m II. vt 1. echar 2. pej perorar sobre III. vi 1. chorrear 2. pej perorar

**sprain** [spreɪn] I. vt torcer II. n torcedura f

**sprang** [spræŋ] vi, vt pt of spring

**sprawl** [sprɔl] vi pej (person) respantigarse; (town) extenderse; to send sb ~ing derribar a alguien

**sprawling** adj (town) de crecimiento descontrolado; (handwriting) irregular

**spray**[1] [spreɪ] I. n 1. (mist) rocío m 2. (device) spray m II. vt rociar III. vi chorrear

**spray**[2] [spreɪ] n rama f; a ~ of flowers un ramo de flores

**spread** [spred] I. n 1. (diffusion) propagación f 2. (range) gama f 3. (meal) comilona f II. <spread, spread> vt (news) difundir; (disease) propagar; (butter) untar; (payments, work) distribuir; (map, blanket) extender III. <spread, spread> vi (news) difundirse; (disease) propagarse; (liquid) extenderse

**spreadsheet** ['spred·ʃit] n hoja f de cálculo

**spree** [spri] n parranda f, tambarria f AmC; to go on a drinking ~ ir de juerga

**sprightly** ['spraɪt·li] <-ier, -iest> adj vivaz

**spring** [sprɪŋ] I. n 1. (season) primavera f 2. (jump) salto m 3. (metal) muelle m 4. (water) manantial m II. <sprang, sprung> vi saltar; to ~ to one's feet levantarse de un salto; to ~ shut/open cerrarse/abrirse de golpe

**springboard** ['sprɪŋ·bɔrd] n trampolín m

**spring-clean** [ˌsprɪŋ·'klin] vt limpiar a fondo

**spring roll** n CULIN rollito m de primavera

**springy** ['sprɪŋ·i] <-ier, -iest> adj elástico, -a

**sprinkle** ['sprɪŋ·kəl] I. vt salpicar II. n salpicadura f

**sprinkling** ['sprɪŋ·klɪŋ] n a ~ unas gotas (of de)

**sprint** [sprɪnt] SPORTS I. vi esprintar II. n (race) esprint m

**sprinter** ['sprɪn·ʈər] n velocista mf

**sprout** [spraʊt] I. n 1. brote m 2. pl (Brussels sprouts) coles m pl de Bruselas II. vi brotar III. vt echar

**spruce**[1] [sprus] n BOT picea f

**spruce**[2] [sprus] adj (neat) aseado, -a

**sprung** [sprʌŋ] pp, Am: pt of spring

**spud** [spʌd] n papa f

**spun** [spʌn] pp, pt of spin

**spur** [spɜr] I. <-rr-> vt fig estimular II. n espuela f; fig estímulo m ▶ on the ~ of the moment sin pensarlo

**spurt** [spɜrt] I. n (jet) chorro m II. vi 1. (gush) salir a chorros 2. (accelerate) acelerar

**spy** [spaɪ] I. n espía mf II. vi espiar (on a); to ~ on sb espiar a alguien

**squabble** ['skwab·əl] I. n riña f II. vi reñir

**squad** [skwad] n (group) pelotón m; (police) brigada f; SPORTS equipo m

**squalid** ['skwal·ɪd] adj 1. (dirty) asqueroso, -a 2. (sordid) sórdido, -a

**squander** ['skwan·dər] vt malgastar, fundir AmL; (opportunity) desperdiciar

**square** [skwer] I. n 1. a. MATH cuadrado m; (in town) plaza f 2. (tool) escuadra f ▶ to go back to ~ one volver al punto de partida II. adj 1. cuadra-

S

do, -a; **forty-three ~ feet** cuatro metros cuadrados; **a ~ deal** un trato justo **2.** (*even*) en paz **3. be there or be ~** si no lo haces, eres un muermo **III.** *vt* cuadrar; (*settle*) acomodar; (*accounts*) saldar; MATH elevar al cuadrado **IV.** *vi* concordar (**with** con)

**square root** *n* raíz *f* cuadrada

**squash**¹ [skwɑʃ] *n* BOT calabaza *f*

**squash**² [skwɑʃ] **I.** *n* **1.** SPORTS squash *m* **2.** (*dense pack*) apiñamiento *m* **II.** *vt* aplastar

**squashy** ['skwɑʃ·i] <-ier, -iest> *adj* blando, -a

**squat** [skwɑt] **I.** <-tt-> *vi* **1.** (*crouch down*) agacharse, ñangotarse *PRico, RDom* **2.** (*property*) ocupar **III.** **1.** (*exercise*) sentadilla *f* **2.** *sl* **to not know ~** no tener ni idea **III.** <-tt-> *adj* (*person*) rechoncho, -a

**squatter** ['skwɑt·ər] *n* ocupador, -a *m, f*

**squeak** [skwik] **I.** *n* chirrido *m* **II.** *vi* chirriar

**squeal** [skwil] **I.** *n* chillido *m* **II.** *vi* **1.** chillar; (*brakes, car*) chirriar **2.** (*inform*) chivarse

**squeamish** ['skwi·mɪʃ] *adj* remilgado, -a; **to feel ~** sentir náuseas

**squeeze** [skwiz] **I.** *n* **1.** estrujón *m*; **to put the ~ on** apretar **2.** ECON restricción *f* **II.** *vt* **1.** (*press together*) estrujar; **freshly ~d juice** zumo recién exprimido **2.** (*force*) presionar; **to ~ sth out of sb** sacar algo a alguien

**squelch** [skwɛltʃ] **I.** *vi* chapotear **II.** *vt* aplastar **III.** *n* chapoteo *m*

**squid** [skwɪd] <-(s)> *n* calamar *m*

**squiggle** ['skwɪg·əl] **I.** *n* garabato *m* **II.** *vi* garabatear

**squint** [skwɪnt] **I.** *vi* (*cross-eyed*) bizquear; (*partly closed eyes*) mirar con los ojos entrecerrados **II.** *n* **1.** bizquera *f AmL* **2.** (*quick look*) mirada *f* furtiva

**squirm** [skwɜrm] *vi* retorcerse; **he ~ed with embarrassment** se le caía la cara de vergüenza

**squirrel** ['skwɜr·əl] *n* ardilla *f*

**squirt** [skwɜrt] **I.** *vt* echar un chorreón de **II.** *vi* chorrear **III.** *n* **1.** chorrito *m* **2.** (*person*) farsante *mf*

**stab** [stæb] **I.** <-bb-> *vt* apuñalar, achurar *CSur*, carnear *Méx*; **to ~ sb in the back** dar a alguien una puñalada trapera **II.** *n* **1.** (*blow*) puñalada *f* **2.** (*pain*) punzada *f* **3. to take a ~ at** (**doing**) **sth** intentar (hacer) algo

**stabbing** **I.** *n* apuñalamiento *m* **II.** *adj* punzante

**stability** [stə·'bɪl·ə·t̬i] *n* estabilidad *f*

**stabilize** ['steɪ·bə·laɪz] **I.** *vt* estabilizar **II.** *vi* estabilizarse

**stable**¹ ['steɪ·bəl] *adj a.* ECON, MED estable; (*structure*) firme

**stable**² ['steɪ·bəl] *n* cuadra *f*

**stack** [stæk] **I.** *vt* apilar; (*shelves*) llenar ▶ **the cards are ~ed against us** la suerte está en contra nuestra **II.** *n* **1.** (*pile*) pila *f* **2.** (*large amount*) montón *m*, ponchada *f CSur* **3.** *pl* (*bookcase*) estantería *f*

**stadium** ['steɪ·di·əm] <-s *or* -dia> *n* estadio *m*

**staff** [stæf] *n* **1.** (*employees*) personal *m*, elenco *m AmL* **2.** (*stick*) bastón *m*; ~ **office** bastón de mando **3.** (*flagpole*) asta *f* **4.** <staves> MUS pentagrama *m*

**stag** [stæg] *n* ZOOL ciervo *m*

**stage** [steɪdʒ] **I.** *n* **1.** (*period*) etapa *f*, pascana *f AmS*; **at this ~ in my life** en esta etapa de mi vida; **in ~s** por etapas **2.** THEAT escena *f*; **the ~** el teatro; **to be on the ~** ser actor/actriz **II.** *vt* **1.** THEAT representar **2.** (*organize*) organizar

**stage fright** *n* miedo *m* escénico

**stagger** ['stæg·ər] **I.** *vi* tambalearse **II.** *vt* **1.** (*amaze*) asombrar **2.** (*work, payments*) escalonar **III.** *n* tambaleo *m*

**staggering** *adj* sorprendente

**stagnant** ['stæg·nənt] *adj* estancado, -a

**stagnate** ['stæg·neɪt] *vi* estancarse

**stain** [steɪn] **I.** *vt* manchar; (*dye*) teñir **II.** *vi* mancharse **III.** *n* **1.** (*mark*) mancha *f*; **grease ~** mancha de grasa **2.** (*dye*) tinte *m*

**stained** *adj* (*marked*) manchado, -a

**stainless** ['steɪn·lɪs] **I.** *adj* sin mancha **II.** *n* acero *m* inoxidable

**stair** [ster] *n* peldaño *m*; *pl* escalera *f*

**staircase** ['ster·keɪs] *n*, **stairway** ['ster·weɪ] *n* escalera *f*

**stake** [steɪk] **I.** *n* **1.** (*stick*) estaca

**2.** (*share*) participación *f*; **to have a ~** tener interés (**in** en) **3.** (*bet*) apuesta *f*; **to play for high ~s** arriesgar mucho; **to be at ~** estar en juego **II.** *vt* (*bet*) apostar; **to ~ one's life** poner la mano en el fuego (**on** por); **to ~ a claim to** reivindicar

**stakeholder** ['steɪk-ˌhoʊl-dər] *n* tenedor(a) *m(f)* de apuestas

**stale** [steɪl] *adj* **1.** (*not fresh*) pasado, -a; (*bread*) duro, -a; (*air*) viciado, -a; (*joke*) viejo, -a **2.** (*tired*) cansado, -a

**stalk**[1] [stɔk] *n* BOT tallo *m*; **her eyes were out on ~s** se le salían los ojos de las órbitas

**stalk**[2] [stɔk] **I.** *vt* (*follow*) acechar **II.** *vi* **to ~ off** marcharse airadamente

**stall** [stɔl] **I.** *n* **1.** (*animals*) establo *m* **2.** (*market*) puesto *m*, tarantín *m* Ven **3.** AUTO calado *m* **4.** shower **~** cabina para ducharse; **toilet ~** urinario *m*. **II.** *vi* **1.** AUTO calarse **2.** (*delay*) ir con rodeos; **to ~ for time** intentar ganar tiempo **III.** *vt* **1.** AUTO calar **2.** *inf* (*keep waiting*) retener

**stamina** ['stæm-ə-nə] *n* resistencia *f*

**stammer** ['stæm-ər] **I.** *vi*, *vt* tartamudear **II.** *n* tartamudeo *m*

**stamp** [stæmp] **I.** *n* **1.** sello *m*, estampilla *f* AmL **2.** (*character*) impronta *f* **3.** (*with foot*) pisotón *m* **II.** *vt* **1.** (*post*) pegar un sello en **2.** (*mark*) estampar **III.** *vi* patalear

**stampede** [stæm-ˈpid] **I.** *n* estampida *f*; (*people*) desbandada *f* **II.** *vi* huir en desbandada

**stance** [stæns] *n* postura *f*

**stand** [stænd] **I.** *n* **1.** (*position*) posición *f*; **to make a ~** oponer resistencia (**against** a) **2.** *pl* (*stadium*) tribuna *f* **3.** (*support, frame*) soporte *m* **4.** (*market*) puesto *m*, trucha *f* AmC **5.** AUTO parada *f*; **taxi ~** parada de taxis **6.** witness **~** estrado *m* **II.** <stood, stood> *vi* **1.** (*be upright*) estar de pie; **to ~ 6 feet tall** medir dos metros; **to ~ still** estarse quieto **2.** (*be located*) encontrarse **3.** (*decision, law*) mantenerse en vigor **III.** <stood, stood> *vt* **1.** (*place*) colocar **2.** (*bear*) aguantar; **I can't ~ her** no la soporto **3.** **to ~ trial** ser juzgado

◆**stand about** *vi*, **stand around** *vi* esperar

◆**stand aside** *vi* **1.** (*move*) apartarse **2.** (*stay*) mantenerse aparte

◆**stand back** *vi* **1.** (*move*) retroceder **2.** (*be objective*) distanciarse

◆**stand by** **I.** *vi* **1.** (*observe*) mantenerse al margen **2.** (*be ready*) estar alerta **II.** *vt* (*support*) apoyar

◆**stand down** *vi* renunciar

◆**stand for** *vt* **1.** (*represent*) representar; (*mean*) significar **2.** (*tolerate*) aguantar

◆**stand in** *vi* suplir (**for** a)

◆**stand out** *vi* destacar

◆**stand over** *vt* vigilar

◆**stand up** **I.** *vi* levantarse, arriscarse *Col*; (*evidence, argument*) ser convincente ▶ **to ~ and be counted** declararse abiertamente **II.** *vt* dar plantón

**standard** ['stæn-dərd] **I.** *n* **1.** (*level*) nivel *m*; (*quality*) clase *f* **2.** (*norm*) norma *f* **3.** (*flag*) estandarte *m* **II.** *adj* normal; (*procedure*) habitual; LING estándar

**standardize** ['stæn-dər-daɪz] *vt* estandarizar; TECH normalizar

**standby** ['stænd-baɪ] **I.** *n* **1.** (*money, food*) reserva *f* **2.** AVIAT lista *f* de espera **II.** *adj* de reserva

**stand-in** ['stænd-ɪn] *n* suplente *mf*; CINE doble *mf*

**standing** ['stæn-dɪŋ] **I.** *n* **1.** (*status*) posición *f* **2.** (*duration*) duración *f*; **of long ~** desde hace mucho **II.** *adj* **1.** (*upright*) vertical **2.** (*permanent*) permanente; (*water*) estancado, -a

**standpoint** ['stænd-pɔɪnt] *n* punto *m* de vista

**standstill** ['stænd-stɪl] *n* paralización *f*; **to be at a ~** estar parado

**stank** [stæŋk] *pt of* stink

**staple**[1] ['steɪ-pəl] **I.** *n* **1.** (*product*) producto *m* principal **2.** (*food*) alimento *m* de primera necesidad **3.** (*component*) elemento *m* esencial **II.** *adj* principal; (*standard*) corriente

**staple**[2] ['steɪ-pəl] **I.** *n* (*fastener*) grapa *f* **II.** *vt* grapar

**stapler** ['steɪp-lər] *n* grapadora *f*

**star** [star] **I.** *n* **1.** ASTRON estrella *f* **2.** TYPO asterisco *m* **3.** (*celebrity*) famo-

S

so, -a *m, f;* **a movie ~** una estrella de cine ▶ **to thank one's lucky ~s** dar las gracias a Dios; **to reach for the ~s** apuntar a lo más alto; **to see ~s** ver las estrellas II. *vt* <-rr-> **1.** THEAT, CINE tener como protagonista **2.** (*mark*) señalar con un asterisco

**starboard** ['star·bərd] I. *n* estribor *m* II. *adj* de estribor

**starch** [startʃ] *n* almidón *m;* CULIN fécula *f*

**starchy** ['star·tʃi] <-ier, -iest> *adj* (*food*) rico, -a en almidón; (*person*) estirado, -a

**stardom** ['star·dəm] *n* estrellato *m,* estelaridad *f* Chile

**stare** [ster] I. *vi* mirar fijamente II. *vt* mirar fijamente; **to ~ sb in the face** *fig* saltar a la vista III. *n* mirada *f* fija

**staring** ['ster·ɪŋ] *adj* que mira fijamente; (*eyes*) desorbitado, -a

**stark** [stark] I. *adj* **1.** (*desolate*) severo, -a; (*landscape*) inhóspito, -a **2.** (*austere*) austero, -a **3.** (*complete*) absoluto, -a; **a ~ contrast** un fuerte contraste II. *adv* **~ naked** en cueros, empelotado, -a *AmL;* **~ raving mad** loco de atar

**starry-eyed** ['star·i,aɪd] *adj* soñador(a)

**star-studded** *adj* (*sky*) estrellado, -a; (*film*) lleno, -a de estrellas; (*cast*) estelar

**start** [start] I. *vi* **1.** (*begin*) comenzar; **to ~ to do sth** empezar a hacer algo **2.** (*begin journey*) salir (**from** de) **3.** (*vehicle, motor*) arrancar **4.** (*begin at level*) empezar **5.** (*jump*) sobresaltarse (**at** con) II. *vt* **1.** (*begin*) comenzar; **we ~ work at 6:30** entramos a trabajar a las 6:30 **2.** (*set in operation*) poner en marcha; (*car*) arrancar; (*business*) abrir ▶ **to ~ something** *inf* crear problemas III. *n* **1.** (*beginning*) principio *m;* **to make an early/a late/a fresh ~** empezar temprano/tarde/de nuevo **2.** (*place*) salida *f;* (*time*) inicio *m* **3.** (*jump*) sobresalto *m;* **to give a ~** dar un respingo; **to give sb a ~** dar un susto a alguien

◆**start back** *vi* **1.** (*jump back*) retroceder de un salto **2.** (*journey*) emprender el regreso

◆**start off** I. *vi* empezar; (*journey*) partir; (*train, plane*) salir II. *vt* empezar; **to start sb off** ayudar a alguien (**on** a)

◆**start out** *vi* **1.** (*begin*) empezar; **to ~ to do sth** ponerse a hacer algo **2.** (*journey*) partir; (*train, plane*) salir

◆**start up** I. *vt* (*organization, business*) fundar; (*vehicle, motor*) arrancar II. *vi* **1.** (*vehicle, motor*) arrancar **2.** (*open*) abrir **3.** (*jump up*) levantarse de un salto

**starter** *n* **1.** AUTO estárter *m* **2.** CULIN entrante *m* **3.** SPORTS titular *mf* ▶ **for ~s** *inf* para empezar

**starting** *adj* de comienzo

**startle** ['star·təl] *vt* sobresaltar

**startling** *adj* asombroso, -a; (*alarming*) alarmante

**starvation** [star·'veɪ·ʃən] *n* hambre *m o f;* **to die of ~** morir de hambre

**starve** [starv] I. *vi* pasar hambre, hambrear *AmL;* (*die*) **a.** *fig* morirse de hambre II. *vt* privar

**stash** [stæʃ] I. *vt* ocultar II. *n* <-es> *inf* **1.** (*place*) escondite *m* **2.** (*cache*) alijo *m*

**state** [steɪt] I. *n* **1.** (*condition*) estado *m;* **~ of mind/war** estado de ánimo/guerra; **solid/liquid ~** estado sólido/líquido **2.** (*nation*) estado *m* **3.** *pl, inf* **the States** los Estados Unidos II. *adj* estatal; (*secret*) de Estado *m* III. *vt* declarar; LAW exponer

**State Department** *n* Departamento *m* de Estado, ≈ Ministerio *m* de Asuntos Exteriores

**stateless** ['steɪt·lɪs] *adj* apátrida

**statement** ['steɪt·mənt] *n* **1.** declaración *f;* **to make a ~** LAW prestar declaración **2.** (*bank*) extracto *m* de cuenta

**state of the art** [,steɪt·əv·ðiˈart] *adj* moderno, -a; (*technology*) punta *inv*

**station** ['steɪ·ʃən] I. *n* **1.** RAIL estación *f* **2.** (*place*) sitio *m;* **police ~** comisaría *f;* **gas ~** gasolinera *f;* **research ~** centro *m* de investigación **3.** RADIO emisora *f;* TV canal *m* II. *vt* colocar; MIL destinar

**stationary** ['steɪ·ʃə·ner·i] *adj* (*not moving*) inmóvil

**stationery** ['steɪ·ʃə·ner·i] *n* artículos *m pl* de papelería

**station wagon** *n* monovolumen *m*

**statistics** [stə'tɪs·tɪks] *n* 1. (*science*) estadística *f* 2. *pl* estadísticas
**statue** ['stætʃ·u] *n* estatua *f*
**Statue of Liberty** *n* the ~ la Estatua de la Libertad
**status** ['ster·təs] *n* 1. (*official position*) estatus *m* 2. (*prestige*) prestigio *m*
**stay** [steɪ] I. *vi* 1. (*not leave*) quedarse; **to ~ in bed** guardar cama 2. (*reside temporarily*) alojarse 3. (*remain*) permanecer; **to ~ friends** seguir siendo amigos II. *vt* (*endure*) resistir; (*hunger, thirst*) aplacar; **to ~ the course** [*or* **distance**] aguantar hasta el final III. *n* estancia *f*, estada *f AmL*
◆**stay away** *vi* ausentarse; **to ~ from** mantenerse alejado de
◆**stay behind** *vi* quedarse
◆**stay in** *vi* quedarse en casa
◆**stay out** *vi* no volver a casa; **to ~ all night** pasar toda la noche fuera
◆**stay up** *vi* no acostarse; **to ~ late** acostarse tarde
**staying power** *n* resistencia *f*
**STD** [ˌes·ti·'di] *n abbr of* **sexually transmitted disease** ETS *f*
**steady** ['sted·i] I. <-ier, -iest> *adj* 1. (*stable*) estable; (*job*) fijo, -a; (*temperature, speed*) constante 2. (*regular*) regular; (*boyfriend*) formal 3. (*hand*) firme 4. (*calm*) sereno, -a II. *vt* 1. (*stabilize*) estabilizar 2. (*calm*) calmar III. *adv* **to be going** ~ ser novios formales IV. *interj* cuidado
**steak** [steɪk] *n* (*fry, grill*) bistec *m*, bife *m AmL*; (*stew, mince*) carne *f* de ternera; (*lamb, fish*) filete *m*
**steal** [stil] I. <stole, stolen> *vt* robar, cachar *AmC*; **to ~ a glance** echar una mirada furtiva (**at** a) ► **to ~ the show** llevarse todos los aplausos II. <stole, stolen> *vi* robar; **to ~ in** entrar a hurtadillas; **to ~ away** escabullirse III. *n* ganga *f*; **to be a ~** ser una ganga
**steam** [stim] I. *n* vapor *m*; **to run out of ~** *fig* perder fuerza ► **to let off** ~ desahogarse II. *adj* de vapor III. *vi* echar vapor IV. *vt* cocer al vapor
◆**steam up** *vi* empañarse; **to get steamed up** *inf* acalorarse (**about** por)
**steamer** ['sti·mər] *n* 1. (*boat*) barco *m* de

vapor 2. CULIN vaporera *f*
**steamy** ['sti·mi] <-ier, -iest> *adj* 1. (*full of steam*) lleno, -a de vapor; (*very humid*) húmedo, -a 2. (*sexy*) erótico, -a
**steel** [stil] I. *n* acero *m*; **nerves of ~** nervios de acero II. *adj* de acero III. *vt* **to ~ oneself** armarse de valor (**for** para)
**steep¹** [stip] *adj* 1. (*sloping*) empinado, -a 2. (*increase, fall*) pronunciado, -a; **that's a bit ~!** ¡no hay derecho! 3. (*expensive*) exorbitante
**steep²** [stip] I. *vt* remojar; **to be ~ed in history** tener mucha historia II. *vi* to **leave sth to ~** dejar algo en remojo
**steeple** ['sti·pəl] *n* torre *f*; **church ~** campanario
**steer¹** [stɪr] I. *vt* (*direct*) dirigir; (*guide*) guiar; (*car*) conducir, manejar *AmL* II. *vi* (*person*) conducir, manejar *AmL*; (*vehicle*) manejarse; NAUT poner rumbo (**for** a); **to ~ clear of** evitar
**steer²** [stɪr] *n* ZOOL novillo *m*; (*castrated*) buey *m*
**steering wheel** *n* (*car*) volante *m*, guía *f PRico*; (*ship*) timón *m*
**stem** [stem] I. *n* 1. (*plant*) tallo *m* 2. (*glass*) pie *m* 3. LING raíz *f* II. <-mm-> *vt* (*stop*) detener III. <-mm-> *vi* to **~ from** resultar de
**step** [step] I. *n* 1. paso *m*; (*footprint*) huella *f*; **to take a ~** dar un paso; *fig* dirigirse (**towards** hacia); **~ by ~** paso a paso; **to be in/out of ~** llevar/no llevar el paso; *fig* estar/no estar al tanto; **to watch one's ~** andar con cuidado; **watch your ~!** ¡mira por dónde pisas! 2. (*stair*) peldaño *m* 3. (*measure*) medida *f*; **to take ~s** tomar medidas (**to** para) 4. MUS **whole/half ~** tono/semitono *m* II. <-pp-> *vi* 1. (*tread*) pisar 2. (*walk*) caminar
◆**step aside** *vi* hacerse a un lado
◆**step back** *vi* 1. (*move back*) retroceder 2. (*gain new perspective*) distanciarse
◆**step down** I. *vi* renunciar (**from** a) II. *vt* reducir
◆**step in** *vi* intervenir
◆**step up** I. *vt* aumentar II. *vi* dar la cara
**stepbrother** *n* hermanastro *m*
**stepchild** *n* hijastro, -a *m, f*

S

**stepdaughter** n hijastra f

**stepfather** n padrastro m

**stepladder** ['step·ˌlæd·ər] n escalera f de mano

**stepmother** ['step·ˌmʌð·ər] n madrastra f

**stepping stone** ['step·ɪŋ·stoʊn] n pasadera f; fig trampolín m

**stepson** ['step·sʌn] n hijastro m

**stereo** ['ster·i·oʊ] I. n (hi-fi) equipo m estéreo; **in** ~ en estéreo II. adj estéreo

**stereotype** ['ster·i·ə·taɪp] I. n estereotipo m II. vt estereotipar

**sterile** ['ster·əl] adj estéril

**sterilize** ['ster·ə·laɪz] vt esterilizar

**sterling** ['stɜr·lɪŋ] I. n (metal) plata f de ley II. adj excelente; **pound** ~ libra esterlina

**stern¹** [stɜrn] adj estricto, -a; (warning) terminante

**stern²** [stɜrn] n NAUT popa f

**stew** [stu] I. n estofado m, hervido m AmS ► **to be in a** ~ sudar la gota gorda II. vt (meat) estofar; (fruit) hacer compota de III. vi cocer

**stick¹** [stɪk] n 1. (wood) a. SPORTS palo m; (celery, rhubarb) tallo f; (deodorant, glue) barra f 2. **walking** ~ bastón m 3. MUS batuta f 4. **in the** ~s en el quinto pino ► **to get the wrong end of the** ~ coger el rábano por las hojas

**stick²** [stɪk] <stuck, stuck> I. vi pegarse; (person) quedarse parado; (door, window) atascarse; (mechanism) bloquearse; **to** ~ **in sb's mind** quedarse grabado a alguien II. vt 1. (affix) pegar 2. inf (put) poner; **to** ~ **one's head out the window** asomar la cabeza por la ventana

◆**stick around** vi acoplarse

◆**stick in** vt meter; (knife, needle) clavar

◆**stick out** I. vt asomar; **to stick one's tongue out** sacar la lengua (at a) ► **to stick one's neck out** arriesgarse II. vi 1. (nail, ears) sobresalir 2. (be obvious) ser evidente; **to** ~ **a mile** [or **like a sore thumb**] saltar a la vista 3. **to stick it out** aguantar

◆**stick together** I. vi 1. (remain loyal) mantenerse unidos 2. (not separate) no separarse 3. (adhere) juntarse II. vt juntar

◆**stick up** I. vt inf (rob) atracar; **stick 'em up!** ¡manos arriba! II. vi sobresalir; (hair) estar de punta

**sticker** ['stɪk·ər] n pegatina f

**stick-on** ['stɪk·ɑn] adj adhesivo, -a

**sticky** ['stɪk·i] <-ier, -iest> adj (label) adhesivo, -a; (surface, hands) pegajoso, -a; (weather) bochornoso, -a

**stiff** [stɪf] I. n fiambre m II. adj 1. (rigid, hard) duro, -a; (shirt) tieso, -a; **to be (as)** ~ **as a board** estar más tieso que un palo 2. (joints) entumecido, -a; (muscles) agarrotado, -a; **to have a** ~ **neck** tener tortícolis 3. (strong) fuerte 4. (strenuous) agotador(a) 5. (price) exorbitante III. adv **to be bored** ~ estar aburrido como una ostra; **to be scared** ~ estar muerto de miedo

**stiffen** ['stɪf·ən] I. vi 1. (get tense: person) ponerse tenso; (muscles) agarrotarse 2. (get dense) espesarse II. vt (penalties) endurecer; (competition) hacer más difícil; (morals) fortalecer

**stifle** ['staɪ·fəl] I. vt sofocar; (yawn, scream, desire) contener; (initiative, opposition) reprimir II. vi sofocarse; (lack of air) ahogarse

**stifling** ['staɪ·flɪŋ] adj (heat) sofocante; (room) agobiante

**still¹** [stɪl] I. adj (calm) tranquilo, -a; (wind, waters) en calma; **to keep** ~ quedarse quieto II. n CINE, PHOT fotograma m III. vt (calm) calmar

**still²** [stɪl] adv 1. aún, todavía; **to be** ~ **alive** seguir vivo; **to want** ~ **more** querer aún más; **better** ~ aún mejor 2. (nevertheless) sin embargo

**still³** [stɪl] n (distillery) destilería f

**stillborn** ['stɪl·bɔrn] adj 1. (born dead) nacido, -a muerto, -a 2. (unsuccessful) malogrado, -a

**stilted** ['stɪl·tɪd] adj (manner, style) forzado, -a

**stimulate** ['stɪm·jə·leɪt] vt a. MED estimular

**stimulus** ['stɪm·jə·ləs] <-li> n estímulo m

**sting** [stɪŋ] I. vt 1. (with poison) picar 2. (goad) incitar II. <stung, stung> vi

1. (*with poison*) picar **2.** (*ache*) escocer; (*criticism*) herir **III.** *n* **1.** (*injury*) picotazo *m* **2.** (*pain*) escozor *m;* ~ **of remorse** remordimientos *mpl*

**stingy** ['stɪn·dʒi] *adj* tacaño, -a, pijotero, -a *AmL*, amarrado, -a *Arg, Par, PRico, Urug*, coñete *Chile, Perú;* (*amount*) mísero, -a

**stink** [stɪŋk] **I.** *n* mal olor *m; fig* escándalo *m;* **to create a ~** montar un escándalo **II.** <stank *or* stunk, stunk> *vi* **1.** (*smell*) apestar, bufar *AmL;* **to ~ of money** estar podrido de dinero **2.** (*be bad*) ser patético, -a **3.** (*business, situation*) oler mal

**stinker** ['stɪŋ·kər] *n inf* asco *m;* (*person*) canalla *mf*

**stipulate** ['stɪp·jə·leɪt] *vt* estipular

**stipulation** [ˌstɪp·jə·'leɪ·ʃən] *n* estipulación *f;* **with the ~ that** a condición de que +*subj*

**stir** [stɜr] **I.** <-ring, -red> *vt* **1.** (*mix*) remover; (*fire*) avivar **2.** (*move*) mover **3.** (*stimulate*) estimular; (*trouble*) provocar **II.** *vi* **1.** (*mix*) mezclarse **2.** (*move*) agitarse **3.** (*rouse*) despertarse **III.** *n* **1.** **to give sth a ~** remover algo **2.** (*excitement*) conmoción *f;* **to cause a ~** causar revuelo

**stir-fry** ['stɜr·fraɪ] <-ied, -ies> *vt* freír en poco aceite y removiendo constantemente

**stitch** [stɪtʃ] **I.** <-es> *n* (*knitting*) *a.* MED punto *m;* (*sewing*) puntada *f;* **cross ~** punto de cruz ▶ **to leave sb in ~es** hacer que alguien se tronche de risa **II.** *vi, vt* coser

**stock** [stak] **I.** *n* **1.** reserva *f* **2.** COM, ECON existencias *fpl;* **to have sth in ~** tener algo en stock; **to be out of ~** estar agotado; **to take ~** hacer el inventario; *fig* hacer un balance **3.** FIN acción *f* **4.** AGR, ZOOL ganado *m* **5.** (*descent*) linaje *m* **6.** (*popularity*) prestigio *m;* **her ~ had fallen/risen** había perdido/ganado prestigio **7. to put (no) ~ in sth** (no) dar crédito a algo **II.** *adj* (*model*) estándar; (*response*) típico, -a **III.** *vt* (*goods*) vender; (*shop*) suministrar; (*shelves*) llenar

**stockbroker** ['stak·broʊ·kər] *n* corredor(a) *m(f)* de bolsa

**stock exchange** *n* bolsa *f*

**stocking** ['stak·ɪŋ] *n* media *f*

**stock market** *n* mercado *m* bursátil

**stockpile** ['stak·paɪl] **I.** *n* reservas *fpl* **II.** *vt* almacenar

**stocky** ['stak·i] <-ier, -iest> *adj* bajo, -a y fornido, -a

**stodgy** ['stadʒ·i] <-ier, -iest> *adj* (*food*) pesado, -a; (*person, book*) aburrido, -a

**stoke** [stoʊk] *vt* (*fire*) atizar; (*furnace*) echar leña; *fig* avivar

**stole**[1] [stoʊl] *pt of* steal

**stole**[2] [stoʊl] *n* FASHION estola *f*

**stomach** ['stʌm·ək] **I.** *n* **1.** estómago *m;* **to have an upset ~** tener mal el estómago; **to have a strong ~** tener estómago **2.** (*belly*) barriga *f* **II.** *vt inf* (*drink, food*) tolerar; (*person, insult*) soportar

**stone** [stoʊn] **I.** *n* **1.** GEO piedra *f;* **to be a ~'s throw (away)** estar a tiro de piedra **2.** MED cálculo *m* **3.** (*jewel*) gema *f* **4.** (*fruit*) hueso *m*, carozo *m CSur* ▶ **to cast the first ~** tirar la primera piedra; **to leave no ~ unturned** no dejar piedra por mover; **to be carved** [*or* **set**] **in ~** estar grabado en piedra **II.** *adv* ~ **hard** duro, -a como una piedra; ~ **crazy** loco de remate

**Stone Age** *n* Edad *f* de Piedra

**stone-cold I.** *adj* helado, -a **II.** *adv* **to knock sb out** ~ dejar de piedra; **to be ~ sober** no haber bebido ni una gota

**stoned** *adj* fumado, -a

**stony** ['stoʊ·ni] <-ier, -iest> *adj* (*beach, ground*) pedregoso, -a; (*expression*) frío, -a; (*silence*) sepulcral; (*feelings*) de piedra

**stood** [stʊd] *pt, pp of* stand

**stool** [stul] *n* (*seat*) taburete *m*

**stoop**[1] [stup] *vi* ARCHIT inclinarse; **to ~ to sth** rebajarse a algo; **to ~ low** caer (muy) bajo

**stoop**[2] [stup] *n* pórtico *m*

**stop** [stap] **I.** *n* **1.** pausa *f;* **to come to a ~** detenerse; **to put a ~ to** poner fin (**to** a) **2.** (*place*) parada *f* ▶ **to pull out (all) the ~s** desplegar todos los recursos **II.** <-ping, -ped> *vt* **1.** (*cease*) parar; (*payment*) suspender **2.** (*switch off*)

S

apagar **3.** (*block*) rellenar; (*hole, ears*) tapar **III.** <- ping, -ped> *vi* pararse; (*car*) detenerse; **to ~ doing sth** dejar de hacer algo; **to ~ and think** (**about**) pararse a pensar

♦**stop by** *vi* pasar por

♦**stop in** *vi* quedarse en casa

♦**stop off** *vi* detenerse un rato

♦**stop over** *vi* pasarse por

♦**stop up** *vt* (*block*) atascar; (*hole*) tapar; (*gap*) rellenar

**stopover** ['stap·ou·vər] *n* parada *f*; AVIAT escala *f*

**stop sign** *n* stop *m*, alto *m* *Méx*

**stopwatch** *n* cronómetro *m*

**storage** ['stɔr·ɪdʒ] *n a.* COMPUT almacenamiento *m*; **to put sth in ~** almacenar algo

**store** [stɔr] **I.** *n* **1.** (*shop*) tienda *f*; **department ~** grandes almacenes *mpl*, emporio *m* *AmC* **2.** (*supply*) provisión *f*; (*wine*) reserva *f* **3.** (*warehouse*) almacén *m*; **what is in ~ for us?** ¿qué nos deparará el futuro? **II.** *vt* **1.** (*into storage*) almacenar **2.** (*for future use*) guardar **3.** COMPUT (*file*) guardar; (*data*) almacenar

**storehouse** ['stɔr·haus] *n* almacén *m*; *fig* mina *f*

**stork** [stɔrk] *n* cigüeña *f*

**storm** [stɔrm] **I.** *n* tormenta *f*; *fig* trifulca *f*; (*protest*) ola *f*; (*political*) revuelo *m*; **to take sth by ~** asaltar algo; **to take sb by ~** cautivar a alguien ▶ **to ride out** [*or* **weather**] **the ~** capear el temporal **II.** *vi* **1.** haber tormenta; (*winds*) soplar con fuerza **2.** (*speak*) bramar

**storm cloud** *n* nubarrón *m*

**stormy** ['stɔr·mi] <-ier, -iest> *adj* tormentoso, -a; (*sea, relationship*) tempestuoso, -a; (*argument*) violento, -a

**story¹** ['stɔr·i] <-ies> *n* (*account*) historia *f*; (*fictional*) cuento *m*; **to tell stories** *a. fig* contar cuentos; **so the ~ goes** dicen ▶ **that's another ~** eso es harina de otro costal; **the same old ~** la misma historia de siempre; **a tall ~** un cuento chino

**story²** ['stɔr·i] *n* piso *m*

**stout** [staut] **I.** *adj* (*person*) robusto, -a; (*shoes, boots*) fuerte **II.** *n* cerve-

za *f* negra

**stoutly** ['staut·li] *adv* (*strongly*) sólidamente; (*firmly*) con firmeza

**stove** [stouv] *n* cocina *f*; (*heater*) estufa *f*

**stowaway** ['stou·ə·wei] *n* polizón, -ona *m, f*

**straggle** ['stræg·əl] *vi* **1.** (*lag behind*) rezagarse **2.** (*come in small numbers*) llegar poco a poco; (*move in a disorganized group*) avanzar desordenadamente

**straggler** ['stræg·lər] *n* rezagado, -a *m, f*

**straight** [streit] **I.** *adj* **1.** (*not bent*) recto, -a **2.** (*honest*) sincero, -a (**with** con) **3.** (*plain*) sencillo, -a; (*gin*) solo, -a **4.** (*consecutive*) seguido, -a **5.** (*heterosexual*) hetero **II.** *adv* **1.** (*direct*) en línea recta; **to go ~ ahead** ir todo recto; **to come/head ~** ir derecho (**at, for** a); **to get ~ to the point** ir directo al grano **2.** *inf* honestamente, con claridad; **to give it to sb ~** ser franco con alguien **3.** (*see, think*) con claridad **III.** *n* recta *f*; **the finishing ~** la recta final

**straightaway** [ˌstreit·ə·'wei] **I.** *adv* enseguida **II.** *n* recta *f*

**straighten** ['strei·tən] *vt* (*hair*) alisar; (*wires*) enderezar; (*body, leg*) estirar

♦**straighten out** *vt* **1.** (*straight*) estirar **2.** (*level*) igualar **3.** (*situation*) arreglar; (*problem*) resolver **4.** (*clarify*) aclarar

♦**straighten up I.** *vi* ponerse derecho, arriscarse *Col* **II.** *vt* **1.** (*tidy*) ordenar **2.** (*level*) igualar

**straightforward** [ˌstreit·'fɔr·wərd] *adj* **1.** (*honest*) honesto, -a **2.** (*easy*) sencillo, -a

**straight-out** [ˌstreit·'aut] *adj inf* (*outright*) redomado, -a; (*refusal*) tajante

**strain¹** [strein] **I.** *n* **1.** (*pressure*) presión *f*; **to be under a lot of ~** tener mucho estrés; **to put a ~** crear tensiones (**on** en) **2.** PHYS deformación *f* **3.** MED torcedura *f* **II.** *vt* **1. to ~ one's eyes/ears** forzar la vista/aguzar el oído **2.** (*relationship*) crear tensiones en; (*credulity*) poner a prueba **3.** CULIN filtrar; (*vegetables*) escurrir

**strain²** [strein] *n* (*virus*) cepa *f*; (*species*) raza *f*; **~ of eccentricity** vena *f* excéntrica; **~ of puritanism** nota *f* de puritanismo

**strained** [streɪnd] adj (relations) tenso, -a; (smile) forzado, -a

**strait** [streɪt] n **1.** GEO estrecho m; **the Bering Strait** el estrecho de Bering **2.** m; **to be in dire ~s** estar en grandes apuros

**strand¹** [strænd] n (wool) hebra f; (rope, string) ramal m; (hair) mechón m; (pearls) sarta f; (plot) hilo m

**strand²** [strænd] vt varar; **to be ~ed** quedarse desamparado

**strange** [streɪndʒ] adj **1.** (peculiar) raro, -a; **I felt ~** me sentía raro; **it's ~ that** es raro que +subj; **~r things have happened** cosas más raras se han visto; **~ to say** aunque parezca mentira **2.** (unfamiliar: face) desconocido, -a; (bed) ajeno, -a

**strangely** adv (behave, dress) de forma rara; **~ enough** aunque parazca mentira

**stranger** ['streɪn·dʒər] n desconocido, -a m, f

**strangle** ['stræŋ·gəl] vt estrangular; (cry) ahogar

**strap** [stræp] **I.** n (bag) correa f; (dress) tirante m **II.** <-pp-> vt sujetar con una correa

**strapless** ['stræp·lɪs] adj sin tirantes

**strapping** ['stræp·ɪŋ] **I.** adj inf robusto, -a **II.** n esparadrapo m

**strategy** ['stræt·ə·dʒi] <-ies> n estrategia f

**straw** [strɔ] n paja f; (drink) pajita f, popote m Méx, pitillo m And ▶ **to be the last ~** ser el colmo; **to draw the short ~** tocarle a uno la china; **to clutch at ~s** agarrarse a un clavo ardiendo

**strawberry** ['strɔ·ber·i] <-ies> n fresa f, frutilla f AmL

**stray** [streɪ] **I.** adj (dog, cat) callejero, -a, realengo, -a Méx, PRico; (hair) suelto, -a **II.** vi (wander) errar; (get lost) perderse; **to ~ from** alejarse de; **to ~ off course** apartarse del camino; **to ~ from the point** divagar

**streak** [strik] **I.** n **1.** (stripe) raya f; (hair) mechón m; (light) rayo m; (lightning) relámpago m **2.** (tendency) vena f; **an aggressive ~** una vena agresiva **3.** (spell)

racha f; **to be on a winning ~** tener una buena racha ▶ **like a ~ of lightning** como un rayo; **to talk a blue ~** hablar como una cotorra **II.** vt rayar; **to have one's hair ~ed** hacerse mechas; **to be ~ed** estar manchado (with de) **III.** vi **1.** (move fast) ir rápido **2.** (naked) correr desnudo en público

**streaky** ['stri·ki] <-ier, -iest> adj rayado, -a

**stream** [strim] **I.** n **1.** (river) arroyo m, estero m Chile, Ecua **2.** (current) corriente f; **to go against the ~** ir a contracorriente **3.** (flow: liquid) chorrito m; (people) torrente m; (insults) sarta f **II.** vi **1.** (flow) fluir; (water) chorrear; (blood) manar; (tears) caer; (sunlight) entrar a raudales; (nose) gotear **2.** (move in numbers) afluir en masa

**streamer** ['stri·mər] n serpentina f

**streamline** ['strim·laɪn] vt (vehicle) aerodinamizar; (method) racionalizar

**streamlined** adj (vehicle) aerodinámico, -a; (method) racionalizado, -a

**street** [strit] n calle f; **in** [or on] **the ~** en la calle ▶ **to be out on the ~** no tener hogar; **to walk the ~s** deambular por las calles; (prostitute) hacer la calle

**streetcar** n tranvía m

**streetwise** ['strit·waɪz] adj espabilado, -a; (politician) astuto, -a

**strength** [streŋkθ] n **1.** (power) fuerza f, ñeque m Chile, Ecua, Perú; (feeling, light) intensidad f; (alcohol) graduación f; (economy) solidez f; (mental) fortaleza f **2.** (members) número m; **to be at full ~** tener el cupo completo; **to be below ~** (office) estar corto de personal **3.** (strong point) punto m fuerte; **one's ~s and weaknesses** sus virtudes y defectos

**strengthen** ['streŋk·θən] **I.** vt (muscles) fortalecer; (wall) reforzar; (financial position) consolidar; (chances) aumentar; (relations) intensificar; (links) estrechar **II.** vi fortalecerse

**strenuous** ['stren·ju·əs] adj (activity) agotador(a); (supporter) acérrimo, -a; (denial) rotundo, -a

**stress** [stres] **I.** n **1.** PSYCH estrés m **2.** (emphasis) énfasis m inv **3.** LING

S

acento m **4.** PHYS tensión f **II.** vt recalcar; LING acentuar

**stressed** adj, **stressed out** adj estresado, -a

**stressful** ['stres·fʊl] adj estresante

**stretch** [stretʃ] **I.** <-es> n **1.** (elasticity) elasticidad f; **at full ~** a todo gas; **not by any ~ of the imagination** ni por asomo **2.** SPORTS estiramiento m **3.** GEO trecho m **4.** (piece) trozo m; (road) tramo m; (time) período m **5.** (race) recta f; **the home ~** la recta final **II.** vi estirarse; (clothes) dar de sí; (sea, influence) extenderse; **to ~ (all the way) back to**) remontarse (**back to**) **III.** vt estirar; **to ~ one's legs/the limit** estirar las piernas/el límite; **to ~ sb's patience** poner a prueba la paciencia de alguien; **to ~ a point** hacer una excepción; **now you're really ~ing it** ahora sí que estás exagerando **IV.** adj elástico, -a

**stretcher** ['stretʃ·ər] n camilla f

**strict** [strɪkt] adj (person) severo, -a, fregado, -a AmC; (control, orders, sense) estricto, -a; (deadline) inamovible; (neutrality) total; (secrecy, confidence) absoluto, -a

**strictly** ['strɪkt·li] adv **1.** (exactly) estrictamente; **not ~ comparable** no del todo comparable; **~ speaking** en rigor **2.** (harshly) severamente; (forbidden) terminantemente

**stride** [straɪd] **I.** <strode> vi andar a trancos; **to ~ ahead** andar dando zancadas; **to ~ across sth** cruzar algo de una zancada **II.** n **1.** (step) zancada f **2.** (progress) progreso m; **to make (positive) ~s forward** hacer grandes progresos; **to make ~s** acercarse (**towards** a) ▸ **to get into** [or **hit**] **one's ~** coger el ritmo; **to take sth in ~** tomarse algo con calma

**strike** [straɪk] **I.** n **1.** MIL ataque m **2.** (workers) huelga f **3.** (discovery) descubrimiento m **4.** (baseball) strike m **II.** <struck, struck or stricken> vt **1.** (collide) golpear; (match) encender; **struck by lightning** alcanzado por un rayo; **to ~ a blow** asestar un golpe (**against** a) **2.** (achieve) conseguir; **to ~ a balance** encontrar un equilibrio; **to ~ a bargain**

hacer un trato **3.** (seem) parecer; **it ~s me that...** se me ocurre que... **4.** (impress) impresionar; **I was struck by the news** la noticia me impactó **5.** (discover) descubrir; (find) encontrar **6. to ~ an attitude** adoptar una actitud; **to ~ fear** infundir miedo (**into** a) **7.** (clock) marcar; **the clock struck three** el reloj dio las tres ▸ **to ~ a chord** llegar a entenderse (**with** con); **to ~ sb dumb** dejar a alguien sin habla; **to ~ it rich** forrarse **III.** <struck, struck or stricken> vi **1.** (hit) golpear; (attack) atacar (**at the heart of** directamente a); **to ~ home** dar en el blanco **2.** (worker) declararse en huelga; **the right to ~** el derecho a la huelga; **to ~ for** hacer una huelga por

♦ **strike back** vi contraatacar; **to ~ at sb** tomar represalias contra alguien

♦ **strike down** vt **1. she was struck down by cancer** fue abatida por el cáncer **2.** LAW revocar

♦ **strike off** vt tachar

♦ **strike out I.** vt **1.** (baseball) eliminar **2.** (delete) borrar **II.** vi **1.** (baseball) ser eliminado; fig fallar **2.** (move off) andar resueltamente; **to ~ on one's own** hacerse independiente

♦ **strike up** vt (conversation, friendship) entablar; (relationship) iniciar

**striker** ['straɪ·kər] n **1.** huelguista mf **2.** SPORTS delantero, -a m, f

**striking** ['straɪ·kɪŋ] adj notable; (result, beauty) impresionante; (resemblance) sorprendente; (contrast) acusado, -a; **visually ~** llamativo

**string** [strɪŋ] **I.** n **1.** (twine) a. MUS cuerda f; (puppet) hilo m; **to pull ~s** fig mover hilos; **with no ~s attached** sin compromiso alguno **2.** (chain) cadena f; (pearls) collar m; (lies) sarta f; (people) hilera f **3.** COMPUT secuencia f **II.** <strung, strung> vt poner una cuerda a; (instrument, tennis racket) encordar; (beads) ensartar

♦ **string along** inf **I.** vi ir/venir también **II.** vt embaucar

♦ **string out** vt (extend) espaciar; (activity) prolongar

♦ **string up** vt inf colgar

**string band** n banda f de cuerda

**strip** [strɪp] I. vt 1. (lay bare) dejar sin cubierta; **to ~ sb of sth** quitar algo a alguien 2. (unclothe) desnudar 3. (dismantle) desmontar II. vi desnudarse III. n 1. (ribbon) tira f; (metal) lámina f; (land) franja f 2. (striptease) striptease m 3. **landing ~** pista f de aterrizaje

**stripe** [straɪp] n 1. (band) raya f 2. (type) **of every ~** de todo tipo; **governments of every ~** gobiernos de todos los colores

**striped** adj rayado, -a; (shirt) a rayas

**stripper** ['strɪp·ər] n 1. (person) stripper mf 2. (solvent) líquido m quitaesmaltes; (wallpaper) líquido quitapapeles

**strive** [straɪv] <strove, striven or strived> vi esmerarse (**to** en, **after, for** por)

**strode** [stroʊd] pt of **stride**

**stroke** [stroʊk] I. vt 1. (caress) acariciar 2. SPORTS golpear suavemente II. n 1. (caress) caricia f 2. MED derrame m cerebral; **to suffer a ~** tener una apoplejía f 3. (pencil) trazo m; (brush) pincelada f 4. SPORTS golpe m; (billiards) tacada f; (swimming style) estilo m 5. (clock) campanada f 6. **by a ~ of fate** por cosas del destino; **a ~ of genius** una genialidad; **a ~ of luck** un golpe de suerte

**stroll** [stroʊl] I. n paseo m; **to go for a ~** ir a dar una vuelta II. vi dar un paseo

**strong** [strɔŋ] I. adj 1. fuerte; (competition) duro, -a; (reason) de peso; (nerves) de acero, fervoroso, -a; (emotion) intenso, -a; (friendship) estrecho, -a; (supporter) acérrimo, -a; (color) llamativo, -a; **to be as ~ as an ox** ser tan fuerte como un toro; **to produce ~ memories** traer muchos recuerdos 2. (very likely) muy probable; **~ chance of success** muchas posibilidades de éxito 3. (high value) de gran valor II. adv inf **to come on ~ to sb** tirar por alguien; **to be still going ~** seguir bien

**strongly** adv fuertemente; (advise) fervorosamente; (condemn, criticize) duramente; **to smell ~** tener un fuerte olor (**of** a); **to be ~ opposed** estar muy en contra (**to** de); **to be ~ biased** tener muchos prejuicios (**against** contra)

**strong-minded** [ˌstrɔŋ·'maɪn·dɪd] adj resuelto, -a

**strove** [stroʊv] pt of **strive**

**struck** [strʌk] pt, pp of **strike**

**structure** ['strʌk·tʃər] I. n estructura f; (building) construcción f II. vt estructurar

**struggle** ['strʌg·əl] I. n 1. (effort) esfuerzo m; **to be a real ~** suponer un gran esfuerzo; **to give up the ~** dejar de esmerarse (**to** en) 2. (skirmish) lucha f; **to put up a ~** oponer resistencia II. vi 1. (effort) esforzarse 2. (fight) luchar

**strung** [strʌŋ] pt, pp of **string**

**stub** [stʌb] I. n (check) talón m; (cigarette) colilla f II. <-bb-> vt **to ~ one's toe** tropezar (**against** con)

**stubborn** ['stʌb·ərn] adj (person, animal) terco, -a; **as ~ as a mule** más terco que una mula; (insistence) tenaz; (problem) persistente; (refusal) rotundo, -a; (resistance) inquebrantable

**stuck** [stʌk] I. pt, pp of **stick** II. adj 1. (jammed) atascado, -a 2. **to be ~** estar loco (**on** por)

**stuck-up** [ˌstʌk·'ʌp] adj inf engreído, -a

**stud**[1] [stʌd] n ZOOL a. fig semental m, garañón m AmL

**stud**[2] [stʌd] n 1. (nail) clavo m 2. **collar ~** gemelo m 3. (tire) taco m 4. (earring) pendiente m

**student** ['stu·dənt] n estudiante mf; **the ~ body** el alumnado

**studied** ['stʌd·id] adj estudiado, -a; (insult) premeditado, -a

**studio** ['stu·di·oʊ] <-s> n a. CINE estudio m; (artist) taller m

**studio apartment** n estudio m

**studious** ['stu·di·əs] adj estudioso, -a

**study** ['stʌd·i] I. vt (subject) estudiar; (evidence) examinar II. vi estudiar III. <-ies> n 1. estudio m; (evidence) investigación f 2. (room) despacho m

**stuff** [stʌf] I. n 1. inf (things) movidas fpl argot; **to know one's ~** conocer su oficio 2. (belongings) cosas fpl 3. (material) material m; (cloth) tela f; **the (very) ~** la esencia (**of** de) II. vt 1. (fill) llenar; **to ~ sth into sth** meter algo en algo; **to ~ sb's head** llenar a alguien la cabeza (**with** de); **to ~ oneself** darse un atracón

S

**2.** (*animal*) disecar

**stuffing** ['stʌf·ɪŋ] *n* relleno *m*

**stuffy** ['stʌf·i] *adj* (*room*) mal ventilado, -a; (*atmosphere*) cargado, -a; (*nose*) taponado, -a; (*person*) tieso, -a

**stumble** ['stʌm·bəl] *vi* **1.** (*trip*) tropezar (**on** con) **2.** (*talking*) balbucear

**stumbling block** *n* obstáculo *m*

**stump** [stʌmp] **I.** *n* (*plant*) tocón *m*; (*arm*) muñón *m* **II.** *vt inf* desconcertar **III.** *vi* **to ~ about** andar pisando fuerte

**stun** [stʌn] <-nn-> *vt* **1.** (*stupefy*) dejar pasmado **2.** (*unconscious*) dejar sin sentido

**stung** [stʌŋ] *pp, pt of* **sting**

**stunk** [stʌŋk] *pt, pp of* **stink**

**stunned** *adj* aturdido, -a

**stunning** ['stʌn·ɪŋ] *adj* **1.** (*surprising*) asombroso, -a **2.** (*impressive*) espléndido, -a; (*dress*) estupendo, -a

**stupendous** [stu·'pen·dəs] *adj* estupendo, -a

**stupid** ['stu·pɪd] *adj* estúpido, -a, cojudo, -a *AmL*, zonzo, -a *AmL*

**stupidity** [stu·'pɪd·ə·t̬i] *n* estupidez *f*, dundera *f AmL*

**sturdy** ['stɜr·di] *adj* **1.** (*robust*) robusto, -a **2.** (*resolute*) decidido, -a; **a ~ defender** un defensor acérrimo

**stutter** ['stʌt̬·ər] **I.** *vi, vt* tartamudear, cancanear *AmL* **II.** *n* tartamudeo *m*

**sty** [staɪ] *n* (*pigsty*) pocilga *f*

**style** [staɪl] **I.** *n* **1.** *a.* ART, ARCHIT estilo *m*; (*management*) modo *f*; (*teaching*) forma *f* **2.** (*elegance*) elegancia *f*; **to have no ~** no ser elegante; **with ~** con estilo; **to live in** (**grand**) **~** vivir a lo grande; **to travel in ~** viajar con todo el confort **3.** (*fashion*) moda *f*; **in ~** de moda **II.** *vt* (*design*) diseñar; (*hair*) peinar

**styling** *n* estilización *f*

**stylish** ['staɪ·lɪʃ] *adj* a la moda; (*elegant*) garboso, -a

**stylist** ['staɪ·lɪst] *n* estilista *mf*

**Styrofoam®** ['staɪ·rə·ˌfoʊm] *n* poliestireno *m*

**sub¹** [sʌb] *n inf* **1.** *abbr of* **substitute** sustituto, -a *m, f* **2.** *abbr of* **submarine** submarino *m* **3.** *abbr of* **sandwich** sándwich *m* mixto

**sub²** [sʌb] <-bb-> *vi abbr of* **substitute**

sustituir

**subconscious** [ˌsʌb·'kan·ʃəs] *adj, n* subconsciente *m*

**subdivide** [ˌsʌb·dɪ·'vaɪd] *vt* subdividir

**subdue** [səb·'du] *vt* (*tame*) someter; (*repress*) reprimir

**subject¹** ['sʌb·dʒɪkt] **I.** *n* **1.** (*theme*) tema *m*; **to change the ~** cambiar de tema; **to wander off the ~** salirse del tema; **on the ~ of** a propósito de **2.** SCHOOL, UNIV asignatura *f*; (*research area*) ámbito *m* **3.** (*citizen*) ciudadano, -a *m, f* **4.** LING, MED sujeto *m* **II.** *adj* **to be ~** estar sujeto (**to** a); **~ to approval** pendiente de aprobación; **to be ~ to colds** ser propenso a acatarrarse; **to be ~ to many dangers** estar expuesto a muchos peligros

**subject²** [səb·'dʒekt] *vt* dominar

**subjective** [səb·'dʒek·tɪv] *adj* subjetivo, -a

**subject matter** *n* tema *m*; (*letter*) contenido *m*

**subjunctive** [səb·'dʒʌŋk·tɪv] *n* subjuntivo *m*

**sublet** [sʌb·'let] <sublet, sublet> *vt* subarrendar

**submarine** ['sʌb·mə·rin] *n* **1.** NAUT, MIL submarino *m* **2.** *inf* sándwich *m* mixto **II.** *adj* submarino, -a

**submerge** [səb·'mɜrdʒ] **I.** *vt* sumergir; **to ~ oneself** *fig* dedicarse de lleno (**in** a) **II.** *vi* sumergirse

**submission** [səb·'mɪʃ·ən] *n* **1.** (*surrender*) sumisión *f* **2.** (*proposal*) presentación *f*; (*document*) entrega *f*

**submissive** [səb·'mɪs·ɪv] *adj* sumiso, -a

**submit** [səb·'mɪt] <-tt-> **I.** *vt* **1.** (*proposal*) presentar; (*document*) entregar **2.** *form* proponer **II.** *vi* (*yield*) someterse

**subordinate¹** [sə·'bɔr·dən·ɪt] **I.** *n* subordinado, -a *m, f* **II.** *adj* (*secondary*) secundario, -a; (*rank*) subordinado, -a

**subordinate²** [sə·'bɔr·də·neɪt] *vt* subordinar

**subscribe** [səb·'skraɪb] **I.** *vi* suscribirse; **to ~ to** suscribir **II.** *vt* (*contribute*) donar

**subscriber** [səb·'skraɪ·bər] *n* (*magazine*) suscriptor(a) *m(f)*; (*phone*) abonado, -a *m, f*

**subscription** [səb·'skrɪp·fən] n suscripción f; **to a ~** suscribirse (**to** a)

**subsequent** ['sʌb·sɪ·kwənt] adj posterior; **~ to** después de

**subsequently** adv después; **~ to** después de

**subside** [səb·'saɪd] vi disminuir; (water) bajar; (ground) hundirse

**subsidiary** [səb·'sɪd·i·er·i] I. adj subsidiario, -a; (reason) secundario, -a; ECON filial II. <-ies> n ECON filial f

**subsidize** ['sʌb·sə·daɪz] vt subvencionar

**subsidy** ['sʌb·sə·di] <-ies> n subvención f; **unemployment ~** subsidio m de desempleo

**subsist** [səb·'sɪst] vi subsistir; **to ~ on sth** sustentarse con [or a base de] algo

**substance** ['sʌb·stəns] n 1. (matter) sustancia f 2. (essence) esencia f 3. (significance) valor m 4. (main point) punto m más importante; **the ~ of the conversation** el punto esencial de la conversación; **in ~** en esencia 5. (possessions) riqueza f; **a man of ~** un hombre acaudalado

**substandard** [ˌsʌb·'stæn·dərd] adj inferior

**substantial** [səb·'stæn·fəl] adj 1. (important) sustancial; (difference, improvement) notable; **to be in ~ agreement** estar de acuerdo en gran parte 2. (large) grande; (meal) copioso, -a; (sum, damage) considerable 3. (sturdy) sólido, -a

**substantially** [səb·'stæn·fə·li] adv (significantly) considerablemente; (in the main) esencialmente

**substantive** ['sʌb·stən·tɪv] n sustantivo m

**substitute** ['sʌb·stə·tut] I. vt sustituir; **to ~ sb for sb** reemplazar a alguien por alguien; **to ~ oil for butter, to ~ butter with oil** sustituir la mantequilla por el aceite II. vi **to ~ for** suplir III. n 1. (equivalent) sustituto m; (milk, coffee) sucedáneo m; **there's no ~ for him** no hay nadie como él 2. SCHOOL, SPORTS suplente mf

**substitution** [ˌsʌb·stə·'tu·fən] n sustitución f

**subtitle** ['sʌb·taɪ·təl] I. vt subtitular II. n subtítulo m

**subtle** ['sʌt·əl] adj sutil; (flavor) suave; (nuance) tenue; (question, suggestion) inteligente; (person) astuto, -a

**subtotal** ['sʌb·tou·təl] n subtotal m

**subtract** [səb·'trækt] vt sustraer; **to ~ 3 from 5** restar 3 a 5

**subtraction** [səb·'træk·fən] n resta f

**subtropical** [ˌsʌb·'trap·ɪ·kəl] adj subtropical

**suburb** ['sʌb·ɜrb] n barrio m periférico; **the ~s** la periferia; **to live in the ~s** vivir en las afueras

**suburban** [sə·'bɜr·bən] adj (area) periférico, -a; (train) de cercanías; (lifestyle) aburguesado, -a

**subvention** [səb·'ven·fən] n subvención f

**subversive** [səb·'vɜr·sɪv] adj subversivo, -a

**subvert** [sʌb·'vɜrt] vt (authority) minar; (principle) debilitar

**subway** ['sʌb·weɪ] n metro m, subte m Arg

**sub-zero** [ˌsʌb·'zɪr·ou] adj bajo cero

**succeed** [sək·'sid] I. vi 1. (be successful) tener éxito; **to ~ in doing sth** lograr hacer algo; **the plan ~ed** el plan salió bien 2. (follow) suceder II. vt suceder

**succeeding** adj siguiente; (generation) venidero, -a; **in the ~ weeks** en las próximas semanas

**success** [sək·'ses] n éxito m; **to meet with ~, to enjoy ~** tener éxito; **to have ~ in doing sth** conseguir hacer algo; **to make a ~ of** tener éxito (of en); **to wish sb ~ with sth** desear a alguien que le vaya bien algo

**successful** [sək·'ses·fəl] adj (business) próspero, -a; (candidate) electo, -a; (solution) eficaz; **to be ~** (person) tener éxito; (business) prosperar

**succession** [sək·'sef·ən] n sucesión f; **in ~** sucesivamente; **a ~ of** una serie de; **an endless ~ of** un sinfín de

**successive** [sək·'ses·ɪv] adj sucesivo, -a; **on ~ occasions** varias veces seguidas

**successor** [sək·'ses·ər] n sucesor/a m(f)

**such** [sʌtʃ] I. adj tal, semejante; **~ great weather/a good book** un tiempo/un libro tan bueno; **~ an honor** tanto honor; **to earn ~ a lot of money** ganar

S

tanto dinero; **or some ~ remark** o un comentario por el estilo; **to buy some fruit ~ as apples** comprar fruta como manzanas **II.** *pron* **~ is life** así es la vida; **people ~ as him** las personas que son como él; **~ as it is** tal como es; **as ~** propiamente dicho

**such and such** ['sʌtʃ·ən·ˌsʌtʃ] *adj* tal o cual; **to arrive at ~ a time** llegar a tal o cual hora; **to see sb in ~ a place** ver a alguien en tal o cual lugar

**suck** [sʌk] **I.** *vt* succionar; (*straw*) sorber; (*air*) aspirar; (*breast*) mamar; (*sweets*) chupar; **to ~ one's thumb** chuparse el dedo **II.** *vi* **1.** chupar **2. this ~s!** ¡vaya mierda! **III.** *n* chupada *f*; (*straw*) sorbo *m*

**sucker** ['sʌk·ər] **I.** *n* **1.** (*person*) imbécil *mf*; (*thing*) mierda *f* **2.** (*device*) *a.* ZOOL ventosa *f* **II.** *vt* *inf* timar (**into** en); **to ~ sb into/out of doing sth** engañar a alguien para que haga/no haga algo

**sudden** ['sʌd·ən] *adj* repentino, -a, sorpresivo, -a *AmL*; (*death*) súbito, -a; (*departure*) imprevisto, -a; (*movement, drop*) brusco, -a; **to put a ~ stop to sth** detener algo de forma repentina; **all of a ~** *inf* de repente

**suddenly** *adv* de repente

**suds** [sʌdz] *npl* **1.** jabonaduras *fpl* **2.** *sl* cerveza *f*

**sue** [su] <suing> **I.** *vt* demandar; **to ~ sb for damages** demandar a alguien por daños y perjuicios; **to ~ sb for divorce** poner a alguien una demanda de divorcio **II.** *vi* presentar demanda; **to ~ for peace** pedir la paz

**suede** [sweɪd] *n* ante *m*

**suffer** ['sʌf·ər] **I.** *vi* sufrir; **the economy is ~ing** la economía se está viendo afectada (**from** por); **to ~ for sth** ser castigado por algo; **to ~ in** [*or* **by**] **comparison** salir perdiendo en comparación **II.** *vt* sufrir; MED padecer de; **to ~ the consequences** sufrir las consecuencias; **to ~ the misfortune of** tener mala suerte de

**suffering** ['sʌf·ər·ɪŋ] *n* sufrimiento *m*; **years of ~** años de penurias

**suffice** [sə·'faɪs] *vi* bastar; **~ (it) to say that** basta decir que

**sufficient** [sə·'fɪʃ·ənt] *adj* suficiente; **to have ~** tener bastante; **to be ~ for** ser suficiente para

**suffix** ['sʌf·ɪks] *n* sufijo *m*

**suffocate** ['sʌf·ə·keɪt] **I.** *vi* asfixiarse **II.** *vt* asfixiar; *fig* sofocar

**suffocating** *adj* asfixiante; *fig* sofocante

**sugar** ['ʃʊg·ər] **I.** *n* **1.** CULIN azúcar *m* **2.** *inf* (*term of affection*) cariño **II.** *vt* azucarar

**sugary** ['ʃʊg·ə·ri] *adj* **1.** azucarado, -a **2.** (*insincere*) meloso, -a

**suggest** [səg·'dʒest] *vt* **1.** (*propose*) proponer; **to ~ doing sth** proponer hacer algo; **to ~** (**to sb**) **that** sugerir a alguien que **+subj; an idea ~ed itself to him** se le ocurrió una idea **2.** (*indicate*) indicar **3.** (*hint*) insinuar; **what are you trying to ~?** ¿qué insinúas?

**suggestion** [səg·'dʒes·tʃən] *n* **1.** (*proposal*) sugerencia *f*; **to make the ~ that** sugerir que **+subj; at Ann's ~** a petición de Ann **2.** (*bit*) pizca *f* **3.** (*insinuation*) insinuación *f*

**suggestive** [səg·'dʒes·tɪv] *adj* **1.** (*lewd*) indecente **2.** (*evocative*) sugestivo, -a

**suicide** ['su·ə·saɪd] *n* **1.** suicidio *m*; **~ bombing** atentado *m* suicida; **to commit ~** suicidarse **2.** (*person*) suicida *mf*

**suit** [sut] **I.** *vt* **1.** (*be convenient*) convenir; **to ~ sb** convenirle a alguien; **that ~s me fine** eso me viene bien; **to ~ oneself** hacer lo que uno quiere; **~ yourself!** ¡haz lo que quieras! **2.** (*be right*) ir [*or* sentar] bien; **they are well ~ed** hacen buena pareja **3.** (*look good*) quedar bien; **this dress ~s you** este vestido te sienta bien **II.** *n* **1.** (*with pants*) traje *m*, terno *m Chile*, flus *m Ant, Col, Ven*; (*with skirt*) traje *m* de chaqueta; **bathing** [*or* **swim**] **~** bañador *m* **2.** LAW pleito *m* **3.** GAMES palo *m*; **to follow ~** seguir el palo; *fig* seguir el ejemplo

**suitable** ['su·tə·bəl] *adj* apropiado, -a (**for** para); **not ~ for children under 14** no apto para menores de 14 años

**suitcase** ['sut·keɪs] *n* maleta *f*, valija *f RíoPl*, petaca *f Méx*

**sulfuric** [sʌl·'fjʊr·ɪk] *adj* sulfúrico, -a

**sulk** [sʌlk] **I.** *vi* enfurruñarse, alunarse *RíoPl*, amurrarse *Chile* **II.** *n* mal humor *m;* **to be in a ~** estar enfurruñado, -a [*or RíoPl* alunado, -a] [*or Chile* amurrado, -a]

**sulky** ['sʌl·ki] <-ier, -iest> *adj* enfurruñado, -a

**sullen** ['sʌl·ən] *adj* malhumorado, -a; (*sky*) sombrío, -a

**sultana** [sʌl·'tæn·ə] *n* pasa *f* sultana

**sultry** ['sʌl·tri] <-ier, -iest> *adj* **1.** (*weather*) bochornoso, -a **2.** (*sensual*) sensual

**sum** [sʌm] *n* **1.** (*money*) cantidad *f* **2.** (*total*) total *m;* **in ~** en resumen **3.** MAT cuenta *f*

**summarize** ['sʌm·ə·raɪz] *vt* resumir

**summary** ['sʌm·ə·ri] *n* resumen *m*

**summer** ['sʌm·ər] **I.** *n* verano *m;* **a ~'s day** un día de verano **II.** *adj* de verano, veraniego, -a

**summertime** ['sʌm·ər·taɪm] *n* verano *m;* **in the ~** en verano

**summit** ['sʌm·ɪt] *n* **a.** *fig* cumbre *f;* **to hold a ~** celebrar una cumbre

**summon** ['sʌm·ən] *vt* llamar; (*meeting*) convocar; LAW citar

**summons** ['sʌm·ənz] *n* llamamiento *m;* LAW citación *f*

**sun** [sʌn] **I.** *n* sol *m;* **the ~'s rays** los rayos del sol; **the rising/setting ~** el sol naciente/poniente; **in the ~** al sol
▶ **everything under the ~** de todo; **to call sb every name under the ~** decir a alguien de todo **II.** <-nn-> *vt* **to ~ oneself** tomar el sol

**sunbathe** ['sʌn·beɪð] *vi* tomar el sol

**sunburn** ['sʌn·bɜrn] *n* quemadura *f* de sol

**sunburned** *adj*, **sunburnt** *adj* quemado, -a por el sol

**sundae** ['sʌn·di] *n* helado con fruta, crema, *etc*

**Sunday** ['sʌn·deɪ] *n* domingo *m; s. a.* **Friday**

**Sunday school** *n* ≈ catequesis *f inv*

**sundial** *n* reloj *m* de sol

**sundown** *n see* **sunset**

**sundry** ['sʌn·dri] *adj* varios, -as; **~ items** objetos varios

**sunflower** ['sʌn·flaʊ·ər] *n* girasol *m*, maravilla *f Chile*

**sung** [sʌŋ] *pp of* **sing**

**sunglasses** ['sʌn·ˌɡlæs·ɪs] *npl* gafas *f pl* de sol

**sunk** [sʌŋk] *pp of* **sink**

**sunken** ['sʌŋ·kən] *adj* sumergido, -a; (*cheeks, eyes*) hundido, -a

**sunlight** ['sʌn·laɪt] *n* luz *f* del sol

**sunlit** ['sʌn·lɪt] *adj* soleado, -a

**sunny** ['sʌn·i] <-ier, -iest> *adj* soleado, -a; (*personality*) alegre

**sunrise** ['sʌn·raɪz] *n* amanecer *m;* **at ~** al alba

**sunroof** ['sʌn·ruf] *n* techo *m* corredizo

**sunset** ['sʌn·set] *n* puesta *f* de sol; **at ~** al atardecer

**sunshade** ['sʌn·ʃeɪd] *n* (*umbrella*) sombrilla *f;* (*awning*) toldo *m*

**sunshine** ['sʌn·ʃaɪn] *n* sol *m;* **in the ~** al sol

**sunstroke** *n* insolación *f*, asoleada *f Col, Chile, Guat;* **to have ~** tener una insolación

**suntan** ['sʌn·tæn] *n* bronceado *m;* **to get a ~** broncearse

**suntan lotion** *n* crema *f* bronceadora

**suntanned** *adj* bronceado, -a

**suntan oil** *n* aceite *m* bronceador

**sunup** ['sʌn·ʌp] *n see* **sunrise**

**super** ['su·pər] **I.** *adj, adv* guay **II.** *n* AUTO súper *f*

**superb** [sə·'pɜrb] *adj* magnífico, -a

**superficial** [ˌsu·pər·'fɪʃ·əl] *adj* superficial

**superfluous** [su·'pɜr·flu·əs] *adj* superfluo, -a; **to be ~** estar de más

**superglue®** ['su·pər·ɡlu] *n* superglue® *m*

**superintendent** [ˌsu·pər·ɪn·'ten·dənt] *n* **1.** director(a) *m(f);* (*building*) portero, -a *m, f* **2.** (*police*) superintendente *mf*

**superior** [sə·'pɪr·i·ər] **I.** *adj* superior; **to be ~** estar por encima (**to** de); **a ~ number** un número mayor (**of** de) **II.** *n* superior *mf*

**superiority** [sə·ˌpɪr·i·'ɔr·ə·ți] *n* superioridad *f*

**superlative** [su·'pɜr·lə·ţɪv] **I.** *adj* excepcional; LING superlativo, -a **II.** *n* superlativo *m*

**supermarket** ['su·pər·ˌmar·kɪt] *n* supermercado *m*

**superpower** ['su·pər·ˌpaʊ·ər] *n* superpotencia *f*

S

**supersonic** [ˌsuˑpərˈsanˑɪk] *adj* supersónico, -a

**superstitious** [ˌsuˑpərˈstɪʃˑəs] *adj* supersticioso, -a

**superstore** [ˈsuˑpərˌstɔr] *n* hipermercado *m*

**supervise** [ˈsuˑpərˌvaɪz] *vt* supervisar; (*thesis*) dirigir

**supervision** [ˌsuˑpərˈvɪʒˑən] *n* supervisión *f*; **under the ~** bajo la supervisión (**of** de)

**supervisor** [ˈsuˑpərˌvaɪˑzər] *n* supervisor(a) *m(f)*; POL alcalde, -esa *m, f*

**supervisory** [ˌsuˑpərˈvaɪˑzəˑri] *adj* de supervisor

**supper** [ˈsʌpˑər] *n* cena *f*; **to have ~** cenar

**supple** [ˈsʌpˑəl] *adj* (*leather, skin*) flexible; (*person*) ágil

**supplement** [ˈsʌpˑləˑmənt] **I.** *n* complemento *m*; (*newspaper*) suplemento *m*; (*book*) apéndice *m* **II.** *vt* complementar

**supplementary** [ˌsʌpˑləˑˈmenˑtəˑri] *adj* adicional

**supplier** [səˈplaɪˑər] *n* proveedor(a) *m(f)*

**supply** [səˈplaɪ] **I.** <-ie-> *vt* suministrar; COM proveer; (*information*) proporcionar; **accused of ~ing drugs** acusado de tráfico de drogas **II.** *n* suministro *m*; ECON oferta *f*; **~ and demand** oferta y demanda; **to be in short ~** escasear

**support** [səˈpɔrt] **I.** *vt* **1.** (*hold up*) sostener; (*weight*) aguantar; **to ~ oneself** apoyarse (**on** en) **2.** (*sustain*) mantener; **to ~ two children** mantener a dos hijos; **to ~ oneself** ganarse la vida **3.** (*pay*) financiar **4.** (*encourage*) apoyar **5.** (*show to be true*) confirmar **II.** *n* **1.** (*help*) apoyo *m*; **moral ~** apoyo moral **2.** (*structure*) soporte *m* **3.** FIN ayuda *f* **4.** confirmación *f*; **to lend ~ to** respaldar; **in ~ of** en apoyo de

**supporter** *n* partidario, -a *m, f*; (*fan*) seguidor(a) *m(f)*

**supportive** [səˈpɔrˑtɪv] *adj* comprensivo, -a; **to be ~ of** apoyar

**suppose** [səˈpoʊz] *vt* **1.** suponer (**that** que); **I ~ not/so** supongo que no/sí; **I don't ~ so** supongo que no; **let's ~ that** supongamos que **2.** (*believe*) creer

**3. to be ~d to do sth** tener que hacer algo; **you are not ~d to know that** no deberías saber eso; **she is ~d to be intelligent** dicen que es inteligente

**supposed** *adj* supuesto, -a; LAW presunto, -a

**supposedly** [səˈpoʊˌzɪdˑli] *adv* supuestamente

**supposing** *conj* **~ that** suponiendo que

**suppress** [səˈpres] *vt* **1.** reprimir; (*evidence, information*) ocultar **2.** MED inhibir

**supremacy** [səˈpremˑəˑsi] *n* supremacía *f*

**supreme** [səˈprim] **I.** *adj* (*authority*) supremo, -a; (*commander*) en jefe; **Supreme Court** Tribunal Supremo; **to show ~ courage** mostrar una gran valentía **II.** *adv* **to reign ~** no tener rival

**surcharge** [ˈsɜrˌtʃɑrdʒ] **I.** *n* recargo *m* **II.** *vt* aplicar un recargo a

**sure** [ʃʊr] **I.** *adj* seguro, -a; **to be ~ of/that** estar seguro de/de que; **to make ~ that** asegurarse de que; **I'm not ~ that/if** no estoy seguro de/de si; **she is ~ to come** vendrá seguro; **I'm not ~ why/how** no sé muy bien por qué/cómo; **~ thing!** ¡claro!; **for ~** seguro; **~ of herself** segura de sí misma **II.** *adv* seguro; **~ I will!** ¡seguro!; **for ~** a ciencia cierta; **~ enough** en efecto ▶ **as ~ as I'm standing here** como me llamo...

**sure-footed** [ˌʃʊrˈfʊtˑɪd] *adj* (*confident*) seguro, -a de sí mismo, -a

**surely** [ˈʃʊrˑli] *adv* **1.** (*certainly*) sin duda **2.** (*astonishment*) claro; **~ you don't expect me to believe that?** ¿no esperarás que me lo crea? **3. ~!** ¡pues claro!

**surf** [sɜrf] **I.** *n* olas *fpl* **II.** *vi* SPORTS hacer surf **III.** *vt* **to ~ the Internet** navegar por internet

**surface** [ˈsɜrˑfɪs] **I.** *n* superficie *f*; **on the ~** *fig* a primera vista; **to scratch the ~ of sth** tratar algo muy por encima **II.** *vi* salir a la superficie

**surface tension** *n* tensión *f* superficial

**surfboard** [ˈsɜrfˌbɔrd] *n* tabla *f* de surf

**surfer** [ˈsɜrˑfər] *n* surfista *mf*; COMPUT internauta *mf*

**surfing** [ˈsɜrˑfɪŋ] *n* surf *m*

**surge** [sɜrdʒ] **I.** *vi* **1.** (*rush*) abalanzarse;

*(waves)* levantarse **2.** *(increase)* aumentar vertiginosamente **II.** n *(waves)* oleaje m; *(indignation)* ola f; *(prices)* aumento m repentino; **power ~** sobrecarga f

**surgeon** ['sɜr·dʒən] n cirujano, -a m, f

**surgery** ['sɜr·dʒə·ri] n cirugía f; **to perform ~** practicar una intervención quirúrgica; **to undergo ~** pasar por el quirófano

**surgical** ['sɜr·dʒɪ·kəl] adj quirúrgico, -a; *(collar, gloves)* ortopédico, -a

**surly** ['sɜr·li] <-ier, -iest> adj hosco, -a

**surname** ['sɜr·neɪm] n apellido m

**surpass** [sər·'pæs] vt sobrepasar; **to ~ oneself** superarse

**surplus** ['sɜr·pləs] **I.** n *(product)* excedente m; FIN superávit m **II.** adj sobrante

**surprise** [sər·'praɪz] **I.** n sorpresa f; **in a ~** con sorpresa; **to sb's ~** para sorpresa de alguien **II.** vt sorprender; **it ~d her that** le sorprendió que +subj; **to ~ sb doing sth** sorprender a alguien haciendo algo

**surprising** adj sorprendente, sorpresivo, -a AmL

**surprisingly** adv sorprendentemente

**surrender** [sə·'ren·dər] **I.** vi rendirse; **to ~ to sb** entregarse a alguien **II.** n *(giving up)* rendición f

**surrogate** ['sɜr·ə·gɪt] n sustituto, -a m, f

**surround** [sə·'raʊnd] **I.** vt rodear **II.** n marco m

**surrounding** adj de alrededor

**surroundings** npl alrededores mpl

**surveillance** [sər·'veɪ·ləns] n vigilancia f; **to be under ~** estar bajo vigilancia

**survey¹** [sər·'veɪ] vt **1.** *(poll)* encuestar **2.** GEO medir **3.** *(research)* investigar **4.** *(watch)* contemplar

**survey²** ['sɜr·veɪ] n **1.** *(poll)* encuesta f **2.** GEO medición f **3.** *(report)* informe m **4.** *(examination)* examen m

**survival** [sər·'vaɪ·vəl] n supervivencia f
▶ **the ~ of the <u>fittest</u>** la ley del más fuerte

**survive** [sər·'vaɪv] **I.** vi *(person)* sobrevivir; *(thing)* conservarse; **to ~ on** vivir a base de **II.** vt sobrevivir a; **to ~ an accident** salir con vida de un accidente

**surviving** adj superviviente

**survivor** [sər·'vaɪ·vər] n superviviente mf

**susceptible** [sə·'sep·tə·bəl] adj susceptible; MED propenso, -a

**suspect¹** [sə·'spekt] vt sospechar; *(person)* sospechar de; **to ~ sb's motives** dudar de los motivos de alguien

**suspect²** ['sʌs·pekt] adj, n sospechoso, -a m, f

**suspend** [sə·'spend] vt **1.** *(stop)* suspender; *(judgment, proceedings)* posponer **2.** SCHOOL, UNIV expulsar temporalmente **3.** *(hang)* colgar

**suspender** [sə·'spen·dər] n pl tirantes mpl, suspensores mpl AmL, calzonarias fpl Col

**suspense** [sə·'spens] n incertidumbre f; CINE suspense m; **in ~** en vilo

**suspension** [sə·'spen·ʃən] n suspensión f; SCHOOL, UNIV expulsión f temporal

**suspension bridge** n puente m colgante

**suspicion** [sə·'spɪʃ·ən] n **1.** *(belief)* sospecha f **2.** *(mistrust)* recelo m

**suspicious** [sə·'spɪʃ·əs] adj **1.** *(arousing suspicion)* sospechoso, -a, emponchado, -a Arg, Bol, Perú **2.** *(lacking trust)* desconfiado, -a

**sustain** [sə·'steɪn] vt **1.** *(maintain)* sostener **2.** *(withstand)* aguantar **3.** *(uphold: conviction)* confirmar; *(objection)* admitir

**sustainable** [sə·'steɪ·nə·bəl] adj *(resources, development)* sostenible

**sustained** [sə·'steɪnd] adj continuo, -a; *(applause)* prolongado, -a

**sustenance** ['sʌs·tə·nəns] n sustento m; **to give sb ~** sustentar a alguien

**swab** [swab] <-bb-> vt fregar; MED limpiar

**swagger** ['swæg·ər] **I.** n arrogancia f **II.** vi pavonearse

**swallow¹** ['swal·oʊ] *(food, drink)* **I.** vt tragar **II.** vi tragar saliva **III.** n trago m
♦**swallow down** vt tragar

**swallow²** ['swal·oʊ] n ZOOL golondrina f

**swam** [swæm] vi pt of **swim**

**swamp** [swamp] **I.** n pantano m, suampo m AmC, wampa f Méx **II.** vt inundar; **to ~ sb** abrumar a alguien *(with con)*; **to**

**be ~ed** estar agobiado (**with** de)

**swan** [swɒn] *n* cisne *m*

**swank** [swæŋk] **I.** *adj* **1.** (*grand*) espléndido, -a **2.** (*pretentious*) fanfarrón, -ona **II.** *n* gran elegancia *f*

**swanky** ['swæŋ·ki] *adj* pijo, -a

**swap** [swɒp] **I.** <-pp-> *vt, vi* cambiar (**for/with** por/a) **II.** *n* cambio *m*

**swarm** [swɔrm] **I.** *vi fig* aglomerarse; **to be ~ing** estar plagado (**with** de) **II.** *n* (*bees*) enjambre *m;* (*people*) multitud *f*

**swastika** ['swɑs·tɪ·kə] *n* cruz *f* gamada

**sway** [sweɪ] **I.** *vi* balancearse **II.** *vt* **1.** (*move*) balancear **2.** (*persuade*) persuadir **III.** *n* **1.** (*influence*) influencia *f;* **under the ~** bajo el influjo (**of** de) **2.** *form* control *m;* **to hold ~ over** dominar

**swear** [swer] <swore, sworn> **I.** *vi* **1.** jurar; **I couldn't ~ to it** no pondría la mano en el fuego **2.** (*curse*) decir palabrotas **II.** *vt* jurar (**to** a); **to ~ sb to secrecy** hacer que alguien jure silencio

◆**swear in** *vt* tomar juramento

**swearing** *n* palabrotas *mpl*

**sweat** [swet] **I.** *n* **1.** sudor *m;* **to break into a ~** romper a sudar **2.** (*effort*) esfuerzo *m;* **no ~** sin problema **3.** *pl inf* chándal *m* ► **it makes me break out in a <u>cold</u> ~** me hace correr un sudor frío por la espalda; **to <u>work</u> oneself into a ~** preocuparse mucho (**about** por) **II.** *vi* sudar (**with** de) **III.** *vt* sudar; **to ~ bullets** sudar la gota gorda

◆**sweat out** *vt* **to sweat it out** *inf* soportar; (*await*) esperar con gran impaciencia

**sweater** ['swet·ər] *n* jersey *m*

**sweatshirt** ['swet·ʃɜrt] *n* sudadera *f*

**sweaty** ['swet·i] <-ier, -iest> *adj* sudado, -a

**Swede** [swid] *n* sueco, -a *m, f*

**Sweden** ['swi·dən] *n* Suecia *f*

**Swedish** ['swi·dɪʃ] **I.** *adj* sueco, -a **II.** *n* **1.** (*person*) sueco, -a *m, f* **2.** LING sueco *m*

**sweep** [swip] <swept, swept> **I.** *n* barrido *m;* **to give sth a ~** barrer algo; **with a ~ of her arm** con un amplio movimiento del brazo; **to make a ~ of an area** rastrear una zona ► **to make a <u>clean</u>**

**~ hacer tabla rasa II.** *vt* **1.** (*floor*) barrer **2.** (*remove*) quitar **3.** (*search*) rastrear **4.** (*win*) aplastar; **to ~ a series** arrasar en una serie ► **to ~ sb off his/her feet** enamorar a alguien **III.** *vi* **1.** (*floor*) barrer **2. to ~ into power** llegar al poder fácilmente; **to ~ into a room** entrar en una sala majestuosamente; **the road ~s around the lake** la carretera rodea el lago **3.** (*extend*) extenderse

◆**sweep aside** *vt* **1.** (*move*) apartar **2.** (*dismiss*) desechar

◆**sweep away** *vt* (*remove*) erradicar

◆**sweep out** *vt* barrer

◆**sweep up** *vt* **1.** (*brush*) barrer **2.** (*gather*) recoger

**sweeper** *n* cepillo *m;* (*person*) barrendero, -a *m, f*

**sweeping I.** *adj* (*gesture*) amplio, -a; (*victory*) aplastante **II.** *npl* basura *f;* **the ~s of society** la escoria de la sociedad

**sweet** [swit] **I.** <-er, -est> *adj* **1.** (*taste*) dulce **2.** (*pleasant*) agradable; (*smile*) encantador(a); **to go one's own way** hacer lo que a uno le da la gana **3.** (*cute*) mono, -a **4. to be ~ on** estar enamorado de **II.** *n pl* caramelos *mpl,* dulce *m Chile*

**sweet-and-sour** [ˌswit·ənˌsaʊ·ər] *adj* agridulce

**sweeten** ['swi·tən] *vt* endulzar; **to ~ sb up** ablandar a alguien

**sweetener** *n* **1.** edulcorante *m* **2.** *inf* incentivo *m*

**sweetheart** ['swit·hɑrt] *n* **1.** (*kind person*) encanto *m* **2.** (*term of endearment*) cariño *m* **3.** (*boyfriend, girlfriend*) novio, -a *m, f*

**sweetie** ['swi·ti] *n inf* cariño *m*

**sweetness** *n* dulzor *m;* **to be all ~ and light** estar de lo más amable

**sweet-talk** *vt* camelar

**sweet tooth** *n* **to have a ~** ser goloso, -a

**swell** [swel] <swelled, swelled *or* swollen> **I.** *vi* **1.** (*bigger*) hincharse **2.** (*louder*) subir **3.** (*more*) aumentar **II.** *vt* **1.** (*size*) hinchar **2.** (*number*) engrosar **III.** *n* (*sea*) oleaje *m;* **a heavy ~** un fuerte oleaje **IV.** <-er, -est> *adj inf* genial

**swelling** *n* hinchazón *f*

**sweltering** *adj* sofocante

**swept** [swept] *vt, vi pt of* **sweep**

**swerve** [swɜrv] **I.** *vi* virar bruscamente; **to ~ from** desviarse de **II.** *n* (*car*) viraje *m* brusco

**swift**[1] [swɪft] *adj* (*fast-moving*) rápido, -a; (*occurring quickly*) súbito, -a

**swift**[2] [swɪft] *n* ZOOL vencejo *m*

**swiftly** *adv* rápidamente

**swig** [swɪg] *inf* **I.** <-gg-> *vt* beber **II.** *n* trago *m*

**swim** [swɪm] **I.** <swam, swum> *vi* **1.** *fig* nadar; **her head was ~ming** la cabeza le daba vueltas **2.** (*full of water*) estar inundado, -a **II.** <swam, swum> *vt* (*cross*) cruzar a nado **III.** *n* nado *m*

**swimmer** [swɪm-ər] *n* nadador(a) *m(f)*

**swimming** *n* natación *f*

**swimming pool** *n* piscina *f*, alberca *f Méx*, pileta *f Arg*

**swimming trunks** *npl* bañador *m*

**swimsuit** [swɪm-sut] *n* bañador *m*

**swindle** [swɪn-dəl] **I.** *vt* estafar **II.** *n* estafa *f*

**swine** [swaɪn] *n* (*mean person*) cabrón, -ona *m, f*

**swing** [swɪŋ] **I.** *n* **1.** (*movement*) vaivén *m* **2.** (*punch*) golpe *m* **3.** (*hanging seat*) columpio *m* **4.** (*sharp change*) cambio *m* drástico; **a mood ~** cambio de humor **5.** MUS swing *m* ▶ **to get (back) into the ~ of things** cogerle el tranquillo **II.** <swung, swung> *vi* **1.** (*move*) oscilar **2.** (*hanging seat*) columpiarse **3.** (*alter*) cambiar **III.** <swung, swung> *vt* (*move*) balancear, chilinguear *Col*

♦**swing around** *vi* dar un giro

**swipe** [swaɪp] **I.** *vt* **1.** (*steal*) mangar **2.** (*card*) pasar; (*car*) dar un golpe a **II.** *n* **1.** (*blow*) golpe *m* **2.** (*criticism*) crítica *f*

**swirl** [swɜrl] **I.** *vi* arremolinarse **II.** *vt* arremolinar **III.** *n* remolino *m*

**Swiss** [swɪs] *adj, n* suizo, -a *m, f*

**switch** [swɪtʃ] **I.** <-es> *n* **1.** ELEC interruptor *m*, suiche *m Méx* **2.** (*substitution*) reemplazamiento *m* **3.** (*change*) cambio *m* **II.** *vi* cambiar (**from/to** de/a); **to ~ with sb** cambiarse con alguien **III.** *vt* cambiar (**for** por)

♦**switch off** **I.** *vt* apagar; (*water, electricity*) cortar **II.** *vi* **1.** apagarse **2.** (*attention*) desconectar

♦**switch on** **I.** *vt* encender **II.** *vi* encenderse

♦**switch over** *vi* cambiar

**switchman** <-men> *n* guardagujas *m inv*

**switchyard** *n* patio *m* de maniobras

**Switzerland** [swɪt-sər-lənd] *n* Suiza *f*

**swivel** [swɪv-əl] <-ll-, -l-> *vt* girar

**swivel chair** *n* silla *f* giratoria

**swollen** [swoʊ-lən] **I.** *pp of* **swell** **II.** *adj* hinchado, -a

**swoop** [swup] **I.** *n* **1.** (*dive*) caída *f* en picado **2.** *inf* (*police*) redada *f* ▶ **in one fell** swoop de un tirón **II.** *vi* (*dive*) *a. fig* caer en picado

**sword** [sɔrd] *n* espada *f*

**swore** [swɔr] *pt of* **swear**

**sworn** [swɔrn] **I.** *pp of* **swear** **II.** *adj* jurado, -a

**swum** [swʌm] *pp of* **swim**

**swung** [swʌŋ] *pp of* **swing**

**syllable** [sɪl-ə-bəl] *n* sílaba *f*; **stressed/ unstressed ~** sílaba tónica/átona; **not a ~** ni media palabra

**syllabus** [sɪl-ə-bəs] <-es, *form:* syllabi> *n* plan *m* de estudios; (*for one subject*) programa *m*

**symbol** [sɪm-bəl] *n* símbolo *m*

**symbolize** [sɪm-bə-laɪz] *vt* simbolizar

**symmetry** [sɪm-ə-tri] *n* simetría *f*

**sympathetic** [ˌsɪm-pə-'θet̬-ɪk] *adj* (*understanding*) comprensivo, -a; (*sympathizing*) receptivo, -a; POL simpatizante (**towards** de)

**sympathize** [sɪm-pə-θaɪz] *vi* (*understand*) mostrar comprensión; (*pity*) compadecerse; (*agree*) estar de acuerdo; **to ~ with** simpatizar con

**sympathy** [sɪm-pə-θi] *n* **1.** compasión *f*; (*understanding*) comprensión *f*; **you have my deepest ~** le acompaño en el sentimiento **2.** solidaridad *f*

**symphony** [sɪm-fə-ni] *n* sinfonía *f*; (*orchestra*) orquesta *f* sinfónica

**symptom** [sɪmp-təm] *n* síntoma *m*

**synagogue** [sɪn-ə-gag] *n* sinagoga *f*

**synchronize** [sɪŋ-krə-naɪz] **I.** *vt* sincronizar **II.** *vi* sincronizarse

**S**

**syndicate**[1] [ˈsɪn·də·kɪt] *n* ECON consorcio *m*; PUBL agencia *f* de noticias

**syndicate**[2] [ˈsɪn·də·keɪt] *vt* ECON agrupar; PUBL vender

**syndrome** [ˈsɪn·droʊm] *n* síndrome *m*; **acquired immune deficiency ~** síndrome de la inmunodeficiencia adquirida

**synonym** [ˈsɪn·ə·nɪm] *n* sinónimo *m*

**synonymous** [sɪˈnɑn·ɪ·məs] *adj* sinónimo, -a

**synopsis** [sɪˈnɑp·sɪs] <-es> *n* sinopsis *f inv*

**synthetic** [sɪnˈθet̬·ɪk] *adj* sintético, -a; (*fake*) artificial

**syringe** [səˈrɪndʒ] *n* jeringuilla *f*

**syrup** [ˈsɪr·əp] *n* **1.** CULIN almíbar *m*, sirope *m AmC, Col* **2.** MED jarabe *m*; **cough ~** jarabe para la tos

**system** [ˈsɪs·təm] *n* **1.** (*set*) sistema *m*; **music ~** equipo *m* de música **2.** (*method, order*) método *m*; POL sistema ▸ **to get something out of one's ~** quitarse algo de encima

**systematic** [ˌsɪs·tə·ˈmæt̬·ɪk] *adj* sistemático, -a

**system error** *n* error *m* en el sistema

**system registry** *n* registro *m* del sistema

# T

**T, t** [ti] *n* **1.** T, t *f*; **~ as in Tango** T de Tarragona **2.** the description fits him to **a ~** la descripción le va perfecta

**tab** [tæb] *n* **1.** (*flap*) solapa *f* **2.** (*label*) etiqueta *f* **3.** *inf* (*bill*) cuenta *f*; **to put sth on the ~** cargar algo a la cuenta **4.** (*ringpull*) anilla *f* ▸ **to keep ~s on sth/sb** no perder de vista algo/a alguien

**tab key** *n* tabulador *m*

**table** [ˈteɪ·bəl] *n* **1.** mesa *f*; **to clear/set the ~** recoger/poner la mesa **2.** MATH tabla *f*; **multiplication ~** tabla de multiplicar **3.** (*list*) lista *f*; **~ of contents** índice *m* ▸ **the ~s have turned** han cambiado las tornas

**tablecloth** [ˈteɪ·bəl·klɔθ] *n* mantel *m*

**tablespoon** *n* cucharón *m*

**tablet** [ˈtæb·lɪt] *n* (*pill*) pastilla *f*

**table tennis** *n* ping-pong *m*

**tabloid** [ˈtæb·lɔɪd] *n* periódico *m* sensacionalista; **the ~ press** la prensa amarilla

**taboo, tabu** [təˈbu] I. *n* tabú *m* II. *adj* tabú *inv*

**tabulate** [ˈtæb·jʊ·leɪt] *vt* COMPUT tabular

**tacit** [ˈtæs·ɪt] *adj* tácito, -a

**tack** [tæk] I. *n* (*approach*) política *f*; **to try a different ~** intentar un enfoque distinto II. *vi* virar

**tackle** [ˈtæk·əl] I. *vt* (*issue, problem*) abordar; (*job*) emprender II. *n* (*equipment*) equipo *m*

**tacky** [ˈtæk·i] <-ier, -iest> *adj* **1.** (*sticky*) pegajoso, -a **2.** *inf* (*showy*) hortera

**tactful** [ˈtækt·fəl] *adj* discreto, -a

**tactic** [ˈtæk·tɪk] *n* ~(**s**) táctica *f*

**tactical** [ˈtæk·tɪ·kəl] *adj* táctico, -a

**tactician** [tækˈtɪʃ·ən] *n* táctico, -a *m, f*

**tactile** [ˈtæk·təl] *adj* táctil

**tactless** [ˈtækt·lɪs] *adj* falto, -a de tacto

**tad** [tæd] *n* **a ~** un poquitín

**tadpole** [ˈtæd·poʊl] *n* renacuajo *m*

**tag** [tæg] I. *n* **1.** **a.** COMPUT etiqueta *f* **2. to play ~** jugar al pillapilla **3. question ~** cláusula final interrogativa II. <-gg-> *vt* etiquetar; **to ~ sth onto sth** añadir algo a algo

◆**tag along** *vi inf* seguir; **to ~ with sb** ir detrás de alguien

**tail** [teɪl] I. *n* **1.** ANAT, AVIAT cola *f*; (*dog, bull*) rabo *m* **2. ~s** (*coin*) cruz *f* **3.** *sl* (*person*) perseguidor(a) *m(f)* **4.** *sl* (*bottom*) trasero *m* ▸ **to chase one's ~** pillarse los dedos; **to turn ~ and run** salir por pies II. *vt* seguir

◆**tail off** *vi* disminuir

**tailgate** I. *n* puerta *f* de atrás II. *vt* AUTO pegarse

**taillight** *n* luz *f* trasera

**tailor** [ˈteɪ·lər] I. *n* sastre *m* II. *vt* (*clothes*) confeccionar

**tailor-made** [ˌteɪ·lər·ˈmeɪd] *adj* hecho, -a a medida; (*perfect*) perfecto, -a

**taint** [teɪnt] I. *vt* (*food*) contaminar; (*reputation*) manchar II. *n* mancha *f*

**take** [teɪk] I. *n* **1.** (*receipts*) ingresos *mpl* **2.** PHOT, CINE toma *f* II. <took, taken>

*vt* 1. (*accept*) aceptar; (*advice*) seguir; (*responsibility*) asumir; **to ~ sth seriously** tomar algo en serio; **to ~ one's time** tomarse su tiempo; **to ~ sth as it comes** aceptar algo tal y como es; **to ~ office** entrar en funciones 2. (*hold*) coger, agarrar *AmL* 3. (*eat*) comer; (*medicine, drugs*) tomar 4. (*use*) necesitar 5. (*bring*) llevar 6. (*decision, bath, holiday, rest*) tomar; (*walk*) dar; (*trip*) hacer; (*photograph*) sacar; (*bus, train*) coger, tomar *AmL* 7. (*feel, assume*) suponer; **to ~ (an) interest** interesarse (**in** por); **to ~ offense** ofenderse ▸ **~ it or leave it** ¡tómalo o déjalo!; **what do you ~ me for?** ¿por quién me has tomado?; **I ~ it that...** supongo que...; **~ that!** ¡toma!

◆**take aback** *vt* sorprender; (*shock*) abatir

◆**take after** *vt* parecerse a

◆**take along** *vt* (*take*) llevarse; (*bring*) traerse

◆**take apart** *vt* 1. (*disassemble*) desmontar 2. (*destroy*) despedazar

◆**take away** *vt* 1. (*remove, subtract*) quitar 2. (*go away with*) llevarse

◆**take back** *vt* 1. (*return*) devolver 2. (*accept back*) aceptar 3. (*repossess*) recobrar

◆**take down** *vt* 1. (*remove*) quitar 2. (*write*) apuntar ▸ **to take sb down** *fig* bajar los humos a alguien

◆**take in** *vt* 1. (*at home*) acoger 2. **to take sb in one's arms** sostener a alguien entre sus brazos; **to take sth in hand** *fig* hacerse cargo de algo 3. (*deceive*) estafar 4. (*understand*) comprender 5. (*include*) englobar

◆**take off** *vt* 1. (*remove*) retirar; (*clothes*) quitarse 2. (*subtract*) descontar II. *vi* 1. *AVIAT* despegar 2. *sl* (*leave*) largarse; (*flee*) salir por pies

◆**take on** *vt* 1. (*acquire*) adoptar 2. (*hire*) contratar II. *vi* apurarse

◆**take out** *vt* 1. (*remove*) quitar 2. (*bring outside*) sacar 3. (*borrow*) coger prestado

◆**take over** *vt* 1. (*buy*) comprar 2. (*control*) tomar el control de 3. (*possess*) tomar posesión de

◆**take to** *vt* (*like*) encariñarse con; **to**

**~ doing sth** aficionarse a hacer algo; **to ~ drink/drugs** darse a la bebida/las drogas

◆**take up** I. *vt* 1. (*bring up*) subir 2. (*start*) empezar 3. (*discuss*) tratar 4. (*accept*) aceptar 5. (*adopt*) adoptar II. *vi* **to ~ with sb/sth** relacionarse con alguien/familiarizarse con algo

**take-home pay** ['teɪk·hoʊm·ˌpeɪ] *n* salario *m* neto

**taken** ['teɪ·kən] *vi, vt pp of* **take**

**takeoff** ['teɪk·ɔːf] *n AVIAT* despegue *m*

**takeout** ['teɪk·aʊt] *n* comida *f* para llevar

**takeover** ['teɪk·ˌoʊ·vər] *n POL* toma *f* del poder; *ECON* adquisición *f*

**taking** ['teɪ·kɪŋ] *n* 1. (*capture*) toma *f*; **it's yours for the ~** es tuyo si lo quieres 2. **~s** ingresos *mpl*

**tale** [teɪl] *n* historia *f*; (*lie*) *a. LIT* cuento *m* ▸ **to tell ~s** chivarse

**talent** ['tæl·ənt] *n* talento *m*

**talented** *adj* con mucho talento

**Taliban** ['tæ·li·bæn] *n* talibán, -ana *m, f*

**talk** [tɔːk] I. *n* 1. (*conversation*) conversación *f*, plática *f Méx* 2. (*lecture*) charla *f* 3. **~s** negociaciones *fpl* ▸ **to be the ~ of the town** andar de boca en boca; **to be all ~ (and no action)** mucho ruido y pocas nueces *prov* II. *vi* hablar ▸ **to ~ dirty** decir obscenidades; **look who's ~ing** ¡mira quién habla!; (*discuss*) hablar de III. *vt* decir;

◆**talk back** *vi* replicar

◆**talk out** *vt* **to talk sb out of sth** disuadir a alguien de algo

◆**talk over** *vt* hablar (**with** con)

◆**talk through** *vt* 1. (*discuss*) discutir 2. (*explain*) explicar

**talkative** ['tɔː·kə·tɪv] *adj* hablador(a)

**talker** *n* hablador(a) *m(f)*

**talking-to** ['tɔː·kɪŋ·tu] *n* sermón *m*

**talk show** *n* programa *m* de entrevistas

**tall** [tɔːl] *adj* alto, -a; **to grow ~(er)** crecer

**tally** ['tæl·i] <-ies> I. *n* cuenta *f*; **to keep a ~** llevar la cuenta (**of** de) II. *vi* coincidir (**with** con)

**tamarind** ['tæm·ə·rɪnd] *n* tamarindo *m*

**tambourine** [ˌtæm·bə·'riːn] *n* pandereta *f*

**tame** [teɪm] I. *adj* 1. (*animal*) manso, -a

**2.** (*unexciting*) soso, -a **II.** vt (*animal*) domesticar

**tamper** ['tæm·pər] vi entrometerse

**tampon** ['tæm·pan] n tampón m

**tan¹** [tæn] **I.** <-nn-> vi broncearse **II.** <-nn-> vt (*leather*) curtir **III.** n bronceado m; **to get a ~** ponerse moreno **IV.** adj marrón claro

**tan²** abbr of **tangent** tg

**tandem** ['tæn·dəm] n tándem m; **to work in ~** trabajar conjuntamente

**tang** [tæŋ] n olor m penetrante

**tangent** ['tæn·dʒənt] n tangente f; **to go off on a ~** salirse por la tangente

**tangerine** [ˌtæn·dʒə·'rin] n mandarina f

**tangible** ['tæn·dʒə·bəl] adj tangible; (*benefit*) palpable

**tangle** ['tæn·gəl] **I.** n maraña f; fig enredo m **II.** vi enredarse

**tank** [tæŋk] n **1.** (*container*) depósito m **2.** MIL tanque m

**tanker** ['tæn·kər] n (*truck*) camión m cisterna; **oil ~** petrolero m

**tanned** [tænd] adj bronceado, -a

**tannery** ['tæn·ə·ri] n curtiduría f

**tantalize** ['tæn·tə·laɪz] vt **1.** (*torment*) atormentar **2.** (*tempt*) tentar

**tantalizing** adj tentador(a); (*smile*) seductor(a)

**tantrum** ['tæn·trəm] n berrinche m, dengue m Méx; **to have** [or **throw**] **a ~** coger [or agarrar AmL] una rabieta

**tap¹** [tæp] n (*water*) grifo m, canilla f Arg, Par, Urug; **to turn the ~ on/off** abrir/cerrar el grifo; **on ~** de barril; fig al alcance de la mano

**tap²** [tæp] **I.** n (*knock*) golpecito m **II.** <-pp-> vi dar golpecitos

**tap dance** ['tæp·dæns] n claqué m

**tape** [teɪp] n (a. *cassette*) cinta f; (*adhesive*) cinta f adhesiva; MED esparadrapo m

**tape measure** n metro m

**taper** ['teɪ·pər] **I.** n (*wick*) cerilla f **II.** vt afilar

**tape recorder** n grabadora f

**tape recording** n grabación f

**tapestry** ['tæp·əs·tri] n tapicería f; (*object*) tapiz m

**tapeworm** ['teɪp·wɜrm] n tenia f

**tap water** n agua f corriente

**tar** [tar] n alquitrán m

**tarantula** [tə·'ræn·tʃə·lə] n tarántula f

**tare** [ter] n ECON tara f

**target** ['tar·gɪt] **I.** n a. ECON objetivo m; **to hit the ~** dar en el blanco; **to be on ~** ir según lo previsto **II.** vt centrarse en

**targeted** ['tar·gɪ·tɪd] adj elegido, -a como objetivo

**target practice** n prácticas f pl de tiro

**tariff** ['ter·ɪf] n (*customs duty*) arancel m

**tarmac®** ['tar·mæk], **tarmacadam®** [ˌtar·mə·'kæd·əm] n asfalto m

**tarnish** ['tar·nɪʃ] **I.** vi deslustrarse **II.** vt deslustrar; (*reputation*) manchar **III.** n mancha f

**tarpaulin** [tar·'pɔ·lɪn] n lona f impermeabilizada

**tart¹** [tart] adj n **1.** (*taste*) agrio, -a; (*acid*) ácido, -a **2.** (*caustic*) cortante

**tart²** [tart] n CULIN tarta f

**tartan** ['tar·tən] n (*design*) tartán m

**tartar** ['tar·tər] n MED sarro m

**tartar(e) sauce** n salsa f tártara

**task** [tæsk] **I.** n tarea f, tonga f Col; **to take sb to ~** llamar la atención a alguien **II.** vt **to be ~ed** estar encargado (**with** de)

**task force** n MIL destacamento m

**taste** [teɪst] **I.** n **1.** sabor m; **sense of ~** sentido del gusto **2.** (*small portion*) bocado m; **to have a ~ of** probar **3.** (*liking*) gusto m; **to get a/lose the ~** coger/perder el gusto (**for** a/por); **to have different ~s** tener gustos distintos ▸ **to leave a** <u>bad</u> **~ (in one's mouth)** dejar un mal sabor de boca fig **II.** vt **1.** (*food, drink*) saborear **2.** (*experience*) experimentar **III.** vi saber (**of, like** a); **to ~ bitter/sweet** tener un sabor amargo/dulce

**taste bud** ['teɪst·bʌd] n papila f gustativa

**tasteful** ['teɪst·fəl] adj con gusto; (*decorous*) con delicadeza

**tasteless** ['teɪst·lɪs] adj soso, -a; (*clothes, remark*) de mal gusto

**tasty** ['teɪ·sti] adj sabroso, -a

**tattle** ['tæt·əl] n chismorreo m

**tattoo** [tæ·'tu] **I.** n (*on skin*) tatuaje m **II.** vt tatuar

**tatty** ['tæt·i] <-ier, -iest> adj estropeado, -a

**taught** [tɔt] *pt, pp* of **teach**

**taunt** [tɔnt] **I.** *vt* burlarse de **II.** *n* insulto *m*

**Taurus** ['tɔr·əs] *n* Tauro *m*

**taut** [tɔt] *adj* (*wire, string*) tensado, -a; (*skin*) terso, -a; (*nerves*) de punta

**tavern** ['tæv·ərn] *n* taberna *f*

**tax** [tæks] *n* <-es> *n* **1.** FIN impuesto *m*; **free of** ~ exento de impuestos **2.** *fig* carga *f* (**on** para) **II.** *vt* FIN gravar con un impuesto

**taxable** ['tæk·sə·bəl] *adj* imponible

**tax allowance** *n* desgravación *f* fiscal

**taxation** [tæk·'seɪ·ʃən] *n* impuestos *mpl*; (*system*) sistema *m* impositivo

**tax avoidance** *n* evasión *f* de impuestos

**tax bracket** *n* categoría *f* impositiva

**tax-deductible** *adj* deducible

**tax dodger** *n,* **tax evader** *n* evasor(a) *m(f)* de impuestos

**tax evasion** *n* evasión *f* de impuestos

**tax exemption** *n* exención *f* fiscal

**tax-free** *adj* libre de impuestos

**tax haven** *n* paraíso *m* fiscal

**taxi** ['tæk·si] *n* taxi *m*

**taxidermist** ['tæk·sɪ·ˌdɜr·mɪst] *n* taxidermista *mf*

**taxi driver** *n* taxista *mf,* ruletero, -a *m, f* *AmC, Méx*

**taxing** *adj* difícil

**taxi stand** *n* parada *f* de taxis

**taxpayer** ['tæks·ˌpeɪ·ər] *n* contribuyente *mf*

**tax rebate** *n* devolución *f* de impuestos

**tax relief** *n* exención *f* de impuestos

**tax return** *n* declaración *f* de la renta

**tax revenues** *n* ingresos *m pl* fiscales

**tax system** *n* sistema *m* impositivo

**tax year** *n* año *m* fiscal

**tea** [ti] *n* té *m*; **strong/weak** ~ té fuerte/flojo; **chamomile** ~ manzanilla *f* ▶ **not for all the** ~ **in China** ni por todo el oro del mundo

**tea bag** *n* bolsita *f* de té

**tea break** *n* descanso *m*

**teach** [titʃ] <taught, taught> **I.** *vt* enseñar; **to** ~ **sb a lesson** dar una lección a alguien **II.** *vi* dar clase(s)

**teacher** ['ti·tʃər] *n* profesor(a) *m(f)*

**teacher training** *n* formación *f* de profesorado

**teaching I.** *n* **1.** docencia *f* **2.** ~s enseñanza *f* **II.** *adj* didáctico, -a

**teaching staff** *n* profesorado *m*

**teacup** *n* taza *f* de té

**team** [tim] **I.** *n* equipo *m* **II.** *adj* de equipo **III.** *vt* asociar

◆**team up** *vi* agruparse; **to** ~ **with** asociarse con

**teammate** *n* compañero, -a *m, f*

**team effort** *n* esfuerzo *m* conjunto

**team spirit** *n* espíritu *m* de equipo

**teamwork** *n* trabajo *m* en equipo

**teapot** ['ti·pat] *n* tetera *f*

**tear¹** [tɪr] *n* (*from crying*) lágrima *f*; **to bring** ~**s to sb's eyes** hacer que a alguien se le salten las lágrimas; **to burst into** ~**s** echarse a llorar; **to not shed (any)** ~**s** no derramar una (sola) lágrima

**tear²** [ter] <tore, torn> **I.** *vt* (*rip*) rasgar; (*ruin*) romper; **to** ~ **a hole** hacer un agujero (**in** en) **II.** *vi* **1.** (*rip*) rasgarse **2.** (*rush*) lanzarse

◆**tear apart** *vt* destrozar; *fig* dividir

◆**tear at** *vt* quitar de un tirón

◆**tear away I.** *vi* salir disparado **II.** *vt* (*pull*) arrancar; **to tear sb/oneself away** sacar a alguien/irse de mala gana

◆**tear down** *vt* derribar

◆**tear into** *vt* arremeter contra

◆**tear off I.** *vt* arrancar **II.** *vi* (*leave*) salir disparado

◆**tear out** *vt* arrancar de cuajo; **to tear one's hair out** *fig* subirse por las paredes (**over** por)

◆**tear up** *vt* despedazar

**teardrop** ['tɪr·drap] *n* lágrima *f*

**tearful** ['tɪr·fəl] *adj* lloroso, -a

**tear gas** *n* gas *m* lacrimógeno

**tease** [tiz] **I.** *vt* **1.** (*make fun*) tomar el pelo (**about** por) **2.** (*provoke*) provocar **II.** *n* bromista *mf*; (*sexually*) provocador(a) *m(f)*

**teaser** ['ti·zər] *n* rompecabezas *m inv*

**teaspoon** *n* cucharilla *f*

**teaspoonful** ['ti·spun·fʊl] *n* cucharadita *f*

**teat** [tit] *n* teta *f*

**teatime** ['ti·taɪm] *n* hora *f* del té

**tea towel** *n* paño *m* de cocina

T

**technical** ['tek·nɪ·kəl] *adj* técnico, -a; **~ term** tecnicismo *m*

**technician** [tek·'nɪʃ·ən] *n* técnico, -a *m, f*

**technique** [tek·'nik] *n* técnica *f*

**technological** [ˌtek·nə·'ladʒ·ɪ·kəl] *adj* tecnológico, -a

**technology** [tek·'nal·ə·dʒi] *n* tecnología *f*

**tedious** ['ti·di·əs] *adj* aburrido, -a

**tee** [ti] *n* SPORTS tee *m*

**◆tee off** *sl* I. *vi* (*start*) arrancar(se) II. *vt* (*anger*) cabrear

**teem** [tim] *vi* rebosar; **to ~/be ~ing with** estar repleto de

**teeming** *adj* muy numeroso, -a

**teenage(d)** ['tin·eɪdʒ(d)] *adj* adolescente

**teenager** ['tin·eɪ·dʒər] *n* adolescente *mf*

**teens** [tinz] *npl* adolescencia *f*

**teensy** ['tin·si] *adj*, **teensy-weensy** *adj*, **teeny** ['ti·ni] *adj* chiquitín, -ina

**tee shirt** ['ti·ʃɜrt] *n* camiseta *f*

**teeth** [tiθ] *pl of* **tooth**

**teethe** [tið] *vi* echar los dientes

**teetotal** [ˌti·'toʊ·təl] *adj* abstemio, -a

**teetotaler** [ˌti·'toʊ·təl·ər] *n* abstemio, -a *m, f*

**telecommunications** ['tel·ɪ·kə·ˌmju·nɪ·'keɪ·ʃənz] *npl* telecomunicaciones *fpl*

**telecommuting** ['tel·ɪ·kə·ˌmju·tɪŋ] *n* teletrabajo *m*

**teleconference** ['tel·ɪ·ˌkan·fər·əns] *n* teleconferencia *f*

**telecopy** ['tel·ɪ·kap·i] *n* fotocopia *f*

**telegram** ['tel·ɪ·græm] *n* telegrama *m*

**telepathic** [ˌtel·ə·'pæθ·ɪk] *adj* telepático, -a

**telepathy** [tə·'lep·ə·θi] *n* telepatía *f*

**telephone** ['tel·ə·foʊn] I. *n* teléfono *m*; **mobile ~** móvil *m* II. *vt, vi* llamar por teléfono III. *adj* telefónico, -a

**telephone book** *n* guía *f* telefónica

**telephone booth** *n* cabina *f* telefónica

**telephone call** *n* llamada *f* telefónica

**telephone conversation** *n* conversación *f* telefónica

**telephone directory** *n* guía *f* telefónica

**telephone exchange** *n* central *f* telefónica

**telephone information service** *n* servicio *m* de información telefónica

**telephone message** *n* mensaje *m* telefónico

**telephone number** *n* número *m* de teléfono

**telephone operator** *n* operador(a) *m(f)* telefónico, -a

**telephone rates** *n* tarifa *f* telefónica

**telephoto lens** ['tel·ə·foʊ·toʊ·'lens] *n* teleobjetivo *m*

**teleprocessing** ['tel·ɪ·pra·ˌses·ɪŋ] *n* teleproceso *m*

**telescope** ['tel·ə·skoʊp] *n* telescopio *m*

**telescopic** [ˌtel·ə·'skap·ɪk] *adj* telescópico, -a; (*folding*) plegable

**teleshopping** ['tel·ə·ˌʃap·ɪŋ] *n* telecompra *f*

**televise** ['tel·ə·vaɪz] *vt* televisar

**television** ['tel·ə·vɪʒ·ən] *n* televisión *f*; (*TV set*) televisor *m*; **to watch ~** ver la televisión; **to turn the ~ on/off** encender/apagar el televisor

**television announcer** *n* locutor(a) *m(f)* de televisión

**television camera** *n* cámara *f* de televisión

**television program** *n* programa *m* de televisión

**television set** *n* televisor *m*

**television studio** *n* estudio de televisión

**tell** [tel] I. <told, told> *vt* 1. (*say*) decir; **to ~ sb of sth** comunicar algo a alguien; **I told you so** te avisé 2. (*narrate*) contar 3. (*command*) mandar; **to ~ sb to do sth** mandar a alguien que haga algo 4. (*make out*) reconocer; **to ~ sth from sth** distinguir algo de algo; **there is no ~ing** no hay manera de saberlo ▶ **to ~ it like it is** las cosas claras; **you're ~ing me!** ¡a mí me lo vas a contar! II. <told, told> *vi* 1. hablar (**of** de) 2. (*know*) saber; **you never can ~** nunca se sabe; **how can I ~?** ¡yo qué sé!; **who can ~?** ¿quién sabe?

**◆tell apart** *vt* distinguir

**◆tell off** *vt* regañar (**for** por)

**teller** ['tel·ər] *n* (*employee*) cajero, -a *m, f*

**telling** ['tel·ɪŋ] I. *adj* (*revealing*) revelador(a) II. *n* narración *f*

**telling-off** [ˌtel·ɪŋ·'ɔf] <tellings-off> *n* Can bronca *f*; **to give sb a ~ for** (*do-*

**ing) sth** echar una bronca a alguien por (hacer) algo

**telltale** ['tel·teɪl] n chivato, -a m, f

**temp** [temp] **I.** vi trabajar temporalmente **II.** n trabajador(a) m(f) temporal

**temper** ['tem·pər] **I.** n temperamento m; (mood) humor m; (bad) ~ (mal) genio; **good ~** buen humor; **to keep one's ~** no perder la calma; **to lose one's ~** perder los estribos **II.** vt (mitigate) atenuar

**temperament** ['tem·prə·mənt] n temperamento m; (moodiness) genio m

**temperamental** [ˌtem·prə·'men·təl] adj temperamental; (unpredictable) caprichoso, -a

**temperate** ['tem·pər·ət] adj moderado, -a

**temperature** ['tem·pər·ə·tʃər] n temperatura f; MED fiebre f; **to run a ~** tener fiebre

**tempest** ['tem·pɪst] n tempestad f

**tempestuous** [tem·'pes·tʃu·əs] adj tempestuoso, -a

**temple¹** ['tem·pəl] n REL templo m

**temple²** ['tem·pəl] n ANAT sien f

**tempo** ['tem·poʊ] <-s or -pi> n **1.** MUS tempo m **2.** (pace) ritmo m

**temporarily** ['tem·pə·rer·ə·li] adv temporalmente

**temporary** ['tem·pə·rer·i] adj (improvement, relief) pasajero, -a; (staff, accommodation) temporal

**tempt** [tempt] vt tentar; **to ~ sb into doing sth** incitar a alguien a hacer algo

**temptation** [temp·'teɪ·ʃən] n tentación f; (tempting thing) aliciente m; **to resist ~** (to do sth) resistir la tentación (de hacer algo); **to succumb to ~** caer en la tentación

**tempting** ['temp·tɪŋ] adj tentador(a)

**ten** [ten] **I.** adj diez inv **II.** n diez m; **~ to one he comes** seguro que viene; s. a. **eight**

**tenacious** [tə·'neɪ·ʃəs] adj firme; (person) tenaz

**tenacity** [tə·'næs·ə·t̬i] n tenacidad f

**tenant** ['ten·ənt] n inquilino, -a m, f

**tend¹** [tend] vi (have tendency) tender; **to ~ to do sth** tender a hacer algo; (usually) soler hacer algo

**tend²** [tend] vt (look after) ocuparse de

**tendency** ['ten·dən·si] <-ies> n tendencia f; MED propensión f

**tender¹** ['ten·dər] adj **1.** (soft) tierno, -a **2.** (easily damaged) vulnerable **3.** (affectionate) cariñoso, -a

**tender²** ['ten·dər] **I.** n COM oferta f **II.** vi hacer una oferta (**for** para)

**tenderize** ['ten·də·raɪz] vt ablandar

**tenderloin** ['ten·dər·lɔɪn] n lomo m

**tenderness** ['ten·dər·nɪs] n **1.** (softness) blandura f **2.** (affection) ternura f **3.** (sensitivity) sensibilidad f

**tendon** ['ten·dən] n tendón m

**tenfold** ['ten·foʊld] adv diez veces

**tennis** ['ten·ɪs] n tenis m inv

**tennis ball** n pelota f de tenis

**tennis court** n pista f de tenis

**tennis racket** n raqueta f de tenis

**tenor** ['ten·ər] n a. MUS tenor m; (of events) curso m

**tense¹** [tens] n LING tiempo m

**tense²** [tens] **I.** adj tenso, -a **II.** vt tensar **III.** vi ponerse tenso

**tension** ['ten·ʃən] n tensión f

**tent** [tent] n (for camping) tienda f de campaña, carpa f AmL; (circus) carpa f

**tentacle** ['ten·tə·kəl] n tentáculo m

**tentative** ['ten·tə·t̬ɪv] adj vacilante; (decision) provisional

**tentatively** adv (suggest) con vacilación; (decide) provisionalmente

**tenth** [tenθ] **I.** adj décimo, -a **II.** n **1.** (order) décimo, -a m, f **2.** (date) diez m **3.** (fraction) décimo m; s. a. **eighth**

**tent peg** n estaquilla f de tienda

**tent pole** n mástil m de tienda

**tenure** ['ten·jər] n (possession) posesión f

**tepid** ['tep·ɪd] adj tibio, -a

**terabyte** ['ter·ə·baɪt] n terabyte m

**term** [tɜrm] n **1.** (label, word, category) término m; **~ of abuse** insulto m; **in glowing ~s** con gran admiración; **in no uncertain ~s** en términos claros; **in simple ~s** en palabras sencillas **2.** **~s** (conditions) condiciones fpl; **to offer easy ~s** ofrecer facilidades de pago **3.** (limit) plazo m; **~ of delivery** plazo de entrega; **in the short/long ~** a corto/largo plazo **4.** UNIV, SCHOOL tri-

**T**

mestre *m* **5. to be on good/bad ~s** llevarse bien/mal (**with** con)

**terminal** ['tɜr·mɪ·nəl] **I.** *adj* terminal; (*extreme*) absoluto, -a **II.** *n* RAIL, AVIAT, COMPUT terminal *f*; ELEC polo *m*

**terminate** ['tɜr·mɪ·neɪt] *vt* poner fin a; (*contract*) rescindir; (*pregnancy*) interrumpir

**termination** [ˌtɜr·mɪ·'neɪ·ʃən] *n* fin *m*; (*contract*) rescisión *f*; (*pregnancy*) interrupción *f*

**terminus** ['tɜr·mɪ·nəs] <-es *or* -i> *n* última parada *f*

**termite** ['tɜr·maɪt] *n* termita *f*

**terrace** ['ter·əs] *n a.* AGR terraza *f*

**terraced house** *n* casa *f* adosada

**terrain** [te·'reɪn] *n* terreno *m*

**terrible** ['ter·ə·bəl] *adj* **1.** (*shocking*) terrible **2.** (*very bad*) espantoso, -a **3.** *inf* fatal

**terribly** ['ter·ə·bli] *adv* terriblemente; (*very*) tremendamente

**terrific** [tə·'rɪf·ɪk] *adj* **1.** (*terrifying*) terrorífico, -a **2.** (*excellent*) estupendo, -a **3.** (*very great*) tremendo, -a

**terrified** *adj* aterrorizado, -a

**terrify** ['ter·ə·faɪ] <-ie-> *vt* aterrar

**terrifying** *adj* aterrador, -a

**territory** ['ter·ə·tɔr·i] <-ies> *n* territorio *m*

**terror** ['ter·ər] *n* terror *m* (**of** a); **to strike ~** infundir terror; **a little ~** un demonio de niño

**terrorism** ['ter·ə·rɪz·əm] *n* terrorismo *m*

**terrorist** ['ter·ə·rɪst] *adj, n* terrorista *mf*

**terrorize** ['ter·ə·raɪz] *vt* aterrorizar

**terror-stricken** ['ter·ər·ˌstrɪk·ən] *adj*, **terror-struck** ['ter·ər·strʌk] *adj* aterrorizado, -a

**terry cloth** [ˌter·i·'klɔθ] *n* felpa *f*

**terse** [tɜrs] *adj* lacónico, -a

**Tertiary** ['tɜr·ʃi·er·i] *n* **the Tertiary** el Terciario

**test** [test] **I.** *n* **1.** SCHOOL, UNIV examen *m*; **to pass/fail a ~** aprobar/suspender un examen; **driving ~** examen de conducir **2.** MED prueba *f*; **blood ~** análisis *m inv* de sangre **3. to put sth to the ~** poner algo a prueba **II.** *vt* **1.** (*examine*) *a.* MED examinar; **to ~ sb for sth** hacer a alguien una prueba de algo **2.** (*meas-*

*ure*) comprobar **3.** (*try to prove*) someter a prueba

**testament** ['tes·tə·mənt] *n* **1.** (*will*) testamento *m* **2.** (*evidence*) testimonio *m* **3. Old/New Testament** Antiguo/Nuevo Testamento

**test bench** *n* banco *m* de pruebas

**test drive** *n* vuelta *f* de prueba

**testicle** ['tes·tɪ·kəl] *n* testículo *m*

**testify** ['tes·tɪ·faɪ] <-ie-> *vi, vt* testificar; **to ~ that...** declarar que...; **to ~ to sth** atestiguar algo

**testimony** ['tes·tɪ·mou·ni] <-ies> *n* testimonio *m*; **to give ~** dar testimonio

**testing I.** *n* experiencia *f* **II.** *adj* duro, -a

**test pilot** *n* piloto *mf* de pruebas

**test stage** *n* período *m* de pruebas

**test tube** *n* probeta *f*

**testy** ['tes·ti] <-ier, -iest> *adj* irritable

**tetanus** ['tet·ə·nəs] *n* tétano(s) *m (inv)*; **~ injection** vacuna *f* antitetánica

**tetchy** ['tetʃ·i] <-ier, -iest> *adj* irritable

**tether** ['teð·ər] **I.** *n* cuerda *f* ▶ **to be at the end of one's ~** no aguantar más **II.** *vt* amarrar; **to be ~ed to sth** *fig* estar atado a algo

**Texan** ['tek·sən] *adj, n* tejano, -a *m, f*

**Texas** ['tek·səs] *n* Tejas *m*

**text** [tekst] *n* texto *m*

**textbook** ['tekst·bʊk] *n* libro *m* de texto

**textile** ['teks·taɪl] **I.** *n pl* tejidos *mpl* **II.** *adj* textil

**than** [ðən, ðæn] *conj* que; **you are taller ~ she (is)** eres más alto que ella; **more ~ 60** más de 60; **more ~ once** más de una vez; **nothing else ~...** nada más que...; **no other ~ you** nadie más que tú; **no sooner had she told him, ~...** en cuanto se lo dijo...

**thank** [θæŋk] *vt* dar las gracias (**for** por); **~ you (very much)** (muchas) gracias

**thankful** ['θæŋk·fəl] *adj* **1.** (*pleased*) aliviado, -a; **to be ~ that...** alegrarse de que... +*subj* **2.** (*grateful*) agradecido, -a

**thankfully** *adv* afortunadamente

**thankless** ['θæŋk·lɪs] *adj* desagradecido, -a

**thanks** [θæŋks] *npl* gracias *fpl* (**to** a); **~ very much** muchísimas gracias; **in ~**

**for...** en recompensa por...

**thanksgiving** [θæŋks·'gɪv·ɪŋ] n acción f de gracias

**Thanksgiving (Day)** n Día m de Acción de Gracias

**that** [ðæt, ðət] I. adj dem <those> ese/esos, esa(s) (more remote) aquel/aquellos, aquella(s) m, f; ~ **table** esa/aquella mesa; ~ **book** ese/aquel libro II. pron 1. rel que; **the woman** — **told me...** la mujer que me dijo...; **all** — **I have** todo lo que tengo 2. dem ése/ésos, ésa(s) m, f, eso(s) neuter; **what is** ~? ¿eso qué es?; **who is** ~? ¿ése/ésa quién es?; **like** ~ así; **after** ~ después de eso III. adv tan; **it was** ~ **hot** hacía tanto calor IV. conj 1. que; **I told you** ~ **I couldn't come** te dije que no podía ir 2. (in order that) para que +subj

**thatch** [θætʃ] n inf (hair) greña f

**thatched roof** n techo de paja

**thaw** [θɔ] I. n (weather) deshielo m II. vi (weather) deshelar; (food) descongelarse III. vt derretir

**the** [ðə, stressed, before vowel ði] I. def art el(la) m(f), los(las) m(f)pl; **from** ~ **garden** del jardín; **at** ~ **hotel** en el hotel; **to** ~ **garden** al jardín II. adv ~ **more one tries,** ~ **less one succeeds** cuanto más se esfuerza uno, menos lo logra; ~ **sooner** ~ **better** cuanto antes mejor

**theater** ['θi·ə·tər] n 1. THEAT teatro m 2. CINE cine m 3. UNIV auditorio m

**theatrical** [θi·'æt·rɪ·kəl] adj teatral; **don't be so** ~ **about it** no hagas tanto teatro por eso

**theft** [θeft] n robo m; **petty** ~ hurto m

**their** [ðer] adj pos su(s); ~ **house** su casa; ~ **children** sus hijos

**theirs** [ðerz] pron pos (el) suyo, (la) suya m, f, (los) suyos, (las) suyas m, fpl; **this house is** ~ esta casa es suya; **they aren't our bags, they are** ~ no son nuestras bolsas, son las suyas; **a book of** ~ un libro suyo

**them** [ðem, ðəm] pron pers pl 1. (they) ellos, -as; **older than** ~ mayor que ellos 2. direct object los(las) m(f); indirect object les; **look at** ~ míralos; **I saw** ~ yo los vi; **he gave** ~ **the pencil** les dio el lápiz 3. after prep ellos, -as; **it's from/**

**for** ~ **es** de/para ellos

**theme** [θim] n a. MUS tema m; **on the** ~ **of** sobre el tema de

**theme music** n sintonía f

**theme park** n parque m temático

**themselves** [ðəm·'selvz] pron 1. subject ellos mismos, ellas mismas m, f 2. object, reflexive se; **the children behaved** ~ los niños se portaron bien 3. after prep sí mismos, sí mismas m, f; **by** ~ solos, -as

**then** [ðen] I. adj **the** ~ **chairman** el entonces presidente II. adv 1. (at that time) entonces; **before/since** ~ hasta/desde entonces; **from** ~ **on(ward)** a partir de entonces; **until** ~ hasta aquel momento; **(every) now and** ~ de vez en cuando 2. (after that) después; **what** ~? ¿y entonces qué? 3. (additionally) además; **but** ~ **(again)** y además 4. ~ **he must be there** entonces debe estar allí

**theologian** [θi·ə·'lou·dʒən] n teólogo, -a m, f

**theology** [θi·'al·ə·dʒi] <-ies> n teología f

**theorem** ['θi·ər·əm] n teorema m

**theoretical** [θi·ə·'ret·ɪ·kəl] adj teórico, -a

**theory** ['θi·ə·ri] <-ies> n teoría f; **in** ~ en teoría

**therapeutic** [θer·ə·'pju·tɪk] adj, **therapeutical** [θer·ə·'pju·tɪ·kəl] adj terapéutico, -a

**therapist** ['θer·ə·pɪst] n terapeuta mf

**therapy** ['θer·ə·pi] <-ies> n terapia f

**there** [ðer] I. adv allí [or allá]; **here and** ~ aquí y allá; ~ **is/are** hay; ~ **will be** habrá; ~ **you are!** ¡ahí lo tienes!; ~**'s the train** ahí está el tren; ~ **is no one** no hay nadie; ~ **and then** en el acto II. interj ¡vaya!; ~, **take this** toma esto; ~, **that's enough!** ¡bueno, basta ya!

**thereabouts** ['ðer·ə·bauts] adv por ahí

**thereafter** [ðer·'æf·tər] adv a partir de entonces

**thereby** [ðer·'bai] adv por eso ▶ ~ **hangs a <u>tale</u>** es una larga historia

**therefore** ['ðer·fɔr] adv por (lo) tanto

**therein** [ðer·'ɪn] adv form ahí dentro; fig en eso

**thereupon** [ˌðer·ə·'pɑn] *adv* acto seguido

**thermal** ['θɜr·məl] *adj* térmico, -a; (*water*) termal

**thermal underwear** *n* ropa *f* interior térmica

**thermodynamic** [ˌθɜr·moʊ·daɪ·'næm·ɪk] *adj* termodinámico, -a

**thermoelectric** [ˌθɜr·moʊ·ɪ·'lek·trɪk] *adj* termoeléctrico, -a

**thermometer** [θər·'mɑm·ə·t̬ər] *n* termómetro *m*

**thermos** ['θɜr·məs] *n* termo *m*

**thermostat** ['θɜr·mə·stæt] *n* termostato *m*

**thesaurus** [θɪ·'sɔr·əs] <-es *or* -ri> *n* diccionario *m* de sinónimos y antónimos

**these** [ðiz] *pl of* **this**

**thesis** ['θi·sɪs] <-ses> *n* tesis *f inv*

**they** [ðeɪ] *pron pers* **1.** (*3rd person pl*) ellos, -as ~ **are my parents/sisters** (ellos/ellas) son mis padres/hermanas **2.** (*people in general*) ~ **say that...** dicen que...

**they'll** [ðeɪl] = **they will** *see* **will**

**they're** [ðer] = **they are** *see* **be**

**they've** [ðeɪv] = **they have** *see* **have**

**thick** [θɪk] **I.** *adj* **1.** (*wall*) grueso, -a; (*coat*) gordo, -a; (*hair*) abundante; (*forest*) denso, -a; (*liquid*) espeso, -a; (*darkness*) profundo, -a **2.** (*stupid*) corto, -a; **to be as ~ as two short planks** no tener dos dedos de frente **3. to be ~ with sb** ser muy amigo de alguien **II.** *n* **to be in the ~ of sth** estar de lleno en algo

**thicken** ['θɪk·ən] *vt, vi* espesar

**thicket** ['θɪk·ɪt] *n* matorral *m*

**thickness** ['θɪk·nɪs] *n* grosor *m*; (*hair*) abundancia *f*; (*sauce*) consistencia *f*

**thick-skinned** ['θɪk·skɪnd] *adj* insensible; **he is ~** todo le resbala

**thief** [θif, θivz] <thieves> *n* ladrón, -ona *m, f*

**thieving** ['θi·vɪŋ] *adj* de dedos largos

**thigh** [θaɪ] *n* muslo *m*

**thimble** ['θɪm·bəl] *n* dedal *m*

**thin** [θɪn] <-nn-> *adj* (*person*) flaco, -a; (*clothes*) fino, -a; (*voice*) débil; (*hair*) ralo, -a; **to be ~ on top** ser calvo

◆**thin out** *vi* disminuir

**thing** [θɪŋ] *n* **1.** cosa *f*; **all my ~s** todas sus cosas; **the lucky/best/main ~** lo

bueno/mejor/principal; **the last ~ she wants to do is...** lo último que quiere hacer es...; **above all ~s** por encima de todo; **if it's not one ~, it's another** cuando no es una cosa es otra **2.** *inf* **the real ~** lo auténtico; **the very ~** lo importante **3.** (*situation*) **as ~s stand, the way ~s are** tal (y) como están las cosas; **the shape of ~s to come** lo que se avecina **4.** *inf* **the poor ~!** ¡el pobre!; (*children, animals*) ¡pobrecito!; **you lucky ~!** ¡qué suerte tienes!; **lazy ~!** ¡vago! ▶ **he won but it was a <u>close</u> ~** ganó por un pelo; **all ~s being <u>equal</u>** si no surge ningún imprevisto; **<u>first</u> ~s first** lo primero es lo primero; **to not know the <u>first</u> ~** no tener ni la más remota idea (about de); **to be onto a <u>good</u> ~** tener un chollo; **to <u>have</u> a ~ about** tener asco a; **to <u>make</u> a (big) ~ about** armar un escándalo (out of por)

**think** [θɪŋk] <thought, thought> **I.** *vt* **1.** (*believe*) pensar; **who would have thought it!** ¡quien lo hubiese pensado! **2.** (*consider*) considerar; **to ~ sb (to be) sth** considerar a alguien (como) algo **II.** *vi* pensar; **to ~ of sb/doing sth** pensar en alguien/hacer algo; **to ~ aloud** pensar en voz alta; **to ~ for/to oneself** pensar por/para sí mismo

◆**think ahead** *vi* pensar de cara al futuro

◆**think back** *vi* **to ~ over/to sth** hacer memoria de/recordar algo

◆**think out** *vt* **1.** (*consider*) pensar muy bien **2.** (*plan*) planear cuidadosamente

◆**think over** *vt* reflexionar sobre

◆**think through** *vt* estudiar detenidamente

◆**think up** *vt* inventar

**thinker** *n* pensador(a) *m(f)*

**thinking** **I.** *n* **1.** (*thought*) pensamiento *m* **2.** (*reasoning*) razonamiento *m* **3.** (*opinion*) opinión *f* **II.** *adj* inteligente

**think tank** *n* gabinete *m* estratégico

**thinner** *n* disolvente *m*

**third** [θɜrd] **I.** *adj* tercero, -a **II.** *n* **1.** (*order*) tercero, -a *m, f* **2.** (*date*) tres *m* **3.** (*fraction*) tercio *m* **4.** MUS, AUTO tercera *f*; *s. a.* **eighth**

**thirdly** *adv* en tercer lugar

**third party** *n* tercero *m*

**Third World** *n* Tercer Mundo

**thirst** [θɜrst] *n a. fig* sed *f*

**thirsty** ['θɜr·sti] <-ier, -iest> *adj* sediento, -a; **to be** ~ tener sed; *fig* estar ansioso (**for** por)

**thirteen** [θɜr·'tin] *adj, n* trece *m; s. a.* **eight**

**thirteenth** [θɜr·'tinθ] I. *adj* decimotercero, -a II. *n* 1. (*order*) decimotercero, -a *m, f* 2. (*date*) trece *m* 3. (*fraction*) decimotercero *m; s. a.* **eighth**

**thirtieth** ['θɜrt̬·i·əθ] I. *adj* trigésimo, -a II. *n* 1. (*order*) trigésimo, -a *m, f* 2. (*date*) treinta *m* 3. (*fraction*) trigésimo *m; s. a.* **eighth**

**thirty** ['θɜr·t̬i] <-ies> *adj, n* treinta *m; s. a.* **eighty**

**this** [ðɪs] I. <these> *adj det* este, -a; ~ **car** este coche; ~ **house** esta casa; ~ **one** éste, -a; ~ **morning/evening** esta mañana/tarde; ~ **time** esta vez; **these days** hoy en día II. <these> *pron dem* éste, -a, esto *f*, esto *neuter*; **what is** ~? ¿esto qué es?; **who is** ~? ¿éste/ésta quién es?; ~ **and that** esto y aquello; ~ **is Ana (speaking)** TEL soy Ana III. *adv* así; ~ **late** tan tarde; ~ **much** tanto; ~ **big** así de grande

**thistle** ['θɪs·əl] *n* cardo *m*

**thong** [θɑŋ] *n* 1. (*of leather*) correa *f* 2. (*G-string*) tanga *m* 3. (*sandal*) chancla *f*

**thorn** [θɔrn] *n* espina *f*

**thorny** ['θɔr·ni] <-ier, -iest> *adj* espinoso, -a, espinado, -a *AmC, CSur, (issue)* peliagudo, -a

**thorough** ['θɜr·oʊ] *adj* 1. (*complete*) absoluto, -a 2. (*detailed*) exhaustivo, -a 3. (*careful*) minucioso, -a

**thoroughbred** ['θɜr·oʊ·bred] I. *n* pura sangre *mf* II. *adj* de pura sangre

**thoroughfare** ['θɜr·oʊ·fer] *n* vía *f* pública

**thoroughly** *adv* 1. (*in detail*) a fondo 2. (*completely*) completamente

**those** [ðoʊz] *pl of* **that**

**though** [ðoʊ] I. *conj* aunque; **as** ~ como si +*subj*; **even** ~ aunque; **even** ~ **it's cold** aunque hace frío II. *adv* sin em-

bargo; **he did do it,** ~ sin embargo, sí que lo hizo

**thought** [θɔt] *n* 1. (*process*) reflexión *f*; **without** ~ sin pensar; **after much** ~ tras mucho reflexionar; **to be deep/lost in** ~ estar ensimismado 2. (*idea, opinion*) pensamiento *m*; **that's a** ~ es posible

**thoughtful** ['θɔt·fəl] *adj* 1. (*pensive*) pensativo, -a 2. (*careful*) cuidadoso, -a 3. (*considerate*) atento, -a

**thoughtless** ['θɔt·lɪs] *adj* irreflexivo, -a; (*tactless*) desconsiderado, -a; (*careless*) descuidado, -a

**thought-out** [,θɔt̬·'aʊt] *adj* planeado, -a

**thought-provoking** *adj* que hace pensar

**thousand** ['θaʊ·zənd] *adj, n* mil *m*

**thousandth** ['θaʊ·zəntθ] *adj, n* milésimo *m*; **the** ~ el número mil

**thrash** [θræʃ] *vt a. fig* dar una paliza

♦**thrash out** *vt inf* (*problem*) discutir; (*agreement*) llegar a

**thrashing** *n* paliza *f*, batida *f AmL*

**thread** [θred] *n* hilo *m* ▶ **to hang by a** ~ pender de un hilo

**threadbare** ['θred·ber] *adj* raído, -a; (*argument, excuse*) trillado, -a

**threat** [θret] *n* amenaza *f*

**threaten** ['θret̬·ən] *vt, vi* amenazar (**to** con)

**threatening** *adj* amenazador(a)

**three** [θri] *adj, n* tres *m; s. a.* **eight**

**three-D** [,θri·'di] *adj abbr of* **three-dimensional** en tres D

**three-dimensional** *adj* tridimensional

**threefold** ['θri·foʊld] I. *adj* triple II. *adv* por triplicado

**three-part** *adj* de tres partes

**three-piece** [,θri·'pis] *adj* de tres piezas

**threshold** ['θreʃ·hoʊld] *n* umbral *m*

**threw** [θru] *pt of* **throw**

**thrice** [θraɪs] *adv* tres veces

**thrifty** ['θrɪf·ti] <-ier, -iest> *adj* ahorrativo, -a

**thrill** [θrɪl] I. *n* estremecimiento *m* II. *vt* estremecer III. *vi* estremecerse

**thriller** ['θrɪl·ər] *n* novela *f* de suspense; CINE película *f* de suspense

**thrilling** ['θrɪl·ɪŋ] *adj* emocionante

**thrive** [θraɪv] <thrived *or* throve, thrived *or* thriven> *vi* crecer mucho; (*business*) prosperar

**thriving** *adj* próspero, -a

**throat** [θrəʊt] *n* (*external*) cuello *m;* (*internal*) garganta *f;* **sore ~** dolor de garganta

**throb** [θrɑb] I. *n* vibración *f;* (*heart*) palpitación *f* II. <-bb-> *vi* vibrar; (*heart*) palpitar

**throne** [θrəʊn] *n* trono *m*

**throttle** ['θrɑt·əl] *n* acelerador *m;* **to open the ~** acelerar; **at full ~** a todo gas

◆**throttle back** *vi* reducir (la velocidad)

**through** [θru] I. *prep* 1. (*place*) a través de, por; **to go right ~ sth** traspasar algo; **to go ~ the door** entrar por la puerta; **to walk ~ a room** atravesar una habitación 2. (*during*) durante; **all ~ my life** durante toda mi vida; **to be ~** acabar (de) 3. (*until*) hasta; **open Monday ~ Friday** abierto de lunes a viernes 4. (*by means of*) por (medio de) II. *adv* 1. (*place*) de un lado a otro; **I read the book ~** leí un libro entero; **to go ~** ir directo (**to** a) 2. (*time*) **all day ~** de la mañana a la noche; **halfway ~** a medio camino 3. **to put sb ~ to sb** poner a alguien con alguien 4. (*completely*) completamente; **to think sth ~** pensarse algo detenidamente ▶ **~ and ~** de cabo a rabo III. *adj* 1. (*finished*) terminado, -a; **we are ~** hemos terminado 2. (*direct*) directo, -a 3. SCHOOL **to get ~** aprobar

**throughout** [θru·'aʊt] I. *prep* 1. (*place*) por todas partes de; **~ the town** por toda la ciudad 2. (*time*) a lo largo de; **~ his stay** durante toda su estancia II. *adv* 1. (*place*) por [*or* en] todas partes 2. (*time*) todo el tiempo

**through traffic** *n* tráfico *m* de tránsito

**through train** *n* tren *m* directo

**throughway** ['θru·weɪ] *n* autopista *f* de peaje

**throw** [θrəʊ] I. *n* 1. (*toss*) lanzamiento *m* 2. *inf* (*chance*) oportunidad *f* II. <threw, thrown> *vi* lanzar III. <threw, thrown> *vt* 1. (*propel, cause to fall*) tirar; (*ball, javelin, glance*) lanzar; **to ~ oneself at sb** tirar los tejos a alguien; **to ~ oneself into sth** entregarse de lleno a algo 2. *inf* (*confuse*) desconcertar 3. **to ~**

**the switch** pulsar el interruptor; **to ~ a party** dar una fiesta

◆**throw away** *vt* 1. (*discard*) tirar 2. (*waste*) malgastar; (*money*) despilfarrar (**on** en) 3. (*say*) soltar

◆**throw back** *vt* 1. (*return*) devolver 2. (*curtains*) correr 3. **to throw sth back** (**in sb's face**) echar algo en cara a alguien

◆**throw down** *vt* 1. (*throw*) tirar 2. (*deposit*) dejar

◆**throw in** *vt* arrojar; (*include*) agregar; (*comment*) soltar

◆**throw off** *vt* 1. (*remove*) quitarse 2. (*escape from*) despistar

◆**throw on** *vt* (*clothes*) ponerse

◆**throw out** *vt* (*heat, light*) despedir; (*person*) echar; (*thing*) tirar

◆**throw together** *vt* (*make quickly*) hacer en un periquete

◆**throw up** I. *vt* 1. (*project upwards*) lanzar al aire 2. (*bring to light*) revelar 3. (*build quickly*) levantar 4. *inf* (*give up*) dejar II. *vi* potar, buitrear *CSur,* revulsar *Méx*

**throwaway** ['θrəʊ·ə·weɪ] *adj* desechable

**throw-in** ['θrəʊ·ɪn] *n* (*soccer*) saque *m* de banda; (*baseball*) lanzamiento *m*

**throwing** *n* lanzamiento *m*

**thrown** *pp of* **throw**

**thru** [θru] *prep, adj see* **through**

**thrush** [θrʌʃ] *n* MED afta *f*

**thrust** [θrʌst] I. <-, -> *vi* (*shove*) empujar II. <-, -> *vt* (*push*) empujar; (*insert*) clavar III. *n* 1. (*shove*) empujón *m* 2. (*impetus*) empuje *m* 3. TECH propulsión *f*

**thrusting** ['θrʌs·tɪŋ] *adj* arribista

**thruway** ['θru·weɪ] *n* autopista *f* de peaje

**thud** [θʌd] <-dd-> *vi* dar un golpe sordo

**thug** [θʌg] *n* matón, -ona *m, f*

**thumb** [θʌm] *n* pulgar *m* ▶ **to be all fingers and ~s to be all ~s** ser un manazas; **to stand out like a sore ~** cantar como una almeja

**thumbnail** ['θʌm·neɪl] *n* uña *f* del pulgar

**thumbnail sketch** *n* pequeña reseña *f*

**thumbtack** *n* tachuela *f*

**thump** [θʌmp] I. *vt* golpear II. *vi*

1. (*heart*) latir con fuerza 2. to ~ on sth aporrear algo III. *n* porrazo *m*

**thumping** *adj inf* descomunal

**thunder** ['θʌn·dər] I. *n* 1. a (clap of) ~ un trueno 2. (*sound*) estruendo *m*

**thunderclap** *n* trueno *m*

**thundercloud** *n* nubarrón *m*

**thundering** ['θʌn·dər·ɪŋ] I. *n* estruendo *m* II. *adj inf* escandaloso, -a; (*very great*) enorme

**thunderous** ['θʌn·dər·əs] *adj* estruendoso, -a

**thunderstorm** ['θʌn·dər·stɔrm] *n* tormenta *f*

**Thursday** ['θɜrz·deɪ] *n* jueves *m inv*; *s. a.* **Friday**

**thus** [ðʌs] *adv form* 1. (*therefore*) por lo tanto 2. (*like this*) de este modo; ~ **far** hasta aquí

**thwart** [θwɔrt] *vt* frustrar

**thyme** [taɪm] *n* tomillo *m*

**thyroid** ['θaɪ·rɔɪd] *adj* tiroides *f inv*

**tick**[1] [tɪk] *n* (*insect*) garrapata *f*

**tick**[2] [tɪk] I. *n* 1. (*sound*) tic-tac *m* 2. (*mark*) visto *m* II. *vt* marcar (*con un visto*)

◆**tick off** *vt* 1. marcar (*con un visto*) 2. (*exasperate*) dar la lata

◆**tick over** *vi fig* ir tirando

**ticket** ['tɪk·ɪt] *n* 1. (*bus, train*) billete *m*, boleto *m AmL*; (*cinema, concert*) entrada *f* 2. (*price, tag*) etiqueta *f* 3. AUTO multa *f* ▶ **just the** ~ justo lo que hacía falta

**ticket agency** *n* taquilla *f*

**ticket counter** *n* mostrador *m* de venta de entradas o billetes

**ticket holder** *n* persona *f* que tiene entrada o billete

**ticket machine** *n* dispensador *m* de billetes

**ticket office** *n* RAIL ventanilla *f* de venta de billetes; THEAT taquilla *f*

**tickle** ['tɪk·əl] I. *vi* hacer cosquillas; (*clothes*) picar II. *vt* hacer cosquillas; (*amuse*) hacer gracia III. *n* cosquilleo *m*; (*tingling*) picor *m*

**ticklish** ['tɪk·lɪʃ] *adj* cosquilloso, -a; (*delicate*) delicado, -a

**tidal** ['taɪ·dəl] *adj* de la marea

**tidal wave** *n* sunami *m*

**tidbit** ['tɪd·bɪt] *n* 1. (*delicacy*) golosina *f* 2. (*information*) noticia *f*; (*gossip*) cotilleo *m*

**tide** [taɪd] *n* marea *f*; (*of opinion*) corriente *f*; **to go against the** ~ ir contracorriente; **to swim with the** ~ seguir la corriente

**tidy** ['taɪ·di] I. *adj* <-ier, -iest> 1. (*orderly*) ordenado, -a; **to have a** ~ **mind** ser metódico 2. *inf* suculento, -a II. *vt* ordenar

**tie** [taɪ] I. *n* 1. (*necktie*) corbata *f* 2. (*cord*) atadura *f* 3. ~s (*bonds*) lazos *mpl* 4. SPORTS empate *m* II. *vi* 1. (*fasten*) atarse 2. SPORTS empatar III. *vt* atar; (*knot*) hacer; **to be ~d by/to sth** estar limitado por/limitarse a algo

◆**tie back** *vt* atar

◆**tie down** *vt* atar; **to tie sb down to sth** *inf* comprometer a alguien a algo

◆**tie in** I. *vt* relacionar II. *vi* coincidir

◆**tie up** *vt* 1. (*bind*) atar; (*hair*) recogerse; **to** ~ **some loose ends** atar cabos sueltos 2. **to be tied up** estar ocupado

**tiebreak** ['taɪ·breɪk] *n*, **tiebreaker** *n* desempate *m*

**tier** [tɪr] *n* (*row*) hilera *f*; (*level*) nivel *m*

**tiff** [tɪf] *n inf* pelea *f*

**tiger** ['taɪ·gər] *n* tigre *m* ▶ **to have a** ~ **by the tail** tener el toro por los cuernos

**tight** [taɪt] I. *adj* 1. (*screw, knot*) apretado, -a; (*clothing*) ceñido, -a; (*rope*) tirante; (*skin*) terso, -a 2. (*condition, discipline*) estricto, -a; (*budget*) restringido, -a; (*situation*) difícil; (*schedule*) apretado, -a; **to be** ~ **for money/time** ir escaso de dinero/tiempo 3. (*hard-fought*) reñido, -a 4. (*drunk*) como una cuba II. *adv* fuerte; **sleep** ~! ¡que duermas bien!

**tighten** ['taɪ·tən] I. *vt* apretar; (*rope*) tensar II. *vi* apretarse; (*restrictions*) intensificarse

**tightrope** ['taɪt·roʊp] *n* cuerda *f* floja

**tights** [taɪts] *npl* medias *fpl*

**tightwad** ['taɪt·wad] *n sl* tacaño, -a *m, f*

**tigress** ['taɪ·grɪs] *n* tigresa *f*

**tile** [taɪl] *n* (*roof*) teja *f*; (*wall, floor*) azulejo *m*

**till**[1] [tɪl] I. *prep* hasta II. *conj* hasta que

**till²** [tɪl] *n* (*cash*) caja *f*

**tiller** ['tɪl·ər] *n* at the ~ al timón

**tilt** [tɪlt] I. *n* inclinación *f* ▶ (at) full ~ a toda máquina II. *vt* inclinar III. *vi* inclinarse; to ~ over volcarse

**timber** ['tɪm·bər] *n* madera *f*; (*beam*) viga *f*

**time** [taɪm] I. *n* 1. tiempo *m*; (*period*) período *m*; to kill/spend/waste ~ matar/pasar/perder el tiempo; to make/save ~ hacer/ganar tiempo; as ~ goes by, in the course of ~ con el paso del tiempo; to be a matter of ~ ser cuestión de tiempo; of all ~ de todos los tiempos; in ~ a tiempo; over/given ~ con el tiempo; free ~ tiempo libre; after a ~ al cabo de un tiempo; all the ~ continuamente; some/a long ~ ago hace algún/mucho tiempo; for the ~ being por ahora; to have a good ~ pasárselo bien; most of the ~ la mayor parte del tiempo; in one week's ~ dentro de una semana; it takes a long/short ~ se tarda mucho/poco; to give sb a hard ~ hacerlas pasar canutas a alguien 2. (*clock*) hora *f*; arrival/departure ~ hora de llegada/salida; train ~s horario *m* de tren; breakfast ~ hora de desayunar; at any ~ a cualquier hora; at any given ~, at (any) one ~ en un momento dado 3. (*moment*) momento *m*; the best ~ of day el mejor momento del día; this ~ tomorrow mañana a esta hora; at all ~s a todas horas; at a different ~ en otro momento; each ~ cada vez; the right ~ el momento oportuno; ahead of ~ con antelación 4. (*occasion*) vez *f*; the last/next ~ la última/próxima vez; ~ and (~) again una y otra vez; lots of ~s muchas veces; from ~ to ~ de vez en cuando; to remember the ~... recordar cuando...; it is about ~ that... ya es hora de que... +*subj* 5. (*right moment*) hora; it's high ~ that... ya es hora de que... +*subj*; right on ~ en el momento preciso 6. to work full/part ~ trabajar a jornada completa/a tiempo parcial; to be on short ~ estar en jornada reducida ▶ ~ is of the essence no hay tiempo que perder; to have ~ on one's <u>hands</u> tener tiempo de sobra; ~ is a great <u>healer</u> el tiempo lo cura todo; ~ is <u>money</u> el tiempo es oro; there's a ~ and a <u>place</u> (for everything) todo a su debido tiempo; there's no ~ like the <u>present</u> no dejes para mañana lo que puedas hacer hoy; ~ and <u>tide</u> wait for no man el tiempo no perdona; in less than no ~ en menos que canta un gallo; to <u>buy</u> ~ ganar tiempo; ~ <u>moves</u> on la vida sigue II. *vt* SPORTS cronometrar III. *adj* SPORTS contrarreloj

**time bomb** *n* bomba *f* de relojería

**timecard** *n* tarjeta *f* de registro horario

**time clock** *n* reloj *m* de control de asistencia

**time-consuming** ['taɪm·kən·ˌsu·mɪŋ] *adj* laborioso, -a

**time difference** *n* diferencia *f* horaria

**timekeeper** *n* (*device*) cronómetro *m*

**time lag** *n* retraso *m*

**timeless** ['taɪm·lɪs] *adj* eterno, -a

**time limit** *n* límite *m* de tiempo

**timely** ['taɪm·li] *adj* <-ier, -iest> oportuno, -a; in a ~ fashion a tiempo

**time-out** [ˌtaɪm·'aʊt] *n* descanso *m*; SPORTS tiempo *m* muerto

**timer** ['taɪ·mər] *n* temporizador *m*

**time sheet** *n* hoja *f* de asistencia

**timetable** *n* (*bus, train*) horario *m*; (*project, events*) programa *m*

**time zone** *n* huso *m* horario

**timid** ['tɪm·ɪd] *adj* <-er, -est> tímido, -a

**timing** ['taɪ·mɪŋ] *n* cronometraje *m*; that was perfect ~ ha sido el momento oportuno

**tin** [tɪn] I. *n* 1. (*metal*) estaño *m*; (*tin-plate*) hojalata *f* 2. (*container*) lata *f* 3. (*for baking*) molde *m* II. *vt* enlatar

**tin can** *n* lata *f*

**tinfoil** *n* papel *m* de aluminio

**tinge** [tɪndʒ] I. *n* tinte *m* II. *vt* teñir; *fig* matizar

**tingle** ['tɪŋ·gəl] I. *vi* estremecerse II. *n* estremecimiento *m*

**tinkle** ['tɪŋ·kəl] *vi*, *vt* tintinear

**tinsel** ['tɪn·səl] *n* oropel *m*

**tint** [tɪnt] I. *n* tono *m*; (*for hair*) tinte *m* II. *vt* teñir

**tiny** ['taɪ·ni] *adj* <-ier, -iest> chiquito, -a, chingo, -a *Col, Cuba*

**tip¹** [tɪp] I. <-pp-> *vt* cubrir II. *n* punta *f*; from ~ to toe de pies a cabeza; **it's on the ~ of my tongue** lo tengo en la punta de la lengua

**tip²** [tɪp] **I.** <-pp-> *vt* (*incline*) inclinar; **to ~ the balance** inclinar la balanza (**against** en contra de, **in favor of** a favor de) **II.** *vi* inclinarse

**tip³** [tɪp] **I.** *n* **1.** (*for service*) propina *f*, yapa *f Méx*; **10 per cent ~** el diez por ciento de propina **2.** (*hint*) aviso *m*; **to give sb a ~** dar a alguien un consejo; **to take a ~ from sb** seguir el consejo de alguien **II.** <-pp-> *vi*, *vt* dejar propina

◆**tip off** *vt* avisar

◆**tip over** *vt*, *vi* volcar

◆**tip up I.** *vt* inclinar **II.** *vi* inclinarse

**tip-off** ['tɪp.ɔf] *n* inf soplo *m*

**tipsy** ['tɪp.si] *adj* <-ier, -iest> bebido, -a, achispado, -a *AmL*

**tiptoe** ['tɪp.toʊ] **I.** *n* on ~(**s**) de puntillas **II.** *vi* ponerse de puntillas

**tiptop** ['tɪp.tap] *adj* de primera

**tirade** ['taɪ.reɪd] *n* diatriba *f*

**tire¹** [taɪr] *n* (*for vehicle*) neumático *m*, llanta *f Méx*, caucho *m Col, Ven*

**tire²** [taɪr] (*become tired*) **I.** *vt* cansar **II.** *vi* cansarse

**tired** ['taɪrd] *adj* <-er, -est> cansado, -a; (*excuse*) trillado, -a; **to be sick and ~** estar aburrido (**of** de)

**tiredness** *n* cansancio *m*

**tire gauge** *n* medidor *m* de presión

**tireless** ['taɪr.lɪs] *adj* incansable

**tiresome** ['taɪr.səm] *adj* molesto, -a; (*person*) pesado, -a, molón, -ona *Guat, Ecua, Méx*

**tiring** ['taɪ.rɪŋ] *adj* agotador(a)

**tissue** ['tɪʃ.u] *n* **1.** (*handkerchief*) pañuelo *m* **2.** ANAT, BIO tejido *m*

**tissue paper** *n* papel *m* de seda

**tit** [tɪt] *n* ANAT teta *f*

**titanium** [taɪ.ˈteɪ.ni.əm] *n* titanio *m*

**titillate** ['tɪt.ə.leɪt] *vt* excitar

**title** ['taɪt.əl] *n* **1.** (*name*) título *m* **2.** (*championship*) campeonato *m*

**titleholder** *n* titular *mf*

**title page** *n* portada *f*

**title role** *n* papel *m* principal

**title track** *n* canción *f* que da nombre al álbum

**titter** ['tɪt.ər] *vi* reírse disimuladamente

**to** [tu] **I.** *prep* **1.** (*direction*) a; **to go ~ Mexico/town** ir a México/a la ciudad; **to go ~ the cinema/the dentist('s)** ir al cine/al dentista; **to go ~ bed** irse a la cama; **~ the left/right** a la izquierda/derecha **2.** (*before*) **a quarter ~ five** las cinco menos cuarto **3.** (*until*) hasta; **to count up ~ 10** contar hasta 10; **~ this day** hasta el día de hoy; **done ~ perfection** hecho a la perfección; **~ some extent** hasta cierto punto **4.** *indirect object* **to show sth ~ sb** mostrar algo a alguien; **to talk ~ sb** hablar con alguien; **this belongs ~ me** esto es mío **5.** (*towards*) con; **to be kind/rude ~ sb** ser amable/grosero con alguien **6.** (*against*) contra; **elbow ~ elbow** codo con codo **7.** (*comparison*) a; **3** (**goals**) **~ 1** 3 (goles) a 1; **superior ~ sth/sb** superior a algo/alguien **8.** (*of*) de; **the top ~ this jar** la tapa de este tarro **9.** (*purpose*) para ▶ **that's all there is ~ it** eso es todo **II.** *infinitive particle* **1.** (*infinitive*) **~ do/walk** hacer/andar **2.** (*command*) **I told him ~ eat** le dije que comiera **3.** (*interrogative*) **she didn't know how ~ say it** no sabía cómo decirlo **4.** (*wish*) **she wants ~ go** quiere irse; **he wants me ~ tell him a story** quiere que le cuente un cuento **5.** (*purpose*) **he comes ~ see me** viene a verme; **to phone ~ ask sth** llamar para preguntar algo **6.** (*intention*) **the work ~ be done** el trabajo que hay que hacer **7.** (*result*) **too tired ~ do sth** demasiado cansado para hacer algo **8.** (*ellipsis*) **he doesn't want ~ eat, but I want ~** él no quiere comer, pero yo sí **III.** *adv* **to push the door ~** cerrar la puerta

**toad** [toʊd] *n* sapo *m*; (*person*) mamarracho, -a *m, f*

**toadstool** ['toʊd.stul] *n* seta *f* venenosa

**toast** [toʊst] **I.** *n* **1. a** (*piece of*) ~ una tostada *f* **2.** (*drink*) brindis *m inv* **II.** *vt* **1.** (*cook*) tostar **2.** (*drink*) brindar **III.** *vi* tostarse

**toaster** *n* tostadora *f*

**tobacco** [tə.ˈbæk.oʊ] *n* tabaco *m*

**tobacconist** [tə.ˈbæk.ə.nɪst] *n* estanquero, -a *m, f*

**to-be** [tə.ˈbi] *adj* futuro, -a

T

**toboggan** [təˈbag·ən] n trineo m

**toboggan run** n, **toboggan slide** n pista f de trineos

**today** [təˈdeɪ] I. adv hoy; (*nowadays*) hoy día II. n hoy m; (*nowadays*) actualidad f

**toddler** [ˈtad·lər] n niño, -a m, f que empieza a caminar

**to-do** [təˈdu] n inf lío m

**toe** [toʊ] I. n dedo m del pie; (*shoe*) puntera f; **on one's ~s** de puntillas ▶ **to step on sb's ~s** pisotear a alguien *fig* II. vt **to ~ the line** conformarse

**toehold** n SPORTS punto m de apoyo

**toenail** n uña f del pie

**toffee** [ˈtɔ·fi] n toffee m

**together** [təˈgeð·ər] adv 1. (*jointly*) juntos, -as **all ~** todos juntos, todas juntas m, f; **~ with** junto con; **to get ~** juntarse; **to get it ~** sl organizarse 2. (*at the same time*) a la vez

**toggle** [ˈtag·əl] I. n COMPUT tecla f de conmutación II. vt pulsar

**toil** [tɔɪl] I. n labor f II. vi (*work hard*) afanarse

**toilet** [ˈtɔɪ·lɪt] n 1. (*room*) cuarto m de baño; (*public*) servicio m 2. (*appliance*) váter m 3. (*process*) aseo m

**toilet paper** n papel m higiénico

**toiletries** [ˈtɔɪ·lɪ·triz] npl artículos m pl de tocador

**toiletries bag** n neceser m

**toilet roll** n rollo m de papel higiénico

**toilet water** n colonia f

**token** [ˈtoʊ·kən] I. n 1. (*sign*) señal f; (*affection*) muestra f; **by the same ~** por la misma razón; **in ~ of** como muestra de 2. (*for machines*) ficha f II. adj simbólico, -a

**told** [toʊld] pt, pp of **tell**

**tolerance** [ˈtal·ər·əns] n tolerancia f

**tolerant** [ˈtal·ər·ənt] adj tolerante

**tolerate** [ˈtal·ə·reɪt] vt 1. (*accept*) a. MED tolerar 2. (*endure*) soportar

**toll¹** [toʊl] n 1. AUTO peaje m 2. TEL tarifa f 3. (*damage*) número m

**toll²** [toʊl] vi doblar

**toll bridge** n puente m de peaje

**toll call** n conferencia f

**toll-free** adv gratis

**toll road** n autopista f de peaje

**tomato** [təˈmeɪ·toʊ] <-es> n tomate m

**tomato ketchup** n ketchup m

**tomb** [tum] n tumba f, guaca f AmL

**tomboy** [ˈtam·bɔɪ] n marimacho m

**tombstone** [ˈtum·stoʊn] n lápida f sepulcral

**tomcat** [ˈtam·kæt] n gato m (macho)

**tomorrow** [təˈmar·oʊ] I. adv mañana; **the day after ~** pasado mañana; **all** (**day**) **~** todo el día de mañana; **~ morning/evening** mañana por la mañana/tarde; **see you ~!** ¡hasta mañana! II. n mañana m ▶ **~ is another day** mañana será otro día; **never put off until ~ what you can do today** no dejes para mañana lo que puedas hacer hoy; **who knows what ~ will bring?** ¿quién sabe qué nos deparará el futuro?

**ton** [tʌn] n tonelada f; **~s of** montones de

**tone** [toʊn] I. n tono m II. vt (*muscles, skin*) tonificar

◆**tone down** vt moderar

**tone control** n control m de tonalidad

**tone-deaf** [ˈtoʊn·def] adj falto, -a de oído musical

**toner** [ˈtoʊ·nər] n 1. (*for skin*) tonificante m 2. (*for printer*) tóner m; PHOT virador m

**tongs** [taŋz] npl tenazas fpl

**tongue** [tʌŋ] n lengua f; **to bite one's ~** morderse la lengua; **to hold one's ~** contenerse (*para no decir algo*); **to have a sharp ~** tener una lengua afilada; **to speak in ~s** hablar en lenguas desconocidas ▶ **have you lost your ~?** ¿te ha comido la lengua el gato?; **to set ~s wagging** dar (de) qué hablar

**tongue-tied** [ˈtʌŋ·taɪd] adj **to be ~** cortarse

**tongue twister** n trabalenguas m inv

**tonic** [ˈtan·ɪk] n tónico m; **~** (**water**) tónica f

**tonight** [təˈnaɪt] adv (*evening*) esta tarde; (*night*) esta noche

**tonne** [tʌn] n tonelada f

**tonsillitis** [ˌtan·sə·ˈlaɪ·tɪs] n amigdalitis f inv

**too** [tu] adv 1. (*overly*) demasiado; **that's ~ much!** ¡es demasiado! 2. (*very*) muy 3. (*also*) también; **me ~!** ¡yo yo!

4. (*moreover*) además

**took** [tʊk] *vt, vi pt of* **take**

**tool** [tul] *n* 1. (*implement*) herramienta *f*, implemento *m AmL* 2. (*instrument*) instrumento *m*

**tool bag** *n* bolsa *f* de herramientas

**toolbar** *n* COMPUT barra *f* de herramientas

**toolmaker** *n* fabricante *mf* de herramientas

**toot** [tut] I. *n* to give a ~ tocar el claxon II. *vi* pitar

**tooth** [tuθ] <teeth> *n* ANAT diente *m*; (*molar*) muela *f*; **he's cutting a ~** está echando un diente ▶ **to set sb's teeth on** <u>edge</u> dar dentera a alguien; **to fight ~ and** <u>nail</u> luchar a brazo partido; **to have a** <u>sweet</u> ~ ser goloso; **to get one's teeth into** hincar el diente a; **to grit one's teeth** apretar los dientes; **in the ~ of sth** (*straight into*) en medio de algo; (*despite*) a pesar de algo

**toothache** ['tuθ·eɪk] *n* dolor *m* de muelas

**toothbrush** ['tuθ·brʌʃ] *n* cepillo *m* de dientes

**toothpaste** ['tuθ·peɪst] *n* pasta *f* de dientes

**toothpick** *n* palillo *m*, pajuela *f Bol, Col*

**toots** [tuts] *n sl* nena *f*

**top** [tap] I. *n* 1. (*highest part*) parte *f* superior; (*mountain*) cima *f*; (*tree*) copa *f*; (*head*) coronilla *f*; (*list*) cabeza *f*; (*bottle*) tapón *m*; (*street*) final *m*; **to get on ~ of sth** llegar a lo más alto de algo; **from ~ to bottom** de arriba a abajo; **from ~ to toe** de la cabeza a los pies; **to feel on ~ of the world** estar loco de contento 2. (*surface*) superficie *f*; **on ~ of** encima de 3. (*highest rank*) lo mejor; **to be at the ~** estar en la cima 4. (*clothing*) top *m* ▶ **at the ~ of one's** <u>voice</u> a grito pelado; **to go** <u>over</u> **the ~** exagerar II. *adj* 1. (*highest, upper*) de arriba 2. (*best*) de primera (calidad) 3. (*successful*) exitoso, -a 4. (*important*) mejor 5. (*maximum*) máximo, -a III. <-pp-> *vt* 1. (*head*) encabezar 2. (*cover*) coronar 3. (*surpass*) superar

◆**top off** *vt* rematar; CULIN coronar

◆**top up** *vt* rellenar

**topcoat** ['tap·koʊt] *n* sobretodo *m*

**top copy** *n* original *m*

**top dog** *n sl* 1. (*boss*) mandamás *mf* 2. (*victor*) ganador(a) *m(f)*

**top executive** *n* ejecutivo, -a *m, f* superior

**top hat** *n* sombrero *m* de copa, galera *f AmL*

**top-heavy** *adj* inestable

**topic** ['tap·ɪk] *n* tema *m*

**topical** ['tap·ɪ·kəl] *adj* de interés actual

**topless** ['tap·lɪs] I. *adj* sin parte de arriba; (*person*) en topless II. *adv* **to go ~** ir en topless

**top-level** ['tap·ˌlev·əl] *adj* (*rank*) de alto nivel; (*importance*) de primera categoría

**topmost** ['tap·moʊst] *adj* más alto, -a

**top-notch** [ˌtap·'natʃ] *adj inf* de primera

**topographer** [tə·'pag·rə·fər] *n* topógrafo, -a *m, f*

**topping** ['tap·ɪŋ] *n* cobertura *f*

**topple** ['tap·əl] I. *vt* derrocar II. *vi* **to ~ (down)** caerse

◆**topple over** *vi* volcarse

**top price** *n* precio *m* máximo

**top priority** *n* prioridad *f* máxima

**top quality** *n* máxima calidad *f*

**top salary** *n* salario *m* máximo

**top-selling** *adj* de mayor venta

**topsoil** *n* capa *f* superior del suelo

**top speed** *n* velocidad *f* máxima

**topsy-turvy** [ˌtap·sɪ·'tɜr·vi] *adj, adv* patas arriba

**torch** [tɔrtʃ] <-es> *n* antorcha *f*; **to carry a ~ for sb** beber los vientos por alguien

**tore** [tɔr] *vi, vt pt of* **tear**

**torment** ['tɔr·ment] I. *n* tormento *m*; *fig* suplicio *m* II. *vt* atormentar

**torn** [tɔrn] *vi, vt pp of* **tear**

**tornado** [tɔr·'neɪ·doʊ] *n* <-(e)s> tornado *m*

**torpedo** [tɔr·'pi·doʊ] <-es> *n* torpedo *m*

**torrent** ['tɔr·ənt] *n a. fig* torrente *m*; **to rain in ~s** llover a cántaros

**torrential** [tɔ·'ren·ʃəl] *adj* torrencial, torrentoso, -a *AmL*

**torso** ['tɔr·soʊ] *n* torso *m*

**tortoise** ['tɔr·təs] *n* tortuga *f*

**tortoiseshell** ['tɔr·təs·ʃel] *n* concha *f*

**torture** ['tɔr·tʃər] I. *n* tortura *f*; (*men-*

*tal*) tormento *m* **II.** *vt* torturar; *fig* atormentar

**torturer** ['tɔr·tʃər·ər] *n* torturador(a) *m(f)*

**toss** [tɔs] **I.** *n* lanzamiento *m* **II.** *vt* lanzar; (*pancake*) dar la vuelta; (*head*) sacudir; **to ~ a coin** echar una moneda al aire **III.** *vi* **to ~ for sth** echar algo a cara o cruz ▶ **to ~ and turn** dar vueltas en la cama

◆**toss about** *vt*, **toss around** *vt* **1.** (*shake*) zarandear **2.** (*consider*) considerar

◆**toss away** *vt* tirar

◆**toss off** *vt* hacer en un periquete; (*drink*) beberse de un trago

◆**toss out** *vt* tirar

◆**toss up** *vi* **to ~ for sth** echar algo a cara o cruz

**toss-up** ['tɔs·ʌp] *n* **it's a ~ between...** la cosa está entre...

**total** ['toʊ·təl] **I.** *adj, n* total *m* **II.** *vt* **1.** (*count*) sumar **2.** (*amount to*) ascender a

**totalitarian** [toʊ·tæl·ə·'ter·i·ən] *adj* totalitario, -a

**totalitarianism** *n* totalitarismo *m*

**totally** ['toʊ·tə·li] *adv* totalmente

**tote¹** [toʊt] *n* SPORTS totalizador *m*

**tote²** [toʊt] *vt inf* (*carry*) llevar consigo [*or* a cuestas]

**tote bag** *n* bolsa *f* grande

**totter** ['tɑt·ər] *vi* tambalearse

**toucan** ['tu·kæn] *n* ZOOL tucán *m*

**touch** [tʌtʃ] <-es> **I.** *n* **1.** (*sense*) tacto *m* **2.** (*act of touching, small amount*) toque *m* **3.** (*communication*) **to be/ get/keep in ~** estar/ponerse/mantenerse en contacto (**with** con); **to be out of/lose ~** no tener/perder el contacto (**with** con) **4.** (*skill*) habilidad *f* ▶ **to be a** <u>soft</u> **~** (*person*) ser un blandengue **II.** *vt* **1.** (*feel*) tocar **2.** (*brush*) rozar **3.** (*reach*) alcanzar; **there's no painter to ~ him** no existe pintor que le iguale **4.** (*emotionally*) conmover **III.** *vi* tocar

◆**touch down** *vi* AVIAT aterrizar

◆**touch off** *vt* hacer estallar

◆**touch on** *vt* tocar

◆**touch up** *vt* retocar

◆**touch upon** *vt* tocar

**touchdown** ['tʌtʃ·daʊn] *n* AVIAT aterri-

---

zaje *m*

**touched** [tʌtʃt] *adj* **1.** (*moved*) conmovido, -a **2.** (*crazy*) tocado, -a

**touching** ['tʌtʃ·ɪŋ] *adj* conmovedor(a)

**touch-sensitive** *adj* sensible al tacto

**touchy** ['tʌtʃ·i] <-ier, -iest> *adj* susceptible (**about** en cuanto a); (*issue*) delicado, -a

**tough** [tʌf] **I.** *adj* **1.** (*strong*) fuerte; (*meat, person*) duro, -a **2.** (*strict*) severo, -a (**on** con) **3.** (*difficult*) difícil; **~ luck** mala suerte **II.** *n* matón, -ona *m, f*

**toughen** ['tʌf·ən] **I.** *vt* endurecer **II.** *vi* endurecerse

**toupee** [tu·'peɪ] *n* peluquín *m*

**tour** [tʊr] **I.** *n* **1.** (*journey*) viaje *m;* **guided ~** visita *f* guiada **2.** MUS gira *f;* **on ~** de gira **II.** *vt* **1.** (*travel*) recorrer **2.** (*visit*) visitar **III.** *vi* ir de viaje

**tourism** ['tʊr·ɪz·əm] *n* turismo *m*

**tourist** ['tʊr·ɪst] *n* turista *mf*

**tourist bureau** *n* oficina *f* de turismo

**tourist class** *n* clase *f* turista

**tourist guide** *n* **1.** (*book*) guía *f* **2.** (*person*) guía *mf*

**tourist industry** *n* industria *f* turística

**tourist information office** *n* oficina *f* de información y turismo

**tourist ticket** *n* pasaje *m* de turista

**tourist visa** *n* visado *m* turístico

**tournament** ['tɜr·nə·mənt] *n* torneo *m*

**tour operator** *n* operador *m* turístico

**tout** [taʊt] *n* revendedor(a) *m(f)*

**tow** [toʊ] **I.** *n* remolque *m; in ~* *fig* a cuestas **II.** *vt* remolcar

**toward(s)** [tɔrd(z)] *prep* **1.** (*time, place*) hacia **2.** (*for*) para **3.** (*regarding*) respecto a; **to feel sth ~ sb** sentir algo por alguien

**tow bar** *n* barra *f* de tracción

**towel** ['taʊ·əl] *n* toalla *f* ▶ **to** <u>throw</u> **in the ~** tirar la toalla

**towel rack** *n* toallero *m*

**tower** ['taʊ·ər] *n* torre *f* ▶ **a ~ of** <u>strength</u> un gran apoyo

◆**tower above** *vi*, **tower over** *vi* ser mucho más alto que

**towering** *adj* (*high*) altísimo, -a; (*large*) inmenso, -a

**town** [taʊn] *n* (*large*) ciudad *f;* (*small*)

pueblo *m;* **the ~** el centro ▶ **to go out** on the ~ to **paint** the ~ **red** irse de juerga

**town council** *n* ayuntamiento *m* concejales

**town hall** *n* ayuntamiento *m edificio*

**townhouse** *n* casa *f* unifamiliar

**town planning** *n* urbanismo *m*

**township** ['taʊn·ʃɪp] *n* municipio *m*

**townspeople** ['taʊnz·ˌpiː·pəl] *npl* ciudadanos *mpl*

**tow truck** *n* grúa *f*

**toxic** ['tak·sɪk] *adj* tóxico, -a

**toxin** ['tak·sɪn] *n* toxina *f*

**toy** [tɔɪ] *n* juguete *m;* **cuddly ~** muñeco *m* de peluche

**toyshop** *n* juguetería *f*

**trace** [treɪs] I. *n* (*sign, amount*) rastro *m;* **to disappear without a ~** desaparecer sin dejar rastro; **~s of a drug/poison** rastros de droga/veneno II. *vt* 1. (*locate*) localizar; **it can be ~d back to...** se remonta a... 2. (*draw*) trazar; (*with tracing paper*) calcar

**trachea** ['treɪ·ki·ə] <-s *or* -chae> *n* tráquea *f*

**tracing** *n* calco *m*

**tracing paper** *n* papel *m* de calco

**track** [træk] I. *n* 1. (*path*) *a. fig* camino *m;* RAIL vía *f;* (*in station*) andén *m;* **to be on the right/wrong ~** ir por buen/mal camino 2. (*mark*) pista *f;* (*animal*) huella *f;* **to be on the ~** seguir la pista (**of** a) 3. (*logical course*) curso *m;* **to get off the ~** salirse del tema 4. SPORTS, MUS pista *f* ▶ **to live on the wrong side** of the **~s** *inf* vivir en los barrios pobres; **to lose/keep ~ of** perder/no perder de vista; **to make ~s** largarse; **to throw sb off the ~** despistar a alguien II. *vt* 1. (*pursue*) seguir la pista de 2. (*trace*) trazar

✦**track down** *vt* localizar

**track and field** *n* atletismo *m*

**track event** *n* carrera *f* de atletismo

**tracking station** ['træk·ɪŋ·ˈsteɪ·ʃən] *n* centro *m* de seguimiento

**track record** *n* historial *m*

**track shoe** *n* zapatilla *f* de atletismo

**tracksuit** *n* chándal *m*

**tract** [trækt] *n* tramo *m;* ANAT tracto *m*

**traction** ['træk·ʃən] *n* (*grip*) adherencia *f*

**tractor** ['træk·tər] *n* tractor *m*

**tractor trailer** *n* camión *m* articulado

**trade** [treɪd] I. *n* 1. (*buying and selling*) comercio *m* (**in** de) 2. (*business activity*) actividad *f* económica 3. (*type of business*) industria *f* 4. (*profession*) oficio *m;* **by ~** de profesión 5. (*swap*) intercambio *m* II. *vi* COM comerciar (**in** en); **to ~ with sb** tener relaciones comerciales con alguien III. *vt* 1. (*exchange*) intercambiar; **to ~ sth for sth** cambiar algo por algo 2. (*sell*) vender

✦**trade in** *vt* aportar como parte del pago

**trade agreement** *n* acuerdo *m* comercial

**trade association** *n* asociación *f* mercantil

**trade fair** *n* feria *f* de muestras

**trade-in** *n* **as a ~** como parte del pago

**trade journal** *n* periódico *m* gremial

**trademark** *n* 1. COM marca *f;* **registered ~** marca registrada 2. *fig* distintivo *m*

**trade name** *n* marca *f;* (*of a firm*) razón *f* social

**trader** ['treɪ·dər] *n* comerciante *mf*

**trade route** *n* ruta *f* comercial

**trade secret** *n* secreto *m* profesional

**tradesman** ['treɪdz·mən] <-men> *n* tendero *m*

**trade union** *n* sindicato *m*

**trade unionist** *n* sindicalista *mf*

**trade war** *n* guerra *f* comercial

**trade wind** *n* viento *m* alisio

**trading** ['treɪ·dɪŋ] *n* comercio *m*

**tradition** [trə·ˈdɪʃ·ən] *n* tradición *f;* **by ~** por tradición; **in the ~ of** del estilo de

**traditional** [trə·ˈdɪʃ·ə·nəl] *adj* 1. (*customary*) tradicional 2. (*conventional*) clásico, -a

**traffic** ['træf·ɪk] I. *n* 1. (*vehicles*) tráfico *m;* **air/commercial/passenger ~** tráfico aéreo/comercial/de pasajeros 2. (*movement*) tránsito *m;* **drug ~** tráfico de drogas II. <trafficked, trafficked> *vi* traficar (**in** con)

**traffic accident** *n* accidente *m* de tráfico

**traffic circle** *n* rotonda *f*

**traffic island** *n* isleta *f*

**T**

**traffic jam** n atasco m

**trafficker** ['træf·ɪk·ər] n traficante mf; **drug/arms ~** traficante de drogas/armas

**traffic light** n semáforo m

**traffic sign** n señal f de tráfico

**tragedy** ['trædʒ·ə·di] <-ies> n tragedia f

**tragic** ['trædʒ·ɪk] adj trágico, -a

**trail** [treɪl] I. n 1. (path) camino m 2. (track) pista f; **to be on the ~** seguir la pista (**of** de) II. vt 1. (follow) seguir la pista de; (animal) seguir el rastro de 2. (drag) arrastrar 3. (be losing) ir perdiendo ante [or contra] III. vi 1. (drag) arrastrarse 2. SPORTS ir perdiendo

♦**trail away** vi esfumarse

♦**trail behind** vi ir detrás

**trailer** n 1. AUTO remolque m; (mobile home) caravana f 2. (advertisement) tráiler m

**trailer park** n cámping m de caravanas

**train** [treɪn] I. n 1. (railway) tren m; **by ~** en tren 2. (series) serie f; **~ of thought** hilo m de pensamiento; **to put in ~** poner en marcha II. vi entrenarse III. vt formar; (animal) amaestrar

**train accident** n accidente m ferroviario

**trained** [treɪnd] adj 1. (educated) formado, -a (**in** en); (animal) amaestrado, -a 2. (expert) cualificado, -a

**trainee** [treɪ·'ni] n aprendiz mf

**trainer** n entrenador(a) m(f)

**training** n 1. (education) formación f; **~ on-the-job** formación laboral 2. SPORTS entrenamiento m (**for** para)

**training camp** n campamento m de instrucción

**training course** n curso m de formación

**training program** n programa m de entrenamiento

**train schedule** n horario m de trenes

**train service** n servicio m de trenes

**trait** [treɪt] n rasgo m

**traitor** ['treɪ·tər] n traidor(a) m(f)

**trajectory** [trə·'dʒek·tə·ri] n trayectoria f; fig camino m

**tram** [træm] n tranvía m; **by ~** en tranvía

**tramp** [træmp] I. vi (walk) ir a pie II. vt (town, miles) patearse inf III. n 1. (sound) ruido m de pasos 2. (walk) caminata f

**trample** ['træm·pəl] vt pisotear

**trampoline** ['træm·pə·lin] n trampolín m

**trance** [træns] n trance m; **to be in a ~** estar en trance

**tranquil** ['træŋ·kwɪl] adj tranquilo, -a

**tranquility** [træŋ·'kwɪl·ə·ţi] n tranquilidad f

**tranquilizer** n tranquilizante m; **to be on ~s** estar tomando tranquilizantes

**transact** [træn·'zækt] vt tramitar

**transaction** [træn·'zæk·ʃən] n transacción f, transa f RíoPl

**transcend** [træn·'send] vt (go beyond) trascender; (surpass) superar

**transcribe** [træn·'skraɪb] vt transcribir

**transcript** ['træn·skrɪpt], **transcription** [træn·'skrɪp·ʃən] n transcripción f

**transfer¹** [træns·'fɜr] I. <-rr-> vt trasladar; (power) transferir; (shop) traspasar II. <-rr-> vi trasladarse; (change train, plane) hacer transbordo

**transfer²** ['træns·fɜr] n traslado m; (information) transmisión f; (shop) traspaso m; (reassignment) transferencia f

**transform** [træns·'fɔrm] vt transformar

**transformation** [ˌtræns·fər·'meɪ·ʃən] n transformación f

**transformer** n transformador m

**transfusion** [træns·'fju·ʒən] n transfusión f; **blood ~** transfusión de sangre

**transient** ['træn·zi·ənt] adj pasajero, -a

**transistor** [træn·'zɪs·tər] n transistor m

**transit** ['træn·zɪt] n tránsito m; **in ~** de paso

**transit business** n negocio m de tránsito

**transition** [træn·'zɪʃ·ən] n transición f

**transitional** [træn·'zɪʃ·ə·nəl] adj transitorio, -a; (government) de transición

**transitive** ['træn·sɪ·ţɪv] adj transitivo, -a

**transit passenger** n pasajero, -a m, f de tránsito

**transit visa** n visado m de tránsito

**translate** [træns·'leɪt] vt LING traducir; **to ~ sth from English into Spanish** traducir algo del inglés al español

**translation** [træns·'leɪ·ʃən] n traducción f

**anslator** n traductor(a) m(f)

**ranslucent** [træns·'lu·sənt] adj translúcido, -a

**ransmission** [træns·'mɪʃ·ən] n transmisión f; **data** ~ transmisión de datos

**ransmission speed** n velocidad f de transmisión

**ransmit** [træns·'mɪt] <-tt-> vt transmitir

**ransmitter** n transmisor m

**ransmitting station** n emisora f

**ransparency** [træns·'per·ən·si] n <-ies> transparencia f

**ransparent** [træns·'per·ənt] adj transparente

**ransplant**[1] [træns·'plænt] vt trasplantar

**ransplant**[2] ['træns·plænt] n trasplante m

**ransport**[1] [træns·'pɔrt] vt transportar

**ransport**[2] ['træns·pɔrt] n transporte m; **public** ~ transporte público

**ransportation** [ˌtræns·pər·'teɪ·ʃən] n transporte m

**ranspose** [træns·'poʊz] vt transponer

**ranssexual** [træns·'sek·ʃu·əl] adj, n transexual mf

**ransvestite** ['træns·ves·taɪt] n travesti mf

**rap** [træp] I. n 1. (device) trampa f; **to set a** ~ poner una trampa 2. sl (mouth) pico m II. vt <-pp-> atrapar

**rapdoor** ['træp·dɔr] n escotillón m

**rapeze** [træ·'piz] n trapecio m

**rapezoid** ['træp·ɪ·zɔɪd] n MATH trapecio m

**rapper** ['træp·ər] n trampero, -a m, f

**rash** [træʃ] I. n 1. (rubbish) basura f; **to take the** ~ **out** sacar la basura 2. sl (people) gentuza f; (book, film) bazofia f 3. inf (nonsense) chorradas fpl II. vt sl 1. (wreck) hacer polvo 2. (criticize) poner por los suelos

**rash can** ['træʃ·kæn] n cubo m de la basura

**rashy** ['træʃ·i] adj cutrísimo, -a

**rauma** ['trɔ·mə] n trauma m

**raumatic** [trɔ·'mæt·ɪk] adj traumático, -a

**raumatize** ['trɔ·mə·taɪz] vt traumatizar

**ravel** ['træv·əl] vi 1. (make trip) viajar; (be away) estar de viaje; **to** ~ **by air/car** viajar en avión/coche; **to** ~ **first-class** viajar en primera 2. (light, sound) pro-

pagarse 3. inf (go fast) ir como una bala II. vt viajar por III. npl viajes mpl

**travel agency** n agencia f de viajes

**travel agent** n agente mf de viajes

**travel card** n bono m de transporte

**traveler** ['træv·ə·lər] n viajero, -a m, f

**traveler's check** n cheque m de viaje

**traveling** n viajar m

**travel expenses** n gastos m pl de viaje

**travel guide** n guía mf turístico, -a; (book) guía f turística

**travel insurance** n seguro m de viaje

**travel sickness** n mareo m

**trawler** ['trɔ·lər] n pesquero m de arrastre

**tray** [treɪ] n bandeja f, charola f AmS

**treacherous** ['tretʃ·ər·əs] adj a. fig traicionero, -a

**treachery** ['tretʃ·ə·ri] n traición f

**treacly** ['tri·kli] adj meloso, -a; (sentimental) empalagoso, -a

**tread** [tred] I. <trod, trodden or trod> vi, vt pisar II. n (step) paso m; (of stair) escalón m

**treadmill** ['tred·mɪl] n SPORTS rueda f de andar; fig rutina f

**treason** ['tri·zən] n traición f

**treasonable** ['tri·zə·nə·bəl], **treasonous** ['tri·zə·nəs] adj traidor(a)

**treasure** ['treʒ·ər] I. n tesoro m; fig joya f; **my assistant is a** ~ mi ayudante es una joya II. vt atesorar

**treasure hunt** n caza f del tesoro

**treasurer** ['treʒ·ər·ər] n tesorero, -a m, f

**treasury** ['treʒ·ə·ri] <-ies> n tesorería f; **the Treasury** Hacienda f

**Treasury Secretary** n ≈ Ministro, -a m, f de Hacienda

**treat** [trit] I. vt 1. a. MED tratar; **to** ~ **badly** tratar mal 2. (pay for) invitar (**to** a) II. vi negociar (**with** con) III. n (event) convite m; (present) regalo m; **it's my** ~ invito yo

**treatment** ['trit·mənt] n 1. trato m; **to give sb the** ~ hacerlas pasar canutas a alguien 2. MED tratamiento m

**treaty** ['tri·ti] <-ies> n tratado m; **peace** ~ tratado de paz

**treble** ['treb·əl] I. vt triplicar II. vi triplicarse

**treble clef** n clave f de sol

**tree** [tri] *n* árbol *m* ▶ **you can't see the** forest **for the ~s** los árboles no te dejan ver el bosque; **to grow on ~s** caer del cielo

**tree-lined** ['tri·laɪnd] *adj* arbolado, -a

**tree surgeon** *n* arboricultor(a) *m(f)*

**tree trunk** *n* tronco *m* del árbol

**trek** [trek] **I.** <-kk-> *vi* caminar **II.** *n* (*walk*) caminata *f*

**trekking** ['trek·ɪŋ] *n* senderismo *m;* **to go ~** hacer senderismo

**trellis** ['trel·ɪs] <-es> *n* espaldera *f;* (*for plants*) enrejado *m*

**tremble** ['trem·bəl] *vi* temblar; **to ~ with cold** tiritar de frío; **to ~ like a leaf** temblar como un flan

**tremendous** [trɪ·'men·dəs] *adj* **1.** (*enormous*) tremendo, -a; (*crowd*) inmenso, -a; (*help*) inestimable **2.** *inf* (*excellent*) estupendo, -a

**tremor** ['trem·ər] *n* temblor *m;* (*of fear, excitement*) estremecimiento *m*

**trench** [trentʃ] <-es> *n* zanja *f;* MIL trinchera *f*

**trend** [trend] **I.** *n* **1.** (*tendency*) tendencia *f* (**toward(s)** hacia); **downward/upward ~** tendencia a la baja/al alza **2.** (*fashion*) moda *f;* **the latest ~s** las últimas tendencias **II.** *vi* tender (**to** a)

**trendsetter** ['trend·set·ər] *n* persona *f* que inicia una moda

**trendy** ['tren·di] **I.** <-ier, -iest> *adj* de moda; (*person*) moderno, -a **II.** <-ies> *n* modernillo, -a *m, f*

**trespass** ['tres·pəs] *vi* LAW entrar ilegalmente

**trespasser** ['tres·pæs·ər] *n* intruso, -a *m, f*

**triad** ['traɪ·æd] *n* tríada *f*

**trial** ['traɪ·əl] *n* **1.** LAW proceso *m;* **~ by jury** juicio *m* con jurado; **to stand ~** ser procesado **2.** (*test*) prueba *f;* **clinical ~s** ensayos *m pl* clínicos; **on ~** a prueba; **to give sb a ~** poner a alguien a prueba

**trial period** *n* período *m* de prueba

**triangle** ['traɪ·æŋ·gəl] *n* triángulo *m*

**triangular** [traɪ·'æŋ·gju·lər] *adj* triangular

**tribal** ['traɪ·bəl] *adj* tribal

**tribe** [traɪb] *n* tribu *f*

**tribesman** ['traɪbz·mən] <-men> *n* miembro *m* de una tribu

**tribeswoman** ['traɪbz·'wʊm·ən] <-women> *n* miembro *m* de una tribu

**tribulation** [ˌtrɪb·jə·'leɪ·ʃən] *n* tribulación *f*

**tribunal** [traɪ·'bju·nəl] *n* tribunal *m*

**tribune** ['trɪb·jun] *n* ARCHIT tribuna *f*

**tributary** ['trɪb·jə·ter·i] <-ies> *adj, n* (*river*) afluente *m*

**tribute** ['trɪb·jut] *n* (*homage*) homenaje *m;* **to pay ~** rendir tributo (**to** a)

**trick** [trɪk] **I.** *n* **1.** (*ruse*) trampa *m;* **dirty ~** una mala pasada; **to play a ~** tender una trampa (**on** a); **to be up to one's (old) ~s again** volver a hacer de las suyas **2.** (*magician*) truco *m* **3.** (*technique*) truquillo *m* **4.** (*illusion*) ilusión *f;* **a ~ of the light** una ilusión óptica ▶ **to try every ~ in the** book intentar todos los trucos habidos y por haber; **the ~s of the** trade los trucos del oficio; **that'll** do **the ~** con eso solucionamos el tema **II.** *adj* **a ~ question** una pregunta con trampa **III.** *vt* (*deceive*) engañar; (*fool*) burlar; (*swindle*) timar

**trickery** ['trɪk·ə·ri] *n* artimañas *fpl*

**trickle** ['trɪk·əl] **I.** *vi* chorrear; (*drops*) gotear; **to ~ in/out** (*people*) ir entrando/saliendo **II.** *n* hilo *m;* (*drops*) *a fig* goteo *m*

◆**trickle away** *vi* consumirse poco a poco

**tricky** ['trɪk·i] <-ier, -iest> *adj* **1.** (*crafty*) astuto, -a **2.** (*difficult*) complicado, -a

**tricycle** ['traɪ·sɪ·kəl] *n* triciclo *m*

**trifle** ['traɪ·fəl] *n* (*thing*) bagatela *f;* (*amount*) insignificancia *f;* **a ~** un poquito

**trifling** *adj* insignificante

**trigger** ['trɪg·ər] **I.** *n* gatillo *m;* *fig* detonante *m* **II.** *vt* desencadenar

**trigonometry** [ˌtrɪg·ə·'nam·ə·tri] *n* trigonometría *f*

**trike** [traɪk] *n* *inf abbr of* **tricycle** triciclo *m*

**trilingual** [ˌtraɪ·'lɪŋ·gwəl] *adj* trilingüe

**trillion** ['trɪl·jən] *n* billón *m*

**trilogy** ['trɪl·ə·dʒi] <-ies> *n* trilogía *f*

**trim** [trɪm] **I.** *n* **1.** (*state*) (buen) estado *m;* **to be in ~** estar listo (**for** para) **2.** (*hair*) **to give a ~** dar un repaso/corte; (*hair*) cortar las puntas **II.** *ad*

muy cuidado, -a; (*person*) esbelto, -a
III. <-mm-> vt (*cut, reduce*) recortar; **to ~ one's beard** recortarse la barba

◆**trim down** vt recortar

◆**trim off** vt cortar

◆**trimming** n 1. (*decoration*) adorno m 2. **~s** CULIN guarnición f

**Trinidad** ['trɪn·ɪ·dæd] n Trinidad f; **~ and Tobago** Trinidad y Tobago

**Trinidadian** ['trɪn·ɪ·dæd·i·ən] I. adj de Trinidad II. n habitante mf de Trinidad

**trinket** ['trɪŋ·kɪt] n baratija f

**trio** ['tri·oʊ] n a. MUS trío m; **string ~** trío de cuerda

**trip** [trɪp] I. n 1. (*journey, drugs*) viaje m; (*shorter*) excursión f; **business ~** viaje de negocios; **to go on a ~** irse de viaje 2. (*fall*) tropezón m II. <-pp-> vi (*stumble*) tropezar (**on** con) III. <-pp-> vt to **~ sb** (**up**) poner la zancadilla a alguien

◆**trip over** vi dar un tropezón

◆**trip up** I. vi tropezar; (*verbally*) equivocarse II. vt 1. (*cause to stumble*) hacer tropezar 2. (*cause to fail*) confundir

**triple** ['trɪp·əl] I. adj triple II. vt triplicar III. vi triplicarse

**triplet** ['trɪp·lɪt] n (*baby*) trillizo, -a m, f

**tripod** ['traɪ·pɑd] n trípode m

**tripping** ['trɪp·ɪŋ] adj ligero, -a

**trite** [traɪt] adj tópico, -a

**triumph** ['traɪ·ʌmf] I. n triunfo m (**over** sobre); **in ~** triunfalmente; **a ~ of medicine** un éxito de la medicina II. vi triunfar (**over** sobre)

**triumphant** [traɪ·ʌm·fənt] adj (*victorious*) triunfante; (*successful*) exitoso, -a; (*return*) triunfal

**trivia** ['trɪv·i·ə] npl trivialidades fpl

**trivial** ['trɪv·i·əl] adj 1. (*unimportant*) irrelevante; (*dispute, matter*) trivial 2. (*insignificant*) insignificante

**trod** [trɑd] pt, pp of **tread**

**trolley** ['trɑl·i] n (*trolley car*) tranvía m

**trombone** [trɑm·ˈboʊn] n trombón m

**troop** [trup] I. n **~s** tropas fpl II. vi to **~ in/out** entrar/salir en tropel

**trooper** ['tru·pər] n (*police*) policía mf

**trophy** ['troʊ·fi] n <-ies> trofeo m

**tropic** ['trɑp·ɪk] n trópico m; **~ of Cancer/Capricorn** Trópico de Cáncer/Ca-

pricornio

**tropical** ['trɑp·ɪ·kəl] adj tropical

**trot** [trɑt] I. n 1. (*horse*) trote m 2. **~s** MED cagalera, obradera Col, Guat, Pan II. vi trotar; (*go busily*) ir apresurado

◆**trot off** vi marcharse

◆**trot out** vt (*excuse, explanation*) soltar

**trotter** ['trɑt·ər] n manita f de cerdo

**trouble** ['trʌb·əl] n 1. (*difficulty*) problema m; **to have ~** tener dificultades; **to be in/get into ~** estar/meterse en un lío; **to be the least of sb's ~s** ser el menor de los males de alguien 2. (*inconvenience*) molestia f; **to go to a lot of ~** tomarse muchas molestias (**for** por); **to go to the ~ of doing sth** tomarse la molestia de hacer algo; **to put sb to the ~ of doing sth** comprometer a alguien para que haga algo; **to be (not) worth the ~ (of doing sth)** (no) merecer la pena (hacer algo) 3. MED enfermedad f; **stomach ~** dolor m de estómago 4. (*malfunction*) avería f II. vt 1. (*bother*) molestar (**for** con) 2. **to ~ oneself** esforzarse (**about** en) 3. (*worry*) preocupar III. vi esforzarse; **to ~ to do sth** molestarse en hacer algo

**troubled** adj 1. (*period, water*) turbulento, -a 2. (*worried*) preocupado, -a; (*look*) de preocupación

**trouble-free** [ˌtrʌb·əl·ˈfri] adj sin problemas

**troublemaker** ['trʌb·əl·ˌmeɪ·kər] n alborotador(a) m(f)

**troubleshooting** ['trʌb·əl·ˌʃu·tɪŋ] n localización f de problemas

**troublesome** ['trʌb·əl·səm] adj molesto, -a

**trouble spot** n centro m de fricción

**trough** [trɒf] n 1. (*receptacle*) abrevadero m; **feeding ~** comedero m 2. METEO, GEO depresión f

**trousers** ['traʊ·zərz] npl pantalones mpl; **a pair of ~** unos pantalones

**trout** [traʊt] n <-(s)> trucha f

**trowel** ['traʊ·əl] n (*building*) llana f; (*gardening*) desplantador m

**truancy** ['tru·ən·si] n falta f injustificada

**truant** ['tru·ənt] I. n persona f que hace novillos II. vi hacer novillos

**truce** [trus] n tregua f

**truck** [trʌk] I. *n* AUTO camión *m* II. *vt* transportar

**truck driver, trucker** *n* camionero, -a *m, f*

**true** [tru] *adj* 1. (*not false*) cierto, -a; **to be ~** ser verdad [*or* cierto] (**that** que); **to ring ~** sonar convincente 2. (*real*) auténtico, -a; **~ love** amor verdadero; **sb's ~ self** la verdadera personalidad de alguien; **to come ~** hacerse realidad 3. (*loyal*) fiel (**to** a)

**truffle** ['trʌf·əl] *n* trufa *f*

**truly** ['tru·li] *adv* 1. (*sincerely*) sinceramente 2. (*as intensifier*) realmente
▶ **yours ~** (*letter*) atentamente

**trump** [trʌmp] GAMES I. *n* triunfo *m* II. *vt* matar
◆ **trump up** *vt* falsificar

**trumpet** ['trʌm·pət] *n* trompeta *f* ▶ **to blow one's own ~** echarse flores

**trumpeter** ['trʌm·pə·tər] *n* trompetista *mf*

**truncate** [trʌŋ·'keɪt] *vt* truncar

**truncheon** ['trʌn·tʃən] *n* porra *f*, macana *f AmL*

**trunk** [trʌŋk] *n* 1. ANAT, BOT tronco *m*; (*elephant*) trompa *f* 2. (*for storage*) baúl *m*; (*car*) maletero *f*, baúl *m AmL* 3. **~s** bañador *m*

**trust** [trʌst] I. *n* 1. (*belief*) confianza *f*; **to gain sb's ~** ganarse la confianza de alguien; **to place one's ~** depositar su confianza (**in** en) 2. (*responsibility*) responsabilidad *f* 3. FIN, COM consorcio *m*; **investment ~** grupo *m* de inversión II. *vt* confiar; **to ~ sb to do sth** confiar a alguien (el) hacer algo; **to ~ sb with sth** confiar la responsabilidad de algo a alguien; **to ~ that...** esperar que... +*subj* III. *vi* confiar (**in** en)

**trusted** ['trʌs·tɪd] *adj* fiable; (*person*) leal

**trustee** [trʌs·'ti] *n* fideicomisario, -a *m, f*; **board of ~s** consejo *m* de administración

**trust fund** *n* fondo *m* de fideicomiso

**trusting** *adj* confiado, -a

**trustworthy** ['trʌst·ˌwɜr·ði] *adj* fiable; (*person*) honrado, -a

**trusty** ['trʌs·ti] <-ier, -iest> *adj* leal

**truth** [truθ] *n* verdad *f*; **in ~** en realidad;
**to tell the ~** decir la verdad (**about** sobre); **to tell the ~,...** a decir verdad,...

**truthful** ['truθ·fəl] *adj* (*true*) veraz; (*sincere*) sincero, -a; (*accurate*) preciso, -a

**truthfulness** *n* (*veracity*) veracidad *f*, (*sincerity*) sinceridad *f*; (*accuracy*) exactitud *f*

**try** [traɪ] I. *n* intento *m*; **to give sth a ~** intentar algo II. <-ie-> *vi* esforzarse; **to ~ and do sth** *inf* intentar hacer algo III. <-ie-> *vt* 1. (*attempt*) intentar; **to ~ one's best** esforzarse al máximo; **to ~ one's luck** probar suerte 2. (*test, sample*) probar 3. LAW juzgar
◆ **try for** *vt insep* tratar de obtener
◆ **try on** *vt* (*put on*) probarse; **to try sth on for size** probarse algo para ver la talla
◆ **try out** *vt* probar; **to try sth out on sb** dar a probar algo a alguien

**trying** *adj* (*exasperating*) irritante; (*difficult*) difícil

**tsar** *n see* **tzar**

**tsarina** *n* zarina *f*

**tsetse fly** ['tse·tsi·flaɪ] *n* mosca *f* tse-tse

**T-shirt** ['ti·ʃɜrt] *n* camiseta *f*, playera *f Guat, Méx*, polera *f Chile*

**tub** [tʌb] *n* 1. (*container*) cubo *m* 2. (*bathtub*) bañera *f* 3. (*carton*) tarrina *f*; **a ~ of ice cream** una tarrina de helado

**tubby** ['tʌb·i] <-ier, -iest> *adj* rechoncho, -a, requenete *Ven*

**tube** [tub] *n* 1. (*hollow cylinder*) tubo *m* 2. ANAT trompa *f*; **Fallopian ~** trompa de Falopio 3. TV tele *f* ▶ **to go down the ~s** irse al traste

**tuberculosis** [tu·ˌbɜr·kjə·'loʊ·sɪs] *n* tuberculosis *f inv*

**tuberculous** [tu·'bɜr·kjʊ·ləs] *adj* tuberculoso, -a

**tuck** [tʌk] I. *n* (*fold*) pliegue *m* II. *vt* (*fold*) plegar
◆ **tuck away** *vt* (*hide*) poner a buen recaudo; **to be tucked away** estar en un sitio seguro II. *vi* comer con apetito
◆ **tuck in** *vt* 1. **to tuck one's shirt in** meterse la camisa 2. (*in bed*) arropar

**Tuesday** ['tuz·deɪ] *n* martes *m inv*; *s. a.* **Friday**

**tuft** [tʌft] *n* (*hair, grass*) mata *f*

**:ug** [tʌg] I. n tirón m II. <-gg-> vt tirar de

**:uition** [tuˈɪʃ·ən] n 1. (fee) tasas fpl 2. (teaching) enseñanza f

**tulip** [ˈtuˈlɪp] n tulipán m

**tumble** [ˈtʌm·bəl] I. n caída f; **to take a ~** caerse II. vi caerse; fig caer

♦**tumble down** vi desplomarse

♦**tumble over** vi caerse

**tumbledown** [ˈtʌm·bəl·ˌdaʊn] adj en ruinas

**tumbler** [ˈtʌm·blər] n vaso m

**tumbleweed** [ˈtʌm·bəl·wid] n planta f rodadora

**tummy** [ˈtʌm·i] <-ies> n childspeak barriguita f

**tummy ache** n childspeak dolor m de tripita

**tumor** [ˈtu·mər] n tumor m; **brain/malignant ~** tumor cerebral/maligno

**tumultuous** [tuˈmʌl·tʃu·əs] adj 1. (noisy) tumultuoso, -a; (applause) apoteósico, -a 2. (disorderly) agitado, -a

**tuna** [ˈtu·nə] n <-(s)> atún m

**tune** [tun] n 1. MUS melodía f; **a catchy ~** una tonada pegadiza 2. (pitch) **to be in/out of ~** estar afinado/desafinado; fig armonizar/desentonar (**with** con) ▶ **to change one's ~** sing another ~ cambiar de parecer; **to the ~ of $100** por valor de 100$ II. vt 1. MUS afinar 2. AUTO poner a punto

♦**tune in** vi 1. **to ~ to a station** RADIO sintonizar una emisora; TV sintonizar un canal 2. fig sl sintonizar (**to** con) II. vt RADIO, TV sintonizar

♦**tune up** vt AUTO poner a punto

**tuner** n (radio) sintonizador m

**tune-up** [ˈtun·ʌp] n AUTO puesta f a punto

**tunic** [ˈtu·nɪk] n FASHION casaca f

**tuning** n AUTO puesta f a punto

**tuning fork** n diapasón m

**tunnel** [ˈtʌn·əl] n túnel m

**turbine** [ˈtɜr·bɪn] n turbina f

**turbocharged** [ˈtɜr·boʊ·ˌtʃɑrdʒd] adj turboalimentado, -a

**turbo engine** n motor m turbo

**turbulence** [ˈtɜr·bju·ləns] n turbulencia f

**turbulent** [ˈtɜr·bju·lənt] adj turbulento, -a

**turd** [tɜrd] n vulg 1. (excrement) zurullo m 2. (person) guarro, -a m, f

**turf** [tɜrf] <-s or -ves> n 1. BOT césped m 2. **the ~** las carreras de caballos 3. (territory) territorio m

**Turk** [tɜrk] n turco, -a m, f

**turkey** [ˈtɜr·ki] n 1. ZOOL pavo m 2. sl (stupid) papanatas mf inv ▶ **to talk ~** hablar claro

**Turkey** [ˈtɜr·ki] n Turquía f

**Turkish** [ˈtɜr·kɪʃ] I. adj turco, -a II. n 1. (person) turco, -a m, f 2. LING turco m

**turmoil** [ˈtɜr·mɔɪl] n 1. (chaos) caos m inv; **to be thrown into ~** estar sumido en el caos 2. PSYCH trastorno m; **to be in a ~** estar desconcertado

**turn** [tɜrn] I. vi 1. (rotate) dar vueltas, girar (**on** sobre) 2. (switch direction) volver; (car) girar; **to ~ around** dar media vuelta, voltearse AmL; **to ~ right/left** torcer a la derecha/izquierda 3. (change) cambiar, transformarse; (for worse) volverse II. vt 1. (rotate) girar 2. (switch direction) volver, voltear AmL; **to ~ one's head** volver la cabeza; **to ~ a page** pasar una página; **to ~ the coat inside out** volver el abrigo del revés 3. (age) cumplir 4. (hour) dar; **it has ~ed three o'clock** dieron las tres 5. **it ~ed my stomach** me revolvió el estómago ▶ **to ~ sth upside down** dejar algo patas arriba III. n 1. (change) giro m; **to make a ~ to the right** girar a la derecha; **to take a ~ for the worse/better** empeorar/mejorar 2. (period of duty) turno m; **in ~** por turnos; **it's your ~** te toca; **to be sb's ~ to do sth** tocar a alguien hacer algo; **to speak out of ~** hablar fuera de lugar 3. (twist) rotación f 4. (service) favor m; **to do sb a good ~** hacer un favor a alguien ▶ **one good ~ deserves another** favor con favor se paga

♦**turn against** vt volverse en contra de

♦**turn around** I. vi volverse II. vt 1. (move) girar 2. (change) transformar

♦**turn away** I. vi apartarse (**from** de) II. vt 1. (refuse entry) no dejar entrar 2. (deny help) rechazar

T

◆**turn back** I. *vi* retroceder II. *vt*
1. (*send back*) hacer regresar 2. (*fold*)
doblar

◆**turn down** 1. (*reject*) rechazar
2. (*volume*) bajar 3. (*fold*) doblar

◆**turn in** I. *vt* (*hand over*) entregar II. *vi*
*inf* (*go to bed*) meterse en la cama

◆**turn off** *vt* ELEC, TECH desconectar;
(*light*) apagar; (*motor*) parar; (*gas, faucet*) cerrar 2. *sl* dar asco

◆**turn on** *vt* 1. ELEC, TECH conectar; (*light*)
encender, prender *AmL*; (*gas, faucet*)
abrir 2. (*excite*) excitar; (*attract*) gustar;
**to ~ the charm** desplegar el encanto

◆**turn out** I. *vi* 1. (*end*) salir 2. (*be
revealed*) resultar; **it turned out to be
true** resultó ser cierto II. *vt* 1. (*light*)
apagar 2. (*kick out*) echar; **to turn
sb out on the street** echar a alguien
a la calle

◆**turn over** *vt* 1. (*reverse*) dar la vuelta
a 2. (*give*) ceder; (*criminal*) entregar
3. (*facts, idea*) dar vueltas a 4. COM, FIN
facturar 5. (*search*) revolver buscando

◆**turn up** I. *vi* 1. (*arrive*) llegar 2. (*become available*) aparecer 3. (*point
upwards*) doblarse hacia arriba II. *vt*
1. (*volume*) subir 2. (*shorten*) acortar
3. (*locate*) localizar

**turnabout** ['tɜr·ə·ˌbaʊt] *n*, **turnaround**
['tɜrn·ə·ˌraʊnd] *n* 1. (*change*) giro *m* en
redondo 2. (*improvement*) mejora *f*

**turnaround time** *n* AVIAT, NAUT tiempo
*m* en puerto; (*of project*) tiempo de
respuesta

**turning** ['tɜr·nɪŋ] *n* giro *m*; (*road*) bocacalle *f*

**turning point** *n* momento *m* decisivo; **a
~ in one's career** un cambio decisivo
en su carrera

**turnip** ['tɜr·nɪp] *n* nabo *m*

**turnout** ['tɜrn·aʊt] *n* 1. (*attendance*) número *m* de asistentes. POL número de
votantes 2. ECON producción *f* 4. FASHION
atuendo *m*

**turnover** ['tɜrn·ˌoʊ·vər] *n* 1. COM, FIN
volumen *m* de negocios; (*sales*) facturación *f* 2. (*in staff*) rotación *f* 3. CULIN
empanada *f*

**turnpike** ['tɜrn·paɪk] *n* AUTO autopista
*f* de peaje

**turnstile** ['tɜrn·staɪl] *n* torniquete *m*

**turntable** ['tɜrn·ˌteɪ·bəl] *n* RAIL plataforma
*f* giratoria

**turpentine** ['tɜr·pən·taɪn] *n* trementina *f*

**turquoise** ['tɜr·kwɔɪz] *n* 1. (*stone*) turquesa *f* 2. (*color*) turquesa *m*

**turret** ['tɜr·ɪt] *n* torreón *m*

**turtle** ['tɜr·təl] <-(s)> *n* tortuga *f*

**turtleneck** ['tɜr·təl·nek] *n* cuello *m* de
cisne

**tusk** [tʌsk] *n* colmillo *m*

**tussle** ['tʌs·əl] I. *vi* pelearse II. *n* pelea *f*

**tutor** ['tu·tər] SCHOOL, UNIV 1. *n* tutor(a) *m(f)*; (*at home*) preceptor(a) *m(f)*
II. *vt* dar clases particulares (**in** de)

**tutorial** [tu·'tɔr·i·əl] *n* COMPUT tutorial *m*

**tux** [tʌks] *inf abbr of* **tuxedo** esmoquin *m*

**tuxedo** [tʌk·'si·doʊ] *n* esmoquin *m*

**TV** [ˌti·'vi] *n abbr of* **television** TV *f*

**tweak** [twik] I. *vt* pellizcar II. *n* pellizco *m*

**tweezers** ['twi·zərz] *npl* (**a pair of**) ~
(**unas**) pinzas

**twelfth** [twelfθ] I. *adj* duodécimo, -a
II. *n* 1. (*order*) duodécimo, -a *m, f*
2. (*date*) doce *m* 3. (*fraction*) duodécimo *m*; *s. a.* **eighth**

**twelve** [twelv] *adj, n* doce *m*; *s. a.* **eight**

**twentieth** ['twen·ti·əθ] I. *adj* vigésimo,
-a II. *n* 1. (*order*) vigésimo, -a *m, f*
2. (*date*) veinte *m* 3. (*fraction*) vigésimo *m*; *s. a.* **eighth**

**twenty** ['twen·ti] <-ies> *adj, n* veinte *m*;
*s. a.* **eighty**

**twerp** [twɜrp] *n sl* capullo, -a *m, f*

**twice** [twaɪs] *adv* dos veces

**twiddle** ['twɪd·əl] I. *vt a.* TECH, ELEC (hacer) girar II. *vi* juguetear (**with** con)
III. *n* giro *m*

**twig** [twɪg] *n* ramita *f*

**twilight** ['twaɪ·laɪt] *n* crepúsculo *m*

**twin** [twɪn] *adj, n* mellizo, -a *m, f;* **identical ~s** gemelos

**twin bed** *n* cama *f* gemela

**twin brother** *n* hermano *m* gemelo

**twine** [twaɪn] I. *vt* 1. (*wind up*) enrollar
2. (*encircle*) rodear II. *n* cordel *m*

**twinge** [twɪndʒ] *n* 1. MED punzada *f*
2. *fig* arrebato *m*; **a ~ of conscience** un
remordimiento de conciencia

**winkle** ['twɪŋ·kəl] I. *vi* brillar II. *n* brillo *m* ▶ **to do sth in a ~** hacer algo en un abrir y cerrar de ojos

**winkling** ['twɪŋ·klɪŋ] I. *adj* brillante II. *n* parpadeo *m* ▶ **in the ~ of an eye** en un abrir y cerrar de ojos

**winning** ['twɪn·ɪŋ] *n* hermanamiento *m* de dos ciudades

**twin sister** *n* hermana *f* gemela

**twirl** [twɜrl] I. *vi* dar vueltas (**around** alrededor de) II. *n* pirueta *f*

**twist** [twɪst] I. *vt* 1. (*turn*) dar vueltas a 2. (*wind around*) enrollar (**around** alrededor de) 3. (*ankle*) torcerse; (*truth*) tergiversar ▶ **to ~ sb's arm** presionar a alguien; **to ~ sb round one's little finger** manejar a alguien a su antojo II. *vi* 1. (*squirm*) (re)torcerse 2. (*river, road*) **to ~ and turn** serpentear III. *n* 1. (*turn*) vuelta *f*; **to give sth a ~** dar un giro a algo 2. (*change*) giro *m* 3. (*hair*) mecha *f*; (*lemon*) rodajita *f*; (*paper*) cucurucho *m* 4. (*dance*) twist *m*

**twisted** ['twɪs·tɪd] *adj* 1. (*cable, metal*) retorcido, -a; (*ankle*) torcido, -a 2. (*perverted*) pervertido, -a; (*logic, humor*) retorcido, -a

**twister** ['twɪs·tər] *n inf* tornado *m*

**twit** [twɪt] *n sl* capullo, -a *m, f*

**twitch** [twɪtʃ] I. *vi, vt* ANAT, MED temblar II. *n* <-es> 1. ANAT, MED tic *m* 2. (*pull*) tirón *m*

**twitter** ['twɪt·ər] I. *vi* gorjear; *fig* parlotear II. *n* gorjeo *m*

**two** [tu] *adj, n* dos *m* ▶ **that makes ~ of us** ya somos dos; **to put ~ and ~ together** sacar conclusiones; *s. a.* **eight**

**two-dimensional** [ˌtu·dɪ·'men·ʃə·nəl] *adj* bidimensional; *fig* superficial

**two-door** *adj* de dos puertas

**two-edged** *adj* de doble filo

**two-faced** *adj* falso, -a, falluto, -a *RíoPl*

**twofold** ['tu·foʊld] I. *adv* dos veces II. *adj* doble

**two-part** *adj* de dos partes

**two-party system** *n* sistema *f* bipartidista

**two-piece** *n* 1. (*suit*) conjunto *m* de dos piezas 2. (*bikini*) bikini *m*

**two-seater** AUTO I. *n* biplaza *m* II. *adj* de dos plazas

**twosome** ['tu·səm] *n* (*duo*) dúo *m*; (*couple*) pareja *f*

**two-way** ['tu·weɪ] *adj* de doble sentido; (*process*) recíproco, -a; (*conversation*) bilateral

**tycoon** [taɪ·'kun] *n* magnate *mf*

**tyke** [taɪk] *n* 1. (*child*) diablillo, -a *m, f* 2. (*dog*) perro *m* callejero

**type** [taɪp] I. *n a.* TYPO tipo *m*; (*machine*) modelo *m*; (*animal, person*) clase *f*; **he's not her ~** no es su tipo II. *vt, vi* escribir con el ordenador

♦**type out** *vt* escribir con el ordenador

♦**type up** *vt* pasar a máquina

**typesetting** ['taɪp·ˌset·ɪŋ] *n* composición *f* tipográfica

**typewriter** ['taɪp·ˌraɪ·tər] *n* máquina *f* de escribir

**typewritten** *adj* mecanografiado, -a

**typhoid** ['taɪ·fɔɪd], **typhoid fever** *n* fiebre *f* tifoidea

**typhoon** [taɪ·'fun] *n* tifón *m*

**typical** ['tɪp·ɪ·kəl] *adj* típico, -a (**of** de); (*symptom*) característico, -a

**typically** *adv* típicamente

**typify** ['tɪp·ɪ·faɪ] <-ie-> *vt* simbolizar

**typing** ['taɪ·pɪŋ] *n* mecanografía *f*

**typist** ['taɪ·pɪst] *n* mecanógrafo, -a *m, f*

**tyranny** ['tɪr·ə·ni] *n* tiranía *f*

**tyrant** ['taɪ·rənt] *n* tirano, -a *m, f*

**tzar** [zar] *n* zar *m*

**tzetze fly** ['te·tsi·ˌflaɪ] *n* mosca *f* tse-tse

# U

**U, u** [ju] *n* U, u *f*; **~ as in Uniform** U de Uruguay

**U[1]** *abbr of* **uranium** uranio *m*

**U[2]** *inf abbr of* **university** universidad *f*

**ubiquitous** [ju·'bɪk·wə·təs] *adj* omnipresente

**udder** ['ʌd·ər] *n* ubre *f*

**UFO** [ˌju·ef·'oʊ] *n abbr of* **unidentified flying object** OVNI *m*

**ugh** [əh] *interj* uf

**ugliness** ['ʌg·lɪ·nɪs] *n* fealdad *f*; (*nastiness*) repugnancia *f*

**ugly** ['ʌg·li] <-ier, iest> *adj* 1. feo, -a, macaco, -a *Arg, Méx, Cuba, Chile*; **to be ~**

**as sin** ser más feo que Pico 2. (*mood*) peligroso, -a; (*look*) repugnante 3. (*violent*) violento, -a; **to turn ~** ponerse violento 4. (*harsh*) desagradable; (*weather*) horroroso, -a; **~ rumors** calumnias

**UHF** [ju·ertf·'ef] *n abbr of* **ultrahigh frequency** UHF *f*

**UK** [ju·'keɪ] *n abbr of* **United Kingdom** RU *m*

**Ukraine** [ju·'kreɪn] *n* Ucrania *f*

**Ukrainian** I. *adj* ucraniano, -a II. *n* 1. (*person*) ucraniano, -a *m, f* 2. LING ucraniano *m*

**ukulele** [ju·kə·'leɪ·li] *n* MUS ukelele *m*

**ulcer** ['ʌl·sər] *n* 1. MED úlcera *f*, chácara *f Col* 2. *fig* llaga *f*

**ulterior** [ʌl·'tɪr·i·ər] *adj* (*secret*) secreto, -a

**ultimate** ['ʌl·tə·mɪt] I. *adj* 1. (*best*) máximo, -a; (*experience, feeling*) extremo, -a 2. (*final*) final; (*cost, consequences, effect*) definitivo, -a 3. (*fundamental*) primordial II. **n the ~** lo último; (*bad taste, vulgarity*) el colmo; **the ~ in fashion** el último grito en moda; **the ~ in stupidity** el colmo de la estupidez

**ultimately** ['ʌl·tə·mɪt·li] *adv* 1. (*in the end*) finalmente 2. (*fundamentally*) fundamentalmente

**ultimatum** [ʌl·tə·'mer·təm] <ultimata *or* -tums> *n* ultimátum *m*

**ultrasound** ['ʌl·trə·saʊnd] *n* ultrasonido *m*

**ultraviolet** [ʌl·trə·'vaɪ·ə·lɪt] *adj* ultravioleta

**umbilical** [ʌm·'bɪl·ɪ·kəl] *adj* umbilical

**umbilical cord** *n* cordón *m* umbilical

**umbrella** [ʌm·'brel·ə] *n* (*rain*) paraguas *m inv*; (*sun*) sombrilla *f*

**umbrella organization** *n* organización *f* paraguas

**umpire** ['ʌm·paɪr] SPORTS I. *n* árbitro *mf* II. *vt, vi* arbitrar

**umpteen** ['ʌmp·tin] *adj inf* innumerable; **~ reasons** múltiples razones

**umpteenth** ['ʌmp·tinθ] *adj* enésimo, -a

**UN** [ju·'en] *n abbr of* **United Nations** ONU *f*

**unabashed** [ʌn·ə·'bæʃt] *adj* desenvuelto, -a; (*behavior*) atrevido, -a

**unable** [ʌn·'eɪ·bəl] *adj* incapaz

**unabridged** [ʌn·ə·'brɪdʒd] *adj* (*whole*) íntegro, -a

**unacceptable** [ʌn·ək·'sep·tə·bəl] *adj* inadmisible

**unaccompanied** [ʌn·ə·'kʌm·pə·nid] *adj* sin compañía; MUS sin acompañamiento

**unaccountable** [ʌn·ə·'kaʊn·tə·bəl] *adj* 1. (*not responsible*) no responsable 2. (*inexplicable*) inexplicable

**unaccustomed** [ʌn·ə·'kʌs·təmd] *adj* raro, -a; (*new*) inusual; **to be ~ to doing sth** no tener costumbre de hacer algo

**unaddressed** [ʌn·ə·'drest] *adj* sin señas

**unadulterated** [ʌn·ə·'dʌl·tə·reɪ·tɪd] *adj* puro, -a; (*alcohol, wine*) no adulterado, -a

**unadventurous** [ʌn·əd·'ven·tʃər·əs] *adj* poco atrevido, -a; (*style*) poco llamativo, -a

**unaffected** [ʌn·ə·'fek·tɪd] *adj* 1. (*not changed*) inalterado, -a 2. (*not influenced*) espontáneo, -a 3. (*down to earth*) sencillo, -a; (*manner, speech*) natural

**unafraid** [ʌn·ə·'freɪd] *adj* sin temor; **to be ~** no tener miedo (**of** de)

**unaided** [ʌn·'eɪ·dɪd] *adj* sin ayuda; **to do sth ~** hacer algo por sí solo

**unaltered** [ʌn·'ɔl·tərd] *adj* inalterado, -a; **to leave sth ~** dejar algo tal como estaba

**unambiguous** [ʌn·æm·'bɪg·ju·əs] *adj* inequívoco, -a; (*statement*) incuestionable

**un-American** [ʌn·ə·'mer·ɪ·kən] *adj* antiamericano, -a

**unanimity** [ju·nə·'nɪm·ə·ţi] *n* unanimidad *f*

**unanimous** [ju·'næn·ə·məs] *adj* unánime

**unannounced** [ʌn·ə·'naʊnst] I. *adj* (*without warning*) inesperado, -a; (*not made known*) fortuito, -a II. *adv* de repente; (*arrive, visit*) sin previo aviso

**unanswerable** [ʌn·'æn·sər·ə·bəl] *adj* (*with no answer*) sin respuesta; (*irrefutable*) irrefutable

**unanswered** [ʌn·'æn·sərd] *adj* sin contestar

**unappetizing** [ʌn·'æp·ə·taɪ·zɪŋ] *adj* poco apetitoso, -a

**unapproachable** [ʌn·ə·'prou·tʃə·bəl] *adj*

**inaccesible;** (*person*) intratable

**unarmed** [ʌnˈɑrmd] *adj* desarmado, -a

**unashamed** [ʌn-ə-ˈʃeɪmd] *adj* desvergonzado, -a; (*greed, selfishness*) descarado, -a; **to leave the children ~ of sth** (*guilt*) no tener remordimientos por algo; (*shame*) no avergonzarse por algo

**unasked** [ʌnˈæskt] *adj* no solicitado, -a; (*spontaneous*) espontáneo, -a

**unassignable** [ʌn-ə-ˈsaɪ-nə-bəl] *adj* LAW intrasferible

**unassuming** [ʌn-ə-ˈsu-mɪŋ] *adj* modesto, -a

**unattached** [ʌn-ə-ˈtætʃt] *adj* 1. (*not connected*) suelto, -a; (*part*) separable 2. (*independent*) libre

**unattainable** [ʌn-ə-ˈteɪ-nə-bəl] *adj* inalcanzable

**unattended** [ʌn-ə-ˈten-dɪd] *adj* 1. (*alone*) sin compañía; **to leave the children ~** dejar a los niños sin vigilancia 2. (*unmanned*) desatendido, -a 3. (*not taken care of*) descuidado, -a

**unattractive** [ʌn-ə-ˈtræk-tɪv] *adj* (*ugly*) poco atractivo, -a; (*unpleasant*) desagradable

**unauthorized** [ʌn-ˈɔ-θə-raɪzd] *adj* no autorizado, -a

**unavailable** [ʌn-ə-ˈveɪ-lə-bəl] *adj* inasequible; (*person*) ocupado, -a

**unavoidable** [ʌn-ə-ˈvɔɪ-də-bəl] *adj* inevitable

**unaware** [ʌn-ə-ˈwer] *adj* ajeno (**of** a)

**unawares** [ʌn-ə-ˈwerz] *adv* desprevenido

**unbalanced** [ʌn-ˈbæl-ənst] *adj* 1. (*uneven*) desnivelado, -a; (*account*) desequilibrado, -a 2. PSYCH trastornado, -a

**unbearable** [ʌn-ˈber-ə-bəl] *adj* insufrible

**unbeatable** [ʌn-ˈbi-tə-bəl] *adj* (*record, team*) imbatible; (*value, quality*) inmejorable; (*meal*) insuperable

**unbeaten** [ʌn-ˈbi-tən] *adj* invicto, -a; (*record*) insuperado, -a

**unbelievable** [ʌn-bɪ-ˈli-və-bəl] *adj* increíble

**unbelieving** [ʌn-bɪ-ˈli-vɪŋ] *adj* incrédulo, -a

**unbending** *adj* firme; (*will*) inquebrantable

**unbiased** [ʌn-ˈbaɪ-əst] *adj* imparcial; (*opinion, report, advice*) objetivo, -a

**unbleached** [ʌn-ˈblitʃt] *adj* sin blanquear; (*flour*) integral

**unbolt** [ʌn-ˈboʊlt] *vt* desatrancar

**unborn** [ʌn-ˈbɔrn] *adj* (*baby*) en gestación

**unbreakable** [ʌn-ˈbreɪ-kə-bəl] *adj* inquebrantable; (*material*) irrompible

**unbroken** [ʌn-ˈbroʊ-kən] *adj* 1. (*not broken*) intacto, -a; **an ~ promise** una promesa cumplida 2. (*continuous*) ininterrumpido, -a

**unbuckle** [ʌn-ˈbʌk-əl] *vt* desabrochar

**unbusinesslike** [ʌn-ˈbɪz-nɪs-laɪk] *adj* poco profesional

**unbutton** [ʌn-ˈbʌt-ən] *vt* desabrochar

**uncalled-for** [ʌn-ˈkɔld-fɔr] *adj* gratuito, -a; (*remark*) fuera de lugar

**uncanny** [ʌn-ˈkæn-i] *adj* <-ier, -iest> 1. (*mysterious*) misterioso, -a 2. (*remarkable*) extraordinario, -a; **to be ~ how...** ser sorprendente cómo...; **an ~ knack** una destreza extraordinaria

**uncared-for** [ʌn-ˈkerd-fɔr] *adj* descuidado, -a

**unceasing** [ʌn-ˈsi-sɪŋ] *adj* incesante; (*support*) incondicional

**uncertain** [ʌn-ˈsɜr-tən] *adj* 1. (*unsure*) dudoso, -a; **to be ~ of/whether/when...** no estar seguro de/de si/de cuándo...; **in no ~ terms** claramente 2. (*chancy*) incierto, -a 3. (*volatile*) volátil

**uncertainty** [ʌn-ˈsɜr-tən-ti] <-ies> *n* incertidumbre *f* (**about** sobre); (*hesitancy*) indecisión *f*

**unchallenged** [ʌn-ˈtʃæl-ɪndʒd] *adj* 1. (*not questioned*) incuestionado, -a 2. (*unopposed*) no protestado, -a; **to go ~** pasar sin protesta

**unchanged** [ʌn-ˈtʃeɪndʒd] *adj* 1. (*unaltered*) inalterado, -a 2. (*not replaced*) no sustituido, -a

**uncharacteristic** [ʌn-ˌkær-ɪk-tə-ˈrɪs-tɪk] *adj* poco característico, -a; **to be ~ of** no ser típico (**of** de)

**uncharitable** [ʌn-ˈtʃær-ɪ-tə-bəl] *adj* (*severe*) severo, -a (**in** en)

**unchecked** [ʌn-ˈtʃekt] *adj* 1. (*unrestrained*) desenfrenado, -a 2. (*not checked*) sin comprobar

**unchristian** [ʌn-ˈkrɪs-tʃən] *adj* indigno, -a de un cristiano

U

**uncivil** [ʌn'sɪv·əl] *adj* grosero, -a (**to** con)

**unclaimed** [ʌn'kleɪmd] *adj* sin reclamar

**uncle** ['ʌŋ·kəl] *n* tío *m*

**unclean** [ʌn'klin] *adj* 1. sucio, -a; (*impure*) impuro, -a 2. (*taboo*) tabú

**unclear** [ʌn'klɪr] *adj* 1. (*not certain*) nada claro, -a; **to be ~** no estar seguro (**about** de) 2. (*vague*) vago, -a

**uncomfortable** [ʌn'kʌm·fər·t̬ə·bəl] *adj* incómodo, -a; **an ~ silence** un silencio incómodo; **it makes me ~ to...** me hace sentir incómodo (el)...

**uncommon** [ʌn'kam·ən] *adj* (*rare*) poco común; **to be not ~** no ser raro (**for** para)

**uncommonly** *adv* raramente; (*extremely*) excepcionalmente

**uncompromising** [ʌn'kam·prə·maɪ·zɪŋ] *adj* intransigente; **to take an ~ stand** adoptar una postura intransigente

**unconcerned** [ʌn·kən'sɜrnd] *adj* 1. (*not worried*) no preocupado, -a; **to be ~** no preocuparse (**about** por) 2. (*indifferent*) indiferente (**with** con respecto a)

**unconditional** [ʌn·kən'dɪʃ·ə·nəl] *adj* incondicional

**unconfirmed** [ʌn·kən'fɜrmd] *adj* no confirmado, -a

**unconnected** [ʌn·kə'nek·tɪd] *adj* desconectado, -a (**to** de)

**unconscionable** [ʌn·kan'tʃə·nə·bəl] *adj* desmedido, -a

**unconscious** [ʌn·kan'tʃəs] I. *adj* 1. MED, PSYCH inconsciente; **to knock sb ~** dejar a alguien inconsciente 2. (*unaware*) no intencional; **to be ~** no ser consciente (**of** de) II. *n* PSYCH inconsciente *m*

**unconsciously** *adv* inconscientemente

**unconsciousness** *n* 1. MED pérdida *f* de conocimiento 2. (*unawareness*) inconsciencia *f*

**unconstitutional** [ʌn·kan·stə'tu·ʃə·nəl] *adj* inconstitucional

**uncontested** [ʌn·kən'tes·tɪd] *adj* (*not disputed*) sin oposición

**uncontrollable** [ʌn·kən'troʊ·lə·bəl] *adj* 1. (*irresistible*) irrefrenable 2. (*frenzied*) incontrolable

**uncontrolled** [ʌn·kən'troʊld] *adj* descontrolado, -a

**unconvinced** [ʌn·kən'vɪnst] *adj* **to be ~** no estar convencido (**of** de)

**unconvincing** [ʌn·kən'vɪn·sɪŋ] *adj* nada convincente; **rather ~** poco convincente

**uncooked** [ʌn'kʊkt] *adj* crudo, -a

**uncooperative** [ʌn·koʊ·'ap·ər·ə·tɪv] *adj* poco cooperativo, -a

**uncork** [ʌn'kɔrk] *vt* descorchar; **to ~ one's feelings** dejar aflorar los sentimientos; **to ~ a surprise** destapar una sorpresa

**uncountable noun** [ʌn·'kaʊn·tə·bəl naʊn] *n* substantivo *m* incontable

**uncouth** [ʌn'kuθ] *adj* basto, -a

**uncover** [ʌn'kʌv·ər] *vt* destapar; (*secret, truth*) desvelar

**uncut** [ʌn'kʌt] *adj* 1. (*not cut*) sin cortar; **an ~ diamond** un diamante en bruto 2. (*not shortened*) sin cortes

**undaunted** [ʌn'dɔn·tɪd] *adj* impertérrito, -a; **to be ~** quedarse impávido (**by** ante)

**undecided** [ʌn·dɪ'saɪ·dɪd] *adj* 1. (*unresolved*) indeciso, -a (**about** ante); **to be ~ as to what to do** no saber qué hacer 2. (*not settled*) no decidido, -a

**undeclared** [ʌn·dɪ'klerd] *adj* 1. FIN no declarado, -a 2. (*not official*) no oficial; **an ~ war** una guerra no declarada

**undeliverable** [ʌn·dɪ·'lɪv·rə·bəl] *adj* que no puede ser entregado, -a

**undelivered** [ʌn·dɪ·'lɪv·ərd] *adj* sin entregar

**undemanding** [ʌn·dɪ·'man·dɪŋ] *adj* sencillo, -a; (*person*) poco exigente

**undeniable** [ʌn·dɪ·'naɪ·ə·bəl] *adj* innegable; (*evidence*) irrefutable

**undeniably** *adv* indudablemente

**under** ['ʌn·dər] I. *prep* 1. (*below*) debajo de; **~ the bed** debajo de la cama; **~ there** ahí debajo 2. (*supporting, governed by*) bajo; **to break ~** romperse bajo el peso; **to be ~ sb's influence** estar bajo la influencia de alguien 3. (*less*) **to cost ~ $10** costar menos de 10$; **those ~ the age of 30** los menores de 30 años 4. **~ the circumstances** dadas las circunstancias; **~ repair** en reparación; **to classify the books ~ fiction** clasificar los libros por ficción **II.** adv **1.** (fewer) menos **2.** to crawl/go ~ meterse debajo **3.** inf to go ~ quedar inconsciente

**underage** [ˌʌn·dər·'eɪdʒ] adj menor de edad

**undercapitalized** [ˌʌn·dər·'kæp·ɪ·tə·laɪzd] adj subcapitalizado, -a; **to be** ~ estar descapitalizado

**undercharge** [ˌʌn·dər·'tʃɑrdʒ] vt, vi cobrar de menos

**underclothes** ['ʌn·dər·klouz] npl, **underclothing** ['ʌn·dər·klou·ðɪŋ] n ropa f interior

**undercoat** ['ʌn·dər·kout] n primera capa f de pintura

**undercover** [ˌʌn·dər·'kʌv·ər] **I.** adj secreto, -a **II.** adv clandestinamente

**undercurrent** ['ʌn·dər·kɜr·ənt] n corriente f submarina; fig trasfondo m

**undercut** [ˌʌn·dər·'kʌt] irr vt (charge less) vender más barato

**underdeveloped** [ˌʌn·dər·dɪ·'vel·əpt] adj **1.** ECON subdesarrollado, -a; (resource) infradesarrollado, -a **2.** BOT inmaduro, -a

**underdog** ['ʌn·dər·dɔg] n desvalido, -a m, f

**underdone** [ˌʌn·dər·'dʌn] adj FOOD poco hecho, -a

**underemployed** [ˌʌn·dər·ɪm·'plɔɪd] adj **1.** subestimado, -a en el trabajo **2.** ECON **to be** ~ ser poco utilizado, -a

**underestimate** [ˌʌn·dər·'es·tə·meɪt] **I.** vt subestimar **II.** n infravaloración f

**underfed** [ˌʌn·dər·'fed] n desnutrido, -a m, f

**underfoot** [ˌʌn·dər·'fʊt] adv bajo los pies; **to trample** ~ a. fig pisar

**undergarment** ['ʌn·dər·gar·mənt] n prenda f interior

**undergo** [ˌʌn·dər·'gou] irr vt experimentar; (change) sufrir; **to** ~ **surgery** ser operado

**undergraduate** [ˌʌn·dər·'græd·ʒ·u·ət] n estudiante mf no licenciado, -a

**underground** ['ʌn·dər·graund] **I.** adj **1.** subterráneo, -a **2.** (clandestine) clandestino, -a **II.** adv **1.** bajo tierra **2.** (clandestinely) en la clandestinidad **III.** n (lifestyle) underground m

**undergrowth** ['ʌn·dər·grouθ] n maleza f

**underhand** [ˌʌn·dər·'hænd], **underhanded** [ˌʌn·dər·'hæn·dɪd] **I.** adj (secret) subrepticio, -a **II.** adv (secretly) subrepticiamente

**underline** [ˌʌn·dər·'laɪn] vt **1.** (word) subrayar; **to** ~ **sth in red** subrayar algo en rojo **2.** (emphasize) enfatizar; **to** ~ **that...** subrayar que...

**underlying** [ˌʌn·dər·'laɪ·ɪŋ] adj subyacente

**undermanned** [ˌʌn·dər·'mænd] adj sin plantilla suficiente

**undermine** [ˌʌn·dər·'maɪn] vt **1.** (damage, sap, weaken) minar; **to** ~ **hopes** desalentar; **to** ~ **sb's confidence** hacer perder la confianza de alguien; **to** ~ **sb's health** perjudicar la salud de alguien **2.** (tunnel under) socavar

**underneath** [ˌʌn·dər·'niθ] **I.** prep debajo de **II.** adv por debajo **III.** adj inferior

**undernourished** [ˌʌn·dər·'nɜr·ɪʃt] adj desnutrido, -a

**underpaid** [ˌʌn·dər·'peɪd] adj mal pagado, -a

**underpants** ['ʌn·dər·pænts] npl calzoncillos mpl

**underpass** ['ʌn·dər·pæs] <-es> n paso m subterráneo

**underpay** [ˌʌn·dər·'peɪ] irr vt pagar un sueldo insuficiente

**underperform** [ˌʌn·dər·pər·'fɔrm] vi rendir por debajo de lo suficiente

**underprivileged** [ˌʌn·dər·'prɪv·ə·lɪdʒd] adj sin privilegios; **the** ~ **class** la clase no privilegiada

**underrate** [ˌʌn·dər·'reɪt] vt subestimar; **to** ~ **the difficulty/importance** infravalorar la dificultad/importancia (of de)

**underrepresented** [ˌʌn·dər·rep·rɪ·'zen·tɪd] adj con mala representación

**undershirt** ['ʌn·dər·ʃɜrt] n camiseta f interior

**underside** ['ʌn·dər·saɪd] n superficie f inferior

**undersigned** ['ʌn·dər·saɪnd] n **the** ~ el/la abajo firmante

**understaffed** [ˌʌn·dər·'stæft] adj falto, -a de personal

**understand** [ˌʌn·dər·'stænd] irr **I.** vt **1.** (perceive) comprender, entender (that **que**); **to make oneself under- stood** hacerse entender; **to not ~ a word** no entender ni una palabra; **to ~ sb's doing sth** entender que alguien haga algo **2.** *form* (*be informed*) quedar informado (**that** de que); **to ~ from sb** saber por alguien (**that** que) **3.** (*believe*) creer; (*infer*) sobreentender; **as I ~** según tengo entendido; **it is understood that...** se sobreentiende que... **II.** *vi* entender (**about** de)

**understandable** [ˌʌn.dərˈstæn.də.bəl] *adj* comprensible; **to be ~ that...** ser comprensible que...

**understanding** **I.** *n* **1.** (*grasp*) entendimiento *m*; **to not have any ~ of sth** no tener ni idea de algo *inf*; **to come to an ~** llegar a entender; **sb's ~** la interpretación de alguien (**of** de) **2.** (*agreement*) acuerdo *m*; **to come to an ~** llegar a un acuerdo **3.** (*rapport*) comprensión *f*; **a spirit of ~** un espíritu de comprensión **4.** (*condition*) condición *f*; **to do sth on the ~ that...** hacer algo a condición de que... **II.** *adj* comprensivo, -a

**understatement** [ˌʌn.dərˈsteɪt.mənt] *n* atenuación *f*

**understood** [ˌʌn.dərˈstʊd] *vt, vi pt, pp of* **understand**

**understudy** [ˈʌn.dərˌstʌd.i] <-ies> *n* THEAT suplente *mf*

**undertake** [ˌʌn.dərˈteɪk] *irr vt* **1.** (*take on*) emprender; **to ~ a journey** emprender un viaje **2.** *form* **to ~ to do sth** comprometerse a hacer algo; **to ~ (that)...** comprometerse a (que)...

**undertaker** [ˈʌn.dərˌteɪ.kər] *n* director(a) *m(f)* de una funeraria

**undertaking** [ˌʌn.dərˈteɪ.kɪŋ] *n* **1.** (*project*) empresa *f* **2.** (*pledge*) promesa *f* (**to** de)

**undervalue** [ˌʌn.dərˈvæl.ju] *vt* infravalorar

**underwater** [ˌʌn.dərˈwɔː.tər] **I.** *adj* submarino, -a **II.** *adv* bajo el agua

**underwear** [ˈʌn.dərˌwer] *n* ropa *f* interior

**underweight** [ˌʌn.dərˈweɪt] *adj* de peso insuficiente

**underworld** [ˈʌn.dərˌwɜːld] *n* **1.** (*criminals*) hampa *m* **2. the Underworld** el inframundo

**underwrite** [ˈʌn.dərˌraɪt] *irr vt* **1.** (*sign*) firmar; **to ~ a contract** firmar un contrato **2.** (*insurance*) asegurar

**undesirable** [ˌʌn.dɪˈzaɪ.rə.bəl] *adj* indeseable; **to be ~ that...** no ser recomendable que...; **an ~ character** un carácter difícil

**undetected** [ˌʌn.dɪˈtek.tɪd] *adj* no descubierto, -a; **to go ~** pasar inadvertido, -a

**undeveloped** [ˌʌn.dɪˈvel.əpt] *adj* **1.** POL, ECON subdesarrollado, -a **2.** (*not used*) poco utilizado, -a **3.** BIO, PSYCH no desarrollado, -a

**undid** [ʌnˈdɪd] *vt, vi pt of* **undo**

**undies** [ˈʌn.diz] *npl inf* paños *m pl* menores

**undisclosed** [ˌʌn.dɪsˈkloʊzd] *adj* no revelado, -a; (*amount*) no desvelado, -a; (*location*) sin desvelar

**undisturbed** [ˌʌn.dɪˈstɜːbd] *adj* **they were ~ by the noise** el ruido no les molestaba

**undivided** [ˌʌn.dɪˈvaɪ.dɪd] *adj* íntegro, -a; **sb's ~ attention** toda la atención de alguien

**undo** [ʌnˈduː] *irr vt* **1.** (*unfasten*) soltar; (*button*) desabrochar; (*zipper*) bajar **2.** (*cancel*) anular; (*damage*) reparar ► **what's** <u>done</u> **cannot be undone** lo hecho, hecho está

**undoing** *n* ruina *f*

**undone** [ʌnˈdʌn] **I.** *vt pp of* **undo** **II.** *adj* **1.** (*unfastened*) desatado, -a; **to come ~** deshacerse, desatarse **2.** (*uncompleted*) por hacer; **to leave sth ~** dejar algo sin hacer

**undoubted** [ʌnˈdaʊ.tɪd] *adj* indudable

**undoubtedly** *adv* sin duda

**undress** [ʌnˈdres] **I.** *vt* desnudar, desvestir *AmL* **II.** *vi* desnudarse, desvestirse *AmL* **III.** *n* **1.** (*informal clothing*) ropa *f* informal **2. to be in a state of ~** estar desnudo

**undressed** *adj* desvestido, -a; **to get ~** desnudarse

**undue** [ʌnˈduː] *adj* indebido, -a

**unduly** [ʌnˈduː.li] *adv* indebidamente

**undying** [ʌnˈdaɪ.ɪŋ] *adj* imperecedero, -a

**unearned** [ʌnˈɜːnd] *adj* **1.** (*undeserved*)

inmerecido, -a **2.** (*not worked for*) no ganado, -a

**unearth** [ʌn·ˈɜrθ] *vt* desenterrar; *fig* sacar a la luz; (*truth*) descubrir

**unearthly** [ʌn·ˈɜrθ·li] *adj* sobrenatural; ~ **noise/scream** ruido/grito aterrador

**unease** [ʌn·ˈiz] *n* malestar *m*; **with growing** ~ con creciente inquietud

**uneasiness** *n* inquietud *f*

**uneasy** [ʌn·ˈi·zi] *adj* <-ier, -iest> **1.** (*uncertain*) intranquilo, -a; **to be/feel** ~ **certain** estar/sentirse inquieto (**about** por) **2.** (*causing anxiety*) ansioso, -a; (*suspicion*) inquietante; (*relationship*) inestable **3.** (*insecure*) dudoso, -a

**uneducated** [ʌn·ˈedʒ·ə·keɪ·t̬ɪd] *adj* inculto, -a

**unemployable** [ʌn·ɪm·ˈplɔɪ·ə·bəl] *adj* incapacitado, -a para trabajar

**unemployed** [ʌn·ɪm·ˈplɔɪd] **I.** *n pl* **the** ~ los desempleados **II.** *adj* parado, -a

**unemployment** [ʌn·ɪm·ˈplɔɪ·mənt] *n* paro *m*

**unemployment benefit** *n* subsidio *m* de desempleo

**unequal** [ʌn·ˈi·kwəl] *adj* **1.** (*inequitable*) desigual **2. to be** ~ **to sth** no estar a la altura de algo; **to be** ~ **to a task** ser incapaz de realizar una tarea

**unequaled** *adj*, **unequalled** *adj* sin igual

**unequivocal** [ʌn·ɪ·ˈkwɪv·ə·kəl] *adj* inequívoco, -a; (*success*) indudable; **to be** ~ **in sth** ser claro en algo

**unethical** [ʌn·ˈeθ·ɪ·kəl] *adj* poco ético, -a

**uneven** [ʌn·ˈi·vən] *adj* **1.** (*not level*) desnivelado, -a **2.** (*unequal*) desigual **3.** (*different*) distinto, -a **4.** (*erratic, fluctuating*) cambiante

**uneventful** [ʌn·ɪ·ˈvent·fəl] *adj* sin acontecimientos; (*unexciting*) tranquilo, -a

**unexceptional** [ʌn·ɪk·ˈsep·ʃə·nəl] *adj* corriente

**unexpected** [ʌn·ɪk·ˈspek·tɪd] *adj* inesperado, -a

**unfair** [ʌn·ˈfer] *adj* injusto, -a

**unfaithful** [ʌn·ˈfeɪθ·fʊl] *adj* **1.** (*adulterous*) infiel **2.** (*disloyal*) desleal **3.** (*not accurate*) inexacto, -a

**unfamiliar** [ʌn·fə·ˈmɪl·jər] *adj* **1.** (*new*) desconocido, -a; **to be** ~ **to sb** no ser familiar a alguien **2.** (*unacquainted*)

ajeno, -a

**unfasten** [ʌn·ˈfæs·ən] **I.** *vt* desatar; (*belt*) desabrochar; (*zipper*) bajar **II.** *vi* soltarse

**unfavorable** [ʌn·ˈfeɪ·vər·ə·bəl] *adj* **1.** (*adverse*) adverso, -a **2.** (*disadvantageous*) desfavorable

**unfilled** *adj* sin llenar [*or* ocupar]

**unfinished** [ʌn·ˈfɪn·ɪʃt] *adj* inacabado, -a

**unfit** [ʌn·ˈfɪt] *adj* **1.** (*unhealthy*) **I'm** ~ no estoy en forma; **to be** ~ **for** no estar en condiciones para **2.** (*incompetent*) incapaz **3.** (*unsuitable*) no apto, -a (**for** para)

**unfold** [ʌn·ˈfoʊld] **I.** *vt* **1.** (*open*) desdoblar; (*arms*) descruzar **2. to** ~ **one's ideas/plans** exponer sus ideas/planes **II.** *vi* **1.** (*develop*) desarrollarse **2.** (*be revealed*) revelarse

**unforeseeable** [ʌn·fɔr·ˈsi·ə·bəl] *adj* imprevisible

**unforeseen** [ʌn·fɔr·ˈsin] *adj* imprevisto, -a

**unforgettable** [ʌn·fər·ˈget̬·ə·bəl] *adj* inolvidable

**unforgivable** [ʌn·fər·ˈgɪv·ə·bəl] *adj* imperdonable

**unfortunate** [ʌn·ˈfɔr·tʃə·nɪt] **I.** *adj* **1.** (*luckless*) desafortunado, -a; **to be** ~ **that...** ser lamentable que... +*subj* **2.** (*regrettable*) deplorable **3.** (*inopportune*) inoportuno, -a **II.** *n* desafortunado, -a *m, f*

**unfortunately** *adv* por desgracia

**unfounded** [ʌn·ˈfaʊn·dɪd] *adj* infundado, -a

**unfriendly** [ʌn·ˈfrend·li] *adj* <-ier, -iest> **1.** (*unsociable*) insociable **2.** (*hard to use*) complicado, -a **3.** (*inhospitable*) hostil

**unfulfilled** [ʌn·fʊl·ˈfild] *adj* **1.** (*unrealized*) incumplido, -a **2.** (*unsatisfied*) insatisfecho, -a **3.** (*frustrated*) frustrado, -a

**unfurnished** [ʌn·ˈfɜr·nɪʃt] *adj* desamueblado, -a

**ungainly** [ʌn·ˈgeɪn·li] *adj* <-ier, -iest> torpe

**ungodly** [ʌn·ˈgad·li] *adj* <-ier, -iest> *inf* atroz; **at this** ~ **hour** a esta hora intempestiva

U

**ungrateful** [ʌnˈɡreɪt·fəl] *adj* ingrato, -a

**unguarded** [ʌnˈɡɑr·dɪd] *adj* **1.** (*not watched*) sin vigilancia **2.** (*careless*) desprevenido, -a; **in an ~ moment** en un momento de descuido

**unhappy** [ʌnˈhæp·i] *adj* <-ier, -iest> **1.** (*sad*) infeliz; **to make sb ~** hacer desdichado a alguien **2.** (*unfortunate*) desafortunado, -a

**unharmed** [ʌnˈhɑrmd] *adj* ileso, -a

**unhealthy** [ʌnˈhel·θi] *adj* <-ier, -iest> **1.** (*sick*) enfermizo, -a **2.** (*unwholesome*) nocivo, -a **3.** (*dangerous*) arriesgado, -a

**unheard** [ʌnˈhɜrd] *adj* desoído, -a; (*ignored*) desatendido, -a

**unheard-of** [ʌnˈhɜrd·ˌʌv] *adj* sin precedentes; (*impossible*) inaudito, -a

**unhelpful** [ʌnˈhelp·fʊl] *adj* de poca ayuda

**unhook** [ʌnˈhʊk] *vt* desenganchar

**unhoped-for** [ʌnˈhoʊpt·ˌfɔr] *adj* inesperado, -a

**unhurt** [ʌnˈhɜrt] *adj* ileso, -a

**unicorn** [ˈju·nɪ·kɔrn] *n* unicornio *m*

**unidentified** [ˌʌn·aɪˈden·tə·faɪd] *n* no identificado, -a; **~ flying object** objeto volante no identificado

**unification** [ˌju·nɪ·fɪˈkeɪ·ʃən] *n* unificación *f*

**uniform** [ˈju·nə·fɔrm] **I.** *n* uniforme *m* **II.** *adj* (*similar*) uniforme; (*constant*) constante

**uniformity** [ˌju·nəˈfɔr·mə·ti] *n* uniformidad *f*

**unify** [ˈju·nə·faɪ] *vt* unificar

**unilateral** [ˌju·nəˈlæt·ər·əl] *adj* unilateral

**unimaginable** [ˌʌn·ɪˈmædʒ·nə·bəl] *adj* inimaginable

**unimportant** [ˌʌn·ɪmˈpɔr·tənt] *adj* sin importancia

**uninformed** [ˌʌn·ɪnˈfɔrmd] *adj* desinformado, -a

**uninhabitable** [ˌʌn·ɪnˈhæb·ɪ·tə·bəl] *adj* inhabitable

**uninhabited** [ˌʌn·ɪnˈhæb·ɪtɪd] *adj* deshabitado, -a; (*deserted*) desierto, -a

**uninhibited** [ˌʌn·ɪnˈhɪb·ɪ·tɪd] *adj* desinhibido, -a

**uninjured** [ˌʌn·ɪnˈdʒərd] *adj* ileso, -a

**uninsured** [ˌʌn·ɪnˈʃʊrd] *adj* sin seguro

**unintelligent** [ˌʌn·ɪnˈtel·ɪ·dʒənt] *adj* poco inteligente

**unintelligible** [ˌʌn·ɪnˈtel·ɪ·dʒə·bəl] *adj* ininteligible

**unintentional** [ˌʌn·ɪnˈten·ʃə·nəl] *adj* involuntario, -a

**unintentionally** *adv* sin intención

**uninterested** [ʌnˈɪn·trə·stɪd] *adj* indiferente

**uninteresting** *adj* aburrido, -a

**uninterrupted** [ʌn·ˌɪn·tər·ˈʌp·tɪd] *adj* ininterrumpido, -a

**union** [ˈjun·jən] *n* **1.** (*act of becoming united*) unión *f* **2.** (*society*) asociación *f* **3.** + *sing/pl vb* (*of employees*) sindicato *m* **4.** (*marriage*) enlace *m*

**Union Jack** *n* bandera del Reino Unido

**unique** [juˈnik] *adj* único, -a; (*exceptional*) excepcional; (*characteristic*) exclusivo, -a

**unisex** [ˈju·nə·seks] *adj* unisex

**unison** [ˈju·nə·sən] *n* **in ~** al unísono; *fig* de acuerdo (**with** con)

**unit** [ˈju·nɪt] *n* **1. a.** COMPUT, COM unidad *f*; **central processing ~** unidad central de proceso; **~ of currency** unidad monetaria **2.** (*furniture*) elemento *m*

**unite** [juˈnaɪt] **I.** *vt* (*join together*) juntar; (*bring together*) unir **II.** *vi* juntarse; **to ~ against sb** unirse para hacer frente a alguien

**united** *adj* unido, -a

**United Arab Emirates** *npl* **the ~** los Emiratos Árabes Unidos

**United Kingdom** *n* **the ~** el Reino Unido

**United Nations** *n* **the ~** las Naciones Unidas

**United States** *n* + *sing vb* **the ~** (**of America**) los Estados Unidos (de América)

**unity** [ˈju·nə·ti] *n* unidad *f*; (*consensus*) consenso *m*

**universal** [ˌju·nəˈvɜr·səl] **I.** *adj* universal; (*agreement*) global **II.** *n* universal *m*

**universe** [ˈju·nə·vɜrs] *n* universo *m*

**university** [ˌju·nəˈvɜr·sə·ti] <-ies> *n* universidad *f*

**unjust** [ʌnˈdʒʌst] *adj* injusto, -a

**unjustifiable** [ʌnˌdʒʌs·tɪˈfaɪ·ə·bəl] *adj* injustificable

**unjustified** [ʌnˈdʒʌs·tɪ·faɪd] *adj* injustificado, -a; (*complaint*) no justificado, -a

**unjustly** *adv* injustamente

**unkempt** [ʌnˈkempt] *adj* descuidado, -a

**unkind** [ʌnˈkaɪnd] *adj* desagradable; **to be ~ to sb** tratar mal a alguien; **to be ~ to animals** ser cruel con los animales; **to be ~ to hair/skin** estropear el pelo/la piel

**unkindly** *adv* cruelmente; **to take sth ~** tomarse algo mal

**unknown** [ʌnˈnoʊn] I. *adj* desconocido, -a; **~ to me** sin saberlo yo II. *n* desconocido, -a *m, f*; **the ~** lo desconocido; MATH la incógnita

**unlawful** [ʌnˈlɔfəl] *adj* ilegal; (*possession, association*) ilícito, -a

**unleaded** [ʌnˈledɪd] *adj* sin plomo

**unleash** [ʌnˈliʃ] *vt* (*dog*) soltar; (*passions*) desatar

**unleavened** [ʌnˈlevənd] *adj* sin levadura

**unless** [ənˈles] *conj* a no ser que +*subj*, a menos que +*subj*; **he won't come ~ he has time** no vendrá a menos que tenga tiempo; **~ I'm mistaken** si no me equivoco

**unlike** [ʌnˈlaɪk] I. *adj* diferente II. *prep* **1.** (*different from*) diferente a; **it's ~ him** no es característico de él **2.** (*in contrast to*) a diferencia de

**unlikely** [ʌnˈlaɪkli] <-ier, -iest> *adj* **1.** (*improbable*) improbable; **it seems ~ that...** parece poco probable; **it's ~ that...** es difícil que... **2.** (*unconvincing*) inverosímil

**unlimited** [ʌnˈlɪmɪtɪd] *adj* ilimitado, -a; (*great*) impresionante

**unlisted** [ʌnˈlɪstɪd] *adj* FIN no cotizado, -a

**unload** [ʌnˈloʊd] I. *vt* **1.** (*goods*) descargar **2.** (*get rid of*) deshacerse de **3.** (*express*) desahogarse II. *vi* **1.** AUTO descargar **2.** (*be emptied*) vaciarse

**unlock** [ʌnˈlɑk] *vt* abrir; *fig* resolver

**unlocked** *adj* abierto, -a; *fig* resuelto, -a

**unlucky** [ʌnˈlʌki] *adj* **1.** (*person*) desgraciado, -a; (*cards, love*) desafortunado, -a; **to be ~ enough to...** tener la mala suerte de... **2.** (*bringing bad luck*) nefasto, -a

**unmanned** [ʌnˈmænd] *adj* no tripulado, -a

**unmarried** [ʌnˈmærɪd] *adj* soltero, -a

**unmentionable** [ʌnˈmenʃənəbəl] *adj* inmencionable; (*disease*) tabú

**unmentioned** [ʌnˈmenʃənd] *adj* indecible

**unmitigated** [ʌnˈmɪtɪˌgeɪtɪd] *adj* absoluto, -a; (*evil*) implacable

**unmoved** [ʌnˈmuvd] *adj* impasible

**unnatural** [ʌnˈnætʃərəl] *adj* **1.** (*not natural*) poco natural; (*affected*) afectado, -a **2.** (*not normal*) anormal

**unnecessarily** [ʌnˌnesəˈserəli] *adv* innecesariamente

**unnecessary** [ʌnˈnesəˌseri] *adj* innecesario, -a; (*uncalled for*) superfluo, -a

**unnerving** *adj* enervante

**unnoticed** [ʌnˈnoʊtɪst] *adj* desapercibido, -a; **to go ~ that...** pasar inadvertido que...

**unobtainable** [ʌnəbˈteɪnəbəl] *adj* inalcanzable

**unobtrusive** [ʌnəbˈtrusɪv] *adj* (*people*) modesto, -a; (*things*) discreto, -a

**unoccupied** [ʌnˈɑkjəˌpaɪd] *adj* deshabitado, -a; (*chair, table*) libre

**unofficial** [ʌnəˈfɪʃəl] *adj* no oficial; (*figures*) oficioso, -a; (*capacity*) extraoficial

**unorganized** [ʌnˈɔrgəˌnaɪzd] *adj* desorganizado, -a

**unorthodox** [ʌnˈɔrθəˌdɑks] *adj* poco ortodoxo, -a; (*approach*) poco convencional

**unpack** [ʌnˈpæk] I. *vt* (*car*) descargar II. *vi* deshacer el equipaje

**unpaid** [ʌnˈpeɪd] *adj* **1.** (*not remunerated*) no remunerado, -a **2.** (*not paid*) pendiente

**unparalleled** [ʌnˈpærəˌleld] *adj* sin precedentes

**unpleasant** [ʌnˈplezənt] *adj* desagradable; (*unfriendly*) antipático, -a

**unpleasantness** *n* antipatía *f*; **the ~** lo desagradable

**unplug** [ʌnˈplʌg] <-gg-> *vt* ELEC desenchufar; (*drain, pipe*) destapar

**unpolluted** [ʌnpəˈlutɪd] *adj* no contaminado, -a

**unpopular** [ʌnˈpɑpjələr] *adj* que gusta poco; **to be ~ with sb** caer mal a alguien

**unpopularity** [ʌnˌpɑpjəˈlerəˌti] *n* im-

U

popularidad f

**unprecedented** [ʌn·ˈpres·ə·den·tɪd] *adj* sin precedentes; (*action*) inaudito, -a

**unpredictable** [ˌʌn·prɪ·ˈdɪk·tə·bəl] *adj* imprevisible

**unproductive** [ˌʌn·prə·ˈdʌk·tɪv] *adj* improductivo, -a; (*negotiations*) infructuoso, -a

**unprofessional** [ˌʌn·prə·ˈfeʃ·ə·nəl] *adj* poco profesional

**unprofitable** [ʌn·ˈprɑf·ɪ·tə·bəl] *adj* (*business*) no rentable; (*investment, meeting*) infructuoso, -a; (*day*) improductivo, -a

**unprompted** [ʌn·ˈprɑmp·tɪd] *adj* espontáneo, -a

**unpublished** [ʌn·ˈpʌb·lɪʃt] *adj* inédito, -a

**unqualified** [ʌn·ˈkwɑl·ə·faɪd] *adj* **1.** (*without qualifications*) sin título; **to be ~ for sth** no estar cualificado para algo **2.** (*unlimited*) incondicional; (*disaster*) absoluto, -a; (*success*) rotundo, -a; (*support*) total

**unquestionable** [ʌn·ˈkwes·tʃə·nə·bəl] *adj* incuestionable; (*fact*) innegable

**unquestionably** *adv* indudablemente

**unquestioning** [ʌn·ˈkwes·tʃə·nɪŋ] *adj* incondicional; (*obedience*) ciego, -a

**unravel** [ʌn·ˈræv·əl] <-ll-, -l-> **I.** *vt* **1.** (*undo*) deshacer **2.** (*solve*) aclarar **II.** *vi* deshacerse

**unreadable** [ʌn·ˈri·də·bəl] *adj* ininteligible; (*text*) ilegible; (*expression, face*) inescrutable

**unreal** [ʌn·ˈril] *adj* **1.** irreal **2.** *sl* impresionante

**unrealistic** [ˌʌn·ˌri·ə·ˈlɪs·tɪk] *adj* poco realista

**unreasonable** [ʌn·ˈri·zə·nə·bəl] *adj* poco razonable; (*unfair*) injusto, -a; (*demands*) excesivo, -a

**unrelated** [ˌʌn·rɪ·ˈleɪ·t̬ɪd] *adj* no relacionado, -a

**unrelenting** [ˌʌn·rɪ·ˈlen·tɪŋ] *adj* **1.** (*not yielding*) implacable (**in** en) **2.** (*not easing*) incesante

**unreliable** [ˌʌn·rɪ·ˈlaɪ·ə·bəl] *adj* informal

**unrepeatable** [ˌʌn·rɪ·ˈpi·t̬ə·bəl] *adj* irrepetible; (*price*) inmejorable

**unreserved** [ˌʌn·rɪ·ˈzɜrvd] *adj* **1.** (*tickets, seats*) no reservado, -a **2.** (*absolute*) incondicional **3.** (*frank*) abierto, -a

**unresolved** [ˌʌn·rɪ·ˈzɑlvd] *adj* sin resolver

**unrest** [ʌn·ˈrest] *n* descontento *m;* (*social*) malestar *m*

**unrestrained** [ˌʌn·rɪ·ˈstreɪnd] *adj* incontrolado, -a; (*criticism, consumerism*) desenfrenado, -a; (*laughter*) desmedido, -a

**unrestricted** [ˌʌn·rɪ·ˈstrɪk·tɪd] *adj* ilimitado, -a; (*access*) libre

**unripe** [ʌn·ˈraɪp] *adj* verde; *fig* inmaduro, -a

**unroll** [ʌn·ˈroʊl] *vt* desenrollar

**unruffled** [ʌn·ˈrʌf·əld] *adj* **1.** (*undisturbed*) sereno, -a; **to be ~** no inmutarse (**by** ante) **2.** (*smooth*) liso, -a

**unruly** [ʌn·ˈru·li] <-ier, -iest> *adj* indisciplinado, -a; (*children*) revoltoso, -a; (*hair*) rebelde

**unsafe** [ʌn·ˈseɪf] *adj* inseguro, -a; (*animal*) peligroso, -a

**unsaid** [ʌn·ˈsed] **I.** *vt pt, pp of* **unsay** **II.** *adj* sin decir; **to leave sth ~** callarse algo; **to be better left ~** mejor no hablar

**unsatisfactory** [ˌʌn·ˌsæt̬·ɪs·ˈfæk·tə·ri] *adj* insatisfactorio, -a; (*answer*) poco convincente; (*service*) poco satisfactorio, -a; (*grade*) insuficiente

**unsatisfied** [ʌn·ˈsæt̬·ɪs·faɪd] *adj* **1.** (*not content*) insatisfecho, -a **2.** (*not convinced*) no convencido, -a

**unsay** [ʌn·ˈseɪ] *irr vt* desdecirse de ▶ **what's underlined cannot be unsaid** lo dicho, dicho está

**unscathed** [ʌn·ˈskeɪðd] *adj* ileso, -a; **to escape ~** escapar ileso

**unscheduled** [ʌn·ˈskedʒ·ʊld] *adj* no programado, -a; (*train, landing*) no previsto, -a

**unscientific** [ˌʌn·ˌsaɪ·ən·ˈtɪf·ɪk] *adj* sin rigor científico

**unscrupulous** [ʌn·ˈskru·pjə·ləs] *adj* sin escrúpulos

**unseat** [ʌn·ˈsit] *vt* POL derrocar

**unsecured** [ˌʌn·sɪ·ˈkjʊrd] *adj* no sujeto, -a; (*stock, funds*) no garantizado, -a; (*loan*) sin aval

**unseemly** [ʌn·ˈsim·li] *adj* impropio, -a

**unseen** [ʌn·ˈsin] *adj* (*unnoticed*) sin ser visto, -a; **to do sth ~** hacer algo inadvertidamente; **sight** ~ a ciegas

**unselfish** [ʌnˈsel·fɪʃ] *adj* generoso, -a

**unsettle** [ʌnˈset·əl] *vt* alterar; (*market*) desestabilizar

**unsettled** [ʌnˈset·əld] *adj* **1.** (*changeable*) inestable **2.** (*troubled*) inquieto, -a **3.** (*unresolved*) no resuelto, -a

**unsettling** [ʌnˈset·əl·ɪŋ] *adj* (*disquieting*) inquietante; (*perturbing*) perturbador(a)

**unshakable** [ʌnˈʃeɪ·kə·bəl] *adj* inquebrantable

**unshaved** *adj*, **unshaven** [ʌnˈʃeɪ·vən] *adj* sin afeitar

**unsightly** [ʌnˈsaɪt·li] <-ier, -iest> *adj* feo, -a

**unsigned** [ʌnˈsaɪnd] *adj* sin firmar

**unskilled** [ʌnˈskɪld] *adj* **1.** (*person*) no cualificado, -a; **to be ~ at** (**doing**) **sth** no estar cualificado para (hacer) algo **2.** (*job*) no especializado, -a

**unsociable** [ʌnˈsou·ʃə·bəl] *adj* insociable

**unsocial** [ʌnˈsou·ʃəl] *adj* insociable

**unsold** [ʌnˈsould] *adj* sin vender

**unsolved** [ʌnˈsalvd] *adj* sin resolver

**unsophisticated** [ʌn·sə·ˈfɪs·tə·keɪ·tɪd] *adj* sencillo, -a; (*machine*) simple; (*person*) ingenuo, -a

**unspeakable** [ʌnˈspi·kə·bəl] *adj* indecible

**unstable** [ʌnˈsteɪ·bəl] *adj* a. PSYCH inestable

**unstuck** [ʌnˈstʌk] *adj* **to** (**be**)**come ~** despegarse; (*fail*) irse al garete

**unsuccessful** [ˌʌn·sək·ˈses·fəl] *adj* sin éxito; (*candidate*) fracasado, -a; **to be ~ in** (**doing**) **sth** fracasar en/no lograr hacer algo

**unsuitable** [ʌnˈsu·tə·bəl] *adj* inapropiado, -a (**for** para); (*moment*) inoportuno, -a *m*; **to be ~ to the occasion** no ajustarse a la ocasión

**unsung** [ʌnˈsʌŋ] *adj* olvidado, -a

**unsure** [ʌnˈʃʊr] *adj* inseguro, -a; **to be ~ how/what...** no ser seguro cómo/qué...; **to be ~ about sth** no estar seguro de algo

**unsuspecting** [ˌʌn·sə·ˈspek·tɪŋ] *adj* confiado, -a; **all ~** nada suspicaz

**unsustainable** [ˌʌn·sə·ˈsteɪ·nə·bəl] *adj*

insostenible

**untangle** [ʌnˈtæn·gəl] *vt* desenredar; (*mystery*) desentrañar

**untapped** [ʌnˈtæpt] *adj* (*resources*) sin explotar

**unthinkable** [ʌnˈθɪŋ·kə·bəl] *adj* inconcebible; (*shocking*) impensable

**unthinking** [ʌnˈθɪŋ·kɪŋ] *adj* **1.** (*thoughtless*) irreflexivo, -a **2.** (*unintentional*) no intencionado, -a

**untidy** [ʌnˈtaɪ·di] <-ier, -iest> *adj* desordenado, -a; (*appearance*) desaliñado, -a

**untie** [ʌnˈtaɪ] <-y-> *vt* desatar; **to ~ one's shoelaces** desatarse los cordones

**until** [ənˈtɪl] **I.** *adv* hasta; **~ then** hasta entonces **II.** *conj* hasta que +*subj*; **~ he comes** hasta que venga; **not ~ sb does sth** no hasta que alguien haga algo

**untimely** [ʌnˈtaɪm·li] *adj* **1.** (*premature*) prematuro, -a **2.** (*inopportune*) inoportuno, -a

**untold** [ʌnˈtould] *adj* **1.** (*immense*) incalculable **2.** (*not told*) nunca contado, -a

**untouched** [ʌnˈtʌtʃt] *adj* **1.** (*not affected*) intacto, -a; **to leave sth ~** dejar algo intacto **2.** (*not eaten*) sin probar; **to leave a meal ~** ni probar una comida **3.** (*not moved*) insensible

**untreated** [ʌnˈtri·tɪd] *adj* no tratado, -a

**untrue** [ʌnˈtru] *adj* **1.** (*false*) falso, -a **2.** (*unfaithful*) infiel (**to** a)

**untrustworthy** [ʌnˈtrʌst·ˌwɜr·ði] *adj* **to be ~** no ser de fiar

**untruthful** [ʌnˈtruθ·fəl] *adj* falso, -a; (*liar*) mentiroso, -a

**unused** [ʌnˈjuzd] *adj* no usado, -a; (*talent, energy*) malgastado, -a; (*goods, clothes*) sin estrenar

**unusual** [ʌnˈju·ʒu·əl] *adj* **1.** (*not usual*) inusual; **to be ~ for sb** ser poco usual en alguien **2.** (*atypically positive*) inusitado, -a **3.** (*atypically negative*) insólito, -a

**unveil** [ʌnˈveɪl] *vt fig* presentar

**unwanted** [ʌnˈwan·tɪd] *adj* no deseado, -a

**unwarranted** [ʌnˈwɔr·ən·tɪd] *adj* **1.** (*not justified*) injustificado, -a; (*criticism*) infundado, -a **2.** (*not authorized*) no autorizado, -a

**unwell** [ʌnˈwel] *adj* indispuesto, -a; **to**

**U**

**feel** ~ sentirse mal

**unwieldy** [ʌnˈwil·di] *adj* abultado, -a; *fig* poco manejable

**unwilling** [ʌnˈwɪl·ɪŋ] *adj* no dispuesto, -a; **to be ~ to do** sth no estar dispuesto a hacer algo; **to be ~ for** sb **to do** sth no querer que alguien haga algo

**unwillingly** *adv* de mala gana

**unwind** [ʌnˈwaɪnd] *irr* I. *vt* desenrollar II. *vi* 1. (*unroll*) desenrollarse 2. (*relax*) relajarse

**unwise** [ʌnˈwaɪz] *adj* imprudente

**unwitting** [ʌnˈwɪt·ɪŋ] *adj* 1. (*unaware*) inconsciente 2. (*unintentional*) involuntario, -a

**unwittingly** *adv* sin darse cuenta

**unworthy** [ʌnˈwɜr·ði] <-ier, -iest> *adj* que no vale la pena; (*person*) indigno, -a

**unwrap** [ʌnˈræp] <-pp-> *vt* desenvolver; *fig* sacar a la luz

**unwritten** [ʌnˈrɪt·ən] *adj* no escrito, -a; (*agreement*) verbal

**unzip** [ʌnˈzɪp] <-pp-> *vt* abrir la cremallera de

**up** [ʌp] I. *adv* 1. (*movement*) (hacia) arriba; ~ **here/there** aquí/allí arriba; **to look** ~ mirar (hacia) arriba; **to stand/get** ~ levantarse; **to go** ~ subir; (**stand**) ~! ¡arriba!; ~ **in Seattle** allá en Seattle 2. **to be ~ all night** no dormir en toda la noche; **with one's head** ~ con la cabeza en alto 3. (*limit*) **time's** ~ se acabó el tiempo; **when 5 hours were** ~ cuando pasaron 5 horas; **from the age of 18** ~ a partir de los 18 años; **to have it** ~ **to one's ears** estar hasta la coronilla (**with** de) 4. SPORTS (*ahead*) por delante ▶ ~ **and down** arriba y abajo; <u>what's</u> ~? ¿qué hay de nuevo?; <u>what's</u> ~ **with him?** ¿qué le pasa? II. *prep* encima de; **to climb** ~ **a tree** subirse a un árbol; **to go** ~ **the stairs** subir las escaleras; **to run** ~ **the slope** correr cuesta arriba; **to go** ~ **the street** ir por la calle III. *n* ~**s and downs** altibajos *mpl;* **to be on the** ~ **and** ~ estar cada vez mejor IV. *adj* 1. (*position:* tent) montado, -a; (*curtains, picture*) colgado, -a; (*hand*) alzado, -a; (*person*) levantado, -a 2. (*ready*) **to be** ~ **and about** [*or* **around**] estar en

buena forma; **to be** ~ **for** (**doing**) sth estar listo para (hacer) algo; ~ **for sale/trial** a la venta/en juicio

**up-and-coming** [ˈʌp·ən·ˈkʌm·ɪŋ] *adj* joven y prometedor(a)

**upbeat** [ˈʌp·bit] *adj* optimista (**about** respecto a)

**upbringing** [ˈʌp·brɪŋ·ɪŋ] *n* educación *f;* **to have a good** ~ tener una buena educación

**upcoming** [ˈʌp·kʌm·ɪŋ] *adj* venidero, -a

**update** [ˈʌp·deɪt] I. *vt* poner al día; COMPUT actualizar II. *n* puesta *f* al día; COMPUT actualización *f;* **to give** sb **an** ~ poner a alguien al día (**on** de)

**upgrade** [ˈʌp·ɡreɪd] I. *vt* mejorar; COMPUT modernizar; **to** ~ sb ascender a alguien (**to** a) II. *vi* mejorar **III.** *n* 1. COMPUT, TECH, COM mejora *f;* **software** ~ modernización del software; **to be on the** ~ ir progresando; MED ir recuperándose 2. (*slope*) cuesta *f*

**upheaval** [ʌp·ˈhi·vəl] *n* 1. sacudida *f;* **political** ~ convulsión *f* política 2. GEO solevamiento *m*

**uphill** [ʌp·ˈhɪl] I. *adv* cuesta arriba; **to run/walk** ~ correr/ir cuesta arriba II. *adj* 1. ascendente 2. (*difficult*) difícil

**uphold** [ʌp·ˈhoʊld] *irr vt* sostener; **to** ~ **the principle that...** defender el principio de que...

**upholster** [ʌp·ˈhoʊl·stər] *vt* tapizar

**upholstery** *n* 1. (*covering*) tapizado *m;* **leather** ~ tapizado de piel 2. (*craft*) tapicería *f*

**UPI** [ju·pi·ˈaɪ] *n abbr of* **United Press International** UPI *f*

**upkeep** [ˈʌp·kip] *n* mantenimiento *m;* (*cost*) gastos *m pl* de mantenimiento

**uplift** [ʌp·ˈlɪft] *vt* elevar; *fig* inspirar

**uplifting** [ʌp·ˈlɪf·tɪŋ] *adj* positivo, -a

**upload** [ˈʌp·loʊd] *vt* subir

**upon** [əˈpɑn] *prep form* 1. (*on top of*) encima de; **to hang** ~ **the wall** colgar en la pared 2. (*around*) en 3. ~ **her arrival** a su llegada; ~ **this** acto seguido; **once** ~ **a time** érase una vez

**upper** [ˈʌp·ər] I. *adj* superior; ~ **management** altos cargos; **the** ~ **Northeast** el alto nordeste II. *n* (*drug*) anfeta *f*

**upper class** <-es> *n* clase *f* alta

**upper-class** *adj* de clase alta

**uppermost** **I.** *adj* más alto, -a **II.** *adv* boca arriba; **to put sth ~** poner algo boca arriba

**upright** [ˈʌp·raɪt] **I.** *adj* recto, -a; (*post, rod*) vertical; (*citizen*) honrado, -a **II.** *adv* verticalmente; **to stand ~** permanecer erguido; **to sit bolt ~** estar muy derecho en la silla **III.** *n* SPORTS poste *m*

**uprising** [ˈʌp·raɪ·zɪŋ] *n* alzamiento *m*

**uproar** [ˈʌp·rɔr] *n* alboroto *m*, batifondo *m CSur*, tinga *f Méx*; **to cause an ~** provocar un escándalo

**uproot** [ʌp·ˈrut] *vt* arrancar de raíz; *fig* desarraigar; **to ~ oneself** perder las raíces

**upset¹** [ʌp·ˈset] **I.** *vt irr* **1.** (*unsettle*) trastornar; (*distress*) afligir **2.** (*untidy*) alborotar **3.** (*overturn*) derrumbar **II.** *adj.* **1.** (*disquieted*) perturbado, -a; (*sad*) apenado, -a; **to get ~** enfadarse (**about** por); **to be ~ (that)...** estar enfadado (porque)...; **don't be ~** no te enfades **2.** **to have an ~ stomach** tener el estómago revuelto **3.** (*overturned*) trastornado, -a

**upset²** [ˈʌp·set] *n* **1.** (*surprise*) sorpresa *f* **2.** **stomach ~** trastorno *m* estomacal **3.** (*trouble*) disgusto *m*

**upside down** [ʌp·saɪd·ˈdaʊn] *adv* al revés; **to turn sth ~** poner algo del revés

**upstage** [ʌp·ˈsteɪdʒ] *vt* eclipsar

**upstairs** [ʌp·ˈsterz] **I.** *adj* de arriba **II.** *adv* arriba; **to go ~** ir arriba; **the people who live ~** los vecinos de arriba **III.** *n* piso *m* de arriba

**upstate** [ˈʌp·steɪt] **I.** *adj* del norte; **in ~ New York** en el norte de Nueva York **II.** *adv* en el norte

**upstream** [ʌp·ˈstrim] *adv* río arriba; **to swim ~** nadar contra la corriente

**upsurge** [ˈʌp·sɜrdʒ] *n* aumento *m* (**in** de)

**uptake** [ˈʌp·teɪk] *n* **to be quick on the ~** cogerlas al vuelo; **to be slow on the ~** ser algo corto

**uptight** [ʌp·ˈtaɪt] *adj* **to be/get ~** estar/ponerse de mala leche (**about** por)

**up-to-date** [ʌp·tə·ˈdeɪt] *adj* **1.** (*contemporary*) moderno, -a; (*book*) actualizado, -a **2.** (*informed*) al día; **to bring sb ~** poner a alguien al corriente

**up-to-the-minute** [ˈʌp·tə·ðə·ˈmɪn·ɪt] *adj* de última hora

**uptown** [ˈʌp·taʊn] *adj* residencial; **in ~ Manhattan** en el norte de Manhattan

**upturn** [ˈʌp·tɜrn] *n* mejora *f*

**upturned** [ʌp·ˈtɜrnd] *adj* vuelto, -a hacia arriba; (*nose*) respingón, -ona

**upward** [ˈʌp·wərd] **I.** *adj* ascendente **II.** *adv* (hacia) arriba; (*in number*) al alza; **to go ~** ir en aumento

**upwards** *adv* (hacia) arriba; **and ~** y más

**uranium** [ju·ˈreɪ·ni·əm] *n* uranio *m*

**urban** [ˈɜr·bən] *adj* urbano, -a; **~ area** zona urbana; **~ decay** deterioro urbano

**urbane** [ɜr·ˈbeɪn] *adj* fino, -a

**urbanization** [ˌɜr·bə·nɪ·ˈzeɪ·ʃən] *n* urbanización *f*

**urchin** [ˈɜr·tʃɪn] *n* iron pilluelo, -a *m*, *f*

**urethra** [jʊ·ˈri·θrə] <-s *or* -e> *n* uretra *f*

**urge** [ɜrdʒ] **I.** *n* (*desire*) ansia *f*; (*compulsion*) impulso *m*; PSYCH instinto *m*; **an ~ to do sth** un impulso de hacer algo; **an ~ for power** un afán de poder; **an irresistible ~** un impulso irresistible; **an uncontrollable ~** un deseo incontrolable; **to control/repress an ~** controlar/reprimir un impulso **II.** *vt* **1.** (*encourage*) fomentar; **to ~ sb to do sth** instar a alguien a hacer algo; **to ~ sb into sth** incitar a alguien a algo **2.** (*recommend*) recomendar ((**up**)**on** a)

◆**urge on** *vt* **to urge sb on** animar a alguien (**to** a)

**urgency** [ˈɜr·dʒən·si] *n* urgencia *f*; **to be a matter of (great) ~** ser un asunto de (gran) urgencia; **to realize/stress the ~** darse cuenta de/remarcar la urgencia (**of** de)

**urgent** [ˈɜr·dʒənt] *adj* urgente; (*insistent*) insistente; **to be in ~ need of sth** necesitar algo urgentemente

**urgently** *adv* urgentemente; (*earnestly*) insistentemente

**urinal** [ˈjʊr·ə·nəl] *n* urinario *m*

**urinate** [ˈjʊr·ə·neɪt] *vi* orinar

**urine** [ˈjʊr·ɪn] *n* orina *f*

**urn** [ɜrn] *n* urna *f*; (*tea*) tetera *f*

**Uruguay** [ˈjʊr·ə·gwaɪ] *n* Uruguay *m*

**Uruguayan** [ˌjʊr·ə·ˈgwaɪ·ən] *adj, n* uru-

U

guayo, -a *m, f*

**us** [əs, *stressed:* ʌs] *pron pers* nos *after prep* nosotros, -as; **it's ~** somos nosotros; **look at ~** míranos; **he saw ~** nos vio; **he gave it to ~** nos lo dio

**USA** [ˌju·es·ˈeɪ] *n abbr of* **United States** EE.UU. *mpl*

**usage** [ˈju·sɪdʒ] *n* **1.** **a.** LING uso *m*; **in common/general ~** de uso común/general **2.** (*treatment*) tratamiento *m*

**use¹** [jus] *n* **1.** (*application*) uso *m*; (*possibility of applying*) empleo *m*; **in ~** en uso; **to be of/no ~** (no) ser de utilidad (**to** para); **it's no ~** es inútil; **there's no ~ doing sth** no sirve de nada hacer algo; **to make ~ of** utilizar; **to be out of ~** estar fuera de servicio; **to come into ~** empezar a utilizarse; **to go out of ~** quedar en desuso **2.** (*consumption*) consumo *m*

**use²** [juz] **I.** *vt* **1.** (*make use of*) usar (**to** para, **against** en contra de); (*skills, training*) hacer uso de; **I could ~ some help** no me vendría mal una mano **2.** (*employ*) emplear; **to ~ discretion** ser discreto **3.** (*consume, manipulate*) utilizar; (*exploit*) explotar; (*energy, drugs*) consumir **II.** *vi* **he ~d to...** solía...; **did you ~ to work in banking?** ¿trabajabas en banca?

♦**use up** *vt* agotar

**used** [juzd] *adj* usado, -a; (*clothes, car*) de segunda mano

**used to** *adj* **to be ~** estar acostumbrado a; **to become ~** acostumbrarse a; **to be ~ doing sth** tener la costumbre de hacer algo

**useful** [ˈjus·fəl] *adj* **1.** (*convenient*) útil (**for** para) **2.** (*beneficial*) beneficioso, -a; (*experience*) positivo, -a **3.** (*effective*) eficaz; (*competent*) competente (**with** en)

**usefulness** *n* utilidad *f*; (*applicability*) aplicabilidad *f*; (*relevance*) relevancia *f*

**useless** [ˈjus·lɪs] *adj* **1.** (*in vain*) inútil; **to be ~ doing sth** ser inútil hacer algo; **to be ~ to do sth** no servir de nada el hacer algo **2.** (*unusable*) inservible; **to be/become ~** no ser/dejar de ser de utilidad (**for** para) **3.** *inf* (*incompetent*) incompetente; **to be worse than ~** no

servir para nada

**user** *n* **a.** COMPUT usuario, -a *m, f*; (*gas, drug*) consumidor(a) *m(f)*

**user-friendly** *adj* COMPUT fácil de usar

**usher** [ˈʌʃ·ər] *n* CINE acomodador(a) *m(f)*

**usual** [ˈju·ʒu·əl] **I.** *adj* habitual; **as ~** como de costumbre; **to be ~ for sb** (**to do sth**) ser habitual para alguien (hacer algo) **II.** *n* **the ~** lo de siempre

**usually** *adv* normalmente

**usurp** [ju·ˈsɜrp] *vt* usurpar

**utensil** [ju·ˈten·səl] *n* utensilio *m*; **kitchen ~s** utensilios de cocina

**uterus** [ˈju·tər·əs] <-ri *or* -es> *n* útero *m*

**utilitarian** [ju·ˌtɪl·ə·ˈter·i·ən] *adj* utilitario, -a

**utility** [ju·ˈtɪl·ə·ti] <-ies> *n* **1.** (*usefulness*) utilidad *f* **2.** (*public service*) empresa *f* de servicio público **3.** COMPUT herramienta *f*

**utilization** [ˌju·tə·lɪ·ˈzeɪ·ʃən] *n* utilización *f*

**utilize** [ˈju·tə·laɪz] *vt* utilizar

**utmost** [ˈʌt·moʊst] **I.** *adj* mayor; **with the ~ care** con sumo cuidado; **the ~ difficulty** la máxima dificultad; **of ~ importance** de primerísima importancia **II.** *n* **the ~** lo máximo; **to the ~** al máximo; **to try one's ~** hacer todo lo posible (**to** para, por)

**utopia** [ju·ˈtoʊ·pi·ə] *n* utopía *f*

**utopian** *adj* utópico, -a

**utter¹** [ˈʌt·ər] *adj* (*complete*) completo, -a; **in ~ despair** en la más absoluta desesperación

**utter²** [ˈʌt·ər] *vt* (*say*) pronunciar; (*warning*) dar; **to ~ a threat** amenazar; **without ~ing a word** sin mediar palabra

**utterance** [ˈʌt·ər·əns] *n* **1.** LING enunciado *m* **2.** (*style*) expresión *f*; **to give ~ to a feeling** manifestar un sentimiento

**utterly** *adv* completamente; (*despise, hate*) profundamente

**U-turn** [ˈju·tɜrn] *n* AUTO cambio *m* de sentido; *fig* giro *m* de 180º

**UV** [ˌju·ˈvi] *abbr of* **ultraviolet** UV

# V

**V, v** [vi] *n* V, v *f*; **~ as in Victor** V de Valencia

**V 1.** *abbr of* **velocity** V **2.** *abbr of* **volt** V **3.** *abbr of* **volume** vol. **4.** *(five)* V

**vac** [væk] *inf* **I.** *n* **1.** *abbr of* **vacuum cleaner** aspirador *m* **2.** *abbr of* **vacuum** vacío *m* **II.** <-cc-> *vt, vi* pasar el aspirador (a)

**vacancy** ['veɪ·kən·si] <-ies> *n* **1.** *(room)* habitación *f* libre; **'~'** 'habitaciones libres'; **'no ~'** 'completo' **2.** *(job)* vacante *f*; **to fill a ~** ocupar una vacante

**vacant** ['veɪ·kənt] *adj* vacío, -a; *(seat, room)* libre; *(job)* vacante; **'~'** 'libre'; **to leave sth/become ~** dejar algo/ quedarse vacante

**vacate** ['veɪ·keɪt] *vt form (place, seat)* dejar libre; *(room, house)* desocupar; *(job, post)* dejar vacante

**vacation** [veɪ·'keɪ·ʃən] *n* vacaciones *fpl*; **on ~** de vacaciones; **to take a ~** tomarse unas vacaciones

**vaccinate** ['væk·sə·neɪt] *vt* vacunar **(against** contra)

**vaccination** [ˌvæk·sə·'neɪ·ʃən] *n* vacunación *f* **(against** contra)

**vaccine** [væk·'sin] *n* vacuna *f*

**vacillate** ['væs·ə·leɪt] *vi* vacilar **(between** entre); **to ~ between hope and despair** oscilar entre la esperanza y la desesperación

**vacuum** ['væk·jum] **I.** *n* vacío *m*; **to fill/ leave a ~** llenar/dejar un vacío; **to live in a ~** vivir en una burbuja **II.** *vt* pasar la aspiradora a

**vacuum cleaner** *n* aspirador *m*

**vacuum-packaged** *adj*, **vacuum-packed** [ˌvæk·jum·'pækt] *adj* envasado, -a al vacío

**vagina** [və·'dʒaɪ·nə] *n* vagina *f*

**vagrant** ['veɪ·grənt] *adj, n* vagabundo, -a *m, f*

**vague** [veɪg] *adj (promise)* vago, -a; *(word)* impreciso, -a; *(outline)* borroso, -a; *(expression)* distraído, -a; *(person)* despistado, -a

**vain** [veɪn] *adj (person)* vanidoso, -a; *(attempt, hope)* vano, -a; **it is ~ to...** es

inútil...; **in ~** en vano; **it was all in ~** todo fue en vano

**valentine** ['væl·ən·taɪn] *n* **1.** *(card)* tarjeta de San Valentín **2.** *(sweetheart)* enamorado, -a *m, f*; **be my ~!** ¿quieres ser mi novio?

**Valentine's Day** *n* día *m* de los enamorados [*or* San Valentín]

**valet** [væ·'leɪ] *n (car parker)* aparcacoches *mf inv*

**valid** ['væl·ɪd] *adj* **1.** válido, -a; **no longer ~** caducado, -a **2.** LAW vigente; *(binding)* vinculante

**validate** ['væl·ə·deɪt] *vt* dar validez a; *(document)* validar; *(ticket)* picar

**validity** [və·'lɪd·ə·ti] *n* validez *f*; *(law)* vigencia *f*

**valley** ['væl·i] *n* valle *m*

**valuable** ['væl·ju·ə·bəl] **I.** *adj (help, ring)* valioso, -a; *(time)* precioso, -a **II.** *n* **~s** objetos *m pl* de valor

**valuation** [ˌvæl·ju·'eɪ·ʃən] *n* valoración *f*; *(estimation)* tasación *f*

**value** ['væl·ju] **I.** *n a.* MATH, MUS valor *m*; **~ judgment** juicio de valor; **set of ~s** escala de valores; **of little ~** de poco valor; **to be of (great) ~** ser (muy) valioso **(to** para); **to be a good ~** estar bien de precio; **to put a ~** poner precio **(on** a); **to place a high ~** dar mucha importancia **(on** a) **II.** *vt* **1.** *(regard highly)* apreciar **2.** FIN tasar **(at** en)

**valued** *adj* apreciado, -a; *(customer)* valioso, -a

**valueless** ['væl·ju·lɪs] *adj* sin valor

**valve** [vælv] *n* **1.** AUTO, ANAT válvula *f* **2.** ELEC lámpara *f*

**vampire** ['væm·paɪr] *n* vampiro *m*

**van¹** [væn] *n* AUTO furgoneta *f*; **delivery ~** furgoneta de reparto; **moving ~** camión *m* de mudanzas

**van²** [væn] *n inf abbr of* **vanguard** vanguardia *f*

**vandal** ['væn·dəl] *n* gamberro, -a *m, f*

**vandalism** ['væn·də·lɪz·əm] *n* vandalismo *m*

**vandalize** ['væn·də·laɪz] *vt* destrozar

**vanguard** ['væn·gard] *n* vanguardia *f*

**vanilla** [və·'nɪl·ə] *n* vainilla *f*

**vanish** ['væn·ɪʃ] *vi* desaparecer **(from** de); **to ~ into thin air** esfumarse

**vanity** ['væn·ə·t̬i] <-ies> n 1. (*pride*) vanidad f 2. (*dressing table*) tocador m

**vanity bag** n, **vanity case** n neceser m

**vantage point** n mirador m; fig posición f ventajosa

**vapor** ['veɪ·pər] n vapor m; **water** ~ vapor de agua; (*on glass*) vaho m, vaporizo m Méx, PRico

**variable** ['vær·i·ə·bəl] adj, n variable

**variance** ['vær·i·əns] n 1. (*disagreement*) discrepancia f; **at** ~ en contradicción; **to be at** ~ discrepar (**with** en); **to set two people at** ~ sembrar la discordia entre dos personas 2. (*variation*) variación f

**variant** ['vær·i·ənt] n variante f

**variation** [,vær·i·eɪ·ʃən] n 1. a. BIO, MUS variación f (**on** de) 2. (*difference*) diferencia f; **wide** ~s grandes diferencias (**in** de)

**varicose** ['vær·ə·koʊs] adj ~ **veins** varices fpl

**varied** ['vær·id] adj variado, -a; (*colors*) multicolor

**variety** [və·raɪ·ə·t̬i] <-ies> n 1. (*diversity*) a. BIO variedad f; **to lend** ~ variar 2. (*assortment*) surtido m; **in a** ~ **of ways** de diversas formas 3. (*sort*) tipo m ▶ ~ **is the spice of life** en la variedad está el gusto

**variety show** n programa m de variedades; THEAT espectáculo m de variedades

**various** ['vær·i·əs] adj 1. (*numerous*) varios, -as; **for** ~ **reasons** por diversas razones 2. (*diverse*) diferentes

**varmint** ['var·mɪnt] n a. fig alimaña f

**varnish** ['var·nɪʃ] I. n barniz m II. vt barnizar

**vary** ['vær·i] <-ie-> I. vi 1. (*change*) variar; **opinions** ~ hay diversidad de opiniones; **to** ~ **between... and...** oscilar entre... y...; **to** ~ **from...** diferenciarse de... 2. (*diverge*) desviarse; **to** ~ **from...** apartarse de... II. vt 1. (*change*) variar 2. (*diversify*) diversificar

**varying** adj variable

**vase** [veɪs] n jarrón m

**vast** [væst] adj enorme; (*area, region*) vasto, -a; (*importance, amount of money*) considerable; (*majority, knowledge*) amplio, -a

**vastly** adv sumamente; ~ **superior** infi-

nitamente superior

**vat** [væt] n tanque m

**Vatican** ['væt̬·ɪ·kən] n Vaticano m

**vault¹** [vɔlt] n 1. ARCHIT bóveda f; (*under churches*) cripta f; (*at cemeteries*) panteón m 2. (*basement*) sótano m; (*bank*) cámara acorazada

**vault²** [vɔlt] (*jump*) I. n salto m II. vi, vt saltar

**vaulting horse** n potro m

**veal** [vil] n ternera f

**veal cutlet** n chuleta f de ternera

**vector** ['vek·tər] n 1. MATH vector m 2. BIO, MED portador(a) m(f)

**veer** [vɪr] vi (*vehicle*) virar; (*wind*) cambiar; (*road, way*) torcer; (*attitude, goal*) cambiar bruscamente; **to** ~ **towards sth** dar un giro hacia algo

**vegan** ['vi·gən] n vegan mf

**vegetable** ['vedʒ·tə·bəl] n vegetal m; (*edible*) hortaliza f; (**green**) ~ verdura f; **seasonal** ~ verdura del tiempo; **root** ~ tubérculo m; ~ **soup** sopa de verduras

**vegetable garden** n huerto m

**vegetable kingdom** n reino m vegetal

**vegetable oil** n aceite m vegetal

**vegetarian** [,vedʒ·ə·ter·i·ən] adj, n vegetariano, -a m, f; **to go** ~ hacerse vegetariano

**vegetate** ['vedʒ·ə·teɪt] vi a. fig vegetar

**vegetation** [,vedʒ·ə·ter·ʃən] n vegetación f

**veg(g)ie** ['vedʒ·i] n inf 1. vegetariano, -a m, f 2. ~s verdura f

**veggieburger** n hamburguesa f vegetariana

**vehemence** ['vi·ə·məns] n vehemencia f

**vehement** ['vi·ə·mənt] adj vehemente

**vehicle** ['vi·ə·kəl] n 1. AUTO vehículo m; **motor** ~ vehículo motorizado 2. (*of expression*) medio m; **to be a** ~ servir de vehículo (**for** para)

**veil** [veɪl] I. n velo m; **a** ~ **of secrecy** un halo de misterio; **under the** ~ bajo el pretexto (**of** de); **to draw a** ~ correr un tupido velo (**over** sobre) II. vt velar; (*disguise*) disimular

**veiled** adj (*wearing a veil*) cubierto, -a con velo; (*thinly* ~ apenas disimulado

**vein** [veɪn] n ANAT, BOT vena f; GEO veta f

**Velcro®** ['vel·kroʊ] n velcro® m

**velocity** [və·'las·ə·t̬i] <-ies> *n* velocidad *f*; **at the ~ of** a la velocidad de; **sound/ light ~** velocidad del sonido/de la luz

**velvet** ['vel·vɪt] I. *n* terciopelo *m* II. *adj* de terciopelo; *fig* aterciopelado, -a

**velvety** ['vel·və·t̬i] *adj fig* aterciopelado, -a

**vendetta** [ven·'det̬·ə] *n* vendetta *f*

**vending machine** *n* máquina *f* expendedora

**vendor** ['ven·dər] *n* vendedor(a) *m(f)*

**veneer** [və·'nɪr] *n* chapado *m*; *fig* apariencia *f*

**venereal** [və·'nɪr·i·əl] *adj* venéreo, -a

**venetian blind** [və·ˌni·ʃən·'blaɪnd] *n* persiana *f* veneciana

**Venezuela** [ˌven·ə·'zwer·lə] *n* Venezuela *f*

**Venezuelan** *adj, n* venezolano, -a *m, f*

**vengeance** ['ven·dʒəns] *n* venganza *f*; **to take ~** vengarse ((up)on de); **with a ~** con ganas

**venison** ['ven·ɪ·sən] *n* venado *m*

**venom** ['ven·əm] *n* veneno *m*; *fig* malevolencia *f*

**venomous** ['ven·ə·məs] *adj* venenoso, -a; *(malicious)* maligno, -a

**vent** [vent] I. *n* conducto *m* de ventilación; **air ~** respiradero *m* II. *vt (feelings)* dar rienda suelta a; *(opinion)* expresar; *(anger)* descargar **(on** contra)

**ventilate** ['ven·t̬ə·leɪt] *vt* ventilar; **artificially ~d** con respiración asistida

**ventilation** [ˌven·t̬ə·'leɪ·ʃən] *n* ventilación *f*

**ventilator** ['ven·t̬ə·leɪ·t̬ər] *n* ventilador *m*; MED respirador *m*

**ventricle** ['ven·trɪ·kəl] *n* ventrículo *m*

**ventriloquist** [ven·'trɪl·ə·kwɪst] *n* ventrílocuo, -a *m, f*

**venture** ['ven·tʃər] I. *n* aventura *f*; COM empresa *f* II. *vt* 1. *(dare)* atreverse **(to** a); *(opinion)* aventurar 2. *(endanger)* arriesgar **(on** en) III. *vi* aventurarse

**venture capital** *n* capital *m* de riesgo

**venue** ['ven·ju] *n* lugar *m*; SPORTS campo *m*

**Venus** ['vi·nəs] *n* Venus *m*

**veranda** *n*, **verandah** [və·'ræn·də] *n* porche *m*

**verb** [vɜrb] *n* verbo *m*

**verbal** ['vɜr·bəl] *adj* 1. *(oral)* verbal; **~ agreement** acuerdo verbal; **~ facility** facilidad de palabra 2. *(word for word)* literal

**verbally** *adv* verbalmente

**verbatim** [vər·'beɪ·t̬ɪm] I. *adj* literal II. *adv* literalmente

**verbose** [vər·'boʊs] *adj* verboso, -a

**verdict** ['vɜr·dɪkt] *n* 1. LAW fallo *m*; *(by jury)* veredicto *m*; **to bring in** [*or* **return**] **a ~** dictar sentencia; *(jury)* emitir un veredicto 2. *(conclusion)* juicio *m* **(on** sobre); **what is your ~?** ¿qué opinas?

**verge** [vɜrdʒ] *n* margen *m*; *fig* borde *m*; **to be on the ~** estar al borde **(of** de); **to be on the ~ of doing sth** estar a punto de hacer algo

♦**verge on** *vt* rayar en; **she is verging on fifty** ronda los cincuenta

**verification** [ˌver·ə·fɪ·'keɪ·ʃən] *n* 1. *(checking)* verificación *f* 2. *(confirmation)* confirmación *f*

**verify** ['ver·ə·faɪ] <-ie-> *vt* 1. *(corroborate)* confirmar 2. *(authenticate)* verificar

**vermicelli** [ˌvɜr·mə·'tʃel·i] *n* fideos *m pl* finos

**vermin** ['vɜr·mɪn] *n* 1. *pl* alimañas *fpl*; *(insects)* bichos *mpl* 2. *(people)* gentuza *f*

**vermouth** [vər·'muθ] *n* vermut *m*

**versatile** ['vɜr·sə·t̬əl] *adj* 1. *(flexible)* versátil; *(mind)* ágil 2. *(multifaceted)* polifacético, -a

**versatility** [ˌvɜr·sə·'tɪl·ə·t̬i] *n* versatilidad *f*; *(mental)* agilidad *f*

**verse** [vɜrs] *n* LIT verso *m*; MUS estrofa *f*; REL versículo *m*

**versed** *adj* **to be (well) ~** estar (muy) versado **(in** en)

**version** ['vɜr·ʒən] *n* versión *f*

**versus** ['vɜr·səs] *prep* frente a; SPORTS, LAW contra

**vertebra** ['vɜr·t̬ə·brə] <-ae> *n* vértebra *f*

**vertebrate** ['vɜr·t̬ə·brɪt] I. *n* vertebrado *m* II. *adj* vertebrado, -a

**vertical** ['vɜr·t̬ə·kəl] *adj* vertical; **~ drop** caída en picado

**vertigo** ['vɜr·t̬ə·goʊ] *n* vértigo *m*

**verve** [vɜrv] *n* ímpetu *m*; **with ~** con brío

**very** ['ver·i] I. adv muy; (not) ~ much (no) mucho; I am ~, ~ sorry de veras lo siento; the ~ best lo mejor de lo mejor; the ~ first el primerísimo; at the ~ most como mucho; at the ~ least por lo menos ▶ to be all ~ **fine**, but... estar muy bien y tal, pero... II. adj at the ~ bottom al final del todo; the ~ fact el mero hecho; the ~ man el mismísimo

**vessel** ['ves·əl] n 1. (boat) embarcación f 2. (container) recipiente m 3. ANAT, BOT vaso m

**vest**[1] [vest] n FASHION chaleco m

**vest**[2] [vest] vt investir (with de, con); (hopes) depositar; to ~ sth in sb conferir algo a alguien

**vestibule** ['ves·tə·bjul] n vestíbulo m

**vet**[1] [vet] inf I. n (animal doctor) veterinario, -a m, f II. vt <-tt-> (examine) examinar

**vet**[2] [vet] n inf MIL veterano, -a m, f

**veteran** ['vet·ər·ən] adj, n veterano, -a m, f

**veterinarian** [,vet·ər·ə·'ner·i·ən] n veterinario, -a m, f

**veterinary** ['vet·ə·rə·ner·i] adj veterinario, -a

**veto** ['vi·t̬ou] I. n <-es> veto m II. vt <vetoed> vetar

**via** ['vaɪ·ə] prep por; ~ Denver/the bridge por Denver/el puente

**viable** ['vaɪ·ə·bəl] adj viable

**viaduct** ['vaɪ·ə·dʌkt] n viaducto m

**vial** ['vaɪ·əl] n ampolla f

**vibrant** ['vaɪ·brənt] adj (personality) enérgico, -a; (color, light) radiante; (economy) en ebullición

**vibrate** ['vaɪ·breɪt] vi vibrar; to ~ with enthusiasm estremecerse de entusiasmo

**vibration** [vaɪ·'breɪ·ʃən] n vibración f

**vicar** ['vɪk·ər] n vicario m

**vicarage** ['vɪk·ər·ɪdʒ] n vicaría f

**vicarious** [vɪ·'ker·i·əs] adj indirecto, -a

**vice** [vaɪs] n vicio m; ~ squad brigada f antivicio

**vice versa** [,vaɪ·sə·'vɜr·sə] adv viceversa

**vicinity** [və·'sɪn·ə·t̬i] <-ies> n inmediaciones fpl; in the ~ of... en los alrededores de...

**vicious** ['vɪʃ·əs] adj (malicious) malicioso, -a; (cruel) despiadado, -a; (fighting) salvaje; (pain) atroz; (wind) devastador(a)

**vicious circle** n círculo m vicioso

**victim** ['vɪk·tɪm] n víctima f; to be the ~ ser víctima (of de) ▶ to **fall** ~ sucumbir (to a)

**victimize** ['vɪk·tə·maɪz] vt discriminar; to be ~d by law ser víctima de la ley

**victor** ['vɪk·tər] n vencedor(a) m(f); to **emerge (as) the** ~ salir victorioso

**Victorian** [vɪk·'tɔr·i·ən] adj victoriano, -a m, f

**victorious** [vɪk·'tɔr·i·əs] adj victorioso, -a

**victory** ['vɪk·tə·ri] <-ies> n victoria f (over sobre); to win a ~ obtener una victoria (in en)

**video** ['vɪd·i·ou] n vídeo m; to come out on ~ salir en vídeo

**video camera** n videocámara f

**video game** n videojuego m

**videophone** n videoteléfono m

**video recorder** n magnetoscopio m

**video surveillance** n vigilancia f con cámaras

**videotape** I. n cinta f de vídeo II. vt grabar en vídeo

**Vietnam** [,vi·et·'nam] n Vietnam m

**Vietnamese** [vi·,et·nə·'miz] I. adj vietnamita II. n 1. (person) vietnamita mf 2. LING vietnamita m

**view** [vju] I. n 1. (opinion) punto m de vista; **exchange of** ~s intercambio m de opiniones; **conflicting** ~s opiniones f pl contrapuestas; to have an optimistic ~ of life ver la vida con optimismo; to hold strong ~s mantener una postura fuerte (about sobre) 2. (perspective) perspectiva f; long-term ~ perspectiva a largo plazo; to take the long ~ of sth considerar algo a largo plazo 3. (sight) vista f; to block sb's ~ estar tapando a alguien; to disappear from ~ perderse de vista ▶ to take a dim ~ of sth ver algo con malos ojos; to have sth in ~ tener algo en mente; in ~ of en vista de; with a ~ to con vistas a; to be on ~ estar expuesto; on ~ to the public abierto al público; with this in ~ con este fin II. vt 1. (consider) considerar; to ~ sth from a different angle

enfocar algo desde un ángulo distinto
2. (*watch*) ver
**viewer** *n* (*person*) telespectador(a) *m(f)*
**viewfinder** ['vju·faɪn·dər] *n* visor *m*
**viewing** *n* visita *f*; **~ figures** índice *m* de audiencia
**viewpoint** ['vju·pɔɪnt] *n* punto *m* de vista
**vigil** ['vɪdʒ·əl] *n* **to keep ~** mantenerse alerta
**vigilance** ['vɪdʒ·ɪ·ləns] *n* vigilancia *f*; **to relax ~** bajar la guardia
**vigilant** ['vɪdʒ·ɪ·lənt] *adj* vigilante; **to be ~ in doing sth** estar atento al hacer algo
**vigor** ['vɪg·ər] *n* vigor *m*; (*energy*) energía *f*
**vigorous** ['vɪg·ər·əs] *adj* enérgico, -a; (*growth*) pujante
**vile** [vaɪl] *adj* **1.** vil **2.** *inf* vomitivo, -a; (*weather*) asqueroso, -a; **~ mood** humor de perros; **to smell ~** apestar
**vilify** ['vɪl·ə·faɪ] <-ie-> *vt* envilecer
**village** ['vɪl·ɪdʒ] **I.** *n* **1.** aldea *f* **2.** + *pl/sing vb* (*populace*) pueblo *m* **II.** *adj* de pueblo
**villager** ['vɪl·ə·dʒər] *n* aldeano, -a *m, f*
**villain** ['vɪl·ən] *n* villano, -a *m, f* ▸ **the ~ of the piece** el malo/la mala de la obra
**vinaigrette** [ˌvɪn·ə·'gret] *n* vinagreta *f*
**vindicate** ['vɪn·də·keɪt] *vt* (*justify*) justificar; (*right*) reivindicar
**vindictive** [vɪn·'dɪk·tɪv] *adj* vengativo, -a
**vine** [vaɪn] *n* vid *f*; (*climbing*) parra *f*
**vinegar** ['vɪn·ə·gər] *n* vinagre *m*
**vineyard** ['vɪn·jərd] *n* viñedo *m*
**vintage** ['vɪn·tɪdʒ] **I.** *n* cosecha *f*; (*season*) vendimia *f* **II.** *adj* **1.** CULIN añejo, -a **2.** ~ **car** coche de época
**vinyl** ['vaɪ·nəl] *n* vinilo *m*
**viola** [vi·'oʊ·lə] *n* MUS viola *f*
**violate** ['vaɪ·ə·leɪt] *vt* **1.** (*break*) violar **2.** (*disturb*) perturbar
**violation** [ˌvaɪ·ə·'leɪ·ʃən] *n* violación *f*; **traffic ~** infracción *f* de tráfico
**violence** ['vaɪ·ə·ləns] *n* violencia *f*
**violent** ['vaɪ·ə·lənt] *adj* **1.** (*cruel*) violento, -a **2.** (*powerful*) fuerte
**violet** ['vaɪ·ə·lɪt] **I.** *n* **1.** BOT violeta *f* **2.** (*color*) violeta *m* **II.** *adj* violeta

**violin** [ˌvaɪ·ə·'lɪn] *n* violín *m*
**violinist** [ˌvaɪ·ə·'lɪn·ɪst] *n* violinista *mf*
**violoncello** [ˌvi·ə·lən·'tʃel·oʊ] *n* violoncelo *m*
**VIP** [ˌvi·aɪ·'pi] *see* **very important person** VIP *mf*
**viper** ['vaɪ·pər] *n a. fig* víbora *f*
**virgin** ['vɜr·dʒɪn] *n* virgen *f*
**virgin forest** *n* selva *f* virgen
**virginity** [vər·'dʒɪn·ə·ti] *n* virginidad *f*; **to lose one's ~** perder la virginidad
**Virgo** ['vɜr·goʊ] *n* virgo *mf*
**virile** ['vɪr·əl] *adj* viril
**virility** [və·'rɪl·ə·ti] *n* virilidad *f*
**virtual** ['vɜr·tʃu·əl] *adj* virtual
**virtually** *adv* prácticamente
**virtue** ['vɜr·tʃu] *n* **1.** (*moral*) virtud *f* **2.** (*advantage*) ventaja *f* ▸ **by ~ of** en virtud de
**virtuous** ['vɜr·tʃu·əs] *adj* virtuoso, -a; (*chaste*) casto, -a
**virulent** ['vɪr·jə·lənt] *adj* MED virulento, -a
**virus** ['vaɪ·rəs] <-es> *n* COMPUT, MED virus *m inv*
**visa** ['vi·zə] *n* visado *m*
**vis-à-vis** [ˌvi·zə·'vi] *prep* con relación a; (*compared to*) en comparación con
**viscosity** [vɪ·'skas·ə·ti] *n* viscosidad *f*
**viscous** ['vɪs·kəs] *adj* viscoso, -a
**vise** [vaɪs] *n* torno *m* de banco
**visibility** [ˌvɪz·ə·'bɪl·ə·ti] *n* **1.** visibilidad *f*; **poor ~** poca visibilidad **2.** (*prominence*) notoriedad *f*
**visible** ['vɪz·ə·bəl] *adj* **1.** visible; **to be barely ~** ser a penas perceptible **2.** (*in the public eye*) notorio, -a
**vision** ['vɪʒ·ən] *n* **1.** (*sight*) vista *f* **2.** (*mental image*) visión *f*
**visit** ['vɪz·ɪt] **I.** *n* visita *f* (**from** de); **to pay a ~ to sb** ir a ver a alguien **II.** *vt* visitar **III.** *vi* ir de visita
**visitation** [ˌvɪz·ə·'ter·ʃən] *n* (*visit*) visita *f*
**visiting hours** *npl* horario *m* de visita
**visitor** ['vɪz·ɪ·tər] *n* visitante *mf*; **~s' book** libro *m* de visitas
**visor** ['vaɪ·zər] *n* visera *f*
**visual** ['vɪʒ·u·əl] *adj* visual; **~ sense** sentido estético; **~ aid** soporte visual
**visualize** ['vɪʒ·u·ə·laɪz] *vt* visualizar
**vital** ['vaɪ·təl] *adj* vital; (*ingredient*) esen-

V

cial; (*part*) crucial; (*statistics*) demográfico, -a

**vitality** [vaɪ·'tæl·ə·t̬i] *n* vitalidad *f*

**vitamin** ['vaɪ·t̬ə·mɪn] *n* vitamina *f*

**vitamin deficiency** *n* avitaminosis *f inv*

**vivacious** [vɪ·'veɪ·ʃəs] *adj* vivaz; (*life*) animado, -a

**vivid** ['vɪv·ɪd] *adj* (*color*) vivo, -a; (*language*) vívido, -a; (*imagination*) fértil

**vixen** ['vɪk·sən] *n* 1. ZOOL zorra *f* 2. *pej* arpía *f*

**vocabulary** [voʊ·'kæb·jə·ler·i] *n* vocabulario *m*; **to widen one's ~** ampliar vocabulario; **the word 'politeness' isn't in his ~** la palabra 'modales' no entra en su vocabulario

**vocal** ['voʊ·kəl] *adj* 1. vocal; (*communication*) oral 2. (*outspoken*) vehemente; **to be ~** armar revuelo (**about** acerca de)

**vocalist** ['voʊ·kə·lɪst] *n* vocalista *mf*

**vocalize** ['voʊ·kə·laɪz] *vi, vt* vocalizar

**vocation** [voʊ·'keɪ·ʃən] *n* vocación *f*; **to miss one's ~** equivocarse de vocación

**vocational** [voʊ·'keɪ·ʃə·nəl] *adj* vocacional; **~ counseling/training** orientación/formación profesional

**vociferation** [voʊ·sɪf·ə·'reɪ·ʃən] *n* vocerío *m*

**vociferous** [voʊ·'sɪf·ər·əs] *adj* vociferante

**vodka** ['vad·kə] *n* vodka *f*

**vogue** [voʊg] *n* moda *f* ▶ **in ~** de moda; **out of ~** pasado de moda

**voice** [vɔɪs] *n* voz *f*; **in a loud ~** en voz alta; **to raise/lower one's ~** levantar/bajar la voz; **to lose one's ~** quedarse afónico/-a; **to listen to the ~ of reason** atender a razones; **to make one's ~ heard** hacerse escuchar

**voice box** <-es> *n* inf laringe *f*

**voiced** *adj* sonoro, -a

**voiceless** ['vɔɪs·lɪs] *adj* LING sordo, -a

**voice mail** *n* mensaje *m* de voz

**voice-over** *n* voz *f* en off

**void** [vɔɪd] I. *n* vacío *m* II. *adj* inválido, -a; **to be ~** estar falto (**of** de) III. *vt* anular

**volatile** ['val·ə·t̬əl] *adj* volátil; (*situation*) inestable

**volcanic** [val·'kæn·ɪk] *adj* volcánico, -a

**volcano** [val·'keɪ·noʊ] <-(e)s> *n* volcán *m*

**vole** [voʊl] *n* ratón *m* de campo

**volition** [voʊ·'lɪʃ·ən] *n* voluntad *f*

**volley** ['val·i] *n* 1. (*salvo*) descarga *f* 2. (*onslaught*) lluvia *f* 3. SPORTS volea *f*

**volleyball** ['val·i·bɔl] *n* voleibol *m*

**volt** [voʊlt] *n* voltio *m*

**voltage** ['voʊl·tɪdʒ] *n* voltaje *m*

**voltage detector** *n* voltímetro *m*

**voltage drop** *n* caída *f* de tensión

**volume** ['val·jum] *n* volumen *m*; **~ of sales** volumen de ventas

**volume control, volume regulator** *n* control *m* de volumen

**volume discount** *n* rappel *m*

**voluntary** ['val·ən·ter·i] *adj* voluntario, -a

**volunteer** [ˌval·ən·'tɪr] I. *n* voluntario, -a *m, f* II. *vt* **to ~ oneself** ofrecerse (**for** para) III. *vi* ofrecerse voluntario

**voluptuous** [və·'lʌp·tʃu·əs] *adj* voluptuoso, -a

**vomit** ['vam·ɪt] I. *vi* vomitar; **it makes me want to ~** me produce náuseas II. *vt* vomitar III. *n* vómito *m*

**voodoo** ['vu·du] *n* 1. vudú *m* 2. *inf* (*jinx*) maldición *f*

**voracious** [vɔ·'reɪ·ʃəs] *adj* voraz

**vortex** ['vɔr·teks] <-es *or* vortices> *n* vórtice *m*

**vote** [voʊt] I. *vi* votar (**for/against** a favor de/en contra de); **to ~ on sth** someter algo a votación II. *vt* votar; **to ~ that...** votar que... +*subj* III. *n* (*choice*) voto *m*; (*election*) votación *f*; **to put sth to the ~** someter algo a votación

◆**vote down** *vt* rechazar (por votación)

◆**vote in** *vt* elegir (por votación)

◆**vote out** *vt* no reelegir (**of** en)

**voter** *n* votante *mf*

**voting** *n* votación *f*

**voting booth** <-es> *n* cabina *f* de voto

**vouch** [vautʃ] I. *vi* **to ~ for sth/sb** responder de algo/por alguien II. *vt* **to ~ that...** confirmar que...

**voucher** ['vau·tʃər] *n* 1. (*coupon*) vale *m* 2. (*receipt*) comprobante *m*

**vow** [vau] I. *vt* hacer voto de II. *n* voto *m*

**vowel** ['vau·əl] *n* vocal *f*

**voyage** ['vɔɪ·ɪdʒ] I. *n* viaje *m* II. *vi* viajar

**(across** por)

**voyeur** [vɔɪ·ˈjɜr] n mirón, -ona m, f

**vulgar** [ˈvʌl·gər] adj 1. (crude) ordinario, -a 2. (commonplace) vulgar

**vulgarity** [vʌl·ˈgær·ə·t̬i] n 1. (crudeness) grosería f 2. (ordinariness) vulgaridad f

**vulnerable** [ˈvʌl·nər·ə·bəl] adj vulnerable

**vulture** [ˈvʌl·tʃər] n a. fig buitre m

**vulva** [ˈvʌl·və] <-s or -e> n vulva f

# W

**W, w** [ˈdʌb·əl·ju] n W, w f; ~ **as in Whiskey** W de Washington

**W** n 1. abbr of **watt** W 2. abbr of **west** O

**wacko** [ˈwæk·oʊ] n sl bicho m raro

**wacky** [ˈwæk·i] <-ier, -iest> adj sl (person) grillado, -a; (thing) estrambótico, -a

**wad** [wad] n (banknotes) fajo m; (cotton) bola f

**waddle** [ˈwad·əl] n andares m pl de pato

**wade** [weɪd] vi andar por el agua; **to ~ into sth** adentrarse en algo; **to ~ into sb** tomarla con alguien

**wader** [ˈweɪ·dər] n 1. (bird) ave m zancuda 2. (boot) bota f de pescador

**wafer** [ˈweɪ·fər] n 1. (biscuit) barquillo m 2. REL hostia f

**waffle**[1] [ˈwaf·əl] n CULIN gofre m, waffle m AmL

**waffle**[2] [ˈwaf·əl] inf I. vi parlotear II. n palabrería f

**waffle iron** n plancha f para gofres [or AmL waffles]

**wag**[1] [wæg] <-gg-> I. vt menear II. n meneo m

**wag**[2] [wæg] n inf (funny person) bromista m f

**wage** [weɪdʒ] n sueldo m; **minimum/living** ~ salario mínimo/de subsistencia

**wage earner** n asalariado, -a m, f

**wage freeze** n congelación f salarial

**wage increase** n aumento m salarial

**wager** [ˈweɪ·dʒər] I. n apuesta f; **to place a** ~ hacer una apuesta II. vt apostar; fig jugarse

**waggle** [ˈwæg·əl] I. vt mover II. vi moverse

**wail** [weɪl] I. vi gemir; (wind) silbar II. vt lamentar III. n lamento m

**wailing** n gemidos mpl

**waist** [weɪst] n cintura f

**waistband** [ˈweɪst·bænd] n cinturilla f

**waist-deep** [ˌweɪst·ˈdip] adj hasta la cintura

**waistline** [ˈweɪst·laɪn] n cintura f; **to watch one's** ~ guardar la línea

**wait** [weɪt] I. vi esperar; **to ~ for sth/ sb** esperar algo/a alguien; **to keep sb ~ing** hacer esperar a alguien; **he cannot ~ to see her** está ansioso por verla; ~ **and see** espera y verás II. vt esperar; **to ~ one's turn** esperar su turno III. n espera f

◆**wait about** vi, **wait around** vi estar a la espera (**for** de)

◆**wait behind** vi esperarse

◆**wait on** vt 1. (serve) servir 2. (expect) estar a la espera de

◆**wait up** vi esperar de pie (**for** a)

**waiter** [ˈweɪ·t̬ər] n camarero m, garzón m AmL, mesero m Méx

**waiting** n espera f

**waiting game** n **to play the** ~ dejar pasar el tiempo

**waiting list** n lista f de espera

**waiting room** n sala f de espera

**waitress** [ˈweɪ·trɪs] n camarera f, garzona f AmL, mesera f Méx

**waive** [weɪv] vt (right) renunciar a; (rule) no aplicar

**waiver** [ˈweɪ·vər] n renuncia f

**wake**[1] [weɪk] n NAUT estela f; **in the ~ of** tras

**wake**[2] [weɪk] n velatorio m

**wake**[3] [weɪk] <woke or waked, woken or waked> I. vi despertarse II. vt despertar

◆**wake up** vi, vt despertar

**walk** [wɔk] I. n 1. (stroll) paseo m; **to take a** ~ ir a dar un paseo; **it's a five minute** ~ está a cinco minutos a pie 2. (gait) andar m 3. (pace) paso m 4. (easy) pan m comido; **to do sth in a** ~ hacer algo con los ojos cerrados ▶ ~ **of life** condición f II. vt andarse; **to ~ sb home** acompañar a alguien a su casa;

to ~ **the dog** sacar a pasear al perro
III. *vi* andar; (*stroll*) pasear ▶ **to ~ on
air** rebosar felicidad
◆**walk about** *vi*, **walk around** *vi* dar
una vuelta
◆**walk away** *vi* irse; **to ~ from** alejarse
de; *fig* desentenderse de
◆**walk back** *vi* volver a pie
◆**walk in** *vi* entrar
◆**walk off** *vi* marcharse
◆**walk on** *vi* seguir andando
◆**walk out** *vi* (*leave*) salir
◆**walk over** *vt* pisotear
◆**walk through** *vt insep* (*part*) ensayar
◆**walk up** I. *vi* 1. (*go up*) subir 2. (*approach*) acercarse (**to** a) II. *vt* subir
**walker** ['wɔ·kər] *n* paseante *mf*; (*as a
hobby*) senderista *mf*
**walkie-talkie** [wɔ·ki·ˈtɔ·ki] *n* walkie-talkie *m*
**walk-in** ['wɔk·ɪn] *adj* empotrado, -a; ~
**closet** vestidor *m*
**walking** I. *n* paseo *m*; SPORTS marcha *f*
atlética; **to do a lot of ~** andar mucho
II. *adj* it is within ~ **distance** se puede
ir a pie; **to be a ~ encyclopedia** ser una
enciclopedia con patas
**walking stick** *n* (*cane*) bastón *m*
**walk-on** ['wɔk·an] *n* THEAT figurante *mf*;
CINE extra *mf*; SPORTS cedido, -a *m, f*
**walkout** ['wɔk·aʊt] *n* salida *f*; (*strike*)
huelga *f*
**walkover** [wɔk·ˌoʊ·vər] *n inf* paseo *m*; **it
was a ~** fue pan comido
**walkway** ['wɔk·weɪ] *n* pasarela *f*
**wall** [wɔl] *n* muro *m*; (*in the interior*) a.
ANAT pared *f*; (*enclosing room*) muralla *f*; (*enclosing house*) tapia *f*; (*barrier*)
barrera *f* ▶ **to have one's back to** [*or*
up against**] the ~** estar entre la espada
y la pared; **to drive sb up the ~** sacar
a alguien de quicio; **to be off the wall**
ser un freaky
◆**wall in** *vt* (*garden*) cercar; *fig* encerrar
◆**wall off** *vt* separar con un muro; **to wall
oneself off** encerrarse en uno mismo
◆**wall up** *vt* (*opening*) tapiar
**wall chart** *n* gráfico *m* de pared
**wallet** ['wal·ɪt] *n* cartera *f*, billetera *f AmL*
**wallflower** ['wɔl·ˌflaʊ·ər] *n* BOT al(h)elí *m*
**wallop** ['wal·əp] *inf* I. *vt* zurrar II. *n* (*hit*)

guantazo *f*; **to pack a ~** causar impacto
**wallow** ['wal·oʊ] I. *n* revolcón *m* II. *vi*
1. (*animal*) revolcarse 2. (*revel*) regodearse; **to ~ in wealth** nadar en la
abundancia
**wallpaper** ['wɔl·ˌpeɪ·pər] I. *n* papel *m*
pintado II. *vt* empapelar
**wall-to-wall** ['wɔl·tə·ˈwɔl] *adj* ~ **carpeting** moqueta *f*
**walnut** ['wɔl·nʌt] *n* nuez *f*; (*tree*) nogal *m*
**walrus** ['wɔl·rəs] <walruses *or* walrus>
*n* morsa *f*
**waltz** [wɔlts] <-es> I. *n* vals *m* II. *vi sl*
ir tan campante
◆**waltz about** *vi*, **waltz around** *vi* dar
vueltas despreocupado
◆**waltz in** *vi sl* entrar como si nada
◆**waltz off** *vi sl* **to ~ with sth** birlar algo
◆**waltz out** *vi sl* salir como si nada
**wand** [wand] *n* varita *f* mágica
**wander** ['wan·dər] I. *vt* vagar por; **to ~
the streets** deambular por las calles,
callejear II. *vi* (*roam*) vagar; (*stroll*) pasearse III. *n inf* paseo *m*
**wane** [weɪn] *vi* menguar
**wangle** ['wæŋ·gəl] *vt inf* agenciarse; **to ~
one's way into sth** arreglárselas para
entrar en algo
**want** [want] I. *vt* querer; **to ~ to do sth**
querer hacer algo; **to ~ sb to do sth**
querer que alguien haga algo; **to ~ sth
done** querer que se haga algo; **you're
~ed on the phone** te llaman por teléfono; **I was ~ing to leave** estaba deseando macharme II. *n* 1. (*need*) necesidad *f*; **to be in ~ of** necesitar 2. (*lack*)
falta *f*; **for ~** por falta (**of** de)
◆**want in** *vi* querer entrar; **do you ~?**
¿te apuntas?
◆**want out** *vi* querer salirse (**of** de)
**wanting** *adj* falto, -a (**in** de); **there is
sth ~** falta algo
**war** [wɔr] *n* guerra *f*; **the Great War** la
Primera Guerra Mundial; **the Second
World War** la Segunda Guerra Mundial;
**to be at ~** estar en guerra; **to declare ~**
*fig* hacer la vida imposible (**on** a)
**war bond** *n* bono *m* de guerra
**war correspondent** *n* corresponsal *mf*
de guerra

**war crime** *n* crimen *m* de guerra

**war criminal** *n* criminal *mf* de guerra

**war cry** *n* grito *m* de guerra

**ward** [wɔrd] *n* **1.** (*wardship*) tutela *f;* **in ~** bajo tutela **2.** (*room*) sala *f;* **maternity ~** sala de maternidad; **geriatric/psychiatric ~** pabellón *m* geriátrico/psiquiátrico

◆**ward off** *vt* evitar

**warden** ['wɔr·dən] *n* guardián, -ana *m, f;* (*prison*) alcaide(sa) *m(f);* **game ~** guardabosque *mf*

**wardrobe** ['wɔrd·roʊb] *n* **1.** (*closet*) ropero *m* **2.** (*clothes*) vestuario *m*

**wardrobe trunk** *n* baúl *m* ropero

**warehouse** ['wer·əhaʊs] *n* almacén *m*

**warfare** ['wɔr·fer] *n* guerra *f*

**warhead** ['wɔr·hed] *n* ojiva *f*

**warily** ['wer·ɪ·li] *adv* cautamente; (*suspiciously*) recelosamente

**warlike** ['wɔr·laɪk] *adj* (*of war*) bélico, -a

**warlord** ['wɔr·lɔrd] *n* jefe *m* militar

**warm** [wɔrm] **I.** *adj* **1.** (*hot*) caliente; (*clothes*) de abrigo; (*day*) caluroso, -a; (*climate, wind*) cálido, -a; (*tracks*) fresco, -a; **to be ~** (*person*) tener calor; (*thing*) estar caliente; (*weather*) hacer calor **2.** (*affectionate*) efusivo, -a; (*welcome*) caluroso, -a ▶ **you're getting ~** ¡caliente, caliente! **II.** *vt* calentar; **to ~ sb's heart** reconfortar a alguien

◆**warm up I.** *vi* calentarse **II.** *vt* calentar; (*food*) recalentar; (*person*) hacer entrar en calor

**warm-blooded** [ˌwɔrm·'blʌd·ɪd] *adj* de sangre caliente

**warm front** *n* frente *m* cálido

**warm-hearted** [ˌwɔrm·'har·tɪd] *adj* bondadoso, -a; (*affectionate*) cariñoso, -a

**warmth** [wɔrmθ] *n* **1.** (*heat*) calor *m* **2.** (*affection*) calidez *f*

**warm-up, warmup** ['wɔrm·ʌp] *n* (pre)calentamiento *m*

**warn** [wɔrn] *vt* advertir; **to ~ sb not to do sth** advertir a alguien que no haga algo; **to ~ sb of a danger** prevenir a alguien de un peligro

**warning** ['wɔr·nɪŋ] *n* aviso *m;* **a word of ~** una advertencia; **to give sb a ~** advertir a alguien; **without ~** sin previo aviso; **~!** ¡atención!

**warning shot** *n* disparo *m* de advertencia

**warp** [wɔrp] *vt* (*wood*) deformar; (*mind*) pervertir

**warpath** ['wɔr·pæθ] *n* **to be on the ~** *fig* buscar pelea

**warped** *adj* deformado, -a; (*mind*) pervertido, -a; **to have a ~ way of looking at things** tener una manera retorcida de ver las cosas

**warrant** ['wɔr·ənt] **I.** *n* **1.** LAW orden *f;* **search ~** orden de registro **2.** COM garantía *f* **II.** *vt* **1.** (*promise*) garantizar **2.** (*justify*) justificar

**warrantee** [ˌwɔr·ən·'ti] *n* beneficiario, -a *m, f* de una garantía

**warranty** ['wɔr·ən·ti] <-ies> *n* garantía *f*

**warren** ['wɔr·ən] *n fig* laberinto *m*

**warring** *adj* en guerra

**warrior** ['wɔr·i·ər] *n* guerrero, -a *m, f*

**warship** ['wɔr·ʃɪp] *n* barco *m* de guerra

**wart** [wɔrt] *n* verruga *f*

**wartime** ['wɔr·taɪm] *n* tiempo *m* de guerra

**wary** ['wer·i] <-ier, -iest> *adj* cauteloso, -a; **to be ~** recelar (**of** de); **to be ~ about** (**doing**) **sth** dudar sobre (si hacer) algo

**war zone** ['wɔr·zoʊn] *n* zona *f* de guerra

**was** [wʌz] *pt of* **be**

**wash** [wɑʃ] **I.** *vt* (*clean*) lavar; (*dishes, floor*) fregar; **to ~ one's hair/hands** lavarse el pelo/las manos **II.** *vi* **1.** (*person*) lavarse; **that excuse won't ~ with me** esa excusa conmigo no cuela **2.** (*do the laundry*) lavar la ropa **III.** *n* **1.** (*cleaning*) lavado *m;* **to have a ~** darse un baño **2.** (*clothes*) **the ~** la ropa para lavar; **to be in the ~** estar en la lavandería **3.** (*layer*) baño *m;* (*painting*) mano *f*

◆**wash away** *vt* **1.** (*clean*) quitar **2.** (*carry away*) arrastrar

◆**wash down** *vt* **1.** (*clean*) lavar **2.** (*carry away*) arrastrar

◆**wash out I.** *vi* quitarse **II.** *vt* (*clean*) lavar; (*remove*) quitar

◆**wash over** *vt* (*not affect*) no afectar

◆**wash up I.** *vt* lavar; **the sea washed it up** el mar lo arrojó sobre la playa **II.** *vi* (*hands, face*) lavarse

**washable** adj lavable

**washbasin** n lavabo m; (bowl) palangana f

**washcloth** n manopla f

**washed-out** ['wɑʃt·'aut] adj 1. (faded) desteñido, -a 2. (tired) cansado, -a

**washer** ['wɑʃ·ər] n (machine) lavadora f

**washing** ['wɑʃ·ɪŋ] n 1. (clothes) ropa f sucia 2. (act) lavado f; (of clothes) colada f; to do the ~ hacer la colada

**washing machine** n lavadora f, lavarropas f inv Arg

**Washington** ['wɑʃ·ɪŋ·tən] n Washington m

**Washington D.C.** n Washington D.C. m

**washout** ['wɑʃ·aut] n inf desastre m; a complete ~ un desastre total

**wasn't** ['wʌz·ənt] = was not see be

**wasp** [wɑsp] n avispa f

**WASP** [wɑsp] n pej inf abbr of White Anglo-Saxon Protestant estadounidense anglosajón, blanco y protestante

**waste** [weɪst] I. n 1. (misuse) derroche m (of de); it's a ~ of time es una pérdida de tiempo; to go to ~ echarse a perder; what a ~! ¡qué pena! 2. (refuse) residuos mpl; to recycle ~ reciclar la basura II. vt (time, opportunity) perder; to ~ one's breath fig gastar saliva; to ~ no time in doing sth apresurarse a hacer algo

♦**waste away** vi consumirse

**wastebasket** ['weɪst·ˌbæs·kət] n papelera m

**wasteful** ['weɪst·fəl] adj derrochador(a)

**wasteland** n yermo m

**waste management** n gestión f de residuos

**wastepaper** n papel m usado

**wastepaper basket** n papelera f

**waste pipe** n tubo m de desagüe

**waste product** n residuos mpl

**wastewater** n aguas f pl residuales

**watch** [wɑtʃ] I. n 1. (on wrist) reloj m (de pulsera) 2. (observation) vigilancia f; to be on the ~ estar pendiente (for de) 3. (period of duty) guardia f; to keep [or be on] ~ estar de guardia II. vt 1. (observe) mirar; (to ~ TV/a film) ver la tele/una película; to ~ sb/ sth do sth mirar a alguien/algo hacer

algo 2. (keep vigil) vigilar; to ~ the kids echar un ojo a los niños 3. (mind) fijarse en; to ~ one's weight cuidar la línea; ~ it! ¡cuidado!, ¡aguas! Méx; to ~ it tener cuidado (with con); ~ yourself cuídate III. vi fijarse

♦**watch out** vi tener cuidado; ~! ¡cuidado!

**watchdog** ['wɑtʃ·dɔg] n (dog) perro m guardián; fig guardián, -ana m, f

**watcher** ['wɑtʃ·ər] n observador(a) m(f)

**watchful** ['wɑtʃ·fəl] adj vigilante; to keep a ~ eye estar pendiente (on de); under the ~ eye bajo la atenta mirada (of de)

**watchman** ['wɑtʃ·mən] <-men> n vigilante m; **night ~** vigilante nocturno

**watchtower** ['wɑtʃ·tau·ər] n atalaya f

**water** ['wɔ·tər] I. n agua f; **bottled/running ~** agua embotellada/corriente; **a drink/glass/bottle of ~** un trago/un vaso/una botella de agua; **territorial ~s** aguas jurisdiccionales; **by ~** por mar ▶ **to be ~ under the bridge** ser agua pasada; **like ~ off a duck's back** como si oyera llover; **to be in deep ~** estar metido en un lío II. vt (plants) regar; (livestock) dar de beber a

**water bottle** n botellín m de agua; (for travelers) cantimplora f

**water cannon** n inv cañón m de agua

**watercolor** n acuarela f

**water-cooled** ['wɔ·tər·kuld] adj refrigerado, -a por agua

**watercress** n berro m

**waterfall** n cascada f

**waterfront** n puerto m

**water heater** n calentador m de agua

**water hose** n manguera f

**watering can** ['wɔ·tər·ɪŋ·kæn] n regadera f

**water level** n nivel m del agua

**water lily** <-ies> n nenúfar m

**water line** n línea f de flotación

**water main** n cañería f principal

**watermark** n línea f del agua; (on paper) filigrana f

**watermelon** n sandía f

**water meter** n contador m de agua

**water pipe** n 1. cañería f 2. (hookah) pipa f de agua

**water pistol** n pistola f de agua

**water polo** n waterpolo m

**water pressure** n presión f del agua

**waterproof** ['wɔ·tər·ˌpruf] adj impermeable

**water-repellent** adj hidrófugo, -a

**watershed** ['wɔ·tər·ʃed] n fig punto m de inflexión

**waterside** n orilla f

**water-ski** ['wɔ·tər·ˌski] vi to go ~ing hacer esquí acuático

**water-skiing** n esquí m acuático

**water softener** n ablandador m de agua

**water-soluble** adj soluble en agua

**water supply** n suministro m de agua

**water tank** n cisterna f; (small) aljibe m

**watertight** ['wɔ·tər·ˌtaɪt] adj hermético, -a; fig irrecusable

**water tower** n depósito f de agua

**waterway** n canal m

**waterworks** n pl reserva f de abastecimiento de agua ► to **turn on** the ~ echarse a llorar

**watery** ['wɔ·tə·ri] <-ier, -iest> adj 1. (bland) aguado, -a 2. (weak) diluido, -a

**watt** [wat] n vatio m

**wattage** ['wat·ɪdʒ] n vatiaje m

**wave** [weɪv] I. n 1. (water) ola f; (surface) ondulación f; to be on the crest of the ~ fig estar en la cumbre 2. PHYS onda f ► to **make** ~s causar problemas II. vi (flag) ondear; to ~ at [or to] sb saludar a alguien con la mano III. vt agitar; to ~ goodbye decir adiós con la mano

◆**wave down** vt hacer señas para que pare

◆**wave on** vt hacer señas para que siga

◆**wave through** vt hacer señas para que pase

**waver** ['weɪ·vər] vi 1. (falter) desfallecer 2. (hesitate) titubear (over acerca de); to ~ between... and... dudar entre... y...

**wavering** adj vacilante; (between two options) titubeante

**wavy** ['weɪ·vi] <-ier, -iest> adj (hair) ondulado, -a; (pattern) ondulante

**wax¹** [wæks] I. n cera f II. vt 1. (polish) encerar; (shoes) lustrar 2. (remove hair from) depilar con cera

**wax²** [wæks] vi (moon) crecer; to ~ and wane crecer y menguar; fig tener altibajos

**waxy** ['wæk·si] <-ier, -iest> adj (shiny) lustroso, -a

**way** [weɪ] I. n 1. (route) camino m; to be (well) on the ~ to doing sth fig ir encaminado a hacer algo; under ~ en curso; on the ~ de camino (to a); to find one's ~ into/out encontrar la manera de entrar/salir (of de); to go out of one's ~ fig tomarse la molestia (to de); to go one's own ~ a. fig irse por su lado; to lose one's ~ perderse; to make one's ~ (progress) progresar; (move) abrirse camino 2. (road) camino m; (name of road) vía f 3. (direction) dirección f; the right/wrong ~ around del derecho/del revés 4. (distance) trayecto m; all the ~ todo el trayecto; (completely) completamente; to be a long ~ off estar muy lejos; to have a long ~ to go tener un largo camino por recorrer; to go a long ~ a. fig llegar lejos 5. (fashion) manera f (to de); in many ~s de muchas maneras; in some ~s en cierto modo; there are no two ~s about it no tiene vuelta de hoja; by ~ of a modo de 6. (manner) modo m; her ~ of life su estilo de vida; in a big ~ a gran escala; either ~ de cualquier forma; no ~! ¡de ninguna manera!; in no ~ para nada; to get one's own ~ salirse con la suya; in a ~ en cierto modo 7. (free space) paso m; to be in sb's ~ estorbar a alguien; in the ~ en medio; to give ~ dar paso; fig dejar hacer (to a); to make ~ abrir paso (for a) 8. (condition) estado m; to be in a bad ~ estar en mala forma ► which ~ the **wind blows** por donde van los tiros; to rub sb the **wrong** ~ caer mal a alguien; **by** the ~ por cierto II. adv sl (very) mogollón de; that's ~ cool! ¡mola mazo!

**way-out** [ˌweɪ·ˈaʊt] adj sl (modern) ultramoderno, -a; (amazing) fuera de serie

**wayside** ['weɪ·saɪd] n borde m del camino

**we** [wi] pron pers nosotros, -as; as ~ say como decimos nosotros

**weak** [wik] adj 1. (not strong) débil; (cof-

**fee, tea**) claro, -a; **to be ~ with desire/thirst** languidecer de deseo/sed; **the ~ link/spot** *fig* el punto débil **2.** (*below standard*) flojo, -a (**at** en)

**weaken** ['wi·kən] **I.** *vi* debilitarse; (*diminish*) disminuir **II.** *vt* debilitar; (*diminish*) disminuir

**weakling** ['wik·lɪŋ] *n* enclenque *mf*

**weakly** ['wik·li] *adv* débilmente; (*unconvincingly*) sin convicción

**weakness** ['wik·nɪs] <-es> *n* **1.** (*lack of strength*) debilidad *f*; **to have a ~** tener debilidad (**for** por) **2.** (*vulnerability*) punto *m* débil; (*flaw in character*) flaqueza *f*

**wealth** [welθ] *n* **1.** (*money*) riqueza *f*; (*fortune*) fortuna *f* **2.** (*large amount*) abundancia *f*

**wealthy** ['wel·θi] <-ier, -iest> *adj* rico, -a

**weapon** ['wep·ən] *n* arma *f*

**wear** [wer] <wore, worn> **I.** *vt* **1.** (*clothes, jewelry, hair*) llevar **2.** (*deteriorate*) desgastar **II.** *vi* desgastarse **III.** *n* **1.** (*clothing*) ropa *f*; **casual/sports ~** ropa informal/deportiva **2.** (*amount of use*) desgaste *m*

◆**wear away I.** *vt* desgastar **II.** *vi* desgastarse; (*person*) consumirse

◆**wear down** *vt* (*reduce*) gastar; (*tire, resistance*) desgastar

◆**wear off** *vi* desaparecer

◆**wear on** *vi* (*time*) pasar lentamente

◆**wear out I.** *vi* gastarse **II.** *vt* gastar; (*patience*) agotar

**wearing** ['wer·ɪŋ] *adj* agotador(a)

**weary** ['wɪr·i] **I.** <-ier, -iest> *adj* **1.** (*tired*) extenuado, -a **2.** (*tiring*) agotador(a) **3.** (*bored*) aburrido, -a; (*unenthusiastic*) desanimado, -a; **to be ~ of** estar harto de **II.** *vt* (*tire*) fatigar; (*bore*) aburrir (**with** con) **III.** *vi* (*get tired*) cansarse; (*get bored*) aburrirse

**weasel** ['wi·zəl] *n* comadreja *f*

**weather** ['weð·ər] **I.** *n* **1.** (*time*) tiempo *m*; (*climate*) clima *m*; **~ permitting** si lo permite el tiempo ▶ **to make heavy ~ of sth** complicar algo **II.** *vt* **1.** (*wear*) desgastar **2.** (*endure*) hacer frente a

**weather-beaten** ['weð·ər·ˌbi·tən] *adj* (*face*) curtido, -a *f*

**weather forecast** *n* previsión *f* meteorológica

**weatherman** ['weð·ər·mæn] <-men> *n* hombre *m* del tiempo

**weathergirl** ['weð·ər·gɜrl] *n* mujer *f* del tiempo

**weatherproof** ['weð·ər·ˌpruf] *adj* impermeabilizado, -a

**weave** [wiv] **I.** <wove *or* weaved, woven *or* weaved> *vt* **1.** (*produce cloth*) tejer **2.** (*intertwine*) entretejer; *fig* tramar; **to ~ sth together** entrelazar algo **II.** <wove *or* weaved, woven *or* weaved> *vi* **1.** (*produce cloth*) tejer **2.** (*twist*) serpentear **II.** *n* tejido *m*

**web¹** [web] *n* **1.** (*woven net*) tela *f*; **spider('s) ~** telaraña *f* **2.** *fig* (*complex network*) trama *f*; (*of lies*) sarta *f*

**web²** [web] COMPUT *n* red *f*; **on the ~** en la red **II.** *adj* de internet

**web-footed** ['web·ˌfʊt·ɪd] *adj* palmípedo, -a

**weblog** ['web·ˌlɔg] *n* blog *m*

**webmaster** *n* administrador(a) *m(f)*

**website** *n* sitio *m* web; **to visit a ~** visitar un sitio web

**webzine** *n* revista *f* electrónica

**wed** [wed] <wedded *or* wed, wedded *or* wed> **I.** *vt* contraer matrimonio con; *fig* casar **II.** *vi* contraer matrimonio

**we'd** [wid] **1.** = **we had** *see* **have 2.** = **we would** *see* **would**

**wedded** ['wed·ɪd] *adj* casado, -a; **lawfully ~ wife** legítima esposa; **to be ~ to** estar unido a; (*opinion*) aferrarse a; (*habit*) tener

**wedding** ['wed·ɪŋ] *n* boda *f*

**wedding anniversary** <-ies> *n* aniversario *m* de bodas

**wedding cake** *n* tarta *f* nupcial

**wedding day** *n* día *m* de la boda

**wedding dress** *n* traje *m* de novia

**wedding ring** *n* alianza *f*

**wedge** [wedʒ] *n* cuña *f*; *fig* porción *f*

**wedlock** ['wed·lak] *n* matrimonio *m*

**Wednesday** ['wenz·deɪ] *n* miércoles *m inv; s. a.* **Friday**

**wee** [wi] *adj* (*tiny*) chiquito, -a

**weed** [wid] *n* **1.** mala hierba *f* **2.** (*marijuana*) maría *f* ▶ **to grow like a ~** crecer como la mala hierba

**weedkiller** ['wid·ˌkɪl·ər] *n* herbicida *m*

**weedy** ['wi·di] *adj* <-ier, iest> lleno, -a de malas hierbas; (*person*) canijo, -a

**week** [wik] *n* semana *f*; **last** ~ la semana pasada; **once a** ~ una vez por semana; **during the** ~ durante la semana; ~ **after/by** ~ semana tras/a semana; **a forty hour** ~ cuarenta horas semanales

**weekday** ['wik·deɪ] *n* día *m* laborable; **on** ~**s** los días laborables

**weekend** ['wik·end] *n* fin *m* de semana; **on/over the** ~ el fin de semana

**weekly** ['wik·li] **I.** *adj* semanal **II.** *adv* semanalmente

**weep** [wip] **I.** *vi, vt* <wept, wept> llorar (**with** de, **for/over** por) **II.** *n* llanto *m*

**weeping** *adj* lloroso, -a

**weeping willow** *n* sauce *m* llorón

**weigh** [weɪ] **I.** *vi* pesar **II.** *vt* **1.** pesar; **to** ~ **oneself** pesarse **2.** (*consider*) sopesar; (*words*) medir; **to** ~ **sth against sth** contraponer algo a algo

◆**weigh down** *vt* doblar del peso; *fig* abrumar

◆**weigh in** *vi inf* (*take part*) intervenir; **to** ~ **to a discussion with one's opinion** intervenir en una discusión dando su opinión

**weigh-in** ['weɪ·ɪn] *n* pesaje *m*

**weight** [weɪt] *n* **1.** (*amount weighed*) peso *m*; **to lift a heavy** ~ levantar algo pesado; **to put on** ~ engordar **2.** (*metal*) pesa *f* **3.** (*importance*) peso; **to carry** ~ tener mucho peso ▶ **to take the** ~ **off one's feet** sentarse y descansar; **to be a** ~ **off sb's mind** ser un alivio para alguien; **it's a great** ~ **off my mind** es un peso que me quito de encima; **to pull one's (own)** ~ poner de su parte

**weightless** ['weɪt·lɪs] *adj* ingrávido, -a

**weightlessness** *n* ingravidez *f*

**weightlifter** *n* levantador(a) *m(f)* de pesas

**weightlifting** ['weɪt·lɪf·tɪŋ] *n* levantamiento *m* de pesas; **to do** ~ hacer pesas

**weighty** ['weɪ·t̬i] *adj* <-ier, -iest> **1.** (*heavy*) pesado, -a **2.** (*important*) importante; (*matter*) de peso

**weir** [wɪr] *n* presa *f*

**weird** [wɪrd] *adj* misterioso, -a; **how** ~ ¡qué raro!; ~ **and wonderful** extraordinario

**welcome** ['wel·kəm] **I.** *vt* **1.** dar la bienvenida a; **to** ~ **sb warmly** recibir a alguien con los brazos abiertos **2.** (*support*) aprobar **II.** *n* **1.** bienvenida *f* **2.** (*approval*) aprobación *f* **III.** *adj* grato, -a; ~! ¡bienvenido, -a!; **to be** ~ ser bienvenido ▶ **you are** ~ de nada; **you're very** ~ no hay de qué; **to be** ~ **to do sth** poder hacer algo; **you are** ~ **to use it** está a su disposición

**welcoming** *adj* acogedor(a)

**weld** [weld] **I.** *vt* (*join metal*) soldar **II.** *n* soldadura *f*

**welfare** ['wel·fer] *n* **1.** bienestar *m* **2.** **social** ~ asistencia *f* social; **to be on** ~ vivir de las ayudas sociales

**welfare state** *n* estado *m* del bienestar

**welfare work** *n* trabajos *m pl* de asistencia social

**welfare worker** *n* trabajador(a) *m(f)* social

**we'll** [wil] = **we will** *see* **will**

**well¹** [wel] **I.** *adj* <better, best> bien; **to feel** ~ sentirse bien; **to get** ~ recuperarse; **to look** ~ tener buen aspecto **II.** <better, best> *adv* **1.** (*satisfactory*) bien; ~ **enough** suficientemente bien; ~ **done** bien hecho *2.* (*thoroughly*) completamente; **that's** ~ **east of here** está muy al este; ~ **enough** suficiente; **pretty** ~ bastante a fondo; **it costs** ~ **over...** cuesta tranquilamente más de... **3.** (*fairly*) justamente; **you may** ~ **think...** bien podrías pensar...; **you might (just) as** ~ **tell her the truth** más valdría que le dijeras la verdad ▶ **all** ~ **and good** muy bien; **that's all very** ~, **but...** todo eso está muy bien, pero...; **as** ~ (*also*) también; **as** ~ **as** así como; **just as** ~ menos mal III. *interj* vaya; **very** ~! ¡muy bien!

**well²** [wel] **I.** *n* (*hole*) pozo *m* **II.** *vi* (*flow*) manar

◆**well up** *vi* brotar

**well-advised** [,wel·əd·'vaɪzd] *adj* bien asesorado, -a; **he would be** ~ **to stay at home** haría bien en quedarse en casa

**well-balanced** [,wel·'bæl·ənst] *adj a.* PSYCH equilibrado, -a

**well-behaved** [,wel·bɪ·'heɪvd] *adj* bien

W

educado, -a; (*child, dog*) obediente
**well-being** ['wel·biˑɪŋ] *n* bienestar *m*;
**a feeling of ~** una sensación de bienestar
**well-bred** [ˌwel·'bred] *adj* bien educado,
-a; (*refined*) refinado, -a
**well-chosen** [ˌwel·'tʃoʊ·zən] *adj* cuidadosamente seleccionado, -a
**well-connected** [ˌwel·kə·'nek·tɪd] *adj* influyente; **to be ~** tener contactos
**well-deserved** [ˌwel·dɪ·'zɜvd] *adj* merecido, -a
**well-developed** [ˌwel·dɪ·'vel·əpt] *adj*
muy desarrollado, -a; (*sense of humor*)
agudo, -a
**well-done** [ˌwel·'dʌn] *adj* bien hecho, -a;
(*meat*) muy hecho, -a
**well-dressed** [ˌwel·'drest] *adj* bien vestido, -a
**well-educated** [ˌwel·'edʒ·ʊ·keɪ·ṭɪd] *adj*
culto, -a
**well-fed** [ˌwel·'fed] *adj* bien alimentado, -a
**well-founded** [ˌwel·'faʊn·dɪd] *adj* fundado, -a
**well-heeled** [ˌwel·'hild] *adj* ricachón, -ona
**well-informed** [ˌwel·ɪn·'fɔrmd] *adj* bien
informado, -a (**about** sobre)
**well-intentioned** [ˌwel·ɪn·'ten·ʃənd] *adj*
**to be ~** tener buenas intenciones
**well-known** [ˌwel·'noʊn] *adj* conocido,
-a (**for** por); **it is ~ that...** es bien sabido que...
**well-mannered** [ˌwel·'mæn·ərd] *adj* con
buenos modales
**well-meaning** [ˌwel·'miˑnɪŋ] *adj* con buenas intenciones
**well-meant** [ˌwel·'ment] *adj* con buenas
intenciones
**well-off** [ˌwel·'ɔf] *adj* acomodado, -a; **the
city is ~ for parks** la ciudad tiene muchos parques
**well-oiled** [ˌwel·'ɔɪld] *adj* **1.** (*functioning smoothly*) eficaz **2.** (*drunk*) como
una cuba
**well-organized** [ˌwel·'ɔr·gə·naɪzd] *adj*
bien organizado, -a
**well-paid** [ˌwel·'peɪd] *adj* bien pagado, -a
**well-placed** [ˌwel·'pleɪst] *adj* situado, -a
**well-read** [ˌwel·'red] *adj* **1.** (*knowledge-*

*able*) culto, -a **2.** (*read frequently*) muy
leído, -a
**well-spoken** [ˌwel·'spoʊ·kən] *adj* bien-
hablado, -a
**well-thought-of** [ˌwel·'θɔt·əv] *adj* de buena reputación; (*school*) de prestigio
**well-timed** [ˌwel·'taɪmd] *adj* oportuno, -a
**well-to-do** [ˌwel·tə·'du] **I.** *adj* de pelas
**II.** *n* **the ~** la gente de pelas
**well-wisher** ['wel·wɪʃ·ər] *n* simpatizante *mf*
**well-worn** [ˌwel·'wɔrn] *adj* raído, -a; *fig*
trillado, -a
**went** [went] *pt of* go
**wept** [wept] *pt, pp of* weep
**were** [wɜr] *pt of* be
**we're** [wɪr] = we are *see* be
**weren't** [wɜrnt] = were not *see* be
**west** [west] **I.** *n* oeste *m;* **in the ~ of
Mexico** en el oeste de México; **to lie 5
miles to the ~ of...** quedar a 8 km al
oeste de...; **to the ~** hacia el oeste; **the
West** el mundo occidental; **the Wild
West** el viejo oeste **II.** *adj* occidental; **~ wind** viento del oeste; **~ coast**
costa oeste; **West Indies** Antillas *fpl*
**III.** *adv* al oeste; **further ~** más al oeste
▶ **to go ~** (*thing*) estropearse; (*person*)
irse al otro mundo
**westbound** ['west·baʊnd] *adj* que va
hacia el oeste
**westerly** ['wes·tər·li] *adj* (del) oeste
**western** ['wes·tərn] **I.** *adj* occidental
**II.** *n* western *m*
**westerner** *n* occidental *mf*; (*western US*)
del oeste de EEUU
**westernize** ['wes·tər·naɪz] *vt* occiden-
talizar
**West Virginia** *n* Virginia *f* Occidental
**wet** [wet] **I.** *adj* <-tt-> **1.** (*soaked*) mojado, -a; (*damp*) húmedo, -a; (*paint*)
fresco, -a; **to get ~** mojarse; **to get sth
~** mojar algo; **~ through** calado hasta los
huesos **2.** (*rainy*) lluvioso, -a ▶ **to be
~ behind the ears** estar con la miel en
los labios; **to be all ~** estar en la parra
**II.** <wet, wet> *vt* humedecer; **to ~ the
bed** mojar la cama
**we've** [wiv] = we have *see* have
**whack** [hwæk] *inf* **I.** *vt* golpear
**II.** *n* (*blow*) golpe *m* ▶ **to be out of ~**

estar fastidiado; **to have a ~ at** intentar
**whacking** n zurra f
**whale** [hweɪl] n ballena f ▸ **a ~ of a...** un(a) enorme...; **to have a ~ of a time** pasarlo bomba
**whaling** n pesca f de ballenas
**wham** [hwæm] interj zas
**wharf** [hwɔrf] <-ves> n muelle m
**what** [hwʌt] **I.** adj interrog qué; **~ kind of book?** ¿qué tipo de libro?; **~ time is it?** ¿qué hora es?; **~ men is he talking about?** ¿de qué hombres está hablando?; **~ an idiot!** ¡qué idiota! **II.** pron **1.** interrog qué; **~ can I do?** ¿qué puedo hacer?; **~ does it matter?** ¿qué importa?; **~'s up?** ¿qué hay?; **~ for?** ¿para qué?; **~ is he like?** ¿cómo es?; **~'s his name?** ¿cómo se llama?; **~'s it called?** ¿cómo se llama?; **~ about Paul?** ¿y Paul?; **~ about a walk?** ¿te va un paseo?; **~ if it snows?** inf ¿y si nieva? **2.** rel lo que; **~ I like is ~ he says** lo que me gusta es lo que dice; **~ is more** lo que es más **III.** interj **~?** ¡qué!; **so ~?** ¿y qué?; **is he coming, or ~?** ¿viene, o qué?
**whatever** [hwʌt·ˈev·ər] **I.** pron **1.** (anything) (todo) lo que; **~ happens, happens** pasará lo que tenga que pasar **2.** (any of them) cualquier(a); **~ you pick is fine** cualquiera que elijas está bien **II.** adj **1.** (being what it may be) cualquiera que; **~ the reason sea** cual sea la razón **2.** (of any kind) de ningún tipo; **there is no doubt ~** no cabe duda
**whatnot** [ˈhwʌt·nɑt] n chisme m; **and ~** y demás
**whatsoever** [ˌhwʌt·soʊ·ˈev·ər] adv sea cual sea; **nothing ~** nada de nada; **to have no interest ~** no tener interés alguno (**in** en)
**wheat** [hwit] n trigo m
**wheat belt** n zona f de cultivo de trigo
**wheel** [hwil] **I.** n **1.** AUTO rueda f; **alloy ~s** llantas f pl de aleación; **front/rear ~** rueda delantera/trasera; **to be on ~s** ir sobre ruedas **2.** (steering wheel) volante m; NAUT timón m; **to be at the ~** ir al volante; **to get behind the ~** ponerse al volante **3.** TECH torno m **4.** **~s** sl carro m ▸ **to be hell on ~s** sl ser un peli-

gro al volante **II.** vt empujar **III.** vi girar ▸ **to ~ and deal** trapichear
◆**wheel around** vi dar media vuelta
**wheelbarrow** [ˈhwil·ˌbær·oʊ] n carretilla f
**wheelchair** n silla f de ruedas
**wheeler-dealer** [ˌhwi·lər·ˈdi·lər] n trapichero, -a m, f
**wheeze** [hwiz] <-zing> vi resollar
**when** [hwen] **I.** adv cuándo; **since ~?** ¿desde cuándo?; **I'll tell him ~ to go** yo le diré cuándo ir **II.** conj **1.** (at which time) en que; **at the moment ~ he arrived** en el momento en que vino **2.** (during) **~ singing that song** cuando cantaba esa canción **3.** (every time) **~ it snows** cuando nieva **4.** (although) **he buys it ~ he could borrow it** lo compra cuando podría pedirlo prestado **5.** (considering) **how can I listen ~ I can't hear?** ¿cómo puedo escuchar si no puedo oír?
**whenever** [hwen·ˈev·ər] **I.** conj **1.** (every time) siempre que; **~ I can** siempre que puedo **2.** (at any time) **he can come ~ he likes** puede venir cuando quiera **II.** adv **~ did I say that?** ¿cuándo he dicho yo eso?; **tomorrow or ~** mañana o un día de estos
**where** [hwer] adv **1.** interrog dónde; **~ does he live?** ¿dónde vive?; **~ does he come from?** ¿de dónde es?; **~ is he going (to)?** ¿adónde va? **2.** rel donde; **the box ~ he puts his things** la caja donde pone sus cosas
**whereabouts** [ˈhwer·ə·baʊts] **I.** n + sing/pl vb paradero m **II.** adv inf dónde; **~ in Caracas do you live?** ¿en qué zona de Caracas vives?
**whereas** [hwer·ˈæz] conj (while) mientras que
**whereby** [hwer·ˈbaɪ] conj por lo cual
**wherein** [hwer·ˈɪn] conj form en donde
**whereupon** [ˈhwer·ə·pɑn] conj con lo cual
**wherever** [ˌhwer·ˈev·ər] **I.** conj dondequiera que; **I am/I go** dondequiera que esté/vaya; **~ he likes** donde le plazca **II.** adv **~ did she find that?** ¿dónde demonios encontró eso?; **or ~** o donde sea

**wherewithal** ['hwer·wɪð·ɔl] *n liter* recursos *mpl*

**whet** [hwet] <-tt-> *vt* 1. (*sharpen*) afilar 2. (*stimulate*) estimular

**whether** ['hweð·ər] *conj* 1. (*if*) si; **to tell/ask ~ it's true** (**or not**) decir/preguntar si es verdad (o no); **I doubt ~ he'll come** dudo que venga 2. (*all the same*) sea; **~ rich or poor** sean ricos o pobres; **~ I go by bus or bike** vaya en autobús o en bici

**whew** [hwu, fju] *interj* uf

**which** [hwɪtʃ] I. *adj interrog* qué; **~ one(s)?** ¿cuál(es)? II. *pron* 1. *interrog* cuál, qué; **~ is his?** ¿cuál es el suyo? 2. *rel* que, el que, la lo que *neuter;* **the book ~ I read/of ~ I'm speaking** el libro que leí/del que estoy hablando; **he said he was there, ~ I believed** dijo que estaba ahí, lo cual creí

**whichever** [hwɪtʃ·'ev·ər] I. *pron* cualquiera que; **you can choose ~ you like** puedes escoger el que quieras II. *adj* cualquier, el que, la que **you can take ~ book you like** puedes coger el libro que quieras

**whiff** [hwɪf] *n* 1. (*smell*) olorcillo *m* (**to a**) 2. (*trace*) indicio *m*

**while** [hwaɪl] I. *n* rato *m;* **a short ~** un ratito; **quite a ~** bastante tiempo; **after/for a ~** después de/durante un rato; **once in a ~** de vez en cuando II. *conj* 1. (*during*) mientras; **I did it ~ he was sleeping** lo hice mientras él dormía; **~ I'm alive** mientras (que yo) viva 2. (*although*) aunque; **~ I like it, I won't buy it** aunque me guste, no lo compraré; **~ I know it's true...** a pesar de que sé que es verdad...

**whim** [hwɪm] *n* capricho *m;* **on a ~** por capricho; **as the ~ takes him** según se le antoja

**whimper** ['hwɪm·pər] I. *vi* quejarse; (*child*) lloriquear II. *n* quejido *m;* **to give a ~** dar un gemido

**whimsical** ['hwɪm·zɪ·kəl] *adj* 1. (*odd*) descabellado, -a 2. (*capricious*) caprichoso, -a

**whine** [hwaɪn] I. <-ning> *vi* gemir; (*cry*) lloriquear; (*engine*) zumbar II. *n* quejido *m;* (*engine*) zumbido *m*

**whip** [hwɪp] I. *n* (*lash*) látigo *m*, fuete *m AmL* II. <-pp-> *vt* 1. azotar; **to ~ sb** *fig* dar una paliza a alguien (**at, in en**) 2. CULIN batir

◆**whip back** *vi* 1. (*bounce back*) rebotar bruscamente 2. (*return*) volverse de golpe

◆**whip off** *vt* (*tablecloth*) sacar de un tirón

◆**whip on** *vt* 1. (*urge on*) animar 2. (*put on quickly*) ponerse rápidamente

◆**whip up** *vt* 1. (*encourage*) avivar; **to ~ support** conseguir apoyo 2. *inf* (*prepare*) improvisar 3. CULIN batir

**whiplash** *n* <-es> 1. (*whip part*) tralla *f* 2. (*blow*) latigazo *m* 3. MED traumatismo *m* cervical

**whipped cream** *n* nata *f* para montar

**whipping** *n* 1. (*punishment*) azotaina *f;* **to give/get a ~** dar/llevarse una paliza 2. (*gusting*) azote *m;* **the ~ of the wind** el azote del viento

**whipping cream** *n* nata *f* para montar

**whir** [hwɜr] <-rr-> I. *vi* hacer ruido II. *n* ruido *m;* (*of wings*) aleteo *m*

**whirl** [hwɜrl] I. *vi* girar rápidamente; **my head ~s** la cabeza me da vueltas II. *vt* hacer girar; **to ~ sb around** dar vueltas a alguien III. *n* torbellino *m;* **a ~ of dust** una polvareda ▶ **to give sth a ~** probar algo

**whirlpool** ['hwɜrl·pul] *n* remolino *m*

**whirlwind** *n* torbellino *m;* **a ~ romance** un idilio relámpago

**whisk** [hwɪsk] I. *vt* 1. CULIN batir 2. (*take quickly*) llevar rápidamente II. *n* 1. (*kitchen tool*) batidora *f;* **electric/hand-held ~** batidora eléctrica/de mano 2. (*movement*) sacudida *f;* (*of tail*) coletazo *m*

**whisker** ['hwɪs·kər] *n* **~s** pelo *m* de la barba; (*of animal*) bigotes *mpl* ▶ **by a ~** por un pelo; **within a ~** (*of doing sth*) a punto (de hacer algo)

**whiskey**, **whisky** ['hwɪs·ki] *n* <-ies> whisky *m*

**whisper** ['hwɪs·pər] I. *vi* cuchichear II. *vt* 1. (*speak softly*) susurrar; **to ~ sth in sb's ear** decir algo al oído 2. *fig* (*gossip*) rumorear; **it is ~ed...** se rumorea... III. *n* 1. (*soft sound or speech*)

**whistle** ['hwɪs·əl] I. <-ling> vi, vt silbar (at a); (bird) trinar II. n 1. silbido m; the ~ of the wind el silbido del viento 2. (device) silbato m; to blow a ~ pitar ▸ to blow the ~ llamar al orden (on a)

**white** [hwaɪt] I. adj blanco, -a; ~ sauce bechamel f; to turn [or go] ~ with fear palidecer de miedo II. n 1. blanco m; (egg) clara f 2. (person) blanco, -a m, f

**White House** n the ~ la Casa Blanca

**white lie** n mentira f piadosa

**whiten** ['hwaɪ·tən] vi, vt blanquear; (go pale) palidecer

**whitewash** ['hwaɪt·waʃ] I. <-es> n 1. (for walls) cal f 2. (coverup) blanqueo m 3. (victory) paliza f II. vt 1. (wall) encalar 2. (conceal) blanquear 3. SPORTS dar una paliza

**white wine** n vino m blanco

**Whitsun** ['hwɪt·sən] n Pentecostés m

**whittle** ['hwɪt̬·əl] <-ling> vt tallar

**whiz** [hwɪz] I. n 1. inf (person) hacha m 2. (noise) silbido m 3. sl to take a ~ echar un meo II. vi ir disparado; to ~ along ir a toda pastilla; to ~ by pasar como una bala

**whizz** [hwɪz] n vi see whiz

**who** [hu] pron 1. interrog quién, quiénes; ~ broke the window? ¿quién rompió la ventana?; ~ were they? ¿quiénes eran? 2. rel que; the people ~ work here la gente que trabaja aquí; all those ~ know her todos los que la conocen; it was your sister ~ did it fue tu hermana quien lo hizo

**whoa** [hwoʊ] interj (to horse) so; (to person) para el carro

**whoever** [hu·'ev·ər] pron 1. rel (who) quien, quienes, quienquiera que, quienesquiera que; ~ said that doesn't know me el que dijo eso no me conoce 2. interrog quién diablos; ~ said that? ¿quién diablos dijo eso?

**whole** [hoʊl] I. adj 1. (entire) todo, -a; the ~ world el mundo entero 2. (in one piece) entero, -a; to swallow sth ~ tragarse algo entero 3. (intact) intacto, -a; (person) ileso, -a II. n 1. (a com-plete thing) todo m; as a ~ en su totalidad; taken as a ~ en conjunto; on the ~ en general 2. (entirety) totalidad f; the ~ la totalidad; the ~ of next week toda la semana que viene III. adv inf completamente; a ~ lot of people un mogollón de gente; to be a ~ lot faster ser mucho más rápido

**wholesale** ['hoʊl·seɪl] I. n venta f al por mayor II. adj 1. COM al por mayor; (business, supplier) mayorista 2. (on a large scale) a gran escala III. adv 1. COM al por mayor 2. (in bulk) en masa

**wholesaler** ['hoʊl·seɪ·lər] n mayorista mf; furniture ~ mayorista de muebles

**wholesome** ['hoʊl·səm] adj sano, -a

**who'll** [hul] = who will see will

**wholly** ['hoʊ·li] adv enteramente; to be ~ aware/different ser totalmente consciente/diferente

**whom** [hum] pron 1. interrog a quién, a quiénes after prep quién, quiénes; ~ did he see? ¿a quién vio?; to ~ did he talk? ¿con quién habló? 2. rel a quien, que after prep quien, que; those ~ I love aquellos a quienes amo; with ~ con quien

**whoop** [hup] I. vi gritar II. vt to ~ it up echar una cana al aire III. n grito m

**whoopee** ['hwu·pi] I. interj estupendo II. n juerga f; to make ~ sl (have sex) echar un polvo; (celebrate) pasárselo de puta madre

**whooping cough** ['hu·pɪŋ·ˌkɔf] n tos f ferina

**whoops** [hwʊps] interj epa

**whopper** ['hwap·ər] n iron 1. (huge thing) cosa f muy grande; a ~ of a fish un cacho pez 2. (lie) embuste m; to tell a ~ contar una mentira como una casa

**whopping** ['hwap·ɪŋ] adj sl enorme; a ~ lie una mentira como una casa

**whore** [hɔr] n puta f

**who's** [huz] 1. = who is see is 2. = who has see has

**whose** [huz] I. adj 1. interrog de quién, de quiénes; ~ book is this? ¿de quién es este libro?; ~ son is he? ¿de quién es hijo? 2. rel cuyo, cuyos, cuya, cuyas; the girl ~ brother I saw la chica cuyo hermano vi II. pron pos de quién, de

**W**

quiénes; **~ is this pen?** ¿de quién es esta pluma?

**why** [hwaɪ] **I.** *adv* por qué; **~ not?** ¿por qué no?; **~'s that?** ¿y eso por qué?; **that's ~ I didn't tell you** por eso no te dije nada; **I want to know ~ you came late** quiero saber por qué llegaste tarde **II.** *n* porqué *m* **III.** *interj* ¡cómo!

**wick** [wɪk] *n* mecha *f*

**wicked** ['wɪk·ɪd] **I.** *adj* **1.** (*evil*) malvado, -a **2.** (*malicious*) retorcido, -a; (*sense of humor*) mordaz **3.** *sl* de puta madre **II.** *n* **the ~** los malos

**wicker** ['wɪk·ər] *n* mimbre *m*

**wicket** ['wɪk·ɪt] *n* (*door*) portillo *m;* **to be in a sticky ~** estar en un apuro

**wide** [waɪd] **I.** *adj* **1.** (*broad*) extenso, -a; (*as a measurement*) ancho, -a; **it is 3 feet ~** tiene 1 m de ancho **2.** (*varied*) amplio, -a; **a ~ range/experience** una amplia gama/experiencia **3.** (*extensive*) grande; **~ support** gran apoyo *m* **II.** *adv* extensamente; (*eyes*) como platos; (*door, window*) de par en par; **to be ~ apart** estar muy lejos (el uno del otro)

**wide-angle** [,waɪd·ˈæŋ·ɡəl] *adj* gran angular

**wide-awake** [,waɪd·ə·ˈweɪk] *adj* bien despierto, -a

**wide-eyed** [ˈwaɪd·aɪd] *adj fig* inocente

**widely** *adv* **1.** (*broadly*) extensamente; (*smile*) ampliamente; (*gesture*) mucho **2.** (*extensively*) ampliamente; **~ accepted/admired** muy aceptado/admirado **3.** (*to a large degree*) considerablemente; **~ differing aims** objetivos muy diferentes

**widen** [ˈwaɪ·dən] **I.** *vt* extender; (*discussion*) ampliar **II.** *vi* ensancharse

**wide-open** [ˈwaɪd·ˌoʊ·pən] *adj* **1.** (*undecided*) abierto, -a **2.** (*exposed*) expuesto, -a; **to be ~** estar expuesto (**to** a)

**widespread** [ˈwaɪd·spred] *adj* extendido, -a; *fig* general

**widow** [ˈwɪd·oʊ] **I.** *n* viuda *f* **II.** *vt* dejar viuda; **to be ~ed** enviudar

**widowed** *adj* viudo, -a

**widower** [ˈwɪd·oʊ·ər] *n* viudo *m;* **to be left a ~** enviudar

**width** [wɪdθ] *n* **1.** (*distance*) extensión *f;* (*clothes*) ancho *m;* **to be 4 inches in**

**~** medir 10 cm de ancho **2.** (*amount, size*) amplitud *f*

**wield** [wild] *vt* manejar; (*weapon*) empuñar; (*power*) ejercer

**wife** [waɪf] <wives> *n* mujer *f;* **my ~** mi mujer

**wig** [wɪɡ] *n* peluca *f*

**wiggle** [ˈwɪɡ·əl] **I.** *vt* menear **II.** *n* (*movement*) meneo *m;* (*walking*) contoneo *m*

**wild** [waɪld] **I.** *adj* **1.** (*animal*) salvaje; (*plant*) silvestre; (*landscape*) agreste **2.** (*unruly*) indisciplinado, -a; (*party*) loco, -a **3.** (*not sensible*) insensato, -a; (*plan*) descabellado, -a; (*guess*) disparatado, -a **4.** (*extreme*) absurdo, -a **5.** METEO tormentoso, -a; (*wind, weather*) furioso, -a **6.** (*angry*) hecho, -a una fiera; **to drive sb ~** sacar de quicio a alguien; **to go ~** ponerse como loco **7.** (*enthusiastic*) loquito, -a; (*applause*) entusiasta **II.** *adv* silvestre; **to grow ~** crecer libre; **to let one's imagination run ~** dejar volar la imaginación

**wild card** *n* GAMES, COMPUT comodín *m*

**wildcat** *n* **1.** ZOOL gato *m* montés **2.** *fig* fiera *f*

**wilderness** [ˈwɪl·dər·nɪs] *n* **1.** (*desert tract*) páramo *m* **2.** (*unspoiled land*) paraje *m* natural

**wildfire** [ˈwaɪld·faɪr] *n* fuego *m* incontrolado ► **to spread like ~** extenderse como un reguero de pólvora

**wild goose** <- geese> *n* ganso *m* salvaje

**wild-goose chase** *n* (*search*) búsqueda *f* inútil

**wildlife** *n* fauna *f* y flora *f*

**wildly** *adv* **1.** (*frantically*) como loco; **to behave ~** portarse como un salvaje; **to talk ~** hablar sin ton ni son **2.** (*haphazardly*) a lo loco; (*shoot, guess*) a tontas y a locas **3.** *inf* (*very*) muy; **~ exaggerated** superexagerado; **~ expensive** carísimo

**wilful** [ˈwɪl·fəl] *adj see* **willful**

**will**[1] [wɪl] <would, would> *aux* **1.** (*future*) **they'll be delighted** estarán encantados; **I'll be with you in a minute** estaré contigo en un minuto; **she ~ have received the letter by now** ya debe haber recibido la carta **2.** (*imme-*

diate *future*) **we'll be off now** ya nos vamos **3.** (*tag question*) **you won't forget, ~ you?** no se te olvidará, ¿verdad? **4.** (*request*) **~ you let me speak!?** ¡déjame hablar!; **give me a hand, ~ you?** échame una mano, ¿quieres?; **~ you be having a slice of cake?** ¿quiere un trozo de tarta? **5.** (*willingness*) **who'll mail this letter for me? — I ~** ¿quién me echa esta carta al buzón? — lo haré yo **6.** (*fact*) **the car won't run without gas** el coche no funciona sin gasolina **7.** (*persistence*) **he ~ keep doing that** se empeña en hacer eso; **the door won't open** no hay manera de abrir la puerta **8.** (*likelihood*) **they'll be tired** estarán cansados

**will²** [wɪl] **I.** *n* **1.** (*faculty*) voluntad *f* (**to** de); (*desire*) deseo *m*; **at ~** a voluntad; **to lose the ~ to live** perder las ganas de vivir **2.** (*testament*) testamento *m* ▸ **where there's a ~, there's a way** querer es poder; **with the best ~ in the world** con la mejor voluntad del mundo; **to have a ~ of one's own** ser cabezón **II.** *vt* **1.** (*try to cause*) sugestionar; **to ~ sb to do sth** sugestionar a alguien para que haga algo **2.** (*bequeath*) legar

**willful** ['wɪl·fəl] *adj* **1.** (*deliberate*) intencionado, -a; (*murder*) premeditado, -a **2.** (*self-willed*) testarudo, -a

**willing** ['wɪl·ɪŋ] *adj* **1.** dispuesto, -a; **to be ~ to do sth** estar dispuesto a hacer algo **2.** (*compliant*) servicial

**willingness** *n* **1.** (*readiness*) disposición *f* **2.** (*enthusiasm*) entusiasmo *m*; **lack of ~** falta *f* de ánimo

**willow** ['wɪl·oʊ] *n* sauce *m*

**willowy** ['wɪl·oʊ·i] *adj* esbelto, -a

**willpower** ['wɪl·ˌpaʊ·ər] *n* fuerza *f* de voluntad

**wilt** [wɪlt] *vi* (*plants*) marchitarse; (*person*) desanimarse

**wily** ['waɪ·li] <-ier, -iest> *adj* astuto, -a

**wimp** [wɪmp] *n sl* endeble *mf*

**win** [wɪn] **I.** *n* victoria *f* **II.** <won, won> *vt* ganar; (*obtain*) obtener; (*recognition, popularity*) ganarse ▸ **to ~ the day** prevalecer; **you can't ~ them all you ~ some, you lose some** no se puede ganar todo **III.** <won, won> *vi* ganar

▸ **to ~ hands down** ganar con mucha facilidad; **you (just) can't ~ with him/her** con él/ella, siempre llevas las de perder; **you ~!** ¡como tú digas!

◆**win back** *vt* recuperar

◆**win over** *vt* ganarse; (*convince*) convencer (**to** para)

**wince** [wɪns] *n* mueca *f* de dolor

**wind¹** [wɪnd] *n* **1.** (*current of air*) viento *m*; **gust of ~** ráfaga *f*; **a breath of ~** un poco de aire **2.** (*breath*) aliento *m*; **to get** (*or* **catch**) **one's ~** recobrar el aliento; **to have the ~ knocked out of sb** parar a alguien los pies ▸ **to take the ~ out of sb's sails** desanimar a alguien; **to sail close to the ~** estar a punto de pasarse de la raya; **to get ~ of sth** enterarse de algo; **to go** (*or* **run**) **like the ~** correr como el viento; **there's sth in the ~** se está tramando algo

**wind²** [waɪnd] <wound, wound> **I.** *vt* **1.** (*coil*) enrollar (**around** alrededor de); (*clock, watch*) dar cuerda a **2.** (*wrap*) envolver **II.** *vi* serpentear

◆**wind down I.** *vt* (*reduce*) reducir; (*business*) limitar **II.** *vi* **1.** (*business*) tocar a su fin **2.** (*relax*) desconectar

◆**wind up I.** *vt* (*finish*) acabar; (*debate, meeting, speech*) concluir **II.** *vi* **to ~ in prison** ir a parar a la cárcel

**windbag** ['wɪnd·bæg] *n* charlatán, -ana *m, f*

**winder** ['waɪn·dər] *n* cuerda *f*

**windfall** ['wɪnd·fɔl] *n* fruta *f* caída; (*money*) ganancia *f* imprevista

**wind farm** *n* granja *f* con energía eólica

**winding** ['waɪn·dɪŋ] *adj* sinuoso, -a

**wind instrument** *n* instrumento *m* de viento

**windmill** *n* molino *m* de viento; (*toy*) molinillo *m*

**window** ['wɪn·doʊ] *n a.* COMPUT ventana *f*; **pop-up ~** ventana emergente; (*shop*) escaparate *m*; (*vehicle*) ventanilla *f*; **rear ~** ventanilla trasera ▸ **to go out (of) the ~** (*plan*) venirse abajo

**window box** <-es> *n* jardinera *f*

**window envelope** *n* sobre *m* de ventanilla

**window-shopping** *n* **to go ~** ir de escaparates

**windpipe** ['wɪnd·paɪp] n tráquea f

**windshield** ['wɪnd·ʃild] n parabrisas m inv

**windsock** n manga f de viento

**windsurfer** ['wɪnd·ˌsɜr·fər] n windsurfista mf

**windsurfing** ['wɪnd·ˌsɜr·fɪŋ] n windsurf m

**wind tunnel** n túnel m aerodinámico

**windward** ['wɪnd·wərd] n barlovento m

**windy**[1] ['wɪn·di] <-ier, -iest> adj (weather) ventoso, -a

**windy**[2] ['waɪn·di] <-ier, -iest> adj (road) sinuoso, -a

**wine** [waɪn] n vino m

**wine cooler** n (drink) ≈ sangría f

**wine list** n carta f de vinos

**winery** ['waɪ·nə·ri] <-ies> n bodega f

**wing** [wɪŋ] I. n 1. ZOOL, AVIAT, ARCHIT, SPORTS, POL ala f; **the west ~ of the house** el ala oeste de la casa; **left/right ~** ala izquierda/derecha 2. ~s THEAT bastidores mpl; **to be waiting in the ~s** estar esperando su oportunidad ► **to** spread [or °stretch] **one's ~s** desplegar las alas; **to** take **sb under one's ~** hacerse cargo de alguien II. vt (fly) volar ► **to ~ it** arreglárselas sobre la marcha

**winger** ['wɪŋ·ər] n SPORTS extremo -a m, f; **left/right ~** extremo izquierdo/derecho

**wing nut** n TECH palomilla f

**wingspan** ['wɪŋ·spæn] n, **wingspread** ['wɪŋ·spred] n envergadura f

**wink** [wɪŋk] I. n 1. guiño m; **to give sb a ~** guiñar el ojo a alguien ► **to have** forty **~s** echarse una siestecita; **to not** sleep **a ~** no pegar ojo; in a **~** en un tris II. vi guiñar el ojo (at a); (light) parpadear

**winner** ['wɪn·ər] n 1. (person) ganador(a) m(f) 2. inf (success) éxito m; (book) obra f premiada; **to be on to a ~** tener mucho éxito (with con)

**winning** ['wɪn·ɪŋ] I. adj 1. ganador(a); (ticket) premiado, -a; (point) decisivo, -a 2. (charming) encantador(a) II. n 1. triunfo m 2. ~s (money) ganancias fpl

**winter** ['wɪn·tər] I. n invierno m II. vi hibernar

**winter sports** npl deportes m pl de invierno

**wint(e)ry** ['wɪn·tri] adj invernal; fig frío, -a

**wipe** [waɪp] I. n 1. limpieza f; **to give the floor a ~** limpiar el suelo 2. (tissue) toallita f II. vt limpiar; (floor) fregar; (one's nose) sonarse; (disk) borrar; **to ~ dry** secar

**wipe down** vt limpiar

**wipe off** vt 1. quitar con un trapo; (data, program) borrar 2. ECON reducir ► **to wipe the smile off sb's** face borrar a alguien la sonrisa de la cara

**wipe out** vt 1. (destroy) exterminar; (economically) arruinar; (debt) liquidar 2. (tire out) dejar hecho polvo

**wipe up** I. vt limpiar II. vi secar

**wire** [waɪr] I. n 1. (metal thread) alambre m 2. ELEC cable m 3. (hidden microphone) micro m (oculto) 4. (prison camp fence) alambrada f 5. inf **to get one's ~s** crossed tener un malentendido; **to** get (sth) **in under the ~** conseguir algo justo a tiempo II. vt ELEC conectar

**wireless** ['waɪr·lɪs] adj inalámbrico, -a

**wiretapping** ['waɪr·ˌtæp·ɪŋ] n escuchas f pl telefónicas

**wire transfer** n transferencia f por cable

**wiring** ['waɪ·rɪŋ] n ELEC 1. (system of wires) cableado m 2. (electrical installation) instalación f eléctrica

**wisdom** ['wɪz·dəm] n 1. sabiduría f; **with the ~ of hindsight** con la sabiduría que da la experiencia; **~ comes with age** más sabe el diablo por viejo que por diablo prov 2. (sensibleness) prudencia f

**wisdom tooth** <- teeth> n muela f del juicio

**wise** [waɪz] adj 1. (having knowledge) sabio, -a 2. (showing sagacity) acertado, -a 3. (sensible) sensato, -a 4. inf (aware) consciente; **to be ~ to sb** tener calado a alguien; **to be ~ to sth** estar al tanto de algo; **to get ~** caer en la cuenta (to de); **to be none the ~r** seguir sin enterarse (for de)

**wise up** sl I. vi ponerse al tanto (to de) II. vt poner al tanto (about de)

**wisecrack** ['waɪz·kræk] I. n coña f II. vi estar de coña

**wise guy** n sl gracioso, -a m, f

**wish** [wɪʃ] I. <-es> n 1. (desire) deseo *m;* **against my ~es** en contra de mi voluntad; **to make a ~** pedir un deseo; **to have no ~** no tener ganas (to de) II. *vt* 1. *(desire)* desear; **I ~ he hadn't come** ojalá no hubiera venido; **I ~ you'd told me** me lo podrías haber dicho 2. *form (want)* **to ~ to do sth** querer algo 3. *(hope)* **to ~ sb luck** desear suerte a alguien; **to ~ sb happy birthday** felicitar a alguien por su cumpleaños; **to ~ sb good night** dar las buenas noches a alguien III. *vi* **to ~ (for)** desear; **as you ~** como usted mande; **if you ~** como quieras; **everything one could ~ for** todo lo que uno podría desear

**wishbone** ['wɪʃ·boʊn] *n* espoleta *f*

**wishful thinking** *n* ilusión *f*

**wishy-washy** ['wɪʃ·i·ˌwɑʃ·i] *adj* insípido, -a; *(drink, soup)* aguado, -a; *(argument)* flojo, -a

**wisp** [wɪsp] *n (hair)* mechón *m*

**wispy** ['wɪs·pi] *adj (hair)* ralo, -a; *(person)* menudo, -a; *(clouds)* tenue

**wistful** ['wɪst·fəl] *adj* nostálgico, -a; *(longing)* añorante

**wit** [wɪt] *n* 1. *(humor)* ingenio *m;* **to have a dry ~** ser mordaz 2. *(intelligence)* inteligencia *f;* **to be at one's ~s' end** estar para volverse loco; **to gather one's ~s** poner las ideas en orden; **to have/keep one's ~s about one** andar con mucho ojo; **to live off one's ~s** vivir del cuento 3. *(person)* chistoso, -a *m, f*

**witch** [wɪtʃ] *n* bruja *f*

**witchcraft** ['wɪtʃ·kræft] *n* brujería *f,* payé *m CSur*

**witch doctor** *n* curandero, -a *m, f,* payé *m CSur*

**witch-hunt** ['wɪtʃ·hʌnt] *n* caza *f* de brujas

**with** [wɪð, wɪθ] *prep* 1. *(accompanied by, by means of)* con; *(together)* **~ sb** (junto) con alguien; **to take sth ~ both hands** tomar algo con las dos manos 2. *(having)* **the man ~ the umbrella** el hombre del paraguas; **~ no hesitation at all** sin ningún titubeo 3. *(manner)*

**~ all speed** a toda velocidad; **~ one's whole heart** de todo corazón; **to cry ~ rage** llorar de rabia 4. *(despite)* **~ all his faults** a pesar de todos sus defectos 5. *(supporting)* **to be ~ sb/sth** estar de acuerdo con alguien/algo; **popular ~ young people** popular entre los jóvenes 6. *(understanding)* **I'm not ~ you** no te sigo; **to be ~ it** estar al tanto; **to get ~ it** ponerse al día

**withdraw** [wɪð·'drɔ] *irr* I. *vt* 1. *(take out)* quitar; *(money)* sacar 2. *(take back)* retirar 3. *(cancel)* cancelar II. *vi* 1. *(leave)* retirarse *(from* de*)* 2. *(socially)* recluirse; *(into silence)* retraerse

**withdrawal** [wɪð·'drɔ·əl] *n* 1. a. MIL retirada *f;* **to make a ~** FIN sacar dinero 2. *(sports)* abandono *m* 3. PSYCH retraimiento *m* 4. MED abstinencia *f;* **to go through ~** presentar síndrome de abstinencia

**wither** ['wɪð·ər] I. *vi* marchitarse; *fig* debilitarse ▶ **to ~ on the vine** desaparecer poco a poco II. *vt (plant)* marchitar; *(strength)* mermar

**withering** ['wɪð·ər·ɪŋ] *adj* destructivo, -a; *(heat, fire)* abrasador(a); *(criticism)* hiriente

**withhold** [wɪð·'hoʊld] *irr vt* ocultar *(from* a*);* *(support)* negar; *(benefits, rent)* retener

**within** [wɪð·'ɪn] I. *prep* 1. *(place)* dentro de, en; **~ the country** dentro del país; **~ sight/easy reach** al alcance de la vista/mano; **~ 5 miles of the town** a menos de 8 km de la ciudad 2. *(time)* en (el transcurso de); **~ 3 days** en (el plazo de) tres días 3. *(according to)* de acuerdo a; **~ the law** dentro de la legalidad II. *adv* dentro; **from ~** desde dentro

**without** [wɪð·'aʊt] *prep* sin; **~ warning** sin previo aviso; **to do ~ sth** apañárselas sin algo

**withstand** [wɪð·'stænd] *irr vt* resistir; *(heat, pressure)* soportar

**witness** ['wɪt·nɪs] I. *n* a. LAW testigo *mf* *(to* de*);* **according to ~es** según testigos II. *vt* 1. *(see)* ser testigo de; *(changes)* presenciar; **to ~ sb doing sth** observar a alguien haciendo algo 2. *(authenticate)* dar fe de

**W**

**witness stand** n tribuna f

**witty** ['wɪt·i] <-ier, -iest> adj ingenioso, -a; (funny) gracioso, -a

**wizard** ['wɪz·ərd] n mago, -a m, f; (expert) genio mf; **to be a ~ at sth** ser un genio haciendo algo

**wobble** ['wab·əl] I. vi tambalearse; (voice) temblar; (prices, shares) fluctuar II. n 1. (movement) tambaleo m 2. (sound) temblor m 3. ECON fluctuación f

**wobbly** ['wab·li] <-ier, -iest> adj tambaleante; (line) zigzagueante; (chair) cojo, -a; (voice) tembloroso, -a

**woe** [wou] n desgracia f; **~s** males mpl

**wok** [wak] n wok m

**woke** [wouk] vt, vi pt of **wake**

**woken** ['wou·kən] vt, vi pp of **wake**

**wolf** [wʊlf] I. <wolves> n 1. lobo m 2. (seducer) donjuán m ▶ **a ~ in sheep's clothing** un lobo disfrazado de cordero; **to cry ~** dar una falsa alarma II. vt engullir

**woman** ['wʊm·ən] <women> n 1. mujer f; **~ candidate/president** candidata/presidenta 2. inf parienta f

**womb** [wum] n útero m; **in the ~** en el seno materno

**women's lib** n inf abbr of **women's liberation** liberación f de la mujer

**won** [wʌn] vt, vi pt, pp of **win**

**wonder** ['wʌn·dər] I. vt preguntarse; **to make sb ~** hacer pensar a alguien; **I ~ why he said that** me extraña que dijera eso II. vi 1. (ask oneself) preguntarse; **to ~ about doing sth** pensar si hacer algo 2. (feel surprise) sorprenderse (at de); **I don't ~** (at it) no me extraña III. n 1. (marvel) maravilla f; **to do** [or **work] ~s** hacer maravillas; **the ~s of modern technology** los prodigios de la tecnología moderna; **it's a ~** (that)... es un milagro que... +subj; **~s** (will) never cease! ¡eso sí es increíble! 2. (feeling) asombro m; **in ~** con asombro; **to listen in ~** escuchar estupefacto

**wonder drug** n remedio m milagroso

**wonderful** ['wʌn·dər·fəl] adj maravilloso, -a

**wonderland** ['wʌn·dər·lænd] n país m de las maravillas

**won't** [woʊnt] = **will not** see **will**

**woo** [wu] vt 1. (attract) atraer 2. (court) cortejar

**wood** [wʊd] n 1. (material) madera f; (for a fire) leña f 2. **~s** bosque m ▶ **to touch** [or **knock] on ~** tocar madera; **to be out of the ~s** estar a salvo

**woodcut** n grabado f en madera

**wooded** ['wʊd·ɪd] adj boscoso, -a

**wooden** ['wʊd·ən] adj 1. (of wood) de madera 2. (awkward) rígido, -a; (smile) inexpresivo, -a

**woodland** ['wʊd·lənd] n bosque m

**woodpecker** n pájaro m carpintero

**woodpile** n montón m de leña

**woodshed** ['wʊd·ʃed] n leñera f

**woodwind** ['wʊd·wɪnd] adj de viento

**woodwork** ['wʊd·wɜrk] n **to come out of the ~** salir de quién sabe dónde

**woodworm** n inv ZOOL carcoma f

**woody** ['wʊd·i] I. <-ier, -iest> adj 1. (tough like wood) leñoso, -a 2. (wooded) boscoso, -a II. n empalmada f

**wool** [wʊl] n lana f ▶ **to pull the ~ over sb's eyes** dar a alguien gato por liebre

**woolen** adj, **woollen** ['wʊl·ən] adj de lana

**woolly** n, **wooly** ['wʊl·i] <-ier, -iest> adj 1. (of wool) de lana 2. (wool-like) lanoso, -a 3. (vague) vago, -a

**word** [wɜrd] I. n 1. palabra f; **of few ~s** de pocas palabras; **to not breathe a ~** no decir ni pío (of de); **in other ~s** en otros términos; **~ for ~** palabra por palabra 2. (news) noticia f; (message) mensaje m; **to get ~** enterarse (of de); **to have ~ from sb** tener un recado de alguien (from de); **to have ~ that...** tener conocimiento de que... 3. (order) orden f; **a ~ of advice** un consejo; **a ~ of warning/caution** una advertencia; **just say the ~** sólo tienes que pedirlo 4. (promise) palabra f (de honor); **to keep one's ~** cumplir su promesa 5. **~s** (lyrics) letra f ▶ **to have a quick ~** hablar en privado (with con); **by ~ of mouth** de viva voz; **to take the ~s (right) out of sb's mouth** quitar a alguien la palabra de la boca; **to put in a good ~** interceder (for por); **~s fail me!** ¡no tengo palabras!; **from the ~ go**

desde el primer momento; **mark** my ~s! ¡toma nota!; **to mince** one's ~s medir sus palabras; **to not mince** one's ~s no tener pelos en la lengua

**wording** n 1. (*words*) términos mpl 2. (*style*) estilo m

**word order** n orden m de las palabras

**word processor** n procesador m de textos

**wordy** ['wɜr·di] <-ier, iest> adj farragoso, -a

**wore** [wɔr] vt, vi pt of wear

**work** [wɜrk] I. n 1. a. PHYS trabajo m; **to be hard** ~ (**doing** sth) (*strenuous*) costar mucho trabajo (hacer algo); **good** ~! ¡bien hecho!; **to be out of** ~ estar en paro 2. (*product*) a. ART, MUS obra f; **reference** ~ obra de consulta 3. ~s + sing/pl vb (*factory*) fábrica f; (*clock*) mecanismo m ► **to get to** ~ on sth ponerse manos a la obra con algo; **the** ~s sl toda la pesca II. vi 1. (*do job*) trabajar (**as** a de) 2. (*be busy*) estar ocupado; **to get** ~ing poner manos a la obra; **to** ~ **hard** ser aplicado; **to** ~ **to do** sth dedicarse a hacer algo 3. (*be successful*) a. TECH funcionar; MED hacer efecto 4. (*affect*) obrar (**against** en contra de); **to** ~ **both ways** ser un arma de doble filo 5. + adj **to** ~ **free/ loose** soltarse/desprenderse ► **to** ~ **like a charm** funcionar de maravilla; **to** ~ **like a dog** [or **slave**] trabajar como un esclavo; **to** ~ **around** prepararse con tranquilidad (**to** para) III. vt 1. **to** ~ **sb hard** hacer trabajar duro a alguien; **to** ~ **oneself to death** matarse trabajando; **to** ~ **a forty-hour week** trabajar 40 horas semanales 2. TECH hacer que funcione; **to be** ~ed ser accionado (**by** por) 3. (*move*) mover; **to** ~ **sth free/loose** liberar/desprender algo; **to** ~ **one's way** abrirse camino (**along** por) 4. (*bring about*) producir; (*cure*) efectuar; **to** ~ **it** [or **things**] **so that...** arreglárselas para que... +subj 5. (*shape*) tallar; (*bronze, iron*) trabajar

◆**work away** vi trabajar sin parar

◆**work in** vt introducir; (*fit in*) colocar; CULIN añadir

◆**work off** vt contrarrestar; (*anger, frus-*

*tration*) desahogar; (*stress*) aliviar; (*debt, loan*) amortizar

◆**work out** I. vt 1. (*solve*) resolver; **to work things out** arreglárselas 2. (*calculate*) calcular 3. (*develop*) desarrollar; (*solution*) encontrar 4. (*understand*) darse cuenta II. vi 1. (*sum*) resultar; (*cheaper*) salir 2. (*be resolved*) resolverse 3. (*be successful*) acabar bien; **to** ~ **for the best** salir perfectamente

◆**work up** vt 1. (*generate*) sacar; (*courage, energy, enthusiasm*) estimular; **to work oneself up** emocionarse; **to work sb up into a rage** sacar a alguien de quicio 2. (*develop*) desarrollar; (*plan*) llevar a cabo; (*interest*) fomentar; **to work one's way up through the company** ir ascendiendo en la empresa

**workaholic** ['wɜrk·ə·hɔ·lɪk] n trabajador (a) m(f) compulsivo

**workbench** <-es> n mesa f de trabajo

**workbook** n cuaderno m de ejercicios

**workday** n (*weekday*) día m laborable; (*time*) jornada f laboral

**worker** ['wɜr·kər] n trabajador(a) m(f); (*in factory*) obrero, -a m, f

**working** adj 1. (*employed*) empleado, -a; (*population*) activo, -a 2. (*pertaining to work*) laboral 3. (*functioning*) que funciona 4. a ~ **knowledge** conocimientos básicos (**of** de)

**working class** ['wɜr·kɪŋ·klæs] <-es> n clase f obrera

**working-class** adj obrero, -a; (*background*) humilde

**workload** ['wɜrk·loʊd] n (volumen m de) trabajo m; **to have a heavy/light/ unbearable** ~ tener mucho/poco/demasiado trabajo

**workman** ['wɜrk·mən] <-men> n obrero m

**workmanlike** ['wɜrk·mən·laɪk] adj profesional

**workmanship** ['wɜrk·mən·ʃɪp] n (*skill*) destreza f; **shoddy** ~ mala calidad; **of fine** ~ de excelente factura

**work of art** n obra f de arte

**workout** ['wɜrk·aʊt] n entrenamiento m

**work permit** n permiso m de trabajo

**workplace** n (lugar m de) trabajo m

**work-sharing** ['wɜrk·ʃer·ɪŋ] n sistema

**W**

*en el cual dos personas comparten un puesto laboral*

**workshop** ['wɜrk·ʃap] *n* taller *m*; UNIV seminario *m*

**workstation** *n* estación *f* de trabajo

**workweek** ['wɜrk·wik] *n* semana *f* laborable

**world** [wɜrld] *n* mundo *m*; **the ~'s population** la población mundial; **the ~ champion** el campeón del mundo; **the best/worst in the ~** el mejor/peor del mundo; **the (whole) ~** over en el mundo entero; **to see the ~** ver mundo; **the ~ of dogs** el mundo del perro; **the animal ~** el mundo animal; **the New/Old/Third ~** el Nuevo/Viejo/Tercer Mundo ▶ **to be a ~ of difference between...** haber un abismo entre...; **he/she has the ~ at his/her feet** the ~ is his/her oyster tiene el mundo a sus pies; **to feel on top of the ~** estar en el séptimo cielo; **that's the way of the ~** así es la vida; **to be for all the ~ like...** ser exactamente como...; **to be ~s apart** ser como la noche y el día; **to be dead to the ~** dormir como un tronco; **to be out of this ~** ser algo nunca visto; **it's a small ~!** ¡el mundo es un pañuelo!; **to move up/down in the ~** *inf* prosperar/venir a menos; **to live in a ~ of one's own** vivir en su mundo; **to mean (all) the ~** serlo todo (to para); **to think the ~** tener un alto concepto (of de); **what/who/how in the ~...?** ¿qué/quién/cómo demonios...?

**World Bank** *n* **the ~** el Banco Mundial

**world-class** *adj* mundialmente reconocido, -a

**World Cup** *n* SPORTS **the ~** la Copa del Mundo; **the ~ Finals** la final de la Copa del Mundo

**world-famous** ['wɜrld·ˌfeɪ·məs] *adj* de fama mundial

**worldly** ['wɜrld·li] *adj* 1. (*goods*) material 2. (*having experience*) mundano, -a; (*manner*) sofisticado, -a; **~ wise** cosmopolita

**world record** *n* récord *m* mundial

**world war** *n* guerra *f* mundial

**worldwide** ['wɜrld·ˌwaɪd] I. *adj* mundial II. *adv* por todo el mundo

**worm** [wɜrm] I. *n* a. COMPUT gusano *m*; (*larva*) oruga *f*; **earth~** lombriz *f*, gusano *m* II. *vt* (*treat for worms*) desparasitar; **to ~ one's way through people** colarse entre la gente; **to ~ a secret** sonsacar un secreto (**out of** a)

**worn** [wɔrn] I. *vt*, *vi pp of* **wear** II. *adj* (*deteriorated*) desgastado, -a; (*clothing*) raído, -a; (*person*) ojeroso, -a; (*expression, news, story*) tópico, -a

**worn-out** [ˌwɔrn·'aʊt] *adj* (*exhausted*) rendido, -a; (*clothing*) raído, -a

**worried** *adj* preocupado, -a (**about, by** por); **~ sick** preocupadísimo; **I am ~ that he may be angry** tengo miedo de que esté enfadado

**worry** ['wɜr·i] I. <-ies> *n* (*anxiety, concern*) preocupación *f*; (*trouble*) problema *m*; **financial worries** problemas económicos; **to be a cause of ~** dar problemas (**to** a); **to have a ~** estar preocupado (**about** por); **it is a great ~ to me** me preocupa mucho II. *vt* <-ie-, -ing> 1. (*concern*) preocupar; **she is worried that she might not be able to find a job** tiene miedo de no encontrar trabajo; **that doesn't ~ me** eso me tiene sin cuidado 2. (*bother*) molestar III. <-ie-, -ing> *vi* preocuparse (**about** por); **don't ~** no te preocupes; **not to ~!** ¡no pasa nada!

**worrying** *adj* preocupante

**worse** [wɜrs] I. *adj comp of* **bad** peor; **to be even/much ~** ser aún/mucho peor (**than** que); **from bad to ~** de mal en peor; **to get ~ and ~** ser cada vez peor; **it could have been ~** podría haber sido peor; **to make matters ~** por si fuera poco; **so much the ~ for her!** ¡peor para ella!; **to get ~** empeorar II. *n* **the ~** el/la peor; **to change for the ~** cambiar para mal; **to have seen ~** haber visto cosas peores; **~ was to follow** lo peor estaba por llegar III. *adv comp of* **badly** peor (**than** que); **to be ~ (off)** estar peor

**worsen** ['wɜr·sən] *vi*, *vt* empeorar

**worship** ['wɜr·ʃɪp] I. *vt* <-pp-, -p-> 1. *a.* REL adorar; **to ~ money/sex** tener obsesión por el dinero/sexo 2. (*admire*) idolatrar ▶ **to ~ the ground sb walks on**

besar el suelo que alguien pisa II. *n a.* REL culto *m*; (*adoration*) adoración *f*

**worst** [wɜrst] I. *adj superl of* **bad**; **the ~** el/la peor; **the ~ soup I've ever eaten** la peor sopa que he comido nunca; **the ~ mistake** el error más grave II. *adv superl of* **badly** peor; **to be ~ affected** ser los más afectados (**by** por) III. *n* **the ~** lo peor; **the ~ of it**, **~ of all** lo peor de todo; **the ~ is over now** ya ha pasado lo peor; **at ~** en el peor de los casos; **at her ~** en su peor momento; **to fear the ~** temerse lo peor ▶ **if** (**the**) **~ comes to** (**the**) **~** en el peor de los casos; **to get the ~ of it** llevarse la peor parte

**worth** [wɜrθ] I. *n* (*value*; (*person*) valía *f*; (*wealth*) fortuna *f*; **to be of great/little ~** tener gran/poco valor (**to** para); **$4,000 ~ of items** objetos por valor de 4.000$; **to get one's money's ~** sacar partido (**from** a) II. *adj* **1.** COM, FIN, ECON **to be ~** valer; **it is ~ about $2,000** está valorado en unos 2.000$; **it's ~ a lot** tiene mucho valor (**to** para) **2.** (*significant, useful*) **to be ~** merecer; **to be ~ a mention/seeing** ser digno de mención/ver; **it's not ~ arguing about** no vale la pena discutir por eso; **it's ~ a try** vale la pena intentarlo ▶ **to be ~ sb's while** compensar; **for all one's ~** con todas sus fuerzas; **for what it's ~** por si sirve de algo; **to be** (**well**) **~ it** valer la pena

**worthless** [ˈwɜrθ·lɪs] *adj* (*no value*) sin ningún valor; (*no use*) inútil

**worthwhile** [ˌwɜrθ·ˈhwaɪl] *adj* **1.** (*beneficial*) que vale la pena; **it's not ~ making such an effort** no merece la pena esforzarse tanto; **it isn't financially ~ for me** no me compensa económicamente **2.** (*useful*) útil

**worthy** [ˈwɜr·ði] <-ier, -iest> *adj* **1.** (*admirable*) encomiable; (*principles*) loable; (*cause*) noble **2.** (*appropriate*) digno, -a (**of** de); **to be ~ of attention** merecer atención

**would** [wʊd] *aux pt of* **will 1.** (*future in the past*) **he said he ~ do it later on** dijo que lo haría más tarde **2.** (*past in the past*) **we thought they ~ have done it before** pensamos que lo ha-

brían hecho antes **3.** (*intention*) **he said he ~ always love her** dijo que siempre la querría **4.** (*possibility*) **I'd go without, but I'm too busy** iría yo, pero estoy muy liado **5.** (*conditional*) **what ~ you do if you lost your job?** ¿qué harías si te quedaras sin trabajo? **6.** (*request*) **~ you phone him, please?** ¿me harías el favor de llamarlo?; **~ you like...?** ¿te gustaría...?; **~ you like me to come with you?** ¿quieres que vaya contigo? **7.** (*regularity*) **they ~ help each other with their homework** solían ayudarse con los deberes; **he ~ say that, wouldn't he?** era de esperar que lo dijera, ¿no? **8.** (*opinion*) **I ~ imagine that...** me imagino que... **9.** (*probability*) **he had an Australian accent — that ~ be Tom** tenía acento australiano — debía de ser Tom **10.** (*preference*) **I ~ rather have water** prefiero beber agua **11.** (*advice*) **I ~n't worry, if I were you** yo que tú no me preocuparía **12.** (*motive*) **why ~ anyone do something like that?** ¿por qué haría nadie algo así?

**would-be** [ˈwʊd·bi] *adj* aspirante a

**wouldn't** [ˈwʊd·ənt] = **would not** *see* **would**

**wound¹** [waʊnd] *vi*, *vt pt*, *pp of* **wind²**

**wound²** [wund] I. *n* herida *f*; **a leg ~** una herida en la pierna/de guerra II. *vt* herir

**wounded** [ˈwun·dɪd] I. *adj* herido, -a II. *npl* **the ~** los heridos

**woven** [ˈwoʊ·vən] I. *vt*, *vi pp of* **weave** II. *adj* tejido, -a

**wow** [waʊ] *inf* I. *interj* hala, caray *AmL* II. *n* exitazo *m*; **I had a ~ of a time** me lo pasé en grande III. *vt* volver loco

**wrap** [ræp] I. *n* **1.** (*robe*) bata *f* **2.** (*shawl*) chal *m* **3.** (*packaging*) envoltorio *m*; **foil ~** papel *m* de aluminio II. *vt* <-pp-> envolver (**in** con); **he ~ped a scarf around his neck** se puso una bufanda; **to ~ one's fingers around sth** agarrar algo con las manos

♦**wrap up** I. *vt* <-pp-> **1.** (*cover*) envolver **2.** *inf* (*finish*) poner fin a; (*deal*) cerrar; **that wraps it up for today** eso es todo por hoy II. *vi* **1. to ~**

**W**

(**well/warm**) abrigarse (bien) **2. to be wrapped up in sth** estar absorto en algo; **to be wrapped up in one's work** vivir para el trabajo **3.** (*finish*) terminar

**wrapper** ['ræp·ər] *n* **1.** (*packaging*) envoltorio *m*; (*book*) sobrecubierta *f* **2.** (*robe*) bata *f*

**wrapping paper** *n* papel *m* de regalo; (*plain*) papel de embalar

**wreath** [riθ] <wreaths> *n* corona *f*

**wreck** [rek] **I.** *vt* (*damage*) destrozar; (*demolish*) derribar; (*hopes, plan*) arruinar **II.** *n* **1.** NAUT naufragio *m*; AUTO accidente *m*; **a ~ of a car** un coche siniestrado; **an old ~** un cacharro **2.** *inf* (*ruin*) ruina *f*; (*mess*) caos *m*; **to feel like a complete ~** estar hecho polvo; **to be a nervous ~** tener los nervios destrozados

**wreckage** ['rek·ɪdʒ] *n* restos *mpl*; (*building*) escombros *mpl*

**wren** [ren] *n* chochín *m*

**wrench** [rentʃ] **I.** *vt* **1.** (*pull*) arrancar (**from** a); (*ankle*) torcerse; (*shoulder*) dislocarse; **to ~ oneself away** soltarse de un tirón **2.** (*take from*) separar (**from** de) **II.** *n* **1.** (*tool*) llave *f* inglesa **2.** (*twist*) tirón *m*, jalón *m* CSur

**wrestle** ['res·əl] SPORTS **I.** <-ling> *vt* **1.** a. SPORTS luchar; **to ~ sb** forcejear con alguien **2.** *fig* lidiar con **II.** <-ling> *vi* luchar **III.** *n* lucha *f*

**wrestler** *n* luchador(a) *m(f)*

**wrestling** *n* lucha *f*; **freestyle ~** lucha libre

**wrestling match** *n* combate *m* de lucha

**wretched** ['retʃ·ɪd] *adj* **1.** (*miserable*) desdichado, -a; (*state*) lamentable; (*house, conditions*) miserable **2.** (*despicable*) despreciable **3.** (*awful*) horrible; (*sick*) mal

**wriggle** ['rɪg·əl] **I.** <-ling> *vi* **1.** (*squirm*) retorcerse **2.** (*move*) deslizarse (**through** por); *fig* escapar (**out of** de) **II.** <-ling> *vt* menear; **to ~ (one's way) out of sth** escaquearse de algo *inf*

**wring** [rɪŋ] <wrung, wrung> *vt* (*twist*) retorcer; (*water*) escurrir

**wrinkle** ['rɪŋ·kəl] **I.** *n* (*crease*) arruga *f*

**II.** <-ling> *vi* (*form folds, creases*) arrugarse; (*apple, fruit*) pasarse **III.** <-ling> *vt* arrugar ▶ **to ~ one's brow** fruncir el ceño

**wrinkled** *adj*, **wrinkly** ['rɪŋ·kli] *adj* arrugado, -a; (*fruit*) pasado, -a

**wrist** [rɪst] *n* muñeca *f*; (*of garment*) puño *m*

**wristband** ['rɪst·bænd] *n* **1.** (*sleeve*) puño *m* **2.** (*strap*) correa *f* **3.** (*sweatband*) muñequera *f*

**wristwatch** <-es> *n* reloj *m* de pulsera

**write** [raɪt] <wrote, written, writing> **I.** *vt* **1.** escribir; **to ~ a check** extender un cheque **2.** MUS componer; (*song*) escribir **3.** COMPUT (*save*) grabar (**to** en) ▶ **to be nothing to ~ home about** no ser nada del otro mundo **II.** *vi* escribir; **to ~ clearly** escribir con letra clara; **to ~ to sb/about sth** escribir a alguien/sobre algo

♦**write away** *vi* **to ~ for sth** solicitar algo por escrito

♦**write back** *vt*, *vi* contestar

♦**write down** *vt* apuntar

♦**write in** *vt* (*insert*) escribir

♦**write off I.** *vi* **to ~ for** solicitar por escrito **II.** *vt* (*attempt*) abandonar; (*project*) dar por perdido; (*debt*) cancelar; **~ as useless** descartar por inútil

♦**write out** *vt* **1.** (*copy*) copiar **2.** (*fill in*) rellenar **3.** (*remove*) suprimir

♦**write up** *vt* redactar; **to ~ a concert** escribir la crítica de un concierto

**write-off** ['raɪt·ɔf] *n* (*beyond repair*) siniestro *m* total; **the camera was a complete ~** la cámara estaba hecha trizas

**write-protected** ['raɪt·prə·'tek·təd] *adj* protegido, -a contra escritura

**writer** ['raɪ·tər] *n* escritor(a) *m(f)*; **~ of children's books** autor(a) *m(f)* de libros infantiles; **DVD ~** grabadora *f* de DVD

**write-up** ['raɪt·ʌp] *n* crítica *f*

**writing** ['raɪ·tɪŋ] *n* **1.** (*handwriting*) letra *f*; **to put sth in ~** poner algo por escrito; **there was some ~ in...** había algo escrito en... **2.** a. LIT escribir *m*; **creative ~** escritura *f* creativa **3.** (*written work*) obra *f*

**writing desk** *n* escritorio *m*

**writing paper** *n* papel *m* de carta

**written** ['rɪt·ən] I. *vt, vi pp of* **write** II. *adj* escrito, -a ▶ **to have guilt ~ all over one's face** llevar la culpa escrita en la cara

**wrong** [rɔŋ] I. *adj* 1. (*not right*) incorrecto, -a; **to be ~ about sth/sb** equivocarse en algo/con alguien; **he is ~ in thinking...** se equivoca si piensa...; **to be in the ~ place** estar mal colocado; **to be plainly ~** estar completamente equivocado; **to get the ~ number** equivocarse de número 2. (*not appropriate*) inoportuno, -a; **this is the ~ time** no es el momento oportuno (**to** para) 3. (*bad*) mal; **it is ~ to...** está mal...; **it was ~ of him** ha hecho muy mal; **what's ~ with that?** ¿qué hay de malo en ello?; **is there anything ~?** ¿te pasa algo?; **what's ~ with you today?** ¿qué te pasa hoy?; **something's ~ with the radio** la radio no funciona bien ▶ **to fall into the ~ hands** caer en manos equivocadas II. *adv* mal; **to get sth ~** equivocarse en algo; **to get it ~** entender mal; **don't get me ~** no me malinterpretes; **to go ~** equivocarse; (*fail*) salir mal; (*machine*) estropearse, descomponerse *Méx* III. *n* mal *m;* **to put sb in the ~** echar la culpa a alguien; **to do sb no ~** no hacer nada malo a alguien; **to suffer a ~** sufrir una injusticia ▶ **to do ~** obrar mal; **he can do no ~** es incapaz de hacer nada malo

**wrongdoing** *n* maldad *f;* LAW delito *m*

**wrongful** *adj* injusto, -a; (*arrest*) ilegal; (*dismissal*) improcedente

**wrongly** *adv* mal; (*believe, state*) erróneamente; (*accuse, convict*) injustamente

**wrote** [roʊt] *vi, vt pt of* **write**

**wrought iron** *n* hierro *m* forjado

**wrung** [rʌŋ] *vt pt, pp of* **wring**

**wry** [raɪ] <wrier, wriest *or* wryer, wryest> *adj* (*dry and ironic*) cáustico, -a; **to make a ~ face** torcer el gesto

**WSW** *abbr of* **west-southwest** OSO

# X

**X, x** [eks] *n* 1. X, x *f;* **~ as in X-ray** X de xilófono 2. MATH x 3. **Mr./Mrs./Ms. ~** el Sr./la Sra. X 4. (*cross*) aspa *f*

**xenophobia** [ˌzen·ə·'foʊ·bi·ə] *n* xenofobia *f*

**xenophobic** [ˌzen·ə·'foʊ·bɪk] *adj* xenófobo, -a

**Xmas** ['krɪs·məs] *n abbr of* **Christmas** Navidad *f*

**X-ray** ['eks·reɪ] I. *n* 1. (*photo*) radiografía *f;* **~s** rayos *m pl* X 2. (*department*) radiología *f* II. *vt* hacer una radiografía de

**xylophone** ['zaɪ·lə·foʊn] *n* xilófono *m*

# Y

**Y, y** [waɪ] *n* 1. Y, y *f;* **~ as in Yankee** Y de yema 2. MATH y

**yacht** [jat] I. *n* yate *m;* (*for racing*) velero *m;* **~ club** club *m* náutico; **~ race** regata *f* II. *vi* navegar

**yachting** *n* **to go ~** navegar

**yachtsman** ['jats·mən] <-men> *n* (*owner*) dueño *m* de un yate; (*sailor*) regatista *m*

**yam** [jæm] *n* ñame *m;* (*sweet potato*) batata *f,* camote *m AmL*

**yank** [jæŋk] *inf* I. *vt, vi* **to ~ (on)** sth tirar de algo, jalar de algo *AmL;* **she ~ed at his hair** le tiró del pelo II. *n* tirón *m,* jalón *m AmL*

◆**yank out** *vt* sacar de un tirón

**Yank** [jæŋk] *n,* **Yankee** ['jæŋ·ki] *n pej inf* yanqui *mf,* gringo, -a *m, f AmL*

**yap** [jæp] I. <-pp-> *vi* 1. (*bark*) ladrar 2. *sl* cotorrear II. *n* 1. (*bark*) ladrido *m* 2. *sl* cotorreo *m*

**yard¹** [jard] *n* yarda *f (0'91 m);* **square ~** yarda cuadrada

**yard²** [jard] *n* 1. (*paved area*) patio *m* 2. (*land*) jardín *m* 3. (*work area*) taller *m* 4. (*storage*) almacén *m* 5. (*livestock*) corral *m*

**yardstick** ['jard·stɪk] *n* (*standard*) criterio *m*

**yarn** [jɑrn] n 1. (thread) hilo m 2. (story) trola f; **to spin a ~** inventarse una trola

**yawn** [jɔn] I. vi bostezar II. n bostezo m; **it was a ~** fig fue un rollo

**yawning** adj 1. (bored) que bosteza 2. (chasm, crater) enorme; **there's a ~ gap** hay un abismo (**between** entre)

**yea** [jeɪ] n voto m a favor

**yeah** [jeə] adv inf sí; **oh ~!** iron ¡no me digas!

**year** [jɪr] n 1. año m; **~ of birth** año de nacimiento; **~ in, ~ out** año tras año; **fiscal ~** ejercicio f fiscal; **leap ~** año bisiesto; **all (the) ~ round** (durante) todo el año; **every other ~** cada dos años; **happy new ~!** ¡feliz año nuevo!; **last/next ~** el año pasado/que viene; **$5000 a ~** 5.000$ al año; **this ~** este año; **I'm eight ~s old** tengo ocho años; **~s ago** hace años; **it's been ~s since...** hacía años que no...; **it'll be ~s before...** pasarán años hasta que...; **over the ~s** con el tiempo 2. SCHOOL, UNIV curso m

**yearbook** ['jɪr·bʊk] n anuario m

**yearly** I. adj anual; **on a ~ basis** cada año II. adv anualmente; **twice ~** dos veces al año

**yearn** [jɑrn] vi ansiar; **to ~ after/for** anhelar/añorar

**yearning** n anhelo m (**for** de); **to have a ~ to do sth** tener ansias de hacer algo

**yeast** [jist] n levadura f

**yell** [jel] I. n chillido m; **a ~ of laughter** una carcajada II. vi chillar; **to ~ at sb (to do sth)** gritar a alguien (que haga algo); **to ~ for sb/help** llamar a alguien/pedir ayuda a gritos III. vt gritar

**yellow** ['jel·oʊ] I. adj 1. amarillo, -a; **golden ~** amarillo canario 2. (cowardly) gallina II. n amarillo m; (egg) yema f

**yellow fever** n fiebre f amarilla

**Yellow Pages®** npl **the ~** las páginas amarillas

**yelp** [jelp] I. vi gritar (**with** de); (dog) aullar II. n grito m; (dog) aullido m

**yen** [jen] inv n yen m

**yep** [jep] adv inf sí

**yes** [jes] adv sí; **~, please** sí, por favor; **to answer ~** contestar que sí (**to** a); **~, indeed** por supuesto que sí; **~, of course** claro que sí; **~?** ¿sí?; **oh ~?** ¿de verdad?

**yesterday** ['jes·tər·deɪ] adv ayer; **~ morning** ayer por la mañana, ayer en la mañana AmL, ayer a la mañana CSur; **the day before ~** anteayer, antes de ayer

**yet** [jet] I. adv 1. (till now) aún; **it's too early to...** aún es muy pronto para...; **not ~** aún no; **as ~** hasta ahora; **have you finished ~?** ¿ya has terminado?; **the best is ~ to come** aún queda lo mejor; **~ again** otra vez más; **~ more food** aún más comida; **~ bigger/more beautiful** aún más grande/bonito 2. (despite that) sin embargo; (in spite of everything) a pesar de todo; **you'll do it ~** ya algún día lo conseguirás II. conj con todo

**yew** [ju] n tejo m

**Yiddish** ['jɪd·ɪʃ] adj, n yiddish m

**yield** [jild] I. n rendimiento m; (production) producción f; COM, FIN beneficio m; (interest) interés m II. vt 1. (results) dar; (information) proporcionar; (profit) proporcionar 2. AGR producir 3. **to ~ ground** ceder terreno; **to ~ responsibility** delegar responsabilidades III. vi AGR, COM, FIN ser productivo; **to ~ to** ceder ante; (give priority) dar prioridad a

**yodel** ['joʊ·dəl] n canción f tirolesa

**yoga** ['joʊ·gə] n yoga m

**yoghourt** n, **yoghurt** ['joʊ·gərt] n see yogurt

**yogi** ['joʊ·gi] n yogui mf

**yogurt** ['joʊ·gərt] n yogur m

**yoke** [joʊk] I. n yugo m; **to throw off the ~** liberarse del yugo II. vt **to ~ two things together** ligar una cosa a otra

**yokel** ['joʊ·kəl] n paleto, -a m, f, pajuerano, -a m, f Arg, Bol, Urug

**yolk** [joʊk] n yema f

**you** [ju] pron pers 1. 2nd pers sing tú, vos CSur, pl: vosotros, -as, ustedes AmL; **I see ~** te/os veo; **do ~ see me?** ¿me ves/veis?; **it is for ~** es para ti/vosotros; **older than ~** mayor que tú/vosotros; **if I were ~** si yo fuera tú/vosotros 2. (2nd person sing, polite form) usted pl: ustedes; **~ have a car** usted tiene/ustedes tienen un coche

**you'd** [jud] = you would see would

**you'll** [jul] = you will see will

**young** [jʌŋ] I. adj joven; **~ children**

niños pequeños; **my ~er brother/son** mi hermano/hijo menor; (*appearance, clothes*) juvenil; (*love*) de juventud
▶ **you live only ~ once!** ¡sólo se vive una vez! II. *n pl* **the ~** jóvenes; zool las crías

**youngster** ['jʌŋ.stər] *n* joven *mf*

**your** [jʊr] *adj pos* **1.** *2nd pers sing* tu(s) *pl:* vuestro(s), vuestra(s) **2.** (*2nd pers sing and pl: polite form*) su(s)

**you're** [jʊr] = **you are** *see* **be**

**yours** [jʊrz] *pron pos* **1.** *sing:* (el) tuyo, (la) tuya, (los) tuyos, (las) tuyas *pl:* (el) vuestro, (la) vuestra, (los) vuestros, (las) vuestras, el/la de ustedes *AmL;* **this glass is ~** este vaso es tuyo/vuestro **2.** *polite form* (el) suyo, (la) suya, (los) suyos, (las) suyas; **~ truly** le saluda atentamente

**yourself** [jʊr.ˈself] *pron reflexive* **1.** *sing:* te *emphatic:* tú (mismo, misma) *after prep:* ti (mismo, misma) **2.** *polite form:* se *emphatic:* usted (mismo, misma) *after prep:* sí (mismo, misma)

**yourselves** *pron reflexive* **1.** os, se *AmL; emphatic, after prep:* vosotros (mismos), vosotras (mismas), ustedes (mismos, mismas) *AmL.* *polite form:* se *emphatic:* ustedes (mismos, mismas) *after prep:* sí (mismos, mismas)

**youth** [juθ] *n* **1.** (*period*) juventud *f* **2.** (*young man*) joven *m* **3.** (*young people*) jóvenes *mpl*

**youthful** ['juθ.fəl] *adj* **1.** (*young-looking*) juvenil **2.** (*typical of the young*) de la juventud **3.** (*young*) joven

**youth hostel** *n* albergue *m* juvenil

**you've** [juv] = **you have** *see* **have**

**yo-yo** ['jou.jou] *n* yo-yo *m*

**yuan** [ju.ˈæn] *n* yuan *m*

**yucky** ['jʌk.i] *adj sl* asqueroso, -a

**yummy** ['jʌm.i] *adj* de rechupete

**yuppie** ['jʌp.i] *n* yuppy *mf*

# Z

**Z, z** [zi] *n* Z, z *f;* **~ as in Zulu** Z de Zaragoza ▶ **to catch some ~'s** echar una cabezada, apolillar un poco *RíoPl*

**zany** ['zeɪ.ni] <-ier, -iest> *adj* (*person*) chiflado, -a; (*idea*) disparatado, -a; (*clothing*) estrafalario, -a

**zap** [zæp] *sl* I. <-pp-> *vt* (*destroy*) liquidar; (*send*) mandar echando leches II. <-pp-> *vi* **to ~ through the channels** hacer zapping; **to ~ somewhere** ir a un sitio echando leches; **to ~ through sth** despachar algo III. *interj* ¡zas!

**zapping** ['zæp.ɪŋ] *n* zapping *m*

**zealot** ['zel.ət] *n* fanático, -a *m, f*

**zealous** ['zel.əs] *adj* ferviente; **to be ~ in** (**doing**) **sth** poner gran celo en (hacer) algo

**zebra** ['zi.brə] *n* cebra *f*

**zero** ['zɪr.ou] I. <-s or -es> *n* cero *m;* **below ~** bajo cero; **to be a ~** ser un cero a la izquierda II. *adj* cero *inv;* (*visibility*) nulo, -a; **my chances are ~** no tengo ninguna posibilidad

**zigzag** ['zɪg.zæg] I. *n* zigzag *m* II. *adj* zigzagueante; (*pattern*) en zigzag III. <-gg-> *vi* zigzaguear

**zinc** [zɪŋk] *n* zinc *m*

**zip** [zɪp] I. *n* **1.** (*ZIP code*) código *m* postal **2.** (*whistle*) silbido *m* **3.** (*vigor*) garra *f* **4.** *sl* (*nothing*) nada; **I know ~ about that** NPI *f.* II. <-pp-> *vt* **to ~ sth open/shut/up** abrir/cerrar/subir la cremallera de algo III. <-pp-> *vi* **to ~ in/past** entrar/pasar volando; **the days ~ped by** los días pasaron volando

**zipper** ['zɪp.ər] *n* cremallera *f*

**zippy** ['zɪp.i] <-ier, -iest> *adj inf* (*fast*) veloz; (*energetic*) enérgico, -a

**zodiac** ['zou.di.æk] *n* zodíaco *m*

**zombie** ['zam.bi] *n* zombi *mf*

**zone** [zoun] I. *n* zona *f;* **time ~** zona horaria II. *vt* dividir en zonas; **to ~ an area for residential use** declarar un lugar zona residencial

**zoning** *n* zonificación *f*

**zoo** [zu] *n* zoo *m*

**zoological** [ˌzou.ə.ˈlɑdʒ.ɪ.kəl] *adj* zoológico, -a; **~ garden** parque *m* zoológico

**zoologist** [zou.ˈɑl.ə.dʒɪst] *n* zoólogo, -a *m, f*

**zoology** [zou.ˈɑl.ə.dʒi] *n* zoología *f*

**zoom** [zum] I. *n* **1.** phot zoom *m* **2.** (*buzz*) zumbido *m* II. *vi* (*move*) ir zumbando; **to ~ away** salir pitando;

Z

**to ~ past** pasar volando; (*costs, sales*) dispararse
◆**zoom in** *vi* enfocar en primer plano
◆**zoom out** *vi* cambiar a un plano general

**zoom lens** *n* zoom *m*
**zucchini** [zu·ki·ni] <-(s)> *n inv* calabacín *m*, calabacita *f AmL.*

# Los verbos regulares e irregulares españoles
# Spanish regular and irregular verbs

**Abreviaturas:**
pret. ind.     pretérito indefinido
subj. pres.    subjuntivo presente

## Verbos regulares que terminan en -ar, -er e -ir

### hablar

| presente | imperfecto | pret. ind. | futuro | subj. pres. |
| --- | --- | --- | --- | --- |
| hablo | hablaba | hablé | hablaré | hable |
| hablas | hablabas | hablaste | hablarás | hables |
| habla | hablaba | habló | hablará | hable |
| hablamos | hablábamos | hablamos | hablaremos | hablemos |
| habláis | hablabais | hablasteis | hablaréis | habléis |
| hablan | hablaban | hablaron | hablarán | hablen |
| **gerundio** hablando | | **participio** hablado | | |

### comprender

| presente | imperfecto | pret. ind. | futuro | subj. pres. |
| --- | --- | --- | --- | --- |
| comprendo | comprendía | comprendí | comprenderé | comprenda |
| comprendes | comprendías | comprendiste | comprenderás | comprendas |
| comprende | comprendía | comprendió | comprenderá | comprenda |
| comprendemos | comprendíamos | comprendimos | comprenderemos | comprendamos |
| comprendéis | comprendíais | comprendisteis | comprenderéis | comprendáis |
| comprenden | comprendían | comprendieron | comprenderán | comprendan |
| **gerundio** comprendiendo | | **participio** comprendido | | |

**recibir**

| presente | imperfecto | pret. ind. | futuro | subj. pres. |
|---|---|---|---|---|
| recibo | recibía | recibí | recibiré | reciba |
| recibes | recibías | recibiste | recibirás | recibas |
| recibe | recibía | recibió | recibirá | reciba |
| recibimos | recibíamos | recibimos | recibiremos | recibamos |
| recibís | recibíais | recibisteis | recibiréis | recibáis |
| reciben | recibían | recibieron | recibirán | reciban |
| **gerundio** recibiendo | | **participio** recibido | | |

## Verbos con cambios vocálicos

**\<e → ie\>  pensar**

| presente | imperfecto | pret. ind. | futuro | subj. pres. |
|---|---|---|---|---|
| pienso | pensaba | pensé | pensaré | piense |
| piensas | pensabas | pensaste | pensarás | pienses |
| piensa | pensaba | pensó | pensará | piense |
| pensamos | pensábamos | pensamos | pensaremos | pensemos |
| pensáis | pensabais | pensasteis | pensaréis | penséis |
| piensan | pensaban | pensaron | pensarán | piensen |
| **gerundio** pensando | | **participio** pensado | | |

**\<o → ue\>  contar**

| presente | imperfecto | pret. ind. | futuro | subj. pres. |
|---|---|---|---|---|
| cuento | contaba | conté | contaré | cuente |
| cuentas | contabas | contaste | contarás | cuentes |
| cuenta | contaba | contó | contará | cuente |
| contamos | contábamos | contamos | contaremos | contemos |
| contáis | contabais | contasteis | contaréis | contéis |
| cuentan | contaban | contaron | contaron | cuenten |
| **gerundio** contando | | **participio** contado | | |

## Verbos con cambios ortográficos

### `<c → qu>`  atacar

| presente | imperfecto | pret. ind. | futuro | subj. pres. |
|---|---|---|---|---|
| ataco | atacaba | ataqué | atacaré | ataque |
| atacas | atacabas | atacaste | atacarás | ataques |
| ataca | atacaba | atacó | atacará | ataque |
| atacamos | atacábamos | atacamos | atacaremos | ataquemos |
| atacáis | atacabais | atacasteis | atacaréis | ataquéis |
| atacan | atacaban | atacaron | atacarán | ataquen |
| **gerundio** atacando | | **participio** atacado | | |

### `<g → gu>`  pagar

| presente | imperfecto | pret. ind. | futuro | subj. pres. |
|---|---|---|---|---|
| pago | pagaba | pagué | pagaré | pague |
| pagas | pagabas | pagaste | pagarás | pagues |
| paga | pagaba | pagó | pagará | pague |
| pagamos | pagábamos | pagamos | pagaremos | paguemos |
| pagáis | pagabais | pagasteis | pagaréis | paguéis |
| pagan | pagaban | pagaron | pagarán | paguen |
| **gerundio** pagando | | **participio** pagado | | |

### `<z → c>`  cazar

| presente | imperfecto | pret. ind. | futuro | subj. pres. |
|---|---|---|---|---|
| cazo | cazaba | cacé | cazaré | cace |
| cazas | cazabas | cazaste | cazarás | caces |
| caza | cazaba | cazó | cazará | cace |
| cazamos | cazábamos | cazamos | cazaremos | cacemos |
| cazáis | cazabais | cazasteis | cazaréis | cacéis |
| cazan | cazaban | cazaron | cazarán | cacen |
| **gerundio** cazando | | **participio** cazado | | |

## \<gu → gü\> averiguar

| presente | imperfecto | pret. ind. | futuro | subj. pres. |
|----------|-----------|-----------|--------|-------------|
| averiguo | averiguaba | averigüé | averiguaré | averigüe |
| averiguas | averiguabas | averiguaste | averiguarás | averigües |
| averigua | averiguaba | averiguó | averiguará | averigüe |
| averiguamos | averiguábamos | averiguamos | averiguaremos | averigüemos |
| averiguáis | averiguabais | averiguasteis | averiguaréis | averigüéis |
| averiguan | averiguaban | averiguaron | averiguarán | averigüen |
| **gerundio** averiguando | | **participio** averiguado | | |

## \<c → z\> vencer

| presente | imperfecto | pret. ind. | futuro | subj. pres. |
|----------|-----------|-----------|--------|-------------|
| venzo | vencía | vencí | venceré | venza |
| vences | vencías | venciste | vencerás | venzas |
| vence | vencía | venció | vencerá | venza |
| vencemos | vencíamos | vencimos | venceremos | venzamos |
| vencéis | vencíais | vencisteis | venceréis | venzáis |
| vencen | vencían | vencieron | vencerán | venzan |
| **gerundio** venciendo | | **participio** vencido | | |

## \<g → j\> coger

| presente | imperfecto | pret. ind. | futuro | subj. pres. |
|----------|-----------|-----------|--------|-------------|
| cojo | cogía | cogí | cogeré | coja |
| coges | cogías | cogiste | cogerás | cojas |
| coge | cogía | cogió | cogerá | coja |
| cogemos | cogíamos | cogimos | cogeremos | cojamos |
| cogéis | cogíais | cogisteis | cogeréis | cojáis |
| cogen | cogían | cogieron | cogerán | cojan |
| **gerundio** cogiendo | | **participio** cogido | | |

**&lt;gu → g&gt;**   **distinguir**

| presente | imperfecto | pret. ind. | futuro | subj. pres. |
|----------|------------|------------|--------|-------------|
| distingo | distinguía | distinguí | distinguiré | distinga |
| distingues | distinguías | distinguiste | distinguirás | distingas |
| distingue | distinguía | distinguió | distinguirá | distinga |
| distinguimos | distinguíamos | distinguimos | distinguiremos | distingamos |
| distinguís | distinguíais | distinguisteis | distinguiréis | distingáis |
| distinguen | distinguían | distinguieron | distinguirán | distingan |
| **gerundio** distinguiendo | | **participio** distinguido | | |

**&lt;qu → c&gt;**   **delinquir**

| presente | imperfecto | pret. ind. | futuro | subj. pres. |
|----------|------------|------------|--------|-------------|
| delinco | delinquía | delinquí | delinquiré | delinca |
| delinques | delinquías | delinquiste | delinquirás | delincas |
| delinque | delinquía | delinquió | delinquirá | delinca |
| delinquimos | delinquíamos | delinquimos | delinquiremos | delincamos |
| delinquís | delinquíais | delinquisteis | delinquiréis | delincáis |
| delinquen | delinquían | delinquieron | delinquirán | delincan |
| **gerundio** delinquiendo | | **participio** delinquido | | |

## Los verbos irregulares

### abolir

| presente | |
|----------|--|
| — | **gerundio** |
| — | aboliendo |
| abolimos | **participio** |
| abolís | abolido |

### abrir

| **participio:** | abierto |
|-----------------|---------|

## adquirir

| presente | |
|---|---|
| adquiero | **gerundio** |
| adquieres | adquiriendo |
| adquiere | |
| adquirimos | **participio** |
| adquirís | adquirido |
| adquieren | |

## andar

| presente | pret. ind. | |
|---|---|---|
| ando | anduve | **gerundio** |
| andas | anduviste | andando |
| anda | anduvo | |
| andamos | anduvimos | **participio** |
| andáis | anduvisteis | andado |
| andan | anduvieron | |

## asir

| presente | |
|---|---|
| asgo | **gerundio** |
| ases | asiendo |
| ase | |
| asimos | **participio** |
| asís | asido |
| asen | |

**aullar**

| presente | |
|---|---|
| aúllo | **gerundio** |
| aúllas | aullando |
| aúlla | |
| aullamos | **participio** |
| aulláis | aullado |
| aúllan | |

**avergonzar**

| presente | pret. ind. | |
|---|---|---|
| avergüenzo | avergoncé | **gerundio** |
| avergüenzas | avergonzaste | avergonzando |
| avergüenza | avergonzó | |
| avergonzamos | avergonzamos | **participio** |
| avergonzáis | avergonzasteis | avergonzado |
| avergüenzan | avergonzaron | |

**caber**

| presente | pret. ind. | futuro | condicional | |
|---|---|---|---|---|
| quepo | cupe | cabré | cabría | **gerundio** |
| cabes | cupiste | cabrás | cabrías | cabiendo |
| cabe | cupo | cabrá | cabría | |
| cabemos | cupimos | cabremos | cabríamos | **participio** |
| cabéis | cupisteis | cabréis | cabríais | cabido |
| caben | cupieron | cabrán | cabrían | |

### caer

| presente | pret. ind. | |
|---|---|---|
| caigo | caí | **gerundio** |
| caes | caíste | cayendo |
| cae | cayó | |
| caemos | caímos | **participio** |
| caéis | caísteis | caído |
| caen | cayeron | |

### ceñir

| presente | pret. ind. | |
|---|---|---|
| ciño | ceñí | **gerundio** |
| ciñes | ceñiste | ciñendo |
| ciñe | ciñó | |
| ceñimos | ceñimos | **participio** |
| ceñís | ceñisteis | ceñido |
| ciñen | ciñeron | |

### cocer

| presente | |
|---|---|
| cuezo | **gerundio** |
| cueces | cociendo |
| cuece | |
| cocemos | **participio** |
| cocéis | cocido |
| cuecen | |

## colgar

| presente | pret. ind. | |
|---|---|---|
| cuelgo | colgué | **gerundio** |
| cuelgas | colgaste | colgando |
| cuelga | colgó | |
| colgamos | colgamos | **participio** |
| colgáis | colgasteis | colgado |
| cuelgan | colgaron | |

## crecer

| presente | |
|---|---|
| crezco | **gerundio** |
| creces | creciendo |
| crece | |
| crecemos | **participio** |
| crecéis | crecido |
| crecen | |

## dar

| presente | pret. ind. | subj. pres. | |
|---|---|---|---|
| doy | di | dé | **gerundio** |
| das | diste | des | dando |
| da | dio | dé | |
| damos | dimos | demos | **participio** |
| dais | disteis | deis | dado |
| dan | dieron | den | |

### decir

| presente | imperfecto | pret. ind. | futuro | subj. pres. |
|---|---|---|---|---|
| digo | decía | dije | diré | diga |
| dices | decías | dijiste | dirás | digas |
| dice | decía | dijo | dirá | diga |
| decimos | decíamos | dijimos | diremos | digamos |
| decís | decíais | dijisteis | diréis | digáis |
| dicen | decían | dijeron | dirán | digan |
| **gerundio** diciendo | | **participio** dicho | | |

### dormir

| presente | pret. ind. | |
|---|---|---|
| duermo | dormí | **gerundio** |
| duermes | dormiste | durmiendo |
| duerme | durmió | |
| dormimos | dormimos | **participio** |
| dormís | dormisteis | dormido |
| duermen | durmieron | |

### elegir

| presente | pret. ind. | |
|---|---|---|
| elijo | elegí | **gerundio** |
| eliges | elegiste | eligiendo |
| elige | eligió | |
| elegimos | elegimos | **participio** |
| elegís | elegisteis | elegido |
| eligen | eligieron | |

## empezar

| presente | pret. ind. | |
|---|---|---|
| empiezo | empecé | **gerundio** |
| empiezas | empezaste | empezando |
| empieza | empezó | |
| empezamos | empezamos | **participio** |
| empezáis | empezasteis | empezado |
| empiezan | empezaron | |

## enraizar

| presente | pret. ind. | |
|---|---|---|
| enraízo | enraicé | **gerundio** |
| enraízas | enraizaste | enraizando |
| enraíza | enraizó | |
| enraizamos | enraizamos | **participio** |
| enraizáis | enraizasteis | enraizado |
| enraízan | enraizaron | |

## erguir

| presente | pret. ind. | subj. pres | subj. imp. |
|---|---|---|---|
| yergo | erguí | irga | **gerundio** |
| yergues | erguiste | irgas | irguiendo |
| yergue | irguió | irga | |
| erguimos | erguimos | irgamos | **participio** |
| erguís | erguisteis | irgáis | erguido |
| yerguen | irguieron | irgan | |

### errar

| presente | pret. ind. | |
|---|---|---|
| yerro | erré | **gerundio** |
| yerras | erraste | errando |
| yerra | erró | |
| erramos | erramos | **participio** |
| erráis | errasteis | errado |
| yerran | erraron | |

### escribir

| participio: | escrito |
|---|---|

### estar

| presente | imperfecto | pret. ind. | futuro | subj. pres. |
|---|---|---|---|---|
| estoy | estaba | estuve | estaré | esté |
| estás | estabas | estuviste | estarás | estés |
| está | estaba | estuvo | estará | esté |
| estamos | estábamos | estuvimos | estaremos | estemos |
| estáis | estabais | estuvisteis | estaréis | estéis |
| están | estaban | estuvieron | estarán | estén |
| **gerundio** estando | | **participio** estado | | |

### forzar

| presente | pret. ind. | |
|---|---|---|
| fuerzo | forcé | **gerundio** |
| fuerzas | forzaste | forzando |
| fuerza | forzó | |
| forzamos | forzamos | **participio** |
| forzáis | forzasteis | forzado |
| fuerzan | forzaron | |

## fregar

| presente | pret. ind. | |
|---|---|---|
| friego | fregué | **gerundio** |
| friegas | fregaste | fregando |
| friega | fregó | |
| fregamos | fregamos | **participio** |
| fregáis | fregasteis | fregado |
| friegan | fregamos | |

## freír

| presente | pret. ind. | |
|---|---|---|
| frío | freí | **gerundio** |
| fríes | freíste | friendo |
| fríe | frió | |
| freímos | freímos | **participio** |
| freís | freísteis | frito |
| fríen | frieron | |

## haber

| presente | imperfecto | pret. ind. | futuro | subj. pres. |
|---|---|---|---|---|
| he | había | hube | habré | haya |
| has | habías | hubiste | habrás | hayas |
| ha | había | hubo | habrá | haya |
| hemos | habíamos | hubimos | habremos | hayamos |
| habéis | habíais | hubisteis | habréis | hayáis |
| han | habían | hubieron | habrán | hayan |
| **gerundio** habiendo | | **participio** habido | | |

### hacer

| presente | imperfecto | pret. ind. | futuro | subj. pres. |
|----------|-----------|-----------|--------|-------------|
| hago | hacía | hice | haré | haga |
| haces | hacías | hiciste | harás | hagas |
| hace | hacía | hizo | hará | haga |
| hacemos | hacíamos | hicimos | haremos | hagamos |
| hacéis | hacíais | hicisteis | haréis | hagáis |
| hacen | hacían | hicieron | harán | hagan |
| **gerundio** haciendo | | **participio** hecho | | |

### hartar

| participio: | hartado – *saturated* |
|-------------|-----------------------|
| | harto (*only as attribute*): estoy harto – *I've had enough* |

### huir

| presente | pret. ind. | |
|----------|-----------|---|
| huyo | huí | **gerundio** |
| huyes | huiste | huyendo |
| huye | huyó | |
| huimos | huimos | **participio** |
| huís | huisteis | huido |
| huyen | huyeron | |

### imprimir

| participio: | impreso |
|-------------|---------|

## ir

| presente | imperfecto | pret. ind. | subj. pres. | |
|---|---|---|---|---|
| voy | iba | fui | vaya | **gerundio** |
| vas | ibas | fuiste | vayas | yendo |
| va | iba | fue | vaya | |
| vamos | íbamos | fuimos | vayamos | **participio** |
| vais | ibais | fuisteis | vayáis | ido |
| van | iban | fueron | vayan | |

## jugar

| presente | pret. ind. | subj. pres. | |
|---|---|---|---|
| juego | jugué | juegue | **gerundio** |
| juegas | jugaste | juegues | jugando |
| juega | jugó | juegue | |
| jugamos | jugamos | juguemos | **participio** |
| jugáis | jugasteis | juguéis | jugado |
| juegan | jugaron | jueguen | |

## leer

| presente | pret. ind. | |
|---|---|---|
| leo | leí | **gerundio** |
| lees | leíste | leyendo |
| lee | leyó | |
| leemos | leímos | **participio** |
| leéis | leísteis | leído |
| leen | leyeron | |

## lucir

| presente | |
|----------|--------------------|
| luzco | **gerundio** |
| luces | luciendo |
| luce | |
| lucimos | **participio** |
| lucís | lucido |
| lucen | |

## maldecir

| presente | pret. ind. | |
|------------|--------------|------------------------------|
| maldigo | maldije | **gerundio** |
| maldices | maldijiste | maldiciendo |
| maldice | maldijo | |
| maldecimos | maldijimos | **participio** |
| maldecís | maldijisteis | maldecido – *cursed* |
| maldicen | maldijeron | maldito – *noun, adjective* |

## morir

| presente | pret. ind. | |
|----------|------------|---------------|
| muero | morí | **gerundio** |
| mueres | moriste | muriendo |
| muere | murió | |
| morimos | morimos | **participio** |
| morís | moristeis | muerto |
| mueren | murieron | |

## oir, oír

| presente | pret. ind. | |
|---|---|---|
| oigo | oí | **gerundio** |
| oyes | oiste | oyendo |
| oye | oyó | |
| oímos | oímos | **participio** |
| oís | oísteis | oído |
| oyen | oyeron | |

## oler

| presente | | |
|---|---|---|
| huelo | **gerundio** | |
| hueles | oliendo | |
| huele | | |
| olemos | **participio** | |
| oléis | olido | |
| huelen | | |

## pedir

| presente | pret. ind. | |
|---|---|---|
| pido | pedí | **gerundio** |
| pides | pediste | pidiendo |
| pide | pidió | |
| pedimos | pedimos | **participio** |
| pedís | pedisteis | pedido |
| piden | pidieron | |

**poder**

| presente | pret. ind. | futuro | |
|----------|------------|--------|---|
| puedo | pude | podré | **gerundio** |
| puedes | pudiste | podrás | pudiendo |
| puede | pudo | podrá | |
| podemos | pudimos | podremos | **participio** |
| podéis | pudisteis | podréis | podido |
| pueden | pudieron | podrán | |

**podrir, pudrir**

| presente | imperfecto | pret. ind. | futuro | |
|----------|------------|------------|--------|---|
| pudro | pudría | pudrí | pudriré | **gerundio** |
| pudres | pudrías | pudriste | pudrirás | pudriendo |
| pudre | pudría | pudrió | pudrirá | |
| pudrimos | pudríamos | pudrimos | pudriremos | **participio** |
| pudrís | pudríais | pudristeis | pudriréis | podrido |
| pudren | pudrían | pudrieron | pudrirán | |

**poner**

| presente | pret. ind. | futuro | |
|----------|------------|--------|---|
| pongo | puse | pondré | **gerundio** |
| pones | pusiste | pondrás | poniendo |
| pone | puso | pondrá | |
| ponemos | pusimos | pondremos | **participio** |
| ponéis | pusisteis | pondréis | puesto |
| ponen | pusieron | pondrán | |

## prohibir

| presente | |
|---|---|
| prohíbo | **gerundio** |
| prohíbes | prohibiendo |
| prohíbe | |
| prohibimos | **participio** |
| prohibís | prohibido |
| prohíben | |

## proveer

| presente | pret. ind. | |
|---|---|---|
| proveo | proveí | **gerundio** |
| provees | proveíste | proveyendo |
| provee | proveyó | |
| proveemos | proveímos | **participio** |
| proveéis | proveísteis | provisto |
| proveen | proveyeron | |

## pudrir *see* podrir

## querer

| presente | pret. ind. | futuro | |
|---|---|---|---|
| quiero | quise | querré | **gerundio** |
| quieres | quisiste | querrás | queriendo |
| quiere | quiso | querrá | |
| queremos | quisimos | querremos | **participio** |
| queréis | quisisteis | querréis | querido |
| quieren | quisieron | querrán | |

**reír**

| presente | pret. ind. | | |
|---|---|---|---|
| río | reí | **gerundio** | |
| ríes | reíste | riendo | |
| ríe | rió | | |
| reímos | reímos | **participio** | |
| reís | reísteis | reído | |
| ríen | rieron | | |

**reunir**

| presente | | |
|---|---|---|
| reúno | **gerundio** | |
| reúnes | reuniendo | |
| reúne | | |
| reunimos | **participio** | |
| reunís | reunido | |
| reúnen | | |

**roer**

| presente | pret. ind. | subj. pres. | |
|---|---|---|---|
| roo/roigo | roí | roa/roiga | **gerundio** |
| roes | roíste | roas/roigas | royendo |
| roe | royó | roa/roiga | |
| roemos | roímos | roamos/roigamos/royamos | **participio** roído |
| roéis | roísteis | roáis/roigáis/royáis | |
| roen | royeron | roan/roigan | |

**saber**

| presente | pret. ind. | futuro | subj. pres. | |
|----------|-----------|--------|-------------|--------|
| sé | supe | sabré | sepa | **gerundio** |
| sabes | supiste | sabrás | sepas | sabiendo |
| sabe | supo | sabrá | sepa | |
| sabemos | supimos | sabremos | sepamos | **participio** |
| sabéis | supisteis | sabréis | sepáis | sabido |
| saben | supieron | sabrán | sepan | |

**salir**

| presente | futuro | |
|----------|--------|--------|
| salgo | saldré | **gerundio** |
| sales | saldrás | saliendo |
| sale | saldrá | |
| salimos | saldremos | **participio** |
| salís | saldréis | salido |
| salen | saldrán | |

**seguir**

| presente | pret. ind. | subj. pres. | |
|----------|-----------|-------------|--------|
| sigo | seguí | siga | **gerundio** |
| sigues | seguiste | sigas | siguiendo |
| sigue | siguió | siga | |
| seguimos | seguimos | sigamos | **participio** |
| seguís | seguisteis | sigáis | seguido |
| siguen | siguieron | sigan | |

### sentir

| presente | pret. ind. | subj. pres. | |
|---|---|---|---|
| siento | sentí | sienta | **gerundio** |
| sientes | sentiste | sientas | sintiendo |
| siente | sintió | sienta | |
| sentimos | sentimos | sintamos | **participio** |
| sentís | sentisteis | sintáis | sentido |
| sienten | sintieron | sientan | |

### ser

| presente | imperfecto | pret. ind. | futuro | subj. pres. |
|---|---|---|---|---|
| soy | era | fui | seré | sea |
| eres | eras | fuiste | serás | seas |
| es | era | fue | será | sea |
| somos | éramos | fuimos | seremos | seamos |
| sois | erais | fuisteis | seréis | seáis |
| son | eran | fueron | serán | sean |
| **gerundio** siendo | | **participio** sido | | |

### soltar

| presente | |
|---|---|
| suelto | **gerundio** |
| sueltas | soltando |
| suelta | |
| soltamos | **participio** |
| soltáis | soltado |
| sueltan | |

**tener**

| presente | pret. ind. | futuro | |
|---|---|---|---|
| tengo | tuve | tendré | **gerundio** |
| tienes | tuviste | tendrás | teniendo |
| tiene | tuvo | tendrá | |
| tenemos | tuvimos | tendremos | **participio** |
| tenéis | tuvisteis | tendréis | tenido |
| tienen | tuvieron | tendrán | |

**traducir**

| presente | pret. ind. | |
|---|---|---|
| traduzco | traduje | **gerundio** |
| traduces | tradujiste | traduciendo |
| traduce | tradujo | |
| traducimos | tradujimos | **participio** |
| traducís | tradujisteis | traducido |
| traducen | tradujeron | |

**traer**

| presente | pret. ind. | |
|---|---|---|
| traigo | traje | **gerundio** |
| traes | trajiste | trayendo |
| trae | trajo | |
| traemos | trajimos | **participio** |
| traéis | trajisteis | traído |
| traen | trajeron | |

**valer**

| presente | futuro | | |
|---|---|---|---|
| valgo | valdré | **gerundio** | |
| vales | valdrás | valiendo | |
| vale | valdrá | | |
| valemos | valdremos | **participio** | |
| valéis | valdréis | valido | |
| valen | valdrán | | |

**venir**

| presente | pret. ind. | futuro | |
|---|---|---|---|
| vengo | vine | vendré | **gerundio** |
| vienes | viniste | vendrás | viniendo |
| viene | vino | vendrá | |
| venimos | vinimos | vendremos | **participio** |
| venís | vinisteis | vendréis | venido |
| vienen | vinieron | vendrán | |

**ver**

| presente | imperfecto | pret. ind. | |
|---|---|---|---|
| veo | veía | vi | **gerundio** |
| ves | veías | viste | viendo |
| ve | veía | vio | |
| vemos | veíamos | vimos | **participio** |
| veis | veíais | visteis | visto |
| ven | veían | vieron | |

# Los verbos irregulares ingleses
# English irregular verbs

| Infinitive | Past | Past Participle |
| --- | --- | --- |
| abide | abode, abided | abode, abided |
| arise | arose | arisen |
| awake | awoke | awaked, awoken |
| be | was *sing*, were *pl* | been |
| bear | bore | borne, born |
| beat | beat | beaten |
| become | became | become |
| beget | begot | begotten |
| begin | began | begun |
| behold | beheld | beheld |
| bend | bent | bent |
| beseech | besought, beseeched | besought |
| beset | beset | beset |
| bet | bet, betted | bet, betted |
| bid | bade, bid | bid, bidden |
| bind | bound | bound |
| bite | bit | bitten |
| bleed | bled | bled |
| blow | blew | blown |
| break | broke | broken |
| breed | bred | bred |
| bring | brought | brought |
| build | built | built |
| burn | burned, burnt | burned, burnt |
| burst | burst | burst |
| buy | bought | bought |

| Infinitive | Past | Past Participle |
|---|---|---|
| can | could | . |
| cast | cast | cast |
| catch | caught | caught |
| choose | chose | chosen |
| cleave *(cut)* | cleft, cleaved, clove | cleft, cleaved, cloven |
| cling | clung | clung |
| come | came | come |
| cost | cost, costed | cost, costed |
| creep | crept | crept |
| cut | cut | cut |
| deal | dealt | dealt |
| dig | dug | dug |
| dive | dived, dove | dived |
| do | did | done |
| draw | drew | drawn |
| dream | dreamed, dreamt | dreamed, dreamt |
| drink | drank | drunk |
| drive | drove | driven |
| dwell | dwelt, dwelled | dwelt, dwelled |
| eat | ate | eaten |
| fall | fell | fallen |
| feed | fed | fed |
| feel | felt | felt |
| fight | fought | fought |
| find | found | found |
| flee | fled | fled |
| fling | flung | flung |
| fly | flew | flown |
| forbid | forbade, forbad | forbidden, forbid |

| Infinitive | Past | Past Participle |
|---|---|---|
| forget | forgot | forgotten |
| forsake | forsook | forsaken |
| freeze | froze | frozen |
| get | got | gotten, got |
| gild | gilded, gilt | gilded, gilt |
| gird | girded, girt | girded, girt |
| give | gave | given |
| go | went | gone |
| grind | ground | ground |
| grow | grew | grown |
| hang | hung, LAW hanged | hung, LAW hanged |
| have | had | had |
| hear | heard | heard |
| heave | heaved, hove | heaved, hove |
| hew | hewed | hewn, hewed |
| hide | hid | hidden |
| hit | hit | hit |
| hold | held | held |
| hurt | hurt | hurt |
| keep | kept | kept |
| kneel | knelt, kneeled | knelt, kneeled |
| know | knew | known |
| lade | laded | laden, laded |
| lay | laid | laid |
| lead | led | led |
| leap | leaped, leapt | leaped, leapt |
| learn | learned, learnt | learned, learnt |
| leave | left | left |
| lend | lent | lent |

| Infinitive | Past | Past Participle |
|---|---|---|
| let | let | let |
| lie | lay | lain |
| light | lighted, lit | lighted, lit |
| lose | lost | lost |
| make | made | made |
| may | might | – |
| mean | meant | meant |
| meet | met | met |
| mistake | mistook | mistaken |
| mow | mowed | mown, mowed |
| pay | paid | paid |
| put | put | put |
| quit | quit, quitted | quit, quitted |
| read [rid] | read [red] | read [red] |
| rend | rent, rended | rent, rended |
| rid | rid, ridded | rid, ridded |
| ride | rode | ridden |
| ring | rang | rung |
| rise | rose | risen |
| run | ran | run |
| saw | sawed | sawed, sawn |
| say | said | said |
| see | saw | seen |
| seek | sought | sought |
| sell | sold | sold |
| send | sent | sent |
| set | set | set |
| sew | sewed | sewn, sewed |
| shake | shook | shaken |

| Infinitive | Past | Past Participle |
|---|---|---|
| shave | shaved | shaved, shaven |
| shear | sheared | sheared, shorn |
| shed | shed | shed |
| shine | shone, shined | shone, shined |
| shit | shit, *iron* shat | shit, *iron* shat |
| shoe | shod | shod, shodden |
| shoot | shot | shot |
| show | showed | shown, showed |
| shrink | shrank, shrunk | shrunk, shrunken |
| shut | shut | shut |
| sing | sang, sung | sung |
| sink | sank, sunk | sunk |
| sit | sat | sat |
| sleep | slept | slept |
| slide | slid | slid |
| sling | slung | slung |
| slink | slunk | slunk |
| slit | slit | slit |
| smell | smelled, smelt | smelled, smelt |
| smite | smote | smitten, smote |
| sow | sowed | sown, sowed |
| speak | spoke | spoken |
| speed | sped, speeded | sped, speeded |
| spell | spelled, spelt | spelled, spelt |
| spend | spent | spent |
| spill | spilled, spilt | spilled, spilt |
| spin | spun | spun |
| spit | spat, spit | spat, spit |
| split | split | split |

| Infinitive | Past | Past Participle |
|---|---|---|
| spoil | spoiled, spoilt | spoiled, spoilt |
| spread | spread | spread |
| spring | sprang, sprung | sprung |
| stand | stood | stood |
| steal | stole | stolen |
| stick | stuck | stuck |
| sting | stung | stung |
| stink | stank, stunk | stunk |
| strew | strewed | strewn, strewed |
| stride | strode | stridden |
| strike | struck | struck |
| string | strung | strung |
| strive | strove | striven, strived |
| swear | swore | sworn |
| sweep | swept | swept |
| swell | swelled | swollen, swelled |
| swim | swam | swum |
| swing | swung | swung |
| take | took | taken |
| teach | taught | taught |
| tear | tore | torn |
| tell | told | told |
| think | thought | thought |
| thrive | thrived, throve | thrived, thriven |
| throw | threw | thrown |
| thrust | thrust | thrust |
| tread | trod | trodden, trod |
| wake | woke, waked | waked, woken |
| wear | wore | worn |

| Infinitive | Past | Past Participle |
|---|---|---|
| weave | wove | woven |
| weep | wept | wept |
| win | won | won |
| wind | wound | wound |
| wring | wrung | wrung |
| write | wrote | written |

# Los numerales

# Numerals

## Los numerales cardinales

## Cardinal numbers

| | | |
|---|---|---|
| cero | 0 | zero |
| uno (*apócope* un), una | 1 | one |
| dos | 2 | two |
| tres | 3 | three |
| cuatro | 4 | four |
| cinco | 5 | five |
| seis | 6 | six |
| siete | 7 | seven |
| ocho | 8 | eight |
| nueve | 9 | nine |
| diez | 10 | ten |
| once | 11 | eleven |
| doce | 12 | twelve |
| trece | 13 | thirteen |
| catorce | 14 | fourteen |
| quince | 15 | fifteen |
| dieciséis | 16 | sixteen |
| diecisiete | 17 | seventeen |
| dieciocho | 18 | eighteen |
| diecinueve | 19 | nineteen |
| veinte | 20 | twenty |
| veintiuno (*apócope* veintiún), -a | 21 | twenty-one |
| veintidós | 22 | twenty-two |
| veintitrés | 23 | twenty-three |
| veinticuatro | 24 | twenty-four |
| veinticinco | 25 | twenty-five |
| treinta | 30 | thirty |

| | | |
|---|---|---|
| treinta y uno (*apócope* treinta y un) -a | 31 | thirty-one |
| treinta y dos | 32 | thirty-two |
| treinta y tres | 33 | thirty-three |
| cuarenta | 40 | forty |
| cuarenta y uno (*apócope* cuarenta y un) –a | 41 | forty-one |
| cuarenta y dos | 42 | forty-two |
| cincuenta | 50 | fifty |
| cincuenta y uno (*apócope* cincuenta y un) ·a | 51 | fifty-one |
| cincuenta y dos | 52 | fifty-two |
| sesenta | 60 | sixty |
| sesenta y uno (*apócope* sesenta y un) –a | 61 | sixty-one |
| sesenta y dos | 62 | sixty-two |
| setenta | 70 | seventy |
| setenta y uno (*apócope* setenta y un) –a | 71 | seventy-one |
| setenta y dos | 72 | seventy-two |
| setenta y cinco | 75 | seventy-five |
| setenta y nueve | 79 | seventy-nine |
| ochenta | 80 | eighty |
| ochenta y uno (*apócope* ochenta y un) –a | 81 | eighty-one |
| ochenta y dos | 82 | eighty-two |
| ochenta y cinco | 85 | eighty-five |
| noventa | 90 | ninety |
| noventa y uno (*apócope* noventa y un) –a | 91 | ninety-one |
| noventa y dos | 92 | ninety-two |
| noventa y nueve | 99 | ninety-nine |
| cien | 100 | one hundred |
| ciento uno (*apócope* ciento un) ·a | 101 | one hundred and one |

| ciento dos | 102 | one hundred and two |
|---|---|---|
| ciento diez | 110 | one hundred and ten |
| ciento veinte | 120 | one hundred and twenty |
| ciento noventa y nueve | 199 | one hundred and ninety-nine |
| dos cientos, -as | 200 | two hundred |
| dos cientos uno (*apócope* doscientos un) –a | 201 | two hundred and one |
| dos cientos veintidós | 222 | two hundred and twenty-two |
| tres cientos, -as | 300 | three hundred |
| cuatro cientos, -as | 400 | four hundred |
| quinientos, -as | 500 | five hundred |
| seiscientos, -as | 600 | six hundred |
| setecientos, -as | 700 | seven hundred |
| ochocientos, -as | 800 | eight hundred |
| nuevecientos, -as | 900 | nine hundred |
| mil | 1 000 | one thousand |
| mil uno (*apócope* mil un) -a | 1 001 | one thousand and one |
| mil diez | 1 010 | one thousand and ten |
| mil cien | 1 100 | one thousand one hundred |
| dos mil | 2 000 | two thousand |
| diez mil | 10 000 | ten thousand |
| cien mil | 100 000 | one hundred thousand |
| un millón | 1 000 000 | one million |
| dos millones | 2 000 000 | two million |
| dos millones quinientos, -as mil | 2 500 000 | two million, five hundred thousand |
| mil millones, un millardo | 1 000 000 000 | one billion |
| un billón | 1 000 000 000 000 | one trillion |
| mil billones | 1 000 000 000 000 000 | one quadrillion |
| un trillón | 1 000 000 000 000 000 000 | one quintillion |

## Los numerales ordinales

### Ordinal numbers

| | | | |
|---|---|---|---|
| primero (*apócope* primer), -a | 1°, 1ª | 1st | first |
| segundo, -a | 2°, 2ª | 2nd | second |
| tercero (*apócope* tercer), -a | 3°, 3ª | 3rd | third |
| cuarto, -a | 4°, 4ª | 4th | fourth |
| quinto, -a | 5°, 5ª | 5th | fifth |
| sexto, -a | 6°, 6ª | 6th | sixth |
| séptimo, -a | 7°, 7ª | 7th | seventh |
| octavo, -a | 8°, 8ª | 8th | eighth |
| noveno, -a | 9°, 9ª | 9th | ninth |
| décimo, -a | 10°, 10ª | 10th | tenth |
| undécimo, -a | 11°, 11ª | 11th | eleventh |
| duodécimo, -a | 12°, 12ª | 12th | twelfth |
| decimotercero, -a | 13°, 13ª | 13th | thirteenth |
| decimocuarto, -a | 14°, 14ª | 14th | fourtheenth |
| decimoquinto, -a | 15°, 15ª | 15th | fifteenth |
| decimosexto, -a | 16°, 16ª | 16th | sixteenth |
| decimoséptimo, -a | 17°, 17ª | 17th | seventeenth |
| decimoctavo, -a | 18°, 18ª | 18th | eighteenth |
| decimonoveno, -a | 19°, 19ª | 19th | nineteenth |
| vigésimo, -a | 20°, 20ª | 20th | twentieth |
| vigésimo, -a primero, -a (o vigesimoprimero, -a) | 21°, 21ª | 21st | twenty-first |
| vigésimo, -a segundo, -a (o vigesimosegundo, -a) | 22°, 22ª | 22nd | twenty-second |
| vigésimo, -a tercero, -a (o vigesimotercero, -a) | 23°, 23ª | 23rd | twenty-third |
| trigésimo, -a | 30°, 30ª | 30th | thirtieth |
| trigésimo, -a primero, -a | 31°, 31ª | 31st | thirty-first |
| trigésimo, -a segundo, -a | 32°, 32ª | 32nd | thirty-second |
| cuadragésimo, -a | 40°, 40ª | 40th | fortieth |

| quincuagésimo, -a | 50°, 50ª | 50th | fiftieth |
|---|---|---|---|
| sexagésimo, -a | 60°, 60ª | 60th | sixtieth |
| septuagésimo, -a | 70°, 70ª | 70th | seventieth |
| septuagésimo, -a primero, -a | 71°, 71ª | 71st | seventy-first |
| septuagésimo, -a segundo, -a | 72°, 72ª | 72nd | seventy-second |
| septuagésimo, -a noveno, -a | 79°, 79ª | 79th | seventy-ninth |
| octogésimo, -a | 80°, 80ª | 80th | eightieth |
| octogésimo, -a primero, -a | 81°, 81ª | 81st | eighty-first |
| octogésimo, -a segundo, -a | 82°, 82ª | 82nd | eighty-second |
| nonagésimo, -a | 90°, 90ª | 90th | ninetieth |
| nonagésimo, -a primero, -a | 91°, 91ª | 91st | ninety-first |
| nonagésimo, -a noveno, -a | 99°, 99ª | 99th | ninety-ninth |
| centésimo, -a | 100°, 100ª | 100th | one hundredth |
| centésimo, -a primero, -a | 101°, 101ª | 101st | one hundred and first |
| centésimo, -a décimo, -a | 110°, 110ª | 110th | one hundred and tenth |
| centésimo, -a nonagésimo, -a quinto, -a | 195°, 195ª | 195th | one hundred and ninety-fifth |
| ducentésimo, -a | 200°, 200ª | 200th | two hundredth |
| tricentésimo, -a | 300°, 300ª | 300th | three hundredth |
| quingentésimo, -a | 500°, 500ª | 500th | five hundredth |
| milésimo, -a | 1 000°, 1 000ª | 1 000th | one thousandth |
| dosmilésimo, -a | 2 000°, 2 000ª | 2 000th | two thousandth |
| millonésimo, -a | 1 000 000°, 1 000 000ª | 1 000 000th | one millionth |
| diezmillonésimo, -a | 10 000 000°, 10 000 000ª | 10 000 000th | ten millionth |

## Numeros fraccionarios (o quebrados)

## Fractional numbers

| | | |
|---|---|---|
| mitad; medio, -a | $^1/_2$ | one half |
| un tercio | $^1/_3$ | one third |
| un cuarto | $^1/_4$ | one quarter |
| un quinto | $^1/_5$ | one fifth |
| un décimo | $^1/_{10}$ | one tenth |
| un céntimo | $^1/_{100}$ | one hundredth |
| un milésimo | $^1/_{1000}$ | one thousandth |
| un millonésimo | $^1/_{1\,000\,000}$ | one millionth |
| dos tercios | $^2/_3$ | two thirds |
| tres cuartos | $^3/_4$ | three quarters |
| dos quintos | $^2/_5$ | two fifths |
| tres décimos | $^3/_{10}$ | three tenths |
| | | |
| uno y medio | $1\,^1/_2$ | one and a half |
| dos y medio | $2\,^1/_2$ | two and a half |
| cinco tres octavos | $5\,^3/_8$ | five and three eighths |
| uno coma uno | $1,1$ | one point one |

## Medidas y pesos

## Weights and measures

### Sistema (de numeración) decimal

### Decimal system

| | | | |
|---|---|---|---|
| giga- | 1 000 000 000 | G | giga- |
| mega- | 1 000 000 | M | mega- |
| hectokilo- | 100 000 | hk | hectokilo- |
| miria- | 10 000 | ma | myria- |
| kilo- | 1 000 | k | kilo- |
| hecto- | 100 | h | hecto- |
| deca- (o decá-) | 10 | da | deca- |
| deci- (o decí-) | 0,1 | d | deci- |
| centi- (o centí-) | 0,01 | c | centi- |
| mili- | 0,001 | m | milli- |
| decimili- | 0,000 1 | dm | decimilli- |
| centimili- | 0,000 01 | cm | centimilli- |
| micro- | 0,000 001 | µ | micro- |

### Tablas de equivalencia

Damos el llamado **imperial system** solamente en los casos en los que en el lenguaje cotidiano éste todavía se sigue usando en los EEUU. Para convertir una medida métrica en la imperial estadounidense, se debe multiplicar por el factor en **negrita**. Asimismo, dividiendo la medida imperial estadounidense por ese mismo factor, se obtiene el equivalente métrico.

### Conversion tables

Only U.S. Customary units still in common use are given here. To convert a metric measurement to U.S. Customary measures, multiply by the conversion factor in **bold**. Likewise dividing a U.S. Customary measurement by the same factor will give the metric equivalent.

## Sistema métrico
## Metric measurement

## Sistema imperial
## U.S. Customary System

### Medidas de longitud

### Length measure

| milla marina | 1 852 m | – | nautical mile | | | |
|---|---|---|---|---|---|---|
| kilómetro | 1 000 m | km | kilometer | **0,62** | mile (=1 760 yards) | m, mi |
| hectómetro | 100 m | hm | hecto-meter | | | |
| decámetro | 10 m | dam | decameter | | | |
| metro | 1 m | m | meter | **1,09** **3,28** | yard (= 3 feet) foot (= 12 inches) | yd ft |
| decímetro | 0,1 m | dm | decimeter | | | |
| centímetro | 0,01 m | cm | centimeter | **0,39** | inch | in |
| milímetro | 0,001 m | mm | millimeter | | | |
| micrón, micra | 0,000 001 m | $\mu$ | micron | | | |
| milimicrón | 0,000 000 001 m | m$\mu$ | milli-micron | | | |
| ángstrom | 0,000 000 000 1 m | Å | angstrom | | | |

### Medidas de superficie

### Surface measure

| kilómetro cuadrado | 1 000 000 m$^2$ | km$^2$ | square kilometer | **0,386** | square mile (= 640 acres) | sq. m., sq. mi. |
|---|---|---|---|---|---|---|
| hectómetro cuadrado | 10 000 m$^2$ | hm$^2$ | square hecto-meter | **2,47** | acre (= 4 840 square yards) | a. |
| hectárea | | ha | hectare | | | |
| decámetro cuadrado | 100 m$^2$ | dam$^2$ | square decameter | | | |
| área | | a | are | | | |

| metro cuadrado | 1 m² | m² | square meter | **1.196** **10,76** | square yard (9 square feet) square feet (= 144 square inches) | sq. yd sq. ft |
| decímetro cuadrado | 0,01 m² | dm² | square decimeter | | | |
| centímetro cuadrado | 0,000 1 m² | cm² | square centimeter | **0,155** | square inch | sq. in. |
| milímetro cuadrado | 0,000 001 m² | mm² | square millimeter | | | |

## Medidas de volumen y capacidad                                   Volume and capacity

| kilómetro cúbico | 1 000 000 000 m³ | km³ | cubic kilo- meter | | | |
| metro cúbico | 1 m³ | m³ | cubic meter | **1,308** | cubic yard (= 27 cubic feet) | cu. yd |
| estéreo | | st | stere | **35,32** | cubic foot (= 1 728 cubic inches) | cu. ft |
| hectolitro | 0,1 m³ | hl | hectoliter | | | |
| decalitro | 0,01 m³ | dal | decaliter | | | |
| decímetro cúbico | 0,001 m³ | dm³ | cubic deci- meter | **0,26** | US gallon | gal. |
| litro | | l | liter | **2,1** | US pint | pt |
| decilitro | 0,000 1 m³ | dl | deciliter | | | |
| centilitro | 0,000 01 m³ | cl | centiliter | **0,338** | US fluid ounce | fl. oz |
| centímetro cúbico | 0,000 001 m³ | cm³ | cubic centimeter | **0,061** | cubic inch | cu. in. |
| mililitro | 0,000 001 m³ | ml | milliliter | | | |
| milímetro cúbico | 0,000 000 001 m³ | mm³ | cubic milli- meter | | | |

**Pesos**                                                     **Weight**

| | | | | | | |
|---|---|---|---|---|---|---|
| tonelada | 1 000 kg | t | ton | **1,1** | [short] ton *Am* (= 2000 pounds) | t. |
| quintal métrico | 100 kg | q | quintal | | | |
| kilogramo | 1 000 g | kg | kilogram | **2,2** | pound (= 16 ounces) | lb |
| hectogramo | 100 g | hg | hectogram | | | |
| decagramo | 10 g | dag | decagram | | | |
| gramo | 1 g | g | gram | **0,035** | ounce | oz |
| quilate | 0,2 g | – | carat | | | |
| decigramo (o deca- gramo) | 0,1 g | dg | decigram | | | |
| centigramo | 0,01 g | cg | centigram | | | |
| miligramo | 0,001 g | mg | milligram | | | |
| microgramo | 0,000 001 g | µg, γ | microgram | | | |

## Temperaturas: Fahrenheit y Celsius

## Temperatures: Fahrenheit and Celsius

Para convertir una temperatura indicada en grados centígrados a Fahrenheit se debe multiplicar por 1,8 y sumar 32; p. ej. 100 °C (el punto de ebullición del agua) × 1,8 = 180; 180 + 32 = 212°F.

Para convertir una temperatura indicada en Fahrenheit a centígrados se deben restar 32 y dividir por 1,8; p. ej. 212°F (el punto de ebullición del agua) − 32 = 180; 180/1,8 = 100 °C.

To convert a temperature from degrees Celsius to Fahrenheit, multiply by 1.8 and add 32; e.g. 100 °C (boiling point of water) × 1.8 = 180; 180 + 32 = 212° F.

To convert a temperature from degrees Fahrenheit to Celsius, deduct 32 and divide by 1.8; e.g. 212° F (boiling point of water) − 32 = 180; 180/1.8 = 100 °C.

|  |  | Fahrenheit | Celsius |
|---|---|---|---|
| el punto de congelación del agua | Freezing point of water | 32° | 0° |
| el punto de ebullición del agua | Boiling point of water | 212° | 100° |
| un día tremendamente frío | An extremely cold day | −40° | −40° |
| un día de frío | A cold day | 14° | −10° |
| un día fresco | A cool day | 50° | 10° |
| un día templado | A mild day | 68° | 20° |
| un día de calor | A warm day | 86° | 30° |
| un día de mucho calor | A very hot day | 104° | 40° |
| la temperatura normal del cuerpo (humano) | Normal body temperature | 98.6° | 37° |

## Símbolos y abreviaturas

| | | |
|---|---|---|
| bloque fraseológico | ▶ | idiom block |
| contracción | = | contraction |
| corresponde a | ≈ | approximate equivalent |
| cambio de interlocutor | – | change of speaker |
| marca registrada | ® | trademark |
| | ◆ | phrasal verb |
| | 1st pers | 1st person |
| | 3rd pers | 3rd person |
| | a. | also |
| abreviación de | abr de, abbr of | abbreviation of |
| adjetivo | adj | adjective |
| administración | ADMIN | administration |
| adverbio | adv | adverb |
| agricultura | AGR | agriculture |
| América Central | AmC | |
| América Latina | AmL | |
| América del Sur | AmS | |
| anatomía | ANAT | anatomy |
| Zona Andina | And | |
| Antillas | Ant | |
| argot | argot | |
| arquitectura | ARCHIT, ARQUIT | architecture |
| República Argentina | Arg | |
| artículo | art | article |
| arte | ART | art |
| astronomía, astrología | ASTR | astronomy, astrology |
| automóvil y tráfico | AUTO | automobile, transport |
| verbo auxiliar | aux | auxiliary verb |
| aviación, tecnología espacial | AVIAT | aviation, aerospace, space technology |
| biología | BIO | biology |
| Bolivia | Bol | |
| botánica | BOT | botany |
| | Can | Canadian English |
| | CHEM | chemistry |
| Chile | Chile | |
| cine | CINE | cinema |
| Colombia | Col | |
| comercio | COM | commerce |
| comparativo | comp | comparative |
| computadores | COMPUT | computing |
| conjunción | conj | conjunction |
| Costa Rica | CRi | |

## Symbols and abbreviations

| | | |
|---|---|---|
| Cono Sur (República Argentina, Chile, Paraguay, Uruguay) | CSur | |
| Cuba | Cuba | |
| culinaria | CULIN | culinary |
| definido | def | definite |
| demostrativo | dem | demonstrative |
| deporte | DEP | |
| República Domenicana | DomR | |
| ecología | ECOL | ecology |
| economía | ECON | economics |
| Ecuador | Ecua | |
| electrotécnica, electrónica | ELEC | electricity, electronics |
| elevado, literario | elev | |
| El Salvador | ElSal | |
| enseñanza | ENS | |
| | EU | European Union |
| feminino | f | feminine |
| | FASHION | fashion and sewing |
| ferrocarril | FERRO | |
| figurativo | fig | figurative |
| Filipinas | Fili | |
| filosofía | FILOS | |
| finanzas, bolsa | FIN | finance, banking, stock exchange |
| física | FÍS | |
| | form | formal language |
| fotografía | FOTO | |
| | GAMES | games |
| geografía, geología | GEO | geography, geology |
| Guatemala | Guat | |
| Guayana | Guay | |
| Guinea Ecuatorial | GuinEc | |
| historia, histórico | HIST | history, historical |
| Honduras | Hond | |
| imperativo | imper | imperative |
| impersonal | impers | impersonal |
| indefinido | indef | indefinite |
| lenguaje informal | inf | informal language |
| infinitivo | infin | infinitive |
| | insep | inseparable |
| interjección | interj | interjection |
| interrogativo | interrog | interrogative |
| invariable | inv | invariable |
| irónico, humorístico | iron, irón | ironic, humorous |
| irregular | irr | irregular |

## Símbolos y abreviaturas

| | | |
|---|---|---|
| jurisdicción, derecho | JUR, LAW | law |
| lingüística, gramática | LING | linguistics, grammar |
| literatura, poesía | LIT | literature, poetry |
| | liter | literary |
| masculino | m | masculine |
| masculino o feminino | m o f | |
| matemáticas, geometría | MAT, MATH | mathematics, geometry |
| medicina, farmacología | MED | medicine, pharmacology |
| metereología | METEO | weather, meteorology |
| México, Méjico | Méx | |
| masculino y feminino | mf | |
| fuerzas armadas | MIL | military |
| minería | MIN | mining |
| música | MUS, MÚS | music |
| | n | noun |
| náutica, navegación | NAUT, NÁUT | nautical, naval |
| negativo | neg | negative |
| Nicaragua | Nic | |
| o | o | or |
| | no art | no article |
| | offensive | insulting language |
| Panamá | Pan | |
| Paraguay | Par | |
| peyorativo | pej, pey | pejorative, disapproving usage |
| persona, personal | pers | person, personal |
| Perú | Perú | |
| | PHILOS | philosophy |
| | PHOT | photography |
| | PHYS | physics |
| plural | pl | plural |
| política | POL | politics |
| posesivo | pos | possessive |
| participio pasado | pp | past participle |
| participio presente | pres p | present participle |
| prensa | PREN | |
| preposición | prep | preposition |
| presente | pres | present |
| pretérito | pret | |
| Puerto Rico | PRico | |
| pronombre | pron | pronoun |
| proverbio | prov | proverb |

## Symbols and abbreviations

| | | |
|---|---|---|
| psicología | PSICO, PSYCH | psychology |
| | pt | past tense |
| | PUBL | publishing, journalism |
| química | QUÍM | |
| radio | RADIO | radio |
| | RAIL | railways |
| República Dominicana | RDom | |
| regional | reg | regional |
| relativo | rel | relative |
| religión | REL | religion |
| Río de la Plata | RíoPl | |
| | s. | see |
| | s. a. | see also |
| | sb | somebody |
| | SCHOOL | school |
| | sep | separable |
| singular | sing | singular |
| | sl | slang |
| sociología | SOCIOL | sociology |
| | SPORTS | sports |
| | sth | something |
| subjuntivo | subj | |
| superlativo | superl | superlative |
| también | t. | |
| tauromaquia | TAUR | |
| teatro | TEAT | |
| técnica | TÉC, TECH | technical |
| teléfono | TEL | telecommunications |
| | THEAT | theater |
| tipografía, imprenta, gráfica | TIPO | |
| televisión | TV | television |
| | TYPO | typography, printing, graphic arts |
| Unión Europea | UE | |
| universidad | UNIV | university |
| Uruguay | Urug | |
| véase | v. | |
| Venezuela | Ven | |
| verbo | vb | verb |
| verbo intransitivo | vi | intransitive verb |
| verbo impersonal | vimpers | |
| verbo reflexivo | vr | |
| verbo transitivo | vt | transitive verb |
| véase también | v.t. | |
| lenguaje vulgar | vulg | vulgar language |
| zoología | ZOOL | zoology |